CHAMBERS
MURRAY

latin-english

DICTIONARY

CHAMBERS
MURRAY
latin-english
DICTIONARY

by Sir William Smith
and Sir John Lockwood

CHAMBERS
EDINBURGH

JOHN MURRAY
LONDON

CHAMBERS
7 Hopetoun Crescent
Edinburgh, EH7 4AY
Larousse Kingfisher Chambers Inc
80 Maiden Lane, New York, New York 10038

First edition 1933

A CIP catalogue record for this book
is available from the British Library

Paperback
ISBN 978-0-550-19003-1 (Chambers)
ISBN 0-7195-3323-6 (Murray)

Printed and bound in Great Britain by Clays Ltd, Elcograf S.p.A.

Preface

Smith's Smaller Latin Dictionary had already had over eighty years of useful life, and had passed through two editions and twenty-seven impressions, when Dr (later Sir John) Lockwood undertook his revision. Published in 1933 and reprinted many times 'Smith and Lockwood' is widely regarded as the best single-volume Latin-English dictionary available.

In his preface Dr Lockwood stressed the effort which he had made to give the meanings of Latin words in their logical order of development: this order, rather than the possibly fortuitous order of their occurrence in surviving literature, is now generally accepted practice. He introduced as an innovation the practice of marking the quantities of long vowels only, and was in advance of most of the custom of his time in marking such long vowels even when they occurred in contexts which in any case (to use an old-fashioned term) 'made position' metrically. The present-day student, properly concerned about pronunciation, will find most of these questions treated in Prof. W. S. Allen's Vox Latina (Cambridge, 1965) — a work which will explain such controversial markings as ĭnicio.

Dr Lockwood was a little tentative in justifying his retention of some derivatives in Romance languages, but they are of value, and have been retained, because some even of the better dictionaries of French, for example, give little help in the matter of derivations.

In this edition the word 'Smaller' has been omitted from the title and the two authors appear *in tandem* — justifiably, since Dr Lockwood found it necessary, as he pointed out, to 'rewrite practically the whole work' in order to achieve his aim, stated in deceptively modest terms, 'to bring up to date the information contained in this dictionary and to provide the student with the means to a better appreciation of the meaning and usage of the words and language which he is handling'.

Abbreviations

abbrev., abbreviation, abbreviated.
ABL., ablative.
Absol., absolute, absolutely, *i.e.* without case or adjunct.
abstr., Abstr., abstract.
ACC., accusative.
acc., according.
Act., active, actively.
adj., *adj.*, Adj., adjective.
adv., *adv.*, Adv., adverb.
Aor., aorist.
ap., apud (*in*).
appl., applied.
appos., apposition.
archit., Archit., architecture, architectural.
b., brother.
beg., beginning.
betw., between.
Botan., botany, botanical.
card., cardinal.
cf., *cf.*, confer (*compare*).
col. Rostr., columnia Rostrata.
Comic., comice *or* in comedy.
Commerc., commerce, in commerce.
comp., *Comp.*, comparative.
concr., Concr., concrete.
conj., *conj.*, conjunction.
conjug., conjugation.
constr., construed, construction.
contr., contracted, contraction.
correl., correlative.
corresp., corresponding.
d., daughter.
DAT., dative.
decl., declension.
def., defective, definite.
demonstr., Demonstr., demonstrative, demonstratively.
dep., deponent.
diff., different.
dim., *dim.*, diminutive (of).
disyl., disyllabic.
dub., doubtful reading.
e.g., *e.g.*, exempli gratiä (*for instance*).
ellipt., elliptically.
Eng., English.
Ep., epistulae (*letters*).
equiv., equivalent.
esp., Esp., especially.
etc., et cetera.
etym., etymological, etymologically.
euph., euphony, euphonic.
euphem., euphemistically.
exc., except.
exclam., Exclamat., exclamation, exclamatory.
f., femine, father.
fem., Fem., feminine.

fin., (ad) finem, *at the end.*
foll., following, followed.
fr., from.
Fr., French.
frag., fragment.
freq., *freq.,* frequent, frequently, frequentative (of.)
Fut., future.
GEN., genitive.
gen., general.
Geom., geometry, geometrically.
Geogr., geography, geographically.
Germ., German.
g.f., grandfather.
g.g.f., great-grandfather.
g.g.m., great-grandmother.
Gk., Greek.
g.m., grandmother.
Gram., Gramm., grammar, in grammar.
h., husband.
i.e., *i.e.*, id est (*that is*).
I.E., Indo-European.
Imp., imperfect.
Imperat., imperative.
Imperf., imperfect.
Impers., impersonal.
inanim., inanimate.
Ind., indicative.
indecl., indeclinable.
indef., *indef.*, indefinite.
Indic., indicative.
Indir., indirect.
Inf., infinitive.
init., (ad) initium, *at the beginning.*
Inscr., inscription.
insep., inseparable.
interj., interjection.
Intrans., intransitive, intransitively.
i.q., idem quod (*the same as*).
It., Italian.
judic., Judic., judicial, judicially.
Lat., Latin.
leg., Leg., legal, legally.
lit., Lit., literal, in a literal sense.
m., masculine, mother.
masc. Masc., masculine.
Merc., mercantile.
metaph., metaphorical, metaphorically.
Mid., middle voice.
milit., Milit., military.
monosyl., monosyllable, monosyllabic.
n., neuter.
negat., negative, negatively.
neut., Neut., neuter.
NOM., nominative.
num., numeral.

obj., Obj., *Obj.*, object, objectively.
occ., occasional, occasionally.
O.F., old French.
O.H.G., old High German.
O.L., old Latin.
opp., opposed (to).
Opt., Optat., optative.
Orat. Obliq., oratio obliqua.
ord., ordinal, ordinary, ordinarily.
Pan., Panegyricus.
Part., participle.
Part., Partit., partitive.
Pass., *Pass.*, passive, passively.
Perf., perfect.
perh., perhaps.
pers., person.
person., Person., personified.
pl., plur., Pl., *Plur.*, plural.
Pluperf., pluperfect.
polit., Polit., political, politically.
Port., Portuguese.
posit., Posit., positive.
prep., *Prep.*, Prep., preposition.
Pres., present.
prob., probably.
pron., Pron., Pron., pronoun.
pronom., pronominal.
prop., Prop., properly.
Prov., proverb, proverbially.
Quest., question.
q.v., quod vide.
R., Romanus, etc.
ref., reference, referring.
refl., Refl., reflexive.
reg., regular., regular, regularly.
relat., Relat., Relat., relative, relatively.
s., sister.
sc., sc., scilicet.
sign., signification.
sing., *sing.*, Sing., singular.
Subj., Subj., subjunctive, subject.
sup., Sup., superlative.
s.v., sub voce.
sync., sync., *syncop.*, syncop., syncopated.
Tab., tabulae (leges XII tabularum).
Trans., transitive, transitively.
transf., Transf., transferred, *i.e.* metaphorical.
trisyl., trisyllable, trisyllabic.
us., usually.
v., vide *or* vox.
v. l., varia lectio (*variant reading*).
VOC., vocative.

Abbreviations
of the names of authors quoted in this dictionary

A SMALLER

LATIN-ENGLISH DICTIONARY

A

A, a, *indecl. f.* (sc. littera), oftener *n.* **I.** The primitive Indo-European *ā* is in Latin, as in Greek, represented by *ă, ĕ,* or *ŏ* (*ā, ε, ο*), and *ā* by *ā, ē,* or *ō* (*ā, η, ω*). *a* has often been retained in Latin where *e* has been substituted in Greek: thus *mag-nus* corresponds to *μέγ-ας, maneo* to *μένω.* So also *a* appears in Latin in some cases where *o* is found in Greek, as in *lavo* beside *λούω* (=*λοϝω*), *da-re* beside *δι-δό-ναι.* Sometimes, however, we have *e* or *o* in Latin for original *a*, where the latter is retained in Greek ; cf. *mol-lis* with *μαλ̣ᾰκός, levis* (=leguis) with *ἐ-λαχ-ύς.* **II.** In Latin compounds *a* long by nature generally remains unchanged, as in *de-labor, e-mano. a* short by nature, followed by a labial or *l*, is sometimes changed to *u*, as in *occupo* (*capio*), *insulto* (*salio*) ; sometimes to *i*, as in *prohibeo* (*habeo*), *dissilio* (*salio*). Before other consonants it generally becomes *i*, as in *reticeo* (*taceo*), *profiteor* (*fateor*). If it is followed by two consonants, as well as preceded by one, it regularly becomes *e*, as in *condemno* (*damno*), *perfectus* (*factus*). **III.** Latin *a*, whether long or short by nature, is, for the most part, represented in French, in an accented syllable, either by *e, cáput* (*chef*), *mărc* (*mer*), *păter* (*père*), *năsus* (*nez*), *amárus* (*amer*), *amăre* (*aimer*), *amătus* (*aimé*), *mortális* (*mortel*), or by *ai*—and this chiefly, though not exclusively, before *m, n* or a guttural, *fămes* (*faim*), *mănus* (*main*), *sănus* (*sain*), *măcer* (*maigre*), *ăcer* (*aigre*), *ăla* (*aile*), *clărus* (*clair*). Sometimes it is not changed, as *quăre* (*car*), *avărus* (*avare*). *a* in position mostly remains unchanged, as *urbor* (*arbre*), *carrus* (*char*), *carmen* (*charme*) ; before *ct* it regularly becomes *ai*, as *factus* (*fait*), *tractus* (*trait*). Unaccented *a* is sometimes unchanged, as *salutem* (*salut*), *parare* (*parer*), *saponem* (*savon*) ; it commonly becomes *e*, as *caballus* (*cheval*). **IV.** As an abbreviation *A* = *Aulus* ; on voting tablets *A* (i.e. *Antiquo*) denoted the rejection of a proposed law ; in judicial trials *A* = *Absolvo*, therefore called by Cicero *lit tera salutaris.* In dates *A.D.* = *ante diem* ; *A.U.C.* = *anno urbis conditae.*

ā, ăb, ăbs (aps, Pl.), (cf. Gk. ἀπό), *Adv.* and *Prep.* **I.** Adverb. Only when compounded with verbs, nouns and adjectives, exc. perh. in phrases like : a milibus passuum quindecim, *fifteen miles away.* ā is found before *m* and *v*, e.g. āmoveo, āverto ; ab before vowels and *d, y, l, n, r, s,* e.g. abdo, abluo, etc. ; abs before *c* and *t*, e.g. abscondo, abstineo ; as before *p*, e.g. asporto ; au before *f* in aufero and aufugio. N.B. the meaning *away* or *off* prominent in verbs, etc., thus compounded, viz. **1.** *away from a place* or *connexion :* abducere, abripere, abicere, aufugere. **2.** *away from one's person :* amittere, aspellere, abruere,

abiurare. **3.** *away,* of source : aboriri. **4.** *away,* of things running away : afluere. abundare. **5.** *away from proper* or *natural direction :* abiungere, absimilis, absonus. **6.** *away,* of destruction or consumption : absorbere, absumere, abuti. **II.** Preposition. (ā before consonants ; ab before vowels and *h*, and before some consonants, esp. *s ;* abs almost only in the phrase abs te.) Always followed by an ABL. of Separation, *away from, off, starting from, beginning from.* **A.** Of Space. **1.** With verbs of motion, rest (esp. distance) : ab urbe discedere, a castris abesse. **2.** Of the starting-point of thought, *the view-point from which :* a tergo, *in the rear ;* ab oriento, *on the east ;* ab decumanā portā, *at the main gate.* **B.** Of Time. **1.** *starting from, reckoning from, since, after :* ab sole orto, ab urbe conditā, ab horā tertiā, a puero (*from childhood*). **2.** *from the age of* (with card. num.) : tirones ab sedecim annis milites scribebat, Liv. **3.** *straight from, immediately after :* recens a vulnere, Verg. ; recens ab incendio, Liv. **C.** Transf. **1.** Denoting *separation, removal, starting from, ceasing from :* a supplicio tuo se continuit populus, Cic. ; a defensione desistere, Caes. ; quartus ab Arcesilā, Cic. ; quantum mutatus ab illo Hectore. Verg. ; initium capit ab aliquā re, Caes. **2.** Denoting *source, origin :* **a.** *parentage :* ortus a Germanis, Caes. ; principum a Corā atque Pometiā, Liv. **b.** *agency, authorship :* translate by, though the real meaning is *from ;* the action of the verb *originates in* or *springs from* the person in the ABL. This usage is restricted to persons and animals, exc. for occasional personifications of things : ab Gallis sollicitarentur, Caes. ; ab elephantis obtriti, Liv. ; ab iniquitate locorum oppugnabantur Poeni, Liv. **3.** Denoting *cause, motive : out of, from, in respect of, from a certain quarter :* ab singulari amore scribo, Balb. ap. Cic. Ep. ; linguam ab inrisu exserens, Liv. ; laborare a re frumentariā, Caes.; aliquid ab liberalitate alicuius exspectare, Caes. ; doleo ab oculis, ab animo, Pl. ; timere, metuere ab aliquo, Ter. **4.** Denoting *point of view ; from the point of view of, on the side of.* Hence of *proximity :* ut nemo a senatu a bonorum causā steterit, *took the side of the senate, etc.*, Cic. ; securior ab Samnitibus agere, Liv. Hence the phrases designating an office or professional post (mostly post-Aug.): servus (or libertus) ab epistulis, a rationibus, *private secretary, accountant, etc.* Also a manu, a balneis, ab actis, etc.

abáctus, a, um, *Part.* abigō.

abacus, ī, *m.* [ᾰβᾰξ], *a tablet or board.* **I.** *for display of cups, vases, etc.*, Cic., Liv. **II.** *for games,* Suet. **III.** *for counting,* Pers. **IV.** in archit. *flat square stone on the top of a column,* Vitr.

1

abaliēnātiō, ōnis, f. a legal transfer of property Cic.

ab-aliēnō, āre. 1. Lit. (legal) to convey, transfer the ownership of : agros, Cic. 2. Transf. a. to separate, deprive : abalienati iure civium, Liv. b. to estrange : Campanos abalienavit, Liv. ; animum a se, Liv.

Abanteus, a, um, belonging to Abas.

Abantiadēs, ae, m. a male descendant of Abas : esp. Acrisius (q.v.).

Abās, antis, m. the twelfth king of Argos, s. of Lynceus and Hypermestra.

ab-avus, ī, m. (avi avus), great-great-grand-father, Cic. (Verg. has quartus pater).

abdicātiō, ōnis, f. [abdicō]. I. Legal, disown-ing, disinheriting : Quint. II. Polit. resig-nation : dictaturae, Liv.

ab-dicō, āre, to disown, reject. Legal : to dis-own, disinherit : patrem, Curt. ; filium, Quint. Polit. to resign (with simple Acc. or reflex. se and ABL.): consulatum, Liv.; se magistratu, Cic. Also absol. : (con-sules) abdicaverunt, Cic.

ab-dicō, dīcere, dīxī, dictum. An augural word (opp. addīcō) ; of an unfavourable omen, to declare against (with Acc.): Cic.

abditus, a, um. I. Part. abdō. II. Adj. put away, hidden, secret : res occultae et abditae, Cic. Poet. : terrai abdita (i.e. secrets), Lucr.

ab-dō, dere, didī, ditum. 1. Lit. a. to put away, remove (with idea of concealment): copias ab eo loco abditas, Caes. ; se in Menapios, Caes. b. to conceal, hide : in suis tectis, Liv. With ABL. of place : speluncis abdidit, Verg. With Instr. ABL. : vultūs frondibus, Ov. 2. Transf. a. to plunge, bury : litteris (ABL.) or in litteris se abdere, Cic. ; lateri abdidit ensem, Verg. b. to keep out of sight : abdenda erat cupiditas, Liv.

abdōmen, -inis, n. [perh. fr. adipomen, adeps], abdomen, paunch, belly : Pl. ; Juv. Transf. : natus abdomini, Ter. ; Cic.

ab-dūcō, dūcere, dūxī, ductum (Imp. abdūc ; also abdūce in Pl. and Ter. ; Perf. sync. abdūxtī, Pl.), to lead away, take away with one. 1. Lit. a. Us. with preps. and ABL. or Acc. : e foro, Cic. ; ex Hispaniā, Liv. ; ad cenam, to invite, Cic. b. Often by force : armenta, Ov. 2. Transf. a. to seduce from allegiance : legiones a Bruto, Cic. b. to divert : homines ab institutis, cogitationem ab consuetudine, Cic.

Abella, ae, f. a town in Campania, abounding in nuts, now Avella ; **Abellāni**, ōrum, m. its inhabitants ; **Abellāna** nux, the filbert.

ab-eō, ire, iī, itum (abin', i.e. abisne, Pl. ; Ter.), to go away, depart. 1. Lit. a. With ABL., with or without ab, ex, de, etc. : ex urbibus, Cic. b. With in and Acc., or with Supine : in Volscos exulatum, Liv. 2. Transf. a. to retire : magistratu, Cic., Liv. b. to pass away : e vitā, Cic. ; Ter. ; vanus terror, Liv. c. to threat, digress (of. aberrare): ab iure, Cic. d. to pass away into, change into : in mores suos, Liv. ; Ov. e. to turn out, result : sic abire, Cic. ; victor, Verg. Colloq. Imper. abi, off with you ; and occ. abin' (for abisne), 2nd Sing.

Pres. Indic. : are you going ? begone ! : in malam pestem, Cic.

ab-equitō, āre, to ride away : Liv.

aberrātiō, ōnis, f. [aberrō], a relief or diversion (from) : a dolore, Cic.

ab-errō, āre, to wander away. 1. Lit. patre, Pl. 2. Transf. a. to digress, de-viate from : a regulā naturae, Cic. With-out ab : coniecturā, Cic. Ep. b. to divert oneself : scribendo aberro, Cic. Ep.

abfore, abforem, abfui, abfuturus. Less correct forms for āfore, etc., v. absum.

ab-hinc, adv. [prep. pleonast. cf. exhinc, deinde], from this time backwards into the past, ago : with Acc. or ABL. and card. num. : abhinc annos quattuordecim, Cic. ; abhine annis quindecim, Cic.

ab-horreō, ēre, to shrink back. 1. Lit. Absol., or with ab and ABL., or occ. with Acc. : abhorret ab hac, Lucr. ; distortos abhorrebat, Suet. 2. Transf. a. to be averse : a scribendo abhorret, Cic. Ep.; Liv. b. to be remote, apart (prep. and ABL.). i. to differ, be inconsistent : ab opinione tuā, Cic. ii. to disagree with (with DAT.): tam pacatae profectioni abhorrens mos, Liv. ; iii. to be free from : ab suspicione, Cic. ; iv. to be unfit, incapable (absol.): sin plane abhorrebit, Cic.

abiciō, icere, iēcī, iectum [iacio]. I. to throw away, cast off or down. 1. Lit.: scutum, Cic. se ad pedes alicuius, prostrate oneself before, Cic. 2. Transf.: vitam, Cic.; versum, pro-nounce carelessly, Cic. Of price: aedes, sold too cheaply, Pl. II. to throw aside, give up, abandon : ista, Cic; abiectis nugis, nonsense apart, Hor. III to let down, humble, degrade: senatus auctoritatem, Cic; se, Cic.

abiectē, adv. 1. despondingly, Cic. 2. Comp: meanly, abjectly, Tac.

abiectiō, ōnis, f. [abiciō], 1. a throwing away or rejecting, Quint. 2. dejection, despondency, animi, Cic.

abiectus, a, um. I. Part. abicio, II. Adj. a. downcast, disheartened, desponding, animo abiecto, Cic. b. low, mean, abject, Cic. Comp: Cic., Liv.; Sup.: Quint.

abiēgnus, a, um [abiēs], made of fir-wood : equus, Prop. ; hastile, Liv.

abiēs, ietis, f. silver-fir. 1. Lit.: Verg. 2. Transf. a. a ship : Verg. b. a spear-shaft : Verg. c. a tablet or letter : Pl. (In verse, the i in abiete, etc., has con-sonantal value.)

ab-igō, igere, ēgī, āctum [agō], to drive away. 1. Lit. to drive off, (steal) : pecus, Liv. 2. Transf. a. to dispel : curas, Hor. b. to keep off : te a cibo, Liv.

abitiō, ōnis, f. [abeō], a going away. Ante-class. for abitus, q.v.

ā-bitō, ere [bītō], to go away : Pl.

abitus, ūs, m. [abeō], a going away, departure. 1. Lit.: Cic. 2. Transf.: outlet : abi-tum custode coronant, Verg. In pl. : Tac.

ab-iūdicō, āre, to take away by judicial sen-tence (opp. adiudico) : Acc. of thing, and ab aliquo or alicui. 1. Lit. Alexandream a populo R. abiudicabit, Cic. ; Pl. 2. Transf.: sibi libertatem, Cic.

ab-iungō, iungere, iūnxī, iūnctum, to unyoke. 1. Lit.: iuvencum, Verg. 2. Transf.: se ab hoc discendi genere, Cic. Ep. ; Caes.

ab-iŭrō, āre, *to deny on oath :* creditum, Sall. ; Pl. *Pass.* : abiuratae rapinae, Verg.

abj-, *v.* abi-.

ab-laqueŏ, āre [laqueus], *to loosen the earth round a tree :* Cato.

ablātivus, ī, *m. sc.* casus [auferō], *the ablative case,* Quint.

ablātus, a, um, *Part.* auferō.

ablēgātiō, ōnis, *f.* [ablēgō], *a sending away :* iuventutis ad bellum, Liv.

ab-lēgō, āre, *to send away :* aliquem foras, Pl. ; pueros venatum ablegavit, Liv.

ab-ligurriō (or **-ligŭriō**), īre, *to lick away, waste :* patria bona, Ter.

ab-locō, āre, *to let out on hire or on lease :* domum, Suet.

ab-lūdō, lūdere, lūsī, lūsum, *to be out of tune with.* Transf. : *to be unlike :* haec a te non multum abludit, Hor.

ab-luō, uere, uī, ūtum. **I.** *to wash away :* **1.** Lit. : abluendo cruori (balneas petit), Tac. **2.** Transf. : sitim, Lucr. ; periuria, Ov. **II.** *to cleanse :* pedes, Cic.

ab-negō, āre. **I.** (poet.) *to refuse :* Verg., Hor. **II.** (post-Aug.) *to deny :* depositum, Plin. Ep.

ab-nepōs, ōtis, *m.* and **ab-neptis**, is, *f. the son and daughter of a great-grandchild :* Suet.

ab-noctō, āre [nox], *to stay out all night :* Sen.

ab-nōrmis, e, *adj.* [ab, nōrma], *deviating from a rule :* sapiens, *a philosopher of no distinct school,* Hor.

ab-nuō, nuere, nuī, nuitum, or nūtum, *to refuse by a nod.* **1.** Lit. : non abnuo, non recuso, Cic. **2.** Transf. **a.** *to refuse, decline.* With Acc. : imperium, pacem, Liv. With *de* (rare) : de ullo negotio, Sall. With *Inf.* : Liv. Of things personified as subjects : spes, Tib. ; Tac. **b.** *to deny* (with Acc. and *Inf.*) : Liv. *Impers. Pass.* : nec abnuitur ita fuisse, Liv.

ab-nūtō, āre [*freq.* abnuō], *tŏ deny (by a nod) often, refuse :* Pl., Enn.

ab-oleō, ēre, ēvī, itum [from the root ol, *to rise, grow, cf.* indolēs], *to destroy the growth, let decay, efface.* **1.** Lit. : monumenta, Verg. ; labem, Tac. **b.** *to abolish :* disciplinam, Liv. With DAT. of person, *to deprive of :* alicui magistratum, Liv.

ab-olēscō, olēscere, olēvī [aboleō], *to decay, wither :* memoria aboleverat, Liv.

abolitiō, ōnis, *f.* [aboleō]. **I.** *an abolishing :* tributorum, Tac. ; legis, Suet. **II.** *an amnesty :* Quint., Suet.

abolla, ae, *f.* [ἀμβολή], *a coarse woollen cloak worn by* **a.** *soldiers :* Suet. **b.** *philosophers :* Juv.

ab-ōminor, ārī, *to deprecate as an ill omen.* **1.** Lit. : Ov., Liv. With *Inf.* : Sen. **2.** Transf. : *to detest, loathe :* Liv. In *Pass.* sense (fr. *Act.* abōmināre in Pl.), abominatus, Liv., Hor. ; abominandus, Liv.

aborigines, um, *m. pl. original inhabitants* (esp. of Italy) : Cic.

ab-orior, orīrī, ortus. **1.** Lit. : *of heavenly bodies :* *to set :* Varr. **2.** Transf. : *to fail :* vox, Lucr.

ab-oriscor, scī [aborior], *to perish :* Lucr.

abortiō, ōnis, *f. miscarriage :* Cic.

abortivus, a, um [aborior], *born prematurely :* Sisyphus, Hor. ; ovum, Mart. *Neut.* Noun.

abortivum, ī, *a means of procuring abortion :* Juv.

abortus, ūs, *m.* [aborior], *miscarriage :* Ter., Cic. Ep.

ab-rādō, rādere, rāsī, rāsum, *to scrape off, shave off.* **1.** Lit. : supercilia, Çic. **2.** Transf. : *to extort :* Ter., Cic.

abreptus, a, um, *Part.* abripiō.

ab-ripiō, ripere, ripuī, reptum [rapiō], *to tear away, carry away.* **1.** Lit. : milites vi fluminis abrepti, Caes. ; de convivio in vincla, Cic. ; Pl. ; Verg. **2.** Transf. : te aestus ingeni tui, Cic.

abrogātiō, ōnis, *f. the repeal of a law :* Cic. Ep.

ab-rogō, āre, *to repeal wholly (vid.* derogo, obrogo). **1.** Lit. : legem, Cic. ; plebiscitum, Liv. **2.** Transf. **a.** *to annul, invalidate, cancel :* tibi magistratum, Cic. **b.** *to take away from, deprive of :* alicui fidem, Pl., Cic.

abrotonum, ī, *n.,* and **abrotonus**, ī, *m. southernwood :* Hor.

ab-rumpō, rumpere, rūpī, ruptum, *to burst off, rend, break, sever.* **1.** Lit. : vincula, Hor. ; abruptis nubibus, Verg. **2.** Transf. : vitam, fas, medium sermonem, Verg. ; se latrocinio, Cic. ; ordines, venas, Tac.

abruptiō, ōnis, *f.* [abrumpō], *a bursting off.* **1.** Lit. : corrigiae, Cic. **2.** Transf. : of divorce : Att. ap. Cic. Ep.

abruptus, a, um. **I.** *Part.* abrumpō. **II.** Adj. *broken away, precipitous.* **1.** Lit. : locus, Liv. ; Tac. *Neut.* Noun, **abruptum**, ī, *an abyss,* Verg. **2.** Transf. *broken, rough, harsh, abrupt :* contumacia, Tac. *Neut. pl. as* Noun : per abrupta, Tac.

abs, *prep. v.* ab.

abs-cēdō, cēdere, cēssī, cēssum, *to go away, withdraw.* **1.** Lit. : e foro, Liv. **2.** Transf. **a.** (with ABL. *Sep.*) *to leave off :* incepto, Liv. **b.** Of places, *to recede, retire :* quantum mare abscedebat, Liv. **c.** Of things : somnus, Ov. ; ira, Tac.

abscēssus, ūs, *m. a going away, withdrawal :* solis, Cic. ; continuus, Tac.

abs-cīdō (**aps-**, Pl.), cīdere, cīdī, cīsum [caedō], *to cut off.* **1.** Lit. : caput, Cic., Liv., Verg. ; Pl. Of *diverting a stream :* Liv. **2.** Transf. : spem, Liv. ; praesidia, Tac.

ab-scindō, scindere, scidī, scissum, *to tear off or away.* **1.** Lit. : tunicam a pectore, Cic. With simple ABL. : umeris vestem, Verg. With *de :* Verg. **2.** Transf. : *to divide, sever :* exercitum, Caes. ; terras, Hor. ; Ov. ; venas, Tac.

abscisus, a, um. **I.** *Part.* abscidō. **II.** Adj. **a.** *cut away, precipitous :* saxum, Liv. **b.** *abrupt, concise :* Quint.

abscondite, *adv.* **I.** *obscurely :* Cic. **II.** *profoundly :* Cic.

absconditus, a, um. **I.** *Part.* abscondō. **II.** Adj. *secret :* insidiae, Cic.

abs-condō, dere, dī (didī, Pl.), ditum. **1.** Lit. *to bury away, conceal :* cadavera foveis, Verg. ; hominem in armamentario, Curt. **2.** Transf. : *to put out of sight:* Phaeacum arces, *bury in the distance,* Verg. ; sidera, Verg. ; fugam furto, Verg.

absēns (aps-, Pl.), entis. **I.** *Part.* absum, *being absent, in absence :* de absente iudicare, Cic. ; Hor. ; consul creari absens, Liv. **II.** Adj. *absent :* conloquia amicorum absentium, Cic. ; Pl., etc.

absentia, ae, *f.* [absēns], *absence :* Cic.

ab-silĭō, īre, iī or uī [saliō], *to leap away :* Lucr. With Acc. : Stat.

ab-similis, e, *adj. unlike :* non absimili formā muralium falcium, Caes.

absinthium (aps-, Pl.), ī, *n. wormwood.* **1.** Lit. : Pl., Lucr. **2.** Transf. : Quint.

absis, or **apsis,** or **hapsis,** īdis, *f.* [ἁψίς]. **I.** *arch. vault :* Plin. Ep. **II.** *orbit of a star :* Plin.

ab-sistō (apsistō, Pl.), sistere, stitī, *to stand away, withdraw.* **1.** Lit. : Pl., Tac. With *ab* or ABL. alone : ab signis, Caes. ; luco, Verg. **2.** Transf. : *to leave off :* obsidione, Liv. With ABL. *Gerund :* sequendo, Liv. With *Inf. :* moveri, Verg.

absolūtē, *adv.* [absolūtus], *unrestrictedly, completely :* vivere, Cic.

absolūtĭō, ōnis, *f.* [absolvō]. **I.** Judic. : *acquittal :* Cic. **II.** Philos. and Rhet. : *perfection, completeness :* Cic.

absolūtōrius, a, um [absolvō], *of acquittal :* tabella, Suet.

absolūtus, a, um. **I.** *Part.* absolvō. **II.** Adj. **a.** *complete, finished :* Cic. *Comp. :* Quint. *Sup. :* Tac. **b.** *unconditional :* officium, Cic.

ab-solvō (apsolvō, Pl.), solvere, solvī, solūtum, *to loosen from, set free, detach.* Transf. **a.** *to free from :* iudicio, Cic. ; Tac. **b.** *to pay off,* Pl., Ter. **c.** Judic. *to acquit.* With *de,* simple ABL., or GEN. : de praevaricatione, Cic. Ep. ; suspicione, Liv. ; improbitatis, Cic. **d.** *to complete, finish off, crown :* rem dissolutam, Cic. ; beneficium, Liv. With *de :* de coniuratione, Sall.

ab-sonus, a, um, *out of tune, discordant, harsh.* **1.** Lit. : vox, Cic. **2.** Transf. : *not in harmony with :* Cic. With DAT., DAT., or *absol. :* absoni a voce motūs, Liv. ; fortunis absona dicta, Hor.

ab-sorbeō (apsorbeō, Pl.), bēre, buī (psī, Lucr.), ptum, *to swallow, gulp down.* **1.** Lit. : placentas, Hor. **2.** Transf. : oceanus tot res, Cic. ; Pl. ; orationem, Cic. ; hunc aestus gloriae, Cic.

absp-, *v.* asp-.

abs-que (apsque, Pl.), *prep.* [abs] with ABL. : *without.* In Pl. and Ter. mostly in conditional clauses containing impersonal *esset* or *foret,* and with a *Pron. me, te,* etc. : apsque eo esset, *if it had not been for him,* Ter. ; absque argumento, Cic.

abs-tēmius, a, um [abs and root of tēmētum, tēmulentus], *sober, temperate.* **1.** Lit. : Ov. **2.** Transf. : *abstinent :* abstemius herbis vivis, Hor.

abstentus, a, um, *Part.* abstineō.

abs-tergeō (aps-, Pl.), tergēre, tārsī, tērsum, *to wipe off, wipe dry.* **1.** Lit. : labellum, Pl. ; fuliginem, Cic. ; fletum, Cic. **2.** Transf. : molestias, Cic. ; Pl. ; dolorem, Cic. Ep.

abs-terreō (aps-, Pl.), ēre, *to scare away.* **1.** Lit. : e turribus hostis, Liv. ; de frumento anseres, Pl. **2.** Transf. **a.** *to deter :* a pecuniis capiendis, Cic. ; Hor. ; Liv. **b.** *to ban, withdraw :* auctum, Lucr.

abstersus, a, um, *Part.* abstergeō.

abstinēns, entis. **I.** *Part.* abstineō. **II.** Adj. *abstinent, temperate :* sociis abstinens eram, *forbearing to,* Cic. With GEN. : pecuniae, Hor. *Sup. :* Plin. Ep.

abstinenter, *adv. incorruptibly :* Cic.

abstinentia, ae, *f.* [abstineō], *abstinence, self-restraint.* **a.** In gen. : Cic. ; Sall. **b.** *From food :* vitam abstinentiā finiit, Tac. ; Sen. Ep.

abs-tineō (aps-, Pl.), tinēre, tinuī, tentum [teneō], *to hold or keep away from.* **A.** *Trans.* and with ABL. *Sep.* or *ab. ; se* cibo, Hirt. ; Pl. ; se dedecore, Cic. ; ab sede ignem, Liv. ; Cic. : aliquos ab legatis violandis, Liv. **B.** *Intrans. : to abstain, hold aloof from :* Pl., Verg. With ABL. : proelio, Caes. ; Pl. ; Cic., etc. With *ab :* Caes. With GEN. : irarum, Hor. With *Inf. :* Pl. ; Suet. With *quin :* aegre abstinent quin castra oppugnent, Liv.

ab-stō, āre, *to stand aloof :* Hor.

abstractus, a, um, *Part.* abstrahō.

abs-trahō, trahere, traxī, tractum (abstrāxe for abstrāxisse, Lucr.), *to drag or pull away.* **1.** Lit. : me a Glycerio, Ter. ; aliquem a conspectu omnium in altum, Cic. ; aliquem ex oculis hominum, Liv. ; navis e portu, Liv. ; liberos in servitutem, Caes. **2.** Transf. : copias a Lepido, Cic. Ep. ; e sinu patriae, Cic. ; a sollicitudine, Cic. ; a rebus gerendis, Cic.

abs-trūdō (aps-, Pl.), trūdere, trūsī, trūsum, *to thrust away.* **1.** Lit. : aurum, Pl. ; me in silvam, Cic. Ep. ; Tac. **2.** Transf. : in profundo veritatem, Cic. ; tristitiam, Tac.

abstrūsus, a, um. **I.** *Part.* abstrūdō. **II.** *Adj. hidden, abstruse, reserved :* insidiae, Cic. ; disputatio paulo abstrusior, Cic. ; terra, Ov. ; homo, Tac.

ab-sum (apsum, Pl.), abesse, āfuī, āfutūrus (*Fut. Inf.* āfore ; *Imp. Subj.* āforem or abessem). **I.** *to be away, absent.* **1.** Lit. : domini ubi apsunt, Pl. With *ab* or *ex :* ex urbe, a foro, Cic., etc. **2.** Transf. **a.** *to be wanting (cf.* desum): Pl. ; Ter. With DAT. : abest historia litteris nostris, Cic. ; Hor. ; Ov. **b.** *to be of no assistance to* (opp. adsum). With DAT. or ABL. or *ab :* longe iis nomen populi Romani afuturum, Caes. ; eo plus aberas a me, Cic. **II.** *to be separated, distant.* **1.** Lit. : non longe a finibus, Caes. With Acc. of extent : magnum spatium, Caes. With ABL. of amount of distance (rare) : aequo fere spatio, Caes. **2.** Transf. **a.** haud permultum a me aberit infortunium, Ter. **b.** *to be free from :* a culpā, Cic. **c.** *to be disinclined to :* toto bello, Caes. ; ab istis studiis, Cic. **d.** *to be different from :* a naturā ferarum, Cic. **e.** *to be unsuitable for :* ab forensi contentione, Cic. **f.** Special phrases. **i.** tantum abest ut . . . ut . . ., *so far from . . . that . . . :* Cic. **ii.** paulum, haud (or non) multum, haud procul abest quin . . . (always *impers.*): legatos nostros haud procul afuit quin violarent, Liv.

ab-sūmō (apsūmō, Pl.), sūmere, sūmpsī, sūmptum, *to reduce by taking away, consume, use up.* **1.** Lit. : virīs in Teucros, Verg. ; absumptis frugum alimentis, Liv. ; Verg. ;

Pl. **2.** Transf. **a,** *to squander, waste :* res paternas, Hor. ; dicendo tempus, Liv.; Cic.; Ov. **b.** *to destroy, ruin :* aliquem ferro, fame, Liv. ; leto, Verg.; Ter.

ab-surdē (apsurdē, Pl.), *adv.* **1.** Lit.: *out of tune :* Cic. **2.** Transf.: *absurdly :* Pl., Cic.

ab-surdus (apsurdus, Ter.), a, um [ab and root of susurrus], *out of tune.* **1.** Lit. (rare) : vox, Cic. **2.** Transf.: *irrational, senseless, absurd* (of persons and things) : Ter., Cic., etc. *Comp. :* Cic. *Sup. :* Cic. Ep.

Absyrtus, i, *m. a son of Acetes, king of Colchis, killed by his sister Medea.*

abundāns, antis. **I.** *Part.* abundō. **II.** Adj. *overflowing.* **1.** Lit.: *Sup. :* amnis, Cic. **2.** Transf.: *abounding, rich, affluent :* oratio, Cic. ; cena, Suet. With Abl.: ingenio, Cic. With Gen.: lactis, Verg. ; rerum, Nep. *Comp. :* Quint. *Sup. :* Suet.

abundanter, *adv. copiously,* Cic.

abundantia, ae, *f.* [abundāns], *abundance.* **a.** Us. with Gen.: Cic. **b.** *affluence :* Cic., Tac.

abundē, *adv. in abundance, amply.* **a.** mala abunde omnia erant, Sall. ; satis facere quaestioni, Cic. ; cavere, Ov. ; satis. Hor. **b.** As *Neut.* Noun with Gen.: terrorum et fraudis abunde est, Verg. ; Suet.

ab-undō, āre [unda], *to overflow.* **1.** Lit.: Tiberis, aqua Albana, Liv. ; Verg. **2.** Transf. **a.** *Absol. : to abound, be rich, grow abundantly :* egentes abundant, Cic.; de terris abundant herbarum genera, Lucr. **b.** With Abl.: *to abound in :* equitatu, Caes.; ornamentis, Cic. ; Ter.

abūsiō, ōnis, *f.* [abūtor]. Rhet. *a misuse* (of tropes), Cic. (*cf.* κατάχρησις).

ab-ūsque, *prep.* [ūsque ab], *all the way from :* with Abl.: Pachyno, Verg.

ab-ūtor, ūti, ūsus, *to use up, consume entirely.* **1.** Lit. With Acc.: aurum, Pl. ; vim, Lucr. With Abl.: otio, Cic. **2.** In bad sense : *to misuse, abuse.* With Acc.: sapientiam, Pl. With Abl.: patientiā. Cic. ; verbis, Cic. *Perf. Part.* abusa used *Passively* in Pl.

āc, *conj., v.* atque.

Acadēmīa, ae, *f.* [ἀκαδήμεια]. **1.** Lit.: *Academy, a gymnasium near Athens, where* Plato taught : Cic. **2.** Transf. **a.** *Platonic philosophy :* Cic. **b,** Cicero's villa near Puteoli. **c,** Part of Cicero's Tusculan estate : Cic.

Acadēmicus, a, um, *relating to the Academy.* As *Masc.* Noun : *a Platonic philosopher :* Cic. Neut. *pl.*: one of Cicero's works, *the Academics.*

Acadēmus, i, a Greek hero, who gives his name to the Academy.

Acalanthis, idis, *f.* [ἀκαλανθίς], *the thistle-finch,* Verg.

Acamās, antis, *m. a son of Theseus and Phaedra.*

acanthus, i, *m.* **I.** *the plant brank-ursine, bear's-breech. Archit.* Corinthian capitals bear representations of this plant. **II.** *a thorny Egyptian evergreen :* Verg.

Acarnānia, ae, *f. a district in W. Greece.* Hence, **Acarnān,** ānis, *m.* and **Acarnānicus,** a, um, *Acarnanian.*

Acastus, i, *m. son of Pelias.*

ac-cēdō, cēdere, cēssi, cēssum (*Perf. sync.* accēstis, Verg.), *to go or to come to* or *near.* **1.** Lit. **A.** With Acc.: fontis, Lucr.; scopulos, Verg. With *ad* or *in* and Acc.: ad oppidum, Caes. ; in Macedoniam, Cic. With Dat. (rare): delubris, Ov. ; muris, Liv. *Absol.,* or with *Adv. :* uccede, lictor, Liv. ; propius, Cic. **B. a.** *to approach in hostility, attack :* ad castra, Caes. **b,** *to go to an auction :* ad illud scelus auctionis, Cic. **2.** Transf. **a.** fama ad nos, Liv. **b.** *to enter upon, undertake :* ad amicitiam Caesaris, Caes.; ad pericula, ad rem publicam, Cic. **c.** *to come over to, assent to :* ad sententiam, Cic. ; Ciceroni, Quint. **d.** *to come near to, resemble :* ad Deos, Cic.; Antonio, Cic. **e.** *to be added.* With Dat., or *ad :* Remis studium oppugnandi accessit, Caes. ; ad virtutis summam, Cic. With *huc, eo,* etc.: huc octodecim naves, Cic. *Absol. :* nisi litterarum lumen accederet, Cic. With noun clause as subj. **i.** with *quod :* accedit quod patrem amo, Cic. **ii.** with *ut :* ad App. Claudi senectutem accedebat ut caecus esset, Cic.

ac-celerō, āre, *to hasten, accelerate.* **1.** Lit.: gradum, Liv.; iter, Caes. **2.** Transf.: mortem, Lucr. Also *Intrans. :* Cic.; Verg.; Liv. *Pass. Impers. :* quantum accelerari posset, Liv.

ac-cendō, cendere, cendi, cēnsum [candō, implied in incendō, etc.], *to light up, set on fire, heat.* **1.** Lit.: lumina, Lucr.; luna radiis solis accensa, Cic.; faces, Cic.; calor oram, Curt. **2.** Transf. **a.** *to fire, inflame :* accensus amore, Liv.; virtutem, Verg. With *ad* or *in* and Acc., *pro* and Abl., or Dat. (of the purpose aimed at) : in rabiem, Liv. ; pro honore, Sall. ; bello, Verg. With *contra* or *in* and Acc. (of the person against whom): contra Marium, Sall. **b.** *to heighten* (*cf.* incendo): discordiam, Liv.

ac-cēnseō, cēnsēre, cēnsui, cēnsum, *to reckon among, assign to :* his cornicines, Liv.; accenseor illi, Ov.

accēnsus, a, um. **I.** *Part.* accendō. **II.** *Part.* accēnseō.

accēnsus, i, *m.* [accēnseō]. **I.** *an attendant, orderly* (attending highest state officials): Cic., Liv. With Dat. or Gen.: accensus Neroni fuit, Cic. ; accensus Gabini, Suet. **II. accēnsi,** ōrum, *m. pl.* **a.** *a class of supernumerary soldiers :* Liv. **b.** perh. the name of the 5th classis of the Servian arrangement.

ac-centus, ūs, *m.* [cantus], *the accentuation of a word :* Graeci προσῳδίας vocant, Quint.

acceptiō, ōnis, *f.* [accipiō], *a taking* or *accepting :* Cic.; frumenti, Sall.

acceptō, āre [*freq.* accipiō] *to accept often :* argentum, Pl.; Quint.

acceptor, ōris, *m.* [accipiō], *one who approves a thing :* Pl. *Fem.* **acceptrix,** icis, *she who receives :* Pl.

acceptus, a, um. **I.** *Part.* accipiō. **II.** *Adj.* **a.** *welcome, acceptable :* plebi acceptus, Caes.; rem acceptam, Cic. **b.** *indebted* (in spec. phrases): mihi vitam suam referret acceptam, lit. *put his life down to my account,* Cic.; omnia mala accepta

referemus Antonio, Cic. **III.** *Neut.* as
Noun, **acceptum,** I (cf. II. b), *the receipt,
credit-side* (of ledgers), opp. expensum :
in acceptum referre alicui, *to place to someone's credit :* Cic.
accersō, ere, *v.* arcessō.
accessiō, ōnis,*f.* [accēdō]. **I.** *a going* or *coming
to, an approach :* in concilium accessio,
Pl. ; suis accessionibus, *by personal applica-
tions,* Cic. ; ut magnas acc. fecerit, *hostile
attacks,* Hirt. **II.** *increasing, addition.* **a.**
pecuniae, Nep. ; fortunae, Cic. **b.** Commerc. : decumae, Cic. ; tritici modium et
accessionem, Cic. **c.** Hence *an appendage :*
Scaurus accessionem adiunxit aedibus.
Cic. ; Punici belli, Liv. **d.** Rhet. : *an
addition that makes a definition complete :* Cic.
accessus, ūs, *m.* [accēdō], *a going* or
coming to, an approach. **1.** L i t. : nocturnus
ad urbem, Cic. ; (aestuum) acc. et recessus,
flow and ebb of tide, Cic. **2.** T r a n s f. **a.**
ad causam facti, Cic. Ep. **b.** *access :*
negare accessum, Ov. **c.** *a passage, entrance :* navibus petere, Liv. ; accessum
lustrare, Verg.
ac-cidō, cidere, cidī, cīsum [caedō], *to cut at
or into, to cut partly.* **1.** L i t. : arbores,
Caes. ; Verg. ; etc. **2.** T r a n s f. : *to
weaken, impair :* res Vestinorum, Liv.
ac-cidō, cidere, cidī [cadō], *to fall at or near,
to reach by falling.* **1.** L i t. : with *ad* or
in and Acc., with D a t., or Acc. (poet.), or
Absol. : ad pedes, Cic. ; in mensas, Ov. ;
genibus praetoris, Liv. ; ut missa tela
gravius acciderent, Caes. **2.** T r a n s f.
a. nihil tam populare ad populi Romani
auris accidisse, Cic. ; auribus, Liv. ; auris,
Pl. **b.** *to happen, fall out (suddenly) :*
contra opinionem, Caes. Often of unfortunate events : detrimentum accidit, Caes.
Hence euphem. for *to die :* si quid mihi
humanitus accidisset, Cic. Also of fortunate events : accidit satis opportune, Caes.
With *ut* or *quod :* accidit ut Hermae deicerentur, Nep. ; accidit perincommode quod
eum nusquam vidisti, Cic. Ep. With *Inf. :*
acciderat mihi opus esse, Cic. Ep.
ac-cieō, ēre, dub. form of acciō : Pl.
ac-cingō, cingere, cīnxī, cīnctum *(Pass. Inf.
accingier,* Verg.), *to gird on or to.* **1.** L i t. :
lateri ensem, Verg. With A b l. *Instr. :* ferro
accincti, Tac. **2.** T r a n s f. **a.** *to equip,
arm :* gladiis accincti, Liv. **b.** *to arm, make
ready for* (esp. accingere se, or accingi).
With *ad* or *in* and Acc., with D a t. or *Inf. :*
ad consulatum, Liv. ; in audaciam, Tac. ;
se praedae, Verg. ; dicere pugnas, Verg.,
Also *Intrans. :* accingunt omnes operi,
Verg.
ac-ciō, cīre, cīvī (or ciī), cītum, *to summon,
fetch.* **1.** L i t. : vocibus Orcum, Lucr. ;
Alexandro doctorem, Cic. ; dictatorem ab
exercitu, Liv. **2.** T r a n s f. : artem haru-
spicum, Tac.
ac-cipiō, cipere, cēpī, ceptum [capiō], *to take
to oneself, receive, accept.* **I.** When the subject is willing, i.e. an active participant : **a.**
arma obsidesque, Caes. **b.** Of money (opp.
expendere), *cf.* acceptus : ei aliquid acceptum referre, *to credit him with something,*
Cic. **c.** *to take over, take upon oneself :*
onera venientum, Verg. T r a n s f. : pro-

vinciam, decumas, Cic. **d.** Hence *to receive
by tradition, news, inheritance, etc. :* a
maioribus, Cic. ; rem rumore, Caes. ;
gloriam a patre, Nep. **e.** *to receive as friend,
guest, ward, to admit to friendship or political
privileges, etc. :* puerum gremio, Verg. ;
Romanos in urbem, Liv. ; in amicitiam,
Cic., Liv. ; in civitatem, Liv. Also with
Adv. : clementer, Cic. ; aliquid in bonam
partem, Cic. ; hospitaliter, Curt. Hence *to
deal with, treat :* sermones militum durius,
Caes. ; aliquid in omen, Liv. **f.** *to take by
hearing, sight, mind, etc., to hear, perceive,
understand :* clamorem, Liv. ; qui haec
putet arte accipi posse, Cic. ; Lucr. ; Verg.
g. *to approve, assent to :* legem, Cic. ;
preces, Liv. **II.** When the subject is unwilling or indifferent, i.e. a passive participant : *to suffer.* **1.** L i t. : ictūs, Lucr. ;
vulnera, Verg. **2.** T r a n s f. : cladem,
detrimentum, Caes. ; calamitatem, Cic.
accipiter, tris, *m. (f.* Lucr.) [perh. fr. ac-
cipiō, i.e. *the seizer :* or fr. ὠκύπτερος, *swift-
winged*], *a bird of prey,* esp. of the falcon kind.
1. L i t. **a.** *common hawk :* Hor. ; Ov.
Called sacer in Verg., as being a bird of
omen. **b.** *sparrow-hawk:* Mart : **2.** T r a n s f.:
pecuniae accipiter, Pl.
accīsus, a, um. **I.** *Part.* accīdō. **II.** *Adj.,
impaired :* Cic., Liv.
accītus, a, um, *Part.* acciō.
accītū, A b l. *sing.* [acciō], *at the summons, call :*
magistratūs accitu istius evocantur, Cic. ;
Verg.
Accius, I, *m. a Roman proper name,* esp. L.
Accius, *a famous Roman poet, the rival of
Pacuvius in tragedy and comedy (fl. c.* 135,
B.C.) ; **Acciānus,** a, um.
acclāmātiō, ōnis, *f.* [acclāmō], *a shouting.* **a.**
a shout of disapproval (esp. in Cic.). **b.**
After Cic. *a shout of approval:* Liv., Suet.
ac-clāmō, āre, *to shout at.* With D a t. **a.**
(with disapprobation) ne mihi acclametis,
Cic. ; Suet. **b.** (with approbation), Tac.,
Suet. With double Acc., *to hail as :* aliquem servatorem liberatoremque, Liv.
ac-clārō, āre [clārus], *to make clear :* an
augural term, Liv.
acclīnis, e, *adj.* [ad-clīnō], *leaning on, inclined to* (with D a t.). **1.** L i t. : arboris
trunco, Verg. **2.** T r a n s f.: falsis, Hor.
ac-clīnō, āre, [*cf.* κλίνω, clīvus, declīnō. etc.],
to lean on or against. **1.** L i t. With *in*
and Acc. : se acclinavit in illum, Ov. With
D a t. : castra tumulo acclinata, Liv. ; Ov.
2. T r a n s f. : *to incline to :* se ad causam
senatūs, Liv.
acclīvis, e (also dub. **-us,** a, um) [ad-clīvus],
sloping upwards, steep : ea viae pars valde
acclivis est, Cic. ; locus paulatim ab imo,
Caes. ; collis placide acclivis, Liv.
acclīvitās, ātis, *f. an upward slope :* pari ac-
clivitate collis, Caes.
accola, ae, *m. f.* [ad, colō], *a dweller near a
place, a neighbour :* pastor accola eius loci,
Liv. ; accolae Cereris, Cic. ; Tiberim ac-
colis fluviis orbatum, Tac.
ac-colō, colere, coluī, cultum, *to dwell by or
near :* illum locum, Cic. ; viam, Liv. ;
Nilum, Verg.
accommodātē, *adv. fittingly, suitably.* Comp.,
Sup. : Cic.

accommodătiŏ, ōnis, f. [accommodŏ], *the fitting of one thing to another.* **1.** L i t. : Cic. **2.** T r a n s f. : *complaisance :* Cic.

accommodătus, a, um. **I.** *Part.* accommodŏ. **II.** *Adj.*, *fitted to, suitable :* with *ad* or DAT. : contionibus, Cic. ; ad persuadendum. Cic. ; ad magnitudinem fluctuum, Caes. *Comp.*: Caes., Cic., etc. *Sup.:* Cic., Plin. Ep.

ac-commodŏ, āre, *to fit one thing to another, adjust.* With *ad* or DAT. **1.** L i t. : coronam sibi ad caput, Cic. ; Pl. ; lateri ensem, Verg. **2.** T r a n s f. **a,** *to adapt :* ad novos casūs temporum novorum consiliorum rationes, Cic. **b,** *to apply, bring to :* testis ad crimen, Cic. ; se ad rem publicam et ad res magnas gerendas, Cic. ; curam pratis, Quint.

ac-commodus, a, um, with DAT. : *fit, convenient :* vallis fraudi, Verg.

ac-congerŏ, gerere, gessi, *to bring together :* huic dona, Pl.

ac-crēdŏ, dere, didi, ditum (*Pres. Subj.* accrēduās. Pl.), *to yield belief to, to credit.* With DAT.: Pl., Hor. With Acc. : Lucr. *Absol. :* Cic. Ep., Nep.

ac-crēscŏ, crēscere, crēvi, crētum, *to grow larger, increase.* **1.** L i t. : flumen, Cic. ; caespes, Tac. **2.** T r a n s f. : fides, Liv. ; invidia, Hor. ; dolores, Nep. ; Pl. With DAT. : *to be added to :* trimetris nomen iambeis, Hor. ; Liv.

accrētiŏ, ōnis, f. *an increasing :* Cic.

accubitiŏ, ōnis, f. [accubŏ], *a lying* or *reclining* at table : epularis, Cic.

ac-cubŏ, āre, *to lie near* or *by :* Furiarum maxima iuxta accubat, Verg. ; alicui custodes, Pl. ; cadus horreis, Hor. Esp. *to recline at table* (*cf.* accumbo) : Pl., Cic., Liv., etc. ; in conviviis, Cic.

ac-cūdŏ, ere, *to strike upon,* colloq. for *to coin :* Pl.

ac-cumbŏ, cumbere, cubui, cubitum [v. cubŏ], *to lay oneself down at* or *near ;* esp. *to take one's place at table* (v. triclinium) : Pl., Cic. ; in convivio, Cic. ; epulis divum, Verg. ; eodem lecto Scipio et Hasdrubal accubuerunt, Liv.

accumulătē, *adv. abundantly :* Cic. Ep.

accumulător, ōris, m. *one who heaps up* or *accumulates :* opum, Tac.

ac-cumulŏ, āre, *to add to a heap, to heap up.* **1.** L i t. : auget, addit, accumulat, Cic. ; confertos acervatim, Lucr. Botan. *to trench up :* Plin. **2.** T r a n s f. : caedem caede, Lucr. ; animam nepotis donis, Verg. ; honorem alicui, Ov.

accūrătē, *adv. carefully :* Cic., Caes.

accūrătiŏ, ōnis, f. [accūrŏ], *carefulness, exactness :* Cic.

accūrătus, a, um. **I.** *Part.* accūrŏ. **II.** *Adj.*, *prepared with care, exact, studied, elaborate :* malitia, Pl. ; commentationes, Cic. ; delectus accuratior, Liv. *Comp.* and *Sup. :* Cic.

ac-cūrŏ, āre (*Perf. Subj.* accūrāssō, Pl.), *to bestow care on, to take pains over, prepare carefully :* Pl., Cic. With *ut* or *ne* and *Subj.*: Pl., Ter.

ac-currŏ, currere, curri (rarely cucurri), cursum, *to run* or *hasten to.* **1.** L i t. : ad praetorem, Cic. ; Caes. ; auxilio suis, Sall. **2.** T r a n s f. : of ideas : Cic.

accursus, ūs, m. *a running* or *hastening to :* populi, Tac. ; Remi, Ov.

accūsābilis, e, *adj.* [accūsŏ], *blameworthy, reprehensible :* turpitudo. Cic.

accūsătiŏ, ōnis, f. [accūsŏ], *an accusation :* accusationem comparare, constituere, instruere, suscipere, Cic. ; capessere, exercere, intentare, Tac. ; factitare, *to urge it,* Cic. ; accusationi respondere, Cic.

accūsātivus, a, um [accūsŏ], with casus, *the accusative case,* Quint.

accūsător, ōris, m. *an accuser, prosecutor, esp.* in a state trial (*petitor,* in a private action) : petitoris personam capere, accusatoris deponere, Cic. Post-Aug. *an informer* (=delator), Juv., Suet.

accūsātōriē, *adv. after the manner of an accuser :* non agam tecum accusatorie, Cic.

accūsātōrius, a, um [accūsător], *of an accuser :* lex, mos, animus, artificium, Cic.

accūsātrix, icis, f. [accūsŏ], *a female accuser :* Pl., Plin. Ep.

accūsitŏ, āre [*freq.* accūsŏ], *to accuse repeatedly :* Pl.

ac-cūsŏ (**accūssŏ**), āre [causa], *to call to account.* **1.** L i t. : Judic. *to arraign, accuse, prosecute.* With Acc. of person and GEN. of crime : ambitūs aliquem, Cic. With other constructions : de vi, de veneficiis, etc., Cic. ; inter sicarios, Cic. ; aliquo crimine, Cic. ; capitis, Nep. **2.** T r a n s f. : *to blame, reprimand.* **a.** With Acc. of person and Acc. *Neut. Pron.,* or *de,* or GEN., or a *quod* clause, of the crime : ipsum vero quid accusas ? Cic. ; me de neglegentiā, Cic. Ep. ; consulem segnitiae, Liv. ; eos, quod ab iis non sublevetur, Caes. **b.** With Acc. of the crime : inertiam adulescentium, Cic.

acer, eris, n. (only in NOM. and GEN. *sing.*), *the maple-tree,* Plin. *The wood :* vile, Ov.

ācer, cris, cre, *adj.* [with lengthened vowel from root ac seen in acuŏ, aciēs, etc.], *sharp, pointed, cutting.* **1.** L i t. : stimuli, Verg. ; ferrum, Tac. **2.** T r a n s f. **A.** Of things affecting the senses : *dazzling, piercing, pungent, stinging.* **a.** Of sight : splendor, Lucr. **b.** Of hearing : flammae sonitum, Verg. ; Cic. **c.** Of smell : acerrimā suavitate, Cic. ; Lucr. **d.** Of taste : umores, Cic. **e.** Of feeling in wide sense : tempestas, Caes. **B.** Of the senses themselves : oculi, Cic. ; sensus videndi, Cic. ; stomachus, Hor. **C.** Of emotions : cupiditas, odium, Cic. ; dolor, metus, Verg. **D.** Of the intellect : *acute, keen, judicious :* vir acri ingenio, Cic. ; memoria, Cic. **E.** Of moral qualities. **a.** In good sense : *keen, spirited, enthusiastic :* milites, Cic. ; equus, Verg. **b.** In bad sense : *fierce, passionate, violent :* uxor, Pl. ; dominos, Lucr. **F.** Of abstract things : *severe, sharp, vigorous :* egestas, Lucr. ; bellum, supplicium, lex, Cic. ; responsum, Liv. *Comp., Sup. :* ācrior, ācerrimus, Cic., Liv. [Fr. *aigre.*]

Acerbās, ae, m.=Sychaeus, *q.v.*

acerbē, *adv. harshly, bitterly.* *Comp., Sup. :* Caes., Cic., Liv.

acerbitās, ātis, f. [acerbus], *harshness, sharpness, sourness.* **1.** L i t. : fructūs magnā acerbitate permixtos, Cic. **2.** T r a n s f. **a,** *bitterness, harshness :* dissensio sine acerbitate, Cic.; severitatem probo, acerbitatem nullo modo, Cic.; Suet. **b.** Esp. of grief : omnis acerbitates perferre, Cic.

acerbō, āre [acerbus]. T r a n s f. : *to embitter, make harsh :* formidine crimen acerbat, Verg.

acerbus, a, um [root *ac*, v. ăcer, aciēs, etc.], *bitter, sour, tart, harsh* (to taste). **1.** L i t : Neptuni corpus acerbum, Lucr.; uva, Phaedr. Hence *unripe.* **2.** T r a n s f. **a.** Of other senses : serrae stridentis acerbum horrorem, Lucr. ; frigus, Hor. *Neut. pl.* as Noun : acerba sonans, Verg. **b.** Of feelings, and things : *severe, biting, painful :* luctus, odium, vexatio, lex, spectaculum, Cic. **c.** Of character : *harsh, rough, crabbed :* inimici, Cic. ; acerbos e Zenonis scholâ exire, Cic. **d.** (From sense *unripe*) *untimely, premature, unready :* impolitae res et acerbae, Cic. ; funere mersit acerbo, Verg. ; partus, Ov.

acernus, a, um [acer], *made of maple :* trabibus acernis, Verg. ; Hor. ; Ov.

acerra, ae, f. [perh. fr. acer=maple], *an incense-box :* Verg., Hor.

acersecomēs, ae, m. [ἀκερσεκόμης, *with unshorn hair*], *a youth :* Juv.

acervālis, e, adj. [acervus], *of the heap :* in logic, argumentatio=Gk. σωρείτης, Cic.

acervātim, adv. *in heaps.* **1.** L i t. : Lucr., Caes. **2.** T r a n s f. : *in a mass, briefly :* Cic.

acervō, āre [acervus], *to heap* or *pile up.* **1.** L i t. : Liv. **2.** T r a n s f. : leges, Liv. ; Quint.

acervus, i, m. [perh. fr. root *ac*, v. ăcer, aciēs, etc.], *a stook* (of corn), *heap.* **1.** L i t. : frumenti, Pl. ; Cic. ; Verg., etc. As illustration in logic, ruentis acervi ratio, *the principle of the diminishing heap,* Hor. **2.** T r a n s f. : facinorum, Cic. ; Ov.

acēscō, acēscere, acui [aceō], *to turn sour :* Hor., Plin.

Acestēs, ae, m. *a mythical king of Sicily.*

acētăbulum, i, n. [acētum], orig. *a vessel for vinegar.* Hence **I.** *a cup-shaped vessel :* Quint., Sen. Ep. **II.** *a measure,* an eighth part of a sextarius : Cato.

acētum, i, n. [orig. *Part.* accō] lit. *become sour ;* hence *sc.* vinum, *sour wine, vinegar.* **1.** L i t : Pl., Hor., Liv. **2.** T r a n s f. : *a pungent wit :* Pl., Hor.

Achaemenēs, is, m. *the first king of Persia, g.f. of Cyrus ;* **Achaemenius**, a, um, *Persian ;* **Achaemenidae**, ārum, m. *pl. the Persian royal family.*

Achaeus, i, m. **I.** *s. of Xuthus, b. of Ion, mythical ancestor of the Achaians.* **II.** *a king of Lydia.*

Achaeus, a, um, *of Achaia, Greek. As noun :* an *Achaian, Greek.*

Achāïa (quadri-syl. in poets), ae, f. **I.** *the district of Achaia in Greece.* **II.** *the name of Greece as a Rom. province.* **Achāïas**, -ădis, f. *an Achaian woman ;* **Achāïcus**, a, um, *Achaian, Greek ;* **Achāïs**, idis, f. *adj. Achaian ;* also as Noun, *an Achaian woman.*

Acharnae, ārum, f. *pl. an Attic deme ;* **Acharnānus**, i, m. *a man of Acharnae.*

Achātēs, ae, m. **I.** *a companion of Aeneas.* **II.** *a river in Sicily.*

Achelōus, i, m. **I.** *a river in Epirus,* now *the Aspropotamo.* **II.** *the river god Achelous.* **Achelōius**, a, um, *of the river Ach. :* pocula Acheloia, *draughts of water,* Verg. **III.** *Aetolian :* heros, i.e. *Tydeus, q.v.* **Achelōias**, adis, and **Achelōis**, idis, f. d. of *Achelous.* In *pl. : the Sirens.*

Acherōn, ontis, or **Acheruns**, untis (esp. in Pl. where it is *fem.*), m., also **Acheros**, i, m. (Liv.). **I.** *a river in Epirus.* **II.** *a river in S. Italy.* **III.** *a river in the Lower World,* or *the Lower World itself.* **Acherontēus**, a, um, **Acherūsius**, a, um, and **Acherunticus**, a, um, *of Acheron, of the Lower World :* senex Ach., *with one foot in the grave,* Hor.

Acheruns, v. Acherōn.

Achillēs, is, m. (poet. N o m. Achilleus, trisyl. ; Voc. Achille ; Acc. Achillea ; Gen. Achillei, and Achilli ; Abl. Achille, rarely i, Ov.), *the famous Greek hero in the Trojan War, s. of Peleus and Thetis.* **Achillēus**, a, um, *of Achilles ;* **Achillidēs**, ae, m. *a descendant of Achilles.* esp. *his son Pyrrhus.*

Achivus, a, um, *Achaian, Greek. Masc. pl.* (Gen. Achīvum, Verg.), *the Greeks.*

Acidalius, a, um, *of Venus ;* **Acidalia**, ae, f. *Venus.*

acidus, a, um [aceō], *sour, tart, acid.* **1.** L i t. : sorba, Verg. **2.** T r a n s f. : *sharp, biting :* invisum acidumque, Hor.; homo acidae linguae, Sen.

aciēs, ēi, f. (Gen. also acii and aciĕ, like dii and diĕ, from diēs) [v. ăcer], *sharpness, cutting edge.* **1.** L i t. : gladiorum, Pl. ; securium, Cic. ; falcis, Verg. **2.** T r a n s f. **A. a.** patimur hebescere aciem auctoritatis, Cic. **b.** Of eyesight, *keenness of vision :* Pl., Cic. **c.** *keenness of the look, glance :* aciem oculorum (non) ferre potuisse, Caes., Lucr. **d.** *the pupil of the eye,* or (poet.) *the eye itself :* acies ipsa quae pupula vocatur, Cic. ; huc geminas nunc flecte acies, Verg. **e.** Of the mind, *sharpness, penetration :* animi, mentis, ingeni, Cic. **B.** Of an army, *the edge, battle-line.* **a.** prima acies hastati erant, Liv. ; Caes. **b.** *the battle-array :* struere, Liv. ; acie triplici instructâ, Caes.; horrida acies, Verg. ; Liv. **c.** *an army in battle-array :* inter duas acies contendebatur, Caes. ; Liv. **d.** *a battle, battlefield :* in acie Pharsalicâ, Cic., Pl. ; in acie vincere, Caes. ; Liv. **e.** Hence *a verbal contest, debate :* philosophos qui in aciem non saepe prodeunt, Cic. **C.** Of a mountain-ridge, *the edge* (*cf.* Wenlock Edge) : hi Fescenninas acies habent, Verg.

acina, v. acinus.

acinacēs, is, m. [ἀκινάκης], *the short straight dagger of the Persians, Medes and Scythians :* Hor., Curt.

acinus, i, m. and **acinum**, i, n. **I.** *a berry,* esp. *the grape :* Plin. Also *the ivy-berry :* Plin. **II.** *the seed in the berry :* Cic.

acipēnser, eris, and **acipēnsis**, is, m., *a fish,* perh. *the sturgeon :* Cic., Hor.

Acis, is, and idis, m. *s. of Faunus, beloved by Galatea, and changed by her after his death to a river in Sicily.*

aclys, ydis, f. [ἀγκυλίς], *small javelin :* Verg.

aconītum, i, n. [ἀκόνιτον], *a poisonous plant, wolf's-bane, monk's-hood.* **1.** L i t. :

Verg., Ov. **2.** Transf.: *a strong poison :* Ov., Juv.

Acontius, I, *m. a lover of Cydippe.*

acor, ōris, *m.* [aceō], *a sour taste, sourness.* **1.** Lit.: Quint. **2.** Transf.: hortor ut iucundissimum genus vitae nonnullis acoribus condias, Plin. Ep.

ac-quiēscō, *v.* adquiēscō.

ac-quīrō, *v.* adquīrō.

acraeus, a, um [ἀκραῖος], *occupying the heights,* epithet of Jupiter and Juno, whose temples stood on heights : Liv.

Acragās, antis, *m.* and **Agrigentum,** i, *n. a mountain on the S.W. coast of Sicily, and a city upon it,* now *Agrigento.* **Acragantinus** (**Agrigent-**) *of Acragas,* esp. of Empedocles who was born there.

acrēdula ae, *f.* Cic. thus translates the ὀλολυγών of Aratus ; perh. *thrush, owl,* or *nightingale.*

ācriculus, a, um [*dim.* ācer], *rather sharp, testy :* senex, Cic.

ācrimōnia, ae, *f.* [ācer], *sharpness, pungency.* **1.** Lit.: of taste : Cato. **2.** Transf.: si patris vim et acrimoniam ceperis, Cic.

Ācrisius, I, *m. king of Argos, f. of Danaë,* unintentionally killed by his g.s. Perseus.

Ācrisiōnē, ēs, *f. d. of Acrisius,* i.e. *Danaë.*

Ācrisiōneus, a, um, *of Acrisius.* **Ācrisiōniadēs,** ae, *m. a descendant of Acrisius,* i.e. *Perseus.*

ācriter, adv. *sharply, keenly, severely* (in all the signif. of the adj. *ācer*): Pl., Lucr., Cic., etc. Comp. ācrius, Sup. ācerrimē, Cic., etc.

ācroāma, atis, *n.* [ἀκρόαμα], *anything heard with pleasure.* **1.** Lit.: quod acroama libentissimo audiret, Cic.; Plin. Ep. **2.** Transf.: *a comic actor:* festivum, Cic. Also *an actor* in general: non solum spectator, sed actor et acroama, Cic.

ācroāsis, is, *f.* [ἀκρόασις, *a hearing*], *a public lecture,* or *recitation :* Cic. Ep.

Ācroceraunia, ōrum, *n. pl. a promontory in Epirus, dangerous to mariners :* hence **ācroceraunius,** a, um, *dangerous :* vita, Ov.

Ācrocorinthus, I, *f. the citadel of Corinth.*

Ācrōn, ōnis, *m. a king of the Caeninenses,* killed by Romulus.

Ācrota, ae, *m. a king of Alba, b. of* Romulus Silvius.

ācta, ōrum, *n. pl. Part.* agō, *deeds.* **1.** Lit.: mortalia, Ov. Esp. *public acts* of magistrates, or *proceedings* of the senate : acta Caesaris defenditis, Cic.; acta tui tribunatūs, Cic.; servare, confirmare, rescindere, convellere, Cic. **2.** Transf.: *report of public proceedings, acts,* or *events :* habebam acta urbana usque ad Nonas Martias, Cic.; acta diurna, Tac.; publica, Tac.

ācta, ae, *f.* [ἀκτή], *the sea-shore, beach.* **1.** Lit.: Cic., Verg. **2.** Transf.: in *pl. laxity of life at the seaside :* Cic.

Actaeōn, onis, *m. g.s. of Cadmus, changed by Diana into a stag and torn to pieces by his hounds.*

āctārius, I, *m.* [ācta], *sc.* scriba. **I.** *a registrar of State documents :* Inscr. **II.** perh. *a shorthand writer :* Suet.

Actē, ae, *f.* (lit. coast-land), early name of Attica ; **Actaeus,** a, um, *of Attica, Attic, Athenian :* **Actias,** adis, *f. adj. Attic.*

āctiō, ōnis, *f.* [agō], *a doing, performance, execution.* **A.** rerum illarum, Cic. **B.** *action, activity :* corporis, mentis, Cic. **C.** Esp. of *public actions, proceedings.* **a.** Of magistrates, etc.: tribunorum, Caes.; consularis, Liv. **b.** Judic.: *an action, suit, process.* With defining GEN. or *de :* actio furti, de repetundis, etc. ; actionem alicui intendere, instituere, Cic. **c.** *permission for a suit* (given by magistrate): actionem alicui dare, Cic. **d.** *forms* or *methods of proceeding :* actiones Hostilianae, Cic. **e.** *pleading, speech of the prosecutor :* instituere litium actiones, Cic.; Quint. **f.** *delivery, gesticulation* (of an orator or actor), often including the voice : Cic. **D.** *the action* or *plot* of a play : Cic. Ep.

āctitō, āre [double *freq.* agō], *to plead or act often* (only of lawsuits and plays) : Cic., Tac.

Actium, I, *n.* **I.** *a promontory and town in Epirus,* near which Octavius defeated Antony and Cleopatra, B.C. 31. Hence **Actiacus,** a, um ; **Actius,** a, um ; **Actias,** adis, *f.* **II.** *a harbour in Corcyra.*

āctiuncula, ae, *f.* [*dim.* āctiō], *a short lawcourt speech :* Plin. Ep.

āctivus, a, um [agō], *active :* philosophia, practical (opp. to *contemplative*), Quint.

āctor, ōris, *m.* [agō]. **I.** *poet. one who drives* or *sets in motion :* pecoris, Ov. **II.** *the doer, accomplisher.* **a.** Lit.: Cato dux, auctor, actor illarum rerum fuit, Cic. ; Caes. **b.** Judic. *one who brings a legal action, plaintiff, pleader. advocate :* Cic. **c.** *an attorney, agent :* Tac.; summarum, *cashier, accountant,* Suet. **III. a.** Rhet.: *one who delivers an oration or recitation :* Cic., Liv. **b.** *a player, actor :* Cic., Hor.

Actor, oris. *m.* **I.** *a companion of Aeneas.* **II.** *g.f. of Patroclus ;* **Actoridēs,** ae, *m. descendant of Actor,* i.e. Patroclus.

āctuāriolum, I, *n.* [*dim.* āctuārius], *a small swift row-boat :* Cic. Ep.

(1) **āctuārius,** a, um [āctus], *easily moved, swift :* navis, navigium, Caes. ; actuaria or actuarium (alone) : Cic. Ep.

(2) **āctuārius,** I, *v.* āctārius.

āctuōsē, adv. *energetically :* Cic.

āctuōsus, a, um [āctus], *full of activity, energetic :* virtus, Cic.; Sen. Ep.

āctus, a, um, *Part.* agō : *v.* ācta.

āctus, ūs, *m.* [agō]. **I.** *a driving.* **a.** levi admonitu, non actu inflectit illam feram, Cic. **b.** *impulse :* magno actu, Verg. **II.** *the doing* or *performing of a thing, an act, performance :* **a.** Lit.: Quint., Suet. **b.** *public* or *state business :* actus rerum, *jurisdiction,* Suet. **c.** Of acting or pantomime, *action in delivery :* carminum, Liv.; histrionum, Quint. **d.** *the delivery itself :* fabellarum, Liv. **e.** *an act* of a play : Hor. Hence transf.: extremus actus aetatis, Cic. : in quarto actu improbitatis, Cic.

āctūtum, adv. *immediately, instantly.* In Pl. *freq.* ; not in Cic. ; once in Liv., Verg.

acula, ae [*dim.* aqua], *a rivulet :* Cic.

aculeātus, a, um [aculeus], *furnished with stings* or *prickles.* Transf. **a.** *stinging,* *sharp*: litterae, Cic. Ep.; Pl. **b.** *subtle :* sophismata, Cic.

aculeus, i, *m.* [*dim.* acus], *a sting, prickle, barb.* **1.** Lit.: apis, Cic.; spinarum, Plin.; sagittae, Liv. **2.** Transf. **a.** Of remarks, etc., *sting, smart :* pungunt quasi aculeis interrogatiunculis, Cic.; Liv.; evellere aculeum severitatis vestrae, Cic. **b.** *spur :* aculeos in animis relinquere, Cic.

acūmen, inis, *n.* [acuō], *a sharpened point.* **1.** Lit. **a.** coni, Lucr.; stili, Cic.; auspicium ex acuminibus, *from spear-points,* Cic. **b.** *the sting of an animal :* scorpi, Cic. **2.** Transf. **a.** Of taste, *pungency:* Plin. **b.** Of the mind, *sharpness, keenness, acuteness :* Cic. **c.** *cunning, artifice, sharp practice :* Hyperidis, Cic.; meretricis acumina, Hor.

acuō, uere, ui, ūtum [v. ācer], *to make sharp or pointed, to whet.* **1.** Lit.: Cic., Verg., etc. **2.** Transf. **a.** *to sharpen by exercise :* mentem, ingenium, prudentiam, linguam, Cic.; Hor. **b.** *to spur on :* aliquem ad crudelitatem, Cic.; Verg. **c.** *to give an edge to, enhance :* studia, curam, iras, Liv.; metum, Verg.

acus, ūs, *f.* [v. ācer], *a needle or pin :* vulnus acu punctum, Cic.; acu pingere, Verg., Ov. Prov.: acu rem tangere, *to hit the nail on the head,* Pl.

acūtē, *adv. sharply, keenly, acutely :* Cic., Lucr. *Comp., Sup. :* Cic.

acūtulus, a, um [*dim.* acūtus], *rather subtle :* Cic.

acūtus, a, um. **I.** *Part.* acuō. **II.** *Adj. sharp, pointed.* **1.** Lit.: Pl., Caes., Verg., etc. **2.** Transf. **a.** Of the objects of sense : *sharp, shrill, keen :* sonus, Cic.; hinnitus, Verg.; stridor, sol, gelu, Hor.; radii solis, Ov. *Neut. pl.* as Noun : acuta belli, Hor. **b.** Of the senses : oculi, Cic., nares, Hor. **c.** Of the intellect : homo acutus magis quam eruditus, Cic. Ep.; homo ingenio prudentiāque acutissimus, Cic.

ad, *adv.* and *prep.* **I.** Adverb. Only when compounded with verbs, etc. (exc. perh. in phrases like : in Aventino ad mille et ducenti erant, Liv., where no Acc. is used after ad). ad remains unchanged in compounds before vowels and *h, b, d, f, g, m, n, q, s,* and commonly before *l, r :* e.g. adesse, adhortari, adbibere, addere, adferre, adgredi, admirari, adnuere, adquiescere, adsequi, adluere, adrogare. ad is assimilated before *c, p, t :* e.g. accipere, apportare, attinere. Before *gn, sc, sp, st,* it is either assimilated or becomes *a :* e.g. adgnoscere or agnoscere, adscribere or ascribere, adsperare, or asperare, adstare or astare. Occasionally for euphony, the form *ar* is used : e.g. arvehere, arcessere. *ar* appears also in the poet. *Inf. Pass.* agier, *cf.* Engl. *to* and Germ. *zu* with *Inf.* The literal meaning of ad is *at* (*cf.* Eng. *aim at, go at,* etc.), and, like our *at,* is used of motion or rest. **1.** *toward, aiming at.* **a.** Lit. : adire, adferre. Hence of *bringing things to one another,* i.e. together (e.g. adstringere), and of *bringing things to oneself.* **b.** Transf.: *towards an end or purpose :* adiurare, adludere, adsoutiri. **2.** *to a certain standard, up to or down to,* so as to

reach. **a.** Lit.: adsequi, adsurgere. **b.** Transf.: adaequare, adfligere. **3.** *of increase* or *addition :* addere, accelerare. **4.** *of intensity, completeness :* addecet. **5.** *at or near* (local) : adesse. **6.** *at,* on the surface merely, tentatively : adbibere, adrodere. **7.** *of beginning* an action : adamare, adurere. **8.** of occasion or circumstances, *at :* acclamare, advigilare. Esp. of mental interest or attention : admirari, approbare. **II.** Preposition with Acc. (exc. in compounds like *adeo, quoad,* etc.). Literally means *at,* and is used of motion or rest, i.e. *towards, in the direction of,* or *near, by, in the neighbourhood of.* **A.** Space. **1.** *at, towards :* ad Capuam profectus sum, Cic. (i.e. *towards* or *to the neighbourhood of Capua ; to the town of Capua* itself would be translated by Capuam alone without ad); ad orientem solem spectat, Caes. **2.** *to* (also with *usque*) : ad eos accedit, Cic.; usque ad castra hostium accessit, Caes.; de meis rebus ad Lollium perscripsi, Cic. Ep. **3.** *reaching to, as far as, even to* (often with *usque*) : ut agmen ad mare extenderet, Curt. Transf.: virgis ad necem caedi. Cic. **4.** *at, near to, by, close to* : pons qui erat ad Genavam, Caes. ; pugna ad Cannas, Liv.; ad dextram, ad laevam, Liv. **5.** *among* (=apud) : neque segnius ad hostis bellum apparatur, Liv.; qui primum pilum ad Caesarem duxerat, *in Caesar's army,* Caes. **B.** Time : **1.** *towards :* ad vesperum, Cic.; ad hiemem, Cic. Ep. **2.** *to, reaching to, as far as, even to, until :* Sophocles ad summam senectutem tragoedias fecit, Cic. **3.** *at, on, by :* ad horam destinatam, Cic. ; ut pecuniam ad diem solverent, Cic. ; ad id tempus, Caes. **C.** Relations of numbers. **1.** *to, even to, up to* (rare) : obsides ad numerum miserunt, Caes.; omnes ad unum idem sentiunt, Cic. **2.** *near, about, almost :* sane frequentes fuimus omnino ad ducentos, Cic. Ep. ad is perhaps adverbial in this sense in phrases like : occisis ad hominum milibus quattuor, Caes. **D.** In various relations. **1.** Final: *with a view to, for the purpose of, with regard to, in relation to :* auxiliaribus ad pugnam non multum confidebat, Caes. ; iuventutem ad facinora incendebant, Sall. Often after utilis, aptus, idoneus ; locus ad egrediendum idoneus, Caes. Hence instead of an *adj.,* to designate a profession : delecto ad navis milite, Liv.; servos ad remum, Liv. **2.** Modal: *at, according to, upon, after* (often of the standard *to which*) ; ad praescriptum agere, Caes. ; ad hunc modum, quem ad modum, Cic., Caes. ; id ad similitudinem panis efficiebant, Caes. **3.** Causal: *on, upon, in consequence of :* ad horum preces in Boeotiam duxit, Liv. **4.** Comparison: *compared with :* homini non ad cetera Punica ingenia callido, Liv. **5.** Addition: ad omnia, *to crown all,* Liv.; ad hoc, ad haec, *besides ;* ad cetera vulnera hanc quoque plagam infligere, Cic. **E.** N.B. the following special phrases : ad me, te, rem, etc., with a negative, or in a virtually negat. clause : *concerning me, thee, the matter, etc. ;* nil ad rem pertinet, *it is not to the purpose* or *point*, Cic. ; quid ad praetorem ? *What has it to do with the praetor ?* Cic. ad tempus : *at a definite, fixed time*, Cic. ; *at a fit, appropriate time*, Caes. ; *for some time, according to circumstances*, Cic. ad praesens : *for the moment*, Cic. Ep., Tac. ; *at present, now* (*cf.* ad praesentiam), Tac. ad locum : *on the spot*, Liv. ad verbum : *word for word, literally*, Cic. ad summam : *on the whole, in general, in a word, in short*, Cic. ad extremum, ad postremum, ad ultimum : *at the end, finally*. **a.** of place, *at the extremity*, etc. : ad extremum unde ferrum exstabat, Liv. **b.** of time, *at last ;* Cic. **c.** of order, *finally, lastly* (=denique) : Cic. **d.** of degree, *to the last degree, quite* (=omnino) : Liv. ad unguem : lit. *to the nail*, hence *exactly :* ad unguem factus homo, *a polished man*, Hor.

adāctiō, ōnis, *f.* [adigō], *a driving to, enforcing :* iuris iurandi, Liv.

adāctus, a, um, *Part.* adigō.

adāctus, ūs, *m. a bringing* or *forcing to :* dentis, Lucr.

ad-aequē, *adv.* Colloq. *equally.* Alw. with negat. : numquam ullo die risi adaeque, Pl.

ad-aequō, āre. **A.** Trans. *to make level.* **1.** Lit. **a.** omnia tecta solo adaequare, Liv. ; Caes. **b.** *to equal, match* (with Acc.) : ut muri altitudinem acervi armorum adaequarent, Caes. **2.** Transf. : *to put on the same level, make equal :* cum virtute fortunam adaequavit, Cic. ; Claudius libertos sibi et legibus adaequaverit, Tac. **B.** Intrans. : *to be on the same level, be equal :* **1.** Lit. : turris quae moenibus adaequaret, Hirt. **2.** Transf. : adaequare apud Caesarem gratiā, Caes.

ad-aggerō, āre, *to heap up :* Cato.

adamantēus, a, um [adamās], *made of steel, iron.* **1.** Lit. : catenae, Manil. **2.** Transf. : nares (taurorum), Ov.

adamantinus, a, um [ἀδαμάντινος], *hard as steel*, etc., *adamantine :* saxa, Lucr. ; clavi, Hor.

adamās, antis, *m.* (Acc. always Gk. adamanta) [ἀδάμας, invincible], *the hardest steel, adamant.* **1.** Lit. : solidoque adamante columnae, Verg. **2.** Transf. : *anything unyielding, inflexible :* in pectore ferrum aut adamanta gerit, *heart of stone*, Ov. [*Fr. diamant.*]

ad-ambulō, āre, *to walk about at*, or *near :* ad ostium, Pl.

ad-amō, āre, *to fall in love with, take a fancy to, covet :* agros et cultūs et copias Gallorum, Caes. ; id concupisti quod numquam videras, id adamasti quod antea non aspexeras, Cic. ; Ov.

ad-aperiō, aperīre, aperuī, apertum, *to uncover, expose to view.* **1.** Lit. **a.** quae velanda essent, Liv. **b.** *to throw open :* forīs portae, Liv. **2.** Transf. : auris ad criminationem, Curt.

adapertilis, e, *adj. that may be opened :* latus tauri, Ov.

adaptātus, a, um [aptō], *fitted, adjusted to* (with DAT.) : Suet.

ad-aquō, āre. **I.** *to water* (plants or animals) : Plin., Suet. **II.** *to get water :* adaquandi causā, Caes.

ad-aquor, MฤฤB. dub. for aquor.

(1) adauctus, a, um, *Part.* adaugeō.

(2) adauctus, ūs, *m. further growth, increase :* Lucr.

ad-augeō, gēre, xī, ctum. **I.** *to make still greater, aggravate :* Ter., Cic. **II.** *to devote* (of sacrifice) : Pl.

ad-augēscō, ere, *to begin to grow* (opp. deperire) : Lucr.

adāxint, *v.* adigō.

ad-bibō, bibere, bibī. **I.** *to begin to drink :* Pl., Ter. **II.** *to drink in.* Transf. : puro pectore verba, Hor. ; Pl. ; Ov.

ad-bītō, ere, *to come near :* Pl.

adc-, for words beginning thus, *v.* acc.

ad-decet, ēre. **I.** *it is also becoming :* me decet, me addecet, Pl. **II.** *it is most becoming, it most befits :* impudentem hominem, Pl.

ad-dēnseō, ēre, or **ad-dēnsō**, āre, *to make compact :* acies, Verg.

ad-dīcō, dicere, dīxī, dictum (Imper. addīce, Pl. for addīc). **1.** Lit. : *to assent to a thing.* **a.** Of omens (us. absol.) *to be favourable :* Fabio auspicanti aves non addixerunt, Liv. **b.** Judic. *to award, adjudge :* creditorem debitoribus addixisti, Cic. ; mihi bona addicat, Cic. ; addictus erat tibi ? (i.e. as your slave, pending payment of the debt), Cic. ; Pl. Hence *to confiscate to the State treasury :* bona in publicum, Caes. **c.** Of auctions, *to knock down to, assign to the highest bidder :* qui bona C. Rabiri sibi addici velit, Cic. **2.** Transf. **a.** *to assign, make over* (of private sales or corrupt transactions) : vendita atque addicta sententia, Cic. ; regna addixit pecuniā, Cic. **b.** *to assign, doom :* aliquem servituti, Caes. ; morti, Cic. **c.** *to dedicate, devote :* senatus cui me semper addixi, Cic. In bad sense, *to surrender :* libidini cuiusque nos addixit, Cic. ; Ov.

addictiō, ōnis, *f.* [addīcō, 1. b.], *the award made by the praetor :* Cic.

addictus, a, um, *Part.* addīcō. **1.** Lit. : *assigned to a creditor pending payment of the debt :* iudicatos addictosque, Liv. **2.** Transf. **a.** *bound over to :* sententiis quasi addicti, Cic. ; nullius addictus iurare in verba magistri, Hor. **b.** *destined to :* gladiatorio generi mortis, Cic.

ad-discō, dīscere, didicī, *to learn in addition :* Cic., Ov.

additāmentum, ī, *n.* [addō], *an addition, increase :* inimicorum, Cic.

ad-dō, dere, didī, ditum [dō]. **I.** *to put or add one thing to another* (opp. adimere, deducere). **1.** Lit. : his paucos equites, Caes. ; Pl. ; Hor., etc. Rarely *to add up :* addendo deducendoque videre quae reliqui summa fiat, Cic. **2.** Transf. : hunc laborem ad opera cottidiana addebant, Caes ; addere gradum (sc. gradui), Liv. ; scelus in scelus, Ov. Esp. in *Imper. :* adde huc fontium perennitates, Cic. ; adde quod in nigras lethargi mergitur undas, Lucr. ; Hor. ; Liv., etc. Of words or new thought : pauca eiusdem generis addit, Cic. Also with Acc. and *Inf. :* se in eam (legem) facere non audere, Cic. **II.** *to give in addition, apply, lay on.* **1.** Lit. : epistulas in eundem fasciculum, Cic. Ep. ; spumantia addit frena feris, Verg. Occas. of persons, *to attach closely to* (as enemy of friend) : Teucris addita Iuno, Verg. ; comitem alicui, Liv., Verg.   **2.** T r a n s f . : animos mihi addidisti, Cic. Ep. ; ardorem mentibus addunt, Verg. ; noctem operi, Verg.

ad-doceō, docēre, docuī, doctum, *to teach in addition :* artis, Hor.

ad-dubitō, āre.   **A.** I n t r a n s . **a.** *to begin to feel doubt :* With *de* or *in* and ABL. : de quo, in his, Cic., Liv. With *Indir. Quest. :* ut addubitet quid potius dicat, Cic. ; addubitavit an tempus esset, Liv. ; Hor.   **b.** *to hesitate :* eos ipsos addubitare coget dissensio, Cic. ; Liv.   **B.** T r a n s . : *to call in question :* re addubitatā, Cic.

ad-dūcō, dūcere, dūxī, ductum, *to draw to.*   **I.** *to lead to, conduct* or *bring to.*   **1.** L i t . : legiones ad urbem, Cic. ; Pl., etc. ; in iudicium adductus, Cic.   **2.** T r a n s f . **a.** *to bring into a situation :* vitam in discrimen, Cic. ; rem in eum locum ut . . ., Liv.   **b.** *to bring to an act or state of mind, to persuade, prompt, induce :* quae causa ad facinus adduxit, Cic. ; in metum, Cic. ; ad suspicandum, Cic. Esp. in *Pass.* with ABL. *Instr. : to be induced :* hac oratione, precibus, timore, Caes. ; misericordiā, Cic. Often with *ut* and *Subj. :* nullo frigore adduci ut capite operto sit, Cic. Rarely *to be induced to believe :* ut iam videar adduci hanc esse patriam, Cic.   **II.** *to draw* or *bring to a destined place (to draw* or *pull ' home '), to draw taut, tighten, contract :*   **1.** L i t . : funem, Caes. ; ballistas, Cic. ; arcum, sagittam, Verg.   **2.** T r a n s f . : habenas amicitiae, Cic. ; sitis miseros adduxerat artūs, Verg.

adductius, *comp. adv.* Only transf. *more severely :* imperitare, Tac.

adductus, a, um.   **I.** *Part.* addūcō.   **II.** Adj., *drawn tight, strained* .   **1.** L i t . : vultus, Suet.   **2.** T r a n s f . : or character : adductum et quasi virile servitium, Tac. Of speech : vis in orationibus adductior, Plin. Ep.

ad-edō, ĕsse, ēdī, ēsum, *to nibble at, gnaw at, eat partly away.*   **1.** L i t . : favos, Verg. ; iecur, Liv.   **2.** T r a n s f . **a.** lapides, Hor.   **b.** of money : non adesā iam, sed abundante etiam pecuniā, Cic. ; Tac.

ademptiō, ōnis. f. [adimō], *a taking away :* civitatis, Cic. ; Tac.

ademptus, a, um, *Part.* adimō.

ad-eō, īre, iī, itum, *to go to, approach.*   **1.** L i t . **a.** si adire non possint, Caes. With Acc. : eas nationes, Caes. ; Ov. With *ad* or *in* and Acc. : ad Caesarem, Caes. ; Pl. ; Cic. ; in ius, Caes., Cic.   **b. i.** *to approach* for the purpose of consulting, entreating, etc. ; *to address :* ad me, Cic. (In *Pass.* neque praetores adiri poterant, Cic.) ; adire deos, aras, deorum sedes, Cic. ; oracula, Verg. ; libros Sibyllinos, Liv.   **ii.** *to go to* (on a visit or to examine) : Pythagoras Persarum magos adiit, Cic. ; Tac.   **iii.** *to go at* (as an enemy) : virum, Verg.   **iv.** manum alicui adire, *to deceive* or *bamboozle some one,* Pl.   **2.** T r a n s f . : *to enter upon, undertake.* With Acc. or *ad :* periculum, hereditatem, Cic. ; Liv. ; Tac. ; adeundae inimicitiae, Cic. ; ad rem publicam, Cic. ; Pl. ; Caes.

ad-eō, *adv.* [v. ad. II. init.], *to this* or *that point, so far* (often with *usque*).   **1.** L i t . **a.** Of space : adeo res rediit, Ter.   **b.** Of time : *so long ;* with *dum, donec* following, and in Cic. with *quoad :* scitis usque adeo hominem in periculo fuisse, quoad scitum sit Sestium vivere, Cic.   **2.** T r a n s f . **A.** *to this point.* **a.** to denote result : non adeo sit imperitus rerum ut confidat, Caes. ; adeo non tenuit iram ut diceret, *so far was he from . . . that,* Liv. ;   **b.** to denote purpose : *to this end :* id ego huic dabo adeo me ut hic emittat manu, Pl.   **B.** Common in all periods of Latin to give emphasis to : **a.** nouns, verbs and adjectives : adeoque inopiā est coactus Hannibal, Liv. ; neminem adeo infaturae potuit, Cic. ; nec sum adeo informis, Verg.   **b.** pronouns, numerals (which *adeo* us. follows), *precisely, exactly, quite, just, chiefly :* id adeo cognoscite, Cic. ; tuque adeo summe Sol, Verg. ; tris adeo incertos soles erramus, Verg.   **c.** si, nisi, nec, nunc, iam, sic, vix, etc. : immemor est nisi adeo monitus, Pl. ; vix adeo, Verg.   **d.** atque, sive, aut, vel ; here it is corrective ; *or rather :* hoc consilio atque adeo hac amentiā impulsi, Cic.   **e.** At beg. of sentence : *thus far, to such an extent :* Liv., Tac.

adeps, ipis, *m.f.* [ἄλειφα, with *d* for *l*], *the soft fat* of animals.   **1.** L i t . : Varr., Plin. Of men : Cassi adipes, Cic.   **2.** T r a n s f . : of earth or trees : Plin. Of oratory : Quint.

adeptiō, ōnis, *f.* [adipīscor], *the obtaining, attainment :* boni, Cic. ; Quint.

adeptus, a, um, *Part.* adipīscor.

ad-equitō, āre, *to ride towards* or *to :* Syracusas, Liv. ; ad nostros, Caes. ; in primos ordines, Curt. With DAT. : portis, vallo, Liv. ; castris, Tac.

adesdum, *v.* dum.

ad-ēsuriō, īre, *to become hungry,* or perh. *to be very hungry :* Pl.

adēsus, a, um, *Part.* adedō.

adfābilis, e, *adj.* [adfārī], *that can be spoken to, courteous :* Ter., Cic., Verg.

adfābilitās, ātis, *f.* [adfābilis], *affability, politeness, courtesy :* Cic.

adfabrē, *adv.* [faber], *skilfully :* Cic.

ad-fātur (of this def. verb the chief forms in use are Pres. Ind. adfātur, adfāminī, adfantur ; Imper. adfāre ; Inf. adfārī ; Perf. Part. adfātus), *to speak to, address :* Cic. ; but chiefly poet. : Verg., Ov. Esp. of prayers and of last words to the dead : adfaturque deos, Verg. ; sic positum adfati discedite corpus, Verg.

adfatim, *adv.* [root of fatiscō, fatīgō], *to weariness, to satiety, sufficiently, enough, abundantly :* iisdem seminibus et homines adfatim vescuntur, Cic. ; parare commeatum adfatim, Sall. With GEN. : divitiarum, adfatim, Pl. ; copiarum, Liv.

adfātus, a, um. *Part.* v. adfātur.

adfātus, ūs, *m.* [adfārī], *a speaking to, address :* reginam ambire adfatu, Verg.

adfectātiō, ōnis, *f.* [adfectō].   **I.** *a striving after, aspiring to* (in good or bad sense) : Nervii circa adfectationem Germanicae originis ultro ambitiosi sunt, Tac. ; imperi, Suet.   **II.** Rhet. *striving after effect, affectation :* Quint.

adfectātus, a, um. **I.** *Part.* adfectō. **II.** *Adj.* Rhet. *studied, far-fetched :* Quint.

adfectiō, ōnis, *f.* [adficiō]. **I.** *the being affected, a disposition or condition of the mind or body.* **a.** Transient : adfectio est animi aut corporis ex tempore aliquâ dē causâ commutatio, ut laetitia, cupiditas, morbus, etc., Cic. **b.** Permanent : *habit, state :* omnes rectae animi adfectiones virtutes appellantur, Cic. ; summum bonum firmâ corporis adfectione contineri, Cic. Of other things : astrorum, *the relative position of the stars,* Cic. **II.** *a favourable disposition, goodwill :* laetas inter audientium adfectiones, *amid the joyous expressions of goodwill of his audience,* Tac.

adfectō, āre [*freq.* adficiō], *to make an effort to do or reach or obtain, to strive after.* **I. a.** Of material things (esp. colloq.) : ad me adfectant viam, Ter. ; quod iter adfectet, videtis, Cic. ; (navem) dextrâ adfectare, Verg. **b.** Of immaterial things : **i.** *to aspire to* (in good or bad sense) : regnum. imperium, Liv. ; famam, Tac. ; caelum, Ov. With *Inf. :* Pl., Ov., Quint. **ii.** *to try to gain over :* civitates, Sall. ; Galliarum societatem, Tac. **II.** *to affect, feign :* studium carminum, Tac. ; Quint.

adfectus, a, um [*Part.* adficiō]. **I.** *disposed, constituted :* oculus conturbatus non est probe adfectus ad suum munus fungendum, Cic. **II.** *furnished with, endowed with, affected by.* **1.** Lit. : omnibus virtutibus, praemiis, laetitiâ, Cic. ; Pl. ; Lucr. **2.** Transf. : *affected by, weakened, impaired :* sollicitudine, Caes. ; vitiis, dolore, senectute, Cic. ; aerumnis, Lucr. ; corpus, vires corporis, Liv. ; res familiaris, Liv. ; bellum adfectum et paene confectum, Cic.

adfectus, ūs, *m.* [adficiō]. **I.** *a state or disposition of mind, feeling :* qualis cuiusque animi adfectus esset, talem esse hominem, Cic. ; Ov. **II.** *a favourable disposition of mind, goodwill, love, desire :* Tac., Juv., Suet. Also of objects of love, *loved ones :* Luc.

ad-ferō, adferre, attuli, adlātum. **I.** *to carry* or *bring to* or *near* (esp. of portable things). **1.** Lit. : litteras ad aliquem *or* alicui, Cic. ; ex urbibus cibaria, Liv. Esp. with *Refl. Pron.,* or with *pedem* or in *Mid. : to bring oneself to, to come to :* huc te adfers, Verg. ; unde malum pedem attulistis, Cat. ; urbem adferimur, Verg. **2.** Transf. **a.** Of news, *to report, announce :* calamitas tanta fuit ut eam ex sermone rumor adferret, Cic. ; nihil novi ad nos adferebatur, Cic. Occas. with Acc. and *Inf.* Often *impers. :* rebellasse Etruscos adlatum est, Liv. **b.** *to bring upon, apply to, lay on :* vim adferre alicui, Cic., Liv., Ov. ; manûs templo, Cic. **c.** *to bring forward* as reason, argument, *or* excuse, *to adduce :* iustas causas adfers, Cic. Ep. Also with sentence as object : et cur credam adferre possum, Cic. ; Lucr. **II.** *to bear* or *bring in addition.* **1.** Lit. : agri qui multo plus adferunt quam acceperunt, Cic. **2.** Transf. : *to contribute, bestow in addition :* adiumentum hominibus nostris, Cic. ; quidquid ad rem publicam attulimus, Cic. **III.** *to bring about, occasion, cause :* ut populo Romano pacem, tranquillitatem, otium,

concordiam adferat, Cic. ; metum, luctum, etc., Cic. ; detrimentum, Caes.

ad-ficiō, ficere, fēcī, fectum [faciō], *to do something to.* **I.** *to influence, affect, work upon the mind or body.* **a.** Mind : sollicitudo de te duplex nos adficit, Cic. : Tac. : varie sum adfectus tuis litteris. Cic. Ep. **b.** Body (rare) : corpus adficere M. Antoni, Cic. ; ut aestus, labor, fames, sitisque corpora adficerent, Liv. ; Ov. Hence *to weaken,* esp. in *Part. Pass.* adfectus, *q.v.* **II.** *to furnish* or *endow with* (with ABL. *Instr.*) : aliquem laude, gloriâ, honore, nomine, praemio, cruciatu, morte, sepulturâ, etc., Cic. ; praedâ, Pl. ; pretio, Verg.

adfictus, a, um, *Part.* adfingō.

ad-fīgō, fīgere, fīxī, fixum, *to fasten to, fix on.* **1.** Lit. : falces longuriis, Caes. ; signa delubris, Hor. ; Verg. ; aliquem cruci, Liv. ; litteram ad caput, Cic. ; Liv. **2.** Transf. : *to fasten permanently :* causa in animo adfixa, Cic. ; iubes eum mihi esse adfixum tamquam magistro, Cic. Ep. ; Tib.

ad-fingō, fingere, fīnxī, fictum. **I.** *to shape* or *fashion one thing to another.* **1.** Lit. : ei manûs adfinxit, Cic. **2.** Transf. : probi orationem adfingit improbo stultovo sapienti, Cic. **II.** *to fashion in addition, add, invent* (esp. in bad sense) : addunt et adfingunt rumoribus (DAT.), Caes. ; ut intellegatis quid error adfinxerit, Cic. ; vitium hoc oculis, Lucr.

adfinis, e, *adj. at the border.* **1.** Lit. : *bordering, adjacent* (with DAT.) : gens adfinis Mauris, Liv. **2.** Transf. **a.** *connected with, implicated in.* With DAT. : culpae, facinori, turpitudini, Cic. ; Pl. ; Liv. With GEN. : suspicionis, rei capitalis, Cic. **b.** *connected by marriage* (mostly as noun) : ex tam multis cognatis et adfinibus, Cic. ; Pl. ; Ov.

adfinitās, ātis, *f.* [adfinis]. **1.** Lit. **a.** *connexion by marriage :* Pl., Ter. ; adfinitate se devincire cum aliquo, Cic. ; cum aliquo adfinitate coniungi, Nep. ; adfinitatem iungere cum aliquo, Liv. **b.** *the persons related by marriage,* Pl. **2.** Transf. : *connexion, union :* litterarum, Quint.

adfirmātē, *adv. with assurance, positively :* promittere, Cic.

adfirmātiō, ōnis, *f.* [adfirmō], *a positive assertion, declaration :* Caes., Cic.

ad-firmō, āre. **I.** *to make firm, strengthen, confirm :* ea res Troianis spem adfirmat, Liv. ; opinionem, dicta alicuius, Liv. ; Tac. **II.** *to present as fixed or true, to assert positively, declare :* dicendum est mihi, sed ita, nihil ut adfirmem, quaeram omnia, Cic. ; quis pro certo adfirmet quot fuerint ? Liv. With Acc. and *Inf. :* Cic., Tac.

adfixus, a, um, *Part.* adfigō.

adflātus, ūs, *m.* [adflō], *a blowing* or *breathing upon, breath, blast.* **1.** Lit. : adflatus ex terrâ, Cic. ; ambusti adflatu vaporis, Liv. ; Ov. **2.** Transf. : *inspiration :* nemo vir magnus sine aliquo adflatu divino unquam fuit, Cic.

ad-fleō, ēre, *to weep at :* Pl., Hor.

adflictātiō, ōnis, *f.* [adflictō], *bodily pain :* Cic.

adflictō, āre [*freq.* adflīgō], *to dash* or *toss about.* **1.** Lit. : navis tempestas adflictabat, Caes. ; Tac. **2.** Transf. : *to* *harass, torment, distress :* adflictatur· res publica, Cic., Tac. Hence adflictare se *or* adflictari (with ABL. *Instr.* or *de*) : de domesticis rebus, Cic. Ep. ; Ter. ; Sall.

adflictor, ōris, *m.* [adflīgō], *a subverter :* dignitatis, Cic.

adflictus, a, um. **I.** *Part.* adflīgō. **II.** Adj. *shattered, distressed :* **a.** Graecia perculsa et adflicta, Cic. ; provinciam adflictam erexisti, Cic. ; Luc. *Comp. :* Cic. Ep. **b.** Of the mind or character : luctu, maerore adflictus, Cic. ; Verg. ; homo adflictus et perditus, Cic.

ad-flīgō, flīgere, flīxī, flīctum, *to dash* or *knock against* or *down* (with DAT. or *ad*). **1.** Lit. : te ad· terram, Pl. ; tempestas navis adflixit, Caes. ; Cic. ; imaginem solo, Tac. **2.** Transf. : *to dash down, prostrate, crush :* senectus enervat et adfligit homines, Cic. ; animos adfligere et debilitare metu, Cic. ; opes hostium, Liv. ; aliquem bello, Liv.

ad-flō, āre, *to breathe* or *blow on.* **A.** Trans. **1.** Lit. : With internal ACC. : calidum membris adflare vaporem, Lucr. With external ACC. : terga adflante vento, Liv. Hence *to blast :* Iuppiter me fulminis adflavit ventis, Verg. ; adflati incendio, Liv. **2.** Transf. : sperat sibi auram posse aliquam adflari voluntatis, Cic. ; laetos oculis adflarat honores, Verg. **B.** Intrans. **1.** Lit. : adflabat frigoris vis, Liv. **2.** Transf. : rumoris nescio quid adflaverat, *had been breathed abroad,* Cic. Ep.

adfluēns, entis. **I.** *Part.* adfluō. **II.** Adj. *abounding in, abundant, rich :* adfluens copiis, studiis, lepore, venustate, scelere, Cic. Also adfluentes copiae, Cic. *Neut.* as Noun : ex adfluenti, *in abundance,* Tac.

adfluenter, *adv. abundantly.* Comp. : Cic., Nep., Tac.

adfluentia, ae, *f.* [adfluō], *a flowing to.* Transf. : *abundance, profusion :* rerum, Cic. ; adfluentiam adfectabat, Nep.

ad-fluō, fluere, fluxī, *to flow towards, to stream.* **1.** Lit. : unguentis adfluens, Cic. **2.** Transf. **a.** *to stream to, flock to :* copiae adfluebant, Liv. ; Tac. ; cum imaginum species ad nos adfluat, Cic. ; incautis amor, Ov. **b.** *to abound* (esp. with ABL.) : ubi effuse adfluunt opes, Liv. ; voluptatibus, Cic. ; Pl. ; Lucr.

adfor, *v.* adfātur.

adfore, adforem, *v.* adsum.

ad-formīdō, āre, *to begin to be afraid :* Pl.

ad-frīcō, cāre, cuī, ctum, *to rub against* (with DAT.). **1.** Lit. : Plin. **2.** Transf. : *to impart by rubbing :* Sen. Ep.

adfrictiō, ōnis, *f.* [adfricō], *a rubbing against :* Phaedr.

ad-fulgeō, fulgēre, fūlsī, *to shine on, beam on.* **1.** Lit. : non Venus adfulsit, Ov. ; Hor. **2.** Transf. : Magoni prima spes adfulsit, Liv.

ad-fundō, fundere, fūdī, fūsum, *to pour to* or *upon.* With ACC. and DAT. **1.** Lit. : Mosae os Rhenum Oceano adfundit, Tac. **2.** Transf. **a.** *to fling towards* or *upon :* equorum tria milia cornibus, Tac. **b.** *Mid. Part. : prostrate :* adfusaeque iacent tumulo, Ov.

ad-gemō, ere, *to groan at, lament :* Ov.

ad-gerō, gerere, gessī, gestum, *to bear* or

carry to. **1.** Lit. : eorum bona ad nos, Pl. ; his aquam, Pl. ; Verg. ; luta et limum adgerebant, Cic. ; Tac. **2.** Transf. : *to bring forward, lay to one's charge :* probra, Tac.

adgestus, ūs, *m.* [adgerō], *a carrying to, accumulation :* Tac.

ad-glomerō, āre, *to wind* (as on a ball), *join to.* Transf. : se lateri nostro, Verg.

ad-glūtinō, āre, *to glue* or *stick on.* **1.** Lit. : Cic. Ep. **2.** Transf. : Pl.

adgn-, *v.* agn-.

ad-gravēscō, ere, *to become heavier.* Transf. : morbus, Ter.

ad-gravō, āre, *to make heavier.* Transf. : *to make worse, aggravate :* quo (bello) si adgravatae res essent, Liv. ; dolorem, Curt.

ad-gredio, ere [Act. form of adgredior], *to go to, approach :* Pl.

ad-gredior, gredī, grēssus [gradior] (Pl. uses irī forms), *to go to, approach* (with ACC. or *ad*). **1.** Lit. **a.** ad hunc, Pl. ; hominem, Pl. **b.** *to approach with words,* etc. : Locustam adgrediar, Cic. ; Pl. ; legatos adgreditur, Sall. ; aliquem dictis, Verg. ; animos largitione, Tac. **c.** *to approach* (as an enemy), *attack :* navem, Caes. ; Hannibalem, Liv. ; Cic. ; Ov. **2.** Transf. : *to go to, enter upon* an undertaking, *undertake* (with ACC., *ad,* or *Inf.*) : causam, Cic. ; Verg., Liv., etc. ; ad petitionem consulatūs, Cic. ; ad dicendum, Cic. ; dicere, Cic. ; Lucr. ; Verg., etc.

ad-gregō, āre [grex], *to bring to the flock, gather, attach to.* **1.** Lit. : quibuscumque signis occurrerat, se adgregabat, Caes. ; si eodem ceteros naufragos adgregaverit, Cic. **2.** Transf. : se ad eorum amicitiam, Caes. ; filium ad patris interitum, Cic.

adgrēssiō, ōnis, *f.* [adgredior], *a going to.* Rhet. : (for prooemium) : *introduction to a speech :* Cic. ; also *a rhetorical syllogism :* Quint.

adgrēssus, a, um, *Part.* adgredior.

ad-haereō, haerēre, haesī, haesum, *to stick* or *cleave to, cling to, hang on.* **1.** Lit. With *ad, in* and ABL., ABL., or DAT. : tragula ad turrim, Caes. ; tela in tuis visceribus, Cic. ; Ov. ; fronte cuspis, Ov. ; tonsis sudor, Verg. ; saxis Galli, Liv. ; navis ancoris, Tac. **2.** Transf. **a.** Of place : Peloponnesus continenti, Liv. **b.** In gen. : in me omnia coniurationis tela adhaeserunt, Cic. **c.** Absol. *to hang on, stick* (sarcastic) : te extremum adhaesisse, Cic.

ad-haerēscō, ere [adhaereō], *to cling to, become attached to.* **1.** Lit. : ne quid emineret, ubi ignis adhaeresceret, Caes. **2.** Transf. **a.** With *ad,* DAT., or *in* and ABL. : ad quamcumque disciplinam, tamquam ad saxum, adhaerescunt, Cic. ; iustitiae honestatique, Cic. ; in his locis, Cic. Ep. **b.** Absol. *to stick, falter, hang fire :* oratio ita libere fluebat ut nunquam adhaeresceret, Cic.

adhaesiō, ōnis, *f.* [adhaereō], *a clinging :* atomorum inter se, Cic.

adhaesus, ūs, *m.* [adhaereō], *a clinging :* pulveris, Lucr.

Adherbal, alis, *m.* **I.** *a Numidian prince, s. of Micipsa.* **II.** *a Carthaginian general in the 2nd Punic War.*

ad-hibeō, ēre [habeō], *to hold a thing towards or to another, to put* or *apply to.* **1.** Lit.: odores ad deos, Cic. ; medicas adhibere manūs ad vulnera, Verg. ; alicui calcaria, Cic. ; manūs genibus, Ov. **2.** Transf. **a.** *to apply, bring, offer :* huc auris, Pl. ; auris ad veram rationem, Lucr. ; Verg. ; alicui voluptates, Cic. ; dis immortalibus cultūs, honores, preces, Cic. **b.** *to add* (rare) : ad maiorum morem hanc doctrinam, Cic. **c.** *to apply* or *use for some purpose, to make use of :* fidem et diligentiam in amicorum periculis, Cic. ; fraudem, dolum, artem, misericordiam, Cic. ; Caes. ; Tib. ; vim, Cic., Liv. ; patientiam, Liv. **d.** *to bring in, call in, summon, invite :* hos ad consilium, Caes. ; consularem, Cic. ; Verg., etc. ; Iovem testem, Cic. ; in *or* ad convivium, Cic., Nep. ; epulis, Verg. ; convivio, Liv. **e.** With *Adv. : to treat :* universos liberaliter, filium severius, Cic. Ep. With *Refl. Pron. : to behave oneself :* sic se adhibere in tantā potestate, Cic. Ep.

ad-hinniō, īre, *to neigh to.* **1.** Lit. : Ov. **2.** Transf. : ad illius orationem, Cic.

adhortātiō, ōnis, *f.* [adhortor], *a cheering on, encouragement :* Cic., Liv., etc.

adhortātor, ōris, *m.* [adhortor], *one who cheers on :* Liv. ; operis, Liv.

ad-hortor, ārī, *to cheer on to* something, *encourage :* Cic., Cat., Tac. ; me ad C. Rabirium defendendum, Cic. ; de re frumentariā Boios, Caes. ; in bellum, Tac. With *Juss. Subj.* (with *or* without *ut or ne*) : Ter., Cic., Liv.

ad-hūc, *adv. to this point.* **I.** Of Place. Only Transf. **a.** conveniunt adhuc utriusque verba, Pl. ; adhuc ea dixi, Cic. **b.** *to this extent :* Caesar erat adhuc impudens, Cic. Ep. ; Liv. **c.** *in addition to this, still further* (chiefly post-Aug.): addam minam adhuc, Pl. ; adhuc sublimia cures, Hor. Esp. with comparatives, *even, still :* Liv., Quint., etc. **II.** Of Time. **a.** *hitherto, until now* (rarely *until then*) : sicut adhuc fecerunt, Cic. ; Pl., etc. Freq. with usque *or* semper : morem qui usque adhuc est retentus, Cic. ; Pl. ; quod adhuc semper tacui, Cic. With *Part.* GEN. : ut adhuc locorum feci. Foll. by *dum :* adhuc dum mihi nullo loco deesse vis, nunquam te confirmare potuisti, Cic. Ep. ; Pl. With negatives : adhuc non venerunt, *not as yet*, Cic. ; nihil adhuc, *nothing as yet*, Cic. Ep. ; Pl. **b.** *still* (=etiam nunc) : adhuc de consuetudine exercitationis loquor, Cic. ; Pl., etc. Rarely=etiam tunc : regem est consecutus fluctuantem adhuc animo, Liv.

ad-iaceō, ēre, *to lie at* or *near, adjoin :* Tac. With DAT., ACC., or *ad :* Tuscus ager Romano, Liv. ; Ov. ; gentes quae mare illud adiacent, Nep. ; mare ad ostium Rhodani, Caes.

ad-iciō, icere, iēcī, iectum [iaciō]. **I.** *to throw to* or *at.* **1.** Lit. : telum in litus, Caes. ; Ov. ; laqueos funium ad saxa eminentia, Curt. **2.** Transf. : ad omnia vestra cupiditatis oculos, Cic. ; animum ad consilium, Liv. ; Ter. ; animum militi, Pl. ; oculum hereditati, Cic. **II.** *to add to.* **1.** Lit. : vallo loricam, Caes. ; legiones ad exercitum, Liv. **2.** Transf. : morem ritūsque sacrorum, Verg. ; Tac. ; ad bellicam laudem ingeni gloriam, Cic. ; aliquantum duci famae et auctoritatis, Liv. Of a speaker, *to add a further point* (with Acc. and *Inf.*) : Liv., Tac. Also with *Indir. Quest. :* Liv., Quint.

adiectiō, ōnis, *f.* [adiciō]. **I.** *a throwing to* or *on, an addition :* Romana res adiectione populi Albani aucta, Liv. **II.** *the permission of adding* (in *pl.*) : Tac. **III.** Archit. *an addition* (for strengthening) : Vitr. **IV.** Rhet. *repetition :* Quint.

adiectus, a, um, *Part.* adiciō.

adiectus, ūs, *m.* [adiciō], *an adding :* Lucr.

ad-igō, igere, ēgī, āctum [agō], (adāxint *Aor. Optat.* in Pl.), *to drive to, force to.* **1.** Lit. : pecore e vicis adacto, Caes. ; Pl. ; me fulmine ad umbras, Verg. Of wounds, *to inflict :* alte vulnus adactum, Verg. ; vulnus Varo adactum, Tac. Occ. *to hurl :* telum, Caes. **2.** Transf. : *to drive* or *force to* something (esp. against the will) : ad mortem, Tac. ; Ter. With *Inf. :* tua imago haec limina tendere adegit, Verg. ; Tac. N.B. **a.** cur non arbitrum adegeris Q. Roscium quaero, *compelled to submit to arbitration*, Cic. **b.** aliquem adigere ius iurandum, Caes., Cic., Liv. ; ad ius iurandum, Caes., Sall. ; iure iurando, Liv., Tac. ; *to put on oath.* **c.** in verba adigere, in verba ius iurandum adigere, *to force to swear allegiance to :* provinciam in sua verba ius iurandum adigebat, Caes. ; neque quemquam Batavum in verba Galliarum adegit, Tac. Absol. : universos adigit, *binds by oath*, Tac.

ad-imō, imere, ēmī, emptum [emō] (ademptsit, *Perf. Subj.* in Pl.), *to take to oneself, withdraw.* **1.** Lit. **a.** Good sense : istas compedes tibi, Pl. ; canibus vincula, Ov. **b.** Bad sense : exercitus adimendus fuit, Cic. ; arma militibus, Liv. **2.** Transf. : alicui vitam, somnum, libertatem, aditum litoris, Cic. ; Liv. ; Tac. Poet. with *Inf.* as obj. : adimam cantare severis, Hor.

adipātus, a, um [adeps], *fatty.* **1.** Lit. *Neut.* as Noun, **adipātum**, *pastry :* Juv. **2.** Transf. of style, *gross :* Cic.

ad-ipiscor, ipisci, eptus [apiscor], *to come up to, reach.* **1.** Lit. : fugientis Gallos adepti ceciderunt, Liv. ; Pl. **2.** Transf. : *to attain, get, obtain :* summos honores, sapientiam, Cic. ; Ter. ; celeritatem, victoriam, Caes. ; ius nostrum, Liv. With GEN. : Galba rerum adeptus est, Tac. With *ut :* adepti sunt ut ceteros dies festos agitare possent, Cic. Used passively (esp. in *Perf. Part.*) : Pl., Cic., Tac., etc.

aditiō, ōnis, *f.* [adeō], *a going to :* quid tibi hanc aditio est ? Pl.

aditus, a, um, *Part.* adeō.

aditus, ūs, *m.* [adeō], *a going to, approach.* **1.** Lit. **a.** urbes uno aditu captae, Cic. ; Lucr. ; Verg. **b.** *permitted approach, access, admittance :* aditus in id sacrarium non est viris, Cic. ; Hor. ; Liv. Hence *means of access, audience :* aditum petentibus non dabat, Nep. **c.** Concrete : *approach, entrance, avenue :* si aditūs cognovisset, Caes. ; in primo aditu templi, Cic. ; Ov. ;

Liv.; ad arcem, Liv. **2.** Transf.: ad ea conanda, Caes.; ad consulatum, Cic.; sermonis, Caes.; laudis, Cic.

ad-iŭdĭcō, āre, *to adjudge, award as arbitrator* (opp. abiūdicō). **1.** Lit.: regnum Ptolemaeo, Cic.; Caes.; Hor.; Liv. **2.** Transf.: *to ascribe, attribute to :* mihi salutem imperi, Cic. Ep.

adiŭĕrō, *v.* adiuvō.

adiŭmentum, ī, *n.* [adiuvō], *a means of aid, help :* consulatūs, petitionis, Cic.; esse alicui magno adiumento ad victoriam, Cic.; mihi honoribus, Cic.; Ov.

adiŭnctĭō, ōnis, *f.* [adiungō]. **I.** *a joining to, union :* verborum, Cic. **II.** *an addition :* virtutis, Cic. **III.** Rhet. *repetition :* Cic.

adiŭnctor, ōris, *m.* [adiungō], *one who joins or unites :* Cic. Ep.

adiŭnctus, a, um. **I.** *Part.* adiungō. **II.** Adj. *connected with :* quae propiora huius causae et adiunctiora sunt, Cic. **III.** *Neut. pl.* as Noun. Rhet. *collateral circumstances :* Cic.

ad-iungō, iungere. iūnxī, iūnctum, *to yoke or harness to.* **1.** Lit.: tauros aratro, Tib.; Hor.; feras, Lucr. **2.** Transf. **a.** Of persons and material things : *to bind, attach to :* beluas humano corpori, Cic.; Pl.; Verg.; Ciliciam ad imperium, Cic.; urbem in societatem, Liv.; sibi aliquem (beneficio), Ter., Tac. **b.** Of immaterial things : fidem rebus, Cic.; animus ad studium, Cic.; suspicionem ad praedam, Cic. **c.** Occ. *to add* (a new thought, etc.): haec quoque opportunitas adiungatur, Cic.; quod cum dicerem, illud adiunxi, Cic. Ep.; Nep.; Verg.

ad-iūrō, āre. **I.** *to swear to, confirm by oath.* With Acc., Acc. and *Inf.*, or *ut :* Pl., Cic., Ov., etc. With Acc., or *per* and Acc., of the thing by which ono swears : adiuro Stygii caput fontis, Verg.; per omnis deos adiuro ut . . ., Pl. **II.** *to swear to in addition :* ut praeter ius iurandum haec adiurarent, Liv.

adiŭtābilis, e, adj. *helping :* Pl.

adiŭtō, āre [freq. adiuvō], *to help :* Pl., Ter., Lucr. [Fr. *aider.*]

adiŭtor, ōris, *m.* [adiuvō], *a helper.* **a.** ad me restituendum, ad praedam, Cic.; honoris, Cic.; Ter.; Liv. **b.** *an assistant, adjutant :* quaestori Fulvium adiutorem submiserat, Caes.; Cic. Ep.; Liv., etc. **c.** *a subordinate actor :* Hor.

adiŭtōrium, ī, *n. help :* Sen. Ep., Quint.

adiŭtrix, īcis, *f.* [adiūtor], *a female helper :* Messana tuorum adiutrix scelerum, Cic.; Pl.; Ter.; legiones adiutrices, *raised in the provinces to strengthen the regulars,* Tac.

adiŭtus, a, um, *Part.* adiuvō.

ad-iuvō, iuvāre, iūvī, iūtum (iuvāvī, Sall., iuerō *or* iūrō=iūverō, Enn., iuerit, Ter. =iūverit), *to give help to, assist.* **1.** Lit.: Pl., Cic., etc. : si nihil ad colendam virtutem litteris adiuvarentur, Cic.; aliquem ad bellum, Liv. **2.** Transf. : *to help, encourage, foster, enhance :* maerorem orationis lacrimis suis, Cic.; clamore Romani adiuvant militem suum, Liv.; ignem, Liv.; quam ad spem multum eos adiuvabat quod Liger ex nivibus crēverat, Caes.; benignitatem, Liv.; formam curā, Ov.

adj-, *v.* adi-.

ad-lābor, lābī, lāpsus, *to slip to or towards, glide to :* umor, Cic.; angues ex occulto, Liv. With Acc. or Dat. : fama adlabitur auris, Verg.; viro sagitta, Verg. With Abl., *glide with :* adlabi classibus aequor, Verg.

ad-labōrō, āre. **I.** *to toil at :* Hor. **II.** *to add to by toil :* simplici myrto nihil adlabores, Hor.

ad-lacrĭmō, āre, *to shed tears at :* Verg.

adlāpsus, a, um, *Part.* adlābor.

adlāpsus, ūs, *m.* [adlābor], *a gliding to :* serpentium, Hor.

ad-lātrō, āre. Lit.: *to bark at.* Transf.: *to rail at :* Africani magnitudinem, Liv.; Mart.

adlaudābilis, e, *praiseworthy :* Pl.

ad-laudō, āre, *to praise much :* Pl.

adlēctĭō, ōnis, *f. promotion, advancement in rank, co-option :* Inscr.

ad-lectō, āre [freq. adliciō], *to allure, entice :* Cic.

adlēctor, ōris, *m.* **I.** *one who promotes, elects, co-opts :* Inscr. **II.** *a tax-collector :* Inscr.

adlēctus, a, um. *Part.* I. adlegō. **II.** adliciō.

adlēgātĭō, ōnis, *f.* [adlēgō], *a despatching, mission :* Cic.

ad-lēgō, āre. **1.** Lit.: *to despatch on private business, commission, depute* (Freq. in Pl.; elsewhere rare) : alium isti rei adlegabo, Pl.; homines nobilis adlegat iis qui peterent, Cic.; adlegati, *deputies,* Cic. **2.** Transf.: *to adduce :* exemplum, Plin. Ep.; (legati) munera preces mandata regis adlegant, Tac.

ad-lĕgō, legere, lēgī, lēctum, *to gather to, elect to* a body: suffragio Druidum adlegitur, Caes.; augures de plebe, Liv.; aliquem in senatum, inter patricios, Suet.

adlĕvāmentum, ī, *n.* [adlevō], *a means of relieving :* Cic.

adlĕvātĭō, ōnis, *f.* [adlevō]. **1.** Lit.: *a raising up :* Quint. **2.** Transf.: *an alleviating, relief :* Cic.

ad-lĕvō, āre, *to lift up, raise.* **1.** Lit.: laqueis adlevati, Sall.; cubito artūs, Ov.; manum, supercilia, Quint. **2.** Transf. **a.** *to lighten, alleviate, relieve :* aliquem, Pl.; onus, sollicitudines, Cic.; corpus, Cic. Ep., Ov. **b.** *to diminish the force of, weaken :* adversariorum confirmatio adlevatur, Cic.; Tac.

adlicĕfacĭō, ere [adliciō, faciō], *to allure :* Sen. Ep.; Suet.

ad-lĭcĭō, licere, lexī, lectum [laciō], *to draw to, attract.* **1.** Lit.: ferrum ad se, Cic. **2.** Transf.: *to entice, allure :* exsules damnatosque ad se, Caes.; Pl.; ad misericordiam, Cic.; mentis hominum dicendo, Cic.; comibus oculis amorem, Ov.; Gallias, Tac.

ad-līdō, līdere, līsī, līsum [laedō], *to dash one thing against another.* **1.** Lit.: (remigum) pars ad scopulos adlisa, Caes.; aliquid trabi, Lucr. **2.** Transf.: Cic. Ep.

ad-lĭgō, āre, *to bind to or up.* **1.** Lit.: Pl.; aliquem ad statuam, Cic.; oculis adligatus, Cic.; vulnus, Liv. **2.** Transf. **a.** *to bind fast, restrain :* navis ancora, Verg.; torpor artūs adligat, Ov. **b.** In moral sense, *to bind, oblige :* caput suum,

Pl. ; beneficio adligari, Cic. ; foedere adligata civitas, Liv. ; adligare se, *to make oneself responsible* (with GEN. or ABL.) : hic furti se adligat, Ter. ; ne se scelere adliget, Cic.

ad-lĭnō, linere, lēvī, litum, *to besmear.* Transf. : nulla nota his sententiis adlini (potest), Cic. ; Hor. ; Sen. Ep.

adlīsus, a, um, *Part.* adllīdō.

adlocūtĭō, ōnis, *f.* [adloquor]. **I.** *a speaking to :* Plin. Ep. **II.** *an address of consolation :* Cat.

adlocūtus, a, um, *Part.* adloquor.

adloquium, ī, *n.* [adloquor], *an address :* adloquio leni perlicere homines, Liv. ; adloquio firmare milites, Tac. ; Ov.

ad-loquor, loquī, locūtus, *to speak to, address :* aliquem. Pl., Cic., Verg., etc. ; adloquendos milites ratus, Liv. ; Suet.

ad-lŭbēscō, ere [lubet], *to begin to please :* Pl.

ad-lūceō, lūcēre, lūxī. **I.** *to shine in addition :* Sen. Ep. **II.** *to shine upon.* Transf. : tibi fortuna faculam lucrificam adlucere vult, Pl.

ad-lūdĭō, āre, *to play, play with :* Pl.

ad-lūdō, lūdere, lūsī, lūsum, *to play with, joke, jest* (esp. post-Aug.). Absol., or with *ad* or DAT. **1.** Lit. : Galba adludens varie, Cic. ; nec plura adludens, Verg. ; Cicero Trebatio adludens, Quint. **2.** Transf. : undae, Ov. ; mare litoribus adludit, Cic. With Acc. : omnia quae fluctūs adludebant, Cat.

ad-luō, luere, luī, *to wash just against :* fluvius latera haec adluit, Cic. ; Verg. ; (Massilia) barbariae fluctibus adluitur, Cic.

adluvĭēs, ēī, *f.* [adluō], *a pool formed by the overflowing of a river :* Liv.

adluvĭō, ōnis, *f.* [adluō]. **I.** *an overflowing :* App. **II.** *alluvial land* (in *pl.*) : Cic.

ad-mātūrō, āre, *to make ripe.* hence *to hasten, expedite :* defectionem civitatis, Caes.

admēnsus, a, um, *Part.* admētior.

ad-mētĭor, mētīrī, mēnsus, *to measure out to :* Cato, Cic.. Suet.

Admētus, ī, *m.* **I.** *a king of Pherae in Thessaly, husband of Alcestis.* **II.** *a king of the Molossi, protector of Themistocles.*

ad-migrō, āre, *to move one's abode to,* hence *to be added to :* Pl.

adminicŭlor, ārī (**adminiculō,** āre, Varr., Plin.), *to prop up* (of vines) : Cic.

adminiculum, ī, *n.* [*ad* and *-mineō* seen in immineō, etc.], lit.. *a projection towards ; a prop, support.* **1.** Lit. : vitis claviculis adminicula apprehendunt, Cic. **2.** Transf.: *support :* nullis adminiculis, sed, ut dicitur, Marte nostro, Cic. ; Pl. ; id senectuti suae adminiculum fore, Liv. ; Tac.

administer, trī, *m.* and **administra,** ae, *f.* **1.** Lit. : *a servant, assistant :* Caes., Cic. **2.** Transf.: audaciae, Cic. ; sunt artes administrae comitesque virtutis, Cic.

administrātĭō, ōnis, *f.* [administrō]. **1.** Lit.: *service, assistance :* Cic. **2.** Transf. **a.** *direction, management :* belli, Caes. ; rerum, mundi, Cic. **b.** In *pl. business* (rare) : portūs, Caes. ; officiis et administrationibus, Tac.

administrātor, ōris, *m.* [administrō], *a manager :* Cic.

ad-ministrō, āre. **1.** Lit.: *to attend upon* (with DAT.) : Pl. **2.** Transf.: *to manage, direct :* navem, classem, imperia, res, Caes. ; bellum, provinciam, rem publicam, iudicia, Cic. Absol. (*cf.* colloq. *to manage*) : milites non sine periculo administrare poterant, Sall.

admīrābilis, e, *adj.* [admīror]. **I.** *worthy to be admired, wonderful :* admirabilis in dicendo vir, Cic. Comp. : Cic., Liv. **II.** *astonishing, surprising, paradoxical :* admirabile genus (causae), Cic. Comp. : Liv.

admīrābilĭtās, ātis, *f. wonderfulness :* Cic.

admīrābilĭter, *adv.* **I.** *admirably:* Cic. **II.** *paradoxically :* dicere, Cic.

admīrandus, a, um [admīror] *to be wondered at :* Cic., Verg., etc.

admīrātĭō, ōnis, *f.* [admīror]. **I.** *a wondering at, wonder, admiration :* Cic. With *Obj.* GEN. : copiose sapienterque dicentis, Cic. ; Liv. ; virtus admirationis plus habet quam gloriae, Cic. ; in *pl. :* Cic. **II.** *astonishment, surprise :* hoc mihi maximam admirationem movet, Cic. With *Obj.* GEN. : divitiarum, Cic. ; ancipitis sententiae, Liv.

admīrātor, ōris, *m. an admirer :* Phaedr., Quint.

ad-mīror, ārī. **I.** *to wonder at, admire :* ingenium tuum, Cic. ; Verg. **II.** *to be surprised at.* With Acc. : Cic. With Acc. and *Inf. :* Cic., Nep. With *quod* clause : Cic. Ep. With *Indir. Quest. :* Ter., Cic., Hor.

ad-mĭsceō, miscēre, miscuī, mixtum, *to add to by mingling, admix, blend.* **1.** Lit. : genus radicis admixtum lacte, Caes. ; Cic. ; aquae (DAT.) admixtum calorem, Cic. ; Ov. **2.** Transf. **a.** his (DAT.) Antonianos milites, Caes. ; Verg. **b.** *to involve, implicate :* ne me admisceas, Ter. ; ad id consilium admiscear ? Cic.

admissārĭus, a, um [admittō], *sc.* equus, *a stallion.* Transf. : Pl., Cic.

admisse for **admīsisse,** *v.* admittō.

admissĭō, ōnis, *f.* [admittō], *a letting in, interview, audience :* Suet. In *pl. :* Plin. Pan.

admissum, ī, *n.* [admittō],*a fault, crime,* Cic., Liv., Tac.

admissus, a, um, *Part.* admittō.

ad-mittō, mittere, mīsī, missum, *to let come or go to, admit.* (With DAT., *ad,* or *in* and Acc.) **1.** Lit. **a.** te ad meas capsas, Cic. ; Pl. ; legatum in cubiculum, Cic. ; Ov. **b.** *to grant an audience :* admissus est nemo, Cic. ; Verg., etc. **c.** *to let go* (of a horse), *put to a gallop :* equites admissis equis refugerunt, Caes. ; Liv. ; Ov. Of hair or water, *to let flow :* Ov. **2.** Transf.: *to allow to come, admit.* **a.** ad consilium, Cic. ; ad colloquium, Caes. ; ad honores, Nep. **b.** Of words, etc.: pacis mentionem auribus, Liv. ; aliquid ad animum, Liv. ; precationem, Liv. **c.** Of an act, etc., *to let it be done, permit :* quod semel admissum coerceri non potest, Cic. ; litem, Cic. **d.** In augury, *to allow, be propitious :* ubi aves non admissisent, Liv., Pl. **e.** *to let come to oneself, become guilty of, commit* (often with *in* and Acc. of *Refl. Pron.*) : quantum in se facinus admisissent, Caes. ;

Pl. ; Cic., etc. ; maleficium, flagitium, fraudem, decus, Cic. ; Ter. ; Liv.

admixtiŏ, ōnis, *f.* [admisceō], *an admixture :* Cic.

admixtus, a, um, *Part.* admisceō.

admoderātē, *adv.* [admoderor], *suitably, appropriately :* Lucr.

ad-moderor, ārī, *to keep within limits, restrain :* Pl.

ad-modum, *adv.* [modus]. Lit.: *up to the measure.* Can usually be translated by *quite.* **A.** Of degree. **a.** With *adj.*, *part.* (often follows its word): admodum magnis itineribus, Caes. ; admodum pauci, Cic. ; pauci admodum, Liv. ; natio admodum dedita religionibus, Caes. ; Ter., etc. Esp. with words denoting age : admodum adulescens, Caes. ; puer admodum, Liv. ; Pl. **b.** With *adv. :* admodum raro, Cic. ; obscure admodum, Cic. ; Ter. ; Liv. **c.** With *verb :* Pl., Cic. Ep. **B.** *fully, completely, quite.* **a.** Of numbers : noctu turres admodum CXX excitantur, Caes. Also *just about :* sex milia hostium caesa, quinque admodum Romanorum, Liv. **b.** With negatives, *at all :* alter non multum, alter nihil admodum scripti reliquit, Cic. ; Pl.; equestris pugna nulla admodum fuit, Liv. **C.** In answers, *exactly, quite, just so ;* Pl., Ter.

ad-moeniŏ, īre, *to build a wall against, besiege :* oppidum, Pl.

ad-mōlior, īrī, *to put a mass against* or *to.* **A.** Trans. **1.** Lit.: *to pile up :* Curt. **2.** Transf.: *to lay violently on :* sacro manūs, Pl. **B.** Intrans. : *to struggle to :* ad nidum, Pl.

ad-moneŏ, ēre. **I.** *to bring to another's mind, remind, advise, warn.* With Acc. of person and various constructions of the thing. **a.** Gen. : aliquem foederis, Liv., Cic., etc. **b.** *de :* ut de doctrinae studiis admoneamur, Cic. **c.** Acc. (us. *Neut. Pron.*): illud te esse admonitum volo, Cic. ; Ter. **d.** Acc. and *Inf. :* admonuisti aliquod dictum in petitionem tuam dici potuisse, Cic. ; Liv. **e.** *Indir. Quest. :* meus me sensus, quanta vis fraterni sit amoris, admonet, Cic. Ep. **f.** *Subj.* (with or without *ut* or *ne*) admonebat me res ut . . ., Cic. ; Caes. ; Tac. **g.** *Inf.* (esp. poet. and post-Aug.): ut eum suae libidines facere admonebant, Cic. ; easdem decedere campis admonuit, Verg. **h.** *ad* and *Gerund. :* ad thesaurum reperiendum, Cic. **II.** *to admonish* by forcible means : telo biiugos, Verg. ; liberos verberibus, Sen. **III.** *to bring to one's own mind, recall* (with Acc. or Gen. of thing) : nomen, Ov. ; dominae, Tib.

admonitiŏ, ōnis, *f.* [admoneō], *a bringing to mind.* **I.** *admonition* (friendly or otherwise) : Cic. **II.** *a reminding :* tanta vis admonitionis inest in locis, Cic. ; Quint.

admonitor, ōris, *m.* (Cic., Ov.) and **admonitrix**, īcis, *f.* (Pl.) [admoneō], *one who admonishes.*

admonitū, Abl. *Sing.* [admoneō], *at the suggestion of :* Cic., Ov., Tac., etc.

admonitum, ī, *n.* [admoneō], *an admonition, suggestion :* Cic.

ad-mordeŏ, mordēre, mōrsum (no perf.), *to bite at.* **1.** Lit.: Verg. **2.** Transf.: *to bleed one* (of money): Pl.

admōtiŏ, ōnis, *f.* [admoveō], *a moving to, an applying :* Cic.

admōtus, a, um, *Part.* admoveō.

ad-moveŏ, movēre, mōvī, mōtum (admōram, admōrim, etc., for admōveram, admōverim, etc. : Verg., Ov.), *to move to* (i.e. into contact with). **1.** Lit. **a.** scalas muris, Caes. ; copias in locum, Liv. **b.** *to move near to :* fasciculum ad narīs, Cic. ; exercitum propius urbem, Cic. ; Hannibalem admotum altaribus, Liv. ; pecus aris, Verg. **2.** Transf.: *to bring to, apply to, lay on.* **a.** manūs vectigalibus, Cic. ; manūs nocentibus, Liv. ; Ov. **b.** Of mind or senses : mentis vestras, non solum auris, ad vocem admovete, Cic. ; Ter. ; Hor. ; spes cupiditati admota, Liv. ; Ov. **c.** *to promote, advance :* Tac. **d.** *to bring on :* leti horas, Lucr.

ad-mūgiŏ, īre, *to low to :* Ov.

admurmurātiŏ, ōnis, *f. a murmuring at :* Cic. In *pl.* : Cic. Ep.

ad-murmurŏ, āre, *to murmur at* (approvingly or disapprovingly) : quam valde universi admurmurarint, Cic. Also *impers. :* Cic.

ad-mutilŏ, āre, *to clip close.* Transf.: *to fleece one* (of money): Pl.

ad-nectŏ, nectere, nexuī, nexum, *to tie* or *bind to.* **1.** Lit.: ad linguam stomachus adnectitur, Cic. ; Liv. **2.** Transf.: rebus praesentibus adnectit futuras, Cic.

adnexus, a, um, *Part.* adnectō.

adnexus, ūs, *m.* [adnectō], *a tying to, connexion :* Tac.

adnisus, a, um, *Part.* adnītor.

ad-nītor, nītī, nīsus or nixus, *to press oneself against, lean against.* **1.** Lit.: natura ad aliquod tamquam adminiculum adnititur, Cic. ; hasta adnixa columnae, Verg. **2.** Transf.: *to take pains about, strive with a view to something :* Sall., Liv. With *de* or *pro :* Cic. Ep. ; Liv. With *ut, ne, ad* and *Gerund. :* omni spe adnisi sunt ut . . ., Liv. ; Sall. ; ad ea patranda omnis civitas adnitebatur, Sall. ; Liv. With *Inf. :* Liv., Tac.

adnixus, a, um, *Part.* adnītor.

ad-nŏ, nāre, *to swim towards, to,* or *near.* **1.** Lit.: Hor. With Acc. : navīs adnare, Caes. With Dat. : Verg., Tac. **2.** Transf.: ad urbem : Cic.

adnotātiŏ, ōnis, *f.* [adnotō], *a comment, remark :* Plin. Ep.

ad-notŏ, āre, *to comment on.* **1.** Lit.: liber adnotabatur, Plin. Ep. ; Quint. **2.** Transf.: *to observe, note :* Plin. Ep., Tac., Suet.

ad-numerŏ, āre. **I.** *to count out to, pay.* **1.** Lit.: Pl., Ter., Cic. **2.** Transf.: verba, Cic. **II.** *to reckon along with, add to.* With Dat.: his libris adnumerandi sunt sex de re publicā, Cic. ; Ov. ; Tac. With *in* and Abl.: in grege adnumeror, Cic. ; Ov.

ad-nūntiŏ, āre, *to bring news, proclaim :* Curt.

ad-nuŏ, nuere, nuī, nūtum. **I.** *to nod at* or *to :* simul ac adnuisset, Cic. ; Pl. ; Verg., etc. **II.** *to nod assent to, show approval of.* **1.** Lit.: Pl., Ter. With Acc. of thing : id quoque toto capite adnuit, Cic. **2.** Transf. **a.** *to assent to, favour :* adnue

coeptis (DAT.), Verg. **b.** *to grant, promise :*
with ACC. of thing and DAT. of person :
caeli quibus adnuis aroem, Verg.; Hor.;
Liv. With ACC. and *Inf. :* Pl., Liv. With
Inf. : Verg. **III.** *to designate by a nod*
(rare) : quos iste adnuerat, Cic.
ad-nŭtō, āre [*freq.* adnuō], *to nod often, nod*
to : Pl.
(1) ad-oleō, olēre, olēvī, ultum [root of alō],
to cause to grow, magnify. Transf.: of
ritual acts, *to pile up on the altar* or *to pile*
up the altar with : verbenasque adole et
tura, Verg.; Iunoni iussos honores, Verg.;
altaria donis, Lucr.; cruore captivo aras,
Tac. Perh. also *to burn* (fr. burnt sacrifices
or adoleo 2) : stipulae adolentur, Ov.
(2) ad-oleō, ēre, *to give out an odour, to smell :*
Pl.
adolēscēns, etc., *v.* adulēscēns, etc.
ad-olēscō, olēscere, olēvī (adolēsse for ado-
lēvisse, Ov.) [adoleō], *to grow up.* **1.** Lit.:
cum liberi adoleverint, Cic.; Pl.; aetas,
Lucr., Verg. **2.** Transf. **a.** *to grow, in-*
crease : cupiditas agendi, Cic.; ingenium,
Sall.; ver, Tac. **b.** *to be piled up with* or
perh. *to be scented with* (cf. adoleō, 2) :
Panchaeis adolescunt ignibus arae, Verg.
Adōnis, is or idis (in Pl. **Adōneus**, eī,
trisyl.) *m.* (Acc. Adōnidem or Adōnim ;
Voc. Adōni), *s. of Cinyras, king of Cyprus,*
loved by Venus on account of his great beauty.
adopertus, a, um [operiō], *covered up.* **1.**
Lit.: capite adoperto, Liv. With *Instr.*
ABL.: purpureo adopertus amictu, Verg.;
aether nubibus, Ov.; lumina somno, Ov.
2. Transf.: *closed up :* foribus adoper-
tis, Suet.
ad-opinor, ārī, *to conjecture further :* Pl.
adoptātiō, ōnis, *f.* [adoptō], *the adopting of a*
child : Cic., Sall.
adoptiō, ōnis, *f.* [adoptō], *a taking of one in the*
place of a child (by fictitious purchase),
adoption : filium in adoptione D. Silano
emancipavit, Cic.; duobus datis in adoptionem, Liv.; asciri per adoptionem, Tac.
adoptivus, a, um [adoptō], *made or acquired*
by adoption. **1.** Lit.: in haec adoptiva
venisti, Cic.; nobilitas, Ov. **2.** Transf.:
of plants : Ov.
ad-optō, āre. **I.** *to take to oneself by choice,*
select : eum sibi patronum adoptarant,
Cic.; Pl.; Etruscas Turnus adoptat opes,
Ov. **II.** Leg. *to adopt as a child* or
grandchild. **1.** Lit.: hunc minorem
Scipionem a Paulo adoptavit, Cic.; Pl.;
Tac.; in regnum, Sall. **2.** Transf.. of
plants, *to graft :* ramum ramus adoptet, Ov.
ador, oris and ōris, *n.* [edō], *a kind of grain :*
Hor.
adōreus, a, um [ador], *of spelt :* liba, Verg.
As Noun **adōrea**, ae, *f. a gift of corn* (as the
reward of valour). **1.** Lit.: Pl. **2.**
Transf.: ille dies qui primus almā
risit adoreā, Hor.
ad-orior, orīrī, ortus (2nd and 3rd pers. *Pres.*
Indic. us. 4th conjug.). Lit.: *to rise up at.*
I. *to accost, address :* Ter. **II.** Esp. of
sudden and unexpected action, *to attack,*
assault. **1.** Lit.: impeditos adori-
ebantur, Caes.; inermem tribunum gladiis,
Cic.; urbem vi, Liv. **2.** Transf. **a.**
fratrem iurgio, Ter.; aliquem minis, Tac.

b. *to venture upon, set about.* With ACC.:
Ov. With *Inf. :* Cic., Ov., Liv., etc.
adōrnō, āre. **I.** *to get ready, equip, fit out.* **1.**
Lit.: navis onerarias, Caes.; maris
classibus et praesidiis, Cic.; Liv. Of an
investiture : flaminem insigni veste, Liv.
2. Transf.: *to prepare :* nuptias, Pl.;
accusationem, Cic. **II.** *to put an orna-*
ment on, decorate. **1.** Lit.: Curt. **2.**
Transf.: adornata verbis, Tac.
ad-ōrō, āre. **1.** Lit.: *to speak to, address,*
make a plea to : sanctum aidus adorat,
Verg. **2.** Transf. **a.** *to entreat :* Iunonis numen, Verg.; Ov.; Liv. **b.** *to ask for*
in prayer. With ACC., or *ut* and *Subj. :*
cum pacem deum (GEN.) adorasset, Liv.;
Ov. **c.** *to worship, reverence :* Phoebum
taciturnus adorat, Ov.; Tac.
adortus, a, um, *Part.* adorior.
adp–, *v.* app–.
ad-quiēscō, quiēscere, quiēvī, quiētum, *to*
repose or rest. **1.** Lit. **a.** In gen.: Pl.,
Cic. Ep.; somno, Curt. **b.** *to rest in*
death : anno adquievit septuagesimo, Nep.
HIC ADQUIESCIT in epitaphs. **2.** Transf.
a. Of things : *to remain undisturbed :*
Liv. **b.** Of feeling : *to find rest or pleasure*
in, acquiesce in : in te uno, Cic. Ep.; P.
Clodi morte, Cic.; cui velut oraculo ad-
quiescebat, Sall.
ad-quīrō, quirere, quisivī, quisitum [quaerō],
to procure or obtain in addition : Cic., Verg.,
etc.
ad-rādō, rādere, rāsī, rāsum, *to shave close.*
1. Lit.: Pl., Hor. **2.** Transf.: Plin.
Ep.
Adrastēa, or **Adrastia**, ae, *f. d. of Jupiter*
and Necessity, the goddess who rewards men
for their deeds.
Adrastus, ī, *m. a king of Argos, father-in-law*
of Tydeus and Polynices ; **Adrastēus**, a,
um ; **Adrastis**, idis, *f. a female descendant*
of Adrastus, esp. *Argia, d. of Adrastus.*
adrēctus, a, um. **I.** *Part.* adrigō. **II.** *Adj.*
steep, precipitous. Comp. : Liv.
ad-rēpo, rēpere, rēpsī, *to creep towards, steal*
upon. **1.** Lit.: Varr. **2.** Transf.:
sensim ad amicitiam, Cic.; in spem, Hor.
With DAT.: animis muliercularum, Tac.
adreptus, a, um, *Part.* adripiō.
Adria, etc., *v.* Hadria, etc.
ad-rīdeō, rīdēre, rīsī, rīsum, *to smile upon*
approvingly (opp. derideo). *Absol.,* with
DAT., or more rarely with ACC. **1.** Lit.:
leniter adridens, Cic.; Pl.; Ov.; vix notis
familiariter adridere, Liv.; Pl.; Hor.;
video quid adriseris, Cic. **2.** Transf.
a. *to be favourable :* cum tempestas adridet,
Lucr. **b.** *to be pleasing* (opp. displiceo).
With DAT.: Cic. Ep., Hor.
ad-rigō, rigere, rēxī, rēctum [regō], *to set*
upright, raise. **1.** Lit.: auris, Pl., Verg.,
etc.; comas, Verg.; adrectis luminibus,
with staring eyes, Verg. **1.** Transf.: *to*
rouse, excite : eos oratione, Sall.; animos,
spes, Verg.; adrectā omni civitate, Tac.;
animos ad bellandum, Liv.
ad-ripiō, ripere, ripuī, reptum [rapiō]. **I.**
to snatch to oneself. **1.** Lit.: *to seize*
hastily or *violently, lay hold of :* aliquem
medium, Ter., Liv.; ipsum pendentem,
Verg.; arma, Caes., Liv.; Ov.; scuta,

Tac.; manu adreptum, Liv.; aliquem barbā, Pl.; Ov. **2.** T r a n s f.: *to seize upon.* **a.** Of persons or material things: patrem familias ex aliquo circulo, Cic.; cohortis, Liv. **b.** Of immaterial things: male dictum ex trivio, Cic.; impedimentum pro occasione, Liv. **c.** Of the mind: *to grasp quickly:* Cic., Nep. **II.** J u d i c.: *to seize.* **1.** L i t. **a.** *to arrest:* adreptus a viatore, Liv.; Cic. **b.** *to bring into court:* ad quaestionem, Cic. **2.** T r a n s f.: *to arraign, satirise:* Hor.

ad-rōdō, rōdere, rōsī, rōsum, *to gnaw* or *nibble at.* **1.** L i t.: Liv. **2.** T r a n s f.: rem publicam, Cic.

adrogāns, antis. **I.** *Part.* adrogō. **II.** *Adj. assuming, arrogant.* **1.** L i t.: Caes., Cic. *Comp.* and *Sup.:* Quint. **2.** T r a n s f.: consilium, dictum, Cic.; crudelitas, Cic. Ep.; Tac.

adroganter, *adv. arrogantly, haughtily:* Caes., Cic. *Comp.:* Suet.

adrogantia, ae, *f.* [adrogō]. **I.** *an assumption, presumption:* ingeni atque eloquentiae, Cic.; sine adrogantiā gravis, Cic.; Tac. **II.** *haughtiness:* licentiam adrogantiamque militum reprehendit, Caes.; Liv.; Tac.

ad-rogō, āre. P o l i t. and L e g. **1.** L i t. **a.** *to put a question to:* aliquem, Pl. **b.** *to associate* (an officer) *with another:* consuli dictatorem, Liv. **2.** T r a n s f. **a.** *to adjudge to, confer upon* (opp. abrogo): Hor. **b.** *to assume, arrogate to oneself, claim* (as by right): mihi nihil adrogo, Cic.; Hor.; Tac.

adrōsus, a, um, *Part.* adrōdō.

adsc-, *v.* asc-.

adsecla, *v.* adsecula.

adsectātiō, ōnis, *f.* [adsector], *an (assiduous, respectful) attendance* (e.g. of clients): in petitionibus, Cic.

adsectātor, ōris, *m.* [adsector], *an attendant, escort:* Cic.

ad-sector, ārī, *to follow constantly after, attend on* (esp. of friends of candidates): Cic., Hor., Tac.

adsecula, ae, *m.* [adsequor], *a follower* (alw. contemptuously), *a hanger-on:* legatorum, Cic.

adsēnsiō, ōnis, *f.* [adsentior], *assent, approval:* Cic., Plin. Ep. In *pl.:* *expressions of approval:* Cic. P h i l o s.: *belief in the reality of sensible appearances:* Cic.

adsēnsor, ōris, *m.* [adsentior], *one who agrees with:* Cic. Ep.

adsēnsus, a, um, *Part.* adsentior.

adsēnsus, ūs, *m.* [adsentior]. **I.** *assent, approval:* adsensu omnium dicere, Cic.; Liv., etc.; cum ingenti adsensu, Liv. In *pl.:* Ov., Tac. **II.** P h i l o s.: *acceptance of the reality of sensible appearances:* Cic. **III.** *an echo:* Verg.

adsentātiō, ōnis, *f.* [adsentor], *assent.* Us. in bad sense: *complaisance:* Pl., Cic. In *pl.:* Cic., Liv.

adsentātiuncula, ae, *f.* [*dim.* adsentātiō], *petty flattery:* Pl., Cic. Ep.

adsentātor, ōris, *m.* (and **adsentātrix,** īcis, *f.*: Pl.), *a flatterer:* Cic., Hor., Liv.

adsentātōriē, *adv. in a flattering manner:* Cic. Ep.

ad-sentiō, sentīre, sēnsī, sēnsum (rarer than dep. adsentior), *to assent to, agree with:* Pl., Verg., Tac. With Acc. of *Neut. Pron.:* Pl. With DAT.: alicui, Cic. Ep., Liv.; precibus, Ov. *Pass. Impers.:* Cic. Ep.

ad-sentior, sentīrī, sēnsus [sentiō], *to assent to, agree with, approve:* Sall., Suet. With DAT.: alicui, Cic.; sententiae, Cic. Ep.; partibus dividundis, Liv. With Acc. of *Neut. Pron.* or *Adj.:* Pl.; aliquid alicui, Cic.

adsentor, ārī [euph. for adsēnsor, fr. adsentior], *to assent always.* **1.** L i t. **a.** In gen.: Ter; aliquid, Ter.; aliquid alicui, Ter., Cic.; alicui, Pl., Cic. **b.** *to flatter:* ipse sibi, Cic. **2.** T r a n s f.: Baiae tibi adsentantur, Cic. Ep.

ad-sequor, sequī, secūtus, *to follow after, overtake, come up with.* **1.** L i t.: Ter., Liv., Tac. With Acc.: Cic., Liv., Tac. **2.** T r a n s f. **a.** *to gain, attain to:* eosdem honorum gradūs, Cic. **b.** Of the mind, *to grasp, comprehend:* ut apertis obscura adsequamur, Cic.

(1) ad-serō, serere, sēvī, situm, *to plant near:* Cato; populus adsita limitibus, Hor.

(2) ad-serō, serere, seruī, sertum. L i t.: *to join or attach to oneself.* **I.** L e g. **a.** aliquem in libertatem *or* liberali causā *or* manu (or without manu) adserere, *to free a slave by the laying on of hands, to liberate:* Pl., Cic., Ov. **b.** aliquem in servitutem, *to declare one to be a slave by the laying on of hands, to claim as a slave:* Liv., Suet. **II.** In wider sense. **a.** *to protect, defend:* se ab iniuriā, Plin. Ep.; dignitatem, Suet. **b.** *to appropriate, claim:* alicui regnum, Liv.; me adsere caelo, Ov.; laudes nostras, Ov.

adsertiō, ōnis, *f.* [adserō], *a formal declaration respecting the freedom or servitude of any person:* Suet.

adsertor, ōris, *m.* [adserō]. **I.1.** L i t.: *one who claims that another is free:* Suet. **2.** T r a n s f.: *a defender, protector, champion:* Ov., Tac., Suet. **II.** *a claimer of a slave:* adsertor puellae, Liv.

ad-serviō, īre, *to serve, assist:* contentioni vocis, Cic.

ad-servō, āre, *to keep or preserve* (fr. destruction, attack, escaping, etc.): Pl., Caes., Cic., Cat., etc.

adsessiō, ōnis, *f.* [adsideō], *a sitting by* (to *console*): Cic. Ep.

adsessor, ōris, *m.* [adsideō], *he who sits by, an assistant:* Cic.

adsevēranter, *adv.* [adsevērō], *earnestly, emphatically:* Cic. Ep. *Comp.:* Cic.

adsevērātiō, ōnis, *f.* [adsevērō]. **I.** *a vehement assertion:* Cic. Ep., Liv., etc. **II.** *firmness,* Tac.

ad-sevērō, āre [sevērus]. **I. A.** I n t r a n s.: *to act seriously or earnestly* (opp. iocari): Cic. **B.** T r a n s.: *to do earnestly:* defensionem, Cic. **II. 1.** L i t.: *to make a positive declaration.* With Acc.: haec, Pl. With *de:* Cic. With Acc. and *Inf.:* Cic., Tac. **2.** T r a n s f.: *to declare, prove:* adseverant magni artūs Germanicam originem, Tac.

ad-sideō, sidēre, sēdī, sēssum [sedeō], *to sit by* or *near.* **1.** L i t. **a.** apud carbones, Pl.; Cic. **b.** *to sit by the sick:* Hor., Tac., etc. With DAT.: Ov., Liv.; valetudini, Tac. **e.** *to sit at, be busy with*: litteris, Plin. Ep. **d.** *to be encamped before, besiege*: prope moenia, Liv.; muros, Verg.; castellum, Tac.; ruinis, Tac. **2. Transf. a.** *to attend upon*: Cic., Liv. With DAT.: Cic., Hor. **b.** *to assist a judge*: Tac. **c.** *to be near to, resemble*: parous insano, Hor.

ad-sīdō, sīdere, sēdī, *to seat oneself by, sit down*: Ter.; esp. of a speaker at the end of a speech: Cic. With *Adv. phr.*: in arā, Pl.; super aspidem, Cic. With Acc.: Hiempsal dextrā Adherbalem adsedit, Sall.

adsiduē, adv. *continually, incessantly*: Ter., Cic., Verg., etc. Sup.: Cic.

adsiduitās, ātis, f. [adsiduus]. **I.** *a constant presence* or *attendance*: medici, Cic. Ep. Esp. of the regular public appearances of candidates for office: Cic. **II.** *persistence.* **a.** Of persons, *unremitting care*: Cic. **b.** Of things, *frequent recurrence*: molestiarum, bellorum, Cic.

adsiduō, adv. *continually*: Pl.

(1) adsiduus, a, um [adsidēo]. **I.** *continually present*: adsiduus in praediis, Cic.; Ov.; adsiduus in oculis hominum, Liv. Hence *in constant attendance*: fuit adsiduus mecum, Cic.; Pl. **II.** *persistent.* **a.** Of persons, *indefatigable*: flagitator, Cic.; custos, Liv. **b.** Of things, *incessant*: foro operam adsiduam dare, Pl.; Lucr.; imbres, motus, etc., Lucr.; labor, Caes., scriptura, Cic. Comp.: Varr.; Sup.: Suet.

(2) adsiduus, i, m. *a taxpayer* (of the upper classes in the Servian constitution): Cic. Hence *a rich man*: Pl.

adsignātiō, ōnis, f. [adsigno], *a marking out* (esp. of allotments of land): agrorum, Cic.; in *pl.*: Cic.

ad-signō, āre. **I.** *to mark out, appoint to a man.* **1. Lit. a.** Of public land allotments, *to assign*: agrum militibus, Cic., Liv. **b.** Of other things: equum publicum, Liv. **2. Transf. a.** *to mark out for, confer upon*: munus humanum adsignatum a deo, Cic.; Liv. **b.** *to put down to, ascribe, impute* (us. in bad sense): id homini, Cic.; Liv.; Tac. In good sense: omnia tuo consilio, Liv.; Tac. **II.** *to make a mark* or *impression on,* or *seal.* **1. Lit.:** tabellas, Pl. **2. Transf.:** verbum adsignatur auditori, Quint.

ad-siliō, silīre, silui, sultum, *to leap to or upon.* **1. Lit.:** moenibus urbis, Ov. Of leaping water: Ov. **2. Transf.:** ad genus illud orationis, Cic.

adsimilātiō, etc., v. adsimulātiō, etc.

ad-similis, e, adj. *similar, like*. With GEN.: Lucr., Ov. With DAT.: Cic., Verg., etc.

adsimiliter, adv. *in like manner*: Pl.

adsimulātiō, ōnis, f. [adsimulo]. **I.** *likeness*: Plin. **II.** *rivalry*: Tac.

adsimulātus, a, um. **I.** Part. adsimulo. **II.** Adj. **a.** *similar*: Cic. With DAT.: montibus adsimulata nubila, Lucr. **b.** *feigned, pretended*: familiaritas, virtus, Cic.; Liv.

ad-simulō, āre, *to make one thing like another.* **1. Lit.:** adsimulata formam Camerti, Verg.; formam totius Britanniae bipenni, Tac.; Lucr. **2. Transf.:** *to imitate, counterfeit, pretend.*

With Acc.: Pl., Verg., etc. With *Inf.*: Pl. With Acc. and *Inf.*: me insanire, Pl.; Ter. Also *Intrans.* (with or without *quasi*): quid si adsimulo? Ter.; adsimulabo quasi nunc exeam, Ter.

ad-sistō, sistere, stitī (or astitī). **I.** *to take one's stand by* or *near*: ad Achillis tumulum, Cic.; Pl.; Verg. **II.** *to stand at* or *by.* **a.** in conspectu patris, Caes.; lecto, Ov.; tribunalibus, Tac. **b.** *to assist in court* (=adesse), *defend*: ut causae suae deprecator adsistat, Tac.; adsistebam Vareno (DAT.), Plin. Ep.

adsitus, a, um, Part. adserō, l.

ad-soleō, ēre, *to be accustomed* (only 3rd *pers. sing.* and *pl.,* and *impers.*): cum multa adsoleat veritas praebere vestigia sui, Liv.; Pl.; ut adsolet, *as is usual*: Cic., Liv., Tac.

ad-sonō, āre, *to sound in response to.* Of Echo: Ov.

adsp-, v. asp-.

ad-sternō, ere, *to strew upon.* In *Mid.*: adsternuntur sepulcro, Ov.

adstipulātor, ōris, m. [adstipulor]. **1.** Lit.: *one who joins another in a contract*: Cic. **2.** Transf.: *one who agrees with*: eorum, Cic.

ad-stipulor, ārī, *to join another in a contract.* Transf.: *to agree with* (with DAT.): Liv.

ad-stituō, uere, uī, ūtum [statuō], *to place near*: Pl.

ad-stō, stāre, stitī, *to stand* or *be standing at* or *by.* **1.** Lit.: Pl.; ante aras, Lucr.; in conspectu meo, Cic.; ante oculos, Verg. **2.** Transf. **a.** *to stand awaiting one* (with DAT.): Lucr. **b.** *to stand by, assist*: Pl. **c.** *to be still standing* or *remaining*: Enn. **d.** *to stand upright*: squamis adstantibus, Verg.

ad-strepō, ere, *to make a noise at* or *to*: Tac. Esp. *to applaud* (with DAT.): Tac. With Acc. of *Neut. Pron.*: eadem, Tac.

adstrictē, adv. *concisely* (opp. remisse), *strictly*: Cic. Comp.: Plin. Ep., Quint.

adstrictus, a, um. **I.** Part. adstringō. **II.** Adj. **1.** Lit.: *drawn close*: soccus, Hor.; limen, Ov. **2.** Transf. **a.** Of style: (opp. remissus) *concise*: Cic. Comp.: Cic. **b.** *tight-fisted*: Prop., Tac.

ad-stringō, stringere, strinxī, strictum, *to draw close, tighten, bind fast.* **1.** Lit.: ad statuam adstrictus est, Cic.; Pl.; vincula, Ov.; frontem, Sen. Ep. Of the effect of cold: vis frigoris (corpora) ita adstringebat, Curt.; Ov. **2.** Transf. **a.** *to draw closer, bind*: fidem iure iurando, Cic.; ne lege et quaestione adstringatur, Cic.; Ter.; orationem numeris, Cic.; inops regio quae parsimoniā adstringeret milites, Liv.; me verbis in sacra iura tuis, Ov.; ad temperantiam, Plin. Ep. **b.** With *Pron. Refl.*: *to become guilty of*: furti sese, Pl.; magno scelere se adstringeret, Cic. **c.** Of style, *to compress*: argumenta, Cic.; Quint.

ad-struō, struere, struxī, structum. **1.** Lit.: *to build near* or *add to a building*: contignationem laterculo, Caes.; huic (villae) quae desunt, Plin. Ep. **2.** Transf.: *to add to*: alicui nobilitatem, Tac.; Ov.

ad-stupeō, ēre, *to be stunned at.* With DAT.: Ov.

ad-sŭŏtus, a, um, *sucked* : Lucr.

adsŭē-făciō, facere, fēci, factum [adsuētus], *to habituate, accustom, train*. With ABL. *Instr.*, DAT., or *ad* : disciplinā, Caes. ; armis, puro sermone, Cic. ; operi, Liv. ; Tac. ; ad supplicia, Liv. ; with *Inf.* : Caes., Cic., Liv.

ad-suēsco, suēscere, suēvī, suētum. **A.** Intrans.: *to become accustomed to*. With ABL. *Instr.*, DAT., *ad* or *in* and ACC., or Inf. : genus pugnae quo adsuerant, Liv. ; Cic. ; Verg. ; quieti, Tac. ; Verg. ; Liv. ; ad hominem, Caes. ; ut fremitum adsuesceret voce vincere, Cic. ; Verg., etc. *Impers. Pass.* : cui longo tempore adsuescitur, Liv. **B.** Trans.: *to accustom* : ne tanta animis adsuescite bella, Verg. Hence the pass. sense of adsuētus, *accustomed, trained*, with ABL. *Instr.*, DAT., *ad* or *in* and ACC., or *Inf.* : labore, Cic. ; frigori, Liv. ; ad controversiam, in iura, Liv. ; muros defendere, Verg.

adsuētŭdō, inis, *f.* [adsuētus], *custom, habit* : mali, Liv. ; Ov. ; Tac.

adsuētus, a, um. **I.** *Part.* adsuēscō. **II.** *Adj.* **a.** *accustomed, customary* : ars, Ov. *Comp.* : Liv. **b.** *familiar with*. With DAT. : Liv. (v. adsuesco, B.)

adsultō, āre (*freq.* adsiliō), *to jump* or *leap at*. **a.** In gen. *to leap about* : per campos, Tac. **b.** Milit.: *to attack*. With DAT.: castris, Tac. With ACC.: latera, Tac.

adsultus, ûs, *m.* [adsiliō], *a leaping upon, attack* (in pl.) : Verg., Tac.

ad-sum, esse, fuī (*Fut. Part.* adfutūrus ; *Fut. Inf.* sometimes adfore, and *Imp. Subj.* adforem ; old *Pres. Subj.* adsiem). **1.** Lit. **a.** *to be at* or *near, be present* : Pl., Cic., Verg., etc. With DAT., *to be present at* : Pl., Cic., Verg., etc. With *preps.* : ad portam, Cic. ; Pl. ; ante oculos, Verg. **b.** *to be present with one's support, stand by* (us. with DAT.) : Camulogenus suis aderat, Caes. ; Ter. ; Cic., etc. Esp. of advocates : absenti adfui Deiotaro, Cic. Of the gods : Verg., Liv. **c.** *to be present as a witness* : (testes) adsunt cum adversariis, Cic. ; Ov. **d.** *to present oneself, come on the scene, appear* : iam adfuturi videntur, Cic. Ep. ; Pl. ; Verg., etc. **e.** *to appear in court* : ad iudicium, Cic. **f.** adesse animo or animis, *to be present in mind, attend to* : adestote omnes animis, Cic. ; also *to be of good courage* : ades animo et omitte timorem, Cic. **2.** Transf.: *to be present, to be at hand*. **a.** Of time : adsunt Kalendae Iuniae, Cic. ; Ov. ; aderat iudicio dies, Liv. **b.** Of other abstract or inanimate things : tanti aderant morbi, Cic. ; quantus adest equis sudor, Hor. ; Ter. ; Verg. ; Tac.

ad-sūmo, sūmere, sūmpsī, sūmptum. **1.** Lit. **a.** *to take to oneself, take up* : id quod alteri detraxerit, sibi adsumat, Cic. ; Lucr. **b.** *to take in addition* : aliam quoque artem, Cic. ; Hor. ; Liv. **2.** **2.** Transf. **a.** *to take up as ally or friend*, etc.: eos in societatem consili adsumunt, Liv. ; uxorem, filium, Plin. Ep. ; Hor. **b.** Of abstract things, *to acquire, derive* : laudem sibi ex aliquā re, Cic. ; Ov. Oce.: *to assume, arrogate to oneself* : neque

mihi quicquam adsumpsi, Cic. Ep. ; Ov. **c.** *to add the minor premiss of a syllogism* : Cic. **d.** Gramm.: adsumpta verba. *epithets*, Cic.

adsūmptiō, ōnis, *f.* [adsūmō]. **I.** *a taking up, adoption* : Cic. **II.** In logic : *the minor premiss of a syllogism* : Cic., Quint.

adsūmptīvus, a, um [adsūmptus]. Rhet. : *causa, which takes its defence from extraneous circumstances*, Cic.

adsūmptus, a, um, *Part.* adsūmō.

ad-suō, suere, *to sew on* : Hor.

ad-sūrgō, sūrgere, surrēxī, surrēctum. **1.** Lit.: **a.** *to rise up, stand up* : dum laudatio recitatur, adsurgite, Cic. ; ex morbo, Liv., Tac. **b.** *to stand up out of respect* (with DAT.) : an quisquam in curiam venienti adsurrexit ? Cic. ; Verg. *Pass. Impers.* : Cic., Liv. **2.** Transf.: *to rise up*. **a.** Of inanimate things : colles adsurgunt, Liv. ; adsurgens fluctu nimbosus Orion, Verg. **b.** Of feelings : adsurgunt irae, Verg. ; querellis haud iustis adsurgis, Verg. **c.** Of style : *to soar* : raro adsurgit Hesiodus, Quint.

adt-, *v.* att.

adūlātiō, ōnis, *f.* [adūlor], *fawning*. **1.** Lit. : canum, Cic. **2.** Transf.: *cringing flattery, servility* : Cic., Liv., Tac. In *pl.* : Liv.

adūlātōrius, a, um, *flattering* : Tac.

adulēscēns, entis [adolēscō], *growing up, young*. **I.** Adj.: Africani filia adulescens, Cic. ; adulescentior, Ter., Sall., Cic. Ep. **II.** Noun : *a young man, young woman* (properly fr. the age of 15 to 30, but sometimes used of older people) : Pl., Caes., Cic., etc.

adulēscentia, ae, *f.* [adulēscēns], *the age of the* adulescens : ineunte adulescentiā, Cic. ; studia adulescentiam alunt, senectutem oblectant, Cic.

adulēscentula, ae, *f.* (term of endearment), *dear little girl* : Pl., Ter.

adulēscentulus, ī, *m.* *a very young man.* Used by Cic. of himself at 27, by Sall. of Caesar at 33 or 35. Also *a recruit* : Cic.

adūlō, āre (rare for adūlor), *to fawn like a dog* : Lucr. *Pass.* : *to be fawned on* : Cic.

adūlor, ārī. **1.** Lit.: *to fawn as a dog* : Ov. **2.** Transf.: *to fawn upon, flatter* in a cringing manner. With ACC.: Cic., Liv., Tac. With DAT.: Nep., Liv. Esp. of servile reverence paid to Eastern kings (= προσκυνεῖν) : Liv.

(1) adulter, erī, *m.* and **adultera**, ae, *f.* *an adulterer* or *adulteress*. **1.** Lit.: sororis, Cic. ; Ov. **2.** Transf.: *paramour* : Hor. Ov.

(2) adulter, era, erum, *adulterous, unchaste* : Hor., Ov.

adulterinus, a, um [adulter], *adulterous.* Transf.: *counterfeit, forged* : Pl., Cic., Sall.

adulterium, ī, *n.* [adulter], *adultery* : Cic., Cat., etc.

adulterō, āre [adulter], *to commit adultery, defile*. **1.** Lit.: Cic., Hor. With ACC.: matronas, Suet. **2.** Transf. **a.** *to defile, prostitute* : ius civile pecuniā, Cic. **b.** *to alter* : faciem, Ov.

adultus, a, um [adoleō], *grown up.* **1.** Lit.: virgo, Cic., Hor., Liv.; fetus apum, Verg.; aetas, Lucr. **2.** Transf. **a.** *matured :* pestis rei publicae, Cic.; coniuratio, Tac. **b.** *fully set in :* aestas, nox, Tac.

adumbrātim, *adv.* [adumbrō], *in sketch or outline :* Lucr.

adumbrātiō, ōnis, *f.* [adumbrō], *a sketch, outline :* Cic.

adumbrātus, a, um. **I.** *Part.* adumbrō. **II.** Adj. *sketched, outlined.* **1.** Lit.: lineamenta virtutum, Cic. **2.** Transf.: **a.** *imperfect :* imago gloriae, Cic. **b.** *fictitious :* comitia, Cic.; laetitia, Tac.

ad-umbrō, āre [umbra]. **1.** Lit.: *to shade or sketch in outline* (=σκιαγραφεῖν): Quint. **2.** Transf. **a.** *to sketch in words or in the imagination :* Cic. **b.** *to copy :* Curt.

aduncitās, ātis, *f.* *hookedness :* Cic.

ad-uncus, a, um, *bent inwards, hooked :* serrula, Cic.; baculum, Liv.; nasus, Hor.

ad-urgeō, ēre, *to press close* (of hot pursuit): Hor.

ad-ūrō, ūrere, ūssī, ūstum, *to scorch, burn on the surface, singe :* **1.** Lit.: capillum, Cic.: vestimenta, Liv., Hor. **2.** Transf. **a.** *to inflame* (of love): Hor., Ov. **b.** Of the action of cold and frost, *to nip, bite :* Verg., Curt.

ad-ūsque, for ūsque ad. **A.** Of place, *all the way up to :* adusque columnas, Verg.; Hor. **B.** Of time, *all the time to :* adusque bellum, Tac.; Ov.

adūstus, a, um. **I.** *Part.* adūrō. **II.** Adj. *burnt, scorched :* panis, Hor.; Ter.; *sunburnt :* Liv.

advectīcius, a, um [advectus], *imported :* vinum, Sall.

advectō, āre [*freq.* advehō], *to convey often :* Tac.

advectus, a, um, *Part.* advehō.

advectus, ūs, *m.* [advehō], *a carrying or conveying :* Tac.

ad-vehō, vehere, vexī, vectum (advextī =advexistī, advexe=advexisse, Pl.), *to carry, transport to :* ex agris frumentum Romam, Cic.; Pl. *Pass.* to be carried by horse, ship, carriage, etc., *to ride, sail, drive* (with *Instr.* ABL.): Pl., Cic., Verg., etc. Also absol. *to sail or ride to* (with ACC.): Verg., Tac.

ad-vēlō, āre, *to wrap up.* Poet. *to veil :* tempora lauro, Verg.

advena, ae, *m./f.* [adveniō], *a newcomer, foreigner, alien* (opp. indigena): Cic. Esp. in appos. to a noun : Ter.; exercitus advena, Verg.; advenae reges, Liv.

ad-veniō, venīre, vēnī, ventum, *to come to, arrive at* (with *ad, in* and ACC., or ACC.). **1.** Lit.: ad forum, Pl.; ad auris, Lucr.; in provinciam, Cic., Ov.; Tyriam urbem, Verg. With *Supine :* Ter. **2.** Transf. Of things : **a.** *to arrive :* dies, Cic.; hora proficiscendi, Tac. **b.** *to come to, accrue to :* Sall., Liv.

adventīcius, a, um [adveniō]. **A.** *coming from abroad, foreign, extraneous :* copiae, Cic. **B.** *coming in addition :* pecunia, Cic.; fructus, Liv.

adventō, āre [*freq.* adveniō], *to come nearer and nearer, be on the point of arriving.*

1. Lit.: Caes., Cic. Ep. With *ad :* Cic. Ep., Verg. With *in* and ACC.: Tac. With ACC.: Tac. With *Supine :* Pl. **2.** Transf.: *to be imminent* (with DAT.): urbi clades, Liv.

adventor, ōris, *m.* [adveniō], *one who arrives.* **a.** *a guest :* Pl. **b.** *a customer :* Pl.

adventus, ūs, *m.* [adveniō]. **1.** Lit. **a.** *arrival :* ad urbem, in urbis, Cic. **b.** *approach :* Caes. **2.** Transf.: malorum, Cic.

adversāria, ōrum, *n. pl.* (*sc.* scripta), *a notebook, day-book, memoranda :* Cic.

adversārius (older **advors-**), a, um [adversus], *turned towards, opposed to* (with DAT): Cic.; Hor. As Noun, *an opponent, enemy :* Pl., Cic., Hor., etc.; *Fem.* **adversāria :** Cic. Ep.

adversātrix, īcis, *f.* [adversor], *a female antagonist :* Pl., Ter.

adversiō, ōnis, *f.* [advertō], *a turning towards :* animi, Cic.

adversor (older **advorsor**), ārī [adversus], *to oppose oneself to, resist :* Curt., Tac. With DAT.: Pl., Cic., Verg., Tac. With ACC.: Tac. With *contra :* Pl.

(1) adversus (older **advorsus**), a, um. **I.** *Part.* advertō. **II.** Adj. *turned towards, facing, opposite.* **1.** Lit.: **a.** *opposite :* antipodes adversis vestigiis stant contra nostra vestigia, Cic.; adversissimi navigantibus venti, Caes.; flumine adverso, Caes., Verg.; in montis adversos, Liv. *Neut.* as Noun : adversa montium, Liv. **b.** *facing, in front :* in adversum os vulnerari, Caes.; dentes, vulnus, Cic. **c.** As Noun with *preps.* : ex adverso, *opposite to* (with DAT.): Liv.; in adversum, *to meet face to face, against :* Verg., Liv. **2.** Transf.: *in hostile opposition to, unfavourable :* omnia nobis secundissima, adversissima illis, Caes. ap. Cic. Ep.; Pl.; Cic.; res adversae, Cic.; valetudo, proelium, Liv.; adversae rerum undae, Hor.; adverso rumore esse, *to be in bad repute,* Tac. *Comp.* : Plin.

(2) adversus or adversum (older **advor-**), *adv. and prep.* **I.** Adv. *opposite to, to meet :* nemo adversus ibat, Liv.; Pl.; adversum ire or venire (with DAT.): Pl., Ter. **II.** Prep. with ACC. **a.** *to the front of, against :* impetum adversus montem in cohortis faciunt, Caes.; Liv. Transf.: adversum leges, rem publicam, Cic.; Pl.; adversus ea respondit, Liv. **b.** *towards, over against, in face of :* adversus advocatos considere, Liv.; Pl. Transf. (esp. of feeling): quonam modo me gererem adversus Caesarem, Cic. Ep.; pietas, iustitia adversus deos, Cic.; adversum divitias animum invictum gerebat, Sall. **c.** *compared with, in comparison with :* adv. veterem imperatorem comparabitur, Liv. N.B. adversus (-um) is rarely placed after the ACC.: quos advorsum, Sall.; hunc adversus, Nep.

ad-vertō (older **advor-**), vertere, vertī, versum, *to turn or direct towards.* **1.** Lit. With ACC., DAT., or *in* and ACC. **a.** urbi agmen, Verg.; sese in hanc nostram plateam, Ter. Esp. nautical : terras proras, Verg.; classem in portum, Liv.; hence aequore cursum, Verg. In *Mid :*

Scythicas advertitur oras, Ov. **b.** *to turn or draw to oneself, attract a man's attention :* adverterat ea res Sabinos tanti periculo viri, Liv.; odia, Tac.; advertit ea res Vespasiani animum ut, etc., Tac. **2.** Transf.: animum, animos, mentem (rare) advertere, *to direct the mind towards.* **a.** *to give attention to :* animos ad religionem, Lucr.; Pl.; Liv.; montis animos, Ov.; Tac. With *ne :* adverterent animos ne quid novi tumultûs oriretur, Liv.; Cic. Sometimes advertere alone : paucis, adverte, docebo, Verg. **b.** *to observe, notice :* With Acc.: postquam id animum advertit, Caes.; Pl.; animum adverti columellam, Cic. With Acc. and *Inf. :* animum advertit magnas esse copias hostium instructas, Caes.; Ter. With *Indir. Quest. :* Liv. Also without animum : quoties novum aliquid adverterat, Tac. **c.** advertere in aliquem (= animadvertere), *to punish :* Tac.

ad-vesperāscit, āscere, āvit [vesper], *evening approaches :* Ter., Cic.

ad-vigilō, āre, *to keep awake by, keep watch by.* **1.** Lit. : ad custodiam ignis, Cic.; parvo nepoti, Tib. **2.** Transf.: Pl., Ter.; pro rei dignitate, Q. Cic.

advocātiō, ōnis, *f.* [advocō], *legal assistance :* tu in re militari multo es cautior, quam in advocationibus, Cic. Ep. Hence, **a.** Concr.: *the counsel, the bar :* Cic., Liv. **b.** *the time allowed for procuring legal assistance :* ut binas advocationes, postulent, Cic. **c.** *delay or adjournment* in gen. : Sen.

advocātus, I, *m.* Lit. : *one called in to aid.* **A.** In law. **a.** Under the Republic, *an assistant* (either as witness or adviser) *in a lawsuit :* Pl., Cic., Liv. **b.** Under the Empire (= patronus, orator), *an advocate, counsel :* Tac., Plin. Ep. **B.** *a helper, friend :* amici advocatique, Cic.

ad-vocō, āre, *to call or summon.* **1.** Lit. **a.** aliquem, Pl.; aliquem ad obsignandum, Cic. Ep.; Liv.; contionem, Cic.; viros in consilium, Cic.; Liv. **b.** *to call in as helper or legal adviser :* viros bonos compluris advocat, Cic.; Pl. **2.** Transf. **a.** animum ad se ipsum advocamus, Cic. **b.** *to call to one's aid :* Verg.; Ov. **c.** *to get a respite, to delay :* Plin. Ep.

advolātū, ABL. *sing. m.* [advolō], *by flying to :* Acc. ap. Cic.

ad-volō, āre, *to fly to or towards.* **1.** Lit. : avis ad eas avis, Cic. **2.** Transf. **a.** vox mihi ad auris, Pl.; imago ad nos, Lucr.; Sestius ad urbem, Cic.; fama advolat Aeneae, Verg. With Acc.: Cic. Ep. **b.** Of a sudden hostile attack (with ad) : Caes.

ad-volvō, volvere, volvī, volūtum, *to roll to or towards :* robora focis, Verg. Of suppliants (with *Refl. Pron.* or in *Mid.*) : *to throw oneself at the feet of, grovel :* us. with DAT. : omnium genibus se advolvens, Liv. With Acc. : cum Tiberi genua advolveretur, Tac.

advorsō, āre [*freq.*, v. advertō], *to turn often to :* animum ne etc., Pl.

advorsum, advorsus, advortō, etc., old forms of adversum, etc.

adytum, I, *n.* [ἄδυτον], *not to be entered, the innermost part of a temple, sanctuary.* **1.** Lit. : Verg., Hor. Hence, cordis, Lucr. **2.** Transf. : of a *tomb :* Verg., Juv.

aedepol, *v.* edepol.

Aeacus, I, *m.* (Gk. Acc. Aeacon), *s. of Jupiter by Aegina ; a king of Aegina,* judge in the Lower World, with Minos and Rhadamanthus. **Aeacidēius,** a, um, and **Aeacidīnus,** a, um, *of the Aeacidae.* **Aeacidēs,** ae, *m.* (Voc. Aeacidā and Aeacidē), *a male descendant of Aeacus,* esp. *his son Phocus.* **II.** *his son Peleus.* **III.** *his g.s. Achilles.* **IV.** *his g.g.s. Pyrrhus, s. of Achilles.* **V.** *his later descendant, Pyrrhus, king of Epirus.* **VI.** *Perseus, king of Macedon.*

Aeaea, ae, *f. an island in the Tyrrhene Sea, home of Circe and Calypso,* now *Monte Circello.*

aedēs, *v.* aedis.

aedicula, ae, *f.* [aedis]. **I.** *a small chapel, shrine :* Cic., Liv. **II.** *a small house* (us. *pl.*) *:* Ter., Cic. **III.** *a small room :* Pl.

aedificātiō, ōnis, *f.* [aedificō]. **I.** *a building of a house :* Cic. **II.** *a building or structure :* Cic. Ep.

aedificātiuncula, ae, *f.* [*dim.* aedificātiō], *a little building :* Cic. Ep.

aedificātor, ōris, *m.* [aedificō], *a housebuilder, architect.* Transf.: opifex aedificatorque mundi, Cic. ; Juv.

aedificium, I, *n.* [aedificō], *a building of any kind :* Caes., Cic., Liv.

aedificō, āre [aedis, faciō]. **1.** Lit. **A.** Intrans.; *to build a house :* Pl., Cic., Hor., etc. **B.** Trans.: *to construct, build :* villam, porticum, hortos, urbem, Cic.; navem, Pl., Cic.; equum, Verg. **2.** Transf.: mundum, Cic.; rem publicam, Cic. Ep.

aedilicius, a, um [aedilis], *of an aedile :* edictiones, Pl.; munus, scriba, repulsa, Cic.; largitio, Liv. As Noun, **aedilicius,** I, *m. sc.* vir, *a past-aedile :* Cic.

aedilis, is, *m.* [cf. aedis. us. aedile) [aedis]. **I.** *an aedile, the superintendent of public and private buildings ; of aqueducts, roads, and sewers ; of the distribution of corn ; of markets, weights, and measures ; of public lands, police, and public spectacles. The aediles also kept the senatus consulta and plebis scita.* The office was created in B.C. 367; at first there were 4 aediles, 2 patrician (aediles curules) and 2 plebeian : Pl., Cic., Liv., Tac., etc. As *Adj. :* aedilis ludi, Pl. **II.** *a magistrate in a municipium* (this office being the first step in the cursus honorum) : Cic. Ep.

aedilitās, ātis, *f.* [aedilis], *the office of an aedile, aedileship :* Cic.

aedis (and **aedēs**), is, *f.* [cf. αἴθω]. Lit. : *a hearth.* **I.** *Sing.* **a.** *a dwelling of the gods, chapel* (a simpler building than a templum) : Cic., Hor., Liv. **b.** *a room :* Pl. **II.** *Plur.* **1.** Lit. : *a house, apartments :* Pl., Cic., Verg. **b.** *a house :* Pl., Cic., Verg., etc. ; liberae, *rent-free,* Liv. For familia : Pl. **2.** Transf.: aurium, Pl. Of a bee-hive : Verg.

aeditimus or **aedituus,** I, *m.* Varr.; **aedituēns,** entis, *m.* Lucr.; **aedituus,** I, *m.* Cic., Hor. [aedis], *a keeper of a temple, sacristan.*

Aeētēs, Aeētās, or **Aeēta,** ae, *m. king of Colchis, f. of Medea.* **Aeētaeus,** a, um, *of Aeetes.* **Aeētias,** iadis, *f.* or **Aeētīnē,** ēs, *f. d. of Aeetes, i.e. Medea.*

Aegaeōn, ŏnis, *m.* **I.** *a giant.* **II.** *a sea-god.*

Aegaeus (Aegēus), a, um, *Aegean, epith. of Neptune and Venus.* **Mare Aegaeum** or **Aegaeum,** I, *n. the Aegean Sea, betw. Greece and Asia Minor, now the Archipelago.*

Aegātēs, um, *f. pl. a group of 3 islands W. of Sicily, near Lilybaeum, where the Carthaginians were defeated by the Romans in a naval battle, which terminated the 1st Punic War,* B.C. 241.

aeger, gra, grum, *sick, ailing, ill.* **1.** Lit.: *of the body.* **a.** With ABL. *of cause:* homines aegri morbo gravi, Cic.; longā navigatione, Tac. Also ex vulnere, Cic. **b.** With ABL. *of part affected:* pedibus, Sall.; oculis, Liv. **c.** Occ. *in agreement with part affected;* corpus, valetudo, Cic. *As* Noun: Cic., Hor. **2.** Transf. **a.** *diseased:* seges, Verg.; maxime aegra rei publicae pars, Cic. **b.** *Of the mind, troubled, distressed:* capellas aeger ago, Verg.; animus, Liv. With LOC.: animi, Liv. With ABL. *of cause:* avaritiā, Sall.; curis, Verg.; amore, Liv. **c.** *Active in sense, causing pain (to body or mind), painful, distressing:* dolores, Lucr.; anhelitus, amor, Verg.

Aegeus (disyl.), eī, *m. king of Athens, f. of Theseus;* **Aegidēs,** ae, *m. Theseus;* **Aegidae,** ārum, *m. pl. descendants of Aegeus.*

Aegēus, *adj. v.* Aegaeus.

Aegialeus (quadrisyl.), eī, *m. s. of Aeetes, b. of Medea, us. called Absyrtus.*

Aegīna, ae, *f.* **I.** *m. of Aeacus.* **II.** *an island off Attica;* **Aegīnēta,** ae, *m. an Aeginetan;* **Aegīnēticus,** a, um, *of Aegina.*

aegis, idis, *f.* [αἰγίς]. **1.** Lit. **a.** *the shield of Jupiter:* Verg. **b.** *the shield of Minerva with Medusa's head:* Verg., etc. **2.** Transf.: *shield, defence:* Ov.

Aegisthus, ī, *m., s. of Thyestes; paramour of Clytemnestra, with whom he murdered Agamemnon, and by whose son Orestes he was killed.*

Aeglē, es, *f. a nymph, daughter of Jupiter and Neaera.*

Aegos flūmen (αἰγὸς ποταμός), *n. a river in the Thrasian Chersonese, where Lysander defeated the Athenians,* B.C. 405.

aegrē, *adv.* [aeger]. **I.** *with pain, displeasure, regret or unwillingness:* esp. in phrase aegre ferre: Cic., Liv. Also aegre pati: Liv.; aegre tolerare, accipere, Tac.; aegre esse alicui, aegre facere alicui, *to hurt, annoy a person,* Pl., Ter. **II.** *with effort or difficulty:* conglutinatio recens aegre divellitur, Cic.; Pl.; Verg. **III.** *hardly, scarcely:* oppugnationem aegre sustentare, Caes.; aegre abstinere quin, etc., Liv. *Comp:* aegrius, Pl., Liv., Tac. *Sup.:* aegerrime, Caes, Cic.

aegreō, ēre [aeger], *to be ill:* morbis corporis, Lucr.

aegrēscō, ere [aeger], *to sicken, fall ill.* **1.** Lit.: morbis, Lucr. **2.** Transf. **a.** *to grow worse:* violentia aegrescit medendo,

Verg. **b.** *to be troubled:* sollicitudine, Tac.

aegrimōnia, ae, *f.* [aeger]. *Of the mind, sorrow, distress:* Pl., Cic. Ep., Hor.

aegritūdō, inis, *f.* [aeger], *sickness, suffering.* **1.** Lit.: *of body:* Tac. **2.** Transf.: *of mind, grief, sorrow:* Pl., Cic., etc. In *pl.:* Ter., Cic.

aegror, ōris, *m.* [aeger], *illness:* Lucr.

aegrōtātiō, ōnis, *f.* [aegrōtō], *sickness, disease.* **1.** Lit.: *of body:* Cic. **2.** Transf.: *of mind:* aegrotationes animi, Cic.

aegrōtō, āre [aegrōtus], *to be sick.* **1.** Lit.: *of body:* Cic.; morbo, Hor. **2.** Transf. **a.** *Of mind:* res ex quā animus aegrotat, Cic.; Hor. **b.** *Of other things, to languish:* artes, Pl.; fama, Lucr.

aegrōtus, a, um [aeger], *sick, diseased.* **1.** Lit.: *of body:* Ter., Hor. As Noun: aegroto, dum anima est, spes esse dicitur, Cic. Ep. **2.** Transf. **a.** *Of mind:* Ter., Cic. With *Inf.:* Pl. **b.** *Of other things:* res publica, Cic.

1. Aegyptus, ī, *f. Egypt;* **Aegyptius, Aegyptiacus,** a, um, *Egyptian.*

2. Aegyptus, ī, *m. a mythical king of Egypt, s. of Belus and b. of Danaus. His 50 sons married the 50 daughters of Danaus.*

aelinos, ī, *m.* [αἴλινος], *a dirge:* Ov.

Aēllō, ūs, *f.* **I.** *one of the Harpies.* **II.** *a swift dog:* Ov.

Aemilius, a, *the name of a famous Roman gens;* **Aemilia via** or **Aemilia,** *a main road in N. Italy;* **Aemiliānus,** a, um, *of the Aemilian gens;* Scipio Africanus Minor, *s. of* L. Aemilius Paulus, *was called* Aemilianus.

Aemilius Macer, *of Verona, a poet, the friend of Vergil and Ovid.*

Aemōnia, *v.* Haemonia, etc.

aemulātiō, ōnis, *f.* [aemulor], *rivalry in anything, emulation.* **A.** *Good sense:* laudis, Nep.; gloriae, Tac. **B.** *Bad sense:* Cic., Tac.

aemulātor, ōris, *m.* [aemulor], *an emulator, keen imitator:* Cic. Ep., Sen. Ep.

aemulātus, ūs, *m.* [aemulor], *emulation, rivalry:* Tac.

aemulor, ārī [aemulus], *to make oneself a rival of, vie with, emulate.* **A.** *Good sense:* Pl.; with ACC.: eius instituta, Cic.; studia, Liv.; Pindarum, Hor. **B.** *Bad sense.* With DAT.: alicui, Cic. With *cum:* mecum, Liv. With *Inf.:* Tac.

aemulus, a, um [fr. root of Gk. ἅμιλλα and Lat. imitor], *striving to equal, emulous, rivalling* (with GEN. or DAT. *of person or thing*). **A.** *Good sense:* laudis, Cic.; Liv.; Hor.; Caesar summis oratoribus aemulus, Tac.; Hor. **B.** *Bad sense:* Verg., Tac.; Karthago aemula imperi Romani, Sall. As Noun, **aemulus,** ī, *m.* and **aemula,** ae, *f. a rival:* Pl., Cic., Ov.

Aenaria, ae (also Pithēcūsa), *f. an island on the Campanian coast, the landing-place of Aeneas; now Ischia.*

Aenēās, ae, *m.* (NOM. occ. Aenēā; GEN. occ. Aenēā; Acc. often Aenēan; VOC. Aenēā), *a Trojan prince, s. of Anchises and Venus; the hero of Vergil's epic, and ancestor of the Romans, worshipped as Iuppiter Indiges.*

Aeneadēs, ae, *m*. (GEN. *pl*. Aeneadum), *a descendant of Aeneas* ; esp. *pl*. **Aeneadae**, ārum and um, *the Trojans*, and hence *the Romans*. Also *epith. of Augustus*. Also **Aenīdēs**, ae, =*Ascanius*. **Aenēis**, idis, or idos, *f*. *Vergil's epic, the Aeneid*. **Aenēius**, a, um (quadrisyl.), *of Aeneas*.

aēneus (or **ahēneus**), a, um [aes], *of bronze*. **1.** Lit.: statua, Cic.; loricae, Nep.; Hor. **2.** Transf. **a.** *bronze-coloured* : barba, Suet. **b.** *hard as bronze* : murus, Hor.; proles, Ov.

aenigma, atis, *n*. [αἴνιγμα], *a riddle, enigma* : Cic.

aēni-pēs, pedis [aēneus, pēs], *adj*. *bronze-footed* : bovis, Ov.

Aēnobarbus, *v*. Ahēnobarbus.

aēnus (or **ahēnus**), a, um [aes], *of bronze*. **1.** Lit.: signa, Lucr.; falx, Verg. Also Noun (*sc*. vas), **aēnum**, I, *n*. *a bronze vessel* or *cauldron* : Verg., Ov. **2.** Transf.: *hard as bronze* : manus, Hor.

Aeolia, ae, *f*. **I.** *a group of islands near Sicily, now the Lipari Islands*. **II.** *the home of Aeolus, the god of the winds*. **III.** *The part of Asia Minor inhabited by the Aeolians*.

Aeolii, ōrum (and **Aeolēs**, um), *m*. *pl*. *the Aeolians of Greece and Asia Minor ; one of the 4 tribes into which the Hellenes are us. divided*.

Aeolis, idis, *f*. *the part of W. Asia Minor inhabited by the Aeolians*.

Aeolius, a, um, *of Aeolus* or *Aeolia, Aeolian*. Esp. appl. to the poetry of Alcaeus and Sappho, who were Aeolians born in Lesbos.

Aeolus, I, *m*. **I.** *the god of the winds, s. of Jupiter, ruler of the Aeolian Islands where he kept the winds imprisoned*. **II.** *king of Thessaly*. **Aeolidēs**, ae, *m*. *a descendant of Aeolus*, esp. his son Sisyphus, Athamas, etc.

aequābilis, e, *adj*. [aequō], *that can be made even*. **a.** *even, uniform* : praedae partitio, motus, tractus orationis, Cic.; Pl. **b.** *consistent* : cunctis vitae officiis aequabilis, Tac. **c.** *impartial* : status rei publicae non in omnis ordines civitatis aequabilis, Cic.; Tac. *Comp.* : Cic. Ep., Sen. Ep.

aequābilitās, ātis, *f*. [aequābilis]. **A.** *evenness, uniformity* : motūs, Cic. Of style : elaborant alii in lenitate et aequabilitate, Cic. **B.** *consistency* : universae vitae, Cic. **C.** *impartiality* : in rebus causisque civium aequabilitatis conservatio, Cic.

aequābiliter, *adv*. *evenly* : Cato ; aequabiliter praedam dispertire, Cic. *Comp.* : Sall, Tac.

aequaevus, a, um [aequus, aevum], *of equal age* : amicus, Verg., Suet.

aequālis, e, *adj*. [aequus]. **1.** Lit.: *of place, even, level* : loca, Sall.; Tac.; terra, Ov. **2.** Transf.: *equal*. **a.** In size, shape, etc. : partem pedis esse aequalem alteri parti, Cic.; chorus Dryadum, Verg. **b.** In character, etc. : virtutes inter se, Cic.; aut linguā aut moribus aequales, Liv. Hence, *even, steady* : imber lentior aequaliorque, Liv.; Ov. **c.** Of age and time : **i.** *equal in age, of the same age* : adulescens ita dilexi senem ut aequalem, Cic.; Ter. **ii.** *coeval, coexistent* : Deiotari benevolentia in populum Romanum est ipsius

aequalis aetati, Cic.; Liv.; aequali tecum aevo, Verg. **iii.** *contemporary* : Philistius aequalis illorum temporum, Cic.; Livius (Andronicus) Ennio aequalis fuit, Cic.; Liv. [Fr. *égal*, Ital. *eguale, uguale*.]

aequālitās, ātis, *f*. [aequālis], *evenness, levelness*. **1.** Lit.: maris, Sen. Ep. **2.** Transf.: *equality, uniformity*. **a.** verborum, Cic. **b.** In age : Cic. **c.** In the State : Tac.

aequāliter, *adv*. *evenly, uniformly* : collis ab summo aequaliter declivis, Caes.; frumentum aequaliter distribuere, Cic. *Comp.* : Tac.

aequanimitās, ātis, *f*. **I.** *goodwill, kindness* : Ter. **II.** *calmness* : Plin.

aequātiō, ōnis, *f*. [aequō], *an equalising, equal distribution* : Cic., Liv.

aequē, *adv*. **I.** *equally* : trabes aeque longae, Caes.; non omnia eadem aeque omnibus suavia esse scito, Pl. ; Cic. ; Verg.; *equally as, just as*, when followed by *et, ac, atque, quam, ut, ac si* and *Subj*., or *cum* : nisi aeque amicos et nosmet ipsos diligamus, Cic.; Pl.; Tac.; nihil aeque eos terruit quam robur imperatoris, Liv.; Pl.; Tac.; nihil aeque ut brevitas placet, Plin. Ep.; aeque enim parabit ac si ipse id bellum gesturus esset, Liv.; Cic. Ep.; novi aeque omnia tecum, Tac.; Pl. With ABL.: Pl. **II.** *justly, fairly*. *Comp*.: Sall.

Aequi, ōrum, *m*. *pl*. *a warlike people of Central Italy*. Hence **Aequiculus** or **-colus**, a, um, and **Aequicus**, a, um.

aequi-lībritās, ātis, *f*. [aequus, lībra], *the equal distribution of the powers of nature* : Cic.

Aequimaelium, I, *n*. *an open space in Rome below the Capitol, on which the house of Sp. Maelius stood, before it was levelled to the ground*.

aequi-noctium, I, *n*. [aequus, nox]. Lit.: *equal night time, the equinox* : Caes., Cic. Ep., Liv.

aequiperābilis, e. *adj*. [aequiperō], *comparable* : Pl. With DAT. or *cum* : Pl.

aequi-perō, āre [aequus, parō]. **I.** *to put on a level, to make equal, compare*. With *cum* : Cic. With *ad* or DAT.: suas virtutes ad tuas, Pl.; Iovis Solisque equis aequiperatum dictatorem, Liv. **II.** *to be on a level with, to equal* : voce magistrum Verg.; ut nemo me aequiperare posset, Liv.

aequitās, ātis, *f*. [aequus]. **1.** Lit.: *evenness, uniformity* : Suet. **2.** Transf. **a.** *fairness, impartiality* : Caes., Cic., Nep. **b.** *equity* (as opposed to *law*) : Cic. **c.** *calmness, equanimity* : animi, Cic.

aequō, āre [aequus]. **I.** *to make level*. **1.** Lit.: aequata agri planities, Cic.; solo (DAT.) templum, Tac. **2.** Transf.: aequandae sunt dictaturae consulatūsque, Liv. **II. a.** *to make equal, equalise* : aequantur sortes, Cic.; Pl.; aequato omnium periculo, Caes.; aequato Marte, Liv.; Lucr. Milit.: aequare frontem, Liv., Tib. With *cum* : opes cum potentissimis, Caes.; Cic.; Verg. With DAT.: dies noctibus, Liv.; Verg. **b.** *to compare* : omnium scelera vix cum huius parvā parte aequari conferrique posse, Cic.; ne aequaveritis Hannibali Philippum, Liv. **III.** *to equal, come up to :* with Dat. or Acc.: qui iam illis fere aequarunt, Cic. ; Ov. ; eā arte aequasset superiores reges, Liv. ; cursum alicuius, Curt. ; sagitta aequans ventos, Verg. ; Hor.

aequor, oris, *n.* [aequus], *a level, flat surface.* **a.** In gen.: speculorum, Lucr. ; camporum patentium aequoribus, Cic. ; campi, Verg. Hence without campi, *a plain :* Verg. **b.** Of water : maris aequor, Verg. ; ponti, Ov. Hence poet. alone in *sing.* and *pl., the sea :* Lucr., Verg., Hor., Ov. Also in prose (rare) : Sall., Curt., Tac.

aequoreus, a, um [aequor], *of the sea :* rex, Ov. ; Britanni, Ov. ; genus, Verg.

aequus, a, um (Aiquos, Inscr., aecus, Lucr. ; aequos, aequom, Cic. ; aecus, aecum, Liv.). **1.** Lit.: of place, *even, level, flat :* Caes., Cic. As Noun, **aequum,** I, *n. a level, a plain :* in aequo campi, Liv. ; Tac. Hence, *favourable, advantageous.* **a.** Of place or time : locum se aequum ad dimicandum dedisse, Caes. ; Tac. ; et tempore et loco aequo, Liv. **b.** Of persons or things : *well-disposed, friendly :* non aequo senatu, Cic. Ep. ; oculis aspicere aequis, Verg. With Dat.: With *in* and Acc.: hoc quod aequum sit in Quinctium, Cic. With *in* and Abl.: aequus in hoste fuit, Prop. As Noun in *pl.* **aequi,** *friends :* Cic. Ep., Liv. **2.** Transf. **a.** *level, equal, like :* aequo censu censeri, Pl. ; dementia, Lucr. ; aequam partem tu tibi sumpseris ac populo Romano miseris, Cic. ; aequo fere spatio, Caes. ; trifariam aequo numero dividere, Liv. ; aequo Marte pugnare, Liv. ; sequiturque patrem non passibus aequis, Verg. With Dat.: urbs nubibus aequa, Ov. As Noun **i.** ex aequo, *on even terms :* disceptatio ex aequo, Liv. ; Ov. **ii.** in aequo *on a level :* aliquem alicui ponere, Liv. **b.** *fair, impartial :* praetor, lex, postulatio, Cic. With Dat.: praebere se aequum alicui, Cic. Ep. ; Tac. As Noun, **aequum,** I, *n. fairness, right :* iniurias gravius aequo habere, Sall. ; Lucr. ; utilitas iusti prope mater et aequi, Hor. Phr. **i.** aequum est, *it is fair, right, just.* With Acc. and *Inf. :* Ter., Lucr., Caes. With Dat. of person and *ut* with *Subj. :* Pl. With Abl.: Pl. **ii.** *Neut.* aequum very freq. with bonum, *what is right and fair :* ex aequo et bono, non ex callido versutoque iure rem iudicari oportere, Cic. ; Pl. ; aequi boni facere, *to consider it right and good,* Ter., Cic., etc. **c.** *calm, composed, balanced* (with *animus* and *mens) :* concedo, et quod animus aequus est, et quia necesse est, Cic. ; Pl. ; aequam memento rebus in arduis servare mentem, Hor. Esp. in Abl. aequo animo, *patiently, with resignation, nonchalantly :* Caes., Cic., etc.

āēr, āeris, *m.* [ἀήρ] (Acc. āēra and āerem ; Dat. *pl.* āeribus, Lucr.), *the air,* prop. *the lower atmosphere* (as opp. to aether, *the upper air*). **1.** Lit.: Cic., Verg. In *pl. :* Lucr. **2.** Transf.: **a.** *atmosphere, climate :* purus et tenuis, Cic. ; Boeotum in crasso aere natus, Hor. **b.** *mist :* Venus obscuro gradientis aere saepsit, Verg.

aerarius, a, um [aes]. **I.** *of bronze :* secturae (*or* structurae), Caes. ; faber, Plin. **II.** *of money :* propter aerariam rationem, Cic. ; tribuni aerarii, *paymasters of the army,* Cic. As Noun. **a. aerarius,** I, *m. a citizen of the lowest class :* referre in aerarios, *to degrade to the lowest rank,* Cic. ; Liv. **b. aerarium,** I, *n. a treasury ;* esp. *the treasury of the Roman people in the temple of Saturn :* referre pecuniam in aerarium, Cic. ; deferre pecuniam in aerarium, Liv. Also *of the money itself :* aerarium sanctius, *a fund in reserve,* not to be touched exc. in time of need, Caes., Liv. In the treasury were kept the public archives and the standards of the legions : Cic., Liv., Tac. : aerarium militare, *the military chest,* Tac.

aerātus, a, um [aes], *fitted with copper* or *bronze :* lecti, *with bronze feet,* Cic. ; naves, *bronze-beaked,* Hor., Ov. ; acies, Verg.

aereus, a, um [aes]. **I.** *made of copper* or *bronze :* galea, cornua, vectis, Verg. **II.** *fitted with copper* or *bronze :* puppis, *bronze-beaked,* Verg.

aerifer, era, erum [aes, ferō], *bearing bronze cymbals :* Ov.

aeri-pes, pedis, *adj.* [aes, pēs], *bronze-footed :* Verg., Ov.

āerius (quadrisyl.), a, um [ἀέριος], *of the air, airy.* **1.** Lit.: volatus avium, Cic. ; volucres, Lucr. ; aerias domos, Hor. ; viae, Ov. ; mel, *sky-dropt,* Verg. **2.** Transf.: *soaring :* Alpes, quercus, arces, Verg.

Āeropē, ēs, and **Āeropa,** ae, *f. the wife of Atreus.*

aerūgo, inis, *f.* [aes]. **1.** Lit.: *rust of copper :* Cic. Hence for *money :* Juv. **2.** Transf.: of passions which corrode the mind. **a.** *envy, malice, ill-will :* Hor. **b.** *avarice :* Hor.

aerumna, ae, *f. hardship, distress, affliction :* Pl., Lucr., Cic., etc.

aerumnābilis, e, *adj. full of trouble :* Lucr.

aerumnōsus, a, um, *full of trouble* or *misery :* Pl., Cic. Comp.: Sen. Sup. : Cic.

aes, aeris, *n.* [cf. Engl. *ore*]. **1.** Lit. **a.** *ore, crude metal :* aes Cyprium, *copper,* Plin. **b.** *an alloy of copper and tin,* i.e. *bronze :* ex aere statuam decerno, Cic. ; ducere, aera, Hor. **2.** Transf. **a.** *things made of copper* or *bronze :* quae ille in aes incidit, *tablets,* Cic. ; Tac. ; excudent alii spirantia mollius aera, *statues,* Verg. ; aere ciere viros, *trumpet,* Verg. ; Ov. ; aera micantia, *weapons,* Verg. **b.** Esp. *copper* or *bronze money :* aes signatum, Cic. ; sometimes in the phrase aes grave = as, i.e. *the standard unit of the coinage :* denis milibus aeris gravis reos condemnavit, Liv. Also aes alone, esp. in Gen. *sing. :* aeris milles, 100 *millions of* asses, Cic. **c.** *money* in general : aes circumforaneum, *borrowed from the bankers in the forum,* Cic. Ep. ; si aes habent, dant mercem, Pl. ; Verg. Phrases. **i.** aes alienum, lit. *the money of another,* hence *a debt :* in aes alienum incidere, *to fall into debt,* Cic. ; aes alienum facere, contrahere, *to run up debts,* Cic. Ep. ; conflare, Sall. ; aes alienum habere, in aere alieno esse, *to be in debt,* Cic. ; dissolvere, Cic., Liv., solvere, persolvere,

Liv. *to pay debts.* **ii.** in aere meo est, *he is among my assets,* Cic. Ep. **d.** *wages, pay :* aere dirutus miles, Cic.; negabant danda esse aera militibus, Liv.; aera, *school-fees,* Hor. In *pl.* (like stipendia), *military service :* Cic., Liv.

Aesar, *an Etruscan name of God.*

Aeschĭnēs, is, *m.* **I.** *a disciple of Socrates.* **II.** *a celebrated Athenian orator, rival of Demosthenes.*

Aeschўlus, I, *m.* **I.** *the first great tragic poet of Greece* (fl. B.C. 480). **II.** *a rhetorician of Cnidus, a contemporary of Cicero.*

Aesculāpĭus, I, *m.* *s. of Apollo and the nymph Coronis, deified on account of his great knowledge of medicine ; the god of medicine.*

aesculētum, i, *n.* [aesculus], *a forest of oaks :* Hor.

aesculeus, i, *f.* *the tallest species of oak, the winter or Italian oak :* Verg., Hor.

Aesōn, onis, *m.* *a Thessalian prince, b. of King Pelias, and f. of Jason ; he was transformed by the magic arts of Medea from an old man into a youth.* **Aesonĭdēs,** ae, *m. Jason ;* **Aesonĭus,** a, um, *Aesonian.*

Aesōpus, i, *m.* **I.** *a Greek fabulist of Phrygia* (about the time of Croesus); **Aesōpēus, Aesōpĭus,** and **Aesōpĭcus,** a, um, *Aesopic.* **II.** *a tragic actor, friend of Cicero.*

aestās, ātis, *f.* [root of Gk. αἴθω], *the hot season* (prop. March to September), *summer.* **1.** Lit.: aestate ineunte, Cic. Ep.; novā, Verg.; mediā, summā, Cic.; iam adultā, Tac.; exactā, Sall. **2.** Transf. **a.** *summer-air :* aestate serenā, Verg.; *summer-heat :* ignea, Hor. **b.** *a year :* te iam septima portat errantem aestas, Verg. Esp. as the season of a campaign : duabus aestatibus gesta, Tac.

aestĭfer, era, erum [aestus, ferō], *bringing heat :* Lucr., Verg.

aestĭmābĭlis, e, *adj.* [aestimō], *valuable :* Cic.

aestĭmātĭō, ōnis, *f.* [aestimō], *the setting a money-value upon, assessment, appraisement.* **1.** Lit.: potestas omnis aestimationis habendae censori permittitur, Cic.; frumenti, Cic.; aequā facta aestimatione, Caes.; poenae, Cic.; litium, *of damages in a suit,* Cic.; possessionum et rerum, *of real estate,* Caes. Hence, praedia in aestimationem accepit, *at such a valuation,* Cic. Ep. **2.** Transf. **a.** *a valuation :* aestimationem arbitriumque eius honoris penes senatum fuisse, Liv.; Cic. **b.** *worth, value :* Cat.

aestĭmātor, ōris, *m.* *a valuer, appraiser.* **1.** Lit.: frumenti, Cic. **2.** Transf.: *an estimator or valuer :* iustus rerum aestimator, Cic.

aestĭmō (aestumō), āre [perh. fr. aes and root of Gk. τίω], *to determine the money-value of a thing, to value, appraise* (with GEN. or ABL. of value or *adv.*). **1.** Lit.: quanti haec aestimentur, Cic.; frumentum III. denariis, Cic.; emit domum prope dimidio carius quam aestimabatur, Cic. In law : litem aestimare, *to assess the damages,* Caes., Cic. **2.** Transf. **a.** *to estimate the moral worth of, to value :* eorum salutem levi

momento, Caes.; tu istā permagno aestimas, Cic.; me esse mortuum nihil aestimo, Cic. With *Indir. Quest. :* Tac., Suet. With *ex, ad,* of the standard used in valuing : ex veritate pauca aestimant, Cic.; ista ad meam rationem usumque non aestimo, Cic.; virtutem annis, Hor.; aliquid vitā, Curt. **b.** *to estimate, reckon :* sicut ego aestimo, *in my estimation,* Sall.; Aegyptios pro sociis, Curt.

aestĭvē, *adv.* *as in summer :* admodum aestive viatici sumus, i.e. *quite scantily,* Pl.

aestĭvō, āre [aestīvus], *to spend the summer :* Varr., Suet.

aestīvus, a, um, [aestās,] *of summer, summer-like, summer :* tempora, dies, Cic.; aves, Liv.; saltūs, *summer-pastures,* Liv.; sol, Verg.; aura, Hor.; umbra, Ov. As Noun, **aestīva,** ōrum, *n.* *pl.* *summer-quarters.* **1.** Lit.: dum in aestivis essemus, Cic.; sub tempus aestivorum, Hirt.; dimittere cohortīs in aestiva, Suet. **2.** Transf. **a.** *a campaign :* nulla ex trinis aestivis gratulatio, Cic. **b.** *summer-pastures :* Plin. Hence, *cattle :* morbi corripiunt tota aestiva, Verg.

aestuārĭum, i, *n.* [aestus], *a tide-place, creek, estuary.* **1.** Lit.: Caes., Plin. Ep., Tac. **2.** Transf.: *an air-shaft* (in mines): Plin.

aestuō, āre [aestus], *to have a surging, undulating movement.* **1.** Lit. **a.** Of fire, *to heave and roar, blaze up :* aestuat, ut clausis rapidus fornacibus ignis, Verg.; Ov. Also of the effects of heat, *to be hot, glow, burn :* exustus ager morientibus aestuat herbis, Verg.; Pl. Of persons : Lycurgi leges erudiunt iuventutem algendo aestuando, Cic.; Ov. **b.** Of water, *to heave and toss, surge, boil :* Verg., Hor. **c.** Of other things, *to heave and toss :* arbor, Lucr.; in ossibus umor, Verg. **2.** Transf. **a.** Of the passions, *to seethe, burn, be passionately inflamed :* desiderio, Cic. Ep.; ingens in corde pudor, Verg. Also *absol. :* Cic. **b.** Of the judgment, *to toss to and fro in perplexity :* dubitatione, Cic.; Hor., etc.

aestuōsē, *adv.* *hotly, impetuously :* Pl. *Comp :* Hor.

aestuōsus, a, um [aestus], *full of agitation or heat.* **a.** *very hot :* aestuosa et pulverentula via, Cic. Ep.; Syrtes, Hor. *Sup. :* Plin. **b.** *seething* (or perh. *tidal*): freta, Hor.

aestus, ūs, *m.* [root of Gk. αἴθω], *a heaving surging movement.* **1.** Lit. **a.** Of fire, *flaring heat, glow :* furit aestus ad auras, Verg. Of heat in general : frigora et aestūs tolerare, Cic.; labore et aestu languidus, Sall.; Hor. Of heat in disease : homines aegri cum aestu febrique iactantur, Cic. **b.** Of water, *seething, surging, boiling :* furit aestus harenis, *the surf,* Verg.; Curt.; exsultant aestu latices, Verg. Esp. of the ebb and flow of the sea, *the tide :* Pl., Caes., Cic.; minuente aestu, *at the ebb of the tide.* Caes. **c.** Of *the stream of atoms in the universe :* Lucr. **2.** Transf. **a.** Of the passions, *seething, ferment, fury :* hunc absorbuit aestus quidam gloriae, Cic.;

comitiorum, Cic. ; civilis belli, Hor. ; Lucr. ;
(amor) irarum fluctuat aestu, Verg. **b.**
Of the judgment, *agitation. restlessness,
anxiety :* qui tibi aestus, qui error, quae
tenebrae, Cic. ; magno curarum fluctuat
aestu, Verg.
aetās, ātis, *f.* [contr. fr. aevitās] (GEN. *pl.*
aetatum, but aetatium in Lucr.). **I. a.**
life-time, life : aetatem gerere, degere, consumere, conterere, Cic. ; aetas acta honeste
et splendide, Cic. ; aetatem used adverbially, *during lifetime,* Pl., Ter. Occ. *a
generation :* haec aetas, Cic. ; hominis
aetatem durare, Liv. **b.** *time of life, age :*
qui valetudine aut aetate inutiles sunt
bello, Caes.; morbo atque aetate confectus
Sall.; id aetatis iam sumus, Cic.; ambo
florentes aetatibus, Verg.; ab ineunte
aetate, Cic.; prima, bona, *youth,* Cic.;
flos aetatis, Cic., Liv.; militaris, Sall.;
media, firmata, constans, *middle age,* Cic.;
consularis, Cic ; provecta, infirma, *old
age,* Cic. So, mala aetas or aetas alone :
Pl. Of things : Falernum hoc bene
aetatem fert, *carries its years well,* Cic. **c.**
the people of a particular age, age : Pl.;
omnes aetates, Cic.; omnis aetas, Liv.,
Tac. **II. a.** *time :* omnia fert aetas, Verg.;
omnis aetatis clarissimus, Curt. **b.** *a
period of time, epoch, age :* heroicis aetatibus, Cic. ; superior, Caes. ; aurea, argentea,
aenea, ferrea, Ov. **c.** *the people living in
such a period :* quid nos dura refugimus
aetas ? Hor. ; impia, Hor.
aetātula, ae, *f.* [*dim.* aetās], *a tender* or
youthful age : Pl., Cic.
aeternitās, ātis, *f.* [aeternus], *eternity.* **a.**
Of the past : ex omni aeternitate fluens
veritas, Cic. **b.** Of the future : animorum,
Cic.; mihi populus Romanus aeternitatem
immortalitatemque donavit, Cic.; Tac.
c. *a courtesy-title of the emperor :* per
aeternitatem tuam, Plin. Ep.
aeternō, āre [aeternus], *to immortalise :*
virtutes in aevum, Hor.
aeternus, a, um [contr. fr. aeviternus].
Lit. *lasting an age, agelong.* **A.** *long-
enduring, lasting, perpetual :* pax, bellum,
aerumna, Cic.; vulnus, Verg. **B.** *enduring from all time :* ex aeterno tempore, Cic.,
Lucr. **C.** *enduring for ever in the future,
immortal :* gloria, memoria, Cic.; Homerus,
urbs, Tib.; nox, Verg.; nihil quod ortum
sit aeternum esse potest, Cic. *Neut.* as
Noun : urbs in aeternum condita, *to all
eternity,* Liv.; sedet aeternumque sedebit
Theseus, *for ever,* Verg.; Hor. **D.** *enduring from all time and for all time, eternal :*
di semper fuerunt, si quidem aeterni sunt
futuri, Cic. ; Verg.
aethēr, eris, *m.* [αἰθήρ] (Gk. Acc. aethera),
the upper, pure air, ether (opp. aēr, *the lower
atmospheric air.*) **1.** Lit. : Cic. **2.**
Transf. **a.** *the air* (esp. of pure air) :
apes liquidum trans aethera vectae, Verg. ;
Lucr.; Hor. **b.** *heaven :* famā super
aethera notus, Verg. **c.** Person. as deity :
pater Aether : Lucr., Verg. **d.** *the upper
world* (opp. Hades), *the earth :* aethere in
alto duros perferre labores, Verg.
aetherius, a, um [αἰθέριος], *of the ether,
ethereal.* **1.** Lit. : altissima aetheriaque

natura, Cic. ; Lucr. ; Hor. **2.** Transf.
a. *of the air :* nubes, Lucr.; nimbi, Verg.
b. *heavenly :* umbrae, Cat. ; arces, Ov. ;
ignes, i.e. *inspiration.* Ov. **c.** *of the upper
world :* vesci aurā aetheriā, Verg.
Aethiopia, ae, *f. a country S. of Egypt, on
both sides of the equator.* **Aethiopicus,** a,
um, *Ethiopian ;* **Aethiops,** opis. **I.** *Masc.*
Noun, *an Ethiopian* or *any black man :*
derideat Aethiopem albus, Juv. **II.** Adj.
stupid : cum hoc homine an cum stipite
Aethiope, Cic.
Aethōn, onis, *m.* [αἴθων], i.e. *burning, the
name of a horse in the chariots of several gods.*
aethra, ae, *f.* [αἴθρα], *the upper air* (*cf.*
aether) : Lucr., Verg.
Aethra, ae, *f.* **I.** *d. of Oceanus and Tethys.* **II.**
d. of Pittheus and m. of Theseus.
Aetna, ae, and **Aetnē,** ēs, *f.* **I.** *the volcano
Etna in Sicily,* now also *Monte Gibello.*
Aetnaeus, a, um, *Etnean.* **II.** *a town
at the foot of Etna ;* **Aetnēnsis,** -e, adj.
Aetōlia, ae, *f. a district in Greece betw. Locris
and Acarnania ;* **Aetōlicus, Aetōlius,
Aetōlus,** a, um, *Aetolian ;* **Aetōlis,** idis, *f.
an Aetolian woman.*
aevitās, ātis, *f.* [aevum], old form of aetas,
occurring in the XII. Tables : Cic.
aevum, i, *n.* (**aevus,** i, *m.* Pl., Lucr.) [αἰϝών,
cf. Eng. *ever*], mostly poet. for aetas. **I.**
a. *life-time :* aevom degere, consumere,
Lucr.; Ov. **b.** *time of life, age, years :*
integer aevi sanguis, Verg. ; maturus aevi,
aevo confectus, Verg. ; flos aevi, Ov. **II.**
a. *time :* vitiata dentibus aevi omnia, Ov. ;
quae per tantum aevi occulta, Tac. **b.**
eternity : in caelo ubi beati aevo sempiterno fruantur, Cic. ; in omne aevum,
for all time, Hor.
Āfer, fra, frum. **I.** Adj. *African.* **II.**
Masc. Noun, *an African.*
aff-, *v.* adf-.
Āfrānius, a, *the name of a Roman gens :*
esp. **I.** L. Afranius, *a celebrated Roman
comic poet* (fl. B.C. 110). **II.** *a general of
Pompey ;* **Āfrāniāni,** orum, *m. pl. soldiers
of Afranius.*
Āfrica, ae, *f.* orig. *the territory of Carthage,
made a Roman province after the 3rd Punic
War,* B.C. 146. Also *the continent of
Africa.* **Āfricānus,** a, um. **I.** Adj. *African.* **II.** *Fem. pl.* as Noun, *panthers :*
Liv. **III.** *Surname of the two most famous
Scipios,* viz. P. Cornelius Scipio, who defeated Hannibal at Zama, B.C. 201; and
his grandson P. Cornelius Scipio Aemilianus,
who was generalissimo in the 3rd Punic
War. **Āfricus,** a, um, *African.* Esp.
Africus ventus or Atricus, i, *m. the S.W.
wind ; the Affrico* or *gherbino :* croberque
procellis Africus, Verg.
āfui, āfore, āforem, āfutūrus, for abf-, *v.*
absum.
Agamēdēs, ae, *m. b. of Trophonius, with
whom he built a temple to the Delphic Apollo.*
Agamēmnōn, onis, *m.* (NOM. also Aga-
mēmnō), *king of Mycenae, commander-in-
chief of the Greek army at Troy.* **Aga-
mēmnonidēs,** ae, *m. his son,* Orestes ;
Agamēmnonius, a, um, *of Agamemnon.*

Aganippē, ēs, *f. a fountain in Boeotia at the foot of Mt. Helicon, sacred to the Muses.*
Aganippēus, a, um, and **Aganippis**, idis, *f. adj. belonging to Aganippe, i.e. sacred to the Muses.*
agāsō, ōnis, *m. an ostler, groom :* Pl., Liv. ; *also a groom acting as footman :* Hor.
Agathoclēs, is, *m.* **I.** *a king in Sicily, son of a potter, famous for his war with Carthage for the possession of Sicily ;* **Agathoclēus**, a, um. **II.** *the author of a history of Cyzicus.*
Agathyrsi, ōrum, *m. pl. a Scythian people in* mod. Transylvania.
Agāvē (-**auē**), ēs, *f. d. of Cadmus, w. of Echion, king of Thebes, m. of Pentheus, whom she tore in pieces, because he despised the Bacchic rites.*
age, agedum, agesis, v. agō.
agellus, i, *m.* [dim. ager], *a small piece of ground, a little field :* Ter., Cic., Hor.
agēma, atis, *n.* [ἄγημα], *a corps in the Macedonian army :* Liv., Curt.
Agēnor, oris, *m., f. of Cadmus and Europa, ancestor of Dido.* **Agēnoreus**, a, um ; **Agēnoridēs**, ae, *m. a descendant of Agenor, esp. Cadmus ; also Perseus, whose g.f. Danaus was descended from Agenor.*
agēns, entis. **I.** *Part.* agō. **II.** Adj. *effective, striking* (rhet.) : imagines, Cic. **III.** agen-tēs, *m. pl. as Noun, secret police under the Empire.*
ager, gri, *m.* [Gk. ἀγρός, *cf.* Eng. *acre*], *land, soil.* **I.** *a field* (pasture or arable): Ter. ; agri cultura, Caes., Cic. ; agri cultio, Cic. ; agri cultor, Liv. ; dives agris, Hor. **II.** *landed property* (of community or individual), *territory, domain :* Pl. ; ager Helvetius, Caes. ; ager privatus, Cic. ; ager publicus, Liv., etc. **III.** Like *rus, the country* (us. in *pl.*). **a.** (opp. town) : homines ex agris concurrunt, Cic. ; Ter. ; Cat. **b.** (opp. mountains) : montis agrosque salutat, Ov. **c.** (opp. seaboard) : pars muri in agrum versa, Liv.
Agēsilāus, i, *m. a celebrated Spartan king, c.* B.C. 400.
agg-, v. adg-.
agger, eris, *m.* [ad gerō], *materials brought to a place and heaped up.* **1.** Lit.: *materials for a rampart, mole, dike, etc. :* milites aggeris petendi causā processerant, Caes. ; aggere paludem explere, Caes. ; fossas aggere complent, Verg. **2.** Transf.: *the pile formed of such material.* **a.** *a mound, rampart for besieging :* iacere, exstruere, instruere, Caes. ; aggere oppidum oppugnare, Cic. Ep. ; aggerem promovere ad urbem, Liv. **b.** *a rampart for defence* (made of earth out of the fossa) : agger ac vallum, rampart and stockade, Caes. ; aggere et fossis et muro circumdat urbem Servius, Liv. ; aggere murorum, Verg. **c.** *a dam, dike, mole :* aggerem iaciebat a litore, Caes. ; aggeribus ruptis exit amnis, Verg. ; incohatus a Druso agger Rheno coercendo, Tac. **d.** *an embankment to carry a road, a causeway, viaduct, road :* viae deprensus in aggere serpens, Verg. ; aggeres umido paludum imponere, Tac. **e.** *any pile* (natural or artificial) : aggeres nivei, Verg. ; aggeres Alpini, Verg. ; armorum, Tac.

aggerō, āre [agger], *to heap or pile up.* **1.** Lit.: cadavera, Verg. ; Tac. **2.** Transf. **a.** iras, Verg. **b.** *to fill up :* spatium, Curt.
agilis, e, *adj.* [agō]. **A.** Pass.: *easily moved, mobile :* classis, Liv. ; remus, rota, Ov. Comp. : Sen. **B.** Act. : *that moves easily, nimble, active.* **1.** Lit.: dea, Ov. **2.** Transf.: *active, busy, quick :* animus, Sen. Masc. as Noun : Hor. Comp. : Sen. Ep., Quint.
agilitās, ātis, *f.* [agilis], *mobility, quickness.* **1.** Lit.: navium, Liv. ; Quint. **2.** Transf.: naturae, Cic. Ep.
Āgis, idis, *m.* (Acc. Agin), *the name of several kings of Sparta.* Esp. *Agis II., b. of Agesilaus and s. of Archidamus ; and Agis IV. who tried to effect reforms, but was put to death by the ephors.*
agitābilis, e, *adj.* [agitō], *easily moved, lightly moving :* aër, Ov.
agitātiō, ōnis, *f.* [agitō], *frequent or violent motion, tossing, etc.* **1.** Lit.: agitationes fluctuum, Cic. ; armorum, Liv. ; lecticae, jolting, Liv. **2.** Transf.: *activity :* nunquam animus agitatione et motu esse vacuus potest, Cic. ; studiorum, Cic. ; Sen. Ep.
agitātor, ōris, *m.* [agito], *a driver, charioteer, etc.* : aselli, equorum, Verg. Esp. of charioteers at the public games : Pl., Cic., Plin. Ep.
agitō, āre [freq. agō], *to put in constant or violent motion.* **1.** Lit.: *to drive, toss.* **a.** Of beasts : biiugos agitare leones, Lucr. ; lanigeros greges hirtasque capellas, Verg. **b.** Of other things : trirerem, *to row*, Nep. ; alas, habenas, hastam, Ov. **c.** Of hunting, *to chase :* feras, avis, Cic. ; onagros, Verg. **d.** Of the motion caused by wind or water, *to sway, toss :* mare ventorum vi agitari, Cic. ; Lucr. ; Verg. ; ventis agitatur pinus, Hor. ; agitata numina Troiae, *storm-tossed*, Verg. **2.** Transf. **A. a.** *to toss :* multis iniuriis iactata atque agitata, Cic. ; Sall. **b.** *to goad, spur :* agitabatur animus inopiā rei familiaris, Sall. ; in furias agitantur equae, Ov. ; plebem, Cic. **c.** *to hunt :* suum quemque scelus agitat, Cic. ; scelerum furiis agitatus Orestes, Verg. **d.** *to hunt or goad with words, deride :* agitat rem militarem, insectatur totam legationem, Cic. ; vesanum poetam agitant pueri, Hor. **B.** *to keep things going.* **a.** In action, *to urge on, be engaged in, celebrate, execute, etc.* : agraria lex a Flavio vehementer agitabatur, Cic. Ep. ; vigilias, custodiam, *to keep guard*, Pl., Tac. ; praesidia, Sall. ; meum natalem, Pl. ; festos dies, Cic. ; pacem, *to be at peace*, Sall. iocos, Ov. Also in *Pass.* : agitatur pax, Sall. ; esp. of time, *to be spent :* vita hominum sine cupiditate agitabatur, Sall. So in *Act.* : agitare aevum, Verg. Also *Absol. to live :* Sall., Tac. **b.** In thought : agitare aliquid or de aliquā re (animo, in animo, in mente, in corde, secum), *to keep a thing moving in the mind, revolve, consider :* eam rem in corde agito, Pl. ; id agitans mecum, Ter. ; Sall. ; quod agitet in mente, Cic. ; in animo bellum, Liv. ; quae omnes animo agitabant, Tac. Without *animo*, etc. : si ille hoc unum agitare

coeperit, Cic. ; Tac. ; de bello, Tac. With *Inf.* as object : ut mente agitaret bellum renovare, Nep. With *Indir. Quest.*, or *ut* (of purpose) : Tac. **c.** In speech, *to discuss, thresh out :* his rebus agitatis, Caes. ; non agitanda res est, Cic. ; de foedere, Liv. ; ut tribuni crearentur, Liv.

Āglaia, ae, or **Āglaiē,** ēs, *f. one of the Graces.*

Aglaophōn, ontis, *m. a celebrated* Greek painter, *f.* and teacher of Polygnotus, c. B.C. 400.

Āglauros, i, *f., d. of Cecrops, changed by Mercury into a stone.*

agmen, inis, *n.* [agō]. **I.** Abstract. **a.** *a moving, movement :* agmine remorum celeri, Verg. ; agmine certo Laocoonta petunt, Verg. **b.** esp. of an army, *marching :* agmine impeditos adoriri, Caes. ; ratio ordoque agminis, Caes. **II.** Concrete. **a.** anything set in motion, *a troop, crowd, train,* etc. : agmen perpetuum, Cic. ; mulierum, Liv. ; Eumenidum, aquarum, corvorum, apium, Verg. ; agmine longo formicas, Ov. Of clouds : Lucr. **b.** Milit. **i.** *an army in motion, an army moving in column :* in itinere agmen nostrum adorti sunt, Caes. ; agmen quadratum erigere, Liv. ; agmen iustum, Tac. ; agmen primum, *the van,* Liv., Tac. ; agmen ducere, *to form the van,* Curt. ; medium, *the centre,* Liv. ; extremum, Caes., Liv., and novissimum, Caes., Liv., *the rear ;* agmen claudere, cogere, *to bring up the rear,* Caes., Liv. ; constituere, *to bring to a halt,* Sall. **ii.** *a fleet moving in column :* navium, Liv. **iii.** Of parts of an army : iumentorum, Caes. ; equitum, Liv. ; impedimentorum, Tac. **iv.** *an army* (rare) *:* instructo agmine, Liv. ; agmina curru proterit, Verg. ; Hor.

agna, ae, *f.* [agnus], *a ewe-lamb :* Varr., Hor., Ov.

agnāscor, nāsci, nātus [ad, gnāscor old form of nāscor], *to be born in addition to.* **A.** Of children born after father's death or after his will was made : constat agnascendo rumpi testamentum, Cic. **B.** Of plants, hair, limbs, etc. : *to grow in addition :* Plin.

agnātiō, ōnis, *f.* [agnāscor], *consanguinity on the father's side :* Cic.

agnātus, a, um. **I.** *Part.* agnāscor. **II.** *Masc. as Noun.* **a.** *a child born into a family where there was already a heres :* Tac. **b.** *a blood relation in the male line :* Cic.

agnellus, i, *m.* [*dim.* agnus], *a lambkin :* Pl.

agnīnus, a, um [agnus], *of a lamb :* lactes, Pl., Varr. *Fem.* as Noun, *flesh of lamb, lamb :* Pl., Hor.

agnitiō, ōnis, *f.* [agnōscō]. **I.** *a recognising :* Quint. **II.** *a perceiving :* animi, Cic.

agnitus, a, um, *Part.* agnōscō.

agnōmen, inis, *m.* [ad, gnōmen old form of nōmen], *a surname,* e.g. Africanus.

agnōscō, nōscere, nōvi, nitum [ad, gnōscō old form of nōscō]. **I.** *to know again, recognise.* **1.** Lit. : cum se conlegit (animus), tum agnoscit illa reminiscendo, Cic. ; aliquem, Verg., Liv., etc. **2.** Transf. : *to express one's recognition, admit, own :* facti gloriam, Cic. ; crimen, Cic., Tac. ;

natum, Nep. ; id ego agnovi meo iussu esse factum, Cic. Ep. ; an me non agnoscetis ducem ? Liv. **II.** *to recognise, realise, perceive :* deum ex operibus eius, Cic. ; Hor. ; Tac. ; accipio agnoscoque deos, Verg.

agnus, i, *m.* (also *fem.* in early Latin), *a lamb :* Pl., Cic., Ov., etc. Prov. : agnum lupo eripere velle, Pl.

agō, agere, ēgi, āctum (agier=agi xii. Tab. ap. Cic.), *to put in motion.* **1.** Lit. : of physical impulse. **a.** *to set moving, drive, whirl,* etc. : vineas turrisque ad oppidum, Caes. ; navis, Liv., Tac. ; turbinem, fundam, nubis, Verg. ; currum, ratem, Ov. With *Refl. Pron.* or in *Pass. :* quo te agis ? Pl. ; Ter. ; is enim se primus agebat, Verg. ; omnis multitudo agebatur, Liv. Without *Pron. :* quo agis ? Pl. **b.** *to make something by driving, push forward, put forth :* aggerem, Caes. ; cuniculos ad aerarium, Cic. ; rimas, Cic. ; cloacam, Liv. ; scintillas, Lucr. ; se ad auras palmes, Verg. ; radices, Ov. **c.** *to drive before one* (cattle, enemies, etc.) : capellas potum, Verg. ; armentum, equum, servum, Liv. ; Germanos in amnem, Tac. **d.** *to hunt, chase :* aliquem praecipitem de fundo, Cic. ; quasdam in exsilium, Liv. ; apros, cervum, Verg. ; piscis in retia, Ov. **e.** *to drive off as booty* (while *ferre* is used of portable things) : impedimenta, Caes. ; praedas, Sall. ; boves, Liv. **2.** Transf. **A.** fr. the above : sitis ignea venis omnibus acta, Verg. ; impetus egit equos, Ov. ; in gloriam praeceps agebatur, Tac. ; animam agere et efflare, Cic. ; gloria radices agit, Cic. ; ferre agere plebem, Liv. **B.** *to keep going, set in motion.* **a.** In action. **i.** *to act* (trans. and intrans.), *do* (esp. with aliquid, nihil, etc.) : Africanus solitus est dicere nunquam se plus agere quam nihil cum ageret, Cic. ; aliud tempus agendi, aliud quiescendi, Cic. ; sine magistratibus, Liv. ; quid agis ? *how do you do ?* Pl. ; nihil agis, *it is of no use,* Ter. **ii.** *to act, deal with, behave* (esp. with adverbs and adv. phrases) : nullo studio, cum simulatione, Caes. ; bene, male, ferociter, praeclare cum aliquo, Cic. **iii.** *to carry out.* With a noun it denotes the action indicated by the noun : bellum agere, *to wage war,* Caes. ; Ov. ; proelium, *to give battle,* Liv. ; triumphum, *to triumph,* Cic. ; vigilias, *to keep watch,* Cic. ; excubias alicui, Ov. ; stationem, Liv., Tac. ; gratias alicui, *to thank :* decima legio ei gratias egit, Caes. ; libera arbitria, *to make free decisions,* Liv. ; silentia, *to keep silence,* Ov. ; forum or conventum, *to hold a court or the assizes,* Cic. ; dilectum, Tac. Of offices, *to administer :* censuram, honorem, Liv. **iv.** *to spend, pass* (of time) : aetatem in litteris, Cic. ; ruri agere vitam, Liv. ; quartum annum ago et octogensimum, *am in my 84th year,* Cic. *Pass. :* melior pars acta diei, Verg. Also *Absol.* (rare) *to live :* Marius apud primos agebat, Sall. ; Gallos trans Padum agentis, Tac. **v.** Of an actor, *to act, play, represent :* primas partis agere, *to play the chief part,* Ter. ; Ballionem illum cum agit, agit Chaeream, Cic. ; gestum in scaenā, Cic. ; hence, senatorem, amicum agere, *to personate,* Tac. Also of an orator's delivery : agere cum dignitate ac venustate, Cic. **vi.** Of sacrificial action, *to act,* i.e. *to despatch the victim :* qui calido strictos tincturus sanguine cultros semper, Agone ? rogat, Ov. **b.** In thought, *to set something moving in thought, to have as one's object,* esp. in phr. id agere ut (or *ne*) : id agunt ut viri boni esse videantur, Cic. ; aliud *or* alias res agere, *not to attend ;* aliud agens ac nihil eius modi cogitans, Cic. **c.** In speech. **i.** *to discuss, treat of, deal with :* is ita cum Caesare egit, Caes. ; egi cum Claudiā et cum vestrā sorore Muciā ut eum ab illā iniuriā deterrerent, Cic. Ep. ; Samnitium bella quae per quartum iam volumen agimus, Liv. **ii.** Hence, often in the sense, *the question at issue is, the matter at stake is :* agitur populi Romani gloria, agitur salus sociorum, aguntur vectigalia, Cic. **iii.** Esp. of public action, in assembly or lawcourt : *to discuss, bring an action, conduct a case :* velim recordere quae ego de te in senatu egerim, Cic. Ep. ; de condicionibus pacis, Liv. Hence, of magistrates : agere cum populo, *to address the people,* Cic. ; rem agere ex iure, ex syngraphā, etc., *or* lege, litibus, causā, etc., *to go to law :* ex iure civili et praetorio agere, Cic. ; tamquam ex syngraphā agere cum populo, Cic. ; agere lege in hereditatem, Cic., Liv. Hence, agere reum, *to accuse one,* Liv. With GEN. of crime : agere furti, *to accuse of theft,* Cic. Ep. **C.** *Imperat.* : age, agite, also with particles, dum, iam, modo, nunc, porro, sane, sis, vero, orig. *up and be doing /* or perh. *lead on (cf.* Gk. ἄγε, ἄγετε), hence, *come !* **i.** In encouragement : agite bibite, Ter. ; Pl. ; dic age, Verg. ; agitedum mecum age, Liv. **ii.** In transitions in discourse, *well then /* freq. in Cic. **iii.** In assent, *very well /* age, sit ita factum, Cic. ; Pl.

agōn, ōnis, *m.* [ἀγών] (Acc. agōna), *a contest :* gymnicus, Plin. Ep. ; musicus, Suet.

agōnālis, e, *adj. belonging to the* agonia : *neut. pl.* as Noun : *festival in honour of Janus.*

agōnia, ōrum, *n. pl.* **I.** *victims.* **II.** *a festival of Janus :* Ov.

agorānomus, ī, *m.* [ἀγορανόμος], *a marketinspector :* Pl.

agrārius, a, um [ager], *of land.* **I.** agrariae leges, Cic., Liv., Tac. ; agrariam rem temptare, Cic. ; triumvir agrarius, *one of 3 commissioners for the division of public lands,* Liv. **II. agrārii,** ōrum, *m. pl.* the *agrarian party :* Cic., Liv.

agrestis, e, *adj. [ager], of the country, rural, rustic.* **1.** Lit. : Musa, Lucr. ; te hospitio agresti accipiemus, Cic. ; poma, Verg. As Noun, **agrestis,** is, *m.* (GEN. *pl.* -ium, Cic. -um, Ov.), *a countryman, a rustic :* Cic., Verg. Also *wild :* palmae, Cic. **2.** Transf. **a.** (opp. the *refined townsman, urbanus), boorish, clownish, uncultured :* Ter., Cic., Ov. **b.** *wild, brutal :* Cic., Ov.

agricola, ae, *m.* [ager colō] (GEN. *pl.* agricolum, Lucr.), *a land-tiller, farmer.* **1.** Lit. : Cic., Verg., etc. **2.** Transf. : of gods, *patrons of farming :* Tib.

Agricola, ae, *m. a Roman family name ;* esp. Cn. Iulius Agricola, *for seven years*

governor of Britain, and father-in-law of Tacitus, who wrote his biography.

agricultiō, agricultor, agricultūra, *v.* ager and cultiō, etc.

Agrigentum, ī, *n., v.* Acragās ; **Agrigentīni,** ōrum, *m. pl. the people of Agrigentum.*

agripeta, ae, *m.* [ager, petō], *one who strives for a plot of land :* Cic.

Agrippa, ae, *m.* **I.** *a Roman family name ;* esp. Menenius Agrippa, *who pacified the plebs in the 1st Secession ;* and M. Vipsanius Agrippa, *son-in-law of Augustus.* **II.** *the surname of several members of the family of Herod, king of Judaea.*

Agrippina, ae, *f.* **I.** *w. of the Emperor Tiberius, g.d. of Atticus.* **II.** *d. of Vipsanius Agrippa and Julia, g.d. of Augustus, w. of Germanicus and m. of the Emperor Gaius.* **III.** *d. of the Preceding and Germanicus, w. of Cn. Domitius Ahenobarbus and m. of the Emperor Nero ;* **Agrippinēnsis,** e, *adj. of Agrippina :* Colonia Agrippinensis, *a colony on the Rhine* (now *Köln or Cologne*) named *after Agrippina* III. **Agrippinēnsēs,** ium, *m. pl. the people of this colony.*

Agyieus (trisyl.), eī or eos, *m. an epith. of Apollo as guardian of the streets and ways* (ἄγυιαί).

ah, ā, *interj. :* Pl., Ter. Verg.

aha, *interj. ah / aha / haha /* an exclamation of reproof or laughter : Pl., Ter.

Ahāla, ae, *m. a family name of the* gens Servilia ; esp. C. Servilius Ahala, *master-of-the-horse to the Dictator Cincinnatus ; the slayer of Maelius.*

ahēneus, ahēnipēs, etc., *v.* aēn-.

Ahēnobarbus (Aēn-), ī, *m. a family name of the* gens Domitia.

ai, *interj.* denoting grief ; *alas !* Ov.

aiēns, *Part.* aiō, =adfirmātivus : *Neut. pl.* as Noun : negantia contraria aientibus, Cic.

ain', =aisne, *v.* aiō.

aiō, *def. verb.* [for agiō, as māior for magior ; *cf.* adagium] (the forms in use are *Pres. Ind.* : aiō, aīs, ait, aiunt ; *Subj.* (rare) : aiās, aiat, aiant ; *Pres. Part.* (raro) aiēns ; *Imp. Ind.* aiēbam, etc., also aibās, aibat, aibant, Pl., Ter. ; ain' is used in familiar dialogue for aisne ?). **I.** *to assent, say* yes (opp. nego) : Diogenes ait, Antipater negat, Cic. ; Pl. **II.** *to say, assert :* with Acc. of Neut. Pron. : Ter., Verg. ; with Acc. and *Inf.* : Pl., Cic., Hor. *Absol. :* ut ait Statius noster, Cic. ; Quint. Transf. : uti mos vester ait, Hor. Esp. in phr. : aiunt, ut aiunt, quo modo or quem ad modum aiunt, in quoting a proverb, etc., *as the saying is :* docebo sus, ut aiunt, oratorem eum, Cic. ; Pl. **III.** *to speak :* esp. in transition : sic ait, et dicto citius tumida aequora placat, Verg. **IV.** Colloq. *ain' ?* (=aisne ?) ; also ain' tu, ain' tute, ain' tandem, ain' vero, quid ais ? *do you really say so ? indeed ? really ?* (expressing surprise, regret, etc.) : ain' tu ? Scipio hic Metellus proavum suum nescit censorem non fuisse ? Cic. ; Pl. Also with *pl.* : ain' tandem ? inquit, num castra vallata non habetis ? Liv.

Aiax, ācis, m. [Ἀίας], the name of 2 Greek heroes famous for bravery. **I.** Ajax, s. of Telamon, who competed with Ulysses for the arms of Achilles. **II.** Ajax, s. of Oileus, king of the Locri.

Aius Loquēns or **Aius Locūtius**, a god who announced to the Romans "the Gauls are coming."

āla, ae, f. [for ax-la, v. axilla; cf. Germ. achsel). **1.** Lit.: a shoulder, armpit. **a.** Of men and animals: Pl.; umbonibus incussāque alā sternuntur hostes, Liv.; sub alā fasciculum portare, Hor. **b.** Of birds, etc. a wing: Pl.; (Harpyiae) magnis quatiunt clangoribus alas, Verg.; apum, Verg.; Mors atris circumvolat alis, Hor.; madidis Notus evolat alis, Ov. **2.** Transf. **a.** Of ships, etc.: velorum pandimus alas, Verg.; remigium alarum, Verg.; alarum insistere remis, Ov.; fulminis ocior alis, Verg. **b.** Of buildings, the wings: Vitr. **c.** Of an army, the wing. Orig. composed of Roman cavalry. but subseq. of the socii, both horse and foot. Still later the alae (or alarii) were composed of foreign troops serving in the Roman armies. Under the Empire alae=foreign cavalry.

Alabanda, ae, f. and ōrum, n.·pl. a town in Caria of great wealth and luxury. **Alabandēnsēs**, ium, or **Alabandēni**, ōrum m. pl. its inhabitants ; **Alabandeus**, a, um, (quadrisyl.), of Alabanda.

alabaster, tri, m. (pl. alabastra) [ἀλάβαστρος]. **1.** Lit.: a perfume-box : Cic. **2.** Transf.: a rose-bud : Plin.

alacer, cris, cre, adj. (Nom. masc. alacris : Enn., Ter., Verg.). **1.** Lit. **a.** lively, brisk, spirited : Cic.; ad bella suscipienda alacer et promptus animus, Caes.; equus, Cic. **b.** lively, gay, cheerful : Ter.; videbant Catilinam alacrem atque laetum, Cic. **2.** Transf.: impetus, Pl.; voluptas, Verg. Comp. : Caes. [It. allegro, Fr. allègre.]

alacritās, ātis, f. [alacer]. **I.** liveliness, briskness, eagerness : alacritas studiumque pugnandi, Caes.; rei publicae defendendae, Cic.; canum in venando, Cic. **II.** cheerfulness, joy, rapture : mihi alacritatem populi concursus adferret, Cic.; with Obj. Gen. : clamor Romanorum alacritate perfecti operis sublatus, Liv.

alapa, ae, f. a box on the ear : Phaedr., Juv.; esp. of the slap given by a master to his slave on emancipation ; hence alapae= freedom : Phaedr.

ālāris, e, adj. (Tac.) and **ālārius**, a, um [āla], of the ala: cohortes, Caes., Liv.; equites, Liv., Tac. Masc. as Noun : Caes., Tac.

ālātus, a, um [āla], winged : plantae, Verg.; pes, equi, Ov.

alauda, ae, f. [a Celtic word]. **I.** the lark : Plin. **II.** the name of a legion raised by Caesar, in Gaul : Suet. In pl. Alaudae, the Larks, i.e. the men of this legion : Cic. [Fr. alouette.]

alazōn, onis, Acc.·ona, m. [ἀλαζών], a braggart : Pl.

Alba, ae, f. **I.** Alba Longa, the mother city of Rome, built by Ascanius, s. of Aeneas, betw. Lucus Albanus and Mons Albanus.

Hence, pax Albana, i.e. betw. Rome and Alba : Liv.; lapis ·Albanus fr. Mons Albanus, It. peperino or piperno ; and so Albanae columnae, Cic. **Albāni**, ōrum, m. pl. its inhabitants. **II.** Alba Fucentia, a town N.W. of Lacus Fucinus on the borders of the Marsi.

albātus, a, um [albus], clothed in white : epuli dominus albatus, Cic.; Hor. In the Circensian games : auriga albatus, Plin.

albeō, ēre [albus], to be white : albente caelo, i.e. at dawn, Caes.; campi ossibus albent, Verg. Esp. Part. as adj. white : albentes rosae, Ov.; spumae, Ov., Tac.; equi, Curt.

albēscō, ere [albeō], to become white : mare albescit, Cic.; Lucr.; fluctus, Verg.; capillus, Hor. Of dawn (cf. albeo): lux, Verg.

albicō, āre [albus], to be white : Cat.; prata canis pruinis, Hor.

albidus, a, um [albus], whitish, white : Ov. Comp. : Plin. Ep.

Albinius, i, m. a· Roman who conveyed the sacred vessels to Caere, after the defeat at the Allia.

Albiōn, ōnis, f. a name of Britain.

albitūdō, inis, f. [albus], whiteness : Pl.

Albius, a, the name of a Roman gens ; esp. Albius Tibullus a Roman elegiac poet ; **Albiānus**, a, um.

Albula, ae, f. (sc. aqua), the old name of the Tiber.

albulus, a, um [dim. albus], whitish : Cat., Mart.

Albunea, and **Albūna**, ae, f. a fountain at Tibur gushing up between steep rocks ; poet. the nymph of the fountain.

albus, a, um [cf. ἀλβός]. **I.** Adj. white (prop. dead white, opp. ater ; candidus =dazzling white, opp. niger). **1.** Lit. **a.** barba, Pl.; plumbum, Caes.; Neut. pl. as Noun : alba et atra discernere, Cic. Also opp. niger : quae alba sint quae nigra dicere, Cic. ; Ov. **b.** pale : corpus, pallor, Hor. **2.** Transf.: bright, clear : sol, Enn.; Lucifer, Ov. Hence, bringing bright weather : Notus, stella, Hor. (cf. clarus aquilo, Verg.). Idiomatic phr. **i.** dentibus albis deridere, i.e. to laugh to scorn, Pl. **ii.** albus an ater sit nescio or ignoro, I know nothing whatever about him, Cic. **iii.** albo rete aliquid oppugnare, to attack skilfully, Pl. **iv.** albā lineā aliquid signare, to make no distinction, Lucil. **v.** alba avis=rara avis, Cic. Ep. **vi.** filius albae gallinae, fortune's favourite child, Juv. **vii.** equis albis praecurrere, to surpass (fr. the white horses in a triumphal chariot), Hor. **viii.** alicui rei album calculum adicere, to approve (fr. the white pebble used in voting and as a sign of acquittal), Plin. Ep. **II.** Neut. as Noun, **album**, i. **1.** Lit.: the colour white, whitening : maculis insignis et albo, Verg.; columnas polire albo, Liv. **2.** Transf.: a white tablet, e.g. **a.** =Annales maximi, the record of the year's events made by the Pontifex Maximus : aliquid in album referre, Cic., Liv. **b.** the tablets on which the Praetor's edicts were posted up in a public place : sedere ad album, Sen. Ep. **c.** a list *of names, register :* aliquem albo senatorio eradere, Tac. ; albo iudicum eradere, Suet.

Alcaeus, i, *m. a famous lyric poet of Mitylene, contemporary with Sappho, inventor of the verse named after him,* Alcaio ; **Alcaicus**, a, um, *Alcaic.*

Alcamenēs, is, *m. a celebrated sculptor, pupil of Phidias.*

Alcathoē, ēs, *f. the acropolis of Megara.* Hence, *Megara itself.*

Alcathous, i, *m. s. of Pelops, founder of Megara.*

alcēdō, inis, *f. the kingfisher :* Pl.

alcēdōnia, ōrum, *n. pl. the winter-days during which the kingfisher broods and the sea was said to be calm.* Transf.: *deep calm:* Pl.

alcēs, is, *f.* [ἄλκη], *the elk :* Caes.

Alcēstis, is, or **Alcēstē**, ēs, *f. d. of Pelias and w. of Admetus, king of Pherae, to save whose life she gave up her own. She was rescued from Death by Hercules, and restored to Admetus.*

Alceus (disyl.), ei and eos, *m. f. of Amphitryo, and g.f. of Hercules ;* **Alcīdēs**, ae, *m. Hercules.*

Alcibiadēs, is, *m.* (Voc. Alcibiadē), *a celebrated Athenian in the time of the Peloponnesian War.*

Alcīdēs, *v.* Alceus.

Alcimedē, *f. w. of Aeson, m. of Jason.*

Alcinoūs, i ,*m. the wealthy king of the Phaeacians,* by whom Ulysses was entertained.

Alcithoē, ēs, *f., d. of Minyas of Thebes, changed into a bat for ridiculing Bacchic rites.*

Alcmaeōn and **Alcmaeō**, onis, and **Alcmaeus**, i, *m. s. of Amphiaraus and Eriphyle ;* at his father's command he killed his mother and was pursued by the Furies ; **Alcmaeonius**, a, um.

Alcmēna or **Alcumēna**, ae, and **Alcmēnē**, ēs, *f., d. of Electryon, w. of Amphitryon and m. of Hercules by Jupiter.*

alcyōn, or **halcyōn**, onis, *f.* [ἀλκυών, Att. ἀλκυών], *the kingfisher, halcyon :* Verg.

Alcyonē (**Halc-**), ēs, *f., d. of Aeolus, w. of Ceyx, changed into a kingfisher ;* **Alcyonēus** and **-nius** (**Halc-**), a, um ; dies Alcyonii = alcedonia.

ālea, ae, *f.* orig. perh. *a die* or *cube ; a dice-game, any game of chance, gambling :* **1.** Lit.: Pl. ; aleā ludere, Cic. ; in aleā aliquid perdere, Cic. ; aleam exercere, Tac. ; aleam ludere, Suet. **2.** Transf.: iacta alea est, *the die has been cast* (the exclamation of Caesar at the Rubicon), Suet. Esp. *a venture, hazard :* aleam inesse hostiis deligendis, Cic. ; Ov. ; dare summam rerum in aleam, Liv. ; in dubiam imperi servitique aleam ire, Liv. ; alea belli, Liv. ; periculosae plenum opus aleae, Hor.

āleātor, ōris, *m.* [ālea], *a dice-player, gambler :* Pl., Cic.

āleātōrius, a, um [āleātor], *of a gambler :* damna, Cic.

ālēc, *v.* allēc.

Alēius, a, um. **I.** *of Ale in Lycia.* **II.** **Alēii** campi, *the Aleian plains in which Bellerophon, thrown by Pegasus and blinded by the lightning of Jupiter, wandered.*

Alemannī or **Alamannī**, ōrum, *m. pl. a German people on the Upper Rhine and*

Danube. **Alemannia**, ae, *f. the country of the Alemanni ;* **Alemannicus**, a, um, *of the Alemanni.*

Alēmōn, onis, *m., f. of Myscelus, who built Croton ;* **Alēmonidēs**, ae, *m. his son Myscelus.*

āleō, ōnis, *m.* [ālea], *a gambler :* Cat.

āles, ālitis (ABL. ālitī, Sen. ; GEN. *pl.* ālitum, Mart. ; ālitium, Lucr., Verg.) [āla]. **I.** Adj. *winged.* **1.** Lit.: avis, Cic. ; equus, deus, Ov. **2.** Transf.: Auster, Verg. ; passu volat alite virgo, Ov. **II.** Noun, *a winged creature.* **1.** Lit. **a.** *a bird, m.* and *f.* : pennis delata ales, Lucr. ; fulvus Iovis ales, *the eagle,* Verg. ; aetheriā lapsa plagā Iovis ales, Verg. ; albus, *the swan,* Hor. ; cristatus, vigil, *the cock,* Ov. **b.** *any winged person or deity :* Cyllenius ales, Mercury, Claud. Of a poet, ales canorus, Hor. ; Maeonii carminis ales, Hor. **c.** In augury, *a bird that gives omens by its flight* (e.g. the aquila), but oscines by their voice (e.g. the corvus) : Cic. **2.** Transf.: *augury, omen* (alw. *f.*) : bona, Cat. ; mala, secunda, Hor.

alēscō, ere [alō], *to grow :* Varr., Lucr.

ālex, *v.* allēc.

Alexander, drī, *m. a Greek name.* Esp. **I.** *s. of Philip II. and Olympias, surnamed the Great.* **II.** *s. of Perseus, king of Macedonia.* **III.** *a tyrant of Pherae in Thessaly.* **IV.** *a king of Epirus.* **V.** *another name of Paris, s. of Priam.*

Alexandrēa (Cic.) and **Alexandria** (later form), ae, *f.* **I.** *a city built by Alexander the Great on the coast of Egypt ;* **Alexandrinus**, a, um, *Alexandrine :* bellum, Cic. ; vita atque licentia, *like that of Alexandria,* i.e. *luxurious,* Caes. **II.** *a town in Troas.*

alga, ae, *f. sea-weed :* Verg., Hor.

algeō, algēre, ālsi, *to be cold, feel chilly.* **1.** Lit.: Of the body : erudiunt iuventutem algendo aestuando, Cic. ; sudavit et alsit, Hor. **2.** Transf.: probitas laudatur et alget, Juv.

algēscō, algēcere, ālsi [algeō], *to catch cold :* ne ille alserit, Ter.

algidus, a, um [algeō]. **I.** Adj. *cold :* loca, Cat. **II.** **Mōns Algidus** (or **Algidus** alone), *a mountain near Rome.* **III.** **Algidum**, *a town on Mons Algidus.* **IV.** Adj. **Algidus**, a, um, *of Algidum.*

algor, ōris, *m.* [algeō], *cold :* Pl., Lucr., Sall., Tac.

algōsus, a, um [alga], *abounding in seaweed :* Plin.

algū, ABL. *sing. m.* [algeō], *by cold :* Pl., Lucr.

ali-, a stem meaning *else, other, different,* e.g. in alius ; but when combined with quis, quam, cubi, etc. is translated *some or other,* e.g. aliquis, *someone or other.*

aliā, ABL. *f.* of alius, *by a different way :* cum aliā evadere nequissent, Liv.

aliās, Acc. *pl. f.* or old GEN. *sing.* of alius, used adv. **1.** Lit.: **a.** Of place, *elsewhere :* in Idā non alias nascitur, Plin. **b.** Of time, past or future, *at another time :* sed plura scribemus alias, Cic. Ep. ; Hor. ; Liv. ; alias . . . alias, *at one time . . . at another time :* alias eruptione temptatā, alius cuniculis actis, Caes.; Pl.; Cic. Often with *saepe, raro :* fecimus et alias saepe, Cic.; ut raro alias quisquam tanto favore sit auditus, Liv. With *non :* non alias militi familiarior dux fuit, Liv.; non alias caelo ceciderunt plura sereno fulgura, Verg. **2.** T r a n s f.: *in other respects, for other reasons :* alias salubri potu aquae, Ter.; non alias magis indoluisse Caesarem ferunt quam quod, etc., Tac.

āliātum, i, *n.* [ālium], *food flavoured with garlic :* Pl.

alibī, *adv.* [alī, -bī as in ibī, ubī], *elsewhere.* **1.** L i t.: nusquam alibi, Cic.; num alibi quam in Capitolio ? Liv.; hic segetes, illic uvae, arborei fetūs alibi, Verg.; alibi . . . alibi, *in one place,* . . . *in another :* alibi pavorem, alibi gaudium ingens fecit, Liv. alibi alius, *one in one place, another in another place :* pecora diversos alium alibi pascere iubet, Liv.; Lucr. **2.** T r a n s f.: **a.** *in other respects, otherwise :* Pl.; Ter.; nec spem salutis alibi quam in pace esse, Liv. **b.** Of persons : *elsewhere, with some other one :* Ter., Liv.

alica, ae, *f. a kind of grain, spelt :* Cato.

alicārius, a, um [alica], *of spelt. Fem.* as Noun, *a prostitute :* Pl.

ali-cubī (older aliquobi), *adv.* [ali- and cubī =ubī, fr. pron. stem quo, *cf.* sicubī], *somewhere or other :* hic alicubi in Crustumenio, Cic.; Ter.

ālicula, ae, *f.* [āla], *a light cape to cover the shoulders :* Mart.

ali-cunde, *adv.* [ali- and cunde=unde, *cf.* alicubī], *from some place or other.* **1.** L i t.: Pl., Lucr.; decedere nos alicunde cogit, Cic. **2.** T r a n s f. (vaguely of persons) : alicunde conradere, Ter.; Pl.; non quaesivit procul alicunde, Cic.

alid for aliud, *v.* alius.

aliēnātiō, ōnis, *f.* [aliēnō], *the transferring of a thing from one person to another.* **1.** L i t.: sacrorum, Cic. **2.** T r a n s f. **a.** Of persons, *a separation, estrangement, desertion :* turpis fugae et alienatio exercitūs, Caes.; tuam a me alienationem, Cic.; in Vitellium alienatio, Tac. **b.** alienatio mentis, *mental aberration,* Tac. Without mentis : Sen. Ep.

aliēnigena, ae, *m.* [aliēnus and root of gignō], *a stranger, a foreigner by birth :* Cic., Liv., etc. As adj. *alien, foreign :* homo longinquus et alienigena, Cic.; hostes, testes, di, Cic.

aliēnigenus, a, um, *of foreign birth or origin :* alienigenis ex partibus, *heterogeneous,* Lucr.

aliēnō, āre [aliēnus], *to make a person or thing another's, to transfer, alienate.* **1.** L i t. **a.** By sale : ea quae accepissent a maioribus vendidisse atque alienasse, Cic. **b.** By ceding : prodita pars insulae atque alienata, Liv. **2.** T r a n s f. **a.** *to estrange, alienate :* legati alienati, Cic. Esp. with animum, voluntatem : omnium suorum voluntates, Caes.; animos eorum a causā, Cic.; a dictatore animos, Liv.; velut alienato ab sensu animo, Liv. Also, voluntate alienati, Sall. **b.** mentem alienare alicui, *to deprive of reason, to drive mad :* paene alienatā mente, Caes.; Iunonis iram alienasse mentem Flacco ferebant, Liv. Also, hostis velut alienatos sensibus, Liv.

c. In *Pass.* with *ab, to recoil from, be averse from :* alienari ab interitu, Cic.

aliēnus, a, um [alius]. **1.** L i t. **a.** *belonging to another person or thing, another's* (opp. suus): Pl.; aliis sua eripere, aliis dare aliena, Cic.; Liv.; pecuniis alienis locupletari, Cic.; alienum vulnus, i.e. *intended for another,* Verg.; of horsemen, suo alienoque Marte pugnare, i.e. *both on horse and on foot,* Liv. For aes alienum, *a debt, v.* aes. **b.** *not related, foreign, strange :* as Noun : se suaque omnia alienissimis crediderunt, Caes.; cives potiores quam peregrini, propinqui quam alieni, Cic.; apud me cenant alieni novem, Pl.; Cic. **2.** T r a n s f.: *foreign to a thing, inconsistent, unsuitable, adverse,* etc. **a.** With GEN.: alienum eius dignitatis, Cic.; Lucr. **b.** With DAT.: quod illi causae maxime est alienum, Cic. **c.** With ABL.: alienum dignitate imperi, Cic.; Hor. **d.** With *ad :* ad iudicium corrumpendum tempus alienum, Cic.; Caes. **e.** With *ab :* humani nihil a me alienum puto, Ter.; Cic. **f.** Alone : alieno loco proelium committunt, Caes.; as Noun : aliena ac nihil profutura petere, Sall. **g.** alienum esse in or ab aliquā re, *to be a stranger to a thing :* in physicis Epicurus totus est alienus, Cic.; homo non alienus a litteris, Cic. **h.** With animus : alieno esse animo in Caesarem milites, Caes.; alieno a te animo, Cic. **i.** With mens, *distracted, insane :* Sall. Comp. : Cic. Sup. : Caes., Cic., etc.

āliger, gera, gerum [āla, gerō], *winged :* amor, Verg.; agmen, *of birds,* Verg.; Ov.

alimentārius, a, um [alimentum], *relating to food :* lex, Cic. Ep.

alimentum, i, *n.* [alō], *nourishment, food.* **1.** L i t. **a.** alimenta corporis, Cic.; Ov. **b.** Of the reward (or aliment) due to parents from children for their rearing : quasi alimenta exspectaret a nobis (patria), Cic. **2.** T r a n s f.: addidit alimenta rumoribus, Liv.; flammae, ignis, furoris, vitiorum, Ov.; famae, seditionis, Tac.

alimōnia, ae, *f.* (Pl.) and **alimōnium,** i, *n.* (Varr., Tac., Juv.) [alō], *nourishment, food.*

aliō, *adv.* [old DAT. of alius, denoting direction to]. **1.** L i t. **a.** Of place : *to another place, elsewhere :* alio transire cogunt, Caes.; alio me conferam, Cic.; Ter.; Hor. With *quo* (indef.) : Arpinumne mihi eundum sit an quo alio ? Cic. Ep.: Liv. **b.** Of persons or things : sermonem alio transferamus, Cic.; Ter.; Ov.; quo alio, nisi ad nos confugerent ? Liv. **2.** T r a n s f.: Of purpose : nusquam alio natam quam ad serviendum, *to no other end,* Liv.; Cic. P h r. **i.** alio . . . alio, *in one direction* . . . *in another :* alio res familiaris, alio ducit humanitas, Cic. **ii.** alius alio, *one in one direction, another in another :* aliud alio dissipavit, Cic.; Liv. **iii.** aliunde alio, *from one place to another :* Sen.

aliōqui or **aliōquin,** *adv.* [prob. ABL. of alius and quis], lit. *in some other way.* **A.** *in other respects :* milites tantum qui sequerentur currum defuerunt ; alioqui magnificus triumphus fuit, Liv.; Lucr.; Hor. **B.** *in general :* non tenuit iram Alexander cuius alioqui potens non erat, Curt.; Caesar

validus alioquin spernendis honoribus, Tac.
C. In arguments, inferences, etc. : *otherwise, else* : credo minimam istius rei fuisse cupiditatem ; alioquin multa exstarent exempla maiorum, Cic. ; Tac., etc.

aliōrsum [contr. fr. aliōvorsum, wh. is also used] and **aliōrsus,** *adv. in another direction.* **1.** Lit. : mater ancillas iubet aliam aliorsum ire, Pl. **2.** Transf. : =in aliam partem *or* rationem, *in another way, in a different sense :* vereor ne aliorsum atque ego feci acceperit, Ter.

ăli-pĕs, pedis, *adj.* [ăla, pĕs], *wing-footed.* **1.** Lit. : deus, equi solis, Ov. **2.** Transf. : cervi, Lucr. ; equi, Verg. *Absol.* for equus, Verg.

aliptēs *or* **aliptă,** ae, *m.* [ἀλείπτης], lit. *the anointer* in the wrestling-schools ; but us. *the trainer* in the gymnasia : Cic. Ep., Juv.

aliquā, *adv.* [orig. ABL. *f.* of aliquis], *by some way or other.* **1.** Lit. : aliquā evadere si posset, Cic. ; Pl. ; Liv. **2.** Transf. : si non aliquā nocuisses, Verg. ; Pl. ; Ter.

aliquam, *adv.* [orig. Acc. *f.* of aliquis], *in some degree* (only used with *diu, multi*). **I.** aliquam diu. **a.** Of time, *for some considerable time :* ut Oppianicum aliquam diu incolumem fuisse miremini, Cic. ; Liv. Often followed by deinde, postea, postremo, tandem, etc. : quos aliquam diu inermes timuissent, hos postea armatos superassent, Caes. ; Liv. **b.** Of place, *for a long distance :* Mela. **II.** aliquam multi, *a considerable number :* sunt vestrum aliquam multi qui Pisonem cognorint, Cic.

aliquandō, *adv.* [ali-, quandō], lit. *at some time or other.* **A.** *some day, one day* (of past or future) : bene cogitasti aliquando, Cic. ; Sall. ; inlucescet aliquando ille dies, Cic. ; si forte aliquando *or* si aliquando, *if perhaps at some time :* Ter., Cic. **B.** *sometimes, at times* (=nonnunquam, interdum) : utilitatem aliquando cum honestate pugnare, Cic. ; Liv. ; Tac. ; aliquando . . . aliquando, *sometimes . . . at other times :* Sen., Quint. **C.** *after some time, at last* (of present or past, often with *Imper.,* or *Juss. Subj.*), Pl., Cic. ; audite quaeso et aliquando miseremini sociorum, Cic. ; Ov. ; quando isti principes fateantur, Cic. ; finem aliquando fecit, Cic. With *tandem :* tandem aliquando Catilinam ex urbe eiecimus, Cic. ; Ter.

aliquantillum, i, *n.* [aliquantulus], *a tiny little bit :* Pl.

aliquantisper, *adv.* [aliquantus], *for a while :* Pl., Ter.

aliquantulus, a, um [*dim.* aliquantus], *some little, just a little :* Hirt. *Neut.* as Noun, with *Partit.* GEN. : aeris alieni aliquantulum, Cic. ; muri, agri, Liv. Acc. *neut.* (of extent) as adv. : aliquantulum progredi, Cic. ; Pl. ; Ter.

aliquantus, a, um [ali-, quantus], lit. *somewhat ; considerable :* armorum aliquanto numero potiti, Sall. ; per aliquantum spatium secuti, Liv. as Noun, esp. with *Partit.* GEN. : aliquantum itineris, Caes. ; agri, auri, animi, temporis, Cic. ; famae, Liv. Acc. *n.* (internal, or of extent) as adv. *to some degree, considerably :* Pl. ; aliquantum commoveri, Cic. ; movit ali-

quantum oratio regis legatos, Liv. Also, like aliquanto, with comparatives : Ter., Liv. ABL. *n.* (of measure) as adv., *by some amount, considerably :* carinae aliquanto planiores quam nostrarum navium, Caes. ; Liv. ; Tac. ; aliquanto prius, *some time before,* Pl. ; post autem aliquanto surrexit, *some time later,* Cic.

aliquātenus, *adv.* [aliquā, tenus]. **1.** Lit. : Of place, *for some distance :* Mela. **2.** Transf. : *to some extent :* illud aliquatenus longe producitur, Sen. Ep. ; Quint.

aliquī, aliqua (orig. aliquae), aliquod, *pl.* aliquī, aliquae, aliqua (orig. aliquae), *indef. adj.* [ali-, quī *indef. adj.*], *some or other, some* (always emphatic) ; opp. *all, much* or *none) :* Pl., Cic., Ov., etc. ; si est aliqui sensus in morte, Cic. ; esse in mentibus hominum tamquam oraculum aliquod, Cic. ; in alicuius certae personae laudem, Cic. ; haec ille aliquā ex parte habebat, *to some extent,* Cic. With numerals (*cf.* τις) to express an indef. number : Cato ; tres aliqui aut quattuor, *some three or four,* Cic. ; aliqui and aliquis are chiefly used in affirmative sentences ; in negative sentences aliqui is stronger than ullus : nec cum aliquā defensione confiteri, *with some available defence,* Cic. ; Pl.

aliquis, aliquid, *pl.* aliquī, aliqua. ABL. *sing.* aliquī, Pl. DAT. and ABL. *pl.* aliquis, Liv., *indef. pron.* [ali-, quis, *indef. pron.*]. **A.** *somebody or other, something.* **a.** aut ipse occurrebat aut aliquos mittebat, Liv. ; fit plerumque ut adfingant aliquid, Cic. ; Pl. ; Hor., etc. With *si, ne,* etc. (*someone,* i.e. stronger than quis, anyone) : si aliquem cui narraret habuisset, Caes. ; Cic. ; Liv. ; Pompeius omnia cavebat ne aliquid vos timeretis, Cic. Occ. with nouns (chiefly a male person ; *cf.* quis) : ut aliquis nos deus tolleret, Cic. ; num igitur aliquis dolor in corpore est ? Cic. **b.** With adjs. : aliquid naturā pulchrum atque praeclarum, Cic. ; aliquid improvisum, Liv. ; Pl. ; Verg. **c.** With *unus* to denote a single, though indef. person : aliquis unus pluresve divitiores, Cic. **d.** With *alius* : ut per alium aliquem te ipsum ulciscantur, Cic. ; Ter. **e.** *Partit.* with *ex, de,* or GEN. : aliquis ex vobis, de tribus nobis, suorum, Cic., etc. **f.** aliquid with GEN. of noun or adj. : Pl. ; aliquid dignitatis, Caes. ; falsi, virium, Cic. ; armorum, Tac. **g.** In Pl. and Ter., with a *pl.* verb (*cf.* Gk. τις) : aperite aliquis actutum ostium, *some one of you,* Ter. **h.** Acc. *n.* (internal, or of extent) as adv., *to some extent :* si in me aliquid offendisti, Cic. ; Verg., etc. **B.** *somebody or something of importance* (*cf.* Gk. τις, τι) : fac ut me velis esse aliquem, Cic. Ep. ; ego quoque aliquid sum, Cic. Ep. ; Pl. ; Ov. ; dicere aliquid, Cic.

aliquō, *adv.* [old DAT. of aliquis], *to some place or other, somewhere :* aliquem aliquo impellere, Cic. ; Pl. With *Partit.* GEN. : aliquo, quo, ubi, etc. : migrandum aliquo terrarum, Brut. ap. Cic. Ep.

aliquot, *indef. indecl. adj.* [ali-, quot], *some or other in number, some :* dies, Ter. ; aliquot de causis, Caes. ; saecula, Cic. Without Noun : ille non aliquot occiderit, Cic. ; Ter.

aliquotiēns (or **-iĕs**), *adv.* [aliquot], *several times* : Cic., Liv.

aliquōvorsum, *adv. towards some place or other* : Pl.

alis, old form of alius, q.v.

Ālis, idis, *f.* =*Ēlis*, q.v. **Ālius** or **Āleus**, a, um=*Ēlius*, q.v.

ālisequos, i, m. [āla sequor, *cf.* pedisequus], *an attendant* : Cat: (ex coni. A. E. Housman.]

aliter, *adv.* [ali-], lit. *by another way.* **A.** Of place (rare): aliter curvantem bracchiu canorum, Ov. **B.** *in another way, otherwise.* **a.** tu si aliter existimes, nihil errabis. Cic. Ep. ; Pl. ; Verg. With negat., *not otherwise* : fieri non potuit aliter, Cic. Ep. ; Ter. ; Verg. ; Tac. aliter . . . aliter, *in one way* . . . *in another* : Pl., Cic. **b.** With ac, atque, quam : *otherwise than* : aliter ac nos vellemus, Cic. ; Pl. Esp. negatively : haud, non, nec, nihil aliter ac, quam, etc. ; i.e. *just as* : nec scripsi aliter ac si, etc., Cic. ; Verg. ; non aliter nisi, *on no other condition than* : non pati C. Caesarem consulem aliter fieri nisi exercitum et provincias tradiderit, Cael. ap. Cic. Ep. ; Liv. ; Tac. **c.** aliter esse or se habere, *to be differently constituted, be differ nt* : rerum longe aliter est, Cic. ; Pl. ; ratio ordoque agminis aliter se habebat ac etc., Caes. **d.** With alius : *one in one way, another in another* : Cic., Liv. **C.** *otherwise than expected, amiss* : ne quid aliter eveniat, Sall. **D.** *in any other case, else* : ius enim semper est quaesitum aequabile ; neque enim aliter esset ius, Cic. ; Verg., etc.

alitus, a, um, *Part.* alō.

aliubi, *adv.* [ali-, ubi] (rare for alibi), *elsewhere* : Plin. aliubi . . . aliubi, *here* . . . *there*, Varr., Plin. aliubi atque aliubi, *now here, now there* : Plin., Sen. Ep.

ālium, i, n. *garlic* : Pl., Hor. ; in *pl.* : Verg.

aliunde, *adv.* [ali-, unde], *from another place or person* : aliunde dicendi copiam petere, Cic. ; aliundo pendere, Cic. ; aliunde . . . aliunde, *from one place* . . . *from another*, Liv. With alius, *one from one place*, . . . *another from another*, Ter., Liv. ; alii aliunde coibant, Liv.

alius, a, ud, *adj.* and *pron.* [ali-]. (Old form alis, Cat. ; alid, Lucr., Cat.) The GEN. *sing.* is us. supplied by alterius or the adj. aliēnus, the DAT. by altorī ; but the GEN. forms alīus, m., aliae, f., DAT. aliī, aliō, and aliae aro found ; *other, different, else* (us. of several, whereas *alter* means *the other* of two). **I. a.** In general : hostes defessi proelio excedebant, alii integris viribus succedebant, Caes. ; bonus augur ' alio die ' inquit, Cic. **b.** Occ. with indef. pron. aliquis, quis, quidam : aliusne est aliquis improbis civibus peculiaris populus ? Cic. **c.** With ac, atque, et, nisi, quam, *other than* : potest non aliud mihi ac tibi videri, Cic. ; lux longe alia est solis et lychnorum, Cic. ; quid aliud temptatur nisi ut id fieri liceat ? Cic. ; simulando aliud quam quod parabatur, Liv. Hence, nihil aliud nisi or quam with a finite verb (an ellipt. constr. in which *fecit* or *factum est, etc.* must be supplied) ; also quid aliud quam ? :

ut nihil aliud nisi do hoste ac de laude cogitet, Cic. ; quibus quid aliud quam admonemus civis nos eorum esse, Liv. **d.** With ABL., *other than* : nec quicquam aliud libertate quaesisse, Cass. ap. Cic. Ep. ; alius Lysippo, Hor. **e.** With praeter, *other than* : nec quicquam aliud est philosophia praeter studium sapientiae, Cic. **II. a.** In distributive clauses alius is repeated, or opposed to nonnulli, quidam, ceteri, partim, etc. Sing., *the one* . . . *the other* ; *pl.*, *some* . . . *others* : quid potes dicere cur alia defendas, alia non cures ? Cic. ; proferebant alii purpuram, tus alii, gemmas alii, vina nonnulli Graeca, Cic. Also opp. aliquis : putat aliquis esse voluptatem bonum ; alius autem pecuniam, Cic. Occ. alius is omitted in one clause : Helvetii eā spe deiecti (*sc.* alii) navibus iunctis, alii vadis Rhodani, etc., Caes. Occ. aliud . . . aliud marks a distinction betw. things, *one thing* . . . *another* : aliud est male dicere . . . aliud accusare, Cic. **b.** alius is repeated (in another Case) or joined with alias, alio, aliter, etc. : legiones aliae in aliā parte resistunt, *some in one place, others in another*, Caes. ; alius in aliā est re magis utilis, Cic. ; iussit alios alibi fodere, Liv. Hence, alius ex alio (Cic.), alius post alium (Sall.), alius super alium (Liv.), *one after another.* **c.** alius atque alius or alius aliusque, *one and another* ; *different* ; *now this, now that* : (res) alio atque alio elata verbo, Cic. **III.** *of another kind, different* : alius nunc fieri volo, Pl. ; homines alii facti sunt, Cic. Ep. ; longe alia mihi mens est, Sall. Hence, in the divisions of the Senate, in alia omnia ire, transire or discedere, *to reject a measure, vote against it* : frequens eum senatus reliquit et in alia omnia discessit, Cic. Ep. **IV.** *the rest, all the others, other* : Diviciaco ex aliis maximam fidem habebat, Caes. Occ. the alius is redundant (*cf.* Gk. ἄλλος), esp. with a negat. and a comparative : non alia ante Romana pugna atrocior, Liv. ; Fama malum quā non aliud velocius ullum, Verg. **V.** Occ.=alter : Gallia est omnis divisa in partis tris, quarum unam incolunt Belgae, aliam Aquitani, tortiam Celtae, Caes. ; ne quis alius Ariovistus regno Galliarum potiretur, Tac.

all- *v.* adl- for words not found here.

allātus, a, um, *Part.* adferō.

allēc, ēcis, n. *fish-pickle* : Hor.

Allectō (NOM. and ACC), *f. one of the three Furies.*

Allia, ae, *f. a small river which flows into the Tiber 11 miles N. of Rome*, on the banks of which the Romans were heavily defeated by the Gauls on the 18th of July, B.C. 390 ; this day, diēs Alliēnsis was considered ever after a dies nefastus.

alliātum, allium, *v.* āliātum, ālium.

Allobrox, ogis, and *pl.* Allobrogēs, um, m. (ACC. *sing.* Allobroga, Juv.), *a Gallic tribe who occupied the country betw. the Rhone and the Isère* ; subdued B.C. 121 by Q. Fabius Maximus ; **Allobrogicus**, a, um.

allūcinātiō, allūcinor, *v.* alūc-.

almus, a, um [alō], *nourishing* : nutrix, Pl. hence, of deities, etc. *life-giving, bountiful* :

Venus, Lucr.; mater terra, Lucr.; Ceres, vites, ager, Verg.; sol, dies, Hor.

alnus, I, *f. the alder.* **1.** L i t.: Cic., Verg. **2.** T r a n s f.: *anything made of alderwood,* esp. boats : tunc alnos primum fluvii sensere cavatas, Verg.; Juv.

alō, alere, aluī, altum (or alitum), *to feed, nourish, rear.* **1.** L i t.: haec (animalia) alunt voluptatis causā, Caes.; quoniam cibus auget corpus alitque, Lucr. Poet.: velut amnis, imbres quem super notas aluere ripas, Hor. With A B L. of means : reliquam partem hiemis so eorum copiis aluerunt, Caes.; Cic. **2.** T r a n s f. **a.** *to maintain, support :* exercitum, milites, nautas, Cic.; Caes.; cum agellus eum non satis aleret, Cic. With A B L. of means : Caes., Sall. **b.** *to rear, bring up :* locus, ubi alitus aut doctus est, Cic.; Pl.; Liv.; haec studia adulescentiam alunt, Cic.; civitas quam ipse semper aluisset, Caes. **c.** *to feed, nourish, strengthen :* controversiam, Caes.; rumores, Liv.; vulnus venis, Verg.

aloē, ēs, *f.* [ἀλόη], *the aloe.* **1.** L i t.: Plin. **2.** T r a n s f.: from its bitterness : Juv.

Alpēs, ium, *f. pl.* (or *sing.* Alpis, is, *f.*), *the Alps :* **Alpicus** (Nep.) and **Alpīnus,** a, um, *Alpine.*

alpha, *n. indecl.* [ἄλφα]. *the Greek name of the 1st letter of the alphabet.* **1.** L i t.: Juv. **2.** T r a n s f.: *the first :* Mart.

Alphēias, adis, *f. the nymph and fountain Arethusa, which unites its waters with the river Alpheus.*

Alphēus (trisyl.) or **Alphēos,** I, *m. the chief river of the Peloponnese, which flows in a W. direction through Arcadia and Elis into the Ionian Sea.* It disappears more than once, and emerges again after flowing some distance underground ; this gave rise to the myth that it flows under the sea, and, reappearing in Sicily, mingles with the waters of Arethusa ; **Alphēus,** a, um, epith. of Pisae (Pisa) in Italy, *founded by a colony from Pisa in Greece.*

alsius or **alsus,** a, um [algeō], *cold, chilly :* corpora, Lucr. alsus only in *Comp. n. :* Antio nihil alsius, nihil amoenius, Cic. Ep.

altāria, ium, *n. pl.* [altus]. **1.** L i t.: *a raised place, a receptacle placed on the altar to hold offerings :* structae diris altaribus arae, Lucr.; cumulatque altaria donis, Verg. **2.** T r a n s f.: *altars* (esp. *high altars*) *:* en quattuor aras ; ecce duas tibi, Daphni, duas, altaria Phoebo, *high altars to Phoebus,* Verg. Of a single altar : Cic., Liv., Tac. [Fr. *autel*].

altē, *adv.* **I.** *high, on high.* **1.** L i t.: cruentum alte extollens pugionem, Cic.; Verg., etc. **2.** T r a n s f.: video te alte spectare, Cic.; altius irae surgunt ductori, Verg.; ingenium altissime adsurgit, Plin. Ep. **II.** *deep, deeply.* **1.** L i t.: petivit suspirium alte, Pl.; sulcus altius impressus, Cic.; alte vulnus adactum, Verg. **2.** T r a n s f.: alte petito prooemio, Cic.; altius aliquam percellere, Tac.; altius omnem expediam famam, Verg.; altius perspiciebant, Cic.; Lucr.; altissime inspexi, Plin. Ep.

alter, tera, terum, *adj.* and *pron.* G E N. us. alterius, but alterīus often in verse. D A T.

alteri, *m.* (rarely alterō) alterae, *f.,* Caes. [ali- and the suffix seen in *uter, neuter*]. **I.** In general, *one of two, the other of two :* Pl.; altera ex duabus legionibus, Caes.; necesse est enim sit alterum de duobus, Cic.; alter ambove, *one or both,* Cic.; alter consulum, Liv. **II.** Distrib. **a.** alter . . . alter, *the one* . . . *the other :* Pl.; alter exercitum perdidit, alter vendidit, Cic.; alteri dimicant, alteri victoriam timent, Cic. Ep. Occ. a noun or pron. stands in place of the second *alter :* Epaminondas . . . Leonidas ; *quorum* alter . . . Leonidas autem, Cic. Occ. the second *alter* is omitted : alter angulus ad orientem solem, inferior ad meridiem spectabat, Caes. **b.** the second *alter* in a diff. Case : alter alterius ova frangit, *each the other's eggs,* Cic. **III.** As a numeral. **a,** *the second :* primo die . . . alter dies . . . , tertius dies, Cic.; se alterā die ad conloquium venturum, Caes.; qui regnabat ulter post Alexandream conditam, Cic.; nunc eris alter ab illo, Verg.; unus alterve (Cic., Tac.) unus et alter (Ter., Hor.), *one or two.* So with tens, hundreds, etc.: accepi tuas litteras quas mihi Cornificius altero vicensimo die reddidit, *on the 22nd day,* Cic. Also of a number collectively : ad Brutum hos libros alteros quinque mittemus, *a 2nd batch of five,* Cic.; alterum tantum, *twice as much, as much again :* Pl.; altero tanto aut sesqui maior, Cic. **IV.** T r a n s f. **a.** *second* (in qualities, power, etc.) : Verres, alter Orcus, Cic.; Hamilcar, Mars alter, Liv.; alter ego (Cic. Ep.), alter idem, *a second self,* Cic. **b.** *another* (opp. to self) as Noun, *a fellow-creature* (*cf.* ὁ πέλας) : qui nihil alterius causā facit, Cic.; Pl.; Hor. **c.** *different* (rare) : quotiens te speculo videris alterum, Hor. **V.** Sometimes = alius (q. v. ad init.) esp. in G E N. D A T. sing.: neque ullius alterius rei memor, Liv.; ne cuius alterius inscitiā rursum peccaretur, Tac.

altercātiō, ōnis, *f.* [altercor], *a dispute, discussion* (esp. in public and consisting of sharp dialogue) : Pl.; dies consumptus est altercatione, Cic.; non tam perpetuae orationes quam altercatio, Liv. Hence of cross-examination : Cic. Ep.

altercō, āre (act. form of altercor), *to wrangle, quarrel :* Ter.

altercor, ārī [alter]. **1.** L i t.: *to dispute, wrangle :* Labienus altercari cum Vatinio incipit, Caes.; esp. *to cross-examine :* Crassus in altercando invenit parem neminem, Cic. **2.** T r a n s f.: *to contend with :* altercante libidinibus pavore, Hor.

alternō, āre [alternus], *to do first one thing, then a second.* **A.** T r a n s.: *to interchange :* alternant spes timorque fidem, Verg.; Suet. **B.** I n t r a n s.: *to change about, alternate :* alternantes proelia miscent, Verg.

alternus, a, um [alter], lit. *every other* (of two), *every second ;* hence, *alternate, one after the other, in turn.* **I.** In general: alternis trabibus ac saxis, Caes.; Pl.; Verg.; ex duabus orationibus capita alterna recitare, Cic.; alternus metus, *mutual fear,* Liv. Of verses (i.e. distichs) : epigramma alternis versibus longiusculis,

Cic.; canere alterno carmine, i.e. *in elegiacs*, Ov. **II.** Judic. of the right of plaintiff and defendant in turn to reject the jurors appointed by the Praetor: alterna consilia *or* alternos iudices reicere, *to reject by turns*, Cic. **III.** *Neut. pl.* alterna (Hor.) and ABL. alternis (freq. in Lucr.; also in Verg., Liv.) as adv. *by turns*.

alter-uter, alterutra (also altera utra), alterutrum (also alterum utrum), GEN. *sing.* alterīus utrīus, Cic., DAT. alterutrī, *the one or the other of two :* si in alterutro peccandum sit, malo videri nimis timidus quam parum prudens, Cic.; Hor.

Althaea, ae, *f.*, *w. of Oeneus, king of Calydon, and m. of Meleager.*

alti-cinctus, a, um [altus, cinctus], *high-girt*, i.e. *active :* Phaedr.

altilis, e. *adj.* [alō], *fattened, fat.* **1.** Lit.: boves, Varr.; altilis (*sc.* avis), *a fattened bird*, esp. of fowls: Hor. Of plants : Plin. **2.** Transf.: dote altili atque opimā, Pl.

alti-sonus, a, um [altus sonus]. **1.** Lit.: *sounding from on high :* Iuppiter, Poet. ap. Cic. **2.** Transf.: Maro, Juv.

alti-tonāns, antis, *adj.* [altus tonāns], *thundering from on high.* **1.** Lit.: Iuppiter, Enn.; pater, Poet. ap. Cic. **2.** Transf.: Vulturnus, Lucr.

altitūdō, dinis, *f.* [altus]. **I.** *height.* **1.** Lit.: Cato; montium, aedium, Cic.; Caes., etc. Concrete: *heights :* altitudines quas cepissent hostes, Liv. **2.** Transf.: orationis, animi, fortunae, Cic.; Liv. **II.** *depth.* **1.** Lit.: fluminis, Caes.; Cic. **2.** Transf.: *reserve* (bad sense): ingeni, Sall.; animi, Tac.

altiusculus, a, um [*dim.* altus], *rather high :* Suet.

alti-volāns, antis, *adj.*[altus volāns], *high-flying :* Enn.; solis rota, Lucr.

altor, ōris, *m.* [alō], *a nourisher, foster-father :* Cic., Ov., Tac.

altrinsecus, *adv.* [*cf.* extrinsecus], *from the other side :* ego adsistam iam hinc altrinsecus, Pl.

altrix, īcis, *f.* [alō], *a nourisher* (fem.): eadem terra parens, altrix, patria dicitur, Cic.; Verg.; Hor.; *a foster-mother*, Ov.

altrōvorsum, contr. altrōrsus, adv. [alterō versum], *on the other side*, Pl.

altus, a, um, orig. *Part.* alō, *grown big.* Hence, **I.** seen fr. below upwards, *high.* **1.** Lit.: Cic., Verg., etc.; ripae, Caes.; columella tribus cubitis altior, Cic. With Acc. of measure : signum septem pedes altum, Liv. *Neut.* as Noun (us. with preps.): editus in altum, *on high*, Cic. Esp. of *the heavens :* Maiā genitum demisit ab alto, Verg. **2.** Transf.: altissimus dignitatis gradus, Cic.; altā mente praeditus, Cic.; *Neut.* as Noun : alta sperare, Sall., Liv.; vox, Cat.; sonus, Quint. Of gods or persons of high rank, birth, etc.: Verg., Hor., Ov. **II.** seen fr. above downwards, *deep.* **1.** Lit.: flumina, aqua, Caes.; Pl.; radices, Cic.; gurges, vulnus, Verg. **2.** Transf. **a.** premit altum corde dolorem, Verg.; somnus, Liv.; sopor, quies, Verg.; artes, Quint.; tranquillitas, Plin.

Ep. Of the past : genus alto a sanguine Teucri, i.e. *remote, ancient*, Verg. **b.** *Neut.* as Noun (us. with preps.) : ingentem molem irarum ex alto animi ciere, Liv. Hence of arguments, etc. : ex alto repetere *or* petere : quid causas petis ex alto ? *far-sought*, Verg. ; Cic. Often of the sea, *deep-water, the deep :* Pl. ; naves nisi in alto constitui non poterant, Caes.; in alto iactari, Cic.; terris iactatus et alto, Verg. Sometimes, however, perh. *the high seas.* Transf.: imbecillitas in altum provehitur imprudens, Cic. *Comp. :* Caes., Cic., etc. *Sup. :* Caes., Cic., etc. [Fr. *haut.*]

alūcinor, ārī [ἀλύω], *to wander in mind, talk idly, dream :* quae Epicurus oscitans alucinatus est, Cic. ; epistulae nostrae debent interdum alucinari, Cic. Ep.

alumnus, a, um [old *Pres. Part. Pass.* of alō], lit. *being nourished, brought up.* Alw. as Noun. **I.** *Masc.* a *foster-son, nursling.* **1.** Lit.: Pl., Verg., Hor.; legionum alumnus, Tac. Of the inhabitants of a country : ut Italia alumnum suum summo supplicio adfixum videret, Cic.; Hor. **2.** Transf.: pacis, Platoniā, Cic. **II.** *Fem. :* a *foster-daughter.* **1.** Lit.: Pl., Suet. **2.** Transf.: bene constitutae civitatis quasi alumna quaedam eloquentia, Cic. **III.** *Neut. :* numen, Ov.

alūta, ae, *f.*, orig. adj. (*sc.* pellis). **1.** Lit.: *soft leather dressed with alum* (alūmen): Caes. **2.** Transf.: of anything made of this. **a.** a *shoe :* Ov., Juv. **b.** a *purse :* Juv. **c.** a *patch for the face :* Ov.

alvearium, ī, *n.* [alveus], lit. a *bellying vessel.* Hence a *beehive :* Cic., Verg. Also a *beehouse, apiary :* Varr.

alveolus, ī, *m.* [*dim.* alveus]. **I.** a *little trough :* Liv., Juv. **II.** a *gaming-board :* Cic. **III.** a *small stream-bed :* Curt.

alveus, ī, *m.* [alvus]. **I.** a *hollow, cavity :* vitiosae ilicis alveo, Verg. **II.** a *hollow vessel, tub, trough :* Liv. **III.** a *bath-tub :* Cic. **IV.** the *hold* or *hull of a ship :* Sall., Liv. Hence, a *boat :* Verg. **V.** a *beehive* (=alvus, alvearium): Plin. **VI.** a *river-bed :* Verg., Hor., Tac. **VII.** a *gaming-board :* Suet.

alvus, ī, *f.* [alō]. **1.** Lit.. **a.** *the belly, bowels :* Cato, Cic. **b.** *the stomach :* Cic., Ov. **c.** *the womb :* Pl., Cic., Hor. **2.** Transf. **a.** a *boat :* Tac. **b.** a *beehive :* Varr., Plin.

Alyattēs, is, *or* eī, *m.* a *king of Lydia, f. of Croesus.*

am-, prefix, *v.* ambi-.

amābilis, e, *adj.* [amō], *lovable, charming :* filiola, Cic. Ep.; Pl.; nodus amicitiae, Cic.; carmen, insania, frigus, Hor.

amābilitās, ātis, *f.* [amābilis], *lovableness, charm :* Pl.

amābiliter, *adv.* [amābilis], *lovingly* (act.): Cic. Ep., Hor. *Comp. :* Ov.

Amalthēa, ae, *f.* **I.** a *nymph, d. of Melissus, king of Crete, who fed the infant Jupiter with goat's milk ;* or *the goat itself*, one of whose horns, accidentally broken off, was placed among the stars as Cornu Amaltheae *or* Cornu copiae. **II.** *the sibyl of Cumae.*

āmandātiō, ōnis, *f.* [āmandō], a *sending away :* rusticana, Cic.

ă-mandō, āre, *to send away.* **1.** Lit.: Cic., Tac. **2.** Transf.: natura res similis procul amandavit a sensibus, Cic.

amāns, antis. **I.** *Part.* amō. **II.** Adj. *loving, fond, affectionate* (esp. with GEN.). **1.** Lit.: cives amantes patriae, Cic. Ep.; Pl.; Ov. **2.** Transf.: nomen amantius indulgentiusque, Cic.; amantissimus verbis utens, Cic. Ep. **III.** Noun, *a lover :* Ter., Verg., etc.

amanter, adv. [amāns], *lovingly :* Cic. Ep. *Comp. :* Tac. *Sup. :* Cic.

āmanuēnsis, is, *m.* [ab, manus], *a secretary :* = a manu servus, Suet.

amāracinum, i, *n.* (*sc.* unguentum) [amāracus], *marjoram ointment :* Lucr.

amāracus, i, *m.f.* and **amāracum**, i, *n.* [ἀμάρακος and -ον], *marjoram :* Cat., Verg.

amarantus, i, *m.* [ἀμάραντος, *unfading*], *amaranth :* Tib., Ov.

amārē, adv. *bitterly :* Pl., Sen. *Sup. :* Suet.

amāritūdō, inis, *f.* (also **amārities**, ēi, *f.* Cat.; **amāror**, ōris. *m.* Lucr., Verg.), *bitterness.* **1.** Lit.: of taste : Varr., Plin. **2.** Transf.: *harshness :* Plin. Ep.; vocis, Quint. [*Fr. amertume.*]

amārus, a, um, *bitter* (opp. dulcis). **1.** Lit.: of taste : Lucr.; salices, Verg. *Neut.* as Noun : sensus iudicat dulce amarum, Cic. *Comp. :* Cat. **2.** Transf. **a.** Of other senses : fumus, Verg.; fructus amarus odore, Plin. **b.** Of the feelings : amores, Verg. *Neut.* as Noun : amara temperet risu, Hor. **c.** Of speech : hostis, Verg.; dicta, Ov.; sales, Quint. **d.** Of conduct, *harsh, morose :* Ter.; amariorem me senectus facit, Cic. Ep.; mulieres, Tac.

Amāsis, is and idis, *m. a king of Egypt,* c. B.C. 500.

amāsius, i, *m.* [amō], *a lover, gallant :* Pl.

Amathūs, ūntis, *f.* (Acc. Amathūnta), *a town on S. coast of Cyprus,* sacred to Venus ; **Amathūsia**, ae, *f. Venus :* **Amathūsiacus**, a, um.

amātiō, ōnis, *f.* [amō]. **I.** *love-making :* Pl. **II.** *an amour, intrigue :* Pl. In *pl. :* Pl.

amātor, ōris, *m.* [amō]. **I.** *a lover* (in good sense) : sapientiae, pacis. Cic.; Hor. **II.** *a gallant, paramour :* Pl., Cic., Hor.

amātorculus, i, *m.* [*dim.* amātor], *a poor little lover :* Pl.

amātōriē, adv. *amorously :* Pl., Cic.

amātōrius, a, um [amō]. **I.** *amorous, erotic :* poesis, voluptas, Cic. **II.** *exciting love :* medicamentum, Suet. As Noun : **amātōrium**, i, *n. a love-philtre :* Sen. Ep., Quint.

amātrix, īcis, *f.* [amō], *a mistress :* Pl., Mart.

Amāzōn, onis, *f. : pl.* Amāzones, *the Amazons, warrior women said to have lived on the R. Thermodon in Pontus ;* **Amāzonicus**, **Amāzonius**, a, um, *Amazonian ;* **Amāzonis**, idis, *f. an Amazon.*

amb-, *v.* ambi.

ambactus, i, *m. a vassal :* Caes.

ambāgēs, is, *f.* (in *sing.* only ABL.; *pl.* complete, GEN. ambāgum) [ambi-, agō], *a going round, roundabout way, a winding.* **1.** Lit.: dolos tecti ambagesque resolvit, Verg.; variarum ambage viarum (of the

labyrinth), Ov. **2.** Transf. **a.** *a rambling story, circumlocution, evasion, quibbles :* Pl., Verg., Liv., etc. **b.** *equivocations, riddle :* immemor ambagum (of the Sphinx), Ov. Of oracles : eā ambage Chalcedonii monstrabantur, Tac.; per ambages, *enigmatically*, Liv.

amb-edō, ēsse, ēdi, ēsum, *to eat or gnaw around.* **1.** Lit.: of locusts, *to eat up :* Tac. **2.** Transf. **a.** Of fire, *to char :* flammis ambesa robora, Verg. **b.** *to waste :* uxoris dotem, Pl.

ambi, abbrev. **amb**, **am**, **an**, *insep.* adv. [cognate with ambō] ; *cf.* Gk. ἀμφι; O.H.G. umpi ; N.H.G. um]. **I.** *twofold, double.* **II.** *around, round about.* Before vowels us. amb : e.g. ambages. Before consonants ambi, am, an : e.g. ambivium, amplector, anquiro.

amb-igō, ere [agō]. **1.** Lit.: *to wander about* (rare) : patriam, Tac. **2.** Transf. **a.** *to waver,* i.e. *to feel doubt, to call in question, to doubt.* With *Indir. Quest. :* haud ambigam hicine fuerit Ascanius an maior, Liv. With Acc. and *Inf. :* Tac. Esp. (in Cic.) in the *Pass. :* quale quid sit ambigitur, Cic.; Hor. **b.** *to argue :* de vero, Cic. Also *to wrangle :* de fundo, Cic.; de regno, Liv.

ambiguē, adv. **I.** *doubtfully :* Cic. **II.** *indecisively :* Tac.

ambiguitās, ātis, *f.* [ambiguus], *double meaning, ambiguity :* Cic., Liv., etc. In *pl. :* Sen. Ep., Quint.

ambiguus, a, um [ambigō], *wavering, changing from one to another.* **1.** Lit.: favor, Liv.; Salamis, Hor.; Proteus, Ov. **2.** Transf. **a.** *doubtful, uncertain :* haud ambiguus rex, Liv.; Pl. Esp. with GEN., *irresolute :* imperandi, pudoris ac metūs, Tac. With *Indir. Quest. :* Ov. *Neut.* as Noun (esp. with preps.) in ambiguo est, Pl. ; in ambiguo relinquere, Lucr.; in ambiguo servare, Hor.; in ambiguo Britannia fuit, Tac. **b.** *disputed :* res possessionis haud ambiguae, Liv. **c.** *causing doubt, unreliable :* esse ambiguā fide, Liv.; domum timet ambiguam, Verg. Of fortune : secundarum ambiguarumque rerum sciens, Tac. **d.** *perplexing, ambiguous* (of speech) : oracula, Cic.; voces, Verg. *Neut.* as Noun, *a riddle :* ambiguorum complura sunt genera, Cic.

amb-iō, īre [fr. eō, but conjug. as 4th, exc. for *Imp.* ambĭbat, Ov.], *to go round or about.* **1.** Lit. (rare) : ut terram lunae cursus proxime ambiret, Cic. ; Ov. **2.** Transf. **a.** *to go about,* esp. of canvassing, *to solicit :* Pl., Cic. With Acc. of persons whose votes are asked : Cic., Sall. With Acc. of the office : magistratum sibi, Pl. **b.** *to court, entreat, solicit :* palmam histrionibus, Pl. ; reginam adfatu, Verg. In *Pass.* with *Inf. :* Tac. With *ut* and Subj.: Suet. **c.** *to surround, encompass :* (clipei) oras ambiit auro, Verg.; ut vallum armis ambirent, Tac.

ambitiō, ōnis, *f.* [ambiō]. **1.** Lit.: *a going about,* esp. of candidates for office ; *canvassing* (by lawful means ; *ambitus* implies unlawful means) : Cic., Liv. **2.** Transf. **a.** *a striving for popular* (or occ.

private) *favour :* ambitione adducti, Cic. ;
commeatibus vulgo datis per ambitionem,
Liv. **b.** *a striving for advancement, ambition* (good or bad) : ambitio honorumque
contentio, Cic. ; Lucr. ; Hor. ; ambitio
mala, Sall. **c.** *a striving for distinction,
self-advertisement, ostentation :* Nep., Hor.,
Tac.

ambitiōsē, *adv.* **1.** Lit.: *in the spirit of
a canvasser :* Cic. Ep., Liv. **2.** Transf.:
with a desire to please. Comp. : Cic. Ep. ;
Sup. : Quint.

ambitiōsus, a, um [ambitiō]. **1.** Lit.:
going round. Hence, *encompassing, turning about :* lascivis hederis ambitiosior,
Hor. Esp. of canvassing : ita ambitiosus,
ut omnis vos nosque cottidie persalutet,
Cic. **2.** Transf. **a.** *courting popular* or
private favour : Liv. ; Ov. ; in Graecos
ambitiosus, Cic. Ep. ; malis artibus
ambitiosus, Tac. **b.** *striving for advancement, ambitious, self-interested :* homo
minime ambitiosus, Cic. Ep. ; Ov. ; Tac.
c. *striving for distinction, ostentatious, self-
advertising :* mors, Tac., Quint. Comp.:
Hor., Suet.

ambitus, ūs, *m.* [ambiō]. **1.** Lit.: *a
going round, revolution, winding :* stellarum,
Cic. ; aquae per amoenos agros, Hor. ;
saeculorum, Tac. **2.** Transf. **a.** *corrupt
practice in canvassing ;* hence *bribery :*
ambitūs or de ambitu aliquem accusare,
Cic. (For leges de ambitu, v. Dict. Ant.)
b. *intriguing for self-interest :* Tac. **c.**
parade, ostentation : Sen. Ep. ; of speech :
Quint. **d.** Of discourse, *a period :* verborum, Cic. Also *circumlocution* (=am-
bages) : multos circa unam rem ambitūs
facere, Liv. **e.** *circumference, border :*
Tac. ; muri, Curt. ; parmae, Plin. Hence,
an open space about : aedium, Cic.

Ambivius, i, *m.* (L. Turpio), *a celebrated
actor in the time of Terence.*

ambō, bae (bō, Pl.), bō and bō, *num.* (DAT.,
ABL. ambōbus, ambābus ; ACC. ambō, Pl.,
Cic., Verg., Liv. ; ambōs, Pl., Sall., Liv.,
Ov.) [ἄμφω]. **I.** *both* (of things naturally
or habitually in pairs) : consules alter ambove, Cic., Liv. ; manūsque ambas, Verg.
II. =uterque : Caesar atque Pompeius
diversa sibi ambo consilia capiunt eodemque die uterque, etc., Caes.

ambrosia, ae, *f.* [ἀμβροσία, *immortality*].
I. *the food of the gods :* Cic., Cat., Ov. **II.**
the unguent of the gods : Verg., Ov.

ambrosius, a, um [ἀμβρόσιος], *immortal,
divine :* comae, Verg.

ambūbāia, ae, *f.* [Syrian word], *a Syrian
flute-player :* Hor., Suet.

ambulātiō, ōnis, *f.* [ambulō]. **I.** *a walking
about, a walk :* ambulationem post-
meridianam conficere, Cic. **II. a.** *place
for walking, a walk :* Cic. Ep.

ambulātiuncula, ae, *f.* [dim. ambulātiō]. **I.**
a short walk : Cic. Ep. **II.** *a small place
for walking :* Cic. Ep.

ambulātor, ōris, *m.* and **ambulātrix,** īcis,
f. [ambulō], *one who walks about.* **I.** *an
idler, lounger :* Cato. **II.** *a pedlar, ,hawk-
ker :* Mart.

ambulātōrius, a, um [ambulō], *moveable :*
turres, Auct. B. Alex.

ambulō, āre [ambi and root of Gk. βαίνω],
to walk. **A.** In general : Pl., Cic., etc. *Pass.*
Impers. satis iam ambulatum est, Cic. **B.**
to walk for pleasure, take a walk : in sole,
in litore, Cic. ; Pl. **C.** *to walk about
importantly :* Hor. **D.** *to travel :* biduo
aut triduo LXX milia passuum ambulare,
Cic. ; bene ambula, *a good journey to you,*
Pl. Hence, with Acc. of via, mare, etc.,
to walk over, travel over : cum Xerxes maria
ambulavisset terramque navigasset, Cic. ;
Ov. Of inanimate things (rare) : amnis
quā naves ambulant, Cato.

amb-ūrō, ūrere, ūssī, ūstum, *to burn around,
to search, char* (opp. exuro.). **1.** Lit.:
Verres sociorum ambustus incendio, Cic. ;
Pl. ; Hor. ; tigna, Liv. **2.** Transf. **a.**
ambustas fortunarum mearum reliquias,
Cic. ; damnatione conlegae prope ambustus
evaserat, Liv. **b.** Of frost-bite, *to nip :*
ambusti artūs vi frigoris, Tac.

ambūstus, a, um. **I.** *Part,* ambūrō. **II.**
Neut. as Noun, *a burn :* Plin.

amellus, i, *m. the purple Italian star-wort :*
Verg.

ā-mēns, entis, *adj. out of one's senses, mad.*
1. Lit.: Ter., Cic., Verg. ; in dies amen-
tior, Suet.; homo amentissimus atque in
omnibus consiliis praeceps, Cic. With
ABL. of cause : metu, terrore amens, Liv. ;
aspectu, Verg. As Noun : erat amentis
cum aciem videres pacem cogitare, Cic.
2. Transf.: *foolish, stupid.* **a.** Of persons, Cic. **b.** Of things : consilium, Cic.
Ep. ; furor, Cat.

āmentia, ae, *f.* [āmēns], *being out of one's
senses, madness.* **1.** Lit.: Ter., Cic., Ov.,
etc. **2.** Transf.: *folly :* Hor.

āmentō, āre [āmentum], *to fit with a strap* or
thong. **1.** Lit.: hastae amentatae, Cic.
2. Transf. **a.** Of discourse : Cic. **b.**
to hurl a javelin by means of a thong :
Luc.

āmentum, i, *n.* [root ap, *cf.* aptus], *a strap*
or *thong* used for giving length or force to
the throw of a spear : epistula ad amentum
deligata, Caes. ; Verg., etc. Also *a shoe-
lace :* Plin.

Ameria, ae, *f. a very ancient town in Umbria,
noted for its osiers,* now *Amelia.* Hence,
Amerinus, a, um.

ames, itis, prob. *m.* [root ap, *cf.* aptus], *a
pole for spreading bird-nets :* Hor.

amethystinus, a, um, *of the colour of amethyst :*
Mart. *Neut. pl.* as Noun (sc. vestimenta) :
Juv.

amethystus, i, *f.* [ἀμέθυστος] *the amethyst :*
Pl.

amfrāctus, *v.* anfractus.

amīcē, *adv. in a friendly way :* Cic. Sup. :
Caes., Cic.

am-iciō, icīre, ixī or icuī, ictum [iaciō], *to
throw around, wrap about.* **1.** Lit.: only
of upper garments : pallium quo amictus
esset, Cic. ; Pl. **2.** Transf. **a.** nube
umeros amictus, Hor. ; Verg. **b.** Of
things : amicitur vitibus ulmus, Ov. ;
Hor.

amīciter, *adv.* [amīcus], *in a friendly way :*
Pl.

amīcitia, ae, *f.* (GEN. *sing.* amīcitāi, Lucr.)
[amīcus], *friendship.* **1.** Lit.: Pl., Lucr.,

Cic., etc. ; amicitiam comparare, contra-here, iungere, gerere, dissociare, dirumpere, etc., Cic. ; in amicitiam incidere, in amicitiā manere, Cic. ; renuntiare alicui, Liv. ; violare, Liv. **2.** T r a n s f. **a.** *a league of friendship* (betw. nations) : amicitiam facere, Caes. ; colere, Sall. ; petere, Liv. ; in amicitiam populi Romani venire, Liv. ; amicitia ac societas, Liv. **b.** Of plants, e.g. of elm and vine : Plin. **c.** Esp. in *pl.* =amici : Tac., Suet.

amĭcĭtĭēs, ēi, *f.* =amicitia, Lucr.

amictus, a, um, *Part.* amicio.

amictus, ūs, *m.* [amicio], prop. *a wrapping around.* **1.** L i t. **a.** *style of dress* : amictum imitari, Cic. **b.** *a wrap, mantle* : Cic. Ep., Verg., Ov. **c.** *a head-dress used in worship* : purpureo velare comas amictu, Verg. **2.** T r a n s f. : nebulae amictu, Verg. ; Lucr.

amicŭla, ae, *f.* [slighting *dim.* amica], *a mistress* : Cic., Plin. Ep.

amicŭlum, i, *n.* [amicio], *a mantle, cloak* : Cic., Liv.

amicŭlus, i, *m.* [*dim.* amicus], *a dear friend* : Cic., Cat., Hor.

amicus, a, um [amo]. **I.** Adj. *friendly, kind,* with DAT. or preps. : mihi nemo est amicior Attico, Cic. Ep. ; erga te esse animo amico, Ter. ; male numen amicum, Verg. Esp. **i.** in politics : tribuni sunt nobis amici, Cic. Ep. **ii.** in foreign politics : Deiotarum, amicissimum rei publicae nostrae, Cic. Ep. ; civitates amicae, Caes. Occ. of things personified : amica silentia lunae, Verg. ; portūs intramus amicos, Verg. Phr. : amicum est mihi, *it pleases me,* Hor. **II.** As Noun. **A. amicus,** i, *m. a friend.* **a.** In gen. : Pl.,· Cic., Verg. ; amicos parare, habere, etc., Cic. ; servare, Hor., Ov. ; aliquo uti amico, Cic. For patronus, *patron* : Hor. For socius, *companion* : Ov. **b.** In foreign politics : Deiotarus ex animo amicus, Cic. ; amici sociique, Liv. **c.** *a courtier, minister* (*cf.* the " King's Friends ") : Nep., Suet. **B. amica,** ae, *f.* **a.** *a lady friend* : Ter., Ov. **b.** *a mistress* : Pl., Ter., Cic. Ep. [Fr. *ami.*]

ā-mĭgrō, āre, *to depart from home, emigrate* : Liv.

āmissĭō, ōnis, *f.* [āmitto], *a losing, loss* : oppidorum, dignitatis, Cic. ; Sen. Ep.

āmissus, a, um. *Part.* āmitto.

āmissus, ūs, *m.* =āmissiō : Nep.

amĭta, ae, *f.* *a father's sister, a paternal aunt* (the mother's sister is called matertera) : Cic., Liv., Tac. ; magna, *great-aunt* : Tac. [O.F. *ante,* Fr. *tante.*]

ā-mittō, mittere, misi, missum (āmisti =āmisisti, Ter. ; āmissis =āmiseris, Pl.), *to let go away, let slip, give up.* **1.** L i t. : stulte feci, qui hunc servum amisi, Pl. ; illam e conspectu amisi meo, Ter. **2.** T r a n s f. : *to let go, let slip, abandon.* **a.** manibus praedam : Pl. ; praeda de manibus amissa, Cic. ; praedam ex oculis manibusque, Liv. **b.** Of abstracta : occasionem : Ter., Caes., Cic., Liv. ; tempus, Cic. Ep. ; fidem, *credit,* i.e. to break one's word, Nep. ; tibi noxiam, *to pardon,* Pl. **b.** *to lose* (by misfortune, folly, etc. ; perdere means *to send to ruin* by criminal or

immoral conduct) : consilium, Ter. ; vitam, Lucr. ; filium, patrem, Cic. ; litem, causam, Cic. ; patriam, Liv. ; milites, Caes., Cic. ; classes amissae, Cic. ; ignominia amissarum navium, Caes. ; colores, Hor.

Ammōn (or **Hammōn**), ōnis, *m. an Ethiopian god, identical with Jupiter ; represented as a ram* : **Ammōnĭacus,** a, um.

amnĭcŏla, ae, *m. f.* [amnis, colō], *a native of the river* : Ov.

amnĭcŭlus, i, *m.* [*dim.* amnis], *a rivulet, brook* : Liv.

amnis, is, *m.* (earlier *f.* ; ABL. amne or occ. amni esp. in poets), *a stream of water, a broad river, torrent.* **1.** L i t. : Pl., Cic., Verg., etc. Also **a.** *the stream, current* in phr. : secundo amni, *downstream,* Verg. ; adverso amne, *upstream,* Curt. **b.** *river-water* : Verg. **2.** T r a n s f. : amnis disciplinarum et artium, Cic.

amō, āre (amāssō, *Aor. Subj.,* Pl.), *to love* (diligo means rather *esteem*). **A.** In general : eum a me non diligi solum, verum etiam amari, Cic. ; amare et diligere, Cic. ; Pl. ; Verg., etc. Also *to have an amour with* : Pl., Ter., Sall., Verg. **II.** Of things. **a.** as obj., *to like, be fond of, take pleasure in* : nomen, orationem, vultum, etc., Cic. ; otia, Verg. **b.** person. as subj. : ianua amat limen, Hor. With *Inf.* (*cf.* Gk. φιλεῖν) : aurum per medios ire satellites amat, *is wont,* Hor. ; with ACC. and *Inf.* : quae ira fieri amat, *delights to have done,* Sall. **III.** Colloq. phr. **a.** In oaths : ita (or sic) me di (bene) ament or amabunt, Pl., Ter. Also ellipt. : ita me Iuppiter, Pl. **b.** te multo amamus quod eto. (=*it is good of you, it is sweet of you*), Cic. Ep. ; et in Attili negotio te amavi, Cic. Ep. ; Pl. **c.** In entreaties : amabo, *please* or *I should like you to,* etc. : amabo te, advola, Cic. With *ut* or *ne* : amabo ut illuc transeas, Ter. ; Pl. ; amabo te ne improbitati meae adsignes, etc., Cic.

amoenē, *adv. charmingly* : Pl. *Sup.*: Plin. Ep.

amoenĭtās, ātis, *f.* [amoenus], *charm* (to the sight). **1.** L i t. : orarum ac litorum amoenitates, Cic. **2.** T r a n s f. **a.** As a term of endearment : uxor mea, mea amoenitas, quid tu agis ? Pl. **b.** amoenitates vitae, Tac. ; Pl.

amoenus, a, um [amo], *charming, pleasing* (to the senses through the sight). **1.** L i t. **a.** Of landscapes : Enn., Cic., Verg., etc. *Neut. pl.* as Noun, *pleasant places* : Tac. **b.** Of other visible things : templum, Liv. ; cultus amoenior quam virginem decet, Liv. *Sup* : Tac. **2.** T r a n s f. : vita, ingenium, Tac. ; aurae, Hor.

ā-mōlĭor, iri. **1.** L i t. : *to clear away, remove* (with effort or difficulty) : onera, Liv., Luc. ; obstantia silvarum, Tac. With *Refl. Pron. to take oneself off* (*cf. to clear off*) : Pl., Ter. **2.** T r a n s f. : *to set aside, put away* : invidiam crimenque ab aliquo, Tac. ; amolior et amoveo nomen meum, Liv. Occ. *to put away, dismiss* : hominem ab oculis, Tac. ; uxorem, Tac.

amōmum or **-on,** i, *n.* [ἄμωμον], *an aromatic shrub, from which the Romans prepared a costly fragrant balsam* : Verg., Ov.

amor (old form amōs, like honōs, labōs, etc.,
Pl.) ōris, m. [amō], *love.* **1.** Lit. (of
natural affection among relations, etc. ;
of sexual passion ; and of a high degree of
friendship) : Pl., Cic., Verg., etc. With *in,
erga,* or GEN. : noster in te amor, Cic. Ep. ;
amoris erga me, Cic. ; ancillae amor, Hor.
In *pl.* : amores hominum in te, Cic. Ep. ;
Pl. ; Verg., etc. **2.** Transf. **a.** *passionate longing* : consulatūs amor, Cic. ; negoti
suscepti, Liv. ; auri, Verg. With GEN. of
Gerund. : Lucr., Hor., Ov. With *Inf.* :
Verg. **b.** *the loved object, one's love* (in
pl.) : Pompeius nostri amores, Cic. Ep. ;
Pl. ; Ov. **c.** *Love* (person.), i.e. Cupid,
Erōs : Cic., Verg., Ov., etc.
Amorgus (-os), i, *f. an island in the Aegean
Sea,* birthplace of the elder Simonides.
amōs, *v.* amor.
āmōtiō, ōnis, *f.* [āmoveō], *a removing, removal* (rare) : doloris, Cic.
āmōtus, a, um, *Part.* āmoveō.
ā-moveō, movēre, mōvī, mōtum, *to put
away, withdraw.* **1.** Lit.: me exinde loco,
Pl. ; testem aps te, Ter. ; virgas a corpore,
Cic. ; alia ab hostium oculis, Liv. With
ex : Cic. Ep. With *Refl. Pron.* : Ter. ;
e coetu se amovissent, Liv. Occ. euph. for
to steal : boves per dolum, Hor. Also *to
banish* : Tac. **2.** Transf. **a.** *to put
away, lay aside* : suspicionem ab aliquo,
Pl. ; socordiam ex pectore, Pl. ; libidinem,
odium, cupidines, Cic. ; bellum, Liv. ;
ludum, Hor. **b.** in *Perf. Part.* : *withdrawn* : locus a conspectu amotus, Liv.
Amphiarāus, i, m. *a famous Greek seer, f. of
Alcmaeon and Amphilochus* ; **Amphia-
rēus** (five syl.), a, um, *Amphiarian* ; **Am-
phiarāidēs,** ae, m. s. *of Amphiaraus,* i.e.
Alcmaeon.
amphibolia, ae, *f.* [ἀμφιβολία], rhet., *ambiguity, double-meaning* : Cic.
Amphictyones, um (Acc. Gk. -as), m. *pl.
the representatives of certain Greek states,
who met at Thermopylae, later at Delphi* ;
the Amphictyons.
Amphilochus, i, m. **I.** s. *of Amphiaraus,
founder of Argos Amphilochium in W.
Greece.* **II.** s. *of Alcmaeon and Manto, who
had a temple at Oropus in Attica.*
Amphiōn, onis, m. s. *of Antiope by Jupiter,
twin-brother of Zethus ; king of Thebes,
husband of Niobe ; famous for his musical
skill* ; **Amphīonius,** a, um.
Amphissus (-os), i, m. s. *of Apollo and
Dryope, founder of the town Oeta at the foot
of Mt. Oeta.*
amphitheātrum, i, n. [ἀμφιθέατρον], lit.
a double theatre, an amphitheatre : Tac.
Amphitrītē, ēs, *f. w.* of Neptune *and goddess
of the sea.*
Amphitryō (-ō) or **ōn,** ōnis, m. s. *of Alceus
and Hipponome, king of Thebes and hus-
band of Alcmene* ; **Amphitryōniadēs,** ae,
m. *Hercules.*
amphora, ae (GEN. *pl.* as a measure, us.
amphorum), *f.* [ἀμφορεύς]. **I.** *an amphora*
(i.e. a large, two-handled, narrow-necked
jar used for wine, oil, honey, etc.) : Cato,
Hor. **II.** *a measure.* **a.** =2 urnae (i.e.
6⅞ gallons) : Cic. **b.** *for a ship's tonnage,
about ₁/₄₀ th ton* : Liv.

Amphrysus (-os), i, m. *a small river in
Phthiotis, on the banks of which Apollo fed
the flocks of Admetus* ; **Amphrysius,
Amphrysiacus,** a, um, *Amphrysian, of
Apollo.*
amplē, adv. *grandly, splendidly* : Cic.
Comp. : amplius, q.v. *Sup.* : amplissime :
Cic., Liv., Suet.
am-plector, plecti, plexus (act. form am-
plectō, Pl.). **1.** Lit.: *to twine oneself
around.* **a.** *to entwine, coil round* : Pl.,
Lucr. Occ. *to embrace* : Pl., Cic., etc.
Also *to clasp* : Liv., Curt. **b.** *to encircle,
enclose* : XV milia passuum circuitu amplexus, Caes. ; Tac. ; locum munimento,
Liv. ; ansas acantho, Verg. **2.** Transf.
a. *to foster, hug, cling to* : plebem, causam
rei publicae, possessiones, virtutem, Cic. ;
aliquem amicissime, Cic. Ep. **b.** *to grasp,
lay hold of* : nomen regium omni vi, Liv. ;
paupertatem, Curt. **c.** *to embrace* with the
mind : omnia consilio, Cic. ; animo rei
magnitudinem, Cic. ; civitates (*sc.* animo),
Tac. **d.** *to embrace in words, comprise,
include* : actio verbis causam et rationem
iuris amplectitur, Cic. ; quod idem interdum virtutis nomine amplectimur, Cic. ;
cuncta versibus, Verg. ; quos lex maiestatis
amplectitur, Tac.
amplexor, āre (old Latin) and **amplexor,**
ārī [*freq.* amplector]. **1.** Lit.: *to entwine oneself about, embrace fondly* : Pl.,
Ter., Cic. Ep. **2.** Transf. ; *to embrace
closely in one's affection, give a warm welcome to* : Cic., Sall.
amplexus, ūs, m. [amplector], *an encircling* :
terrarum, Lucr. ; serpentis, Cic. ; Liv.
Occ. *an embrace* : Verg., Ov., Tac.
amplificātiō, ōnis, *f.* [amplificō], *an extending, enlarging.* **1.** Lit.: rei familiaris,
Cic. **2.** Transf. **a.** gloriae, Cic. **b.**
Rhet. *a heightened description* : Cic.,
Quint.
amplificātor, ōris, m. [amplificō], *an enlarger, an amplifier* : Cic.
amplificē, adv. *splendidly* : Cat.
amplificō, āre [amplus facio], *to widen, to
extend, enlarge.* **1.** Lit.: divitias, Cic. ;
urbem, Cic., Liv. **2.** Transf. **a.** *to increase* : auctoritatem, sonum, Cic. **b.**
Rhet.: *to heighten, amplify* : Cic.
ampliō, āre [amplius], *to make wider, to
extend, enlarge.* **1.** Lit.: rem, Hor. **2.**
Transf. **a.** Hannibalis bellicis laudibus
ampliatur virtus Scipionis, Quint. ; Mart.
b. In law : *to adjourn the hearing of a case* :
potestas ampliandi, Cic. ; with Acc. of
person, *to defer his case* : Liv.
ampliter, adv. **1.** Lit.: *largely* : Lucil.
2. Transf.: *grandly, splendidly* : Pl.
amplitūdō, inis, *f.* [amplus], *width, extent,
size, bulk.* **1.** Lit.: cornuum, Caes. ;
urbis, Liv. ; corporis, Plin. Ep. In *pl.*:
Cic. **2.** Transf. **a.** animi, Cic. **b.**
grandeur, importance : hominum, in quibus
summa auctoritas est et amplitudo, Cic. ;
civitatis, Caes. ; Liv. **c.** Rhet.: *copiousness* or *dignity of expression* : Platonis,
Cic. Of metre : Quint.
amplius. **I.** Adj. [*Comp.* of amplus], *more,
larger, additional* (chiefly with *quid, nihil*) :
quid faciam amplius ? Ter., Cic. ; nihil

dico amplius, Cic. Hence, the ellipt.
phr. nihil amplius, Cic. **II.** Neut. Noun.
A. more, a larger amount or number :
Pl. ; temporis, obsidum, Caes. ; negoti,
Cic. ; Cat. **B. a.** Judic.: the president
of the court said 'amplius' when ad-
journing the hearing of a case : Cic. **b.**
Judic.: amplius non potere, to bring no
further action, make no further claim : Cic.
c. Polit.: of an addition to a motion in
the senate ; hoc amplius censeo, Cic. **III.**
Adv. **A.** more, to a larger extent. **a.** Without quam (the case not being affected by
the omission): amplius centum cives
Romani, Cic. ; pugnatum duas amplius
horas, Liv. **b.** Less often with ABL.:
amplius horis quattuor, Caes. ; Liv. **c.**
With quam (Aug. and post-Aug.) : Liv.,
Suet. **B.** further, longer (chiefly with
negatives) : non luctabor tecum amplius,
Cic. ; Caes. ; Verg. **C.** more times (rare) :
felices ter et amplius, Hor.

amplus, a, um. **1.** Lit.: of space : large,
wide, spacious : curia, gymnasium, domus,
signum, Cic. ; collis, Sall. ; porticus, Verg.
2. Transf. **A. a.** Of quantity or amount,
etc. ; large, great : res familiaris, Cic. ;
exercitus, Sall., Plin. Ep. ; pabula, Lucr. ;
lucrum, Pl. **b.** Of internal force or power,
great, strong, powerful : irae, Ter. ; vires,
Lucr. ; spes, Sall., Prop. ; metus, Cic. ;
animus, Sall. **B.** great, grand, lordly,
splendid, imposing (esp. in the superlative).
a. Externally : munera, Caes. ; honores,
verba, beneficia, laudes, Cic. ; spolia, Verg.
b. Rather on the internal side, great, i.e.
high, eminent : familia, Cic. ; amplissimo
genere natus, Caes. Hence (cf. Eng. 'his
Eminence '), amplissimus as a title for
persons in high office : ordo amplissimus
(of the senate), Cic., Plin. Ep. **c.** Rhet. :
amplus orator, Cic. ; amplum orationis
genus, Cic. Here amplus includes the ideas
of dignity and fulness. Comp : freq. in all
periods. Sup. : from Cicero onwards.

Ampsanctus, I, m. a valley and lake in Italy,
dangerous from their pestilential exhalations,
now Le Mofete.

ampulla, ae, f. a small amphora (q.v.), flask,
jar, pot, etc. **1.** Lit.: Pl., Cic. **2.**
Transf. (fr. a painter's colour-pot), highly-
coloured language, bombast : Hor.

ampullārius, I, m. a flask-maker ; Pl

ampullor, āri [ampulla], to be bombastic : Hor.

amputātiō, ōnis, f. [amputō], a pruning.
1. Lit.: sarmentorum, Cic. **2.** Transf.:
a cutting (i.e. the part cut off) : Plin.

am-putō, āre, to cut around, trim, prune. **1.**
Lit.: esp. of plants : vitem ferro, Cic. ;
capillos, Plin. Ep. **2.** Transf. : to prune
away : amputata inanitas omnis, Cic. ;
numerum legionum, Tac.

Ampyx, ycis, m. **I.** one of the Lapithae. **II.**
a companion of Phineus, changed by Perseus
into a stone.

Amūlius, I, m. s. of Procas, king of Alba ;
he ordered Romulus and Remus, the grand-
sons of his brother Numitor, to be thrown into
the Tiber.

amurca, ae, f. [Gk. ἀμόργη] pronounced
amurga ; the watery matter from an olive-
press, oil-dregs : Cato, Verg.

amussis, is, f. (Acc. amussim), a carpenter's
rule or square or plumb-line : Varr. Hence,
examussim (Pl.) **adamussim** (Varr.)
according to rule, exactly.

amussitō, āre [amussis] to adjust to the
plumb-line. Transf : Pl.

Amyclae, ārum. f. pl. **I.** a town in Laconia,
the home of Tyndareus, and the birthplace of
Castor and Pollux. **II.** a town in Latium ;
Amyclaeus, a, um.

Amyclīdēs, ae, m. a descendant of Amyclas,
founder of Amyclae, i.e. Hyacinthus.

amygdalum, I, n. und -a, ae, f. (Cato)
[ἀμύγδαλον], an almond : Ov.

Amýmōnē, ēs, f. **I.** d. of Danaus and g.m. of
Palamedes. **II.** a fountain near Argos.

Amyntās, ae, m. **I.** f. of Philip II. of Macedon ; **Amyntiadēs**, ae, m. Philip. **II.** a
shepherd in Verg.

Amyntor, oris, m. king of the Dolopians, and
f. of Phoenix, who is called **Amyntoridēs**, ae.

amystis, idis, f. [ἀμυστί, without closing the
mouth], the emptying of a cup at one draught :
Hor.

Amythāōn, onis, m. s. of Cretheus and f. of
Melampus, who is called Amythāonius.

an, conj. It introduces the second and succeeding members in a disjunctive question,
or in an expression of irresolution ; or, or
whether, or perhaps, or rather. N.B. that
the first member can be introduced by
utrum, -ne, nonne, num (in direct questions),
an (rare), or by no interrog. particle. **A.**
Direct (negat. an non). **a.** utrum defenditis an impugnatis plebem ? Liv.;
Pl. ; Cic. ; custosne urbis an direptor est
Antonius ? Cic. ; Pl. **b.** N.B. that as the
opinion of the speaker or the probability
of the case often leans to the second of such
alternatives, this inclination is occ. emphasised (e.g. in Pl., Ter.) by potius, rather ;
or we find the first member omitted, so that
an often appears to introduce a single
question, when it may be rendered or is it
the case that, or is it rather that (sometimes
showing surprise) : Cic., Hor. **B.** Indirect
(negat. necne ; rarely an non). **a.** id
agitur bonisne an malis moribus vivamus,
Sall. ; vivat an mortuus sit quis aut curat ?
Cic. Occ. anne : interrogetur tria pauca
sint anne multa, Cic. **b.** With the first
member omitted (cf. A.b.) : quaesivi an
misisset, Cic. **c.** Esp. in dependence on
expressions of irresolution, e.g. dubito, haud
scio, nescio, incertum : an dolo malo
factum sit ambigitur, Cic. ; Ov. ; certe est,
et id incertum an hoc ipso die, Cic. N.B.
with regard to haud scio an, nescio an (cf.
A.b.) that, in the clause introduced by an,
the tone is often, if not always, that of a
strong assertion, and we must translate not
merely by or as I am inclined to believe, but
by or as I feel sure, or as I feel convinced :
testem non mediocrem, sed haud scio an
gravissimum, Cic. ; ingens eo die res, ac
nescio an maxima illo bello gesta sit, Liv.

an-, v. ambi.

anabathrum, I, n. [ἀνάβαθρον], a raised seat
at the public games : Juv.

Anaces, um, m. pl. [Gk. ἄνακες], an epithet
of the Dioscuri : Cic.

Anacharsis, is, m. a famous Scythian philosopher in the time of Solon.

Anacreōn, ŏntis, m. a famous lyric poet of Teos (c. B.C. 540). **Anacreōntius**, a, um.

anadēma, atis, n. [ἀνάδημα], a band for the head, a wreath : Lucr.

anaglypta, ōrum, n. pl. work in bas-relief : Plin., Mart.

anagnōstēs, ae, m. [ἀναγνώστης], a reader : Cic. Ep.

anancaeum, I, n. [ἀναγκαῖον, compulsory], a large drinking cup, which had to be drained at a draught : Pl.

anapaestus, a, um [ἀνάπαιστος], pes, the metrical foot, anapaest ‿ ‿ –, Cic. Neut. as Noun (sc. carmen), an anapaestic poem : Cic.

anas, anatis, f. a duck : Cic., Ov.

anaticula, ae, f. [dim. anas], a duckling : Cic. As term of endearment : Pl.

anatinus, a, um [anas], of a duck : Pl.

anatocismus, I, m. [ἀνατοκισμός, breeding on breeding], interest on interest, compound interest : Cic. Ep.

Anaxagorās, ae, m. [Ἀναξαγόρας], a famous philosopher of Clazomenae, teacher of Pericles and Euripides.

Anaxaretē, ēs, f. a maiden of Cyprus, who, refusing the love of Iphis, was changed into a stone.

Anaximander, drī, m. a famous philosopher of Miletus.

Anaximenēs, is, m. a famous philosopher of Miletus who taught that air is the first-principle of all things.

Ancalītēs, um, m. pl. a tribe in Britain.

anceps (ancipes, Pl.), cipitis, adj. [amb-, caput]. **1.** Lit.: two-headed : Ianus, Ov. **2.** Transf. **a.** acumen (montis), Ov.; ferrum, Lucr.; securis, Ov.; Pl. **b.** having two fronts, twofold, on both sides : cum anceps hostis et a fronte et a tergo urgeret, Liv.; ancipiti proelio pugnatum est, Caes.; ancipiti contentione (i.e. terrā marique) distracti, Cic.; metus et ab cive et ab hoste, Liv.; odium (transfugarum), Liv. Occ. of double nature, amphibious : bestiae, Cic. **c.** doubtful, uncertain, undecided : fortuna belli, Cic.; ancipiti Marte pugnare, Liv.; fides, Curt. **d.** of double meaning or interpretation, equivocal : oraculum, sententia, Liv.; ius, Hor. **e.** precarious, critical, risky (' between two fires '), mostly post-Aug.: cos revocare anceps erat, Liv.; viae, Ov.; adulatio, Tac. Neut. as Noun (in sing. or pl.): danger, risk, peril (mostly with preps.) : Tac.

Anchisēs, ae, m. s. of Capys, f. of Aeneas ; carried by Aeneas on his shoulders from the flames of Troy ; **Anchisēus**, a, um ; **Anchisiadēs**, ae, m. s. of Anchises, i.e. Aeneas.

ancile, is, n. (GEN. pl. anciliōrum, Hor.), a small oval shield ; esp. the shield said to have fallen from heaven in the reign of Numa : Verg., Liv., Tac. As adj. : Juv.

ancilla, ae, f. dim. a maid-servant, female slave : Pl., Cic.. Hor., etc.

ancillāris, e, adj. [ancilla], of female servants : Cic.

ancillula, ae, f. [dim. ancilla], a little serving-maid. **1.** Lit.: Ter., Ov. **2.** Transf.: Cic.

ancipes, v. anceps.

ancisus, a, um [amb, caedō], cut around : omnia ancisa recenti vulnere, Lucr.

ancora, ae, f. [ἀγκύρα], an anchor : ancoras iacere, to cast anchor, Caes.; ponere, Liv.; navis deligare ad ancoras, Caes.; consistere ad ancoram, to lie at anchor, Caes.; solvere, to weigh anchor, Cic.; tollere, Caes.; moliri, vellere, Liv.; praecidere, Cic. Transf.: as a symbol of security : refuge, hope, support : Ov.

ancorāle, is, n. [ancora], a cable : Liv.

ancorārius, a, um [ancora], of an anchor : funes, cables, Caes.

Ancus Marcius, I, m. the fourth king of Rome.

Ancyra, ae, f. a town in Galatia, now Angora ; **Ancyrānus**, a, um. Monumentum Ancyranum, an important record of the reign of Augustus found at Ancyra.

andabata, ae, m. a gladiator, whose helmet was without openings for the eyes, a blindfold gladiator : Cic. Ep.

Andēs, ium, f. pl. a village near Mantua, birthplace of Vergil ; **Andīnus**, a, um.

Andraemōn (or -ēmōn), onis, m. **I.** f. of Amphissus and h. of Dryope, changed into a lotus. **II.** f. of Thoas.

Andria, ae, v. Andros.

Andriscus, I. m. a slave who proclaimed himself s. of king Perseus, and thus brought about the 3rd Macedonian War.

Androclēs, is (-us, I), m. a slave who healed the injured foot of a lion, and was afterwards recognised, and saved from death by the lion.

Androgeōs (-eus), I (or -ōn, ōnis, Acc. Androgeōna, m. s. of Minos, king of Crete, killed by the Athenians and Megarians ; **Androgeōnēus**, a, um.

androgynus, I, m. [ἀνδρόγυνος], and -gynē, ēs, f. a man-woman, hermaphrodite : Cic.

Andromachē, ēs, and -a, ae, f. d. of king Eëtion and w. of Hector.

Andromeda, ae, and -ē, es, f. d. of Cepheus and Cassiope rescued from a sea-monster by Perseus, and after death placed in heaven as a constellation.

andrōn, ōnis, m. [ἀνδρών, men's quarters in a house], a corridor : Plin. Ep.

Andronicus, I. m. the surname of several Romans, esp. L. Livius Andronicus, the first dramatic and epic poet of the Romans ; ob. B.C. 204.

Andros (or -us). I, f. an island in the Aegean Sea, now Andro ; **Andrius**, a, um ; **Andria**, ae, f. a woman of Andros, title of a comedy by Terence.

ānellus, I, m. [dim. ānulus], a little ring : Pl., Lucr., Hor

anēthum, I, n. dill, anise : Verg.

an-frāctus, ūs, m. [amb, frangō], a bend. **1.** Lit.: Cic. Also orbit : solis, Cic. Esp. of roads, bend, winding : Caes., Liv. **2.** Transf.: of discourse (= ambages), circumlocution, digression : Cic., Quint. Also of legal proceedings : iudiciorum, Cic.; iuris, Quint.

angellus, ī, m. [dim. angulus], small corners or points : Lucr.

angina, ae, f. [angō], quinsy : Pl., Plin.

angiportus, ūs, m. and **angiportum**, I, n. [ang-, cf. angustus, and portus], a narrow street, lane, alley : Pl., Cic., Hor., etc.

Angitia, ae, *f. a goddess worshipped by the Marsi ; s. of Medea and Circe.*

ango, ere [*cf.* ἄγχω], *to press tight.* **1.** L i t . : *to throttle, strangle :* Verg. **2.** T r a n s f . : *to torture, distress, pain.* **a.** Of body : Plin. **b.** Of mind : cura angit hominem, Ter. ; Lucr. ; Hor. ; cruciatu timoris angi, Cic. ; Liv. ; angi animi, Pl., Cic. ; angi animo, Cic. With *de :* de Statio manu misso angor, Cic. Ep.

angor, ōris, *m.* [angō]. **1.** L i t . : *a compression* (of the neck). **a.** *suffocation :* Liv. **b.** *quinsy :* Plin. **2.** T r a n s f . : *anguish, torment, distress* (of a transitory nature, whereas *anxietas* is of a lasting nature) : angorem capere pro amico, Cic. ; Tac. ; confici angoribus, Cic.

anguicomus, a, um [anguis, coma], *snakehaired* (i.e. having snakes for hair) : Gorgon, Ov.

anguiculus, ī, *m.* [*dim.* anguis], *a small snake :* Cic.

anguifer, era, erum [anguis, ferō], *snakebearing :* caput, Ov.

anguigena, ae, *m.* [anguis and root of gignō], *snake-born :* epith. of the Thebans who sprang from dragons' teeth : Ov.

anguilla, ae, *f.* [anguis], *an eel :* Juv. ; T r a n s f . : anguilla est, elabitur (as proverb) : Pl.

angui-manus, a, um [anguis, manus], *snake-handed, with serpent arm* (i.e. the trunk) : of the elephant : Lucr.

anguineus, a, um, [anguis] *snaky :* Gorgonis comae, Ov.

anguinus, a, um [anguis], *snaky :* Cato ; Cat. *Neut.* as Noun (*sc.* ovum), *a snake's egg :* Plin.

angui-pēs, pedis, *adj.* [anguis, pēs], *snakefooted :* of the giants : Ov.

anguis, is (ABL. angue or -i), *m.f. a snake, serpent.* **1.** L i t . : Pl., Cic., Verg., etc. P r o v . : latet anguis in herbā (i.e. concealed danger) : Verg. Also for something odious : odisse aliquem aeque atque anguis, Pl. ; Hor. **2.** T r a n s f . **A.** Myth. as an emblem. **a.** of terror : of the head of Medusa : Ov. **b.** of rage : of the serpentgirdle of Tisiphone, Ov. **c.** of art and wisdom : of the serpent-team of Medea (Ov.), and of the inventive Ceres, Ov. **B.** Astron. **a.** =draco, *the Dragon,* betw. the Great and the little Bear : Cic., Verg., Ov. **b.** hydra, *the Hydra :* Ov. **c.** *the Serpent,* which Anguitenens carries in his hand : Ov.

angui-tenēns, entis, adj. [anguis, teneō], *serpent-holding.* As Noun : *the constellation Ophiuchus :* Cic.

angulāris, e, *adj.* [angulus], *having angles or corners :* lapis, Cato.

angulātus, a, um [angulus], *having angles or corners :* Cic.

angulus, ī, *m. an angle, a corner.* **1.** L i t . : obtusus, Lucr. ; ad parīs angulos, *at right angles,* Cic. ; castrorum, Caes. ; muri, Alpium, Liv. ; Ov. **2.** T r a n s f . : *a corner* (as being a retired or unfrequented place) : nec ullo in angulo totius Italiae, Cic. ; angulus hic mundi nunc me accipit, Prop. ; Ter. ; Hor. Hence opp. to life of town or business : Cic., Hor.

angustē, *adv. in narrow limits, in close proximity.* **1.** L i t . : sedere, Cic. ; Pompeium angustissime continere, Caes. ; transportare milites, *by packing them close,* Caes. **2.** T r a n s f . **a.** *within narrow limits :* quod angustius apud Graecos valet, Cic. **b.** *concisely, briefly :* dicere, scribere, Cic.

angustiae, ārum, *f. pl.* [angustus], *a narrow place, a strait, defile.* **1.** L i t . : Corinthus posita in angustiis, Cic. ; Hellesponti, Suet. ; itineris, Caes. ; Tac. **2.** T r a n s f . : *shortness, narrowness.* **a.** Of time : in his angustiis temporis, Cic. **b.** Of money, supplies, etc. : rei frumentariae, Caes. ; aerari, Cic. ; Tac. ; spiritūs (of breath in speaking), Cic. **c.** *limitations, restrictions* (of circumstances, etc.) : pectoris tui, Cic. ; hence, *difficulties, perplexities :* in summas angustias adduci, Cic. ; Caes. **d.** Of verbal subtlety : Cic.

angusticlāvius, a, um [angustus, clāvus], *wearing a narrow stripe of purple, as a* plebeian tribune : Suet.

angustō, āre [angustus], *to make narrow :* Cat., Luc., Sen.

angustus, a, um [angō]. **1.** L i t . : of space, *narrow, strait, close together, limited :* fauces portūs, fines, Caes. ; pontes, Cic. ; rima, Hor. *Neut.* as Noun : per angustum, Lucr. ; angusta viarum (i.e. *narrow ways*), Verg., Tac. Also transf. *a narrow compass, straits, a critical position :* res est in angusto, Caes. ; Ter. ; in angustum rem concludere, adducere, deducere, Cic. **2.** T r a n s f . : *short, limited.* **a.** Of time : Verg., Ov. **b.** Of money, supplies, etc. : res frumentaria, fides (*financial credit*), Caes. ; spiritus (breath in speaking), Cic. **c.** *limited* in circumstances, hence, **i.** *base, petty :* animus, Cic. **ii.** *subtle, petty :* minutae angustaeque concertationes, Cic. **iii.** Of style, *brief :* Cic., Prop. *Comp.* and *Sup. :* Caes.

anhēlitus, ūs, *m.* [anhēlō], *quick breathing, panting, puffing.* **1.** L i t . **a.** ex cursurā anhelitum ducere, Pl. ; aeger, Verg. In *pl. :* Cic. **b.** *breathing, breath :* recipere, *to take breath,* Pl. ; vini (i.e. breath smelling of wine), Cic. ; Ov. **2.** T r a n s f . : *an exhaling, exhalation :* terrae, Cic.

anhēlō, āre [anhēlus], *to breathe hard, pant, puff, gasp.* **1.** L i t . : Ter., Lucr., Verg. **2.** T r a n s f . **a.** fornacibus ignis anhelat, Verg. **b.** With Acc. : verba quasi anhelata, Cic. ; Catilinam scelus anhelantem, Cic. ; anhelati ignes, Ov.

anhēlus, a, um [an (=dvá), hālō]. **A.** *panting, puffing :* Verg. **B.** *causing one to pant or gasp :* sitis, Lucr. ; tussis, Verg.

Anicius, a, *the name of a Roman gens ;* **Aniciānus**, a, um : Aniciana nota, *the Anician brand* (of wine dating from the consulship of L. Anicius Gallus, B.C. 159).

anicula, ae, *f.* [*dim.* anus], *a silly old woman, old wife :* Ter., Cic.

Aniēn, *v.* Aniō.

anīlis, e, *adj.* [anus], *of an old woman :* Cic., Verg., etc.

anīlitās, ātis, *f.* [anīlis], *old age of a woman :* Cat.

anīliter, *adv. like an old woman :* superstitiose atque aniliter dicere, Cic.

anima, ae, *f.* (GEN. animāī, Lucr.) [root of Gk. ἄημι], lit. *that which breathes* or *blows*. **1.** Lit. **a.** *air, a breeze, wind* : Pl., Verg., etc.; aurarum, Lucr. **b.** *the air* (as an element) : Lucr., Cic., Verg. **c.** *air* (in respiration or expiration), *the breath*. animam recipere, *to take breath*, Ter.; excipere, Pl.; continere, Cic.; comprimere, *to hold the breath*, Ter.; intercludere, *to stop the breath*, Tac. In *pl.* : Verg., Ov. **2.** Transf. **a.** *fumes* : amphorae, Phaedr. **b.** *breath as the breath of life, life* ; animam adimere, Pl.; exstinguere, relinquere, Ter.; efflare, agere, edere, Cic.; exhalare, expirare, Ov.; amittere, Lucr.; emittere, Nep.; proicere, Verg. Also of the blood as the life : purpuream vomit ille animam, Verg. Prov.: animam debere (of a man deeply in debt), Ter. As a term of endearment, *my life, my soul* : Cic. Ep. **c.** *a living being* (as we say *souls* for *persons*) : Verg., Tac. **d.** *souls separated from the body, manes* : Enn., Verg., Suet., etc. **e.** rarely = animus, *the rational soul* : anima rationis consilique particeps, Cic.; Sall.

animadversiō, ōnis, *f.* [animadvertō]. **I.** *a heeding, attention, observation* : notatio naturae et animadversio, Cic.; animadversio et diligentia, Cic.; quaestio atque animadversio in civem quid fecerit, Liv. **II.** **a.** *censure, reproach* : Cic. **b.** *chastisement, punishment* : paterna, censoria, Cic.; Tac.; Dolabellae in audacis servos, Cic.

animadversor, ōris, *m.* [animadvertō], *an observer* : Cic.

animadvertō (older **-vortō**), tere, tī, sum [animum, adverto] (rare in poets exc. Ter. and Verg.), lit. *to turn the mind to*. **I.** *to give heed to, attend to* : Liv. With Acc. : horum dolorem, Cic.; Ter. With *ne* and *Subj.* : animadvertant ne adsentatione capiantur, Cic. **II.** *to remark, notice, observe* (as the result of attention). With Acc. : Cic., Verg., etc. With Acc. and *Inf.* : Ter., Cic., etc. With *Indirect Quest.* : Cic. **III. a.** *to censure, reproach* : Ter., Cic. **b.** *to punish, chastise*, esp. in aliquem animadvertere : Caes., Cic., Liv., etc. Also *in* or *aliquem animadvertere*, Cic., Tac. Also absol. *to punish with death* : Tac.

animal, ālis, *n.* [anima], *a living being, an animal* : Lucr., Cic.; animalia inanimaque omnia, Liv. Of man : animal providum et sagax homo, Cic.; Ov. Of the universe : hunc mundum animal esse, Cic. Opp. to man : alia animalia gradiendo, alia serpendo ad pastum accedunt, etc. Cic.; Quint. Hence, contemptuously of a man, *a brute* (so pecus, udis : q.v.) : Cic.

animālis, e, *adj.* [anima]. **I.** *of air* : natura vel terrena, vel ignea, vel animalis, vel umida, Cic. **II.** *animated, living* : corpora, Lucr.; quaedam animalis intellegentia, Cic.

animāns, antis. **I.** Part. animō, *animate, living* : Cic. **II.** Noun, *m.f.n. any living being ; an animal* : animantium genera quattuor, Cic.; Lucr.; Ov. Poet.: of man : hic stilus haud petet ultro quemquam animantem, Hor.

animātiō, ōnis, *f.* [animō], lit. *the bestowal of life*. Transf.: *the living being itself* : Cic.

animātus, a, um. **I.** *Part.* animō. **II.** *Adj.* **a.** *disposed, minded ;* animatus melius quam paratus, Cic.; sic in amicum sit animatus, Cic.; Liv. With *Inf.* : si quid animatus es facere, Pl. **b.** *courageous, stout-hearted* (= animosus) : more fully animatus probe, Pl.

animō, āre. **I.** [anima]. Lit.: *to fill with breath* or *air* : hence, *to make alive, animate* : Lucr., Cic. Poet.: guttas animavit in anguis, Ov. **II.** [animus]. *to endow with spirit, temperament* or *courage* : utcumque temperatus sit aër, ita pueros orientis animari, Cic.; ipso terrae suae solo ac caelo acrius animantur, Tac.

animōsē, *adv.* **I.** *courageously* : Cic. **II.** *ardently, eagerly* : Cic. *Comp.* : Sen. *Sup.* : Suet.

animōsus, a, um. **I.** [anima], *full of air* or *breath, airy* : guttura, Ov. Of the wind : Eurus, Verg. **II.** [animus]. **a.** *full of courage, spirited* : Cic., Hor.; joined with fortis, Cic., Hor. Of a horse : Verg., Ov. Also bella, Ov. **b.** Poet.: *proud*, with *Causal* ABL.: en ego (Latona) vestra parens, vobis animosa creatis, Ov. **c.** *spirited, fearless* (of expense or danger) : corruptor, Tac.

animula, ae, *f.* [*dim.* anima], *a little soul, life, piece of soul* : quae (litterae) mihi quiddam quasi animulae restillarunt, Cic. Ep.

animulus, I. *m.* [*dim.* animus] only Voc.: mi animule, *dear heart !* : Pl.

animus, I, *m.* [*v.* anima]. **I.** In a general sense, *the rational soul in man* (opp. to the body, *corpus*, and to the physical life, *anima*) : credo deos sparsisse animos in corpora humana, Cic.; Lucr.; Hor. Also of animals : Cic., Verg., Ov. **II.** In a more restricted sense, *the soul as thinking, feeling, willing* : hence, **A.** *the intellect, understanding, mind, reason, thought* : recordari cum animo, Cic.; Pl.; rem agitare animo or in animo, Cic., Liv., Tac.; Occ. mens et animus without distinction of meaning : Cic., Verg.; and often animum rebus advertere, adiungere, adhibere, applicare, attendere, intendere, etc.; animo rem comprehendere, complecti, lustrare, etc., Cic., etc. Transf.: of particular faculties of the mind. **a.** *memory* : Ter.; ex animo effluere, Cic.; omnia fert aetas, animum quoque, Verg. **b.** *sense, consciousness* : reliquit animus Sextium, Caes.; Pl.; Verg. **c.** *knowledge* : quos conscius animus exagitabat (guilty knowledge, i.e. consciousness of guilt), Sall.; Lucr. **d.** *opinion, judgment* (mostly in ABL.) : meo quidem animo, *in my opinion*, Pl., Cic.; ex animi tui sententiā, Cic. So too LOCAT. or GEN.: animi pendere, Cic., Liv.; dubius, incertus animi, Sall., Curt. **e.** *imagination, fancy* : cerno animo sepultam patriam, Cic.; fingite animis, Cic. **B.** *the sensibility ; the heart, feelings, affections, passions*. In general, *heart, soul, feeling, spirit* : Pl.; animus aeger, Cic.; animum offendere, comprimere, Cic.; aequo animo ferre, Cic., Liv. Occ. in LOCAT. or GEN.: illam animi excrucias,

Pl. ; Verg. ; infelix animi, Verg. ; ferox animi, Tac. ; and often the phr. ex animo, *from the heart, sincerely* : Cic., Hor. Occ. opp. to mens, *heart* contrasted with *mind* : omnium mentis animosque perturbare, Caes. ; Pl. As a term of endearment : Pl., Ter. Also *disposition, attitude of mind, character* : animus vultu aestimatur, Curt. Often with Adj., e.g. bonus, fortis, iracundus, magnus, liber, simplex, etc. : alacer et promptus, Caes. ; Pl. ; Cic. ; Hor. Transf. : of particular emotions or passions. **a.** *courage, spirit* : animum addere, Pl., Cic. ; bono animo esse, Pl., Cic. ; augere, Caes., Liv. ; also in *pl.* : Liv. Of a top : dant animos plagae, Verg. **b.** *arrogance, pride* (esp. *pl.*) : Cic., Liv., Ov. **c.** *ill-humour, wrath, violent passion* : Cic., Hor. In *pl.* : Pl., Ov. Of the winds : Verg. **d.** *feelings of pleasure, delight* : Pl. ; in *pl.* : Ov. In phr. animi causā : Pl., Caes., Cic. **e.** *proud, confident or high hopes* (esp. *pl.*) : Liv., Tac. **C.** *the will ; desire, inclination, wish* : ad omnia et animo et consilio paratus, Cic. ; hos auctores ut sequar inclinat animus, Liv. Hence, esp. *purpose, intention* : hostes in foro constiterunt hoc animo ut, etc., Caes. Phr. : in animo habere, set alicui in animo, *to purpose, intend* (with *Inf.*) ; *also* est animus, animum *or* in animum inducere (*v.* inducere), *to purpose, resolve* : istum exheredare in animo habebat, Cic., Ov., etc.

Aniō (orig. Aniēn), ēnis, and **Aniēnus**, i, *m.* *a tributary of the Tiber into which it flows a few miles above Rome,* now *the Teverone ;* **Aniēnsis**, e, and **Aniēnus**, a, um.

Anius, i, *m.* *a king and priest at Delos who entertained Aeneas.*

ann-. For verbs and derivatives beg. thus, *v.* adn-.

Anna Perenna, *a native Italian goddess.*

annālis, e, *adj.* [annus]. **I.** *lasting a year :* tempus, cursus, Varr. **II.** *relating to the year :* esp. in the phr. lex annalis, *a law fixing the youngest age at which a man was eligible for a magistracy,* Cic. **III.** *m. pl.* as Noun, *yearly records, chronicles :* Cic., Liv., etc.

anne, *v.* an.

anniculus, a, um [annus], *a year old, yearling :* Cato, Varr., Nep.

Annius, a, *name of a Roman gens ;* esp. T. Annius Milo (*v.* Cicero, pro Milone) ; **Anniānus,** a, um.

anniversārius, a, um [annus vertō], *returning every year, annual, yearly :* Cic., Liv.

annōn, *v.* an.

annōna, ae, *f.* [annus]. **1.** Lit. : *the year's produce ;* esp. *agricultural produce, grain :* Cic., Liv., Tac. Also of other produce : salaria, Liv. Hence, *the price of corn or other things, market rate :* cara, *high prices* (opp. vilitas, *low prices*), Pl., Cic. ; ad denarios L in singulos modios annona pervenerat, Caes : nihil mutavit annona, Liv. ; acris, Tac. **2.** Transf. : vilis amicorum est annona, Hor. ; cena hac annonā est sine sacris hereditas, Pl.

annōsus, a, um [annus], *full of years, old :* Verg., Hor., etc.

annōtinus [annus, *cf.* diutinus], *a year old, last year's :* naves, Caes.

annus, i, *m.* [perh. for annus fr. am=ambi]. **1.** Lit. : **a.** *a circuit* (of a heavenly body, e.g. of a planet) : Lucr., Cic., Verg. **b.** *a circuit of the sun, a year :* Pl., Cic., Hor., etc. ; anno exeunte, *at the end of the year,* Cic. ; anno circumacto, Liv. ; annus solidus, *a full year,* Liv. ; initio, principio anni, Liv. ; anno pleno, *at the year's close,* Hor. ; Pl. ; extremo anno, Liv. ; extremo anni, Tac. Of age : annos LX natus (*v.* natus). **c.** *the world-year* (c. 25,800 ordinary years) : Cic. **d.** *a period* (indefinite) : differs curundi tempus in annum ? Hor. **2.** Transf. **a.** *the season of the year :* nunc formosissimus annus, Verg. ; Hor. **b.** *the produce of the year :* Luc., Tac. **c.** *age, time of life :* Prop. **d.** *the year of office or the legal age for an office :* is erat annus in quo per leges ei consulem fieri liceret, Caes. ; anno meo, Cic. Adv. phr. **i.** anno, *a year ago, last year :* Pl. ; *for a whole year :* Liv. ; *in each year, yearly :* bis anno, Liv. ; with *in :* ter in anno, Cic. **ii.** annum, *for a whole year :* Liv. **iii.** ad annum, *for the coming year, a year hence :* Cic. **iv.** in annum, *for a year :* Liv., Hor. **v.** per annos, *year by year :* Tac.

annuus, a, um [annus]. **I.** *lasting a year :* penus, Pl. ; magistratus, Caes. ; tempus, Cic. Ep. ; Hor. **II.** *recurring every year, yearly, annual :* Lucr., Verg. ; commutationes, *the changes of the season,* Cic. ; ludi, Tac. *Neut. pl.* as noun, *yearly pay, pension,* Plin. Ep.

an-quīrō, quirere, quisivi, quisitum [quaerō], *to seek on all sides, search for.* **1.** Lit. : ad vivendum necessaria, Cic. **2.** Transf. : *to make inquiries.* **a.** In gen. : Cic., Tac. **b.** Judic. : *to institute an inquiry* (with de) *or a prosecution* (with ABL. or GEN.) : de perduellione, Liv. ; Tac. Impers. Pass. : pecuniā (i.e. in a case for a *fine*). capitis (in a capital case), Liv.

ānsa, ae, *f.* *a handle, haft.* **1.** Lit. : poculi, Verg. ; urcei, Ov. ; Cato. **2.** Transf. : *a handle* (i.e. opportunity or excuse) : reprehensionis ansa, Cic. ; ansas ad reprehendendum dare, Cic.

ānsātus, a, um [ānsa], *having a handle.* Transf. : homo, *with his arms a-kimbo,* Pl.

ānser, ēris. *m.* (*f.* Varr.) [Gk. χήν ; Germ. Gans ; Eng. gander], *a goose :* Cic., Liv., Hor.

Ānser, eris, *m.* *a poet, friend of the triumvir Antonius.*

Antaeus, i, *m.* *a Libyan giant killed by Hercules.*

ante (old form **anti**) [connected with Gk. ἀντί], *adv.* and *prep.* **I.** Adverb : *before.* **A.** Place : *before, in front,* occ. *forwards :* ante aut post pugnare, Liv. ; ingredi non ante sed retro, Cic. ; Verg. Also in compounds, e.g. antesignani, antecedo, etc. **B.** Time : *before, previously.* **a.** ut ante dixi, Cic. ; Ter ; Verg. Rarely with nouns : ignari sumus ante malorum (=*priorum malorum,* τῶν πρὶν κακῶν), Verg. Also in compounds, e.g. antecapio, antelucanus, etc. **b.** Esp. with ABL. of measure or difference (e.g. multo, paulo,

tanto, etc.) : multo ante prospexi tempestatem futuram, Cic. ; multis ante saeculis,
Cic. ; Liv. (N.B. ante is usually placed
after at least one such ablative.) **c.** Occ.
with Acc. : ante quadriennium, Tac. **d.**
ante . . . quam *or* ante quam, *v.* antequam.
II. Preposition : *before.* **A.** Place :
before, in front of. **1.** Lit. : ante suum
fundum insidias conlocavit, Cic. ; ante
oculos versari, Cic. ; Pl. ; Verg. Occ. with
verbs of motion : equitatum ante se mittit,
Caes. ; Pl. **2.** Transf. : *before* (in superiority or preference : = *prae* of Caes., Cic.) :
Sall. Esp. with alios, omnis, etc. : Pl.,
Verg., Liv., etc. : longe ante alias pulchritudine insignis, Liv. **B.** Time : *before, previous to* : ante lucem, Pl. ; ante
noctem, Hor. ; ante Verrem praetorem,
Cic. ; ante Iovem, Verg. ; ante urbem conditam, Liv. Also with Abl. of measure :
a^liquanto ante adventum meum, Cic. ; tot
annis ante civitatem datam, Cic. Phrases.
i. *before the due time* : ante tempus, Cic.,
Liv. ; ante diem, Verg., Ov. ; ante annos,
Verg., Ov. **ii.** *up till now* (with negat.) :
ante hunc diem crimen inauditum, Cic. ; Pl.
iii. Esp. of dates of the month : ante diem
quartum Idūs Martias (instead of die quarto
ante Id. Martias), or abbrev. a.d. IV. Id.
Mart., *on the fourth day* (or in Eng. *three
days*) *before the Ides of March.* N.B. that
this phrase may be treated as a single word
and be preceded by the preps. *in, ad,* or
ex : nuntii venerunt ex a.d. III. Non.
Iun. usque ad prid. Kal. Sept., Cic. Ep.

anteā, *adv. before* (ref. to any time, past or
pres., whereas antehac means *before this
present time*), *before this* or *that* : Ter. ; et
antea laudatus, et hoc tempore laudandus,
Cic. ; clipeis antea Romani usi sunt : deinde
scuta pro clipeis fecere, Liv. With *quam
v.* antequam.

ante-ambulō, ōnis, *m. a fore-runner* : Mart.,
Suet.

ante-capiō, capere, cēpi, ceptum. **1.** Lit. :
to take or *occupy beforehand* : locum
castris, Sall., Liv. **2.** Transf. **a.** *to have
an innate conception of* : rei informatio
animo antecepta, Cic. **b.** *to provide for
beforehand* : multa quae bello usui forent,
Sall. **c.** *to take measures against beforehand, anticipate* : famem, noctem, Sall.

antecēdēns, entis. **I.** Part. antecēdō. **II.**
Neut. pl. as Noun : *antecedent causes* :
Cic.

ante-cēdō, cēdere, cēssi, cēssum. **1.** Lit. :
to go before (in space) : with Acc., or
absol. : Pompeius expeditus antecesserat
legiones, Cic. Ep. *Absol.* : qui anteces-
serant, suos ascendentis protegebant, Caes. ;
Liv. ; Hor. **2.** Transf. **a.** *to precede* (in
time) : Ter. **b.** *to have precedence, to
excel, surpass.* With Dat. or Acc. of thing or
person surpassed, and Abl., or *in* and Abl.
of thing *in which* : natura hominis pecudi-
bus antecedit, Cic. ; Veneti usu nauticarum
rerum ceteros antecedunt, Caes. ; eum in
amicitiā, Nep. ; honore et aetate, Cic.

ante-cellō, ere (*cf.* excellō, etc. ; fr. root seen
in celsus and Gk. κολώνη]. Lit. : *to
project before.* Transf. : *to be prominent,
excel.* With Abl. of thing *in which* : hu-

manitate, Cic. With Dat. of thing surpassed : Cic. ; with Acc. : Tac.

anteceptus, *v.* antecapiō.

antecēssiō, ōnis, *f.* [antecēdō]. **1.** Lit. : *a
going before* : Cic. **2.** Transf. : *that
which goes before, the antecedent cause* :
antecessiones (= antecedentia), Cic.

antecēssor, ōris, *m.* [antecēdō], *he who goes
before.* Milit., antecessores, *the advanced
guard* : Auct. Bell. Afr. ; Suet.

antecursor, ōris, *m. a forerunner.* Milit.,
antecursores, *the advanced guard* : Caes.

ante-eō, īre, iī. (Old forms, antideō = anteeō
like antidea for anteā, Pl. ; antidit = anteit,
Pl. N.B. anteire as trisyl., Lucr. ; anteis,
anteit, disyl., Hor. *Pres. Subj. sync.* anteat,
Ov. ; so also antibō, Tac. ; antīssent, an-
tisse, Tac.), *to go before, precede.* **1.** Lit. :
a. Of space : Cic., Hor., etc. With Dat. :
Lucr., Cic. With Acc. : Hor. **b.** Of time,
to anticipate : aetatem meam honoribus
vestris anteistis, Liv. ; Tac. **2.** Transf.
a. *to excel, surpass.* With Abl. of thing *in
which* : operibus, Cic. With Dat. of thing
or person surpassed : alicui aetate, Cic. ;
virtus omnibus rebus, Pl. With Acc. :
aliquem sapientiā, Ter. ; Nep. ; Verg. In
Pass. : se abs te anteiri putant, Cic. ; Tac.
b. *to take precedence of, to set aside* : auctoritati parentis, Tac.

ante-ferō, ferre, tuli, lātum. **1.** Lit. : *to
carry* or *bear before* : fascis, Caes. ; Tac. **2.**
Transf. **a.** *to set before, prefer* : with
Dat. and Acc. : longe omnibus unum
Demosthenem, Cic. **b.** *to bring before-
hand* : Cic. Ep.

antefixus, a, um [ante, fīxus *Part.* fīgō],
fastened before : truncis arborum ora, Tac.
Hence, *Neut. pl.* as Noun, *small ornaments
fixed to the edge of the roofs, etc. of temples* :
Liv.

ante-gredior, gredi, grēssus [gradior], *to go
before, to precede.* **1.** Lit. : with Acc. :
Cic. **2.** Transf. : of time : Cic.

ante-habeō, ēre, *to prefer* : incredibilia veris,
Tac.

ante-hāc (disyl., Hor.), *before this* (present)
time, formerly, previously : Pl., Cic. Ep.,
Hor., Tac. Sometimes = antea : *previously, before that time* : Pl., Sall.

ante-lātus, a, um, *Part.* anteferō.

antelogium, i, *n.* [ante λόγος], *a prologue* :
Pl.

ante-lūcānus, a, um [lūx], *before daybreak* :
Cic. ; cenae, i.e. *lasting until daybreak,* Cic.

ante-merīdiānus, a, um, *before mid-day, in
the forenoon* : Cic.

ante-mittō, mittere, mīsi, missum, *to send
before* or *forwards* (rare for praemitto) :
Caes.

antemna (or **antenna**), ae, *f. a sail-yard* :
Caes., Liv., Verg., etc.

Antēnor, oris, *m. a Trojan, who after the fall
of Troy went to Italy and founded Patavium*
(Padua) ; **Antēnoreus,** a, um, *of Antenor* ;
Patavian ; **Antēnoridēs,** ae, *m. a male
descendant of Antenor.*

ante-occupātiō, ōnis, *f.,* lit. *fore-grasping.*
Rhet. : *an exception, objection* (= προ-
κατάληψις) : Cic.

ante-perta, ōrum, *n. pl.* [ante, pariō], *things
previously acquired* : Pl.

ante-pēs, pedis, *m. the fore-foot* : Cic. poet.

ante-pīlāni, ōrum, *m. pl.* [pīlum], *the two acies of the army in front of the pilani* (=triarii), i.e. *the hastati and principes* : Liv.

ante-pōnō, pōnere, posuī, positum, *to set one thing before another* (with ACC. and DAT.). **1.** Lit. : equitum locos sedilibus plebis, Tac. ; prandium pransoribus, Pl. ; Hor. **2.** T r a n s f. : *to prefer one thing to another* : amicitiam omnibus rebus humanis, Cic. ; Tac.

ante-potēns, entis, *adj. rich beyond all others* (with ABL. of respect) : Pl.

antequam (and **ante . . . quam**), *conj.* (*ante* properly belonging as an adv. to the antecedent clause, *quam* to the temporal clause) *before* (Old Eng. *before that*). **A.** With Indic. : Cic., Liv., etc. **B.** With Subj. (here there is always implied a notion of anticipating, forestalling, preventing, or intentionally delaying) : antequam de meo adventu audire potuissent, in Macedoniam perrexi, Cic. ; antequam obsiderem Syracusas, temptavi pacem, Liv. ; Ter. ; Verg.

Anterōs, ōtis, *m.* (an opponent of Eros), *an avenger of slighted love*.

antēs, ium, *m. pl. rows or ranks*, of vines, Verg. ; of soldiers, Cato.

ante-sīgnāni, ōrum, *m. pl.* [signum], *a picked body of Roman soldiers who preceded the standards in battle or on the march* : Caes., Liv. T r a n s f. : in *sing.*, *a prominent man* : Cic.

ante-stō (or **anti-stō**), stāre, stetī. Lit. : *to stand before.* T r a n s f. : *to excel.* With ABL. of the thing *in which* and DAT. of thing excelled : Cic. With DAT. alone : Cato, Nep. With ACC. : Lucr.

antestor, ārī [contr. from antetestor]. Judic. *to call as a witness* : licet antestari ? (the formula used in asking a man to be a witness) : Pl., Hor. Also non-judic. : Cic.

ante-veniō, venīre, vēnī, ventum, *to come before* or *in front.* **1.** Lit. : Liv. With DAT. : tempori, Pl. With ACC. : exercitum, Sall. **2.** T r a n s f. **a.** *to anticipate, thwart, prevent* (with ACC.) : insidias, Sall. **b.** *to exceed, surpass* : Tac. With DAT. : Pl. With ACC. : Sall.

ante-vertō (**vortō-**), vertere, vertī, versum (as *dep.* : Pl.), *to go* or *come before.* **1.** Lit. : Cic. With DAT. : Pl. **2.** T r a n s f. **a.** *to anticipate, prevent* : with DAT. : Cic., Ter. With ACC. : damnationem, Tac. **b.** *to put before, give precedence* (with *ut*-clause as object) : omnibus consiliis antevertendum existimavit ut Narbonem proficisceretur : Caes. ; Pl.

anticipātiō, ōnis, *f.* [anticipō], *a preconception, an innate idea* (=πρόληψις) : Cic.

anti-cipō, āre [ante, capiō], *to take before, anticipate* : Lucr. ; anticipata via, Ov. ; eius rei molestiam, Cic. Ep. Of knowledge : anticipatum mentibus nostris (*cf.* anticipatio), Cic.

anticus, a, um [ante], *in front, foremost* (opp. posticus) : Cic. (*v.* also antiquus).

Anticyra, ae, *f.* **I.** *a town in Phocis on the Corinthian gulf*, now *Aspra Spitia.* **II.** *a town in Thessaly.* **III.** *a town in Locris.*

All three towns were noted for the production of hellebore.

antideā, antideō, antidhāc, old forms of anteā, anteō, antehāc.

antidotum, I, *n.* (and **-us** or **-os**, ĭ, *f.*) [ἀντίδοτον (-ος)]. **1.** Lit. : *a counterpoison* : Phaedr., Suet. **2.** T r a n s f. : adversus Caesarem, Suet.

Antigonē, ēs (**-a**, ae), *f.* **I.** *d. of Oedipus.* **II.** *d. of Laomedon, changed into a stork.*

Antigonēa (**-ia**), ae, *f.* **I.** *a town in Epirus* ; **Antigonēnsis**, e. **II.** *a town in Macedonia.*

Antigonus, ĭ, *m.* **I.** '*king of Asia*' ; *a general and successor of Alexander the Great* ; *f. of Demetrius Poliorcetes* ; *died* B.C. 301. **II.** Antigonus Gonatas, *king of Macedon* ; *s. of Demetrius Poliorcetes* : *died* A.D. 239. **III.** Antigonus Dōsōn, *b. of Gonatas* ; *died* B.C. 320. **IV.** *a writer on agriculture.*

Antilochus, ĭ, *m. s. of Nestor, killed at Troy.*

Antimachus, ĭ, *m. a Greek poet of Colophon, contemporary with Socrates and Plato.*

Antiochīa (**-ēa**), ae, *f. The name of several cities* ; esp. *Antioch on the R. Orontes, the capital of the Greek kings of Syria* ; now *Antakieh* ; **Antiochēnsis**, ium, *m. pl. its inhabitants.*

Antiochus, ĭ, *m.* **I.** *the name of several Syrian kings* ; esp. *Antiochus the Great, who fought against Rome* ; *died* B.C. 187 ; **Antiochīnus** (**-ēnus**), a, um and **Antiochēnsis**, e. **II.** *an Academic philosopher, teacher of Cicero and Brutus* ; **Antiochīnus, Antiochēus** (**-īus**), a, um.

Antiopē, ēs (**-a**, ae), *f.* **I.** *d. of Nycteus, w. of Lycus, king of Thebes, m. of Amphion and Zethus.* **II.** *the title of a tragedy by Pacuvius.*

Antipater, trī, *m.* **I.** *a general and successor of Alexander the Great, f. of Cassander.* **II.** *his grandson, s. of Cassander, and son-in-law of Lysimachus.* **III.** *the name of several philosophers.* **IV.** *a distinguished lawyer, friend of the orator, L. Crassus.*

Antiphatēs, ae, *m.* **I.** *king of the Laestrygones.* **II.** *s. of Sarpedon, killed by Turnus.*

Antiphōn, ōntis, *m.* **I.** *the first of the* '*Attic Orators,*' *born* B.C. 480. **II.** *a sophist, contemporary with Socrates.*

antipodes, um, *m. pl.* [ἀντίποδες], *the antipodes* : Cic. (as a Gk. word).

antiquārius, ĭ, *m.* (Tac.) and **antiquāria**, ae, *f.* (Juv.) *an antiquary.*

antiquē, *adv. like the ancients* : Hor. Comp. : Tac.

antiquitās, ātis, *f.* [antīquus]. **1.** Lit. **a.** *former time, antiquity* : fabulae ab ultimā antiquitate repetitae, Cic. **b.** *ancientness* : generis, Cic. ; Nep. **2.** T r a n s f. **a.** *the history of ancient times* : Cic., Nep., Tac. **b.** abstr. for concr., *men of former times, the ancients* : Cic. **c.** *primitive virtue, integrity, etc.* : Cic., Plin. Ep.

antiquitus, *adv.* [antīquus]. **I.** *from ancient times* : with inde : Liv., Plin. Pan. Occ. : *for a long time past* : Caes. **II.** *in former times, long ago* : Caes.

antiquō, āre [antīquus], lit. *to make old or obsolete.* In law : *to reject* : legem, Cic., Liv. (The letter A was used = Antiquo, *I vote against the bill.*)

antiquus (antīcus), a, um [ante], lit. *coming before* (in place or time). **A.** Place: Only transf. (in comp. and sup.) *more* or *most important, preferable* : antiquior ei fuit laus et gloria quam regnum, Cic. ; Liv.: iudiciorum causam antiquissimam se habiturum, Cic. ; Liv. **B.** Time. **a.** *previous, former, earlier, of a former time* : Pl., Cic., Ov., etc. *Masc. pl.* as Noun, *the ancients* : Cic., Hor. **b.** *ancient, primeval, primitive* : Pl., Cic., Verg., etc. Also like vetus, *old* : Ter., Cic., Verg. ; and (rarely) *aged* : Verg., Ov. Transf.: *of the old stamp*, i.e. *simple, upright, honest* : Pl., Cic., Tac. *Neut.* as Noun, **antiquum**, i, *an old custom* : Pl., Ter. *Comp.* : Cic., Liv. *Sup.* : Cic. Ep., Hor., Liv.

antistes, stitis, *m.* and *f.* (also **antistita**, ae, *f.* Pl., Cic., Ov.). **1.** Lit.: *a foreman, an overseer* ; esp. *a president of a temple, a high-priest* : caerimoniarum et sacrorum, Cic. ; Liv.; Juv. As *fem.* : *a chief priestess* : adsiduae templi antistites, Liv. **2.** Transf.: *a master in any science or art* : artis dicendi, Cic. ; Ov.

Antisthenēs, is and ae, *m. a pupil of Socrates ; founder of the Cynic Philosophy ; teacher of Diogenes.*

antistita, v. antistes.

antistō, v. antestō.

antitheton, i, n. [ἀντίθετον], Rhet. *opposition, antithesis* : Cic., Pers.

Antōnīnus, i, *m. the name of several Roman emperors* ; esp. Antoninus Pius (A.D. 138–161), and M. Aurelius Antoninus (A.D. 161–180).

Antōnius, a, *the name of a Roman gens* ; esp. **I.** M. Antonius, *a famous orator just before the age of Cicero.* **II.** C. Antonius, *Cicero's colleague in the consulship.* **III.** M. Antonius, *the triumvir, defeated by Octavianus at Actium*, B.C. 31 ; **Antōnius, Antōniānus**, a, um.

antrum, i, n. [ἄντρον], *a cave, grotto.* **1.** Lit.: Verg., Hor., Suet. **2.** Transf.: *a hollow or hole* : Verg. Of a sedan : Juv.

Anūbis, is (or idis), *m.* (Acc. Anūbin or -im), *the Egyptian dog-headed god of hunting.*

ānulārius, i, *m.* [ānulus], *a ring-maker* : Cic.

ānulātus, a, um [ānulus], *wearing a ring* : Pl.

ānulus, i, *m. a finger-ring, signet-ring* : Pl., Cic., Liv. The right to wear a gold ring belonged in the time of the Republic to the equites only : Liv. ; hence anulus equestris : Hor. ; anulum invenit, i.e. he has been promoted to the equestrian order, Cic. ; ius anulorum, *equestrian rank* : Suet. Also *any ring-like article* : Plin., Mart.

(1) ānus, i, *m. the fundament* : Cic. Ep.

(2) ānus, i, *m. a ring* : Pl.

anus, ūs (also -uis, Ter.), *f. an old woman, old wife, old maid* : Pl., Cic., Ov., etc. For *the Sibyl* : Hor., Ov. As Adj. *old, aged* : anūs matronae, Suet. Also of animals and things : Cat., Ov., Plin.

ānxiē, *adv. anxiously* : Sall., Suet.

ānxiĕtās, ātis, *f.* [ānxius]. **I.** *mental trouble, anxiety* (strictly a lasting condition of mind, while *angor* is temporary): Cic., Juv. Sometimes =angor, *anguish, trouble* : anxietas animi, Ov. ; Curt. **II.** *scrupulous care, carefulness* : quaerendi, Quint.

ānxifer, era, erum [ānxius ferō], *causing anxiety* : Cic. poet.

ānxitūdō, inis, *f.* [ānxius], *anxiety* : prona ad luctum, Cic.

ānxius, a, um [angō]. **1.** Lit.: *anxious, solicitous, uneasy, disquieted, troubled* (mostly of a permanent habit of mind) : anxio animo esse, Cic. ; mentes, Hor. ; anxius animi, Sall. The source or cause of the feeling. **a.** In ABL. : gloriā eius, *troubled by the renown of the other*, Liv. ; Ov. **b.** In GEN.: inopiae, Liv. ; furti, Ov. ; potentiae, Tac. **c.** In ABL. with *de* or *pro* : Curt., Plin. Ep. **d.** With *ad* : Luc. **e.** With *ne* or *an* and *Subj.* : Sall., Tac. **2.** Transf.: *tormenting* : angor, Lucr.; aegritudines, Cic. ; curae, Liv. ; timor, Verg.

Anytus, i, *m.*, *one of the accusers of Socrates.*

Aones, um, *m. pl.* (Acc. Aonas), *the Boeotians.*

Aonia, ae, *f. a part of Boeotia, in which are Mt. Helicon and the fountain Aganippe* ; **Aonis**, idis, *f. a Boeotian woman* ; **Aonides**, *f. pl. the Muses* ; **Aonius**, a, um, *Boeotian* ; *of the Muses* ; Aonius vir, i.e. Hercules, Ov. ; deus, i.e. Bacchus, Ov. ; **Aonidēs**, ae, *m. a Theban.*

Aornos, i, *m. Lake Avernus.*

apage, *interj.* [ἄπαγε], lit. *take away!* **a.** With Acc., *away with!* : te a me, Pl., Ter. **b.** Intrans.: *away! begone!* Pl., Ter.

Apella, ae, *m. a credulous Jew, who lived in the time of Horace.*

Apellēs, is, *m.* (Voc. Apella), *a famous Greek painter of the time of Alexander the Great* ; **Apellēus**, a, um.

aper, prī, *m. a wild boar* : Cic., Verg., etc. Prov.: uno saltu duos apros capere (*cf. to kill two birds with one stone*), Pl. ; apros immittere liquidis fontibus (used of very perverse action), Verg.

aperiō, aperīre, aperuī, apertum (*Fut.* aperibō, Pl.). **I.** *to uncover, disclose to view.* **1.** Lit.: patinas, Pl. ; ut corporis partes quaedam aperiantur, Cic. ; dispulsa nebula diem aperuit, Liv. ; dies faciem victoriae, Tac. ; ramum qui veste latebat, Verg. Poet.: *to open out to view* (by the movement of a ship, etc.) : aperientibus classem promunturiis, Liv. ; formidatus nautis aperitur Apollo, Verg. **2.** Transf.: *to uncover* (what is or should be concealed), *unveil, reveal* : probra tua, Pl. ; maleficium non occultari sed aperiri debet, Cic. ; futura, Tac. ; Ov. With Acc. and *Inf.* : Liv. With *Indir. Quest.* : Nep. With *Refl. Pron.* or in *Pass.*, *to reveal one's true character*, Ter. ; Ov. ; Quint. **II.** *to open, unclose.* **1.** Lit.: ostium, Ter. ; foris, Ter., Ov., Suet. ; viam, Verg. ; epistulam, Cic. Ep. **2.** Transf.: amicitiae foris, Cic. Ep. ; apertus cursus ad laudem, Cic. ; ventus incendio viam, Liv. ; aperire locum (populum, gentem, etc.), *to open up, make accessible* : armis orbem terrarum, Liv.; Tac. ; locum suspicioni, Cic. ; occasionem ad invadendum, Liv. Occ. *to open, start* : scholam, Cic. ; annum, Verg. ; locum asylum, Liv. [Fr. ouvrir.].

apertē, *adv. openly, clearly, frankly, without disguise* : Ter., Cic., Hor., etc. *Comp.* and *Sup.* : Cic., etc.

apertō, āre [aperiō], *to keep on laying bare*: Pl.

apertus, a, um. **I.** *Part.* aperiō. **II.** Adj. **A.** *uncovered.* **1.** Lit.: lectica, Cic.; corpora, Liv.: naves, i.e. *without decks*, Cic., Liv.; loca, i.e. *without cover*, Caes.; caelum, i.e. *unclouded*, Verg. **2.** Transf. **a.** *unveiled, not hidden*: simultates partim obscurae, partim apertae, Cic.; Liv. **b.** Of style, *clear, unvarnished*: narratio, Cic. **c.** Of character, *open, frank, candid*: animus apertus et simplex, Cic. Ep. **B.** *open.* **1.** Lit.: ostium, Cic. Also opp. to clausus, *not obstructed, open*: oculi, Lucr.; caelum, Cic., Ov.; mare, oceanus, Caes.; aequor, Ov.; campus, Liv.; iter, vis, Liv. Esp. **apertum**, i, as *neut.* Noun, *the open* (us. with *preps.*): in aperto communire castra, Liv.; Lucr.; Hor. In *pl.*: Tac. **2.** Transf.: haec apertiora sunt ad reprehendendum, Cic.; res, Lucr.; Liv. As Noun: omnia in aperto sunt, Sall.; Tac. *Comp.* and *Sup.*: Caes., Cic., etc.

apex, icis, m. **1.** Lit.: *the conical cap of a flamen, ornamented at the top with a piece of olive wood*: Liv. **2.** Transf. **a.** *a hat, cap, crown, tiara*, etc.: Cic., Verg., Hor. **b.** *the highest ornament or honour*: Cic., Hor. **c.** *the tip or top of a thing, the point, summit*: lauri, Verg.; flammae, Ov.

Aphareus (trisyl.), el, m. *a king of Messenia*; **Aphareïus**, a, um: proles, i.e. *Lynceus and Idas, the sons of Aphareus.*

aphractus, i, f. [ἄφρακτος], *a long vessel without a deck* (=navis aperta): Cic. Ep.

apiānus, a, um [apis], *of bees*: Plin.

apiārius, i, m. [apis], *a bee-keeper*: Plin.

apicātus, a, um [apex], *adorned with the priest's cap*: Ov.

apicius, a, um [apis], *liked by bees*; hence *sweet, dainty*: uvae, Cato; Varr. *Neut.* as Noun (sc. vinum): Cato, Varr.

Apicius, i, m. *a notorious epicure under Augustus and Tiberius*; **Apiciānus**, a, um.

apicula, ae, f. [dim. apis], *a little bee*, Pl. [It. *pecchia*; Fr. *abeille.*]

Apina, ae, f. *a small town in Apulia.* In *pl. trifles*: Mart.

apis (-ēs), is, f. (GEN. *pl.* apium, Cic.; apum, Ov.; apium and apum, Liv.), *a bee*: Cic., Verg., etc.

Apis, is, m. *a god in the form of an ox, worshipped by the Egyptians.*

apiscor, apisci, aptus [apō, *cf.* adipiscor, which is commoner], lit. *to begin to attach to oneself*; hominem, Pl.; contagia morbi, Lucr.; hence *to reach after, attain, gain* (by effort). Hence, transf.: hereditatem, Pl.; maris apiscendi causā, Cic. Ep.; spes apiscendi summi honoris, Liv.; Tac. With GEN.: Tac. Also *Pass.*: ingenio sapientia apiscitur, Pl.

apium, i, n. the name of certain umbelliferous plants, *parsley, celery*, etc. **a.** Used for garlands: Verg., Hor. **b.** Used for prize-wreaths in the Isthmian and Nemean games: Plin., Juv. [It. *appio*; Fr. *ache.*]

aplustre, is, n. (NOM. *pl.* aplustria, DAT. aplustris, Lucr.) [ἄφλαστον], *the curved stern of a ship, with its decorations*: Cic.

apō (or **apiō**), ere, *to fasten, attach*; found only in *Part.* **aptus.** **I.** *fastened, attached.* **1.** Lit.: gladius saetā equinā aptus, Cic. **2.** Transf. With *ex*: *fastened from*; *depending on*: rerum causae aliae ex aliis aptae, Cic. With ABL. alone: Cic. **II.** *joined together.* **1.** Lit.: omnia inter se apta et conexa, Cic. *Neut.* as Noun: apta dissolvere, Cic. **2.** Transf. **a.** *connected*: apta inter se et cohaerentia dicere, Cic. **b.** *fitted* or *furnished*: omnibus rebus aptus, Caes.; naves aptae instructaeque remigio, Liv.; caelum stellis fulgentibus aptum, Verg.; Lucr. **c.** *adapted*: initia apta et accommodata naturae, Cic.; fornices in muro apti ad excurrendum, Liv. (*v.* Adj. aptus).

apoclēti, ōrum, m. *pl.* [ἀπόκλητοι, *selected*], *the select committee* of the Aetolian League: Liv.

apodytērium, i, n. [ἀποδυτήριον], *the undressing-room in a bathing-house*: Cic. Ep., Plin. Ep.

apolactizō, āre [ἀπολακτίζω], *to kick away, spurn, scorn*: Pl.

Apollō, inis, m. *s. of Jupiter and Latona, twin-brother of Diana*; *the sun-god*; **Apollināris**, e, and **Apollineus**, a, um, *of Apollo.*

Apollodōrus, i, m. **I.** *a famous rhetorician, teacher of Augustus*; **Apollodōreī**, ōrum, m. *pl. his pupils.* **II.** *a famous grammarian of Athens.* **III.** *an Academic philosopher.* **IV.** *a tyrant of Cassandrea.*

Apollōnius, i, m. **I.** **Apollōnius Rhodius,** *a Greek poet of Rhodes, author of the 'Argonautica.'* **II.** *a famous rhetorician in Rhodes.*

apologus, i, m. [ἀπόλογος]. **I.** *a narrative*: Pl. **II.** *a fable*: Cic.

apophorēta, ōrum, n. *pl.* [ἀποφόρητα], *presents received by guests at table to take home with them*: Suet.

apoproegmenon, i, n. [ἀποπροηγμένον], Stoic term for *that which is to be rejected* (opp. proegmenon): Cic.

aposphragisma, atis, n. *the figure on a signet-ring, seal*: Plin. Ep.

apothēca, ae, f. [ἀποθήκη], *a place where a thing is laid up, storehouse*: Cic. Esp. for wine: Hor. [It. *bottega*; Sp. *bodega*; Fr. *boutique.*]

apparātē, adv. *with great preparation, sumptuously*: apparate edere et bibere, Cic.Ep.; Liv. *Comp.*: Plin. Ep.

apparātiō, ōnis, f. [apparō], *a preparing, preparation*: Cic.

apparātus, a, um. **I.** *Part.* apparō. Of persons: *prepared*: Pl., Cic. **II.** Adj. of things: *well supplied*: domus omnibus instructior rebus et apparatior, Cic. Hence *magnificent, splendid, sumptuous*: ludi apparatissimi, Cic.; Liv.

apparātus, ūs, m. [apparō]. **I.** *a getting or making ready, a preparing, providing*: operum ac munitionum, Liv.; Cic. **II.** Concr. *apparatus* (*instruments, furniture, machines*, etc.): omnem commeatum, totiusque belli apparatum (*munitions of war*), Caes. Also *pl.*: Caes.; oppugnandarum urbium, Liv. Of men: auxiliorum, Liv. **III.** *display, pomp, magnificence, state*:

regio apparatu, Cic.; Liv.; in *pl.*, Persicos odi apparatūs, Hor.; fortunae, Liv.

ap-pāreō, ēre. **I.** *to come in sight, become visible.* **1.** Lit.: Pl.; cum lux apparuit, Caes.; equus demersus rursus apparuit, Cic.; apparent rari nantes, Verg. With DAT.: anguis ille, qui Sullae apparuit immolanti, Cic. **2.** Transf. **a.** *to show oneself*: promissa, Ter.; quo studiosius absconditur, eo magis apparet, Cic.; rebus angustis animosus appare, Hor. **b.** *to be visible* or *discernible :* nihil apparet in eo ingenuum, nihil moderatum, Cic.; Ov. **c.** *to be apparent, to be certainly coming,* etc. : apparebat atrox cum plebe certamen, Liv. Esp. *impers.* apparet, *it is plain, manifest, certain :* with Acc. and *Inf.*: Ter., Cic., Liv.'; with *Indir. Question :* Cic., Liv.; occ. with DAT.: Liv., Nep. **II.** *to appear as the attendant of any public officer, the priest of a deity,* etc., *to attend, serve* (with DAT.) : Cic., Liv., Verg. (*v.* apparitor).

ap-pariō, ere, *to gain, acquire :* Lucr.

appāritiō, ōnis, *f.* [appāreō], *service, attendance.* **1.** Lit.: in longā apparitione singularem fidem cognovi, Cic. Ep. **2.** Transf.: *household servants* (only *pl.*): ex necessariis apparitionibus, Cic. Ep.

appāritor, ōris, *m.* [appāreō], *a servant,* esp. *an attendant on a public official* (e.g. *an orderly, lictor, scribe,* etc.) : Cic., Liv.

ap-parō, āre, *to prepare* or *make ready, arrange, put in order, provide,* etc. **1.** Lit.: prandium, convivium, Cic.; nuptias, Ter.; bellum, Cic., Liv.; aggerem, Caes. With *in :* in Sestium apparabantur crimina, *against Sestius,* Cic. With *ad :* bellum ad hostis, Liv. **2.** Transf.: fabricam, Pl. With *Inf.* as object : Pl., Caes. Also se apparare with *Inf.* : Pl., Ter. With *ut* and *Subj.* : Pl. *Absol.* : dum apparatur, Ter.; Nep.

appellātiō, ōnis, *f.* [appellō]. **I.** *an addressing, accosting :* hanc nactus appellationis causam, Caes. Hence *an appeal to a tribune for assistance, and from one magistrate to another of equal or higher rank* (*provocatio* and *provoco,* of an appeal to the populus in a matter affecting life) : intercessit appellatio tribunorum, i.e. ad tribunos, Cic.; appellationem et tribunicium auxilium, Liv. **II.** *a naming, a calling by name.* **1.** Lit.: nominum ullorum inter eos, Plin. **2.** Transf.: *name, title :* Cic., Tac. In gram., *pronunciation :* lenis appellatio litterarum, Cic.; Quint.

appellātor, ōris, *m.* [appellō], *one who appeals, an appellant :* Cic.

appellitō, āre [*freq.* appellō], *to name often, to be accustomed to call* or *name :* Tac.

ap-pellō, āre [*cf.* compellāre ; prob. from the same root as pellō ; *cf.* Gk. πέλας, πελάζειν], lit. *to go up to.* Hence, **I.** *to accost, address, speak to :* aliquem, Pl., Cic., Ov., etc.; centuriones nominatim, Caes. **II. a.** *to address in entreaty :* vos imploro et appello, Cic. With *ut* and *Subj.* : Nep. With Acc. of person and *ut* and *Subj.* : Nep.; so too with *Indir. Quest.* : te appello . . . sciatisne, etc., Liv. **b.** *to appeal to the magistrates,* esp. to a tribune for assistance (*v.* appellatio) : procurator a praetore tribu-

nos appellare ausus, Cic., Liv. **c.** *to address with a view to inciting to something (bad), to make overtures to :* aliquem de proditione, Liv. **d.** *to address with a view to demanding something,* e.g. money ; *to dun :* appellatus es de pecuniā, Cic. Occ. with Acc. *to apply for :* mercedem, Juv. **e.** *to summon to court, to sue :* Cic. **III.** *to name* or *call :* Celtae nostrā linguā Galli appellantur, Caes.; Pl.; Cic.; Ov., etc. Hence, *to designate, salute by a certain title :* rex a suis appellatur, Caes.; Verg. Occ. *to mention by name :* quos non appello hoc loco, Cic. **IV.** *to pronounce :* litteras, Cic.

ap-pellō, pellere, pull, pulsum. **I.** *to drive, move* or *bring to* (with *ad* or DAT.). **1.** Lit.: turris ad opera Caesaris appellebat, Caes.; Pl.; Ov. **2.** Transf.: me ad mortem, Pl.; animum ad scribendum, Ter.; mentem ad philosophiam, Cic. **II.** Nautical, *to bring* (a ship) *to land.* **a.** With Acc. of navis, classis, etc. : cum Persae classem ad Delum appulissent, Cic.; navigia litori, Cic.; Liv. Occ. of persons : alios ad Siciliam appulsos esse, Cic.; me vestris deus appulit oris, Verg. Transf.: rationes ad scopulos appellere, Cic. **b.** With ABL.: cum Rhegium onerariā nave appulisset, Suet. **c.** Without *navem,* etc. or *nave :* ad insulam appulerunt, Liv.; ad eum locum, Caes.; huc, Hor. **d.** With *navis* as subj. (rare): Germanici triremis Chaucorum terram appulit, Tac.

appendicula, ae, *f.* [*dim.* appendix], *a small appendage :* Cic.

appendix, icis, *f.* [ad pendeō], *that which hangs to anything, an appendage.* Transf.: *an addition, supplement :* appendicem animi esse corpus, Cic.; belli, Liv.

ap-pendō, pendere, pendī, pēnsum. **1.** Lit.: *to weigh out, pay :* aurum alicui, Cic., Liv. **2.** Transf.: verba tamquam appendere, Cic.

Appennīnus, ī, *m. the Appennine Mts. ;* **Appennīnicola**, ae, *m.f. an inhabitant of the Appennines ;* **Appennīnigena**, ae, *m. adj. born on the Appennines.*

appetēns, entis. **I.** *Part.* appetō. **II.** Adj.: *craving for, eager for* (with GEN.) : gloriae, Cic., Tac. Esp. of money (=*avarus*), *grasping, avaricious :* Sall., Cic.

appetenter, *adv.* [appetēns], *eagerly, graspingly :* Cic.

appetentia, ae, *f.* [appetēns], *a craving for :* laudis, Cic. Without GEN.: effrenata, Cic.

appetitiō, ōnis, *f.* [appetō]. **1.** Lit. *a grasping at :* solis, Cic. **2.** Transf. *a craving for :* alieni, Cic.

appetītus, ūs, *m.* [appeto]. **I.** *a craving* or *desire :* voluptatis, Cic. **II.** *passion* or *desire,* as a faculty of the soul : in *pl. the appetites* or *passions* (opp. *ratio, reason*) : Cic.

ap-petō, petere, petīvī (or petiī), petītum. **1.** Lit. **a.** *to make for, try to reach :* Europam, Cic.; mare terram appetens, Cic.; Liv. **b.** *to make for* (as an enemy), *assail :* umerum gladio, Caes.; insidiis, Cic.; Liv.; Verg. **c.** *to lay hold of, grasp :* salutari, appeti, etc., Cic. **2.** Transf. **a.** me amor, Pl.; fata Veios appetebant, Liv. **b.**

to strive after, crave for : amicitiam, Caes.; bona, Cic.; Lucr. With *Inf.*: Cic. **c.** **Intrans.** (in expressions of time), *to draw near, approach* (freq. in Liv.) : dies appetebat, Caes.; Pl.; iam ver appetebat, Liv.

ap-pingō, ere. **I.** *to paint in or among :* Hor. **II.** *to add in writing :* Cic. Ep.

Appius, a, *a Roman praenomen,* esp. of members of the gens Claudia ; **Appius, Appiānus,** a, um. **Appia via** (or **Appia** alone), *the Appian road, leading S. from Rome through Capua to Brundisium, made by the censor Ap. Claudius.* **Appia aqua,** *the aqueduct made by the same censor.*

ap-plaudō plaudere, plausī, plausum. **I.** *to strike against :* Tib., Ov. **II.** *to clap the hands in approbation, to applaud :* Pl.

applicātiō, ōnis, *f.* [applicō], *an attaching or applying :* animi, Cic.

applicātus, a, um. **I.** *Part.* applicō. **II.** Adj. *laid upon ; lying upon or close to :* Leucas colli applicata, Liv.

applicitus, a, um. **I.** *Part.* applicō. **II.** Adj. *lying upon or close to, attached to :* Quint., Plin. Ep.

applicō, āre, āvī (Ter., Cic., etc.) and uī (Liv., etc.), ātum (Cic., Liv.) and itum (Quint., etc.). **1.** Lit.: *to bring into close contact :* **a.** In general (with *ad* or **Dat.** : se ad arborem, Caes.; Ov.; se ad flammam, Cic.; sinistrum cornu ad oppidum, Liv.; corpora corporibus, Liv.; Verg. **b.** Esp. of ships, *to lay alongside* (the quay or land, etc.) : navis ad terram, Caes.; Liv.; navim ad naufragium, Cic.; ad (*or* in) oras applicor, Ov. **2.** Transf. **a.** *to bring into union or connexion :* ut ad honestatem applicetur voluptas, Cic.; verba verbis, Quint. **b.** *to apply, devote* (oneself or the mind) *to :* se ad amicitiam, Cic.; Ter.; se ad Siculos, Cic.; Pl.; Ter.; se ad scribendam historiam, Cic.

ap-plōrō, āre, *to deplore in addition :* Hor.

ap-pōnō, pōnere, posuī, positum (*Perf.* apposivī, Pl.; *cf.* pōnō) *to put,* or *lay near,* or *beside, to apply to, etc.* **1.** Lit. **a.** mensulam, Pl.; omnes columnae machinā appositā deiectae, Cic.; scalis appositis urbem defenderunt, Liv.; appositā velatur ianua lauro, Ov.; lumen in mensā, Tac.; paenulam ad vulnus, Suet. **b.** *to lay before* a person, *to serve up :* patellam, Cic.; pabula, Verg.; cenam, Pl. *Impers. Pass.* : Pl. **2.** Transf. **a.** With Acc. and Dat.: *to attach to any service* or *duty, to appoint :* custodem Tullio me, Cic.; accusator apponitur civis Romanus, Cic.; moderator et magister consulibus appositus, Liv. **b.** With Dat.: *to put down to* (as an accountant): appone lucro, Hor.; Ter. **c.** *to add to :* tibi annos, Hor.; Pl.

ap-porrēctus, a, um [ad porrēctus], *stretched beside* or *near :* draco, Ov.

ap-portō, āre, *to carry, bring, convey to.* **1.** Lit.: divitias domum, Pl.; signa populo Romano apportavit, Cic. **2.** Transf.: morbos, Lucr.; insolitam rem auribus, Lucr.; adventum (= advenire), Pl.

ap-pōscō, ere, *to demand in addition :* Ter., Hor.

appositē, *adv. pertinently, appropriately :* ad persuadendum, Cic.

appositus, a, um. **I.** *Part.* appōnō. **II.** Adj., *situated at* or *near to, contiguous* (with Dat.). **1.** Lit.: castellum flumini, Tac. **2.** Transf. **a.** audacia fidentiae non contrarium, sed appositum ac propinquum (*cf.* Eng. ' next door to '), Cic. **b.** *fit, suitable, appropriate,* etc. With *ad :* menses ad agendum maxime appositi, Cic. *Comp.* and *Sup.*: Cic.

ap-pōtus, a, um, *intoxicated :* Pl.

ap-precor, ārī, *to worship, pray to :* Deos, Hor.

ap-prehendō (also **apprendō**), endere, endī, ēnsum, *to grasp, take hold of.* **1.** Lit.: eos manu, Pl.; Tac. Of the tendrils of the vine, Cic. Of atoms : Cic. **2.** Transf. **a.** *to take possession of :* Hispanias, Cic. Ep. **b.** Of discourse : *to lay hold of and bring forward :* quidquid ego apprehenderam, statim accusator extorquebat e manibus, Cic. **c.** Of disease, etc., *to lay hold of :* Cato, Luc.

apprendō, *v.* apprehendō.

apprimē, *adv. especially :* Pl., Ter., Nep.

ap-primō, primere, pressī, pressum, *to press to :* scutum pectori, Tac.

approbātiō, ōnis, *f.* [approbō]. **I.** *an approving, assenting to :* Cic., Liv. In *pl.* : Cic. **II.** In logic: *proof :* Cic.

approbātor, ōris, *m.* [approbō], *one who gives his approval :* Cic. Ep.

approbē, *adv. very well :* Pl.

ap-probō, āre, lit. *to make good.* So **I.** *to approve* (the act of another): Pl. With Acc. : Ter.; orationem, Caes.; sententiam, Cic.; donum, Liv. With Acc. and *Inf.* : ita fieri oportere, Cic. **II.** *to make good* (in the eyes of another), *to win approval.* **a.** *to prove :* innocentiam, Tac. **b.** *to win approval for :* opus approbavit, Phaedr.; with Dat. of person who approves : castrorum rudimenta Paulino approbavit, Tac.

ap-prōmittō, ere, *to promise in addition* (with Acc. and *Fut. Inf.*) : Cic.

ap-properō, āre. **A.** Trans.: *to give additional speed to, to hasten :* opus approperatum est, Liv.; Tac. **B.** Intrans.: *to make haste :* Pl., Ter., Cic. Ep. Transf.: ad facinus, Cic.

appropinquātiō, ōnis, *f. an approach* (in time): mortis, Cic.

ap-propinquō, āre, *to approach, come,* or *draw near to.* **1.** Lit.: of place : ad aquam, Cic.; Liv. With Dat.: Caes. **2.** Transf. **a.** In gen.: nobis libertas, Cic. **b.** Of rank : centuriones, qui iam primis ordinibus appropinquabant, Caes. **c.** Of time : hiems appropinquabat, Caes.; Cic. Ep.; Liv.

ap-pugnō, āre, *to fight against, attack, assault :* castra, Tac.

Appulēius (Āpul-), ī, *m.* **I.** *the name of several Romans ;* esp. L. Appuleius Saturninus, *a turbulent tribune of the people,* B.C. 102. **II.** *the African author of the ' Golden Ass '* (fl. A.D. 160).

appulsus, a, um, *Part.* appellō.

appulsus, ūs, *m.* [appellō]. **I.** *a landing, bringing to land :* ab litorum appulsu arcere, Liv.; Tac. **II.** *an approach,* in general : pars terrae appulsu solis exarsit, Cic.; frigoris et caloris appulsūs sentire, Cic.

apricātiŏ, ōnis, *f.* [apricor], *a basking in the sun :* Cic.

apricitās, ātis, *f.* [apricus], *sunniness, sunshine :* Plin.

apricor, āri [apricus], *to sun oneself, bask in the sun :* Cic.

apricus, a, um [aperiō], *lying open to the air, exposed :* aprico Lare, Prop. Hence, esp. *exposed to the sun, sunny; basking in the sun, bathed in sunlight.* **1.** Lit.: loci opaci an aprici, Cic.; colles, Liv.; mergi, Verg. *Neut.* as Noun, *a sunny spot :* Plin. **2.** Transf.: in apricum proferet aetas, Hor.

Aprīlis, is [aperiō]. **I.** Adj. mensis Aprilis, *the month April,* Cic.; Idūs Apriles, Cic., Ov. **II.** *Masc.* as Noun (*sc.* mensis): Ov.

aprūgnus (also aprūnus), a, um [aper and root of gignō], *of the wild boar :* Pl.

aps and **aps-**, *v.* abs (ab) and abs-.

apsis, *v.* absis.

apsūmēdŏ, inis, *f.* [absūmō], *a consuming, devouring :* Pl.

aptē, *adv. closely, so as to fit.* **1.** Lit.: mundi corpus apte cohaeret, Cic.; capiti pileum apte reponit, Liv. **2.** Transf.: *suitably, fitly, duly :* Cic., Ov., Liv. With *ad :* ad rerum dignitatem apte loqui, Cic.; Liv. With DAT.: Quint. *Comp.* ; Quint., Mart. *Sup.* : Cic.

aptō, āre [aptus], *to fasten, fit, adjust.* **1.** Lit. **a.** arma corpori, Liv.; sagittas nervo, Verg. **b.** *to make fit or suitable, to make ready, equip :* arma, Liv.; trabes, Verg. With *ad :* ad pugnam classem, Liv.; ad arma manūs, Ov. With DAT.: arma pugnae, Liv.; se pugnae, Verg. With *Instr. ABL.*: se armis, Liv.; classem velis, Verg. **2.** Transf.: *to adapt, adjust :* animos armis, Verg.; Hor.; verbum ad id aptatum quod ante dixerat, Cic.

aptus, a, um. **I.** *Part.* apō. **II.** Adj. **1.** Lit.: *fitting :* calcei habiles et apti ad pedem, Cic.; formas deus aptus in omnīs, Ov. **2.** Transf.: *fitted, suited, adapted, appropriate.* With *ad :* castra ad bellum ducendum aptissima, Caes.; Liv.; locus ad insidias aptior, Cic. With DAT.: non omnia rebus sunt omnibus apta, Lucr.; venti aptiores Romanae classi, Liv.; Cic.; Ov., etc. With *in* and ACC.: in quod (genus pugnae) minime apti sunt, Liv. With *qui :* nulla videbatur aptior persona, quae de aetate loqueretur, Cic.; Ov. With *Inf.*: aetas mollis et apta regi, Ov. Absol.: iar aptus, Hor.; aptus exercitus, Liv.; tempus aptum, Liv.

apud, *prep.* with ACC. (also **aput**, Inscr.) *at, beside, by, near* (and with a *pl.* word *among*), always of rest, and principally of persons. **1.** Lit. **a.** cum apud eum Sulpicius sederet, Cic.; Pl. **b.** *at the house of :* apud te cenavit, Cic.; fuisti apud Laecam, Cic.; Pl., etc. **c.** *in the hands of :* (obsides) apud eum sint, Caes.; Pl., etc. **d.** *among :* apud eos erat rex Diviciacus, Caes.; Pl.; Cic.; Verg., etc. **e.** *before, in the presence of* (=coram): apud iudices reus est factus, Cic.; Caesar apud milities contionatur, Caes.; Pl.; Ov.; apud praetorem profiteri, Cic. **f.** *Of place, near :* apud oppidum morati, Caes.; Pl.; Cic.; Verg.;

2. Transf. **a.** With *pers. pron.* : colloq. *to be at home,* i.e. in one's senses : Pl., Ter. **b.** *in the writings of (authors) :* apud Xenophontem moriens Cyrus maior haec dicit, Cic.; apud Solonem, *i.e. in his laws,* Cic. **c.** *in the hands of :* par gloria apud Hannibalem hostīsque Poenos erat, Liv.; Ter.; Cic.; Verg. **d.** *among* (mentally or morally) : auctoritatem apud omnīs Belgas amplificat, Caes.; apud viros bonos gratiam consecuti sumus, Cic. (apud is occ. placed after its Noun : Lucr., Tac.)

Āpūlia, ae, *f. a region in S.W. Italy,* now *Puglia ;* **Āpūlicus, Āpūlus,** a, um.

aqua, ae (aquāī, Lucr., etc.), *f. water.* **I.** In gen.: Pl.; pluvia, profluens, Cic.; flumen aquae, Verg.; marina, Cic. Ep.; caelestis, Liv., Hor.; intercus, *dropsy,* Cic. In *pl.* : Cic., Verg. Phrases: **a.** praebere aquam, i.e. *to invite to a feast, to entertain,* Hor. **b.** aquam aspergere alicui, i.e. *to revive,* Pl. Cic. **c.** aquam liberam, servam bibere, i.e. *to be in freedom, in slavery,* Ov. **d.** in aquā scribere (of vain or resultless actions), Cat. **e.** aqua et ignis, to denote the necessaries of life : non aquā, non igni, ut aiunt, pluribus locis utimur quam amicitiā, Cic. Hence, aquā et igni interdicere alicui, *to exclude from fire and water,* Cic. So the bride, on the day of marriage, received from the bridegroom aqua et ignis (*v.* Dict. Ant.). **f.** aquam et terram petere (as a token of submission), Liv. **II.** In more restricted senses : *water.* **a.** Of the sea : Cic., Ov. **b.** Of lakes and rivers : Cic., Liv., Ov. **c.** Of rain : cornix augur aquae, Hor.; Ov.; hence, *a flood, inundation :* aquae magnae, Liv. **d.** In *pl.* of watering-places and medicinal springs ; *the waters :* ad aquas venire, Cic. Hence, often as the name of a place, Aquae Sextiae, etc. **e.** Of a waterclock : certis ex aquā mensuris, Caes.; hence =*a measured time for speaking, allowance of time :* aquam dare, Plin. Ep.; aquam perdere, Quint.; aqua haeret, *the water stops,* to denote a difficulty in explaining one's meaning, Cic. [Fr. *eau* from older *eave,* orig. *ève ;* also O. Fr. *aigue.*]

aquaeductus *v.* ductus.

aquāliculus, i, *m.* [aquālis], lit. *a small water-vessel :* hence, *the stomach :* Sen. Ep. ; *the belly, paunch :* Pers.

aquālis, e, *adj.* [aqua], *of water :* Varr. As Noun, *m.f.* (*sc.* urceus or hama), *a basin, ewer :* Pl.

aquārius, a, um [aqua], *of or relating to water :* rota, *for drawing water,* Cato; provincia, *superintendence of the supply of water,* Cic. As Noun, **aquārius,** i, *m.* **a.** *a water-carrier :* Juv. **b.** *an inspector of the conduits or water-pipes :* Cael. ap. Cic. Ep. **c.** *the water-bearer,* one of the sig. of the Zodiac : Hor.

aquāticus, a, um [aqua]. **I.** *found in or by the water, aquatic :* lotos, Ov. **II.** *watery, moist :* Auster, Ov.

aquātilis, e, *adj.* [aqua]. **I.** *found in or near water, aquatic :* bestiae, Cic. As Noun, **aquātilia,** n. *pl. aquatic animals :* Plin. **II.** *having a watery taste, watery :* cucurbitae, Plin.

aquātiō, ōnis, *f.* [aquor]. **I.** *a fetching of water :* esp. *on the part of troops,* Caes. **II.** *a place whence water is brought, a watering-place :* Cic.

aquātor, ōris, *m.* [aquor], *a water-fetcher* (milit.) : Caes.

aquila, ae, *f.* [aquilus], *an eagle.* **1.** Lit. : Cic., Verg., etc. **2.** Transf. **a.** Milit. *the eagle,* i.e. *the principal standard of a Roman legion* (while signa are the standards of the cohorts) : Caes., Cic., etc. **b.** Archit. (=ἀετός), *the gable of a house,* or *the pediment of a temple* (so-called from its resemblance to an eagle with outspread wings) : sustinentes fastigium aquilae, Tac. [Fr. *aigle.*]

aquilex, ecis (or -egis) *m.* [aqua legō], *a finder or engineer of springs :* Plin. Ep.

aquilifer, erī, *m.* [aquila ferō], *an eagle-* or *standard-bearer :* Caes.

aquilīnus, a, um [aquila], *of the eagle :* ungulae, Pl.

Aquilius (-illius). **a,** *the name of a Roman gens ;* esp. C. Aquilius Gallus, *a famous jurist, and friend of Cicero ;* **Aquiliānus,** a, um.

aquilō, ōnis, *m.* **1.** Lit. **a.** *the N.N.E. wind :* Liv., Ov. ; *in pl. :* Cic., Hor. **b.** *a stormy wind :* Verg. **2.** Transf. : *the North :* spelunca conversa ad aquilonem, Cic.

Aquilō, ōnis, *m. h. of Orithyia, f. of Calais and Zetes ;* **Aquilōnius,** a, um.

aquilōnius, a, um [aquilō], *northerly :* Cic., Plin.

aquilus, a, um, *dark-coloured, dun, swarthy :* color, Pl., Suet.

Aquīnum. ī, *n. a town of the Volsci, now Aquino,* birth-place of the poet Juvenal ; **Aquīnās,** ātis, adj. *of Aquinum ;* **Aquinātēs,** ium, m. *pl. its inhabitants.*

Aquitānia, ae, *f. a province in S. Gaul.* **Aquitānī,** ōrum, *m. pl. its inhabitants.*

aquola, *v.* aquula.

aquor, ārī [aqua], *to bring* or *fetch water* (milit.) : Caes., Sall. Of bees : Verg.

aquōsus, a, um [aqua], *abounding in water, humid, rainy :* campus, Liv. ; hiems, Verg. ; nubes, Ov. ; languor (*dropsy*), Hor. ; mater, i.e. *Thetis,* Ov. ; Piscis, Ov. *Comp. :* Plin. *Sup. :* Cato.

aquula (aquo-), ae, *f.* [dim. aqua], *a tiny stream of water :* Pl., Cic.

ar, an old form for ad, *q.v.*

āra, ae, *f.* (old form āsa), *an altar.* **1.** Lit. **a.** In gen. : Pl., Cic., Verg., etc. **b.** In the phr. arae et foci, arae means either *the altars of the Penates* or *the public altars :* pro aris et focis pugnare, Cic., Liv. **c.** *the altar as a sanctuary* (of protection) : in aram confugere, Cic. ; Pl. ; Tib. **d.** *an altar tomb :* āra sepulcri, Verg. **2.** Transf. **a.** ad aram legum confugere, Cic. ; Ov. **b.** As a proper name. **i.** *certain rocks in the sea :* Verg. **ii.** Ara Ubiorum (from an altar erected to Augustus), now *Godesberg :* Tac. **iii.** *a constellation :* Cic.

arabarchēs, ae, *m.* [ἀραβάρχης], *an officer of customs in Egypt :* Juv. ; applied to Pompeius, Cic. Ep.

Arabia, ae, *f. a country of W. Asia. anciently divided into Petraea, Deserta, and Felix ;*

Arabicus, Arabius, Arabus, a, um. **Arabs,** abis (Gk. Acc. *pl.* Arabas), adj. *Arabian.* As Noun, *an Arab ;* **Arabī,** ōrum, m. pl. *the Arabs.*

Arachnē, ēs, *f. a Lydian maiden who challenged Minerva to a trial of skill in spinning, and, as a punishment, was changed by her into a spider.*

arānea, ae, *f.* [ἀράχνη]. **I.** *a spider :* Pl., Verg., Sen. Ep., etc. **II.** *a spider's web, cobweb :* (aedes) oppletae araneis, Pl. ; Lucr. ; Ov. [It. *aragna ;* Fr. *araignée ; cf.* also It. *ragnatela,* 'cobweb.']

arāneola, ae, *f.* (Cic.) and **arāneolus,** ī, *m.* (Verg.) [dim. arānea], *a small spider.*

arāneōsus, a, um [*v.* arāneus, adj.], *full of spiders' webs :* Cat.

arāneus, ī, *m.* [ἀράχνης], *a spider :* Lucr. [It. *ragno.*]

arāneus, a, um [arāneus], *of the spider :* Plin. As Noun in *neut. pl. : a spider's web :* Phaedr.

Arar (Araris, Claud.), aris, *m.* (Acc. Ararim), *a tributary of the Rhodanus,* now the *Saône.*

arātiō, ōnis, *f.* [arō], *ploughing ;* and in gen. *the cultivation of the ground, farming.* **1.** Lit. : Cic. **2.** Transf. : *arable land :* arationes, *the public allotments farmed out for a tenth of the produce :* Cic.

arātiuncula, ae, *f.* [dim. arātiō], *a small arable plot* or *estate :* Pl.

arātor, ōris, *m.* [arō]. **I.** *a ploughman, husbandman, farmer :* Cic., Verg., etc. **II.** In *pl.* aratores, *the cultivators of public lands* (cf. aratio) : Cic.

arātrum, ī, *n.* [arō], *a plough :* Cic., Verg., etc.

Arātus, ī, *m.* **I.** *a Greek poet of Soli in Cilicia, author of an astronomical poem, entitled Φαινόμενα ;* **Arātēus,** a, um. **II.** *of Sicyon, a famous Greek general, founder of the Achaian League.*

Araxēs, is, *m.* **I.** *a river in Armenia Maior.* **II.** *a river in Persia.*

Arbacēs, is, *m. the first king of Media.*

Arbēla, ōrum, *n. pl. a town in Assyria,* now *Arbil,* where Alexander the Great defeated Darius, B.C. 331.

arbiter, trī, *m.* [ar = ad, bītō]. **1.** Lit. : *one who visits something* (as a hearer or spectator). **a.** *an intruder, bystander, witness :* Pl., Cic., Ov., etc. **b.** In law : *an intervener, umpire, arbiter, a judge* (one who decides acc. to equity, while the *iudex* decides acc. to strict law) : Caesar constituit ut arbitri darentur ; per eos fierent aestimationes, Caes. ; Pl. ; Cic. **2.** Transf. **a.** *umpire :* arbiter inter antiquam Academiam et Zenonem, Cic. ; pugnae, Hor. **b.** *a ruler, controller, director :* arbiter bibendi, Hor ; Petronius elegantiae arbiter, Tac. ; imperii (Augustus), Ov. ; armorum, (Mars), Ov. ; Hadriae, Hor.

arbitra, ae, *f.* [arbiter], *a female witness :* Hor.

arbitrārius, a, um [arbiter], *uncertain, not fixed :* Pl. ABL. **arbitrāriō** as Adv. *uncertainly :* Pl.

arbitrātus, us, *m.* [arbitror] *a decision :* Pl. Us. in ABL. with meo, tuo, eius, etc. *just as I, etc., decide, choose, direct, etc. :* Pl., Cic.

arbĭtrĭum, ĭ, n. [arbiter]. **I.** *intrusion, presence.* Concr.: locus ab omni arbitrio liber, Sen.Trag. **II. 1.** Lit.: *the award or decision of an arbitrator,* which was to be given in accordance with 'equity' (v. arbiter): iudicium est certae pecuniae, arbitrium incertae, Cic. **2.** Transf. **a.** *the award, decision* of any umpire: libera arbitria agere, *to exercise free choice* (with *de* or GEN.), Liv.; ad iudicium arbitriumque alicuius redire, Caes.; res ab opinionis arbitrio seiunctae, Cic.; Hor. **b.** *the decision* of any matter, *control, direction,* etc.: suo nomine atque arbitrio, Caes.; vixit ad aliorum arbitrium, non suum, Cic.; Lucr.; Hor.; salis vendendi arbitrium, *monopoly,* Liv.

arbĭtrō, āre (a rare active form of arbitror): Pl.; Cic. *Pass.*: cum ipse praedonum socius arbitraretur, Cic.

arbĭtror, ārī [arbiter]. **I. a.** *to be a witness of*: Pl., Cic. **b.** *to give evidence as a witness*: Liv. **II. a.** *to award as an arbiter*: fidem alicui, Pl. **b.** *to decide as an arbiter, to come to a conclusion, to infer, have a well-founded opinion* (usual meaning): Pl., Caes., Cic., etc. (us. in phr. ut arbitror, or with Acc. and *Inf.*).

arbor, oris (older form **arbōs**, like labōs, etc., with Acc. ARBOSEM), *f. a tree.* **1.** Lit.: Cic., Verg., etc.; freq. with GEN. of the species: fici, the *fig-tree,* Cic.; abietis, *fir-tree,* Liv.; etc. Poet.: arbor Iovis, the *oak,* Ov.; arbor Phoebi, the *laurel,* Ov.; arbor Palladis, the *olive,* Ov.; Herculea, the *poplar,* Verg. **2.** Transf.: *things made of wood.* **a.** *a mast*: with mali (' the trunk of the mast '), Verg.; also alone, Luc. **b.** *an oar*: Verg. **c.** *a ship*: Pelias arbor, Ov. **d.** *a gallows, gibbet*: arbori infelici suspendito, Cic.; Liv.

arbŏrārĭus, a, um [arbor], *of trees*: falx (*for pruning trees*), Cato.

arbŏrĕus, a, um [arbor]. **1.** Lit.: *of trees*: frondes, Ov.; fetus, Verg. **2.** Transf.: *treelike, branching*: cornua cervorum, Verg.

arbōs, *v.* arbor.

arbuscŭla, ae, *f.* [*dim.* arbor], *a small tree, shrub*: Varr.

Arbuscŭla, ae, *f. an actress in the time of Cicero.*

arbustus, a, um [arbor], *planted with trees, wooded*: Cic. Neut. as Noun. **a.** *a plantation, a vineyard planted with trees*: Cato, Verg.; expressa arbusto convicia, *that smacked of the vineyard,* Hor. **b.** in *pl.* arbusta = arbores: arbusta diruta ripis, Verg.; Lucr.

arbŭtĕus, a, um [arbutus], *of the wild strawberry-tree*: Verg., Ov.

arbŭtum, ī, n. [arbutus], *the fruit of the wild strawberry-tree*: Lucr., Verg.; also used in pl. for *the leaves and foliage of the arbutus*: frondentia capris arbuta sufficere, Verg.

arbŭtus, ī, *f.* [cognate with arbor], *the wild strawberry-tree* or *arbutus*: Verg., Hor., Curt.

arca, ae, *f.* [arceō], *a place for keeping any thing.* **1.** Lit. **a.** *a chest, cupboard*: Cato, Cic. Esp. *a box for money, a coffer*: Hor. Also of *the money in it*: arcae

nostrae confidito, Cic.; Cat.; ex arcā absolvere aliquem (*to pay 'spot' cash*), Ter. **b.** *a coffin*: Hor., Liv. **2.** Transf.: any closed or confining place: *a close prison, a cell*: Cic.

Arcădes, *v.* Arcas.

Arcădĭa, ae, *f. a mountainous inland district of Peloponnesus.* Hence, **Arcădĭcus, Arcădĭus**, a, um.

arcānus, a, um [arca]. Lit.: *shut up, closed.* **A.** Of things: *secret, private, hidden, concealed*: Cic., Verg., Tac., etc. Esp. of things *sacred and mysterious*: arcana sacra, Hor., Ov. and (poet.), the deity presiding over such mysteries: Ceres, Ov. Neut. as Noun, *a secret*: Cic., Hor., Liv. Esp. in *pl.*: fatorum arcana, Verg.; imperi, Tac. ABL. **arcānō** as adv. *in secret, privately*: Pl., Caes., Cic. Ep. **B.** Of persons: *that keeps a secret, trusty*: as Noun: dixisti arcano satis, Pl. Transf.: arcanā nocte, Ov.

Arcas, adis, m. **I.** *s. of Jupiter and Callisto, progenitor of the Arcadians.* **II.** *an Arcadian.* In *pl.* **Arcădes**, um, m. (Acc. Arcadas), *Arcadians.*

arcātus, ī, m. [arcus], *jaundice*: Lucr.

arcĕō, ēre, uī [cf. ἀρκέω, ἀλαλκεῖν]. **I.** *to shut up, enclose*: alvus arcet et continet quod recipit, Cic. **II.** *to keep off, keep at a distance, prevent.* With Acc. only: pluvias aquas, Cic.; vulgus, Hor.; somnos, Ov. With *Inf.* as obj.: *to hinder, prevent*: Ov., Tac. With *ne* or *quin*: Liv. With *ab*: tu Iuppiter hunc a tuis aris ceterisque templis arcebis, Cic.,; Verg., etc. With simple ABL. (not with persons): Verginiam matronae sacris arcuerant, Liv.; hostis transitu (amnis), Liv.; Cic.; Ov., etc. Poet.: *to keep safe from*: classem aquilonibus, Hor. With DAT.: oestrum pecori, Verg.; Ov.

Arcĕsĭlās, ae (Acc. -lam), m. *a Greek philosopher, founder of the Middle Academy.*

Arcĕsĭus, ī, m. *s. of Jupiter, father of Laertes.*

arcessītū, ABL. *sing. m.* [arcessō]. *at the summons*: tuo, Pl.; Cic.

arcessītus, a, um. **I.** Part. arcessō. **II.** Adj. *far-fetched*: dicta, Cic.; frigidi et arcessiti ioci, Suet.

arcessō, ere, īvī, ītum (*Inf.* also arcessīre and arcessīrī: we also find a form, *accerso*, which arose from a transposition of letters, freq. used by Sall.). [ar = ad, -cessō from cēdō]. Lit. (causative of accēdō): *to make to come to one*). Hence, **1.** Lit. **a.** *to send for, fetch, summon*: Pl., Caes., Cic., etc. **b.** Judic. *to summon, arraign before a court of justice*: hence, in gen. *to accuse* (with Acc. of person and GEN. or ABL. of charge): aliquem capitis, Cic.; Sall.; Tac.; innocentem iudicio capitis, Cic.; Suet. **2.** Transf. **a.** *to fetch, bring here* or *to oneself*: quies molli strato arcessita, Liv.; si quid melius habes, arcesse, Hor. **b.** *to fetch, derive*: a capite (*fountain-head*) quod velimus, Cic.; gloriam a periculo, Curt.

Archĕlāus, ī, m. **I.** *a philosopher of the Ionian school, pupil of Anaxagoras and teacher of Socrates.* **II.** *a king of Macedonia, friend of Euripides.* **III.** *s. of a* *general of Mithridates, killed by Gabinius.* **IV.** *a king of Cappadocia in the time of Tiberius.*

archetypus, a, um [ἀρχέτυπος], *original* : archetypos Cleanthas, Juv. *Neut.* as Noun : Plin. Ep.

Archilochus, ī, m. *a Greek poet of Paros, the originator of iambic verse, and . the author of bitter satires* (7th cent. B.C.). **Archilochīus,** a, um, *Archilochian ; sarcastic, bitter.*

archimagīrus, ī, m. [ἀρχιμάγειρος] *a chief cook,* Juv.

Archimēdēs, is (GEN. -mēdī, Cic. ; ACC. -em and -ēn), m. *the most famous mathematician of antiquity, killed at the taking of Syracuse ;* **Archimēdēus,** a, um.

archipīrāta, ae, m. [ἀρχιπειρατής], *a leader of pirates :* Cic., Liv.

architectōn, onis, m. [ἀρχιτέκτων], *a master-builder, architect.* **1.** Lit. : Pl., Sen. Ep. **2.** Transf. : *a master in cunning :* Pl.

architector, ārī [architectus], *to build, construct.* Transf. : *voluptates,* Cic.

architectūra, ae, f. [architectus], *the art of building, architecture :* Cic.

architectus, ī, m. [ἀρχιτέκτων]. **1.** Lit. *a master-builder, architect :* Cic. **2.** Transf. : *a deviser, author :* sceleris, Cic.

archōn, ontis [ἄρχων], *a magistrate at Athens, an archon :* Cic.

Archȳtās, ae, m. *a Pythagorean philosopher of Tarentum and friend of Plato, drowned off Italy.*

arci-tenēns, entis, adj. [arcus teneō], *holding a bow, bow-bearing.* Of Apollo and of Diana : Verg., Ov. As Noun : a constellation : *the Archer :* Cic. poet.

arctophylax, acis, m. [ἀρκτοφύλαξ], *the Bear-keeper (a constellation),* us. called Bootes : Cic. poet.

arctos (ACC. arcton, Verg., Ov. Nom. pl. arctoe, Cic.), ī, f. [ἄρκτος]. **1.** Lit. : *the Great and Little Bear* (ursa maior et minor), *a double constellation :* Verg., Ov. **2.** Transf. **a.** *the north pole :* Ov. **b.** *the coolness of the North :* Hor. **c.** *the night :* Prop.

arctūrus, ī, m. [ἀρκτοῦρος], *bear-keeper, the brightest star in the constellation, Bootes :* Cic. Also *the whole constellation* (= arctophylax, q.v.) : Verg. ; *sub ipsum Arcturum, just about the rising of Arcturus,* Verg.

arctus, arctō, etc. Incorrect forms of artus, artō, etc.

arcuātus, a, um. **I.** Part. arcuō. **II.** Adj. *bent like a bow, curved :* arcuatus currus, Liv.

arcuō, āre [arcus], *to curve,* Plin. Ep.

arcula, ae, f. [dim. arca]. **1.** Lit. : *a small box, a casket for perfumes, ornaments,* etc. : Pl., Cic. **2.** Transf. : *a pigment-box* (for rhetoricians) : Cic.

arculārius, ī, m. [arcula], *a maker of little boxes or jewel-caskets :* Pl.

arcus, ūs, m. (earlier arquus). **I.** *a bow :* Pl. ; arcus intentus in aliquem, Cic. ; Verg. ; incurvare, adducere, Verg. ; remissus, Hor. **II.** *the rainbow :* Enn., Cic., Verg., etc. ; pluvius arcus, Hor. **III.** *anything arched or curved.* Of waves : aquarum, Ov. Of a serpent : immensos sinuatur in arcūs,

Ov. Of a curve in flight : secuit sub nubibus arcum, Verg. Of a bay or harbour : falcatus in arcūs, Ov. ; curvatus in arcum Verg. Of the boughs of trees : Verg. Of the zones : via quinque per arcūs, Ov. Archit. : *an arch, vault, triumphal arch,* etc. : Ov. ; marmoreus, Suet.

ardea, ae, f. *a heron :* Verg.

ardeliō, ōnis, m. *a busybody, a meddler :* Phaedr., Mart.

ardēns, entis. **I.** Part. ārdeō. **II.** Adj. **1.** Lit.: *blazing, burning :* oppidani cupas ardentis in opera provolvunt, Hirt. Hence, *hot, fiery :* quinta (zona) est ardentior illis, Ov. Sup. : Plin. **2.** Transf. **a.** *flaming, gleaming :* stella, clipeus, oculi, Verg. ; apes ardentes auro, Verg. **b.** Of sensation : *fiery, burning, smarting :* Lucr. ; Cic. ; Falernum, Hor. *Neut.* Comp. as Noun : ardentius sitire, Cic. **c.** Of emotions, etc. : *glowing, hot, ardent :* animus, ira, odium, studium, oratio, orator, Cic. ; studia, Ov.

ardenter, adv. *burningly :* Cic. Comp. and Sup. : Plin. Ep.

ārdeō, ārdēre, ārsī, and Fut. Part. ārsūrus. **1.** Lit. : *to be on fire, to burn, blaze :* taedae, Enn. ; domus ardebat in Palatio, Cic. ; ardet Carthago, Liv. Occ. to emit *rays of fire :* puero caput arsisse, Liv. ; Cic. ; comae, Verg. **2.** Transf. **a.** *to radiate light, flash, glow :* Tyrio ardebat murice laena, Verg. ; oculi, Pl., Cic. **b.** Of sensation, *to burn, smart :* fauces siti, Liv. ; podagrae doloribus, Cic. **c.** Of emotion. **i.** *to be ablaze* (i.e. in a state of turmoil) : Galliam ardere, Caes. ; bello sociorum Italia, Cic. **ii.** *to burn* (with eagerness), *to be at fever heat, to be eager ;* omnium animi ad ulciscendum ardebant, Caes. ; in arma, Verg. ; Tac. ; flagitio, Pl. ; iracundiā, Ter. ; Liv. ; studio pugnae, Caes. ; cupiditate, Cic. With *Inf.* as object : Sall., Verg. Esp. *to burn with love :* ex aequo captis ardebant mentibus ambo, Ov. ; with ABL. of the object of passion : non aliā magis arsisti, Hor. ; also ACC. : Verg. ; Hor. **d.** Occ. of the sensation or emotion itself : furor, Cic. ; dolor, Verg.

ārdēscō, ārdēscere [ārdeō]. **1.** Lit. : *to take fire, to kindle, to become inflamed :* Lucr., Ov. **2.** Transf. **a.** *to gleam, glitter :* fulmineis ignibus undae, Ov. ; Tac. **b.** ardescit pugna (*waxes hotter*), Tac. ; Verg. **c.** Of the emotions and passions : cuppedine, Lucr., Verg. ; in iras, Ov.

ārdor, ōris, m. [ārdeō]. **1.** Lit. : *a burning fire, heat, flame :* ardor, Lucr. ; Cic. **2.** Transf. **a.** *flashing, brightness :* ille imperatorius ardor oculorum Cic. ; Lucr. **b.** Of the emotions and passions : *heat, ardour, eagerness :* Lucr. ; mentis ad gloriam, Cic. ; armorum, Liv. Esp. of *love :* Ov. ; Hor. ; and occ., *the beloved object :* tu primus, et ultimus illi ardor eris, "*flame,*" Ov.

Arduenna, ae, f. *the Ardennes.*

ardus, a, um, v. āridus.

arduus, a, um [cf. ὀρθός]. **1.** Lit. **a.** *erect* (freq. in Verg.) : (coluber) arduus ad solem, Verg. ; campo sese arduus infert, Verg. ; equo ardua cervix, Verg. ; Hor. Hence,

b. *steep, lofty :* Enn.; mons, Ov.; difficili ascensu et arduo, Cic.; collis aditu
arduo, Liv. *Neut.* as Noun : per arduum
scandere, Hor.; in arduo, Tac.; ardua
terrarum, Verg.; Lucr.; Tac. **2.** T r a n s.
a. *steep, difficult to reach, laborious :* opus,
Cic.; virtus, Hor.; victoria, Ov.; arduum
factu, Liv. *!Neut.* as Noun : nec fuit in
arduo societas, Tac. **b.** *trying, adverse :*
aequam rebus in arduis servare mentem,
Hor.; onus, Tac.

āre, *v.* ārefaciō.

ārea, ae, *f. a level* or *clear* or *open space* (esp.
in a town), *vacant ground.* **a.** *the site for a
house :* praeclara area, *a desirable building
plot,* Cic. Ep.; Hor.; Liv. **b.** *the site of a
house* now pulled down : Liv. **c.** *open
space* (about a house), *courtyard :* Liv.,
Plin. Ep. **d.** *the site* (of a temple, etc.) *and
the space about it, place, piazza :* area Concordiae, Liv. **e.** *a playground :* Hor.
Hence, transf. : area scelerum, Cic.; teritur nostris area maior equis, Ov. **f.** *a
threshing floor :* Cic., Verg., etc. **g.** *a
fowling-ground :* Pl.

Arectaeus, a, um, *Babylonian.*

āre-faciō (**ārfaciō,** Cato), (*per anastrophen,*
facit āre, Lucr.), facere, fēcī, factum [āreō
faciō], *to make dry, to dry up :* Cato, Lucr.,
Suet.

āreō, ēre. **1.** L i t. : *to be dry :* Pl.; tellus,
Ov. **2.** T r a n s f. : *to be dry from thirst* or
drought : Liv., Verg., etc. (mostly in *Part.*

ārēns, ārentis.

āreola, ae, f. [dim. ārea] *a small open space :*
Plin. Ep.

Arēopagus (**-os**), I, *m.* (or **Arēus pagus**)
*Mars' Hill at Athens, seat of the criminal
court of the same name :* **Arēopagītēs,** ae,
m. a member of this court.

Arēs, is, *m. the Greek name of the war-god
Mars :* **Arēus,** a, um, *of Mars.*

ārēscō, ārēscere [āreō], *to become dry, to dry
up :* vestimenta, Pl.; lacrima, Cic.; unda,
Tac. Also of trees, etc. : Cic., Tac.

Arestoridēs, ae, *m. s. of Arestor,* i.e. *Argus.*

aretālogus, I, *m.* [ἀρεταλόγος], *a babbler
about virtue, a boaster.* Of a Cynic or Stoic :
Juv., Suet.

Arethūsa, ae, *f. a fountain near Syracuse.*
She was a nymph pursued by the river-god
Alpheus in Peloponnesus, and changed by
Diana into a fountain which flowed under
the sea, appearing again near Syracuse :
Arethūsis, idis, *adj.* a poet. epith. of Syra-
cuse ; **Arethūsius, Arethūsaeus,** a, um.

Argēi, ōrum, *m. pl.* **I.** *certain consecrated
places in Rome ascribed to Numa.* **II.**
*figures of men made of rushes thrown annually
into the Tiber to take the place of earlier
human sacrifices.*

argentārius, a, um [argentum]. **I.** *of silver :* metalla, Plin. **II.** *of money :* inopia,
auxilium, Pl.; cura, Ter.; taberna, Liv.
As Noun. **A. argentārius,** I, *m. a money-
changer, banker :* Pl., Cic., Liv. **B. ar-
gentāria,** ae, *f.* **a.** *a banking-house, bank :*
Pl., Liv. **b.** (*sc.* ars) *the business of a
banker* or *money-changer :* argentariam
facere, Cic. **c.** (*sc.* fodina) *a silver-mine :*
Liv.

argentātus, a, um [argentum], *plated* or

ornamented with silver : milites, Liv.
T r a n s f. : argentata querimonia (i.e. *backed
up with money*), Pl.

argenteolus, a, um [*dim.* argenteus], *of
pretty silver :* Pl.

argenteus, a, um [argentum]. **1.** L i t. : *of
silver, made of silver :* aquila, Cic.; Hor.;
salus, *a silver greeting* (i.e. a present), Pl.
As Noun (*sc.* nummus) : Liv. **2.** T r a n s f.
a. *adorned with silver* = argentatus : scaena,
Cic.; Liv. **b.** *of a glittering white colour,
silvery :* ales, Ov.; anser, Verg. **c.** Of
the silver age : subiit argentea proles, Ov.

Argentiexterebrōnidēs [argentum extere-
brō], a name coined by Plautus, *extortioner,
sponger.*

argentum, I, *n.* [ἀργός, ἀργυρίον], **1.** L i t. :
the white metal ; silver : Pl., Cic., etc.
2. T r a n s f. **a.** *silver plate :* purum, caelatum, Cic.; Lucr.; Hor., etc. **b.** *silver
money :* argentum aere solutum est, Sall.;
also, *money in gen.* : argenti sitis, Hor.;
Pl.; Ter.

Argēus, Argī, *v.* Argos.

Argia, ae, *f. d. of Adrastus and w. of Polynices.*

Argīlētum, I, *n. a part of Rome* inhabited
chiefly by *workmen and booksellers ;* **Ar-
gīlētānus,** a, um.

argilla, ae, *f.* [ἄργιλλος or ἄργιλος], *white
clay, potter's earth :* Cic.

Argīvus, a, um, *v.* Argos.

Argō, ūs (Acc. Argō), *f. the ship in which the
Greek heroes under Jason sailed to Colchis
for the golden fleece ;* **Argonautae,** ārum,
m. pl. the Argonauts ; **Argōus,** a, um.

Argos, *n.* (only Nom. and Acc.), more freq.
as *pl.* **Argī,** ōrum, *m. Argos, in the Peloponnesus ;* **Argīvus, Argēus, Argus,
Argolicus,** a, um ; **Argīvi,** ōrum, *m. pl. the
Argives* or *Greeks ;* **Argolis,** idis, *f. adj.*

argūmentātiō, ōnis, *f.* [argūmentor], *an adducing of proof, an argumentation :* Cic.,
Quint.

argūmentor, ārī [argūmentum], *to adduce
proof, bring evidence :* Cic., Liv. With
Acc. *neut. to adduce something as proof :* illa,
Cic.; Liv. With *de, to argue from, conclude from :* Cic.

argūmentum, I, *n.* [arguō], *a means of making something clear ; evidence, indication,
proof, argument :* Pl., Lucr.; argumentis
refellere, Cic.; litteras ad senatum missae
argumentum fuere, Liv. Of outward indication : animi laeti argumenta, Ov.
T r a n s f. **a.** *the subject of any written composition ; theme, argument, plot :* argumentum est fictae rei, quae tamen fieri
potuit, Cic.; epistulae, Cic. Ep.; Pl.;
Livius Andronicus ab saturis ausus est
primus argumento fabulam serere, Liv.;
Pl. Occ. the composition itself : Liv., Ov.
b. *the subject* or *motif* of artistic representations (sculpture, painting, embroidery, etc.) :
Cic., Verg., Ov.

arguō, uere, uī [ἀργός], *to make clear.* Hence,
I. *to declare, prove.* **1.** L i t. (with Acc.
and *Inf.* : Pl., Cic., Liv. **2.** T r a n s f. : *to
reveal* or *betray :* degeneres animos timor
arguit, Verg.; laudibus arguitur vini
vinosus Homerus, Hor. **II.** With Acc.
of the person, *to accuse, charge ;* servos ipsos
neque arguo, neque purgo, Cic.; Pl. The

offence charged is expressed by **a.** Gen.
(the usual constr.) : viros summi sceleris,
Cic. ; Pl. ; Verg., etc. **b.** Abl. : prob.
only in case of crimen : te hoc crimine non
arguo, Cic. **c.** *de :* de eo crimine, quo de
arguatur, Cic. **d.** Acc. and *Inf. :* me
arguit hanc domo ab se subripuisse, Pl. ;
Ov. In *Pass.* with *Inf. :* patrem occidisse
arguitur, Cic. **III.** With Acc. of things :
to find fault with, censure : ea culpa, quam
arguo, Liv. ; with Acc. and *Pass. Inf.* : Ov.
Argus, i, *m. the hundred-eyed keeper of Io,
killed by Mercury at the command of Jupiter.*
argūtē, *adv.* **I.** *subtly, acutely :* Cic. *Comp.*
and *Sup. :* Cic. **II.** *craftily :* Pl.
argūtiae, ārum, *f. pl.* [argūtus], *clear-cut or
expressive movements.* **A.** Physical : digitorum, Cic. Of chattering : Pl. **B.** Mental. **a.** *acuteness, subtlety :* Demosthenes
nihil argutiis et acumine Hyperidi cedit,
Cic. **b.** *excessive nicety, over-refinement :* Cic.
argūtulus, a, um [*dim.* argūtus], *somewhat
subtle :* Cic.
argūtus, a, um [arguō]. **1.** Lit. (physical).
a. to the sight, *clear, bright, distinct, clear-
cut* (perh. with idea of *expressive, graceful*) :
oculi, Cic. ; solea, Cat. ; caput, Verg. ;
manus (of expressive action), Cic. **b.** to
the hearing : *clear-toned, penetrating piercing* (of pleasant or unpleasant sounds) ;
tuneful or *grating :* hirundo, olores, ilex,
serra, Verg. ; forum, Ov. Occ. of a person :
Neaera, poetae, Hor. In bad sense, *prating, chatty :* Pl., Cic. Ep. **2.** Transf.
(mental) : *clear-cut, acute, subtle.* **a.** In
good sense, *bright, witty :* orator, poema,
Cic. ; Hor. **b.** In bad sense, *cunning, sly :*
meretrix, Hor. **c.** Of omens, *distinct :*
Cic., Prop. *Comp.* and *Sup. :* Cic.
argyraspis, idis, *adj.* [ἀργύρασπις], *having a
silver shield :* Liv.
Ariadna, ae, *f. d. of Minos, king of Crete ;
she extricated Theseus from the Labyrinth,
and accompanied him on his return to Greece.
She was deserted by Theseus at Naxos, where
Bacchus fell in love with her, and placed her
crown as a constellation in the sky ;* **Ariad-
naeus,** a, um.
Arīcia, ae, *f.* **I.** *an old town in Latium, on
the Appia via, now la Riccia ;* **Arīcīnus,** a,
um. **II.** *w. of Hippolytus and m. of Virbius.*
āriditās, ātis, *f. dryness :* Plin.
āridulus, a, um [*dim.* aridus], *dry :* labella,
Cat.
āridus (contr. **ārdus**), a, um [āreō], *dry,
parched.* **1.** Lit. : ligna, Lucr., Hor. ;
folia, Cic. ; Pl. *Neut.* as Noun, after
prep., dry land : in aridum, in arido, ex
arido, Caes. Poet. : febris, *parching,*
Verg. ; fragor. *the crackling of dry wood,*
Verg. ; sitis, Lucr., Verg. **2.** Transf. **a.**
withered : crura, Ov. **b.** *meagre :* victus,
Cic. **c.** *dry, dull, flat :* genus sermonis,
Cic. ; magister, Quint. ; libri, Tac. **d.**
niggardly : Pl., Ter.
ariēs (in poets the *i* is occ. consonantal ; so
ariete becomes a dactyl), ietis, *m.* **1.** Lit. :
Pl., Varr. **2.** Transf. **a.** *the Ram, a sign
of the zodiac :* Ov. **b.** *a battering-ram :*
Pl., Caes., Liv. **c.** *a projecting beam shaped
so as to break the force of a current :* Caes.

arietō, āre (arietat as a dactyl, Verg.) [ariēs],
to butt like a ram, to strike violently. **A.**
Trans. : qui tam proterve nostras aedis
arietat ? Pl. ; arietata inter se arma, Sen.
Ep. **B.** Intrans : arietat in portas,
Verg. ; in me, Att. ap. Cic. Ep.
Ariobarzānēs, is, *m. a king of Cappadocia.*
Ariōn, onis, *m.* (Acc. Ariona). **I.** *a famous
lyric poet of Lesbos, rescued from drowning
by a dolphin.* Hence, **Ariōnius,** a, um.
II. *a horse with the gift of speech and
prophecy sent by Neptune to Adrastus.*
arista, ae, *f.* **1.** Lit. : *the awn or beard of
an ear of grain :* munitur vallo aristarum,
Cic. ; Ov. **2.** Transf. **a.** *an ear of corn :*
Verg , Ov. **b.** *a harvest of corn :* post
aliquot aristas, Verg. Also, *an ear of
spikenard :* Ov.
Aristaeus, i, *m. s. of Apollo and Cyrene ;
said to have taught men the management of
bees, and to have been the first to plant olive
trees.*
Aristarchus, i, *m. a famous grammarian and
critic at Alexandria.*
Aristīdēs, is, *m.* **I.** *an Athenian famous for
his integrity ; a contemporary and rival of
Themistocles.* **II.** *a poet of Miletus.*
Aristippus, i, *m. a philosopher of Cyrene, disciple of Socrates, and founder of the Cyrenaic
school ;* **Aristippēus,** a, um.
Aristius, *v.* Fuscus.
Aristogītōn, onis, *m. an Athenian who conspired against the Pisistratidae.*
Aristō, ōnis, *m. a philosopher of Chios, disciple of Zeno ;* **Aristōnēus,** a, um.
Aristophanēs, is, *m.* **I.** *the most famous
Athenian comic poet ;* **Aristophanēus,** a,
um. **II.** *a famous grammarian of Byzantium, teacher of Aristarchus.*
Aristotelēs, is, *m.* (Gen. Aristotelī, Cic.), *a
famous philosopher, born at Stagira, pupil of
Plato, teacher of Alexander the Great, and
founder of the Peripatetic school ;* **Aristo-
telēus** and **-īus,** a, um.
Aristoxenus, i, *m. a Peripatetic philosopher
and musician.*
arithmēticus, a, um [ἀριθμητικός], *of numbers.* As Noun, **arithmētica,** ōrum, *n. pl.
arithmetic :* in arithmeticis satis exercitatus,
Cic. Also **arithmetica,** ae, *f.* Sen. Ep.
āritūdō, inis, *f.* [āridus], *dryness :* Pl., Varr.
Ariūsius, a, um, *of Ariusia in Chios.*
arma, ōrum, *n. pl.* **1.** Lit. **a.** *armour,
defensive arms :* induere, detrahere, Liv.
Occ. *a shield :* caelestia, Liv. ; so conlegit in arma, Verg. **b.** *arms, weapons*
(both of defence and offence, but of the
latter only in close combat) : Pl. ; arma
alia ad tegendum, alia ad nocendum,
Cic. ; esse in armis, Caes. ; vocare ad arma,
Cic. ; vocare in arma, Verg. ; capere,
sumere, Cic. ; aptare, induere, Liv. ; descendere ad arma, Caes. ; accingi armis,
Verg. ; ponere, Cic. Ep. ; relinquere,
tradere, Liv. Freq. with other words, e.g.
vi atque armis, Liv. ; armis et castris,
Cic. **2.** Transf. **a.** *warfare, camp-life :*
rem ad arma deducere, Caes. ; Galli inter
arma nati, Liv. ; silent leges inter arma,
Cic. ; nulla nisi in armis relinquitur spes,
Liv. ; in arma feror, Verg., Tac. **b.** *soldiers,
armed men :* Liv., Verg., Tac. **c.** *means*

of protection, defence, weapons : ille spoliatus armis audaciae, Cic. ; arma senectutis, Cic. ; Ov. **d.** *equipment, tools.* **i.** of agriculture : Verg. Also for grinding corn : Verg. **ii.** of a ship : Caes. **iii.** of the wings of Daedalus : Ov.

armamaxa, ae, *f.* |ἁρμάμαξα], *a Persian travelling-carriage* (esp. for women) : Curt.

armāmenta, ōrum, *n. pl.* [armō], *fittings,* esp. *the tackle of a ship :* Pl., Caes., Ov., etc.

armāmentārium, ī, *n.* [armāmenta], *an arsenal, armoury :* publicum, Cic. ; Liv.

armāriolum, ī, *n.* [*dim.* armārium], *a little chest or closet :* Pl.

armārium, ī, *n.* [arma], *a cupboard, chest, safe* (for stores, clothing, money, etc.) : Pl., Cic.

armātūra, ae, *f.* [armō], *an outfit, equipment, armour.* **1.** Lit. : Numidae levis armaturae, Caes. ; Cic. Ep. Hence, *light-armed troops :* Cic., Liv. **2.** Transf. : of discourse : tamquam levis armaturae prima orationis excursio, Cic.

armātus, a, um. **I.** *Part.* armō. **II.** Adj. *equipped, armed.* **1.** Lit. : Cic., Liv., Verg., etc. Reg. superl. : Cic. As Noun, **armātus,** ī, *m. an armed man :* Enn., Caes., Liv. **2.** Transf. : armati animis, Cic.

armātū, ABL. *sing. m.* [armō], *in the manner of arming.* **1.** Lit. : Cretico, Liv. **2.** Transf. : like armatura, *troops, armed in a certain way :* (relicto) omni graviore armatu, Liv.

Armenia, ae, *f. a country in W. Asia.* Hence, **Armeniacus,** a, um ; **Armeniaca,** ae, *f. the apricot tree ;* **Armeniacum,** ī, *n. the Armenian apple,* i.e. *the apricot ;* **Armenius** a, um.

armentālis, e, *adj.* [armentum], *of a herd :* equa, Verg.

armentārius, ī, *m. a herdsman, neatherd :* Varr., Lucr., Verg.

armentum, ī, *n.* [arō], lit. *cattle for ploughing,* most freq. in *pl.* **I. a.** Of oxen : Cic. **b.** Of horses : Verg. **c.** Transf. : of sea-monsters : Ov. **II.** *a herd.* **a.** Of oxen : Liv., Verg., Ov. **b.** Of horses : Verg. **c.** Transf. of stags : Verg.

armifer, era, erum [arma ferō], *armour-bearing, armed :* Ov.

armiger, era, erum. **I.** Adj. [arma gerō] **a.** *armour-bearing, armed :* Prop. **b.** *producing warriors :* Prop. **II.** Noun. **a.** *an armed person :* cum paucis armigeris, Curt. **b.** Us. *an armour-bearer, esquire :* Pl., Cic., Verg. ; armiger Iovis (i.e. aquila), Verg., Ov.

armilla, ae, *f.* [armus], *an armlet, arm-ring, bracelet :* Pl., Cic., Liv.

armillātus, a, um [armilla], *ornamented with a bracelet :* Prop., Suet.

Armilūstrum, ī, *n.* [arma, lūstrō], *a place in Rome, where the festival of the purification of arms was celebrated.*

Arminius, ī, *m. a German prince who defeated Varus,* A.D. 9, *and saved the independence of Germany.*

armi-potēns, entis, *adj.* [arma potēns], *powerful in arms, warlike :* Mavors, Lucr. ; diva, Verg.

armi-sonus, a, um [arma sonō], *resounding with arms :* Verg.

armō, āre [arma]. **1.** Lit. : *to furnish or*

equip with arms : pastores, Caes. ; Cic. Poet. : manūs armat sparus, Verg. With *Instr.* Abl. : Liv., Verg. Poet. : calamos veneno, Verg. With *in, contra, adversus :* servi in dominos armabantur, Cic. ; in proelia fratres, Verg. ; iuventus contra Milonis impetum armata est, Cic. *Pass.* in *Refl. sense :* milites armari iubet, Caes. **2.** Transf. **a.** *to arm* (as with weapons) : temeritatem multitudinis auctoritate publicā, Cic. ; Ov., etc. **b.** *to rouse to arms :* in hunc unum tota res publica armata est, Cic. ; pudor armat in hostis, Verg., Liv., etc. **c.** *to fit out* (esp. for war), *equip :* navis, Caes. ; classem, Liv., Verg. ; muros propugnaculis, Liv.

Armoricae, ārum, *f. pl. the district of N.W. Gaul,* now *Brittany and a part of Normandy.*

armus, ī, *m.* [ἁρμός]. **I.** *the shoulder where it is fitted to the shoulder-blade, the fore-quarter* (us. of an animal) : ex umeris armi fiunt, Ov., Hor. Of men : Verg. **II.** *the side of an animal :* Verg.

Arnē, ēs, *f. a woman who betrayed her country* (*the island Siphnos*), *and was changed into a jackdaw.*

arō, āre [ἀρόω], *to plough, till.* **1.** Lit. : Pl., Cic., Hor., etc. With Acc. : agrum, Cic. ; campum, Ov. ; Capuam, Verg. Prov. of useless labour : litora bubus arat, Ov. Also *to live by farming :* cives Romani qui arant in Siciliā, Cic. With Acc. : Hor. **2.** Transf. **a.** Of a ship : aequor, Verg., Ov. **b.** Of age : iam venient rugae, quae tibi corpus arent, Ov.

Arpīnum, ī, *n. a town in Latium, birthplace of Marius and Cicero,* now *Arpino.* Hence, **Arpīnās,** ātis, *adj.* ; **Arpīnātēs,** ium, *m. pl. its inhabitants.*

arqu-, *v.* arc-.

arr-, *v.* adr-.

Arria, ae, *f. the wife of Paetus, famous for her fortitude.*

ars, artis, *f. method, way, means.* **A.** Of dealing with material things. **a.** *handicraft, trade ;* hence, the division into liberales, ingenuae, etc., i.e. those befitting a freeman or gentleman, and inliberales, sordidae, etc., i.e. those of slaves and the lower classes : Cic. **b.** esp. *skilled work, craftsmanship, art :* Cic. ; arte laboratae vestes, Verg. **c.** *artificial means :* locus et naturā et arte munitus, Caes. **d.** Transf. : *a work of art :* clipeum efferri iussit Didymaonis artis, Verg. ; Hor. **B.** Of action, in which the mind is more especially concerned. **a.** *skill in the liberal arts* (combining *theory* and *practice*), *any such art or profession :* ars gubernatoris, gubernandi, disserendi, etc., Cic. ; ars duellica, Pl. ; artes militares et imperatoriae, Liv. ; artes civiles, Tac. ; ars musica, Ter. ; rhetorica, Quint. ; magica, Verg. ; centum puer artium, *accomplishments,* Hor. Cic. ol *theory* as opposed to *practice* (facultas) : Cic. Also person. : Artes, *the Arts :* Phaedr. **b.** *methods, devices, cunning :* suis artibus, fraude et insidiis circumventus, Liv. ; dolis instructus et arte Pelasgā, Verg. ; Ter. **c.** Of moral action ; *moral attitude* or *conduct, moral qualities* or *character* (in good or bad sense) : Pl. ; artes eximiae, huius administrae virtutis, Cic. ; insolens malarum artium, Sall. ; Tac. ; eā arte (i.e. constantiā) Pollux arces attigit igneas, Hor.

Arsacēs, is, *m. first king of the Parthians ;* **Arsacidae**, ārum, *m. pl. his successors ;* **Arsacius**, a, um, *Parthian.*

Arsinoē, ēs, *f.* **I.** *the name of several Egyptian queens.* **II.** *the name of several towns in Egypt, Cyrene, Cilicia ;* **Arsinoëticus**, a, um.

Artabānus, ī, *m.* **I.** *a Parthian king.* **II.** *a general of Xerxes.*

Artaxata, ōrum, *n. pl.* (-a, ae, *f.*), *the capital of Armenia, on the R. Araxes.*

Artaxerxēs, is, *m. the name of several Persian kings ;* esp. Artaxerxes I, *s. and successor of Xerxes ;* and Artaxerxes II, *b. of Cyrus the younger.*

artē, *adv. closely, tightly.* **1.** Lit.: arte continentur trabes, Caes. ; Pl. ; Hor. ; quam artissime, ire, Sall. ; artius complecti aliquem, Cic. **2.** Transf.: arte contenteque aliquem habere, Pl.; dormire, Cic. ; rationem adstringere, Cic. ; appellare aliquem (i.e. by abbreviating his name), Ov. ; diligere aliquem, Plin. Ep.

Artemis, idis, *f. the Greek name of Diana.*

artēria, ae, *f.* (**artēria**, ōrum, *n. pl.* : Lucr.). **I.** [ἀρτηρία], *the windpipe.* Also called arteria aspera : Cic. **II.** *an artery :* Cic.

arthriticus, a, um [ἀρθριτικός] *gouty, arthritic :* Cic.

articulātim, *adv.* [articulātus], *joint by joint, piecemeal.* **1.** Lit.: aliquem concidere Pl. ; poet. ap. Cic. **2.** Transf.: of speech : *with proper divisions ; distinctly :* Lucr., Cic.

articulō, āre [articulus]. Lit.: *to divide into joints.* Transf.: of speech, *to utter distinctly, to articulate :* Lucr.

articulōsus, a, um [articulus], *full of joints.* Transf.: of style : *full of divisions;* Quint.

articulus, ī. *m.* [*dim.* artus]. **1.** Lit. a *small joint* (e.g. of the finger), *knuckle, joint :* Caes., Ov., etc. Hence, **a.** *the finger :* quid sit utile supputat articulis, Ov. **b.** *the whole limb :* Lucr. **2.** Transf. **a.** Of plants : sarmentorum, Cic. **b.** Of discourse : *a member, division :* Cic. Also the *article* as a part of speech : Quint. **c.** Of time : *a turning-point, a critical moment :* Pl. ; in ipso articulo temporis,, *at the very nick of time,* Cic. ; in ipso articulo, Ter. ; in articulo rerum, Curt. **d.** *a turning-point, a stage* (in the cursus honorum) : Augustus ap. Suet.

artifex, icis, *m.* [ars faciō]. **I.** Adj. **A.** Act., *contriving means, skilful, ingenious* (with GEN. or Absol.): homines talis negoti artifices, Sall. ; stilus, Cic. ; manus, **B.** Pass.: *skilfully made, artistic :* boves, Prop. ; motus, Quint. Of a horse, *broken, trained :* Ov. **II.** Noun. **a.** *a worker, craftsman, artist* (us. with a qualifying word): artifices scaenici, *actors,* Cic. Absol. of a *physician :* Liv. ; of a *builder,* Liv. ; of an *orator* or *writer :* Cic. **b.** *a deviser, master :* si pulcher est hic mundus, si probus eius artifex, Cic. ; Liv. In bad sense : artifices ad corrumpendum iudicium, Cic. ; Ter. ; Verg.

artificiōsē, *adv. skilfully :* Cic. Comp.: Cic. *Sup. :* Auct. ad Her.

artificiōsus, a um [artificium]. **A.** Act.: *full of contrivances, ingenious, accomplished :* rhetores artificiosissimi, Cic. **B.** Pass.: **a.** *made with art, ingenious :* artificiosi operis divinique, Cic. **b.** *made according to the rules of an art, artificial* (opp. *naturalis*) : Cic.

artificium, ī, *n.* [artifex], *a contriving of means.* **I.** *workmanship, skill in handicraft :* singulari opere artificioque perfectum, Cic. Hence, **a.** *an industry, profession, art :* Cic., Tac. **b.** Concr., *work done, artistic work, work of art :* Cic. **II.** *dexterity, adroitness, clever manœuvring :* Caes., Cic. In bad sense, *cunning* (in *pl.*) : Cic. Ep. **III.** *rules of art, theory of an art :* non esse eloquentiam ex artificio, sed artificium ex eloquentiā natum, Cic.

artō, āre [artus], *to pack closely, compress.* **1.** Lit.: Lucr. **2.** Transf.: *to limit, contract :* Pl., Liv.

artolaganus, ī, *m.* [ἀρτολάγανον], *a kind of bread or cake (made of meal, wine, milk, oil, lard, pepper) :* Cic. Ep.

artopta, ae, *m.* [ἀρτόπτης]. **I.** *a baker :* Juv. **II.** *a vessel to bake in, a breadpan :* Pl.

artua, *v.* artus.

artus, a, um [root seen in ἀραρίσκω, arma, etc.], *fitted, fitting.* Hence, **1.** Lit. **a.** *close, tight :* claustra, Lucr. ; Cic. ; compages, Verg. ; toga, Hor. ; catena, Ov. **b.** *confined, compact* (and so *narrow, dense*) : silvae, Caes. ; vallis, Liv. ; fauces, Tac. ; theatrum, Ov. Hence, *crowded :* convivia, Hor. *Neut.* as Noun *in phr. in artum, in* arto), *a close or confined space :* Lucr., Hor., Liv. Hence, in arto commeatus, Tac. ; spem sibi ponere in arto, Ov. ; Liv. **2.** Transf. **a.** *close, tight :* nullum vinculum iure jurando artius esse, Cic. ; vincula amoris artissima, Cic. Ep. ; somnus, Cic. **b.** *limited, straitened :* commeatus, Liv. ; petitio, Liv. (*cf.* **1.** b.). Of fortunes : res, Ov., Tac. ; tempora, Curt. **c.** *strict, severe :* iura, Lucr.

artūs, uum, *m. pl.* (artua, n. Pl. ; DAT. and ABL. artubus : *sing.* Luc.) [root seen in ἀραρίσκω, arma, etc.]. **1.** Lit.: *joints* (=articuli) : digitorum, Cic. ; Tac. ; per membra, per artūs, Lucr. ; Pl. ; Suet. **2.** Transf.: *the limbs :* Enn., Lucr., Cic.. Verg., etc.

ārula, ae, *f.* [*dim.* āra], *a small altar :* Cic.

arund-, *v.* harund-.

Arūns, ūntis, *m. an Etruscan name for the younger son of a king (while the elder was called Lar or Lars) :* esp. **I.** b. of Lucumo (*Tarquinius Priscus*). **II.** *a younger son of Tarquinius Superbus.* **III.** *s. of Porsenna.*

aruspex, *v.* haruspex.

arvīna, ae, *f. grease, fat :* Verg.

arvus, a, um [arō], *that has been ploughed, arable :* ager, Pl., Cic. As Noun, **arvum**, ī, *n. arable land.* **1.** Lit. : Cic. Also in gen. sense, *soil, land* (esp. in *pl.*) : Lucr., Verg. ; Ov. ; Tac. **2.** Transf. **a.** *region, country :* aspicis en, praeses, quali iaceamus in arvo, Ov. ; arva Neptunia (*the sea*), Verg.

arx, arcis, *f.* [*cf.* arceō], *a keep, stronghold, citadel :* Pl., Lucr., Cic., etc. Esp. the citadel of Rome, on the N. peak of the Capitoline hill : Cic., Caes., Liv. P r o v. : arcem facere e cloacā (*cf.* ' to make a mountain out of a molehill'), Cic. Hence, poet. **a.** of a mountain or hill : Romae septem arces, Verg. ; Hor. ; Ov. **b.** of heaven : arces igneae, Hor. ; Ov. **2.** T r a n s f. **a.** *bulwark, protection, refuge :* hic portus, haec arx, haec ara sociorum, Cic. ; tribunicium auxilium et provocationem, duas arces libertatis tuendae, Liv. ; ad excursiones faciendas, Liv. **b.** *stronghold, mainstay :* in arcem illius causae invadere, Cic. ; ubi Hannibal sit, ibi caput atque arcem totius belli esse, Liv.

as, assis, *m. a unit.* **I.** As a standard of weight, *a pound*, divided into 12 parts, or *ounces* (*v.* Tables of weight and money at the end of the volume.) **II.** As a coin, the *as* was, acc. to the ancient custom of weighing money, originally *a pound weight of uncoined copper* (asses librales or aes grave), afterwards gradually reduced in weight, till at the close of the Punic War it was about 1 ounce. The small value of the *as* after the last reduction led to the word being used in various phrases to denote a paltry coin : quod (*sc.* pondus auri) si comminuas, vilem redigatur ad assem, Hor. ; viatica ad assem perdiderat, *to the last farthing*, Hor. **III.** In divisions of money among heirs, *etc.*, the *as*, with its parts, was used to designate the portions. Thus, heres ex asse, *sole heir ;* heres ex semisse, *he who receives half ;* heres ex dodrante, *he who receives three-fourths of the inheritance :* and so heres ex besse, triente, quadrante, sextante, *etc.:* Cic. [F*r.* as; Eng. ace, in dice and cards.]

āsa, *v.* āra.

Ascalaphus, ī, *m. s.* of *Acheron and Orphne, changed into an owl.*

Ascānius, ī, *m. s.* of *Aeneas and Creüsa, and founder of Alba Longa.*

a-scendō, scendere, scendī, scēnsum [scandō], *to climb up, mount up, ascend.* **A.** T r a n s. **1.** L i t. : murum, Caes. ; Verg.; ripam, Cic. ; equum, Liv. ; Ter. ; classem, Tac. **2.** T r a n s f. : unum gradum dignitatis, Cic. **B.** I n t r a n s. (mostly with *in* and Acc. or Absol.). **1.** L i t. With *in :* Pl., Cic., Verg., etc. With *ad :* Liv. Absol. : quā fefellerat ascendens hostis, Liv.; Caes. ; Sall. **2.** T r a n s f. **a.** *to rise in* rank, etc. ; with *in :* in summum locum civitatis, Cic. ; with *ad :* ad hunc gradum amicitiae, Curt. ; Cic. ; Lucr. Absol. : gradatim ascendit vox, Cic. **b.** With *super* or *supra, to rise above, surpass :* supra praeturas, Tac. With *supra* as Adv. : usque ad nos contemptus Samnitium pervenit, supra non ascendit, Liv.

ascēnsiō, ōnis, *f.* [ascendō], *a climbing up, an ascending, ascent.* **1.** L i t. : Pl. **2.** T r a n s f.: oratorum, Cic.

ascēnsus, ūs, *m.* [ascendō]. **I.** *a climbing up, an ascending, ascent :* primos prohibere ascensu coeperunt, Caes. ; Cic. ; Verg., etc. Also in *pl.* : scalis ascensūs temptant, Liv. ; Cic. T r a n s f.: ad honoris amplioris

gradum, Cic. **II.** Concr. : *a place for ascending, an ascent ;* difficilis atque arduus, Cic. ; qualis esset natura montis, et qualis in circuitu ascensus, Caes. ; Ov. T r a n s f.: in virtute multi ascensūs, Cic.

ascia, ae, *f.* [*cf.* ἀξίνη]. **I.** *an axe or hatchet :* ROGVM ASCIA NE POLITO, Fragm. XII. Tab. ap. Cic. **II.** *a mason's trowel :* Vitr. Phrases—sub asciā posuit ; consummatum hoc opus sub asciā est ; sub asciā or ad asciam dedicatum ; — occur often in sepulchral inscriptions, and mean that the tomb was consecrated before its building was finished.

a-sciō, scīre [perh. formed from ascīvī, perf. of asciscō, by analogy with scīvī from sciō], *to take to, or associate with oneself :* socios, Verg. ; aliquem in societatem, per adoptionem, Tac.

a-sciscō, sciscere, scīvī, scītum. **1.** L i t. **a.** Of public measures : *to approve or adopt anything :* cum iussisset populus Romanus aliquid, si id ascivisset socii populi ac Latini, Cic. **b.** Of persons in public matters : *to receive or admit a person in some capacity* (as *citizen, ally*), *to adopt :* Numam Pompilium regem alienigenam sibi ipse populus ascivit, Cic. ; socios, Caes. With *in* (in civitatem, societatem, senatum, nomen, *etc.*) : asciti simul in civitatem et patres, Liv. ; Tac. **2.** T r a n s f. **a.** Of persons, *to adopt, admit into one's society, associate :* aliquem ad sceleris foedus, Cic. ; ad spem praedae, Liv. ; in conscientiam facinoris, Liv. ; dominos, Lucr. ; aliquem generum, Liv., Verg., Tac. **b.** Of things, *to adopt, appropriate :* ritūs peregrinos, Liv.; nova verba, Hor. ; sacra a Graecis, Cic. ; sibi oppidum, Cic. ; Lucr. **c.** *to assume, arrogate to oneself* (with *sibi*) : prudentiam, Cic. ; Liv. ; Tac.

ascītus, a, um. **I.** *Part.* asciscō. **II.** *Adj.*, acquired (opp. to what comes by nature) : Nep., Ov., Curt.

Asclēpiadēs, ae, *m.* **I.** *a famous physician of Prusa in Bithynia, friend of Crassus.* **II.** *a blind philosopher of Eretria.* **III.** *a Greek poet, inventor of the Asclepiad metre.*

ascopēra, ae, *f.* [ἀσκοπήρα], *a leathern sack or wallet :* Suet.

Ascra, ae, *f. a village in Boeotia, birthplace of Hesiod ;* **Ascraeus**, a, um, *of Hesiod ;* **Ascraeus**, ī, *m.* the *Ascraean, i.e. Hesiod.*

a-scrībō, scrībere, scrīpsī, scrīptum. **I.** *to add to or insert in a writing* (*absol.;* with DAT., *ad* or *in* with Acc. or *in* and ABL.). **1.** L i t. : non solum illud perscribunt, sed etiam causam ascribunt, Cic. ; diem in epistulā, Cic. Ep. ; Suet. Esp. of s u p e r-s c r i p t i o n s and i n s c r i p t i o n s : non credo ascripturum esse MAGNO, Cic. ; etc. **2.** T r a n s f. : *to ascribe, assign :* hoc incommodum Scipioni ascribendum videtur, Cic. ; alicui legatum (i.e. to bequeath), Plin. Ep. P o e t. : ascriptus poenae dies, *the appointed day*, Phaedr. ; ascribere sibi exemplum, *to apply* (an *illustration*) *to oneself*, Phaedr. **II.** *to add to a list, enrol* (as *citizen, soldier, colonist,* etc.). **1.** L i t. : ascribi se in eam civitatem voluit, Cic. ; colonos Venusiam ascripserunt, Liv. With DAT. : urbanae militiae, Tac. **2.** T r a n s f.

ascribe me talem in numerum, Cic.; aliquem ordinibus deorum, Hor.; Tac.

ascripticius, a, um [ascribō], *enrolled* or *received in any community* (*as citizen, soldier*, etc.) : Cic.

ascriptiō, ōnis, *f.* [ascribō], *an addition in writing* : Cic.

ascriptivus a, um, [ascribō], *enrolled as a* (*supernumerary*) *soldier* (*cf.* ascripticius and accensus) : Pl.

ascriptor ōris, *m.* [ascribō], *one who subscribes to* or *approves anything* : legis agrariae, Cic.

ascriptus, a, um. **I.** *Part.* ascribō. **II.** *Adj.,* civis, *a naturalised citizen,* Cic. (see ascribo II.).

asella, ae, *f.* and **asellus**, ī, *m.* [*dim.* asina and -us], *a little ass, an ass's colt* : Cic., Verg., etc. Prov.: narrare fabulam surdo asello (*to preach to the deaf*), Hor.

Aselliō, ōnis, *m. an early Roman historian.*

Āsia, ae, *f.* (poet. **Āsis**, idis, *f.*). **I.** orig. *a town in Lydia,* and later *the country around it* ; **Āsius**, a, um, *of Asia.* **II.** *the kingdom of Troy.* **III.** *the Roman province of Asia.* **IV.** *Asia Minor.* **V.** *the kingdom of Pergamum.* **VI.** *the continent of Asia ;*

Āsiānus, a, um, *of the Roman province of Asia* ; **Āsiānī**, ōrum, *m. pl. the inhabitants of this province* ; **Āsiāticus**, a, um, *Asiatic* ; transf.: genus dicendi, *a florid, Oriental style of speaking,* Cic. ; **Āsiāticus**, ī, *m. a surname of Cornelius Scipio, who conquered Antiochus.*

asilus, ī, *m. a gad-fly, horse-fly,* us. called tabanus : Verg.

asina, ae, *f.* (Varr.) and **asinus**, ī, *m.* [*cf.* ὄνος], *an ass.* **1.** Lit.: Cato ; Cic. **2.** Transf.: *an ass, a fool* : Pl., Ter., Cic. [Fr. *âne.*]

Asinius, ī, *m. a Roman name ;* esp. Asinius Pollio, *a friend of Augustus, founder of the first library in Rome, author of a history* (*now lost*) *of the Civil War between Caesar and Pompeius, and a writer of tragedies.*

Āsōpus, ī (Acc. Āsōpon), *m. a river in Boeotia ;* person. *f. of Aegina, Euboea,* and *Euadne. g.f. of Aeacus ;* **Āsōpiadēs**, ae, *m. g.s. of Asopus, i.e. Aeacus ;* **Āsōpis**, idis (or idos), *f.* (Acc. -ida), *d. of Asopus.*

asōtus, ī, *m.* [ἄσωτος], *a sensualist, debauchee* : Cic.

asparagus, ī, *m.* [ἀσπάραγος], *asparagus* : Cato ; in *pl.* : Juv., Suet.

a-spargō, *v.* aspergō.

Aspāsia, ae, *f. an accomplished Greek woman in the time of Pericles.*

aspectābilis, e, *adj.* [aspectō], *that may be seen, visible* : Cic.

aspectō, āre [*freq.* aspiciō], *to look at repeatedly* or *attentively, to gaze at.* **1.** Lit.: quid me aspectas ? Pl. ; Cic. ; Lucr. ; immensam silvam. Verg. **2.** Transf. **a.** *to observe, pay attention to* : iussa principis. Tac. **b.** Of site : *to face, look towards* : collis adversas desuper arces, Verg. ; Tac.

aspectus, a, um, *Part.* aspiciō.

aspectus, ūs, *m.* [aspiciō]. **A.** Act. **a.** *a seeing* or *looking at, a look, view, sight* : uno aspectu iudicare, Cic. ; also, primo aspectu, Cic. ; urbs situ est praeclaro ad aspectum, Cic. With Gen. or Adj.: aspectum hominum vitare, Cic. ; Tac. ; Verg. In *pl.* : mortalis aspectūs reliquit, Verg. **b.** *a glance of the eye, look* : lubricos oculos fecit (natura) et mobilis ut aspectum, quo vellent, facile converterent, Cic. **c.** *range of sight* (us. con-spectus) : prope in aspectu urbis, Cic. **d.** *eyesight* : Enn. ; aspectum omnino amittere, Cic. **B.** Pass. **a.** *a coming into sight, appearance* : eius aspectus nobis seditiones adferebat, Cic. **b.** *physical appearance, look, mien* : Lucr. ; horridiores aspectu, Caes. ; Tac. ; Cethegi, Cic. ; Hor.

as-pellō, ere, *to drive away* : Pl., Ter. Transf.: metum alicui, Pl.

asper, era, erum (aspra = aspera, Enn.; aspris = asperis, Verg.). **1.** Lit. Of touch : *rough, uneven* (opp. to *lēvis* or *lēnis*) : saxa, Enn.; lingua aspera tactu, Lucr. ; loca, Caes.; frena, Liv. : quid iudicant sensūs ? dulce, amarum : lene, asperum, Cic. ; rubus, sentes (i.e. prickly), Verg. *Neut.* as Noun (esp. in *pl.*): Lucr., Hor., Tac., etc. Of carvings : aspera signis pocula, Verg. **2.** Transf. **A.** Of other senses. **a.** Of taste : *harsh, bitter* : sapor maris, Plin. ; of wine, Ter. **b.** Of sound : *harsh, grating,* etc.; pronuntiationis genus, Cic. ; Ov. **c.** Of smell : *pungent* : Plin. **d.** Of climate, weather, etc., *rough, severe, wintry* : mare, Liv. ; aspera caelo Germania, Tac. ; hiems, Verg. **B.** Of character. **a.** Of persons and animals, *rough, harsh, savage, hard, severe* : homines asperi et montani, Caes. ; homo asper et durus, Cic. ; Liv. ; Verg., etc. ; asperrimos illos ad condicionem pacis, Liv. With causal ABL. : Verg., Ov. Of animals : Verg., Hor., etc. **b.** Of discourse : *severe, caustic, biting* : asperioribus facetiis perstringere, Cic. ; Ov., etc. **c.** Of principles, tenets, etc., *harsh, hard, austere* : doctrina (sc. Stoicorum) non moderata nec mitis, sed paulo asperior et durior, Cic. ; sententia, mimus, Liv. ; studiis asperrima belli, Verg. **d.** Of circumstances or situations : *rough, difficult* : tempora, Cic. ; in dies gravior atque asperior oppugnatio erat, Caes. ; bellum, labores, etc., Sall. ; pugna, odia, fata, Verg. [Fr. *âpre.*]

asperē, *adv.* [asper], *roughly.* Transf.: *harshly, severely* : Cic., Sall., Liv.

a-spergō (**aspargō**), spergere, spērsi, spērsum [spargō], *to scatter* or *sprinkle upon ; to besprinkle, bespatter* : aquam, Pl. ; aequor Ionium glaucis virus ab undis, Lucr. The constr. is (a) *to sprinkle* one thing (Acc.) on another (DAT.). (b) *to besprinkle* one thing (Acc.) with another (ABL. *Instr.*). **1.** Lit. **a.** Guttam Bulbo, Cic. ; pecori virus, Verg. Sometimes *in* with ABL. instead of DAT.: pigmenta in tabulā, Ci c. **b.** ne aram sanguine aspergeret, Cic. ; Pl. ; Ov., etc. **2.** Transf. **a.** sales orationi, Cic. ; illius comitatem tuae gravitati, Cic. **b.** infamiā aspergi, Cic., Nep. ; suspicione, Liv. ; Hor.

aspergō (or **aspargō**), inis, *f.* [aspergō, v.]. **I.** *a sprinkling ;* aquarum, Ov. **II.** *a spray :*

nimborum, Luer. ; salsa, Verg. ; flummifera, Ov.

asperitās, ātis, *f.* [asper], *unevenness, roughness* (opp. *lēvitas*). **1.** Lit.: of touch: saxorum, Cic. ; locorum, Sall. ; Liv. **2.** Trans f. **A.** Of other senses. **a.** Of taste: *harshness* : Plin. **b.** Of sound : *harshness of tone* : vocis, Lucr. ; Tac. **c.** Of climate, etc.: *severity* : hiemis, Tac. ; frigorum, Tac. ; Ov. **B.** Of character : *roughness, severity, harshness, fierceness.* **a.** Of persons : Stoicorum, Cic. ; patris, Ov. **b.** Of things : orationis, Cic. ; Ov.; remedi, Tac. **C.** Of circumstances : *hardness, difficulty* : belli, Sall. ; asperitates rerum, Cic.

āspernātiō, ōnis, *f.* [āspernor], *contempt, disdain* (rare) : Cic., Sen. Ep.

āspernor, ārī [ab spernor ; *v.* spernō], lit. *to kick away from oneself.* Hence, **a.** *to reject with scorn or aversion, spurn, repel* : Ter. ; preces, querimonias, Cic. ; Verg. ; placamina irae, Liv. ; furorem alicuius a suis aris atque templis, Cic. ; militiam, disciplinam, Tac. **b.** *to reject, refuse* ; consilia, Liv. ; Tac. ; honorem, Tac. With *Inf.* as object : dare aspernabantur, Tac.

asperō, āre [asper], *to make rough, to roughen.* **1.** Lit.: Varr., Verg. **2.** Trans f. **a.** (*cf.* rubus asper, Verg.), *to make prickly, give a point to* : sagittas ossibus, Tac. ; Luc. **b.** *to make severe, fierce* ; *to excite* : hunc in saevitiam, Tac. ; iram victoris, Tac.

aspersiō, ōnis, *f.* [aspergō], *a sprinkling* : aquae, Cic. Of *the laying on of colours* : Cic.

aspersus, a, um, *Part.* aspergō.

a-spiciō, spicere, spexī, spectum [ad, speciō]. **I.** *to catch sight of, descry* : Pl. ; respexit et equum alacrem laetus aspexit, Cic. ; Hor. ; Ov. **II. 1.** Lit. **a.** *to look at, behold* : Ter. With *ad* : ad me, Pl. ; Varr. With *contra* : Pl. With *Acc.*: Cic., Verg., etc. ; lumen aspicere, i.e. *to be born*, Cic. Also of looking boldly at : Lacedaemonios in acie, Nep. ; hostem, Tac. In *Pass.*, *to be in sight* : pars fori aspici potest, Cic. With *Indir. Quest.* : *behold / see /* : aspice qui coeant populi, Verg. ; Pl. ; also parenth. : quantas ostentant, aspice, viris, Verg. **b.** *to inspect, examine closely* : opus admirabile, Ov. ; Boeotiam atque Euboeam, Liv. **2.** Trans f. **a.** Of the mind, *to observe, consider* : res (obscuras) aspicere, Cic. ; Pl. ; Ov. ; with *Indir. Quest.* : Verg., Hor., Ov. **b.** Of locality, *to look upon, face* : ea pars Britanniae Hiberniam, Tac.

aspīrātiō, ōnis, *f.* [aspīrō]. **I.** *a breathing to* or *upon* : aëris (i.e. of the air upon us), Cic. **II.** *evaporation, exhalation* : terrarum, Cic. **III.** Gram. : *a rough breathing, aspiration* : Cic., Quint.

a-spīrō, āre. **A.** Intrans. **1.** Lit.: *to breathe* or *blow upon, to breathe* (with *ad*, DAT., or Absol.) : ad quae (granaria) nulla aura umida aspirat, Varr. ; nautis lenius aura, Cat. ; pulmones se contrahunt aspirantes, Cic. Of the fragrance of a plant : amaracus dulci umbrā, Verg. Of musical instruments : tibia choro, Hor. Gram. : *to give the aspirate to* : Quint. **2.** Trans f. **a.** *to breathe upon with favour, to assist* :

fortuna labori, Verg. ; Ov. **b.** *to pant after, aspire to, come near to reaching* or *attaining* (with *ad*, *in* and Acc., local Adv.) : ad meam pecuniam, Cic. ; bellicā laude ad Africanum, Cic. ; in curiam, Cic. Poet. with DAT. : equis aspirat Achillis, Verg. **B.** Trans. **1.** Lit.: *to breathe* or *blow upon* : Iuno ventos aspirat eunti, Verg. **2.** Trans f.: dictis amorem, Verg. ; Quint.

aspis, idis, *f.* [ἀσπίς] (Acc. sing. -ida ; *pl.* -idas), *the asp, viper* : Cic.

asportātiō, ōnis, *f.* [asportō], *a carrying away* : signorum, Cic.

as-portō, āre [abs], *to carry away.* Of things : Cic., Liv. Of persons : Pl., Ter., Cic.

asprēta, ōrum, *n. pl.* [asper], *rough places* : Liv.

ass-, *v.* ads-.

āssa, *v.* āssus, a, um.

Assaracus, ī, *m. king of Phrygia* ; *s. of Tros, b. of Ganymede and Ilus, f. of Capys, g.f. of Anchises.*

asser, eris, *m.* [related to adserere (2)]. **I.** *a pole, stake, post* : Pl., Caes. As a missile : Liv. **II.** *a pole on which a litter was carried* : Juv., Suet.

assula, ae, *f. a splinter* : Pl., Cat.

assulātim, *adv.* [assula], *in splinters* : Pl.

āssus, a, um [perh. for ārsus, cogn. with āreō]. **1.** Lit.: *roasted* : Pl., Hor. Neut. as Noun, *roast meat* : vitulinum, Cic. Ep **2.** Trans f.: *dry* : sol (i.e. a basking in the sun without previous anointing), Cic. Ep. ; femina or nutrix, *a dry-nurse*, Juv. Neut. pl. as Noun, *a sweating-bath* (*cf.* our ' dry shampoo '), Cic. Ep.

Assyria, ae, *f. a country in Asia, between Media, Mesopotamia, and Babylonia ;* **Assyrius,** a, um ; **Assyriī,** ōrum, *m. pl. the Assyrians ;* or *the eastern peoples.*

ast-. For verbs and derivatives beginning thus, *v.* adst-.

ast, *conj.* (*cf.* at), used in laws and vows ; also occ. in Pl., Cic. Ep., Verg., Juv. ; us. before vowels and with pronouns, to make a contrast : Bellona, si hodie nobis victoriam duis, ast ego templum tibi voveo, *then I for my part*, Liv.

Astacidēs, ae, *m. s. of Astacus, i.e. Melanippus.*

Astartē, ēs, *f. a Syro-Phoenician goddess ;* acc. to Cic. *the fourth Venus.*

Asteria, ae, (-ē, ēs), *f.* **I.** *d. of Polus and Phoebe, m. of the Tyrian Hercules.* **II.** *d. of the Titan Coeus, changed by Jupiter into a quail* (ὄρτυξ) *and thrown into the sea ;* hence *the island Ortygia* (later *Delos*) *which arose in the place where she fell.*

Astraea, ae, *f.* **I.** *the goddess of Justice.* **II.** *the constellation Virgo.*

Astraeus, a, um, *of Astraeus, a Titan, h. of Aurora and f. of the winds* : fratres, i.e. *the winds,* Ov.

astrologia, ae, *f.* [ἀστρολογία], *astronomy* : Cic.

astrologus, ī, *m.* [ἀστρολόγος]. **I.** *an astronomer* : Cic. **II.** *a star-interpreter, astrologer* : Enn., Cic., Juv.

astrum, ī, *n.* [ἄστρον], *a star, constellation.* **1.** Lit. (poet. and in elevated prose) : Cic., Verg., etc. **2.** Trans f. **a.** Of great height : turrim sub astra eductam, Verg. ;

Ov. **b.** *heaven, immortality, glory :* sic itur ad astra, Verg. ; educere in astra, Hor. ; tollere ad astra, Cic. Ep. ; Verg. ; Hor.

astu, *n. indecl.* [ἄστυ], *a city,* esp. *Athens* (as urbs for Rome) : Ter., Cic., Nep.

astula, *v.* assula.

Asturia, ae, *f. a district in Hispania Tarraconensis ;* **Asturicus,** a, um ; **Asturica,** ae, *f. the capital of Asturia, now Astorga ;* **Astur,** uris, *adj. ;* as Noun, *an Asturian.*

astus, ūs, *m.* (mostly in ABL. *sing.*), *cleverness, craft, cunning* (shown in a single act ; astutia denotes character) : Pl., Verg., Tac. In *pl. :* Tac.

astūtē, *adv. cunningly :* Pl., Ter., Cic. Ep.

astūtia, ae, *f.* [astūtus]. Orig. perh. *dexterity, adroitness.* In bad sense, *cunning, slyness :* Pl., Ter., Cic. In *pl.: sly tricks :* Pl., Ter., Cic.

astūtus, a, um [astus], *artful, clever ;* us. in bad sense, *sly, cunning :* Pl., Cic., Hor., etc. *Comp. :* Pl., Cic.

Astyagēs, is, *m.* **I.** *king of Media, f. of Mandane, and g.f. of Cyrus.* **II.** *an enemy of Perseus changed by him into stone by means of Medusa's head.*

Astyanax, actis, *m.* (ACC. -acta, Verg.). **I.** *s. of Hector and Andromache.* **II.** *a tragic actor in the time of Cicero.*

Astylos, I, *m. a centaur and soothsayer, who warned his fellow-centaurs against the war with the Lapithae.*

asylum, I, *n.* [ἄσυλον], *a place of refuge, sanctuary :* Cic. ; Liv. ; asylum Iunonia, Verg. ; asyli ius, Tac.

asymbolus, a, um [ἀσύμβολος], *contributing nothing to an entertainment* (=immunis, Hor.), *scot-free :* Ter.

at, *conj. moreover, but, yet :* i.e. it denotes transition from one thought to another, sometimes contrasting, sometimes opposing or contradicting, sometimes limiting, but almost always adding something. (sed is a word of opposition ; *at* a word of addition and always at the beginning of a sentence or clause.) **I.** C o n t r a s t i n g. In general : una navis profugit, at ex reliquis una Massiliam praemissa est, Caes. ; non placet M. Antonio consulatus meus, at placuit M. Servilio, Cic. **b.** Esp. of transition to a new narrative, to a sudden occurrence, to a passionate appeal, etc., *but lo ! :* dapibus epulamur opimis, at subito adeunt Harpyiae, Verg. ; me Notus obruit, at tu, nauta, etc., Hor. **II. a.** O p p o s i n g, o b-j e c t i n g or c o n t r a d i c t i n g: *but on the contrary, but also :* dices, ' quid postea, si Romae adsiduus fui ? ' respondebo, ' at ego omnino non fui,' Cic. Strengthened by *pol, hercle,* etc. ; Pl. ; by *contra, e contrario, potius, etiam, vero :* L. Opimius eiectus est e patriā, at contra his Catilina absolutus, Cic. **b.** Introducing an objection, real or imaginary, of an opponent ; *but it may be objected :* prudentia est senescentis aetatis ; at memoria minuitur, Cic. Also in introducing the answer to an objection : quid porro quaerendum est ? factumne sit ? at constat, *why, it is agreed* . . ., Cic. Esp. with *enim ; but surely,* etc. : at enim cur a me potissimum hoc praesidium petierunt ? *but, it will be asked,* Cic. **III.** L i m i t i n g :

but yet, but at least (with a negative preceding, or in the apodosis of a conditional sentence) : causam, si non commode, at libere dici, Cic. : consules, si minus fortes, at tamen iusti, Cic. ; si tu oblitus es, at di meminerunt, Cic. **IV.** Occ. of m e r e t r a n s i t i o n : comminus gladiis pugnatum est ; at Germani etc. ; Caes.

Atābulus, I, *m. a scorching wind, blowing in Apulia, now Sirocco.*

Atalanta, ae, (-ē, ēs), *f.* **I.** *d. of king Schoeneus, famous for her speed in running ;* **Atalantaeus** (-eūs), a, um. **II.** *d. of Iasius of Arcadia, loved by Meleager.*

atat or **attat,** also repeated atatatae, attatatatae, *or* atatte, atattate, etc., *interj.* An exclamation of joy, pain, wonder, fright, warning, etc. : Pl., Ter.

at-avus, I, *m. the father of a great-great-grandfather, or great-great-grandmother,* opp. to adnepos. **1.** Lit.: Pl., Cic. **2.** Transf.: like avus, abavus, etc.: *ancestor, forefather :* Verg., Hor.

Atella, ae, *f. an old town in Campania ;* **Atellānus,** a, um ; Atellana fabula, *a popular kind of force which originated at Atella.* Also **Atellāna,** ae, *f.* Hence, **Atellānicus,** **Atellānius,** a, um, *of the Atellan farce ;* **Atellānus,** I, *m. an actor in an Atellan farce.*

āter, tra, trum, *black (dead black, simple black* as opp. to *white ;* v. albus : diff. from niger, *glossy black).* **1.** Lit. **a.** In gen.: Pl., Cic., Verg., etc. *Comp. :* Pl. **b.** *dark, dirty :* ater pulvere, Hor. ; dens, *dirty,* Hor. Also = atratus : *clothed in black :* lictores atri, Hor. **2** Transf. **a.** *dark, gloomy, dismal,* etc.: funus, formido, Lucr. ; cupressus, timor, Verg. ; mors, Hor. ; Esquiliae (as a burying-place), Hor. **b.** *black, unlucky :* dies atri are the days on which the state experienced some calamity : si atro die faxit insciens, probe factum esto, Liv. ; Ov. **c.** *malevolent, malicious :* versus, Hor. ; atro dente, (i.e. the venomous tooth of malice), Hor.

Athamās, antis, *m. s. of Aeolus, g.s. of Hellen, king in Thessaly ; f. of Helle and Phrixus by Nephele, and of Learchus and Melicerta by Ino.* In a fit of madness he pursued Ino, who, with Melicerta, threw herself into the sea, and both became sea-deities, Ino becoming Leucothea (Matuta) and Melicerta becoming Palaemon (Portunus) ; **Athamantēus,** a, um ; **Athamantiadēs,** ae, *m. s. of Athamas, i.e. Palaemon ;* **Athamantis,** idis, *f. d. of Athamas, i.e. Helle.*

Athēnae, ārum, *f. pl. Athens, the capital of Attica, in Greece ;* **Athēniēnsis,** e, *adj. :* **Athēniēnsēs,** ium, *m. pl. the Athenians ;* also **Athēnaeus,** a, um ; **Athēnaeum,** I, *n.* **I.** *a fortress in Athamania.* **II.** *a temple of Minerva at Athens, in which scholars and poets used to read their works.* **III.** *a similar temple at Rome, built by the emperor Hadrian.*

Athēnio, ōnis, *m. a leader in the slave rebellion in Sicily, c.* B.C. *100.*

atheos, I, *m.* [ἄθεος], *one who does not believe in the gods, an atheist :* Cic.

Athesis, is, *m.* (ACC. Athesim, ABL. Athesi),

one of the chief rivers of N. Italy, now the Adige.

athlēta, ae, *m.* [ἀθλητής], *an athlete :* Cic., Liv.

athlēticē, *adv. athletically :* Pl.

Athōs, or **Athō** or **Athōn** (no GEN.; ACC. Athō, Athon, Athōnem; DAT. Athō; ABL. Athōne), *m. a high mountain in Macedonia, on the Strymonian gulf, now Monte Santo.*

Atīlius, a, *the name of a Roman gens ;* esp. M. Atilius Regulus, who was defeated and captured by the Carthaginians in the first Punic War; **Atīliānus,** a, um.

Atlās, antis, *m.* **I.** *a mythical king of Mauretania, s. of Iapetus and Clymene, and f. by Pleione of the Pleiades, and by Aethra of the Hyades.* He was changed by Perseus, with the aid of Medusa's head, into Mt. Atlas for refusing him a hospitable reception. **II.** *a name given to a man of colossal height, and* (ironically) *to a dwarf* (Juv.). **III.** *the Atlas Mts. in N. Africa.* **Atlantiadēs,** ae, *m. a male descendant of Atlas.* **a.** *Mercury, g.s. of Atlas.* **b.** *Hermaphroditus, s. of Mercury, g.g.s. of Atlas ;* **Atlantis,** idis, *f. a female descendant of Atlas.* **a.** *Electra.* **b.** *Calypso ;* **Atlanticus,** a, um, *of Mt. Atlas ; mare, the Atlantic Ocean ;* **Atlantiacus, Atlantēus,** a, um, *African, Libyan.*

atomus, I, *f.* [ἄτομος], *an indivisible element, atom :* from these, acc. to Democritus, all things are composed : Cic.

atque (before vowels, *h*, and sometimes consonants) or **ac** (us. before consonants), *conj.* [from adqua]: a copulative particle, denoting a closer internal connexion than is implied by *et : and also, and besides, and even, and.* **I.** Used in joining single words. **A.** In general. **a.** Esp. where these express ideas closely related to each other : ex animo ac vere dicere, Ter.; copia sententiarum atque verborum, Cic. Often the ideas are related by contrast : omnia honesta atque inhonesta ; divina atque humana, Sall. With simul, *at once . . . and :* Britannorum acies in speciem simul ac terrorem editioribus locis constiterat, Tac. **b.** In adding a more important word : *and indeed, and in particular :* magna dis immortalibus habenda est gratia atque huic ipsi Iovi Statori, Cic. ; hebeti ingenio atque nullo,' Cic. **c.** In this sense sometimes strengthened by *adeo : and actually, and further :* non petentem atque adeo etiam absentem, Liv. By *etiam :* id iam populare atque atque etiam plausibile factum est, Cic. **B.** In comparisons. **a.** With par, idem, item, aequus, similis, iuxta, talis, totidem, etc., *as :* neque enim mihi par ratio cum Lucilio est ac tecum fuit, Cic.; pariter patribus ac plebi carus, Liv. **b.** With adverbs of time, esp. simul ; simul ac or atque, *as soon as,* v. simul. Also with principio, statim ; principio atque=simul atque : Pl. **c.** With alius, dissimilis, contra, contrarius, secus, etc. : than, to, from : illi sunt alio ingenio atque tu, Pl. ; contrario motu atque caelum (versatur), Cic. ; quod iste aliter atque ut edixerat decrevisset, Cic. **d.** With comparatives (for *quam*), *than :* haud minus ac iussi faciunt, *no less*

than, Verg. **II.** To connect whole clauses : *and indeed, and yet, and further.* **A.** In general : Africanus indigens mei ? minime hercle. ac ne ego quidem illius, Cic. **B. a.** To add something emphatic or important (*cf.* I. A. b.) hoc enim spectant leges, hoc volunt. . . . atque hoc multo magis efficit ipsa naturae ratio, Cic. **b.** In expressing a wish, us. with utinam : videmus enim fuisse quosdam, . . . atque utinam in Latinis talis oratoris simulacrum reperire possemus ! Cic. **c.** To introduce an abrupt statement : *and instantly, and lo :* vir gregis ipse caper deerraverat ; atque ego Daphnim aspicio, Verg. **C.** To connect an adversative clause : **a.** *and consequently, but :* impetum ferre non potuerunt ac terga verterunt, Caes. **b.** (occ. with *tamen*) *and yet, nevertheless :* nihil praeterea est magnopere dicendum ; ac tamen pauca dicam, Cic. **D.** In introducing a final clause, positive or negative : atque ut, ac ne : ac ne sine causā videretur edixisse, Cic.

at-quī, *conj.,* lit. *but anyhow.* **I.** In general. To connect an emphatic adversative assertion or clause : *but yet, and yet.* Cl. satis scite promittisti tibi. *Sy.* atqui tu hanc iocari credis ? Ter.; magnum narras, vix credibile. atqui sic habet, Hor. ; tum, ut me vidit, peropportune, inquit, venis ; atqui mihi quoque videor, inquam, venisse opportune, Cic. **II.** Esp. **A.** Sometimes to introduce emphatically a new or confirmatory clause : *but indeed, yet certainly :* hunc ego non diligam ? atqui sic a summis hominibus accepimus, Cic. With *pol :* atqui pol hodie non feres, Pl. **B.** In conditional sentences : atqui si : *but if, if indeed :* sine veniat ; atqui, si illam digito attigerit, oculi illi ilico effodientur, Ter. **C.** To modify a preceding negation or negative interrogation : *still, nevertheless, but rather : Ni.* numquam auferes hinc aurum. *Ch.* atqui iam dabis, Pl. ; o rem, inquis, difficilem et inexplicabilem ; atqui explicanda est, Cic. Ep. **D.** In logic : To connect a minor premiss, whether affirmative or negative (while atque connects only an affirm. proposition) : *well but, but now :* (mors) aut plane neglegenda est . . . aut etiam optanda . . . ; atqui tertium certe nihil inveniri potest ; quid igitur timeam, etc., Cic.

ātrāmentum, i, *n.* [āter], *blacking ;* hence, *black juice :* sepiae, Cic. ; *writing-ink :* temperatum, Cic. Ep. ; *black lacquer :* Pl. ; Vitr., Plin. ; *blacking* (for leather) : sutorium, Cic. Ep., Plin.

ātrātus, a, um [āter], *clothed in black* or *mourning :* Cic. ; Tac. Of the sun in eclipse : Prop. Of suppliants : Suet.

Atrax, acis, *f. a town in Thessaly ;* hence, **Atracidēs,** ae, *m. the Thessalian Caeneus ;* **Atracis,** idis, *f. the Thessalian Hippodamia.*

Atreus (disyl.), ei, *m.* (Acc. Atrea, Voc. Atreu), *s. of Pelops and Hippodamia,* **b.** *of Thyestes and f. of Agamemnon and Menelaus ;* **Atrīdēs (-da),** ae, *m. a male descendant of Atreus,* esp. *Agamemnon :* **Atrīdae,** ārum, *m. pl. Agamemnon and Menelaus.*

ātriēnsis, is, *m.* [ātrium], *the overseer of the*

atrium : in gen. *of the house, a majordomo :* Pl., Cic., Plin. Ep.

ātriolum, ī, *n.* [*dim.* ātrium], *a small hall, an ante-chamber :* Cic. Ep.

ātritās, ātis, *f.* [āter], *blackness :* Pl.

ātrium, ī, *n. the hall.* **I.** *principal room in a Roman house,* Cic., Hor., etc. In *pl.* of a single atrium : Verg.; Ov. **Transf.** *the whole house:* nec capient Phrygias atria nostra nurūs, Ov. Of *the entrance rooms in the dwellings of the gods :* dextrā laevāque Deorum atria nobilium valvis celebrantur apertis, Ov. **II.** *a hall* or *court* (in a sanctuary): in atrio Libertatis, Cic.; atrium regium, Liv. So atrium auctionarium, *an auction-room,* Cic.

atrōcitās, ātis, *f.* [atrōx]. **1.** Lit.: *horribleness, heinousness :* sceleris, Sall.; rei atrocitatem levare, Cic.; temporum, Suet. **2.** Transf. **a.** Of character and disposition : *brutality, savagery :* morum, Tac.: non atrocitate animi moveor, Cic. **b.** Philos. and judic.: *severity, rigour :* Cic., Quint.

atrōciter, *adv. horribly, fiercely, cruelly :* Cic., Liv., etc. Comp. : Liv., Tac.

Atropos, ī, *f.* one of the three Parcae or *Fates who was supposed to cut the thread of human life.*

atrōx, ōcis, *adj. horrible, abominable, fierce* (both of things and persons : saevus, us. only of persons). **1.** Lit.: tempestas, Liv.; hora Caniculae flagrantis, Hor.; proelium, periculum, Liv.; res scelesta, atrox, Cic., Ter. **2.** Transf.: of character or disposition : *savage, fierce, unrelenting :* genus orationis, Cic.; astutia, Pl.; imperium, ingenium, Liv.; odium, Ov.; atrox longo dolore, Tac.; animus Catonis, Hor. With GEN.: atrox odi Agrippina, Tac. Comp. and Sup., atrōcior, atrōcissimus : Cic. Ep., Quint.

Atta, ae, *m.* **I.** *the comic poet.* T. Quīntus Atta. **II.** Atta Clausus, *the ancestor of the* gens Claudia.

attāctū, ABL. *sing. m.* [attingō], *by a touching :* Verg., Varr.

attāctus, a, um, *Part.* attingō.

attagēn, ēnis, *m.* (Hor.); **attagēna,** *f.* (Mart.), *a heath-cock* [Gk. ἀτταγήν].

Attalus, ī, *m. the name of several kings of Pergamum, the most famous of whom was Attalus III, who made the Roman People the heir of his vast riches.* **Attalicus,** a, um. **1.** Lit.: urbes, i.e. Pergamean, Hor. **2.** Transf.: *worthy of an Attalus,* i.e. **a.** *richly ornamented with gold :* tori, vestes, Prop. **b.** *opulent, with oriental splendour :* Attalicis condicionibus, Hor. **Attalica,** ōrum, *n. pl.* (*sc.* vestimenta), *garments of woven gold,* Plin.

attamen, *adv.* (better as two words, **at tamen**), *but yet, but however, nevertheless :* Caes., Cic., Ov.

attat and **attate,** *v.* atat.

attegia, ae, *f. a cottage, hut :* Juv.

attemperātē, *adv. opportunely, in the nick of time :* Ter.

at-temptō, āre. **I.** *to make trial of, test :* inimicos, Cic. **II.** *to tamper with* (a person's loyalty, etc.): ne sua fides attemptetur, Cic.; Hor. **III.** *to assail* (of a military attack): Tac.; Phaedr.

at-tendō, tendere, tendī, tentum. Orig., *to stretch* or *bend* (*e.g.* the bow). **Transf.:** alone or with animum or animos : *to direct the attention, bend the mind, to attend to, notice,* (*cf.* advertere animum, and animadvertere). **A.** attendite animos ad ea, etc., Cic. With *Indir. Quest. :* quid velim animum attendite, Ter.; Liv. **B.** Without animum, etc.: rem gestam vobis dum breviter expono, diligenter attendite, Cic.; Ter.; Juv. **i.** With Acc. *of the thing* or *person* to which the attention is directed : sed stuporem hominis attendite, Cic.; Lucr., etc. Pass.: versūs aeque prima et media et extrema pars attenditur, Cic. With Acc. and *Inf. :* Cic. With *Indir. Quest. :* Cic., Juv., etc. **ii.** With *de :* Cic. **iii.** With DAT.: sermonibus malignis, Plin. Ep.; eloquentiae plurimum attendit, Suet.

attentē, *adv. attentively, carefully :* Ter., Cic. Comp. : Cic., Hor. Sup. : Cic.

attentiō, ōnis, *f.* [attendō], *attention, application,* with or without animi : Cic., Quint.

at-tentō, *v.* attemptō.

(1) attentus, a, um. **I.** *Part.* attendō. **II.** Adj. **a.** *strained :* animus in spe, Ter. **b.** *attentive :* animus, Cic.; Lucr.; Hor.; acerrima atque attentissima cogitatio, Cic. **c.** *intent on* (business, etc.), *industrious, careful* (colloq.) : ad rem attentiores sumus Ter.; paterfamilias prudens et attentus, Cic.; quaesitis attentus, Hor.; vita, Cic.

(2) attentus, a, um, *Part.* attineō.

attenuātē, *adv. without rhetorical ornament, simply :* Cic.

attenuātus, a, um. **I.** *Part.* attenuō. **II.** Adj. transf. in Cic. of style. **a.** *shortened, concise.* **b.** *meagre, insipid, without ornament.* **c.** *too refined, affected.*

at-tenuō, āre. **1.** Lit. **a.** *to make thin :* Lucr.; falx arboris umbram, Cat. **b.** *to thin, reduce :* vires morbo attenuatae, Liv.; legio proeliis attenuata, Caes.; bellum expectatione Pompei attenuatum est, Cic. **2.** Transf. **a.** *to diminish :* curas, Ov. **b.** *to humble :* insignem attenuat Deus, Hor.

at-terō, terere, trīvī, trītum (*Perf.* atteruī, Tib.). **I.** *to rub at :* Cerberus leniter atterens caudam, Hor. Of the action of a running stream upon sand : Ov. **II.** *to rub at, wear away.* **1.** Lit.: bucula herbas, Verg. **2.** Transf.: postquam alteri alteros aliquantum attriverant, Sall.; Italiae opes bello, Sall.; famam atque pudorem, Sall.; nec publicanus atterit (Germanos), Tac. Pass. atteri, *to lose dignity by being outdone,* Tac.

at-testor, ārī, *to bear witness to, attest, confirm :* Phaedr.

at-texō, xere, xuī, xtum, *to weave* or *plait on* or *to.* **1.** Lit.: pinnae loricaeque ex cratibus attexuntur, Caes. **2.** Transf.: Cic., Varr.

Atthis, idis, *f.* **I.** *a female friend of Sappho.* **II.** *a name for Attica.*

Attica, ae, *f.* **I.** *a district of Greece, the capital of which was Athens.* **II.** *d.* of *Atticus.*

atticē, *adv. in the Attic* or *Athenian manner :* Cic.

atticissō, āre [ἀττικίζω], *to imitate the Athenian manner :* Pl.

Atticus, a, um ['Ἀττικός], *of Attica or Athens, Attic, Athenian.* Also, *a surname of T. Pomponius, the friend of Cicero.*

attigō, *v.* attingō.

at-tineō, tinēre, tinuī, tentum [teneō]. **A.** Trans. **a.** *to hold to, hold fast,* etc. : aliquem ante oculos, Pl. ; prensam dextram, Tac. So too, ripam Danuvi, Tac. Transf.: aliquem spe pacis, Sall. ; Tac. **b.** *to reach for :* cultros, Pl. **B.** Intrans.: *to pertain to or concern* (ordinary sense of the word): nihil ad Pamphilum quicquam attinere, Ter. ; quid istuc ad me attinet ? Pl. ; nil ad nos de nobis attinet, Lucr. ; quod ad eam civitatem attinet, *as far as relates to,* Cic. ; Liv. With Acc. and Inf. as subject : dici plura non attinet, Cic. ; Hor. ; Liv. ; neque quemquam attinebat id recusare, Cic. Absol.: dicere quae nihil attinet, Hor.

at-tingō (attigō, Pl.), tingere, tigī, tāctum [tangō], *to come in contact with, touch.* **1.** Lit. **a.** In gen.: prius quam aries murum attigisset, Caes. ; Lucr. ; Cic., etc. **b.** *to put hand to :* arma, Nep. **c.** *to lay hand on, assault :* Pl., Cat., Liv. **d.** *to touch* in eating : Verg. **e.** *to touch* (land) : Caes., Cic. Ep. Also *to reach* any place : Pl., Tac. **f.** *to touch* (geogr.) : Caes., Cic., Cat. **2.** Transf. **a.** *to touch, affect :* erant perpauci, quos ea infamia attingeret. Liv. ; Lucr., Cic. **b.** *to touch upon (in speaking), to mention slightly :* paucis rem, Pl. ; Lucr. ; quod quicquam breviter perstrinxi atque attigi, Cic. **c.** *to handle, deal with :* rem militarem, Caes. ; orationes, Cic. ; forum, Cic. Ep. With *ad :* Ov. **d.** *to come near to,* hence *to concern, resemble :* labor non attingit deum, Cic. ; Pl. ; quae non magis legis nomen attingunt, quam si latrones aliqua sanxerint, Cic. With *ad :* quae nihil attingunt ad rem, Pl.

Attis, idis (also **Atthis** or **Atys,** yos), *m. a young Phrygian shepherd, whom Cybele loved.*

at-tollō, tollere, *to lift or raise up, elevate.* **1.** Lit. **a.** super limen pedes, Pl. ; regem apes umeris, Verg. ; manūs ad caelum, Liv. ; se in femur, Verg. ; se in auras, Ov. ; se ab casu, Liv. ; mare ventis, Tac. **b.** oculos humo, Ov. **c.** Of buildings : *to erect :* immensam molem, Verg. ; turris, Tac. **2.** Transf. **a.** *to lift up, raise:* animos ad spem consulatūs, Liv. ; nomen alicuius ad sidera, Luc. ; Punica se quantis attollens gloria rebus, Verg. **b.** *to exalt, extol :* hominem praemiis, laudibus attollere, Tac.

at-tondeō, tondēre, tondī, tōnsum. **1.** Lit.: *to clip.* **a.** *to prune :* vitem, Verg. **b.** *to crop, nibble at :* virgulta, Verg. **2.** Transf. **a.** *to lessen :* laus est attonsa Laconum, poet. ap. Cic. **b.** *to fleece* (colloq.) : Pl.

attonitus, a, um. **I.** *Part.* attonō. **II.** *Adj., infuriated, inspired, frantic :* vates, Hor. ; domus, Verg. ; as Noun : mater attonitae diu similis fuit, Ov.

at-tonō, tonāre, tonuī, tonitum, *to thunder at ;* hence, *to stun, stupefy :* quis furor vestras attonuit mentis ? Ov. ; most freq.

in *Part.* attonitus, *thunder-uck, bewildered :* talibus attonitus visis ac voce deorum, Verg. ; novitate ac miraculo, Liv. ; Tac. ; vultus, Tac.

attōnsus, a, um, *Part.* attondeō.

at-torqueō, ēre, *to hurl up :* iaculum in auras, Verg.

attractus, a, um, *Part.* attrahō.

at-trahō, trahere, trāxī, tractum, *to draw*.*or drag to or towards, to attract.* **1.** Lit.: adducitur atque adeo attrahitur Lollius, Cic. ; tribunos attrahi ad se iussit, Liv. Poet.: quae causa attraxerit Arpos, Verg. Of the magnet : ferrum, *to attract,* Plin. **2.** Transf.: *to draw, attract :* me ad hoc negotium provincia attraxit, Cic. ; Ov.

at-trectō, āre [tractō], *to take and handle, to finger.* **1.** Lit.: esp. in an *unlawful or violent manner :* libros contaminatis manibus, Cic. ; signum (Iunonis), Liv. ; Verg. ; aliquem nimium familiariter, Pl. ; Cic. Occ. *to appropriate to oneself :* fascī securisque, Liv. **2.** Transf.: blanditia popularis aspicitur non attrectatur, Cic.

at-trepidō, āre, *to hobble to a place :* Pl.

at-tribuō, uere, uī, ūtum, *to allot, assign, bestow.* **1.** Lit. **a.** In gen.: equos gladiatoribus attribuit, Caes. ; Liv. **b.** Of quarters, etc. : alteram partem vici cohortibus ad hibernandum, Caes. **c.** Of public money : Cic., Liv. Also of private money : Cic. Ep. **d.** Of persons for a particular work : Commio Morinos, Caes. **e.** Of business, etc., to particular persons : video cui sit Apulia attributa, Cic. Also of people : *to annex, subject :* insulae Rhodiis attributae, Cic. Ep. **2.** Transf. **a.** *to assign, bestow :* timor quem mihi natura pudorque meus attribuit, Cic. ; Cat. **b.** *to attribute or impute to :* aliis causam calamitatis, Cic. **c.** *to lay as a tax :* Liv. **d.** *to add :* ad amissionem amicorum miseriam nostram, Cic.

attribūtiō, ōnis, *f.* [attribuō]. **I.** *the assignment of a debt :* Cic. Ep. **II.** Gramm.: *a predicate,* attribute=attributum, Cic.

attribūtum, ī, *n.* **I.** *money assigned from the public treasury :* Varr. **II.** Gramm.: *a predicate, attribute :* Cic.

attritus, a, um, *Part.* atterō, *worn away :* ansa, Verg. ; vomer, Verg. *Comp. :* Cic. Transf.: attrita frons (*a shameless, impudent face*), Juv.

Attys, *v.* Attis and Atys.

Atys or **Attys,** yos. *m.* **I.** *s. of Hercules and Omphale :* ancestor *of the 1st dynasty of Lydian kings.* **II.** *s. of Alba, king of the Albani.* **III.** *ancestor of the gens Atia.*

au, *interj.,* an exclamation of pain, surprise, or deprecation : Pl., Ter.

auceps, cupis, *m.* [contr. for aviceps, from avis capiō], *a birdcatcher, fowler.* **1.** Lit.: *a poulterer :* Pl., Hor. **2.** Transf. **a.** *an eavesdropper :* Pl. **b.** *a caviller :* auceps syllabarum, Cic.

auctārium, ī, *n.* [augeō], *an addition, over-weight* (in a purchase): Pl.

auctificus, a, um [auctus, faciō]. *increasing :* motus, Lucr.

auctiō, ōnis, *f.* [augeō], *an increasing, increase.* Transf.: *an increasing* of the price by bidding ; hence *a sale by auction, an auction :* facere, *to hold,* Pl., Cic. ; pracdicare, *to proclaim*, Pl. ; constituere, Cic. ; proscribere, *to advertise*, Cic. ; proferre, *to defer, to adjourn*, Cic. Ep.

auctiōnārius, a, um [auctiō], *of an auction :* atria, Cic. ; tabulae, *sale-catalogues*, Cic.

auctiōnor, ārī [auctiō], *to hold an auction :* Caes., Cic.

auctitō, āre [*freq.* auctō], *to increase much :* pecunias faenore, Tac.

auctō, āre [*freq.* augeō], *to increase or enlarge much :* Pl., Lucr. T r a n s f. : Cat.

auctor, ōris, *m.f.* [augeō], *one who promotes increase.* **I.** *an originator, author.* **1.** L i t. **a.** *progenitor :* L. Brutus, praeclarus auctor nobilitatis tuae, Cic. ; Verg., etc. **b.** *founder :* Troiae Cynthius auctor, Verg. ; Ov. ; Suet. **c.** *author* (of a work of art, etc.), esp. *a writer, historian :* rerum Romanarum auctores, Cic. ; Ov., etc. **2.** T r a n s f. **a.** In gen. : *an originator, cause, doer :* auctores belli esse nolebant, Caes. **b.** Of news, *author, reporter, informant :* haec se certis auctoribus comperisse, Caes. ; legati auctores sunt concilia haberi, Liv. Hence, *an authority* or *person responsible for a statement :* Polybius haud spernendus auctor, Liv. ; or for a doctrine : non sordidus auctor naturae verique, Hor. ; in antiquissimā philosophiā Cratippo auctore versaris, Cic. **c.** *an instigator, proposer of a measure :* Cotta profectionis auctor, Caes. ; deditionis, Cic. ; legibus ferendis auctor, Cic. Often in ABL. *Absol.* : me, te, eo auctore, *at my, your, his suggestion :* Pl., Cic., etc. **II.** *an enlarger, supporter, backer.* **a.** Of a law or other public measure (opp. to *lator* = the proposer), *a seconder, supporter :* isti rationi neque lator quisquam est inventus neque auctor unquam bonus, Cic. ; Liv., etc. P h r. : auctor fieri, *to give consent, to approve :* ut nemo civis Romanus libertatem possit amittere nisi ipse auctor factus sit, Cic. ; Liv. **b.** More gen. : *seconder, backer :* ut auctore populo Romano maneas in sententiā, Cic. ; si probat auctor Acestes, Verg. **c.** *voucher, surety, bail, guarantor :* plures auctores eius rei videbantur, Caes. ; fama nuntiabat te esse in Syriā ; auctor erat nemo, Cic. Ep. ; si mihi Iuppiter auctor spondeat, Verg. With Acc. and *Inf.* : Pl. ; auctorem esse with Acc. and *Fut. Inf.* : Liv. Occ. in law, **i.** *a representative* (of women and children), *trustee :* Cic., Liv. T r a n s f. : **ii.** *a seller, vendor :* Pl., Cic. T r a n s f. : benefici, Cic. **d.** *a spokesman, champion :* suae civitatis, Cic. ; meae salutis, Cic.

auctōrāmentum, ī, *n.* [auctōrō]. **I.** *a contract, engagement :* esp. *of gladiators :* Sen. Ep. **II.** *the wages agreed upon, pay, hire :* servitutis, Cic. T r a n s f. : Sen. Ep.

auctōritās, ātis, *f.* **I.** *an originating, producing.* Only T r a n s f. **a.** In gen. : *origination, a lead in any action, responsibility :* auctoritatis eius et inventionis comprobatores, Cic. ; auctoritatem defugere, Pl., Ter., Cic. **b.** Of news, etc., *source of origin, basis :* si exquiratur usque ab stirpe auctoritas (rumoris), Pl. ; ne parum auctoritatis esset in fabulā, Cic. Hence, *records for verifying statements :* legationes cum publicis auctoritatibus convenisse, Cic.

c. *instigation, advice :* auctoritate Orgetorigis permoti, Caes. ; cum (Reguli) valuisset auctoritas, Cic. **d.** In matters of state, *authority to act :* qui habet imperium a populo R., auctoritatem legum dandarum a senatu, Cic. Also *leading, guidance :* (*cf.* **a.** supra) quarta legio Caesaris auctoritatem exercitumque persecuta est, Cic. ; auctoritatem praerogativae omnes centuriae secutae sunt, Liv. **e.** In law, *title* to property, *right* of ownership : lex usum et auctoritatem fundi iubet esse biennium, Cic. **II.** *a supporting, seconding, backing.* **a.** Of public measures (esp. of *the sanction of the senate*) : sine auctoritate senatūs foedus facere, Cic. ; ex auctoritate patrum, Liv. Hence, *a resolution* or *proposal supported by a majority of the senate* (less formal and authoritative than a senatūs consultum) : si quis intercedat senatūs consulto, auctoritate se fore contentum, Liv. **b.** Of authoritative support given to an opinion or judgment, *sanction, approval :* do Catuli auctoritate et sententiā dicendum esse, Cic. **c.** *a vouching, guarantee, security :* quid vero habet auctoritatis furor iste, quem divinum vocatis ? Cic. Hence, **i.** the names of the witnesses to the drawing up of a senatūs consultum : senatūs consulti auctoritates, Cic. **ii.** More gen. : cum auctoritates principum coniurationis conligeret, Cic. **III.** *influence, weight, prestige, authority* (very freq.). **a.** Of persons : aequitate causae et auctoritate suā commovet, Cic. : habere, facere (*to obtain*), adripere, imminuere, etc., Cic. **b.** Of things : utilitatis species falsa ab honestatis auctoritate superata est, Cic.

auctōrō, āre [auctor]. **I.** L i t. : *to be an auctor* in a sale : hence *to purchase* or *secure for oneself :* Vell. **II.** With *Refl. Pron.* or in *Mid.* : *to bind oneself, to hire oneself out :* esp. of gladiators : quid refert, uri virgis ferroque necari auctoratus eas, Hor. T r a n s f. : eo pignore velut auctoratum sibi proditorem ratus est, Liv.

auctumnālis, auctumnus, *v.* autumnālis, autumnus.

auctus, a, um. **I.** *Part.* augeō. **II.** *Adj.* (only in *Comp.* made greater, *enlarged*) : maiestas, Liv. ; Pl. ; Caes. ; Lucr.

auctus, ūs, *m.* [augeō], *an increasing, increase, growth.* **1.** L i t. : corporis, Lucr. Concr. *a growth :* (in *pl.*) : Liv. **2.** T r a n s f. : civitatis, Liv. ; imperi, Tac. In *pl.* : Tac.

aucupium, ī, *n.* [auceps], *bird-catching, fowling.* **1.** L i t. : Cic., Prop. T r a n s f. : *a snaring, lying in wait for :* hoc novum est aucupium, Ter. ; delectationis, Cic. Also (*cf.* auceps). **a.** *eavesdropping :* facere aucupium auribus, Pl. **b.** *cavilling, quibbling :* aucupia verborum, Cic.

aucupō, āre = aucupor, *to lie in wait for, to watch for :* num quis est, sermonem nostrum qui aucupet ? Pl. With *Indir. Quest.* : Pl.

aucupor, ārī [auceps], *to go bird-catching* or *fowling.* **1.** L i t. : Varr. **2.** T r a n s f. : *to lie in wait for, to snatch at,* etc. : viden' scelestus ut aucupatur ? Pl. ; aliouius imbecillitatem, Cic. ; tempus, Cic. ; somnos, Ov.

audācia, ae, *f.* [audāx], *boldness.* **A.** In good sense : *courage, intrepidity, daring :* audacia in bello, Sall. ; summae hominem audaciae mittit, Caes. ; Ov. T r a n s f. : *a bold deed, daring enterprise :* Liv. **B.** In bad sense (most freq.) : *recklessness, audacity, presumption, effrontery :* Pl., Cic., etc. In *pl.* : *audacious actions :* Cic., Tac.

audācter (rarely audāciter) [audāx], *adv. boldly, courageously, audaciously :* Pl., Lucr., Cic., etc. *Comp.* audācius, Pl., Caes., Cic. *Sup.* audācissimē (-umē, Ter.), Caes., Liv.

audāx, ācis, *adj.* [audeō]. **A.** in good sense, *daring, bold :* Pl. ; coepta, Verg. **B.** in bad sense (most freq.), *reckless, venturesome, audacious, presumptuous.* **a.** Of persons : Ter. ; Ov. ; Verres homo audacissimus, Cic. With *ad :* ad facinus audacior, Cic. With ABL. of respect : viribus audax, Verg. With *Inf.* : Hor. **b.** T r a n s f. : to things : audax facinus, Ter. ; negotium, Cic. ; consilium, Liv. ; paupertas, dithyrambi, Hor.

audēns, entis. **I.** *Part.* audeō. **II.** *Adj. daring* (in good sense). *Comp.* : Verg. *Sup.* : Tac. As Noun : Ov., Tac.

audentia, ae, *f.* [audēns], *boldness, courage,* in good sense : Tac. In the use of words : Plin. Ep.

audentius, *comp. adv. more boldly* or *fearlessly :* Tac.

audeō, ēre (*Perf.* ausī, Cato. Old *Optat.* freq. as *Pot. Subj.* ausim) [avidus]. **1.** L i t. : *to be eager, have a mind to :* audere in proelia, Verg. ; aude contemnere opes, Verg. **2.** Hence, *to venture, make bold to do, presume :* With ACC. (esp. of *Neut. Pron.*) : facinus, Ter., Tac., Liv. ; plebs per se nihil audet, Caes. ; Verg. ; castrorum oppugnationem, Tac. Hence, *Pass.* (rare exc. in *Gerund.*) : agenda res est audendaque, Liv. With *Inf.* (the usual constr.) : Pl., Cic., Hor., etc. *Absol. to show daring or audacity :* audendo atque agendo res Romana crevit, Liv. ; Verg. With *quin :* ut non audeam quin promam omnia, Pl.

audiēns, entis. **I.** *Part.* audiō. **II.** *Adj. obedient :* with GEN. : Pl. Esp. in phr. dicto audientem esse (Pl., Cic.), and also with DAT. of person, *to be obedient to* any *one's command :* Ser. Tullio populum dicto audientem esse, Liv. ; Caes. ; Cic. **III.** As NOUN (but not in NOM. *sing.*) : *a hearer, auditor :* Cic., Liv.

audientia, ae, *f.* [audiēns], *a hearing, a listening :* facere alicui, *to secure for someone,* Pl., Liv. T r a n s f. : facit ipsa sibi audientiam oratio, Cic.

audiō, īre, īvī or iī, ītum (*Imperf.* audībat, Ov. ; *Fut.* audībō, Pl. ; audīn'=audīsne, as ain'=aisne ; *Inf. Perf.* audīsse better than audīvisse) [aus=auris, dō]. **I.** *to hear.* **a.** Of the sense of hearing : audiendi sensus, Cic. **b. i.** *to hear, apprehend with the sense of hearing :* Pl. ; Verg., etc. ; neque eum querentem quisquam audierit, Nep. ; Cat. **ii.** *to be spoken of, hear* something *about oneself* (esp. with *bene* or *male*) : bene audire a parentibus, Cic. ; Ter.; Hor. **iii.** *to hear, be told, learn by hearing* (what is heard is in ACC., ACC. and *Inf.*, or object clause ; the source of the information is in ABL. with *ex* (most

freq.), *ab,* or *de*) : quae vera audivi, taceo, Ter. ; audivi ex maioribus natu hoc idem fuisse in Scipione, Cic. ; Pl. ; Verg., etc. Hence, also *Pass.* with NOM. and *Inf.* : Bibulus nondum audiebatur esse in Syriā, Cic. Ep. ; Caes. N.B. To be carefully distinguished from preced. constr. is audire de aliquo (aliquid) : *to hear or be told* (any *thing*) *concerning any one :* de psaltriā hac audivit, Ter. ; Cic. audito as ABL. *Absol.* : *it being heard,* i.e. *when news came that :* audito, Q. Marcium in Ciliciam tendere, Sall. ; Liv. **II.** *to listen, listen to, to hear with attention.* **a.** In gen. : benigne, attente, Cic., etc. T r a n s f. : neque audit currus habenas, Verg. **b.** *to give an audience to :* Archias audiebatur a Marcello, Cic. **c.** Of an examining judge, *to hear and question :* Caes., Cic. T r a n s f. : dolos, Verg. ; de pace, Liv. **d.** Of pupils : *to hear a teacher, attend his lectures :* Zenonem audiebam frequenter, Cic. **e.** Of prayer or entreaty : *to listen to, grant :* in quo di immortales meas preces audiverunt, Cic. ; Caes., etc. Also of persons : puellas ter vocata audis, Hor. ; Verg. **f.** Of arguments, narrations, etc. ; *to approve :* nec Homerum audio, qui Ganymedem a Dis raptum ait, Cic. ; audio, nunc dicis aliquid quod ad rem pertinet, Cic. **III.** (cf. I. b. ii.), *to hear oneself called or to allow oneself to be called :* recte vivis, si curas esse quod audis, Hor. ; Matutine pater seu Iane libentius audis, Liv.

audītiō, ōnis, *f.* [audiō]. **A.** A c t. : *a hearing, a listening to :* fabellarum, Cic. **B.** P a s s. : *hearsay :* hoc solum auditione expetere coepit, Cic. T r a n s f. : *report :* levem auditionem pro re compertā habent, Cic. In *pl.*, *reports :* Caes., Cic., Tac.

audītor, ōris, *m.* [audiō]. **I.** *a hearer :* Cic. **II.** *a pupil, disciple :* Cic.

audītōrium, ī, *n.* [audiō, auditor]. **I.** *a lecture-room, hall of justice :* Quint., Tac. Of the forum : Tac. **II.** *the audience :* Plin. Ep.

audītus, ūs, *m.* [audiō]. **I.** *the sense of hearing :* Cic. **II.** *a hearing :* Cic., Tac. T r a n s f. : *a rumour, report :* occupaverat animos prior auditus, Tac.

auferō, auferre, abstulī (apstulī), ablātum [ab-ferō], *to bear away, to carry off.* **I. 1.** L i t. **a.** In gen. : aurum aps te, Pl. ; vos istaec intro auferte, Ter. ; multa domum suam auferebat, Cic. **b.** In *Mid.* or *Pass.* or with *Pron. Refl.* : *to take oneself off, be borne away :* te opsecro, hercle, aufer te modo, Pl. ; pennis aufertur Olympum, Verg. ; e conspectu terrae ablati sunt, Liv. **2.** T r a n s f. **a.** *to carry off, obtain :* id inultum nunquam auferet, Ter. ; responsum ab aliquo, Cic. Also with *ut :* ut in foro statueret (statuas), abstulisti, Cic. **b.** *to carry away, divert :* ne te auferant aliorum consilia, Cic. Ep. ; Liv. ; Ov. **c.** Chiefly, colloq. *to lay aside, cease from :* aufer abhunc lacrimas, Lucr. ; Liv. ; Pl. With *Inf.* as object : Hor. **II.** In bad sense. **1.** L i t. **a.** *to carry off* (plunder, etc.), with ACC. and DAT. or ABL. and prep. : aliquid eris, Pl. ; Cic., etc. ; pecuniam de aerario, Cic. Ep. **b.** *to extort :*

n Leonidā nummorum aliquid, Cic. **c.** *to remove with violence :* caput domino, Verg. **2. Transf. a.** auferat omnia invita oblivio, Liv. ; Verg. ; abstulit mors Achillem, Hor. ; Liv. **b.** spiritum alicui, Cic. ; spem defensionis, Cic. ; Liv. ; somnos, Hor. In good sense : metūs, Verg.

Aufidius, a, *the name of a Roman gens :* esp. **I.** Cn. Aufidius, *who wrote a Greek history.* **II.** T. Aufidius, *an orator ;* **Aufidiānus,** a, um.

Aufidus, i, *a river in Apulia, remarkable for its rapid and violent stream,* now the *Ofanto.*

aufugiō, fugere, fūgī [ab-fugiō], *to flee away or from :* Pl., Cic., Tac. ; ex eo loco, Liv. With Acc. : aspectum parentis, Cic. ; Prop.

Augē, ēs, *f. d. of Aleus and Neaera, and m. by Hercules of Telephus.*

Augēās, ae, *m. a king of Elis, whose stable containing 3000 head of cattle, and uncleansed for 30 years, was cleaned out in one day by Hercules, who turned through it the R. Alpheus ;* **Augēus,** a, um.

augeō, augēre, auxī, auctum (old *Optat.* auxitis in a prayer, Liv.) [*cf.* Gk. αὔξω]. **I.** *to enlarge, make greater, increase.* **1.** Lit. : cibus auget corpus, Lucr. ; rem publicam agris, Cic. ; aerarium, Tac. ; turris, Tac. ; amnis nimbis auctus, Ov. **2. Transf. a.** In gen. : morbum, suspicionem, Ter. ; spem, metum, etc., Caes. ; molestiam, improborum animos, etc., Cic. **b.** *to magnify, exalt, extol :* Cic. **II.** *to enrich* (mostly with *Instr.* ABL.). **1.** Lit. : aer terram auget imbribus, Cic. ; Lucr. **2. Transf.:** aliquem, Pl., Cic. Ep. ; aliquem divitiis, scientiā, honore, etc., Cic. ; honoribus, Hor., Tac. ; largitione, Tac. ; damno, Ter. Relig.: aram, Pl. ; si quā ipse meis venatibus auxi, Verg. **III.** Intrans. : *to become greater, grow, increase :* Lucr., Cat., Sall.

augēscō, ere [augeō], *to begin to grow, to become greater.* **1.** Lit. : Lucr., Cic. **2.** Transf. : Ter., Sall., Liv., Tac.

augmen, inis, *n.* [augeō], *an increase, growth;* hence *bulk :* Lucr. In *pl.* : Lucr.

augur, uris [avis]. **I.** *an augur, i.e. a member of a college of priests at Rome, who foretold the future by observing the flight* or *notes of birds, the feeding of the sacred fowls, lightning, certain appearances of quadrupeds, and any unusual occurrences,* Cic. The augur is said to have been orig. called *auspex :* and the scientific term for observation continued to be auspicium and not augurium. **II.** *any interpreter* (of signs), *soothsayer, diviner, seer :* augur Apollo, Hor. : veri providus augur Thestorides, Ov. ; nocturnae imaginis augur, Ov.

augurālis, e, *adj.* [augur], *of augurs, of soothsaying* or *prophecy :* libri, Cic. ; cena. *which the augur gave on his entrance into office,* Cic. Ep. Noun, **augurāle,** is, *n.* **a.** *the part of a Roman camp where the general took the auspices :* Tac. Hence, *the general's tent :* Quint. **b.** *the augur's wand* or *staff* = lituus : Sen.

augurātiō, ōnis, *f.* [auguror]. *a divining, a soothsaying :* Cic.

augurātō, *adv. after taking the auguries :* Liv.

augurātus, ūs. *m.* [auguror]. *the office of augur :* Cic., Tac., Plin. Ep.

augurium, i, *n.* [augur]. **I.** *the profession of an augur, the watching and explanation of the flight of birds,* etc., *augury* (v. augur). **a.** augurium agere, *to take an augury,* Cic. ; augurium salutis, *an augury taken to ascertain whether one might pray to the gods for the prosperity of the state* (de salute), Cic. **b.** *a sign given in augury, an omen :* accipere, Cic. ; nuntiare. Liv. **II. a.** *interpretation* (of signs), *divination, prophecy, soothsaying :* cui laetus Apollo augurium citharamque dabat, Verg. ; coniugis augurio, Ov. **b.** *presentiment, foreboding :* inhaeret in mentibus quasi saeculorum quoddam augurium futurorum, Cic. ; Ov. ; Plin. Ep.

augurius, a, um [augur], *of the augurs, augural :* ius, Cic.

augurō, āre [augur] (rarer than auguror). **1.** Orig. *to augur ; to consecrate by auguries :* augurato templo ac loco, Cic. ; see also augurato. **2. Transf. a.** *to play the augur :* oculis investigans astute augura, Pl. **b.** *to presage, forebode :* si quid veri mens augurat, Verg. ; Cic.

auguror, ārī [augur]. **1.** Lit. **a.** *to act as augur, take auguries :* Cic. **b.** *to predict by augury,* Cic. **2.** Transf. in gen. **a.** *to predict :* Cic. ; with Acc. : Cic. **b.** *to conjecture, forebode :* quantum ego opinione auguror, Cic. With Acc. : Tac. With Acc. and *Inf.* : Caes., Ov. With *Indir. Quest.* : Cic.

Augusta, ae. *f.* **I.** *in the time of the emperors, a title of the mother, wife, daughter, or sister of the emperor.* **II.** *the name of several towns,* esp. **Augusta Taurinōrum,** *Turin ;* **Augusta Praetōria,** *Aosta.*

Augustālis, e, *adj. of the emperor Augustus :* ludi Augustales (or AUGUSTALIA), *games in honour of Augustus :* Tac. ; Augustales sodales, *a college of 25 priests, instituted by Tiberius in honour of Augustus :* Tac.

Augustānus, (Augustiānus, Suet.), a, um [Augustus]. **I.** *of Augustus.* **II.** *of an emperor, imperial :* Augustani, *Roman Knights appointed by Nero,* Tac. **III.** *inhabitants of Augusta :* Plin.

augustē, *adv. reverentially, sacredly :* venerari deos, Cic. *Comp. :* Cic.

Augustīnus, a, um [Augustus], *of Augustus :* currus, Suet.

augustus, a, um [augeō]. **1.** Lit. : *consecrated, sacred, venerable :* sancta vocant augusta patres ; augusta vocantur templa, sacerdotum rite dicata manu, Ov. ; Verg. ; Liv. ; Eleusis sancta et augusta, Cic. *Sup.* : Liv. **2.** Transf. : *majestic, grand :* forma amplior augustiorque humanā, Liv. ; primordia urbium augustiora reddere, Liv. ; tectum, Verg. *Sup.* : Liv.

Augustus, i, *m.* a name of honour given first to Octavianus and then to the Emperors after him (*cf.* Augusta, a name given first to Livia, wife of Octavianus): Hor., Tac. As *Adj.* **Augustus,** a, um, *of Augustus* or *the emperor, Augustan, imperial :* Ov. Esp. mensis Augustus, *the month August,* named after Octavianus. [It. *agosto,* Fr. *août*.]

(1) aula, ae. *f.* (GEN. aulāī, Verg.) [αὐλή], *the court of a Greek house.* **1.** Lit. **a.** *the court-yard :* Prop., Hor. **b.** *the inner court* (= atrium) : Verg., Hor. **2.**

Transf. **a.** *a palace, royal court :* illā se iactet in aulā, Verg. ; Hor. ; aulas et cerea regna refingunt (of bees), Verg. **b.** *the people of the royal court, the court :* Tac. **c.** *royal power :* Cic. Ep., Tac.
(2) **aula** = olla, q.v.
aulaeum, i, n. [αὐλαία], more freq. used in *pl.* **I.** In gen. **a.** *hangings, curtains :* Curt. **b.** *a canopy :* Hor. **c.** *coverings of a bed :* Verg. **d.** (of dress): Juv. **II.** Esp. *the curtain of a theatre* = siparium (Verg., Ov.) ; which was let down below the stage when the play began, and raised again when the performance was concluded. Hence the expressions, aulaea premuntur (Hor.), or aulaeum mittitur (Phaedr.), to denote the opening of the scene ; and aulaeum tollitur (Cic.), to signify the conclusion.
Aulētēs, ae, m. [Αὐλητής, *the flute-player*], *surname of an exiled Egyptian king, one of the Ptolemies.*
aulicus, a, um [αὐλικός], *of a princely court, princely :* apparatus, Suet. As Noun **aulici,** ōrum, *m. pl. courtiers :* Nep.
Aulis, is *or* idis (Acc. -idem, Liv. ; -ida, Ov. ; -in, Luc.), f. *a port in Boeotia from which the Greek fleet set sail for Troy.*
auloedus, i, m. [αὐλῳδός], *one who sings to the flute :* Cic.
Aulōn, ōnis. m. *a vine-bearing mountain and valley in Calabria.*
aulula, ae, f. [dim. aula = olla], *a small pot or pipkin.* Hence Aulularia, *sc.* fabula, *the play relating to the pot* (of treasure): Pl.
aura, ae (Gen. *sing.* aurāī, Verg.), f. [οὖρα]. **I.** *the wafting air, a gentle breeze, a breath of air.* **1.** Lit. : et me nunc omnes terrent aurae, Verg. ; Plin. Ep. **2.** Transf. **a.** Of odour : Lucr., Verg. **b.** Of the voice : Prop. **c.** Of light (*a shimmer*) : Verg. **II.** *a breeze, wind, gale.* **1.** Lit. (esp. in navigation): Lucr. ; nocturna, Caes. ; aurae vela vocant, Verg. **2.** Transf. **a.** neque periculi tempestas neque honoris aura, Cic. ; famae, Verg. **b.** Of a shifting wind : aura popularis, Cic. ; Liv. ; Hor. ; aurā non consilio, Liv. ; in *pl. :* Verg. **III.** *air* (mostly poet. and *pl.*). **A.** *the air.* **1.** Lit. : captare naribus auras, Verg. ; Lucr. ; esp. *the air of life :* vitales aurae, Lucr., Verg. **2.** Transf. : auram libertatis captare, Liv. **B.** *the region of air, heaven.* **1.** Lit. : dum se laetus ad auras palmes agit, Verg. Hence, *the upper world* (as opp. to *the lower*), *light of day :* Eurydice superas veniebat ad auras, Verg. ; Ov. **2.** Transf. : *daylight* (i.e. *publicity*) : ferre sub auras, fugere auras, Verg.
aurārius, a, um [aurum], *of gold, golden :* negotium, Pl. ; metalla, *gold mines,* Plin. As Noun, **aurāria,** ae, f. (*sc.* fodina), *a gold mine :* Tac.
aurātus, a, um [aurum]. **I.** *ornamented with gold, gilded :* Enn. ; tecta, Cic. ; tempora, Verg. ; milites, Liv. **II.** *made of gold, golden* (= aureus): monilia, Ov. ; Cat. **III.** *consisting of gold :* metalla, Lucr.
Aurēlius, a, *the name of a Roman gens :* esp. **I.** L. Aurelius Cotta, *author of an important law concerning the iudicia.* **II.** *Roman Emperor* (v. Antoninus). **III.** Sex. Aurelius Victor, *a Roman historian* (4th cent. A.D).

aureolus, a, um [dim. aureus], *of gold, golden.* **1.** Lit. : applied to small things : anellus, *a pretty little gold ring,* Pl. ; Cat. **2.** Transf. : *golden, very precious :* aureolus et ad verbum ediscendus libellus, Cic. ; pedes, Cat.
aureus, a, um (disyl. in Verg., Ov.) [aurum], *of gold, golden.* **1.** Lit. **a.** In gen. : patera, Pl. ; funis, Lucr. ; corona (a reward of valour), Liv. ; nummus (and *absol.* aureus, i, m.), *a gold coin* (Cic., Juv.), of the value of 25 denarii or 100 sestertii, i.e. about 1*l.* 1*s.* 1½*d.* (but see Dict. Ant. aurum). Poet. : aurea vis, *the power of changing everything to gold,* Ov. **b.** *wrought* or *ornamented with gold, gilded* (= auratus): sella, Cic. ; cingula, Verg. ; Ov. **c.** *of the colour of gold, glittering with gold :* lumina solis, Lucr. ; sidus, caesaries, Verg. **2.** Transf : *golden* (of physical and moral excellence): aurea Venus, Verg. ; qui nunc te fruitur aureā, Hor. ; mediocritas, Hor. ; aetas, Ov.
aurichalcum, i, n. **I.** *a fabulous metal superior to gold :* Pl. **II. a.** *superior kind of copper :* Plin., Suet.
auricomus, a, um [aurum coma], *golden-haired :* poet. *with golden foliage :* fetus (arboris), Verg.
auricula, ae, f. [dim. auris]. **I.** *the external ear, the ear-lap, lobe of the ear :* Pl. ; auriculam opponere, *to offer one's ear* (in token of readiness to appear as a witness in court), Hor. Prov. : auriculā infimā mollior, Cic. Ep. **II.** In gen., *the ear :* Lucr., Hor. [It. orecchio / Fr. oreille.]
aurifer, era, erum [aurum ferō], *gold-carrying, gold-bearing,* arbor (of the Hesperides), Cic. ; amnis, (i.e. *Pactolus*), Tib.
aurifex, icis, m. [aurum faciō], *a worker in gold, a goldsmith :* Pl., Cic.
auriga, ae, m.f. [aurea = reins, agō]. **1.** Lit. **a.** *a driver, charioteer,* Caes., Verg. Esp. *a charioteer in the games of the circus :* Cic. **b.** *a groom :* Verg. **2.** Transf. **a.** A constellation : *the Waggoner,* Cic. **b.** *a helmsman :* Ov.
aurigārius, i, m. [auriga], *a charioteer in the circus races :* Suet.
aurigātiō, ōnis, f. [aurigō], *a driving of a chariot in the races :* Suet.
aurigena, ae, m.f. [aurum and gen- in gignō], *gold-born, sprung from gold :* Ov.
auriger, era, erum [aurum gerō], *gold-bearing :* tauri (i.e. *with gilded horns*), Cic.
aurigō, āre [auriga], *to drive a chariot in the chariot-race :* Suet.
Aurinia, ae, f. *a prophetess reverenced by the Germans.*
auris, is, f. [For ausis ; *cf.* Gk. οὖς], *the ear* (us. in *pl.*). **1.** Lit. : auris adhibere, *to give ear, listen,* Pl. ; auribus accipere, *to hear,* Pl., Cic., Ov., etc. ; adrigere, Ter., Verg. ; erigere, dedere, admovere, Cic. ; applicare, Hor. ; praebere, Liv. ; Ov. ; implere, Tac. ; auribus haurire, Ov. ; bibere aure, Hor. Phr. : in *or* ad aurem, *also* in aure, dicere, admonere, etc., i.e. *to whisper in the ear :* in aurem dicere nescio quid puero, Hor. ; ad aurem admonere, Cic. ; in aure, Juv. ; Cynthius aurem vellit et admonuit, Verg. ; in utramvis *or* in dextram aurem dormire, *to sleep soundly* (i.e. *to be*

unconcerned), Ter. **2.** T r a n s f. **a.** *the sense of hearing, the ear* (e.g. for music): aures, quarum est iudicium superbissimum, Cic.; Hor. **b.** *hearers, auditors*: Hor. **c.** *the ear of a plough, the mould or earthboard*: Verg.

aurĭtŭlus, ī, *m.* [*dim.* aurĭtus], '*little Long Ears*' (i.e. the ass): Phaedr.

aurītus, a, um [auris], *eared*; hence, *long-eared, large-eared*. **1.** L i t.: lepores, Verg.; asellus, Ov. **2.** T r a n s f. **a.** *attentive, listening*: Pl.; quercus (of the trees following Orpheus), Hor. **b.** *by hearsay*: Pl.

aurōra, ae, *f.* [root of Gk. ἠώς], *the dawn, daybreak*. **1.** L i t.: Pl. Lucr.; ad primam auroram, Liv. P e r s o n.: *the goddess of the morning*; *d. of Hyperion and w. of Tithonus*. **2.** T r a n s f.: *the East*: Verg., Ov.

aurum (rustici ōrum dicebant, Fest.), ī, *n. gold*. **1.** L i t.: Lucr., Cic., etc. P r o v.: montis auri polliceri, *to promise mountains of gold*, Ter. **2.** T r a n s f. **a.** *things made of gold*. **i.** *gold plate, ring, cup*, etc.: Ter.; argento auroque, Lucr.; pleno auro, Verg.; aestivum, Juv.; fulvum mandunt sub dentibus aurum, Verg.; auro heros Aesonius potitur, Ov. **ii.** *coined gold, money*: Pl.; vide, quaeso, ne qua lacuna sit in auro, Cic. Ep.; aurum signatum, Liv.; Verg. **b.** Of colour or lustre: auro squamam incendebat fulgor, Verg.; Ov. **c.** *the Golden Age*: redeant in aurum tempora priscum, Hor.; Ov.

Aurunca, ae, *f. Suessa Aurunca, an old town in Campania, birthplace of C. Lucilius*; **Auruncus**, a, um.

Auruncī, ōrum, *v.* Ausones.

auscultātĭō, ōnis, *f.* [auscultō]. **I.** *a listening, attending to*: Sen. **II.** *an obeying*: Pl.

auscultātŏr, ōris, *m.* [auscultō], *a hearer, listener*: Cic.

auscultō, āre (colloq.), perh. lit. *to apply the ears*; hence *to hear with attention, to listen to*. **1.** In gen.: ausculto atque animum adverto sedulo, Pl. With A c c.: Pl., Ter., Cat. **2.** E s p. **a.** *to give credit to*: crimina, Pl. **b.** *to listen in secret, to overhear*: omnia ego istaec auscultavi ab ostio, Pl. **c.** Of servants: *to attend or wait at the door for orders*: Pl., Hor. **d.** With D a t.: *to give heed, obey*: mihi ausculta: vide, ne tibi desis, Cic.; Pl.; Ter. *Impers. Pass.*: Pl.

ausim, *v.* audeō.

Ausones, um, *m. pl. an old name of the primitive inhabitants of Central Italy*; **Ausonĭa**, ae, *f.* poet. for *Italy*; **Ausonĭus**, a, um, *Ausonian*; **Ausonĭī**, ōrum, and **Ausonĭdae**, ārum, *m. pl. the inhabitants of Ausonia or Italy*; **Ausonis**, idis, *f. adj.* Italian.

auspex, icis, *m.f.* [contr. of avispex, from avis and speciō: cf. augur.]. **1.** L i t.: *a bird-seer, one who observes the flight, singing, or feeding of birds, and from them predicts future events*: *an augur, soothsayer*: Cic., Hor. Later, of the birds observed for such purposes; *ominous, prophetic*: (galli gallinacei) victoriarum omnium auspices, Plin. **2.** T r a n s f. **a.** *the person who witnessed the marriage ceremony, and who in ancient times took the auspices at the ceremony*: nubit

genero socrus nullis auspicibus, nullis auctoribus, Cic.; Liv.; Juv., etc. **b.** *a director, commander*: divis auspicibus, Verg.; auspice Teucro, Hor.

auspicātō, *adv. after taking the auspices* (*cf.* augurato), Cic., Liv., Tac.

auspicātus, a, um. **I.** *Part.* [auspicor], *consecrated by auguries*: auspicato in loco, Cic.; Hor.; Liv. **II.** Adj. *fortunate, favourable, auspicious*. *Comp.*: Venus, Cat. *Sup.*: initium, Tac.; Plin. Ep.

auspicĭum, ī, *n.* [auspex]. **1.** L i t.: *a bird-seeing, a bird-watching*: *divination from birds, auspices*: Enn., Cic., Liv. The auspicia were divided into *maxima* or *maiora*, and *minora*: the former were possessed by dictators, consuls, censors, and praetors: the latter by curule aediles and quaestors. Magistrates, on their entrance upon office, received the auspices: while their office lasted, they were said, habere auspicia (Cic., Liv.), i.e. *to have the right of taking the auspices*; at the expiration of their office, they laid them down. In war the commander-in-chief (and under the Empire the Emperor) alone had the right of taking the auspices: ductu auspicioque alicuius res gerere, Liv.; Pl.; Tac. **2.** T r a n s f. **a.** *the chief command, direction, control*: tuis auspiciis totum confecta duella per orbem, Hor.; meis auspiciis, Verg. **b.** *a sign, omen*: Pl., Cic., Verg.; auspicium facere, *to give a sign*, Pl., Cic., Liv. P o e t.: cui (diviti) si vitiosa libido fecerit auspicium, Hor.

auspicō, āre (for auspicor): *to take the auspices*: Pl.

auspicor, ārī [auspex]. **1.** L i t.: *to take the auspices*: Cic., Liv. **2.** T r a n s f.: *to make a good beginning* (*of*): esp. in phr. auspicandi causā or gratiā: non auspicandi causā sed studendi, Plin. Ep.; auspicandi gratiā tribunal ingredi, Tac.; with A c c.: militiam, Suet.; with *Inf.*: Suet. T r a n s f.: senatorium gradum, Sen. Ep.

auster, trī, *m. the south wind*. **1.** L i t.: fulmine pollens, Lucr.; validus, Hor.; vehemens, Cic. Ep.; plumbeus, Hor.; umidus, frigidus, Verg. P r o v.: floribus austrum immittere (said of those who bring evil upon themselves), Verg. **2.** T r a n s f.: *the south country, the south*: in aquilonis austrive partibus, Cic.

austērē, *adv. rigidly, severely*: Cic.

austērĭtās, ātis, *f. severity*: Quint., Plin. Ep.

austērus, a, um [αὐστηρός]. **1.** L i t.: of the senses. **a.** Prop. of taste, *harsh, sour*: Plin. **b.** Of smell: *pungent*: Plin. **c.** Of colour: *drab*: Plin. *Comp.*: Plin. **2.** T r a n s f. **a.** Of character, *harsh, severe, stern*: Cic., Prop. **b.** Of style, *severe*: Hor., Quint. **c.** Of circumstances, treatment: *gloomy, hard, severe*: Hor., Prop., Plin.

austrālis, e, *adj.* [auster]. **I.** *of the south wind*: nimbi, Ov. **II.** *southern*: regio, Cic.; cingulus, Cic.; Ov.

austrīnus, a, um, *of or brought by the south wind*: calores, Verg.

ausum, ī, *n.* [audeō], *a daring attempt, enterprise*: fortia ausa, Verg.; in bad sense, pro talibus ausis, Verg.

ausus, a, um, *Part.* audeō.

aut, *conj.* [*cf.* Gk. αὖ], *or*, introduces a real or important alternative or one that excludes the other ; whereas *vel* introduces an alternative that is merely a matter of choice or that is unimportant. **I.** Of equal things absolutely opposed. **a.** a single aut, *or :* verum aut falsum, Cic. ; ut iuraret aut obsides daret, Caes. **b.** repeated aut, *either . . . or :* aut invitus dimicare aut magnā cum infamiā castris se continere, Caes. ; omne corpus aut aqua aut aer aut ignis aut terra est aut id quod est concretum ex his, Cic. (Occ. poet. aut . . . vel, and vel . . . aut). **II.** To introduce a new alternative, supposing the first to fail : *or else otherwise* (*cf.* alioquin) : reduc uxorem, aut quam ob rem non opus sit cedo, Ter. ; Cic. ; omnia bene sunt ei dicenda, qui hoc se posse profitetur, aut eloquentiae nomen relinquendum est, Cic. ; res ipsa et rei publicae tempus aut me ipsum, quod nolim, aut alium quempiam aut invitabit aut dehortabitur, Cic. ; nec intellegi nec quaeri aut disputari, Cic. **III.** In a limiting sense, to subjoin a less important alternative : *or at least.* **a.** Alone : truncis arborum aut admodum firmis ramis, Caes. **b.** With a particle (e.g. *certe*) : video hanc primam ingressionem meam aut reprehensionis aliquid, aut certe admirationis habituram, Cic. **IV.** In an augmenting sense, to subjoin a more important or correcting alternative, *or even, or indeed, or rather.* **a.** Alone : Graeci aut ullae exterae gentes, Cic. **b.** With a particle (e.g. *etiam, vero, omnino, potius*) : quid ergo aut hunc prohibet, aut etiam Xenocratem, Cic. ; proditores aut potius aperti hostes, Cic. ; ego iam aut rem, aut ne spem quidem exspecto, Cic. Ep.

autem, *conj.* (never used at the beginning of a clause) [*cf.* Gk. αὖ], *again, moreover ;* like *at* it adds a new thought. **I.** Antithetical, *on the other hand, but :* Gyges a nullo videbatur, ipse autem omnia videbat, Cic. **II.** Adding something different. **A.** In gen.: *moreover, and* (emphatic) : unum (iter) angustum et difficile erat ; mons autem altissimus pendebat, Caes. **B.** Esp. **a.** In transitions, *and. now :* totos dies (Cleomenes) perpotabat ; ecce autem nuntiatur, Cic. So with interjections : Pl., Ter. Also in connecting a parenthetical clause : quod vitium effugere qui volet (omnes autem velle debent), etc., Cic. **b.** In continuing a train of thought, a word being sometimes repeated from a previous clause, *now, and, well but, well then :* in Africam transcendes ; transcendes autem ? Liv. In dialogue for surprise or correction, *indeed :* num quis testis Postumum appellavit ? testis autem ? num accusator ? Cic. Also in arguments, to indicate the steps by which the conclusion is reached, *now, well but ;* aut hoc, aut illud ; hoc autem, non igitur illud, Cic. Also in resuming after a parenthesis : Cic. **c.** Poet.: sed and autem are connected in questions : sed quid ego haec autem revolvo ? Verg.

authepsa, ae, *f.* [αὐθέψης], *a self-cooker,* a utensil for cooking : Cic.

autographus, a, um [αὐτόγραφος], *written with one's own hand, autograph :* epistula, Suet.

Autolycus, i, *m. s. of Mercury and Chione ; a clever thief who could transform himself into various shapes.*

automaton, or **-um**, i, *n.* [αὐτόματον], *a self-moving machine, an automaton :* Suet.

Automedōn, ontis, *m. the charioteer of Achilles.* Transf.: *any charioteer :* Cic., Juv.

Autonoē, ēs, *f. d. of Cadmus and m. of Actaeon ;* **Autonēius**, a, um, epith. of Actaeon in Ov.

autumnālis, e, adj. [autumnus], *of the autumn, autumnal :* lumen, Cic. poet. ; aequinoctium, Varr., Liv. ; corna, Ov.

autumnus, i, *m. the autumn.* **1.** Lit.: pomifer, Hor. ; gravis, Caes. ; autumno adulto, *about the middle of autumn,* Tac. ; vergente, *drawing to a close,* Tac. In *pl.* : Hor., Ov. **2.** Transf.: *year :* Ov.

autumnus, a, um, *autumnal :* frigus, Ov.

autumō, āre. **I.** perh. orig. *to suppose, believe :* poet. ap. Cic. **II.** *to assert, aver* (of questionable assertions ; opp. nego, *to say no*), poet., and chiefly in Pl.: si vera autumas, Pl. With Acc. and *Inf.* : Pl., Cat., Hor. In *Pass.* : Pl.

auxiliāris, e, adj. [auxilium], *suitable for aid, helpful, helping.* **I.** In gen.: undae, Ov. ; carmen (of an incantation), Ov. **II.** Milit.: milites, cohortes, etc., or absol. auxiliares, *auxiliary troops, auxiliaries,* supplied by the allies (freq. opp. to legiones) : Caes., Liv., Tac. Hence, *of auxiliaries :* stipendia, Tac.

auxiliārius, a, um [auxilium], *bringing aid, helping, auxiliary.* **I.** In gen. : Pl. **II.** Milit.: cohors, Cic. ; equites, Sall. ; milites, Liv.

auxiliātor, ōris, *m.* [auxilior], *a helper, assistant :* Quint., Tac.

auxiliātus, ūs, *m.* [auxilior], *a helping, aid :* Lucr.

auxilior, āri [auxilium], *to give aid, to assist, succour, help* (rare in class. prose) : with DAT. : Pl., Caes., Cic. Ep. Transf.: Ov.

auxilium, i, *n.* [augeō], *help, aid, assistance.* **I.** In gen. **a.** argentarium, Pl. : expetere, Ter. ; petere ab aliquo, Cic. ; dare, Verg. ; ferre alicui, Pl., Cic., Ov., etc. **b.** *a source of help :* auxilium esse alicui, Pl. ; more freq.: auxilio esse alicui, Pl., Nep., Ov., etc.; rei auxilium reperire, Caes. In *pl.* : Liv., Ov. ; auxilia bene beateque vivendi, Cic. **II.** Milit.: us. in *pl.* auxilia. **a.** *auxiliary troops, auxiliaries :* mostly composed of foreign allies and light-armed troops (while the Italian allies were usually called *socii*). Hence, opp. to the legions : sex legiones et magna equitum ac peditum auxilia, Cic. ; Caes., etc. In *sing.* (rare) : Tac., Ov. **b.** In gen.: *military force, power :* Caesar confisus famā rerum gestarum, infirmis auxiliis proficisci non dubitaverat, Caes.

auxim, is, it, etc., v. augeō.

avārē, adv. greedily : Ter., Cic., etc. Comp. : Col. Sup.: Sen.

avāriter, adv. greedily : Pl.

avāritia, ae, *f.* [avārus], *greediness, a craving,* esp. after wealth, *avarice.* **1.** Lit.: inhians et imminens, Cic. Opp. to abstinentĭa, Sall. In *pl.* : omnes avaritiae, *all instances or degrees of avarice*, Cic. **2.** Transf. **a.** In gen. : gloriae, Curt. **b.** Of *gluttony* : Pl.

avārĭtĭēs, ēī, *f. avarice* : Lucr.

avārus, a, um [aveō], *eagerly desirous of, greedy* (esp. of wealth), *avaricious, grasping.* **1.** Lit. : Ter., Cic., Hor. With GEN. : publicae pecuniae, Tac. Occ. not in a bad sense : agricola, Verg. ; with GEN. : Hor. *Comp. :* Cic., Hor. *Sup. :* Cic. Poet. of inanimate things : fuge litus avarum (shore of the covetous), Verg. **2.** Transf. : Acheron, Verg. ; mare, spes, Hor.

ā-vehō, vehere, vexī, vectum, *to carry off or away* (on carts, ships, horses, etc.) : frumentum navibus avexerunt, Caes. ; aliquem a patriā, Pl. ; domum, Liv. ; in finitimas urbīs, Liv. ; Tac. ; with Acc. of the place whither : penitusque alias avexerat oras, Verg. *Pass. :* to ride, *be carried away, sail away :* citato equo ad cohortīs avehitur, Liv.: creditis avectos hostīs, Verg.

Avella, *v.* Abella.

ā-vellō, vellere, vellī *or* vulsī (volsi), vulsum (volsum), *to pull or pluck away, to tear off or away.* **1.** Lit. **a.** tigna trabisque, Lucr. ; avulsum umeris caput, Verg. ; silices a montibus, Lucr. ; poma ex arboribus, Cic. **b.** Of violent action in gen., *to take away by force, tear away :* rus ab aliquo, Ter. ; pretium alicui, Hor. ; aliquem de matris complexu, Cic. With *Pron. Refl.* or in *Mid. : to tear oneself away :* Ter., Verg. **2.** Transf. : hunc a tanto errore, Cic.

avēna, ae, *f.* **I. a.** *oats :* Verg. **b.** *wild oats,* a weed : infelix lolium et steriles avenae, Verg. ; Cato ; Cic. **II.** In gen. **a.** *a stem or stalk, a straw,* etc. : fistula surgit disparibus avenis, Ov. **b.** *a shepherd's pipe, an oaten pipe :* silvestrem tenui Musam meditaris avenā, Verg. ; Ov. [Fr. *avoine.*]

Aventīnus, ī, *m.* **I.** Also **Aventīnum,** ī, *n. the Aventine,* one of the seven hills of Rome ; **Aventīnus,** a, um. **II.** *s. of Hercules.*

(1) aveō, ēre, *to be eager to do, to long for.* **1.** Lit. With *Inf. :* Cic., Ov., etc. With *Acc.* : aveo genus legationis. Cic. Ep. **2.** Transf. (with things as subject) : Cat., Hor., Tac.

(2) aveō *or* **haveō,** ēre, *to fare well. Inf.* and *Imper.* used as a form of salutation. **a.** At meeting, *hail !* : Caesar simul atque, have, mihi dixit, etc., Cael. ap. Cic. Ep. **b.** At parting, *farewell !* : haveto at the end of Catilino's letter in Sall. ; Marcus avere iubet, Mart. As a farewell to the dead : in perpetuum, frater, ave atque vale, Cat.

Avernus lacus, or absol. **Avernus,** ī, *m. a lake near Cumae* (now *Lago d' Averno*) *whose exhalations were said to kill birds flying over it, and from which there was a descent to the Lower World ;* **Avernus,** a, um, and **Avernālis,** e. **Averna,** ōrum, *n. pl.* (*sc. loca*).

ā-verruncō, āre, an ancient religious term : *to avert :* (prodigiorum) averruncandorum causā supplicationes senatus decrevit, Liv. ; Cato.

āversābĭlis, e, *adj.* [āversor]. *abominable :* Lucr.

ā-versor, ārī, *to turn oneself away.* **1.** Lit. : Cic. With Acc. : *to turn oneself away from,*

repel *from one's presence :* filium (consul) aversatus, Liv. ; Ov. **2.** Transf. ; preces, Liv. ; honorem, Ov. ; scelus, Tac.

āversor, ōris, *m.* [āvertō], *an embezzler :* pecuniae publicae, Cic.

āversus, a, um. **I.** *Part.* āvertō. **II.** *Adj.* **1.** Lit. : *turned round, hind-foremost, belonging to the hinder or after part :* ne aversi (i.e. in the rear) ab hoste circumvenirentur, Caes. ; Liv. ; aversos boves caudis in speluncam traxit, i.e. *backwards,* Liv. *Neut.* as Noun, us. in *pl. :* per aversa urbis, Liv. **2.** Transf. : *estranged, hostile.* With *ab :* aversus a Musis, Cic. With DAT. : aversus mercaturis, Hor. *Absol. :* aversa Deae mens, Verg. ; animus, Tac. *Comp.* and *Sup. :* Sen.

ā-vertō (avor-), vertere, vertī, versum, *to turn away, to turn aside, to avert,* etc. **1.** Lit. **A. a.** Trans. : aliquid ab oculis, Cic. ; Pl. ; iter ab Arari Helvetii averterant, Caes. ; Italiā Teucrorum regem, Verg. ; locis seminis ictum, Lucr. With *in :* in fugam classem, Liv. With Acc. of place *to which :* Verg. *Absol. :* mille acies avertit, avertetque (*sc.* in fugam), Liv. **b.** Mid. (with reflex. sense) : aversi (*turning away*) omnes ad Tarquinium salutandum, Liv. With Acc. of object from which : equus fontis avertitur, Verg. **c.** Intrans. : *to turn oneself away, retire :* Pl., Verg. **B.** *to turn anything aside* from its proper channel, *to divert, embezzle, appropriate to oneself :* pecuniam publicam, Cic. ; quattuor a stabulis tauros, Verg. ; piscis mensā, Hor. ; praedam domum, Caes. **2.** Transf. **a.** *to divert a person* from a course of action, purpose, etc. : populi opinionem a spe (alicuius rei) avertere, Cic. ; Liv. **b.** *to turn one from you, estrange :* ipso Pompeius totum se ab eius (*sc.* Caesaris) amicitiā averterat, Caes. ; Cic. ; animos, Sall. ; nobis mentem deorum, Cat. **c.** *to avert :* quod omen Iuppiter avertat, Cic.

avĭa, ae, *f.* [avus], *a grandmother :* Pl., Curt. Transf. : *old wives' fables, prejudices :* Pers.

avĭārĭus, a, um [avis] *cf birds :* Varr. *Neut.* as Noun, *an aviary :* Cic. Ep. ; also, *a haunt of wild birds :* Verg.

avĭdē, *adv. eagerly, greedily :* Cic., Hor., etc. *Comp. :* Liv., *Sup. :* Cic.

avĭdĭtās, ātis, *f.* [avidus], *eagerness, longing, vehement desire* (in both good and bad sense). **I.** In gen. : potionis et cibi, Cic. ; sermonis, Cic. ; imperandi, Tac. ; Liv. **II.** Esp. *eagerness for money, avarice :* Pl., Cic.

avĭdus, a, um [aveō], *longing eagerly for* (in either good or bad sense ; avarus, strictly in bad sense only), *desirous, eager, greedy.* **1.** Lit. **A.** In gen. : With GEN. (the us. constr.) : cibi, Ter. ; gloriae, Cic. ; novarum rerum, Liv. ; belli gerundi, Sall. ; Ov. *Sup. :* Sall. With *in* and Acc. : avida in novas res ingenia, Liv. With DAT. : servorum manūs subitis avidae, Tac. With *Inf. :* Ov. *Absol.,* and transf. to things : sunt avidae (aures meae), Cic. ; amor, Cat. ; cor, Ov. **B.** Esp. **a.** For money, *greedy, avaricious* (= avarus) : Pl., Cic., Hor. ; aliquantum ad rem avidior, Ter. **b.** For food, *hungry greedy, gluttonous :* convivae, Hor. **2.**

Transf.: mare, Lucr., Hor.; ignis, Ov.
Of space: complexus, Lucr.
avis, is, *f.* (ABL. *sing.* both avi and ave, but
the former more usual), *a bird.* **1.** Lit.
a. In gen.: Pl., Lucr., Cic. Prov.: avis
alba, for *something rare, unusual* : Cic. Ep. ;
so, rara avis, Juv. **b.** Esp., *a bird of omen*
(*v.* augurium and auspicium), Ov. **2.**
Transf.: *a sign, omen* : avi sinistrā, Pl. ;
malā avi, Hor.; secundis avibus, Liv. ;
bonis avibus, Ov.
avītus, a, um [avus], *of a grandfather, ancestral.* **1.** Lit.: Cic., Verg., etc. **2.**
Transf.: *very old* or *ancient* : merum,
Ov.
ā-vius, a, um [via], *out of the way, lonely* :
also, *trackless, pathless.* **1.** Lit.: Pl. ;
avia peragro loca, *untrodden*, Lucr. ; itineribus, Sall. ; montes, Hor.. Liv. Also, *Neut.*
as Noun.: us. in *pl.*, *pathless, lonely places* :
avia cursu dum sequor, Verg. ; avia Ar-
meniae, Tac. Poet. of persons: *wandering, straying* : in montis sese avius abdidit
altos, Verg. **2.** Transf.: *going astray* :
avius a verā longe ratione vagaris, Lucr.
āvocāmentum, ī, *n. diversion, recreation* :
Plin. Ep. In *pl.* : Plin. Ep.
āvocātiō, ōnis, *f.* [āvocō], *a calling off, a
diverting of the attention, diversion* (*v.* rare) :
Cic. ; Sen. Ep.
ā-vocō, āre, *to call off* or *away.* **1.** Lit.:
partem exercitūs ad bellum, Liv. ; pubem
in arcem obtinendam, Liv. **2.** Transf.
a. *to withdraw, divert, remove* : aliquem ab
industriā ad desidiam, Cic. ; senectus avo-
cat a rebus gerundis, Cic. ; animos ad
Antiochum, Liv. **b.** *to divert, amuse* :
Plin. Ep.
ā-volō, āre, *to fly away.* **1.** Lit.: velut
avium examina, Liv., Cat. **2.** Transf.:
to fly, hasten away : experiar certe, ut hinc
avolem, Cic. Ep. ; Verg. ; Liv.
āvulsus, a, um, *Part.* āvellō.
avunculus, ī, *m.* [avus], *a mother's brother,
maternal uncle* (*a father's brother* = patruus) :
Cic., Verg. ; avunculus magnus, *a grandmother's brother* (aviae frater), *great-uncle*,
Cic. ; avunculus maior, *a brother of the
great-grandmother, great-great-uncle* (proaviae
frater), Gai. Occ. avunculus maior =
avunculus magnus, *brother of the grandmother*, Suet. ; and avunculus, *absol.* =
avunculus maior, Tac. [Fr. oncle.]
avus, ī, *m. a grandfather.* **1.** Lit.: Pl.,
Cic., Hor. **2.** Transf.: *ancestor, forefather* : Verg., Hor.
Axenus, ī, *m. adj.* [ἄξενος], *inhospitable*, an
early name of the sea later called Pontus
Euxinus (*hospitable*).
axicia, ae, *f. a pair of scissors* : Pl.
axilla, ae, *f.* [āla], *the arm-pit* : Cic. [Fr.
aisselle. Germ. *Achsel.*]
axim, *v.* agō.
axis (also assis), is, *m.* [Gk. ἄξων]. *an axle.*
I. Of a wheel: faginus axis, Verg. und
Transf.: *a chariot, waggon*, Ov. **II.** *the
axis of the world* : mundum versari circum
axem caeli, Cic. ; Lucr. Transf. **a.** *the
pole* : Luc. ; and *the north pole* : Lucr..
Cic., Verg., etc. **b.** *the whole sky* : maximus Atlas axem umero torquet stellis ar-
dentibus aptum, Verg. ; Ov. **c.** *a region,*

climate, country : boreus, *the north*, Ov. ;
Gallicus, Juv. **III.** *a board, plank* : Caes.,
Luc.

B

B, b, indecl. *n.* **I.** The Romans probably gave
the sound *p* in many cases where they wrote
b, especially when the *b* was final, as in ab,
ob, sub, before *p* or *t*, or when those preps.
were used in comp., before the same letters,
when no assimilation took place in writing.
Quintilian says ' cum dico *obtinuit*, secundam *b* litteram ratio poscit, aures magis
audiunt *p.*' Hence, we find variations
between *bs* and *ps* : cf. *Absyrtus* and *Apsyr-
tus, opsonium* and *obsonium* : gen., however, the Gk. ψ was rendered by *ps.* **II.**
Latin initial *b* corresponds in only a few
words to Greek β, as in *balbus* (βάρβαρος),
balo (βλη-χή), *bos* (βοῦς), *bito* (βαίνω),
(ἔ-βη-ν). In *bibo* it corresponds irregularly
to π ; in *balaena*, initial *b* represents φ. *b*
in the middle of words corresponds to Indo-
European *bh*, and therefore to Greek φ ;
as in *albus* (ἀλφός), *ambo* (ἄμφω), *nebula*
(νέφος), *umbilicus* (ὀμφαλός) ; in a few
instances it corresponds to *dh*, and so to
Greek θ, as in *ruber* (ἐ-ρυθ-ρός), *uber* (οὖθαρ).
In words *borrowed from* the Greek, *b* sometimes represents π, as in *buxus* (πύξος),
Burrus (Πύρρος), *carbasus* (κάρπασος). **III.**
In *bis, bellum, bonus, b* has arisen from an
earlier Latin *du.* In *publicus* (= populicus), it has taken the place of *p.* In *as-
pello, asporto* (absp.), the *b* is omitted : in
aufero, aufugio (abf.), it is changed to *u.*
IV. Latin *b* most commonly remains unchanged in French, esp. at the beginnings
of words, as *bonus* (bon), *bibere* (boire) ; but
in a good many instances turns to *v*, as
cubare (couver), *ebrius* (ivre), *habere* (avoir),
subinde (souvent). So also in Italian *avere.*
V. In Inscr., B generally denotes *bonus* or
bene : thus B. D. = *Bona Dea* ; B. M. =
Bene Merenti.
babae or **papae**, *interj.* [βαβαί or παπαί], an
exclamation of wonder or joy : *wonderful !
strange !* Pl., Ter.
Babylōn, ōnis, *f.* (Gk. Acc. -ōna), *the ancient
Chaldean city on the Euphrates ;* **Baby-
lōnius**, a, um (with ref. to astronomy and
astrology), Hor. ; **Babylōnii**, ōrum, *m. pl.
the Babylonians ;* **Babylōnia**, ae, *f. the
country of Babylon ;* **Babylōnicus**, a, um
(with ref. to tapestry), Lucr. ; **Babylōni-
ēnsis**, e, *adj.*
bāca (less correctly bacca), ae, *f. a berry.* **1.**
Lit. **a.** In gen.: Cato, Verg. **b.** Esp.
the olive : Cic., Ov. Absol. (poet.) for the
olive-berry : quot Sicyon bacas, quot parit
Hybla favos, Ov. **2.** Transf. **a.** *the
fruit of any tree* : Cic. **b.** Of things like a
berry : e.g. *a pearl* : aceto diluit insignem
bacam, Hor. ; circum cava tempora bacae,
Ov. [Fr. *baie.*]
bācātus, a, um [bāca, 2. b.], *set with pearls,
beaded* : monile, Verg.
baccar (bacchar), aris. *n.* [βάκχαρις], *a plant
having a fragrant root, from which an oil was
pressed* : Verg.

Baccha (BACA, Inscr.), ae, *f. a Bacchante, a female devotee of Bacchus ; the Bacchae conducted their frantic revels with an ivy crown upon the head, hair loose and flying, a fawn-skin upon the shoulder, and a thyrsus in the hand.*

bacchābundus, a, um [bacchor], *revelling like Bacchantes :* agmen, Curt.

bacchānal (BACANAL, Inscr.), ālis, n. **I.** *a place devoted to Bacchus :* Pl., Liv. **II.** In gen., in pl.: **Bacchānālia**, ium and iōrum : *a feast of Bacchus, the orgies of Bacchus :* Cic., Liv. In sing. (rare) : Baccanal facere, Pl., Juv.

bacchātiō, ōnis, *f.* [bacchor], *a revelling, raving, in the manner of the Bacchae :* Cic.

Bacchiadae, ārum, m. pl. *an ancient royal family of Corinth, which, being dethroned by Cypselus, migrated to Sicily, and founded Syracuse,* B.C. 734.

bacchor, ārī [Bacchus], *to celebrate the festival of Bacchus.* **1.** Lit.: Pl., Cat. Hence, **bacchantēs**, um or ium, *f.* = Bacchae, *the Bacchantes :* Ov., Curt. Poet. of a place personified : virginibus bacchata Taygeta, i.e. scene of the Bacchic rites, Verg. **2.** Transf. **a.** *to revel or rave like the Bacchae :* in voluptate, Cic.; totam incensa per urbem bacchatur, Verg. Of poetic recitation : carmen (i.e. declaim wildly), Juv. **b.** Of things personified : aula (= olla), Pl.; bacchatur fama, Verg.; ventus, Hor. **c.** Of discourse : Cic.

Bacchus, ī, m. [βάκχος, adj. raving], *e. of Jupiter and Semele, Dionysus, the god of vegetation and esp. of vine-culture :* **Bacchēus, Bacchicus, Bacchius**, a, um; **Bacchis**, idis, *f.* = Baccha. Transf. **a.** *the vine :* Verg. **b.** *wine :* Verg. **c.** *the cry ' Bacche ' :* Verg.

bācifer, era, erum [bāca ferō]. **I.** *bearing berries :* taxus, Plin. **II.** Esp. : *bearing olives :* Ov.

bacillum, ī, n. [dim. baculum], *a small staff, a wand :* Cic., Juv. In particular, *the wand or staff of the lictor,* Cic.

baculum, ī, n. (**baculus**, ī, m. Ov.) [βάκτρον], *a stick, a walking stick :* Cic., Liv., Ov. Also *the augural staff or lituus :* Liv.; *a sceptre :* Curt.

Bactra, ōrum, n. pl. *the chief city of Bactria* (now *Balkh*) ; **Bactriānus, Bactrius**, a, um ; **Bactriāni**, ōrum, m. pl. *its inhabitants.*

badissō, āre [βαδίζω], *to go, walk :* Pl.

Baetis, is (ACC. -tin, Mart. ; ABL. te, Liv., -ti, Plin.), m. *a river in S. Spain, now the Guadalquivir ;* **Baeticus**, a, um ; **Baetica**, ae, *f. a Roman province, now Andalusia ;* **Baetici**, ōrum, m. pl. *the people of Baetica ;* **Baeticātus**, a, um, *clothed in Baetican wool ;* **Baeticola**, ae, adj. *dwelling on the R. Baetis ;* **Baetigena**, ae, adj. *born on the R. Baetis.*

baetō, v. bītō.

Bagōus, ī (-ās, ae), m. *an eunuch at the Persian court.* Transf.: *any guard of women :* Ov.

Baiae (disyl.), ārum, *f. pl. a town on the coast of Campania, famous as a watering-place and holiday resort ;* **Baiānus**, a, um.

bāiulō, āre [bāiulus], *to bear a burden :* Pl.; asinus baiulans sarcinas, Phaedr. [Fr. bailler.]

bāiulus, ī, m. *a carrier of a burden, a porter, carrier :* Pl., Cic.

bālaena, ae, *f.* [φάλαινα], *a whale :* Pl., Ov. [Fr. baleine.]

balanātus, a, um [balanus], *perfumed with balsam :* Pers.

balanus, ī, *f.* (m., Plin.) [βάλανος = glāns]. **1.** Lit.: *an acorn,* Plin. **2.** Transf. **a.** *any fruit of similar form.* Esp. *a nut yielding a balsam, the Arabian ben-nut :* Hor. **b.** A species of shell-fish : Pl., Plin.

balatrō, ōnis, m. [cogn. with blaterō], Lit.: *a babbler ;* hence, *a jester, a buffoon :* Hor.

bālātus, ūs, m. [bālō], *the bleating of sheep :* Lucr., Verg. Of goats : Plin.

balbē, adv. *stammeringly :* Lucr.

balbus, a, um [βάρβαρος], *stammering, stuttering* (opp. planus) : Lucr., Cic., Hor.

Balbus, a, *a Roman cognomen, esp. of L. Cornelius Balbus, a native of Gades, whom Cicero defended.*

balbūtiō, īre [balbus]. **1.** Lit.: *to stammer :* with Acc.: Hor. **2.** Transf.: *to speak obscurely* (opp. aperte or clarā voce dicere) : Cic. With Acc.: Cic.

balineum and contr. **balneum**, ī, n. [βαλανεῖον], *a bath :* both forms in Cic. Ep. Mostly in pl. **balinea** (Liv.) and **balnea** (Aug. and post-Aug.), ōrum, n. or **balineae** (Pl., Tac.) and **balneae** (Pl., Cic., Tac.), ārum, *f.* [It. bagno ; Fr. bain.]

Balliō, ōnis, m. *a worthless fellow in the Pseudolus of Plautus ; hence any worthless fellow :* Cic.

ballista, ae, *f.* [βάλλω], *a large military engine for hurling stones and other missiles, the ballista* (orig. dist. from catapulta, which discharged arrows : Caes., Cic., Liv. Transf. **a.** *a missile :* Pl. **b.** iam infortuni intenta ballista probe, Pl.

ballistārium, ī, n. = ballista : Pl.

balneae, v. balineum.

balneārius, a, um [balneum], *of the baths :* Cat. As Noun, **balneāria**, ōrum, n. pl. *a bath room, bath :* Cic. Ep.

balneātor, ōris, m. [balneum], *the keeper of a bath :* Pl., Cic. Comic.: of Neptune : Pl.

balneolum, ī, n. [dim. balneum], *a small bath-room :* Juv.

balneum, v. balineum.

bālō, āre [cf. Gk. βληχή], *to bleat :* Pl., Ov., Quint. Poet.: pecus balans, Juv.; and absol. balantum grex, Verg.; Lucr. [Fr. bêler.]

balsamum, ī, n. [βάλσαμον]. **I.** *a fragrant gum of the balsam-tree, balm of Gilead :* Verg., Tac. **II.** *the balsam-tree itself :* Plin., Tac. [Fr. baume.]

balteus, ī, m. (and **baltea**, n. pl.). **1.** Lit.: **a.** *a girdle, belt :* esp. *a shoulder-belt or sword-belt :* Caes., Verg. **b.** *a woman's girdle :* Ov. **2.** Transf. **a.** As an instrument of punishment, *a strapping :* Juv. **b.** *the edge, crust of a cake :* Cato.

Bambaliō, ōnis, m. *cognomen of M. Fulvius, f.-in-law of M. Antonius.*

Bandusia, ae, *f. a pleasant fountain,* (probably) *near Venusia.*

Baptae, ārum, m. pl. priests of Cotytto, the goddess of lewdness.

baptistērium, ī, n. [βαπτιστηρίον], a bathing-tank : Plin. Ep.

barathrum, ī, n. [βάραθρον], a deep pit, a gulf, abyss. **1.** Lit.: Pl., Cat., Lucr. Of a whirlpool : Verg. Of the infernal regions : Verg. **2.** Transf. **a.** the maw, stomach : Pl. Of a greedy man : barathrum macelli, Hor. **b.** aliquid barathro donare (i.e. to squander), Hor.

barba, ae, f. the beard. **1.** Lit.: **a.** Of men : Pl., Cic., Verg., etc. ; barbam promittere, Liv. ; also barbam submittere (as a sign of mourning), Suet. ; barbam vellere alicui (i.e. to insult), Hor. ; barbam pascere sapientem (i.e. study the Stoic Philosophy), Hor. **b.** Of animals : Verg., Hor. **2.** Transf. : of plants : Plin.

barbarē, adv. in the manner of a foreigner. **1.** Lit.: of Latin (as opp. to Greek): Demophilus scripsit, Marcus vortit barbare (= Latine), Pl. **2.** Transf. **a.** in an uncivilised way : Cic. **b.** Of manners : rudely, roughly : Hor.

barbaria, ae (rarely **barbariēs**, Acc. -em), f. [barbarus]. **1.** Lit. **a.** an outlandish or foreign country, i.e. outside of Greece or Italy : Cic., Hor., Ov. **b.** Applied (in the mouth of a Greek) even to Italy, as opp. to Greece : Pl. **2.** Transf.: barbariem. **a.** Mental : Cic. **b.** Of language : Cic. **c.** Of manners : Cic., Ov.

barbaricus, a, um [βαρβαρικός], outlandish, foreign, strange, barbarous, opp. to Greek or Roman : with the accessory idea of splendour : Enn., Lucr., Verg. Also (in the mouth of a Greek) for Italian, Roman : urbes, Pl. Also for German : Suet.

barbariēs, v. barbaria.

barbarus, a, um [βάρβαρος], foreign, strange, barbarous : and as Noun, a foreigner, stranger, barbarian. **1.** Lit. **a.** opp. to Greek or Roman : Pl., Cic., Verg., etc. **b.** Of Latin as opp. to Greek (but seldom so in the mouth of a Roman) : cum alienigenis, cum barbaris aeternum omnibus Graecis bellum est eritque, Liv. ; Pl. ; Cic. in barbarum, adv. after the manner of barbarians or foreigners, Tac. **2.** Transf. **a.** Of manners : uncultivated, unpolished : inhumanus ac barbarus (opp. to commodus ac disertus), Cic. ; of verses : Ov. **b.** Of character : wild, savage, cruel : barbari quidam et immanes, Cic. ; libidines, Hor. ; ignis, Ov. Comp. : Ov.

barbātulus, a, um [dim. barbātus], having a small or foppish beard. **a.** Of men : Cic. Ep. **b.** Of fishes : Cic.

barbātus, a, um [barba], having a beard, bearded. **1.** Lit. **A.** Of men and gods. **a.** dicere licebit Iovem semper barbatum, Apollinem semper imberbem, Cic. Hence, an adult : Pl., Hor. **b.** an ancient Roman (because unshaven): Cic., Juv. **c.** With magister = a philosopher : Pers., Juv. **B.** Of animals : barbati mulli, Cic. Ep. ; Cat. **2.** Transf. **a.** Of plants : Plin. **b.** Of cloth : Mart.

barbiger, era, erum [barba gerō], bearded : capellae, Lucr.

barbiton, n. (v. rarely) and **barbitos**, m. and f. (only in Nom. Acc. and Voc ; pl. barbita, n.) [βάρβιτον (-ος)], a lyre, a lute : Hor. Transf.: the music of the lute : Ov.

barbula, ae, f. [dim. barba]. **1.** Lit.: a little beard : Cic. **2.** Transf. : of plants : Plin.

Barcās, ae, m. ancestor of the Barcine family at Carthage, to which Hamilcar and Hannibal belonged ; **Barcinus**, a, um ; **Barcini**, ōrum, m. pl. the Barcine faction.

Barcē, ēs, f. **I.** a city in Cyrenaica ; **Barcaei**, ōrum, m. pl., its inhabitants. **II.** the nurse of Sychaeus.

Bardaei (**Vardaei**, Cic.), ōrum, m. pl. an Illyrian tribe; **Bardaicus**, a, um : calceus (or Bardaicus alone), a soldier's boot ; poet. for the soldiers themselves : Juv.

bardus, a, um [cf. Gk. βραδύς], stupid, dull of apprehension (v. rare) : Pl., Cic.

baritus (also **barritus, barditus**), ūs, m. the war-cry of the Germans : Tac.

bārō, ōnis, m. blockhead : Cic., Pers.

barrus, ī, m. an elephant : Hor.

basanītēs (us. with lapis) [βασανίτης], a touch-stone : Plin.

bascauda, ae, f. a basket : Juv.

bāsiātiō, ōnis, f. [bāsiō], a kissing, kiss : Cat.

basilica, v. basilicus.

basilicē, adv. royally, splendidly, magnificently : exornatus, Pl. ; ut ego interii basilice ! Pl.

basilicus, a, um [βασιλικός], kingly, royal, splendid, magnificent : Pl. As Noun. **I.** **basilicus**, ī, m. (sc. iactus), the king's throw (of dice) : Pl. **II.** **basilica**, ae, f. [βασιλική (sc. οἰκία or στοά), a public building with double colonnades, which was used both as a court of justice and as an exchange ; a basilica (pure Lat. regia) : Cic., Tac., etc. **III.** **basilicum**, ī, n. a princely robe : Pl.

bāsiō, āre [bāsium], to kiss : Cat., Mart.

basis, is, f. [βάσις, a stepping, going]. **I.** a pedestal, foot, base : statuarum, Cic. ; Ov. **II.** Math. base : trianguli, Cic.

bāsium, ī, n. a kiss : Cat., Phaedr., Juv.

Bassareus (trisyl.), eī, m. [βασσάρα, a fox-skin], a title of Bacchus ; hence **Bassaricus**, a, um.

Bastarnae (or **-ernae**), ārum, m. pl. a powerful German tribe on the Lower Danube.

Batāvi (-āvī, Luc.), ōrum, m. pl. the inhabitants of the present Holland ; **Batāvus**, a, um.

Bathyllus, ī, m. **I.** a Samian boy, loved by Anacreon. **II.** a freeedman of Maecenas famous as a pantomimist.

batillum (or **vatillum**), ī, n. **I.** a shovel, fire-shovel, etc.: Plin. **II.** a fire-pan, chafing-dish : Hor.

batiola, ae, f. a drinking-cup : Pl.

battuo (or **bātuō**), uere, uī, to strike, beat, pound : battuatur tibi os, Pl. Absol.: of fencing : Suet. [It. battere ; Fr. battre.]

Battus, ī, m. the founder of Cyrene ; **Battiadēs**, ae, m. an inhabitant of Cyrene, esp. the poet Callimachus.

baubor, ārī [cf. Gk. βαΰζω]. Of dogs, to bark gently : Lucr.

Baucis, idis, f. w. of Philemon, who entertained Jupiter and Mercury.

Bavius, ī, m. a dull poet, hostile to Vergil and Horace.

beātē, *adv. happily :* vivere, Cic. *Comp. :* Sen. Ep. *Sup. :* Sen.

beātĭtās, ātis, and **beātĭtūdō**, inis, *f.* [beātus], *happiness ;* words coined by Cic.

beātŭlus, a, um [*dim.* beātus]. As Noun, *the blessed creature :* Pers.

beātus, a, um. **I.** *Part.* beō. **II.** *Adj.* **a.** *blessed, prosperous, happy* (opp. miser) : Ter., Cic., Hor. ; virtus efficit vitam beatam, Cic. As Noun, **beātum**, ĭ, *n. happiness :* Cic. ; **beātī**, ōrum, *m. pl.* the *blessed* or *fortunate persons :* Cic., Hor. **b.** Of outward prosperity, *prosperous, wealthy :* opulentissimae et beatissimae civitatis, Cic. ; Pl. ; Hor. ; Liv. Poet. : of inanimate things : arces, rus, Hor. ; Eurotas, Verg. ; sedes beatae (i.e. beatorum), Verg.

Bēbryces, um, *m. pl. a people of Bithynia ;* **Bēbrycia**, ae, *f. their district,* also *Bithynia ;* **Bēbrycius**, a, um.

Bēdriācum (-ăc-, Juv.), ĭ, *n. a village in N. Italy betw. Verona and Cremona, scene of two battles betw. the armies of Otho, Vitellius, and Vespasian ;* hence, **Bēdriācēnsis**, e.

Belgae, ārum, *m. pl. a Germano-Celtic people of N. Gaul and S. Britain ;* **Belgicus**, a, um : Gallia Belgica, *the district betw. the Seine, Marne, Rhine, and North Sea ;* **Belgium**, ĭ, *n. this district.*

bellāria, ōrum, *n. pl.* [bellus] *: dessert fruits, nuts, confectionery,* etc. : Pl.

bellātor, ōris (ancient form duellātor, Pl.), *m.* [bellō]. **I.** *a warrior, soldier* (dist. fr. miles, a *professional* soldier) : Pl., Cic., Ov., Liv. **II.** As *Adj. warlike, valorous :* Turnus, equus, Verg., Ov., Tac.

bellātrix, īcis, *f.* [bellātor], *a female warrior ;* or as *Adj. warlike.* **1.** *Lit. :* Camilla, Verg. ; diva, Ov. **2.** *Transf. :* ista bellatrix iracundia, Cic.

bellē, *adv.* [bellus], colloq. *finely, prettily, neatly, excellently, well,* etc. : Pl., Lucr., Cic. ; belle habere, *to be in good health,* Cic. Ep. ; cetera belle, *the rest is all right,* Cic. Ep.

Bellerophōn (**-ontēs**), ontis, *m. s. of Glaucus and g.s. of Sisyphus ; the slayer of Chimaera, and rider of Pegasus ;* **Bellerophontēus**, a, um.

belliatulus, a, um [*dim.* bellus], humorously for bellulus : Pl.

bellicōsus, a, um [bellicus], *fond of war, warlike, martial.* **1.** *Lit. :* gentes, Cic. ; Hor. ; provincia, Caes. **2.** *Transf. :* bellicosior annus, Liv. **2.** *Transf. : Sup. :* Cic., Tac.

bellicus (old form, duellicus, Pl.), a, um [bellum], *of war, military :* ars, Pl. ; laus, Cic. ; tubicen, Ov. ; gloria, Tac. ; caerimoniae, Liv. ; maxime in res bellicas potens, Liv. Of the gods : Ov. As Noun : **bellicum**, ĭ, *n. a signal for march or for the beginning of an attack* (given by the trumpet). **1.** *Lit. :* Philippum, ubi primum bellicum cani audisset, arma capturum, Liv. ; Cic. **2.** *Transf. :* iidem me bellicum cecinisse dicunt, Cic.

belliger, era, erum [bellum gerō]. *waging war, warlike, martial :* gentes, Ov. ; manus, Ov.

belligerō, āre [bellum gerō], *to wage or carry on a regular war* (rare). **1.** *Lit. :* Pl. ;

cum Gallis tumultuatum verius quam belligeratum erat, Liv. **2.** *Transf. :* cum fortunā, Cic. ; Pl.

belli-potēns, entis, *adj.* [bellum potēns], *powerful in war :* Enn. As Noun : magne Bellipotens, Verg.

bellō, āre (**bellor**, ārī, Verg.) [bellum], *to wage* or *carry on war, to war.* **1.** *Lit. :* Caes., Cic., Hor., etc. With *cum :* Cic., Liv., etc. With *adversus :* Liv. *Impers. Pass. :* si cum Alexandro foret bellatum, Liv. ; quoad bellatum esset, Liv. **2.** *Transf. : to fight, contend :* Ov.

Bellōna, ae, *f. the goddess of war, s. of Mars.*

bellŭa, etc., *v.* bēlua, etc.

bellŭlus, a, um [*dim.* bellus], *pretty, sweet :* Pl.

bellum, ĭ, *n.* (old and poet. form duellum) [fr. duo : hence prop., *a contest between two, a duel*) *war* (as opp. to *peace,* pax and dist. from tumultus, q.v.). **1.** *Lit. :* iam aes atque ferrum, duelli instrumenta, Cic. ; bellum ita suscipiatur ut nihil aliud nisi pax quaesita videatur, Cic. ; belli eventus, exitus, fortuna, iura, Cic., etc. ; belli artes, Liv. ; iustum bellum, *a regular war* (entered on with due formality), Cic., Ov., etc. ; bellum Helveticum or Helvetiorum, *against the H.,* Caes. For *against,* cum with ABL. ; *adversus, contra,* in with ACC. ; and with some verbs DAT. Phr. (Caes., Cic., Liv.) : bellum parare, *to arm ;* movere, *to stir up ;* ciere, Verg. ; denuntiare or indicere or iubere, *to declare ;* inferre alicui, *to make war upon :* facere, sumere, suscipere, *to undertake ;* alicui bellum mandare, or deferre bellum ad aliquem, or dare alicui bellum, *to entrust with the management of a war ;* agere, *to carry on, wage ;* administrare cum aliquo, i.e. contra aliquem, *to conduct as general ;* gerere, *to wage war ;* ducere or trahere, *to protract ;* continuare bellum, *to continue without interruption ;* conficere, perficere, *to bring to a close by victory ;* componere, *to terminate by agreement or treaty ;* deponere, ponere, *to give up ;* exstinguere, Pl. ; proficisci, mittere ad bellum, Cic., etc. ; bellum serere, alere, fovere, Liv. ; circumferre, Liv., Tac. ; spargere, exercere, Tac. Adv. phr. : bello, but oftener in bello : *in war, in time of war :* Pl., Liv. ; esp. in connexion with Adj. or GEN. : Veienti bello, Cic. ; bello Latinorum, Cic. ; bello domique, Liv. Contrasted with proelium : Hannibal fassus in curiā est non proelio modo se, sed bello victum, Liv. ; belli (LOCAT. *sing.*), *in war, abroad :* belli domique, Pl., Cic., Liv., etc. **2.** *Transf.* **a.** *combat, fight :* hic vero ingentem pugnam, ceu cetera nusquam bella forent, Verg. ; etc. **b.** *contention : aeternum bellum cum improbis,* Cic. ; tribunicium, Liv. Person. : mortiferumque averso in limine Bellum, Verg.

bellus, a, um [contr. fr. benlus, fr. benus = bonus], colloq. *fine, handsome, pretty,* etc. **a.** Of persons : Pl., Cic. Ep., Ov., etc. **b.** Of places and things : Pl., Ter. ; copia, Cic. ; locus pueris bellissimus, *a very nice place for the boys,* Cic. Ep. ; Hor. ; recordor, quam bella paulisper nobis gubernantibus civitas fuerit, Cic. Ep. With *Inf. :* bellum est cavere malum, Cic. [Old Fr. *bel ;* mod. : *beau, bel, belle.*]

bēlua, ae, *f. a beast*, esp. of large size, *a monster* (*v.* bestia). **1.** Lit.: Pl., Cic., Ov., etc. ; of the sea-monster slain by Perseus, Ov. Esp. *the elephant :* Ter., Cic. ; Gaetula belua, Juv. **2.** Transf. **a.** avaritia, belua fera, Sall. ; Cic. **b.** As a term of reproach : *beast, brute :* Pl., Cic., Liv. [It. *belva.*]

bēluātus, a, um [bēlua], *embroidered with figures of animals :* Pl.

bēluōsus, a, um [bēlua], *abounding in monsters :* Oceanus, Hor.

Bēlus, i, *m.* = *Baal, an Asiatic deity, identified with Hercules ; builder of Babylon and founder of the Babylonian empire. In myth he appears as king of Tyre and f. of Dido ; also as an ancient king of Egypt, f. of Danaus and Aegyptus ;* **Bēlidēs**, ae, *m. s. of Belus ; or descendant of Belus, e.g. Lynceus and Palamedes ;* **Bēlis**, idis, *f. a female descendant of Belus, us. pl.* **Bēlidēs**, um, *the grand-daughters of Belus, i.e. the Danaides.*

Bēnācus, i, *m. a large lake in N. Italy, through which the Mincius (Mincio) flows, now Lago di Garda.*

bene, *adv.* (*comp.* ınelius : *sup.* optimē) [benus = bonus], *well* (in all its senses). **A.** In gen. **a.** With verbs and participles, *well, rightly, kindly, prosperously :* Pl., Cic., Verg., etc. ; villa bona beneque aedificata, Cic. ; bene morati reges, Cic. ; bene mereri de re publicā, Cic. ; rem gerere, Caes., Cic., etc. ; mori, Liv., Ov. ; emere, vendere, Cic. **b.** With *Adj.* or *Adv. : quite, properly, very* (colloq.) : bene magna caterva, Cic. ; bene penitus, Cic. **B.** Phr. **a.** bene agere cum, *to deal well with :* Cic. **b.** bene dicere, *to speak well, correctly, sensibly, to the point :* Cic. With DAT. *to speak kindly to, praise :* Cic. **c.** bene facere, *to do or act well :* Cic. ; bene facis, bene fecisti, bene factum, i.e. *thank you*, Pl., Ter., Cic. ; bene facere alicui, *to do someone a kindness*, Liv. ; bene sibi facere, ' *to do oneself well*,' Pl. ; bene facta, *n. pl. good deeds, benefits, or meritorious acts*, Cic. **d.** bene esse alicui, *to be well with one, be fortunate for :* iurat bene solis esse maritis, Hor. So bene est, bene habet (= εὖ ἔχει), bene agitur, *it is well, I am satisfied*, etc. Thus in letters, si vales, bene est ; or abbreviated S. V. B. E., Cic. : bene habent tibi principia, *you have made a good beginning*, Ter. ; bene habet ; *it's all right*, Juv. **e.** non bene, vix bene, *hardly :* vix bene desieram, Ov. ; satis bene, *fairly well*, Cic. **f.** As an exclamation : *good, excellent*, etc. : Cic. ; and with ACC. or DAT. : *your health !* etc. ; bene te, Pl. ; bene mihi, bene vobis, Pl. [Fr. *bien.*]

benedicē, *adv.* [bene and dīc in dīcō, q.v.], *affably, kindly :* Pl.

bene-dīcō, bene-faciō, etc., *v.* bene.

beneficentia, ae, *f. active kindness, beneficence :* Cic., Tac.

beneficentior, *v.* beneficus.

beneficiārius, a, um [beneficium], *of a favour :* Sen. Ep. As Noun, **beneficiāriī**, ōrum, *m. pl. privileged soldiers who were*

exempt from menial service : Caes., Plin. Ep.

beneficium, i, *n.* [beneficus], *a well-doing, good conduct :* Cato. But gen. **I.** *kindness done, favour done, benefit, good turn :* Pl. ; pro maleficio beneficium reddere, Ter. ; conlocare, dare, deferre, Cic. ; conferre in aliquem, Cic. ; accipere, Ter. ; beneficio adligari, vinci, Cic. In ABL. : beneficio tuo (*thanks to you*) salvus, Cic. ; hoc beneficio, Ter. ; sortium beneficio, Caes. **II.** In public life : *a distinction, favour.* **1.** Lit. : *promotion* to the public offices conferred by the Roman people : cooptatio conlegiorum ad populi beneficium transferebatur, i.e. the offices became the gift of the people, Cic. Also of military promotions : quae antea dictatorum et consulum ferme fuerant beneficia, Liv. ; Cic. Ep. ; Tac. **2.** Transf. : *the persons promoted :* magna esse Pompei beneficia et magnas clientelas in citeriore provinciā sciebat, Caes.

beneficus, a, um [bene faciō]. Lit. : *well-doing ;* hence, *generous, liberal, beneficent, obliging :* Pl., Cic. ; beneficia voluntas, *readiness to oblige*, Cic. Comp. : beneficentior : Sen. ; Sup. : beneficentissimus : Cic.

bene-fiō, *v.* bene faciō.

benevolē, *adv. kindly :* Cic.

bene-volēns, entis, *adj.* [bene volō], *well-wishing, kind-hearted*, Pl. Comp. benevolentior : Cic. Ep. ; *Sup.* benevolentissimus : Cic.

benevolentia, ae, *f.* [bene volēns], *good-will, good-feeling, kindness :* foll. by erga, *towards*, Cic. ; also, *in* and Acc. : Caes. Or *absol. :* Ter. ; benevolentiā sempiternā aliquem colere, complecti, Cic. ; benevolentiam imperatoribus conciliare, Caes. ; capere, movere, comparare, sibi adiungere, Cic.

benevolus, a, um [volō], *well-wishing, kind, friendly :* Cic. ; erga aliquem, Pl. ; alicui, Ter., Cic. Ep. Of servants : *devoted :* servus domino benevolus, Cic. Comp. and Sup. from benevolens, q.v.

benignē, *adv.* **1.** Lit. **A.** Of feeling : **a.** *kindly, in a friendly way :* facere, Pl. ; Cat. ; Occ. *with right good will :* arma capere, Liv. Comp. : Pl. **b.** Phr. : benigne dicis *or* facis, *or absol.* benigne (colloq.), both in accepting and declining an offer : *I thank you, I am much obliged ; no, I thank you*, etc. : benigne dicis, Pl. ; dic ad cenam veniat . . . benigne, respondet, Hor. ; Cic. Also benigne facere alicui, *to do a favour to someone*, Ter., Cic., Liv. **B.** Of action : *liberally, generously :* benigne pecuniam praebere, Pl. ; iis ipsis quibus benigne videbitur fieri, Cic. Comp. : Hor. **2.** Transf. : of the yield of trees, etc. : si benigne corna vepris et pruna ferant,

benignitās, ātis, *f.* [benignus]. **I.** Of feeling or behaviour : *good-heartedness, kindness, friendliness :* etsi me attentissimis animis summā cum benignitate auditis, Cic. ; animī, Tac. **II.** Of action : *beneficence, liberality, bounty :* ne maior benignitas sit, quam facultates, Cic. ; Pl. ; Hor., etc. In *pl. :* vides, benignitates hominum ut periere, Pl.

benignus, a, um [beno- (= bon-) and gen-
in gignō]. **1.** Lit. **A.** Of feeling, behaviour, words, looks, etc.: *kind-hearted,
kindly, friendly* : oratio, Cic.; verba,
Prop., Liv.; vultus, Liv.; Hor. **P o e t.** =
faustus, *propitious, favourable* : quas benigno numine Iuppiter defendit, Hor.;
fati benigni, Juv. **B.** Of action : **a.** *beneficent, liberal, bounteous*, etc. (opp.
malignus): erga te benignus fui, Pl. ¦ Cic. ;
Hor. **b.** *lavish* (colloq.): Pl. **P o e t.**
with GEN.: vini somnique benignus, Hor.
2. T r a n s f.: of things, *bounteous, generous* : ager, Ov.; cornu, Hor.; benigna
materia gratias agendi Romanis, Liv.
Comp.: Cic., Liv. *Sup.:* Sen.

beō, *to make happy, to bless, gladden* (colloq.) :
Pl., Ter. Hence, beas or beasti, i.e. *I'm
delighted at that* : Pl. With ABL. *Instr.* :
caelo Musa beat, Hor.

bĕrbĕx, *v.* vervēx.

Berecyntus, ī, m. a mountain in Phrygia,
sacred to the Magna Mater (*v.* Cybele);
Berecyntius, a, um ; **Berecyntia**, ae,
f. the Magna Mater.

Berenīcē, ēs, *f.* **I.** *d. of Ptolemy Philadelphus
and Arsinoe, w. of her own brother Ptolemy
Euergetes ; her beautiful hair was placed as
a constellation in the heavens* (Coma Bere-
nīcēs) ; **Berenīcēus**, a, um. **II.** *d. of
Herod Agrippa I.* **III.** *the name of several
towns,* esp. *of one in Cyrenaica* ; **Berenīcis**,
idis, *f. the region around Berenice.*

Beroē, ēs, *f.* **I.** *nurse of Semele.* **II.** *one
of the Oceanides.* **III.** *w. of Doryclus of
Epirus.*

bērÿllus, ī, *f.* [βήρυλλος], *beryl* : Juv.
T r a n s f.: *a beryl ring* : Prop.

bēs, bēssis, m. [du-cssis, fr. as], properly
two-thirds of the as ; hence, *two-thirds of
a unit ;* used esp. in reckoning monthly
interest, and so ⅔% per month, i.e. 8% per
annum : faenus ex triente factum erat
bessibus, Cic. Ep.

bēstia, ae, *f. a beast* (opp. to man: the
generic name for beast). **I.** In gen. **1.**
L i t.: Pl., Cic., Liv. **2.** T r a n s f.: as
a term of reproach : mala tu es bestia, Pl.
II. Esp. *a wild beast destined to fight with
gladiators and criminals in the public
spectacles :* ad bestias mittere, Cic.; Suet.
[Fr. *bête.*]

bēstiārius, a, um [bēstiā], *of beasts* : ludus,
Sen. As Noun: **bēstiārius**, ī, m. *one who
fought with wild beasts in the public spectacles :* Cic., Sen. Ep.

bēstiola, ae, *f.* [*dim.* bēstia], *a little beast* or
animal ; an insect : Cic., etc.

bēta, *n. indecl.* [βῆτα], *the second letter of the
Greek alphabet* (pure Lat. *be*, B) : Juv.

bēta, ae, *f.* a vegetable, *the beet* : Cic. Ep.,
Cat. [Fr. *bette.*]

bētāceus, a, um [bēta], *of beet :* pedes, *beet-
roots*, Varr. As *masc.* Noun : Plin. Ep.

bētō, *v.* bītō.

bi-, *two ;* found in composition only [Gk. δι-] :
the older form was *dui* or *du*, as dui-dens for
bi-dens.

Biānor, ŏris, *m.* **I.** *a centaur.* **II.** *a hero,
founder of Mantua.*

Biās, antis, *m. a Greek philosopher, one of the
seven wise men.*

Bibāculus, ī, m. *a Roman cognomen,* e.g. of
the poet M. Furius.

bibliopōla, ae, m. [βιβλιοπώλης], *a bookseller* : Mart., Plin. Ep.

bibliothēca, ae, *f.* [βιβλιοθήκη], *a library,*
both as *a room* and as *a collection of books* :
Cic., Ov., etc.

biblus, ī, *f.* [βίβλος] poet. for papyrus . Luc.

bibō, bibere, bibī [for pibō, *cf.* Gk. πίνω],
to drink. **1.** L i t. **a.** In gen.: aquam,
Pl., Cic.; lac, Ov. Hence, cyathos, Pl.;
pocula, Tib. *Absol.* : Pl., Cic., Ov., etc.
Also, de vino, Cato ; ex aquā, Prop. ;
a fonte, Mart.; ex solido auro, Prop. ; in
gemmā, Mart. ; gemmā, Verg. *Impers.
Pass.* : Pl., Cic. **b.** P h r.: bibere Graeco
more, i.e. *propinando, to drink to one's
health,* Cic. ; aut bibat aut abeat, *let him
quaff or quit !* Cic. ; bibere flumen, poet. of
a dweller or new arrival on the banks, Verg.
Ov. ; bibere aquas, i.e. to be drowned, Ov.
2. T r a n s f.: **a.** Of things: *to imbibe,
drink in, absorb :* (terra) bibit umorem,
Verg.; fumum amphora bibit, Hor.;
hasta cruorem, Verg. **b.** *to drink in :*
longum amorem, Verg. ; bibere aure or
auribus, Hor. [It. *bevere* ; Fr. *boire.*]

bibulus, a, um [bibō], *drinking freely,
thirsty.* **1.** L i t. : Hor. With GEN.:
Falerni, Hor. **2.** T r a n s f.: to things:
harena, Lucr. ; favilla, Verg. ; lanae, Ov. ;
charta, Plin. Ep.

Bibulus, ī, m. *a Roman cognomen,* esp. M.
Calpurnius Bibulus, *consul with Caesar,*
B.C. 59.

biceps, cipitis, *adj.* [bi-, caput], *having two
heads, two-headed :* puella, Cic. ; Parnasus,
Ov.

biclinium, ī, *n. a dining-couch for two persons :* Pl.

bi-color, ōris, *adj. two-coloured :* equus,
Verg. ; baca, Ov.

bi-corniger, erī, m. *two-horned :* an epithet
of Bacchus : Ov.

bicornis, e [bi-, cornu], *adj. two-horned.*
1. L i t. : caper, Ov. **2.** T r a n s f. : furca,
Verg. ; luna, Hor. Of rivers : Rhenus,
Verg.

bicorpor, oris, *adj.* [bi-, corpus], *having two
bodies :* Cic. poet.

bi-dēns, entis, *adj. with two teeth.* **1.** L i t. :
hostia, Plin. **2.** T r a n s f. : ancora, Plin.
As Noun : **a.** m. *a two-pronged fork :* Lucr.,
Verg. **b.** *f. an animal for sacrifice whose
two rows of teeth are complete,* esp. a sheep :
Verg., etc. Hence, *a sheep :* Phaedr.

bidental, ālis, *n. a place struck by lightning :*
Hor. (The spot was consecrated by the
sacrifice of a sheep [bidens] ; whence the
name ; but perh. derived fr. bidens,
pronged fork, *cf.* ' forked lightning ' and the
trident mark at Athens.) Also of the
corpse that has been struck : Pers.

biduum, ī, *n.* [bi-, diēs], *a period of two days :*
Ter., Cic., Liv., etc.

biennium, ī, *n.* [bi-, annus], *a period of two
years :* Pl., Cic., Liv., etc.

bifāriam, *adv.* [*cf.* Gk. διφάσιος], *in two
directions, on two sides :* distribuere, Cic. ;
Pl. ; castra bifariam facta, Liv.

bifer, era, erum [bi-, ferō], *bearing twice* (a
year) : Varr., Verg.

bifidus, a, um [bi-, and *fid* root of findō], *cleft into two parts* : Ov.

biforis, e, *adj.* [bi-, foris], *having two* (i.e. *folding*) *doors* : valvae, Ov. Hence, *double* : cantus, i.e. from a double flute, Verg.

bi-fōrmātus, a um, poet. ap. Cic. and **bifōrmis**, e, *adj.* [bi-, fōrma], *double or two-formed, two-shaped* : Verg., Ov. ; hominum partus, Tac. Of a poet (as man and swan) : vates, Hor.

bi-frōns, ontis, *adj.* *with two foreheads or faces* : bifrons Ianus, Verg.

bifurcus, a, um [bi-, furca], *two-forked* : valli, Liv. ; ramus, Ov.

bigae, ārum, *f. pl.* (*sing.* biga, ae, Tac., Suet.) [contr. from biiugae, *sc.* equae], *a pair of horses* (rarely *of other animals*), *a two-horsed chariot* : Cat., Verg.

bigātus, a, um [bigae], *bearing the figure of a pair of horses* : argentum, Liv. As *masc.* Noun, *a silver coin thus stamped* : Liv., Tac.

biiugis, e, *adj.* (Verg.), and **biiugus**, a, um [bi-, iugum], *yoked two together* : leones, Lucr. ; certamine biiugo (= bigarum), *the contest between the* bigae, Verg. As Noun **biiugī**, ōrum, *m. pl. sc.* equi : *two horses yoked abreast*, hence, *a two-horsed chariot* : desiluit Turnus biiugis, Verg.

bi-libra, ae, *f. two pounds* : Liv.

bilibris, e, *adj.* [bilibra]. **I.** *weighing two pounds* : offae, Plin. **II.** *containing two pounds* : cornu, Hor. ; Pl.

bilinguis, e, *adj.* [bi-, lingua], *two-tongued.* Of persons kissing voluptuously : Pl. Also, *speaking two languages, bilingual* : Canusinus, Hor. T r a n s f. : *double-tongued* (i.e. treacherous) : Pl., Verg.

bilis, is (ABL. bilī, Pl., Cic. ; later, bīle), *f. gall, bile.* **1.** Lit. : Cato, Lucr., Cic. **2.** T r a n s f. **a.** *anger, choler* : bilem movere, Pl. ; bilem id commovet, Cic. Ep. ; bile tumet iecur, Hor. ; effundere, Juv. **b.** atra (or nigra) bilis, *black bile* (for *melancholy*), Cic. Also *of madness*, Pl., Sen. Ep.

bilix, īcis, *adj.* [bi-, and the root of licium], *with a double thread or wire* : lorica, Verg.

bilustris, e, *adj.* [bi-, lūstrum], *lasting two lustra,* i.e. *of ten years' duration* : bellum, Ov.

bimaris, e, *adj.* [bi-, mare], *situated between two seas* : Corinthus, Hor. ; Ov.

bi-maritus, ī, *m. the husband of two wives* : Cic.

bimātris, e, *adj.* [bi-, māter], *having two mothers.* Of Bacchus : Ov.

bimātus, ūs, *m.* [bīmus], *the age of two years* : Varr.

bimembris, e, *adj.* [bi-, membrum], *having limbs of two kinds* : Verg., Ov. As Noun : Ov.

bimēstris, e (ABL. bimēstrī ; bimēstre, Ov.), *adj.* [bimēnsis], *of two months' duration* : stipendium, Liv. ; porcus, *two months old*, Hor.

bimulus, a, um [*dim.* bīmus], *only two years old* : Cat., Suet.

bīmus, a, um [bi-himus, *of two winters,* fr. hiems], *two years old, lasting two years* : Cato ; merum, Hor. ; nix, Ov. ; sententia, i.e. a vote for the continuance of a government for two years, Cic. Ep.

binī, ae, a (in *sing.* Lucr. ; GEN. *pl.* freq.

binum) [bi-, with the distributive term. -nus ; so ter-nī, quaternī], *a pair, brace.* **I.** Properly : boves, Pl. ; aures, Verg. ; scyphi, Cic. **II. a.** As *card. num.* with a *pl.* noun with *sing.* meaning : castra, litterae, ludi, Cic. **b.** *two at a time, two each* : describebat censores binos in singulas civitates, Cic. ; Ter., etc. A b s o l. : bis bina, i.e. *two pairs or twice two,* Cic. ; so, bini consules, Liv.

binoctium, ī, *n.* [bi-, nox], *a space of two nights* : Tac.

binōminis, e, *adj.* [bī-, nōmen], *having two names,* Ov.

Biōn, ōnis, *m. a philosopher of the Academic and later of the Cynic school, born in Scythia* (fl. c. B.C. 300), *a witty satirist* : **Biōnēus**, a, um.

bipālium, ī, *n.* [bi-, pāla], *a double mattock* : Cato, Varr.

bipalmis, e, *adj.* [bi-, palmus], *two spans long or broad* : spiculum, Liv.

bi-partītus (Cic.) and **bipertītus** (Plin.), a, um [bi-, partiō], *in two divisions.* But mostly in ABL. bipartītō (Caes., Cic.), and bipertītō (Liv.) : insidias conlocare, Caes. ; classem distribuere, Cic. ; equites emittere, Liv.

bi-patēns, entis, *adj.* *doubly opened* : portis alii bipatentibus adsunt, Verg.

bi-pedālis, e, *adj. two feet long, broad, or thick* : Cato, Cic., Hor., etc.

bipennifer, era, erum [bipennis, ferō], *bearing a two-edged axe* : Ov.

bipennis, e, *adj.* [bi-, penna], *having two edges, two-edged* : ferrum, Verg. ; Ov. As Noun (more freq.), **bipennis**, is, *f.* (*sc.* securis), *an axe with two edges, battle-axe* : Verg., Tac., etc.

bi-pertītus, *v.* bipartītus.

bi-pēs, edis, *adj. two-footed* : equi, Verg., Quint. As Noun : *a biped* (esp. contemptuously *of men*) : Cic., Plin. Ep.

birēmis, e. **I.** *Adj.* [bi-, rēmus], *two oared* : lembi, Liv. ; scapha, Hor. Also *with two 'banks' of oars* : Caes. **II.** as Noun, **biremis**, is, *f.* **a.** *a small two-oared boat* : Luc. **b.** *a galley with two 'banks' of oars* : Caes., Cic., etc.

bis, *adv. num.* [for duis, as bellum for duellum], *twice* : bis consul, Cic. ; bis in die, Cic. ; bis die, Hor. ; cottidie bis, Liv. ; bis improbus, Cic. With numerals, prop. for multiplying (e.g. bis bina, Cic.), otherwise chiefly poet. : bis quinos dies, Verg. ; bis quinque, Hor Phr. : bis terque, i.e. *several times,* Cic. Ep. ; bis terve, i.e. *not often,* Cic. Ep. ; bis tanto *or* tantum, *twice as much* : bis tanto amici sunt inter se quam prius, Pl. ; Verg.

Bisaltis, idis (Gk. Acc. -ida), *f. Theophane, d. of Bisaltes, epon. hero of the Thracian Bisaltae* ; *changed by Neptune into a ewe.*

Bistones, um, *m. pl. a Thracian tribe* ; **Bistonius**, a, um. T r a n s f. : *Thracian* ; **Bistonis**, idis, *f. adj. Thracian* ; as Noun, *a Thracian woman, a Bacchante.*

bisulci-lingua, ae, *f. adj.* [bisulcus lingua], *with a cloven tongue.* T r a n s f. : *of a hypocrite* : Pl.

bi-sulcus, a, um, *two-furrowed* ; hence, *cloven* : Ov.

Bithȳnī, ōrum, *m. pl. a people of Thracian origin in N. Asia Minor :* **Bithȳnus**, **Bithȳnicus**, a, um ; **Bithȳnia**, ae, *f. their country ;* **Bithȳnis**, idis, *f. a Thracian woman.*

bitō (**baetō, bētō**), ere *[cf. Gk. βαίνω], to go or come :* Pl.

Bitō (**-ōn**), ōnis, *m. s. of the Argive priestess, and b. of Cleobis, famous for his filial affection.*

bitūmen, inis, *n. bitumen, asphalt :* Lucr., Verg., Tac., etc.

bitūmineus, a, um [bitūmen], *of bitumen :* Ov.

bivius, a, um, *having two ways or passages :* fauces, Verg. As Noun, **bivium**, ī, *n. a place with two ways or where two ways meet :* in bivio portae, Verg. T r a n s f. : ad bivia consistere, Liv. ; *a twofold means :* Varr. Of *a twofold love :* Ov.

blaesus, a, um, *lisping, stammering, speaking indistinctly :* Ov., Juv.

blandē, adv. *in a winning manner, coaxingly, soothingly, flatteringly :* Pl., Lucr., Cic., etc. Comp. : Cic., Hor. Sup. : Cic.

blandidicus, a, um [blandus, dīcō], *smooth-speaking, fair-spoken :* Pl.

blandiloquentia, ae, *f.* [blandus loquor], *coaxing language :* Enn.

blandiloquentulus (Pl.) and **blandiloquus**, a, um [blandus loquor], *of coaxing speech, smooth-tongued :* Pl.

blandimentum, ī, *n.* [blandior], *coaxing address, blandishment, flattery* (gen. in pl.). **1.** Lit. : minis aut blandimentis, Cic. ; Pl. ; Ov., etc. ; in *sing.* : Tac. **2.** T r a n s f. : *anything that pleases the senses, an allurement, charm :* multa nobis blandimenta natura ipsa genuit, Cic. ; sine apparatu, sine blandimentis, expellunt famem, *without whets to the appetite,* Tac.

blandior, īrī [blandus], *to coax, soothe, caress, flatter.* **1.** Lit. : Cic., Ov., etc. With DAT. : Pl., Cic., Ov., etc. With DAT. of person and *ut* with *Subj.* : Liv. **2.** T r a n s f. : of things : *to please, attract :* blandiente inertiā, Tac. ; Ov. With DAT. : voluptas sensibus nostris, Cic. ; Tac. With *Subj.* : Lucr.

blanditer, adv. *winningly, flatteringly :* Pl.

blanditia, ae, *f.* [blandus], *winning address, coaxing, wheedling, flattery ;* nearly = blandimentum, but more abstract. **1.** Lit. : of persons : Pl., Cic. Often in pl. : Pl., Cic., Ov., etc. **2.** T r a n s f. : of things : *charm, seduction :* praesentium voluptatum blanditiis deleniri, Cic.

blanditim, adv. [blandior], *in a coaxing, caressing manner :* Lucr.

blandus, a, um, *smooth-tongued, having a winning address, coaxing, flattering.* **1.** Lit. : of living beings : Pl., Cic., Verg., etc. With *Inf.* : blandum ducere, Hor. **2.** T r a n s f. : *winsome, seductive, flattering :* inlecebris blandae voluptatis, Cic. ; flores, voces, Verg. Comp. : Pl., Cic., Ov., etc. Sup. : Stat.

blaterō, āre, *to prate, to babble :* Hor.

blatiō, īre [akin to blaterō], *to talk foolishly, babble :* nugas blatis, Pl.

blatta, ae, *f. a kind of beetle :* Verg., Hor., Plin.

blennus, ī, *m.* [βλεννός], *a blockhead, dolt :* Pl.

blīteus, a, um [blitum], *tasteless, silly :* Pl.

blitum, ī, *n.* [βλίτον], *a pot herb, a kind of orache :* Pl., Plin.

Boadicēa, *v.* Boudicca.

boārius (**bovārius**), a, um [bōs], *of neat cattle :* forum, Cic., Liv.

Bocchar, aris, *m. a king of Mauretania at the time of the second Punic war.* T r a n s f. : *any African :* Juv.

Bocchus, ī, *m. a king of Mauretania, f.-in-law of Jugurtha, whom he betrayed to Sulla ;* **bocchus**, ī, *m. a plant named after him :* Verg.

Bodotria, ae, *f. the Firth of Forth, on the E. coast of Scotland.*

Boeōtī, ōrum or um, and **Boeōtiī**, ōrum, *m. pl. the inhabitants of a district betw. Attica and Phocis in Greece ;* **Boeōtius**, **Boeōtus**, a, um ; **Boeōtia**, ae, *f. this district.*

bois, ae, *f. a collar :* Pl. More freq. *pl.* **boiae**, ārum, Pl.

Boiī, ōrum, *m. pl. a people of Gaul ;* some migrated to N. Italy, others to Germany, where they were called **Boiēmī**, **Boihēmī** or coll. **Boihēmum** (whence *Bohemia*) ; **Boius**, ī, *m.* and **Boia**, ae, *f. a Boian.*

bōlētus, ī, *m.* [βωλίτης], *a mushroom :* Pl., Juv., Suet.

bolus, ī, *m.* [βόλος], *a throw or cast.* **1.** Lit. **a.** Of dice (ante- and post-class. for iactus) : Pl. **b.** *a cast of a fish-net ;* hence *the catch, haul* (of fish) : Suet. **2.** T r a n s f. *a haul or win.* **a.** *gain, profit :* Pl., Varr. **b.** *a choice titbit :* Ter.

bombax, interj. [βομβάξ], *an exclamation of surprise : strange ! Oh, indeed !* Pl.

bombus, ī, *m.* [βόμβος], *a hollow, deep sound, a booming or humming.* Of a trumpet : Lucr., Cat. Of bees : Varr.

bombȳcinus, a, um [bombȳx], *of silk, silken :* Juv. ; Neut. pl., **bombȳcina**, ōrum, *silken clothes :* Mart.

bombyx, ȳcis, *m.* [βόμβυξ]. **1.** Lit. : *the silk-worm :* Plin. **2.** T r a n s f. : *a silken garment, silk :* Prop., Plin.

Bona Dea, *the Good Goddess, worshipped by Roman women as the goddess of chastity and fertility.*

bonitās, ātis, *f.* [bonus], *good quality, goodness.* **A.** Of things : terrae, Lucr. ; agrorum, Caes. ; praediorum, vocis, Cic. **B.** Of a person's moral qualities. **a.** *goodness* in gen. : ingeni, naturae, Cic. **b.** *goodness, excellence, honesty :* alicuius fidem bonitatemque laudare, Cic. ; bonitas et iustitia, Cic. ; Ov. **c.** *goodness, kindness :* bonitas et beneficentia, Cic. ; Tac. [It. *bontà ;* Fr. *bonté.*]

bonus, a, um (old form duonus) ; comp. melior ; sup. optimus : *good.* **A.** *good* as fulfilling one's function. **a.** Of things : ager, Ter. ; domicilia, Cic. ; vinum, Hor. **b.** Of persons : servus, Pl., Cic. ; uxor, imperator, Cic. ; gladiator, Ov. **c.** *good = clever,* etc. **i.** With ABL. : iaculo, remis, Verg. ; bello, Liv. **ii.** With *Inf.* : calamos inflare, Verg. **iii.** With GEN. of Ger. : furandi, Tac. **iv.** With DAT., *good for, i.e. suitable for :* ager pecori alendo,

Liv. **v.** With *ad :* ad proelium, Tac. **d.** Of race, birth, material circumstances (*cf.* our 'good family,' 'good society,' etc.): bonorum, id est lautorum et locupletium, Cic. ; bonis rebus meis, Cic. **e.** Of other circumstances, *good,* i.e. *favourable, opportune, right, sound :* occasio, Pl. ; condicio, navigatio, rumores, valetudo, sententia, Cic. **B.** Of moral qualities. **a.** *good = virtuous, honourable,* etc.: Pl., Cic., Hor. ; optimi mores, Cic. **b.** *good = brave :* boni ignavique Sall. **c.** Of behaviour to others, *gracious, bountiful, kind* (with Dat., or *in* and Acc., or *Absol.*) : bono animo in populum R., Caes., Cic. ; vos o mihi manes este boni ! Verg. ; Acestes, Verg. Esp. of the gods, *v.* Iuppiter, Bona Dea, etc. **Phr. i.** bona verba, *words of good omen,* Tib. ; *civil language,* Ter. **ii. b.** dicta, *witty sayings,* Cic. **iii. b.** aetas, *the prime of life,* Cic. **iv. b.** pars, *a good* (i.e. *a large*) *portion,* Hor. **v. b.** vir, esp. in political sense, *a loyal citizen* (*cf.* optimates), Cic. **vi.** bono animo esse, *or* bonum animum habere, *to be of good cheer,* Cic. Ep., Liv. ; also *to be well-disposed,* Cic. **vii.** bona *or* cum bonā veniā tuā, *with your kind permission,* Cic., Liv. **viii.** bonae artes, *liberal education, liberal arts,* Cic. ; also *honourable dealing,* Sall., Tac. **ix.** bona fides, *good faith,* Cic. As Noun, **bonum,** i, *n. good, a good thing.* **A.** Opp. to what is bad ; i.e. *what is morally good, a moral good ;* non est igitur voluptas bonum, Cic. Often with aequum (q.v.), *what is right and proper,* Cic. **B.** Opp. to what is harmful ; i.e. *what is materially good,* i.e. *what is valuable, advantageous,* etc., *a good :* **a.** ornatissimus omnibus fortunae bonis, i.e. *blessings,* Cic. ; esp. in phr. bono esse alicui, *to be for profit, be profitable to one :* cui bono ? *who was the gainer ?* Cic. **b.** In *pl.* bona, *goods, effects, property :* Cic., Liv. **boni,** ōrum, *m. pl.* **a.** (*morally*) *good men :* Pl., Cic., Hor. **b.** *brave men :* Sall., Hor. In *sing. :* Cic. **c.** (*cf.* B. v.), *loyal citizens, patriots :* Cic., Sall. **d.** *the better classes :* Pl., Sall. **meliōrēs,** um, *m. pl.* one's *betters :* Pl., Ter.

boŏ, āre [orig. bovŏ ; cf. Gk. βοάω], *to roar, cry aloud :* Pl., Ov.

Boōtēs, ae (also Gen. -ti ; Acc. -tēn ; Voc. -tē), *m.* the *constellation Boŏtes, the Waggoner* or *Bear-keeper.*

Boreās, ae, *m.* [βορέας *or* βορρᾶς] (Acc. -ean or eam). **I.** *the north wind* (pure Lat. aquilo) : **Borēus** (**-ius**), a, um. **II.** Transf. : *the North.* **III.** Person. : *s. of the river-god Strymon, and f. of Calais and Zetes by Orithyia.*

bōs, bovis (Gen. *pl.* : boum ; also bovum, Cic. ; and boverum, Cato ; Dat. *pl.* contr. bōbus *or* būbus) : *m. f. an ox or cow :* Pl., Cic., Verg., etc. ; bos Lucas (because the Romans first encountered elephants in Lucania), *the elephant,* Lucr. Prov. : bovi clitellas imponere (i.e. to impose upon a person a duty for which he is not qualified), Poet. ap. Cic. ; optat ephippia bos (of a discontented person), Hor. Transf. : *a whip cut from neat's leather :* Pl. [It. *bove ;* Fr. *bœuf ;* Eng. *beef.*]

Bosporus (and **Bosphorus**), i, *m.* [βόσπορος, ' heifer's ford,' from Io's passage as a heifer]. **I.** Thrācius, *the strait which unites the Euxine and the Propontis ;* **Bosporius,** a, um. **II.** Cimmerius, *the strait connecting the Lake Maeotis with the Euxine ;* **Bosporānus,** i, *m. a dweller by it ;* also *Adj.*

botulus, i, *m. a sausage :* Mart.

Boudicca (wrongly Boadicēa), ae, *f. queen of the British tribe Iceni in the time of Nero.*

bovārius, *v.* boārius.

bovile, *v.* bubile.

bovillus, a, um, old form = bubulus [bōs], *of oxen* or *kine :* grex, in an old religious formula, Liv.

brācae, ārum, *f. pl.* (*sing.* brāca, ae, Ov.), *trousers, breeches,* orig. worn only by non-Roman and non-Greek nations : Tac.

brācātus [brācae], a, um, *wearing trousers* or *breeches.* **1.** Lit. : Cic., Ov. **2.** Transf. for trans-alpinus, in opp. to togatus (q.v.) : Gallia Brācāta, afterwards called Gallia Narbōnēnsis : Cic., Plin. As *masc.* Noun : Juv.

bracchiālis, e, *adj.* [bracchium], *of the arm :* nervus, Pl.

bracchium, i, *n.* (less correctly, brāchium) [βραχίων]. **1.** Lit. **a.** Properly *the forearm* (while lacertus is the upper arm) : Lucr., Ov., Curt. **b.** In gen. *the whole arm :* Caes., Cic. ; collo dare bracchia circum, Verg. ; derexit bracchia contra torrentem, Lucr. Prov. : levi *or* molli bracchio agere (i.e. to act without energy), Cic. ; praebere bracchia sceleri (i.e. to lend aid), Ov. **2.** Transf. **a.** *claws :* of *Cancer,* Ov. ; *Scorpio,* Verg. **b.** *branches of trees :* Cato ; (arbor) ramos et bracchia tendens, Verg. **c.** *an arm of the sea :* Ov. ; Curt. **d.** *the sailyards of ships :* iubet intendi bracchia velis, Verg. **e.** Milit. : *an outwork* or *a dam :* muro bracchium iniunxerat, Liv. **f.** *the side-works, moles of a harbour :* Liv., Plin. Ep. [Fr. *bras.*]

branchiae, ārum, *f. pl.* [τὰ βράγχια], *gills,* e.g. of a fish : Plin.

Branchus, i, *m. s. of Apollo ;* hence, **Branchidae,** ārum, *m. pl. his descendants ; hereditary priests of the temple and oracle of Apollo at Miletus.*

brassica, ae, *f. a cabbage :* Pl. In *pl.* : *varieties of cabbage :* Cato.

brattea, *or* **bractea,** ae, *f. a thin plate of metal, gold leaf :* Lucr., Verg., etc.

bratteola, ae, *f.* [*dim.* brattea], *a fine thin leaf of gold :* Juv.

Brennus, i, *m.* **I.** *leader of the Gauls, who defeated the Romans at the Allia.* **II.** *leader of the Gauls who invaded Macedonia and Greece* (2nd cent. B.C.).

breviārium, i, *n.* [brevis], *a summary, abridgment, abstract :* rationum, imperi, officiorum, Suet. ; Tac.

breviculus, a, um [*dim.* brevis], *somewhat short, shortish :* homo, Pl.

brevi-loquēns, entis, *adj.* [brevis loquor], *brief in speaking :* Cic. Ep.

brevis, e, *adj. short, confined,* of space and of time. **A.** Space. **1.** Lit. **a.** In distance, extent, *short, small :* via, Liv. ;

cursus, Verg.; caput, Verg. **b.** In height: Cic., Ov., etc.; brevis corpore, Suet. **c.** Of depth: *shallow*: vada, Verg. As Noun, **brevia**, ium, *n. pl.*; *shallow places, shoals*: Verg., Tac. In metaph.: Sen. Ep. **2.** T r a n s f. **a.** *small, unimportant*: cena, Hor.; impensa, Ov. **b.** Of speech, *short, concise*: narratio, Cic.; Hor.; as Noun: in breve causas cogere, Liv.; hence, brevi (ABL.) *in short, briefly*: brevi exponere, persoribere, Cic. **B.** T i m e. **1.** L i t.: *short*: vitae brevis cursus, Cic.; dies, Pl., Verg.; ad breve tempus, *for a short while*, Cic.; brevi tempore, brevi, *in a short while, soon*: brevi postea, Cic.; Caes. **2.** T r a n s f. **a.** *of brief duration, short-lived, transient*: dolor, Cic.; dominus, flos rosae, aevum, ira, Hor. **b.** In metric, *short*: syllaba, Hor.; Quint. Comp.: Pl., Cic., Ov., etc. Sup.: Cic., Verg., etc. [Fr. *bref*.]

brevitās, ātis, *f.* [brevis], *shortness*. **A.** Of space or bulk. **1.** L i t.: brevitas nostra, *smallness of stature*, Caes.; Lucr. **2.** T r a n s f. of discourse, *brevity, conciseness*: Cic., Hor., etc. **B.** Of time, *shortness*. **1.** L i t.: vitae, temporis, Cic.; imperi, Tac. **2.** T r a n s f. (in metric): pedum, syllabarum, Cic. In *pl.*: Cic.

breviter, *adv. shortly, briefly, concisely*. **A.** Of space. **1.** L i t.: Tib., Tac. **2.** T r a n s f.: of discourse: Cic., Verg., etc. **B.** Of time. T r a n s f.: of syllables, breviter dicitur, *is pronounced short*, Cic. Comp.: Cic., Quint. Sup.: Cic., Quint.

Briareus (trisyl.), eī, *m.* a hundred-armed giant, also called *Aegaeon*.

Brigantes, um (ACC. -tas, Tac.), *m. pl. a powerful tribe in Britain*; **Briganticus**, a, um.

Brimō, ūs (ACC. -īda, Ov.; VOC. -ī, Ov.), *f. a name of Proserpina*.

Brisēis, idos (ACC. -ida, Ov.; VOC. -i, Ov.), *f. Hippodamia, d. of Brises, slave of Achilles.*

Britannī, ōrum, *m. pl. the Britons*, the name of the inhabitants of **a.** the British Isles. **b.** Great Britain. **c.** England; **Britannus**, **Britannicus**, a, um; **Britannia**, ae, *f. their country*. As Noun, **Britannicus** was a surname of the emperor Claudius, given to him for victories in Britain, and borne also by his son Germanicus.

Britomartis, is, *f. d. of Zeus and Carme*; *when pursued by Minos, she cast herself into the sea and was made a goddess.*

Bromius, ī, *m.* [βρέμω], '*the roaring god,*' epith. of Bacchus.

Broteās, ae, *m.* **I.** *one of the Lapithae.* **II.** *twin-brother of Ammon, and with him killed by Phineus.*

Brundisium, ī, *n. a town with an excellent harbour on the Adriatic coast of Calabria*, now *Brindisi*; **Brundisinus**, a, um; **Brundisinī**, ōrum, *m. pl. its inhabitants.*

brūma, ae, *f.* [contr. from brevima, old *sup.* of brevis]. **I.** *the shortest day in the year, the winter solstice*; opp. to solstitium (the *summer solstice*): Ter., Luor., Cic.; sub brumā, *at midwinter*, Caes. **II.** *the winter time, winter*: Cic., Verg., Hor.

brūmālis, e. *adj.* [brūma]. **I.** *of the winter solstice or shortest day*: dies, Cic.; signum,

---

i.e. Capricorn, Cic.; so, flexus, Lucr. **II.** *wintry, of winter*: tempus, Cic. poet.; frigus, Verg.; horae, Ov.

Bruttii, ōrum, *m. pl. the inhabitants of the S. extremity of Italy*; also *their district*; **Bruttius**, a, um.

brūtus, a, um [*cf.* Gk. βαρύς], *heavy, unwieldy*. **1.** L i t.: pondus, Lucr.; tellus. Hor. **2.** T r a n s f.: *heavy, dull, stupid, imbecile, irrational*: Sen., Plin.

Brūtus, ī, *m. a Roman surname*; esp. **I.** L. Iunius Brutus, *liberator of Rome from regal dominion*. **II.** M. Iunius Brutus, *nephew of Cato Uticensis; one of the murderers of Julius Caesar*. **III.** D. Iunius Brutus, *one of Caesar's murderers*; **Brūtinus**, a, um.

Bubastis, *f. a goddess worshipped at Bubastis in Egypt.*

bubīle (also bovīle), is, *n.* [bōs], *a stall for oxen*: Pl., Cato, Phaedr.

būbō, ōnis, *m.* (*f.* Verg.) [cf. Gk. βύας], *an owl, the horned owl* (with cry of ill-omen): Lucr., Verg.

bubulcitor, ārī [bubulcus], *to keep or drive oxen*: Pl.

bubulcus, ī, *m.* [bōs; cf. būbulus], *one who ploughs with oxen, a ploughman* (= arator): Cic., Ov.

būbulus, a, um [bōs], *of oxen*: pecus, Varr.; corii, *straps of ox-hide*, Pl.; fimum, Liv. As Noun, **būbula**, ae, *f.* (*sc.* caro), *beef*: Pl.

būcaeda, ae, *m.* [bōs caedō], *one who is whipped with thongs of ox-hide*: Pl.

bucca, ae, *f. the cheek, the chops or jowl.* **1.** L i t.: inflare, Pl., Hor.; sufflare buccas, Pl. Hence, *the mouth*: dicere quod or quidquid in buccam venerit (colloq.), Cic. Ep., Mart. Also ellipt.: garrimus quidquid in buccam, Cic. Ep. **2.** T r a n s f. **a.** *a puff-cheek, i.e. a bawler, ranter*: Juv.; also *of horn-blowers*: Juv. **b.** *a mouthful*: Mart. [It. bocca; Fr. bouche.]

buccō, ōnis, *m.* [bucca], lit. '*fat-cheeks*'; hence, *a silly babbler*: Pl.

buccula, ae, *f.* [*dim.* bucca]. **1.** L i t.: *a little cheek*: Suet. **2.** T r a n s f. In *pl.*: *the beaver of a helmet*: Liv., Juv.

bucculentus, a, um [buccula], *full-cheeked*: Pl.

Būcephalās, ae, *m.* [βοῦς, κεφαλή, '*bull-head*'], *the horse of Alexander.*

būcina, ae, *f. a crooked horn or trumpet* (while tuba is us. straight). **1.** L i t. **a.** *a herdsman's horn*: Varr., Prop. **b.** *a war-trumpet*: Cic., Verg.; used to proclaim the watches of the day and night; hence = vigilia: ad tertiam bucinam, Liv. **c.** *a trumpet for summoning a public meeting*: Cic., Prop. **2.** T r a n s f. **a.** Of Triton's trumpet-shell: Ov. **b.** Of rumour: Juv.

būcinator, ōris, *m.* [būcina], *a trumpeter*. **1.** L i t.: Caes. **2.** T r a n s f.: Cic. fil. ap. Cic. Ep.

būcolica, ōrum, *n. pl.* [βουκολικός], *pastoral poetry, bucolics*: Ov.

būcula, ae, *f.* [*dim.* bōs], *a young cow, a heifer*: Cic., Verg.

būfō, ōnis, *m. a toad*: Verg.

bulbus (-os), ī, *m.* [βολβός]. **I.** *a bulb*: Plin. **II.** *an onion*: Cato, Ov.

būlē, ēs, *f.* [βουλή], *the (Greek) council*: Plin. Ep.

būleuta, ae, m. [βουλευτής], a councillor :
Plin. Ep.

būleutērion, ī, n. [βουλευτήριον], a Greek
senate-house : Cic.

bulla, ae, f. **I.** a bubble : perlucida, Ov.
Transf.: si est homo bulla, Varr. **II.** a
boss, knob, stud (upon a door, girdle, etc.) :
Pl., Cic., Verg. **III.** the bulla, an amulet us.
of gold worn by generals in a triumph and
by noble youths : Pl., Cic., etc. Also hung
upon the forehead of favourite animals :
Ov.

bullātus, a, um [bulla], wearing the bulla :
heres, Juv.

bullō, āre, to bubble : Cato.

būmastus, ī, f. [βούμαστος, cow-breasted], a
species of grape with large clusters : Verg.

Būpalus, ī, m. a statuary of Chios attacked
by the poet Hipponax in revenge for the
sculptor's exhibition of his deformity.

būris, is, m. (Acc. -im), the crooked hinder
part of the plough, the plough-tail : Varr.,
Verg.

Burrus, an old form of Pyrrhus.

Busīris, idis (Acc. -in, Ov.), m. a king of
Egypt who sacrificed strangers and was himself slain by Hercules.

būstirapus, ī, m. [bustum rapiō], a tomb-
robber : Pl.

būstuārius, a, um [bustum], connected with
funeral rites : gladiator, Cic.

būstum, ī, n. [perh. fr. root of ūrō, cf. Vesta.]
1. Lit. **a.** a place where dead bodies were
burned and buried : Lucr. Also the pyre
after burning : Verg. **b.** In gen.: a
tomb, barrow : Cic., Verg., etc. ; Gallica
busta (i.e. of the Gauls slain in Rome
by Camillus), Liv. **2.** Transf.: bustum
legum omnium ac religionum, Cic. ; Lucr.,
Ov.

Būtēs, ae (Acc. -ēn, Verg.), m. **I.** s. of
Amycus, king of the Bebrycians, slain by
Dares at the tomb of Hector. **II.** name of
several men in Verg., Ov.

buxifer, era, erum, bearing box-trees : Cat.

buxus, ī, f. (buxum, ī, n., Verg.) [πύξος]. **1.**
Lit.: the box-tree : Ov. **2.** Transf.:
box-wood : rasile, Verg. Hence for things
made of box-wood : a pipe or flute : Verg. ;
a whipping-top : volubile buxum, Verg. ;
a comb : Ov. [Fr. buis.]

Byblis, idis (Acc. -ida, Ov. ; Voc. -i, Ov.),
f. d. of Miletus and Cyanē, changed into a
fountain.

Byrsa, ae, f. the citadel of Carthage.

Byzantium, ī, n. a Greek colony on the
Thracian Bosporus ; later Constantinopo-
lis, now Constantinople ; **Byzantius**, a, um ;
Byzantiī, ōrum, m. pl. its inhabitants.

C

C, c, the third letter of the Latin alphabet, corresponding originally in sound to the Greek
Γ. **I.** The Duilian inscription gives LECIONES
for legiones ; and even to the latest times
C. and Cn. stood for Gaius and Gnaeus. But
from an early period there was a tendency
to give to C the sound of K : in inscriptions
Consul is represented by the abbreviation

Cos. not Kos. ; and K was retained as a
written symbol only before a, as in KAL
for Kalendae and Calumnia. **II.** c in Latin
corresponds regularly to Gk. κ. Sometimes
where π is found in Greek, Latin, following
the orig. Indo-European, has c (or qu) :
thus coquo, πέπτω ; linquo, λείπω ; voco,
Ϝέπος ; oculus, ὄφομαι. In the Germanic
languages it is represented by h and sometimes, in the middle of a word, by g : cf.
calamus, O. H. G. halm. **III.** Changes of
c in French. **1.** of c into ch : cf. Lat.
caballus, calidus, canis, etc., with Fr. cheval,
chaud, chien, etc. **2.** Of c into s : cf. Lat.
facimus, licere,- placere, etc. with Fr.
faisons, loisir, plaisir, etc. **3.** Of c into g :
cf. Lat. acer, etc.: with Fr. aigre, etc. **4.**
Omission of c : **i.** Between two vowels : cf.
Lat. focus, nocere, etc. : with Fr. feu, nuire,
etc. **ii.** followed by t : cf. Lat. dictus :
Fr. dit. lectus : Fr. lit. **iii.** followed by r :
cf. Lat. lacrima, with Fr. larme. **IV.** as an
abbrev. C stands for Gaius, and reversed,
Ͻ. for Gaia. Upon voting tablets it meant
condemno. As a numeral it denotes centum.

caballus, ī, m. [καβάλλης], an inferior sad-
dle- or pack-horse ; a nag, hack : Lucil.,
Hor., Sen. Ep. ; of Pegasus (in jest) : Juv.
Prov.: optat arare caballus (of discon-
tent with one's own work), Hor.

Cabīrus, ī, m. a deity of Lemnos and Samothrace.

cachinnātiō, ōnis, f. [cachinno], loud and
vulgar laughter : Cic.

cachinnō, āre [cachinnus], to laugh aloud,
burst out laughing immoderately : Lucr., Cic.

cachinnō, ōnis, m. one who laughs loudly, a
scoffer : Pers.

cachinnus, ī, m. a loud or merry laugh :
tollere, Cic., Hor. ; commovere, Cic. ; edere,
Suet. Transf.: of the ripple and plash
of waves : Cat.

cacō, āre, to go to stool. **A.** Intrans.: Cat.,
Hor. **B.** Trans.: to defile : Cat.

cacoëthes, is, n. [κακόηθες, of bad habit], an
obstinate, malignant disease. **a.** Physical,
e.g. an ulcer : Plin. **b.** Mental: scribendi
cacoëthes, Juv.

cacula (cācula in Pl. Pseud. Arg. 4), ae, m.
a servant, esp. the servant or slave of a soldier :
Pl.

cacūmen, inis, n. the tip, end, or point of a
thing ; the peak, summit. **1.** Lit.: ram-
orum, Caes., Lucr. ; montium, Liv. ; Lucr. ;
Verg. Of tree-tops : Lucr., Verg., etc. **2.**
Transf.: the end, limit : donec alescundi
summum tetigere cacumen, Lucr.

cacūminō, āre [cacūmen], to point, make
pointed : Ov.

Cācus, ī, m. s. of Vulcan, a giant who dwelt on
Mons Aventinus ; he was killed by Hercules.

cadāver, eris, n. [cadō], a dead body, a corpse,
carcase. **1.** Lit.: Lucr., Cic., Verg., etc.
Ep. **b.** Of a vile wretch : Cic.
2. Transf. **a.** Of ruins : Sulp. ap. Cic.

cadāverōsus, a, um [cadāver], like a corpse,
cadaverous : Ter.

Cadmus, ī, m. **I.** s. of the Phoenician king
Agenor, b. of Europa, h. of Harmonia, f. of
Polydorus, Ino, Semele, Autonoë, and
Agave ; founder of Thebes in Greece ;
Cadmēus (-ēius), a um, Cadmean, Theban ;

Cadmēa, ae, f. (sc. arx), *the citadel of Thebes* ; **Cadmēis**, idis. f. adj., *Cadmean, Theban*, and as NOUN, *a female descendant of Cadmus*. **II.** *an executioner in the time of Horace.*

cadō, cadere, cecidī, (cāsum), *to fall.* **1.** Lit. **A.** Of falling from a height, *to fall down.* **a.** In gen. : arbores in te, Pl. ; (aves) praecipites cadunt in terram, Lucr. ; Liv. The place *from which* is in the ABL. with a *prep.* : ex equo, de equo, Pl. ; Cic. ; de montibus, Verg., or in ABL. without a *prep.* : lapides caelo cadunt, Liv. **b.** Of the heavenly bodies, *to set* : Verg. **c.** Of hair, leaves, etc., *to fall off, be shed* : folia, Pl., Verg. ; dentes, Lucr. ; barba, Verg. **d.** Of fluids : imbres, Lucr., Verg. ; flumen, Liv. ; amnis in sinum maris, Liv. **B.** Of drooping from weakness, etc., *to fall, droop, sink* : Pl., Ov., Liv., etc. ; oculi, vultus, Cic. ; manus, Verg. Esp. in death, *to droop and die, fall dead, be killed* : Pl. ; pauci de nostris cadunt, Caes. ; Cic. ; Ov. ; in acie, Liv. With *ab* : ab hoste, Ov. ; Tac. With *Instr.* ABL. : Ov., Tac. Of victims, *to be sacrificed* : Verg., etc. **2.** Transf. **A.** *to fall and perish* (from violence, etc.) : labentem et prope cadentem rem publicam, Cic. **B.** Of the wind, anger, courage, etc. : *to fail, abate, drop, subside, etc.* : vis venti, Liv. ; Ov. ; ira, Liv. ; animi, Cic., Liv. ; cunctus pelagi fragor, Verg. ; cadere animis, Cic. **C.** *to fail,* i.e. *to be unsuccessful* : With ABL. of causa or formula, *to lose one's case* : Cic., Quint. ; also *absol.* : Tac. With ABL. of crimen, *to fall by an accusation, be condemned* : Tac Of theatrical shows : *to fall flat, fail* (opp. stare) : Hor. **D.** *to fall under, become subject to* (with *sub, in,* or *ad,* and ACC. : sub sensūs nostros, Lucr. ; Cic. ; sub imperium R., Cic. ; in potestatem alicuius, in morbum, Cic. ; ad servitia, Liv. Of dates : in id saeculum, Cic. **E.** *to fall in with, agree with, be suitable to* (with *in* or *sub* and ACC.) : non cadit in hunc hominem ista suspicio, Cic. ; Verg. **F.** With DAT., *to fall to one, happen, occur,* and *absol.*, *to turn out* : nihil ipsis incommodi cadere possit, Cic. ; Verg. ; si non omnia caderent secunda, Caes. ; Cic. ; Verg., etc. Of dice : Ter., Liv. Hence, cadere in (ad) invitum or cassum, *to fail* : Pl., Lucr., Liv. **G.** Rhet. of words and periods, *to close, end* : Cic. [Fr. *choir, chance.*]

cādūceātor, ōris, m. [cādūceum], *an officer sent with a flag of truce* : Liv.

cādūceum, ī, n. [κηρύκειον] (strictly adj. : sc. sceptrum or baculum). or **cādūceus**, ī, m. (sc. scipio). **I.** *the herald's staff* (emblem of peace) : Cic., Liv. **II.** *the wand of Mercury,* as messenger of the gods : Suet.

cādūcifer, era, erum [cādūceus ferō], *bearing a herald's staff* : Ov.

cādūcus, a, um [cadō]. **1.** Lit. **a.** *falling, fallen* (mostly poet.) : oleae, Cato ; frondes, Verg. ; aqua, Ov. ; caduco fulmine, Hor. ; caduci bello, Verg. **b.** *inclined* or *destined to fall* (rare) : (vitis) naturā caduca est, Cic. ; iuvenis, Verg. **2.** Transf. **a.** *fleeting, frail, perishable* : res humanae, corpus, Cic. ; spes, fama, Ov. **b.** In law :

caduca bona, *an estate without an heir* : Cic. As Noun, **cādūcum**, ī, n. *an unowned estate* : Juv.

Cadurci, ōrum, m. pl. *a tribe in Gallia Narbonensis* ; **Cadurcum**, ī, n. *a Cadurcian coverlet,* and Transf. : *a bed having a Cadurcian coverlet* : Juv.

cadus, ī, m. [κάδος], *a large vessel* (mostly of earthenware), *for containing liquids.* **a.** For wine : Pl., Verg. ; hence = *wine* : Hor. **b.** For other liquids : Plin., Mart. **c.** For the ashes of the dead (= urna) : Verg.

caecigenus, a, um [caecus and *gen.* in gignō], *born blind* : Lucr.

Caecilius, a, *name of a Roman gens* ; esp. Caecilius Statius, *a Roman comic poet, a contemporary of Ennius* ; hence **Caeciliānus**, a, um.

caecitās, ātis, f. [caecus], *blindness.* **1.** Lit. : Cic. **2.** Transf. : Cic.

caecō, āre [caecus], *to make blind, to blind.* **1.** Lit. : Lucr. **2.** Transf. **a.** mentis imperitorum, Cic. **b.** *to render obscure* : celeritate caecata oratio, Cic.

Caecubus ager, *a marshy district in S. Latium, famous for its wine* ; **Caecubus**, a, um ; **Caecubum**, ī, n. (sc. vinum), *this wine.*

Caeculus, ī, m. s. of Vulcan, and founder of Praeneste.

caecus, a, um, *blind.* **I.** *unseeing, blind.* **1.** Lit. : Cic., Lucr. ; corpus, i.e. *the back*, Sall. As Noun : ut si caecus iter monstrare velit, Hor. ; apparet id quidem etiam caeco, Liv. **2.** Transf. : *blind* (mentally or morally). **a.** Of persons : caecus atque amens tribunus, Cic. ; caecus furore, Verg. With *ad* : caecus ad has belli artis, Liv. **b.** Of the passions : cupiditas, Cic. ; Lucr. **c.** *random, indiscriminating, vague, aimless* : fortuna, suspicio, Cic. ; exsecrationes, Liv. ; caeco Marte resistunt, Verg. ; pavor, Tac. **II.** *not allowing sight, without light, blinding.* **1.** Lit. : nox, Lucr., Cic. ; domus (i.e. without windows), Cic. ; caligo, Verg. **2.** Transf. : *obscure* : exspectatio, Cic. ; crimen (i.e. without evidence), Liv. ; vestigia, Verg. **III.** *unseen, invisible, hidden.* **1.** Lit. : vallum, Caes. ; vulnus, Lucr. (also = a tergo, Verg.) ; fores, eventus, Verg. ; fata, Hor. **2.** Transf. : of mental objects : caecas exponere causas, Lucr. ; Cic. Verg. Comp. : Hor.

caedēs, is (GEN. pl. caedium), f. [caedō], *a cutting.* **1.** Lit. : of men, *a cutting down, slaughtering, carnage,* esp. in battle or by an assassin ; *murder* : Cic., Verg., etc. ; caedem facere, Caes. ; edere, perpetrare, Liv. ; committere, Ov., Quint. ; facere in aliquem, Sall., Tac. Also. *Pass : the slaughter* : Caes., Liv. Of beasts, in sacrifice or hunting : boum, Verg. ; studiosus caedis ferinae, Ov. **2.** Transf. **a.** *the persons slain* or. *murdered, the slain* : caedis acervi, Verg. **b.** *the blood shed, gore* : Verg. ; in pl. : Tac.

caedō, caedere, cecidī, caesum [cf. Gk. σχίζω], *to strike, beat, cut, kill.* **a.** *to strike, beat* : aliquem pugnis, Pl. ; ianuam saxis, Cic. ; calcibus arva, Verg. Esp. of flogging : virgis, Cic. ; Hor. **b.** *to cut* : lignum, Pl. ;

arbores, Cic.; silvam, materiam, Caes.; Verg. c. *to strike mortally, to kill, murder.* i. Of men : Cic., Ov.; esp. in war : Cic., Liv.; also *to cut to pieces* : exercitus caesus fususque, Cic.; Liv. ii. Of beasts, esp. in sacrifice : Cic., Verg.

caeduus, a, um [caedō], *fit for cutting* : silva, Cato; Varr.

caelāmen, inis, n. [caelō], *engraved work, a bas-relief* (rare) : Ov.

caelātor, ōris, m. [caelō], *a carver or engraver in bas-relief* : Cic., Juv.

caelātūra, ae, f. [caelō]. **1.** Lit.: *the art of carving or engraving in bas-reliefs,* esp. *in metals* : Quint. **2.** Transf.: *the engraved figures, carved work* : Sen. Ep., Quint.

caelebs, libis, adj. *unmarried, single* (i.e. a bachelor or a widower) : Pl., Cic., Ov.; vita, Hor., Tac. Of animals : columba, Plin. Of trees on which no vine has been trained : Hor., Ov.

caeles, itis, us. in pl. **caelĭtēs**, itum, adj. [caelum], *heavenly, celestial* (poet. for caelestis), Enn., Ov. As Noun : *an inhabitant of heaven* : Pl., Cic., Ov.

caelestis, e (ABL. *sing.* -te for -tī, Ov.; GEN. pl. -tum for -tium, Verg.), adj. [caelum]. **1.** Lit.: *of the sky or heaven, celestial* : ignis fulminis, Lucr.; Tac.; orbes, Cic.; aquae, Hor., Liv.; aerii mellis dona, Verg.; prodigia, Liv. As Noun, **caelestia**, n. pl., *the heavenly bodies* : Cic., Tac. **2.** Transf. **a.** *of the gods, divine* : numen, Cat.; animi, Vorg.; irae, Liv. As Noun (mostly pl.), *the gods* : Lucr., Cic., Verg., etc. Neut. pl. : *heavenly things* : Cic., Tac. **b.** In gen.: *divine, god-like* : legiones, Cic.; quos Elea domum reducit palma caelestis, Hor.; mens, Liv.

caelĭbātus, ūs, m. [caelebs], *celibacy* : Suet.

caelĭcola, ae (GEN. pl. caelicolum, Verg.), adj. [caelum colō], *dwelling in heaven, a god* : Enn., Verg.

caelĭfer, era, erum [caelum ferō], *supporting the heavens* : Verg.

caeli-potēns, entis, adj. [caelum potēns], *powerful in heaven* : Pl.

Caelius, a, *name of a Roman gens* ; esp. **I.** M. Caelius Rufus, *whom Cicero defended* ; **Caeliānus**, a, um. **II.** L. Caelius Antipater, *a historian of the time of the Gracchi.* **Caelius Mōns,** *one of the seven hills of Rome.*

caelō, āre [caelum], *to engrave in relief upon metals, to carve, engrave, chase.* **1.** Lit.: hanc speciem Praxiteles caelavit argento, Cic.; vasa caelata, Cic.; Verg., etc. **2.** Transf. **a.** Upon wood : Verg. **b.** Of poetry : caelatum musis opus, Hor.

(1) **caelum**, ī, n. [for caed-lum from caedō], *the chisel or burin of a sculptor or engraver* : Quint., Stat.

(2) **caelum**, ī, n. (old form **caelus**, ī, m. *in pl.* only caelī, Lucr.) [for cavilum, fr. cavus], *the sky, heaven, the heavens, the vault of heaven.* **1.** Lit. **a.** In gen.: Pl., Lucr., Cic., etc.; caelo albente, Caes. Phr.: de caelo tangi, i.e. *by lightning,* Cato, Verg., Liv.; also, e caelo ictus, Cic.; de caelo servare (i.e. in augury) : Cic.; de caelo fieri (of celestial signs), Cic. **b.** *Heaven* (as the abode of gods): Pl., Cic.,

Verg., etc. **c.** *the air, atmosphere, weather, climate* : serenum, Verg.; salubre, Cic.; palustre, Liv.; foedum (of the climate of Britain), Tac.; caelum non animum mutant, Hor. Of the upper air (of earth) opp. to the Lower World : falsa ad caelum mittunt insomnia Manes, Verg. **2.** Transf.: *the summit of prosperity, happiness, honour,* etc. : Caesar in caelum fertur, Cic.; in caelo sum, Cic. Ep.; exaequare aliquem caelo, Lucr.; Tac.; de caelo aliquem detrahere, Cic.; accipere, Ov.; recludere, Hor. [It. *cielo* ; Fr. *ciel.*]

caementum, ī, n. [caedō], *rough unhewn stone, rubble* (used for walls), us. in pl. : Cato, Cic., Hor., etc.

Caeneus, (disyl.), eī and eos, (voc. -neu or -ni) m. *orig. a girl, but later changed by Neptune into a boy.*

caenōsus, a, um [caenum], *muddy, boggy* : Juv.

caenum, ī, n. *dirt, filth, mud, mire* (alw. with idea of loathsomeness). **1.** Lit.: Pl., Cic., Verg., etc. **2.** Transf. **a.** *filth* (social and moral): Pl., Lucr., Liv. **b.** Of a man (in abuse): Pl., Cic.

caepa, ae, f. and **caepe**, is, n. (pl. caepae, ārum, f.), *an onion* : Enn., Hor., Ov. [It. *cipolla.*]

Caere, n. *indecl.* (f. GEN. -ritis, ABL. -ōte, Verg.), *an old city in Etruria, now Cervetri* ; hence, **Caeres**, itis and ētis, adj.: dignus Caerite cerā (i.e. without the right of voting), Hor.; **Caerĭtēs** (-ētēs), um, m. pl. *its inhabitants.*

caerimōnia, ae, f. **1.** Lit. (only in *sing.*). **a.** Subjectively, *reverence, veneration* (shown by external acts): Cic., Liv. **b.** Objectively, *sacredness, sanctity* (attaching to a person or thing) : Cic., Tac. **2.** Transf. (mostly in pl.) : *a solemnity, religious usage, sacred ceremony* (whilst *ritus* designates both sacred and profane rites) : Caes., Cic., Liv.

caeruleus (poet. also **caerulus**), a, um [for caeluleus, fr. caelum], *azure, blue.* **a.** *sky-blue* : Enn. As Noun in n. pl.: per caeli caerula, Lucr.; Ov. **b.** Of the sea, water, ice, etc.: Lucr., Verg., Ov. Of sea-deities : Prop., Hor. Of ships : Ov. As Noun in n. pl. (= the sea): Verg. **c.** *blue, dark blue* : oculi, Cic., Tac.; color (of woad), Caes.; serpens, draco, Ov.; Verg. **d.** *blue-green* : Palladis arbor, Ov. **e.** *blue-black, leaden* : imber, nubes, Verg.; hence, *dark, dun, dusky* : puppis Charonis, Verg.; equi Plutonis, Ov.

Caesar, aris, m. *a surname in the gens Iulia* ; esp. **I.** C. Iulius Caesar, *the famous statesman, general, orator, and author, assassinated by Brutus and Cassius,* B.C. 44. **Caesareus, Caesariānus, Caesarīnus,** a, um ; **Caesariānī,** ōrum, m. pl. *the adherents of Caesar in the Civil War.* **II.** C. Iulius Caesar Octavianus Augustus (q.v.), *after whom all the emperors bore the name Caesar, with the title Augustus, until, under Hadrian, Augustus was used to denote the ruling emperor, and Caesar, the heir to the throne.*

Caesariō, ōnis, m. *s. of Caesar by Cleopatra.*

caesariātus, a, um [caesariēs], *covered with hair* : Pl.

caesariēs, ēī, f. **I.** *a head of hair, hair* :

(mostly poet. and only *sing.*). Us. of men : Pl., Verg., Liv., etc. Also of women : Verg., Ov. **II.** *the hair of the beard* : Ov.

caesicius, a, um [caesius], *bluish, dark blue* : linteolum, Pl.

caesim, *adv.* [caedō], *by cutting, with cuts*. **1.** Lit. : Milit., *with the edge of the sword*, opp. to punctim: Liv. **2.** Transf. : of language : *in a clipped style* : Cic., Quint.

caesius, a, um, *bluish grey* (us. of the eyes): caesios oculos Minervae, Cic. ; hence, *grey-eyed* : Ter., Lucr., Cat.

caespes, itis, *m. a turf, sod.* **1.** Lit. : Caes. Used for altars, mounds (of tombs), for covering huts, sheds, etc. : Cic., Verg., etc. **2.** Transf. **a.** *the turf, sward* : Verg., Suet. **b.** *a hut or cot of turf* : Hor. **c.** *an altar of turf* : Hor., Tac.

caestus, ūs, *m.* [caedō], *a strap of bull's hide loaded with lead or iron, wound around the hands and arms, a boxing-glove* : Cic., Verg., etc.

caetra (or **cētra**), ae, *f. a short Spanish shield* : Verg., Liv., etc.

caetrātus, a, um [caetra], *armed with a caetra* : Caes., Liv. As Noun, **caetrātī**, ōrum, *m. pl. troops so armed* : Caes., Liv.

Caïcus, i, *m. a river in Mysia*.

Caïēta, ae (-ē, ēs), *f.* **I.** *the nurse of Aeneas*. **II.** *a town on the coast of Latium, now Gaeta*.

Caïus, *v.* Gāius.

Calabria, ae, *f. the S.E. peninsula of Italy* ; **Calaber**, bra, brum.

Calaïs, is, *m. the winged s. of Boreas and Orithyia, and b. of Zetes*.

Calamis, idis, *m. a famous Greek sculptor* (5th cent. B.C.).

calamister, trī, *m.* (**-um**, i, *n.* Pl., Varr.) [calamus], *a curling iron, crisping-pin*. **1.** Lit. : Pl., Cic. **2.** Transf. : of style : Cic., Tac.

calamistrātus, a, um [calamister], *curled with the iron* : Pl., Cic.

calamitās, ātis, *f.* perh. orig. *a blight*. **1.** Lit. : in farming, *damage, harm, loss* : fructuum, Cic. ; Pl. ; Ter. **2.** Transf. : *damage, mishap, injury*. **a.** In gen. : Pl. ; calamitates perferre, Caes. ; Cic. **b.** Esp. in war, *disaster, defeat* : calamitatem inferre alicui, Caes. ; Sall.

calamitōsē, *adv. disastrously* : Cic.

calamitōsus, a, um [calamitās]. **A.** Act. : *blighting*. **1.** Lit. : Cato, Cic. **2.** Transf. : *disastrous, destructive* : plebi incendium, Sall. ; bellum, Cic. *Sup.* : Cic. **B.** Pass. : *blighted, suffering great damage*. **1.** Lit. : agri, Cic. ; Cato. **2.** Transf. : otium, Cic. ; homines, Cic. Ep. *Comp.* : Cic. *Sup.* : Sen. Ep.

calamus, i, *m.* [κάλαμος], *a reed, cane* (pure Lat. harundō). **1.** Lit. : Cato. **2.** Transf. **a.** Of things of similar form, *any straw of grain, a stalk, stem* : Verg. **b.** Of objects made of reeds : *a reed-pen*: Cato, Cic. Ep., Hor. ; *a reed-pipe*: Lucr., Verg. ; *a dart, arrow*: Hor., Verg. ; *a fishing-rod* : Ov. [Fr. *chaume*.]

Calānus (Call-), i, *m. an Indian gymnosophist in the time of Alexander the Great ; in old age he burned himself on his funeral pile*.

calathiscus, i, *m.* [καλαθίσκος], *a small wicker basket* : Cat.

calathus, i, *m.* [κάλαθος], *a wicker basket, a hand-basket* (= quasillum). Acc. to diff. uses, *a flower-, wool-, thread-,* or *fruit-basket*, etc. : Verg., Ov. **2.** Transf. : *a bowl* of similar form, of metal or wood, for milk or wine : Verg.

calātor, ōris, *m.* [calō] (lit. *a servant for calling*, etc., *a crier* ; hence, in gen.), *any servant, attendant* : Pl.

calcāneum, i, *n.* [calx], *the heel* : Verg. [It. *calcagno*.]

calcar, āris, *n.* [calx], *a spur.* **1.** Lit. : Pl. ; incendere equum calcaribus, Hirt. ; subdere equo calcaria, Liv. ; equi fodere calcaribus armos, Verg. **2.** Transf. : calcaribus ictus amoris, Lucr. ; calcaribus uti, Cic. Prov. : addere calcaria sponte currenti, i.e. *to spur a willing horse*, Plin. Ep.

calcārius, a, um [calx, 2], *of lime* : Cato. *Masc.* as Noun, *a lime-burner* : Cato.

calceāmentum, i, *n.* [calceō], *shoeing, shoes* in gen. : Cic., Suet.

calceārium, i, *n.* [calceus], *shoe-money* : Suet.

calceātus, ūs, *m.* [calceō], *a shoe or sandal* : Plin., Suet.

calceō, āre [calceus], *to furnish with shoes, to shoe* : Cic., Suet. ; pedes, Phaedr. Of animals : Suet. Comic. : dentes calceati, Pl. [Fr. *chausser*.]

calceolārius, i, *m. a shoemaker* : Pl.

calceolus, i, *m.* [*dim.* calceus], *a small shoe, a half-boot* : Cic.

calceus, i, *m.* [calx], *a walking shoe, a half-boot* : Cic., Hor., etc. ; calceos poscere (*v.* solea), *to rise from table* (since the Romans took off their shoes at meals), Plin. Ep. ; calceos mutare, i.e. *to become a senator* (from the peculiar shoes worn by senators), Cic.

Calchās, antis (Acc. -anta, Verg. ; Abl. Calchā, Pl.), *m. s. of Thestor, the most famous Greek seer at Troy*.

calcitrō, āre [calx], *to strike with the heels, to kick.* **1.** Lit. **1.** Of animals : Plin. **2.** Transf. : *to resist, to be stubborn or refractory* : Cic. **II.** *to strike convulsively with the feet, to writhe*, of one dying : Ov.

calcitrō, ōnis, *m. a kicker.* **1.** Lit. : equus, Varr. **2.** Transf. : of men : *a boisterous fellow, a blusterer* : Pl.

calcō, āre [calx], *to tread upon, to trample under foot, to walk over.* **1.** Lit. : uvam, Cato ; Ov. ; Verg. ; morientem acervos, Ov. ; Tac. ; scopulos, litora, Ov. ; calcanda semel via leti, Hor. **2.** Transf. **a.** *to trample upon, oppress* : libertatem, Liv. ; amorem, Ov. **b.** *to spurn* : Prop., Quint.

calculus, i, *m.* [*dim.* calx, 2]. **I.** *a small stone, a pebble* : Cic., Verg. **II.** *a counter used in playing draughts* : Ov., Quint. ; hence, calculum reducere, *to take back a move*, i.e. *retrace one's steps*, Cic. **III.** *a pebble used for reckoning* ; hence, *a reckoning, computing, calculating* : calculum alicuius rei subducere, *to compute*, Cic. ; ad calculos vocare aliquid, *to subject to an accurate reckoning*, Cic. ; aliquem ad calculos vocare, *to settle accounts with any one*, Liv. ; cum aliquā re parem calculum ponere, i.e. *to return equal for equal*, Plin. Ep. **IV.** *a pebble used in voting* : Ov., Plin. Ep.

Cal 91 Cal

caldārius, a, um [calda], *having warm water : cella*, Plin. Ep.

caldus, a, um, *v.* calidus.

Calēdonia, ae, *f. the N. part of Britannia*, now *the Highlands of Scotland ;* hence **Calēdonius**, a, um.

calefaciō (contr. **calfaciō**), facere, fēci, factum : *Inf. Pass.* calefieri and calfieri [caleō faciō], *to make warm or hot, to warm, heat.* **1.** Lit.: corpus, Cic.; Pl.; Ov. **2.** Transf.: *to heat, to anger, excite, etc. :* hominem, Cic. Ep.; calefactaque corda tumultu, Verg.

calefactō, āre [*freq.* calefaciō], *to make warm, to warm, heat.* **1.** Lit.: aquam, Pl.; Hor. **2.** Transf.: aliquem virgis, Pl.

calefieri, *v.* calefaciō.

Calendae, *v.* Kalendae.

caleō, ēre (calitūrus, Ov.; *impers.* calētur, Pl.), *to be warm or hot, to glow with heat* (opp. frigere): **1.** Lit.: Pl., Cic.; Sabaeo ture calent arae, Verg. Comic. of persons : *to feel warm :* Pl. **2.** Of persons : Cic. Ep.; Romani calentes ab recenti pugnā, Liv.; amore, Ov.; feminā, Hor.; morbo mentis, Hor.; scribendi studio, Hor. Of animals: (leones) caede calentes, Lucr. **b.** Of abstract things : *to be urged on hotly, i.e. enthusiastically :* illud crimen caluit re recenti, nunc in causā refrixit, Cic.; Tib. **c.** *to be yet warm, new, or fresh :* at enim nihil est, nisi dum calet hoc agitur, Pl.

Calēs, ium, *f. pl. a town in N. Campania, famous for its wine,* now *Calvi ;* **Calēnus**, a, um ; **Calēnum**, i, *n. its wine.*

calescō calēscere, caluī [caleō], *to grow or become warm or hot* (opp. refrigescere). **1.** Lit.: Cic., Ov., etc. **2.** Transf.: *to become inflamed with love, etc. :* Ter., Ov.

calfaciō and **calfieri**, *v.* calefaciō.

calidē, *adv. promptly*, Pl.

calidus (Cic., and us. in poets). and **caldus** (in Aug. prose), a, um. (*Comp.* caldior, Hor.) [caleō], *warm, hot.* **1.** Lit.: Cato, Lucr., Cic., etc. As Noun : **calida** (**calda**), ae, *f. warm water :* Cato, Tac.; **calidum**, i, *n. a warm drink* (of wine and water) : Pl. **2.** Transf. **a.** *hot, fiery, impetuous.* Of living beings : Verg., Hor. Hence, consilium, Ter., Cic., Liv. **b.** *brisk, prompt :* consilium, mendacium, Pl. *Comp. :* Hor., Liv. [It. caldo ; Fr. chaud.]

caliendrum, i, *n.* [καλλυντρον, *ornament*], *woman's headdress made of false hair :* Hor.

caliga, ae, *f.* [*cf.* calceus], *a strong and heavy shoe, studded with iron nails, worn by Roman soldiers.* **1.** Lit.: Cic. Ep. **2.** Transf.: *the soldiers :* offendere tot caligas, Juv.

caligātus, a, um [caliga], *wearing heavy shoes :* Juv.

cālīginōsus, a, um [cālīgō], *covered with mist, foggy, murky.* **1.** Lit.: caelum, Cic. **2.** Transf.: of obscurity : nox, Hor.

cālīgō, inis, *f.* **1.** Lit. **a.** *mist, fog :* Lucr., Verg., Liv. **b.** *darkness, gloom :* Pl., Cic., Ov., etc. **c.** *mistiness* before the eyes, caused by dizziness : Liv. **2.** Transf. **a.** *mental fogginess, obtuseness :* Cic., Cat. **b.** Of *affliction and trouble, gloom :* Cic., Quint.

cālīgō, āre [cālīgō]. **A.** Intrans.: *to be wrapped in mist* or *darkness.* **1.** Lit.: Verg. **2.** Transf.: Sen. **B.** Trans. (v. rare). **a.** *to veil in darkness, obscure :* Verg. **b.** *to cause mistiness and dizziness to :* Juv.

caligula, ae, *f.* [*dim.* caliga], *a small military boot :* Tac.

Caligula, ae, *m.* the pet name given by the soldiers to Gaius (q.v.) s. of Germanicus.

calix, icis, *m.* [κυλιξ]. **I.** *a cup, goblet :* calix mulsi, Cic.; Pl.; Hor.; hence = wine : Cat., Hor. **II.** *a cooking vessel, pot :* Cato, Ov. [Fr. *calice* ; Eng. *chalice.*]

calleō, ēre [callum]. **A.** Intrans.: *to be thick-skinned.* **1.** Lit.: plagis costae callent, Pl. **2.** Transf. **a.** *to be hardened, callous, insensible :* Sulpic. ap. Cic. Ep. **b.** *to be practised, to be wise by experience :* omnes homines ad suum quaestum callent, Pl.; ea quorum usu calleret, Liv. **B.** Transf.: *to know by experience* or *practice, to be versed in :* Pl.; iura, Cic.; Hor., etc. With *Inf.* : duramque callet pauperiem pati, Hor.; Lucr. With *Indir. Quest. :* Ter.

Callicratidās, ae, *m. a Spartan commander, defeated and killed in the naval battle of Arginusae,* B.C. 406.

callidē, *adv.* [callidus]. **I.** *skilfully, expertly :* Pl., Cic. *Comp. :* Tac. *Sup. :* Nep. **II.** *cunningly, craftily :* Pl., Cic., Sall.

calliditās, ātis, *f.* [callidus]. **I.** *skilfulness, dexterity, expertness :* Cic., Ov., etc. **II.** *cunning :* Cic., Ov. In war : Liv. In *pl., sly tricks :* Ter.

callidus, a, um [calleō]. **I.** *worldly-wise, experienced, expert, skilful :* Pl., Lucr., Cic. With GEN.: rei militaris, Tac. With ABL.: Pers. With *Inf.* : Hor. Also of things : artificium (naturae), Cic.; Hor. *Comp.* and *Sup. :* Cic. **II.** In bad sense : *crafty, cunning, artful, sly :* Pl., Cic., Tac.; ad fraudem callidi, Cic. Also of things : doli, Pl.; audacia, Cic. *Comp. :* Ter.

Callimachus, i, *m. a distinguished Greek poet and grammarian at Alexandria* (c. B.C. 270) ; *born at Cyrene.*

Calliopē, ēs (-pēa, ae), *f. the chief of the Muses, goddess of Epic poetry, and, in the poets, sometimes of every other kind of poetry.*

Calliphōn, ōntis (ACC. -ōntem, DAT. -ōnī, Cic.), *m. a Greek ethical philosopher who made the 'chief good' to consist in virtue with pleasure.*

Callirrhoē (poet. **Callirhoē**), ēs, *f.* **I.** *d. of R. Acheloüs, and second w. of Alcmaeon.* **II.** *a famous spring at Athens.*

callis, is, *m.* (*f.* Liv.), *a cattle-track, mountain-track, forest-path.* **1.** Lit.: Liv., Verg. **2.** Transf.: *hill-* or *forest-pastures :* Cic., Liv., Tac.

Callisthenēs, is, *m. a philosopher of Olynthus, pupil of Aristotle and friend of Alexander the Great, by whom he was finally put to death.*

Callistō, ūs (DAT. -ō, Cat.), *f. d. of an Arcadian king, Lycaon, m. of Arcas by Jupiter ; changed into a she-bear and placed in the heavens by Jupiter as the constellation Helice* or *Ursa Maior.*

callōsus, a, um [callum], *with a hard skin, thick-skinned*. Hence, *solid, fleshy :* ova, Hor.

callum, i, *n. hardened skin* (esp. on the feet or hands). **1.** Lit.: Lucr., Cic. In *pl.* Suet. Hence, **a.** *firm flesh :* aprugnum, Pl. ; for which also absol. callum, Pl. **b.** Of the hard skin of plants, etc.: Plin. **2.** Transf.: *hardness, callousness, insensibility :* ipse labor quasi callum quoddam obducit dolori, Cic. ; Quint.

calō, or **kalō**, āre (an old word) [*cf.* Gk. καλέω], *to call out, proclaim, convoke* (only in religious matters): calata comitia, *comitia called for consecrating a priest or a king,* Gell. Hence, calatis granis, Cic.

cālō, ōnis, *m. an army servant, soldier's servant :* Caes., Liv. Hence, *any groom, a drudge :* Cic., Hor.

calor, ōris, *m.* [caleō], *warmth, heat, glow.* **1.** Lit. **a.** In gen.: Pl., Cic., Verg., etc. In *pl.* : Cic. **b.** *vital heat :* Cic., Verg. **c.** *summer heat :* vitandi caloris causā Lanuvi tris horas adquieveram, Cic. Ep. Hence, also *summer,* Lucr. ; esp. in *pl.* : mediis caloribus, Liv. ; Cic. **d.** Of winds : calores austrini, Verg. **e.** Of fever : Tib. **2.** Transf.: *the heat of passion, ardour, impetuosity :* calor ac spiritus, Quint. ; dicendi, Quint. Poet.: *the fire of love :* trahere calorem, Ov. In *pl.* : Hor., Ov. [Fr. *chaleur.*]

Calpurnius, a, *name of a Roman gens, which includes the Bestiae, Bibuli, Pisones ;* **Calpurniānus**, a, um.

caltha, ae, *f. a yellow flower,* prob. *pot marigold :* Verg.

calthula, ae, *f.* [caltha], *a yellow robe* (for women) : Pl.

calumnia (or **kalumnia**), ae, *f. trickery, chicanery.* **I.** In gen. **a.** *sharp practice :* cum calumniā senatūs auctoritas impediretur, Cic. ; Sall. In *pl.* : Cic. Ep. **b.** *subterfuge, pretext :* religionis calumnia, Cic. Ep. ; in calumniā delitescere, Cic. **c.** *misrepresentation, perversion of the truth :* haec effugiunt Academicorum calumniam, Cic. **II.** In law. **a.** *a false accusation, dishonest legal procedure :* Cic., Liv. ; in *pl.* : Cic. ; calumniam iurare, *to swear that one did not bring a malicious accusation,* Cael. ap. Cic. Ep. ; Liv. **b.** *an action for malicious accusation :* Cic., Phaedr., Tac.

calumniātor (**kal-**), ōris, *m.* [calumnior], mostly in law, *a false accuser, perverter of law :* Cic., Mart.

calumnior (and **kalumnior**), ārī [calumnia]. **I.** In gen.: *to misrepresent, censure unfairly :* Cic. Ep. With *Refl.* Pron. : *to misrepresent* or *depreciate oneself :* Quint. Absol. : Cic. Ep. **II.** In law : *to make a false accusation, misrepresent :* Cic., Liv.

calva, ae, *f. the skull without hair :* Liv., Mart.

calvitiēs, ēī, *f.* (Suet) and **calvitium**, i, *n.* (Cic.) [calvus], *baldness.*

calvor, i, *to devise tricks, use artifice, to deceive :* Pl.

calvus, a, um, *bald, without hair :* Pl., Suet. Of plants : Cato, Mart. [Fr. *chauve.*]

(1) calx, calcis, *f. the heel.* **1.** Lit.: calces deteris, Pl. ; ferratā calce, Verg. ; certare pugnis, calcibus, unguibus, Cic. ; *caedere* calcibus, *to kick,* Pl. Prov.: adversus stimulum calces (*sc.* iactare, etc.), Ter. **2.** Transf.: *a kick :* Juv.

(2) calx, calcis, *f.* (sometimes *m.*). **1.** Lit. **a.** *a small stone :* hence *a counter* or *draught* (rare for *dim.* calculus, *q.v.*) : Pl. **b.** *lime-stone, lime,* whether slaked or unslaked : Cato, Lucr., Cic. ; viva, *quicklime,* Vitr. **2.** Transf.: *the line marked with lime* or *chalk* (i.e. the goal in a race-course ; opp. to carceres, *q.v.*) : ad calcem pervenire, Cic. ; Lucr. Prov.: ad carceres a calce revocari, i.e. to have to do a thing all over again, Cic. [Fr. *chaux.*]

Calydōn, ōnis, *f. an ancient town in Aetolia, on the R. Evenus, the residence of Oeneus, f. of Meleager and Deianira, g.f. of Diomedes ; famous for the hunt of the boar sent by Diana and killed by Meleager ;* **Calydōnius**, a, um, heros, i.e. *Meleager ;* **Calydōnis**, idis, *f. adj.* ; *as Noun =* Deianira.

Calypsō, ūs (Acc. -ō), *f. a nymph, d. of Atlas* (or *of Oceanus*)*, who lived in the island of Ogygia.*

calyx, ycis, *m.* [κάλυξ]. **I.** *the calyx of a flower :* Plin. **II.** *shell* (of shell-fish, etc.) : Plin.

camara, ae, *v.* camera.

Cambysēs, is, *m. s. and successor of the elder Cyrus ; king of Persia.*

camella, ae, *f.* [*dim.* camera], *a kind of drinking vessel, a goblet :* Ov.

camēlus, i, *m. a camel, a dromedary :* Cic., Hor., etc. [Fr. *chameau.*]

Camēna, ae, *f.* [orig. casmēna ; fr. root meaning *to relate, sing*], *a* (Latin) *muse :* Verg., Liv., etc.

camera (also **camara**), ae, *f.* [καμάρα]. **I.** *a vault, an arched roof, an arch :* Cic. Ep., Lucr. **II.** *a flat ship with an arched covering :* Tac. [Fr. *chambre.*]

Camerinum, i, *n. a town in Umbria,* now *Camerino ;* hence **Camers**, ertis, *adj.* ; **Camertēs**, ium, *m. pl. its inhabitants ;* **Camertinus**, a, um.

Camilla, ae, *f. a Volscian heroine who was killed in the war between Aeneas and Turnus.*

Camillus, i, *m. a cognomen of several persons in the gens Furia ;* esp. M. Furius Camillus, *who took Veii and freed Rome from the Gauls.*

caminus, i, *m.* [ἡ κάμινος]. **I.** *a furnace, fire-place :* Cic. Ep. ; Hor. **II.** *a smelting furnace, a forge :* Verg., Ov., Juv. Prov.: oleum addere camino, i.e. *to aggravate an evil,* Hor. [Fr. *cheminée* and from it Eng. *chimney.*]

cammarus (**gamm-**), i, *m.* [κάμμαρος], *a kind of lobster :* Varr., Juv.

Campānia, ae, *f. a region on the E. coast of central Italy ; chief city, Capua ;* **Campānicus, Campānius, Campānus,** a, um ; **Campāns,** antis, *adj.* ; **Campāni,** ōrum, *m. pl. the Campanians* or *Capuans.*

campē, ēs, *f.* [κάμπη], *a winding, writhing :* campas dicere, i.e. *to seek evasions,* Pl.

campester, tris, tre [campus]. **I.** *of a plain, flat, champaign. level :* opp. montanus and collinus : campestres ac demissi loci, Caes.; iter, Caes. ; urbs, barbari, Liv. ; Hor. ; hostis, i.e. *fighting in a plain,* Liv. As

Noun: **campestria**, ium, *n. pl.*, *flat land, level ground :* pauca campestrium, Tac. **II.** *relating to* or *held in the Campus Martius :* ludus, Cic.; proelia, Hor. As Noun. **campestre**, is, *n. (sc. velamentum), a loin-cloth, apron* (worn for sports): Hor. **III.** *pertaining to the comitia held in the Campus Martius :* gratia, Liv.; Cic.

campus i, *n. an even, flat space, a plain.* **1.** Lit. **a.** In gen.: Cic., Verg., etc. **b.** Esp. *the Campus Martius* at Rome. **i.** As a place of assembly for the Roman people : Cic., Hor., etc.; e campo comitia ad patres translata sunt, Tac. Hence, *the comitia themselves :* curiam pro senatu, campum pro comitiis, Cic. **ii.** As a place for games, exercise, recreation, military drills, etc. : Cic., Hor. (There were other *campi* at Rome, as the Campus Esquilinus, etc.) **c.** In *pl.*, of certain regions, e.g. Campi Aleii (in Lycia), Campi Lapidei (in S. Gaul), Campi Macri (in N. Italy), Campi Magni (in Africa), Campi Veteres (in Lucania). **2.** Transf. **a.** *a field of action, subject of debate*, etc. : magnus est in re publicā campus, Cic. **b.** Poet. : *any level surface* (as of the sea): Pl., Lucr.; campos salis aere secabant, Verg. [Fr. *champ*.]

Camulodūnum, i, *n. a town of the Trinobantes in Britain*, now *Colchester.*

camur, ura, urum [*cf.* camera], *crooked, bent inwards :* cornua, Verg.

Canacē, ēs, *f. d. of Aeolus and s. of Macareus.*

canālis, is, *m. a channel, conduit, gutter, waterpipe :* Cato, Caes., Verg., etc.

cancelli, ōrum, *m. pl.* [*dim.* cancer, 2]. **1.** Lit. : *an enclosure of wood, a railing, grating, balustrade by which a place is enclosed and protected :* fori, Cic.; *the barrier in the public spectacles :* Cic.; circi, Ov. **2.** Transf. : *boundaries, limits :* extra hos cancellos egredi, Cic.

(1) cancer, crī (GEN. canceris, Lucr.), *m. a crab.* **1.** Lit. : Pl., Verg. **2.** Transf. **a.** A sign of the Zodiac, the Crab : Cic., Lucr., Ov. Hence, *the south :* Ov. and *great heat:* Ov. **b.** *cancer :* Cato, Ov. [It. *granchio, cancro ;* Fr. *cancre, chancre.*]

(2) cancer, crī, *m.* [cogn. with κιγκλίς], *a lattice :* Fest.

cande-faciō, facere, fēci, factum [candeō faciō], *to make dazzlingly white :* Pl.

candēla, ae, *f.* [candeō]. **I.** *a wax-light, tallow candle, torch, taper* (used by the poor, and in funeral processions): Juv. Prov.: candelam apponere valvis, i.e. to set the house on fire, Juv. **II.** *a waxed cord :* Liv.

candēlābrum, i, *n.* [candēla], *a candlestick, a chandelier :* Cic., Mart.

candēns, entis. **I.** *Part.* candeō. **II.** *Adj. : shining white, glittering :* marmor, Lucr.; taurus, elephantus, Verg.; lilia, Ov.

candeō, ēre, *to be of brilliant whiteness, to shine, glitter* (mostly poet). **1.** Lit. : ubi canderet vestis, Hor.; Cat. **2.** Transf. : *to be white hot, to be glowing hot :* ut calidis candens ferrum e fornacibus stridit, Lucr.; Dionysius candente carbone sibi adurebat capillum, Cic.; Hor.

candēscō, candēscere, candui [candeō], *to become glittering white, to glisten.* **1.** Lit. : ut solet aer candescere solis ab ortu, Ov.

2. Transf. : *to grow white-hot :* ferrum candescit in igni, Lucr.; Ov.

candidātōrius, a, um [candidātus], *of a candidate :* Cic. Ep.

candidātus, a, um [candidus], *clothed in pure white :* Pl., Suet. Hence, **candidātus**, ī, *m. a candidate for office* (lit. clothed in a white toga). **1.** Lit. : Cic., etc. **2.** Transf. : candidatus immortalitatis et gloriae, Plin. Pan.

candidē, adv. *in dazzling white :* vestitus, Pl. Transf. : *clearly, simply :* Quint.

candidulus, a, um [*dim.* candidus], *beautifully white :* only of small objects : dentes, Cic.

candidus, a, um [candeō], *of a dazzling white, gleaming* (opp. to *niger*, a glistening or lustrous black : while *albus* is a dead white, opp. to *ater*, a dead black). **1.** Lit. **a.** In gen.: stella, Pl.; sidera, Lucr.; vela, Cat.; vestis, Liv.; luna, barba, populus, avis, Verg.; equi, Tac. **b.** Of the complexion or personal beauty. *fair, lustrous, radiant :* Daphnis, Dido, Verg.; cervix, Hor. Prov. : candida de nigris facere, Ov. Poet. for candidatus, *clothed in white :* pompa, Ov.; candida sententia = candidi lapilli, i.e. *a sentence of acquittal*, Ov. **2.** Transf. **a.** Of conditions of life : *bright, clear, serene :* pax, fata, Tib.; nox, Prop.; dies, Ov. **b.** Of mind and character, *frank, sincere, open, candid :* Hor., Ov., Plin. Ep. **c.** Of style, *clear, perspicuous, unaffected :* genus dicendi, Cic.; Quint. Of the orator himself : Quint. Comp. : Verg., Plin. Ep. Sup. : Varr., Quint.

candor, ōris, *m.* [candeō], *a dazzling, glossy whiteness, radiance, brightness*, etc. **1.** Lit. **a.** In gen.: solis, Cic.; Lucr.; nivali candore equi, Verg; tunicarum, Liv. **b.** Of complexion : Cic., Tib., Prop. In *pl.* : Pl. **2.** Transf. **a.** Of mind or character, *frankness, sincerity, candour :* Ov., Plin. Pan. **b.** Of style, *simplicity, naturalness :* Quint. **c.** Of discourse, *brilliance :* fucatus, Cic.

canēns, entis, *Part.* canō.

cānēns, entis. **I.** *Part.* cāneō. **II.** *Adj. grey, greyish :* Verg., Ov.

cāneō, ēre, uī [cānus], *to be white* or *hoary :* temporibus geminis canebat sparsa senectus, Verg.; pruina, Ov.

canēs, is, *v.* canis.

cānēscō, ere [cāneō], *to grow white* or *hoary.* **1.** Lit.: pubula canescunt, Ov. **2.** Transf. **a.** *to grow old :* Cic., Ov. **b.** *to grow feeble* (of discourse): cum ipsa oratio iam nostra canesceret, Cic.; Quint.

canicula, ae, *f.* [*dim.* canis], *a small dog* or *bitch.* **1.** Lit. : Plin. As a term of abuse : Pl. **2.** Transf. : *the Dog-star, Sirius :* flagrans, Hor.; Ov.

canīnus, a, um [canis], *of a dog, canine.* **1.** Lit.: dentes, Varr.; lac, Ov.; scaeva canina, *a favourable augury from a dog*, Pl. **2.** Transf.: littera, *the letter R*, Pers.; eloquentia, *snarling*, Quint.; verba, *biting words*, Ov.

canis (also **canēs**, apēs, apēs, *for* aedis, apis, etc., Pl.), is, *m.f.* [*cf.* κύων stem κυν-], *hound.* **1.** Lit. : Pl.; canum fida custodia, Cic.; vigiles, Hor.; obscenae, Verg. **2.** Transf. **a.** Of a shameless or enraged person : Pl., Hor., Suet. **b.** Of a hanger-on or parasite : multa sibi opus esse, multa canibus suis, quos circa se haberet, Cic. **c.** Of dice, *the worst throw :* damnosi canes, Ov. ; mittere, Suet. **d.** *a constellation,* Canis Maior, whose brightest star is the Dog-star (canicula or Sirius) : Cic., Verg., etc. ; and Minor, commonly called Ante-canis (hence *pl.* canes) : Ov. **e.** *the sea-dog :* Plin. ; and mythically, of *the dogs of Scylla :* Lucr., Cic., Verg. [It. *cane ;* Fr. *chien.*]

canistra, ōrum, *n. pl.* [κάναστρα], *wicker baskets for bread, fruit, flowers,* etc. (esp. for religious use in sacrifices) : Cic. Ep., Verg., etc.

cānitiēs, em, ē (other cases not used), *f.* [cānus], *a grey* or *greyish-white colour, hoari-ness.* **1.** Lit.: Ov. Esp. of *grey hair :* Cat., Verg., Ov. **2.** Transf.: *old age :* Hor.

canna, ae, *f.* [κάννα], *a reed, cane.* **1.** Lit.: palustris, Ov. **2.** Transf.: of *things made of reed.* **a.** *a reed pipe, flute :* Ov. **b.** *a small vessel, gondola :* Juv.

cannabis, ae, *f.* (and less freq. **cannabum,** i, *n.*) [κάνναβις and κάνναβος], *hemp :* Varr., Pers. [It. *canape ;* Fr. *chanvre.*]

Cannae, ārum, *f. pl. a village in Apulia, on the S. bank of the R. Aufidus, famous for a great victory won by Hannibal over the Romans near it,* B.C. 216 ; **Cannēnsis,** e, *adj.*

canō, canere, cecinī [*cf.* καναχή], *to produce (musical) notes ; to sing* or *play.* **A.** Intrans. **a.** Of men : absurde, Cic. ; imitabere Pana canendo, Verg. ; tibiā, Lucr. ; Cic. ; citharā, Tac. Also of faulty delivery : *to speak in a sing-song tone :* Cic. **b.** Of birds, etc. : galli, Cic. ; Ter. ; volu-cres, Prop. ; ranae, Verg. **c.** Of instru-ments, etc. : *to sound, resound :* tibiae, Cic. ; Prop. Of the music of the spheres : (nisi putamus) ad harmoniam canere mun-dum, Cic. **d.** Milit. *to sound.* **i.** With person as subject : Hasdrubal receptui cecinit, Liv. Transf.: revocante et receptui canente senatu, Cic. **ii.** With instrument as subject : classicum apud eos cecinit, Liv. ; Verg. **iii.** Impers.: nisi receptui cecinisset, Liv. **B.** Trans. **a.** With Acc.: carmen, cantilenam, versūs, verba, etc. : carmina, quae in epulis can-untur, Cic. ; praecepta canere, Hor. ; carmen, Verg. ; verba ad certos modos, Ov. Prov.: carmen intus canere (of one who thinks only of his own advantage), Cic. ; cantilenam eandem canis, *always the same old song,* Ter.: canere aliquid surdis auribus, i.e. *to preach to deaf ears,* Liv. **b.** *to sing of, to celebrate in song :* clarorum virorum laudes atque virtutes, Cic. ; deos regesve, Hor. ; Verg. With Acc. and *Inf.:* Verg. With *Indir. Quest. :* Lucr. **c.** *to foretell, pre-dict* (since the responses of oracles were usually in verse) : Cic., Verg., etc. **d.** *to sound* or *play an instrument,* esp. milit. : classicum cani iubet, Caes. ; bellicum canere, Cic. ; (dea) pastorale signum canit, Verg. Poet.: cecinit iussos receptūs, Ov.

canor, ōris, *m.* [canō]. **I.** *tune, song :* cycni, Lucr. ; Quint. **II.** *sounding :* Martius aeriā rauci canor, Verg.

canōrus, a, um [canor], *tuneful, melodious, harmonious.* **A.** Act. **a.** Of persons or living things producing sound : orator, Cic. ; aves, Verg. ; Triton, vox, Ov. As a fault in delivery, *in a sing-song, droning tone :* sine contentione vox, nec languens, nec canora, Cic. **b.** Of instruments : fides, Verg., Hor. ; aes, Verg. **B.** Pass.: of things uttered : versus, Hor. ; nugae, *mere jingling,* Hor. ; Suet. *Neut.* as Noun, *melodious style :* omnino canorum illud in voce splendescit, Cic.

Cantaber, brī, and *pl.* **Cantabrī,** ōrum, *m. the people of the district* **Cantabria** (ae, *f.*) *in N.W. Spain ;* **Cantabricus,** a, um.

cantāmen, inis, *n.* [cantō], *a spell, incanta-tion :* Prop.

cantātor, ōris, *m.* [cantō], *a singer :* Mart.

cantharis, idis, *f.* [κανθαρίς], *a genus of beetles :* of several species, freq. used in medicine, Plin. ; esp. *the* (poisonous) *Spanish fly :* Cic., Ov.

cantharus, i, *m.* [κάνθαρος]. **I.** *a large, wide-bellied drinking vessel with handles, a tankard, pot :* Pl. ; potare modicis can-tharis, Hor. ; gravis pendebat cantharus ansā, Verg. **II.** *a kind of sea-fish :* Ov., Plin.

canthērīnus, a, um [canthērius], *of a horse :* Pl.

canthērius (cant-), i, *m.* [κανθήλιος], *a gelding :* Pl., Cic. Prov.: minime can-therium in fossam. Liv.

canthus, i, *m.* [κανθός], *a wheel-tire :* Quint. Transf.: *a wheel :* Pers.

canticum, i, *n.* [cantus], *a song.* **I.** *the lyrical passage in the Roman comedy, sung by one person, and accompanied by music and dancing ; a solo :* Cic. Ep. ; agere, Liv.; desaltare, Suet. **II.** *a song,* in gen. : Phaedr., Quint. **III.** *a singing tone in the delivery of an orator :* Cic., Plin. Ep.

cantilēna, ae, *f.* [cantus], *an old song,* colloq. for *silly prattle, gossip :* Cic. Prov.: cantilenam eandem canis, Ter.

cantiō, ōnis, *f.* [canō]. **I.** *a singing, a song :* Pl., Suet. **II.** *an incantation, charm, spell :* Cic. [It. *canzone ;* Fr. *chanson.*]

cantitō, āre [freq. cantō], *to sing* or *play re-peatedly :* Ter., Cic.

Cantium, i, *n. a district in Britain, now Kent.*

cantiuncula, ae, *f.* [dim. cantiō], *an alluring song :* Cic.

cantō, āre [freq. canō], *to sing, play,* etc. **A.** Intrans. **a.** Of men : Ter., Cic., Verg., etc. ; cantare ad manum histrioni (the actor accompanied the song with gestures or dancing, Liv. ; fidibus, Pl. ; avenis, Ov. Prov.: ad surdas auris, Ov. Of faulty delivery : *to declaim in a singing tone, to drawl :* si cantas, male cantas, si legis, cantas, Caes. ap. Quint. ; Juv. So of any monotonous sound : ocima, *to cry herbs* (*for sale*), Pers. **b.** Of birds : deos gallis sig-num dedisse cantandi, Cic. ; Pl.; Prop. **c.** Of instruments : tibia, Ov. Transf. for fiction : non est cantandum, res vera agitur, Juv. **B.** Trans. with Acc. of car-men, versus, etc. **a.** *to sing, play, recite :* Hymenaeum, Ter. ; carmina non prius audita canto, Hor. ; Ov. **b.** *to sing of, to celebrate* or *praise in song :* Caesarem,

Cic.; Verg.; Augusti tropaea, Hor. **c.**
to harp on, i.e. *repeat, reiterate :* Pl. **d.** Of
an actor : *to enact, represent a part :* fabulam, Orestem, Suet. **e.** *to predict :* vera
cantas ? vana vellem, Pl.; Tib. **f.** *to use
charms, incantations, to enchant :* Cato ;
frigidus in pratis cantando rumpitur anguis,
Verg.; cantatum carmen, Ov. [Fr. *chanter.*]

cantor, ōris, *m.* [canō]. **I.** *a musician,
singer, poet.* **1.** Lit.: Hor., Suet. **2.**
Transf. **a.** (*cf.* canto, B.c.): cantor
formularum, Cic. **b.** With GEN. of the
person : *an extoller, eulogist :* cantores
Euphorionis, Cic. **II.** *an actor, player :*
Cic., Hor. [Fr. *chanteur.*]

cantrix, īcis, *f.* [canō], *a female musician or
singer :* Pl. As *fem. Adj. :* Varr.

cantus, ūs, *m.* [canō]. **I.** *tone, melody,
singing, playing.* **a.** Of men and instruments : cantus vocum et nervorum et
tibiarum, Cic.; Verg.; lugubres cantūs,
Hor.; est autem in dicendo etiam quidam
cantus obscurior, Cic. **b.** Of animals :
Lucr.; Cic.; sub galli cantum, Hor.;
Enn.; Cic. **II.** *a prophecy, prediction :*
Cat. **III.** *an incantation :* Verg., Ov.
[Fr. *chant.*]

Canulēius, a, *name of a Roman* gens;
esp. C. Canuleius (*trib. pleb.* B.C. 445),
*author of a law permitting intermarriage of
patricians and plebeians.*

cānus, a, um, *white, hoary, grey.* **1.** Lit.:
fluctus, nix, Lucr.; gelu, montes, Verg.;
lupus, aqua, Ov. Esp. of *white* or *grey
hair' :* cano capite atque albā barbā, Pl.;
Hor.; Ov. As Noun, **cānī,** ōrum, *m. pl.*
(*sc.* capilli), *grey hairs :* non cani, non
rugae repente auctoritatem adripere possunt, Cic.; Ov. **2.** Transf.: *hoary,
ancient :* senectus, Cat.; Fides, Verg.

Canusium, I, *n. a Greek town in Apulia,
famous for its wool, now Canosa :* **Canusīnus,** a, um ; **Canusīnus,** ī, *m.* an inhabitant of the town; **Canusīna,** ae, *f. a
garment of its wool :* **Canusīnātus,** a, um,
clothed in its wool.

capācītās, ātis, *f.* [capāx], *a capability of
holding, capacity :* Cic.

Capaneus (trisyl.), eī (Voc. -eu, Ov.), *m.
one of the seven heroes who attacked Thebes.*

capāx, ācis, *adj.* [capiō], *able to hold much,
wide, spacious, roomy.* **1.** Lit.: mundus,
Lucr.; capaciores scyphi, Hor.; pharetra,
urbs, Ov.; domus, Plin. Ep.; moles, Tac.
With GEN.: cibi vinique capacissimus,
Liv.; Ov. **2.** Transf. **a.** In gen.: aures
avidae et capaces, i.e. not easily satisfied,
Cic. **b.** Of the mind : *able to grasp, receptive, capable, qualified :* ingenium, Ov. With
GEN.: animal mentis capacius altae, Ov.;
imperi, Tac.; molis tantae mens, Tac.

capēdō, inis, *f.* [capis], *a bowl* or *cup used in
sacrifices :* Cic.

capēduncula, ae, *f.* [dim. capēdō], *a small
bowl used in sacrifices :* Cic.

capella, ae, *f.* [dim. caper]. **1.** Lit.: *a
she-goat :* Verg., Hor. As a work of art :
Cic. **2.** Transf.: *a star in the constellation Auriga* (us. called capra), *Capella :*
sidus pluviale Capellae, Ov.

Capēna, ae, *f. an old town in Etruria, now
San Martino ;* hence, **Capēnās,** ātis, *adj. ;*

Capēnātēs, um, *m. pl. its inhabitants ;*
Capēna, a, um ; **Capēna Porta,** *a gate
in the Servian Wall, S.E. of Rome, from
which the Via Appia starts.*

caper, prī, *m.* [*cf.* κάπρος]. **1.** Lit.: *a
he-goat, a goat :* Verg., Hor., Ov. **2.**
Transf.: *the odour of the arm-pits :*
Cat., Ov.

caperrō, āre. **A.** Trans.: *to wrinkle, to
contract :* App. **B.** Intrans.: *to be
wrinkled :* Pl.

capessō, ere, ivī (rarely, iī), ītum (*Part.
Fut.* capessītūrus, Tac.) [capiō : *cf.* lacessō],
*to seize, catch at eagerly, snatch at, lay hold
of.* **1.** Lit. **a.** In gen.: cibum dentibus
ipsis, Cic.; arma, Verg. Of relations of
place : *to strive to reach, to make for :*
Italiam, Verg. With *Pron. Refl.* and *in*
or *ad : to take oneself to :* quam magis te
in altum capessis, Pl.; also transf.: Pl.
2. Transf.: *to take in hand, undertake,
enter upon, engage in :* rem publicam,
Cic.; Liv.; libertatem, Cic., Sall.; viam,
fugam, Liv.; iussa, Pl., Verg.; magistratūs, inimicitias, Tac.

Caphāreus or **Caphēreus** (trisyl.), eī (Acc.
-rea, Ov.), *m. a rocky peninsula on the S.
coast of Euboea, where the Greek fleet was
wrecked on its return from Troy, now Capo
d'Oro ;* hence, **Caphārēus,** (-eus, Prop.), a,
um.

capillātus, a, um [capillus], *having hair,
hairy.* **1.** Lit.: adulescens bene capillatus, Cic. **2.** Transf.: *old-fashioned ;*
hence of *long ago :* (vinum) capillato diffusum consule, Juv.

capillus, ī, *m.* (**capillum,** ī, *n.* Pl.) [caput].
1. *the hair of the head* (sometimes *of the
beard*) : compositus, Pl., Cic.; promiscus
Caes.; tonsus, Ov. **II.** *a hair : sing. :*
Juv.; *pl. :* compti, Cic.; intonsi, Ov.
[Fr. *cheveu.*]

capiō, capere, cēpī, captum (old *Fut.* form
capsō : Pl.), *to take.* **I. A.** *to take hold of,
grasp, seize.* **1.** Lit. **a.** fustem, Pl.; arma,
Caes., Cic.; saxa manu, Verg.; pignora,
Liv. **b.** *to occupy :* montem, loca superiora, Caes.; terras, Verg. **c.** *to reach
land, gain the harbour,* etc. : insulam, Caes.;
Cic.; Verg.; also transf.: oti portum et
dignitatis, Cic. **2.** Transf. **a.** *to take,
adopt,* etc. : consilium, fugam, Caes.;
mediam viam consili, Liv.; ex aliquā re
exemplum, consuetudinem, etc., Cic.;
impetum capere, *to gather momentum,* Liv.
b. Of an office, *to take up, assume :* honorem, Pl.; consulatum, Cic.; moderamina
navis, Ov. **B.** *to take by force, guile,* etc., *to
capture, catch, appropriate.* **1.** Lit.:
legiones, Pl.; Orgetorigis filiam, Caes.;
Cic.; Hor.; castra, Caes., Cic.; oppidum,
Caes., Liv.; agros de hostibus, Cic.; uros,
Caes.; iaculo piscis, Ov.; Cic.; also
transf. oppressā captāque re publicā, Cic.
2. Transf. **a.** *to seize upon, take possession of :* cupido cepit me, Enn.; nos
servitutis oblivio ceperat, Cic.; dementia
cepit amantem, Verg. **b.** Of the bodily
or mental powers (in *Pass.*), *to be seized,
injured, weakened :* oculis et auribus captus, Cic., Liv.; Verg.; mente, Cic. Also
with *Part.* agreeing with the part affected :

velut mente captā, Liv. **c.** Of the will, *to take in, ensnare, captivate, charm :* Ter. ; subdolā oratione civitates capere, Caes. ; errore captus, Cic., Liv. ; amore captivae, Liv. ; dolis lacrimisque, Verg. **d.** *to cast in a law-suit, convict :* Pl., Cic. **C.** *to take by choice, choose, select, elect :* de istac sum iudex captus, Pl. ; locum castris, Caes. ; me augurem, Cic. ; Palatium Romulus, Remus Aventinum capiunt, Liv. **D.** *to take as a recipient, receive.* **1.** L i t. : of income, taxes, etc. ; capit ille ex suis praediis sescenta sestertia, Cic. ; Ter. ; stipendium, Caes. ; vectigal ex agro, Liv. ; ex hereditate nihil, Cic. *Absol. : to inherit :* Juv. With pecuniam, *to take a bribe :* Cic., Liv., etc. **2.** T r a n s f. **a.** Of benefits *or* harm, etc. : virtutis opinionem, Hirt. ; ne quid res publica detrimenti capiat, Caes. ; utilitates ex amicitiā, Cic. **b.** Of feelings, passions, etc. : plus voluptatis ex adventu viri, Pl. ; Liv. ; laetitiam, dolorem, Cic. ; timorem, Verg. **c.** Of external form, shape ; etc. : figuras novas, Ov. ; Pl. **II.** *to take, hold, contain* (*cf.* capax). **1.** L i t. : Pl. ; cum unā domo iam capi non possint, Cic. ; plenos capit alveus amnis, Ov. ; Verg. **2.** T r a n s f. **a.** *to contain, hold in :* non capiunt angustiae pectoris tui (tantam personam), Cic. ; irarum fluctūs in pectore, Lucr. ; Ov. **b.** Of the mind, *to take in, comprehend, grasp :* quod mentes eorum capere possent, Liv. ; Cic.

capis, idis, *f.* [capiō], *a bowl with one handle* (used in sacrifices) : Liv.

capistrō, āre [capistrum], *to tie with a halter, to muzzle :* Ov.

capistrum, i, *n.* [capiō]. **I.** *a halter, a muzzle.* **1.** L i t. : Varr., Verg. **2.** T r a n s f. : maritale, Juv. **II.** *a band for the wine-press :* Cato. [It. *capestro* ; Fr. *chevêtre.*]

capitālis, e, *adj.* [caput]. **1.** L i t. **a.** *of the head or life, mortal :* periculum, Pl. **b.** In law : *affecting a man's caput,* i.e. either his life or civil position : flagitia, Ter. ; reus rerum capitalium, Cic. ; capitali poenā adficere aliquem, Suet. **2.** T r a n s f. **a.** *deadly, mortal, dangerous :* inimicus, Pl. ; hostis, odium, oratio, Cic. **b.** *chief, preeminent :* Cic. Ep., Ov. ; *Comp. :* Cic. As Noun, **capital** *or* **capitāle**, is, *n. a capital crime :* Cic., Liv., Tac.

capitō, ōnis, *m.* [caput], *a big-headed person :* Cic. (*cf.* fronto, naso).

Capitōlium, i, *n.* **1.** L i t. : *the Capitol at Rome.* **a.** In a restricted sense, *the temple of Jupiter on the Mons Tarpeius.* **b.** In a wider sense, *the whole hill, including the temple and the* arx (q.v.). P o e t. : sometimes in *pl.* ; **Capitōlīnus**, a, um ; **Capitōlīni**, ōrum, *m. pl. persons who had charge of the Capitoline games.* **2.** T r a n s f. : *the citadel* of any town.

capitulātim, *adv.* [capitulum], *by heads, summarily :* Nep.

capitulum, i, *n.* [*dim.* caput], *a small head.* **1.** L i t. : Pl. **2.** T r a n s f. **a.** Comic. for *a man* (Pl.) or as a term of endearment (Ter.). **b.** A r c h i t. : *the capital of a column :* Plin., Vitr. [It. *capitolo ;* Fr. *chapitre.*]

Cappadocia, ae, *f. a province of Asia Minor, north of Cilicia ;* **Cappadocus**, a, um ; **Cappadox**, ocis, *m. a Cappadocian.*

capra, ae, *f.* [caper], *a she-goat.* **1.** L i t. : Cic. ; fera, Verg. **2.** T r a n s f. **a.** *a bright star in the constellation Auriga, Capella :* Hor. **b.** *the smell of the arm-pits :* Hor. [Fr. *chèvre.*]

caprea, ae, *f.* [capra], *a roe :* Verg. P r o v. : iungere capreas lupis (of something impossible), Hor.

Capreae, ārum, *f. pl. an island off Surrentum, at the S. end of the Bay of Naples,* now *Capri.*

capreolus, i, *m. a chamois, roebuck.* **1.** L i t. : Verg. **2.** T r a n s f. : capreoli, in mechanics : *supports, props, stays :* Caes.

Capricornus, i, *m.* [caper, cornu], *Capricorn, a sign of the Zodiac :* Cic., Ov.

capri-ficus, i, *f.* [caper ficus : lit. *the goatfig,* as we say dog-rose, etc.], *the wild fig-tree, the wild fig :* Ter., Hor.

caprigenus, a, um [caper and *gen* in gignō], *of goat-breed :* Pl., Verg.

caprinus, a, um [caper], *of goats :* stercus, Cato ; pellis, Cic. ; grex, Liv. P r o v. : de lanā caprinā rixari, i.e. to wrangle about trifles, Hor.

capri-pēs, pedis, *adj.* [caper pēs], *goat-footed, a poet.* epithet of rural deities : capripedes Satyri, Lucr., Hor.

capsa, ae, *f.* [capiō], *a holder, case, box,* esp. for book-rolls and law-papers : Cic., Hor. [It. *cassa ;* Fr. *caisse.*]

capsārius, i, *m.* [capsa], *a slave who took care of the* capsae *and carried those of school-boys :* Suet.

capsō, is, it, etc., *v.* capiō.

capsula, ae, *f.* [*dim.* capsa], *a small box* or *chest :* Cat.

Capta, ae, *f. a cult-name of Minerva.*

captātiō, ōnis, *f.* [captō], *a catching at :* verborum, Cic. ; Quint.

captātor, ōris, *m.* [captō], *one who grasps at :* aurae popularis, Liv. *Esp. a legacy-hunter :* Hor.

captiō, ōnis, *f.* [capiō], *a taking, catching.* T r a n s f. **a.** *a deceiving, trickery, fraud :* si in parvulā re captionis aliquid vererere, Cic. ; Pl. **b.** In dialectics : *a fallacy, a sophism :* captionos discutere, Cic. ; Pl. **c.** *a disadvantage, loss :* ne quid captioni mihi sit, Pl., Cic. Ep.

captiōsē, *adv. captiously, insidiously :* interrogare, Cic.

captiōsus, a, um [captiō]. **I.** *fallacious, deceptive :* societas, Cic. *Comp. :* Cic. **II.** *captious, sophistical :* probabilitas, Cic. *Sup. :* Cic. *Neut. pl.* as Noun, *sophisms :* Cic. **III.** *dangerous, hurtful :* quam captiosum est populo ! Cic.

captiuncula, ae, *f.* [*dim.* captiō], *a quirk, quibble, sophism :* Cic. Ep.

captivitās, ātis, *f.* [captīvus]. **I.** *a state of bondage, captivity :* Tac. Collect., *a crowd of captives :* Tac. **II.** Of countries, towns, etc. : *a taking, capture :* urbium, Tac. Also in *pl.* : Tac.

captivus, a, um [captus, capiō]. **I.** *caught, taken prisoner, taken in war.* **1.** L i t. : naves, Caes. ; cives, Cic. ; pecunia, Liv. ; vestis, Verg. As Noun : *a prisoner, cap-*

tive : Cic., Verg., etc. In *fem. :* captiva, Ov., Curt. **2.** T r a n s f. : *in bondage (to love)* : mens, Ov. **II.** *of prisoners :* sanguis, Verg. ; cruor, Tac. [It. *cattivo ;* Fr. *chétif,* ' *wretched, mean.* ']

captō, āre [*freq.* capiō], *to catch at frequently* or *eagerly, endeavour to catch, etc.* **1.** L i t. : Tantalus fugientia captat flumina, Hor. ; Verg. **2.** T r a n s f. : *to try to catch, to court, etc. ;* consilium, sermonem, Pl. ; adsensionem alicuius, Cic. ; plausūs, misericordiam, Cic. ; occasionem, Liv. ; testamenta, Hor. ; homines, Plin. Ep. ; Juv. With *Inf.* as object : prendi et prendere captans, Ov. **b.** *to entrap, outwit, deceive, etc. :* Pl., Cic. ; hostem insidiis, Liv. With G e n. of crime in which one is caught : me impudicitiae, Pl.

captūra, ae, *f.* [capiō]. **1.** L i t. : *a taking, catching (of animals) :* Plin. **2.** T r a n s f. : concr. : *takings.* **a.** *that which is taken, quarry, draught of fishes, etc. :* Suet. **b.** *gain (by an immoral employment) :* Suet.

captus, a, um. **I.** *Part.* capiō. **II.** N o u n : **captus,** ī, *m.* (Verg., Liv., Tac.) and **capta,** ae, *f.* (Ter.), *a captive, prisoner.*

captus, ūs, *m.* [capiō] *a taking, seizing ; that which is taken.* **1.** L i t. : trium digitorum captus, Plin. **2.** T r a n s f. : *mental grasp, capacity, notion :* ut captus est Germanorum, Caes. ; Ter. ; Cic.

Capua, ae, *f. the chief city of Campania* (q.v.), *famous for its wealth and luxury, now Santa Maria di Capua.*

capulāris, e, *adj.* [capulus], *of or fit for a coffin:* homo, Pl.

capulus, ī, *m.* or **capulum,** ī, *n.* [capiō]. **I.** *coffin, sarcophagus, bier :* Pl., Lucr. **II.** *a handle:* aratri, Ov. Esp. *the hilt of a sword:* Cic., Verg., etc.

caput, itis, *n. the head.* **1.** L i t. : of men and animals : Pl., Cic., Verg., etc. ; capite operto, obvoluto, Cic. ; caput aperire, Cic. ; demittere, Caes. ; extollere, Cic. ; efferre, Verg. P h r. : supra caput esse, *to be over our very heads,* i.e. to be imminent, Cic., Liv. P r o v. : nec caput nec pedes. i.e. neither beginning nor end, Cic. Ep. ; capita conferre, i.e. to confer in secret, Liv. **2.** T r a n s f. **A.** *the head, top, extremity* (beginning or end), *of anything :* ulpici, Cato ; papaveris, Liv. ; Verg. ; tignorum, Caes. Of rivers : *fountain-head, source :* Lucr., Verg., Liv., etc. ; also *the mouth :* Caes., Liv. Hence, si quid sine capite manabit, Cic. Of plants, sometimes *the root :* vitis, Cato ; also *vine-branches :* Cic. **B.** a. *an individual, a person :* ridiculum caput ! Ter. ; Pl. Also in elevated style, tam cari capitis ! Hor. ; Verg. ; liberum, Cic. ; quot capitum vivunt, totidem studiorum milia, Hor. ; Liv. So in numbering : capite censi (*reckoned by the head, cf.* ' *poll-tax* '), Cic., etc. ; in capita, *to or for each person,* Liv. ; capitum Helvetiorum milia CCLXIII, Caes. Of animals : sus triginta capitum fetūs enixa, Verg. **b.** P o e t. : *the head,* as the seat of the understanding, *the judgment, sense :* incolumi capite es ? Hor. ; caput insanabile, Hor. **c.** *the head,* hence, *life :* Ov. ; capitis periculum adire, Ter., Liv. ; capitis poena, Caes. ; certamen capitis, Cic.

Hence, *civil existence, political status* (including the rights of liberty, citizenship, and family : its loss or deprivation was called deminutio *or* minutio capitis) : capitis accusare, *to accuse on a capital charge,* Nep. ; capitis damnare, *to condemn to death,* Cic. **C.** *the head,* hence *the chief.* **a.** Of persons, *the leader of anything, the chief person :* caput scelerum, Pl., Ter. ; Graecorum concitandorum, Cic. : belli, consili, Liv. : capita nominis Latini, Liv. ; ego caput fui argento reperiundo (D a t.), Pl. **b.** Of *the capital on which interest was paid :* Hor. Of any total : demit de capite medimna DC., Cic., Liv. [It. *capo ;* Fr. *chef.*]

Capys, yos, *m.* **I.** *s. of Assaracus, and f. of Anchises.* **II.** *a companion of Aeneas.* **III.** *the eighth king of Alba.* **IV.** *a king of Capua.*

Cār, Cāris (Acc. *pl.* Cāras), *m. a Carian;* **Cāricus,** a, um ; **Cāria,** ae, *f. the district in S.W. Asia Minor inhabited by the Carians ;* **Cārica,** ae, *f.* (*sc.* ficus), *a Carian dried fig,* hence, *any dried fig.*

Caracalla, ae, *m. the Emperor* Antoninus Caracalla (A.D 211–217).

Caratacus, ī, *m. Caradoc, king of the Silures in Britain, defeated and taken prisoner to Rome* (A.D. 51).

carbaseus, a, um [carbasus], *of or made of* carbasus : vela, Cic. ; Verg.

carbasus, ī, *f.* [κάρπασος] (*pl. neut.* carbasa), *very fine Spanish flax.* **1.** L i t. : Plin. **2.** T r a n s f. : of *things made of it.* **a.** *a linen garment :* Verg., Curt. In *pl.* : Ov. **b.** *a sail, canvas :* tumidoque inflatur carbasus austro, Verg. ; Enn. **c.** *a curtain* or *awning :* Lucr.

carbatina, *v.* carpatina.

carbō, ōnis, *m. a piece of burning* or *charred wood, charcoal, embers :* Ter. ; qui apud carbones adsident, semper calent, Pl. ; Lucr. ; Cic. P h r. : cretā an carbone notandi ? i.e. as sane or insane ? Hor. [Fr. *charbon.*]

Carbō, ōnis, *m. a Roman cognomen in the* gens Papiria.

carbōnārius, ī, *m.* [carbō], *a charcoal-burner :* Pl.

carbunculus, ī, *m.* [*dim.* carbō], *a small coal.* T r a n s f. **a.** Of sorrow : amburet misero ei corculum carbunculus, Pl. **b.** *a reddish, bright kind of precious stone :* Plin. **c.** *a friable sandstone :* Varr. [Fr. *escarboucle.*]

carcer, eris, *m. an enclosure :* ventorum, Verg. ; hence, **I.** *a prison, jail.* **1.** L i t. : me in carcerem compingere, Pl. ; Lucr. ; in carcerem conici, Cic. ; in carcerem condi, Liv. In a simile : ex corporum vinculis tamquam e carcere, Cic. (*v.* also lautumiae, Tullianum.) **2.** T r a n s f. : *the criminals* *confined* : in me carcerem effudistis, Cic. As term of reproach : *jail-bird* : Ter. **II.** *the barrier* or *starting place in the circus* : Enn., Verg., Suet.; us. in *pl.* : Lucr., Cic., Verg. T r a n s f. : of a starting-point of action : ad carceres a calce revocari, Cic.

carcerārius, a, um [carcer], *of a prison* : quaestus, Pl.

Carchēdonius, a, um [Καρχηδόνιος], *Carthaginian.*

carchēsium, ī, *n.* [Καρχήσιον], *a Greek beaker or cup slightly contracted in the middle* : **1.** L i t. : Verg., Ov. **2.** T r a n s f. (in *pl.*), *the similarly-formed upper part of a mast* : Lucil., Luc.

Cardaces, um (Acc. -as), *m. pl. a class of Persian soldiers* : Nep.

cardiacus, ī, *m.* [καρδιακός]. *one who is suffering from heart-burn* : Cic., Hor., etc.

cardō, inis, *m.* [*cf.* Gk. κραδαίνω], *a pivot- hinge.* **1.** L i t. : *the hinge of a door* : Pl. ; vellere postis a cardine, Verg. ; versato cardine, Ov. **2.** T r a n s f. **a.** Astron., *a pole* : Varr., Ov. **b.** *that on which all de- pends, the turning-point* : haud tanto cessa- bit cardine rerum, Verg.

carduus, ī, *m. the thistle* : Verg. [Fr. chardon.]

cāre,a *dv.* **1.** L i t. : Varr. *Comp.* : Cic., Suet. *Sup.* : Sen. Ep. **2.** T r a n s f. : *dearly, highly* : carius aestimare, Planc. ap. Cic. Ep.

cārectum, ī, *n.* [cārex], *a rush-plot* : Verg.

careō, ēre (*Pres. Subj.* carint = careant, Pl. ; carendus, Ov.), constr. with ABL. ; in earlier poets also with GEN. or ACC. : *to be without,* **A.** With a living subject. **a.** *to be free from, not to have* : carere culpā, Pl. ; dolore, Cic. ; invidendā aulā, Hor. ; morte, Hor. **b.** *to hold aloof* or *keep away from, deny one- self* : vino, Pl. ; Veneris fructu, Lucr.; foro, senatu, aspectu civium, Cic. **c.** *to be destitute of, to want* (the thing wanted being *desirable,* but not indispensable) : egere, *to want what is necessary*) : patriā, Ter. ; commodis omnibus, Cic. ; tali munero, Verg. With GEN. : Ter. With ACC. : Pl. **B.** With an inanimate subject, *to be without* : haec duo tempora carent crimine, Cic. ; aditu carentia saxa, Ov. ; Verg.

cārex, icis, *f.* some kind of *rush* : acuta, Verg.

Cārica, *v.* Cār.

cariēs, em, ē (other cases not in use), *f. dry rot* : Lucil., Varr., Ov.

carīna, ae, *f. the bottom of a ship, the keel.* **1.** L i t. : Pl., Caes., Ov., etc. **2.** T r a n s f. *a ship* : Enn., Verg., etc. [Fr. *carène ;* Eng. verb. *careen.*]

Carīnae, ārum, *f. pl.* the *Keels ; a district in Rome between the Caelian and Esquiline Hills.*

carīnārius, ī, *m. a dyer of yellow* : Pl.

cariōsus, a, um [cariēs], *decayed, rotten, crumbling.* **1.** L i t. : terra, Cato ; dentes, Plin. ; vina, Mart. **2.** T r a n s f. : senec- tus, *withered,* Ov.

cāris, idis, *f.* [καρίς], *a kind of sea-crab* : Ov.

cāritās, ātis, *f.* [cārus], *dearness, high price.* **1.** L i t. : annonae, *high price of corn,* Cic., Liv. ; primum caritas nata est, deinde in- opia, Cic. **2.** T r a n s f. : *high regard, es- teem, affection* : in aliquem, Cic. ; erga patriam caritas, Liv. With *Obj.* GEN. :

love for : patriae et suorum, Cic. ; rei pub- licae, Cic., Liv. With *Subj.* GEN. (rarer) : civium, Cic., Liv. ; necessitudinis, Cic. In *pl.* : Cic. [Fr. *cherté, charité.*]

carmen, inis, *n.* **I.** *a tune, song, strain* (vocal or instrumental, mostly poet. for cantus) : Enn., Cic., Verg., etc. **II.** Of a composition in verse (epic, lyric, or dra- matic) : Cic., Lucr., Verg., etc. A b s o l. for *lyric poetry* : carmine tu gaudes, hic delectatur iambis, Hor. ; and for *drama* : Liv. **III.** *a prophetic or oracular utterance, prediction* : Verg., Liv., etc. **IV.** *a magic formula, an incantation, charm* : per libros carminum valentium, Hor. ; Verg. ; Tac., etc. **V.** *a formula in religion* or *law, a formulary* : Cic. ; lex horrendi carminis erat, Liv. **VI.** *moral saws* (*in verse*) : Cic. **VII.** *a poetic inscription* : Verg., Ov. [Fr. *charme, charmer.*]

Carmenta, ae, and **Carmentis,** is, *f. an ancient prophetic deity of Rome, m. of Euander ; the chief of the Camenae ;* **Car- mentālis,** e, *adj.* : Porta Carmentalis, *a gate at Rome, near her temple, through which the Fabii went to their destruction, hence called* Porta Scelerata.

Carna (or **Carda,** or **Cardea**), ae, *f. the god- dess, guardian of door-hinges* [cardō], i.e. of family life.

carnārium, ī, *n.* [carō]. **I.** *a flesh-hook* : Pl., Cato. **II.** *a larder* : Pl.

Carneadēs, is, *m. a famous philosopher, born at Cyrene, the founder of the New Academy* (B.C. 215–130) ; **Carneadēus,** a, um.

carnifex, icis, *m.* (old form, **carnufex**) [carō, faciō], *an executioner, hangman.* **1.** L i t. : Pl., Lucr., Cic. ; rapere ad carnuficem, Pl. **2.** T r a n s f. **a.** *a murderer* : Ter., Cic., Liv. **b.** As a term of abuse : Pl., Ter., Cic.

carnificīna, ae, *f.* [carnifex]. **1.** L i t. **a.** *the work of hangman* : carnuficinam facere = carnificem esse, Pl. **b.** *execution, tor- ture* : subire, Cic. ; ductum in ergastulum et carnificinam, Liv. **2.** T r a n s f. : carni- ficina est aegritudo, Cic.

carnificō, āre [carnifex] : *to mangle, mutilate* : Liv.

carnivorus, a, um [carō vorō], *feeding on flesh, carnivorous* : Plin.

carnōsus, a, um, *fleshy, pulpy* : Plin.

carō, carnis, *f.* [*cf.* Gk. κρέας], *flesh.* **1.** L i t. : Pl., Cic. ; lacte et carne vivere, Caes. In *pl.* : carnes vipereae, Ov. ; Enn. **2.** T r a n s f. **a.** Of fruit : Plin. **b.** Of style : Quint. **c.** In contempt : istius pecudis ac putidae carnis consilium, Cic. [Fr. *chair.*]

cārō, ere, *to card* : lanam, Pl.

Carpathus, ī, *f. an island between Crete and Rhodes, now Skarpanto* ; **Carpathius,** a, um ; vates, senex, i.e. *Proteus,* Ov.

carpatina, ae, *f.* [καρπατίνη], *a kind of rustic shoe* : Cat.

carpentum, ī, *n. a two-wheeled covered car- riage or chariot,* esp. used by women on festal occasions : Liv., Ov., Tac.

carpō, pere, psī, ptum [*cf.* καρπός], *to pluck, pluck off, cull, crop, gather.* **1.** L i t. **a.** Of flowers, fruit, etc. : rosam, poma, Verg. ; vindemiam de palmite, Verg. ; flores ab arbore, Ov. **b.** Of other things : *to pluck,* *tear off, tear away* : summas carpens media inter cornua saetas, Verg. Of wool : *to pluck* : vellera, Verg. Hence, *to card for spinning* : pensum, Verg. **c.** Of animals : *to graze on, browse,* etc. : Cic. ; carpunt gramen equi, Verg. Occ. of men : prandium, Ter. Poet. of Envy : summa cacumina carpit, Ov. **2.** Transf. **a.** *to call, gather* : omnis undique flosculos (orationis), Cic. ; gaudia, Ov. **b.** *to take and enjoy, make use of* : diem, Hor. ; somnos sub dio, Verg. ; auras vitalis, Verg. **c.** *to wear away, consume, weaken* : caeco carpitur igni, Verg.; viris, Verg. ; Liv. ; tuos labores, Hor. Milit. : *to wear down, harass* : agmen adversariorum, Caes. ; novissimos, Liv. **d.** *to pluck to pieces, hence, to slander, calumniate* : aliquem vocibus, Caes. ; sermonibus, Liv. ; maledico dente, Cic. **e.** *to separate into parts, to cut to pieces, divide* : saepe carpenda membris minutioribus oratio est, Cic. ; in multas parvasque partis carpere exercitum, Liv. **f.** *to enter upon a journey, pass over, navigate, to take or pursue one's way* : viam ; Verg. ; iter, Hor. ; supremum iter (= mori), Hor. ; gyrum, prata, Verg. ; litora curru, Ov. ; pede campos, Ov. [It. *carpia* ; Fr. *charpie,* ' lint.']

carptim, *adv.* **I.** *by pieces, in detached parts* : res gestas persoribere, Sall. ; Plin. Ep. **II.** *at different places* or *points* : carptim adgredi, Liv. **III.** *at different times, separately* : dimissi carptim ac singuli, Tac. ; Liv.

carptor, ōris, *m.* [carpō], *a carver of food* : Juv.

carptūra, ae, *f.* [carpō], *a gathering from flowers (by bees)* : Varr.

Carrhae, ārum, *f. pl. a town in Mesopotamia, where Crassus was defeated and killed by the Parthians* (B.C. 53).

carrūca, ae, *f.* [carrus], *a four-wheeled travelling carriage* : Mart., Suet. [Fr. *charrue.*]

carrus, I, *m. a four-wheeled waggon or car* : Caes., Liv. [Fr. *char.*]

Carthāgō (also **Karth-**), inis, *f.* **I.** *Carthage, a city in N. Africa near Tunis ; a Phoenician colony* (9th cent. B.C.) ; **Carthāginiēnsis,** e, *adj.* **II.** **Carthāgō Nova,** *a town on the S.E. coast of Spain founded by Hasdrubal* (B.C. 242).

Cartimandua, ae, *f. queen of the Brigantes in Britain.*

caruncula, ae, *f.* [dim.`carō], *a little piece of flesh* : Cic.

cārus, a, um, *dear, high priced* (opp. vilis). **1.** Lit. : pisces, agnina, bubula, Pl., Cic. Comp. : Cic. ; Sup. : Pl., Cic. With ABL. of price : asse carum est, Cato ; Pl. **2.** Transf. : *dear, precious, beloved* : Pl., Cic., Verg., etc. Comp. : Ter., Cic., etc. Sup. : Cic. [Fr. *cher.*]

Cārus, I, *m. a Roman cognomen,* esp. **I.** *of the poet* T. Lucretius Carus. **II.** *of the Emperor* M. Aurelius Carus (A.D. 282–3).

Caryae, ārum, *f. pl. a village in Laconia, with a temple of Diana* ; **Caryātides,** um, *f. pl.* (*sc.* virgines). **I.** *the maidens of Caryae, serving in the temple of Diana.* **II.** Archit.: *female figures used instead of columns.*

Carystos, I, *f. a town in Euboea, famous for its marble* ; **Carystēus,** a, um ; **Carystii,** ōrum, *m, pl. its inhabitants.*

casa, ae, *f. a hut, cottage, cabin* : Cic., Verg., etc. [Fr. *chez, caserne.*]

cascus, a, um, *old, primitive* : an Oscan word : Cic. [Lit. ' grey.']

cāseolus, I, *m.* [cāseus], *a small cheese* : Verg.

cāseus, I, *m. cheese* : Pl., Cic., Verg., etc. [It. *cacio* ; Eng. *cheese* ; Germ. *Käse.*]

casia, ae, *f.* [κασία]. **I.** *a fragrant, shrublike plant, mezereon* : Verg., Ov. **II.** *a tree with aromatic bark* : Pl., Verg.

Caspii, ōrum, *m. pl. a people inhabiting N. Media* ; **Caspius,** a, um ; **Caspium mare,** *the Caspian Sea* ; **Caspiae portae** or **pylae,** *narrow passes in Mt. Taurus.*

Cassander, drī, *m. s. of Antipater, and king of Macedonia after the death of Alexander the Great.*

Cassandra, ae, *f. d. of Priam and Hecuba* ; *she received the gift of prophecy from Apollo, but with the condition of being believed by no one.*

cassēs, ium (*sing.* ABL. casse, Ov.), *m. pl.* **I.** *a hunting-net, snare* : Verg. ; decidere in casses, Ov. **II.** *a spider's web* : Verg. Transf.: Ov.

Cassiopē, ēs, **Cassiopēa** and **Cassiepēa,** ae, *f., w. of Cepheus, and m. of Andromeda, afterwards made a constellation.*

Cassiterides, um, *f. pl. tin-islands,* perh. *the Scilly Isles.*

Cassius, a, *name of a Roman gens* ; esp. **I.** Sp. Cassius, *author of the first agrarian law,* B.C. 485. **II.** L. Cassius Longinus Ravilla, *a strict judge, author of the lex Cassia tabellaria,* B.C. 137. **III.** L. Cassius, *defeated and killed by the Helvetii,* B.C. 106. **IV.** C. Cassius Longinus, *one of the murderers of Caesar* ; **Cassiānus,** a, um.

Cassivellaunus, I, *m. a British chieftain, defeated by Caesar.*

cassis, idis (**cassida,** ae, Verg.), *f, a helmet* (prop. *of metal,* while galea was of leather) : Pl., Caes., Verg. Sometimes = galea : Ov.

cassō, āre [cadō], *to be ready to fall, totter* : Pl.

cassus, a, um, *empty* (mostly poet.). **1.** Lit. : nux, Pl., Hor. With ABL. *devoid of, deprived of* : virgo dote cassa, Pl. ; lumine aer, lumine corpus, Lucr. ; cassus lumine, i.e. dead, Verg. **2.** Transf.: *empty, vain* : Cic. ; formido, Lucr. ; vota, Verg. ; labores, Plin. Ep. *Neut.* as Noun : cassa memorare, Pl. ; in cassum, or in one word incassum, *adv. in vain, uselessly, to no purpose.* Pl., Lucr., Verg., Liv., etc.

Castalia, ae, *f. a spring on Parnassus, sacred to Apollo and the Muses* ; **Castalius,** a, um ; **Castalis,** idis, *f. adj. epith. of the Muses* ; **Castalides,** um, *f. pl. the Muses.*

castanea, ae, *f.* [κάστανον]. **I.** *the chestnut-tree* : Verg., Plin. **II.** *a chestnut* : Verg., Plin. [Fr. *chataigne.*]

castē, *adv.* **I.** *purely, without stain, uprightly* : Pl., Cic. **II.** *chastely, modestly* : Cic. **III.** *devoutly* : Cic., Ov. Comp. : Liv. ; Sup. : Cic. Ep.

castellānus, a, um [castellum], *of a castle or fortress* : triumphus, Cic. As Noun, **castellāni,** ōrum, *m. pl. the occupants of a castle, the garrison* : Sall., Liv. [Fr. *châtelain.*]

castellātim, adv. [castellum], *by castles, castle by castle :* dissipati, *in different fortresses,* Liv.

castellum, i, n. [dim. castrum], *a castle, fort, stronghold.* **1.** Lit.: Cic., Verg., etc. **2.** Transf.: *stronghold, shelter :* latrocini, Cic.; Liv. [Fr. *château.*]

castēria, ae, f. *a part of a ship, where the rowers used to rest :* Pl.

castigābilis, e, adj. [castigō], *deserving punishment :* Pl.

castigātiō, ōnis, f. [castigō], *a correcting, chastising with words ; reproof,* etc.: Cic., Liv. In *pl. :* Cic., Liv.

castigātor, ōris, m. [castigō], *a corrector, reprover :* Pl., Hor., Liv.

castigātōrius, a, um [castigātor], *reproving :* Plin. Ep.

castigātus, a, um, **I.** *Part.* castigō. **II.** *Adj. small, delicate :* pectus, Ov.

castigō, āre [castus, agō]. Lit.: *to make clean ;* hence, **I.** *to correct, chastise, punish :* verberibus, Cic.; Pl.; Liv.; hence, *to reprove, censure* (v. punire): pueros verbis, Cic.; Pl.; Verg.; Pompeius segniores castigat, Caes.; Liv. **II.** *to hold in check, to rein in, to restrain.* **1.** Lit.: Ter., Liv. **2.** Transf.: animi dolorem, Cic.; carmen, Hor.; plebem, Tac. [Fr. *châtier.*]

castimōnia, ae, f. [castus], *purity.* **I.** In gen. *purity of morals, morality :* Cic. **II.** *chastity, abstinence* (esp. of the ministers of religion): Cic., Liv.

castitās, ātis, f. [castus], *chastity, purity of body :* Cic., Hor., Tac.

castor, oris, m. [κάστωρ], *a beaver :* pure Lat. fiber (Acc. castora, Juv.), Ov.

Castor, oris, m. *s. of Tyndareus, twin-brother of Pollux and b. of Helen ;* the two brothers became the constellation Gemini, and served as a guide to sailors.

castoreum, i, n. [castor], *a secretion of the beaver ; castor :* Lucr. In *pl. :* Verg.

castra, ōrum, *v.* castrum.

castrēnsis, e, adj. [castra], *of the camp :* ratio, Cic.; Prop.

castrō, āre, *to geld, castrate.* **1.** Lit.: Pl., Varr., Suet. **2.** Transf.: Maecenatem felicitas, Sen. Ep. ; libellos, Mart.

castrum, i, n. **I.** In *sing. : any fortified place, a castle, fort, fortress* (rare for castellum): Nep., Liv. More us. in a proper name, e.g. Castrum Altum, Liv.; Castrum Inui, Verg. **II.** In *pl. :* **castra**, ōrum, n. *a military camp, an encampment.* **1.** Lit.: Enn.; ponere, *to pitch,* Caes.; munire, Caes.; communire, Liv.; facere, habere castra, *to encamp,* Caes.; castra movere, *to break up,* Caes.; promovere, Caes.; movere retro, Liv.; castra stativa, Cic.; aestiva, Suet.; hiberna, Caes., Liv.; navalia, Caes.; nautica, Nep. With numerals: una, Tac.; bina, Cic.; Liv. In a proper name : Castra Cornelia or Corneliana, etc., Caes. **2.** Transf. **a.** (mostly in ABL.) *a day's march :* Caes.; secundis castris pervenit ad Dium, Liv. **b.** *military service :* qui magnum in castris usum habebant, Caes.: Tib. **c.** Of a philosophical school or political party : Epicuri castra, Cic. Ep.; Hor. **d.** Of a beehive : Verg.

castus, a, um [cf. καθαρός]. Lit.: *clean.*

I. In gen. *morally pure,* etc. **a.** Of persons : Cic., Verg., etc. With *a* and ABL.: a culpā, Pl. **b.** Of things : res familiaris casta a cruore civili, Cic.; vita, animus, Cic.; signa, *signs, indications of innocence,* Ov. **II.** Of sexual morality, *pure, chaste.* **a.** Of persons : Latona, Enn.; Minerva, Hor.; matres, Verg.; Cic. **b.** Of things : Veneris conubia, Lucr.; domus, Cat.; vultus, Ov. **III.** In religion, *godly, holy.* **a.** Of persons : contio, Cic.; sacerdotes, Verg. **b.** Of things : donum, Cic.; taedae, Verg.; nemus, Tac. *Comp.* and *Sup. :* Cic. [Fr. *chaste.*]

casula, ae, f. [dim. casa], *a little cottage or hut, a small house :* Juv.

cāsus, ūs, m. [cadō], *a falling.* **1.** Lit.: nivis, Liv.; Lucr.; Hor.; in *pl. :* Lucr. In battle : Epaminondae, Nep. **2.** Transf. **A.** *a fall.* **a.** In gen. *the end, overthrow, downfall :* Gracchorum, Caes.: Enn.; Cic.; hiemis, urbis, Verg.; in *pl. :* Ov. **b.** In morality (rare) : Cic. **c.** Gramm. *a case* (= πτῶσις) : Cic. **B.** *that which befalls, a happening, chance, event, issue,* etc. (good or bad). **a.** calamitosus, Cic.; varii, Liv., Verg.; secundi et adversi, Nep.; meum casum luctumque, Cic.; casūs cognoscere nostros, Verg.; bellorum, Tac. Esp. in ABL.: *by chance, by accident :* sive casu sive consilio deorum, Caes.; non consulto, sed casu, Cic. **b.** Occ. *an opportunity ;* navigandi, Caes.; victoriae, Sall.; Tac.; facinoris casum dare, Sall.; mortis, Verg.; casum adferre, Quint.

Catadūpa, ōrum, n. *pl. the cataracts of the Nile, near Syene.*

catagelasimus, a, um [καταγελάσιμος], *serving for ridicule ; a banterer, jeerer :* a pun on the name of the parasite Gelasimus, Pl.

catagraphus, a, um [κατάγραφος], *painted, coloured :* Cat.

Catamītus, v. Ganymēdes.

cataphractēs, ae, m. [καταφράκτης], *a coat of scale-armour :* Tac.

cataphractus, a, um [κατάφρακτος], *mailclad, mailed* (pure Latin, loricatus): Liv., Prop.

cataplus, i, m. [κατάπλους], *the arrival of a ship.* Transf.: *a ship or fleet that arrives :* Cic., Mart.

catapulta, ae, f. [ὁ καταπέλτης], *an engine of war for throwing arrows, lances,* etc., *a catapult :* Lucil., Caes., Liv. Transf.: *a missile :* Pl.

catapultārius, a, um [catapulta], *thrown by a catapult :* Pl.

cataracta (also **catarracta**), ae, f. and **catarractēs**, ae, m. [ὁ καταρράκτης]. **I.** *a waterfall :* esp. *that of the Nile :* Plin. **II.** *a portcullis :* Liv. **III.** *a flood-gate :* Plin. Ep.

cataractria, ae, f. a word coined to designate a kind of spice : Pl.

catasta, ae, f. [κατάστασις], *a stage on which slaves were exposed for sale :* Tib., Pers.

catē, adv. *wisely, skilfully :* Pl., Cic. poet.

catēia, ae, f. [a Celtic word], *a kind of javelin :* Verg.

catellus, i, m. (and **catella**, ae, f. Juv.) [dim. catulus], *a puppy, whelp :* Pl., Cic.,

Juv. As a term of endearment : Pl., Hor.

catellus, i, *m*. (and **catella**, ae, *f.* Cato, Liv., Hor.) [*dim.* catēna], *a small chain :* Pl. [Fr. cadeau.]

catēna, ae, *f. a chain, a fetter.* **1.** Lit. : catenis vincire aliquem, Pl. ; catenas indere alicui, Pl. ; in catenas conicere, Caes. ; catenas inicere alicui, Cic. ; serā domitus catenā, Hor. ; in catenis aliquem Romam mittere, Liv. ; eximere se ex catenis, Pl. ; rumpere catenas, Hor. ; catenas alicui exsolvere, Tac. **2.** Transf. **a.** *a chain*, i.e. *a series of things connected together,* Lucr. **b.** *a barrier, restraint, bond :* legum, Cic. ; Hor. ; Liv. [Fr. chaine.]

catēnātus, a, um [catēna], *chained.* **1.** Lit. : Hor., Ov., Quint. **2.** Transf. : versus, Quint.

caterva, ae, *f. a crowd, a troop.* **I.** Us. of men : testium, Cic. ; comitum, Lucr. ; iuvenum, Verg. Occ. **a.** *a body* of irregular or foreign soldiers : tumultuariae catervae Germanorum, Tac. ; Verg. **b.** *a company of actors* (us. grex) : Pl., Cic. **II.** Of animals : pecudum, Lucr. ; Verg.

catervārius, a, um [caterva], *in a crowd or troop :* Suet.

catervātim, *adv.* [caterva]. **I.** *in companies :* Sall., Liv. **II.** *in crowds* or *heaps* (of the plague-stricken) : Lucr., Verg.

cathedra, ae, *f.* [καθέδρα], *an arm-chair :* Hor., Prop. ; also, *a sedan-chair :* Juv. ; also *a teacher's chair :* Juv. [Fr. chaire.]

Catilīna, ae, *m.* L. Sergius, a Roman patrician, whose conspiracy was detected and defeated by Cicero, B.C. 63 ; **Catilīnārius**, a, um.

catillō, āre [catillus], *to lick a plate :* Pl.

catillus, i, *m.* [*dim.* catīnus], *a small dish, bowl,* or *plate :* Cato, Hor.

catīnus, i, *m.* [κάτινον], *a deep vessel* for serving up or cooking food, *a bowl, dish, pot :* Varr. ; Hor. For incense : Suet.

Catō, ōnis, *m.* [catus], *a cognomen in the gens Porcia* ; esp. **I.** M. Porcius Cato (B.C. 235-149), *the accepted type of old Roman, and famous for his hatred of Carthage, Greek, and Scipio Africanus ; author of the* Origines (*the Early History of Italy*) *and De Re Rustica ;* **Catōniānus**, a, um. **II.** *his g.g.s.* M. Porcius Cato Uticensis (B.C. 95-46), *famous for his rigid Stoicism and hostility to Caesar`; he committed suicide at Utica after the battle of Thapsus ;* **Catōnini**, ōrum, *m. pl. his supporters. Also a cognomen in the gens Valeria ;* esp. M. Valerius Cato, *a grammarian and poet of the time of Sulla.*

catōnium, i, *n.* [κάτω], *the lower world :* Cic. Ep. (humorously).

Catullus, i, *m.* C. Valerius Catullus, *a famous Latin lyric and elegiac poet* (ob. B.C. 54).

catulus, i, *m.* **I.** *a puppy :* Pl., Cic., Verg., etc. **II.** *a whelp, cub,* etc. : Pl., Lucr., Verg., etc.

Catulus, i, *m. a cognomen in the gens Lutatia ;* esp. **I.** C. Lutatius, *consul* B.C. 241, *who defeated the Carthaginians at Aegates Insulae.* **II.** Q. Lutatius, *consul* B.C. 102 *with Marius.* **III.** Q. Lutatius (s. of II.), *consul* B.C. 78.

catus, a, um [Sabine = acūtus], *sharp ;*

hence, **I.** *clear-sounding, shrill :* Enn. **II.** *sharp,* of the intellect. **a.** In a good sense : *keen, shrewd, sagacious :* Pl., Cic., Hor. With *Inf. :* iaculari, Hor. **b.** In a bad senso : *crafty, cunning :* cata est et callida, Pl. ; Hor.

cauda (or **cōda**), ae, *f. the tail of animals :* Lucr., Cic. Prov. : caudam iactare popello, i.e. *to flatter, fawn upon,* Pers. ; caudam trahere, *to have a tail stuck on,* i.e. *to be an object of derision,* Hor. Humorously : *the end of Verres' name,* alluding also to the tail of a boar, Cic. [It. coda ; Fr. queue.]

caudeus, a, um [caudex], *of wood, wooden :* cistella, Pl.

caudex, *v.* cōdex.

caudicālis, e, *adj.* [caudex], *of tree-trunks :* Comic. : provincia, *the employment of wood-splitting,* Pl.

Caudium, i, *n. a town in Samnium, near which was the mountain-pass (Furculae Caudinae) where the Roman army was shut in by the Samnites,* B.C. 321 ; **Caudīnus**, a, um.

caulae, ārum, *f. pl.* [cavus]. **I.** *an opening, hole, passage :* per caulas corporis, Lucr. **II.** *a sheep-fold, pen, cote :* Verg.

caulis (or rustic **cōlis**), is, *m.* [*cf.* καυλός], *the stalk* or *stem of a plant.* **a.** In gen. : brassicae, Cato ; dictamni, Verg. **b.** Esp. *a cabbage-stalk, a cabbage :* Cic., Hor. [It. cavolo ; Fr. chou.]

Caunus (-os), i, *f. an old town on the coast of Caria ;* **Cauneus (-ius)**, a, um ; **Caunea, ae**, *f. a Caunian dried fig ;* **Caunei (-ii)**, ōrum, *m. pl. its inhabitants.*

caupō, ōnis, *m.* [*cf.* κάπηλος], *a petty tradesman, huckster, innkeeper :* Pl., Cic., Hor.

caupōna, ae, *f.* [caupō]. **I.** *a female shop-keeper, inn-keeper :* App. **II.** *a retail shop, inn, tavern :* Cic., Hor.

caupōnius, a, um [caupō], *of a shop* or *tavern :* puer, Pl.

caupōnor, āri [caupō], *to traffic* or *trade in anything :* non cauponantes bellum, sed belligerantes, Enn.

caupōnula, ae, *f.* [*dim.* caupōna], *a small inn* or *tavern :* Cic.

Caurus (Lucr., Verg.) or **Cōrus**, i, *m.* (Caes.), *the north-west wind.*

causa (older **caussa**), ae, *f.* [O.L. caudō, *cf.* incūdō], lit. 'a cutting.' *cf.* 'decision.' Hence, **1.** Lit. : in law, *a process of law, a law-suit, case :* causae privatae, publicae, Cic. ; causam dicere, agere, orare, *to plead a case,* Cic., Liv. ; defendere, Cic. ; constituere, Cic. ; causam cognoscere, *to examine* (as a judge), Caes. ; causā cadere, *to lose an action,* Cic. ; causam perdere, Cic. ; indictā causā, *without pleading,* Cic. **2.** Transf. **A.** *a discussion, a matter of discussion :* disserendi, Cic. ; Juv. **B.** *a matter in hand, business, concern,* etc. **a.** *a commission, charge :* cui senatus dederat causam ut etc., Cic. **b.** *political* or *party interests :* in causam plebis inclinatus, Liv.; Cic. **c.** *condition, position, case :* in eādem causā fuerunt Usipetes, Caes. ; Cic. **d.** *personal relations, connexion :* explicare breviter quae mihi sit ratio et causa cum Caesare, Cic. N.B. esp. the ABL. with a GEN. (which it us. follows) or *Pron.*

Possess. : nostrā causā, *in our interests,* Cic. ; patris causā, Pl. ; hence, *for the sake of :* emolumenti, honoris, Cic. ; sui muniendi, Caes. **C.** *the grounds or cause of something.* **a.** In gen. *an effective cause, inducement, motive, purpose, cause, reason :* causa ea est quae id efficit cuius est causa, Cic. ; appellationis, Caes. ; belli, Liv. ; rerum, Verg. ; explicandae philosophiae, Cic. ; ad obiurgandum, Ter. With *Inf.* : Verg. **Prep. phr.** : quā de causā, Cic. ; ob (*or* propter) eam causam, Cic., etc. With *conjs.* : quid est causae, quae est causa, quin, Ter., Cic. ; Hor., etc. ; nulla causa quo minus, Sall., Liv. ; cur, quā re, quam ob rem, quod, ut, ne, Pl., Cic., Hor., etc. **b.** In partic. **i.** *good reason, just cause :* cum causā accedere ad accusandum, Cic. ; sine causā, Cic. **ii.** *a feigned cause, pretext, pretence :* Pl. ; causam inferre, Caes. ; tumultūs, Liv. ; per causam (with Gen.), *under the pretext (of) :* Caes. **iii.** *an excuse* (i.e. for not doing something) : Pl. ; causas dare, accipere, Cic. Ep. ; nectere, Verg. [It. *cosa ;* Fr. *chose.*]

causāriī, ōrum, *m. pl. invalids :* Liv. Hence, **causārius,** a, um, *sick, diseased :* Plin., Sen.

causīa, ae, *f.* [καυσία], *a Macedonian white hat with a broad brim :* Pl.

causidicus, ī, *m.* [causa and dic, *v.* dīcō], *a pleader, advocate at law* (often contemptuously) : Lucr., Cic., Juv.

causificor, ārī [causa faciō], *to make a pretext :* Pl.

causor, ārī [causa], *to plead as an excuse, to urge as a pretext :* multa, Lucr. ; Hor. ; animi perturbationem, Liv. ; valetudinem, Tac. ; *Absol.* : causando nostros in longum ducis amores, Verg. With *Inf.* : causatus consulere velle, Liv. With Acc. and *Inf.* : Liv., Tib. With *quod* clause : Suet.

caussa, *v.* causa.

causula, ae, *f.* [*dim.* causa]. **I.** *a petty lawsuit :* Cic. **II.** *a slight cause :* Auct. Bell. Afr.

cautē, *adv.* **I.** *cautiously, carefully :* Pl., Caes., Cic. *Comp.* : Cic., Hor. *Sup.* : Cic. Ep. **II.** *with security :* Cic.

cautēla, ae, *f.* [cautus, caveō], *precaution :* Pl.

cautēs, is, *f. a rough, pointed rock :* Caes., Verg.

cautim, *adv.* [cautus, caveō], *cautiously, warily* = caute : Ter.

cautiō, ōnis, *f.* [caveō]. **I.** *wariness, heedfulness, caution, circumspection,* Cic. ; mihi cautio est = cavendum est, *I must beware* (colloq.) : Pl., Ter. ; mea cautio est, *I must see to it,* Cic. ; res cautiones habet, *the matter requires caution,* Cic. ; also, *admits of caution :* Cic. Ep. **II.** *provision, security pledge, guarantee.* **a.** In gen. : hunc Pompeius omni cautione devinxerat, Cic. **b.** In business or law, *a security, bond :* Cic. Ep. With Acc. and *Inf.* : Suet.

cautor, ōris, *m.* [caveō]. **I.** *one who is on his guard :* Pl. **II.** *a surety :* Cic.

cautus, a, um. **I.** *Part.* caveō. **II.** *Adj.* **A.** *wary, cautious, provident :* Ter., Cic., Ov., etc. With *in* and ABL. : Cic., Hor. With *ad* or *adversus* and Acc. : Liv. With

Inf. : Hor. Of things : consilium, Cic., Tac. ; manus, timor, Ov. **B. Pass:** *made safe, secured :* quo mulieri esset res cautior, Cic., Hor. *Comp.* : Cic., Liv. : *Sup.* : Tac.

cavaedium, ī, *n.* [cavum aedium], *inner court of a house :* Plin. Ep.

cavea, ae, *f.* (Gen. caveāī, Lucr.)·[cavus], *an excavated place, a cavity.* **I.** In gen. : Plin. **II.** Esp. **a.** *an enclosure for animals ; a stall, cage, den, coop, bee-hive,* etc. : Pl., Cic., Verg., etc. **b.** *the auditorium of a theatre :* Cic., Verg. ; cavea ima *or* prima (*the seats of the nobility*), media, summa, *or* ultima (*the seats of the lower classes*) : Cic. **Transf.** : *a theatre :* Pl., Cic. [It. *gaggia, gabbia ;* Fr. *cage.*]

caveō, cavēre, cāvī, cautum (*Imper.* regul. cavē ; but also cave, Pl. ; Hor.) [*cf.* ἀκούω]. **I.** *to be on one's guard, to take care, beware, guard against.* **a.** In gen. : Pl. ; non fuisse difficile cavere, Caes. ; cave ! Hor. *Impers. Pass.* satis cautum est, Cic. ; Hor. ; ut ipsis ab invidiā caveatur, Liv. **b.** With *ab, to be on one's guard against :* a me, Cic., Pl. ; ab insidiis, Sall. Also with *simple* ABL. : malo, Pl. **c.** With Acc. *to beware of :* aliquid, Pl. ; vallum caecum, Caes. ; inimicitias, Cic. ; iurgia, Ov. *Pass.* : quod multis rationibus caveri potest, Cic. ; Pl. ; Liv. **d.** With *ne : to take heed lest, to guard against :* cavete ne nova proscriptio instaurata esse videatur, Cic. ; Pl. ; Ov., etc. Occ. with *ut ne :* Cic. N.B. *Imper.* with *Subj.* without *ne : take care not to :* ignoscas, Cic. ; Pl. ; Verg., etc. **e.** With *ut : to take care that :* caveamus, ut ea moderata sint, Cic. ; Pl. **f.** With *Inf.* : Cic. Ep., Verg. **II.** *to make provision.* **A.** In gen. : *to give protection, take care for* (us. with DAT.) : mihi meisque, Cic. ; Ov. ; sociis nihil cautum, Liv. **B.** In law or business. **a.** *to look after the legal or pecuniary interests of any one* (with DAT.) : Cic. Hence, duae leges quarum altera privatorum aedificiis cavet, etc., Cic. **b.** *to give security, to stand security for* (with ABL. of security given) : civitates obsidibus de pecuniā cavent, Caes. **c.** *to get security* = ab aliquo, Cic. **d.** *to stipulate :* Tauromenitanis cautum est foedere ne navem dare debeant, Cic. ; sociis Samnitium nihil cautum, Liv.

caverna, ae, *f.* [cavus], *a hollow, cavity, cave,* etc. : Verg. ; terrae, Lucr., Cic. ; navium, *the hold,* Cic. ; caeli, *the vault,* Lucr.

cavilla, ae, *f. jeering, scoffing, banter :* Pl.

cavillātiō, ōnis, *f.* [cavillor], *raillery, scoffing, gibe, banter.* **1.** Lit. : Pl., Cic., Liv. **2.** **Transf.** : *sophistry, quibbling :* Quint.

cavillātor, ōris, *m.* [cavillor], *a jeerer, scoffer.* **1.** Lit. : Pl., Cic. Ep. **2.** **Transf.** *a quibbler :* Sen. Ep.

cavillātrix, īcis, *fem. adj.* [cavillor], *sophistical :* Quint.

cavillor, *to jeer, scoff.* **1.** Lit. : Cic. Ep., Liv. With Acc. *to chaff, jeer at :* Cic. Ep., Liv., Tac. With Acc. and *Inf.* : Cic. **2.** **Transf.** : *to quibble :* Liv.

cavō, āre [cavus], *to make hollow, to hollow out, excavate :* lapidem, Lucr. ; navis ex arboribus, Liv. ; arbore lintris, Verg. ; oculi cavati, Lucr. ; alni cavatae, Verg.

cavum, ĭ, *n.* (Pl., Verg., Liv., etc.) and **cavus**, ĭ, *m.* (Varr., Hor.), *a hole, a hollow, a cavity.*

cavus, a, um [*cf.* κοῖλος], *hollow, hollowed,* vena, Cic. ; rupes, Liv. ; nubes, Lucr., Verg. Hence, **a.** *vaulted :* aedes, Verg. **b.** *deep-channelled :* flumina, Verg.

Caystros (-us), ĭ, *m. a river in Lydia, famous for its swans :* **Caystrius**, a, um.

ce, an inseparable demonstrative particle [*cf.* ci-tra and Gk. ἐ-κεῖ]. ce is appended to pronouns and adverbs, though the final *e* is often dropped. **1.** To pronouns : e.g. hi-c, illi-c, isti-c : sometimes the ce is doubled, e.g. hancce ('this here'), hacce, istaecce. When ce is doubled and followed by *ne*, it becomes *ci*, as in hicine, isticine, illicine. **2.** The adverbs hīc, hūc, hāc, hīnc, illūc, illīnc, illāc, istinc, etc., which already have the particle ce, are strengthened by its reduplication, as hicce, hūcce, hincce, illicce : so sic and sicine. ce occurs also in nunc, tunc, from num and tum.

Cēa (Cĭa), ae, or **Ceōs**, ō, *f.* (Acc. Ceō, Cic.), *one of the Cyclades, now Zia ;* **Cēus** (Cī-), a, um, esp. of Simonides, and **Cōae Camēnae**, *his poems ;* **Cēī**, ōrum, *m. pl. its inhabitants.*

Cebrēnis, idos (Acc. -ida), *f. Hesperie, d. of Cebren, a river-god in Troas.*

Cecrops, opis, *m. the first king of Attica ;* **Cecropius**, a, um ; **Cecropia**, ae, *f. the citadel of Athens ;* Athens ; **Cecropidēs**, ae, *m.* (Voc. -idē), *a male descendant of Cecrops, i.e.* Theseus : Transf. *one of noble birth,* Juv. ; **Cecropidae**, ārum, *m. pl.* Athenians ; **Cecropis**, idis, *f.* **I.** *a female descendant of Cecrops :* esp. Aglauros ; in *pl.* Procne and Philomela. **II.** *an Athenian woman ;* as *Adj., Attic, of Attica.*

cedo and *pl.* **cette** [prob. from ce, dŏ = dā], *give here, bring me* (colloq.). **1.** Lit.: cedo aquam manibus! Pl. ; senem, Ter ; cedo alteram (*sc.* virgam), Tac. **2.** Transf. **a.** *tell me, let's hear :* unum cedo auctorem tui facti, Cic. ; Ter. In Ter. also cedodum. **b.** To call attention, *behold !* cedo mihi leges Atinias, Cic. **c.** *let me :* cedo ut inspiciam, Pl.

cēdō, cēdere, cessi, cessum. **I.** *to go, move, walk along.* **1.** Lit.: retrorsus cedit, Pl. ; Hor. **2.** Transf. **a.** Like ire : *to come to something, to have some result, to turn out :* prospere, Sall., Tac. ; bene, Hor. ; malo, Ov. ; Verg. ; Quint. **b.** cedere pro aliquā re : *to go for something* (as of equal value), *to be the price of :* epulae pro stipendio cedunt, Tac. ; Cato. **c.** With Dat. or *in* and Acc., *to fall to one's lot or share, accrue :* ut is quaestus huic cederet, Cic. ; Verg. ; arma Antoni in Augustum cessere, Tac. ; in Romanum imperium, Liv. ; in dicionem Antoni, Tac. ; aurum in praedam, Liv. ; praedae, Liv. ; praeda alicui, Hor. **d.** With *in* and Acc. (like abire), *to be changed into, become :* poena in vicem fidei cessit, Liv. ; cedere in unum, *to be of one opinion,* Tac. **II. A.** Intrans. : *to go away, to withdraw, depart, retire.* **1.** Lit.: Pl., Cic. ; quoquam, Lucr. ; de caelo, Enn. ; e corpore anima, Lucr. ; e patriā, Cic. ;

patriā, Cic. ; coma de vertice, Cat. Esp. milit. *to retreat, withdraw, evacuate :* de oppidis, Cic. ; ex loco. Liv. ; loco, Liv., Tac. Mercant : cedere foro, i.e. *to become bankrupt,* Juv. **2.** Transf. **a.** In gen.: horae quidem cedunt et dies, Cic. ; cedere e vitā, Cic. ; vitā, Cic., Hor. ; non cessit fiducia Turno, Verg. ; memoriā, Liv. **b.** With Dat. or implied Dat. : *to yield, give place to, submit :* Viriatho nostri exercitūs cesserunt, Cic. ; fortunae, Caes. ; malis, Cic., Verg. ; precibus, Cic. **c.** *to give place to* (i.e. *to be inferior to*), *to yield to* (with or without Abl. of Manner) : neque multum cedebant virtute nostris, Caes. ; Cic. ; salix cedit olivae, Verg. Pass. Impers. : ut non multum Graecis cederetur, Cic. ; Liv. **d.** In law : alicui bonis *or* possessione cedere, *to relinquish property in favour of somebody :* Cic., Liv. **B.** Trans. **a.** With Acc. of obj. (rare except in case of *Neut. Pron.,* etc.), and Dat. : *to concede, give up, yield :* aliquid cedo amicitiae, tribuo parenti, Cic. ; cedere currum ei, Liv. **b.** With *ut* clause : Liv. ; Caesar cessit ut Nero consulatum iniret, Tac. ; Liv.

cedrus, ĭ, *f.* [κέδρος], *the cedar.* **1.** Lit.: Plin. **2.** Transf. **a.** *cedar-wood :* Verg., Curt. **b.** *cedar-oil* (used to preserve books) : Hor., Ov., etc. [It. cedrato : Fr. cédrat.]

Celaenae, ārum, *f. pl. a town in Phrygia, on the R. Maeander,* scene of the contest of Apollo and Marsyas ; **Celaenaeus**, a, um.

Celaenō, ūs, *f.* **I.** *d. of Atlas, one of the Pleiades.* **II.** *one of the Harpies ;* hence, *an avaricious woman :* Juv.

cēlātum, ĭ, *n.* [cēlō], *a secret :* Pl.

celeber, bris, bre, *adj.* (*masc.* celebris, Tac.), *crowded,* us. in Sup. **celeberrimus** : *crowded, populous, frequented, resorted to* (opp. desertus). **1.** Lit.: via, Cato ; urbs, Cic. ; in celeberrimo urbis loco, Cic. ; forum, Cic. With Abl. Instr. : fontibus Ide, Ov. **2.** Transf. **a.** Of festivals ; *largely attended :* Cic., Hor., Liv. Hence, dies, Cic. **b.** Of persons, etc. : *much spoken of, famous :* Tiresias famā, Ov. ; vir ingenio, Tac. ; res totā Siciliā, Cic. ; fama inter barbaros, Liv. ; nomen ad posteros, Liv. ; dea, Ov. ; responsum, Liv. Sup. : Liv. **c.** *crowded,* in quick succession : verba, Ov.

celebrātiō, ōnis, *f.* [celebrō]. **I.** *a gathering in crowds, a large assembly :* Cic. In *pl.* : Cic. **II.** *a festal celebration, a festival :* ludorum, Cic. Ep. ; annua, Tac.

celebrātus, a, um. **I.** Part. celebrō. **II.** Adj. : **a.** *much-frequented :* forum, Sall. ; hence, *much-used, frequent :* Cic. **b.** *attended by crowds, solemnised :* supplicatio, Liv. ; dies, Ov. **c.** *much-spoken of, famous :* Tac. Comp. : Liv., Ov.

celebrĭtās, ātis, *f.* [celeber]. **1.** Lit.: *a crowding, crowd* (with the idea of *bustling*) : iudiciorum, Cic. Ep. ; viae, Cic. Ep. ; Tac. ; virorum, Cic. **2.** Transf. **a.** *large attendance at or celebration of* a festival : ludorum, supremi diei, Cic. **b.** *fame, renown :* sermonis hominum, Cic.

celebrō, āre [celeber]. **I.** *to go in great numbers or often to.* **1.** Lit.: delubra, Lucr. ; viam, Cic. ; forum, silvas, Ov.

2. Trans f. **a.** *to crowd, fill :* contiones convicio cantorum, Cic. ; ripas carmine, Ov. ; cuius nuntiis celebrantur aures cotti die meae, Cic. **b.** *to do frequently,* *practise often, exercise, repeat :* ad eas artis celebrandas, Cic. ; popularem potestatem, Liv. ; seria et iocos cum aliquo, Liv. ; Pl. ; nuptias, Liv. ; coetum, Verg. ; convivium omnium sermone laetitiâque, Cic. **c.** *to escort, attend :* Cic., Tac. Trans f. : avus laude celebratus, Cic. **d.** *to make widely known, advertise, broadcast, honour :* laudem carminibus, Cic. ; honores alicuius, Verg. ; memoriam, Tac. ; sententiam magno sensu, Tac. ; aliquem admiratione, Tac.

celer, celeris, celere, *swift, fleet, quick, rapid, speedy, hurried, fast.* **1.** Lit. **a.** Of living beings : Pl., Hor., Ov., etc. With *Inf.:* Hor. **b.** Of things : curriculum, Pl.; flamma, Lucr. ; motus, Lucr., Caes. ; receptus, Caes. ; navis, Cat. ; turbo, Verg. ; venti, rivi, Hor. **2.** Trans f. : consilium, Ter. ; mens, oratio, Cic. ; victoria, Caes. : remedia, Nep. ; fata, Verg. In bad sense : *hasty, precipitate, rash :* iambi, Hor. ; con silia, Liv. ; desperatio rerum, Liv. Comp. : celerior, Cic. Sup. : celerrimus, Cic., Verg. As Noun, **celerēs,** um, *m. pl. the mounted bodyguard of the Roman kings :* Liv.

celere, adv. *quickly :* Enn., Pl.

celeri-pēs, pedis, adj. [celer pēs], *swift footed :* Cic. Ep.

celeritās, ātis, f. [celer], *swiftness, quickness, speed, rapidity.* **1.** Lit. : equitum, Caes. ; equorum, pedum, navis, Cic. ; in capiendis castris, Cic. In *pl. :* Cic. **2.** Trans f. **a.** Of news : Caes. **b.** In gen. : ani morum, ingeni, orationis, syllabarum, Cic. ; dicendi, Cic. ; veneni, Cic.

celeriter, adv. *quickly, speedily :* Pl., Caes., Cic. Ep. Comp. : celerius, Caes., Cic. Sup. : celerrimē, Caes., Cic.

celerō, āre [celer]. **A.** Trans. : *to quicken, hasten, speed up, accelerate :* casūs, Lucr. ; gradum, viam, Verg. ; fugam in silvas, Verg. ; celerandae victoriae intentior, Tac. **B.** Intrans. : *to make haste, hasten, speed, accelerate :* Lucr., Cat., Tac.

Celeus (trisyl.), eī, m. *king of Eleusis, f. of Triptolemus.*

cella, ae, f. [perh. fr. cēlō]. **I.** *a store-room, a place for grain or fruits, a granary,* etc. : Cato, Cic., Verg., etc. ; apium, *bee-cells,* Verg. Hence, dare, emere, imperare ali quid in cellam, Cic., etc. **II.** *a mean apart ment or garret,* etc. : Ter., Cato ; esp. of slaves : Cic., Hor. **III.** *the part of a temple in which the image of the god stood, the sanctuary :* Cic., Liv. **IV.** *a room in a bathing-house :* Plin. Ep. **V.** *a room in a brothel :* Juv.

cellārius, a, um [cella], *of a store-room :* sagina, Pl. As Noun, **cellārius,** ī, m. *one who has charge of stores, a steward, butler :* Pl.

cellula, ae, f. [dim. cella], *a small store-room, or apartment :* Ter.

Celmis, is, m. *one of the Idaean Dactyli, priests of Cybele.*

cēlō, āre [cf. καλύπτω, oc-culō], *to hide, cover.* **1.** Lit. **a.** fontium origines, Hor. ; Lucr. ; Ov. **b.** *to hide* (by putting into a place of concealment). **i.** Of persons :

plerosque hi qui receperant celant, Caes.; se tenebris, Verg. Pass. : diu celari virgo non potest, Ter. **ii.** Of things : Caes. ; sacra alia terrā, Liv. **2.** Trans f. **A.** *to avoid revealing, hide, veil* (feelings, etc.) : gaudium, Ter. ; consilia, Cat. ; Ov. **B.** Of facts, words, etc. : *to keep secret, be silent about.* **a.** With Acc. of object : senten tiam, Cic. ; Caes. ; factum, Verg. Pass. ut celetur consuetio, Pl. ; Lucr. **b.** With Acc. of object and Acc. of person (from whom one conceals), *to hide something from one, to keep one in the dark about* or in *ignorance of something :* te sermonem, Cic. Ep. ; Liv. ; Ov. O c c. with Acc. of object omitted or implied : nec venditor celare emptores debuit, Cic. ; Ov. Pass. : cela bar, Cic. Esp. Pass. with de and ABL. : credo celatum esse Cassium de Sullā, Cic. ; also in Act. : Liv.

celōx, ōcis, m. and f. [same root as celer]. **I.** Adj. *swift, quick :* Pl. **II.** Noun : *a swift-sailing ship, cutter :* Pl., Liv.

celsus, a, um [-cellō, seen in excellō, etc.], *projecting, erect, prominent, lofty, tall* (celsus, high, in comparison with something else, altus, high *absolutely*). **1.** Lit. : (Deus homines) celsos et erectos constituit, Cic. ; celsus haec dicebat, Liv. ; Verg. **2.** Trans f. (morally). **a.** In good sense : *lofty, elevated :* celsus et ea, quae homini accidere possunt, omnia parva ducens, Cic. Also of *rank* or *station :* celsissima sedes dignitatis, Cic. **b.** In bad sense (rare) : *haughty, proud :* celsi et spe haud dubiā feroces, Liv. ; Cic. ; Hor. Comp. : Ov., Quint.

Celsus, ī, *m. a Roman cognomen ;* esp. A. Cornelius, *the chief Roman writer on medi cine* (A.D. 50).

Celtae, ārum, *m. pl. the Celts,* who occupied most of W. Europe ; esp. *the inhabitants of central Gaul :* **Celticus,** a, um ; **Celticum,** ī, n. (*sc.* imperium), *the Celtic nation :* **Celticē,** adv. *in the Celtic language.*

Celtibērī, ōrum, *m. pl. a people in central Spain ; sing.* **Celtibēr,** ērī, Cat. ; **Celti bēria,** ae, *f. their country ;* **Celtibēricus,** a, um ; **Celtibēr,** ēra, ērum.

cēna, ae, f. *the principal meal of the Romans* taken about 3–4 p.m. **1.** Lit. : Pl., Cic., Hor., etc. ; curare, Pl. ; apparare, Ter.; facere, Cic. Ep. ; invitare or vocare ad cenam, Cic. Ep.; anteponere, Pl. ; ap ponere, Ter. ; cenam dare alicui, Pl., Cic. Ep. ; cenae aliquem adhibere, Plin. Ep.; cenae caput, *the principal dish,* Cic. ; cena prior, i.e. *a previous invitation,* Hor. ; cenam condicere alicui, *to engage oneself to any one as a guest,* Suet. ; inter cenam, *at table,* Cic. Esp. of festal occasions : auguralis, Cic. ; nuptialis, Pl. **2.** Trans f. **a.** *a dish, course,* at dinner : Mart. **b.** *a company at table :* ingens cena sedet, Juv.

cēnāculum, ī, n. [cēna], *orig. a dining-room,* us. in an upper story ; hence, *an upper story, an upper room, a garret :* Pl., Cic., Hor., etc. Of the lodgings of the poor : Juv.

cēnāticus, a, um [cēna], *of a dinner :* Pl.

cēnātiō, ōnis, f. [cēnō], *a dining-room :* Plin. Ep., Juv.

cēnātus, a, um, *Part.* [cēnō]. **I,** *having dined :* cur te cenatum noluerit occidere, Cic.; Pl.; Hor. **II.** Of time : *spent in feasting :* noctes, Pl.

Cenchrēis, idis, *f. w. of Cinyras and m. of Myrrha.*

Cenimagni, ōrum, *m. pl. a British tribe in East Anglia.*

cēnĭtŏ, āre [*freq.* cēnō], *to be accustomed to dine :* Cic. Ep., Suet.

cēnō, āre [cēna]. **A.** Intrans.: *to take a meal, dine, eat :* Pl., Cic., Hor. **B.** Trans.: *to make a meal of, to eat, dine upon :* cenam, Pl.; avis, Hor.; septem fercula, Juv. Transf.: magnum malum, Pl. (See also cenatus.)

cēnseō, cēnsēre, cēnsui, cēnsum. Polit. **I.** *to appraise, assess, value, rate* (of persons and property). **1.** Lit. **a.** *to take account of the names and property of Roman citizens* (the office of the censors), *to take the census :* Pl.; censores populi aevitates, subolis, familias, pecuniasque censento, Cic.; Liv.; esse consui censendo, *to become a fit subject for the censor's list,* Cic.; is censendo finis factus est, Liv.; capite censi, *rated or counted by the head* (= the lowest class of citizens), Sall. **b.** *to give an account or return of one's property* (also as *depon.* cēnseor, cēnsus) : censendi causā, Cic.; in quā tribu ista praedia censuisti? Cic. **2.** Transf. In gen.: *to estimate, esteem, value :* Pl.; si res cenaenda sit, Cic.; censendum nil nisi dantis amor, Ov.; unā victoriā Carius censebatur, Tac. With GEN. of price: Pl. **II.** *to deliver an opinion, be of opinion.* **a.** Of an official, senator, etc.: *to state as one's opinion, vote* (with ACC. and *Gerund.,* or ACC. and *Inf.* or with *ut* or *ne* and *Subj.*) : captivos reddendos in senatu non censuit, Cic.; Liv., etc.; plerique censebant, ut noctu iter facerent, Caes.; Cic.; Tac. With ellipsis : pars deditionem, pars eruptionem censebant (*sc.* faciendam), Liv.; mitiora censuit, *proposed a mitigated sentence,* Tac. Also *absol. :* Tac. **b.** Of the Senate : *to express an opinion, vote.* With ACC. and Gerund. or ACC. and *Inf. :* iungendum foedus cum Lucanis censuerunt, Liv.; Caes.; Cic.; censuere patres duas provincias Hispaniam rursus fieri . . . et Macedoniam Illyriamque eosdem obtinere, Liv. With *ut* or *ne* and *Subj. :* Caes., Cic., Liv. With DAT. and ACC. : bellum Samnitibus et Patres censuerunt et populus iussit, Liv. **c.** Of the populus (with ACC. and *Fut. Inf.*) : Liv. **d.** In gen.: *to be of opinion, think, judge :* quid censetis, nullasne insidias pertimescendas? Cic.; Pl.; Hor.; Liv. *Absol.* censeo, *as affirmative or encouraging answer :* Pl., Ter. **e.** *to advise,* esp. with *Subj. :* magnopere censeo desistas, Cic.; Pl.; Hor.; Liv.; quid nunc consili captandum censes? Pl.; Cic.

cēnsĭō, ōnis, *f.* [cēnseō], *an estimating, taxing, rating, assessing :* Pl.

cēnsŏr, ōris, *m.* [cēnseō], *a censor.* **1.** Lit.: the title of two Roman magistrats, who presided over the rating of the citizens, punished moral or political misdemeanour with degradation, and performed other functions : Cic., Liv. **2.** Transf.: *a rigid judge of morals, a censurer, critic :* pertristis, Cic.; Hor.; Ov.

cēnsōrĭus, a, um [cēnsor], *of the censors.* **1.** Lit. : tabulae, *the lists of the censors,* Cic.; lex, *a contract for leasing buildings,* Cic.; *for the public revenues,* Cic.; sometimes, also, *the orders,* or *decisions of the censors* (concerning the divisions of the people, taxes, public buildings, etc.), Cic.; nota (i.e. degradation by a censor), Liv.; opus, a *fault or crime punished by the censors,* Cic.; censorius homo, *one who had been censor,* Cic. **2.** Transf.: *rigid, severe :* gravitas, Cic.; Mart.

cēnsūra, ae, *f.* [cēnseō], *the office of censor, censorship.* **1.** Lit.: Cic., Ov., Liv. **2.** Transf.: *decision, criticism :* libellorum, Ov.; vini, Plin.

cēnsus, a, um, *Part.* cēnseō.

cēnsus, ūs, *m.* [cēnseō], *a registering and rating of Roman citizens, their property,* etc., *a census.* **1.** Lit.: censum habere, Cic.; agere, Liv. Less exactly, censum habere, *to make a formal counting,* Caes. **2.** Transf. **a.** *the register of the census, the censors' lists :* in censum referre, Liv.; censu prohibere, Cic. **b.** *the sum assessed :* senatorum, *a senator's fortune,* Suet.; equester, *a knight's fortune,* Suet. **c.** *wealth, property,* in gen.: homo egens, sine censu, Cic.; Liv.; Hor.; Ov.

centaurēum (or **-ium**, Lucr.), i, *n.* [κενταύρειον or κενταύριον], *the herb centaury :* Lucr.; in *pl. :* Verg.

Centauromachia, ae, *f. the name of a fictitious country :* Pl.

Centaurus, i, *m.* [Κένταυρος], *a Centaur. The Centaurs were fabled monsters of Thessaly, part man and part horse, who had a fierce conflict with the Lapithae ;* **Centaurēus, Centauricus**, a, um. Transf.: *a constellation in the S. hemisphere.*

centēnārĭus, a, um, *of the number* 100 : numerus, Varr.; Plin.

centēni, ae, a (GEN. centēnum), *a group of a hundred :* viciens centena milia passuum, Caes.; Cic.; in *sing. :* centenā arbore fluctum verberat, Verg. Hence, *a hundred each :* Hirt., Verg.

centēsĭmus, a, um [centum], *the hundredth :* Pl., Cic. As Noun **centēsĭma**, ae, *f.* (*sc.* pars), *the hundredth part, a percentage.* Of a tax : centesima rerum venalium, Tac. Of interest ; 1% monthly (12% per annum): Cic.

centĭceps, cipitis *adj.* [centum caput], *hundred-headed :* belua, Hor.

centiēs (earlier **centiēns**), *adv.* [centum], *a hundred times.* **1.** Lit.: Cic. **2.** Transf. *a great many times :* Pl., Ter.

centi-manus, a, um [centum manus], *hundred-handed :* Hor., Ov.

centō, ōnis, *m.* [κέντρων], *cloth composed of pieces sewed together, patch-work,* etc.: Cato, Juv.; used in war to ward off missiles or to extinguish fires : centones insuper iniecerunt : Caes. Prov.: centones sarcire alicui, i.e. *to impose upon by falsehood,* Pl.

centum, *indecl. adj.* [*cf.* ἑκατόν], *a hundred.* **1.** Lit.: Cic. **2.** Transf.: *an indefinitely large number :* Verg., Hor.

centum-gemĭnus, a, um, *a hundred-fold* : Verg.

centumplex, ĭcis, *adj.* [centum plicō], *a hundred-fold* : murus, Pl.

centumpondĭum, ĭ, *n.* [centum, pondō], *a hundred pounds in weight* : Pl., Cato.

centumvĭrālis, e, *adj.* [centum viri], *pertaining to the centumviri* : iudicium, Cic. ; Quint., Suet.

centum vĭri, ōrum, *m. pl. a bench of judges chosen annually for civil suits* : Cic., Quint., Suet.

centunculus, ĭ, *m.* [*dim.* centō], *a piece of patch-work* : Sen. Ep. ; *a party-coloured horse-cloth* : Liv.

centurĭa, ae, *f.* [centum], *orig. a parcel or division of a hundred things of one kind* : hence, in gen., *any division.* Esp. **A.** Milit.: *a division.* **a.** of the legion, *a century* (= ⅓ maniple, ⅓ cohort, ₆₀ legion): Caes., Liv. **b.** *a division of cavalry under the kings* : Liv. **B.** Constit. *a century,* i.e. one of the 193 groups into which Servius Tullius divided the Roman people : Cic., Liv.

centurĭātĭm, *adv.* [centuria], *by centuries.* Milit.: Caes., Liv. Constit.: Cic.

centurĭātus, a, um, *Part.* centuriō, *divided into centuries* : comitia centuriata, Cic., Liv. Comic.: Pl. O c c. *passed in the* com. cent.: lex, Cic.

centurĭātus, ūs, *m.* [centuriō]. **I.** *a division into centuries* : Liv. **II.** *the post of centurion* : Cic.

centurĭō, āre [centuria], *to divide into centuries.* **A.** Of the infantry : iuventutem centuriare, Liv. ; Cic. **B.** Of the people in the comitia, *v.* centuriatus.

centurĭō, ōnis, *m.* [centuria], *the commander of an infantry century* ; *centurion* : Caes., Cic., Liv., Hor.

centurĭōnātus, ūs, *m.* [centuriō], *an election of centurions* : Tac.

centussis, is, *m.* [centum as], *a hundred asses* : Pers.

cēnŭla, ae, *f.* [*dim.* cēna], *a little dinner* : Cic., Mart.

Ceōs, *v.* Cēa.

Cephalus, ĭ, *m. h. of Procris.*

Cēphēnes, um, *m. pl. an Ethiopian people, called after their king Cepheus* ; **Cēphēnus**, a, um.

Cēpheus (disyl.), eī (Acc. -ea), *m. king of Ethiopia, h. of Cassiope, f. of Andromeda* ; **Cēphēĭus** (-ēus), a, um ; **Cēphēĭs**, ĭdis, *f. d. of Cepheus, esp. Andromeda.*

Cēphīsus (-os), ī, *m.* **I.** *a river in Phocis and Boeotia, the deity of which was f. of Narcissus* ; **Cēphīsĭus**, i. m. *Narcissus* ; **Cēphīsĭs**, ĭdis, *f. adj.* **II.** *a river in Attica* ; **Cēphīsĭas**, adis, *f. adj.*

cēra, ae, *f.* [*cf.* κηρός], *wax.* **1.** L i t.: Lucr., Cic., Verg. In *pl.* of the cells of bees : Verg. **2.** T r a n s f. **a.** *a writing-tablet covered with wax* : Pl., Cic., Ov., etc. ; prima cera, *the first page,* Hor. ; Cic. Of wills : Juv., Suet. **b.** *a wax seal* : Pl., Cic., Ov. **c.** *a waxen image of an ancestor* : Sall., Ov. [Fr. *cire.*]

Cerāmīcus, ī, *m. the name of two cemeteries, one inside, the other outside, the walls of Athens.*

cērārĭum, ī, *n. a fee for affixing a seal* : Cic.

Cerastae, ārum, *m. pl. a horned people in Cyprus, changed into bullocks.*

cerastēs, ae, *m.* [κεράστης], *a horned serpent* : Prop.

cerăsus, ī, *f.* [κέρασος]. **I.** *the cherry-tree* : Varr., Ov. **II.** *a cherry* : Prop. [It. *ciriegia* or *ciliegia* ; Fr. *cerise.*]

cērātus, a, um [cēra], *waxed* : tabula, Pl. ; tabella, Cic. ; taedae, Ov. ; Hor.

Cerberus, ī, *m. the three-headed or hundred-headed dog, which guarded the entrance to Hades* ; **Cerbereus**, a, um.

cercŏpĭthēcus, ī, *m.* [κερκοπίθηκος], *a long-tailed monkey* : Varr., Juv.

cercūrus, ī, *m.* [κέρκουρος], *a kind of light vessel peculiar to the Cyprians* : Pl., Liv. ; also, *a sea-fish,* Ov.

Cercyōn, ŏnis (Acc. -ona, Stat.), *m. a cruel tyrant at Eleusis, killed by Theseus* ; **Cercyonēus**, a, um.

cerdŏ, ōnis, *m.* [κέρδων, κέρδος], *a hireling, journeyman* : Juv.

Cerĕālis, e, *adj. of Ceres* : sulci, papaver, Verg. ; nemus, Ov. ; also *fit for Ceres* : cenae, Pl. ; hence, *of corn* : arma, *implements for grinding corn and preparing it for food* : Verg. As Noun, **Cerĕālĭa**, ium, *n. pl. the festival of Ceres (April 10th).*

Cerĕālis (-ĭālis), is, *m. a Roman cognomen* ; esp. Petilius Cerealis, *governor of Britain,* A.D. 71.

cerebellum, ī, *n.* [*dim.* cerebrum], *a small brain* : Plin. [It. *cervello* ; Fr. *cervelle, cerveau.*]

cerebrōsus, a, um [cerebrum], *hot-headed* : Lucil., Hor.

cerebrum, ī, *n. the brain.* **1.** L i t.: Pl., Cic., Verg., etc. ; alii in cerebro dixerunt animi esse sedem, Cic. Poet. for *head, skull* : Hor. **2.** T r a n s f. **a.** *understanding* : Pl., Hor., Suet. **b.** *hot temper, passion* : o te, Bolane, felicem cerebri, Hor. ; Pl.

Cerēs, eris, *f. d. of Saturn and Ops, m. of Proserpine* ; *goddess of agriculture.* T r a n s f.: *bread, grain* : Cic., Verg., Hor.

cēreus, a, um [cēra], *waxen, of wax.* **1.** L i t.: Cic. ; effigies, Hor. ; castra, Verg. **2.** T r a n s f. **a.** *wax-coloured* : pruna, Verg. ; Hor. **b.** *like wax, easily moulded* : cereus in vitium flecti, Hor. As Noun, **cēreus**, ī, *m. a wax-light, taper* : Pl., Cic. [Fr. *cierge.*]

cērārĭa, ae, *f.* [cēra], *a female maker of wax-lights* : Pl.

cērintha, ae, *f.* [κηρίνθη], *a plant of which bees are fond, wax-flower* : Verg.

cērinus, a, um [κήρινος], *wax-coloured* : Neut. *pl.* as Noun, *wax-coloured garments* : Pl.

cernō, cernere, crēvī, crētum (orig. *Part.* certus, q.v.) [*cf.* κρίνω], *to separate, sift.* **1.** L i t.: Cato, Ov. **2.** T r a n s f. *to distinguish, discern.* **a.** With the eye (freq. but only in present-stem) : *to perceive, see distinctly* : Enn. ; estne hic Hegio I si satis cerno, is hercle'st, Ter. ; vis magna pulveris cernebatur, Caes. ; ego Cumanum ex hoc loco cerno, Pompeianum non cerno, Cic. ; Lucr. ; Verg. With Acc. and *Inf.* : Caes., Sall. With *Indir.* Quest. : Cic., Verg., etc. **b.** With the mind, *to perceive,* *see clearly :* vis et natura deorum non sensu, sed mente cernitur, Cic. ; in voluptate spernendā virtus cernitur, Cic. ; cerno animo, Cic. **c.** *to decide what is doubtful.* **i.** Judicially, etc.: *to decree, determine* (= decernere) : quodcumque senatus creverit agunto, Cic. ; priusquam id sors cerneret, Liv. **ii.** *to decide by fighting :* cernere ferro, Enn., Verg. ; certamen, Pl. ; Lucr. **iii.** *to decide* (after consideration), *resolve :* with *Inf.* : Lucil., Cat. ; with Acc. and *Inf.* : Pl. **iv.** In law : of inheritances : *to decide upon,* i.e *to decide to take up ;* hereditatem, Cic., Liv.

cernuus, a, um [*cf.* κάρα, cerebrum]́, *head foremost, headlong :* Lucil., Verg.

cērōma, atis, n. [κήρωμα], *an ointment or liniment for wrestlers :* Juv.

cērōmaticus, a, um [κηρωματικός], *smeared with* ceroma : Juv.

cerrītus, a, um, *having a crazed brain, frantic, mad :* Pl., Hor.

certāmen, inis, n. [certō], *that which decides, a contest, match* (cf. 'test match'). **1.** Lit.: **a.** In gen.: Cic. ; biiugum, Verg. ; pedum, Ov. ; certamina ponere (Verg.), instituere, *to order* or *arrange a contest,* Suet. **b.** Milit. *a battle, combat :* Enn., Lucr. ; varium, navale, Caes. ; inire certamen, Liv. ; Ov. **2.** Transf. **a.** In gen. *rivalry :* est mihi tecum pro aris et focis certamen, Cic. ; verborum linguaeque, Liv. ; honoris, Cic. ; Prop. **b.** In law : pugna forensium certaminum, Quint.

certātim, adv. [certō], *with contest or struggle, in rivalry :* Cic., Verg., etc.

certātiō, ōnis, *f.* [certō], *a contending, contest,* etc. **1.** Lit. : Ter. ; corporum, Cic. In *pl.* : Suet. **2.** Transf. **a.** *rivalry :* Cic. **b.** *a discussion* (with GEN. *about something*) : multae, Cic. ; Liv.

certē, adv. [certus], *certainly, unquestionably, assuredly, undoubtedly* (*cf.* certo). **A.** In gen.: Pl. ; certe scio, Cic. ; ea certe vera sunt, Cic. ; Ov. **B.** In confirmation of a previous statement : at licuit ut certe licuit, Cic. ; o dea certe, Verg. **C.** In answers : *yes certainly,* etc. : Pl., Cic. **D.** To restrict an assertion : *surely, at least, at all events* (alone or with particles) : Pl. ; ego certe meum officium praestitero, Caes. ; Cic. ; Ov. ; certe quidem vos estis Romani, Liv. *Comp.* : Liv., Ov. [Fr. *certes.*]

certō, adv. *with certainty, for certain.* **A.** Esp. in phr. certo scio, Pl., Cic., Sall., etc. **B.** In answers : *yes certainly :* Pl., Ter. **C.** In other usages : nihil ita exspectare quasi certo futurum, Cic. ; perii certo, Pl.

certō, āre [cernō], *to decide by contest.* **1.** Lit. **a.** *to contend, compete :* cursu cum aequalibus certare, Sall. ; sagittā, Verg. **b.** Esp. in war (us. with armis, bello, etc.) : *to fight out an issue :* armis cum hoste certare, Cic. ; proelio, Sall. ; acie, Verg. *Impers. Pass.* : Verg., Tac. **2.** Transf. **a.** *to contend* (in a friendly or unfriendly way), *emulate, vie with :* minis mecum, Pl. ; certare ingenio, contendere nobilitate, Lucr. ; cum aliquo dissacitate, Cic. ; officiis inter se, Cic. ; ioco, Hor. *Impers. Pass.* : certatum inter conlegas male dictis, Liv. Occ. with DAT. for *cum* and ABL. : solus tibi

certat Amyntas, Verg. ; certantem uvam purpurae, Hor. Poet. in *Pass.* sense : certatam lite Deorum Ambraciam, *contended for,* Ov. With *Inf.* : Lucr., Verg. **b.** In law, *to dispute, debate :* Cic. ; ita de provocatione certatum ad populum est, Liv. ; si quid se iudice certes, Hor. Hence, in gen. (with *Indir. Deliberative*) : Enn.

certus, a, um [orig. *Part.* of cernō, but us. *adj.*]. **I.** *determined, resolved, settled.* **a.** Impers.: certum est, with DAT. of person resolving : *it is determined, it is one's decision :* Pl. ; us. *with Inf.* : certum est deliberatumque ... omnia dicere, Cic. ; Verg. ; certum atque decretum est, Liv. **b.** Personal. With *Inf.* : certa mori, Verg. ; Tac. With GEN. : certus eundi, Verg. ; Tac. ; consili, Tac. ; fugae, Plin. Ep. **II.** *determined, appointed, settled, definite :* concilium in diem certam indicere, Caes. ; Verg. ; domicilium, lex, tribunal, Cic. ; certi fines, Hor. ; certo aere, Ov. Occ. = *certain* (indef. but more emphatic than *quidam*), *some particular ; esp.* in *pl.* : habet certos sui studiosos, Cic. **III.** *sure, unerring, to be depended upon, trusty, faithful,* etc. **a.** Of persons : Pl., Cic., Verg., etc. **b.** Of things : receptus, Caes. ; animo certo voluntas, Verg. ; sagitta, Hor. ; agmine certo, Verg. *Neut. pl.* as Noun : certa maris, Tac. **IV.** Of the understanding and knowledge : *certain, sure, known as true :* res, Caes., Liv. ; certo patre nasci, Cic. ; rumorque per barbaros manavit certior, Liv. ; nihil certius ex eo auditum est, Liv. *Neut.* as Noun : certum scire, *to know for a certainty :* Ter., Cic. Ep., Liv. ; certum habere, Cic. Ep., Liv. ; pro certo habere, *to hold or regard as certain,* Cic. Ep. ; certum or certius facere alicui, *to make a thing certain for a person,* Pl. **b.** Of persons : *certain, sure, possessed of knowledge :* Pl. ; certus de suā geniturā, Suet. ; exiti, Tac. With Acc. and *Inf.* : Cic. Ep. esp. in phr. (aliquem) certiorem facere, *to inform, make acquainted :* Pl., Ter. With *de* : de his rebus, Caes. With GEN. : certiorem me sui consili fecit, Cic. With Acc. *and Inf.* : Caes. With *Indir. Quest.* : Caes., Cic. Ep. With *Juss. Subj.* : Caes. In *Pass.* certior fio, *I am informed* : de Caesaris adventu Helvetii certiores facti sunt, Caes. ; Cic. Ep., etc. Also, with *Posit.* : Anchisen facio certum, Verg. ; Pl. *Sup.* : Caes., Verg.

cērula, ae, *f.* [*dim.* cēra], *a small piece of wax :* miniata, i.e. *a critic's red pencil :* Cic. Ep.

cērussa, ae, *f. white-lead,* used by painters, etc. ; as a cosmetic : Pl., Ov.

cērussātus, a, um [cērussa], *painted with white lead :* Cic., Mart.

cerva, ae, *f.* [cervus], *a hind :* Ov. Poet.: *deer* in gen. : Ter., Cat., Verg., etc.

cervical, ālis, n. [cervix], *a pillow or bolster :* Juv. In *pl.* : Plin. Ep.

cervicula, ae, *f.* [*dim.* cervix], *a small or elegant neck :* Cic., Quint.

cervīnus, a, um [cervus], *of a stag or deer :* Varr. ; pellis, Hor. ; Ov. ; senectus (i.e. of great age), Juv.

cervix, īcis, *f. the neck ; the nape, the back of*

the neck with the parts touching it (collum, *the neck* simply) ; alw. *pl.* in Sall., Cic. **1.** L i t. : Enn., Cic., Verg., etc. ; sextā cervice ferri (i.e. on the necks of six men), Juv. Of execution : cervices alicui dare, Cic. ; cervices securi subicere, Cic. Of animals : Cic., Verg. **2.** T r a n s f. (from bearing the yoke). **a.** Bad sense, i.e. of involuntary, apathetic, etc. conduct : imposuistis in cervicibus nostris dominum, Cic. ; regno in cervices accepto, Liv. ; bellum ingens in cervicibus erat, Liv. **b.** Good sense, i.e. of voluntary, etc. action : suis cervicibus rem publicam sustinent, Cic.

cervus (older **cervos**), i, *m.* [*cf.* cornu], *a stag, a deer.* **1.** L i t. : Cic., Verg. ; vincere cervum cursu, Pl. **2.** T r a n s f.: cervi, *forked stakes :* milit. *chevaux-defrise :* Caes., Tib., Liv.

cessātiō, ōnis, *f.* [cēssō] **I.** *a hanging back, delaying :* Pl. **II.** *inactivity, idleness :* Cic.

cessātor, ōris, *m.* [cēssō], *a loiterer, an idler :* Cic. Ep., Hor.

cessiō, ōnis, *f.* [cēdō]. Legal : *a giving up, surrendering :* Cic.

cessō, āre [*freq.* cēdō], lit. *to give way often ;* hence, **a.** *to hang back, slacken off, become remiss :* ab opere, ab apparatu munitionum, Liv. With *Inf.* : Pl., Cic. Ep., Verg., Liv. Impers. Pass. : Liv. **b.** *to hang back, be remiss :* Ter., Cic. ; nullo officio, Liv. ; in studio atque opere, Cic. ; also with in and Acc. : in vota precesque, Verg. Impers. Pass. : Verg. **c.** *to rest, be inactive, idle :* nihil agere et cessare (of the gods of Epicurus), Cic. ; Verg. Impers. Pass. : Ter. Of land, *to lie fallow :* Verg. ; cessata arva, Ov. Of altars, *to be unvisited by worshippers :* Ov. **d.** In law : *to default* by non-appearance : Suet.

cestrosphendonē, ēs, *f.* [κεστροσφενδόνη], *a military engine for hurling stones :* Liv.

cestus and **cestos**, i, *m.* [κεστός] (lit. *worked with a needle*), *a girdle, girth :* Cato. Esp. *the charmed embroidered girdle of Venus :* Mart.

cēstus, ūs, *m.* wrongly for caestus.

cētārium, i, *n.* [cētus], *a fish pond :* Hor.

cētārius, i, *m.* [cētus], *a fish-monger :* Ter., Cic.

cētē, *v.* cētus.

cēter-, cētera, cēterum (Nom. *sing. m.* not in use], *adj. the other, the remaining. the rest of.* In *sing.* : a pecu cetero apsunt, Pl. ; vestem et ceterum ornatum, Cic. ; multitudo, Liv. ; silva, Verg. In *pl., all the other, the rest of :* Ter., Cic., Hor. ; Aedui ceterique amici populi Romani, Caes. As Noun (esp. in *pl.*), *the rest :* Pl. ; ceterum omne incensum, Liv. ; et tu et ceteri, Cic. ; ut omittam cetera, Cic. ; Hor. **cēterum**, Acc. *n. sing.* as adv. **a.** *for the rest, in other respects, otherwise :* Pl. ; foedera alia aliis legibus, ceterum eodem modo omnia fiunt, Liv. **b.** In passing to a new point, *besides, for the rest, further* (freq. in Liv.) : ceterum ex aliis negotiis quae impensio exercentur, Sall. ; Pl. **c.** With a restricting force, *but, yet, still, on the other hand :* avidus potentiae, ceterum vitia sua occultans, Sall. ; Liv. ; Tac. **cētera**, Acc. *n.*

pl. as adv. *in all other respects :* vir cetera egregius, Liv. ; cetera laetus, Hor. ; quiescas cetera, Pl. ; Verg.

cēterōqui or **-quin** [cēter qui], adv. *for the rest, in other respects, otherwise :* Cic.

Cethēgus, i, *m. a Roman cognomen in the gens* Cornelia ; esp. **I.** M. Cornelius, *a famous orator.* **II.** C. Cornelius, *one of Catiline's fellow-conspirators.*

cētos, *v.* cētus.

cētra, cētrātus, *v.* caetr-.

cette, *v.* cedo.

cētus, i, *m.* and **cētos**, *n. (pl.* cētē, Verg.) [κῆτος], *any large sea-animal, a whale, a shark, dog-fish, seal, dolphin, etc.* : Pl., Plin.

ceu, adv. *as, like as, just as.* In comparisons : tenuis fugit ceu fumus in auras, Verg. ; Cat. ; Hor. ceu cum, *as when :* Verg., Sen. : ceu si, *as if, as it were, like as if :* Lucr. Also as *conj. as though, as if :* Enn. ; ceu cetera nusquam bella forent, Verg.

Cēyx, ȳcis (Acc. ȳca), *m. s. of Lucifer, king of Trachis, h. of Alcyone ; he and his wife were changed into kingfishers.*

Chabriās, ae, *m. a famous Athenian general* (ob. B.C. 357).

Chalciopē, ēs, *f. s. of Medea, and w. of Phrixus.*

Chaldaei, ōrum, *m. pl. a people of Assyria, early famous in astrology and astronomy ;* hence, *astrologers :* Cic. ; **Chaldaeus, Chaldāicus**, a, um.

Chalybes, um, *m. pl. a peopl. of Pontus, noted as workers of iron.*

chalybēius, a, um [χαλυβήϊος], *of steel :* massa, Ov.

chalybs, ybis, *m.* [χάλυψ], *steel :* Verg. Of *a horses's bit :* Luc. ; of *a rail :* Luc.

Chāones, um, *m. pl. a people of Epirus ;* **Chāonius**, a, um ; **Chāonis**, idis, *f. adj.* **Chāonia**, ae, *f. their land.*

Chaos (Nom. and Acc. ; Abl. Chaō), *n.* [χάος], *infinite empty space.* **A.** *the gulf of the Lower World :* Verg. ; Ov. **B.** *the confused, shapeless mass out of which the universe was made :* Verg., Ov. ; a Chao, *from the beginning of the world,* Verg.

chara, ae, *f. an edible root found in Spain :* Caes.

charactēr, ēris, *m.* [χαρακτήρ]. L i t. *a marker for branding.* T r a n s f. *a mark, character, style, etc. :* Varr.

charistia, ōrum, *n. pl.* [χαρίστια], *a family banquet* (after the Parentalia, Feb. 20), *at which family feuds were settled :* Ov.

Charites, um, *f. pl.* [χάριτες, pure Lat. Gratiae], *the Graces.*

Charōn, ontis, *m. the ferryman of the Lower World.*

Charōndās, ae, *m. a legislator of Catana.*

charta, ae, *f.* [χάρτης], *a leaf of the Egyptian papyrus, paper.* **1.** L i t. : Lucr., Plin. ; dentata, *smoothed* (*with ivory*), *fine paper,* Cic. Ep., Hor. ; soluta, *an undone wrapper,* Juv. **2.** T r a n s f. **a.** *the papyrus plant,* Plin. **b.** *a writing, letter, poem, etc.* : Lucr., Cic., Hor. **c.** *any thin leaf, plate :* plumbea, Suet.

chartula, ae, *f.* [*dim.* charta], *a little paper, a bill :* Cic. Ep. [Fr. *chartre*.]

Charybdis, is, *f. the whirlpool in the straits of Messina.* T r a n s f. : Cic., Hor.

chēlē, ēs, f. [χηλή, the *claw* of an animal]. Pl. chēlae, astron : Lit. *the arms of Scorpio.* Transf.: *the constellation Libra, into which Scorpio extends* : Verg.

chelydrus, ī, m. [χέλυδρος], *a fetid water-snake* : Verg.

chelys (Acc. -yn, Voc. -y), f. [χέλυς], *the tortoise.* Transf.: *a musical instrument (a sort of lyre) made of the shell of a tortoise* (pure Lat. testudo) : Ov.

cheragra, ae, f. [χειράγρα], *gout in the hand* : Hor.

Cherronēsus (**Cherson-**), ī, f. Lit.: *a peninsula;* esp. **I. Ch. Thrācia,** *the Chersonese,* now *Gallipoli.* **II. Ch. Taurica,** *the Crimea.*

chīliarchēs, ae, and **-us**, ī, m. [χιλιάρχης and -ος]. **I.** *the commander of a thousand men* : Curt. **II.** In Persia, *the chancellor* or '*grand vizier*' : Nep.

Chīlō, ōnis, m. *a Lacedaemonian, one of the Seven Wise Men.*

Chimaera, ae, f. (χίμαιρα). **I.** *a fire-breathing monster killed by Bellerophon.* **II.** the name of *a ship* : Verg.

Chionē, ēs, f. **I.** d. *of Daedalion,* m. *of Autolycus.* **II.** m. *of Eumolpus.*

Chios or **Chīus**, ī, f. *an island in the Aegean Sea, famous for wine and marble,* now *Scio* : **Chīus,** a, um ; **Chīum,** ī, n. *Chian wine* ; n. pl. *fine Chian cloth.*

chīrographum, ī, n. [χειρόγραφον], *hand-writing* (pure Lat. manus). **1.** Lit.: *autograph* : Cic. **2.** Transf. **a.** *the writing or document itself* : Cic., Suet. **b.** *a bond, surety,* or *obligation under one's own hand* : Suet.

Chīrōn, ōnis (Acc. -ōna), m. *a centaur famous for his knowledge of plants, medicine, and divination ; s. of Saturn and Philyra ; tutor of Aesculapius, Hercules and Achilles ; became a constellation.*

chīronomos, ī, m.f. and **chīronomōn**, ūntis, m. [χειρονόμος or χειρονομῶν], *one who moves his hands according to the rules of art : a gesticulator* : Juv.

chīrūrgia, ae, f. [χειρουργία], *surgery.* Transf.: *violent remedies* : chirurgiae taedet, Cic. Ep.

chlamydātus, a, um [chlamys], *dressed in a military cloak* : Cic., Pl.

chlamys, ydis, f. [χλαμύς], *a Greek military cloak* : Pl., Cic., Verg.; embroidered or inwrought with gold-thread, Verg. ; purple, Ov. Worn also by non-military persons : Verg., Tac. ; by children : Verg.

Choerilus, ī, m. *an incompetent Greek epic poet who accompanied Alexander the Great.*

chorāgium, ī, n. [Dor. χοραγία], *the training and production of a chorus* : Pl.

chorāgus, ī, m. [Dor. χοραγός], *one who defrays the cost of production of a chorus,* the *choregus* : Pl.

choraulēs, ae, m. [χοραύλης], *a flute-player who accompanied the chorus-dance* : Juv., Suet.

chorda, ae, f. [χορδή], *a gut, gut-string,* esp. **a,** *catgut, a string (of a musical instrument)* : Lucr., Cic., Hor. **b.** *a rope, cord* : Pl.

chorēa (**-rēa,** Verg.), ae, f. [χορεία] (us. in pl.), *a dance in a ring, a dance* : Lucr., Verg., etc.

chorēus or **-īus,** ī, m. [χορεῖος, sc. πούς,

pēs], in prosody, *a trochee,* i.e. the foot — ᵕ : Cic.

chorocitharista, ae, m. [χοροκιθαριστής], *one who plays the cithara to accompany a chorus* : Suet.

chorus, ī, m. [χορός], *a dance in a ring, a round dance* = chorea. **1.** Lit.: agitare, exercere, Verg.; Hor. **2.** Transf. **a.** *a band of singers and dancers, a chorus, choir* : Cic., Verg. Esp. in tragedy : Hor. **b.** Of others, *a choir, troop* : philosophorum, Cic. ; Dryadum, Verg. [Fr. choeur.]

Chremēs, ētis or is or ī (Acc. -ēta, -ētem, -em or -ēn ; Dat. -ēti ; Voc. -es, -ē), m. *an old miser* : Ter., Cic., Hor.

Christus, ī, m. [χριστός, anointed], *Christ* : Plin. Ep. ; **Christiānus,** ī, m. *a Christian.*

chrysanthus, ī, m. [χρυσός ἄνθος], *gold-flower* ; perh. *ivyflower* or *marigold* : Verg.

Chrysēs, ae, m. *a priest of Apollo* : **Chrysēis,** idis, f. *his daughter, a captive of Agamemnon.*

Chrysippus, ī, m. *a famous Stoic philosopher, pupil of Cleanthes and Zeno,* B.C. 290–210 ;

Chrysippēus, a, um.

chrysolithos, ī, m.f. [χρυσόλιθος, gold-stone], *chrysolite, topaz* : Prop., Ov.

chrysos, ī, m. [χρυσός], *gold* : Pl.

cibārius, a, um [cibus], *of food.* **1.** Lit.: res, Pl. ; Cato. As Noun, **cibāria,** ōrum, n. pl. *rations, food-allowance* : Pl., Caes., Cic., Hor., etc. Of provincial governors : Cic. **2.** Transf.: *of the food of slaves, coarse, ordinary* : panis, *black-bread,* Cic.

cibātus, ūs, m. [cibō], *food, victuals, nutriment* : Pl., Lucr., Varr.

cibō, āre [cibus], *to feed, fodder* (of animals) : Suet.

cibōrium, ī, n. [κιβώριον], *a drinking-cup* (made like the large *pod* of the Egyptian bean) : Hor.

cibus, ī, m. *food* for man and beast, *victuals.* **1.** Lit. (in *sing.* or *pl.*) : cibum capere, Pl. ; petere, Ter. ; capessere (of animals), Cic. ; Ov. **2.** Transf.: *food, nourishment.* **a.** cibus animalia, *the nourishment afforded by the air,* Cic. Of plants : Lucr. **b.** quasi quidam humanitatis cibus, Cic. ; furoris, Ov.

cicāda, ae, f. *the cicada, tree-cricket* : Lucr., Verg.

cicātricōsus, a, um [cicātrīx], *full of scars, covered with scars* : Pl., Quint.

cicātrīx, īcis, f. *a scar, a cicatrice.* **1.** Lit. : Ter. ; cicatrices adversae, Cic. ; Ov. ; Hor. **2.** Transf. **a.** Of plants : *a mark of incision* : Verg. **b.** Of a patched shoe : Juv. **c.** refricare obductam iam rei publicae cicatricem, Cic. ; Ov.

ciccus, ī, m. [κίκκος], *the core of a pome-granate ;* hence *something unimportant, worthless, a trifle* : Pl. [It. cica, cigolo ; Fr. chiche, chiquet.]

cicer, eris, n. *the chick-pea* : Pl., Hor. [It. cece ; Fr. chiche.]

Cicerō, ōnis, m. *a cognomen in the gens Tullia* ; esp. **I.** M. Tullius, *orator and statesman* (B.C. 106–43) ; **Cicerōniānus,** a, um. **II.** Q. Tullius, *his brother, legatus of Caesar.*

cichorēum, ī, n. [κιχόριον], *succory* or *endive* : Hor.

cicilendrum and **cicimandrum**, ī, n. *fanciful names for spice* : Pl.

Ciccones, um, *m. pl. a Thracian tribe near the R. Hebrus.*

ciconia, ae, *f. a stork, the white stork :* Cic., Hor. [It. *cicogna ;* Fr. *cigogne.*]

cicur, uris, *adj. tame :* bestiarum vel ciourum vel ferarum genera, Cic.

cicuta, ae, *f. hemlock.* **1.** Lit.: Ov. **2.** Trans f. **a.** *the poison extracted :* Cato, Lucr., Hor.; in *pl. :* Hor. **b.** *a pipe or flute made from it :* Lucr., Verg.

cieo, ciēre, cīvī, cītum [*cf. κίω, κινέω*], *to move, to put in motion, to stir.* **1.** Lit. **a.** calcem, Pl.; (animal) motu cietur interiore, Cic.; puppes citae, Hor. Occ. *to stir, agitate :* mare venti cient, Liv.; imo Nereus ciet aequora fundo, Verg. **b.** *to rouse or excite to or against something ; to call or send for, to summon :* ad sese aliquem, Cat.; ad arma, Liv.; aere ciere viros, Verg. Esp. *to summon to help :* Liv., Tac.; hence, *to invoke, appeal to :* nocturnos manis, Verg.; foedera et deos, Liv. **2.** Trans. **a.** *to call upon by name, mention by name :* erum, Pl.; Verg.; Tac.; triumphum nomine ciere, Liv. Hence, patrem, i.e. show one's free birth, Liv. **b.** *to set in motion, start, bring about :* often used with a Noun periphrastically : motūs, Cic.; varias voces, Lucr.; ciere simulacra pugnae, Verg.; also *to renew* a combat, i.e. give new impulse to a fight : consul pugnam ciebat, Liv.

Cilicia, ae, *f. a province in S. Asia Minor ;* **Cilix,** icis, *adj. ;* **Cilices,** um, *m. pl.* (Acc. -as, Ov.), *the Cilicians ;* **Cilissa,** ae, *f. adj. ;* **Cilicius,** a, um; **Cilicium,** i, *n.* (*sc.* vestimentum), *a garment, orig. of Cilician goats' hair, worn by soldiers and sailors* [Fr. *cilice*] ; **Ciliciēnsis,** e.

Cimber, brī, *m.* **I.** Esp. pl. **Cimbri,** ōrum, *a people of N. Germany who invaded Italy and were defeated by Marius,* B.C. 101 ; hence, **Cimbricus,** a, um. **II.** *cognomen of L. Tillius, one of the murderers of Caesar.*

cimex, icis, *m. a bug :* Plin. As a term of reproach : Hor.

Cimmerii, ōrum, *m. pl* **I.** *a Thracian people in the Crimea ;* **Cimmerius,** a, um. **II.** *a fabulous people, living in caves between Baiae and Cumae, in perpetual darkness.*

Cimon, ōnis, *m.* **I.** *f. of Miltiades.* **II.** *s. of Miltiades, a famous Athenian general* (ob. B.C. 449).

cinaedicus, a, um [cinaedus], *lewd :* Pl.

cinaedus, i, *m.* [*κίναιδος*]. **I.** *a sodomite :* Pl., Juv. **II.** *a wanton dancer :* Pl.

cincinnātus, *adj.* [cincinnus], *with curled hair :* Pl., Cic.

Cincinnātus, i, *m. a cognomen in the gens Quinctia ;* esp. L. Quinctius, dictator, B.C. 458.

cincinnus, i, *m. curled hair, a lock or curl of hair.* **1.** Lit.: Pl., Cic. **2.** Trans f. : *too elaborate oratorical ornament* (*cf.* calamister) : in oratoris cincinnis ac fuco, Cic.

Cincius, a, *name of a Roman gens ;* esp. **I.** L. Cincius Alimentus, *a Roman historian.* **II.** M. Cincius *a plebeian tribune,* B.C. 204, *author of the lex de donis et muneribus.*

cincticulus, i, *m.* [*dim.* cinctus], *a little girdle :* Pl.

cinctūra, ae, *f.* [cingō], *a girding, a girdle :* Quint., Suet. [It. *cintura ;* Fr. *ceinture.*]

cinctus, a, um, *Part.* cingō.

cinctus, ūs, *m.* [cingō], *a girding.* **1.** Lit.: cinctus Gabinus, *a peculiar manner of girding the toga on solemn occasions :* incinctus cinctu Gabino, Liv.; Verg. **2.** Transf.: *a girdle, belt :* Suet.

cinctūtus, a, um [cinctus], *girded, girt :* Hor., Ov.

Cineās, ae, *m. a friend of King Pyrrhus of Epirus, who advised Pyrrhus to make peace with the Romans.*

cinefactus, a, um [cinis, faciō], *reduced to ashes :* Lucr.

cinerārius, i, *m.* [cinis], *a hair-curler* (with irons heated in hot ashes) : Cat.

cingō, cingere, cīnxī, cinctum, *to gird, encircle.* **1.** Lit. **a.** quasi zonā liene cinctus, Pl. Hence, of the sword, *to gird on* (the verb often being *Middle*) : Hispano cingitur gladio, Liv.; Verg.; inutile ferrum cingitur, Verg. **b.** Of garments, *to gird up, tuck up :* Gabino cinctu cinctus, Liv.; puer alte cinctus, Hor. Hence, *to prepare or gird oneself for :* Pl.; cingitur in proelia Turnus, Verg. **c.** *to encircle, wreathe* (the head) : caput coronā, Lucr.; tempora pampino, Hor.; cinctum nubibus atris caput (Atlantis), Verg. **2.** Transf. **a.** Of places : *to surround, encircle, enclose, encompass :* flumen Dubis oppidum cingit, Caes.; montes Thessaliam cingunt, Caes.; Lucr.; provincia mari cincta, Cic.; cinxerunt aethera nimbi, Verg. Rarely of immaterial things : diligentius urbem religione quam ipsis moenibus cingitis, Cic. **b.** Milit. **i.** *to beset, to beleaguer, to invest a place,* etc.: Nervii vallo et fossā hiberna cingunt, Caes.; Liv.; urbem obsidione, Verg. Rarely of immaterial things : Sicilia cincta periculis, Cic. **ii.** *to cover,* i.e. *protect :* equitatus latera cingebat, Caes.; Liv.; castra vallo, Liv. **iii.** Of fortifications : *to man,* i.e. *to surround with men :* praesidi tantum est, ut ne murus quidem cingi possit, Caes. **c.** *to escort, form a ring round :* Ov., Liv., Tac. [Fr. *ceindre.*]

cingula, ae, *f.* [cingō], *a girdle, belt, girth :* Ov.

cingulum, i, *n.* [cingō], *a girdle, belt :* Petr. More freq. *pl.;* cingula, *a sword-belt,* Verg. [It. *cingolo ;* Fr. *sangle.*]

cingulus, i, *m.* [cingō], *a girdle of the earth, a zone :* Cic.

cinifiō, ōnis, *m.* [cinis flō] = cinerārius, *a hair-curler :* Hor.

cinis, eris, *m.* (*f.* in *sing. :* Lucr., Cat.), *ashes.* **1.** In gen. **1.** Lit.: Lucr.; cinerem immundum iactare, Verg.; fer cineres, Verg.; Suet. Prov.: huius sermones cinerem haud quaeritant (i.e. require no ornament or polishing), Pl. **2.** Transf.: omne verterat in fumum et cinerem, Hor.; Pl. **II.** Esp. *the ashes of something that has been burnt.* **1.** Lit. **a.** Of a corpse : dare poenas cineri atque ossibus clarissimi viri, Cic.; ut mutam nequiquam adloquerer cinerem, Cat.; Verg., etc. **b.** Of a city : cineres patriae, Verg. **2.** Transf.: of death : Troia virum. acerba cinis, Cat. [It. *cenere ;* Fr. *cendre.*]

Cinna, ae, *m. a Roman cognomen ;* esp. **I.** L. Cornelius, *consul* B.C. 87–84, *a supporter* *of Marius :* **Cinnānus**, a, um. **II.** *his son* L. Cornelius, *one of the murderers of Caesar.* **III.** C. Helvius, *a poet, friend of Catullus.*

cinnamōmum or **cinnamum**, ī, n. [κιννάμωμον or κίνναμον], *cinnamon.* As term of endearment : Pl. In *pl. ; twigs of cinnamon :* Ov.

Cinyps, yphis, m. a river in Libya, famous for the long-haired goats on its banks ; **Cinyphius**, a, um.

Cinyrās, ae (Acc. -an, Voc. -ā), *m. f. of Myrrha and Adonis ;* **Cinyrēius**, a, um : virgo, Myrrha ; iuvenis, Adonis.

cippus, ī, m. **I.** *a stake, post,* etc. : esp. *a gravestone :* Hor. **II.** Milit. cippi, *palisades :* Caes. [Fr. cep.]

circā, adv. and prep. = circum. **I.** Adv. : *around, round about, all around, in the environs :* gramen erat circa, Ov. ; Verg. ; ex montibus, qui circa sunt, Liv. Often attributively with a noun in Liv. : multarum circa civitatum. **II.** Prep. with Acc. **A,** Of place. **a.** Extent : circa Hennam lacūs lucique sunt plurimi, Cic. ; Ov. Also *in the neighbourhood of :* detrimentis circa montem Amanum acceptis, Caes. ; Liv. Of attendants, etc. *around, about :* trecentos iuvenis circa se habebat, Liv. ; Cic. **b.** Motion, *to . . . round about,* to *. . . all around,* etc.. Romulus legatos circa vicinas gentis misit, Liv. **B.** Of time : *about, towards :* postero die circa eandem horam, Liv. ; Hor. ; circa Ciceronem, *about Cicero's time,* Sen. **C.** Of number : *about, nearly, almost* (= ad or circiter) : ea fuere oppida circa septuaginta, Liv. ; Suet. **D.** Transf. : *about, concerning :* Quint., Tac., Suet.

circāmoerium, ī, n. [circa moerus, for mūrus], *space about a wall* (v. pomerium): Liv.

Circē, ēs (Acc. -am, Pl., -ēn, Cic. ; Gen. -ae, Verg. ; Abl. -ā, Hor.), *f. d. of the Sun and Perse, famous for her magic ;* **Circaeus**, a, um.

circēnsis, e, adj. [circus], *of the circus :* ludi, Cic., Liv. As Noun, **circēnsēs** (sc. ludi), *the games in the circus :* Verg., Suet.

circinō, āre [circinus]. *to make round.* Transf. : *to make a circle* (by movement) : Ov.

circinus, ī, m. [κίρκινος], *a pair of compasses :* Caes. [It. cercine ; Fr. cerne.]

circiter, adv. and prep. : *about, near.* **A.** Adv. of time and number : mediā circa nocte, Caes. ; Pl. ; circiter ccxx naves eorum paratissimae, Caes. ; Liv. **B.** Prep. with Acc. of extent. **a.** Of place : loca haec circiter, Pl. **b.** Of time : circiter meridiem, Pl., Caes. ; Cic. Ep. ; Hor.

circlus, v. **circulus.**

circueō, circuitiō, v. circum-.

circuitus (**circumitus**), ūs, m. [circumeō], *a going round, a circuit.* **1.** Lit. **a.** In gen. : solis, *revolution,* Cic. **b.** *a detour,* or *road round :* Caes. ; Cic. ; Verg. **c.** *circumference :* collis, Caes. **2.** Tr ansf. **a.** Rhet. *a period :* Cic., Quint. **b.** *a circumlocution, a periphrasis* = circumitio (2) : Quint. **c.** Of action : *a roundabout way :* gloriam circuitu petis, Curt.

circulātim, adv. [circulor], *in groups :* Suet.

circulātor, ōris, m. [circulor], *a pedlar :* auctionum, Asin. Poll. ap. Cic. Ep. Of quack-philosophers : Sen. Ep.

circulor, ārī [circulus]. **I.** *to form in groups for conversation :* Caes. **II.** *to stroll about :* Cic. **III.** Of 'tub-thumping' quacks : *to collect a crowd :* Sen. Ep.

circulus, ī, m. (**circlus**, Verg.) [circus], *a circular figure, a circle, circuit* **1.** Lit. **a.** In gen. \ Cic. ; muri, Liv. **b.** Astron.: *a circular path, orbit :* Cic., Ov. **2.** Transf. **a.** *any circular body ; a ring, hoop :* auri, Verg. ; Suet. **b.** *a circle or company for social intercourse* (mostly *pl.*) : in conviviis rodunt, in circulis vellicant, Cic. ; Liv. ; Mart., etc. [It. *circolo* ; Fr. cercle.]

circum, adv. and prep. [prob. Acc. of circus], *round, about, all around* (not used of time or number). **I.** Adv. **a.** Pl. ; quae circum essent opera tueri, Caes. ; matres stant circum, Verg. Attributively with a Noun (= *neighbouring*) : portis circum omnibus instant, Verg. ; hostilibus circum litoribus, Tac. Also with undique ; circum undique convenere, Verg. **b.** In composition : circum is unchanged, e.g. circumago ; though circu-eo, circu-itus are found for circum-eo and circum-itus. **II.** Prep. **a.** With Acc. of extent : Cato ; terra circum axem se summā celeritate convertit, Cic. ; varios hic flumina circum fundit humus flores, Verg. Also *in the neighbourhood of :* urbes quae circum Capuam sunt, Cic. ; Tac. Of attendants, etc. *around, about :* Ter. ; eos equites circum se habere consuerat, Caes. ; Hectora circum, Verg. **b.** With Acc. of motion to : Pl ; Naevius pueros circum amicos dimittit, Cic. ; Hor. (circum is sometimes placed after its Noun, even in prose : Cic.).

circum-agō, agere, ēgī, āctum, *to set in circular motion, to drive or turn in a circle.* **I.** *to turn round, wheel.* **1.** Lit. : Cato ; equos frenis, aciem, signa, navis, Liv. ; Tac. ; circumagente se vento, Liv. **2.** Transf. **a,** Of time (with *Reft. Pron.* or in *Mid.*), *to revolve, pass away :* in ipso conatu rerum circumegit se annus, Liv. ; circumactus est annus, Liv. ; Lucr. **b.** Of the feelings : *to bring round, to change the temper of :* unā voce, quā *Quirites* eos pro *militibus* appellarat facile circumegit et flexit, Suet. ; quo te circumagas ? Juv. **II.** *to move about, drive to and fro.* **1.** Lit. : (milites) huc illuc clamoribus hostium circumagi, Tac. ; nil opus est te circumagi, Hor. **2.** Transf. Of the feelings, *to sway to and fro* (us. *Pass.*) : rumoribus vulgi circumagi, Liv.

circum-arō, āre, *to plough around :* Liv.

circum-caesūra, ae, f. *the external contour or outline :* Lucr.

circum-cīdō, cīdere, cīdī, cīsum [caedō], *to cut around, clip, trim.* **1.** Lit. : aciem, Lucr. ; Cic. ; caespitem gladiis, Caes. Of circumcision : Tac. **2.** Transf. : *to cut short, cut down :* sumptūs, Liv. Of wordiness in style : Cic., Quint.

circum-circā, adv. *all around :* Pl., Sulp. ap. Cic. Ep.

circumcisus, a, um. **I.** *Part.* circumcīdō. **II.** *Adj.* **a.** *steep, precipitous, inaccessible* : collis, Caes. ; Cic. **b.** *shortened, abridged, short* : orationes, vita, Plin. Ep.

circum-clūdō, clūdere, clūsī, clūsum [claudō], *to shut or hem in, enclose on every side.* **1.** Lit. : duobus exercitibus, Caes. ; cornua ab labris argento circumcludunt, Caes. **2.** Transf. : consiliis meis circumclusus, Cic.

circum-colō, ere, *to dwell round about* : Liv.

circum-cursō, āre, *to run round or about* : Ter., Lucr. With Acc. : Pl., Cat.

circum-dō, dāre, dedī, datum, *to put or place round.* **A.** With Acc. (or in *Pass.*, Nom.) and Dat. of ind. object : *to put, place, or set round.* **1.** Lit. : satellites armatos contioni, Liv. ; equites cornibus circumdat, Liv. ; Cic. ; Verg. With Dat. implied : ligna et sarmenta circumdare, Cic. ; Caes., etc. In *Mid.* with Acc. : chlamydem circumdata, Verg. **2.** Transf. : cancelli, quos mihi ipse circumdedi, Cic. ; egregiam famam paci circumdedit, Tac. **B.** With Acc. and *Instr.* Abl. : *to surround with, encompass, enclose, encircle with.* **1.** Lit. : me bracchiis, Pl. ; animum (deus) corpore, Cic. ; oppidum quinis castris, Caes. ; taurino quantum possent circumdare tergo, Verg. **2.** Transf. : exiguis finibus oratoris munus, Cic. ; pueritiam robore, Tac. **c.** With double Acc. : terram radices, Cato. So in *Pass.* : infula virgineos circumdata comptūs, Lucr.

circum-dūcō, dūcere, dūxī, ductum (*Imper.* circumdūce, Pl.), *to lead or draw around.* **1.** Lit. **a.** Pl. : cohortibus longiore itinere circumductis, Caes. ; aratrum, Cic. ; flumen Dubis, circino circumductum, Caes. Rarely with obj. implied (*sc.* agmen) : praeter castra hostium circumducit, Liv. **b.** *to lead about* (from place to place) : with *two* Acc. : Pl. ; aliquem omnia sua praesidia, Caes. **2.** Transf. **a.** *to cheat or defraud of* : with Abl. : quadringentis Philippis me circumduxerunt, Pl. **b.** Of discourse, etc. *to lengthen out* : Quint. Also *to drawl out* : Quint.

circumductiō, ōnis, *f.* [circumdūcō]. **I.** *a cheating, defrauding* : argenti, Pl. **II.** Of style : *a period* : Quint.

circum-eō or **circueō**, circu(m)īre, circu(m)iī, circuitum, *to go round.* **1.** Lit. **a.** hostium castra, Caes. ; aras, Ov. ; Pl. ; Liv., etc. (Also intrans. : per hortum, Pl.). Esp. milit. *to march round, enclose, encompass* : sinistrum cornu, Caes. ; hostem a fronte et a tergo, Curt. ; sese circumiri arbitrabantur, Caes. ; Liv. **b.** *to go about, go the round of, visit* : manipulos, Caes. ; praedia, Cic. ; vigilias, Liv. Esp. *to go about canvassing, etc.* : Quinctilius circumire aciem Curionis coepit, Caes. ; Cic. Ep. ; Liv. ; Tac. **2.** Transf. **a.** totius belli fluctibus circumiri, Cic. ; Tac. **b.** *to get round, circumvent, get the better of* : Pl. ; multā prior arte Camillam circuit, Verg. **c.** Of discourse : *to express by circumlocution* : Vespasiani nomen, Tac.

circum-equitō, āre, *to ride round* : moenia, Liv.

circum-ferō, ferre, tulī, lātum, *to carry round, hand round.* **1.** Lit. **a.** In gen. : mulsum, Pl. ; codicem, Cic. ; poculum, Liv. ; tegmine silvam (iaculorum), Verg. In *Mid.* : *to revolve* : Cic. Of the eyes, *to turn or direct about* : acies, Verg. ; oculos, Liv. **b.** Esp. relig. *to carry round in order to purify* : Pl. ; idem ter socios purā circumtulit undā, i.e. sprinkled them in turn, Verg. **2.** Transf. **a.** *to carry about, spread abroad* : bellum, Liv. ; clamorem, incendia, Tac. **b.** Of news : Plin. Ep. With Acc. and *Inf.* : Ov. **c.** Of books (in *Pass.*) : *to be circulated* : Quint.

circum-flectō, flectere, flexī, flexum, *to wheel about* : cursūs, Verg.

circum-flō, āre, *to blow round about.* Transf. : ab omnibus ventis invidiae circumflari, Cic.

circum-fluō, fluere, fluxī, *to flow round.* **A.** Intrans. **1.** Lit. : Curt. **2.** Transf. *to be overflowing, abound* : oratio, Cic. With *Instr.* Abl. : *to overflow with* : omnibus copiis, Cic. ; exercitu, Cic. **B.** Trans. **1.** Lit. : utrumque latus circumfluit aequoris unda, Ov. ; Sen. **2.** Transf. **a.** *to stream or flock round* : Varr., Luc. **b.** secundae res vos circumfluunt, Curt.

circumfluus, a, um [circumfluō]. **A.** Act. : *flowing around, circumfluent* : umor, Ov. **B.** Pass. : *surrounded with water* : insula, Ov. ; campi Euphrate, Tac.

circum-fodiō, fodere, fōdī, fōssum, *to dig round.* **A.** Intrans. : Cato. **B.** Trans. : Sen. Ep.

circum-forāneus, a, um [circum, forum]. **I.** *all around the market* or *forum* : aes, i.e. *money borrowed from the bankers of the forum* : Cic. Ep. **II.** *going from market to market, itinerant* : pharmacopola, Cic. ; Suet.

circum-fundō, fundere, fūdī, fūsum, *to pour around.* **A.** With the Acc. (or Nom. in *Pass.*) of that which is poured. **1.** Lit. **a.** circumfusa nubes, Verg. ; igni circumfuso, Liv. **b.** With Dat. of the obj. around which : mare circumfusum urbi, Liv. With *ad* : amurcam ad oleam, Cato. **2.** Transf. **a.** magna multitudo circumfundebatur, Caes. ; iuventus circumfusa, Verg. ; undique circumfusae molestiae, Cic. **b.** With Dat. : cedentibus circumfusi, Cic. ; Liv. **c.** In Act. without *Refl. Pron.* : circumfudit eques, Tac. **B.** With Acc. of the obj. around which (us. with Abl. *Instr.* of the thing poured). **1.** Lit. : terra circumfusa mari, Cic. ; (eos) multo nebulae amictu, Verg. Without Abl. : terram circumfundit aer, Cic. **2.** Transf. : copiis circumfusus, Cic. ; densis circumfundimur armis, Verg. Without Abl. : praefectum milites circumfundunt, Tac.

circum-gemō, ere, *to growl around* : ovile, Hor.

circum-gestō, āre, *to bear* or *carry about* : epistulam, Cic. Ep.

circum-gredior, gredī, grēssus [gradior], *to walk round, surround* (esp. with the view of attacking) : Tac.

circum-iaceō, ēre, *to lie round about, to border upon* : with Dat. : Lycaonia et Phrygia Europae, Liv. Absol. : circumiacentes populi, Tac.

circum-iciō, icere, iēcī, iectum [iaciō], *to cast, throw,* or *place around.* **a.** With Acc. of thing thrown and Dat. of thing round which : multitudinem hominum moenibus, Caes. ; Liv. With Acc. alone : fossam, Liv. ; vallum, Liv., Tac. **b.** With Acc. of thing round which and *Instr.* Abl. of thing thrown : extremitatem caeli rotundo ambitu, Cic. ; planities saltibus circumiecta, Tac. Also, quod anguis vectem circumiectus fuisset, *had wound itself round a bar,* Cic.

circumiectus, a, um. **I.** *Part.* circumiciō. **II.** *Adj.* : of localities : *lying around, surrounding* : Liv., Tac. With Dat. : aedificia circumiecta muris, Liv. ; Tac. *Neut. pl.* as Noun : Tac.

circumiectus, ūs, *m.* [circumiciō], *a surrounding, encompassing* : munita arx circumiectu arduo, Cic.

circumitiō, ōnis, *f.* [circumeō], *a going round, circuit.* **1.** Lit. : esp. milit., *the rounds, the patrol* : vigiliarum, Liv. **2.** Transf. : Of discourse : *a roundabout way* : circumitione et anfractu, Cic. ; Ter.

circumitus, *v.* circuitus.

circumlātus, a, um, *Part.* circumferō.

circum-ligō, āre. **A.** With Acc. and Dat. : *to bind* or *fasten round* or *to* : habilem (natam) hastae, Verg. **B.** With Acc. and Abl. *Instr.* ; *to bind round with* : ferrum stuppā, Liv. ; Cato. ; Cic.

circum-linō, linere, *no perf.,* litum (**circumliniō,** īre, Quint.). **A.** With Acc. and Dat. *to smear all over* : circumlita taedis sulfura, Ov. **B.** With Acc. and Abl. *Instr.* : *to besmear, to bedaub, to anoint* (us. in *Perf. Part.*) : circumliti mortui cerā, Cic. With Abl. understood : oculum, Plin. Ep. Transf. : circumlita saxa musco, Hor. ; Ov.

circumlocūtiō, ōnis, *f.* [circum, loquor], *circumlocution* : Quint.

circum-luō, ere, *to wash* or *flow around* : pars arcis circumluitur a mari, Liv. ; Tac.

circum-luviō, ōnis, *f.* [luō], *alluvial land* (in *pl.*) : Cic.

circum-mittō, mittere, mīsī, missum, *to send around* : praecones, Caes. ; milites post montis, Liv. ; iugo (Abl.) circummissus Veiens, Liv.

circum-moeniō (Pl.), *v.* circummūniō.

circum-mūniō, īre, *to wall around, to fortify* : Uticam vallo, Caes.

circummūnitiō, ōnis, *f.* [circummūniō], *an investing of a town, circumvallation* : Caes.

circum-padānus, a, um [circum Padus], *situated around* or *near the R. Po* : campi, Liv.

circum-pendeō, ēre, *to hang around* : Ov., Curt.

circum-plaudō, ere, *to applaud on all sides* : Ov.

circum-plector, plectī, plexus (Act. *Imper.* circumplecte, Pl.), *to clasp around, embrace.* **1.** Lit. : Cic. ; pharetram auro, Verg. **2.** Transf. : collem opere, Caes.

circum-plicō, āre, *to fold* or *twine around* : Cic.

circum-pōnō, pōnere, posuī, positum, *to put* or *place around* : with Acc. and Dat. : nemus stagno, Tac. ; Hor. Absol. : Hor.

circumpōtātiō, ōnis, *f.* [pōtō], *a drinking round in succession* : XII. Tab. ap. Cic.

circum-rētiō, īre [circum and rēte], *to enclose with a net, ensnare.* Transf. : aliquem, Lucr. ; cum te circumretitum frequentiā populi Rom. esse videam, Cic.

circum-rōdō, rōdere, rōsī, *to gnaw* or *nibble all round.* Transf. : dudum enim circumrodo, quod devorandum est (i.e. I have long hesitated to speak out), Cic. Ep. ; dente Theonino circumroditur (i.e. is slandered), Hor.

circum-saepiō, saepīre, saepsī, saeptum, *to fence round, enclose.* **1.** Lit. : Suet. **2.** Transf. : corpus armatis, Liv. ; Cic.

circum-scindō, ere, *to rend around, strip off* : Liv.

circum-scrībō, scrībere, scrīpsī, scriptum, *to draw a line around, to enclose.* **1.** Lit. : virgā regem, Liv. ; Cic. ; orbem, Cic. **2.** Transf. : *to mark the boundary of, limit, bound.* **a.** vitae spatium, Cic. ; uno genere genus aratorum, Cic. **b.** Of the powers of public officials, *to limit, restrict* : senatus praetorem circumscripsisset, Cic. ; Caes. **c.** *to mark off for the purpose of excluding, to set aside* : hoc omni tempore Sullano ex accusatione circumscripto, Cic. **d.** *to set aside, defeat the purpose of* (by a legal quibble) : testamentum, Plin. Ep. **e.** *to circumvent, entrap* : captiosis interrogationibus, Cic. ; pupillos, Juv.

circumscriptē, *adv.* [circumscrībō]. **I.** Rhet. : *in periods* : Cic. **II.** *comprehensively* : Cic.

circumscriptiō, ōnis, *f.* [circumscrībō]. Lit. : *an encircling* ; and concr. *a circle* : Cic. **2.** Transf. **a.** *a boundary, limit, circuit* : terrae, temporum, Cic. **b.** Rhet. : verborum, *a period,* Cic. Also *a comprehensive statement* : Quint. **c.** *a circumventing, deceiving* : Cic. In *pl.* : Cic.

circumscriptor, ōris, *m.* [circumscrībō], *a deceiver* : Cic., Juv.

circumscriptus, a, um. **I.** *Part.* circumscrībō. **II.** *Adj.* Rhet. **a.** *rounded into periods, periodic* : verborum ambitus, Cic. **b.** *limited, concise* : Cic. *Comp.* : Plin. Ep.

circum-secō, āre, *to cut* or *pare around* : Cato ; aliquid serrulā, Cic.

circum-sedeō, sedēre, sēdī, sĕssum, *to sit around, beset.* **1.** Lit. **a.** In gen. : aliquem, Sen. Ep. **b.** *to besiege, blockade, invest* : Mutinam, Cic. ; Liv. ; Tac. **2.** Transf. : lacrimis me circumsessum videtis, Cic. ; Liv.

circum-sēpiō, *v.* circumsaepiō.

circumsēssiō, ōnis, *f.* [circumsedeō], *a besieging* : Cic.

circum-sīdō, ere, *to set oneself down about a place, besiege* : Liv., Tac.

circum-siliō, īre [saliō], *to hop round.* **1.** Lit. : passer, Cat. **2.** Transf. : morborum omne genus, Juv.

circum-sistō, sistere, stetī, *to take one's stand round, to surround.* **1.** Lit. : With Acc. : Caes., Liv., Verg., etc. *Absol.* : Pl., Cic., Tac. In *Pass.* : Caes. **2.** Transf. : with Acc. : Liv., Tac.

circum-sonō, āre. **A.** Intrans. : *to resound on every side, to ring again with* : (locus) circumsonat ululatibus, Liv. ; Cic.

B. Trans. **a.** *to sound around* : clamor hostis circumsonat, Liv. ; Ov. **b.** *to make to ring all about* : murum armis, Verg. ; Cic. In *Pass.* : Ov.

circum-sonus, a, um, *sounding on every side* : turba canum, Ov.

circum-spectātrix, īcis, *f. a woman-spy* : Pl.

circumspectiō, ōnis, *f.* [circumspiciō], *a looking about.* T r a n s f. : *circumspection, caution* : Cic.

circum-spectō, āre, *to look round often or anxiously (at or for), to watch for.* **1.** L i t. : With Acc. : Pl., Cic., Liv. With *Indir. Quest.* : Liv. With Acc. and *ut* and *Subj.* : alius alium ut proelium ineant circumspectant, Liv. *Absol.* : Pl., Cic., Liv. **2.** T r a n s f. with Acc. : defectionis tempus, Liv. ; Tac. *Absol.* : Cic.

circumspectus, a, um. **I.** *Part.* circumspiciō. **II.** *Adj. well considered, guarded, circumspect.* **1.** L i t. : verba, Ov. ; Quint. **2.** T r a n s f. : of persons : *circumspect* : Quint., Suet. *Comp.* : Sen. *Sup.* : Suet.

circumspectus, ūs, *m.* [circumspiciō]. *a looking around.* **A.** A b s t r. **1.** L i t. : Plin. **2.** T r a n s f. : *consideration* : rerum, Liv. ; Ov. **B.** C o n c r. : *a view around* : Cic., Liv.

circum-spiciō, spicere, spexī, spectum [speciō]. **A.** I n t r a n s. : *to look about, to cast a look around.* **1.** L i t. : Pl., Cic., Verg. **2.** T r a n s f. : *to look round, to be on the watch, be cautious* : Cic. **B.** T r a n s. *to look round upon, view on all sides, to survey.* **1.** L i t. **a.** sua quisque miles, Caes. ; Liv. ; oculis Phrygia agmina circumspexit, Verg. ; se circumspicere, *to look around oneself,* Pl. **b.** *to look round and see, descry* : saxum ingens, Verg. **2.** T r a n s f. **a.** *to* view mentally, *to ponder, examine* : consilia, Caes. ; nunquamne, homo amentissime, te circumspicies, Cic. **b.** *to look about for or to find* : externa auxilia, Liv. With *Indir. Quest.* : Cic., Liv.

circum-stō, stāre, stetī, *to stand round, be stationed round.* **1.** L i t. : Enn., Caes., Verg., Curt. (Hence as Noun, circumstantēs, *the bystanders,* Tac.) With Acc. : Cic., Verg., Liv. E s p. in a hostile manner : Cic., Verg., Liv. **2.** T r a n s f. : terrores, Liv. ; odia, Verg. With Acc. : Romanos terror circumstabat, Liv. ; Cic. ; Verg.

circum-strepō, ere, *to make a noise around, to shout clamorously round. Absol.* or with Acc. : Tac. With *Jussive Subj.* : Tac.

circum-surgēns, entis [surgō], *rising all around* : iuga, Tac.

circum-tentus, a, um [tendō], *stretched* (hence, *bound*) *round* : corio, Pl.

circum-tergeō, ēre, *to wipe around* : Cato.

circum-terō, ere, *to rub around ;* hence, *to crowd round* : Tib.

circum-textus, a, um [texō], *woven all round* : Verg.

circum-tonō, tonāre, tonuī, *to thunder around. Of the din of arms* : hunc circumtonuit Bellona, Ov.

circum-tōnsus, a, um [tondeō], *shorn all round* : Suet. T r a n s f. : of style : Sen. Ep.

circum-vādō, vādere, vāsī, *to encompass* or *assail on all sides.* **1.** L i t. With Acc. : Liv. ; aliquem clamoribus, Tac. **2.** T r a n s f. : terror aciem, Liv.

circum-vagus, a, um, *roaming* or *flowing around* : oceanus, Hor.

circum-vallō, āre, *to surround with a rampart, circumvallate, blockade* : Caes., Liv. T r a n s f. : Ter.

circumvectiō, ōnis, *f.* [circumvehō]. **I.** *a carrying around* (of merchandise) : Cic. Ep. **II.** *a revolution* : solis, Cic.

circum-vector, ārī, *to be carried around ;* and as *Mid., to cruise* or *ride round* : Ligurum oram, Liv. ; Hor. T r a n s f. = *to describe* : singula, Verg.

circum-vehor, vehī, vectus, *to be carried round ;* and as *dep., to sail* or *ride round.* **1.** L i t. : Pl., Caes., Liv. With Acc. of place : Liv. **2.** T r a n s f. : = *to describe* : Verg.

circum-vēlō, āre, *to veil around* : Ov.

circum-veniō, venīre, vēnī, ventum, *to come round, encircle, encompass.* **1.** L i t. : Cocytos sinu labens circumvenit atro, Verg. With Acc. : Rhenus insulas circumveniens, Tac. In *Pass.* : Sall. E s p. in a hostile manner, *to surround, encompass, invest* : ex itinere nostros adgressi circumvenere, Caes. ; montem opere, Caes. ; moenia exercitu, Sall. ; legio circumventa, Liv. **2.** T r a n s f. **a.** *to beset, oppress* : circumventus morbo, exsilio atque inopiā, Enn. ; te non Siculi circumveniunt, Cic. ; Hor. ; falsis criminibus circumventus, Sall. ; Cic. ; Tac. **b.** *to get round, defraud* : circumventus pecuniā, Cic.

circum-vertōr (vortor), vertī, *to turn oneself round* : Pl. With Acc. : Ov.

circum-vestiō, īre, *to clothe* or *cover round.* T r a n s f. : se circumvestire dictis, poet. ap. Cic.

circum-vinciō, īre, *to bind around* : aliquem virgis, Pl.

circum-vīsō, ere, *to look* or *glare around at* : Pl.

circum-volitō, āre, *to fly round and round.* **1.** L i t. : Liv., Tac. With Acc. : lacūs circumvolitavit hirundo, Verg. ; Hor. **2.** T r a n s f. *Absol.* : circumvolitant equites, Lucr.

circum-volō, āre, *to fly round.* **1.** L i t. : with Acc. : Verg., Hor., Quint. **2.** T r a n s f. : nox caput circumvolat, Verg.

circum-volvor, volvī, *to roll oneself round, to revolve round.* With Acc. : Verg., Ov.

circus, ī, *m.* [κίρκος, κρίκος], *a ring, a hoop.* **I.** Astron. *an orbit, circle* : circus lacteus, *the Milky Way,* Cic. **II.** *an oval space for chariot races,* etc. E s p. **a.** *the Circus Maximus at Rome* : Enn., Cic., Liv., Ov., etc. **b.** *the Circus Flaminius in the Campus Martius* : Cic., Liv., Ov. **c.** *the Circus Maritimus* : Liv. [It. *cerco ;* Fr. *cirque.*]

ciris, is, *f.* [κεῖρις], *a sea-bird, into which Scylla, the daughter of Nisus, was changed* : Verg., Ov.

cirrātus, a, um [cirrus], *with curled hair, curly-haired* : Mart.

cirrus, ī, *m.* (mostly *pl.*). **I.** *a curl, ringlet, or tuft of hair* : Juv. **II.** *a fringe* (on dress) : Phaedr.

cis, prep. *on this side, on the near side of.* **A.** With Acc. **a.** Of space : cis Taurum, Cic., Ep. ; cis Rhenum, Caes. With verb of motion : cis Tiberim redire, Liv. **b.** Of time : *within :* cis dies paucos, Pl. **B.** In Compos. : Cisalpinus, Cispadanus, etc.

cisium, ī, n. *a light two-wheeled car :* Cic., Verg.

Cisseus (disyl.), eī, m. *a king of Thrace,* f. *of Hecuba ;* **Cissēis**, idis, f. *his daughter Hecuba.*

cista, ae, f. [κίστη], *a chest, box* (for money, clothes, etc.) : Cic., Hor. ; for sacred objects : Cat., Ov.

cistella, ae, f. [dim. cistula], *a small chest or box :* Pl., Ter.

cistellātrix, īcis, f. [cistella], *a woman-keeper of the money-box :* Pl.

cistellula, ae, f. [dim. cistella], *a little box or chest :* Pl.

cisterna, ae, f. [cista], *a subterranean reservoir for water :* Varr., Mart., Tac.

cistophorus, ī, m. [κιστοφόρος, box-bearer], *an Asiatic coin, of the value of about four drachmas, on which a cista was stamped :* Cic., Liv.

cistula, ae, f. [dim. cista], *a little box or chest :* Pl.

citātim, adv. [citātus], *quickly, hastily :* Auct. B. Afr.

citātus, a, um. **I.** Part. citō. **II.** Adj. *quick, rapid, speedy :* citato equo, Caes. ; Liv. ; pede, Cat. ; gradu, agmine, Liv. Instead of adv., *hastily :* ferunt citati signa, Liv. ; Caes. Comp. : Liv. ; Sup. : Liv. Transf. : of gestures, etc. : Quint.

citerior us, adj. [comp. of adj. : citer, from cis], *on this side, hithermost :* Gallia, Caes. ; Cic. Transf. : *nearer to earth, more mundane :* deduc orationem de caelo ad haec citeriora, Cic.

Cithaerōn, ōnis, m. *a range of mountains dividing Boeotia from Attica.*

cithara, ae, f. [κιθάρα], *the cithara, lyre or lute :* Lucr., Verg., Tac. Transf. : *the art of cithara-playing :* Verg., etc. [It. cetera ; Sp. guitarra.]

citharista, ae, m. [κιθαριστής], *a player on the cithara :* Cic.

citharistria, ae, f. [κιθαρίστρια], *a woman cithara-player :* Ter.

citharizō, āre [κιθαρίζω], *to play on the cithara :* Nep.

citharoedus, ī. m. [κιθαρῳδός], *a player of the cithara, with voice-accompaniment :* Cic., Hor.

citimus, a, um [cf. citerior], *nearest to us :* (stella) ultima a caelo, citima terris, Cic.

citō, adv. [citus], *soon, speedily, quickly,:* Pl., Cic., Hor. Ov. Comp.: citius: Pl., Cic., Verg., etc. Sup. : citissimē : Caes. Phr. **a.** dicto citius, *sooner than one can speak :* Hor., Verg. **b.** serius aut citius, *sooner or later,* Ov. **c.** With a negative (= non facile), *not easily :* neque verbis aptiorem cito alium dixerim, Ter. **d.** citius (= potius), *sooner, rather :* ut vicinum citius adiuveris quam fratrem, Cic. ; Hor.

citō, āre [freq. cieō]. **I.** *to put into quick motion,* hurry. **1.** Lit. (mostly post-Aug., exc. in Pl. * Part.). **2.** Transf. : motum (animi), *to excite,* Cic. **II.** *to call or summon.* **1.** Lit. : patres in curiam, sena-

tum in forum, Liv. ; reum, accusatorem, Cic. Of 'witnesses : in hanc rem testem totam Siciliam citabo, Cic. Comic.: Pl. Of an appeal to a god : Cat., Ov., etc. Also of a victor at the games, etc., *to summon by proclamation,* etc. : victorem Olympiae citari, Nep. ; Cic. ; Liv. **2.** Transf. : *to call to witness, to appeal to, cite :* quamvis citetur Salamis clarissimae testis victoriae, Cic. ; libri, quos Licinius citat auctores, Liv.

citrā [ABL. f. of old adj. citer, v. citerior], adv. and prep. **I.** Adv. : *on this side, on the near side :* Ov. ; hence, *short of, short :* paucis citra milibus occurrunt, Liv. ; tela citra cadebant, Tac. **II.** Prep. with Acc. *on this side of, on the near side of.* **1.** Lit. **a.** Of space : citra flumen intercepti, Liv. ; Caes. ; Hor. With verbs of motion : Caes., Cic., Hor. After its case : Hor. **b.** Of time = *since :* citra Troiana tempora, Ov. **2.** Transf. **a.** *short of, less than :* nec virtus citra genus est, Ov. **b.** *short of, without* (= sine) : Quint., Tac., Suet.

citreus, a, um [citrus], *of citrus-wood :* mensa, Cic.

citrō, adv. [DAT. of old adj. citer, v. citerior], *to the near side, to this side* (alw. with ultro, *to the further side, to that side*) : cursare ultro et cito, Cic. ; qui ultro citroque navigarent, Cic. ; Liv. ; ultroque citroque, Lucr. ; ultro citro commeantibus, Cic. Hence = *reciprocally :* datā ultro citroque fide, Liv.

citrus, ī, m. **I.** *an African tree with fragrant wood :* Varr., Luc. **II.** *the citron-tree :* Plin.

citus, a, um. **I.** Part. cieō. **II.** Adj. *quick, swift, rapid* (opp. tardus). **1.** Lit.: bigae, Cat., Verg. ; navis, Ov. ; venator, Hor. ; agmen, cohortes, Tac. **2.** Transf.: ad scribendum, Pl. ; fama, Pl. ; vox, Cic. ; mors, Ov. ; pes (i.e. iambus), Hor. ; via, Liv. Comp. : Pl. Instead of the adv. citō : citi solvite vela, Verg. ; Pl. ; Tac., etc.

civicus, a, um [civis], *of citizens, civil, civic* (more rare than civilis, and, exc. in phr. civica corona, mostly poet.): iura, Hor. ; arma, Ov. ; corona, *the civic crown, made of oak leaves, given for saving the life of a fellow-citizen in war,* Cic., Liv. Hence, without corona : Quint., Tac.

civilis, e, adj. [civis]. **I.** *of citizens or fellow-countrymen ; civic, civil :* sanguis, Lucr. ; conciliatio et societas, Cic. ; bellum, Cic. ; Romani civilem esse clamorem inter se gratulantes, Liv. ; acies, Ov. ; irae, Tac. ; quercus (= corona civica), Verg. Esp. ius civile. **a.** *rights as a citizen, civil rights :* Cic. **b.** *the body of Roman law relating to civil rights, Civil Law :* Cic. **c.** *the form of procedure in Roman law :* Liv. **II.** *of public or political life, political, public :* civilis ratio, *politics, political science,* Cic. ; civilium rerum peritus, Tac. ; Hor. Esp. civil as opp. to *military :* Cic., Liv. **III.** *like a citizen ; befitting a citizen ; courteous, gracious, affable :* sermo, Liv. ; animus, Liv., Tac., Suet. Comp. : Ov. Esp. of distinguished men : civile rebatur misceri voluptatibus vulgi, Tac.

civilitas, ātis, f. [civilis]. **I.** *the art of gov-*

ernment : Quint. **II.** *courteousness, graciousness :* Suet.

cīvīlĭter, *adv.* **I.** *citizen-like :* civiliter opibus utebantur, Liv. ; Juv. Also *as an ordinary citizen would :* Tac. **II.** *courteously, graciously :* Ov., Tac.

cīvīs, *is* (ABL. us. cīve), *m. f.* [*cf.* κεῖμαι]. Lit. : *a resident ;* hence, *a citizen, fellow-citizen.* **I.** **Esp.** civis Romanus, opp. peregrinus, advena, hospes, hostis : Pl., Cic., Ov., etc. **II.** In gen. : Attica, Pl. ; imperare corpori, ut rex civibus suis, Cic. Hence, civis totius mundi, Cic.

cīvĭtās, *ātis, f.* [cīvis]. **I.** Lit. : *citizenship, rights of a Roman citizen, freedom of the city :* civitatem alicui dare, Cic., Liv. ; civitate aliquem donare, Cic., Suet. ; accipere *or* ascribere aliquem in civitatem, Cic. ; asciscere aliquem in civitatem, Liv. ; civitatem habere, consequi, deponere, amittere, adimere, retinere, etc., Cic. **2.** Transf. **a.** *the citizens united in a community, the body politic, the state :* conventicula hominum quae civitates nominatae sunt, Cic. ; omnis civitas Helvetia, Caes. ; Liv., etc. ; condere, administrare, Cic. ; una civitas communis deorum atque hominum, Cic. **b.** *the citizens, the townsfolk :* Orgetorix civitati persuasit, Caes. ; Cic. ; Nep. **c.** *a city* (as a collection of houses) : civitatem incendere, Enn. ; muri civitatis, Tac. ; Quint. [It. *città ;* Fr. *cité.*]

clādēs, *is, f.* [*cf.* κλάω, per-cellō], *damage, loss.* **1.** Lit. : (material) : dextrae manūs, Liv. ; plus populationibus quam proeliis cladium fecit, Liv. ; dare late cladem, Lucr. **2.** Transf. **a.** In gen. : *damage, loss, disaster, ruin :* illam meam cladem maximum esse rei publicae vulnus iudicastis, Cic. ; Pl. ; Hor., etc. In *pl. :* Lucr., Cic., Ov. **b.** Esp. in war : *defeat, discomfiture, overthrow :* cladem alicui adferre, Cic. ; inferre, facere, Liv. ; accipere, Cic., Liv. ; Hor. **c.** *a destroyer, a scourge :* geminos Scipiadas, cladem Libyae, Verg.

clam, *adv.* and *prep.* [*cf.* cēlō] (opp. palam). **I.** Adv. : *secretly, privately.* **a.** In gen. : Pl., Cic., Verg., etc. **b.** As predicate, with *esse : secret, unknown :* nec id clam esse potuit, Liv. ; Pl. ; Ter. With Acc. and *Inf. :* Pl. **II.** (mostly in the comic poets), *Prep.* us. with ABL. or ACC. : *without the knowledge of, unknown to.* With ABL. : clam vobis salutem petivit, Caes. ; Pl. ; Lucr. ; with ACC. : clam matrem, Pl. ; clam me est, *it is unknown to me.* Ter. ; clam aliquem habere, *to keep* (a thing) *secret from someone,* Ter.

clāmātor, *ōris, m.* [clāmō], *a bawler, noisy declaimer :* Cic.

clāmĭtātĭō, *ōnis, f.* [clāmĭtō], *a bawling noise :* Pl.

clāmĭtō, *āre* [*freq.* clāmō], *to cry aloud frequently, cry out, yell.* **1.** Lit. : Cic., Phaedr. With quoted words : Ter., Cic., etc. With Acc. : Cic. With Acc. and *Inf. :* Caes., Cic., etc. Impers. Pass. : Liv. With *Juss. Subj. :* clamitans aspiceret verberum notas, Tac. So with *ut* or *ne :* Pl., Ter., Tac. **2.** Transf. : *to cry aloud* (i.e. proclaim). With Acc. : supercilia clamitare calliditatem videntur, Cic.

clāmō, *āre* [*cf.* καλέω, calō], *to call, shout aloud, cry out.* **1.** Lit. : Ter., Cic. Of snoring : Pl. Of geese : Cic. Of a cricket : Phaedr. With quoted words : Cat., Ov., Sen. Ep., etc. With Acc. and *Inf. :* Ter., Cic., Verg. With *ut* and *Juss. Subj. :* Cic. With Acc. of person or thing called to : Pl., Verg., Liv., etc. **2.** Transf. : *to cry out* (i.e. proclaim). With Acc. or Acc. and *Inf. :* quid enim restipulatio clamat ? Cic. ; quae (tabulae) se corruptas atque interlitas esse clamant, Cic. ; Pl. ; Cat. [It. *chiamare.*]

clāmor (old form **clāmōs**), *ōris, m. a loud call, a shout, yell, cry, noise.* **1.** Lit. **a.** In gen. : edere, Cic. ; facere, tollere clamorem, Pl. ; Cic. ; Verg. **b.** Of approval : clamore consensuque populi, Cic. Ep. ; Tac. In *pl. :* Cic., Phaedr., etc. **c.** Of disapproval (us. *pl.*) : clamoribus et conviciis, Cic. **d.** In battle : clamorem tollere, Caes. ; Liv. **e.** Of grief or pain : Verg., Liv. **f.** Of birds : Lucr., Verg. **2.** Transf. Of the reverberation of inanimate things : ter scopuli clamorem inter cava saxa dedere, Verg. ; Hor.

clāmōsus, a, um [clāmor], *full of clamour or noise.* **A.** Act. : *noisy, bawling :* Quint., Juv. **B.** Pass. : *filled or accompanied with noise or clamour :* circus, Juv. ; actio, Quint.

clanculum, *adv.* and *prep.* [dim. clam]. **I.** Adv. : *secretly, privately :* Pl., Ter. **II.** Prep. with Acc. : *unknown to :* Ter.

clandestīnō, *adv. secretly :* Pl.

clandestīnus, a, um [clam], *secret, hidden :* suspicio, Pl. ; introitus, conloquia, Cic. ; consilia, Caes. ; natura, Lucr.

clangō, *ere, to clang, resound :* Stat.

clangor, *ōris, m.* [clangō], *clang, din, bray, shrill cry :* Of trumpets, etc. : Verg. Of birds : Liv., Verg. **clārē**, *adv.* **1.** Lit. Of sound, *loudly, aloud, distinctly, clearly :* Pl., Ter., Cic. Ep., etc. Comp. : Suet. **2.** Transf. **a.** To the sight, *distinctly, clearly :* claro oculis video, Pl. Comp. : Plin. Also *brightly :* Cat. **b.** To the mind, *distinctly, clearly :* Quint. ; eo clarius id periculum apparet, Cael. ap. Cic. Ep. Sup. : Quint. **c.** Of moral distinction, *illustriously.* Comp. : Nep.

clārĕō, *ēre* [clārus], *to be distinct, clear* (lit. of sound). Transf. **a.** To the sight, *to be clear, bright :* Enn. ; claret ille Canis, Cic. poet. **b.** To the mind : *to be clear, manifest :* quod in primo carmine claret, Lucr. **c.** Of character : *to be distinguished, illustrious :* Enn.

clārēscō, clārescere, clāruī [clārĕō]. **1.** Lit. Of sound, *to become distinct, clear :* sonitus armorum, Verg. ; Quint. **2.** Transf. **a.** To the sight : *to become clear, bright :* Tac. **b.** To the mind : *to become clear, manifest :* Lucr., Quint. **c.** Of character : *to become illustrious :* Lucr., Tac.

clārĭgātĭō, *ōnis, f.* [clārigō]. **1.** Lit. *a challenge or solemn demand for compensation, an ultimatum :* Quint. **2.** Transf. : *the exaction of a fine for transgression of prescribed limits :* Liv.

clārĭgō, *āre* [clārus]. Of the fetiales, *to*

make a solemn demand for compensation, deliver an ultimatum : Plin.

clāri-sonus, a, um [clārus sonō], *clear-sounding :* vox, Cat.

clāritās, ātis, *f.* [clārus], *distinctness.* **1.** Lit. of sound : claritas in voce, Cic. **2.** Transf. **a.** To the sight : Plin. **b.** Of style : *clearness, perspicuity :* Quint. **c.** *distinction :* num te fortunae tuae, num claritatis, paenitebat ? Cic. ; Tac., etc.

clāritūdō, inis, *f.* [clārus]. **I.** *brightness :* fulgor et claritudo, Tac. **II.** *distinction :* Sall., Tac.

clāro, āre [clārus]. **I.** *to make bright or clear :* Poet. ap. Cic. **II.** *to make clear* (to the mind) : Lucr. **III.** *to make famous :* illum non labor Isthmius clarabit pugilem, Hor.

Claros, i, *f. a town in Ionia, near Colophon, famous for a temple and an oracle of Apollo ;* hence **Clarius,** a, um, esp. *as epith. of Apollo ;* also *of Antimachus of Colophon.*

clārus, a, um [*cf.* calō, καλέω]. **1.** Lit. : of sound, *clear, loud, distinct :* clamor, Pl. ; vox, Caes., Cic., Liv. ; tuba, Verg. ; plangor, Ov. **2.** Transf. **a.** To the sight : *distinct, clear, bright :* lux, Pl., Cic. ; lumen, color, etc., Lucr. ; clarissima mundi lumina Verg. ; clarissimae gemmae, Cic. ; caelum, nox, Tac. With ABL. : argento clari delphines, Verg. ; Lucr. ; Ov. Of the wind : *making clear, bringing fair weather :* aquilo, Verg. **b.** To the mind, *clear, manifest, plain :* clara res est, totā Siciliā celeberrima, Cic. ; clara et certa, Ter., Liv. *Comp. :* Cic., Ov. **c.** Of character : *distinguished, renowned, famous,* etc. (opp. obscurus). **i.** In good sense : nobilitas, Pl. ; pugna, Pl. ; exempla, Cic. ; pax clarior quam bellum fuerat, Liv. ; Ov. ; vir fortissimus et clarissimus, Cic. With ABL. : clariores gloriā, Cic. ; bello, Tac. ; agendis causis, Hor. With ABL. of Cause : giganteo triumpho, Hor. With *ex :* ex doctrinā nobilis et clarus, Cic. With *ob :* ob id factum, Hor. ; Liv. With *in* and ABL. : in litteris, Quint. With *ab :* Verg. Esp. in *Sup.,* of distinguished personages : clarissimus vir, Cic. Ep. ; Plin. Ep. **ii.** In bad sense : *notorious :* populus (*sc.* Campanus) luxuriā superbiāque clarus, Liv. ; Cic. [It. *chiaro ;* Fr. *clair.*]

classiārius, a, um [classis], *of the navy :* Quint. ; centurio, Tac. More freq. as Noun in *pl. :* **classiāriī,** ōrum, *m. naval forces, marines :* Caes., Tac.

classicula, ae, *f.* [*dim.* classis], *a little fleet, flotilla :* Cic. Ep.

classicus, a, um [classis]. **I.** *of or relating to a classis of the Roman people :* Varr. Esp. *of the first classis :* Cato. Transf. : classicus scriptor, Gell. **II.** *relating to the army* in gen., but as *Adj.* only of *the naval forces :* classici milites, Liv. Also as Noun. **a. classici,** ōrum, *m. pl. marines :* Tac. **b. classicum,** i, *n., a signal of battle* given by the trumpet : classicum cecinit, Liv. ; Caes. Hence, *the war-trumpet itself :* Verg., Liv.

classis, is, *f.* (ABL. classī or more freq., classe) [*cf.* calō, καλέω]. Lit. : *a sum-*

moning. Hence, **I.** In the Servian constitution, *a class* or *division of the Roman people :* Cic. ; Liv. Transf. : qui (philosophi) mihi, cum illo conlati, quintae classis videntur, Cic. **II.** *an army.* **a.** On land (very ancient) : Liv. ; Hortinae classes, Verg. **b.** At sea, *a fleet :* nomina in classem dare, Liv. ; facere, Caes. ; classe navigare, Cic. ; armare, deducere, Verg.

clātri (**clāthri**), ōrum, *m. pl.* [κλῇθρα], *a trellis, grate,* esp. *to the cages of animals :* Cato, Hor.

clātrō (**clāthrō**), āre [clātri], *to provide with a grating* or *bars :* Pl., Cato.

claudeō, ēre (Cic.) or **claudō,** ere (Sall.) [claudus], *to limp, be lame.* Transf. : beatam vitam, etiam si ex aliquā parte claudĕret, Cic. ; Liv.

claudicātiō, ōnis, *f.* [claudicō], *a limping :* Cic.

claudicō (**clōdicō**), āre [claudeō], *to limp, halt, be lame.* **1.** Lit. : Carvilio graviter claudicanti ex vulnere, Cic. ; Ov. **2.** Transf. **a.** Of the wings of birds : Lucr. ; of the *deflexion* of a balance : Lucr. ; of the *inclination* of the earth's axis : Lucr. **b.** *to be lame, to halt, waver :* tota res vacilla et claudicat, Cic. Of discourse : si quid in nostrā oratione claudicat, Cic. ; Quint.

clanditās, ātis, *f. lameness :* Plin. In *pl. :* Plin.

Claudius (**Clōdius**), *a name of two famous Roman gentes, one patrician, the other plebeian :* esp. **I.** Appius Claudius, *the decemvir* (B.C. 450). **II.** App. Claudius, *censor* B.C. 212, *builder of the Via Appia.* **III.** P. Clodius, *the enemy of Cicero.* **IV.** Clodia, *sister of III, the ' Lesbia ' of Catullus ;* **Claudiālis,** e ; **Claudiānus** and **Clōdiānus,** a, um. *v.* also Nero and Marcellus.

(1) claudō, *v.* claudeo.

(2) claudō (also **clūdō,** *cf.* exclūdō, etc.), claudere, clausi, clausum [*cf.* κλείς, clāvis]. **I.** *to bolt, bar, barricade, shut, close.* **1.** Lit. : portas, Caes., Cic. ; ostia, Cat. ; pars clausa fenestrae, Ov. **2.** Transf. **a.** pupulas, auris, Cic. ; lumina, Verg. ; os cludere, Tac. **b.** Of closing the free passage : aditūs, Liv., Tac. ; viam, transitum, Liv. ; fugam hostibus, Liv. ; rivos (by damming), Verg. Often in *Pass.* (of closing a way against someone) : clausa nobis erant omnia maria, Caes. ; Cic. ; Liv. **c.** *to bring to a close, conclude :* Hor., Ov., Quint. Esp. milit. : agmen claudere, i.e. *to bring up the rear,* Caes. **II.** *to lock up, shut in, imprison.* **a.** In gen. : in curiā vos, Liv. ; stabulis armenta, Verg. ; aliquem domo, Tac. ; quae urbs terrā marique clauderetur, Cic. ; Tusco claudimur amni, Verg. Without ABL. : Cic., Ov., etc. **b.** Esp. in war, *to blockade, hem in,* etc. : oppidum operibus, Caes., Liv. ; urbem obsidione, Nep. Also in hunting. [It. *chiudere ;* Fr. *clore,* etc.]

claudus (**clūdus,** Pl.), a, um, *limping, halting, lame.* **1.** Lit. : Pl. ; Volcanus, Cic. ; Verg. ; pede Poena claudo, Hor. ; Verg. **2.** Transf. : *crippled :* naves, Liv. ; Lucr. ; Tac. Of the elegiac metre : clauda carmina alterno versu, Ov.

claustra (**clōstra**), ōrum, *n. pl.* (*sing.* claustrum, I, Curt.) [claudō]. **I.** *a bar, bolt, lock, fastening.* **1.** Lit.: claustra revellere, Cic.; laxare, Verg. **2.** Transf. **a.** nobilitatis, Cic.; portarum naturae, Lucr. **b.** *barriers* (preventing a free passage), *barricades :* loci, Cic.; Liv.; montium, Tac. Hence, *a dam* or *dike :* Verg., Liv. **II.** *barricades* (to prevent egress), *enclosures.* **a.** In gen.: claustris feras retinere, Liv.; Cic.; Verg. **b.** Esp. in war, *blockading lines :* contrahere claustra, Tac. [Fr. *cloître.*]

clausula, ae, *f.* [claudō], *a close, conclusion, ending:* edicti, epistulae, mimi, Cic.; Suet. Rhet.: *the close of a period :* clausulae quae numerose et iucunde cadunt, Cic.; Quint.

clausus, a, um. **I.** *Part.* claudō. **II.** *Neut.* as Noun, **clausum**, I, *a locked place or an enclosure :* Verg. In *pl. :* Lucr., Sall.

Clausus, I, *m. a Sabine name ;* esp. Clausus, *ancestor of the gens Claudia.*

clāva, ae, *f. a knotty branch* or *stick, a club, cudgel :* Pl., Cic., Verg., etc. Also *a foil :* Cic.

clāvārium, I, *n.* [clāvus], *money given to soldiers for the purchase of shoe-nails :* Tac.

clāvātor, ōris, *m.* [clāva], *a cudgel-bearer :* Pl.

clāvicula, ae, *f.* [*dim.* clāvis], *the tendril of a vine :* Cic.

(1) **clāviger**, erī, *m.* [clāva gerō], *the club-bearer :* Ov.

(2) **clāviger**, erī, *m.* [clāvis gerō], *the key-bearer :* Ov.

clāvis, is, *f.* (Acc. -em or -im, Abl. -I or -e) [*cf.* κλείς], *a key :* Pl.; portarum, Sall.; horreorum, Cic.; Ov.; clavis adimere uxori, i.e. *to part from a wife :* Cic. [It. *chiave ;* Fr. *clef.*]

clāvulus, I, *m.* [clāvus], *a small nail :* Cato, Varr.

clāvus, I, *m.* [*cf.* κλείς]. **I. 1.** Lit.: *a nail* (us. of metal: sometimes of hard wood): Pl., Caes., Liv.; clavum pangere *or* figere, *to fix a nail* (*in the wall of the temple of Jupiter in order to mark the year*), Liv. Hence, ex hoc die clavum anni movebis (i.e. *reckon the beginning of the year*), Cic. And as *a symbol of immovable firmness :* saeva Necessitas clavos trabalis manu gestans, Hor. (*v.* trabalis) ; beneficium trabali clavo figere, Cic. **2.** Transf.: *the handle* or *the tiller of a rudder :* and *the rudder itself* (only *sing.*) *:* Enn.; clavumque ad litora torquet, Verg. Transf.: clavum tanti imperi tenere, Cic. **II.** *a purple stripe on the tunica*, which for the senators was broad (latus), for the equites, narrow (angustus): Ov., Liv., etc.; latum clavum ab Caesare impetrare, i.e. to become a senator, Plin. Ep. Hence = *a tunic :* Hor. [It. *chiovo ;* Fr. *clou.*]

Cleanthēs, is (Acc. -em and -ēn, Voc. -e), *a Stoic philosopher, pupil of Zeno ;* **Cleanthēus**, a, um.

clēmēns, entis (Abl. us. -tī), *adj.* **1.** Lit.: of the character. **a.** *gentle, tranquil, mild :* Ter., Cic., Liv. **b.** On particular occasion, *gentle, forbearing, merciful* (of men and their actions) *:* Pl., Cic., Liv., Hor. **2.** Transf. **a.** Of the wind, weather, etc. *:* Cat., Ov.,

Curt. **b.** Of other things, *toned down :* rumor, Sall. Comp. *:* Liv., Stat.; *Sup. :* Cic., Ov.

clēmenter, *adv.* **1.** Lit. **a.** *gently, placidly, calmly :* aliquem accipere, Cic.; ferre aliquid, Cic. Ep.; Pl.; Lucr. **b.** *mercifully :* Caes., Cic., Liv. **2.** Transf.: *gently, not abruptly, gradually :* collis clementer adsurgens, Tac. Comp. *:* Lucr., Liv. *Sup. :* Pl., Sen.

clēmentia, ae, *f.* [clēmēns]. **1.** Lit.: of the character, etc., *mildness, humanity, mercy :* Ter.; illam clementiam mansuetudinemque nostri imperi, Cic.; Ov. **2.** Transf.: of the weather: *calmness, mildness :* aestatis, Plin. Ep.

Cleobis, is, *m. b. of Bito.*

Cleōn, ōnis, *m. the leader of the Athenian democracy after Pericles.*

Cleōnae, ārum, *f. pl. a town in Argolis near Nemea ;* **Cleōnaeus**, a, um.

Cleopatra, ae, *f.* **I.** *s. of Alexander the Great.* **II.** *d. of Ptolemy Auletes and queen of Egypt* (ob. B.C. 31).

clepō, clepere, clepsī, cleptum (clepsō, clepsim, old *Fut.* and *Optat.* in old laws, Cic., Liv.) [*cf.* κλέπτω], *to steal :* Pl. ; poet. ap. Cic.

clepsydra, ae, *f.* [κλεψύδρα]. **1.** Lit. **a.** *water-clock, clepsydra ;* used *to regulate the time allotted to speakers and declaimers :* ad clepsydram latrare, Cic. **2.** Transf.: *the time measured by the clepsydra :* petere, dare, Cic.; Mart.

clepta, ae, *m.* [κλέπτης], *a thief :* Pl.

cliēns, entis, *m.f.* [clueō, *hear*]. **1.** Lit.: *a client.* **a.** At Rome (*v.* also patrōnus): Pl., Cic., Liv. **b.** In Gaul and Germany, *a vassal, retainer :* Caes., Tac. **c.** Of whole nations : *allies* or *vassals :* Caes. **2.** Transf.: cliens Bacchi, Hor.

clienta, ae, *f.* [cliēns], *a female client :* Pl., Hor.

clientēla, ae, *f.* [cliēns], *clientship, dependence.* **a.** At Rome (opp. patrocinium, *patronage, protection*): Ter.; esse in fide et clientelā, Cic. Hence, concr. (us. *pl.*), *bodies of clients, dependants :* magnas esse Pompei clientelas in citeriore provinciā sciebat, Caes.; Cic.; Tac. **b.** Abroad : *vassals :* Caes. Hence, concr. : Tac.

clientulus, I, *m.* [*dim.* cliēns], *an insignificant client :* Tac.

clīnāmen, inis, *n.* [*cf.* clīnātus], *inclination* (of atoms) *:* Lucr.

clīnātus, a, um, *Part.* [clīnō, as in dē-clīnō, etc., *cf.* κλίνω], *inclined, bent, sunk :* Cic. poet.

Cliō, ūs, *f. the Muse of history.*

clipeātus, a, um [clipeus], *armed with a shield :* Verg., Ov. As Noun : Pl., Liv.

clipeus, I, *m.* (occ. **clipeum**, I, *n.*). **1.** Lit.: *the* (*round*) *bronze shield of Roman soldiers* (*v.* also scutum): Pl., Verg., etc. Prov. : clipeum post vulnera sumere, Ov. **2.** Transf. **a.** *a shield-shaped metal surface engraved with a bust* or *medallion :* Liv., Tac. **b.** *the sun's disk :* Ov. **c.** *the vault of heaven :* Enn.

Clisthenēs, is, *m. an Athenian statesman* (fl. B.C. 510).

Clitarchus, I, *m. a historian, biographer of Alexander the Great.*

clitellae, ārum, f pl. a pack-saddle, pannier : Pl., Hor. P r o v. : bovi clitellas imponere : Cic. Ep.

clitellārius, a, um [clitellae], of a pack-saddle, bearing a pack-saddle : homines, Pl. ; asini, Cato.

clivōsus, a, um [clivus], hilly, full of slopes, steep : Verg. ; Ov.

clivus, ī, m. [clīnō, v. clīnātus], a slope, an ascent : Pl. ; milites ex inferiore loco adversus clivum incitati cursu, Caes. ; lenis, Liv. ; mollis, Verg. T r a n s f. **a.** mensae, Ov. **b.** an ascending road, esp. clivus Capitolinus, Cic. Ep., Liv. ; Tac. ; clivus sacer, Hor. **c.** P r o v. : clivo sudamus in imo, Ov.

cloāca, ae, f. [cluō, i.e. pūrgō], a sewer, drain : Cic., Liv., Hor. Comic : Pl. E s p. cloaca maxima, a brook which was shut in and used to drain the forum : Liv. P r o v. : arcem facere e cloacā, Cic. [It. chiavica.]

clōd-, **clūd-**, v. claud-.

Cloelia, ae, f. a Roman girl, one of the hostages given to Porsenna, who made her escape back to Rome.

clōstra, v. claustra.

Clōthō, f. (only in Nom. and Acc.), ' the spinner,' one of the three Parcae or Fates.

cluĕō, ēre, and **clueor**, ērī [cf. κλύω], to hear oneself called, to be spoken of, reputed ; ut meus victor vir belli clueat, Pl. ; quaecumque cluent, Lucr.

clūnis, is m. and f. (mostly pl.) [cf. κλόνις], a buttock, haunch : Pl., Hor., Liv., etc.

clūrinus, a, um [clūra, an ape], of, or belonging to, apes : Pl.

Clūsius, ī, m. [claudō], a cognomen of Janus.

clūsus, v. clausus.

Clymenē, ēs (Acc. -ēn, Ov.), f. w. of Merops and m. of Phaëthon by Sol ; **Clymenēius**, a, um.

Clymenus, ī, m. a cognomen of Pluto.

clystēr, ēris, m. [κλυστήρ], a clyster, an injection (pure Lat. lotio) : Suet. T r a n s f. : a clyster-pipe, syringe : Suet.

Clytaemēstra (and **Clutēm-**), ae, f. d. of Tyndareus and Leda ; sister of Helen, Castor, and Pollux ; w. of Agamemnon and m. of Orestes, Iphigenia and Electra. Having murdered her husband, she was killed by Orestes.

Clytiē, ēs, f. d. of Oceanus, changed into the plant heliotropium.

Cnaeus, v. Gnaeus.

Cnōssus (Gnōssus, and **-os**), ī, f. a town in n. Crete, centre of the Minoan empire ; **Cnōssius (Gn-)**, a, um ; **Gnōsiī**, ōrum, m. pl. ; **Gnōssius (Cn-)**, ae, **Gnōssias**, adis, **Gnōssis**, idis, f. = Ariadne ; **Gnōssias**, adis, f. adj. ; **Gnōssiacus**, a, um.

co- in comp., v. cum.

Coa, v. Cous.

coacervātio, ōnis, f. [coacervō], a heaping together. R h e t. : a heaping up of proofs : Cic., Quint.

co-acervō, āre, to heap together. **1.** L i t. : Caes., Cic., Cat. **2.** T r a n s f. : argumenta, Cic. ; luctūs, Ov.

co-acēscō, acēscere, acuī, to become acid or sour : Cic. T r a n s f. : Cic.

coāctio, ōnis, f. [cōgō], a collecting, calling in of money : Suet.

coāctō, āre [freq. cōgō], to constrain, force (with Inf.) : Lucr.

coāctor, ōris, m. [cōgō]. **I.** a collector of money from auctions, rents, etc. : Cato, Cic., Hor. **II.** erant agminis coactores, i.e. brought up the rear, Tac. **III.** one who forces to an action : Sen. Ep.

coāctū, Abl. sing. m. [cōgō], by or under compulsion : coactu meo, Cic. ; civitatis, Caes. ; Lucr.

coāctum, ī, n. [cōgō], a coverlet of thick, fulled cloth ; a felt : Caes.

coāctus, a, um, Part. cōgō.

co-aedificō, āre, to build up together, build upon : Cic.

co-aequō, āre, to make uniformly level. **1.** L i t. : aream, Cato ; montis, Sall. **2.** T r a n s f. : ad libidines tuas omnia coaequasti, Cic.

coagmentātiō, ōnis, f. [coagmentō], a joining together ; a union : corporis, Cic.

coagmentō, āre [coagmentum], to join, glue, cement together. **1.** L i t. : Caes., Cic. **2.** T r a n s f. : pacem, Cic.

coagmentum, ī, n. [cōgō], a joining together ; a joint (mostly in pl.) : Pl., Cato, Caes.

coāgulum, ī, n. [cōgō], a means of coagulation ; rennet : Varr., Ov. [It. caglio, gaglio.]

co-alēscō (cŏlēscō, Lucr.), alēscere, aluī, alitum [cf. alō]. **I.** to grow together. **1.** L i t : Varr. ; saxa vides solā colescere caloe, Lucr. **2.** T r a n s f. : to unite, agree together, coalesce (freq. in Liv., Tac.) : ut cum Patribus coalescerent animi plebis, Liv. ; in huno consensum, Tac. ; Liv. **II.** to strike root, take firm root, thrive. **1.** L i t. : grandis ilex coaluerat inter saxa, Sall. Ov. **2.** T r a n s f. : dum Galbae auctoritas fluxa, Pisonis nondum coaluisset, Tac. In Perf. Part. : coalitam libertate inreverentiam ne prorupisse, Tac. ; libertas, Tac.

coalitas, a, um, Part. coalēscō.

co-angustō, āre, to contract, compress. **1.** L i t. : alvos, Varr. **2.** T r a n s f. : to limit, restrict : Cic.

coarct-, v. coart-.

co-arguō, uere, uī. **I.** (With Acc. of thing), to prove conclusively, demonstrate. **1.** L i t. : errorem, crimen, Cic. ; Tac. **2.** T r a n s f. : fuga laboris desidiam coarguit, Cic. **II.** (With Acc. of person) to refute, prove wrong or guilty. **1.** L i t. : criminibus coarguitur, Cic. ; Ov. With Gen. of the crime : aliquem avaritiae, Cic. **2.** T r a n s f. : of things : quam (legem) coarguit usus, Liv.

coartātio, ōnis, f. [coartō], a crowding together : Liv.

co-artō, āre, to crowd up, throng, narrow. **1.** L i t. : forum, Tac. ; Gnaeus in oppidis coartatus, Cic. Ep. ; angustae fauces coartant iter, Liv. **2.** T r a n s f. **a.** Of time : to abridge : consulatūs aliorum, Tac. **b.** Of discourse : to abridge, compress : Crassus haec coartavit in oratione suā, Cic. ; plura in unum librum, Plin. Ep.

coaxō, āre [κοάξ, the sound made by frogs], to croak : Suet.

Cōcalus, ī, m. a mythical king in Sicily who protected Daedalus.

Coccēius, a, name of a Roman gens, to which Nerva (q.v.) belonged.

coccinātus, a, um [coccinus], *clothed in scarlet* : Mart. ; puerulus, Suet.

coccineus, and **coccinus**, a, um [coccum], *scarlet-coloured* : Mart., Juv. [It. *cocciniglia* ; Fr. *cochenille*.]

coccum, i, n. [κόκκος, a berry], *the kind of berry* (now known to be an insect, *cochineal*, *kermes*) *found upon the scarlet dye oak* : Plin. Transf. **a.** *scarlet dye* : Verg., Hor., Quint. **b.** *scarlet garments*, etc. : Suet.

coclea (cochlea), ae, f. [κοχλίας], *a snail* : Pl., Cic., Hor. [It. *chiocciola*.]

cocleāre, is, n. [coclea, from the form of a snail-shell], *a spoon* ; Mart.

cocles, itis, m. *a person blind of one eye* : Pl. As a Roman surname ; esp. Horatius Cocles, *who, in the war with Porsenna, defended the Tiber-bridge.*

coctilis, e, adj. [coquō], *baked, burned* : lateres, Varr. ; hence, muri (Babylonis), i.e. *built of bricks*, Ov.

coctūra, ae, f. *a style of cooking* : Plin.

coctus, a, um, *Part.* coquō.

cocus, v. coqūus.

Cōcўtus (-os), i, m. [κωκυτός, wailing], *a river in the Lower World* ; **Cōcўtius**, a, um. **cōda**, v. cauda.

cōdex (older **caudex**), icis, m. *the trunk of a tree, the stock.* 1. Lit. : Verg., Ov. 2. Transf. **a.** *the block of wood to which criminals were bound for punishment* : Pl., Prop. **b.** A term of abuse, *blockhead* : Ter. **c.** *a block*, consisting of several tablets : Varr., Sen. ; hence, *a book* : Cato, Cic., Quint. ; also *a ledger* (dist. fr. adversaria, q.v.) : Cic.

cōdicilli, ōrum, m. pl. [dim. cōdex], *small trunks of trees, fire-logs.* 1. Lit. : Cato. 2. Transf. **a.** *small tablets for writing* : Plin. **b.** *a short writing, note, petition*, etc. : epistulam hanc convicio efflagitarunt codicilli tui, Cic. ; Tac., etc. **c.** *an imperial rescript, a diploma* : Suet. **d.** *an addition to a will, a codicil* : Tac., Plin. Ep.

Codrus, i, m. **I.** *an Athenian king who sacrificed his life for an Athenian victory over the Dorians.* **II.** *a poet, ridiculed by Vergil.*

coel-, v. cael-.

co-emō, emere, ēmī, emptum, *to buy up* : Ter., Cic., Hor., etc.

coēmptiō, ōnis, f. [coemō]. In law. **I.** *a pretended sale of an estate* (for the purpose of relieving it from the burden of certain sacrificial rites) : Cic. **II.** *a marriage contracted by a mock sale of the parties* (by which the wife was freed from the tutela legitima and the family sacra) : Cic.

coēmptiōnālis, e, adj. [coemptiō], *of a sham marriage* : senex, *one used on such an occasion* ; hence, *poor, worthless* : Pl.

coēmptus, a, um, *Part.* coemō.

coen-, v. caen-.

co-eō, īre, iī, itum. 1. Lit. : *to go or come together, to meet, assemble.* **a.** In gen. : matronae ad Veturiam coeunt, Liv. ; Ov., etc. ; in porticum, Plin. Ep. *Impers. Pass.* : Tac. **b.** In a hostile manner : inter se coiisse viros, Verg. ; Ov. **c.** *to form a union by coming together, unite* : qui unā coierint, Caes. ; reliqui coeunt inter se, Caes. ; in unum, Verg., Liv. **d.** Of the sexes : *to have connexion, cohabit* : Lucr., Ov., Curt. 2. Transf. **a.** Of things : semina, Lucr. ; iac, Varr. ; gelidus coit formidine sanguis, Verg. Of wounds : Ov. **b.** In feeling, will, or judgment : *to combine, agree, conspire* : principes tum unā coierunt, Caes. ; coeant in foedera dextrae, Verg. ; conubio, Curt. ; taedae iure, Ov. **c.** With societatem (cum aliquo or *Absol.*), *to enter into an alliance, to make a compact, form a league* : Cic.

coepiō, coepere, coepī (coēpit, Pl., Lucr.), coeptum [for co-apiō, v. apō]. (The tenses of the Present-stem are ante-class., incipiō being the class. Present ; coeptūrus, Liv., Quint. The class. tenses are those of the Perfect- and Supine-stems). **A.** Act. : **coepī**, *I have laid hold of, I have begun, I began* : Enn. ; pugna coepit, Liv. ; Ov., etc. With Acc. : orationem, Tac. ; Pl. With *Inf. Act.* : Enn. ; fugere coepit, Caes. ; ver esse coeperat, Cic., Ov. With ellipsis of dicere : Liv., Verg. With *Inf. Pass.* : iudicia fieri coeperunt, Cic. ; Hor. ; Ov. **B.** Pass. : **coeptus est** : amicitia coepta est, Liv. ; Cic. In the *Part.* : consilium fraude coeptum, Liv. ; coepti fiducia belli, Verg. With *Inf. Pass.*, or *Inf. Act.* of Intrans. verb : pons institui coeptus est, Caes. ; Pl. ; Cic. ; Cat. ; mitescere discordiae coeptae, Liv.

coeptō, āre [freq. coepiō]. **A.** Trans. : *to begin eagerly, to attempt.* **a.** us. with *Inf.* : Lucr., Cic., Tac. With Acc. : insidias, Tac. ; Ter. **B.** Intrans. : *to begin, commence, make a beginning* : coniuratio, Tac.

coeptus, a, um. **I.** *Part.* coepiō. **II.** Noun : **coeptum**, i, n. *a beginning, undertaking* : Lucr., Verg., Liv., etc. With adv. : bene coeptum, Liv. In *pl.* : Verg., Liv., etc.

coeptus, ūs, m. [coepiō], *a beginning* (only in *pl.*) : appetenti : Cic.

co-epulōnus, i, m. [epulō], *a companion at a feast* : Pl.

coerātor, v. cūrātor.

co-erceō, ēre [arceō], *to shut up together* or *closely.* 1. Lit. **a.** *to close round, form bounds to, enclose* : mundus omnia complexu suo coercet, Cic. ; Lucr. ; Ov. **b.** *to hem in, confine* : operibus intra muros coercetur hostis, Liv. ; mortuos Styx coercet, Verg. **c.** *to keep in order* : virgā turbam, Hor. ; primas acies, Verg. **d.** *to keep from straggling* (by pruning) : Cato ; vitem, Cic. 2. Transf. **a.** *to limit* : faenus, Liv. ; verba numeris, Ov. **b.** Of discourse, *to confine* : nos quasi extra ripas diffluentis, Cic. ; Ov. **c.** Of moral restraint : *to restrain, repress* : audaciam, cupiditates, etc., Cic. ; suppliciis civem, Cic. ; Caes. ; Hor., etc. **d.** Of the critic's pruning : Hor.

coercitiō, ōnis, f. [coerceō], *coercion, compulsion* (by exercise of punishment) : Liv., Tac. Hence, *the right of coercing* : Suet.

coerō, v. cūrō.

coerul-, v. caer-.

coetus (coïtus), ūs, m. [coeō]. 1. Lit. : *a coming* or *meeting together* : Pl., Lucr., Curt. Of the sexes (form coitus) : Ov., Suet. **II.** *an assemblage, crowd, company* : Cic., Verg., etc.

Cŏeus (disyl.), ī, *m. u Titan, f. of Latona.*

cōgĭtātē, *adv. deliberately, with mature reflexion* : Pl., Cic.

cōgĭtātĭō, ōnis, *f.* [cōgĭtō]. **1.** Lit.: *a thinking, considering, deliberating ; reflexion, meditation* (often opp. to sensus, sensation) : belli, Caes. ; cogitatione complecti, comprehendere, Cic. ; tacita, Quint. With *Indir. Quest.* : Cic. **2.** Transf. **a.** *a thought, plan, design* : meas cogitationes in rem publicam conferebam, Cic. ; posteriores enim cogitationes (ut aiunt) sapientiores solent esse, Cic. ; Liv., etc. **b.** *the faculty of thought, the reasoning power* : vim cogitationis habere, Cic.

cōgĭtātus, a, um. **I.** *Part.* cōgĭtō. **II.** *Adj. well-considered ; thought out, deliberate* : scelus, Cic. **III.** Noun, **cōgĭtāta**, ōrum, *n. pl. reflexions, thoughts, ideas* : Ter., Cic. In *sing.* : Nep.

cōgĭtō, āre [contr. fr. co-agitō], *to turn over thoroughly* (in the mind). **I.** In gen.: *to consider thoroughly, to ponder, reflect upon, think* (puto = simply, *to be of opinion*) : cum meo animo, Pl. ; in animo, Ter. ; toto animo, Cic. Ep. With *de :* de gloriā suā, Cic. With Acc. : mecum aliam rem, Ter. ; Pl. ; pacem, Cic. ; Lucr. With *Indir. Quest.* : Pl., Cic. With *Indir. Deliberative*: Pl., Ter. Also *to have in one's thoughts, picture to oneself :* Scipionem, Laelium, Cic., Tac. **II.** Of more settled thought. **a.** With *Adv.* : *to think of, to be disposed towards* : male, Cato, Cic. ; amabiliter in aliquem, Anton. ap. Cic. Ep. **b.** *to have in mind, to intend, meditate, design*, etc. With *Inf.* : impeditos adoriri cogitabant, Caes. ; Pl. ; Hor., etc. With Acc. : Cic., Tac., etc. ; and esp. with Acc. of *Neut. Pron. :* Verg., Hor., Liv. With *de :* Suet. With *ut* and *Subj.* : Caes., Cic. With ellipsis of ire *or* manere : Cic. Ep.

cognātĭō, ōnis, *f.* [cognātus]. **1.** Lit.: *relationship by birth* : Cic., Liv. With GEN. or *cum* : Cic., Liv. **2.** Transf. **a.** *affinity, agreement, resemblance*, etc. : Cic., Quint. **b.** Concr.: *relatives, family* : cum tibi tota cognatio sarraco advehatur, Cic. ; in *pl.*, Caes.

co-gnātus, a, um [nātus, *v.* nāscor], *related by birth,* and as Noun, *m.* and *f. a relation by birth* (on either the father's or the mother's side ; contrast *agnatus*). **1.** Lit. **a.** Pl. ; tot propinqui cognatique, Cic. ; Hor. ; amicae et cognatae, Ter. With DAT. : is mihi cognatus fuit, Ter. **b.** Of objects relating to kindred : urbes, Verg. ; cineres, Cat. Of animals : anguilla longae cognata colubrae, Juv. Of other things : recens tellus cognati retinebat semina caeli, Ov. **2.** Transf.: *kindred, related, connected, similar :* nihil est tam cognatum mentibus nostris quam numeri ac voces, Cic. ; Hor.

cognĭtĭō, ōnis, *f.* [cognōscō], *a becoming acquainted with, a learning, investigation, acquiring of knowledge ;* hence occ. *knowledge, acquaintance.* **I.** In gen. **a.** naturae, animi, Cic. ; cognitione atque hospitio dignus, Cic. ; Quint. **b.** Concr.: *a conception, notion, idea* : innatas cognitiones (deorum) habemus, Cic.. **II.** Legal : *a judicial investigation, inquiry* : agrorum,

Cic. ; cum dies cognitionis esset, Cic. ; inter patrem et filium, Liv. ; de libellis, Tac. ; Cic. **III.** *recognition* : Ter.

cognĭtor, ōris, *m.* [cognōscō], *one who knows;* hence, **1.** In law. **a.** *a witness* or *guarantor of identity* : Cic. **b.** *a representative, attorney, advocate* : Cic. **2.** Transf.: *an advocate, defender* (in gen.): sententiae, Cic. ; Liv. ; Hor.

cognĭtū, ABL. *sing. m.* [cognōscō], dignum cognitu, *worth knowing :* Suet.

cognĭtus, a, um, *Part.* cognōscō.

co-gnōmen, ĭnis, *n.* [gnōmen = nōmen]. **1.** Lit.: *a surname, distinguishing members of the same gens, derived from the name of a place, e.g. Africanus, or occ. from a nickname, e.g.* Cursor, Calvus, etc. : Cic., Liv. **2.** In gen. *a name* : cognomina locorum, Verg.

cognōmentum, ī, *n.* **1.** Lit.: *a surname :* Pl., Tac. **2.** Transf.: *a name*, in gen.: Tac.

cognōmĭnātus, a, um. **I.** [gnōmen = nōmen], *of the same name, synonymous* : verba, Cic. **II.** [cognōmen] *surnamed :* Suet.

cognōmĭnis, e, *adj.* [cognōmen], *of the same name* : Pl., Liv., Verg.

co-gnōscō, gnōscere, gnōvī, gnĭtum (*Perf. tenses,* contr. cognōstī, cognōram, cognōrō, cognōssem, etc.) [gnōscō = nōsco], *to investigate for the purpose of knowing ; to become acquainted with, learn ;* and in *Perf. tenses, to know.* **I.** In gen. **A.** By the senses. **a.** Enn. ; regiones, Caes. ; totum amnem, Verg. Occ. of the sexes : Cat., Ov., Tac. Also = *to read :* Nep. **b.** *to recognise, identify :* Ter., Lucr., Cic. **B.** By the understanding. C o n s t r.: the source of information is expressed by *ab* or *ex,* the ABL. alone, or *per ;* what the information relates to by *de ;* the facts learnt by **a.** Acc. : Caes., Cic., Verg. **b.** Acc. and *Inf.* : Lucr., Caes., Liv. Also after ABL. *Absol.* cognito, Liv. **c.** Acc. and *Pres. Part.* : Nep. **d.** *Indir. Quest.* : Ter., Sall., Tac. **II.** Esp. **a.** In law, *to examine a case, to investigate judicially* : Cic. With Acc. : causam, Caes., Cic., Liv. With *de :* Cic., Suet. **b.** Milit. *to reconnoitre :* qualis esset natura montis cognoscere, Caes. [It. *conoscere ;* Fr. *connaître.*)

cōgō, cōgere, coēgī, coāctum [contr. fr. co-agō], *to move, bring, drive together to one point ; to gather together, collect.* **1.** Lit. **A.** In gen. : of cattle, men, money, etc.: Pl., Cic., Verg. **B.** Esp. *to bring into close connexion.* **a.** Of fluids : *to thicken, curdle, condense* : mella frigore, Verg. ; in nubem cogitur aer, Verg. **b.** Of places (*in Perf. Part*) : *straitened, contracted :* saltus in artas coactus fauces, Liv. **c.** Milit.: agmen cogere, *to keep the column together,* hence *to bring up the rear,* Cic., Liv. **2.** Transf.: *to bring pressure upon.* **a.** *to confine, restrict :* cogere in ordinem, i.e. *to set to rights,* hence (v. ordo): Liv. ; me in semihorae curriculum coegisti, Cic. ; verba in alternos pedes, i.e. *to write in elegiac verse,* Ov. **b.** Most freq. *to constrain, compel, force* to some action. With Acc. of pers.: Ter., Liv. ; and with *Inf.* : Lucr., Verg., Liv. With *ut* and *Subj.* :

Ter., Lucr., Cic., etc. With *ad* : Pl. ; ad bellum, Liv. ; ad proelia, Verg. With *in* and Acc. : Hirt., Ov., Liv. With double Acc. : Ter. ; quid non mortalia pectora cogis ? Verg. ; cogi aliquid, Liv. With Acc. of thing alone : Nep., Ov. **c.** In logic : *to infer, conclude* : ex quibus id quod volumus cogitur, Cic.

cohaerentia, ae, *f.* [cohaereō], *a clinging together, coherence* : Cic.

co-haereō, haerēre, haesī, *to stick or cling together, cohere.* **1.** Lit. **a.** mundus ita apte cohaeret, Cic. ; Lucr. ; Tac. ; partibus inter se cohaerentibus, Cic. **b.** Occ. *to cling closely to* : scopuloque adfixa cohaesit, Ov. ; Curt. **2.** Transf. **a.** *to cohere, harmonise, be consistent* : Ter. ; non modo non cohaerentia inter se, sed maxime disiuncta, Cic. ; virtutes sine vitā beatā cohaerere non possunt (i.e. *hold together, exist*), Cic. **b.** *to be consistent or in agreement with* : illa cohaerent cum causā, Cic. ; moribus nobiscum cohaerentes, Curt. **c.** Of relationship : alicui sanguine, Quint.

co-haerēscō, haerēscere, haesī [cohaereō], *to cling together, cohere* : atomi inter se, Cic.

co-hērēs, ēdis, *m. f. a co-heir* : Cic., Hor.

co-hibeō, ēre [habeō], *to hold together, to hold close, confine.* **1.** Lit. **a.** universa natura omnīs naturas ipsa cohibet, Cic. ; nodo cohibere crinem, Hor. ; auro lacertos, Ov. **b.** *to hold back, repress, check*, etc. : muris Ardea Turnum, Verg. ; carcere ventos, Ov. ; cervos arcu, Hor. ; ab licentiā praedandi hostem, Liv. ; Tac. **2.** Transf. : esp. of the senses and passions : *to repress, restrain*, etc. : manūs, oculos, animum ab auro gazāque regiā, Cic. ; Pl. ; furorem, temeritatem, Cic. ; iras, Verg. ; bellum, Liv. With *Refl. Pron.* : Ter., Sulp. ap. Cic. Ep.

co-honestō, āre, *to honour fully, celebrate* : exsequias, Cic. ; Liv. ; Tac.

co-horrēscō, horrēscere, horruī, *to start shuddering all over* : Cic.

cohors, rtis, *f.* **1.** Lit. [*cf.* χορτός, hortus], *a court-yard, yard*, esp. for cattle or poultry : Cato, Ov. **2.** Transf. **a.** *a suite, escort* : praetoria, Cic. ; reginae, Verg., Tac., etc. **b.** Milit. *a cohort* (the tenth part of a legion, comprising 3 manipuli or 6 centuriae) : Milit. *a cohort* : Caes., etc. Occ. opp. to legiones ; *auxiliary troops, allies* ; Sall., Tac. [It. *corte* ; Fr. *cour.*]

cohortātiō, ōnis, *f.* [cohortor], *an encouraging, encouragement* : iudicum, Cic. ; legionis, Caes. In *pl.* : Cic.

cohorticula, ae, *f.* [cohors], *a small cohort* : Cael. ap. Cic. Ep.

co-hortor, ārī, *to cheer up, encourage, incite.* **A.** In gen. : hac (eloquentiā) cohortamur, Cic. ; aliquem ad virtutem, Cic. ; ad libertatem recuperandam, Cic. With *Inf.* : Tac. **B.** Esp. of military addresses : Caes. With *ad* : ad pugnam, Caes. ; Quint. With *ut* or *ne* : Caes., Tac.

cō-iciō, *v.* cōniciō.

co-inquinō, āre, *to defile wholly, contaminate* : Acc.

coitiō, ōnis, *f.* [coeō]. **I.** *a coming* or *meeting together* : Ter. **II.** In bad sense, *a conspiracy, coalition* : Cic., Liv. ; facere, Cic. ; dirimere, Cic. Ep. In *pl.* : Liv.

coitus, *v.* coetus.

colaphus, ī, *m.* [κόλαφος], *a blow with the fist, a cuff* : icere, Pl. ; Quint, etc. [It. *colpo* ; Fr. *coup.*]

Colchis, idis, *f. a country on the E. side of the Black Sea* ; **Colchis**, idis, *f. adj.* ; and as Noun, esp. *Medea* ; **Colchicus, Colchus**, a, um ; **Colchus**, ī, *m. a Colchian.*

colēns, entis. **I.** *Part.* colō. **II.** Adj. (with GEN.) *devoted to* : Cic.

coleus, *v.* culleus.

cōliphia (coll-), *v.* cōlyphia.

cōlis, is, *v.* caulis.

col-l (for compounds of con + l), *v.* con-l.

collāre, is, *n.* [collum], *a band or chain for the neck* : Pl., Varr. [Fr. *collier.*]

Collātia, ae, *f. an old town in Latium* ; **Collātīnus**, a, um, esp. *as cognomen of* L. Tarquinius, *h. of Lucretia* ; **Collātīnī**, ōrum, *m. pl. the inhabitants of Collatia.*

Collīna Porta, *the Colline Gate of Rome near the Quirinal Hill (called also* Agōnēnsis *and* Quirīnālis Porta*.*)

collis, is (ABL. -e or -ī), *m.* [*cf.* κολωνός], *high ground, hill* (opp. campus and mons) : Cic., Verg., etc. [It. *collina* ; Fr. *colline.*]

collum, ī, *n.* (-us, ī, *m.* Pl.), *the neck*, of men and animals (*v.* cervix). **1.** Lit. **a.** In gen. : Pl. ; proceritas collorum, Cic. ; collum in laqueum inserere, Cic. ; in collum invasit, Cic. ; Verg. ; Ov. ; etc. **b.** Esp. **i.** As symbol of subjection : colla adsuescere servitio, Verg. **ii.** As symbol of life : actum 'st de collo meo, Pl. **iii.** Of arresting : collum alicui optorquere (Pl.), opstringere (Pl.), torquere (Liv.). **2.** Transf. : *the neck.* Of a flask or bottle : Cato, Phaedr. Of a poppy : Verg. [Fr. *col, cou.*]

collybus, ī, *m.* [κόλλυβος]. **1.** Lit. : *exchange* : Cic. Ep. **2.** Transf. : *the rate of exchange* : Cic.

collyra, ae, *f.* [κολλύρα], *vermicelli* : Pl.

collyricus, a, um ; -ius, *vermicelli-soup* : Pl.

collyrium, ī, *n.* [κολλύριον], *a liquid eye-salve* : Hor.

colō, colere, coluī, cultum [earlier quolō, *cf.* inquilīnus, βουκολέω], *to till, tend, take care of.* **1.** Lit. **a.** Of agriculture, *to till, cultivate* : Cato ; praedia, vitem, Cic. ; Verg. ; arbores, Hor. **b.** *to live in a place, inhabit.* With Acc. (= incola) : Pl., Cic. Ep., Verg., etc. Absol. : Pl. ; prope Oceanum, Liv. ; Tac. **2.** Transf. : *to tend, take care about, foster, cultivate, promote.* **a.** Of the action of gods : ille (Iuppiter) colit terras, Verg. ; Pl. ; Liv. **b.** Of abstract qualities, feelings, etc. : amicitiam, Pl. ; iustitiam, virtutem, Cic. ; memoriam alicuius, Cic. ; fidem. Liv. ; amorem, Verg. **c.** Of a manner of life : servitutem apud aliquem, Pl. ; vitam, Pl. ; vi aevom, Lucr. ; vitam illam, Cic. Ep. **d.** Of the body (esp. of dress) : formam augere colendo Ov. ; lacertos auro, Curt. In *Pass.* with *Refl.* sense : Liv. **e.** *to worship, honour, pay honour to* (of gods, etc., and men) : deos, caerimonias, Cic. ; Ov. ; religiones, aram, Liv. ; Africanum, Cic. ; Pl. ; numina (Augusti), Verg. ; aliquem donis, Liv. ; poetarum nomen, Cic.

colocāsia, ōrum, *n. pl.* [κολοκάσιον],

Egyptian bean (a kind of water-lily) : Verg.,
Mart.

colōna, ae, *f.* [colōnus], *a country-woman :*
Ov.

colōnia, ae, *f.* [colōnus]. **I.** *an abode, dwell-ing :* Pl. **II.** *a colony, colonial settlement.*
1. Lit.: coloniam conlocare idoneis in
locis, Cic. ; in colonias mittere, Liv. **2.**
Transf.: *the colonists themselves, out-settlers :* coloniam deducere aliquo, Cic. ;
Liv. ; Galli trans Rhenum colonias mitte-bant, Caes. As the name of towns, *v.*
Agrippina, etc.

colōnicus, a, um [colōnus]. **I.** *of agri-culture :* Varr. **II.** *of a colony :* Caes.,
Suet.

colōnus, i, *m.* [colō], *a cultivator of the
ground ; a farmer.* **I.** In gen. : Cato, Cic.,
Verg. ; *ruris, countryman,* Hor. Occ.:
farm-tenants : Domitius navis servis, liber-tis, colonis compleverat, Caes. ; Cic. **II.**
Esp. *an outsettler, a colonist :* delectum
colonorum, qui Capuam deducti erant,
habere instituunt, Caes. ; Cic. ; Verg., etc.
Of *an inhabitant* in gen.: Verg. [Fr.
colon.]

color (old form **colōs**), ōris, *m. colour, tint,
hue.* **1.** Lit. **a.** In gen. : Pl., Cic., Verg.,
etc. Of grapes : ducere, *to gather colour,*
Verg. **b.** Esp. *the colour of the skin ; the
complexion :* venusti oculi, color suavis,
Cic. ; verus (opp. to paint), Ter. ; niveo
colore, Hor. ; colorem mutare, Hor. ; per-dere, Ov. ; crebra coloris mutatio, Cic. ;
robur et colos, Liv. Prov.: homo nullius
coloris, i.e. unknown, Pl. Also *beauty,
lustre,* etc.: o formose puer, nimium ne
crede colori, Verg. ; nullus argento color
est, Hor. **2.** Transf.: *colour,* i.e. **a.**
external condition, outward appearance :
amisimus omnem non modo succum ac
sanguinem, sed etiam colorem et speciem
pristinam civitatis, Cic. ; Hor. **b.** Of
style : *colouring, complexion,* i.e. *tone,
style :* qui est, inquit, iste tandem urbanita-tis color ? Cic. ; tragicus, Hor. In *pl.* :
Hor. Also *lustre, grace :* Cic. **c.** *a
colourable pretext, excuse :* dic aliquem,
Quintiliane, colorem, Juv. ; Quint. [Fr.
couleur.]

colōrātus, a, um. **I.** *Part.* colōrō. **II.** *Adj.*
a. *coloured, tinted :* arcus, Cic. **b.** *having
a healthy colour :* corpora, Quint. **c.**
swarthy : Verg., Tac.

colōrō, āre [color], *to colour, paint, tinge, dye,
tan,* etc. **1.** Lit.: corpora, Cic. ; Ov.
2. Transf.: *of the mind, style,* etc. : *to
give a certain complexion to :* Cic., Sen. Ep.

colōs, *v.* color.

colosserōs, ōtis, *m.* [Κολοσσός Ἔρως, the
Colossal-love], *an appellation of a large and
handsome man :* Suet.

colossēus, a, um [κολοσσαῖος], *colossal,
gigantic :* statua, Plin., Suet.

colossus, i, *m.* [κολοσσός], *a gigantic statue,
a colossus :* Plin., Suet. Esp. *the famous
Colossus at Rhodes.*

colostra, ae, *f.* (**colostrum,** i, n., also in *pl.*,
Mart.), *the first milk after delivery, beestings :*
Plin. As a term of endearment : Pl.

colpa, *v.* culpa.

coluber, bri, *m. a serpent, snake, adder :* Verg.

Ov. Of the hair of the Furies : Lucr., Ov.
[Fr. *couleuvre.*]

colubra, ae, *f.* [coluber], *a (female) snake* or
adder : Lucil., Hor., Ov. Of the hair of the
Furies : Pl., Ov.

colubrifer, era, erum [coluber ferō], *snake-bearing.* Of Medusa : Ov.

colubrinus, a, um [coluber], *snaky, cunning,
wily :* Pl.

cōlum, i, *n. a strainer :* Cato, Verg.

columba, ae, *f. a dove, pigeon :* Pl., Cic.,
Ov., etc. As a term of endearment : Pl.

columbar, āris, *n.* [columba], *a kind of collar
like a pigeon-hole :* Pl.

columbārium, i, *n.* [columba]. **1.** Lit.:
a dove-cote, pigeon-hole : Varr. **2.** Transf.
a tomb with niches for the urns : Inscr.

columbinus, a, um [columba], *of a dove* or
pigeon : Cic. Ep., Hor. As Noun, *a little
dove :* Mart.

columbus, i, *m. a male dove* or *pigeon :* Pl.,
Hor. ; *a dove* in gen. : Plin.

columella, ae, *f.* [*dim.* columna], *a small
column, a pillar :* Cato, Caes., Cic.

columen, inis, *n.* [root cel-, *cf.* excellō, etc.],
a height, summit, peak. **1.** Lit. **a.** Of
mountains : Cat. **b.** Of walls or buildings,
the coping, roof, gable ; gable-pillar : Cato,
Varr. **2.** Transf. **a.** *the summit, head,
chief,* etc. : columen amicorum Antoni,
Cic. ; audaciae, Pl. **b.** *a support, stay :*
senati, Pl. ; rei publicae, Cic. ; mearum
rerum, Hor.

columna, ae, *f.* [root cel-, *cf.* excellō, etc.], *a
column, pillar, post.* **1.** Lit.: Cic., Ov.,
etc. Esp. columna rostrata, *a column orna-mented with beaks of ships,* columna Mae-niana, also *Absol.* columna, *a pillory* in the
forum Rom.: Cic. Pl., as the sign of a
bookseller's shop ; hence, *the booksellers :*
non concessere columnae, Hor. **2.** Transf.
a. *a pillar, support :* iniurioso ne pede
proruas stantem columnam, Hor. **b.** Of
the arm : Pl. **c.** *a water-spout :* Lucr. **d.**
columnae Herculis, Tac. ; Protei, Verg.
[It. *colonna ;* Fr. *colonne.*]

columnārium, i, *n.* [columna], *a tax on
house-pillars :* Caes., Cic. Ep.

columnārius, i, *m.* [columna], *one condemned
at the* Columna Maeniana : *a criminal* or
debtor : Cael. ap. Cic. Ep.

columnātus, a, um [columna], *supported by
pillars :* Varr. Comic : os, i.e. *supported
upon the hand,* Pl.

colurnus, a, um [for corulnus, from corulus
= corylus], *made of hazel-wood :* Verg.

colus, I and ūs, *f.* (also *m.* Cat., Prop., Ov.),
a distaff : Verg., etc.

colūtea, ōrum, *n. pl.* [κολουτέα], *a pod-like
kind of fruit :* Pl.

colyphia (**-liphia**), ōrum, *n. pl.* [κωλήφια],
the food of athletes : Pl., Juv.

coma, ae, *f.* [κόμη], *the hair of the head.* **1.**
Lit. **a.** Of men : Verg. ; calamistrata,
Cic. ; flava, Hor. ; componere, comere,
Ov. ; rutilare et summittere, Suet. In
pl. : Verg. ; promissae comae, Liv., Tac.
b. Of sheep : Acc. **2.** Transf. **a.** Of
trees, *foliage,* etc. : Cat., Verg., etc. **b.**
Of rays of light : Cat.

comāns, antis, *adj.* [coma], *hairy, covered
with hair.* **1.** Lit.: colla equorum, Verg. ;

galea, Verg. **2.** T r a n s f. **a.** Of plants, etc.: Verg. **b.** Of rays of light : stella (i.e. a comet), Ov.

cŏmarchus, ī, *m.* [κώμαρχος], *a governor of a village :* Pl.

comātus, a, um [coma], *having much or long hair.* **1.** L i t. : Cat., Suet. (*cf.* Gallia Comata, *v.* Gallia). **2.** T r a n s f. : of trees : Cat.

com-bibō, bibere, bibī. **I.** *to drink with any one :* Sen. Ep. **II.** *to drink up, drink the full draught, absorb.* **1.** L i t. **a.** Of persons : succos, Ov. ; atrum venenum corpore, Hor. ; lacrimas, Sen. Ep. **b.** Of things : metreta amuream, Cato ; ara cruorem, Ov. **2.** T r a n s f. : artis, Cic.

combibō, ōnis, *m.* [combibō], *a pot-companion :* Cic. Ep.

comb-ūrō, ūrere, ūssī, ūstum, *to burn up, consume.* **1.** L i t. : Pl., Lucr. ; frumentum, Caes. ; aliquem vivum, Cic. **2.** T r a n s f. : *to consume, ruin :* aliquem iudicio, Cic. Ep. ; diem, Pl. Of love : Prop.

combūstus, a, um, *Part.* combūrō.

com-edō, ēsse, ēdī, ēsum or ēstum (comēsus, a, um, the more usual form ; comēsūrus, Pl. ; comēstus, Cic. Usual forms of *Pres. Ind.,* comēs, comēst, comēstis, Pl. ; *Imperf. Subj. :* comēsset, Cic. ; *Optat.* comedim, īs, etc., Pl., Cic.), *to eat up, to eat.* **1.** L i t. : Pl., Cic., Hor. Prov. : tam facile vinces quam pirum vulpes comest, Pl. **2.** T r a n s f. **a.** *to devour* (i.e. *squander*) : patrimonium, Cic. ; Hor. **b.** comedere aliquem, *to eat a man out of house and home,* Pl. **c.** Of grief : se comedere, Pl. **d.** aliquem oculis, Mart.

comes, itis, *m.f.* [con and i, root of eō], *one who goes with another ; companion on a journey, fellow-traveller.* **1.** L i t. **a.** Pl., Cic., Verg., etc. ; comes ire alicui, Verg. ; fugae, Cic. Ep., Liv. ; itinerum, Cic. Ep. **b.** In wider sense, *a sharer, associate :* victoriae, Caes. ; furores, Cic. ; mortis, Lucr. ; in ulciscendis quibusdam, Cic. Ep. ; aliquem comitem habere consiliis, Pl. **c.** Special senses : **i.** *a guardian, tutor :* Verg., Suet. **ii.** *one of the suite, retinue which accompanied magistrates,* etc. : Cic., Hor., Suet. **iii.** *one of the imperial retinue or court :* Suet. **2.** T r a n s f. : *attendant :* mortis comes gloriae, Cic. ; Hor. ; with D a t. : Lucr. [It. *conte ;* Fr. *comte.*]

comēs, comēsse, *v.* comedō.

comēstus, a, um, *Part.* comedō.

comēsus, a, um, *Part.* comedō.

comētēs, ae, *m.* [κομήτης, *cf.* coma], *a comet :* Cic., Verg. In app. to sidus : Tac.

cōmicē, *adv. in the manner of comedy :* Cic.

cōmicus, a, um [κωμικός], *of comedy, comic :* poeta, Cic. ; res, Hor. ; senes, Caecil. ap. Cic. ; aurum (= lupina), *stage-money,* Pl. As Noun, **cōmicus,** ī, *m.* **a.** *an actor of comedy :* Pl. **b.** *a writer of comedy :* Cic.

cōmis, e, *adj. courteous, affable ; kind, friendly* (*v.* cōmitās) : Cic., Hor. ; erga aliquem, Cic. ; in uxorem, Hor. ; bonis, Tac. *Comp. :* Cic.

cōmissābundus, a um [cōmissor], *going in a riotous bacchanalian procession, revelling :* Liv.

cōmissātiō, ōnis, *f.* [cōmissor]. *a riotous Bacchanalian procession, a revelling :* Cic., Liv. In *pl. :* Cic., Liv.

cōmissātor, ōris, *m.* [cōmissor], *one who joins in a festive procession, a reveller :* Cic., Liv. Hence, in contempt : nostri isti comissatores coniurationis, Cic.

cōmissor (**cōmīsor**), ārī [κωμάζω], *to go in festive bacchanalian procession, to revel, make merry :* Pl., Hor., Liv.

cōmitās, ātis, *f.* [cōmis], *courteousness, kindness, friendliness, affability, gentleness :* Cic. ; in socios, Tac. Disparagingly (*cf.* 'good nature') : rem bene paratam comitate perdidit, Pl. ; Suet.

comitātus, a, um, *Part.* comitor.

comitātus, ūs, *m.* [comitor], *an escort, a train, retinue.* **1.** L i t. **a.** ancillarum puerorumque, Cic. ; equitum triginta, Caes. ; Verg. Esp. *the imperial retinue, court, suite :* Tac. **b.** *a company* (of people travelling together), *a party, caravan :* Caes., Cic., Liv. **2.** T r a n s f. : virtutum, Cic.

cōmiter, *adv.* [cōmis], *kindly, courteously, civilly :* Pl., Cic., Ov., etc. *Sup. :* comissume, Pl.

comitia, ōrum, *v.* comitium, no. II.

comitiālis, e, *adj.* [comitia], *of the comitia :* dies, Cic. Ep., Liv. ; biduum, Caes. ; homines, i.e. who were always at the comitia, and sold their votes, Pl. ; morbus, *the falling-sickness, epilepsy* (so called because its occurrence broke up the comitia), Sen.

comitiātus, ūs, *m.* [comitia], *an assembly of the people in the comitia :* dimittere, Cic.

comitium, ī, n. [con and i, root of eō]. **I.** In *sing.* **1.** L i t. : *a place of assembly* (at the end of the forum) : Cic., Liv. **2.** T r a n s f. : *a place of assembly elsewhere,* e.g. the Ephoreum at Sparta : Nep. **II.** In *pl. :* **comitia,** ōrum, n. **1.** L i t. **a.** *the assembly of the Romans for electing magistrates,* etc. ; *the comitia, the elections.* The comitia were of three kinds : comitia curiata, centuriata, and tributa. Most often comitia = comitia centuriata ; and, when held for elections, are often defined, as consularia, praetoria, i.e. for the election of consuls, etc. ; so, comitia consulum habere, Liv. ; comitia regi creando, Liv. ; and even comitia mea, i.e. *at which I am* a candidate, Cic. ; habere, Cic. ; edicere, differre, Liv. ; conficere, dimittere, Cic. Ep. **b.** *elections* out of Rome : Cic., Liv. **2.** T r a n s f. : ubi de capite meo sunt comitia, Pl.

comitō, āre [comes], *to accompany, attend :* castra, Prop. ; funera, Ov. E s p. in *Perf. Part. :* alienis viris comitata, Cic. ; parum comitatus, Cic. ; Ov. *Comp. :* comitātior, Cic.

comitor, ārī [comes], *to accompany, follow, attend.* **1.** L i t. : magnā comitante catervā, Verg. ; Tac. With Acc. : comitati eos ex civitate excessere, Caes. ; Verg., etc. **2.** T r a n s f. **a.** With Acc. : Verg. **b.** With D a t. : Tarquinio Superbo prospera fortuna comitata est, Cic. ; tardis mentibus virtus non comitatur, Cic. *Absol. :* Tac.

com-maculō, āre, *to spot all over, stain, pollute.* **1.** L i t. : manūs sanguine, Verg. ; Tac. **2.** T r a n s f. : se ambitu, Cic. ; Tac

com-manipulāris, is, *m. a comrade in the same* manipulus : Tac.

com-marītus, ī, *m. a fellow-husband* : Pl.

commeātus, ūs, *m.* [commeō], *a going to and fro, passing freely.* Hence, **I.** *a free passage, thoroughfare* : perfodi parietem quā commeatus esset, Pl. **II.** Milit. : *a leave of absence, furlough* : dare, Cic., Liv. ; sumere, Liv. ; in commeatu esse, *to be on furlough*, Liv. **III.** *a carrying over, transport, passage.* **a.** Of troops : duobus commeatibus exercitum reportare, Caes. **b.** Of merchandise : Londinium copiā negotiatorum et commeatuum maxime celebre, Tac. **IV.** Milit. (very freq.) *lines of communication* : Pl. ; commeatu nostros intercludere, prohibere, Caes. ; maritimi, Liv. Also non-milit. : Cic. **V.** Milit. (very freq.), *supplies*, esp. *provisions* : supportare, Caes. ; portare, advehere, convehere, invehere, subvehere, Liv. Also non-milit. : Cic. [Fr. *congé*.]

com-meditor, ārī, *to practise thoroughly* ; hence, *to imitate* : Lucr.

com-meminī, isse, *to recollect thoroughly, to remember* : hominem probe commeminisse, Cic. ; Pl. With GEN. or *Inf.* : Pl. *Absol* : Pl., Ov.

commemorābilis, e, *adj.* [commemorō], *worth mentioning, memorable* : Pl., Cic.

commemorātiō, ōnis, *f.* [commemorō], *a reminding, mentioning, recital* : Ter. With *Obj.* GEN. : Cic., Liv. With *Subj.* GEN. : posteritatis, Cic. Ep.

com-memorō, āre, *to call to mind, recall completely.* **A.** To one's self (rare). With *Indir. Quest.* : Cic. With Acc. and *Inf.* : Cic. Ep., Suet. **B.** To others : Pl. ; officia, Cic. ; amicitiam, Liv. Hence, often *to mention, recount.* With Acc. : Pl., Lucr., Cic., etc. With Acc. and *Inf.* : Caes., Cic. With *Indir. Quest.* : Pl., Ter., Cic. With *de* : Cic., Nep.

commendābilis, e, *adj.* [commendō], *praiseworthy, commendable* : Liv.

commendātīcius, a, um [commendātus], *recommending, giving recommendation or introduction* : tabellae, Cic. ; litterae, Cic. Ep.

commendātiō, ōnis, *f.* [commendō]. **I.** *a recommending, recommendation* : Cic., Sall., etc. With *Obj.* GEN. : Cic. In *pl.* : Cic. Ep. T r a n s f. (with *Subj.* GEN.) : oculorum, Cic. **II.** *that which recommends, excellence or worth* : ingeni, Cic. ; Quint.

commendātor, ōris, *m.* (Plin. Ep.) and **commendātrix**, īcis, *f.* (Cic., Plin. Ep.) [commendō], *one that commends.*

commendātus, a, um. **I.** *Part.* commendō. **II.** *Adj. recommended* : quae res commendatior erit memoriae hominum sempiternae ? Cic. *Sup.* : Cic. Ep.

com-mendō, āre [mandō], *to entrust or commit entirely to one's charge or care.* **1.** L i t. **a.** Of physical delivery : librum meum Sabino tuo, Cic. Ep. **b.** Of putting under someone's protection : mē tuae fidei, Ter. ; Cic. ; se civitatesque suas Caesari, Caes. ; Ov., etc. **2.** T r a n s f. : **a.** nomina memoriae, Cic. ; aliquid litteris, Brut. ap. Cic. Ep. **b.** *to recommend* a person for

office, etc. : se civibus, Cic. ; candidatos, Tac. **c.** *to recommend, render agreeable* : verborum splendore et copiā, Cic. ; Hor.

commēnsus, a, um, *Part.* commētior.

commentāriolum, ī, *n.* [*dim.* commentārius], *a short treatise* : Cic., Quint.

commentārius, ī, *m.* (*sc.* liber) and less freq., **commentārium**, ī, *n.* (*sc.* volumen) [commīniscor]. **I.** *a note-book, memorandum* : orationis, Cic. ; Liv. ; diurni, *a day-book, journal*, Suet. **II.** As the title of a book (mostly *pl.*) *memoirs, notes, memoranda* (for use in a more formal treatise or history) : thus, Caesaris Commentarii, Cic. ; Commentarios Numae, Liv. **III.** In law : *a brief* : Cic. **IV.** *an abstract, memorandum* : do apparatibus belli facere, Liv. **V.** *lecture-notes* : Quint.

commentātiō, ōnis, *f.* [commentor], *diligent meditation, a studying, a careful preparation* : sese cottidianis commentationibus exercuit, Cic. T r a n s f. : tota philosophorum vita commentatio mortis est, Cic.

commentīcius, a, um [commentus], *thought out, devised.* **A.** Opp. to what is already existing : *newly invented* : nominibus novis et commenticiis appellata, Cic. ; Suet. **B.** Opp. to what is actual : *fictitious, imaginary, ideal* : commenticii et ficti Dei, Cic. Opp. to that which is true : *fabricated, forged, false* : crimen, Cic. ; ficta et commenticia fabula, Cic.

commentor, ārī [*freq.* commīniscor]. **1.** In gen. *to think over, consider thoroughly, study* : Pl., Cic. With Acc. : Cic. With *de* : de libertate, Cic. With *Indir. Quest.* : Cic. Ep. *Perf. Part.* in *Pass.* sense : *studied, carefully prepared* (opp. to extemporary) : Cic. **2.** T r a n s f. **a.** *to devise, invent, contrive* : ut cito commentatus est (*sc.* mendacium) ! Pl. **b.** *to sketch out, work up, write, compose* : mimos, Cic. ; aliquid in reum, Cic.

commentor, ōris, *m.* [commīniscor], *one who devises something, an inventor* : uvae, i.e. Bacchus, Ov.

commentus, a, um. **I.** *Part.* commīniscor. **II.** Noun, **commentum**, ī, *n.* **I.** *an invention, fabrication, fiction.* Ter. With *Obj.* GEN. : Cic., Liv., Ov. **II.** *a contrivance, device* : Suet.

com-meō, āre, *to go and come, pass to and fro.* **I.** In gen. **a.** Of living beings : fossam perduxit ut tuto etiam singuli commeare possent, Caes. ; Cic. ; Liv., etc. **b.** Of inanimate objects : Cic., Tac. **II.** Esp. with reference to the place, *to visit often, resort to.* **a.** Of living beings, e.g. of traders : in urbem, Pl. ; Caes. ; Cic. **b.** Of things : crebro illius litterae ad nos commeant, Cic. Ep. ; Pl.

commercium, ī, *n.* [commercor], *trade, commerce, commercial intercourse.* **1.** L i t. **a.** In gen. : Sall. ; annonae, Liv. ; Tac. **b.** Esp. *the right to trade* : Cic. ; ceteris Latinis populis commercia inter se ademerunt, Liv. **2.** T r a n s f. : *intercourse, communication, dealings* : commercium habere cum Musis, Cic. ; Pl. With GEN. of the person with whom : plebis, Liv. With GEN. of the thing in which : sermonum, Liv. ; belli, i.e. *ransom*, Verg. ; loquendi audiendique, Tac.

com-mercor, ari, *to trade together, purchase* : captivos, Pl. ; Sall.

com-mereō, ēre (also **commereor**, Pl., Ter.), *to entirely merit, richly deserve.* **1.** Lit. : aestimationem, Cic. ; poenam, Ov. **2.** Transf. : *to be guilty of an offence or crime* : noxiam, Pl. ; Ter. ; Ov.

com-mētior, mētīri, mēnsus, *to measure* : porticūs, Pl. Transf. : *to measure with or by something* : negotium cum tempore, Cic.

commētō, āre [*freq.* commeō], *to go frequently* : Pl., Ter.

commictus, a, um, *Part.* commingō.

com-migrō, āre, *to go off in a body, migrate* : Pl., Cic. Ep., Liv., etc.

com-milĭtĭum, ī, *n.* [con and milit- (miles)], *companionship in war.* **1.** Lit. : in commilitium ascisci, Tac. **2.** Transf. : *fellowship, companionship* : studiorum, Ov.

com-milĭtō, ōnis, *m.* [con and miles], *a fellow-soldier* : Caes., Cic., Suet.

comminātĭō, ōnis, *f.* [comminor], *a violent threatening, menacing* : Cic. In *pl.* : *violent threats* : Liv.

com-mingō, mingere, minxi, mictum, *to defile* (with urine) : Cat., Hor. ; commictum caenum (as a term of abuse), Pl.

com-miniscor, minisci, mentus [root as in reminiscor], *to devise by careful thought, to contrive, invent.* **A.** Of something to meet a difficulty : Liv., Suet. With *Indir. Quest.* : Pl. **B.** Of something imaginary : Cic. **C.** Of something untrue : Pl., Cic. Ep., Liv. **D.** Of something hostile : Liv. *Part.* commentus sometimes in *Pass.* sense (= commenticius) : *feigned, fictitious* : funera, Ov. ; Liv.

com-minor, āri, *to threaten violently, menace* : pugnam, Liv. ; necem alicui, Suet. ; alicui cuspide, Suet.

com-minuō, uere, uī, ūtum, *to lessen considerably, break up, split up, shatter.* **1.** Lit. : Pl. ; statuam, Cic. ; Ov. **2.** Transf. : *to fritter away, impair.* **a.** argenti pondus et auri, Hor. **b.** opes civitatis, Cic. ; Ov. **c.** Of persons : re familiari comminuti sumus, Cic. Ep. ; Viriathum, Cic. ; Ov.

com-minus, *adv.* [manus], *hand to hand.* **I.** Of fighting. **1.** Lit. : Enn. ; nec eminus hastis aut comminus gladiis uteretur, Cic. ; Caes., Ov., etc. **2.** Transf. : of contention in words : agere, Cic. ; in agriculture : Verg. **II.** Without the idea of contest : *nigh at hand, hard by* : Lucr., Ov., Tac.

com-misceō, miscēre, miscuī, mixtum, *to mix or mingle together, to intermingle.* **1.** Lit. : mulsum, Pl. ; Suet. With Acc. and *cum* : amurcam cum aquā, Cato ; Lucr. ; Cic. With ABL. : frusta cruento mero, Verg. ; Pl. ; Suet. With *in* and Acc. : fumus in auras commixtus, Verg. **2.** Transf. : temeritas cum sapientiā commiscetur, Cic. ; terroribus commixtum clamorem, Verg. ; tecum aliquid consili, Pl.

commiserātĭō, ōnis, *f.* [commiseror], *a pitying.* Rhet. : *a passage intended to excite compassion* : Cic.

com-miserēscō, ere, *to commiserate* : Enn. *Impers.* : Ter.

com-miseror, āri, *to commiserate, bewail.* **I.** In *gen.* : Acc. ; fortunam Graeciae, Nep. **II.** Rhet. : *to try to excite compassion* : Cic.

commissĭō, ōnis, *f.* [committō]. **1.** Lit. *a letting go together* : hence, *the beginning of a fight, game,* etc. : *the celebration of games* : Cic. Ep. ; Plin. Ep. **2.** Transf. : *a prize declamation* (*cf.* ἀγώνισμα, Thucyd.) : Suet.

commissūra, ae, *f.* [committō], *a joining together, union, joint* : funis, Cato ; digitorum (ossium), *joints,* Cic. ; Caes. Transf. : verborum, Quint.

commissus, a, um. **I.** *Part.* committō. **II.** Noun, **commissum**, ī, *n.* **I.** *a thing undertaken* : with *Adv.* : Liv. Esp. of bad action, *an offence, crime* : Pl., Cic., Verg. In law *an offence* with its necessary penalties : Suet. **II.** *that which is entrusted, a secret, trust* : Cic., Hor.

com-mitigō, āre, *to make thoroughly soft* : Ter.

com-mittō, mittere, misī, missum, *to let go together* : hence, **I.** *to put together, connect, unite.* **1.** Lit. **a.** In *gen.* : commissis mālis, Caes. ; Ov. ; Liv. ; commissa inter se munimenta, Liv. ; caudas utero, Verg. ; vir equo commissus, Ov. ; Liv. **b.** For fighting, etc., *to match* : Juv. ; pugilis Latinos cum Graecis, Suet. **2.** Transf. : *to bring together* : acies, Prop. ; hence, **a.** With proelium, etc., *to join battle,* etc., *to set going, begin* : proelium, Caes., Liv. ; pugnam, Cic. ; bellum, rixam, Liv. **b.** In gen. *to start* : iudicium, Cic. ; ludos, Pl., Cic. Ep., Verg. **c.** *to set about, undertake,* hence, *commit, perpetrate* : delictum, Caes. ; facinus, flagitium, Caes. ; fraudem, Hor. With contra legem : Cic. ; multa nefario in deos, Cic. ; Verg. **d.** Phr. **i.** With *ut,* *to be guilty of so acting that* . . . : Pl., Cic., etc. **ii.** With *cur* or *quāre* : Caes., Liv. **iii.** With *Inf.* : Ov. **iv.** With poenam, multam, etc., *to incur a penalty* : Cic. Hence, in *Pass.,* *made liable to penalties, forfeited* : hereditas, Cic. ; sponsio (Caudina), Liv. **II.** *to put a thing somewhere for protection,* etc., *to entrust, commit.* **a.** me vestrae fidei commisit, Caes. ; Ter. ; his salutem nostram rectissime committi arbitramur, Cic. ; Pl. ; Hor. ; semina sulcis, Verg. ; Hor. ; commissi calores fidibus, Hor. Prov. : ovem lupo committere, Ter. **b.** With *Refl. Pron., to commit oneself, venture* : se in id conclave, Cic. ; se ventis, Caes. ; se urbi, Cic. ; se mortis periculo, Cic. ; se proelio, Liv. ; se ponto, Verg. **c.** With rem (instead of *Refl. Pron.*), *to commit one's fortunes* : rem proelio, Caes. ; rem in aciem, Liv. ; rem publicam in discrimen, Liv. **d.** With DAT. alone : Pl., Ter.

commixtus, a, um, *Part.* commisceō.

commodē, *adv. in due or proper measure* ; hence **A.** *fitly, aptly, suitably* : Pl., Ter., Cic. **B.** *conveniently, easily, comfortably* : Caes., Cic. Ep., Hor. **C.** *opportunely* : Caes., Cic. **D.** *kindly, obligingly* : Pl., Ter. *Comp.* : Cic., Hor. ; *Sup.* : Caes., Cic. Ep.

commodĭtās, ātis, *f.* [commodus], *just proportion, symmetry* : membrorum, Suet. Hence, **a.** Of style : *fitness, aptness of* *expression* : Cic. **b.** *fitness* (in time), *a favourable moment* : ad faciendum, Cic. ; Pl. **c.** *convenience, pleasantness, comfort* : vitae, Cic. ; itineris, Liv. In *pl.* : Ter., Cic. **d.** Of persons : *pleasantness, obligingness* : Pl., Ov. As term of endearment : Pl.

commŏdō, āre [commodus]. **I.** *to adjust to measure, to adapt one thing to another.* **1.** Lit. : Cato. **2.** Transf. : Pl. ; orationi vocem, Plin. Pan. ; also with *ad* : Plin. Ep. **II.** *to adapt (oneself), to be serviceable, obliging*, etc. *Absol.* or with DAT. of person benefited : Pl., Cic. With ABL. or *in* and ABL. of the thing in which : Cic. Ep. Hence, with Acc. of thing : *to oblige by supplying something, to bestow, supply, lend* : Pl. ; aurum alicui, Cic. ; culturae patientem aurem, Hor. ; Ov. ; peccatis veniam, Tac. ; falsos testis, Sall.

commŏdŭlē [*dim.* commodē], and **commŏdŭlum**, *adv. nicely, conveniently, suitably* : Pl.

com-mŏdus, a, um, *having due* or *right measure* ; hence, **I.** *of full measure* or *weight* : talentum argenti, Pl. ; cyathus, Hor. **II.** *fitted, adapted, suitable, fit, convenient.* **A.** Of things. **a.** *adapted to circumstances, suitable* : defensio, Cic. ; sibi ratio belli, Caes. ; Ter. ; omnia commoda curationi, Liv. ; seges commoda Baccho, Verg. Rarely with *ad* : Ov. **b.** *opportune* (in time) : anni tempus, Cic. Ep. ; Ter. **c.** *convenient, advantageous, easy, comfortable* : in Britanniam traiectus, Caes. ; iter, Liv. ; hiberna, Liv. ; in commodiorem statum pervenire, Liv. Of health : Plin. Ep. Phr. : commodum est, *it pleases, is agreeable* : Pl., Ter. ; quod commodum est, *just as you please*, Cic. **B.** Of persons : *agreeable, obliging, friendly*, etc. : Pl., Ter., Cic., Hor. Transf. : (iambus) spondeos stabilīs in iura paterna recepit commodus, Hor. *Comp.* : Cic., etc. ; *Sup.* : Caes., etc. As Noun, **commŏdum**, *ī, n.* etc. [commodus]. **I.** *a convenient opportunity, favourable circumstances, convenience* : cum erit tuum commodum, Cic. Ep. Phr. : commodo meo, tuo, etc. : *at my, thy*, etc., *convenience, at one's leisure* : quod commodo tuo fiat, Cic.Ep. ; also, per commodum, Liv. ; naves quas sui quisque commodi fecerat, Caes. **II.** *advantage, profit, interest* : Ter. ; rei familiaris commoda, Caes. ; contra valetudinis commodum, Cic. ; Hor. ; quod commodo rei publicae facere possis (*as far as consistent with the interests of the state*), Cic. ; in same sense, si per commodum rei publicae posset, Liv. **III.** In *pl., remuneration for public services* : *pay, gratuities*, etc. : veteranorum, Br. et Cass. ap. Cic. Ep. ; emeritae militiae, Suet. ; tribunatūs (militum), Cic. Ep. ; Ov. **IV.** *a loan* : Cic.

commŏdum, *n.* Acc. of commodus as adv. **I.** *opportunely, seasonably, in the nick of time* (colloq.) : ecce autem commodum aperitur foris, Pl. ; Cic. Ep. **II.** *just at the moment* : ad te ibam commodum, Pl. ; esp. followed by a *cum* clause : *just . . . when* : commodum discesseras heri, cum Trebatius venit, Cic. Ep. ; Ter.

Commodus, ī, *m. a Roman emperor*, A.D. 180–192.

com-mōlior, īrī, *to set in motion* : tempestas fulmina, Lucr.

commone-faciō, facere, fēcī, factum. **I.** With Acc. of person : *to remind forcibly* : Pl., Cic. Ep. ; and with GEN. of thing : Cic., Sall. ; also with *ut* and *Juss. Subj.* : Cic. **II.** With Acc. of thing : *to call to mind fully* or *clearly* : Caes., Cic. With Acc. and *Inf.* : Cic.

com-moneō, ēre. **I.** *to remind fully, to put in mind of.* With Acc. of person : Pl., Cic., Quint. ; and with GEN. of thing : Pl., Quint. ; or with *de* : aliquem de avaritiā tuā, Cic. ; or with *Neut.* Acc. of *Pron.* : Pl. ; or with *Indir. Quest.* : Pl., Quint. With *ut* or *ne* and *Juss. Subj.* : Ter., Quint. **II.** *to bring fully to one's recollection* : aliquid, Quint.

com-mōnstrō, āre (commōnstrāssō = commōnstrāverō, Pl.), *to point out distinctly* : Pl., Ter., Cic. With *Indir. Deliberative* : Pl.

commŏrātiō, ōnis, *f.* [commoror], *a considerable tarrying, delaying* or *staying* : Cic. Ep. Rhet. : *a dwelling upon some important point* : Cic., Quint.

com-morior, morī, mortuus, *to die together* : with DAT. : Sen. Ep. Commorientēs (a lost play of Pl.) : Ter.

com-moror, ārī. **A.** Intrans. : *to stay* or *wait for some time* : Caes., Cic. Rhet. : in eādem sententiā, Cic. **B.** Trans. : *to stop, detain, retard* : Pl.

commŏtiō, ōnis, *f.* [commoveō], *a violent moving.* Transf. : *a rousing, excitement* : animi, Cic. In *pl.* : Cic.

commŏtiuncula, ae, *f.* [*dim.* commōtiō], *a slight indisposition* : Cic. Ep.

commōtus, a, um. **I.** *Part.* commoveō. **II.** *Adj.* **a.** *impassioned, lively* : genus dicendi, Cic. **b.** *impassioned ; angry, excited* : animus commotior, Cic. ; Liv. ; Drusus commotior animo, Tac. **c.** *disordered, deranged, insane* : commotus ille, Ter. ; Hor. ; commotus mente, Plin. ; ingenio, Tac.

com-moveō, movēre, mōvī, mōtum (contr. forms : commōrunt, Lucr. ; commōrat, Ter. ; commōrit, Hor. ; commōssem, Cic., etc.) : *to set in motion violently.* **1.** Lit. : *to stir up, agitate, displace, dislodge, drive backwards* or *forwards* : Pl. ; magni commorunt aequora venti, Lucr. ; castra ex eo loco, Cic. ; se domo, Cic. Ep. ; hostem, Liv. : cervum, Verg. ; alas, Verg. Occ. *to carry to and fro* : sacra, Verg. Hence, humorously : mea si commovi sacra, Pl. **2.** Transf. : *to stir up, agitate*, etc. **A.** Of the body, mind, and emotions ; with ABL. or *in* (or rarely *ex*) and ABL. of the cause : *ad* and Acc., or *ut* and *Subj.* of the object aimed at. **a.** *to disorder, trouble* : *v.* commotus. **b.** *to stir, incite* : Ter., Cic. ; dulcedine gloriae commoti, Cic. ; Lucr. ; Caes. ; commoveor animo ad ea quae etc., Cic. Ep. With *ut* : Ter. **c.** *to trouble, disquiet* : Caes., Cic. **d.** *to stir up, rouse to anger* : Hor., Verg. **B.** *to set in motion, arouse* (i.e. *cause*) : tumultum, bellum, dolorem, misericordiam, Cic. ; lacrimas, Curt. ; iram, Ov. **C.** *to drive off* (in argument) : Cic.

commūne, is, *v.* commūnis.

commūnicătĭŏ, ōnis, *f*. [commūnicŏ], *an imparting, communicating :* civitatis, sermonis, Cic. Rhet. *a figure of speech in which the speaker appears to give his hearers a share in the discussion :* Cic.

commūnicŏ, āre [commūnis], *to make common, put into a common stock, share.* With Acc. of thing shared, and *cum* with Abl. (also Dat. : Caes.) of person or thing with whom it is shared or united. **A.** By giving. **a.** With a thing : (pecunias) cum dotibus communicant, Caes. ; aliquid cum meā laude, Cic. **b.** With a person : gloriam cum legionibus, Caes. ; civitatem nostram vobiscum, Cic. Also, te mensā meā, Pl. **c.** Also by telling, *to confer with, communicate with :* quibuscum communicare de maximis rebus Pompeius consuerat, Caes. ; Cic. With Acc. of thing discussed : Caes., Cic. **B.** By receiving : mecum meam provinciam, Pl. ; inimicitias mecum, Cic. Ep.

commūnicor, ārī, = commūnicŏ, once in Liv.

com-mūnĭŏ, īre, *to make and fortify strongly :* castra, Caes., Liv. T r a n s f. : causam testimoniis, Cic.

commūnĭŏ, ōnis, *f*. [commūnis], *a sharing in common, mutual participation :* legis, iuris, sanguinis, Cic. ; victoriae, Tac.

com-mūnis, e, *adj*. [root seen in mūnus], *shared together, common to several or to all, common, general, universal.* **1.** Lit. : communia esse amicorum inter se omnia, Ter. ; aliquid cum aliquo commune habere, Cic. ; non proprium senectutis est vitium sed commune valetudinis, Cic. ; Lucr. ; commune periculum miserabantur, Caes. ; existimatio communis omnibus est, Liv. ; Martem communem belli (i.e. *the general chances*), Liv. ; communis vitae ignarus (i.e. *of the customs of society*), Cic. ; communi sensu caret (i.e. *of a sense of propriety*), Hor. P h i l o s. : loci, *common-places, common topics :* Cic. R h e t. : exordium, *one that suits either side of a case,* Cic. As Noun, **commūne**, is, *n*. **a.** *common property* (in *pl.*) : Cic., Hor. **b.** *a community, state :* Cic., Ov. Hence, **in commūne** : **i.** *for a common object, advantage,* etc. : consulere, Ter. ; Pl. ; Cic. **ii.** *equally :* vocare honores, Liv. Also, libertatem in communi ponere, Tac. **iii.** *in general :* haec in commune de omnium Germanorum origine accepimus, Tac. **iv.** As exclam. : in commune : *shares !* Phaedr., Sen. Ep. **2.** T r a n s f. : of manners : *putting oneself on an equality with others ; free from snobbishness, affable :* Cyrum minorem communem erga Lysandrum fuisse, Cic. ; communis infimis, Nep. Comp. : Cic.

commūnĭtās, ātis, *f*. [commūnis]. **I.** *community, fellowship :* deorum et hominum, Cic. With Obj. Gen. : condicionis cum aliquo, Cic. **II.** *sense of fellowship :* Cic. **III.** *affability :* Nep.

commūnĭter, *adv*. *in common, jointly :* Cic., Hor., Ov.

commūnĭtĭŏ, ōnis, *f*. [com-mūnĭŏ], *the making of a road.* R h e t. = *an introduction :* Cic.

com-murmurŏ, āre (Plin.), and **-or**, ārī (Cic.), *to murmur, mutter to one's self.*

commūtābĭlis, e, *adj*. [commūtŏ]. *subject to change, changeable :* cera, Cic. Rhet. *interchangeable* (i.e. *suitable for either side of the case*) : exordium, Cic.

commūtătĭŏ, ōnis, *f*. and **commūtātus**, ūs, *m*. (Lucr.) [commūtŏ], *a changing, change :* aestuum, Caes. ; caeli, Cic. ; rerum, fortunae, etc., Cic.

com-mūtŏ, āre. **I.** *to change entirely, alter.* **a.** signa rerum, Cic. ; Lucr. ; iter, consilium, voluntatem, opinionem, Caes. In *Mid.* : *to become changed :* tempora commutantur, Cic. **b.** With Abl. or *cum* and Abl. : *to exchange* (*for*): studium belli gerundi agriculturā, Caes. ; Pl. ; Lucr. ; Cic. ; gloriam constantiae cum caritate patriae, Cic. **II.** *to interchange, exchange with somebody :* captivos, Cic. ; Pl. Of conversation : unum verbum tecum, Ter.

comŏ, āre, *v*. comāns.

cŏmŏ, cŏmere, cŏmpsī, cŏmptum [con, emŏ], *to put together, arrange.* **A.** In gen. (only in *Part.* comptus) : Lucr. ; ramos vittā comptos (i.e. *bound about*), Verg. **B.** Esp. of the hair : *to braid, dress :* Pl. ; capillos, Cic. ; Verg. ; comas, Ov. **C.** Of rhet. ornament : Cic., Quint.

cŏmoedia, ae, *f*. (Gen. cōmoediāī, Pl.) [κωμῳδία], *a comedy :* facere, agere, exigere, spectare, Ter. ; legere, Plin. Ep. ; vetus, Cic. ; prisca, Hor.

cŏmoedĭcē, *adv*. *as in comedy :* Pl.

cŏmoedus, ī, *m*. [κωμῳδός], *a comedian, comic actor :* Cic. Juv., etc. As *Adj*. : Juv.

cŏmōsus, a, um [coma], *hairy, with much or long hair :* frons, Phaedr. Of plants, *leafy :* Plin.

compāctĭŏ, ōnis, *f*. [compingŏ], *a joining together :* membrorum, Cic.

compactum, ī, *n*. and **compactus**, a, um, *v*. compectum and compectus.

compāctus, a, um. **I.** *Part*. compingŏ. **II.** *Adj*. *compact, strongly built :* compactis membris, Suet.

compāgēs, is, *f*. [con, pangŏ], *a joining or fastening together.* **1.** Lit. : Lucr. ; lapidum, Ov. ; scutorum, Tac. T r a n s f. **a.** *joints, seams :* Verg., Liv., Tac. **b.** *a fabric, framework :* corporis, Cic. Of the State : Tac.

compāgŏ, inis, *f*. [con, pangŏ], *a fastening, connexion :* Ov.

com-păr, aris (Abl. -parī, Liv. ; -pare, Ov.), *properly a Noun, a perfect match.* **I.** As Noun. **a.** *a comrade :* Pl., Hor. **b.** *a mate :* Pl., Cat., Ov. **II.** As *Adj*. *fully equal, on an equal level :* consilium consilio (Dat.), Liv. ; Lucr. ; compari Marte concurrunt, Liv.

compărābĭlis, e, *adj*. [comparŏ], *that may be compared, comparable :* Cic., Liv.

compărătĭŏ, ōnis, *f*. [comparŏ]. **I.** *a bringing together.* **a.** *a comparison :* orationis suae cum scriptis alienis, Cic. **b.** *relative position :* e.g. *of sun, moon, and planets :* Cic. **c.** *arrangement :* provincia sine comparatione data, Liv. **II.** *a putting together, a making ready, a providing for* or *of :* novi belli, Cic. ; veneni, Liv. ; testium, Cic.

compărātīvus, a, um [comparŏ], *of* or *suitable for comparison, comparative :* Cic., Quint.

com-pāreō, ēre. **I.** *to become quite visible, put in an appearance :* Pl., Lucr., Cic. **II.** *to be visible, be forthcoming, be extant :* Pl., Cic., Liv.

com-parō, āre. **I.** [con, parō], *to put together.* **1.** Lit. **a.** labella cum labellis, Pl. ; res inter se, Cic. ; Liv. **b.** *to get together, provide :* Pl. ; praesidium Genabi tuendi causā comparabant, Caes. ; nautas gubernatoresque, Caes. ; Liv. ; convivium, Cic. **2.** Transf. **a.** In gen. *to arrange, prepare :* omnis res ad profectionem, Caes. ; Cic. **b.** With *Refl. Pron. : to make oneself ready, to prepare :* se uxor, ut fit, comparat, Cic. ; se ad respondendum, Cic. ; se ad iter, Liv. Occ. in *Mid. :* legati in Boeotiam comparati sunt, Liv. **c.** Of abstracts : auctoritatem sibi, Caes. ; fugam, Caes. ; amicitias, Cic. ; tribunicium auxilium sibi, Liv. With *ut* clause : Cic., Liv. With *Inf. :* Ter., Ov. *Impers. Pass. :* Cic. Ep., Liv. **d.** Of public affairs : *to arrange in detail :* consules inter se provincias comparaverant, Liv. ; consules comparant inter se ut se consul devoveret, Liv. **II.** [compǎr] *to match together.* **1.** Lit. : ut ego cum patrono disertissimo comparer, Cic. ; Scipio et Hannibal ad extremum certamen comparati duces, Liv. ; se mihi comparat Aiax ? Ov. **2.** Transf. : of moral qualities : ne se quidem ipsi cum illis virtute comparant, Caes. ; neminem tibi, Cic. ; Hor. ; Liv. With *ad :* Ter. With *Indir. Quest. : to show by comparing :* Cic., Liv.

com-pāscō, pāscere. **I.** *to feed (cattle) together :* Cic. **II.** *to consume by feeding :* Varr.

com-pāscuus, a, um, *of a common pasturage :* ager, Cic.

compectus, a, um [con, paciscor], *in agreement, agreed :* Pl.

compectum, i, n. *an agreement ;* esp. in ABL. *by agreement, according to agreement :* Cic., Liv. So, de compecto, Pl. ; ex compecto, Suet.

compĕdiō, īre [compēs], *to fetter, shackle :* Pl., Varr.

compellātiō, ōnis, f. [compellō]. **I.** *an accosting :* Auct. Her. **II.** *a reprimanding, rebuke :* Cic. In *pl. :* Cic. Ep.

(1) compellō, āre [root seen in appellāre, etc.], *to summon, call upon by name.* **1.** Lit. **a.** blande hominem, Pl. ; aliquem voce, Verg. ; Tourcam nomine, Liv. **b.** In law, *to summon, call to account :* Cic., Liv., Tac. **2.** Transf. : *to upbraid, arraign :* pro cunctatore segnem, Liv. ; ne compellarer inultus, Hor.

(2) com-pellō, pellere, pull, pulsum. **1.** Lit. **a.** Of cattle, etc. : Cic., Verg., etc. With DAT. : (imaginem) gregi, Hor. **b.** *to gather together by force, to crowd :* Lucr. ; navis hostium in portum, Caes. ; dispersos homines unum in locum, Cic. ; Liv. **2.** Transf. **a.** amores nostros dispulsos, Pl. **b.** *to drive on, urge, force, constrain :* minis compulsus, Cic. ; aliquem tantas in angustias, Cic. ; aliquem ad virtutem, Pl. ; ad arma, Cic. ; Ov. ; Suet. With *ut* and *Subj. :* Pl., Tac. With *Inf. :* Ov., Tac.

compendiārius, a, um [compendium],

---

short, abridged : via quasi compendiaria, Cic. *Fem.* and *Neut.* as Noun, *a short method :* Sen. Ep.

compendium, i, n. [con and pendō]. Lit. : *a careful weighing ;* hence **1.** Lit. **a.** Of money, etc. ; *a saving, profit acquired by saving,* etc. : ego hodie compendi feci binos panis, Pl. ; suo etiam privato compendio servire, Caes. ; aliquem cum quaestu compendioque dimittere, Cic. ; Tib. **2.** Transf. **a.** *a shortening, abbreviating :* verba confer maxume ad compendium, Pl. Hence, facere compendi, *to shorten, abridge :* Pl. **b.** In *pl.* of a journey, *short cuts :* propioribus compendiis ire, Tac. ; per compendia montis, Ov.

compēnsātiō, ōnis, f. [compēnsō], *a weighing together.* Transf. : *compensation :* Cic.

com-pēnsō, āre, *to weigh together, to weigh one thing against another.* Transf. : *to counter-balance ; compensate :* laetitiam cum doloribus, Cic. ; laetitiam cum doloribus, Cic. ; bona cum vitiis, Hor. With simple ABL. : labores gloriā, Cic ; Catonis est dictum, pedibus compensari pecuniam (i.e. *in shoe-leather*), Cic. ; Ov.

com-percō, percere, persī. **I.** *to save carefully :* with Acc. : Ter. **II.** *to be sparing, refrain :* with *Inf. :* Pl.

comperendinātiō, ōnis, f. (Tac.) and **comperendinātus**, ūs, m. (Cic.) [comperendinō], *a deferring of a trial to the next day but one.*

comperendinō, āre [perendinus]. Judic. *to cite a defendant to a new trial on the next day but one, to defer the day of trial :* Cic. With Acc. of person : reum, Cic.

com-periō, perīre, perī, pertum (**comperior**, Ter., Sall., Tac.) [pariō], *to find out, obtain sure information of, ascertain, learn,* etc. : certo comperire, Ter. ; ex captivis, per exploratores, Caes. ; certis auctoribus, Cic. ; indicia mortis, Cic. ; Cat. ; nihil de Sullā, Cic. With Acc. and *Inf. :* Ter., Cic., Hor, etc. With *Indir. Quest. :* Sall. N.B. esp. in Perf. Part. *discovered, well-authenticated.* **a.** facinus, Cic. ; compertā et explorata, Liv. ; pro comperto polliceri, Suet. In ABL. *Absol.,* with *Indir. Quest. :* nondum comperto quam regionem hostes petissent, Liv. **b.** Phr. : compertum habeo *and* compertum mihi est, *I have ascertained, I know quite well :* Cic., Sall. **c.** With GEN. : *detected, convicted :* compertus probri, Liv. ; Tac.

compertus, a, um, *Part.* comperiō.

com-pēs, edis, f. *a fetter or shackle for the feet* (us. in *pl.*). **1.** Lit. : Pl., Ov., etc. **2.** Transf. : Liv. ; compedes corporis, Cic. ; grata (of love), Hor. ; nivali compede vinctus Hebrus, Hor.

compēscō, ere [root seen in paciscor] *to confine, curb, restrain.* **1.** Lit. : ramos fluentis, Verg. ; mare, Hor. ; hunc catonā, Hor. ; Quint. ; incendia, Plin. Ep. **2.** Transf. : linguam, Pl. ; Lucr. ; sitim multā undā, Ov. ; seditionem, Tac. With *Inf. to forbear :* Pl.

com-petitor, ōris, m. and **competitrix**, īcis, f. [competō], *a rival, competitor* (esp. for office) : Cic., Liv., etc.

com-petō, ere, īvī or īre, ītum, *to coincide, go or come together, meet.* **1.** Lit. : ubi

viae competunt, Varr. **2.** T r a n s f. **a.**
Of time : *to coincide, agree, etc.* : (tempus)
cum Othonis exitu competisse, Tac. ; with
DAT. : Suet. **b.** Of other things : *to agree
with, answer to :* animo nequaquam corpus
competiit, Suet. Hence, *to be fit, capable,
competent* (esp. in negative sentences) : ut
vix ad arma capienda competeret animus,
Liv. ; neque animo neque auribus, Sall. ; Tac.
compĭlātĭō, ōnis, *f.* [compīlō], *a general pillaging, plundering :* hence contemptuously
of a collection of documents, *a compilation :*
Cic.
com-pīlō, āre, *to cram together hastily;* hence,
to seize and collect hastily, to plunder, pillage.
1. L i t. : aedis, Pl. ; fana, Cic. ; Hor. ;
templa ornamentis, Liv. **2.** T r a n s f. :
sapientiam, Cic. ; scrinia Crispini, Hor.
com-pingō, pingere, pēgi, pāctum [pangō], *to
fix together, unite, frame, compose.* **1.** L i t. :
Lucr., Cic. ; aedificia, Sen ; septem com-
pacta cicutis fistula, Verg. **2.** T r a n s f. :
to fasten up, lock up, confine : aliquem in
carcerem, Pl. ; se in Apuliam, Cic. Ep. ; in
iudicia compingi, Cic.
compĭtālis, e, *adj.* [compitum], *of cross-roads :*
Lares, Suet. As Noun, **compĭtālĭa,** ium
and iōrum, *n. pl. a festival, annually celebrated at cross-roads in honour of the Lares
compitales :* Cato, Cic. Ep.
compĭtālĭcius, a, um [compĭtālis], *of* or
belonging to the compitalia : dies, Cic. Ep. ;
ludi, Cic.
compĭtum, ī, *n.* (mostly in *pl.*) [*cf.* competō],
the meeting-place of roads, cross-roads :
Cato, Cic., Verg., etc.
com-placeō, ēre, uī, and complacitus sum.
With DAT. **I.** *to be at once pleasing to
several persons :* Ter. **II.** *to be very
pleasing :* Pl., Ter.
com-plānō, āre, *to make even* or *level :* terram, Cato ; Suet. ; domum, i.e. *pull down,*
Cic.
complector, plectī, plexus [con, plectō]. *to
fold closely to* or *about oneself, to fold oneself
closely about* a thing, *to clasp around, embrace.* **1.** L i t. : aliquem, Pl., Cic., Verg.,
etc. ; dextram, Verg. ; membra, Ov. ;
genua, Quint. ; (vitis) claviculis suis quidquid est nacta complectitur, Cic. ; amaracus illum floribus complectitur, Verg. **2.**
T r a n s f. **A.** sopor complectitur artūs,
Verg. ; (philosophiae) vis valet multum, cum
est idoneam complexa naturam, Cic. **B.**
to embrace, comprise. **a.** In discourse, writing, etc. : omnia istius facta oratione, Cic. ;
libro rerum memoriam, Cic. **b.** *to comprise, include :* mundus omnia complexus
est, Cic. ; Britannia insularum quas
Romana notitia complectitur, maxima, Tac.
Perf. Part. in *Pass.* sense : quo uno maleficio scelera omnia complexa esse videantur,
Cic. **C.** *to enclose* an area : collem opere,
Caes. ; Liv. **D.** Of the intellect : *to grasp,
comprehend, understand :* deum cogitatione,
Cic. ; aliquid memoriā, mente, Cic. ;
animo, Ov. ; formam animi magis quam
corporis, Tac. ; Cic. **E.** Of the affections :
to display affection, or *esteem for,* etc. : aliquem caritate, benevolentiā, Cic. ; Liv. ;
quos fortuna complexa est, Cic. ; artis in-
genuas, Ov.

complēmentum, ī, *n.* [compleō], *that which
fills up* or *completes, a complement :* Cic.,
Tac.
com-pleō, ēre, ēvī, ētum, *to fill full, fill up.*
1. L i t. **A.** Lucr. ; hostes fossam complent, Caes. ; paginam templa, Cic. ; navigia,
Liv. ; urnam, Ov. ; litora, Verg. With
Instr. ABL. : Caes., Cic., Hor., etc. Esp. of
food and drink : me complevi flore Liberi,
Pl. ; Cic. With GEN. (rare) : urbis ararum,
Lucr. ; completus mercatorum carcer, Cic.
B. Milit. **a.** *to occupy with large numbers,
to man,* etc. : montem hominibus, Caes. ;
loca milite, Verg. ; navis colonis pastoribus-
que, Caes. ; Liv. **b.** *to complete, fill up :*
legiones, Caes. ; cohortis, Sall. ; decem
milia armatorum completa sunt. Also of
provisions, etc. : complere exercitum omni
copiā, Caes. **2.** T r a n s f. **A. a.** Of sound :
omnia clamore, Caes. ; Lucr., Liv. ; sonus
auris complet, Cic. ; nemus voce, Hor. **b.**
Of light : sol cuncta suā luce complet, Cic. ;
Verg. **c.** Of feeling, passion, etc. : reliquos bonā spe complet, Caes. ; Cic. ;
omnia terrore, Liv. With GEN. : aliquem
dementiae, Pl. **B.** *to fulfil, complete.* **a.**
Of time : Gorgias centum et septem complevit annos, Cic. ; Verg. ; sua fata, Ov.
b. Of promises, etc. : summam promissi,
Cic. ; his rebus completis, etc., Caes. ;
sacrum, Liv.
complētus, a, um. **I.** *Part.* compleō. **II.**
Adj. complete, perfect : completus verborum ambitus, Cic.
complexĭō, ōnis, *f.* [complector], *a combination, close connexion.* **1.** L i t. : atomorum,
Cic. **2.** T r a n s f. **a.** In gen. : bonorum,
Cic. **b.** verborum, Cic. ; brevis complexio
totius negoti, Cic. **c.** R h e t. : *a period :*
unā complexione multa devincire, Cic.
d. In logic. **i.** *the full statement of a syllogism :* Cic. **ii.** *a dilemma :* Cic.
complexus, a, um, *Part.* complector.
complexus, ūs, *m.* [complector], *an enfolding,
embrace.* **1.** L i t. : **a.** complexum ferre, accipere, Liv. ; Ov. ; in *pl.* : Cic., Verg., etc. ;
liberos a parentum complexu divellere,
Sall. ; mundus omnia complexu suo coercet,
Cic. ; Lucr. **b.** In hostile sense, *a grappling :* in Caesaris complexum venire, *to
come to grips with C.,* Caes. ; armorum, Tac.
2. T r a n s f. **a.** res publica Pompei filium
suo sinu complexuque recipiet, Cic. **b.** *a
connexion* (in discourse) : Quint.
complĭcātus, a, um. **I.** *Part.* complicō. **II.**
Adj. complicated, confused : notio, Cic.
com-plĭcō, āre, *to fold together, to fold up :*
rudentem, Pl. ; epistulam, Cic. Ep. ; se in
dolio, Sen. Ep.
complōrātĭō, ōnis, *f.* and **complōrātus,** ūs,
m. [complōrō], *a loud* or *general groaning,
lamentation* (esp. for the dead) : mulierum,
Liv. With *Obj.* GEN. : sui patriaeque, Liv.
complōrātus, ūs, *m.* [complōrō], *a loud wailing* for the dead : Liv.
com-plōrō, āre, *to bewail together* or *violently,
to mourn for* (as dead) : desertos penatis,
Ov. ; complorata res est publica, Liv. ; Cic.
com-plūres, a (GEN. -ium), *adj. several,* a
good many : Ter., Cic., Hor., etc. As
Noun : Cic., Suet. ; complures hostium,
Hirt.

complūriēs or **-iēns**, *adv.* [complūrēs], *several times, a good many times :* Pl.
complūsculi, ae, a, *adj., pl.* [*dim.* complūrēs], *a pretty good number :* Pl., Ter.
compluvium, I, *n.* [con, pluō], *a quadrangular open space in the middle of a Roman house towards which the roof sloped so as to throw the rain water into a cistern in the floor,* termed impluvium : Varr., Suet.
com-pōnō, pōnere, posuī, positum (*Perf. Part.* syncop. compostus, Verg.). **I.** *to lay by together, store up, hoard.* **1.** L i t. : uvas in cratibus, Cato ; Cic. ; ligna in caminum, Cato ; munera, Cic. ; aridum lignum, Hor. ; Verg. Of the ashes of the dead : Prop., Ov. **2.** T r a n s f. : compono quae mox depromere possim, Hor. **II.** *to put* or *place together.* **A. a.** In gen. : Lucil. ; manibusque manūs atque oribus ora, Verg. **b.** In hostile sense, *to match :* Lucil. ; cum Bitho Bacchius, Hor. ; Quint. **c.** In law, *to confront :* Epicharis cum iudice composita, Tac. **d.** Of comparison, *to compare.* With *cum :* dicta cum factis, Sall. ; Quint. With D a t. : Cat. ; parva magnis, Verg. **e.** Of friendship, etc., *to unite :* genus indocile ac dispersum, Verg. Also *to reconcile :* aversos amicos, Hor. **B.** *to put together, construct, compose.* **a.** In gen. : qui cuncta composuit, Cic. ; genus hominum compositum ex corpore et animā, Sall. ; urbem, Verg. T r a n s f. : mendacia, Pl. ; insidias, Tac. **b.** Of writings, etc. : edictum, librum, carmen, Cic. ; litteras, orationem, Liv. ; versūs, Hor. ; orationem ad conciliandos plebis animos, Liv. ; aliquid de ratione dicendi, Quint. **c.** Of other things, *to arrange, settle, agree upon :* pacem, Pl., Liv., Verg. ; consilium, Liv. ; foedus, Verg. ; leges, Verg. ; locum tempusque, Tac. E s p. in phr. ex composito, *in accordance with a pre-arranged plan :* Liv., Tac. Without *ex :* Verg. With *ut* and *Subj. :* compositum erat inter ipsos ut . . ., Tac. ; Liv. With *Inf. :* Tac. **C.** *to put in order, compose.* **a.** Of hair, dress, etc. : capillum, Cic. ; comas, Ov. ; togam, Hor. ; verba, Cic. T r a n s f. : composita et constituta res publica, Cic. With *ad* or *in* and occ. D a t. *to adapt, suit :* auspicia ad utilitatem rei publicae composita, Cic. ; Tac. ; Luc. Of hypocrisy : vultum, Tac., Suet. ; in ostentationem virtutum compositus, Liv. ; compositus ad maestitiam, Tac. ; compositus in tristitiam, Tac. **b.** Of troops : Liv. ; Verg. ; agmen ad pugnam, Liv. ; exercitum pugnae, Tac. **c.** In bed : defessa membra, Verg. ; se thalamis, Verg. ; quiete compositus, Quint. So perh., ante diem clauso componat vesper Olympo, Verg. Hence, *to lay out a corpse, to bury :* Cat., Hor., Ov., Tac. **d.** *to lay, settle, allay, calm.* **1.** L i t. : motos fluctūs, Verg. ; mare, Ov. **2.** T r a n s f. : Daciam, Tac. ; controversias, Caes. ; bellum, Nep. ; Verg. ; Tac. ; litis, Verg. ; Pl. *Pass. Impers. :* ut componatur, *that peace should be restored,* Cic.
com-portō, āre, *to carry* or *bring together :* Caes., Cic., Verg., etc.
com-pos, otis, *adj.* [for *com-pot-s, v.* potis]. **I.** *possessing fully,* etc. : us. with G e n.,

more rarely with A b l. : laudis, Pl. ; animi, Ter. ; mentis, consili, virtutis, Cic. ; voti, Hor., Liv. ; patriae. Liv. With A b l. : praedā, Liv. ; animo, Cic., Liv. ; mente, Verg. **II.** *sharing in* (with G e n.) : Pl., Quint.
compositē, *adv. in an orderly* or *regular manner, in elegant style :* dicere, Cic. ; Sall. *Comp. :* Tac.
compositiō, ōnis, *f.* [compōnō], *a putting together.* **A. a.** Of combatants, *a matching :* Cic. Ep. **b.** Of friendship : *a reconciliation :* Caes., Cic. **B.** *a putting together, compounding :* unguentorum, Cic. T r a n s f. : pacis, bonorum, Cic. **C.** *an orderly arrangement* (of words) : Cic., Quint.
compositor, ōris, *m.* [compōnō], *an orderer, arranger :* Cic., Ov.
compositūra, ae, *f.* [compōnō], *a joining together, connexion :* Cato ; oculorum, Lucr.
compositus, a, um. **I.** *Part.* compōnō (v. compono. II. B.c.). **II.** Adj. **A. a.** *compound :* opp. simplex : verba, Quint. **b.** *made up,* i.e. *invented, false, feigned :* mendacia, Pl. ; crimen, Cic. **B. a.** *fitly ordered, prepared, well arranged :* Ter. ; res publica, Tac. ; compositior pugna, Liv. ; litterulae tuae compositissimae, Cic. Ep. **b.** *adapted :* in ostentationem, Liv. ; alius historiae magis idoneus, alius compositus ad carmen, Quint. ; adliciendis moribus alicuius, Tac. **c.** *affected, assumed :* vultus, Tac. **d.** *composed, settled, calm, sedate :* adfectūs mites atque compositi, Quint. ; aetas, Tac.
com-pōtātiō, ōnis, *f. a drinking together* (=συμπόσιον) : Cic.
compotiō, īre [compos], *to put in possession of, to make master of.* With A c c. of pers. and A b l. of thing : me piscatu novo compotivit, Pl. *Pass. :* locis compotita sum, Pl.
com-pōtor, ōris, *m.* (Cic.), and **compōtrīx**, īcis, *f.* (Ter.), *a drinking-companion.*
com-prānsor, ōris, *m. a table-companion :* Cic.
comprecātiō, ōnis, *f.* [comprecor], *a united supplication :* deorum, Liv.
com-precor, ārī. **I.** *to pray earnestly to, supplicate, implore :* Iovi molā salsā, Pl. ; deos, Ter. ; fidem caelestum, Cat. **II.** *to pray earnestly for :* mortem sibi, Sen. Ep. ; Plin. Ep.
com-prehendō, prehendere, prehendī, prehēnsum, *and* **comprendō**, prendere, prendī, prēnsum. **I.** *to grasp, grip together, unite.* **1.** L i t. : navis funibus, Liv. **2.** T r a n s f. *to unite, comprise, include.* **a.** In a list, in words, in thought : in formulam iudicia, Cic. ; omnis scelerum formas, Verg. ; aliquid numero, Verg. ; aliquid dictis, Ov. ; Lucr. ; Cic. **b.** In affection : aliquem humanitate, amicitiā, Cic. **c.** In space : circuitus eius xxxiii stadia comprehendit, Curt. **II.** *to grasp, lay hold of, seize firmly.* **1.** L i t. : **a.** funis, Caes. ; comprehendunt utrumque et orant, Caes. ; Cic. ; comprensa manūs effugit, Verg. **b.** Of fire : casae ignem comprehenderunt, *caught fire,* Caes. ; ignis robora comprendit, Verg., Liv. **c.** *to seize, arrest :* hominem, Cic. ; Ter. ; Caes. ; Liv. Of things : equos, raedas, collis, Cic. ;

Liv. **d.** *to catch in an act*: aliquem in furto, Caes.; fures, Cat. Transf. to the crime: adulterium, Cic. **2.** T r a n s f.: of the intellect, *to grasp, comprehend* : omnis animo virtutes, Cic.; aliquid memoriā, Cic. [Fr. *comprendre*.]

comprehēnsibilis, e, *adj.* [comprehēnsus], *that can be laid hold of.* T r a n s f.: *apprehensible by the senses or the mind, comprehensible* : Cic.

comprehēnsiō, ōnis, *f.* [comprehendō]. **I.** *a grouping together.* **a.** Of words in a period : Cic., Quint. **b.** Of ideas : rerum, Cic. **II.** *a grasping, seizing.* **1.** L i t. **a.** (rare) : Cic. **b.** Of arresting : sontium, Cic. **2.** T r a n s f.: of the mind or senses, *comprehension* : Cic.

comprehēnsus, a, um. *Part.* comprehendō.

comprēndō and **comprēnsus**, *v.* comprehendō.

compressiō, ōnis, *f.* [comprimō], *a pressing together or closely.* **1.** L i t.: *an embracing* : Pl. **2.** T r a n s f.: of style : *condensation*, Cic.

compressius, *comp. adv. in a rather condensed manner* : loqui, Cic.

compressū, ABL. *sing. m.* [comprimō]. **I.** *by pressing together or closely* : Cic. **II.** *by embracing* : Pl., Ter.

compressus, a, um, *Part.* comprimō.

com-primō, primere, pressī, pressum [premō]. **I.** *to press or squeeze together, clench, grit* : dentis, Pl.; (digitos) compresserat pugnumque fecerat, Cic.; labra, Hor.; compressis ordinibus, Liv.; versūs ordinibus, Ov. P r o v.: compressis manibus sedere, Liv. **II.** *to press closely.* **1.** L i t. **a.** *to embrace*, etc.: Pl., Ter., Liv. **b.** *to close* : oculos (morientis), Ov. **c.** *to hold in, keep in, restrain* : animam, Ter.; manum, Ter.; vocem, Pl.; linguam alicui, *to silence someone*, Pl.; gressum, Verg. Of persons, *to give a check to* : cuius adventus Pompeianos compressit, Caes. **2.** T r a n s f. **a.** Of passions, desires, etc.: *to check, repress, suppress* : cupiditatem, Cic.; nefarios conatūs alicuius, Cic.; seditionem, Liv.; Pl. Of persons : Pl.; exasperatos Ligures, Liv. **b.** Of other things : *to suppress* : frumentum, Cic. Ep.; famam captae Carthaginis, Liv.

comprobātiō, ōnis, *f.* [comprobō], *full approval* : Cic.

comprobātor, ōris, *m.* [comprobō], *a wholehearted approver* : Cic.

com-probō, āre. **I.** *to make quite good, to establish, confirm* : comprobat hominis consilium fortuna, Caes.; Cat.; rem testimonio, Cic.; Pl. **II.** *to approve heartily* : sententiam, Cic.; Liv.

comprōmissum, ī, *n. a mutual engagement to abide by the award of an arbiter* ; Cic.

com-prōmittō, mittere, misī, missum. In law : *to engage mutually to abide by the decision of an arbiter* : Cic. Ep.

cōmptus, a, um. **I.** *Part.* cōmō. **II.** *Adj.* *adorned, elegant, neat* : pueri, Hor. Esp. of style : oratio, Cic. Of the orator himself : Quint. *Comp.* : Tac.

cōmptus, ūs, *m.* **I.** [cōmō], *an ornament for the hair or head* : Lucr. **II.** = coemptiō : Lucr.

compulsus, a, um, *Part.* compellō.

com-pungō, pungere, pūnxī, pūnctum, *to prick or puncture all over or severely.* **1.** L i t.: collum dolone, Phaedr. O c c.: *to tattoo* : barbarus compunctus notis Threīciis, Cic. **2.** T r a n s f. **a.** (dialectici) ipsi se compungunt suis acuminibus, Cic. **b.** Of bright colours : aciem, Lucr. **c.** Of heat and cold : sensūs corporis, Lucr.

computātiō, ōnis, *f.* [computō]. **I.** *a reckoning, computing, computation* : Sen. Ep.; Plin. Pan. **II.** *niggardliness* : Sen.

com-putō, āre, *to sum up, reckon up, compute* : suos annos, Juv.; Quint. With *Indir. Quest.* : Quint. With *Instr.* ABL.: rationem digitis, Pl. *Absol.* : Cic. [Fr. *compter*.]

com-putrēscō, ere, *to become wholly putrid, to rot* : Lucr.

con- in composition, *v.* cum.

cōnāmen, inis, *n.* [cōnor]. **I.** *an effort, exertion, struggle* : Lucr., Ov. **II.** Concr.: *support* : Ov.

cōnātum, ī, *n.* [cōnor], *an undertaking, effort, venture* : Pl.; Lucr.; perficere, Caes.; Cic.; Ov., etc.

cōnātus, ūs, *m.* [cōnor]. **I.** *an exertion, effort.* **1.** L i t.: Ter.; conatu desistere, Caes.; in ipso conatu, Liv.; maiore conatu studioque aguntur, Cic. **2.** T r a n s f.: *an impulse, instinctive movement* : Cic. **II.** Concr.; conatūs tuos compressi, Cic.; Caes.; Liv.

con-cacō, āre, *to defile with ordure, to pollute* : Phaedr.

con-caedēs, ium, *f. pl. an abattis barricade of felled trees* : Tac.

con-calefaciō, facere, fēcī, factum and *Pass.* **con-calefiō**, fierī, factus, *to warm thoroughly* : Lucr., Cic.

con-caleō, ēre, *to be thoroughly warm* : Pl.

con-calēscō, calēscere, caluī, *to become thoroughly warm, to glow.* **1.** L i t.: Pl.; corpora nostra ardore animi concalescunt, Cic. **2.** T r a n s f. (with love) : Ter.

con-callēscō, callēscere, calluī [calleō], *to become hard or callous all over.* T r a n s f. **a.** Of the feelings, *to become insensible* : Cic. Ep. **b.** Of the intellect, *to become expert and shrewd* : animus usu concalluit, Cic.

concamerātus, a, um [camera], *vaulted, arched* : Suet.

Cōncanus, ī, *m. one of a savage tribe in Hispania Tarraconensis, who drank horses' blood.*

con-castigō, āre, *to chastise severely* : Pl.

concavō, āre [concavus], *to curve, bend* : bracchia in arcūs, Ov.

con-cavus, a, um, *hollow, concave* : *vaulted, arched, curved, bent* : cymbala, Lucr.; altitudines speluncarum, Cic.; saxa, Verg.; bracchia cancri, Ov.; vallis, Ov.

con-cēdō, cēdere, cēssī, cēssum. **A.** I n t r a n s.: *to go quite away, take oneself off, go away, retire, withdraw.* **1.** L i t.: de viā, Pl.; ex aedibus, Ter.; a parentum oculis, Cic.; oculis, Pl.; in hiberna, Liv.; dies caelo, Verg.; ad Manis, Verg.; vitā, Tac.; and without vitā : Tac. **2.** T r a n s f. **a.** With *in* and ACC., *to go or pass over to, yield to, submit, be merged in* :

in sententiam alicuius, in condiciones, in deditionem, Liv. ; Lucr. ; in gentem nomenque imperantium, Sall. **b.** With DAT. or *Absol.* : *to give way, yield, submit, retire before.* **i.** Under compulsion, etc. : alicui, Pl., Ov. ; naturae (i.e. *to die*), Sall. ; cedant arma togae, Cic. **ii.** To wishes, demands, etc. : postulationi tuae, Cic. ; tibi, Ter. Hence = *to pardon* : temere dicto, Cic. ; vitio, Hor. **iii.** In rank, precedence, etc. : nemini studio et cupiditate, Cic. ; Liv. ; Verg. **B.** T r a n s. : *to retire from, yield, give up* (freq. with DAT.). **a.** *to give up, hand over* : militibus praedam, Caes. ; his libertatem, Caes. ; Pl. ; Hor. ; hoc pudori meo, Cic. **b.** *to give up, relinquish, cede* : petitionem tibi, Cic. ; Siciliam, Liv. **c.** *to yield as a favour* (*to a person or feeling*, etc.), *pardon, overlook out of regard for* : omnia ista tibi, Cic. ; amicitias meas rei publicae, Cic. ; multa virtuti eorum, Caes. **d.** *to allow, permit.* With DAT. of person and *Inf.* : Caes., Hor., Cic. In *Pass.* : fatis nunquam concessa moveri Camarina, Verg. With *ut* and *Subj.* : Lucr., Cic. With *Subj.* alone : Cat., Ov. **e.** *to admit, grant* : with Acc. and *Inf.* : Lucr., Cic. *Impers. Pass.* : Caes., Cic., Hor.

con-celebro, āre. **I.** *to go in great numbers to, to people, fill with life, go frequently to.* **1.** L i t. : mare, terras, Lucr. ; variae volucres loca aquarum concelebrant, Lucr. **2.** T r a n s f. : *to pursue or prosecute vigorously* : studia per otium, Cic. **II.** *to throng to.* **1.** L i t. : of shows, festivals, etc. : *to celebrate* : Pl. ; convivia, triumphum, Cic. ; spectaculum, Liv. **2.** T r a n s f. : *to celebrate, make widely known* : famā ac litteris victoriam, Caes. ; Cic. ; Tib.

con-cēnātio, ōnis, *f.* *a dining together* : Cic.

concentiō, ōnis, *f.* [concino], *a singing together, harmony* : Cic.

con-centuriō, āre, *to assemble by centuries* ; hence, *to amass* : Pl.

concentus, ūs, *m.* [concino], *a singing together, a blending of voices or sounds.* **1.** L i t. **a.** avium, Cic., Verg. **b.** tubarum, Liv. ; Ov. **2.** In harmony or symphony : Cic. **2.** T r a n s f. : *harmony, concord, agreement* : doctrinarum, Cic. ; Hor. ; Tac.

conceptiō, ōnis, *f.* [concipiō]. **I.** *conception of off-spring* : Cic. **II.** *drawing up of juridical formulas* : Cic.

conceptus, a, um, *Part.* concipiō.

conceptus, ūs, *m.* [concipiō]. **I. A.** *a taking, catching* (*cf.* concipere ignem) : flagrante triclinio ex conceptu camini, Suet. **B.** Esp. *conception of offspring.* **a.** hominum pecudumve, Cic. **b.** Of plants : *budding, sprouting* : Plin. **c.** *the fetus* : Suet. **II. a.** *a collecting* : Plin. **b.** *a collection, conflux* : Sen.

con-cerpo, cerpere, cerpsi, cerptum [carpō], *to tear up, tear in pieces.* **1.** L i t. : epistulas, Cic. Ep. ; Liv. **2.** T r a n s f. : *to abuse, revile* : Curio concerpitur, Cael. ap. Cic. Ep.

concertātiō, ōnis, *f.* [concerto], *a strife of words, dispute, controversy* : concertationis studium, Cic. ; magistratuum, verborum, Cic. In *pl.* : Cic.

concertātor, ōris, *m.* [concerto], *one who vies with another, a rival* : Tac.

concertātōrius, a, um [concerto], *of controversy, controversial* : Cic.

con-certō, āre. **I.** *to contend keenly* : cum aliquo, Ter. ; proelio, Caes. ; de regno, Suet. **II.** *to dispute, quarrel* : cum inimico, Cic. ; Nep.

concessiō, ōnis, *f.* [concēdō], *an allowing, conceding.* **a.** In gen. : agrorum, Cic. **b.** R h e t. : *a concession (made to an opponent)*, Quint. **c.** *an admission (of a fault, with an appeal for indulgence)* : Cic.

con-cessō, āre, *to leave off, cease* (with *Inf.*) : Pl.

concessus, a, um. **I.** *Part.* concēdo. **II.** *Neut.* as Noun : *a thing permitted* : Cic.

concessū, ABL. *sing. m.* [concēdō], *by permission* : Caesaris, Caes. ; Cic. ; Tac.

concha, ae, *f.* [κόγχη]. **I. a.** *a bivalve shell-fish, mussel* : Pl., Cic., Verg. **b.** *a mussel-shell* : Cic. **II. a.** *a pearl-oyster* : Plin. **b.** *a pearl* : Ov. **c.** *an oyster-shell* : Ov. **III. a.** *the murex* : Lucr. **b.** *the purple-dye* : Ov. **IV. a.** *Triton's trumpet* : Verg., Ov. **b.** *a trumpet* : Verg. **c.** *a vessel for holding oil, unguents*, etc. : Cato, Hor. [It. *cocca* ; Sp. *coca* ; Fr. *coque* and *coche*.]

conchis, is, *f.* [κόγχος], *a kind of bean boiled with the pods* : Juv.

conchīta, ae, *m.* [κογχίτης, κόγχη], *a catcher of shell-fish* : Pl.

conchyliātus, a, um [conchylium]. **I.** *dyed with purple* : Cic. **II.** *dressed in purple.* As Noun : Sen. Ep.

conchylium, I, n. [κογχύλιον]. **I.** *a shell-fish, small mussel* : Cic. **II.** *an oyster* : Cic., Hor. **III.** *the murex* : Lucr. Hence, **a.** *purple dye, purple* : Cic. **b.** *purple garments, purple* : Quint., Juv. [It. *cochiglia* ; Fr. *coquille*.]

con-cido, cidere, cidi [cadō], *to fall in a heap, to collapse, to tumble to the ground.* **1.** L i t. **a.** conclave illud concidit, Cic. ; pronus in fimo, Verg. **b.** *to fall lifeless, fall in battle* : Pl. ; concidit pugnans, Caes. ; in proelio, Cic. ; Verg. Of victims : vitulus mactatus concidit, Lucr. ; Ov. **2.** T r a n s f. : *to collapse, sink down, fall to ruin, perish* : si unus ille occidisset, gentes omnes concidissent, Cic. ; crimen, Cic. ; Ilia tellus, Verg. ; auguris Argivi domus, Hor. ; scimus solutione impeditā fidem concidisse (*credit collapsed*), Cic. ; venti, Hor. ; vita, Lucr. ; opes Persarum, Tac. ; hostes animis, Hirt. ; bellum, Tac. Of the wind, *to subside* : Hor.

con-cīdo, cidere, cidi, cisum [caedō], *to cut up, cut to pieces, destroy*, etc. **1.** L i t. **a.** In gen. : nervos, Cic. ; navis, Liv. ; ligna, Ov. **b.** In battle : Caes., Cic. **c.** By flogging : aliquem virgis, Cic. ; Juv. **2.** T r a n s f. **a.** *to cut up* (i.e. *to make breaks in*) : itinera concisa aestuariis, Caes. ; Verg. **b.** *to cut up, ruin* : Pl. ; auctoritatem ordinis, Cic. **c.** By argument : Timocratem totis voluminibus, Cic. **d.** Of style : *to divide minutely, dismember, render feeble* : nec minutos numeros sequens, concidat delumbetque sententias, Cic.

con-cieo, ciēre, civi, citum, and **concio**, Ire (Lucr., Liv., Tac.). **I.** *to move together, bring or assemble together* : homines miraculo rei novae, Liv. ; donis auxilia, Tac. **II.** *to move violently, to shake, stir up.* **1.** L i t. :

Lucr.; concitus imbribus amnis, Ov.; murali concita tormento saxa, Verg. **2.** T r a n s f. **a.** *to rouse, stir up, excite :* milites ad recuperandam libertatem, Liv.; hostem, Tac. Esp. in *Perf. Part. :* immani concitus irā, Verg.; pulso Thyias concita tympano, Hor.; divino concita motu, Ov. **b.** *to stir up,* i.e. *to cause :* uxori turbas, Pl.; bellum, Liv.; seditionem, Tac.

conciliābulum, ī, *n.* [conciliō], *a public meeting-place :* Liv., Tac. Comic.: damni, Pl.

conciliātiō, ōnis, *f.* [conciliō], *a bringing together ;* hence, **I.** *a union :* totius generis hominum conciliatio, Cic. **II.** *a uniting in feeling, a conciliating, making friendly, a gaining over :* gratiae, Cic.; conciliationis causā, Cic.; Quint. Rhet.: *the gaining over of hearers :* Cic. **III.** P h i l o s.: *an inclination, bent, desire :* prima est enim conciliatio hominis ad ea, quae sunt secundum naturam, Cic.

conciliātor, ōris, *m.* [conciliō], *he who brings together or about ; a mediator, promoter :* nuptiarum, Nep.; proditionis, Liv.; Tac.

conciliātrīcula, ae, *f.* [*dim.* conciliātrīx], *a dear match-maker :* Cic.

conciliātrīx, īcis, *f.* [conciliō], *she who brings together or about ; a female mediator or promoter :* Pl.; quam blanda conciliatrix sit natura (i.e. *a matchmaker*), Cic.; humanae societatis, amicitiae, Cic.

conciliātū, ABL. *sing. m.* [conciliō], *by a union (of atoms), by a connexion (of bodies) :* Lucr.

conciliātūra, ae, *f.* [conciliō], *the profession of pander :* Sen. Ep.

conciliātus, a, um. **I.** *Part.* conciliō. **II.** *Adj. favourably inclined, favourable to* (with *ad* and Acc.): *Comp. :* Quint.

conciliō, āre [concilium], *to call together, to bring together ; to unite, connect.* **1.** L i t.: primordia non ex ullorum conventu conciliata, Lucr. **2.** T r a n s f. **a.** *to unite in thought or feeling, to make friendly, to bring or win over :* homines inter se, Cic.; reliquas civitates Caesari, Caes.; Cic.; deos homini, Ov.; animos hominum, Cic., Liv. P o e t.: artis conciliare, i.e. *to commend,* Ov. **b.** *to bring about or win* (by mediation): Pl.; pacem inter civis, Cic.; se illis regna conciliaturum confirmat, Caes.; nuptias, Nep. **c.** In gen. *to bring about, procure, acquire :* pecuniam, gloriam, Cic.; famam clementiae, Liv.; arma sibi, Verg.; risūs, Quint.

concilium, ī, *n.* [con, calō], *a calling or bringing together.* **I.** Of things, *a combination, union :* virtutum, Cic.; Lucr. **II.** Of persons, *a meeting, assembly.* **a.** In gen.: Pl.; pastorum, Cic.; Verg.; but freq. as a term of dignity, *an assemblage, conclave :* deorum, Cic.; piorum, Verg. **b.** *a public assembly for consultation, a council :* commune concilium Belgarum, Caes.; plebis, Liv.; habere, inire, Pl.; convocare, dimittere, Cic.; diem concilio constituere, Caes.; concilium legatis dare, Liv.; cogere, vocare, Verg.; indicere, Liv.

concinnē, *adv. elegantly :* Pl., Cic.

concinnitās, ātis, *f.* [concinnus], *elegance, neatness :* Sen. Ep., Suet. Of style : *symmetry, correct arrangement :* Cic.

concinnitūdō, inis, *f.* [concinnus], *elegance of style :* Cic.

concinnō, āre [concinnus]. **1.** L i t. : *to make regular or symmetrical, to adjust, get right :* pallam, Pl.; lutum, Pl.; vinum, Cato. **2.** In gen. : *to bring about :* multum mihi negoti, Sen. Ep.; consuetudo amorem, Lucr.; vis venti hiatum, Lucr. With *Predic. Adj.* (= reddere), *to make, render, cause to be :* me insanum verbis concinnat suis, Pl.

concinnus, a, um, *regular, symmetrical, shapely.* **1.** L i t.: concinna est (virgo) facie, Pl.; Samos, Hor.; tectorium, Cic. Ep. **2.** T r a n s f. **a.** Of style, *well-arranged, elegant, neat :* oratio, sententia, Cic.; versus, Hor. **b.** Of a person : *elegant, refined :* Cic. **c.** Of a person's behaviour : *courteous, agreeable :* concinnus amicis, Hor.; Lucr.; tibi concinnum est, i.e. *it suits you :* Pl. *Comp. :* Cic., Lucr.

con-cinō, cinere, cinuī [canō]. **A.** I n t r a n s.: *to sing, play, or sound together.* **1.** L i t.: cornua ac tubae concinuere, Tac.; ubi signa concinuissent, Liv. Hence, concinit albus olor, Ov. **2.** T r a n s f.: *to agree together, harmonise :* inter se, Liv.; cum aliquo, Cic. *Absol.:* videsne ut haec concinant, Cic. **B.** T r a n s.: *to join in singing or playing, sing about, celebrate :* haec cum concinuntur, Cic.; carmina, Cat.; festos dies, Hor. Of ill-omened birds : tristia omina, Ov.

conciō, īre, v. concieō.

conciō, concīon-, v. contiō, contiōn-, etc.

concipilō, āre, *to seize and carry off :* Pl.

con-cipiō, cipere, cēpī, ceptum [capiō]. **I.** *to take or lay hold of completely, take to oneself, to take in,* etc. **1.** L i t.: of material things. **a.** Of moisture, *to absorb :* marinum umorem, Lucr.; Varr.; terra caducas concepit lacrimas, Ov.; Curt. **b.** Of fire, *to catch :* flammam, Caes.; ignem, Lucr., Cic., Ov., etc. **c.** Of aïr : aera, Ov.; auram, Curt. **d.** Of seed : semina terra concipit, Cic. Hence, *to conceive :* Lucr.; cum concepit mula, Cic.; aliquem ex aliquo, Cic.; a captivā, de lupo, Ov. T r a n s f. : conceptum periculum res publica parturit, Cic. **2.** T r a n s f. : *to take in.* **a.** Of the senses, i.e. *to perceive :* haec oculis, Pl. **b.** Of the intellect, i.e. *to comprehend, understand :* aliquid animo ac mente, Cic. With Acc. and *Inf. :* Cic. **c.** Of the mind, *to conceive, imagine :* aliquid mente, Cic., Liv. With Acc. and *Inf. :* Ov. **d.** Of feeling, passion, etc. ; *to conceive, devise :* inimicitias, Caes.; aliquid spe, Liv.; fraudes inexpiabilis concepissent, Cic.; scelus in se, Cic.; nefas, Hor.; animo iras, Ov. **II.** *to take together, comprise.* **1.** L i t.: ignem trullis, Liv. **2.** T r a n s f.: of formal language, documents, etc., *to comprise, draw up in formal words :* vadimonium, Cic. Ep.; ius iurandum, Liv.; iuris iurandi verba, Liv., Tac.; foedus, Verg.; vota, Ov. Hence, *to announce in formal language :* Cato; Latinas ferias, Liv.; auspicia nova, Liv.

concisē, *adv. concisely :* Quint.

concisiō, ōnis, *f.* [concīdō]. Rhet. *a cutting up of a clause into short divisions :* Cic.

concisus, a, um. **I.** *Part.* concīdō. **II.**

Adj.: *cut up, short, concise* : sententiae, Cic. ; Quint. Transf. to the orator : Cic.

concitātē, *adv.* [concitātus], *in an impassioned manner* : Quint. *Comp.* : Quint.

concitātiō, ōnis, *f.* [concitō], *a setting in violent motion.* **1.** Lit.: *rapid movement* : remorum, Liv. **2.** Transf. **a,** *an excitement of the passions, lively emotion* : animi, Cic. ; animorum, Liv. **b,** *sedition, tumult* : concitationes crebrae fiebant, Caes. ; Cic.

concitātor, ōris, *m.* [concitō], *one who excites or rouses, an exciter, instigator* : seditionis, Cic. ; Liv. ; Tac.

concitātus, a, um. **I,** *Part.* concitō. **II.** Adj.: *violently moved,* **a.** *rapid, swift* : quam concitatissimos equos immittere iubet, Liv. ; *Comp.* : Cic. **b.** *excited* : testimonia non concitatae contionis sed iurati senatūs, Cic. ; oratio, Quint. ; clamor concitatior, Liv.

concitō, āre [*freq.* conciō], *to put in violent or quick motion* : *to stir up, rouse.* **1.** Lit.: artūs, Lucr. ; equum calcaribus, Liv. ; (montem) magno cursu concitatos iubet occupare, Caes. ; agmen, Ov. ; se in hostem, Liv. ; tela, Verg., Liv. **2.** Transf. **a.** Of persons : *to rouse, urge,* etc. : suos, Caes. ; multitudinem spe, Liv. ; Cic. ; Tac. ; concitari ad studium, Cic. ; ad arma, Caes., Hor. ; in te, Cic. ; Etruriam omnem adversus nos, Liv. With *Inf.* : Ov. **b.** Of things : *to stir up, excite* (i.e. *to cause* any *disturbance,* passion, evil, etc.) : tumultum, Caes., Liv. ; iram, risum, Cic. ; bellum Romanis, Liv. ; invidiam in aliquem, Cic. ; Ov.

concitor, ōris, *m.* [conciō], *he who rouses or excites, an exciter* : belli, Liv., Tac. ; vulgi, Liv.

concitus and **concĭtus,** a, um, *Part.* conciō and conciō.

conclāmātiō, ōnis, *f.* [conclāmō], *a loud shouting* or *crying,* or *of many persons together* : Caes. ; in *pl.*: Tac.

conclāmitō, āre [*freq.* conclāmō], *to keep on bawling* : Pl.

con-clāmō, āre. **I.** *to call* or *cry aloud, shout out, yell.* **a.** Of a body of men : conclamare gaudio, Liv. ; victoriam, Caes. ; Cic. ; paeana, Verg. With Acc. and *Inf.* : Caes., Cic., Verg. With *ut,* or *Subj.* alone : Caes. **b.** Of one person : Caes. With quoted words : Pl., Ov. With Acc. : Verg. With Acc. and *Inf.* : Tac. With *Indir. Quest.* : Caes. Esp. *to call* a dead person by name in lamentation : suos, Liv. ; Luc. **II.** *to call together.* **a.** *to call to one's help* : duros agrestis, Verg. ; Ov. **b.** Milit.: conclamatur ad arma, Caes., Liv. ; conclamare vasa, i.e. *to give orders* to break camp, Caes.

conclāve, is, *n.* [clāvis], *a room that may be locked up* : Pl., Cic., Hor., etc.

con-clūdō, clūdere, clūsī, clūsum [claudō], *to shut up together* or *closely, enclose.* **1.** Lit.: me in cellam cum illā, Pl. ; locus conclusus, Lucr., Hor. ; bestias delectationis causā, Cic. ; animum in corpore, Cic. ; with *Instr.* ABL.: locum sulco, Verg. ; Suet. **2.** Transf. **a.** *to include, compress, comprise* : ius civile in parvum et angustum locum, Cic. ; Ter. ; in hanc formulam omnia

iudicia, Cic. **b.** *to round off, conclude* : epistulam, perorationem, senteutiam, Cic. Rhet.: *to close rhythmically* : versum, Hor. ; Cic. **c.** Philos.: *to round off* with a deduction : argumentum, Cic. ; Quint. ; hence, *to deduce, conclude.* With Acc. and *Inf.* : Cic.

conclūsē, *adv. with periods rhetorically rounded off* : dicere, Cic.

conclūsiō, ōnis, *f.* [conclūdō], *a shutting up.* **1.** Lit.: Milit. *a siege, blockade* : Caes. **2.** Transf. **a.** *a conclusion, end* : muneris ac negoti, Cic. Ep. **b.** Rhet. *the conclusion of a speech, peroration* : orationis, Cic. Also, *a period* : Cic., Quint. **c.** In logic : *the conclusion* in a syllogism : Cic., Quint.

conclūsiuncula, ae, *f.* [*dim.* conclūsiō], *a futile* or *captious inference* : Cic.

conclūsus, a, um. **I.** *Part.* conclūdō. **II.** *Adj. confined* : concluso mari (opp. to vastissimo oceano), Caes.

concoctus, a, um, *Part.* concoquō.

con-color, ōris, *of the same colour* (in the poets used only in NOM. *sing.*), candida cum fetu concolor albo procubuit sus, Verg. ; Ov. With DAT.: Ov.

con-comitātus, a, um, *attended* : Pl.

con-cōpulō, āre, *to join, unite* : argentum auro, Lucr.

con-coquō, coquere, coxī, coctum. **1.** Lit.: *to cook thoroughly* : Sen. Ep. Occ. **a.** *to boil down* : odores, Lucr. **b.** *to digest* : Lucr. ; cibus facillimus ad concoquendum, Cic. **2.** Transf. **a.** Comic. (with *Refl. Pron.*) : *to waste, pine away* : Pl. **b.** Like our *digest* or *swallow* or *stomach* = *to endure, suffer, put up with* : odia, Cic. Ep. ; Liv. **c.** *to reflect maturely upon, to mature* : tibi diu deliberandum et concoquendum est utrum etc. ; Cic. clandestina consilia, Liv.

concordia, ae, *f.* [concors], *a union of feeling, union.* **1.** Lit.: of persons : Pl. ; ex dissensione ad concordiam revocare, Cic. ; ordinum, Cic. Ep. ; Liv. ; Ov. **2.** Transf.: of things : rerum, Hor. ; Quint. ; formae atque pudicitiae, Juv.

concorditer, *adv.* [concors], *harmoniously, in union* : Pl., Ov., Suet. *Comp.* : Liv. *Sup.* : Cic.

concordō, āre [concors], *to be of one mind, to agree together, to harmonise.* **1.** Lit.: cum aliquo, Ter. **2.** Transf.: of things : iudicia opinionesque, Cic. With DAT.: Ov. With *cum* : Quint.

con-cors, cordis, *adj.* [cor], *of the same mind, united, agreeing, harmonious.* **1.** Lit.: of persons : secum, Liv. ; civitas concordior, Pl. ; concordissimis fratribus, Cic. ; Parcae, Verg. With DAT.: Tac. **2.** Transf.: of things. **a.** regnum, Liv. ; amicitia, Cic. ; pax, Ov. ; Verg. **b.** Of sound : Cic., Ov.

con-crēbrēscō, brēscere, bruī, *to become frequent, increase* : Verg.

con-crēdō (-crēduō, Pl.), crēdere, crēdidī, crēditum, *to entrust wholly, consign, commit to* : rem et famam alicui, Cic. ; Pl. ; Hor. With Acc. understood : Pl.

con-cremō, āre, *to burn to ashes, consume* : urbem igni, Liv. ; Suet.

con-crepō, crepāre, crepuī, crepitum, *to rattle, creak, clash loudly* or *together*. **A.** Intrans.: ostium, Pl.; manūs, Ov.; armis concrepare, Caes.; arma concrepuere, Liv.; gladiis ad scuta, Liv.; digitis, Pl., Cic. **B.** Trans.: *to cause to sound* or *rattle* : aera, Ov.

con-crēscō, crēscere, crēvī, crētum. (*Inf. sync.* -crēsse, Ov.) **I.** *to grow together*. **1.** Lit.: Verg.; *de terris terram concrescere posse*, Lucr.; in this sense, chiefly in *Perf. Part.* concretus, *compounded, composed* : aut simplex est natura animantis aut concreta ex pluribus naturis, Cic. **2.** Transf.: illud funestum animal, ex civili cruore concretum, Cic.; labes, Verg. **II.** *to become condensed, curdle, congeal, clot* : Cic., Lucr., Verg., Ov.

concrētiō, ōnis, *f.* [concrēscō]. **I.** *a uniting, condensing, congealing* (opp. liquor): Cic. **II.** *any material compound* : Cic.

concrētus, a, um. **I.** *Part.* concrēscō, *grown together, compounded.* **II.** *Adj.* **a.** *compounded* : Cic. **b.** *condensed, thick, curdled, congealed*, etc.: aer (opp. fusus, extenuatus), Cic., Lucr.; pingue et concretum esse caelum, Cic.; lac, Verg.; glacies, Liv.

con-criminor, ārī, *to bring a bitter complaint* : Pl.

con-cruciō, āre, *to torture severely* : Lucr.

concubīna, ae, *f.* [concumbō], *a concubine* : Pl., Cic. Also *a wanton* : Tac.

concubīnātus, ūs, *m.* [concubīnus], *cohabitation without marriage, concubinage* : Pl. Of adultery : Suet.

concubīnus, ī, *m.* [concumbō], *one who lives in concubinage* : Cat., Tac.

concubitus, ūs, *m.* [concumbō]. **1.** Lit.: *a lying* or *reclining together* : Prop. **2.** Transf.: *sexual intercourse* : Cic., Verg., etc.

concubius, a, um [concumbō], *of* or *belonging to the time of sleep* : only in the phrase concubiā nocte, *in the first sleep*, Cic., Liv.; noctu concubiā, Enn. As Noun, **concubium**, ī, n. *the time of the first sleep* : Pl.

con-culcō, āre [calcō], *to heel thoroughly* ; *to crush under the heel.* **1.** Lit.: Cato. **2.** Transf.: *to trample underfoot.* **a.** *to maltreat* : istum, Cic.; Italiam, Cic. Ep. **b.** *to treat with contempt* : lauream, Cic.; Lucr.

con-cumbō, cumbere, cubuī, cubitum. **1.** Lit.: *to lie* or *recline together* : Prop. **2.** Transf. (sexually): cum aliquā, Ter.; Cic., Ov.; with DAT.: Ov.

con-cupiēns, entis [cupiō], *warmly desiring, coveting* : with GEN.: Enn.

con-cupiscō, cupiscere, cupīvī (or -iī), cupītum, *to long much for, to covet* ; *to aspire to, strive after* : signa, tabulas, gloriam, Cic.; Hor.; Liv., etc. With *Inf.* : Cic., Tac. With Acc. and *Inf.* : Suet. *Absol.* : Tac.

con-cūrō, āre, *to care for suitably, attend to* : Pl.

con-currō, currere, currī (and -cucurrī), cursum. **I.** *to run together.* **A.** *to run in a body, to assemble in haste* : Ter.; ad arma milites, Caes.; domum tuam, Cic.; Lucr.; ad me restituendum, Cic. *Impers. Pass.* : concurritur undique, Cic.; Caes.; Liv.

B. *to run upon one another, to meet* or *dash together.* **1.** Lit. **a.** Of things : concurrunt nubes ventis, Lucr.; ne prorā concurrerent, Liv. Of the Symplegades : Ov. With DAT.: concurrit dextera laevae, Hor. **b.** Milit. *to rush together, meet in battle, join issue* : Sall., Liv., Tac.; concurrunt equites inter se, Caes.; Verg.; vexilla cum vexillis, Liv.; Ov.; adversus fessos, Liv. With DAT.: audet viris concurrere virgo, Verg.; Liv. **2.** Transf.: of abstract objects : *to meet, concur, happen at the same time* : multa concurrunt simul, Ter.; res concurrent contrariae, Cic. **II.** *to run eagerly, resort to* : ad Druides, Caes.; ad C. Aquilium, Cic.; nulla sedes quo concurrant (i.e. for refuge), Cic. Ep.

concursātiō, ōnis, *f.* [concursō]. **I.** *a running together*. **1.** Lit.: Liv. **2.** Transf. *a coincidence* : somniorum, Cic. **II. 1.** Lit. **a.** *an eager* or *excited* or *active running about* : Cic., Liv. **b.** Milit. *a skirmishing* : leviter armatorum, Liv.; Curt. **2.** Transf.: exagitatae mentis, Sen. Ep.

concursātor, ōris, *m.* [concursō]. Milit. *a skirmisher* (opp. statarius) : Liv.

concursiō, ōnis, *f.* [concurrō]. **I.** *a running* or *meeting together, a concourse* : atomorum, Cic. In *pl.* : Cic. **II.** Rhet. *an emphatic repetition of certain words* : concursio in eadem verba, Cic.

con-cursō, āre [*freq.* concurrō], *to rush about excitedly* or *actively, run hither and thither.* **a.** In gen.: Lucr., Caes., Cic., etc. Of the sea : undis concursantibus, Acc. *Impers. Pass.* : Caes. With Acc.: cum iam omnia fere domos concurrent, *go about from house to house*, Cic. **b.** Milit. *to skirmish* : Liv.

concursus, ūs, *m.* [concurrō]. **I.** *a running together, a concourse, assembly.* **1.** Lit.: fit concursus per vias, Pl.; Caes.; Verg.; in *pl.* : incredibilem in modum concursūs fiunt ex agris, Cic.; Hor. **2.** Transf.: of abstr. objects : *union, combination, concurrence* : studiorum, Cic. **II.** *a violent rushing together, collision.* **1.** Lit. **a.** navium, Caes.; Ov. Of atoms : Lucr., Cic. **b.** Milit. *an onset, rush, charge* : Caes., Cic. **2.** Transf.: asper concursus verborum, Cic.

concussū, ABL. *sing. m.* [concutiō], *by a shaking* : Lucr.

concussus, a, um, *Part.* concutiō.

con-cutiō, cutere, cussi, cussum [quatiō]. **I.** *to shake* or *strike together* : Ov., Tac. **II.** *to shake violently, convulse.* **1.** Lit.: Ter.; corpora risu, Lucr.; concussae cadunt urbes, Lucr.; terra ingenti motu concussa est, Liv.; lora, Verg.; arietibus munimenta, Curt. **2.** Transf. **a.** Of the feelings, *to convulse, agitate* : barbarus pavor concusserat, Curt.; Sall.; casu concussus acerbo, Verg.; metu concussus, Verg. **b.** Of power, etc., *to convulse, shatter, throw into violent disorder* : rem publicam, Cic.; regnum, Liv.; concusso Hannibale, Liv.; fidem, Tac. **c.** *to agitate* (i.e. *to rouse*) : fecundum pectus, Verg. **d.** With *Refl. Pron.* : *to shake up*, hence, *search, examine oneself* (*cf.* excutio) : Hor.

condalium, ī, n. [κονδύλιον, κόνδυλος], *a little ring for slaves* : Pl.

con-decet, āre, *impers. it is (quite) becoming, seemly :* capies quod te condecet, Pl. ; aurum gerere, Pl.

con-decŏrŏ, āre, *to adorn gracefully :* ludos scaenicos, Ter.

condemnātor, ōris, *m.* [condemnō], *one who causes a condemnation :* Tac.

con-demnŏ, āre [damnō], *to sentence, condemn, doom* (opp. absolvo, *to acquit*) : **1.** Lit. **a.** The crime is expressed by the GEN., ABL., or *de* and ABL. ; the damages by the GEN., ABL. (rare), or *ad* and ACC. : aliquem rerum capitalium, iniuriarum, ambitūs, Cic. ; eodem crimine, Cic. ; de aleā, Cic. ; capitis, sponsionis, Cic. ; capitali poenā, Suet. ; ad mortem, Tac. **b.** Occ. : of the prosecutor, *to urge or effect the condemnation of a person :* istum omnium mortalium sententiis condemnavi, Cic. ; Pl. **2.** Transf. : *to condemn, blame severely :* me inertiae, Cic. ; se iniquitatis, Caes.

condēnsŏ, āre (condēnseat, Lucr.) [condēnsus], *to make dense, press close together :* Varr.

con-dēnsus, a, um, *very dense, close together, thick :* corpora, Lucr. ; puppes, Verg. ; vallis arboribus condensa, Liv. ; acies, Liv.

condiciŏ, ōnis, *f.* [condīcō], *an arrangement, settlement, agreement.* **1.** Prop. **a.** *Absol. :* condicionem alicui ferre, Pl. ; sub condicione, *conditionally,* Liv. ; arma per condicionem ponere, Tac. ; condicione, non bello, Curt. **b.** *Partic. terms, agreement :* ista condicio respuatur, Cic. ; aequitate condicionum perspectā, Caes. ; eā condicione ut . . . *or* ne . . ., Cic., etc. ; sub condicionibus iis pacem agere, Liv. ; Ov. **c.** *a marriage-contract, hence, marriage, match :* Pl. ; condicionem filiae quaerendam esse, Liv. ; filiam eius eiecisti, aliā condicione quaesitā, Cic. **2. a.** Of persons and things : *situation, circumstances, condition, rank, place,* etc. : infima condicio servorum, Cic. ; vitae, Caes., Cic. ; cura condicione super communi, Hor. ; iuris libertatisque, Caes. **b.** *circumstances, terms, conditions* (under which one acts) : condicione aequā (*or* iniquā) pugnare, Caes.

con-dīcō, dīcere, dīxī, dictum, *to talk over together, arrange together, to agree upon :* sīc condicunt, Tac. ; quarum rerum . . . condixit pater patratus P.R. patri patrato Latinorum, Liv. Phr. : alicui ad cenam *or* cenam condicere, *to engage oneself to supper :* Pl., Suet. Without cenam : Cic. Ep.

condignē, *adv. very worthily :* Pl. With ABL. ; Pl.

con-dignus, a, um, *wholly deserving, very worthy.* With ABL. : *worthy of :* Pl.

condimentum, ī, *n.* [condiō], *spice, seasoning, relish.* **1.** Lit. : cibi, Cic. ; Pl. **2.** Transf. : omnium sermonum facetiae, Cic. ; Pl.

condiŏ, īre [perh. an access. form from condō]. **1.** Lit. : of fruits, etc., *to preserve, pickle :* oleas albas, Cato. Hence, *to embalm :* mortuos, Cic. **2.** Transf. **a.** Of food, etc., *to make savoury, to season :* cenam, Pl. ; ius, Hor. ; unguenta, Cic. **b.** Of language, etc., *to season :* duo sunt, quae

---

condiant orationem, verborum numerorumque iucunditas, Cic. ; hilaritate tristitiam temporum, Cic. Ep.

condiscipulātus, ūs, *m.* [condiscipulus], *companionship at school :* Nep.

con-discipulus, ī, *m. a school-fellow :* Cic., etc.

con-disco, discere, didicī, *to learn thoroughly :* modos, Hor. ; Suet. With *Inf.* : Pl., Cic., Hor. With *Indir. Quest.* : Cic.

conditiŏ, *v.* condiciŏ.

conditiŏ, ōnis, *f.* (condiŏ), *a preserving.* **1.** Lit. : of fruits, etc. : Varr. In *pl.* : Varr. **2.** Transf. : of food, etc. : *a spicing, seasoning, flavouring :* Varr. In *pl.* : Cic.

conditor, ōris, *m.* [condō], *a builder, founder.* **1.** Lit. : urbis, Liv., Nep. ; Romanae arcis, Verg. **2.** Transf. **a.** *founder, author :* Romani iuris, Liv. ; totius negoti (in a pun on sense of condio), Cic. **b.** *author, composer :* Tib., Ov.

conditōrium, ī, *n.* [conditus], *a place where anything is laid up.* **I.** *a coffin, urn for ashes,* etc. : Suet. **II.** *a tomb :* Plin. Ep.

conditus, a, um, *Part.* condō.

conditus, a, um, **I.** *Part.* condiō. **II.** Adj. **a.** *seasoned :* Cic. **b.** Of style : *polished :* oratio lepore et festivitate conditior, Cic. Of the orator : Cic.

con-dŏ, dere, didī, ditum. **I.** *to put together.* **1.** Lit. **a.** *to build :* aram, Liv. ; arcem, moenia, Verg. **b.** Of cities, etc., *to build, found :* Romam, Enn. ; urbem, Lucr., Cic. ; arces, Verg. ; Romanam gentem, Verg. ; post urbem conditam, Cic. **2.** Transf. **a.** Of written productions, *to build, compose :* carmen, Lucr. ; Liv. ; poëma, Cic. Ep. ; Caesaris acta, Ov. ; bella, Verg. **b.** *to found, establish :* ius iurandum, Pl. ; conlegium, Liv. ; mores gentis, Curt. ; aurea saecula, Verg. **II.** *to put by.* **1.** Lit. **a.** Of things, *to store, hoard,* etc. : frumentum, fructūs, pecuniam, Cic. ; Verg. With *in* and ACC. : minas in crumenam, Pl. ; Suet. With *in* and ABL. : in aerario, Cic. With ABL. alone : Hor., Suet. **b.** Of persons (with *in* and ACC.) : aliquem in custodiam, Liv. ; in carcerem, Cic. **c.** Of the dead, *to lay :* aliquem sepulcro, Cic. ; ossa terrā, Verg. **2.** Transf. **a.** *to lay up, store :* mandata corde memori, Cat. ; Cic. ; Verg., etc. **b.** *to lay to rest :* (fulgur conditum, *v.* fulgur) ; hence, of time : longos soles cantando, Verg. ; Lucr. ; Hor. ; diem, Plin. Ep. ; condere lustrum, *to close,* Liv. **III.** *to put away* or *out of sight, hide.* **1.** Lit. **a.** Sibyllam, Cic. ; lumen, Lucr. ; oculos, Ov. ; milites in silvis, Curt. ; Liv. ; Verg. ; se portu, Verg. **2.** Transf. : iram, Tac. ; ensem in pectore, Ov. ; in pectus, i.e. *to bury,* Verg.

condoce-faciŏ, facere, fēcī, factum. **I.** *to train together :* beluas, Cic. **II.** *to train thoroughly :* animum ut etc., Cic.

con-docĕŏ, docēre, docuī, doctum, *to train, instruct fully :* Pl.

condoctus, a, um. **I.** *Part.* condoceŏ. **II.** Adj. *comp. :* Pl.

con-dolēscŏ, dolēscere, doluī [doleō], *to begin to feel (great) pain.* **a.** Physical : mihi condoluit caput, Pl. ; dens, latus, pes condoluit, Cic. ; Hor. **b.** Mental : Cic., Ov.

condōnātiō, ōnis, *f.* [condōnō], *a giving away :* Cic.

con-dōnō, āre, *to give as a present, to present, give up.* **1.** Lit. **a.** Pl. ; apothecas hominibus nequissimis, Cic. **b.** *to remit :* aliis condonantur pecuniae, Cic. **2.** Transf. **a.** *to surrender, sacrifice :* aliquid iudicio potestatique, Cic. ; seque vitamque suam rei publicae, Sall. ; Caes. **b.** *to remit* (a debt), *forgive, pardon* (an offence, etc.). With Acc. of thing and Dat. of person : pecunias creditas debitoribus, Cic. ; Iugurthae scelus, Sall. With Acc. of thing or person pardoned and Dat. of person for whose sake pardon is given : praeterita fratri, Caes. ; Cic. ; Liv. With *two* Acc. : *to present with, make a present of :* argentum quod habes condonamus te, Ter. ; Pl. *Impers. Pass. :* habeo multa (*many complaints against you*), quae condonabitur, Ter.

con-dormiō, īre, *to sleep soundly :* Curt., Suet.

con-dormiscō, īscere, iī [dormiō], *to fall soundly asleep :* Pl.

condūcibilis, e, *adj.* [condūcō], *advantageous, expedient :* consilium ad eam rem, Pl.

con-dūcō, dūcere, dūxī, ductum. **A.** Trans. **a.** *to draw or lead together, to assemble, collect :* exercitum in unum locum, Caes. ; Cic. ; auxilia, Liv. Occ. *to connect, unite :* Lucr., Cic., Ov. **b.** Commerc. **i.** *to hire, take on lease :* aedis mihi, Pl. ; hortum, Cic. Ep. ; mercede aliquem, Cic. ; Hor. ; homines, Caes. ; conductis nummis (i.e. on mortgage), Hor. **ii.** *to contract for, farm :* columnam conduxerat faciendam, Cic. ; Pl. ; vectigalia, Cic., Liv. **B.** Intrans. : *to be of use or profit to, to profit, conduce to,* etc. (only in 3rd pers. *sing.* and *pl.*). With *ad :* ad vitae commoditatem, Cic. ; Pl. With *in* and Acc. : in commune, Tac. ; Pl. With Dat. : rei publicae, Cic. ; Pl. ; Hor. *Absol. :* Cic.

conducticius, a, um [condūcō], *hired :* Pl., Nep.

conductiō, ōnis, *f.* [condūcō]. **I.** *a connecting :* Cic. **II.** *a hiring, farming :* fundi, Cic. ; vectigalium, Liv.

conductor, ōris, *m.* [condūcō]. **I.** *a lessee, tenant :* agri, Caes. **II.** *a contractor :* histrionum, Pl. ; operis, Cic. Ep.

conductus, a, um. **I.** *Part.* condūcō. **II.** Noun **a.** **conductī**, ōrum, *m. pl. mercenary soldiers :* Nep. Of *hired mourners :* Hor. **b.** **conductum**, ī, *n. anything hired,* esp. a house : Cic.

conduplicātiō, ōnis, *f.* [conduplicō], *a doubling :* humorously, for *embracing :* Pl.

con-duplicō, āre, *to double :* divitias, Lucr. ; Ter. Humorously, of a loving embrace : corpora, Pl.

con-dūrō, āre, *to make very hard :* ferrum, Lucr.

condus, ī, *m.* [condō], *one who lays up provisions* (opp. promus) : Pl.

cō-nectō, nectere, nexuī, nexum, *to tie, bind, link.* **1.** Lit. : Pl., Verg., Tac. Occ. *to make by tying :* nodum, Cic., Ov. **2.** Transf. **a.** amicitiam cum voluptate, Cic. ; omnia inter se conexa, Cic. ; filiam discrimini patris, Tac. **b.** In discourse : Cic., Hor. **c.** Philos. = concludo, *to subjoin a logical conclusion :* Cic.

cōnexiō, ōnis, *f.* [cōnectō], *a binding together, a conclusion, logical sequence :* Quint.

cōnexus, a, um. **I.** *Part.* cōnectō. **II.** *Adj. connected, joined :* Silanum per adfinitatem conexum Germanico, Tac. *Comp. :* Lucr. Of time : conexos his funeribus dies, i.e. *following :* Cic. **III.** *Neut.* as Noun : *logical connexion, necessary inference :* Cic.

cōnexus, ūs, *m.* [cōnectō], *a joining together, combination :* Lucr. ; in *pl. :* Lucr.

cōn-fābulor, ārī, *to talk together, discuss :* Pl., Ter. With Acc. : Pl.

cōnfarreātiō, ōnis, *f. an ancient solemn marriage-ritual among the Romans :* Plin.

cōn-farreō, āre [farreus, fr. far], *to unite in marriage by the rite of* confarreatio : Tac.

cōn-fātālis, e, *adj. bound by the same fate :* res, Cic.

cōnfectiō, ōnis, *f.* [cōnficiō]. **I.** *a complete making, a carrying through :* libri, Cic. **II.** *a (successful) completion :* belli, Cic. **III.** *a using up, chewing :* escarum, Cic.

cōnfector, ōris, *m.* [cōnficiō]. **I.** *one who carries through :* negotiorum, Cic. **II.** *one who (successfully) completes :* totius belli, Cic. Ep. **III.** *one who uses up, a destroyer :* confector omnium ignis, Cic. ; ferarum, Suet.

cōnfectus, a, um, *Part.* cōnficiō.

cōn-ferciō, fercīre (no *Perf.*), fertum [farciō], *to stuff or cram together :* Lucr., Varr. Rare exc. in *Perf. Part.* confertus : **a.** *stuffed full :* cibo conferti, Cic. ; ingenti turbā conferta templa, Liv. Transf. : voluptatibus conferta vita, Cic. **b.** *close-packed :* plures simul conferti, Liv. (*v.* confertus II.).

cōn-ferō, ferre, tulī, lātum. **I.** *to bring or carry together.* **1.** Lit. **a.** signa in unum locum, Caes. ; multa ex agris in urbem, Caes. ; Ov. ; conferre viris in unum, Liv. Phr. : conferre pedem, *to go or come with one*, Pl. ; conferre gradum, *to walk by anyone's side*, Pl., Verg. ; capita conferre, *to put heads together*, Cic., Liv. **b.** Of money, offerings, etc., *to contribute :* Pl. ; ad tuum honorem pecunias, Cic. ; aurum argentumque in publicum, Liv. ; frumentum, Caes. **c.** *to bring together, condense, compress :* Pl. ; rem in pauca, Cic. ; totam Academiam ex duobus libris in quattuor, Cic. Ep. ; Ov. **2.** Transf. **a.** *to bring together* (ideas, plans, etc.), *to consult together, confer, consider, or talk over together :* sermones, consilia, etc., Ter., Cic. ; iniurias, Tac. ; si quid res feret, coram inter nos conferemus, Cic. Ep. With *Indir. Quest. :* Cic., Liv. Without *Obj. :* Pl. **b.** *to bring together, compare :* With *cum, inter* with *Refl. Pron.*, Dat. or *Absol. :* hanc pacem cum illo bello, Cic. ; Caes. ; vitam inter se utriusque, Cic. ; parva magnis, Cic. ; Hor. ; rationes, Cic. ; Pl. ; Ov. **II.** Milit. (with arma, castra, signa, etc.), (*to set together :* hence, *to join battle, engage.* **1.** Lit. : castra castris hostium, Caes., Liv. ; conlatis signis depugnare, Pl. ; Liv. ; signa cum Alexandrinis, Cic. ; pedem cum pede, *to fight foot to foot*, Liv. ; certamina pugnae manu, Lucr. ; seque viro contulit, *matched himself*, Verg. *Absol. :* mecum confer, Ov. **2.** Transf. : of a *legal contest :* non possum magis pedem conferre, ut niunt, Cic.; litâ, Hor. **III.** *to bring or direct to a centre.* **1.** Lit. **a.** *to carry over, transfer :* copias in provinciam, Cic.; quos eodem audita clades (i.e. the news of the defeat) contulerat, Liv. Most freq. with *Refl. Pron., to direct one's course, transfer oneself :* qui se suaque omnia in oppidum contulissent, Caes.; se Rhodum, se in fugam, Cic.; Liv.; so ad pedes, Pl. **b.** *to transform :* corpus in albam volucrem, Ov. **2.** Transf. **a.** *to devote time, etc.,* to a certain object : with *ad* or *in :* omne tempus ad aliquam rem, Cic.; quo mortuo, me ad pontificem Scaevolam contuli, i.e. became his disciple, Cic.; se ad studium scribendi, Cic.; omne studium ad gloriam celebrandam, Cic.; omnīs curas cogitationesque in rem publicam, Cic. **b.** *to attribute, impute, ascribe to, etc. :* permulta in Plancium, Cic.; eius rei culpam in multitudinem, Caes.; culpam in aliquem, Pl.; Cic. Ep.; res ad imperium deorum, Lucr. **c.** *to put off, postpone :* = differre : omnia in mensem Martium, Cic. Ep.; Caes.; Liv.

cōnfertim, *adv.* [cōnfertus] *in a compact body :* pugnare, Liv.; Sall.

cōnfertus, a, um. **I.** *Part.* cōnferciō. **II.** Adj. : *close-packed, crowded* (opp. rarus) : Enn., Cic., Verg., etc. *Comp. :* Liv. *Sup. :* Caes., Liv., etc.

cōn-fervēfaciō, facere, *to make glowing* or *melting :* Lucr.

cōn-fervēscō, fervēscere, ferbuī, *to begin to boil.* Transf. : mea cum conferbuit ira, Hor.

cōnfessiō, ōnis, *f.* [cōnfiteor] *an acknowledgment, admission, confession :* errati sui, Cic.; culpae, Liv.; Quint. In *pl. :* Cic. With Acc. and *Inf. :* ea erat confessio caput rerum Romam esse, Liv.

cōnfessus, a, um. **I.** *Part.* cōnfiteor. **II.** Adj. in *Pass.* sense *acknowledged, hence, undoubted, incontrovertible :* res, Cic. **III.** As Noun. **a.** Act. : **cōnfessus,** ī, *m.* *one who has admitted* (his guilt) : Sall. **b.** Pass. : **cōnfessum,** ī, *n.* *an admitted thing :* in confessum venire, *to be generally admitted,* Plin. Ep.; ex confesso, *confessedly, beyond doubt,* Quint.

cōnfestim, *adv.* [*cf.* festinus], *speedily, without delay :* Pl., Cic., Verg., etc.

cōnficiēns, entis. **I.** *Part.* cōnficiō. **II.** Adj. : *producing, productive, efficient :* causae, Cic.; civitas conficientissima, litterarum, *most thorough in its accounts,* Cic.

cōn-ficiō, ficere, fēcī, fectum. (*Pass.* forms freq. from cōnfiō, as well as from the regular form cōnficior : cōnfit, Pl.; cōnfieret, Liv.; cōnfierī, Lucr.) [faciō], *to put together.* **I.** **a.** *to make up, manufacture, construct :* Pl.; anulum, pallium, Cic.; tabulae litteris Graecis confectae, Caes.; libros Graeco sermone, Nep. **b.** *Of a business, etc. : to bring into effect, carry through, complete :* nuptias, Ter.; bellum (i.e. successfully), Caes., Hor.; legationem, mandata, facinus, Cic. *Absol.* (rare) : tu cum Apellā Chio confice de columnis, Cic. Ep. **c.** Of time and space, *to complete :* sexaginta annos, Cic.; Caes.; iter, Caes.; Cic.; cursum, Cic. Ep.; Verg. **d.** Of mental effects, *to bring about, cause :* Ter.; motūs animorum,

Cic.; animum auditoris mitiorem, Cic. **e.** Philos. in *Pass. : to be brought about, deduced :* Cic. **II.** Of number, *to make up, get together.* **1.** Lit. **a.** Of money, troops, etc. : pecuniam ex illā re, Cic.; Liv.; legiones ex dilectu novo, Caes.; (Bellovacos) posse conficere armata milia centum, Caes. **2.** Transf. : *to get together, secure, obtain :* virginem, Ter.; hortos mihi, Cic. Ep.; of votes : suam tribum necessariis suis, Cic.; Liv. **III.** *to work out, use up, wear out, exhaust.* **1.** Lit. **a.** Of persons : Pl.; confectus senectute, Cic.; itinere, vulneribus, Caes.; aevo, Verg.; fame, Liv. So *to despatch* (= to kill) : Cic. Liv. **b.** Of property, *to exhaust :* patrimonium, Cic. **c.** Of food, *to chew :* Cic., Liv. **d.** Of other things : Cic., Lucr. **2.** Transf. : me angoribus, Cic.; Liv.

cōnfictiō, ōnis, *f.* [cōnfingō], *an inventing, fabrication :* criminis, Cic.

cōnfictus, a, um, *Part.* cōnfingō.

cōnfīdēns, entis. **I.** *Part.* cōnfīdō. **II.** Adj. : *trustful,* hence, *self-confident.* **a.** Good sense : Pl., Ter. *Comp. :* Pl. **b.** Bad sense : *bold, undaunted :* *presumptuous, full of assurance :* Ter., Cic., Hor. *Sup. :* Verg.

cōnfīdenter, *adv.* [cōnfīdēns], *confidently, fearlessly.* **a.** Good sense : Pl. *Comp. :* Cic. **b.** Bad sense : Ter.

cōnfīdentia, ae, *f.* [cōnfīdēns]. **I.** *firm trust, confidence :* Pl. With *Obj.* GEN. : Pl. With *Acc.* and *Inf. :* Pl. **II.** *self-confidence.* **a.** Good sense : Pl., Cic. **b.** More freq. in bad sense : Pl., Cic., Quint., etc.

cōnfīdentiloquus, a, um [cōnfīdēns loquor], *speaking confidently.* *Comp. :* Pl.

cōnfīdō, fīdere, fīsus sum, *to have full or complete faith* or *trust, feel confidence* (us. with DAT.) : huic legioni Caesar confidēbat maximē, Caes.; sibi, Caes., Cic.; virtuti militum, Caes.; Liv., etc. With ABL. of cause or ground of confidence : corporis firmitate aut fortunae stabilitate, Cic.; naturā loci, Caes. With Acc. and *Inf. :* Pl., Cic., Ov., etc. *Absol. :* Pl., Cic.

cōn-fīgō, fīgere, fīxī, fīxum. **I.** *to fix, fasten, nail together :* Cato, Caes. **II.** *to pierce all over.* **1.** Lit. : Lucil.; capras sagittis, Cic.; Verg. **2.** Transf. : cornicum oculos, i.e. *to paralyse* or *render powerless,* Cic.; eius sententiis confixum Antonium, Cic.

cōn-fingō, fingere, finxī, fictum, *to form, shape, fabricate completely.* **1.** Lit. : nidos, Plin. **2.** Transf. : aliquid criminis, Cic.; Liv.; Ter. With Acc. and *Inf. :* Cic.

cōnfīnis, e, *adj.* [finis], *having common borders, adjoining.* **1.** Lit. : in confinem agrum, Liv. With DAT. : confines erant hi Senonibus, Caes.; Liv., Ov. **2.** Transf. : *nearly related, akin :* studio confinia carmina vestro, Ov.; Quint.

cōnfīnium, ī, *n.* [cōnfīnis], *a common boundary, frontier.* **1.** Lit. : Cic. Also in *pl.* (= *neighbours*), Cic. **2.** Transf. : Aurora tenet confinia lucis et noctis, Ov.; Tac.

cōn-fīō, fierī, *v.* cōnficiō.

cōnfirmātiō, ōnis, *f.* [cōnfirmō], *a full strengthening.* Transf. **a.** *a securing,* re-

inforcing : libertatis, Cic. **b.** *a reinforcing,
encouragement* : animi, Caes. ; Cic. Ep. **c.**
a confirmation (of a fact or statement), *corroboration* : Caes., Cic. Rhet., *an adducing of proofs* : Cic.

cōnfirmātor, ōris, *m.* [cōnfirmō], *cne who
confirms or reinforces* : pecuniae (*a surety,
security*), Cic.

cōnfirmātus, a, um. **I.** *Part.* cōnfirmō. **II.**
Adj. **a.** *resolute* : animus, Cic. ; confirmatiorem exercitum efficere, Caes. **b.**
certain, proved. Comp. : Cic.

cōn-firmitās, ātis, *f. firmness :* in a bad
sense, *obstinacy :* Pl.

cōn-firmō, āre, *to make quite firm, strengthen,
reinforce.* **1.** Lit. : stipites, Caes. ; hoc
nervos confirmari putant, Caes. ; se confirmare, *to recover strength,* Cic. Ep. **2.**
Transf. **A.** *to reinforce, secure.* **a.** pacem
et amicitiam cum proximis civitatibus, Caes.
b. Of the disposition, e.g. in loyalty :
homines, Caes., Nep. **c.** Of public affairs,
to ratify, sanction : acta Caesaris, Cic. Ep. ;
Nep. **B.** *to reinforce* by encouragement, *to
encourage :* animum, Pl., Caes., Lucr. ;
suos ad dimicandum, Caes. ; se confirmare,
Caes., Cic. **C.** *to reinforce* a statement.
a. *to corroborate, confirm :* rem, Caes., Cic.
With Acc. and *Inf. :* Lucr. **b.** *to assert
positively :* With Acc. and *Inf. :* Caes.,
Cic. With *de :* Cic.

cōn-fiscō, āre [fiscus]. **I.** *to store in a chest :*
Suet. **II.** *to put into the common chest, to
seize upon for the public treasury, to confiscate :* Suet. **III.** *to deprive a person of
his property in this way :* Suet.

cōnfīsiō, ōnis, *f.* [cōnfīdō], *confidence, assurance :* animi, Cic.

cōnfīsus, a, um, *Part.* cōnfīdō.

cōnfiteor, fitēri, fessus [fateor]. **I.** *to acknowledge fully, admit, confess, own, avow*
(us. unwillingly and with ref. to an error,
etc., previously denied or hidden): confiteor
et genus et divitias meas, Pl. ; peccatum
suum, Cic. ; Ov. With Acc. and *Inf. :*
Ter., Cic., Lucr., etc. With *Indir. Quest. :*
Quint. Rarely with *de :* Cic., Tac. **II.**
Of one's identity, *to reveal, manifest oneself*
or *a fact about oneself :* confessa vultibus
iram, Ov. ; alma parens, confessa deam,
i.e. se deam esse, Verg.

cōnfixus, a, um, *Part.* cōnfīgō.

cōn-flagrō, āre, *to be in a general blaze.* **1.**
Lit. : impedimenta, Caes. ; incendio conflagrare, Cic. **2.** Transf. : invidiae incendio conflagrare, Cic. ; Liv.

cōnflictiō, ōnis, *f.* [cōnflīgō], *a striking together, a collision :* Quint. Transf. : *a
contest, conflict :* Cic.

cōnflictō, āre [*freq.* cōnflīgō], us. in *Pass.* **I.**
In *Mid.* sense : *to come into violent collision.*
Transf. : *to contend or struggle with :* qui
cum ingeniis conflictatur eiusmodi, Ter. ;
Nep. *Act.* in same sense : ut conflictares
malo, Ter. **II.** *to be beaten down violently.*
Transf. : *to be severely buffeted : to be
severely harassed, afflicted,* etc. : nos duriore
(fortunā) conflictati videmur, Cic. ; magnā
inopiā necessariarum rerum, Caes. ; multis
difficultatibus, Liv. ; milites tantum conflictati sunt, Tac. Also A cт. *to beat down :*
rem publicam, Tac.

cōnflictū, ABL. *sing. m.* [cōnflīgō], *by a striking together :* lapidum, Cic.

cōn-flīgō, flīgere, flīxī, flīctum. **A.** Trans. :
to throw or dash together. **1.** Lit. : corpora,
Lucr. **2.** Transf. : *to set one thing
against another :* factum cum scripto, Cic.
B. Intrans. : *to dash together, to come into
collision* or *conflict.* **1.** Lit. : hiemes
aestatibus, Lucr. ; armis, Cic. ; adversi
venti confligunt, Verg. With *cum, contra,
adversus, inter* (and *Refl. Pron.*) : equites
hostium proelio cum equitatu nostro conflixerunt, Caes. ; Cic. ; Liv. ; contra conspirationem hostium, Brut. ap. Cic. Ep. ;
adversus classem, Nep. ; naves inter se
conflixerunt, Caes. Impers. *Pass. :* cum
in loco aequo atque aperto confligeretur,
Caes. **2.** Transf. : copia cum egestate,
Cic. ; causae inter se, Cic.

cōn-flō, āre, *to blow up* or *together.* **I.** *to
blow into flame, kindle.* **1.** Lit. : incendium, Liv. ; Pl. **2.** Transf. : of the
passions : invidiam inimico, Cic. ; Lucr. ;
coniurationem, Suet. **II.** *to smelt, fuse,
forge, melt down.* **1.** Lit. : falces in
ensem, Verg. ; Suet. **2.** Transf. : *to fabricate, forge, manufacture* (often contemptuously) : exercitum perditorum, Cic. ; mendacium, Cic. ; aes alienum grande, Sall. ;
iudicia, Liv. ; alicui periculum, Cic. ; Ter. ;
Lucr. [*It. gonfiare ; Fr. gonfler.*]

cōnfluēns, entis. **I.** *Part.* cōnfluō. **II.** Adj.
flowing together ; flowing into : a confluente
Rhodano castra movi, *from the confluence
of the Rhone* (with the Arar), Lepidus ap.
Cic. Ep. **III.** Noun : **cōnfluēns,** entis,
or **cōnfluentēs,** ium, *m. pl. the meeting of
rivers, the confluence :* Caes., Liv. Hence,
Cōnfluentēs, *f. pl.* Koblenz.

cōn-fluō, fluere, fluxī (cōnflūxet = cōnflūxisset, Lucr.), *to flow together.* **1.** Lit. :
Lucr. ; Fibrenus divisus aequaliter in
duas partis cito in unum confluit, Cic. ; Liv. ;
Tib. **2.** Transf. : *to stream or pour in
together, to come together in crowds.* **a.** ad
eum, Caes. ; Cic. **b.** ad ipsos laus, honos,
dignitas confluit, Cic. ; Lucr. ; Ov. ; Tac.

cōn-fodiō, fodere, fōdī, fōssum. **I.** *to dig
up :* hortum, Pl. ; Cato. **II.** *to pierce,
stab, transfix.* **1.** Lit. : Sall., Liv., Verg.,
etc. **2.** Transf. : tot iudiciis confossus,
Liv. ; quaedam scripta notis, Plin. Ep.

cōnfore, *v.* cōnsum.

cōnfōrmātiō, ōnis, *f.* [cōnfōrmō], *a symmetrical forming* or *fashioning ; a shape,
form.* **1.** Lit. : lineamentorum, Cic. ;
corporis, Cic. **2.** Transf. **a.** vocis, *expression of voice,* Cic. ; verborum, *arrangement,* Cic. ; conformatio et moderatio continentiae et temperantiae, *shaping and regulation,* Cic. ; animi, *an idea, notion, concept,*
Cic. **b.** Rhet. : *a figure of speech :* Cic.,
Quint.

cōn-fōrmō, āre, *to shape, form, fashion, put
together, make.* **1.** Lit. : mundum a
naturā conformatum, Cic. ; Cat. **2.**
Transf. : mores, Cic. ; Tac.

cōnfōssus, a, um, **I.** *Part.* cōnfodiō. **II.**
Adj. *well-drilled, full of holes :* te faciam
confossiorem, Pl.

cōnfrāctus, a, um, *Part.* cōnfringō.

cōn-fragōsus (and **cōnfragus,** Lucr.), a, um

[con, frag-], *broken, rough, rugged.* **1.**
Lit.: Varr.; via, Liv. *Neut. pl.* as Noun,
broken ground : Liv. **2.** Transf.: condiciones, Pl.

cŏn-frĕmŏ, ere, uī, *to murmur together or
loudly :* Ov.

cŏn-fricŏ, āre, *to rub vigorously or all over, rub
in.* **1.** Lit.: caput unguento, Cic. **2.**
Transf.: genua (i.e. to touch the knees
in earnest entreaty), Pl.

cŏn-fringŏ, fringere, frēgī, frāctum [frangō],
to break in pieces. **1.** Lit.: foris, Pl.,
Liv.; digitos, Cic. Prov.: tesseram (i.e.
to break friendship), Pl. **2.** Transf.: *to
break down, bring to naught, destroy :* naturae
portarum claustra, Lucr.; rem (i.e. to
dissipate), Pl.; consilia, Cic.

cŏn-fŭgiŏ, fugere, fūgī, *to flee to for refuge
or help.* **1.** Lit.: Ter.; in aram, Cic.;
Verg., etc. **2.** Transf.: *to have recourse
to.* **a.** ad florentis Etruscorum opes, Liv.;
ad meam fidem, Cic. **b.** Of *artifices and
evasions :* confugit illuc ut neget, Cic.;
Ter.

cŏnfŭgium, ī, *n.* [cōnfugiō], *a place of refuge,
a refuge :* Ov.

cŏn-fulgĕŏ, ēre, *to shine brightly, to glitter :*
Pl.

cŏn-fultus, a, um [fulciō], *supported by one
another :* Lucr.

cŏn-fundŏ, fundere, fūdī, fūsum. **I.** *to pour
together, mingle, blend, mix.* **1.** Lit.: of
liquids : Pl., Cic., Verg., etc. **2.** Transf.
a. In gen.: vera cum falsis, Cic.; tantā
confusā multitudine, Caes.; sermones in
unum, Liv; rusticus urbano confusus, Hor.
b. *to jumble together, disorder, mix up :*
Cic.; corporis atque animi sensūs, Lucr.;
signa et ordines peditum atque equitum,
Liv.; foedus, Verg.; proelia confundere
cum aliquo, Hor. **c.** Of mental disorder,
to perturb : maerore confusa Fabia, Liv.;
Plin. Ep. Also, *to bewilder, perplex :*
audientium animos, Liv.; Tac. **II.** *to
pour into, diffuse, spread.* **1.** Lit.: cibus
in eam venam confunditur, Cic.; Hor. **2.**
Transf.: aliquid confundere in totam
orationem, Cic.

cŏnfūsē, *adv. confusedly, in disorder :* Cic.
Comp. : Cic.

cŏnfūsiŏ, ōnis, *f.* [cōnfundō]. **I.** *a mingling,
mixing, blending :* virtutum, Cic. **II.** *confusion, disorder, trouble, distress :* temporum, Cic.; Liv.; Tac. Of mental confusion (shown on the face): oris, Tac.

cŏnfūsus, a, um. **I.** *Part.* cōnfundō. **II.**
Adj. : *confused, perplexed, disorderly :*
oratio, Cic.; verba, Ov.; confusissimus
mos, Suet.: memoria, Liv. Of mental confusion (esp. as shown on the face), *troubled :*
confuso vultu, Ov., Liv.; ore, Curt.; facies
confusior, Tac.

cŏnfūtŏ, āre [*cf.* fūtis, *a water-vessel*], *to prevent water from boiling over.* Transf. **a.**
to check, repress : dolores, Cic.; Cato. **b.**
Esp. *to put to silence* (by words, etc.), *confute :* Pl., Lucr.; argumenta Stoicorum,
Cic.; verba magnifica rebus, Liv.

cŏn-gelŏ, āre. **A.** Trans.: *to cause to
freeze up, to congeal.* **1.** Lit.: mare con-
gelatum, Varr.; Mart. **2.** Transf.: in
lapidem (i.e. *to petrify*), Ov. **B.** Intrans.

to become frozen up. **1.** Lit.: Ister con-
gelāt, Ov. **2.** Transf.: lingua, Ov.;
congelasse nostrum amicum otio (i.e. completely numbed), Cic. Ep.

congĕminātiŏ, ōnis, *f.* [congeminō], *a doubling ;* Comic. for *embracing :* Pl.

con-gĕminŏ, āre, *to double :* Pl.; ictūs cre-
bros, Verg.

con-gĕmŏ, ere, uī. **A.** Intrans.: *to gasp,
sigh* or *groan deeply or loudly :* congemuit senatus frequens, Cic.; arbor
supremum congemuit, Verg. **B.** Trans.:
to deplore deeply, bewail : mortem, Lucr.

conger, grī, *m.* [γόγγρος], *a sea-eel, conger-
eel :* Pl.

congĕriēs, ēī, *f.* [congerō], *that which is
brought together ;* hence , *a heap, pile, mass :*
lapidum, Liv.; silvae, Ov.; armorum,
Tac. Of *chaos :* Ov. Of a *funeral-pile :*
Ov. Rhet.: *accumulation :* Quint.

con-gerŏ, gerere, gessī, gestum, *to bear, carry,*
or *bring together ;* hence, *to heap* or *build
up,* etc. **1.** Lit. **a.** undique saccos, Hor.;
epulas alicui, Pl.; grana in os, Cic.; laticem in vas, Lucr.; aram sepulcri arboribus,
Verg.; oppida manu, Verg. **b.** Of hostile
action, *to shower :* tela, Tac.; tela in aliquem, Curt. **2.** Transf. **A.** *to heap upon,
shower.* **a.** In kindness : Cic.; ingentia
beneficia in aliquem, Liv.; congestos iuveni
triumphos, Tac. **b.** In hostility: male
dicta in Caesarem, Cic.; Liv.; iuveni
triumphos, Tac. **B.** In discourse. **a.** *to
mass together, comprise :* operarios omnis in
sermonem, Cic. **b.** *to keep up, multiply,
repeat :* argumenta, Quint.; Mart.

con-gerŏ, ōnis, *m. a thief :* Pl.

con-gerrŏ, ōnis, *m. a jolly companion, a
play-fellow :* Pl.

congesticius, a, um [congestus], *heaped* or
piled up : agger ex materiā, Caes.

congestus, a, um, *Part.* congerō.

congestus, ūs, *m.* [congerō]. **I.** *a carrying*
or *bringing together, an accumulating :* Cic.,
Tac. **II.** *a heap, pile, mass :* Lucr., Tac.

congiālis, e, *adj.* [congius], *holding a congius :*
fidelia, Pl.

congiārius, a, um [congius], *of* or *holding a
congius :* us. as Noun, **congiārium**, ī, *n.*
(*sc. donum*), *a gift to the people, each individual receiving a congius,* e.g. of oil : Liv.
Transf.: *a largess in money divided
among the soldiers :* Cic.; *among the
people :* Tac.; or *among private friends :*
Cael. ap. Cic. Ep.; Liv.

congius, ī, *m. a Roman liquid-measure* (= 6
sextarii, i.e. about 6 pints): Liv. (*v.* table
at end of volume).

con-glaciŏ, āre, *to freeze up.* **1.** Lit.:
aqua conglaciaret frigoribus, Cic. **2.**
Transf.: Curioni nostro tribunatus con-
glaciat, Cael. ap. Cic. Ep.

con-gliscŏ, ere, *to burn* or *blaze up.* Transf.:
Pl.

conglŏbātiŏ, ōnis, *f.* [conglobō], *a massing
together :* Tac.

con-glŏbŏ, āre. *to gather into a ball, make
round* or *spherical.* **1.** Lit. **a.** Cic.; esp.
in *Perf. Part. :* terra undique ipsa in sese
conglobata, Cic. **b.** *to group together :* of
the *atoms of Epicurus :* corpuscula conglobata, Lucr. **2.** Transf. **a.** Of people,

to gather or *group together :* uti quosque fors conglobaverat, Sall ; se in forum, Liv. ; se in unum, Liv. ; se in templo, Tac. ; eos fortuna similis conglobaverat Agathyrnam, Liv. **b.** Philos.: definitiones conglobatae, Cic.

con-glomerō, āre, *to roll together, wind up, conglomerate :* Lucr. Transf.: omnia mala in aliquem, Enn.

conglūtinātiō, ōnis, *f.* [conglūtinō], *a gluing* or *cementing together.* **1.** Lit.: Cic. **2.** Transf.: verborum, Cic.

con-glūtinō, āre, *to glue, cement,* or *join together.* **1.** Lit.; Varr. **2.** Transf. **a.** *to cement, unite closely :* amicitias, rem dissolutam, Cic. ; Ter. **b.** *to devise, contrive.* With *ut* and *Subj. :* Pl.

congraecō, āre [graecus], *to lavish on banquests like the Greeks* (i.e. *to squander in luxury*) : aurum, Pl.

con-grātulor, ārī, *to congratulate one another :* Pl. ; with Acc. and *Inf. :* Liv.

con-gredior, gredī, grěssus [gradior], *to go* or *come together, to meet :* luna tum congrediens cum sole, tum digrediens, Cic. Esp. **A.** In a friendly way, *to meet, address, accost, associate with :* Pl., Cic., Liv. With Acc.: Pl. With *prep. :* cum Caesare, Caes. ; Cic. ; in conloquium, Liv. **B.** In a hostile way, *to meet, fight, contend, engage, etc.* **1.** Lit.: Caes., Verg., etc. : cum finitimis proelio, Caes. ; Pl. ; Liv. ; contra Caesarem, Cic. With Dat.: puer Achilli, Verg.: Curt. **2.** Transf. Of forensic strife, etc. : tecum luctari et congredi, Cic.

congregābilis, e, *adj.* [congregō], *easily brought together, gregarious :* examina apium, Cic.

congregātiō, ōnis, *f.* [congregō], *a flocking together, a natural union, association :* hominum, Cic. Transf.: argumentorum, Quint.

con-gregō, āre [grex]. **I.** Of birds, beasts, etc.. *to collect into a flock* or *herd :* in *Mid. :* apium examina congregantur, Cic. **II.** Of men (in natural gatherings), *to collect ; to unite, associate :* dispersos homines in unum locum, Cic. ; se cum aequalibus, Cic. ; Tac. In *Mid.:* pares cum paribus facillime congregantur, Cic. ; unum in locum, Cic. ; ad aliquem, Liv. ; inter se, Tac. Transf.: Quint.

congrěssiō, ōnis, *f.* [congredior]. **I.** *a coming together, a meeting :* Cic. **II.** *association, friendly meeting :* Cic. In *pl. :* familiarum, Cic.

congrěssus, a, um, *Part.* congredior.

congrěssus, ūs, *m.* [congredior]. **I.** *a friendly meeting, association, society, etc. :* omnes aditum, sermonem, congressum tuum fugiunt, Cic. ; Liv., etc. In *pl. :* Cic., Verg., etc. Of animals : Cic. Transf. *a close union, combination :* materiāī, Lucr. **II.** *a hostile encounter, a contest, fight :* in primo congressu circiter septuaginta ceciderunt, Caes. ; Cic. ; Verg., etc.

congruēns, entis. **I.** *Part.* congruō. **II.** *Adj.* **a.** *coinciding,* hence *corresponding, agreeing, suitable, consistent :* vita cum disciplinā, Cic. ; congruens actio menti, Cic. ; saturas motu congruenti peragebant, Liv. ;

Cic. Phr. : congruens est or videtur, *it is* (or *seems) appropriate :* with *Inf. :* Tac. ; with Acc. and *Inf. :* Plin. Pan. **b.** *self-consistent, uniform, harmonious :* concentus, Cic. ; clamor, Liv.

congruenter, *adv. consistently, in conformity with.* With *ad* and Acc. : ad aliquid congruenter dicere, Cic. With Dat. : congruenter naturae vivere, Cic.

congruentia, ae, *f.* [congruō], *consistency, symmetry :* corporis, Plin. Ep. ; morum, Suet.

congruō, uere, uī, *to run together ; to coincide.* **1.** Lit.: ut ad metam eandem solis dies congruerent, Liv. **2.** Transf. **a.** *to coincide* (in time) : tempus ad id ipsum, Liv. ; dies mensesque cum solis lunaeque ratione, Cic. ; forte congruerat ut etc. ; Tac. **b.** *to correspond, agree, be consistent with.* With *cum :* Cic., Liv. With *inter :* Cic., Liv. With Dat. : Cic., Liv., Tac. *Absol. :* Liv., Tac. **c.** *to agree* (in feeling or opinion): inter se, Pl. ; alicui, Ter. ; linguā, moribus, etc., Liv. ; de ceteris (rebus) mirifice congruunt, Cic. Rarely with *in* and Acc. : omnium in unum sententiae, Liv.

congruus, a, um [congruō], *agreeing, corresponding :* sermo cum illā, Pl.

con-iciō, icere, iēcī, iectum [iaciō]. **I.** *to throw together.* **1.** Lit. : Pl. ; sarcinas in medium, Liv. ; Verg. **2.** Transf. In thought or speech, *to cast together,* hence, **a.** *to conclude, infer, conjecture :* Ter. ; aliquid ex aliquā re, Lucr. ; de futuris, Nep. With Acc. and *Inf. :* Cic. Ep. With *Indir. Quest. :* Pl., Cic. **b.** *to divine from omens, foretell ; to interpret* an omen, dream, etc. : somnium huic, Pl. ; de aliquā re ex oraculo, Cic. With *Indir. Quest. :* Cic. **II. 1.** Lit. **a.** *to throw, hurl in a mass :* (of missiles, etc.) : tela in nostros, Caes. ; Liv. ; spolia igni, Verg. **b.** *to throw forcibly* or *violently, fling, thrust, impel, etc. :* gladium in os adversum, Caes. ; Ov. ; facem iuveni, Verg. ; aliquem in vincula, Caes. ; in carcerem, Cic. ; auxilia in mediam aciem, Caes. ; navem in portum, Cic. With *Refl. Pron. :* se in pedes (= *to take to one's heels*), Ter. ; se in signa, Caes. ; se in latebras, Verg. **2.** Transf. : *to throw, cast, fling.* **a.** oculos in aliquem, Cic. ; crimina in tuam diligentiam, Cic. ; culpam in vigilem, Liv. **b.** hostis in fugam, Caes. ; hostis in terrorem ac tumultum, Liv. ; Pl. ; rem publicam in perturbationes, Cic. With *Refl. Pron. :* se in latebram (in disputing), Cic. ; se in noctem (of starting on a night-journey), Cic. ; se in versum, Cic.

coniectiō, ōnis, *f.* [coniciō]. **1.** Lit. : *a hurling, throwing* (esp. *on the part of a number together*) : telorum, Cic. **2.** Transf. *a conjecture, interpretation :* somniorum, Cic.

coniectō, āre [freq. coniciō], *to throw, cast together.* Transf. *to put together* or *turn over in the mind ; to conjecture, infer ; to conclude, guess.* With Acc. : Ter. ; rem eventu, Liv. ; iter, Liv. ; valetudinem exeo quod etc., Tac. ; animos militaris altius, Tac. With Acc. and *Inf. :* Caes., Tac. With *Indir. Quest. :* Liv., Quint. With *de :* de imperio, Tac.

coniector, ōris, *m.* and **coniectrix**, īcis, *f.* (Pl.) [coniciō], *one who interprets dreams :* Pl., Cic. ; *or who solves a riddle :* Pl.

coniectūra, ae, *f.* [coniciō]. **I.** *a putting together* (of various apparently unconnected circumstances) ; *a conjecture, inference, conclusion, guess :* Pl. ; (ex aliquā re) facere, Ter., Cic. ; capere, Cic. With *Obj.* GEN. : Liv. **II.** *a divining, an interpreting of dreams or omens :* Pl., Cic., Ov.

coniectūrālis, e, *adj.* [coniectūra]; *of conjecture, conjectural :* Cic., Quint.

coniectus, a, um, *Part.* coniciō.

coniectus, ūs, *m.* [coniciō]. **I. a.** *a throwing* or *casting together :* terrae, Liv. **b.** *concourse, union :* materiāl, Lucr. **II.** *a throwing* or *casting* (by many or in a mass). **1.** Lit. : lapidum, Cic. Ep. ; telorum, Nep. Liv. ; ad (or intra) teli coniectum venire (i.e. within range) : Liv., Tac. **2.** Transf. **a.** oculorum in me, Cic. **b.** animorum in me, Cic. ; minarum, Plin. Pan.

cōnifer, era, erum [cōnus, ferō], *cone-bearing :* cyparissi, Verg.

cōniger, era, erum [cōnus, gerō], *cone-bearing :* pinus, Cat.

cō-nitor, nītī, nīxus or nīsus **I.** *to press against for support, lean firmly on :* genu flexo, Cic. poet. **II.** *to make a strong effort, exert oneself.* **1.** Lit. Physically. **a.** *Absol.* or with *Instr.* ABL. : omnes conisi hostem avertunt, Liv. ; spem grąǵis, ah ! silice in nudā conixa reliquit, Verg. ; omnibus regni viribus conixus, Liv. ; toto corpore, umeris, Verg. **b.** The obj. of the effort is expressed by *in* and ACC. : in summum iugum, Caes. ; Liv. ; Lucr. ; by the *Inf.* : Liv., Tac. ; by *ad* and *Ger.* : Curt. ; by *ut* and *Subj.* : Cic. **2.** Transf. Mentally : animo, Cic. With *ad* and *Gerund.* : Tac.

coniugālis, e, *adj.* [coniūnx], *relating to marriage, conjugal :* amor, Tac.

coniugātiō, ōnis, *f.* [coniugō], *a combining.* Rhet. : *the etymological relationship of words :* Cic. [Fr. *conjugaison.*]

coniugātor, ōris, *m.* [coniugō], *one who joins, unites :* Cat.

coniugiālis, e, *adj.* [coniugium], *of marriage :* foedus, Ov.

coniugium, ī, *n.* [coniūnx], *a connexion, union.* **1.** Lit. : corporis atque animae, Lucr. **2.** Transf. Of the sexes, *marriage, wedlock :* Ter., Cic., Verg., etc. Of animals : Verg., Ov. Also concr. = coniunx : *a husband :* Prop. ; *a wife :* Verg., Tac.

con-iugō, āre. **I.** *to form by union :* amicitiam, Cic. **II.** coniugata verba, i.e. *etymologically related*, Cic.

coniūnctē, *adv.* [coniūnctus]. **I.** *in connexion, conjointly :* Cic. In logic : *hypothetically* (opp. simpliciter, *categorically*) : efferre aliquid, Cic. **II.** *in a friendly way :* vivere, Cic. ; Nep. *Comp.* : Cic. Ep., Plin. Ep. ; *Sup.* : Cic.

coniūnctim, *adv.* [coniūnctus], *unitedly, jointly :* Caes., Nep., Liv.

coniūnctiō, ōnis, *f.* [coniungō], *a joining together, union, combination.* **1.** Lit. : portuum, Cic. **2.** Transf. **a.** In gen. : *union, association*, etc. : hominum, Cic. ;

mentis cum externis mentibus (i.e. *sympathy*), Cic. **b.** By blood or marriage : Cic., Nep. Also of sexual union : Cic. **c.** In friendship, politics, etc. : Cic. **d.** Philos. and Rhet. : *a connexion of ideas* or *propositions :* Cic. **e.** Gramm. : *a connecting particle, a conjunction :* Cic.

coniūnctus, a, um. **I.** *Part.* coniungō. **II.** Adj. **1.** Lit. **a.** Of places : *bordering upon, near :* with DAT. : Caes., Nep. ; with ABL. : Verg. **2.** Transf. **a.** *connected with, agreeing with, conforming to.* Us. with *cum :* hoc iudicium cum illo, Cic. ; prudentia cum iustitiā, Cic. With DAT. : praecepta naturae coniuncta, Cic. With ABL. : libido scelere coniuncta, Cic. **b.** *connected by blood or marriage :* With *Instr.* ABL. : Caes., Cic. **c.** By friendship, politics, etc. With *Instr.* ABL., and DAT. : Caes., Cic., Ov. With *cum* and ABL. : Pl., Cic. *Comp.* : Cic. ; *Sup.* : Cic. **III.** *Neut.* as Noun. **a.** In physics : *an essential* or *inherent property of bodies* (opp. eventum, *accident* or *external condition*) : Lucr. **b.** Rhet. *connexion :* Cic.

con-iungō, iungere, iūnxī, iūnctum, *to join together.* **1.** Lit. **a.** boves, Cato ; duas domos, Cic. With *Instr.* ABL. : turris pontibus, Caes. ; calamos cerā, Verg. **b.** *to unite, bring close.* With DAT. or *cum* and ABL. : castra oppido, Caes. ; castra castris, Liv. ; montem cum oppido, Caes. ; dextrae dextram, Ov. **2.** Transf. **a.** In gen. *to join together, unite :* noctem diei, Caes. ; Liv. ; Tac. ; cohortis cum exercitu, Caes. ; dedecus cum probro, Cic. Also *to make in union, unite in :* bellum, Caes., Cic. **b.** By blood or marriage : With *Instr.* ABL. and DAT., or *cum* with ABL. : Cic., Ov., Tac. Also *to form by union :* conubia, Cic., Liv. **c.** By friendship, politics, etc. With *Instr.* ABL. : Caes., Cic. Ep., Verg. With *cum* and ABL. : Nep. Also *to form by union :* amicitias, Cic. Also *to continue uninterrupted :* Tac., Suet.

coniūnx, iugis, *m.f.* [con, iungō], *a spouse, wife :* Lucr., Cic., Hor., etc. ; more rarely, *a husband :* Cic., Verg., etc. In *pl.* for the *married pair :* Cat. Of animals : Ov. Also *a betrothed, a bride :* Verg., Ov.

coniūrātiō, ōnis, *f.* [coniūrō], *a swearing together*, hence, **a.** *a union confirmed by oath, an oath-fellowship :* Ter., Caes., Liv. **b.** Most freq. in bad sense, *a conspiracy, plot :* Caes., Cic., etc. **c.** *the conspirators themselves :* Cic.

coniūrātus, a, um. **I.** *Part.* coniūrō. **II.** Adj. *united by oath :* Cic., Verg., Ov. **III.** Noun, **coniūrāti**, ōrum, *m. pl. conspirators :* Cic.

con-iūrō, āre (*Perf. Part.* coniūrātus in Act. sense : *v. infr.*), *to swear together, to combine together by an oath.* **I.** Good sense. **1.** Lit. : Pl., Caes., Verg. With Acc. and *Fut. Inf.* : Liv. With *Inf.* : Hor. *Perf. Part. Mid.* : consul coniuratos dimittit (*after they had taken the oath*), Liv. **2.** Transf. **a.** In gen. : *to unite, conspire* (in *spirit* or *feeling*) : Hor. **b.** *to assent to by an oath :* quae iurat, mens est ; nil coniuravimus illā, Ov. **II.** Bad sense : *to*

form a conspiracy or plot (very freq.) : inter
se, Sall. ; cum aliquo in omne flagitium et
facinus, Liv. ; contra rem publicam, Cic. ;
de Pompeio interficiendo, Cic. Also with
ut and Subj. : Liv. ; and less freq. Inf. :
patriam incendere, Sall. ; Verg.

coniux, v. coniūnx.

cō-nīveō, nīvēre, nīvī or nīxī [cf. nicō, nictō],
to close the eyes, to blink, wink. **1**. L i t. **a**.
Of the person : Cic., Tac. **b**. Of the eyes :
Cic. **2**. T r a n s f. **a**. Of the sun and moon
in eclipse : Lucr. **b**. Of the mind, to be
not wide-awake : Cic. **c**. to wink at (i.e.
leave uncensured), connive at : with in and
A b l. : Cic., Pers.

conj-, v. coni-.

con-labāscō, ere [labō], to begin to fall, to
totter along with. T r a n s f. : Pl.

con-labefactō, āre, to make to reel violently :
Ov. Of liquefying metals : Lucr.

con-labefīō, fierī, factus, to be made to reel or
totter, to be brought to utter ruin. **1**. L i t. :
navis, Caes. ; Lucr. **2**. T r a n s f. **a**. Of
the melting of metals : Lucr. **b**. In
politics : Nep.

con-lābor, lābī, lāpsus, to fall in a heap or
in complete ruin, to collapse. **1**. L i t. :
Verg. ; pons, Liv. ; urbes, Tac. Of persons : Verg., Tac., etc. **2**. T r a n s f. :
ossa morbo, Verg. ; in corruptelam, Pl.

con-lacerātus, a, um [lacero], torn all to
pieces, lacerated : corpus, Tac.

conlacrimātiō, ōnis, f. [con-lacrimō], a
weeping together : Cic.

con-lacrimō, āre, to weep together or very
much, to bewail, deplore. **A**. I n t r a n s. :
Pl., Cic. **B**. T r a n s. : Cic., Liv.

conlacteus, ī, m. ; and **conlactea**, ae, f.
[con-, lact-, v. lac], a foster-brother : foster-
sister : Juv.

conlāpsus, a, um, Part. conlābor.

conlātiō, ōnis, f. [cōnferō], a bringing together.
1. L i t. **a**. In war : signorum (i.e. an engagement), Cic. **b**. Of money : a contribution, collection : stipis aut decimae, Liv. ;
Tac. **2**. T r a n s f. **a**. a combination : malitiarum, Pl. **b**. a bringing together for
comparison. **i**. R h e t. : Cic., etc. **ii**.
Philos. : conlatio rationis (analogy), Cic.

conlātīvus, a, um [conlātus], brought together,
collected : Pl.

conlātor, ōris, m. [cōnferō], a contributor :
symbolarum, Pl.

conlātus, a, um, Part. cōnferō.

conlaudātiōne, A b l. sing. f. [conlaudō], by
warm praise : Cic.

con-laudō, āre, to praise greatly : Pl., Cic.,
Hor., etc.

con-laxō, āre, to widen, to make loose or porous :
lateramina, Lucr.

conlēcta, ae, f. (orig. adj. : sc. pecunia)
[conligō], a pecuniary contribution : conlectam exigere, Cic.

conlēctāneus, a, um [conlēctus], collected
together : Suet.

conlēcticius [conlēctus], a, um, gathered
together hastily : exercitus (opp. dilectus),
Cic. Ep.

conlēctiō, ōnis, f. [conligō], a gathering
together : membrorum (Absyrti), Cic. Rhet.
a. a summing up, recapitulation : Cic. **b**.
a conclusion, inference : Sen. Ep., Quint.

conlēctīvus, a, um [conlēctus], syllogistic :
Quint.

conlēctus, a, um, Part. conligō.

conlēga, ae, m. [legō], one chosen at the same
time with another. **1**. L i t. In office, a
colleague : bis unā consules, conlegae in cen-
surā, Cic. ; Hor. ; Tac. **2**. T r a n s f. In
gen. **a**. comrade, associate. Metrodorus,
Epicuri conlega sapientiae, Cic. ; a fellow-
slave : Pl. ; a fellow-actor : Juv.

conlēgium, ī, n. [conlēga]. **I**. a union or
association in any office, colleagueship : P.
Decius consul per tot conlegia expertus,
Liv. ; Tac. **II**. C o n c r. : a body of persons
united by the same office or calling ; a college, guild, corporation, brotherhood : pontificum, Caes. ; Liv. ; praetorum, etc., Cic. ;
ambubaiarum, Hor.

con-lēvō, āre, to make quite smooth : Sen. Ep.

con-lībertus, ī, m. a fellow-freedman : Pl.

con-lībrō, āre, to weigh or measure off : Cato.

con-libuit or **conlibitum est** (conlu-), it
thoroughly pleased, it was quite agreeable.
A. A c t. form : impers. : Hor. ; with
impers. Subj. and D a t. : Sall. **B**. P a s s.
form : impers. with D a t. : Pl., Cic. ; with
impers. Subj. : Ter.

con-līdō, līdere, līsī, līsum [laedō], to clash,
strike, dash, or crush together. **1**. L i t. :
Lucr., Cic., Ov. **2**. T r a n s f. : to bring
into collision, to set at variance : Graecia
barbariae lento conlisa duello, Hor. ; Quint.

conligātiō, ōnis, f. [conligō], a binding
together. T r a n s f. : societatis, Cic. ; causarum, Cic.

(1) **con-ligō**, āre, to bind together. **1**. L i t. :
manūs, Pl., Cic., Liv. O c c. : to fasten or
pin together : pluribus scutis uno ictu pilorum transfixis et conligatis, Caes. **2**.
T r a n s f. **a**. homines in terse, Cic. **b**.
sententias verbis, Cic. **c**. to restrain, stop,
hinder : impetum furentis (Antoni), Cic.

(2) **con-ligō**, ligere, lēgī, lēctum [legō], to pick
up or gather together, collect. **1**. L i t. **a**.
Of things : Pl. ; sarmenta, Caes. ; aer
umorem, Cic. ; vasa (milit. to pack up),
Liv. ; luna revertentis ignis, Verg. ; flores,
uvas, Ov. **b**. Of persons : milites, exercitum, Cic. ; Liv. Also to rally troops : se
conligere, Caes. ; ex fugā reliquos, Nep. **c**.
to gather or draw together, contract, compress,
concentrate : pallium, Pl. ; sinūs fluentis,
Verg. ; in spiram se conligit anguis, Verg. ;
se in arma, Verg. ; cogebantur breviore
spatio et ipsi orbem conligere, Liv. ; equos,
to pull up, stop, Ov. **2**. T r a n s f. **a**. In
gen. : to bring together, collect : Pl. ; resun-
dique, Cic. ; rumorum ventos, Cic. ; Lucr.
O c c. : to accumulate, acquire gradually :
benevolentiam civium, Cic. ; auctoritatem,
Caes. ; famam clementiae, Liv. ; sitim,
Verg. **b**. With Refl. Pron., or animum,
mentem, etc., to collect or recover oneself :
Cic., Ov., etc. **c**. to gather, put together in
the mind : Cic., Hor., hence, to infer, conclude. With A c c. : Liv. With A c c. and
Inf. : Cic., Ov., Tac. With Indir. Quest. :
Cic. Ep., Hor. With ex and A b l., or A b l.
alone of that from which the conclusion is
drawn : Cic., Quint.

con-līneō, āre. **A**. T r a n s. : to direct
something in a straight line, to aim straight :

hastam aut sagittam, Cic. **B.** Intrans.: *to hit the mark* : Cic.

con-linō, linere, lēvī, litum. With Acc. and *Instr.* ABL.: *to besmear.* **1.** Lit.: ora venenis, Ov.; Hor. **2.** Transf.: *to defile* : Pl.

con-liquefactus, a, um [liquefiō], *made liquid, dissolved, melted* : venenum in potione, Cic.

conlīsus, a, um, *Part.* conlīdō.

conlītus, a, um, *Part.* conlinō.

conlocātiō, ōnis, *f.* [conlocō]. **I.** *a placing together, arrangement* : verborum, Cic. **II.** filiae, *a giving in marriage*, Cic.

con-locō, āre, *to place together, put in order, arrange* ; *to put into position, station, establish*, etc. **1.** Lit. **a.** In gen.: cruminam in collo, Pl.; impedimenta in tumulo, Caes.; exercitum in hibernis, Caes.; aliquem in cubili, Cic.; me in gremio, Cat.; iuvenem in latebris, Verg.; comites apud ceteros hospites, Cic.; ut ante suum fundum Miloni insidias conlocaret, Cic.; se Athenis (*Locat.*), Cic. With *Locat.* ABL.: Ov. With *in* and Acc.: Pl., Sall. **b.** Of women, *to give in marriage* : matrem homini nobilissimo, Caes.; in matrimonium, Cic.; Pl.; in conlocandā filiā, Tac. **c.** Of money, *to lay out, invest*, etc.: in eā provinciā pecunias magnas conlocatas habent, Cic.; Pl.; Tac. **2.** Transf. **a.** *to arrange, establish* : multa in pectore suo, Pl.; has res, Caes.; verba, Cic.; philosophiam in urbibus, Cic. **b.** *to lay out, employ*, etc.: se in cognitione et scientiā, Cic.; adulescentiam in voluptatibus, Cic.; in otium se, Pl.; melius apud bonos beneficium conlocari (i.e. *put out to interest*), Cic.; spem dignitatis in aliquo (i.e. *to stake*), Cic.

con-locuplētō, āre, *to make quite rich, to enrich* : Ter.

conlocūtiō, ōnis, *f.* [conloquor], *a (familiar or private) conversation, conference* : Cic. In *pl.* : Cic.

conloquium, ī, *n.* [conloquor], *n. a talking together, conversation, conference* : ad (or in) conloquium (alicuius) venire, Caes., Cic.; with pervenire, Cic.; with convenire, Nep.; cum se immiscuissent conloquiis montanorum, Liv.; cum aliquo habere, Liv.; conloquia amicorum absentium, Cic.; Ov.; Tac.

con-loquor, loquī, locūtus, *to talk together, to hold a conversation or conference* : Pl., Caes., Liv. With *cum* and ABL.: Ter., Caes., Cic. With *inter* and *Refl. Pron.* : Cic. With Acc. (of person): Pl.

conlub-, *v.* conlib-.

con-lūceō, ēre, *to be lighted up, to shine brightly, to be entirely illuminated.* **1.** Lit.: Lucr., Cic., Verg., etc. With ABL.: candelabri fulgore, Cic.; flammis, Verg. With *ab* : mare a sole, Cic. **2.** Transf.: *to be resplendent* : Cic., Ov.

con-lūdō, lūdere, lūsī, lūsum, *to play or sport together, play with.* **1.** Lit.: (puer) gestit paribus conludere, Hor.; summā in aquā plumae, Verg. **2.** Transf. (in law): *to act in fraudulent collusion* : Cic.

con-luō, luere, luī, lūtum. *to wash out, rinse* : metretam amurcā, Cato; os de oleo, Plin. Transf.: ora (i.e. *to quench thirst*). Ov.

conlūsiō, ōnis, *f.* [conlūdō], *a secret fraudulent understanding, collusion* : Cic.

conlūsor, ōris, *m.* [conlūdō], *play fellow, fellow-gambler* : Cic., Plin. Ep.

con-lūstrō, āre. **I.** *to light up, illumine* : Cic. Transf. In painting, *to represent in bright colours, light up* : conlustrata (opp. opaca), Cic. **II.** *to examine on all sides, to survey, inspect* : omnia oculis, Cic.; Verg.

con-lutulentō, āre, *to soil* (with mud); hence, *to defile much* : Pl.

conlūtus, a, um, *Part.* conluō.

conluviō, ōnis (Cic., Liv.), and **conluviēs**, em, ē (Atticus ap. Cic. Ep.; Tac.), *f.* [conluō], *washings, rinsings* ; *sweepings, a mass of filth.* Transf.: *off-scourings, vile medley* : conluvio mixtorum omnis generis animantium, Liv.; cum ex hac turbā et conluvione discedam, Cic.; in multā conluvie rerum, Tac.

conm-, *v.* comm-.

conn-, *v.* cōn-.

Conōn, ōnis (Acc. -ōna), *m.* **I.** *a famous Athenian admiral* (c. 400 B.C.). **II.** *a famous mathematician and astronomer of Samos* (c. 230 B.C.).

cōnōpēum (**cōnōpium**), ī, *n.* [κωνωπεῖον], *a net of fine gauze to keep off mosquitoes*, etc.: Varr., Hor., Juv.

cōnor, ārī, *to try, endeavour, venture.* With Acc.: quicquam fallaciae, Ter.; opus magnum et arduum, Cic.; tantam rem, Liv.; plurima, Verg. With *Inf.* : Caes., Cic., Hor., etc. With *si* (= *in the hope that*) : Caes. *Absol.* : Ter., Caes., Liv.

conquassātiō, ōnis, *f.* [conquassō], *a severe shaking* : valetudinis, Cic.

con-quassō, āre. **I.** *to shake often or severely.* **1.** Lit.: Apuliam maximis terrae motibus, Cic.; Lucr. **2.** Transf.: conquassatur mens, Lucr.; civitatem, Cic. **II.** *to shatter in pieces* : Cato.

con-queror, querī, questus, *to complain of passionately or much* : Ter., Cat., Ov. With Acc.: iniuriam, Liv.; Ov.; Tac.; esp. Acc. of *Neut. Pron.* : aliquid pro re publicā, Cic. With Acc. and *Inf.* : Lucr., Suet. With *de* : Cic. With *cur* and *Indir. Quest.* : Tac.

conquestiō, ōnis, *f.* [conqueror]. **I.** *a violent complaining, complaint* : Cic.; with *de* or *adversus* : Quint.; with *Obj.* GEN. : Sen. Ep. **II.** Rhet.: *an appeal to compassion* : Cic.

conquestū ABL. *sing. m.* [conqueror], *by an outcry* : Liv.

conquestus, a, um, *Part.* conqueror.

con-quiēscō, quiēscere, quiēvī, quiētum (*Perf. syncop.* conquiēstī, Cic.; conquiēsse, Liv.), *to be wholly at rest, to take rest, to repose.* **1.** Lit. Physically: Cic.; sub armis, Caes.; a continuis bellis, Cic. Prov.: de istac re in oculum utrumvis conquiescito, i.e. *be quite easy, untroubled*, Pl. **2.** Transf. **a.** Mentally : *to find rest, recreation* : habebam ubi conquiescerem, Cic.; Liv. With *in* : in nostris studiis, Cic. Ep. **b.** In purpose, will, etc., *to keep quiet, remain inactive, flag* : Cic., Liv. **c.** Of things, *to lie dormant, slacken*, etc.: navigatio, Cic.; imber, Liv.

con-quinisco, quiniscere, *to cower, squat, stoop down :* Pl.

con-quiro, quirere, quisivi, quisitum. **1.** Lit. **A.** *to search for, seek out* (in order to bring together). **a.** Of things : frumentum, navis, Caes. ; scuta, Cic. ; pecuniam, Liv. **b.** Of persons : Caes., Liv. **B.** *to search for thoroughly* (in order to find) : (of persons) : Cic., Liv. **2.** Transf. : voluptates, Caes. ; Lucr. ; Liv. ; suavitates undique, Cic. [Fr. *conquérir*.]

conquisitio, onis, *f.* [conquiro], *a search for* (in order to bring together or obtain). **1.** Lit. : librorum, Liv. ; Tac. Milit. *a levying, levy :* Cic., Liv. **2.** Transf. : piaculorum, Liv.

conquisitor, oris, *m.* [conquiro]. **I.** *a recruiting officer :* Cic., Liv. **II.** *a claqueur :* Pl.

conquisitus, a, um. **I.** *Part.* conquiro. **II.** Adj. *sought out, selected, recherché :* coloni, Cic. ; mensae conquisitissimis epulis exstruebantur, Cic.

con-rado, rädere, räsi, räsum, *to scrape or rake together.* **1.** Lit. : corpora, Lucr. Esp. of money : Pl., Ter. **2.** Transf. : fidem dictis, Lucr.

conre-, conri-, *v.* corre-, corri-.

con-roboro, are, *to strengthen fully, invigorate.* **1.** Lit. Physically : Cic., Suet. **2.** Transf. : coniurationem nascentem, Cic. ; virtutem, Cic. ; eloquentiae famam, Tac.

con-rodo, rodere, rosi, rosum, *to gnaw to pieces :* Cic., Juv.

con-rogo, are, *to collect by asking* or *invitation :* suos necessarios, Cic. ; pecuniam, Caes. ; auxilia ab sociis, Liv. [Fr. *corvée*, fr. conrogata.]

conrosus, a, um, *Part.* conrodo. [Fr. *creux.*]

conru-, *v.* corru-.

con-saepio, saepire, saepsi, saeptum, *to fence round, hedge in closely :* Suet. Esp. in *Perf. Part.* consaeptus : Cic. With *Instr.* ABL. : Liv. Hence, **consaeptum**, i, *n. an enclosure :* Varr., Liv.

consalutatio, onis, *f.* [consaluto], *a mutual greeting, salutation :* forensis, Cic. Ep. ; Tac.

con-saluto, are, *to greet, hail, salute* (of the action of several persons) : inter se amicissime, Cic. Esp. by title, name, etc., *to hail* (as king, etc.) : eum regem, Liv. ; Cic. ; Tac.

con-sanesco, sänescere, sänui, *to become quite sound* or *healed :* Cic. Ep.

consanguineus, a, um (GEN. *pl.* consanguineum, Lucr.) [con, sanguis], *related by blood :* Verg., Ov. Mostly as Noun, brother, sister : Cic. Ep., Cat., Verg. Most freq. in *pl.*, *relatives :* Pl., Caes., Cic.

consanguinitas, ätis, *f.* [consanguineus], *blood relationship :* Verg., Liv.

con-saucio, are, *to wound severely :* caput, Suet.

consceleratus, a, um. **I.** *Part.* conscelero. **II.** Adj. : *utterly wicked, depraved :* Cic. Sup. : Cic. **III.** Masc. as Noun : Cic.

con-scelero, are, *to stain* or *dishonour utterly :* domum, Cat. ; oculos videndo, Ov. ; auris paternas, Liv.

con-scendo, scendere, scendi, scensum

[scando], *to climb up, mount, ascend.* **A.** Of several together. **a.** In gen. With ACC. : vallum, Caes. ; equos, Liv. ; navibus aequor, Verg. ; montis, Cat. With *in :* in equos, Ov. ; Lucr. **b.** Nautical : *to go on board a ship, to embark.* With ACC. : navem, Caes. ; Liv. ; classem, Verg. With *in :* in navem, Caes. **B.** Occ. of an individual : equum, Liv. ; Pompeius navem conscendit, Caes. With LOCAT. or ABL. (of separation) of the starting-point, and *in* with ACC. of the destination : Thessalonicae, Liv. ; Epheso, Cic. Ep. ; ab eo loco, Cic. ; in Siciliam, Liv.

conscensio, onis, *f.* [conscendo], *an embarking :* in navis, Cic.

conscientia, ae, *f.* [consciens, conscio]. **I.** *a joint knowledge, a being privy to, a witnessing,* etc. : Cic., Liv. With *Subj.* GEN. : Cic., Liv., Tac. With *Obj.* GEN. : Tac. **II.** *consciousness, knowledge, a sense.* **a.** In gen. : Cic., Sall., Tac. With *Obj.* GEN. : Cic., Liv., Tac., etc. With *de :* Sall. With *Indir. Quest. :* Liv. With *ne* and *Subj. :* Tac. **b.** *a consciousness* of right or wrong, *the moral sense, conscience :* conscientia recta, Cic. ; mala, Sall. ; egregia, Liv. ; bona, Sen. Ep. Without *Adj.* **i.** *a good conscience :* magna vis est conscientiae, Cic. ; Sen. Ep. **ii.** *a bad conscience :* is recitatis litteris conscientiä convictus repente reticuit, Cic. ; Liv. ; conscientiä vecordes, Tac. In *pl.* : suae (quemque) malae cogitationes conscientaeque animi terrent, Cic.

con-scindo, scindere, scidi, scissum, *to tear up* or *rend to pieces.* **1.** Lit. : pallulam, Pl. ; Ter. ; epistulam, Cic. Ep. **2.** Transf. : sibilis conscissus, Cic. Ep. ; is me ab optimatibus ait conscindi, Cic. Ep.

con-scio, scire, *to be conscious* of wrong : nil conscire sibi, Hor.

con-scisco, sciscere, scivi or scii, scitum (*Perf. Inf.* conscisse, Cic., Liv.). **I.** *to approve* or *decide upon* in common. Esp. of public action. With ACC. : Cic., Liv. With *ut* and *Subj. :* Liv. **II.** *to decide upon for oneself* (us. with *Refl. Pron.*), *to inflict* or *bring upon oneself :* sibi mortem consciscere, Cic. ; letum, Lucr. ; exsilium et fugam, Liv. ; facinus in se et suos, Liv. Without sibi : letum, Pl. ; mortem, Cic. Ep. ; Liv. ; Tac.

conscissus, a, um, *Part.* conscindo.

conscitus, a, um, *Part.* conscisco.

conscius, a, um [scio]. **I.** *sharing knowledge with another : cognisant, privy ;* Pl., Cic., Verg., etc. With *Obj.* GEN. : Ter. ; consilii, Caes. ; officiorum, Cic. Ep. ; ante actae vitae, Liv. ; interficiendi Postumi, Tac. Poet. : fati sidera, Verg. With DAT. : huic facinori tanto, Cic. ; coeptis, Ov. Poet. : sacris nox, Ov. With *in :* mihi in privatis omnibus conscius, Cic. Ep. ; Prop. With *de :* his de rebus, Cic. Ep. With *Indir. Quest. :* Nep. As Noun. With GEN. : Nep. **II.** Masc. as Noun, conscius, i, *m.* and **conscia**, ae, *f. a partner, accomplice, confidant, joint-conspirator :* Cic., Nep. With GEN. : rebellionis, Othonis, Tac. With DAT. : matri, Juv. **II.** *conscious to oneself, sensible, aware.* Without *Refl. Pron. :* conscia virtus, Verg. ; audacis

facti (lupus), Verg. With *Refl. Pron.* **i.**
With Gen. : iniuriae sibi, Caes., Cic. ; mens
sibi conscia recti, Verg. **ii.** With Dat. : sibi
factis mens, Lucr. **iii.** With *in :* nullā
sibi turpi in re, Lucr. **iv.** With Acc. and
Inf. : Cic. **v.** With *Indir. Quest. :* Hirt.
O c c. : *having a sense of guilt :* quos conscius animus exagitabat, Sall. ; Pl. ; Lucr. ;
Verg.

cŏn-screor, āri [screō], *to clear the throat
loudly :* magnifice, Pl.

cŏn-scribo, scribere, scripsi, scriptum. **I.**
to write together in a list, enlist, enrol (of the
levying of troops, enrolling of citizens, etc.) :
legiones, Caes. ; Collinam novam (tribum)
conscribebat, Cic. ; ut in senatum vocaren-
tur qui patres quisque conscripti essent,
Liv. Hence, for the senate as a whole,
patrēs cŏnscripti (for patres et conscripti, *heads of families and the newly
elected*) : Cic., Liv. Also in *sing.* **cŏn-
scriptus,** i, m. *a senator :* Hor. **II.** *to draw
up in writing ; to compose, write.* **1.** L i t. :
librum de consulatu, Cic. ; epistula Graecis
conscripta litteris, Caes. ; legem, Cic. ;
foedus, Liv. ; litteras ad Hannibalem, Liv.
With *de :* Cic. With *Indir. Quest. :* Cic.
With Acc. and *Inf. :* Suet. **2.** T r a n s f. :
epistolium lacrimis, Cat. ; mensam vino,
Ov. ; aliquem stilis, Pl.

cŏnscriptiŏ, ōnis, *f.* [cōnscrībō]. L i t. : *a
drawing up in writing, draft :* in *pl.*,
quaestionum, Cic.

cŏn-secŏ, secāre, secui, sectum, *to cut into
small pieces, to dismember :* brassicam,
Cato ; membra, Ov.

cŏnsecrātiŏ, ōnis, *f.* [cōnsecrō], *a religious
dedication, consecration :* cápitis, Cic. Of
the *deification* of Roman emperors : Tac.

cŏn-secrŏ, āre [sacrō], *to make holy, dedicate
to a deity.* **1.** L i t. **a.** Of things : locum
certis circa terminis, Liv. ; lucos ac nemora,
Tac. ; locus consecratus, Caes. ; (opp. profanus), Cic. ; candelabrum Iovi, Cic. Also
to dedicate to the gods below, hence, *to devote
to destruction :* te tuumque caput sanguine
hoc consecro, Liv. ; Cic. **b.** Of persons,
etc., *to deify :* Liberum, Cic. ; Tac. ; omne
fere genus bestiarum, Cic. **2.** T r a n s f. **a.**
to consecrate, hallow : artem deorum inventioni, Cic. ; origines suas, Liv. **b.** *to
make immortal, immortalise :* Socratis ratio
disputandi Platonis litteris consecrata,
Cic. ; Quint. ; more fully, ad immortalitatis et religionem et memoriam consecrare,
Cic.

cŏnsectārius, a, um [cōnsector], *that follows
logically, consequent :* Cic. As Noun in
n. pl. conclusiones, *inferences :* Cic.

cŏnsectātiŏ, ōnis, *f.* [cōnsector], *an eager
pursuit, a striving after :* concinnitatis, Cic.

cŏnsectātrix, icis, *f.* [cōnsector] = *Adj.*,
eagerly pursuing. With Gen. : consecta-
trices voluptatis libidines, Cic.

cŏnsectiŏ, ōnis, *f.* [cōnsecō], *a cutting to
pieces :* arborum, Cic.

cŏn-sector, āri [*freq.* cōnsequor], *to follow* or
go after eagerly or *continuously.* **I.** In gen.
1. L i t. : hos, Ter. ; Pl. **2.** T r a n s f. :
rivulos, Cic. E s p. : *to go after, strive
after, emulate, imitate :* potentiam, Cic. ;
benevolentiam Macedonum largitione, Cic.

II. In hostility, *to chase eagerly* or *closely,
hunt down.* **1.** L i t. : equites, Caes. ;
latrones, Cic. ; pecora, Liv. ; Lucr. **2.**
T r a n s f. : Fufium conviciis, Cic. Ep. ;
Tac. ; Pl.

cŏnsecūtiŏ, ōnis, *f.* [cōnsequor], *an effect,
consequence.* **I.** rerum consecutiones videre, Cic. **II.** Rhet. : *connexion, sequence :*
verborum, Cic.

cŏn-senēscŏ, senēscere, senui, *to grow old
together.* **1.** L i t. **a.** Hor., Ov., Liv. Also
of a single person : Liv. **b.** *to become en-
feebled, to decay, lose strength,* etc. : (filia)
maerore et lacrimis consenescebat, Cic. ;
Pl. ; veru in manibus, Pl. ; vires, Cic. **2.**
T r a n s f. : veteres leges ipsā suā vetustate
consenuisse, Cic. ; Liv.

cŏnsensiŏ, ōnis, *f.* [cōnsentiō], *a feeling* or
thinking together ; agreement, unanimity.
1. L i t. **a.** omni in re consensio omnium
gentium, Cic. With *de :* Cic. With
Subj. and *Obj.* Gen. : universae Galliae consensio libertatis vindicandae, Caes. **b.**
Bad sense, *a plot, conspiracy :* scelerata,
Cic. ; Nep. In *pl. :* Cic. **2.** T r a n s f. :
the conspirators themselves : Nep.

cŏnsensus, ūs, *m.* [cōnsentiō], *a common
feeling, agreement, unanimity, concord.* **1.**
L i t. **a.** vester, Cic. ; omnium, Cic. ; inter
malos ad bellum, Tac. ; in rem publicam,
Cic. ; ad rem publicam recuperandam, Cic.
With *Obj.* Gen. : attemptatae defectionis,
Liv. Adverbially : consensu, *unanimously,
with general consent,* etc. : bellum erat consensu, Liv. ; Tac. **b.** Bad sense, *a conspiracy :* Cic. **2.** T r a n s f. Of things :
agreement, harmony : omnium doctrinarum,
Cic. ; Lucr.

cŏnsentāneus, a, um [cōnsentiō], *agreeing
with, consistent with :* with *cum :* Cic. Ep. ;
With Dat. : consentanea mors eius vitae,
Cic. ; Quint. P h r. : consentaneum est,
it is consistent, reasonable : with *ut* and
Subj. : Pl. ; with *Inf. :* Cic.

cŏnsentiēns, entis. **I.** *Part.* cōnsentiō. **II.**
Adj. : agreeing, accordant, harmonious : of
the order of nature : Cic. ; clamor, unanimous, Liv.

cŏn-sentiŏ (later **cōsentiŏ**), sentire, sensi,
sēnsum, *to agree in feeling* or *thought, to be
of one opinion ; to determine in common,
decree,* etc. **1.** L i t. Of persons. **a.** In
gen. : consentiente populo, Cic. ; cum
bonis, Cic. ; cum aliquā re, Cic. ; de amicitiae utilitate, Cic. ; sibi ipse, Cic. ; Hor. ;
ad rem publicam conservandam, Cic. ;
Liv. ; in adserendā libertate, Suet. With
Inf. : Cic., Tac. With *ut* or *ne* and *Subj. :*
Liv. With Acc. and *Inf. :* Cic., Tac.
With Acc. : bellum (i.e. *to vote war*), Liv.
Pass. Impers. : de prioribus consentitur,
Tac. In bad sense, *to plot together, conspire,* etc. : cum Belgis, Caes. ; belli faci-
endi causā, Cic. ; urbem inflammare, Cic. ;
ad prodendam Hannibali urbem Romanam,
Liv. ; de urbe tradendā, Nep. **2.** T r a n s f.
Of things : *to accord, agree, harmonise, be
consistent,* etc. : cum vultus cum oratione
non consentiret, Caes. ; ratio nostra con-
sentit, pugnat oratio, Cic. ; Lucr. ; Hor.
With Dat. : Cic., Quint. ; inter se, Cic.

cŏn-sēp-, *v.* cŏn-saep-.

cōnsequēns, entis. **I.** *Part.* cōnsequor. **II.** Adj.: *following on, coherent ; agreeable to reason, logically consequent :* hoc probato consequens est beatam vitam virtute esse contentam, Cic. **III.** *Neut.* as Noun, *a logical consequence :* Cic.

cōnsequentia, ae, *f.* [cōnsequor], *a natural sequence :* eventorum, Cic.

cōnsequia, ae, *f.* [cōnsequor] = cōnsequentia : Lucr.

cōn-sequor, sequi, secūtus. **I.** *to follow closely.* **1.** Lit. **a.** In gen.: Lentulum, Caes. ; Pl. ; litteras suas, Liv. ; comitibus non consecutis, Cic. **b.** In hostility : copias Helvetiorum, Caes. ; Liv. **2.** Transf. **a.** In time : *to follow, come after :* hunc Cethegum consecutus est aetate Cato, Cic. ; nox consequitur diem, Cic. ; consequitur tempestas, Caes. **b.** In action : *to follow as an effect, to result from :* pudorem rubor, terrorem pallor consequitur, Cic. ; rebus ab ipsis sensus, Lucr. Of a logical consequence : fit quod consequitur necessarium, Cic. **c.** In a course of action or an opinion : *to adopt :* sententias (principum), Cic. ; Pl. ; eum morem, Cic. ; Chrysippum, Cic. ; mediam consili viam, Liv. **II.** *to come after and join, to come up with, overtake.* **1.** Lit.: novissimum agmen, Caes. ; aliquem in itinere, Cic. ; Verg. ; Ov. *Absol. :* Cic., Liv. **2.** Transf.: *to reach or attain to.* **a.** fructum amplissimum ex vestro iudicio, Cic. ; fortitudinis gloriam, Cic. ; Ov. ; regna, Caes. With *ut* or *ne* and *Subj. :* Cic. Ep. ; Quint. **b.** With a personal object : *to overtake, happen to, befall :* Ter. ; prosperitas Caesarem est consecuta, Nep. **c.** *to attain, come up to the standard of :* aliquem maiorem, Cic. **d.** *to attain to* (in language), *do justice to :* laudes eius verbis, Cic. ; Ov. **e.** *to attain to* intellectually, *grasp, understand :* Cic.

(1) cōn-serō, serere, sēvī, situm, *to sow closely* or *together.* **I.** Of the thing planted. **1.** Lit.: Cato, Curt. Also *to plant firmly :* Liv. **2.** Transf.: stilos caecos, Auct. B. Afr. **II.** Of the ground. **1.** Lit.: Cato, Cic., Verg. **2.** Transf.: consitus senectute, Pl. ; lumine arva (sol), Lucr.

(2) cōn-serō, serere, serui, sortum. **I.** *to string together, twine, fasten together.* **1.** Lit. **a.** In gen.: scuta super capita, Curt. ; tegimen spinis, Verg., Tac. Poet.: nocti diem, Ov. **b.** In hostility (with manūs, pugnam, inter se, etc.) : Pl. ; *to engage in close combat, to join hand to hand, to join battle :* manum cum aliquo, Cic., Caes. ; manūs inter se, Liv. ; pugnam inter se, Liv. ; proelia, Verg. ; pugnam seni, Pl. Rarely *Absol. :* levis armatura cum levi armaturā conseruit, Liv. In *Mid. :* navis conseritur, Liv. **2.** Transf. **a.** haud ignotas belli artis inter se conserebant, i.c. *they brought into collision,* Liv. **b.** In law, manum conserere, *to make a joint seizure of* (by the litigant parties laying their hands upon it before the praetor) : Cic. **II.** *to make by stringing* or *fastening together.* **1.** Lit.: loricam hamis auroque, Verg. **2.** Transf.: exodia conserta fabellis Atel-

lanis, i.e. *formed by union with,* Liv. ; sermonem, Curt.

cōnsertē, *adv. connectedly :* Cic.

cōnsertus, a, um, *Part.* cōnserō.

cōn-serva, ae, *f. a female fellow-slave.* **1.** Lit.: Pl. **2.** Transf.: Ov.

cōnservātiō, ōnis, *f.* [cōnservō], *a keeping, preserving.* **1.** Lit.: frugum, Cic. **2.** Transf.: aequabilitatis, Cic.

cōnservātor, ōris, *m.* [cōnservō], *a keeper, preserver :* di immortales, conservatores huius urbis, Cic.

cōn-servitium, i, *n. joint servitude :* commune, Pl.

cōn-servō, āre (*Inf. Perf.* us. cōnservāsse). **1.** Lit. **a.** *to keep close watch over, guard, preserve closely :* Ter. ; rem familiarem, Cic. **b.** *to keep safe, keep from harm :* Nervios, Caes. ; Cic. ; aras, Nep. ; civis incolumis, Cic. **2.** Transf.: *to keep fully, maintain,* etc.: Lucr. ; ordines, Caes. ; ius iurandum, Cic. ; pristinum animum erga nos, Cic. ; imperium, Liv.

cōn-servus, i, *m. fellow-slave :* Pl., Cic., Hor.

cōnsessor, ōris, *m.* [sedeō], *one who sits with* or *near, an assessor :* in a court of justice, Cic. ; at a feast, Cic. ; at public exhibitions, Cic. Ep., Liv.

cōnsessus, ūs, *m.* [sedeō], *a sitting together.* Concr. *an assembly, a court,* etc. : Cic., Verg., etc. In *pl. :* Cic.

cōnsīderātē, *adv. with caution* or *deliberation, deliberately :* agere, Cic. *Comp. :* Liv. *Sup. :* Cic. Ep.

cōnsīderātiō, ōnis, *f.* [cōnsīderō], *an examination :* naturae, Cic.

cōnsīderātus, a, um. **I.** *Part.* cōnsīderō. **II.** Adj. **a.** Of things, *well-considered, deliberate :* Cic. **b.** Of persons, *circumspect, cautious :* Cic., Liv. *Comp. :* Cic. Ep.

cōnsīderō, āre [perh. fr. sīdus, *cf.* dēsīderō], *to look at carefully, to inspect, to examine.* **1.** Lit.: candelabrum etiam atque etiam, Cic. ; spatium, Ov. With *Indir. Quest. :* Ov. **2.** Transf. Of the mind, *to consider maturely, to contemplate, ponder on,* etc. With Acc.: Ter., Cic., Tac. With *de :* Cic. With *Indir. Quest. :* Cic., Sall., Liv. With *ne* and *Subj., to take care* (rare) : Cic. *Absol. :* Cic. Ep. *Impers. Pass. :* Cic.

cōn-sīdō, sidere, sēdī (less freq. sīdī), sessum, *to sit down, take a seat, to settle.* **1.** Lit. **a.** In gen.: Liv., Plin. Ep. With *in* and ABL.: Caes., Cic., Verg., etc. With ABL. alone : Verg., Ov. With other *preps. :* Liv., Verg., Ov. *Impers. Pass. :* Cic. **b.** Of courts, etc. : *to sit, hold sessions, to be in session :* Druides in loco consecrato, Caes. ; in theatro imperiti homines consederant, Cic. ; Ov. ; ad ius dicendum, Liv. **c.** Milit.: *to encamp, take up a position :* sub monte, trans flumen, quo in loco, Caes. ; pro castris, Liv. ; tumulis, Liv. **d.** *to settle, take up one's abode, establish oneself :* Caes., Cic. Ep. ; Verg. **2.** Transf. **a.** Of things : *to settle, sink down, subside,* etc. : terra ingentibus cavernis consedit, Liv. ; Cic. ; omne mihi visum considere in ignis Ilium, Verg. ; Tac. ; ignis, Ov. ; pulvis, Curt. **b.** Of excited feelings : *to subside, abate :* furor, Cic. ; ferocia ab re bene gestā, Liv. ; primus terror, Liv. **c.** In gen. *to settle down permanently in, sink in* : iustitia in mente, Cic. ; urbs luctu, Verg. ; nomen utriusque in quaesturā (i.e. *sank and was not heard of again*), Cic. **d.** Of discourse, *to sink*, i.e. *to conclude, end* : Cic.

cŏn-signō, āre, *to seal up, seal, sign, subscribe.* **1.** Lit. : Pl. ; tabulas signis, Cic. ; decretum, Liv. **2.** Transf. **a.** *to attest, authenticate, vouch for* : monumentis consignata antiquitas, Cic. **b.** *to record* : litteris aliquid, Cic. ; rerum quasi consignatae in animis notiones, Cic.

cŏn-sĭlēscō, sĭlēscere, sĭlui, *to become perfectly still or quiet* : Pl.

cōnsĭlĭārĭus, a, um [cōnsilium], *suitable for counsel, counselling* : senatus, amicus, Pl. As Noun. **a.** *a counsellor, adviser* : Cic. **b.** *an assessor in a court of justice* : Suet. **c.** Of an augur, as *the interpreter* of the divine will : Cic.

cōnsĭlĭātor, ōris, m. [cōnsilior], *a counsellor* : Phaedr., Plin. Ep.

cōnsĭlĭor, ārī [cōnsilium]. **I.** *to take counsel, to consult* : cum suis, Caes. Absol. : Cic. Ep., Hor., Tac. **II.** *to give counsel, to advise* (with Dat.) : Hor.

cōnsĭlĭum, ī, n. [sed-, seen in sedeō]. **I.** Act. : *a taking counsel, consultation, united deliberation.* **1.** Lit. : Pl. ; cum aliquo consilia conferre, Cic. ; ad consilium rem deferre, Caes., Cic. ; quasi vero consili sit res, Caes. ; Liv. ; Verg. With *Indir. Quaest.* : Cic. Ep. **2.** Transf. **a.** Concr. *the body deliberating together, a council of advisers, a council of war* : Caes., Cic., Liv., Hor. **b.** Abstr. of the mental quality, *deliberation, insight, sagacity, judgment*, etc. : Ter., Cic., Hor., etc. **II.** Pass. *a resolution, decision, purpose, policy*, etc. **1.** Lit. : in consilio permanere, Caes. ; consilio desistere, Caes. Esp. capere or inire consilium : With *de* : Caes., Liv. With Gen. : Cic. With Gerund. in Gen. : Caes., Cic. Ep., Liv., Tac. ; with *Inf.* : Caes., Cic., Liv. With *ut* and *Subj.* : Pl., Cic., etc. With *Indir. Quaest.* : Caes. Absol. consilio, *intentionally* : Cic. Ep., Liv., Verg. ; privato consilio, *for private purposes*, Caes., Cic. **2.** Transf. : *a help in forming a resolution*, i.e. *advice, counsel* : Pl. ; consilium dare, Cic., Hor. ; consiliis alicuius uti, Cic. ; consiliis parere, Cic. ; sequi, Liv. ; hoc fecit de eius consilio, Caes. Also = *an adviser* : Ov. [It. *consiglio* ; Fr. *conseil.*]

cŏn-sĭmĭlis, e, adj. *like in all respects, entirely similar* : Pl., Lucr., Tac. With Gen. : causa consimilis causarum earum, Cic. ; Pl. ; Lucr. With Dat. : cui homini erus est consimilis, Pl. ; Caes. ; Cic. With *atque* or *ac* : Lucr. ; Pl. With *quasi* : Pl.

cŏn-sĭpĭō, sipere [sapiō], *to be of sound mind* : mentibus, Liv.

cŏn-sistō, sistere, stitī, stitum. **I.** In relation to others, *to take up a position, station oneself, be posted.* **1.** Lit. : Caes., Cic., Liv. Also of individuals : Pl., Cic., Verg. **2.** Transf. **a.** *to come and rest upon, fall on* : in quo (viro) non modo culpa nulla sed ne suspicio quidem potuit consistere, Cic. ; Liv. ; Ov. **b.** *to take its stand in, depend on, consist of.* With *in* and Abl. : Lucr., Caes., Cic. With *ex* : Lucr. With Abl.

alone : Lucr., Quint. With *circa* or *inter* : Quint. **II.** With idea of firmness, stability, etc., *to come to a standstill, take a firm stand, stop, halt*, etc. **1.** Lit. **a.** In gen. : Cic., Verg., etc. Esp. milit. : Caes., Liv. ; a fugā, Liv. Of ships, *to come to anchorage* : in ancoris, Caes. ; also *to ground* : in vadis, Caes. **b.** Of travellers, *to halt on a journey* : Cic. **c.** Of traders, etc., *to settle, take up residence* : Caes. **2.** Transf. **a.** Of concr. things, *to come to a standstill, stop, come to rest* : rota, flumina, Verg. ; Ov. **b.** Of abstr. things, *to come to a standstill, stop, cease* : Pl. ; omnis administratio belli, Caes. ; forensium rerum labor, Cic. ; bellum, Liv. ; ira, Ov. **c.** With idea of permanence, *to last, endure, be steadfast, stand one's ground* : mente, Cic. ; in dicendo, Cic. ; constitit in nullā qui fuit ante color, Ov. ; Hor. **d.** *to exist, take place* : vix binos oratores laudabilis constitisse, Cic. ; non in te quoque constitit idem exitus, Ov.

cōnsĭtĭō, ōnis, f. [cōnserō], *a sowing, planting* : Cic.

cōnsĭtor, ōris, m. [cōnserō], *a sower, planter* : uvae, i.e. *Bacchus*, Ov.

cōnsĭtūra, ae, f. [cōnserō], *a sowing, planting* : agri, Cic.

cōnsĭtus, a, um, *Part.* cōnserō.

cŏn-sōbrīnus, ī, m. and **cŏn-sōbrīna**, ae, f. **I.** *a first-cousin* (prop. *the child of a mother's sister*) : Cic., Nep. **II.** *a distant-cousin* : Suet. [It. *cugino* ; Fr. *cousin.*]

cŏn-sŏcer, erī, m. *a joint father-in-law* : Suet.

cōnsŏcĭātĭō, ōnis, f. [cōnsociō], *a union, association* : Cic., Liv.

cōnsŏcĭātus, a, um. **I.** *Part.* cōnsociō. **II.** Adj. : *held in common, shared* : di, Liv. ; consociatissima voluntas, Cic. Ep.

cŏn-sŏcĭō, āre. **I.** *to enter into partnership, hold or enjoy in common, share* : consociare mihi tecum licet, Pl. ; motūs, Lucr. ; imperium, Liv. ; Tac. ; cum amicis iniuriam, Cic. ; Liv. ; Tac. ; Patres rem inter se consociant, Liv. ; Cic. **II.** *to unite in making, make by uniting* : umbram consociare ramis, Hor.

cōnsōlābĭlis, e, adj. [cōnsolor], *that may be consoled* : dolor, Cic. Ep.

cōnsōlātĭō, ōnis, f. [cōnsolor]. **I.** *a strengthening, encouragement, soothing, consolation, comfort* : Cic. With *Subj.* Gen. : Cic. With *Obj.* Gen. : malorum, Cic. Ep. ; timoris, Cic. Ep. In *pl.* : Cic. **II.** *a consolatory discourse or treatise* : Cic., Quint.

cōnsōlātor, ōris, m. [cōnsolor], *one who consoles, a comforter* : Cic.

cōnsōlātōrĭus, a, um [cōnsolor], *of consolation* : litterae, Cic. Ep. ; Suet.

cōn-sōlor, ārī, *to strengthen fully*, hence, *to cheer up, encourage, reassure, soothe, console, comfort.* **a.** Of persons : aliquem, Ter., Caes. ; Ov. ; aliquem de miseriis communibus, Cic. ; aliquem in miseriis, Cic. With Acc. and *Inf.* : his me consolor victurum suavius, Hor. **b.** Of things, *to soothe, alleviate, relieve* : magnitudinem doloris, Cic. ; cladem, Liv.

cōn-somnĭō, āre, *to dream of* : Pl.

cōn-sŏnō, āre, uī. **I.** *to sound together.* **1.** Lit. : Varr. ; consonante clamore, Liv. **2.** Transf. : *to harmonise, agree* : with *cum*,

DAT., or *inter se* : Sen. Ep. **II.** *to sound loudly, resound, echo* : contra consonat terra, Pl. ; ululatibus theatrum, Tac. ; omne nemus strepitu, Verg.

cŏn-sŏnus, a, um, *sounding together.* **1.** Lit. : clangor, Ov. **2.** Transf. : *in keeping, suitable* : Cic. Ep.

cŏn-sŏpĭo, īre, *to put fast asleep* : somno consopiri sempiterno, Cic. ; Lucr.

cŏn-sors, ortis, adj. (or Noun), *of a common lot.* **A.** Act. : *having a common lot, partaking in common with.* **a.** consortes tres fratres, Cic. ; consors censoris, Liv. ; consortem sociam fallere, Hor. **b.** With esp. ref. to brothers and sisters : consors Phoebi, Ov. ; consortia pectora, Ov. **c.** With *Obj.* GEN. : consors mecum temporum illorum, Cic. ; laboris, Cic. ; culpae, Ov. ; thalami, Ov. ; filius consors tribuniciae potestatis adsumitur, Tac. With *in* : in lucris atque furtis, Cic. **B.** Pass. : *shared in common.* (Of bees), consortia tecta urbis habent, Verg. ; Prop.

cŏnsortĭo, ōnis, f. [cōnsors], *fellowship, community, partnership* : Cic., Liv.

cŏnsortĭum, ĭ, n. [cōnsors], *partnership* : Suet. With *Obj.* GEN. : Liv., Tac. In *pl.* (concr.) : Tac.

cŏnspectus, a, um. **I.** *Part.* cōnspĭcĭo. **II.** Adj. **a.** *in sight, visible* : tumulus conspectus hosti, Liv. **b.** *gazed at, striking, conspicuous* : Pallas chlamyde et pictis conspectus in armis, Verg. ; Liv., etc. Comp. . Liv., Ov., Tac.

cŏnspectus, ūs, m. [cōnspĭcĭo]. **A.** Act. : *a looking at, a look ; sight, view, the range of sight, power of seeing.* **1.** Lit. : conspectum alicuius perferre, Caes. ; fugere conspectum alicuius, Caes. Ov. ; e conspectu alicuius fugere, Ter. ; Cic. ; fugare aliquem e conspectu, Lucr. ; prodire ad aliquem in conspectum, Pl. ; sese dare in conspectum (alicui), Enn., Ter. ; castra in conspectum hostibus data, Liv. ; in conspectum alicuius venire, Cic. ; in conspectu ponere, Liv. ; in conspectu imperatoris, Caes. ; in conspectu, Verg. Of inanimate and abstract things : procul a conspectu imperi, Cic. **2.** Transf. : *the mental view, the mind's eye* : quae ponunt in conspectu animi, Cic. ; Liv. **B.** Pass. : *a being seen, appearance in the scene* : conspectu suo proelium restituit, Liv.

cŏn-spergo, spergere, spěrsī, spěrsum [sparg-]. **I.** *to besprinkle, bespatter all over.* **1.** Lit. : aras sanguine, Lucr. ; me lacrimis, Cic. ; Pl. **2.** Transf. : oratio conspersa quasi verborum sententiisque floribus, Cic. ; caput Tauri stellis, Cic. **II.** *to sprinkle* : Pl.

cŏnspĭcĭendus, a, um. **I.** *Gerund.* cōnspĭcĭō. **II.** *Adj.* : *worth gazing at* : opus, Liv. ; eques, Ov.

cŏnspĭcillum, ī, n. [cōnspĭcĭō], *a keeping (a person) in sight* : Pl.

cŏn-spĭcĭo, spicere, spexī, spectum, *to get a full sight of, catch sight of,* and *Pass.*, *to come* or *be in sight.* **1.** Lit. **a.** Pl. ; nostros equites, Caes. ; Cic. ; Verg. ; inter se conspecti, Liv. ; conspicitur, Hor. With *Part.* : aliquos ex navi egredientis, Caes. ; Liv. ; loca multitudine armatorum com-

pleta, Caes. ; Cic. ; Lucr. With Acc. and *Inf.* : Caes., Lucr. **b.** *to look at intently, look at with admiration* : Pl. ; Demetrium cum ingenti favore, Liv. ; bene notum te, Hor. Esp. in *Pass.* : *to attract attention* (in good or bad sense) : Cic., Liv., Ov., etc. **2.** Transf. Of the mind : aliquem mentibus, Cic. ; corde, Pl. With *Indir. Quest.* : Pl.

cŏnspĭcor, ārī [specĭō], *to get a full sight of, descry.* With Acc. : Pl., Caes., Liv., etc. With Acc. and *Part.* : Pl., Caes., Liv. With Acc. and *Inf.* : Pl., Ter. With *Indir. Quest.* : Caes.

cŏnspĭcŭus, a, um [cōnspĭcĭō]. **I.** *in sight, visible* : Hor., Ov., Tac. **II.** *looked at with admiration, remarkable, striking, distinguished* : Ov., Tac. With DAT. (of person) : Liv., Tac. With ABL. (of *Cause*) : Tib., Ov., Tac.

cŏnspīrātĭo, ōnis, f. [cōnspīrō], *a blowing or breathing together.* Transf. : *concord, unison* (of feeling or opinion). **a.** Good sense : bonorum omnium, Cic. **b.** Bad sense : *a plotting, plot, conspiracy* : Cic., Tac.

cŏnspīrātus, a, um. **I.** *Part. Mid.* cōnspīrō : *having agreed* or *conspired ; all together* : Caes., Phaedr. **II.** Noun, **cŏnspīrāti**, ōrum, m. *pl.* conspirators : Suet.

cŏn-spīro, āre, *to breathe* or *blow together, sound together.* **1.** Lit. : aereaque adsensu conspirant cornua rauco, Verg. **2.** Transf. : *to act in unison, to agree.* **a.** Good sense : omnium generum ordinumque consensus ad liberandam rem publicam conspiravit, Cic. **b.** Bad sense : *to plot together, conspire* : priusquam plures civitates conspirarent, Caes. With *in* : in iniuriam, Liv. ; Tac. ; in Augustum, Suet. With *ad* : ad res novas, Suet. With *ut* or *ne* and *Subj.* : Liv., Suet. With *Inf.* : Suet. *Impers. Pass.* : Suet.

cŏn-spōnsor, ōris, m. *a joint surety* : Cic. Ep.

cŏn-spŭo, uere, *to cover with spit.* **1.** Lit. : Pl., Petr., Juv. **2.** Transf. : canā nive Alpis, Hor. (parodying a line of Bibaculus.)

cŏn-spurco, āre, *to defile all over, pollute* : Lucr., Suet.

cŏn-spūto, āre [*freq.* cōnspŭo], *to spit upon in contempt* : Cic. Ep.

cŏn-stabĭlĭo, īre, *to confirm, establish securely* : rem meam, Pl. ; Ter.

cŏnstāns, antis. **I.** *Part.* cōnstō. **II.** *standing firm, fixed, steady.* **1.** Lit. : gradus, Liv., Hor. **2.** Transf. **a.** *steady, firm, set* : aetas, Cic. ; pax, vultus, Liv. **b.** *stable, steady, invariable* (of things) : cursus, Cic. ; motus (mundi), Cic. ; fides, Hor. **c.** *of firm character, stable, steadfast* (of persons) : Cic., Ov., etc. With GEN. : fidei, Tac. **d.** *agreeing with itself, consistent* : rumores, Cic. Ep. ; memoria huius anni, Liv. Comp. : Cic., Lucr., Hor., etc. *Sup.* : Cic.

cŏnstanter, adv. *firmly, steadily.* **1.** Lit. : Cic. **2.** Transf. **a.** *firmly, steadily* : constanter ac non trepide pugnare, Caes. **b.** *with stability, invariably* (of things) : Cic., Sall. **c.** *with firmness of character, with unruffled calm, sedately* (of persons) : Cic. **d.** *consistently, uniformly* (of actions or words): Caes., Cic., Hor., etc. *Comp.:* Cic., Tac. *Sup.:* Cic., Suet.

cōnstantia, ae, *f.* [cōnstāns]. Lit.: *a standing firmly.* Transf. **a.** *steadfastness, firmness, steadiness, persistence :* vocis atque vultūs, Nep.; oppugnandi, Auct. B. Alex. **b.** *stability, unchangeableness :* (stellarum) perennes cursūs cum admirabili constantiā, Cic. **c.** *firmness of character, stability, steadfastness, constancy, selfpossession :* Caes., Cic., Ov., etc. In *pl.: different kinds of constancy :* Cic. **d.** *consistency, uniformity* (of actions or words): inter augures, Cic.; constantiae causā, Cic.

cōnsternātiō, ōnis, *f.* [cōnsternō], *a shying, stampede.* **1.** Lit.: quadrigarum, Liv. **2.** Transf. **a.** *stampede, dismay, alarm :* mentis, Tac.; Liv. **b.** *a wild rush, tumult :* muliebris, Liv.; Curt.; Tac.

(1) cōnsternō, āre, *to startle, make to shy, stampede.* **1.** Lit.: equos, Sall.; Ov., Liv. **2.** Transf. **a.** *to stampede, terrify, alarm :* pecorum in modum consternatos caedunt fugantque, Caes.; sunt animo consternati, Caes. **b.** *to alarm* (and drive to some excited action): Ov.; metu servitutis ad arma consternati, Liv.; in fugam, Liv.

(2) cōn-sternō, sternere, strāvi, strātum, *to strew all over, spread out, cover over.* With Acc. of the thing covered and *Instr.* ABL. **1.** Lit. **a.** Of the ground : viam lauro, Tac.; Cic.; Verg., etc. **b.** Of a couch, etc.: Cat. **c.** Of a roof, *to thatch :* Caes. **d.** Of a floor : Caes. **e.** Of a ship : constrata navis, *a decked ship,* Caes., Cic. **2.** Transf.: forum corporibus civium, Cic.; maria navibus, Liv.; Sall.; Hirt.

cōn-stīpō, āre, *to press* or *crowd closely together :* Caes., Cic.

cōn-stituō, uere, uī, ūtum [statuō], *to make to stand, to set up, erect, to set, plant, establish firmly.* **A.** Of objects already existing. **1.** Lit. **a.** hominem ante pedes Q. Manili constituunt, Cic.; vobis ego taurum ante aras constituam, Verg.; impedimenta, Liv. **b.** Milit. *to station* or *post :* legionem passibus CC ab eo tumulo constituit, Caes.; Liv.; navis ad latus apertum hostium, Caes. Rarely *to bring to a halt :* agmen, Sall., Liv. **c.** *to settle, establish* (of people in a home, etc.): Helvetios, Caes.; plebem in agris publicis, Cic.; hiberna in Belgis, Caes. **2.** Transf. **a.** Of persons in authority, etc., *to set up, establish :* curatores legibus agrariis, Cic.; patronum huic causae, Cic.; Commium regem, Caes. **b.** Of a date, price, penalty, etc., *to settle, determine :* diem concilio, Caes.; Pl.; in diem tertium aliquid, Sall.; Ter.; Liv.; praemia, Caes.; poenam, Caes.; Cic.; pretium frumento, Cic.; aetatem ad consulatum, Cic. With *Indir. Quest. :* Cic., Nep. With *de :* Caes. **c.** Of a course of action, *to settle, determine, resolve.* With Acc. and *Inf. :* Cic. Ep. With *Inf. :* Lucr., Caes., Nep. With *ut* and *Subj. :* Pl., Cic., Sall. **d.** *settle, set in order, arrange, regulate, organise :* rem publicam, rem familiarem, Cic.; has res, Caes.; res divinā providentiā constitutas, Cic.; Nep. **B.** Of an object made by the action. **1.** Lit.: *to set up, erect, construct, etc. :* Lucr.; op-

pidum, turris, Caes.; nova moenia, Verg.; sepulcrum, Ov. **2.** Transf.: concordiam, libertatem, legem, etc., Cic.

cōnstitūtiō, ōnis, *f.* [cōnstituō]. **I.** *a setting in order, regulating, settlement :* religionum, Cic. **II.** *settled condition :* corporis, Cic. **III.** *a regulation, order, ordinance :* senatūs, Liv. **IV.** Rhet.: *the discussion :* Cic.

cōnstitūtus, a, um. **I.** *Part.* cōnstituō. **II.** Adj. **a.** *ordered, disposed :* bene constitutum corpus, Cic. Of character : Cic. **b.** *fixed, established :* cursus siderum, Quint. **III.** *Neut.* as Noun. **a.** *a fixed order :* Sen. **b.** *an arrangement, agreement :* cum aliquo habere, Cic. Ep.; facere, Cic.; ad constitutum venire, Cic.

cōn-stō, stāre, stitī, stātum. **I.** *to stand with* or *together.* **1.** Lit.: Pl. **2.** Transf. **a.** *to stand together, be put together, be composed of, consist of* (with *ex* and ABL. alone): homo ex animo constat et corpore, Cic.; Lucr.; Hor.; constat materies solido corpore, Lucr.; Quint.; Plin. Ep. With *in* and ABL. *to depend on :* Caes. **b.** *to stand together, agree, tally, correspond :* constetne oratio aut cum re aut ipsa secum, Cic.; sibi constare, Cic., Hor.; constat idem omnibus sermo, Liv. **c.** Commerc.: *to tally, correspond, agree,* esp. in phr. ratio constat, *the account tallies, is correct :* Cic., Tac. Hence, with ABL. (of price), *to cost :* Pl.; quanto detrimento necesse sit constare victoriam, Caes.; Cic.; Ov. [Fr. *coûter.*] **II.** *to stand firm, stand still.* **1.** Lit.: prius quam constaret hostium acies, Liv. **2.** Transf. **a.** *to stand firm, remain unchanged, be constant :* mente, Cic.; in sententiā, Cic.; animo sententia, Verg.; uti numerus legionum constare videretur, Caes.; non color, non vultus ei constabat Liv.; Verg.; Ov. **b.** *to have existence* or *be in existence :* si ipsa mens constare potest vacans corpore, Cic.; Lucr.; Juv. **c.** Of facts, reports, etc.: *to be established, settled, undisputed, well-known :* quae cum constent, perspicuum debet esse, Cic. Esp. *impers. : it is well known, is agreed on as a fact, is established :* us. with Acc. and *Inf.:* omnibus constabat, hiemari in Galliā oportere, Caes.; cum inter augures constet imparem numerum debere esse, Liv.; cum de Magio constet, Cic. Ep. With *Indir. Quest. :* Cic. Ep., Liv. Hence, with DAT. *pers.* = certum est, *one is determined, resolved :* with *Indir. Deliberative :* neque satis Bruto neque tribunis militum constabat, quid agerent, Caes.

cōnstrātus, a, um. **I.** *Part.* cōnsternō, 2. **II.** *Neut.* as Noun : *a flooring :* pontium, Liv.

cōn-stringō, stringere, strīnxī, strīctum. **1.** Lit. **a.** *to draw* or *bind together :* sarcinam, Pl.; Cato. **b.** *to draw* or *bind tightly :* Pl., Cic., Hor. **2.** Transf.: *to bind tight, to keep in restraint.* **a.** fidem religione potius quam veritate, Cic.; orbem terrarum novis legibus, Cic.; Liv.; Tac. **b.** In rhet. and logic : *to compress :* (sententia) aptis constricta verbis est, Cic.; Quint. **c.** *to condense :* nives perpetuo rigore constrictae, Curt.

constructiŏ, ōnis, *f.* [cōnstruŏ], *a heaping up together,* hence, **I.** *an erecting, building :* hominis, Cic. **II.** R h e t. : *arrangement, fit connexion :* verborum, Cic. ; Plin. Ep.

cŏn-struŏ, struere, struxī, structum. **I.** *to heap up together, pile up :* Cic., Hor., Ov. **II.** *to make by heaping things together, build :* navem, aedificium, Cic. ; Verg. ; Liv. ; nidum, Cic., Ov.

cōnstuprātor, ōris, *m.* [cōnstuprŏ], *a debaucher :* Liv.

cŏn-stuprŏ, āre, *to debauch utterly.* **1.** L i t. : matronas, virgines, Liv., etc. **2.** T r a n s f. : iudicium, Cic. Ep.

cŏn-suādeŏ, ēre, *to advise strongly.* With DAT. of person and ACC. of thing advised : Pl.

cōnsuāsor, ōris, *m.* [cōnsuādeŏ], *one who advises strongly :* Cic.

cŏn-sūcidus, a, um, *quite juicy :* Pl.

cŏn-sūdŏ, āre, *to sweat profusely :* Pl., Cato.

cōnsuē-faciŏ, facere, fēcī, factum [cōnsuēscŏ], *to accustom, inure, habituate.* With *Inf.* : Gaetulos consuefacit ordines habere, Sall. ; Ter. With *ut* or *ne* and *Subj.* : Ter., Varr.

cŏn-suēscŏ, suēscere, suēvī, suētum (the *Perf.* forms are us. sync., e.g. cōnsuēstī, cōnsuēram, etc.). **A.** Intrans. **a.** In gen. *to accustom oneself, to become accustomed :* esp. in *Perf. tenses* : *to be accustomed.* With *Inf.* : Caes., Cic., Hor. Rarely *impers.* : sicuti in sollemnibus sacris fieri consuevit, Sall. *Absol.* : Cato, Cic., Verg. **b.** With *cum :* *to cohabit with :* Ter., Cic. **B.** Trans. (rare) *to accustom, inure, habituate :* tum bracchia consuescunt firmantque lacertos, Lucr. In *Perf. Part.* : Pl., Lucr., Liv. With *Inf.* : Lucr. (*v.* also consuētus).

cōnsuētiŏ, ōnis, *f.* [cōnsuēscŏ], *carnal intercourse :* Pl.

cōnsuētūdŏ, inis, *f.* [cōnsuēscŏ], *custom, habit.* **a.** In gen. : Pl., Cic., Hor., etc. ; in eam se consuetudinem adduxerant, *they had formed the habit* (with *ut*), Caes. ; est autem hoc Gallicae consuetudinis, Caes. ; loquendi, vivendi, Cic. ; ad consuetudinem Graecorum, Cic. ; ex consuetudine, pro consuetudine, and *Absol.* consuetudine, *according to custom, from habit,* etc. : ex consuetudine suā phalange factā, Caes. ; pro meā consuetudine, *according to my custom,* Cic. ; consuetudine suā, Caes. ; ut fert consuetudo, *as the manner is, as is usual :* Cic. ; maiorem pulverem quam consuetudo ferret, Caes. **b.** *a usage* or *idiom of language* (for consuetudo loquendi) : Cic., Varr. **c.** *social intercourse, intimacy :* cum Scipionibus erat ei domesticus usus et consuetudo, Cic. ; dare or immergere se in consuetudinem (alicuius), Cic. ; epistularum, Cic. Ep. In *pl.* : Cic. **d.** *intercourse in love* (in an honourable sense, but more freq. in a dishonourable sense), *an amour, illicit intercourse :* Ter., Sall., Liv., etc. [Fr. *coûtume.*]

cōnsuētus, a, um. **I.** *Part.* cōnsuēscŏ. **II.** A d j. *usual, customary :* Ter., Sall., Verg., etc. *Sup.* : Ov.

cōnsul, ulis, *m.* (in old inscr. **cōnsol**, once **cōsol** : often abbreviated, *sing.* cos., *pl.* coss.) [con, sed- seen in sedeŏ], *a consul ;* one of the two highest magistrates of the Roman republic : consul ordinarius, *who entered office on the first of January,* Liv. (opp. suffectus, *one chosen in the course of the year in the room of another,* Liv.) ; consul designatus, *consul elect* (so called in the interval betw. election and entrance on office), Cic. ; consul maior, *the consul who had the larger number of votes ;* or *the senior consul,* Gell. ; consulem dicere, creare, facere, etc., *to elect,* Cic., etc. ; declarare, Cic., Liv. ; renuntiare, sufficere, Cic. P h r. : *to date the year :* M. Messalā et M. Pisone Coss. coniurationem fecit, *in the consulship of* (i.e. A.U. 693), Caes. ; motum ex Metello consule civicum, Hor. ; pro consule (as NOM. or other cases), *acting in the place of a consul :* Caes., Cic., Liv. ; cos. primum, iterum, tertium, etc., *consul for the first, second, third time,* etc., Cic., Liv.

cōnsulāris, e. *adj.* [cōnsul]. **I.** *of a consul, consular :* aetas, *the age required by law for the consular office* (viz., the 43rd year), Cic. ; comitia, *for the choice of consul,* Cic. ; exercitus, Liv. ; lictor, Hor. ; res, *worthy of a consul,* Liv. **II.** *having held the office of consul :* vir, homo, Cic. As Noun, **cōnsulāris**, is, *m.* *one who has been consul, ex-consul :* Sall., Cic. Esp. under the empire, *a man of consular rank sent by the emperor into a province as governor :* Tac.

cōnsulāriter, *adv. like a consul, in a manner worthy of a consul :* Liv.

cōnsulātus, ūs, *m.* [cōnsul], *the office of consul, the consulship :* consulatu peracto, Caes. ; consulatum petere, adipisci, obtinere, Cic. ; gerere, Cic., Liv. ; inire, ingredi, accipere, Suet. ; consulatu fungi, Suet. ; se consulatu abdicare, Cic. ; consulatum abdicare, Liv. In *pl.* : Liv., Tac.

cōnsulŏ, sulere, suluī, sultum, [con and *sed* seen in sedeŏ]. **I.** *to deliberate, take counsel ; to consider, reflect :* **1.** L i t. **a.** In gen. : Pl., Cic., etc. ; in commune, *for the common good,* Ter., Liv., Tac. ; in medium, Verg. ; ad summam rerum consulere, Caes. With *de :* *de salute suorum,* Cic. ; *Impers. Pass.* : consultum est de Rhodiis, Sall. With ACC. : rem delatam, Liv. With *Indir. Deliberat.* : quid agant consulunt, Caes. **b.** With DAT. of person or object considered : *to consult the interests of :* Pl. ; sibi consulere, Caes., etc. ; saluti, Caes., Cic. ; timori magis quam religioni, Caes. ; Hor. **2.** T r a n s f. **a.** *to come to a decision ; to decide on a certain course :* also, *to take measures accordingly :* aliquid male consulere, Sall. ; Pl. ; Cic. ; ex re consulere (*according to the necessities of the case*), Tac. Esp. *of passing sentence on* or *inflicting punishment :* with *de* or *in* and ACC. : de perfugis gravius quam de fugitivis consultum, Liv. ; crudeliter in victos consulere, Liv. **b.** With boni, optimi, and ACC. : *to take in good part, interpret favourably :* tu haec quaeso consule boni, Ov. ; Cato ; Quint., etc. **c.** *to advise (something) :* with ACC. of *Neut. Pron.* : tun' consulis quicquam ? Ter. ; Pl. **II.** *to consult, ask advice of.* **a.** In gen. with ACC. of the person or thing (personified) that is consulted : si me consulis, suadeo, Cic. ; speculum

suum, Ov. **i.** With *de* and ABL. of the thing
asked about : de parvis rebus consulimur,
Cic. ; Ov. **ii.** With ACC. of *Neut. Pron.*,
or *Indir. Quest.* : nec te id consulo, Cic. Ep. ;
Pl. ; cum te consuluissem quid censeres,
Cic. Ep. With rem : rem nullam obscuram
(nos) consulis, Verg. **iii.** *Absol.* (esp. in
Supine) : nuntios misit consultum, Nep.
b. In religion, etc. : Apollinem de re, Cic. ;
aliquem de sortibus, Caes. ; vates nunc
extis, nunc per avis consulti, Liv. ; exta,
Verg., Ov. With *Indir. Quest.* : Liv.,
Tac. **c.** In law : (te) de iure, Cic. With
ACC. of thing : si ius consuleros, Liv. **d.**
In politics : populum de eius morte, Cic. ;
Liv. With *Indir. Quest.* : Cic., Liv.
cōnsultātiō, ōnis, *f.* [cōnsultō]. **1.** Lit.
a. *a mature deliberation, consideration* :
Ter., Cic. With *ne* and *Subj.* : Liv. With
Indir. Quest. : Liv. **b.** *an asking of advice, consultation* : Cic. Ep. **2.** Transf. :
a theme or *matter for discussion* (esp. in law) :
Cic.
cōnsultō, *adv. deliberately, after due consideration* : Pl., Liv. Comp. : Liv., Tac.
cōnsultō, āre [*freq.* cōnsulō]. **I.** *to reflect,
consider maturely ; to take counsel, deliberate.*
a. In gen. : Pl., Sall., Liv. With *de* :
Caes., Cic., Liv. With *super* and ABL. :
Tac. With *Indir. Quest.* : Cic., Liv. With
ACC. of the thing considered : quid con-
sultant ? Pl. ; eam rem, Liv. **b.** With
DAT. *to consult the interests of* : rei publicae,
Sall. **II.** *to consult, ask advice of* : quid me
consultas quid agas ? Pl. ; Liv. ; Tib. ;
avis, Plin. Ep.
cōnsultor, ōris, *m.* [cōnsulō]. **I.** *a counsellor, adviser* : Sall., Tac. **II.** *he who asks
advice of one, a consulter, client* : Cic., Hor.
cōnsultrix, īcis, *f.* [cōnsulō], *she who has a
care for* : natura, Cic.
cōnsultus, a, um. **I.** *Part.* cōnsulō.
II. Adj. *skilled, experienced.* With GEN. :
iuris, Cic., Liv. ; eloquentiae, Liv. ; sapientiae, Hor. Sup. : Cic., Liv. **III.** As
Noun. **a.** iuris consultus, *a lawyer, a
consulting barrister* : Cic. Without iuris :
Hor. **b.** *Neut.* **i.** In phr. consulto opus est,
there is need of deliberation, Sall. **ii.** *a
decree, decision, resolution* : Cic., Verg., etc.
Esp. senatūs consultum or in one word
senatūsconsultum (abbrev. s.c.), Cic., etc. ;
cf. consulta Patrum, Hor. **iii.** *a consultation, inquiring of a deity* : Tac. **IV.** ABL.
cōnsultō as Adv., *deliberately, on purpose* :
Pl., Cic., Hor., etc.
[cōn-sum], futūrum, fore, only in *Fut.*
forms, *to be, to happen* : confido confu-
turum, Pl. ; spero confore, Ter.
cōnsummātus, a, um. **I.** *Part.* cōnsummō.
II. Adj. *perfect, consummate* : Sen. Ep.,
Quint. Sup. : Plin. Ep.
cōnsummō, āre [summa]. **I.** *to cast* or
sum up, Transf. : velut consummata
eius belli gloria, Liv. ; Ov. **II.** *to bring
to completeness* or *perfection* : Liv., Curt.,
Quint.
cōn-sūmō, sūmere, sūmpsī, sūmptum, *to
take up entirely.* **I.** *to use up, exhaust, consume.* **1.** Lit. **a.** In gen. : consumptis
telis gladiis impetum faciunt, Caes. ; lacrimas, Cic. **b.** Of food, *to consume, devour* :

Caes., Cic., Verg., etc. **c.** Of money, etc.,
to exhaust, squander : Caes., Cic., Ov., etc.
2. Transf. **a.** Of persons, *to exhaust,
wear out, destroy* : si me vis aliqua morbi
consumpsisset, Cic. ; exercitum fame paene
consumptum, Caes. ; Liv. ; Ov. **b.** Of
things : flammam concipiunt haec et con-
sumuntur, Caes. ; nihil est quod non con-
sumat vetustas, Cic. ; vocem metus con-
sumit, Tac. **II.** *to use up completely,
employ, spend, devote* to some object. **a.**
Of money, labour, etc. : pecuniam in agrorum emptionibus, Cic. ; operam in agris
colendis, Cic. ; Hor. ; Liv. With *in* and
ACC. ; tota ubera in natos, Verg. ; Quint.
b. Of time, *to use up, spend* : Lucr., Caes.,
Cic. ; dicendo tempus, Cic. ; Ov. ; tota
nox in exinaniendā nave consumitur, Cic. ;
Caes. ; multos dies per dubitationem, Sall.
cōnsūmptiō, ōnis, *f.* [cōnsūmō], *a consuming,
wasting* : Cic.
cōnsūmptor, ōris, *m.* [cōnsūmō], *a consumer,
destroyer* : ignis consumptor omnium, Cic.
cōnsūmptus, a, um, *Part.* cōnsūmō.
cōn-suō, suere, suī, sūtum, *to stitch together,
to sew up.* **1.** Lit. : tunicam, Varr. **2.**
Transf. : consutis solis, Pl. ; os, Sen. Ep.
[It. *cucire* / Fr. *coudre*.]
cōn-surgō, surgere, surrēxī, surrēctum, *to
rise up together* or *in a body, to stand up.* **1.**
Lit. **a.** Of persons : consurgunt triarii,
Caes., Liv. ; ex insidiis, Caes. ; senatus, Cic.
Ep. ; consurgitur ex consilio, Caes. ; toro
consurgere, Ov. Esp. out of respect : Cic.
Impers. Pass. : honorifice consurgitur.
Occ. of one person : Liv., Ov. **b.** Of
things : de terrā ignis corpora, Lucr. ;
quercus, Verg. ; mare imo fundo ad aethera,
Verg. ; villa, Plin. Ep. **2.** Transf. **a.** Of
persons, *to rise up* or *be roused* for some
object (with *ad* or *in* and ACC.) : ad
bellum, ad gloriam, Liv. ; ad iterandum
ictum, Liv. ; in arma, Verg. ; Ov. **b.** Of
things, *to arise, be raised* : venti, remi,
bellum, Verg. ; ira, Quint.
cōnsurrēctiō, ōnis, *f.* [cōnsūrgō], *a general
rising* or *standing up* : Cic.
cōn-susurrō, āre, *to whisper together* : Ter.
cōnsūtus, a, um, *Part.* cōnsuō.
con-tābēfaciō, ere, *to waste, to wear out completely* : Pl.
con-tābēscō, tābēscere, tābuī, *to waste away
gradually* : Pl., Cic.
contābulātiō, ōnis, *f.* [contabulō], *a joining of
boards together, a flooring, a floor* or *storey* :
Caes.
contabulō, āre [con tabula], *to board over, to
build with floors* or *stories* : turris, Caes.,
Liv. ; totum murum turribus, Caes. ; mare
molibus, Curt.
contāctus, a, um, *Part.* contingō.
contāctus, ūs, *m.* [contingō], *a touching,
touch, contact.* **1.** Lit. **a.** contactu omnia
foedant, Verg. ; Liv. In *pl.* : viriles, Ov.
b. With ref. to disease : *contagion* : vul-
gati contactu morbi, Liv. **2.** Transf. :
contagion, infection (in gen.) : Sall., Tac. [It.
contatto.]
contāgēs, is, *f.* [contingō], *contact, touch* :
Lucr.
contāgiō, ōnis, *f.* [contingō], *a touching ; contact, touch.* **1.** Lit. **a.** Cato ; corporis,

Cic. **b.** With ref. to disease : *contagion, infection :* Liv. **2.** Transf. **a,** *contact, intercourse :* contagione Romanorum abstinere, Liv. **b.** Of moral contamination, *contagion, infection, bad example :* sceleris, Cic. ; criminis, mali, Liv. ; traxerat contagio proximos populos, Liv. In *pl. :* Cic.

contāgĭum, ĭ, *n.* [contingō]. **1.** L i t. **a.** *touch, contact :* Lucr. **b.** *contagion :* morbi Lucr. ; Curt. ; in *pl. :* vicini pecoris contagia, Verg. ; Ov. **2.** T r a n s f. Of moral contamination : aegrae mentis, Ov. ; lucri, Hor.

contāmĭnātus, a, um. **I.** *Part.* contāminō. **II.** A d j. : *polluted, impure, defiled :* Liv., Hor. *Sup. :* Cic. **III.** *Masc.* as *Noun :* Tac.

contāmĭnō, āre [for contagminō, fr. *tag* root of tangō]. **I.** *to bring into contact ; to mingle, blend :* multas Graecas fabulas, Ter. **II.** More freq., *to defile, stain, pollute.* **1.** L i t. : spiritum, Cic. **2.** T r a n s f. : gaudium aegritudine, Ter. ; sese maleficio, Cic. ; Liv., etc. ; mentem scelere, Liv. ; veritatem mendacio, Cic.

con-technor, ārī [techna], *to devise plots :* Pl.

contēctus, a, um, *Part.* contegō.

con-tĕgo, tegere, tēxī, tēctum, *to cover up* or *over.* **1.** L i t. : coria centonibus, Caes. ; Cic. ; Verg., etc. **2.** T r a n s f. : *to cover up,* hence, **a.** *to protect,* quidam servili habitu contecti, Tac. **b.** *to hide, conceal :* eas partis corporis contexit, Cic. ; Caes. T r a n s f. : libidines, Cic. ; Ter. ; Tac.

con-tĕmĕro, āre, *to pollute :* Ov.

con-temnō, temnere, tēmpsī, temptum, *to hold cheaply, to slight, belittle, depreciate, disparage.* **a.** Of things : Romam prae suā Capuā, Cic. ; dolorem, voluptatem, Cic. ; Ter. ; Hor., etc. With *Inf.* as *Obj. :* Hor. **b.** Of persons : Pl., Caes., Cic., etc. Of things personified : Lucr., Verg. **c.** *Absol. :* Cic., Nep.

contemplātĭo, ōnis, *f.* [contemplor], *a viewing, surveying.* **1.** L i t. : caeli, Cic. **2.** T r a n s f. (mental) : with *Obj.* G E N. : Cic., Curt., Tac. *Absol. :* Cic., Plin. Ep.

contemplātor, ōris, *m.* [contemplor], *a contemplator, an observer :* caeli ac Deorum, Cic.

contemplātū, A B L. sing. *m.* [contemplor], *by a survey :* Ov.

contemplātus, a, um, *Part.* contemplor.

contemplō = contemplor : Pl.

contemplor, ārī [templum]. **1.** L i t. *to mark out an augural* templum : Varr. Hence, *to look at attentively, survey, gaze upon :* Pl., Verg., etc. With A c c. : Pl., Cic., Hor., etc. **2.** T r a n s f. Of the mind : *to observe, survey :* Cic. With A c c. : Cic.

contemptim, *adv.* [contemnō], *slightingly :* Pl., Lucr., Liv., etc.

contemptĭo, ōnis, *f.* [contemnō], *a slighting, belittling, despising :* Cic., Liv. P h r. : hostibus in contemptionem venire, *to become despised by the enemy,* Caes.

contemptĭus, *adv. comp., more slightingly :* Sen., Suet.

contemptor, ōris, *m.* and **contemptrix,** īcis, *f.* (Pl.) [contemnō], *a slighter :* Verg.,

Liv., etc. As *Adj.* T r a n s f. : lucis animus, Verg. ; Sall.

contemptus, a, um. **I.** *Part.* contemnō. **II.** *Adj. of little value, despicable, contemptible :* vita, Cic. ; res, Hor. With D A T. : Trebellius contemptus exercitui, Tac. *Comp. :* Cic. ; *Sup. :* Cic., Quint.

contemptus, ūs, *m.* [contemnō]. **A.** A c t. : *a slighting, belittling, despising :* Liv., Tac. In *pl. :* Liv. **B.** P a s s : *a being slighted* or *scorned :* Lucr., Liv., Ov. P h r. : contemptui esse, *to be an object of scorn :* Caes., Suet.

con-tendō, tendere, tendī, tentum. **I.** *to strain together.* **A.** I n t r a n s. : *to match oneself, compete :* cum Sequanis bello, Caes. ; Cic. Ep. ; Hor. ; contra populum armis, Caes. ; Cic. ; Cat. ; de potentatu inter se, Caes. ; Lucr. With D A T. : Lucr., Prop. *Absol. :* Caes., Nep. *Pass. Impers. :* Caes., Cic. **B.** T r a n s. : *to compare, contrast :* id cum defensione nostrā, Cic. ; vellera Sidonio ostro, Hor. ; ipsas causas, Cic. ; Tac. **II.** *to strain tightly.* **A.** I n t r a n s. : *to make a strong effort, exert oneself.* **1.** L i t. : labore, Cic. With *ut* and *Subj.* : Caes., Cic. With *Inf.* (esp. of travelling or marching) : Caes., Cic., Verg. Without *Inf.,* *to hurry :* in Italiam magnis itineribus, Caes. ; domum, Caes. ; ad occupandum Vesontionem, Caes. **2.** T r a n s f. **a,** *to strive for :* ad summam gloriam, Cic. ; Caes. **b.** *to strive to effect* by entreaty, influence, etc. With *ut* or *ne* and *Subj. :* Caes., Cic. With *Neut. Pron.* and *ut* clause : Caes. **c.** *to strive* in argument, etc., *to maintain firmly.* With A c c. and *Inf. :* Cic., Lucr., Ov., etc. With *Neut. Pron.,* and A c c. and *Inf. :* Cic., Liv. **B.** T r a n s. : *to strain* or *draw tight, stretch out fully.* **1.** L i t. : Lucil. ; arcum, vincla, Verg. ; navem funibus, Caes. ; tormenta, Cic. ; pontem, Enn. ; oculi contendunt se, Lucr. Hence, telum in auras, Verg. **2.** T r a n s f. : corpora, Cic. ; nervos, Lucr., Cic. ; cervicem, Verg.

(1) contentē, *adv.* [contendō], *with great exertion, earnestly :* Cic. *Comp. :* Cic.

(2) contentē, *adv.* [contineō], *closely, sparingly, scantily :* Pl.

contentĭo, ōnis, *f.* [contendō]. **I. a.** *a competing, struggle, dispute,* etc. : proeliorum contentiones, Cic. ; cum aliquo habere, Caes. ; facere, Cic. ; deponere, Liv. ; inter aliquos de aliquā re, Cic. **b.** *a comparing, contrasting :* Cic. R h e t. antithesis : Cic. **II.** *a straining, exertion, effort ; a straining to obtain.* **1.** L i t. : remittere, Caes. ; vocis, Cic. **2.** T r a n s f. : Cic., Liv. ; honorum, Cic. ; libertatis, Liv.

(1) contentus, a, um. **I.** *Part.* contendō. **II.** *Adj.* **1.** L i t. : *strained, tense, tight :* Lucr., Cic., Verg. **2.** T r a n s f. : *eager, intent :* ad tribunatum contento studio veniamus, Cic. ; Lucr.

(2) contentus, a, um. **I.** *Part.* contineō. **II.** *Adj. contented, satisfied :* Pl., Cic. With *Instr.* A B L. : Lucil., Cic., Verg., etc. With *Inf. :* Ov., Quint. *Comp. :* Pl.

con-terminus, a, um, *bordering upon, neighbouring.* With D A T. : Ov. *Neut. pl.* as *Noun :* Tac.

con-terŏ, terere. trīvī, trītum, *to grind to powder, destroy by friction, pulverise, crumble.* **1.** Lit.: Lucr., Varr., Ov. **2.** Transf.: *to wear away, wear out, use up.* **a.** In gen.: operam, Pl.; Ter.; me tuā oratione, Pl.; se in negotiis, Cic.; contritum praemium, Cic. **b.** Of time, *to use up, consume, waste* : aetatem in litibus, Cic.; Pl.; Prop. With ABL.: diei brevitatem conviviis, Cic.; Ter.; Lucr., etc.

con-terreŏ, ēre, *to frighten, scare completely* : Lucr., Verg., Liv. Transf.: loquacitatem nostram vultu ipso, Cic.

con-testor, ārī, *to call to join as witness* : deos, Caes.; deos hominesque, Cic. In law: litem, *to enter on a lawsuit by calling witnesses*, Cic. *Perf. Part.* in *Pass.* sense: contestatā lite, Cic. Transf.: ab hac contestatā virtute maiorum, *accredited, proved*, Cic.

con-texŏ, texere, texui, textum, *to entwine, weave together, interweave.* **1.** Lit.: contexta viminibus membra, Caes.; Cic.; Tib. **2.** Transf. **a.** Of woodwork, *to brace together* : Caes. Hence, *to construct by bracing together* : Verg., Tac. **b.** Of writings, etc., *to weave or join together* : Cic., Hirt., Quint. Hence, *to construct by so joining* : crimen, Cic.

contextē, *adv. in a connected manner, in close connexion* : Cic.

contextus, a, um. **I.** *Part.* contexŏ. **II.** *Adj.* : *cohering, connected* : contexta condensaque corpora, Lucr.; Quint.

contextus, ūs, *m.* [contexŏ], *a weaving or bracing together, connexion.* **1.** Lit.: corporum (i.e. atomorum), Lucr. **2.** Transf. *connexion, coherence* : rerum, Cic.; operis, Tac.; dicendi, Quint.

conticēscŏ (conticiscŏ, Pl.), ticēscere, ticuī [taceŏ]. **I.** *to become quite still, silent, hushed.* **1.** Lit. **a.** Of many together : Verg. **b.** Of one: Pl., Cic., Hor. **2.** Transf.: artes nostrae, Cic.; tumultus, Liv.; undae, Ov. **II.** *to keep silence* : Liv.

conticinnŏ, *adv.* [conticēscŏ], *in the evening* : Pl.

conticiscŏ, *v.* conticēscŏ.

contignātiŏ, ōnis, *f.* [contignŏ], *a joining of beams or boards, a storey, floor* : Caes. Concr.: Liv.

contignŏ, āre [tignum], *to join together with beams, to floor* : Caes.

contiguus, a, um [contingŏ]. **A.** Act.: *touching together, adjoining, bordering upon, neighbouring, near* : Ov., Tac. With DAT.: Ov. **B.** Pass.: *that may be touched, within reach* : hunc contiguum hastae, Verg.

continēns, entis. **I.** *Part.* continēŏ. **II.** *Adj.* : Lit. *holding together.* **A.** *bordering upon, contiguous, adjacent* : aer mari, Cic.; Caes.; Cappadociae pars ea, quae cum Ciliciā continens est, Cic. Ep.; tecta continentia, Liv. Transf.: diebus, i.e. *successive*, Caes.; Cic.; Liv. **B.** *holding together, unbroken, uninterrupted.* **1.** Lit.: continentis silvas ac paludes habebant, Caes.; cursus, Caes.; uno continenti agmine, Liv. Esp. continens terra, *the main land, continent*, Nep.: us. *Absol.* (without terra): Caes., Liv. **2.**

Transf.: labor, bellum, Caes.; e continenti genere, Cic.; imber, memoria, Liv. **C.** *holding oneself in, self-controlled* : in vitā, Caes.; in pecuniā, Caes.; Cic. Ep.; Nep. *Comp.* : Caes.; *Sup.* : Cic., Suet. **III.** Rhet. as Noun, **continēns**, entis, *n. the chief point, hinge* : causae, Cic., Quint.

continenter, *adv.* **I.** *in unbroken succession.* **1.** Lit.: sedetis (i.e. *close together*), Cat. **2.** Trans. Of time: *without interruption* : continenter totā nocte ierunt, Caes.; Liv. **II.** *temperately, moderately* : vivere, Cic.

continentia, ae, *f.* [continēns], *a holding in, repressing.* **1.** Lit.: Suet. **2.** Transf.: *a holding in, or curbing of oneself, self-control, continence* (opp. libido): Caes., Cic., Sall.

con-tineŏ, tinēre, tinuī, tentum [teneŏ]. **I.** *to hold*, or *keep together, to keep in company or in a mass.* **1.** Lit. **a.** Pl.; aggerem, Caes. **b.** *to keep in one loco*, Caes.; exercitum, Liv. **c.** oppidum pons fluminis continet, Caes.; Cic. **2.** Transf.: haec virtus amicitiam et gignit et continet, Cic.; Liv. **II.** *to hold* or *keep within bounds, to confine.* **1.** Lit.: mundus omnia complexu suo continet, Cic.; Ov., etc.; Pompeium quam angustissime, Caes.; se vallo, Caes.; Ov.; se domi, Cic.; sese intra silvas, Caes.; agricolam continet imber, Verg. **2.** Transf. **a.** civitates in amicitiā, Caes.; te in studiis, Cic.; suos silentio, Liv. **b.** *to hold within self, to comprise, include* : ut omnia contineant in se vim caloris, Cic.; Lucr.; talis res hic liber continet, Caes.; Hor.; comitia curiata rem militarem continent, Liv. Occ. in *Pass. to be composed of* : non venis et nervis et ossibus continentur (di), Cic.; Lucr. **III.** *to hold* or *keep fast, to hold in, control, repress.* **1.** Lit.: navis copulis, Caes.; suos a proelio, Caes.; Sall.; Cic.; gradum, Verg.; Hor. **2.** Transf.: animum a libidine, Sall.; risum, Cic.; dolorem, Liv.; se, Ter., Cic., Ov. With *ne* and *Subj.* : Caes.; vix me contineo quin etc., Ter.; Pl.; Ov.

con-tingŏ, tingere, tigī, tāctum [tangŏ]. **A.** Trans. **I.** *to touch closely, come into contact with* : terram osculo, Liv.; funem manu, Verg.; sidera comā, Ov. Sexually : Pl. **II.** *to touch one thing with another, to affect by touching.* **1.** Lit.: lac sale, Verg.; ora sacro medicamine, Ov.; Lucr.; Hor. **2.** Transf.: *to touch, affect* : quos publica contingebat cura, Liv.; me manifesta libido contigit, Ov. *Perf. Part.*, *polluted, defiled by touch* : contacta civitas rabie iuvenum, Liv.; dies religione, Liv.; Tac. **III.** *to touch, border on.* **1.** Lit.: Helvii finis Arvernorum contingunt, Caes.; Liv. Also with DAT.: Caes.; inter se, Caes. **2.** Transf.: *to touch, be close, near to* : aliquem sanguine ac genere, Liv.; deos quoniam propius contingis, Hor.; Sabinum modico usu, Tac. **IV.** *to reach* (to). **1.** Lit.: avem ferro, Verg.; hostem, Liv. Also of place : Italiam, Verg.; Hor.; Ov. **2.** Transf.: aevi florem, Lucr.; nostras infamia temporis contigit, Liv. Intrans.: *to reach, come to* (v. III. 1); hence, *to happen to, befall* (with DAT.), or

Absol. to turn out, happen, succeed (mostly in good sense): hoc contigit nomini, Cic.; Ter.; Ov., etc. With *Inf.:* non cuivis homini contingit adire Corinthum, Hor.; Quint. With *ut* and *Subj.:* volo hoc oratori contingat ut etc., Cic.; Pl. *Absol. :* Ter., Cic., Hor.

continuātiō, ōnis, *f.* [continuō], *an unbroken series, succession :* rerum, Cic.; imbrium, Caes. Rhet.: verborum, *a period :* Cic., Quint.

continuō, āre [continuus], *to make continuous, make all in one, join on without break.* **1.** Lit.: fundos, Cic.; Liv.; pontem, Tac.; aedificia moenibus, Liv.; latus lateri, Ov. In *Mid. (join on to) :* atomi cohaerescunt inter se et continuantur, Cic.; Tac. **2.** Transf.: magistratum, Sall.; iter die et nocte, Caes.; diem noctemque potando, Tac.; Cic.; Hor.; paci externae confestim continuatur discordia domi, Liv.; hiemi continuatur hiems, Ov.

continuus, a, um [continueō], *holding together, unbroken, continuous.* **1.** Lit.: montes, Hor.; Liv.; Rhenus uno alveo continuus, Tac. **2.** Transf. **a.** Of time : *unbroken, successive :* dies continuos quinque, Caes.; Pl.; annos prope quinquaginta continuos, Cic.; postulandis reis tam continuus annus fuit, Tac.; Ov. **b.** Of events, etc. : *incommoda*, Caes.; bella, obsidio, Liv.; Ov. Abl. **continuō** as *Adv. without break, immediately, without delay :* Pl., Cic., Verg., etc.; often as correl. to ubi, ut, postquam, simul ac, cum, etc.: ubi primum terram tetigimus, continuo . . ., Pl.; quod continuo consilium dimiserit, simul ac me viderit, Cic.; Lucr. Occ. in argument, with a negative, actual or implied : *necessarily, as an immediate consequence :* si quis non sit avarus, continuo sanus ? Hor.; Cic.

cōntiō, ōnis, *f.* [old form **cōventiō**, *a coming together*]. **1.** Lit.: *a meeting* convened by a magistrate, priest, or commander : advocare contionem, Caes., Cic., Liv.; habere, Liv.; advocare populum in contionem, Liv.; plebem ad contionem vocare, Liv.; frequentis contionis modo, Liv.; laudare aliquem pro contione, Sall. **2.** Transf. **a.** *the people thus assembled :* Cic. **b.** *the speech delivered to such a meeting, popular address, harangue :* contionem apud milites habuit, Caes.; Cic.; Liv., etc. **c.** *the speaker's platform :* Cic., Liv.

cōntiōnābundus, a, um [cōntiōnor], *haranguing at a popular meeting, playing the demagogue :* Liv.

cōntiōnālis, e, *adj.* [cōntiō], *belonging to or suitable for a public assembly :* clamor, Cic. Ep.; senex, Cic.

cōntiōnārius, a, um [cōntiō], *of or suited to a public assembly :* populus, Cic. Ep.

cōntiōnātor, ōris, *m.* [cōntiōnor], *an haranguer of the people :* in a bad sense, *a demagogue, an agitator :* Cic.

cōntiōnor, ārī [cōntiō]. **I.** *to be convened or come to a meeting :* Liv. **II.** *to address a meeting, harangue :* apud milites, Caes.; ex turri, Cic.; adversus aliquem, Liv. Occ.: *to declare at a meeting.* With Acc. and *Inf. :* Cic. Ep. Also with quoted words : Cic.

cōntiuncula, ae, *f.* [*dim.* cōntiō], *a short harangue :* Cic.

con-tollō, ere (*cf.* conferō), *to bring together :* gradum, Pl.

con-tonat, *v. impers. it thunders heavily :* Pl.

con-torqueō, torquēre, torsī, tortum, *to whirl, twist,* or *twirl about vigorously.* **1.** Lit. **a.** Esp. of sea and wind : Lucr., Cic., Verg. **b.** Of missiles, *to hurl vigorously :* Lucr., Verg., Curt. **2.** Transf. **a.** Of forcible language: verba, Cic.; Plin. Ep. **b.** *to twist, involve* an argument : Cic.

contortē, *adv. in involved language :* Cic. Comp. : Cic.

contortiōnēs, um, *f. pl.* [contorqueō], *involvings, intricacies :* orationis, Cic.

contortor, ōris, *m.* [contorqueō], *a twister, perverter :* legum, Ter.

contortulus, a, um [*dim.* contortus], *somewhat involved :* Cic.

contortuplicātus, a, um [contortus plicō] *twisty-tangled :* Pl.

contortus, a, um. **I.** *Part.* contorqueō. **II.** *Adj. :* **a.** *whirling, vehement :* oratio, Cic.; Quint. **b.** *involved, intricate :* contortae et difficiles res, Cic.

contrā, *adv.* and *prep.* (from con, like in-trā, ex-trā, ci-trā, ul-trā, etc.). Originally, *over against :* hence, **I.** Adv.: *over against, facing, fronting, opposite to.* **1.** Lit. **a.** In rest : omnia contra circaque, Liv.; Pl.; Ov. **b.** Of direction, motion: adi contra, Pl.; contra intueri, Liv. **c.** Of opposition, etc. : contra obniti, Verg.; Lucr.; Tac. **2.** Transf. **a.** Correspondence : *in return, in reply*, etc. : amare, Pl.; dicere, Cic.; agedum, pauca accipe contra, Hor. **b.** Equivalence in weight : iam mihi auro contra constat filius (*is worth his weight in gold*), Pl. **c.** Direct or diametrical opposition : *on the contrary, exactly the reverse :* ut hi sunt miseri, sic contra illi beati, Cic.; quin contra, Liv.; cognoscere quid boni utrisque aut contra esset, Sall. With *atque* (ac) or *quam : otherwise than, contrary to what :* contra atque erat dictum, Caes.; factum est meā culpā contra quam tu mecum egeras, Cic.; Liv. **d.** Rhetorical antithesis : *on the other hand :* Cic.; o fortunati mercatores ! miles ait; contra mercator, militia est potior, Hor. **e.** Opposition in gen. : si quā ex parto obviam contra veniretur, Caes.; dicere, iudicare, Cic. In compounds, contra gen. contains the idea of hostile opposition, e.g. contradico. **II.** Prep. with Acc. : *over against, opposite to, facing.* **1.** Lit.: unum latus est contra Galliam, Caes.; castellum loco edito contra arcem obiecit, Liv. **2.** Transf. **a.** Of actions, *against, to meet, to attack, in opposition to*, etc. : contra vim fluminis, Caes.; nautas contra Carthaginem duxit, Caes. **b.** Of opinions, etc. : *against, contrary to, counter to, in defiance of*, etc. : spem, Caes., Liv.; opinionem, Caes., Cic.; ius gentium, Liv.

contractiō, ōnis, *f.* [contrahō], *a drawing together, contraction.* **1.** Lit.: digitorum (opp. porrectio), Cic.; frontis, Cic. Occ.: *a shortening :* syllabae, Cic. **2.** Transf.: animi (in dolore), *depression*, Cic.

contractiuncula, ae, f. [dim. contractiō], a slight depression : animi, Cic.

contractus, a, um. I. Part. contrahō. II. Adj. drawn together or close, contracted. 1. Lit. a. nares contractiores introitūs habent, Cic.; Juv. b. narrowed, limited (in space): locus, Verg.; Hor. 2. Transf. a. oratio, studia, Cic.; vox, Quint. b. Act. pinching : paupertas, Hor. Comp. : Cic., Lucr.

contractus, ūs, m. [contrahō]. I. a drawing together, shrinking : Varr. II. a transacting : rei, Quint.

contrā-dīcō, dicere, dixī, dictum, to gainsay, contradict. With Dat. : sententiis aliorum, Tac. Used impers. with quin : Liv.

contrādictiō, ōnis, f. [contrādīcō], a gainsaying, objection, refutation : Quint., Tac. In pl. : Quint., Tac.

con-trahō, trahere, traxī, tractum. I. to draw together into one place. 1. Lit.: exercitum in unum locum, Caes.; Cic. Ep.; classem, Nep.; utrumque ad conloquium, Liv.; Ov. 2. Transf. a. to draw together, hence, to bring about, cause, contract, incur : amicitiam, Cic.; bellum Saguntinis, Liv.; culpam, Cic. Ep.; aliquid damni, Cic.; Pl.; Ov.; porca contracta (due for the expiation of a crime), Cic. b. In business, to make a contract, conclude a bargain : rationem, rem, negotium cum aliquo, Cic.; hence, to have dealings with : contrahere nihil cum populo, Cic. II. to draw close, tighten, narrow. 1. Lit. : contract, abridge, pulmones se contrahunt aspirantes, Cic.; vela, Hor.; frontem, Cic.; castra, Caes.; si contrahit orbem (luna), Ov. Poet. of bees : contracto frigore pigrae, Verg. 2. Transf. a. to draw in, narrow, limit : appetitūs, verba, Cic.; Hor. b. to pinch, depress : animus incommodis amici contrahitur, Cic.; Lucr.

contrāriē, adv. in an opposite direction or manner : Cic., Tac.

contrārius, a, um [contrā], lying over against, fronting, opposite. 1. Lit. a. collis adversus huic et contrarius, Caes.; Cic.; Tac.; ictus, Liv. b. coming to meet : classi contraria flamina, Ov. c. opposite (the action being in opposite directions): in contrarias partis fluere, Cic.; Ov. 2. Transf. a. opposite, contrary, opposed : ardor, Lucr.; studia, Cic. With Gen.: huius igitur virtutis contraria est vitiositas, Cic. With Dat. : Cic., Ov. With inter and Refl. Pron. : orationes inter se contrariae Aeschinis Demosthenisque, Cic.; Quint. With ac : contrarium decernebat ac paulo ante decreverat, Cic. As Noun, **con-trārium**, I, n. : decernere, Cic.; vocant animum in contraria curae, Verg.; in contraria versus, Ov.; ex contrario, on the contrary, on the other hand : Caes., Cic.; and e contrario : Nep. b. opposed, hence, hostile, inimical : Lucr., Verg., Quint. c. in opposite balance : fatis contraria fata, Verg.

contrectābiliter, adv. so as to be felt : Lucr.

contrectātiō, ōnis, f. [contrectō], a touching, handling : Cic. In pl. : Cic.

con-trectō, āre [tractō], to touch, handle closely. 1. Lit. : pectora, Ov. Esp. of frequent handling : liber manibus vulgi contrectatus (well-thumbed), Hor. Also of defiling touch : Pl., Tac. 2. Transf. a. to defile with the eyes : Tac. b. to handle or dwell upon mentally : mente voluptates, Cic.

con-tremiscō, tremiscere, tremuī. A. Intrans.: to begin to tremble all over. 1. Lit.: Lucr., Cic., Verg. 2. Transf.: fides, Cic. B. Trans.: to tremble at : periculum, Hor.

con-tremō, ēre, to tremble all over : tellus, Lucr.

con-tribuō, uere, uī, ūtum, to put in the same tribe, list, lot, etc.; incorporate. 1. Lit. With cum : Calaguritani erant cum Oscensibus contributi, Caes. With Dat.: Ambracia contribuerat se Aetolis, Liv. With in : in unam urbem contributi, Liv. 2. Transf.: to bring into a common stock : Ov.

contristō, āre [tristis], to make quite sad, to cover with gloom. 1. Lit.: Cael. ap. Cic. Ep. 2. Transf.: to overcast with gloom : Verg.; annum, Hor.

contritus, a, um, Part. conterō.

contrōversia, ae, f. [contrōversus]. I. a civil lawsuit, litigation, dispute : Pl.; magnae rei, Cic.; de fundo habere, Cic.; ager in controversiā erat, Liv.; rem in controversiam adducere, vocare, Cic.; controversiam alere, componere, Caes.; constituere, tollere, distrahere, etc., Cic. II. a subject of litigation : Caes. III. Rhet.: dispute, debate : Cic., Tac. IV. contradiction, question : vicimus sine controversiā, etc.; Ter.; nihil controversiae fuit quin etc., Liv.; Cic.

contrōversiōsus, a, um [contrōversia], much controverted : res, Liv.

contrō-versus, a, um [contrā ; cf. intrō and intrā]: that is the subject of dispute, controverted, disputed (opp. certus): Cic., Liv. Neut. pl. as Noun : Quint.

con-trucīdō, āre, to hew or cut to pieces. 1. Lit.: corpus, Cic.; Sen. Ep. 2. Transf. rem publicam, Cic.

con-trūdō, trūdere, trūsī, trūsum, to thrust or mass together : Lucr., Cic.

con-truncō, āre, to hack to pieces : filios, Pl.

contrūsus, a, um, Part. contrūdō.

contubernālis, is, m.f. [contubernium]. 1. Milit. a. a tent-companion or comrade (there were us. ten men and a decanus in one tent): Cic., Tac. b. a young man who accompanied a general in order to learn the art of war, a junior staff-officer : Cic. 2. Transf. a. a comrade, mate : in consulatu, Cic. b. husband or wife of a slave (comic.): Pl.

contubernium, i, n. [taberna]. I. Abstr. 1. Lit. a. tent-companionship : Tac. b. a serving as a junior staff-officer : Cic., Liv., etc. 2. Transf. a. In gen.: companionship, intercourse : Tac. b. marriage among slaves : Curt. Hence, concubinage : Cic. II. Concr. a. a common war tent : Caes., Tac. b. In gen.: a common dwelling : Suet. Esp.: the dwelling of a male and female slave : Tac.

con-tueor, tuērī, tuitus (Pres. contuimur, Lucr.; Inf. contuī, Pl.). I. to look on, survey, consider attentively. 1. Lit.:

totam terram eiusque situm, Cic.; Suet.
2. Transf. Of the mind: Lucr., Cic.
II. *to get a view of, descry* : Pl.

contŭĭtū (contūĭtū, Pl.), ABL. *sing. m.* [contueor] (*by*) *an attentive looking at* : Curt.

contŭmācia, ae, *f.* [contumāx], *wilfulness, defiance, stubbornness :* Cic., Liv., Tac. In good sense : libera, Cic.

contŭmācĭter, *adv.* *stubbornly, defiantly* : Cic. Ep., Liv., Quint. *Comp. :* Nep. In good sense : Sen. Ep., Quint.

contŭmāx, ācis, *adj. stubborn, defiant :* Cic., Tac.; voces, preces, Tac. In good sense: Tac. *Comp.:* Cic.; *Sup.:* Sen. Ep.

contŭmēlĭa, ae, *f.* **1.** Lit. *outrage, ill-treatment* (physical). **a.** Of persons: Pl., Liv., Tac. **b.** Of things, *buffeting, knocking-about :* Caes. **2. Transf.:** *outrage, affront.* **a.** In gen.: aliquid in suam contumeliam vertere, Caes.; Cic. **b.** Of language, *affront, insult, abuse :* verborum, Cic., Liv.; Hor.; dicere alicui, Pl.; imponere alicui, Sall.; in aliquem contumeliam iacere, Cic.; ingerere, Tac.

contŭmēlĭōsē, *adv. abusively :* Cic., Quint. *Comp.:* Ter., Liv. *Sup.:* Cic.

contŭmēlĭōsus, a, um [contumēlĭa]. **1.** Lit.: *doing outrage, bringing dishonour :* Caes., Cic., etc. **2. Transf.** Of language, *insulting, abusive :* Cic., Sall., Liv. *Comp. :* Cic. Ep.; *Sup. :* Quint.

con-tŭmŭlō, āre, *to entomb :* Ov.

con-tŭndō, tundere, tudĭ, tūsum, *to beat small, grind, crush, pound to pieces* or *powder.* **1.** Lit.: Pl., Cic., Ov., etc. **2. Transf.:** facta alicuius, Pl.; audaciam, Cic.; animum, Cic. Ep.; populos ferocis, Verg.; Hannibalem, Liv.

con-tŭor, tuī, *v.* contueor.

contŭrbātĭō, ōnis, *f.* [conturbō], *utter disorder :* mentis, Cic.

contŭrbātus, a, um. **I.** *Part.* conturbō. **II.** *Adj. quite disordered :* Cic.; animus, Cic. *Comp. :* Cic. Ep.

con-turbō, āre, *to derange utterly, throw into disorder* or *confusion.* **1.** Lit.: Romanorum ordines, Sall.; Cat. **2. Transf. a.** Of the mind, etc.: animum, Lucr., Cic.; vocem, Lucr.; rem publicam, Sall. **b.** Of money matters, *to derange one's accounts* (i.e. *become bankrupt*): With or without rationes *or* rationem: Cic., Juv. Transf.: conturbasti mihi rationes, Ter.

contus, ī, *m.* [κοντός], *a pole :* Verg., Tac.

contūsus, a, um, *Part.* contundō.

contūtū, *v.* contuitū.

cōnūbĭālis, e, *adj.* [cōnūbĭum], *of wedlock:* iura, Ov.

cōnūbĭum, ī, *n.* [nūbō], *alliance by marriage, intermarriage.* **a.** Prop.: patrum et plebis, Liv.; ius conubi, Cic.; Verg.; Ov. **b.** = ius conubi, *the civil right of inter-marriage according to Roman law :* Cic., Liv. In *pl.* : Cic. **c.** = coniugium, *marriage :* Lucr., Verg. In *pl. :* Verg.

cōnus, ī, *m.* [κῶνος], *a cone :* Cic., Lucr. Transf.: *the apex of a helmet :* Verg., Ov.

con-vădor, ārī, *to bind over to appear before a court* (comic.) : Pl.

con-vălēscō, valēscere, valuī. **I.** *to grow quite strong.* **1.** Lit.: Varr. **2.** Transf.: fides, Milo, Cic.; ignis, Ov. **II.** *to regain*

strength, recover. **1.** Lit.: ex morbo, Cic.; Ov. **2. Transf.:** civitas, Cic., mens, Ov.

con-vallis, is, *f.* (ABL. convalle), *a valley enclosed on all sides :* Lucr., Cic., Verg., etc.

convāsō, āre [vāsa], *to pack up baggage, etc.* : Ter.

convectō, āre [*freq.* convehō], *to carry* or *bring together in abundance :* Verg., Tac.

convector, ōris, *m.* [convehō], *a fellow-passenger :* Cic. Ep.

con-vehō, vehere, vexī, vectum, *to carry* or *bring together ;* esp. *in vehicles, boats, etc.* : Caes., Cic., Liv.

con-vellō, vellere, vellī, vulsum, *to drag violently, tear up, rend away, pull* or *pluck up, wrench off,* etc. **1.** Lit.: Cato, Cic., Verg., etc. (Milit.: convellere signa, Cic., Liv.) With *prep.* or ABL.: simulacrum e sacrario, Cic.; silvam ab humo, Verg.; (turrim) altis sedibus, Verg.; Cic. **2. Transf.:** rem publicam, Cic.; iudicia Cic.; verbis convellere pectus, Ov.; instituta omnium, Cic.; acta Dolabellae, Cic.; fidem legionum, Tac.

convena, ae, *adj. m.* and *f.* [conveniō], *coming together :* amantis facere convenas, *to bring them together,* Pl. As Noun in *pl.* only: convenae, *assembled strangers, refugees :* Cic.

convĕnĭēns, entis. **I.** *Part.* conveniō. **II.** *Adj.* **a.** *agreeing, consistent, harmonious :* amici, Cic.; motūs, Lucr. **b.** *fitting, appropriate, suitable.* With *cum :* Ov. With DAT.: Cic., Ov., etc. With *ad,* *to denote an end in view :* Cic., Ov. With *inter se:* Lucr. *Absol. :* Ov., Quint. *Comp. :* Suet. *Sup. :* Plin. Ep.

convĕnĭenter, *adv.* **I.** *agreeably to, conformably, consistently.* With *cum* and ABL.: Cic. With DAT.: Cic., Hor. **II.** *suitably, aptly.* With *ad :* Liv.

convĕnĭentĭa, ae, *f.* [conveniēns], *agreement, accord, harmony :* naturae convenientia cum extis, Cic.; partium, Cic.

con-vĕnĭō, venīre, vēnī, ventum (*Fut.* convenibō, Pl.). **I. A. Intrans.:** *to come together, come in a body, meet together, assemble.* **1.** Lit. **a.** Of persons: Cic., Verg., etc. **b.** Of towns united for jurisdiction in one centre : ex civitatibus quae in id forum convenirent, Cic. **c.** Of woman's marriage : viro in manum, Cic., Liv. **2. Transf.:** *to unite, coincide :* multae causae convenisse in unum locum videntur, Cic.; Pl. **B. Trans.:** *to meet, go to meet :* eum in itinere, Caes.; Cic.; Pl.; etc. *Pass.:* ab nuntio uxoris erat conventus, Liv. **II.** *to come together, unite, combine, harmoniously.* **1.** Lit.: atomi, Lucr. **2. Transf. a.** Of persons: *to agree, be of one mind, harmonise :* de re inter nos, Pl. **b.** More freq. with *Pass. sense : to be agreed upon :* Pl.; quod tempus inter eos committendi proeli convenerat, Caes. ; Cic ; ardentia vidit castra ; id convenerat signum, Liv.; pax quae cum T. Quinctio convenisset, Liv. *Pass. :* pacem conventam, Sall.; Liv. Oftener *Impers. :* mihi cum Deiotaro convenit, ut . . ., Cic.; Pl.; ne inter consules quidem ipsos satis conveniebat, Liv. ; de facto convenit, Cic. With DAT. of thing :

pacto convenit, Liv. With Acc. and *Inf.*:
Liv.· **III.** *to fit, suit, be adapted to.* **1.**
Lit.: ad pedem apte convenire (of a shoe),
Cic. **2.** Tr an s f. **A.** *to fit, be applicable,
suitable.* With *ad* or *in* and Acc.: Cato,
Cic. With *cum* : Cic. With Dat.: Ter.,
Cic., Sall. With Acc. and *Inf.*: Pl. **B.**
Impers. it is fitting, becoming, proper. **a.**
With *Inf.*: Lucr., Caes., Hor. **b.** With
Acc. and *Inf.*: Ter., Verg. **c.** With
Subj.: Hor.
conventiculum, ī, *n.* [*dim.* conventus]. **I.**
a small assembly : Cic. **II.** *a place of
assembly* : Tac.
conventicius, a, um [conventus], *of coming
together* : Pl. *Neut.* **conventicium** (*sc.*
aes) : *a fee for attendance at the assembly* (in
Greek towns) : Cic.
conventiō, ōnis, *f.* [conveniō], *an agreement,
compact* : Liv., Tac.
conventus, a, um, *Part.* conveniō. *Neut.* as
Noun, *an agreement, pact* : Cic., Liv.
conventus, ūs, *m.* [conveniō]. **I.** *a coming
together* : only concr. *a gathering, assembly.*
a. In gen.: Ca Cic., Verg.; indicere,
indicere, Liv. **b.** *an assembly at a certain
place in a province* (for the administration
of justice, business, etc.), *a district court* :
hence, conventūs agere, *to hold the circuits* or
assizes : Caes., Cic., Liv. Hence, *the commune* or *corporation* in such a district : Caes.
II. *a coming together in union, a combination.* **1.** Lit.: atomorum, Lucr. **2.**
Tr an s f.: *agreement* : ex conventu, Cic.
con-verrō (-vorrō), verrere, verrī, versum.
I. *to sweep* or *brush together, to sweep up.*
1. Lit.: Pl., Cato. **2.** Tr an s f.: hereditates omnium, Cic. **II.** *to brush thoroughly:*
aliquem totum cum pulvisculo (i.e. *give him
a good dusting*), Pl.
conversātiō, ōnis, *f.* [con-versor], *intercourse,
society* : Quint., Tac.
conversiō, ōnis, *f.* [convertō]. **I.** *a turning
round, revolving, revolution.* **1.** Lit.: caeli,
Cic.; in *pl.*: Cic. Hence, *the periodical
return of the seasons* : mensium annorumque
Cic. **2.** Tr an s f. **a.** Rh et.: *the rounding of a period* : Cic.; also *the repetition of
the same word at the end of a clause* : Cic.
b. *a complete* or *violent change* : Cic.
con-versō, āre [*freq.* convertō], *to turn round
frequently* : animus se ipse conversans, Cic.
Mid. **conversor,** ārī, *to associate with* :
Sen. Ep.
(1) conversus, a, um, *Part.* converrō.
(2) conversus, a, um, *Part.* convertō.
con-vertō (vortō), vertere, vertī, versum.
A. Tr an s. **I.** *to make to turn completely
round* or *back* (and *Mid.* **convertor,** *to turn
oneself round, wheel round*). **1.** Lit.:
terra circum axem se convertit, Cic.;
Lucr.; aciem in fugam, Caes.; Liv. In
Mid. as *Act.* : fugam in se, Pl. Esp.
Milit. : signa convertere, Caes., Liv. **2.**
Tr an s f. **a.** *to turn completely* : animos
ad deorum cultum a vitae pravitate, Cic. ;
gemitu conversi animi, Verg. **b.** *to change
completely, transform* : Pl.; Hecubam in
canem, Cic.; Verg.; castra castris, Caes. ;
crimen in laudem, Cic. **c.** *to translate* :
orationes e Graeco, Cic.; in Latinum, Cic.
II. *to turn intently* in a certain direction,

direct to an object. **1.** Lit.: navis in eam
partem, Caes.; ferrum in me, Verg.; iter
in provinciam, Caes.; oculos in aliquem,
Cic.; also, virgo adeo eximiā formā ut
converteret omnium oculos (i.e. *attracted*),
Liv.; ad hunc se multitudo convertit,
Caes.; Cic.; Nep.; tigna contra vim fluminis, Caes.; aciem eo, Caes. With Dat.:
Lucr. **2.** Tr an s f.: risum in iudicem,
Cic.; studium ad causas agendas, Tac. **B.**
Intr an s.: *to turn round* or *back, return.*
1. Lit.: Sall. **2.** Tr an s f. **a.** in amicitiam, Pl.; ad aliquem, Cic.; ad sapien-
tiora, Tac.; eodem, Lucr. **b.** *to change,
be transformed* : vitium in bonum, Cic. ;
Sall.
con-vestiō, īre, *to clothe completely* : Enn.
Tr an s f.: domum lucis, Cic.; omnia suā
luce sol, Lucr.
convexus, a, um [convehō], *carried round,
rounded off; vaulted, arched, convex* (sometimes *concave*). **1.** Lit.: Verg., Ov.
Neut. pl. as Noun, *vault, arch* : Verg. **2.**
Tr an s f.: *sloping downwards* : Verg. ;
ad aequora, Ov.
conviciātor, ōris, *m.* [convicior], *a railer, re-
viler* : Cic., Suet.
convicior, ārī [convicium], *to revile, rail at* :
Varr., Liv., etc.; with Dat.: Quint.
convicium, ī, *n.* [cogn. with vōx, vōc-is].
I. *a loud noise, a cry, clamour* : Pl., Cic.
Of birds: Ov. Of frogs and cicadae :
Phaedr. **II.** *loud, violent outcry, abuse, invective* : conviciis consectari aliquem, Cic. ;
alicui facere, Pl., Cic., Ov., etc.; ingerere
convicia alicui, Hor.; acerbior in conviciis,
Tac. **III.** *a loud outcry of protest.* **1.**
Lit.: Cic. **2.** Tr an s f.: aurium (*the
protest of the ears against harsh sounds*),
Cic. **IV.** *rebuke, reprimand* : Cic.
convictiō, ōnis, *f.* [convīvō], *companionship* :
Cic. fil. ap. Cic. Ep. Concr. (in *pl.*) =
convictores : Cic. Ep.
convictor, ōris, *m.* [convīvō], *he who lives
with one, a familiar friend* : Hor., Plin. Ep.
convictus, a, um, *Part.* convincō.
convictus, ūs, *m.* [convīvō], *a living together,
social intercourse.* **1.** Lit.: Cic., Ov. **2.**
Tr an s f. *a banquet, feast* : Tac., Juv.
con-vincō, vincere, vīcī, victum, *to overcome,
beat down* (in argument). **I.** *to refute, confute, prove wrong* (of persons or things) :
Pl., Lucr., Cic., etc. **II.** *to convict, prove
guilty.* With Gen. of the charge (most
freq.) : Cic. With *in* and Abl.: Cic., Tac.
With Abl.: Cic., Suet. With *Inf.*: Liv.,
Tac. **III.** *to prove true* : facinus, Cic. ;
avaritiam, Caes.; furorem, Ov. With
Acc. and *Inf.* : Cic., Quint.
con-visō, ere, *to look all over, to search thoroughly.* **1.** Lit.: Lucr. **2.** Tr an s f.
Of light, *to pervade,* Lucr.
conviva, ae, *m.* [con, vīvō]: *a table-companion, guest* : Pl., Cic., Hor., etc.
convivalis, e, *adj.* [conviva], *of a feast,
convivial* : oblectamenta, Liv.; ludi, Curt.;
fabulae, Tac.
convivātor, ōris, *m.* [convivor], *the master of
a feast* : Hor., Liv.
convivium, ī, *n.* [convivor]. Lit.: *a living
together,* hence, *a social meal, banquet* : ornare, Cic.; agitare, Pl.; facere, Cat.;

curare, Verg. **Concr.** (in *pl.*) = convivae, *guests*, Ov., Sen.

con-vīvō, vīvere, vīxī, victum. **I.** *to live with :* avaro, Sen. Ep. **II.** *to feast with :* cum aliquo, Quint.

convīvor, ārī [conviva], *to feast together :* Ter., Cic., Suet.

con-vocō, āre, *to call together, to convoke, assemble.* **1.** Lit.: homines ad societatem vitae, Cic. ; ad concilium, Caes. ; ad contionem, Liv. ; concilium, Cic. ; convocat hic amnis, Ov. **2.** Transf.: sibi consilia in animum, Pl.

con-volō, āre, *to fly* or *flock together ;* hence, *to assemble hastily :* Ter., Cic., Liv.

con-volvō, volvere, volvī, volūtum. **I.** *to roll together :* Lucr. **II.** se sol, *to roll along* (in its orbit): Cic. **III.** Of a snake : *to move in coils* or *to coil up :* Verg. Of a book, *to roll up :* Sen. **IV.** *to strengthen with coils, intertwine :* Caes.

con-vomō, ere, *to vomit all over :* mensas hospitum, Cic. ; Juv.

con-vortō, *v.* converto.

con-vulnerō, āre, *to wound severely :* Curt., Plin. Pan.

convulsus, a, um, Part. convellō.

co-olēscō, *v.* coalēsco.

co-operiō, operīre, operuī, opertum, *to cover completely.* **1.** Lit.: Lucr. Hence, *to overwhelm :* aliquem lapidibus, Cic., Liv. ; Tac. **2.** Transf.: aliquem nefariis sceleribus, Cic. ; Sall. ; Hor. [It. *coprire ;* Fr. *couvrir.*]

cooptātiō, ōnis, *f.* [cooptō], *an election of a colleague, by vote of existing members :* conlegiorum, Cic. ; censoria, Cic. ; in Patres, Liv.

co-optō, āre, *to choose, to elect as a colleague :* senatores, Cic. ; senatum, Liv. ; aliquem in amplissimum ordinem, Cic.

co-orior, orīrī, ortus, *to arise all together* or *all at once, suddenly.* **1.** Lit.: Lucr.; montani ad pugnam, Liv. ; in nos gentes, Tac. **2.** Transf.: dolores, Pl. ; bellum, Caes. ; ventus, Caes., Sall. ; seditio, Verg. ; ignes pluribus simul locis, Liv. ; subito tempestates, Cic.

coortus, ūs, *m.* [coorior], *a rising, originating :* Lucr.

cōpa, ae, *f.* [v. caupō], *hostess of a wine-shop :* Verg., Suet.

cophinus, ī, *m.* [κόφινος], *a basket :* Juv. [It. *cofano ;* Sp. *cofre, cofin ;* Fr. *coffre.*]

cōpia, ae, *f.* [for co-op-ia, fr. *ops, cf.* in-op-ia], *abundance, ample stock, supply, store, plenty.* **1.** Lit. **a.** In *sing. :* Pl. ; frumenti, pabuli, Caes. ; agri, pecuniae, Cic. ; lactis, Verg. ; omnis copia narium, Hor. **b.** Esp. in *pl.* **i.** *means of living, resources :* exercitum suis copiis sustentavit, Cic. ; Caes. **ii.** *military stores, supplies :* Caes., Liv. **iii.** *private means, property, wealth :* conferre suas copias in provinciam, Cic. ; familiares, Liv. ; Hor. **2.** Transf. **a.** Of living beings : *a multitude, large supply, plenty :* Pl., Cic., Ov., etc. Esp. milit. (us. *pl.*), *troops, forces :* Caes., Cic., Liv., etc. **b.** Of abstract things, *stores, abundance, richness :* Lucr. ; verborum, Cic., Quint. ; in dicendo, Cic. **c.** With ref. to action ; *means, opportunity, facility.* With GEN. :

Liv. ; facere copiam frumenti alicui, Caes. ; facere civibus consili sui copiam, Cic. ; dare copiam pugnae, Verg. ; senatūs copiam dare, Tac. (Rarely of persons, *opportunity of approaching, access to :* eius, Pl., Ter.). With GEN. of Gerund. : Pl., Sall., Verg., etc. With *Inf. :* Sall., Cat. With *ut* and *Subj. :* Pl., Ter. Phr.: pro copiā, *according to opportunity, ability,* etc. : Pl., Cato, Liv. ; pro temporis huius copiā, Liv. ; pro rei copiā, Sall.

cōpiolae, ārum, *f. pl.* [*dim.* cōpia], *a small force of troops :* Brut. ap. Cic. Ep.

cōpiōsē, *adv. abundantly, plentifully.* **1.** Lit.: in provinciam copiose profectus erat, *well supplied*, Cic. **2.** Transf. Of style : *fully, at length :* Cic. Comp. and *Sup. :* Cic., Quint.

cōpiōsus, a, um [cōpia]. **1.** Lit. **a.** *being in abundance, plentiful :* Caes., Phaedr. **b.** *having in abundance, well-supplied, rich, wealthy,* etc. (of persons and things ; opp. inops): Caes., Cic., Liv. With ABL.: Cic., Tac. **2.** Transf. **a.** *a being in abundance :* supellex verborum, Quint. **b.** *rich, copious, fertile,* etc. : ad dicendum, Cic. ; vir, Liv. ; lingua, Cic. Comp. and *Sup. :* Caes., Cic., etc.

cōpis, is *adj.* [for co-op-is, fr. *ops*], *abundantly supplied, wealthy :* Pl. ; pectus, Pl.

cōpula, ae, *f.* [for co-ap-ula ; *cf.* apiscor], *that which binds fast, a band, cord, rope.* **1.** Lit.: Pl., Nep., Ov. **2.** Transf.: *a tie, bond :* Hor., Nep. Of words : Quint. [It. *coppia ;* Fr. *couple.*]

cōpulātiō, ōnis, *f.* [cōpulō], *a coupling, joining.* **1.** Lit.: atomorum inter se, Cic. **2.** Transf. Of *social union :* Cic. Of words : Quint.

cōpulātus, a, um. **I.** Part. cōpulō. **II.** Adj.: *joined together, connected :* Cic. Comp. (= *more binding*) : Cic.

cōpulō, āre (Part. Perf. cōplāta, Lucr.) [cōpula], *to bind* or *tie fast, unite.* **1.** Lit.: hominem cum beluā, Cic. ; Pl. With DAT.: Lucr., Liv. **2.** Transf.: sermonem cum aliquo, Pl. ; honestatem cum voluptate, Cic. ; an haec inter se copulari possint, Cic. With DAT. : Cic. With ACC. alone : concordiam, Liv.

cōpulor, ārī, *to unite closely, clasp :* dexteras, Pl.

coqua, ae, *f.* [coquus], *a female cook :* Pl.

coquinō, āre [coquus], *to cook :* Pl.

coquinus, a, um [coquus], *of cookery :* forum, Pl.

coquō, coquere, coxī, coctum [*cf.* πέπτω, πέσσω] (Pres. Opt. coquint, Pl.), *to cook ; to boil, fry, bake,* etc. ; *to prepare by cooking,* etc. **1.** Lit.: Pl., Cic., Ov., etc. **2.** Transf. **a.** Of action by heat, *to bake, burn, parch :* Cato, Hor., Verg. **b.** *to ripen, mature :* poma matura et cocta, Cic. ; vindemia, Verg. **c.** *to digest :* Cic. **d.** Of the mind : *to mature, concoct, prepare :* Pl., Cic., Liv. **e.** Of action on the mind : *to worry, disquiet :* ardentem curaeque iraeque coquebant, Verg. ; Pl. ; Quint. [It. *cuocere ;* Fr. *cuire.*]

coquus (cocus), ī, *m.* [coquō], *a cook :* Pl., Cic., Liv.

cor, cordis, *n.* [*cf.* κῆρ, καρδία], *the heart.*

1. Lit.: Pl., Lucr., Cic., etc. Of persons (as a term of affection or admiration): Pl., Verg. **2.** T r a n s f. **a.** *the heart*, as the seat of the emotions : Pl., Cic., Verg., etc. P h r.: cordi esse alicui, *to be in one's heart ; to be agreeable, dear, pleasing to one :* Pl., Cic., Hor. With *Inf. :* Pl., Liv. **b.** *the heart*, as the seat of wisdom : *mind, judgment,* etc.: Pl., Lucr., Cic. [It. *cuore ;* Fr. *coeur.*]

cŏram, adv. and prep. [for co-ŏr-am, fr. ŏs, ŏris, *the face*]. **I.** A d v. **a.** *in person, personally :* Pl., Cic., Verg., etc. **b.** *openly, publicly, in someone's presence :* Ter., Cic., Hor., etc. Rarely with verb of motion : Hor. **II.** P r e p. (with ABL.). **a.** *Before* its Noun, etc.: Cic., Hor., Tac. **b.** *After* its Noun, etc.: Hor., Tac.

corbis, is, *m.f. a wicker basket :* Pl., Cic., Ov.

corbita, ae, *f.* [corbis], *a slow-sailing merchant-vessel :* Pl., Cic. Ep. [Sp. *corbeta ;* Fr. *corvette.*]

corbŭla, ae, *f.* [dim. corbis], *a little basket :* Pl., Cato, Varr., Suet.

corcŭlum, i, *n.* [dim. cor]. **I.** *dear heart :* Pl. **II.** *miserable heart :* Pl.

cordātē, adv. *prudently, wisely :* Pl.

cordātus, a, um [cor], *wise, prudent :* egregie cordatus homo, Enn.

cor-dŏlium, i, *n.* [cor, doleō], *heart-ache :* Pl. [It. *cordoglio ;* Sp. *cordojo.*]

coriandrum, i, n. ; also, **-us,** i, *f.* [κορίαννον], *coriander :* Pl., Cato.

coriārius, i, *m.* [corium], *a tanner, currier :* Plin., Inscr.

Corinthus, i (Also NOM. **-os,** ACC. **-on**), *f. a city in Greece on the isthmus named after it ;* **Corinthiacus,** a, um ; **Corinthiēnsis,** e ; **Corinthius,** a, um : aes, *an alloy of gold, silver, and copper, used for costly ornaments,* etc.: Cic. Hence, vasa Corinthia, Cic. ; Corinthia supellex, Cic. ; **Corinthia,** ōrum, *n. pl.* (sc. vasa) : Cic. ; **Corinthii,** ōrum, *m. pl. the people of Corinth.*

Coriŏli, ōrum, *m. pl. a town in Latium ;* hence, **Coriŏlānus,** a, um ; also as cognomen of C. Marcius.

corium, i, *n.* (**corius,** i, *m.* Pl.) [orig. scorium, *cf.* scortum]. **I.** *skin, hide.* **1.** Lit.: Lucr., Caes., Cic. ; alicui corium concidere, Pl. P r o v.: canis a corio nunquam absterrebitur uncto, Hor. **2.** T r a n s f. Of plants : *bark, rind :* Plin. **II.** *dressed hide, leather :* Sall. O c c. *strap :* Pl. Also *a layer* in building : Cato. [It. *cuoio ;* Fr. *cuir.*]

Cornēlia, ae, *f. daughter of Scipio Africanus the elder, and mother of the Gracchi.*

Cornēlius, a, *the name of a gens, to which belonged some of the most celebrated Romans, the Scipios, Sulla, the Gracchi, etc. ;* **Cornēliānus,** a, um.

corneŏlus, a, um [dim. corneus], *rather horny :* Cic.

(1) corneus, a, um [cornū], *of horn, horny :* Cic., Verg., Ov.

(2) corneus, a, um [cornus], *of the cornel tree ; of cornel-wood :* Cato, Verg., Ov.

cornĭcen, inis, *m.* [cornū, canō], *a horn-blower :* Cic., Liv., Juv.

cornĭcor, āri [cornix], *to caw like a crow :* Pers.

cornĭcŭla, ae, *f.* [dim. cornix], *a (poor) little crow :* Hor. [It. *cornacchia ;* Fr. *corneille.*]

cornĭcŭlārius, i, *m.* [corniculum], *a soldier who has been promoted by the gift of a corniculum : an adjutant of a centurion,* etc. : Suet.

cornĭcŭlum, i, *n.* [dim. cornū], *a little horn.* **1.** Plin. **2.** T r a n s f.: *a horn-shaped decoration given as a reward for bravery :* Liv.

corniger, era, erum [cornū, gerō], *horn-bearing, horned :* Lucr., Verg., Ov.

corni-pēs, edis, *adj. horn-footed, hoofed :* Cat., Verg., Ov.

cornix, icis, *f.* [*cf.* cor-vus ; κόρ-αξ], *a crow : the carrion crow :* Lucr., Cic., Verg., etc. Its appearance on the left side was considered as a favourable omen : Pl., Cic. ; and its cries as a sign of rain : Verg., Hor. P r o v.: cornicum oculos configere, i.e. *to bite the biters,* Cic.

cornū, ūs, *n.* (**cornum,** i, *n.,* Ov.), *a horn* (of cattle). **1.** Lit.: Cic., Verg., etc. E s p. cornu copiae, *the horn of plenty,* the horn of the goat Amalthea placed among the stars : Pl., Hor., Ov. **2.** T r a n s f. **A.** Abstr. *strength, might :* tu (sc. amphora) addis cornua pauperi, Hor. ; Ov. **B.** Concr. **a.** Of things made of horn. **i.** *a bow :* Verg., Ov. **ii.** *a horn, trumpet :* Cic., Verg., etc. **iii.** *a lantern :* Pl. **iv.** *an oil cruet :* Hor. **v.** *a funnel :* Verg. **b.** Of things resembling a horn. **i.** *a wart :* Hor. **ii.** *a hoof :* Cato, Verg. **iii.** *the bill of a bird :* Ov. **iv.** *the horns of the moon :* Verg., Ov. **v.** *the branches of a river :* Ov. **vi.** *the arm of a bay ; a tongue of land :* Caes. ap. Cic. Ep., Ov. **vii.** *the ends of the sailyards :* Verg., Ov. **viii.** *the cone of a helmet in which the crest was placed :* Verg., Liv. **ix.** *the end of a stick round which books were rolled :* Ov. **x.** *the tip of a bow :* Ov. **xi.** *the horn-shaped side of the cithara* (perh. the sounding-board): Cic. **xii.** *the point or extremity of a place :* Liv., Tac. **xiii.** *the wing of an army* (one of the three main divisions ; of which ala *the extreme wing,* consisting of cavalry, was only a part): Caes., Liv. T r a n s f.: cornua disputationis tuae commovere, Cic. [It. *corno ;* Fr. *corne.*]

1. cornum, i, *n.* v. cornū.

2. cornum, i, *n.* [cornus]. **I.** *the cornel-cherry :* Verg. **II.** = cornus, 2, b.: Ov.

cornus, i, *f. a cornel-cherry, dogwood tree.* **1.** Lit.: Verg. **2.** T r a n s f. **a.** *(something)* made of cornel-wood : Ov. **b.** *a spear-shaft, lance :* Verg., Ov.

cornūtus, a, um [cornū], *horned : animalia,* Varr. As NOUN : Acc.

Coroebus, i, *m. a young Phrygian who fought for Priam against the Greeks.*

corŏlla, ae, *f.* dim. [for corŏn-ula, fr. corōna], *a little garland :* Pl., Cat.

corŏllārium, i, *n.* [corŏlla], orig. *a garland of flowers ;* later, **a.** *a wreath of thin metal silvered or gilt, given as a reward to actors,* etc.: Cic. **b.** *a gift, douceur :* Cic.

corōna, ae, *f.* [*cf.* κυρ-τός, κορωνίς, cur-vus, etc.], *a garland, wreath, chaplet.* **1.** Lit. **a.** With ref. to religious or festal rites : Pl.,

Cic., Hor., etc. **Phr.** : sub coronā vendere : *to sell captives as slaves* (since they were crowned with a chaplet), Caes., Liv. So, sub coronā venire, *to be sold by public auction*, Caes., Liv. ; sub coronā venum dari, Tac. **b.** As reward given to soldiers (*v.* civicus, muralis, navalis, etc.). **c.** As emblem of sovereignty : Verg. **d.** *a constellation, Ariadne's Crown* : Verg., Ov. **2.** Transf. Of objects in the form of a crown. **a.** *a circle of men, bystanders in a court of justice*, etc. : Cic., Hor., Ov. **b.** Milit. *the besiegers round a hostile place* : Caes., Liv. **c.** *a circle of men, for the defence of a place* : Cic., Liv. [Fr. couronne.]

corōnāmentum, ī, *n.* [corōnō], *flowers for garlands* : Cato.

corōnārius, a, um [corōna], *of a wreath* : Plin. ; aurum, *a present of gold collected in provinces for a victorious general* : Cic.

Corōneus (trisyl.), eī, *m.* *a king of Phocis, father of a daughter who was changed into a crow.*

Corōnis, idis, *f. d. of Phlegyas, m. of Aesculapius.* **Corōnidēs**, ae, *m. son of Coronis*, i.e. *Aesculapius.*

corōnō, āre [corōna], *to garland, wreathe.* **1.** Lit. : Cic., Verg., etc. **2.** Transf. : *to garland, encircle* : Lucr. ; omnem abitum custode, Verg. ; silva aquas, Ov.

corporeus, a, um [corpus]. **I.** *corporeal* : Lucr., Cic. **II.** *composed of flesh, fleshly* : Ov.

corpulentus, a, um [corpus], *corpulent, fleshy* : Pl., Quint.

corpus, oris, *n.* *any object perceptible by the senses, form, matter, body, substance.* **1.** Lit. **A.** (opp. mens, animus, anima) : tangere aut tangi nisi corpus nulla potest res, Lucr. ; corpus intellegi sine loco non potest, Cic. ; aquae, Lucr. **B.** *the animal body* : Pl., Cic., Ov., etc. **C.** Esp. **a.** *the flesh* : Lucr., Cic., Ov. **b.** *a lifeless body, a corpse* (= cadaver) : Caes., Liv., Ov. Hence, *the forms of the dead* (as still having substance) : Verg. **c.** *the trunk*, as opp. to the head : Verg., Ov. **2.** Transf. **a.** *a person, being, creature*, etc. : Cic., Verg., Ov., Liv., etc. **b.** *a totality, complete whole*, esp. *a body politic, a corporate body, community, corporation* : rei publicae, Cic. ; civitatis, Liv., Tac. **c.** *the body, general frame* (e.g. of ships, etc.) : Caes. [It. corpo ; Fr. corps, and, from it, Eng. corpse ; also Fr. corsage.]

corpusculum, ī, *n.* [*dim.* corpus]. **I.** *a small body of matter, an atom* : Lucr., Cic. **II.** *a puny body* : Juv. **III.** *a dear little body* : Pl.

cor-rādō, *v.* conrādō.

corrēctiō, ōnis, *f.* [corrigō]. **I.** *a making straight ; an amendment, improvement, correction* : vitiorum, Cic. ; Suet. **II.** Rhet. : *a correction of what has been said* : Cic.

corrēctor, ōris, *m.* [corrigō], *a corrector, reformer* : Ter., Cic., Hor., etc.

cor-rēpō, rēpere, rēpsī, *to creep or slink* : Lucr., Cic.

correptius, *comp. adv. in a shorter way* : Ov.

correptus, a, um, *Part.* corripiō.

cor-rīdeō, ēre, *to laugh aloud.* Transf. : Lucr.

corrigia, ae, *f.* [corrigō], *a shoe-tie, shoe-latchet* : Cic. [It. coreggia, scoreggia ; Sp. correa ; Fr. courroie.]

cor-rigō, rigere, rēxī, rēctum [regō], *to put quite straight, put in line with.* **1.** Lit. : Plin. Ep. **2.** Transf. : *to set right.* **a.** Of physical error : (navium) cursum, Cic. ; Ov. **b.** Of mental or moral error : Pl., Cic., Ov., etc. **c.** Of a composition : Cic. Ep., Hor., Quint. [It. scorgere, and corgere in accorgersi.]

cor-ripiō, ripere, ripuī, reptum [rapiō], *to seize, snatch up, carry off quickly or violently.* **1.** Lit. **a.** In gen. : Cic., Verg., etc. With Refl. Pron. : Pl., Ter., Verg. With viam, gradum, etc., *to set out quickly on, to hasten* : viam, Verg., Plin. Ep. ; gradum, Hor. **b.** Of robbery, etc. : Cic., Verg., Tac. **2.** Transf. **a.** Of death, disease, fire, etc. : fiamma corripuit tabulas, Verg. ; Lucr. ; Ov. ; nec singula morbi corpora corripiunt, Verg. ; Lucr. ; Ov. **b.** Of the passions, emotions, etc. : hunc plausus hiantem corripuit, Verg. ; correpta cupidine, Ov. ; Suet. **c.** *to seize upon* (with abuse, censure, etc.) : convicio, Caes. ; Ov. ; Liv., etc. Often in Tac. of accusation : a delatoribus corripitur, Tac. **d.** *to shorten, cut short* : moras, Ov. ; Tib. Of syllables : Quint.

cor-ro-, *v.* con-ro-.

cor-rūgō, āre, *to make full of wrinkles, to wrinkle* : ne sordida mappa corruget naris (i.e. in disgust), Hor.

cor-rumpō, rumpere, rūpī, ruptum, *to burst, break to pieces* ; hence, **I.** *to destroy utterly, ruin, waste.* **1.** Lit. : frumentum flumine atque incendio corruperunt, Caes. ; Sall. ; Prop. **2.** Transf. : diem, Pl. ; se suosque, Sall. ; voluptatem, Hor. ; libertatem, Tac. **II.** *to destroy* (the essence of a thing), *taint, ruin, corrupt, mar, adulterate*, etc. **1.** Lit. : cenam, Pl. ; conclusa aqua facile corrumpitur, Cic. ; Hor. ; Verg. **2.** Transf. **a.** Morally : filium, Pl. ; mulierem, Ter. ; milites licentiā, Sall. ; mores civitatis, Cic. ; disciplinam, Tac. Esp. of bribery : aliquem pecuniā, Cic. ; Sall. ; Liv. ; fidem nutricis, Ov. ; Hor. **b.** Of documents, etc. : *to corrupt, falsify* : Cic. Also of pronunciation : Quint.

cor-ruō, ruere, ruī. **A.** Intrans. : *to fall in a heap or in ruins, collapse, sink to the ground.* **1.** Lit. **a.** Of things : Cic., Ov. **b.** Of persons : Cic., Verg., etc. **c.** Of animals : Prop. **2.** Transf. : opes, Cic. ; histriones, Cic. ; Liv. In a law-suit : Plin. Ep. **B.** Trans. **a.** *to shatter* : Lucr., Cat. **b.** *to heap up* : Pl.

corruptē, *adv.* **I.** *corruptly* : Cic. **II.** *in lax discipline* : Comp. : Tac.

corruptēla, ae, *f.* [corrumpō], *a means of ruining ; corruption, seduction.* **A.** Abstr. : Pl., Cic., Liv. **B.** Concr. : *a corrupter, seducer* : Pl., Ter.

corruptiō, ōnis, *f.* [corrumpō], *a breaking up, ruining.* **A.** Act. : Tac. **B.** Pass. : *a corrupt condition* : Cic. Transf. : opinionum, Cic. [It. corruzione.]

corruptor, ōris, *m.* (Pl., Cic., Hor.) and **cor-ruptrix**, īcis, *f.* (Cic. Ep.) [corrumpō], *a corrupter, seducer, briber.* [It. corruttore.]

corruptus, a, um. **I.** *Part.* corrumpō. **II.**
A d j. : *ruined, tainted, bad :* caelum, Lucr.,
Verg. ; aqua, Auct. B. Alex. ; *iter factum
corruptius* imbri, Hor. ; *homines corruptis-
simi*, Sall.

cortex, icis, *m.* and *f., the bark, rind.* **a.** Of
trees and plants : Cic., Verg., etc. **b.** *the
bark of the cork-tree, cork :* Cato, Hor., Ov.
P r o v. : nare sine cortice, Hor.

cortīna, ae, *f.* **I.** *a round vessel, a kettle,
caldron :* Pl., Cato. **II.** *the tripod of
Apollo in form of a caldron :* Verg. ; *a
tripod as sacred offering :* Suet. T r a n s f. :
of the vault of heaven : Enn.

corūlus, *v.* corylus.

cōrus, *v.* caurus.

coruscō, āre [*cf.* κορύσσω]. **1.** Lit. : *to
swing rapidly, oscillate, quiver.* **A.** T r a n s. :
Cic., Verg., etc. **B.** I n t r a n s. : Lucr.,
Verg. **2.** T r a n s f. Of the tremulous
vibration of light : Pac., Verg.

coruscus, a, um [coruscō]. **1.** Lit. : *swinging rapidly, oscillating, waving :* silvae,
Verg. Also *quivering :* Pl. **2.** T r a n s f.
Of the tremulous vibration of light, *shimmering :* Lucr., Verg., etc.

corvus, i, *m.* [*cf.* κορώνη], *a raven :* Pl., Cic.,
Ov., etc. P r o v. : in cruce corvos pascere,
Hor. T r a n s f. : *a military implement, a
grapnel :* Curt.

Corybantes, ium, *m. pl.* *the priests of Cybele ;*
Corybantius, a, um.

Cōrycius, a, um, *belonging to the Corycian
mountain-caves on Parnasus ;* **Cōrycius**,
a, um ; **Cōrycides** Nymphae, *the Muses.*

cōrycus, i. *m.* [κώρυκος], *a sack filled with
sand, flour, etc. on which the athletae practised
with their fists.* Comic. : corycus laterum et
vocis meae Bestia, Cic.

corylētum, i, *n.* [corylus], *a copse of hazel-
trees :* Ov.

corylus (corulus), i. *f.* [κόρυλος], *a hazel or
filbert tree :* Cato, Verg., Ov.

corymbifer, eri, *m.* [corymbus, ferō], *bearing
clusters of ivy berries,* an epithet of Bacchus :
Ov.

corymbus, i, *m.* [κόρυμβος], *a cluster of ivy-
berries :* Verg., Ov. Also of fruit or
flowers.

coryphaeus, i, *m.* [κορυφαῖος], *a leader,
chief, head :* Cic.

cōrytos, i, *m.* [γωρυτός], *a quiver :* Verg.,
Ov.

cōs, **cōss** = cōnsul, cōnsulēs.

cōs, **cōtis**, *f.* *a whetstone, hone, grindstone.*
1. L i t. : Cic., Hor., Liv. **2.** T r a n s f. :
Cic., Hor. (v. also cautēs).

Cōs or **Cous (Coos)**, Coi, *f. a small island in
the Aegean Sea, celebrated for the cultivation
of the vine and for weaving very fine linen ;*
Cōus, a, um ; **Cōum**, i. *n.* (*sc.* vinum) :
Hor.; **Cōa**, ōrum. *n. pl.* Coan garments :
Hor., Ov.

cosmēta, ae, *m.* [κοσμητής], *an adorner :* a
slave who had charge of the wardrobe of his
mistress : Juv.

costa, ae, *f. a rib.* **1.** L i t. : Pl., Lucr., Verg.
2. T r a n s f. : *a side, a wall :* costae aeni,
Verg. ; navium, Plin. [It. *costa ;* Sp.
cuesta ; Fr. *côte.*]

costātus, a, um [costa], *having ribs, ribbed :*
Varr.

costum, i, *n.* [κόστος], *an oriental aromatic
plant :* Hor., Ov.

cothurnātus, a, um [cothurnus], *wearing the
cothurnus ;* hence, *of or suitable to tragedy,
tragic :* Ov., Sen. Ep. ; hence, *elevated :*
Ov.

cothurnus, i, *m.* [κόθορνος], *a high boot.*
I. In gen. : Cic. **II.** *a Greek hunting-boot*
(laced up in front and reaching to the middle
of the leg) : Verg., Juv. **III.** *the buskin
worn by tragic actors* (soccus by comic actors).
1. L i t. : Cic., Hor. **2.** T r a n s f. **a.**
tragedy : Hor. **b.** *a subject of tragedy :*
Juv. **c.** *the elevated style of Greek tragedy :*
Verg., Quint., etc.

cōtid-, *v.* cottid-.

cottabus, i, *m.* [κότταβος], *a game which con-
sisted in flicking a drop of wine, etc., on a
brazen vessel.* Comic. : Pl.

cottana (cotona, coctona, and **coctana)**,
ōrum, *n. pl.* [a Syrian word], *a kind of small
fig :* Juv., Mart.

cottidiānus (cōtid-), a, um [cottidiē], *of every
day, daily.* **1.** L i t. : Ter., Caes., Cic.,
Liv. A d v. **cottidiānō :** Pl., Cic.
2. T r a n s f.: *everyday, ordinary :* verba,
Cic. Ep. ; Ter., Cic.; Mart.

cottidiē (cōtid-), adv. [quot, diēs], *daily,
every day :* Ter., Cic.

coturnix, icis, *f. a quail :* Pl., Lucr., Ov.,
etc.

Cotys, yis, *m.* [Acc. us. -tyn], the name of
several Thracian kings.

Cotyttō, ūs, *f. the Thracian goddess of
lewdness.*

Coüs and **Cōus**, *v.* Cōs.

covinnārius, i, *m.* [covinnus], *a soldier who
fought from a chariot :* Tac.

covinnus, i, *m. a war-chariot of the Britons and
Belgae :* Luc. Of a *travelling-chariot :*
Mart.

coxa, ae, *f. the hip-bone :* Plin. Ep. [It.
coscia ; Fr. *cuisse.*]

coxendix, icis, *f.* [coxa], *the hip :* Pl., Varr.,
Suet.

crābrō, ōnis, *m. a hornet :* Verg., Ov. P r o v. :
irritare crabrones, Pl. [It. *calabrone.*]

crambē, ēs, *f.* [κράμβη], *a kind of cabbage :*
Plin. T r a n s f. : crambe repetita, i.e. *a
réchauffé, stale repetitions,* Juv.

crāpula, ae, *f.* [κραιπάλη], *drunkenness, debauch,* esp. in its consequences, *the next day's
sickness, headache :* Pl., Cic., Liv. [Fr.
crapule.]

crāpulārius, a, um [crāpula], *for* (i.e. to prevent) *intoxication :* Pl.

crās, adv. *to-morrow.* **1.** L i t. : Pl., Cic.,
Hor., etc. **2.** T r a n s f. : *in the future :*
Hor., Ov.

crassē, adv. *thickly.* T r a n s f. **a.** *grossly,
rudely :* Hor. **b.** *not clearly, confusedly :*
Sen. Ep.

crassitūdō, inis, *f.* [crassus]. **I.** *thickness :*
Pl., Cic., etc. **II.** *density :* Cic. **III.**
Concr. *dregs :* Cato.

crassus, a, um. **1.** Lit. **a.** *thick :* Pl.,
Cic. Ep., Ov., etc. **b.** *thick, dense.* Of
soil : Cic., Verg. Of liquids : Verg., Hor.,
Ov. Of the atmosphere : Lucr., Cic., Verg.,
etc. **2.** T r a n s f. **a.** infortunium, i.e. *a
round beating,* Pl. **b.** *dense, dull :* Hor.,

Quint. *Comp. :* Lucr., Quint.; *Sup. :*
Cic. [It. *grasso ;* Sp. *graso :* Fr. *gras,*
graisse : Eng. *grease.*]
Crassus, a, *a family name in the gens* Licinia;
esp. **I.** L. Licinius Crassus, *a famous*
orator. **II.** M. Licinius Crassus, *the trium-*
vir, killed at Carrhae, B.C. 53.
crăstĭnus, a, um [crās], *to-morrow's :* Pl.,
Cic., Verg., etc.; Old ABL. (or LOCAT.) :
die crastini, *to-morrow,* Pl. As Noun : in
crastinum differre, Cic.
crătēra, ae, *f.* (Cic., Hor., Liv.) and **crătēr,**
ēris, *m.* (Lucr., Verg., Ov.; Acc. -ēra, Verg.;
Acc. *pl.* -ēras, Verg.) [κρατήρ], *a bowl for*
mixing wine. **1.** Lit. : Verg., Ov. **2.**
Transf.: *a bowl :* for oil, Verg.; for
water : Plin. Ep.; an opening in the earth :
Lucr., Ov.; the name of a constellation :
Cic., Ov.
crātis (Acc. -im, Pl.), is, *f.* wicker- *or hurdle-*
work (mostly in *pl.*). **1.** Lit. **a.** *a hurdle :*
Cato, Verg., Hor. **b.** *a hurdle* (for punishing criminals) : Pl., Liv., Tac. **c.** *a*
harrow : Verg. **d.** *the ribs* of a shield :
Verg., Curt. **e.** Milit. : *fascines* (for filling
up trenches, etc.) : Caes., Liv. **2.** Transf.:
spinae, Ov.; pectoris, Verg.; favorum,
Verg. [It. *grada ;* Sp. *grada.*]
creătĭō, ōnis, *f.* [creō], *a choosing to an office,*
election : magistratuum, Cic.
creātor, ōris, *m.* (Cic., Ov.), and **creātrix,**
īcis, *f.* (Lucr., Cat., Verg.) [creō], *a begetter,*
father ; mother. Hence, *founder :* urbis,
Cic.
crēber, bra, brum [cogn. with crē-scō]. **I.**
Of growth, *dense-grown, luxuriant, prolific.*
1. Lit. : Pl.; arbores, Caes.; silva, Lucr.;
Ov. **2.** Transf.: creber procellis Africus, Verg. Of writings : Thucydides creber
rerum frequentiā, Cic. **II. a.** Of material
things, *dense, crowded, numerous :* Pl.;
aedificia, Caes.; Cic., etc. **b.** Transf.
Of immaterial things, *repeated, frequent :*
itiones, Ter.; Lucr.; anhelitus, Verg.;
rumores, litterae, Caes.; sermones, Cic.;
ignes, Sall. Hence, in scribendo, Cic.
Comp. : crēbrior : Caes., Cic.; *Sup. :*
crēberrimus : Caes., Sall.
crēbrēscō (crēbēscō), brēscere, bruī (buī)
[crēber], *to thicken, become frequent, increase,*
gain strength : crebrescunt optatae aurae,
Verg.; bellum, Tac.; sermo, Verg. With
Acc. and *Inf.* clause as subject : per idoneos socios crebrescit vivere Agrippam, Tac.
crēbrĭtās, ātis, *f.* [crēber], *frequency :* litterarum, Cic.
crēbrō, *adv. repeatedly, frequently, again and*
again : Pl., Cic. Ep. *Comp. :* crēbrius,
Pl., Cic. Ep. *Sup. :* crēberrimē, Cic.
crēdĭbĭlis, e, *adj.* [crēdō], *trustworthy, worthy*
of belief, credible : Cic., Ov., etc.; credibile
est, with Acc. and *Inf. :* Tac.
crēdĭbĭlĭter, *adv. credibly :* Cic.
crēdĭtor, ōris, *m.* [crēdō], *an entruster, lender,*
creditor : Cic., Liv., Hor.
crēdō, dere, dĭdī, dĭtum (*Pres. Subj.* crēduam,
creduās, Pl. *Opt. :* creduim, īs, it, etc. Pl.)
I. *to entrust, consign,* etc. : Pl.; alicui
grandem pecuniam, Cic.; militi arma, Liv.;
se suaque omnia alienissimis, Caes.; per-
fidis se credidit hostibus, Hor.; pennis se
caelo, Verg.; arcana libris, Hor.; Pl. **II.**

to put faith in, have trust or *confidence in*
(with DAT.). **a.** Of persons : Cic., Liv.,
Hor. **b.** Of things : Sall., Liv., Verg. **III.**
to trust the words of any one, give credence
to, believe. **a.** Of persons (with DAT.) :
Pl., Ter., Cic. Esp. in phr. mihi credo,
mihi credite, Cic., Hor. *Pass. Impers. :*
Juv. *Pass. Pers. :* Verg., Ov. **b.** Of
words, etc. (with DAT.) : orationi, promissis, Cic.; Liv. **c.** Of facts (with Acc.) :
homines id quod volunt credunt, Caes.; in
Pass. : res tam scelesta credi non potest,
Cic. **IV.** *to believe, to be of opinion, to*
think, suppose. With Acc. and *Inf. :* Pl.,
Cic., Hor., etc. Hence, in *Pass.* with NOM.
and *Inf. :* navis creditur ire, Lucr.; Quint.
Often in parenthesis (polite or ironical) : si
te iam, Catilina, interfici iussero, credo, erit
verendum mihi, Cic. Phr. : crederes, *you*
(*i.e. any one*) *would have thought,* Liv.; so,
credas, *one would imagine,* Juv. *Pass.*
Impers. : satis creditum est, *it is believed*
on good evidence, Liv.; credito, *it being be-*
lieved (with Acc. and *Inf.*) : Tac. [Fr.
croire.]
crēdŭlĭtās, ātis, *f.* [crēdulus], *trustfulness,*
credulity : Ov., Tac.
crēdŭlus, a, um [crēdō], *trustful, credulous, too*
confiding. **1.** Lit. Of living creatures :
Cic., Ov., etc. With DAT. : Verg., Tac.
With *in* and Acc. : in vitium, Ov. **2.**
Transf. : credula res amor est, Ov.;
fama, Tac.; spes animi mutui, Hor.
cremō, āre, *to burn to ashes, consume by fire :*
urbem, Liv.; Caes.; Lucr., etc. Esp. of
the burning of the dead : Cic. Of *victims in*
sacrifices : Ov.; of *things devoted :* Liv.
cremor, ōris, *m.* *thick juice obtained from*
animal or *vegetable substances ; pulp, broth,*
etc. : Pl., Cato, Ov.
creō, āre. **I.** *to create, produce.* **1.** Lit. :
genus humanum, fruges, Lucr.; arbores,
Verg.; Cic. **2.** Transf. **a.** Of abstract
things, *to bring into being, produce, cause :*
Pl.; luxuriam, periculum, Cic.; dictaturam, Liv. **b.** Of election to office, *to*
make, create : consules, Caes., Cic.; dictatorem, Liv. **II.** *to beget, bear :* Hor., Liv.,
Ov. Poet. : in *Part. Perf.* with ABL. :
sprung from, begotten by, born of : Ov.
Creō or **Creōn,** ontis, *m. king of Corinth, who*
betrothed his daughter Creusa to Jason.
creper, era, erum [*cf.* κνέφας], *dark.* Transf.
uncertain, obscure, doubtful : creperi certamina belli, Lucr.
crepĭda, ae, *f.* [κρηπίς], *a slipper* or *sandal,*
consisting only of a sole : Cic., Liv., Hor.
Prov. : ne sutor supra crepidam, *let the*
cobbler stick to his last, Plin.
crepĭdātus, a, um [crepida], *wearing san-*
dals : Cic.
crepĭdō, inis, *f.* [κρηπίς]. **I.** *a ground,*
basis, foundation, pedestal : Plin. **II.** *an*
elevated enclosure ; a quay, pier, dam, dike,
etc. : Cic., Verg., Liv.
crepĭdŭla, ae, *f.* [*dim.* crepida], *a small san-*
dal : Pl.
crepĭtācillum, ī, *n.* [*dim.* crepităculum], *a*
small rattle : Lucr.
crepĭtācŭlum, ī, *n.* [crepitō], *a rattle :* Mart.,
Quint.
crepĭtō, āre [*freq.* crepō], *to rattle, crackle,*

clatter, rustle repeatedly or *intensely* : Pl., Luer., Verg., etc. [Sp. *grietar*.]

crepitus, ūs, *m.* [crepō], *a rattling, creaking, clattering, clashing, rustling*, etc. : cardinum, Pl. ; dentium, Cic. ; armorum, Liv. ; carbasi, Lucr. Of a noisy breaking of wind : Pl., Cic. Ep., etc.

crepō, āre, uī, itum. **A.** Intrans.: *to rattle, crack, creak, clatter*, etc.: foris, Pl., Ter. ; remi, Verg. ; catena, Sen. Ep. ; sonabile sistrum, Ov. ; crepante pede, Hor. ; nubes subito motu, Ov. ; crepat ingens Seianus, Juv. **B.** Trans.: *to cause to sound.* **1.** Lit.: populus frequens laetumter crepuit sonum, Hor. **2.** Transf.: *to talk noisily* or *chatter about* : publicas res, Pl. ; gravem militiam, Hor.

crepundia, ōrum, *n. pl.* [crepō]. Lit.: *a rattle* ; *toys* (as amulets), *hung round infants' necks* : Pl., Cic.

crepusculum, ī, *n.* [*cf.* creper], *partial night, twilight, dusk of the evening.* **1.** Lit.: Pl., Ov. **2.** Transf.: *darkness*, in *pl.* : Ov.

crēscō, crēscere, crēvī, crētum (*Inf.Perf.sync.* crēsso, Lucr.). **I.** *to come into being, arise, spring* : Lucr., Verg. Esp. in *Part.Perf.* cretus : *arisen, sprung, born of* (with ABL.) : corpore materno, Lucr. ; Troiano a sanguine, Verg. **II.** Of things already in existence : *to grow, thrive, increase in bulk*, etc. **1.** Lit.: arbores, Lucr. ; (ostrea) cum lunā pariter, Cic. ; Verg. **2.** Transf. **a.** *to grow in bulk* : Liger ex nivibus, Caes. ; crescit et invito lentus in ore cibus, Ov. **b.** Of number : non mihi absenti crevisse amicos, Cic. ; Ov. **c.** Of immaterial things : hostium opes animique, Cic. ; inopia omnium, Liv. ; fuga atque formido latius, Sall. ; crescit amor nummi quantum ipsa pecunia crescit, Juv. **d.** Esp. in honour or distinction : accusarem alios potius, ex quibus possem crescere, Cic. ; ille (Dumnorix) per se (Diviciacum) crevisset, Caes. ; crescendi in curiā occasio, Liv. ; posterā laude, Hor. ; Quint. [Fr. *crotre*.]

crēta, ae, *f. Cretan earth*, i.e. *chalk or a similar kind of earth* : Plin. ; used for whitening garments, Pl. ; as a cosmetic : Hor. ; for seals : Cic. (*cf.* cretula) ; for marking *the goal in a race-course* : Plin. ; used to make *a white* or *favourable mark* : sani ut cretā an carbone notandi, Hor. [Sp. *greda* ; Fr. *craie, crayon.*]

Crēta, ae, *f.* (Acc. -am or -ēn), *an island in the Mediterranean, now Candia* : **Crētaeus, Crēsius, Crēticus, Crētānus**, a, um ; **Crētēnsis**, e ; **Crēs**, Crētis, *m.* and **Cressa**, ae, *f. a Cretan.*

crētātus, a, um [crēta], *marked with chalk* : fascine, Cic. Ep. ; bos, Juv. Transf.: ambitio (of candidates clothed in white), Pers.

crēteus, a, um [crēta], *made of chalk* or *clay* : persona, Lucr.

crētiō, ōnis, *f.* [cernō]. In law, *a formal declaration respecting the acceptance of an inheritance* : Cic.

crētōsus, a, um [crēta], *abounding in chalk* or *clay* : Cato, Ov.

crētula, ae, *f.* [*dim.* crēta], *white clay used for seals* : Cic.

(1) crētus, a, um, *Part.* cernō.

(2) crētus, a, um, *Part.* crēscō.

Creūsa, ae, *f.* **I.** *d. of Creon, king of Corinth, and w. of Jason ; killed by Medea.* **II.** *d. of Priam and w. of Aeneas.*

cribrum, ī, *n.* [*cf.* κρίνω, cernō], *a sieve* : Cic. Prov.: imbrem in cribrum gerere, Pl.

crimen, inis, *n.* [cernō]. **I.** *a charge or accusation.* **a.** Judic. or public : Pl., Cic., Verg., etc. ; oft. with defining GEN.: crimen malefici, ambitūs, avaritiae, etc., Cic. ; esse in crimine, *to be accused*, Cic. ; crimen inferre, adferre, offerre, Cic. ; intendere, Liv. ; defendere, propulsare, Cic. ; Ov. **b.** Nonjudic.: *charge, reproach* : adrogantiae, Cic. **II. a.** *the ground* or *matter of a charge* : crimina belli (i.e. *charges of acts of war*), Verg. ; Liv. **b.** *crime, guilt* : Liv., Ov., Tac. **c.** *the guilty cause* : se causam clamat crimenque caputque malorum, Verg.

criminātiō, ōnis, *f.* [criminor], *an accusation* ; esp. in bad sense, *slander, calumny* : Cic., Liv. In *pl.* : Cic., Liv., Tac.

criminor, *an accuser* ; esp. in bad sense, *a slanderer* : Pl. ; in alios, Tac.

criminō = criminor, *to accuse* : Pl.

criminor, ārī [crimen], with personal object : *to bring a charge against* ; esp. in bad sense, *to slander, calumniate.* **a.** With Acc. of person : me tibi, Ter. ; C. Marius Q. Metellum apud populum R. criminatus est, bellum illum ducere, Cic. ; Liv. ; Tac. **b.** With Acc. of thing : potentiam meam invidiose criminabatur, Cic. ; Tac. With Acc. and *Inf.* : de amicitiā, quam a me violatam esse criminatus est, Cic. ; Liv. With *de* : nescio quid de illā tribu, Cic.

criminōsē, *adv. by way of accusation* ; *slanderously*, etc.: Cic., Liv., etc. *Comp.* : Cic., Tac. *Sup.* : Suet.

criminōsus, a, um [crimen], *accusatory, slanderous* : orationes, Liv. ; iambi, Hor. ; acerbus, criminosus, popularis homo ac turbulentus, Cic. *Sup.* : Suet.

crinālis, e. *adj.* [crinis], *of the hair* : Verg., Ov. *Neut.* as Noun, **crināle**, *a hair-band* : Ov.

crinis, is, *m. hair* ; esp. *the long hair of women* (*cf.* capillus). **1.** Lit. **a.** In *pl.*: Pl., Cic., Verg., etc. **b.** In *sing.* (in collect. sense) : Hor., Ov., Tac. **2.** Transf.: of object resembling hair, *e.g. the tail of a comet* : Verg., Ov.

crinitus, a, um [crinis], *having long hair* or *locks.* **1.** Lit.: Enn., Verg. ; Ov. **2.** Transf.: galea, *crested*, Verg. ; stella, i.e. *a comet* : Cic.

crisō, āre, *to move the haunches* : Lucil., Juv.

crispisulcāns, antis [crispus sulcō], igneum fulmen, *the forked, furrowy lightning* : Poet. ap. Cic.

crispō, āre [crispus]. **A.** Trans. **1.** Lit. (of the hair), *to curl, wave* : Plin. **2.** Transf.: *to wave, swing, brandish* : Verg. **B.** Intrans. (only in *Part.* **crispāns**, *curled, wrinkled* : Plin., Pers.

crispus, a, um. **1.** Lit. (of the hair), *curled, waved* : Pl. Of persons : *having curled hair, curly-headed* : Pl., Ter. **2.** Transf. **a.** *curled, wrinkled* : Enn. ; brassica, Cato. **b.** *in tremulous motion, quivering* : Verg., Juv. [Fr. *crêpe.*]

crista, ae, f. [perh. fr. same root as crinis].
1. Lit.: *a tuft on the head of animals*, esp.
a cock's comb : Varr., Juv.; *crest* of a lap-
wing, Ov.; of a serpent, Ov. Prov.: illi
surgunt cristae, Juv. 2. Transf.: *the
crest of a helmet, plume* : Luor., Verg., Liv.
[It. *cresta* ; Fr. *crête*.]

cristātus, a, um [crista]. 1. Lit.: *tufted,
crested* : ales, Ov. 2. Transf.: *plumed* :
galeae, Liv.; Achilles, Verg.

criticus, i, m. [κριτικός, *capable of judging*],
a critic : Cic. Ep., Hor., Quint.

croceus, a, um [crocus]. I. *of saffron* :
odores, Verg. II. *saffron-coloured, yellow,
golden* : acanthus, Verg.; Ov.

crocinum, i, n. *saffron* ; as term of endearment : Pl.

crōciō, īre, *to cry or croak like a raven* : Pl.

crocodīlus, i, m. [κροκόδειλος], *a crocodile* :
Cic. [It. *coccodrillo*.]

crocōtārius, a, um *of or belonging to the preparation of saffron-coloured garments* : in-
fectores, Pl.

crocōtula, ae, f. [dim. crocus], *a saffron-
coloured dress* : Pl., Verg.

crocus, i, m. (Verg., Prop., Ov.) and **crocum**,
i, n. (Sall., Plin.) [κρόκος]. 1. Lit.: *the
crocus.* 2. Transf. a. *saffron*, made
from the plant, used as a perfume : Lucr.,
Hor., Sen. Ep. b. *saffron-colour* : Verg.

Croesus, i, m. *king of Lydia, famous for his
wealth.*

crotalistria, ae, f. [crotalum], *a castanet-
dancer* : Prop.

crotalum, i, n. [κρόταλον], *a rattle, castanet* :
Cic.

cruciābilitātēs, um, f. pl. [cruciābilis], *tortures, torments* : animi, Pl.

cruciābiliter, adv. *with torture* : Pl., Auct.
B. Afr.

cruciāmenta, ōrum, n. pl. [cruciō], *tortures* :
Pl., Cic.

cruciātus, ūs, m. [cruciō], *torture, torment, a
torturing.* 1. Lit. (of the body): Pl.,
Cic., Ov., etc. 2. Transf. a. Of the
mind : Cic. b. Comic. = *calamity, ruin* :
Pl. c. In pl. : *instruments of torture* :
Cic.

cruciō, āre [crux], *to rack, torture, torment.*
1. Lit. (of the body): Pl., Cic., Ov., etc.
2. Transf. (of the mind): Pl., Cic. Ep.,
Hor. In Middle : miserae matres cruci-
antur, Pl.; Cic.; with Acc. and Inf.,
crucior bolum tantum mihi ereptum, Ter.;
Pl.

crucisalus, i, m. [crux, saliō], *a gallows- or
cross-dancer* : Pl.

crūdēlis, e, adj. [crūdus], *cruel, unfeeling.*
1. Lit. Of persons : Cic., Sall. With *in*
and Acc. : in liberos, Cic.; in plebem, Liv.
2. Transf. Of things : bellum, Cic.;
facinora, Sall.; poena, Verg., Ov. Comp. :
Cat., Ov., Quint. Sup. : Nep., Suet.

crūdēlitās, ātis, f. [crūdēlis], *cruelty, barbarity* : Caes., Cic., Liv.; in nostros
homines, Cic.; exercere in vivo, Cic.

crūdēliter, adv. *cruelly, in a cruel manner* :
Caes., Cic. Comp. : Cat., Liv., Ov. Sup. :
Caes., Cic.

crūdēscō, dēscere, duī [crūdus], *to become
harsh or violent* : morbus, Verg.; pugna,
Verg.; seditio, Tac.

crūditās, ātis, f. [crūdus], *repletion, indigestion* : Cic.

crūdus, a, um [cf. κρύος, cruor]. 1. Lit.
a. *bloody, bleeding* : vulnera, Ov., Plin. Ep.
b. *raw, uncooked* : Pl., Liv., Suet. 2.
Transf. A. *raw, undressed* (of hide, etc.) :
Varr., Verg. B. *unripe, immature.* a.
Of fruit : Cic. b. Of age : equa, Hor.;
puella, Mart.; senectus (i.e. *fresh, not fully
matured*), Verg., Tac.; diem crudi adhuc
serviti, Tac. c. Of food, *hard, undigested* :
Juv. Of persons, *suffering from indigestion,
dyspeptic* : Cic., Hor., Quint. d. Of feeling, *hard, harsh, merciless* : Pl., Verg., Ov.
e. Of the voice, *harsh* : Cic. Comp. : Cic.
Sup. : Suet. [Fr. *cru*.]

cruentō, āre [cruentus], *to make bloody, to
stain with blood.* 1. Lit.: Enn., Cic., Ov.
2. Transf.: haec te lacerat, haec cru-
entat oratio, Cic.

cruentus, a, um [fr. root of cruor], *gory,
bloody, bloodstained.* 1. Lit. : Cic., Hor.,
Liv., etc. Hence, *blood-red* : Verg. 2.
Transf. a. Of abstr. things : victoria,
Sall.; ira, Hor.; pax, Tac. b. *bloodthirsty,
cruel* : Hor., Ov.

crumēna (**crumina**), ae, f. *a small pouch or
purse* (for money) ; us. hanging from the
neck). 1. Lit.: Pl. 2. Transf.: non
deficiente crumenā (= *money*), Hor.; Juv.

cruor, ōris, m. [cf. κρέας, κρύος, crūdus]. I.
gore, blood from a wound (whilst *sanguis* is
blood in gen.). 1. Lit. : Lucr., Cic., Verg.,
etc. In pl. : Verg. 2. Transf.: *bloodshed, murder* : castus a cruore civili, Cic.;
adde cruorem stultitiae, Hor. In pl.:
Hor. II. = *sanguis, the blood in the body* :
Lucr.

cruppellāriī, ōrum, m. pl. [a Celtic word],
mail-clad combatants (among the Gauls) :
Tac.

crūricrepida, ae, m. [crūs crepō], *Fitzrattle-
shin* (*a fictitious name of a slave*) : Pl.

crūrifragius, i, m. [crūs frangō], *one whose
legs or shins are broken* : Pl.

crūs, ūris, n. *a leg, shank, shin.* 1. Lit.
Of animals and men : Cic., Verg., etc. 2.
Transf. Of a bridge : Cat.

crūsta, ae, f. I. *the hard surface of a body ;
rind, shell, crust, bark,* etc. : luti, Lucr.;
fluminis, Verg. II. Of plastic art : *plaster-
work, stucco, inlaid work on walls* or *vessels.*
1. Lit.: Cic., Juv. 2. Transf.: *stucco*
("whitewash"): Sen. [It. *crosta* : Fr.
croûte.]

crūstulum, i, n. [dim. crūstum], *small pastry* : Hor., Sen. Ep.

crūstum, i, n. [crūsta], *pastry, anything
baked* : Verg., Hor.

crux, ucis, f. *a pole or cross* (on which slaves
were impaled or hanged). 1. Lit.: Ter.;
tollere in crucem, Cic.; in cruce suffigere,
Hor.; in crucem agere, Cic.; cruci adfigere,
Tac. 2. Transf. a. Comic. (= *destruction, ruin,* etc.) : abi in malam crucem (*go
and be hanged*), Pl.; quaerere in malo crucem, Ter. b. Of persons : *a gallows-bird* :
Pl. ; *a torment* (i.e. *a tormentor*) : Ter. Also
in pl. : Ter. [It. *croce* ; Fr. *croix*.]

crypta, ae, f. [κρύπτη], *a covered gallery, a
subterranean passage* : Juv., Suet. [It.
grotta ; Sp. *gruta* ; Fr. *grotte*.]

crypto-porticus, ūs, *f. a covered gallery* or *passage* : Plin. Ep.

crystallinus, a, um [κρυστάλλινος], *made of crystal.* N o u n : **crystallina,** ōrum, *n. pl.* (*sc.* vasa), *crystal vases* : Mart., Juv.

crystallus, i, *f.* and **-um,** i, *n. rock-crystal.* **1.** Lit. : Curt., Sen. **2.** T r a n s f. **a.** *anything made of crystal* : Mart. **b.** *a precious stone, clear as crystal* : Prop.

cubiculāris, e, *adj.* [cubiculum], *of a bed-chamber* : Cic.

cubiculārius, a, um [cubiculum], *of a sleeping-chamber* : Mart. N o u n : **cubiculārius,** i, *m. a chamberlain* : Cic., Suet.

cubiculum, i, *n.* [cubō]. **I.** *a lying-* or *sleeping-room, bed-chamber* : Pl., Cic., Liv., etc. **II.** *the elevated seat of the emperor in the theatres* : Suet.

cubile, is, *n.* [cubō], *a place of rest, a couch, bed.* **1.** Lit. **a.** Of men : Lucr., Cic., Hor., etc. Esp. *a marriage-bed* : Verg., Ov. **b.** Of animals : *a nest, lair, etc.* : Cic., Verg., etc. **2.** T r a n s f. **a.** Of the sun : Hor. **b.** avaritiae non iam vestigia, sed ipsa cubilia videre, Cic.

cubital, ālis, *n.* [cubitum], *an elbow-cushion* : Hor.

cubitālis, e, *adj.* [cubitum], *of the elbow* ; hence, as a measure, *a cubit long* : Liv.

cubitō, āre [*freq.* cubō], *to lie in bed* (as a habit) : Pl., Cic. Also *to lie resting* : Tac.

cubitum, i, *n.* [cubō], *the elbow.* **1.** Lit. : Pl., Verg., Quint., etc. **2.** T r a n s f. : *a cubit* : Pl., Cic. [It. *cubito* ; Sp. *codo* ; Fr. *coude*.]

cubitus, ūs, *m.* [cubō], *a lying down* : Verg. ; in *pl.* (= concubitus), Pl.

cubō, āre, uī (rarely āvī), itum [*cf.* κύπτω], *to lie, lie recumbent.* **1.** Lit. **a.** In gen. : Cic., Suet. **b.** *to recline at table* : Cic., Hor., Suet. **c.** *to lie in bed* : Pl., Cic., Ov., etc. Of illness : Pl., Lucr., Hor., Ov. **2.** T r a n s f. Of inanimate objects : esp. of places : *to lie at an incline, to slope* : Lucr., Hor. [It. *covare* ; Fr. *couver*.]

cucullus, i, *m. a cowl* or *hood fastened to a garment* : Mart., Juv.

cucūlus, i, *m. a cuckoo* : Plin. As a term of reproach : Pl. ; as nickname, esp. of dilatory husbandmen who defer pruning until the cuckoo is heard : Pl., Hor. [Fr. *coucou*.]

cucumis, eris, *m. a cucumber* : Verg. [It. *cocomero* ; Fr. *concombre*.]

cucurbita, ae, *f. a gourd.* **1.** Lit. : Plin. **2.** T r a n s f. : in medic. : *a cupping-glass* : Juv. [It. *cucuzza* ; Fr. *courge* and *gourde*.]

cūdō, ere, *to strike, beat, pound.* In gen. : Lucr., Plin. P r o v. (*v.* faba) : istaec in me cudetur faba, Ter. **b.** Of metals : *to prepare by beating, to forge* ; and of money, *to stamp, coin* : Pl., Ter., Quint. T r a n s f. : quas tu mihi tenebras cudis ? Pl.

cuicuimodi (quoiquoimodi), GEN. of quisquis and modus, *of whatever kind, sort, etc.* : Pl., Cic.

cūiās, ātis [cūius], pron. interrog., *of what country* or *town* ? (old NOM. cūiātis or quoiātis) : Pl., Cic., Liv.

cūius (older **quōius**), a, um. **I.** Pron. inter. [fr. the stem quo-], *of whom* ? *whose* ? Pl. ; cuium pecus ? Verg. With -nam (pray),

subjoined : cuianam vox prope me sonat ? **II.** As Pron. relat. adj. : *of whom, whose* : is Helenam abduxit, quoiā causā nunc facio opsidium Ilio, Pl. ; Cic.

cūiuscemodi, cūiusmodi, etc. *v.* modus.

cūiusnam, v. cūius.

culcita, ae, *f.* [perh. fr. calcō], *a cushion, pillow* : Cic. Comic. : gladium faciam culcitam eumque incumbam, Pl. [It. *coltrice, coltre* ; Sp. *colcha*.]

culcitella, ae, *f.* [*dim.* culcita] : Pl.

cūleus, *v.* culleus.

culex, icis, *m.* (*f.* Pl.) *a gnat, midge* : Pl., Verg., Hor.

culīna, ae, *f. a kitchen.* **1.** Lit. : Pl., Cic. Ep., Hor., etc. **2.** T r a n s f. : *food, victuals* : Hor., Juv.

culleus (less correctly **cūleus,** and in signif. 2. **cōleus,** i, *m.* [κολεός, Ion. κουλεός, *a sheath*]. **1.** Lit. : *a leather bag, a sack for holding liquids* : Pl. ; Nep. ; for parricides : Cic. ; Juv. **2.** T r a n s f. **a.** *a large measure for liquids, holding 20 amphorae* : Cato. **b.** (also coleus) *the scrotum* : Cic. Ep., Mart.

culmen, inis, *n.* [*cf.* columen, fr. root cel seen in excellō, etc.]. **I.** *any upstanding thing* ; *the stalk* : fabae, Ov. **II.** *the top, summit.* **1.** Lit. Of a building : *a roof, etc.* : Verg., Liv. Of *mountain summits* : Alpium, Caes. Of *the summit of the clouds* : Lucr. Of *the crown of the head of men* : Liv. **2.** T r a n s f. : *the pinnacle, acme, height* ; a summo culmine fortunae, Liv. ; ruit alta a culmine Troia, Verg.

culmus, i, *m. a stalk, stem,* esp. of grain. **1.** Lit. : Cic., Verg. **2.** T r a n s f. : *straw* (as thatch) : Verg.

culpa, ae, *f. liability, fault, blame.* **1.** Lit. : abest a culpā, Cic. ; penes aliquem culpa est, Ter., Liv., Sen. ; in culpā esse, Ter., Cic., Hor. ; in culpā versari, Cic., Liv. ; extra culpam esse, Cic., Liv. ; culpam in aliquem conferre, Ter., Caes. ; Cic. ; transferre in aliquem, Cic. ; aliquid culpae dare alicui, Cic. With defining GEN. : Cic., Liv., etc. Euphemist. for *unchastity* : Verg., Tac., etc. **2.** T r a n s f. : continuo culpam ferro compesce, Verg. [It. *colpa*.]

culpitō, āre [*freq.* culpō], *to blame* or *rate bitterly* : Pl.

culpō, āre [culpa], *to hold liable, blame, condemn,* etc. With pers. Obj.: Ov., Quint. ; in Pass. : Hor., Quint., etc. With thing as Obj. : Pl., Hor., Ov., Quint. Of lifeless things : arbore aquas culpante, Hor.

cultē, adv. *elegantly, with refinement* : Ov., Quint. Comp. : Tac.

cultellus, i, *m.* [*dim.* culter], *a small knife* : Varr., Hor. [It. *coltello* ; Fr. *couteau*.]

culter, tri, *m.* **I.** *a knife of any kind* : Pl., Cic., Liv. **II.** *a ploughshare, coulter.* **1.** Lit. : Plin. **2.** T r a n s f. : Hor. [It. *coltro* ; Fr. *coutre*.]

cultiō, ōnis, *f.* [colō] *cultivation* : agri, a *tilling of the ground, agriculture,* Cic.

cultor, ōris, *m.* [colō] *a tiller, planter, husbandman, cultivator, etc.* **1.** Lit. : Sall., Verg., Liv., etc. ; agrorum, Liv. ; agelli, Hor. ; terrae, Cic. Hence, *an inhabitant, a dweller* : eius terrae, Sall. ; collis eius (sc. Ianiculi), Liv. ; nemorum, Verg. **2.**

Transf. **a.** *a fosterer, supporter* : fautor et cultor bonorum, Liv. ; veritatis, Cic. ; Ov. **b.** *a worshipper, reverencer* : Verg. ; deorum, Hor. ; Ov.

cultrārius, I, *m.* [culter], *he who slew the victim* (for sacrifice) : Suet.

cultrix, īcis, *f.* [colō]. **I.** *she who tends or takes care of* : Cic. **II.** *a female inhabitant* : nemorum, Verg. ; Cat. ; Ov.

cultūra, ae, *f.* [colō], *a tilling, cultivating, tending.* **1.** Lit.: agri, Cic. In *pl.* : agri culturas docuit usus, Lucr. Without defining GEN. : *agriculture, husbandry* : Varr., Hor. **2.** Transf. **a.** Of the mind : *care, culture, cultivation* : animi, Cic. Without defining GEN. : Hor. **b.** *a courting* : potentis amici, Hor.

cultus, a, um. **I.** *Part.* colō. **II.** Adj. : *cultivated, tilled.* **1.** Lit. : ager cultior, Varr. ; cultissimus, *highly cultivated*, Cic. *Neut. pl.* as Noun : culta, *cultivated lands, tilth* : Lucr., Verg., Liv. **2.** Transf. **a.** (with or without *bene*), *well-dressed, neat, trim,* etc. : Ov., Suet. **b.** Of the mind, *cultivated, refined* : Cic., Ov.

cultus, ūs, *m.* [colō]. Lit. : *a tilling, tending, keeping, care.* **1.** Lit. **a.** Of agriculture : *cultivation, culture* : agricolarum, Cic. ; agrorum. Liv. **b.** Of cattle-keeping : *care,* etc. : Cic., Verg. **c.** Of the body : *care,* etc. : Caes., Cic. **2.** Transf. **a.** Of Abstract qualities : *care, training, education* : Sall., Cic., Hor. **b.** Of manner of life (opp. *state of nature*) : *culture, refinement, civilisation* ; *style of living, degree of civilisation,* etc. : homines a ferā agrestique vitā ad humanum cultum civilemque deducere, Cic. ; Caes. ; Verg. : in *pl.* : cultūsque artesque virorum, Ov. In bad sense : *luxury:* Sall., Liv. **c.** *style of dress,* etc. : Sall., Ov., Liv., etc. **d.** *care, attention.* **i.** to the gods, *worship, reverence* : Cic., Ov. **ii.** to men, *reverence, honouring* : Tac.

culullus, I, *m. a goblet, beaker* : Hor.

cūlus, I, *m. the buttocks* : Cat., Mart.

(1) cum (orig. form com) [*cf.* Gk. ξύν and ξυνός], *adv.* and *prep., together.* **I.** Adv. : only in Comp. (e.g. con-, co-, etc.). **A.** Meaning. **a.** *together* ; of union, sympathy, closeness, etc., e.g. coniungo, complector, consentio, etc. : occ. hostile, e.g. configo, etc. ; freq. with nouns of fellowship, e.g. conlega, coheres, etc. **b.** *together* ; of convergence, e.g. contraho, conlabor, etc. **c.** *completely, in a mass, entirely,* e.g. concremo, conterreo, etc. **d.** *in conformity, on a level,* e.g. coaequo, comparo, etc. **e.** *mutually* : e.g. conloqui, commercium, contexo, etc. **B.** Forms. *cum* appears : **a.** as con before c, d, g, l, q, ra, ro, t, v and consonantal i, e.g. concutio, conicio, etc. ; as cōn before f, s, e.g. cōnfero, cōnsequor. It is assimilated to r in re, ri, ru, e.g. corrumpo, etc. **b.** as co before vowels, h, n, gn, e.g. coalesco, conecto, etc. ; exc. comes, comitium. **c.** as com before b, m, p, e.g. comparo, etc. **II.** Prep. *together* : with Instr. ABL. = *together with, in company with, in connexion with, in common with, with.* **A.** Prop. **a.** With persons : cum legionibus tribus profectus est, Caes. **b.**

With things : the being *accompanied with* or the being *furnished with* : optabilis est mors cum gloriā, Cic. ; onerariae naves cum commeatu, Liv. **N.B.** the position of *cum* with *pers. Pron.* and *relat. Pron.* : mecum, tecum, secum, nobiscum, etc. ; quocum (quicum), quācum, quibuscum. **B.** Used to complete the sense with verbs, etc., which denote action, contention, comparison, agreement, difference, deliberation, etc. : agere cum aliquo, Caes., Cic. ; bellum gerere cum aliquo, Caes., Cic., Liv. ; conferre pacem cum bello, Cic. ; consentire, dissentire cum aliquo, Cic., etc. ; secum reputare, Cic. **C.** To indicate the circumstances, accompaniments, results, or the way and manner, of an action : *with, in, under, among, to,* etc. (often used for an adverb) : illa illud cum malo fecit meo, Pl. ; cum lucro, Hor. ; cum magno provinciae periculo, Caes. ; cum summā tuā dignitate, Cic. ; multis cum lacrimis aliquem obsecrare, Caes. ; pars cum cruciatu necabatur, Caes. ; cum virtute vivere, Cic. **Phr.** : **1.** cum eo quod *or* ut (ne), to add, qualify, *or* limit : *under the condition, with the exception, that,* etc. : sit sane, quoniam ita tu vis ; sed tamen cum eo, credo, quod sine peccato meo fiat, Cic. ; Antium nova colonia missu, cum eo ut Antiatibus permitteretur, si et ipsi ascribi coloni vellent, Liv. **2.** cum dis volentibus, etc., *with the goodwill or consent of the gods* : volentibu' cum magnis dis, Enn. ; cum dis bene iuvantibus arma capite, Liv. **3.** With an ordinal number (cum octavo, cum decimo, etc.) for our *fold* : cum octavo, cum decimo, *eight-fold, ten-fold,* Cic. **D.** To denote action in time, *simultaneously with* **a.** a person : exit Crassus cum nuntio, Cic. Hence, cum primis, *ranking with the first ; especially, particularly* : Cic. **b.** a stated time : cum primā luce, Cic.

(2) cum (older **quom**), *conj.* **I.** With Indicative. **a.** *when,* i.e. *at the time when* (no causal relation being implied) : haec cum facta sunt in concilio, magnā spe et laetitiā omnium discessum est, Caes. **b.** *since,* i.e. *since the time when* : nondum centum et decem anni sunt cum de pecuniis repetundis lata lex est, Cic. **c.** *while,* i.e. *during which* (if verb in main clause is *Pres. Indic.* ; otherwise, usually *Subj., v.* II. b.) : vicensimus annus est cum omnes scelerati me unum petunt, Cic. **d.** *whenever* : cum eius generis copia defecit, ad innocentium supplicia descendunt, Caes. ; cum comminus venerant, gladiis a velitibus trucidabantur, Liv. (*v.* also II. e.). **e.** In inverted sentences : nondum lucebat cum Ameriae scitum est, Cic. ; iamque hoc facere noctu apparabant cum matres familiae repente procucurrerunt, Caes. **II.** With Subjunctive. **a.** *at a time when* (consecutive) : Crassus hodie, cum vos non adessetis, posuit idem, Cic. **b.** *when, while, as* (i.e. to express the situation, or the circumstances as well as the date) : accepit agrum temporibus eis, cum iacerent pretia praediorum, Cic. ; tum cum bello sociorum tota Italia arderet, C. Norbanus in summo otio fuit, Cic. (*v.* also I. c.). **c.** *since,* i.e. *now that* (of causal relation) : cum esset egens, sumptuosus, audax, ad omnem fraudem versare suam mentem coepit, Cic. **d.** *when, although :* patrem meum, cum proscriptus non esset, iugulastis, Cic. **e.** *whenever :* cum cohortes ex acie procucurrissent, Numidae effugiebant, Caes. (often in Liv.). **f.** If the cum clause is equivalent to a participle : Caesarem saepe accusavit cum adfirmaret (= adfirmans), illum nunquam, dum haec natio viveret, sine curā futurum, Cic. **g.** Often in historians, in summing events just described : cum haec in Achaiā gererentur, Caesar mittit etc., Caes. **h.** If the verb in the main clause is a potential or consecutive Subjunctive : quis tam dissoluto animo est qui, haec cum videat, tacere ac neglegere possit ? Cic. **Phr.** : cum primum, etc., *as soon as* (mostly with *Indic.*) : Pompeius cum primum contionem habuit, . . . ostendit etc., Cic. ; praesertim cum *or* cum praesertim, *especially as* (with *Subj.*) : Cic. ; quippe cum, *since of course* (usually with *Indic.*) : Cic. ; utpote cum, *seeing that* (with *Subj.*) : Cic. ; cum . . . tum, *while . . . so too, not only . . . but also* (the verb in the cum clause being frequently in *Subj.*) : cum plurimas et maximas commoditates amicitia contineat, tum illā nimirum praestat omnibus, quod bonā spe praelucet in posterum, Cic.

cum maximē, a, With *ut*, and verb understood : Bacchidem amabat, ut quom maxime, tum Pamphilus, Ter. **b.** nunc cum maxime *or* cum maxime alone, *now especially, just now :* Ter., Cic. **c.** cum maxime (with verb, usually in *Subjunctive*) : *especially when, just while :* freq. in Liv.

Cūmae, ārum, *f. pl.* an ancient city on the coast of Campania, renowned for its Sibyl. **Cūmānus,** a, um ; **Cūmāni,** ōrum, *m. pl.* the inhabitants ; **Cūmānum** ; i, *n. an estate (of Cicero's) near Cumae.* Also **Cūmaeus,** u, um.

cumba (cymba), ae, *f.* [κύμβη], *a boat, skiff.* **1.** Lit. : Cic., Ov. Esp. *Charon's boat :* Verg., Hor. **2.** Transf. : ingenii, Prop. ; Ov. ; Quint.

cumera, ae, *f. a grain-bin :* Hor.

cumīnum (cym-), i, *n.* [κύμινον], a plant used in medicine, and said to produce paleness of face ; hence, exsangue cuminum, Hor. ; Pers.

cum maximē, v. cum (2).

cum prīmis, v. cum (1) II. D. a.

cumque (quomque and **cunque),** adv. Lit.: *any when, at any time.* **I.** Rarely used alone : Lucr., Hor. **II.** Us. as an affix attached to relat. pronouns and pronom. adverbs : quicumque, *whoever ;* ubicumque, *wherever,* etc.

cumulātē, adv. **I.** *in increased measure :* Cic. **II.** *fully, completely :* Cic. Comp. : Cic. Sup. : Cic. Ep.

cumulātus, a, um. **I.** *Part.* cumulō. **II.** Adj. **a.** *increased, augmented :* Cic., Liv. **b.** *crowned, complete, perfect :* Cic., Verg. Comp. : Cic., Liv. Sup. : (with GEN.) : scelerum, Pl.

cumulō, āre [cumulus]. **I.** *to heap or pile up.* **1.** Lit. : materiem, Lucr. ; arma in ingentem acervum, Liv. **2.** Transf. **a.**

bene facta, Pl. ; Liv. ; Tac. **b.** *to increase by piling up, amass, accumulate :* funus funere, Lucr. ; aes alienum usuris, Liv. ; haec aliis nefariis cumulant, Cic. ; eloquentiā bellicam gloriam, Cic. **II.** *to pile up* (so as to fill), *to fill full, overload, etc.* **1.** Lit. : fossas corporibus, Tac. ; Verg. ; Liv., etc. **2.** Transf. **a.** cumulari voluptatibus, Cic. ; omni laude, Cic. ; Tac. **b.** *to make complete or perfect, to crown :* gaudium, Cic. ; (summum bonum) cumulatur ex integritate corporis et ex mentis ratione perfectā, Cic.

cumulus, i, *m.* [*cf.* κυέω, κῦμα]. *a heap, pile.* **1.** Lit. **a.** Of water : Verg., Ov. **b.** Of other things : Verg., Ov., Liv. **2.** Transf. **a.** *a heap, mass :* legum coacervatarum, Liv. **b.** *a crowning addition, increase, completion :* pro mercedis cumulo, Cic. Ep. ; Ov. ; ad summam laetitiam meam magnus ex illius adventu cumulus accedet, Cic. Ep. ; aliquem cumulum artibus adferre, Cic. ; addit perfidiae cumulum, Ov. [Fr. *comble*.]

cūnābula, ōrum, *n. pl.* [cūnae], *a cradle.* **1.** Lit. : Cic. Of the bed of young animals : Verg. **2.** Transf. : qui non in cunabulis sed in campo sunt consules facti, Cic. ; gentis nostrae, Verg.

cūnae, ārum, *f. pl. a cradle.* **1.** Lit. : Pl., Cic., Ov., etc. Of the nests of young birds : Ov. **2.** Transf. : Ov.

cunctābundus, a, um [cunctor], *hanging back, hesitating :* Liv., Tac.

cunctāns, antis. **I.** *Part.* cunctor. **II.** Adj. *shrinking, hesitating, reluctant.* **a.** Of persons : Verg., Tac. **b.** Of things : Lucr., Verg. Comp. : Lucr., Tac., etc.

cunctanter, adv. *with hesitation or delay :* Liv. Comp. : Tac.

cunctātiō, ōnis, *f.* [cunctor], *hesitation, delay.* With *Subj.* GEN. : Caes. With *Obj.* GEN. : Cic., Liv. Without GEN. : Cic., Plin. Ep., Tac. In *pl.* : Tac., Quint.

cunctātor, ōris, *m.* [cunctor], *one who holds back or hesitates :* Liv., Tac. As cognomen of Q. Fabius Maximus in 2nd Punic War.

cunctō = cunctor : Pl.

cunctor, āri, *to hang back, hesitate, be reluctant, delay.* **a.** Of persons : Enn., Cic., Verg., etc. With *Inf.* : Cic., Sall., Liv., Tac. With *Indir. Deliberative* : Sall., Suet. With *quin-* clause : non cunctandum existimavit quin pugnā decertaret, Caes. *Impers. Pass.* : nec cunctatum apud latera, Tac. **b.** Of things : tardum cunctatur olivum, Lucr. ; amnis, Verg.

cūnctus, a, um [contr. fr. coniunctus *or* coiünctus], *all together, all in a body, the whole, all, entire :* Gallia, Caes. ; senatus, Cic. ; orbis terrarum, Verg. ; gratia, Pl. In *pl.* : Pl., Cic., Hor., etc. With GEN. : hominum cunctos ingenti corpore praestans, Ov. ; Tac. ; esp. in *neut. pl.* : viāi cuncta, Lucr. ; terrarum, Hor. ; Tac.

cuneātim, adv. [cuneus], *in the form of a wedge.* Milit. : Caes.

cuneātus, a, um [cuneus], *wedge-shaped :* collis acumine longo, Ov. ; Liv. Comp. : Liv.

cuneō, āre [cuneus], *to unite by a wedge* (of the keystone in building). **1.** Lit. : Sen. Ep. **2.** Transf. : Quint.

cuneus, i, m. *a wedge.* **1.** Lit.: Cato,
Verg., Tac., etc. **2.** Transf. **a.** Milit.:
troops drawn up in the form of a wedge, or
column with narrow front : Caes., Verg.,
Liv., etc. **b.** *the wedge-form division of the*
rows of seats in a theatre : Verg., Suet.
Poet.: *the spectators :* Phaedr. [It.
conio ; Fr. *coin.*]

cuniculus, i, m. *a rabbit, coney.* **1.** Lit.:
Varr., Mart. **2.** Transf.: *a burrowing,*
underground passage : Cic. Milit. *a mine :*
Caes., Cic., Liv. Transf.: res occulte
cuniculis oppugnatur, Cic. [It. *coniglio.*]

cunnus, i, m. *the female pudenda.* **1.** Lit.:
Cat., Mart. **2.** Transf. *an unchaste*
woman : Hor.

cunque, v. cumque.

(1) cūpa, ae, f. *a tun, vat, etc. :* Caes., Cic.,
Luc. [It. *coppa ;* Fr. *coupe.*]

(2) cūpa, ae, f. [κώπη], *the handle of an oil-*
mill : Cato.

cūpēd-, v. cuppēd-.

cūpēdō, v. cupīdō.

cupidē, adv. *eagerly, passionately* (in good and
bad sense): Pl., Cic., Hor., etc. *Comp. :*
Caes., Liv. *Sup. :* Caes., Sall.

cupidĭtās, ātis, f. [cupidus], *eagerness,*
passion, enthusiasm, desire (in good, bad, or
indifferent sense). **a.** In gen.: Ter., Caes.,
Cic. With GEN.: pecuniae, Caes. ; gloriae,
Cic. ; cognoscendi, Cic. ; Liv. Also, ad
reditum, Cic. ; ad venandum, Curt. **b.** For
power, etc.: ambition : Cic., Plin. Pan. **c.**
For money, etc.: *greed, avarice :* cupiditas
et avaritia, Cic. ; Sall. **d.** Of the senses :
vini, Curt. **e.** *partiality, party-spirit :* Cic.,
Liv.

cupīdō (**cūpēdō** or **cuppēdō,** Lucr.), inis, f.
(in Hor. alw. m. and occ. in Ov.) [cupiō], *a*
desire, lust, longing, eagerness. **a.** In gen.
With GEN.: urbis condendae, Liv. ; Sall. ;
without GEN.: Lucr., Hor., Ov., Tac.
With *Inf. :* Enn., Curt. **b.** For money,
etc.: *greed, avarice.* With GEN.: Ov.
Without GEN.: Hor., Tac. **c.** For power,
etc.: honoris, Sall. ; Liv. ; Tac. **d.** Of
the senses: aquae, Pl. ; Lucr. ; virginis,
Pl., Ov. *Person.* **Cupīdō,** *the god of love,*
s. of Venus ; hence, **Cupīdineus,** a, um.

cupidus, a, um [cupiō], *desirous, longing,*
eager, enthusiastic. **a.** In gen. With
GEN.: bellandi, Caes. ; Ter. ; Liv. ; novarum rerum, Caes., Cic. ; Lucr. ; Hor.
With *Inf. :* Prop., Ov. Also, in perspici-
endā rerum naturā, Cic. **b.** For money, etc.
With or without GEN.: Pl., Cic. **c.** For
power, etc.: *ambitious.* With GEN.:
Caes. **d.** Of the senses : vini, Pl. ; without GEN.: Cat., Tib. Esp. *of lovers :*
Ter., Cat., Ov. **e.** With ref. to persons :
partial, fond of, attached to : homo cupidissimus nostri, Cic. In bad sense : iudex,
testes, Cic. *Comp. :* Cic. *Sup. :* Cic.,
Nep.

cupiēns, entis. **I.** *Part.* cupiō. **II.** *Adj.:*
desirous, eager, enthusiastic : with GEN.:
Pl., Tac. Without GEN.: Tac. *Sup. :*
Sall.

cupienter, adv. *eagerly, etc. :* Pl.

cupiō, cupere, cupīvī (or -iī), cupītum
(*Imperf. Subj.* cupiret, Lucr.), *to be eager*
for, long for, desire (denoting inclination

merely). With ACC. : Pl., Cic., Hor., etc.
With GEN. of person : Pl. With *Inf. :*
Ter., Lucr., Cic., etc. With ACC. and *Inf. :*
Cic., Nep. With *ut* or *ne* and *Subj. :* Pl.,
Cic., Ov., Plin. Ep. With *Subj.* alone :
Plin. Ep. Occ. **a.** Of a lover : Ov. **b.** *to*
be favourable or *inclined to, to favour, to*
wish well to, etc.: cuius causā omnia cum
cupio, tum mehercule etiam debeo, Cic. ;
cupio omnia quae vis, Hor. With DAT.:
Ter., Caes., Cic. Ep.

cupītor, ōris, m. [cupiō], *one who desires :* in-
credibilium, Tac.

cuppēdia (**cūp-**), ae, f. [cuppes], *daintiness,*
lickerishness : Cic.

cuppēdia (**cūp-**), ōrum, n. pl. *dainty dishes,*
tit-bits, delicacies : Pl.

cuppēdinārius (**cūp-**), i, m. cuppēdia], *a*
confectioner : Ter.

cuppēdō, v. cupīdō.

cuppes (**cūpes**), edis, m. *adj., fond of*
delicacies : Pl.

cupressētum, i, n. [cupressus], *a grove of*
cypress-trees : Cato, Cic.

cupresseus, a, um [cupressus], *made of*
cypress-wood : Liv.

cupressifer, era, erum [cupressus, ferō],
cypress-bearing : Ov.

cupressus, i (ūs), f. (ABL. cupressō, Verg. ;
cupressū, Ov. ; NOM. pl. cyparissi, Verg.)
[κυπάρισσος], *the cypress :* sacred to
Pluto, and used at funerals. **1.** Lit.: Cato,
Verg., etc. **2.** Transf.: *a box of cypress-*
wood : Hor.

cūpula, ae, f. [dim. cūpa (2)], *a small crooked*
handle : Cato.

cūr (older **quor,** Pl.), *interrog. adv. : for*
what reason, why ? **A.** Direct question :
cur senatum cogor reprehendere ? Cic. ;
Pl. ; Hor., etc. **B.** Indirect question :
quid sit cur etc., Caes., Cic., Ter., Ov., etc. ;
non est causa cur etc., Cic., etc.

cūra, ae, f. [caveō], *watchfulness, care, soli-*
tude, concern, etc. **I.** *care bestowed on any-*
thing, attention, pains, etc. **1.** Lit. **A.**
In gen.: in aliquā re curam ponere, Cic. ;
rem cum curā parare, Sall., Liv. ; cum
magnā curā, Caes., Cic., Liv. In pl. :
omnis meas curas in rem publicam conferebam, Cic. With *Subj.* GEN.: Liv., Hor.
With *Obj.* GEN.: Cic., Liv., Ov. With *de*
and ABL.: Cic. ; curam agere de aliquā re,
Liv. With *pro* and ABL.: Liv., Ov.
Phr. : curae (alicui) esse, *to be an object of*
concern or *attention (to somebody) :* Caes.,
Cic., Hor., etc. ; (*cf.* II. 2.). Also : ut
petitionem suam curae haberent, Sall. **B.**
In partic. **a.** Of public business : *ad-*
ministration, charge, management : rerum
publicarum, Sall. ; urbis, Liv. ; peditum,
Tac. ; legionis armandae, Liv. **b.** In law,
guardianship, trusteeship : sororis filios in
curā habere, Liv. **c.** In medicine : saucios
curā sustentare, Tac. So a *means of healing,*
cure : doloris, Cic. Ep. ; Prop. **d.** In
farming : boum, Verg. **2.** Transf. **a.**
an object of care, a charge : Anchises, cura
deum, Verg. **b.** Of writings, *a study,*
effort : Tac. In pl. : Tac. **c.** *a guardian :*
Ov. **II.** *anxiety, worry, concern.* **1.** Lit.
a. In gen. : Pl., Cic., Hor., etc. **b.** In
partic. of love : Verg., etc. **2.** Transf. :

the object of love, one's love : Verg., Hor. [Fr. cure.]

cŭrābĭlis, e, adj. [cūrō], anxious, troublesome : Juv.

cŭrālĭum, ĭ, n. [Ion. κουράλιον], red coral : Ov. In pl. : Ov.

cŭrātĭō, ōnis. f. [cūrō], a taking care of, management. **A.** In gen. : corporis, Cic. ; Liv. ; curatio et administratio rerum, Cic. ; quid tibi hanc curatio est rem ? what does this concern you ? Pl. **B.** In partic. **a.** management of State affairs, administration, office, etc. : Cic., Liv. **b.** In medic. : healing, cure : Cic., Liv., Tac.

cŭrātĭus, comp. adv. more carefully : Tac., Plin. Ep.

cŭrātor (older COERATOR), ōris, m. [cūrō], he who takes charge, a manager, overseer, superintendent. **a.** In public matters : ludorum, Pl. ; suntoque aediles coeratores urbis annonae ludorumque sollemnium, Old Law in Cic. ; muris reficiendis, Cic. **b.** In law : a guardian, keeper : Hor., Quint.

cŭrātūra, ae, f. [cūrō], attention, attentiveness (to the body) : Ter.

cŭrātus, a, um. **I.** Part. cūrō. **II.** Adj. **a.** anxious, earnest : preces, Tac. ; Plin. Ep. **b.** cared-for, attended-to : Cato, Cic., Hor. Comp. : Cato ; Sup. : Tac.

curcŭlĭō (**gurg-**), ōnis, m. a cornworm, weevil : Pl., Cato, Verg. [It. gorgolione ; Sp. gorgojo.]

curcŭlĭuncŭlus, ĭ, m. [dim. curculiō], a little weevil : i.e. something trifling, worthless : Pl.

Cŭrētes, um, m. pl. a mythical race in Crete who attended the birth of Jupiter and worshipped him with noisy music.

cŭria, ae, f. **I. a.** a curia ; one of the 30 parts into which Romulus divided the Roman people : Liv. **b.** a place of meeting for the curiae : Varr., Ov., Tac. **II. a.** a meeting of the senate, the senate : Varr., Hor. **b.** the senate-house : Cic., Liv., Hor., Ov. Also of similar buildings in other cities : Cic., Ov.

cŭriālis, is, m. [cŭria], a member of the same curia : Pl., Cic.

cŭriātim, adv. [cŭria], by curiae : Cic.

cŭriātus, a, um [cŭria]. **I.** made by, composed of the curiae : comitia, Cic., Liv. **II.** passed by the comitia curiata : lex, Cic., Liv.

(1) cŭrĭō, ōnis, m. [cŭria], the priest or president of a curia : Varr. ; maximus (over all the curiae), Liv.

(2) cŭrĭō, ōnis, m. adj. [cŭra], wasted by sorrow, lean, emaciated : Pl.

cŭrĭōsē, adv. **I.** with care, carefully, etc. : Suet. Of style : too nicely, affectedly : Quint. **II.** curiously, inquisitively : Suet. Comp. : Cic.

cŭrĭōsĭtās, ātis, f. [cŭriōsus], desire of knowledge, curiosity : Cic. Ep.

cŭrĭōsus, a, um [cŭra]. **I.** careful, painstaking, diligent : with in or ad : in omni historiā, Cic. ; ad investigandum, Cic. Hence, consilia, Quint. **II.** inquiring, curious, inquisitive, prying : (in good or bad sense) : Cic., Hor., Quint. ; oculi, Cic. As Noun : Cat. ; also a spy or scout : Suet. **III.** care-worn : Pl.

curis (quiris), f. a spear : Ov.

Curius, a, name of a Roman gens, esp. M'. Curius Dentatus, conqueror of the Samnites, Lucanians and Pyrrhus.

cūrō (older COERO), āre [cūrā]. **I.** to give care or attention to, take charge of, care for, take care of, look after, attend to, trouble oneself about, etc. In gen. **1.** Lit. (with person as subject). With Acc. : Pl., Cic., Hor., etc. With Acc. and Gerund. : to take charge of, see to : obsides dandos, Caes. ; Cic. ; Liv. With Inf. (most freq. with a negative) : Cic., Hor., Ov. With ut or ne and Subj. : Pl., Cic. So in concluding letters, cura ut valeas, Cic. Ep. With simple Subj. : Cic. Ep., Phaedr. With de and ABL. : Cic. Ep. With DAT. : Pl. Absol. : Pl., Ter. Pass. Impers. : Ter. **2.** Transf. (with thing as subject) : Lucr., Hor. **B.** In partic. **a.** Of public affairs : to be in charge ; take charge of, administer, etc. Absol. : Sall., Tac. With Acc. : Sall., Liv., Tac. **b.** Of religious matters : to take charge of, attend to. With Acc. : Liv. **c.** Of the body : to attend to (with food, rest, cleansing, etc.) : corpora, Cic. ; vulnus, Liv. ; cutem, Hor. ; with medicine, etc. : aegrum, Liv. **d.** In farming : vineam, Cato. **e.** Of money : to see about, provide for payment of. With Acc. : Cic. Ep., Liv. **II.** to worry or bother about, trouble about (colloq.). With Acc. : aliud (Ter.), alia (Pl.) cura (worry about other things, i.e. don't worry about this ; never mind) ; viri nihil periuria curant, Cat.

curricŭlum, ĭ, n. [currō]. **I.** a running : conicere se in curriculum, Pl. ABL. : curriculo, as Adv. : at full speed, swiftly : Ter. **II.** a racing, running-match. **1.** Lit. : Hor., Liv. **2.** Transf. **a.** a course, a lap of the course : Liv. Transf. : solis et lunae, Cic. ; medium noctis, Verg. ; vitae, gloriae (career), Cic. **b.** the course, the raceground : Cic., Hor. Transf. : mentis, Cic. **c.** (perh. dim. of currus), a chariot for racing : Tac. Hence, a chariot in gen. : Curt.

currō, currere, cucurri, cursum, to hasten, hurry, run. **1.** Lit. Of living beings. **a.** On land : Pl., Cic., Verg., etc., Pass. Impers. : Pl., Cic. Rarely with Acc. : qui stadium currit, Cic. ; aequor, Verg. Prov. : currentem incitare or instigare, etc., to spur a willing horse, Cic. **b.** On sea, etc. : Hor. **2.** Transf. Of things. **a.** Concrete : sol currens, Lucr. ; amnes in aequora currunt, Verg. ; currentem undam, Verg. ; rubor per ora, Verg. **b.** Abstract : proclivus currit oratio, Cic. ; currit ferox aetas, Hor. With Acc. : talia saecla currite, Verg. [It. correre, Fr. courir.]

currus, ūs, m. [currō], a chariot, car, wain. **1.** Lit. **A.** In gen. : Lucr., Cic., etc. **B.** In partic. **a.** a war-chariot : Caes., Tac. **b.** a triumphal car : Cic., Ov., etc. Hence, a triumph : quam ego currum cum tuā laudatione conferrem ? Cic. ; Prop. **c.** a racing-car : Verg. **d.** a plough with wheels : Verg. **2.** Transf. **a.** the team : Verg. **b.** a ship : Cat.

cursim, adv. [currō], by running, at the double. **1.** Lit. : Pl., Liv. **2.** Transf. : dicere, Cic.

cursĭtō, āre [*freq.* cursō], *to keep on running about :* Ter., Cic., Hor., etc.

cursō, āre [*freq.* currō], *to run about :* Ter., Cic., Tac. *Pass. Impers. :* Ter.

cursŏr, ōris, m. [currō], *a runner.* **a.** In a race : *a racer :* Lucr., Cic. Also of *a chariot-racer :* Ov. **b.** *a courier :* Nep., Plin. Ep., etc. **c.** *a slave who ran before the chariot of a grandee :* Sen. Ep., Mart.

cursūra, ae, f. [currō], *a running, haste, speed :* Pl., Varr.

cursus, ūs, m. [currō], *a running, hastening, speeding.* **1.** Lit. Of living beings. **A.** Properly : Cic., Verg., etc. ; cursu in hostem feruntur, Liv. Occ. **a.** *speed :* Liv., Verg. **b.** *journey* (by land, sea, or air) : Cic., Hor., Ov., etc. **c.** *suitable time* or *weather for a voyage :* cursum exspectare, Cic. Ep. **B.** *course, direction :* tenere cursum, *to keep one's course,* Caes., Cic. ; cursum corrigere, Liv. **2.** Transf. Of things *rapid movement, speed, flow,* etc. **A.** Concrete. **a.** Properly : navium, Caes. ; stellarum, Cic. ; lunae, Lucr., Liv. ; Aquilonis, Lucr. **b.** *course, direction :* ut nulla earum navium cursum tenere posset, Caes. In *pl. :* Ov. **B.** Abstract. **a.** *speed, flow, (rapid) progress :* verborum, orationis, Cic. ; honorum, Cic., Tac. ; vitae, Cic. ; in cursu mens dolor est, Ov. **b.** *course, direction :* vitae, Cic. ; rerum, Cic., Tac. [It. *corso ;* Fr. *cours.*]

Curtius, a, *name of a Roman gens :* esp. Q. Curtius Rufus, *the historian, who wrote the history of Alexander the Great.*

curtō, āre [curtus], *to shorten.* Transf. : Hor.

curtus, a, um, *shortened, docked, broken.* **1.** Lit. **a.** In gen.: dolia, Lucr. ; vasa, Juv. **b.** In partic. : *gelded :* Prop. ; *circumcised :* Hor. ; *bob-tailed :* Hor. **2.** Transf. : *defective :* oratio, Cic. ; res, Hor. [Fr. *court.*]

curūlis, e, *adj.* [currus], *of a chariot.* **a.** In gen.: equi, Liv. ; triumphus (opp. ovatio), Suet. **b.** In partic. : sella curulis, *the curule chair* (inlaid with ivory, used by the consuls, praetors, curule aediles, etc.); Cic., Liv., Ov., etc. ; called curule ebur, Hor. ; curulis sedes, Tac. ; and as Noun, **curūlis**, is, f. : Tac., Suet. Hence, of the magistrates : aedilis, Liv. ; aedilitas, Cic., Liv.

curvāmen, inis, n. [curvō] *a bend, curve :* Ov.

curvātūra, ae, f. [curvō], *a bend, curve :* Ov.

curvō, āre [curvus], *to crook, bend, arch, curve.* **1.** Lit. : portus curvatus in arcum, Verg. ; Ov., etc. ; curvata senio membra, Tac. In *Mid. :* Verg. **2.** Transf. : *to bend, to move :* nec (te) vir Pieriā paelice saucius curvat, Hor.

curvus, a, um, *crooked, bent, curved.* **1.** Lit. **a.** Of things : Lucr., Varr., Verg., etc. **b.** Of persons : *bent* (with age, toil, etc.) : Pl., Verg., Ov. **2.** Transf. **A.** Concrete. **a.** *concave, hollow, arched,* etc. : Verg., Ov. **b.** *winding, curved :* litus, Hor., Verg. ; flumina, Verg., Ov. **B.** Abstract. : *crooked :* mores, Pers. *Neut.* as Noun, *what is crooked :* Hor., Plin. Ep. [Fr. *courbe.*]

cuspis, idis, f. *a point, spike.* **1.** Lit. : asseres cuspidibus praefixi, Caes. ; of *the point of a spear,* Liv., Ov. ; *of a punt pole,* Verg. ; *of a reed :* Ov. ; *of a sting :* Ov. **2.** Transf. **a.** *a spear, lance :* tremendā cuspide pugnax, Hor. ; Verg. ; Liv. **b.** *the trident of Neptune :* Ov. **c.** *a pointed tube :* Varr.

custōdēla, ae, f. [custōs], *a watch, guard,* etc. : Pl.

custōdia, ae, f. [custōs], *a watching, guarding,* etc. **1.** Lit. **a.** In gen. : in custodiam aliquem recipere, Pl. ; agitare custodiam, *to keep guard,* Pl. ; ponere in alicuius custodiā, Cic. ; aliquid custodiā continere, Cic. With *Subj. Gen.* : Caes., Hor., Liv. With *Obj. Gen.* : Cic., Liv., Verg. **b.** In partic. of *imprisonment* or *other restraint* : habere aliquem in custodiā, Liv., Tac. ; aliquem servare liberā custodiā (i.e. *confinement in one's own home*), Liv. **2.** Transf. **A.** With abstract *Obj. Gen.* : salutis, etc., Cic. ; libertatis, etc., Liv. **B.** Concrete. **a.** us. in *pl.* : *persons who serve as guards, a guard :* colonia meis custodiis munita, Cic. ; Caes. In *sing. :* abest custodia regis, Ov. **b.** *a place where guard is kept, a watch-* or *guard-house :* haec (urbs) mea sedes est, haec vigilia, haec custodia, Cic. In *pl. :* Cic. **c.** *a place of confinement, a prison :* Caes., Cic. **d.** *persons in confinement, captives, prisoners :* Sen. Ep. In *pl. :* Sen. Ep., Suet.

custōdiō, īre [custōs], *to watch over, guard, protect,* etc. **1.** Lit. **A.** In gen.: corpus domumque, Cic. ; maritimam oram xx longis navibus, Liv. ; se custodire, Cic. ; poma ab insomni dracone, Ov. ; Nep. *Impers. Pass. :* Suet. **B.** In partic. **a.** *to hold in custody :* Pl., Cic., Verg., etc. **b.** *to keep watch on :* Cic., Liv. **c.** *to keep carefully, preserve :* Cic. Ep. **2.** Transf. : memoriā aliquid custodire, Cic. ; teneriores annos ab iniuriā sanctitas docentis custodiat, Quint.

custōs, ōdis, m.f. [*cf.* κεύθω], *a keeper, guardian, warder, watchman.* **1.** Lit. **A.** In gen.; Pl., Cic., Verg., etc. **Esp.** in military and civil matters, *sentinel, watchman :* Caes., Cic., Nep. Of *a garrison* (in *pl.*) : Caes., Cic., Liv. Of the gods (freq.) : nemorum Diana, Verg. ; Hor. ; Cic. **B.** In partic. **a.** Of teachers of youth : Ter., Hor. **b.** *a spy :* Caes., Curt. **2.** Transf. **a.** Of dogs : Verg. **b.** In moral matters : cupiditatum, Cic. ; virtutis verae, Hor. With abstr. Subject : sapientia custos totius hominis, Cic. **c.** *a receptacle for safe-keeping.* Of *a quiver :* telorum, Ov. ; of *an incense box :* turis, Ov.

cuticula, ae, f. [*dim.* cutis], *the thin external skin* or *cuticle :* Juv.

cutis, is, f. *the skin.* **1.** Lit. : *living skin,* esp. of man (opp. pellis, *dead, coarse* or *withered skin*) : Hor., Quint., etc. Prov. : cutem curare, *to look after one's skin.* Hor. **2.** Transf. **a.** tenerā quādam elocutionis cute, Quint. **b.** *skin, rind :* Plin. **c.** *leather :* Mart.

Cyanē, ēs, f. *a nymph who was changed into a fountain,* in Ov.

Cyaneae, ārum, f. pl. *two small rocky islands at the entrance of the Pontus Euxinus,* also called Symplēgades (q.v.); **Cyaneus**, a, um.

Cўaneē, ēs, *f. d. of Maeander, and m. of Caunus and Byblis.*

cyathissō, āre [κυαθίζω], *to fill a cup, to act as cup-bearer :* Pl.

cyathus, i, *m.* [κύαθος], *a ladle (for pouring wine into the cups) :* Pl., Hor., Suet. As a measure, *one-twelfth part of a sextarius :* Hor.

cybaea, ae, *f.* [κυβή], *a merchant ship :* Cic.; also with navis : Cic.

Cybelē (Cybēbē), ēs, *f. a goddess, originally Phrygian, subsequently worshipped in Rome also as Ops or Mater Magna;* **Cybelēius**, a, um.

cybiosactēs, ae, *m.* [κυβιοσάκτης], *a dealer in salt-fish ;* a nickname of the thirteenth Ptolemy, and afterwards of the Emperor Vespasian : Suet.

cyclas, adis, *f.* [κυκλάς, *circular*], *a state-robe of women, with a border running round it :* Prop., Juv.

cyclicus, a, um [κυκλικός], *scriptor, a cyclic poet :* Hor.

Cyclōps, ōpis (Acc. Cyclōpa, Hor.), *m. a Cyclops ; pl.* Cyclōpes, um, *a fabulous one-eyed race of giants in Sicily, who were Vulcan's workmen ;* esp. *the Cyclops Polyphemus ;* **Cyclōpius**, a, um, *Cyclopian.*

cycnēus (cygn-), a, um [κύκνειος], *of a swan :* Cic., Ov.

cycnus (cygnus), i, *m.* [κύκνος], *a swan.* **1.** Lit.: Cic. Prov.: quid enim contendat hirundo cycnis, Lucr.; certent cycnis ululae, Verg. **2.** Transf.: *a poet :* Dircaeus, i.e. Pindar, Hor. [It. *cigno ;* Fr. *cygne*.]

Cycnus (Cyg-), i, *m.* **I.** *king of the Ligurians s. of Sthenelus, changed to a swan and placed among the stars.* **II.** *s. of Neptune, changed to a swan.*

Cўdippē, ēs, *f. the wife of Acontius.*

cylindrus, dri, *m.* [κύλινδρος]. **I.** In geom. *a cylinder :* Cato, Verg. **II.** *A roller for levelling the ground :* Cato, Verg.

Cyllarus, i, *m.* **I.** *a centaur in* Ov. **II.** *the war-horse of Castor in* Verg.

Cyllēnē, ēs and ae, *f. a mountain in Arcadia, on which Mercury was born.* **Cyllēnius**, a, um ; and **Cyllēnius**, i, *m. Mercury ;* also **Cyllēnēus**, a, um, and **Cyllēnis**, idis, *f. adj.*

cymba, *v.* cumba.

cymbalum, i, *n.* [κύμβαλον], *a cymbal (us. pl.*) : Lucr., Cic., Verg., etc.

cymbium, i, *n.* [κυμβίον], *a small drinking vessel :* Verg.

cyminum, *v.* cuminum.

Cynicē, adv., *after the manner of the Cynics :* Pl.

Cynicus, a, um [κυνικός, *dog-like ;* Diogenes was called ὁ κύων], *Cynic, relating to the Cynic philosophy :* institutio, Tac. More freq. as Noun, **Cynicus**, i, *m. a Cynic :* Cic., Hor., Juv.

cynocephalus, i, *m.* [κυνοκέφαλος], *an African ape with a dog's head :* Cic. Ep.

Cynosūra, ae, *f.* [Κυνόσουρα, *dog's tail*], *a constellation near the north pole, Ursa Minor.* Hence, **Cynosūris**, idis, *f. adj.*

Cynthus, i, *m. a mountain of Delos, celebrated as the birth-place of Apollo and Diana ;* **Cynthius**, a, um, *Cynthian ;* **Cynthius**, i, *m. = Apollo ;* **Cynthia**, ae, *f. = Diana.*

cyparissus, *f. v.* cupressus.

Cyprus (-os), i, *f. a large island in the Mediterranean Sea, off the coast of Asia Minor, renowned for its fruitfulness, and for the worship of Venus ;* **Cyprius**, a, um; **Cypria**, ae, *f. = Venus.*

Cypselus, i, *m. a despot of Corinth.*

Cyrēnē, ēs, and **Cyrēnae**, ārum, *f. the chief city of a flourishing Greek colony in north-eastern Africa, founded by the Theraeans ; the birth-place of Aristippus, founder of the Cyrenaic philosophy ;* **Cyrēnaicus**, **Cyrēnaeus**, a, um, and **Cyrēnensis**, e ; **Cyrēnaici**, **Cyrēnaei**, ōrum, *m. pl. adherents of the Cyrenaic philosophy ;* **Cyrēnenses**, ium, *m. pl. inhabitants of Cyrene.*

Cyrnos, i, *f. the Greek name of Corsica ;* **Cyrnēus**, a, um.

Cyrus, i, *m.* **I.** *the founder of the Persian monarchy,* B.C. 560. **II.** *Cyrus Minor, a brother of Artaxerxes Mnemon, killed at Cunaxa,* B.C. 401. **III.** *an architect of the time of Cicero.*

Cytae, ārum, *f. pl. a town in Colchis, said to have been the birth-place of Medea ;* **Cytaeaeus**, **Cytaeus**, a, um, *Colchian ;* **Cytaeis**, idis, *f. Medea.*

Cythēra, ōrum, *n. pl. an island in the Aegean Sea, celebrated for the worship of Venus, now Cerigo.* Hence, **1.** **Cythērēus**, a, um. As Noun : **Cythērēa**, ae, *f. Venus.* **2.** **Cythērēus**, a, um : heros, i.e. Aeneas. As Noun : **Cythērēis**, idis, *f. Venus.* **3.** **Cythēriacus**, a, um. **4.** **Cythērēis**, idis, *f. i.e. Venus.* **5.** **Cythērēias**, adis, *f. adj. belonging to Venus.*

cytisus, i, *m. f.* [κύτισος], *a plant :* prob. *shrubby lucerne or clover :* Verg.

Cytōrus (-os), i, *m. a mountain of Paphlagonia, famous for its box-wood ;* **Cytōriacus (-ius)**, a, um.

D

D, d, the fourth letter of the Latin alphabet, corresponding to the Greek Delta (Δ). **I.** Changes of *d* to other letters and *v. v.* **1.** *d* to *t.* At the end of words *t* was frequently substituted for it in early times ; e.g. haut for haud in Plautus. *t* is sometimes changed to *d* in the derivation of words : *e.g.* from *mentior* comes *mendax.* **2.** *du* to *b.* At the beginning of some words, *du* followed by a vowel has been changed into *b :* e.g.: *duellum, bellum ; duis, bis ; duonus, bonus.* In (*d*)*uiginti,* the *d* has been dropped. **3.** *d* to *r :* e.g.: *ar* for *ad* (*v.* arbiter). **4.** *d* to *l :* e.g. : *dingua, lingua ; odor* (ὄζειν), *oleo.* **5.** In compound words, *d* at the end of the first portion of the compound is assimilated to the initial consonant of the second portion if this is *c, p,* or *t ;* e.g. *accedo, ap-parare, at-tingo ;* and occasionally to *q,* e.g. *quic-quam* for *quid-quam.* When, in such cases, *d* is followed by *s* and another consonant, it is sometimes omitted altogether : e.g. *a-scendo, a-stringo ;* and also when *d* is followed by the nasal *gn :* e.g. : *a-gnatus, a-gnosco.* **6.** In inflexion, *d* is omitted before *s,* or (rarely) assimilated :

e.g. : *custos* for *custod-s* : *lae-si*, for *laed-si* : but *ces-si* for *ced-si*. **II.** Changes of *d* in the Romance languages : **1.** *d* into *s* : especially *di* into *z*: e.g. : Lat. *ardens, pendulus*, It. *arzente, penzolo* ; Lat. *medius, radius*, It. *mezzo, razzo*. **2.** *di* into *g* or *j* : e.g.; Lat. *hodie*, It. *oggi* ; Lat. *dies, diurnus*, Fr. *jour*. **3.** *d* into *l* : e.g. : Lat. *cicada, hedera*, It. *cicala, ellera* ; Lat. *cauda*, Sp. *cola*. **4.** *d* into *r* (rare): e.g. : Lat. *lampas, lampadis*, Sp. *lampara*. **5.** *d* into *n* : e.g. : Lat. *lampas, lampadis* ; It. *lampana* ; Lat. *perdix*, It. *pernice*. **6.** Omission of *d* : in French, between two vowels : e.g.: Lat. *audire, fides, nudus, videre*, Fr. *ouir, foi, nu, voir*. In Italian at the end of words : e.g.: Lat. *ad, modo, fides*, It. *a, mò, fè*. **III.** In the oldest period of the Latin language, the ABL. *sing.* ended in *d* : MARID, DICTATORED, IN ALTOD MARID, on the Col. Rostr. Several prepositions and other prefixes originally ended in *d*, which *d* was afterwards usually dropped : *e.g.* prod in *prod-ire, prod-esse* ; red in *red-ire, red-dere*. **IV.** As an abbreviation, D usually stands for the praenomen Decimus ; also for Deus, Divus, Dominus, Decurio, *etc.* ; in epitaphs, D. M. = Dis Manibus. **N.B.**—The use of the symbol D as the representative of 500 is a modern corruption : the original mark was the half of the original Tuscan numeral ⓪ or CIꝹ = 1000, which printers have found it convenient to represent by D.

Daae, *v.* Dahae.

Dăci, ōrum, *m. pl. a warlike people living on both sides of the lower Danube* ; **Dăcia,** ae, *f. their country* ; **Dăcus,** I, *m. a Dacian* ; **Dăcicus,** I, *m. a gold coin struck under Domitian, conqueror of the Dacians.*

dacrima, *v.* lacrima.

dactylicus, a, um [δακτυλικός], *dactylic* : numerus, Cic.

dactylus, i, *m.* [δάκτυλος, *a finger*], in metre, *the foot* — ‿ ‿ (called after the three joints of the finger) : Cic.

daedalus, a, um [δαίδαλος, *cf.* Daedalus]. **A.** A c t. : *skilful, cunning in workmanship* : Verg. With GEN. : verborum, Lucr. **B.** P a s s. : *curiously wrought, skilfully made, variously adorned, gay* (δαιδάλεος) : Lucr., Verg.

Daedalus, I, *m. an Athenian architect of prehistoric times* ; **Daedalēus (-ius),** a, um.

Dahae, ārum, *m. pl. a Scythian tribe beyond the Caspian Sea.*

damma (older **dāma**), ae, *f.* (*m.* Verg.). **1.** L i t. : *a fallow-deer, buck or doe* : Verg., Hor., Ov. **2.** T r a n s f. : *venison* : Ov., Juv. [It. *daino, daina* ; Fr. *daim, daine*.]

Damascus, i, *f. the capital of Coele-Syria* ; **Damascēnus,** a, um ; **Damascēnum,** i, *n. a Damascene plum, a damson.*

damnātĭō, ōnis, *f.* [damnō], *condemnation* : Cic. With GEN. of the offence : Cic. ; of the criminal : Cic. ; of the penalty : pecuniae, Cic. In *pl.* : Cic.

damnātōrius, a, um [damnō], *damnatory, condemnatory* : Cic.

damnātus, a, um. **I.** *Part.* damnō. **II.** *Adj.* **a.** *criminal* : quis te damnatior ? Cic. **b.** *hateful* : Prop.

damnĭfĭcus, a, um [damnum faciō], *hurtful, injurious, pernicious* : Pl.

damnĭgĕrŭlus, a, um [damnum gerō], *harmbringing, pernicious* : Pl.

damnō, āre [damnum], *to cause loss to, harm, damage.* **A.** In gen. : Pl. **B.** Esp. in law, *to impose damages or fine or penalty on* ; *to condemn.* **1.** L i t. With ACC. of person : Caes., Cic., Liv. With ACC. of thing : causam, Cic. With ACC. of person and GEN. of crime or penalty : Cic., Verg., etc. With *de* and ABL. of crime : Cic., Tac. With *ob* and ACC. of crime : Liv. With *quod* and *Subj.* of crime : Liv. With ABL. : eo nomine, Caes. ; eo crimine, Cic. ; Verg. Esp. of the penalty : Cic., Liv. With *ad* and ACC. of penalty : Tac., Suet. **2.** T r a n s f. **a.** Of the plaintiff : *to effect a person's condemnation* : Pl., Liv. **b.** With ref. to a will, *to bind an heir to certain conditions* (with *Inf.*) : Hor. **c.** In gen. *to condemn* : aliquem stultitiae, Cic., Lucr. P h r. : aliquem voti or votorum, *to condemn someone to the amount of what he has vowed* : Liv. With votis : Verg. **d.** *to devote* : caput Orco, Verg. [Sp. *danar*.]

damnōse, *adv. with much loss, ruinously* : bibere, Hor.

damnōsus, a, um [damnum]. **A.** A c t. : *causing much loss, ruinous* : societatibus damnosus, Liv.; Hor.; Ov. *Sup.* : Pl. **B.** P a s s. : *wronged, injured* : Pl. **C.** R e f l. : *ruining oneself* : Pl. *Comp.* : Suet.

damnum, i, *n.* [for dapnum, *cf.* δαπανή], *loss incurred, damage* (opp. lucrum). **A.** In gen. : Pl. ; dare alicui, Pl., Cato, Cic. ; exercitum Caesar duarum cohortium damno reducit, Caes. ; facere, *to sustain*, Pl., Cic. ; contrahere, Cic. ; pati, Liv. ; ferre, Ov. (*v.* freq.) ; explere, sarcire, *to repair*, Caes. ; naturae damnum, *natural defect*, Liv. Abusively of persons : Pl., Ov. **b.** In law, *damages, fine, penalty* : Pl., Cic., Liv. [Fr. *dommage*.]

Dāmōn, ōnis, *m.* **I.** *a Pythagorean, famous for his friendship with Phintias.* **II.** *an Athenian musician.*

Danaē, ēs, *f. d. of Acrisius and m. of Perseus by Jupiter* ; **Danaēïus,** a, um.

Danaus, I, *m. s. of Belus and b. of Aegyptus* ; *he came from Egypt to Greece and became king of Argos* ; **Danaus,** a, um ; **Danai,** ōrum (or -um), *m. pl. the Greeks.*

danista, ae, *m.* [δανειστής], *a money-lender, usurer* : Pl.

danisticus, a, um [δανειστικός], *money-lending, usurious* : Pl.

danō, *v.* dō, *ad init.*

Danuvius, I, *m. the upper Danube.* (Hister = the lower Danube.)

Daphnē, ēs, *f. d. of the river-god Peneus* ; *pursued by Apollo, she was changed into a laurel.*

Daphnis, idis (ACC. -im or -in), *m. a Sicilian shepherd, s. of Mercury.*

dapĭnō, āre [daps], *to serve up*, as food : Pl.

daps, dapis (GEN. *pl.* and DAT. *sing.* not found), *f.* [*cf.* δαπανή], *a feast for religious purposes, a sacrificial feast* (thus dist. fr. convivium, epulae, epulum). **1.** L i t. : Cato, Verg., Liv., etc. **2.** T r a n s f. : *a feast* (in gen.), *banquet.* In *sing.* : Cat.,

Ov., Liv., etc. In *pl.* : Verg., Ov., Tac., etc.

dapsilis, ɘ· (ABL. *pl.* ·Is : Pl.), *adj.* [δαψιλής, daps], *sumptuous. bountiful, plentiful* : sumptus, Pl. ; dotes, Pl. *Neut.* Acc. as Adv. : Suet.

Dardanus, ĭ, *m. s. of Jupiter and Electra, ancestor of the royal family of Troy ;* **Dardanus, Dardanius**, a, um ; **Dardania**, ae, *f. a city founded by Dardanus on the Hellespont,* but oftener = Troia ; **Dardanidēs**, ae, *m. a male descendant of Dardanus ; pl.* **Dardanidae**, ārum or um, *the Trojans ;* **Dardanis**, idis, *f. adj. Trojan.*

Darēus, ĭ, *m.* the name of several Persian kings ; esp. **I.** D. Hystaspis, *f. of Xerxes.* **II.** D. Nothus, *f. of Artaxerxes and Cyrus the younger.* **III.** D. Codomannus, *overthrown by Alexander the Great.*

datārius, a, um [datus, *Part.* dŏ], *to be given away* : Pl.

datātim, *adv.* [datŏ], *by giving in turn or tossing from one to the other* : isti qui ludunt datatim, Pl.

datiō, ōnis, *f.* [dŏ], *a giving, allotting, making over.* **1.** Lit. : legum datio, Cic. **2.** Transf. : *the right of alienation* : Liv. [It. *dazio* ; Sp. *dacio.*]

dativus, a, um [dŏ], *relating to giving* : casus (or simply, dativus, as Noun), *the dative case,* Quint.

datō, āre [*freq.* dŏ], *to give frequently, give away* : Pl.

dator, ōris, *m.* [dŏ], *a giver* : laetitiae, Verg. In playing ball, the slave who hands the ball to the player is called *dator,* and the player himself *factor* : Pl.

datū, ABL. *sing. m.* [dŏ], *by giving* : Pl.

Daulis, idis, *f. a city in Phocis, scene of the fable of Tereus, Procne, and Philomela ;* **Daulius**, a, um ; **Daulias**, adis, *f. adj. :* ales (i.e. *Procne*) ; Dauliades puellae (i.e. *Procne and Philomela.*)

Daunus, ĭ, *m. king of Apulia, ancestor of Turnus ;* **Daunius**, a, um, *Daunian ; or Italian.*

dē, *adv.* and *prep.* **I.** *Adv.* only in compounds. **A.** Form and Quantity : the *e* becomes short before a vowel or *h,* e.g. dĕhisco, dĕinde, and coalesces with it in verse; *v.* deinceps, dehinc ; sometimes contraction occurs, e.g. dēbeo, dēgo, fr. dehabeo, deago. **B.** Meaning. **a.** *down* (literally) : defluo. **b.** *down from a superior position,* hence, *with authority ; down from the right source or to the right person or place ; down home, duly :* denuntio, dedo, dedico, defero, decedo. **c.** *down, deviating from the right path or state, awry :* decipio, declino, depravo. **d.** *down, left behind, left in misfortune :* destituo, derelinquo. **e.** *down to the end :* defleo, degrandinat. **f.** *down over, from top to toe :* dealbare, deamare. **g.** *down, below the mark, less than right :* deficio, desum. **h.** *down from* (with idea of stripping) : dearmare. **i.** *down from off, away :* deripio, derogo, denudo. **j.** *down, wrongways* (reversing the meaning) : dedecorare, dediscere. **II.** *Prep.* : *down.* With ABL. *down from, down away ; derived from, starting from, taken from,* etc. **A.** Of Place. **1.** Lit. *down from* :

de muro deicere, Caes. ; labi de caelo, Verg. ; anulum de digito detrahere, Cic. ; de castris procedere, Sall. ; decedere de provinciā (*cf.* to '*go down*' from Oxford), Cic. ; proles suscepta de te, Verg. **2.** Transf. **a.** Of origin : *from, descended from, derived from* : homo de plebe, Cic., Liv. ; de Argolicā gente esse, Verg. **b.** Of separation : *from among, from out of :* pauci de nostris cadunt, Caes. ; unus de illis, Cic. ; de servis fidelissimus, Nep. **c.** Of orig. form or material from which a thing is made : *from, of :* de templo carcerem fieri, Cic. ; nil posse creari de nilo, Lucr. ; in deum de bove versus, Ov. **d.** Of stock or source from which a thing is taken : *from, out of :* aliquid dare de communi aerario, Nep. ; de suo, Cic., Liv. ; de praedā, Liv. *Cf.* phr. de novo, *anew ;* de integro, *afresh ;* de improviso, *unexpectedly.* **e.** Of person as source of news, etc. : hoc de patre audivi, Cic. ; discere id de me, Ter. **B.** Of Time. **a.** Of point of departure, *after* (rare) : statim de suctione, Cic. Ep. Hence, diem de die, *day after day,* Liv. **b.** In Phr. de nocte, de vigiliā, etc. to denote the period in *the course of* which the action occurs (= Gk. GEN. of time) ; less precise than the ABL. alone, which denotes the exact time : surgunt de nocte latrones, Cic. ; de die, Liv. ; de mense Decembri, Cic. **C.** Of mental operations. **a.** Of the starting-point (i.e. the subject-matter) of thought or action : *about, concerning, of, with respect to :* multa narrare de Laelio, Cic. ; de Dionysio sum admiratus, Cic. ; de aliquā re timere, dimicare, Nep. ; triumphare de hostibus, Caes. **b.** Of that which starts or causes action : *for, on account of, because of :* quā de causā, Caes. ; fiere de supplicio suo, Cic. **c.** To denote that in conformity with which a thing is done : *according to, after, in imitation of :* de propinquorum sententiā, Cic. ; de more maiorum, Liv. Phr. de industriā, *on purpose,* Cic. [It. *di* ; Fr. *de.*]

dea, ae (DAT. and ABL. *pl.* deābus in the phrase dīs deābusque, Cic.), *f.* [deus], *a goddess* : Cic., Verg., etc. (v. diva).

de-albō, āre [albus], *to whiten all over, whitewash, plaster* : Cic.

deambulātiō, ōnis, *f.* [deambulō], *a walking about, a promenading* : Ter.

de-ambulō, āre, *to walk about, to take a walk* : Ter., Cato, Cic.

de-amō, āre, *to love downright* or *out and out* : illam, Pl. Of things : munera, Pl. Also (*cf.* amo), *to be exceedingly obliged to* : deamo te, Syre, Ter.

de-armō, āre, *to disarm* : exercitum, Liv.

de-artuō, āre [artus], *to tear limb from limb.* Transf. : opes, Pl.

de-asciō, āre [ascia], *to polish down with an axe.* Transf. : aliquem, Pl.

dēbacchor, ārī, *to revel like Bacchantes to the end, revel unchecked.* **1.** Lit. : Ter. **2.** Transf. : ignes, Hor.

dēbellātor, ōris, *m.* [dēbellō], *a conqueror* : ferarum, Verg.

dē-bellō, āre, *to war to the end.* **A.** Intrans. : *to bring a war to an end* : Liv. Most freq. in *Pass. Impers.* : Liv., Tac. ; and in

Part. Perf. absol. debellato, *after the war was ended :* Liv. **B.** Trans. : **a.** *to war down, subdue.* With Acc. of person : Verg., Tac. **b.** *to fight out.* With Acc. of thing : rixa debellata, Hor.

dēbeō, ēre, uī, itum [dē, habeō]. Lit. *to have or hold from* another man ; *to owe, to be in debt.* **1.** Lit. Of money and money's worth. With Acc. of thing and Dat. of person : Pl., Cic., etc. Pass. *to be due :* quam ad diem legioni frumentum deberi sciebat, Caes. ; Cic. Also absol. *to owe money, be in debt :* ut illi (Dat.) quam plurimi deberent, Sall. Without indirect obj. : Kal. Ian. debuit, Cic. **2.** Transf. **A.** Of things not estimated in money. **a.** In gen. with Acc. : *to owe, to be bound* or *liable to do* or *render :* Pl. ; maiorem ei res publica gratiam debet, Cic. ; hoc munus patriae debere, Cic. ; Turnum haec iam mihi sacra, Verg. Pass. : *to be due* or *owing :* Veneri reliquum tempus deberi arbitrabatur, Cic. ; honores quasi debitos repetere, Sall. ; praemia reddant debita ! Verg. **b.** Of moral or other obligation : (*one*) *ought.* With *Inf. :* Pl. ; num ferre contra patriam arma debuerant ? Cic. ; dici beatus ante obitum nemo debet, Ov. Poet. : *must of necessity* (freq. in Lucr.) : omnia debet cibus integrare novando, Lucr. **c.** *to owe* with ref. *to* necessity or destiny ; *to be destined to something :* urbem cerno Phrygios debere nepotes, Ov. More freq. in Pass. *to be due* (by destiny) : cui regnum Italiae Romanaque tellus debentur, Verg. *Absol. :* tempora Parcae debita complerunt, Verg. ; morbo naturae debitum reddiderunt, Nep. Hence, phr. ludibrium alicui debere (cf. Gk. γέλωτα ὀφλεῖν), *to be fated to become the sport of,* Hor. **B.** Esp. of thanks : *to owe thanks for, be under obligation for, be indebted for :* fac (*suppose*) me multis debere, Cic. With Acc. : hoc beneficium alicui, Cic. ; alicui salutem, Ov. [It. *dovere* ; Fr. *devoir.*]

dēbilis, e, *adj. wanting strength ; powerless, feeble, paralysed.* **1.** Lit. Of living beings : Cato, Cic., Verg., etc. **2.** Transf. **a.** Chiefly of things used by living beings : Ter. ; corpus, Lucr. ; ferrum, Verg. ; manus, Ov. **b.** Of mind, character, etc. : memoriā debilis, Cic. ; ingenio, Tac. ; praetura, Cic. *Comp. :* Tac.

dēbilitās, ātis, *f.* [dēbilis], *state of being disabled, powerlessness, feebleness, paralysis.* **1.** Lit. : Cic., Liv., etc. With Gen. : membrorum, Liv. ; linguae, Cic. In *pl. different kinds of debility :* Cic. **2.** Transf. Of the mind : animi, Cic.

dēbilitātiō, ōnis, *f.* [dēbilitō], *a disabling, paralysing :* animi, Cic.

dēbilitō, āre [dēbilis], *to render powerless, disable, enfeeble.* **1.** Lit. : membra, Cic. ; Lucr. ; aliquem, Liv., Tac., Ov. Poet. : hiems nunc oppositis debilitat pumicibus mare Tyrrhenum, Hor. **2.** Transf. : *to paralyse, crush, break down :* debilitatus metu, Cic. ; fortitudinem, Cic. ; membrum rei publicae debilitatum, Cic. ; nec tarda senectus debilitat viris animi, Verg. ; veritatem, Cic.

dēbitiō, ōnis, *f.* [dēbeō], *an owing, debt :* Cic.

dēbitor, ōris, *m.* [dēbeō], *a debtor.* **1.** Lit. Of money, etc. : Caes., Cic., Hor., etc. **2.** Transf. **a.** Non-pecuniary sense : Ov. **b.** *one indebted for, under obligation for :* vitae, Ov. ; Plin. Ep.

dēbitum, ī, *n.* [dēbeō], *what is owed, a debt.* **1.** Lit. Of money, etc. : Cic. **2.** Transf. : *any obligation :* vitae, Curt. [It. *detta* ; Sp. *deuda* ; Fr. *dette, débit.*]

dē-blaterō, āre, *to prate all about,* with Acc. and *Inf. : to blab out :* Pl.

dē-cantō, āre, *to sing off,* **I.** *to sing* or *repeat monotonously all through over and over again* (cf. *cantilena*) : pervulgata praecepta, Cic. ; elegos, Hor. **II.** *to sing on to the end, to leave off singing :* hi iam decantaverant, Cic.

dē-cēdō, cēdere, cessī, cessum. **I.** *to move down duly, withdraw, retire,* '*clear out*' (with idea of making way for another). **1.** Lit. **a.** decedamus, Pl. ; de parte (agri) decedere, Caes. ; Cic. ; Verg., etc. Esp. of *making way.* **i.** out of respect : with Dat. of person and often with de viā or viā : Pl., Hor., Suet, etc. **ii.** in abhorrence : Caes., Cic., Verg. Pass. *to be made way for :* Cic. **b.** Milit. *to withdraw, to evacuate :* de colle, Caes. ; nisi decedat atque exercitum deducat ex his regionibus, Caes. **c.** In official lang. : *to retire* on the expiration of a term of office : de provinciā, Liv. ; e provinciā, Cic., Liv. ; provinciā, Cic., Liv. ; Albinus Romam decessit, Sall. ; Romam ad triumphum, Liv. **2.** Transf. **a.** *to retire* (in favour of another), *to give up* rights, possessions, etc. : de suo iure, Cic. ; iure suo, Liv. ; de possessione, de suis bonis, Cic. **b.** *to give place, yield to.* With Dat. : Hor. **c.** Of living beings : *to depart* (from life), *to die :* de vitā, Cic. ; cum paterfamilias decessit, Caes. ; Liv. **d.** Of things : *to abate, subside, cease :* corpore febres, Lucr. ; decessisse inde aquam, Liv. ; decedere aestum, Liv. ; invidia decesserat, Sall. ; de summā nihil decedet, Ter. ; ut de causā eius periculi nihil decederet, Cic. With Dat. : ea cura patribus, Liv. ; quidquid libertati plebis caveretur, id suis decederē opibus credebant, Liv. ; Tac. Occ. of the sun : *to withdraw, set :* Verg., Tac. **II.** *to go awry ; go wrong, depart, swerve.* **1.** Lit. : quae naves paululum suo cursu decesserint, Caes. **2.** Transf. Of duty, faith, etc. : se nullā cupiditate inductum de viā decessisse, Cic. ; de officio, Cic. ; officio, fide, Liv. *Impers. Pass. :* de officio deceasum, Liv.

decem, *indecl. adj.* [Gk. δέκα], *ten.* **1.** Lit. : Ter., Cic., etc. **2.** Transf. : for large number : Pl., Hor.

December, bris, *m.* [decem], *of the tenth month of the Roman year,* reckoned from March, *of December.* **1.** Lit. : Kalendae, Cic. ; Nonae, Hor. ; libertas (i.e. of the Saturnalia), Hor. As Noun (*sc.* mensis) : Cic., Ov., etc. **2.** Transf. As closing the year, *a* (past) *year :* undenos implevisse Decembris, Hor.

decem-iugis, is, *m.* [iugum] (with *currus* understood), *a ten-horse chariot :* Suet.

decem-peda, ae, *f.* [pēs], *a ten-foot measuring rod :* Cic., Hor.

decempedātor, ōris, m. [decempeda], *a land-surveyor :* Cic.

decem-plex, icis, adj. [plicŏ], *tenfold :* numerus, Nep.

decemprimi, ōrum (or **decem primi**), m. pl. *the ten chief men in the body of decuriones (or senate) in the municipia and colonies :* Cic.

decem-scalmus, a, um, *having ten tholepins :* actuariola, Cic.

decemvirālis, e, adj. [decemviri], *decemviral : belonging to or made by the decemviri :* leges, Liv.; potestas, Tac.; annus, Cic.; certamina, Liv.

decemvirātus, ūs, m. [decemviri], *the decemvirate, the office of decemvir :* Cic., Liv.

decem-viri, ōrum, m. pl. *a commission of ten,* appointed at diff. times for diff. purposes, e.g. **a.** decemviri legibus scribundis (B.C. 461, *for compilation of the laws*), Cic., Liv. **b.** decemviri stlitibus (litibus) iudicandis (*a permanent board for deciding private cases*), Cic. **c.** decemviri sacris faciundis (*for attending to religious matters*, e.g. the Sibylline books ; orig. 2 in number, later 15), Liv. **d.** decemviri agris dividundis, *for dividing public lands*, Cic., Liv. *Sing.* decemvir : Cic., Liv.

decennis, e, adj. [decem annus], *of ten years, lasting ten years :* Quint.

decēns, entis. **I.** *Part.* decet. **II.** *Adj.* **a.** In gen.: *becoming, seemly, proper :* amictus, Ov.; motus, Hor.; Quint. **b.** Of bodily symmetry : *comely, handsome, well-formed :* Hor., Ov., Tac., etc. **c.** In moral sense : *becoming, right, proper :* Hor. *Comp. :* Ov., Tac., etc. *Sup. :* Quint.

decenter, adv. [decēns], *becomingly, fitly, with propriety :* Hor., Ov., Plin. Ep. *Comp. :* Hor.

decentia, ae, f. [decēns], *becomingness, propriety :* colorum, Cic.

deceptus, a, um, *Part.* dēcipiō.

dē-cernō, cernere, crēvī, crētum (the sync. forms *decrēram, decrērim, decrēsse*, etc., are freq. and class.): Lit. *to sift, separate thoroughly or finally ; to decide, settle, determine.* **1.** Lit. **A.** Properly of an arbitrator, public official, public body, etc. **a.** Of facts : *to sit de hereditate controversia est*, Druides decernunt, Caes.; rem dubiam, Liv. **b.** Of policy, *to decide on, decide.* With Acc.: Caes., Cic., Liv. With *ut* and *Subj. :* Cic. Ep. With *Indir. Quest. :* Liv. Also *absol., to put forward a proposal :* Liv. **B.** In private matters, *to decide.* **a.** Of facts. With Acc. and *Inf. :* Ter., Cic. Ep. With *Indir. Quest. :* Pl. *Absol. :* Ter. **b.** Of a course of action, *to resolve, determine,* mostly with *Inf. :* Ter., Caes., Liv. With Acc. and *Inf. :* Pl., Sall. With *ut* and *Subj. :* Cic. **2.** T r a n s f.: *to settle* by combat. **a.** Of actual fighting. With Acc.: Cic., Liv. With ABL. *Instr. :* Cic., Liv., Verg., etc. With *Indir. Quest. :* Liv. *Absol. :* Caes. **b.** Of legal combats, etc. With *de* or *pro* and ABL. : Cic.

dē-carpō, cerpere, cerpsī, cerptum [carpō], *to pluck down ; to gather.* **1.** Lit.: acina de uvis, Cato ; novos flores, Lucr.; arbore pomum, Ov.; Verg. **2.** T r a n s f. **a.** *to cull, gather :* oscula, Cat.; ex re fructūs,

Hor.; Cic. **b.** *to derive :* humanus animus decerptus ex mente divinā, Cic. **c.** *to pluck away* (with idea of loss to the original): ne quid iocus de gravitate decerperet, Cic.

dēcertātiō, ōnis, f. [dēcertō], *a putting to the issue :* rerum omnium, Cic.

dē-certō, āre, *to fight out, fight to a finish, contest to the end.* **a.** Milit. with proelio, Cic., Caes. (freq.); and less freq. pugnā, Caes.; ferro, Ov. *Absol. :* Caes., Tac. *Pass. Impers. :* Cic. **b.** Non-milit. : inter se decertare (of rival orators), Cic.; iure, legibus, Cic.; contentione dicendi, Cic. Of things (with DAT.): Africum decertantem Aquilonibus, Hor.

dēcessiō, ōnis, f. [dēcēdō], *a withdrawing.* **a.** In gen. : Cic. Ep. **b.** *the retirement* (of an official) *from a province :* Cic. **c.** *diminution, deduction :* de summā, Cic.

dēcessor, ōris, m. [dēcēdō], *one who retires from* (a province, government, etc.), *a retiring official, a predecessor in office* (opp. successor): Cic., Tac.

dēcessus, ūs, m. [dēcēdō], *withdrawal.* **a.** *retirement* of an official or ruler from a province : Cic. **b.** Of the tide : ebb : Caes. **c.** *decease, death :* Cic. [Fr. *décès.*]

decet, ēre, uit [*cf.* δοκεῖν, decus], *it is seemly, becoming ; it beseems, is fitting, proper* (very freq. and class., not in Caes.): minus severe quam decuit, Cic.; Ter., etc. With Acc. of Obj. (if expressed) : facis ut te decet, Ter.; Pl.; Quint. With Noun or Pron. as Subject : omnis Aristippum color decuit, Hor.; Cic., etc.; id maxime quemque decet, Cic.; Pl., etc. In *pl.* : neo velle experiri, quam se aliena deceant, Cic. With DAT. of the Object : istuc facinus nostro generi non decet, Pl.; Sall. With Acc. of person and *Inf.,* or *Inf.* alone : oratorem irasci minime decet, Cic.; Pl.; Verg., etc.; exemplis grandioribus decuit uti, Cic.; Pl.; Ov., etc.

dē-cidō, cidere, cidī [cadō], *to fall down.* **1.** Lit. **a.** In gen. : de lecto, Pl.; poma ex arboribus, Cic.; Ov.; equo, Caes.; ex equo, Nep.; toro, Ov. **b.** Esp. *to fall down dead, to die :* Verg., etc.; morbo, Pl. **2.** T r a n s f.; *to fall, fall off or away,* etc.: quantā de spe decidi ! Ter.; a spe societatis alicuius, Liv.; ficta omnia celeriter tamquam flosculi decidunt, Cic. [It. *decadere ;* Fr. *déchoir.*]

dē-cīdō, cidere, cīdī, cisum [caedō], *to cut down ; to cut short.* **1.** Lit.: collum, Pl.; auris, Tac.; pennas, Hor.; virgam arbori, Tac. **2.** T r a n s f. **a.** *to cut short, put an end to ; to settle :* res, Cic.; negotia, Hor. Comic.: Pl. **b.** *to settle :* cum aliquo, Cic.; de rebus, Cic.; decidere iactu coepit cum ventis, Juv. [It. *decidere ;* Fr. *décider.*]

deciēns (later **deciēs**), adv. [decem], *ten times.* **1.** Lit.: deciens seni, Cic.; HS. deciens centena milia, Cic.; without *centena milia :* HS. deciens, *a million sesterces,* Cic.; ad deciens aeris, *up to a million,* Liv. **2.** T r a n s f. Of indef. number : Hor.

decima, v. decuma.

decimānus, v. decumānus.

decimus (older **decumus**), a, um [decem],

the tenth : mensis, Pl. ; hora, Cic. ; legio,
Caes. ; unda, Ov. ; pars praedae, Liv.
Phr. : cum decimo efficit ager, *yielded a
ten-fold return*, Cic. *Neut.* Acc. as adv.
decimum, *for the tenth time*, Liv.
dē-cipiō, cipere, cēpī, ceptum [capiō], Lit.
*to catch down, catch and make to fall ; to de-
ceive, cheat* (us. of *deliberate deception ;*
contr. fallo, deludo). **1.** Lit.: ita deci-
piemus foveā lenonem, Pl. ; homines per
conloquium deceptos, Caes. **2.** Transf.
a. In gen. *to snare, mislead, beguile :* esp.
in *Pass.* : Caes., Hor., Liv. **b.** Of things :
aliquem exspectationes, Cic. ; Verg. ; iudicium error, Ov. **c.** *to charm to sleep, lull :*
diem, laborem, Ov. ; laborum decipitur,
is beguiled of his labour, Hor. **d.** *to escape
one's notice* (= fallere) : amatorem amicae
decipiunt vitia, Hor. *Absol. :* Liv.
dēcīsiō, ōnis, *f.* [dēcīdō], *a cutting short, a
settlement, decision :* Cic.
dēcīsus, a, um, *Part.* dēcīdō.
Decius, a, *name of a Roman plebeian gens ;*
esp. P. Decius Mus, *who devoted himself to
death in the Latin war* (B.C. 340), *and his
son and grandson, who fell at Sentinum*
(B.C. 295) *and at Asculum* (B.C. 279) ;
Deciānus, a, um.
dēclāmātiō, ōnis, *f.* [dēclāmō]. **I. 1.** Lit.:
exercise in speaking, declamation : Cic.,
Quint. **2.** Transf.: *a theme, subject for
declamation :* Quint., Juv. **II.** *loud, eager
speaking, shouting :* vulgari declamatione
contendere, Cic,
dēclāmātor, ōris, *m.* [dēclāmō], *one who
trains himself in public speaking, a declaimer :* Cic., Quint., Juv.
dēclāmātōrius, a, um [dēclāmātor], *of or
belonging to practice in public speaking ;
declamatory, rhetorical :* opus, Cic. ; studium, Tac.
dēclāmitō, āre [*freq.* dēclāmō]. **I.** *to practise public speaking frequently or intensely :*
Cic., Hor., Juv. With Acc.: causas,
Cic. **II.** *to talk violently, to bluster :* de
aliquo, Cic.
dē-clāmō, āre. Lit. *to shout down* (i.e. from
a platform, etc.). **I.** *to practise public
speaking, declaim :* Cic., Hor., etc. With
Acc.: aliquid ex aliā oratione declamare,
Cic. **II.** *to speak violently, to bawl, to bluster :*
vehementissime contra aliquem declamare,
Cic.
dēclārātiō, ōnis, *f.* [dēclārō], *a making clear
or known, an expression :* animi, amoris,
Cic. Ep.
dē-clārō, āre [clārus]. Lit. *to make clear
from above, with authority ; to make clear
from full knowledge, announce with full
authority.* **1.** Lit. Of public or official
announcements : *to proclaim, announce,
declare :* declaratus consul, Cic. ; Liv. ;
victorem magnā praeconis voce Cloanthum
declarat, Verg. **2.** Transf. **a.** Of facts,
to make known, announce, reveal, declare.
With Acc.: Cic., Nep. With Acc. and
Inf. : Pl., Lucr., Cic. With *Indir. Quest. :*
Ter., Caes., Cic. Ep. **b.** Of feelings, etc. :
animi magnitudinem, Cic. ; Cat. **c.** By
reasoning or explanation : propriam (alicuius) rei vim definitione declarare, Cic. ;
Lucr. [It. *dichiarare.*]

dēclīnātiō, ōnis, *f.* [dēclīnō], *a leaning from
or away, a bending aside ; a slanting movement.* **1.** Lit.: atomorum, Cic. ; quot
ego tuas petitiones parvā quādam declina-
tione effugi, Cic. ; Curt. **2.** Transf. **a.**
a turning aside, a shunning, an avoiding :
(ab aliquā re), Cic. ; opp. appetitio, Cic.
b. Rhet. *digression :* declinatio brevis a
proposito, Cic. **c.** Gramm., *declension, inflexion* (formerly including *conjugation,
comparison, derivation,* etc.) : Cic.
dē-clīnō, āre [lost verb clīnō = Gk. κλίνω].
A. Trans.: *to make to lean from the true
line or direction ; to deflect.* **1.** Lit. **a.** In
gen. : se extra viam, Pl. ; sese rectā regione
viāī, Lucr. ; ex illo lumina, Cat. ; agmen,
Liv. Poet.: *to let droop :* nec dulci
declinat lumina somno, Verg. **b.** Of
weapons or attacks, *to parry, shun, avoid :*
ictum, Liv. **2.** Transf. **a.** *to deflect,
divert* (only in *Pass.*) : metu declinatus
animus, Quint. ; Ter. **b.** Gramm., *to
decline, conjugate :* Quint. **c.** *to shun,
avoid :* urbem, Cic. ; vitia, Cic. ; invidiam,
Tac. **B.** Intrans. : *to turn aside from
the true course, deviate.* **1.** Lit.: de viā,
Cic. ; Liv. **2.** Transf.: a religione
offici, Cic. ; ab rerum ordine, Liv. ; in
Italiam bellum, Liv. ; in peius, Quint. ;
amor, Ov.
dē-clīvis, e, *adj.* [clīvus], *sloping downwards,
steep* (as regarded *from above ; acclivis,* as
viewed *from below*). **1.** Lit.: collis ab
summo aequaliter declivis, Caes. ; locus,
Caes. ; Hor. ; flumina, Ov. *Neut.* as
Noun, **dēclīve,** is, *n.,* *a declivity or slope :*
si per declive sese reciperent, Caes. ; Ov.
2. Transf.: iter declive senectae, Ov. ;
Plin. Ep.
dēclīvitās, ātis, *f.* [dēclīvis], *a sloping place,
declivity :* Caes.
dēcocta, ae, *f.* (sc. aqua) [dēcoquō], *a cold
beverage,* invented by Nero : Juv., Suet.
dēcoctor, ōris, *m.* [dēcoquō], *a bankrupt :*
Cic., Cat.
dēcoctus, a, um. **I.** *Part.* dēcoquō. **II.**
Adj. boiled down. Transf. (of style)
luscious, over-sweet : Cic. Comp. : Pers.
dē-collō, āre [collum], *to take* (the head) *off
from the neck, to behead :* homines, Sen. ;
Suet.
dē-cōlō, āre [cōlum], *to come down through a
sieve, trickle or filter away.* Transf.: si
spes decolabit, Pl.
dē-color, ōris, *adj.* [color]. **I.** *off-colour,
faded, pale.* **1.** Lit.: sanguis, Poet. ap.
Cic. **2.** Transf.: aetas, Verg. **II.** *dis-
coloured.* **1.** Lit.: sanguine decolor, Ov. ;
India (i.e. *browned*), Ov. **2.** Transf.:
fama (i.e. *by lies*), Ov.
dēcolōrātiō, ōnis, *f.* [dēcolōrō], *a discolouring :*
Cic.
dē-colōrō, āre, *to discolour :* Suet. : mare,
(i.e. *ensanguine*), Hor.
dē-coquō, coquere, coxī, coctum. **I.** *to boil
down, boil away.* **1.** Lit. : Varr. ; pars
quarta (argenti) decocta erat, Liv. **2.**
Transf. **a.** *to waste, ruin :* Quint. ; hunc
alea decoquit, Pers. **b.** Without object
expressed, *to become bankrupt ;* Cic. **II.**
to boil thoroughly : olus, Hor.
decor, ōris, *m.* [*cf.* decet], *comeliness, grace,*

beauty. **a.** Of the person : Hor., Ov., Tac. **b.** In gen.: mobilibusque decor naturis dandus et annis, Hor. ; divini signa decoris, Verg. ; Ov. Of style : Quint. In *pl.* : orationem plenam veris decoribus, Liv. **c.** *ornament :* Ov.

decŏrē, *adv.* **I.** *gracefully, beautifully* (of person): Poet. ap. Cic. **II.** *becomingly, gracefully :* Cic., Sall.

decorō, āre [decus], *to beautify, adorn, embellish.* **1.** Lit.: Larem coronā, Pl. ; oppidum monumentis, Cic. ; pyram fulgentibus armis, Verg. **2.** T r a n s f.: *to embellish, honour :* me lacrumis, Enn. ; aliquem honoribus, Cic. ; muneribus, Verg. ; versibus, Hor.

decŏrus, a, um [decor], *graceful, beautiful, adorned, bedecked.* **a.** Of outward appearance : delubra deum, Lucr. ; galeae, Verg. ; caput, Ov. ; arma, Liv. ; iuventa, Tac. With ABL. *Instr. :* Verg., Hor., Ov. **b.** Of inward matters, *graceful, beautiful, becoming :* senis sermo, Cic. ; silentium, Hor. With ABL. *Instr. :* Liv., Tac. With DAT.: Cic., Liv. With *ad* and ACC.: ad ornatum, Cic. With *pro* and ABL.: Tac. As Noun, **decŏrum**, ī, n. *propriety, grace :* Cic., Tac.

dē-crepitus, a, um [crepō], *broken down, worn out, decrepit :* senex, Pl. ; Cic.

dē-crescō, crēscere, crēvī, crētum, *to grow down, grow less, grow shorter, wane, decrease, diminish :* ostreae cum lunā, Cic. ; Lucr. Of water, *to subside :* Hor., Ov. Occ. *to disappear :* cornua descrescunt, Ov. [Fr. *décroître.*]

dēcrētus, a, um. **I.** *Part.* dēcernō. **II.** Noun, **dēcrētum**, ī, n. *a decision, resolution* (of persons in authority). **1.** Lit.: praetoris, decurionum, etc., Cic. ; pontificum, Liv. ; perfringere, evertere, Cic. ; stare decreto, Caes., Cic., Liv. **2.** T r a n s f.: Philos. *a principle, tenet, doctrine* (*cf.* δόγμα) : Cic.

decuma (decima), ae, f. (*sc.* pars) [decimus], *the tenth part, tithe.* **a.** As offering to gods : Liv. **b.** As a tax on landholders in the provinces : Cic. ; us. in *pl.* : Cic., Liv. **c.** *a largess bestowed on the people :* Cic., Tac., Suet. [Fr. *dîme.*]

decumānus (decimānus), a, um [decima], *of or belonging to the tenth.* **a.** *paying tithes :* Lucil. ; ager, Cic. As Noun, **decumānus**, ī, m. *a farmer of tithes :* Cic. ; **decumāna**, ae, f. *the wife of a tithe-farmer :* Cic. **b.** *of the tenth cohort :* porta decumana, *the gate of the quarters of the 10th cohort of each legion* (the main entrance of a Roman camp, on the side turned away from the enemy): Caes., Liv. **c.** *of the tenth legion :* miles, Auct. B. Afr. In *pl.* **decumānī**, ōrum, m. Auct. B. Afr., Auct. B. Hisp., Tac., Suet.

decumātēs, ium, *adj. pl.* [decuma], *subject to tithes :* agri, Tac.

dēcumbō, cumbere, cubuī, *to lie down.* **a.** *to go to bed :* Cato, Suet. **b.** *to lie at table :* Pl., Ter., Cic. **c.** *to fall :* gladiatores honeste, Cic.

decumō (decimō), āre [decuma], *to tithe, take a tenth ;* esp. Milit. of punishment, *to decimate :* legiones, Tac. ; Suet.

decuria, ae, f. [decem], *a group of ten.* **1.**

Lit.: Esp. polit. *a tenth part* of a curia (*cf.* decurio): Sen. Ep. **2.** T r a n s f.: *a division, class,* without ref. to number. **a.** Most freq. *a panel of judges* (three of these, till Augustus added a fourth, and Caligula a fifth): Cic., Suet. **b.** scribarum, viatorum, lictorum, Tac. ; Liv. **c.** *a club* of boon companions : Pl.

decuriātiō, ōnis, f. [decuriō], *a dividing into* decuriae : Cic.

decuriātus, ūs, m. [decuriō], *a dividing into* decuriae : Liv.

decuriō, āre [decuria]. **1.** Lit.: Polit. *to divide into tens* or decuriae : equites decuriati, Liv. **2.** T r a n s f.: *to make into groups :* Cic.

decuriō, ōnis, m. [decuria], *the head of ten, the chief of a decuria, a decurion.* **a.** In the army, *the commander of a decuria of cavalry :* Caes., Liv., Tac. **b.** *a member of the senate of a municipium, or a colony :* Caes., Cic. **c.** *a head-chamberlain :* cubiculariorum, Suet.

dē-currō, currere, cucurrī and currī, cursum. **I.** *to run down, hasten down.* **1.** Lit. **a.** de tribunali decurrit, Liv. ; Laocoon ardens summā decurrit ab arce, Verg. ; Caesar ad cohortandos milites decucurrit, Caes. Esp. of military movements from higher ground : Caes., Liv. **b.** Milit. (etc.) *to parade, manœuvre :* Liv., Verg., Tac. **c.** Down to the sea (of rivers, ships, etc.) : Hor., Liv., Tac. **d.** Down to land (of ships) : Liv. **2.** T r a n s f.: *to run for help* or *refuge, have recourse to :* ad haec extrema iura, Cic. ; ad preces, Hor., Ov. *Pass. Impers.:* Liv. **II.** *to hasten to the goal:* ad calcem, Cic. With ACC. of extent, *to traverse rapidly.* **1.** Lit. : spatium ad carceres, Cic. ; vada, Cat. **2.** T r a n s f.: aetatis spatium, Pl. ; aetatem, Cic. ; laborem, Verg. ; lumen vitae, Lucr. ; vitam, Phaedr. ; per totas quaestiones, Quint. ; ad consulendum te, Plin. Ep.

dēcursiō, ōnis, f. [dēcurrō]. Milit. **I.** *a raid, descent :* Brut. ap. Cic. Ep. ; Hirt. **II.** Of *military evolutions or the sake of exercise or show :* Suet.

dēcursus, ūs, m. [dēcurrō]. **I.** *a running down.* **a.** *fall, downward course :* montibus ex altis magnus decursus aquāī, Lucr. ; rapidus (amnium), Verg. **b.** Milit. *a raid, descent :* ex collibus, Liv., Tac. Milit. *parade, manœuvre :* Liv., Tac. **II.** *a complete course.* **1.** Lit.: *end of the course* (in games): Suet. **2.** T r a n s f. **a.** *a complete course :* honorum, Cic. **b.** R h e t.: *the rhythmical run of a verse :* Quint.

dēcurtātus, a, um [curtus], *cut down, cut off short, mutilated.* **1.** Lit.: amicus, Sen. **2.** T r a n s f. Of style : Cic.

decus, oris, n. [*cf.* decet, δοκεῖν, δόξα]. Lit. *brightness.* **1.** Lit. **a.** Of outward distinctions, *grace, beauty :* regium, Sall. ; Liv. ; decus enitet ore, Verg. Hence, vitis ut arboribus decori est, tu decus omne tuis, Verg. **b.** Of qualities, actions, etc. : *honour, glory :* ad decus et ad laudem civitatis, Cic. ; virtutem esse militis decus, Liv. ; pudoris, Ov. **c.** Occ. of persons, *shining light, glory :* Hor., Cat. **2.** T r a n s f. :

titles to honour. **a.** *virtue :* decus et hones-tas, Cic. ; Liv. **b.** *great deeds, distinctions* (in *pl.*) *:* militiae, Liv. **c.** *distinctions* (inherited) : Tac.

decussō, āre [decussis = the figure X], *to divide crosswise, in the form of an X :* Cic.

dēcussus, a, um, *Part.* **dēcutiō.**

dē-cutiō, cutere, cussī, cussum [quatiō], *to shake, beat, or cast down or off.* **1.** Lit. : Verg., Liv., etc. ; mella foliis, Verg. Comic. : ex armario argenti tantum, Pl. **2.** Transf. : Cael. ap. Cic. Ep.

dē-decet, decēre, decuit (used only in 3 *pers. sing.* and *pl.*) *; it misbecomes, is unseemly, unsuitable, unbecoming* (us. with Acc.). **a.** With Noun or Pron. as subject : si quid dedeceat, Cic. ; vox, Quint. With Acc. of person : neque te ministrum dedecet myrtus, Hor. ; Tac. In *pl. :* nec dominam dedecuere comae, Ov. **b.** With *Inf.* as subject, and Acc. of pers. : oratorem irasci simulare non dedecet, Cic. **c.** With subject implied : ut iis, quae habent, modice et scienter utantur, et ut ne dedeceat, Cic.

dē-decorō, āre, *to disgrace, dishonour, bring to shame :* Pl., Cic., Prop., etc.

dē-decōrus, a, um, *disgraceful, dishonourable :* Pl., Tac.

dē-decus, oris, n. *disgrace, dishonour, infamy, shame.* **1.** Lit. **a.** Of appearance : Ov., Phaedr. Abstract : Pl. ; cum ignominiā et dedecore perire, Cic. ; dedecus admittere, *to incur,* Caes. Hence, *a cause of dishonour :* dedecori esse (alicui), Cic. ; Ter. ; Hor. **2.** Transf. : *acts causing dishonour.* **a.** *moral turpitude, vice :* Ov., Tac. **b.** *disgrace in war, i.e. culpable defeats* (in *pl.*) : militiae, Liv.

dēdicātiō, ōnis, f. [dēdicō], *a dedicating :* aedis, Liv. ; celebrare, Liv.

dē-dicō, āre. **I.** *to set down for a definite purpose.* **1.** Lit. : Relig. **a.** *to set apart to a deity, dedicate :* aedem Castori ac Polluci, Cic. ; loca sacris faciendis, Liv. **b.** Of the deity : Fidem et Mentem in Capitolio dedicatas (*installed*), Cic. ; Hor. ; Liv. **2.** Transf. : equi memoriae urbem, Curt. ; Phaedr. **II.** *to specify clearly, declare.* **1.** Lit. Of property : praedia in censum, Cic. **2.** Transf. : Lucr.

dē-dignor, ārī, *to regard as unworthy ; to disdain, scorn :* Tac. With double Acc. : aliquem maritum (i.e. as a husband), Ov. ; Verg. ; Curt. With *Inf. :* Ov., Tac.

dē-discō, dīscere, didicī, *to unlearn, to forget.* With Acc. : Pl., Caes., Cic. With *Inf. :* Cic., Ov.

dēditicius, ī, m. [dēditus] *relating to the condition of* dediti ; as Noun in *pl. : surrendered persons, subjects :* Caes., Liv.

dēditiō, ōnis, f. [dēdō], *a giving up, an unconditional surrender; a capitulation :* in deditionem venire, Liv. ; aliquem in deditionem accipere, Caes., Liv. With *Obj.* GEN. : Liv., Tac. In *pl.* : Tac.

dēditus, a, um. **I.** *Part.* dēdō. **II.** Adj. : *devoted, absorbed, addicted.* With DAT. : Cic., Hor., etc. With *in* and ABL. : Lucr., Cat. *Sup.* : Dolab. ap. Cic. Ep. Phr. : **dēditā operā**, *purposely, intentionally :* Pl., Cic., Liv.

dē-dō, dere, didī, ditum, *to give up, surrender, yield.* **1.** Lit. : aliquem hostibus in cruciatum, Caes. ; Ter. ; aliquem alicui, Cic. ; Hor. ; reum telis militum, Cic. ; aliquem ad necem, Liv. ; neci, Verg., Liv. Esp. milit. : Pl., Caes., Liv. ; urbem, agros in populī Romani dicionem, Liv. ; Pl. Hence, res dedere, *to make restitution, give satisfaction,* Liv. **2.** Transf. : *to give up, devote.* **a.** se amicitiae eorum, Caes. ; se doctrinae, Cic. ; animum sacris, Liv. ; se ad audiendum, Cic. ; se totum alicui, Cic. ; auris poetis, Cic. ; membra somno, Lucr. ; ubi spectaculi tempus venit deditaeque eo (*sc.* ad spectacula) mentes cum oculis erant, Liv. **b.** Bad sense : se desidiae, libidinibus dedere, Cic.

dē-doceō, ēre, *to unteach, to teach the contrary* (with double Acc.) : aliquem geometriam, Cic. With Acc. (of personal object) and *Inf. :* Hor. Pass. : Cic.

dē-doleō, ēre, *to come to an end of grieving, grieve no more :* Ov.

dē-dolō, āre, *to chop downwards, hack or hew away.* Comic. : Pl.

dē-dūcō, dūcere, dūxī, ductum. **I.** *to lead or draw down.* **1.** Lit. **a.** In gen. : ut elephanti etiam deduci possent, Liv. ; eum de rostris, Caes. ; Pl. ; summā vestem deduxit ab orā, Ov. ; ornos montibus, Verg. ; Ov. **b.** Milit. : copias ex superioribus locis, Caes. ; Sall. **c.** *to draw down to the water, launch :* Caes., Liv., Verg., etc. (*v.* also II. 1. d.). **2.** Transf. **a.** From a higher standard, *to seduce :* aliquem vero, Lucr. ; aliquem a pietate, Cic. ; aliquem de fide, Cic. (*cf.* II. 2. a.). **b.** Of pedigree, derivation, etc. : nomen ab Anco, Ov. ; carmen ab origine mundi, Lucr. ; Hor. **II.** *to lead or draw away from its original place or to a determined place, to divert, withdraw.* **1.** Lit. **a.** In gen. : pecora ex agris, Caes. ; legionem ab opere, Caes. ; aquam Albanam, Cic. ; atomos de viā, Cic. ; hunc ad militem, Ter. ; Cic., etc. ; aliquem in conspectum Caesaris, Caes. ; Liv., etc. ; aliquem ad iudicium, Cic. **b.** Milit. : legiones in hiberna, Caes., Liv. ; impedimenta in proximum collem, Caes. **c.** Of colonists, *to lead out, plant :* colonos or coloniam in aliquem locum, Cic., Liv. ; colonia in agro Gallorum deducta, Liv. **d.** Naval, *to bring* (into port) : navem in portum, Caes. **e.** As a mark of respect (to magistrates, candidates, etc.), *to conduct, escort* (down to the forum or back home) : Cic., Liv., Hor. Esp. : *to conduct a bride* (to her new home) : uxorem domum, Ter. ; quo primum virgo quaeque deducta est, Caes. ; Pl. ; virginem ad aliquem, Liv. ; in domum, Tac. **f.** Of weaving, *to draw out, spin out :* filum, Ov., Cat. **g.** Of diminution, *to deduct, diminish :* cibum, Ter. In arithm. : *to subtract :* Cic., Liv. **h.** In law : *to lead away a person from a disputed possession in the presence of witnesses in order to procure him the right of action :* Cic. **2.** Transf. **a.** *to divert, dissuade :* aliquem de sententiā, Cic. **b.** *to bring* (into some state or situation) : aliquem ad eam sententiam, Caes. ; in periculum, Caes. : rem in controversiam,

Cic.; aliquem in societatem belli, Liv.; Aeolium carmen in Italos modos, Hor. **c.** Of curing illness : Cato ; corpore febris, animo curas, Hor. ; Cic. **d.** Of compositions: *to draw out, spin out, elaborate :* Hor., Ov., Quint. [It. *dedurre ;* Fr. *déduire.*]

dēductiō, ōnis, *f.* [dēdūcō]. **I.** *a leading down, drawing off :* rivorum a fonte, Cic. **II.** *a leading away.* **1.** L i t. **a.** Of colonists : militum in oppida, Cic. **b.** *a reduction :* Cic. **c.** In law : *the eviction of a person from an estate, as a form of beginning a lawsuit* (*v.* deduco, II. l. h.), Cic. **2.** T r a n s f. : *a deducing, an inference :* rationis, *train of reasoning,* Cic.

dēductus, a, um. **I.** *Part.* dēdūcō. **II.** Adj. **a.** *drawn down, bent inwards.* Comp. : nasus, Suet. **b.** *spun out ; fine, subtle :* carmen, Verg.

de-errō (in the poets, disyl.), āre, *to wander away, go astray.* **1.** L i t. : Pl., Cic., Verg. **2.** T r a n s f. : a vero, Luor. ; significatione, Quint. *Absol. :* quia sors deerrabat ad parum idoneos, Tac.

dēfaecō, āre [faex], *to cleanse from dregs.* T r a n s f. **a.** *to cleanse, to wash :* Pl. **b.** *to clear up, make clear :* quidquid ambiguum fuit, nunc defaecatum est, Pl.

dēfatīgātiō (**dēfet-**), ōnis, *f.* [dēfatīgō], *a wearing down, exhaustion :* Caes., Cic.

dē-fatīgō (**dēfetīgō**), āre, *to wear down, out, exhaust* (of the body or of the mind): Pl., Caes., Cic.

dēfatiscor, *v.* dēfetiscor.

dēfectiō, ōnis, *f.* [dēficiō], *an acting ineffectively, failure.* **A.** *defection, desertion.* **1.** L i t. : Galliae, Caes. ; Tac. ; ab Romanis ad Hannibalem, Liv. **2.** T r a n s f. : a rectā ratione, Cic. **B.** *a gradual weakening, exhaustion.* **1.** L i t. **a.** virium, Cic. **b.** Of an eclipse : solis, lunae, Cic., Tac. **c.** *a breakdown :* Tac. **2.** T r a n s f. : animi, Cic. Ep.

dēfector, ōris, *m.* [dēficiō], *a deserter, a rebel :* Tac., Suet.

dēfectus, a, um. **I.** *Part.* dēficiō. **II.** Adj. : *failing, wanting.* **a.** Physically : Ov. **b.** In courage : Tac.

dēfectus, ūs, *m.* [dēficiō], *a failing, failure.* **a.** aquarum, Liv. **b.** *desertion, revolt :* Curt. **c.** Of eclipses : Lucr., Cic., Verg.

dē-fendō, fendere, fendī, fēnsum [*cf.* offendō] **I.** *to beat* or *knock down, thrust off.* **1.** L i t. : Enn. ; ictūs, lapides, etc., Caes. ; hostem a fossā, Hirt. ; Ov. **2.** T r a n s f. : noxiam, Ter. ; vim inlatam, Cic. ; iniuriam, Caes., Cic. ; crimen, Cic., Liv. With DAT. : solstitium pecori, Verg. ; aestatem capellis, Hor. ; iniuriam foribus, Pl. **II.** *to defend, protect.* **1.** L i t. : oppidum, castra, Caes. ; se ab finitimis, Caes. ; se adversus aliquam, Liv. ; se contra aliquem, Cic. With thing as subject : Caes. Without object, *to act as defender :* Caes., Cic., Liv. **2.** T r a n s f. **a.** In gen. : *to defend* ab iniuriā, Caes. ; provinciam a calamitate, Cic. ; Sall. ; Liv. ; myrtos a frigore, Verg.; auctoritatem contra invidiam, Cic. **b.** In public life, *to champion, defend :* parricidi reum, Cic. Without object : Cic. **c.** Of an argument, etc., *to uphold, support, maintain.* With

Acc. : Cic. With Acc. and *Inf. :* Cic., Tac. **d.** Of a rôle (as actor, etc.), *to sustain :* actorum partis, Hor.

dēfēnsiō, ōnis, *f.* [dēfendō]. **I.** *a warding off.* T r a n s f. : criminum, Liv. : Quint. **II.** *a defending.* **1.** L i t. : urbium, Caes. **2.** T r a n s f. : dignitatis, Cic. Ep. With *ad :* ad istam omnem orationem, Cic.

dēfēnsitō, āre [*freq.* dēfēnsō], *to defend often, to practise defending :* Cic.

dēfēnsō, āre [*freq.* dēfendō], *to defend* or *protect diligently :* Pl., Ov., Liv.

dēfēnsor, ōris, *m.f.* [dēfendō]. **I.** *one who wards* or *keeps off :* necis, Cic. **II.** *a warder, guardian, protector* (freq. in a judicial sense) : murus defensoribus nudatus, Caes. ; Verg. ; Ov. ; paterni iuris defensor, Cic. ; illius, Hor. T r a n s f. : *the guards* (sublicae) of a bridge : Caes.

dē-ferō, ferre, tulī, lātum. **I.** *to bear, carry, bring down.* **1.** L i t. : Pl., Liv., Verg. **2.** T r a n s f. : eum ex tanto regno fortuna detulit, Nep. **II.** *to bear off* or *away, carry off, bring away to.* **1.** L i t. **a.** In gon. : epistulas alicui, Pl. ; Germani in castra delati, Caes. ; fuga regem eo defert, Liv. ; natos ad flumina, Verg. ; ramalia arida tecto, Ov. ; iacula in Idam error detulit, Ov. **b.** In public affairs : pecuniam in aerarium, Liv. ; senatûs consulta in aedem Cereris, Liv. **c.** Of ships, *to carry out of the course :* longius aestu delatus, Caes. ; Cic. **2.** T r a n s f. **a.** In gen. : fato in nostrum aevum delatus, Hor. **b.** *to offer, confer, grant, lay at the feet of* someone (of power, rank, etc.): ad hunc totius belli summam, Caes. ; imperium ad aliquem, Cic. ; palmam Crasso, Cic. ; pacem hostibus, Liv. ; Hor. **c.** *to report* (esp. *to superiors*) : rem ad consilium, Caes. ; rem ad senatum, Cic. ; eam vocem ad Catonem, Cic. ; Liv. **d.** In law, *to report* to the praetors, etc. : esp. deferre nomen and (post-Aug.) aliquem, *to inform against, indict :* nomen alicuius de ambitu, Cic. ; rem ad populum, Cic. ; crimina de Perseo, Liv. ; reos ad praetorem, Tac. ; maiestatis deferri, Tac. ; Drusus defertur moliri res novas, Tac. **e.** *to report* for services to the State, *recommend :* in beneficiis ad aerarium delatus, Cic. ; horum nomina ad aerarium, Cic.

dē-fervēfaciō, facere, fēcī, factum, *to make boil thoroughly :* brassicam, Cato.

dē-fervēscō, fervēscere, fervī and ferbuī, *to cease boiling, cool down.* **1.** L i t. : Cato. **2.** T r a n s f. **a.** Of passion : Cic. **b.** Of speech : quasi defervorat oratio, Cic.

dēfessus, a, um, *Part.* dēfetiscor.

dē-fetiscor (rarely dēfat-), fetīscī, fessus [fatīscor], *to become utterly weary, faint, tired* (very rare except in *Part. Perf.*). **1.** L i t. : adgerundā aquā defessi, Pl. ; Ov.; diuturnitate pugnae defessi, Caes. ; cultu agrorum, Cic. With *Inf. :* Pl., Lucr. *Absol. :* Cic., Verg. T r a n s f. Of things : defessa accusatio, Cic.

dē-ficiō, ficere, fēcī, fectum (old *Opt.* dēfexit, in old formula in Liv.). **A.** I n t r a n s. : *to act ineffectively* (esp. polit. and milit.), *fail, desert, secede.* **1.** L i t. : ab amicitiā populi Rom., Caes.; (consules) a senatu, a re publicā, a bonis omníbus defecerant, Cic.; quod primus a patribus ad plebem defecisset, Liv. *Absol.* : Caes. **2.** T r a n s f. **a.** pugnando deficere, Caes.; animo deficere, Caes.; a virtute, Cic. With *Inf.* : Lucr. **b.** Of things (esp. of arms, food, etc.): *to fail, run short* : materia, frumentum, Caes.; copiae, Cic.; arma, Curt.; cum tela nostris deficerent, Caes.; tempus anni ad bellum gerendum, Caes.; luna, sol, Cic.; oratio, Liv. **c.** *to fail, grow weak, droop, fall* : vita, Pl.; manus ad coepta, Ov.; mores, Hor. **B.** T r a n s. : *to fail, secede from, desert, abandon* : me civitas, Cic. But us. with *neut.* or *abstr.* subject: quem iam sanguis viresque deficiunt, Caes.; Hor.; aliquem fides, vox, dies, etc., Cic. Rarely in *Pass.* : cum aquilifer a viribus deficeretur, Caes.; sanguine defecti artūs, Ov.; consilio deficitur, *is deficient in*, Cic. (*v.* also **defit**).

dē-fīgŏ, figere, fīxī, fixum, *to fix down, fix firmly, fix on one object.* **1.** L i t. **a.** In gen.: asseres in terrā, Caes.; Cic.; Liv.; ad tectum regulas, Caes.; terrā hastas, Liv.; Verg.; arborem terrae, Verg.; te in terram, Pl. **b.** Of weapons: cultrum in corde, Liv.; Caes.; Cic.; gladium iugulo, Liv. **2.** T r a n s f. **a.** Of moving things: sidera, Hor.; lumina regnis Libyae, Verg.; oculos in te, Ov.; Cic.; Tac. Of persons: defixus lumina, Verg.; defixi et Neronem intuentes, Tac. **b.** Of attention, etc., *to fix, concentrate* : animos in eas res, Cic.; in eo mentem orationemque, Cic. **c.** *to strike motionless, root to the spot, astound, etc.* : pavor cum admiratione Gallos, Liv.; obtutu haeret defixus in unō, Verg. **d.** Of *witchcraft* : regis animum, Verg.

dē-fīngŏ, fingere, fīnxī, *to mould after a pattern* (perh. in Hor. *to mould awry*) : panem, Cato; defingit Rheni 'luteum' caput, Hor.

dē-fīniŏ, īre. **I.** *to mark down, mark out, set precise limits to.* **1.** L i t. : imperium populi Romani, Cic. **2.** T r a n s f. **a.** In time, *to limit* : potestatem in quinquennium, Cic.; Caes. **b.** In degree, range, etc., *to limit, prescribe, define, etc.* : Pl.; tempus adeundi, Caes.; ante quem diem iturus sit, Caes.; oratoris vim, Cic. **c.** *to mark down, determine, assign* : sibi hortos, Cic.; ut suus cuique locus erat definitus, Caes. **d.** In language, *to limit, define* (the use of a term) : amicitiam paribus officiis, Cic. **II.** *to bring to a finish, to end* : orationem, Cic.

dēfīnītē, *adv. precisely* : Cic.

dēfīnītiŏ, ōnis, *f.* [dēfīniŏ]. **1.** L i t. : *a limiting, a boundary* : Inscr. **2.** T r a n s f. **a.** *a marking out, prescribing* : Cic. **b.** *a definition* : Cic., Quint.

dēfīnītīvus, a, um [dēfīniŏ], *definitive, explanatory* : constitutio, Cic.

dēfīnītus, a, um. **I.** *Part.* dēfīniŏ. **II.** A d j. : *definite, precise* : Cic.

dēfit, **dēfīunt** (*Inf.* dēfierī), *fails, is lacking* : causa defiet cur etc., Liv.; lac mihi non defit, Verg.; Pl.; Ter.

dēflagrātiŏ, ōnis, *f.* [dēflagrŏ], *a burning up, destruction by fire.* **1.** L i t. : Cic. **2.** T r a n s f. : Cic.

dē-flagrŏ, āre, *to burn down.* **A.** I n t r a n s. : *to burn itself out, be consumed by fire.* **1.** L i t. : Cic., Liv. **2.** T r a n s f. **a.** *to be destroyed* (as by fire) : Cic., Liv. **b.** Of the passions : *to burn out* : Liv., Luc., Tac. **B.** T r a n s. (mostly in *Part.*), *to burn down.* **1.** L i t. : Enn. **2.** T r a n s f. : in cinere deflagrati imperi, Cic.

dē-flectŏ, flectere, flexī, flexum. **A.** T r a n s.: *to bend down, bend or turn aside* (from the straight, etc.). **1.** L i t. : amnis in alium cursum, Cic.; ad Romanos cursum, Liv.; tela, Verg. **2.** T r a n s f. **a.** Of the eyes : oculos ab eo, Liv. **b.** *to deflect, pervert* : principes aliqua pravitas de viā deflexit, Cic.; tragoediam in risūs, Ov.; ad verba rem, Cic. **B.** I n t r a n s. : *to turn off, aside.* **1.** L i t. : *to deviate* : viā, Tac.; in Tuscos, Plin. Ep. **2.** T r a n s f. : Cic.

dē-fleŏ, ēre, ēvī, ētum, *to weep over utterly or despairingly, mourn as lost.* With Acc. of person : Lucr., Ov. With Acc. of thing : Cic., Verg. *Absol.* : Tac., Plin. Ep.

dēflexus, a, um, *Part.* dēflectō.

dē-floccātus, a, um [floccus], *stripped of its wool.* Comic. = *bald* : Pl.

dē-flōrēscŏ, flōrēscere, flōruī, *to shed blossoms, droop.* **1.** L i t. : Cat. **2.** T r a n s f. : Cic., Liv.

dē-fluŏ, fluere, fluxī. **I.** *to flow down.* **1.** L i t. : Cato; Ov.; flamma ex Aetnā, Liv.; saxis umor, Hor. **2.** T r a n s f. **a.** *to stream or slip down, drop* : iam ipsae defluebant coronae, Cic.; pedes vestis defluxit ad imos, Verg.; tota cohors relictis ad terram defluxit equis, Verg.; ex equo, Curt.; moribundus ad terram, Liv. **b.** Of origin, *to be derived* : hoc totum e sophistarum fontibus, Cic. **II.** *to flow quite away.* **1.** L i t. : rusticus exspectat dum defluat amnis, Hor. **2.** T r a n s f. : ex novem tribunis unus defluxit, Cic. Ep.; vires, tempus, ingenium, Sall.; succus, Hor. **III.** *to drop or slip out of right place.* T r a n s f. : toga, Hor.

dē-fodiŏ, fodere, fōdī, fossum. **I.** *to dig down, dig out* : terram, Hor. **II.** *to make by digging down, to hollow out* : specus, Verg. **III.** *to bury in the earth.* **1.** L i t. : Pl., Cic., Ov., etc. **2.** T r a n s f. : defodiet aetas nitentia, Hor.

dēfore, *v.* dēsum.

dē-fōrmātiŏ, ōnis, *f.* [dēfōrmŏ], *a disfiguring, degradation* : Liv.

dē-fōrmis, e, *adj.* [fōrma]. **I.** *formless, shapeless* : animae, Ov. **II.** *ill-formed, disfigured, ugly* : **1.** L i t. : (homo), Cic.; iumenta, Caes.; opus, Caes.; aspectus, Cic.; solum patriae belli malis, Liv. **2.** T r a n s f. (moral). **a.** P a s s. : *degraded* : agmen, Liv. **b.** A c t. : *degrading* : spectaculum, oratio, blanditiae, Liv.; obsequium, Tac.; Hor. *Neut. pl.* as Noun : Tac. *Comp.* : Cic.

dēfōrmitās, ātis, *f.* [dēfōrmis], *unshapeliness, ugliness.* **1.** L i t. (physical) : Cic., Liv. **2.** T r a n s f. (moral) : Cic., Quint.

dēfōrmiter, *adv. without grace or beauty, inelegantly* : Quint., Suet.

dē-fōrmŏ, āre [fōrma]. **I.** *to shape from a pattern.* **1.** L i t. : areas, Cato; marmora, Quint. **2.** T r a n s f. : *to sketch, delineate* : Pl., Cic. **II.** *to shape away from a pattern*

or *its proper form : to disfigure, mar.* **1.**
Lit. (physical, of persons and things) : Cic.,
Verg., eto. **2. Transf.** (moral) : causam,
Cic. ; victoriam clade, Liv. ; domum, Verg.

dēfossus, a, um, *Part.* dēfodiō.

dē-fraudō (dēfrūdō), āre, *to cheat, rob utterly*
(esp. of money), *defraud.* **1.** Lit. With
Acc. of person : Pl., Ter. With double
Acc. : Pl. **2. Transf.** : Cic. ; genium
suom, i.e. *to deny oneself some pleasure*, Pl.,
Ter.

dē-frēnātus, a, um [frēnum], *unbridled, unrestrained* : Ov.

dē-fricō, fricāre, fricuī, frictum (and fricātum, Cat.), *to rub down.* **1.** Lit. : Cat.,
Ov., Suet. **2. Transf.** : sale multo urbem
defricuit, Hor.

dē-fringō, fringere, frēgī, frāctum [frangō], *to
break down* or *off* : crura sibi, Pl. ; ramum
arboris, Cic. ; ferrum ab hastā, Verg.

dēfrūdō, *v.* dēfraudō.

dēfrutō, āre [dēfrutum], *to boil down to*
defrutum : Cato.

dēfrutum, ī, *n.* [ferveō], *sc.* mustum, *new
win-boiled down, mead* : Pl., Verg.

dē-fugiō, fugere, fūgī, *to run away from,
shirk, avoid.* **A. Trans. 1.** Lit. : proelium, Caes. ; aditum alicuius sermonemque,
Caes. **2. Transf.** : auctoritatem, Pl. ;
patriam, inimicitias, Cic. **B. Intrans.** :
Caes., Liv.

dēfūnctus, a, um, *Part.* dēfungor.

dē-fundō, fundere, fūdī, fūsum, *to pour out.*
1. Lit. : aquam, Cato ; vinum, Hor.
2. Transf. : fruges pleno cornu, Hor.

dē-fungor, fungī, fūnctus, *to work out fully,
discharge, perform, finish* (esp. of things
troublesome or unpleasant) ; *to have done
with, get rid of* : Ter., Ov. ; with ABL. :
studio, Lucr. ; periculis, Cic. ; Verg. ;
proelio, morbis, imperio regis, Liv. ; laboribus, Hor., Ov. ; vitā, Verg., Curt. Without
vitā, *to die* : Ov., Tac.

dē-futūtus, a, um [futuō], *after copulation* :
Cat.

dēgener, eris (ABL. -erī, Tac.), *adj.* [genus],
*falling off from one's stock, unworthy of one's
race, degenerate.* **1.** Lit. : Verg., Liv.,
Tac. With GEN. : patriae artis, Ov. **2.**
Transf. : *morally degenerate, base, ignoble* :
animus, Verg. ; vultus, preces, insidiae,
Tac. Of persons : Liv., Tac.

dēgenerō, āre [genus]. **A. Intrans.** : *to
fall off from one's stock, to become unlike
one's race, to fall off, to degenerate.* **1.**
Lit. : qui a vobis nihil degenerat, Cic. ;
Liv. ; Macedones in Syros, Liv. ; poma,
Verg. **2. Transf.** : a Stoicis, Cic. ; ab
hac virtute, Cic. ; Tac. ; ad theatralis
artis, Tac. **B. Trans.** : *to enervate.*
Transf. : *to disgrace* (by degeneracy) :
Prop., Ov. Hence, Noun, **dēgenerātum**,
degeneracy of character : Liv.

dē-gerō, ere, *to carry off* : ornamenta ad aliquem, Pl. ; Cato.

dēgō, dēgere, dēgī [dē agō], *to keep moving
to the end, to spend* or *pass.* With Acc. :
diem, Pl. ; aetatem, Pl., Ter., Cic. ; aevom,
bellum, Lucr. ; otia, Cat. ; senectam, Hor.
Without aetatem, *to live* : Hor., Tac.

dē-grandinat, *v. impers. it leaves off hailing*
or *hails violently* : Ov.

dē-gravō, āre, *to weigh* or *press down, to overpower.* **1.** Lit. : altam ulmum vitis, Ov.
Milit. : (hostes) degravabant prope cir-
cumventum cornu, Liv. **2. Transf.** :
peritos nandi lassitudo et pavor degravant,
Liv. ; Ov.

dē-gredior, gredī, grēssus [gradior], *to step
down, march down, descend* : monte, Sall. ;
Liv. ; Tac. ; de montibus, Liv. ; ex arce,
Liv. ; ad pedes, Liv. ; in campum, Liv. ;
Tac.

dē-grunniō, īre, *to grunt violently* or *hard* :
Phaedr.

dē-gustō, āre, *to take a taste of, to taste.* **1.**
Lit. : vinum, Cato, Varr. **2. Transf. a.**
Of fire, *to lick* : ignes degustant tigna, Lucr.
b. Of a weapon, *to graze* : Verg. **c.** *to taste*
(i.e. have experience of) : eandem vitam,
Cic. ; imperium, Tac. ; litteris primis labris,
Quint.

de-hauriō (dehōriō), haurīre, hausī, haustum, *to skim off* : Cato.

de-hinc (poet. sometimes monosyl.), *adv.* **A.**
Of space : *from this place, from here* :
Plin. **B.** Of time : *from this time forward.* **a.** *henceforth* : dehinc postulo, ut
redeat iam in viam. Ter. ; Pl. ; Liv. **b.**
thenceforwards : omnes dehinc Caesares,
Suet. **c.** *afterwards, then, thereupon* : ut
speciosa dehinc miracula promat, Hor. ;
Verg. ; Tac. Rarely in enumerations
(= deinde) : primum . . . dehinc, *first
. . . . then* or *next*, Sall., Verg.

de-hiscō, hīscere (*Perf. Inf.* dehīsse, Varr.),
to gape down from above, gape open : terrae
dehiscunt, Verg. ; cumba rimis, Ov. ; Sen.
Ep. ; intervallis acies, Liv.

dehonestāmentum, ī, *n.* [dehonestō], *dis-
figurement, blemish.* **1.** Lit. : Sall., Tac.
2. Transf. : amicitiarum, Tac. Without GEN. : Tac.

de-honestō, āre, *to disgrace, dishonour* :
famam, Liv. ; Tac.

de-hortor, ārī, *to urge off from, discourage,
dissuade* : res ipsa me aut invitabit aut
dehortabitur, Cic. ; multa me dehortantur
a vobis, Sall. With *Inf.* : Cato, Sall., Tac.
With *ne* and *Subj.* : Enn., Ter.

Dēianira, ae, *f. d. of Oeneus and w. of Hercules.*

dē-iciō, icere, iēcī, iectum [iaciō]. **I.** *to
cast, throw, fling down* ; *to fell, overthrow.*
1. Lit. **a.** In gen. : aliquem equo, Caes. ;
se de muro, Caes. ; Pl. ; Cic. ; Liv. ; equum
e campo in viam, Liv. ; Lucr. ; se a montibus, Liv. ; Cic. ; turrim, Caes. ; statuas,
Cic. ; arbores, Liv. ; monumenta, Hor. ;
sortem (in urnam), Caes., Liv., Verg. **b.**
to fell by a mortal blow, to kill : Caes., Verg.
2. Transf. a. From a high public position : Aeduos principatu, Caes. ; de possessione imperi, Liv. **b.** Of the eyes, etc. :
oculos de isto, Cic. ; vultum, Verg. **II.**
to cast, fling out of a place or *position.* **1.**
Lit. **a.** Milit. : *to drive out, dislodge* :
hostis muro, Caes. ; Cic. ; praesidium ex
saltu, Caes. ; Liv. **b.** Of ships, *to drive
out of the course* : Caes., Liv., Tac. **2.**
Transf. **a.** In law, *to eject, evict, dispossess* : de possessione fundi, Cic. **b.**
From a resolution, etc. : eum de sententiā,
Cic. ; studio feriendi, Tac. **c.** From hopes,

prospects, etc. : spe, Caes. ; aedilitate, Cic. ;
certo consulatu, Liv. ; coniuge tanto,
Verg. ; de honore, Cic. **d.** With abstr.
Noun as object : metum, Cic. ; vitia a se,
Cic.

Dēidamīa, ae, *f. d. of Lycomedes, m. of
Pyrrhus or Neoptolemus.*

dēiectiō, ōnis, *f.* [dēiciō], *a throwing down or
out, eviction :* Cic.

dēiectus, a, um. **I.** *Part.* dēiciō. **II.** Adj.
a. *sunken, low :* loca, Caes. **b.** *disheartened, dispirited :* Verg., Quint.

dēiectus, ūs, *m.* [dēiciō]. **I.** *a casting
down :* arborum, Liv. ; Ov. **II.** *a steep
slope :* collis, Caes. In *pl.* : Caes.

dē-ierō, āre [*cf.* pēierō, iūrō], *to swear fully or
solemnly :* per omnis deos et deas, Pl. ; Ter.

dein, *v.* deinde.

dein-ceps (disyl. Hor. ; *cf.* dehinc, deinde),
adv. [orig. declinable Adj. ; formed from
deinde on analogy of princeps, q.v.], *one
after another, successively, in turn.* **A.** Of
space : alias deinceps ratis iungebat, Caes. ;
Cic. ; Liv. **B.** Of time : Caes., Cic., Liv.
C. In enumerations : Cic., Tac. With
deinde or *inde ;* deinde etiam deinceps
posteris prodebatur, Cic. ; Liv. ; deinceps
inde multae, Cic. ; Liv.

deinde, and abbrev. **dein** (in both forms *ei* is
very often monosyl. in the class. poets), *adv.*
[dē, inde]. **A.** Of place (rare) : *from
that or this place :* via interest perangusta,
deinde paulo latior patescit campus, Liv.
Of local succession : *e.g.* of military order :
auxiliares in fronte . . . post quos . . .
dein . . . exin, *next ; after these,* Tac. ; Liv.
B. Of time : *thereafter, thereupon, afterwards, then :* complures ex iis occiderunt ;
deinde se in castra receperunt, Caes. ; Cic. ;
Pl. ; Verg., etc. Of successive events, in
correlation with *primum, inde, postea,
postremo* (very freq.) : primum suo, deinde
omnium remotis equis, Caes. ; Pl. ; Cic., etc.
C. Of order. **a.** In enumerating facts
or arguments : *afterwards, next in order,
in the next place, then :* hoc apparet in
bestiis ; primum ut se ipsae diligant ;
deinde ut . . . , Cic. With deinde repeated : Cic. **b.** Of rank : excellente
tum Crasso et Antonio, deinde Philippo,
post Iulio, Cic.

Dēionidēs, ae, *m. Miletus, s. of Deïone by
Apollo.*

Dēiotarus, ī, *m. a king of Galatia ; defended
by Cicero in an oration delivered before
Caesar.*

Dēiphobus, ī, *m. s. of Priam and Hecuba ;
h. of Helen after death of Paris.*

dē-iungō, ere, *to unyoke.* Transf. : se a
forensi labore, Tac.

dē-iūrō, *v.* dēierō.

dē-iuvō, āre, *to fail to help :* Pl.

dēj-, *v.* dēi.

dē-lābor, lābī, lāpsus, *to slip down ; sink,
glide, or fall down.* **1.** Lit. : in scrobes,
Caes. ; Lucr. ; Cic. Ep. ; signum de caelo
delapsum, Cic. ; aetheriis ab astris, Verg. ;
Ov. ; ex equo, Liv. ; caelo, Verg. ; Ov.
With DAT. : serta capiti delapsa, Verg. **2.**
Transf. **a.** *to sink :* ad inopiam, Tac. ;
Cic. ; in aliquam turpitudinem, Cic. ; Tac.
b. *to come unawares :* in hostis, Verg.

dē-lacerō, āre, *to tear in pieces.* Transf. :
Pl.

dē-lāmentor, ārī, *to lament utterly :* natam
ademptam, Ov.

dēlapidō, āre [lapis], *to clear of stones :* Cato.

dēlāpsus, a, um, *Part.* dēlābor.

dēlassō, āre, *to weary or tire quite out :* Pl.,
Hor.

dēlātiō, ōnis, *f.* [dēlātus], *a reporting.* **a.**
With nominis, *an accusing, indicting* (*v.*
defero) : Cic. **b.** *an informing, denuncia-
tion :* Tac. In *pl.* : Tac.

dēlātor, ōris, *m.* [dēlātus], *a reporter* (*v.* defero). **a.** criminum, Liv. ; maiestatis, Tac.
b. *an informer, denouncer :* Tac., Suet.

dēlectābilis, e, *adj.* [dēlectō], *able to delight,
delightful :* Tac.

dēlectāmentum, ī, *n.* [dēlectō], *a delight,
pastime :* Ter., Cic.

dēlectātiō, ōnis, *f.* [dēlectō], *a delighting,
delight, pleasure, charm :* Ter., Cic. ; in
pl. : Cic. With defining GEN. : videndi,
Cic.

dē-lectō, āre [dē and lactō, *freq.* of laciō seen
in perliciō, etc. ; *cf.* oblectō], *to draw away*
(from serious business), *attract, allure,
charm :* Enn., Ter. ; ab aliquo, Cic. ; de-
lectati re suā familiari, Cic. ; iumentis,
Cic. ; imperio, Caes. ; iambis, Hor. *Absol. :*
Cic. Elliptically as *impers. verb :* me magis
de Dionysio delectat, Cic. With a sentence
as subject : me pedibus delectat claudere
verba, Hor. ; Cic. ; Ov. In *Pass. :* vir
bonus et prudens dici delector, Hor. [It.
dilettante.]

dēlēctus, a, um, *Part.* dēligō.

dēlēctus, ūs, *m. a choosing for a purpose :*
with defining GEN. : Cic. (*v.* also dilectus).

dēlēgātiō, ōnis, *f.* [dēlēgō], *the making over
or assignment* of a debt : Cic. Ep., Sen.

dē-lēgō, āre, *to assign or commit from one
place or sphere to another, to transfer, commit.*
1. Lit. Of place : Pleminium in Tullianum, Liv. ; Tac. **2.** Transf. **a.** *to assign, make over, commit :* laborem alteri,
Cael. ap. Cic. Ep. ; fortunae spes suas, Liv. ;
Tac. ; Quinto delegabo, si quid aeri meo
alieno superabit, Cic. Ep. ; obsidionem in
curam conlegae, Liv. ; rem ad senatum,
Liv. **b.** *to assign, attribute, impute :* hoc
crimen optimis nominibus, Cic., Tac. ;
servati consulis decus ad servum, Liv.

dēlēnificus, a, um [dēlēniō faciō], *soothing,
seductive :* facta, Pl.

dēlēnīmentum, ī, *n.* [dēlēniō], *what soothes.*
a. *a palliative, solace :* Liv. With *Obj.*
GEN. : Tac. **b.** *allurement, bait, seduction :*
Liv. With *Subj.* GEN. : Liv., Tac.

dē-lēniō (**dēliniō**), īre. Lit. *to smooth down.*
a. *to soothe, appease, calm, console :* milites,
Cic. ; Hor. **b.** *to allure, win over, seduce :*
Pl. ; muneribus multitudinem, Cic. ; Liv. ;
Ov. ; animos hominum praedā, Liv.

dēlēnitor, ōris, *m.* [dēlēniō], *one who smooths
down, wins over :* iudicis, Cic.

dēleō, ēre, ēvī, ētum. **I.** Of writing : *to
blot out, wipe out, efface.* **1.** Lit. : epistulas, Cic. Ep. ; digito legata, Cic. ; Hor. ;
Ov. **2.** Transf. : Ter. : turpitudinem
fugae, Caes. ; omnem memoriam discordiarum, Cic. ; ignominiam, Liv. **II.**
In gen. *to destroy, annihilate.* **1.** Lit. **a.**

Of things as objects : Caes., Cic., Ov., etc.
b. Of personal objects : Caes., Cic., Verg.,
etc. **2.** Transf. : *opinionum commenta
delet dies*, Cic.

dēlētrix, īcis, *f.* [dēleō], *a destroyer :* Cic.

Dēliacus, a, um [Δηλιακός], *of Delos,
Delian :* aes, celebrated like the Corinthian,
Plin. ; vasa, Cic.

dēlīberābundus, a, um [dōlīberō], *weighing
well, reflecting :* Liv.

dēlīberātiō, ōnis, *f.* [dēlīberō], *a weighing,
considering ; deliberation, consultation.* **1.**
Lit. : deliberationes habere de re publicā,
Cic. ; Liv. ; habet res deliberationem, *needs
consideration*, Cic. **2.** Rhet. = causa de-
liberativa : Cic.

dēlīberātivus, a, um [dēlīberō]. Rhet. :
relating to deliberation, deliberative : genus,
Cic. ; Quint.

dēlīberātor, ōris, *m.* [dēlīberō], *one who de-
liberates :* Cic.

dēlīberātus, a, um. **I.** *Part.* dēlīberō. **II.**
Adj. : *resolved upon, determined. Comp. :*
Cic. Ep.

dē-lībero, āre [libra, *balance*], *to weigh well
in the mind, ponder.* **1.** Properly :
Caes., Cic. With *de* and ABL. : Caes., Cic.,
Liv. With rem or *Neut.* of demonstr.
pron. : Ter., Caes., Cic. With *Indir.
Quest.* : Caes., Cic., Liv. *Pass. Impers.*
Caes., Cic., Liv. Occ. (esp. in *Pass.*) *to
resolve, determine* (after deliberation) : deliberatum est omnia dicere, Cic. ; sic
habuisti deliberatum (with *Inf.*), Cic. ;
deliberatā morte, Hor. **2.** In partic. *to
consult* (an oracle) : Delphos, Nep.

dē-lībo, āre, *to take a taste* or *sip of.* **1.** Lit. :
Varr., Lucr. **2.** Transf. **a.** Enn. : no-
vum honorem, Liv. ; flosculos (orationis),
Cic. ; oscula, Verg. **b.** With idea of mar-
ring or diminishing : aliquid de honestate,
Cic. ; Lucr.

dē-lībro, āre [liber], *to take off the bark, to
peel :* arborum cacumina, Caes.

dēlībūtus, a, um [*cf.* λείβω], *well-drenched,
steeped :* Pl., Cic., Hor. Transf. : Ter.

dēlīcātē, adv. *softly, luxuriously :* vivere,
Cic. *Comp. :* Sen.

dēlīcātus, a, um [dēliciae]. **I.** *soft, tender,
dainty.* **1.** Lit. : Of living beings : Pl.
Cat., Plin. Ep. **2.** Transf. : Of things :
litus, sermo, versus, Cic. ; versiculi, Cat. ;
amnis, Plin. Ep. **II.** *dainty, pampered,
spoiled with indulgence.* **1.** Lit. : Of persons : Pl., Cic., Quint. **2.** Transf. Of
things : voluptates, Cic. ; convivium, Cic.
Ep. ; navigia, Suet. **III.** (rare) *dainty,
nice, fastidious :* Pl. ; aures, Quint. *Comp. :*
Cic., Cat. *Sup. :* Cic., Plin. Ep. [Fr.
délié.]

dēlīciae, ārum, *f. pl.* (*sing.* **dēlicia**, ae, *f. :*
Pl. ; **dēlicium**, ī, *n. :* Phaedr.) [dē, laciō
seen in ēliciō, etc.], *allurements, enticements,
delights ; passing fancies, whims, pet in-
dulgences, tastes, extravagances.* **A.** Abstract. **a.** In gen. : Sall., Cic., Hor.
b. Of taste in art, style, etc. : *fanciful
ideas, extravagant forms of expression :* Cic.,
Hor. **c.** Of behaviour : *jocose or whimsi-
cal frolics, sport :* Cic. Phr. : facere delicias, *to make sport, play tricks*, Pl., but in
Cat. facere delicias aliquo, *to centre one's*

fancies on someone ; esse in deliciis alicui
and aliquid in deliciis habere, *to have as a
pet fancy*, Lucr., Cic. **B.** Concrete :
pet, favourite, darling : Pl., Cic., Cat., Verg.
[Fr. *délices.*]

dēliciolae, ārum, *f. pl.* [*dim.* dēliciae], *a little
pet :* Cic.

dēlicium, *v.* dēliciae, *ad init.*

dēlicō, *v.* dēliquō.

dēlictum, ī, *n.* [dēlinquō], prop. *something
left undone, a fault of omission ;* hence, *a
fault, offence, wrong :* Pl., Cic., Hor., etc. ;
delictum in se admittere, Ter. ; committere,
Caes. In *pl. :* Cic., Sall., Hor.

dēlicuus, a, um [dēlinquō]. *wanting, lacking :*
Pl.

dē-ligō, āre, *to bind fast :* aliquem, Cic. ;
homini rostrum, Pl. ; aliquem ad palum,
Liv. ; epistulam ad amentum, Caes.

dē-ligō, ligere, lēgī, lēctum [legō]. **I.** *to
choose for a purpose :* aliquem ad res con-
ficiendas, Caes. ; aliquem ex senatu in hoc
consilium, Cic. ; Liv. ; ab omni ordine
centum oratores, Verg. ; locum castris,
Caes., Liv. ; aliquem inter duces bello, Tac.
Esp. of soldiers : Caes., Sall., Verg. Rarely
to choose, set aside (for leaving behind) :
Verg. **II.** In farming, *to gather in :* Cato.
Hence, in gen. *to gather :* Hor., Ov. (*v.* also
diligo.)

dē-lingō, ere, *to have a lick of ;* *to lick off :*
salem, Pl.

dēlīni-, *v.* dēlēni-.

dē-linquō, linquere, liquī, lictum (alw. intrans., but occ. with Internal Acc., us.
Neut. Pron.), *to fail, be wanting,* or *lacking*
(in duty, etc.), *to do wrong, commit a fault* or
crime, to offend : Ter., Cic. ; in bello miles,
Cic. ; in ancillā, Ov. ; per ambitionem,
Sall. With Acc. of *Neut. Pron.* and like
words : ne quid delinquat, Pl. ; si quid
deliquero, Cic. ; maiora, Liv. ; quae libidine deliquerant. Tac. *Pass. Impers. :* ut
nihil a me adhuc delictum putem, Cic.
Ep.

dē-liquēscō, liquēscere, licuī, *to melt down* or
away, liquefy, dissolve. **1.** Lit. : Pl., Ov.
2. Transf. : qui alacritate futili gestiens
deliquescat, Cic.

dēliquiō, ōnis, *f. failure, despair of getting :*
libertatis, Pl.

dēliquium, ī, *n.* [dēlinquō], *a falling away,
failure :* solis, Plin.

dē-liquō *and* **dē-licō**, āre, *to clarify completely, to strain.* **1.** Lit. : Varr. **2.**
Transf. : *to clear up, explain :* Pl.

dēlīrāmentum, ī, *n.* [dēlīrō], *nonsense, absurdity :* Pl.

dēlīrātiō, ōnis, *f.* [dēlīrō], *silliness, infatua-
tion, dotage :* Cic., Plin. Ep.

dē-līrō, āre [lira]. Lit. *to draw the furrow awry in ploughing.* Transf. : *to leave
the track of sense, act as a dotard, drivel :*
Pl., Cic., Hor., etc. ; delirat linguaque mens-
que, Lucr. With Acc. *of Neut. Pron. :*
quidquid delirant reges, Hor.

dēlīrus, a, um [dē, lira], *astray, demented,
doting.* **a.** Of persons : Cic., Hor. **b.** Of
things : Lucr.

dē-lītēscō, lītēscere, lituī [latēscō], *to lie
down in hiding, hide oneself, to lie hid, to
lurk.* **1.** Lit. : Pl., Cic., Verg., etc.

2. Transf. : *to skulk behind, take shelter under :* in alicuius auctoritate, Cic. ; in dolo malo, Cic.

dē-lītigō, āre, *to dispute thoroughly ;* hence *to scold roundly :* Hor.

Dēlius, *v.* Dēlos.

Dēlos, ī (Acc. -um or -on), *f. the smallest of the Cyclades, birthplace of Apollo ;* **Dēliacus, Dēlius,** a, um, esp. *of Apollo,* and (in *fem.*), *of Diana.*

Delphi, ōrum, *m. pl. a small town in Phocis, famous for the oracle of Apollo,* now *Kastri ;* also *the inhabitants of Delphi :* **Delphicus,** a, um, *of Delphi* or *Apollo ; like the tripod of Apollo.*

delphīnus, ī, *m.* (Cic., Hor., etc.) and **delphīn,** īnis, *m.* (Acc. -īna, Ov. ; Abl. īne, Pl., Ov.; *pl.* Nom. -īnes, Verg., Ov.; Acc. -īnas, Verg. ; Gen. -īnum, Verg., Prop.) [δελφίς, δελφίν], *a dolphin.* **1.** Lit. : Cic., Verg., etc. **2.** Transf. : *the Dolphin,* a constellation : Varr., Ov. [Fr. *dauphin.*]

deltōton, ī, *n.* [Δελτωτόν], *the Triangle,* a constellation : Cic. poet.

dēlūbrum, ī, *n.* [dē luō], *a place of purification ; a shrine, sanctuary,* (*v.* templum) : in *pl.* : Cic., Liv.; in *sing. :* Liv. Freq. in gen. sense, *a temple* (= aedes) : in *pl. :* Lucr., Cic., Verg., etc.; in *sing. :* Cic., Verg.

dē-luctor, āri, and **dē-luctō,** āre, *to have a wrestling-bout :* Pl.

dē-lūdificō, āre, *to make great game of :* aliquem, Pl.

dē-lūdō, lūdere, lūsī, lūsum, *to play one false, dupe :* aliquem, Cic., Verg., Ov.; aliquem aliquā re, Ter., Verg.; somnia sensūs, Verg.

dēlumbis, e [lumbus], *loinless,* hence, *enervated, feeble :* Pers.

dē-lumbō, āre [lumbus]. **1.** Lit. : *to lame in the loins :* Plin. **2.** Transf.: *to weaken, enervate :* sententias, Cic.

dē-mandō, āre, *to hand over* or *entrust to someone's charge :* aliquem alicuius curae, Liv.; aliquem (or aliquid) alicui, Suet.; curam sauciorum legatis, Liv.

dēmarchus, ī, *m.* [δήμαρχος], *the chief official of a demus* or *village, a demarch ; a tribune of the people :* Pl.

dē-mēns, entis, *adj. mindless, insane, mad* (denoting a permanent state : āmēns us. refers to temporary distraction). **1.** Lit. Of persons : Cic., Verg., Hor. **2.** Transf. Of things : discordia, Verg.; strepitus, Hor. *Comp. :* Cic.; *Sup. :* Cic.

dēmēnsum, ī, *n.* [dēmētior], *a ration, allowance :* Ter.

dēmēnsus, a, um, *Part.* dēmētior.

dēmenter, *adv.* [dēmēns], *insanely :* Cic. *Sup. :* Sen.

dēmentia, ae, *f.* [dēmēns], *defectiveness of mind, insanity, madness :* Ter., Cic., Verg., etc. In *pl. : mad acts :* Cic. Ep.

dēmentiō, īre, *to be mad :* Lucr.

dē-mereō, ēre, and **dēmereor,** ērī, *to earn duly.* **a.** With Acc. of thing : *to earn, merit, deserve :* aliquid mercedis domino, Pl. **b.** With Acc. of person : *to deserve well*

---

of, to oblige (us. demereor): aliquem, Ov., Tac.; etc. ; beneficio civitatem, Liv.

dē-mergō, mergere, mērsī, mērsum, *to sink, dip under, plunge into* (esp. *the water,* but sometimes *the earth,* etc., i.e. *to bury, plant*). **1.** Lit. : ferrum in imbrem, Lucr. ; demersis aequora rostris ima petunt, Verg.; corpus paludibus, Cic. ; plebem in fossas cloacasque exhauriendas, Liv. ; dapes in alvum, Ov. **2.** Transf. : est animus caelestis quasi demersus in terram, Cic. ; domus ob lucrum demersa exitio, Hor. ; plebs aere alieno demersa, Liv.

dēmessus, a, um, *Part.* dēmetō.

dē-mētior, mētīrī, mēnsus, *to measure out* or *allot duly :* cibum, Pl. ; verba, Cic.

dē-metō, metere, messuī, messum, *to mow, reap, cut down, crop.* **1.** Lit. : frumentum, Caes. ; fructūs, agros, Cic. **2.** Transf. : pollice florem, Verg. ; caput, Ov.

Dēmētrius, ī, *m. a Greek name,* esp. **I.** D. Poliorcētēs, *s. of Antigonus, and king of Macedonia.* **II.** D. Phalēreus, *a famous orator, governor of Athens.* **III.** D. Magnēs, *a contemporary of Cicero.*

dēmigrātiō, ōnis, *f.* [dēmigrō], *an emigration :* Nep.

dē-migrō, āre, *to move off, depart, emigrate.* **1.** Lit. : loco, Pl. ; de oppidis, Caes. ; ex agris in urbem, Liv. ; ad virum optimum, Cic. **2.** Transf. : ex hominum vitā ad deorum religionem, Cic.

dē-minuō, uere, uī, ūtum, *to lessen down,* i.e. *to lessen by taking something away, to make smaller, diminish.* **1.** Lit. : Pl., Lucr., Cic., etc. With Abstr. *Subject :* Lucr., Caes. **2.** Transf. : potentiam, Caes. ; dignitatem conlegi, Cic. ; aliquid de libertate meā, Cic. ; Caes. ; ex regiā potestate, Liv.; alicui timor studia deminuit, Caes. ; se capite deminuere, *to forfeit one's civil rights,* Cic., Liv.

dēminūtiō, ōnis, *f.* [dēminuō], *a lessening, diminution, decrease, abridging.* **1.** Lit. : luminis, vectigalium, Cic. ; de bonis privatorum, Cic. **2.** Transf. **a.** In gen. : alicuius libertatis, Cic. ; provinciae (i.e. *period of office*), Cic. ; Tac. ; capitis, *the loss of civil rights,* Caes. **b.** In law, *right of alienation :* Liv.

dē-miror, ārī, *to wonder greatly at, to be amazed.* With Acc. and *Inf. :* Pl., Cic. Mostly colloq. (in *1st pers. sing.*) : *I wonder, I am at a loss to imagine,* etc. (often with *Indir. Quest.*): demiror qui sciat, Pl. ; Ter. ; Cic. Ep.

dēmissē, *adv. low* (opp. alte). **1.** Lit. *Comp. :* Ov. **2.** Transf. : (in good or bad sense) : *humbly, modestly ; abjectly :* Cic. *Sup. :* Caes.

dēmissiō, ōnis, *f.* [dēmittō], *a letting down, sinking, lowering.* **1.** Lit. : storiarum, Caes. **2.** Transf. : animi, *low spirits, depression :* Cic.

dēmissicius, a, um, *allowed to hang down, flowing :* tunica, Pl.

dēmissus, a, um. **I.** *Part.* dēmittō. **II.** Adj. : *sunken, low-lying.* **1.** Lit. **a.** Of ground : Caes. **b.** Of dress, hair, etc. : *allowed to hang down, long and loose :* Hor., Ov. **c.** Of other things, *downcast, droop-*

ing : Ter. ; capite demisso, Caes., Cic. ;
vultu, Sall. ; oculis, Liv. **2.** T r a n s f.
a. demissâ voce, Verg. **b.** animo demisso,
Cic. ; Liv. *Absol.* : quis P. Sullam nisi
maerentem demissum adflictumque vidit ?
Cic. **c.** Of manners : *lowly, humble, unassuming* (opp. elatus) : Cic., Hor. **d.**
Of condition : *poor, humble* : Sall. **e.** Of
birth, *descended* : ab alto Aeneâ, Hor. ;
Verg. ; Troiâ, Tac. *Comp.* : Cic., Liv.

dē-mītīgō, āre, *to make quite mild* : Cic. Ep.

dē-mīttō, mittere, mīsī, missum, *to let go
down, to drop, let sink, lower.* **1.** L i t. **a.**
In gen. : aliquem *or* aliquid with or without
ABL. (of separation *or* instrument) *or* pre-
positional phrase : Cic., Verg., etc. **b.**
With idea of violence : sublicas in terram,
Caes. ; Ov. ; aliquem in carcerem, Liv. ;
Hor. **c.** Nautical. **i.** *to lower* : antennas,
Sall. ; cornua, Ov. **ii.** *to bring downstream* : navem, Liv. ; *to land* : Verg. **d.**
Milit. **i.** *to move soldiers into a lower country* : in loca plana agmen, Liv. ; Caes.
ii. *to lower in salute* : arma, Auct. B. Afr.
2. T r a n s f. ; *to let sink* (esp. with *Refl.
Pron.*). **a.** In gen. : hoc in pectus tuum
demitto, Sall. ; dignitatem in discrimen,
Liv. ; se in causam, Cic. ; Tac. **b.** Of
spirits : se animo demittere, i.e. *to become
depressed,* Caes. ; animos, Cic. **c.** Of descent, *v.* demissus.

dēmiūrgus, or **dāmiūrgus,** ī, *m.* [δημιουρ-
γός], *the chief magistrate in some of the
Greek states* : Liv.

dēmō, dēmere, dēmpsī, dēmptum [contr.
from dē-emō], *to take away ; withdraw, subtract.* **1.** L i t. : clipea de columnis, Liv. ;
Cic. ; succum a vellero, Ov. ; fetūs arbore,
Ov. ; with DAT. : vincla pedibus, Ov. ;
Pl. ; Ter. ; Hor. **2.** T r a n s f. : mihi
molestiam, Ter. ; sollicitudinem, Cic. ;
curas, Verg. ; ex dignitate populi, Liv. ;
partem de solido die, Hor. ; Lucr.

Dēmocritus, ī, *m. a famous philosopher of
Abdera, originator of the atomic theory ;*
Dēmocriticus (-tius, -tēus). **a,** um ;
Dēmocritiī, ōrum, *m. pl. his followers.*

dē-mōlior, īrī, *to pull down, demolish.* **1.**
L i t. : statuas, Cic. ; Lucr. ; templa, Liv.
2. T r a n s f. : de me culpam hanc demoli-
bor, Pl. ; Bacchanalia, Liv. ; Ov.

dēmōlītiō, ōnis, *f.* [dēmōlior], *a pulling down :*
statuarum, Cic.

dēmōnstrātiō, ōnis, *f.* [dēmōnstrō], *a pointing
out* (as with the finger). **1.** L i t. : Cic. ;
in *pl.* : Cic. **2.** T r a n s f. : *full explanation* : Cic.

dēmōnstrātīvus, a, um [dēmōnstrō]. Rhet.:
designed for display : causa, Cic.

dēmōnstrātor, ōris, *m.* [dēmōnstrō], *one
who points out :* Cic.

dē-mōnstrō, āre, *to point straight at, point
out clearly.* **1.** L i t. With ACC. : Pl.,
Cic., Liv. With *Indir. Quest.* : Ter., Cic.
In law : finis, to deliver a piece of land to the
purchaser (*pointing out its boundaries*), Cic.
2. T r a n s f. : *to point out by speech or
writing ; to state precisely, explain, describe.*
With ACC. : Caes., Cic., etc. With ACC.
and *Inf.* : Caes., Cic. With *Indir. Quest.* :
Caes., Quint. Often in Caes. with *supra* :
ad ea castra quae supra demonstravimus ;

ut supra demonstravimus. *Pass. Impers.* :
Caes. [I t. *dimostrare ;* Fr. *démontrer.*]

Dēmophoön, ontis, *m. s. of Theseus and
Phaedra.*

dē-morior, morī, mortuus. **I.** *to die* (leaving a vacancy) : chiefly in *Perf. Part. :* in
demortui locum censor sufficitur, Liv. ; cum
esset ex veterum numero quidam senator
demortuus, Cic. Comic. : potationes plurimae demortuae, Pl. **II.** *to be dying utterly.*
1. L i t. : Pl. **2.** T r a n s f. : With Acc.
to be dying for love of : Pl.

dē-moror, ārī. **A.** I n t r a n s. : *to delay,
wait :* Pl., Tac. **B.** T r a n s. : *to delay,
retard, hinder :* aliquem, Pl., Cic. ; Teucros
armis, Verg. ; iter. eruptiones, agmen,
Caes. ; annos, Austros, Verg. [Fr. *demeurer.*]

Dēmosthenēs, is (GEN. also -ī, Cic.), *m. the
greatest of the Athenian orators.*

dē-moveō, movēre, mōvī, mōtum, *to move
away, displace, dispossess.* **1.** L i t. With
ACC. of person or thing and ABL. (Cic., Liv.,
Tac.) or *de* and ABL. (Cic.) or *ex* and ABL.
(Cic.) of thing from which. Without ABL.
(Caes.). **2.** T r a n s f. : aliquem a causâ ali-
cuius, Cic. ; Ter. ; aliquem de verâ sen-
tentiâ, Cic. ; Burrum praefecturâ, Tac.

dē-mūgītus, a, um [mūgiō], *filled with bellowing, lowing :* paludes, Ov.

dē-mulceō, mulcēre, mulsī, *to stroke down, to
stroke caressingly :* caput tibi, Ter. ; dorsum,
Liv.

dēmum, adv. [Neut. of old superl. adj. dēmus
from dē, *cf.* summus from sub]. **I.** In all
periods of Latin. **A.** Of time, *at length,
at last ; then and not till then :* quartâ vix
demum exponimur horâ, Hor. Enclitically
with the adverbs nunc, tum or tunc, post,
modo, iam : nunc demum rescribo iis litteris, Cic. ; heu nunc misero mihi demum
exsilium infelix! Verg. ; tum demum Lis-
cus oratione Caesaris adductus, Caes. ;
utrâque re satis expertâ tum demum consules . . ., Liv. ; post eum demum huc
cras adducam, Pl. ; modo demum, *only now,
now for the first time :* Ter. ; iam demum,
now at last, now : Ov. **B.** To give emphasis, *precisely, exactly, just, indeed.* **a.**
Enclitically with Pronouns : sic sentio, id
demum aut potius id solum esse miserum,
quod turpe sit, Cic. ; idem velle atque idem
nolle, ea demum firma amicitia est, Sall. ;
illa seges demum, Verg. **b.** Emphasising
the whole sentence : ea sunt enim demum
non ferenda in mendacio quae etc., Cic.
II. In post-Aug. period. **a.** *exclusively,
only, solely :* adeo suis demum oculis
credidit, Quint. **b.** = denique, *finally, in
short :* Tac.

dē-murmurō, āre, *to mutter right through :*
carmen, Ov.

dēmūtātiō, ōnis, *f.* [dēmūtō], *a changing :*
Cic.

dē-mūtō, āre. **A.** T r a n s. : *to change,
alter.* **a.** Pl., Cato, Tac. **b.** *to change for
the worse :* Pl. **B.** I n t r a n s. **a.** *to change
one's mind :* Pl. **b.** *to become different*
(with atque) : Pl.

dēnārius, a, um [old Noun dēnum, *cf.* dēnī],
containing a set of 10. **I.** A d j. : *containing*
10, *worth* 10 (*asses*) : numerus digitorum,
Vitr. ; nummi, Liv. **II.** Noun, **dēnārius,**

I, *m.* (*n.* : Pl.) : *a Roman silver coin, which originally contained ten, and afterwards eighteen asses, equivalent in value to an Attic drachma.* **1.** Lit.: Caes., Cic. GEN. *pl.* dēnārium, Cic. ; also, dēnāriōrum, Cic. Ep. **2.** T r a n s f.: *money in gen.* : Cic. Ep. [It. *danaro* ; Sp. *dinero* ; Fr. *denier*.]

dē-nārrō, āre, *to tell, relate, recount fully* : Ter., Hor.

dē-nāsō, āre [nāsus], *to denose, to deprive of the nose* : Pl.

dē-natō, āre, *to swim down* : Hor.

dē-negō, āre. **I.** *to say no, deny positively* : aliquid, Pl., Tac. **II.** *to refuse flatly* : conloquia, Caes. ; aliquid alicui, Pl., Cic., Ov., etc. Of things personified : Ov., Tac. With *Inf.* : Ter., Hor. With Acc. and *Inf.* : Pl., Ter., Prop. [Fr. *dénier*.]

dēni, ae, a (GEN. *pl.* dēnum, Cic. ; dēnōrum, Liv.) [old Noun dēnum]. **1.** Lit.: *in a set or sets of* 10, *a half-score* : uxores habent deni duodenique inter se communis, Caes. ; bis denis navibus (lit. *with two half-score ships*), Verg. Hence, *ten each* : denos ut ad conloquium adducerent (lit. *that they (each) should bring a half-score men*), Caes. **2.** T r a n s f.: dēnus, a. um = decimus. *tenth* : Ov.

dēnicālis (**dēnec-**), e. *adj.* [nex], *freeing from death, purifying from death* : feriae, Cic.

dēnique, *adv.* [for dēne-que ; dēne fr. dē as superne fr. super ; -que as in quisque, ûsque]. Lit. *all the way down.* **A.** Of time : *finally, lastly, at last* : mori me denique coges, Ter. Often with ad extremum, ad postremum, and tandem : ad extremum ipsâ denique necessitate excitantur. Cic. With the particles tum, nunc, or an ABL. of time (= tandem *or* demum) : quo cum venerimus, tum denique vivemus, Cic. ; nunc denique amare videor, Cic. Ep. ; multo denique die Caesar cognovit montem a suis teneri, Caes. Like demum with *is* and *vix*, to add to the force of the expression (= Gk. γέ) : is denique honos mihi videri solet, Cic. Ep. **B.** In enumeration. **a.** To end an enumeration, *finally, in fine* : mathematici, poetae, musici, medici denique, Cic. After preceding primum . . . deinde, Cic. **b.** Freq. to close an enumeration by ascending to a climax or more general expression : *in short, in a word, in general* : pernegabo atque obdurabo, peiierabo denique, Pl. ; omnia municipia, praefecturae, coloniae, tota denique Italia, Cic. **c.** Occ. with enumeration implied : *briefly, at least* : nostros crediderant praesidia deducturos aut denique (*not to mention other possibilities, at least*) indiligentius servaturos, Caes.

dē-nōminō, āre. **I.** *to call by a derived name* : Hor. **II.** *to give a precise name to* : Quint.

dē-nōrmō, āre [norma], *to bend from the straight, to make crooked or irregular* : Hor.

dē-notō, āre. **I.** *to mark down, specify* : Cic., Liv. **II.** *to mark down, take careful note of* : Cic., Tac. **III.** *to brand, stigmatise* : Suet.

dēns, dentis, *m.* [orig. *Pres. Part.* of edō], *a tooth.* **1.** Lit.: primores, *the front teeth,* Plin.; also called adversi acuti, Cic, ; maxillares, *the jaw-teeth, grinders,* Cels. ;

called also genuini, *cheek-teeth,* Cic. ; dens Indus, *the elephant's tusk,* Ov.; also = *ivory,* Ov. P r o v.: albis dentibus deridere aliquem, *to laugh heartily at* (so as to show one's teeth), Pl. **2.** T r a n s f. **a.** *a point, spike, prong, fluke,* etc.: aratri, Verg.; ancorae, Verg.; curvo Saturni dente = falce, Verg. **b.** Of that which *gnaws at, eats away or destroys* : leti, Lucr.; aevi, Ov. **c.** Of calumny : maledico dente carpunt, Cic. ; invido dente, Hor.; atro dente aliquem petere, Hor. [It. *dente* ; Fr. *dent, dentelle.*]

dēnsē, *adv. thickly, closely.* **A.** In space : Plin. **B.** In time, *closely, in quick succession, repeatedly. Comp.* : Cic., Ov.

dēnsitās, - atis, *f.* [dēnsus]. *closeness. thickness:* Liv., Quint.

dēnsō, āre (Verg., Liv., etc.), and **dēnseō**, ēre (Lucr., Verg., Tac., etc.) [dēnsus], *to thicken, to make thick, to press close together.* **1.** Lit.: ignem, aëra, Lucr.; ordines, aggerem, Liv.; catervas, hastilia, Verg. **2.** T r a n s f. **a.** ictūs, Tac. **b.** Of speech, *to condense* : orationem, Quint.

dēnsus, a, um [*cf.* Gk. δασύς], *having its parts near together* ; *close, crowded, thick, dense* (opp. rarus). **1.** Lit.: silvae, Caes.; terra, Verg ; hostes, Verg.; densum umeris vulgus, Hor. ; litus, Ov. ; aër, Hor. With ABL.: lucus iuncis et harundine, Ov.; acies densa armis virisque, Tac. **2.** T r a n s f. **a.** *frequent, continuous* : ictūs, Verg.; plagae, Hor. **b.** *intense* : amores, Verg.; frigoris asperitas, Ov. **c.** Of style : *condensed, with the matter compressed* : Quint. Of the author himself: Quint. *Comp.*: Caes.. Verg.. etc. *Sup.*: Caes.. Verg.. etc.

dentālia, ium, *n. pl.* [dēns], *the share-beam of a plough* : Verg. Hence, *a plough* : Pers.

dentātus, a, um [dēns]. **I.** *toothed, having teeth.* **1.** Lit.: Ov. **2.** T r a n s f.: vir (i.e. mordax), Pl. ; of cold and heat : Lucr. **II.** *worked with teeth* : in phr., charta dentata, i.e. *polished,* Cic.

dentifrangibulus, I, *m.* and **-um**, i, *n.* [dēns frangō], *a tooth-breaker* ; *m.* : *one who knocks out teeth,* Pl. : *n. pl. the fist,* Pl.

dentilegus, I, *m.* [dēns legō], *tooth-collector, one who picks up his teeth* after they have been knocked out : Pl.

dentiō, īre [dēns], *to cut teeth* : ne dentes dentiant, *lest they should grow* (because not worn off by eating), Pl.

dē-nūbō, nūbere, nūpsī, nūptum, *to marry beneath one* (of a woman) : in domum alicuius, Tac. ; Ov. Of a mock marriage : Tac.

dē-nūdō, āre, *to lay quite bare, strip naked.* **1.** Lit.: Enn., Cic., Suet. **2.** T r a n s f.: **a.** Of facts, *to lay bare* : suum consilium alicui, Liv. **b.** *to strip bare, strip of one's all* : aliquem, Lentulus ap. Cic. Ep.

dēnūntiātiō, ōnis, *f.* [dēnūntiō], *an intimation, announcement, warning, threat* : Cic. With *Obj.* GEN.: periculi, Caes. ; calamitatum, belli, testimoni, Cic. ; armorum, Liv. With *Subj.* GEN. : Cic.

dē-nūntiō, are, *to announce with authority* ; *to give notice, to announce, intimate officially, to give official warning.* **1.** Lit. **A.** Polit. and Milit. **a.** With Acc. and *Inf.* : Caes.,

Liv. **b.** With Acc.: bellum, Caes., Cic., Liv. **c.** With *Jussive Subj.* (very freq.): nationibus ut auxilia mittant, Caes.; Liv.; Fabio ne saltum transiret, Liv.: Gallicis populis multitudinem domi contineant, Liv. With *Inf.*: Tac. **B.** Relig. (of portents, omens, etc.): *to give intimation, threaten.* **a.** With Acc.: Cic., Verg. **b.** With *Jussive Subj.*: ut exeamus e vitā, Cic. **C.** Legal. **a.** denuntiare testimonium, with Dat., *to summon as a witness, to give someone notice that his evidence will be required*: Cic., Quint., Plin. Ep. **b.** *to give notice of a suit*: de isto fundo, Cic. **2.** Transf. **a.** *to announce, intimate, warn* (with assumption of authority or superiority). With Acc. and *Inf.*: Cic., Liv. With *Jussive Subj.* (with or without *ut*): Cic. **b.** *to warn, threaten.* **i.** Of persons: mihi inimicitias, Cic.; mortem, Liv. With Acc. and *Fut. Inf.*: Liv. **ii.** Of things as subject: illa arma non periculum nobis denuntiant, Cic.; Verg.; Tac. [Fr. *dénoncer.*]

dēnuō, *adv.* [for dē novō]. Lit. *down from, starting from what is new; anew, afresh, again, once more*: Pl., Ter., Cic., Liv.

dēnus, a, um; *v.* dēnī.

Dĕōis, idis, *f. d. of Deo (Ceres),* i.e. *Proserpine*; **Dĕōius,** a, um, *of Deo.*

de-onerō, āre, *to disburden, unload.* Transf.: ex illius invidiā aliquid, Cic.

deorsum and **deorsus,** *adv.* [for dēvorsum, *turning downwards*], *downwards* (opp. sursum): cuncta feruntur, Lucr.; Pl.; Cic., etc.; sursum deorsum commeare, Cic.; Ter.

de-ōsculor, āri, *to kiss warmly*: Pl.

dē-paciscor, better dēpeciscor.

dēpactus, a, um [dē, pangō], *fastened or fixed down*: vitae terminus, Lucr.

dē-parcus, a, um, *excessively niggardly*: Suet.

dē-pāscō, pāscere, pāvi, pāstum (Cic., Verg., etc.) and **dēpāscor,** pāscī (Lucr., Verg.). **I.** *to eat down, pasture.* **1.** Lit.: saltūs, Ov.; luxuriem segetum, Verg. **2.** Transf. = *to prune away*: luxuriem orationis stilo depascere, Cic. **II.** *to consume by feeding on, eat up.* **1.** Lit.: altaria (*the flesh on the altars*), Verg.; miseros depascitur artūs, Verg. **2.** Transf.: aurea dicta, Lucr.; veterem possessionem Academiae, Cic.; artūs depascitur arida febris, Verg.

dē-peciscor, pecisci, pectus [paciscor], *to settle by bargaining.* **1.** Lit.: tria praedia sibi, Cic.; aliquid cum aliquo, Cic.; ad condiciones alicuius, Cic. **2.** Transf. (with Abl. of price): Ter., Cic. Ep.

dē-pectō, pectere, pexum, *to comb down, comb off*: vellera, Verg.; Ov. Comic. *to curry* (one's hide), Ter.

dēpeculātor, ōris, *m.* [dēpeculor], *a plunderer, embezzler*: aerari, Cic.

dē-peculor, āri [peculium], *to embezzle.* **1.** Lit.: Apollonium omni argento spoliasti ac depeculatus es, Cic. **2.** Transf.: laudem honoremque alicuius, Cic.

dē-pellō, pellere, pulī, pulsum. **A.** Trans.: *to drive or cast down, to drive out or away; to expel.* **1.** Lit. **a.** In gen.: simulacra deorum depulsa sunt, Cic.; stellas Aurora,

Ov.; Verg.; aliquem de loco, Cic.; Cato; iugum a civibus, Cic.; Liv.; aliquem urbe, Tac.; Cic.; Verg., etc. **b.** Milit.: defensores vallo munitionibusque depellere, Caes.; loco editiore depelli, Sall. **c.** Of weaning: agnos a matre, Varr.; ab ubere, Hor. *Absol.*: Verg. **2.** Transf. **a.** *to avert*: morbum, Caes., Cic. Ep.; famem, Cic., Hor.; pestem, Verg.; auditiones falsas, Tac.; turpitudinem alicui, Cic.; mortem fratri, Ov. **b.** *to avert, deter, dissuade from*: aliquem de susceptā causā propositāque sententiā, Cic.; Caesar ab superioribus consiliis depulsus, Caes.; Cic., etc.; te ex illā actione, Cic.; aliquem spe, Liv.; Cic. With *quin* and *Subj.*: Pl., Tac. **B.** Intrans.: *to deviate*: Lucr.

dē-pendeō, ēre, *to hang down, to hang down from.* **1.** Lit.: sordidus ex umeris nodo dependet amictus, Verg.; Lucr.; serta tectis, Ov.; Verg.; Quint.; laqueo dependentem, Liv. **2.** Transf. **a.** *to depend upon*: fides a veniente die, Ov. **b.** *to be derived from*: huius augurium dependet origine verbi, Ov.

dē-pendō, pendere, pendī, pēnsum, *to weigh or pay down as due; to pay up.* **1.** Lit. Of bail forfeited: Pl., Cic. Ep. **2.** Transf.: rei publicae poenas praesenti morte dependere, Cic.; Luc. [Fr. *dépens.*]

dē-perdō, perdere, perdidī, perditum. **I.** *to lose utterly*: paucos ex suis, Caes.; nihil de iure civitatis, Cic., gratiam, Pl.; bona, honestatem, Cic.; Ov., etc. **II.** *to destroy, ruin* (in *Perf. Part.*): Prop., Suet.

dē-pereō, perīre, periī, *to go to utter ruin, to perish; to be lost, undone*: tempestate naves, Caes.; illius exercitus magna pars deperiit, Caes.; Lucr.: Cic., etc. Transf.: amore mulierculae, Liv. With Acc., *to be dying with love for*: Pl., Ter., Cat.

dēpexus, a, um, *Part.* dēpectō.

dē-pingō, pingere, pinxī, pictum (*Perf. sync.* dēpinxtī, Pl.), *to represent in painting, paint, portray.* **1.** Lit.: pugnam Marathoniam, Nep.; Prop. **2.** Transf. **a.** Of dress, *to embroider*: Suet. **b.** In words or thought: *to portray, to represent, describe*: in illā (*sc.* re publicā), quam sibi Socrates depinxerit, Cic.; formam verbis, Pl.; quidvis cogitatione, Cic.

dē-plangō, plangere, plānxī, *to bewail deeply* (strictly, *with beating of the breast*): palmis domum, Ov.

dē-pleō, ēre, ēvī, *to empty out*: oleum, Cato.

dē-plexus, a, um [plector], *gripping firmly*: Lucr.

dēplōrābundus, a, um [dēplōrō], *weeping bitterly*: Pl.

dē-plōrō, āre. **A.** Intrans.: *to weep or wail bitterly*: Cic. **B.** Trans. **a.** *to weep over or bewail bitterly*: damnationem illam, Cic.; Liv.; Ov.; multa de Gnaeo deplorabo, Cic. Ep. **b.** *to mourn as lost, despair of*: agros, Liv.; Ov.; Quint.

dē-pluit, ere, *rains down*: multus lapis, Tib.

dē-pōnō, pōnere, posuī, positum (*Perf.* dēposivī, Pl., Cat.). **I.** *to lay down.* **a.** In gen.: caput, Pl.; lecticam, Cic.; corpora sub ramis arboris, Verg.; Hor.; arma in contubernio, Caes.; Cic.; caput terrā, Ov.;

Verg. **b.** *to lay down as a wager, stake :* vitulam, Verg. **c.** In *Perf. Part., laid on the ground, dying, despaired of, dead :* ut depositi proferret fata parentis, Verg. ; Ov. T r a n s f. : mihi videor aegram et prope depositam rei publicae partem suscepisse, Cic. **II.** *to lay down* (in a place or with a person, esp. for safety), *to deposit ; commit to the care of, entrust.* **1.** L i t. : gladium apud aliquem, Cic. ; Pl. ; Liv. ; obsides apud eos, Caes. ; pecuniam in templo, Liv. ; Caes. **2.** T r a n s f. : P. Romani ius in vestrā fide ac religione depono, Cic. ; aliquid in aure, Hor. **III.** *to lay down, lay aside, get rid of.* **1.** L i t. : arma, Caes., Liv. ; crinem, Tac. ; onera iumentis, Caes. ; Verg. ; aliquid de manibus, Cic. ; coronam in arā, Liv. **2.** T r a n s f. : imperium, Caes. ; amicitias, maerorem, etc., Cic. ; bellum, Ov., Liv., Tac. ; contentionem, Liv. ; omnem spem contentionis, Caes.

dēpopulātiō, ōnis, *f.* [dēpopulor], *a laying waste, ravaging :* Cic., Liv. In *pl. :* Cic.

dēpopulātor, ōris, *m.* [dēpopulor], *one who lays waste, a marauder :* Cic.

dē-populō, āre (Enn. ; Auct. B. Hisp., and in *Perf. Part.*, Caes., Liv.) and **dēpopulor**, ārī (Caes., Cic., Liv., Ov.) [populus], *to unpeople, depopulate ; lay waste, devastate.* **1.** L i t. Of territory : Caes., Cic.. Ov. ; etc. **2.** T r a n s f. : *to waste, spoil, destroy :* domos, fana, Cic. ; Cerealia dona, Ov. ; omne mortalium genus vis pestilentiae depopulabatur, Tac.

dē-portō, āre. **I.** *to carry or convey down :* argentum ad mare ex oppido, Cic. E s p. of conveyance by water : Caes., Liv. **II.** *to convey away to a place.* **1.** L i t. : frumentum in castra, Caes. E s p. *to bring home :* victorem exercitum, Cic. ; Nep. ; Liv. **2.** T r a n s f. Of abstract and mental objects : *to carry off, win, bring home :* tertium triumphum, Cic. ; lauream, Tac. ex Asiā dedecus, Cic. **III.** *to convey away* (from home) : Agyrio vasa Syracusas, Cic. ; Nep. E s p. *to banish, transport for life ;* a frequent sentence under the Empire (attended with loss of citizenship) : aliquem in insulam, Tac.

dē-pōscō, pōscere, popōsci, *to demand, require for some object.* **a.** In gen. : unum ab omnibus ad id bellum imperatorem deposci, Cic. **b.** For punishment : Cic., Ov. ; ducem ipsum in poenam, Liv. ; aliquem ad mortem, Caes. ; aliquem morti, Tac. **c.** *to demand* (as due or needed), *claim :* sibi provinciam, Cic. ; Caes. ; Liv. ; pericula, Tac.

dēpositus, a, um. **I.** *Part.* dēpōnō. **II.** Noun, **dēpositum**, i, *n. what is entrusted, a deposit :* reddere depositum, Cic. ; infitiari, Juv.

dēprāvātē, *adv. perversely, wrongly :* iudicare, Cic.

dēprāvātiō, ōnis, *f.* [dēprāvō], *a making crooked, distorting.* **1.** L i t. : membrorum, Cic. ; Sen. Ep. **2.** T r a n s f. : animi, verbi, Cic.

dē-prāvō, āre [pravus], *to make crooked, to pervert, distort.* **1.** L i t. : Varr., Cic. **2.** T r a n s f. **a.** *to distort, pervert by words* (i.e. *to misrepresent*) : aliquid, Ter., Cic.

b. Morally, *to pervert, corrupt, seduce :* aliquem, Caes., Cic., Liv. ; mores, Cic.

dēprecābundus, a, um [dēprecor], *earnestly entreating :* Tac.

dēprecātiō, ōnis, *f.* [dēprecor], *supplication, intercession against* (rarely *for*) *something.* **I. a.** *an averting by prayer, deprecation :* periculi, Cic. **b.** *a begging off ; an asking for pardon :* eius facti, Cic. ; meis perfidiis, Pl. R h e t. *a plea for indulgence :* Cic. **II.** *an earnest entreating, invocation (cf.* detestatio) : deorum, Cic.

dēprecātor, ōris, *m. an intercessor.* **a.** *against* something : Caes., Cic., Liv. With G e n. : Cic., Tac. **b.** *for* something : Caes., Cic., Liv. With G e n. : Cic.

dē-precor, ārī. **I.** *to pray against, avert or ward off by prayer ; to deprecate ;* (with Acc. of person if expressed) : Enn. ; mortem, Caes. ; Cic. ; Liv. ; Quint. ; ab sese calamitatem, Cic. With *ne* and *Subj. :* Pl., Cic., Ov., etc. With *quo minus* and *Subj. :* Liv. With *quin* and *Subj. :* Cat. *Absol. :* Cic., Verg. With Acc. and *Inf.*, *to plead in excuse :* Sall. **II.** *to supplicate, entreat for* something : pacem, Cic. Ep. ; vitam alicuius ab aliquo, Cic. ; paucos dies exsolvendo donativo, Tac. ; a vobis custodem salutis meae, Cic.

dēprehēnsiō, ōnis, *f.* [v. dēprendō], *a catching, detection :* veneni, Cic.

dē-prendō (and **dēprehendō**), endere, endī, ēnsum, *to clutch hold of ; arrest, intercept, surprise, seize.* **1.** L i t. **A.** In gen. : onerarias navis, Caes. ; internuntios, Caes. ; Liv. ; litteras, Liv. ; deprensus in aggere serpens, Verg. Of action by things (esp. by storms) : deprensa navigia, Lucr. ; Verg. ; Curt., etc. **B.** Of crime or fault, *to catch, arrest, surprise, detect.* **a.** Of persons : aliquem in manifesto scelere, Cic. ; Sall. ; Quint. ; percussorem cum sicā, Cic. ; aliquem, Pl., Hor., Quint. **b.** Of things : venenum, Cic., Liv. **c.** *to discover :* nummos in circo, Cic. ; Ov. **2.** T r a n s f. Of mental action, *to detect, find out, discover :* facinora oculis prius quam opinione, Cic. ; si me stultior ipso deprenderis, Hor. ; in Livio Patavinitatem, Quint.

dēprēnsus (and **dēprehēnsus**), a, um. *Part.* dēprendō.

dēpressus, a, um. **I.** *Part.* dēprimō. **II.** Adj. **a.** *lying low. Comp. :* Plin. Ep. **b.** Of the voice : *low. Sup. :* Auct. Her.

dē-primō, primere, pressī, pressum [premō], *to press or weigh down, sink down.* **1.** L i t. **a.** In gen. : Pl. ; terram et maria deprimere, Cic. ; depresso aratro (*sc.* in terram), Verg. **b.** *to plant deep, to dig deep :* vitis in terram, Cato ; fossam, Hirt., Tac. **c.** *to sink* a ship : Caes., Cic., Ov., etc. **2.** T r a n s f. : *to press down, keep down, trample on :* improbitate depressā veritas emergit, Cic. ; ita se quisque extollit, ut deprimat alium, Liv.

dēproeliāns, antis [proelior], *battling fiercely :* Hor.

dē-prōmō, prōmere, prōmpsī, prōmptum, *to take down or out from ; produce.* **1.** L i t. : cibum servis, Pl. ; pecuniam ex arcā, Cic. ; tela pharetris, Verg. ; Hor. ; Ov. **2.**

Transf.: Pl.; quasi e thesauris argumenta, Cic.; iuris utilitatem de libris, Cic.

dē-prŏperō, āre. **A.** Intrans.: *to make great haste :* Pl. **B.** Trans.: *to hasten to prepare :* čoronas, Hor. With *Inf.* as object : Pl.

depsō, sere, suī, stum [δεψέω], *to knead :* Cato.

dē-pŭdēre, puduit, *to put off all sense of shame :* Ov., Sen.

dē-pūgis (or **dēpȳgis**), is, *adj.* [pūga], *without buttocks*, or *thin-buttocked :* Hor.

dē-pugnō, āre, *to fight hard, fight to a finish.* **1.** Lit.: Pl., Lucr., Caes., Cic., etc.; cum aliquo, Cic. Of gladiatorial combats, Cic. *Pass. Impers. :* Pl., Cic. Ep., Liv. **2.** Transf.: cum fame, Pl. In a figure borrowed from gladiators : voluptas cum honestate, Cic.; indocti stolidique et depugnare parati, Hor.

dēpulsiō, ōnis, *f.* [dēpellō], *a driving off, averting :* mali, Cic. Rhet. *a defence :* Cic.

dē-pulsō, āre [*freq.* dēpellō], *to thrust away :* aliquem de viā, Pl.

dēpulsor, ōris, *m.* [dēpellō], *one who thrusts aside :* dominatūs, Cic.

dēpulsus, a, um, *Part.* dēpellō.

dē-pungō, ere, *to prick or mark down* (with *Indir. Deliberative*) *:* Pers.

dē-pūrgō, āre, *to clean out thoroughly :* piscem, Pl.; prata, Cato.

dē-putō, āre. **1.** Lit.: *to cut off, prune :* vineam, Cato. Poet.: umbras (i.e. ramos), Ov. **2.** Transf.: *to calculate out, reckon.* With Acc.: operam alicuius parvi preti, Ter. With Acc. and *Inf.* : Pl., Ter.

dē-pȳgis, *v.* dēpūgis.

dēque, *v.* susque, dēque.

Dercetis, is, or **Dercetō**, ūs, *f. a Syrian goddess.*

dērēctus, a, um, *Part.* dērigō.

dērelictiō, ōnis, *f.* [dērelinquō], *an abandoning, neglecting :* communis utilitatis, Cic.

dē-relinquō, linquere, līquī, lictum, *to leave behind in misfortune, to forsake :* aliquem, Pl., Cic.; castra, Liv.; agros, Cic.

dē-repente, *adv.* [*cf.* dēsubitō, dēnuō, *etc.*], *suddenly :* Tac.

dē-rēpō, rēpere, rēpsī, *to creep down :* Phaedr.

dēreptus, a, um, *Part.* dēripiō.

dē-rīdeō, rīdēre, rīsī, rīsum, *to laugh to scorn, deride :* aliquem, Pl., Cic., Hor.; aliquid, Hor., Juv. Prov.: albis dentibus aliquem deridere, Pl. *Absol. :* Pl., Cic., etc.

dē-rīdiculus, a, um [rīdiculus], *very laughable, very ridiculous :* Pl., Varr., Liv. As Noun, **dērīdiculum**, i, n. **I.** *derision, mockery :* Pl. **II.** *an object of derision :* deridiculo fuit senex, Tac. **III.** *ridiculousness, absurdity :* corporis, Tac.

dē-rigō, rigore, rēxī, rēctum [regō], *to give a particular direction to, to direct, aim.* **1.** Lit.: vela ad castra Corneliana, Caes.; cursum ad litora, Caes.; Cat.; equum in consulem, Liv.; Ov.; maritimos cursūs, Cic.; huc gressum, Verg.; navem eo, Nep. Esp. of weapons : spicula, Verg.; Hor.; Suet.; tela in corpus Aeacidae, Verg.; vulnera, Verg., Tac. With Dat.: Ilo hastam, Verg. **2.** Transf.: *to direct,*

aim, regulate. With *ad* and Acc. of the object aimed at or standard : vitam ad certam rationis normam, Cic.; Quint.; Tac. With *in* and Acc.: Quint. With Abl. *Instr. :* utilitatem honestate, Cic. (*v.* also dirigo).

dē-rigui (*Perf.*), *became* or *grew stiff :* formidine sanguis deriguit, Verg.; oculi, Verg.; comae, Ov.

dē-ripiō, ripere, ripui, reptum [rapiō], *to snatch, pull, tear down or away.* **1.** Lit.: aliquem de arā, Pl.; Ov.; velamina ex umeris, Ov.; ramos arbore, Ov.; Verg.; Tac.; pellem leoni, Ov.; Pl. **2.** Transf.: quantum de meā auctoritate deripuisset, Cic.

dērisor, ōris, *m.* [dērīdeō], *a mocker, scoffer :* Pl., Hor., Quint.

dērīsus, a, um, *Part.* dērīdeō.

dērīsus, ūs, *m.* [dērīdeō], *mockery, scorn, derision :* Phaedr., Tac.

dērīvātiō, ōnis, *f.* [dērīvō], *a turning off into another channel, diversion :* fluminum, Cic.; Liv.

dē-rīvō, āre [rīvus], *to draw away down,* as water from a river, etc.; *to draw off, divert.* **1.** Lit.: de fluvio aquam. Pl.; aqua ex flumine derivata, Caes. **2.** Transf. **a.** nihil in suam domum inde, Cic.; Ter.; Quint.; hoc fonte derivata clades, Hor.; derivare animum, curāque levare, Lucr.; alio responsionem suam derivavit, Cic. **b.** Gramm. (= ducere), *to derive* (words) : Quint.

dē-rogō, āre, *to propose* (some removal) *from a law, propose a partial repeal.* **1.** Lit.: do lege aliqua, Cic.; legem, Cic. **2.** Transf.: *to detract from the force or dignity of* a thing : ubi certam derogat vetustas fidem, Liv. With *de :* de honestate quiddam, Cic. With *ex :* Cic. With Dat. of person: mihi tantum, Cic.; fidem alicui, Cic.; Luc. With Dat. of thing: Tac.

dē-rōsus, a, um [rōdō], *gnawed away* clipeos derosos a muribus, Cic.

dē-runcinō, āre [runcina], *to plane off.* Comic. : militem, Pl.

dē-ruō, ruere, ruī, *to make to tumble or fall down.* **1.** Lit.: Sen. **2.** Transf.: cumulum de laudibus alicuius, Cic.

dē-ruptus, a, um [rumpō], *broken down or off, steep, precipitous :* Lucr., Liv., Tac. *Comp. :* Liv. *Neut. pl.* as Noun : in derupta praccipitati, Liv.; Tac.

dē-saeviō, īre, iī, *to rage violently :* toto Aeneas desaevit in aequore, Verg.; pelago hiems, Verg.; tragicā desaevit in arte, Hor.

dē-saltō, āre, *to dance duly, to represent in a dance:* Suet.

dē-scendō, scendere, scendī, scēnsum [scandō], *to climb, go,* or *come down, descend* (opp. ascendo). **1.** Lit. **a.** In gen.: ex equo, Cic.; Caes.; Tib.; de rostris, Cic.; Lucr.; Liv.; ab Alpibus, Liv.; Verg.; caelo, Hor.; Verg.; Ov.; in campos, Liv.; Lucr.; Cic.; Verg.; ad umbras, Verg.; Cic.; Ov. *Absol. :* Pl., Lucr., Verg., Suet. **b.** In partic., *to go down,* sc. from the dwelling-houses (which in Rome were mostly situated on eminences) to the forum, the comitia, etc.: de palatio et

aedibus suis, Cic. ; ad forum, Cic., Liv. ;
Hor. *Absol.* : Cic., Liv. **c.** M i l i t. *to
march down, sc.* from a higher into a lower
position : ex superioribus locis in planitiem
descendere, Caes. ; Liv. *Impers. Pass.* :
Liv. Hence, descendere in aciem, Liv. ;
in certamen, Cic. **d.** Of falling things, e.g.
weapons : ferrum in corpus, Liv. ; Ov. ;
toto corpore pestis, Verg. **2.** T r a n s f.
a. *to sink into, penetrate* : si quid tamen
olim scripseris, in Maeci descendat iudicis
auris, Hor. ; quod verbum in pectus
Iugurthae descendit, Sall. ; Liv. *Impers.
Pass.* : Cic., Tac. **b.** *to lower oneself, descend
to ; to stoop to any act* : ad vim atque arma,
Caes. ; senes ad ludum adulescentium, Cic. ;
Hor. ; preces in omnis, Verg. *Absol.* : Cic. **c.**
to descend, be derived : a vitā pastorali ad
agri culturam, Varr. ; usus in nostram
aetatem, Quint.

dē-scēnsus, ūs, m. [dēscendō]. **I.** *a climbing
down, descent* : Sall. **II.** *a descent, slope
down* : Hirt. ; facilis descensus Averno,
Verg.

dē-sciscō, sciscere, scii (or scivi), scitum, *to
break allegiance.* **1.** L i t. : *to revolt, desert,
go over to another party* : ab aliquo, Caes.,
Cic., Liv. ; ad aliquem, Liv. *Impers.
Pass.* : Liv. *Absol.* : Nep., Liv., Tac.
2. T r a n s f. : *to desert, fall away, deviate.*
a. Of persons : a veritate, Cic. ; Quint. ;
Plin. Ep. ; ad saevitiam, Suet. ; Cic. Ep.
b. Of things : quis ignorat eloquentiam
descivisse ab istā vetero gloriā ? Tac.

dē-scribō, scribere, scripsi, scriptum. **I.**
to write out, copy, transcribe : librum, Cic. ;
carmina, Verg. ; praecepta, Cic. **II.** *to
design, portray, represent, describe, draw.*
1. L i t. : eius formam, Pl. ; geometricas
formas, Cic., Liv. ; caeli meatūs, Verg. ; Hor.
2. T r a n s f. In words : mulierem, Cic. ;
hominum sermones moresque, Cic. ; Pl. ;
lucum, etc., Hor. ; facta versibus, Nep. ;
Hor. ; Quint. With Acc. and *Inf.* : Ov.
(*v.* also discribo).

dēscriptē, *v.* discriptē.

dēscriptiō, ōnis, *f.* [dēscribō]. **1.** L i t. **a.**
a copy : tabularum, Cic. **b.** *a representation* (e.g. *a diagram, plan, map, etc.*) :
descriptionibus aliquid explicare, Cic. ;
aedificandi, Cic. **2.** T r a n s f. **a.** *a representation, description* : nominis, Cic. ;
regionum, Quint. (*v.* also discriptio).

dēscriptus, a, um. **I.** *Part.* dēscribō. **II.**
A d j. *v.* discriptus.

dē-secō, secāre, secui, sectum, *to cut away, to
lop off, crop.* **1.** L i t. : auris, Caes. ;
partis ex toto, Cic. ; spicas fascibus, Liv. ;
hordeum, pabulum, herbas, Caes. ; collum,
Verg. **2.** T r a n s f. : prooemium, Cic. Ep.

dē-serō, serere, serui, sertum, *to disconnect ;
to forsake, abandon, desert.* **1.** L i t. **a.**
M i l i t. : exercitum, duces, oppidum, Caes. ;
locum, Tac. *Absol.* : Nep., Quint., Tac.
b. In gen. : aliquem, Pl., Cic., Verg. ;
pignus, Pl. **2.** T r a n s f. : sese, Caes. ;
vadimonia, Cic. ; officium, Caes., Cic. ;
causam, Cic., Liv. ; locum virtutis, Hor. ;
Quint. Of things : genua cursorem, Pl. ;
aliquem vires, Tac. ; donec te deseret aetas,
Hor. *Pass.* : deseremur a re familiari, Cic.
Ep. ; Caes.

dēsertor, ōris, m. [dēserō], *one who forsakes,
an abandoner.* **1.** L i t. : amicorum, Cic.
Ep. ; salutis, Cic. M i l i t. *a deserter* :
Caes., Liv., Tac. **2.** T r a n s f. : Asiae,
Verg. ; amoris, Ov.

dēsertus, a, um. **I.** *Part.* dēserō. **II.** A d j. :
deserted ; unfrequented, unpopulated. **1.**
L i t. : loca, Caes. ; urbes, via, Cic. ; vicus,
Hor. ; ager, Liv. As Noun, **dēserta**,
ōrum, *n. pl. desert places* : Verg. **2.**
T r a n s f. : res, vita, Cic. *Comp.* : Cic.,
Hor. *Sup.* : Cic.

dē-serviō, īre, *to serve devotedly, be an absolute slave* : amicis, Cic. ; corpori, Cic. ;
Quint. ; Plin. Ep. Of things as subject :
si officia (mea) deserviunt amicis, Cic. ;
Quint.

dēses, idis (Nom. *sing.* not used), *adj.* [dē-
sideō], *sitting down, sitting at ease ; apathetic, indolent.* **1.** L i t. : Liv., Tac. **2.**
T r a n s f. : nec rem Romanam tam de-
sidem unquam fuisse, Liv. ; Luc.

dē-siccō, āre, *to dry up completely, to drain* :
Pl.

dē-sideō, sidēre, sēdi [sedeō], *to remain sitting,
to sit idle, remain inactive* : Pl., Phaedr.,
Sen. Ep., etc.

dēsiderābilis, e, *adj.* [dēsiderō], *worthy of
desire, desirable* : Cic., Liv., Tac. *Comp.* :
Suet.

dēsiderātiō, ōnis, *f.* [dēsiderō], *a longing for ;
sense of want* : voluptatum, Cic.

dēsiderium, I, *n.* [dēsiderō], *a longing for ;
sense of want ; grief for the absence or loss
of anyone or anything.* **1.** L i t. With
Obj. G e n. : Ter., Lucr., Cic., Ov., etc.
Absol. : Ter., Cic., Quint. In *pl.* : Cic.,
Hor. P h r. : me desiderium tenet alicuius, Cic. Ep. ; alicuius desiderio moveri,
Cic. ; ex desiderio laborare, Cic. ; desideria
alicuius commovere, Cic. As term of endearment : Cic. Ep., Cat. **2.** T r a n s f.
a. *want, appetite* : cibi potionisque, Liv.
b. *a request, petition* : desideria militum
ad Caesarem ferre, Tac. [It. *desio* ; Fr.
désir.]

dē-sīderō, āre [sīdus ; Lit. *to watch for a
constellation in vain*]. **I.** *to miss, feel the
want of.* **a.** In gen. : aliquem, Pl., Ter.,
Cic. ; aliquid, Cic., Tac. **b.** M i l i t. : *to
lose ;* and more freq. *Pass.* ; *to be missing,
to be lost* : in eo proelio non amplius cc.
milites desideravit, Caes. ; Cic. **II.** *to
need, look for, long for* : aliquid, Caes., Cic.,
Hor. With Acc. of object and *Inf.* : Pl.,
Caes. With *ab* : ab Chrysippo nihil magnum desideravi, Cic. ; Caes. ; Quint. With
in : in Catone eloquentiam, Cic. ; Quint.
Absol. : Pl., Ter. [Fr. *désirer.*]

dēsidia, ae, *f.* [dēsideō], *a sitting still or idle.*
1. L i t. : Prop. **2.** T r a n s f. : *idleness,
inactivity, apathy* : Pl., Cic., Verg., etc. In
pl. : Lucr., Verg.

dēsidiābulum, I, *n.* [dēsidia], *a lounging-
place* : Pl.

dēsidiōsē, *adv. idly* : Lucr.

dēsidiōsus, a, um [dēsidia], *indolent, lazy.* **1.**
L i t. : Varr., Plin. Ep. **2.** T r a n s f. :
spent in idleness ; causing idleness : otium,
Cic. ; delectatio, Cic. ; puer (*sc.* Cupido),
Ov. *Comp.* : Varr. *Sup.* : Cic., Plin.
Ep.

dē-sīdŏ, sīdere, sēdī, *to settle* or *sink down.*
1. Lit.: ut multis locis terrae desederint,
Cic.; Liv. **2.** Transf.: *to sink* (i.e.
deteriorate) : mores, Liv.
dēsignātiŏ, ōnis, *f.* [dēsignō], *a marking
down for a purpose, a designation, specifica-
tion.* Transf. **a.** *specific mention :* personarum et temporum, Cic. **b.** *an appointing, nomination* (for office) : Tac., Suet.
(*v.* also dissignatio.)
dēsignātor, *v.* dissignātor.
dē-signō, āre. **I.** *to mark out* for a purpose, *to
plan.* **1.** Lit.: urbem aratro, Verg.;
Tac. With DAT. of purpose : locum circo,
Liv. **2.** Transf. **a.** *to mark down, mark
out, point clearly to, indicate :* oratione
fratrem, Caes.; oculis ad caedem unum-
quemque nostrum, Cic.; aliquem notā ignaviae, Cic.; aliquem digito, Ov.; decumam ex praedā, Liv.; turpitudinem,
Cic.; Caes. **b.** Polit.: of nomination
to an office : *to elect, choose :* ab plebe
designari, Cic. Esp. **dēsignātus**, as a title
applied to a magistrate who has been
elected, but has not yet entered upon the
duties of his office : consul, aedilis, tribunus
plebis, Cic. **II.** *to portray :* Europen, Ov.
(*v.* also dissigno.) [It. *disegnare, designare ;*
Fr. *désigner, dessiner.*]
dē-silĭō, silīre, siluī (suluī, Pl.; siliī, Curt.)
[salĭō], *to leap down, alight.* **1.** Lit.:
Caes., Ov.; de navibus, Caes.; Pl.; ex
equis, Caes., Liv.; Pl.; Ov.; ab equo,
Verg.; curru, Verg.; Ov.; Tac.; ad
pedes, Caes., Liv.; in aquam, Caes., Ov.
2. Transf. **a.** nec desilies imitator in
artum, Hor. **b.** Of things : lympha, Hor.;
Ov.; fulmina, Prop.
dē-sĭnō, sinere, sĭī (contr. *Inf.* dēsīsse, Cic.),
situm, *to leave off, give over, cease, abandon.*
A. Trans. **a.** With *Inf.* (*v.* freq.): Pl.,
Caes., Cic. **b.** With ACC.: artem, Cic. Ep.;
versūs, Verg. **c.** With *Obj. Inf.* implied :
Pl.; desine plura (loqui), Verg. **d.** In *Pass.*
(us. in *Perf.* tenses, and foll. by *Pass. Inf.*) :
veteres orationes a plerisque legi sunt de-
sitae, Cic.; Liv.; tunc bene desinitur, Ov.
B. Intrans.: bellum, Sall.; ferrea gens,
Verg.; ira, Hor.; imbres, Ov. With *in*
and ACC. *to end in :* cauda desinit in piscem, Ov.; Verg.; Sen. Ep.; Rhet. of the
close of a period : Cic., Quint. With ABL. :
communibus locis, Cic. With GEN.: querellarum, Hor.
dēsĭpĭentĭa, ae. *f.* [dēsipiō], *want of understanding, foolishness :* Lucr.
dē-sĭpĭō, sipere [sapĭō], *to be without sense or
understanding ; to act foolishly :* dulce est
desipere in loco, Hor.; Pl.; Cic.
dē-sistō, sistere, stitī, stitum, *to come to a
standstill ; cease from effort or resistance.* **I.**
to abandon (the society of) a person : aps te,
Pl. **II.** *to abandon* action begun. With
ABL., or *de* or *ab* and ABL. : de petitione,
Liv.; Cic.; a defensione, Caes.; Liv.;
oppugnatione, Caes.; Cic.; Verg., etc.
With DAT.: Verg. With *Inf.* : Caes.,
Cic., Hor. With *quin* : Pl. With *Obj.
Inf.* implied : Pl., Caes., Ov., etc.
dēsĭtus, a, um, *Part.* dēsinō.
dē-sōlō, āre [sōlus], *to leave lonely.* **a.** Of
land, *to desolate, strip* (of inhabitants) :

agros, Verg.; desolatae terrae, Ov. **b.**
Of persons (us. in *Perf. Part. ; left in the
lurch*): Verg., Plin. Ep., Tac. With ABL. :
desolatus servilibus ministeriis, Tac.
dēspectŏ, āre [*freq.* dēspiciō], *to gaze down
upon.* **1.** Lit.: ex alto terras, Ov.; Verg.
2. Transf. **a.** Of situation, *to look down
on, command a view of :* quos despectant
moenia Abellae, Verg. **b.** *to look down
upon, to despise :* liberos ut multum infra,
Tac.
dēspectus, a, um, *Part.* dēspiciō.
dēspectus, ūs, *m.* [dēspiciō]. **I.** *a looking
down upon ; a commanding view :* erat ex
oppido Alesia despectus in campum, Caes. ;
sub terras, Lucr. In *pl.* : cum ex omnibus
partibus despectūs haberet (oppidum),
Caes. **II.** *an object of contempt* (in *Predic.*
DAT.) : Auct. Her. [It. *dispetto ;* Sp. *des-
pecho ;* Fr. *dépit.*]
dēspēranter, *adv. hopelessly, despairingly :*
loqui secum, Cic. Ep.
dēspērātiŏ, ōnis, *f.* [dēspērō], *hopelessness,
despair :* Caes., Cic., Liv., etc. With *Obj.*
GEN. : Caes., Cic., Liv. In *pl.* : Cic. Ep.
dēspērātus, a, um. **I.** *Part.* dēspērō. **II.**
Adj.: *given up, despaired of ; in a hopeless
state :* aegrota ac prope desperata res publica, Cic.; exercitum conlectum ex senibus
desperatis, Cic.; desperatas pecunias exigere, Cic. *Comp.* : Cic. Ep. *Sup.* : Cic.
dē-spērō, āre. **A.** Intrans. : *to be hopeless, despair :* Cic., Ov. With *de* and ABL. :
Caes., Cic. Ep., Liv. With DAT. : Caes.,
Cic. **B.** Trans.: *to despair of, give up in
despair.* With ACC. : Cic., Hor., Liv.; in
Pass. : Cic. Ep., Hor., Liv. In Caes. only
in *Perf. Part.* **N.B.** the phrase desperatis
hominibus, *reduced to despair, desperate,*
Caes. With ACC. and *Inf.* : Cic., Hor., Ov.
dēspĭcātĭŏ, ōnis, *f.* [dēspicor], *contempt.* In
pl. (*contp. amicitiae*) : Cic.
dēspĭcātuī, *Predic.* DAT. *m.* [dēspicor], *for
(or as) an object of contempt :* si quis despicatui ducitur, Cic ; Pl.
dēspĭcātus, a, um [dēspicor], *despised, contemptible. Sup.* : Cic.
dēspĭcĭēns, ntis. **I.** *Part.* dēspiciō. **II.** Adj.
contemptuous ; with GEN. : Cic.
dēspĭcĭentĭa, ae, *f.* [dēspiciō], *a looking
down upon, despising, contempt ;* with *Obj.* GEN. :
Cic.
dē-spĭcĭō, spicere, spexī, spectum (*Inf. Perf.*
dēspexe, Pl.) [speciō]. **I.** *to look down.*
A. Intrans. : ad te, Pl.; de vertice
montis in vallis, Ov.; Hor. *Impers. Pass.* :
Caes., Liv. **B.** Trans. : *to look down
upon.* **1.** Lit.: aethere summo mare,
Verg.; Cic.; Ov. **2.** Transf.: *to look
down upon, to despise* (opp. suspicere) : suos,
Caes.; Cic.; Verg.; laborem, Caes.; Cic.
II. perh. *to look away :* Cic.
dēspĭcor, ārī [speciō], *to despise, disdain :*
Pl. *Perf. Part.* in *Pass.* sense : Pl.
dēspŏlĭātor, ōris, *m.* [dēspolĭō], *a robber,
plunderer :* Pl.
dē-spŏlĭō, āre, *to strip, rob, plunder.* **1.**
Lit.: aliquem, Pl., Ter., Cic. Ep.; se
armis, Caes.; templum, Cic. **2.** Transf.:
despoliari triumpho, Liv.
dē-spondeŏ, spondēre, spondī, spōnsum (*Perf.
Inf.,* dēspopondisse, Pl.). **I.** *to pledge or*

promise *solemnly* or *fully*. **1.** L i t. **a.** In gen. : librum alicui, Cic. Ep. ; Liv. ; Luc. ; consulatum, Liv. **b.** Esp. *to promise in marriage, to betroth* : filiam alicui, Pl. ; Cic. ; Ov., etc. *Impers. Pass.* : Ter. C o m i c. : bibliothecam tuam cave cuiquam despondeas, Cic. Ep. **2.** T r a n s f. : *to pledge, devote* : spes rei publicae despondetur anno consulatūs tui, Cic. Ep. **II.** *to pledge away.* T r a n s f. : with animum or animos, *to lose courage, to despair, despond* : Pl., Liv.

dēspōnsō, āre [*freq.* dēspondeō], *to betroth* : Suet. [It. *disposare.*]

dēspōnsus, a, um, *Part.* dēspondeō.

dē-spūmō, āre [spūma], *to skim off, to skim.* **1.** L i t. **a.** undam aeni, Verg. **b.** I n - t r a n s. : *to froth down* : Luc. **2.** T r a n s f. *to work off* (i.e. *digest*) : Falernum, Pers. Intrans. : Sen.

dē-spuō, ere, *to spit (on the ground).* **1.** Lit. : Tib., Liv. **2.** T r a n s f. : *to reject with contempt* : preces, Cat. ; Pl. ; Sen. Ep.

dē-squāmō, āre [squāma], *to take the scales off, to scale.* **1.** L i t. : piscīs, Pl. **2.** T r a n s f. : *to peel off* : Lucil. ; corticem, Plin.

dē-stillō, āre, *to drip* or *trickle down, to distil.* **1.** L i t. (Trans.) : Verg. **2.** T r a n s f. (Intrans.) : destillant tempora nardo, Tib.

dē-stimulō, āre, *to worry to death, waste away* : Transf. : bona, Pl.

dēstinātiō, ōnis, *f.* [dēstinō], *a settlement, appointment* : partium quibus cessurus esset, Liv. ; consulum, Tac. ; Stat.

dēstinātus, a, um. **I.** *Part.* dēstinō. **II.** Adj. *fixed, determined* : Cic. Hence, destinatum est alicui, *it is one's decision or intention* (with *Inf.*) : Liv., Plin. Ep. **III.** *Neut.* as Noun : *a thing marked down.* **a.** *a mark* : velut destinatum petentibus, Liv. ; Curt. **b.** In *pl.* : *designs, intentions* : Phaedr., Tac. ABL. *sing.* as Adv. **dēstinātō,** *intentionally* : Suet. P h r. **ex dēstinātō,** *intentionally* : Sen., Suet.

dē-stinō, āre [*cf.* στάνω, stō], *to fasten down ; secure.* **1.** L i t. : antemnas ad malos, Caes. : ratis ancoris, Caes. **2.** T r a n s f. : *to fix, determine beforehand, intend, appoint* (in Livy freq. with animo or animis). **A.** In gen. With double Acc. : aliquem consulem, Liv., Tac. With *Inf.* : Caes., Liv., Ov., etc. With DAT. of person or thing: alteri diem necis, Cic. ; Pl. ; Hor. ; nostros operi, Caes. ; Verg. With *ad* : aliquem ad mortem, Liv. ; Curt. ; consilia ad bellum, Liv. ; Quint. With *in* : saxo in aliud destinato, Tac. **B.** In partic. **a.** Of archers, etc., *to mark in aiming, take aim at* (with Acc.) : Liv. **b.** Of traders, *to mark down, fix upon* (for purchase) : sibi aliquid, Pl., Cic. Ep.

dē-stituō, uere, uī, ūtum [statuō]. **I.** *to set aprat in a place, set persons by themselves* : Mucium ante tribunal, Liv. ; cohortis extra vallum, Liv. ; signa hic, Pl. ; alios in convivio, Cic. With thing as subject : alveum in sicco aqua destituit, Liv. ; Verg. **II.** *to leave apart, leave in the lurch, forsake, abandon.* **1.** L i t. : aliquem, Caes., Cic., Liv. **2.** T r a n s f. With thing as sub-

ject : ventus aliquem, Liv. ; destitutus ab unicā spe, Liv. ; Curt. With thing as object : spem, Liv. : fugam, Ov. ; consilium, Suet. With ABL. of separation : eius consiliis destitutus, Cic. Ep. ; Quint. ; destituit deos mercede pactā, Hor.

dēstitūtiō, ōnis, *f.* [dēstituō], *a forsaking, deserting* : Cic., Suet. With *Subj.* GEN. : Cic.

dēstitūtus, a, um, *Part.* dēstituō.

dēstrictus, a, um. **I.** *Part.* dēstringō. **II.** Adj. *strict, severe.* Comp. : Tac.

dē-stringō, stringere, strinxī, strictum. **I.** *to strip.* **1.** L i t. **a.** Of leaves, etc. : Cato, Luc., Quint. **b.** Of clothes : Phaedr. **c.** Esp. of unsheathing a sword : gladium, Caes., Cic., Liv. ; ensem, Hor. **d.** Of *rubbing* the body in the bath : Plin. Ep. **2.** T r a n s f. Of criticism, censure : Ov. **II.** *to brush gently against, to graze* : aequora alis, Ov. ; corpus harundo, Ov.

dēstructiō, ōnis, *f.* [dēstruō], *a pulling down.* **1.** L i t. : murorum, Suet. **2.** T r a n s f. : sententiarum, Quint.

dē-struō, struere, struxī, structum, *to unbuild, pull down.* **1.** L i t. : navem, aedificium, Cic. ; Verg. **2.** T r a n s f. : ius, Liv. ; Ov. ; Quint. ; hostem, Tac.

dē-subitō (and **dē subitō**), *adv. on a sudden, suddenly* : Pl., Lucr., Cic.

dē-sūdāscō, ere, *to begin to sweat all over.* *Impers. Pass.* : Pl.

dē-sūdō, āre, *to sweat all over.* T r a n s f. : in his (*sc.* exercitationibus ingeni), Cic.

dēsuē-fīō, fierī, factum, *to be (made) unaccustomed* : multitudo a contionibus, Cic. ; Varr

dē-suēscō, suēscere, suōvī, suētum, *to grow unaccustomed to.* Rare except in *Perf.* *Part.* **dēsuētus,** a, um. **A.** Act. : *unaccustomed* : desueta triumphis agmina, Verg. With *Inf.* : Liv. **B.** P a s s. : *disused, out of use* : arma, Vorg. ; res, Liv. ; verba, Ov.

dēsuētūdō, inis, *f.* [dēsuēscō], *discontinuance, disuse* : armorum, Liv. ; Ov.

dēsuētus, a, um, *v.* dēsuēscō.

dēsultor, ōris, *m.* [dēsiliō], *a leaper* : esp. *one who in the games of the circus vaulted from one horse to another, a circus-rider.* **1.** L i t. : Varr., Liv. **2.** T r a n s f. Of an inconstant person : amoris, Ov., Sen.

dēsultōrius, a, um [dēsultor], *of a desultor* : equus, Suet. *Masc.* as Noun (*sc.* equus) : Cic.

dēsultūra, ae, *f.* [dēsiliō], *a leaping down* from a horse (opp. insultura) : Pl.

dē-sum, esse, fuī, futūrus (Poet. ee as one syll., e.g. in dēest, dēerat), *to be below* (the due level) ; *to fall short, fail, be wanting.* **A.** In gen. **a.** *Absol.* (esp. of things : Ter., Cic., Hor., etc. ; paulum ad (*to complete*) summam felicitatem defuisse, Caes. **b.** Mostly with DAT. of person disappointed : Pl., Caes., Cic. **c.** With *in* and ABL. : Cic. **d.** With quo minus and *Subj.* : Cic., Tac. **e.** With *Inf.* : Prop., Tac. **B.** In partic. *to fail in one's duty or service.* With DAT. (of person or thing) : Caes., Cic., Hor., Liv. *Absol.* : Cic., Tac.

dē-sūmō, sūmere, sūmpsī, *to take for oneself from a quantity ; to pick out, choose* : hostem sibi, Liv. ; sibi vacuas Athenas, Hor. ; sibi pugnas, Tac.

dē-super, *adv. from above :* Caes., Verg., Ov.

dē-surgō, ere, *to rise and get down* (from one's couch) for a purpose, *leave the room :* cenā, Hor. ; Lucr.

dē-tegō, tegere, tēxī, tēctum, *to uncover, unroof.* **1.** Lit. **a.** Of buildings and the head : aedem, Liv. ; Pl. ; Verg. ; caput detectus, Verg. **b.** Of other things : Cic., Verg., etc. **2.** Transf. **a.** *to disclose* (by uncovering) : iuga montium nebula, Liv. ; cladem, Liv. ; formidine detegi, Tac. **b.** *to disclose, reveal* (a secret, etc.) : Liv., Ov., Quint.

dē-tendō, tendere, tēnsum, *to unstretch* (in striking camp) : tabernacula, Caes. ; Liv.

dētentus, a, um, *Part.* dētineō.

dē-tergeō, tergēre, tērsī, tērsum (also inflected by 3 *conj.*, dētergunt, Liv. 36, 44). **I.** *to wipe off, wipe away.* **1.** Lit. : lacrimas pollice, Ov. ; Suet. **2.** Transf. **a.** *to wipe, sweep away :* nubila caelo, Hor. ; navibus remos, Caes. ; ab utroque latere remos, Liv. **b.** *to cleanse by wiping, clean out :* caput pallio, Pl. ; cloacas, Liv. Transf. : *to clean up, sweep clear* (colloq.) : mensam, Pl. ; primo anno octoginta, Cic. Ep.

dēterior, ius, *adj. comp.* (*sup.* dēterrimus) [double comparative of stem seen in dē-mum ; *cf.* inferior, exterior], *lower in order, inferior.* **a.** Of things : Pl., Cic. Ep., Verg., etc. *Sup. :* Cic., Verg., etc. *Neut. pl.* as Noun : Ov. **b.** Of persons (opp. melior, optimus) : Pl., Cic., Liv. *Sup. :* Cic.

dēterius, *adv. worse :* Pl., Cic., Tac. ; spe deterius nostrā, Hor.

dēterminātiō, ōnis, *f.* [dēterminō], *a boundary, conclusion, end :* mundi, Cic. Transf. : orationis, Cic.

dē-terminō, āre, *to bound precisely ; to limit, prescribe.* **1.** Lit. : augur regiones ab oriente ad occasum determinavit, Liv. ; Pl. **2.** Transf. : id quod dicit, spiritu non arte determinat, Cic. ; Lucr. ; Tac.

dē-terō, terere, trīvī, trītum, *to rub down* or *away, to wear away, to wear out.* **1.** Lit. : strata saxea viarum pedibus, Lucr. ; detrita tegmina, Tac. Comic. : calces deteris (i.e. you tread on my heels), Pl. **2.** Transf. : laudes alicuius culpā ingeni, Hor. ; Quint. ; ardorem ac ferociam militis, Tac.

dē-terreō, ēre, *to scare off, frighten away, deter, discourage from.* **1.** Lit. With *ab :* eum ab instituto consilio, Caes. ; Cic. ; Liv. With *de :* aliquem de sententiā, Cic. ; Pl. With Acc. and Abl. : homines caedibus, Hor. ; Sall. With Acc. and Abl. *Instr. :* reliquos magnitudine poenae, Caes. ; Ov. With *ne, quin, quo minus* and *Subj.* (quin, quo minus only in negative sentences) : Pl., Caes., Cic. With Acc. of Object and *Inf. :* Cic. **2.** Transf. **a.** With thing as subject : alium pudor, Cic. **b.** With thing as object (like defendere, prohibere, etc.) : *to avert, ward off :* vim a censoribus, Liv.

dētersus, a, um, *Part.* dētergeō.

dētestābilis, e, *adj.* [dētestor], *execrable,*

abominable, detestable : omen, Cic. ; Liv. ; homo, Cic. *Comp. :* Cic.

dētestātiō, ōnis, *f.* [dētestor]. **I.** *a solemn execrating, cursing :* Liv., Hor. **II.** *an averting :* scelerum, Cic.

dē-testor, ārī. **I.** *to invoke the gods against something.* **1.** Lit. **a.** *to pray for deliverance from :* te tamquam auspicium malum, Cic. **b.** *to avert at one's prayer :* o di immortales, avertite et detestamini hoc omen, Cic. **2.** Transf. : *to deprecate, plead against, avert :* a me patriae querimoniam, Cic. ; invidiam, Cic. **II.** *to call down in cursing :* minas periculaque in caput eorum, Liv. ; Plin. Ep. **III.** *to call down a curse upon, to curse, execrate solemnly.* **1.** Lit. : omnibus precibus aliquem, Caes. ; Ov. **2.** Transf. : *to loathe, abhor :* auctorem cladis, Tac. *Pass. :* bella matribus detestata, Hor.

dē-texō, texere, texuī, textum, *to weave off, to plait ; to finish* or *make by weaving* or *plaiting.* **1.** Lit. : telam, Pl. ; aliquid viminibus mollique iunco, Verg. Comic. : pallium, *to steal,* Pl. **2.** Transf. : exorsa et potius detexta, Cic.

dē-tineō, tinēre, tinuī, tentum [teneō], *to hold* or *keep back from something, to hold up.* **1.** Lit. (from going or coming) : Pl. ; Verg. ; novissimos proelio, Caes. ; Liv. ; naves tempestate detinebantur, Caes. ; Ov. **2.** Transf. **a.** In gen. : nos de nostro negotio, Cic. ; aliquem ab incepto, Sall. **b.** *to keep occupied* (with *in* and ABL.) : in negotiis detineri, Cic. ; Ov. ; Tac. **c.** Of things : diem sermone, Ov. ; animum studiis, Ov. ; Quint.

dē-tondeō, tondēre, totondī and tondī, tōnsum, *to shear off, clip thoroughly.* **1.** Lit. : Pl. ; ovis, Cato ; crinis, Ov. **2.** Transf. : detonsae frigore frondes, Ov.

dē-tonō, āre, uī, *to cease thundering.* **1.** Lit. : Ov. **2.** Transf. : nubes belli, Verg. ; Quint.

dētōnsus, a, um, *Part.* dētondeō.

dē-torqueō, torquēre, torsī, tortum. **I.** *to twist, turn,* or *bend aside, to turn away.* **1.** Lit. : ponticulum, Cic. ; habenas, vulnus, Verg. ; (orbis partem) a latere in dextram partem, Cic. ; proram ad undas, Verg. ; Hor. **2.** Transf. : voluptates animos a virtute detorquent, Cic. ; animum in alia, Tac. ; Hor. **II.** *to twist out of shape, to distort.* **1.** Lit. : Vatinius corpore detorto, Tac. **2.** Transf. : omnia detorquendo suspecta efficere, Liv. ; verba in crimen, Tac. ; Quint.

dētractātiō and **dētractātor,** *v.* detrect—.

dētractiō, ōnis, *f.* [dētrahō], *a drawing off, taking away :* doloris, Cic. Rhet. : *ellipsis :* Quint.

dētractō, *v.* dētrectō.

dētractor, ōris, *m.* [dētrahō], *a disparager :* sui, Tac.

dētractus, a, um, *Part.* dētrahō.

dē-trahō, trahere, traxī, tractum (*Inf. Perf. sync.* dētraxe, Pl.). **I.** *to drag,* or *to draw, pull down.* **1.** Lit. : aliquem de curru, Cic. ; aliquem ex cruce, Cic. Ep. Occ. Of buildings : muros, castella, Tac. **2.** Transf. **a.** *to induce to come down, draw down :* aliquem ad aequum certamen, Liv. ; ab arce hostem, Liv. **b.**

Of loss of dignity: regum maiestatem ab summo fastigio ad medium, Liv. **II.** *to drag, draw off* or *away, tear off.* **1.** Lit.: soccos, Ter.; vestem, Cic.; anulum de digito, Ter.; stramenta e mulis, Caes. With DAT.: torquem alicui, Cic.; Pl.; Verg., etc.; frenos equis, Liv.; Caes.; Hor. **2.** Transf. **a,** *to force* or *induce to leave* or *come ; to withdraw:* Hannibalem ex Italiā, Liv.; Cic.; ex tortiā acie cohortis, Caes.; Clodium in iudicium, Cic.; aliquem ad accusationem, Cic. **b.** Of opinions, etc.: opinionem alicui, Cic.; Ov. **c.** *to withdraw, diminish, detract from :* tantum de facultate, Cic.; Nep.; honorem debitum ordini, Cic.; Quint.; errorem animis, Ov. Hence, *to disparage ; to* absentibus, Cic. [It. *detrarre.*]

dētrectātiō, ōnis, *f.* [dĕtrectō], *a drawing back from, shirking :* militiae, Liv.

dētrectātor, ōris, *m.* [dĕtrectō], *a disparager :* laudum suarum, Liv.

dē-trectō (or **dētractō**), āre. **I.** *to avoid handling, draw back from, shirk, fight shy of.* **1.** Lit.: iuga, Verg.; aratrum, Ov. **2.** Transf.: militiam, Caes., Liv.; pugnam, certamen, Liv., Tac.; iussa, Tac. *Absol.:* Liv. **II.** *to mishandle* (or *to lower in dignity*) *; disparage, depreciate :* virtutes, Liv.; ingenium Homeri, Ov.; Tac.; aliquem, Sall. With DAT.: Suet. *Absol.:* Ov.

dētrīmentōsus, a, um [dētrīmentum], *hurtful, detrimental :* Caes.

dētrīmentum, ī, *n.* [dēterō], *a rubbing off.* Transf.: *loss, damage, detriment.* **a.** In gen. (opp. emolumentum): inferre, adferre, Caes.; importare, Cic.; accipere, capere, Cic. Esp. in the formula by which unlimited power was conferred on the consuls: videant consules (dent magistratūs operam), ne quid res publica detrimenti capiat, Caes., Cic., Liv. **b.** In war, *loss, defeat :* accipere, Caes.; detrimentum acceptum sarcire, Caes.; reconciliare, Caes.

dētrītus, a, um, *Part.* dēterō.

dē-trūdō, trūdere, trūsī, trūsum, *to thrust* or *push down.* **1.** Lit. **a.** In gen.: aliquem ad molas, Pl.; Verg.; in pistrinum, Cic.; Pl.; Ov.; sub Tartara, Ov.; navis scopulo, Verg. **b.** Milit.: *to dislodge :* Verg., Liv., Tac. **c.** Legal, *to evict :* Cic. **2.** Transf. **a.** With non-personal subject : Vatin. ap. Cic. Ep.; Tac. **b.** *to force* or *induce a person against his will :* aliquem de suā sententiā, Cic. Ep. With *ab :* Suet. With *ex :* Nep.; ad mendicitatem, Pl.; Cic.; Tac. With *in :* Cic. Ep., Tac. **c.** Of time, *to thrust aside* (i.e. *forcibly postpone*) *:* comitia in mensem Martium, Cic. Ep.

dē-truncō, āre, *to lop* or *cut off.* **1.** Lit.: caput, Ov.; arbores, Liv. **2.** Transf.: *to lop away, mutilate :* corpora, Liv.

dētrūsus, a, um, *Part.* dētrūdō.

dē-turbō, āre, *to hustle down, dash down, expel.* **1.** Lit. **a.** In gen.: aliquem in viam, Pl.; Lucr.; Trebonium de tribunali, Caes.; Menoeten in mare puppi ab altā, Verg.; caput terrae, Verg.; statuam, Cic. **b.** Milit. (with *de* or *ex*): Pl., Caes., Cic., etc. **2.** Transf.: verecundiam mi, Pl.;

aliquem de sanitate, Cic.; aliquem possessione, Cic. Ep.

Deucaliōn, ōnis, *m. s. of Prometheus, king of Phthia. He and his wife Pyrrha were the only survivors of a great deluge ;* **Deucaliōnēus,** a, um.

de-ūnx, ūncis, *m.* [ūncia], *eleven twelfths :* heres ex deunce, Cic.; avidi deunces (i.e. *eleven per cent.*), Pers.

de-ūro, ūrere, ūssī, ūstum, *to burn down* or *up, consume.* **1.** Lit.: vicum, Liv.; Caes.; Tac. **2.** Transf. Of cold : *to nip, destroy :* hiems arbores deusserat, Liv.

deus, ī, *m.* [cf. Δῖος, GEN. of Ζεύς, adj. δῖϝος, dīvus, diēs] (No Voc. *sing.* ; Nom. *pl.* dī or dīī; DAT. and ABL. *pl.* ; dīs or diīs; deī and deīs are rarer; GEN. *pl.* deōrum or deum), *a god, a deity.* **1.** Lit. **A.** Prop.: Enn., Cic., etc. Occ. *the deity* or *deity :* Cic., Verg. **B.** Special combinations. **a.** Forms of ejaculation: di, Ter.; dii immortales, Cic.; pro di immortales, Pl.; di magni, Ov.; pro deum atque hominum fidem, Ter.; and ellipt., pro deum immortalium (fidem), Ter. **b.** Forms of wishing (well or ill), greeting, asseveration, etc. : di bene vortant, *the gods grant it good issue!* Pl.; ita di deaeque faxint, *the gods grant it may be so,* Ter.; and in negative sense, di faciant ne etc., Cic.; di meliora velint, Ov.; and ellipt., di meliora, *God forbid!* Cic., Liv.: di te ament (amabunt), as a form of greeting, *God bless you!* Pl.; ita me di ament (amabunt), *so help me God!* Pl.; per deos, *by the gods!* Cic.; dis volentibus, *God willing,* Sall.; di hominesque, *all the world,* Cic. **2.** Transf. Of highly distinguished or fortunate persons : te in dicendo semper putavi deum, Cic., Pl.; Verg., etc. [It. *dio ;* Fr. *dieu.*]

de-ūstus, a, um, *Part.* deūrō.

de-ūtor, ūtī, *to ill-treat.* With ABL.: victo, Nep.

dē-vastō, āre, *to lay waste completely :* finīs, Liv.; agmina, Ov.

dē-vehō, vehere, vexī, vectum. **I.** *to carry* or *convey down :* carinas, Caes.; Verg.; Liv. **II.** *to convey to an appointed place :* eo frumentum, Caes. With *ad :* Liv. With *in :* Pl., Liv. In Mid. : *to travel* (by sea or water), *to sail down* or *to :* Tiberi devectus, Tac.; Veliam devectus, Cic. **III.** *to carry away :* sarmenta, Verg.

dē-vellō, vellere, vellī (volsī, Cat.), vulsum, *to pluck* or *pull off :* aliquid, Pl., Cat., Tac.

dē-vēlō, āre, *to unveil :* ora sororis, Ov.

dē-veneror, ārī. **I.** *to reverence, worship fully:* deos prece, Ov. **II.** *to avert by worship:* somnia, Tib.

dē-veniō, venīre, vēnī, *to come to, go to, arrive at, reach.* **1.** Lit. With *ad :* Pl., Caes. With *in* and Acc. : Pl., Lucr., Caes., Liv. With simple Acc. : Verg.; Numa quo devenit, Hor. **2.** Transf. **a.** ad iuris studium, Cic. **b.** *to happen :* tantum devenisse ad eum mali, Ter.

dē-verberō, āre, *to thrash soundly :* hominem usque ad necem, Ter.

dē-versor, ārī [*freq.* dēvertō], *to lodge* (as a guest) : apud aliquem, Cic.; Liv.; in domo aliquā, Cic.

dēversor, ōris, *m*. [dēvertō], *a guest* : Cic.
dēversōriolum, ĭ, *n*. [*dim*. dēversōrium], *a small lodging* : Cic. Ep.
dēversōrius (dēvōrs-, Pl.), a, um [dēvertō], *fit to lodge in* : taberna, Pl. ; Suet. *Neut*.
dēversōrium, ĭ, as Noun, *an inn or lodging* : Cic., Liv. Transf. : flagitiorum, Cic.
dēverticulum (older **dēvort-**), ĭ, *n*. [dēvertō]. **I.** *a by-road, by-path*. **1.** Lit. : Ter., Cic., Curt. **2.** Transf. : *a digression* : legentibus velut deverticula amoena quaerere, Liv. ; Quint. ; Juv. **II.** *a place for travellers to put up at ; an inn, a lodging*. **1.** Lit. : Ter., Liv., Tac. **2.** Transf. : fraudis, Cic. ; dolis, Pl.
dē-vertō (older **-vortō**), vertere, vertī, versum (Trans. : Luc. Intrans. : Cic., Liv., Tac.) and **dēvertor**, vertī, versus (Pl., Ter. ; rare in Cic., Liv., etc.), *to turn aside ; to turn to ; to put up at, lodge*. **1.** Lit. : apud aliquem, Pl., Liv. ; ad aliquem, Pl., Cic. ; in tabernam, Pl., Cic., Tac. ; Massiliam, Cic., Tac. *Absol.* : Cic. **2.** Transf. : *to have recourse to* : ad magicas artis, Ov. **II.** *to turn aside and leave, digress*. **1.** Lit. : viā, Liv. **2.** Transf. : *to digress* : Cic. Ep., Liv.
dēvexus, a, um [dēveho], *moving downwards, inclining downwards, sloping, shelving, steep*. **1.** Lit. **a.** Of stars : Cic., Hor. **b.** Of places : Caes., Cic., Verg., Ov. **2.** Transf. : aetas iam a diuturnis laboribus devexa ad otium, Cic. Ep. ; aetas, Sen. Ep.
dē-vinciō, vincīre, vīnxī, vīnctum (*Perf. sync.* dēvīnxtī, Pl.), *to bind fast, tie up*. **1.** Lit. : servom, Pl. ; aliquem fasciis, Cic. ; Liv. ; Dircam ad taurum, Pl. **2.** Transf. : se vino, Pl. ; Sen. Ep. ; membra sopore, Lucr. ; beneficio devinctus, Caes., Cic., etc. ; caritate, Cic. ; suos praemiis, Caes. ; aliquem omni cautione, foedere, Cic. ; animos centurionum pignore, Caes. ; se cum aliquo adfinitate, Cic.
dē-vincō, vincere, vīcī, victum, *to conquer entirely, overcome, subdue*. **1.** Lit. Of cities or countries : Caes., Cic. Of persons : Cic. Of things : Ov. ; devicta bella, Verg. **2.** Transf. : bonum publicum privatā gratiā devictum, Sall. ; Pl.
dēvinctus, a, um. **I.** *Part.* dēvinciō. **II.** Adj. : *strongly attached, devoted to*. With DAT. : Cic., Tac. *Comp.* : Hor.
dēvītātiō, ōnis, *f*. [dēvītō], *an avoiding* : Cic.
dē-vītō, āre, *to avoid, shun* : procellam temporis, Cic. ; Pl. ; Hor., etc.
dē-vius, a, um [via], *lying off the high-road, out of the way, devious*. **1.** Lit. : iter, *a by-way*, Cic. Ep. ; oppidum, Cic. ; saltus, Liv. ; rura, Ov. *Neut.* as Noun : per devia, Suet. **2.** Transf. **a.** Of living beings : *living apart, solitary, retired, sequestered* : Cic., Hor., Liv. ; avis, *the owl* (from its lonely habits), Ov. **b.** *erroneous, inconsistent*. Of persons : Cic., Ov. Of speech : Plin. Ep.
dē-vocō, āre, *to call down, off or away ; to call, to fetch by calling*. **1.** Lit. : aliquem de provinciā ad gloriam, Cic. ; suos ab tumulo, Liv. ; ex praesidiis, Liv. ; sidera caelo, Hor. **2.** Transf. : aliquem ab

instituto cursu ad praedam, Cic. ; suas fortunas in dubium, i.e. *to imperil*, Caes.
dē-volō, āre, *to fly down*. **1.** Lit. : Pl., Verg., Liv., etc. **2.** Transf. : ad florentem amicitiam, Cic. ; de tribunali, Liv. ; in forum, Liv. ; Lucr.
dē-volvō, volvere, volvī, volūtum, *to roll down*. **1.** Lit. **a.** saxa in musculum, Caes. ; Ov. ; clipeos e muris, Curt. ; Cat. ; auratas trabis, Verg. ; fusis mollia pensa, *to spin off*, Verg. **b.** Mid. *to roll down, to fall headlong* : Liv., Curt. **2.** Transf. **a.** aliquem vitā suā, Pl. ; per audacis nova dithyrambos verba devolvit (like a torrent), Hor. **b.** Mid. : *to sink down, fall back upon* : ad spem inanem pacis, Cic. ; Liv.
dē-vorō, āre, *to swallow or gulp down, to devour*. **1.** Lit. : aliquid, Cat., Cic. **2.** Transf. **a.** *to engulf, swallow up* (as the sea, earthquakes, etc.) : Ov., Plin. **b.** *to seize greedily, take to oneself* : lucrum, Cic. ; Pl. **c.** *to swallow* (i.e. only half utter) : verba, Sen., Quint. **d.** *to consume, waste, squander* : pecuniam publicam, Cic. ; Quint. **e.** *to repress* : lacrimas, Ov. ; Sen. Ep. Hence, *to bear with patience* : homĭnum ineptias, Cic. ; Quint.
dēvors-, **dēvort-**, *v*. dēvers-, dēvert-.
dēvortia, ōrum, *n. pl.* [dēvertō], *by-ways* : itinerum, Tac.
dēvōtiō, ōnis, *f*. [dēvoveō]. **I.** *a devoting, consecrating* : Deciorum devotiones, Cic. **II.** *a cursing, execration* : Nep. **III.** *sorcery, enchantment ; concr. an incantation, spell* : Tac., Suet.
dēvōtō, āre [*freq.* dēvoveō], *to enchant, bewitch* : sortis, Pl.
dēvōtus, a, um. **I.** *Part.* dēvoveō. **II.** Adj. **a.** *devoted, attached*. With DAT. : Juv. With *in* and Acc. : Luc. *Sup.* : Suet. *Masc.* as Noun : Caes. **b.** *devoted to destruction, accursed* : arbos, Hor.
dē-voveō, vovēre, vōvī, vōtum, *to vow, dedicate conditionally to a deity*. **1.** Lit. : aliquid Marti, Caes. ; Cic. ; Hor. Esp. se dis or simply se, *to devote oneself to death* : Enn., Cic., Liv., Verg. ; devotis corporibus, Liv. ; Hor. **2.** Transf. **a.** *to devote, give up* : vobis animam hanc, Verg. ; se amicitiae alicuius, Caes. ; Curt. **b.** *to devote to the infernal gods* : hence, *to curse, to execrate* : aliquem, Nep., Ov., Quint. ; arma, Ov. **c.** *to bewitch* : Tib., Ov.
dēvulsus, a, um, *Part.* dēvellō.
dextāns, antis, *m*. [de, sextāns : lit. *less one-sixth*], *five-sixths* : Suet.
dextella, ae, *f*. [*dim*. dextra], *a little right hand* : Quintus filius, ut scribis, Antoni est dextella, Cic. Ep.
dexter, tera, terum, and tra, trum, *to or on the right side, right*. **1.** Lit. : manus, Pl., Cic. ; umerus, Caes. ; latus, Hor. ; cornu, Ter., Caes., Liv. ; ala, Liv. In Adv. sense, dexter abis, Verg. *Comp.* dexterior : Varr., Ov., Suet. *Sup.* dextimus : Sall. **2.** Transf. **a.** *handy, dexterous, adroit* : rem dexter egit, Liv. **b.** *lucky, favourable, propitious* (acc. to the Gk. interpretation of omens on the right) : Cat., Verg., Quint., etc. **c.** *opportune, right* : rebus dexter modus, Verg. ; tempus, Hor. As Noun, **dextera** or **dextra**, ae, *f*. (*sc.* manus), *the*

right hand. **1.** ´Lit.: Pl., Cic., Verg., etc. **Phr.**: ad dexteram specta, Pl.; Caes.; Cic.; a dextrā laevāque, Ov.; Pl.; Cic.; dextrā, Caes.; Pl.; Liv. **2.** Transf. **a.** *a solemn pledge:* tendere, Cic.; dare, Nep.; fallere, Verg., Liv.; renovare, Tac. **b.** *the hand:* Hor. [It. *destra*.] Hence, **ABL.**, *f.* as *prep.* (with Acc.), **dexterā** and **dextrā**, *to the right of:* Sall., Liv.

dexterē and **dextrē**, *adv. adroitly, skilfully:* Liv. *Comp.:* dexterius, Hor.

dexteritās, ātis, *f.* [dexter], *adroitness, readiness:* Liv.

dextrōrsum (Hor.) or **dextrōrsus** (Liv.), and uncontracted, **dextrōvorsum** (Pl.), *adv. towards the right side, to the right.*

(1) **di**, *inseparable prefix: v.* dis.

(2) **di**, *v.* deus.

Dia, ae, *f.* **I.** *old name of Naxos.* **II.** *m. of Mercury.*

diabathrārius, i, *m.* [διάβαθρα], *a maker of slippers or shoes:* Pl.

diadēma, atis, *n.* [διάδημα], *a royal head-band:* Cic., Hor., etc.

diaeta, ae, *f.* [δίαιτα]. **I.** *a mode of living prescribed by a physician, diet:* Cic. Ep. **II.** *a chamber, living-room:* Plin. Ep., Suet.

dialecticē, *adv. logically:* Cic.

dialecticus, a, um [διαλεκτικός], *of dis-putation, dialectical:* Cic., Quint. *Nouns:* **dialecticus**, i, *m. a dialectician, logician:* Cic., Quint.; **dialectica**, ae, *f.* (Cic.), and **dialecticē**, ēs, *f.* (Quint.) *sc.* ars, *dialectic, logic:* **dialecta**, ōrum, *n. pl. logical ques-tions, dialectics:* Cic.

dialectos, i, *f.* [διάλεκτος], *a manner of speaking, a dialect:* Suet.

diālis, e, *adj.* [*cf.* Iuppiter, diēs], *of Jupiter:* flamen dialis (the most distinguished of the flamines): Liv.; also called sacerdos, Suet.; and *absol.* Dialis, Tac.; coniux sancta Dialis, Ov.; diale flaminium, Suet.; apex dialis, Liv.

dialogus, i, *m.* [διάλογος], *a conversation, a dialogue:* Cic.

Diāna (older **Diāna**), ae, *f. an ancient Italian deity, identified with Greek Artemis, sister of Apollo; the virgin moon-goddess* (Luna), *patroness of virginity; presiding over child-birth* (Lucina), *the chase, and nocturnal in-cantations* (v. Hecate). Transf.: *the moon:* Ov.; **Diānius**, a, um; **Diānium**, i, n. **I.** *an enclosure sacred to Diana.* **II.** *a promontory in Spain, now Denia.*

diāria, ōrum, *n. pl.* [diēs], *a daily allowance of food, or pay:* Cic. Ep.; Hor.

dibaphus, a, um [δίβαφος]; *twice dyed* (viz. with scarlet and purple): Plin. As Noun, **dibaphus**, i, *f. a State-robe with purple stripe* (worn by Roman magistrates): Cic. Ep.

dica, ae, *f.* [δίκη], *a lawsuit, judicial process in a Greek court:* ua. in phr., dicam scribere (alicui), *to bring an action against any one* (= Gk. δίκην γράφεσθαι): Pl., Ter., Cic.; supscribere, Pl.; impingere, Ter.; e lege Rupiliā sortiri dicas, i.e. *to select the jury by lot,* Cic.

dicācitās, ātis, *f.* [dicāx], *witty repartee, pungent wit, banter:* Cic., Quint.

dicāculus, a, um [*dim.* dicāx], *ready with an answer:* Pl.

Dicaearchus, i, *m. a famous philosopher and geographer, pupil of Aristotle.*

dicātiō, ōnis, *f.* [dicō], *a declaration of inten-tion to become a citizen of* a State: Cic.

dicāx, ācis, *adj.* [root of dicō, q.v.], *ready or sharp in speech; witty, sharp-tongued, satirical:* Pl., Cic., Hor. *Comp.:* Cic., Liv.

dichorēus, i, *m.* [διχόρειος], *a double trochee:* Cic.

diciō, ōnis, *f.* (only in Acc., Gen., Dat., Abl. *sing.*) [root of dicō, *cf.* regiō fr. regō]. *control, dominion, sovereignty, power.* **1.** Lit.: Acc.: dedunt se in dicionem populo, Pl.; civitatem in dicionem populi Romani redigere, Caes., Cic., Liv.; aliquem sub dicionem p. R. subiungere, Cic.; in dicionem venire (or cadere, Cic.), Liv. Gen.: suae dicionis agrum facere, *to make oneself master of,* Liv.; Curt. Dat.: gentem dicioni nostrae subicere, Tac. Abl.: in dicione alicuius esse, Cic., Liv.; sub ali-cuius dicione esse, Caes., Ov.; dicione tenere, Verg.; in dicione alicuius teneri, Caes. **2.** Transf.: auris meas dedo in dicionem tuam, Pl.; aliquem in suā potestate ac dicione tenere, Cic.

dicis causā or **grātiā** [root of dicō], orig. legal, meaning " for the sake of judicial form "; hence, in gen., *for form's sake, for the sake of appearance:* Cic.

dicō, āre [root of dicō]. **I.** Relig., *to dedicate, consecrate, devote* (*cf.* dedico): aram, Liv.; Cic.; Ov., etc. Occ. **a.** With personal object: *to deify* (*cf.* dedico): inter numina dicatus Augustus, Tac. **b.** *to consecrate by its first use, to inaugurate:* nova signa, Tac. **II.** In gen.: *to set apart, dedicate, devote:* aurium operam tibi, Pl.; hunc totum diem tibi, Cic.; tuum studium meae laudi, Cic.; Verg.; se Remis in clientelam, Caes.; se alii civitati, *or* in aliam civitatem, Cic.

dicō, dīcere, dīxī, dictum [older deicō, deicere, deixi, dictum, *cf.* δείκνυμι] (*Perf. sync.* dīxtī, Cic.; old *Fut.* dīxō, Pl.; *Aor. Opt.* dīxim, Pl.). **I.** *to show, indicate, point out.* **A.** *to appoint, fix.* **a.** Legal: diem (day *for trial*) alicui, Cic.; multam, Cic.; iudi-cem, Liv.; fugam, Ov. **b.** In gen.: diem operi, Cic., Caes., Ter.; pecuniam doti, Cic.; Hor.; Ov.; Liv.; diem ad conveniendum, Liv. **B.** *to nominate, ap-point:* dictatorem, Cic., Liv.; dictatorem T. Manlium, Liv.; arbitrum bibendi, Hor. **II.** *to indicate by words; to say, tell, speak, declare, specify.* **A.** In gen. **a.** Without object: ut ante dixi, Cic.; de aliquā re, pro aliquo, contra aliquem, Cic.; dixi (at end of speech), Cic. Also *Pass.* ut dictum est, Caes., Cic., etc. **b.** With object. **i.** *to say* (the exact words): crudelem, ne dicam 'sceleratum,' Cic.; fortasse dices 'quid ergo ?' Cic.; or with *Pron.*, etc.: haec cum dixisset, Cic., etc.; orationem versūs, *to speak, deliver, recite,* Cic.; Hor.; Liv., etc. **ii.** With person or thing as object, *to indicate, specify, mention:* quos supra dixi, Caes., Cic., etc. Also *to set forth, express in words:* sententiam, Caes.; quod sentio, Cic.; causam, Caes., Cic., Liv.; ius, Caes., Cic. **Phr.** dictum (ac) factum, *no sooner said than done,* Ter.; *cf.* dicto

citius, Verg., Hor., Liv. **iii.** With clause as
object : *to say, assert, declare.* With Acc.
and *Inf. :* Cic., etc. With *Indir. Quest. :*
Cic., etc. In *Pass. :* dicitur Aristaeus
olivae inventor esse, Cic. ; dicar princeps
Aeolium carmen ad Italos deduxisse modos,
Hor. ; *Impers.* (us. when there is a reference to a previous statement or current
saying), with Acc. and *Inf. :* Caes., Cic.,
etc. **B.** In partic. **a.** *to tell of* (in verse) :
Dianae laudes, Hor. ; bella, Hor. ; Tac.
b. *to call, name :* Chaoniam a Chaone,
Verg. ; Quint. ; amens dicitur, Hor. **c.**
to tell, warn. With DAT. and *ne* with *Subj. :*
Pl., Ter., Nep., Ov. **d.** *to pronounce,
articulate :* Cic., Quint. **e.** *to mean* (by
one's words) : Platonem videlicet dicis,
Cic. ; Pl. [It. *dire ;* Fr. *dire.*]

dicrotum, i, *n., sc.* navigium (Cic. Ep.) and
dicrota, ae, *f. sc.* navis (Auct. B. Alex.)
[δίκροτος], *a galley with two banks of oars.*

dictamnus, i, *f. the plant dittany,* which grew
in great abundance on Mt. Dicte and Mt.
Ida : Cic., Verg.

dictāta, ōrum, *n. pl.* [dictō], *things dictated,
lessons, rules :* Cic., Hor. For gladiators :
Suet. For actors : Juv.

dictātor, ōris, *m.* [dictō], *a dictator.* **a.** an
extraordinary magistrate at Rome, elected
in times of emergency, and armed with
absolute authority ; formerly called Magister populi, and also Praetor Maximus : Cic.,
Liv. **b.** *the chief magistrate of other cities
of Italy :* Cic., Liv.

dictātōrius, a, um [dictātor], *of a dictator,
dictatorial :* gladius, Cic. ; maiestas, Liv. ;
invidia, Liv.

dictātrix, īcis, *f.* [dictō], *a mistress* (of the
feast) : Pl.

dictātūra, ae, *f.* [dictō], *the office of a dictator,
dictatorship :* Caes., Cic., Liv.

Dictē, ēs, *f. a mountain in E. Crete, where
Jupiter was reared ;* **Dictaeus,** a, um,
Dictaean or *Cretan.*

dictiō, ōnis, *f.* [dīcō]. **I.** *a setting forth in
words, stating, declaring :* iuris, Cic., Liv. ;
sententiae, Cic. ; testimoni, Ter. ; causae,
Caes., Cic., Liv. **II.** Rhet. **a.** *speaking,
oratory :* Cic. **b.** *style in speaking :* Cic.
c. *expression, diction :* Quint. **d.** Concr.
speech, utterance : Cic., Quint. **III.** *a
warning* (by an oracle) : Liv. **IV.** *conversation, discussion :* Tac.

dictitō, āre [*freq.* dictō]. **I.** *to say often* or
emphatically ; to declare, assert repeatedly.
With Acc. and *Inf. :* Ter., Caes., Cic., etc.
Absol. : ut dictitabat, Caes. *Pass. Impers. :* Pl. **II.** Legal : causas, *to plead
frequently :* Cic.

dictō, āre [*freq.* dīcō]. **I.** *to say often ; to
tell repeatedly :* Cic. ; mercemur servum qui
dictet nomina, Hor. **II. a.** *to dictate for
writing :* with DAT. of person : Tironi, Cic.
Ep. ; Hor. ; Quint. Of the dictating of
teachers : memini quae mihi parvo Or-
bilium dictare, Hor. **b.** (From the practice of dictating to *amanuenses*) *to put in
writing* (by dictation) : carmina, Hor. ;
non unus tibi rivalis dictabitur heros, Juv. ;
codicillos, Suet.

dictū, ABL. *sing. m.* [dīcō], *in the telling :*
mirabile dictu, Verg. ; Cic.

dictus, a, um. **I.** *Part.* dīcō. **II.** Noun,
dictum, i, *n. something said ; a saying, a
word.* **A.** In gen. (oft. opp. factum) : Cic.,
Verg., etc. ; dicta dicere, Pl., Lucr. Used
both with *adj.* and with *adv. : ridiculum,*
Pl. ; Cic. ; etc. ; breviter, commode dicta,
Pl., Cic., etc. **B.** In partic. **a.** *a saying,
maxim, proverb :* aurea dicta, Lucr. ;
Catonis est dictum, Cic. **b.** *a witty saying,
bon-mot :* haec (dicta) bona, Cic. ; Hor. ;
Liv. **c.** In *pl. : poetical diction, verse :*
rerum naturam expandere dictis, Lucr. ;
Prop. **d.** *a prediction, prophecy,* Lucr. ;
Verg. **e.** *an order, command :* dicta dare,
Liv. ; dicto parere, Verg., Ov., Liv. ; dicto
audientem esse, Pl., Cic., Liv. [Sp.
dicho.]

Dictynna, ae, *f. a name of* **I.** *Britomartis.*
II. *Diana ;* **Dictynnāeum,** i, *n. a place
sacred to Dictynna, near Sparta.*

Didius, a, *name of a Roman plebeian gens ;*
esp. D. Iulianus, Roman emperor, A.D. 193.

di-dō (or **disdō**), dere, didī, ditum, *to put
asunder ; distribute, disseminate.* **1.** Lit. :
argentum, Cato ; in venas cibum, Lucr.
2. Transf. : dum munia didit (*sc.* servis),
Hor. ; tua terris didita fama, Verg. ;
Lucr. ; Tac.

Dīdō, ūs (Acc. Dīdō, Verg.), *f. the foundress of
Carthage, called also Elisa or Elissa.*

di-dūcō, dūcere, dūxī, ductum, *to lead* or
draw apart ; to separate. **1.** Lit. **a.** digitos (opp. comprimere), Cic. ; rictum risu,
Hor. ; diductis terris hauriebantur (of an
earthquake), Tac. ; Verg. ; Ov. **b.** Milit.
to divide, distribute, disperse : copias, Caes. ;
navis, Caes. ; cornua, Liv. ; aciem in
cornua, Liv. ; hostem, Tac. Poet. :
choros, Verg. **2.** Transf. : cum didu-
caris ab eo, quicum libentissime vixeris,
Cic. ; diductam civitatem ut civili bello,
in studia senatum, Tac. ; assem in partis
centum, Hor.

diēcula, ae, *f.* [*dim.* diēs], *one little day, a
little while :* Ter., Cic. Ep.

di-ērēctus, a, um (only in Pl. and Varro, as
an abusive expression, equiv. to the English,
go and be hanged /). **1.** Lit. Of persons :
i hinc dierectus, Pl. ; also in Voc. : abi
dierecte, Pl. **2.** Transf. Of things :
ducit lembum dierectum navis praedatoria,
Pl.

diēs, ēī (old NOM. dius ; old LOCAT. diūs, Pl. ;
old GEN. and DAT. diē ; GEN. diī, Verg.),
m. (*f.* in sense 2. A. a.) [*cf.* Iuppiter, deus,
Διός, GEN. of Ζεύς]. **1.** Lit. **a.** *daylight :* iam dies caelo concesserat, Verg. ;
Ov. ; Plin. **b.** *a natural day, a day* as
opp. to night : Pl. ; die, *in the daytime,*
Cic. ; also *in a day,* Verg. ; diem noctemque, i.e. *without ceasing,* Caes. ; Verg. ; diem
ac noctem, Liv. ; and in *pl. :* Ter., Cic. ;
de die, *by day, in the daytime,* Suet. ; longo
die, *throughout the long day,* Hor. ; diem
totum, Hor. **c.** *the civil day* of twenty-
four hours : paucos dies ibi morati, Caes. ;
dies continuos xxx. sub brumā esse noctem,
Caes. *Fem.* occ. in sense 2. A. a. ; once
in Sall. Phr. : postridie eius diei, *on the
day after that day,* Caes. ; post diem tertium
eius diei, *the next day but one,* Cic. ; diem
ex die, *from day to day,* Caes., Liv. ; in dies,

day by day, *daily* (esp. with words denoting increase or decrease), Pl., Caes., Cic., Liv. ; in diem vivere, *to live for the day*, Cic. **2.** Transf. **A.** *a set day, date.* **a.** *a set day, appointed time*, (us. *fem.*)*; date* (for appearing before court, making a payment, *etc.*) : dies conloquio dictus est ex eo die quintus, Caes. ; dicta, Cic. ; edicta ad conveniendum, Liv. ; in diem differre, Liv. ; pacta et constituta, Cic. ; Caes. ; caecā die emere, occultā vendere, i.e. to buy on credit and sell for cash, Pl. **b.** *an anniversary :* dies Alliensis, Liv. ; dies natalis urbis, Cic. Without natalis : diem meum scis esse III. Non. Ian., Cic. **c.** = dies mortis, *last day :* quandocumque fatalis et meus dies veniet, Tac. ; supremus dies vitae, Cic. ; diem suum obire, *to die,* Sulpic. ap. Cic. Ep. ; obire diem supremum, Nep. ; obire diem, Nep., Suet. **B.** *a day* with especial ref. to what is done in it. **a.** is dies honestissimus nobis fuerat, Cic. ; hic dies et Romanis refecit animos et Persea perculit, Liv. ; diem exercere, Verg. **b.** *a day's journey :* hanc regionem, dierum plus triginta in longitudinem patentem, Liv. **c.** Of a man's mood or temper on any day : qualem diem Tiberius induisset, Tac. **C.** In gen.: *time, space of time, period :* te ipsum dies leniet, Cic. ; iram nec longa dies pietas nec mitigat ulla, Verg. ; Ov. ; Pl. ; Ter.

Diēspiter, tris, *m.* [diēs and pater ; *v.* Iuppiter.]

dif-fāmō, āre [fāma], *to spread by evil report, to defame :* Ov., Tac.

differentia, ae, *f.* [differō], *a difference, diversity.* **a.** In gen. : with GEN.: honesti et decori, Cic. ; Quint. With *in :* quanta differentia est in principiis naturalibus, Cic. In *pl. :* Quint. **b.** *specific difference* (in logic), *species :* Cic.

differitās, ātis, *f.* [differō] = differentia, *a difference :* Lucr.

dif-ferō, differre, distulī, dīlātum. **A.** Trans. : *to bear* or *carry apart, different ways ; to spread, scatter, disperse.* **1.** Lit. : favillam, Lucr. ; nubila, Lucr., Verg. ; ignem, Caes. ; Pl. ; Hor. **2.** Transf. **a.** *to distract, disquiet, disturb :* miser exanimor, differor, distrahor, Pl. **b.** *to spread abroad, publish, divulge :* with Acc. of thing : commissam libertatem populo Rom. sermonibus, Liv. With Acc. and *Inf. :* no mi hanc famam differant, me dedidisse, Pl. ; Nep. *Impers. Pass. :* differtur per manipulos, Tac. With Acc. of the person : *to defame :* dominos variis rumoribus, Tac. ; Prop. **c.** With ref. to time : *to defer, put off, delay :* horam, Cic. ; tempus, Cic. ; Liv. ; Ov. ; concilium, Verg. ; gaudia, Ov. ; iter in praesentia, Caes. ; reliqua in crastinum, Cic. Rarely with *ad :* Cic. With *Inf. :* Hor., Liv. With *quin* and *Subj. :* Liv. **d.** With Acc. of person : *to put off, amuse with promises, get rid of :* aliquem in tempus aliud, Cic. ; Liv. ; Verg. ; legati ad novos magistratūs dilati, Liv. **B.** Intrans. : *to differ, be different, be distinguished from* (no *Perf.* or *Supine* in this sense) : qui re consentientes vocabulis differebant, Cic. ; in aliquā re, Lucr., Nep. With *ab : multum a Gallicā*

consuetudine, Caes. ; Pl. ; Cic. With *inter se :* hi omnes legibus differunt, Caes. ; Cic. ; Quint. With *cum :* occasio cum tempore differt, Cic. With DAT. : nisi quod pede certo differt sermoni, Hor. ; Quint. As *Impers.* verb. : Cic. Hor.

dif-fertus, a, um [dis-farciō], *stuffed out, crammed.* **1.** Lit. : corpus odoribus, Tac. **2.** Transf. : provincia exactoribus, Caes. ; Hor.

dif-ficilis, e, *adj.* (Comp. difficilior, Caes. ; *Sup.* difficillimus, Caes., Cic., etc. [dis facilis] *not easy, hard to do, difficult, troublesome.* **1.** Lit. Of things. **a.** In gen. : Pl. ; iter, Caes. ; Cic. ; Hor. ; tempus anni. Caes. ; Cic. ; difficile est ad fidem, Liv. ; ad perdocendum, Cic. ; difficile factu, dictu, Cic. ; *Neut.* as Noun : in difficili esse, Liv. **b.** Of lie of land : loci, Sall. ; valles, Caes. **2.** Transf. Of character : *hard to manage* or *to please ; intractable, harsh, surly :* Ter., Cic., Ov., etc. ; terrae, Verg. *Neut.* Acc. **difficile** as Adv., *with difficulty :* Suet.

difficiliter, adv. *with difficulty :* Cic. *Comp.:* difficilius, Caes., Quint. *Sup.* difficillimō, Cic.

difficultās, ātis, *f.* [difficilis, *cf.* facultās], *difficulty, embarrassment, trouble.* **1.** Lit. Of things. **a.** res erat in magnis difficultatibus, Caes. ; res habet difficultatem, Cic. ; magnam res ad receptum difficultatem adferebat, Caes. With GEN. : belli gerendi, Caes. ; Cic. ; Tac. **b.** *embarrassment* (due to scarcity) : nummaria, domestica, Cic. With GEN. : Caes., Suet. **2.** Transf. of character : *intractability, surliness :* Cic.

difficulter, adv. *I.* *with difficulty :* Caes., Liv., Tac., etc. *II.* *grudgingly :* Liv.

diffīdēns, entis. *I.* *Part.* diffīdō. *II.* Adj.: *diffident, anxious :* Suet.

diffīdenter, adv. *without self-confidence, diffidently :* Cic., Liv.

diffīdentia, ae, *f.* [diffīdō], *want of confidence ; mistrust, diffidence* (opp. fidentia) : Cic., Ov., Quint. With *Obj.* GEN. : Sall., Plin. Ep., Tac.

dif-fīdō, fīdere, fīsus sum, *to be distrustful, to distrust, despair :* Pl., Cic. With DAT. (of person or thing) : Caes., Cic., Ov., etc. *Pass. Impers. :* Liv., Tac. With Acc. and *Inf. :* Caes., Cic., Liv., etc. With *Inf. :* Cato, Nep. With *ne* and *Subj. :* Lucr. With ABL. : Tac., Suet.

dif-findō, findere, fidī, fissum, *to cleave asunder, to split.* **1.** Lit. : malos, Enn. ; terram, Lucr. ; saxum, Cic. ; Hor. ; Verg. **2.** Transf. **a.** urbium portas muneribus, Hor. **b.** Legal : diem diffindere, *to break off the day's business :* Liv. Hence, diem somno, Varr.

dif-fingō, ere, *to form differently, to remodel, reshape.* **1.** Lit. : ferrum, Hor. **2.** Transf. : neque diffinget infectumque reddet, Hor.

diffissus, a, um, *Part.* diffindō.

diffīsus, a, um, *Part.* diffīdō.

dif-fiteor, ērī [fateor], *to disavow, to deny :* Planc. ap. Cic. Ep., Ov. With Acc. and *Inf. :* Quint.

dif-flō, āre, *to blow apart, disperse by blowing :* legiones spiritu, Pl.

dif-fluŏ, ere, *to flow in different directions*.
1. Lit.: Lucr., Caes., Cic. Occ. of a person, *to stream, drip all over* : sudore diffluentes, Phaedr.; Plin. **2.** Transf.: *to melt away, dissolve*. **a.** Physically: privata cibo natura animantum diffluit, Lucr. **b.** Morally: luxuriā, Ter., Cic.; otio, luxu, Cic. **c.** Rhet. (*Pres. Part*) = *not periodic* : Cic.

diffrāctus, a, um, *Part.* diffringō.

dif-fringō, fringere, frāctum [frangō], *to break asunder, to shatter* : crura, Pl.; axe diffracto, Suet.

dif-fŭgiŏ, fugere, fŭgī, *to flee apart* or *in different directions, to disperse*. **1.** Lit.: Lucr., Cic., Verg., etc. With *in* and Acc.: Lucr., Liv. With *ad* : Hirt., Verg. **2.** Transf.: stellae, Ov.; nives, Hor.; sollicitudines, Hor.

diffŭgium, ī, *n.* [diffŭgiŏ], *a fleeing in different directions* ; *a dispersion* ; in *pl.* : Tac.

diffundĭtŏ, āre [*freq.* diffundō], *to pour out, scatter*. Transf.: Pl.

dif-fundŏ, fundere, fŭdī, fŭsum, *to pour in different directions*. **1.** Lit.: undam, Cat.; Ov.; sanguis per venas in omne corpus, Cic.; vina diffusa (in amphoras), Hor.; Ov. **2.** Transf. **a.** Of light, scents, etc., *to spread, diffuse* : Lucr., Cic., Verg. **b.** Of solids: rami late diffunduntur, Caes.; comam, Verg., Ov.; equitem, Verg. **c.** Of abstract things: error longe lateque diffusus, Cic.; laudem alicuius, Cic.; bella longum in aevum, Hor.; Verg., etc. **d.** *to expand, unbend* (*cf.* dissolvere, solvere, remittere, *etc.*) ; *to cheer up, gladden* : vultum, animos, Ov.; Sen. Ep.; ut ex bonis amici quasi diffundantur, Cic.

diffŭsē, *adv. diffusely, expansively, amply* : res dicere, Cic.; *Comp.* : Cic.

diffŭsilis, e, *adj.* [diffundō], *expanding, diffusive* : aether, Lucr.

diffŭsus, a, um. I. *Part.* diffundō. II. Adj.: *spread abroad, spread out, extended, wide*. **1.** Lit.: platanus patulis diffusa ramis, Cic. *Comp.* : Plin. Ep. **2.** Transf.: ius civile, i.e. *loose, not systematised*, Cic.; opus, Plin. Ep.

diffŭtūtus, a, um [futuŏ], *exhausted by promiscuous sexual union* : Cat.

Digentia, ae, *f. a small stream that ran through Horace's Sabine farm, now Licenza*.

di-gerŏ, gerere, gessī, gestum, *to carry apart, spread about, distribute*. **1.** Lit. **a.** In gen.: inque canis totidem trunco digestus ab uno Cerberus, Ov.; Nilus septem in cornua, Ov.; Plin. Ep. **b.** Of orderly distribution : tabulas, Cic.; arborem per agros, Verg.; capillos, Ov. Hence, of the body, *to digest* : Sen. **2.** Transf. **a.** In gen.: poenam in omnis, Ov.; mala per annos, Ov. **b.** Of orderly distribution : *to catalogue, assort* : Cic., Verg., Liv., etc. With *Indir. Quest.* : Cic., Liv.

digestiŏ, ōnis, *f.* [dīgerŏ], *an (orderly) arrangement*. Rhet. = μερισμός, *enumeration of parts* : Cic., Quint.

digestus, a, um, *Part.* dīgerŏ.

digĭtŭlus, ī, *m.* [*dim.* digitus], *a little finger*, i.e. *mere touch of a finger* : Pl., Ter., Cic.

digĭtus, ī, *m.* I. *a finger*. **1.** Lit.: Pl., Cic., Ov., etc.; digitus pollex, *the thumb* ; index

or salutaris, *the forefinger* ; medius (infamis), *the middle finger* ; minimo proximus or medicinalis, *the ring-finger* ; minimus, *the little finger*. Phr.: attingere digito (uno), *to touch lightly, gently*, Pl., Ter., Cic.; attingere extremis digitis (us. with a neg.), *with the tips of the fingers*, Cic.; attingere caelum digito, *to attain the height of felicity*, Cic. Ep.; concrepare digitos or digitis, *to snap the fingers* (as a signal), Pl., Cic.; liceri digito, *to bid with the finger* (at an auction), Cic.; monstrari digito, *to be pointed out*, Hor.; with demonstrari, Cic., Tac.; porrigere digitum, *to stretch out a finger, to give oneself ever so little trouble*, Cic. **2.** Transf. As a measure of length : *an inch*, the sixteenth part of a Roman foot (pes) : Caes. Prov.: digitum (transversum) non discedere ab aliquā re, *not to swerve a finger's breadth from*, Cic. II. *a toe* (*cf.* Gk. δάκτυλος, Fr. doigt): Lucr., Verg., Quint. [It. *dito* ; Fr. *doigt*.]

digladior, ārī [gladius], *to flourish a sword wildly*. **1.** Lit.: inter se sicis, Cic. **2.** Transf.: de quibus inter se (philosophi) digladiari solent, Cic.

dignātiŏ, ōnis, *f.* [dignor]. **1.** Lit.: *a thinking worthy, esteem, respect* : Suet. **2.** Transf.: *dignity, honour* (for dignitas) : Liv., Tac., Suet.

dignē, *adv. worthily, fitly, becomingly* : Pl., Cic., Hor. *Comp.* : Hor.

dignĭtās, ātis, *f.* [dignus], *worthiness, worth, merit*. **1.** Lit.: Cic., Nep. **2.** Transf. **a.** *dignity* of appearance, bearing, etc.: formae, Cic.; corporis, Nep.; ludos cum dignitate facere, Cic. **b.** *moral dignity, honour, esteem* : retinere in rebus asperis dignitatem, Cic.; cum dignitate otium, Cic.; Liv.; Tac. **c.** *dignity, rank, position* (due to office, age, etc.) : Caes., Cic., Liv., etc. **d.** *official dignity* (i.e. of public office) : Cic. Ep., Quint. **e.** *men of position, officials* (in *pl.*) : Liv., Quint. **f.** Of things, *dignity of appearance* : domūs, Cic.; urbis, Nep., g. Rhet. *dignity of style* : verborum, Cic.; Quint.; Tac.

dignŏ, āre (for dignor) : *to think worthy* : res consimili laude dignantur, Cic.; Verg. With *Inf.* : Acc., Lucr.

dignor, ārī [dignus], *to think worthy*, or *deserving* ; with Acc. and ABL.: haud equidem tali me dignor honore, Verg.; Ov.; Tac. With double Acc. : regem nostrum filium, Curt.; Ov. With *Inf.* as Obj., *to deign* : Lucr., Verg., Curt., etc. [Fr. *daigner*.]

di-gnōscŏ (later **dĭnōscŏ**), ere, *to distinguish, discern, know the difference*. With Acc. and ABL.: civem dignoscere hoste, Hor. With Acc. only, or with ABL. *Instr.* : dominum ac servum, Tac.; vocem auribus, Quint. Absol. : inter se similes, vix ut dignoscere possis, Ov.; Suet.

dignus, a, um [*cf.* decet]. I. Of things, *fit, adequate, suitable, deserved* : supplicium, Cic.; praemia, Verg.; causa, Liv.; Pl.; Hor., etc.; dignum est, *it is fit, proper* : Pl., Cic., Verg., etc. II. Of persons, *worthy, deserving* : Pl., Cic., Verg., etc. With ABL. *Instr. Assoc.* : *worthy of* : Pl., Cic., Verg., etc. With ABL.: dignum

dictu, Liv.; Sen. Ep.; Tac. With GEN.:
Pl., Cic. Ep., Ov. With *ad*: Pl., Cic.
With *pro* and ABL.: Cic., Sall., Hor. With
relat. and *Subj.*: Pl., Cic., Quint. With
ut and *Subj.*: Pl., Liv. With *Inf.*: Cat.,
Verg., Liv., etc. *Comp.*: Hor., Liv., etc.
Sup.: Cic.

di-gredior, gredī, grēssus [gradior], *to step
or go apart or asunder, to separate.* **1.** Lit.
a. Cic., Verg., etc. **b.** *to move apart,
separate*: a me, Cic.; Caes.; Liv.; a
conloquio Canini, Caes.; Liv.; ex conloquio, Liv.; Caes.; viā, Liv.; Sall.; in
castra, Sall.; Tac. **2.** Transf.: *to
deviate, swerve from*: nostro officio, Ter.
Esp. of speech, *to digress*: a causā, Cic.;
de causā, Cic.; ex eo, Quint. *Absol.*:
Cic., Quint.

dīgrēssiō, ōnis, *f.* [dīgredior], *a parting,
separating.* **1.** Lit.: Cic. Ep. **2.** Transf.:
a deviation: Cic. Esp. of speech, *digression*: a propositā oratione digressio,
Cic.; Quint.

dīgrēssus, a, um, *Part.* dīgredior.

dīgrēssus, ūs, *m.* [dīgredior], *a parting,
separating.* **1.** Lit.: Cic. **2.** Transf.:
a digression: Quint.

dīiūdicātiō, ōnis, *f.* [dīiūdicō], *a judging,
deciding between people*: Cic.

di-iūdicō, āre. **I.** *to judge between, to decide,
determine between.* **1.** Lit.: verbis controversias, Cic.; Ter.; Hor., etc. With
Indir. Quest.: Caes. **2.** Transf.: belli
fortunam, Caes. **II.** *to discriminate
between, to distinguish*: vera et falsa, Cic.;
inter has sententias, Cic.; vera a falsis,
Cic. With *Indir. Quest.*: Plin. Ep.

dīiūnct-, dīiung-, *v.* disiūnct-, disiung-.

di-lābor, lābī, lāpsus, *to slip, glide apart or
asunder.* **1.** Lit. **a.** Of solids: *to fall in
pieces, break up*: Lucr., Verg., Liv., etc.
b. Of snow, ice, clouds, etc., *to break up,
dissolve*: Cic., Verg., Liv. **c.** Of water
and fire, *to stream in different directions*:
Cic., Hor., Tac.; *cf.* Proteus in aquas dilapsus, Verg. **2.** Transf. **a.** Of groups of
persons, esp. soldiers: *to break up, disperse.* With *ab* or *ex*: Liv. With *in*
and ACC.: Liv. *Absol.*: Sall., Nep., Liv.
b. *to break up, decay*: omnia, Cic.; divitiae ac vis corporis, Sall.; Cic.; Liv.;
curae, Ov. **c.** Of time, *to slip away*:
Sall.

di-lacerō, āre, *to tear to pieces.* **1.** Lit.:
Cat., Ov., Tac. **2.** Transf.: rem publicam, Cic., Sall.; opes, Ov.; Tac.

di-lāminō, āre [lāmina], *to split in two*:
nuces, Ov.

di-laniō, āre, *to tear to pieces*: cadaver, Cic.;
Lucr.; Ov., etc.

di-lapidō, āre, *to demolish* (a structure of
stone). Transf.: xxx minas, Ter.

dīlāpsus, a, um, *Part.* dīlābor.

di-largior, īrī, *to bestow liberally, to broadcast*: pecuniam Magis, Tac.; Cic.

dīlātiō, ōnis, *f.* [differō], *a putting off, delaying, deferring.* With GEN.: Cic., Liv.,
Tac. *Absol.*: Liv., Suet.

dīlātō, āre [dīlātus, differō], *to broaden out,
widen, expand* (opp. contrahō). **1.** Lit.:
fundum. Cic.; castra, aciem, Liv.; rictūs,
Ov. **2.** Transf.: orationem, Cic.;

gloriam, Cic.; litteras (i.e. in pronunciation), Cic. [Fr. *délayer.*]

dīlātor, ōris, *m.* [differō], *a dilatory person*:
Hor.

dīlātus, a, um, *Part.* differō.

di-laudō, āre, *to praise wildly or extravagantly*: libros, Cic. Ep.

dīlēctus, ūs, *m.* [dīligō], *a choosing apart,
a selecting from several, a selection.* **A.**
In gen.: Pl., Caes., Cic., Verg., etc. **B.**
Milit. **1.** Lit.: *a picking* (men for
service): dilectum habere, *to hold a levy*,
Caes., Cic.. Liv., etc.; conficere, Liv.;
legiones ex novo dilectu conficere, Caes.
2. Transf. (concr.) *the troops raised by
levy, the levy*: Tac.

dīlibūtus, *v.* dēlibūtus.

dīligēns, entis. **I.** *Part.* dīligō. **II.** Adj.
discriminating; *careful, conscientious, strict,
accurate* (opp. neglegens). **A.** In gen. **1.**
Lit.: Cic., Quint. With *in* and ABL.; or
ad with ACC.: Cic., Quint. With GEN.:
= *carefully observant of*: Cic., Nep., Quint.
With DAT.: Cic. **2.** Transf. Of things:
scriptura, Cic.; remedia, Sen. Ep.; stilus,
Tac. **B.** In partic. *thrifty, economical*:
Cic., Quint., Plin. Ep. *Comp.*: Cic., Plin.
Sup.: Cic., Suet.

dīligenter, *adv. carefully, strictly, conscientiously*: Pl., Ter., Caes., Cic. *Comp., Sup.*:
Caes., Cic.

dīligentia, ae, *f.* [dīligēns], *carefulness,
conscientiousness.* **a.** In gen.: adhibere
ad (or *in*) rem, Cic. Ep.; conferre in aliquid,
Cic.; in re publicā, Cic.; Quint.; Plin.
Ep.; erga pecuniam alienam, Tac. With
Obj. GEN.: Cic., Quint. **b.** In partic.
thrift, economy: Cic., Suet.

di-ligō, ligere, lēxī, lēctum [legō], *to choose
apart from others, distinguish by choosing*;
to value, esteem, regard above others, to love.
1. Lit.: aliquem, Pl., Cic., Verg., etc.
2. Transf. Of things: Caesaris consilia, Cic.; Cypron, Hor.

di-lōricō, āre [lōrīca], *to tear apart, tear
open*: tunicam, Cic.

di-lūceō, ēre, *to be distinct in the light*: fraus,
Liv.

dīlūcēscō, lūcēscere, lūxī [dīlūceō], *to begin
to shine clearly, to grow light, dawn.* **1.**
Lit. **a.** Us. without subject: iam di-
lucescebat, Liv.; Cic. **b.** With subject:
dies, Hor. **2.** Transf.: discussa est
illa caligo: diluxit, patet, videmus omnia,
Cic.; rerum genitalis origo, Lucr.

dīlūcidē, *adv.* **I.** *clearly, brightly.* **1.** Lit.:
Comp.: Plin. **2.** Transf.: *clearly, distinctly*: explicare, Cic.; Quint.

dīlūcidus, a, um [dīlūceō], *clear, bright.* **1.**
Lit.: Plin. **2.** Transf. Of speech:
clear, plain, distinct: Cic., Quint. *Comp.*:
Cic.

dīlūculum, ī, n. [dīlūcēscō], *daybreak, dawn*:
Pl., Cic.

di-lūdium, ī, n. [lūdus], *an interval between
plays, games,* etc.: Hor.

di-luō, uere, uī, ūtum. **I.** *to wash asunder,
flood, break up, separate.* **1.** Lit.:
lateres, Caes.; sata laeta, Verg.; unguenta
lacrimis, Ov. **2.** Transf. **a.** molestias,
Cic.; crimen, Cic., Liv.; curas, Ov. **b.**
to solve, explain (*cf.* dissolvo): quod rog-

avi, Pl. **II.** *to temper, dilute.* **1.** Lit.: absinthia, Lucr.; Verg.; Liv., etc. **2.** Transf.: *to weaken, impair :* adfectuum viris, Quint.; eius auctoritatem, Sen. Ep.

dīluviēs, ēī, *f.* [dīluō], *a flooding, inundation, flood :* Lucr., Hor.

dīluviō, āre [dīluviēs], *to flood, inundate, deluge :* Lucr.

dīluvium, ī, *n.* [dīluō], *a flood, deluge.* **1.** Lit.: Verg., Ov., Plin. Ep. **2.** Transf.: *desolation, destruction :* Verg. [Fr. *déluge.*]

dīmachae, ārum, *m. pl.* [δίμαχαι], *Macedonian soldiers who fought both on foot and on horseback :* Curt.

dī-mānō, āre, *to flow different ways ; to spread abroad.* Transf.: meus forensis labor dimanavit ad existimationem hominum, Cic.

dīmēnsiō, ōnis, *f.* [dīmētior], *a measuring.* **1.** Lit.: Cic. **2.** Transf.: versuum, Quint.

dī-mētior, mētīrī, mēnsus, *to measure out.* **1.** Lit.: terram, Cic.; Verg.; Quint. *Perf. Part.* in *Pass.* sense : Caes., Cic., Verg., etc. **2.** Transf.: syllabas, Cic. (*v.* also dēmētior.]

dī-mētō, āre (Liv.) and **dīmētor**, ārī (Cic.), *to measure or mark out :* locum castris, Liv.; eorum cursūs, Cic.

dīmicātiō, ōnis, *f.* [dīmicō], *a fighting, struggle, tussle.* **1.** Lit.: Caes., Liv., Suet. In *pl.* : Caes. With GEN.: proeli, Cic.; universae rei, Liv. **2.** Transf.: (e.g. *in an election*) : non modo contentione, sed etiam dimicatione elaborandum, Cic.; Liv.; Quint. With GEN.: vitae, Cic.

dī-micō, āre (but *Perf. Inf.* dīmicuisse, Ov.). Lit.: *to brandish, flourish about on all sides ;* hence, *to fight, struggle, contend.* **1.** Lit. Us. with ABL.: armis, Caes.; acie *and* in acie, Caes.; acie cum aliquo, Liv.; proelio, Cic.; ferro pro patriā, Liv. *Impers.* *Pass.* (with or without proelio) : Caes., Cic. Of gladiatorial combats: Suet. **2.** Transf.: de vitā, capite, etc., Cic.; de famā, Nep., Cic.; de liberis, etc., Liv.

dīmidiātus, a, um [dīmidius], *halved, half.* **1.** Lit.: procumbunt dimidiati, dum appetunt, Pl.; luna, Cato; mensis, Cic. **2.** Transf.: dimidiate Menander (Terence), Caes. ap. Suet.

dī-midius, a, um [medius], lit. *through the middle ;* hence, *half.* **a.** In ante-Aug. period. only with *pars* : Pl., Caes., Cic., Ov., etc. **b.** From Aug. period, with other nouns (= dimidiatus) : spatium, Nep.; luna, Ov.; vectigal, Liv.; crus, Juv. **c.** Of person of mixed blood : dimidius patrum, dimidius plebis, Liv. As Noun, **dīmidium**, ī, *n. the half.* With GEN.: Pl., Hor., Liv.; dimidio minus, *less by one half*, *half the size of* : Pl., Caes., Cic., Hor. Hence (like a comparative) with *quam* : vix dimidium militum quam quod acceperat successori tradidit, Liv. [Fr. *demi.*]

dīminūtiō, better dēminūtiō.

dīmissiō, ōnis, *f.* [dīmittō]. **I.** *a sending out in different directions :* libertorum ad faenerandas provincias, Cic. **II.** *a dismissing, discharging :* propugnatorum, Cic.

dīmissus, a, um, *Part.* dīmittō.

dī-mittō, mittere, mīsī, missum. **I.** *to let*

go or send different ways : *to send about or round.* **1.** Lit.: Naevius pueros circum amicos dimittit, Cic.; litteras circum municipia, Caes.; Liv. With *ad, in* and ACC.: Caes. With ABL., or *per* and ACC.: nuntios totā civitate Aeduorum, Caes.; haec equites dimissi passim imperabunt, Caes.; Verg. Without ACC. expressed : dimisit circum omnis propinquas regiones, Caes.; per provincias, Liv. **2.** Transf.: animum ignotas in artis, Ov. **II.** *to break up* (any meeting *or* body), *to dismiss :* senatu dimisso, Cic.; concilium, Cic., Caes.; conventum, Sall.; convivium, Liv., Tac. Esp. milit. *to disband ; to send out in detachments, to detach :* Pl., Caes., Cic. **III.** *to let go apart, discharge, dismiss, release.* **1.** Lit.: aliquem ab se, Cic.; aliquem incolumem, Caes.; Hor., etc.; hostem ex manibus, Caes.; Cic.; eum ex custodiā, Liv.; Suet. **2.** Transf. **a.** *to let go apart, to abandon, leave, desert :* eum locum, Caes.; provinciam, Liv.; Ov.; fortunas morte, Cic. praedam ex manibus, Caes. **b.** *to give up, renounce, forsake, forgo :* philosophiam, libertatem, suum ius, etc., Cic.; occasionem, oppugnationem, etc., Caes.; iracundiam suam rei publicae dimittere, Caes.; tributa alicui, Tac.

dim-minuō, ere, *to dash to pieces :* homini caput, Pl.; Ter.

dīmōtus, a, um, *Part.* dīmoveō.

dī-moveō (dism-), movēre, mōvī, mōtum. **I.** *to move apart or asunder, to part, make a way through :* terram aratro, Verg.; Lucr.; undas, Lucr.; Ov.; aera, aquas, Verg.; rubum lacertae, Hor.; obstantia propinquos, Hor.; turbam, Tac. **II.** *to move apart, separate from something.* **1.** Lit.: umbram caelo, Verg.; sacra suo statu, Liv. **2.** Transf.: quos spes societatis a plebe dimoverat, Sall.; terror fide socios dimovit, Liv.; te lucro, Hor. **III.** *to break up, disperse :* Bacanalia, Inscr.

Dindymus (-os), ī, *m.* and **Dindyma**, ōrum, *n. pl. a mountain in Mysia, sacred to Magna Mater ;* **Dindymēnē**, ēs, *f. this goddess.*

dī-nōscō, *v.* dignōscō.

dīnumerātiō, ōnis, *f.* [dīnumerō], *a counting one by one, an enumeration :* noctium, Cic. Rhet. : *an enumeration of particulars :* Cic.

dī-numerō, āre, *to count out separately or one by one.* **1.** Lit.: viginti minas illi, Ter.; Pl. **2.** Transf.: stellas, annos, Cic.; tempora, Verg.; Ov.; syllabas, Cic.

diōbolāris, e, *adj.* [διώβολον], *costing two oboli :* Pl.

Diodotus, ī, *m. a Stoic philosopher, teacher of Cicero.*

dioecēsis, is, *f.* [διοίκησις], *a district, government :* Cic. Ep.

dioecētēs, ae, *m.* [διοικητής], *an overseer of the revenue, treasurer :* Cic.

Diogenēs, is, *m.* **I.** *an Ionian philosopher, pupil of Anaximenes.* **II.** *the Cynic philosopher of Sinope, 4th cent. B.C.* **III.** *a Stoic philosopher, teacher of Carneades and Laelius.*

Diomēdēs, is, *m. s. of Tydeus and king of Argos ; a famous hero at Troy ;* **Diomēdēus (-īus)**, a, um.

Diōn (Diō), ōnis, *m. brother-in-law of the*

elder Dionysius of Syracuse, the pupil and friend of Plato.

Diōnē, ēs (-**a**, -**ae**), *f.* **I.** *m. of Venus.* **II.** *Venus ;* **Diōnaeus,** a, um, *of or sprung from Venus.*

Dionȳsius, ī, *m.* **I.** *the name of two tyrants of Syracuse.* **II.** *D. of Heraclea, a pupil of Zeno.* **III.** *a Stoic of Cicero's time.*

Dionȳsus (-**os**), ī, *m. the Greek god Bacchus* (called Liber or Bacchus in Roman poetry) ; **Dionȳsia,** ōrum, *n. pl. the festival of Dionysus.*

diōta, ae, *f.* [διώτη], *a two-handled wine-jar :* Hor.

Diphilus, ī, *m. a Greek comic writer of Sinope, used by Plautus.*

diplōma, ătis, *n.* [δίπλωμα], *a letter folded double.* **I.** *a State letter of recommendation given to persons travelling :* Cic., Tac. **II.** *a document drawn up by a magistrate, granting some privilege ; a diploma :* Suet.

Dipylon, ī, *n. N.W. gate at Athens.*

Dircē, ēs (Acc. -am, Pl.), *f.* **I.** *a fountain in Boeotia ;* **Dircaeus,** a, um, *Dircean, Boeotian :* cycnus, i.e. Pindar, Hor. **II.** *w. of Theban Lycus, killed by being tied to a bull.*

dirēct-, *v.* dērēct-.

diremptus, a, um, *Part.* dirimō.

diremptus, ūs, *m.* [dirimō], *a separation :* Cic.

direptiō, ōnis, *f.* [dīripiō], *plundering :* urbis, Cic., Caes. ; sociorum, Cic. In *pl. :* Cic. Ep. ; Liv.

direptor, ōris, *m.* [dīripiō], *a plunderer :* Cic., Tac.

direptus, a, um, *Part.* dīripiō.

diribeō, ēre, itum [dis habeō], *to separate or sort the tablets when taken out of the cistae or ballot-boxes, to ascertain the majority :* tabellas, Cic.

diribitiō, ōnis, *f.* [diribeō], *a sorting of the tablets used in voting :* Cic.

diribitor, ōris, *m.* [diribeō], *a sorter of the tablets when taken out of the ballot-boxes :* Cic.

diribitōrium, ī, *n.* [diribeō], *the place where the voting tablets were sorted :* Plin., Suet.

dirigēscō, *v.* dērigui.

dī-rigō, rigere, rēxī, rēctum (*Perf.* dīrēxtī, Verg.) [regō], *to put into line or order by arranging the parts, to arrange.* **1.** Lit.: aciem, Caes., Liv. ; navis ante portum, Liv. ; in pugnam navis, Liv. ; regiones lituo, Cic. ; vicos, Liv. **2.** Transf.: materias divisione, Quint. (*v.* also derigo).

dir-imō, imere, ēmī, emptum [dis, emō], *to take asunder ; to part by coming between, separate, break off.* **1.** Lit.: corpus, Cic. ; Lucr. ; urbs flumine dirempta, Liv. **2.** Transf.: *to break off, interrupt.* **a.** proelium diremit nox, Pl., Caes., Liv. ; comitia, Liv. **b.** *to break off and end :* conloquium, Caes. ; societatem, controversiam, etc., Cic. ; bellum, Liv., Verg. ; amicitias, Tac. ; auspicium, Liv. ; pacem, conubium, Liv.

dī-ripiō, ripere, ripuī, reptum [rapiō], *to snatch or tear asunder, tear in pieces.* **1.** Lit. **a.** dapes, Verg. ; membra, Ov. ; Pl. ; Lucr. **b.** Milit. *to lay waste, ravage, pillage :* bona alicuius, Caes. ; castra, Liv. ; provincias, Cic. **c.** *to snatch away :* vaginā ensem, Ov. ; ferrum a latere, Tac. Hence,

to make a raid on, to scramble for : talos (in medium iactos), Quint. ; editum librum, Suet. **2.** Transf. Of the mind : diripior, Pl.

dīritās, ātis, *f.* [dīrus]. **I.** *fatal mischief, misfortune :* Poet. ap. Cic., Suet. **II.** *fierceness, cruelty :* Cic., Suet.

dī-rumpō (**dirr-**, Pl., and **disr-**), rumpere, rūpī, ruptum, *to burst or break asunder or in pieces.* **1.** Lit.: caput, Pl. ; Cic. ; Tac. **2.** Transf. **a.** *to break off, sever :* amicitias, Cic. **b.** In *Pass. to burst* with envy, indignation, laughter, etc. : dirumpor dolore, Cic. Ep. With Acc. and *Inf.* : Cic. Ep.

dī-ruō, ruere, ruī, rutum, *to pull asunder or to pieces, demolish.* **1.** Lit.: Ter. ; urbem, Cic. ; Ov., etc. ; arbusta, Verg. **2.** Transf. **a.** *to break up* (in gen.) : agmina vasto impetu, Hor. ; Bacchanalia, Liv. **b.** In finance : homo diruptus dirutusque, Cic.

diruptiō, ōnis, *f.* [dīrumpō], *a tearing to pieces :* Sen.

diruptus, a, um, *Part.* dīrumpō.

dīrus, a, um, *fearful, awful.* **1.** Lit. In augury and the language of augurs : ill-omened, ominous, boding : Cic., Verg., etc. As Noun, **dīra,** ōrum, *n. pl.* and **dīrae,** ārum, *f. pl.* **a.** (sc. res), *ill-boding portents, unlucky signs :* Cic., Hor., Tac. **b.** As appellation of the Furies : Verg. **2.** Transf. : *abominable, fell, dreadful, awful.* **a.** Of persons : Verg., Hor., Ov. **b.** Of things : venena, Verg. ; bellum, Verg. ; amores, Ov. ; quies, Tac.

dīrutus, a, um, *Part.* diruō.

dīs, dīte, Gen. dītis [contr. fr. dīves], *rich.* **1.** Lit. Of people : Ter., Hor., Liv., etc. **2.** Transf. **a.** Of offerings, ornaments, etc. : Ov. **b.** Of land, etc., *rich, fertile :* Curt., Tac. **c.** Of the mind : Lucr. **d.** Of military service, *profitable :* Liv. *Comp.* : Hor., Liv. *Sup.* : Caes., Verg., Ov., Liv.

Dis, Dītis, *m.* a name of Pluto.

dis-, *adv.* only in compounds (= Gk. δίς, *cf.* διά]. **A.** Forms: unchanged before *c, p, q, t ;* discedo, dispar, disquiro, distendo, and before *s* with a vowel following ; dissentio ; assimilated before *f ;* differo ; dī-before other consonants ; diduco, dilabor, etc. ; dī- or dis- before consonantal *i* ; diiudico, disiungo, disicio ; dir- before vowels ; dirimo, diribeo ; *exc.* dishiasco.

B. Meaning. **a.** *asunder, in several parts or directions :* dimoveo, divido. **b.** *asunder* (of one person or thing), *apart, away :* discedo. **c.** Of separation in time ; differo, adjourn. **d.** *separately, in detail, distinctly :* distinguo, diluceo. **e.** *sundering* what has been or should be united : dissocio. **f.** *dividing ruinously :* dirimo, diruo **g.** *freely, bountifully :* diffundo. **h.** *wildly, extravagantly :* discupio. **i.** *not, un-,* reversing the meaning : dispar. [It. *dis-*, Fr. *dés-*, Eng. *dis-*.]

dis-cēdō, cēdere, cēssī, cēssum (*Perf. sync.* discēstī, Pl.). **I.** *to go or part asunder, to separate, be severed.* **1.** Lit. **a.** terra, Cic. ; caelum, Cic., Verg. ; Numidae in duas partis, Sall. ; Tac. **b.** *to disperse, scatter* (intrans.) : fumus in aras, Lucr. ; palus

multos in amnĭs, Luc. **Esp. milit.**: in
silvas, Caes.; **ex fugā** in civitates, Caes.
Absol.: Nep. **c.** Of breaking old ties, *to
part from, forsake*: ab amicis, Cic.; Caes.;
Liv. **2. Transf.** Of classification: di-
visio in tris partis, Quint. **II.** *to go away
from, to leave, depart.* **1. Lit. A.** In gen.
With *ab*: Pl., Caes., Cic. With *ex*: Caes.,
Cic., Ov. With *de*: Cic., Liv. With *in*
and Acc.: Caes., Sall. With *ad*: Verg.
With simple Acc.: domum, Caes.; Nep.;
Capreas, Tac. *Absol.*: Caes., Cic., Hor.
Impers. Pass.: Caes., Liv., Tac. **B.**
Milit. a. *to march off, decamp*: ab Ger-
goviā, Caes.; ab signis, Caes., Liv.; ab armis,
Caes., Sall., Liv.; ex hibernis, Caes. *Absol.*:
Caes. **b.** Denoting the result of a battle: *to
get away, come off* (victorious, conquered,
wounded, *etc.*): superiores, Caes.; victor
ab hoste, Hor.; aequo Marte cum Volscis,
Liv.; ut spoliis Sexti Rosci hoc iudicio ornati discedant, Cic. **2. Transf. a.** *to
depart, deviate, swerve from*; *to leave, give
up*: a fide iustitiāque, Cic.; ab oppugnatione, Caes.; a suā sententiā, Caes. **b.**
discedere in sententiam, a phrase of the
senate-house: *to vote or divide with any
one*, by going over to his side of the house:
in hanc sententiam, Liv.; discedere in alia
omnia, *to vote or divide against any one*, Cic.
Ep. *Impers. Pass.*: Caes., Liv. **c.** *to
pass away, to vanish*: modo audivi, quarta-
nam a te discessisse, Cic. Ep.; hostibus spes
potiundi oppidi discessit, Caes.; Liv.; ex
animo memoria alicuius, Cic. **d.** discedere
ab aliquo, *to leave out of consideration,
except*: Cic. Ep.

disceptātĭō, ōnis, *f.* [disceptō], *a dispute, debate, discussion*: Cic., Liv., Quint. Freq.
in law: iuris, iudici, Cic., Quint. In *pl.*:
Cic., etc.

disceptātor, ōris, *m.* (and **disceptātrix**, īcis,
f. Cic.) [disceptō], *an arbitrator*: Pl., Cic.,
Liv. With *Obj.* GEN.: Cic. With *de*:
Caes. With *inter*: Liv.

dis-ceptō, āre [dis captō]. **Lit.**: *to take to
pieces*; *to discuss* before an arbitrator. **I.**
In law: *to decide, settle.* **1. Lit.**: res,
Cic.; controversias, Liv.; bella, Cic. With
inter: Liv., Plin. Ep. *Absol.*: Cic., Liv.
2. Transf.: cum Academici eorum controversias disceptarent, Cic. **II.** In gen.:
to debate, dispute, discuss, treat. With *de*:
Caes., Cic., Sall., Liv. Also, ob rem pe-
cuniariam cum aliquo, Tac. With *apud*
se or inter se, Caes. With *ad*: ad aliquem,
Liv. With Instr. ABL.: armis, Caes., Tac.
Absol.: Cic., Hirt., Tac. *Impers. Pass.*:
Liv., Tac.

dis-cernō, cernere, crēvī, crētum. **1. Lit.**:
to separate, keep apart: discreta tellus,
Lucr.; telas auro, Verg.; ordines, Liv.;
Sall.; improbus a nobis, Cic.; limes agro
positus, litem ut discerneret arvis, Verg.;
septem discretus in ostia Nilus, Ov. **2.**
Transf.: *to distinguish between*: alba
et atra, Cic.; Hor., etc.; suos, Caes.;
Cic.; verba articulatim, Lucr. With
Indir. Quest.: Cic., Liv., etc.

dis-cerpō, cerpere, cerpsī, cerptum [carpō],
to pluck, tear in pieces. **1. Lit.**: Lucr.;
animum, Cic.; iuvenem, Verg.; Liv., etc.

2. Transf.: quasi discerpta contrectare,
Cic.; me infestis diotis, Cat.

discēssĭō, ōnis, *f.* [discēdō]. **I. a,** *a separation*; of married persons: Ter. **b.**
Esp. in the senate-house: *a division* (for
voting): facere, Cic., Hirt., Tac. **II.** *a
going away, departure*: Tac.

discēssus, ūs, *m.* [discēdō]. **I.** *a going
asunder, separation, parting*: caeli, Cic.;
partium, Cic. **II.** *a going away, departure.*
a. In gen.: Cic., Verg. **Euphem.** for
exile: Cic. **Euphem.** for death: Cic.
In *pl.*: Cic. **b.** Milit. *a marching off, de-
camping*: Caes., Tac.

discīdĭum, ī, *n.* [discindō], *a tearing asunder.*
1. Lit.: corporis, nubis, Lucr. **2.**
Transf. a. *a severing, separation*: cor-
poris atque animāī, Lucr.; adfinitatum,
Cic. Occ. = *separation, divorce*: Ter.,
Cic. Ep., Ov., Tac. **b.** *discord, disagree-
ment*: amicorum, Cic.; belli, Cic.; civile,
Cic.; Liv.; Tac.

dis-cīdō, ere [caedō], *to cut in pieces*: Lucr.

discinctus, a, um. **I.** *Part.* discingō. **II.**
Adj. a. *ungirt*: Verg. **2. Transf. a.**
at one's ease, negligent: Hor., Ov. **b.** *dissolute, reckless*: Hor.

di-scindō, scindere, scidī, scissum, *to tear* or
cleave asunder; *to split, rend, divide.* **1.**
Lit.: vestem, Ter.; Cic.; Verg.; etc.
2. Transf.: discissa vis animāī, Lucr.;
amicitias, Cic.; orationem (i.e. interrupt),
Sen. Ep.

dis-cingō, cingere, cīnxī, cinctum, *to ungird, take off the girdle.* **1. Lit.**: tunicam,
Hor. As a milit. punishment: destrictis
gladiis discinctos destituit, Liv.; Afros, i.e.
stripped of their all, Juv. **2.** in metaphor:
Cic. Ep.

disciplīna (and **discipulīna**, Pl.), ae, *f.*
[discipulus], *learning, teaching.* **1. Lit.**:
alicui in disciplinam tradi, Cic.; accipere
ab aliquo disciplinam, Cic.; Caes. **2.**
Transf. A. *learning, knowledge, science*:
Cato; iuris civilis, rei publicae, militiae,
Cic.; bellica, Cic. **Esp.**: *system of edu-
cation or philosophy, school, doctrines*: Cic.
B. *regulation of life, training, discipline.* **a.**
Prop. at home: Cic., Liv. **b.** Milit.:
Caes., Cic., Liv., Tac. **c.** National: populi
Romani, Caes., Liv.; Lycurgi, Cic. **d.** Of
manners or ways of living; *custom, ways,
habit*: Pl., Ter., Cic.

discipulus, ī, *m.* (Pl., Cic.) and **discipula**,
ae, *f.* (Pl., Hor.) [discō], *a learner, pupil.*
a. In gen.: Pl., Cic., Hor. **b.** *an ap-
prentice*: Pl.

discissus, a, um, *Part.* discindō.

dis-clūdō, clūdere, clūsī, clūsum, *to shut up
separately, to keep apart by some barrier.*
1. Lit.: mons Arvernos ab Helviis dis-
cludit, Caes.; Nerea ponto, Verg.; ossa ac
nervos, Lucr.; tigna, Caes.; morsūs roboris, Verg. **2. Transf.**: Cic.

discō, discere, didicī [fr. root of διδάσκω or
of δείκνυμι], *to learn.* **a.** By study: litteras Graecas, ius civile, etc., Cic.; Pl.;
Hor.; Cic.; dialectica ab aliquo, Cic.;
Quint.; virtutem ex me, Verg.; aliquid de
aliquo, Ter. With *Inf.*: Pl., Cic., Verg.,
etc. With *Indir. Quest.*: Cic., Hor.,
Ov. *Absol.*: Caes., Cic., Quint. **b.** *to

learn to know or recognise : haec certis signis, Verg. ; succos nectaris, Hor. ; crimine ab uno omnia, Verg. **c.** to learn, receive information, be told. With Acc. and Inf. : Caes., Cic., Hor. With Indir. Quest. : Cic., Liv. **d.** With things as subject : Pl., Verg.

discobolus, ī, m. [δισκόβολος], a thrower of the discus : Quint.

dis-color, ōris, adj. [color], of different colour. **1.** Lit. **a.** (different fr. surrounding objects) : Cic., Verg., Ov. With Dat. : vestis fatis discolor alba meis, Ov. **b.** (different in itself), parti-coloured, variegated : Ov., Curt. **2.** Transf. Of character, different : matrona meretrici dispar erit atque discolor, Hor.

dis-condūcō, ere, to be unprofitable or injurious. With Dat. : Pl.

dis-conveniō, īre, to disagree ; to be inconsistent : vitae disconvenit ordine toto, Hor. Impers. : Hor.

discordābilis, e, adj. [discordō], disagreeing, discordant : ingenium, Pl.

discordia, ae, f. [discors], disagreement, dissension, discord. **1.** Lit. Of persons. **a.** In gen. : Pl., Cic., Verg., etc. In pl. : Cic. **b.** Of soldiers, a mutiny : Tac. **2.** Transf. Of things : principiorum, Lucr.

discordiōsus, a, um [discordia], prone to discord : vulgus, Sall.

discordō, āre [discors], to be at variance, to quarrel, to disagree. **1.** Lit. : inter se, Ter. ; inter se cupiditates, Cic. ; cum Cheruscis, Tac. ; animus secum, Cic. **2.** Transf. : to be out of harmony with, be opposed to : ab oratione vox, Quint. With Dat. : Hor. Absol. : Pl., Hor., Tac.

dis-cors, cordis, adj. [cor], discordant, disagreeing, at variance (opp. concors). **1.** Lit. **a.** Of persons : Cic., Liv., Tac. ; civitas secum, Liv. ; Tac. With Dat. : Tac. **b.** Of things : inter se membra, Lucr. ; arma, venti, animi, Verg. ; Hor. ; Ov. **2.** Transf. : disagreeing, out of harmony, inconsistent : inter se responsa, Liv. ; ora sono discordia, Verg. ; hostes moribus, Curt.

discrepantia, ae, f. [discrepō], discordance, disagreement : rerum et verborum, Cic.

discrepātiō, ōnis, f. [discrepō], a difference, dispute : inter consules, Liv.

discrepitō, āre [freq. discrepō], to be altogether different : Lucr.

dis-crepō, āre, ui, to differ in sound, to be out of tune or unison. **1.** Lit. : in fidibus aut in tibiis, quamvis paulum discrepent, Cic. **2.** Transf. **a.** to disagree, be different. With ab or cum and Abl. of that from which : Cic. ; also with Dat. : Cic., Hor. With Abl., de or in and Abl. of that in which : Cic. With inter se : Cic. **b.** res discrepat, and more freq. Impers., discrepat, there is a difference of opinion, (it) is a matter of dispute : id quod haud discrepat, Liv. ; Ov. Impers. With de : Liv. With Indir. Quest. : Liv. With quin and Subj. : Liv. With inter : Liv.

discrētus, a, um, Part. discernō.

di-scrībō, scrībere, scrīpsī, scrīptum, to mark out in sections or portions ; to apportion out in a plan, scheme, etc. ; to classify ; to dis-

tribute according to a schedule : urbis partis ad incendia, Cic. ; milites in legiones, Liv. ; Cic. ; centurias ex censu, Liv. ; vim frumenti vicatim populo, Liv. ; vecturas frumenti civitatibus, Caes. ; Ter. ; Italiae regiones, Cic. Ep. ; sedes deorum, Hor.

discrīmen, inis, n. [dis, cernō : cf. crīmen], lit. that which separates ; a dividing-line, means of separation. **1.** Lit. : dare discrimina costis, Verg. ; quos inter et hostem discrimen murus facit, Ov. ; leti, Verg., Ov. ; cum duo maria pertenui discrimine separarentur, Cic. Occ. = a space between, interval : aequo discrimine, Lucr., Verg. **2.** Transf. **A.** a distinction, difference : Lucil. ; omni discrimine remoto, Cic. ; nullo discrimine, Verg. ; Tac. With Obj. Gen. : Cic., Verg., Liv., etc. **B.** the dividing-line (sc. rerum), the critical moment. **a.** res in id discrimen adducta est, utrum . . . an etc., Cic. ; Liv. ; aliquid in magno ponere discrimine (i.e. as being important), Liv. ; belli, Liv. **b.** a dangerous crisis, crisis, danger, risk : in summo rem esse discrimine, Caes. ; in discrimen capitis aliquem adducere, vocare, Cic. ; rem publicam in discrimen committere, Liv. ; aliquid in discrimen deferre, Liv. ; per tot discrimina rerum, Verg. ; periculi, Liv.

discrīminō, āre [discrimen], to divide, separate. **1.** Lit. : Etruriam, Cic. ; agros, Verg. **2.** Transf. : Liv., Sen. Ep.

discriptē, adv. with good arrangement, in good order : Cic.

discriptiō, ōnis, f. [discribō], a classification, distribution. With Obj. Gen. : Cic., Liv., Suet.

discriptus, a, um. I. Part. discribō. II. Adj. well-arranged, scientifically classified, kept apart : Cic., Hor. Comp. : Cic.

discruciātus, a, um, Part. discruciō.

dis-cruciō, āre, to torture by dragging apart. **1.** Lit. : aliquem discruciatum necare, Cic. **2.** Transf. : with Pron. Refl. or in Mid. : to torment oneself : Pl., Cic. ; animi (Loc.), Pl., Ter. With Acc. and Inf. : Pl., Cic. Ep., Cat.

dis-cumbō, cumbere, cubuī, cubitum, to lie down severally. **a.** For a meal, to take their several places at table : Lucr., Cic. Ep., Verg., etc. Impers. Pass. : Cic., Verg. Of a single person : Curt., Juv., Tac. **b.** to go to bed : Pl., Cic.

dis-cupiō, cupere (colloq.), to desire wildly, be keen. With Inf. : Pl.

dis-currō, currere, cucurrī and currī, cursum, to run different ways, to run to and fro, dash about. **1.** Lit. : in muris armata civitas, Caes. ; circa deum delubra, Liv. ; per omnis silvas, Ov. ; ad rapiendas virgines, Liv. ; ad arma, Liv. ; ad portas, Verg. ; in muros, Verg. Pass. Impers. : Verg. **2.** Transf. Of things : (Nilus) septem discurrit in ora, Verg. ; fama totā urbe, Curt. ; mens utroque, Ov.

discursus, ūs, m. [discurrō], a running to and fro, a running about : Hirt., Liv., Ov., etc.

discus, ī, m. [δίσκος], a quoit : Hor., Ov. Prov. : qui discum audire quam philosophum malunt, Cic.

discussus, a, um, Part. discutiō.

dis-cŭtĭō, cutere, cussī, cussum [quatiō], *to strike asunder, smash to pieces, shatter.* **1.** Lit.: Lucr., Caes., Verg., Liv., etc. **2.** Transf.: *to break up, scatter, disperse.* **a.** With concr. object: illos coetūs, Liv.; Boeoticum consilium, Liv.; nivem, Caes.; caliginem, Liv.; sol umbras, Verg. **b.** With abstr. object: terrorem animi tenebrasque, Lucr.; periculum, Cic., Liv.; famam, Tac.; caliginem, Cic.

disertē (and **disertim**, Pl.), adv. *clearly, expressly, distinctly*: Pl., Cic., Liv., etc. Comp.: Mart. Sup.: Liv., Quint.

disertus, a, um [disserō]. **A.** Act.: *arranging or setting things forth well; fluent, eloquent*: Ter., Cic., Ov., etc. With GEN.: Cat. Comp.: Cic. Sup.: Cic., Cat. **B.** Pass. *well-arranged, explicit*: oratio, Cic.; verba, Ov., Quint. Comp.: Sen. Ep. Sup.: Cic. Ep.

dis-hĭāscō, ēre [hiō], *to gape open*: Cato.

dis-ĭcĭō, icere, iēcī, iectum [iaciō], *to fling apart* or *asunder*. **1.** Lit. **a.** Milit.: phalangem, Caes., Liv.; agmen, Liv.; Sall.; Nep. **b.** Of the forces of Nature as agents: Lucr., Verg., Liv., Tac. **c.** Of buildings, etc., as object: *to scatter, break up, lay in ruins*: Nep., Verg., Ov., Liv. **2.** Transf.: *to break up*: compositam pacem, Verg.; consilia ducis, Liv.

dĭsiectō, āre [freq. disiciō], *to toss hither and thither*: Lucr.

dĭsiectus, a, um. **I.** Part. disiciō. **II.** Adj. *scattered, lying apart*: Caes., Liv.

dĭsiectus, ūs, m. [disiciō], *a casting asunder, scattering*: Lucr.

dĭsiūnctĭō (or **dĭiūnctĭō**), ōnis, f. [disiungō]. **I.** *a disjoining, a separation, alienation*: in tantā diiunctione meorum, Cic.; animorum, Cic. **II.** In dialectics: *a statement of an argument by contradictory propositions, one or the other of which must be accepted; a dilemma*: Cic. **III.** Rhet. *a disjunctive proposition*: Cic.

dĭsiūnctĭus, comp. adv. *rather in the manner of a dilemma*: Cic.

dĭsiūnctus, a, um. **I.** Part. disiungō. **II.** Adj.: *separate, distinct; distant, remote.* **1.** Lit.: Aetolia procul a barbaris gentibus, Cic. Sup.: Cic. **2.** Transf. **a.** *remote, apart*: vita maxime disiuncta a cupiditate, Cic. Comp.: Cic. **b.** Of speech: *disjointed, disconnected, abrupt*: Cic. Of the orator himself: Tac. **c.** In dialectics: *logically opposed; partaking of the nature of a dilemma*: Cic.

dĭs-iungō (or **dī-iungō**), iungere, iūnxī, iūnctum, *to unyoke.* **1.** Lit. **a.** bovem, Cic.; Hor.; Ov. **b.** *to wean*: Varr. **2.** Transf. **a.** Geogr. *to separate*: Sall. In Pass. with *ab* and ABL. of separation: Cic., Liv.; with ABL.: Verg.; with *inter se*: Lucr. **b.** In gen.: Pompeium a Caesaris amicitiā, Cic.; Ter.; honesta a commodis, Cic.; Quint.; veterem amicitiam sibi ab Romanis, Liv.

dĭspālēscō, ere [dispālor], *to be divulged, noised abroad*: Pl.

dĭs-pālor, ārī, *to straggle or stray in different directions*: Nep.

dĭs-pandō (**dispennō**, Pl.), pandere, pān-

sum (Lucr., Suet.) and pessum (Pl., Lucr.), *to stretch out, to extend, expand*: hominem divorsum, Pl.; manūs, Pl.; Suet.; membra, vestis, hiatum, Lucr.

dĭs-pār, aris, adj. *differently* (i.e. *imperfectly*) *matched, unequal, unlike*: male dispar, Hor.; Liv.; proelium, Caes.; Ov.; calami, Ov.; Verg.; fortuna, studia, tempora, Cic.; habitus animorum, Liv. With DAT.: Lucr., Cic., Hor. With GEN.: sui, Cic.

dĭsparātus, a, um. **I.** Part. disparō. **II.** Noun, **disparātum**, ī, n. Rhet. *that which is negatively opposed*; e.g. sapere, non sapere: Cic.

dĭs-parĭlis, e, adj. *dissimilar, different*: aspiratio terrarum, Cic.

dĭsparĭlĭter, adv. *differently*: Varr.

dĭs-parō, āre, *to disjoin, separate*: alium aliā, Pl.; eos, Cic.; Caes.

dĭspartĭō, -tĭor, v. dispertiō.

dĭs-pellō, pellere, pulī, pulsum, *to drive asunder; to disperse*. **1.** Lit.: pecudes, Cic. Ep.; ater quos aequore turbo dispulerat, Verg.; Lucr.; Liv. **2.** Transf.: ab animo tamquam ab oculis caliginem, Cic.; Phaedr.

dispendium, ī, n. [dispendō] (opp. compendium), *expense, cost, loss.* **1.** Lit.: sine dispendio, Pl., Ter.; dispendia comae, Ov.; silvae, Luc. **2.** Transf.: morae dispendia, Verg.

dĭs-pendō, ere, *to weigh out*: Varr.

dĭspennō, colloq. form of dispendō = dispandō (q.v.).

dĭspēnsātĭō, ōnis, f. [dispēnsō], *a weighing or doling out.* **1.** Lit.: inopiae (i.e. *of a scanty store*), Liv. **2.** Transf. **a.** *control, management, superintendence*: aerari, Cic.; annonae, Liv. **b.** *the office of a dispensator; stewardship*: Cic., Suet.

dĭspēnsātor, ōris, m. [dispēnsō], *a superintendent, steward, treasurer*: Juv., Suet.

dĭs-pēnsō, āre [freq. dispendō], *to weigh out, pay out.* **1.** Lit. **a.** Of money: Pl., Nep. **b.** Of household stores, *to distribute, manage*: Cic. Ep., Mart. Absol.: Hor. **2.** Transf. **a.** *to dispense, distribute*: oscula suprema natos per omnis, Ov.; laetitiam inter impotentis populi animos, Liv. **b.** *to regulate, arrange*: annum, Liv.; inventa, Cic.; victoriam, Liv.; fata, Ov. [Fr. dépenser.]

dĭs-percŭtĭō, cutere, *to dash completely out and scatter*: cerebrum, Pl.

dĭs-perdō, dere, didī, ditum, *to waste by dispersal, squander away.* **1.** Lit.: rem, Pl.; possessiones, Cic. **2.** Transf.: *to destroy, ruin utterly.* **a.** With personal object: Pl., Vatin. ap. Cic. Ep. **b.** stridenti miserum stipulā disperdere carmen, Verg. (For Pass. sense, v. dispereō.)

dĭs-pereō, īre, iī, *to go to ruin; to be wasted, squandered*: fundus, Cic.; cibus, Lucr.; tui labores, Cat. Prov.: male partum male disperit, Pl. In exclamations: disperii! Pl., Ter.; dispeream! Pl.; dispeream, si or nisi, Cat., Hor., Prop.

dĭ-spergō, spergere, spersī, spērsum [spargō], *to scatter about, disperse.* **1.** Lit. **a.** Of things: Ter., Lucr., Cic.; nubes venti, Lucr. **b.** Of persons: *to spread over, dis-*

tribute : evocatos totā acie, Caes. ; Tac. *Perf. Part.* dispersi, freq. in *Mid.* sense (esp. of soldiers), *spreading over, scattered :* Cic. ; in opere, in omnis partis, Caes. ; toto campo, Liv. **2.** T r a n s f. : *to spread out, spread over :* bellum, Cic. ; plebis vis dispersa in multitudine, Sall. ; vitam in auras, Verg. ; rumorem, Tac.

dispērsē, *adv. dispersedly, here and there :* disperse et diffuse dictae res, Cic.

dispērsus, a, um, *Part.* dispergō.

dis-pertiō, īre (and **dispertior,** īrī, once each in Cic., Liv.) [partiō], *to separate into parts, portion out, distribute.* **1.** L i t. : pecuniam iudicibus, Cic. ; Sall. ; Tac. ; funditores inter manipulos, Sall. ; coniuratos municipiis, Cic. ; exercitum per oppida, Liv. *Mid. :* Pl. **2.** T r a n s f. : tempora voluptatis laborisque, Cic. ; administrationem inter se, Liv.

dispessus, a, um, *v.* dispandō.

di-spiciō, spicere, spexī, spectum [specio], *to see distinctly.* **A.** I n t r a n s. **1.** L i t. : Pl., Cic., Suet. **2.** T r a n s f. *to consider carefully :* Pl. **B.** T r a n s. : *to see distinctly.* **1.** L i t. : nubila, rem, Lucr. ; dispecta Thule, Tac. **2.** T r a n s f. Of the mind. **a.** *to see distinctly, make out :* verum, Cic. ; Ter. ; eorum nil, Liv. ; mentem principis, Tac. **b.** *to distinguish* (in thought) : insidiatorem et petitum insidiis, Liv. ; lumina mundi, Cat. **c.** *to look into, consider :* res Romanas, Cic. Ep. With *Indir. Quest. :* Plin. Ep.

dis-pliceō, ēre [placeō], *to displease.* **a.** In gen. With DAT. : Pl., Cic., Ov., etc. Without DAT. : Ter., Cic., Hor., etc. With *Inf.,* or ACC. and *Inf.* as Subject : Cic. **b.** With *Pron. Refl.* in DAT. : *to be displeased, dissatisfied with oneself :* Ter., Hor. In gen. : *to be out of humour :* Cic. [It. *dispiacere,* Fr. *déplaire.*]

dis-plōdō, plōdere, plōsum [plaudō], *to burst asunder with a noise :* Varr. In *Perf. Part. :* Lucr., Hor.

dis-pōnō, pōnere, posuī, positum (contr. dispostum, Lucr.), *to place here and there, to set in different places ; to distribute* or *arrange regularly.* **1.** L i t. **a.** libros, Cic. ; cippos obliquis ordinibus in quincuncem, Caes. ; ensīs per herbam, Verg. ; Ov. ; aciem, Tac. **b.** Milit. *to station at intervals, to arrange, set guards,* etc. : custodias, exploratores, praesidia, etc., Caes. ; Liv. ; equos (i.e. *in relays*), Liv. **2.** T r a n s f. : verba ita disponunt ut pictores varietatem colorum, Cic. ; Quint. ; Tac. ; consilia, Liv. ; diem (i.e. *the day's work*), Tac.

dispositē, *adv. orderly, methodically :* Cic., Quint.

dispositiō, ōnis, *f.* [dispōnō], *a regular arrangement :* in oratory : Cic., Quint.

dispositū, ABL. *sing. m.* [dispōnō], *in the orderly arranging :* Tac.

dispositūra, ae, *f.* [dispōnō], *an orderly arrangement :* Lucr.

dispositus, a, um. **I.** *Part.* dispōnō. **II.** A d j. **a.** *properly arranged :* studia ad honorem disposita, Cic. **b.** *orderly, methodical :* vir, Plin. Ep. *Comp. :* Sen.

dis-pudet, ēre, uit, (*it*) *is a great shame.* With

Inf. as subj. : Pl. With ACC. and *Inf.* as subj. : Ter.

dispulsus, a, um, *Part.* dispellō.

dis-pungō, pungere, pūnxī, pūnctum. In trade, *to examine, check, balance,* or *audit an account :* rationes expensorum et acceptorum, Sec.

disputābilis, e, *adj.* [disputō], *that may be disputed, disputable :* Sen. Ep.

disputātiō, ōnis, *f.* [disputō], *an arguing.* C o n c r. : *an argument, debate :* Caes., Cic., Quint.

disputātor, ōris, *m.* [disputō], *a disputant :* Cic.

dis-putō, āre. **1.** L i t. In trade, *to reckon up ; to estimate, compute :* rationem cum aliquo, Pl. **2.** T r a n s f. : *to examine, investigate, discuss.* With ACC. of *Neut. Pron.* (or the like) : Pl., Cic. ; rem alicui, Pl. With *de :* Caes., Cic. With ACC. and *Inf. :* Ter. *Impers. Pass. :* Caes., Cic.

dis-quīrō, ere [quaerō], *to investigate in detail :* Hor.

disquisītiō, ōnis, *f.* [disquīrō], *a* (judicial) *inquiry :* Cic., Liv., Tac. In *pl. :* Cic.

disrumpō, *v.* dirumpō.

dis-saepiō, saepīre, saepsī, saeptum, *to separate by a hedge, etc. ; to fence off.* **1.** L i t. : Ov. **2.** T r a n s f. : Lucr., Cic.

dis-saeptum, ī, *n.* [dissaepiō], *a barrier, partition :* Lucr.

dis-sāvior, ārī [suāvior], *to kiss wildly :* Q. Cic. ap. Cic. Ep.

dis-secō, secāre, secuī, sectum, *to cut asunder, cut up :* Plin., Suet.

dis-sēminō, āre, *to scatter seed.* T r a n s f. : *to spread abroad, disseminate :* sermonem, Cic.

dissēnsiō, ōnis, *f.* [dissentiō], *difference of opinion, disagreement ; dissension, disunion.* **1.** L i t. : inter homines de iure, Cic. ; civilis, Caes. ; ordinum, Tac. ; Zenonis a superioribus, Cic. In *pl. :* Caes., Cic., Tac. **2.** T r a n s f. Of things, *conflict, incompatibility :* utilium cum honestis, Cic.

dissēnsus, ūs, *m.* [dissentiō], *dissension, disagreement :* Verg.

dissentāneus, a, um [dissentiō], *contrary* (opp. consentaneus) : Cic.

dis-sentiō, sentīre, sēnsī, sēnsum, *to differ in feeling* or *opinion, disagree, dissent* (opp. consentio). **1.** L i t. : Caes., Cic., Ov., etc. With *ab :* Caes., Cic., etc. With *inter se :* Cic. With *cum :* Cic., Sen. Ep. ; secum, Quint. With DAT. : Hor. With ACC. and *Inf. :* Lucr. **2.** T r a n s f. Of things, *to differ, be in conflict, be inconsistent :* Sen. Ep. With *ab :* Cic., Quint. With *cum :* Auct. Her. With DAT. : Sen. Ep.

dissēp-, *v.* dissaep-.

dis-serēnat, āre, *it grows fine in all directions, it is clearing up :* Liv.

(1) dis-serō, serere, sēvī, situm, *to scatter seed, to sow.* T r a n s f. : Lucr., Caes.

(2) dis-serō, serere, seruī, sertum. L i t. : *to arrange in order.* T r a n s f. : *to examine, argue, discuss.* **A.** With *de :* Cic., Liv. With Internal ACC. of *Pron.* (or the like) : aliquid, Cic., Sall. ; nihil de eā re, Tac. ; Cic. With ACC. of the matter discussed : bona libertatis, Tac. ; Sall. ; Liv. With

Acc. and *Inf.* : Cic. With *Indir. Quest.* :
Sall., Quint. **B.** With *cum* : Cic. With
contra : Cic. With *inter* : Cic. **C.** *Absol.* :
Cic., Quint.

dis-serpō, ere, *to creep about ; to spread* :
Lucr.

dissertiō, ōnis, *f.* [serō], *a disconnecting, severance.* Transf. : iuris humani, Liv.

dissertō, āre [*freq.* disserō 2.], *to set forth at
length, to debate ; dispute, treat of* : haec,
Tac. ; Pl. ; pacis bona, Tac. *Absol.* :
Tac.

dis-sīdeō, sīdēre, sēdī, sēssum [sedeō], *to sit
apart, be remote, distant.* **1.** Lit. **a.**
Geogr. (with ABL. of separation) : Verg.,
Prop. **b.** Of a garment, *to sit awry* : Hor.
2. Transf. **a.** Of persons, *to be at variance, to disagree.* With *ab* : Cic., Ov. With
inter se : Cic. Ep. With *cum* : Cic. With
de (concerning) : Cic. *Absol.* : Hor., Tac.
b. Of things, *to differ, disagree.* With *ab* :
Cic., Quint. With *inter se* : Cic. With
cum : Cic. With DAT. : Hor. *Absol.* :
Quint.

dis-sīdō, sīdere, sōdī, *to settle apart,* hence, *to
fall into disagreement, fall out* : a Pompeio,
Cic. Ep. *Absol.* : Suet. With *in* and
Acc., *to divide off to* : Tac.

dissignātiō, ōnis, *f.* [dissignō], *a regulation,
arrangement* : totius operis, Cic. (*v.* also
designatio.)

dissignātor, ōris, *m.* [dissignō], *one who arranges, a master of ceremonies, marshal.* **a.**
In the theatre : Pl. **b.** At funerals : Hor.,
Sen.

dis-signō, āre, *to mark as different.* Hence,
a. *to regulate, marshal, arrange* : rem
publicam disciplinā, Cic. **b.** *to arrange,
contrive* : aliquid, Pl., Ter., Hor. (*v.* also
designo.)

dis-silīō, silīre, silui [saliō], *to leap, start,
spring asunder.* **1.** Lit. : de concursu
corpora, Lucr. ; vox in multas, Lucr. ;
saxa, Lucr. ; Verg. ; Ov. ; mucro ictu,
Verg. **2.** Transf. : risu, Sen. Ep. ; gratia
fratrum geminorum dissiluit, Hor.

dis-similis, e, *adj. unlike, dissimilar* (opp.
similis : cf. dispar). With GEN. : Cic.,
Hor., Ov. With DAT. : Cic., Verg., Hor.
With *atque* or *ac* : Lucr., Cic. With *ac
si* : Liv. With *inter se* : Lucr., Cic.,
Quint. *Absol.* : Cic., Hor., Quint., Plin.
Ep. *Sup.* dissimillimus, Cic., etc.

dissimiliter, *adv. differently* : Cic., Sall.
With DAT. : Liv.

dissimilitūdō, inis, *f.* [dissimilis], *unlikeness,
difference* : Cic., Quint. In pl. : Cic.

dissimulanter, *adv. dissemblingly, secretly,*
etc. : Cic., Liv., Ov.

dissimulantia, ae, *f.* [dissimulō], *a dissembling* : Cic.

dissimulātiō, ōnis, *f.* [dissimulō], *a disguising.* **a.** Of appearance : Tac. **b.** Of acts,
thoughts, etc. : Cic., Quint., Tac. **c.** *the
Socratic εἰρωνεία* : Cic., Quint.

dissimulātor, ōris, *m.* [dissimulō], *a dissembler* : Hor., Tac. As *Adj.* with animus, *able to disguise* : Sall.

dis-simulō, āre, *to pretend away, to conceal deceptively what exists, to pretend that a thing
is not what it is.* **I.** *to dissemble, disguise ;
hide, keep secret.* With Acc. : Ter., Cic.,

Ov., etc. With Acc. and *Inf.* : Pl., Cic.
Ep., Ov., Suet. With *Indir. Quest.* : Verg.,
Quint. With *quasi* and *Subj.* : Pl. With
ne : Sall. *Absol.* : Pl., Cic., Verg., etc.
II. *to pretend not to see, ignore* : Liv. In
Pass. : Sacrovir diu dissimulatus, Tac.
[Fr. *dissembler*.]

dissipābilis, e, *adj.* [dissipō], *that can be
dispersed* : ignis et aēr, Cic.

dissipātiō, ōnis, *f.* [dissipō], *a scattering, dispersing.* **1.** Lit. : civium, Cic. **2.**
Transf. Rhet. : corporum, Cic.

dis-sipō (dissupō), āre, *to throw asunder,
scatter, disperse.* **1.** Lit. **a.** In gen. :
Lucr., Cic., Ov., etc. In Mid. : Hirt. **b.**
Milit. : *to disperse, break up :* phalangem, Liv. ; hostis, Caes., Cic. Ep. ; in
fugam, Liv. Hence, fuga dissipata, Liv.
c. *to destroy by scattering, squander away* :
possessiones, Cic., Tac. ; rem publicam, Liv.
2. Transf. **a.** *to scatter, spread abroad* :
famam, sermones, Cic. ; bellum, Liv. **b.**
Rhet. (of speech or speaker) in *Perf. Part.* :
Cic. **c.** *to drive away* : curas, Hor.

dissitus, a, um, *Part.* disserō, 1.

dissociābilis, e, *adj.* [dissociō]. **A.** Act.
separating, estranging : oceanus, Hor. **B.**
Pass. that cannot be united ; incompatible :
res olim dissociabilis miscere, Tac.

dissociātiō, ōnis, *f.* [dissociō], *a separation* :
Tac.

dis-sociō, āre, *to separate from fellowship ;
to disjoin, disunite.* **1.** Lit. : artas partis,
Lucr. ; dissociata locis concordi pace ligavit,
Ov. ; montes dissociantur opacā valle, Hor.
2. Transf. : *to estrange, detach* : amicitias,
Cic. ; barbarorum copias, Tac. ; legionem a
legione, Tac. ; Cic.

dissolūbilis, e, *adj.* [dissolvō], *that can be
dissolved or separated* : Cic.

dissolūtē, *adv.* **I.** Of style : *disconnectedly* :
Cic. **II.** *negligently, carelessly* : Cic.

dissolūtiō, ōnis, *f.* [dissolvō], *a breaking up,
a loosening, dissolving, destroying, dissolution.* **1.** Lit. : navigi, Tac. ; naturae,
Cic. **2.** Transf. **a.** legum, Cic. ; imperi,
Tac. **b.** *a refutation* : criminum, Cic. **c.**
Of discourse : *want of connexion, disconnexion* : Cic. Ep. ; Sen. Ep. **d.** Of character, *weakness* :
animi, Cic. Ep. ; Sen. Ep.

dissolūtus, a, um. **I.** *Part.* dissolvō. **II.** *Adj.*
a. Of style, *disconnected* : Cic., Quint.
Neut. as Noun, *asyndeton* : Cic., Quint. **b.**
Of character : *lax, remiss, negligent* : Cic.
Sup. : Cic. **c.** *licentious, dissolute* : mens
luxu dissoluta, Tac. ; Cic. *Comp.* : Sen.

dis-solvō, solvere, solvi, solūtum, *to unloose,
dissolve, break up.* **1.** Lit. **a.** In gen. :
navigium, Cic. Ep. ; Ov. ; nodos, glaciem,
Lucr. ; pontem, Nep. ; apta, Cic. Hence,
animam, i.e. to die, Lucr. ; Cic. **b.** Of
persons, *to release from bonds* : Pl. **2.**
Transf. **a.** In gen. *to break up* : amicitias,
leges, acta Caesaris, etc., Cic. ; religiones,
rem publicam, Liv. ; Sall. ; frigus, Hor.
b. *to smash, refute* : criminationem, Cic. ;
Quint. ; Tac. **c.** *to get quittance* (of a debt),
discharge, pay : pecuniam alicui, Cic. ;
Ter. ; Caes. ; aes alienum or nomen, Cic. ;
vota, Cic. ; Cat. In *Mid.* of the person, *to
free oneself* from debt : Cic. **d.** *to free* from
anxiety : Pl. ; from some occupation : Ter.

dis-sonus, a, um (opp. consonus), *dissonant, discordant, confused.* **1.** Lit.: clamores, Liv.; questus, Tac. **2.** Transf.: *disagreeing, different :* gentes sermone moribusque, Liv.; Luc.; Quint. With *ab :* Liv.

dis-sors, sortis, adj. *having a different fate ; not shared with others* (opp. consors): ab omni milite dissors gloria, Ov.

dis-suādeō, suādēre, suāsi, suāsum, *to urge differently ; to advise against ; dissuade.* With Acc. of thing : legem agrariam, Cic.; pacem, Liv.; poenam, Tac.; Pl. With *de :* Cic. With Acc. and *Inf. :* Cic., Quint. With *Inf. :* Quint., Suet. *Absol. :* Pl., Cic., Ov., etc.

dissuāsiō, ōnis, f. [dissuādeō], *an advising to the contrary ; a dissuasion :* rogationis, Cic. In *pl. :* Sen. Ep.

dissuāsor, ōris, m. [dissuādeō], *one who advises to the contrary :* Cic., Liv., Luc.

dis-suāvior, v. dissāvior.

dissultō, āre [freq. dissiliō], *to leap apart, to fly or burst asunder :* dissultant ripae, Verg.

dis-suō, suere, sūtum, *to unstitch ; to undo, unfasten.* **1.** Lit.: sinum, Ov. **2.** Transf.: amicitias, Cic.

dissupō, v. dissipō.

dis-taedet, ēre, *tires (one) out.* With Acc. of person and Nom. of *Neut. Pron. :* Pl. With *Inf.* as subject : Ter.

distantia, ae, f. [distō], *distance, remoteness.* **1.** Lit.: Plin. **2.** Transf.: *difference, diversity :* inter eos morum studiorumque, Cic.; Quint.

dis-tendō (and **distennō**), tendere, tendī, tentum, *to stretch asunder ; stretch out, extend.* **1.** Lit. **a.** aliquem, Pl., Ov., Liv.; aciem, Caes.; Liv. **b.** *to swell out, distend :* ubera cytiso, Verg.; Pl.; Tib. **c.** Of torture : tormento aliquem, Suet. **2.** Transf.: in duo pariter bella curas hominum, Liv.; ea res animos, Liv.

distennō, v. distendō.

(1) distentus, a, um. **I.** *Part.* distendō. **II.** Adj.: *filled, full :* Hor., Ov., Suet. *Comp. :* Hor.

(2) distentus, a, um. **I.** *Part.* distineō. **II.** Adj. *distracted, occupied.* With *circa :* Tac. *Sup.* (with *de*) : Cic. Ep.

dis-terminō, āre, *to separate by a boundary, to divide.* **1.** Lit.: quas (stellas) intervallum binas disterminat unum, Cic. poet.; Asiam ab Europā, Lucan. **2.** Transf.: Lucr.

distichon, ī, n. [δίστιχον], *a poem of two verses, a distich :* Mart., Suet.

distinctē, adv. **I.** *distinctly, clearly :* dicere, Cic. *Comp. :* Plin. Ep. **II.** *lucidly :* dicere, Cic. *Comp. :* Plin. Ep.

distinctiō, ōnis, f. [distinguō], *a distinguishing, distinction.* **A.** In gen. **a.** Act. *a differentiation* (with *Obj.* Gen.) : Cic., Quint. **b.** Pass. *a difference, distinction* (with *Subj.* Gen.) : Cic. **B.** Rhet. **a.** *a separation, division in discourse :* Cic. **b.** *a mark of separation, a stop :* Cic., Quint. **c.** A figure of speech : *a distinction between the same word repeated in a different sense, or between two allied words :* Cic., Quint.

distinctus, a, um. **I.** *Part.* distinguō. **II.** Adj. **1.** Lit. **a.** *separate, distinct :* Cic. **b.** *marked at different points, pricked out,*

set off, spangled (esp. with gems or the like) : pocula gemmis distincta, Cic.; Ov.; caelum astris distinctum et ornatum, Cic.; Ov. **c.** *diversified, varied.* *Comp. :* Liv. **2.** Transf. **a.** Of style, *set off, adorned :* oratio expolitione distincta, Cic.; Quint. **b.** Of the speaker himself : *lucid :* Cic. *Comp. :* Tac.

distinctus, ūs, m. [distinguō], *a distinguishing, distinction ; variety (of colour-scheme) :* Stat., Tac.

dis-tineō, tinēre, tinuī, tentum [teneō], *to hold* or *keep asunder.* **1.** Lit. **a.** tigna, Caes.; duo freta Isthmos, Ov.; Lucr. **b.** Milit. *to prevent (troops) from uniting* or *acting together :* Caes., Liv. **c.** In civil life : duae factiones senatum distinebant, Liv. **2.** Transf. **a.** *to keep asunder, stand in way of :* victoriam, Caes.; pacem, Liv.; hostem, Verg.; quem Notus distinet a domo, Hor. **b.** *to keep divided :* duae factiones senatum, Liv. **c.** Mentally : *to prevent concentration (of thought) ; to distract :* distineor dolore, Cic. Ep.; in multitudine iudiciorum distineri, Cic. Ep.; Nep. With *quo minus* and *Subj. :* Tac. With *ad* and *Gerund. :* Liv.

di-stinguō, stinguere, stīnxī, stīnctum [stinguō for stingō, cf. στίζω]. **1.** Lit.: *to mark off ;* hence, **a.** In gen. : *to separate, divide, part :* onus inclusum numero distinxit eodem, Ov.; Curt. **b.** Esp. by colour, gems, etc. : *to set off :* Hor., Ov. **2.** Transf. **a.** In gen. *to distinguish, discriminate :* crimina, Cic.; Quint.; fortis ignavosque, Tac.; somnia a falsis, Cic.; Liv.; Quint.; vero falsum, Hor. *Impers. Pass.* (with *Indir. Quest.*) : Cic., (Abl. *Absol.* of *Perf. Part.*) Tac. **b.** Rhet. and Gramm. : *to mark the pauses, to punctuate :* Cic., Quint. **c.** Of style, *to set off :* varietatibus opus, Liv.; Cic. So, voluptatem, Cic.; cenam comoedis, Plin. Ep.

di-stō, āre, *to stand apart, to be separate, distant.* **1.** Lit. **a.** *Absol.* (or freq. with Intern. Acc.) : multum, tantum, etc.) : Caes., Cic., Liv., Ov. With *inter se :* Cic., Liv. With *ab :* Luor., Caes., Cic. With Abl.: Hor., Ov. **b.** Of time : aetate, Quint.; haud multum distanti tempore, Tac. With *inter se* (and tempore) : Quint. With *ab :* Hor. **2.** Transf. Of quality : *to differ, be different :* Cic., Quint. With *inter se :* Cic., Quint. With *ab :* Cic., Hor., Quint. With Dat.: Hor., Quint. *Impers.* distat (with *Indir. Quest.*) : Hor.

dis-torqueō, torquēre, torsī, tortum, *to turn different ways ; to twist, distort.* **1.** Lit.: os, Ter.; Hor.; Ov.; Quint. **2.** Transf. Of torture : Sen., Suet.

distortiō, ōnis, f. [distorqueō], *a distorting, contortion.* With Gen. : Cic.

distortus, a, um. **I.** *Part.* distorqueō. **II.** Adj.: *distorted, misshapen, deformed.* **1.** Lit. : Cic., Hor., Quint. *Sup. :* Cic. **2.** Transf.: genus enuntiandi distortius, Cic.

distractiō, ōnis, f. [distrahō], *a drawing asunder.* Transf. **a.** *severance :* animorum, Cic.; Pl.; Sen. Ep. **b.** nulla nobis societas cum tyrannis, et potius summa distractio est, Cic.

distractus, a, um. **I.** *Part.* distrahō. **II.**
Adj.: *severed, separate* : inter se dis-
tractior, Lucr.
dis-trahō, trahere, traxi, tractum, *to drag,
draw* or *pull asunder* or *in pieces* ; *to
separate forcibly.* **1.** Lit. **a.** In gen. : aliquid : Caes., Cic., Liv. ; aliquem, Pl., Cic.,
Verg., etc. **b.** *to sell in lots, to retail* : Lucil.
Tac., Suet. **2.** Transf. **a.** *to break up,
sever, dissolve* : amorem, Ter. ; hanc rem,
Caes. ; aciem, Caes. ; haec natura cohaerentia, Cic. ; controversias (i.e. *to settle*), Cic. ;
omnem societatem civitatis, Cic. ; concilium
Boeotorum, Liv. ; aliquem famā, Tac. **b.**
to break off, estrange, alienate : aliquem ab
aliquo, Cic., Ter. ; sapientiam a voluptate,
Cic. **c.** *to distract, perplex* : in contrarias
sententias distrahitur animus, Cic. ; Tac.
obsessos egestas inter decus ac flagitium,
Tac. ; res publica distracta lacerataque,
Liv. [It. *distrarre*.]
dis-tribuō, uere, uī, ūtum, *to portion out,
distribute.* **1.** Lit. : argentum, Ter. ; exercitum, Caes. ; milites in legiones, Caes. ;
Cic. ; Numidas in hiberna, Liv. ; pecuniam
in iudices, Cic. ; equos Germanis, Caes. ;
pecus viritim, Caes. ; Suet. **2.** Transf.
a. Of civil liabilities : quod civitatibus
aequaliter esset distributum, Cic. **b.** In
gen. : rationem in quinque partis, Cic. ;
vitae opera, Sen.
distribūtē, *adv. orderly, methodically* : scribere, Cic. *Comp.* : Cic.
distribūtiō, ōnis, *f.* [distribuō], *an apportioning, distribution.* **a.** In gen. : criminum,
Cic. ; Quint. In *pl.* : Cic. **b.** Rhet. :
Cic.
districtus, a, um. **I.** *Part.* distringō. **II.**
Adj.: *with attention diverted, occupied,
engaged.* With ABL. *Instr.* : Cic., Nep., Hor.
Comp. : Cic. Ep.
di-stringō, stringere, strinxi, strictum, *to
press, draw tight apart* or *in different directions.* **1.** Lit. : radiis rotarum districti
pendent, Verg. ; canum rabies districta,
Lucr. **2.** Transf. : *to distract* or *divert
the attention of.* **a.** Milit. : Romanos,
Liv. **b.** In gen. : distringor officio, Plin.
Ep. ; Phaedr.
dis-truncō, āre, *to hack asunder* : aliquem
medium, Pl.
disturbātiō, ōnis, *f.* [disturbō], *demolition* :
Corinthi, Cic.
dis-turbō, āre, *to drive in rout.* **1.** Lit.:
vidistis contionem gladiis disturbari, Cic.
2. Transf. **a.** Of material things : *to
demolish* : domos, Lucr., Cic. ; opera,
Caes. **b.** Of immaterial things : *to demolish, ruin, smash up* : machinas, Pl. ;
legem, vitae societatem, Cic. ; nuptias,
Ter. ; rem, Cic. Ep.
disyllabus, a, um [δισύλλαβος], *disyllabic* :
Lucil., Quint.
ditēscō, ere [dis, ditis], *to grow rich* : Lucr.,
Hor.
dithyrambicus, a, um [διθυραμβικός], *dithyrambic* : poema, Cic.
dithyrambus, ī, *m.* [διθύραμβος], *a dithy-
ramb, dithyrambic poem* (in honour of Bacchus) : Cic., Hor.
ditiae, ārum, *f.* [contr. for divitiae], *wealth* :
Pl.

ditiō, wrongly for diciō.
ditō, āre [dis, ditis], *to enrich.* **1.** Lit. :
socios praemiis belli, Liv. ; me benignitas
tua ditavit, Hor. ; Liv. In *Mid.* : *to become rich* : Liv. **2.** Transf. : cum lingua
Catonis et Enni sermonem patrium dita-
verit, Hor.
diū, *adv.* [LOCAT. of dius,' old NOM. of diēs].
1. Lit. : *in the day-time* (mostly with
noctu) : Pl., Sall., Hor., Tac. **2.** Transf.
a. *in a long time* ; *for a long while, long* :
Pl., Cic., Hor., etc. *Comp.* **diūtius**, **i.**
longer, still longer : Pl., Ter., Caes., Cic.
ii. *longer than right, too long* : Caes., Sall.,
Tac. *Sup.* **diūtissimē,** *for a very long
time, longest* : Caes., Cic. **b.** *long ago.*
With *iam* : Pl., Ter., Cic. Ep. With negative : Pl., Ter. Alone : Varr., Verg.
diurnus, a, um [dius, *v.* diēs]. **I.** *by day,
the day's* : itinera, Caes. ; labores, Cic. ;
lumen, Lucr., Ov. ; horae, Verg. **II.** *lasting a day, daily* : cibus, Liv. ; mercede
diurnā conductum, Hor. ; aetatis fata
diurna, Ov. ; diurnis urbis actis mandare,
Tac. As Noun, **diurnum,** ī, *n.* **a.** *a day-
book, account-book* : Juv. Mostly in *pl.*
(*sc.* acta), *daily records, journal* : populi
Romani, Tac. **b.** = diārium, *daily allowance* of rations : Sen., Suet. [It. *giorno* ;
Fr. *jour.*]
(1) dius, a, um [*cf.* Gk. δῖος], *godlike, divine* :
orae luminis, otia, Lucr. ; dius fidius, Cic. ;
Camilla, Verg. ; sententia Catonis, Hor. ;
indigetes, Liv.
(2) diūs, old LOCAT. of dius (diēs) : Pl.
diūtinē, *adv. for a long time* : Pl.
diūtinus, a, um [diū], *lasting, long* : supplicium, Pl. ; servitus, Cic. ; laetatio, Caes. ;
pax, Liv.
diūtius ; **diūtissimē,** *v.* diū.
diūturnitās, ātis, *f.* [diūturnus], *length of
time, long duration.* With GEN. : temporis,
Cic. ; belli, Caes. ; Sall. *Absol.* : Cic.
diūturnus, a, um [diū], *of long duration,
lasting, long* : bellum, pax, etc., Cic. ;
labor, Caes. ; quies, Sall. ; obsidio, Ov.
Comp. : Caes., Cic. Ep., Ov.
dīva, *ae, v.* dīvus.
di-vāricō, āre, *to spread asunder, to stretch
apart.* **A.** Trans.: hominem, Cic. ; Cato.
B. Intrans. : Varr.
di-vellō, vellere, vellī, vulsum (or volsum), *to
pluck* or *pull asunder, to tear in pieces.* **1.**
Lit. : res a natura copulatas, Cic. ; corpus, Verg. ; Tac., etc. ; moenia mundi,
Lucr. **2.** Transf. **a.** With abstr. obj. :
adfinitatem, Cic. ; commoda civium, Cic. ;
amorem, Hor. **b.** Mentally : distrahor
dolore, Cic. **c.** *to tear away* : aliquem ab
aliquo, Cic. ; liberos a parentum complexu, Sall. ; aliquem dulci amplexu, Verg. ;
Damalin adultero, Hor. **d.** *to estrange* :
aliquem ab aliquo, Cic. ; sapientiam a
voluptate, Cic.
di-vēndō, vēndere, vēnditum, *to sell in lots* :
bona, Cic., Liv., Tac.
di-verberō, āre, *to lash asunder* ; hence, *to
cleave* : aërias undas, Lucr. ; fluctūs,
Curt. ; umbras ferro, Verg.
di-verbium, ī, *n.* [verbum], *the dialogue of a
comedy* : Liv.

diversē (dīvorsē), adv. in different places or directions, hither and thither. **1.** Lit.: Auct. B. Afr.; Suet. Comp.: Sall. **2.** Transf.: curae meum animum divorse trahunt, Ter.; de eādem re dicere, Cic. Sup.: Suet.

diversitās, ātis, f. [dīversus]. **I.** contradiction, direct contrast or opposition: naturae, Tac.; inter exercitum imperatoremque, Tac. **II.** diversity, difference: consiliorum, Tac.; Quint.; Plin. Ep.

diversōrium, v. dēversōrium.

diversus (dīvorsus), a, um. **I.** Part. dīvertō. **II.** Adj.: turned different ways; hence, **A.** in different directions or places, apart, separate (most freq.). **1.** Lit.: divorsae state, Pl.; diversi pugnabant, Caes.; Liv.; Verg.; quo diversus abis ? Verg.; diversam aciem in duas partis constituit, Caes.; Liv.; loca, Caes., Cic., Liv.; itinera, Caes.; flumina diversa locis, Verg., Ov. Sup.: Liv. Occ. = individuals; Cic. Neut. pl. as Noun: fugam per diversa petunt (i.e. by different routes), Liv. **2.** Transf. **a.** different, unlike: varia et diversa genera, Cic.; Cat.; Quint.; morum diversus, Tac. With ab: Cic., Sall., Quint. With DAT.: Quint. **b.** distracted, fluctuating: metu ac libidine divorsus agebatur, Sall.; Pl.; vulgus, Tib.; diversus animi, Tac. **B.** remote, sequestered: litus, Verg.; pascua, Ov.; oppida, Tac. **C.** set over against each other, opposite, contrary. **1.** Lit.: equos in diversum iter concitatos, Liv.; diversis ab flumine regionibus, Caes.; iter a proposito diversum, Caes.; procurrentibus in diversa terris, Tac.; cinguli inter se diversi, Cic. **2.** Transf. **a.** opposite, conflicting, diametrically opposed: consilia, Caes.; Cic.; Sall. With DAT.: Hor. With inter se: Sall., Liv. Comp.: Lucr. Sup.: Sall. Neut. as Noun: nullo in diversum auctore, Tac.; ex diverso, Quint., Tac. **b.** hostile, inimical: amantes, Prop.; acies, Tac.; subsellia, Quint. With ab: Cic., Liv.

di-vertō (vortō), vertere, vertī, versum, to turn or go different ways. Transf. to differ: Pl.

dives, itis, adj. (NOM. and ACC. of Neut. pl. do not occur; ABL. sing. us. divite; rarely dīvītī) [perh. fr. dīvum, the sky, the home of gods. Lit.: a heavenly-being], rich. **1.** Lit. Of people: Pl., Cic. With ABL. (of material): Hor., Ov., Liv. With GEN.: Verg., Hor., Ov. **2.** Transf. Of things: animus hominis, Cic.; ager, ramus, Capua, Verg.; Hor.; Ov. With ABL.: Verg., Ov., Liv. With GEN.: Hor. Comp.: Pl., Cic., Ov., etc. Sup.: Cic., etc. (v. also dīs, dīte.)

di-vexō, āre, to pull or haul asunder. **1.** Lit.: meam rem, Pl.; omnia, agros, Cic. **2.** Transf.: to worry to distraction: Suet.

dividia, ae, f. [dīvidō]. division. **I.** dissension, discord: in pl.: Acc. **II.** care, trouble, vexation: Acc. **III.** a cause of trouble or worry (in Pred. DAT.): Pl.

di-vidō, videre, visī, visum (Perf. sync. divisse, Hor.) [fr. root seen in viduus], to part asunder. **I.** to separate a whole into parts,

to divide, bisect, cleave. **1.** Lit. **a.** In gen.: animal, Cic.; Hor.; Verg.; muros, Verg.; Lucr.; aerem, Cic.; nubila, Hor. **b.** Geogr.: flumen vallem, Caes.; Enn.; Liv.; Galliam in partīs tris, Caes.; Cic.; civitatem in quattuor pagos, Caes. **c.** to make one's way through: caelum, Cic. **d.** to divide among several ; to distribute, apportion: agros, Lucr., Cic., Verg.; nummos in viros, Pl.; Tac.; praedam per milites or inter milites, Liv.; Pl.; equitatum in omnis partīs, Caes.; exercitum omnem passim in civitates, Liv.; agros viritim civibus, Cic.; loca praefectis, Liv.; Hor. With cum: praemia mecum, Ov.; Pl. Absol.: Pl., Ov., Liv. **2.** Transf. **a.** In gen. to separate into parts, divide: bona tripartito, Cic.; genus universum in species certas, Cic.; Suet.; animum nunc huc celerem, nunc dividit illuc, Verg.; Cat. **b.** In partic. **i.** sententiam, to take the vote separately on different parts of a motion: Cic., Plin. Ep. **ii.** Of the parts of a discourse, or in the logical treatment of a subject: to distribute: Cic. **iii.** In music, to take part in, accompany: citharā carmina, Hor. **c.** to sell in lots: Suet. **d.** to apportion: belli rationem, Caes.; Tor.; Sall. **II.** to separate two wholes, to keep apart, separate, sever. **1.** Lit. **a.** In gen.: seniores a iunioribus, Cic.; a corpore capita, Liv.; Tac. With ABL. (of separation): Prop. **b.** Geogr. With ab: Caes., Liv. With ABL. of separation: Verg., Ov. **2.** Transf. **a.** to separate, distinguish: tempora curarum remissionumque, Tac.; dignitatem ordinum, Tac.; legem bonam a malā, Cic.; diversis, Hor. **b.** to set off: gemma fulvum quae dividit aurum, Verg.

dividuus, a, um [dīvidō]. **1.** Lit. **a.** divisible: animal, Cic. **b.** divided, separated: Pl., Ov., Sen. Ep., etc. **2.** Transf.: dividuum (me) tenent alter et alter amor, Ov.

divīnātiō, ōnis, f. [dīvīnō]. **I.** the faculty of foreseeing, predicting, divination: Cic., Nep. **II.** In law: the selecting of the most suitable person to conduct a prosecution: Cic. Ep., Quint., Suet.

divīnē, adv. **I.** through divine power: Pl. **II. a.** by divine inspiration, prophetically: Cic. Comp.: Cic. **b.** in a superhuman, marvellous manner; divinely, admirably: Cic., Quint.

divīnitās, ātis, f. [dīvīnus]. **I.** godhead, divinity: Cic. Of the deified Romulus: Liv.; of Augustus: Suet. **II. a.** power of divining, divination: Cic. **b.** divine quality, godlike excellence: Cic., Quint.

divīnitus, adv. [dīvīnus]. **I.** from god, by divine providence: Pl., Cic., Verg., etc. **II. a.** by inspiration, prophetically: Pl., Lucr., Cic. **b.** divinely, admirably, excellently: Cic.

divīnō, āre [dīvīnus], to foretell by soothsaying, guess. With Acc.: Cic., Ov., Liv. With Acc. and Inf.: Cic., Liv. With Indir. Quest.: Liv. Absol.: Pl., Cic., Ov., etc. [Fr. deviner.]

divīnus, a, um [dīvus (or dīvum, sky)]. **I.** of a deity (or of heaven), divine (or heavenly). **a.** In gen.: Pl.; numen, Cic.; ratione ac

mente divinā, Cic. ; stirps, Verg. ; origo,
Liv. ; non sine ope divinā, Caes. ; divinis-
sima dona, Cic. ; res divina, *divine worship,*
sacrifice, Pl., Cic., etc. ; in *pl.* : Pl., Cic.,
Liv. In *pl.* also = *religious affairs* : Caes.,
Cic. ; divina verba, *a form of prayer* :
Cato ; religiones (opp. fides humana), Liv.
b. **Esp.** with *humanus,* as a comprehensive expression : *all things, human and
divine* (*cf.* di hominesque) : Pl., Caes., Cic.,
etc. But in definition of philosophia (by
scientia divinarum humanarumque rerum),
divinae res prob. = *nature, physics,* as dist.
from humanae res, *morals* : Cic., Sen. Ep.,
Quint. So in law, divinae res signifies
natural laws, opp. humanae res, *positive
laws* : Cic. As Noun **divīnum,** i, *n.* **i.**
offering : facere, Liv. **ii.** *that which is
under divine sanction* (e.g. an oath) : Pl.
II. a. *divinely inspired, prophetic* : Pl.,
Cic., Hor., etc. With GEN. : Hor. *Comp.* :
Cic. As Noun, **divīnus,** i, *m. a soothsayer,
diviner, prophet* : Cic., Hor., Liv. **b.**
superhuman, admirable, unrivalled : Cic.,
Phaedr., Quint. *Comp.* : Cic.

divīsiō, ōnis, *f.* [dīvidō], *a division.* **1.**
Lit. : *a distribution* : agrorum, Tac. **2.**
Transf. : *a logical* or *rhetorical division* :
Cic., Quint.

divīsor, ōris, *m.* [dīvidō], *distributor* : Italiae,
Cic. **Esp.** : *a person hired by a candidate
to bribe the electors* : Cic., Suet.

divīsui, DAT. *sing. m.* [dīvidō], *for dividing* :
Macedonia divisui facilis, Liv.

divīsus, a, um. **I.** *Part.* dīvidō. **II.** Adj. :
separate, distinct. Comp. : Lucr.

divitiae, ārum, *f. pl.* [dīves], *riches, wealth.*
1. **Lit.** : Pl., Cic., Hor. **Prov.** : superare Crassum divitiis, Cic. Ep. **2.** **Transf.**
a. *costly offerings, ornaments, etc.* : Liv.,
Hor., Ov. **b.** Of soil, *richness* : Ov. **c.**
Of style, *richness, copiousness* : Cic., Quint.

dīvolg-, *v.* dīvulg-.

dīvor-, *v.* dīver-.

divortium, i, *n.* [dīvertō], *a separation.* **I.**
In gen. : inter nos, Pl. **II. a.** *divorce* :
Pl., Cic. ; facere cum aliquā, Cic., Quint.,
Suet. **b.** *a parting* of ways, water, etc. :
itinerum, Liv. ; Verg. ; aquarum, Cic. Ep.,
Liv. ; Tac. In simile : Cic.

dīvulgātus, a, um. **I.** *Part.* dīvulgō. **II.**
Adj. : *widespread, common* : Lucr., Tac.
Sup. : Cic. Ep.

dī-vulgō, āre, *to spread among the people,
make common* ; *publish, divulge* : librum,
Cic. ; consilium, Caes. ; aliquid turpi famā,
Tac. With Acc. and *Inf.* : Cic. Ep., Suet.

dīvulsus, a, um, *Part.* dīvellō.

dīvus, a, um. [*cf.* deus, diēs, Iuppiter, Ζεύς,
Διός]. **I.** *of a deity, divine* : Cat., Verg.
II. *deified* : divus Iulius, Cic. ; Liv. As
Noun, **dīvus,** i, *m.* (GEN. *pl.* us. dīvom or
dīvum), and **dīva,** ae, *f. a god, goddess,
deity* : Pl., Cic., Verg., etc. **Esp.** of some
deceased Emperors : Tac., Suet. **dīvum,**
i, *n. the sky* : sub dīvo (*cf.* sub Iove), *under
the open sky, in the open air,* Cic., Verg.,
Hor. ; sub divum rapere, Hor. (*v.* also dius.)

(1) dŏ, dare, dedī, datum (also danit, danunt,
Pl. ; *Optat.* duim, etc., Pl., Ter., Liv. ; also
duās, Pl. ; dane = dasne, Pl.) [fr. same
root as Gk. δίδωμι, *give,* but confused with

-dō (2) which is derived fr. same root as Gk.
τίθημι, *put,* e.g. in senses I. 2. c., I. 2. e.,
II. a.]. **I.** *to offer, give.* **1.** **Lit. A.** *to
offer* : aliquid, Pl. ; fabulam, Ter., Cic. ;
hosti terga, Caes. ; iugulum Clodio, Cic. ;
vela ventis, Verg. **B.** *to give.* **a.** In gen. :
aliquid, or aliquid alicui, Pl., Cic., Verg., etc.
With persons as object : ei filiam suam in
matrimonium, Caes., Liv. ; iudicem, vadem,
testem, Cic. ; milites, Liv. **b.** In partic.
i. *to offer, dedicate* : aliquid deo, Hor., Ov.,
Liv., Tac. **ii.** Of letters, *to give* (to a
messenger) *for delivery* : litteras ad te, Cic.
Ep. **iii.** Of money, *to pay* : ut ratio acceptorum et datorum par sit, Cic. So in
phr. : dare poenas alicui, *to pay the
penalty,* Sall., Ov. ; dare verba, *to pay in
words* (i.e. *to cheat*), Pl., Cic., Hor. **2.**
Transf. **a.** In gen. *to give, bestow, confer* :
auctoritatem, honorem, imperium, civita-
tem alicui, Cic., Liv. ; victoriam nobis,
Liv. ; augurium huic, Ov. ; fidem inter
se, Caes. **b.** *to grant, concede, allow, permit* : iis iter per provinciam, Caes. ; Liv. ;
tempus alicui ut etc., Cic. ; tris horas exercitui ad quietem, Caes. ; Cic. ; indutias,
Liv. Of a person pardoned, aliquem alicui
dare, Cic. ; alicuius veniam alicui dare,
Liv. With DAT. of person, and *ut* and
Subj. : Liv. With DAT. of person and
Inf. : Hor., Ov. With *ne* and *Subj.* : Ov.
In law : do, dīco, addīco, a formula used
by the praetor : viz. do, *in the granting of
judges, actions, exceptions, etc.* : dico, *in
pronouncing sentence* : addico, *in adjudging
property in dispute* : Varr. ; called the tria
verba, Ov. **c.** *to give up, hand over, deliver, devote* : se studiis, Cic., Hor. ; se
fugae, gemitui, labori, Cic. ; urbem militibus
diripiendam, Liv. ; urbem exitio, Verg.,
Liv. ; se in fugam, Cic. ; incolas in deditionem, Liv. ; animum in luctum, Ov. ;
se ad defendendos homines, Cic. **Phr.** :
operam dare, *to bestow attention.* With
DAT. : Cic., Nep. With *ut* and *Subj.* :
Caes., Cic. ; pessum dare, *to deliver to
destruction, v.* pessum. **d.** *to give* by word
of mouth or writing, *communicate, tell* :
paucis dabo, Ter. ; nomina (for enlistment),
Caes., Cic. ; da mihi nunc, satisne probas ?
Cic. ; fata data, Verg. With *Indir. Quest.* :
Verg. **e.** *to impute, ascribe, assign* : hoc
vitio datur, Ter. ; hoc Metello laudi datum
est, Cic. **II.** *to cause, bring about, produce,
make.* **a.** In gen. : spem, Cic., Liv. ;
stragem, Verg., Liv. ; impetum in hostem,
Liv. ; sibi dubitationem, Caes. ; legiones
stratas, Liv. **b.** Of audible, visible, con-
ceivable objects : *to utter, make, etc.* : clamorem, sonitum, etc., Verg. ; dicta, Verg. ;
Liv. ; ex fumo lucem, Hor. ; documentum,
Cic., Liv.

(2) dō, dare, dedī, datum, *to put.* This is
found in compounds, e.g. abdo, circumdo,
etc. *v.* also do (1) *ad init.*

docĕō, docēre, docuī, doctum [*cf.* decet ; Gk.
δοκεῖν. **Lit.** *to make bright* or *clear*], *to make
to know.* **I.** *to teach, instruct.* With Acc.
of person and Acc. of thing taught : Pl.,
Cic., Hor. ; in *Pass.* with Acc. of thing :
Hor., Quint. With Acc. of person and *Inf.* :
Cic., Liv., Tac., etc. With Acc. of person

or Acc. of thing alone : Caes., Cic., Hor.,
etc. **II.** *to show, inform.* With Acc. and
Inf. : Caes., Cic., Hor., etc. With Acc.
of person and *Indir. Quest. :* Cic., Quint.
With Acc. of person and *de :* Caes., Cic.,
etc. **III.** docere fabulam. Li t. *to teach a
play* (to the actors) ; hence, *to bring out,
exhibit :* Cic., Hor.

dochmius, i, *m.* [δόχμιος (*sc.* πούς], *the doch-
miac foot in poetry,* ⌣ ⌣ ⌣ ⌣ ⌣ : Cic.

docilis, e, *adj.* [doceō], *easily taught,
tractable, docile.* **a.** Of living beings : Cic.,
Hor., etc. *Comp. :* Quint. With *ad :*
Varr., Cic., Curt. ; in *Comp. :* Pl. With
ABL. : Juv. With GEN. : Hor. **b.** Of
things : capilli, Ov.

docilitās, ātis, *f.* [docilis], *aptness for being
taught :* Cic. With *ad :* Suet.

doctē, *adv.* **I.** *learnedly, skilfully. Comp. :*
Hor. *Sup. :* Sall. **II.** *shrewdly, cunningly :* Pl. *Comp. :* Pl.

doctor, ōris, *m.* [doceō], *a teacher, instructor :*
Cic., Hor., Quint.

doctrīna, ae, *f.* [doceō], *teaching, instruction,
education.* **1.** Lit. : Cic., Hor., Quint.
2. Transf. **a.** Objective : *learning, knowledge, science* (in *sing.* or *pl.*): Cic., Quint.
b. Subjective : *the possession of knowledge,
learning, erudition, principles ;* in *sing. :*
Nep. ; in *pl. :* Cic.

doctus, a, -um. **I.** *Part.* doceō. **II.** Adj.
A. *learned, skilled, versed, experienced.* **1.**
Lit. Of persons : Cic., Tib., etc. With
GEN. : Verg., Hor. With ABL. : Cic., Sall.,
Mart. With *ex :* Cic. With *ad,* or *in* and
ABL. : Ov. With *Inf. :* Hor. *Comp. :*
Cat., Ov. *Sup. :* Cic., Verg. *Masc.* as
Noun (us. in *pl.*) ; Cic., Phaedr. **2.**
Transf. Of things : frontes, Hor. ;
voces, Cic. ; Ov. ; falx, Prop. **B.** *know-
ing, cunning, shrewd :* Pl., Ter. ; dolus, Pl.

documen, inis, *v.* documentum.

documentum, i, *n.* (also **documen,** Lucr.)
[doceō], *a lesson, example ;* a *pattern,
warning.* With GEN. : Cic., Liv., Tac.
With *Indir. Quest. :* documentum capere,
quid esset victis extimescendum, Cic. ;
quantum in bello fortuna posset, iam ipsi
essent documento, Caes. ; Liv. ; docu-
menta damus quā simus origine nati, Ov.
With *ne* and *Subj. :* documentum esse, ne
quis fidei Romanae confidat, Liv. ; Pl. ;
Hor. *Absol. :* alicui documento esse,
Caes., Liv., Quint.

Dōdōna, ae, *f. a city in Epirus, famous for its
ancient oracle of Zeus.* Transf. : *the oak-
grove of D. :* Verg. ; **Dōdōnaeus,** a, um ;
Dōdōnis, idis, *f. adj.*

dōdrāns, antis, *m.* [dē quadrāns. Lit. *a
fourth off*], *three-fourths :* aedifici reliquum
dodrantem emere, Cic. ; (agri), Liv. ; Mart.;
heres ex dodrante, Nep. As a measure of
length, *nine inches :* Suet.

dogma, atis, *n.* [δόγμα], *a philosophical tenet,
doctrine :* Cic., Juv.

Dolabella, ae, *m. a Roman cognomen in the
gens* Cornelia ; esp. P. Cornelius, *Cicero's
son-in-law.*

dolābra, ae, *f.* [dolō], *a pick-axe, mattock :*
Liv., Tac., Juv.

dolēns, entis. **I.** *Part.* doleō. **II.** *Adj.
causing pain, painful. Comp. :* Ov.

dolenter, *adv. painfully, with sorrow :* Cic.
Comp. : Cic.

doleō, ēre, uī (dolitūrus, Liv., Verg., etc.)
[perh. fr. same root as dolō], *to feel pain,
suffer pain, smart with pain, ache.* **A.**
Physically : doleo ab oculis, Pl. ; pes,
oculi, caput, latera, pulmones, Cic. ; Pl. ;
Lucr. *Impers. :* mihi dolet, cum ego
vapulo, Pl. **B.** Mentally. **a.** Of personal
subjects : *to be pained, grieved, indignant,
chagrined :* Ter., Verg., Quint., etc. With
ABL. of cause : Cic., Verg., etc. With *de :*
Cic. Ep., Hor., Ov. With *ex :* Caes., Cic.
Ep. With *quod* or *id quod :* Caes., Ov.
With Acc. and *Inf. :* Lucr., Cic., Verg., etc.
With *Inf. :* Hor. With Acc. (freq.) :
Caes., Cic., Verg., etc. **b.** Of subjects not
personal : *to give pain.* With DAT. :
animus mihi dolet, Pl. ; Ter. ; Cic. *Impers. :* mihi dolebit, non tibi, si quid ego
stulte fecero, Pl. ; Ter. ; Cic.

dōliāris, e, *adj.* [dōlium], *cask-like, tubby :*
anus, Pl.

dōliolum, i, *n.* [*dim.* dōlium], *a small cask :*
Liv.

dōlium, i, *n.* [perh. fr. root of dolō], *a very
large jar* (for storing wine) : Pl., Cato, Hor.,
etc. ; de dolio haurire, Cic. Prov. : in
pertusum ingerimus dicta dolium, Pl.

dolō, āre, *to lop with an axe, to hew.* **1.** Lit. :
robur, Cic. ; Cat., etc. **2.** Transf. :
caput fuste, Hor. ; opus, sicut potuit, dola-
vit, Cic. ; hodie hunc dolum dolamus, Pl.

dolō or **dolōn,** ōnis, *m.* [δόλων]. **I.** *a pike :*
Verg. **II.** *a swordstick :* Suet. Transf. :
a fly's sting : Phaedr. **III.** *the fore-topsail*
or perh. *the sail on the bowsprit :* Liv.

Dolō, ōnis, *m. a Trojan spy.*

Dolopes, um (Acc. sing. -em, Liv.), *m. pl. a
warlike people in Thessaly ;* **Dolopia,** ae, *f.
their country.*

dolor, ōris, *m.* [doleō], *pain, smart, ache.* **A.**
Physical : Pl., Cato, Cic. With GEN. of
part affected : Lucr., Cic., Hor. **B.**
Mental : *pain, grief, anguish.* **1.** Lit. :
Pl., Caes., Cic., Hor. ; commovere, accipere,
Cic. Esp. *indignation, chagrin, resentment :* Caes., Cic., Verg., Hor. With *Obj.*
GEN. : Caes., Cic., Ov., Liv. With *ex :* Cic. ;
iustus, Liv., Tac. **2.** Transf. **a.** *an object or cause of grief :* Prop., Ov. ; magno
esse Germanis dolori Ariovisti mortem,
Caes. **b.** Rhet. *passionate expression,
pathos :* Cic., Quint. [Fr. *douleur*.]

dolōsē, *adv. craftily :* Pl., Cic.

dolōsus, a, um [dolus], *crafty, cunning, deceitful.* **a.** Of persons : Pl., Hor., Ov.
With *Inf. :* Hor. **b.** Of things : taurus,
cinis, Hor. ; vulpes, Phaedr.

dolus, i, *m.* [*cf.* Gk. δόλος, δέλεαρ], *wile, artifice, stratagem.* **A.** Unqualified, in bad
sense, *trickery, guile* (in *sing.* or *pl.*): Pl.,
Cic., Verg., etc. ; dolos conserere, Pl. ;
versare, Verg. ; nectere, Liv. **B.** Qualified by *malus,* the legal phr. for *deliberate
fraud :* Pl., Ter., Cic., Liv.

domābilis, e, *adj.* [domō], *tameable :* Hor.,
Ov.

domesticātim, *adv.* [domesticus], *in the
house, at home :* Suet.

domesticus, a, um [domus]. **I.** *of the house :*
parietes, Cic. ; vestis, Cic. ; in Adv. sense

domesticus otior, Hor. **II.** *of one's family ;*
domestic, household, private : in luctu domestico, Cic.; praedones, Cic.; clades,
Liv.; iudicium, Caes.; usus cum aliquo,
Cic. As Noun, **domestici**, ōrum, *m. pl. the*
members of a family or household : Cic.,
Liv., Suet. Also, *domestica, household*
slaves : Suet. **III.** *home-, native, belonging*
to one's own country : domesticae copiae rei
frumentariae, Caes.; bellum (*civil*), Caes.,
Cic.; castra (= praetoria cohors), Juv.;
domestica facta celebrare, Hor.

domī, *adv.* [old LOCAT. of domus]. **I.** *at*
home : Pl., Ter., Cic., Hor., etc. **II.** *in*
one's own country, at home : Pl., Caes., Cic.,
etc. (*v.* also domus.)

domicilium, I, *n.* [domus and root of cēlō], *a*
settled dwelling-place, home, abode. **1.** Lit.:
Pl., Caes., Cic. **2.** Transf.: superbiae,
gloriae, etc., Cic.; carcer, domicilium
plebis, Liv.

domina, ae, *f.* [dominus]. **1.** Lit.: *the*
mistress of a house, household or family
(= era, materfamilias) : Pl., Ov., Quint.,
etc. **2.** Transf. **a.** *a wife :* Verg., Ov.
Also *a mistress :* Tib., Prop. **b.** Of a goddess, *Our Lady :* Verg., Prop., Ov. **c.** Of
members of the Imperial family : Suet.
d. Of abstracts : Fors domina campi, Cic.
[It. *donna ;* Sp. *doña, dueña ;* Fr. *dame.*]

domināns, antis. **I.** *Part.* dominor. **II.**
Adj. **a.** *bearing sway.* *Comp. :* Lucr. **b.**
literal : nomina, Hor.

domĭnātĭō, ōnis, *f.* [dominor], *lordship,*
mastery ; esp. *absolute dominion, tyranny,*
despotism (dist. fr. regnum and imperium:
opp. to libertas). **1.** Lit.: Cic., Liv., Tac.
In *pl.*: Cic., Tac. **2.** Transf.: iudiciorum, Cic.

domĭnātor, ōris, *m.* [dominor], *ruler, lord :*
rerum Deus, Cic.; and **dominātrix**, īcis, *f.*
mistress. Transf.: dominatrix animi
cupiditas, Cic.

domĭnātus, ūs, *m.* [dominor], *lordship, mas-*
tery ; esp. *absolute rule, sovereignty, tyranny.*
1. Lit.: Cic., Caes. In *pl.*: Cic. **2.**
Transf.: cupiditatum, Cic.; omnium
rerum, Cic.

domĭnĭcus, a, um [dominus], *of a lord or mas-*
ter : Varr., Sen. Ep. As Noun, **dominicum**,
ī, *n. a collection of poems by the emperor*
Nero : Suet.

domĭnĭum, ī, *n.* [dominus]. **I.** In law, *lord-*
ship, absolute ownership : Liv. **II.** *a*
feast, banquet : Lucil., Cic.

domĭnor, ārī [dominus], *to be or play*
the master, to have dominion, bear rule,
tyrannise. **1.** Lit. Of persons: Cic.,
Verg., etc. With *in* and ABL.: Cic.,
Verg., Ov., Liv. With *in* and ACC.: Ov.,
Liv. With *inter :* Caes. With ABL.:
Verg. **2.** Transf. Of things: sol. Cic.;
mare, Tac.; consilium, Cic. With *in* and
ABL.: Cic., Ov., Quint. With *in* and ACC.:
Cic. With *inter :* Verg. **Pass.:** Enn.

domĭnus, ī, *m.* [*v.* domus], *a master of a*
house or household. **1.** Lit.: Cic., etc.
Occ. *the young master :* Pl. **2.** Transf.
a. Of a husband or lover : Ov. **b.** *a*
master, owner : Cato, Cic., Hor. As Adj.
asserting ownership : manus, Ov. **c.** *mas-*
ter, employer : Pl., Cic. Ep. **d.** *a master,*

lord; esp. *a despot :* Cic., Verg. Transf. of
emotions : Cic. Also, rerum temporumque,
Liv. **e.** With or without convivi or epuli
(like rex) : *the master of a feast, the host :*
Cic., Liv. **f.** *a title of the emperors :* Suet.

domiporta, ae, *f.* [domus, portō], *she that*
carries her house on her back ; of *the snail,*
Poet. ap. Cic.

Domitiānus, ī, m. ; T. Flavius D.; *Roman*
Emperor, A.D. 81–96.

Domitius, a, *name of a Roman plebeian gens ;*
esp. L. D. Aenobarbus, *general of Pompey*
in the civil war ; **Domitiānus**, a, um.

domĭtō, āre [*freq.* domō], *to tame, break in :*
boves, currūs, Verg. [Fr. *dompter.*]

domĭtor, ōris, *m.* and **domĭtrix**, īcis, *f.*
(Verg., Ov.) [domō], *a tamer, breaker.* **1.**
Lit.: equorum, Cic., Verg. **2.** Transf.:
a subduer, vanquisher. With *Obj.* GEN.:
Cic., Verg., etc.

domĭtus, a, um, *Part.* domō.

domĭtus, ūs, *m.* [domō], *a taming ;* quadrupedum, Cic.

domō, āre, uī, itum [fr. same root as domus],
to tame, to break in. **1.** Lit.: feras
beluas, Cic.; Pl.; Verg., etc. **2.** Transf.:
to subdue, vanquish, conquer. **a.** Of
physical force : Cic., Hor., Liv., Tac.
b. Of moral control : Pl.; libidines, Cic.;
invidiam, Hor.; with abstr. subject : Sall.;
Hor. **c.** Poet. uses : vino domiti, Enn.;
terram rastris, Verg.; uvam prelo, Hor.;
Ov.; *cf.* vim fluminis, Liv.

domus, *f.* (Voc. domus ; Acc. domum ;
GEN. domūs ; domī in Pl., Ter.; LOCAT.
domī, q.v. ; DAT. domuī ; occ. domō and
domū ; ABL. domō ; rarely domū. NOM.
pl. domūs ; Acc. domōs ; also domūs ;
GEN. domōrum and domuum ; DAT. and
ABL. domibus) [fr. same root as Gk. δέμειν,
build ; dominus comes fr. old LOCAT. in
-n]. **1.** Lit.: *house, home :* in alicuius
domum venire, Cic.; in domos refugere,
Liv.; in nostrā domō, Pl.; Quint., etc.;
domum, *homewards, to the house :* Pl., Cic.,
Verg., etc. In *pl.* : domos, Pl., Liv., etc.;
domo, *from home, from the house :* Pl., Ter.,
Cic.; also *at home :* Nep., Suet.; domi, *at*
home, in the house : Pl., Cic., Verg., etc.;
domi meae, *at my house.* **2.** Transf. **a.**
any sort of building or abode ; of the winds,
animals, the Minotaur, etc. : Verg.; of
the gods : Verg., Ov.; of the body as the
home of the soul : Ov. **b.** In gen.: *one's*
native place, country, home : Pl., Cic., Verg.,
etc. Hence, the phr. belli domique, and
domi militiaeque, *in war and peace* (*v.* bellum
and militia) : noster populus in pace et
domi imperat, Cic. **c.** *a household, family,*
race : Cic. Ep., Verg., etc. **d.** *a philosophi-*
cal school, sect : Cic., Sen. Ep. [It. *duomo ;*
Fr. *dôme.*]

dōnābĭlis, e, *adj.* [dōnō], *worthy to receive a*
present : Pl.

dōnārĭum, ī, *n.* [dōnum], *the place in a temple*
where votive offerings were kept. **1.** Lit.:
Luc. **2.** Transf. **a.** *a temple, sanctuary,*
altar : Verg., Ov. **b.** *a votive offering :*
Liv.

dōnātĭō, ōnis, *f.* [dōnō], *a giving, a dona-*
tion : Cic.

dōnātīvum, ī, *n.* [dōnō], *a largess, donative*

given by emperor to his soldiers (*v.* congiarium) : Tac., Suet.

dōnec (dōnicum, Pl., Cato ; **dōnique,** Lucr.), *conj.* [dōnec, contr. fr. dōnique, wh. is fr. dō-ne (= up to) and que ; dōnicum is fr. dō-ne and cum ; Lit. *up to whenever*]. **I.** *up to the time when, until* (not in Caes., 4 times in Cic.). **a.** With *Indic.* : Pl., Cic., Verg., etc. **b.** With *Subj.* : Verg., Tac., etc. With usque, usque adeo, usque eo, eo usque, in tantum preceding : **i.** With *Indic.* : Pl., Ter., Cic., Liv. **ii.** With *Subj.* : Pl., Hor., Quint. **II.** *so long as, while.* **a.** With *Indic.* : Hor., Ov., Liv., Tac. **b.** With *Subj.* : Liv., Tac.

dōnicum, *v.* dōnec.

dōnō, āre [dōnum]. **1.** Lit. **a.** *to make a gift of, bestow* (with Acc. of gift and Dat. of person) : Pl., Cic., Verg., etc. **b.** *to present* a person (Acc.) *with a gift* (Abl.) : Pl., Cic., Hor., etc. With *Inf.* as *Obj.* : Verg., Hor. **2.** Transf. **a.** alicui aeternitatem, Cic. **b.** *to give up, sacrifice* : amicitias rei publicae, Cic. Ep. **c.** *to remit, forgive* a debt, obligation, *etc.* : aliquid alicui, Caes. **d.** (*cf.* condonare), *to forgive, pardon* (for another's sake) : noxae damnatus donatur populo Romano, Liv. ; Ov. [Fr. donner.]

dōnum, i, *n.* [dō], *a gift, present* (*a voluntary gift*). **1.** In gen. : Pl., Cic., Verg., etc. ; ultima *or* suprema dona, *the last honours, funeral rites,* Ov. ; dona praesentia cape laetus horae, Hor. **2.** In partic. : *a votive offering to a deity, sacrifice* : Pl., Cic., Verg., etc. [Fr. don.]

Dōrēs, um, *m. pl.* the Dorians, one of the four Hellenic tribes ; **Dōricus (-ius),** a, um, *Dorian or Grecian.*

Dōris, ĭdis, *f.* **I.** *the country of the Dorians.* **II.** *d.* of *Oceanus, w. of Nereus, and m. of* 50 *sea-nymphs.* Transf. *the sea* : Verg., Ov.

dormiō, īre (Fut. dormībō, Pl.) [*cf.* Gk. δαρθάνω], *to sleep.* **1.** Lit. : Pl., Cic., Hor., etc. Pass. : tota mihi dormitur hiems, Mart. ; Cat. Pass. Impers. : Juv. Prov. : non omnibus dormio, *not asleep to everybody,* Cic. **2.** Transf. **a.** Of death : Pl., Cat. **b.** *to be asleep, inactive, or unconcerned* : Pl., Cic., Prop., etc.

dormītātor, ōris, *m.* [dormītō], *a dreamer* (or perh. *a sleeper by day,* i.e. *a burglar*) : Pl.

dormītō, āre [*freq.* dormiō], *to be drowsy with sleep or want of sleep.* **1.** Lit. : Pl., Cic., Hor. **2.** Transf. **a.** oscitans et dormitans sapientia, Cic. ; quandoque bonus dormitat Homerus, Hor. ; Pl. ; Quint. **b.** Of a lamp (= *go out*) : Ov.

dormītōrius, a, um [dormiō], *of or for sleeping* : cubiculum, Plin. Ep.

dorsum, i, *n.* (*m.* **dorsus,** Pl.) [perh. contr. of deorsum, q.v. as *Neut.* Noun], *the back* of a man or beast (opp. venter). **1.** Lit. : Pl., Verg., Liv., etc. **2.** Transf. Of a mountain ridge : Caes., Liv., Verg., etc. Of a reef : Verg. Of the back of the sharebeam : Verg. [It. *dosso ;* Fr. *dos.*]

dōs, ōtis, *f.* [dō ; *cf.* Gk. δωτίνη], *a marriage portion, dowry.* **1.** Lit. : Pl., Cic., Hor., etc. **2.** Transf. : (iuris civilis) artem

verborum dote locupletasti, Cic. ; formae, Ov. ; naturae fortunaeque, Plin. Ep.

Dossennus, i, *m. Hunchback, a burlesque character* in *Atellane farces.* Transf. : Hor.

dossuārius, a, um [dorsum], *that carries* (burdens) *on its back :* asellus, Varr.

dōtālis, e, *adj.* [dōs], *of or forming a dowry :* aedes, Pl. ; praedia, Cic. Ep. ; agri, Hor. ; Tyrii, Verg.

dōtātus, a, um. **I.** *Part.* dōtō. **II.** Adj. : *endowed.* **1.** Lit. : Pl., Cic. Ep., Hor., etc. **2.** Transf. : Chione dotatissima formā, Ov.

dōtō, āre [dōs], *to endow, to portion :* Suet. ; sanguine dotabere, virgo, Verg. [Fr. douer.]

drachma (drachuma, Pl.), ae, *f.* [δραχμή], *a drachma,* a Greek silver coin of about the same value as the Roman denarius : Pl., Cic., Hor.

dracō, ōnis, *m.* [δράκων], *a sort of serpent, a dragon.* **1.** Lit. : Cic., Suet. As the guardian of treasures : Cic., Phaedr. **2.** Astron. : *the constellation, Draco :* Cic. poet.

Dracō, ōnis, *m. an Athenian lawgiver, notorious for his severity,* c. B.C. 620.

dracōnigena, ae, *m.f.* [dracō and *gen.* in gignō], *sprung from the* (*teeth of the*) *dragon :* urbs, i.e. Thebes, Ov.

drāpeta, ae, *m.* [δραπέτης], *a runaway slave :* Pl.

dromas, adis, *m.* [δρομάς, *the running beast*], *a dromedary :* Liv.

dromos, i, *m.* [δρόμος], *the Spartan racecourse :* Liv.

Druĭdēs, um (**Druidae,** ārum, Cic.) [Celtic word ; *cf.* Gk. δρῦς. Lit. : *priests of the oaks*], *m. pl. the Druids, the priests and wise men of the Gauls and Britons :* Caes., Luc., Tac.

Drūsilla, ae, *f.* **I.** Livia D., *the second wife of Augustus, m. of Tiberius.* **II.** *d. of Drusus Germanicus.*

Drūsus, i, *m. a cognomen in the gens Livia ; esp.* **I.** M. Livius, B.C. 91, *who renewed several of the proposals of the Gracchi.* **II.** Claudius Drusus Nero, *s. of Livia Drusilla and Tiberius Claudius Nero ; f. of Germanicus.*

Dryantĭdēs, is, *m. Lycurgus, king of Thrace, s. of Dryas.*

Dryas, adis, *f. a Dryad, a wood-nymph :* us. in *pl.* **Dryades.**

Dryopē, ēs, *f.* **I.** *m. of Amphissus.* **II.** *m. of Tarquitus.*

Dryopes, um, *m. pl.* (*sing.* **Dryops,** Ov.), a *people of Epirus.*

duālis, e, *adj.* [duo], *that contains two.* Gramm. : numerus, *the dual,* Quint.

dubiē, *adv. doubtfully :* Cic. Freq. with negatives : non *or* haud dubie, *undoubtedly, indisputably :* Cic. Ep., Liv., etc.

dubitābilis, e, *adj.* [dubitō], *doubtful :* nec erit dubitabile verum, Ov.

dubitanter, *adv.* **I.** *doubtingly :* Cic. **II.** *hesitatingly :* Cic.

dubitātiō, ōnis, *f.* [dubitō], *a wavering.* **1.** Lit. In opinion or judgment : *a doubting, uncertainty, doubt.* **a.** In gen. : adferre alicui, Cic. ; eo sibi minus dubitationis dari, quod etc., Caes. ; sine ullā dubitatione, Cic. With *Obj.* GEN. : Caes., Cic., Quint. With *de :* Cic. With *Indir. Quest. :* Cic., Quint. With *quin,* after negatives : Cic. **b.** Rhet. a figure of speech, *(assumed)* embarrassment ; Cic. **2.** Transf. : *a wavering* (in action or decision), *hesitation, irresolution :* aestuabat dubitatione, Cic. ; sine ullā dubitatione, Cic. ; inter dubitationem senati, Sall. ; (Caesar) nullā interpositā dubitatione legiones ex castris educit, Caes.

dubito, āre [*freq.* of old Lat. dubāre, *v.* dubius], *to halt between two opinions, waver.* **1.** Lit. In opinion or judgment : *to be uncertain, to doubt.* **a.** In gen. : Cic., Verg., Quint. With *de :* Caes., Cic., Quint. *Pass. Impers.* de armis dubitatum est, Cic. With Acc. (in prose only with *Neut. Pron.*) : Pl., Cic., Ov., etc. In *Pass. :* dubitati tecta parentis, Ov. ; Cic. ; Liv. With *Indir. Quest.* or *Deliberative :* Pl., Cic., Hor., etc. Poet. in *Pass. :* an dea sim, dubitor, Ov. With negative (or in interrog.) and *quin :* Pl., Cic., Ov., etc. With Acc. and *Inf. :* Lucr., Liv., etc. **b.** Of inanim. and abstr. subjects : *to be uncertain, waver :* si fortuna dubitabit, Liv. ; manus, oratio, Quint. **2.** Transf. In action or decision, *to stop to think, to be irresolute, to hesitate* (us. with negat.) : Pl., Caes., Verg., etc. With *Inf.* (most freq.) : Pl., Cic., Verg., etc. ; rare affirmatively : Cic., Sall., Curt. With negat. (or in interrog.) and *quin :* Caes., Cic. With Acc. of *Neut. Pron. :* Ter., Cic., Verg. [Fr. douter.]

dubius, a, um [fr. old Lat. dubāre, formed fr. root of duo and of fuī, *I was.* Lit. of *double nature, ambiguous*]. **A.** Act. : *wavering.* **1.** Lit. In opinion : *doubting, uncertain :* Pl., Cic. With GEN. : sententiae, Liv. ; mentis, salutis, Ov. With *Indir. Quest.* or *Deliberative :* Lucr., Verg., Liv., etc. With Acc. and *Inf. :* Liv. With negat. and *quin :* Liv., Curt. **2.** Transf. In action or decision : *irresolute, vacillating, undecided.* **a.** In gen. : Caes., Ov., etc. **b.** Of inanim. subjects : fluctibus dubiis volvi coeptum est mare, Liv. **B.** Pass. : *that is doubted of, doubtful, uncertain.* **a.** In gen. : victoria, Caes. ; salus, Cic. ; Lutati nomen haud dubium est, Liv. ; haud dubii hostes, Liv. ; proelia, Tac. ; dubiae crepuscula lucis, Ov. ; caelum, Verg. **b.** Phr. **i.** With *Neut.* Adj. **dubium :** dubium est, esp. freq. with negatives : Pl., Ter., Cic. Ep. With *de :* Cic., Quint. With *Indir. Quest. :* Caes., Cic., Quint. Without verb : dubium est, esp. freq. with negatives : dubium pius an sceleratus Orestes, Ov. ; Tac. With negat. and *quin :* Ter. With Acc. and *Inf. :* Pl., Ter., Liv., etc. ; aliquid dubium habero, *to regard anything as uncertain :* Cic. **ii.** With **dubium** as *Neut.* Noun : in dubium vocare, *to call in question,* Cic. ; venire, *to be called in question,* Cic., Liv. ; in dubio : in dubio est animus, Ter. ; Lucr. ; in dubio ponere (with *Indir. Quest.*), Liv. ; sine dubio, *without doubt, doubtless, certainly :* Ter., Cic., Quint. ; procul dubio, *beyond doubt :* Lucr., Liv. ; haud pro dubio *and*

haud pro dubio habitum est, *as beyond doubt,* Liv. **C.** Causative. **a.** *causing doubt or uncertainty :* cena, Ter., Hor. **b.** *dangerous, critical, difficult :* res, Pl., Verg., Liv., etc. ; pericla, Lucr. ; tempora, Hor. ; alicuius fortunas in dubium devocare, Caes.

ducatus, ūs, *m.* [dux], *military leadership, command :* Suet. [Sp. *ducado ;* It. *ducato ;* Fr. *duché.*]

ducenarius, a, um [ducēnī], *containing* or *relating to two hundred :* procuratores, i.e. *who received a salary of 200 sestertia,* Suet. ; iudices, *petty judges* (chosen from persons possessed of 200 sestertia), Suet.

duceni, ae, a [for *ducentēnī*], *a group of 200;* also 200 *each :* Pl., Hirt., Liv.

ducentesima, ae, *f.* (*sc.* pars) [ducentī], *a two-hundredth part, one-half per cent. :* Tac., Suet.

ducenti, ae, a, *pl. num.* (duo centum), *two hundred.* **1.** Lit. : Pl., Liv., etc. **2.** Transf. : *an indefinitely large number :* Pl., Cat., Hor. **ducentiens** or **ducenties,** *adv.* [ducentī], *two hundred times.* **1.** Lit. : Cic. **2.** Transf. : *many times :* Cat.

duco, dūcĕre, dūxī, ductum (*Imper.* us. dūc ; dūce in Pl.) [*cf.* Germ. *ziehen, zuck, zeugen ;* Eng. *tow, tug*]. **I. A.** *to draw, draw along, haul, pull, draw out.* **1.** Lit. **a.** In gen. : carros, Caes. ; plaustra, Ov. ; curru victorem, Hor. **b.** Of parts of the body, *to draw into a strained position :* os, Cic. ; vultum ad suspiria, Ov. ; ilia (i.e. *to become broken-winded*), Hor. **c.** *to draw* (so as to make, shape, construct). **i.** vallum, fossam, Caes. ; parietem, Cic. ; viam, Liv. ; murum, Liv.. Hor. **ii.** Of spinning : stamina, fila, lanas, Ov. In metaph. : epos, Hor. ; carmina, Ov. **iii.** Of other things : lineam, litteram, orbem, Ov. ; vivos vultūs de marmore, Verg. **2.** Transf. *to draw out, prolong.* **a.** In gen. : longas voces in fletum, Verg. **b.** In time : bellum, Caes. ; rem leniter, Liv. Of time itself : tempus, Cic. ; diem ex die, Caes. ; noctem ludo, Verg. Also, *to put off* a person : aliquem, Caes. Hence, *to pass, spend :* aetatem in litteris, Cic. **B.** *to draw to oneself, pull at.* **1.** Lit. **a.** remos, Ov. ; frena manu, Ov. **b.** Of shape, colour, etc. ; *to draw on, take on :* senectam, Verg. ; pallorem, Ov. ; nomina, Hor. **c.** *to draw, attract :* silvas carmine, Ov. **2.** Transf. : ducit te species, Hor. In *Pass. :* honore aut gloriā duci, Cic. Hence colloq. *to draw, deceive :* me dictis, Ter. **C.** *to draw out* (from its place), *draw off.* **1.** Lit. **a.** ferrum vaginā, Ov. ; sortem, Cic. (Hence, of person : sorte ductus, Verg.) ; aquam, Cato, Cic. ; gemitum pectore, Ov. **b.** Of stealing : Sall. ; Juv. ; Colloq. *to take oneself off :* me ad regem, Pl. **2.** Transf. : *to derive, trace from its source :* genus Olympo, Verg. ; belli initium a fame, Cic Ep. (Mostly *Pass.* in prose, *to spring from.* **D.** *to draw in, take in, suck in, quaff, inhale.* **1.** Lit. : animam spiritu, Cic. ; succos nectaris, Hor. ; pocula, Hor. **2.** Transf. : oblivia vitae, Hor. ; pocula, Hor. **II.** *to lead, conduct.* **A.** In gen. **1.** Lit. : illos in carcerem, Cic. ; pecudes, Verg. **2.** Transf. Of a road: via ducit in urbem, Verg. **B.** In partic. **a.** *to bring* or *take (with one):* reliquos obsidum loco secum, Caes.; sua praemia, Ov. **b.** *to bring home (as wife):* aliquam in matrimonium, Caes.; aliquam, Cic.; ex plebe, Liv. **c.** *to have a train of, conduct as leader:* pompas, Verg., Ov.; choros, Hor. **C.** M i l i t. **a.** *to lead, march:* exercitum in Segusianos, Caes.; Liv. Without Obj.: Hannibal ad Hiberum ducit, Liv. **b.** *to lead, march* or *order to march in the van.* **i,** Of the commander: legiones ducere, Caes. **ii.** Of the troops: agmen ducere, Curt. Without Obj.: Tac. **c.** *to lead, command, be in command of:* exercitum, Cic.; ordinem, Caes., Liv.; turmas, Verg. **III.** M e r c a n t. (*cf.* Gk. ἡγεῖσθαι), *to calculate, compute, reckon.* **1.** L i t.: Lucil.; XC medimnum milia, Cic. **2.** T r a n s f. **a.** alicuius rationem ducere, *to consider, calculate someone's advantage:* Cic.; rationem offici, Cic. **b.** *to account, esteem, reckon, consider:* aliquid pro nihilo, Pl.; parvi id ducebat, Cic.; aliquid honori, Sall.; aliquem despicatui, Cic.; aliquem in numero hostium, Cic.; tutelae nostrae duximus, Liv. With Acc. and *Inf.:* Caes., Cic., Verg., etc.

ductim, *adv.* [dūcō], *by drawing off, in a continuous stream:* invergere in me liquores tuos, Pl.

ductĭtō, āre [*freq.* ductō]. **1.** L i t. **a.** *to lead about:* Pl. **b.** *to lead home a wife:* Pl. **2.** T r a n s f.: *to cheat:* ego follitim ductitabo, Pl.

ductō, āre [*freq.* dūco]. **1.** L i t. **a.** *to draw, trail:* restim, Ter. **b.** *to lead about:* exercitum, Sall., Tac.; Pl. **c.** *to take home:* Pl., Ter. **2.** T r a n s f.: *to deceive, cheat:* Pl.

ductor, ōris, *m.* [dūcō], *a leader.* **a.** *commander, general:* exercitūs, Cic.; apum (in their battles), Verg.; and of the leaders in warlike games, Verg., Suet. **b.** *a guide:* itineris, Liv.

ductus, a, um, *Part.* dūcō.

ductus, ūs, *m.* [dūcō]. **I.** *a drawing, tracing.* **a.** C o n c r. *the lines, form:* oris, muri, Cic.; Luer.; Quint. **b.** *a drawing off from its source:* aquarum, Cic. **II.** *generalship, command:* Pl., Caes., Cic., etc.

dūdum, *adv.* [fr. dum and old adv. meaning *long,* fr. wh. comes Gk. δήν]. L i t. *a while ugo* (mostly colloq.). **I.** *a short while ago, just now:* Pl., Ter., Cic., Verg. With *ut* or *cum: as* or *when just now:* Pl., Cic. **II.** *a long while ago, long ago.* With *haud:* Pl. With *quam* (mostly in exclam.): Pl., Ter., Cic. Ep. Oftenest with *iam:* Cic., Verg.

duidēns, *v.* bidēns.

Duillius (or **Duilius**), ī, *m. a Roman consul who defeated the Carthaginians in the first naval battle ever won by the Romans,* B.C. 260.

duim, *v.* dō.

dulcēdō, inis, *f.* [dulcis], *sweetness.* T r a n s f.: *pleasantness, charm:* aquarum, Luer.; orationis, Cic.; irae, Liv.; oti, Tac.; praedandi, Liv.

dulcēscō, dulcēscere, dulcuī [dulcis], *to become sweet:* Cic.

dulciculus, a, um [*dim.* dulcis], *delightfully* or *rather sweet:* Pl., Cic.

dulcifer, era, erum [dulcis ferō], *containing sweetness, sweet:* Pl.

dulcis, e, *adj.* [*cf.* Gk. γλυκύς] (in taste; opp. amarus). **1.** L i t.: Pl., Cic., Hor., etc. *Comp.:* Ov. *Sup.:* Plin. **2.** T r a n s f. **a.** In gen.: *pleasant, delightful, charming:* Pl.; vita, Luer.; orator, Cic.; nomen libertatis, Cic.; otium, amores, poemata, Hor. *Comp.:* Cic. **b.** Esp. of friends, lovers, *etc.: charming, loved, dear:* Cic., Hor. Hence, in addresses: optime et dulcissime frater, Cic. Ep.; Hor. *Neut.* Acc. **dulce** as *Adv., sweetly, pleasantly:* dulce ridentem, Cat., Hor. [It. *dolce;* Fr. *doux.*]

dulciter, *adv. sweetly, delightfully:* Cic., Quint. *Comp.:* Prop., Quint. *Sup.:* Cic.

dulcitūdō, inis, *f.* [dulcis], *the quality of sweetness:* Cic.

dūlicē, *adv.* [δουλικῶς], *like a slave, servilely:* Pl.

Dūlichium, ī, *n.* (or **Dūlichia,** ae, *f.*), *an island in the Ionian Sea, belonging to the kingdom of Ulysses:* **Dūlichius,** a, um.

dum, *adv.* and *conj.* (prob. Acc. of duration, fr. root seen in preps. dē, dō (*v.* dōnec). Lit. *during all this time, this while, up to now*]. **I.** A d v e r b. **a.** *up to now, yet,* in combination with negatives, nōn, nē, nec, nēmō, nihil, nūllus, haud. **b.** As enclitic, *now.* **i.** With Imperative, esp. age, agite (colloq.): *a moment:* Pl., Ter., Cic., Cat., etc. Occ. agedum with a *pl.* verb: Cic., Liv. **ii.** In enumeration (= Gk. μέν): primumdum, Pl. **c.** As Demonstr. Adv. = usque eo or tamdiu, *so long:* Cat. **II.** *Conjunction, whilst, so long as, during the time when, at the time when, to the time when.* **A.** With Indic. **a.** *whilst, while, during the time when.* Mostly with *Pres.:* Pl., Cic., Verg., etc. With *Imperf.:* Cic., Liv., Tac. Freq. with *Historic Pres.:* Ter., Caes., Cic., Verg., etc. With *Perf.:* Cic., Nep. With *Pluperf.* (rare): Liv. With *Fut.* (rare) = Pl. (In *Orat. Obliq.* the Indic. is occ. kept by poets and post-Aug. writers: Ov., Tac., etc.) **b.** *so long as, during all the time that.* With *Pres.:* Cato, Cic. With *Imperf.:* Caes., Cic. With *Perf.:* Liv. With *Fut.:* Pl., Cic., Verg. Often with tam diu, tantum, tantum modo, tantisper, usque: Pl., Cic., Liv., etc. **c.** *until, to the time when.* Mostly with *Perf.:* Cic., etc. With *Fut. Perf.* (rare): Cic. Ep., Verg. With *Pres.* (prob. *dum* = *whilst*): Ter., Verg., Liv. After exspectare: Ter. After morari: Verg., Liv. **B.** With *Subj.* **a.** *during a time when, during such a time as* (*Subj.* here is consecutive): *v.* rare (many exx. us. quoted are really due to attraction to another *Subj.,* or to some obliqueness): Verg., Liv. **b.** *during all a time when, so long as, i.e. provided that, if only.* (*Subj.* here is Jussive): Pl., Cic., etc. Often with dum modo: Pl., Cic., Ov., etc. and negatively dum ne: Pl., Cic. Ep., Ov., etc.; or dum modo ne: Cic. **c.** *until,* with *Pres.* and *Imperf. Subj.:* prob. *dum* here = *whilst.* (*Subj.* is Consecutive, Jussive, or Final): Pl., Caes., Cic., Verg., etc. Often

after unspectate : Caes., Cic., Hor., Liv.,
Tac. ; and after morari : Hirt., Liv.
dūmētum, i. *n.* [dūmus], *a thorn-brake,
thicket.* **1.** Lit. : Cic., Verg., Hor. **2.**
Transf. : Stoicorum, Cic.
dum modo, *v.* dum.
dūmōsus, a, um [dūmus], *full of thorns :*
rupes, Verg. ; saxa, Ov.
dumtaxat, *adv.* [fr. old legal phr., where dum
taxat (*v.* taxō) meant ' *so long as (the
magistrate) estimates*' (e.g. a fine at less or
more than half a man's property)]. **I.** *not
less than, at least.* **a.** Numerically : dumtaxat ad prid. Non. Mai., Cic. Ep. ; Pl.
b. In gen. : nos animo dumtaxat vigemus,
Cic. ; Hor. ; Quint. ; Suet. **c.** O c c. =
provided that at least : Cic. **II.** *not more
than, just so much as, merely.* **a.** Numerically : Cato, Cic., Liv. **b.** In gen. : pedi-
tatu dumtaxat procul ad speciem utitur,
equites in aciem mittit, Caes. ; Luor. ; Cic.,
etc.
dūmus, i, *m. a bramble :* Cic., Verg.
duo, ae, o (Acc. *masc.* duo or duōs : Gen.
duum Sall., Liv.) [*cf.* Gk. δύο, δύω]. **I.**
two (with or without a Noun) : Pl., Cic.,
Verg., etc. **II.** *the two, both :* Pl., Cic., Ov.,
etc. [It. *due, duo ;* Fr. *deux.*]
duodeciēns (-ēs), *adv. twelve times :* Cic.,
Liv.
duodecim [duo decem], *twelve :* Pl., Caes.,
Cic. ; duodecim (and more freq. XII.)
Tabulae, *the laws of the Twelve Tables,* Cic.
[It. *dodici,* Sp. *doce,* Fr. *douze.*]
duo-decimus, a, um [duodecim], *the twelfth :*
legio, Caes.
duo-dēnī, ae, a, *a dozen, a group* (or *groups*) *of
twelve.* **1.** Lit. : uxores habent deni duodenique inter se communis, Caes. ; duodena discribit in singulos homines iugera,
Cic. ; duodena mundi astra, Verg. ; Ov. ;
Liv. **2.** Transf. : *a dozen each :* fossa
duplex duodenum (Gen.) pedum, Caes.
duo-dē-quadrāgēsimus (or **-gēns-**), a, um,
adj. the thirty-eighth : Liv.
duo-dē-quadrāgintā, *indecl. adj. thirty-
eight :* Cic., Liv.
duo-dē-quinquāgēsimus (or **-gēns-**), a,
um, *adj. the forty-eighth :* Cic.
duo-dē-triciēns (-ēs), *adv. twenty-eight
times :* Cic.
duo-dē-trigintā, *indecl. adj., twenty-eight :*
Liv.
duo-dē-vicēnī, ae, a, *adj. a score save two, a
group* (or *groups*) *of eighteen ;* hence, *eighteen
each :* Liv.
duo-dē-viginti, *indecl. adj., eighteen :* Pl.,
Caes., Cic.
duo-et-vicēsimānī, ōrum, *m. pl.* [duo et
vicēsimus], *soldiers of the twenty-second
legion :* Tac.
duo-et-vicēsimus (or **-cēns-**), a, um, *the
twenty-second :* legio, Tac.
duoviri, *v.* duumviri.
duplex, icis (ABL. us. duplicī ; -ice, Hor.),
adj. [*cf.* Gk. διπλαξ], *two-fold, double.*
A. In number. **1.** Lit. : Lucr. ; omnis
de officio duplex est quaestio, Cic. ;
quem locum duplici altissimo muro munierat, Caes. ; tabellae, Suet. ; dorsum, Verg.
Hence, *cloven, divided into two :* ficus, Hor.
2. Transf. (= ambo or uterque), *both :*

oculi, Lucr. ; palmae, Verg. **B.** In degree.
1. Lit. : *thick, strong, stout :* amiculum,
Nep. ; pannus, Hor. **2.** Transf. : *double,*
i.e. *false :* Ulixes, Hor. ; Cat. ; also *ambiguous :* verba, Quint.
duplicārius, i, *m.* [duplex], *a soldier who receives double pay :* Liv.
dupliciter, *adv. doubly, on two accounts :*
Lucr., Cic.
duplicō, āre [duplex], *to double.* **A.** In
number. **1.** Lit. : numerum obsidum,
Caes. ; Cic., etc. **2.** Transf. **a.** *to bend
double :* Naev. ; virum dolore, Verg. **b.**
to make a compound of two : verba, Liv.
B. In degree. **1.** Lit. : iter eius diei,
Caes. **2.** Transf. : *to enlarge, lengthen :*
sol crescentis decedens duplicat umbras,
Verg. ; Lucr. ; Cic. ; Ov.
duplus, a, um [*cf.* Gk. διπλόος], *double, twice
as large, twice as much :* dupla et tripla
intervalla, Cic. ; pecunia, Liv. As Noun,
duplum, i, *n. the double :* decrevit ut in
duplum iret, i.e. *he would have to pay double,*
Cic. ; Pl. Also, **dupla,** ae, *f.* (*sc.* pecunia)
a double price : Pl., Varr. [It. *doppio ;*
Fr. *double.*]
dupondius, *m.* (or **-dium,** *n.*), I [duo pondō],
the sum of two asses : a coin, Cic.
dūrābilis, e, *adj.* [dūrō], *lasting, durable :*
Ov., Quint.
dūrāmen, inis, *n.* [dūrō], *hardness :* aquarum,
ice, Lucr.
dūrateus, a, um [δουράτεος], *wooden* (of the
Trojan horse) : Lucr.
dūrē (Ter., Hor., Quint.), **dūriter** (Ter.,
Lucr.), *adv. hardly.* Transf. **a.** Physically : *hardily :* Ter. **b.** *boorishly, awkwardly, stiffly :* Lucr., Hor., Quint. Comp. :
Hor., Ov., Quint. **c.** *harshly, roughly,
unkindly :* Ter. Comp. : Caes., Cic.,
Tac. **d.** *hardly, unfortunately.* Comp. :
Suet.
dūrēscō, dūrēscere, dūruī [dūrus], *to grow
hard, to harden :* umor, Cic. ; limus, Verg. ;
Ov. ; Tac. Transf. : Quint.
dūrēta, ae, *f.* [a Span. word], *a wooden
bathing-tub :* Suet.
dūritās, ātis, *f.* [dūrus], *hardness, harshness :*
orationis, Cic.
dūriter, *adv. ; v.* dūrē.
dūritia, ae, *f.* (and **dūritiēs,** Cels. ; Acc.
-tiem, Lucr., Cat., Ov. ; ABL. -tiē, Suet. ;
[dūrus], *hardness.* **1.** Lit. : saxi, Lucr. ;
pellis, Ov. **2.** Transf. **a.** *hardiness, aus-
terity* in living : Pl., Caes., Cic., etc. **b.**
harshness, strictness, rigour, cynicism :
Ter. **c.** *hardness, oppressiveness, severity ;*
opp. lenitas : imperi, Tac. ; Suet. **d.** *insensibility :* animi, Cic. ; Ov.
dūriusculus, a, um [*dim. comp.* of dūrus],
somewhat harsh : versus, Plin. Ep.
dūrō, āre [dūrus]. **A.** Trans. *to harden,
make hard.* **1.** Lit. (us. in *Perf. Part.*) :
Lucr., Hor., Ov., Liv. **2.** Transf. : *to
harden, toughen, make hardy, inure.* **a.**
Physically : se labore, Caes. ; Lucr. ;
umeros ad vulnera, Verg. ; usu armorum
durati, Liv. **b.** Mentally and morally :
cor, Pl. ; animum, Hor. ; mentem, Tac. ;
vitia, Quint. ; ad omne facinus durato, Tac.
B. Intrans. : *to harden, become hard, dry.*
1. Lit. : solum, Verg. **2.** Transf. **a.**

to be hardy, tough, inured ; to hold out, en-dure. **i.** Physically : Pl., Verg., Liv., etc. *Impers.* Pass.: Liv. Occ. with Acc.: laborem, Verg. ; and of ships : aequor, Hor. **ii.** Mentally and morally, *to be hard, callous, steeled ; to have the strength of will* : in alicuius necem, Tac. ; nequeo durare quin intro eam, Pl. **b.** *to hold out, last out, live on* (of persons and things) : Pl., Cato, Lucr., Verg., Tac. With *Inf.:* vivere, Luc. T r a n s f.: *of hills, to continue un-broken* : Tac. Of things, *to last, continue* : bellum, odium, etc., Tac.

dūrus, a, um [perh. cf. Gk. δηρόν, *long-lasting ;* or δόρυ, *timber,* δρύς, *oak*], *hard.* **1.** L i t. **a.** To the touch : ferrum, Lucr., Hor. ; cautes, Verg. ; pellis, Lucr., Verg. **b.** To other senses ; *harsh, rough.* To taste : Verg. To the ear : Cic., Quint. **2.** T r a n s f. **A.** Physically, *hard, tough, hardy :* Cic., Verg., etc. **B.** In culture, *rustic, rough, rude, untrained :* Cic., Verg., etc. **C.** Of character. **a.** *hard, parsi-monious :* durus nimisque attentus, Hor. **b.** *shameless, brazen :* os, Ter. **c.** *harsh, stern, cruel, inflexible, unfeeling :* Ter., Cic., Ov., etc. **D.** Of things and circumstances. **a.** Of weather, *severe :* Caes. **b.** In gen. *hard, severe, harsh, cruel, oppressive :* morbus, lex, servitus, Pl. ; labor, Lucr. ; condicio, Cic. ; dolores, Verg. ; Hor. ; Quint. *Neut. pl.* as Noun : Verg., etc. *Comp. :* Lucr., Caes., Cic. *Sup. :* Caes., Cic.

duumvir, v. duumviri.

duumvirātus, ūs, m. [duumviri], *the office of a duumvir :* Plin. Ep.

duumviri, ōrum, m. pl. [GEN. of duo, and vir. Lit. (*in sing.*) *one man of two*] or **duoviri,** *a commission of two* (the name of various extraordinary magistrates). **a.** perduellionis, *a criminal court* (specially created by the king or people) : Cic., Liv. **b.** sacrorum, *the keepers of the Sibylline books* (superseded by the decemviri sacris faciundis) : Liv. **c.** navales, *magistrates created for the purpose of equipping fleets :* Liv. **d.** aedi faciendae (dedicandae, locandae). *for building (dedicating, con-tracting for*) *a temple,* Liv. ; in *sing. :* duum-vir, Liv. **e.** iuri dicundo, *the highest magis-trates in the municipia ; justices :* Caes., Cic.

dux, ducis, m.f. [pr. short form of root seen in dūcō]. **A.** In gen. : *a conductor, guide.* **1.** L i t.: itinerum, Caes. ; locorum, Liv. **2.** T r a n s f. (in any action) : Cic., Verg., etc. With GEN. : Cic., Verg. With *ad* : Cic. **B.** In Partic. *a leader* (of a train). **a.** Of per-sons : Liv. Of animals : pecoris, Tib. ; Hor. ; Ov. **C.** M i l i t. **1.** L i t. **a.** *leader, commander ;* Caes., Cic., Liv. **b.** *a lieuten-ant-general* (as opp. imperator) : Caes., Cic. **2.** T r a n s f. : of the leader of a philosophi-cal school : Lucr., Hor., Quint. [It. *duce, duca, doge ;* Fr. *duc.*]

Dymās, antis, m. f. of *Hccuba,* who is called **Dymantis,** idis.

dynamis, is, f. [δύναμις], *store, plenty* (as *vis* in Lat.) : Pl.

dynastēs, ae, m. [δυναστής]. *a ruler, prince* (of a small foreign district) : Caes., Cic. T r a n s f.: of the triumvirs : Cic. Ep.

E

E, e, *indecl. n.* (or *sc. littera*), f. the fifth letter of the Latin alphabet, corresponding to both the ε and the η of the Greeks. **I.** *e* is sub-stituted for *a :* **1.** in compounds of roots which contain *a* before a double consonant : e.g. : scando, descendo. It sometimes, but rarely, takes the place of *ă :* e.g. : gradior, progredior. In some cases double forms exist, the one with the substituted, the other with the original vowel : e.g. : conspergo and conspargo from spe̅rgo. **2.** in the re-duplication of roots with *a :* e.g. : cado, ce-cidī ; tango (root tag-), te-tigi. **3.** in the perfect of some verbs which have *d* in the present : e.g. : iacio, ie̅ci ; facio, fe̅ci. **II.** *e* is changed into *i.* **1.** in a few com-pound verbs : e.g. : specio, conspicio ; premo, imprimo : but generally the *e* of the simple verb remains unchanged. **2.** in the inflexions of substantives : e.g. : nomen, nominis. **III.** *e* takes the place of *i.* **1.** in the neuter forms of adjectives in *is ;* e.g. facilis, facile ; similis, simile. **2.** in the NOM. and ACC. sing. of a class of neut. substantives : e.g. : ovile (stem ovili-). **3.** in the NOM. forms aedes, canes, etc., for aedis, canis, etc. **IV.** *e* in verbal roots is sometimes changed into *o* in derived sub-stantives : e.g. : tego, toga ; pendo, pon-dus. The formative suffix *os* (orig. *as*) of neuter nouns (which in the nom. has be-come *us*), sinks in the oblique cases to *es ;* as opos (opus), operis (for opes-is). *e* takes the place of *o* also in velle from volo. **V.** *e* is rarely found instead of *u ;* thus from iūro are formed deiero, and peiero. **VI.** *e* is omitted in the inflexions of many nouns, which in the NOM. sing. end in e̅r : e.g. mater, matris ; magister, magistri ; pul-cher, pulchra, pulchrum. **VII.** changes of *e* in the Romance languages. **1.** *e* long or before double consonant generally remains unchanged, as spero, Fr. espère ; crudelis, Fr. cruel ; ferrum, It. ferro, Fr. fer ; terra, It. terra, Fr. terre, but is sometimes changed **i.** into *oi* in French : cf. avena, credo, with Fr. avoine, crois ; **ii.** into *i* in French : cf. cera, ecclesia, temo, with Fr. cire, église, timon ; **iii.** into *ei* in French before *n ;* cf. frenum, Fr. frein ; plenus, Fr. plein ; serenus, Fr. serein. **2.** short *e* is generally changed **i.** into *ie ;* cf. fel, gelu, with It. fiele, gielo ; fel, ferus, hedera, with Fr. fiel, fier, lierre. **ii.** sometimes into *i ;* cf. deus, ego, meus, with It. dio, io, mio ; decem, nego, with Fr. dix, nier.

ē, *prep. v.* ex.

eā, *v.* is.

eādem, *v.* idem.

eāpropter (= proptereā) : Ter.

eapse, *v.* ipse.

eā-tenus, adv. [ABL. f. of is, and tenus], *so far* (rare) : foll. by quoad or ut, *so far . . . as (that)* . . . , Cic.

ebenus, *v.* hebenus.

ē-bibō, bibere, bibī (*Perf. Part.* ēpōtus), *to drink up, drain.* **1.** L i t.: sanguinem, Pl. ; also, poculum, Pl. ; Ter. ; ubera, Ov. ; Nestoris annos, i.e. *as many cups as to equal*

Nestor's years, Ov. Also *to squander in drink* : Hor. **2.** Transf. of things : *to suck in, absorb* : (fretum) peregrinos ebibit amnis, Ov.

ē-bītō, ere, *to go out* : Pl.

ē-blandior, īri, *to coax or wheedle out, to obtain by flattery or coaxing* : unum consulatūs diem, Tac. ; Cic. Ep. ; Liv. Perf. Part. in Pass. sense : *obtained by flattery* : eblandita suffragia, Cic.

Eborācum (Ebur-), ī, *n. a town of the Brigantes in Britain, now York.*

ēbrietās, ātis, *f.* [ēbrius], *drunkenness* : Cic., Ov., etc.

ēbriolus, a, um [*dim.* ēbrius], *tipsy* : Pl.

ēbriōsitās, ātis, *f.* [ēbriōsus], *drunken habit, sottishness* : Cic.

ēbriōsus, a, um [ēbrius], *addicted to drunkenness.* **1.** Lit. : Cic., Sen. Ep. **2.** Transf. : acina, Cat. Comp. : Cat.

ēbrius, a, um. **1.** Lit. **a.** *who has drunk his fill* ; corresp. with satur (*who has eaten his fill*) : Ter. Hence, cena, Pl. ; lucerna, Mart. **b.** *drunk, intoxicated* : Pl., Cic., Ov., etc. **2.** Transf. **a.** Of the words, acts of a drunkard : *drunken* : Tib., Prop. **b.** *drunk, intoxicated* with love, success, etc. : Cat., Hor. [Fr. *ivre.*]

ē-bulliō, īre [bulla], *to bubble out.* Transf. : virtutes (i.e. *to babble about*) : Cic.

ebulum, ī, *n.* and **-lus**, ī, *m. dane-wort, dwarf-elder* : Pl. [It *ebbio* ; Sp. *yedgo, yezgo* , Fr. *hiéble.*]

ebur, oris, *n. ivory.* **1.** Lit. : Cic., Verg., etc. **2.** Transf. **a.** *anything made of ivory* : a statue : Verg., Ov. ; a flute : Verg. ; a scabbard : Ov. ; a State-chair : Hor., Ov. **b.** *an elephant* : Juv.

eburātus, a, um [ebur], *adorned or inlaid with ivory* : Pl.

eburneolus, a, um [*dim.* eburneus], *of ivory* : fistula, Cic.

eburneus (Cic., Suet.) and **eburnus** (Verg., Hor., Ov.), a, um [ebur], *of ivory.* **1.** Lit. : signum, Cic. ; Suet. ; pecten, porta, etc., Verg. ; Hor. ; Ov. ; ensis (*with ivory hilt*), Verg. **2.** Transf. **a.** *white as ivory* : bracchia, Ov. **b.** *of the elephant* : dentes, Liv.

ēcastor [ē is old *exclam.*], *by Castor ! faith !* Pl., Ter.

ecca, eccam, *v.* ecce, *no.* B.

ecce [-ce is particle meaning *here, cf.* cedŏ ; first part uncertain ; but the word was felt to be equiv. to an *imperat.*], *see! behold! here he comes! here I am!* Occ. with NOM. or ACC. : **A.** In gen. **a.** qui venit, ecce, Palaemon, Verg. ; Pl. ; Ter. ; Ov. ; quid me quaeris ? ecce me, Pl. **b.** In lively enumerations, to introduce something new : ecce trahebatur passis capillis, Verg. ; Cic. ; Hor. **B.** Colloq. combined with the pronouns is, ille, and iste, into one word ; as : NOM., ecca, Ter. ; eccilla, Pl. ; eccillud, Pl. ; Acc. *sing.* : ellum, Ter. ; eccum, Pl. ; eccam, Ter. ; *pl.* : eccos, Pl.

eccerē [either invocation of Ceres ; or ecce rē, *here in fact* ; or ecce rem, *there's the point, voilà*] : Pl., Ter.

eccheuma, atis, *n.* [ἔκχευμα]. *a pouring out* : Pl.

ecclēsia, ae, *f.* [ἐκκλησία], *a Greek assembly of the people* : Plin. Ep.

ecdicus, ī, *m.* [ἐκδικός], i.e. cognitor or defensor civitatis, *a legal agent of a community* : Cic. Ep.

ecfātus, ecferŏ *etc., v.* eff-.

ecfertus, a, um. **I.** Part. effarciō. **II.** Adj. *stuffed out, bulging* ;' fame, Pl. Sup. : Pl.

ecflictim, adv. [effligō], *to death, desperately* (with amaro, etc.) : Pl.

ecflictŏ, āre [*freq.* effligō], *to strike dead* : Pl.

Echidna, ae, *f.* **I.** the Lernaean hydra, killed by Hercules. **II.** *a monster, half woman, half serpent, m. of Cerberus* : **Echidnaeus**, a, um.

Echinades, um, *f. pl. a group of small islands off Acarnania.*

echinus, ī, *m.* [ἐχῖνος], *a hedgehog* ; *edible sea-urchin.* **1.** Lit. : Hor. **2.** Transf. *a copper vessel or rinsing bowl* (from its shape) : Hor.

Echiŏn, onis, *m.* **I.** *a hero who sprang from the dragon's teeth sown by Cadmus* ; **Echionidēs**, ae, *m. Pentheus, s. of Echion* ; **Echionius**, a, um, *Cadmean, Theban.* **II.** *s. of Mercury* ; *one of the hunters of the Calydonian boar* ; **Echionius**, a, um.

Echō, us, *f. a nymph who was changed by Juno into an echo.*

ecloga, ae, *f.* [ἐκλογή]. **I.** *a selection of passages from a book* : Varr. **II.** *a short poem*, like the Bucolica of Vergil, or the Silvae of Statius : Stat.

eclogārii, ōrum, *m. pl.* [ecloga], *select passages from a work* : Cic. Ep.

ecquandŏ, interr. adv. [perh. for et and quandŏ], *ever, at any time ?* (in passionate interrogations) : ecquando unam urbem habere licebit ? Liv. ; Cic. Also ecquandone ? Cic., Prop.

ecquī, ecqua or ecqua, ecquod, *interr. adj.* [v. ecquis], *any, is there any ?* **a.** With a Noun : ecqui pudor est, Verres ? Cic. ; Pl. ; Verg., etc. In Indir. Quest. : Ter., Liv. With suffix -nam : ecquaenam origo, Lucr. ; Cic. **b.** Rarely without a Noun : ecqui poscit prandio ? Pl. In Indir. Quest. : Liv.

ecquis, ecquid (ABL. ecquī), interr. pron. [perh. for et-quis. Lit. *is there any one further, anyone at all ?*]. **a.** Without a Noun : *any one, any body ? any thing ?* in animated interrogations : heus ecquis hic est ? ecquis aperit hoc ostium ? Pl. ; Cic. ; Verg., etc. In Indir. Quest. : Cic. With suffix -nam : ecquidnam adferunt ? Pl. ; Cic. **b.** With a Noun (rare) : Pl., Verg., Liv. Adverbial uses. **i.** ecquid (*n.* ACC.). *in any respect ? is it that ? whether ?* (in Direct or Indir. Quest.) : Pl., Cic., Hor., etc. **ii.** ecqui (ABL.), *in any way ? whether ?* (in Indir. Quest.) : Pl. **iii.** ecquŏ, *anywhither ? anywhere ?* (in Direct Quest.) : Cic.

eculeus, ī, *m.* [*dim.* equus], *a young horse* ; *colt, foal.* **1.** Lit. : Liv. **2.** Transf. **a.** Of works of art : Cic. **b.** *an instrument of torture* ; *a wooden rack* : Cic., Sen. Ep.

edācitās, ātis, *f.* [edāx], *voracity, gluttony* : Pl., Cic. Ep.

edāx, ācis, *adj.* [edŏ], *voracious, gluttonous.*
1. Lit.: Pl., Cic., Ov., etc. *Sup.*: Sen.
Ep. **2.** Transf.: *devouring*: ignis,
Verg., Ov.; imber, Hor. With GEN.:
Ov.

ē-dentō, āre [dēns], *to unteeth, make toothless*: malas alicui, Pl.

ē-dentulus, a, um [ē dēns]. *toothless.* **1.**
Lit.: Pl. **2.** Transf. Of old wine:
Pl.

edepol, used by way of oath or exclamation
[etym. uncertain, but pol. is fr. Pollux], *by
Pollux! faith! truly! indeed!* Pl., Ter.

edera, ae, and its derivatives, *v.* hed-.

ē-dicō, dicere, dixi, dictum (*Imperat.* ēdīce,
Verg.). Lit.: *to show forth or say out.*
A. Of a magistrate. **a.** *to publish a decree
or edict, proclaim, announce.* With Acc.:
diem comitiis, Liv.; diem exercitui ad
conveniendum, Liv.; senatum in diem
posterum, Liv.; iustitium, Cic. With
Acc. and *Inf.*: Cic., Liv. With *de*: Tac.,
Suet. With *Subj.*: Cic. Ep., Verg. With
ut or *ne* and *Subj.*: Cic., Liv. *Impers.*
Pass. (in ABL. of *Perf. Part.*): Liv. **b.**
Esp. of the praetor's edict on entering
office: Cic.: *v.* edictum. **B.** In gen. *to
speak out, declare.* With Noun-object: Pl.,
Cic. With Acc. and *Inf.*: Ter. With
Indir. Quest.: Cic., Sall. With *ut* or *ne*
and *Subj.*: Pl., Ter., Hor. With DAT.
and *Pass. Inf.*: Verg.

ēdictiō, ōnis, *f.* [ēdĭcŏ], *an order, edict,* for
edictum: Pl.

ēdictō, āre [*freq.* ēdĭcŏ], *to proclaim exactly*:
facta tua, Pl.

ēdictum, ī, *n.* [ēdĭcŏ], *a proclamation, ordinance, edict.* **A.** of a Roman magistrate.
a. In gen.: Cic., Liv. **b.** Esp. *the edict
of a praetor upon entering office, laying down
the rules by which he would be guided in the
exercise of his judicial functions*: Cic. **B.**
In gen. **a.** *an order, command*: Ter. **b.**
a play-bill, placard: Sen. Ep. [Fr. *édit.*]

ē-discō, discere, didicī. **I.** *to learn off, learn
thoroughly, commit to memory*: poetas, Cic.;
magnum numerum versuum, Caes.; Quint.
II. In gen.: *to learn thoroughly*: istam
artem (iuris), Cic.; Hor.; Ov. With *Inf.*:
Ov. With *Indir. Quest.*: Ov., Liv.

ē-disserō, serere, seruī, sertum, *to analyse
fully, explain in full detail.* With Acc.:
Cic., Verg., etc. With *Indir. Quest.*: Pl.,
Cic., Liv. *Pass. Impers.*: Cic., Liv.
Absol.: Cic.

ē-dissertō, āre [*freq.* ēdisserŏ], *to explain in
very full detail.* With Acc.: Pl., Liv.

ēditīcius, a, um [ēdŏ]. In law, *put forth,
proposed*: iudices, *chosen by the plaintiff in
the* causa sodaliciorum, Cic.

ēditiō, ōnis, *f.* [ēdŏ]. **1.** Lit.: *a putting
forth ; a publishing (of literary works)*:
Sen., Plin. Ep. Hence, *an edition*: Quint.
2. Transf. **a.** *a published statement*:
Liv. **b.** In law, *a designation*: tribuum,
Cic.

ēditus, a, um. **I.** *Part.* ēdŏ. **II.** Adj.:
standing out, elevated: collis paululum ex
planitie editus, Caes.; Cic.; Liv., etc.
Comp.: Caes., Sall. *Sup.*: Sall., Liv.
Transf.: viribus editior, Hor. **III.** *Neut.*
as Noun. **a.** *a high place*: in edito. Suet.;

edita montium, Tac. **b.** *an ordinance*: in
pl.: Ov.

edŏ, ēsse (later edere), ēdī, ēsum (in best
period, *Pres. Indic.* ēs, ēst, ēstis; *Imperf.*
Ov. *Subj.* ēssem. Old forms of *Pres.* (*Opt.*)
Subj. edim, edīs, edit, etc.: Pl., Cic.,
Hor.) [*cf.* Gk. ἐσθίειν, ἔδομαι, Germ.
essen], *to eat.* **1.** Lit.: aliquid, Pl., Cic.,
Verg., etc. Prov.: multos modios salis
simul edisse, *to have eaten many a peck of
salt together,* i.e. *to have been very much
together,* Cic.; de patellā, *to dine off a consecrated salver ;* hence, *to show contempt
for religion,* Cic.; pugnos, *to taste one's
fists,* i.e. *to get a good drubbing,* Pl. **2.**
Transf.: *to devour.* **a.** Of reading : sermonem tuom, Pl. **b.** Of wasting, consuming. **i.** Of personal subjects : bona, Pl.
ii. Of inanimate subjects : ut mala culmos
esset robigo, Verg.; corpora virus, Ov. **iii.**
Of abstract subjects : si quid est animum,
Hor.; nec te tantus edat tacitam dolor,
Verg.

ē-dŏ, dere, didī, ditum, *to put forth.* **1.** Lit.
A. In gen. **a.** *to put forth, send forth, discharge* : Maeander in sinum maris editur,
Liv.; clanculum ex aedibus me edidi foras,
Pl. **b.** *to emit, utter* (of breath, sounds,
etc.): Lucr., Cic., Ov. **B.** Of birth: *to
bring forth, to give birth to, to produce* :
progeniem in oras luminis, Lucr.; partum,
Cic.; Liv.; edidit geminos Latona, Ov.;
Verg. In *Pass.*: Venus aquis edita, *sprung
from,* Ov.; Maecenas atavis edite regibus,
Hor. Ooo. *to beget*: Verg. **C.** Of writings,
to publish : Cic., Hor., etc. **2.** Transf.:
to publish, proclaim, divulge, spread abroad.
A. Of public proclamations and statements.
a. In gen. With Acc.: Caes., Cic., Ov., etc.
With *Indir. Quest.*: Cic. With Acc. and
Inf.: Cic., Liv. **b.** Of oracles : Cic., Ov.,
Liv. **c.** In law, *to promulgate, proclaim,
ordain* : verba, Cic.; tribūs (said of the
plaintiff in a causa sodaliciorum), *to name
the tribes,* Cic.; mandata, Liv. With
Indir. Quest.: Liv. **B.** *to produce, cause.*
a. In gen.: proelia pugnasque, Lucr.;
caedem, etc., Liv.; ruinas, Cic.; exempla
cruciatūs in aliquem, Caes.; scelus in aliquem, Cic. **b.** Of public shows : *to produce* : Liv., Tac., Suet.

ē-dŏceō, docēre, docuī, doctum, *to teach or
inform thoroughly.* **1.** Lit. **a.** *to teach
thoroughly, instruct clearly.* With two Acc.:
one of the person, other of thing, and in
Pass. with the latter : Pl., Cic., Liv., etc.
With Acc. of person and *Inf.*: Ov. With
Acc. and *Inf.*: Liv. **b.** *to inform.* With
Acc. of person and of thing : Cic., Sall.,
Liv. With Acc. of person and *Indir. Quest.*:
Caes., Liv. With Acc. and *Inf.*: Verg.,
Liv. With Acc. of person and *ne* with
Subj. (*Juss.*): Ter., Liv. **2.** Transf.:
of abstract subjects : fama Punici belli
satis edocuerat, viam tantum Alpis esse,
Liv. With *ut* and *Subi.*: Cic.

ē-dolō, āre, *to hew out.* Transf.: *to work
out, finish*: Enn., Varr.

ē-domō, āre, uī, itum, *to tame completely, subdue.* **1.** Lit.: orbem, Ov. **2.** Transf.:
vitiosam naturam, Cic.; nefas, Hor.

Edōni, ōrum, *m. pl. a Thracian tribe, much*

given to revelry ; **Ēdōnus,** a, um ; **Ēdōnis,** idis, *f. adj.* ; as Noun, *a Bacchante.*

ē-dormiō, īre, *to sleep out to a finish.* **A.** Without Obj.: Cic. **B.** With Obj.: **a.** *to sleep off :* crapulam, Cic. **b.** *to sleep right through :* Hor. In *Pass. :* Sen. Ep.

ēdormiscō, ere [ēdormiō], *to sleep off :* crapulam, Pl.; Ter.

ēducātiō, ōnis, *f.* [ēducō], *a rearing, bringing up, education :* us. of human beings, Cic., Quint., Tac. Of animals : Cic. Of plants : Plin.

ēducātor, ōris, *m.* [ēducō], *a rearer, bringer up :* of a *foster-father :* Cic., Quint.; of *tutors, instructors :* Tac.; and **ēducātrix,** īcis, *f. a nurse.* Transf.: educatrix sapientia, Cic.

ēducō, āre [root duc, *v.* dūcō], *to draw out, train ; to bring up* a child physically or mentally; esp. the latter. **1.** Lit.: aliquem, Pl., Cic., Ov., etc.; liberaliter educatus, Cic. **2.** Transf. **a.** neque hac nos patria lege educavit, Cic. **b.** Of animals or plants : lepores, apros, Hor.; florem imber, Cat.; herbas humus, Ov.

ē-dūcō, dūcere, dūxī, ductum (*Imper.* ēdūce, Pl.). **I.** *to lead* or *draw out, bring away.* **a.** Pl.; uxorem ab domo secum, Caes.; medicum secum, i.e. from Rome, Cic.; gladium, Caes.; sortem, Cic.; telum corpore, Verg. Hence, aura educit colores, Cat. Occ. *to drain :* lacum, Cic. Transf.: of time, *to draw out, spend :* Prop. **b.** Milit.: *to lead* or *march out* troops : praesidium ex oppido, Caes.; Pl.; exercitum ab urbe, Liv.; copias castris, Caes.; Verg. Without ABL.: exercitum in expeditionem, Cic.; Caes.; Liv. Without *Obj. : to march out :* ex hibernis educere, Caes.; in aciem, Liv. **c.** Naut.: navis ex portu, *to put to sea,* Caes. **d.** In law, *to summon :* aliquem in ius, Cic.; ad consules, Cic.; aliquem ad tintinnaculos, Pl. **II.** *to hatch :* pullos, Pl. Hence, *to rear, bring up, educate* (either bodily or mentally, but for the latter sense *v.* ēducāre): aliquem, Pl., Cic., Verg., etc.; aliquem severā disciplinā, Cic. **III.** *to draw up, raise, erect :* turrim summis sub astra eductam tectis, Verg.; Ov.; Hor.; molem caelo, Verg.; turrim, Tac.; molem in Rhenum, Tac.

edūlis, e, *adj.* [edō], *edible :* capreae, Hor. *Neut. pl.* as Noun, **edūlia,** ium, *eatables :* Varr., Suet.

ē-dūrō, āre, *to last out, continue :* solis fulgor in ortūs edurat, Tac.

ē-dūrus, a, um, *very hard.* **1.** Lit.: pirus, Verg. **2.** Transf.: eduro ore negare, Ov.

Ēetiōn, ōnis, *m. f.* of Andromache, *king of Thebe in Cilicia ;* **Ēetiōnēus,** a, um.

ef-farciō, *v.* efferciō.

effātus, a, um. **I.** *Part.* effor. **A.** Act., *v.* effor. **B.** Pass. **a.** *solemnly pronounced :* verba longo carmine, Liv. **b.** *solemnly dedicated :* locus templo, Liv. **II.** *Neut.* as Noun. **a.** *sing.* (in logic), *an axiom :* Cic. **b.** *pl. solemn pronouncements, predictions :* Varr., Old Law in Cic.

effectiō, ōnis, *f.* [efficiō], *a doing completely, accomplishment.* **1.** Lit.: artis, Cic. **2.**

Transf. (= causa efficiens) : *the producing* or *efficient cause,* Cic.

effectīvus, a, um [efficiō], *producing, practical :* ars, Quint.

effector, ōris, *m.* and **effectrix,** īcis, *f.* [efficiō], *a producer, author :* Cic.

effectus, a, um. **I.** *Part.* efficiō. **II.** Adj., *finished, complete :* Quint. Comp. : Quint. *Neut.* as Noun, *an effect :* Cic., Quint.

effectus, ūs, *m.* [efficiō]. **I.** *a completing, effecting, completion :* operis, Liv.; ad effectum aliquid adducere, Liv.; esse in effectu, Cic., Liv.; sine effectu, Cic., Liv. **II.** *result, effect :* (herbarum) vim et effectum videres, Cic.; eloquentiae, Cic.; Quint. In *pl. :* Quint.

effēmināte, *adv. in a womanish manner :* Cic.

effēminātus, a, um. **I.** *Part.* effēminō. **II.** Adj.: *womanish, effeminate :* Cic., Quint. *Sup. :* Q. Cic. *Masc.* as Noun : Cic.

ef-fēminō, āre [fēmina], *to make a woman of.* **I.** *to represent as a woman :* aërem, Cic. **II.** *to make womanish, enervate :* corpus animumque virilem, Sall.; animos, Caes.; virum, Cic.; Caes.

efferātus, a, um. **I.** *Part.* efferō. **II.** Adj.: *brutal, savage :* Cic. Comp. : Liv. Sup. : Sen. Ep.

ef-ferciō (ecf-, Pl.), fercīre, fertum [farciō], *to stuff, cram, fill out :* intervalla grandibus saxis, Caes.; Pl.

efferitās, ātis, *f.* [efferō], *wild* or *savage state :* Cic.

(1) ef-ferō, āre [ferus], *to make wild* or *savage, to brutalise.* **a.** Physically : speciem oris, Liv.; terram immanitate beluarum, Cic. **b.** Mentally and morally : gentem, Cic.; militem, animos, Liv.; efferavit ea caedes Thebanos ad exsecrabile odium Romanorum, Liv. [Fr. *effarer.*]

(2) ef-ferō (older ecf-), efferre (ecf-), extulī, ēlātum. **I.** *to carry, bring out* or *forth.* **A.** In gen. **1.** Lit.: tela ex aedibus, Cic.; Pl.; cistellam domo, Ter.; Caes.; frumentum ab Ilerdā, Caes.; pedem portā, Cic. Ep.; Pl.; se tectis, Verg.; Lucr.; Tac. **2.** Transf.: of news, etc., *to publish, divulge :* Caes., Cic., Tac. Occ.: *to utter :* clamorem, Pl.; verba, Ter., Varr.; sententias, Cic. **B.** *to carry out for burial, bury :* Pl., Cic., Hor., etc. Transf.: meo unius funere elata populi Romani esset res publica, Liv. **C.** Of the soil : *to bring forth, bear, produce :* id quod agri efferunt, Cic. Poet.: (Italia) genus acre virum (GEN.) extulit, Verg. **II.** *to carry away.* **1.** Lit.: Furium longius extulit cursus, Liv. **2.** Transf.: comitia ista praeclara me laetitiā extulerunt, Cic. Ep. Mostly in *Pass. : to be carried away* (by passion, etc.), *to be transported, hurried away :* cupiditate, Cic.; vi naturae atque ingeni, Cic.; laetitiā, Cic.; Lucil.; Caes., etc. **III.** *to lift off the ground, lift up, raise, carry off one's feet.* **1.** Lit.: aliquem in murum, Caes.; super caput scutum, Liv., Tac.; pulvis elatus, Liv.; corvus e conspectu elatus, Liv.; Verg.; Tac. **2.** Transf. **a.** caput Autumnus agris extulit, Hor. **b.** pretia, Varr. **c.** ad summum imperium per omnis honorum gradūs, Cic.; supra leges, Tac.; pecuniā aut

honore, Sall. ; maximis laudibus, Cic., Tac. ;
virtus se extulit et ostendit suum lumen,
Cic. **d.** In bad sense: res gestae meae me
nimis extulerunt, Cic. ; Liv. ; with *Pron.*
Refl.: *to exalt oneself ;* or *Pass.*: *to be
exalted, puffed up, haughty, proud* : se
efferre insolenter, Cic. ; superbiā se ecferens,
Sall. ; Cic. Esp. freq. in *Part. Perf.*:
stultā ac barbarā adrogantiā elati, Caes. ;
recenti victoriā, Caes. ; Cic. ; ad iustam
fiduciam, Liv. ; Curt. **IV.** *to bear to the end,
endure* : laborem, Acc. (perh. in Lucr.).

effertus, *v.* ecfertus.

ef-ferus, a, um, *very wild, savage* : iuventus,
Verg. ; Lucr.

ef-fervēscō, fervēscere, fervī, *to begin to boil
over.* **1.** Lit.: aquae, Cic. ; Cato. **2.**
Transf.: Pontum armatum, efferves-
centem in Asiam, Cic. ; huius vis, Cic. ;
verba, Cic. ; in irā, Lucr. ; Tac. ; vulneribus, terrore, Lucr.

ef-fervō, ere, *to boil over or up.* **1.** Lit. Of
Etna: Verg. **2.** Transf.: cf worms:
Lucr. ; of bees: Verg.

ef-fētus, a, um, *exhausted, worn out by bearing.* **1.** Lit.: Plin. Of the earth: Lucr.
2. Transf.: corpus, Cic. ; vires (corporis),
Verg. With GEN.: veri effeta senectus,
past the power of conceiving truth, Verg. ;
Sall.

efficācitās, ātis, *f.* [efficāx], *efficacy, power* :
Cic.

efficāciter, adv. *effectually* : Quint. *Comp.* :
Quint., Tac., Plin. Ep. *Sup.* : Plin. Ep.

efficāx, ācis, adj. [efficiō], *efficacious, effectual,
capable* : tardus et parum efficax, Cael. ap.
Cic. Ep. ; preces ad muliebre ingenium,
Liv. ; Hercules, Hor. ; Sen. Ep. ; continua-
tio in rebus peragendis, Liv. With *Inf.* :
Hor. *Comp.* ; Quint. *Sup.* : Liv.

efficiēns, entis. **I.** *Part.* efficiō. **II.** Adj.:
effecting, effective, efficient : res efficientes,
i.e. causae ; opp. res effectae, *effects,* Cic.
With GEN.: Cic.

efficienter, adv. *efficiently* : Cic.

efficientia, ae, *f.* [efficiō], *efficacy, efficiency,
influence* : Cic.

ef-ficiō (older **ecf-**), ficere, fēcī, fectum
(*Aor. Opt.* ecfexis, Pl. ; *Pass. Inf.* ecfieri,
Pl., Lucr.), *to do or work out.* **A.** As an
act of intention, *to make, build, form.* **1.**
Lit.: Pl. ; pontem, castella, Caes. ; columnam, Cic. ; unam ex duabus legionibus,
Caes. **2.** Transf. **a.** Of non-material
things : officium, munus, Cic. ; Pl. ; nuptias alicui, Ter. ; magnas rerum commutationes, Caes. ; civitatem, Cic. **b.** With
2nd Acc., *to make, create* : aliquem consulem, Cic. **c.** With Acc. and *Inf. to make
out, try to prove* : Cic. *Impers. Pass.* :
Cic. **B.** As a result, *to make, bring about,
cause.* **1.** Lit. **a.** In gen.: haec insula
portum efficit, Caes. ; Cic. **b.** Of the soil,
etc.: *to produce, bear, yield* : Cic. ; cum
decimo, *ten-fold,* Cic. **2.** Transf. **a.** Of
non-material things : tantam vilitatem
pax efficit, Cic. ; Nep. **b.** With *ut* and
Subj. : Pl., Caes., Cic. With Acc. preceding : hanc mulierem tibi, tua ut sit, Pl.
With *ne* and *Subj.* : Cic., Verg., Liv., Tac.
With *quo minus* and *Subj.* : Quint. With
quo magis and *Subj.* : Liv. **c.** With 2nd

Acc.: fortuna eos caecos, Cic. ; Pl. ; hunc
montem murus arcem efficit, Caes. **d.** Of
numbers, *to make up, amount to, yield :*
Caes., Cic. Ep., Liv. So, *to make up a sum
of money, recoup oneself :* Cic.

effictus, a, um, *Part.* effingō.

effigia, ae, *v.* foll. art.

effigiēs, ēī (**effigia,** ae, Pl. ; Acc. pl. -iās,
Lucr.), *f.* [effingō], *a copy or imitation.* **1.**
Lit. **a.** formarum, Lucr. ; deus effigies
hominis et imago, Cic. ; Verg. **b.** *a
phantom :* Ov. In a dream : Plin. Ep. In
contemptuous sense : Liv. **c.** *a statue or
portrait :* Cic., Verg., etc. **2.** Transf.:
*a perfect expression or copy, an ideal form or
model :* humanitatis, Cic. ; Liv. ; eloquentiae, Cic.

ef-fingō, fingere, fīnxī, fīctum, *to mould out.
to work or press as in moulding.* **A.** *to
press out.* **a.** In cleansing : fiscinas spon-
giā, Cato ; spongiis sanguinem, Cic. ;
manūs, Ov. **b.** *to press, fondle :* manūs,
Ov. **B.** *to mould.* **1.** Lit.: Veneris pul-
chritudinem, Cic. ; deum (GEN.) imagines
in hominum species, Tac. ; casūs in auro,
Verg. **2.** Transf.: *to express, represent,
portray :* mores, Cic. ; imaginem virtutis,
Quint. ; sensūs mentis, Tac.

effiō (**ecf-**), *v.* efficiō.

efflāgitātiō, ōnis, *f.* [efflāgitō], *an urgent demand, entreaty :* Cic. Ep.

efflāgitātū, ABL. sing. *m.* [efflāgitō], *at the
urgent request :* meo, Cic.

ef-flāgitō, āre, *to demand or ask urgently :*
epistulam, Cic. Ep. ; Liv. ; Verg. ; misericordiam alicuius, Cic.

efflic-, *v.* ecflic-.

ef-flīgō (**ecf-,** Pl.), flīgere, flīxī, flīctum, *to
dash out, exterminate :* Pompeium, Cic. Ep. ;
Pl. ; viperas, Sen.

ef-flō (older **ecflō**), āre, *to blow, breathe out or
forth.* **A.** Trans.: (sol) suos efflavit
ignīs, Lucr. ; ignis Aetnaeos faucibus, Verg. ;
Ov. ; mare naribus, Ov. ; animam, *to expire,*
Cic., Pl. **B.** Intrans.: flamma, Lucr.

ef-flōrēscō, flōrēscere, flōruī, *to begin to blossom forth.* Transf.: ingeni laudibus,
Cic. ; utilitas ex amicitiā, Cic.

ef-fluō (**ecfl-**), fluere, fluxī, *to flow or run
out, to flow forth.* **1.** Lit.: imbres,
Lucr. ; unā cum sanguine vita, Cic. ; ne
quā levis effluat aura, Ov. **2.** Transf.
a. Of non-fluids: *to slip away, drop
off :* manibus opus, Lucr. ; de pectore
caedis notae, Ov. ; Quint. Of persons:
Cic. Ep. **b.** *to pass away :* praeterita aetas
Cic. Hence (= *to be forgotten*) : antequam
ex tuo animo effluam, Cic. Ep. ; also with
subject mens : dicenti mens effluit, Cic. **c.**
Of rumour, *to get abroad :* Ter., Quint.

effluvium, i, n. [effluō], *a flowing out, an outlet :* laoūs, Plin.

ef-fodiō (**ecf-,** Pl.), fodere, fōdī, fōssum (*Inf.
Pass.* ecfodīrī, Pl.). **I.** *to dig out, dig up.*
1. Lit.: aulam auri plenam, Pl. ; ferrum,
Cic. ; Ov. ; signa, Liv. ; sepulcra, Verg.
2. Transf. **a.** *to gouge out :* oculos or
oculum (alicui), Pl., Caes., Cic. ; lumen,
Verg. In metaph.: oculos orae maritimae, Cic. **b.** *to root out, gut :* domos,
Caes. **II.** *to excavate, make by digging :*
lacum, Suet.

ef-for (older **ecfor**), fāri, fātus. **A.** In gen. : *to speak* or *say out, to utter* : Lucr. ; celanda, Liv. ; Verg. ; Hor. **B.** In partic. **a.** In logic : *to state a proposition* : Cic. **b.** *to dedicate by solemn pronouncement* : templum, Cic. Ep.

effossus, a, um, *Part.* effodiō.

effrēnātē, *adv. unrestrainedly* : Cic. *Comp.* : Cic.

effrēnātiō, ōnis, *f.* [effrēnō], *unbridled impetuosity* : animi, Cic.

effrēnātus, a, um, **I.** *Part.* effrēnō. **II.** A dj. : *unbridled, unrestrained* : cupiditas, Cic. ; Liv. ; Plin. Ep. *Comp.* : Cic., Liv., Quint. *Sup.* : Sen. Ep.

ef-frēnō, āre, *to unbridle, let loose.* **1.** Lit. : rare exc. in *Perf. Part.* : effrenati equi, Liv. **2.** Transf. : secundis rebus effrenatus, Cic.

ef-frēnus, a, um [frēnum], *unbridled.* **1.** Lit. : equus, Liv. **2.** Transf. : gens, Verg. ; amor, Ov.

ef-fringō (**ecfr-**, Pl.), fringere, frēgī, frāctum [frangō], *to break out, to break off, break open* : cardines foribus, Pl. ; foris, Cic., Pl., Ter. ; cistam, Hor. ; cerebrum, Verg. ; carcerem, Tac.

ef-fugiō, fugere, fūgī, **A.** Intrans. : *to flee out* or *away, to escape.* With *ab* : Pl., Cic. With *ex* : Pl., Cic., Liv. With Abl. : Pl., Ter., Liv. *Absol.* : Pl., Caes., Cic. Ep., Verg. With *ne* and *Subj.* : Liv., Tac. **B.** Trans. : *to flee from, escape.* **1.** Lit. : impias propinquorum manūs, Cic. ; mortem, Caes. ; equitatum, Caes. ; scopulos, Verg. ; Hor. **2.** Transf. **a.** infortunium, Pl. ; mortem, Caes. ; cupiditates adulescentiae, Tac. **b.** *to escape the attention of* : nihil te effugiet, Cic. ; Hor. ; Liv.

effugium, i, *n.* [effugiō], *escape, flight.* **1.** Lit. : Lucr. ; mortis, Cic. In *pl.* : Verg., Tac. **2.** Transf. : *a means* or *way of escape* : habere effugia pennarum, Cic. ; Tac. ; dare alicui, Liv.

ef-fulgeō, fulgēre, fūlsī (*inf.* effulgere, Verg.), *to shine forth.* **1.** Lit. **a.** Of light : tres simul soles, Liv. ; nova lux oculis effulsit, Verg. **b.** auro, Verg. ; ornatu, Tac. **2.** Transf. : *to be conspicuous* : Liv. ; audaciā, Tac.

ef-fultus, a, um [fulciō], *propped up, supported* : effultus stratis velleribus, Verg.

ef-fundō (**ecf-**, Pl.), fundere, fūdī, fūsum, *to pour out* or *forth.* **1.** Lit. **a.** Of liquid : Pl., Cic., Liv., Verg., etc. Poet. : tempestas effusa, Verg. **b.** Of non-liquids : *to pour forth, shower out, fling forth* : saccos nummorum, Hor. ; tela, Verg., Liv. ; effusum tam late incendium, Liv. **2.** Transf. **A. a.** *to pour forth, send out with a rush, fling violently* : iuvenem harenā, Verg. ; equus consulem lapsum super caput effudit, Liv. ; auxilium castris, Verg. With *Pron. Refl.*, or *Pass.* in *Mid.* sense ; *to pour forth, rush out* : Caes., Verg., Liv., etc. **b.** Of utterance, *to pour out, give vent to* : Cic., Verg., etc. **c.** Of feeling, *to vent, discharge* : iram in aliquem, Liv. ; Cic. ; Quint. **B. a.** *to pour forth bountifully, produce abundantly* : fruges, Cic., Hor. **b.** *to lavish, waste, run through* : patrimonium, Cic. ; conlectam gratiam floren-

tissimi nominis, Cic. Ep. ; viris, Liv. ; fortunas, Tac. ; laborem, Verg. ; viris in ventum, Verg. **C. a.** *to let go freely, slackly, without restraint* : habenas, Verg. Esp. in *Perf. Part.* : habenae, Verg., Liv. ; comae, Ov. ; sinus togae, Liv. ; caedes, agmen, Liv. **b.** With *Pron. Refl.* or in *Mid.* : *to let oneself go, give oneself up* ; se in aliquā libidine, Cic. ; Pompeius in nos suavissime effusus, Cic. Ep. ; in socordiam, ad preces, Liv. ; in lacrimas, Tac.

effūsē, *adv.* **I.** *spreading far and wide* : ire, Sall. ; Liv. *Comp.* : Liv. **II.** *lavishly* : donare, Cic. ; Liv. *Comp.* : Tac. **III.** *unrestrainedly* : exsultare, Cic. *Comp.* : Tac., Plin. Ep. *Sup.* : Plin. Ep.

effūsiō, ōnis, *f.* [effundō], *a pouring out, pouring forth.* **1.** Lit. : aquae, Cic. **2.** Transf. **a.** (in *pl.*) : Of people : hominum ex oppidis, Cic. **b.** *profusion, prodigality* : Cic., Liv. In *pl.* : Cic. **c.** *unrestrained outburst* : animi in laetitiā, Cic.

effūsus, a, um. **I.** *Part.* effundō. **II.** Adj. **1.** Lit. **a.** *spread out, extensive* : Lucr., Hor. ; Tac. **b.** *loose, unrestrained* (of things, or behaviour) : quam posset effusissimis habenis, Liv. **2.** Transf. : *prodigal, lavish* : Cic., Liv., Plin. Ep. *Comp.* : Cic., Quint. *Sup.* : Liv., Suet.

effūtiō, īre [v. fundō], *to dribble out at random, to blab out, prate, chatter* : Lucr., Cic., Hor. Intrans. : Ter., Cic.

ef-futuō (**ecf-**), futuere, futuī, futūtum, *to waste in debauchery* : Cat.

ē-gelidus, a, um, *with the chill off, lukewarm* : tepores, Cat. ; Notus, Ov. ; aqua, Suet. Also perh. *chill* : flumen, Verg.

egēns, entis. **I.** *Part.* egeō. **II.** Adj. : *needy, necessitous* : Pl., Caes., Cic., etc. With Gen. : Ov. *Comp.* : Cic. Ep. *Sup.* : Cic., Liv. As Noun : Caes.

egēnus, a, um [egeō], *in want of, destitute of.* With Gen. : Verg., Liv., Tac. With Abl. : Tac. *Absol.* : Pl., Verg.

egeō, ēre, uī, *to be needy, suffer want.* **1.** Lit. **a.** Pl., Cic., Hor. *Impers. Pass.* : Pl. **b.** *to need, lack, be destitute of.* With Abl. : Caes., Cic., Sen. Ep. ; of inanimate subjects : opus eget exercitatione non parvā, Cic. ; Quint. With Gen. : Pl., Caes., Ov., etc. ; of inanim. subjects : Lucr., Quint. With Acc. (of *Neut. Pron.*) : Pl. **2.** Transf. **a.** *to be without* : auctoritate, Cic. ; res proprio nomine, Lucr. ; audaciae, Sall. **b.** *to want, wish for.* With Gen. : Pl., Hor. With Abl. : Hor.

Ēgeria, ae, *f.* *a nymph* or *Camena, instructress of Numa.*

ē-gerō, gerere, gessī, gestum, *to carry* or *bear out* or *away.* **1.** Lit. **a.** praedam ex tectis, Liv. ; humanas opes a Veiis, Liv. ; fluctūs, Ov. ; nivem, Liv. ; bona fortunasque in tributum, Tac. **b.** *to discharge, emit* : lacus bitumen, Tac. ; Ov. **2.** Transf. : dolorem, Ov. ; sermones, Sen. Ep. ; Luc.

egestās, ātis, *f.* [egeō], *indigence, destitution.* **1.** Lit. **a.** In gen. : Pl., Caes., Cic., Verg. In *pl.*, *cases of destitution*, Cic. **b.** In partic. : cibi, Tac. ; Sall. ; Suet. **2.** Transf. : linguae, Lucr. ; animi, Cic.

ēgestiō, ōnis, *f.* [ēgerō], *a wasting* or *squandering :* Plin. Ep.

ēgestus, a, um, *Part.* ēgerō.

ego (for *pl.* v. nōs) [*cf.* Gk. ἐγώ], *pron. I* (and in oblique cases *me*). N.B. **a.** With emphat. suffixes ; in NOM. and ACC. -met ; in DAT. and ABL. -pte = *myself.* **b.** mihi, nōbis as *Ethic* DAT. = *pray, say I,* etc. ; quid mihi Celsus agit ? Hor. ; Cic. ; etc. **c.** ad mē = *to my house :* Cic. Ep. : **d.** apud mē, *at my house, at home with me.* T r a n s f. : vix sum apud me, *in my right mind,* Ter. **e.** ABL. with *cum :* mēcum, nōbiscum. **f.** GEN. meī, nostrī (really from meus, noster. L i t. : *of my, our interest*) are mostly objective : immemor mei ; odium nostri. **g.** O c c. : nōs = ego ; absente nobis, Ter. ; nobis consulibus, Cic. [It. *io ;* Span. *yo ;* Fr. *je.*]

egomet, *v.* ego.

ē-gredior, gredī, grĕssus [gradior]. **I.** *to step, march, go* or *come out.* **1.** L i t. **a.** In gen. With *ex :* Pl., Caes., Cic., Liv. With *ab :* Pl., Caes., Cic., Liv., Hor. **b.** Milit. *to march out.* With *ex :* Caes. With *extra :* Caes., Liv. With ABL. : Caes., Sall. With *ad :* Caes., Sall., Liv. With *in* and ACC. : Liv. *Absol. :* Caes., Sall. **c.** Naut. : *to disembark, land :* ex navi, Cic., Caes. ; navi, Caes., Liv., Ov. ; in terram, Cic. *Absol. :* Caes., Liv., Ov. ; e portu, or *absol. : to set sail :* Cic. Ep., Ov. **2.** T r a n s f. of discourse : *to digress, wander :* a proposito, Cic. **II.** *to go up, ascend :* ad summum montis, Sall. ; in vallum, Tac. ; Liv. ; Ov., etc. **III.** With ACC. *to overstep, pass.* **1.** L i t. : finis, Caes. ; flumen, Liv. **2.** T r a n s f. : *to overstep, surpass :* relationem, praeturam, Tac. ; Quint. **IV.** With ACC. : *to go out from, quit shelter of :* tentoria, Tac., Luc. ; portum, Quint. ; tecta, Plin. Ep.

ēgregiē, *adv. uncommonly well, specially, excellently.* **a.** With verbs : Ter., Cic., Liv. **b.** With Adj. : Caes., Cic. **c.** As expression of assent, applause, etc. ; *very good !* Plin. Pan. *Comp. :* ēgregius, Juv.

ē-gregius, a, um [grex]. L i t. : *picked out of the flock ;* hence *uncommon, distinguished, pre-eminent.* **a.** In gen. : forma, facies, Ter. ; vir, Cic. ; corpus, Hor., Ov. ; virtus, Caes. ; victoria, Liv. With *in* and ABL. : Cic., Sall. With GEN. : animi, Verg. ; Sall. *Neut.* as Noun (*in pl.*) : Sall., Tac. **b.** During the empire : *of distinguished rank, illustrious, honourable :* Tac. ; and *Neut.* as Noun, *honour :* Tac.

ēgressus, a, um, *Part.* ēgredior.

ēgressus, ūs, *m.* [ēgredior], *a going out, egress, departure.* **1.** L i t. **a.** In gen. : Cic., Tac. ; in *pl., times* and *places of going out,* Sall. **b.** Of birds : *a flight :* Ov. **c.** *a disembarking, landing :* Caes. **2.** T r a n s f. **a.** *a passage out, exit :* Tac. ; *of the mouths of the* Hister : Ov. **b.** R h e t. : *a digression :* Quint., Tac.

ē-gurgitō, āre [gurges], *to pour out, lavish :* argentum domo, Pl.

ehem, *interj.* An exclamation of joyful surprise : Pl., Ter.

ēheu, *interj.* An exclamation of pain : *ah ! alas !* Pl., Ter., Hor., Ov.

eho, *interj. ha ! hi ! oho !* (of vehement questions, commands, remonstrances) : Pl., Ter. With affixed *dum :* Ter.

(1) eī, DAT. of is, q.v.

(2) eī, *interj.* an exclamation of grief or fear ; *ah ! woe !* Pl., Ter., Verg.

ēia (also **hēia**), *interj.* **I.** An exclamation of joy or surprise : *ah ! ah ha ! indeed ! ;* Pl., Ter. ; eia vero, *oh yes, no doubt !* Pl. **II.** Of exhortation : *ho ! quick ! come on !* Pl., Hor. ; eia age, *come then ! up then !* Verg.

ē-iaculor, ārī, *to shoot* or *spout forth :* aquas, Ov. ; se in altum sanguis, Ov.

ē-iciō, icere, iēcī, iectum [iaciō], *to fling* or *cast out.* **1.** L i t. **a.** cadaver domo, Cic. ; Pl. ; navigantem de navi, Cic. ; equitem, *to throw,* Verg. **b.** Of parts of the body : linguam, *to thrust out,* Cic. ; armum, *to dislocate,* Verg. **c.** N a u t. : *to drive, run a ship ashore :* navem in terram, Caes. ; ad Chium, Liv. Also *to run aground,* and in *Pass. to be stranded, castaway :* Pl., Caes., Liv., Tac. Also of persons : Pl., Cic., Verg., etc. **d.** With *Refl. Pron. to fling oneself out, rush out, sally forth :* se ex castris, Caes. ; Cic. ; Liv. **2.** T r a n s f. : *to expel, banish, eject.* **a.** Of persons : aliquem e senatu, Cic. ; Caes. ; Liv. ; de senatu, Liv. ; Cic. Ep. ; finibus, Sall. ; Pl. ; ex oppido, Caes. ; in exsilium, Cic. **b.** Of things : curam ex animo, Pl. ; Cic. ; Liv. **c.** With *Refl. Pron.,* of the passions, *to break out :* Cic. **d.** Of actors, public speakers, etc. *to hiss off :* Cic. Hence, *to reject :* Cynicorum rationem, Cic.

ēiectāmenta, ōrum, *n. pl.* [ēiectō], *what is cast out, refuse :* Tac.

ēiectiō, ōnis, *f.* [ēiciō], *a casting out, banishment :* Cic. Ep.

ēiectō, āre [*freq.* ōiciō], *to cast out repeatedly* or *violently :* cruorem ore, Verg. ; Ov.

ēiectus, a, um, *Part.* ēiciō.

ēiectus, ūs, *m.* [ēiciō], *a casting out, emission :* animai, Lucr.

ēierō (later **ēiūrō**), āre. **I.** In law, *to swear off, reject by oath.* **1.** L i t. : forum or iudicem iniquum sibi eierare, Cic. **2.** T r a n s f. As to one's solvency : bonam copiam (i.e. to swear that one is insolvent), Cic. **II.** In State affairs : magistratum, imperium eiurare, *to lay down, resign an office :* Tac. ; Plin. Ep. *Absol. :* Tac. **III.** *to forswear, disown :* patriam, Tac.

ēiulātiō, ōnis, *f.* [ēiulō], *a yelling, lamenting :* Pl., Cic.

ēiulātus, ūs, *m.* [ēiulō], *a wailing, lamenting :* Cic.

ēiulō, āre [*cf.* ei, ēia], *to wail, moan, utter lamentations :* Pl., Cic.

ēiūrō, *v.* ēierō.

ēj-, *v.* ēi-.

ē-lābor, lābī, lāpsus. **I.** Of things, *to glide, slip forth.* **1.** L i t. : Pl., Cic., Verg., etc. With *ex :* Liv. With *de :* Cic. **2.** T r a n s f. **a.** *to pass away insensibly :* vita, Lucr. ; ignis in frondes, Verg. ; adsensio omnis illa, Cic. **b.** *to fall insensibly :* in servitutem, Liv. **II.** *to slip, glance off.* With ABL. : Caes. With *super :* Liv. **III.** Of persons, *to slip away, escape.* **1.** L i t. With *ex :* Caes., Cic. Ep. With *de :* Verg. With *inter :* Liv. With DAT. : Verg., Tac.

2. Transf. a. animi corporibus, Cic.; Ter.; aliquid memoriâ, Cic. **b.** *to get off*, *escape* : ex criminibus, Cic.; causa e manibus, Cic. Occ. with Acc.: pugnam aut vincula, Tac.

ēlăbŏrātus, a, um. **I.** *Part.* ēlăbŏrō. **II.** Adj.: Rhet.: *studied, elaborate*; us. of what is *overdone* : concinnitas, Cic.; Quint.

ē-lăbŏrō, āre. **A.** Intrans. : *to exert oneself to the utmost, use every effort.* With *ut* and *Subj.* : Cic. *Impers. Pass.* : Cic. With *in* and Abl. : Cic., Quint. *Impers. Pass.* : Tac. With *in* and Acc. : Quint. **B.** Trans. : *to labour on, take pains with, to work out, elaborate* (in Cic. mostly *Pass.*) : Cic., Hor., Tac., etc. With *Inf.* : Quint.

ē-lāmentābilis, e, *adj. very lamentable* : gemitus, Cic.

ēlanguēscō, languēscere, langui, *to grow utterly faint, feeble* ; *to slacken.* **1.** Lit. : Liv., Tac. **2.** Transf. : differendo elanguit res, Liv.

ēlāpsus, a, um, *Part.* ēlābor.

ēlātē, *adv.* [efferō], *loftily, proudly* : Cic. *Comp.* : Nep.

Elatēïus, a, um, *of Elatus, a prince of the Lapithae* ; *v.* Caeneus.

ēlātiō, ōnis, *f.* [efferō], *a carrying out.* Transf. **a.** *excitement* : voluptaria, Cic. **b.** *exaltation, elevation* : animi, Cic.

ē-lātrō, āre, *to bark out.* Transf. : aliquid acriter, Hor.

ēlātus, a, um. **I.** *Part.* efferō. **II.** Adj.: *elevated.* Transf. : animus magnus elatusque, Cic.

ē-lavō, lavāre, lāvī, lautum and lōtum, *to wash out, wash clean.* Transf. : in mari elavare, i.e. *to be cleaned out, wrecked*, Pl. Hence, elavare bonis, Pl.

Elea (or **Velia**), ae, *f. a city in Lucania, birthplace of Parmenides and Zeno, founders of the Eleatic philosophy* ; **Eleātēs,** ae, *a native of Elea* ; **Eleātici,** ōrum, *m. pl. the Eleatics.*

ēlecebra, ae, *f.* [ēliciō], *a female allurer, wheedler* : Pl.

ēlectē, *adv. choicely* : Cic.

ēlectilis, e, *adj.* [ēligō], *choice, dainty* : Pl.

ēlectiō, ōnis, *f.* [ēligō], *a choice* : Cic., Quint., Tac. In *pl.* : Tac.

ēlectō, āre [*freq.* ēliciō], *to wheedle out* (a secret) : Pl.

ēlectō, āre [*freq.* ēligō], *to choose, select* : Pl.

Electra, ae, (Acc. -an, Ov.), *f.* **I.** *d. of Atlas and Pleione, and m. of Dardanus by Jupiter.* **II.** *d. of Agamemnon and Clytaemnestra, and s. of Orestes.*

ēlectrum, ī, *n.* [ἤλεκτρον]. **I.** *amber* (pure Lat. succinum). **1.** Lit. : Ov. In *pl.* : Verg. **2.** Transf. (in *pl.*) : *amber beads or balls* : Ov. **II.** *an alloy of gold and silver.* **1.** Lit. : Verg. **2.** Transf. : *articles made of electrum* (or *of amber ?*) : Juv.

ēlectus, a, um. **I.** *Part.* ēligō. **II.** Adj.: *select, choice* : Cat. *Comp.* : Auct. Her. *Sup.* : Cic., Cat., Suet.

ēlectus, ūs, *m.* [ēligō], *a choice* : Ov.

ēlegāns, antis, *adj.* [as fr. ēlegō, āre, another form of ēligēns from ēligo]. **I.** In good sense : *choice, nice* (i.e. *discriminating, particular*), *tasteful, elegant.* **a.** Of persons : Cic., Nep., Quint. *Comp.* : Cic. *Sup.* :

Nep. **b.** Of things : *refined* : Ter., Cic., Liv., etc. *Comp.* : Cic. *Sup.* : Cic. Ep., Quint. **II.** In bad sense : *dainty, fastidious* : Pl., Ter., Cato.

ēleganter, *adv.* [ēlegāns], *with discrimination, with good taste and propriety* : Cic., Liv. *Comp.* : Cic., Liv., etc. *Sup.* : Cic., Quint.

ēlegantia, ae, *f.* [ēlegāns]. **I.** *discrimination, taste, refinement, elegance.* With Gen. : doctrinae, Cic.; vitae, Tac.; verborum Latinorum, Cic.; Quint.; scriptorum, Cic. *Absol.* : Cic. **II.** In bad sense : *daintiness, fastidiousness, aestheticism* : Pl.

ēlegī, ōrum, *m. pl.* [ἔλεγοι], *elegiac verses* : Hor., Ov., Tac., etc.

ēlegīa (also **elegēa**), ae, *f.* [ἐλεγεία], *an elegy* : Ov., Quint.

Eleleus, eī, *m.* (trisyl. fr. ἐλελεῦ, the cry of the Bacchantes), *a surname of Bacchus* ; **Eleleïdes,** um, *f. pl. Bacchantes.*

elementārius, a, um, *learning the elements* : senex, Sen. Ep.

elementum, ī, *n.* [perh. fr. ole- seen in adolēscō], us. *pl.* : *first principles, elements.* **1.** Lit. : Lucr., Cic., Ov., etc. In *sing.* of the "*element*" *of fire* : Juv. **2.** Transf. **a.** *first principles, rudiments of an art or science* : Cic., Ov., Quint., etc. **b.** *the beginnings of other things* : prima Romae, Ov.; cupidinis pravi, Hor.

elenchus, ī, *m.* [ἔλεγχος]. **I.** *a rare kind of pearl* : Plin., Juv. **II.** **elenchī,** ōrum. *m.* [ἔλεγχοι], perh. *criticisms* (title of a work) : Suet.

elephantomacha, ae, *m. one who fights from an elephant* : Liv.

elephantus, ī, *m.* (rarely *f.*) (**elephās,** antis, Lucr., Sen. Ep., Luc.) [ἐλέφας], *an elephant.* **1.** Lit. : Pl., Cic., Verg., etc. **2.** Transf. **a.** *ivory* : Verg. **b.** *elephantiasis* : Lucr.

Eleusin, īnis, *f. Eleusis, an old city in Attica, famous for its mysteries of Demeter (Ceres)* ; **Eleusīnus (-sīnius),** a, um.

elephās, *v.* elephantus.

eleutheria, ae, *f.* [ἐλευθερία], *liberty* : Pl.

ē-levō, āre, *to lift up, raise.* **1.** Lit. : contabulationem, Caes. **2.** Transf. **a.** *to lighten, alleviate* : aegritudinem, Cic. **b.** *to lessen, diminish, impair* : perspicuitatem, Cic.; auctoritatem, Liv. **c.** *to make light of, disparage* : causas offensionum, Cic.; res gestas, Liv.; Etruscos, Liv.; Prop.

ē-liciō, licere, licuī, licitum [laciō], *to draw out, entice out, lure out.* **1.** Lit. : aliquem hinc foras, Pl.; hostem ex paludibus silvisque, Caes.; Cic.; ad pugnam, Caes.; Cic.; Liv.; ad subeunda pericula, Cic.; in proelium, Tac.; Caes.; aliquem ut etc., Liv. **b.** By religious or magic rites : Cic., Ov., etc. **2.** Transf. : of inanimate objects : lacrumas, Pl.; terra elicit herbescentem ex semine viriditatem, Cic.; etiam ex infantium ingeniis voces, Cic.; responsum, misericordiam, Liv.; cadum, Hor.; veritatem, Tac.

Elicius, ī, *m.* [ēliciō], *surname of Jupiter* (in connexion with *rites of incantation*) : Liv., Ov.

ēlicitus, a, um, *Part.* ēliciō.

ē-līdō, līdere, līsī, līsum [laedō]. **I.** *to knock, dash,* or *crush out.* **1.** Lit. : oculos,

Pl., Verg.; aurigam e curru, Cic.; Tac.; ignis nubibus, Ov. **2.** Transf.: (imago) recta retrorsum eliditur, Lucr.; morbum, Hor.; vocem, Quint. **II.** *to break or dash to pieces, to shatter, to crush.* **1.** Lit.: talos alicui, Pl.; navis, Caes.; anguis, Verg.; caput saxo, Liv. **2.** Transf.: aegritudine elidi, Cic.

ē-ligō, ligere, lēgī, lēctum [legō], *to pick out* (with the fingers), *pluck out.* **1.** Lit.: Varr. **2.** Transf. **a.** *to pluck out* : nervos coniurationis, Liv.; nervos urbis, Cic. **b.** *to pick out, choose* : locum ad pugnam, Cic.; urbi locum, Liv.; ex malis minima, Cic.; de tribus, Cic.; a multis commodissimum quodque, Cic. With *Indir. Quest.* : Liv.

ē-līminō, āre [līmen], *to turn out of doors* : se, Enn., Varr. Transf.: *to carry out of doors* : dicta foras, Hor.

ē-līmō, āre, *to file out, make by filing.* **1.** Lit.: Ov. **2.** Transf.: *to elaborate, perfect* : σχόλιον aliquod, Att. ap. Cic. Ep.; Quint.

ē-linguis, e, adj. [lingua]. **1.** Lit. *without tongue, speechless* : Cic., Liv. **2.** Transf.: *without eloquence* : Cic., Tac.

ē-linguō, āre [lingua], *to de-tongue* : Pl.

Ēlis, (or **Ālis**), Ālidis (Acc. -in or idem ; ABL. -ide, sometimes -ī), *f. a country (and town) on the W. coast of Peloponnesus, in which Olympia is situated* ; **Ēlēus**, a, um, *Elean* or *Olympian* ; **Ēleī** (**Ēliī**), ōrum, *m. pl. the Eleans* ; **Ēlias**, adis, *f. adj. Elean or Olympian.*

Elissa (-īsa), ae, *f. another name for Dido.*

ēlīsus, a, um, *Part.* ēlīdō.

ēlixus, a, um, *boiled.* **1.** Lit.: Pl., Varr., Hor., Juv. **2.** Transf. (comic.) *sodden* : Mart., Pers.

elleborōsus, a, um, *needing much hellebore, i.e. very mad* : Pl.

elleborus (hell-), i, *m.* and **elleborum**, i, *n.* [ἐλλέβορος and ἐλλ-], *hellebore,* a name of poisonous plants used for mental diseases : Pl., Verg., Sen. Ep., etc.

ellipsis, is, *f.* [ἔλλειψις]. Rhet : *an ellipsis* : pure Lat. detractio : Quint.

ellum, ellam, v. ecce.

ē-locō, āre, *to let or hire out, to farm out* : fundum, Cic.

ēlocūtiō, ōnis, *f.* [eloquor]. Rhet. *oratorical delivery* ; *style* : Cic., Quint.

ēlogium, i, *n.* [ἐλεγεῖον]. **I.** *a short saying, sentence, maxim* : Cic. **II.** Most freq.: *an inscription* (on a tombstone) : Cic.; (on the images of ancestors) : Suet.; (on votive tablets) : Suet.; (on doors) : Pl. **III.** *a clause in a will* : Cic. **IV.** *a record, report* in criminal cases : Suet.

ēloquēns, entis. **I.** *Part.* ēloquor. **II.** Adj.: *eloquent* : Cic., Quint., Plin. Ep. *Comp.* : Quint. *Sup.* : Cic., Quint., Tac.

ēloquenter, *adv. eloquently.* *Comp.* and *Sup.* : Plin. Ep.

ēloquentia, ae, *f.* [ēloquor], *eloquence* : Cic.

ēloquium, i, *n.* [ēloquor], *eloquence* : Verg., Hor., Ov.

ē-loquor, loquī, locūtus, *to speak out, declare, state clearly.* **1.** Lit. With Acc.: Pl., Caes., Cic., Hor. *Absol.* : Pl., Ter., Verg.

2. Transf. (Intrans.) : *to speak* in an oratorical or eloquent manner : Cic., Quint.

ēlōtus, a, um, *Part.* ēlavō.

ēluācrus, a, um [ēluō], *for washing out* : labrum, Cato.

ē-lūceō, lūcēre, lūxī, *to shine out, shine forth.* **1.** Lit.: Cic. Of *the glitter* of bees, Verg. **2.** Transf.: ex quo elucebit omnis constantia, Cic.; Lucr.; Quint.

ē-luctor, ārī. **A.** Intrans.: *to struggle out, force a way through.* **1.** Lit.: aqua omnis, Verg. **2.** Transf.: eluctantium verborum (homo), Tac. **B.** Trans. **a.** *to struggle out of* : tot ac tam validas manūs, Liv.; nivis, Tac. **b.** *to surmount by effort* : locorum difficultates, Tac.

ē-lūcubrō, āre (Cic., Tac.) and **ēlūcubror**, ārī (Cic. Ep.), *to compose by lamplight (at night)* : epistulam, Cic. Ep.; Tac.

ē-lūdō, lūdere, lūsī, lūsum. **I.** *to play out* or *to the end, end the bout* : Ter. Of the sea : Cic. **II.** In boxing, etc., *to play off, parry* (a weapon or blow). **1.** Lit.: hastas, Mart. *Absol.* : oratio, Cic. With Acc. of person, *to baffle, foil* : Caes., Verg., Tac., etc. **2.** Transf.: *to parry, ward off* : bellum quiete, Liv.; Tac.; ultionem praevaricando, Tac. **III.** *to outplay, beat in play.* **1.** Lit.: militem in aleā, Pl. Also with Acc. of thing won: anulum te elusit, Pl. **2.** Transf. **a.** tibi tuas palmas, Prop. **b.** *to outmanœuvre, get the better of, delude* : Pl., Ter., Cic., Liv. **c.** *to make sport of, mock at* : aliquem, Cic., Tac.; nos contumeliis, Liv.; artem auguris, Liv.

ē-lūgeō, lūgēre, lūxī, *to mourn the full time.* **A.** Trans.: Cic. Ep. **B.** Intrans.: Liv.

ē-lumbis, e, adj. [lumbus], *loinless* : of style, *wanting in vigour, emasculated* : Tac.

ē-luō, luere, luī, lūtum. **I.** *to wash or rinse out* ; *wash clean.* **1.** Lit.: vascula, Pl.; purpureum colorem, Lucr.; corpus, Ov. **2.** Transf. **a.** *to get rid of, squander* : Pl. **b.** *to wash away* : scelus, Verg.; Cic.; Ov.; Quint.

ēlūsus, a, um, *Part.* ēlūdō.

ēlūtus, a, um. **I.** *Part.* ēluō. **II.** Adj.: *watery, insipid. Comp.* : Hor.

ēluviēs, em, ē, *f.* [ēluō]. **I.** *a washing away, a flowing off, discharge* : Lucil., Juv. **II.** *an overflowing, an inundation* : Ov., Tac. Transf.: civitatis, Cic. **III.** *ravine* : Curt.

ēluviō, ōnis, *f. an overflowing, a deluge* : Cic.; *in pl.* : Cic.

Ēlvīna (Hēl-), ae, *f. a surname of Ceres* in Juv.

Ēlysium, i, *n. the abode of the blessed in the lower world* ; **Ēlysius**, a, um; campi, Verg.

(1) em, old Acc. of is.

(2) em, interj. v. hem.

(3) em, interj. [older eme, *Imper.* of emō, *take it !*], *here ! there !* Pl., Ter., Cic. Esp. with *Imper.* : Pl., Ter.

ēmācitās, ātis, *f.* [emāx], *a fondness for buying* : Plin. Ep.

ēmancipātiō (ēmancup-), ōnis, *f.* [ēmancipō]. In law **a.** *the releasing of a son from the patria potestas, emancipation* (v. emancipo); Quint **b.** any *formal conveyance of property* : fundorum, Plin. Ep.

ēmancipātus, a, um. **I.** *Part.* ēmancipō. **II.** Adj. *conveyed, made over.* Transf.: tribunatus, Cic.

ē-mancipō (**ēmancupō**), āre, *to put out of the hand* (*ownership*), *to transfer.* **1.** Lit. In law. **a.** Of a son : *to declare free and independent, to emancipate from the patria potestas,* Liv. ; filium in adoptionem, Cic. **b.** Of property, *to make over ownership to another, convey :* Quint., Suet. **2.** Transf.: *to make over, convey* (i.e. *enslave*) : nunc ego, mulier, tibi me totum emancupo, Pl. ; nemini emancipata (senectus), Cic. ; Hor.

ē-mānō, āre, *to ooze or flow out.* **1.** Lit. : Lucr. **2.** Transf. **a.** *to spring from :* ex fonte (aliquo), Cic. **b.** Very freq. *to trickle out, leak out ; to spread abroad, become known ;* in vulgus, Cic. ; fama, sermo, Cic. ; Liv. *Impers. :* emanabat (with Acc. and *Inf.*) : Liv.

Ēmathia, ae, *f. a district in Macedonia :* hence *Macedonia* or *Thessaly* (*Pharsalus*) ; **Ēmathius**, a, um, *Macedonian* or *Thessalian* (*Pharsalian*) ; **Ēmathis**, idis, *f. adj. Macedonian* or *Thessalian* ; **Ēmathĭdes**, um, *f. pl. the daughters of the Macedonian king Pierus ; the Pierides.*

ē-mātūrēscō, mātūrēscere, mātūruī, *to come to maturity.* **1.** Lit. : Plin. **2.** Transf. *to soften, be mitigated :* ira, Ov.

emāx, ācis [emō ; cf. edāx], *very fond of buying :* Cato, Cic., Ov.

emblēma, ātis, n. (Abl. *Pl.* -matis, Cic.) [ἔμβλημα]. **I.** *tesselated work, mosaic :* vermiculatum, Lucil. **II.** *inlaid work :* Cic.

embolium, ī, n. [ἐμβόλιον], *something inserted ; an interlude, ballet.* Transf.: sororis, Cic.

ēmendābilis, e, adj. [ēmendō], *capable of correction :* error, Liv.

ēmendātē, adv. *faultlessly :* Cic., Hirt., Quint. *Comp. :* Quint.

ēmendātiō, ōnis, f. [ēmendō], *a correction, emendation :* Cic., Quint.

ēmendātor, ōris, m. and **ēmendātrix**, īcis, f. [ēmendō], *a corrector :* Cic.

ēmendātus, a, um. **I.** *Part.* ēmendō. **II.** Adj.: *faultless :* mores, locutio, Cic., Hor., etc. ; Plin. *Sup. :* Plin. Ep.

ē-mendicō, āre, *to obtain by begging :* Suet.

ē-mendō, āre [mendum], *to free from faults, correct, reform, improve.* **a.** In gen. : civitatem, Cic. ; Quint. ; vitia adulescentiae, Nep. ; Ov. ; Hor. **b.** language : Cic., Quint.

ēmēnsus, a, um, *Part.* ēmētior.

ē-mentior, īrī, *to lie, fabricate, feign :* Cic., Suet. With Acc. : Pl., Cic., Liv. ; aliquem, i.e. to personate, Pl. With Acc. and *Inf. :* Cic., Liv., Tac. *Perf. Part.* in *Pass.* senso : Cic.

ē-mercor, ārī, *to buy up, purchase :* aditum principis, Tac.

ē-mereō, ēre, and **ē-mereor**, ērī, *to obtain by service, to merit, earn fully.* **1.** Lit. **a.** In gen. With Acc. : Pl., Prop., Quint. With *Inf. :* Ov. With Acc. of person : *to earn* (*the favour*) *of, to lay under obligation :*

Tib., Ov. **b.** Milit. *to serve out, complete one's term of service,* mostly with stipendia (*pay*) : Cic., Sall., Liv. ; also militiam, Suet. ; annos, Ov. **2.** Transf. **a.** annuum tempus (*sc.* magistratūs), Cic. Ep. **b.** emeritis stipendiis libidinis, Cic.

ē-mergō, mergere, mērsī, mērsum. **A.** Trans.: *to raise from a dive, plunge, etc. : to raise from the water.* **1.** Lit. : e gurgite vultūs Nereides, Cat. ; montes nullos apertos rivos, Liv. Mostly in *Perf. Part. :* e flumine emersus, Cic. ; Liv. ; paludibus, Tac. **2.** Transf. : sese ex malis, Ter. Mostly in *Perf. Part. :* emersus ex diuturnis tenebris, Cic. ; velut emerso ab admiratione animo, Liv. **B.** Intrans. : *to rise* or *come forth from the water, come up.* **1.** Lit. : e flumine, Cic. ; de paludibus, Liv. ; ab infimā arā, Cic. ; ex Antiati in Appiam, Cic. ; Liv. *Impers. Pass. :* Ter. *Absol. :* Cic., Tac. **2.** Transf. **a.** Of the sun, etc. : Cic., Tac. ; in suam lucem luna, Liv. **b.** Of plants, etc. : viriditas e vaginis, Cic. **c.** *to raise or extricate oneself from ; to emerge, get clear :* ex miserrimis sordibus, Cic. ; ex obnoxiā pace, Liv. **d.** *to rise* (in power, position) : ad summas opes, Lucr. *Absol. :* Juv. **e.** *to come out, appear :* ex quo magis emergit, quale sit decorum illud, Cic.

ēmeritus, a, um. **I.** *Part.* ēmereor. **II.** Noun, **emeritus**, ī, m. *a soldier who has served his time ; a veteran ;* only in *pl. :* Tac. **III.** Adj. : *that has become unfit for service, worn out :* equi, Ov. ; Prop. ; Juv.

ēmersus, a, um, *Part.* ēmergō.

emetica, ae, f. [ἐμετική], *an emetic :* Cael. ap. Cic. Ep.

ē-mētior, mētīrī, mēnsus, *to measure out.* **1.** Lit. : spatium oculis, Verg. **2.** Transf. **a.** *to pass through, pass over, traverse :* freta, terras, sidera, tot inhospita saxa, Verg. ; ingens spatium uno die, Liv. Of a lifetime : quinque principes emensus, Tac. **b.** *to impart, bestow :* aliquid patriae, Hor. ; Cic. *Perf. Part.* in *Pass.* sense : *traversed, passed through :* Caes., Verg., Liv.

ē-metō, ere, *to reap from :* plus frumenti agris, Hor.

ē-micō, micāre, micuī, micātum. **I.** *to leap, dart, spring out, spring forth :* cor in pectus, Pl. ; e corpore sanguis, Lucr. : Ov. ; saxa tormento, Liv. ; Ov. ; iuvenum manus emicat in litus, Verg. ; Lucr. ; ante omnia corpora, Verg. **II.** *to dart forth, gleam out.* **1.** Lit. : ex oculis flamma, Ov. ; Curt. **2.** Transf. : *to shine forth, be conspicuous :* Agrippinae pavor emicuit, Tac. ; Hor.

ē-migrō, āre, *to move out, depart :* ex illā domo, Cic. ; e vitā, Cic. ; domo, Caes. *Absol. :* Pl.

ēminēns, entis. **I.** *Part.* ēmineō. **II.** Adj. *standing out, projecting, lofty.* **1.** Lit. : saxa, Sall. ; Caes. ; oculi, Cic. *Comp. :* Caes., Quint., Sall. *Sup. :* Quint. **2.** Transf.: *distinguished, eminent :* ingenium, Quint. ; Cic. *Comp. :* Tac. *Sup. :* Quint. As Noun, **ēminentēs**, ium, m. *pl. :* Tac. ; **ēminentia**, ium, n. *pl. :* Quint.

ēminentia, ae, f. [ēminēns], *projection, standing out, prominence :* Cic. In painting, *the lights* (opp. umbrae, *the shades*) : Cic.

ē-mineō, ēre [cf. mentum, mōns], to stand out, project. **1.** Lit.: stipites ex terrā, Caes.; Cic.; stipites ab ramis, Caes.; Liv.; belua ponto, Ov.; Curt.; ferrum per costas, Liv. Absol.: Caes., Ov., etc. Of the lights in painting: to stand out, be prominent: Cic., Quint. **2.** Transf.: to be conspicuous or remarkable (of persons or things): Cic., Ov., Liv., etc.; Demosthenes unus eminet inter omnis in omni genere dicendi, Cic.; Quint.; ante alios, Liv.

ē-minor, āri, to threaten: Pl.

ē-minus, adv. [manus] (opp. comminus), out of the reach of hands; at a distance, from a distance. **1.** Lit.: pugnare, Caes.; Verg.; Liv., etc. **2.** Transf.: Lucr., Ov.

ē-miror, āri, to wonder greatly at: aequora, Hor.

ēmissārium, ī, n. [ēmittō], an outlet: lacūs, Cic. Ep.; Suet.

ēmissārius, ī, m. [ēmittō], an emissary, scout, spy: Cic., Suet.

ēmissīcius, a, um [ēmittō], prying about, spying: oculi, Pl.

ēmissiō, ōnis, f. [ēmittō], a letting go forth or escape, discharge: telorum, Cic.: anguis, Cic.

ēmissus, a, um, Part. ēmittō.

ēmissus, ūs, m. [ēmittō], a sending forth, emission: Lucr.

ē-mittō, mittere, mīsī, missum, to let go forth, let loose, send forth. **1.** Lit. **A.** By intention. **a.** Of troops: equites, Caes.; essedarios ex silvis, Caes.; aliquem pabulatum, Caes. **b.** At the games: ex portā leporem, Pl.; Cic. **c.** Of water: aquam ex lacu, Liv.; Cic. Ep.; Curt. **d.** Of missiles. to let fly, discharge: Caes., Sall., Liv. **B.** By sufferance, accident, carelessness, to allow to go forth, discharge. **a.** From prison, to let out: aliquem e custodiā, etc., Cic.; Pl. **b.** From slavery, debt, etc., to release, free: manu emittere aliquem, Pl., Liv., Tac.; librā et aere liberatum emittit, Liv. **c.** to let slip, allow to escape: Catilinam e urbe, Cic.; Hannibalem e manibus, Liv.; Licinium de manibus, Cic. Of things: scutum manu, Caes.; Phaedr. Also, animam, i.e. to expire, Nep. **2.** Transf. **a.** to put forth, publish: librum, Suet.; aliquid dignum, Cic. **b.** to fling out, give utterance to, let slip: vocem caelo, Liv.; Lucr.; Cic., etc.

emō, emere, ēmī, emptum [orig. to take, receive, cf. compounds, adimō, etc.], to buy. **1.** Lit.: aliquid de aliquo, Cic.; minoris aut pluris, Cic.; tanti, quanti, Pl., Cic.; bene, cheaply, Cic.; male, dearly, Cic.; also, care, Hor.; in diem, on credit, Nep. With Instr. ABL. (of purchase-money): Pl., Cic.; magno, parvo, Cic. Ep. **2.** Transf.: to purchase, bribe: sententias (iudicum), Cic.; militem, Tac.; aeternum nomen sanguine, Ov.

ē-moderor, āri, to set bounds to and so end: dolorem verbis, Ov.

ē-modulor, āri, to attune all through: Musam, Ov.

ē-mōlior, īri, to accomplish with great effort: negotium, Pl.

ē-molliō, īre, to make quite soft. **1.** Lit.:

Liv. **2.** Transf. **a.** to make mild, gentle: mores, Ov. **b.** to enervate, render effeminate: exercitum, Liv.; Luc.; Tac.

ē-molō, ere, to grind out and so use up: granaria, Pers.

ēmolumentum, ī, n. [ēmolō], what is got by grinding: hence, results, gain, profit: Lucr., Cic., Liv., etc. In pl.: Cic. With GEN.: pacis, Tac.; Pl.; Cic.; Juv. Also a cause of profit: Liv.

ē-moneō, ēre, to advise fully (with Acc. of person and ut and Subj.): Cic. Ep.

ē-morior, morī (morīrī, Pl., Ter.), mortuus, to die right out, die off. **1.** Lit.: Pl., Cic., Ov., etc. **2.** Transf.: to perish, pass away: eorum laus, Cic.; Quint.; amor, Ov.; auxilium, Pl.

ēmortuālis, e, adj. [ēmorior], of death: dies. Pl.

ēmortuus, a, um, Part. ēmorior.

ēmōtus, a, um, Part. ēmoveō.

ē-moveō, movēre, mōvī, mōtum (Perf. sync. ēmōstis, Liv.), to move out, move away, force away. **1.** Lit.: multitudinem e foro, Liv.; plebem de medio, Liv.; aliquos senatu, Liv.; postis cardine, Verg. **2.** Transf.: morbum pestilentiamque ex agro Romano, Liv.; nomen ex pectore, Pl.; curas dictis, Verg.

Empedoclēs, is, m. a famous natural philosopher of Agrigentum, c. B.C. 450; Empedoclēus, a, um.

emphasis, is, f. [ἔμφασις]. Rhet.: emphasis, stress: Quint.

empīricus, ī, m. [ἐμπειρικός], a physician whose knowledge is gained merely from experience: Cic.

emplastrum, ī, n. [ἔμπλαστρον], a plaster: Cato.

emporium, ī, n. [ἐμπόριον], a place of trade, a market-town, market: Pl., Cic. Ep., Liv.

emptiō, ōnis, f. [emō], a buying. **1.** Lit.: Cic., Tac. **2.** Transf.: a thing purchased (in pl.): Cic. Ep., Plin. Ep.

emptitō, āre [freq. emō], to be in the habit of buying: Tac., Plin. Ep.

emptor, ōris, m. [emō], a buyer, purchaser: Pl., Cic., Hor., etc.

emptus, a, um, Part. emō.

ē-mūgiō, īre, to bellow out: Quint.

ē-mulgeō, mulgēre, mūlsum, to drain out: paludem, Cat.

ēmūnctus, a, um. **I.** Part. ēmungō. **II.** Adj., clean-nosed: hence, keen-nosed, of fine discernment: naris emunctae senex, Phaedr.; Hor. Of orators: Quint.

ē-mungō, mungere, mūnxī, mūnctum [cf. ἀπομύσσειν, mūcus], to wipe the nose clean. **1.** Lit. with Acc. of Pron. Refl.: Suet. Also in Mid.: Varr., Juv. **2.** Transf.: to cheat: Pl., Hor. With ABL., to cheat of: auro, Pl.; Ter.

ē-mūniō, īre. **I.** to build up: supra modum ceterae altitudinis, Liv. **II.** to fortify, secure strongly: murum opere, Liv.; Verg. **III.** to clear, make roads through: silvas, Tac.

ēn (ĕm, Pl.), interj. **A.** Interrogative [fr. est-ne?], is it so? really? then? : Pl., Cic., Verg., etc. **B.** [Gk. ἤν, ἠνίδε]. **a.** Demonstrative: there! see there! en Priamus, Verg.; Pl.; Cic.; etc.; consul en!

hic est, Liv. With *Pres.* : eu ego vester Ascanius, Verg. ; Hor. ; en hic, Cic. Ep. ; Pl. ; Ov. Rarely with Acc. : en causam cur, Cic. ; Juv. With whole sentences : Pl., Verg., Liv. **b.** With *Imperat.* : come/ come then/ Pl., Verg., etc.

ēnărrăbilis, e, adj. [ēnărrō], *that may be related, described* (only with a negative) : Verg., Sen. Ep., Quint.

ēnărrătiō, ōnis, f. [ēnărrō]. **I.** *a detailed description* : Quint. **II.** In metre, *a scanning* : Sen. Ep.

ē-nărrō, āre, *to explain or relate in full* : res gestas, Cic. ; Pl. ; Liv., etc.

ē-nāscor, nāscī, nātus, *to sprout or spring up, arise.* **1.** Lit. : rami, Caes. ; capillus, Liv. ; Lucr. **2.** Transf. : insula medio alveo, Curt.

ē-natō, āre, *to swim out, to escape by swimming.* **1.** Lit. : Hor. **2.** Transf. : Cic.

ēnātus, a, um, *Part.* ēnāscor.

ē-nāvigō, āre. **I.** *to sail out, sail away* : Curt., Suet. With Acc. of extent : undam, Hor. **II.** *to escape by sailing.* Transf. : e cotibus oratio, Cic.

Enceladus, ī, m. *one of the giants whom Jupiter buried under Etna.*

endō, v. in-.

endromis, idis, f. [ἐνδρομίς], *a wrap (sweater) for athletes* : Mart., Juv. ; also for the sportswoman : Juv.

Endymiōn, ōnis, m. *a beautiful youth, with whom Luna fell in love as he lay asleep on Mt. Patmos in Caria.*

ē-necō (-nicō), necāre, necuī (-nicāvī, Pl.), nectum (later necātum), (*Fut. Perf.* ēnicāssō, Pl.), *to kill completely, to kill off.* **1.** Lit. : Pl. **2.** Transf. **a.** *to exhaust, wear out* : fame, Pl., Cic., Liv. ; arando, Hor. **b.** Colloq., *to torture, plague to death* : amando, Pl. ; rogitando, Ter. Without Abl. : Pl., Ter.

ēnervātus, a, um. **I.** *Part.* ēnervō. **II.** Adj. *without sinews.* **1.** Lit. : Cic. **2.** Transf. : *without energy, forceless* : Cic., Sen.

ēnervis, e, adj. [nervus], *nerveless, forceless* : Quint., Tac.

ēnervō, āre [nervus], *to take out the sinews, weaken physically.* **1.** Lit. : aliquem, Cic.; corpora animosque, Liv. ; Hor. ; Ov. **2.** Transf. : orationem, Cic.

ēnicō, v. ēnecō.

enim, conj. [a demonstrative particle, perh. orig. meaning *just then, just so, just as you say, yes indeed*]. **A. a.** To corroborate a preceding assertion : *yes, indeed, truly, certainly* : ego enim vocari iussi, *yes, I did,* Pl. ; ille (Dumnorix) enim revocatus resistere ac se manu defendere coepit, *in fact,* Caes. ; Cic. ; Verg. ; Liv., etc. In ironical or indignant discourse : tu enim repertu's Philoctetem qui superes veriverbio ! *you indeed/* Pl. **b.** Strengthened by *vero,* and written as one word **enimvērō**, *in very truth, to be sure, certainly* : enimvero ferendum hoc quidem non est, Cic. ; enimvero manifesta res est, Liv. ; Ter. ; tum enimvero, Liv. In corroborating replies : *Me.* ain vero ? *So.* aiio enimvero, Pl. In ironical or indignant discourse : *Da.* ubi voles, arcesse. *Si.* bene sane :

id enimvero hic nunc abest, Ter. **c.** *at enim* (v. also *at*), in stating an opponent's objection, *but it will be said,* Cic. **d.** *sed enim ; but indeed, but in truth* : Cic., Verg. ; also *sed enimvero* : Liv. **B.** Explaining a previous assertion ; *namely, for instance, I must tell you, now* : Pl., Ter., Cic. **C.** Giving a reason (most freq.) : *in fact, for.* Often ref. to some assertion which is to be mentally supplied : Epicurus multa praeclare saepe dicit ; (*I say* ' praeclare ') quam enim sibi constanter dicat non laborat, Cic. ; Ov., etc. So in the common expression : quid enim dicam ? *or* quid enim ? i.e. *are not these examples enough?* Cic., Hor., Liv., etc.

enimvērō, v. enim.

Enipeus (trisyl.), eī (Voc. -eu, Ov.), m. *a tributary of the R. Peneus ; also the river-god.*

ēnisus, a, um, *Part.* ēnītor.

ē-nĭteō, ēre, uī, *to shine out, gleam forth.* **1.** Lit. : Acc. ; campus, Verg. ; Cat. ; decus enitet ore, Verg. **2.** Transf. : *to shine out, be conspicuous* : virtus in bello, Cic. ; Liv. ; in eis oratoribus Demosthenes, Cic. Ep.

ē-nĭtēscō, ere, *to begin to shine forth, to brighten.* **1.** Lit. : oculi hilaritate, Quint. ; Hor. **2.** Transf. : virtus, Sall. ; Quint. ; Tac.

ē-nitor, nītī, nīsus (older -nixus). **I.** *to force or work one's way out or up, to mount up, climb.* **1.** Lit. : in ascensu, Caes. ; Hor. ; Ov. ; Liv. ; in editiora, Tac. Of vines, *to climb* : Verg. With Acc. (rare) : aggerem, Tac. **2.** Transf. : Hor., Curt. **II.** *to exert oneself, make a great effort, struggle.* **1.** Lit. : per adversos fluctus, Liv. ; Tac. **2.** Transf. **a.** In gen. With Acc. of *Neut. Pron.* and *ne* with *Subj.* : Cic. Ep. ; Sall. With *ut* and *Subj.* : Caes., Cic., Liv., etc. With *Inf.* : Ter., Sall., Hor. Absol. : Ter., Cic., Quint. *Perf. Part.* in *Impers. Pass.* sense : ab iisdem summā ope enisum, Sall. **b.** With Acc. : *to bring forth, give birth to* : Verg., Liv., Tac., etc. ; also Absol. : Quint., Tac., Suet.

ēnixē, adv. *strenuously* : Pl., Caes., Cic., Liv. *Comp.* : Liv. *Sup.* : Suet.

ēnixus, a, um. **I.** *Part.* ēnītor. **II.** Adj. : *strenuous, earnest* : studium, Liv. ; virtus, Liv. *Comp.* : Sen.

Ennius (Q.), ī, m. *the greatest Latin poet before the classical period, writer of tragedy, comedy, satire, and epic history* ; *a native of high rank of Rudiae in Calabria* (B.C. 239–169).

Ennosigaeus, ī, m. = Ἐννοσίγαιος, ' *the earthshaker,*' i.e. *Neptune.*

ē-nō, nāre, *to swim out, escape by swimming* : e conchā, Cic. ; in terram, Liv. Of flying : Lucr., Verg.

ēnōdātē, adv. *without knots ; clearly, plainly* : narrare, Cic. *Comp.* : Cic.

ēnōdātiō, ōnis, f. [ēnōdō], *an unknotting, explanation* : Cic.

ēnōdis, e, adj. [nōdus], *without knots.* **1.** Lit. : trunci, Verg. **2.** Transf. : of speech : *clear, plain* : Plin. Ep.

ē-nōdō, āre, *to free from knots.* **1.** Lit. : *to explain, elucidate* : Cic.

ē-ˈrmis, e, adj. [nōrma]. **I.** *out of rule,*

irregular, unshapely : toga, Quint. ; vici,
Tac. **II.** *of unusual size, enormous* :
spatium, hastae, Tac.

ēnormĭtās, ātis, *f.* [ēnōrmis], *irregular shape* :
Quint.

ē-nōtēscō, nōtēscere, nōtuī, *to become generally known* : Tac., Plin. Ep.

ē-nŏtŏ, āre, *to take notes of, note down* :
Quint., Plin. Ep.

ensĭculus, ī, *m.* [*dim.* ēnsis], *a little sword,
rapier* : Pl.

ensĭfer, era, erum [ēnsis ferō], *sword-bearing,*
epith. of Orion : Luc.

ensĭger, era, erum [ēnsis gerō], *sword-
bearing* : epith. of Orion : Ov.

ensis, is, *m. a sword* ; chiefly poet. : Lucr.,
Verg., etc. Of a Gallic sword : Liv.

enthȳmēma, atis, *n.* [ἐνθύμημα]. **I.** In
gen. *a thought, reflexion,* Cic., Quint. **II.**
a kind of argument : Cic., Quint.

ē-nūbŏ, nūbere, nūpsī. **I.** *to marry out (of
her rank)* : e patribus, Liv. **II.** *to marry
(and leave the town)* : Liv.

ēnucleātē, *adv. simply* : Cic.

ēnucleātus, a, um. **I.** *Part.* ēnucleō. **II.**
Adj. **a.** *simple, straightforward* : suffragia, Cic. **b.** Of style, *simple, plain,
clear* : Cic.

ē-nucleō, āre, *to take out the kernels, to clear
from the husks.* Transf. : *to make clear,
explain* : Cic.

ēnumerātĭō, ōnis, *f.* [ēnumerō], *a counting
out fully or in detail, enumeration* : malorum,
Cic. ; Quint.

ē-numerŏ, āre, *to count out fully or in detail,
reckon up.* **1.** Lit. : peculium, Pl. ; Ter. ;
dies, Caes. Hence, *to pay* (*count out the
money*) : pretium, Cic. **2.** Transf. : *to recount, relate* : stipendia, Liv. ; Cic. ; Verg.,
etc.

ēnūntĭātĭō, ōnis, *f.* [ēnūntiō]. In rhet. and
logic : *a declaration, enunciation, proposition* : Cic., Quint.

ēnūntĭātīvus, a, um [ēnūntiō], *declarative,
enunciative* : Sen.

ēnūntĭātum, ī, *n.* [ēnūntiō], *a proposition* :
Cic.

ē-nūntĭŏ, āre, *to report, divulge, disclose.* **1.**
Lit. : Pl. ; sociorum consilia adversariis,
Cic. ; Caes. ; Liv. With Acc. and *Inf.* :
Pl. Transf. **a.** *to declare plainly* :
sententias, Cic. ; Quint. In logic, *to state* a
proposition : (aliquid), Cic. **b.** *to articulate,
pronounce clearly* : litteras, Quint.

ēnūptĭō, ōnis, *f.* [ēnūbō], *the right of marrying
out* : Liv.

ē-nūtrĭŏ, īre, *to nourish, bring up to the end.*
1. Lit. : puerum, Ov. **2.** Transf. : ingenia, Quint.

eŏ, īre, iī, itum [for eiō, *cf.* Gk. εἶμι, ἰέναι]
(īssem, īsse, for iissem, iisse, Ter., Cic., Ov.,
etc.), *to go.* **1.** Lit. **a.** In gen. (of movement of every kind) ; hence, acc. to context,
to walk, ride, sail, pass, etc. : Pl., Cic., Verg.,
etc. ; ire pedibus, Liv. ; equis, Liv. ; curru,
Liv. ; puppibus, Ov. With Acc. of goal :
Verg., Ov., etc. With ABL. of way by
which : ibam forte Viā Sacrā, Hor. ; Cic. ;
Liv. With cognate or internal Acc., ire
exsequias, Ter. With *Inf.* visere, Ter. ;
videre, Prop. **b.** Milit. : *to go or march* :
infestis signis ad aliquem ire, Caes. ; Liv. ;

contra hostem, Caes. ; in hostem, Liv. ;
Verg. **c.** Polit. : pedibus ire, or ire in aliquam
sententiam, in voting, *to go over or accede to
any opinion* : Liv. *Impers.* : ibatur in
eam sententiam, Cic. And ire in alia
omnia, *to vote against a bill, v.* alius. **2.**
Transf. **A.** Of persons. **a.** *to go, pass,
proceed,* etc. ; in dubiam imperi servitique
aleam, Liv. ; Pl. ; in lacrimas, Verg. ; in
poenas, Ov. **b.** *to go and set about* something (esp. with Supine in -um) : cubitum
ire, Cic. ; ultum iniurias, Liv. ; Verg., etc.
Hence the constr. of *Inf. Pass.* iri with
Supine. as *Fut. Inf. Pass.* Lit. (*that*) *there
is a going* (to do something). Also *Imper.*
I, eās, eat, etc. as a mocking or indignant
exclamation : Verg., Ov., etc. ; in *Orat.
Obliq.* : irent crearent consules ex plebe,
Liv. **B.** Of things : *to go,* etc. **a.** In
gen. : Cato ; Euphrates ibat iam mollior
undis, Verg. ; Lucr. ; it clamor caelo, Verg.
b. Of time : *to pass away* : it dies, Pl. ;
anni, Hor. **c.** Of the turn of affairs : *go
on, turn out, happen* : incipit res melius ire
quam putaram, Cic. Ep. Hence (a wish) :
sic eat, *so may it fare,* Liv.

eŏ, *adv.* [is]. **I.** Old Dative, or Directive.
A. *thither, thereto.* **1.** Lit. : Pl. ; eo
coloniam deducere, Cic. ; Caes. ; Liv., etc. ;
ibit eo quo vis, Hor. ; Cic. ; Liv., etc.
Occ. : instead of a case of the Pron. *is* :
eo milites imponere, i.e. equis, Caes. **2.**
Transf. **a.** With idea of addition : *thereto* : accedit eo quod etc., Cic. Ep. **b.** Of
tendency, *to that end or purpose, to this
result* : hoc eo spectabat ut etc., Cic. **c.**
Of degree or extent : *so far, to that extent,
to such a point* : eo aliquem redigere, Ter. ;
eo res crevit, Liv. ; eo rem adducam ut etc.,
Cic. Often with GEN. : eo magnitudinis
procedere, Sall. ; Liv. ; etc. Strengthened
with usque : usque eo despicere, Nep. **B.**
Of time, with dum, donec, quamdiu, etc. :
so long, until : usque eo . . . dum . . .,
Cic. **II.** Locatival ABL. (rare) : *there, at
that place.* **1.** Lit. : cum tu eo quinque
legiones haberes, Cic. Ep. Esp. with loci :
ut templum exstrueretur eo loci, Tac. **2.**
Transf. : res erat eo iam loci ut etc., Cic.
III. *Instr.* ABL. **a.** Of Measure with
Comparatives : *the* (i.e. *by that amount*), *by
so much* : eoque maior gloria paritur, Cic.
Esp. with corresponding quo : *the* (relat.)
. . . *the* (demonstr.), *by as much . . . by
so much* : Cic. With eo understood : quo
plures erant, maior caedes fuit, Liv. **b.** Of
Cause : *on that account, with that in view, therefore* : eo ero brevior, Cic. ; so maxime quod
sermo inter omnis congruebat, Liv. ; Pl.,
Cic., etc. Occ. with *magis* or *minus* : quae
eo magis praetereo quod vereor, Cic. With
ut or *ne* and *Subj.* : Pl., Ter., Cic. With
quo and *Subj.* : Ter., Cic.

eŏdem, *adv.* [idem]. **I.** Old Dative or Directive, *to the same place.* **1.** Lit. : Pl., Caes.,
etc. **2.** Transf. **a.** *to the same point,
matter,* etc. : eodem accedit ut *or* quod etc.,
Pl., Cic. ; eodem pertinet quod etc., Caes.
b. *to the same person* : Cic., Liv. **II.**
Locatival ABL. *in the same place.* **1.** Lit.
(rare) : Liv. **2.** Transf. (rare) : *in the
same position* : res eodem est loci, Cic. Ep.

Ēōs (only in Nom.), *f. the dawn* (pure Lat.,
Aurora); **Ēōus** (poet. **Ēŏus**), a, um. **a.**
of the dawn or *at dawn :* Verg. **b,** *eastern,
orient :* Verg., etc., **Ēōus,** i, m. *f. the
morning-star :* Verg. **b,** *an Eastern :* Ov.

Epamīnōndās, ae, m. *a famous Theban
general who defeated the Spartans at Leuctra*
(B.C. 371) *and Mantinea* (B.C. 362), *where
he was killed.*

Epaphus, i, m. *s. of Jupiter and Io.*

Epēus (-īus), i, m. *inventor and builder of the
Trojan horse.*

ē-pāstus, a, um [pāscō], *eaten up :* Ov.

ephēbus, i, m. [ἔφηβος], *a male youth* (18 to
20 years of age) : Ter., Cic., Ov., etc. ; exire
ex ephebis (i.e. *to attain to manhood*), Ter.,
Cic.

ephēmeris, idis, *f.* [ἐφημερίς], *a day-book,
diary, journal :* Cic., Ov., etc.

Ephesus, i, *f. the chief of the 12 Ionian cities
in Asia Minor, with a famous temple of
Artemis* (Diana) ; **Ephesius,** a, um ;
Ephesii, ōrum, m. pl. *the Ephesians.*

ephippiātus, a, um, *mounted on a saddled
horse :* Caes.

ephippium, i, n. [ἐφίππιον]. Lit. *anything
placed on a horse's back ; a saddle* (pure Lat.
stragulum) : Caes., Cic. P r o v. : of discontented persons : optat ephippia bos
piger, Hor.

ephorus, i, m. [ἔφορος, *overseer*], *a Spartan
magistrate, an ephor :* Cic.

Ephorus, i, m. *of Cyme in Aeolis, a famous
Greek historian.*

Ephyra, ae (-ē, ēs), *f. the ancient name of
Corinth ;* **Ephyrēius,** a, um, *Corinthian.*

Epicharmus, i, m. *a Pythagorean philosopher*
(B.C. 540–450), *one of the chief founders of
comedy.*

epichysis, is, *f.* [ἐπίχυσις], *a vessel for pouring :* Pl.

epicrocus, a, um [ἐπίκροκος], *transparent,
fine, thin :* Pl.

epicus, a, um [ἐπικός], *epic :* poëta (Ennius), Cic. ; poëma, Cic.

Epicūrus, i, m. *a famous Greek philosopher of
Samos who spent most of his life at Athens ;
founder of the Epicurean philosophy* (B.C.
342–270) ; **Epicūrēus,** a, um ; **Epicūrēi,**
ōrum, m. pl. *the Epicureans.*

epidicticus, a, um [ἐπιδεικτικός], *for display :* genus dicendi, Cic.

epidipnis, idis, *f.* [ἐπιδειπνίς]. *a dessert :*
Mart.

epigramma, atis, *n.* (Dat. pl. -atīs, Cic.)
[ἐπίγραμμα]. **1.** Lit. : *an inscription :*
Cic., Nep. **2.** T r a n s f. : *a short poem, an
epigram :* Cic., Quint.

epilogus, i, m. [ἐπίλογος], *the peroration of
a speech, epilogue* (pure Lat. peroratio or
conclusio) : Cic., Quint.

epimēnia, ōrum. n. pl. [ἐπιμήνια], *a month's
rations :* Juv.

Epimētheus, ei, m. (*afterthought*) *s. of Iapetus
and b. of Prometheus* (*forethought*) ; **Epi-
mēthis,** idis, *f. his daughter,* Pyrrha.

epinicia, ōrum, n. pl. [ἐπινίκια], *songs of
victory :* Suet.

epirēdium, i, n. [raeda], *a thong to fasten a
horse to a carriage :* Quint., Juv.

Epirus (-os), i, *f. a district in N.W. Greece ;*

Epīrōtēs, ae, m. *a native of Epirus ;* **Epīrō-
ticus,** a, um ; **Epīrēnsis,** e.

epistolium, i, n. [ἐπιστόλιον], *a short letter,
note :* Cat.

epistula, ae, *f.* [ἐπιστολή]. **I.** *a written
communication, a letter, epistle :* Cic., Ov.,
etc. ; dare, *to send a letter* (lit. *to give it* to the
tabellarius or letter-carrier), Cic. ; ab
epistulis (sc. libertus or servus), *secretary,*
Suet. **II.** *a sending of letters :* venio nunc
ad tuas litteras, quas pluribus epistulis accepi, Cic. Ep.

epitaphium, i, n. [ἐπιτάφιον], *a funeral
oration, eulogy :* Cic.

epithalamium, i, n. [ἐπιθαλάμιον], *a nuptial
song :* Quint.

epithēca, ae, *f.* [ἐπιθήκη], *an addition, increase :* Pl.

epitoma, ae, (-ē, ēs), *f.* [ἐπιτομή] *an abridge-
ment, epitome :* Cic. Ep.

epityrum, i, n. [ἐπίτυρον], *an olive-salad,
eaten with cheese :* Pl., Cato.

epodes, um, m. pl. *sea-fish :* Ov.

epōdos, i, m. [ἐπωδός], *a species of lyric invented by Archilochus, in which a longer
verse is followed by a shorter one, e.g. the
Epodes of Horace :* Quint.

Epona, ae, *f. the protecting goddess of asses and
horses.*

epops, opis, m. [ἔποψ], *a hoopoe :* Verg., Ov.

epos (only in Nom. and Acc. sing. ; pl. epē,
Prop.), n. [ἔπος, *word ; saga*], *an heroic
poem, an epic :* Hor.

ē-pōtus (exp-, Pl.), a, um, *drained to the
dregs, drunk off.* **1.** L i t. : Cic., Liv., Ov.,
etc. **2.** T r a n s f. *a. wasted in drink :* Pl.
b. *absorbed, swallowed up :* umores, Lucr. ;
Ov.

epulae, ārum, *f. pl.* [cf. epulum]. **I. 1.**
L i t. : *dishes of food, food :* Pl., Cic., Verg.,
etc. P o e t. : vestis blattarum epulae,
Hor. **2.** T r a n s f. : oculis epulas dare,
Pl. ; Cic. **II. a.** *sumptuous meals, ban-
quets :* Caes., Cic., Verg., etc. **b.** *ban-
quets at relig. or public festivals :* Cic.,
Hor.

epulāris, e, adj. [epulum], *of a banquet, at
banquets :* Cic.

epulātiō, ōnis, *f. feasting :* Lucil., Suet.

epulō, ōnis, m. [epulum], *a guest at a meal,
feast* or *banquet ;* Cic. Esp. Tresviri or
Septemviri Epulones : *a college of priests
who superintended the sacrificial banquets
to the gods :* Cic., Liv., etc. In sing. :
Triumvir Epulo, Liv.

epulor, ārī. **I.** [epulum], *to be present at a
banquet :* Saliarem in modum (i.e. *sumptuously*), Cic. ; Tac. With Abl., dapibus
opimis, Verg. **II.** [epulae], *to eat :* praedam divisit ad epulandum militibus, Liv. ;
aliquem epulandum ponere mensis, Verg.
Also *to dine* (intrans.) : Liv.

epulum, i, n. [edō, cf. epulae], *a sumptuous
meal, a banquet, feast.* **a.** On relig., solemn,
or public occasions : Cic., Liv. **b.** *a feast*
in gen. : Juv., Suet.

equa, ae, *f.* [equus], *a mare :* Cic., Verg., Hor.

eques, itis, m. [equus], *a horseman, rider.*
A. In gen. : Cic., Verg., etc. **B.** In
partic. **a.** *a horse-soldier, trooper :* Caes.,
Liv., etc. Sing. or pl. for *horse-soldiers,
cavalry :* Liv., Tac. **b.** Equites, *the order*

of knights, the equites, who, among the Romans, held a middle rank between the senate and the populace Cic., Ov., etc. In collect. sing. : the equestrian order : Hor., Tac., Suet.

equester, tris, tre (equestris also m. in Liv.), adj. [eques]. **I.** of a horseman, equestrian : statua, Cic.; Suet. **II.** of cavalry : proelium, Caes.; Cic.; Liv.; etc. **III.** belonging to the order of knights, of equestrian rank : Cic.; census, Liv.; anulus (i.e. aureus, worn by the equestrian order), Hor. Neut. pl. : equestria, ium (sc. loca), the seats of the knights in the theatre : Sen., Suet.

equidem, adv. [e- (seen in e-depol, e-n-im) and quidem], a strengthening particle : verily, truly, indeed, at all events, etc. (usually connected with 1 pers. sing. or pl.) for my part, as far as I am concerned. **A.** In gen. **a.** Without other particles : equidem me Caesaris militem dici volui, Caes.; Cic. With 1 pers. pl. : Ter., Cic. With other pers. : Pl.; scitis equidem milites, Sall.; vanum equidem hoc consilium est, Sall. **b.** With certe, edepol, etc. : certe equidem noster sum, Pl.; Ter.; Verg. **B.** In a concessive sense, with sed, tamen, or verum in the apodosis : vellem equidem vobis placere, sed multo malo vos salvos esse, Liv.; Pl.; Cic., etc.

equile, is, n. [equus : cf. ovile, etc.], a stable for horses : Cato; Suet.

equinus, a, um [equus], of horses : Varr., Cic., Hor.

Equiria, orum, n. pl. [equus], the annual horse-race in the Campus Martius in honour of Mars : Varr., Ov.

equitabilis, e, adj. [equito], that may be ridden over : planities, Curt.

equitatus, us, m. [equito], a body of horsemen, cavalry : Caes. In pl. : Caes., Cic., Sall.

equito, are [eques], to ride. **a.** In gen.: Cic., Liv., etc.; in harundine longa (to ride a hobby horse), Hor. **b.** Of cavalry : to make raids : Cic. Transf.: Cic., Hor.

equuleus, v. eculeus.

equus, i, m. (equos and equom in pre-Aug. period, ecus and ecum, Aug. to end of 1st cent. A.D., equus and equum after that) [cf. Attic ἵππος (Aeolic ἴκκος)], a horse, steed. **1.** Lit.: Pl.; equo vehi, Caes.; equo uti, Cic.; ex equo pugnare, Liv.; equis virisque, with horse and foot (i.e. with might and main), Liv.; also equis viris, Cic.; equo merere, to serve as a horse-soldier, Cic. **2.** Transf. **a.** equus ligneus = navis, Pl. **b.** In pl. equi = currus : Verg. **c.** equus bipes, a sea-horse, Verg. **d.** the constellation Pegasus : Cic. poet.

era, ae, f. [v. erus], the mistress of a house. **1.** Lit.: Pl., Ter. **2.** Transf. **a.** Of a goddess, the Lady : Pl., Cat. **b.** Of a sweetheart : Cat., Ov.

e-radico (**exr-**), are, to pluck up by the roots, to root out. **1.** Lit.: Varr. **2.** Transf.: Pl., Ter. [Fr. arracher.]

e-rado, radere, rasi, rasum, to scrape (or scratch) out. **1.** Lit.: terram, Varr. **2.**

Transf. **a.** aliquem senatorio albo, Tac. **b.** elementa cupidinis pravi, Hor.; Sen. Ep.

eranus, i, m. [ἔρανος], a fund for mutual protection against want (a friendly society) : Plin. Ep.

Erato (only in Nom.), f. the Muse of lyric and love-poetry. Transf.: Muse in gen.

Eratosthenes, is, m. a famous geographer, poet, and philosopher of Alexandria.

erc-, v. herc-.

Erebus, i, m. [ἔρεβος], god of darkness, s. of Chaos and b. of Nox. Transf.: the Lower World ; **Erebeus**, a, um, of the Lower World.

Erechtheus (trisyl.), ei, m. a mythical king of Athens ; **Erechtheus**, a, um ; **Erechthidae**, arum, m. pl. the Athenians ; **Erechthis**, idis, f. d. of Erechtheus, viz. Orithyia or Procris.

erectus, a, um. **I.** Part. erigo. **II.** Adj.: upright, erect, lofty. **1.** Lit.: (homines) humo excitatos celsos et erectos constituit, Cic.; vultus, Ov.; prorae, Caes. Comp. : Caes. **2.** Transf. **a.** elevated, lofty, noble ; esp. with some similar adj. : celsus et erectus, Cic.; sublime et erectum ingenium, Tac. Comp. : Cic. In bad sense : haughty : Cic. **b.** alert, attentive : Cic., Liv., Tac. With ad : Cic. Comp. : Quint. **c.** courageous, resolute : Cic., Tac.

e-repo, repere, repsi (erepsemus = erepsissemus, Hor.). **I.** to creep out, crawl forth : Pl., Varr. **II.** to creep or climb up : Suet. With Acc. : to creep over : Hor., Juv.

ereptio, onis, f. [eripio], a forcible taking away, seizure, robbery : Cic.

ereptor, oris, m. [eripio], a robber, plunderer : bonorum, libertatis, Cic.; Tac.

ereptus, a, um, Part. eripio.

erga [perh. fr. e and obsolete rega (cf. rego), ruling. Lit. from the direction ; in the line], prep. with Acc., towards, over against. **1.** Lit. Of place : Pl. **2.** Transf. Of feelings and conduct towards a person. **a.** Friendly : benevolentia amicorum erga nos, Cic.; Caes.; Pl., etc. **b.** Unfriendly: against : ne malus item erga me sit, ut erga illum fuit, Pl.; Ter.; Nep.; Tac. **c.** In post-Aug. writers (esp. Tac.) of every kind of mental relation : anxii erga Seianum, Tac.; erga Germanicos exercitus laudes, Tac.

ergastulum, i, n. [ἐργάζεσθαι, 'to work'], a private prison or workhouse for debtors or offending slaves. **1.** Lit.: Cic., Liv., Suet. **2.** Transf. (in pl. only; cf. servitia) : the inmates of an ergastulum : Caes., Juv.

ergo (in Ov. and poets sometimes ergo), prep. and adv. [ex and obsol. rogus ; orig. laying straight ; hence, **a.** With Gen., from the line of, in connexion with, for the sake of. **b.** As adv. straight on, consequently, therefore]. **I.** Prep. (with Gen. preceding) : in consequence of, on account of, because of (archaic) : quoius rei ergo, Cato ; funoris ergo, Lex ap. Cic. ; formidinis ergo, Lucr.; illius ergo, for his sake, Verg. **II.** Adv.: consequently, therefore. **a.** Esp. in a logical conclusion : negat haec filiam me suam esse ; non ergo haec mater mea est, Pl.; Cic.; Liv.; itaque ergo, Liv. **b.** In interrogative **argumentation :** *so, so then :* ergo haec veteranus miles facere poterit, doctus vir sapiensque non poterit ? Cic. **c.** In questions where a consequence is asked for ; *then :* dedemus ergo Hannibalem ? Liv. ; Pl. ; Cic., etc. Esp. *quid ergo ? why then ? :* quid ergo hanc dubitas conloqui ? Pl. ; Caes. ; Cic., etc. **d.** With imperatives, *then, now :* vide ergo, hanc conclusionem probaturusne sis, Cic. ; Pl. ; Verg., etc. **e.** Resumptive (like *igitur*), with dicere expressed or understood : *as I was saying, I say, well then :* tres viae sunt ad Mutinam, quo festinat animus, ut etc. tres ergo ut dixi viae, Cic. So (like *igitur* and *inquam*) after parentheses : Cic.

Erichthō, ūs, *f. a Thessalian witch consulted by Pompey.* T r a n s f. : *any witch.*

Erichthonius, ī, *m.* **I.** a mythical king of Athens, s. of Vulcan ; **Erichthonius,** a, um, *Athenian.* **II.** *s. of Dardanus, f. of Tros, and king of Troy ;* **Erichthonius,** a, um, *Trojan.*

ēricius, ī, *m.* [hēricius], *a hedgehog.* **1.** L i t. : Varr. **2.** Milit. *chevaux-de-frise :* Caes.

Ēridānus, ī, *m. the Greek name of the river Padus,* now *Po.*

erifuga, ae, *m.* [erus, fugiō], *a runaway slave :* Cat.

ē-rigō, rigere, rēxī, rēctum [regō], *to put up straight, to raise or set up, to erect.* **1.** L i t. **a.** arborem, Cic. ; mālum de nave, Verg. ; scalas ad moenia, Liv. ; oculos, Cic. **b.** With *Pron. Refl.,* or in *Mid. : to raise oneself, to rise :* Caes., Cic., Verg., etc. **c.** *to build, erect :* turris, Caes. **d.** *to put troops up* (sloping ground) : aciem in collem, Tac. ; Liv. **2.** T r a n s f. **a.** *to arouse, excite :* mentis, aurīsque, Cic. ; paululum se erexit et addidit historiae maiorem sonum vocis, Cic. **b.** *to raise up, cheer up, encourage :* animum demissum et oppressum, Cic. ; rem publicam ex tam gravi casu, Liv. ; se erigere, Cic. ; se in spem, Liv. ; se ad cupidinem, Liv. ; Tac. ; spem, Tac.

Ērigonē, ēs, *f. d. of the Attic Icarus, translated to the sky as the constellation Virgo ;* **Ērigonēius,** a, um.

erīlis, e, *adj.* [erus, era], *of a master or mistress :* Pl., Verg., etc.

Ērinna, ae (-ē, ēs), *f. a Lesbian poetess, contemporary with Sappho.*

Erinȳs, yos (Acc. -yn, Ov.), *f. one of the Furies.* T r a n s f. **a.** Of Helen, *curse.* **b.** *frenzy.* **Erinyes** (*pl.*), *the Furies.*

Eriphȳla, ae (-ē, ēs), *f. d. of Talaüs and w. of Amphiaraus, whom she betrayed ; killed by her son Alcmaeon.*

ē-ripiō, ripere, ripuī, reptum [rapiō], *to snatch, tear or pull out and away, take away violently or by force.* **1.** L i t. **a.** In gen. : vela armamentaque eripere, Caes. ; hirundines ex nido, Pl. ; torrem ab igne, Ov. ; ensem vaginā, Verg. ; caelum diernque ex oculis, Verg. ; prospectum oculis, Verg. With D a t. of person *from whom :* Pl., Ter., Cic. ; also with *ab :* Caes., Cic. With D a t. *of thing from which :* eum morti, Verg. **b.** *to deliver, rescue :* aliquem ex periculo, Caes. ; Cic. ; Liv. ; istum de vestrā severitate, Cic. With *Pron. Refl. : to rescue*

oneself, *to escape :* se flammā, Cic. ; Caes. ; Verg. ; se ex pugnā, Cic. ; Caes. ; Liv. With D a t. of person *from whom :* Liv. With D a t. of thing *from which :* Verg., Hor., Sen. Ep. P r o v. : lupo agnum eripere (for an impossible feat), Pl. **c.** In *Perf. Part. snatched away by death, having died suddenly :* fato ereptus, Verg., Liv. ; Ov. **2.** T r a n s f. With A c c. of thing taken : omnem usum navium, Caes. ; Cic. ; fugam, Verg. ; Hor. Also with D a t. of person *from whom :* Pl. ; alicui errorem, etc., Cic. ; Ov., etc.

ērogātiō, ōnis, *f.* [ērogō], *a paying out :* pecuniae, Cic. Ep. ; Tac.

ē-rogitō, āre [*freq.* ērogō], *to try to find out by asking :* ex aliquo (with *Indir. Quest.*), Pl.

ē-rogō, āre, *to entreat successfully.* **1.** P o l i t. *to ask for and obtain a grant of public money :* hence, *to expend such money :* pecunias ex aerario, Cic., Liv. ; in aliquam rem, Cic., Liv. **2.** T r a n s f. **a,** Of private expenditure : Cic. Ep. **b.** *to bequeath :* grandem pecuniam in Tigellinum, Tac.

Erōs, ōtis, *m.* [ἔρως], *Love* (or *Cupid*).

errābundus, a, um [errō], *wandering, straggling :* Liv. P o e t. : odor, Lucr. ; vestigia bovis, Verg.

errāticus, a, um [errō], *wandering, roving, erratic :* Cato ; cursus (of the gadding vine'), Cic. ; Delos, Ov.

errātiō, ōnis, *f.* [errō], *a wandering, roving about :* Pl., Ter., Cic.

errātum, ī, *n.* [errō], *an error, mistake, blunder.* **a.** Cic. **b.** In moral sense : Cic. In *pl.* : Cic. Ep., Sall., Ov.

errātus, ūs, *m.* [errō], *a wandering about :* longis erratibus actus, Ov.

errō, āre, *to wander, stray, rove, roam.* **1.** L i t. **a.** Of living creatures : Ter., Cic., Verg., etc. Impers. *Pass.* : Verg. With Acc. of ground covered : Verg., Ov. **b.** Of things : stellae, Cic. ; Cocytus flumine languido, Hor. ; Verg. ; ignis, Ov. *c. to lose one's way, go astray :* errare viā, Verg. **2.** T r a n s f. **a.** *to wander, waver :* oratio, Cic. ; dubiis adfectibus errat, Ov. ; ne tuus erret honos, Ov. **b.** *to wander from the truth, to err, mistake :* totā re errare, Cic. ; Lucr. With A c c. of *Neut. Pron. :* mone, quaeso, si quid erro, Pl. ; Ter. ; Quint. With A c c. of Noun : errabant tempora, *in chronology,* Ov. *Impers. Pass. :* si erratur in nomine, Cic. ; Liv. **c.** Morally (but pardonably) : Sall.

errō, ōnis, *m.* [errō], *a wanderer, vagabond, vagrant :* Hor., Ov., etc.

error, ōris, *m.* [errō], *a wandering or straying about.* **1.** L i t. **a.** Of living creatures : Cic., Verg., Ov. With *Obj.* G e n. : pelagi (on or over the sea), Verg. **b.** Of things : of atoms, Lucr. ; of the labyrinth, Ov. **2.** T r a n s f. **a.** *a wavering, uncertainty, perplexity :* Pl., Lucr., Liv. With *Obj.* G e n. : Liv., Tac. **b.** *a departing from the truth, an error, delusion :* Pl. ; rapi in errorem, Cic. ; deponere, Cic. ; demere, Hor. ; mentis, Cic. ; Verg., etc. Also *a cause of error, deception :* Verg., Liv., Tac. **c.** Morally : Pl., Ov., Curt.

ē-rubēscō, rubēscere, rubuī, *to redden all over, blush.* **1.** L i t. **a.** saxa roratis erubuere rosis, Ov. **b.** *to redden* or *blush with shame, to feel ashamed :* erubui mecastor propter clamorem tuom, Pl. ; in aliquā re, Cic. ; aliquā re, Liv. **2.** T r a n s f. **a.** *to be ashamed of.* With Acc. : Prop. ; in *Gerund. Adj. :* Hor. With *Inf.* as Obj. : Verg., Liv., Quint., etc. With Acc. and *Inf. :* Liv. **b.** *to have respect for.* With Acc. : Verg.

ĕrūca, ae, *f. a colewort :* Hor.

ē-ructō, āre, *to belch* or *vomit forth, to throw up.* **1.** L i t. : saniem, Verg. ; Cic. **2.** T r a n s f. **a.** *to talk of drunkenly :* caedem sermonibus suis, Cic. **b.** Of volcanoes, rivers, etc. : *to throw up :* Varr., Lucr., Verg.

ĕrūdĭō, īre [rudis], *to bring out of the rough* or *natural state ; to polish, educate, train.* **a.** aliquem artibus, Cic. ; aliquem in iure civili, Cic. ; aliquem ad Graecorum disciplinam, Cic. **b.** *to teach, instruct* (in looser sense). With *Indir. Quest. :* Ov. With *de :* me omni de re publicā, *keep me informed about,* Cic. Ep. Of objects not personal : ut florent oculos erudiere suos, Ov.

ĕrūdĭtē, *adv. learnedly. Comp. :* Cic., Quint. *Sup. :* Cic., Plin. Ep.

ĕrūdītĭō, ōnis, *f.* [ĕrūdĭō], *instruction, education.* **1.** L i t. : Cic. Ep., Quint. **2.** T r a n s f. : *learning, knowledge, erudition :* Cic., Quint.

ĕrūdītŭlus, a, um [*dim.* ĕrūdītus], *rather skilled :* Cat.

ĕrūdītus, a, um. **I.** *Part.* ĕrūdĭō. **II.** A d j. : **a.** P r o p. *accomplished, educated, trained :* Cic., Quint. ; artibus militiae, Liv. ; Cic. ; ad rei militaris scientiam, Cic. With *Inf. :* Tac. Hence, oratio, aures, Cic. ; gustus, Tac. **b.** *instructed, learned :* iuris civilis doctrinā, Cic. *Comp. :* Cic. ; *Sup. :* Cic., Liv., Quint.

ē-rumpō, rumpere, rūpī, ruptum. **A.** T r a n s. : *to make to break* or *burst out* or *open.* **1.** L i t. : Cato ; ignis, Lucr. ; nubem, Verg. With *Pron. Refl. :* portis se foras erumpunt, Caes. : Verg. **2.** T r a n s f. : gaudium, Ter. ; ne in me stomachum erumpant, Cic. Ep. ; iram in hostis, Liv. **B.** I n t r a n s. : *to break out, to burst* or *sally forth.* **1.** L i t. : ex castris, Caes. ; ignes ex Aetnae vertice, Cic. ; a portā, Liv. ; per hostis, Liv. ; tempestates, Hirt. **2.** T r a n s f. : furor, Cic. ; seditio, Liv. ; Tac. ; vera vox, Cic. ; lacrimae, adfectus, Quint. ; illa coniuratio ex latebris, Cic. ; vitia in amicos, Cic. ; aliquid in omnium perniciem, Liv. ; Tac. : res ad ultimum seditionis, Liv.

ē-ruō, ruere, ruī, rutum, *to tear up* or *out, uproot, pluck up, stir up.* **1.** L i t. **a.** In gen. : aliquid, Cic., Ov. ; aurum terrā, Ov. ; Hor. ; Tac. ; segetem ab radicibus, Verg. ; aquam romis, Ov. **b.** In partic. *to root out, to demolish ;* urbem totum a sedibus, Verg. **2.** T r a n s f. **a.** *to dig out, draw forth* (i.e. with effort) : scrutari locos, ex quibus argumenta eruamus, Cic. ; sacra recognosces annalibus eruta priscis, Ov. ; veritatem, Quint. **b.** *to uproot, destroy :* regnum, Verg. ; civitatem, Tac.

ēruptĭō, ōnis, *f.* [ērumpō], *a breaking out,*

bursting forth. **a.** Of volcanoes : Aetnaeorum ignium, Cic. **b.** Milit. *a sally :* ex oppido eruptionem fecerunt, Caes. ; in hostis, Liv.

ēruptus, a, um, *Part.* ērumpō.

erus, ī, m. **1.** L i t. : *the master of a house* or *family :* Pl., Cic., Verg., etc. O c c. : *the young master :* Pl. **2.** T r a n s f. **a.** *master, owner* (= dominus) : Cat., Hor. **b.** Of the gods, *Lord :* Cat.

ērutus, a, um, *Part.* ēruō.

ervum, ī, *n. the bitter vetch :* Verg., etc. [Fr. *ers.*]

Erycīnus, *v.* Eryx.

Erymanthus, ī, m. **I.** *a chain of mountains in Arcadia :* **Erymanthis,** a, um ; **Erymanthis,** idis, *f. :* ursa, i.e. *Callisto of Arcadia, who was changed into a bear and placed by Jupiter as a constellation in the sky.* **II.** *a river in Arcadia.*

Erysichthōn, onis, m. *s. of the Thessalian king Triopas ; punished with raging hunger for cutting down a grove of Ceres.*

Erythēa (-ĭa), ae, *f. a small island in the Bay of Gades, home of the giant Geryon ;* **Erythēis,** idis, *f. adj.*

erythinus, ī, m. [ἐρυθῖνος], *a red mullet :* Ov.

Eryx, ycis, (-cus, ī), m. *a high mountain on W. coast of Sicily, famous for its temple of Venus, with a city of the same name.* **Erycīnus,** a, um ; **Erycīna,** ae, *f. Venus.*

esca, ae, *f.* [for *ed-ca,* from edō], *food.* **I.** In gen. **1.** L i t. (in *sing.* or *pl.*) : Pl., Cic., Verg., etc. **2.** T r a n s f. : *tit-bits, tasty bits* (of gossip) : Pers. **II.** *bait.* **1.** L i t. : Pl. **2.** T r a n s f. : divine Plato escam malorum appellat voluptatem, Cic.

escārĭus, a, um [esca]. **I.** *of food, eating :* Varr., Juv. **II.** *of a bait :* Pl.

ē-scendō, scendere, scendī, scēnsum [scandō], *to climb up, mount up, ascend.* **a.** ex alto puteo ad summum, Pl. ; in equum, Liv. ; in navem, Nep. ; in rostra, Cic. O c c. with Acc. : Sall., Liv., Tac. **b.** From the sea-coast to any place : Delphos, Liv.

ēscēnsĭō (exsc-), ōnis, *f.* [ēscendō], *a hostile raid, invasion from the coast :* in agrum, ad urbem, ad populandum facere, Liv. In *pl. :* Liv.

esculentus, a, um [esca], *good to eat, eatable, esculent :* frusta, Cic.

ēsculētum, ēsculus, *v.* aesc-.

ēsĭtō, āre [*freq.* edō], *to eat habitually :* Pl., Cato.

Esquĭlĭae, ārum, *f. pl.* [Lit. *out-settlements*], *one of the seven hills of Rome, the Esquiline ;* **Esquĭlīnus,** a, um ; **Esquĭlīna** (sc. porta), ae, *f.*

essedārĭus, ī, m. [essedum]. **I.** *a fighter in a* (Gallic or British) *war-chariot :* Caes., Cic. Ep. **II.** *a kind of gladiator :* Suet.

essedum, ī, n. [Celtic word], *a two-wheeled war-chariot of the Gauls and Britons :* Caes., Cic., Verg., etc.

essentĭa, ae, *f., the being* or *essence of a thing* (= Gk. οὐσία) : Quint.

ēstrix, īcis, *f.* [edō], *a female glutton :* Pl.

ēsŭ, ABL. *sing. m.* [edō], *in the eating :* herbae formidolosae esu, Pl.

ēsŭrĭālis, e, *adj.* [ēsŭriō], *of hunger :* feriae, *hunger-holidays,* Pl.

ēsūriō, īre [edō], *to desire to eat, be hungry, to hunger.* **1.** Lit.: Pl., Cic., Hor. etc. **2.** Transf. (with ACC.): *to hunger for :* Curt. In *Pass.* : Ov.

ēsūrītiō, ōnis, *f.* [ēsūriō], *a hungering, hunger :* Cat. In *pl.* : Cat.

ēsus, a, um, *Part.* edō.

et [orig. *further, also ; cf.* Gk. ἔτι]. **I.** Adv. **a,** *thereto, besides, also :* Caes., Cic., Verg. **b,** *even, actually :* timeo Danaos et dona ferentis, Verg. **c,** *even, that is, I mean :* cernes urbem et promissa Lavini moenia, Verg. ; Liv. **d.** In combination with simul (Cic., Sall.), etiam (Cic., Liv.), quoque (Cic., Liv.), quidem (Cic., Liv.), nec non (Verg.) ; also, non modo . . . sed et (Tac.). **II.** Conj. **A. a,** Merely adding : *and* (connecting words or sentences) : Pl., Cic., Verg., etc. **b,** Strengthening : *and indeed, and moreover, and even, yes and :* errabas, Verres, et vehementer errabas, Cic. ; Liv. ; Tac., etc. **c,** Explanatory : *for* (in a parenthesis, *cf.* etenim) : Cic., Verg., etc. **d.** Logical : *now, but* (adding the minor premiss) : Cic. **e,** Temporal. **i,** *when :* vix prima inceperat aestas, et pater Anchises . . . iubebat, Verg. ; Liv., etc. **ii,** *and then :* dixit, et in silvam refugit, Verg. ; Tac., etc. **f,** Circumstantial : *in these circumstances.* **i,** With *Imper. : and then :* dic mihi . . . et eris mihi magnus Apollo, Verg. ; Sen., etc. **ii,** With indignant question or exclamation : *and yet :* et quisquam dubitabit quin etc. ? Cic. ; Verg., etc. **g,** Antithetical : *however, but :* severus et saepius misericors, Tac. ; Liv. **B.** In combination. **a,** With aeque, par, similis, alius, etc. : *as, than :* nisi aeque amicos et nosmet ipsos diligamus, Cic. ; aliter docti loquuntur et indocti, Cic. ; Ter., etc. **b,** When repeated, et . . . et, it serves to connect two ideas more closely : *both . . . and, as well . . . as, not only . . . but also :* et audax et malus, Pl. ; Cic., etc. Similarly with -que, in Pl., Sall., Liv., Tac. (not Caes., Cic.) : signaque et ordines, Liv. ; et . . . -que is v. rare (but in Cic.). **c,** Rarely tum . . . et, *both . . . and* (also et . . . tum) : Cic. **d,** With negative. **i,** et . . . et non, or et non . . . et, when only a single word is negatived : Cic. **ii,** et . . . neque, or neque . . . et, mostly when a clause is negatived : Cic., Liv. (In some cases this results in antithesis *not . . . but.*)

et-enim, *conj.* introduces a reason or explanation : *and in fact, for :* praeclaro quidem dicis ; etenim video iam quo pergat oratio, Cic. ; Pl. ; Lucr., etc. In parentheses : Cic., Liv.

ĕtēsiae, ārum, *m. pl.* [ἐτησίαι], *periodic winds* (in the Aegean Sea) ; *Etesian winds, monsoons :* Lucr., Cic., etc.

ĕtēsius, a, um [ἐτήσιος, *annual*], *Etesian :* flabra aquilonum, Lucr.

ēthĭcē, ēs, *f.* [ἠθική], *moral philosophy, ethics :* Quint.

ēthŏlŏgia, ae, *f.* [ἠθολογία], *the art of character-sketching :* Quint.

ēthŏlŏgus, ī, *m.* [ἠθολόγος], *a character-sketcher, mimic :* Cic.

ĕtiam, *conj.* [eti, orig. form of et, and iam, seen in quoniam, etc.]. **I.** Of time. **a,**

yet, *as yet, still :* quam diu etiam furor iste tuus nos eludet ? Cic. ; Pl. ; Verg., etc. With negatives : nec plane etiam abisse ex conspectu, Caes. ; Pl. ; Cic., etc. Often with *dum, nunc, tunc :* neque etiam dum scit pater, Ter. ; vixdum etiam coetu vestro dimisso, Cic. ; so with nondum : Ter., Cic. *v.* also etiamnunc, etiamtunc. **b,** etiam atque etiam, *repeatedly, again and again ;* hence also *pressingly, urgently :* Pl., Lucr., Cic., etc. **II. a,** Merely adding : *also, furthermore, too, likewise, besides :* atque alias etiam dicendi quasi virtutes sequetur, Cic. ; Pl. ; Verg., etc. Esp., non modo (solum) . . . sed (verum) etiam : *not only . . . but also :* tenebat non modo auctoritatem, sed etiam imperium in suos, Cic. ; Caes., etc. **b,** Intensive : *even, nay even :* quae omnes docti atque sapientes summa, quidam etiam sola bona esse dixerunt, Cic. After negative sentences (for *immo*) : *nay, indeed, nay rather :* Mamertina civitas improba antea non erat ; etiam erat inimica improborum, Cic. ; Ter. Emphatically with comparatives : *yet, still :* sunt autem etiam clariora, Cic. ; Ter., etc. **c,** Affirmative : *certainly, granted, by all means, yes indeed, yes :* Zeno in unā virtute positam beatam vitam putat, quid Antiochus ? etiam, inquit, beatam, sed non beatissimam, Cic. ; *yes, happy, but not perfectly happy,* Cic. ; Pl., etc. **d,** Declamatory (mostly colloq.). **i,** In statements : *actually ! just look !* heus etiam mensas consumimus, Verg. **ii,** In questions : *what ! pray ! really ?* quam diu etiam etc. ? Cic. ; etiam clamas, carnufex ? Pl. ; etc. And in questions that imply a command : scelerate, etiam respicis ? *you are looking round, are you ?* Pl. ; Ter. **iii,** With emphatic imperatives : *but, indeed, but just, etc. :* etiam tu hoc responde, Ter. ; Pl.

ĕtiam-nunc (alw. in Caes., Cic.) or **ĕtiamnum** (also separately, etiam nunc and etiam num), *adv.* [num, q.v. = nun (*cf.* Gk. νῦν) now], *even at the present time, yet till now, still* (us. with present tenses). **A.** Prop. : de materiā loquor orationis etiamnunc, non ipso de genere dicendi, Cic. ; Pl., etc. With negatives : nec Telamoniades etiam nunc hiscere quicquam audet, Ov. ; Pl. ; Cic. **B.** Wrongly. **a,** Of past time (for *etiamtunc*) : Cic., Verg., etc. **b,** For *etiam : also, besides, moreover :* Plin., Sen. Ep.

ĕtiam-sī, *conj.* (also separately), *even if, although* (used like *si*). **a,** With *Indic. :* Pl., Cic., etc. **b,** With *Subj. :* Pl., Cic., Liv. **c,** With verb understood : Pl., Cic., Quint.

ĕtiam-tum (less freq. **ĕtiam-tunc**), *adv. even then, till that time, till then, still* (always with *past* tenses) : Ter., Cic., Tac., etc.

Ĕtrūria, ae, *f. a district in N.W. Italy :* **Etruscus**, a, um, *Etruscan :* aurum, *a golden amulet worn by Roman boys of noble birth :* Juv. ; **Etrusci**, ōrum, *m. pl. the Etruscans.*

et-sī, *conj. even if, although* (used like *si*). **a,** With *Indic. :* Pl., Cic., Verg., etc. **b,** With *Subj. :* Pl., Cic., Liv. **c,** Ellipt. **i,** With verb understood : crudelitati etsi seras, non levis tamen venire poenas, Liv.; Cic. **ii.** With Apodosis suppressed or obscured (*cf.* quamquam): *although, yet, but :* vale atque salve; etsi aliter ut dicam meres, Pl.; Cic. Ep.; Liv., etc.

etymologia, ae, *f.* [ἐτυμολογία], *etymology :* Cic.

eu [εὖ], *well done! bravo!* Pl., Ter., Hor.

Euadnē, ēs, *f. d. of Iphis and w. of Capaneus.*

Euan (or **Euhan**) [εὐάν], *m. a name of Bacchus ;* **euāns** (or **euhāns**), antis, *crying Euan :* Cat. With Acc.: orgia, Verg.

Euander (or **-drus**), drī, *m. s. of Carmenta ; an Arcadian who emigrated to Italy and founded Pallanteum, at the foot of the Palatine hill ;* **Euandrius**, a, um.

euax, a cry of delight; *hurrah !* Pl.

Euēnus, ī, *m.* **I.** *a king of Aetolia, f. of Marpessa.* **II.** *a river in Aetolia ;* **Euēninus**, a, um.

euge and **eugepae** [εὖγε and εὐγέπαι], *well done! good! cheers!* Pl., Ter. Ironically: Pl., Ter.

Euha-, *v.* Eua-.

Euhēmerus, ī, *m. a Greek philosopher, noted for his rationalising of the popular myths and religion.*

Euhi-, Euhoe, *v.* Eui-, Euoe.

Euius, ī, *m. a name of Bacchus ;* **Euias**, adis, *f. a Bacchante.*

Eumenides, um, *f. pl.* [Εὐμενίδες, *the gracious ones*], *a euphemistic name for the Erinyes or Furies.*

Eumolpus, ī, *m.* **I.** *a priest of Ceres, who brought the Eleusinian mysteries to Attica ;* **Eumolpidae**, ārum, *m. pl. his descendants who had charge of the Eleusinian festival.* **II.** *s. of Musaeus, a descendant of I.*

eumpse, old Acc. of ipse: Pl.

eunuchus, ī, *m.* [εὐνοῦχος], *a eunuch :* Cic., Juv.

euoe [εὐοῖ], *a joyous cry in Bacchic rites :* Pl., Verg., etc.

Euphorbus, ī, *m. s. of Panthus, a brave Trojan, whose soul Pythagoras asserted had descended to himself by transmigration.*

Euphrātēs, is, *m. the river Euphrates in W. Asia.* Transf.: *the people living by the river :* Verg.

Eupolis, idis, *m. a famous Athenian comic poet* (fl. B.C. 420).

Euripidēs, is, *m. a famous Athenian tragic poet* (B.C. 480-405); **Euripidēus**, a, um.

Euripus, ī, *m.* εὐρῖπος, [*a narrow strait*], *the strait between Boeotia and Euboea.* Transf. **a.** *a canal, conduit :* Cic. **b.** *a trench round the Circus :* Suet.

Eurōpa, ae (-ē, ēs), *f.* **I.** *d. of Agenor and m. of Sarpedon and Minos by Jupiter, who, in the shape of a bull, carried her off to Crete ;* **Eurōpaeus**, a, um. **II.** *the continent of Europe, named after her ;* **Eurōpaeus**, a, um.

Euröus, *v.* Eurus.

Eurus, ī, *m.* [εὖρος], *the S.E. wind* (Lat. Vulturnus). **1.** Lit.: Verg. In *pl. :* Verg., Ov. **2.** Transf. **a.** *the east wind :* Ov. Hence, **Euröus**, a, um, *eastern :* Verg. **b.** *wind in gen. :* Verg.

Euryalus, ī, *m. friend of Nisus.*

Eurydicē, ēs, *f. w. of Orpheus.*

Eurypylus, ī, *m.* **I.** *s. of Neptune and king*

---

of Cos ; **Eurypylis**, idis, *f. adj. Coan.*

Eurysthenēs, is, *m. twin-brother of Procles and king of Sparta, the ancestor of one of the two royal families at Sparta.*

Eurystheus (trisyl.), eī (Acc. -ea, Verg.), *m. s. of Sthenelus and g.s. of Perseus, a king of Mycenae, who, at the command of Juno, imposed on Hercules his twelve labours.*

Eurytus, ī, *m. king of Oechalia and f. of Iole ;* **Eurytis**, idis, *f. his daughter Iole.*

euschēmē, *adv.* [εὐσχήμως], *becomingly, gracefully :* Pl.

Euterpē, ēs, *f. the Muse of music.*

Eutrapelus, ī, *m.* [εὐτράπελος, *witty*], *P. Volumnius, friend of Antony, so called because of his wit.*

Euxīnus Pontus (also **Euxinus**, ī, *m.* or **Pontus**, ī, *m.*), *the Black Sea.*

ē-vādō, vādere, vāsī, vāsum. **I.** *to go out or forth.* **1.** Lit. With *ex :* Pl., Cic. With Abl.: Sall., Verg. With *in* and Acc.: Liv. With Acc. of Extent, *to go out through, to pass through :* Verg., Ov., Liv., Tac. With *per* and Acc.: Liv. **2.** Transf.: *to come out, turn out, result in (becoming).* **a.** Of persons: perfectus Epicureus evasit, Cic.; iuvenis evasit vere indolis regiae, Liv. Also, quo evadas nescio, i.e. *what you are driving at,* Pl.; Ter. **b.** Of things: quoniam primum vanum inceptum evasisset, Liv.; aliquando id, quod somniavimus, evadere, Cic.; pestilentia in morbos, Liv.; Pl. **II.** *to go up, ascend.* **1.** Lit. With *ex :* Cic. With *ad :* Verg., Suet. With *in* and Acc.: Liv., Curt. With *super* and Acc.: Curt. With Acc. of Extent : Verg., Liv. **2.** Transf.: Quint. **III.** *to get away, escape.* **1.** Lit. With *ex :* Caes., Cic., Liv. With Abl.: Sall., Liv. With Dat.: Verg. With Acc. of Extent, *to pass through, escape :* Verg., Ov., Liv., etc. **2.** Transf.: e morbo, e periculo, ex iudicio, Cic.; Liv. With Acc.: Lucil.; casūs omnis, Verg.; Phaedr.

ē-vagor, āri, *to wander forth, to roam, range.* **1.** Lit. **a.** In gen.: Liv. **b.** Milit.: *to manœuvre :* Liv. **2.** Transf.: late evagata est vis morbi, Liv.; Cic.; Quint. With Acc. (rare): *to stray beyond :* rectum ordinem, Hor.

ē-valēscō, valēscere, valuī, *to become quite strong, to increase, grow fully.* Transf. **a.** In Perf. *to have power or ability.* With *Inf. :* Verg., Hor. Absol.: Quint. **b.** With *in* and Acc., *to grow, strengthen into :* adfectatio quietis in tumultum evaluit, Tac. **c.** Of a word or expression : *to prevail, get into vogue :* Quint., Tac.

ē-vānēscō, vānēscere, vānuī, *to vanish, pass away, die away, disappear.* **1.** Lit. Of objects of the senses: Bacchi flos, Lucr.; vinum et salsamentum vetustate, Cic.; cornuaque extremae lunae, Ov.; in tenuem ex oculis evanuit auram, Verg. **2.** Transf.: omnis eorum memoria evanuit, Cic.; rumor, ingenium, Liv.; vis herbarum, Ov.; bella per moras, Tac. [It. *svanire ;* Fr. *évanouir.*]

ēvānidus, a, um [ēvānēscō], *vanishing, passing away.* **1.** Lit.: pectora, Ov. **2.** Transf.: gaudium, Sen. Ep.; amor, Ov.

ḗvāns, v. euāns.

ē-vāstō, āre, to lay utterly waste, to devastate : Liv.

ḗvax, v. euax.

ḗvectus, a, um, Part. ēvehō.

ē-vehō, vehere, vexī, vectum. I. to carry out. or forth, to convey out. 1. Lit. : Cato ; omnia (signa) ex fanis plaustris, Cic. With Pron. Refl., or in Mid. : to rush forth ; ride, drive, or sail forth : evectus effreno equo, Liv. ; Tac. ; in altum, Liv. ; resolutis oris in ancoras evehuntur, Liv. With Acc. of end of motion : Curt. 2. Transf. : e Piraeeo eloquentia, Cic. ; Tac. ; spe vanā evectus, Liv. II. to carry upwards. 1. Lit. : aliquem ad auras, Ov. ; carpento in Collem Esquiliarum evehi, Liv. 2. Transf. : aliquem ad aethera, Verg. ; Hor. ; pericula sua ad consulatum, Tac. ; privatum supra modum evectae opes, Tac.

ē-vellō, vellere, vellī (vulsi, Flor.), vulsum, to pull, pluck, or tear out. 1. Lit. : linguam alicui, Cic. ; ferrum, Caes. ; arborem, Liv. ; spinas agro, Hor. Poet. : odorem e turis glaebis, Lucr. 2. Transf. : radicitus mala, Lucr. ; scrupulum ex animo, Cic. [It. svellere, svegliere.]

ē-veniō, venīre, vēnī, ventum (Pres. Subj. ēvenat, Pl.), to come out, come forth. 1. Lit. : Pl., Hor. 2. Transf. a. to result (as a consequence), to turn out, issue, end (only of things) : quae (auspicia) sibi secunda evenerint, Cic. ; Pl. ; si adversa pugna evenisset, Liv. With Adv. : feliciter, Caes. ; bene ac feliciter, Cic., Liv. ; praeter spem, Ter. ; nostrā ex sententiā, Pl. ; contra ac dicta sint, Cic. b. to come to pass, happen : ut plerumque evenit, Cic. ; maxime id in rebus publicis evenit, Cic. ; Pl. ; ubi pax evenerat, Sall. ; vereor, ne idem eveniat in meas litteras, Cic. Ep. Impers. with ut and Subj. : Ter., Cic., Quint. c. With Dat., to befall, happen to : Pl. ; cum mihi nihil improviso evenisset, Cic. ; L. Genucio consuli ea provincia sorte evenit, Liv. ; si quid sibi eveniret (i.e. if he should die), Suet.

ḗventum, ī, n. [ēveniō]. I. issue, consequence, result : Lucr. ; consilia eventis ponderare, Cic. II. an occurrence, event : eventorum memoria, Cic. III. With Gen. of person or Pron. Adj. : the sum of what happens to anyone ; experience, fortune : ut te ex nostris eventis admonendum putares, Cic. Ep. ; aliorum eventis doceri, Tac.

ḗventus, ūs, m. [ēveniō]. I. an issue, consequence, result : eventum pugnae expectare, Caes. ; Tac. ; dicendi, Cic. ; ex eventu (iudicare), Cic. ; eventus stultorum magister est, Liv. ; semper ad eventum festinat (poeta), Hor. In pl. : Cic. II. an occurrence, accident, event : Cic. In pl. : rerum, Cic. III. experience, fortune, fate (esp. of death) : Scipionis eventu maerere, Cic. ; militum, Liv. ; navium, Caes. ; patriae, Liv. In pl. : Caes.

ē-verberō, āre, to flog or beat violently : os oculosque hostis, Quint. ; clipeum alis, Verg. ; Ov. ; Curt.

ḗverriculum, ī, n. [ēverrō], a dragnet, seine. 1. Lit. : Varr. 2. Transf. a. Pun-

ningly of Verres' plunderings, a very clean-sweep : Cic. b. a clean-sweep (i.e. sweep-ing away) : malitiarum omnium, Cic.

ē-verrō, verrere, verrī, versum, to sweep out, sweep clean. 1. Lit. : stercus ex aede Vestae, Varr. 2. Transf. : to sweep clean (i.e. to plunder thoroughly) : Pl. Pun-ningly of Verres : o Verria praeclara ! quod fanum non eversum atque extersum reliqueris ? Cic.

ḗversiō, ōnis, f. [ēvertō], an overthrowing. 1. Lit. : columnae, Cic. ; Quint. 2. Transf. : rerum publicarum eversiones, Cic., Tac.

ḗversor, ōris, m. [ēvertō], a subverter, de-stroyer : civitatis, Cic. ; regnorum Priami, Verg. ; Quint.

(1) ḗversus, a, um, Part. ēverrō.

(2) ḗversus, a, um, Part. ēvertō.

ē-vertō (-vortō), vertere, vertī, versum. I. to turn out : pupillum fortunis patriis, Cic. ; Pl. ; cervices, to dislocate, Ter. II. to turn upwards. a. Of the sea, to upheave : evertit aequora ventis, Verg. ; Ov. ; Sen. Ep. b. to overturn, overthrow : navem, Cic. ; arborem, Verg. Hence, to destroy : urbes, Cic. ; castellum, Hor. ; Ov. Transf.: to overthrow, ruin, destroy : civitatem, Cic. ; res Asiae, Verg. ; aliquem non iudicio sed vi evertere, Cic. ; leges, testamenta, Cic. ; spem, Ov. ; Lucr. ; disciplinam militarem, Cic.

ē-vestīgātus, a, um [vestīgō], tracked out : Ov.

ḗvias, v. euias.

ḗvictus, a, um, Part. ēvincō.

ē-vidēns, entis, adj. [intrans. use of stem vidē], of things (like perspicuus) : clear to view, prominent, plain, evident : Cic., Quint., Suet. Comp. : Cic., Liv., etc. Sup. : Liv., etc.

ḗvidenter, adv. clearly, plainly : Liv., Quint. Sup. : Suet.

ḗvidentia, ae, f. [ēvidēns], clearness in speech : Cic., Quint.

ē-vigilō, āre. I. to wake up, awake : Quint., etc. II. A. Intrans. : to be fully wake-ful, vigilant. Transf. : in quo evigila-verunt curae et cogitationes meae, Cic. With Acc. (of Time) : to watch through : noctem, Tib. B. Trans. : to compose, elaborate untiringly : libros, Ov. ; consilia evigilata cogitationibus, Cic. Impers. Pass. Cic.

ē-vilēscō, vilēscere, viluī, to become quite worthless, despicable : pericula, Tac. ; Suet.

ē-vinciō, vincīre, vinxī, vinctum, to bind round, to entwine : diademate caput Tiri-datis evinxit, Tac. In Part. Perf. : viridi Mnestheus evinctus oliva, Verg. ; Ov. ; suras evincta cothurno, Verg.

ē-vincō, vincere, vicī, victum, to overcome completely, to vanquish utterly. 1. Lit. : evicit omnia miles, Liv. ; Aeduos, Tac. 2. Transf. a. to prevail over things : su-perbiam miseratio, Liv. ; solis imago evincit nubis, Ov. ; platanus caelebs evincet ul-mos, Hor. So of difficult places (i.e. to get through) : remis Charybdin, Ov. b. to prevail over persons : lacrimis evicta, Verg. ; evincunt instando ut etc., Liv. c. to *prevail* by argument, *prove.* With Acc. and *Inf.*: Hor.

ēvinctus, a, um, *Part.* ēvinciō.

ē-vīrō, āre [vir], *to castrate :* Cat., Varr.

ē-viscerō, āre, *to disembowel.* **1.** Lit.: Enn. **2.** Transf.: columbam, Verg.

ēvītābīlis, e, *adj.* [ēvītō], *avoidable* (with negative) : Ov.

ēvītātiō, ōnis, *f.* [ēvītō], *an avoiding :* malorum, Quint.

(1) ē-vītō, āre, *to escape, avoid.* **1.** Lit.: Cat., Hor., Ov. **2.** Transf.: casum, Caes. ; causas suspicionum, Cic. ; Quint.

(2) ēvītō [vīta], *to deprive of life :* vidi Priamo vi vitam evitari, Enn.

ēvocāti, ōrum, *m. pl.* [ēvocō], *veteran and discharged soldiers, again called to the colours :* Caes., etc.

ēvocātor, ōris, *m.* [ēvocō], *one who calls to arms :* servorum, Cic.

ē-vocō, āre, *to call out or forth.* **1.** Lit. **A.** In gen. : aliquem foras, Pl. ; (Tullia) evocavit virum e curiā, Liv. ; nostros ad pugnam, Caes. **B.** In partic. **a.** the gods from a conquered city : Liv. **b.** spirits : Metellos ab inferis, Cic. ; animas Orco, Verg. **c.** In public and military affairs : *to call out, summon :* senatum omnem ad se, Caes. ; Cic. ; magnam partem oppidanorum ad bellum, Caes. **2.** Transf. **a.** *to call forth, draw out, draw on :* cupiditas praedae milites longius evocabat, Caes. ; Liv. ; ad aliquem honorem, Caes. **b.** *to evoke, awake, excite :* misericordiam nullius oratione, Cic. ; Liv. ; risum lugentibus, Sen. Ep.

ēvoe, *v.* euoe.

ē-volgō, *v.* ēvulgō.

ē-volō, āre, *to fly out or forth.* **1.** Lit.: ex quercu (aquila), Cic. ; Ov. **2.** Transf. **a.** Of rapid movement : *to rush or spring forth :* (hostes) subito ex omnibus partibus silvae evolaverunt, Caes. ; Cic. ; Ov. ; ut, lapidem ferro quom caedimus, evolat ignis, Lucr. **b.** In gen. : ex poenā, Cic. ; oratio, Cic.

ēvolūtiō, ōnis, *f.* [ēvolvō], *an unrolling or opening* of a book ; hence, *a reading :* poëtarum, Cic.

ēvolūtus, a, um, *Part.* ēvolvō.

ē-volvō, volvere, volvī, volūtum, *to make to roll out or forth or away ;* also with *Refl. Pron.* or in *Mid.* *to glide forth.* **1.** Lit. Mostly of water : Verg., Liv., etc. ; vis venti arbusta, Lucr. ; silvas, montis, Ov. ; per humum evolvuntur, Tac. **2.** Transf.: ad auris militum ea dicta evolvebantur, Liv. **II.** *to unroll, roll out, unfold.* **1.** Lit. **a.** In gen. : vestis, Ov. **b.** Of a book-roll : Cic. Ep. Also *to unroll and read :* Cic., Ov., Tac., etc. **2.** Transf. **a.** *to unfold and disclose, strip off :* evolutis integumentis dissimulationis, Cic. ; aede patriā rebusque summis, Tac. ; ex praedā clandestinā, Liv. **b.** *to unfold, disentangle :* me ex his turbis, Ter. ; animi complicatam notionem, Cic. **c.** *to unfold and disclose, to unravel :* Enn. ; naturam rerum omnium, Cic. ; seriem fati, Ov. ; Verg., etc.

ē-vomō, vomere, vomuī, vomitum, *to vomit forth.* **1.** Lit.: Cic., Tac., Suet. ; tantam

pestem (with ref. to Catiline), Cic. **2.** Transf.: in me orationem ore impurissimo evomuit, Cic. ; Ter.

ē-vulgō, āre, *to make public, publish, divulge :* civile ius, Liv. ; arcanum, Tac. *Impers. Pass.* (with Acc. and *Inf.*) : Tac.

ēvulsiō, ōnis, *f.* [ēvellō], *a pulling out :* dentis, Cic.

ēvulsus, a, um, *Part.* ēvellō.

ex, **ec**, or **ē**, *adv.* and *prep.* [the form ē is not used before vowels ; ec is not used before vowels ; in old Latin (e.g. in Plautus) it is used in compounds before *f*, e.g. ecferre ; ex is used in compounds before consonants *c, h, p, q, s, t* regularly and assimilated before *f* ; but with nouns, the use of ex before these and other consonants is variable ; some set expressions have the same form invariably, as ex parte, ex sententiā, ex tempore, ē regione, ē re publicā, used adverbially.] **I.** Adv. (only in compounds). **a.** *out or forth* from confinement, protection, a number of persons or things, or a centre : eripere, exire, expandere, etc. **b.** *out from the ground, upwards :* erigere, escendere, eniti, etc. **c.** *out and off :* exuere, evanescere, etc. **d.** *out into the open, out so as to be perceptible, clearly, loudly :* edicere, exclamare, exaudire, etc. **e.** *out of restraint, difficulties or due bounds :* effugere, evadere, egredi, etc. **f.** *out to the end, thoroughly, perfectly :* efficere, enumerare ; often with idea of *creation* or *artificial result :* elaborare, effingere, efferare, etc. **g.** *out to exhaustion,* often *prodigally* or *wastefully :* effetus, ebibere, effundere, etc. **h.** *out, so as to remove :* properly in denominative adjectives and verbs, e.g. expers, enervare ; but also in denominative verbs which were orig. formed without a preposition, e.g. exarmare (as contrasted with armare). Hence, ex comes to be felt as expressing a reverse meaning : emergere, expedire, excludere (contrasted with immergere, impedire, includere). **II.** Prep. (with ABL. of Separation), *out from, forth ;* hence, *from, off.* **1.** Lit. Of space. **a.** In gen. : ex silvis, Caes. ; e curiā, Liv. ; ex equis desilire, Caes. ; globum terrae eminentem e mari, Cic. **b.** To indicate the place *from* which any thing is done (but Eng. says *on*) : ex equo (ex equis) pugnare, Caes. ; ex itinere, Caes., Cic. **c.** In phrases to denote direction *from* which : reliquis ex omnibus partibus colles oppidum cingebant, *on all the other sides,* Caes. Hence, the adverbial expressions, ex adverso, ex diverso, ex contrario, e regione, ex parte, etc. (*v.* adversus, etc.). **2.** Transf. **A.** Of time. **a.** In gen. : from and after a given point of time : *from, since :* bonus volo iam ex hoc die esse, Pl. ; ex quo (*sc.* tempore), Verg. ; Liv. **b.** *immediately after, directly after, after :* Cotta ex consulatu est profectus in Galliam, Cic. So the phrase, aliud ex alio, *one thing after another :* me cottidie aliud ex alio impedit, Cic. Ep. So, diem ex die exspectabam, *one day after another, from day to day,* Cic. Ep. ; Caes. Less freq. in specifying a future date : *from, after :* hunc iudicem ex Kal. Ian. non habemus, Cic. **B.** Of other relations.

a. With verbs which denote taking, receiving (both physically and mentally, as perceiving, learning, hoping, *etc.*) : *from, out of, of :* solem e mundo tollere ; amicitiam e vitā tollere, Cic. ; intellexi ex tuis litteris te ex Turannio audisse, Cic. Ep. ; ex captivis comperit, Caes. **b.** With words denoting the whole from which something is taken. Esp. with *numerals : out of, of :* ex omnibus saeculis vix tria aut quattuor nominantur paria amicorum, Cic. ; ex tribus istis modis rerum publicarum velim scire quod optimum iudices, Cic. **c.** To denote the material of which anything is made : *of :* statua ex aere facta, Cic. **d.** To indicate the cause or origin : *from, through, by, by reason of, on account of :* cum esset ex aere alieno commota civitas, Cic. ; ex Transalpinis gentibus triumphare, Cic. Esp. to indicate that *from* which anything derives its name : *from, after, an account of :* cui postea Africano cognomen ex virtute fuit, Sall. **e.** To indicate transition : *from, out of ; from being :* di ex hominibus facti, Cic. ; nihil est tam miserabile quam ex beato miser, Cic. **f.** ex (e) re, ex usu, *or* ex iniuriā, *to anyone's advantage or injury :* aliquid facere bene e re publicā, *for the good of the State*, Cic. ; ex usu terrae Galliae, *for the good of Gaul*, Caes. ; ex nullius iniuriā, *without injustice to anyone*, Liv. **g.** To denote conformity : *according to, after, in conformity with :* ex litteris Caesaris supplicatio decreta est, Caes. ; ex conlegi sententiā, Liv. ; ex senatūs consulto, Cic. ; ex foedere, Liv. ; ex sententiā, *as one could wish*, Ter. **h.** In adverbial expressions : *e.g.* ex aequo, ex commodo, ex diverso, ex facili, ex adfluenti, ex continenti, ex confesso, ex improviso, ex inopinato, *etc. : v.* these words. N.B.—*ex* placed after its noun (rare) : terris ex omnia surgunt, Lucr.

ex-acerbō, āre, *to exasperate, make thoroughly angry :* Liv., etc.

exāctiō, ōnis, *f.* [exigō]. **I.** *a driving out, expelling :* regnum, Cic. **II.** *a demanding, exacting ;* esp. **a.** *supervision :* operum publicorum, Cic. **b.** *a calling in, collecting of debts :* Cic., Liv. **c.** *a tax :* Cic. ; capitum atque ostiorum, Cic. Ep. ; Tac.

exāctor, ōris, *m.* [exigō]. **I.** *a driver-out :* regum, Liv. **II.** *a demander, exactor.* **a.** *a task-master, superintendent :* supplici, Liv. ; Tac. ; studiorum, Quint. **b.** *a collector of taxes :* Caes.

exāctus, a, um. **I.** *Part.* exigō. **II.** Adj. : *precise, accurate, exact :* numerus, Liv. ; fides, Ov. ; vir, Plin. Ep. With GEN. : morum, artis, Ov. *Comp. :* Ov., Suet. ; *Sup. :* Plin. Ep.

ex-acuō, uere, uī, ūtum, *to make quite sharp, keen, or pointed.* **1.** Lit. : vallos furcasque, Verg. **2.** Transf. **a.** Of sight : oculorum, ingeni aciem, Cic. **b.** Of feelings : *to sharpen, stir up, etc. :* aliquem, Cic. ; animos in bella, Hor. ; se ad amorem immortalitatis, Plin. Ep.

ex-adversum (**-advorsum**) and **ex-adversus**, *adv.* and *prep. exactly over against, opposite.* **I.** Adv. : apud ipsum lacum est pistrilla, et exadvorsum fabrica, Ter. ;

Pl. **II.** Prep. : with Acc. : ara exadversus eum locum consecrata est, Cic. ; Nep.

exaedificātiō, ōnis, *f.* [exaedificō], *a complete building up.* Transf. : of a speech : Cic.

ex-aedificō, āre. **I.** *to finish building.* **1.** Lit. : oppidum, Caes. ; Capitolium, Cic. **2.** Transf. : incohatam ignaviam, Pl. ; opus, Cic. Comic. : me ex his aedibus, Pl. **II.** *to build up :* templa deorum, Liv. ; Sall.

exaequātiō, ōnis, *f.* [exaequō], *levelling.* Transf. : *a levelling (of ranks), an equality :* Liv.

ex-aequō, āre, *to make quite equal or level.* **1.** Lit. **a.** Of ground : tumulos tumulis exaequabant, Auct. B. Hisp. **b.** Of balance : argentum argento exaequabitur, Pl. **2.** Transf. : *to place on a level, regard as equal, to equal :* neminem secum dignitate, Caes. ; Cic. ; vetus miles tironi sese exaequari aineret, Liv. ; Lucr. ; facta dictis, Sall. ; libertatem, Liv. ; Lucr. ; Cic.

ex-aestuō, āre. **1.** Lit. **A.** Of things. **a.** Of water, *to boil up, foam up :* Verg., Liv., etc. **b.** Of land, *to glow with heat :* Lucr. **B.** Of persons, *to be overheated :* Suet. **2.** Transf. : mens exaestuat irā, Verg. ; dolor, Ov.

exaggerātiō, ōnis, *f.* [exaggerō], *a heaping up.* Transf. : *elevation, exaltation :* animi, Cic.

ex-aggerō, āre, *to complete or raise up a mound, to pile up.* **1.** Lit. : aggesta humo planitiem Curt. **2.** Transf. **a.** *to enlarge, increase by heaping up :* rem familiarem, Cic. ; Phaedr. **b.** *to exalt, enhance, heighten the effect of :* orationem, Cic. ; tanto opere virtutem, Cic. ; Quint.

exagitātor, ōris, *m.* [exagitō], *a censurer, reprehender :* rhetorum, Cic.

ex-agitō, āre, *to keep thoroughly driven or on the move, to stir up thoroughly, rouse fully, harass.* **1.** Lit. : Lucr. ; leporem, Ov. Occ. *to drive or scare away :* Ov. **2.** Transf. **a.** In gen. : ab Suebis exagitati bello premebantur, Caes. ; Cic. ; at omnes di exagitent me, Hor. ; exagitari verberibus Furiarum, Suet. **b.** *to abuse roundly, censure severely, etc. :* aliquem convicio, Caes. ; cum etiam Demosthenes exagitetur ut putidus, Cic. Of feelings : *to stir up, irritate, excite :* plebem, Sall. ; tanta vis hominis leniunda quam exagitanda videbatur, Sall. ; Tac. ; maerorem, Cic. Ep. ; Cat. In good sense : huius disputationibus exagitatus maxime orator est, Cic.

exagōga, ae. *f.* [ἐξαγωγή], *an exportation of goods, export :* Pl.

ex-albēscō, albēscere, albuī, *to become quite white :* esp. *to turn very pale :* Enn., Cic.

ex-āmen, inis, n. [ex, agō, for ex-ag-men]. **I.** *a drove or thing led out.* **1.** Prop. : *a swarm*, esp. of bees : Cic., Verg., etc. ; of wasps and locusts : Liv. **2.** Transf. : pullorum, Lucr. ; servorum, Cic. ; iuvenum, Hor. ; servorum, Cic. **II.** *the tongue of a balance.* **1.** Lit. : Iuppiter ipse duas aequato examine lances sustinet, Verg. **2.** Transf. : *a weighing :* legum, Ov. [It. *sciame, sciamo :* Sp. *enjambre ;* Fr. *essaim.*]

examĭnō, āre [exāmĕn], *to weigh, test.* **1.** Lit.: (aēr), tamquam paribus examinatus ponderibus, Cic.; ad certum pondus, Caes. **2.** Transf.: omnia verborum mŏmentis, non rerum ponderibus, Cic.; Hor.; Quint.

ex-amussim, *adv. to rule or measure, exactly :* Pl., Varr. (v. amussis).

ex-anclō, āre [ex and Gk. ἄντλος, *hold of a vessel :* ἀντλεῖν, *to clear the hold*], *to draw off, drain.* **1.** Lit.: vinum poculo, Pl. **2.** Transf.: *to drain to the dregs :* cum aerumnis diem, Enn.; labores, Lucil., Cic.

ex-animālis, e, *adj.* **I.** *lifeless, dead :* Pl. **II.** *deadly :* curae, Pl.

exanimātĭō, ōnis, *f.* [exanimō], *want of breath, a feeling of suffocation :* Cic. In *pl. :* Cic.

exanimis, e, and **exanimus**, a, um (the latter form most common in plur.), *adj.* [anima]. *breathless, lifeless, dead.* **1.** Lit.: Lucr., Verg., Liv., etc. **2.** Transf.: *breathless* (with fear), *frightened to death* (rare, and only in form exanimis) : Verg., Hor., Liv.

exanimō, āre [anima], *to deprive of breath.* **1.** Lit. **a.** *to put out of breath, to wind :* fore ut duplicato cursu Caesaris milites exanimarentur, Caes.; Pl. **b.** *to deprive of breath* (i.e. *of life*): taxo se exanimavit, Caes.; gravi vulnere exanimari, Cic.; Lucr.; Hor.; Liv., etc. **2.** Transf.; *of the effect of emotions, esp. fear :* oratio haec me miseram exanimavit metu, Ter.; Pl.; adulescentulus sic initio accusationis exanimatus sum, Cic.; te metūs exanimant iudiciorum atque legum, Cic.; cur me querellis exanimas tuis ? Hor.; Verg.

exanimus, a, um, v. exanimis.

ex-ārdēscō, ārdēscere, ārsī, ārsum, *to burst out into a blaze, take fire.* **1.** Lit.: materies facilis ad exardescendum, Cic. Occ.: *to become heated :* exarsit sidere limus, Ov. **2.** Transf.: Indutiomarus multo gravius hoc dolore exarsit, Caes.; Cic., etc.; hodierno die ad spem libertatis exarsimus, Cic.; Liv.; Tac.; in seditionem, Liv.; Verg.; amor, amicitia, iniuria, Cic.; novum proelium, Liv.; dolor, Verg.; iracundia in eum, Tac.

ex-ārēscō, ārēscere, āruī, *to become quite dry.* **1.** Lit.: vestimenta uvida, Pl.; amnes, Cic.; Caes.; fauces siti, Cic. **2.** Transf.: vetustate opinio, Cic.; facultas orationis, Cic. Ep.

ex-armō, āre. **I.** *to deprive of arms, to disarm :* cohortis, Tac.; Luc. Transf.: accusationem, Plin. Ep. **II.** *to lose the rigging :* Sen. Ep.

ex-arō, āre. **I.** *to plough out, dig up in ploughing :* radices, Cato; sepulcra, Cic. **II.** *to plough out, i.e. thoroughly.* **1.** Lit.: Varr. Hence *to raise by ploughing, cultivate :* tantum frumenti, Cic. **2.** Transf. **a.** Of wrinkles : rugis vetus frontem senectus, Hor. **b.** Of writing with a stilus on wax tablets : exaravi nescio quid ad te, Cic. Ep.; Plin. Ep.; librum, Phaedr.; Suet.

ex-asciātŏ, a, um [ascia], *hewn out.* Comic. : opus, Pl.

ex-asperō, āre. **I.** *to make quite rough :* vocem, Quint. **II.** *to roughen up.* **1.**

Lit.: undas, Ov.; mare fluctibus, Liv. **2.** Transf.: *to irritate. exasperate :* aliquem, Liv.; animos, Liv.; rem verbis, Quint.

ex-auctōrō, āre (a soldier's word and mostly in *Pass.*), *to release from oath, to discharge from service, to dismiss.* **a.** Liv., Tac., Suet. **b.** *dismiss in disgrace, cashier :* Tac., Plin. Ep., Suet.

ex-audĭō, īre, *to hear clearly.* **a.** Prop.: nec satis exaudibam, Pl.; maximā voce, ut omnes exaudire possint, dico, Cic.; id clariore voce (dixit) ut maxima pars militum exaudiret, Caes.; Liv. With Acc. and *Inf.* : Caes. **b.** (*cf.* audio) *to listen to* (and so *grant, obey*) : vota precesque, Verg.; Ov.; Liv., etc.; ridebit monitor non exauditus, Hor.

ex-augeō, ēre, *to enlarge fully :* bene facta, Pl.; opinionem, Ter.

exaugurātĭō, ōnis, *f.* [exauguro], *a desecrating, profaning :* in *pl. :* Liv.

ex-augurō, āre, *to desecrate, profane :* fana, Cato; Liv.

ex-auspicō, āre, *to take a good augury from a thing :* ex vinculis, Pl.

ex-ballistō, āre [ballista], *to finish off with the ballista :* Ballionem, Pl.

exbibō, v. ēbibō.

ex-caecō, āre, *to make quite blind.* **1.** Lit.: Cic. **2.** Transf. **a.** *to stop up, choke* (a river, channel, etc.): Ov. **b.** *to darken :* fulgor argenti excaecatus, Plin.

excalceātus, a, um. **I.** *Part.* excalceō. **II.** *Adj. unshod :* Suet. Esp. of an actor, *not wearing the buskin* (cothurnus) ; *acting in comedy :* and as *pl.* Noun, *comic actors :* Sen. Ep.

ex-calceō (-calciō), āre, *to take off the shoes from.* With Acc.: pedes, Suet. Esp. of tragedians : *to take off the cothurni :* Sen. Ep. (*cf.* excalceatus).

ex-calfaciō, facere, factum, *to heat thoroughly :* Plin.

excandēscentia, ae, *f.* [excandēscō], *growing anger :* Cic.

ex-candēscō, candēscere, canduī, *to grow white hot.* **1.** Lit.: Cato. **2.** Transf.: *to rise to white heat :* haec nullam habent vim, nisi irā excanduit fortitudo, Cic.; in aliquem, Suet.

ex-cantō, āre, *to charm forth :* Pl., Hor., Sen., etc.

ex-carnificō, āre, *to tear piecemeal, rack to death.* **1.** Lit.: aliquem, Cic., Sen. Ep., Suet. **2.** Transf.: Ter., Sen.

ex-cavō, āre, *to hollow-out :* trullam, Cic.

ex-cēdō, cēdere, cēssī, cēssum (*Perf. Subj.* syncop. excēssis, Ter.). **I.** *to go out, go away, retire, withdraw.* **1.** Lit. With *ex :* Pl., Cic., Liv., etc. With Abl. : Cic.; Verg., Liv., etc. With *in* and Acc. : Cic., Liv. With Acc. (of place left) : Liv.; also *Impers. Pass.* : Liv. *Absol.* : Cic., Liv., Tac. **2.** Transf. **a.** From life : e (or ex), vitā, Cic.; e medio, Ter.; vitā, Cic., Curt., Tac. Without vitā : Curt., Sen. Ep., Tac., Suet. **b.** In gen. : ex magisterio alicuius, Pl.; palma, Verg.; ex pueris (i.e. from childhood), Cic.; id e memoriā excessit, Liv.; Ter.; cupiditatum dominatus excessit, Cic. **II.** *to go,* *pass out* from surrounding objects. **1.** Lit.: rupes quattuor stadia in altitudinem excedit, Curt. **2.** Transf. **a.** *to go beyond ordinary bounds, to proceed to :* tantum illa clades excessit, Tac.; Liv.; eo laudis excedere, Tac.; ad publicam querimoniam excessit res, Liv.; paululum ad enarrandum (i.e. *digress*), Liv.; in aliquid, Liv., Plin. Ep. **b.** *to go beyond, surpass, exceed* (with Acc.): modum, Liv.; finitum tempus, Liv.; summam octoginta milium, Liv.; Tac., etc.; fastigium equestre, Tac.; Suet.; fidem, Ov.; decretum, Tac.

excellēns, entis. **I.** *Part.* excellō. **II.** *Adj.* : *standing out, lofty.* **1.** Lit.: loca, Auct. B. Hisp. **2.** Transf.: *eminent, distinguished, surpassing, excellent :* excellens omni genere laudis, Cic.; in omni genere, Cic.; studium, Caes.; natura, Cic.; ingenium, Liv.; cycnus, Verg. *Comp. :* Nep., Plin. *Sup. :* Caes., Plin., etc.

excellenter, *adv. eminently, admirably :* Cic., Nep. *Comp. :* Cic.

excellentia, ae, *f.* [excello] *eminence, superiority, excellence.* With *Obj.* or *Subj.* Gen.: Cic. In *pl. :* Cic.

ex-cellō, cellere [v. antecellō], *to stand up prominently, stand out, be eminent, to distinguish oneself, to surpass, excel* (mostly in good sense). With Dat. of person surpassed : Cic., Quint. Also with *prep. :* inter aliquos, Cic.; praeter omnis, Cic.; super ceteros, Liv. *Absol. :* Cic., Tac. With *Instr.* Abl., whereby one surpasses : Caes., Cic. Also with *in* and Abl. : Cic.

excelsē, *adv. high, loftily.* Transf.: Plin. Ep. *Comp. :* Cic.

excelsitās, ātis, *f.* [excelsus], *loftiness.* Transf.: animi, Cic.

ex-celsus, a, um, *lofty, high, elevated.* **1.** Lit.: mons, Caes.; Cic.; Verg.; cornu (bovis), Caes. *Comp. :* Caes. *Sup. :* Caes. Hirt. As Noun, **excelsum**, i, *n. a height :* simulacrum Iovis in excelso conlocare, Cic.; Ov. **2.** Transf.: homo, orator, animus, Cic.; gloria, Tac. *Neut.* as Noun : in excelso aetatem habere, Sall; excelsa spectare, Liv. *Comp. :* Cic., Quint.

exceptiō, ōnis, *f.* [excipiō], *an exception, restriction, limitation.* **a.** In gen.: consiliorum sine ullā exceptione communitas, Cic.; neque te patior cum exceptione laudari, Cic. In *pl. :* unus imperitat nullis iam exceptionibus, Tac. **b.** In law: *the exception* or *objection of the defendant to the plaintiff's statements :* Cic.

exceptō, āre [*freq.* excipiō]. **a.** *to catch, take up repeatedly :* barbatulos mullos exceptans de piscinā, Cic.; equae exceptant levis auras, Verg. **b.** *to receive in succession :* hos singulos, Caes.

exceptus, a, um, *Part.* excipiō.

ex-cernō, cernere, crēvī, crētum, *to sift out, separate :* a matribus haedos, Verg.; ex captorum numero Saguntinos, Liv. [It. *scernere.*]

ex-cerpō, cerpere, cerpsī, cerptum [carpō], *to pick* or *take out.* **1.** Lit.: semina pomis, Hor. **2.** Transf. **a.** *to pick out, choose, select :* etiam excerpere ex ipsis

(malis) si quid inesset boni, Cic. E s p. *to make extracts from, copy from* (e.g. a book in course of reading); quod quisque commodissime praecipere videbatur, excorpsimus, Cic.; Plin. Ep., etc.; nomina ex tabulis, Liv. **b.** *to take out, leave out, except :* de numero, Cic.; numero, Hor.; Ter. **c.** *to withdraw oneself :* se consuetudini hominum, Sen. Ep.

excerptus, a, um. **I.** *Part.* excerpō. **II.** *Neut.* as Noun, **excerptum**, *an extract :* Sen. Ep., Quint.

excēssus, ūs, *m.* [excēdō]. **I.** *a departure* (from life), *death :* e vitā, Cic., Sen. Ep.; vitae, Cic.; Romuli, Cic. Alone : Tac., Suet. **II.** *a digression :* Quint., Plin. Ep.

excetra, ae, *f. a snake, serpent.* **1.** Lit.: Pl., Cic. poet. **2.** Transf.: as term of reproach : Pl., Liv.

excidiō, ōnis, *f.* [v. excidium], *a destroying, destruction :* Pl.

excidium, i, *n.* [for exscidium, fr. exscindō], *overthrow, demolition, destruction :* urbis, Liv.; Verg. Also *a cause of destruction :* seditio prope urbi excidio fuit, Tac. In *pl. :* Verg., Liv., Tac.

ex-cidō, cidere, cidī [cadō], *to fall out* or *from.* **1.** Lit. With *ex :* Cic., Ov. With *de :* Cic. With Dat. (*from which*) : Verg. With *in* and Acc. : Liv. Esp. of the lots cast in a vessel : ut cuiusque sors exciderat, Liv. **2.** Transf. **a.** Of utterance : *to drop out unawares, to slip out, escape :* verbum ex ore alicuius, Cic.; vox ore, Verg.; Ov.; verbum tibi (*from you*), Cic.; libellus, Cic. **b.** From the memory or mind ; *to fall, slip out, escape :* de memoriā, Liv.; ex animis, Liv.; Ov.; animo, Verg. With Dat. of person : at mihi ista exciderant, Cic. *Absol. :* Quint. *Impers. :* excidit ut peterem, Ov. **c.** *to pass away, be lost, perish :* aliquid, Cic.; virtus, Hor.; luctus, Ov. **d.** *to drop* (from a standard), *degenerate :* in vitium libertas excidit, Hor. **e.** *to fail in ;* hence *to lose, be deprived of.* With *ex :* Pl. With Abl. : Ter., Ov., Curt., etc.

ex-cidō, cidere, cidī, cisum [caedō], *to cut out* or *off, to quarry, fell,* etc. **1.** Lit.: Enn.; lapides e terrā, Cic.; arbores, Caes.; excisum latus rupis in antrum, Verg.; columnas rupibus, Verg.; rubos arvis, Quint. **2.** Transf. **a.** *to raze, demolish :* domos, Cic.; Troiam, Verg.; Hor.; Tac. **b.** *to extirpate, banish :* aliquid ex animo, Cic.; Hor.; causas bellorum, Tac.

ex-cieō, v. exciō.

ex-ciō, īre, īvī or iī, ītum or itum (*Imperf.* exoībat, Liv.); also fr. **-cieō**, exciet, Pl.; (*Inf.* excière, Liv.), *to stir, rouse out.* **1.** Lit. **a.** In gen.: me ante aedīs, Pl.; consulem ab urbe, Liv.; suem latebris, Ov.; Liv. **b.** From sleep, *to rouse, awaken :* somno excitus, Sall.; sopore, Lucr.; aliquem ex somno, Liv. **c.** *to summon forth :* auxilia, Liv.; Tac.; animas sepulcris, Verg.; principes Romam, Liv.; Volscos ad expugnandam secum Ardeam, Liv. **2.** Transf. **a.** *to set in motion, awaken* (i.e. *cause*): lacrimas alicui, Pl., Tac.; molem in undis, Verg.;

tumultum, terrorem, Liv. **b.** *to rouse* (with anger, fear, etc.), *excite :* conscientia mentem excitam vastabat, Sall. ; commotis excita sacris, Verg. ; Liv. ; excivit ea caedes Bructeros, Tac.

ex-cipiō, cipere, cēpī, ceptum [capiō]. **I.** With Activity of Subject predominating : **A.** *to take from a person or place, to lay hold of and bring out, remove.* **1.** Lit. : vidulum e mari, Pl. ; clipeum sorti, Verg. **2.** Transf. **a.** *to free, deliver :* servitute exceptus, Liv. ; nihil cupiditati, Tac. **b.** *to except, make an exception of :* Pl. ; excepi de antiquis praeter Xeno- phanem neminem, Cic. ; excepto, quod non simul esses, cetera laetus, Hor. **Esp.** *in agreement, law, etc., to except by name, to make a formal exception :* in Hasdrubalis foedere nec exceptum tale quicquam fuerit, Liv. Also *to mention specially :* Saguntini excipiuntur, Liv. **B.** *to take hold of, inter- cept, catch on its way.* **1.** Lit. **a.** In gen. *to catch, intercept, surprise :* servos in pabulatione, Caes. ; uros, Caes. ; Verg. ; Hor. ; incautum, Verg. ; speculatorem, Liv. **b.** Of things falling : sanguinem paterā, Cic. ; imbrem armis suis, Liv. ; tela clipeo, Curt. Transf. of the aspect of a building ; porticus arcton, Hor. **c.** Of persons or things roaming or fleeing : multos ex fugā dispersos, Caes. ; fugientis feras, Phaedr. ; vagos per hiberna milites, Liv. **2.** Transf. **a.** In gen. *to catch, pick up, intercept, surprise :* rumores, Cic. ; sermonem eorum e servis, Liv. ; motūs futuros, Verg. With Acc. and *Inf.* (*cf.* accipio) : Liv. **b.** *to receive with favour, welcome,* etc. ; benigno vultu eos, Liv. ; adsensu populi excepta vox consulis, Liv. **Esp.** *to welcome, entertain* a person in time of need : Cic., Verg. ; aliquem hospitio, Ov. ; epulis, Tac. Also of inanimate subjects : patenti itinere Priaticus campus eos excepit, Liv. **c.** Of an event, fortune, etc., *taking hold of* or *receiving next a person :* qui quosque eventūs exciperent, Caes. ; quis te casus excipit ? Verg. ; excepit deinde eum bellum, Liv. **II.** With Passivity of Subject predominat- ing. **A.** Of blows and the like, *to receive from another, intercept on its way ; to receive, withstand.* **1.** Lit. : tela, Caes., Cic. ; impetūs, Caes. ; plagae genus in se, Lucr. ; vulnera, Cic. ; Quint. ; equitem, Verg. **2.** Transf. : vim frigo- rum hiememque, Caes ; pericula, labores, Cic. Of things as Subject : sublicae vim fluminis, Caes. **B.** *to receive in succession.* **1.** Lit. : Romulus gentem, Verg. **2.** Transf. : *to come next to, follow after, succeed :* hunc locutum Labienus, Caes. ; Herculis vitam immortalitas, Cic. ; tristem hiemem pestilens aestas. Liv. Without *Obj.* expressed : turbulentior inde annus excepit, Liv. ; Caes.

excisiō, ōnis, *f.* [excidō], *a destroying :* Cic.

excisus, a, um, *Part.* excidō.

excitātus, a, um. **I.** *Part.* excitō. **II.** Adj. : *vigorous, strong, loud :* sonus, Cic. ; lumina, Quint. *Comp. :* Liv., Quint. *Sup. :* odor, Plin.

excitō, āre [*freq.* exciō], **I.** *to rouse out* or

forth, *scare out, wake up.* **1.** Lit. : feras, Cic. ; aliquem a portu, Pl. ; e somno, Cic. ; Pl. ; somno, Liv. ; a mortuis (ab inferis), Cic. **2.** Transf. : *to awaken, rouse :* plausum, discordiam, risūs, etc., Cic. ; Verg. ; suspicionem alicui, Cic. **II.** *to make to rise or stand up, raise up.* **1.** Lit. : aliquem, Cic. So in court of law or senate : *to call upon :* reos, testis, Cic. ; Liv. ; Quint. **2.** Transf. : **a.** Of buildings : *to raise, erect :* Cic., Verg., etc. **b.** Of fire : *to raise :* Lucr., Caes., Cic. **c.** Of dejected spirits, etc. : *to arouse, cheer up, inspire, revive :* studia hominum, Caes. ; senatum abiectum, Cic. ; animos omnium ad laetitiam, Caes. ; aliquem ad laborem et ad laudem, Cic. ; Quint.

excitus, a, um, *Part.* exciō.

ex-clāmātiō, ōnis, *f.* [exclāmō]. Rhet., *an exclamation :* Cic., Quint., Tac.

ex-clāmō, āre. **I.** Intrans. : *to call* or *cry aloud, to call* or *cry out :* Pl., Cic., Quint. **II.** *to shout out, exclaim.* **a.** With quoted words : Pl., Cic., Ov., etc. **b.** With Acc. and *Inf. :* Pl., Liv., etc. With *Neut.* Acc. of adjective : Quint. With *ut* and *Subj. :* when a command or exhortation is implied : Cic., Liv. **III.** With personal object : *to call upon by name :* Pl., Anton. ap. Cic.

ex-clūdō, clūdere, clūsī, clūsum (*Perf. sync.* exclūstī, Ter.) [clūdō, claudō], *to shut out, exclude, not to admit.* **1.** Lit. : aliquem, Pl., Ter., Hor. ; aliquem a domo, Cic. ; moenibus, Cic., Verg. **Occ. a.** Of birds, *to hatch :* ex ovis pullos, Cic. ; Cato ; Lucr., etc. (v. also excudo). **b.** *to knock out :* oculum, Pl., Ter. **2.** Transf. **a.** *to shut out, keep off :* ictus solis, Hor. **b.** *to shut off, keep away, prevent :* aliquem ab re frumentariā, Caes. ; a navigatione, Caes. ; Cic. ; a re publicā, Cic. ; ab omni doctrinā, Cic. ; reditu, Nep. ; Liv. Without *Abl.* of Separation : Caes., Cic.

exclūsiō, ōnis, *f.* [exclūdō], *a shutting out, exclusion :* Ter.

exclūsus, a, um, *Part.* exclūdō. Comic. *Sup. :* Pl.

excoctus, a, um, *Part.* excoquō.

excōgitātiō, ōnis, *f.* [excōgitō], *a thinking out, contriving :* Cic.

excōgitātus, a, um. **I.** *Part.* excōgitō. **II.** Adj. : *sought out, choice. Sup. :* Suet.

ex-cōgitō, āre, *to consider thoroughly, to con- trive, devise :* aliquid mali aut sceleris, Cic. ; multa ad avaritiam excogitabantur, Caes. ; ferreas manūs tuendis urbibus, Caes. *Impers. Pass.* (with *ut* and *Subj.*) : Nep.

ex-colō, colere, coluī, cultum, *to tend, culti- vate, work carefully.* **1.** Lit. : vineas, Plin. ; lanas, Ov. **2.** Transf. **a.** Of things, *to improve, polish, adorn :* urbem, Suet. ; Plin. Ep. **b.** Of manners or charac- ter : *to improve, civilise, refine :* ex agresti immanique vitā exculti ad humanitatem sumus, Cic. ; vitam per artis, Verg. ; animos doctrinā, Cic. ; orationem, Cic., Quint., Tac. **c.** *to honour :* deos, Phaedr. ; Ov.

ex-coquō, coquere, coxī, coctum. **I. a.** *to*

boil away : Cato. **b.** *to remove by heat :* Verg., Ov. **II. A.** *to cook, bake thoroughly, dry up.* **1.** Lit.: terram sol, Lucr.; Verg. Comic.: aliquam, Ter. Hence *to harden :* ferrum, Ov. **2.** Transf.: *to cook up :* malum alioui, Pl. **B.** *to make by thorough heating :* harenas admixto nitro in vitrum, Tac.

ex-cors, cordis, *adj.* [cor], *without intelligence, without understanding, senseless :* Pl., Cic., Hor.

excrēmentum, ī, *n.* [excernō], *excrement, ordure :* Plin.; oris, *spittle,* Tac.; narium, *mucus of the nose,* Tac.

excreō, v. exscreō.

ex-crēscō, crēscere, crēvī, crētum. **I.** *to grow out* or *forth, to grow up, rise up.* **1.** Lit. In gen.: solum tumulo in altum, Luc.; in hos artūs, in haec corpora excrescunt, Tac. **2.** Transf. Of morbid excrescences: Suet. **II,** *to grow exceedingly, increase :* litium series, Suet.; Quint.

(1) excrētus, a, um, *Part.* excernō.

(2) excrētus, a, um, *Part.* excrēscō.

excruciābilis, e, *adj.* [excruciō], *deserving of torture :* anus, Pl.

ex-cruciō, āre, *to torment greatly, torture to death.* **1.** Lit. (physically): Pl.; servos fame vinculisque, Caes.; Cic.; frigus nudos, Lucr. **2.** Transf. (mentally): Pl., Cic. With animi (Locatival GEN.): Pl., Ter.

excubiae, ārum, *f. pl.* [excubō], *a lying out.* **1.** Lit. **a.** In gen.: foris, Pl. **b.** Milit.: *a watching, keeping watch* (esp. by day): Cic., Verg., Tac., etc. **2.** Transf. **a.** *watchfires :* excubias divum aeternas, Verg. **b.** *the persons keeping watch ; a watch :* Tac., Suet.

excubitor, ōris, *m.* [excubō], *one who keeps watch, a watchman, sentinel :* Caes., Suet. Of a cock : Verg.

ex-cubō, cubāre, cubuī, cubitum, *to lie* or *sleep out of doors.* **1.** Lit. **a.** In gen.: Cic. **b.** Milit.: *to keep watch :* Caes., Verg., etc. Of non-personal subjects : naves ad portum excubabant, Caes. **2.** Transf.: *to be watchful* or *attentive :* excubabo vigilaboque pro vobis, Cic.; animo, Cic.; cupido pulchris in genis, Hor.; ad opus, Caes.

ex-cūdō, cūdere, cūdī, cūsum, *to strike* or *beat out.* **1.** Lit. **a.** silici scintillam, Verg. **b.** Of metal work, *to hammer out, forge, mould :* excudent alii spirantia mollius aera, Verg. **c,** *to hatch out :* pullos, ova, Varr., Cic., etc. (v. also excludo). **2.** Transf. **a.** Of the work of bees : ceras, Verg. **b.** Of writings : Cic. Ep., Tac., Plin. Ep.

ex-culcō, āre [calcō]. **I.** *to tread* or *beat out :* furfures, Pl. **II.** *to tread down, to stamp firm* or *close :* singuli ab infimo solo pedes terrā exculcabantur, Caes.

excultus, a, um, *Part.* excolō.

excūrātus, a, um, [cūrō], *carefully attended to :* Pl.

ex-currō, currere, cucurrī (rarely -currī), cursum, *to run, hasten out* or *forth.* **1.** Lit. **a.** In gen.: Pl., Cic.; excurro in Pompeianum, Cic. Ep. Comic.: in crucem, i.e. go to the devil, Pl. **b.**

Milit. : *to sally forth, to make a sortie :* omnibus portis, Liv.; also, *to make an inroad :* in finis Romanos, Liv. **2.** Transf. **a.** In gen.: animi foras, Cic.; fons ex summo montis cacumine, Curt. **b.** Geogr.: ab intimo sinu paeninsula excurrit, Liv.; Ov.; Curt. **c,** *to run out, expand, move freely :* campus, in quo excurrere virtus posset, Cic.; ne oratio excurrat longius, Cic. **d.** With Acc. of Extent : **i.** *to run out over :* spatium, Ter. **ii.** *to run over, omit :* multa, Sen.

excursiō, ōnis, *f.* [excurrō], *a running out* or *forth.* **1.** Lit. **a.** Of stepping forward in speaking : excursio moderata eaque rara, Cic. **b.** Milit.: (i) *a sally, sortie ; an inroad, invasion ;* crebras ex oppido excursiones faciebant, Caes.; oram maris infestam excursionibus crebris faciebant, Liv.; Cic. (ii) *the advance of skirmishers at the beginning of a battle :* Cic. **2.** Transf.: In a speech. **a.** *outset, start :* Cic., Quint. **b.** *room for launching out :* Quint.

excursor, ōris, *m.* [excurrō], *a skirmisher, a scout,* Cic.

excursus, ūs, *m.* [excurrō], *a running out* or *forth.* **1.** Lit. Milit.: *a sally, charge, attack, an inroad, invasion :* militum, Caes.; Tac. Of bees : Verg. **2.** Transf. (in speech) *a digression :* Quint.

excūsābilis, e, *adj.* [excūsō], *that may be excused, excusable :* Ov.

excūsātē, *adv. without blame, excusably :* Quint. Comp. : Tac., Plin. Ep.

excūsātiō, ōnis, *f.* [excūsō], *a giving reason for exemption* or *acquittal, an excusing, excuse, plea :* dare, accipere, Cic. With *Obj.* GEN.: Cic. With *Subj.* and *Obj.* GEN. combined: excusatio Ser. Sulpici legationis obeundae, Cic. With *Causal* GEN.: excusatio necessitatis, vel aetatis, Cic.; Caes.; Pl. With Acc. and *Inf.* : Cic. With *cur* (and *Subj.*): Cic. Ep. With *quo minus* (only after a negative): Cic. *Absol.* : Cic.

excūsātus, a, um. **I.** *Part.* excūsō. **II.** Adj.: *free from blame, exempt.* Comp. : Plin. Ep. Sup. : Sen.

ex-cūsō, āre [causa : cf. accūsō, from ad and causa], *to release from a charge, to exempt, free from blame ; to excuse.* **A.** With personal Object : aliquem quod etc., Caes., Cic.; se de aliquā re, Caes.; Atticae meae velim me ita excuses, ut . . ., Cic. Ep.; se apud aliquem, Cic. In *Pass.* : dixi, cur excusatus abirem, Hor.; with DAT. (*from* which): Tac.; with *Inf.* : Liv. **B.** With ref. to the fault committed : *to make excuses for, apologise for :* tarditatem litterarum mearum, Cic. Ep.; missos ignis excusat, Ov.; Quint.; Tac. **C.** *to allege in excuse, to plead as an excuse.* With Acc. : propinquitatem, morbum, Cic.; inopiam, Caes.; valetudinem, Liv.; Ov.; Tac., etc. With Acc. and *Inf.* : Pl., Liv., Suet. In *Pass.* with *Inf.* : Cic.

excussus, a, um, *Part.* excutiō.

excūsus, a, um, *Part.* excūdō.

ex-cutiō, cutere, cussī, cussum (*Aor. Opt.* excussit, Pl.) [quatiō], *to shake out* or *off.* **1.** Lit. **A.** In gen.: **a.** crinom, Verg.; poma venti excutiunt Ov.; hastam clipeo,

Verg. ; Ov. ; litteras in terram, Cic. **b.** *to knock, fling, hurl out* or *off :* dentis, cerebrum alicui, Pl. ; equus excussit equitem Liv. ; excussus curru, Verg. **Poet.:** navis excussa magistro, Verg. ; excussos laxare rudentis, Verg. ; Teucros vallo, Verg. ; ignem de crinibus, Ov. Hence (from a sling or bow): glandem, Liv. ; fundis lapides, Curt. ; and so, tela, Liv. So also, lacertum excutere, of the action of *throwing out the arm* in hurling, swimming, etc. : Ov., Sen. **B.** In partic. *to shake out* a person's garments for anything concealed : pallium, Pl. ; Suet. With personal Object : Cic., Phaedr. **2. Transf. a.** In gen. *to shake off,* or *out, get rid of, discard, banish :* metum corde, Ov. ; conceptum foedus, Verg. ; excussus patriā, Verg. ; Ter. ; lectis utrumque, Hor. ; sibi opinionem, Cic. ; studia de manibus excutiuntur, Cic. ; aliena negotia curo, excussus propriis, Hor. ; si flava excutitur Chloe, Hor. ; risum sibi, Hor. ; excutior somno, Verg. **b.** *to search, examine, investigate :* verbum, Cic. With *Indir. Quest. :* Quint. [It. *scotere ;* and fr. Part. excussa, It. *scossa ;* Fr. *escousse.*]

ex-dorsuō, āre [dorsum]. Of fishes : *to take out the backbone, to fillet :* Pl.

exec-, v. exsec-.

ex-edō, ēsse, ēdī, ēsum (*Pres. Opt.* exedint, Pl.), *to eat up, devour, consume.* **1.** Lit. : frumentum, Varr. ; Pl. **Prov.:** tute hoc intristi, tibi omne est exedendum, Ter. **2. Transf. a.** Of the action of rust, decay, water, etc. : exesa scabrā robigine pila, Verg. ; epigramma exesis posterioribus partibus versiculorum, Cic. ; exesae arboris antrum, Verg. ; Curt. ; of fire : Lucr. ; exesa vis luminis, Tac. **b.** Of the action of grief, anxiety, etc. : *to prey upon, consume :* aegritudo exest animum, Cic. ; Cat. ; exspectando exedor miser, Pl. **c.** In gen. *to destroy :* rem publicam, Tac.

exedra, ae, *f.* [ἐξέδρα], *a hall (with seats) for conversation* or *discussion ; a lecture-room :* Cic., Quint.

exedrium, ī, *n.* [ἐξέδριον], *a sitting-room :* Cic. Ep.

exemplāris, e, *adj.* [exemplum], *following a model :* (litteras) exemplaris omnium litterarum, Tac. As *Neut.* Noun, **exemplar,** āris (also **exemplāre,** is, *n.* Lucr.) **I.** *a transcript, copy* (more freq. exemplum : q.v.). **1.** Lit. : rerum magnarum, Lucr. ; litterarum, Pollio ap. Cic. Ep. ; librum in exemplaria transcriptum mille, Plin. Ep. **2. Transf.:** *a copy, likeness :* alicuius, Cic. **II.** *a pattern, model, ideal :* utile proposuit nobis exemplar Ulixen, Hor. ; exemplar formaque rei publicae, Cic. ; Quint. ; Tac., etc. In *pl. :* Hor.

exemplum, ī, *n.* [exemō (later eximō) ; *cf.* templum fr. tem-], *that which is taken out of a larger quantity, a sample.* **1.** Lit. : purpurae, tritici, Auct. Her. **2. Transf. A.** *a sample.* **a.** *an example, typical instance :* divinare morientis etiam illo exemplo confirmat Posidonius, Cic. ; proponere exempla iracundiae, Cic. ; proferre, Cic. So with causā or gratiā ; exempli causā paucos nominavi, Cic. ; Quint. **b.**

character, make, tenor, pattern : isto exemplo vivere, Pl. ; testamentum eodem exemplo, Caes. ; litterae uno exemplo, Cic. ; eodem exemplo quo etc., Liv. **c.** *a precedent :* exemplo Pompili, Cic. ; Liv., etc. ; omnia mala exempla ex bonis orta sunt, Sall. **d.** *a pattern, model (for imitation), example (to follow) :* exemplum habere ad imitandum, Cic. ; exemplum a me petere, Liv. ; ab aliquo capere, Cic. ; Liv. ; sumere, Cic. ; probitatis, Cic. **e.** *an object-lesson* (to advise or warn) *:* magister equitum creatus exemplo fuit conlegas eumque intuentibus, Liv. Often *a warning :* clades eorum exemplo fuit, Caes. ; esse in exemplo, Ov. ; arcendis sceleribus exemplum nobile, Liv. ; **f.** *a warning,* i.e. *punishment :* habet aliquid ex iniquo omne magnum exemplum, Tac. ; meritum quidem novissima exempla, Tac. **B.** *a transcript, copy :* Pl. ; litterarum, Cic. Ep. ; ea pluribus exemplis scripta, Ov. [It. *esempio, scempio ;* Sp. *ejemplo.*]

exemptus, a, um, *Part.* eximō.

exenterō, āre [ἐξεντερίζω], *to disembowel.* **Transf. a.** *to empty :* marsuppium alicuius, Pl. **b.** *to torture, torment :* Pl.

ex-eō, īre, iī (rarely-īvī), itum. **A.** **Intrans.** *to go out* or *forth.* **1.** Lit. **a.** In gen. : Pl., Caes., Cic. With *ex :* Pl., Caes., Cic. With *ab :* Ter., Liv., Quint. With *de :* Cic. With ABL. domo : Caes., Cic. ; also portā, Pl. ; castris, Caes. With *ad :* Ter. With *in :* Lucr., Caes. Cic., Liv. Of non-personal subjects : de consularibus mea prima sors, Cic. ; Hor. ; (Nilus) in maris exit aquas, Ov. *Pass. Impers. :* Pl., Cato. **b.** Naval and Milit. *to disembark, march out :* in terram, Cic. ; de nave, Cic. ; ad pugnam, Liv., Verg. ; ad bellum, Cic. Ep. *Absol. :* Caes. *Pass. Impers. :* Caes. **2. Transf. a.** In gen. : *to pass out of a condition :* ex potestate, e vitā tamquam e theatro, Cic. ; de vitā, Cic. ; Plin. Ep. ; studio gloriae, Cic. **b.** Of time : *to run out, end, expire :* indutiarum dies exierat, Liv. ; Cic. ; Sen. Ep. **c.** *to exceed, pass over, pass into, digress :* vestra vita, licet supra mille annos exeat, Sen. ; Quint. ; Plin. Ep. **d.** *to issue, come out in such and such a form :* currente rotā cur urceus exit ? Hor. ; libri ita exierunt, Cic. Ep. **e.** *to get out* or *abroad ; become public :* exire atque in vulgus emanare, Cic. ; exit opinio (with Acc. and *Inf.*): Suet. **B.** **Trans.** **1.** Lit. **a.** *to go* or *pass beyond ; to cross :* limen, Ter. ; Avernas vallis, Ov. **Transf.:** lubricum iuventae, Tac. **b.** *to avoid, parry, ward off :* corpore tela, Verg. ; Lucr. **2. Transf.:** *to exceed :* modum, Ov. **C.** *to go forth from the land, rise up :* e terrā hordeum, Varr. ; in auras ignis, Lucr. ; ad caelum arbos, Verg. ; colles, Ov. [It. *uscire.*]

exeq-, v. exseq-.

ex-erceō, ēre [Lit. *to make strong enough* or *thoroughly effective : cf.* Gk. ἀρκεῖν]. **1.** Lit. **a.** Milit. : *to drill, train, exercise :* copias, Caes. **b.** In gen. *to train, exercise :* in gramineis exercent membra palaestris, Verg. ; corpus, Cic. ; se saliendo, Pl. ; se genere venationis, Caes. ; so in *Mid. :* Cic. **c.** *to keep busy, work :*

tauros, Verg.; ego te exercebo hōdie, Ter.
2. Transf. **a.** *to keep busy, work :* collis,
flumina, Verg.; rura, Hor.; metalla,
Tac. Of abstracts, *to employ to the full,
exploit :* diem, Verg.; victoriam in plebem,
Sall.; victoriam in captis, Liv.; in pugnā
Fortuna opes, Liv. **b.** Of the mind: *to
train, school, discipline :* ad hanc te amentiam voluntas, Cic.; ingenium, Quint.; se
in subitis dictionibus, Cic. **c.** *to practise,
exercise, work, busy oneself with :* medicinam,
Cic.; arma, Verg.; iudicium, Cic.; quaestiones, Liv.; leges, Tac.; odium in aliquo,
Ov.; scelus, libidinem, avaritiam in socios,
Liv.; pacem et hymenaeos, Verg. **d.** *to
work to excess, worry, harass :* hominum
vitam curis, Lucr.; me fortuna exercuit,
Cic.; te exercent numinis irae, Verg.;
Sall.

exercĭtātĭō, ōnis, *f.* [exercito]. **I.** *an
exercising, practising, training.* **1.** Lit.:
Cic.; Liv.; in armis, Caes.; iuventutis in
gymnasiis, Cic. **2.** Transf. of the
mind: Cic.; iuris civilis, Cic.; dicendi,
Cic.; Quint. **II.** *(practical) experience :*
Cic.; superiorum pugnarum, Caes.

exercĭtātus, a, um. **I.** *Part.* exercito. **II.**
Adj. **a.** *practised, trained, experienced :*
in aliquā re, Caes., Cic., Quint.; in pro-
pagandis finibus, Cic.; bello, Liv.; Caes.,
Cic. *Comp. :* Cic., Liv. *Sup. :* Caes.,
Cic. **b.** *harassed, disturbed :* curis de salute
patriae, Cic.; Syrtes Noto, Hor. *Comp. :*
Tac.

exercĭtĭum, ī, *n.* [exerceō], *exercising,
exercise :* equitum, Tac.

exercĭtō, āre [*freq.* exerceō], *to keep in training :* corpus atque ingenium, Sall.; Quint.

exercĭtor, ōris, *m.* [exerceō], *a trainer :* Pl.

exercĭtus, a, um. **I.** *Part.* exerceō. **II.**
Adj. **a.** *harassing, vexatious :* militia,
Tac.; Cic.; Plin. Ep. **b.** *harassed :* Cic.
Ep., Tac. **c.** *disciplined :* Cic., Tac.

exercĭtus, ūs, *m.* (DAT. *sing.* occ. -ū, Caes.,
Liv.) [exerceō]. **1.** Lit. *training :* Pl.
2. Transf. **a.** *a disciplined body of
men, an army :* Pl.; exercitum conscribere,
comparare, conficere, Cic.; scribere, Liv.;
contrahere, cogere, Caes. Comic.: noli
mihi exercitum imperare (i.e. *do not burden
me beyond endurance*), Pl. **b.** As *infantry,*
in opp. to cavalry: (Caesar) exercitum
equitatumque castris continuit, Caes. **c.**
*the assembly of the people in the Comitia
Centuriata :* Pl. **d.** *a troop of attendants :*
Pl. **e.** *a host, swarm, flock,* etc. : corvorum,
Verg.

exerō, v. exserō.

exēsor, ōris, *m.* [exedō], *that eats away :* murorum, Lucr.

exēsus, a, um, *Part.* exedō.

exhālātĭō, ōnis, *f.* [exhālō], *an exhalation,
vapour :* Cic.

ex-hālō, āre. **I. A.** Trans.: *to breathe
out, exhale :* nebulam, Lucr., Verg. **B.**
Intrans. : *to steam, reek :* Lucr. **II.**
to breathe out to a finish : edormi crapulam
et exhala, Cic.; animam, Ov.; vitam,
Verg. Without animam *or* vitam : Ov.,
Sen. Ep.

ex-haurĭō, haurīre, hausī, haustum. **I.** *to
draw, drain off.* **1.** Lit.: sentinam, Cic.

2. Transf. **a.** Of material things, *to draw
off, remove :* terram, Caes.; Hor.; pecuniam
ex aerario, Cic. **b.** Of immaterial things :
sibi manu vitam Cic.; alicui dolorem, Cic.;
vim ingentem aeris alieni, Liv. **II.** *to
draw off to exhaustion, drain dry.* **1.**
Lit.: vinum, Cic.; flumen, Prop. **2.**
Transf. **a.** Of persons and things,
to drain dry, gut completely, clear out :
plebem impensis, Liv.; Cic. Ep.; tecta,
Liv.; aerarium, Cic.; pharetram, Ov.
b. *to exhaust, drain to the lees* (i.e. *bear to the
end) :* laborem, periculum, Liv.; bella,
Verg. **c.** *to exhaust, bring to an end :*
amorem, Cic.; sermonem, Cic. Ep.; aliquid
sermone, Cic.

exhērēdō, āre [ex and hērēs], *to disinherit :*
aliquem, Cic., Quint.

ex-hērēs, ēdis, *adj. disinherited :* with
GEN. **1.** Lit.: paternorum bonorum,
Cic.; Pl.; Quint. **2.** Transf.: vitae,
Pl.

ex-hĭbeō, ēre [habeo], *to hold out, produce in
public, present.* **1.** Prop. of witnesses,
documents, etc.: testem, Curt.; fratres,
Cic.; exhibe librarium illud, Cic.; omnia
integra, Cic. **2.** Transf. **A.** *to display,
present, offer to view.* **a.** With *Refl. Pron. :*
se ministratorem alicui, Suet.; Plin. Ep.
Hence, querulos sonos, Ov. **b.** exhibuit
gemino praesignia tempora cornu, Ov.
c. Of abstracts: humanitatem, Plin. Ep.;
Suet. **B.** *to offer,* and so *to cause :* **a.**
molestiam tibi, Cic. Ep.; Pl.; Tib. Of a
benefit : Liv. **b.** With *Predic. Adj. to set*
a thing *out* to be such : rem salvam exhi-
bebo (i.e. I will put it all right), Pl.

ex-hĭlarō, āre, *to gladden :* servitutem nostram, Cic. Ep.

ex-horrēsco, horrēscere, horruī, *to shudder
exceedingly, to be terrified :* Cic., Ov. With
Acc., *to shudder at :* Verg., Liv.

exhortātĭō, ōnis, *f.* [exhortor], *an encouraging :* Planc. ap. Cic. Ep.; Quint.,
Tac. In *pl.* : Quint.

exhortātīvus, a, um [exhortor], *of encouragement, exhortative :* Quint.

ex-hortor, ārī, *to encourage strongly :*
trepidos, Ov.; sese in arma, Verg. With
ut and *Subj. :* Quint., Tac. Transf.:
virtutes, Sen. Ep.

ex-ĭgō, igere, ēgī, āctum [agō]. **I.** *to move,
keep going, drive out.* **A.** Of physical
force. **1.** Lit.: *to drive out or forth :*
virum a se, Pl.; reges ex civitate, Cic.;
uxorem, Ter.; sacer admissas exigit Hebrus
aquas, Ov.; exigit ensem per medium
iuvenem, Verg. **2.** Transf. **a.** Of a
play : fabulam, Ter. **b.** lassitudinem ex
corpore, Pl. **B.** *to force out, exact* (payment, penalty). **1.** Lit.: pecunias, Caes.,
Cic.; obsides, Caes.; poenas, Ov. **2.**
Transf.: litteras, Cic. Ep.; ex omnibus
rebus voluptatem, Cic.; piacula ab aliquo,
Liv.; viam (i.e. the construction of a road),
Cic., Liv.; rationem, Sen. Ep.; Plin. Ep.
With *ut* or *ne* and *Subj. :* Cic., Juv. **C.** *to
dispose of* (by sale) : agrorum fructūs, Liv.
II. *to keep going to the end.* **1.** Lit.: *to
complete, finish :* Verg.; monumentum,
Hor.; opus, Ov.; commentarios, Quint.
2. Transf. **a.** aerumnam, Pl.; aetatem,

Pl., Cic., Liv., etc.; annos, Hor.; Verg., etc.; ante exactam hiemem, Caes. **b.** Of time : *to use up, spend, pass* : aevum, Verg., Lucr., etc.; diem supremum, Tac.; Ov. **c.** *to turn over in the mind, consider fully* : secum aliquid, Verg.; Liv.; de his rebus cum eo, Planc. ap. Cic. Ep.; Plin. Ep. Hence **i.** *to determine, estimate, regulate* to a standard : ad perpendiculum columnas, Cic.; opus ad viris, Ov.; Sen. Ep.; Tac.; plagas, Tac. **ii.** *to determine, ascertain* (facts) : aliquid, Verg.; rationem, Hor. *Impers. Pass.* (with *Indir. Quest.*) : Ov.

exiguē, *adv. stingily, meagrely* : Ter., Cic.; dicere, Cic. With numbers, *barely* : Caes.

exiguitās, ātis, *f.* [exiguus]. *meagreness, shortness, smallness* : Caes. With GEN. : Caes., Cic., etc.; temporis, Caes., Liv.

exiguus, a, um [exigō], *meagre, scanty, small.* **a.** Of extent : Caes., Cic., Hor. **b.** Of physical size : Verg., Hor. **c.** Of time : Caes., Cic., Verg. **d.** Of quantity : Caes., Cic., Hor. **e.** In quality : facultates, Caes.; ingenium, Cic.; solacia, Verg. *Sup.* : Ov., Plin. Ep. *Neut.* as Noun with GEN. : exiguum campi ante castra erat, Liv.; temporis, Plin. Ep.

exiliō, v. exsiliō.

exilis, e, *adj.* [ex īle, *loinless*], *feeble, meagre, small, thin.* **1.** Lit. : femur, Hor.; digiti, Ov.; solum, Cic. **2.** Transf. **a.** In wealth, *straitened, poor* : Nep., Hor. Hence *cheerless* : via, Ov. **b.** Of style : *meagre, jejune, dreary* : Cic., Quint. **c.** With GEN., *free from* : Pl. *Comp.* : Plin.

exilitās, ātis, *f.* [exilis], *thinness* : vocis, Quint. Of style : *meagreness, dreariness* : Cic.

exiliter, *adv. meagrely, jejunely, drearily* (of style) : Cic. *Comp.* : Varr.

exilium, v. exsilium.

exim, v. exinde.

eximiē, *adv. exceptionally* : Cic., Liv., Juv.

eximius, a, um [eximō], *taken out, excepted.* **1.** Lit. **a.** tu unus eximius es, Liv., Cic.; Ter. **b.** For sacrifice : *choice, selected* : Verg., Liv. **2.** Transf. : *exceptional, special, eminent* : mulier facie eximiā, Cic.; opinio virtutis, Caes.; virtus, Caes.; animus in rem publicam, Cic.; ignes Aetnae, Lucr.

ex-imō, imere, ēmī, emptum [emō], *to take out, take away, remove.* **1.** Lit. : spinis de pluribus unam, Hor.; Cato; rem acervo, Ov.; telum, Quint. **2.** Transf. **a.** *to remove* from a list or category. With *ex* : Cic. With *de* : Cic., Nep. With ABL. : Hor., Liv., Quint. **b.** *to free, release* : aliquos ex obsidione, Cic. Ep. : ex servitute, Liv.; urbem obsidione, Liv.; aliquem metu, Pl.; servitute, Liv.; morti, Tac. **c.** *to take away, remove, banish* : hic dies atras eximet curas, Hor.; religionem, Liv.; Cic.; alicui lassitudinem, Pl.; Romanis dubitationem, Liv. *Pass. Impers.* : plurimis mortalium non eximitur, quin eto., Tac. **d.** Of time : *to take away* from the main business : Cic., Liv., Suet.

exin, *adv.* v. exinde.

ex-ināniō, īre, *to empty completely.* **1.** Lit. : navem, Cic. **2.** Transf. : *to clean out, plunder completely* : Pl., Caes., Cic.

ex-inde, exim, and **exin,** *adv.* **A.** In space : *out from that place, thence.* **1.** Lit. : Pl., Tac. **2.** Transf. (in enumerating a series in local succession) : *after that, next* : Cic., Tac. **B.** In time : *after that, thereafter, then* (freq.) : Enn., Cic., Verg., Liv. With *ubi* or *postquam* : ostium ubi conspexi, exinde me ilico protinam dedi, Pl. Transf. (in enumerating a succession of events) : *furthermore, next* : Verg., Liv., Tac. **C.** Of other relations : to indicate a rule, standard, or measure : *hence, accordingly* : proinde ut quisque fortuna utitur, ita praecellit ; atque exinde sapere eum omnes dicimus, Pl.

existimātiō, ōnis, *f.* [existimō], *a valuing, appraising.* **A.** Prop. **a.** *public opinion* : vulgi, Caes.; hominum, Caes., Cic.; militis de imperatore, Liv. **b.** *a valuing of evidence, or the means or right of forming an opinion* : communis omnibus, Liv. **B.** With *Obj.* GEN. (expressed or implied) : *the public estimation in which a man is held.* **a.** In gen. : *reputation, good name, character* : offendere, oppugnare, Cic.; Suet. **b.** In finance, *credit* : Caes.

existimātor, ōris, *m.* [existimō], *an appraiser, critic* : Cic.

existimātū, ABL. *Sing. m.* [existimō], *in the judging* : existimatu facile est (with ACC. and *Inf.*) : Liv.

ex-istimō (existumō), āre [aestimō], *to appraise or value completely* (morally). **1.** Lit. : vitam tanti, Cic.; Pl.; Nep.; utcumque haec existimata erunt, Liv. **2.** Transf. : *to appraise, estimate, form an opinion or judgment.* **A.** *to form an opinion about.* With Acc. of *Obj.* : Ter. With *Predic.* Noun or Adj. : eum avarum, Cic.; Quint. With *Predic. Descript.* GEN. : Nep. With ACC. and *Inf.* : Pl., Cic., etc. So in *Pass.* : disciplina in Galliam translata esse existimatur, Caes.; Cic.; Quint. With *Indir. Quest.* : Ter., Sall. *Impers. Pass.* (with ACC. and *Inf.*) : Caes.; (with *Indir. Quest.*) : Caes., Quint. **B.** *to form an opinion, judge* : Quint. With *de* : Cic. *Impers. Pass.* (*Absol.* or with *de*) : Cic.

existō, v. exsistō.

exitiābilis, e, *adj.* [exitium], *destructive, fatal, deadly* : Ov., Liv., Tac. With DAT. : Pl., Cic. Ep., Tac.

exitiālis, e, *adj.* [exitium], *destructive, fatal, deadly* : Cic., Verg.

exitiō, ōnis, *f.* [exeō], *a going or coming out* : ex utero, Pl.

exitiōsus, a, um [exitium], *destructive,* Cic., Tac. With DAT. : Cic., Tac. *Comp.* : Tac.

exitium, ī, n. [exeō], *a going off* (at the end). **1.** Lit. : Pl. **2.** Transf. : *destruction, ruin* : Pl., Lucr., Cic., etc.; ad exitium dare, Tac. In *pl.* : Pl., Cic., Verg. Also *a cause of ruin* : ego omnibus meis exitio fuero, Cic. Ep.; Hor.

exitus, ūs, *m.* [exeō], *a going out or forth, egress, departure.* **1.** Lit. : Lucr., Caes., Cic. In *pl.* : Caes. **2.** Transf. **a.** *place of egress, outlet, passage* : portarum,

Caes. ; Juv. In *pl.* : Cic., Liv. **b.** *end,
close, conclusion, termination :* orationis,
Cic. ; quaestionem ad exitum adducere,
Cic. ; ita magnarum initia rerum celerem et
facilem exitum habuerunt, Caes. ; Hor. ;
verba quae casūs habent in exitu similīs,
Cic. ; in exitu iam annus erat, Liv. ; foedum
exitu, Liv. Also *end of life, fate :* natura
ad humanum exitum abripuit,
Cic. ; Ov. ; Liv. In *pl.* : Cic. **c.** *issue,
result, event :* de exitu rerum sentire,
Caes. ; Cic. ; Liv. ; futuri temporis exitus,
Hor. In *pl. :* Cic., Hor.

exlecebra, ae, v. ēlecebra.

ex-lēx, ēgis, *adj. without law.* **a.** *bound by
no law :* Lucil., Cic., Liv. **b.** *heedless of
laws, reckless :* Hor.

exmoveō, v. ēmoveō.

ex-obsecrō (exops-), āre, *to entreat
earnestly.* With *ut* and *Subj. :* Pl.

ex-oculō, āre *(Aor. Opt.* exoculāssitis, Pl.)
[oculus], *to deprive of eyes :* Pl.

exodium, ī, *n.* [ἐξόδιον], *a comic after-piece
or interlude :* Liv., Juv., Suet.

ex-olēscō, olēscere, olēvī, olētum [v. ado-
lēscō], *to grow out to rankness or weakness.*
T r a n s f. : *to decay, weaken, fade (from age) :*
litterae, Suet. ; patris favor, Liv. ; disciplina, rumor, dolor, Tac. In *Pass. :*
exoletum vetustate odium, Liv. ; Pl. ;
Suet.

exolētus, a, um. **I.** *Part.* exolēscō. **II.** As
Noun, **exolētus,** ī, *m. : a vile person of
mature age :* Pl., Cic., Tac., etc.

ex-onerō, āre, *to free from a burden, to disburden, unload.* **1.** L i t. : navem, Pl. ;
plenas colos, Ov. **2.** T r a n s f. : *to relieve.*
a. In respect of population : plebem
exoneratam deducta in colonias multitudo
praestabat, Liv. ; multitudinem proximas
in terras, Tac. C o m i c. : eam ex hoc agro,
Pl. **b.** In gen. : civitatem vano metu,
Liv. ; fidem, Liv. ; laborum meorum
partem, Tac. ; aliquid in quaslibet auris,
Sen. Ep.

exoptābilis, e, *adj.* [exoptō], *desirable,
desired :* nuntius, Pl.

exoptātus, a, um. **I.** *Part.·* exoptō. **II.**
A d j. : *desired much, longed for, welcome :*
Pl., Cic., Verg. *Comp. :* Cic. Ep. *Sup. :*
Pl., Cic. Ep.

ex-optō, āre, *to wish or desire much, to long
for.* With Acc. : Pl., Cic., Liv. With
Inf. : Ter., Cic. Ep. With *ut* and *Subj. :*
Pl., Cic. Ep.

exōrābilis, e, *adj.* [exōrō], *that may be en-
treated, placable :* Pl., Liv. ; non exorabilis
auro, Hor. ; iracundiae, Cic. Ep. ; in
aliquem, Cic. Ep. *Comp. :* Sen.

exōrābula, ōrum, *n. pl.* [exōrō], *means of
winning over :* Pl.

exōrātor, ōris, *m.* [exōrō], *a successful
pleader :* Ter.

ex-ōrdior, ōrdīrī, ōrsus, *to begin a web, to lay
the warp.* **1.** L i t. : Pl., Cato. In metaph. :
Cic. **2.** T r a n s f. : *to begin, start.* With
Acc. : Pl., Ov., Liv., etc. With *Inf.* :
Cic., Nep. With *loqui* understood : Cic.,
Quint., Tac. With *ab : to start from, begin
with :* Cic., Liv. *Perf. Part.* in *Pass.* sense :
Pl., Cic.

exōrdium, ī, *n.* [exōrdior], *the beginning, the

warp of a web. **1.** L i t. : Quint. **2.**
T r a n s f. : *a beginning, prelude.* **a.** In
gen. With GEN. : Enn., Cic., Verg., etc.
In *pl.* : Lucr., Verg. **b.** Rhet. : dicendi,
Cic. Hence : *the exordium, introduction :*
Cic., Quint. In *pl.* : Verg., Quint.

ex-orior, orīrī, ortus *(Pres. Indic.* and
Imper. are of 3rd *Conjug. :* Ter., Lucr.,
Verg., Ov. ; also *Imperf. Subj.:* exoreretur,
Lucr., Liv.) *to rise and come out or forth*
(esp. suddenly). **1.** L i t. Of persons : Ter.,
Lucr., Cic., Liv. Of stars, etc. : Cic., Verg.
Of trees, rivers, etc. : e terrā arbusta, Lucr. ;
Nilus mediā ab regione diei, Lucr. **2.**
T r a n s f. : *to arise, issue* (from some origin
or cause) : utero dolores, Pl. ; exoritur
Antipatri ratio ex alterā parte, Cic. ;
repente Gyges rex exortus est Lydiae, Cic. ;
horum ex iniustitiā maxima perturbatio,
Cic. ; mora, Caes. ; clamor, discordia, Verg. ;
fama, bella, Liv.

exōrnātiō, ōnis, *f.* [exōrnō], *a thorough
equipping or dressing.* T r a n s f. *a dress-
ing-up* (of style), *embellishment :* Cic.

ex-ōrnō, āre, *to put into order ; to equip,
furnish thoroughly ; to dress, fit out.* **1.**
L i t. : **a.** navem, mulierem, Pl. ; nuptias,
Pl. ; aciem, Sall. ; aliquem aliquā re, Sall.
C o m i c. : *to dress down :* Ter. **b.** *to
adorn, embellish :* domum, Cic. ; me, Pl. ;
aliquem veste regiā, Curt. **2.** T r a n s f. :
to adorn, give lustre to : te moribus lepidis,
Pl. ; philosophiam falsa gloria, Cic. ;
orationem, Cic.

ex-ōrō, āre, *to beg successfully, prevail upon,
win over by entreaty ; to gain or obtain by
entreaty.* With *ut* (or *ne*) and *Subj.* : Pl.,
Cic. With Acc. of person : Pl., Cic., Ov.,
etc. With Acc. of thing obtained : Pl.,
Verg., etc. With double Acc. : Pl. With
thing as subject : Ov. In *Pass.* : opem
exorata fero, Ov. *Absol. :* Pl., Tac.

exors, ortis, v. exsors.

exōrsus, a, um. **I.** *Part.* exōrdior. **II.**
Noun, **exōrsa,** ōrum, *n. pl. beginning,
preamble :* Verg.

exōrsus, ūs, *m.* [exōrdior], *a beginning :*
orationis, Cic.

exortus, a, um, *Part.* exorior.

exortus, ūs, *m.* [exorior], *a rising.* **1.** L i t. :
solis, Suet. **2.** T r a n s f. : *the East :* in
pl. : ab occasu solis ad exortūs, Liv.

ex-os, ossis, *adj. without bones, boneless :*
Lucr.

ex-ōsculor, ārī, *to kiss fondly :* Tac., Plin.
Ep., Suet.

exossō, āre [ex os], *to deprive of the bones, to
bone :* Pl., Ter., Lucr.

exōstra, ae, *f.* [ἐξώστρα], *a machine thrust
out* (in theatres a device for showing an
interior). T r a n s f. Of anything public :
Cic.

ex-ōsus, a, um [ex, ōsus (ōdī]. **A.** A c t.
hating exceedingly, detesting : exosus
Troianos, Verg. ; Ov. ; as *finite verb :*
patrios mores exosus es, Curt. **B.** P a s s. :
hated exceedingly, hateful : ob scelera universis exosus, Eutr.

exōticus, a, um [ἐξωτικός], *foreign, exotic :*
Pl. As Noun, **exōticum,** ī, *n. a foreign
garment :* Pl.

ex-pallēscō, pallēscere, palluī, *to grow* or

turn very pale : Pl., Ov., Plin. Ep. With
Acc. : Hor.

ex-palliātus, a, um [pallium], *robbed of his
cloak :* Pl.

ex-pallidus, a, um, *exceedingly pale :* ex-
pallido colore, Suet.

ex-palpō, āre, *to coax out :* Pl.

expalpōnidēs, ae, v. nummōsexpalpōnidēs.

ex-pandō, pandere, pandī, pānsum, *to spread
out, unfold, expand.* In *Mid. :* Nilus, Plin.
Ep. T r a n s f. : rerum naturam dictis,
Lucr. [It. *spandere.*]

ex-papillātus, a, um [papilla], *bared to the
breast :* Pl. (dub.).

expatior, v. exspatior.

ex-pavēscō, pavēscere, pāvī, *to become very
much afraid :* ad id, Liv. With Acc. :
Hor., Tac., etc.

expectā-, v. exspectā-.

expectorō, āre [pectus], *to drive from the
breast ; to banish from the mind :* Enn.

expecūliātus, a, um [pecūlium], *stripped of
property :* servi, Pl.

expediō, īre, iī (or īvī), ītum (*Fut.* expedībō,
Pl.) [ex and ped-, cf. impedīre], *to free from
a fetter or snare, to unfetter, free, extricate,
disentangle.* **1.** L i t. : ex laqueo se expedire, Cic. ; mortis laqueis caput, Hor.
In *Mid. :* Verg. Also, *to send clear :*
trans finem iaculum, Hor. **2.** T r a n s f.
a. *to free, clear, extricate.* **a.** Of things
(from entanglements, covers, etc.) : *to get
out, get ready :* Caes., Cic., Liv., Verg., etc.
b. Of persons, *to prepare for action :* se ad
pugnam, Cic., Liv. ; legiones, Caes. ; Liv. ;
Tac. So, navis, *to clear for action,* Caes.
c. Of roads, *to clear* of obstacles, attacks,
etc. : aditūs, Caes. ; commeatūs, Liv. ;
iter fugae, Liv. **B.** Of immaterial things,
to extricate, free. **a.** From troubles, etc.
With Acc. of person : ex servitute filium,
Pl. ; Ter. ; se ab omni occupatione, Cic.
Ep. ; se stultitiā, Cic. ; Ter. With Acc.
of thing : rationem salutis, Cic. ; victoriam, Caes. With Acc. of thing cleared
away : curas, Hor. **b.** In money-matters,
etc. : *to clear, set right :* nomina mea, Cic.
Ep. ; rem frumentariam, Caes. **c.** By
speech, *to clear up, set forth clearly :* Pl.,
Ter. ; omnem famam, Verg. ; rei initium,
Sall. With *de :* Tac. With *Indir. Quest. :*
Tac., Juv. P h r. **rēs expedit** or *expedit,
the matter clears, develops* (favourably) ;
hence *it is advantageous, useful, expedient :*
nihil nec expedire nec utile esse, quod sit
iniustum, Cic. With *Inf.,* or Acc. and *Inf.*
clause as Subject : Ter., Cic., Hor., Quint.
With *ut* and *Subj. :* Tac. With *adv. :* si
ita expedit, Cic. Ep.

expeditē, adv. *without obstruction or hindrance,
freely :* Pl., Cic., Suet. *Comp. :* Cic.
Sup. : Cic. Ep.

expeditiō, ōnis, *f.* [expediō]. Milit. : *a
special mission of lightly-equipped troops,
special service :* milites in expeditionem
misit, Caes. ; Cic. ; facere, Liv.

expeditus, a, um. **I.** *Part.* expediō. **II.**
A d j. **a.** *unfettered, unhampered, unobstructed.*
1. Lit. Mostly of persons. **A.** In gen. :
Caes., Cic., Hor. **B.** M i l i t. **a.** *cleared, free,
ready for action :* Caes., Cic., Liv., etc. ; as
Noun, in expedito habere integras copias

ad opem ferendam, Liv. **b.** *without baggage :* Caes., Liv. **c.** *lightly equipped :*
Caes., Sall., Liv. *Masc.* as Noun : Caes.,
Liv. **2.** T r a n s f. **a.** Of persons : *ready,
prompt :* ad dicendum, Cic. **b.** Of things,
clear, without obstruction : iter, Caes., Liv. ;
locus, Caes. ; via ad honores, Cic. Also
ready to hand : res frumentaria, Caes. ;
pecunia, Cic. *Neut.* as Noun : hoc in
expedito positum, Quint. *Comp. :* Cic.
Sup. : Cic., Plin.

ex-pellō, pellere, pulī, pulsum, *to drive* or
thrust out or *away, to eject, expel.* **1.** L i t.
Of persons or material things. With Abl.
of separation : Cic., Verg., etc. With *ex :*
Cic. With *ab :* Cic., Liv. With *in* and
Acc. : Cic., Ov., Liv. **2.** T r a n s f. : ali-
quem vitā, Cic. ; aevo, Lucr. ; periculo,
Pl. ; haec ex animo, Lucr. ; Cat. ; corde
desidiam, Pl. ; somnos, quietem, spem,
Ov. ; dubitationem, Caes. ; vitam, Tac.

ex-pendō, pendere, pendī, pēnsum, *to weigh
out from a stock.* **1.** L i t. **a.** *to weigh out,
weigh :* aliquem, Pl. ; pecunias, Cic. **b.**
to weigh out money in payment, *to pay down :*
Cic. **c.** *to lay out, expend :* Hor. (See
also expensus.) **2.** T r a n s f. **a.** *to estimate,
rate, value at :* hominem auro, Pl. **b.** *to
weigh mentally, ponder, estimate, consider :*
testem, Cic. ; aliquid, Cic. ; Verg. ; Tac. ;
aliquid animo, Ov. With *Indir. Quest. :*
Cic., Juv. **c.** *to pay a penalty* (*to the full*),
suffer a punishment : Acc. ; scelerum
poenas, Verg. ; poenas capite, Tac. [It.
spendere.]

expēnsus, a, um [*Part.* expendō], *paid out,
spent.* In phr. : ferre alicui expensum
aliquid (*or* pecuniam expensam), *to charge
as paid out* to, *carry to the debt of* (opp.
acceptum *or* receptum) : Cic., Liv. ; also
t r a n s f. *to lend :* Cael. ap. Cic. Ep. As
Noun, **expēnsum,** ī, *n. money paid, payment :* bene ratio accepti atque expensi
inter nos convenit, Pl. ; in codicem expensum et receptum referre, Cic.

expergē-faciō, facere, fēcī, factum [expergō],
to awaken, rouse. **1.** L i t. : aliquem e
somno, Suet. **2.** T r a n s f. : caput, Lucr. ;
se. Cic. ; mele. Lucr. ; probrum, Pl.

expergiscor, pergīscī, perrēctus, *to awake.*
1. L i t. : Cic., Hor. **2.** T r a n s f. : Pl.,
Cic., etc.

ex-pergō, pergere, pergī, pergitum, *to awaken.*
1. Lit. : Acc., Tac. **2.** T r a n s f. : *to
awaken* from death : Lucr.

experiēns, entis, **I.** *Part.* experior. **II.**
A d j. **a.** *enterprising, active :* Cic., Ov.,
Liv. ; ingenium, Ov. *Sup. :* Cic. **b.**
With Gen., *ready to undergo :* Ov.

experientia, ae, *f.* [experior], *a trial, testing.*
1. L i t. **a.** aliquid experientiā temptare,
Varr. ; veri, Ov. **b.** *trial, endeavour :*
patrimoni amplificandi, Cic. **2.** T r a n s f. :
experimental knowledge, practical experience :
hominum, Verg. ; rerum, Tac. Without
Gen. : Verg., Tac.

experimentum, ī, *n.* [experior], *actual proof
from experience.* **a.** hoc maximum est
experimentum (with Acc. and *Inf.*), Cic. ;
lenitatis, Tac. **b.** *practical experience* (in
this sense us. *pl.*) : Metello experimentis
cognitum erat (with Acc. and *Inf.*), Sall. ;

nullis castrorum experimentis, Tac. ; experimento meo, Quint.

ex-perior, perīrī, pertus [cf. Gk. πεῖρα (for περ-ι-α), πειράω, periculum, comperire, reperire], to try fully, put to the test. **1.** Lit. **a.** In gen. : Cic. With Acc. of thing : eandem belli fortunam, Caes. ; vim veneni in servo, Cic. ; imperium, Liv. ; avis, Ov. ; iudicium discipulorum, Quint. With Acc. of person : Pl., Cic., Verg., etc. With Indir. Quest.: Pl., Cic., Liv. **b.** In law : to try or test by law, to go to law : aut intra parietes aut summo iure experietur, Cic. ; Liv. **c.** In Perf. tenses : to have tested and so learnt, to know by experience : Cic., Verg. With Acc.: Pl., Cic., Hor. With Acc. and Inf.: Pl., Caes., Liv., etc. **2.** Transf.: to try to do, attempt : istuc, Pl. ; omnia de pace, Caes. ; extremum auxilium, Caes. ; libertatem, Sall. ; ultima, Liv. With Inf.: Quint. With ut and Subj.: Cic. Ep., Nep. ; in me ut etc., Cic.

experrēctus, a, um, Part. expērgiscor.

ex-pers, tis, adj. [pars], having no part in, not sharing in. **1.** Lit.: Liv. With Gen.: Ter., Cic. **2.** Transf.: destitute or devoid of, free from, without. With Gen.: Pl., Cic., Ov., etc. With Abl.: Pl., Lucr., Sall.

expertus, a, um. **I.** Part. experior. **II.** Adj. **a.** Pass.: tried, proved, tested : virtus, Cic., Liv. ; artes, Tac. Sup.: Suet. **b.** Act.: experienced. With Gen.: Verg., Tac. With Abl.: Liv.

expetessō, ere [expetō], to desire, long for: Pl.

ex-petō, ere, īī or īvī, ītum, to make for earnestly, aim at, strive to reach, strive after eagerly. **1.** Lit. **a.** Trans.: Asiam, Cic. ; mare medium terrae locum expetens, Cic. **b.** Intrans.: to aim at, assail, fall upon. Transf.: ira in hanc, Pl. ; in eum omnes clades huius belli, Liv. ; id innocenti, Pl. **2.** Transf. **A.** Of time: to reach, attain to : bono si quid male facias, aetatem expetit, Pl. **B.** Of things as object : to aim at, long for, desire keenly. **a.** In gen.: Cic. With Acc.: Pl., Cic. With Inf.: Pl., Ov., Liv., etc. With Obj. Acc. and Pass. Inf.: Enn., Cic. Ep. With ut and Subj.: Pl. **b.** Of penalties, payments, etc : to require, demand, exact: pecuniam, Cic. ; mortem pro vitā civium, Cic. ; poenas ab aliquo, Cic. ; Liv. ; ius ab invitis, Liv.

expiātiō, ōnis, f. [expiō] satisfaction, atonement, expiation: scelerum, Cic. ; foederis rupti, Liv.

expictus, a, um, Part. expingō.

expīlātiō, ōnis, f. [expīlō], a pillaging, plundering: expilationes sociorum, Cic.

expīlātor, ōris, m. [expīlō], a pillager, plunderer, Cic. Ep.

ex-pīlō, āre, to pillage, rob, plunder thoroughly. **1.** Lit.: socios, Cic. ; thesauros, Liv. ; Cic. **2.** Transf.: to plagiarise from : aliquem, Cic.

ex-pingō, pingere, pīnxī, pictum. **I.** to paint out, paint over with paint : Plin., Mart. **II.** to paint exactly, paint to the life. Transf. (in words) : Cic.

ex-piō, āre, to purify from taint, reconcile after

pollution, cleanse ritually. **1.** Lit.: forum R. a sceleris vestigiis, Cic. ; fani religionem, Cic. ; puerum, Pl. **2.** Transf. **a.** Of bad omens, etc.: to avert their threat : prodigia, Cic., Liv. ; manis, Cic. ; iram caelestium, Liv. ; detestationem, Hor. **b.** Of crimes, etc.: to atone for, expiate : Caes., Cic., Liv., etc. ; tua scelera di immortales in nostros milites expiaverunt, Cic.

expīrō, v. exspīrō.

ex-piscor, ārī [ex, piscis : Lit. to fish out], to search out, ferret out : Ter. ; nihil, Cic. ; ab illo omnia, Cic. Ep.

explānātiō, ōnis, f. [explānō], a making plain, an explanation. **a.** In gen.: somniis explanationes adhibere, Cic. ; Quint. **b.** As a fig. of speech : Cic., Quint. **c.** clear pronunciation : verborum, Quint.

explānātor, ōris, m. [explānō], an explainer : Cic.

explānātus, a, um. **I.** Part. explānō. **II.** Adj.: plain, distinct : Cic.

ex-plānō, āre, to make completely level and plain. Transf. **a.** to set forth clearly or plainly : aliquid, Cic. ; pauca de illius moribus, Sall. With Indir. Quest.: Cic. **b.** to expound, make clear, explain : rem obscuram interpretando, Cic. ; carmen, Liv. **c.** to pronounce or utter clearly : verba, Plin. Pan.

explaudō, v. explōdō.

explēmentum, ī, n. [expleō], that which fills up. Of food : a filling, stuffing : Pl., Sen. Ep.

explendēscō, v. exsplendēscō.

ex-pleō, ēre, ēvī, ētum (contr. forms: explēris, Cic. ; explēssent, Liv.) [cf. plēnus, compleō, etc.]. **I.** to fill out or up. **1.** Lit.: aliquid, Pl., Lucr., Caes., Cic. ; aliquid aliquā re, Caes., Cic., Hor. **2.** Transf. **a.** to fill up, complete : numerum, Caes., Verg., Liv. **b.** to make good, repair (losses, deficiencies, etc.) : partem relictam, Cic. ; damna, Liv. **c.** Of wants, desires: to glut, satisfy, sate · sitim, Cic. ; ieiunam cupidinem, Lucr. ; desiderium, iram, Liv. ; Cic. ; Tac. ; animum gaudio, Ter. ; avaritiam pecuniā, Cic. ; se caede, Liv. ; Sall. ; corda tuendo, Verg. ; animum ultricis flammae, Verg. **d.** Of time, to fulfil, complete : annum, Cic. ; Tib. ; Tac. **e.** In measure, to complete : iustam muri altitudinem, Caes. ; quinque orbis cursu, Verg. ; summam talenti, Liv. ; centurias non explere (i.e. to fail to bring all to the poll), Liv. Also, sementis mollioribus numeris, Cic. **f.** to fulfil, discharge · amicitiae munus, Cic. **II.** to unload: navibus se, Enn.

explētiō, ōnis, f. [expleō], a satisfying : Cic.

explētus, a, um. **I.** Part. expleō. **II.** Adj.: full, complete : Cic.

explicātē, adv. plainly, clearly : dicere, Cic.

explicātiō, ōnis, f. [explicō], an unfolding, uncoiling. **1.** Lit.: rudentis, Cic. **2.** Transf. **a.** analysis : naturae, Cic. **b.** solution, interpretation : fabularum, Cic.

explicātor, ōris, m. and **explicātrix**, īcis, f. [explicō], an expounder, explainer : Cic.

explicātus and **explicitus**, a, um. **I.** Part. explicō. **II.** Adj. **A.** **explicātus**. **1.** Lit.: spread out : Cic. **2.** Transf.: plain, clear in detail : causa, Cic. Comp.:

Cic. Ep. **B. explicitus**, *disentangled, un-impeded :* hence *easy, simple. Comp. :* Caes.

explicātus, ūs, *m.* [explico], *an unfolding.* Transf.: *solution, interpretation* (in *pl.*) *:* Cic.

ex-plico̅, āre, āvī and ui (the latter in Verg., Hor., Liv., and post-Aug.), ātum or itum (Cic. uses mostly ātum, Caes. ātum and itum), *to unfold, unroll, unfurl.* **1.** Lit. **a.** velum. Pl. ; vestem, Cic. ; volumen, Cic. ; orbis serpens, Ov. ; frontem solli-citam, Hor. **b.** *to extend, display :* frondes (pampinus), Verg. ; ut forum usque ad atrium Libertatis explicaremus, Cic. Ep. In *Mid. :* Sall. **c.** Milit. *to extend, deploy :* ordinem, Liv. ; equites se turma-tim explicare coeperunt, Caes. ; aciem, Liv. ; cohortis, Verg. ; Hor. **2.** Transf. **a.** *to unravel* a complicated or difficult matter, *to disentangle, set in order, settle, adjust :* Pl., Cic., Hor., etc. **b.** By words : *to develop, unfold, set forth in detail,* and so, *to make clear and intelligible.* With Acc. : Cic., Verg., Liv. With *de :* Cic. With *Indir. Quest. :* Quint. **c.** *to disentangle, set free* (as from snares, etc.) : Siciliam, Cic. ; legatos fugā, Liv.

ex-plōdo̅ (explaudo̅), plōdere, plōsī, plōsum, *to drive out or off by clapping.* **1.** Lit. Of an actor, *to hoot off :* Cic., Hor. ; e scaenā, Cic. **2.** Transf. **a.** *to scare away :* noc-tem, Lucr. **b.** *to reject, discredit :* sen-tentiam, Cic. ; hoc genus divinationis vita explosit, Cic.

explo̅rātē̆, *adv. after careful investigation, on good grounds ; with certainty :* Cic. *Comp. :* Cic. Ep.

explo̅rātio̅, ōnis, *f.* [explōro], *espionage :* Tac.

explo̅rātor, ōris, *m.* [explōro]. **a.** In gen.: *a tracker, spy :* Pl. As Adj.: foci, Mart. **b.** Milit. : *a spy, scout, one of a reconnoitring party :* Caes., Tac. **c.** explorator viae : *one who ran before the emperor to clear the way :* Suet.

explo̅rāto̅rius, a, um [explōrātor], *given to scouts :* corona, Suet.

explo̅rātus, a, um. **I.** *Part.* explōro. **II.** Adj.: *established by investigation ;* hence *reasonably certain, sure :* victoria, Caes. ; exploratam habere pacem, Cic. ; pro explorato aliquid habere, Caes. ; explo-ratum habere (with Acc. and *Inf.*) : Cic. alicui est exploratum (with Acc. and *Inf.*): Cic. *Comp. :* Cic. Ep.

ex-plo̅ro̅, āre [Lit. : *to feel out the ground*], *to search out, investigate.* **1.** Lit. **a.** In gen.: caecum iter, Ov. ; locum castris, Caes. ; fugam, Cic. ; insidias, Verg. **b.** Milit.: *to spy out, reconnoitre :* loca atque tempora cuncta explorat, Sall. ; occulte explorare loca, Caes. ; Cic. With *Indir. Quest. :* Caes. ; ante explorato et subsidiis positis, Liv. **2.** Transf. **a.** rem totam, Cic. Ep. ; animum regis, Liv. With *de :* Nep. With *Indir. Quest. :* Liv. Esp. : in *Perf. Part.* ascertained *by investiga-tion, found out* (v. exploratus) : explorato (ABL. *Absol.*) iam profectos amicos, Tac. **b.** *to probe, search, put to the proof :* portas, Verg. ; robora fumus, Verg. ; secundae res animos, Tac. ; Ov.

explōsio̅, ōnis, *f.* [explōdo̅], *a driving off by clapping :* Cael. ap. Cic. Ep.

explōsus, a, um, *Part.* explōdo̅.

ex-polio̅, īre, īvī or ii, ītum, *to smooth off, polish.* **1.** Lit. : aedis, Pl. ; libellum pumice, Cat. **2.** Transf. **a.** *to polish, embellish, refine :* Dionem Plato doctrinis omnibus, Cic. ; Pl. ; Plin. Ep. ; orationem, Quint. ; consilium, Pl.

expolītio̅, ōnis, *f.* [expolio̅], *a complete smooth-ing off, rubbing up, polishing.* **1.** Lit. : urbana (*of a house in town*), Cic. Ep. **2.** Transf. of style : Cic.

expolītus, a, um. **I.** *Part.* expolio̅. **II.** Adj.: *polished, clean :* dens expolitior, Cat.

ex-po̅no̅, pōnere, posuī, positum (*perf.* exposuit, Pl. : *Part.* expostus, Verg.). **I.** *to put out or forth.* **a.** By force : ali-quem ictu, Pl. Of children : *to expose :* puellam ad necem, Pl. ; Cic. ; Liv. **b.** From a ship : *to set on shore, disembark :* milites ex navibus, Caes. ; de puppibus, Verg. ; in terram, Caes., Liv.; ad eum locum, Caes. ; in Africā, Liv. ; Sen. Ep. ; Suet. With ABL. : Caes., Ov. **c.** In situation (mostly in *Perf. Part.*), *exposed, abandoned :* rupes exposta ponto, Verg. ; ad ictūs, Liv. ; ne inermes provinciae bar-baris nationibus exponerentur, Tac. Transf.: ad pericula, Liv. ; ad invidiam, Tac. **II.** *to put forth, expose to view, dis-play.* **1.** Lit. **a.** In gen.: Caes., Cic., Verg., etc. **b.** Mercant. : rem venditioni, Tac. ; ei DCCC exposuisti (*offered*), Cic. Ep. **2.** Transf. **a.** *to set forth, pub-lish :* totam causam ante oculos, Cic. ; orationem, praemium, Cic. **b.** By words : *to set forth, exhibit, state :* obscura dilucide, Cic. ; Tac. ; narrationem, Cic. ; eadem multitudini, Caes. With Acc. and *Inf. :* Cic. With *Indir. Quest. :* Cic. ; also in ABL. *n.* of *Perf. Part. :* Caes., Liv. With *de :* Cic.

exporrēctus, a, um, *Part.* exporrigo̅.

ex-porrigo̅, rigere, rōxī, rēctum (contr. *Imper.* expōrge, Ter.), *to stretch out, spread out :* labellum, Pers. Comic.: exporge frontem, *smooth out your brow,* Ter. [It. *sporgere :* Sp. *espurrir.*]

exportātio̅, ōnis, *f.* [exporto̅], *exportation :* Cic.

ex-porto̅, āre, *to carry out.* **a.** In gen.: corpora luce carentum tectis, Verg.; Pl.; Cic., etc. **b.** *to export :* aurum ex Italiā, Cic.

ex-po̅sco̅, pōscere, popōscī, *to ask earnestly, beg, implore.* **a.** In gen.: misericordiam, Cic. ; signum proeli, Caes. ; pacem precibus, Liv. ; victoriam ab diis, Caes. With *ut* and *Subj. :* Liv. With Acc. of person and *Subj. :* Liv. With *Inf. :* Verg. **b.** In partic. : *to demand the surrender of :* aliquem, Nep., Liv. ; eum ad poenam, Tac.

expositīcius, a, um [expōno̅], *exposed* (of a foundling) : Pl.

expositio̅, ōnis, *f.* [expōno̅], *an exposing.* Rhet.: *a setting forth, narration :* Cic., Quint. In *pl. :* Cic.

expositus, a, um. **I.** *Part.* expōno̅. **II.** Adj.: *accessible.* Transf. **a.** *accessible, affable :* Plin. Ep. ; Luc. **b.** In a bad sense : *common, vulgar :* Juv. **c.** Of authors : *lucid :* Quint.

expostulātiō, ōnis, *f.* [expostulō], *an expostulation, complaint :* Cic., Tac. In *pl. :* Cic. Ep., Liv.

ex-postulō, āre. **I.** *to demand vehemently* or *urgently, to lay claim to :* auxilium, Pl. ; primas sibi partis, Tac. With *ut* and *Subj. :* Tac. With Acc. and *Pass. Inf. :* Tac. **II.** *to claim the surrender of :* aliquem ad supplicium, Tac. ; Suet. **III.** *to make a demand* or *claim against, hence to expostulate.* With *cum* and Abl. of person, and *de* and Abl. of thing : Ter., Cic. ; or Acc. of thing : Ter. ; or Acc. and *Pass. Inf. :* Pl. ; or *cur* and *Subj. :* Tac. ; with *quia* clause : Pl.

expostus, a, um. *Part.* expōnō.

expōtus, v. ēpōtus.

expressus, a, um. **I.** *Part.* exprimō. **II.** Adj. : *prominent, distinct, clear.* **1.** Lit. : Cic., Quint. **2.** Transf. : non expressa signa, sed adumbrata virtutum, Cic. ; Plin. Ep. *Comp. :* Cic. Of pronunciation : expressior sermo, Quint. ; litterae, Cic.

ex-primō, primere, pressī, pressum [premō]. **I.** *to press* or *squeeze out.* **1.** Lit. : lacrimulam, Ter. ; sudorem de corpore, Lucr. ; nubium conflictu ardor expressus, Cic. ; liquorem, Ov. Occ. of the object pressed or squeezed : Venus madidas exprimit imbre comas, Ov. **2.** Transf. : *to squeeze* or *wring out, extort :* ab aliquo nummulorum aliquid, Cic. Ep. ; ullam vocem, Caes. ; sponsionem nobis, Liv. ; confessionem, Liv. ; deditionem, Liv. With *Indir. Quest. :* Liv. With *ut* and *Subj. :* Cic., Liv. **II.** *to press upwards, elevate :* turris cottidianus agger, Caes. **III.** *to form by pressure, to model, form.* **1.** Lit. : expressa in cerā ex anulo imago, Pl. ; Hor. ; vestis singulos artūs exprimens, Tac. **2.** Transf. : *to represent, portray, imitate.* **a.** In words : Mithridaticum bellum, Cic. ; mores alicuius oratione, Cic. ; oratorem, Cic. With *Indir. Quest. :* Cic., Plin. Ep. **b.** Of translations : verbum de verbo expressum extulit, Ter. ; fabellae Latinae ad verbum de Graecis expressae, Cic. ; Cat. ; Plin. Ep. **c.** Of pronunciation : litteras, Cic. ; verba, Quint.

exprobrātiō, ōnis, *f.* [exprobrō], *a reproaching :* alicui alicuius rei, Liv. ; immemoris beneficî, Ter.

ex-probrō, āre [probrum], *to make quite into a reproach, to reproach, censure.* **a.** In gen. : Pl., Cic., Liv., etc. With Dat. of person and Acc. of thing : Cic., Ov., Liv. Occ. with *de :* mihi de uxore, Nep. With Acc. and *Inf. :* Pl., Liv. **b.** Sometimes the Acc. represents the person's own acts, etc., which have been insufficiently recognised by the person reproached ; *to blame for forgetting, etc. ; to bring up against* another : officia, Cic. ; virtutem suam in Philippi bello, Liv.

ex-prōmō, prōmere, prōmpsī, prōmptum, *to take forth* or *out (as from a store), to fetch out, bring forth.* **1.** Lit. : heminas octo in urceum, Pl. ; omnis apparatūs supplici, Liv. **2.** Transf. **a.** *to bring forth, give vent to* feelings : mente querellas, Cat. ; maestas voces, Verg. ; benignum ex tete

ingenium, Pl. ; in meo inimico crudelitatem, Cic. **b.** Of acts : *to exhibit, display :* supplicia in civis Romanos, Cic. ; laborem in cenis, Cic. **c.** *to disclose, declare, state :* occulta apud amicum, Ter. ; originem sacrorum, Liv. ; sententiam, Tac. With *Indir. Quest. :* Cic., Liv. With Acc. and *Inf. :* Tac.

expugnābilis, e, *adj.* [expugnō], *that may be taken by storm :* Liv. With Dat. : Tac.

expugnātiō, ōnis, *f.* [expugnō], *a taking by storm :* urbis, Caes. ; Cic. In *pl. :* nocturnae aedium (i.e. burglaries), Cic. Ep.

expugnātor, ōris, *m.* [expugnō], *one who takes by storm.* **1.** Lit. : urbis, Cic. **2.** Transf. : pudicitiae, Cic.

expugnācior, *comp. adj.* [expugnō], *more successful* or *effective :* herba, Ov.

ex-pugnō, āre, *to take by assault, to storm.* **1.** Lit. **a.** Of things : moenia mundi, Lucr. ; oppidum, Caes., Sall., Liv. ; navis, Caes. ; carcerem, Pl. ; Ter. ; Sall. **b.** Of persons : *to conquer in war :* Liv., Curt., Tac. **2.** Transf. **a.** *to conquer, subdue, overcome :* sapientis animum, Cic. ; pertinaciam legatorum, Liv. **b.** *to gain by contention, wrest, extort :* sibi legationem, Cic. ; quae tua virtus, expugnabis, Hor. With *ut* and *Subj. :* Cic. **c.** With *Cogn.* or *Internal Acc. : to carry to a successful finish :* coepta, Ov.

expulsiō, ōnis, *f.* [expellō], *a driving out, expulsion :* Cic. In *pl. :* Cic.

expulsō, āre [*freq.* expellō], *to drive out, to expel :* Mart.

expulsor, ōris, *m.* [expellō], *one who drives out, an expeller :* Cic., Nep.

expulsus, a, um, *Part.* expellō.

expultrix, īcis, *f.* [expellō], *she that drives out* or *expels :* Cic.

expūmō, v. exspūmō.

expūnctus, a, um, *Part.* expungō.

ex-pungō, pungere, pūnxī, pūnctum. **1.** Lit. : *to prick out :* Pl. **2.** Transf. **a.** *to prick out :* to cancel (by pricking out) : nomen, Pl. ; decurias iudicum, Suet. **b.** *to cancel, remove :* pupillum, Pers.

expuō, v. exspuō.

expūrgātiō, ōnis, *f.* [expūrgō], *a justification, vindication, excuse :* Pl.

expūrgātū, Abl. *sing. m.* [expūrgō], *in the exculpating :* non facile est expurgatu, Ter.

ex-pūrgō, āre, *to purge out, cleanse, purify.* Transf. **a.** *to cure :* me cicutae, Hor. **b.** *to purify :* sermonem, Cic. **c.** *to exculpate, vindicate, justify, excuse :* aliquem, Pl. ; Ter. ; Sall. ; aliquid, Tac.

ex-pūtēscō, ere, *to rot away :* Pl.

ex-putō, āre, *to lop off, clear up, prune.* Transf. **a.** *to consider well, to examine :* utramque rem simul, Pl. **b.** *to fathom, comprehend* (with *Indir. Quest.*) : Planc. ap. Cic. Ep.

exquaerō, v. **exquīrō.**

ex-quīrō, quīrere, quīsīvī, quīsītum (exquaeris, Pl. ; exquaesīverō, Pl.) [quaerō], *to search out thoroughly* or *carefully ; to seek for.* **1.** Lit. : iter, Caes. ; Sall. ; antiquam matrem, Verg. **2.** Transf. **a.** *to search out, inquire into, ascertain by inquiry :* sententias, Caes. ; veritatem, Cic. ; aliquid ex (or *de* or *ab*) aliquo, Cic. With *Indir.*

Quest. : Cic. *Impers. Pass.* with Acc. and *Inf.* : Pl. **b.** *to search fully, examine* : tabulas eorum, Cic. ; eius facta, Cic. ; aliquem, Pl., Ter. **c.** *to seek out, devise* : eis honores, Cic.

exquisītē, *adv. with studied care or close examination* : Cic., Quint. *Comp.* : Cic., Quint.

exquisītus, a, um. **I.** *Part.* exquīrō. **II.** A d j. **a.** *carefully studied or considered, choice, refined* : sententiae, verba, doctrina, munditia, Cic. ; iudicium litterarum, Cic. *Comp.* : Cic., Quint. *Sup.* : Cic. **b.** *carefully devised* : supplicia, Cic.

ex-rādīcitus, *adv. from the very roots* : Pl.

ex-sacrificō, āre, *to sacrifice fully* : hostiis, Enn.

ex-saeviō, īre, *to rage itself out, cease raging* : tempestas, Liv.

ex-sanguis, e, *adj.* **A.** P a s s. : *bloodless.* **1.** L i t. : Lucr., Cic., Verg., etc. Hence *pale* : metu, Ov. ; Verg. **2.** T r a n s f. Of style : Tac. **B.** A c t. : *making pale* : cuminum, Hor.

ex-sarciō (**-serciō**, Ter.), sarcīre, sartum, *to patch up.* T r a n s f. : *to repair, restore* : sumptum, Ter. ; Q. Cic.

ex-satiō, āre, *to satisfy fully, satiate, glut.* **1.** L i t. : exsatiati cibo vinoque, Liv. **2.** T r a n s f. : morte Scipionis exsatiari, Liv. ; Ov. ; Tac.

exsaturābilis, e, *adj.* [exsaturō], *that may be satiated* : nec exsaturabile pectus, Verg.

ex-saturō, āre, *to satisfy completely, satiate* : eius cruciatu animum, Cic. ; Verg. ; Ov.

exscendō, v. ēscendō.

exscēnsiō, v. ēscēnsiō.

exscidium, v. excidium.

ex-scindō, scindere, scidī, scīsum, *to tear out.* T r a n s f. : *to extirpate, destroy.* Of things : Cic., Verg., Liv. Of persons : Tac.

ex-screō, āre, *to cough up, to spit out* : Pl., Ov., Suet.

ex-scrībō, scrībere, scrīpsī, scrīptum. **I.** *to write out, make as a written extract* : complura de libris, Varr. **II.** **a.** *to note down* : nomina, Pl. ; sacra omnia, Liv. **b.** *to write out in full, copy out* : tabulas, Cic. Of paintings, *to copy* : Plin. Ep. T r a n s f. : *to copy or take after, to resemble* : filia totum patrem mirā similitudine exscripserat, Plin. Ep.

ex-sculpō, sculpere, sculpsī, sculptum [scalpō]. **I.** *to carve out, dig out* : foramina arborum, Cato ; aliquid e quercu, Cic. Ep. ; Quint. T r a n s f. : *to dig out, extort* : ex aliquo verum, Ter. With *ut* and *Subj.* : Pl. **II.** *to scratch out, erase* : hos versūs, Nep.

ex-secō (**exsicō**, Pl.), secāre, secuī, sectum *to cut out or away.* **1.** L i t. **a.** In gen. : Cic., Hor., Sen. Ep. **b.** *to castrate* : Cic., Luc. **2.** T r a n s f. **a.** *to cut out* (i.e. *exclude*) : Plin. Ep. **b.** *to cut out, deduct* : quinas hic capiti mercedes exsecat, Hor.

exsecrābilis, e, *adj.* [exsecror], *imprecatory* : carmen, Liv. ; *odium*, i.e. *bitter, merciless,* Liv.

exsecrātiō, ōnis, *f.* [exsecror], *execration, curses.* **1.** L i t. : Cic., Tac. In *pl.* : Cic. **2.** T r a n s f. : *a solemn oath combined with*

imprecations : Cic., Liv., Tac., etc. In *pl.* : Cic., Tac.

exsecrātus, a, um. **I.** *Part.* exsecror. **II.** A d j. : *accursed, execrable, detestable* : Cic. *Sup.* : Plin.

exsecror, ārī [ex and sacra, *to banish from sacred rites*]. **I.** *to curse, execrate* : aliquem, Cic. ; Liv. ; aliquid, Cic., Verg., Liv., etc. With *ut* and *Subj.* : Cic. With *in* and Acc. of person and *quod*-clause : in se ac suum ipsius caput exsecratus, quod etc. ; Liv. ; verba exsecrantia, Ov. **II.** *to take an oath with imprecations on oneself* : omnis exsecrata civitas, Hor.

exsectiō, ōnis, *f.* [exsecō], *a cutting out* : linguae, Cic.

exsectus, a, um, *Part.* exsecō.

exsecūtiō, ōnis, *f.* [exsequor]. **I.** *an accomplishing, performance* : negoti, Tac. **II.** Of discourse : *a discussion* : Quint., etc.

exsecūtor, ōris, *m.* [exsequor]. In law : *a prosecutor, an avenger* : offensarum, Suet.

exsecūtus, a, um, *Part.* exsequor.

exsequiae, ārum, *f. pl.* [exsequor]. L i t. : *the following of a corpse beyond the walls ; a funeral procession, funeral obsequies* : cohonestare, prosequi, Cic. ; iusta exsequiarum, Cic. ; exsequiis rite solutis, Verg. ; exsequias ire, Ter., Ov.

exsequiālis, e, *adj.* [exsequiae], *of a funeral* : carmina, Ov.

ex-sequor, sequī, secūtus (3rd pers. pl. *Pres. Indic.* exsecuntur, Liv.). **I.** *to follow out or accompany to the grave* : aliquem omni laude et laetitiā, Poet. ap. Cic. **II.** *to follow, accompany to the end.* **1.** L i t. : Pl. ; cladem illam fugamque, Cic. ; sectam, Cat. ; Tarquinium igni ferro, Liv. **2.** T r a n s f. **a.** *to prosecute, continue, maintain* : id usque ad extremum, Cic. ; ius suum, Caes. ; incepta, Liv. ; obsidiones, Tac. ; sermonem cum aliquo, Pl. ; orationem, Cic. ; suam spem, sua consilia, Liv. With *Inf.* : Pl. With *ut* and *Subj.* : Pl. With ABL. *gerund* : percontando or quaerendo, i.e. *to follow up with a question,* Liv. Colloq. *to go through with, undergo* : egestatem, aerumnam, mortem, etc., Pl. ; fatum Pompei, Cic. Ep. **b.** *to follow up, carry out* (commands, duties): mandata, Cic. ; iussa, praecepta, Verg. ; regis officia, Cic. **c.** *to go through, relate, describe* : Cic. Ep., Verg., Liv., etc. **d.** *to follow up, pursue* with vengeance : violata iura, Liv. ; dolorem, Liv. ; Tac. ; Plin. Ep.

ex-serō, serere, seruī, sertum, *to undo, disconnect, hence to put forth, thrust out.* **1.** L i t. : bracchia aquis, Ov. ; manum ad mentum, Liv. ; linguam ab inrisu, Liv. Esp. in *Perf. Part.* : *thrust out, protruding from the body, uncovered* : dextris umeris exsertis, Caes. ; unum exserta latus Camilla, Verg. **2.** T r a n s f. **a.** *to put forth, exercise* : exseram in librum tuum ius, quod dedisti, Plin. Ep. **b.** *to reveal, show.* With Acc. and *Inf.* : Phaedr. With *Predic. Noun* : Suet.

exsertō, āre [*freq.* exserō], *to thrust forth repeatedly* or *fiercely* : Scyllam ora exsertantem, Verg.

exsertus, a, um, *Part.* exserō.

ex-sībilō, āre. **I.** *to hiss out* or *forth* :

aliquid, Sen. **II.** *to hiss off an actor :*
Cic., Suet.

exsiccātus, a, um, **I.** *Part.* exsiccō. **II.**
Adj. (of style): *dry, jejune :* orationis
genus, Cic.

ex-siccō, āre. **I.** *to dry up :* arbores, Cic.
II. *to drain dry* (a bottle): Q. Cic. ; vina
cutullis, Hor.

exsicō, v. exsecō.

ex-signō, āre, *to mark out, record exactly :*
omnia, Pl. ; sacra omnia, Liv.

ex-siliō, silīre, silui [saliō], *to spring out or
forth, to spring or leap up, to start up.* **1.**
Lit. Of living beings : Pl., Cic., Ov. With
ex : Pl. With *de :* Cic. With ABL.:
Hor., Ov. With *ad :* Ter. With *in* and
ACC.: Verg. **2.** Transf. Of things :
lumen, Lucr. ; oculi, Ov. ; a Cicerone
eloquentia, Sen. Ep.

exsilium, i, *n.* [for exsulium, fr. exsul], *banishment, exile* (voluntary or involuntary).
1. Lit.: in exsilium ire, proficisci, exigere,
eicere, pellere, expellere, Cic. ; in exsilium
mittere, Liv. ; de exsilio reducere, Cic. Ep. ;
so with revocare, Liv. ; with redire, Pl. ;
ab exsilio revocare, Tac. **2.** Transf. **a.**
a place of exile, a retreat : Cic., Tac. ; in
pl. : Verg. **b.** In *pl. : those who are
banished, exiles :* Tac.

ex-sistō, sistere, stitī, stitum. **I.** *to step out
or forth, to come forth.* **1.** Lit.: e latebris,
Liv. ; ab inferis, Cic., Liv. ; speluncā, Cic. ;
Ov. ; vox ab aede Iunonis ex arce, Cic.
2. Transf. *to appear, exist, be :* in animis
maiores varietates, Cic. ; timeo ne in eum
exsistam crudelior, Cic. Ep. **II.** *to come
into being, arise suddenly, spring forth,
become.* **1.** Lit.: vermes de stercore,
Lucr. ; palma ex pavimento, Caes. ; a
mediā fronte cornu, Caes. ; fiamma, Cic.
2. Transf.: bellum, Cic., Liv. ; malacia,
Caes. ; ex luxuriā avaritia, Cic. ; ex amicis
inimici, Cic. ; magna inter eos controversia,
Caes. ; ex quo exsistet ut etc., Cic.

exsolūtus, a, um, *Part.* exsolvō.

ex-solvō, solvere, solvī, solūtum (exsoluā-
tur, Lucr. ; exsoluisse, Ov.). **I.** *to loose,
unloose, unbind, undo completely.* **1.** Lit.
a. restim, Pl. ; nexūs, Lucr. ; nodum,
Liv. ; catenas, Tac. ; pugionem a latere,
Tac. **b.** *to dissolve :* (ignis) exsolvit
glaciem, Lucr. ; exsoluta alvo, Tac. **c.** *to
break open, wound :* bracchia ferro, Tac.
d. With ACC. of person and ABL. of thing :
to set free, release : Pl., Lucr., Verg., Tac.
2. Transf. **a.** *to loosen, throw off the
restraint of :* legis nexūs, Tac. ; obsidium
(i.e. *to raise*), Tac. **b.** *to solve, explain :*
with *Indir. Quest. :* Lucr. **c.** *to release,
free :* artis religionum animos nodis, Lucr. ;
animos religione, Liv. ; curis, Verg. ;
Cic. Ep. ; Tac., etc. **II.** *to discharge, pay
in full :* pretium, Pl. ; mea nomina, Cic.
Ep. ; multiplicem sortem, Liv. ; legata,
Tac. Transf.: exsolvit quod promi-
serat, Cic. ; ius iurandum, fidem, Liv. ;
beneficia, Tac. ; poenas alicui, Liv. [It.
sciogliere, sciorre.]

exsomnis, e, *adj.* [somnus], *sleepless, wakeful :*
Verg.

ex-sorbeō, ēre, *to suck up, suck dry.* **1.** Lit.:
pectora, Ov. **2.** Transf.: civilem san-

guinem, Cic. ; difficultates, Cic. ; animam
amborum, Pl.

ex-sors, sortis, *adj.*, *without a lot.* **a.** *given
or chosen without the drawing of lots :* Verg.
b. With GEN.: *having no share in, free
from :* Verg., Hor., Liv., Tac.

ex-spatior, ārī, *to go out of the course.* **1.**
Lit.: flumina, equi, Ov. **2.** Transf.:
to digress : Quint.

exspectābilis, e, *adj.* [exspectō], *to be looked
for.* With neg.: Tac.

exspectātiō, ōnis, *f.* [exspectō], *a looking for,
awaiting, expecting, expectation :* praeter
exspectationem, Cic. ; in exspectatione
esse, Pl., Caes. ; exspectationem facere,
sustinere, Cic. ; destituere, Liv. ; decipere,
Cic. ; aliquem in summam exspectationem
adducere, Cic. ; caecā exspectatione pendere, Cic. With *Obj.* GEN.: Caes., Cic.,
Quint. In *pl. :* Cic. With *de :* Cic. Ep.
With *Indir. Quest. : a waiting to see :* Cic.

exspectātus, a, um. **I.** *Part.* exspectō.
II. Adj.: *looked for, awaited, longed for,
welcome :* Pl., Cic., Verg., etc. Phr.:
ante exspectatum, *sooner than was looked
for :* Verg., Ov., Sen. Ep. *Comp. :* Pl.
Sup. : Cic. Ep., Hirt.

ex-spectō, āre. Lit.: *to look out.* Hence,
to wait and watch. **a.** In gen.: *to want to
see, to wait.* With *Indir. Quest. :* Pl.,
Caes., Cic., etc. With *si* (and *Subj.*) : Pl.,
Caes. With *dum* (and *Subj.*) : Pl., Caes.,
Cic., Hor., etc. With *ut* (and *Subj.*) : Pl.,
Caes., Cic., Liv., etc. *Impers. Pass.* :
Caes., Tac. With *quin* (after neg.) : Caes.
With ACC. *to await* (with persons or things as
Object) : Pl., Cic., Ov., etc. With abstract
Subject : Hor. **b.** *to expect with desire,
fear, etc.* ; *to look for, long for ; to
apprehend.* With ACC. (of thing) : Pl.,
Caes., Cic., Liv., etc. With ACC. (of
person) : Pl., Cic., Ov., etc. With *ab* (or
ex) and ABL. of source *from which :* aliquid
ab aliquo, Cic., Liv. ; aliquid ab liberalitate
alicuius, Caes. ; aliquid ex aliquo, Cic.
With *Obj.* ACC., and *Pres. Inf. :* Cic. With
ACC. and (*Fut.*) *Inf. :* Ter., Liv. **c.**
Poet.: almost *to have need of, require :*
neque illae (oleae) exspectant falcem,
Verg.

ex-spergō, spergere, spērsum [spargō], *to
sprinkle all over.* **1.** Lit.: sanie, Verg.
2. Transf.: *to diffuse :* exspergi quo
possit vis animal, Lucr.

ex-spēs, *adj.* (only in NOM. *sing.*), *without
hope:* Hor., Ov. With GEN.: Acc., Tac.

exspīrātiō, ōnis, *f.* [exspīrō], *a breathing out,
exhalation :* terrae, Cic.

ex-spīrō, āre. **A.** Trans.: *to breathe out,
to exhale.* **1.** Lit.: animam medios in
ignis, Ov. ; fiammas pectore, Verg. ;
odorem de corpore, Lucr. **2.** Transf.:
to emit, cause to spring forth : cadavera
vermis, Lucr. **B.** Intrans. **a.** *to blow
forth :* vis, Lucil. ; ignis, Lucr. ; vis fera
ventorum, Ov. **b.** *to breathe one's last, to
expire :* Verg., Hor., Liv., etc. In metaph.:
res publica, Liv.

ex-splendēscō, splendēscere, splenduī, *to
shine forth, glitter.* Transf.: Nep., Suet.

ex-spoliō, āre, *to strip, pillage, plunder completely.* **1.** Lit.: fana atque domos, Sall. ;

sese, Cic. **2. Transf.**: exercitu et provinciā Pompeium, Cic. Ep. ; Caes. **Comic.**: inprobis se artibus, Pl.

ex-spuŏ, spuere, spuī, spūtum, *to spit out, to spit.* **1.** Lit.: Varr. ; vina, Juv. **2.** Transf.: *to cast out, eject, emit.* **a.** mare (te) spumantibus undis, Cat. ; piscis humum, Ov. Comic.: lacrumam unam, Pl. **b.** *to banish :* miseriam ex animo, Ter., Lucr.

ex-sternŏ, ĕre [*cf.* cōnsternāre], *to startle, scare, stampede; to terrify, affright:* aliquem adsiduis luctibus, Cat. ; equos, Ov.

ex-stillŏ, āre, *to drop or trickle out :* Pl., Ter.

exstimulātor, ōris, m. [exstimulŏ], *an inciter :* alicuius, Tac. ; rebellionis, Tac.

ex-stimulŏ, āre, *to prick, to goad hard.* Transf.: *to excite, stimulate :* aliquem dictis, Ov. ; animum, Tac. ; exstimulatur a libertis, ut ostenderet, Tac.

exstinctiŏ, ōnis, f. [exstinguŏ], *extinction, annihilation,* Cic.

ex-stinctor, ōris, m. [exstinguŏ]. **I.** *an extinguisher :* incendi, Cic. Transf.: belli, Cic. **II.** *an annihilator, destroyer :* patriae, Cic.

ex-stinguŏ, stinguere. stinxī, stinctum (*Aor. Opt.* exstinxit, Pl. ; *Perf. contr.* exstinxtī, Verg.), *to put out, quench, extinguish.* **1.** Lit.: lumen, Lucr. ; incendium, Cic. Ep. ; ignem, Ov. ; sol exstinguitur, Cic. **2.** Transf. **a.** *to deprive of life or strength, to kill, destroy :* aliquem, Cic., Verg., etc. ; animam alicui, Ter. ; iuvenem fortuna morbo exstinxit, Liv. **b.** *to abolish, destroy :* rumores, Caes. ; gloriam rei militaris, Caes. ; leges, amicitias, invidiam, etc., Cic. ; famam, veritatem, Liv. [*Fr. éteindre.*]

exstirpŏ, āre [stirps], *to pluck up by the root, to root out.* **1.** Lit.: arbores, Curt. ; pilos de corpore, Mart. **2.** Transf.: vitia, Cic. ; ex animo humanitatem, Cic.

ex-stŏ, stāre (*Fut. Part.* exstātūrus, Plin.), *to stand out or forth.* **1.** Lit.: capite solo ex aquā, Caes. ; cervi vix cornibus, Verg. ; altius ab aquā, Liv. ; scopulus aquis, Ov. ; super aequora, Ov. **2.** Transf. **a.** id quod est inluminatum, Cic. *Impers.*: with *Indir. Quest.* or *Acc.* and *Inf.*; rare): Cic. **b.** *to be visible ; to be extant, to exist still.* Of persons : Pl., Hor., Liv. Of things (concr. or abstr.): Cato, Cic., Quint.

exstrūctiŏ, ōnis, f. [exstruŏ], *a building up, erecting :* tectorum, Cic.

exstrūctus, a, um, *Part.* exstruŏ.

ex-strūŏ, struere, struxī, structum. **I.** *to pile or heap up.* **1.** Lit.: mensas opulis, Cic. ; Pl. ; Hor. ; canistra, Hor. ; aggerem, Caes. ; mare (aedificiis), Sall. **2.** Transf.: animo altitudinem excellentiamque virtutum, Cic. **II.** *to make by piling up, build up, raise :* tumulos, Caes. ; acervum, aedificium, sepulcrum, etc., Cic. ; Tac.

exsūctus, a, um. **I.** *Part.* exsūgŏ. Adj.: *dried up :* Sen. Ep. *Comp.* : Varr.

ex-sūdŏ, āre. **A.** *Intrans.* *to come out by sweating, to exude :* umor, Verg. **B.** Trans.: *to discharge by sweating.* Transf.: *to toil over :* causas, Hor. ; certamen, Liv.

ex-sūgŏ, sūgere, sūxī, sūctum (*Fut.* exsūgēbō, Pl.), *to suck out :* umorem, Varr. ; sanguinem alicui (alicuius), Pl.

ex-sul, ulis, m. f. [ex, solum], *a banished person, exile.* **1.** Lit.: Caes., Cic., Ov., etc. With GEN. : Hor. With ABL. : Sall. **2.** Transf.: exsul mentis, Ov.

exsulŏ, āre [exsul], *to be an exile, to live in banishment.* **1.** Lit.: Pl., Cic., Liv. **2.** Transf. **a.** Of things : avaritia ex urbe, Pl. ; res publica, Cic. **b.** Of persons : animo, Cic.

exsultātiŏ, ōnis, f. [exsultŏ], *a springing up.* Transf.: *excessive rejoicing, exultation :* Tac.

exsultim, adv. [exsiliŏ], *with frolic or frisking :* Hor.

exsultŏ, āre [*freq.* exsiliŏ], *to spring vigorously, leap or jump about.* **1.** Lit.: Lucr., Cic., Ov., etc. **2.** Transf. **a.** Of inanimate subjects : sanguis, Verg. ; latices aestu, Verg. ; breves (syllabae), si continuantur, exsultant, Quint. **b.** *to exult, rejoice exceedingly ; to run riot :* laetitiā, gaudio, insolentiā, victoriā, Cic. ; Verg. ; Liv. ; Tac. ; in ruinis alicuius, Cic. ; furor, oratio, laetitia, Cic. **c.** Of speech, *to range freely, or at liberty :* Cic., Quint., Tac.

exsuperābilis, e, adj. [exsuperŏ], *that can be overcome :* non exsuperabile saxum, Verg.

exsuperantia, ae, f. [exsuperŏ], *pre-eminence, superiority :* virtutis, Cic.

ex-superŏ, āre. **A.** *Intrans.*: *to mount up, tower on high.* **1.** Lit.: flammae, Verg. **2.** Transf.: *to get the upper hand, to prevail, excel.* Of persons : Ov. ; virtute, Verg. Of things : sol, vapor, dolor, Lucr. **B.** *Trans.*: *to surmount.* **1.** Lit.: iugum, Verg. ; Sen. Ep. **2.** Transf. **a.** *to surpass, exceed :* Tarquinios superbiā, Liv. ; Ov. ; laudes alicuius, Liv. **b.** *to overpower, overcome :* materiā viris exsuperante meas, Ov. ; caecum consilium, Verg.

ex-surdŏ, āre [surdus], *to deafen.* Transf. of taste : *to dull, blunt :* palatum, Hor.

ex-sūrgŏ, sūrgere, surrēxī. **I.** *to stand up and go out :* foras, Pl., Cic. Milit.: ex insidiis, Liv. **II.** *to rise up.* **1.** Lit.: a genibus, Pl. ; Cic. ; altior, Verg. ; acies in collis, Tac. **2.** Transf. **a.** In revolt : Liv., Tac. **b.** *to rise up, recover :* causa, Cic. ; res publica, Cic. Ep.

ex-suscitŏ, āre, *to rouse from sleep, awaken thoroughly.* **1.** Lit.: Pl. ; te gallorum cantus, Cic. **2.** Transf. **a.** Of fire : *to fan, kindle :* flammas exsuscitat aura, Ov. ; Liv. **b.** Of the mind : *to stir up, rouse :* quae cura exsuscitat animos, Cic.

exta, ōrum, n. pl. [prob. *Neut. pl.* of old *Part.* of exsecŏ], *the important organs of the body* (the heart, lungs, liver): Pl. ; interpretari, Cic. ; reddere Marti, Verg. ; dare, Liv. ; spectare, Curt. (It was from the *exta* of animals sacrificed that the haruspices drew their divinations.)

ex-tābēscŏ, tābēscere, tābuī, *to waste or pine away.* **1.** Lit.: fame, Suet. **2.** Transf.: opiniones diuturnitate, Cic.

extāris, e, adj. [exta], *used for cooking the exta :* aula (i.e. olla), Pl.

extemplō (extempulo, Pl.), *adv.* [ex templō. Lit. *on the spot ; cf.* ex tempore], *straightway, forthwith, on the spur of the moment* (once in Cic.) : Pl., Verg., Liv. ; quom extemplo, etc., *as soon as,* Pl. ; èxtemplo . . . mox . . . postremo, Liv. Correl. with *quando :* Pl., Ter. ; with *ut* (= *when*) : Verg. ; with *ubi :* Pl.

extemporālis, e, *adj.* [ex tempore], *on the spur of the moment, extemporary :* oratio, Quint. ; facultas, Suet.

extemporālitās, ātis, *f.* [extemporālis], *the faculty of extemporaneous speaking or versifying :* Suet.

extempulō, v. extemplō.

ex-tendō, tendere, tendī, tentum and tēnsum, *to stretch out, spread out, extend.* **1.** Lit. **a.** vincla escaria, Pl. ; bracchium, Cic. ; capita tignorum, Caes. ; pennas, funem, Hor. ; eum moribundum, Verg. In *Mid.* : Verg., Ov. **b.** *to widen, broaden, enlarge :* agros, stagna, Hor. ; itinera, Liv. ; munimenta, Curt. ; epistulam, Plin. Ep. **2.** Transf. **a.** *to extend, increase, enlarge :* famam factis, Verg. ; cupiditatem gloriae, Liv. ; spem in Africam, Liv. ; nomen in ultimas oras, Hor. **b.** *to strain* (*one's powers*) : se supra viris, Liv. ; cum se magnis itineribus extenderet, Caes. **c.** In time : *to extend, prolong :* aetatem, Pl. ; pugnam ab horā tertiā ad noctem, Liv. ; Suet. ; aevum, Hor. ; curas venientem in annum, Verg. [It. *stendere, stendardo ;* Sp. *estandarte ;* Fr. *étendard.*]

extēnsus, a, um, *Part.* extendō.

extentō, āre [*freq.* extendō], *to strain.* **1.** Lit. : nervos, Lucr. **2.** Transf. : viris, Pl. ; se, Pl.

extentus, a, um. **I.** *Part.* extendō. **II.** Adj. : *extensive, wide :* Lucr., Quint. *Sup. :* Liv.

extenuātiō, ōnis, *f.* [extenuō], *a thinning out.* Transf. : *a lessening* (as figure of speech) : Cic., Quint.

extenuātus, a, um. **I.** *Part.* extenuō. **II.** Adj. : *thinned, reduced :* copiolae meae sunt extenuatissimae, Brut. ap. Cic. Ep.

ex-tenuō, āre, *to thin out, make thoroughly thin, fine, or small.* **1.** Lit. **a.** dentibus extenuatur cibus, Cic. ; aër extenuatus, Cic. ; extenuari in aquas, Ov. **b.** Milit. : mediam aciem, Liv. **2.** Transf. : *to make light of, lessen, diminish :* suum munus, Cic. ; crimen, Cic. ; viris, Hor. ; curas, Ov. ; famam belli, Liv.

exter or **exterus,** tera, terum [ex, with compar. suffix], *on the outer side, outward, external, foreign, strange.* **A.** Posit. : vis, Lucr. ; hostis, Cic. ; esp. in phr. exterae nationes, exterae civitates, Caes., Cic., etc. **B.** *Comp. :* **exterior,** ius, *outer, exterior :* Cic., Hor., Liv. **c.** *Sup. :* **extrēmus** and **extimus.** Form **extrēmus,** a, um, *outermost, utmost, extreme, at the end.* **1.** Lit. Of place or position : Caes., Cic., Hor., Liv. *Neut.* as Noun : finitum est, habet extremum, Cic. With *Part.* GEN. : in extremo montis, Sall. ; Caes. ; Cic. In *pl.* : extrema agminis, Liv. **2.** Transf. **a.** Of time or order : *latest, last :* Cic., Hor., Liv., etc. ; *Neut.* as Noun : extrema pati (*to bear the final doom*), Verg., Tac. ; die

(= diei) extremum erat, Sall. *Neut.* Acc. as *Adv. :* **extrēmum :** *for the last time :* adloquor extremum maestos amicos, Ov. ; **ad extrēmum,** *at last,* Caes. ; Cic. ; Ov. **extrēmō** (LOCAT. as Adv.), *at last, finally :* Nep. **b.** Of quality or degree. (i) *utmost, extreme :* extremam famem sustentare, Caes. ; extremae dementiae est, Sall. ; ad extrema iura decurrere, Cic. As Noun : ad extrema descendere, Pollio ap. Cic. Ep. ; res publica in extremo sita, Sall. ; ad extrema ventum foret, ni etc., Liv. Adv. : improbus homo, sed non ad extremum perditus, Liv. (ii) '*vest, vilest, meanest :* mancipia, Sen. Ep ; alimenta vitae, Tac. ; ingenium, Liv. Form **extimus,** a, um, *outermost, farthest, most remote* (rare) : orbis, Cic. ; Pl. ; Lucr.

ex-terebrō, āre, *to bore out.* **1.** Lit. : ex auro aliquid, Cic. **2.** Transf. : *to extort :* istuc ut etc., Pl.

ex-tergeō, tergēre, tērsī, tērsum, *to wipe thoroughly, clean.* **1.** Lit. : Pl., Cato. **2.** Transf. : *to clean out, plunder :* fanum, Cic.

exterior, ius, v. exter.

exterius, adv. v. extrā.

ex-terminō, āre [terminus], *to drive beyond the boundaries ;* hence **1.** Lit. : *to drive out or away :* aliquem ex urbe, Cic. ; de civitate, Cic. ; a suis dis penatibus, Cic. ; urbe atque agro, Cic. **2.** Transf. : *to put aside :* quaestiones physicorum, Cic. ; auctoritatem vestram e civitate, Cic.

externus, a, um [exter], *outward, external, coming from outside.* **a.** In gen. : Cic., Hor., Ov. **b.** Esp. with respect to family or country : *foreign, strange :* auxilia, Caes. ; bella, Liv., Quint. ; religio, Cic. ; gens, Verg. ; amor, Ov.; mores, gratiae, Tac. As Noun : canum odium in externos, Cic. ; externa moliri, Tac. ; Cic.

ex-terō, terere, trivī, trītum. **I.** *to rub out, get by rubbing :* extritus viribus ignis, Lucr. **II.** *to wear away.* **a.** *by rubbing :* Varr. Transf. : Quint. **b.** *by treading :* Varr., Ov. Transf. : Sen. Ep.

ex-terreō, ēre. **I.** *to frighten out :* somno, Enn. **II.** *to frighten, scare thoroughly ; to terrify, affright* (most freq. in *Pass.*) : praeter modum exterreri, Cic. ; repentino periculo exterriti, Caes. ; legiones exterruit vultur, Tac. ; novitate exterritus, Lucr. ; anguis exterritus aestu (*frenzied, dazed*), Verg.

extērsus, a, um, *Part.* extergeō.

exterus, v. exter.

ex-texō, ere. Lit. : *to unweave ;* hence, *to plunder, cheat :* Pl.

ex-timēscō, timēscere, timui, *to become greatly afraid of, to await with fear, to dread.* **A.** Intrans. : Ter. With *de :* Cic. With ABL. of Cause : Cic. With *ne* and *Subj.* : Cic., Hor. *Impers. Pass. :* Tac. **B.** Trans. : patrem, Ter. ; rerum casūs, Caes. ; magistrum, Hor. ; periculum ab aliquo, Cic.

extimus, v. exter.

extispex, icis, *m.* [exta speciō], *one who inspects the entrails, a diviner :* Cic.

extispicium, i. *n.* [extispex], *an inspection of entrails for the purpose of divination :* Suet.

ex-tollō, ere, *to lift up.* **1.** Lit. **a.** in gremium liberorum genus, Enn. ; onera in iumenta, Varr. ; alte pugionem, Cīc. **b.** Of building : *to raise up, erect :* Pl. **2.** Transf. **a.** *to raise, lift up :* meritum alicuius verbis, Cic. ; Pl. ; hostem verbis, Liv. ; animos honoribus ad superbiam, Tac. ; hortos insigni magnificentiā, Tac. ; aliquem supra ceteros, Tac. ; aliquid in maius, Liv. **b.** *to put off, defer :* res serias ex hoc die in alium diem, Pl.

ex-torqueō, torquēre, torsī, tortum, *to twist out, wrench out, wrest away.* **1.** Lit. **a.** In gen. : arma e manibus, Cic. ; tibi sicam de manibus, Cic. **b.** *to wrench out, put out of joint, dislocate :* articulum, Sen. Ep. ; membris extortus, Plin. Ep. ; Juv. ; in servilem modum extorti, Liv. ; extorque, nisi ita factum'st, Ter. **2.** Transf. **a.** *to take away by force, to extort :* obsides, Caes. ; pecuniam, Cic. ; nihil a miseris, Cic. **b.** Of abstract things : ex animis cognitiones verborum, Cic. ; alicui errorem, Cic. ; Hor. ; ei regnum, Liv. ; sententias de manibus iudicum, Cic. ; suffragium populi, Liv. ; vitam vis morbida membris, Lucr. With *ut* and *Subj. :* Cic.

extorris, e, *adj.* [ex and terra], *driven out of one's country, exiled, banished :* Cic., Liv With ABL. of separation : Sall., Liv.

extortor, ōris, *m.* [extorqueō], *an extorter :* bonorum, Ter.

extortus, a, um, *Part.* extorqueō.

extrā (old Lat. extrād), *adv.* and *prep.* [old ABL. *sing. fem.* fr. ex and suffix -tero-, *cf.* intrā, etc. ; but also perh. ABL. *fem.* of exterus]. **A.** Adv. : *on the outside, without.* **1.** Lit. Of place : Caes., Cic., Hor., etc. With verbs of motion : Cic., Quint. *Comp. :* extērius, Ov. **2.** Transf. : *except :* esp. with quam, or quam si : *except that, unless that :* extra quam in reum capitis praeiudicium fiat, Cic. ; Liv. **B.** Prep. with Acc.: *outside of, without, beyond.* **1.** Lit. of place : Caes., Cic., Hor. ; after its Noun in Tac. With verbs of motion : Pl., Caes., Cic. **2.** Transf. **a.** With abstracts, *outside, free from, out of :* esse extra noxiam, Ter. ; extra famam noxae, Liv. ; extra vitia, Tac. ; extra numerum, Pl., Cic., Hor. ; extra ordinem, Cic. ; extra cottidianam consuetudinem, Caes. ; extra iocum, Cic. Ep. **b.** Colloq. : *excepting, except* (for praeter) : extra unum te, Pl. ; extra ducem paucosque praeterea, reliqui in bello rapaces, Cic. Ep. ; Liv.

extractus, a, um, *Part.* extrahō.

ex-trahō, trahere, traxī, tractum, *to draw, drag, pull out.* **1.** Lit. **a.** Of things : rete ex aquā, Pl. ; telum e corpore, Cic. ; Liv. ; de vulnere, Ov. **b.** Of persons : extrahitur domo, Cic. ; aliquem vi in publicum, Liv. ; aliquem cubili, Tac. **2.** Transf. **a.** Of things : urbem ex periculis, Cic. ; (scelera) ex tenebris in lucem, Liv. ; ex animis radicitus religionem, Cic. **b.** Of persons : hostis invitos in aciem, Liv. ; rure in urbem, Hor. **c.** In time : *to drag out, prolong :* res variis calumniis, Cic. Ep. ; certamen usque ad noctem, Liv. ; pugnam in posterum, Tac. ; bellum in tertium annum, Liv. Occ. : *to waste :* triduum disputa-

tionibus, Caes. ; tempus morando, Liv. ; aestatem, Caes., Liv.

extrāneus, a, um [extrā], *that which is outside, external, extraneous, strange.* **a.** In gen. : Cic. **b.** In partic. : *foreign, strange, not related :* as Noun, *a stranger :* Liv., Tac., Suet. [Fr. *étrange.*]

extra-ōrdinārius, a, um, *out of the usual course, unusual, special.* **1.** Lit. : imperium, petitio, pecuniae, etc., Cic. ; honos, Caes. ; cohortes, cura, etc., Liv. **2.** Transf. : cupiditates, Cic.

extrārius, a, um [extrā], *outward, external.* **a.** In gen. : lux, Lucr. ; res, Cic. **b.** Of family relationship : *strange, unrelated :* Ter., Quint.

extrēmitās, ātis, *f.* [extrēmus], *the extremity, end :* Cic. Rhet. as figure of speech : Quint.

extrēmus, a, um, v. exter.

ex-trīcō, āre (and -or, ārī, Pl.) [trīcae], *to disentangle, extricate.* **1.** Lit. : extricata cerva plagis, Hor. **2.** Transf. **a.** *to unravel, clear up :* Pl., Varr., Vatin. ap. Cic. Ep. **b.** *to get with difficulty :* mercedem, Hor.

extrin-secus, *adv.* [LOCAT. Adv. extrim (fr. exter), and secus]. **I.** *from outside, from abroad :* in dicendo aliquid extrinsecus alicunde quaerere, Cic. ; imminens bellum, Liv. **II.** *on the outside :* animum circumdedit corpore et vestivit extrinsecus, Cic. ; Suet.

extritus, a, um, *Part.* exterō.

ex-trūdō, trūdere, trūsī, trūsum, *to thrust out or forth, to drive out, drive away.* **1.** Lit. : aliquem ex aedibus, Pl. ; aedibus, Pl. ; foras, Pl., Ter. ; a latebris, Tac. ; Cic. ; te in viam, Cic. **2.** Transf. **a.** *to force out, keep out by force :* saxa, Lucr. ; rerum novitate extrusa vetustas, Lucr. ; mare molibus, Caes. **b.** *to push off, get sold :* merces, Hor.

ex-tumeō, ēre, *to swell up :* Pl.

ex-tundō, tundere, tudī, tūsum. **I.** Of violence : *to beat out, strike out.* **1.** Lit. : calcibus frontem, Phaedr. **2.** Transf. **a.** labor fastidia, Hor. **b.** (= *to extort*) : Pl., Suet. **II.** Of the smith's work : *to beat out, hammer out.* **1.** Lit. : ancilia, Verg. **2.** Transf. : nobis hanc artem, Verg. ; aliquem continuatio, Quint. ; librum, Tac.

ex-turbō, āre, *to hustle out or off, to drive or thrust out or away.* **1.** Lit. **a.** (mostly of persons) : homines e possessionibus, Cic. ; Pl. ; cunctos aedibus, Pl. ; Cic. Occ. : *to put away* (a wife) : Tac. With matrimonio, Tac. **b.** Of things : *to knock out, tear away :* alicui oculos, Pl. ; pinum radicibus, Cat. **2.** Transf. **a.** *to expel :* aegritudinem ex animo, Pl. ; spem pacis, Liv. **b.** *to harass :* mentem, Cic. Ep. ; Stat.

ex-ūberō, āre, *to grow luxuriantly ; to be abundant, to abound.* **1.** Lit. : luxuriā foliorum umbra, Verg. ; spumis amnis, Verg. ; pomis annus, Verg. **2.** Transf. : eloquentia, Tac. ; Quint.

ex-ulcerō, āre, *to make sore, to cause to ulcerate.* Transf. : *to make to smart, exasperate :* ea, quae sanare nequeunt, exulcerant, Cic. ; exulcerati ignominiā animi, Liv. ; dolorem, Plin. Ep.

ex-ululō, āre, *to howl* or *cry out aloud :* Ov. *Perf. Part. ; invoked with loud cries :* Cybeleia mater Phrygiis exululata modis, Ov.

exūnctus, a, um, *Part.* exungō.

ex-undō, āre, *to flow out or over, to stream out.* **1.** L i t . : tura balsamaque in adversa litora exundant, Tac. **2.** T r a n s f . : ingenii fons, Juv. ; eloquentia, Tac.

ex-ungō, ungere, ūnctum, *to anoint freely :* Pl.

ex-uō, uere, uī, ūtum [ex and root meaning, *to put on, cover*], *to put off, strip off.* **A.** With Acc. of thing taken off. **1.** L i t . : serpens vestem, Lucr. ; alas, Verg. ; umero ensem, Verg. ; Hor. ; Ov. In *Mid. :* cornua exuitur, Ov. **2.** T r a n s f . : *to lay aside, cast off, divest oneself of :* humanitatem, Cic. ; silvestrem animum, Verg. ; mores antiquos, Liv. ; iugum, Liv. ; fidem, patriam, Tac. *Pass.* with Acc. and *Inf.* as subject : mihi quidem ex animo exui non potest, esse deos, Cic. **B.** With Acc. of that from which a thing is taken, and ABL. of thing taken : *to strip bare, despoil.* **1.** L i t . : Caes., Verg., etc. **2.** T r a n s f . : se iugo, Liv. ; hostem impedimentis, Caes. ; hostem castris, Liv. ; aliquem bonis, Tac. ; ex his te laqueis, Cic.

exurgeō, ēre, *to squeeze out :* Pl.

ex-ūrō, ūrere, ūssi, ūstum (-ūssum, Pl.). **I.** *to burn up.* **1.** L i t . **a.** *to burn up, burn to ashes :* oculos, Pl. ; aliquem vivum, Cic. ; vicos, Cic. ; classem, Verg. **b.** *to dry up :* agrum, Verg. ; Lucr. ; Sall. ; aliquem sitis, Lucr. ; Curt. **2.** T r a n s f . : *to consume, dry up :* exustus flos veteris ubertatis, Cic. **II.** *to burn out, remove by burning :* aliis infectum scelus, Verg. **III.** *to heat thoroughly :* antra caminis, Ov. T r a n s f . : *to heat, incense greatly :* divos, Tib.

exūssus, a, um, *Part.* exūrō.

exūstiō, ōnis, *f.* [exūrō], *a burning up :* exustiones terrarum, Cic.

exūstus, a, um, *Part.* exūrō.

exūtus, a, um, *Part.* exuō.

exuviae, ārum, *f. pl.* [exuō], *what is stripped or taken off.* **a.** *clothing :* Pl., Verg.. Suet. **b.** *the* (*stripped off*) *skin, hide of an animal ;* leonis, Verg. ; *the slough of a snake ;* Verg. C o m i c . : bubulae (*a whip of*), Pl. **c.** *spoils* stripped from an enemy, as armour, etc. : exuvias indutus Achilli, Verg. ; (locus) exuvias nauticis ornatus, Cic. In metaph. : tu ornatus exuviis huius, Cic.

F

F, f, the sixth letter of the Latin alphabet, occupies the same place as digamma in the Greek alphabet, to which it corresponds in form, though entirely different in phonetic character. **I.** Initial *f* in Latin takes its rise from I. E. *bh* or (less frequently) from *dh*, sometimes irregularly from I. E. *gh* (which is properly represented by Latin *h*). Hence it corresponds to Gk. φ or θ, and at times to Gk. χ. Thus we have Gk. φέρω

beside Lat. *fero.* On the other hand we have Gk. θήρ beside Lat. *ferus ;* Gk. θύρα Lat. *fores.* And again we have Gk. χρίω beside Lat. *frio. f* occurs but little in the middle of Latin words, in which place *b* usually corresponds to φ, as in *ambo* (ἀμφω), *nebula* (νέφος). Though *f* most commonly represents Gk. φ (when initial), it was phonetically different, and was not, like φ, an aspirate. Assimilation is seen in *offero, differo, effero,* for *obfero, dis-fero, ec-fero.* **II.** According to Grimm's law, Latin *f,* from *bh,* corresponds to *b* in Gothic, and to *p* (or *b*) in Old High German ; thus, Lat. *frater,* Goth. *brōthar,* O. H. G. *bruodar;* whilst, when it arises from *dh,* it corresponds to Goth. *d* and O. H. G. *t ;* thus, Lat. *fores,* Goth. *daúr* and Eng. *door,* O. H. G. *tor ;* and, when it arises from *gh,* to Goth. *g* and O. H. G. *k* (or *g*); thus Lat. *fel,* Eng. *gall,* O. H. G. *galla.* **III.** In the Romance languages *f* in general remains unchanged ; sometimes, however, it changes : (i) (when it begins a word) to *h ;* this occurs chiefly in Spanish, in which it is very common ; thus, Lat. *ferrum,* Sp. *hierro ;* Lat. *filius,* Sp. *hijo ;* Lat. *fabulari,* Sp. *hablar ;* Lat. *facere,* Sp. *hacer ;* it also appears in Fr. *hors* from Lat. *foris.* (ii) Rarely into *b :* Lat. *flocculus,* It. *bioccolo ;* Lat. *forfex,* It. *forbice.*

faba, ae, *f.* [*cf.* Gk. φακός, and perh. φαγεῖν], *the broad bean :* Pl., Cic., Verg., etc. ; istaec in me cudetur faba, i.e. I shall smart for it, Ter. [It. *fava ;* Fr. *fève.*]

fabālis, e, *adj.* [faba], *of beans, bean-*stipulae, Ov.

fabella, ae, *f.* [*dim.* fābula], *a brief narrative, a short story.* **a.** In gen. : Cic., Sen. Ep. **b.** *a short fable, a tale :* aniles, Hor. **c.** *a short play :* haec tota fabella, quam est sine argumento ! Cic. [It. *favella.*]

faber, bra, brum, *workmanlike, skilful :* ars, Ov. As Noun, **faber,** brī, *m.* (GEN. *pl.* us. fabrum : Caes., Cic. ; but also fabrōrum : Pl., Cic., *etc.*), *a workman.* **A.** In gen. : Pl., Caes., Cic. P r o v . : faber est quisque fortunae suae, Appius ap. Sall. **B.** In partic. : **a.** *a smith, carpenter :* Pl., Cic. With qualifying terms : faber tignarius, *carpenter,* Cic. ; fabri ferrarii, *blacksmiths,* Pl. ; marmoris aut eboris aut aeris, Hor. **b.** M i l i t . (in *pl.*): *sappers, engineers :* ex legionibus fabros delegit, Caes. ; praefectus fabrum, Caes. [Fr. *-fèvre* in *orfèvre.*]

fabrē, *adv. in a workmanlike manner ; skilfully :* Pl.

fabrē-faciō, facere, fēcī, factum, *to carpenter, build :* navigia, Liv. ; also *to forge :* argentum, Liv.

fabrica, ae, *f.* [faber], *the art, trade, or profession* of fabri : pictura et fabrica (*architecture*) ceteraeque artes, Cic. ; aeris et ferri, Cic. T r a n s f. **a.** *a work of skill :* membrorum animantium, Cic. C o m i c . : *a smart dodge :* facere, fingere, Pl., Ter. **b.** *a workshop, smithy,* Ter., Cic. [Sp. *forja ;* Fr. *forge, fabrique.*]

fabricātiō, ōnis, *f.* [fabricor], *a making, framing, construction with skill.* **1.** L i t . : hominis, Cic. **2.** T r a n s f. Cf style : Cic.

fabricātor, ōris, *m.* [fabricor], *an artificer,*

maker, *deviser*. **1.** L i t. : tanti operis (mundi), Cic. ; Ov. ; doli, Verg. **2.** T r a n s f. : morbus leti fabricator est, Lucr.

fabricor, ārī (Pl., Lucr., Cic., Tac.) and **fabricō**, are (Verg., Hor., Ov., Liv., etc.) [fabrica], *to construct, build, forge, create*. **1.** L i t. : Acc. ; gladium, signa, etc., Cic. ; navis, pontis, etc., Tac. ; cratera, tela, Ov. ; aliquid ad usum hominum, Cic. ; in nostros fabricata est machina muros, Verg. ; arma fabricaverat usus, Hor. **2.** T r a n s f. : verba, Cic. ; Pl. ; philosophia animum fabricat, Sen.

fabrilis, e, *adj.* [faber], *of or belonging to an artificer* : opera, Verg. ; scalprum, Liv. ; dextra, Ov. ; erratum, Cic. Ep. As Noun, **fabrīlia**, ium, *n. pl. tools* : Hor.

fābula, ae, *f.* [fārī], *a tale, story, subject of talk.* **A.** In gen. **1.** L i t. : poeticae, Liv. ; de te fabula narratur, Hor. ; fabula fias, Hor. ; Ov. **2.** T r a n s f. **a.** *conversation, talk* (in *pl.*) : Tac. P r o v. : lupus in fabulā, of a person who comes just as we are talking about him (*cf.* Eng. *talk of the devil*), Ter., Cic. Ep. ; lupus in sermone, Pl. **b.** Colloq. : *affair, concern, matter* : sed quid ego aspicio ? quae haec est fabula ? Pl. ; Ter. **B.** In partic. : **a.** *mere chatter, idle talk* : fabulae *! stuff ! nonsense !* Ter. **b.** *fiction, fictitious tale, myth* : Pl., Cic., Ov., etc. **c.** *a dramatic poem, drama, play* : Cic., Hor. ; facere, Varr. ; docere, Cic. ; dare, Ter., Cic. T r a n s f. : non solum unum actum, sed totam fabulam confecissem, Cic. **d.** *an apologue, fable* : Cic., Quint., Phaedr. **e.** *chatter, news* (in *pl.*) : Plin. Ep. [It. *favola* ; Sp. *fabla, habla* ; Fr. *fable*.]

fābulāris, e, *adj.* [fābula], *fabulous, legendary* : historia, Suet.

fābulātor, ōris, *m.* [fābulor], *a narrator, a story-teller* : Sen. Ep., Suet.

fābulor, ārī [fābula], **I.** *to speak, converse, talk, chat* : Pl., Suet. **II.** *to invent, say falsely* : aliquid, Liv. [Sp. *hablar*.]

fābulōsus, a, um [fābula], *fabulous, legendary* : Hor., Tac., etc. *Comp.* and *Sup.* : Plin.

fabulus, ī, *m.* [*dim.* faba], *a small bean* : Pl., Cato, Varr.

facessō, facessere, facessīvī, facessītum [*intens.* faciō]. **A.** T r a n s. : *to do eagerly or earnestly.* **a.** In gen. : *to despatch, perform, accomplish* : Enn. ; iussa, Verg. ; mille iocos, Ov. **b.** In bad sense : *to bring on, cause, occasion, create* : alicui negotium, Cic. ; innocenti periculum, Cic. ; Tac. ; rem, Pl. **B.** I n t r a n s. : *to hasten away, retire, depart* : Pl. ; ex urbe, ab ore atque oculis populi Romani, Liv. ; Cic. ; urbe, Liv. ; operae facessant, Cic.

facētē, *adv.* **I.** *brilliantly, elegantly* : Pl., Ter. ; Cic. **II.** *brilliantly, wittily, humorously* : Cic., Quint. *Comp.* : Cic. *Sup.* : Cic., Plin. Ep.

facētia, ārum, *f. pl.* (*sing.* **facētia**, ae, Pl.), [facētus]. **a.** *a brilliant, sprightly, or clever thing* : Pl. **b.** *brilliant remarks, witticisms, pleasantry, drollery, humour* : Cic., Tac.

facētus, a, um [*Act. Part.* fr. old verb formed fr. root of fax]. **A.** Of things : *brilliant,*

fine, elegant : facetis victibus vivere, Pl. **B.** Of behaviour : *fine, courteous, polite, genteel* : Pl., Ter., Hor. **C.** Of style : **a.** *fine, elegant* : molle atque facetum Vergilio adnuerunt Camenae, Hor. ; Quint. **b.** Of persons or their words : *elegant* : Cic. ; more freq. *witty, humorous* : Cic., Juv. *Comp.* : Lucil. *Sup.* : Cic.

faciēs, ēī, *f.* [perh. fr. faciō], *make, form, shape.* **1.** L i t. **A.** In gen. : **a.** Of persons : Pl., Lucr., Hor., Sen. Ep. In *pl.* : Verg. **b.** Of things : curvata in montis faciem circumstetit unda, Verg. ; haec facies Troiae erat, Ov. ; antequam Vesuvius mons ardescens faciem loci verteret, Tac. In *pl.* : Ov. **B.** In partic. : *face, visage, countenance* : Cic. ; de facie nosti, Cic. ; curvo nec faciem litore dimovet, Hor. ; quam liberali facie, Ter. ; torva, Verg., Ov. ; hispida, Hor. P o e t. : cura dabit faciem, facies neglecta peribit, *beauty*, Ov. **2.** T r a n s f. **a.** *external form, look, appearance, aspect* : urbis, Sall. ; Plin. Ep. ; senatūs, Cic. ; senum, Juv. **b.** *external appearance* (as opposed to reality) : *pretence, pretext* : publici consili facie, Tac. **C.** *aspect, nature, character* : ad istam faciem est morbus, Pl. ; honesti, Cic., Quint. ; scelerum, laborum, Verg. ; in hederae faciem frondescere, Ov. ; nuli, Curt. [It. *faccia* ; Sp. *faz* ; Fr. *face*.]

facilis, e, *adj.* [faciō : L i t. *that which can be done or made*], *easy to do, easy, free from difficulty.* **1.** L i t. **A.** In gen. : Pl., Cic., Verg., etc. *Comp.* : Cic. *Sup.* : facillimus, Pl., Cic., Quint. With *ad* (us. foll. by *Gerund*) : haec ad iudicandum sunt facillima, Cic. With ABL. of verbal Nouns in -u : facilia factu, Cic., Liv., Ter. ; cognitu, dictu, Cic. ; visu, Verg. *Comp.* : Ter. ; *Sup.* : Sall. With *Inf.* as Subject : quod illis prohibere erat facile, Caes. ; Ter. ; Quint. *Comp.* and *Sup.* : Quint. **B.** Of routes, sites, etc. : *easy, negotiable, suitable, convenient, well-adapted* : iter facilius atque expeditius, Caes. ; ascensus, aditus, etc., Caes. ; descensus Averno (DAT.), Verg. With *ad* : angustiae ad receptum faciles, Liv. ; materies ad exardescendum, Cic. ; credulitas feminarum ad gaudia, Tac. With DAT. : terra pecori, Verg. ; campus operi, Liv. With ABL. of verbal Noun : facilis victu gens, Verg. As Noun in phr. : in facili esse, *to be easy* : Liv. **C.** Of movement : *easy, mobile, nimble* : oculi, Verg. ; manus, corpus, Ov. **2.** T r a n s f. **a.** Of persons : *ready, quick* : facilis et expeditus ad dicendum, Cic. ; in excogitando, Quint. **b.** Of persons and character : *easy, good-natured, affable, tractable* : Ter., Cic., Verg., etc. With *in* and ABL. : Cic. With *ad* and Acc. : Cic. With *in* and Acc. : Ov. With GEN. of *Gerund.* : Liv. *Comp.* : Quint., Suet. *Sup.* : Cic. As Noun in *Adv. phr.* : ex facili : Tac. ; e facili : Ov. **c.** Of fortune, etc. : *favourable, prosperous* : res et fortunae tuae, Cic. Ep. ; Liv.

facile, *Neut.* Acc. as *Adv.* **A.** P r o p. : *easily, without trouble or difficulty* : Ter., Caes., Cic., etc. *Comp.* and *Sup.* : Caes., Cic. **B.** Less prop. : **a.** *easily, certainly, unquestionably, beyond dispute* (esp. with

superlatives and words denoting superiority):
Pl., Cic., Quint. Also of a sum of money :
huic hereditas facile ad HS. triciens venit
testamento propinqui sui, Cic. **b.** *readily,
willingly, without hesitation* : Ter., Cic.
Esp. in phr. : facile pati, Ter., Cic. *Comp.* :
Cic. Ep. **c.** *agreeably, well* : *Comp.* : Pl.
Sup. : Ter., Suet. [It. *facile* ; Sp. *facil* ;
Fr. *facile.*]

facilĭtās, ātis, *f.* [facilis], *easiness, ease,
facility, readiness.* **1.** Lit. **a.** In gen. :
Cic., Quint. **b.** Of speech : *facility* or
fluency : verborum, Quint. ; oris, Tac.
c. Of sites, etc. : *suitability* : camporum,
Tac. **2.** Transf. : of character. **a.** In
good sense : *readiness, willingness to oblige ;
good nature, affability* : Ter., Cic. ; sermonis, Cic. ; morum, Cic. **b.** In bad
sense : *levity, heedlessness* : Suet.

facinorōsus (or **facinerōsus**), a, um
[facinus], *criminal* (of persons) : Cic., Liv.
Sup. : Cic.

facinus, oris, *n.* [faciō], *a deed, action.* **A.** In
gen. (the nature of the deed being defined
by *Adj.*) : Pl., Ter., Caes., Cic., Tac. In
pl. : Cic., Sall., Liv. Colloq. : for res
or negotium ; quod facinus video ? Pl.
B. Of bad deeds. **1.** Lit. : *villainy,
crime* : facinus est vincire civem Romanum,
Cic. ; nihil facinoris praetermittere, Liv. ;
facere, committere, obire, Cic. ; in se
admittere, Caes. ; patrare, suscipere, Sall.
In *pl.* : Cic., Sall. **2.** Transf. **a.** *an
instrument of villainy,* said of a poisoned
cup : facinus excussit ab ore, Ov. **b.** In
pl. : *criminals, scoundrels* : Sall.

faciō, facere, fēcī, factum (*Imper.* face or fac ;
old *Fut.,* orig. *Aor. Subj.,* faxō, Verg., Liv. ;
Pass. faxitur, Liv. ; *Aor. Subj.,* orig. *Aor.
Opt.* faxim, Pl., Ter., Cic., Hor. For *Pass.*
v. fīō, fierī, factus) [fr. root seen in Gk.
τί-θη-μι, ἔ-θη-κα], *to do, make.* **I.** Intrans.
A. *to act.* **a.** *Absol.* : Nep., Ov. **b.** With
Adv., to act, behave, deal : Pl., Ter., Caes.,
Cic., Liv. **c.** With *cum* or *ab aliquo, to
act with* or *on the side of* : Cic. ; also *adversus
aliquem* : Nep. **d.** *to benefit, be of use* :
nec caelum nec aquae faciunt, Ov. Often
with alicui, ad aliquid (*cf.* Eng. *to do for*) :
nihil facit incolumi Rhodus, Hor. ; Prop. ;
frena minus sentit (equus) quisquis ad arma
facit, Ov. **e.** *to offer sacrifice* : Liv. With
Abl. of offering : Pl., Verg. With *Dat.*
of deity : Cic. Occ. with Acc. of offering :
Cic., Liv. Also in *Pass.* : cum pro populo
fieret, Cic. Ep. ; Liv. **f.** Instead of another
verb used in same sentence : diligenter,
sicut adhuc fecistis, attendite, Cic. ; Nep. ;
Hor. **B.** With *Internal* or *Cogn. Acc., to
do, take a line of action.* **a.** With *Neut.
Pron.* or *Adj.* (mostly *Interrog.*) : Cic.,
Verg., etc. Often with *Abl.* (rarely with
de), or *Dat.* : quid hoc homine facias ?
Cic. ; Pl. ; quid tu huic homini facias ?
Cic. ; Hor. ; quidnam facerent de rebus
suis, Nep. Also in *Pass.* : quid Tulliolā
meā fiet ? Cic. Ep. ; Pl. ; quid mihi fiet ?
Ov. ; de fratre quid fiet ? Ter. ; Pl.
b. Mercant. : *to carry on a trade or profession* : mercaturas, argentariam, Cic.
c. *to suffer, experience* : iacturam, detrimentum, naufragium, Cic. ; ne facias quod

Ummidius, Hor. **II.** Trans. (i.e. with
Acc. of what is made, produced or effected).
1. Lit. Of material things, *to make, form,
create* : pontem, castra, classem, Caes. ;
vasa, signa, carcerem, etc., Cic. ; tumulum,
horrea, Verg. ; tabernas, Liv. ; candelabrum e gemmis, Cic. ; signum de marmore,
Ov. Also of written compositions : epigramma, syngrapham, testamentum, Cic. ;
librum, Nep. ; carmen, Verg. And of
milit., polit., mercant. matters : cohortis,
Caes. ; centurias, Liv. ; auxilia mercede,
Tac. ; exercitum, Tac. ; comitia, iudicia,
Cic. ; pecuniam ex aliquā re, Cic. **2.**
Transf. **A.** *to make, form, create, perform,
carry into effect.* **a.** iter, Cic., Liv. ; fugam,
Sall., Liv. ; impetum in hostem, Cic., Liv. ;
eruptiones ex oppido, Caes. ; verba, Cic. ;
initium, finem, etc., Cic., etc. **b.** *to carry
out, perform, commit* : divinas res, sacra,
promissa, Cic. ; scelus, Tac. In *Pass.* : ut
fit, *as usually happens, as is commonly the
case* : Cic., Liv. ; so, qui fit ? how does it
happen ? Hor. ; fiat (an expression of
assent), *so be it,* Pl. Ter. **c.** *to make, cause, do,
bring about,* etc. **i.** With *Nouns* : coniura-
tiones, iniuriam, Caes. ; laetitiam, admirationem, etc., Cic. ; metum, timorem, Liv.,
Tac. ; silentia, Verg. ; amorem, somnos,
Ov. Freq. with *Dat.* : fidem alicui, Cic. ;
audaciam alicui, nomen alicui, Liv. ; umbram nepotibus, Verg. ; orationi audientiam, Cic. Esp. in phr. copiam or potestatem (alicui) facere, *to give opportunity* or
permission. **ii.** With *Subj., ut* or *ne* and
Subj., or *quin* (after negat.) : Pl., Ter.,
Cic. **iii.** With *Obj. Acc.* and *Inf.* : Varr.,
Verg., Ov. **B.** With Predic. extension,
to make a person or thing something. **a.**
With Noun or Adj. : aliquem reum, etc.,
Cic. ; Pl. ; Verg., etc. ; vectigalia sibi
deteriora, Caes. ; Cic., etc. Esp. in *Pass.* :
hi consules facti sunt, Cic., Liv. ; Tatius
ex hoste rex, Liv. **b.** With *Gen.* : *to
make* a thing *belong to* someone or something,
to put a thing *into a category* or *position* :
omnia quae mulieris fuerunt viri fiunt, Cic. ;
omnem oram Romanae dicionis fecit, Liv. ;
sui muneris rem publicam, Tac. **C.** Of
mental action. **a.** With *Gen.* : *to put into*
a category, to regard, value at such : *to*
pluris, Cic. Ep. ; rem aequi bonique, Cic. ;
dolorem nihili, Cic. ; Pl. ; Sall. ; Quint.
b. *to make, represent* to oneself or to hearers
or to readers : Xenophon facit Socratem
disputantem, Cic. ; se locupletem, Cic. ;
abominandam eam curiam facit, Liv. ;
me unum ex iis feci qui etc., Cic. With
Obj. Acc. and *Inf.* : Cic. Esp. in *Imper.* :
fac, *suppose* : fac animos non remanere
post mortem, Cic. ; fac potuisse, Cic. ;
fac velle, Verg. [It. *fare* ; Sp. *hacer* ;
Fr. *faire.*]

facteon, jestingly formed by Cicero, after the
analogy of the Greek verbals, for *faciendum.*

facticius, a, um [faciō], *made, artificial* :
colores, Plin.

factiō, ōnis. *f.* [faciō]. **I. a.** *a doing* : quae
haec factio est ? Pl. **b.** *a making, right of
making* : testamenti, Cic. **II.** *a company*

of persons acting together. **a.** In gen. : *a social group, set* : Pl. **b.** *a political party, clique, following* : Caes., Cic., Liv., Tac. **c.** *a party of charioteers and their supporters in the Circus* (of these there were four, named after their colours : albata, prasina, russata, veneta) : Suet. [It. *fazione* ; Sp. *faccion* ; Fr. *façon*.]

factiōsus, a, um [factiō]. **I.** *fond of doing, busy* : linguā factiosi, Pl. **II.** *connected with* or *favouring a party* or *faction* ; *supported by a party, having a large following* : Cic., Sall., Nep. *Sup.* : Plin. Ep.

factitō, āre. **1.** Lit. : *to make* or *do frequently, to be accustomed to make* or *do.* **a.** In gen. : vitium, Pl. ; haec, Cic. ; versūs, Hor. **b.** *to practise a trade* or *profession* : accusationem, Cic. ; delationem, Tac. ; coactiones argentarias, Suet. **2.** Transf. : *to make* or *declare a person something* : aliquem heredem, Cic.

factor, ōris, m. [faciō]. **I.** In ball-playing, *he who strikes the ball, the striker-out, batsman* (*cf.* datores, *servers, bowlers*) : Pl. **II.** *an oil-presser* : Cato.

factū, ABL. *sing.* m. [faciō] *in the making* : Varr. (v. also facilis, l. A.).

factus, a, um. **I.** *Part.* faciō. **II.** Adj. : factius nihilo facit, *he is no nearer bringing it to pass,* Pl. **III.** Noun : **factum,** i, n. *an accomplished fact ; a deed, act, exploit* (v. facinus) : Pl., Cic., Verg., etc. With *Adv.* (here factum is strictly a Participle) : neque recte ac turpiter factum celari poterat, Caes. ; recte, male facta, Cic. ; Sall. ; Liv. ; Quint. [It. *fatto* ; Sp. *hecho* ; Fr. *fait.*]

facul, *adv.* [facilis], *easily* : Acc., Lucil.

facula, ae, f. [*dim.* fax], *a little torch.* **1.** Lit. : Cato, Varr., Prop. **2.** Transf. : Pl. [It. *flaccola* ; Sp. *hacha*.]

facultās, ātis, f. [facul, *adv.* of facilis], *feasibility, practicability, power, means, opportunity.* **1.** Lit. : abite dum est facultas, Caes. ; facultatem dimittere, Caes. ; facultate uti, Cic. With GEN. : fugae, Caes. ; Cic. ; Quint. ; sui conligendi facultatem hostibus relinquere, Caes. ; facultatem iudicandi facere, Cic. ; facultatem dicendi parare, Quint. With *ad* : ad ducendum bellum, Caes. ; Cic. With *ut* and *Subj.* : Cic. **2.** Transf. **a.** *capacity, ability, mental resources* : ex his studiis haec crescit facultas, Cic. ; ingeni facultates, Cic. Ep. **b.** *material resources, means, supplies, abundance, stock, store* : omnium rerum, quae ad bellum usui erant, summa erat in eo oppido facultas, Caes. ; Cic. Esp. in *pl.* (often concr., *means*) : videndum ne maior benignitas sit quam facultates, Cic. ; singulorum facultates et copiae divitiae sunt civitatis, Cic. ; Italiae, Caes. ; comparare, Caes.

fācundē, *adv. eloquently* : Pl., Liv., Tac. *Sup.* : Sen.

fācundia, ae, f. [fācundus], *eloquence* : Pl., Sall., Hor., Tac., etc. (Fr. *faconde*).

fācunditās, ātis, f. [fācundus], *eloquence* : Pl.

fācundus, a, um [fāri], *having power of speech, speaking with natural fluency, fluent in speech.* **1.** Lit. : Pl., Sall., Ov. Tac.,

etc. *Comp.* and *Sup.* : Quint. **2.** Transf. Of things : oratio, Sall. ; vox, Ov. ; ingenia humana, Liv. ; libertas, Quint. *Sup.* : Quint.

faeceus, a, um [faex], *impure* : only in metaph. : mores, Pl.

faecula, ae, f. [*dim.* faex], *the lees of wine* (salt of tartar) : Lucr., Hor.

faenebris, e, adj. [faenus], *of interest* or *usury* : leges, Liv. ; Tac.

faenerātiō, ōnis, f. [faeneror], *a lending at interest, usury* : Cic.

faenerātō, *adv. with interest* : Pl.

faenerātor, ōris, m. [faeneror], *one who lends at interest, a money-lender, usurer* : Cato, Cic., Hor., etc.

faeneror, āri (and **faenerō,** āre, Ter., Liv., etc.) [faenus], *to lend at interest.* **1.** Lit. : binis centesimis faenerari (at 2 per cent. per month, 24 per cent. per annum), Cic. **2.** Transf. **a.** *to drain by usury* : provincias, Cic. **b.** *to loan on interest, trade in* : beneficium. Ter., Cic.

faeneus, a, um [faenum], *made of hay* : Cic.

faenīlia, ium, n. *pl.* [faenum], *hay-loft* : Verg., Ov.

faeniseca, ae, m. *a rustic* : Pers.

faenisex (**fēn-**), ecis, m. [faenum, secō], *a mower* : Varr.

faenum (**fēn-**), i, n. *hay* : Varr., Ov. Prov. : faenum habet in cornu (i.e. he is a dangerous fellow ; fr. the custom of binding the horns of vicious cattle with hay), Hor. [It. *fieno* ; Sp. *heno* ; Fr. *foin*.]

faenus (**fēn-**), oris, n. [perh. fr. root of fēcundus], *what is bred* ; hence *interest on money lent.* **1.** Lit. : et sors (*capital*) et faenus, Pl. ; pecunias faenori dare, Cic. ; pecuniam faenore accipere, occupare, Cic. ; solvent tolerabili faenore, Cic. ; nummos in faenore ponere, Hor. ; faenore omni solutus, Hor. Occ. **a.** *a debt* (due to excessive interest charged) : Sall., Liv. **b.** *capital lent on interest* : Pl., Cic. Ep., Tac. **c.** *putting out money to interest* : pecunias faenore auctitare, Tac. **2.** Transf. : *gain, profit, advantage* : Cic., Tib., etc.

faenusculum (**fēn-**), i, n. [*dim.* faenus], *a little interest* : Pl.

faex, faecis, f. *grounds, sediment, lees, dregs* of liquids. **1.** Lit. **a.** In gen. : poti faece tenus cadi, Hor. ; Lucr. **b.** Of wine : Hor. **c.** *the liquor* or *brine of pickles* : Ov. **2.** Transf. **a.** *sediment, impurity* : Ov. **b.** Socially : res itaque ad summam faecem turbasque residit, Lucr. ; populi, Cic. Ep. ; legationis, Cic. ; Juv. [It. *feccia* ; Sp. *hez* ; Fr. *fèces*.]

fāgineus (Cato, Ov.), **fāginus** (Verg., Ov.), **fāgeus** (Plin.), a, um [fāgus], *of beech, beechen.* [Fr. *faine*.]

fāgus, i, f. [*cf.* Doric φᾱγός, Attic φηγός], *a beech-tree* : Caes., Verg., Ov. [It. *faggio* : Sp. *haya*.]

fāla (**phala**), ae, f. **I.** *a wooden scaffolding used in sieges* : Enn. Prov. : isti, qui hastis trium nummorum causā subeunt sub falas (i.e. run a great risk for a slight gain), Pl. **II.** In *pl.* : *certain towers* or *pillars in the Circus* : Juv.

falārica (**phal-**), ae, f. [perh. fr. fala], *a sort*

of missile, covered with tow and pitch : Enn., Verg., Liv.

falcārius, ī, *m.* [falx]. *a sickle-maker :* Cic.

falcātus, a, um [falx]. **I.** *fitted with sickles, scythed :* currus, quadrigae, Liv. **II.** *sickle-shaped, curved :* ensis, Ov.

falcifer, era, erum [falx ferō], *scythe-bearing :* Ov. Epith. of Saturn : Ov.

Falernus, a, um [conn. with Faleriī in Etruria, Falisci], *Falernian :* ager (a district in N. Campania famous for its wine), Cic. As Noun : Falernum (*sc.* vinum), *Falernian wine :* Hor.

fallācia, ae, *f.* [fallāx], *deceit, trick, treachery :* Pl., Ter., Phaedr., Suet. In *pl.* : *tricks, stratagems :* Pl., Cic.

fallāciloquus, a, um [fallāx loquor], *speaking deceitfully* or *falsely :* malitiae, Acc.

fallāciter, *adv. deceitfully, fallaciously :* Cic. Sup. : Plin.

fallāx, ācis, *adj.* [fallō], *deceitful, treacherous, deceptive, fallacious.* **a.** Of persons : Cic., Ov. **b.** Of things : ut tamquam in herbis non fallacibus fructus appareat, Cic. ; arva, Ov. ; spes, Cic. ; nuntius, Liv. ; sensus oculorum, Cic. With GEN. : homines amicitiae fallaces, Tac. *Comp.* : Ov. *Sup.* : Cio.

fallō, fallere, fefellī, falsum [perh. conn. with Gk. σφάλλω, or with φηλήτης, *deceiver*]. **I.** *to set* or *put wrong.* **a.** In gen. : *to lead into error, make to err :* Euryalum fallit timor, Verg. **b.** *to put wrong in judgment, expectation, lead into (mental) error ; to blind, deceive, disappoint :* nisi me fallit animus, Caes. ; Liv. With *Refl. Pron.* or in *Pass.,* *to be wrong :* nisi me forte fallo, Cic. ; nisi (ni) fallor, Cic., Verg., etc. Also *Impers.* : fallit me, *I am mistaken,* Varr., Cic. **c.** With thing as Object : *to lead wrong, to disappoint :* meam spem vis improborum, Cic. ; Liv. ; opinionem alicuius, Caes., Cic. Ep. O cc. : *to fail to fulfil :* fidem hosti datam, Cic. ; Liv. ;. si sciens (fidem) fallo, Liv. ; mandata, Ov. ; promissum, Curt. **II.** *to deceive* (deliberately), *cheat, trick, dupe* (with or without dolo, fraude, etc.). **a.** Mostly in bad sense : Pl., Cic., Verg., etc. **b.** Poet. (bad faith implied) : dominum sterilis ager, Ov. ; Hor. **c.** *to beguile, cheat, wile away :* amorem, Verg. ; somno curam, Hor. ; medias sermonibus horas, Ov. **d.** *to cheat, prove treacherous to :* glacie pedes fallente, Liv. ; Curt. **III.** *to escape notice* or *observation, to lie concealed.* **a.** speculator, insidiae, Liv. With ACC. : Cic., Liv., Ov., etc. With *Part.* agreeing with Subject : ne hostis falleret ad urbem incedens, Liv. ; Verg. **b.** *Impers. :* fallit me (but us. with negat.), *I do not know,* Pl. Also with clause as Subject : **i.** With ACC. and *Inf.* : Ter., Cic. Ep., Liv. **ii.** With *Indir. Quest.* : Cic. **iii.** With *quin* (after negat.) : Caes. **IV.** Rare poet. usages : tu faciem illius tabe dolo (*counterfeit*), Verg. ; matris cineres operatos fallere (*to swear falsely by*), Hor. [It. *fallire ;* Fr. *faillir.*]

falsē, *adv.* (v. rare), *falsely, untruly :* Pl., Cic.

falsidicus, a, um [falsus dīcō], *speaking falsely, lying :* fallaciae, Pl.

falsificus, a, um [falsus faciō], *acting falsely, working deceit :* Pl.

falsiiūrius, a, um [falsus iūrō], *that swears falsely :* glossema, Pl.

falsiloquus, a, um [falsus loquor], *falsespeaking, lying :* Pl.

falsimōnia, ae, *f.* [falsus], *a trick, imposition :* Pl.

falsi-parēns, entis, *adj. having a pretended father :* Cat.

falsō, ABL. as *adv.* **I.** *by mistake, erroneously, wrongly :* Cic., Liv., etc. **II.** *by deceit, with fraud, falsely, untruly :* Pl., Caes., Cio., etc.

falsus, a, um. **I.** *Part.* fallō. **II.** Adj. **A.** *mistaken, wrong, erroneous.* **a.** Of persons : Sall., Liv. **b.** Of things : *mistaken, groundless, vain, empty :* opinio, spes, timor, etc., Cic. ; formido, gaudia, Verg. ; Hor. ; Ov. *Neut.* as Noun, *an error :* falsum de iure respondere, Cic. ; telis in falsum iactis (i.e. *without aim*), Tac. ABL. as *Adv.* : Cic., Liv., etc. **B.** Act. : *lying, deceiving :* testes, Cic. ; lingua, verba, avis, etc., Ov. ; vates, Liv. *Neut.* as Noun, *lying, falsehood, perjury :* falsi damnatus, Tac. ABL. as *Adv.* : Pl., Caes., Cio., etc. **C.** Pass. **a.** *falsified, false, feigned, untrue :* testamenta, etc., Cic. ; litterae, Cic., Liv. ; rumores, Caes. ; crimina, Hor. **b.** *spurious, unreal, sham* (of things) : Verg., Ov. **c.** Of persons : *sham, pretended, fictitious :* Cic., Ov. *Neut.* as Noun, *a lie, falsehood, untruth :* Cic., Ov., etc. [Fr. *faux.*]

falx, falcis, *f.* [cogn. with flec-tō]. **I.** *a sickle, reaping-hook :* Cato, Cic., Verg. **II.** *a pruning-hook* or *-knife :* Verg., Hor. **III.** *a hook used for pulling down walls :* Caes., Curt., Tac. [It. Sp. *falce ;* Fr. *faux.*]

fāma, ae, *f.* [fārī]. **I.** *mere talk ; the purport* or *substance of the common talk ; a report, rumour, saying, tradition :* Pl., Cic., Verg., etc. ; fama ferebat, Cic., Ov., Liv. ; fama adfertur, Caes. ; famam perferre ad aliquem, Caes. With *de :* Caes., Cic. With *Obj.* GEN. : Cic., Liv. With ACC. and *Inf.* : Pl., Caes., Cic. Liv. **II.** *public opinion :* Caes., Verg., Liv., Quint. **III.** *reputation* (defined) : bona, Pl., Cic. ; mala, Sall. ; obliti melioris famae, Verg. **IV.** *reputation* (undefined). **a.** In good sense : *fair fame, reputation, renown :* fama et existimatio, Cic. ; fama liberalitatis, Cic. ; Hor. ; belli, Liv. **b.** In bad sense (= infamia) : *ill fame, infamy :* Ter., Sall., Verg., Tac. **c.** *fame, glory, a name :* Nep., Verg., Liv., etc.

famēlicus, a, um [famēs], *hungry, famished, starved :* Pl., Ter., Juv.

famēs, is, *f.* [*cf.* Gk. χαίνω], *hunger.* **1.** Lit. **a.** Prop. : fame confici, famem tolerare, Caes. ; levare, Cic. ; fame interficere, Caes. ; Ov. ; propulsare, Tac. ; explere, Cic. **b.** *famine* (rare) : Cic., Curt. **2.** Transf. **a.** *poverty, indigence :* aliquem ad famem reicere, Ter. **b.** *poverty of expression* (opp. ubertas and copia) : Cic. **c.** *hunger* (or in Engl. *thirst*), i.e. *greed :* auri sacra fames, Verg. ; argenti, Hor. ; Curt. [It. *fame ;* Sp. *hambre ;* Fr. *faim.*]

fāmigerātiō, ōnis, *f.* [fāma gerō], *tale-bearing, hence a report, rumour :* Pl.

fāmigerātor, ōris, *m.* [fāma gerō], *a tale-bearer :* Pl.

familia, ae, (with pater, māter, fīlius, and fīlia, the archaic GEN. *sing.* familiās is more usual than familiae), *f.* [famulus], *the slaves in a household, a household-establishment, domestics.* **1.** L i t. : Pl., Caes., Cic., Quint. Of *slaves* belonging to a particular temple : Martis, Cic. Of *serfs* or *vassals :* Caes. E s p. : pater familias, mater familias, etc. (or as one word), *the master, mistress, etc. of a household :* Cato, Cic., Tac., etc. In *pl.* patres, etc., familias (or familiarum) : Caes., Cic., etc. **2.** T r a n s f. **a.** *a house and all belonging to it, a family-estate :* Ter., Cic. **b.** *a house, a family as part of a gens :* Pl., Cic., Sall., Liv. **c.** *a brotherhood, a fraternity, sect, troop, school :* Peripateticorum, gladiatorum, Cic. ; Pl. ; Suet. ; Fausti, Cic. ; ducere familiam, *to be the head* or *founder of a sect, etc.,* Cic.

familiāris, e, *adj.* [familia]. **1.** L i t. **a.** *of slaves* or *servants :* only as Noun, **familiāris**, is, *m. a slave, servant :* Pl., Liv., Sen. Ep. **b.** *of a house, household,* or *family ; domestic :* esp. in phr. res familiaris, *property,* Pl., Caes., Cic., etc. ; copiae, Liv. ; pecuniae, Tac. ; maeror, Pl. ; consilium, Liv. **2.** T r a n s f. **a.** *familiar, intimate, friendly.* Of persons : Cic., Plin. Ep. Of things : sermones, Cic. ; vultus, Cic. Ep. ; conloquium, Liv. *Comp. :* Cic., Nep., Liv. *Sup. :* Cic. As Noun, *a familiar acquaintance, intimate friend :* Caes., Cic. **b.** In divination, of those parts of the animal, *which related to the person sacrificing* (opp. hostilis) : Cic., Liv.

familiāritās, ātis, *f.* [familiāris], *familiarity, intimacy ; familiar intercourse, friendship.* **1.** L i t. : in alicuius familiaritatem venire, intrare, se insinuare, sese dare, Cic. ; in familiaritatem aliquem recipere, Cic. ; cum hospite, Cic. ; inter mulieres, Liv. In *pl. :* Cic. **2.** T r a n s f. : in *pl. :* for familiares, *intimate acquaintances, friends :* Suet. In *sing. :* Tac.

familiāriter, *adv. familiarly, on friendly terms :* Pl., Cic., Quint. *Comp. :* Cic., Quint. *Sup. :* Cic., Nep.

fāmōsus, a, um [fāma]. **A.** P a s s. : *much talked of.* **a.** In good or colourless sense : *celebrated, renowned :* Hor., Tac., etc. **b.** In bad sense : *infamous, notorious :* Pl., Sall., Ov., Tac., etc. **B.** A c t. : *defamatory, slanderous, libellous :* carmen, i.e. *a lampoon,* Hor. ; Tac. ; Suet. [Fr. *fameux*.]

famula, ae, *f.* [famulus], *a female slave, hand-maid, maidservant.* **1.** L i t. : Lucr., Verg. **2.** T r a n s f. : si virtus famula fortunae est, Cic.

famulāris, e, *adj.* [famulus], *of slaves* or *servants :* vestis, Cic. ; iura, Ov.

famulātus, ūs, *m.* [famulor], *servitude, slavery.* **1.** L i t. : Cic. **2.** T r a n s f. **a.** *a slave-establishment :* Tac. **b.** virtutis servientis voluptati, Cic.

famulor, āri [famulus], *to serve, attend upon* (rare) : Cic.

famulus, i, *m.* (older **famul**, Lucr.), *a house-slave, servant, house-carle.* **1.** L i t. : Pl., Cic., Verg., etc. **2.** T r a n s f. : *attendant, minister* (of the gods) : Idaeae matris

famuli, Cic. ; Liv. ; sacrorum, Ov. Also as *adj.* **famulus**, a, um, *serving, serviceable :* Ov., Luc.

fānāticus, a, um [fānum], *inspired, enthusiastic.* **1.** L i t. : Liv., Juv. **2.** T r a n s f. : *frantic, wild, frenzied :* philosophi, Cic. ; error, Hor. ; cursus, Liv.

fandus, a, um, v. fātur.

fānum, i, *n.* [for fas-num, fr. root seen in fēstus, fēriae], *a place consecrated to a deity* (by public pronouncement of the augurs) ; *a sanctuary, temple :* Lucr., Cic., etc.

fār, farris, *n.* spelt. **1.** L i t. : Cato, Ov., Liv., etc. In *pl. : grain :* Verg., Ov. **2.** T r a n s f. : *meal, grits :* Cato, Hor., Ov., etc.

farciō, farcīre, farsī, fartum [for fraciō, *cf.* Gk. φράσσω], *to fill full, stuff, cram :* pulvinus rosā fartus, Cic. ; Cato ; Cat., etc.

farfarus (**farferus**, Pl.), i, *m., the plant colt's-foot :* Plin.

farina, ae, *f.* [fār]. *ground corn ; meal, flour.* **1.** L i t. : Plin. **2.** T r a n s f. : **a.** *any powder :* Plin. **b.** *character, quality :* Pers. ; in metaph. : Suet.

farrāgō, inis, *f.* [fār], *mixed fodder for cattle, mash.* **1.** L i t. : Varr., Verg. **2.** T r a n s f. **a.** *a medley, hodge-podge :* nostri libelli, Juv. **b.** *a trifle :* Pers.

farrārius, i, *m.* [fār], *a hand-mill for corn :* Cato.

farrātus, a, um [fār]. **I.** *filled with corn :* Pers. **II.** *made of corn :* Juv.

fartim (or **fartem**), Acc. *sing.* as fr. fartis [farciō]. **I.** *stuffing :* vestis, Pl. **II.** *mincemeat :* fartem facere ex hostibus, Pl. **III.** *Adv. by stuffing :* App.

fartor, ōris, *m.* [farciō], *crammer* or *fattener of fowls, poulterer :* Ter., Cic., Hor.

fartus, a, um, *Part.* farciō.

fās, *indecl. n. divine word, law* (disting. from ius, *human law*). **1.** L i t. : contra fas, Cic., Sall. ; ius ac fas omne delere, Cic. Ep. ; exuere, Tac. ; fas et iura sinunt, Verg. ; leporem gustare fas non putant, Caes. ; sicut fas iusque est, Liv. O c c. **a.** *a sacred duty :* Liv. Personified : Liv. **b.** *divine will* or *ordinance, fate :* non esse fas Germanos superare, si etc., Caes. ; fas obstat, Verg. **2.** T r a n s f. : *right* (opp. *wrong*), esp. in phr. : fas est, *it is right, lawful :* Pl., Cic., Hor., etc. ; fas prohibet, Ov. ; ultra fas, Hor. ; fas omne abrumpit, Verg. ; fas gentium, Tac.

fascia, ae, *f.* [cogn. with fascis], *a band, bandage, swathe.* **1.** L i t. Of surgical bandages : Cic., Quint., etc. Of stockings : Cic. Of swaddling clothes : Pl. Of a breast-band : Ov. Of a bed-girth : Cic. **2.** T r a n s f. : *a swathe* or *streak of cloud in the sky :* Juv.

fasciātim, *adv. in bundles :* Quint.

fasciculus, i, *m.* [dim. fascis], *a small bundle, packet :* Cic. ; Hor.

fascinō, āre [fascinum], *to cast an evil eye upon, bewitch.* **1.** L i t. : Verg. **2.** T r a n s f. : *to envy, speak with envy of :* Cat.

fascinum, i, *n.* (**-inus**, i, *m.* Verg.) [*cf.* Gk. βάσκανος], *the evil eye, a bewitching, witchcraft.* **1.** L i t. : Plin. **2.** T r a n s f. : *a charm, amulet against the evil eye ;* hence for pēnis (fr. such use of its image) : Verg., Hor.

fasciola, ae, f. [dim. fascia], a small bandage : Cic., Hor.

fascis, is, m. **I.** a bundle, pack : Hirt., Verg., Tac., etc. **II.** In pl. **fascēs**: a bundle consisting of rods and (originally) an axe (carried by lictors before dictator, consul, and praetor). **1.** Lit.: Pl., Cic., Liv., Tac., etc.; cedere fascisque summittere, (i.e. acknowledge oneself inferior), Cic. **2.** Transf.: a supreme office, esp. the consulship : Lucr., Verg., etc. [It. fascio ; Sp. fajo, haz ; Fr. faix.]

fassus, a um, Part. fateor.

fasti, ōrum, v. fāstus.

fastidiō, ire [fastidium], to feel disgust or nausea ; to be squeamish, turn from anything unpleasant to the senses. **1.** Lit.: Pl., Hor., Sen. Ep. With Acc.: num fastidis omnia praeter pavonem ? Hor.; Quint. **2.** Transf. Of mental aversion : to be disdainful, scornful, haughty : Pl., Cic. With GEN. (like taedet): fastidit mei, Pl. With ACC.: to disdain, despise, scorn, turn from : Hor., Liv., Tac., etc. Of things : somnus agrestium lenis virorum non humilis domos fastidit, Hor. With Inf.: ne fastidieris nos in sacerdotum numerum accipere, Liv.; Ov., etc.

fastidiōsē, adv. squeamishly, fastidiously ; scornfully, disdainfully : Cic., Phaedr. Comp. : Cic.

fastidiōsus, a, um [fastidium], that feels disgust, squeamish, fastidious, **1.** Lit.: Pl., Varr. **2.** Transf.: fastidious, nice, disdainful, scornful : Antonius facilis in causis recipiendis erat, fastidiosior Crassus, Cic.; dominus terrae fastidiosus, Hor. Sup. : Plin. Ep. In good sense : very refined and delicate. Sup..: aurium sensus, Auct. Her. In Act. sense : cloying, tiring : fastidiosam desere copiam, Hor.

fastidium, i, n. [fr. fasti-tidium, earlier, taedium], distaste, disgust, squeamishness, loathing. **1.** Lit. **a.** Of taste : cibi satietas et fastidium, Cic. In pl. : magna movet stomacho fastidia, Hor. **b.** Of sight : oculorum in hominum insolentium indignitate fastidium, Cic. Ep. **2.** Transf. **a.** distaste, aversion ; fastidiousness, disgust : ab aliquā re fastidio quodam et satietate abalienari, Cic.; Quint., etc. In pl. : spectatoris fastidia ferre superbi, Hor. **b.** scornful contempt, haughtiness, disdain ; fastidium adrogantiamque fugiamus, Cic. In pl. : Verg., Tib.

fastigātē, adv. in a sloping position : Caes.

fastigātus, a, um. **I.** rising to a point : collis in acutum cacumen fastigatus, Liv. **II.** sloping down : collis leniter fastigatus, Caes. ; Liv.

fastigium, i, n. in arch., a pediment, the gable end of a roof. **1.** Lit.: Cic., Verg., Liv. **2.** Transf. **A.** a slope. **a.** Upwards : Caes., Liv. **b.** Downwards : Caes., Cic., Liv. **B.** In regard to measurement. **a.** From below, elevation, height : colles pari altitudinis fastigio, Caes. Of the top of a shield : Liv. In pl. : Lucr. **b.** From above, the depression, depth : forsitan et scrobibus quae sint fastigia quaeras, Verg. **C.** the highest point : exalted rank, dignity ; dictaturae semper altius fastigium fuit, Liv. ;

(M. Laetorio) curatio altior fastigio suo data est, Liv. ; tamquam mortale fastigium egressus, Tac. ; eloquentiae, Quint. **D.** a leading or chief point, head in a discourse : summa sequar fastigia rerum, Verg. **E.** a leading sort or kind : Varr. [Fr. faîte.]

fastus, ūs, m. scornful contempt, haughtiness, arrogance, disdain : Cat., Ov., Tac. In pl. : arrogant deeds : Verg., etc.

fāstus, a, um [fās], with dies : a day on which courts could be held ; a court-day. **1.** Lit.: Varr., Ov. In pl. : without dies : Cic., Liv. **2.** Transf. (in m. pl.) **a.** a register of court-days, festivals ; a calendar, almanac : Cic., Liv., Suet. As title of a poem : a poetical calendar, Ov. **b.** a register of the year's events, the records : Cic., Hor. **c.** a register of magistrates' names : Cic., Liv.

fāstūs, uum, m. pl. : a calendar (= fasti : v. fāstus, 2) : Varr., Luc.

fātālis, e, adj. [fātum], of fate or destiny ; preordained, fateful. **a.** continuatio ordinis sempiterni, Cic. ; deae, i.e. the Fates, Ov.; hora, Liv. ; libri, i.e. Sibyllini, Liv. ; iudex, Hor. ; ad salutem rei publicae, Cic. ; fatale est (with Acc. and Inf.) : Suet. **b.** In bad sense, bringing doom, deadly : vincla, Lucr.; telum, Verg.; monstrum (ref. to Cleopatra), Hor.

fātāliter, adv. according to fate, by fate : Cic., Ov., Tac., etc.

fateor, fatēri, fassus, [cf. fāri], to admit, own, acknowledge. **1.** Lit.: Pl., Cic., Verg., etc. With Acc. and Inf.: Pl., Cic., Hor., etc. With Acc.: Pl., Cic., Ov., etc. With de : Cic. With Indir. Quest.: Verg. **2.** Transf.: to make known, reveal : vultu iram, Ov.; Quint. With Indir. Quest. : Juv. With thing as subject : Juv.

fāticanus (and **-cinus**), a, um [fātum canō], fate-telling, prophetic : Ov.

fātidicus, a, um [fātum dīcō], that predicts fate, prophetic : Cic., Verg., etc. As Noun, **fātidicus**, a prophet : Cic.

fātifer, era, erum [fātum ferō], death-bringing, deadly : Verg., Ov.

fatigātiō, ōnis, f. [fatigō], weariness, exhaustion : Liv., Quint., Tac.

fatigō, āre [cf. adfatim], to weary, tire, exhaust. **1.** Lit.: (milites) magno aestu fatigati, Caes. ; Cic. ; Verg., etc. Of inanimate objects : navis fluctūs fatigat, Verg.; Ov., etc. **2.** Transf. **a.** to weary (with importunity), worry : aliquem precibus, Hor., Liv., Tac. **b.** to wear down, worry, harass, torment : aliquem vinclis et carcere, Cic. ; aliquem suppliciis, Sall. ; animam curis, Lucr. ; terrasque metu caelumque, Verg.

fātiloqua, ae, f. [fātum loquor], a prophetess : Liv.

fatiscō, ere (**fatiscor**, Lucr.), [cf. Gk. χαίνω, χάσμα, χατέω]. **I.** to gape, crack, split, give way : naves rimis, Verg. ; delubra deum, Lucr. **II.** to grow weary, become exhausted, droop from exhaustion (perh. fr. connexion of ideas of dissolution and exhaustion) : Acc., Lucr., Tac. With Inf. : Stat.

fātū, ABL. sing. m. [v. fātur], in the telling : haud mollia fatu, Verg.

fatua, ae, f. v. fatuus.

fatuitās, ātis, f. [fatuus], foolishness, silliness : Cic.

fātum, i, n. [v. fātur], *what is said, an utterance.* **1.** Lit.: *a divine utterance, oracle :*
Pac.; ex fatis Sibyllinis haruspicumque
responsis, Cic.; Liv.; Verg. **2.** T r a n s f.
a, *destiny, fate :* in philos. language, *the
eternal, immutable law of nature* (as dist.
fr. fors, *mere chance*) : fieri omnia fato ratio
cogit fateri, Cic.; fuit hoc sive meum sive
rei publicae fatum, Cic. In *pl. :* Verg.,
Hor., Ov. **b.** *the will or decree of the gods :*
huic fato divum proles virilis nulla fuit,
Verg. **c.** *that which causes the fate* of a
person or thing : Ilio tria fuisse audivi
fata, quae illi forent exitio, Pl.; duo illa rei
publicae paene fata, Gabinium et Pisonem,
Cic.; **Fata** (personified), *the Fates :* Prop.
d. *doom, fate, natural death :* sic Hortensi
vox exstincta fato suo est, Cic.; Liv.; fato
functus, Quint., Tac.; perfunctus fato,
Liv. In *pl. :* Ov., Quint. **e.** *bad fortune,
calamity, mishap :* suum fatum quere-
bantur, Caes.; quod si iam fatum extremum
rei publicae venit, Cic.

fātur, fantur, fāri, fātus (*Fut., fābor ;
Imper.,* fāre ; *Gerund,* fandī, fandō ; *Pres.
Part.,* fāns, fantem, fantis ; old *Inf.,* fārior
in Verg.) [*cf.* Gk. φημί, φάσκω], *to speak :*
ficto pectore fatur, Verg.; sic fatus, Verg.;
ne fando quidem auditum est, Cic.; Pl.;
Verg.; data copia fandi, Verg. With Acc. :
animus dementit deliraque fatur, Lucr.;
vix ea fatus eram, Verg.; Cic. With
Indir. Quest. : Verg.

fatuus, a, um [fr. root of fatīscō]. *gaping ;*
hence *idiotic, foolish, silly :* Pl., Ter., Cic.
As Noun, **fatuus,** i, m., **fatua,** ae, f. *a fool
or jester* (kept by Romans of rank) : Sen.
Ep. [Fr. *fat.*]

faucēs, ium, f. *pl.* (poet. also in the ABL.
Sing. : fauce, Ov.; Hor.) [fr. root of Gk.
χαῦνος, *gaping*], *the throat, pharynx, gullet.*
1. Lit.: Pl., Hor., Ov., Quint. **2.**
T r a n s f. **a.** *throat, jaws* (in metaph.) :
Timarchides premit fauces defensionis tuae,
Cic.; urbem belli ore ac faucibus ereptam
esse, Cic. **b.** Of a *chasm* : patefactis
terrae faucibus, Cic.; vorago aperit fauces,
Verg. **c.** Of a narrow way by land or sea,
neck, gorge, pass, isthmus, channel : Corinthus posita in angustiis atque in faucibus
Graeciae, Cic.; quā fauces erant angustissi-
mae portus, Caes.; Lucr.; Verg., etc. **d.**
Of the place from which the chariots were
started in races : Enn. [It. *fauci, foce ;*
Sp. *hoz.*]

Faunus, i, m. *a mythic personage, s. of Picus ;
institutor of tillage and grazing, and after his
death the deity of agriculture and of shepherds,
and also a giver of oracles :* **Faunī,** ōrum,
m. *pl. woodland gods, part human and part
animal ;* Fauns.

faustē, adv. *favourably, auspiciously :* evenire,
Cic.

faustitās, ātis, f. [faustus], *good fortune,
happiness ;* personified as a goddess :
Ceres almaque Faustitas, Hor.

Faustulus, i, m. *the shepherd who brought up
Romulus and Remus.*

faustus, a, um [for faves-tus from favor,
favōs, like hones-tus from honōs]. Lit. :
favourable ; hence *of favourable omen ;
fortunate, auspicious* (rare, exc. in formulae

of prayers) : quod bonum faustum felix
fortunatumque esset, Cic.; o nox illa fausta
huic urbi ! Cic.; tempus, Lucr.; omen,
Ov., Liv.

fautor (favitor, Pl.), ōris, m. [faveō], *a
favourer ; supporter, partisan, patron :* Pl.,
Hor., Suet. With *Obj.* GEN. (of person or
thing) : Cic., Hor., etc. With DAT. :
Lucil., Cic.

fautrix, īcis, f. [faveō], *a patroness, protectress.*
With GEN. : regio fautrix suorum, Cic.;
Ov. With DAT. : Thais nostrae omni est
fautrix familiae, Ter.

favea, ae, f., *a pet girl :* Pl.

faveō, favēre, fāvi, fautum, *to be favourable,
to be well-disposed towards ; to favour,
support, befriend.* **1.** Lit. : Cic., Verg.,
etc. With DAT. (of person) : Enn., Caes.,
Cic., etc. With DAT. (of thing) : Caes.,
Cic., Ov., etc. *Pass. Impers. :* Cic., Quint.
2. T r a n s f. **a.** In sacrifices and religious
ceremonies, favere linguis (rarely linguā),
ore, *to speak words of good omen only*
(= Gk. εὐφημεῖν) ; hence to *refrain from all
speech ; to be silent :* Cic., Hor., Ov.; ore
favete omnes, Verg.; Enn.; linguā, Juv.
b. With *Inf., to be eager :* Enn., Ov.

favilla, ae, f. [*cf.* foveō]. **1.** Lit. **a.** *glowing
ashes, embers :* Ter., Lucr., Verg., Suet.
b. *the still glowing ashes of the dead :* Verg.,
Hor., etc. **2.** T r a n s f. **a.** *ashes :* Verg.,
Ov. **b.** *spark* (i.e. beginning) : Prop.

favitor, ōris, v. fautor.

Favōnius, i, m. [prob. fr. root of foveō], *the
warming wind, the west wind* (also called
Zephyrus), which blew at the beginning of
spring, and promoted vegetation : Cic., Hor.

favor, ōris, m. [faveō], *favour, goodwill, support, partiality* (esp. of a party). **1.** In
gen. : favore populi tenetur, Cic.; amplecti
aliquem favore, Liv.; in aliquem, Tac. ;
in gratiam et favorem nobilitatis Iugurtha
venit, Sall.; conciliare, Suet. **2.** Partic.
a. *favour* as shown by applause : quem
favorem secum in scaenam attulit Panurgus,
Cic.; Verg., etc.; facere, emereri, promere,
Quint. **b.** *religious silence :* Ov.

favōrābilis, e, adj. [favor], *in favour, popular,
agreeable :* oratio, Tac.; Quint., etc.
Comp. : Plin. Ep.

favus, i, m. *a honeycomb :* Cic., Verg., etc.

fax, facis, f. [perh. *cf.* Gk. παι-φάσσω, *flash,
lighten*]. **I.** *a torch, flambeau, link.* **1.**
Lit. **a.** In gen. : Cic., Hor., etc. Also of
an *unlighted torch :* Verg., Liv., etc. **b.** At
weddings : *the torch carried before the
bride :* Pl., Cic., Verg., etc. Hence as a
symbol of Cupid : Tib., Prop., Ov. **c.**
Carried at funerals : Verg., Sen. Ep., etc.
Also used to light the pyre : Prop. **2.**
T r a n s f. **a.** In gen. : alicui ad libidinem
facem praeferre (*to act as torch-bearer,* i.e.
guide), Cic. **b.** *marriage :* Hor., Ov.
c. *death :* inter utramque facem (*between
marriage and death*), Prop. **II.** *a firebrand.*
1. Lit. **a.** In gen. : Caes., Cic., Tac.
b. As symbol of the Furies : Verg., Ov.
2. T r a n s f. : *firebrand.* **a.** Of *persons*
(i.e. *inciter, instigator*) : omnium incendiorum, Cic.; huius belli, Liv. **b.** Of
things (i.e. *incitement, stimulus*) : subicere
faces invidiae meae, Cic.; duas faces ad

plebem in optimatis accendandam, Liv. ;
Tac. **III.** *flame* or *light*. **1.** Lit. **a.** Of
the heavenly bodies (poet.) : canentes rite
crescentem face noctilucam, Hor. ; Lucr.
b. *a fiery meteor, shooting-star* : Lucr., Cic.,
Verg., etc. **2.** Transf.: me torret face
mutuā Calais, *flame of love*, Hor. ; dicendi
faces, *fire of eloquence*, Cic. ; dolorum faces,
agonies, Cic.

faxim, faxō v. faciō.

febrĭcŭla, ae, *f.* [*dim.* febris], *a slight fever* :
febriculam habere, Cic. Ep.

febris, is (Acc. *Sing.* febrem and febrim :
Abl. most freq. febri), *f.* [for ferbris, from
ferveō], *a fever*. **1.** Lit.: febrem habere,
Cic. ; aestu febrique iactari, Cic. In *pl.* :
Lucr., Cic., Hor. **2.** Transf.: nunc certe
scio, hoc febrim tibi esse, Pl.

februa, ōrum, v. februum.

februālis, e. v. februum.

Februārius, ĭ, *m.*, or **Februārius mēnsis**
[februum], *the month of expiation* (v. Februa,
s.v. februum), *February* : until the time of
the decemvirs the last month of the Roman
year, afterwards the second : Cic., Ov.,
etc.

februāta, ae, v. februum.

februum, ĭ, *n.* in the Sabine and old Lat.
lang. *a purgation* : Februa Romani dixere
piamina patres, Ov. Hence **Februa**,
ōrum, *n. pl.* *the Roman festival of purification
and expiation* (the Lupercalia), *celebrated
on the 15th of the month, hence called February*
(v. Februārius) ; whence **Februālis, Feb-
rūlis**, and **Februāta**, *surnames of Juno,
who was worshipped at this festival* ; **Feb-
ruātus (diēs)**, *the festival itself* ; and **Feb-
ruus**, *a surname of Lupercus, who presided
over it.*

fēciālis, wrongly for fētiālis.

fēcundĭtās, ātis, *f.* [fēcundus], *fruitfulness,
fertility, fecundity*. **1.** Lit. (of living
beings or soils) : Cic. Personified : Tac.
2. Transf.: *luxuriance of style* : volo se
efferat in adulescente fecunditas, Cic.

fēcundō, āre [fēcundus], *to make fruitful, to
fertilise* : viridem Aegyptum nigrā fecundat
harenā, Verg.

fēcundus, a, um [fr. root of fētus], *fruitful,
fertile, teeming* (of persons, animals, soils,
plants). **1.** Lit.: Lucr., Verg., etc.
Comp. : Cic. With Gen.: Tac. **2.**
Transf. **A. a.** *rich, copious, abundant* :
fons, Ov. ; calices, Hor. *Comp.* : Ov.
With Abl. : Ov. **b.** *rich, abounding in.*
With Gen.: fecunda culpae saecula, Hor. ;
Aemilium genus fecundum bonorum civium, Tac. With Abl. : amor felle, Pl. ;
Verg. *Comp.* : Juv. *Sup.* : Pl., Tac.,
etc. **B.** *making fruitful, fertilising* : imber,
Verg.; excipe fecundae patienter verbera
dextrae (the blows given to women by the
luperci to promote fruitfulness), Ov.

fel, fellis, *n.* [*cf.* Gk. χόλος and helus (= holus)],
the gall-bladder, gall, bile. **1.** Lit.: Cic.,
Ov., etc. ; Alcidae furiis exarserat atro
felle dolor (because the bile was thought
to be the seat of anger), Verg. **2.** Transf.
a. *poisonous liquid, poison* : Verg., Ov.
b. *bitterness, acrimony* : amor et melle et
felle est fecundissimus, Pl. ; Tib. ; Ov.
[It. *fiele* ; Sp. *hiel* ; Fr. *fiel.*]

fēles, is, *f.* **1.** Lit.: *a cat* : Cic., Ov., etc.
2. Transf.: *a thief* : Pl.

fēlīcĭtās, ātis, *f.* [fēlix], *fruitfulness, fertility*.
1. Lit.: Plin. Ep. **2.** Transf.: *good
fortune* : Caes., Cic. In *pl.* : Ter., Cic.
Fēlicitās personified : Cic., Suet.

fēlīcĭter, *adv. fruitfully, abundantly.* **1.**
Lit.: Verg. **2.** Transf. **a.** *auspiciously,
favourably* : Pl., Caes., Cic. In wishes and
exclamations: *good luck* : Cic. Ep., Phaedr.,
etc. **b.** *luckily, happily, successfully* : Pl.,
Cic., Ov., etc. *Comp.* : Ov. *Sup.* : Caes.,
Cic., etc.

fēlix, īcis, *adj.* [perh. *cf.* Gk. θήλη, θάλλειν].
1. Lit. **a.** *fruit-bearing* : arbor, Liv. ;
Lucr. ; Verg., etc. **b.** *fruitful, fertile* :
felicior regio, Ov. **2.** Transf. **a.** *of good
omen* ; *auspicious, favourable, propitious* :
Pl., Verg., Liv., etc. **b.** *lucky, fortunate,
successful.* Of persons : Cic., Verg., etc.
Comp. and *Sup.* : Cic. Of things : saecula,
Ov. ; Quint. ; cursus, Ov. ; mendacium.
seditio, Liv. ; sermo, Quint. *Comp.* and
Sup. : Quint. With Gen.: te cerebri
felicem, Hor. ; Ov. ; felices operum dies,
Verg. With *in* and Abl. (of *Ger.*) : Cic.
With *Inf.* : quo non felicior alter unguere
tela manu, Verg.

fēlix, v. filix.

fēmen, inis, v. femur.

fēmĭna, ae, *f.* [orig. *fem. Part.* fr. root of
fētus]. Lit.: *one who brings forth*. **1.**
Lit.: *a female*. **a.** Of human beings, *a
woman* (with reference to sex) : Cic., Verg.,
etc. As a term of reproach to effeminate
men : Ov., Suet. **b.** Of animals and gods
(us. as *Adj.*): Enn., Cic., Ov., etc. **2.**
Transf. **a.** Of plants and minerals : Plin.
b. *the feminine gender* : Quint. [Fr.
femme.]

fēminālĭa, ium, *n. pl.* [femen], *thigh-coverings,
drawers* : Suet.

fēminātus, a, um [fēmina], *womanish,
effeminate* : Poet. ap. Cic.

fēmineus, a, um [fēmina]. **I.** *of a woman* :
manus, Cic. poet. ; femineae sortis, Ov. ;
amor, Ov. ; poena, Verg. ; vox, Ov.,
Quint. ; Kalendae (the first of March, on
which the Matronalia were celebrated).
Juv. **II.** *womanish, effeminate, unmanly* :
pectus, Ov. ; amor praedae, Verg.

fēminīnus, a, um [fēmina]. Gramm., *of
feminine gender* : Varr., Quint.

femur, oris *or* inis (the latter from a Nom.
femen : Abl. us. femore, but feminibus in
pl.), *n. the thigh* : Pl., Cic., Verg., etc.

fēn-, v. faen-.

fenestra, ae, *f.* [perh. fr. root of Gk. φαίνω],
*an opening in a wall to admit the light, a
window*. **1.** Lit.: Pl., Cic. Ep., Verg.,
etc. ; fenestras indere, Pl. ; iungere, Hor.
2. Transf. (of other openings). **A.**
Material. **a.** *a loop-hole* : Caes. **b.** *a
hole, breach* : Verg. **c.** *a hole through the
ear* : Juv. **B.** Immaterial. **a.** *an opening, opportunity* : fenestram ad nequitiam
patefacere, Ter. **b.** *windows* (of the soul) :
animi, Cic.

fera, ae, *f.* [ferus], *a wild animal, wild beast* :
Caes., Cic., Hor. Of *a sea-monster* : Ov.
Of the constellations of the *Great* and *Little
Bear* : magna minorque ferae, Ov.

ferācius, comp. adv. more fruitfully : laetius feraciusque renata urbs, Liv.

fērālis, e, adj. of the dead or corpses. **1.** Lit. **a.** In gen.: funeral : cupressus, Verg. ; munera, Ov. ; sacra, Luc. ; reliquiae, Tac. **b.** relating to the festival of the dead : dies, tempus, Ov. In n. pl. **Fērālia,** ium (Fĕr- in Ov.), the festival of the dead (celebrated annually on the 17th or the 21st of February): Cic. Ep., Liv., Ov. **2.** Transf. **a.** deadly, fatal : dona, papilio, Ov. ; annus. bellum, Tac. **b.** doleful, gloomy : ferali carmine bubo, Verg. ; tenebrae, Tac.

ferāx, ācis [ferō], fruit-bearing, fruitful, fertile. **1.** Lit. Of land : Cic., Hor., Suet. Sup. : Caes. With GEN. : Hor., Ov., Plin. Ep. With ABL. : Verg., Ov. Of plants : Verg. **2.** Transf. : nullus feracior in philosophiâ locus est, Cic. ; aetas virtutum ferax, Liv. ; ferax saeculum bonis artibus, Plin. Ep.

ferculum, i, n. [ferō]. Lit.: a carrier. **a.** a portable frame, barrow : (for carrying spoils, the images of the gods, in public processions, etc.): Cic., Liv., Suet. **b.** a dinner tray ; a course or service ; also, a single dish : Hor., Suet., etc.

ferē, adv. [cogn. with firmus]. **I. a.** nearly, almost, about : quintâ fere horâ, Cic. ; Pl. ; semper fĕre, Cic. ; tantum fere, Cic. ; totius fere Galliae, Caes. ; eodem fere tempore, Liv. ; fere mediam caeli metam, Verg. Hence with negatives to limit or qualify them : scarcely anybody, anything, etc. : nemo fere, nihil fere, Cic., etc. **b.** just, quite : iam fere, Enn. ; qui tum fere multis erat in ore, Cic. ; paria esse fere peccata, Hor. ; cum circa hanc fere consultationem disceptatio omnis verteretur, Liv. **II.** as a rule, in general, for the most part, usually : ruri fere se continebat, Ter. ; illud iter pedibus fere confici solet, Cic. ; ut fere fit, Cic. ; nigra fere terra, Verg. Also with plerumque : Ter. ; with plerique : Cic.

ferentārius, i, m. [perh. fr. feriō], a sort of light-armed soldier, either horse or foot, who fought with missiles. **1.** Lit.: Sall., Tac. **2.** Transf.: one who is active or ready : Pl.

Feretrius, i, m. an epithet of Jupiter (either the Striker [feriō] or derived from feretrum, (bier).

feretrum, i, n. [φέρετρον], a bier : Verg., Ov., etc.

fēriae, ārum, f. pl. [cf. fēstus], holidays, festivals. **1.** Lit.: Pl., Cic., Liv. **2.** Transf.: rest, leisure : praestare Hesperiae longas ferias, Hor. Comic.: venter gutturque resident esurialis ferias, Pl.

fēriātus, a, um [fēriae], keeping holiday, idle. Of persons: Pl., Cic. Of things: machaera, Pl. ; dies, toga, Plin. Ep.

ferīnus, a, um [ferus], of wild beasts : vestis, Lucr. ; caro, Sall. ; vultus, Ov. ; lac, Verg. Hence **ferīna,** ae, f. (sc. carō), the flesh of wild animals, game, venison : Verg.

feriō, īre, to strike, smite (the forms of the Perf., Sup., and Part. supplied by percutiō, q.v.). **1.** Lit. **a.** In gen.: foris, Pl. ; parietem, Cic. ; murum arietibus, Sall. ; stricto ferit retinacula ferro, Verg. ; socii feriunt mare, Verg. P o e t.: sublimi

feriam sidera vertice, Hor. Absol. : cornu ferit ille, Verg. ; Quint. **b.** Of vibrations of light and sound : corpora quae feriant oculos, Lucr. ; Cic. Ep.; feriuntque summos fulgura montis, Hor. ; sole fere radiis feriente cacumina primis, Ov. ; ferit aethera clamor, Verg. **c.** to give a death-blow ; to slay, kill : Enn. ; aliquem securi, Cic. ; Verg., etc. Hence of slaughtering for sacrifice : Verg., Liv., etc. Whence the phrase, foedus ferire, to make a covenant, to strike a treaty : Enn., Cic., Verg., etc. **2.** Transf. **a.** to strike, hit : minus multa patent in eorum vitâ, quae fortuna feriat, Cic. ; verba palato, Hor. ; feriunt animum sententiae, Quint. **b.** Colloq.: to give a knock to. i.e. to gull, cheat : aliquem, Pl., Ter., Prop. [It. ffedere ; Sp. herir.]

feritās, ātis, f. [ferus], wildness, savageness, roughness. **1.** Lit.: beluae, Cic. ; tauri, Ov. Of men : Cic., Verg., etc. **2.** Transf. Of things: Scythici loci, Ov.

fermē, adv. [perh. for ferimē, superl. of ferē]. **I. a.** nearly, almost, about : duodequa-dragesimo ferme anno, Liv. ; Pl. ; erant eiusmodi ferme situs oppidorum, Caes. ; Tac. With negatives : to limit or qualify them : scarcely, hardly anybody, anything, etc. : nemo ferme, Pl. ; nihil ferme, Cic. ; nec ferme res antiqua alia est nobilior, Liv. ; haud ferme ulla civitas intacta seminibus eius motūs fuit, Tac. **b.** just, quite : iam ferme moriens me vocat, Ter. ; Pl. **II.** usually, for the most part, mostly : quod ferme evenit, Cic. ; Pl. ; ferme in omnibus proeliis, Sall. ; Liv. ; Tac.

fermentō, āre [fermentum], to cause to rise : panem, Plin. ; terram, i.e. to break up, Varr.

fermentum, i, n. [fervō, ferveō]. **1.** Lit. **a.** that which causes fermentation, leaven, yeast : Tac. **b.** Perh. a drink made of fermented barley ; malt liquor, beer : Verg. **2.** Transf.: anger, passion, ferment : uxor nunc in fermento tota est, Pl. Also of the cause of anger or vexation : Juv.

ferō, ferre (with perf. tulī, orig. tetulī, wh. is freq. in Pl., Ter. ; and Sup. lātum ; both tetulī and lātum, orig. tlātum are connected with tollō) [cf. Gk. φέρω]. **I.** to bear, carry. **1.** Lit. **a.** In gen.: oneris quidvis, Ter. ; arma, Caes. ; Cic. ; Verg., etc. **b.** to bear (fruit, etc.); hence to bring forth, produce : rami poma ferentes, Ov. ; terra fruges, Cic. ; florem, Hor. ; ventrem ferre, Varr., Liv. **2.** Transf.: to bear. **a.** In gen.: sororis filium nomen suum ferre voluit, Cic. ; eam laudem Africanus cognomine ipso prae se ferebat, Cic. ; ille finis Appio alienae personae ferendae fuit, Liv. ; censûs suos corpore ferre, Ov. **E s p.:** with or without Adv. : to bear, support, endure : aliquid, Cic., Hor., etc. ; aliquem, Ter., Cic., Quint. ; aliquid aegre, aequo animo, Cic., Liv. ; with Acc. and Inf. : Cic., Ov., etc. ; with quod-clause : Cic., Ov., Quint. **b.** to bear, produce : haec aetas prima Athenis oratorem prope perfectum tulit, Cic. **II.** to bear, bring (with one), proffer. **1.** Lit. Of offerings, presents, etc.: haec tibi victor Romulus arma fero, Liv. ; imperat dona ad

navis ferri, Verg.; Baccho liba, Verg.
2. Transf. **a.** *to bring, proffer :* auxilium
alicui, Pl., Ter., Caes., Cic.; condicionem,
Caes.; preces Iunoni, Verg.; matri obviae
complexum, Liv. **b.** *to bring, cause :*
fastidia, Verg.; fidem operi, Verg.; vulnera membris, Ov.; alicui luctum lacri-
masque. Liv. **c.** *to bring* into publicity, *to
show, present, exhibit :* dolorem paulo
apertius, Cic.; Liv. Esp. in phr.; prae
se ferre, *to display, show, make no secret of :*
with Acc.: Cic. Ep., Quint.; with Acc. and
Inf. : Cic. **d.** Of discourse, *to publish,
report :* hence *to talk about :* haec omnibus
ferebat sermonibus, Caes.; nostra laus
semper feretur, Cic.; carmine laudes ferre,
Verg.; aliquam ad caelum laudibus ferre,
Liv.; without laudibus, Cic.; without
ad caelum, Liv. With Acc. and *Inf.*:
Lucr., Verg., Liv., Tac. With *pers.*
Subj. in *Pass.* : vivus per ora feror, Verg.;
famā fertur, Verg. Hence, *to declare,
report, assert, boast* (esp. in 3rd *pers. pl.*
as ferunt, and 3rd *pers. sing. Pass.* fertur,
men say, it is said, cf. Fr. *on dit*): hunc
omnium inventorem artium ferunt, Caes.;
Cic.; Hor., etc.; is regem interemisse
fertur, Cic.; Verg.; se quisque belli ducem
potiorem fert, Liv.; non sat idoneus pugnae
ferebaris, Hor. **e.** Polit. and Leg.: suffragium *or* sententiam ferre, *to give a vote, to
vote :* Cic.; legem (privilegium, rogationem)
ad populum, *or Absol. : to propose a law,*
etc.: Cic., Liv.; ferre iudicem, *to offer or
propose* (*to the defendant*) *as judge :* Cic.
Hence, iudicem alicui ferre, *to propose a
judge to* (i.e. *to bring a suit against, to sue a
person*): Liv. **f.** Mercant.: *to enter in
a ledger or account book :* quod minus
Dolabella Verri acceptum rettulit, quam
Verres illi expensum tulerit, *set down as
paid,* Cic. **III.** *to bear, carry away, bear
off.* **1.** Lit. **a.** In gen.: aliquid, Pl., Cic.,
Verg., etc. **b.** *to carry off* as plunder (esp.
in phr. ferre et agere, v. agō): Verg., Liv.
c. Of things person. as Subjects, *to carry off,
sweep away :* te fata tulerunt, Verg.;
armenta fert aqua, Verg.; Ov.; omnia
fert aetas, Verg. **2.** Transf. **a.** *to carry
off, win, gain, get :* maximas laudes inter
suos, Caes.; eorum suffragia, centuriam,
Cic.; responsum, Caes., Cic.; victoriam
ex inermi, Liv.; honorem virtutis, Ov.
b. *to plunder :* hi ferre agere plebem, Liv.;
cuncta, Tac. **IV.** *to bear, carry, move, set
in motion, move on or forward,* etc. **1.** Lit.
a. omnia ferri et fluere adsimili nobis
ratione videntur, Lucr.; signa ferri iussit,
Caes., Liv. **b.** With pedem, gressum, etc.:
Ter., Lucr., Verg., etc. **c.** With *Refl.*
Pron., or in *Mid., to move, go :* esp. *to move
hastily, rush, hasten :* alicui sese obviam
ferre, Cic.; Verg.; alii aliam in partem
perterriti ferebantur, Caes.; Cic.; Verg.,
etc. **2.** Transf. (of inanimate subjects):
a. quo ventus ferebat, Caes.; Verg.; quo
fata ferant, Verg.; te rursus in bellum
unda tulit, Hor. **b.** With pedes, vestigia,
iter, via, etc., as Subject: Caes., Verg.,
Liv., etc. **c.** Of mental influences: ut
mea fert opinio, Cic.; quā quemque animus
fert, Liv.; ira Romanos per hostium aciem

tulit, Liv.; Hor.; odio ferri in Ciceronem,
Nep.
ferōcia, ae, *f.* [ferōx], *untamed spirit ; warlike temper.* **I.** In good sense : Romana
virtus et ferocia, Liv.; Sall.; Cic.; Tac.
II. In bad sense: *overbearingness, presumption :* quae haec, malum, ferocia est. Pl.;
adrogans atque intoleranda ferocia, Cic.;
Ov.; Tac.
ferōcitās, ātis, *f.* [ferōx], *wild or untamed
courage ; high spirit, fierceness.* **I.** In good
sense : corporis viribus et animi ferocitate
ceteris praestare, Cic. **II.** In bad sense:
presumption : Pl., Cic., Suet.
ferōciter, *adv.* **I.** *courageously, bravely :*
Liv., Tac. *Comp. :* Sall. *Sup. :* Liv.
II. *defiantly ; presumptuously, haughtily :*
Pl., Cic., Liv. *Comp. :* Cic. Ep. *Sup. :*
Curt.
Ferōnia, ae, *f., an old Italian deity, patroness
of freedmen.*
ferōx, ōcis, *adj.* [ferus]. **I.** In good sense :
high-spirited, dauntless, daring, warlike :
equi, Pl.; Aequorum magna gens et ferox,
Cic.; Tullus ferox, Liv.; adversus singulos
ferox, Liv.; Latium, Hor. *Sup. :* Liv.,
Tac. **II.** In bad sense : *headstrong, untameable, haughty, defiant, insolent :* Pl.,
Verg., Liv., Tac., etc. *Comp. :* Pl., Cic.
Ep., Quint. With *Gen.:* linguae feroces,
Tac.; Ov. With *Inf. :* Pl. [Fr. *farouche.*]
ferrāmenta, ōrum, *n. pl.* [ferrātus], *implements or tools made of,* or *shod with, iron,*
esp. agricultural : Caes., Hor., Tac., etc.
ferrārius, a, um [ferrum], *of iron :* fabri,
blacksmiths, Pl.; as Noun: **ferrārius,** i,
m. a blacksmith : Sen. Ep.; **ferrāriae,**
ārum, *f. pl.* (*sc.* fodinae), *iron-mines, iron-
works :* Caes., Liv. [Eng. *farrier.*]
ferrātilis, e, *adj.* [ferrātus], *fit or fetters :* Pl.
ferrātus, a, um [ferrum], *furnished, covered,*
or *shod with iron :* servi, i.e. *in irons,* Pl.;
hasta, Liv.; sudes, Verg.; agmina, Hor.;
belli ferratos postis, Enn. As Noun,
ferrāti, ōrum, *m. pl.* (*sc.* milites), *soldiers in
armour :* Tac.
ferreus, a, um [ferrum], *made of iron, iron.*
1. Lit. : Lucr., Caes., etc. Poet. : ferrea
telorum seges, Verg. **2.** Transf. **a,** *hard,
unfeeling, hard-hearted, cruel :* qui virtutem
duram et quasi ferream esse quandam
volunt, Cic.; os ferreum, Cic.; praecordia,
Ov. **b.** *firm, rigid, unyielding, immoveable :*
(Cato) ferrei prope corporis animique, Liv.;
vox, somnus, iura, Verg.
ferricrepinus, a, um [ferrum crepō], *fetters-
clanking :* insulae, i.e. ergastula, Pl.
ferriterium, I, *n.* [ferrum terō], *a fetters-gall-
house,* comically for ergastulum : Pl.
ferriterus, I, *m.* [ferrum terō], *a slave who is
galled with fetters :* Pl.
ferritrībāx, ācis, *adj.* [fr. ferrum and τρίβω],
galled with fetters : of slaves, Pl.
ferrūgineus (-**ginus,** Lucr.), a, um [fer-
rūgō], *of the colour of iron-rust, rusty, dusky :*
Pl., Verg.
ferrūgō, inis, *f.* [ferrum], *iron-rust.* **1.** Lit.:
Plin. **2.** Transf. **a.** *the colour of iron-
rust, a dirty red* (robigo) *or dusky colour,
murky gloom :* Verg. **b.** *dark colour* (in
general) : Verg., Ov.
ferrum, I, *n.* [perh. = Gk. χέρσον], *iron.* **1.**

Lit.: Lucr., Cic., etc. Poet.: gerere ferrum in pectore, Ov.; Hor. **2. Transf.**: any iron instrument : *a plough :* ferro scindimus aequor, Verg.; *a crow-bar :* turrim ferro adgressi, Verg.; *a spade :* ferro mitiget agrum, Hor.; *an axe :* mordaci velut icta ferro pinus, Hor.; *a dart :* petita ferro belua, Hor.; *the point of an arrow :* exstabat ferrum de pectore aduncum, Ov.; *an iron stilus :* dextra tenet ferrum, Ov.; *hair-scissors :* solitus longos ferro resecare capillos, Ov.; *curling-irons :* crinis vibratos calido ferro, Verg. Esp.: *a sword :* Caes., Cic., Hor., Liv. So, ferrum et ignis, like our *fire and sword*, to denote utter destruction : hostium urbes agrique ferro atque igni vastentur, Liv.; Cic.; Ov., etc. So, ferro flammāque : Cic. Hence *force of arms :* decernere ferro, Cic.; Verg.; Liv. [Sp. *hierro* ; Fr. *fer*.]

ferrūmĭnō, āre, *to cement, glue :* Plin.

fertĭlis, e, *adj.* [ferō], *able to bear, fruitful, fertile.* **1. Lit.:** agri, Cic., Ov., Liv.; oliveta, Hor.; herba, Ov. *Comp. :* Ov., Quint. *Sup. :* Caes., Liv. With GEN.: Cic., Hor., etc. **2. Transf. a.** *abundant, productive :* pectus, Ov. **b.** *making fruitful, fertilising :* dea (i.e. *Ceres*), Ov.; Tib.

fertĭlĭtās, ātis, *f.* [fertilis], *fruitfulness, fertility :* loci, Caes.; Cic.; Ov. Of animals: Ov.

ferŭla, ae, *f.* **I.** *a teacher's stick :* Hor., Juv.; *a goad :* Ov. **II.** *a hollow stalk, fennel :* Verg.

fĕrus, a, um [*cf.* Gk. θήρ], *wild* (of animals and plants), *in a wild state.* **1. Lit.:** varia genera bestiarum vel cicurum vel ferarum, Cic.; fructus, Verg. Of places : Varr., Hor. As Noun, **fĕrus**, i, *m. a wild animal,* of *a horse :* Verg.; of *a goat :* Verg. (v. also fera). **2. Transf. a.** *wild, savage, uncivilised ; barbarous :* nulla gens est neque tam immansueta neque tam fera, Cic.; fera Numantia, Hor. **b.** Of manners, *savage, uncivilised :* vita, victus, mores, Cic. **c.** *inhuman, cruel, savage :* visam Britannos hospitibus feros, Hor.; moenera belli, Lucr.; hiems, Ov. [It. Sp. *fiero* ; Fr. *fier*.]

fervē-făcĭō, facere, fēci, factum [ferveō], *to make boiling hot, to heat, boil :* patinae sese fervefaciunt, Pl.; pix fervefacta, Caes.; fervefacta iacula, Caes.

fervēns, entis. **I.** *Part.* ferveō. **II.** *Adj.:* *boiling hot ; seething, burning.* **1. Lit.:** Pl., Lucr., Cic., etc. **2. Transf.:** *heated, inflamed, impetuous :* ferventior animus, Cic.; rapido ferventius amni ingenium, Hor.; ira, Ov.

ferventer, *adv. hotly, warmly :* loqui, Cael. ap. Cic. Ep. *Sup. :* Cic. Ep.

fervĕō, vēre, buī (also **fervō**, vĕre, vī, in Pl., Lucr., Verg), *to boil, seethe, steam.* **1. Lit.:** quaecumque immundis fervent allata popinis, Hor. Hence *to burn, seethe with heat :* solis vapore bracchia Cancri, Ov. **2. Transf. A.** Of agitated movement : *to be in a ferment.* **a.** Of water : *to boil, seethe, foam :* Cato, Lucr., Verg., etc. **b.** Of bees, etc., *to move excitedly, briskly :* Verg., Ov. Of bees and men at work : fervet opus, Verg. Of armies : Lucr.,

Verg. Of flames : litora flammis, Verg. **B.** Of heated, excited feelings : *to be heated,* or *agitated, to rage :* Ter.; caede, Verg.; avaritiā, Hor.; avaritia, Cic.

fervēscō, ere [ferveō], *to begin to boil, to grow hot.* **1.** Lit.: Pl., Lucr. **2. Transf.:** animus in irā, Lucr.

fervĭdus, a, um [ferveō], *boiling, seething, hot, fiery.* **1.** Lit.: quarta pars mundi, Cic.; sol, Lucr.; Aetna, aestus, sidus, Hor. *Sup. :* Curt. **2. Transf. a.** *boiling, seething, foaming :* vada, aequor, Hor. **b.** Of grapes, *fermenting :* Ov. **c.** To the taste : *hot, fiery. Comp. :* Hor. **d.** In character, etc., *hot, hot-blooded, in a ferment, impetuous :* virtus, Cat.; florente iuventā fervidus, Hor.; mortis fraternae fervidus irā, Verg.; ingenia, Liv.; oratio, Cic.; dicta, Verg. *Comp. :* Cic.

fervor, ōris, *m.* [ferveō], *seething ; fermenting ; violent heat.* **1.** Lit.: mundi, Cic.; coruscus, Lucr.; solis fervores, Lucr.; medii, Verg.; sicci, Ov. Also *fever :* Lucr. **2. Transf. a.** *seething* (of water) : Lucr.; hence *commotion* (caused by pirates) : maris, Cic. **b.** *heat, vehemence, passion :* animi, Cic.; pectoris, Hor.; aetatis, Cic.

Fescennia, ae, *f. a town in Etruria, famous for its licentious dialogues in verse ;* **Fescenninus**, a, um; **Fescennini**, ōrum, *m. pl.* (*sc.* versūs), *Fescennine verses, Fescennines :* nuptiales, Sen.

fessus, a, um [connected with fatiscō], *wearied, tired, exhausted :* **1.** Lit.: de viā fessus, Cic.; plorando, Cic. Ep.; itinere et proelio, Liv.; aetate, Verg.; valetudinibus, Tac. With GEN.: Verg. **2. Transf. a.** Of the body: *exhausted, worn out :* Verg., Liv., etc. **b.** Of age : aetas, Tac. **c.** Of things : domus aetatis spatio fessa, Lucr.; naves, Verg.; res, Verg., Tac.

festīnanter, *adv. hastily, speedily, quickly :* Cic. *Comp. :* Tac., Suet.

festīnātĭō, ōnis, *f.* [festīnō], *a hastening ; hurrying :* Cie., Liv. In *pl. : times of hurry,* Cic.

festīnātō, *adv.* [festīnō], *hurriedly :* Quint., Suet.

festīnō, āre. **A. Intrans. :** *to hasten, make haste, hurry.* **1.** Lit.: Pl., Cic. Ep., Verg., etc. **2. Transf.:** ad singulare Antoni factum festinat oratio, Cic. **B. Trans.:** *to hasten, hurry on.* **1.** Lit. With *Inf.:* Sall., Verg., etc. With Acc.: Enn., Verg., Ov., Tac. **2. Transf.** With *Inf.:* defungi proelio, Liv.; componere litis, Hor. With ACC.: poenas, Hor.; mortem, Tac; nec virgines festinantur (into marriage), Tac.

festīnus, a, um [festīnō], *hasty, hastening :* cursu festinus anhelo, Ov.; veste quam festina urgebam, Verg.

festīvē, *adv. with jollity, gaily.* **1.** Lit.: Pl. **2. Transf.:** *humorously, smartly, prettily :* Cic.

festīvĭtās, ātis, *f.* [festīvus], *jollity, merriness.* **1.** Lit.: Pl. As term of endearment : Pl. **2. Transf. a.** Of speech : *gaiety, pleasantry, humorous fancy :* Cic. In *pl. :* Cic. **b.** Of behaviour : mei patris festivitas et facilitas, Ter.

festīvus, a, um [fēetus], *of a holiday or festival, festal.* **1.** Lit.: ludi, Pl. **2.** Transf. **a.** *merry, jolly, gay, sprightly:* femina, opera, Pl.; homo, Cic. *Comp.:* Cic. Ep. *Sup.:* Pl. **b.** Of speech: sermo, oratio, poema, Cic.

festūca, ae, *f.* **I.** *a stalk, stem, blade:* Varr., Plin. **II.** *a rod with which slaves were touched in the ceremony of manumission* (called also vindicta): Pl.

festus, a, um [fr. root seen in fēriae], *full of rejoicing, festal.* **1.** Lit.: dies, Pl., Cic., Hor., etc.; dapes, Hor.; fronde, Verg.; vestitus, Tac. **2.** Transf.: *keeping holiday:* plebs, domus, Tac. *Neut.* as Noun, **fēstum**, ī, *n. a holiday, festival; a festal banquet, a feast:* agere, celebrare, Ov.; in *pl.:* Hor., Ov. [Fr. *fête.*]

fēteō, fētidus, wrongly for foeteō, foetidus, etc.

fetiālis, is, *m. a member of the Roman college of priests that attended to the due forms in making peace or war:* Cic., Liv. As *Adj.:* fetiali religione sancire, Cic.; ius, Cic.; caerimoniae, Cic.

fētūra, ae, *f.* [fētus], *a bringing forth, bearing, breeding.* **1.** Lit.: aetas (bovis) feturae habilis, Verg.; Varr. **2.** Transf.: *young, offspring, brood:* Cic., Ov. Of plants: Plin.

fētus, a, um. **I.** *pregnant, breeding.* **1.** Lit.: pecus, Verg.; vulpes, Hor. **2.** Transf.: *teeming, fruitful, productive.* Of the earth: terra feta frugibus, Cic.; Ov. Of other things: loca furentibus austris, Verg.; machina feta armis, Verg. **II.** *with a brood of cubs:* Verg., Ov.

fētus, ūs, *m.* [fētus 1.], *a bringing forth, breeding.* **1.** Lit.: Pl., Cic. Of plants: *a bearing, producing:* Cic. **2.** Transf. **a.** *young ones, offspring, progeny, brood:* Cic.; apium, avium, ovium, Verg.; cervae, Ov.; Germania quos horrida parturit fetūs, Hor. Of plants: *fruit, produce, shoots:* Cic., Verg., etc. **b.** In gen.: nec ullā aetate uberior oratorum fetus fuit, Cic.; dulcis Musarum expromere fetūs, Cat.

fi, *interj. pah! foh!* at a bad smell: Pl.

fiber, brī, *m. a beaver:* Pl.

fibra, ae, *f.* [cf. fimbriae]. **1.** Lit. **a.** *a fibre, filament,* in plants or animals: Cic., Verg., Ov. **b.** *lobe or segment, of the lungs or liver;* esp. with ref. to omens: quid fibra valeat, accipio, Cic. **2.** Transf.: *entrails:* caesorumque boum fibris de more crematis, Ov.; nec fibris requies datur ulla renatis, Verg.

fibula, ae, *f.* [fīvō, old form of fīgō]. Lit.: *a fastener.* **a.** *a brooch* (of the safety-pin type), *a clasp:* Verg., Liv., etc. **b.** *a clamp, brace:* trabes binis utrimque fibulis distinebantur, Caes.

ficedula (ficēd-, Mart.), ae, *f.* [ficus edō], *the fig-pecker or becafico:* Juv.

ficedulēnsēs, ium, *m. pl.* [ficedula], *a comic name for a class of soldiers:* Pl.

fictē, *adv. feignedly:* Cic. Ep.

fictilis, e, *adj.* [fīctus, fingō]. Lit.: *that can be shaped;* of pottery, hence alw. *made of clay, earthen:* Cic., Liv., Ov. *Neut.* as Noun (mostly in *pl.*), *an earthen vessel:* Ov., Juv.

fictiō, ōnis, *f.* [fingō]. **I.** *a fashioning, forming:* Phaedr., Quint. **II.** *a feigning, counterfeiting:* Quint.; in *pl.:* Quint. **III.** In rhet. and law: *an assumed or fictitious case, a supposition:* Quint.

fictor, ōris, *m.* [fingō], *one who makes images of clay, wood, wax,* etc.; *a moulder.* **1.** Lit.: Cic. **2.** Transf.: vitae agundae, Pl.; fandi fictor Ulixes, Verg.

fictrix, īcis, *f.* of fīctor. Transf.: Cic.

fictūra, ae, *f.* [fingō], *a forming, fashioning:* Pl. Transf.: fortunae, Pl.

fictus, a, um. **I.** *Part.* fingō. **II.** *Adj.:* *feigned, fictitious, false:* in amicitiā nihil fictum est, Cic.; dii, Cic.; amor, Lucr.; pectus, Verg.; gemitus, Ov.; cunctatio, Tac. Of persons: Hor., Plin. Ep. As Noun, **fictum**, ī, *n. fiction, falsehood:* Verg., Ov.

ficulus, ī, *m.* [*dim.* ficus], *a little fig:* Pl.

ficulnus (-neus, Varr.), a, um, *of the fig-tree:* Hor.

ficus, ī and ūs, *f.* (us. 2nd decl.). **I.** *a fig-tree:* Cato, Cic., Hor. **II.** *the fruit of the fig-tree, a fig:* Pl., Cic., Hor. [Sp. *higo.*]

fidē-commissum (also **fidei-**), ī, *n. a trust, feoffment* (i.e. a bequest made nominally to one person, for the benefit of another): Quint., Suet.

fidēlia, ae, *f.* [cf. Gk. πίθος], *an earthen vessel, pot:* Pl. *Prov.:* duo parietes de eādem fideliā dealbare, Cur. ap. Cic. Ep.

fidēlis, e, *adj.* [fīdēs], *trusty, faithful, loyal.* **1.** Lit.: Cic., Hor., etc. With *Dat.:* Pl., Cic., Hor., etc. With *in* and *Acc.:* Ter., Cic., Sall. *Comp.:* Pl., Cic. *Sup.:* Cic. As Noun, **fidēlis**, is, *m. a trusty person, confidant:* Cic. Ep. **2.** Transf. **a.** Of the action: opera, Caes., Cic.; consilium, Cic.; silentium, Hor.; cura, Ov. **b.** Of things: *trustworthy, trusty, sure:* navis, Cic.; lorica, Verg.; portus, Ov. *Neut.* Acc. as *Adv.* **fidēle**, *faithfully:* Pl. [Sp. *fiel;* Fr. *féal.*]

fidēlitās, ātis, *f.* [fidēlis], *faithfulness, trustiness, fidelity, loyalty:* Cic.; fidelitas amicum erga, Pl.

fidēliter, *adv.* **I.** *faithfully, loyally:* Cic., Ov., etc. *Comp.:* Ov., Plin. Ep. *Sup.:* Plin. Pan. **II.** *securely:* per quorum loca fideliter mihi pateret iter, Planc. ap. Cic. Ep.; Quint. *Comp.:* Quint. *Sup.:* Plin.

fidēns, entis. **I.** *Part.* fīdō. **II.** *Adj.:* *confident, courageous, resolute:* Cic., Verg., Tac.

fidenter, *adv. confidently, boldly:* Cic. *Comp.:* fidentius, Cic. Ep.

fidentia, ae, *f.* [fīdēns], *self-confidence* (philos. term): Cic.

1. fidēs, eī (Gen. *sing.* fidēī, Lucr.; Gen. and Dat. *sing.* fidē, Pl., Hor., etc.), *f.* [fr. weakest form of root of fīdō; *cf.* Gk. πιθεῖν and πείθω], *trust* (in person or thing); *faith, confidence, reliance; belief.* **1.** Lit. **a.** In gen.: fidem habere alicui (or rei), Pl., Lucr., Cic., etc.; rei fidem adiungere, adferre, tribuere, Cic.; fidem facere, *to produce belief,* Caes., Cic.; with *Acc.* and *Inf.:* fac fidem, te nihil nisi populi utilitatem et fructum quaerere, Cic.; fidem

imminuere, abrogare, derogare, Cic. ; decipere, Liv. ; levare, Hor. **b.** *commercial
credit :* cum fides totā Italiā esset angustior,
Caes. ; scimus, Romae, solutione impeditā,
fidem concidisse, Cic. ; agrariis legibus fidem
moliri, Liv. ; res fidesque, Pl., Sall. Poet. :
segetis certa fides meae, Hor. **2.** Transf. :
that which creates confidence. **A.** Of
character, attitude, etc. : *trustworthiness.*
a. Of persons : *honour, loyalty, allegiance,
honesty, integrity :* Pl., Cic., Ov., etc. ; in
fide esse, manere, Caes. ; de pace cum fide
agere, Liv. ; Hor. ; erga populum Romanum, Caes. ; Cic. Ep. **b.** Of things :
trustworthiness, credibility : Cic., Quint.
c. *loyal fulfilment :* dicta fides sequitur,
Ov. ; Verg. **d.** In law : ex fide bonā, *in
good faith,* Cic. ; de malā fide, Cic. **B.** *a
promise, pledge, oath, one's word.* **a.** In
gen. : dare, Pl., Cic., Verg., etc. ; accipere,
Verg. ; servare, Pl., Cic., Tac., etc. ;
liberare, Cic., Liv. ; exsolvere, Liv. ;
violare, frangere, Cic. ; abrumpere, Tac.
b. *a promise of protection or safe-conduct ;*
hence *protection :* fidem ei publicam iussu
senatūs dedi, Cic. ; fide acceptā ab legatis
vim afuturam, Liv. ; se suaque omnia in
fidem atque potestatem populi Romani permittere, Caes. ; deorum fidem opsecrare,
Pl. ; implorare, Cic. ; in fidem alicuius se
conferre, Cic. [It. *fede ;* Sp. *fe ;* Fr. *foi.*]
2. fidēs, is, and more freq. in *pl.* **fidēs,** ium,
f. [*cf.* Gk. σφίδη]. Lit. *a gut-string, string*
of a musical instrument. Transf. **a.** *a
stringed instrument, lyre, lute, cithara :* Pl. ;
fidibus canere praeclare, Cic. ; fidibus
canoris ducere quercūs, Hor. ; Verg. ;
fidibusne Latinis Thebanos aptare modos
studet, Hor. In *sing. :* Hor., Ov. **b.** *the
Lyre* (a constellation) : Varr., Cic. poet.
fidicen, inis, *m.* [fidēs canō]. **I.** *a lutist,
lyrist :* Cic. **II.** *a lyric poet :* Hor., Ov.
fidicina, ae, *f.* [fidicen], *a female lutist :* Pl.,
Ter.
fidicinus, a, um [fidicen], *for lute-playing :*
ludus, Pl.
fidicula, ae, and more freq. **fidiculae,** ārum,
f. [*dim.* fidēs]. *a small lute or cithara.* **1.**
Lit. : Cic. **2.** Transf. : an instrument
of torture : Suet.
fidissimē, *sup. adv., most faithfully :* Cic.
Ep.
Fidius, I, *m.* [fidēs], an epithet of Jupiter¯ ;
esp. in phr. : medius fidius ! (Cic. Ep.,
Sall., Plin. Ep.) ; per deum fidium ! (Pl.) ;
by the god of truth ! as true as heaven !
fidō, fidere, fisus sum [older feidō, by vowel-
extension fr. *fid,* root of fidēs, 1.], *to trust,
confide, put confidence in :* with DAT. : sibi,
Cic. Ep., Hor. ; nocti, Verg. ; pestilentiae,
Liv. With ABL. : prudentiā, Cic. ; fugā,
Verg. ; arcu, Ov. With *Inf. :* Hor., Caes.
fidūcia, ae, *f.* [fidō]. **1.** Lit. : *trust, confidence, reliance, assurance.* **a.** In gen. :
spes atque fiducia, Caes. ; us. with *Obj.*
GEN. of that on which reliance is placed :
Cic., Verg., etc. **b.** With or without sui or
other *Refl.* Pron. (or with *Possess.* Pron. :
Pl.), *self-confidence, self-reliance :* Pl.,
Caes., Ov., etc. **2.** Transf. **a.** *trustworthiness :* Pl. **b.** *sense of security,
security :* Ov. **c.** In law : *a trusting,*

trust : accipere, alicui committere. Cic. ;
iudicium fiduciae, Cic.
fidūciārius, a, um [fidūcia], Leg. : *relating
to a thing held in trust.* In gen. : *given,* or
held in trust : urbem alicui veluti fiduciariam
dare, Liv. ; Caes.
fidus, a, um [fīdō], *trusty, to be depended on,
sure (cf.* fidēlis). **1.** Lit. Of persons : Pl.,
Cic., Hor., etc. Sup. : Cic. Ep., Verg.,
Liv. With DAT. of person *to whom* one is
faithful : Liv., Ov. With GEN. : Verg.
2. Transf. Of things : *sure, certain, safe :*
vis canum, Lucr. ; familiaritates, Cic. ;
ensis, spes, litora, Verg. ; pax, Liv. ; pons,
provinciae, potentia, Tac. ; statio male
fida carinis, Verg. ; Tac., etc. *Comp. :*
Liv. *Sup. :* Verg., Ov., Tac.
figlīnus (figulīnus), a, um [figulus], *a
potter's :* creta, Varr. As Noun, **figlīna,**
ae, *f.* **a.** (*sc.* ars) *the potter's art :* Varr.
b. *a potter's workshop :* Plin.
figō, figere, fixi, fixum (*Part. Perf.* ficta,
Lucr.). **I.** *to fix, fasten, affix.* **1.** Lit. :
arma in parietibus, Cic. ; arma thalamo,
Verg. ; spolia eo loco, Liv. ; ancoram in
prato, Ov. ; arma ad postem, Hor. **2.**
Transf. : oculos solo, Verg. ; oculos in
terram, Liv. ; Verg. ; oculos in virgine,
Verg. ; oscula terrae, Ov. ; Lucr. ; in
silentium fixus, Tac. : vestigia, Verg. ;
domos, Tac. Of abstract things : omnia
mea studia in consulatu, Cic. Ep. **II.** *to
fix, fasten* (by driving or thrusting in). **1.**
Lit. **a.** palum in parietem, Pl. ; mucrones
in cive, Cic. ; Ov. ; clavos in templo, Liv. ;
unguis cervicibus, Ov. **b.** *to pierce,
transfix :* cervos, Verg. ; hunc telo, Verg. ;
Ov. **2.** Transf. : adversarios, Cic. ; aliquem maledictis, Cic.
figulāris, e, *adj.* [figulus], *a potter's· :* rota,
Pl.
figulus, I, *m.* [fingō]. Lit. : *a shaper ;* esp.
a potter : Varr. ; *a builder* (in brick) :
Juv.
figūra, ae, *f.* [fingō], *a shape, figure, form.*
1. Lit. **a.** hominum, corporis, oris, formae,
Cic. ; navium, Caes. ; lapidis, Ov. **b.** In
art : fictilis, Cic. ; signatur cera figuris,
Ov. **c.** Of *the Epicurean atoms or ultimate
parts of bodies :* Lucr., Quint. **d.** *a shade
or phantom of the dead :* Lucr., Verg. **2.**
Transf. **a.** *form, nature, kind :* ex figurā
negoti, Cic. ; pereundi mille figurae, Ov.
b. Rhet. : *a figure of speech :* Cic. **c.**
Gramm. : *form* of a word by inflexion :
Varr., Quint.
figūrātus, a, um. **I.** *Part.* figūrō. **II.** Adj. :
Of speech, *figurative :* Quint.
figūrō, āre [figūra], *to form, mould, shape.*
1. Lit. : boum terga ad onus accipiendum,
Cic. ; anūs in volucris, Ov. ; signum in
modum Liburnae, Tac. **2.** Transf. **a.**
voces lingua, Lucr. ; os tenerum pueri,
Hor. **b.** Rhet. : *to adorn with rhetorical
figures :* orationem, Quint.
filātim, *adv.* [filum], *thread by thread :* distrahere, Lucr.
filia, ae (DAT. and ABL. *pl.* filiābus and
filiis), *f.* [filius], *a daughter.* **1.** Lit. : Pl.,
Cic., Hor., etc. In apposition : virginem
filiam, Cic., etc. ; **filia familiās,** or (as one
word) **filiafamiliās ;** v. familia. **2.**

Transf.: *female offspring, offshoot :* Pontica pinus, silvae filia nobilis, Hor. [Sp. *hija.*]

filicātus, a, um [filix], *engraved with fernfronds :* paterae, Cic.

filiola, ae, *f.* [*dim.* filia], *a little daughter :* Pl., Cic.

filiolus, i, *m.* [*dim.* filius], *a little son :* Pl., Cic. Ep.

filius, i (Voc. fili), *m., a son.* **1.** Lit.: Pl., Cic., Hor., etc. In *pl.* often means *children :* Cic., Quint. For **filius familiās**, or **filiusfamiliās** ; v. familia. **2.** Transf.: terrae filius, *a son of mother earth, a nobody :* Cic. Ep. ; fortunae filius, *a child of fortune, fortune's favourite,* Hor. [Sp. *hijo.*]

filix, icis, *f. fern :* Verg., Hor. [Sp. *helecho ;* It. *felce.*]

filum, i, *n.* **1.** Lit. **a.** Of flax or wool ; *a thread :* Varr., Verg., Ov. Poet.: *the thread of life* spun by the Fates : sororum fila trium, Hor. Prov.: pendere filo (tenui), *to be hanging by a thread,* Ov. **b.** *the fillet* or *thin band of wool* round the upper part of a flamen's cap ; *a priest's* or *ambassador's fillet :* Tib., Liv. **c.** In gen.: *a string, cord, filament, fibre :* aranei, web, Lucr. ; fila lyrae, *the strings,* Ov. ; candelae, *wick,* Juv. ; porri, *shreds,* Juv. **2.** Transf. **a.** Of speech : *texture, quality :* argumentandi tenue filum, Cic. ; orationis, Cic. ; tenui deducta poemata filo, Hor. **b.** *figure, contour :* mulieris, Pl. ; solis, Lucr.

fimbriae, ārum, *f. pl.* [*cf.* fila, fibra], *the extremity of anything,* esp. if separated into shreds and filaments ; *a border, edge, fringe :* cincinnorum, Cic.

fimbriātus, a, um [fimbriae], *fringed :* lato clavo ad manūs fimbriato, Suet.

fimus, i, *m.* [*cf.* fūmus, suffire], *dung :* Verg., Liv. Also *mire :* Verg.

findō, findere, fidi, fissum, *to cleave, split.* **1.** Lit.: hoc quasi rostro finditur Fibrenus, Cic. ; hasta fisso transit praecordia ligno, Verg. ; hiulca siti findit Canis aestifer arva, Verg.; patrios findere sarculo agros, Hor. ; cor meum et cerebrum finditur, Pl. **2.** Transf.: *to part, halve :* qui dies mensem Veneris marinae findit Aprilem, Hor. [Fr. *fendre.*]

fingō, fingere, finxi, fictum [*cf.* Gk. τεῖχος], *to mould, shape, form.* **1.** Lit. **a.** In gen.: volucres nidos, Cic. ; esse aliquam vim, quae finxerit hominem, Cic. ; corpora fingere linguā, Verg. **b.** Of the plastic arts : *to shape* or *form* in wax, clay, stone, etc. ; *to mould* or *model :* e cerā, Cic. ; e luto fictus Epicurus, Cic. ; pocula de humo, Ov. Often alone of statuary : Cic., Quint. Poet.: mella tenacia, Verg. **c.** *to arrange, dress :* of the hair : Verg., etc. ; of the vine : Verg. **2.** Transf. **a.** In gen.: *to form, shape, mould :* fortunam sibi, Pl. ; vultum, Caes. ; Cic. ; Ov. ; vitam, Cic. ; carmina, Hor. **b.** With double predicate : *to form into something :* finxit te natura ad honestatem magnum hominem, Cic. ; si miserum fortuna Sinonem finxit, Verg. ; (illum) spissae nemorum comae fingent Aeolio carmine nobilem, Hor. **c.** By instruction : hence *to train :* os rabidum premendo, Verg. ; voce paternā

fingeris ad rectum, Hor. **d.** Mentally or in speech : hence *to represent, imagine, sketch out :* fingite cogitatione imaginem huius condicionis meae, Cic. ; ex suā naturā ceteros fingere, Cic. ; aliquid animo, Cic. ; aliquid sibi, Cic. With Acc. and *Inf.:* Lucr., Cic., Quint. **e.** Falsely : hence *to invent, forge, fabricate, feign :* fallaciam, Pl., Ter. ; crimina in aliquem fingere, Cic. ; Hor. [Fr. *feindre.*]

finiēns, entis. **I.** *Part.* finiō. **II.** Adj.: finiens orbis (= finiens circulus, Sen.), *the horizon :* Cic.

finiō, īre [finis], *to set bounds to, to limit, bound, enclose within boundaries.* **1.** Lit.: populi Romani imperium Rhenum finire, Caes. ; in ore sita lingua est, finita dentibus, Cic. ; clausas margine aquas, Ov. ; signum animo, Liv. **2.** Transf. **a.** *to set bounds to ; to limit, restrain :* cupiditatem, Cic. ; imperium, Liv. **b.** *to mark out, fix, define, determine :* silvae latitudinem, Caes.; spatia omnis temporis numero noctium finiunt, Caes. ; sepulcris modum, Cic. *Pass.*: de pecuniā finitur, ne maior causā ludorum consumeretur, Liv. **c.** *to put an end to ; finish, terminate, complete ;* in *Pass. to come to an end, to end :* bellum, Caes. ; dolores morte, Cic. ; amores, labores, sitim, Hor. ; censuram, odium, Liv. ; vitam mihi ense, Ov. ; ut sententiae verbis finiantur, Cic. **d.** Without *Obj. : to end,* i.e. *come to an end :* of speaking : Ov., Quint. ; of life : Tac.

finis, is (ABL. regularly fīne ; but fīnī, Cato, Lucr.), *m.* (occ. *f.* in *sing.*) [perh. *cf.* findō]. **1.** Lit. **a.** Ter.: Rubico finis est Galliae, Cic. ; fere ad extremum finem provinciae Galliae, Liv.; finis proferre, propagare, Cic. ; arbitri finis regemus, Cic. Of *the barrier* or *starting point in a race* (in *pl.*) : Verg. **b.** (In *pl.*) *the area enclosed within boundaries, the territory, domains :* Pl., Cic., Verg., etc. **2.** Transf. **a.** *a limit, bound :* finem et modum transire, Cic. ; officiorum finis protulisse, Cic. ; iuris, Lucr. ; Hor. ; sedecim stipendiorum, Tac. Phr.: fine with GEN.: *up to, as far as :* Cato, Ov. **b.** *an end :* finem facere laborum, proeli, pugnandi, Caes. ; Cic. ; finem facere libidini, Cic. ; Ter. : Caes. ; vitae finem adferre alicui, Cic. ; imperium sine fine dedi, Verg. , finem dare malis, Verg. Of *the end of life :* Hor., Tac., etc. **c.** *extreme limit, ultimate point, summit :* licebit etiam finem pro extremo aut ultimo dicere, Cic. ; fines bonorum et malorum, Cic. ; honorum populi finis est consulatus, Cic. ; aequi iuris, Tac. **d.** *end, purpose, final cause :* domūs finis est usus, Cic. ; quod ad eum finem memoravimus, Tac. **e.** Rhet. (= finitio and definitio) : *a definition, explanation :* Quint.

finitē, *adv. to a limited extent, with restrictions :* Cic.

finitimus (older **-tumus**), a, um [finis], *bordering upon, neighbouring.* **1.** Lit.: provincia, bellum, Caes. ; Hor. ; Liv., etc. With DAT.: Caes., Cic., Hor. As Noun, **finitimi**, ōrum, *m. pl. neighbours :* Caes., Cic., Liv. **2.** Transf.: *bordering upon ; nearly related, akin to :* malum, Cic. With

DAT.: metus aegritudini, Cic. ; poeta oratori, Cic.

finītiō, ōnis, f. [fīniō], *a defining :* Quint.

finītor, ōris, m. [fīniō], *one who determines boundaries, a surveyor.* **1.** Lit.: Cic. Comic.: eius (argumenti) nunc regiones, limites, confinia determinabo : ei rei ego sum factus finitor, Pl. **2.** Transf.: *the horizon :* Sen., Luc.

finītus, a, um. **I.** *Part.* fīniō. **II.** Adj.: Rhet., *of phrases that end well : well-rounded, full :* Cic.

fīō, fieri [*cf.* Gk. φύναι and Lat. ful]. **I.** Lit.: *to come into being, arise :* omnia fiunt ex ipsis elementis, Ov. ; Pl. **2.** Transf. **a.** *to come about, be made, become :* fit clamor, Cic. ; impetus, Caes., Liv. ; nomen loco, Liv. ; manceps fit Chrysogonus, Cic. ; certior fit, Cic., etc. **b.** *to come about, happen :* si fieri potest, Cic. ; quid illo fiet ? Cic. ; ita fit ut etc., Cic. ; quo fit ut etc., Hor. ; ut (fere) fit, *as (commonly) happens :* Cic., etc. **II.** *to become, be made ;* hence used as *Pass.* of faciō, q.v.

firmāmen, inis, n. [firmō], *a prop, support :* Ov.

firmāmentum, I, n. [firmō], *a means of strengthening ; support, prop.* **1.** Lit.: transversaria tigna, quae firmamento esse possint, Caes. **2.** Transf. **a.** *a support, prop, stay :* ceterorum ordinum, Cic. ; dignitatis, Cic. ; legionem ex subsidiis in primam aciem firmamentum ducit, Liv. **b.** Rhet.: *the chief support of an argument, the main point :* Cic.

firmātor, ōris, m. [firmō], *a confirmer, establisher :* paci, Tac. ; disciplinae militaris, Plin. Ep.

firmē, adv. *firmly, steadily :* Pl., Cic.

firmitās, ātis, f. [firmus], *stability, firmness, strength.* **1.** Lit.: materiae, Caes. ; corporis, Cic., Quint. **2.** Transf.: animi, Cic. ; imperi, Suet. *Absol. :* Cic.

firmiter, adv. *strongly, solidly ; with steadiness :* Pl., Caes., Cic. *Comp. :* Ov., Plin. *Sup. :* Cic. Ep.

firmitūdō, inis, f. [firmus], *stability, firmness, strength.* **1.** Lit.: tanta in navibus erat firmitudo, Caes. **2.** Transf.: animi, Pl., Cic., Tac., etc. ; haec constitutio habet firmitudinem, Cic.

firmō, āre [firmus], *to make strong, firm, or steady ; to strengthen, fortify, support.* **1.** Lit. **a.** corpora iuvenum labore, Cic. ; corpora cibo, Liv. **b.** Milit.: locum magnis munitionibus, Caes. ; urbem colonis, Cic. ; subsidiis aciem, Liv. ; aditum urbis, Verg. **2.** Transf. **a.** pacem, Caes., Liv. ; provinciam pace praesidiisque, Cic. ; opes, Cic. ; firmatā iam aetate, Cic. *Part.* as Noun : non tamen pro firmato stetit magistratūs eius ius, Liv. **b.** *to strengthen* in resolution ; *to encourage, animate :* cuius adventus nostros firmavit, Caes. ; animum, Verg. ; labantis consilio, Hor. ; cunctos adloquio, Tac. **c.** *to confirm, prove :* fidem, Pl., Ter. ; aliquid iure iurando, Cic. ; omina, Verg. **d.** *to assert positively* (= adfirmō). With Acc. and *Inf. :* Lucr., Hirt., Tac. [It. *fermare ;* Fr. *fermer.*]

firmus, a, um, *firm, stable, strong, stout.* **1.**

Lit. **a.** rami, Caes. ; robora, Verg. ; firmissima vina, Verg. ; carina, Ov. ; area firma templis sustinendis, Liv. ; Tac. **b.** Of health and physique : effice ut ad nos firmus ac valens venias, Cic. ; non Hydra secto corpore firmior crevit in Herculem, Hor. **2.** Transf. **a.** In general power : *firm, firmly-rooted, powerful, strong :* cohortes minime firmae ad dimicandum, Caes. ; Cic., etc. ; res publica, spes, candidatus, etc., Cic. With *Inf. :* Hor. *Comp. :* Cic. *Sup. :* Cic. **b.** Morally : *strong, unyielding :* in causā firmissimus, Cic. ; in sententiā firmiores, Cic. ; firmissimus in irā, Ov. ; pectus, Verg. With *contra* or *adversus :* Sall., Liv., Tac. **c.** In loyalty : fides firma nobis, Pl. ; amici, Pl., Cic. [It. *fermo ;* Fr. *ferme.*]

fiscālis, e, adj. [fiscus], *of the imperial treasury, fiscal :* calumniae (*the resulting fines went to the treasury*), Suet.

fiscella, ae, f. [*dim.* fiscina], *a small basket :* Varr., Verg., etc.

fiscina, ae, f. [fiscus], *a small basket :* Pl., Cic., Verg., etc.

fiscus, I, m. **1.** Lit.: *a basket used for olives in the oil-press.* Hence, *a money-bag* or *-box :* Cic., Phaedr. **2.** Transf. **a.** *the State-treasury, public revenues :* Cic. **b.** Under the Empire : *the imperial treasury* (opp. to aerarium, *the public chest* or *treasury*), *emperor's privy purse* (but distinct from his *private* property) : Tac., Suet. **c.** *cash :* Juv.

fissilis, e, adj. [fissus]. **I.** *easily cleft* or *split :* robur, Verg. **II.** *cleft, split :* comic.: ad focum si adesses, non fissile haberes caput, Pl.

fissiō, ōnis, f. [findō], *a cleaving, dividing :* glaebarum, Cic.

fissus, a, um. **I.** *Part.* findō. **II.** Adj.: *cloven :* ungula, Lucr. **III.** Noun, **fissum**, I, n., *a cleft, fissure :* Pl. ; but almost confined to augury, and used of a divided liver : fissum in extis, Cic.

fistūca, ae, f. *a rammer, beetle (pavior's tool) :* Cato, Caes.

fistula, ae, f. [perh. fr. findō], *a pipe, tube.* **1.** In gen.: *a water-pipe* (usually of lead) : Cic., Ov., Liv. **2.** Mostly *a hollow reedstalk ;* hence **a.** *a reed-pipe, a shepherd's pipe, pipes of Pan :* Verg., etc. ; eburneola (*a pitch-pipe,* for giving the tone to an orator), Cic. **b.** *a writing-reed :* Pers. **c.** *a sort of ulcer, a fistula :* Cato, Nep. **d.** farraria, *a hand-mill for grinding corn :* Cato. [It. *fischio.*]

fistulātor, ōris, m. [fistula], *a player on the shepherd's pipe, a pipe :* Cic.

fistulātus, a, um [fistula], *provided with pipes :* tabulae, Suet.

fisus, a, um, *Part.* fīdō.

fixus, a, um. **I.** *Part.* fīgō. **II.** Adj.: *fixed, fast, immoveable.* **1.** Lit.: Cic., Ov. **2.** Transf.: decretum, Cic. ; animo fixum immotumque, Verg.

flābellifera, ae, f. [flābellum ferō], *a fanbearer, a female slave :* Pl.

flābellum, I, n. [*dim. cf.* flābra], *a small fan* or *fly-flap.* **1.** Lit.: Ter. **2.** Transf.: *a fan* (to excite) : seditionis, Cic.

flābilis, e, adj. [flō], *airy :* Cic.

flābra, ōrum, *n. pl.* [flō], *blasts*, esp. of wind ; *breezes, winds :* Lucr., Verg.

flacceō, ēre [flaccus], *to be flabby.* T r a n s f. : *to flag, lose courage :* Cic. Ep. ; condiciones, Enn.

flaccēscō, flaccēscere, flaccuī [flacceō], *to become flabby, to flag.* T r a n s f. : oratio, Cic.

flaccidus, a, um [flaccus], *flabby.* T r a n s f. : *languid, feeble :* flaccidiore turbine fertur, Lucr.

flaccus, a, um [perh. *cf.* Gk. βλάξ], *flabby.*
1. L i t. : auriculae, Varr. **2.** T r a n s f. Of persons : *flap-eared :* Cic. Hence **Flaccus** as cognomen (e.g. of Horace). [It. *fiacco.*]

flagellō, āre [flagellum], *to whip, lash.* **1.** L i t. : Ov., Suet. **2.** T r a n s f. : colla comae, Mart. ; opes arca, Mart.

flagellum, ī, *n.* [*dim.* flagrum], *a whip.* **1.** L i t. **a.** *a scourge :* Cic., Verg., etc. **b.** *a riding-whip :* Verg. **2.** T r a n s f. **A.** Material. **a.** *the thong of a javelin :* Verg. **b.** *a young branch or shoot, a vine-shoot :* Varr., Verg. **c.** *the arm of a polypus :* Ov. **B.** I m m a t e r i a l : *the lash or sting* **a.** of conscience : Lucr., Juv. **b.** of love : Hor. [Fr. *fléau.*]

flāgitātiō, ōnis, *f.* [flāgitō], *an earnest request or demand :* Cic. In *pl. :* Tac.

flāgitātor, ōris, *m.* [flāgitō], *a persistent demander ; a dun :* Pl., Cic. With GEN. : triumphi, Liv.

flāgitiōsē, *adv. shamefully, infamously :* Cic. *Sup. :* Cic.

flāgitiōsus, a, um [flāgitium], *shameful, infamous, profligate :* vita, Cic. ; civitas, Sall. ; fama, Tac.

flāgitium, ī, *n.* [*cf.* flāgitō, flagrō, and Eng. " *a burning shame* "], *a shamefully vicious or disgraceful act ; a shame, scandal.* **1.** L i t. **a.** domesticis stupris flagitiisque, Cic. ; flagrantissima flagitia et adulteria, Tac. **b.** In gen. : *anything shameful or disgraceful, scandalous conduct :* Pl. ; praeesse agro colendo flagitium putes, Cic. ; illa militiae flagitia, Tac. **2.** T r a n s f. **a.** *shame, disgrace :* Pl. ; magnum dedecus et flagitium, Cic. ; flagitium imperio demere, Liv. **b.** As a term of reproach, like scelus : *shame, disgrace,* hence *rascal, scoundrel :* flagitium illud hominis ! Pl. ; Sall.

flāgitō, āre [*freq.* perh. fr. root of flagrō], *to demand* or *press persistently ; to dun.* **1.** P r o p. With Acc. of thing : stipendium, Caes. ; crimen, auxilium, etc., Cic. ; pugnam, Liv. ; res ipsa severitatem flagitat, Cic. With *ab* and ABL. of person *from whom :* mercedem gloriae ab iis, Cic. ; Caes. With Acc. of person and of thing : haec me Crassus flagitabat, Cic. ; Caes. ; Hor. With *ut* and *Subj. :* Cic. With *Inf. :* Hor. With *Indir. Quest. :* Verg. With Acc. and *Inf. :* a delatoribus revocanda praemia, Suet. **2.** *to summon before court, to accuse :* ut peculatorem flagitari iussit, Tac.

flāgrāns, antis. **I.** *Part.* flagrō. **II.** A d j. : *flaming, blazing.* **1.** L i t. : telum, Verg. ; Canicula, Hor. ; flagrantissimo aestu, Liv. **2.** T r a n s f. **a.** Of lustre : *glistening, lustrous :* flagrans clipeo, Verg. **b.** Of feeling : *hot, passionate, vehement :* cupiditas, Cic. ;

oscula, Hor. ; cupido, flagitia, Tac. *Comp. :* Juv., Tac. *Sup. :* Tac., Plin. Ep.

flagranter, *adv. passionately, vehemently :* Tac.

flagrantia, ae, *f.* [flagrō], *a burning, blazing.* T r a n s f. **a.** oculorum, Cic. **b.** As a term of reproach : flagiti flagrantia, Pl.

flagritrība, ae, *m.* [flagrum τρίβω], *a whip-waster,* i.e. *with being flogged :* Pl.

flagrō, āre [*cf.* Gk. φλέγω], *to blaze, flame, be on fire, glow with heat.* **1.** L i t. : Lucr., Cic., Verg., etc. **2.** T r a n s f. **a.** With passion or ardour : odio, cupiditate, etc., Cic. ; bello Italia, Cic. ; Liv. ; amore, Cic., Hor. **b.** *to suffer severely, be the victim* (with Abl. of cause) : invidiā et infamiā, Cic. ; Tac. ; rumore malo, Hor. **c.** With thing as subject : vitia libidinis apud illum, Cic. ; Sall.

flagrum, ī, *n. a whip, scourge.* **1.** L i t. : Pl., Liv. **2.** T r a n s f. : ad sua qui domitos deduxit flagra Quiritis, Juv. C o m i c. : of a slave : gymnasium flagri, Pl.

(1) flāmen, inis, *m. a priest of one particular deity :* Cic., Liv. ; flamen Dialis, *priest of Jupiter :* Liv., Tac.

(2) flāmen, inis, *n.* [flō], *a blowing,* (us. in *pl.*). **a.** *a blast, gale :* Enn., Lucr., Verg., etc. **b.** Of *wind-music :* Berecyntiae flamina tibiae, Hor.

flāminica, ae, *f.* [flāmen], *the wife of a flamen,* who assisted at the sacrifices : Ov. ; Dialis, Tac.

Flāminīnus, ī, *m. a cognomen in the gens* Quinctia ; esp. T.Q. Flamininus, *conqueror of King Philip of Macedonia.*

flāminium (older -**ōnium**), ī, *n.* [flāmen], *the office of flamen :* Cic., Liv., Tac.

Flāminius, a, *name of a Roman gens* ; esp. C. F. Nepos, *who was defeated and killed by Hannibal at Lake Trasimenus* ; **Flāminius**, a, um ; hence **via Flāminia**, *leading from Rome to Ariminum.*

flamma, ae, *f.* [flagrō], *a blazing fire ; blaze, flame.* **1.** L i t. : Enn. ; solis, Lucr. ; flammam concipere, Caes. ; sedare, Cic. ; mox cum somno et flammam abisse, Liv. ; ferro flammāque, also flammā ferroque, Liv. P r o v. : flamma fumo est proxima (i.e. it is dangerous to trifle with temptation), Pl. ; e flammā cibum petere (from the famished wretches who snatched the meat offered on a funeral pile), Ter. ; prius undis flamma miscebitur (of any thing impossible), Poet. ap. Cic. **2.** T r a n s f. **a.** *that which produces light ; a star, torch,* etc. : erat is splendidissimo candore inter flammas circulus elucens, Cic. ; flammam media ipsa tenebat ingentem, Verg. **b.** *heat :* mixta cum frigore, Ov. **c.** Of colour and lustre : stant lumina flammā, Verg. ; rubrā suffusus lumina flammā, Ov. **d.** Of passion : esp. of love : Cic., Ov., etc. **e.** Of destruction, disaster, etc. : civilis belli, Cic. Ep. ; invidiae, Cic. ; implacatae flamma gulae, Ov. [It. *fiamma ;* Sp. *llama.*]

flammārius, ī, *m.* [*cf.* flammeum], *a maker of bridal veils :* Pl.

flammeolum, ī, *n.* [*dim.* flammeum], *a dainty bridal veil :* Juv.

flammēscō, ere [flamma], *to become inflamed :* Lucr.

flammeus, a, um [flamma], *flaming, fiery.* **1.**
Lit.: Acc.; sunt stellae naturā flammeae,
Cic. **2.** Transf. **a.** Of the eyes : *blazing,
flaming :* Ov. **b.** *flame-coloured. Neut.*
as Noun, **flammeum,** ī, a (*flame-coloured*)
bridal-veil : Cat., Juv. ; flammea conterit
(i.e. changes husbands repeatedly), Juv.

flammĭfer, era, erum [flamma ferō], *flame-
bearing,* i.e. *flaming, fiery :* crinis (stellae),
Ov.

flammō, āre [flamma]. **A.** Intrans.: *to
flame, blaze, burn* (perh. only in *Pres. Part.*) :
flammantia lumina, Verg. **B.** Trans.:
to inflame, set on fire, burn : in *Pass.* also
to burn. **1.** Lit.: Lucr., Tac. **2.**
Transf.: of passion : flammato corde,
Verg. ; omnis exercitūs flammaverat adrogantia venientium a Vitellio militum, Tac.

flammŭla, ae, f. [*dim.* flamma], *a little flame :*
Cic.

flātus, ūs, m. [flō], *a blowing, breathing.* **1.**
Lit.: flatibus Euri, Verg. ; Notus invido
flatu, Hor. ; equi umescunt spumis flatuque
sequentum, Verg. **2.** Transf. **a.** Of fortune, etc. : prospero flatu fortunae utimur,
Cic. **b.** *inflation, haughtiness* (mostly *pl.*) :
Verg., Ov. [It. *flato*.]

flāvēns, entis [flāvus], *yellow* or *gold-coloured :*
cerae, Ov. ; culta, Verg.

flāvēscō, ere [*cf.* flāvēns], *to become yellow*
or *gold-coloured, to turn a light yellow :*
campus aristā, Verg. ; ebur, Ov.

Flāvius, a, name of a Roman gens, to which
belonged the emperors, Vespasian, Titus,
and Domitian ; **Flāvius, Flāviānus,** a,
um ; **Flāviālis,** e.

flāvus, a, um [*cf.* flagrō], *yellow, flaxen, gold-
coloured :* Enn. ; arva, aurum, crines (?),
Verg. ; mellis liquor, Lucr. ; coma, Tiberis,
Hor. ; mella, harena, Ov.

flēbĭlis, e, adj. [fleō]. **A.** Pass.: *to be
wept over ; lamentable :* species, Cic. ;
Hector, Ov. ; nulli flebilior, Hor. **B.**
Act.: *ready to weep.* **a.** *weeping, doleful :*
sponsa, Ino, Hor. ; Ov. **b.** Of things :
doleful, pathetic : vox, gemitus, Cic. ;
modi, Hor. ; elegia, Ov. ; questus, Liv.
[It. *fievole* ; Sp. *feble* ; Fr. *faible*.]

flēbĭlĭter, adv. **I.** *with tears :* Cic., Liv.
II. *dolefully :* Cic., Hor.

flectō, flectere, flexī, flexum [*cf.* Gk. φάλκης,
and Lat. falx]. **I.** *to bend, curve, crook.*
1. Lit.: arcūs, Verg., Ov. ; artūs, Liv. ;
ulmus flexa in burim, Verg. ; anguis
flectit sinūs, Ov. **2.** Transf. **a.** (in
opinion or will) : aliquem, Enn. ; sententiam dictis, Enn. ; aliquem oratione, Cic. ;
animos, Cic. ; quibus rebus flectebar
animo, Cic. ; aliquem precibus, donis,
precando, Liv. ; superos, Verg. **b.** In
Gramm. : *to mark with a circumflex accent :*
Quint. **II.** *to turn the course of, to wheel.*
1. Lit.: equos, Cic., Hor. ; currum, Cic. ;
plaustrum, Ov. ; membra, Cic. With
Refl. Pron., or in *Mid. :* hinc silva se
flectit sinistrorsus, Caes. ; milvus flectitur in
gyrum, Ov. **2.** Transf. **a.** Of the route :
with *iter, viam, cursum :* Verg., Liv., etc. ;
hence *to double* a cape : in flectendis promunturiis, Cic. ; without *iter, viam, cursum :*
Verg., Liv., Tac. **b.** In gen. (esp. of eyes,
voice, mind) : *to turn, direct :* with *Obj. :*

suam naturam huc et illuc, Cic. ; animum
a vero, Liv. ; oculos, Verg. ; vocem, Ov.:
primos ad deditionem, Liv. ; without
Obj. : ad providentiam flectere, Tac.
c. In Gramm.: *to form* a word from
another language : Quint.

flēmĭna, n. *pl.* [Gk. φλεγμόνη], *an inflamed
swelling* about the ankles : Pl.

fleō, flēre, flēvī, flētum (contr. forms flēsti,
Ov. ; flērunt, Verg. ; flēsse, Ov.) [*cf.* Gk.
φλέω]. **A.** Intrans.: *to weep.* **1.** Lit.:
Pl., Cic., Hor., etc. *Pass. Impers. :* Ter.
2. Transf. of inanimate things : *to drop,
trickle :* uberibus flent omnia guttis, Lucr.
B. Trans.: *to weep for ; bewail, lament :*
aliquem, Pl., Cat., Hor. ; meum casum,
Cic. ; Tac. ; amissas amicitias, Cat. In
Part. Perf. : multum fleti ad superos, Verg.

flētus, a, um, *Part.* fleō.

flētus, ūs, m. [fleō], *a weeping.* **1.** Lit.:
Enn. ; ut urbe totā fletus fieret, Cic. ; haec
magnā cum misericordiā fletuque pronuntiantur, Caes. : fletum populo movere, Cic. ;
reprimere, Cic. In *pl. :* Verg., Quint.
2. Transf.: *tears :* Ov.

flexănimus, a, um [flectō animus]. **A.**
Act.: *that bends* or *sways the soul ;* oratio,
Pac. ; amor, Cat. **B.** *swayed in soul :* Pac.

flexĭbĭlis, e, adj. [flexus], *that may be bent ;
pliant, flexible.* **1.** Lit.: materia rerum,
Cic. ; arcus, Ov. **2.** Transf. **a.** *tractable :*
of the voice, etc. (opp. durus), Cic. **b.**
fickle : animus, Cic.

flexĭlis, e, adj. [flectō], *pliant, pliable, supple :*
cornu, Ov.

flexĭloquus, a, um [flexus loquor], *ambiguous,
equivocal :* oracula, Cic.

flexĭō, ōnis, f. [flectō], *a bending, turning.*
1. Lit.: laterum, Cic. **2.** Transf. **a.**
quae deverticula flexionesque quaesisti,
Cic. **b.** Of the voice : *a modulation :*
Cic. In *pl. :* Cic.

flexĭ-pēs, pedis, adj. [flexus], *with twining
feet :* hederae, Ov.

flexŭōsus, a, um [flexus], *full of turns* or
windings : iter, Cic. *Sup. :* Plin.

flexūra, ae, f. [flectō], *a bending, winding,
turning :* laterum, Lucr. ; vicorum, Suet.
Transf.: Sen. Ep.

flexus, a, um, *Part.* flectō.

flexus, ūs, m. [flectō], *a bending, turning,
winding.* **1.** Lit.: of *the passages* of the
ears, Cic. ; in aliquo flexu viae, Liv. ; Cic.
Ep. ; labyrinthei, Cat. ; modico flexu
Rhenus, Tac. **2.** Transf. **a.** (political)
change : itinera flexūsque rerum publicarum,
Cic. **b.** *an artful turning :* Quint. **c.** Of
the voice : *a modulation :* Quint.

flīctus, ūs, m. [flīgō, *to strike,* Liv. Andron.],
a striking, dashing together, collision :
Pac., Verg.

flō, flāre, flāvī, flātum [*cf.* Gk. φλέω and Lat.
fleō], *to blow.* **A.** Intrans. **a.** Of the
wind or breath : Pl., Caes., Ov., etc. **b.** Of
a wind-instrument : Ov. **B.** Trans. **a.**
Chimaera acrem flaret de corpore flammam,
Lucr. ; pulvis vento flatus, Auct. B. Afr.
b. tibia flatur, Ov. **c.** Of metal : *to
smelt, cast :* Liv. ; hence *to coin :* Cic.

floccus, I. m. *a flock* of wool, etc. **1.** Lit.:
Varr. **2.** Transf.: *anything trifling, of
small account, a straw* (esp. with negatives) :

ceterum qui sis, floccum non interduim, Pl.
Mostly in CEN. (of price) with facere, *to
account of slight value :* deos flocci facere,
Pl., Ter. ; rem publicam flocci non facere,
Cic. Ep. ; Pl. ; Ter. [It. *flocco ;* Sp.
flueco, fleco.]

Flōra, ae, *f. the goddess of flowers and spring ;*
Flōrālis, e.

flōrēns, entis. **I.** *Part.* flōreō. **II.** A d j. :
blooming, enflowered. **1.** L i t. : cytisus,
Verg. ; arva, Hymettus, Ov. **2.** T r a n s f.
a. In age, beauty, etc. ; *fresh and charming*
(with ABL.) : aetate, opibus, honoribus, etc.,
Cic. ; Verg., etc. ; aetas, Lucr., Cic., Liv. ;
iuventa, Hor. *Sup. :* Liv. **b.** In means,
power, or repute : *flourishing* : civitas, Caes. ;
res publica, Cic. ; urbs, Liv. *Sup. :* Cic.,
c. Of speech : Cic. *Comp. :* Cic. **d.** Of
light : *glittering, gay :* Lucr. ; catervae
aere, Verg.

flōreō, ēre [flōs], *to blow, bloom, blossom,
flower.* **1.** L i t. **a.** Of plants : Lucr., Cic.,
Verg., etc. **b.** Of land, crops, etc. : Cic.,
Ov. **2.** T r a n s f. : *to be in the heyday.*
a. In age or beauty : annis equus, Lucr. ;
Hor. **b.** In means, power, or repute ; *to
be prosperous, be eminent, be in good repute :*
in Graeciâ musici floruerunt, Cic. ; florentis
domûs amicus, Tac. With ABL. : Sicilia
opibus et copiis, Cic. ; lepore dicendi, Cic.
With *in* and ABL. : Cic., Nep. **c.** Of
various things : *to be gay, to swarm :* mare
velivolis puppibus, Lucr. ; laetas urbes
pueris florere videmus, Lucr. ; meus ad
urbem accessus hominum gratulatione
florebat, Cic. **d.** Of wine : *to froth, foam,
ferment :* Ov.

flōrēscō, flōrēscere, flōruī [flōreō]. **1.** L i t. :
to begin to blossom or flower : Lucr., Cic.
2. T r a n s f. **a.** Of persons : Cic. **b.** patria,
Plin. Ep. ; Lucr.

flōreus, a, um [flōs]. **I.** *made of flowers :*
coronae, Pl. ; Tib. **II.** *flowery :* rura,
Verg.

flōridus, a, um [flōs]. **1.** L i t. **a.** *made of
flowers :* Ov. **b.** *flowery :* Lucr., Cic.,
Ov. **2.** T r a n s f. **a.** *blooming, fresh, beautiful :* Galatea floridior prato, Ov. ; novitas
mundi, Lucr. **b.** Of discourse : *ornate :*
Quint. *Comp. :* Cic.

flōrifer, era, erum, [flōs ferō], *bearing flowers,
flowery :* Lucr., Cic.

flōrilegus, a, um [flōs legō], *flower-culling :*
apes, Ov.

flōrus, a, um [flōs], *bright* or *rich :* crines,
Verg.

flōs, ōris, *m.* [perh. fr. same root as flō].
1. L i t. : Lucr., Cic., Verg., etc. **2.**
T r a n s f. **a.** *the juice of flowers :* fucoque
et floribus oras explent (of bees), Verg.
b. *the prime* or *best of anything, the first
bloom ;* esp. of youth : Pl. ; prima genas
vestibat flore iuventas (*downy hair*), Verg. ;
flos aetatis, *prime of life,* Lucr. ; also *youthful beauty, innocence,* Liv. ; Cat. ; vini, *the
bouquet,* Pl., Lucr. **c.** *the crown, glory,
heyday* of anything : Pl. ; quod floris, quod
roboris in iuventute fuerat, amiserant, Liv. ;
vitae, Cic. ; dignitatis, Cic. ; legatorum,
Cic. **d.** Of speech : *a flower, ornament :*
quasi verborum sententiarumque flores,
Cic. ; Quint. [It. *flore ;* Fr. *fleur.*]

flōsculus, i, *m.* [*dim.* flōs], *a little flower,
floweret.* **1.** L i t. : Cic. **2.** T r a n s f. **a.**
vitae, Juv. **b.** Of style : Cic., Quint.

flūctifragus, a, um [flūctus frangō], *wave-
breaking :* litus, Lucr.

flūctuātiō, ōnis, *f.* [flūctuō], *a movement of
waves.* T r a n s f. of the mind : *wavering,
vacillation :* Liv.

flūctuō, āre, or (later) **flūctuor**, ārī [flūctus],
to move like the waves ; to toss about. **1.**
L i t. : Pl., Lucr., Cic. **2.** T r a n s f. **a.** Of
light : fluctuat omnis aere renidenti tellus,
Verg. **b.** Of the emotions : *to toss about,
be restless, to waver :* animus, Pl. ; animo,
Verg. ; ira, Verg. ; magnoque irarum
fluctuat aestu, Verg.; inter spem metumque,
Liv. ; utrius populi mallet victoriam esse,
fluctuatus animo fuerat, Liv. ; fluctuantem
sententiam confirmare, Cic. Ep.

flūctuōsus, a, um [flūctus], *billowy :* mare,
Pl.

flūctus, ūs, *m.* [fluō]. **1.** L i t. : *a flowing,
undulating :* Lucr. Hence *a wave, billow,
surge* (freq. in *pl.*): Enn., Cic., Verg., etc.
P r o v. : fluctus in simpulo (" tempest in a
tea-cup "), Cic. **2.** T r a n s f. : *turbulence,
commotion, disturbance :* in hac tempestate
populi et fluctibus, Cic. ; rerum fluctibus
in mediis, Hor. ; irarum, Lucr., Verg.
[It. *fiotto ;* Fr. *flot.*]

flūēns, entis. **I.** *Part.* fluō. **II.** A d j. **a.**
lax, loose, enervated : Campani fluentes luxu,
Liv. **b.** Of style : *flowing, fluent :* oratio,
Cic. ; Quint. ; also in bad sense : *loose :*
Cic., Quint.

fluenta, ōrum, *n. pl.* [fluō], *a flow, flood,
running water, a stream :* Lucr., Verg.

fluenter, *adv. in a flowing manner :* Lucr.

fluidus (**flūvidus**, Lucr.), a, um [fluō],
flowing, fluid. **1.** L i t. : Lucr., Verg.,
Ov. **2.** T r a n s f. **a.** *soft, slack, lax :* Gallorum corpora, Liv. ; Ov. **b.** A c t. : *relaxing :* calor, Ov.

fluitō (contr. **flūtō**, Lucr.), āre [*freq.* fluō].
1. L i t. **a.** *to float, swim, sail :* Cic., Liv.,
Ov., etc. **b.** *to move with the water, toss
about :* Verg. **2.** T r a n s f. **a.** *to move
unsteadily, hang loose, flap in the wind :*
aplustra, Lucr. ; amictus, Cat. ; vela, Ov. ;
vestis, Tac. ; miles, *staggering :* Tac. **b.**
In mind : *to waver :* Lucr., Hor. ; fides,
Tac.

flūmen, inis, *n.* [fluō], *a flowing (of water) ;
the flood, stream.* **1.** L i t. **a.** Of water :
flumine adverso, *against the stream ;* secundo
flumine, *down stream,* Caes. ; rapidus mon-
tano flumine torrens, Verg. ; Tiberine pater,
hunc militem propitio flumine accipias, Liv.
In *pl.* : Varr., Verg., etc. **b.** Of other
things which flow : *a stream, flood :* sanguinis, Lucr. ; largoque umectat flumine
vultum, Verg. ; lactis, Ov. **2.** T r a n s f. **a.** *a
river* (the usual word) : Enn., Cic., Verg.,
etc. ; flumen Rhodanus, Garumna flumen,
Caes. **b.** Of words : verborum, orationis
Cic., Quint. [It. *fiume.*]

flūmineus, a, um [flūmen], *of rivers, river- :*
aqua, Ov. ; volucres, Ov.

fluō, fluere, fluxī, fluxum [*cf.* Gk. ἀνα-φλύω,
Lat. fleō], *to flow (in a stream).* **1.** L i t.
a. Of water : Enn., Cic., Ov., etc. **b.** Of
other things : sudor, mella, Verg. ; aes

rivis, Verg.; cruor, Hor.; fluit ignibus aurum, Ov. **2. Transf. a.** *to flow, overflow, run down, drip* with any fluid: with ABL.: sudore et lassitudine membra, Liv.; Ov. Without ABL.: buccae, Cic.; Menoetes, Verg. **b.** *to stream* (like water), *flow :* fluctus odorum, Lucr.; rami, Verg.; tunici, Ov.; relictis turba fluit castris, Verg. **c.** Of language: *to flow on* (in good or bad sense): oratio, Cic.; carmen venā pauperiore fluit, Ov.; Herodotus quasi sedatus amnis fluit, Cic.; facetiis, Pl. **d.** Of fortune: in rebus prosperis et ad voluntatem nostram fluentibus, Cic.; res fluit ad interregnum, Cic. Ep.; rebus prospere fluentibus, Tac. **e.** *to flow away* (and perish); *to sink, droop, drop :* excident gladii, fluent arma de manibus, Cic.; luxu, mollitiā, Cic., Liv.; vires lassitudine, Liv.; ad terram cervix, Verg.; sic mihi tarda fluunt ingrataque tempora, Hor.

flūtō, v. fluitō.

fluviālis, e, *adj.* [fluvius], *of rivers, river- :* undae, harundo, Verg.; anas, Ov.

fluviātilis, e, *adj.* [fluvius], *of rivers, river- :* testudines, Cic.; Liv.

flūvidus, v. fluidus.

fluvius (older **flovios**), ĭ, *m.* [fluō], *a river.* **1.** Lit.: Pl., Cic., Verg., etc. (not in Caes.); apud Hypanim fluvium, Cic. **2. Transf.:** *running water, a stream :* Verg. [Fr. *fleuve.*]

fluxus, a, um [fluō]. **1.** Lit.: *flowing, fluid ;* hence *leaky :* vas, Lucr. **2. Transf. a.** Physically: *loose, slack :* crinis, Tac.; habena, Liv.; corpora (i.e. flabby), Tac. **b.** Morally or mentally: *lax, loose, dissolute, careless :* animi molles et aetate fluxi, Sall.; duces, Tac.; animi fluxioris esse, Suet. **c.** *unstable, weak, fleeting :* huius belli fortuna, Cic.; res humanae, Sall.; fides, Pl., Sall., Liv., etc.; studia, Tac.; fluxa senio mens, Tac.

fōcāle, is, *n.* [vulgar form of faucāle, fr. faucēs], *a neck-cloth, cravat,* worn by sick or effeminate persons: Hor., Quint.

fōcillō, āre [fōcula], *to revive* or *refresh* by warmth. **1.** Lit.: aegre focillatus, Plin. Ep. **2. Transf.:** te remediis, Sen. Ep.; societatem, Suet.

fōcula, ōrum *n. pl.* [foveō], *stoves :* Pl. Comic.: iam intus ventris fumant focula, Pl.

foculus, ĭ, *m.* [*dim.* focus], *a fire-pan, chafing-dish, brazier.* **1.** Lit.: Cato, Liv. **2. Transf.:** *fire :* bucca foculum excitat, Juv.

focus, ĭ, *m.* [*cf.* fax], *a place* or *apparatus for heating.* **I.** *a fire-place, hearth* (consecrated to the Lares). **1.** Lit.: Pl., Cic., Verg., etc.; ad focum sedere, Cic. **2. Transf. a.** *hearth* (i.e. home): domi focique, Ter.; nudum eicit domo atque focis patriis, Cic.; agellus, quem tu fastidis, habitatum quinque focis, Hor. So esp. in phr.: pro aris et focis, Liv.; Cic., etc. **b.** *a funeral pyre :* Verg. **c.** *an altar-fire :* Ov., etc. **II.** *a fire-pan, brazier :* Cato, Sen. Ep.

fodicō, āre [fodiō], *to prod, nudge.* **1.** Lit.: mercemur servum, laevum qui fodicet latus, Hor. **2. Transf.:** *to jog the memory :* Pl., Cic.

fodiō, fodere, fōdi, **fōssum** (*Inf. Pass.* fodiri, Pl.), *to dig, delve.* **1.** Lit. **a.** fodit; invenit auri aliquantum, Cic.; hortum, Pl.; arva, Ov. **b.** *to make by digging, to dig out :* puteum, Pl., Caes.; fossam, Liv.; cubilia, Verg.; vallum, Tac. **2. Transf.:** *to prod, prick, goad.* **a.** Physically: te stimulis, Pl.; equi armos calcaribus, Verg.; ora hastis, Liv.; multos pugionibus, Tac. **b.** Mentally: cor stimulo, Pl.; te stimulis, Cic. [Fr. *fouir.*]

foecund-, v. fēcund-.

foedē, *adv. foully, cruelly, horribly :* Pl., Verg., Liv., etc. *Comp. :* Liv., *Sup. :* Cic. Ep.

foederātus, a, um [foedus], *leagued together, federated :* civitates, Cic. *Masc. pl.* as Noun : Cic.

foedifragus, a, um [foedus frangō], *league-breaking, perfidious :* Cic.

foedītās, ātis, *f.* [foedus, *adj.*], *foulness, horror, hideousness.* **1.** Lit. (physical): odoris, Cic.; Alpium, Liv.; spectaculi, Liv. **2.** Transf. (moral): animi, Cic.; Quint.

foedō, āre [foedus, *adj.*], *to make foul, horrible, hideous.* **1.** Lit. (physical): hostium copias (i.e. with wounds), Pl.; Harpyiae contactu omnia foedant immundo, Verg.; pectora pugnis, Verg.; ora, Tac.; foedati agri, Liv. **2. Transf.** (morally): *to pollute, disgrace, blacken :* gloriam maiorum, Pl.; foedati crimine turpi, Lucr.; Romam ipsam foedavit adventus tuus, Cic.; multiplici clade foedatus annus, Liv.

foedus, a, um, *foul, filthy, disgusting , abominable, horrible, shocking.* **1.** Lit. (physical): Ter.: sapor, species, Lucr.; foedissimum monstrum, Cic.; tempestates, Verg., Liv.; res foeda aspectu, Liv.; volucris (*sc.* bubo), Ov.; victus, Hor. With DAT.: pestilentia foeda homini, Liv. *Comp. :* Liv. **2. Transf.** (moral): amor, Lucr.; bellum, Cic. Ep.; ministeria, Verg.; condiciones, carmen, Hor.; consilium, Liv.; foedum exitu, Liv.; scriptores carmine foedo splendida facta linunt, Hor. *Comp. :* Cic.; *Sup. :* Cic., Quint.

foedus, eris, *n.* [fr. root of fidēs], *a league, treaty, charter, compact.* **1.** Lit. **a.** Polit.: aliquem sibi foedere adiungere, Caes.; foedus facere, Caes., Cic.; ferire, icere, pangere, Cic., Liv.; foedera neglegere, violare, rumpere, Cic.; solvere, turbare, Verg. **b.** Private: *a compact, covenant, agreement :* foedus fecerunt cum tribuno plebis, Cic.; frangere, Cic.; thalami, Ov. **2. Transf.** of things: *a law :* naturae, Lucr.; Verg.; Ov.; Parcarum, Ov.

foen-, v. faen-.

foeteō, ēre, *to have a bad smell, to stink.* **1.** Lit.: Pl. **2. Transf.:** fī ! fī ! foetet tuos mihi sermo, Pl.

foetidus, a, um [foeteō], *stinking :* Pl., Cic., Suet.

foetor, ōris, *m.* [foeteō], *a bad smell, a stench.* **1.** Lit.: iacebat in foetore atque vino, Cic. **2. Transf.:** reconditorum verborum foetores, Aug. ap. Suet.

foetu-, v. fētu-.

foliātus, a, um [folium], *leaved, leafy. Neut.* as Noun (*sc.* unguentum), *an unguent* or *oil made of the leaves of spikenard,* etc. (also called nardinum); *nard-oil :* Juv.

folium, ī, n. [cf. Gk. φύλλον], a leaf : Pl., Cic., Verg., etc. [It. foglia ; Sp. hoja ; Fr. feuille.]

folliculus, ī, m. [dim. follis], a small bag or sack. **1.** Lit. **a.** In gen. : folliculis frumentum vehere, Liv. ; Cic. **b.** a ball to play with, inflated with air : Suet. **2.** Transf.: a husk, pod, shell, skin, follicle : Varr., Sen. Ep. ; the shell of an egg : Lucr. [Sp. hollejo.]

follis, is, m. [cf. flō]. **I.** a pair of bellows : Cic., Verg., etc. **II.** a boxer's punch-ball : Pl. **III.** a leather money-bag : Juv. **IV.** puffed cheeks : Juv.

follitim, adv. wallet by wallet, by walletfuls : Pl.

fōmentum, ī, n. [foveō], a warm lotion or poultice, fomentations. **1.** Lit.: Hor. **2.** Transf. **a.** cold fomentation, bandage : Tac., Suet. ; cf. frigida curarum fomenta, Hor. **b.** a mitigation, alleviation : summorum malorum, Cic. ; Hor. ; Tac.

fōmes, itis, m. [foveō], touchwood, tinder : Verg., Luc.

fōns, fontis, m. a natural spring. **1.** Lit.: Enn., Cic., Hor., etc. **2.** Transf. **a.** spring-water, water : Pl., Verg. In pl. : Verg. **b.** a stream : Verg. **c.** a fountainhead, source ; origin : amicitiae, maeroris, dicendi, Cic. ; scribendi, Hor. ; mali, Liv.

fontānus, a, um [fōns], of or from a spring, spring- : aqua, Ov.

fonticulus, ī, m. [dim. fōns], a little spring or fountain : Hor.

for, v. fātur.

forābilis, e, adj. [forō], that may be pierced : Ov.

forāmen, inis, n. [forō], an opening produced by boring. **a.** a hole : inventa sunt in eo (scuto) foramina ccxxx, Caes. ; tibia pauco foramine, Hor. ; operculi, Liv. **b.** an aperture, opening : foramina illa quae patent ad animum a corpore, Cic. ; terrae, Ov.

forās, adv. [orig. Acc. pl. of old Noun fora, cf. θύρα], out of doors, (to) outside, abroad. **1.** Lit.: foras perferre, Cic. ; (scripta) foras dare, Cic. ; ambo se foras eiciunt, Liv. ; Pl. ; Verg., etc. **2.** Transf.: si (animus) eminebit foras, Cic. [It. fuora ; Sp. fuera.]

forceps, cipis, m. f. [formus, hot, and capiō], a pair of tongs, pincers, forceps : Lucil., Verg., Ov.

forda, ae, f. [ferō], a cow in calf : Ov.

fore and **forem**, v. sum.

forēnsis, e, adj. [forum]. **I.** of the market or markets : factio, Liv. ; Quint. **II.** of the Forum (Romanum) and public business conducted there ; public, forensic : vestitus, Cic., Liv. (Neut. pl. as Noun : State-dress : Suet.) ; sententia, Cic., res, Cic. Masc. as Noun, a city-man : Quint. Esp. of speech-making : dictio, strepitus, certamen, Cic. ; Marte forensi florere, Ov.

forfex, icis, f. scissors : Mart.

forīs, is, and more freq. pl. **forēs**, um, f. [fr. root seen in forās], a door, gate ; in pl. folding or double doors. **1.** Lit.: foris crepuit, Pl. ; Ter. ; ut lictor forem virgā percuteret, Liv. ; forem cubiculi clauserat, Cic. ; Ov. In pl. : Pl., Cic., Hor., etc.

2. Transf.: in gen. **a.** an opening, entrance : aeneus equus, cuius in lateribus fores essent, Cic. **b.** quasi amicitiae foris aperire, Cic. Ep.

forīs, adv. [Loc. and Abl. pl. of old Noun fora, v. forās]. **I.** Locative : at the doors ; hence not in the house, outside, out of doors, abroad, without : Pl., Ter. ; haec studia delectant domi, non impediunt foris, Cic. Occ.: in foreign countries : parvi sunt foris arma, nisi est consilium domi, Cic. ; Tac. **II.** Ablative (of separation): from without, from abroad : consilium petere forie potius quam domo, Cic. Occ.: from foreign countries : verba petita foris, Hor.

fōrma, ae, f. form, contour, figure, shape. **1.** Lit. **a.** Pl. ; falcium, Caes. ; corporis, Cic. ; eximiā formā pueros, Cic. ; igneae formae, Cic. ; aratri, Verg. ; agri, Hor. **b.** beauty : di tibi formam dederunt, Hor. ; spretae iniuria formae, Verg. **c.** form, shape, image : formae pictae caelataeque, Cic. ; Liv. ; clarissimorum virorum, Cic. Hence plan, stamp, mould : cum formam videro, quale aedificium futurum sit, scire possum, Cic. Ep. ; pecuniae, Tac. ; a shoe-maker's last : Hor., Quint. **2.** Transf. **a.** outline ; general idea (of anything) : viri boni, ingeni, dicendi, Cic. ; rei publicae, Cic., Liv. ; scelerum, Verg. ; formam vitae inire, Tac. **b.** Philos. (like species), a sort, kind : Cic., Quint. **c.** Gramm.: the quality of a word ; also, its form, declension, conjugation, etc. : Varr., Quint. [Sp. horma.]

fōrmālis, e, adj. [fōrma], having a set form (like a rescript or circular), formal : Suet.

fōrmāmenta, ōrum, n. pl. [fōrmō], shapes, forms : Lucr.

fōrmātor, ōris, m. [fōrmō], a former, fashioner. Transf.: morum, Plin. Ep.

fōrmātūra, ae, f. [fōrmō], a forming, fashioning : labrorum, Lucr.

fōrmīca, ae, f. an ant : Pl., Cic., Verg., etc. [Sp. hormiga ; Fr. fourmi.]

fōrmīcīnus, a, um [fōrmīca], ant-like : gradus, Pl.

fōrmīdābilis, e, adj. [fōrmīdō], causing fear, terrifying : Ov., Sen. Ep.

fōrmīdō, āre [fōrmīdō, noun], to dread ; to be greatly afraid, to be terrified (expressing fear, esp. of the unknown, in its strongest form): Pl. With Acc.: Pl., Cic., Hor. With Inf. : Pl., Hor. With ne and Subj. : Pl. With si and Subj.: Pl. Pass. : Verg., etc.

fōrmīdō, inis, f. fearfulness ; fear, terror, dread. **1.** Lit. (subjectively) : Pl., Cic. ; formidinem alicui iniicere, Cic. ; facere, inferre, intendere, Cic. With Obj. Gen.: Cic., Hor. In pl. : Cic. **2.** Transf. (objectively) : that which produces fear. **a.** awe, awesomeness : caligantem nigrā formidine lucum, Verg. ; Tac. **b.** Of a scarecrow : furum aviumque maxima formido, Hor. ; Verg. **c.** = threats : ostentare, Sall.

fōrmīdōlōsē, adv. dreadfully, terribly : Cic.

fōrmīdōlōsus, a, um [fōrmīdō], full of dread. **A.** Act.: terrifying, terrible : facinus, Pl. ; ferae, Hor. ; tempora, Cic. ; id erat formidolosissimum hosti, Liv. ; in vulgus,

Tac. **B.** Pass.: *frightened* : Ter., Varr.
Comp. : Tac.

fŏrmō, āre [fōrma], *to shape, fashion, mould*.
1. Lit.: materiam effectio, Cic.; classem
in Idā, Verg. **2.** Transf.: orationem,
Cic.; consuetudinem ratione formare,
Cic.; personam novam, Hor.; puerum
dictis, Hor.; se in mores alicuius, Liv.;
mores, eloquentiam, etc., Quint.

fŏrmōsē, *adv. beautifully* : Quint.

fŏrmōsĭtās, ātis, f. [fōrmōsus], Philos. *beauty* :
Cic.

fŏrmōsĭus, *comp. adv.*, *more beautifully* :
Quint.

fŏrmōsus, a, um [fōrma], *finely formed ;
beautiful, handsome, shapely* (denoting
beauty of form). **1.** Lit. of persons and
things : Cic., Verg., etc. *Comp.* : Cic.,
Ov. *Sup.*: Cic., Nep. **2.** Transf.: nihil est virtute formosius, Cic. Ep.; nunc
formosissimus annus, Verg.; Ov.

fŏrmŭla, ae, f. [dim. fōrma]. **I.** Physical:
dainty form or beauty : Pl. **II.** Leg.: *a
regular form* of language or procedure ;
a form, formula. **a.** In judicial proceedings : testamentorum, iudiciorum, Cic.; de
dolo malo, Cic.; cognitionis, Liv.; formulā
cadere, Quint. **b.** *the form* or *condition* of
alliance, etc., *charter, status according to
charter* : milites ex formulā paratos, Liv.;
aliquos in sociorum formulam referre,
Liv. **III.** Ethic.: *a rule, principle* :
Stoicorum, Cic.

fornācālis, e, *adj.* [fornāx], *of an oven* : dea,
the goddess Fornax, Ov.

fornācŭla, ae, f. [dim. fornāx], *a small furnace or oven* : Juv.

fornāx, ācis, f. [fornus = furnus], *a furnace,
oven, kiln.* **1.** Lit.: Cato, Lucr., Cic.,
Verg. **2.** Transf. of Etna: Lucr., Verg.,
Ov.

fornĭcātus, a, um [fornix], *vaulted, arched* :
paries, Cic.; via, Liv.

fornix, icis, m. *an arch or vault.* **1.** Lit. **a.**
Cic., Sall., Verg. **b.** *a series of arches, an
arcade* : Liv. **c.** *an arched opening in
walls, a sally-port* : Liv. **2.** Transf. **a.**
caeli, Enn. **b.** *a brothel* : Hor., Juv.,
Suet.

fornus, ī, m. v. furnus.

fŏrō, āre, *to bore, pierce.* Comic.: Pl.

forpex, icis, f. *fire-tongs* : Cato, Suet.

fors, fortis, f. [ferō], *chance, hap, luck,
hazard* (opp. consilium). **I.** Ter.; ut fors
tulerit, Cic.; Liv.; o si urnam argenti
fors quae mihi monstret ! Hor. **II.**
Adv. **A.** Nom. **fors** (for fors est, sit,
etc.), *the chances are, would be,* etc. ; *perchance, perhaps, peradventure* : Verg. Esp.
a. fors et, *perhaps too* : Verg., Hor.
b. forsit (= fors sit), *there may be a chance ;
perhaps* : Hor. **c. fors-an** [for fors (sit)
an], *perhaps, perchance, peradventure* : Ter.,
Verg., Liv., etc. **d. forsitan** [from fors
sit an] *there may be a chance whether ; perhaps, peradventure* : strictly, with *Subj.* :
Ter., Cic., Verg., etc. With *Indic.* : Ov.,
Liv. As ordinary *Adv.* : Liv. **B.** Abl.
(*Instr.*) **forte**, *as it happens* or *happened* :
Pl., Cic., Verg., etc. ; forte temere, Liv.
Phr. with *ne, si, nisi ; lest, if, unless per-
haps,* or *it so happens that* : Pl., Cic., Tac., etc.

fortasse (also **fortassis**), *adv. perhaps, per-
adventure, possibly, probably.* **a.** Pl., Cic.,
Hor. **b.** With Acc. and *Inf.* : Pl., Ter.,
Cic. **c.** Ironically in replies : *perhaps so !
very likely !* Pl., Ter. **d.** In designating
numbers or amount : elegit ex multis
Isocratis libris triginta fortasse versūs,
Cic.; nemo, nonnulli, satis, nimis fortasse,
Cic.

forte, v. fors **II. B.** [Cic.

forticulus, a, um [dim. fortis], *somewhat bold
or resolute* : Cic.

fortis, e, *adj.* (Old Lat. **forctis**). **I.**
Physically: *strong, stout, sturdy* : mulier, Pl.; equus, Lucr., Verg.; castra, Cic.;
tauri, coloni, umeri, etc., Verg.; remedia,
Tac.; testudo facta ex fortissimis lignis,
Caes. **II.** Morally: *stout-hearted, resolute, spirited, brave,* etc. **a.** Of persons :
Ter., Cic., Verg., etc. With *Inf.* : Hor.
Comp. : Cic., Hor. *Sup.* : Cic., Hor., etc.
b. Of things : animus, Cic. Ep., Hor.;
senectus, consilia, oculi, oratio, etc., Cic.;
factum, Cic., Liv., etc.; pectus, Hor.;
placidis miscentem fortia dictis, Ov.
Comp. : Caes., Cic. *Sup.* : Cic. **III.** In
bad sense : *bold, hardened* : tam fortes ad
sanguinem civilem, Liv.; facinus, Ov.
[Sp. *fuerte*.]

fortĭter, *adv.* **I.** Physically: *strongly,
stoutly, vigorously* : adstringere, Pl.; for-
tius attrahere lora, Ov. **II.** Morally:
bravely, valiantly, manfully : Caes., Cic.,
Hor., etc. *Comp.* : Caes., Hor. *Sup.* :
Caes., Cic.

fortĭtūdō, inis, f. [fortis]. **I.** Physical:
strength : Phaedr. **II.** Moral: *courage,
resolution, bravery, intrepidity* : Caes., Cic.,
etc. In *pl.* : Cic.

fortŭītus (scanned as trisyl. in Juv.), a, um
[forte, analog. with grātuītus], *casual, un-
premeditated, accidental, fortuitous* : concursio rerum fortuitarum, Cic.; subita et
fortuita oratio, Cic.; iacere fortuitos sermones, Tac.; caespes, Hor. *Neut. pl.* as
Noun : nihil tam capax fortuitorum quam
mare, Tac.; Quint. Abl. *sing.* **fortuītō**
Adv., by chance, accidentally : Pl., Cic.,
etc.

fortūna, ae, f. [fors], *chance, hap, luck, fate,
fortune* (good or ill) : plus fortunam quam
consilium valere, Cic.; rei publicae fortuna
fatalis, Cic.; belli fortuna, Caes.; fortunae
rota, Cic.; se fortunae committere, Cic.
Ep.; suas fortunas eius fidei permittere,
Caes.; secunda, adversa, Cic., etc. Personified : Pl., Cic., Hor., etc. Often
good luck or *ill fortune,* acc. to the context.
a. *good luck, good fortune, prosperity* : a
Fortunā deseri, Caes.; Pl.; Cic.; Hor.;
imperium in tam paucorum virtute atque
fortunā positum, Liv.; dum fortuna fuit,
Verg.; fortunam sibi facere, Liv. **b.** *ill
luck, misfortune, adversity* (rare) : eis multa
ademisset fortuna, Cic.; arte emendare
fortunam, Hor. **2.** Transf. **a.** *state, condition, circumstances, lot* : condicio et fortuna servorum, Cic.; mulieres omnis
fortunae ac loci, Cic.; Liv.; homines
infimā fortunā, Cic.; fortunae commuta-
tionem, Caes. **b.** (us. in *pl.*) *property,
possessions, goods, fortune* : Caes., Cic.,
etc. In *sing.* : Hor., Ov., Quint.

fortūnātē, *fortunately, prosperously :* Pl., Cic., Liv.

fortūnātus, a, um. **I.** *Part.* fortūnō. **II.** Adj. [fortūna] **a.** *fortunate, blessed :* Pl., Cic., Verg., etc. *Comp. :* Ter., Cic., Hor. *Sup. :* Cic. With GEN.: fortunatus laborum, Verg. **b.** *in good circumstances, well off, wealthy, rich :* Cic. *Sup. :* Caes.

fortūnō, āre [fortūna], *to make prosperous or fortunate ; to prosper, bless :* Pl., Cic. Ep., Liv., Hor.

forulī, ōrum, *m. pl.* [dim. forus], *a book-case :* Juv., Suet.

forum, i, *n.* *a public place, market-place.* **1.** Lit. **a.** *a market,* as a place for buying and selling : piscarium, Pl. ; piscatorium, Liv. ; holitorium, Liv., Tac. ; boarium, Cic., Liv. ; hence of places where markets were held, *a market-town, market :* Cic., etc. **b.** *the forum,* as the place of meeting, where public affairs were discussed, courts of justice held, money transactions carried on, etc. In Rome **i. Forum Rōmānum** or *absol.* **Forum,** *an open place between the Capitoline and Palatine hills,* in which were the Curia, Rostra, halls of justice, temples, and orig. shops : Pl., Cic., Hor., etc. **ii.** the Imperial extensions, Forum Iulium, Augusti, etc. : Ov., Suet., etc. **2.** Transf. **a.** *a court, assizes* (esp. in provinces) : in id forum convenire, Cic. ; forum agere, Cic. Ep. ; Verg. **b.** *public life, duties :* ut forum et iuris dictionem cum ferro et armis conferatis, Cic. ; ut primum forum attigerim, Cic. Ep. **c.** *the money-market, the exchange :* haec fides atque haec ratio pecuniarum quae in foro versatur, Cic. ; sublata erat de foro fides, Cic.

forus, i, *m.* **1.** Lit. **a.** *a gangway in a ship :* Enn., Cic., Verg. **b.** *a block of* (lit. the passages through) *seats* in the circus : Liv. **2.** Transf. **a.** *the tiers* of a hive : Verg. **b.** *the interior of a dice-box :* aleatorius, Aug. ap. Suet.

fossa, ae, *f.* [fodiō], *a ditch, trench, fosse :* Lucr., Cic., Verg., etc. : ducere, praeducere, Cic. ; fodere, Liv. ; deprimere, Hirt., Ov., Tac.

fossiō, ōnis, *f.* [fodiō], *a digging :* Cic. In *pl. :* Cic.

fossor, ōris, *m.* [fodiō], *a digger, delver.* **1.** Lit. : Verg., Hor., etc. **2.** In contemptuous sense : *a hind, lout :* Cat., Pers.

fossūra, ae, *f.* [fodiō], *a digging.* In *pl. :* Suet.

fossus, a, um, *Part.* fodiō.

fōtus, a, um, *Part.* foveō.

fovea, ae, *f. a small pit.* **1.** Lit. **a.** In gen. : Lucr., Verg. **b.** *a pitfall :* Lucr., Cic., Hor. **2.** Transf. : *a snare :* Pl. [It. *foggia.*]

foveō, fovēre, fōvi, fōtum [*cf.* Gk. τέφρα], *to warm, keep warm.* **1.** Lit. : epulas foculis, Pl. ; pennis pullos, Cic. ; ignibus aras, Ov. ; corpus refoventque foventque, Ov. ; coluber fovit humum, Verg. ; castra fovere (i.e. *cling to the camp*), Verg. **b.** *to keep warm by fomentations :* vulnus lymphā, Verg. **2.** Transf. **A.** Physical. **a.** *to fondle, caress :* gremio puerum, Verg. **b.** *to attend to :* animas et olentia ora illo flore (*cure*), Verg. **B.** Moral : *to foster, ani-*

mate, keep alive : sensūs hominum, Cic. ; spem, patrum voluntatem, Liv. ; vota animo, Ov. ; consilia alicuius, Tac. ; ingenia et artis, Suet. Occ. with personal Object, *to encourage :* Cic. Ep., Liv.

fracēs, um, *m. pl.* [*cf.* frangō], *grounds* or *dregs of oil :* Cato.

fracēscō, fracēscere, fracui, *to become broken ; to become soft* or *mellow :* Cato, Varr.

frāctūra, ae, *f.* [frangō], *a fracture :* Cato.

frāctus, a, um. **I.** *Part.* frangō. **II.** Adj. : *weak, feeble, faint :* me audis fractiorem esse animo, Cic. Ep. ; spes, Cic. ; vox, Juv.

frāga, ōrum, *n. pl. strawberries :* Verg., Ov. [Fr. *fraises.*]

fragilis, e, *adj.* [fr. root of frangō]. **I.** *crackling* (*cf.* fragor) : sonitus chartarum, Lucr. ; lauri, Verg. **II.** *easily broken, brittle, fragile.* **1.** Lit. : cadi, Ov. ; rami, Verg. ; myrtus, Hor. Of ice : aquae, Ov. **2.** Transf. **a.** *frail, feeble :* corpus, Cic. ; Lucr. ; Hor. **b.** *unstable, fleeting :* fortuna, Cic. ; res humanae, Cic. ; gloria, Sall. [It. *frale ;* Fr. *frêle.*]

fragilitās, ātis, *f.* [fragilis], *brittleness.* Transf. : *weakness, frailness, frailty :* humani generis, Cic. ; mortalitatis, Plin. Ep.

frāglō, v. frāgrō.

fragmen, inis, *n.* [fr. root of frangō], *a fracture.* Mostly in *pl. : pieces broken off, fragments ; ruins, wreckage :* silvarum, Lucr. ; remorum, Verg. ; telorum, Tac. ; taedas et fragmina poni imperat, Ov. *Sing. :* saxo atque ingenti fragmine montis, Verg.

fragmentum, i, *n.* [fr. root of frangō], *a piece broken off, a piece, remnant, fragment* (mostly in pl.) : saeptorum, Cic. ; tegularum, Liv. ; Verg. *Sing. :* Cic.

fragor, ōris, *m.* [fr. root of frangō]. **I.** *a crashing ; crash, noise, din :* Cic. ; Lucr. ; tectorum, Liv. ; pelagi, Verg. **II.** *a breaking, fragility :* Lucr.

fragōsus, a, um [fragor]. **I.** *crashing, roaring :* torrens, Verg. **II.** **a.** *broken, breakable, fragile :* Lucr. **b.** *broken, rugged :* silvis horrentia saxa fragosis, Ov. Transf. of style : oratio, Quint.

frāgrō (**frāglō,** Cat.), āre, *to emit a scent, to smell.* **a.** *to be fragrant :* cubile sertis, Cat. ; Verg. ; Mart. **b.** *to reek :* Mart. [Fr. *flairer.*]

framea, ae, *f. a spear, javelin,* used by the Germans : Tac., Juv.

frangō, frangere, frēgi, frāctum, *to break, break in pieces, wreck, shiver.* **1.** Lit. **a.** ova, Cic. ; compluribus navibus fractis, Caes. ; Ter. ; cervicem, Cic. ; gulam, Sall. ; guttur, Hor. ; crura, Cic. ; Hor. ; corpora ad saxum, Verg. **b.** *to break up :* glaebam, Verg. ; fluctum, Lucr., Cic. **c.** *to crush, grind, crunch :* fruges saxo, Verg. ; glandem sues, Verg. **2.** Transf. **a.** In gen. : fidem, foedus, Cic. ; mandata, Hor. **b.** Mostly of *breaking* a man's spirit, resolution, etc. : aliquem auctoritate, Cic. ; furorem alicuius, Cic. ; proeliis calamitatibusque fracti, Caes. ; te ut ulla res frangat ? Cic. ; animo fracto, Cic. ; ingenium mala, Ov. Hence, bellum proeliis, Cic. ; dolorem, Plin. Ep. ; frigora se, Varr. **c.** vox fractos sonitūs imitata, Verg.; frangitur vox, Quint.

frāter, tris, *m.* [*cf.* Gk. φράτωρ], *a brother.* **1.** Lit. **a.** *a (full) brother:* Pl., Cic., Verg., etc.; fratres gemini, Cic.; fratres gemelli, Ov. **b.** *a cousin :* Cic., Ov., Tac.; frater patruelis, Cic.; perh. *also for levir* (*cf.* Fr. *beau-frère*), *a brother-in-law, sister's husband :* gratias de fratris filio remisso agit, Liv. **2.** Transf. **a.** Of members of the same nation : Lucr., Verg. **b.** *a comrade, dear friend :* Cic., Hor. **c.** An honorary title given to allies : Caes., Cic. Ep. **d.** Of things of a like kind : aspicies illic positos ex ordine fratres (i.e. libros), Ov. [Fr. *frère*.]

frāterculus, ī, *m.* [*dim.* frāter], *a little brother.* **1.** Comic. of the Giants: Juv. **2.** Transf. of a friend : Cic.

frāternē, *adv. in a brotherly manner :* Cic. Ep.

frāternitās, ātis, *f.* [frāternus] *brotherhood* (v. frater, 2. c.): Tac.

frāternus, a, um [frāter], *of* or *for a brother, brotherly, fraternal.* **1.** Lit. **a.** amor, Caes.; parricidium, Cic.; invidia, Sall.; sanguis, Hor. **b.** *of a cousin* (v. frater, 1, b.): frater erat, fraterna peto, Ov. **2.** Transf.: *a brother's.* **a.** propter amorem in nos fraternum, Cic.; foedus, Hor. **b.** Of animals yoked together : it tristis arator maerentem abiungens fraternā morte iuvencum, Verg.

frātricīda, ae, *m.* [frāter caedō], *the murderer of a brother, a fratricide :* Cic., Nep.

fraudātiō, ōnis, *f.* [fraudō], *a cheating, swindling :* Pl., Cic.

fraudātor, ōris, *m.* [fraudō], *a cheat, swindler :* Cic.

fraudō, āre (old Aor. Opt. fraudāssis, Pl.; and in the depon. form, frausus siet, Pl.) [fraus], *to cheat, swindle, defraud.* With Acc. of pers. and Abl. of thing : cum Caecilius a Vario magnā pecuniā fraudaretur, Cic.; milites praedā, Liv.; pueros somno, Ov. With Acc. of Pers. only : fidentem, Pl.; creditores, Cic.; so, lucernas, Hor. With Acc. of thing only : *to embezzle, purloin :* stipendium equitum, Caes.; Pl.

fraudulentia, ae, *f.* [fraudulentus], *a disposition to swindle :* Pl.

fraudulentus, a, um [fraus], *prone to swindling.* **a.** In private life : *knavish, fraudulent :* Pl., Cic.; venditiones, Cic. **b.** In public life : *deceptive, treacherous :* Cic., Hor. Sup. : Pl.

fraus, fraudis, *f.* (Gen. *pl.* fraudium, Cic.; fraudum, Tac.) [*cf.* frustum, Gk. θραύω]. Orig. (*undeserved*) *hurt ;* hence *deception.* **1.** Lit. **A.** Act. : *trickery, fraud, imposition :* socios omni fraude fefellit, Cic.; sese dedere sine fraude constituunt, Caes.; legi fraudem facere, Pl., Cic. Ep., Liv. In *pl.* : Cic., Hor. **B.** Pass. : *deception, delusion, error :* me in hanc inlexit fraudem, Pl.; Cic.; Verg., etc. **2.** Transf. **A.** Act **a.** *a deceiver, cheat :* Pl., Ter. **b.** *a bad action, offence, crime, wrongdoing :* in fraudem incidi, Pl.; fraudem capitalem admittere, Cic.; fraudem committere, Hor. In *pl.* : fraudes inexpiabiles, Cic. **c.** Of things : caeli sereni fraude deceptus, Verg. **B.** Pass. : *detriment, damage,*

harm : Pl.; id mihi fraudem tulit, Cic. Ep.; esse alicui fraudi aut crimini, Cic. Esp. in phr. sine fraude, *without harm* or *hurt :* quod sine fraude meā populique Romani Quiritium fiat, facio, Liv.; ceterae multitudini diem statuit, ante quam sine fraude liceret ab armis discedere, Sall.; nodo coerces viperino Bistonidum sine fraude crinis, Hor.

frausus, v. fraudō, *ad init.*

fraxineus (and **-nus**, Ov.), a, um [fraxinus], *of ash-wood, ashen :* Verg., Ov.

fraxinus, ī, *f. an ash-tree, ash.* **1.** Lit. : Enn., Verg., Hor. **2.** Transf. : *an ashen spear* or *javelin :* Ov. [Sp. *fresno ;* Fr. *frêne.*]

fremebundus, a, um [fremō], *roaring, snorting :* Acc., Ov.

fremitus, ūs, *m.* [fremō], *a dull roaring* or *murmuring sound ; snorting, roaring, growling, din :* silvāi, imbrium, Enn.; terrae, maris, Cic.; marinus, Verg.; clamor fremitusque, Caes.; plausi fremituque virum (Gen.) consonat omne nemus, Verg.; castrorum, Liv.; equorum, Caes., Liv. In *pl.* : Lucr., Quint.

fremō, fremere, fremuī, fremitum [*cf.* Gk. βρέμω], *to make a low roaring* or *murmuring sound, to make a din, to roar, growl, snort, mutter, grumble :* venti, Ov.; Lucr.; equus, leo, Verg.; fremant omnes licet, Cic. With Acc. : *to murmur out something ; to grumble, growl :* uno omnes eadem ore fremebant, Verg. With Acc. and *Inf.* : Cic. Ep., Liv., Tac.

fremor, ōris, *m.* [fremō], *a low roaring, murmuring :* Verg.

frēnātor, ōris, *m.* [frēnō], *a curber, tamer.* **1.** Lit. : equorum, Stat. **2.** Transf. : infinitae potestatis animus, Plin. Pan.

frendō, ere [perh. *cf.* Gk. χρεμίζω, or χραίνω, χονδρός], *to gnash :* dentibus, Pl.; frendens aper, Ov.; Hannibal frendens gemensque, Liv. With Acc. : *to crunch, crush :* Acc.; fabam, Varr.

frēnī, ōrum, v. frēnum.

frēniger, era, erum [frēnum gerō], *bridle-bearing :* Stat.

frēnō, āre [frēnum], *to bridle, curb.* **1.** Lit. : equos, Verg.; Hirt.; Liv.; ora cervi capistris, Ov. **2.** Transf. in gen. : gentis iustitiā, Verg.; (Aeolus ventos) vinclis et carcere frenat, Verg.; furores alicuius, Cic.; voluptates suā temperantiā, Liv. With *quo minus* and *Subj.* : Liv.

frēnum, ī, *n.* (more freq. in *pl.* **frēna**, ōrum ; and **frēnī**, ōrum, *m.*) [fr. root of frendō], *a bridle, curb.* **1.** Lit. In *pl.* : Lucr., Cic., Verg., etc. In *sing.* : Hor. Prov. : frenum mordere, *to take the bit between one's teeth :* Cic. Ep. **2.** Transf. : *curb, restraint,* etc. (us. *pl.*) : alicui frenos adhibere, Cic.; date frenos impotenti naturae, Liv.; frena licentiae inicere, Hor.; Cic.; frena imperii moderari, Ov.; tenere, capere, Ov.; accipere, Liv. *Sing.* : frenum accipere, Verg.; voluptates tenere sub freno, Sen. Ep. [Fr. *frein.*]

frequēns, entis, *adj.* [fr. root of farciō], *crowded, in crowds.* **1.** Lit. **a.** Of persons : frequens senatus, Cic.; Equites Romani frequentissimi in gradibus Concordiae

steterunt, Cic. ; frequentior legatio, Liv. ;
populus, Hor. **b.** Of places : *filled, full,
crowded ; populous, well stocked :* frequen-
tissimum theatrum, Cic. ; nulla (praefectura) totā Italiā frequentior dici possit,
Cic. ; celebre et frequens emporium, Liv. ;
compita, Hor. ; via, Ov. With ABL. : loca
aedificiis, Liv. ; terra colubris, Ov. With
GEN. : silvae frequens (mons), Tac. **2.**
Transf. in time-relation : *repeated, frequent, constant, regular.* **a.** Of persons
(often best rendered by *Adv. ; often,
repeatedly*) : frequens Platonis auditor,
Cic. ; filium frequentiorem prope cum illis
quam secum cernebat, Liv. ; adesse frequens senatui, Tac. ; in ore frequens posteritatis eris, Ov. **b.** Of things : pocula Cic. ;
opera, Pl. ; frequentior fama, Liv. ; sententia, Plin. Ep.

frĕquentātĭō, ōnis, *f.* [frequentō]. Rhet. :
a crowding, piling up : argumentorum, Cic.

frĕquenter, *adv. numerously, in great numbers.*
1. Lit. : Cic. Ep., Liv. **2.** Transf. :
often, repeatedly : Cic., Quint. Comp. :
Ov., Quint., Suet. Sup. : Cic., Quint.,
Suet.

frĕquentĭa, ae, *f.* [frequēns], *an assembling
in great numbers ; a numerous attendance,
concourse ; and hence a numerous assembly,
multitude, crowd, throng.* **a.** Of persons :
Caes., Cic. With GEN. : Cic., Sall., Quint.
b. Of things : magna frequentia sepulcro-
rum, Cic. ; creber rerum frequentiā, Cic.

frĕquentō, āre [frequēns]. **1.** Lit. **a.** With
ACC. of persons : *to bring together in crowds :*
Cic. **b.** *to fill with a great number ; to
crowd, people :* urbes sine hominum coetu
non potuissent frequentari, Cic. ; templa
frequentari nunc decet, Ov. **2.** Transf.
a. luminibus sententiarum orationem, Cic.
b. In time-relation : *to visit or resort to
repeatedly, to frequent ; to do or make use of
frequently ; to repeat :* domum alicuius,
Cic. Ep., Sall., Quint. ; aliquem, Tac. ;
Hymen ! clamant, Hymenaee ! frequen-
tant, Ov. ; coniugia et educationes liberorum frequentabantur, Tac. **c.** *to join in
a throng at, attend at* (used of a single person) :
sacra, Ov. ; festos dies, Tac.

frĕtensis, e, *adj.* [fretum], *of the straits (of
Sicily) :* mare, Cic.

frĕtum, i, *n.* [perh. fr. root of ferveō]. **1.**
Lit. : *foaming water ;* hence applied to
shore-water, straits, estuaries : fervet fretis
spirantibus aequor, Verg. ; quid de fretis
aut de marinis aestibus plura dicam ? Cic. ;
fretum Siciliense, *the Straits of Messina,*
Cic. ; also fretum Siciliae, Caes. ; and sometimes fretum, *the Straits :* Cic., Liv. ;
fretum nostri maris et Oceani, *the Straits of
Gibraltar,* Sall. **2.** Transf. **a.** Esp. in
pl. the sea : in freta dum fluvii current,
Verg. ; Ov. ; fretum Euxinum, Ov. **b.**
seething flood : aetatis freta, Lucr. **c.** Also :
caeli, Enn.

frĕtus, ūs, *m. a strait* (= fretum). **1.** Lit. :
angusto fretu, Lucr. **2.** Transf. **a.** per-
angusto fretu divisā servitutis ac libertatis
iura, Cic. **b.** Of spring : fretus ipse anni,
Lucr.

frētus, a, um [fr. root seen in ferō], *supported,
relying ;* hence *trusting, confident.* With

ABL. : virtute et viribus, Pl. ; intellegentiā
vestrā, Cic. ; iuventā, Verg. With DAT. :
discordiae hostium, Liv.

frĭcō, cāre, cuī, ctum (and -cātum) [friō], *to
rub, rub down :* lavari aut fricari, Pl. ;
(sus) fricat arbore costas, Verg. ; frictus
ocelli angulus, Juv.

frĭctus, a, um, *Part.* fricō.

frĭctus, a, um, *Part.* frīgō.

frĭgĕ-factō, āre [frīgeō, faciō], *to make cold,
to cool :* os, Pl.

frīgĕō, ēre [Gk. ῥῑγέω], *to be cold.* **1.** Lit. :
Ter., Verg. **2.** Transf. **a.** *to be numbed,
dull, spiritless :* sine Cerere et Baccho friget
Venus, Ter. ; valde metuo ne frigeas in
hibernis, Cic. Ep. ; quod tibi supra scripsi,
Curionem valde frigere, iam calet, Cael. ap.
Cic. Ep. ; vires in corpore, Verg. ; senis
consilia, Liv. **b.** *to be coldly received,
coldly treated, fall flat :* Ter. ; friget patronus Antonius, Cic. ; prima contio Pompei
frigebat, Cic. Ep.

frīgēscō, ere [frīgeō], *to become cold, to be
chilled.* **1.** Lit. : Lucr., Tac. **2.** Transf.
a. *to become dull* or *torpid :* si Parthi vos
nihil calfaciunt, nos hic frigore frige-
scimus, Cael. ap. Cic. Ep. **b.** *to grow cold
towards any one :* Pers.

frīgĭdārĭus, a, um [frīgidus], *for cooling :*
cella balinei, Plin. Ep.

frīgĭdē, *adv.* **I.** *inactively, feebly :* Cael. ap.
Cic. Ep. **II.** *dully, insipidly, frigidly :*
quae sunt dicta frigidius, Quint. Sup. :
Quint.

frīgĭdŭlus, a, um [*dim.* frīgidus], *rather cold.*
1. Lit. : puella, Verg. **2.** Transf. :
faint or *shivering :* singultus, Cat.

frīgĭdus, a, um [frīgeō], *cold, cool, chill.*
1. Lit. : Lucr., Cic., Verg., etc. Comp. :
Cic., Hor. Sup. : Caes. Prov. : aquam
frigidam suffundere (of slandering), Pl.
(As Noun, **frīgida**, ae, *f. cold water :* Pl.,
Plin. Ep., etc.) Occ. : of a dead person,
or one stiffened with fright : illa (Eurydice)
Stygiā nabat iam frigida cumbā, Verg. ;
membra nati, Ov. ; frigida mens criminibus,
Juv. **2.** Transf. **a.** *cold, numbed, torpid,
dull, spiritless :* nimis lentus in dicendo et
paene frigidus, Cic. ; in Venerem, Verg. ;
accusatoribus frigidissimis utitur, Cic. Ep. ;
cura, Lucr. ; virgo, Ov. ; bello dextera,
Verg. ; (apes) contemnuntque favos et
frigida tecta relinquunt, Verg. **b.** Of
words : *flat, dull, frigid :* cave in istā tam
frigidā, tam ieiunā calumniā delitescas,
Cic. ; ioci, Suet. ; Quint. **c.** *chilling, benumbing.* Of actual cold : aquilo, auster,
Verg. ; sidera, Ov. Of fear : rumor, Hor.
[It. *freddo ;* Fr. *froid.*]

frīgō, frīgere, frīxī, frīctum [*cf.* Gk. φρύγω],
to roast, parch, fry : frictae nuces, Pl. ;
frictum cicer, Hor. [It. *friggere, fritto ;*
Sp. *freir ;* Fr. *frire.*]

frīgus, oris, *n.* [Gk. ῥῖγος], *cold, coldness,
coolness.* **1.** Lit. : Pl., Cic., Ov., etc. ;
opacum (i.e. *the cool shade*), Verg. In *pl. :
frosts, cold season, cold spell :* ut tectis saepti
frigora caloresque pellamus, Cic. ; propter
frigora frumenta in agris matura non erant,
Caes. ; Verg., etc. **2.** Transf. **a.** (*the
cold of*) *winter :* lac mihi non aestate novum
non frigore defit, Verg. ; Hor. In *pl. :*

Verg. **b.** (*the coldness of*) *death :* ast illi solvuntur frigore membra, Verg.; Lucr.; Ov. **c.** *a cold shudder*, produced by fear : Aeneae solvuntur frigore membra, Verg. **d.** *coldness in action, inactivity, dulness :* Cael. ap. Cic. Ep., Ov. **e.** *a cold or frigid reception* of a person or thing, esp. a discourse ; *chilliness, coldness :* maiorum ne quis amicus frigore te feriat, Hor. ; Quint., etc.

friguttiō, īre, *to stammer, stutter :* quid friguttis ? Pl.

friō, āre, *to rub, break, crumble:* glaebas terrarum, Lucr.; Varr.

fritillus, ī, *m. a dice-box :* Juv.

frivolus, a, um (fr. root of friō]. *sorry, paltry :* sermo, Auct. Her. ; aura, Phaedr. ; auspicium, Suet. ; Quint. As Noun, **frivola,** ōrum, *n. pl., trifles :* inter frivola mea, Sen. ; Juv.

frondātor, ōris, *m.* [frōns], *a leaf-stripper, a dresser, pruner* of trees : Verg., Ov.

frondeō, ēre [frōns], *to be in leaf :* Lucr., Verg., Ov.

frondēscō, frondēscere [frondeō], *to become leafy ; to put forth leaves :* Enn., Cic., Verg., etc.

frondeus, a, um [frōns], *leafy :* nemora, Verg. ; tecta, Verg. ; casa, Ov.

frondifer, era, erum [frōns ferō], *leaf-bearing, leafy :* nemus, Lucr.

frondōsus, a, um [frōns], *full of leaves* or *foliage, leafy :* silva, Enn. ; montes, Varr. ; vertex collis, Verg. ; ramus, Ov.

1. frōns (frūns, Enn. ; **frūs,** Enn.), ondis, *f.* [perh. *cf.* Gk. θρόνα] *a leaf, foliage.* **1.** L i t.: Cato, Lucr., Ov. In *pl.* : Enn., Cic., Verg., etc. **2.** T r a n s f.: *a festoon* or *chaplet of leaves :* Verg., Hor., Ov. In *pl.* : Ov.

2. frōns, frontis, *f.* [*cf.* Gk. ὀ-φρύς], *the forehead, brow* (of men or animals). **1.** L i t.: Pl., Cic., Verg., etc. ; sollicitam explicare frontem, Hor. ; frontem contrahere, Cic. ; frons urbana (i.e. impudence), Hor. ; salvā fronte (i.e. without blushing), Ov. In *pl.* : Lucr., Cic. **2.** T r a n s f. **a.** *the forepart* of *anything, the front, façade, van, etc. :* (navium), Verg. ; ianuae, Ov. ; fronte sub adversā, Verg. ; copias ante frontem castrorum struit, Caes. ; aequā fronte ad pugnam procedebat, Liv. ; dextrā fronte prima legio incessit, Tac. Esp. a front, adverbially, *in front, before, in the van :* a tergo, a fronte, a lateribus, Caes., Cic. **b.** *the outer end* of a book-roll : Tib., Ov. **c.** In measuring land, *breadth* or *frontage :* mille pedes in fronte, Hor. **d.** *the outside, exterior ; external appearance :* utrum fronte an mente, Cic. Ep. ; Phaedr. ; Juv.

frontālia, ium, *n. pl.* [frōns], *an ornament for the forehead, frontlet,* of horses : Liv.

frontō, ōnis, *m.* [frōns], *one who has a large* or *broad forehead :* Cic.

frūctuārius, a, um [frūctus]. **I.** *productive :* Varr. **II.** *liable to payment out of produce :* agri, Cael. ap. Cic. Ep.

frūctuōsus, a, um [frūctus], *productive, fruitful.* **1.** L i t.: Varr., Cic. *Sup.* : Caes., Cic. **2.** T r a n s f.: philosophia, Cic. ; vita fructuosior hominum generi, Cic. ; Quint.

frūctus, a, um, *Part.* fruor.

frūctus, ūs (old GEN. *sing.* frūctī, Ter.) [fruor]. **I.** A b s t r a c t : *a using and enjoying* (v. ūsusfrūctus). **1.** L i t.: Ol. mea est haec. *St.* scio, sed meus fructus est prior, Pl. ; Lucr. **2.** T r a n s f.: ad animi mei fructum atque laetitiam, Cic. **II.** C o n c r e t e : *proceeds, returns* in relation to outlay ; *produce, profit, income.* **1.** L i t.: praediorum, Cic. ; pecuniae, Caes., Cic. ; aurum ex fructu metallorum coacervatum, Liv. **2.** T r a n s f. **a,** *the produce* itself of land, trees, etc. ; *the fruits* of the earth, etc.: Cato ; fructūs serere, percipere, condere, demetere, comportare, Cic. ; fructum ferre, Varr., Quint. ; rami fructūs tulere, Verg. ; necessarii fructūs, Liv. **b.** A b s t r a c t : *the results* of any action, *fruit, consequence, benefit, reward :* fructūs ex aliquo (or ex aliquā re) capere, ferre, Cic. ; ex re decerpere, Hor. ; virtutis, vitae, animi, etc.. Cic. ; magno fructui esse alicui, Liv. [It. *frutto ;* Sp. *fruto ;* Fr. *fruit.*]

frūgālis, e, *adj.* [frūx], *thrifty, orderly, honest* (only in *Comp.* and *Sup.*): Comp. : Pl., Ter., Varr. ; *Sup.* : Cic. (For *Posit.* v. frūgī.)

frūgālitās, ātis, *f.* [frūgālis], *thriftiness, orderliness, restraint, honesty.* **1.** L i t.: Cic., Quint., etc. **2.** T r a n s f. of style : *restraint :* Quint.

frūgāliter, *adv.* in a *thifty, orderly, temperate way :* Pl., Cic., Hor.

frūgēs, um, v. frūx.

frūgī (orig. DAT. of frūx), used as *indecl. adj.* : **I.** *useful, serviceable :* Pl. **II.** *virtuous, honest, temperate, upright, orderly :* Ter., Cic., Hor. Strengthened with *bonae :* permodestus ac bonae frugi, Cic. Ep. ; Pl. **III.** *discreet, temperate, thrifty :* Cic., Hor., Quint., etc.

frūgifer, era, erum [frūx ferō], *fruitful, productive, fertile.* **1.** L i t.: Enn. ; agri, Cic. ; messes, Ov. ; Liv. **2.** T r a n s f.: philosophia, Cic. ; Liv.

frūgiferēns, entis, *adj.* [frūx ferō], *fruitful :* Lucr.

frūgilegus, a, um [frūx legō], *grain-gathering :* formicae, Ov.

frūgiparus, a, um [frūx pariō], *fruitful :* fetus, Lucr.

frūtus, a, um, *Part.* fruor.

frūmentārius, a, um [frūmentum], *of corn, corn- :* lex, *respecting the distribution of grain,* Cic. ; loca, *abounding in corn,* Caes. ; provinciae, Caes. ; navis, *a corn ship,* Caes. Milit.: res, *commissariat,* Caes., Cic. As Noun, **frūmentārius,** ī, *m. a corn-dealer :* Pl., Cic., Liv.

frūmentātiō, ōnis, *f.* [frūmentor]. **I.** *a providing* of corn. Milit.: *a foraging :* Caes., Suet. In *pl.* : Caes. **II.** *a distribution of corn :* Suet.

frūmentātor, ōris, *m.* [frūmentor]. **I.** *a provider* of corn, *a public corn-agent :* Liv. **II.** *a forager :* Liv.

frūmentor, ārī [frūmentum]. Milit.: *to fetch corn, to forage :* Caes., Sall., Liv.

frūmentum, ī, *n.* [frūgmentum, from *frug* in frūx, fruor], *produce,* esp. of the various kinds of cereals ; hence, *corn, grain :* Caes.,

Cic., Hor., etc. In *pl.* : *crops, standing corn* : Cato, Caes., Cic., Hor., etc. [Fr. froment.]

frūniscor, frūnīscī, frūnītus [for *frūg-nī-scor*, fr. *frūg* in frūx], *to have the enjoyment or profit of* : hinc tu, nisi malum, frunisci nihil potes, ne postules, Pl.

fruor, fruī, frūctus and fruitus [for frūgor ; for the root *cf.* frūx], *to have at one's disposal, to have the enjoyment or profit of.* *Constr.* mostly with ABL. (with ACC. in Cato, Ter., Lucr.). **1.** Lit. : *of material things as object.* **a.** In gen. : Pl., Cic. *Absol.* : Ter., Cic., Hor. **b.** Of personal objects : Pl., Cic., Tib., etc. **c.** Legal : *to have the use and enjoyment of a thing, to have the usufruct* : certis fundis patre vivo frui solitum esse, Cic. ; Liv. **2.** Transf. *of immaterial things,* **a.** *to possess, enjoy* : immortali aevo, Lucr. ; otio. voluptatibus, Cic. ; Ov. ; vitā, Cic., Tac. ; iustitiae fruendae causā, Cic. **b.** *to find pleasure in, to delight in* : recordatione nostrae amicitiae, Cic. ; res fruenda oculis, Liv.

frūstillātim, *adv.* [frūstillum], *little bit by little bit* : Pl.

frūstrā, *adv.* [perh. orig. a *Neut. pl.* ACC.; for root *cf.* fraus]. **1.** Lit. : *in deception, in error* : iam hi ambo et servos et era frustra sunt duo, Pl. ; Sall. **2.** Transf. **a.** *without effect, to no purpose, uselessly, in vain* : Pl., Cic., Verg., etc. ; *to baffle* aliquem, *to baffle*, Tac. As exclam. : *in vain* ! Hor. **b.** *without reason or cause, groundlessly* : frustra eo sine causā, Cic. ; Verg. ; Suet.

frūstrāmen, inis, *n.* [frūstror], *deception* : Lucr.

frūstrātiō, ōnis, *f.* [frūstror], *a deceiving, deception.* **1.** Lit. : Pl. **2.** Transf. : *a baffling by underhand means* (= *obstruction*) : Liv., Quint.

frūstrātus, ūs, *m.* [frūstror], *a means of deceiving* (in Predic. DAT.) : Pl.

frūstror, ārī (and **frūstrō**, āre, Pl.) [frūstrā], *to deceive ; disappoint* (one's expectations), *trick* : ego me frustro, Pl. ; alios, Cic. ; nec Tarquinios spe auxili frustrabor, Liv. ; inceptus clamor frustratur hiantis, Verg. *Absol.* : Lucr., Cic.

frūstulentus, a, um [frūstum], *full of crumbs* : Pl.

frūstum, ī, *n.* [*cf.* Gk. θραύω], *a piece, bit* (of food). **1.** Lit. : Cato, Cic., Verg., etc. Comic. : frustum pueri, *you bit of a boy* ! Pl. **2.** Transf. : philosophiam in frusta dividere, Sen. Ep. ; Quint.

frutex, icis, *m.* *a shrub, bush.* **1.** Lit. : Varr., Lucr., Verg., etc. **2.** Transf. : *as a term of reproach, like caudex, stipes* : *blockhead* : Pl.

fruticētum, (also **frutectum**), ī, *n.* [frutex], *a shrubbery, thicket* : Hor., Suet.

fruticō, āre, and **fruticor**, ārī (Cic. Ep.) [frutex], *to put forth shoots, to sprout out ; to become bushy.* **1.** Lit. : Cic. Ep. **2.** Transf. : *of the hair* : fruticante pilo, Juv.

fruticōsus, a, um [frutex]. **I.** *full of shrubs or bushes* : litora, Ov. **II.** *bushy* : vimina, Ov.

frūx, frūgis, and more freq. in *pl.* **frūgēs**, um, *f.* [*cf.* fruor], *fruits of the earth, produce of the fields ; grain, vegetables,* and in gen. *produce* (rarely of trees). **1.** Lit. **a.** In gen. : in *pl.* : Enn., Cic., Verg., etc. ; in *sing.* : Cic., Hor., Ov. **b.** Of trees : Hor. **2.** Transf. (*cf.* fructus) : *result, success, value* : quae virtutis maturitas et quantae fruges industriae sint futurae, Cic. ; bonam frugem libertatis ferre, Liv. ; ad (bonam) frugem se recipere, *to reform oneself,* Cic. ; aliquem ad frugem corrigere, Pl. ; centuriae seniorum agitant experta frugis, Hor. ; facere frugem, Pl.

fūcātus, a, um. **I.** *Part.* fūcō. **II.** Adj. : *dyed, coloured ; hence falsified, counterfeit* : candor, nitor, etc., Cic.

fūcō, āre [fūcus], *to redden, to paint or dye red.* **1.** Lit. **a.** In gen. : alba nec Assyrio fucatur lana veneno, Verg. **b.** Of cosmetics : *to rouge* : Ov., Quint. **2.** Transf. **a.** *to paint, dye* (of any colour) : Verg., Hor., Tac. **b.** *to falsify, misrepresent* : Cic.

fūcōsus, a, um [fūcus], *painted, coloured.* Transf. : *counterfeit, spurious* : merces fallaces quidem et fucosae, Cic. ; ambitiosae fucosaeque amicitiae, Cic.

1. fūcus, ī, *m.* [φῦκος], *sea-weed or rock-lichen* (used for dyeing or painting red). **1.** Lit. : Hor., Quint. **2.** Transf. **a.** *red paint* (esp. as a cosmetic) : Pl., Cic. Of other colours : Prop. **b.** *red or purple colour* : Hor., Ov. **c.** *a kind of red-glue secreted by bees ; bee-glue* (= *propolis*) : Verg. **d.** *disguise, deceit, dissimulation* : Pl., Ter. ; sine fuco et fallaciis, Cic. ; sine fucis, Hor.

2. fūcus, ī, *m.* *a drone, the male of the honey-bee* : Varr., Verg.

fue or **fu**, *interj.* denoting aversion, *foh* ! Pl.

fuga, ae (old GEN. *sing.* fugāī, Lucr.), *f.* [*cf.* fugiō], *a running away, flight.* **1.** Lit. **a.** In gen. : fuga ab urbe turpissima, Cic. Phr. : (i) *to take to flight* : dare sese in fugam, se conferre, se conicere, Cic. ; fugae se mandare, Caes. ; fugam capere, petere, Caes. ; capessere, Liv. ; facere, Sall., Liv. (ii) *to put to flight* : in fugam aliquos dare, conicere, convertere, Caes. ; fugam facere, Liv. (iii) reprimere fugam, Caes., Cic. Ep. ; esse in fugā, Cic. Ep. In *pl.* : Cic., Hor. **b.** *flight from one's native land ; expatriation, exile, banishment* (v. exsilium) : Enn. ; sibi exsilium et fugam deprecari, Cic. ; dura fugae mala, Hor. In *pl.* : Tac. **c.** Of rapid movement : *flight, speed* : expectet facilemque fugam ventosque ferentis, Verg. ; fuga temporum, Hor. **2.** Transf. **a.** *a means of flight, opportunity for flight* : alicui fugam dare, Verg., Hor. ; fugam reperire, Verg. ; alicui fugam claudere, Liv. **b.** *a fleeing from, avoiding.* With *Obj.* : GEN. : laborum et dolorum, Cic. ; pericli, Verg. ; Hor.

fugācius, *comp. adv.* *with a greater inclination towards flight* : bellum gerere, Liv.

fugāx, ācis, *adj.* [fugiō], *ready or apt to take flight ; fugitive, timid.* **1.** Lit. **a.** *caprea,* Verg. ; mors et fugacem persequitur virum, Hor. ; fugacissimus hostis, Liv. Of a woman : *coy, shy* : Hor. **b.** *speeding*

swiftly away, fleeting : volucrique fugacior
aurā, Ov. **2.** Transf. **a.** With GEN.:
shunning, avoiding : ambitionis, Ov. **b.**
fleeting, transitory : haec omnia contemne :
brevia, fugacia, caduca existima, Cic. Ep. ;
fugaces labuntur anni, Hor.

fŭgĭens, entis. **I.** *Part.* fugiō. **II.** Adj.:
fleeing. **1.** Lit.: *scared :* Lucr. **2.**
Transf. **a.** *retreating :* portus ad litora,
Prop. **b.** With *Obj.* GEN.: *averse from,
shunning :* laboris, Caes. **c.** *fleeting* (i.e.
spoiling) *:* vinum, Cic.

fŭgĭō, fugere, fūgī, fugitum [*cf.* Gk. φεύγω].
A. Intrans.: *to flee, to take flight, run
away, make off.* **1.** Lit.: Pl., Cic., Hor.,
etc. Occ.: *to escape* (as the result of
flight) : ex proelio, Cic. Ep. **b.** *to go into
exile :* Cic., Ov. **c.** *to go off in flight, to
speed, to hasten away :* tenuis fugiens per
gramina rivus, Verg. ; nubes, Hor. ; Tantalus a labris sitiens fugientia captat
flumina, Hor. **2.** Transf. **a.** *to have an
aversion from :* omne animal appetit quaedam et fugit a quibusdam, Cic. ; Quint.
b. *to fly, pass quickly away :* de corpore
vires, Verg. ; ore color, Hor. Esp. of the
flight of time : irreparabile tempus, Verg. ;
annus, Hor. **B.** Trans.: *to flee from,
avoid, shun.* **1.** Lit. **a.** concilia conven-
tūsque hominum, Caes. ; Cic. ; Verg., etc.
Esp. *to leave one's country ; to be exiled
from :* nos patriam fugimus, Verg. ; Hor.
Occ.: *to escape from* (by flight) : Acheronta, Hor. ; Verg. **2.** Transf. **a.** *to
shun, avoid, forgo :* conspectum multitudinis, Caes. ; superbiam adrogantiamque
magno opere fugiāmus, Cic. ; laborem, Ter.,
Verg. ; quod si curam fugimus, virtus
fugienda est, Cic. With *Inf.* : Lucr., Cic.,
Verg., etc. **b.** *to be averse from, avoid with
scorn* or *dislike :* nuptias, Ter. ; Nep.
c. *to escape, fail :* vox Moerim fugit, Verg. ;
quos viros vigilantia, Verg. **d.** *to escape*
(one's notice, etc.): tanta est animi
tenuitas, ut fugiat aciem, Cic. Esp. with
Acc. of person : *to escape one's notice ;
not to be known to,* etc. : hominem amentem
hoc fugit, Cic. , Quint. With *Inf.* or
Indir. Quest. as *Subject :* Cic. Ep. [It.
fuggire ; Sp. *huir ;* Fr. *fuir.*]

fŭgĭtans, antis. **I.** *Part.* fugitō. **II.** Adj.:
fleeing, avoiding : with *Obj.* GEN.: litium,
Ter.

fŭgĭtīvus, a, um [fŭgĭō]. **I.** *runaway, truant,
fugitive :* canis, Pl. ; servi, Liv. ; Hor.
With *prep.* : a domino, Cic. **II.** More
freq. as Noun, *a runaway slave :* Pl., Cic.,
Hor., etc. As a term of abuse: Pl., Ter.

fŭgĭtō, āre [*freq.* fugiō]. **A.** Intrans.:
to flee hastily : Ter. **B.** Trans.: *to flee
from, avoid, shun.* **1.** Lit.: erum, Pl. ;
Ter. ; Lucr. **2.** Transf.: quaestionem,
Cic. ; tuom conspectum, Ter. With *Inf.* :
Ter., Lucr.

fŭgĭtor, ōris, *m.* [fugiō], *one who runs away :*
Pl.

fŭgō, āre [fuga], *to put to flight, drive* or *chase
away.* **1.** Lit. **a.** exercitum, Liv. ; Cic.,
etc. ; aliquem, Cic., Hor. **b.** *to send into
exile :* Lucr., Ov. **2.** Transf. **a.** astra
Phoebus, Hor. ; flammas a classe, Ov.
b. *to drive away, avert :* audacem fugat

hoc poetam, Hor. ; multos a proposito,
Quint.

fulcĭmen, inis, *n.* [fulciō], *a prop, support,
pillar :* Ov.

fulcĭō, fulcire, fulsī, fultum, *to prop up, to
stay, support.* **1.** Lit.: vitem, Cic. ;
Atlas, caelum qui vertice fulcit, Verg. ;
Scaurum pravis fultum male talis, Hor.
2. Transf. **a.** Materially: *to support,
secure, strengthen :* fultosque emuniit
obice postis, Verg. ; ianua fulta serā, Ov. ;
stomachum cibo, Sen. Ep. **b.** Immaterially : labantem rem publicam, Cic. ; fulcire
putatur porticum Stoicorum, Cic. ; his
fultus societatibus atque amicitiis, Liv. ;
subsidiis fulta prima acies fuit, Liv. ; serie
genus, Prop.

fulcrum, i, *n.* [fulciō], *the post* or *foot of a
couch, a bed-post.* **1.** Lit. : Verg., Suet.,
etc. **2.** Transf.: *a couch, bed :* Juv.

fulgeō, fulgēre, fūlsī (acc. to the 3rd conj.:
fulgit, Lucr. ; fulgere, Verg.) [v. flagrō], *to
flash* (with light), *to lighten.* **1.** Lit.: si
fulserit, si tonuerit, Cic. ; Lucr. ; fulsere
ignes et aether, Verg. **2.** Transf. **a.** *to
flash, glitter, shine :* Enn. ; unguentis,
purpura, Cic. ; micantes fulsere gladii,
Liv. ; arma, Verg. ; oculi, Hor. ; caelo
luna, Hor. ; Cyclades (on account of their
white marble), Hor. **b.** fulgere, tonare,
permiscere Graeciam (of the eloquence of
Pericles), Cic. **c.** *to shine, to be distinguished :* M. Claudium fulgentem Siciliā
domitā, Liv. ; honoribus, Hor. ; sacerdotio,
Tac. ; indoles virtutis in adulescentulo, Nep.

fulgĭdus, a, um [fulgeō], *flashing, glittering,
shining :* Lucr.

fulgō, v. fulgeō.

fulgor, ōris, *m.* [fulgeō], *lightning* (mostly
poet. for fulgur). **1.** Lit.: Lucr., Verg.,
Ov. In *pl.* : Cic. **2.** Transf. **a.** *flash,
glitter, brightness, splendour :* candelabri,
Cic. ; armorum, Hor. ; vestis, Ov. In *pl.* :
stupet insanis acies fulgoribus (*glittering
plate*), Hor. **b.** *a bright star :* salutaris
ille fulgor, qui dicitur Iovis, Cic. **c.** *splendour, glory :* nominis et famae, Ov. ; Hor. ;
Quint.

fulgur, uris, *n.* [fulgeō], *a flash of lightning,
lightning, levin.* **1.** Lit. : Cic., Ov., Tac.,
etc. **2.** Transf. **a.** (for fulmen) *a stroke
of lightning :* Lucr., Verg., Hor. **b.** *a
thing struck by lightning, a levin-spot :* aliquis senior qui publica fulgura condit, Juv.
c. *brightness, splendour :* solis, Lucr. [Fr.
foudre.]

fulgŭrālis, e, *adj.* [fulgur], *treating of lightning :* libri, Cic.

fulgŭrātor, ōris, *m.* [fulgur], *a priest who
interprets and propitiates lightning :* Cic.

fulgŭrītus, a, um [fulgur], *struck by lightning :*
arbores, Pl.

fulgŭrō, āre [fulgur], *to send lightning, to
lighten.* **1.** Lit.: Iove tonante, fulgu-
rante, comitia populi habere nefas, Cic.
Impers. : Plin. **2.** Transf. of oratory:
Quint., Plin. Ep.

fŭlĭca, ae (also **fŭlix,** icis, Cic. poet.), *f. the
coot,* a water-fowl : Verg., Ov.

fūlĭgō, inis, *f. soot.* **1.** Lit. : Pl., Cic.,
Verg., etc. **2.** Transf.: *black paint*
(= stibium), Juv.

fulix, icis, v. fulica.

fullō, ōnis, *m. a fuller, cloth-fuller :* Pl., Plin.

fullōnica, ae, *f.* [fullō], (*sc.* ars) *the fuller's craft ; fulling :* Pl.

fullōnius, a, um [fullō], *of a fuller :* Pl.

fulmen, inis, *n.* [for fulg-men, fr. root of fulgeō], *a stroke of lightning, a thunderbolt* (dist. fr. fulgur, *the flash*). **1.** Lit.: Lucr., Cic., Verg., etc. **2.** Transf. **a.** *a bolt* (*cf.* Eng. *a bolt from the blue*), i.e. a sudden disaster : fulmina fortunae contemnere, Cic.; duo fulmina meam domum per hos dies perculerunt, Liv. **b.** Of force like lightning : fulmen habent acres in aduncis dentibus apri, Ov.; duo fulmina belli Scipiadas, Verg.; Lucr.; Cic.

fulmenta, ae, *f.* [for fulc-menta, fr. root of fulciō]. **I.** *a prop support* of a building ; Cato. **II.** Comic.: *of the heel of a shoe :* Pl.

fulmineus, a, um [fulmen], *of lightning.* **1.** Lit.: ignis, Lucr., Ov.; ictus, Hor. **2.** Transf.: *with the force of lightning :* ensis, Verg.; Mnestheus, Verg.; os apri, Ov.; dentes apri, Phaedr.

fulminō, āre [fulmen], *to hurl lightnings.* **1.** Lit.: Hor. Impers. : Verg. **2.** Transf.: Caesar dum magnus ad altum fulminat Euphratem bello, Verg.; oculis, Prop.

fultūra, ae, *f.* [fulciō], *a prop, stay.* Transf.: accedit stomacho fultura ruenti, Hor.; corporis fulturis animus sustinetur, Plin. Ep.

fultus, a, um, *Part.* fulciō.

fulvus, a, um, *dun, tawny, bronze, red-brown, yellow-brown :* corpora fulva leonum, Lucr.; tegmen lupae, Verg.; harena, Verg., Ov.; aurum, Verg., Ov.; lumen, nubes, Verg.

fūmeus, a, um [fūmus], *full of smoke, smoking :* lumina taedis, Verg.

fūmidus, a, um [fūmus], *full of smoke, smoking, steaming :* templa caeli, Lucr.; taeda, Verg.; altaria, Ov.; amnis, Verg.

fūmifer, era, erum [fūmus ferō], *producing smoke ; smoking :* Verg.

fūmificō, āre [fūmus faciō], *to cause smoke ; to burn incense :* Pl.

fūmificus, a, um [fūmus faciō], *causing smoke ; smoking, steaming :* mugitus (taurorum), Ov.

fūmō, āre [fūmus], *to smoke, steam, reek, fume :* agger, Caes.; summa villarum culmina, Verg.; domus, Cic.; recenti fossione terram fumare calentem, Cic.; fumantis pulvere campos, Verg.; altaria donis, Lucr.; equos fumantis sudore, Verg.

fūmōsus, a, um [fūmus], *smoked :* imagines, Cic.; magistri equitum, Juv.; perna, Hor.; cadus, Ov.

fūmus, i, *m.* [*cf.* Gk. θυμός, θύος]. **1.** Lit. **a.** *smoke :* Pl., Cic., Verg., etc. In *pl.* : Caes. **b.** *steam* (in *pl.*) : Verg. **2.** Transf.: omne verterat in fumum et cinerem (i.e. had consumed), Hor. [Sp. *humo.*]

fūnālis, e, *adj.* [fūnis], *attached to a rope or cord ;* equus, *a trace-horse,* Suet. As Noun, **fūnāle**, is, *n.* **I.** *a cord or thong of a sling :* Liv. **II.** *a waxed cord ; a wax-torch.* **1.** Lit.: Cic., Verg., Hor. **2.** Transf.: *a chandelier :* Ov.

fūnambulus, i, *m.* [fūnis ambulō], *a rope-dancer :* Ter., Suet.

fūnctiō, ōnis, *f.* [fungor], *a discharging ; a performance :* with both *Obj.* and *Subj.* GEN.: labor est functio quaedam vel animi vel corporis gravioris operis et muneris, Cic.

fūnctus, a, um, *Part.* fungor.

funda, ae, *f.* [*cf.* Gk. σφενδόνη], *a sling.* **1.** Lit.: Pl., Caes., Verg., etc. **2.** Transf. **a.** *a sling-stone :* Caes., Liv. **b.** *a casting-net, drag-net :* Verg. [Sp. *honda.*]

fundāmen, inis, *n.* [fundō, āre], *a foundation* (mostly in *pl.*) : ponere fundamina, Verg.; Siculae terrae, Ov.

fundāmentum, i, *n.* [fundō, āre], *a foundation, ground-work, basis* (mostly in *pl.*). **1.** Lit. In *sing.* : Pl. In *pl.* : Caes., Verg., etc. ; a fundamentis diruere, proruere, Liv. ; *to lay the foundations :* agere, Cic. ; locare, Verg. ; iacere, Liv. **2.** Transf. In *sing.* : pietas fundamentum est omnium virtutum, Cic. ; imperi, Sen. Ep. In *pl.* : libertatis, Cic. ; Quint.

fundātor, ōris, *m.* [fundō, āre], *a founder :* urbis, Verg.

fundātus, a, um. **I.** *Part.* fundō. **II.** *Adj.* : *on firm foundations.* Transf. (in *Sup.*) : familia, Cic.

funditō, āre [funda], *to ply the sling, to sling or fling about.* **1.** Lit.: globos, Pl. **2.** Transf.: verba, Pl.

funditor, ōris, *m.* [funda], *a slinger :* Caes., Sall.

funditus, *adv.* [fundus]. **I.** *from the very bottom, from the foundations.* **1.** Lit.: monumentum funditus delere, Cic.; perire, Hor. **2.** Transf.: belli commovit funditus aestūs, Lucr.; rem publicam evertere, Cic.; iustitiam funditus tollere, Cic.; abolitae leges et versae funditus, Tac. **II.** *at the bottom, below :* subsedit funditus, ut faex, Lucr.

fundō, āre [fundus], *to lay the bottom, keel, foundation,* etc.; *to found.* **1.** Lit.: Pl.; mea puppis erat validā fundata carinā, Ov.; Erycino in vertice sedes fundatur Veneri Idaliae, Verg. **2.** Transf. **a.** *to secure to the ground :* dente tenaci ancora fundabat navis, Verg. **b.** *to lay or make secure the foundations of* (esp. in *Perf. Part.*): illud vero maxime nostrum fundavit imperium, Cic. With *Abl.* of basis : bonorum coniunctione fundatus, Cic. Ep. ; qui legibus urbem fundavit, Verg. ; nitidis fundata pecunia villis, Hor.

fundō, fundere, fūdi, fūsum [*cf.* Gk. χέω, *Perf.* κέ-χυ-κα], *to pour, pour out.* **1.** Lit. **a.** sanguinem e paterā, Cic. ; vina paterā in aras, Ov. ; lacrimas, Verg. With *Refl. Pron.* or in *Mid.* : *to pour, stream, gush forth :* Cic., Liv. **b.** Of metals : *to melt ; hence to cast, found in metal :* Hor., Quint. **2.** Transf. of things non-fluid. **A.** With idea of abundance, etc. **a.** *to pour forth in abundance or in streams, to shower* (esp. of light, odour, etc.) : luna se plena fundebat per fenestras, Verg. ; a vertice flamma funditur, Verg. ; Liv. ; odores in pectora, Ov. ; animam, Lucr. ; vitam, Verg. ; tela, Verg. ; picem, Caes. ; hostis de iugis, Liv. **b.** *to bring forth, bear, produce in abundance :*

Lucr., Cic., Verg. **c.** Of words, etc. :
mendacia, Pl. ; vocem, carmen, etc., Cic. ;
has ore loquellas Verg. **B.** With idea of
spreading out. **a.** *to pour forth, spread out
or abroad :* ne vitis in omnis partis nimia
fundatur, Cic. ; homines fusi per agros
vagantur, Cic. ; tum se latius fundet
orator, Cic. **b.** Milit. : *to scatter in rout :*
hostium copias, Caes. ; Cic. ; Liv. **c.** *to
spread out, extend* on the ground : corpora
(cervorum) humi, Verg. ; duos diverso
vulnere, Ov. Esp. in *Part.* (Pass. or
Mid.) : corpora ferro fusa iacebant, Verg. ;
fusus in herbā, Ov.

fundus, ī, m. [*cf.* Gk. πυθμήν], ground. **I.**
the bottom. **1.** Lit. : armari fundum
exsecuit, Cic. ; dolium a fundo pertusum,
Liv. ; (Aetna) fundo exaestuat imo, Verg.
2. Transf. **a.** largitio fundum non habet,
Cic. ; fluxas Phrygiae res vertere fundo,
Verg. **b.** Legal : *the ultimate approver
or sanctioner :* nisi is populus fundus factus
esset, Cic. ; Pl. **II.** Of land : *farm,
estate :* Pl., Cic., Hor., etc. [Sp. *hondo ;*
It. *fondo ;* Fr. *fond, fonds.*]

fūnebris, e, *adj.* [fūnus], *of a funeral, funereal.*
1. Lit. : contio, epulum, Cic. ; cupressi,
Hor. ; pompa, Tac. **2.** Transf. : *deadly,
murderous :* bellum, Hor. ; sacra, Ov.

fūnerātus, a, um [fūnus ; but regarded as
Part. fūnerō], *done to death :* Hor.

fūnereus, a, um [fūnus], *of a funeral, funeral-.*
1. Lit. : faces, Verg. **2.** Transf. :
deadly, fatal : torris, Ov.

fūnerō, āre [fūnus], *to bury with funeral rites,
to inter :* Plin., Suet.

fūnestō, āre [fūnestus], *to pollute or contaminate with death.* **1.** Lit. : aras humanis hostiis, Cic. **2.** Transf. : gentem,
Juv.

fūnestus, a, um [fūnus]. **A.** Act. : *causing
death or destruction : deadly, fatal :* ad
eius funestam securim servati, Cic. ; arma,
Ov. ; taeda, Verg. *Comp. :* funestior
dies, Cic. With DAT. : o diem illum
funestum senatui bonisque omnibus ! Cic.
B. Pass. : *filled with death or grief for
death, in mourning :* agri, Lucr. ; familia,
Cic., Liv. ; annales velut funesti, Liv. ;
utque manūs funestas arceat aris (i.e.
blood-stained), Ov.

fungīnus, a, um [fungus], *of a mushroom :*
Pl.

fungor, fungī, fūnctus, *to satisfy or employ
oneself* (with *Instr.* ABL.) ; *to discharge,
perform, execute, undergo :* munere, Cic.,
etc. ; officio, Cic. ; Liv. ; sacris, Hor. ;
laboribus, Hor. ; vice cotis, Hor. ; ter
aevo functus senex (Nestor), Hor. ; dapibus, Ov. ; eo sumptu, Tac. With ACC. :
Pl., Ter., Lucr. ; *cf.* use of *Gerundive :*
muneris fungendi gratiā, Cic. ; spes facta
militiae fungendae potioribus ducibus, Liv.
Absol. : facere et fungi sine corpore nulla
potest res, Lucr.

fungus, ī, m. [Gk. σφόγγος, σπόγγος]. *a mushroom, fungus.* **1.** Lit. : Pl., Hor. **2.**
Transf. **a.** *a dolt :* Pl. **b.** *a mushroom-
like formation* on the wick of a candle or
lamp burning ; *a clot :* Verg.

fūniculus, ī, m. [*dim.* fūnis], *a slender rope,
a cord :* Cic., Quint.

fūnis, is, m. (*f.,* Lucr.), *rigging ; a rope,
cable, cord :* Cato, Caes., Verg., etc.
Phr. : funem ducere *or* sequi (i.e. to command or serve), Hor. ; funem reducere
(i.e. to change one's mind), Pers.

fūnus, eris, *n. a burial, funeral.* **1.** Lit. :
Cic., Hor., etc. In *pl. :* Cic., Verg., etc.
Phr. : iusta funera conficere, Caes. ; funere
efferri, Cic. ; funus ornare, facere alicui,
Cic. (Comic. : funus facere prandio,
Pl.) ; celebrare, Liv. ; funus militare
alicui facere, Liv. ; funeri omnia iusta
solvere, Cic. **2.** Transf. **a.** *death,* esp.
violent death, murder : exstinctum Nymphae crudeli funere Daphnin flebant, Verg. ;
Hor. In *pl. :* Verg., Hor. ; edere, Liv.
b. *a corpse :* lacerum, Verg. **c.** *destruction, ruin, fall :* rei publicae, Cic. ; dum
regina funus imperio parabat, Hor. In
pl. : Troiae, Hor. Of persons : Gabinium
et Pisonem, duo rei publicae portenta ac
paene funera, Cic.

fuō, v. sum.

fūr, fūris, m. *f.* [Gk. φώρ], *a thief :* Pl., Cic.,
Hor., etc. As term of abuse towards slaves :
thief, knave : Pl., Ter., Verg.

fūrācissimē, adv. [fūrāx], *most thievishly :*
Cic.

fūrāx, ācis, adj. [fūror], *given to stealing,
thievish :* Cic. *Comp. :* Mart. *Sup. :*
Cic.

furca, ae, *f. a fork* (us. *two-pronged*). **1.**
Lit. : Caes., Verg., Liv. Prov. : naturam
expellas furcā, tamen usque recurret,
Hor. **2.** Transf. **a.** *a fork-shaped prop
or pole for supporting vines :* Verg. ; *a
fork-shaped prop, pole for supporting the
seats of a theatre,* Liv. : *for the gable of a
house,* Ov. ; *for pushing off a scaling-party :*
Liv. **b.** *a (rough) pillory for punishing
slaves :* Pl., Cic., Hor., etc. **c.** *a narrow
pass or defile :* Furcae Caudinae (us. Furculae), Luc. [Sp. *horca ;* Fr. *fourche ;* also
It. *forcone ;* Sp. *hurgon ;* Fr. *fourgon.*]

furcifer, erī, m. [furca ferō], *bearing the
furca ;* as a term of abuse applied **a.** to
slaves ; *gallows-rogue, rascal :* Pl., Cic.,
Hor. **b.** to free persons : Cic.

furcilla, ae, *f.* [*dim.* furca], *a little fork :*
Cic. Ep., Cat.

furcillō, āre [furcilla], *to support.* Transf. :
meam fidem, Pl.

furcula, ae, *f.* [*dim.* furca], *a forked prop.*
1. Lit. : suspenso furculis ab hostibus
muro, Liv. **2.** Transf. : Furculae Caudinae, *a double fork-shaped defile near Caudium* where the Roman army was hemmed
in by the Samnites (B.C. 321) ; *the Caudine
Forks :* Liv.

furenter, adv. *furiously :* Cic. Ep.

furfur, uris, m. bran. **1.** Lit. : Pl. In
pl. : Pl., Varr., Phaedr. **2.** Transf. :
scurf on the skin, head, etc. : Plin. In a
pun : Phaedr.

Furia, ae, oftener in *pl.* **Furiae,** ārum, *f.*
[furō], *the spirits of frenzy and madness.*
1. Lit. **a.** *the (avenging) spirits (of the
dead) urging to frenzy and madness :* Liv.
b. *the avenging goddesses, the Furies :* Cic.,
Verg., Hor. **2.** Transf. **a.** Of a person
acting like a Fury : *evil spirit :* Cic., Hor.,
Liv. **b.** *frenzy, madness of spirit leading

to destruction : Cic., Verg., Liv. O c c. of sexual frenzy : Verg., Ov. **c.** *frenzy of wrath and thirst for vengeance :* Verg. **d.** *frenzy foretelling evil :* Cassandrae, Verg.

furiālis, e, *adj.* [furia]. **I.** *belonging to the Furies :* Cic., Verg., Ov. **II.** *like the Furies.* **a.** P a s s.: *frenzied, maddened, frantic :* vox, Cic. ; caput Cerberi, Hor. ; arma (i.e. *of the Bacchantes*), Ov. ; carmen, Liv. **b.** A c t.: *making mad, infuriating :* vestis, Poet. ap. Cic.

furiāliter, *adv. in a frenzied or frantic way :* odit, Ov.

furibundus, a, um [furō], *frenzied, frantic, mad.* **a.** In gen.: homo, impetus, Cic. ; aer, Lucr. ; Leo, Hor. **b.** Of prophetic inspiration : praedictiones, Cic.

furīnus, a, um [für], *of thieves :* Pl.

furiō, āre [furiae], *to madden :* matres equorum, Hor. ; furiata mens, Verg. ; furiati ignes (amoris), Ov.

furiōsē, *adv. in frenzy, madly :* Cic. Ep.

furiōsus, a, um [furia], *full of madness or frenzy ; mad, frenzied, frantic.* **1.** L i t. of persons : Cic., Hor. **2.** T r a n s f. of things : cupiditas, contiones, genus dicendi, Cic. ; inceptum, Liv. ; vultus, Lucr. ; amor, vota, Ov. *Comp. :* Hor., Ov. *Sup. :* Cic.

furnāria, ae, *f.* [furnus], *the trade of a baker :* furnariam exercere, Suet.

furnus (**fornus**, Varr.), i, *m. an oven :* Pl., Hor., Ov.

furō, ere [*cf.* Gk. φύρω], *to rage, rave : to be out of one's mind, distracted, mad, frantic.* **1.** L i t. Of persons. **a.** In gen.: Cic., Hor. With Acc. and *Inf. :* Cic. Ep. **b.** Of the passions : libidinibus, audaciā, Cic. ; dolore, irā, Ov. ; Inachiā furere (*to be madly in love* with), Hor. With *Cogn.* or *Intern.* Acc.: Verg., Liv. With *Inf. :* Hor. **2.** T r a n s f. Of things : ventus, nubes, Lucr. ; aether, aestus, tempestas, flammae, Verg. ; ardor edendi, Ov.

furor, ārī (*Supine* fūrātum, Pl.) [für], *to thieve, steal, purloin, pilfer.* **1.** L i t. **a.** In gen.: Pl. With Acc.: Cic., Quint. **b.** Of military pillage : Tac. **c.** Of literary plagiarism : Cic. Ep. **2.** T r a n s f. **a.** *to steal away :* pone caput fessosque oculos furare labori, Verg. **b.** *to steal,* i.e. *falsely adopt, personate :* civitatem, Cic. ; speciem Iacchi, Prop.

furor, ōris, *m.* [furō], *a raving ; madness, frenzy, wild excitement, delirium.* **1.** L i t. **a.** In gen.: Cic., Hor., etc. **b.** Of the passions (esp. of love) : Verg., Ov., etc. ; of lust of battle : Verg. ; hence personified : Verg. ; of political excitement : Caes., Liv. **c.** Of the *inspired frenzy* of prophets and poets : Cic., Prop. In *pl. :* Ov. **2.** T r a n s f.: furores caeli marisque, Verg. ; Cat.

furtificus, a, um [fūrtum faciō], *that commits theft, thievish :* Pl.

furtim, *adv.* [fūrtum], *by stealth, secretly, clandestinely, privily :* Pl., Cic., Hor., Liv., etc. ; furtim magis quam bello, Tac.

furtīvē, *adv. stealthily, secretly :* Pl., Ov., Sen.

furtivus, a, um [fūrtum], *stolen, purloined, pilfered.* **1.** L i t.: Pl., Hor., Liv., etc.

2. T r a n s f.: *secret, hidden, concealed, furtive :* iter, Cic. ; amor, Verg. ; nox, mens, libertas, Ov.

fūrtum, i, *n.* [für], *theft, robbery.* **1.** L i t.: facere, Pl., Cic., etc. ; furti aliquem adstringere, Pl. ; in furto comprehensus, Caes. ; oves furto periere, Hor. **2.** T r a n s f. **a.** (in *pl.* only) : *stolen goods,* Cic., Hor. **b.** *a secret action ; trick, artifice, stratagem :* haud furto melior, Verg. ; furto et fraude, Liv. In *pl. :* furta belli, Verg. ; Sall. ; Ov. **c.** *stolen or secret love, intrigue :* Verg., Ov. In *pl. :* Cat., Verg., Ov. ABL. *sing.* **fūrtō** as *Adv., by stealth, in secret :* Ov., Liv.

fūrunculus, i, *m.* [*dim.* für], *a petty thief, pilferer :* Cic.

furvus, a, um [*cf.* fuscus], *black.* **1.** L i t.: nubes, Lucr. ; equus, Ov. ; gens (Maurorum), Juv. **2.** T r a n s f. of the nether world : *black, dark, obscure :* ex Acheronte suo furvis peperisse sub antris, Ov. ; furvae regna Proserpinae, Hor.

fuscina, ae, *f. a three-pronged spear, a trident :* Juv. ; of Neptune : Cic., Suet.

fuscō, āre [fuscus], *to blacken, darken :* fuscentur corpora campo, Ov. ; Luc.

fuscus, a, um [*cf.* furvus], *dark, swarthy, dusky.* **1.** L i t.: purpura, Cic. ; nubila, Ov. ; alae (noctis), Verg. ; Andromede, Ov. *Comp. :* Plin. **2.** T r a n s f. of the voice : *indistinct, muffled, low :* Cic., Quint.

fūsē, *adv.* **I.** *widely :* manus fusius resolvitur, Quint. **II.** *copiously, diffusely :* aliquid disputare, Cic. *Comp. :* Cic., Quint.

fūsilis, e, *adj.* [fundō, ere], *molten, softened, liquid :* argilla, Caes. ; aurum, Ov.

fūsio, ōnis, *f.* [fundō, ere], *a pouring out, efflux :* animi, Cic. [Fr. *foison*.]

fūstis, is (ABL. regularly fūsti ; fūste, Hor.), *m. a knobbed stick, a stick :* Pl., Varr., Hor. E s p. for *cudgelling :* male mulcati clavis ac fustibus, Cic. ; Pl. ; Hor., etc. And for *beating to death* as a milit. punishment : decimum quemque fusti necat, Tac. ; Sall. [Fr. *fût*.]

fūstitudinus, a, um [fūstis tundō]. C o m i c.: *cudgel-bang-ian :* insulae (i.e. ergastula), Pl.

fūstuārium, i, *n.* [fūstis], *a cudgelling to death,* a military punishment : Cic., Liv.

fūsus, a, um. **I.** *Part.* fundō. **II.** *Adj.: spread out ;* hence *expanded, broad, wide.* **1.** L i t.: aer, Cic. ; Gallorum corpora, Liv. ; toga, Suet. ; fusior terra, Luc. **2.** T r a n s f. of style : *copious, diffuse :* Cic., Quint. *Comp. :* Quint.

fūsus, i, *m. a spindle :* Verg., Ov.

fūtātim, *adv.* [*cf.* cōnfūtō], *abundantly, frequently :* Pl.

fūtilis (earlier **fūttilis**), e, *adj.* [fr. root of fundō], *that easily pours out, leaky.* **1.** L i t.: canes, Phaedr. **2.** T r a n s f.: *ready to bend or break.* **a.** *brittle :* glacies, Verg. **b.** *untrustworthy, worthless, futile :* servos, Ter. ; haruspices, sententiae, alacritas, Cic. ; auctor, Verg. Neut. Acc. as *Adv. in vain :* Pl.

fūtilitās, ātis, *f.* [fūttilis], *worthlessness, futility :* Cic.

fŭtŭō, uere, uī, ūtum, *to have connexion with a female :* Cat., Mart.

futūrus, a, um. I. *Fut. Part.* sum [fuŏ, fuĭ]. II. Adj.: *future, coming, imminent :* res, tempus, Cic.; mors, soccr, Ov. III. As Noun, futūrum, ĭ, *n. the future :* futurum prospicere, Cic.; ignarus futuri, Liv.; Verg.; in futurum videre, Liv.

fŭvī, old *Perf.* of sum [fuŏ].

G

G, g, *indecl. n.*, or (*sc.* littera), *f.* the seventh letter of the Roman alphabet. I. a. C, not G, at first represented the guttural media in Latin; the pronunciation of C subsequently became identical with that of K; and the new symbol G was introduced. The earliest inscription in which it is found is the epitaph of Scipio Barbatus, which is not later than 234 B.C.
b. As an initial, *g*, in pure Latin words, enters into consonantal combination with *l* and *r* only; hence in roots which originally began with *gn*, the *g* was dropped in the classical period; thus gnascor, gnatus, gnosco, gnomen, became nascor, natus, nosco, nomen; but in compounds the *g* often reappears, as in cognatus, ignosco, agnomen. c. With *s*, *g* combines to form *x*; e.g. the stem *reg*- has Nom. *sing.* rex. Similarly in the perfect tenses of verbs, as *rego, rexi.* But sometimes the *g* disappears between two consonants, as in *mulgeo, mulsi*, fulgeo, fulmen. II. Latin *g* usually corresponds to orig. Indo-European *g*, and therefore to Greek γ, as in Lat. *genus*, Gk. γένος. Orig. *gh* (Gk. χ) is also represented in Latin by *g* when not initial, as in Lat. *anguis*, Gk. ἔχις. Initial *g* from *gh* appears not to be found in Latin except where the *g* is followed by *r*, as in *gratus*, Gk. χαίρω. In a few words Latin *g* has arisen from orig. *k* : as in *digitus*, Gr. δάκτυλος. III. According to Grimm's law, Latin *g*, from Indo-European *g*, corresponds to *k* in Gothic and to *ch* in Old High German; thus we have Lat. *genus* beside Goth. *kuni*, Eng. *kin*, O. H. G. *chind*. IV. *g* before a, o, u, remains unchanged in French; before *e* and *i* it sometimes becomes *s* or *c* ; thus Lat. *fragea* (from *fragum*), Fr. *fraise* ; Lat. *gingiva*, Fr. *gencive*. It becomes *j* in *jaune* from Lat. *galbinus*, and *jumeau* from Lat. *gemellus*. It is sometimes omitted in French between vowels, as in *nier* from Lat. *negare* ; *trente* from Lat. *triginta* ; *août* from Lat. *augustus*. In Spanish, initial *g* sometimes becomes *h*, as in *hermano* from Lat. *germanus*.

gaesum, ĭ, *n.* [Celtic word], *a long heavy javelin :* of the Gauls: Caes., Liv., Verg.; of Roman skirmishers: Liv.

Gaetūlī, ōrum, *m. pl. a people of N.W. Africa bordering on the Sahara ;* Gaetŭlus, a, um ; Gaetūlicus, a, um.

Gāius (or in short C), *a Roman praenomen.* a. *The names* Gaius *and* Gaia *were used formally of a bridegroom and bride.* b. In partic.: i. Gaius Caesar, v. Caligula. ii. *an eminent jurist* (A.D. 110-180).

Galatae, ārum, *m. pl. a Celtic people who migrated from Gaul into Asia Minor in the 3rd century* B.C.; *the Galatians ;* Galatia, ae, *f. their country.*

galba, ae, *f.* [Celtic word]. In Gallic a nickname, *Fat-paunch :* Suet. As *a cognomen in the gens* Sulpicia ; esp. Ser. Sulpicius Galba, *Roman emperor*, A.D. 68-69.

galbaneus, a, um [galbanum], *of galbanum :* odores, Verg.

galbanum, ĭ, *n.* [χαλβάνη], *galbanum, the resinous sap of a Syrian plant :* Suet.

galbeum, ĭ, *n.* or galbeus, ĭ, *m. a kind of arm-band* (worn as an ornament, or for medical purposes): Luc., Suet.

galbinus, a, um [*cf.* gilvus], *greenish-yellow, yellowish.* 1. Lit.: avis, Mart. Neut. *pl.* as Noun (*sc.* vestimenta), *pale-green clothes* (of aesthetes): Juv. 2. Transf.: *effeminate :* mores, Mart.

galea, ae, *f. a helmet, morion.* a. Prop. of leather: Pl., Caes., Verg., etc. b. Of metal: galeae aeneae, Cic.; aerea, Verg. c. *a cap :* venatoria, Nep.

galeātus, a, um [galea], *helmeted :* Cic. As Noun: Juv. Hence galeāri, *Inf. Pass. :* milites galeari iubet, Auct. B. Afr.

galēriculum, ĭ, *n.* [*dim.* galērum], *a small covering for the head.* a. *a cap :* Mart. b. *a wig :* Suet.

galērītus, a, um [galērum], *wearing a hood or bonnet* (as country folk do) : Prop.

galērum, ĭ, *n.* (also galērus, ĭ, *m.* Verg.) [galea], *head-dress, cap.* 1. Lit.: *a cap made of undressed leather :* Verg., Juv., Suet. 2. Transf.: *a wig :* Juv., Suet.

galla, ae, *f. a gall-nut, oak-apple :* Verg.

Gallī, ōrum, *m. pl. a widely diffused race, the* Galli *or* Gauls, *whose principal abodes were* Gallia Trānsalpīna, *now* France, *and* Gallia Cisalpīna, *the northern part of Italy ;* Gallia, ae, *f.* Gaul, *the country of the Gauls ;* Gallicus, a, um, *Gallic :* canis, *a greyhound* (Ov.); Gallica (*sc.* solea), ae, *f. a kind of slipper* (Cic.); Gallicānus, a, um.

gallīna, ae, *f.* [gallus], *a hen :* Pl., Cic., Hor. As term of endearment: Pl. Phr.: gallina scripsit (of a scrawler, i.e. hentracks), Pl. Prov.: gallinae albae filius (i.e. fortune's favourite), Juv.

gallīnāceus (or -ācius), a, um [gallīna, gallus], *of domestic fowls* or *poultry :* gallus, *a poultry-cock*, Pl., Cic.

gallīnārius, ĭ, *m.* [gallīna], *a poultry-farmer :* Cic., Varr.

Gallograecī, ōrum, *m. pl.* (= Galatae), *Gauls who migrated into Asia Minor ;* Gallograecia, ae, *f.* = Galatia.

Gallus, ĭ, *m.* I. a *Roman cognomen.* Esp. C. Cornelius Gallus, *a Roman poet, friend of Vergil.* II. Gallī, ōrum, *m. pl. the priests of Cybele, so called because of their frenzy.* In *Sing.*: Gallus, ĭ, *m. a priest of Cybele.* Gallicus, a, um, *belonging to the priests of Cybele.* Transf. *of the priests of Isis.*

gallus, ĭ, *m. a cock, domestic-cock :* Cic., Hor., etc.

gānea, ae, *f.* (Cic., Liv., Tac., etc.) and gāneum, ĭ, *n.* (Pl., Ter.), *a disorderly house* or *a low eating-house.*

gāneō, ōnis, *m.* [gānea], *a debauchee :* Ter., Cic., Tac.

gāneum, v. gānea.

gangaba, ae, m. [a Persian word], *a porter* : Curt.

Gangaridae, ārum (GEN. *pl.* Gangaridum, Verg.), m. *pl. an Indian people on the Ganges.*

gannĭō, īre [perh. *cf.* Gk. γάνυμαι], *to yelp.* Transf. of persons : *to snarl* : Ter., Cat., Juv.

gannītus, ūs, m. [gannĭō], *a yelping, snarling, whining.* **1.** Lit. of dogs : Lucr. **2.** Transf. of persons : Mart.

Ganymēdēs, is, m. *a beautiful youth who was carried off by Jupiter's eagle from Mount Ida to Olympus, and there made cup-bearer in place of Hebe* ; **Ganymēdēus**, a, um.

Garamantes, um, m. *pl.* (ACC.—as, Verg.), *a nation of Africa (in the modern Fezzan).*

Garamantis, idis, f. adj.

Gargaphiē, ēs, f. *a valley of Boeotia sacred to Diana, where Actaeon was torn to pieces by his own hounds.*

garrĭō, īre [*cf.* Doric γᾶρυς, Att. γῆρυς], *to chatter, prate, tattle.* **1.** Lit. : nugas, Pl. ; aniles fabellas, Hor. ; Cic. Ep. Absol. : Ter., Cic. **2.** Transf. of frogs : *to croak*, Mart.

garrulĭtās, ātis, f. [garrulus], *talkativeness, chattering, prattle* : Ov., Quint., etc.

garrulus, a, um [garrĭō], *chattering, prattling, talkative, garrulous.* **1.** Lit. of persons : Pl., Hor. ; lingua, Ov. **2.** Transf. **a.** Of animals or inanimate things : hirundo, cicada, Verg. ; cornix, rivus, Ov. **b.** Of a time *for chatting* : hora, Prop. **c.** Of subjects of talk : garrula narrare pericula nautae, Juv.

garum, i, n. [Gk. γάρος], *a fish-sauce* : Hor., Sen. Ep., etc.

gaudēns, entis. **I.** Part. gaudeō. **II.** Adj. : *cheerful, glad* : gaudenti animo, Cic. Ep.

gaudeō, gaudēre, gāvīsus sum, [for gāvideō, *cf.* Gk. γηθέω], *to rejoice, be glad, be pleased.* **1.** Lit. of persons. **a.** In gen. : Pl., Cic., Hor. With ACC. (mostly *Intern.* or of *Neut. Pron.*) : gaudium, Ter., Cat. ; nil scio quod gaudeam, Pl. With ACC. and *Inf.* : Pl., Caes., Cic. With *Inf.* : Hor., Quint., Tac. With *quod, at the fact that* : sane gaudeo, quod te interpellavi, Cic. ; Hor. With *quom* or *quia* : Pl. With *si* : Hor. With ABL. *Instr.* : Cic., Hor., Liv., etc. With *in* and ABL. : Lucr., Prop. **b.** Esp. in phrase, in sinu or in se gaudere, *to feel a quiet joy* : in sinu, Cic., Tib ; in se, Cat. **c.** Like salvēre (*cf.* Gk. χαίρειν) in salutation : Celso gaudere refer, Hor. **2.** Transf. of inanim. and abstr. subjects : *to rejoice in, delight in* : Phoebo gaudet Parnasia rupes, Verg. ; gaudentia bracchia loris, Prop. ; laudes, quibus gaudent militum animi, Liv. [It. *godere, gioire* ; Fr. *jouir.*]

gaudium, i, n. [gaudeō], *joy, gladness* : esp. *the feeling of joy.* **1.** Lit. **a.** Mental : exclamare gaudio, Ter. ; gaudium atque laetitiam agitare, Sall. ; triumphare gaudio, Cic. ; missa legatio quae gaudio fungeretur, Tac. With *Obj.* GEN. : gaudium periculosi saltūs superati, Liv. In *pl.* : Pl., Cic., Hor., etc. **b.** Sensual : (us. in *pl.*) :

Lucr., Sall., Hor., etc. In *sing.* : Liv. **2.** Transf. : *the object which produces joy* : gaudio esse alicui, Pl. ; Clytium, nova gaudia, Verg. ; Ov. ; hoc gaudium clade foedatum est, Liv. ; fugiunt tua gaudia, Ov. [It. *gioia* ; Sp. *gozo* ; Fr. *joie.*]

gaulus, i, m. [γαυλός], *a bucket* : Pl.

gausape, is, and **gausapum**, i, n. [γαυσάπης], *a shaggy woollen cloth, frieze, felt*, used for clothing, etc. : *a garment or cover of frieze.* **1.** Lit. : Lucil., Hor. In *pl.* : gausapa, Ov. **2.** Transf. : *a shaggy beard* : Pers.

gāvīsus, a, um, Part. gaudeō.

gāza, ae, f. [Persian word ; Gk. γάζα], *the royal treasure.* **1.** Lit. : Cic., Liv., Tac., etc. **2.** Transf. : *treasure, riches, wealth* : Syriae, Cic. ; agrestis, Verg. In *pl.* : Lucr., Hor.

gelidē, adv. *coldly, frigidly* : Hor.

gelidus, a, um [gelū], *icy-cold, icy, frosty.* **1.** Lit. : aqua, Lucr., Cic. ; pruina, Lucr., Verg. ; nives, Lucr. ; valles, nox, aether, Verg. ; loca, Liv. As Noun, **gelida**, ae (*sc.* aqua), *cold water* : Hor., Juv. **2.** Transf. **a.** *cold, stiff, numbed* with death, old age, or fright : (Niobe) corporibus gelidis incumbit, Ov. ; gelidus tardante senectā sanguis hebet, Verg. **b.** Act. : *making cold, freezing* : letum, Lucr. ; tremor, Verg. ; mors, Hor. ; metus, Ov.

Gellius, a. *the name of a Roman gens.* Esp. Aulus Gellius, *a grammarian of the latter half of the second century*, A.D., *author of the "Attic Nights."*

gelō, āre [gelū]. **A.** Trans. : *to freeze, to congeal.* **1.** Lit. : fluvius, qui ferrum gelat, Mart. **2.** Transf. (of effect of fright, etc.) : pavidoque gelantur pectore, Juv. ; Luc. **B.** Intrans. : *to freeze, become frozen* : Luc. [Sp. *helar.*]

Gelōnī, ōrum, m. *pl. a Scythian people in the S. of what is now Russia* ; **Gelōnus**, i, m. *a Gelonian.*

gelū, ūs, n. (**gelum**, i, n. Varr., Lucr.; **gelus**, ūs, m. Acc.), *icy coldness, frost, cold.* **1.** Lit. (mostly in ABL.) : membra torrida gelu, Liv. ; geluque flumina constiterint acuto, Hor. ; rura gelu tum claudit hiems, Verg. **2.** Transf. : *coldness, chill* produced by death, old age, fright : sed mihi tarda gelu saeclisque effeta senectus, Verg. ; Luc.

gemebundus, a, um [gemō], *groaning or sighing* : Ov.

gemellipara, ae, f. [gemellus parĭō], *mother of twins* : Ov.

gemellus, a, um [*dim.* geminus], *paired, double.* **1.** Lit. **a.** In gen. : legio, Caes. **b.** *twin-born* : fratres, proles, Ov. As Noun, *twin-brother* : Cat. In *pl.* : Verg., Hor., Ov. **2.** Transf. : *resembling each other*, or *alike*, as twins : par nobile fratrum, nequitiā et nugis pravorum et amore gemellum, Hor. [Fr. *jumeau.*]

gemĭnātĭō, ōnis, f. [geminō], *a doubling* : verborum, Cic.

geminō, āre [geminus]. **A.** Trans. : *to double.* **1.** Lit. : victoriae laetitiam, Liv. ; decem frater geminaverat annos, Ov. In Part. Perf. : sole geminato, Cic. ; victoria, Liv. ; urbs, Liv. **2.** Transf. **a.** *to pair, join*, or *unite* : ut geminentur tigribus agni,

Hor. ; geminant Corybantes aera, Hor.
b. *to repeat, reproduce.* In *Part. Perf.* :
prope geminata cacumina montium, Liv. ;
plausus, Verg. ; vulnus, Ov. ; consulatus,
Tac. **B.** I n t r a n s.: *to be double* : Lucr.
geminus, a, um [*cf.* Gk. γάμος], *paired,
double, two-fold, both, two.* **1.** L i t. **a.** In
gen.: nuptiae, Ter. ; nomen, Cic. ; Somni
portae, Verg. ; geminae acies, Verg. ;
aures, Ov. ; Chiron (as being half-man,
half-horse), Ov. **b.** *twin :* fratres, Cic. ;
sorores, Ov. ; pueri, proles, Verg. As
Noun, **gemini,** órum, *m. pl. twins :* Cic.,
Liv. As name of a constellation : *Gemini :*
Varr. **2.** T r a n s f.: *resembling, similar,
like,* as twins : geminum in scelere par,
Cic. ; audacia, Cic.
gemitus, ûs (old Gᴇɴ. *sing.* gemiti, Pl.),
m. [gemō], *a sighing, sigh, groan.* **1.** L i t.
Of persons : Cic., Verg. ; ut gemitus
fieret, Cic. ; gemitum dare, tollere, Verg.
In *pl.* : Ter., Cic., Verg., etc. ; gemitūs
edere, Lucr. ; ciere, Verg. ; excitare, Liv.
2. T r a n s f. of things : *a groaning, roaring,
roar :* dat tellus gemitum, Verg. In *pl.* :
plaga facit gemitūs, Cic.
gemma, ae, *f.* [fr. root gen- of gignō], *a bud
or eye on a plant.* **1.** L i t. : Cic., Verg.
2. T r a n s f. **a.** *a precious stone,* esp. one
already cut, *a jewel, gem :* Cic., Ov., etc.
Hence of *things made of precious stones.*
(i) *a goblet :* ut gemmā bibat, Verg. ; Ov.
(ii) *a seal-ring, signet :* impressā gemmā
signare, Ov. ; Juv. Comic.: Pl. (iii) *a
pearl :* Prop. **b.** Of *things resembling
gems :* e.g. *the eyes of the peacock's tail :*
Ov. **c.** In literary sense, like *gem* in
English : *ornament, beauty :* in carmine
gemmas invenies, Mart.
gemmātus, a, um [gemma], *bejewelled :*
anuli, Liv. ; monilia, Ov. ; pocula, Juv.
gemmeus, a, um [gemma], *composed of, set,
or adorned with precious stones ; jewelled.*
1. L i t. : Cic., Ov. **2.** T r a n s f. **a.** *adorned
with what look like jewels :* cauda (of a
peacock), Phaedr. **b.** *glittering, sparkling :*
euripus, Plin. Ep. **c.** *brilliant :* rumor,
Mart.
gemmifer, era, erum [gemma ferō], *bearing
gems :* mare, Prop.
gemmō, āre [gemma], *to bud, sprout.* **1.**
L i t. : Varr., Cic. **2.** T r a n s f. (only in
Pres. Part.) **a.** *set with precious stones :*
gemmantia sceptra, Ov. **b.** *sparkling* as
with jewels : herbae gemmantes rore,
Lucr. ; gemmantis explicat alas (pavo),
Mart.
gemō, ere, uī, itum [*cf.* Gk. γέμω]. **A.**
I n t r a n s.: *to sigh, groan.* **1.** L i t. Of
persons : Pl., Cic., Prop., etc. **2.** T r a n s f.
a. Of animals : (leones), Lucr. ; turtur ab
ulmo, Verg. **b.** Of inanimate subjects, *to
moan, groan :* gementis litora Bospori,
Hor. ; malus antemnaeque gemant, Hor. ;
gemuit sub pondere cumba, Verg. ; rota,
Verg. ; gubernacula, Plin. Ep. **B.**
T r a n s.: *to sigh over, bemoan, bewail.*
With Acc. : Lucr., Cic., Verg., etc. In
Pass. : status qui voce omnium gemitur,
Cic. Ep. With *Inf.* : paucis ostendi gemis,
Hor. With Acc. and *Inf.* : Hor., Mart.
[Fr. *geindre*.]

Gemōniae (with or without **scālae**), ārum.
f. pl. : *steps up the Capitoline hill, on which
the bodies of criminals were thrown out from
the Carcer :* Juv., Tac., etc.
gena, ae, *f.,* mostly in *pl.* (orig. Dual), **genae,**
ārum [*cf.* Gk. γένυς]. **1.** L i t.: *chin, or
cheeks and chin :* pilosae, Cic. ; mihi prima
genas vestibat flore iuventa, Verg. **2.**
T r a n s f. **a.** *the cheek-bone, cheek :* Lucr.,
Cic., Ov., etc. **b.** *the sockets of the eyes :*
Ov. **c.** *the eye,* or *eyes :* cornicum eruit
ungue genas, Prop. ; restiterim fixis in tua
membra genis, Ov. [It. *ganascia ;* and,
from it, Fr. *ganache*.]
geneālogus, ī, *m.* [γενεαλόγος], *a genea-
logist :* Cic.
gener, erī, *m.* [root *gen* in gignō], *a son-in-
law.* **1.** L i t. : Pl., Cic., Ov., etc. Also,
a daughter's betrothed, or *suitor :* Verg.,
Hor. **2.** In less exact sense : **a.** *the husband of a grand-daughter* or *great-granddaughter,* for progener : Tac. **b.** *a brother-
in-law :* Nep. **c.** *a daughter's paramour :*
Hor. [Sp. *yerno ;* Fr. *gendre*.]
generālis, e, *adj.* [genus]. **I.** *belonging to*
or *distinctive of a class :* Lucr., Cic. **II.**
relating to all, general, universal : Cic.,
Quint., Sen. Ep.
generāliter, *adv. in general, generally :* Cic.,
Quint., Plin. Ep.
generāscō, ere [generō], *to be generated, produced :* Lucr.
generātim, *adv.* [genus]. **I.** *by kinds,
classes,* or *nations :* Lucr., Cic., Verg., etc.
II. *generally, in general :* singillatim potius
quam generatim loquar, Cic. ; Quint.
generātor, ōris, *m.* [generō], *a maker* or
breeder of a stock : Cic. ; equorum, Cic.
generō, āre [genus], *to beget, procreate, breed.*
1. L i t. of living beings : Enn., Cic., Verg.,
etc. Poet.: Troiā generatus Acestes,
Verg. **2.** T r a n s f. **a.** Of inanimate
things : generandi gloria mellis, Verg. ;
terra rubos, Quint. **b.** virtutes, Quint. ;
poema, Quint.
generōsius, *comp. adv. more nobly :* Hor.
generōsus, a, um [genus]. *of good stock, high-
bred.* **I.** Of horses, cattle, cultivated
fruits, etc. **1.** L i t. : equus, Quint. ;
pecus, Verg. ; pruna, Ov. ; arbor, Quint. ;
vinum, Hor. *Sup.* : Quint. **2.** T r a n s f. :
well-stocked, or *bearing good stock :* insula
generosa metallis, Verg. ; Ov. **II.** Of
men. **1.** L i t. : Cic., Verg., etc. *Comp.* :
Hor. *Sup.* : Sall., Suet. **2.** T r a n s f. **a.**
Of moral character : *noble-minded, chival-
rous, generous :* Cic., Quint., Juv. **b.** Of
things : *noble, high-toned :* ortus amicitiae,
Cic. ; virtus, forma, Cic. ; animus, Quint. ;
generosos vestis honores (i.e. *the dress of
honour* of a mother of three children),
Prop. *Comp.* : Quint.
genesis, is, *f.* [γένεσις], *generation, birth,
creation.* T r a n s f. *the constellation in the
ascendant at one's birth ; horoscope :* Juv.,
Suet.
genesta, v. genista.
genetivus, a, um [*gen* in gignō]. **I.** *inborn,
belonging to one from birth :* imago, Ov. ;
notae, Suet. **II.** G r a m m. : *casus, the
genitive case,* Suet. Without *casus* : Quint.
genetrix, īcis, *f.* [*fem.* form of genitor], *a*

mother, ancestress. **1.** L i t.: Verg., Hor.; Aeneadum genetrix (i.e. Venus), Lucr.; Suet.; magna deum (GEN.) genetrix (i.e. Magna Mater), Verg. **2.** T r a n s f.: patria, o mea genetrix, Cat.; frugum (i.e. *Ceres*), Ov.

geniālis, e, *adj.* [genius], *devoted to* or *connected with one's* genius. **a.** *nuptial, bridal :* lectus, Cic., Hor., Liv.; torus, Verg.; ducuntur raptae, genialis praeda, puellae, Ov. **b.** *joyous, blithesome, festive :* festum, Ov.; hiems, Verg.; rus, Ov.

geniāliter, *adv., joyously, merrily :* festum genialiter egit, Ov.

geniculātus, a, um [geniculum], *with knee-joints.* T r a n s f.: *having knots, jointed :* culmus, Cic.

geniculum, i, n. [*dim.* genū]. **I.** *a little knee, a knee :* Varr. **II.** *a joint in a plant :* Plin.

genista and **genesta,** ae, f. *the broom-plant, broom :* Verg. [It. *ginestra ;* Sp. *hiniesta ;* Fr. *genêt ;* Eng. *Planta-genet.*]

genitābilis, e, *adj.* [root gen in gignō], *fruitful, generative :* Lucr.

genitālis, e, *adj.* [root gen in gignō ; *cf.* Gk. γενετή]. **I.** *fruitful, generative :* semina, Lucr., Verg.; arvum, Verg.; membra, Ov. **II.** *relating to birth, birth- :* dies, Tac. **III.** *presiding over birth :* Diana, Hor.

genitāliter, *adv. in a fertilising manner :* Lucr.

genitīvus, v. genetīvus.

genitor, ōris, m. [genō, gignō ; Gk. γενέτωρ], *father, creator.* **1.** L i t.: Enn., Cic., Verg., etc. **2.** T r a n s f.: asciscet nova, quae genitor produxerit usus, Hor.; urbis, Ov.

genitrix, v. genetrix.

genitūra, ae, f. [root gen in gignō], *a begetting.* T r a n s f. in astrology : *natal star, nativity :* Suet.

genitus, a, um, *Part.* gignō.

genius, i, m. [root gen in gignō ; properly *generative power, vital energy, creative spirit,* closely associated with physical well-being, marriage, birth, birthdays, and occasions of personal rejoicing]. **1.** L i t. **A.** *the genius.* **a.** Of a person : te per genium obsecro, Hor.; Sen. Ep.; cras genium mero placabis, Hor.; Ov. **b.** Of a place : loci, Verg.; urbis Romae, Liv. **B.** *the spirit of social enjoyment, fondness for good living, taste, appetite, inclination :* isti qui cum geniis suis belligerant, parcipromi, Pl.; indulge genio, Pl.; suom defrudans genium, Ter. **2.** T r a n s f. C o m i c.: used by parasites for their *entertainer, patron :* ecquis est, qui mihi commonstret Phaedromum genium meum ? Pl. **b.** *wit, talent, genius :* Juv.

genō, v. gignō.

gēns, gentis, f. [root gen in gignō]. **I.** *gens, stock, clan* (consisting of families united together by a common name and by certain religious rites). **1.** L i t.: L. Tarquitius patriciae gentis, Liv.; gens Tarquiniorum, Cic.; sine gente, Hor.; patricii minorum gentium, Cic. Ep., Liv. **2.** T r a n s f. **a.** Of the gods and great men : maiorum gentium dii qui habentur, Cic.; Cleanthes, qui quasi maiorum est gentium Stoicus, Cic.

b. Of beasts : *a race, stock :* in spem gentis, Verg.; Ov. **II.** In more extended sense : *a tribe, folk* (mostly of sections of a larger nation or people). **1.** L i t.; homines, civitates, nationes, gentes, Cic.; omnes exterae gentes ac nationes, Cic.; Nerviorum, Caes.; nationis nomen, non gentis evaluisse paulatim, Tac. **2.** Loosely : *a region, country :* quae gens iacet supra Ciliciam, Nep. Also, gentes (opp. to Romani) : *foreign nations, foreigners :* Tac. P h r. (colloq.) : gentium with adverbs such as *ubi : among the tribes, in the world, on earth :* ubi gentium ? Pl.; unde, nusquam gentium, Pl., Liv.; ubivis, quovis gentium, Ter.; ubicumque gentium, Cic.; tu autem abes longe gentium, Cic. Ep. **III.** Of a single offspring : *offspring, scion :* deum (GEN.) gens, Aenea, Verg.

genticus, a, um [gēns], *tribal, national :* mos, Tac.

gentilicius, a, um [gentilis], *of a particular* gens : sacra, Liv.; nomen, Suet.

gentīlis, e, *adj.* [gēns], *of* or *belonging to the same* gens or race, *hereditary.* **1.** L i t.: nomen, Suet.; monumentum Domitiorum, Suet.; gentile domus nostrae bonum, Tac. As Noun : *a person belonging to the same* gens : Cic., Liv., Suet. **2.** In a more extended sense : *tribal, national :* imperium religio, utilitas, Tac.

gentīlitās, ātis, f. [gentilis]. **I.** *the relationship of those who belong to the same* gens: gentilitatum, agnationum iura, Cic.; Plin. Pan. **II.** *relatives bearing the same name* (in pl.) : Plin. Pan.

genū, ūs, n. (in the Neut. NOM. and ACC. *sing.* genus, Cic. poet.; *pl.* genua, as a disyllable gonva, Verg.) [*cf.* Gk. γόνυ], *the knee :* Pl., Cic., Verg., etc.; genuum iunctura (*knee-joint*), Ov.; genibus minor (*kneeling*), Hor.; genibus advolvi, Liv., Tac.; so, se advolvere, Tac.; niti genibus, Liv.

genuālia, ium, n. *pl.* [genū], *garters :* Ov.

(1) genuīnus, a, um [root gen in gignō, *cf.* ingenuus], *innate, native, natural :* genuinae domesticaeque virtutes, Cic.

(2) genuīnus, a, um [genu-, Gk. γένυς, Lat. gena], *belonging to the jaw :* dentes, *jaw-teeth,* Cic.; as Noun, **genuīni,** ōrum, m. *pl. :* Verg.; and *Sing.* **genuīnus,** i, m. : quae genuinum agitent, Juv.

genus, eris, n. [root gen in gignō ; *cf.* Gk. γένος], *breed, stock, kind* (us. devoid of the dignity implied in gens ; hence its wide extension to mean merely *class, category*). **1.** L i t. **A.** *breeding, birth, breed, stock, family :* **a.** In gen. : ii, qui nobili genere nati sunt, Cic.; amplisimo genere natus, Caes.; patricium, Liv.; Atys, genus unde Atii duxere, Verg. **b.** E s p. *birth, for high* or *noble birth :* et genus et virtus, Hor. **B.** **a.** *race, stock :* in famam generis ac familiae, Quint.; fortuna non mutat genus, Hor. **b.** *a descendant, child :* and collect., *offspring, race :* credo equidem genus esse deorum, Verg.; audax Iapeti genus, Hor.; sive neglectum genus et nepotes respicis, Hor. **2.** T r a n s f. **A.** Of living creatures having like characteristics : *a race, class species, kind.* **a.** Of men : ex infinitā societate generis humani, Cic. ; implacidum genus (Genauni), Hor. ; stabiles (amici), cuius generis est magna penuria, Cic. ; genus inritabile vatum, Hor. In *pl.* : eorum hominum genera sunt duo, Caes. **b.** Of other animals : ferarum, Caes. ; piscium, Hor. ; silvestre, Lucr. In *pl.* : varia genera bestiarum, Cic. **B.** Of lifeless or abstract things having like characteristics : omnis generis tormenta, Liv. ; naves omni genere armorum ornatissimae, Caes. ; genus pugnae, Caes. ; frugum omne genus, Liv. ; materiā̆, Lucr. ; dicendi, Cic., Quint. In *pl.* : genera munitionis, Caes. ; furandi, Cic. The Acc. *sing.* is sometimes used adverbially, instead of the GEN. of Quality : aliquid id genus, *something of that sort*, Cic. ; Lucr. ; Hor., etc. **C. a.** In a still more general sense : *matter, respect, way* : = res, aliquid : in omni genere, Cic. ; qui in aliquo genere inconcinnus est, Cic. **b.** Philos : (opp. *species or partes*, and comprising them) : *a general term, logical genus* : Varr., Cic. **c.** Gramm. : *gender* : in nominibus tria genera, Quint. [Fr. *genre*.]

genus, *the knee* : v. genū.

geōgraphia, ae, *f.* [γεωγραφία], *geography* : Cic. Ep.

geōmetrēs, ae (ō in Vulg. Lat. and Juv.), *m.* [γεωμέτρης, lit. *earth-measurer*], *a geometer, a mathematician* : Cic., Quint., Juv.

geōmetria, ae, *f.* [γεωμετρία], *geometry* : Cic., Quint.

geōmetricus, a, um [γεωμετρικός], *belonging to geometry, geometrical* : Cic. As Noun, **a. geōmetricus,** i, *m. a geometer, geometrician* : Quint. **b. geōmetrica,** ōrum, *n. pl. geometry* : Cic.

geōrgicus, a, um [γεωργικός], *belonging to husbandry, agricultural* : carmen, *the Georgics, the title of an agricultural poem by Vergil.* As Noun, **geōrgica,** ōrum, *n. pl. : the Georgics* (of Verg.), Gell. : Gk. GEN. *pl.* Geōrgicōn : Gell.

gerēns, entis. **I.** *Part.* gerō. **II.** Adj. : with GEN. : *managing* : rei, Pl. ; negoti, Cic.

germānē, *adv. sincerely* : Cic. Ep.

Germāni, ōrum, *m. pl. the Germans* ; **Germānus,** a, um, *German* ; **Germānia,** ae, *f. Germany. The Germans on the west of the Rhine were divided into two Roman provinces, called Germania Superior and Germania Inferior, and together Germaniae, the two Germanies* ; **Germānicus,** a, um ; **Germānicus,** I, *m. the personal cognomen of Tiberius Drusus, son-in-law of Augustus* ; *of Drusus' son, known by this name ; and of several emperors, e.g. Domitian ; also the name of a gold coin struck by Domitian* ; **Germāniciānus,** a, um, *stationed or serving in Germany* : exercitus (Suet.) ; **Germāniciāni,** ōrum, *m. pl., Roman soldiers stationed in Germany.*

germānitās, ātis, *f.* [germānus], *brotherhood, sisterhood.* **1.** Lit. : Cic., Liv. **2.** Transf. **a.** *the relationship of the various colonists from one mother-city* : Liv. **b.** Of things : *union, similarity* : Pl.

germānus, a, um [*cf.* germen], *having the same parents.* **1.** Lit. : fratres, Pl. ; Ter. ;

Cic. As Noun, **germānus,** i, *m.,* and **germāna,** ae, *f. : full brother, full sister* : Ter., Ov. Also *a half-brother* : Verg. **2.** Transf. **a.** *brotherly, sisterly* : in germanum modum, Pl. **b.** *genuine, sincere, true* : nomen, gerrae, Pl. ; Campani, Cic. ; iustitia, Cic. ; asinus (comic.), Cic. Ep. *Sup.* : Cic. [Sp. *hermano.*]

germen, inis, *n.* [fr. root gen of gignō ; or fr. gerō]. **1.** Lit. : *embryo, unborn child* : Ov. **2.** Transf. **a.** *a bud, shoot* : Verg. **b.** *a bud, graft* : ex arbore germen, Verg. **c.** *a germ* (of frenzy) : Lucr.

germinō, āre [germen]. **A.** Intrans. : *to sprout, bud* : Plin. **B.** Trans. and Transf. : *to put forth* (*wings, hair*) : Plin.

gerō, gerere, gessi, gestum [earlier gesō]. **I.** *to bear on or about oneself.* **1.** Lit. **a.** *to bear, wear* : Pl. ; vestem, Ov. ; coronam, Suet. ; spolia ducis caesi, Liv. **b.** (rare) *to bear, carry, bring to a place* : saxa in muros, Liv. ; imbrem in cribrum gerere, Pl. **2.** Transf. **a.** Of bodily features, etc. : *to wear, bear, display* : virginis os habitumque gerens, Verg. ; barbam, Verg. ; cornua fronte, Ov. ; distentius uber, Hor. ; virginis arma, Verg. **b.** *to sustain* a part : personam, Cic. **c.** *to bear* (*and present to view*) : fortem animum, Sall. ; Liv. ; Verg. With prae se : *to display, exhibit* : prae se gerere coniecturam, Cic. ; utilitatem, Cic. With Refl. Pron. and an *Adv.* or *Adj.* : *to bear, deport, behave, or conduct oneself* : se liberius, Cic. ; se inconsultius, Liv. ; sic me in hoc magistratu, Cic. ; me medium (i.e. be *neutral*), Liv. ; dis te maiorem, Hor. ; ut seque et exercitum more maiorum gereret, Sall. **d.** gerere morem alicui, *to comply with, gratify, humour* : Pl., Cic., Ov. In *Pass.* : ut utrique a me mos gestus esse videatur, Cic. Ep. ; Pl. ; Ter. **II.** Of maternity : *to bear, carry in oneself.* **1.** Lit. : uterum, partum, Plin. **2.** Transf. **a.** Of the earth, trees, etc. : semina rerum tellus, Lucr. ; India lucos, Verg. Also *to bear and produce* : violam terra, Ov. ; malos platani, Verg. **b.** Of feelings : iras, Pl., Ter. ; cum multis inimicitias, Cic. ; Caes. ; in Romanos odium, Liv. ; pro me curam, Verg. **III.** Of military and civil and other important matters : *to bear the weight or responsibility of* ; hence *to administer, conduct, manage.* **a.** Of public affairs : bellum gerere, Caes.. Cic., Liv. ; negotium, Caes. ; rem publicam, magistratum, consulatum, res, Cic. ; res gestae, *great public events* or *exploits* : Cic., etc. In *Sing.* res gesta : Cic. **b.** Of private affairs (of importance) : rem gerere, Pl. ; negotium meum, Cic. Ep. Of a period of life : *to pass, spend* : Suet.

gerō, ōnis, *m.* [gerō], *a carrier, porter* : Pl.

gerrae, ārum, *f. pl.* [γέρρα], *wattles* ; hence *trifles,* Pl. As interj. : gerrae ! *stuff ! nonsense !* Pl.

gerrō, ōnis, *m.* [gerrae], *a trifler, idle fellow* : Ter.

gerulifigulus, i, *m.* [gerulus figulus], *an abettor* : flagiti, Pl.

gerulus, ī, *m.* [gerō], *a bearer, carrier* : Pl., Hor., Suet.

Gēryōn, onis and **Gēryonēs**, ae (archaic GEN. *sing.* Gēryonāī, Lucr.), *m. a mythic king in Spain who had three bodies, and who was slain by Hercules* ; **Gēryonāceus**, a, um.

gestāmen, inis, *n.* [gestō]. **A**. Pass.: *that which is carried* or *worn* ; *ornaments, accoutrements,* etc.: clipeus, gestamen Abantis, Verg. ; Priami (i.e. *sceptre,* etc.), Verg. ; Juv. In *pl.* : clipeum laevae gestamina, Ov. **B**. Act.: *that which carries.* **a**. *a carriage* : Tac. **b**. With lecticae or sellae : *a litter, sedan-chair* : lecticae gestamine, Tac.

gestātiō, ōnis, *f.* [gestō]. **I**. *a being carried* or *conveyed about* (in a litter, carriage, boat, etc.) ; *a riding, driving,* or *sailing for pleasure* : Sen. Ep., Suet. **II**. *a drive* (i.e. the place where one drives) : Plin. Ep.

gestātor, ōris, *m.* [gestō]. **I**. *a bearer, carrier* : Plin. Ep. **II**. *a rider* (to take the air) : Mart.

gestātōrius, a, um [gestātor], *that serves for carrying* : sella, *a sedan-chair,* Suet.

gesticulātiō, ōnis, *f.* [gesticulor], *pantomimic action, gesticulation* : Quint., Suet.

gesticulor, ārī [gesticulus, *dim.* gestus], *to make mimic gestures, to gesticulate* : Suet.

gestiō, ōnis, *f.* [gerō], *a doing, performing* : negoti, Cic.

gestiō, īre [gerō], perh. orig. of female animals, 'to be in heat' ; hence **I**. *to itch.* i.e. *to be eager, to long* : gestiunt pugni mihi, Pl. With *Inf.* : Pl., Cic., Hor. **II**. *to be excited, run riot, gambol.* **a**. Through desire or its realisation (mostly physically) : quid est quod sic gestis ? Ter. ; laetitia, Cic. With ABL. (of cause): cur non gestiret taurus equae contrectatione, Cic. ; laetitiā, Cic. ; cycnos studio videas gestire lavandi, Verg. But, gestientes otio, *impatient from being (so long) inactive,* Liv. **b**. Rhet.: *to run riot, expatiate freely* : Quint.

gestitō, āre [*freq.* gestō], *to be in the habit of bearing* or *wearing:* anulum, machaeram, Pl.

gestō, āre [*freq.* gerō], *to bear about, to carry* (us. on one's person). **1**. Lit. **a**. crepundia, Pl. ; caput in pilo, Cic. ; arma umeris, Liv. ; cuneos manu, Hor. ; obtusa pectora, Verg. **b**. In *Mid.* or *Pass.*: *to be carried about* (in a litter, carriage, boat, etc.), *to take the air, to ride, drive, sail,* etc., *for pleasure* : Sen. Ep., Juv., Suet. **2**. Transf. **a**. *to carry fondly, cherish, preserve* : gestandus in sinu, Ter. ; meum animum, Pl. ; testem suum in pectore, Juv. **b**. *to carry about, blab, tell* : Pl., Sen. Ep.

gestor, ōris, *m.* [gerō], *a tale-bearer, tattler* : Pl.

gestus, a, um, *Part.* gerō.

gestus, ūs, *m.* [gerō], *the carriage* (of the body or some part of it), *posture, motion, gesture.* **1**. In gen.: gestus voltusque, Ter. ; gestum imitari, Lucr. ; vitium in gestu, Cic. In *pl.* : nec flecti cervix nec bracchia reddere gestūs, Ov. **2**. *the artificial gesture of an actor* or *orator, gesticulation* : Cic., Quint. In *pl.* : Cic., Quint., Juv.

Geta and **Getēs**, ae, *m.*, us. *pl.* **Getae**, ārum, *m. a people on the Lower Danube* ; **Geticus**, a, um, *of the Getae* ; ο c c. *Thracian* ; **Geticē**, *in Getic* : Ov.

gibba, ae, *f.* [cf. gibbus], *a hump on the back, hunch* : Suet.

gibber, era, erum [gibbus], *crook-backed, hunch-backed, hump-backed* : Varr., Suet.

gibbus, ī, *m.* [cf. Gk. κυφός], *a hump* : Juv. [It. *gobbo*.]

Gigantes, um, *m. pl. a fabulous race of monsters, sons of Earth and Tartarus, who endeavoured to storm Olympus, but were smitten by Jupiter with lightning and buried under Etna and other volcanoes* ; **Gigantēus**, a, um.

gignō, gignere, genuī, genitum (old form of the *Pres.* genō, Varr., Cic. ; *Inf. Pass.* genī, Lucr.), *to beget, bear, bring forth, produce.* **1**. Lit.: Enn. ; (Hercules) quem Iuppiter genuit, Cic. ; deus vos huic urbi genuisse videatur, Cic. ; deus animum ex suā mente genuit, Cic. In *Pass.* : Pl., Ov., Suet. With ABL. : paelice genitus, Liv. ; Suet. ; Verg. With *de* : de quo sunt geniti, Ov. ; with *ex* : e terrā gonita, Ov. ; Curt. ; with *ab* : Tac. *Neut. pl.* of *Pres. Part.* as Noun, **gignentia**, ium, *things that produce,* as *plants* ; *vegetation* : Sall. **2**. Transf.: virtus amicitiam gignit, Cic. ; ludus genuit trepidum certamen, Hor. ; perturbationes (mentis) gignuntur ex intemperantiā, Cic.

gilvus, a, um [cf. helvus], *pale yellow* : equi (perh. *dun*), Verg.

gingīva, ae, *f. a gum (of the mouth)* : Cat., Juv. [Fr. *gencive*.]

glaber, bra, brum, *without hair, smooth, bald* : Pl., Varr. Comp. : Pl. Masc. as Noun, **glaber**, *a young (beardless) slave, a page* : Cat., Phaedr., Sen. Ep.

glaciālis, e, *adj.* [glaciēs], *icy, frozen, full of ice* : hiems, Verg. ; frigus, Ov. ; Scythia, Ov.

glaciēs, ēī, *f.* [cf. gelū], *ice.* **1**. Lit. : Lucr., Verg. In *pl.* : Verg. **2**. Transf.: *hardness* : aeris, Lucr.

glaciō, āre [glaciēs], *to make* or *turn into ice* ; *to freeze* : positas ut glaciet nives Iuppiter, Hor.

gladiātor, ōris, *m.* [gladius], *a swordsman, fighter* in the public games, *a gladiator* : Cic. As term of reproach: applied to M. Antonius, Cic. Ο c c. in *pl.* : *a combat of gladiators, gladiatorial exhibition* : Liv. ; gladiatores dare, Ter. ; Cic. ; edere, Tac. ; locum gladiatoribus dare, Cic. ; gladiatoribus, *at a show of gladiators,* Cic. Ep.

gladiātōrius, a, um [gladiātor], *belonging to gladiators* : animus, Ter. ; ludus, familia, consessus, locus, Cic. ; munus, Liv., Suet. ; spectaculum, Liv., Tac. *Neut.* as Noun, **gladiātōrium** (*sc.* praemium, auctoramentum), *the hire* or *pay of gladiators* : gladiatorio accepto decem talentis, Liv.

gladiātūra, ae, *f.* [gladius], *the profession of a gladiator* : Tac.

gladius, ī, *m.* [fr. same root as glaber], *a sword.* **1**. Lit.: stringere, Caes., Cic. ; Verg. ; destringere, Caes., Cic., Liv. ; educere, Caes., Cic. Ep. ; nudare, Ov. ; con ere, Tac. ; recondere in vaginam

Cic.; gladio comminus rem gerit Varenus, Caes. Prov.: suo sibi hunc gladio iugulo, (i.e. beat him at his own weapons), Ter. Phr.: plumbeo gladio iugulatum iri, Cic.; ignem gladio scrutari (i.e. to go from bad to worse), Hor.; gladium alicui dare (to help a man to ruin), Pl. **2.** Transf. **a.** *murder, death :* gladiorum impunitas, Cic. **b.** *a gladiatorial combat :* dubitat, utrum se ad gladium locet an ad cultrum, Sen. Ep. [Fr. *glaive.*]

glaeb-, better than glēb-.

glaesum, v. glēsum.

glandifer, era, erum [glāns ferō], *acorn-bearing :* Cic.

glandiōnida, ae, *f.* [glandium], *a savoury, glandulous morsel :* Pl.

glandium, i, *n.* [glāns], *a delicate kernel or glandule* in meat, esp. in pork : Pl.

glāns, glandis, *f.* [*cf.* Gk. βάλανος], *mast, the the nut-like fruit of forest-trees :* an acorn, beech-nut, chestnut, etc. **1.** Lit.: Pl., Cic., Verg., etc. **2.** Transf. *an acorn-shaped ball* of lead or clay which was slung at the enemy ; *a bullet :* Caes., Verg., etc.

glārea, ae, *f.* *gravel :* Cic. Ep., Verg., Liv., etc.

glāreōsus, a, um [glārea], *full of gravel, gravelly :* Varr., Liv.

glaucōma, atis, *n.* (also, ae, *f.* : Pl.) [γλαύκωμα], *a clouding or opacity of the crystalline lens or its capsule, cataract.* Comic.: alicui glaucomam ob oculos obicere (i.e. to throw dust into his eyes), Pl.

glaucus, a, um [γλαυκός], *greenish or bluish grey :* undae, Lucr.; amictus (Nymphae), Verg.; salix, Verg.

Glaucus, i, *m.* **I.** *s.* of Sisyphus, devoured by his own horses. **II.** *the commander of the Lycians in the Trojan war ; who fought with Diomede and exchanged arms with him.* **III.** *a fisherman of Anthēdon, in Euboea, who was changed into a sea-god.*

glēba (glaeba), ae, *f. a lump of earth, a clod.* **1.** Lit.: Lucr., Cic., Verg., etc. Used as missiles : Cic. **2.** Transf. **a.** *land, soil :* terra potens ubere glaebae, Verg. **b.** Of other things : *a lump :* turis, Lucr.; sevi ac picis, Caes.

glēbula (glaeb-), ae, *f.* [*dim.* glēba], *a small clod.* Transf. **a.** *a little piece of land :* Juv. **b.** *a little lump :* ex metallo, Plin. Ep.

glēsum (and glaesum), i, *n. amber :* Tac.

glīs, glīris, *m. a dormouse :* Varr., Mart. [It. *ghiro* ; Fr. *loir* ; also Sp. and Fr. *liron.*]

gliscō, ere, *to swell up, grow, blaze up.* **1.** Lit.: ignis Alexandri sub pectore gliscens, Lucr. **2.** Transf.: rabies, proelium, Pl.; gliscit, ut ignis oleo, Cic.; furor, clamor, Lucr.; violentia, Verg.; invidia, seditio, Liv.; multitudo, saevitia, gloria, etc., Tac.

globōsus, a, um [globus], *round as a ball, spherical :* Pac., Cic., Liv.

globus, i, *m.* [*cf.* glomus], *a round, solid body, ball, sphere, globe.* **1.** Lit.: globus, quae terra dicitur, Cic.; terrae, Cic.; stellarum, Cic.; visci, Pl.; solis, lunae, Lucr.; nubium, Tac.; flammarum globos, Verg.; sanguinis, Ov. **2.** Transf. **a.** *a crowd, mass* of men : globus increpabat

dictatorem, Liv.; virum (GEN.) densissimus, Verg.; militum, Tac. **b.** *a clique :* ex illo globo nobilitatis, Sall.; Nep.

glomerāmen, inis, *n.* [glomerō], *a round body, ball :* lunae, Lucr.

glomerō, āre [glomus], *to form into a ball, gather into a round heap, to gather up.* **1.** Lit.: offas ex ficis et farre, Varr.; terram deus, Ov.; lanam in orbis, Ov. **2.** Transf. **a.** *to gather together in a mass, to huddle :* agmina cervi glomerant, Verg.; manum bello, Liv. In *Mid.* : legiones in testudinem glomerabantur, Tac.; glomerantur aves, Verg. **b.** tempestatem nubes glomerant, Verg.; venti grandinem glomeratam in terras agunt, Liv.; gressūs glomerare superbos (i.e. bring the feet together), Verg.

glomus, eris, *n.* [*cf.* globus], *a ball or clue* of yarn or thread : lanae, Lucr., Hor.

glōria, ae, *f. glory, fame, renown.* **1.** Lit.: Pl., Cic., Hor., etc.; capere, consequi, Cic.; esse in maximā gloriā, Cic. With *Subj.* GEN.: armenti gloria, taurus, Ov.; frontis, Tac. In *pl.* : veteres Gallorum glorias, *glorious deeds,* Tac. With *Obj.* GEN.: gloria belli, Caes.; legum et publicae disciplinae, Cic.; carminum, Tac. **2.** Transf.: *thirst for glory, ambition ; vain-glory ; pride, boasting :* ostentatio et gloria, Cic.; quem tulit ad scaenam ventoso gloria curru, Hor.; vana gloria, Liv.; iactantia gloriaque, Tac. With *Obj.* GEN.: generandi mellis, Verg.

glōriātiō, ōnis, *f.* [glōrior], *a glorying, boasting, vaunting :* Cic.

glōriola, ae, *f.* [*dim.* glōria], *a little glory :* Cic. Ep.

glōrior, āri [glōria], *to glory, pride oneself* (both in good and in bad sense), *to boast, vaunt, brag :* Caes., Cic. Constr. **a.** Of thing boasted about : with *ABL.*: Caes., Cic., Liv., Ov.; with *de :* Cic.; with *in* and *ABL.*: Cic.; with *Acc.* and *Inf.* : Caes., Cic., Hor.; with *Indir. Quest.* : Suet.; with *Acc.* of *Neut. Pron.,* or *Nom.* of *Gerund. Adj.* : vellem idem posse gloriari quod Cyrus, Cic.; Liv.; beata vita glorianda est, Cic. **b.** Of person against whom : with *adversus* and *Acc.* : Liv.

glōriōsē, *adv.* **I.** *gloriously :* Cic. Ep. *Comp.* : Sall. *Sup.* : Cic. Ep. **II.** *boastfully, vauntingly, pompously :* Pl., Cic., Sall.

glōriōsus, a, um [glōria]. **I.** *full of glory, famous, renowned :* de clarorum hominum factis gloriosis, Cic.; Liv., etc.; dies gloriosissimus, Tac. **II.** *vain-glorious, boasting, bragging :* gloriosa ostentatio civitatis, Cic.; (vir) mendax et gloriosus, Pl.; miles, Ter., Cic.; esse gloriosi animi, Suet.

glōssēma, atis, *n.* [γλώσσημα], *an antiquated or foreign word needing explanation :* Varr., Quint.

glūbō, ere [*cf.* Gk. γλύφω], *to bark, peel, skin :* salictum, Cato ; ramos, Varr.; Remi nepotes, Cat.

glūma, ae, *f.* [glūbō], *a peeling, husk* of corn: Varr.

glūten, inis, *n.* [*cf.* Gk. γλοιός], *glue :* Lucr. Of bees : Verg.

glūtinātor, ōris, *m.* [glūtinō], *a gluer to-gether, a bookbinder :* Cic. Ep.
glūtinō, āre [glūten], *to glue, glue together :* chartas, Plin.
gluttiō (glūtiō), īre [fr. root seen in gula], *to swallow or gulp down :* collyras, Pl. ; epulas, Juv. [It. *inghiottire ;* Fr. *en-gloutir*.]
gluttō, ōnis, *m.* [gluttiō], *a glutton* (colloq.) : Pers. [It. *ghiottone ;* Sp. *gloton ;* Fr. *glouton*.]
glūtus (and **gluttus**), a, um [*cf.* glūten], *tenacious, holding :* locus bene glutus siet, Cato.
gnārus, a, um (also **gnāruris**, e, Pl. Another form is nārus, like nāvus, nōtus, acc. to Cic.) [fr. root of gnōscō], *adj.* **A.** Act. : *knowing or acquainted with* a thing ; *skil-ful, practised, expert.* With GEN. : loci, Pl. ; rei publicae, Cic. With ACC. and *Inf. :* Liv., Tac. With *Indir. Quest. :* Cic., Suet. With ACC. alone : simul gnaruris vos volo esse hanc rem mecum, Pl. **B.** Pass. : *known ,* Tac.
Gnaeus or **Gneus** (or Cn-) i., *m* (abbrev. Cn.) a *|Roman praenomen.*
gnātus, *v.* nātus.
gnāv-, *v.* nāv-.
gnōbilis, *v.* nōbilis.
gnōscō, *v.* nōscō.
Gnōssus or **Gnōsus**, I, *f.* [Κνωσσός], *the ancient capital of Crete, the residence of Minos ;* **Gnōsius**, a, um, *Gnosian, Cretan :* **Gnōsia**, ae, *f. the Cretan (princess),* i.e. *Ariadne :* **Gnōsii**, ōrum, *m. pl. the in-habitants of Gnosus ;* **Gnōsiacus**, a, um, *Gnosian, Cretan :* rex, i.e. *Minos ;* **Gnōsias** (**Gnōss-**), adis, *f. adj. Gnosian, Cretan :* **Gnōsias**, adis, *f.* i.e. *Ariadne :* **Gnōsis**, idis, *f. adj.* Gnosian : corona, i.e. *the con-stellation of Ariadne's Crown :* **Gnōsis**, idis, *f.* i.e. *Ariadne.*
gnōtus, *v.* nōscō.
gōbius (also cōb —), I, and **gōbiō**, ōnis, *m.* [κωβιός], *a fish of small value,* prob. *the gudgeon :* Ov., Juv. [Fr. *goujon*.]
Gordius, I, *m. king of Gordium, famous for the inextricable knot on the yoke of his chariot, which was cut by Alexander the Great.*
Gorgiās, ae. *m. a famous Greek sophist in the time of Socrates, native of Leontini (Sicily).*
Gorgō, onis, *f. d. of Phorcus, also called Medusa, whose head was covered with snakes instead of hair, and who turned all she looked upon to stone ; she was killed by Perseus. She had two sisters like herself ;* **Gorgo-neus**, a, um.
grabātus, I, *m.* [κράβατος], *a small couch, camp-bed, pallet :* Cic., Cat., Verg.
Gracchus, i, *m. a cognomen in the gens* Sempronia ; E s p : Ti. Sempronius Gracchus *the elder, aad his two sons* Ti. and C. Sem-pronius Gracchus, *tribunes of the plebs, the former,* B.C. 133, *and the latter,* B.C. 123 ; **Gracchānus**, a, um.
gracilis, e (**gracilus**, a, um, Ter.), *adj. slender.* **1.** Lit. **a.** *slender, slim, slight :* hibiscus, Verg. ; puer, Hor. ; Ter. ; ca-pella, Ov. **b.** *meagre, thin, lean :* equi hominesque, Liv. ; Hor. ; crura, Suet. *Comp. :* Plin. *Sup. :* Suet. **2.** Transf. **a.** *meagre, scanty, poor :* vindemiae, Plin.

Ep. **b.** Of style : *simple, plain, un-adorned :* Ov., Quint. Of the speaker : Quint. [Fr. *grêle.*]
gracilitās, ātis, *f.* [gracilis], *thinness, lean-ness.* **1.** Lit. : corporis, Cic. ; crurum, Suet. In *pl. :* Cic. **2.** Transf. Of style : *simplicity, plainness, absence of ornament :* Quint.
grāculus (colloq. **graccŭlus**), i, *m.* [from its note gra gra, acc. to Quint.], *a jackdaw :* Phaedr., Mart. [It. *gracchia ;* Sp. *grajo ;* old Fr. *graille.*]
gradārius, a, um [gradus], *going step by step.* Transf. Of a deliberate speaker : Sen. Ep.
gradātim, *adv.* [gradus], *step by step, by de-grees :* Cic., Varr., Plin. Ep.
gradātiō, ōnis, *f.* [gradus], *a series of steps.* Rhet. : *a gradation or climax,* Cic., Quint.
gradior, gradī, grēssus [fr. root seen in gradus], *to step, pace, walk.* **1.** Lit. : Pl., Cic., Verg., etc. **2.** Transf. Of things : foras gradiens clamor, Lucr.
Grādīvus (Grād-, once in Ov.) [perh. fr. gradior ; so *the Marcher*], *a name of Mars.*
gradus, ūs, *m.* **I.** The movement of the foot ; *a step, pace.* **1.** Lit. : proferre, Enn. ; suspenso gradu, *on tiptoe,* Ter. ; presso gradu, *slow march,* Liv. ; citato gradu in hostem ducere, *quick march,* Liv. ; pleno gradu, i.e. "*at the double,*" Liv. ; facere, Cic. ; addere, Liv. ; celerare, sis-tere, revocare, Verg. **2.** Transf. **A.** *step, stage :* gradum mei reditūs esse, Cic. Ep. ; gradum facere ex aedilitate ad cen-suram, Cic. ; notitiam primosque gradūs (amoris) vicinia fecit, Ov. **B.** *stance, foot-ing.* **a.** Milit. : stabili gradu impetum hostium excipere, Liv. ; hence *position, the ground on which one stands :* in suo quis-que gradu obnixi, Liv. ; hostes gradu de-moti, Liv. ; in gradu stetimus certi non cedere, Ov. **b.** In gen. : fortis et con-stantis est, non de gradu deici, Cic. ; si gradum *(standing)* apud te haberem, Liv. **II.** That on which one steps in ascending : *a step, stair.* **1.** Lit. (us. *pl.*) : gradūs templorum, Cic. ; per gradūs deieci Ser-vium, Liv. ; postīs sub ipsos nituntur gradibus, Verg. **2.** Transf. **A.** Of things resembling steps. **a.** *a braid of* hair : Quint, Juv., Suet. **b.** *a degree of* a circle : Manil. **B.** Of abstract things : *a step, degree ; rank :* nostri quoque san-guinis auctor Iuppiter est, totidemque gradūs distamus ab illo, Ov. ; per omnis bonorum gradūs, Cic. ; magistratuum, Cic. In *sing. :* summum gradum tenere digni-tatis, Cic. ; ad hunc gradum amicitiae, Liv.
Graeci, ōrum, *m. pl. the Greeks* (this was a Roman name, the people called themselves *Hellenes*). Also in *Sing.* **Graecus**, i, *m.*, **Graeca**, ae, *f.;* **Graecum**, i, *n. Greek language ;* **Graecus**, a, um ; **Graecē**, *in Greek ;* **Graecia**, ae, *f. Greece ;* also ap-plied to Lower Italy, called Magna Graecia, Maior Graecia. **Graeculus**, a, um, *in contemptuous sense ;* and **Graeculus**, i, *m. a paltry Greek ;* **Graecānicus**, a, um, *of Greek origin, in Greek fashion.*
graecissō, āre [Graecus], *to ape the Greek fashion :* Pl.

graecor, āri [Graecus], *to play the Greek* : Hor.

Grāii (Grāi), ōrum (GEN. also Grāium), *m. pl.* mostly poet. for Graeci, *the Greeks* ; **Grāius**, a, um.

Grāiugena, ae (GEN. *pl.* Grāiugenum, Verg.), *m. a Greek by birth.*

grallae, ārum, *f.* [gradior], *stilts* : Varr.

grallātor, ōris, *m.* [grallae]. *a walker on stilts* : Pl., Varr.

grāmen, inis, *n.* [cf. Gk. γράστις, γράω], *grass.* **1.** Lit. : Lucr., Verg., Liv., etc. In *pl.* : Lucr., Verg., Hor. **2.** Transf. : *any plant or herb* : non illa feris incognita capris gramina, Verg. ; mala gramina, Verg. ; Ov. ; Quint.

grāmineus, a, um [grāmen], *of grass, covered with grass, grassy.* **1.** Lit. : campus, Verg. ; corona obsidionalis, Liv. **2.** In partic. : *of Indian reed, cane* : hasta (Minervae), Cic.

grammaticus, a, um [γραμματικός], *dealing with reading and writing, with letters in* gen. ; *literary, philological* : ars, Auct. Her. ; grammaticas ambire tribūs et pulpita, Hor. As Noun. **a. grammaticus**, i, *m. a philologist, a teacher of literature and literary language* : Cic., Hor., Quint. **b.** **grammatica**, ae, *f.* (sc. ars) (Cic., Suet.), **grammaticē**, ēs, *f.* [γραμματική] (Quint.), **grammatica**, ōrum, *n. pl.* [τὰ γραμματικά] (Cic.), *grammar, philology, literature and language.*

grammatista, ae, *m.* [γραμματιστής], *a teacher of grammar or language* : Suet.

grānāria, ōrum, *n. pl.* [grānum], *a granary* : Pl., Cic., Hor., etc. [Fr. grenier.]

grandaevus, a, um [grandis aevum], *of great age* : Nereus, Verg. ; apes, Verg. ; pater, Ov. ; senes, Tac.

grandēscō, ere [grandis], *to become great, to grow* : Lucr.

grandiculus, a, um [dim. grandis], *fairly large or tall* : globi, Pl. ; virgo, Ter.

grandifer, era, erum [grandis ferō], *large-bearing, productive* : arationes, Cic.

grandiloquus, i, *m.* [grandis loquor], *speaking grandly or loftily* : Cic. ; in a bad sense, as Noun : *a boaster* : Cic.

grandinat, āre, *impers.* [grandō], *it hails* : Sen. Transf. : saxis, Pac.

grandiō, īre [grandis]. **A.** Trans. : *to make great, increase, enlarge* : Pl. **B.** Intrans. : *to become great, to grow* : fruges, Cato.

grandis, e, *adj. full-grown* (prop. of adolescence). **1.** Lit. **a.** Of stature : *grown up, tall* : Ter., Cic., Hor. **b.** *advanced in years, aged, old* ; often with natu or aevo : grandis natu, Cic., Hor. ; grandior natu, Pl.; grandis aevo, Tac. ; grandior aevo, Ov. ; grandior aetas, Cic., Ov. ; aevum, Lucr. **c.** Of produce : *well-grown, large* : fetus, Cic. ; seges, Varr. ; frumenta, Verg. **2.** Transf. **a.** In size, amount, quantity : saxa, Lucr., Caes. ; corpora, Lucr. ; libri, Cic. ; epistula, Cic. Ep., Juv. ; ossa, Ov. ; pecunia, Cic., Liv. ; aes alienum, Sall. ; faenus, Cic. Comp. : Cic. ; Sup. : Plin. **b.** Of the voice : *loud, strong* : Quint. Comp. : Cic. Neut. Acc. : grande sonare, Juv. **c.** Of quality : *great, important,*

strong, powerful : grande decus rerum, Hor. ; ingenium, Ov. As Noun : metit Orcus grandia cum parvis, Hor. Esp. of style : *great, grand, lofty, sublime* : genus dicendi grandius, Cic. ; Quint. Of the speaker : Cic., Quint. Comp. : Cic.

granditās, ātis, *f.* [grandis]. Of style : *grandeur, sublimity* : verborum, Cic. ; Plin. Ep.

grandius, comp. adv. [grandis], *more sublimely* : sonat Alcaeus, Ov.

grandō, inis, *f.* hail, *a hail-storm* : Pl., Cic., Verg., etc. In *pl.* : Cic.

grānifer, era, erum [grānum ferō], *grain-carrying* (of ants) : agmen, Ov.

grānum, i, *n. a grain, seed, small kernel* : tritici, Pl. ; uvae, Ov. ; fici, Cic. [Fr. grain.]

graphiārius, a, um [graphium], *of writing-stiles* : theca, Suet.

graphicē, adv. *skilfully, finely, smartly* : Pl.; sonat Alcaeus, Ov.

graphicus, a, um [γραφικός]. **1.** Lit. : only as Noun, **graphicē**, ēs, *f.* (sc. τεχνή), *the art of painting* : Plin. **2.** Transf. of persons : *masterly, skilful* : Pl.

graphium, i, *n.* [γραφεῖον], *a writing stilus*, Ov., Suet.

grassātor, ōris, *m.* [grassor]. **I.** *a vagabond, idler* : Cato. **II.** *a waylayer, street-robber, foot-pad* : Cic., Juv., Suet.

grassātūra, ae, *f.* [grassor], *a waylaying* : Suet.

grassor, āri [freq. fr. old Part. of gradior], *to walk about.* **1.** Lit. **a.** In gen. : Pl., Ov. **b.** *to loiter about, prowl about* (esp. with mischievous intent), *play the highwayman* : Liv., Tac. **2.** Transf. Of a course or method of action. **a.** *to proceed* : animus ad gloriam virtutis viā grassatur, Sall. ; ait, se iure grassari, Liv. : cupidine atque irā, Sall. ; artibus, veneno, Tac. ; obsequio, Hor. **b.** *to attack, proceed against* : with adversus or in and ACC. : ut in te hac viā grassaremur, Liv. ; in externos, Suet. Without Prep. phr. : sagittarii eminus grassabantur, Tac. With abstract thing as Subject : Tac.

grātē, adv. **I.** *with pleasure, willingly* : Cic. **II.** *thankfully, gratefully* : Cic., Hor., Suet. Sup. : Plin.

grātēs (us. only in NOM. and ACC. : in ABL. gratibus, Tac.), *f. pl.* [grātus], *thanks, thanksgiving* (esp. to the gods), mostly with agere (*to pay, give thanks*) : ut Dianae laudes gratisque agam, Pl. ; diis laudes gratisque agunt, Liv. ; gratis tibi ago, summe Sol, Cic. ; o decus Italiae, virgo, quas dicere gratis quasve referre parem ! Verg. With habere, *to feel gratitude* : vobis gratis ago atque habeo, Pl. ; Liv. ; Tac.

grātia, ae, *f.* [grātus], *pleasingness.* **I.** *the quality of being pleasing.* **A.** Physical : *agreeableness, pleasantness, charm, loveliness, grace* : formae, Ov. ; corporis, Suet. ; in vultu, Quint. Personif. : **Grātia** : us. *pl.* **Grātiae**, ārum (= Gk. Χάριτες), *the three Graces* : Hor., Quint. Sing. : Ov. **B.** Mental : *favour, esteem, regard* : o c c. *liking, love, friendship* (felt by another) : nihili facere alicuius gratiam, Pl. ; gratiā atque hospitiis florens hominum nobilissimorum, Cic. ; alicuius gratiam sequi, Caes.;

quantam eo facto ad plebem inierat gratiam,
Liv. ; cum aliquo in gratiam redire, Cic.
Ep. ; so, reverti, Liv. ; ab aliquo in gratiam
inire, Cic. ; gratiā plurimum possunt, Caes. ;
gratiā valere, Caes. ; id gratiā Luculli im-
petravit, Cic. ; summā nobilitate et gratiā
inter suos, Caes. In *pl.* : L. Murenae provincia multas bonas gratias attulit, *tokens of
favour,* Cic. **II.** As a feeling shown in word
or act towards another. **A.** *a favour, kindness, service, approval :* gratiam a patre
petere, Pl. ; petivit in benefici loco et
gratiae, Cic. ; gratiam dicendi facere, Liv.
Hence : **a.** In ABL. *sing.* **grātiā** (after a
GEN.) : *in favour of, for the sake of, on
account of :* negoti gratiā properare, Sall. ;
dolorum effugiendorum gratiā, Cic. ; exempli gratiā, Quint. ; with *Pronom. Adj. :*
meā gratiā, *for my sake,* Pl. ; eā gratiā, *on
that account,* Sall. **b.** in gratiam with GEN. :
to please, win the approval of : Liv. **c.** cum
gratiā with GEN. : *with the approval of,
to the joy of :* Cic., Liv. **B.** With facere :
grace, pardon, excuse : iuris iurandi volo
gratiam facias, Pl. ; alicui delicti gratiam
facere, Sall. ; Liv. **C.** Most freq. : *thanks,
thankfulness, gratitude ; acknowledgment :*
pro beneficio gratiam repetere, Liv. : est
dis gratia, Ter. ; populo Romano gratiam
referre, Cic. ; gratiam rei ferre, Liv. In
pl. (mostly with agere, *to give thanks,* and
often with habere, *to feel gratitude*) : alicui
gratias agere, Cic., Liv., etc. ; alicui gratias
habere, Pl., Liv. ; alicui gratias et agere
et habere, Cic. **Phr.** : bene vocas ; tam
gratia est (like benigne, *no, thank you*), Pl.
ABL. *pl.* **grātiīs** (Pl., Ter.) and **grātis,**
for thanks (merely), *out of kindness, without
recompense or reward, for nothing, gratuit-
ously, gratis :* honoris causā gratiis dabo,
Pl. ; gratis rei publicae servire, Cic. ;
gratis praetor factus est, Cic.
grātĭfĭcātĭō, ōnis, *f.* [grātĭficor]. **I.** *a showing kindness, readiness to oblige :* Cic. **II.**
*complaisance in giving favours, freehanded-
ness :* Cic.
grātĭfĭcor, āri, [grātus faciō]. **I.** With DAT. :
to do a favour, gratify : gratificatur mihi
gestu accusator, Cic. ; Tac. **II.** With Acc.
of *Neut. Pron. :* deus nihil cuiquam gratificans, Cic. ; Liv. **III.** Rarely with Acc. :
to make a present of : populo gratificans et
aliena et sua, Cic. ; potentiae paucorum
decus atque libertatem suam gratificari, Sall.
grātĭīs, *v.* grātia, II. C.
grātĭōsus, a, um [grātia]. **I.** PASS. : *held
in favour, popular.* Of persons : Cic.
Sup. : Cic. ; foll. by *Prep. :* apud omnis
ordines, Cic. ; in suā tribu, Cic. Of things :
causas apud te rogantium gratiosiores esse
quam vultūs, Cic. ; rogatio gratiosissima,
Cic. **II.** Act. (rare) : *that shows favour,
obliging :* gratiosi scribae sint in dando et
cedendo loco, Cic. **III.** *won by favour*
(rare) : missio, Liv.
grātis, *v.* grātia, II. c.
grātor, āri [grātus]. **I.** *to wish joy, to rejoice
with, to congratulate :* invicem inter se
gratantes, Liv. ; nescia, gratentur consolen-
turne parentem, Ov. With DAT. : Verg.,
Ov. With Acc. and *Inf. :* Verg., Tac. **II.**
to express thanks : Ov., Liv.

grātuītus, a, um [grātēs], *earning* (merely)
thanks ; done for favour or *friendship,
spontaneous, gratuitous.* In gen. : si
sine praemio (liberalitas) benigna est,
gratuita, Cic. ; comitia, Cic. Ep. ; furor,
Liv. ; parricidia, Liv. ABL. *Sing. n.*
grātuītō as *Adv., without pay* or *profit :*
Cic., Sall., Tac. Occ. **a.** *without interest :*
pecunia, Plin. Ep. ; faenus, Suet. **b.**
unprovoked : odium, Sen. Ep. ; Liv.
grātŭlābundus, a, um [grātulor], *congratu-
lating :* quo se omnis multitudo gratula-
bunda effudit, Liv. ; Suet.
grātŭlātĭō, ōnis, *f.* [grātulor]. **I.** *a manifesta-
tion of joy, rejoicing :* Cic., Liv. ; inter
gratulationes amicorum, Suet. **II.** *an expression of joy, congratulation :* tantam isti
gratulationem esse factam, Cic. In *pl. :*
Caes. **III.** *a religious festival of joy and
thanksgiving :* Cic., Liv.
grātŭlātor, ōris, *m.* [grātulor], *a congratula-
tor :* Cic.
grātŭlor, āri [grātus]. **I.** *to express one's
joy :* gratulatum satis suo ac patris
nomine esse, Liv. **II.** *to wish* a person *joy,
to congratulate.* With DAT. of person :
nescio, gratulerne tibi, an timeam, Cic. ; de
iudicio, Cic. ; de victoriā, Liv. ; tibi in
hoc, Cic. ; alicui victoriam gratulari, Cic. ;
tibi gratulor quod te summa laus prosecuta
est, Cic. With Acc. and *Inf. :* ei recupera-
tam libertatem est gratulatus, Cic. ; Ov. ;
Liv. Also, ad me venerunt gratulatum,
Cic. ; felicitati tuae, Cic. Ep. **II.** *to give
thanks :* Ter. ; dis immortalibus, Cato ap.
Cic. Ep. ; illi dolori, Quint.
grātus, a, um. **I.** *causing joy ; hence,
pleasing, agreeable, welcome, dear.* **a.** Of
things : tibi mea officia, Cic. Ep. ; hedera
est gratissima Baccho, Ov. ; dapibus supremi grata testudo Iovis, Hor. ; gratae in
vulgus leges, Liv. ; alicui gratum facere,
to do someone a favour, Caes., Cic. *Comp. :*
Caes., Cic., Liv. *Sup. :* Cic. **b.** Of persons : Hor., Plin. Ep. *Sup. :* Ov. With
DAT. : donec gratus eram tibi, Hor. ; Ov.,
Suet. **II.** *causing* or *earning gratitude :*
cum gratum mihi esse potuit, Ter. *Comp. :*
officia, Cic. Ep. **III.** *thankful, grateful :*
Cic., Hor., Quint. ; se alicui gratum praebere, Cic. ; pro beneficiis vix satis gratus
videar, Sall. ; gratissimis animis, Cic.
[Fr. *gré* in *de bon gré, malgré ;* It. *malgrado.*]
grăvantĕr, *adv. reluctantly :* Liv.
grāvastellus, i, m. [*cf.* rāvus], *a rather grey-
headed fellow :* Pl.
grăvātē, *adv. with difficulty* or *reluctance, unwillingly, grudgingly :* respondere, Cic. ;
venire, Liv.
grăvātim, *adv. with difficulty, unwillingly :*
Lucr., Liv.
grăvēdĭnōsus, a, um [gravēdō], *subject to
colds* or *influenza :* Cic.
grăvēdō, inis, *f.* [gravis], *heaviness* in the
head, *cold, influenza :* Pl., Cic. Ep., Cat.
grăvēscō, ere [gravis], *to become burdened* or
heavy. **1.** Lit. : fetu nemus omne gravescit, Verg. **2.** Transf. : *to be aggravated,
to grow worse :* aerumna gravescit, Lucr. ;
valetudo Augusti, Tac.
grăvĭdĭtās, ātis, *f.* [gravidus], *pregnancy :*
Cic.

gravĭdō, āre [gravidus], *to burden, load ;* hence, *to impregnate.* T r a n s f. : terra gravidata seminibus, Cic.

gravĭdus, a, um [gravis]. L i t. *making* or *being heavy ;* hence, *pregnant, with child, with young.* **1.** L i t. : gravida puero, Pl. ; gravida esse ex aliquo viro, Pl. ; uxor, Cic. ; pecus, Verg. ; Ov., etc. **2.** T r a n s f. : manus, Pl. ; nubes, Lucr. ; tellus, Poet. ap. Cic. ; culmus, Verg. ; aristae, Ov. With A b l. : ubera gravida vitali rore, Cic. ; gravidae semine terrae, Ov. ; pampineo gravidus ager, Verg. ; tempestas fulminibus atque procellis, Lucr. ; urbs bellis, Verg. ; pharetra sagittis, Hor.

gravis, e, *adj. [cf.* Gk. βαρύς], *heavy, weighty* (opp. levis). **I.** In gen. (as a natural quality). **1.** L i t. : corpora, Lucr. ; ·tellus, Ov. ; aureum amiculum, Cic. ; navigia, Caes. ; robur aratri, Verg. So with respect to weight or value : aes grave (money of the oldest standard, in which an *as* weighed a full pound), Liv. **2.** T r a n s f. **a.** Of persons (in respect to character) : *weighty, influential, venerable, dignified :* ordo, consilium, Cic. ; civitas, Cic., Liv. ; senatus, Ov. ; pietate gravem ac meritis virum, Verg. **b.** Of persons and things (as affecting a partic. matter) : *weighty, important :* testis, auctor, Cic. ; testimonium, oratio, verbum, auctoritas, etc., Cic. ; sine gravi causā, Caes. ; exemplum, Hor. **c.** Of sound : *deep, grave, low, bass* (opp. acutus, treble) : vocem ab acutissimo sono usque ad gravissimum sonum recipiunt, Cic. ; sonus, Ov. ; vox, Quint. **II.** P a s s. *heavy-laden, loaded.* **1.** L i t. **a.** In gen. : naves spoliis graves, Liv. ; graves imbre nubes, Liv. ; gravis aere dextra, Verg. ; armis miles, Liv. ; miles, Tac. **b.** *pregnant :* regina Marte gravis, Verg. **2.** T r a n s f. Of the body (as affected by food, drink, age, etc.) : somno epulisque, Liv. ; vulnere, Liv. ; morbo, Verg. ; annis, Verg., Liv. ; mero somnoque, Ov. With L o c a t. A b l. : aetate et viribus gravior, Liv. Without A b l. : abit in somnum gravis, Lucr. ; Verg. **III.** A c t. **1.** L i t. Of things causing physical effects : *heavy, oppressive, injurious, noxious, severe :* cibus, Cic. ; autumnus, Caes. ; anni tempus, Cic. Ep., Liv. ; gravis cantantibus umbra, Verg. ; solum caelumque, Tac. ; vulnus, Liv. Of smell or flavour : *offensive, noisome, bitter, harsh :* grave olentia centaurea, Verg. ; Hor. **2.** T r a n s f. : *heavy, oppressive, severe, harsh,* etc. : miserior graviorque fortuna, Caes. ; velim, si tibi grave non erit, me certiorem facias, Cic. ; verbum gravius, Cic. ; ne quid gravius in fratrem statueret, Caes. ; gravior hostis, Liv. ; senes ad ludum adulescentium descendant, ne sint iis odiosi et graves, Cic. ; supplicium, Cic. ; contumelia, Liv. C o m p. : Pl., Cic., Hor., etc. S u p. : Caes., Cic., etc.

gravĭtās, ātis, *f.* [gravis], *weight, heaviness.* **I.** As a natural quality. **1.** L i t. : Lucr., Cic., Ov. ; armorum, navium, Caes. ; oneris, Ov. **2.** T r a n s f. **a.** Of personal character : *dignity, seriousness, influence :* Cic., Liv. **b.** Of persons and things (as affecting a partic. matter) : *weight, im-*

portance : civitatis, provinciae, Caes. ; sententiarum, artium, Cic. **II.** P a s s. : *the state of being burdened or loaded.* **a.** *pregnancy :* Ov. **b.** Of bodily affections : *weakness, faintness :* corporis, linguae, Cic. ; membrorum, Lucr., Cic. **III.** A c t. : *heaviness, pressure.* **1.** L i t. Of physical effects : *heaviness, severity, noxiousness :* morbi, Cic. ; caeli, Cic. Ep., Liv. ; aquarum, Liv. ; soporis, Ov. Of smell : odoris, Tac. **2.** T r a n s f. : *severity, harshness,* etc. : belli, Liv. ; annonae, Tac. ; censor summā gravitate, Cic.

gravĭter, *adv. weightily, heavily.* **I.** In gen. **1.** L i t. : cadere, Lucr. ; Caes. ; Verg. ; Ov. ; Liv. **2.** T r a n s f. **a.** *with weight, influence, dignity :* vivere, agere, Cic. **b.** *with weight, authority* (as affecting a partic. matter) : res gestas narrare, Cic. **c.** Of sound : *deeply :* Lucr., Cic. **II.** P a s s. : *with vexation, chagrin, indignation* (in phr. with accipere, ferre) : aliquid accipere, Cic., Liv., Tac. ; aliquid ferre, Cic. ; senatum graviter ferre quod (*the fact that*) nihil facerem, Cic. ; ferebat graviter illam sibi ab isto provinciam datam, Cic. **III.** A c t. : *heavily, severely.* **1.** L i t. (physically) : Ter. ; ictus, Caes. ; saucius, Liv. ; ferire, Verg. ; gravissime adflictae naves, Caes. ; spirantibus flabris, Lucr. ; aegrotare, dormitare, Cic. Of smell : *strongly, offensively :* spirantes hydri, Verg. **2.** T r a n s f. : *severely, deeply, vehemently,* etc. : irasci, Ter. ; dissentire, dicere, angi, Cic. ; decernere, Caes.

gravō, āre [gravis], *to make heavy ; to load, burden, weigh down.* **1.** L i t. **a.** gravantur arbores fetu, Lucr. ; praefectum castrorum sarcinis gravant, Tac. ; poma gravantia ramos, Ov. **b.** Of other physical effects : gravatus, *weighed down, heavy :* gravatus cibo, Liv. ; vino somnoque, Liv. ; choreis somnoque, Verg. **2.** T r a n s f. **a.** *to burden, be oppressive to :* nil moror officium, quod me gravat, Hor. ; militiā gravari, Liv. **b.** *to make more severe, aggravate :* fortunam meam, Ov. ; invidiam matris, Tac. ; iniusto faenore gravatum aes alienum, Liv. **c.** E s p. **gravāri** as *Dep. : to count or think heavy ; to feel burdensome, to feel vexed, or annoyed at anything :* Pl., Cic., Tac., etc. With *Inf. : to be loth, disdain :* Caes., Cic., Liv. With A c c. : Pegasum equitem, Hor. ; aspectum civium, Tac. With *quod* clause : *to raise objections :* Cic.

gregālis, e, *adj.* [grex], *of or belonging to a herd or flock.* **1.** L i t. : equi, Varr. **2.** T r a n s f. **a.** *belonging to the same body :* only as Noun in *pl. : comrades, companions :* Cic. **b.** *of the common sort, common :* sagulum, Liv. ; habitus, Tac.

gregārius, a, um [grex], *of or belonging to a flock or herd.* T r a n s f. Of soldiers : *in the ranks, rankers :* Cic., Liv., Tac.

gregātim, *adv. flock by flock, herd by herd.* T r a n s f. Of men : *in troops or crowds :* civis Romanos gregatim coniectos in lautumias, Cic.

gremĭum, I, *n.* **1.** L i t. **a.** *the lap, bosom :* Cic. Cat., Verg. **b.** *womb :* Ter. **2.** T r a n s f. : **a.** terra gremio semen accipit,

Cic. **b.** Of a mother's loving care:
gremio ac sinu matris educabatur, Tac. **c.**
In gen.: Aetolia medio fere Graeciae
gremio continetur, Cic.; abstrahi e sinu
gremioque patriae, Cic.; (omnia) in vestris
pono gremiis, Verg. [It. *grembo.*]

grēssus, a, um, *Part,* gradior.

grēssus, ūs, *m.* [gradior], *a stepping, step.*
1. Lit.: tendere gressum ad moenia,
Verg.; inferre, Verg.; premere, Ov. In
pl.: Verg. **2.** Transf.: *course* (of a
vessel): huc dirige gressum, Verg.

grex, gregis, *m.* (*f.* Lucr.), *a flock, herd,
drove, swarm.* **1.** Lit. Of cattle, birds,
etc.: Cic., Verg., etc. Occ. of small
cattle: non ego sum pastor, non hic armenta gregesve observo, Ov. **2.** Transf.
of persons: *a company, troop, band.* **a.**
In gen.: Epicuri de grege porcus, Hor.;
venalium, Pl.; amicorum, philosophorum,
Cic.; grege facto, Sall., Liv.; scribe tui
gregis hunc, Hor. **b.** Of players or
charioteers: Pl., Ter. **c.** Of things
(comic.): virgarum, Pl. [It. *gregge.*]

grossus, ī, *m. f.* (sc. ficus), *a heavy fig that
falls unripened:* Cato.

gruis, *v.* grūs.

grūmus, ī, *m. a small heap of earth:* Acc.,
Auct. B. Alex.

grunniō (and **grundiō**), īre, *to grunt,* of
swine: Varr., Juv. [It. *grugnire;* Sp.
gruñir; Fr. *grogner.*]

grunnītus, ūs, *m.* [grunniō], *a grunting* of
swine: Cic.

grūs (**gruis**, Phaedr.), gruis, *f.* and *m.* [*cf.*
Gk. γέρανος], *a crane:* Lucr., Cic., etc.; as
a delicacy: Hor.

grȳ, *n. indecl.* [Gk. γρῦ], *a tiny scrap, crumb:*
Pl.

grȳps, grȳpis, *m.* [γρύψ], *a fabulous animal*
(*having the body and feet of a lion, with the
head and wings of an eagle*), *a griffin.*
Prov.: iungentur iam grypes equis,
Verg.

gubernāculum (gubernāclum, Lucr., Verg.),
ī, *n.* [gubernō], *a helm, rudder.* **1.** Lit.:
Cic., Verg., etc. **2.** Transf. (in *pl.*;
of State-government) *the helm:* gubernacula rei publicae tractare, Cic.; ad
gubernacula rei publicae sedere, Cic.; ad
gubernacula rei publicae accedere, Liv.
[It. *governale;* Fr. *gouvernail.*]

gubernātiō, ōnis, *f.* [gubernō], *a steering,
navigating* of a ship. **1.** Lit.: Cic. **2.**
Transf.: civitatis, Cic.; tantarum rerum,
Cic.

gubernātor, ōris, *m.* [gubernō], *a steersman,
navigator.* **1.** Lit.: Pl., Cic., Verg., etc.
2. Transf.: rei publicae, Cic. Also
gubernātrix, īcis, *f.* : gubernatrix civitatum eloquentia, Cic.; Ter.

gubernō, āre [κυβερνῶ], *to steer* or *navigate*
a ship. **1.** Lit.: Cic. Prov.: gubernare e terrā (i.e. to direct others when
in safety oneself), Liv.; quilibet nautarum tranquillo mari gubernare potest, Liv.
2. Transf.: ex sermone hoc guberna-
bunt doctius, Pl.; aliquem animus, Ter.;
rem publicam, Cic.; sed haec fortuna
viderit, quoniam ratio non gubernat, Cic.
[It. *governare;* Sp. *gobernar;* Fr. *gouverner.*]

gubernum, ī, *n.* [gubernō], *a helm, rudder:*
Lucil., Lucr.

gula, ae, *f.* [fr. root seen in gluttiō], *the gullet,
throat.* **1.** Lit.: Pl.; alicui inter-
stringere gulam, Pl.; contorquere, Cic.;
frangere, Sall. **2.** Transf.: *the palate*
(i.e. appetite, gluttony): o gulam insulsam,
Cic.; inritamenta gulae, Sall.; gulae
parens, Hor.; intempestivae ac sordidae
gulae homo, Suet. [Fr. *gueule.*]

gulōsus, a, um [gula], *gluttonous, dainty.* **1.**
Lit.: fictile, Juv. **2.** Transf.: lector,
Mart.

gumia, ae, *m. f.* [perh. *cf.* Gk. γόμος], *a glutton, gourmand:* Lucil.

gurdus, ī, *m.* [a Spanish word], *a numskull:*
Quint. [Sp. *gordo;* Fr. *gourd.*]

gurges, itis, *m.* [fr. root seen in Gk. βορά,
βάραβρον, Lat. vorō], *an abyss, gulf,
swirl* (of water), *raging current.* **1.** Lit.:
Verg., Ov., Juv. In *pl.*: Cic., Liv. **2.**
Transf. **a.** Of violent water: *flood,
depths:* Euboicus, Ov.; Carpathius, Verg.;
Herculeus, Juv. **b.** *a bottomless abyss:*
divitias in profundissimum libidinum gurgitem profundit, Cic.; Liv. Of persons:
gurges vitiorum turpitudinumque, Cic.
[Fr. *gorge.*]

(1) gurguliō, ōnis, *m.* [perh. by redupl. fr.
root of gula], *the gullet, weasand, windpipe:*
Pl., Cic. [It. *gorgoglio.*]

(2) gurguliō, *v.* curculio.

gurgustium, ī, *n.* [colloq., fr. gurges], *hole
and corner, dark hovel:* Cic.

gustātōrium, ī, *n.* [gustō], *a first course,
whet:* Plin. Ep.

gustātus, ūs, *m.* [gustō], *the sense of taste.*
1. Lit.: Cic. **2.** Transf. **a.** *the taste*
or *flavour of anything:* uva primo est perac-
erba gustatu, Cic. **b.** *taste, appetite* for
anything: verae laudis, Cic.

gustō, āre [*cf.* Gk. γεύω], *to taste,* to *partake
of.* **1.** Lit. **a.** ne aquam quidem, Cic.
Ep.; anserem gustare fas non putant,
Caes.; aliquid de sanguine, Juv. **b.** *to
eat a little, have a snack:* post solem lava-
batur, deinde gustabat, Plin. Ep. **2.**
Transf. **a.** Of speech: civilem sanguinem,
Cic.; amorem vitae, Lucr.; partem ullam li-
quidae voluptatis, Cic.; praecepta, Cic. **b.**
to get a taste or *snack of:* sermonem alicuius, Pl.; lucellum, Hor.

gustus, ūs, *m.* [*cf.* gustō], *a tasting, a partaking* or *eating a little of.* **1.** Lit. **a.** epulas
explorare gustu, Tac. **b.** *a light dish at the
beginning of a Roman meal, a whet, relish:*
Mart., Juv. **2.** Transf. **a.** Of speech:
flavour: sermo praeferens proprium quendam gustum urbis, Quint. **b.** Of a
specimen: *a foretaste:* gustum tibi dare
volui, Sen. Ep.; Plin. Ep. [F. *goût.*]

gutta, ae, *f. a drop.* **1.** Lit.: vini, Pl.;
sanguinis, Pl., Verg.; imbrium, Cic.; of
tears: Ov.; of *a blush:* sanguinis in
facie, Juv. **2.** Transf. **a.** *natural spots* or
specks: on bees: Verg.; on snakes: Ov.
b. *a drop* (i.e. a little): certi consilii, Pl.;
dulcedinis, Lucr. [It. *gotta;* Sp. *gota;* Fr.
goutte.]

guttātim, *adv. drop by drop:* Pl.

guttula, ae, *f.* [dim. gutta], *a tiny drop:* Pl.

guttur, uris, *n.* (also *m.* : Acc. *sing.* gut-

turem, Pl.), *the gullet, throat.* **1.** Lit.:
Pl., Ov.; guttur frangere, Hor. In *pl.*:
fodere guttura cultro, Ov. **2.** Transf.:
gluttony : vitium ventris et gutturis, Cic.;
Juv. [Fr. *goitre.*]

gūtus (and **guttus**), ī, *m.* [gutta], *a narrow-
necked vessel, cruse* (for oil, etc.): Hor.,
Varr., Juv. [It. *gotto ;* Fr. *godet,* dim. of
O. F. *got.*]

Gȳās, ae, *m. a giant with a hundred arms.*

Gȳgēs, is or ae, *m. a king of Lydia* (B.C. ? 716–
678), *famous for his ring ;* **Gȳgaeus**, a, um.

gymnasiarchus, ī, *m.* [γυμνασίαρχος], *the
master of a gymnasium :* Cic.

gymnasium, ī, *n.* [γυμνάσιον], *a public place
of training in wrestling and other physical
exercises.* **1.** Lit.: Pl., Cic., Ov., etc.
Comic.: gymnasium flagri (*whip's practice-
ground,* i.e. one who is often flogged). Pl.
2. Transf.: *a place for philosopher's
lectures :* omnia gymnasia atque omnes
philosophorum scholae, Cic.; Liv.; Juv.

gymnasticus, a, um [γυμναστικός], *gymnastic :* Pl.

gymnicus, a, um [γυμνικός], *gymnastic :*
ludi, Cic.; Suet.

gymnosophistae, ārum, *m. pl.* [γυμνοσο-
φισταί (*naked philosophers*)], *gymnoso-
phists,* Indian ascetics : Plin.

gynaecēum (Pl., Ter.) or **gynaecium** (Cic.),
ī, *n.* [γυναικεῖον], among the Greeks, *the
women's apartments.*

gynaecōnītis, idis, *f.* [γυναικωνῖτις], *the
women's apartments in a Greek house :* Nep.

gypsātus, a, um [gypsum], *covered or coated
with gypsum :* manibus gypsatissimis, Cic.
Ep.; of slaves marked for sale : gypsati
pedes, Tib., Ov.

gypsum, ī, *n.* [γύψος], *plaster of Paris,
gypsum.* **1.** Lit.: Cato. **2.** Transf. :
a plaster figure : Juv. [It. *gesso.*]

gȳrus, ī, *m.* [γῦρος], *a ring, curve, coil.* **1.**
Lit. **a.** anguis septem gyros traxit, Verg.;
gyros ducere, Ov.; in gyrum flecti, Ov.
b. Of horses' movements (perh. *curvetting*):
gyros ire, Ov.; gyros dare, carpere, Verg.;
equi variare gyros docentur, Tac. **2.**
Transf. **a.** *a place where horses are
trained, a course :* Cic., Prop. **b.** (as
metaph. of **a**) ex ingenti campo oratorem
in exiguum gyrum compellere, Cic. **c.**
orbit, course : seu bruma nivalem interiore
diem gyro trahit, Hor. [It. Sp. *giro.*]

H

H, h, the eighth letter of the Latin alphabet,
has the place and form of the Greek Eta,
which originally stood for the rough breathing. The Latin H, however, was quite
different in phonetic character from the
Greek *spiritus asper,* to which it never
(except in borrowed words) corresponds.
I. Lat. *h,* has its origin regularly from initial
gh (Gk. χ), as in Lat. *hortus,* Gr. χόρτος; and
sometimes from *bh* (Gr. φ), as in Lat. *herba,*
compared with Gr. φορβή. Medial *h* in *mihi*
is for *b* from *bh.* In *traho, veho, h* (from *gh*)
occurs at the end of a root and it must have

had a strong guttural sound. The combinations *th, ph, ch,* to represent θ, φ, χ, in words
borrowed from the Greek, were of comparatively late introduction in Latin ; they
rarely appear in inscriptions before B.C. 94 ;
in earlier periods the Greek aspirates were
represented by *t, c, p* ; and φ was sometimes represented by *b,* as in *Bruges* (Enn.)
from Φρύγες. **II.** In the Romance languages initial *h* is often dropped ; thus from
Lat. *habere* we have It. *avere,* Fr. *avoir ;*
from Lat. *hora,* It. *ora,* Fr. *or* (adv.) ; from
Lat. *homo,* Fr. *on ;* from Lat. *hordeum,* Fr.
orge ; from Lat. *haustare,* Fr. *ôter.* **III.**
a. As an abbreviation HH. stands for
heredes. **b.** In HS for sestertius, H is not
the letter of that shape, but the numeral
II crossed, v. sestertius.

ha, hahae, hahahae, an exclamation. **a.**
Of joy, satisfaction, exultation : Pl., Ter.
b. Of laughter and esp. of derisive laughter : Pl., Ter.

habēna, ae, *f.* [habeō] Lit. that by which a
thing is held]. **I.** Us. in *pl.* : *a halter,
bridle, rein.* **1.** Lit. : effusissimis habenis stationem hostium invadit, Liv.;
habenas effundere, dare, immittere, adducere, premere, Verg.; exhortatur equos,
quorum per colla iubasque excutit habenas,
Ov.; habenis flectit equos, Verg. **2.**
Transf. **a.** Of a ship : classi immittit
habenas, Verg.; vincitur ars vento, nec
iam moderator habenis utitur, Ov. **b.** In
gen. fluminibus vestris totas immittite
habenas, Ov.; habere profundi habenas,
Lucr.; amicitiae, Cic.; rerum, Verg.;
irarum, Verg.; crescendi immissis certamen
habenis, Lucr. **II.** *a holder.* **1.** Lit.:
the strap : of a sling : fundae, Verg.; of a
javelin : Luc. **2.** Transf.: *a strap :* for
a whip-top : Verg.; for flogging : Hor.

habeō, ēre, uī, itum [fr. root seen in Gk.
κώπη, Lat. *capiō*]. *Aor. Opt.* habēssit,
Cic.). **I.** *to hold, keep.* **1.** Lit. **a.** *to
hold, handle, wield :* ensem aptat habendo,
Verg.; iaculum manibus, Ov.: vestem,
Ov.; hastas, Tac. **b.** *to hold, keep :* qua
regio Anchisen habet, Verg.; Ov. Often
with DAT. of *Refl. Pron.* : habeant sibi
arma, Cic.; tibi habe Canephoros, Cic.;
in formula of divorce : valeas, res tuas tibi
habeas, Pl. ; Cic. **c.** *to hold, keep* (in any
position) : aliquem in obsidione, Caes.;
aliquem in liberis custodiis, Sall. ; milites in
castris, Liv. Esp. with *Part. Perf.* (to
express a past action whose effects continue) : segregatum habui a me Pamphilum,
Ter. ; inclusum in curiā senatum habuerunt,
Cic.; equitatum quem coactum habebat,
praemittit, Caes. **2.** Transf. **A.** *to hold,
handle, use, manage, treat :* uti tu me hic
habueris, Pl. ; sine imperio et modestiā
exercitus habitus, Sall. ; exercitum luxu-
riose habere, Sall. ; saucii maiore curā
habiti, Liv.; equitatu agmen adversariorum
male habere et carpere, Caes. Also of
power, wealth : *to use, manage :* magnae
opes modeste habitae, Tac. **B.** *to hold,
control, keep.* **a.** In gen.: regnum, Ov. ;
urbem Romam reges, Tac. ; nos Amaryllis
habet, Verg.; Thaida habeo, Cic. Ep.;
animus habet cuncta, Sall. Occ. with

Refl. Pron. : secreto hoc audi, tecum habeto, Cic. Ep.; pacem sibi habeat, Liv. **b.** Of levies, meetings, etc.: *to hold, direct, arrange :* dilectum, contionem, comitia, senatum, Caes., Cic., Liv.; concilia, Caes.; censum, Cic.; conquisitionem, Liv. **c.** Of other things: *to carry on, make,* etc.: disputationem, Caes., Cic.; orationem, Caes., Cic., Liv., etc.; preces, Liv.; sermonem, verba, Cic.; rationem, Caes.; iter, Ter., Caes., Cic. **C.** *to hold, keep* (in any condition). **a.** In gen.: reliquas civitates stipendiarias, Caes.; aliquem in honore, Caes.; aliquem suspectum, Sall.; alios in eâ fortunâ ut etc., Liv.; milites in otio, Liv.; milites per otium habebantur, Tac.; Hadriaticum mare in potestate, Caes. **b.** Esp. with *Perf. Part. :* hoc compertum habeo, Sall.; domitas habere libidines, Cic.; habere cognitum aliquem, Cic. **c.** With *Refl. Pron.,* or in *Mid.,* or *Intrans. : to be in a certain condition of circumstances, health,* etc. With *Refl. Pron. :* videbatur se non graviter habere, Cic.; ut meae res sese habent, Ter.; ut nunc res se habet, Liv.; ratio ordinis aliter se habebat ac Nervii detulerant, Caes. In *Mid. :* virtus clara aeternaque habetur, Sall.; sicuti pleraque mortalium habentur, Sall. *Intrans.* (*cf.* ἔχειν with *Adv.*) *:* ut bene haberem filiae nuptiis, Pl.; bene habet; iacta sunt fundamenta defensionis, Cic.; atqui sic habet, Hor. **D.** *to hold in any category or class ; to classify, regard as, to account, esteem, consider ; to think* or *believe so and so :* Considius rei militaris peritissimus habebatur, Caes.; parentem Asiae et dici et haberi, Cic.; id obliviscendum, pro non dicto habendum, Liv.; aliquem in hostium numero, Caes.; aliquem pro hoste, Caes., Liv.; pro certo, explorato, re compertâ habere, Caes., Cic.; Achivos uno ordine, Verg.; Cic.; ludibrio, Ter. Hence, sic habeto or sic habeas, with Acc., or Acc. and *Inf. : be convinced, believe, know :* Cic. Also without sic: Cic. **E.** With *Adv. : to take, accept* (a situation of things), *submit to :* iniurias gravius aequo, Sall.; ea civiliter, Tac.; aegre habere with Acc. and *Inf. :* Liv. **II.** *to have, possess.* **1.** Lit. (with personal *Subject*). **a.** Without *Obj. :* amor habendi, Verg., Hor.; in nummis, Cic.; in Bruttiis, Cic. Hence, perh. habere = habitare: Syracusis habet, Pl.; Liv. **b.** With material *Obj. :* aurum, Pl.; pecuniam, navis, etc., Cic.; magnum numerum equitatûs circum se, Caes.; secum senatorem, Cic.; muros, Verg.; vos conscios habeo, Liv.; decemviris consules similis, Liv. **2.** Transf. **a.** With inanimate or abstract *Subject :* locus ille nihil habet religionis, Cic.; animalia somnus habet, Verg.; me habuit thalamus, Verg.; ira me habet, Ov.; latrocinia nullam habent infamiam, Caes. **b.** With personal *Subject* and abstract *Object :* quem usum belli haberent, Caes.; gratiam, Caes., Cic.; invidiam, spem, Cic.; vitae necisque potestatem, Cic.; vim dicendi, Cic.; neque modestiam neque modum, Sall. **c.** With verbals or verbal clauses as *Object :* to

have ; hence, occ. *to be able, to know,* etc. With *Inf. :* haec dicere, Cic.; Liv.; Hor. With a *relat. clause :* nihil habeo quod cum amicitiâ Scipionis possim comparare, Cic.; Hor. With *Indir. Quest. :* nec quid faceret habebat, Cic. With *Gerund. Adj. :* praesertim cum enitendum haberemus ut etc., Plin. Ep.; Tac. **3.** Phr. **a.** *to have in one's mind, to know :* si quidem istius regis (Anci) matrem habemus, ignoramus patrem, Cic.; habes consilia nostra; nunc cognosce de Bruto, Cic. Ep. **b.** *to have as a habit, peculiarity,* or *characteristic :* habebat hoc omnino Caesar, Cic. **c.** habere in animo: with *Inf. : to intend, to be disposed, inclined :* Caes., Cic. **d.** Gladiatorial phrase, of a wounded combatant, hoc habet or habet, *he has it, he is hit:* Verg. Comic.: hoc habet: repperi, qui senem ducerem, Pl.; Ter. [It. *avere* ; Sp. *haber* ; Fr. *avoir.*]

habilis, e, adj. [habeō], *easily handled* or *managed, handy.* **1.** Lit.: gladii, Liv.; ensis, arcus, Verg.; currus, Ov.; frameae, Tac. As *Predic. Adj. :* membris venit habilis vigor (i.e. making his limbs pliant), Verg. **2.** Transf.: *suitable, well-adapted.* **a.** Of things: calcei, Cic.; figuram corporis habilem et aptam ingenio humano, Cic.; bos feturae habilis, Verg.; ingenium ad res habilius, Liv.; naves velis, Tac. **b.** Of persons: in aliquâ re, Cic.; Numidarum gentem equis tantum habilem, Liv.; vicina seni non habilis Lyco. Hor.

habilitās, ātis, *f.* [habilis], *aptitude, suitability.* In *pl. :* Cic.

habitābilis, e, adj. [habitō], *habitable :* Cic., Hor., Ov.

habitātiō, ōnis, *f.* [habitō], *a dwelling, inhabiting ;* hence, *a place to dwell in.* **1.** Lit.: Pl., Cic. In *pl. :* Caes. **2.** Transf. *house-rent :* Suet.

habitātor, ōris, *m.* [habitō], *a dweller, occupant, tenant :* Cic., Liv., Juv.

habitō, āre [*freq.* habeō], *to dwell, reside, live.* **1.** Lit. **a.** Without *Obj. :* in aedibus, Pl.; in Siciliâ, Cic.; in viâ, Cic.; ruri, Cic.; Romae, Liv.; vallibus imis, Verg.; sub rupe, Ov.; sub terrâ, Cic.; habitandi causâ, Caes. *Pass. Impers. :* vicorum, quibus frequenter habitatur, Liv. **b.** With Acc.: casas, urbes, collem, Verg.; locum, Tac. As Noun, **habitantēs,** *occupants, inhabitants :* Ov., Quint. In *Pass. :* colitur ea pars (urbis) et habitatur frequentissime, Cic.; (agellus) habitatus quinque focis, Hor.; raris habitata mapalia tectis, Verg.; campi magnis urbibus habitati, Tac. **2.** Transf. (without *Obj.*) *:* in oculis, Cic.; in foro, Cic.; in hac unâ ratione tractandâ, Cic.; omnibus in terris gloria nominis mei, Cic.; cum his curis, Cic.

habitūdō, inis, *f.* [habitus], *condition, habit* of the body (for habitus): corporis, Ter., Auct. Her.

habituriō, īre [habeō], *to desire to have, to long for :* Pl.

habitus, a, um. **I.** *Part.* habeō. **II.** Adj. **1.** Lit. Of the body: *in good condition :* virgo habitior, Ter.; Pl. **2.** Transf. Of character: *of a certain humour :* ut patrem tuom vidi esse habitum, diu etiam duras (litīs) dabit, Ter.

habitus, ūs, m. [habeō], *the condition or state of the body, habit, bearing.* **1.** Lit.: Cic.; oris, Cic.; hominis, Hor.; corporum, Tac.; virginalis, Cic. **2.** Transf.: *character, quality, style.* **A.** *Of things.* **a.** *In gen.*: (praediscere) patrios cultūsque habitūsque locorum, Verg.; Italiae, pecuniarum, armorum, temporum, Liv. **b.** *style of dress*: Punicus, Liv.; Romanus, Hor.; Suet.; pastorum, Liv. **B.** *Mental and moral.* **a.** *In gen*: *quality, nature, character*: servos is habitu haud probo est, Pl.; orationis, Cic.; naturae ipsius, Cic.; novae fortunae, Liv.; suo habitu vitam degere, Phaedr. **b.** *a state of feeling* (at a partic. moment), *temper, disposition*: praeteritus, praesens, Liv.; provinciarum, Tac. **c.** Philos. *a completed and fixed state* or *condition* (acquired by custom or practice), *habit*: animi aut corporis, Cic. [It. *abito.*]

hāc [ABL. *fem.* of hīc, used as *Adv.*] *by this way, on this side*: Pl., Cic., Verg., etc.

hāc-tenus (sometimes separated), *adv.* lit. *as far as this.* **A.** *Of space*: *to this place, thus far.* **1.** Lit.: Verg., Ov., Tac. **2.** Transf.: to indicate the limit of anything: *thus far*: hactenus mihi videor de amicitiā quid sentirem potuisse dicere, Cic.; Quint. Often in ellipse: sed. si placet, in hunc diem hactenus, Cic.; hactenus arvorum cultūs (*sc.* cecini), Verg.; hactenus haec, Hor. **B.** *Of time*: *up to this time, hitherto*: Verg., Ov., Liv., Tac. **C.** *In extent* (with sense of restriction). **a.** *so much, so far only*: Burrum sciscitanti hactenus respondisse: 'ego me bene habeo,' Tac. **b.** *so much, so far.* With correlatives. **i.** *quoad, quod*: hactenus existimo nostram consolationem recte adhibitam esse, quoad certior ab homine amicissimo fieres iis de rebus, Cic. Ep.; Plin. Ep. **ii.** *ut, ne, si*: artem hactenus requirunt ut certis dicendi luminibus ornentur, Cic.; Hor.; Ov.; hactenus addito discrimine, ne auctor dubitaretur, Tac.: Cic. Ep.; Quint.; hactenus utilia si praeparant ingenium, Sen. Ep.

Hadria, ae, f. *a city in Northern Italy, on the coast of the sea named after it,* now *Adria*; **Hadriāticus**, a, um: Hadriaticum mare, or Hadriaticum, *the Adriatic Sea*; **Hadriacus**, a, um; **Hadria**, ae, m. *the Adriatic Sea.*

Hadriānus, P. Aelius, Roman emperor, A.D. 117–138.

haedilia, ae, f. [dim. haedus,] *a little kid*: Hor.

haedillus, i, m. [dim. haedus,] *a little kid, as* a term of endearment · Pl.

haedīnus, a, um [haedus], *of a kid, kid's*: pellicula, Cic.

haedulus, i, m. [dim. haedus], *a little kid*: pinguissimus, Juv.

haedus (older **aedus**; rustic **ēdus**), i, m. *a young goat, a kid.* **1.** Lit.: Cic., Verg., etc. **2.** Transf.: Haedi, *a pair of stars in the hand of the Waggoner* (Auriga): Varr., Verg., Ov. In *sing.*: Prop.

Haemonia, ae, f. *a poetical name of Thessaly*; **Haemonius**, a, um, *Thessalian*; **Haemonis**, idis, f. *a Thessalian woman.*

Haemus or **Haemos**, i, m. *an extensive range of mountains in Thrace,* now *the Great Balkan.*

haereō, haerēre, haesi, haesum, *to cling, cleave, stick, hold fast, be fixed or attached.* **1.** Lit.: scalarum gradūs male haerentes, Cic. Ep.; frondes male haerentes, Ov. With *in* and ABL.: pugnus in mālā haereat, Ter.; male laxus in pede calceus haeret, Hor.; in corpore ferrum, Verg.; in equo, Cic.; in tergo, Liv. With ABL.: equo, Hor.; tergo volueres haesere sagittae, Verg.; adverso litore naves, Hor.; pede pes, Verg.; terra imā sede, Cic. With DAT.: haerentem capiti coronam, Hor. **2.** Transf. **a.** *to hang about, linger, stay, remain fixed*: hi in oculis haerebunt, Cic.; in medullis populi R. ac visceribus, Cic.; in omnium gentium sermonibus ac mentibus, Cic.; visceribus civitatis tyrannus, Liv. Occ. with idea of wasting time: Athenis, Ter.; in iure ac praetorum tribunalibus, Cic.; in obsidione, Curt. **b.** *to remain close, cling, hang on*: in te omnis haeret culpa, Ter.; in sententiā, Cic.; haerent infixi pectore vultūs, Verg.; homini huic peccatum, Cic.; criminibus, Tac.; haesserat Euandro, Verg.; Plin. Ep.; ut haeream apud Thaidem, Ter.; apud fidicinam, Pl. Milit.: tergis, in tergis, or in terga, *to hang on the rear of* an enemy, Liv., Curt., Tac. With *ad*: ad impedimenta nostra exercitus barbarorum, Liv. **II.** *to come to a standstill, stiffen, stick fast.* **1.** Lit.: ipse evasit, duo turmae haesere, Liv.; aspectu territus haesit, Verg.; vox faucibus haesit, Verg. Phr.: tali ut in luto haeream, Pl.; (of a speaker): haeret in salebrā, Cic.; aqua haeret, *the water* (clock) *stops* (of one at a loss for a word), Cic. **2.** Transf. **a.** *to be brought to a standstill, be checked*: in iis poenis, Cic.; fama adulescentis ad metas, Cic.; criminibus, Tac.; Hectoris manu victoria Graium haesit, Verg. **b.** *to stick, perplexed*: Pl., Cic., Hor., etc.; in multis nominibus, Cic.; circa formas litterarum par, Quint.; in hac difficultate rerum consilium, Liv. **c.** *to be inexplicable*: haeret haec res, Pl.

haerēscō, ere [haereō], *to stick, adhere*: Lucr.

haeresis, is, f. [αἵρεσις], *a philosophical sect*: Cic.

haesitābundus, a, um [haesitō], *hesitating, faltering*: Plin. Ep.

haesitantia, ae, f. [haesitō], *a faltering, stammering*: linguae, Cic.

haesitātiō, ōnis, f. [haesitō], *a sticking fast.* **I.** *Of speech*: *a stammering*: Cic., Quint. **II.** *Of mind*: *indecision, hesitation*: Cic. Ep., Tac., etc.

haesitātor, ōris, m. [haesitō], *one who hesitates, is undecided*: Plin. Ep.

haesitō, āre [freq. haereō], *to stick fast, remain fixed in a place.* **1.** Lit.: in palude, Caes.; in vadis, Liv.; sub terris iubar haesitat ignis, Lucr. Prov.: haesitas in eodem luto, Ter. **2.** Transf. **a.** *Of speech*: *to hesitate, stammer*: linguā, Cic. **b.** *Of mind*: *to be undecided, to be at a loss, to hesitate*: Cic., Liv., Quint.; in maiorum institutis, Cic. *Impers. Pass.*: de mutando rei publicae statu haesitatum erat, Suet.

hahae, hahahae, v. ha.

Halaesus, i, *m. a son of Agamemnon ; the founder of Falisci, an ally of Turnus.*

halagora, *f.* [ἅλς ἀγορά], *the salt market :* Pl.

hālāns, antis. **I.** *Part.* hālō. **II.** Adj.: *breathing* (fragrantly) : croceis halantes floribus horti, Verg.

hālēc, *v.* ālēc.

haliaeetos, i, *m.* [ἁλιαίετος], *the sea-eagle, or osprey :* Verg., Ov.

hālitus, ūs, *m.* [hālō], *exhalation.* **I.** *breath :* Lucr., Juv. Hence, *fumes :* terrae, Quint. **II.** *mist, vapour :* Verg.

hallex, icis, *m. the thumb* or *great toe.* Comic.: Pl.

hallūcinor, āri [perh. *cf.* Gk. ἀλύω], *to wander in mind, talk idly* (better spelt ālūcinor, q.v.).

hālō, āre, *to breathe, breathe out, exhale.* **A.** Intrans.: de gelidis vallibus aurae, Ov.; arae sertis, Verg. **B.** Trans.: nardi florem, nectar qui naribus halat, Lucr.

halophanta, ae, m. [ἀλοφάντης], *a salt-informer,* i.e. *a rascal, scoundrel :* Pl.

hālūcinor, *v.* ālūcinor.

hama (**ama**), ae, *f.* [ἅμη], *a water-bucket* (for extinguishing fires), Plin. Ep., Juv.

Hamādryas, adis (Gk. Dat. *pl.* Hamādryasin, Prop.), *f. a wood-nymph.*

hāmātilis, e, *adj.* [hāmātus], *performed by hooks :* piscatus, Pl.

hāmātus, a, um [hāmus], *having a hook, hooked.* **1.** Lit.: ungues, harundo, Ov. Hence, viscata hamataque munera, Plin. Ep. **2.** Transf.: *shaped like a hook, hooked, crooked :* Cic., Ov.

hamaxagōga, ae, *m.* [ἁμαξαγωγός], *one who carries off anything in a waggon :* bonorum, Pl.

hamaxō, āre [ἅμαξα, a waggon], *to yoke to a waggon :* Pl.

Hamilcar (**Am-**), aris, *m. a celebrated Carthaginian general in the first Punic war, surnamed Barca ; father of Hannibal.*

hāmiōta, ae, *m.* [hāmus], *a man of hooks, a hookite* (of an angler) : Pl., Varr.

hāmulus, i, *m.* [*dim.* hāmus], *a small hook :* piscarius, Pl.

hāmus, i, *m.* [*cf.* χαμός, "bent"], *a hook* **1.** Lit. **a.** In gen.: Caes., Verg. **b.** *a fish-hook :* Pl., Cic. In metaph.: occultum decurrere ad hamum, Hor.; meus hic est: hamum vorat, Pl. **2.** Transf. Of hooked or crooked things: *the talons of a hawk :* Ov.; *thorns :* Ov.

Hannibal, alis, *m. a Punic name.* Esp. *Hannibal, son of Hamilcar, the leader of the Carthaginians in the second Punic war.*

Hannō, ōnis, *m. a Punic name.* Esp. *a Carthaginian general who explored the W. coast of Africa* (c. B.C. 500).

hara, ae, *f. a pen* or *coop for animals.* **1.** Lit.: anserum, Varr.; *a hog-stye :* Varr. **2.** Transf.: Epicure noster, ex harā producte non ex scholā, Cic.; as abusive term, hara suis, Pl.

harēna, ae, *f.* **1.** Lit. **A.** *sand :* Lucr., Verg., etc. Prov.: harenae semina mandare (i.e. to begin a fruitless work), Ov. In *pl.* : *grains of sand :* Verg., etc. **B.** *a stretch of sand.* **a.** Of the seashore: Lucr., Verg., Ov. **b.** Of a desert (in *pl.*): Ov., Tac. **c.** Of a sandy or poor soil :

Cic., Verg. **d.** *the place of combat* (strewn with sand) *in the amphitheatre, the arena :* Sen. Ep., Juv., Suet. **2.** Transf. **a.** *combats in the arena :* operas harenae promittere, Tac.; Suot. **b.** *the combatants :* Juv. **c.** *the fighting ground, the scene* or *theatre of any contest :* of the law-courts: Plin. Ep.; of the civil war: Luc. [It. rena.]

hariolātiō, ōnis, *f.* [hariolor], *a divining, divination, soothsaying :* Enn.

hariolor, āri [hariolus], *to divine, foretell.* **1.** Lit.: Cic. **2.** Transf. in a bad sense (like vaticinor): *to speak foolishly, to talk nonsense :* Pl., Ter.

hariolus, i, *m.* (and **hariola**, ae, *f.*, Pl.), *a diviner, soothsayer :* Pl., Ter., Cic.

Harmodius, i, *m. a famous Athenian, who, with Aristogiton, killed Hipparchus, b. of Hippias.*

harmonia, ae, *f.* [ἁρμονία], *an agreement of sounds, in succession rather than consonance ; melody :* pure Lat. concentus. **1.** Lit.: Cic. **2.** Transf. *concord, harmony,* in gen.: neque harmoniā corpus sentire solere, Lucr.

harpagō, āre [ἁρπάζω], *to rob, plunder :* aurum, Pl.

harpagō, ōnis, *m.* [ἁρπάγη], *a grappling-hook, grapple, drag.* **1.** Lit.: Caes., Liv. **2.** Transf. *a rapacious person :* Pl.

Harpalycē, ēs, *f. d. of a Thracian king, and brought up as a warrior.*

harpē, ēs, *f.* [ἅρπη], *a sickle-shaped sword, falchion, scimitar :* Ov., Luc.

Harpocratēs, is, *m. the Egyptian god of light ; but regarded as the god of silence.*

Harpȳiae (trisyl.), ārum, *f. pl.* (*sing.* Harpȳia, Verg.) [Ἅρπυιαι], *the Harpies, rapacious monsters, half-bird, half-woman.*

harundifer, era, erum [harundō ferō], *reed-bearing :* Ov.

harundineus, a, um [harundō], *made of* or *abounding in reeds, reedy :* silva, Verg. Poet.: carmen, *on a reed-pipe,* i.e. *pastoral,* Ov.

harundinōsus, a, um [harundō], *abounding in reeds :* Cat.

harundō, inis, *f. a reed, cane* (slenderer and taller than canna), *the common reed.* **1.** Lit.: Cato, Caes., Verg., etc. **2.** Transf. *anything made of reed : an angling rod :* Pl., Ov.: *limed twigs for catching birds :* Prop., Mart.; transf.: Pl.; *the shaft of an arrow :* Ov.; hence, *an arrow :* Verg., Ov.; *a pen :* Pers.; *a reed-* or *Pan-pipe :* Verg., Ov.; *a flute :* Ov.; *a weaver's comb :* Ov.; *a reed for brushing down cobwebs :* Pl.; *a rod along which vines were trained :* Varr.; *a splint for holding together injured limbs :* Suet.; *a hobby-horse :* Hor.

haruspex [haru (*v.* hira) and spec in speciō], *a soothsayer, diviner* (among the Etruscans) *who foretold future events from the inspection of the entrails of victims.* **1.** Lit.: Pl., Cic., Verg., etc. **2.** Transf. *a prophet* in gen.: Prop., Juv.

haruspica, ae, *f.* [haruspex], *a female soothsayer :* Pl.

haruspicinus, a, um [haruspex], *dealing with divination by the inspecting of victims :*

libri, Cic. As Noun, **haruspicina**, ae, *f.*
(*sc.* ars), *the art of such divination :* Cic.
haruspicium, i, *n.* [haruspex], *inspection of
victims, divination :* Cat.
Hasdrubal (As-), alis, *m.* **I.** *son-in-law of
Hamilcar, whom he succeeded as general in
Spain.* **II.** *brother of Hannibal, defeated
and killed at the battle of the Metaurus,*
B.C. 207.
hasta, ae, *f. a spear, pike, javelin.* **I.** In
gen. : Pl., Cic., Verg., etc. ; hasta pura
(i.e. without iron), as a reward to soldiers :
Suet. ; without pura : Sall., Tac. **II.**
a spear as a sign. **a.** Of a public auction
(orig. of booty in the camp) : hastam in
foro ponere et bona civium voci subicere
praeconis, Cic. ; comitibus eorum sub hastā
venditis, Liv. ; ius hastae, Tac. **b.** Of the
centumviral court : Suet. **III.** *a hair-
comb of a bride :* Ov.
hastātus, a, u.. [hasta], *armed with a spear.*
I. In gen. : Tac. As Noun, **hastāti**,
ōrum, *m. pl. the first line of a Roman army
drawn up in order of battle :* Liv., Ov. **II.**
With ord. num. in agreement with ordo ;
or more freq. without ordo, to designate the
companies of hastati : mihi T. Quinctius
decimum ordinem hastatum adsignavit,
Liv. ; signifer primi hastati, Cic. ; Fulgi-
nius ex primo hastato, Caes.
hastile, is, *n.* [hasta], *the shaft of a spear or
javelin.* **1.** Lit. : Cic., Nep., Liv. **2.**
Transf. **a.** *the spear itself, javelin :* Verg.,
Ov., Juv. **b.** *a stick, shaft :* virgae, Verg.
Of a *vine-prop :* Verg.
hau or **au**, a cry of pain or grief : Pl., Ter.
haud or **haut**, sometimes **hau** before consonants, *adv.* An emphatic particle used
to negative single words : *not at all, by no
means.* **a.** Most freq. with *Adv.* : haud
sane diu est, Pl. ; haud sane intellego, Cic. ;
haud temere est visum, Verg. ; haud pro
dubio, Liv. **b.** With *Adj.* : haud mediocris vir, Cic. ; bene dicere haud absurdum
est, Sall. ; haud ignotae belli artes, Liv. **c.**
With *Pron.* : haud quisquam, Pl. ; hic se
ipsus fallit, haud ego, Ter. **d.** With
verbs (less freq.) : Pl., Lucr., Cic., Tac.,
etc. For the phr., haud scio an, *v.* an.
Pleonastic with another neg. : neque ego
haud committam ut, si peccatum siet, Pl.
e. haud dum, or, **hauddum**, an emphatic
nondum, not at all as yet, not just yet : Liv.
f. haud quāquam, or, **handquāquam**, *by
no means whatever, not at all :* Ter., Cic.,
Verg., etc.
hauriō, haurīre, hausi, haustum (*Fut. Part.*
hausūrus, Verg.). **I.** *to draw off* (liquids,
esp. water). **1.** Lit. : aquam de puteo,
Cic. ; limo turbatam haurit aquam, Hor. ;
palmis hausta duabus aqua, Ov. ; de dolio
sibi hauriendum putet ? Cic. Occ. of
blood : Cic., Ov., Liv. **2.** Transf. **a.**
to draw off as from a fount or source, *to
derive :* hausta a fontibus naturae, Cic. ;
ex vano hauriunt scriptores, Liv. ; ex
parvo, Hor. ; fontis adire et praeceptis
haurire, Hor. ; ex divinitate animos, Cic. ;
sumptum ex aerario, Cic. **b.** *to sweep,
scrape up, gather, pick up :* ventus arbusta
radicibus ab imis, Lucr. ; pulverem, Ov.
II. *to draw off* (all), *drain dry, drain, empty.*

A. The vessel. **1.** Lit. : pateram, Verg. ;
Ov. Occ. of blood : quos hauserit ensis,
Verg. With ABL. *Instr. :* latus gladio,
Verg. ; ventrem ictu, Liv. ; iugulum
gladio, Tac. **2.** Transf. : Italiam faenore, Tac. ; medium orbem sol, Verg. ;
pavor corda, Verg. **B.** The draught. **1.**
Lit. : Ov. Occ. of blood : Liv. **2.**
Transf. **a.** Of property : sua, Tac. ;
Mart. **b.** Of pleasure and pain : voluptates, calamitates, Cic. ; supplicia, Verg.
III. *to draw, drink, suck in, swallow.* **1.**
Lit. : lacūs faucibus, Ov. Of things :
alveus aquas, Ov. **2.** Transf. **a.** Of
light, air, sound : lucem, Verg. ; oculis
ignem, Verg. ; caelum, Verg. ; auram
communem, Quint. ; suspiratūs, Ov. ;
vocem auribus, Verg. **b.** In gen. : oculis
auribusque gaudium, Liv. ; animo spem
inanem, Verg. ; meram libertatem, Liv. ;
studium philosophiae, Tac. **c.** *to swallow
up destructively :* cum paludibus arma
haurirentur, Tac. ; altitudine nivis hauriebantur, Tac. ; aggerem incendium, Liv. ;
Tac. ; puppis hausta perit, Ov.
haustrum, i, *n.* [hauriō], *a scoop, bucket for
drawing water :* Lucr.
haustus, a, um, *Part.* hauriō.
haustus, ūs, *m.* **I.** *a drawing off* (water) :
Juv. ; aquae ductus, haustus (i.e. *right of
drawing*), Cic. **II.** *a drinking ;* concr. *a
draught. drink.* **1.** Lit. (mostly *pl.*) :
Lucr., Verg., Ov. **2.** Transf. **a.** caeli,
Curt. ; esse apibus partem divinae mentis
et haustūs aetherios, Verg. **b.** Pindarici
fontis, Hor. ; iustitiae, Quint.
haut, *v.* haud.
haveō, *v.* aveō.
Heautontīmōrūmenos (Hautont-), i, *m.*
[ἑαυτόν τιμωρούμενος], *a self-tormentor :*
the title of a comedy of Terence, rendered
by Cicero, *Ipse se puniens.*
hebdomas, adis, *f.* [ἑβδομάς], *a period of
seven days* (in relation to sickness) : Cic.
Ep.
Hēbē, ēs, *f. the goddess of youth* (pure Lat.
Iuventas), *daughter of Juno, cup-bearer to
the gods, and wife of Hercules, after his
deification.*
hebenus, i, *f.* [ἔβενος], *the ebon-tree, ebony :*
Verg., etc.
hebeō, ēre [hebes], *to be blunt* or *dull.* **1.**
Lit. : ferrum, Liv. **2.** Transf. *to be
dull, sluggish :* gelidus tardante senectā
sanguis hebet, Verg. ; ipsi hebent mirā
diversitate naturae, Tac.
hebes, etis, *adj. blunt, dull.* **1.** Lit. :
machaera, Pl. ; mucro, Lucr. ; tela, Cic.
Hence, ictus, Ov. **2.** Transf. **a.** Physically : *dim, faint, sluggish :* populi Romani aures, Cic. ; os, color, Ov. ; exercitus,
Sall. ; ad sustinendum laborem miles, Tac.
Comp. : Cic. **b.** Mentally : *dull, obtuse,
sluggish :* sensus, Cic. ; me hebetem molestiae reddiderunt, Cic. ; Tac. ; hebetiora
hominum ingenia, Cic. ; memoria, Cic. ;
oratio, Quint.
hebēscō, ere [hebeō], *to grow blunt.* Transf.
a. Physically : *to grow dim :* sidera, Tac. ;
oculi, Suet. **b.** Mentally : *to grow blunt,
dull* or *dim :* mentis acies, Cic. ; acies
auctoritatis, Cic. ; illi per fastidium et

contumaciam hebescunt, Tac. ; virtus (in
repute), Sall.
hebetō, āre [hebes], *to make blunt.* **1.** Lit.:
hastas, Liv. **2.** Transf.: *to blunt, dull,
dim.* **a.** Physically: visūs alicui, Verg. ;
dies hebetarat sidera, Ov. ; vos mihi
taurorum flammas hebetastis, Ov. **b.**
Mentally: ingenium, Plin. Ep. ; animo
simul et corpore hebetato, Suet.
Hebrus, ī, *m. the principal river of Thrace,
now Maritza.*
Hecalē, ēs, *f. a poor old woman who kindly
received Theseus.*
Hecatē, ēs, *f. d. of Perses* (or *Persaeus*) *and
Asteria ; goddess of magic and witchcraft :
she is often identified with Diana and Luna
in their chthonic or underworld aspect, and is
therefore represented with three heads ;*
Hecatēius, a, um, and **Hecatēis**, idos, *f.
adj.*
hecatombē, ēs, *f.* [ἑκατόμβη], *a hecatomb ;
a sacrifice on a large scale :* Juv.
Hector, oris, *m. s. of Priam and Hecuba, husband of Andromache ; the bravest of the
Trojans, slain by Achilles ;* **Hectoreus**,
a, um, *of Hector.* Transf. *Trojan.*
Hecuba, ae, and **Hecubē**, ēs, *f. wife of
Priam : after the destruction of Troy she
became a captive, and was ultimately
changed into a dog.*
Hecyra, ae, *f.* [ἑκυρά], *a mother-in-law, the
title of a comedy by Terence.*
hedera, ae, *f. ivy :* sacred to Bacchus ; also
made into garlands for poets : Verg., Hor.,
Ov. In *pl.* : *ivy-trails :* Verg. [It. *ellera ;* Sp. *hiedra ;* Fr. *lierre,* earlier
l'ierre.]
hederāceus, a, um [hedera], *of ivy, ivy-:* Cato.
hederiger, era, erum [hedera], *ivy-wearing :*
Maenades, Cat.
hederōsus, a, um [hedera], *covered with ivy :*
antrum, Prop.
hēdychrum, ī, n. [ἡδύχρουν], *a perfume for
the skin :* Cic.
hei, hēia, *v.* ei, ēia.
Helena, ae, or **Helenē**, ēs, *f. d. of Jupiter and
Leda, s. of Castor and Pollux and of Clytaem-
estra (and wife of Menelaus) : she was carried off by Paris to Troy, and thus became the
cause of the Trojan war.*
Helenus, ī, *m. son of Priam and Hecuba, a
celebrated soothsayer.*
Hēliades, um, *f. pl. daughters of Helios* (Sol)
*and sisters of Phaëthon, who were changed into
poplars* (or *alders*), *and their tears into
amber.*
Helicē, ēs, *f.* [ἑλίκη], *a constellation ; the
Great Bear :* Cic., Ov.
Helicōn, ōnis, *m. a mountain in Boeotia,
sacred to Apollo and the Muses ;* now
Zagara ; **Helicōnius**, a, um ; **Helicō-
niades, Helicōnides**, um, *f. pl. the Muses.*
Hellas, adis, *f. Greece.*
Hellē, ēs, *f. d. of Athamas and Nephele, s.
of Phrixus : while fleeing from her step-
mother on a ram with a golden fleece, she was
drowned in the strait called after her, Hellē-
pontus.*
hellebor-, *v.* ellebor-.
Hellēn, ēnis, *m. a son of Deucalion, and king
of Thessaly, from whom the Greeks were
supposed to have been called Hellenes.*

Hellēspontus, ī, *m. the strait connecting the
Propontis (Sea of Marmora) with the
Aegean,* now *the Dardanelles :* cf. Helle ;
Hellēspontius, a, um ; **Hellēspontiacus**,
a, um.
helluō, ōnis, *m. a glutton, squanderer :* Ter., Cic.
helluor, ārī [helluō], *to be a glutton.* **1.** Lit.:
Cic. **2.** Transf.: libris, Cic. ; rei publicae sanguine, Cic. ; in exostrā, Cic. *Perf.
Part.* used Passively : Verg.
helops (also **elops** and **ellops**), opis, *m.*
[ἕλλοψ], *a very savoury fish,* perh. *sturgeon:*
Enn., Varr., Ov., etc.
helvella, ae, *f.* [*dim.* helus = holus]. *a
savoury potherb :* Cic. Ep.
helveolus, a, um [*dim.* helvus], *yellowish :*
Cato.
Helvētii, ōrum, *m. pl. a people of Gallia Lug-
dunensis* (in mod. *Switzerland*) ; **Helvētius,
Helvēticus**, a, um.
helvus, a, um [*cf.* gilvus], *light bay :* color,
Varr.
hem, *interj.* An expression of pleased or
displeased surprise : Pl., Ter., Cic.
hēmerodromus, ī, *m.* [ἡμεροδρόμος], one
who runs all day], *a scout, courier :* Nep.,
Liv.
hēmicillus, ī, *m.* [ἡμίκιλλος], *a mule* (as a
term of reproach) : Cic.
hēmicyclium, ī, n. [ἡμικύκλιον], *a semi-
circle.* Transf. Of anything semi-
circular. **a.** *a row of seats :* Cic. **b.** *a
place furnished with rows of seats* (*for dis-
cussions*) : Suet.
hēmina, ae, *f.* [ἡμίνα], *a measure.* **I.** *the
half of a sextarius :* for liquids : Pl., Cato.
II. *a measure,* in gen. : Pers. [Fr. *mine,* six
bushels.]
hēminaria, ōrum, n. *pl.* [hēmina], *presents of
the measure of a hemina :* Quint.
hendecasyllabi, ōrum, *m. pl.* [ἑνδεκα-
σύλλαβοι], *verses of eleven syllables* (— — |
— ◡ ◡ | — ◡ | — ◡ | — ◡̄) : Cat., Plin.
Ep.
hēpatārius, a, um [Gk. ἧπαρ, ατος], *of the
liver :* morbus (comically for love), Pl.
heptēris, is, *f.* [ἑπτήρης (ναῦς)], *a galley with
seven banks of oars :* Liv.
hera, *v.* era.
Hēra, ae, *f. the Greek goddess Hera,* identified
with Juno of the Romans ; **Hēraea**, ōrum,
n. *pl. her festival.*
Hēraclitus, ī, *m. a celebrated Greek philosopher of Ephesus, called* "The Obscure"
and also "The Weeping Philosopher,"
fl. c. B.C. 500.
herba, ae, *f.* [*cf.* Gk. φορβή], *springing vegetation.* **I.** *a blade, stalk.* **1.** Lit.: frumenta in herbis erant, Caes. ; herbae gemmantes rore, Lucr. ; ut sulcis frumenti
quaereret herbam, Verg. ; primis segetes
moriuntur in herbis, Ov. ; prodit seminis
herba, Ov. **2.** Transf.: tua messis in
herbā est, Cic. ; laus velut in herbā vel
flore praecerpta, Tac. **II.** *a plant, herb :*
Pl., Cic., Verg., etc. **III.** *grass, sward :*
Lucr., Cic., Verg. In *pl.* : Ov. **IV.** *grass*
(as weed) or *weeds* in gen. (in *pl.*) : Verg.
herbēscō, ere [herba], *to grow into blades :*
viriditas, Cic.
herbeus, a, um [herba], *grass-coloured, grass-
green :* oculi, Pl.

herbidus, a, um [herba], *full of grass, grassy* : campi, Varr. ; Liv. ; Ov. ; insulae herbidae harundine, Plin. Ep.

herbifer, era, erum [herba ferō], *grassy* : colles, Ov. ; Plin.

herbigradus, a, um [herba gradior], *that moves in the grass* : Poet. ap. Cic.

herbōsus, a, um [herba]. **I.** *grassy* : Verg., Hor., Ov. *Sup.* : Cato. **II.** *made of turf* : arae, Ov. **III.** *made of herbs* : moretum, Ov.

herbula, ae, *f.* [dim. herba], *a little herb* : Cic., Quint.

Hercēus, i, m. [ἑρκεῖος], *an epithet of Jupiter, as the protector of the house and its enclosure* ; **Hercēus**, a, um.

herciscō (erciscō), ere. In law : *to divide an inheritance* : familiam, Cic.

herctum (erctum), i, n. In law : *an inheritance* (only used with ciere, *to divide an inheritance*) : Cic.

Herculāneum, ei, n. *a town of Campania, situated on the sea-coast* ; *it perished with Pompeii in an eruption of Vesuvius,* A.D. 79 ; **Herculāneus**, a, um ; **Herculānēnsis**, e.

Herculēs, is and ī (Voc. Hercules, Hercule and Hercle, as an oath : v. infra), *m. son of Jupiter and Alcmena, husband of Deianira, and, after his deification, of Hebe ; the poplar was sacred to him* ; **Herculeus**, **Herculāneus**, a, um : Herculanea pars, *the tenth part* (dedicated to H.).

hercules, voc. (Cic.), also **hercule** (Cic., Quint.), **hercle** (Pl., Ter., Cic.), an oath or asseveration : *by Hercules !* Similarly : **mehercules** (Cic., Phaedr.), **mehercule** (Cic., Quint.), **mehercle** (Ter.).

here, *adv. v.* heri.

hērēditārius, a, um [hērēditās]. **I.** *relating to an inheritance* ; auctio, Cic. ; lites, Quint. **II.** *inherited, hereditary* : cognomen, Cic. ; imperium, Curt.

hērēditās, ātis, *f.* [hērēs], *heirship, an inheriting.* **1.** Lit. : Varr., Cic. **2.** Transf. **a.** Material goods : *the thing inherited, an inheritance* : Pl. ; hereditates mihi negasti venire, Cic. ; capere hereditatem ab aliquo, Cic. ; cernere, adire, obire, tradere, Cic. ; usurpare, Tac. ; transmittere, Plin. Ep. Prov. : hereditas sine sacris (Lit. *without the sacred rites of the family,* i.e. *without vexatious obligations*), Pl. **b.** Characteristics, etc. : huius gloriae, Cic. ; cupiditatum, Cic.

hērēdium, i, n. [hērēs], *an hereditary estate* : Varr., Nep.

hērēs, ēdis, m. f. *an heir, heiress.* **1.** Lit. : me nemo nisi amicus fecit heredem, Cic. ; Ov. ; aliquem scribere, instituere ; aliquem testamento relinquere, Cic. ; omnium bonorum, Liv. ; ex asse heres, *sole heir*, Quint. ; heres secundus, *the second heir, next heir* (failing the first), Cic., Hor., Quint. ; possessio heredum secundorum, *a reversionary estate*, Cic. **2.** Transf. **a.** *owner, possessor, master* : Pl. **b.** *after-growth, successor* : of the heads of the Hydra, Ov. **c.** Academiae, Cic. ; regni, Liv. ; laudis, fraudis, criminis, Ov.

heri (Pl., Ter., Cic., Ov.) and **here** (Pl., Hor., Ov., Juv.), *adv.* [cf. Gk. χθές. Lat. hesternus], *yesterday.*

herif-, heril-, *v.* erif-, eril-.

hermāphrodītus, ī, m. [ἑρμαφρόδιτος], *an hermaphrodite, a person who has the characteristics of both sexes* (called after the son of Hermes and Aphrodite ; since he and the nymph Salmacis became one person) : Ov.

Hermathēna, ae, *f.* ['Ερμῆς-'Αθηνᾶ], *a double bust of Hermes and Athena* : Cic. Ep.

Hermēraclēs, is, m. ['Ερμῆς-'Ηρακλῆς], *a double bust of Hermes and Hercules* : Cic. Ep.

Hermēs or **Herma**, ae, m. *a Greek god identified by Romans with Mercury* ; hence, *a Hermes-pillar,* i.e. *a carved head on a pedestal* ; these pillars stood at street-corners, etc.

Hermionē, ēs, and **-a**, ae, *f. d. of Menelaus and Helen, and w. of Orestes.*

Hērō, ūs, *f. a priestess of Aphrodite in Sestos, loved by Leander of Abydos.*

Hērōdēs, is, m. *Herod ; the name of several kings of Palestine.*

Hērodotus, ī, m. *the father of Greek history, a native of Halicarnassus, born* B.C. 484.

hērōicus, a, um [ἡρωϊκός], *of demigods, heroic* : tempora, aetates, Cic. ; carmen, Quint., Tac.

hērōīna, ae, *f.* [ἡρωίνη], *a demi-goddess* : Prop.

hērōïs, idis, *f.* (DAT. *pl.* hērōïsin, Ov.) [ἡρωΐς], *a demi-goddess* : Ov., Suet.

hērōs, ōis, m. [ἥρως], *a demi-god, hero.* **1.** Lit. : Cic., Verg., etc. ; Laertius heros (*i.e. Ulysses*), Ov. **2.** Transf. **a.** Of illustrious men : Cic. **b.** As *adj.*, heroas sensūs, Pers.

hērōus, a, um [ἡρῷος], *relating to a demigod, heroic* : versus, pes (i.e. epic), Cic. ; carmen, Quint. ; as Noun : apte iungitur herous cum breviore modo, Ov. ; Quint.

herus, v. erus.

Hēsiodus, ī, m. *Hesiod, an early Greek poet, born at Ascra in Boeotia, author of ' Works and Days ' and ' The Generation of the Gods '* ; **Hēsiodēus**, or **-ius**, a, um.

Hēsionē, ēs, and **Hēsiona**, ae, *f. d. of Laomedon king of Troy ; rescued by Hercules from a sea-monster.*

Hesperus (**-os**), ī, m. In myth: *s. of Cephalus and Aurora* ; or *of Iapetus and Asia, and b. of Atlas* ; **Hesperius**, a, um, *Western, Hesperian* ; **Hesperia**, ae, *f. the land of the evening star, the western land* (i.e. *Italy and Spain*) : **Hesperis**, idis, *f. adj. Western* : **Hesperides**, um, *f. pl. the Hesperides, daughters of Hesperus* (or *of Erebus and Nox*), *who, beyond Mount Atlas, watched a garden with golden apples. Also a group of islands in the Atlantic.*

hesternus, a, um [cf. heri], *of yesterday, yesterday's* : disputatio hesterni et hodierni diei, Cic. ; reliquiae, Pl. ; ius, Ter. ; Iacchus, Verg. ; coma, Ov. ; sneeringly, of freedmen : hesterni Quirites (i.e. mushroom-citizens), Pers.

hetairia, ae, *f.* [ἑταιρία], *a secret society* : Plin. Ep.

hetairicē, ēs, *f.* [ἑταιρική], *a troop of friends* (name of a troop in the Macedonian army) : Nep.

heu ! exclamation of grief or pain, *oh ! ah ! alas !* heu me miserum, Pl., Ter., Cic. ; heu me, Hor. ; heu nefas ! Hor. ; heu edepol, heu hercle, Pl. ; heu, Pl., Verg., Hor., Juv.

hourotēs, ae, *m.* [εὑρετής], *an inventive person :* (as Greek) : Pl.

heus ! *interj.* used to call attention : *ho ! ho there !* Pl., Cic., Verg., etc.

hexameter, trī, *m.* [ἑξάμετρος] (of six measures) : Cic., Hor.

hexēris, is, *f.* [ἑξήρης (ναῦς)], *a vessel with six banks of oars :* Liv.

hiāscō, ere [hiō]. *to begin to open :* Cato.

hiātus, ūs, *m.* [hiō], *an opening, aperture, abyss.* **1.** L i t. : oris, Cic. ; terrarum, Cic. ; caeli, Lucr. Hence, *the open mouth, gaping jaws :* Lucr., Ov., Quint. In *pl. :* Verg. **2.** T r a n s f. **a.** Of style : *gaping jaws, mouthing :* quid dignum tanto feret hiatu ? Hor. **b.** Of greed : praemiorum, Tac. **c.** G r a m m. : *hiatus* (i.e. two vowels esp. in diff. words, in sequence, e.g. conati imponere, Verg.) : Cic., Quint.

Hiber, ēris, *m.* and *pl.* **Hibērēs**, ērum, *Iberians,* the Gk. name for *Spaniards ;* **Hibērus**, a. um, **Hibērus**, ī, *m. the river Ebro ;* **Hibērī**, ōrum, *m. pl. the Spaniards ;* **Hibēria**, ae, *f. Spain ;* **Hibēricus**, a, um ; **Hibērina**, ae, *f. a Spanish woman.*

hībernācula, ōrum, *n. pl.* [hiberna], *tents or huts for winter-quarters :* Liv. Also *winter-quarters :* Caes., Liv., Tac. Hence, in *sing. : a winter-residence, winter-apart-ment :* Plin. Ep.

Hibernia, ae, *f. Hibernia or Ireland.* Also called **Iūverna**, ae : Juv. ; and **Iernē**, ēs : Claud.

hībernō, āre [hibernus], *to winter.* **1.** L i t. : Varr. Milit. : *to keep in winter-quarters* (intrans.) : Cic., Liv. **2.** T r a n s f. *to rest, repose :* Pers. [It. *vernare.*]

hībernus, a, um [v. hiems], *of or in winter.* **1.** L i t. : tempus, Lucr., Cic. ; tempora, menses, Cic. ; annus, Hor. ; navigatio, Cic. Ep. ; expeditio, Liv. ; pulvis, Verg. **2.** T r a n s f. **a.** *like winter, wintry, cold :* flatus, noctes, Verg. ; Alpes, mare, Hor. **b.** *wintering, in winter-quarters :* legiones, Suet. Neut. *pl.* as Noun, **hiberna** (*sc.* castra), *winter-quarters :* Caes., Liv. ; also (*sc.* tempora), *winters :* Verg. [It. *inverno, verno ;* Sp. *invierno ;* Fr. *hiver.*]

hibiscum, ī, *n.* [ἰβίσκος], *the marsh-mallow :* Verg.

hibrida (**hybrida**), ae, *m. f.* Prop. of beasts from two different species, *a mongrel, crossbreed, hybrid.* T r a n s f. Of men : Hor., Suet., etc.

hic, haec, hōc, *pron.* or *pronom. adj.* refers to what is either actually, or is conceived of as being, near to or closely connected with the speaker : *this.* **I.** In gen. **a.** Ref. to someone or something near : hic homo sanus non est, Pl. ; haec deorum regna, Cic. ; hi domum me ad se auferent, Pl. ; audebat haec dicere, Cic. **b.** Of the speaker himself : hic homo, i.e. ego, Pl. ; hunc hominem, i.e. me, Hor. ; si Pergama dextrā defendi possent, etiam hac (i.e. meā) defensa fuissent, Verg. **c.** hic . . . hic of things taken in succession : hic versus Plauti non est. hic est, Caes. ap. Cic. Ep. **II.** With other pronouns : hoc idem fit in reliquis civitatibus, Caes. ; hoc ipsum civile ius, Cic. ; hic est ille vultus quem etc., Cic. **III.** Opp. to *ille, iste,* as denoting what

is or is regarded as nearer. **a.** *my client* or *the defendant* (opp. *iste, the opponent*) : Cic. **b.** *the latter* (ille, *the former*) : Caesar magnus habebatur et Cato ; ille misericordiā clarus factus, huic severitas dignitatem addiderat, Sall. O c c. *the former :* melior est certa pax quam sperata victoria ; haec in tuā, illa in deorum manu est, Liv. **c.** Similarly it refers mostly to what has been said ; *ille* often (esp. in Cic.) to what follows : haec Scipio cum dixisset, Cic. ; verum illud addit, ' non possidebat,' Cic. **d.** Often it refers to what is explained by a Relat. (qui, quod, or ut) Clause or by Acc. and *Inf. :* quam quisque norit artem, in hac se exerceat, Cic. ; id hoc facilius eis persuasit, quod etc., Caes. ; hoc animo in nos esse debebis, ut aetas nostra in adulescentiā tuā conquiescat, Cic. Ep. ; unum hoc definio, tantam esse necessitatem virtutis, Cic. ; o c c. ref. to what follows in *Orat. Rect. :* sic hoc proloquar ; continuo Amphitruo delegit viros, Pl. **IV.** Of time. **a.** *the present, living, modern :* haec annonā, Pl. ; huius nostri Catonis, Cic. **b.** *the last :* his annis viginti, Cic. ; hoc triduo, Cic. **V.** Special uses. **A.** Of Nom. for huius rei : causa haec est quod etc., Liv. **B.** Of hoc (*Neut. sing.* Nom.). **a.** With Gen. : hoc commodi est quod etc., *there is this advantage,* etc., Cic. **b.** hoc est (pointing an explanation) : *that is, that is to say, namely :* quadriennium, hoc est, ex quo tempore fundus veniit, Cic. **c.** hoc est *or* erat, quod ? indignant or reproachful : *is or was it for this that,* etc. ? : hoc erat, alma parens, quod me per tela, per ignis eripis ? Verg. **d.** With *Impers. verbs,* pleonastically as Subject : lucescit hoc iam, Pl., Ter. **VI. a.** Strengthened with -ce : **hice, haece, hōce** (Nom. *pl. masc.* sometimes hisce, Nom. *pl. fem.* haec for haece, and in Gen. *pl.* hōrunc, hārunc, for hōrunce, hārunce) : hoce haud dubium, Ter. ; huiusce rei, Cic. ; apud hasce aedis, Pl. **b.** Also with the *Interrog.* particle *-ne,* as **hicine, haecine, hōcine** ? hicin'Achilles est ? Pl. ; hancine impudentiam ! iudices, hanc audaciam ! Cic.

hic, old form **heic** (also with *demonstr.* suffix -ce, **hice** or with *interrog.* -ne, **hicine**), *adv.* [Locat. of hīc], *in this place, here.* **1.** L i t. Of place : Pl., Cic., Verg., etc. ; with Gen. : hic viciniae, Pl., Ter. ; with -ne : hicine libertatem aiunt esse aequam omnibus ? Ter. **2.** T r a n s f. **a.** *in this affair, in this particular, herein, here :* hic, quantum in hoc fortuna possit, cognosci potuit, Caes. ; hic tu tabellas desideras publicas, Cic. Of time : *hereupon, here* (rare) : hic regina poposcit pateram, Verg. ; hic Postumius ait, Liv. ; hic Scipio, Cic.

hice, haece, hōce, hicine, haecine, hōcine, *v.* hic.

hicine, *adv. v.* hic.

hiemālis, e, *adj.* [hiems]. **1.** L i t. *of or in winter :* tempus, vis, Cic. ; aquae, Sall. ; nimbi, Ov. **2.** T r a n s f. *like winter, stormy :* navigatio, Cic. Ep.

hiemō, āre [hiems]. **I.** Of persons, *to pass the winter, to winter :* Caes., Cic., Hor. **II.** Of things : *to be wintry, cold, stormy :*

mare, Hor.; tempestas, annus, Aquilo, Sen. Ep.

Hiempsal, alis, *m. son of Micipsa and king of part of Numidia.*

hiems (hiemps), emis, *f.* [*cf.* Gk. χιών, χειμών], *winter.* **1.** Lit.: modestia hiemis, Tac.; prodit hiems, Lucr.; hiems summa, Cic.; gravissimā hieme, Caes.; hiems appropinquabat, Caes.; hiems iam praecipitaverat, Caes.; initā hieme, Caes.; iam prope hieme confectā, Caes.; ante exactam hiemem, Caes. In *pl.* : Lucr., Cic., Hor., etc. **Hiems** personified: Verg., Ov. **2.** Transf. **a.** *stormy weather* : Cic., Verg., etc. **b.** *coldness* (of death): letalis hiems in pectora venit, Ov. **c.** Of love: *the winter* : mutati amoris hiem, Ov. **d.** Of ' a bad time ': suae senectuti acriorem hiemem parat, Pl.

Hierō, ōnis, *m.* **I.** *ruler of Syracuse, a friend of the poet Simonides of Ceos, about* 478 B.C. **II.** *a later ruler of Syracuse, in the latter half of the third century* B.C., *a friend of the Romans* ; **Hierōnicus**, a, um.

hieronica, ae, *m.* [ἱερονίκης], *a conqueror in the sacred games* : Suet.

Hierosolyma, ōrum, *n. pl. Jerusalem* ; also **Solyma**, ōrum, *n. pl.* ; **Hierosoly-mārius**, i, *m. a name given to Pompeius from his taking Jerusalem* ; **Solymus**, a, um, *belonging to Jerusalem.*

hietō, āre [*freq.* hiō], *to keep yawning* : Pl.

hilaris, e, and **hilarus**, a, um, *cheerful, gay, blithe, merry.* **i.** Form *hilaris* : of persons : Cic., Hor., Quint.; of things : ingenium, Pl.; dies, Pl., Ter.; vultus, Cic.; animus, Cic. Ep.; vox, oratio, etc., Quint. *Neut.* Acc. **hilare** as *Adv.* : Cic., Tac., etc. *Comp.* : Cic., Suet. **ii.** Form *hilarus* : of persons : Pl., Ter., Cic. Ep.; of things : vita, vultus, Cic.; adauctus, Lucr.; Saturnalia, Cic. Ep. *Comp.* : Pl., Cic., etc. *Sup.* : Pl.

hilaritās, ātis, *f.* [hilaris], *cheerfulness, gaiety, merriment* : Cic., Quint. In *pl.* : Sen. Ep.

hilaritūdō, inis, *f.* [hilaris], *cheerfulness, merriment* : Pl.

hilarō, āre [hilarus], *to make cheerful, to cheer, gladden :* Periclis suavitate maxime hilaratae sunt Athenae, Cic. ; Ov.

hilarulus, a, um [*dim.* hilarus], Attica (*a merry little soul*), Cic. Ep.

hilarus, a, um, *v.* hilaris.

hillae, ārum, *f. pl.* [*dim.* hīra], *the smaller intestines of animals* (other than men and sheep). Transf. *a kind of smoked sausage :* Hor.

Hilōtae (Il-), ārum, *m. pl. the original inhabitants of Laconia, afterwards the slaves of the Spartans, the Helots.*

hilum, i, *n.* [whence nihilum for ne-hilum], *a little thing, a trifle ;* us. with neg., *not in the least, nothing at all :* Sisyphu' vorsat saxum neque proficit hilum, Lucil. ; nec defit ponderis hilum, Lucr.

hinc, *adv.* [hīc], *from this place, hence.* **1.** Lit. Of place : Pl., Ter., Cic. In a book (*from this point onward*) : maiora iam hinc bella dicentur, Liv. **2.** Transf. **A. a.** *from this side, on this side, here :* hinc fides pugnat, illinc fraudatio, Cic. ; multis hinc

atque illinc vulneribus acceptis, Liv.; hinc . . . hinc, Liv.; hinc atque hinc vastae rupes, Verg.; Liv. **b.** Denoting origin or cause : *from this source or cause, hence :* hinc illae lacrimae ! Ter.; Cic.; Verg., etc. **B.** Of time. **a.** *henceforth, after this :* Tac. **b.** For abhinc, *ago :* hinc ducentos annos, Pl.

hinniō, īre, *to neigh :* Lucr., Quint.

hinnītus, ūs, *m.* [hinniō], *a neighing :* Lucr., Cic., Verg. In *pl.* : Ov.

hinnuleus, i, *m. a young roebuck, a fawn :* Hor.

hinnulus, i, *m.* [*dim.* hinnus], *a young mule :* Maecen. ap. Suet.

hinnus, i, *m.* [ἴννος], *a mule :* ex equo et asinā, Varr. (*v.* mūlus.)

hiō, āre, *to open, be open, to gape.* **1.** Lit.: oculi, Pl.; concha, Cic.; venae, Verg.; lilia, Ov. Of the mouth: leo immane hians, Verg.; clamor frustratur hiantis, Verg.; aquam hianti ore captantes, Curt. **2.** Transf. **a.** Of speech, *to be badly connected, to leave an hiatus :* hiantia loqui, Cic.; oratio, Quint.; compositio, Tac. **b.** *to gape with greedy longing :* avaritiā, Cic.; corvum deludet hiantem, Hor.; canis ad spem futuri, Sen. Ep. **c.** *to gape with wonder :* Verg.; vulgus ad magnitudinem praemiorum, Tac. **d.** With Acc.: carmen lyrā, Prop.

hippagōgi, ōrum, *f. pl.* [ἱππαγωγοί], *cavalry-transports :* Liv.

Hipparchus, i, *m. son of Pisistratus, slain by Harmodius and Aristogiton,* B.C. 514.

Hippiās, ae, *m. the son of Pisistratus ; tyrant of Athens,* B.C. 527-510.

hippocentaurus, i, *m.* [ἱπποκένταυρος], *half-horse, half-man :* Cic.

Hippocratēs, is, *m. a celebrated Greek physician of Cos, about* 430 B.C.

Hippocrēnē ēs, *f.* (ἵππου κρήνη), *a spring on Mount Helicon, sacred to the Muses ; produced by a stroke from the hoof of Pegasus.*

Hippodamē ēs (-ēa, -ia, ae), *f.* **I.** *d. of Oenomaus, king of Elis, and wife of Pelops.* **II.** *d. of Adrastus and wife of Pirithous.*

Hippolytē, ēs, and -a, ae, *f.* **I.** *an Amazon, taken captive in war by Theseus.* **II.** *the wife of Acastus, king of Magnesia.*

Hippolytus, i, *m. son of Theseus and Hippolyte : in consequence of a false accusation brought against him by his step-mother Phaedra, he was torn to pieces by horses, but was restored to life by Aesculapius.*

hippomanes, is, *n.* [ἱππομανές, *horse-heat, horse-rage*]. **I.** *a slimy humour that flows from a mare when in heat :* Verg., Tib., Prop. **II.** *a small black membrane on the forehead of a new-born foal, used in making love-potions :* Juv.

Hippomenēs, ae, *m. son of Megareus, who, beating Atalanta in a race, won her as his wife.*

hippōnactēus, i, *m.* (*sc.* versus) [Hippōnax], *the sort of iambic verse invented by Hipponax :* Cic.

Hippōnax, actis, *m. a Greek poet of Ephesus, about* 540 B.C., *celebrated for the bitterness of his satires.*

hippotoxotae, ārum, *m. pl.* [ἱπποτοξόται], *mounted archers :* Caes.

hippūrus, i, m. [ἵππυρος], a fish, perh. golden carp, gold-fish : Ov.

hir, indecl. n. [cf. χείρ], a hand : Lucil.

hira, ae, f. the empty gut (called, also, intestinum ieiunum) : Pl.

hircīnus (hirquīnus), a, um [hircus], of a goat, goat's : Pl., Hor.

hircōsus, a, um [hircus], that smells like a goat, goatish : senex, Pl.

hircus (hirquos, Sab. **fircus)**, i, m. a he-goat. **1**. Lit.: Verg., Hor. **2**. Transf. **a**. goatish smell : ab alis, Pl.; alarum, Cat.; in alis, Hor. **b**. Of a filthy person : Pl. **c**. Of sensual persons : Pl., Cat.

hirnea, ae, f. a jug for holding liquids : Pl., Cato.

hirq-, v. hirc-.

hirsūtus, a, um [fr. root of horreō], rough, shaggy, bristly, prickly. **1**. Lit.: quarum (animantium) aliae spinis hirsutae, Cic.; supercilium, Verg.; glacialis hiems canos hirsuta capillos, Ov.; castaneae, Verg. **2**. Transf. rude, unpolished : sumpserit annalis : nihil est hirsutius illis, Ov.

Hirtius, a, the name of a Roman gens. Esp. A. Hirtius, consul B.C. 43, and author of the eighth book of the Commentaries on Caesar's Gallic wars ; **Hirtinus**, a, um.

hirtus, a, um [fr. root of horreō], rough, hairy, shaggy. **1**. Lit.: oves, Varr.; saetae in corpore, Ov.; os, comae, Curt.; toga, Quint. **2**. Transf. rough, rude : ingenium, Hor. [It. irto ; Sp. yerto.]

hirūdō, inis, f. (also called sanguisuga), a leech, bloodsucker. **1**. Lit.: Pl. **2**. Transf.: aerari, Cic. Ep.; Hor.

hirundininus, a, um [hirundō], of swallows : nidus, Pl.

hirundō, inis, f. [cf. χελιδών], a swallow : Pl., Verg., etc. As a term of endearment : Pl. Prov.: quid contendat hirundo cycnis ? Lucr. [It. rondine, rondinella ; Fr. aronde, hirondelle.]

hiscō, ere [hiō]. **I.** to open slightly, to gape : aedes, Pl.; venae tabularum, Lucr.; tellus, Ov. **II.** to open the mouth : Cic., Verg., etc. Always with negat. in Liv. With Intern. Acc.: nec quicquam, Ov.; Prop.

Hispāni, ōrum, m. pl. the Spaniards ; **Hispānus**, a, um, Spanish ; **Hispānia**, ae, and (because divided into two parts, Citerior and Ulterior), **Hispāniae**, ārum, f. pl. the country of the Spaniards, Spain ; **Hispāniēnsis**, e, and **Hispānicus**, a, um.

hispidus, a, um, hairy, bristly. **1**. Lit.: frons, Verg.; facies, Hor. **2**. Transf.: agri, Hor.

Hister (Ister), trī, the lower Danube.

hister, v. histriō.

historia, ae, f. [ἱστορία], inquiry, investigation, learning. **1**. Lit. (rare): est in omni historiā curiosus (ethnological inquiry), Cic. Prov.: historiam scribere, (cf. "have a thing down in black and white"): Pl. **2**. Transf. **a**. a narrative of past events, history : Cic., Quint., Juv. **b**. any kind of narrative : account, tale, story : si quid in eā epistulā fuit historiā dignum, Cic. Ep.; amarae, Hor. **c**. the subject of a story : Prop. [It. storia ; Fr. histoire.]

historicus, a, um [ἱστορικός], belonging to history : sermo, genus, Cic.; homines, Cic.; fides, Ov.; nitor, Quint. As Noun, **historicus**, i, m. one versed in or one who studies history ; a writer of history, historian : Cic., Quint., Juv.

histricus, a, um [hister, histriō], of stage-players : inperator, stage-manager, Pl.

histriō, ōnis, m. [Etruscan form hister, Liv.], a stage-player, actor either of tragedy or comedy : Pl., Cic., Liv., etc.

histriōnālis, e, adj. [histriō]. **I.** of a stage-player, actor : studium, Tac. **II.** for an actor : favor, Tac.

histriōnia, ae, f. [histriō], the art of acting, dramatic art : Pl.

hiulcē, adv. Of speech : with a hiatus : Cic.

hiulcō, āre [hiulcus], to cause to gape or split open : Cat.

hiulcus, a, um [hiō], gaping, split, opened. **1**. Lit.: siti arva, Verg. **2**. Transf. **a**. Of speech : gaping, with hiatus : Cic., Quint. **b**. gaping with greed : genus, Pl.

hōc. **I.** Nom. and Acc. Neut. and Abl. Masc. and Neut. sing. of hīc. **II.** v. hūc.

hodiē, adv. [hōc diē], on this day, to-day. **1**. Lit.: Pl., Cic., Hor., etc. **2**. Transf. **a**. at this time : Cic., Quint., Juv. **b**. up to the present time, still : Cic., Quint., Tac., etc.; hodie quoque, Cic., Liv. **c**. now, at once : hodie itura, Ter.; Pl.; Cic.; Hor.; also, nunquam hodie, colloq. for in no wise now : Pl., Ter., Verg. [It. oggi ; Sp. hoy ; Fr. hui in aujourd'hui.]

hodiernus, a, um [hodiē], of this day, to-day's. **1**. Lit.: dies, edictum, Cic.; summa, Hor. **2**. Transf. (rare) of the present time, present, modern : ad hodiernum diem, Cic.

holitor, ōris, m. [holus], a kitchen- or market-gardener : Pl., Cic. Ep., Hor.

holitōrius, a, um [holitor], used by market-gardeners : forum, Liv.

holus, eris, n. pot-herbs, vegetables ; esp. cabbage, colewort, turnip : Varr., Verg., etc.

Homērus, i, m. Homer, the earliest of Greek poets ; **Homēricus**, **Homērius**, a, um ; **Homērōnidēs**, ae, m. an imitator of Homer.

homicida, ae, m.f. [homō caedō]. **I.** a man-slayer, a murderer, murderess : Cic., Quint., Juv. **II.** as transl. of ἀνδροφόνος (epithet of Hector), slayer of men : Hor.

homicidium, i, n. [homicida], manslaughter, murder : Quint., Tac.

homō, inis (old Gen. homōnis), m.f. [fr. root of humus], a human being, and in pl., men, mankind. **1**. Lit. **A.** Pl., Cic., Verg., etc.; inter homines esse (Cic.), agere (Tac.), to be alive or also to see the world. In apposition : oculi hominis histrionis, Cic.; nemo homo, Pl., Cic. Of females : eam nemo hominem appellare possit, Cic.; quae (Io) bos ex homine est, Ov. **B.** With special implication. **a.** In a good sense : a man, as a reasonable or moral being : si homo esset, eum potius legeret, Cic.; Nero dicebat se quasi hominem tandem habitare coepisse, Suet.; Pl.; Ter. **b.** In a bad sense : a man, as a weak being, subject to error : te ut hortarer rogaremque, ut et hominem te et virum esse meminisses, Cic.;

Quint. **2.** Transf. **a.** *a man, a person ;* and in *pl.*, *persons, people, folk :* homo omni doctrinā eruditus, Cic. ; homines doctissimi, Cic. ; homo novus, *v.* novus. Prov. : quot homines, tot sententiae, Ter., Cic. ; ut homines sunt, ita morem geras (i.e. take every man in his humour), Ter. ; homo nulli coloris (i.e. a man one cannot make out), Pl. **b.** Milit. : homines, opp. to equites, *foot-soldiers, infantry :* capti homines equitesque producebantur, Caes. **c.** Occ. in Liv. of *members* of the senate. **d.** More or less slightingly : *the man, the fellow :* ibi homo coepit me obsecrare, Ter. ; ei medico imperasti ut venas hominis incideret, Cic. ; Hor. **e.** *a man,* as opp. to a woman : mi homo et mea mulier, vos saluto, Pl. [It. *uomo ;* Sp. *hombre ;* Fr. *homme.* on.]

homullus, i, *m.* [*dim.* homō] (Lucr., Cic.), also **homuncio**, ōnis, *m.* (Ter., Cic., etc.) and **homunculus**, i, *m.* (Pl., Cic.) *a little man, manikin, poor mortal, sorry creature,* etc.

honestāmentum, i, *n.* [honestō], *an ornament, grace :* Sen. Ep. In *pl. :* Sall.

honestās, ātis, *f.* [honestus]. **I.** *honourableness, honourable consideration* (which one receives), *reputation, esteem, respectability.* **1.** Lit. : Cic., Liv. In *pl. :* Cic. **2.** Transf. (in *pl.*) : *respectable persons :* omnes honestates civitatis, Cic. **II.** *honourableness* of character, *honourable feeling, sense of honour, probity.* **1.** Lit. : Cic. **2.** Transf. of things : *beauty, grace :* Cic.

honestē, *adv.* **I.** *honourably, respectably :* honeste natus, Suet. **II.** *decently, becomingly, with propriety :* Pl., Cic., Hor., etc. *Comp. :* Cic., Juv., Suet. *Sup. :* Cic. **III.** In moral sense, *honourably, virtuously :* Ter., Cic., Quint.

honestō, āre [honestus], *to honour, dignify, grace :* aliquem honore, Pl., Sall. ; laude, Cic. ; nec domo dominus, sed domino domus honestanda est, Cic. ; ingens corpus arma honestabant, Liv.

honestus, a, um [honōs]. **I.** *regarded with honour, enjoying respect or esteem, honourable, well-bred, of gentle birth, gentlemanly :* familia, Cic. ; honestus homo et nobilis, Cic. ; parentis honestos fascibus et sellis, Hor. ; genus et fortuna, Liv. ; honesto loco natus, Cic. ; milites honestissimi sui generis, Caes. ; omnium honestarum rerum egens, Sall. *Comp. :* Pl., Cic., Liv. *Sup. :* Caes., Cic., Quint. As Noun, **honestus**, i, *m. a gentleman :* Hor. ; **honesta**, ae, *f. a gentlewoman, lady :* Ter. **II.** *deserving of honour, honourable, virtuous, proper, becoming.* **1.** Lit. : causae, Lucr. ; vita, homines, testimonia, etc., Cic. ; soror, Hor. ; mores, Juv. *Comp. :* Cic., Quint. *Sup. :* Cic. As Noun, **honestum**, i, *n. virtue, the good* (opp. *turpe, the bad,* and *utile, expediency*) : Cic., Hor., Quint. **2.** Transf. of things (esp. of personal appearance) : *handsome, fine :* homo, forma, Ter. ; facies, Ter., Suet. ; asini, ager, Varr. ; caput, equi, Verg. *Comp. :* Varr.

honor (Hor., Ov., Tac.) or **honōs** (Caes., Cic., Verg., etc.), ōris, *m.* **1.** Lit. *a mark of honour, respect, or esteem* (for merit).

A. In gen. : **a.** Given to persons : alicui honorem reddere, Cic., Liv. ; tribuere, Cic. ; aliquem praecipuo honore habere, Caes. ; summo (tanto, magno, etc.) in honore esse, Caes., Cic., Liv., etc. ; magno esse honore, Caes., Liv., Tac. ; gratiā, dignitate, honore auctus, Caes. ; honoribus et praemiis decorari, Cic. ; rite suum Baccho dicemus honorem, Verg. ; his laetus donis honoribusque dimissus (*compliments*), Liv. ; *cf.* addit verbis honorem, Liv. **b.** Given to things : *honour, esteem, value :* physicae tributus est honos, Cic. ; quae nunc sunt in honore vocabula, Hor. **c.** Phr. : honoris causā. **i.** *with all respect :* quem honoris causā nomino, Cic. **ii.** *to honour :* honoris Diviciaci causā, Caes. ; Liv. **iii.** *for the sake of :* mei honoris causā, Pl. ; praefari *or* dicere honorem, to make an excuse for using any phrase = *by your leave,* or *saving your presence :* si dicimus : ille patrem strangulavit, honorem non praefamur. sin de Aureliā aliquid aut Lolliā, honos praefandus est, Cic. Ep. **B.** Personified : aedem Honoris et Virtutis, Cic., Liv. **C.** In partic. **a.** (very freq.) *public honour, official dignity, office, post, preferment* (the high offices being called honores) : tribunicius, Caes. ; honoris gradus, Cic. ; petere, Cic. ; extraordinarium honorem appetere, Caes. ; honores alicui mandare, Cic. ; capere, Suet. ; honoribus uti, Cic., Sall., Liv. ; perfungi, Cic. ; honores dare, Hor. **b.** Relig. : *offering* (to the gods or the dead), *due service, rites :* divum templis indicit honorem, Verg. ; dis habere, Liv. ; honore sepulturae carere, Cic. ; aris mactavit honores, Verg. ; adolere, Ov. **c.** Of military, athletic, etc. awards : *award, distinction, prize :* militaris, Liv. ; pugnae, Verg. ; Ov. ; medico honorem habere, Cic. Ep. **2.** Transf. **a.** *glory, fame, renown :* Cic. ; also *a cause of fame :* honori summo esse alicui, Cic. **b.** *ornament, grace, charm, beauty :* silvis Aquilo decussit honorem, Verg., Hor. In *pl. :* laetos oculis adflarat honores, Verg. ; Hor. [It. *onore ;* Fr. *honneur.*]

honōrābilis, e, *adj.* [honōrō], *showing respect :* Cic.

honōrārius, a, um [honōs], *given or done for the sake of conferring honour :* frumentum, Cic. ; tumulus, Suet. ; arbiter, Cic. As Noun, **honōrārium**, i, *n. a fee or present given on promotion to an office :* Traj. ap. Plin. Ep.

honōrātē, *adv. with honour, honourably :* Tac.

honōrātus, a, um. **I.** *Part.* honōrō. **II.** Adj. **A.** Pass. *honoured, highly regarded or esteemed or respected.* **a.** In gen. : Cic., Hor., Ov. ; praefectura, Cic. ; militia, Liv. ; amici (i.e. courtiers), Liv. *Comp. :* Cic. Ep., Liv. *Sup. :* Pl., Liv., Tac. **b.** *in high position :* praetor, consul, Ov. **B.** Act. *conferring honour :* honoratissimo decreto, Liv. ; rus, Ov. ; sedes, Tac.

honōrificē, *adv. in an honourable* (i.e. *honouring) or respectful manner :* aliquid de aliquo honorifice praedicare, Cic., Liv. *Comp. :* honorificentius, Cic. *Sup. :* honōrificentissimē, Cic. Ep.

honōrificus, a, um [honōs faciō], *that confers*

honour, honourable : mentio, Cic. ; facta,
Caes. Comp. : honŏrificentior, Nep. Sup. :
honŏrificentissima verba, Cic.

Honōrius, I, m. son of the emperor Theodosius,
and Roman Emperor of the West, A.D. 395–
423.

honōrō, āre [honōs]. I. to honour, respect :
mortem luctu publico, Cic. ; virtutem,
Cic. ; tumulum, Ov. II. to award honour
or distinction to : aliquos coronā triumph-
ali, Liv.

honōrus, a, um [honōs], bringing honour :
quae in Drusum honora et magnifica
Augustus fecisset, Tac. ; oratio, Tac. ;
Stat.

honōs, v. honor.

hoplomachus, I, m. [ὁπλομάχος], a heavy-
armed combatant, a sort of gladiator : Mart.,
Suet.

hōra, ae (old GEN. sing. hōrāī, Lucr.), f.
[ὥρα], an hour (among the Romans, this
varied in length, acc. to the time of year, fr.
sunrise to sunset being reckoned as 12
hours). 1. Lit. : hora hiberna, Pl. ; ternas
epistulas in horā dare, Cic. ; quattuor horarum spatio antecedens, Caes. ; quintā fere
horā, Cic. ; hora quota est ? Hor. ; horam
de legitimis horis remittere, Cic. ; hora
partūs, Suet. Phr. : in horas, every hour,
hourly, Hor. ; Plin. Ep. ; ad horam,
punctually, Sen. ; in horam vivere, to care
only for the passing hour, to live from hand
to mouth : Cic. ; omnium horarum homo
(amicus, etc.), ready, active, well disposed at
all times : Suet. 2. Transf. a. time :
crastina, Verg. ; Hor. ; Ov. b. season of
the year : sub verni temporis horam, Hor.
c. In pl. hōrae, ārum, a horologue, clock :
Cic. [It. ora / Fr. heure.]

Hora, ae, f. w. of Quirinus (Romulus), worshipped as a goddess ; called before her death
Hersilia.

Hōrae, ārum, f. pl. the Hours, daughters of
Jupiter and Themis, goddesses who presided
over the changes of the seasons and kept
watch at the gates of heaven.

hōraeum, I, n. [ὡραῖον, sc. τάριχος], a
pickle made of young fishes : Pl.

Horātius, a, the name of a Roman gens.
Esp. I. Horatii, the three brothers who
fought against the Alban Curiatii. II.
Horatius Cocles, who, in the war with Porsenna, defended single-handed the bridge
over the Tiber. III. Q. Horatius Flaccus,
the celebrated Augustan poet, B.C. 65–8 ;
Horātius, a, um.

hordeāceus (Cato) and hordeārius (Plin.),
a, um [hordeum], of barley, barley-.

hordēia, ae, f. perh. the name of a fish : Pl.

hordeum, I, n. barley : Cato, Liv., Suet. In
pl. : Verg. [It. orzo / Fr. orge.]

horia, ae, f. a fishing-smack : Pl.

horiola, ae, f. [dim. horia], a tiny fishing-
smack : Pl.

hornō, adv. during this year : Pl.

hornŏtinus, a, um [hornus], this year's :
nuces, Cato ; frumentum, Cic.

hornus, a, um [perh. fr. ὥρινος], this year's :
fruge, Hor.

hōrologium, I, n. [ὡρολόγιον], a clock, either
a sun-dial, or a water-clock : Varr., Cic. Ep.
[It. oriuolo / Sp. reloj / Fr. horloge.]

hōroscopus, I, m. [ὡροσκόπος], a nativity,
horoscope : Pers.

horrendus, a, um. I. Gerund. horreō. II.
Adj. awesome ; hence a. dreadful, terrible :
monstrum, Verg. ; silva, Liv. ; nox, Ov. ;
rabies, Hor. Neut. Acc. as Noun : horrendum stridens, Verg. b. wondrous, awesome : Sibylla, Verg. ; virgo (Camilla),
Verg.

horrēns, entis. I. Part. horreō. II. Adj. :
rigid ; hence, bristling, bristly, rough,
shaggy : sus, Lucr. ; rupes, rubi, Verg. ;
Marte Latini, Verg. ; horrenti nemus umbrā, Verg.

horreō, ēre, to stand on end, stand rigid, to
bristle. 1. Lit. A. saetae densis similes
hastilibus horrent, Ov. ; horret capillis ut
marinus asperis echinus, Hor. ; cautibus
Caucasus, Verg. B. In partic. a. From
cold : to stiffen, be numbed ; hence, perh.
to shudder, shiver : terra, Cic. ; manus,
Ov. ; horrenti tunicam non reddere servo,
Juv. b. From fear : to be numbed, shudder,
quake, shiver : corpus, Pl. ; totus tremo
horreoque, Ter. ; quadrupedes, Ov. ; membra timore, Ov. With Acc. : to shudder at,
shrink from : ursos, Ov. ; aciem ac tela,
Liv. 2. Transf. A. In gen. : to bristle :
horrebant saevis omnia verba minis, Ov.
B. In partic. a. From fear : to shrink
from, dread. With Acc. : Ariovisti crudelitatem, Caes. ; dolorem, Cic. ; pauperiem,
Hor. With Inf. : Cic., Liv. ; horret animus referre, Liv. With Indir. Quest. :
Cic. With ne and Subj. : Liv. b. From
amazement : to be amazed : quae mehercule
ego, Crasse, cum tractantur in causis, hor-
rere soleo, Cic. ; animo, Cic.

horrēscō, horrēscere [horreō], to rise on end,
bristle up. 1. Lit. A. In gen. : segetes,
Verg. ; bracchia villis, Ov. ; mare, Cic.
B. From awe or fear : to begin to shake or
quake, start : ferae iniecto terrore mortis
horrescunt, Cic. 2. Transf. A. In gen. :
to become wild or fearsome : fulmina, Lucr.
B. In partic. a. From fear : to begin to
quake, shudder, to become terrified : Pl.,
Verg. With Acc. : morsūs futuros, Verg. ;
procellas, Hor. b. From amazement : hor-
rescit visu subito Aeneas, Verg.

horreum, I, n. a barn, shed, storehouse. 1.
Prop. for grain : a granary : Cic., Verg.,
etc. 2. Transf. : for wine : Hor. ;
storehouses of bees : Verg. ; of ants : Ov.

horribilis, e, adj. [horreō]. I. terrifying : rei
publicae pestis, Cic. ; species, Caes. ; tempestas, Cic. ; libellus, Cat. Comp. : Cic.
II. Colloq. : amazing, astounding : hoc
τέρας (i.e. Caesar) horribili vigilantiā, celeritate, diligentiā est, Cic. Ep.

horridē, adv. uncouthly, roughly : Cic.,
Quint. Comp. : Cic., Tac.

horridulus, a, um [dim. horridus]. 1. Lit.
a. gently swelling or firm : papillae, Pl.
b. rather shaggy, bristly : caput, Lucil.
2. Transf. a. rather unkempt, shabby :
comes, Pers. b. In speech : rather uncouth, rugged : orationes Catonis, Cic.

horridus, a, um [horreō], standing up, rough,
shaggy, bristly. 1. Lit. a. In gen. : barbula, Cic. ; caesaries, Ov. ; sus, Verg. ;
densis hastilibus myrtus, Verg. Comp. :

Verg. **b.** From cold : *numbed* or *shivering* : si premerem ventosas horridus Alpis, Ov. ; horrida cano bruma gelu, Verg. **2. Transf. a.** In dress, etc. : *rough, rugged, wild* : Lucr., Verg., Liv., etc. Of land : campus, Cic. ; silva fuit, late dumis atque ilice nigrā horrida, Verg. **b.** Of weather : *rough, wild* : Iuppiter horridus austris, Verg. ; grando, Verg. ; tempestas, fluctus, Hor. **c.** In character, manners, or speech : *uncouth, rude, rough* : Enn. ; ut vitā sic oratione horridus, Cic. ; oratio, Cic. ; gens, Verg. ; numerus Saturnius, Hor. ; ita de horridis rebus nitida est oratio tua, Cic. ; modus dicendi, Liv. *Comp.* : Cic., Plin. Ep. **d.** *wild, frightening, frightful* : vis teli, Lucr. ; paupertas, Lucr. ; horridiore aspectu esse, Caes. ; acies, Verg. ; virga (mortis), Hor. With *Pass. Inf.* : cerni, Sen.

horrifer, era, erum [horror ferō], *causing shudders.* **a.** Of cold : *chilling, freezing* : Acc. ; Boreas, Ov. **b.** Of fear : *terrifying* : Pac. ; aestus (Tartari), Lucr. ; aegis, Verg.

horrificē, *adv., in a manner to cause awe or dread* : Lucr.

horrificō, āre [horrificus]. **I.** *to make rough, ruffle* : mare Zephyrus, Cat. **II.** *to cause dread* : vatum praedicta monitu horrificant, Verg.

horrificus, a, um [horror faciō], *terrifying, appalling* : bustum, Lucr. ; letum, Verg. ; lapsus (of the Harpies), Verg.

horri-sonus, a, um [horreō sonus], *dreadsounding* : fragor, Lucr. ; fremitus, Verg.

horror, ōris, m. [horreō], *a bristling up, stiffening, rigidity.* **I.** Lit. **A.** In gen. **a.** comarum, Luc. **b.** *a shivering, quivering* : ramos horrore moveri, Ov. **B.** In partic. **a.** From cold : *a shuddering, shivering, cold-fit, ague-fit* : Cic. Ep., Verg. **b.** From fear : *a shuddering, quaking* : ea res me horrore adficit, Pl. ; horror ingens spectantis perstringit, Liv. ; Lucr. **2. Transf. a.** Of speech : *roughness, rudeness* : Quint. **b.** From fear : *dread, fright* : qui me horror perfudit ! Cic. Ep. **E s p.** from relig. fear : *awe, reverence* : fusus horrore venerabundusque, Liv. ; Luc. **c.** From joy : *a thrill* : me quaedam divina voluptas percipit atque horror, Lucr. **d.** *that which causes shivering or dread* : *that horror* : serrae stridentis, Lucr. ; Scipiades, Carthaginis horror, Lucr.

horsum, *adv.* [contr. from hō-vorsum ; *ho-* is stem of hīc], *hither, this way* : horsum pergunt, Ter. ; Pl.

hortāmen, inis, *n.* [hortor], *an incitement, exhortation* : Ov. With *ad* and Acc. : Liv. In *pl.* : *encouragement* : Tac.

hortāmentum, i, *n.* [hortor], *an incitement, encouragement* : ea cuncta Romanis hortamento erant, Sall. In *pl.* : animi, Liv. ; victoriae, Tac.

hortātiō, ōnis, *f.* [hortor], *encouragement, exhortation* : Cic. Ep., Sall., Liv. ; ad philosophiam (the title of a treatise by Augustus), Suet.

hortātivus, a, um [hortor], *suitable for encouragement or exhortation* : genus (dicendi), Quint.

hortātor, ōris, *m.* [hortor], *an inciter, encourager* : Pl. ; studi, Cic. ; scelerum, Verg. ; animorum, Ov.

hortātus, ūs, *m.* [hortor], *incitement, encouragement* : in ABL. *sing.* : Caes., Cic., Ov. In *pl.* : Ov., Tac.

hortor, ārī, *to urge strongly, to incite, instigate, encourage, exhort.* **1.** Lit. (with personal *Subject*). **a.** With man or beast as *Obj.* : with Acc. only : aliquem, Pl., Cic. Ep., Ov. ; vitulos, Verg. P r o v. : hortari currentem (i.e. to spur a willing horse), Cic. E s p. *to address soldiers, issue 'general orders'* : Sabinus suos hortatus, cupientibus signum dat, Caes. ; and with *Intern.* Acc. : pauca pro tempore milites hortatus, Sall. ; with the matter urged expressed by *ad* or *in* and Acc. : ad laudem milites hortari, Cic. ; in amicitiam iungendam, Liv. ; in proelia, Verg. ; or by *de* : aliquem de concilianda pace, Caes. ; Cic. Ep. ; or by *ut* or *ne* and *Subj.* : Pl., Caes., Cic., etc. ; or by *Subj.* alone : Caes., Liv., Suet. **b.** With thing as *Obj.* : in Acc. : pacem, Cic. Ep., Nep. ; Ov. ; in *Inf.* : Nep., Hor., Ov., Suet. **2. Transf.** Of inanimate or abstract subjects : pol bene facta tua me hortantur, tuo ut imperio paream, Pl. ; multae res ad hoc consilium Gallos hortabantur, Caes ; rei publicae dignitas haec minora relinquere hortatur, Cic.

hortulus, i, *m.* [*dim.* hortus], *a little garden.* **1.** Lit. : Cat., Juv. In *pl.* : hortuli, *garden-grounds,* Cic. **2.** T r a n s f. : Democriti fontibus Epicurus hortulos suos irrigavit, Cic.

hortus, i, *m.* [*cf.* Gk. χόρτος], *an enclosed place for plants,* hence, *a garden, a pleasure-garden, fruit-garden, kitchen-garden, vineyard.* **1.** Lit. **a.** In *sing.* : Pl., Cic., Plin. Ep. **b.** In *pl.* : *park, pleasuregrounds* : Cic., Juv., Tac., etc. **2. Transf.** (for holera) : *garden-stuff, vegetables, greens* : Cato, Hor.

hospes, itis, *m.* and **hospita,** ae, *f.* **I.** *one who entertains a stranger, a host, hostess.* **a.** Prop. opp. to caupo, *inn-keeper* : Cic., Hor., Juv. **b.** Of an inn : Hor. **c.** Of a billet : Tac. **II.** *one who is entertained, a guest.* **1.** L i t. : per dexteram istam te oro, quam regi Deiotaro, hospes hospiti, porrexisti, Cic. ; non hospites, sed peregrini atque advenae, Cic. ; Pl. ; Hor., etc. ; Iuppiter Hospes, *Jupiter the (ideal) Guest,* Ov. **2.** T r a n s f. **A.** *a friend by ties of hospitality* : id factum ex suis hospitibus Caesar cognoverat, Caes. ; Cic. **B.** Opp. to a native. **a.** *a stranger, foreigner* : nec peregrinus atque hospes in agendo, Cic. ; Pl. ; Hor. **b.** Of things (practically an *Adj.*) : *strange, foreign* : terra hospita, Verg. ; hospita navis, Ov. ; hospita aequora, Verg. [It. *oste* ; Sp. *huesped* ; Fr. *hôte.*]

hospita, *v.* hospes.

hospitālis, e, *adj.* [hospes], *of or relating to a guest* or *host.* **1.** L i t. : tessera, Pl. ; mensa, Cic. ; Iuppiter, Cic. ; deversorium, cubiculum, beneficia, caedes, Liv. **2.** T r a n s f. : *hospitable* : Cic. ; tibi pectus, Hor. *Sup.* : Cic. As Noun, *a former*

host, a *guest-friend* : Liv. [It. *ospitale,
spedale* ; Fr. *hôtel*.]

hospĭtālĭtās, ātis, *f.* [hospitālis], *hospitality* :
Cic.

hospĭtālĭter, *adv. hospitably, as a guest* :
invitare, accipere, Liv., Curt.

hospĭtĭum, ĭ, *n.* [hospes]. **1.** L i t. **a.**
*hospitality, friendship established by hospital-
ity* : facere cum aliquo, Cic., Liv. ; vetus
hospitium renovare, Cic. ; hospitia iungere,
Liv.; qui hospitio Ariovisti usus erat, Caes. ;
iungimus hospitio dextras, Verg. ; renuntiare, Liv. **b.** *a hospitable reception* : alicui
hospitium praebere, Pl. ; aliquem hospitio
accipere, invitare, Cic. ; hospitio excipere, Liv. **2.** T r a n s f. **a.** *a place where
strangers are entertained, a lodging, chambers
for guests, an inn* : Cic., Liv., Juv., etc. ;
hospitio prohibemur harenae (*shelter*), Verg.
b. *shelter* (for animals) : in *pl.* : Verg.
[It. *ospizio* ; Fr. *hospice*.]

hospĭtor, ārī [hospes], *to be a guest, to lodge.*
T r a n s f. : deum in humano corpore
hospitantem, Sen. Ep.

hostĭa (also **fostĭa**), ae, *f.* [hostiō, *to strike,*
Enn.], *an animal sacrificed, a victim,
sacrifice* : immolare, Pl., Cic. ; hostiis
sacrificare, Liv. ; mactata hostia, Hor. ;
hostiis humanis litare, Tac. ; hostiis piare
prodigia, Tac.

hostĭātus, a, um [hostia], *provided with
victims* : Pl.

hostĭcus, a, um [hostis]. **I.** *foreign, strange* :
domicilium, Pl. **II.** *of an enemy* : ager,
Liv. ; moenia, Hor. ; Pl. ; Ov. As Noun,
hostĭcum, ī, *n. the enemy's territory* : Liv.

hostīlis, e, *adj.* [hostis]. **I.** *of an enemy* :
Pl., Cic., Hor., etc. **II.** *for an enemy* :
metus, Sall. **III.** *like an enemy, hostile* :
hostilem in modum, Cic. ; legati rettulerunt
omnia hostilia esse, Liv. ; ne quid ab se
hostile timeret, Sall. ; Liv. ; Tac. *Neut.
pl.* as Noun : hostilia facere, Sall. ; audere,
loqui, etc. Tac.

hostīlĭter, *adv. like an enemy, in a hostile
manner* : Cic., Liv., Ov., etc.

Hostīlĭus, a, *the name of a Roman gens.*
Esp. **I.** Hostus Hostilius, *victorious against
the Sabines.* **II.** *his grandson*, Tullus Hostilius, *third king of Rome* : **Hostīlĭus**, a, um.

hostĭmentum, ī, *n.* [hostiō], *a recompense,
requital* : Pl.

hostĭō, īre, *to return like for like, to make
requital* : Pl.

hostis (fostis), is, *m. f.* **I.** Orig. *a stranger,
foreigner* : hostis apud maiores nostros is
dicebatur quem nunc peregrinum dicimus,
Cic. **II.** *a foreign enemy in arms, foe* (dist.
fr. inimicus, *a personal enemy*.) **1.** L i t.
(in *sing.* or *pl.*) : Pl., Cic., Verg., etc. **2.**
T r a n s f. (of one's own nation). **a.** *a declared public enemy* : Caes., Cic. **b.** In
gen. *an enemy, foe, opponent* : dis hominibusque hostis, Cic. ; Verg., etc. In *fem.* :
hostis est uxor, invita quae ad virum nuptum datur, Pl. ; certa hostis, Ov. **c.** Of
animals or things : in ovilia demisit hostem
vividus impetus, Hor. ; (in backgammon)
unus cum gemino calculus hoste perit, Ov.

hūc (older **hōc**, e.g. in Pl., Verg., etc.), *adv.*
[hīc], *to this place, hither.* **1.** L i t. : Pl.,
Cic., Verg., etc. With *Part.* G e n. : com-

migravit huc viciniae, Ter. Contrasted
with *illuc* : huc et illuc rapit, Cic. ; ne cur-
sem huc illuc viā deterrimā, Cic. Ep. ; Liv. ;
huc atque illuc intuentem, Cic. ; tum
huc, tum illuc volant alites, Cic ; huc
et huc euntium, Hor. **2.** T r a n s f. **a.** *to
this, to these* : accedebat huc quod Dumnorix dixerat, *to this was added, that* . . .,
Caes. ; Cic. ; huc natas adioe septem, Ov.
b. *to this* or *such a pitch* : huc unius
mulieris libidinem esse prolapsam, Cic.
With *Part.* G e n. : huc adrogantiae venerat,
Tac. **hūcĭne**, *interrog., to this pitch ?*
hucine tandem omnia reciderunt ? Cic. ;
Sall. With G e n. : hucine rerum venimus ?
Pers.

hui ! exclamation of astonishment or admiration : Pl., Ter., Cic. Ep.

hūiusce modĭ, **hūius modĭ**, G e n. of hīce
or hīc and modus, *of this kind.*

hūmānē (Ter., Cic., Hor.) and **hūmānĭter**
(Cic. Ep.), *adv.* **I.** *agreeably to human
nature, as a man should* : Ter., Cic., Hor.
Comp. : Cic. **II.** *courteously, politely* :
Cic. Ep. *Sup.* : Cic. Ep.

hūmānĭtās, ātis, *f.* [hūmānus], *human
nature, the condition of being a man.* **1.**
L i t. : magna est vis humanitatis, Cic. ;
humanitatis societas, Cic. ; communis humanitatis ius, Cic. ; humanitatis non parum
habere, Cic. **2.** T r a n s f. Of the higher
side of human nature. **a.** *humane conduct,
kindness, courtesy* : Caes., Cic., etc. **b.**
liberal education, culture, refinement : Cic.

hūmānĭtus, *adv.* [hūmānus]. **I.** *in accordance with human nature* : Enn., Cic. **II.**
humanely, kindly, tenderly : Ter.

hūmānus, a, um [homō], *belonging to man,
of man, human.* **1.** L i t. : facinus, Pl. ;
esse aliquem humanā specie et figurā, Cic. ;
caput, Hor. ; hostiae, Cic. ; res, Cic. ;
amor, Cic. ; scelus (i.e. *against men*), Liv. ;
As Noun, **hūmānus**, ī, *m. mortal man* :
Ov. ; in *pl.* : Lucr. ; **hūmānum**, ī, *n.
humanity, human nature, feeling, lot, etc.* :
homo sum ; humani nihil a me alienum
puto, Ter. ; Pl. ; Liv. ; in *pl.* : Cic., Liv.
2. T r a n s f. Of the higher side of human
nature. **a.** *humane, kind, courteous* : Cic. ;
ingenium, Pl., Ter. ; sensus, Cic. *Sup.* :
Cic. Ep. **b.** *well-educated, cultured, refined* : gens, Cic. ; homo doctissimus atque
humanissimus, Cic. ; humanissimus sermo,
Cic. Ep.

hūmātĭō, ōnis, *f.* [humō], *a burying* : Cic.

hūmātor, ōris, *m.* [humō], *one who buries* :
Luc.

hūme-, v. ūme-.

hŭmī, *adv.* [L o c a t. of humus], *on* or *in the
ground* : iacere humi, Cic. ; humi requies-
cere, Sall. ; stratus humi, Liv., Juv. ;
quousque humi defixa tua mens erit ? Cic. ;
te mater condet humi, Verg. ; locus in
carcere duodecim pedes humi depressus,
Sall.

hūmĭd-, **hūmĭf-**, v. ūmid-, ūmif-.

hŭmĭlis, e, *adj.* [humus]. **1.** L i t. : *on the
ground.* **A.** *lying near the ground, low-
lying* : et vites et ea quae sunt humiliora
neque se tollere a terrā altius possunt, Cic. ;
myricae, Verg. ; turrim humilem parvam-
que fecerant, Caes. ;· casa, Verg. **B.** Less

prop. **a.** In relation to sea-level : *near or just above the surface* : humilis volat aequora iuxta, Verg. ; Italia, Verg. **b.** In relation to normal : *shallow* : naves, Caes. ; fossa, Verg., Tac. ; *stunted* : ex humili corpusculo, Sen. Ep. **2. Transf. a.** Of birth or importance : *low, humble, weak* : ut si parentibus nati sint humilibus, Cic. ; humillimus homo de plebe, Liv. ; civitas ignobilis atque humilis, Caes. *Comp.* : Caes. As Noun : ex humili potens, Hor. ; ex humili extollit Fortuna, Juv. **b.** Of mind or character : *low, mean, base, abject* : Cic., Hor., Quint. ; animus, Lucr., Cic. ; preces, Cic., Suet. ; pavor, Verg. *Sup.* : Suet. **c.** Of dress or style of living : *mean* : vestitus, Nep. ; domus, Juv. **d.** Of language : *mean* : oratio, Cic. ; sermo, Cic., Hor., Quint. [It. *umile* ; Fr. *humble.*]

humilitās, ātis, *f.* [humilis]. **1.** L i t. **a.** *nearness to the ground* : animalium, Cic. ; lunae, Cic. ; arborum, Sall. **b.** *shallowness* : navium, Caes. **2. Transf. a.** Of condition in life : *lowness, meanness, insignificance* : Caes., Cic., Liv. ; generis, Sall., Suet. **b.** Of mind or character : *meanness, abjectness* : Cic., Liv., Quint. ; opp. to adrogantia : Caes.

humiliter, *adv.* **I.** *low, deeply* (opp. alte) : *Sup.* : Plin. Ep. **II.** *basely, meanly, abjectly* : Cic., Liv., Sen. Ep.

humō, āre [humus], *to put into the ground, to inter, bury.* **1.** L i t : Cic., Verg. **2. Transf.** *to perform funeral rites* : militari honestoque funere, Nep.

humus, i, *f.* [*cf.* Gk. χαμαί], *the ground.* **1.** L i t : Enn., Cic., Verg., etc. ; ab humo attollit amicum, Verg. ; ventus harenam humo excitat, Sall. ; surgit humo, Ov. ; sodit humo, Ov. *v.* also humi, Ov. **2. Transf. a.** *land, region* : Punica, Ov. **b.** Of what is common or ordinary : ne dum vitat humum nubes et inania captet, Hor.

hyacinthinus, a, um [ὑακίνθινος], *of the hyacinthus* : flos, Cat. T r a n s f. : *hyacinthus-coloured* : Pers.

hyacinthus or **-os,** i, *m,* perh. *corn-flag,* or *blue iris* : Verg.

Hyacinthus or **-os,** i, *m. a Spartan youth, loved by Apollo, but accidentally killed by him ; from his blood sprang the flower of the same name ;* **Hyacinthia,** ōrum, *n. pl. the Hyacinthia, a spring-festival at Sparta in honour of Hyacinthus.*

Hyades, um, *f.* L i t. *the Rainers ; a group of seven stars in the head of the constellation Taurus.*

hyaena, ae, *f.* [ὕαινα], *the striped hyena* : Ov.

hyalus, i, *m.* [ὕαλος], *glass* : Verg.

Hyantēus, Hyantius, a, um, *Boeotian.*

Hybla, ae, and **Hyblē,** ēs, *f. a mountain-range in E. Sicily, famous for its honey ;* **Hyblaeus,** a, um ; **Hyblēnsēs,** ium, *m. pl. the inhabitants of several towns, called Hybla, in Sicily.*

hybrida, *v.* hibrida.

Hydaspēs, is, *m. a large tributary of the Indus, now the Jelum.*

Hydra, ae, *f.* [Ὕδρα, *water-snake*]. **I.** *the Hydra : a seven-headed dragon killed by Hercules.* **II.** *the constellation Water-snake,*

---

also called Anguis. **III.** *a fifty-headed hydra in the infernal regions.*

hydraula, ae, or **hydraulēs,** ae, *m.*[ὑδραύλης], *one who plays on the water-organ* : Suet.

hydraulicus, a, um [ὑδραυλικός], *of the water-organ, hydraulic* : Suet.

hydraulus, i, *m.* [ὕδραυλος], *a water-organ* : Cic.

hydria, ae, *f.* [ὑδρία, a water-pot], *a jug, ewer, urn* : Cic.

Hydrochous, i, *m.* [Ὑδροχόος, water-pourer], *the constellation* Aquarius : Cat.

hydrōpicus, a, um [ὑδρωπικός], *dropsical, suffering from dropsy* : Hor.

hydrōps, ōpis, *m.* [ὕδρωψ], *the dropsy* : Hor.

hydrus, or **-os,** i, *m.* [ὕδρος], *a water-serpent* : Verg., Ov., Juv.

Hylās, ae, *m. a youthful companion of Hercules in the Argonautic expedition ; landing for water on the coast of Mysia, he was carried off by the nymphs.*

Hyllus (**Hylus**), i, *m. son of Hercules and husband of Iole.*

Hymēn, enis, and **Hymenaeus** or **-os,** i, *m.* [Ὑμήν, Ὑμέναιος], *the god of marriage,* Hymen. **1.** L i t : Pl., Cat., Ov. **2.** T r a n s f. **a.** *nuptials, a wedding* (in form Hymenaeus) : Verg. ; in *pl.* : Lucr., Verg. **b.** Of animals : *pairing* : Verg. **c.** *a wedding-hymn* : in form Hymen : Ter. ; in form Hymenaeus : Pl., Ov.

Hymēttus, or **-os,** i, *m. a mountain-range near Athens, famed for its honey and its marble ;* **Hymēttius,** a, um.

Hypanis, is, *m. a river of Sarmatia, now the Bug.*

hyperbaton, i, *n.* [ὑπέρβατον], R h e t. : *transposition of words* : pure Lat., transgressio : Quint.

hyperbolē, ēs, *f.* [ὑπερβολή], R h e t. : *exaggeration, hyperbole* : pure Lat., superlatio and superiectio : Quint.

Hyperborei, ōrum, *m. pl. a fabulous people, living in the extreme north ;* **Hyperboreus,** a, um.

Hyperidēs, is, *m. a celebrated Athenian orator, contemporary with Demosthenes.*

Hyperion, onis, *m.* **I.** *son of a Titan and the Earth, father of the Sun.* **II.** *the Sun himself ;* **Hyperionis,** idis. *f. daughter of the Sun, i.e. Aurora.*

Hypermēstra, ae, (**-ē, ēs**), *f. one of the daughters of Danaus, who alone saved her husband's life.*

hypocaustum or **-on,** i, *n.* [ὑπόκαυστον], *a bathing-room heated from below, a sweating-room* (pure Lat., vaporarium) : Plin. Ep.

hypocrita or **-ēs,** ae, *m.* [ὑποκριτής], *a mime who accompanied the delivery of an actor by gestures* : Suet.

hypodidascalus, i, *m.* [ὑποδιδάσκαλος], *an under-teacher* : Cic. Ep.

hypomnēma, atis, *n.* [ὑπόμνημα], *a memorandum, note* : Cic. fil. ap. Cic. Ep.

Hypsipylē, ēs, *f. d. of Thoas, Queen of Lemnos in the time of the Argonauts ;* **Hypsipylēus,** a, um.

Hyrcani, ōrum, *m. pl. a people who dwelt on the Caspian Sea ;* **Hyrcānus,** a, um.

Hyrtacus, i, *m. father of Nisus* in Verg. ; **Hyrtacidēs,** ae, *m. son of Hyrtacus, i.e. Nisus.*

I

I, i, the ninth letter of the Latin alphabet.
I. On the substitution of *i* for *a* and *e*, vide
those letters. *i* takes the place of *o* in oblique cases from noun-stems in *on*, as
cardo(n), *cardinis*, and *hominis* ; in derivatives from stems in *o*, as *multi-tudo* and
publi-cus ; at the end of the first stem in
compounds like *multi-sonus* ; and in a few
special instances, as in *cognitus*, and *ille*
from *ollus*, *olle*. It is substituted for *u* in
the DAT. and ABL. *pl.* of noun-stems in
u, as *fructi-bus*, *geni-bus* ; at the end of
the first stem in compounds like *aesti-fer* ;
in superlatives, as well as in positive adjs.
of similar form, as *optimus* (from optumus),
finitimus. Long *i* has in some Latin words
arisen from the diphthong *ai*, e.g. in the
compounds of *caedo*, *quaero*, as *occido*, *in-
quiro*, and in *iniquus* from *aequus* ; also
from *ei*, as in *dico*, *divus*, *liber*. **II.** Consonantal *i* (formerly and wrongly written as
j) represents a sound which corresponds in
Latin to the orig. Indo-European and San-
skrit spirant *y*, as well as to the German *j*,
and the English *y* (before a vowel). It
must not be supposed similar to the French
j, though the latter regularly represents it in
derivatives from the Latin. There is no
corresponding consonant in Greek. In
several Latin words consonantal *i* corresponds to a Greek ζ, which arose from *y*
preceded by a parasitic δ ; thus, Lat.
iugum, Gk. ζυγόν ; Lat. *ius* (sauce), Gk.
ζύ-μη, ζω-μός. In at least one instance
the I. E. *y* retained in Lat. *i* is represented
by the rough breathing in Greek ; Lat.
iecur, Gk. ἧπαρ. The ancient grammarians state that the *i*-sound between two
vowels was pronounced double ; and hence,
in such cases, some authors (as Cicero) repeated the *i* in writing, e.g. aiio (aio),
Maiia (Maia), peiius (peius), etc. Sometimes in like cases a tall I was written. **III.**
In the Romance languages. **A.** Simple *i*.
1. accented *i long* is usu. unchanged ; e.g.
Lat. *amicus*, It. amico, Sp. amigo, Fr. ami ;
Lat. *spina*, It. spina, Sp. espina, Fr. épine.
2. accented *i short* us. changes to *e* in Italian
and Spanish, but in French to *oi* ; e.g. Lat.
niger, It. nero, Sp. negro, Fr. noir ; Lat.
minus, It. meno, Sp. menos, Fr. moins.
3. accented *i* before a double consonant
commonly becomes *e* ; e.g. Lat. *siccus*, It.
secco, Sp. seco, Fr. sec ; Lat. *crista*, It. Sp.
cresta, Fr. crête. But *i* followed by *ng* or
gn generally becomes *ei*, and sometimes *a*,
in French ; e.g. Lat. *pingere*, *cingere*, *lingua* ;
Fr. peindre, ceindre, langue. Unaccented *i*
is most commonly unchanged ; it sometimes
becomes *oi*. When a short vowel in Latin
immediately precedes the accented syllable,
it is lost in French ; *i* is often in this
position, and disappears accordingly ; e.g.
Lat. *sanitatem*, *positura*, *septimana* ; Fr.
santé, posture, semaine. **B.** Consonantal *i*.
1. into *g*, *gi*, or *gg* : e.g. Lat. *Ianuarius*,
iam, *maius*, *peius* ; It. gennaio, già, maggio,
peggio. Lat. *iuniperus*, *iunix*, Fr. genièvre,

génisse. **2.** into *i* : e.g. Lat. *maior*,
baiulare, *adiutare* ; Fr. maire, bailler, aider.
3. into *y* : e.g. Lat. *iam*, *maior* ; Sp. ya,
mayor. **4.** irregularly into *l* : e.g. Lat.
Iulius ; It. luglio. **5.** Omission of *i* : e.g.
Lat. *ieiunare* ; Fr. jeûner. **IV.** As an
abbreviation I.O.M. signifies Iovi Optimo
Maximo ; I. R. Iuno Regina'; I. V. T. Iulia
Victrix Togata.

Iacchus, i, m. ["Ἴακχος]. **I.** *a male deity connected with the mysteries at Eleusis.* **II.**
Bacchus. **Transf.** *wine* : (Silenum) inflatum hesterno Iaccho, Verg.

iaceō, iacēre, iacuī [intrans. fr. root of iaciō],
to lie. **1.** Lit. **A.** Simply : humi, Lucr.,
Cic., etc. ; in limine, Cic. ; in lecto, Cic. ;
in harenā, Verg. ; alicui ad pedes, Cic. ;
sub arbore, Verg. ; campo, Verg. ; lecto,
Ov. **B.** In partic. **a.** *to lie* in bed : Cic.
Ep., Hor., Ov., etc. **b.** *to lie low, lie dead,
to have fallen :* proximi iacentibus insiste-
rent, Caes. ; Liv. ; Ov. ; telo iacet Hector,
Verg. So *to lie in ruins :* Troia iacet certe,
Ov. ; Juv. **2.** Transf. **A.** Physically. **a.**
to be or stay long at a place : Pl., Cic. Ep.
b. Geogr. : *to lie, be situated :* Nep. But
us. *to lie flat, level, or low :* in vertice montis
planities, Verg. ; ponti aequora, Lucr. ;
campi Faesulae inter Aretiumque, Liv. ;
urbis loca, Tac. **c.** *to lie spread out :*
terrae, Verg., Ov. ; vagi crines per colla,
Ov. ; vestis, Ov. **B.** Mentally or immaterially : **a.** *to lie idle* or *neglected.* **i.** *to
be idle, indolent, inactive :* Cic. ; pecunia,
Cic., Plin. Ep. ; ars tua, Ov. ; mea numina,
Verg. **ii.** *to lie dormant, be disused; neglected,* or *despised :* iudicia, virtutes, iustitia, Cic. ; pauper ubique iacet, Ov. So
of prices : pretia praediorum, Cic. **b.** *to
lie prostrate.* **i.** *to be overthrown :* humana
vita, Lucr. ; pietas, Ov. **ii.** *to fall, be
refuted :* conclusio, Cic. ; iacent suis testibus qui etc., Cic. **iii.** *to lie dejected, be
cast down :* animum amici iacentem excitare, Cic. ; Liv. ; iacet in maerore meus
frater, Cic. Ep. [It. giacere, Fr. ci-gît.]

iaciō, iacere, iēcī, iactum [perh. fr. root of
ἵημι, Aor. ἧκα]. **I.** *to lay.* **1.** Lit. :
aggerem, molem, Caes. ; fundamenta, Cic.,
Liv. ; vallum, Liv. ; muros, Verg. ; molem
in altum, Hor. **2.** Transf. : fundamenta causae, defensionis, pacis, Cic. ;
odia in longum, Tac. **II.** *to throw, cast,
fling.* **1.** Lit. **A.** In gen. : iacula in
casas, Caes. ; se in profundum, Cic. ;
saxeam pilam ponto. Verg. ; coniugem in
praeceps, Tac. Simply : talos, Pl., Cic. ;
lapides, Cic. Occ. *to throw away :* scuta,
Pl. ; vestem, Ov. **B.** In partic. **a.** Of
a sower : semina, Verg., Ov. **b.** Of a
tree : *to throw* (its produce) : iacturas
poma myricas, Ov. So of other things : de
corpore odorem, Lucr. **c.** Of stags : *to
cast* or *shed :* cornua, Ov. **2.** Transf.
a. In gen. : *to cast, throw* (abuse, accusations, etc.) : contumeliam in aliquem, Cic. ;
adulteria, Cic. ; minas, Liv. ; probra in
feminas, Tac. **b.** Of hints, innuendoes :
to throw out, let drop : suspicionem, Cic. ;
vera an vana, Liv. ; fortuitos sermones,
Tac. ; de lacu Albano, Liv. With Acc.
and *Inf.* : Sall.

iactāns, antis. **I.** *Part.* iactō. **II.** *Adj.* : *bragging, boastful* : Cic., Plin. Ep. *Comp.* : Verg., Hor. With GEN. : sui, Quint.

iactanter, *adv. boastfully, ostentatiously*. *Comp.* : Tac.

iactantia, ae, *f.* [iactō], *bragging, ostentation* : militaris, Tac. ; privata, Plin. Ep. ; sui, Tac.

iactātiō, ōnis, *f.* [iactō], *a tossing to and fro, jolting, shaking*. **1.** **L i t. a.** In gen. : vulneris (of a wounded man), Liv. ; maritima, Liv. ; Cic. **b.** In speaking : *swaying, gesticulation* : corporis, Cic. ; manūs, Quint. **2.** **T r a n s f. a.** In *pl.* : *agitation* : animorum, Cic. **b.** *boasting, bragging, ostentation* : Cic. ; popularis (i.e. based on popular applause), Cic. ; animi, Liv. ; cultūs, Tac.

iactātor, ōris, *m.* [iactō], *a braggart* : rerum a se gestarum, Quint. ; Suet.

iactātus, ūs, *m.* [iactō], *a tossing, quivering* : pennarum, Ov.

iactĭtō, āre [*freq.* iactō], *to toss about*. Transf.: *to bandy* : inter se ridicula, Liv. ; Phaedr.

iactō, āre [*freq.* iaciō], *to throw, cast, fling energetically, repeatedly*, or *excitedly*. **I.** *to toss to and fro* or *violently, to swing, make to quiver* or *vibrate*. **1.** **L i t. a.** In gen. : bracchia in numerum, Lucr. ; cerviculam, Cic. ; manūs, Quint. ; corpus in suo sanguine, Ov. **b.** Of an orator (with *Refl. Pron.* or in *Mid.*) : *to fling oneself about, gesticulate* : se suo more, Cic. ; exsultare immoderateque iactari, Cic. **c.** Of the sea, etc. : iactati forma profundi, Ov. ; Lucr. ; ut Aeneas pelago iactetur, Verg. ; iactata flamine navis, Ov. **2.** **T r a n s f.** (mostly in *Pass.* or *Mid.*). **a.** *to harass, disquiet, disturb* : iactor crucior agitor, Pl. ; iactari morbis, Lucr. ; clamore et convicio, Cic. Ep. ; per labores, Liv. As in a storm : qui in hac tempestate populi iactemur, Cic. **b.** Of opinions (in *Mid.*) : *to totter, waver, fluctuate* : Cic. Of money (in *Mid.*): *to fluctuate in value* : Cic. **c.** With *Refl. Pron.* or in *Mid.* : *to strut about, make a display, be officious* or *active* : intolerantius se iactare, Cic. ; iactare se in causis centumviralibus, Cic. ; de aliquo, Cic. ; se actionibus, Liv. ; luco, Verg. ; forensi labore iactari, Cic. In spending money : se in pecuniis, Cic. **II.** *to toss off* : *toss* or *fling away, fling in showers, scatter*. **1.** **L i t. a.** *to toss off*: talos adripio, iacto basilicum, Pl. ; vestem argentumque de muro, Caes. **b.** *to fling in showers* : hastas, Cic. ; lapides vacuum in orbem, Verg. ; semina, Ov. ; basia, Juv. Occ.: arma multa passim, Liv. ; lucem de corpore, Lucr. **2.** **T r a n s f. a.** *to toss, scatter in rout* : iactatos aequore toto Troas, Verg. **b.** Of words : *to fling out* : voces pro umbram, Verg. ; terrorem (i.e. threats), Cic. ; probra in quempiam, Liv. Oftener *to bandy about* (in discussion) : eas res, Caes. ; in senatu aliquid, Cic. ; rem sermonibus, Liv. ; ultro citroque querimonias, Liv. ; iactamus omnis te Roma beatum, Hor. Similarly : pectore curas, Verg. *Impers. Pass.* with *de* and ABL. : Liv. **c.** *to fling about* in boasting, *advertise,*

boast of, vaunt : urbanam gratiam et dignitatem, Caes. ; genus et nomen, Hor. ; Ov. ; se alicui ultorem, Hor. With Acc. and *Inf.* : Liv. [It. *gettare* ; Fr. *jeter*.]

iactūra, ae, *f.* [iaciō], *a throwing away* ; esp. *a throwing overboard*. **1.** Lit. : in mari iacturam facere, Cic. ; Curt. **2.** Transf. : *loss, sacrifice*, etc. : vitae iacturam facere, Caes. ; rei familiaris, Cic. ; dignitatis, Caes. ; Cic. ; equitum, Liv. ; suorum, Caes. ; temporis, Liv. ; sepulcri, Verg. In *pl.* : Caes., Cic.

iactus, a, um, *Part.* iaciō.

iactus, ūs, *m.* [iaciō], *a throwing* ; *a throw, cast* : fulminum, Cic. ; talorum, Cic., Ov. ; tesserarum, Liv. ; intra teli iactum (i.e. within range), Verg. ; se iactu dedit aequor in altum, Verg.

iaculābilis, e, *adj.* [iaculor], *that can be thrown* or *hurled* : telum, Ov.

iaculātor, ōris, *m.* and **iaculātrix**, īcis, *f.* (Ov.) [iaculor], *a thrower, shooter, hurler* : Hor. E s p. *a soldier armed with darts* or *javelins* : Liv. Transf.: Juv.

iaculor, ārī [iaculum]. **1.** Lit. **a.** *to throw the javelin* : Cic., Liv. ; or *other missiles* : Liv. **b.** With Acc.: *to hurl, shoot at, shoot* : cervos, Hor. ; aliquem ferro, Ov. **c.** With Acc. of thing thrown : *to throw, cast, hurl, fling* : puppibus ignis, Verg. ; missilem ignem, Tac. **2.** Transf. **a.** *to aim at* (i.e. strive after) : multa, Hor. **b.** With words : *to fling at* : probris in aliquem, Liv. ; Quint. With Acc. : verbum, Lucr. [Fr. *jaillir*.]

iaculum, i, *n.* [iaculus]. **I.** *a dart, javelin* : Caes., Cic., Ov. **II.** *a cast-net* : Pl., Ov.

iaculus, a, um [iaciō], *what is thrown* or *what darts out* : rete iaculum, *a cast-net*, Pl. ; of a serpent : Luc.

iäient-, *v.* iënt-.

iäiūn-, *v.* iëiūn-.

iam, *adv.* **I.** Of time. **A.** *already, by now* (*then*), *now* (*then*) *at last* : iam vesperascit, Ter. ; obsolevit iam ista oratio, Cic. ; iamque dies, ni fallor, adest, Verg. ; septingentos iam annos vivunt, Cic. ; iamque ab eo non longius biduo viā aberant, Caes. ; ubi iam se paratos esse arbitrati sunt, Caes. With *Future* : *now at once, even now* : iam aderunt, Cic. Ep. Strengthened by *nunc, tum, tunc*, or *tandem* : nunc iam nobis vobisque consulatus patet, Liv. ; iam nunc timeo, Cic. ; se iam tum gessisse pro cive, Cic. ; regnum Dea iam tum tenditque fovetque, Verg. ; Baebius Massa iam tunc optimo cuique exitiosus, Tac. ; Liv. ; iam tandem ades, Pl. ; Verg. ; Liv. **B.** *from now* (*then*), *henceforth* (*thenceforth*), *forthwith, straightway* : Ter., Cic., Verg., etc. Rarely with *Present* : Cic., Verg. **II.** In other relations. **A.** In transition and enumeration (*cf.* iam . . . iam) : *now, henceforth, next, moreover* : Cic., Verg., etc. ; also iam vero, Cic. **B.** In emphasis. **a.** *now, actually, even further* : non cum senatu modo sed iam cum diis bellum gerere, Liv. **b.** *precisely, indeed, quite* : quem iam our Peripateticum appellem, nescio, Cic. **C.** In a conclusion : *then surely, then at once it follows* : si hoc dixissem, iam mihi optimo iure senatus vim attulisset, Cic. **iam iam**, *instantly, now at this very moment, every moment :* iam iam intellego quid dicas, Cic.; iam iam futurus rusticus, Hor.; Verg. Also iam iamque : Caesar adventare iam iamque et adesse eius equites nuntiabantur, Caes.; iam iamque tenet, Verg.; iam . . . iam, *now — now, at one time — at another :* Verg., Hor. **iam diū** and **iam dūdum** (or **iamdūdum**), *now for a long time.* **a.** With *Pres.* or *Imperf.* (translate by *Perf.* and *Pluperf.* of the Eng. verb): iam diu flagitat populus, Cic.; te iam dudum hortor, Cic.; iam dudum flebam, Ov. **b.** With *Perf. : for a long time now, for a long time past, long ago :* nemo iam dudum litore in isto constitit, Ov.; iam dudum audivi, Pl.; inimicitiae iam diu susceptae, Cic. **c.** With *Imperat. : now at last :* iam dudum sumite poenas, Verg. **iam pridem** (or **iampridem**), *this long time, for a long time.* **a.** With *Pres.* or *Imperf.* (v. iam dūdum): *now and for a long time past, for a long time now :* iam pridem cupio, Cic.; iam pridem resides animi, Verg.; ad mortem te duci iam pridem oportebat, Cic. **b.** With *Perf. : long ago :* is iam pridem mortuus est, Cic. [It. *già, di già,* Fr. *déjà ;* iam magis, It. *giammai,* Fr. *jamais.*]

Iambēus, a, um [ἰάμβειος], *iambic :* trimetri, Hor.

Iambus, I, *m.* [ἴαμβος], an iambic foot, an iambus, ‿ ⟋ . **1.** Lit. : Cic., Hor., Quint. **2.** Transf. *an iambic poem, iambic poetry :* Cic., Hor., Quint. In *pl. :* Hor., Quint.

Iāniculum, I, *n. a hill of Rome on the right bank of the Tiber.*

Iānigena, ae, *m.f. child of Janus.*

iānitor, ōris, *m.* and **iānitrix**, icis, *f.* (Pl.) [iānus], *a doorkeeper, porter :* carceris, Cic.; (inferorum), Verg.; Ov., etc.

ianthina, ōrum, *n. pl.* [ἰάνθινος], *violet-coloured garments :* Mart.

iānua, ae, *f.* [iānus], *a door, house-door.* **1.** Lit.: occludere, pultare, Pl.; claudere, Cic.; reserare, Ov.; frangere, Hor.; inferni regis, Verg. **2.** Transf. **a.** Milit.: *the key* (i.e. commanding the entrance to a territory): urbs Asiae ianua, Cic.; Ov. **b.** *an entrance, approach :* quā nolui ianuā sum ingressus in causam, Cic.; Famae, Plin. Ep. **c.** *index :* vultus animi ianua, Q. Cic.

iānus, I, *m.* [fr. root seen in ire ; *lit. a way in* or *out, doorway, arch.*] **I.** *a covered passage, arcade :* Cic., Liv., Suet. **II.** one of the three arched passages in the Roman Forum (where the merchants and money-changers had their stand): Cic., Hor., Ov. **III.** Personified, **Iānus**, *an old Italian deity,* perh. mostly represented with two faces: **Iānālis**, e, *adj. ;* **Iānuālis**, e, *adj. ;* **Iānuārius**, a, um. *of Janus :* mensis, Cic. **b.** *of January :* Caes., Cic., etc.; also as Noun (sc. mensis), *January :* Caes., etc. [It. *gennaio ;* Sp. *enéro ;* Fr. *janvier.*]

Iapetus, I, *m. a Titan, f. of Atlas, Prometheus, and Epimetheus.* **Iapetionidēs**, ae, *m. s. of Iapetus,* i.e. *Atlas.*

Iāpydes, um, *m. pl. a people in Illyria ;* **Iāpys**, ydis, *adj. ;* **Iāpydia**, ae, *f. their country.*

Iāpyx, ygis, *m. s. of Daedalus who ruled in S. Italy.* **Iāpyx**, ygis, *adj. ; (sc. ventus), a wind that blows from Apulia* (W.N.W.) *towards Greece :* Verg., Hor.; **Iāpygia**, ae, *f. S. Apulia.*

Iasius, I, *m. s. of Jupiter and Electra, loved by Ceres ;* called also **Iasiōn**, ōnis.

Iāsōn, onis, *m.* **I.** *Jason, a famous Greek hero, s. of Aeson, king of Thessaly ; the leader of the Argonauts, husband of Medea, and afterwards of Creüsa ;* **Iāsonius**, a, um. **II.** *tyrant of Pherae, in Thessaly* (ob. B.C. 370).

iaspis, idis, *f.* [ἴασπις], *a green precious stone, jasper :* Verg. [It. *diaspro ;* Sp. *diaspero ;* Fr. *jaspe.*]

Ibēr-, v. Hibēr-.

ibi (older **ibī**), *adv. in that place, there :* referring, like *is,* to the immediate context. **1.** Lit. Of space : in Italiam contendit, duasque ibi legiones conscribit, Caes.; Cic.; Ov., etc. With corresp. *Rel. Adv.,* ubi, unde, *etc. :* ubi tyrannus est, ibi nulla est res publica, Cic.; Pl., etc. **2.** Transf. **A.** Of time : *then, thereupon :* Pl.; Verg.; Liv. With corresp. *Rel. Adv., cum, ubi, postquam :* Pl., Ter., Liv. **B.** Of other relations. **a.** *there, therein, therewith :* si quid est, quod ad testis reservet, ibi nos quoque paratiores reperiet, Cic.; ibique iuventutem suam exercuit (caedes, rapinae, etc.), Sall.; ibi imperium fore, unde victoria fuerit, Liv.; Pl., etc. **b.** Of persons : *in him, in her,* etc. : duxi uxorem ; quam ibi miseriam vidi ! Ter.; Liv.; Juv. [It. *vi ;* Fr. *y.*]

ibidem, *adv.* [old Lat. **ibī** and **-dem**, as in **idem**], *in the same place, in that very place, just there.* **1.** Lit. Of space : cenati discubuerunt ibidem, Cic.; Verg. With corresp. *ubi :* ubi amici, ibidem opes, Pl. With GEN.: ibidem loci, Pl. For *eōdem, to the same place :* Pl. **2.** Transf. **a.** Of time : *at that very moment :* Cic. **b.** Of other relations : *in the same matter :* laesit in eo Caecinam, sublevavit ibidem, Cic.; Pl.; Juv.

Ibis, is and idis, *f.* [ἴβις], *a bird held sacred by the Egyptians, which lived on water-animals, the ibis :* Cic., Ov., etc.

ibus, v. is.

Ibycus, I, *m. a Greek lyric poet of Rhegium, whose murder was brought to light by the cranes who witnessed it.*

Icarus, I, *m.* **I.** *a son of Daedalus, who, on his flight from Crete with his father, fell into the sea ;* **Icarius**, a, um : esp. *epithet of part of the Aegean Sea, into which he fell ; the Icarian Sea.* **II.** **Icarus** or **Icarius**, I, *m. s. of Oebalus king of Sparta, f. of Erigone and Penelope, placed in the heavens as the constellation Boötēs ;* **Icarius**, a, um ; **Icaris**, idis, and **Icariōtis**, idis, *f. the daughter of Icarus* or *Icarius,* i.e. *Penelope.* As *Adj. : of Penelope.*

iccircō, v. idcircō.

Icēni, ōrum, *m. pl. a British people dwelling in Suffolk and Norfolk, who revolted from the Romans under Boudicca.*

ichneumōn, onis, *m.* [ἰχνεύμων], *an animal which tracks out and devours crocodiles' eggs, Pharaoh's rat* : Cic., Mart.

(icō or iciō), ici, ictum. *to strike, hit, smite* (mostly in *Perf. Part.* ictus). **1.** Lit. : colapho me icit, Pl. ; icimur ictu, Lucr. ; telo venenato ictus, Cic. ; lapide ictus, Caes. ; Summanus e caelo ictus, Cic. ; Ov. **2.** Transf. **a.** With ref. *to striking the* victim sacrificed in making a covenant : cum Gaditanis foedus icisse dicitur, Cic. ; Tac. **b.** Of emotion : novā re consules icti, Liv. ; conscientiā, metu, Liv. ; desideriis icta, Hor. ; domestico vulnere, Tac.

icōn, onis, *f.* [εἰκών], *an image* : Plin.

iconicus, a, um [εἰκονικός], *of an image, copied from life* : Plin., Suet.

ictericus, i, *m.* [ἰκτερικός], *jaundiced* : Juv.

ictis, idis, *f.* [ἰκτίς], *the common weasel* : Pl.

ictus, a, um, *Part.* Icō.

ictus, ūs, *m.* [icō]. **1.** Lit. *a blow, stroke,* occ. *a wound* : pilorum, Caes. ; scorpionis, Caes. ; fulminis, Cic. ; pilum, haud paulo quam hasta vehementius ictu missuque telum, Liv. ; obliquus, Hor. ; caecis ictibus procul vulnerabantur, Liv. ; arboris, Hor. **2.** Transf. **a.** Of the sun's rays : ramis laurea fervidos excludet ictūs, Hor. ; solis, Ov. **b.** In prosody or music, *a beating time, a beat* : Hor. ; et pedum et digitorum ictu intervalla signant, Quint. **c.** Abstract : *stroke* : calamitatis, Cic. ; singulis veluti ictibus bella transigere, Tac. Also *range* : sub ictum dari, Tac. ; stare sub ictu Fortunae, Luc.

icuncula, ae, *f.* [*dim.* Icōn], *a small image or figure* : puellaris, Suet.

Ida, ae, or **Idē,** ēs, *f.* **I.** *a mountain in Crete, where Jupiter was brought up* ; **Idaeus,** a, um. **II.** *a mountain range near Troy* ; **Idaeus,** a, um, *Idaean,* also *Phrygian.*

Idalium, i, *n. a mountain city in Cyprus, sacred to Venus* ; *called also* **Idalia,** ae, *f.* **Idalius,** a, um, *Idalian,* also *Cyprian* ; **Idaliē,** ēs, *f. Venus.*

idcircō or iccircō, adv. [id circō, *v.* circā], *on that account, for this reason, therefore.* **I.** Ref. to previous statement : neque idcirco Caesar opus intermittit, Caes. ; Pl. ; Hor. etc. **II.** Ref. to a clause : **a.** With *quod* or *quia* : idcirco arcessor, nuptias quod mihi apparari sensit, Ter. ; Cic. ; Hor. ; quia natura mutari non potest, idcirco verae amicitiae sunt, Cic. **b.** With *si* : non, si Opimium defendisti, idcirco te isti bonum civem putabunt, Cic. ; Hor. **c.** With *ut, ne, quo* (of purpose) : quae ut fieret, idcirco pugnatum esse arbitror, Cic. ; Juv. ; sese idcirco ab suis discedere noluisse, quo facilius civitatem in officio contineret, Caes.

idea, ae, *f.* [ἰδέα], *a (Platonic) idea* ; *archetype* : Sen. Ep.

idem, eadem, idem, pron. [for is-dem ; -dem is a demonstr. suffix]. Lit. *this very, exactly this ;* hence, *the very same, the same.* **A.** In gen. **a.** Most commonly as an emphasising *Adj.* : idem iste Mithridates, Cic. **b.** To emphasise an additional fact : *that also, also, at the same time, likewise* : cum Academico et eodem rhetore congredi, Cic. ; musici qui erant quondam iidem poetae, Cic. **c.** Simil. with *unus* . *and that the same* : uno eodemque tempore, Cic. **d.** In making a contrast : *yet, nevertheless* (cf. " all the same ") : Epicurus cum optimam naturam dei dicat esse, negat idem esse in deo gratiam, Cic. **e.** As Noun : amicus est tamquam alter idem (cf. alter ego), Cic. ; idem velle atque idem nolle, Sall. *Neut. sing.* with *Partit.* GEN. : Cic., Ov. *v.* also under eōdem, eādem. **B.** In comparisons, with various *Conj., Pron.,* etc. which may be rendered by *as.* **a.** With *et* or oftener *atque, ac* : Gallorum eadem atque Belgarum oppugnatio est, Caes. ; Cic. **b.** With *Relat. qui* : servi iisdem moribus erant quibus dominus, Cic. **c.** With *cum* and ABL. : in eādem mecum Africā geniti, Liv. ; Cic. ; Tac. **d.** With DAT. : Lucr., Cic. Ep., Ov., etc.

identidem, adv. [related to *idem* as *itidem* to *is*], *repeatedly, several times, every moment, over and over again* : Pl., Cic., Cat., etc.

ideō, adv. [id eō. Lit. that for that purpose], *for that reason, on that account, therefore.* **A.** Causal, i.e. ref. to a clause which states *cause* or *reason.* **a.** Simply : atque ideo ad Pompeium contendit, Caes. ; Lucr., etc. **b.** With *quod, quia, quoniam* : hunc iudicem fugiebant ideo quod naturā non propensus ad misericordiam videbatur, Cic. ; Hor., etc. **B.** Ref. to a clause which states *purpose* : ideoque decemviros conubium diremisse ne etc., Liv. ; Cic. ; Tac. **C.** Occ., when negatived, to denote a *consequence* or *result that does not follow* : with *si* : non, si causa iusta est, ideo etc., Cic. ; with ABL. *Absol.* : talibus recitatis non ideo Thrasea decessit sententiā, Tac.

idiōta, ae, *m.* [ἰδιώτης], *an uneducated, inexperienced, ordinary person* : Cic.

idōlon, i, *n.* [εἴδωλον], *a spectre, apparition* : Plin. Ep.

idōneē, adv. *fitly, suitably* : Cic.

idōneus, a, um, *fit, meet, proper, suitable* (of persons and things) : minus idoneis verbis uti, Cic. ; homo, Cic. ; auctor, Quint. (As Noun : in deligendis idoneis, Cic. ; Liv. ; Tac. ; apud idonea provinciarum, Tac.) Constr. : with *ad* and ACC. : Pl., Caes. Cic. ; with *in* and ACC. : Quint. ; with DAT. : Caes., Hor., etc. ; so too, perferendis militum mandatis habebatur idoneus, Tac. ; with *Relat.* clause : idoneus non est qui non impetret, Cic. ; Pl. ; Ter. ; with *Inf.* : Hor.

Idūmaea, ae, *f. a region to the S. of Palestine* ; **Idūmaeus,** a, um.

Idūs, uum, *f. pl.* [prob. an Etruscan word]. *the fifteenth day of March, May, July, and October, and the thirteenth of the other months ; the Ides* : Caes., Cic., Tac. (*v.* calendar at end of volume) ; (interest and school-fees were paid on the Ides) : diem pecuniae Idūs Novembris esse, Cic. Ep. ; faenerator Alphius redegit Idibus pecuniam, Hor. ; (pueri) ibant octonis referentes Idibus aera, Hor.

iecur, iecoris (also iocineris, Liv.) *n.* [cf. Gk. ἧπαρ], *the liver.* **1.** Lit. : Cic., Liv., Hor., etc. **2.** Transf. (as the seat of the passions). **a.** Of love : Hor. **b.** Of anger : Hor., Juv.

iecusculum, ī, *n.* [*dim.* iecur], *a little liver* : Cic.

iēiūnē, *adv. meagrely, with poverty of language or ideas* : Cic., Plin. Ep. *Comp.* : Cic.

iēiūniōsior (iāiūn-, Pl.) ius, *comp. adj.* [iēiūnus], *fasting more, more hungry* : dies, Pl.

iēiūnitās (iāiūn-, Pl.), ātis, *f.* [iēiūnus], *a fasting, emptiness of stomach.* **1.** L i t. : Pl. **2.** T r a n s f. **a.** Of style : *emptiness, meagreness* : Cic. **b.** Of knowledge : bonarum artium, Cic.

iēiūnium, ī, *n.* [iēiūnus], *a fasting, fast.* **1.** L i t. : Cereri instituere, Liv.; ieiunia indicere, Hor. ; ponere, solvere, Ov. ; servare, Suet. **2.** T r a n s f. Of its effects. **a.** *hunger* : Ov. **b.** *leanness* : Verg. [Fr. *jeûne*.]

iēiūnus (iāiūnus, Pl.), a, um, *fasting, empty.* **1.** L i t. : Pl., Cic., Liv. **2.** T r a n s f. **A.** Of its effects : *hungry* : Cic. Ep. ; dentes, Hor. **B.** Of material things. **a.** Of land : *hungry, poor* : Cic., Verg. **b.** Of other things : *thin, meagre* : sanies, Verg. **C.** Of immaterial things. **a.** Of desire : *hungering for* (with GEN.) : aures ieiunae huius orationis, Cic. **b.** Of spirit or action : *feeble, poor, mean* : animus, cognitio, calumnia, Cic. **c.** Of style : *meagre, starved. Comp.* : Cic. [**Sp.** *ayúno* ; Fr. *jeûne*.]

iēntāculum (iāient-, Pl.), ī, *n.* [iēntō], *an early light meal, breakfast* : Pl., Mart., Suet.

iēntō, āre [prob. for iāientō, conn. with iēiūnus], *to breakfast* : Suet.

Iernē, *v.* Hibernia.

igitur, *adv.* (avoided by Caesar ; rarely first in sentence in Cic.) *in these circumstances, then.* **A.** Of the natural result. **a.** In gen. : cetera peragrans invenies igitur etc., Lucr. ; Pl. **b.** In questions : *then as a result, things being so* : Pl., Cic., Liv. **c.** In commands : Cic. **B.** In logic, to mark the conclusion : *then, therefore, accordingly, consequently* : Pl., Cic., Quint. **C.** In speeches. **a.** Resumptive after parentheses : *then, as I was saying* : Cic. **b.** Summarising after an enumeration : *I may say in short* : Cic. **c.** Emphasising : ea vis, ea igitur ipsa quae etc., Cic.

ignārus, a, um [in gnārus]. **A.** A c t. : *ignorant, unacquainted, inexperienced, unaware.* **1.** L i t. : Cic., Verg., etc. *Sup.* : Pl. With GEN. : huius oppidi, Pl. ; facundiae ac poliendae orationis, Cic. ; mali, Verg. : Pisonis, Tac. With *Indir. Quest.* : Cic., Liv., Quint. With Acc. and *Inf.* : Cic., Ov., etc. **2.** T r a n s f. Of inanim. and abstr. subjects : quae flumina lugubris ignara belli, Hor. ; non ignara philosophae grammatice, Quint. **B.** P a s s. : *not known* : lingua, Sall. ; fors, Ov. With DAT. : regio hostibus ignara, Sall. ; Ov. ; Tac.

ignāvē, *adv. without energy* or *spirit, slackly, listlessly, lackadaisically* : Cic., Hor. *Comp.* : Verg.

ignāvia, ae, *f.* [ignāvus]. **I.** *slackness, listlessness* : Pl., Sall. **II.** *faintheartedness, cowardice* : Cic., Verg.

ignāviter, *adv. without energy* or *spirit* : Lucil., Hirt. ap. Cic. Ep.

ignāvus, a, um [in gnāvus]. **1.** L i t. (of living beings). **a.** *without energy* or *spirit, slack, listless, spiritless* : Pl., Cic., Verg., etc. *Comp.* : Cic. ; *Sup.* : Pl. With GEN. : legiones operum et laboris ignavae, Tac. With *ad* : ignavus ad muniendum hostis, Liv. **b.** *faint-hearted, cowardly* : Cic., Hor., etc. *Sup.* : Sall., Liv. *Masc.* as Noun : Cic., Ov., etc. **2.** T r a n s f. (of inanimate and abstr. things). **a.** *slack, lazy, idle* : senectus, Cic. ; nemora (i.e. *unfruitful*), Verg. ; anni, Ov. ; septima lux, Juv. **b.** *causing inactivity* or *indolence* : frigus, Ov.

ignēscō, ere [ignis], *to take fire, to become inflamed.* **1.** L i t. : Cic., Ov. **2.** T r a n s f. : Rutulo ignescunt irae, Verg.

igneus, a, um [ignis]. **1.** L i t. **a.** *of fire, fiery, on fire, burning* : sidera tota, Cic. ; vis caeli, Ov. ; ignea vis (i.e. *fire*, as the primary creative element, acc. to Heraclitus), Cic. **b.** *burning-hot, fiery* : sol, Verg. ; aestas, arces, Hor. **2.** T r a n s f. Of emotion and energy : furor, Ov. ; vigor, Verg. ; Tarchon, Verg.

igniculus, ī, *m.* [*dim.* ignis], *a small fire, a little flame, a spark.* **1.** L i t. : Quint., Juv. **2.** T r a n s f. : desideri, Cic. Ep. ; virtutum, Cic. ; viriles, Cic. Ep.

ignifer, era, erum [ignis ferō], *fire-bearing, fiery* : aether, Lucr. ; axis, Ov.

ignigena, ae, *m.* [ignis and gen in gignō], *fire-born,* epith. of Bacchus : Ov.

igni-pēs, pedis, *adj.* [ignis pēs], *fiery-footed* : equi, Ov.

igni-potēns, entis, *adj.* [ignis potēns], *ruler of fire,* epith. of Vulcan : deus, Verg. As Noun : Verg.

ignis, is, *m. fire* (both as an element, and as matter in combustion ; in former sense us. *sing.*). **1.** L i t. **A.** In gen. : Pl., Cic., Verg., etc. ; ignem concipere, Cic. ; pati ab igne ignem capere, Cic. ; lapidum conflictu atque tritu elici ignem videmus, Cic. ; ignem accendere, Verg. ; ignem comprehendere, Caes. P h r. (of banishment) : aquā et igni interdicere, Cic. **B.** In partic. **a.** *conflagration* : ignis auditur, Verg. ; pluribus simul locis ignes coorti, Liv. **b.** *a beacon, watch-fire* (in *pl.*) : fumo atque ignibus significabatur, Caes. ; facere, Caes. **c.** *funeral-pyre* : Caes. ; supremi ignes, Ov. **d.** *fire-brand* : ignem operibus inferre, Caes. ; ignibus armata multitudo, Liv. ; Cic. Of brands for torture : aliquem igni excruciare, Caes. ; in *pl.* : Cic. **e.** Of lightning : fulsere ignes et aether, Verg. ; in *sing.* : Hor., Juv. **f.** Of the stars : Cic., Verg., etc. **2.** T r a n s f. **A.** Of what is destructive : *flame, fire* : quom ille obrutum ignem (i.e. of war) reliquerit, Liv. ; of persons, *a firebrand* : ne parvus hic ignis (i.e. Hannibal) incendium ingens exsuscitet, Liv. **B.** *light, brightness, splendour, lustre, redness.* **a.** In gen. : oculorum, Cic. ; Ov. ; fronte curvatos imitatus ignis (Lunae), Hor. ; ob os offusus, Cic. **b.** *sacer ignis* (i.e. *erysipelas*), Verg. C. Of emotions (e.g. anger, love) : exarsere ignes animo, Verg ; caeco carpitur igni, Verg. ; in *sing.* and *pl.* : Hor., Ov. Hence, *a flame* (i.e. the loved one) : Verg., Hor.

ignōbilis, e, *adj.* [in and gnōbilis, older form of nōbilis], *unknown to fame, insignificant,* *undistinguished, obscure.* **1.** Lit. **a.** Of persons : Pl., Cic., Verg. ; civitas, Caes. **b.** Of things : argentaria, Cic. **2.** Transf.: *obscure* (in origin), *of humble birth :* Ter., Cic., Hor., etc.

ignōbilitās, ātis, *f.* [ignōbilis], *want of fame, obscurity.* **1.** Lit. : Cic., Ov. **2.** Transf.: *obscurity* (of origin), *humble birth :* generis, Cic. ; Liv.

ignōminia, ae, *f.* [in and gnōmen, older form of nōmen], *public degradation.* **1.** Lit. **a.** Milit.: signiferos ignominiā notavit ac loco movit, Caes. ; sine ignominiā domum reverti, Caes. ; cum ignominiā dimittere, Liv. **b.** Civil: (by act of the censors): ignominiā notare, Cic. ; in *pl.* : Suet. **2.** Transf. (in gen.): *dishonour, disgrace :* Lucil. ; aliquem ignominiā adficere, Cic. ; ignominiam fugiunt ac dedecus, Cic. In *pl.* : iudiciis ignominiisque concisus, Cic. With *Subj.* GEN. : ignominia senatūs, Cic. With *Obj.* GEN. : cum summā ignominiā familiae, Nep. With defining GEN. : ignominia amissarum navium, Caes.

ignōminiōsus, a, um [ignōminia]. **I.** Of persons : *disgraced, degraded :* Liv., Quint. As Noun : Quint., Tac., Suet. **II.** Of things : *disgraceful :* dominatio, Cic. ; dicta, Hor. ; fuga, Liv.

ignōrābilis, e, *adj.* [ignōrō], *unknown :* Cic.

ignōrantia, ae, *f.* [ignōrāns], *want of knowledge, ignorance :* Quint., Tac. With *Obj.* GEN. : Caes., Ov., Tac., etc. With *Indir. Quest. :* Tac.

ignōrātiō, ōnis, *f.* [ignōrō], *want of knowledge or acquaintance, ignorance :* with *Obj.* GEN. : Cic., Curt. ; with *de :* Cic.

ignōrō, āre [perh. fr. old *adj.* ignōrus]. **I.** *not to know, to have no knowledge of, to be unacquainted with, ignorant of :* Pl., Cic., Hor. With Acc. : Pl., Cic., Prop., etc. With *de :* Cic. Ep. With Acc. and *Inf. :* Cic., Quint. With *Indir. Quest. :* Caes., Cic., Ov. With *quin* (after negat.) : Cic., Quint. In *Pass.* **a.** *to be unknown :* Ter., Cic., Hor. **b.** *unobserved, unnoticed :* Sall. **c.** *unrecognised :* Ter., Tac. **II.** *to take no notice of, disregard* (rare) : with Acc. : Pl., Cic.

ignōscēns, entis. **I.** *Part.* ignōscō. **II.** Adj. : *forgiving, placable :* animus ignoscentior, Ter.

ignōscō, nōscere, nōvī, nōtum [in and gnōsco, older form of nōscō, lit. *not to try to ascertain,* with esp. reference to a fault or crime], *to overlook, pardon, forgive, excuse :* Ter., Cic., Juv. *Impers. Pass. :* Ter., Cic. Usual constr. **a.** With DAT. of person and Acc. or depend. clause of the offence : ut eis delicta ignoscas, Pl. ; Cic. ; velim mihi ignoscas, quod ad te scribo tam multa totiens, Cic. Ep. ; mihi ignoscite si appello etc., Cic. *Impers. Pass. :* deprecatores, quibus non erat ignotum, Cic. Ep. ; Suet. **b.** With DAT. of offence : Pl., Cic. Ep., Hor. *Impers. Pass. :* peccato mi ignosci aequom est, Ter. **c.** With Acc. alone (only of *Neut. Pron.* in Cic.) : hoc, Cic. ; peccatum, Pl. ; Verg. Also in *Ger. Adj. :* dementia ignoscenda quidem, scirent si ignoscere Manes, Verg. ; Ter.

(1) ignōtus, a, um, *Part.* ignōscō.

(2) ignōtus, a, um [in and gnōtus, older form of nōtus). **A.** Pass.: *unknown.* **1.** Lit. (of persons and things) : Pl., Cic., Hor., etc. With DAT. : Cic., Curt. *Comp. :* Liv., Quint. ; *Sup. :* Cic. **2.** Transf. **a.** *obscure :* homo, Cic. ; *Sup. :* Cic. **b.** *obscure* (in origin), *low-born :* Hor., Ov. **B.** Act. *not knowing :* as Noun : aliquem producere ad ignotos, Cic. ; Nep. ; Phaedr.

īle, is, *n.* mostly in *pl.* **īlia,** ium [Gk. ἴλια], *guts, intestines.* **1.** Lit.: Verg., Hor., Ov. ; ilia omnium rumpere, Cat. ; invidiā ilia (sua) rumpere, Verg. **2.** Transf. **a.** *the loin, groin, flanks :* ilia ducere, Hor. ; equis ilia suffodere, Liv. **b.** In *sing. : testicle :* Cat.

īlex, icis, *f.* *the holm-oak or evergreen oak :* Verg., Hor., Ov. [It. *elce* ; Fr. *yeuse.*]

Īlia, ae, *f.* *a poetical name of Rhea Silvia, m. of Romulus and Remus;* **Īliadēs,** ae, *m. s. of Ilia,* i.e. *Romulus or Remus.*

Īlias, adis, *f.* *the Iliad of Homer, v.* also under Ilium.

īlicet, *adv.* [īre and licet, *cf.* scīlicet and vidēlicet ; hence anciently, a form of dismissing an assembly or funeral-party ; *we* or *you may go, it is over.*] **I. a.** *let us go, let us be gone :* ilicet ; quid hic conterimus operam frustra ? Ter. **b.** *all is over :* actum est, ilicet, peristi, Ter. ; Pl. **II.** *immediately, forthwith :* Verg.

īlignus (īligneus, Cato), a, um [īlex], *of holm-oak, oaken :* Ter., Verg.

Īlios, ī, *v.* Īlium.

Īlithyia (quadrisyl.), ae, *f.* *a goddess of the Greeks who aided women in child-birth.* (Lat. Iuno Lucina.)

Īlium or Īlion, ī, *n.* *a poetical name for Troy.* Also **Īlios,** ī, *f. ;* **Īlius, Īliacus,** a, um ; **Īliēnsēs,** ium, *m. pl. the Trojans :* **Īliadēs,** ae, *m. son of Troy :* esp. Ganymede : **Īlias,** adis, *f. a Trojan woman ;* **Īlias,** adis, *f. is also the name of the epic poem on the Trojan war, the Iliad. On account of the great extent of the poem,* Ilias *is used to represent a great quantity* (Ov.).

il-l-, for words thus compounded, *v.* inl-.

illā, *adv. by that way :* Pl., Tac.

illāc, *adv.* [orig. *Neut.* ABL. *fem.* of ille], *by that way, on that side :* Pl., Ter. ; illac facere (i.e. to belong to that party), Cic. Ep.

ille, a, ud (older **olle** and **ollus,** a, um) (NOM. *pl.* and DAT. *sing. m.* olli, Verg.), *demonstr. pron.* and *adj. ; that, that yonder, that more remote in space, time, or thought.* **A.** In gen. **a.** With Nouns : Pl. ; sol me ille admonuit, Cic. ; in illā tranquillitate vivere, Cic. ; ex illo tempore, Verg., Ov. ; so without tempore, Verg., Ov. **b.** With another *Pron.* : Pl. ; est idem ille tyrannus deterrimum genus, Cic. ; cum primum audivi, ego ille ipse factus sum, Cic. **c.** Without a Noun or *Pron.* **1.** Strong : *that person or thing ; he, she, it* (with some emphasis) : illum ab Alexandreā discessisse, nemo nuntiat, Cic. Ep. ; multum ille et terrā iactatus et alto, Verg. So with *quidem :* philosophi quidam, minime mali illi quidem, sed non satis acuti, Cic. ; Ov. **ii.** Weak : *he, she, it* (mostly of a person or thing just named) : Cic., Verg., etc. **B.** Strongly emphatic :

that famous : illa Medea, Cic.; tune ille Aeneas ? Verg.; Antipater ille Sidonius, Cic.; illud Solonis (dictum), Cic.; Papirius illo corporis robore, Liv. **C.** Ref. to what follows (wh. is mostly expressed by a *quod* clause (*the fact that*), or by Acc. and *Inf.*, or by direct words) : unde ergo illud ' aspicite, o cives,' etc., Cic.; illud acerbissimum est quod, etc., Cic. **D.** Contrasted with *hic : that more remote, the former, that more remote in time or thought :* non antiquo illo more sed hoc nostro eruditus, Cic. (see also under *hic*). **E.** Phr.: non dicam illinc hoc signum ablatum esse et illud, *not merely this or that particular statue,* Cic.; ille aut (or et) ille, *this or that, such and such :* Cic., Suet.

illi, *v.* illic.

illic, illaec, illūo [ille and -ce], *he, she, or it yonder, that yonder :* Pl., Ter. With the interrog. particle *-ne,* in the form **illicine :** Pl., Ter.

illic, illi (Pl., Ter., Verg.), *adv.* [LOCAT. fr. root of ille], *in that place, there, yonder.* **1.** Lit.: Pl., Ter., Caes., Verg., etc. **2.** Transf.: *in that matter, therein :* res publica et milite illic et pecuniâ vacet, Liv.; ego illi maximam partem feram, Ter.

illim, *adv.* **I.** *from that place :* Pl., Ter., Lucr., Cic. Ep. **II.** *from that person :* Cic.

illinc, *adv.* [illim and -ce]. **I.** *from that or yonder place :* Pl., Ter., Ov. **II.** *on that side :* hinc pudicitia illinc stuprum, Cic.; Pl.; Juv.

illō, *adv.* *to that place.* **1.** Lit.: Pl., Caes., Cic. **2.** Transf. *to that point :* haec omnia Caesar eodem illo pertinere arbitrabatur, Caes.

illōc, *adv.* [illō and -ce], *to that place yonder :* Pl.

(1) illūc, *neut. v.* illic.

(2) illūc, *adv.* **1.** Lit. **a.** *to that place yonder, in that direction :* Pl., Cic., Juv. Esp. in phr. : huc illuc : Ter., Sall., Quint.; huc et illuc, Cic., Hor. **b.** *to that person :* Pl.; illuc (i.e. to Nero) cuncta vergere, Tac. **2.** Transf. *thereto, to that matter :* illuc redeat oratio unde deflexit, Cic.; quo res haec pertinet ? illuc, Hor.; Juv.

Illyrii, ōrum, *m. pl. a people on the Adriatic Sea, in Jugo-Slavia and Albania ;* **Illyrius,** a, um ; **Illyria,** ae, *f.* and **Illyricum,** i, *n. their country,* and (as consisting of two parts, one Greek, the other Roman) **Illyriae,** ārum, *the (two) Illyrias ;* **Illyricus,** a, um, and **Illyris,** idis, *f. adj. Illyrian ;* and **Illyris,** idis, *f. the country.*

Ilōtae, *v.* Hīlōtae.

Ilus, i, *m.* **I.** *s. of Tros, f. of Laomedon, and founder of Ilium.* **II.** *a name of Ascanius.*

im, *v.* is.

imāginārius, a, um [imāgō], *that exists only in imagination, seeming, fancied, imaginary :* fasces, Liv.; militia, Suet.

imāginātiōnēs, um, *f. pl.* [imāginor], *fancies, dreams :* Plin., Tac.

imāginor, āri [imāgō], *to picture to oneself, to fancy, imagine :* pavorem eorum, Tac.; with *Indir. Quest. :* Quint. Of dreams : with Acc. and *Inf. :* Suet.

imāgō, inis, *f.* [*cf.* imitor], *an imitation, copy : an image, likeness.* **1.** Lit. **a.** In gen. :

in a picture, statue, mask, apparition, etc. : Agesilaus neque pictam neque fictam imaginem suam passus est esse, Cic.; cerae, Hor.; epistula atque imago me certum fecit, Pl. Esp. of ancestral images, us. made of wax, which were placed in the atria of Roman houses, and carried in funeral processions : ius imaginis, Cic.; vir honoratissimae imaginis futurus, Liv. Hence, *noble ancestry :* (mihi) nullae sunt imagines, Cic.; homo multarum imaginum, Sall.; Hor. **b.** *a phantom, apparition :* Verg., Tac., etc. Of phantoms in dreams : Hor., Suet., etc. **c.** In sound : *an echo :* Varr., Verg., etc. **2.** Transf. **A. a.** *a mental picture of real persons, things, or events ;* hence occ. *recollection :* Scipionis memoriam atque imaginem sibi proponere, Cic.; expressam imaginem vitae videre, Cic.; illius noctis, Ov. Also of the *actual appearance* of the object of thought : imago Turni venientis, Verg.; caesorum, Tac. **b.** *a conception, idea of immaterial or abstract things :* naturae urbis et populi, Cic.; proconsularis, Liv.; iustitiae, virtutis, Quint. Also *the materialisation of a conception, the realisation, the very incarnation :* te imaginem antiquitatis, Cic.; tantae pietatis, Verg. **B.** Rhet. *a figure of speech, simile, metaphor :* Cic., Hor., etc. **C.** *a mere phantom or ghost, a shadowy form :* iustitiae umbrâ et imaginibus utimur, Cic.; iudiciorum, civitatis, rei publicae, etc., Cic.; iuris, Liv.; pacis, Tac.

imāguncula, ae, *f.* [*dim.* imāgō], *a little image :* aerea, Suet.

imbēcillius, *comp. adv. more weakly, feebly, faintly :* Cic.

imbēcillitās, ātis, *f.* [imbēcillus], *weakness, feebleness.* **1.** Lit. (physically) : materiae, Caes.; corporis, Cic.; Suet. **2.** Transf. **a.** Mental : animi, Caes.; consili, Cic.; ingeni, Plin. Ep. **b.** Of general ability : *helplessness :* humani generis, Cic.

imbēcillus, a, um, *weak, frail, feeble.* **1.** Lit. (of the body) : Cic. *Comp. :* Quint. *Masc.* as Noun : Lucr. **2.** Transf. **a.** Of mental qualities : animus, Cic.; imbecilliores vel animo vel fortunâ, Cic.; suspiciones, Tac. *Masc.* as Noun : Cic., Sen. Ep. **b.** Of general ability : *helpless, impotent :* natura generis humani, Sall.; medicina, Cic. Ep.; regnum, Sall.; aetas, Hor. *Comp. :* Cic. Ep.

imbellis, e, *adj.* [bellum], *non-combatant.* **1.** Lit. **A.** Of living beings : Ov., Liv. *Comp. :* Tac. **B.** Of things. **a.** *free from themes of war :* lyra, cithara, Hor.; Ov. **b.** Of a period of time : *free from war :* triennium, Liv. **2.** Transf. **a.** *disliking war, unwarlike, peaceful, cowardly :* imbelles timidique, Cic.; ignavi et imbelles, Liv.; Asia, Liv.; Tarentum, Hor.; cervi, Verg. **b.** Of actions : res, Cic. **c.** Of a weapon thrown by an old man : Verg.

imber, bris, *m.* [*cf.* Gk. ὄμβρος] (ABL. us. imbri), *rain, a shower of rain, heavy or pouring rain* (pluvia is rain in gen.). **1.** Lit. : venit imber, Pl.; maximus, Cic.; magni et adsidui, Cic. Ep.; iter factum corruptius imbri, Hor.; lapideus aut sanguineus, Cic.; grandinis, Lucr.; imbri lapidavit, Liv. **2. Transf. a.** *a rain-cloud :* caeruleus supra caput adstitit imber, Verg. **b.** *rainwater* (in *pl.*) *:* cisternae servandis imbribus, Tac. **c.** *water or liquid in* gen. : Lucr., Verg., Ov. **d.** *a stream of tears :* imbre per indignas usque cadente genas, Ov. **e.** Like the Eng. *shower,* of things that fall fast like rain : ferreus ingruit imber, Verg. ; aureus, Ter.

imberbis, e (Cic., Hor.) and **imberbus,** a, um (Cic., Hor.) [barba], *without a beard, beardless.*

im-bĭbō, bibere, bibi, *to drink in, imbibe.* **Transf.** (mentally). **a.** *to conceive :* de aliquo malam opinionem animo imbibere, Cic. ; certamen animis, Liv. **b.** *to determine, resolve steadfastly.* With Acc. of *Neut. Pron. :* Liv. With *Inf. :* Lucr., Cic.

im-bĭtō, v. inbĭtō.

imbrex, icis, *f.* [imber], *a fluted tile, guttertile, pan-tile.* **1.** Lit. : Pl., Verg. **2. Transf. a.** *a (water-) trough :* Cato. **b.** *a mode of applauding with the hands :* Suet.

imbrĭcus, a, um [imber], *rainy :* Auster, *rain-bringing,* Pl.

imbrĭfer, era, erum [imber ferō], *rain-bringing, rainy :* Austri, Ov. ; ver, Verg.

im-bŭō, buere, buī, būtum [perh. connected with bibō], *to wet, soak, steep, saturate.* **1.** Lit. : imbuti sanguine gladii legionum, Cic. ; sanguis novus imbuit arma, Verg. ; oscula Venus quintā parte sui nectaris imbuit, Hor. ; alium imbuta colorem, Lucr. **2. Transf. a.** (mostly in bad sense) *to steep, stain, taint :* gladium scelere, Cic. Esp. in *Part. Perf. :* hac ille crudelitate imbutus, Cic. ; imbutae caede manūs, Ov. ; Acc. : imbutae praedā manūs, Tac. **b.** (in simple sense) *to steep, fill :* mentem imbuit deorum opinio, Cic. ; religione, superstitione imbutus, Cic. ; admiratione, Liv. ; favore Othonis, Tac. **c.** *to steep, train, educate, accustom :* animum tenerum opinionibus, Cic. ; Pl. ; liberaliter educatos servilibus vitiis, Liv. ; aliquem ad officia legum, Tac. ; imbuuntur contemnere deos, Tac. ; nos ita a maioribus instituti atque imbuti sumus, Cic. ; litterulis Graecis imbutus, Hor. **d.** Of beginning an action : bellum sanguine, Verg. ; terras vomere, Ov. ; opus, Ov. ; cursu Amphitriten, Cat.

imĭtābĭlis, e, adj. [imitor], *that can be imitated :* Cic., Verg., etc.

imĭtāmen, inis, *n.* [imitor], *imitation :* Ov. In *pl.* (concr.) *likeness, image :* Ov.

imĭtāmenta, ōrum, *n. pl.* [imitor], *imitations, mimicry, pretence :* peractis tristitiae imitamentis, Tac.

imĭtātĭō, ōnis, [imitor]. **I.** *imitation :* virtutis, Cic. ; Quint. **II.** *simulation, pretence :* nihil ostentationis aut imitationis adferre, Cic.

imĭtātŏr, ōris, *m.* and **imĭtātrīx,** īcis, *f.* (Cic.) [imitor], *an imitator, copyist :* Cic., Hor. With *Obj.* GEN. : Cic., Ov., Quint.

imĭtātus, a, um, *Part.* **A.** Act. : *v.* imitor. **B.** Pass. *copied :* simulacra, Cic. ; voluptas, Ov. ; adfectus, Quint.

imĭtor, ārī [perh. fr. same root as aemulus], *to imitate, represent, copy, portray.* **a.** In some external form : aere capillos, Hor. ;

populi speciem et nomen, Cic. ; heroum veteres casūs dicendo, Cic. Poet. : putre solum imitamur arando (i.e. make loose or friable), Verg. ; robore duro ferrum, Verg. **b.** In action or conduct ; *to act like, copy, counterfeit :* nepam, Pl. ; Aratum, Cic. ; populi consuetudinem, Cic. ; mutatā iuvenem figurā imitaris, Hor. ; maestitiam, Tac.

im-maduisse, *Perf. Inf., to have become moist :* lacrimis genas, Ov.

immānis (inm-, Pl.), e, adj. [in, *not,* and O.L. mānus, *good*], *enormous, portentous, monstrous.* **1.** Lit. : ponti aequora, Lucr. ; corporum magnitudo, Caes. ; praeda, Cic. ; antrum, barathrum, telum, Verg. *Neut. :* immane quantum (like Gk. θαυμαστὸν ὅσον), *prodigiously,* Hor., Tac. *Neut.* Acc. as *Intern.* Acc. : leo hians immane, Verg. **2. Transf.** Of character : *unnatural, monstrous, inhuman, savage, gross :* Pl. ; belua, hostis, Verres, Cic. ; crudelitas, facinus, natura, animus, Cic. ; orae, Verg. ; coeptis immanibus effera Dido, Verg. ; vitium, Raeti, Hor. *Comp. :* Verg. ; *Sup. :* Cic. *Neut. pl.* as Noun : Tac., Juv.

immānĭtās, ātis, *f.* [immānis]. **1.** Lit. *monstrous size, vastness, excess :* vitiorum, Cic. **2. Transf.** Of character, *etc. : enormity, savageness, barbarism :* Cic. ; tanti facinoris, Cic. ; morum, naturae, Cic. ; parricidii, Quint.

im-mānsuētus, a, um, *untamed, wild, savage :* Cyclops, ingenium, ventus, Ov. *Comp. :* Sen. ; *Sup. :* Ov.

immātūrĭtās, ātis, *f.* [immātūrus]. **I.** *unripeness, immaturity :* sponsarum, Suet. **II.** *untimely haste :* Cic.

im-mātūrus (inm-, Pl.), a, um, *unripe, immature, premature.* **1.** Lit. Of plants : Plin., Quint. **2. Transf.** Of other things : vomica, Pl. ; infans immaturus est editus, Suet. ; mors, Cic., etc. ; filius obiit, Hor. ; amor, consilium, Liv.

im-medĭcābĭlis, e, adj. *incurable :* vulnus, Ov. ; telum, Verg.

im-memor (inm-, Pl.), oris, adj. *unmindful, forgetful, heedless :* Cat., Ov. ; ingenium, Cic. ; mens, pectus, Cat. With GEN. : benefici, Ter. ; rerum gestarum, Cic. ; coniugis, Hor. ; Verg. ; quietis immemor nox traducta est, Liv. With *Inf. :* Pl. With Acc. and *Inf. :* Suet.

im-memorābĭlis, v. immemor-.

im-memorāta, ōrum, *n. pl. things unrecorded :* iuvat immemorata ferentem legi, Hor.

immensĭtās, ātis, *f.* [immēnsus], *immeasurableness :* latitudinum, longitudinum, Cic. In *pl. : immense stretches :* camporum, Cic.

im-mēnsus (inm-), a, um, *immeasurable, boundless, unfathomable, vast, immense :* magnitudo regionum, Cic. ; in mari immenso vehi, Cic. ; iacuitque per antrum immensus, Verg. ; tempus, Cic. ; nox, Ov. ; immensus ruit profundo Pindarus ore, Hor. *Neut.* Acc. as *Adv. :* creverat immensum, Ov. ; immensum attolli, Tac. *Neut.* Noun, **immensum,** i, *n. boundless extent, infinite space, immensity :* loci, Liv. ; per immensum ventis actus, Ov. ; Lucr. ;

proruta por immensum aedificia, Tac. ;
mons in immensum editus, Sall.
im-merēns (inm-), entis, adj. undeserving,
innocent : Ter., Hor., Suet. As Noun : Pl.
im-mergō mergere, mĕrsī, mĕrsum (Perf.
sync. immĕrstī, Pl.), to dip or plunge into ;
to immerse. **1.** Lit. : immersus in flumen,
Cic. ; nautas pelago, Ov. ; Verg. **2.**
T r a n s f. with Refl. Pron. **a.** Physically :
to throw or plunge oneself into : sese in
ganeum, Pl. **b.** se in alicuius consuetudinem, Cic.
im-meritō (inm-), adv. undeservedly, unjustly, without cause : Ter., Cic., Quint.
With neque or haud : Ter., Liv., Luc., etc.
im-meritus (inm-), a, um. **A.** A c t. :
undeserving, guiltless, innocent : Verg.,
Hor., Ov. With Inf. : Hor. As Noun :
inmerito meo, for no fault of mine, Pl. **B.**
P a s s. : undeserved, unmerited : laudes,
Liv. ; ope, Ov.
im-mersābilis, e, adj. [mĕrsō], that cannot
be sunk. T r a n s f. : (Ulixes) adversis
rerum immersabilis undis, Hor.
immersus, a, um, Part. immergō.
im-mētātus, a, um [metō], unmeasured :
iugera, Hor.
im-migrō (inm-), āre, to go or remove into.
1. Lit. : et in domum et in paternos
hortos, Cic. ; Pl. **2.** T r a n s f. : nulla res
publica fuit, in quam tam serae avaritia
luxuriaque immigraverint, Liv. ; Pl. ; Cic.
im-mineō (inm-), ēre, to project over or towards,
to overhang. **1.** Lit. : choros ducit Venus
imminente lunā, Hor. ; nemus, Verg. With
D a t. : collis urbi, Verg. ; imminens prope
ipsis moenibus tumulus, Liv. ; caelum orbi,
Ov. **2.** T r a n s f. **A.** to be near to, adjoin.
a. In space : imminet hic, sequiturque
parem, Ov. ; carcer imminens foro, Liv.
b. In time : to be near at hand, to impend :
sunt qui ea, quae imminent, non videant,
Cic. **B.** to threaten by nearness, to menace :
propter propinquitatem Aegina Piraeeo,
Cic. ; Parthi Latio, Hor. ; instabat agmen
Caesaris atque universum imminebat, Caes.
Of things : turris, Liv. ; bellum, Quint. ;
periculum, insidiae, Suet. **C.** to be grasping, come open-mouthed at : huius mendici-
tas aviditate coniunctā in nostras fortunas
imminebat, Cic. ; in exercitūs opprimendi
occasionem, Liv. ; exitio coniugis, Ov. ;
rebus, Tac. ; Verres avaritiā semper hiante
atque imminente fuit, Cic.
im-minuō (inm-), uere, uī, ūtum, to lessen,
diminish, impair. **1.** Lit. : exiguas copias, Cic. Ep. ; numerum, Liv. ; aestivorum tempus comitiorum mora imminu-
erat, Sall. ; verbum imminutum, Cic. **2.**
T r a n s f. **a.** to weaken, impair : vīrīs,
Lucr. ; mentem, Sall. ; corpus otio, animum libidinibus, Tac. **b.** to infringe,
impair (cf. Eng. ' make a hole in '), en-
croach upon : pudicitiam, Pl. ; bellum, ius
legationis, libertatem, Cic. ; auctoritatem,
Cic. Ep. ; suas res, Liv. ; pacem Bocchi,
Sall. ; Agrippa discidio domum imminu-
erat (i.e. the honour of), Tac.
imminūtiō, ōnis, f. [imminuō], a lessening,
mutilation. **1.** Lit. : corporis, Cic. **2.**
T r a n s f. : dignitatis, Cic. ; criminis, Quint.
R h e t. meiosis : Cic., Quint.

im-misceō (inm-), miscēre, miscuī, mixtum,
to mix in, intermix, intermingle, blend. **1.**
Lit. : inmixta corporibus semina, Lucr. ;
se nubi, Verg. ; manūs manibus, Verg. ;
summis ima, Ov ; immixti turbae militum togati, Liv. **2.** T r a n s f. : non fugienda petendis inmiscere, Hor. With
Refl. Pron. or in Mid. : ne adfinitatibus
immisceamur, Liv. ; Tac. ; se bello, Liv. ;
se conloquiis montanorum, Liv.
im-miserābilis, e, adj. unpitied : Hor.
immisericorditer, v. inmis-.
im-misericors, ordis, adj. pitiless, merciless : Cic.
immissiō, ōnis, f. [immittō], a letting grow :
sarmentorum, Cic.
immissus, a, um, Part. immittō.
im-mitis, e, adj. not soft or mellow, unripe.
1. Lit. Of fruits : uva, Hor. **2.** T r a n s f.
harsh, severe, stern, pitiless : naturā et
moribus immitis, Liv. ; Achilles, Verg. ;
caedes, Liv. ; mors, Tib. ; mandata, Tac. ;
insula, Tac. ; caelum, Plin. Ep. Neut.
pl. as Noun : Ov. Comp. : Ov., Tac.
Sup. : Plin.
im-mittō (inm-), mittere, mīsī, missum.
I. 1. Lit. to insert, let in, put in position.
a. tigna in flumen, Caes. ; aquam canali-
bus, Caes. ; coronam (of Ariadne) caelo,
Ov. **b.** to engraft : feracis plantas, Verg.
c. to let go free, let loose, launch : frena, habenas, Verg. ; immissae ferae silvis et sidora
caelo, Verg. In Mid. : se ad auras palmes
agit laxis per purum immissus habenis,
Verg. ; immissorum aliorum in alios ram-
orum, Liv. Of the hair : let grow : barba
immissa, Verg., Quint. ; capilli, Ov. **2.**
T r a n s f. to let pass : aliquid in auris (i.e.
to listen to), Pl. ; also without in : Pl. ;
corrector imprudens senarium (i.e. over-
looks), Cic. **II.** to let go against, let loose
at, launch against ; and with Refl. Pron.
to plunge into. **1.** Lit. : pila in hostis,
Caes. ; navis in classem, Caes. ; equos in
eos, Liv. ; servos ad spoliandum fanum,
Cic. ; scilicet tu praetor in mea bona, quos
voles, immittes ? Cic. ; corpus in undas,
Ov. ; armaturam levem in stationes, Liv. ;
in medios se immisit hostis, Cic. **2.**
T r a n s f. to let go against, set on, incite :
alii Tarquinium a Cicerone immissum aiebant, Sall. ; immissis qui monerent, Tac. ;
invidiā delator immissus, Plin. Ep. Of
feelings, to instil : fugam Teucris atrumque
timorem, Verg.
immixtus, a, um, Part. immisceō.
immo (older **immō**), a particle used in
making a correction of a previous question
or statement ; it is us. placed first in
the sentence. **I.** In a n s w e r s. **A.** Con-
firming and strengthening a preceding
question of negative colouring : yes, yes
indeed, certainly : G. haec tibi iam aderit
supplicans ultro. T. credin' ? G. immo
certe ; novi ingenium mulierum, Ter. ;
quaesivi viveretne ipse et ceteri ; immo
vero, inquit, ii vivunt, Cic. ; quid tu ?
nullane habes vitia ? immo alia et fortasse
minora, Hor. **B.** Denying and rejecting
with correction. **a.** Mostly after a preceding affirmative statement : no, nay
rather : ' e provinciā decedo ' ; ' ut opinor

ex Africâ'; 'immo ex Siciliâ,' Cic.; *T.* etiam fatetur de hospite ? *Th.* immo pernegat, Pl. **b.** To retort or reject a question : *nay rather, let me say rather, on the contrary : Me.* quid apud hasce aedis negoti est tibi ? *So.* immo quid tibi'st ? Pl.; causa igitur non bona est ? immo optima, Cic. Ep. **c.** Elliptically with *si : ah ! but if only :* immo si scias, Pl. **II.** In the middle of a sentence (correcting oneself) : *nay rather, or rather :* simulacra deum, deos immo ipsos convulsos ex sedibus suis ablatos esse, Liv.; Quint.

im-mŏbĭlis, *unshaken, motionless.* **1.** Lit.: terra, Cic.; obiecta res immobilis eos defixit, Liv. Also *hard to move or not moving easily ;* hence, *unwieldy :* arma, hasta, agmen, phalanx, Liv. *Comp. :* Ov. **2.** Transf.: ardet Ausonia immobilis ante, Verg.; stetit una integra atque immobilis virtus populi Romani, Liv.; immobilem se precibus ostendit, Tac.; adversum lasciviam vulgi, Tac.

immŏdĕrātē, *adv. without measure or limit.* **1.** Lit.: vox profusa, Cic. **2.** Transf.: iactari, Cic. *Comp. :* Cic. Ep.

im-mŏdĕrātĭō, ōnis, *f. want of moderation, excess :* verborum, Cic.

im-mŏdĕrātus (inm-), a, um, *unbounded, limitless.* **1.** Lit.: (of space) : Lucr. **2.** Transf. *unbounded, uncontrolled :* homo, intemperantia, oratio, tempestates, Cic.; potestas, Liv.; luxuria, Suet. *Sup. :* Suet.

immŏdestē (inm-, Pl.), *adv. immoderately, extravagantly :* amare, Pl.; gloriari, Liv.; Quint.

im-mŏdestĭa (inm-, Pl.), ae, *f. lack of restraint, license :* eri, Pl.; publicanorum, Tac.

im-mŏdestus (inm-), a, um, *unrestrained, uncontrolled :* in vino, Ter.; genus iocandi, Cic.; fautores histrionum, Tac.

immŏdĭcē, *adv. beyond measure, excessively :* Liv., Luc., Quint.

im-mŏdĭcus, a, um, *unbounded, unmeasured, excessive.* **1.** Lit.: rostrum, Ov.; tempestates, Suet. **2.** Transf. **a.** Of persons : in numero augendo, Liv.; immodicus linguâ, Liv.; saevitiâ, Tac. With GEN.: laetitiae et maeroris, Tac. **b.** Of things : lingua, imperia, cupido, Liv.; fastus, Ov.; oratio, Plin. Ep.

im-mŏdŭlātus, a, um, *unrhythmical, inharmonious :* Hor.

immŏlātĭō, ōnis, *f.* [immolō], *a sacrificing, sacrifice :* Cic. In *pl. :* Tac.

immŏlātor, ōris, *m.* [immolō], *a sacrificer :* Cic.

immŏlītus, a, um [mōlior], *built up, erected :* Liv.

immŏlō (inm-, Pl.), āre [mola], orig. *to sprinkle meal* (mola salsa) *on a victim ;* hence *to sacrifice, immolate.* **1.** Lit.: Cic., Suet. With ACC.: homines, Cic.; agnum, Hor.; dis magnis, Pl.; Musis bovem, Cic.; bovem Dianae, Liv. With ABL.: hostiis immolandum cuique deo, Cic.; Liv. *Impers. Pass. :* pluribus diis immolatur, Cic. **2;** Transf. *to immolate, slay :* Pallas ta hoc vulnere immolat, Verg.

im-morior, mori, mortuus, *to die upon.* **1.**

Lit.: illa sorori immoritur, Ov. **2.** Transf.: studiis, Hor.

im-moror, āri, *to stay in, upon, or at.* Transf.: *to dwell upon :* ne terrenis immorer, Quint.; cogitationibus, Plin. Ep.

immŏrsus, a, um [mordeō], *bitten into.* **1.** Lit.: Prop., Stat. **2.** Transf.: *stimulated :* stomachus, Hor.

im-mortālis (inm-), e, *adj. not subject to death, immortal.* **1.** Lit.: corpus, Cic.; dii (or di), Cic., Liv., etc.; genus, Verg.; pro di inmortales ! Ter.; Cic. As Noun (mostly in *pl.*) : Lucr., Cic., Liv. **2.** Transf. (of fame) : memoria, Cic.; opera, Liv.; immortalia ne speres, monet annus, Hor. ; of happiness : Prop.

immortālĭtās (inm-, Pl.), ātis, *f.* [immortālis], *exemption from death, immortality.* **1.** Lit.: Pl.; animorum, Cic. In *pl. :* Cic. **2.** Transf. (of fame) : mortem, quam immortalitas consequatur, Cic.; aliquid immortalitati commendare, tradere, Cic.; Liv.; Quint.; of happiness : Ter.

immortālĭter, *adv. infinitely :* gaudeo, Cic. Ep.

immortŭus, a, um, *Part.* immorior.

im-mōtus, a, um, *unmoved, immoveable, motionless.* **1.** Lit.: arbor immota manet Verg.; aquae, Ov.; mansit immota acies, Liv.; legio, dies, Tac. **2.** Transf.: mens, Verg.; immotas praebet mugitibus auris, Ov.; animus, vultus, Tac.; pax, Liv. In the *Neut. :* si mihi non animo fixum immotumque sederet, Verg.; Tac.

im-mūgĭō, ire, *to bellow, roar in or at :* Aetna cavernis, Verg.

im-mulgĕō, ēre, *to milk into :* teneris ubera labris, Verg.

immundĭtĭa, v. inmunditia.

im-mundus (inm-, Pl.), a, um, *unclean, dirty, filthy, foul.* **1.** Lit.: homo, Pl.; humus, Cic.; sues, Verg. *Comp. :* Cat. Sen. *Sup. :* Sen. Ep., Plin. Ep. **2.** Transf.: pauperies, dicta, Hor.

im-mūnĭō, ire, *to fortify in* a place : praesidium, Tac.

immūnis, e, *adj.* [mūnus], *without office or duty ; free or exempt from a public service, untaxed.* **1.** Lit.: civitates, Cic.; agri, Cic.; fucus, Verg. With ABL.: militiâ, Liv. With *ab :* ab omni onere, Suet. With GEN.: portoriorum, Liv.; Tac. **2.** Transf. **a.** *free or exempt* in gen. (but with idea of obligation), *not contributing a due share or what is expected :* virtus, Cic.; te meis immunem tingere poculis (i.e. without bringing your share), Hor.; quem scis immunem Cynarae placuisse rapaci (i.e. without presents), Hor. With GEN.: operum, Ov. **b.** *exempt, free* (without idea of obligation) : immunis aram si tetigit manus (i.e. exempt from dues in expiation of wrongdoing), Hor. With GEN.: urbem immunem tanti belli, Verg.; sequoris (Arctos), Ov.; caedis manus, Ov. With ABL.: animus tristitiâ, Sen. Ep. (v. also inmoenis.)

immūnĭtās, ātis, *f.* [immūnis], *freedom or exemption from public services or taxes, privilege.* **1.** Lit.: (Druides) militiae vacationem omniumque rerum habent immunitatem, Caes.; Cic.; Tac., etc. In *pl. :* Cic., Tac., Suet. **2.** Transf. (in

gen.): *freedom, exemption, immunity :*
magni muneris, Cic.

im-mūnītus, a, um. **I.** *unfortified, unde-*
fended : oppida, Liv.; Sparte, Ov. **II.**
unpaved : via, Cic.

im-murmurō, āre, *to murmur at* or *against :*
totumque immurmurat agmen, Ov.; with
Dat.: silvis Auster, Verg.; Ov.

(1) immūtābilis, e, *adj.* [immūtō], *v.* inmūtābilis.

(2) im-mūtābilis, e, *adj. unchangeable,*
unalterable : causae, res, spatia, Cic.;
ratio, Liv.; necessitas, Quint. *Comp. :*
Cic.

im-mūtābilitās, ātis, *f. unchangeableness,*
fixity : in factis, Cic.

immūtātiō, ōnis, *f.* [immūtō], *an exchanging,*
substitution. **a.** In gen.: ordinis, verborum, Cic. **b.** Rhet.: *metonymy :* Cic.,
Quint.

(1) immūtātus, a, um, *Part.* immūtō.

(2) im-mūtātus (inm-), a, um, *unchanged,*
unaltered (rare): id mutavit, quia me in-
mutatum videt, Ter.; Cic.

im-mūtō (inm-), āre, *to change, alter.* **a.**
In gen.: Pl.; vultum, Ter.; prosperis
rebus immutari, Cic.; aliquid de institutis
priorum, Cic. **b.** Rhet.: *to put one*
word for another by metonymy : pro Afris
immutat Africam, i.e. says 'Africa' when
he means the people of Africa, Cic.

im-pācātus, a, um, *restless :* Hiberos, Verg.

impactus, *Part.* impingō.

im-pallēscō, pallēscere, palluī, *to grow* or
turn pale at : with Abl.: Stat., Pers.

im-pār, aris, *adj. not paired ;* hence, **A.**
uneven, odd (as the numbers 3, 5, 7): stellarum numerus par an impar sit, nescitur,
Cic.; Verg.; ludere par impar, *to play at*
odd and even, Hor. **B.** *not equal* (in number, size, or length), *greater,* or *less :* congressus impari numero, Caes.; imparibus
intervallis, Cic.; imparibus carmina facta
modis, Ov.; mensae pes tertius, Ov.; toga
dissidet impar, Hor. **C.** *not matching, un-*
like in colour or appearance: acer coloribus
impar, Ov.; boves et uri, Verg.; hence,
inconsistent in conduct: nil fuit unquam sic
impar sibi, Hor. **D.** *not a match, unequal,*
inferior, weaker. **a.** In point of strength,
etc.: consilio et viribus impar, Liv.; Ov.
With Dat.: Achilles (Apollini) miles impar,
Hor.; dolori, Suet. **b.** In point of rank:
iuncta impari, Liv.; maternum genus, Tac.
c. Of a situation: *uneven :* videbam quam
impar esset sors (*the conditions*), Liv.; certamen, Ov.; pugna, Verg.

im-parātus (inp-), a, um, *not ready, un-*
provided, unfurnished : Pl., Ter., Cic. *Sup. :*
Caes. *Masc.* as Noun : Cic.

impariter, *adv. unequally :* versibus impariter iunctis (i.e. in hexameters and penta-
meters), Hor.

im-pāstus, a, um, *unfed, hungry :* leo, Verg.

im-patiēns, entis, *adj. that cannot bear, en-*
dure, or *suffer, impatient* (with Gen.) **a.**
Of persons: vulneris, Verg.; laborum,
Ov.; solis, pulveris, tempestatum, Tac.;
irae (i.e. of restraining anger), Ov. **b.** Of
things: cera impatiens caloris, Ov.; Luc.
Sup. : Plin.

impatienter, *adv. impatiently, intolerably :*

Tac., Plin. Ep. *Comp.* and *Sup. :* Plin.
Ep.

im-patientia, ae, *f. unwillingness* or *inability*
to bear, want of endurance : Tac. With *Obj.*
Gen.: Tac., Suet.

impavidē, *adv. fearlessly :* exhausto poculo,
Liv.

im-pavidus, a, um, *adj. fearless, undaunted.*
Of persons: Verg., Hor., Ov.; peditum
acies inter perculsos, Liv.; pectora, Liv.
Of things: leo, Verg.; stabant equi, Liv.

impedimentum (inp-), I, *n.* [impediō], *that*
which entangles or *hampers, a hindrance, im-*
pediment. **a.** In gen.: Cic., Liv., etc.;
impedimenta naturae, Cic.; also in *pl. :*
Liv.; alicui esse impedimento, Pl., Ter.;
alicui esse impedimento ad pugnam, Caes.;
ad dicendum, Cic.; Liv.; alicui inferre,
Cic.; adferre, Tac. With *quo minus* and
Subj. : Liv. **b.** (In *pl.*): *baggage, lug-*
gage : Cic. Milit. *the baggage, baggage-*
train : Caes., etc. Occ. *the pack-horses :*
Caes.

impediō (inp-), īre [root of pēs], *to entangle,*
ensnare, to shackle, hamper. **1.** Lit.:
sese in plagas, Pl.; reti piscis, Pl.; impediunt teneros vincula nulla pedes, Ov.;
sinistrā impeditā, satis commode pugnare
non poterant, Caes.; equos frenis, Ov. *v.*
also impeditus. **2.** Transf. **A.** Physically. **a.** *to entwine, encircle :* aliquem
amplexu, Ov.; caput myrto, Hor.; orbis
orbibus, Verg. **b.** *to obstruct, make im-*
passable : munitionibus saltum, Liv. **B.**
Immaterially. **a.** *to entangle, embarrass :*
stultitiā suā impeditus, Cic.; qui me et se
hisce inpedivit nuptiis, Ter. **b.** *to ob-*
struct, check, prevent, impede : Cic., Quint.;
studiis impediri, Cic.; rationem belli impedire, Cic.; navigationem (Corus), Caes.;
aliquem a vero bonoque, Sall.; Cic.; in
suo iure impediri, Caes.; quem dignitas
fugā impediverat, Tac.; with *ne* and
Subj. : id casus quidam, ne facerem, im-
pedivit, Cic.; Liv.; etc.; with *quo*
minus : Cic.; with *quin* (after negat.):
Cic. Ep.; with *Inf. :* Cic., Verg., Ov.

impeditiō, ōnis, *f.* [impediō], *a hindrance,*
obstruction : Cic.

impeditus (inp-), a, um. **I.** *Part.* impediō.
II. Adj. *hampered, obstructed, in difficul-*
ties. **A.** Physically. **a.** Of persons: Pl.;
impeditos adgredi, Caes.; itinere impediti,
Caes.; agmen, Liv. **b.** Of places: *ob-*
structing or *obstructed, blocked :* silvae,
locus, itinera, Caes.; saltus, Liv. *Comp. :*
Caes., Liv.; *Sup. :* Caes. **B.** Of immaterial things. **a.** *hampered, intricate, diffi-*
cult : navigatio, Caes.; disceptatio, Liv.;
bellum, Tac. **b.** *obstructed, obsessed, busily*
occupied : Ter.; omnium impeditis animis,
Caes., Cic.; solutione impeditā fides concidit, Cic.

impēiūrātus, *v.* imperūirātus.

im-pellō (inp-), pellere, pulī, pulsum. **I.** *to*
push, drive, or *strike against.* **1.** Lit.:
cuspide montem impulit in latus, Verg.;
aequora remis, Verg.; arbores, Liv. **2.**
Transf.: maternas auris luctus, Verg.;
auras mugitibus, Ov. **II.** *to drive on, set in*
motion, impel. **1.** Lit.: biremis vectibus,
Caes.; impellunt animae lintea Thraciae,

Hor. ; navem triplici versu, Verg. ; aciem, Liv. ; aequor velis, Tac. ; aliquem in fugam, Cic., Liv. **2.** T r a n s f. **a.** *to give a push to* (anything tottering, etc.) : praecipitantem impellamus, Cic. ; animum labantem, Verg. ; ruentem, Tac. ; animus huc illuc inpellitur, Ter. **b.** *to drive on, urge on, impel* (in gen.) : Cic., Quint. With *in* and Acc. : nisi eum di immortales in eam mentem impulissent, Cic. ; Quint. With *ad* : ad memoriam comprehendendam impulsi, Cic. ; Quint. With *ut* and *Subj.* : Germanos facile impelli ut in Galliam venirent, Caes. ; Cic. ; Hor. With *Inf.* : Verg., Liv., Tac., etc. With simple Acc. : Hor., Tac., etc. ; so in *Pass.* : amentiā impulsus, Caes. ; impulsus furiis, Verg.

im-pendeŏ (inp-), ēre, *to hang over, to overhang.* **1.** L i t. With DAT. : saxum Tantalo, Cic. ; mons altissimus (itineri), Caes. With Acc. : mare impendent saxa, Lucr. *Absol.* : Lucr. **2.** T r a n s f. *to hang over, to be near or imminent, to threaten.* With *in* and Acc. : in me terrores, Cic. ; Pl. With DAT. : omnibus terror, Cic. ; Pl. With Acc. : te mala, Ter. *Absol.* : vento impendente, Verg. ; magnum bellum impendet a Parthis, Cic. ; formidinis ora, Lucr.

impendiōsus (inp-), *v.* inpendiōsus.

impendium (inp-), i, *n.* [impendŏ]. **I.** In gen. : *deliberate outlay, cost, expense* (mostly in ABL.) : qui quaestum sibi instituisset sine impendio, Cic. ; tantulo impendio ingens victoria stetit, Curt. ; Liv. In *pl.* : reposcere rationem impendiorum, Quint. ; Cic. ABL. *sing.* as *Adv.* : l i t. *at a cost,* hence colloq. : *by a great deal, very much* (with comparatives) : at ille impendio nunc magis odit senatum, Cic. Ep. ; Pl. ; Ter. **II.** *interest paid on a loan.* **1.** L i t. : faenus et impendium recusare, Cic. Ep. In *pl.* : Cic. **2.** T r a n s f. : ut impendiis augere possimus largitatem tui muneris, Cic.

im-pendŏ (inp-), pendere, pendī, pēnsum, *to weigh out upon ; hence to spend (money) on.* **1.** L i t. : pecuniam in aliquam rem, Cic. ; certus sumptus impenditur, Cic. ; Pl. ; Liv. **2.** T r a n s f. : operam, curam in aliquid, Cic. ; nihil sanguinis in socios, Ov. ; vitam usui alicuius, Tac. ; curas (foll. by *Inf.*), Verg.

im-penetrābilis e, *adj. that cannot be penetrated.* **1.** L i t. : silex ferro, Liv. ; accipiendis ictibus, Tac. **2.** T r a n s f. : pudicitia, Tac.

impēnsa, ae, *f.* [impendŏ], *outlay, expense.* **1.** L i t. : impensam fecimus in macrocolla, Cic. Ep. ; sine impensā, Cic. ; arationes magnā impensā tueri, Cic. ; parcere impensae, Liv. ; cenarum, Hor. In *pl.* : Hor., Tac., etc. ; also *forms of expenditure* : Cic. **2.** T r a n s f. : operum, Verg. ; cruoris, Ov. ; officiorum, Liv.

impēnsē (inp-), *adv. at great cost, expensively.* **1.** L i t. : *Comp.* : Pers. *Sup.* : Suet. **2.** T r a n s f. *with great effort, eagerly* : retinere, Liv. ; petere, Quint. C o l l o q. : inprobus, Pl. ; aliquid cupore, Ter. *Comp.* : eo facio id impensius, Cic. Ep. ; consulere, Verg. ; agere gratias, Liv.

impēnsus (inp-), a, um. **I.** *Part.* impendŏ.

II. A d j. : (*freely*) *expended ; hence high, dear.* **1.** L i t. : impenso pretio, Caes., Cic. Ep., Liv. ; without pretio : Hor. **2.** T r a n s f. *earnest, eager :* libido, Lucr. ; voluntas, Cic., Liv. ; cura, Ov. ; preces, Suet. *Comp.* : Pl., Ov. *Sup.* : Suet.

imperātŏr (inp-), ōris, *m.* [perh. fr. O:L. induperātor : Lucr.], *a commander.* **1.** L i t. **a.** Orig. a milit. term, *a commander-in-chief, general :* Caes., Cic., etc. **b.** Esp. in the time of the republic, a title of honour conferred on a general after an important victory : Caes., Cic., Liv. Hence, placed after the name as a title : Cicero Imp. s. d. Caesari Imp., Cic. Ep. **c.** *the title of the Roman emperors* (which always preceded their names) as having absolute control of the military and naval forces : Suet. **2.** T r a n s f. **a.** In gen. *any commander, chief, director :* histricus, *stage-manager, director*, Pl. ; familiae, Pl. ; nolo eundem populum imperatorem et portitorem esse terrarum, Cic. ; imperator vitae mortalium animus est, Sall. **b.** In partic. of Jupiter : Cic., Liv. [Fr. empereur.]

imperātŏrius, a, um [imperātŏr]. **I.** *of a general :* consilium, laus, labor, Cic. ; partes, Caes. nomen, Cic. Ep. ; Tac. **II.** *imperial :* Suet.

imperātrix, īcis, *f. fem.* of imperātŏr : of Clodia : fortis viros ab imperatrice in insidiis locatos, Cic.

imperātum, I, *n.* [imperŏ], *a command, order :* imperatum (oftener imperata) facere, Caes. ; detrectare, Suet. ; ad imperatum, Caes.

im-perceptus, a, um, *unperceived, unknown :* Ov.

im-percŏ, *v.* inpercŏ.

im-percussus, a, um, *not striking loudly, noiseless :* pedes, Ov.

im-perditus, a, um, *not destroyed, not slain :* vos o Graiis imperdita corpora, Teucri, Verg.

im-perfectus (inp-), a, um, *unfinished, incomplete, imperfect :* vita, Lucr. ; pons, Caes. ; corpus, Cic. Ep. ; pars, Verg. ; sermo, Quint. ; cibus, Juv.

im-perfōssus, a, um, *unpierced, unstabbed :* Ov.

imperiōsus (inp-), a, um [imperium], *possessed of command.* **1.** L i t. : *imperial :* populi, Cic. ; dictatura, Liv. **2.** T r a n s f. **a.** Of self-control : sapiens, sibi qui imperiosus, Hor. **b.** *magisterial :* virga, Ov. **c.** *imperious, domineering, tyrannical :* Hor., Quint. ; cupiditas, Cic. ; aequor, Hor. *Comp.* : Pl., Hor. *Sup.* : Liv.

imperītē, *adv. unskilfully, ignorantly :* Cic. *Comp.* and *Sup.* : Cic.

im-perītia, ae, *f. inexperience, ignorance :* Sall., Quint., Tac., etc.

imperītŏ (inp-), āre [imperŏ]. **I.** *to exercise lordship :* Sall., Liv., Tac. With DAT. : gentibus, Lucr. ; nemori, Verg. ; alteri populo, Liv. ; equis, Hor. ; legionibus, Hor. *Impers. Pass.* : quod superbe avareque crederent imperitatum victis esse, Liv. ; quanto sit angustius imperitatum, Tac. **II.** *to order* (with *Intern.* Acc.) : aequam rem imperito, Hor. ; Pl.

im-perītus (inp-), a, um, *inexperienced, un-*

acquainted, unskilled, ignorant : Ter., Cic.,
Liv.; initium (poematis), Quint. With
GEN.: rerum, Ter.; nostrae consuetudinis,
Caes.; iuris, Cic.; morum, Cic.; nandi,
Liv., Tac. With *in :* in verbis, Quint.
Comp. : Cic., Quint. *Sup. :* Cic. As
Noun : Sall., Cic.

imperium (inp-), I, *n.* [imperō], *command,
order, exercise of authority.* **1.** Lit.:
inpera ; inperium exsequar, Pl.; imperio
parebant, Caes.; imperia iniusta, Sall.;
imperio Iovis huc venio, Verg.; imperiis
deum expositis, Liv. **2.** Transf. *the
power* or *right of commanding.* **A.** In gen. :
control, sovereignty, mastery : tenebat imperium in suos, Cic.; Pl.; Hor.; imperium iudiciorum tenere, Cic.; animi imperio, corporis servitio utimur, Sall.; imperia legum potentiora quam hominum,
Liv. **B.** Of political power. **a.** *sovereignty* (of individual or community):
totius Galliae imperio potiri, Caes.; civitatis imperium obtinere, Caes.; Numa de
suo imperio curiatam legem tulit, Cic.; sub
populi Romani imperium dicionemque
cadere, Cic.; cum duobus ducibus de imperio in Italiā decertatum est, Cic.; regere
imperio populos, Verg. **b.** Concr.
dominion, realm, empire : Cic., Verg., Tac.,
etc. **C.** Of political power delegated to
Roman officials. **a.** *the imperium,* the old
royal sovereignty temporarily held **i.** regularly by consuls and praetors (outside
Rome, except on occasion of a triumph),
ii. extraordinarily by dictators (inside and
outside Rome); it was dist. fr. other commands by its military powers: imperium,
sine quo res militaris administrari, teneri
exercitus, bellum geri non potest, Cic.;
de imperio Caesaris gravissime decernitur,
Caes.; alicui imperium dare, Cic.; mandare, deponere, Cic. Often opposed to
magistratus (*civil command*) : mandant
(cives) imperia, magistratūs, Cic. **b.**
period of office : continuare, Cic.; proro-
gare, Suet.; in istius imperio, Cic. **c.**
*an official holding the imperium, a com-
manding officer* (only in pl.) (*cf.* Eng. ' the
authorities,' 'High Command,' etc.) : imperia, potestates, legationes ex urbe exe-
unto, Cic.; erat plena lictorum et imperi-
orum provincia, Caes. **d.** (*cf.* B.) *the
supreme power :* tandem quasi coactus
recepit imperium, Suet. [Fr. *empire.*]

im-periūrātus, a, um, *that is never sworn
falsely by,* epithet of the Styx : aquae, Ov.

im-permissus, a, um, *unlawful, forbidden :*
gaudia, Hor.

im-perō (inp-), āre (old *Aor. Opt.* imper-
āssit, Cic.) [parō], *to impose as a burden or
tax,* etc.; hence, *to requisition, give orders
for.* **1.** Lit.: milites, frumentum, Caes.;
frumentum, stipendium, Liv.; obsides,
Caes., Cic. With Acc. of thing demanded
and DAT. of person *from whom :* mihi
exercitum (*trouble*), Pl.; obsides civitatibus, Caes.; Iugurthae pecuniam, Sall.;
frumentum civitati, Cic. **2.** Transf. **A.**
to command, order, enjoin : Pa. iubesne ?
Ch. iubeo, cogo atque impero, Ter.; fac
quod inperat, Pl.; Caes.; Hor. With
DAT. of person : si huic inperabo, Pl.;

and *ut* or *ne* and *Subj. :* Pl., Caes., Liv.,
etc.; with *Subj.* (without *ut*) : Caes., Ov.
With *Indir. Quest. :* Pl., Ter. With *Inf.*
(in Caes. and Cic. only *Pass. Inf.*): mihi
omnia adsentari, Ter.; has actuarias imperat fieri, Caes.; iungere equos Horis, Ov.;
Tac. In *Pass. :* in lautumias deduci im-
perantur, Cic.; haec procurare imperor,
Hor.; imperato quod res poposcisset, Liv.
Phr.: ad imperandum, *to receive orders :*
nunc ades ad imperandum, Cic. Ep.; ad
imperandum vocari, Sall. **B.** *to command,
govern, rule over.* **a.** Of nations, public
officers : magistratus, populus, Cic.; Hor.;
Quint. With DAT.: omnibus gentibus,
Cic.; Caes.; omni Numidiae, Sall. **b.**
In gen. *to command, master, govern :* liberis,
Ter.; cupiditatibus, Cic.; sibi, Sen. Ep.;
imperat arvis, Verg.; irae, Ov.; animo,
Liv.; dolori, Plin. Ep.; animum rege, qui,
nisi paret, imperat, Hor.

im-perterritus, a, um, *undaunted, unterri-
fied :* Verg.

im-pertiō (inp-), īre [pars; orig. = in
partem ducere]. **I.** With Acc. of person
and ABL. of thing : *to make one a sharer in,
to present with :* aliquem salute, Pl., Ter.;
aliquem donis, Suet. **II.** With Acc. of
thing and DAT. of person : *to give a share,
communicate, impart :* populo potestatis
aliquid, Cic.; Hor.; talem te nobis, Cic.;
aliis gaudium suum, Liv.; tantum temporis
huic studio, Cic.; auris studiis honestis,
Tac.; Terentia impertit tibi multam salutem, Cic. Ep. In *Pass. :* viro forti conlegae meo laus impertitur, Cic.; pro his
impertitis oppugnatum patriam nostram
veniunt, Liv.

im-perturbātus, a, um, *unruffled, calm.* Of
persons : Sen. Ep., Plin. Ep. Of things : im-
perturbato ore, Ov.; occupationibus quies,
Sen. Ep.

im-pervius, a, um, *impassable, impervious.*
1. Lit.: amnis, Ov.; itinera, Tac. **2.**
Transf.: lapis ignibus, Tac.

im-petibilis, e, *adj.* [patior], *insufferable :*
dolor, Cic.

im-petō, ere, *to make for ; to assail, attack :*
fuci, Varr.; aliquem arcu, Luc.

impetrābilis (inp-), e, *adj.* [impetrō]. **A.**
Pass.: *obtainable :* triumphus, venia,
pax, Liv.; votum, Prop. *Comp. :* Liv.
B. Act.: *able to obtain, successful .* orator,
Pl. Transf.: dies, Pl.

impetrātiō, ōnis, *f.* *an obtaining by request :*
in *pl. :* Cic.

impetriō (inp-), īre [impetrō]. Relig. *to
seek to obtain by favourable omens :* Pl., Cic.

im-petrō (inp-), āre (old *Inf. Fut.* inpetrās-
sere, Pl.) [patrō]. **I.** *to accomplish, effect,
bring to pass :* incipere multo est quam in-
petrare facilius, Pl. **II.** *to get, obtain, pro-
cure* (by asking or entreating). With
Acc.: quod volui, ut volo, inpetravi a
Philocomasio, Pl.; a me istam exceptionem
nunquam impetrabunt, Cic.; Caes.; Hor.
With *ut* or *ne* and *Subj. :* Pl., Cic. Ep.,
Caes., etc. With *Subj.* (without *ut*) : Pl.
Impers. Pass. : Caes.; in ABL. of *Perf.
Part. :* impetrato, ut maneret, Liv. With
Acc. and (*Pass.*) *Inf. :* Tac. *Absol. :* Pl.,
Caes., Cic.

11*

impetus (inp-), ūs, *m.* (old GEN. *sing.* impetis, Lucr.: ABL. impete, Lucr., Ov.) [impetō], lit. *a making for,* hence, *an attack, assault, charge, onset.* **1.** Lit.: armatorum, Cic.; facere in aliquem, Caes.; ad aliquem, in agros, Liv.; dare impetum in aliquem, Liv.; ferre, sustinere, excipere, Caes.; propulsare, Cic.; frangere, Cic. Ep. **2.** Transf. (without ref. to an object), *violent impulse, violent or rapid motion, rush, violence.* **a.** Physical: in magno impetu maris atque aperto, Caes.; impetus caeli, Lucr., Cic.; tantos impetūs ventorum, Caes. **b.** Mental: *impulse, vehemence, passion,* etc. *Sing.*: addere, Liv.; repentino quodam impetu animi incitatus, Cic.; divinus, Cic.; dicendi, Cic.; est mihi per saevas impetus ire feras, Ov.; impetu magis quam consilio, Liv.; famae, Tac. *Plur.*: animalia habent suos impetūs, Cic.; insanos impetūs vulgi cohibere, Cic.

im-pexus, a, um, *uncombed.* **1.** Lit.: barba, Verg.; porrigo, Hor. **2.** Transf.: antiquitas, Tac.

impiē, *adv. impiously, undutifully, disloyally :* Cic., Quint., Suet.

im-pietās, ātis, *f. want of right feeling towards.* **a.** *parents : unfilial conduct :* Ov., Quint. **b.** *the State* (or *Emperor*) *: disloyalty :* duces impietatis, Cic.; impietas in principem, Tac. **c.** *the gods : impiety :* in deos, Cic.

im-piger, gra, grum, *not indolent ; active, energetic, indefatigable.* **1.** Lit. Of persons : Cic., Hor., etc. With *in* and ABL.: in scribendo, Cic. Ep. With ABL.: impiger manu, Tac. With *ad :* ad labores belli, Cic.; Luc. With a limiting GEN.: militiae, Tac. With *Inf.:* Hor. **2.** Transf. Of things: equus, Lucr.; mens, Lucr.; militia, Liv.

impigrē (inp-), *adv. actively, energetically :* Pl., Sall., Liv.

impigritās, ātis, *f.* [impiger], *activity, energy :* Cic.

im-pingō (inp-), pingere, pēgī, pāctum [pango]. **I.** *to make fast on :* huic compedes, Pl. **II.** *to pin against, to force, thrust,* or *dash against.* **1.** Lit. **a.** In gen.: pugnum in os inpinge, Pl.; in vallum impingerentur, Tac.; hostem in aciem, Liv.; agmina muris, Verg. **b.** *to force upon a person :* huic calix mulsi impingendus est, Cic.; clitellas ferus, Hor. **2.** Transf. *to dash* or *fling at :* dicam tibi grandem, Ter.; aliquem in litem, Sen. Ep.

impiō (inp-), āre [impius], *to make impious* or *undutiful :* erga parentem aut deos me, Pl.

im-pius (inp-), a, um, *without right feeling towards parents and relations, country* or *king,* or *gods.* **1.** Lit. **a.** *unfilial, undutiful :* Cic., Hor., Suet. **b.** *unpatriotic, disloyal :* Cic. **c.** *impious :* Caes., Cic., Hor. Masc. *pl.* as Noun : *unscrupulous rogues :* Pl. **2.** Transf. **a.** Of things: propinquorum manus, Cic.; bellum, Cic.; furor, Verg.; Tartara (occupied by impii), Verg.; fama, Verg.; caedes, tumultus, Hor. **b.** *invoked in curses :* dii, Tac. **c.** *without natural love for* (his farm) : miles, Verg.

im-plācābilis, e, *adj. unappeasable, implacable :* inimicitiae, Cic. Ep.; Turnus, Verg.; numen, Ov.; implacabilis esse alicui, Cic., Liv.; in aliquem, Cic. Ep., Liv.; veteri delicto, Liv.

implācābilius, *comp. adv. more implacably :* Tac.

im-plācātus, a, um, *unappeased, unsatisfied :* Verg., Ov.

im-placidus, a, um, *ungentle, savage :* genus, Hor. *Sup.* : Stat.

im-pleō (inp-), ēre, ēvī, ētum (*syncop.* forms, implērunt, implēssem, etc. are not uncommon), *to fill in, fill up.* **1.** Lit. **a.** In gen.: de iustitiā quattuor libros, Cic.; fusti caput, Pl.; gremium frustis, Cic.; mero pateram, Verg.; cibis venas, Liv.; navis sociis, Liv.; navibus omnem oram Italiae, Liv. Occ. with GEN. of material : ollam denariorum, Cic. **b.** *to fill* with food, *to satisfy, satiate ;* esp. in Mid. : implentur veteris Bacchi pinguisque ferinae, Verg.; Juv. **c.** *to fill out, fatten :* nascentes implent conchylia lunae, Hor. **d.** *to impregnate :* (Peleus Thetidem) implet Achille, Ov. **2.** Transf. **a.** In gen. : acta Herculis implerant terras, Ov.; vestigia alicuius, Plin. Ep.; orbem terrarum nominis sui gloriā, Cic.; scopulos vocibus, Verg.; urbem nomine meo, Hor.; urbem tumultu, Liv.; omnia terrore, Liv.; maria terrasque fugā, Liv. With GEN. of abstr. noun : adulescentem temeritatis, Liv. **b.** *to fill, satisfy :* non semper Demosthenes auris meas, Cic.; milites praedā, Liv.; desideria naturae, Curt.; dolorem lacrimis, Tac. **c.** *to fill up* a portion of time or a number, *to complete :* puer, qui nondum impleverat annum, Ov.; Hor.; impleta si essent sex milia, Liv.; numerum, Juv.; finem vitae, Tac. **d.** *to fulfil, discharge :* ne id profiteri videar, quod non possim implere, Cic.; fata, Liv.; partis offici, Plin. Ep.; consilium, Tac.; munia sua, Tac. **e.** *to contaminate :* urbs impletur (contagione morbi), Liv.; medullas (nequitia), Juv. [It. *empiere.*]

implexus, a, um [plexus, plectō], *enfolded, entwined.* **1.** Lit.: caeruleos implexae crinibus anguis, Verg. **2.** Transf.: vidua implexa luctu, Tac.

implicātiō, ōnis, *f.* [implicō], *an entwining, entanglement.* **1.** Lit.: nervorum, Cic. **2.** Transf.: rei familiaris, Cic.

implicātus, a, um. **I.** *Part.* implicō. **II.** *Adj. involved, confused :* nec in sermone quicquam implicatum fuit, Cic.

implicīscor, ī [implicō], *to grow confused, disordered :* Pl.

implicitē, *adv. intricately :* Cic.

implicitus, a, um, *Part.* implicō.

im-plicō (inp-), āre, āvī, ātum, and (esp. post-Aug.) āre, uī, itum, *to enfold, involve, entangle, entwine, envelop.* **1.** Lit.: involvulus in folio se, Pl.; nunc huc, inde huc incertos implicat orbis, Verg.; materno bracchia collo, Ov.; comam laevā, Verg.; crinem auro, Verg.; dextrae se parvus Iulus, Verg.; implicare ac perturbare aciem, Sall. In *Perf. Part.* : quini erant ordines coniuncti inter se atque implicati, Caes. **2.** Transf. **a.** In gen.: *to en-*

tangle, involve, develop : di immortales vim suam hominum naturis implicant, Cic. ; multis implicari erroribus, Cic. ; bello, Verg. In *Perf. Part.:* Deus nullis occupationibus est implicatus, Cic. ; morbo implicitus, Lucr., Caes., Liv., etc. ; also, in morbum, Nep., Liv. **b.** *to attach closely, connect intimately, to unite, join :* omnes qui nostris familiaritatibus implicantur, Cic. In *Perf. Part. :* implicatus familiaritate, Cic. ; amicitiā, benevolentiā, Cic. Ep. [It. *impiegare,* Fr. *employer.*]

implōrātiō, ōnis, *f.* [implōrō], *a beseeching for help, imploring :* deorum et hominum, Cic. ; Quint.

im-plōrō, āre, *to invoke with tears, call to one's assistance, call upon for aid.* **A.** With personal objects : quem implorem ? Cic. ; Caes. ; aliquem auxilium implorare, Liv. ; a Veiis exercitum Camillumque ducem implorabunt, Liv. **B.** With inanim. or abstr. objects : *to beseech, entreat, appeal to or for :* misericordiam, fidem, dignitatem, etc., Cic. ; auxilium a populo Romano, Caes. ; leges, Liv. ; caelestis aquas, Hor.

implūmis, e, *adj.* [plūma], *without feathers, unfledged :* Hor., Ov.

im-pluō (inp-), uere, uī, ūtum, *to rain into* or *upon.* Transf. : Peneus summas aspergine silvas, Ov. With *Intern.* Acc. : malum quom inpluit ceteris, ne inpluat mihi, Pl.

impluviātus, *v.* inpluviātus.

impluvium (inpl-), ī, *n.* [impluō]. **I.** *an opening in the roof of the atrium of a Roman house :* Pl., Ter. **II.** *a rectangular basin in the atrium which received the rain-water.* **1.** Lit. : Cic., Liv. **2.** Transf. *the uncovered space in the atrium, including the* impluvium : Liv.

impolītē, *adv. without ornament :* dicere, Cic.

im-polītus, a, um, *unpolished, rough.* **1.** Lit. : lapis, Quint. **2.** Transf. : genus (magistrorum), Cic. ; Quint. ; forma (orationis), Cic.

im-pollūtus, a, um, *unstained :* virginitas, Tac.

im-pōnō (inp-), pōnere, posuī, positum (old forms of *Perf.* inposīvit, inposīsse, Pl. Syncop. *Part.* impostus, Lucr., Verg.), *to place, put, set,* or *lay upon* or *in.* **1.** Lit. **a.** In gen. : pedem in undam, Pl. ; aliquem in rogum, Cic. ; aliquid in foco, Pl. With *supra :* Ter., Ov., Liv., etc. With *insuper :* Verg., Liv. Mostly with DAT. of thing *on which :* conlegae diadema, Cic. ; pondera nobis, Liv. ; iuvenis rogis, Verg. ; Pelion Olympo, Hor. ; raptos caelo, Ov. Sometimes with an *Adv.* instead of DAT. : eo mulieres imposuerunt, Caes. **b.** *to put on board ship, to embark :* aliquid in navem, Pl. ; legiones in navis, Caes. ; deprehensis navibus circiter L atque eo militibus impositis, Caes. ; nos cumbae, Hor. **2.** Transf. **a.** In gen. : *to lay* or *put upon :* onus observantiae Bruto, Cic. Ep. ; rei publicae vulnera, Cic. ; labores sibi, Caes. ; leges civitati per vim, Cic. ; cognata vocabula rebus, Hor. ; finem spei, Liv. ; modum dolori, Plin. Ep. **b.** *to set over, as overseer, commander, etc. :* vilicum,

Cic. ; devictis triginta viros, Sall. ; Macedoniae regem, Liv. **c.** *to lay* or *impose a tax, etc. :* stipendium victis, Caes. ; agris vectigal, Cic. ; tributa genti, Suet. **d.** With DAT. of pers. only : *to put upon,* i.e. *palm something off upon anyone ; to impose upon, deceive :* Catoni egregie imposuit Milo noster, Cic. Ep. ; Juv., etc. ; (eis) luxuria specie liberalitatis, Tac.

im-portō, āre, *to bring, carry,* or *convey in, import from abroad.* **1.** Lit. : vinum ad se, Caes. ; commeatūs in oppidum, Caes. **2.** Transf. **a.** *to bring in* or *upon :* calamitatem alicui, Cic. ; odium libellis, Hor. ; fraudem aut periculum, Liv. **b.** *to import :* importantur non merces solum adventiciae, sed etiam mores, Cic.

importūnitās (inp-), ātis, *f.* [importūnus]. **I.** *annoying insistence :* Ter. **II.** Of character : *want of consideration* (for others), *ill-nature, ruthlessness :* Pl., Cic., Sall.

importūnus (inp-), a, um [cf. opportunus]. **1.** Lit. : *unsuitable, inconvenient.* **a.** Of place : aggeribus turribusque locus, Sall. ; sedes huic sermoni, Cic. ; Tac. **b.** Of time : tempus, Cic. **2.** Transf. **a.** *ill-omened :* bubo, Verg. ; Hor. **b.** *troublesome, distressing :* tempestas, Pl. ; pauperies, Hor. **c.** Of character : *wanting in consideration* or *respect for others : ill-natured, cross-grained, harsh, bullying, ruthless :* **i.** Of persons : Pl., Cic., Hor., etc. *Sup. :* Liv. **ii.** Of things : natura, libidines, Cic. ; mors, Ov. ; sitis famesque argenti, Hor.

im-portuōsus, a, um, *without a harbour :* mare, Sall., Tac. ; litus, Liv.

impos, otis, *adj.* [cf. compos], *not master, without control :* homo, animi impos, Pl. ; sui, Sen. Ep.

impositus, a, um, *Part.* impōnō.

im-possibilis, e, *adj. impossible :* Quint.

impostus = impositus.

im-potēns (inp-), entis, *adj. powerless, impotent, feeble.* **I.** In gen. : Cic., Hor. With GEN. : gens impotens rerum suarum, Liv. ; amoris, Tac. ; regendi (equos), Liv. **II.** *having no control over oneself* (sc. sui), *headstrong, wild, violent, ungovernable.* **1.** Lit. Of persons : Ter., Cic., Quint. *Comp. :* Cic. Ep. *Sup. :* Cic. With *Inf. :* Hor. **2.** Transf. Of things : animus, laetitia, Cic. ; dominatus, Cic. Ep. ; rabies, postulatum, Liv. ; iussa mulierum, Tac. ; amor, Cat. ; Aquilo, Hor. *Comp. :* Liv. *Sup. :* Cic. Ep., Quint.

impotenter, *adv.* **I.** *powerlessly :* elephantos impotentius regi, Liv. **II.** *passionately, violently, intemperately :* aliquid facere, dicere, Quint.

impotentia (inp-), ae, *f.* [impotēns]. **I.** *want of means, poverty :* Ter. **II.** *want of self-control, ungovernableness, violence :* animi, Cic. ; muliebris, Liv., Tac.

impraesentiārum, *adv.* prob. for in praesentiā hārum (rerum), *for the present, in present circumstances :* Cato, Nep., Tac.

im-prānsus (inp-), a, um, *without breakfast, fasting :* Pl., Hor.

imprecātiō, ōnis, *f.* [imprecor], *an invoking of evil, curse :* Sen. Ep.

im-precor, ārī, *to invoke* (a curse) : alicui

diras, Tac.; litora litoribus contraria, fluctibus undas imprecor, Verg.

impressiō, ōnis, *f*. [imprimō], *a pressing into or upon*. **1.** Lit. (in hostile sense): *thrust, pressure :* Cic.; facere, Varr., Hirt., Liv.; dare, ferre, Liv.; impressione pulsi, Liv. **2.** Transf. **a.** *an impression* (made on the mind by phenomena): Cic. **b.** *emphasis :* vocum, Cic. **c.** *a beat, time-division* in rhythm : Cic.

impressus, a, um, *Part.* imprimō.

imprīmīs [later spelling for **in prīmīs**], *adv. in the first place, chiefly, especially :* ut erat in primis inter suos copiosus, Cic.; in primis arduum videtur res gestas scribere, Sall.

im-prīmō, primere, pressi, pressum [premō]. **I.** *to press into* or *upon*. **1.** Lit.: muris aratrum, Hor.; impresso genu nitens, Verg.; Dido os impressa toro, Verg.; signo impressae tabellae, Liv. **2.** Transf.: flagitiorum vestigiis Italiam, Cic.; quasi ceram animum, Cic. **II.** *to make by pressing, imprint.* **1.** Lit.: vestigium, Cic.; in eius modi cerā centum sigilla hoc anulo, Cic.; notam labris dente, Hor. **2.** Transf.: fortitudinis impressa vestigia, Cic.; quorum lectione duplex imprimeretur rei publicae dedecus, Cic.; menti impressa, Cic.; in omnium animis eorum notionem, Cic. [Fr. *empreindre.*]

im-probābilis, e, *adj. not deserving of approbation :* motus animi, Sen. Ep.

improbātiō, ōnis, *f.* [improbō], *disapprobation, blame :* Cic.

improbē, *adv. not according to standard.* **1.** Lit. *Comp. :* Suet. **2.** Transf. **a.** *badly, wrongfully :* Cic., Quint. *Comp.* and *Sup. :* Cic. **b.** *persistently, pressingly :* Quint. *Comp. :* Cat.

improbitās, ātis, *f.* [improbus], *bad quality.* **a.** Of persons : *depravity :* Cic., Ov., etc. **b.** Of animals : *rascality :* simiae Dodoneae, Cic.

improbō, āre [improbus], *to think bad : to disapprove, blame, condemn, reject :* consilium, Caes.; ista studia, iudicium, Cic.; (Nymphas) pastor, Ov. Without Acc. : Caes., Quint.

improbulus, a, um [*dim.* improbus], *roguishly inclined :* Juv.

im-probus (inp-), a, um, *not good, below standard, of poor quality.* **I.** Of wares, building materials, etc. : Pl., Mart. *Comp. :* Pl. **II.** Of living beings and their acts, words, etc. : *bad* (as not conforming to social and political standards of respe atability, right conduct, and sense of order; the exact sense being given by the context). **a.** In gen. : *bad, perverse, shameless :* Pl., Cic., Ov., etc. *Sup. :* Cic. **b.** Polit. : *disloyal, rebellious, unruly, unpatriotic :* improbi as Noun, freq. opp. to boni, Cic.; *cf.* improbo iracundior Hadriā (*unruly*), Hor. **c.** *bad, unfeeling, cruel, merciless :* Cic. Ep., and very freq. in Verg. (*cf.* also mons, Verg.). **d.** *persistent, self-willed :* Verg. (*cf.* labor, almost personified : Verg.; divitiae, *insatiate*, Hor.) Of feelings : *importunate :* Verg., Quint. **e.** Applied playfully (*cf.* Eng. 'rascal,' 'naughty') : perh. in puer (Amor) improbus ille, Verg.; freq. in Ov. and Mart.

im-procērus, a, um, *not tall, undersized :* pecora, Tac.

im-prōdictus, a, um, *not postponed :* dies, Cic.

im-professus, a, um, *that has not openly declared himself :* Suet.

im-prōmptus, a, um, *not ready :* Tac.; linguā impromptus, Liv.

im-properātus, a, um, *not hurried, lingering :* vestigia, Verg.

im-proprius, a, um, *unsuitable :* nomen, verba, Quint. *Neut.* as Noun, *impropriety :* Quint.; in *pl. :* Quint.

im-prosper, era, erum, *unfortunate, unprosperous :* fortuna, Tac.

improsperē, *adv. unfortunately :* Tac.

imprōvidē, *adv. without foresight, recklessly :* Liv.

im-prōvidus, a, um, *not foreseeing, not anticipating, not providing for something :* senes, Cic.; aetas puerorum, Lucr.; Cic.; improvidos hostis opprimere, Liv.; pectora, Verg.; festinatio, Liv. With GEN. : improvidus futuri certaminis, Liv.; Tac.

im-prōvisus, a, um, *unforeseen, unexpected :* pericula, bella, etc., Cic.; improvisior postis, Tac.; improvisi aderunt, Verg. *Neut. pl.* as Noun, *emergencies :* Tac. Phr. : **dē imprōvisō** (Ter., Caes., Cic.), **ex imprōvisō** (Pl., Cic., Liv.), **imprōvisō** (Pl., Cic., Verg., etc.), *unexpectedly.*

im-prūdēns (inp-), entis, *adj.* **I.** *not foreseeing, not anticipating* or *expecting :* equites imprudentis atque inopinantis hostis adgrediuntur, Caes.; Pl.; nunquam imprudentibus imber obfuit, Verg. **II.** *not knowing, ignorant, unaware :* haec omnia imprudente L. Sullā facta esse, Cic.; Ter. With GEN. : legis, Cic.; laborum, Verg.; maris, Liv. **III.** *without prudence* or *wisdom :* Quint. *Comp.* and *Sup. :* Sen.

imprūdenter, *adv.* **I.** *without foresight :* Nep. **II.** *unknowingly, unawares. Comp. :* Ter. **III.** *without consideration, unwisely :* Caes. ap. Cic. Ep.

im-prūdentia (inp-), ae, *f.* **I.** *want of foresight, inadvertence :* Caes. **II.** *want of knowledge :* Ter., Cic. With GEN. : Liv. **III.** *want of consideration, want of wisdom* or *purpose :* Cic. With GEN. : imprudentia teli emissi, Cic.

im-pūbes, eris (Caes., Cic.) and **im-pūbēs**, is (Lucr., Verg., Liv., etc.), *adj.* **I.** *under the age of puberty.* **1.** Lit. : Cic., Verg., etc. Often as Noun. **2.** Transf. Of things : *youthful :* corpus, Hor.; malae, Verg.; anni, Ov. **II.** *virgin, unmarried :* qui diutissime impuberes permanserunt, Caes.

im-pudēns (inp-), entis, *adj. without shame, shameless.* **1.** Lit. : Pl., Cic., Hor. *Comp. :* Cic. **2.** Transf. Of things : audacia, Pl.; Ter.; mendacium, Cic. *Comp. :* Pl. *Sup. :* oratio, Ter., Cic.; calumniae, Liv.

impudenter, *adv. shamelessly :* Pl., Ter., Cic. *Comp. :* Cic. Ep.; *Sup. :* Cic.

impudentia (inp-), ae, *f.* [impudēns], *shamelessness, impudence :* Pl., Caes., Cic.

impudīcitia (inp-), ae, *f.* [impudicus], *unchasteness, immodesty, lewdness :* Pl., Tac., Suet.

im-pudicus (inp-), a, um. **I.** *shameless :* facinus, Pl. **II.** *unchaste, immodest, lewd :* Pl., Cic. *Comp. :* Pl. ; *Sup. :* Cic.

impugnātĭō, ōnis, *f.* [impugnō], *an attack, assault :* Cic. Ep.

im-pugnō, āre, *to attack, assail.* **1.** L i t. (milit.) : nostri acrius impugnare coeperunt, Caes. ; terga hostium, Liv. **2.** T r a n s f. (non-milit.) : Cic. ; dignitatem alicuius, Cic. ; acerrime regem, Sall. ; meritum et fidem, Ov. ; sententiam, Tac.

impulsĭō, ōnis, *f.* [impellō], *a pushing against, pressure.* **1.** L i t. : Cic. **2.** T r a n s f. **a.** Mental : *incitement, impulse :* Cic. **b.** R h e t. : ad hilaritatem, Cic.

impulsor (inp-), ōris, *m.* [impellō], *an inciter :* Ter. With GEN. : sceleris, Cic. ; pravi, Tac.

impulsus, a, um, *Part.* impellō.

impulsus ūs, *m.* [impellō], *a pushing* or *striking against, a pressure, shock, impulse* (almost alw. in ABL. *sing.*) : sonus qui impulsu et motu orbium conficitur, Cic. ; scutorum, Cic. T r a n s f. : *incitement :* vostro impulsu, Ter. ; eorum impulsu, Caes. ; Cic.

impūne (inp-), *adv. without punishment, without fear of punishment, with impunity.* **1.** L i t. : Pl., Cic., Tac., etc. *Comp. :* Pl., Cic. *Sup. :* Pl. **2.** T r a n s f. *safely, without restraint :* Verg., Hor. *Comp. :* Cic.

impūnĭtās, ātis, *f. freedom* or *safety from punishment, impunity :* alicui dare, Cic. ; concedere, Caes. With GEN. : flagitiorum, peccandi, Cic. ; Tac.

impūnĭtē, *adv. with impunity :* Cic.

im-pūnītus, a, um, *unpunished.* **1.** L i t. **a.** Of persons : *Comp. :* Hor. **b.** Of things : iniuria, scelera, etc., Cic. ; fuga, Liv. ; Tac. *Comp. :* Liv. **2.** T r a n s f. *unrestrained :* mendacium, libertas, Cic.

impūrē, *adv. impurely, vilely :* vivere, Cic. *Sup. :* Cic. Ep.

im-pūrĭtās, ātis, *f.* (moral), *impurity :* in *pl. :* Cic.

im-pūrus (inp-), a, um, *unclean, filthy, foul.* **1.** L i t. : Ov. **2.** T r a n s f. (morally) *impure, filthy, infamous, vile.* **a.** Of persons : Pl., Ter., Cic. *Comp.* and *Sup. :* Cic. **b.** Of things : animus, Sall. ; mores, Cat. ; historia, Ov.

im-putātus, a, um, *unpruned, untrimmed :* vinea, Hor.

im-putō, āre, *to bring into reckoning, enter in an account, to reckon, charge.* T r a n s f. (with DAT. of person). **a.** *to put down to a person's account, to ascribe as a merit or fault, to give the credit or blame for :* alicui moras belli, Tac. ; Ov., etc. **b.** *to put down to a person's charge,* i.e. *as a favour granted to him ; to expect a person to be grateful for a thing* (*cf.* obligare) : noli imputare vanum beneficium mihi, Phaedr. ; gaudet muneribus sed nec data imputant nec accepti obligantur, Tac. **c.** *to take the credit of :* alii transeunt quaedam imputantque quod transeant, Plin. Ep. ; Suet.

imulus, a, um [*dim.* imus], imula oricilla, *dainty little ear-tip,* Cat.

imus, a, um [*Sup.* of inferus], *deepest, undermost.* **1.** L i t. : terra imā sede semper

haeret, Cic. ; in fundo imo, Verg. ; vox or chorda (= *highest*), Hor. ; conviva (*v.* triclinium), Hor. But, ad imam quercum, *at the foot of the oak,* Phaedr. ; so, ab imo pectore, Verg. *Neut.* as Noun, *the bottom :* locus erat paulatim ab imo acclivis, Caes. ; murum ab imo ad summum, Liv. ; ima summis mutare, Hor. With, GEN. : inter ima pedis, Verg. **2.** T r a n s f. Of time : *the last :* mensis, Ov. *Neut.* as Noun : servetur ad imum, Hor. ; also as *Adv. Phr.,* ad imum, *at last,* Hor.

(1) in-, *not* (found only in compounds ; in form it follows the lines of the *prep.* in) [*cf.* Gk. ἀ-]. N.B. three types of negative formation. **a.** Purely negat. words, e.g. insons, *not guilty,* from in and sons, *guilty.* **b.** When the second part of the compound is a participle, a notion of continuation arises, e.g. invictus, *unconquered,* comes to mean *unconquerable.* **c.** Mutilated words, e.g. inermis, from in and arma : *not having any weapons.*

(2) in (old forms endo and indu, Enn., Lucr.) [*cf.* Gk. ἐν], *adv.* and *prep.* **I.** A d v. only in compounds. **A.** F o r m. **a.** ind- and indu- are seen in indigere, indipisci, indigena and O.L. induperator. **b.** *in* before *gn* or *n* representing gn loses its *n :* ignoscere. **c.** *in* before *b, m, p,* becomes *im* (exc. occasionally in early Latin) : imbibere, immittere, imponere. **d.** *in* before *l* and *r* remains unchanged : inrumpere, inlatus. **e.** *in* before *f* and *s* becomes in : inferre, inserere. **f.** *in* before other letters is unchanged. **B.** M e a n i n g. **a.** *in* or *into :* inesse, inire. **b.** *in* or *into* (with added notion of limited space) : inhibere, includere. **c.** *on* or *on to, at, over :* inniti, incidere ; metaph. indormitare. **d.** *towards, in direction of :* incedere, intendere. **e.** Often implies hostility : *against :* invadere, incurrere, invidere, imprecari. **f.** Of *causation : bringing into a state, developing towards* (*cf.* Eng. *en-,* esp. in denominal verbs. e.g. *enslave, ennoble*). **i.** In denominal verbs : inescare, instaurare, incusare, impedire, infuscare ; also in a few *Adj. :* incanus, inclutus. **ii.** On pattern of these verbs : incendere and occ. intendere. **g.** Hence, esp. with verbs of inceptive meaning, *tending to, working up to, starting on ;* very freq. after Cic., e.g. inlucescere, Liv. (lucescere, Cic.), innotescere ; occ. of partial or limited action : intremere, immutare, incipere. **II.** P r e p. (with LOCAT. ABL., or ACC.). **A.** With LOCAT. ABL. to denote a fixed point or place. **1.** L i t. Of space : *in, on, among :* plures in eo loco sine vulnere quam in proelio aut fugā intereunt, Caes. ; sedere in equo, Cic. ; in eo flumine pons erat, Caes. With names of places : navis in Caietā est parata nobis, Cic. Ep. **2.** T r a n s f. **a.** Of time, indicating a fixed or limited point or period : *in, during, in the course of :* feci ego istaec itidem in adulescentiā, Pl. ; in omni aetate, Cic. P h r. : in tempore, *at the right* or *proper time, in time :* Ter., Liv., Tac. ; in praesentiā *and* in praesenti, *at present, now, at this moment, under these circumstances :* vestrae quidem cenae non solum in praesentiā, sed etiam postero die iucundae sunt, Cic. **b.** In other relations it denotes the being *in* a certain situation, condition or occupation. **i.** In gen. *a.* magno in aere alieno, Cic.; summā in sollicitudine ac timore, Caes.; in summā, *on the whole*, Cic. *β.* As regards the opinion of others: in odio esse, Cic.; in honore esse, Cic.; in amore, etc., Cic. *γ.* Of persons: *in the case of, as regards, in dealing with*: in Nerviis, Caes.; in bono servo dici, Cic.; non talis in hoste fuit Priamo, Verg. *δ. on the ground* or *score of* : vexatur in eo libro quem scripsit, Cic. *ε.* With ref. to dress, arms, etc.; *arrayed in, set in* : homines in catenis Romam mittere, Liv.; in armis, Caes. **ii.** To denote that a person or thing is to be found in, or belongs to, any body or collection: *in, among* : Thales, qui sapientissimus in septem fuit, Cic. **iii.** With *Gerunds* and *Gerundives*, to indicate the being employed or busy upon some *present* act: *in* : ne in quaerendis suis pugnandi tempus dimitteret, Caes.; in excidendā Numantiā, Cic. **B.** With Acc. of direction or place reached : *into, on to, towards, against.* **1.** Lit. **a.** Of space. **i.** With verbs of motion, *into* or *to* : in foveam decidi, Pl.; equitatus noster in conspectum venit, Caes.; in Britanniam traiectus, Caes. Of hostile action : exercitum in Bellovacos ducere, Caes. Sometimes with *versus* : castra ex Biturigibus movet in Arvernos versus, Caes. Rarely with the verbs ponere, conlocare, etc. (for *in* with ABL.): in eculeum impositus, Cic.; sororem et propinquas suas nuptum in alias civitates conlocasse, Caes. Of motion upwards : in caelum ascendere, Cic. **ii.** Denoting mere direction towards, without motion: *towards* : Belgae spectant in septentriones et orientem solem, Caes. Hence, also to denote dimension in any given direction; *in* : sex pedes in altitudinem, Caes. **2.** Transf. **a.** Of time (reaching or tending to some period of time) : *till* : dormiet in lucem, Hor.; or meant to apply to a date or period (transl. by *for*) : indutiae in triginta annos impetraverunt, Liv.; ad cenam hominem in hortos invitavit in posterum diem, Cic. Phr.: in posterum (posteritatem) or in futurum, *in future, for the future* : Cic.; in praesens, *for the present* : Liv.; in perpetuum or in aeternum, *for ever* : Cic.; in tempus, *for the occasion* : Tac.; in diem vivere, *to live only for the day, regardless of the future,* Cic.; in diem (oftener in dies) with comparatives or words denoting increase : *day by day, daily* : Cic., Liv.; so also, in horam and in horas, *every hour* : Hor. **b.** In other relations. **i.** To denote tendency or direction towards or against, progress, inclination, aim, purpose, etc. : *on, with reference to, with a view to, respecting ; towards, against* : id, quod apud Platonem est in philosophos dictum, Cic.; num etiam in deos immortalis inauspicatam legem valuisse ? Liv.; ardere in proelia, Verg.; venerat in funus, Cic.; quae in rem sunt, *of use,* Liv.; servilem in modum, *in the*

manner of slaves, Cic. **ii.** With verbs of dividing : in partis tris, Caes.; Macedonibus treceni nummi in capita statutum est pretium, *a head, for each person,* Liv. **iii.** To denote change into something : in villos abeunt vestes, Ov. **iv.** In adverb. expressions : in universum, *in general,* Liv.; in tantum, *to such an extent,* Verg., Liv.; in deterius, *for the worse,* Tac.

in-accessus, a, um, *unapproachable, inaccessible* : lucus, Verg.; vertex, Tac.

in-acēsco, acēscere, acui, *to turn sour.* Transf.: haec tibi per totos inacescant omnia sensūs, Ov.

Inachus or **-os,** i, m. *the first king of Argos, f. of Io and Phoroneus* ; **Inachius,** a, um, *Inachian,* also *Argive, Grecian* : iuvenca, i.e. *Io* (Verg.). **Inachidēs,** ae. m. *a male descendant of Inachus,* and **Inachis,** idis, *f. adj. Inachian* : as Noun. **I.** *a female descendant of Inachus* : esp. *Io.* **II.** *a river in Argolis, named after Inachus.*

in-adc-, *v.* inacc-.

in-adfectātus, a, um, *unaffected, natural* : oratio, Quint.; Plin. Pan.

in-adsc-, *v.* inasc-.

in-adsuētus, a, um, *unaccustomed* : equi, Ov.

in-adt-, *v.* inatt-.

in-adūstus, a, um, *unsinged* : corpus, Ov.

in-aedifico, āre. **I.** *to build on* : inaedificata in muris moenia, Caes.; Cic.; inaedificata superne multa multis nubila, Lucr.; aliquid in locum publicum, Liv. **II.** *to build up so as to obstruct, to wall up, block up* : vicos plateasque, Caes.; Cic.; portas, Liv.

in-aequābilis, e, *adj. uneven.* **1.** Lit.: locus, Varr.; Liv. **2.** Transf.: haec inaequabili varietate distinguimus, Cic.

inaequābiliter, adv. *unevenly, unequally* : Varr., Suet.

in-aequālis, e, *adj.* **A.** Pass.: *uneven, unequal.* **1.** Lit.: loca, Tac.; portūs, Ov.; calices, Hor. *Comp.* : Plin. Ep. *Sup.* : Suet. **2.** Transf. Of persons: *uneven, capricious* : Hor. **B.** Act.: *that makes uneven* : tonsor, Hor.

in-aequālitās, ātis, *f. unevenness, unlikeness* : Quint.

inaequāliter, adv. *unevenly, unequally* : Liv., Tac.

in-aequātus, a, um, *unequal* : Tib.

in-aequo, āre, *to bring to a level, to level up* : Caes.

in-aestimābilis, e, *adj.* **I.** *that cannot be estimated* : Liv. **II.** *that cannot be valued, invaluable* : imperator, Liv. **III.** *not worthy to be esteemed, valueless* : Cic.

in-aestuo, āre, *to boil or rage within* : Hor.

in-aff-, *v.* inadf-.

in-amābilis, e, *adj. unworthy of love, hateful* : Pl.; Plin. Ep.; palus, Verg.; regnum (of the Lower World), Ov.

in-amārēsco, ere, *to become bitter* : inamarescunt epulae, Hor.

in-ambitiōsus, a, um, *unambitious, unassuming* : rura, Ov.

in-ambulātio, ōnis, *f. a walking, parading* (on the rostra), Cic. Transf.: tremuli lecti, Cat.

in-ambulo, āre, *to walk up and down, parade* : Pl., Cic., Liv.

in-amoenus, a, um, *unlovely* : regna (of the Lower World), Ov.

ināniae, ārum, *f. pl.* [inānis], *emptiness* : Pl.

inānilogista, ae, *m.* [inānis and λογιστής], *an idle talker* : Pl.

inānimantum, I, *n.* [ināniō], in *pl. empty spaces* : Pl.

inanimus, a, um [anima], *lifeless, inanimate* : Cic., Liv., Tac.

ināniō, īre [inānis], *to make empty* : hoc ubi inanitur spatium, Lucr. ; Plin.

inānis, e, *adj. empty, void.* **1**. Lit. **A**. In gen. : aequalis, Pl. ; spatium, Lucr. ; domus, Cic. ; naves inanes ad eum remitterentur, Caes. ; cerae, galea, Verg. ; venter, funus, Hor. ; currus, Ov. With GEN. : dolium lymphae, Hor. ; corpus animae, Ov. As Noun, **ināne**, is, *n. an empty space, vacuum* : Lucr., Cic., Verg. **B**. In partic. **a**. *without money, poor* : Pl., Cic., Prop. ; civitas, Cic. *Comp.* : Cic. *Sup.* : Apulia pars inanissima Italiae, Cic. **b**. *without life* or *substance* : umbra, imago, Ov. ; regna Ditis (as inhabited by inanes), Verg. ; Tartara, Ov. **2**. Transf. *empty, hollow, idle, worthless.* **a**. In gen. : cogitatio, cupiditates, crimen, etc., Cic. ; spes, Cic., Verg. ; causae, Verg. ; minae, Hor. With GEN. : omnia plena consiliorum, inania verborum, Cic. ; inanissima prudentiae, Cic. With ABL. : nulla epistula inanis aliquā re utili, Cic. Ep. **b**. Of time : unoccupied, idle : Verg. **c**. Of men : empty and vain, hollow : Lucr., Liv., etc. ; inaniora ingenia, Liv. As Noun, **ināne**, *n. emptiness, worthlessness, vanity* : Hor., Pers. ; in *pl.* : Hor. ; inania belli, inania famae, Tac.

inānitās, ātis, *f.* [inānis], *emptiness, empty space.* **1**. Lit. : Pl., Cic. **2**. Transf. *uselessness* : Cic.

ināniter, *adv. vainly, idly, uselessly* : Cic., Hor., Ov.

(1) **inarātus**, a, um, *Part.* inarō.

(2) **in-arātus**, a, um, *unploughed, fallow* : terra, Verg. ; Hor.

in-ārdēscō, ārdēscere, ārsī, *to become kindled, take fire.* **1**. Lit. : nubes solis radiis, Verg. ; Hor. **2**. Transf. (of the passions) : cupidine vindictae, Tac. ; specie praesentis inarsit, Ov.

in-ārēscō, ere, *to become dry, to dry up* : Quint., Tac. Transf. : liberalitas, Plin. Ep.

in-arō, āre, *to plough in* : sarmenta, Cato.

in-ascēnsus, a, um, *not climbed* or *mounted* : locus, Plin. Ep.

in-ass-, *v.* inads-.

in-attenuātus, a, um, *undiminished, unweakened* : fames, Ov.

in-audāx, ācis, *adj. not daring, cowed* : raptor, Hor.

in-audiō, īre, *to hear in confidence, have inside information of* : rem, Cic. ; aliquid de aliquā re, Pl., Cic. Ep.

(1) **inaudītus**, a, um. *Part.* inaudiō.

(2) **in-audītus**, a, um. **1**. Lit. **a**. *unheard* : nemini, Cic. **b**. Of persons on trial : *unheard, without a hearing* : Tac., Suet. **2**. Transf. *unheard of, unusual* : Cic.

inaugurātō, *adv. after consulting the auguries* : Liv.

in-augurō, āre, *to introduce by augury.* **A**. Without *Obj.* expressed : *to take the auguries* : Liv. *Impers. Pass.* : Pl. **B**. With *Obj.* : *to augur in, consecrate a place or (official) person by augury, to install* : augur in locum eius inauguratus est filius, Liv. ; aliquem flaminem, Liv. ; Cic. ; locum, Liv.

inaurātus, a, um. **I**. *Part.* inaurō. **II**. Adj. : *gilded, gilt* : statua, Cic. ; vestis, Ov.

inaurēs, ium, *f. pl.* [auris], *ear-rings* : Pl.

in-aurō, āre, *to cover* or *overlay with gold, to gild.* Transf. *to gild,* i.e. *to make rich* : Cic. Ep., Hor.

in-auspicātō, *adv. without consulting the auspices* : Cic.

in-auspicātus, a, um. **I**. *at which no auspices were taken, without auspices* : lex, Liv. **II**. *unlucky* : Plin.

in-ausus, a, um, *not ventured, unattempted* : scelus, Verg. ; nobis, Tac.

inb-, *v.* imb-.

in-bītō, ere, *to go into* : domum, Pl.

in-caeduus, a, um, *uncut, unhewn* : lucus, Ov.

in-calēscō, calēscere, caluī, *to grow warm* or *hot.* **1**. Lit. : incalescente sole, Liv. ; incaluit vis illa mali, Ov. ; lacrimis incaluisse togam, Prop. ; vino, Liv. **2**. Transf. **a**. With passion : Ov. ; laetitiā, Tac. **b**. In speaking : Cicero raro incalescit, Tac.

in-calfaciō, facere, *to warm, to heat* : culmos, Ov.

in-callidē, *adv. unskilfully, awkwardly* : Cic.

in-callidus, a, um, *unskilful, not shrewd, guileless* : Cic., Tac.

in-candēscō, candēscere, canduī. **I**. *to become white* : spumis unda, Cat. ; pulvere, Plin. Pan. **II**. *to grow white-hot* : ara ignibus, Ov. ; (tempestas) toto autumni aestu, Verg.

in-cānēscō, cānēscere, cānuī, *to grow grey* : ornus albo flore piri, Verg.

in-cantātus, a, um, *sung over, enchanted* : vincula, Hor.

in-cānus, a, um, *grown grey* : Pl., Verg., Suet., etc.

in-cassum, *v.* cassus.

in-castīgātus, a, um, *unreproved* : Hor.

in-cautē, *adv. incautiously, negligently* : Cic. Ep., Liv. *Comp.* : Caes., Liv., Plin. Ep.

in-cautus, a, um. **A**. Act. : *incautious, negligent, heedless, hasty* : Caes., Cic., Liv. ; incautos ad credendum pavor, Liv. *Comp.* : Cic. Ep., Liv. With *ab* : incautus a fraude, Liv. With GEN. : futuri, Hor. **B**. Pass. **a**. *not guarded against, unforeseen* : scelus, Lucr. **b**. *unguarded* : agri, Sall. ; Liv. ; iter hostibus incautum, Tac.

in-cēdō, cēdere, cēssī, cēssum, *to go, step,* or *march along, to parade.* **1**. Lit. **a**. In gen. (but esp. of pompous or majestic movement) : ut ovans praedā onustus incederem, Pl. ; Liv. ; quam taeter incedebat ! Cic. ; ego quae divum incedo regina, Verg. ; totā in urbe, Ov. With ACC. : maestos locos, Tac. **b**. Milit. : *to move forwards, advance, march* : Sall., Liv., Tac. **2**. Transf. **a**. *to advance, proceed* : malitiae lenonis contra incedam, Pl. **b**. Of inanim. and abstr. subjects : ad inventionem animus, Cic. ; tenebrae, Tac. ; rumor, Tac.

Of sudden emotions, *to come upon* : tantus timor, Caes. ; religio, Liv. ; ambitio, suspicio, Tac. With *in* and Acc. : nova nunc religio in te istaec incessit, Ter. ; pestilentia in Romanos, Liv. With Dat. : exercitui dolor, Caes. ; mulieres, quibus belli timor insolitus incesserat, Sall. ; cura patribus, Liv. With Acc. : timor patres, Liv. ; adversa valetudo aliquem, Tac.

in-celebrātus, a, um, *not spread abroad*: Tac.

in-cēnātus, a, um, *that has not dined* : Pl., Cato.

incendiārius, ī, *m.* [incendium], *an incendiary* : Tac., Suet.

incendium, ī, *n.* [incendō], *a burning, fire, conflagration.* **1.** Lit. : Caes., Cic., Tac. ; facere, excitare, restinguere, Cic. In *pl.* : Caes., Cic., Verg., etc. **2.** Transf. **a.** *burning, heat* : stomachi, Lucr. **b.** *a firebrand, torch* : Verg., Ov. **c.** *fire* (of passion) : invidiae incendio conflagrare, Cic. ; cupiditatum incendiis inflammatus, Cic. ; Pl. ; Ov. **d.** As destructive : in suas fortunas incendium excitatum, Cic. ; incendio alieni iudici conflagrare, Liv.

incendō, cendere, cendī, cēnsum [*cf.* accendō]. **1.** Lit. **a.** *to kindle, light up* : cupas, Caes. ; tus et odores, Cic. ; lychnos, Verg. Also, aras, altaria, Verg. **b.** *to set on fire, burn* : oppida, aedificia, etc., Caes. ; classem, tabularium, Cic. ; urbem, Cic., Liv. ; vepres, agros, Verg. **2.** Transf. **a.** *to light up, make bright, brighten, illumine* : solis incensa radiis luna, Cic. ; auro squamam incendebat fulgor, Verg. **b.** Of the feelings : *to kindle, inflame, excite* : loquarne ? incendam, Ter. ; Ov. ; ut mihi non solum tu incendere iudicem, sed ipse ardere videaris, Cic. ; aliquem querellis, Verg. ; plebem largiundo, Sall. ; iuventutem ad facinora, Sall. ; Cic. ; bonorum animos, Cic. Ep. ; luctūs, Verg. ; vīris pudor, Verg. ; incendor irā, Ter. ; Pl. ; (mulier) incensa odio, Cic. **c.** *to fire, enhance, raise* (the price of) : annonam, Varr. **d.** *to destroy, ruin* : tuom genus, Pl.

incēnis, e, *adj.*, *that has not dined* : Pl.

incēnsiō, ōnis, *f.* [incendō], *a setting on fire, burning* : Cic.

(1) incēnsus, a, um, *Part.* incendō.

(2) in-cēnsus, a, um, *not registered, not assessed* : hominem incensum vendere, Cic. ; populus, Liv.

inceptiō, ōnis, *f.* [incipiō]. **I.** *a beginning* : operis, Cic. **II.** *an undertaking, enterprise* : Ter.

inceptō, āre [*freq.* incipiō]. **I.** *to begin.* With *Inf.* : Pl. **II.** *to undertake, attempt* : quid inceptas ? Ter.

inceptor, ōris, *m.* [incipiō], *a beginner or originator* : Ter.

inceptus, a, um. **I.** *Part.* incipiō. **II.** Noun, **inceptum,** ī, *n.* **I.** *a beginning* : Hor. **II.** *an attempt, undertaking* : Ter., Cic., Verg. ; perficere, Sall. ; peragere, Verg. ; haerere in incepto, Verg. ; desistere incepto, Verg. ; absistere incepto, Liv. In *pl.* : Sall., Verg., etc. ; inceptis adnue meis, Ov.

in-cernō, cernere, crēvī, crētum, *to sift over or upon*: terram cribro, Cato ; piper album cum sale nigro, Hor.

in-cērō, āre, *to smear or cover over with wax* : genua deorum (perh. with waxen tablets inscribed with vows), Juv.

incertō, āre [incertus], *to render doubtful* : animum, Pl.

in-certus, a, um. **I.** *not decided, not settled, not fixed, unsteady, uncertain, doubtful* : of *things* thought about) : amicus certus in re incertā cernitur, Enn. ; spes, Ter., Cic. ; sedes, Sall. ; rumores, Caes. ; exitus pugnarum, Cic. ; aetas, dominatus, Cic. ; conligere incertos, et in ordine ponere crinis, Ov. ; lunam, Verg. ; incertis mensibus (i.e. in weather), Verg. *Comp.* and *Sup.* : Cic. With *Indir. Quest.* : incerti socii an hostes essent, Liv. ; incertum est ab utro factum sit, Cic. Parenthetically (without est) : incertum vi an voluntate, Liv. ; Tac. *Neut.* as Noun, *uncertainty, insecurity* : in incerto esse, Sall. ; in incerto habere, Sall. ; aliquid in incertum vocare, Cic. ; quae omnia ex incerto maiora territis ostentat, Liv. ; also *Sup.* : ex incertissimo, Liv. ; ne cuius incerti vanique auctor esset, Liv. ; incerta belli, Liv. ; incerta maris et tempestatum, Tac. ; praefectus annonae in incertum creatus, *for an indefinite time*, Liv. *Abl.* **incertō** as *Adv.*, *not certainly* : id admodum incerto scio, Pl. **II.** *undecided, irresolute, not sure.* **1.** Of persons : Pl., Sall., Cic. With *Indir. Quest.* : Ter., Cic. Ep., Verg., etc. With *Gen.* : incertus sententiae, Liv. ; meae salutis, Ov. ; ultionis, Tac. With *de* : de fide sociorum, Liv. ; Plin. Ep. **2.** Transf. Of things personified or by transference of epithet from persons : tris incertos caligine soles erramus, Verg. ; incertam excussit securim, Verg. ; vultus, Sall.

incessō, cessere, cessīvī [*freq.* incēdō], *to assault, assail, attack.* **1.** Lit. : vagos lapidibus, Liv. ; telorum lapidumque iactu, Ov. **2.** Transf. (with words) : reges dictis protervis, Ov. ; aliquem suspicionibus, Tac.

incessus, ūs, *m.* [incēdō]. **1.** Lit. **a.** *a marching, stepping, stately step, pace, gait* : fingere, Cic. ; incessus, citus modo, modo tardus, Sall. ; erectus, Tac. ; vera incessu patuit dea, Verg. ; hominum iumentorumque incessu, *trampling*, Liv. **b.** *a hostile attack, invasion* : Tac. **2.** Transf. : *an entrance, approach* : incessūs claudere, Tac.

incestē, *adv.* **I.** *uncleanly, impurely* (ceremonially) : facere sacrificium Dianae, Liv. ; ut casta inceste hostia concideret, Lucr. **II.** *unchastely, impurely* : Cic., Suet.

incestō, āre [incestus]. **I.** *to make unclean* (ceremonially), *to pollute, defile* : totam funere classem, Verg. **II.** *to defile* : puellam, Pl. ; Tac. ; thalamos novercae, Verg.

in-cestus, a, um [castus], *unclean* : hence, *impure, polluted, defiled.* **I.** In religion : Hor., Liv., Tac. **II.** In morals : *defiled, polluted, unchaste, lewd* : os, Cic. ; amores, Hor., Tac. ; voces, Ov. ; sermo, Liv. ; nuptiae, Tac. *Neut.* as Noun, *unchastity, incest* : Cic., Liv., Quint., etc. ; in *pl.* : Cic., Suet.

incestus, ūs, *m.* [incestus], *unchastity, incest* : Cic., Liv.

incho-, *v.* incoh-.

in-cĭdŏ, cidere, cidi, cāsum [cadō], *to fall into* or *upon*. **1.** L i t. **a.** In gen.: in foveam, Cic.; Lucr.; Verg., etc.; saxum in crura, Cic.; ad terram Turnus, Verg.; (turris) super agmina late incidit, Verg. With DAT.: Lucr.; caput arae, Ov.; ruinae nostris capitibus, Liv. **b.** Of strong or violent movement: in latrones, Cic.; in hostem, Liv. With DAT.: exercitus portis, Liv.; duo amnes flumini, Liv. **2.** Transf. (of chance occurrences). **A.** With personal Subject: *to come upon unexpectedly, fall in with :* nonnullae cohortes in agmen Caesaris incidunt, Caes.; in insidias, Cic.; inter catervas armatorum, Liv.; in morbum, Cic. Ep., Liv.; in miserias, in gloriae cupiditatem, in sermonem, etc., Cic.; in eorum mentionem, Cic., Tac.; in amicitiam eius, Sall. With DAT.: homini, Cic.; Verg. **B.** With inanim. Subject. **a.** Mentally : *to come to* or *occur to one :* redeunti ex ipsā re mihi incidit suspicio, Ter.; incidit de uxoribus mentio, Liv.; aliquid in mentem, Cic. **b.** Of external events : *to fall upon :* pestilentia in urbem, Liv. With DAT.: tantus terror exercitui, Caes.; ut nihil incidisset civitati mali, Cic. Also simply *to happen, occur :* aliquod bellum incidit, Caes.; forte ita inciderat ne etc., Liv.; incidunt saepe tempora cum etc., Cic. **c.** Of coincidence in time : *to fall on, happen in :* cum in Kalendas Ianuarias Compitaliorum dies incidisset, Cic.

in-cĭdŏ, cidere, cĭdi, cisum [caedō], *to cut into.* **1.** Lit. **a.** In gen.: arboribus incisis, Caes.; vitis, Verg. **b.** *to carve, engrave, inscribe.* With *in* and ABL.: id in aere incisum nobis tradiderunt, Cic.; Suet. With *in* and ACC.: leges in aes incisae, Liv.; Cic.; Suet. With DAT.: amores arboribus, Verg.; Ov.; Plin. Pan. With ABL.*Instr.*: tabula his incisa litteris, Liv. **c.** *to sever by cutting into :* linum, Cic.; funem, Verg.; venam, Tac. **d.** *to form by cutting, to cut :* faces, Verg.; Ov. **2.** Transf. *to cut into, cut short :* hence, *to put an end to :* poēma, Cic.; litis, Verg.; ludum, Hor.; spe incisā, Liv.

incĭēns, entis, *adj.* [For *in-cu-iēns, cf.* Gk. ἐγ-κυ-ος], *pregnant, with young :* Varr.

incĭle, is, *n.* [perh. fr. incīdō], *a ditch, trench.* **1.** Lit.: aperire, Cato. **2.** Transf.: in incili omnia adhaeserunt, Cael. ap. Cic. Ep.

incīnctus, a, um, *Part.* incingō.

in-cingŏ, cingere, cīnxī, cīnctum, *to engird, gird about.* **1.** Lit. (mostly in *Mid.*): sese serpentibus, Cat.; incingi zonā, Ov.; (Tisiphone) torto incingitur angue, Ov.; incinctus cinctu Gabino, Liv.; pellibus, Verg. **2.** Transf. **a.** *to drape, wreathe :* aras verbenis, Ov. **b.** *to girdle :* urbes moenibus, Ov.

in-cĭnŏ, ere [canō], *to sing* or *play :* varios ore modos, Prop.

incĭpessŏ, *v.* incipissō.

in-cĭpĭŏ, cipere, cēpi, ceptum. (Rarely used in *Perf. tenses,* which in the class. per. are supplied by coepio. The *Perf. Pass.* however is common.) [capiō], *to take in hand, take on.* **A.** Trans. *to take in hand, begin.* With ACC.: facinus, Pl., Sall.;

bellum, Sall., Liv.; iter, Pl.; sementem, Verg.; opus, Liv.; mandata, Tac. Without ACC.: a Iove incipiendum putat, Cic.; Ter., etc. With *Inf.*: Pl., Caes., Cic., Ov., etc. *Pass.*: proelium incipitur, Sall., Tac.; Victoria, Tac.; incepta oppugnatio, Caes.; iter, labor, furor, Verg.; Pl.; Ter. O c c. *to begin (to speak*): unde potius incipiam, Cic.; Ov., etc. **B.** I n t r a n s. *to begin to be, to begin :* annus, Pl.; cum rosam viderat, tum incipere ver arbitrabatur, Cic.; prima quies mortalibus aegris incipit, Verg.; clamor et pugna, Liv.

incĭpissŏ, ere [incipiō], *to begin :* orationem, Pl. With *Inf.*: Pl.

incīsē and **incīsim**, *adv.* [incīdō], *in short clauses :* Cic.

incīsĭŏ, ōnis, *f.* and **incīsum**, ī, *n.* [incīdō]. Rhet. *a division, clause* of a sentence : Cic.

incīsus, a, um, *Part.* incīdō.

incĭtāmentum, ī, *n.* [incitō]. **I.** *an inducement, incentive :* laborum, Cic. In *pl.* : incitamenta victoriae, Tac. **II.** Of persons : uxor, quae incitamentum mortis fuit, Tac.

incĭtātĭŏ, ōnis, *f.* [incitō]. **A.** A c t. *an inciting, rousing :* languentis populi, Cic. **B.** P a s s. *rapidity, vehemence.* **1.** L i t.: (sol) tantā incitatione fertur, Cic. **2.** T r a n s f.: animi, Caes.; mentis, orationis, Cic.

incĭtātĭus, *comp. adv. more* (or *rather) impetuously :* Cic.

incĭtātus, a, um. **I.** *Part.* incitō. **II.** A d j. : *rapid, swift.* **1.** L i t.: equo incitato (*at full gallop*), Caes., Cic., Liv.; cursu incitato, Caes. *Sup.* : Cic. **2.** T r a n s f.: cursus in oratione incitatior, Cic.

in-cĭtŏ, āre, *to set in rapid motion, to hasten, to urge forwards.* **1.** L i t.: equos, Caes., Liv.; navis remis, Caes.; se ex castris, Caes.; ex alto se aestus, Caes.; stellarum motūs incitantur, Cic.; amnis hibernis incitatus pluviis, Liv. P r o v. : incitare currentem (*cf.* 'to spur a willing horse '), Cic. **2.** T r a n s f. **a.** *to rouse, spur, stimulate :* aliquem imitandi cupiditate, Cic.; multa Caesarem ad id bellum incitabant, Caes.; aliquem ad laborem, Cic.; aliquem ad servandum genus hominum, Cic.; animos, Cic. **b.** *to inspire* (with frenzied utterance): terrae vis Pythiam, Cic.; Cat. **c.** *to augment, increase :* eloquendi celeritatem, Cic.; metum, Ov.; caelibum poenas, Tac. **d.** In bad sense, *to excite, arouse, stir up :* tribunus populum in consules incitabat, Liv.; Cic.; civitas ob eam rem incitata, Caes.

(1) in-cĭtus, a, um, *set in rapid motion, rapid, violent :* venti vis, Lucr.; hasta, Verg.

(2) in-cĭtus, a, um, *not moved* of a piece in a game. T r a n s f.: ad incita or ad incitas (*sc.* calces) aliquem redigere, deducere (i.e. to bring to a standstill, reduce to extremity), Pl.

in-cīvīlĭus, *comp. adv. more irregularly* (in law): Suet.

inclāmĭtŏ, āre [*freq.* inclāmō], *to exclaim against strongly, to abuse violently :* inclamitor quasi servos, Pl.

in-clāmŏ, āre, *to cry out at.* **I.** Without Object : Cic., Quint. **II.** *to cry out at, chide, abuse, scold.* With ACC.: Pl., Hor.,

Liv. With Dat.: Ov., Liv. **III.** *to call out to, hail.* With Acc.: Cic., Liv.

in-clārēscō, clārēscere, clāruī, *to become famous or celebrated :* mea fortuna, Tac.

in-clēmēns, entis, *adj. unmerciful, rigorous, harsh :* dictator, Liv.; verbo inclementiori appellari, Liv.

inclēmenter, *adv. rigorously, harshly :* Pl., Liv. *Comp. :* Ter., Liv.

in-clēmentia, ae, *f. unmercifulness, harshness :* divum, Verg.

inclīnātiō, ōnis, *f.* [inclīnō], *a leaning, bending.* **1.** Lit.: corporis, Cic. In *pl. :* variis trepidantium inclinationibus, Tac. **2.** Transf. **a.** *an inclination, tendency :* ad meliorem spem, Cic. **b.** *inclination, bias, favour :* voluntatis, Cic.; animorum, Liv.; iudicum ad aliquem, Quint.; principum in hos, Tac. **c.** *a change :* temporis, Cic.; rerum inclinationes, Cic. **d.** *inflexion :* vocis, Cic., Quint.

inclīnātus, a, um. **I.** *Part.* inclīnō. **II.** Adj.: **a.** *inclined, leaning, prone :* plebs ante inclinatior ad Poenos fuerat, Liv.; eius animus ad pacem inclinatior erat, Tac. **b.** *sinking, falling :* fortuna, Cic. Ep.; domus, Verg.; res, Liv. **c.** *Of the voice : low, deep :* Cic.

in-clīnō, āre [*cf.* acclīnō]. **A.** Trans. **1.** Lit. **a.** *to bend, turn in some direction :* Pl.; inclinato in postmeridianum tempus die, Cic.; sol meridie se inclinavit, Liv.; aquas ad litora, Ov.; genua harenia, Ov.; mālos (*to lower*), Liv.; inclinato in dextrum capite, Quint.; aestu fretum inclinatum est, Liv. **b.** Milit. (*Mid.* or *Pass.*) *: to fall back or give way :* Romana inclinatur acies, Liv.; acies inclinatas, Tac.; inclinari rem in fugam apparuit, Liv. **2.** Transf. *: to turn or incline in some direction.* - **a.** In gen. (with *Refl. Pron.* or in *Mid.*) *:* se ad Stoicos, Cic.; inclinari opes ad Sabinos videbantur, Liv.; so also, haec animum inclinant ut credam, Liv. **b.** *to divert, transfer :* culpam in aliquem, Liv.; in ditis a pauperibus inclinata onera, Liv. Hence, *to change, alter,* esp. for the worse: se fortuna inclinaverat, Caes.; ut me paululum inclinari timore viderunt, Cic. Ep.; omnia fortuna, Liv. **B.** Intrans. *to bend, turn in some direction.* **1.** Lit. **a.** paulum corpora, Lucr.; meridies, Hor.; dies, Tac.; sol, Juv. **b.** Milit.: *to yield, give way :* Tac.; in neutram partem acies, Liv.; in fugam, Liv. **2.** Transf. *to turn, incline in some direction.* **a.** In gen.: suā sponte quo impellimus inclinant, Cic.; hos ut sequar inclinat animus, Liv.; sententia senatūs ad pacem faciendum, Cic.; hisce, Hor. With *Inf.*: inclinavit sententia suum in Thessaliam agmen demittere, Liv. **b.** *to change for better or worse :* omnia repente ad Romanos, Liv.; fortuna belli, Liv.; magistratuum finis, Tac.

inclitus, *v.* inclutus.

in-clūdō, clūdere, clūsī, clūsum, *to shut in, confine, keep in.* **1.** Lit. **A.** In gen. With *in* and Abl. or Acc.: armatos in cellā Concordiae, Cic.; aliquem in custodias, Cic.; Liv. With Locat. or Locat. Abl.: aliquid domi, Cic.; minora castra maioribus, Caes.; inclusi parietibus, Cic.; ali-

quem carcere, Liv.; se moenibus, Liv.; suras auro, Verg.; hunc domo, Ov. With Dat.: corpora caeco lateri, Verg. **B.** In partic. **a.** *to set :* zmaragdos auro, Lucr.; ebur buxo, Verg. **b.** *to engraft, bud :* huc ex arbore germen, Verg. **c.** *to shut, shut off, obstruct, block :* a tergo viam, Cic.; includi vento in hostium orā, Liv.; limina portis, Ov.; iter vocis, Verg.; spiritum, Liv. **2.** Transf. **A.** In gen.: *to include, enclose, insert :* senatūs consultum in tabulis, Cic.; in huius me consilii societatem, Cic.; orationem in epistulam, Cic. Ep.; sententiam versibus, Hor.; oratio libro inclusa, Liv. **B.** In partic. **a.** *to block, obstruct, confine :* verba versu, Cic.; dolor vocem, Cic.; nullis neque temporis neque iuris inclusus angustiis, Liv. **b.** Of time: *to close, end :* includet crastina fata dies, Prop.; huius actionem vespera, Plin. Ep.

inclūsiō, ōnis, *f.* [inclūdō], *confinement :* Cic.

inclūsus, a, um, *Part.* inclūdō.

inclutus and **inclitus,** a, um [*cf.* Gk. κλυτός fr. κλύω], *celebrated, renowned.* **a.** Of persons : Pl., Lucr., Liv., etc. **b.** Of things : moenia bello, Verg.; gloria Palamedis famā, Verg.; leges Solonis, Liv.

(1) incoctus, a, um, *Part.* incoquō.

(2) in-coctus, a, um, *uncooked, raw :* Pl.

in-cōgitābilis, e, *adj. thoughtless, inconsiderate :* Pl.

in-cōgitāns, antis, *adj. thoughtless, inconsiderate :* Ter.

incōgitantia, ae, *f.* [incōgitāns], *thoughtlessness, inconsiderateness :* Pl.

in-cōgitātus, a, um. **I.** *not thought over, unstudied :* opus, Sen. **II.** *thoughtless, inconsiderate :* animus, Pl.

in-cōgitō, āre, *to contrive, scheme against :* fraudem socio, Hor.

in-cognitus, a, um. **I.** *not investigated :* res, Cic.; causa, Cic. **II.** *not known, unknown :* res, lex, etc., Cic. *Neut. pl.* as Noun : Cic.; incognita (i.e. *not identified ;* hence, *unclaimed*) sub hastā veniere, Liv. With Dat. of pers.: quae omnia fere Gallis erant incognita, Caes.; palus oculis nostris, Ov.

incohātus, a, um. **I.** *Part.* incohō. **II.** Adj.: *unfinished, incomplete :* rem incohatam relinquere, Cic.; Pl.

incohō, āre, *to take in hand, take on, begin, start :* Lucr.; Phidias potest signum ab alio incohatam absolvere, Cic.; templum, Liv.; Stygio regi nocturnas aras, Verg.

incola, ae, *m. f.* [incolō], *an inhabitant, a resident.* **I.** In gen. **a.** Of men : Cic., Sall.; (Socrates) totius mundi se incolam arbitrabatur, Cic.; Pergama incola captivo bove victor arat, Ov. **b.** Of animals and inanim. things : aquarum incolae, Cic.; (aliquem) obicere incolis aquilonibus, Hor. **II.** *a foreign resident,* as opp. to *a citizen :* peregrini atque incolae, Cic.; cives atque incolae, Cic.; Pl.; Liv.

in-colō, colere, coluī. **A.** Trans.: *to dwell in, inhabit :* urbem, Cic.; ea loca, Caes.; ferae terras, Liv. *Pass. :* e locis quoque ipsis, qui a quibusque incolebantur, Cic. **B.** Intrans.: *to dwell or reside :* Neptuno, qui salsis locis incolit, Pl.; trans Rhenum, Caes.; cis Hiberum, Liv.

in-columis, e, adj. [perh. fr. same root as calamitās], unharmed, unimpaired, safe and sound, alive : argentum, Pl.; exercitum transducere, Caes.; urbs, arx, cives, etc., Cic.; genae, Hor.; summa, Lucr. With ab : equestrem splendorem a calamitate iudici retinere, Cic.

incolumitās, ātis, f. [incolumis], freedom from harm, safety, life : Cic.; incolumitatem deditis pollicebatur, Caes. In pl. : Cic.

in-comitātus, a, um, unaccompanied, unattended. **1.** Lit.: virgines, Varr.; funera, Lucr.; incomitata videtur ire viam, Verg. **2.** Transf.: externis virtus bonis, Ov.

in-commendātus, a, um, not entrusted to somebody ; hence, unprotected : tellus, Ov.

incommodē, adv., unseasonably, inconveniently, not agreeably : Pl., Caes., Liv., etc. Comp. : Cic. Sup. : Cic. Ep.

incommodesticus, a, um, comically for incommodus : Pl.

incommoditās, ātis, f. **I.** unsuitableness. **a.** Of conduct : incommoditate apstinere, Pl.; alienati animi, Cic. Ep. **b.** Of time : temporis, Liv. **II.** damage, disadvantage : Ter.

incommodō, āre, to be troublesome, annoying : alicui, Ter.; alicui nihil, Cic.

in-commodus, a, um, unseasonable, troublesome, disagreeable. **a.** Of things : iter, Ter.; non incommoda aestate statio, Caes.; valetudo, Cic.; ne voce quidem incommodā, Liv. Sup. : in rebus eius incommodissimis, Cic. **b.** Of persons : ne incommodus nobis sit, Pl.; Cic. As Noun, **incommodum**, I, n. inconvenience, trouble, disadvantage, disaster : Pl.; incommodi nihil capere, Cic.; incommodo adfici, Cic.; quae res magnum incommodum nostris attulit, Caes.; ut acceptum incommodum virtute sarciretur, Caes.; locus plus habet adiumenti quam incommodi, Cic. Of the health : with GEN.: valetudinis, Cic. Ep. In pl. : tot incommodis conflictati, Caes.; Cic.; vitae, Juv.

in-commūtābilis, e, adj. unchangeable : status rei publicae, Cic.

in-comparābilis, e, adj. that cannot be equalled, incomparable : Quint.

in-compertus, a, um, lost to knowledge, unknown : inter cetera vetustate incomperta, Liv.

incompositē, adv. without order, in disorder : hostis veniens, Liv. Of discourse : Quint.

in-compositus, a, um, not carefully arranged. **a.** in disorder : agmen, Liv. **b.** unstudied, artless : motus, Verg. **c.** irregular, rugged : incomposito pede currere versūs, Hor.; oratio, Quint. Of the author : Quint.

in-comprehēnsibilis, e, adj. that cannot be seized or held. Transf. **a.** (metaph. fr. wrestling) in disputando, Plin. Ep. **b.** Mentally : that cannot be grasped ; praecepta, Quint.; opus, Sen. Ep.

in-cōmptus, a, um, unadorned, undressed, unkempt. **1.** Lit. (of the hair) : incomptis Curium capillis, Hor.; incompta nudis capillis, Ov. Comp. : Suet. Hence, caput,

Hor.; homo, Tac. **2.** Transf.: oratio quasi incompta, Cic.; oratio incompta, Liv.; versus, Verg., Hor.; apparatus, Tac.

in-concessus, a, um, not allowed, forbidden : hymenaei, Verg.; spes, Ov.; Quint.

in-conciliō, āre. **I.** to ensnare, deceive : aliquem, Pl. **II.** to get by trickery : copias alicuius, Pl. **III.** to bring trouble upon : ne inconciliare quid nos porro postules, Pl.

in-concinnitās, ātis, f. incongruity, absurdity : sententiarum, Suet.

in-concinnus, a, um, inharmonious, absurd, awkward : qui in aliquo genere inconcinnus aut multus est, is ineptus dicitur, Cic.; personam feret non inconcinnus, Hor.

in-concussus, a, um, unshaken, stable. **1.** Lit.: sidera, Luc. **2.** Transf.: otium, Sen. Ep.; pax, Tac.

incondite, adv. confusedly : Cic.

in-conditus, a, um. **I.** not (carefully) put together, unorganised, undisciplined, disorderly. **1.** Lit.: multitudo, acies, Liv.; homines, agmen, Tac. **2.** Transf. **a.** ius civile, Cic.; libertas, barbaria, Liv. **b.** Of language : without art, rough, unformed : genus dicendi, Cic.; ioci militares, Liv.; Verg. Neut. pl. as Noun, impromptus : Liv. **II.** unburied : corpora, Luc.

in-congruēns, entis, adj. inconsistent, incongruous : Plin. Ep.

inconsiderātē, adv. without reflexion or circumspection : Cic.

in-consīderātus, a, um. **A.** Act.: thoughtless, not circumspect : Cic. Comp. : Nep.; Sup. : Quint. **B.** Pass.: reckless : cupiditas, Cic. Sup. : Cic.

in-cōnsōlābilis, e, adj. inconsolable. Transf.: incurable : vulnus, Ov.

in-cōnstāns, antis, adj. changeable, inconsistent, fickle. **a.** Of persons : Cic. Sup. : Sen. Ep. **b.** Of things : litterae, Cic. Ep.; Comp. : Cic.

inconstanter, adv. changeably, inconsistently : Cic., Liv. Sup. : Cic.

in-cōnstantia, ae, f. changeableness, inconsistency, fickleness. **a.** Of persons : Cic. **b.** Of things : mentis, Cic.; frontis ac luminum, Quint.

inconsultē, adv. indiscreetly : Caes., Cic., Liv. Comp. : Liv.

in-cōnsultus, a, um. **A.** Act. **a.** without receiving advice : Verg. **b.** imprudent, indiscreet : of persons : Cic., Hor., Suet.; of things : Pl.; ratio, Cic.; largitio, pavor, pugna, Liv. **B.** Pass. not consulted : Liv., Plin. Ep., Suet.

in-cōnsultū, ABL. sing. m. : meo, without consulting me, Pl.

in-cōnsūmptus, a, um. **I.** unconsumed : Ov. **II.** imperishable : iuventa, Ov.

in-contāminātus, a, um, untainted : Varr., Liv.

in-contentus, a, um, unstretched : fides (lyre-string), Cic.

in-continēns, entis, adj. not retaining. Transf. not keeping within due bounds. incontinent : homo, Pl.; Tityos, Hor.; manus, Hor.

incontinenter, adv. without due self-control : Cic.

in-continentia, ae, f. inability to retain or

hold. Transf. *inability to restrain one's desires, lack of self-control* : Cic.

in-conveniēns, entis, *adj. not matched, dissimilar* : corpus, Phaedr.

in-coquō, coquere, coxī, coctum, *to boil in.* **1.** Lit.: radices Baccho, Verg.; cruorem herbis, Hor. **2.** Transf. **a.** *to dye* : vellera Tyrios incocta rubores, Verg. **b.** *to imbue* : incoctum generoso pectus honesto, Pers.

in-corporālis, e, *adj. bodiless, incorporeal* : ius, Quint.

in-corrēctus, a, um, *unimproved* : opus, Ov.

incorruptē, *adv. uncorruptly, justly* : iudicare, Cic. *Comp.* : Cic.

in-corruptus, a, um. **1.** Lit. *untainted, uninjured* : succus et sanguis, Cic.; virgo, Cic.; templa, Liv.; praeda,. Tac. **2.** Transf. *uncorrupted* (by bribery, flattery, etc.). **a.** Of persons : testis, Cic.; adversus blandientis, Tac. *Sup.* : custos, Hor. **b.** Of things : sensus, animus, Cic.; iudicium, Liv.; fides, Tac.

incrēbrāvit, 3rd *Pers. Perf.* (as fr. a form incrēbrāscō), *has got into the habit of visiting* : Pl.

in-crēbrēscō, crēbrēscere, crēbruī and **in-crēbēscō**, crēbēscere, crēbuī, *to become frequent or strong, to increase, spread* : mores deteriores, Pl.; Auster, Caes.; ventus, Cic. Ep.; consuetudo, Cic.; nemorum murmur, Verg.; fama belli, Liv.; proverbio increbruit, Liv.

in-crēdibilis, e, *adj. beyond belief, marvellous, extraordinary* : Pl., Caes., Cic. With ABL.: incredibile memoratu, Sall.

incrēdibiliter, *adv. extraordinarily* : delectari, consentire, Cic.

in-crēdulus, a, um, *unbelieving, incredulous* : Hor.

incrēmentum, ī, n. [incrēscō], *growth, increase.* **1.** Lit. Of plants and animals : in *pl.* : Cic. **2.** Transf. **a.** urbis, multitudinis, Liv.; iniuriarum in dies, Liv. **b.** Rhet.: *an ascending towards a climax* : Quint. **c.** *that which will grow into* : dentes, populi incrementa futuri, Ov.; magnorum ducum haec incrementa sunt, Curt. **d.** Concr. (of recruits) : incremento novare exercitum, Curt.; so also, summo bono adferre incrementum, Cic. **e.** *scion, progeny* : Iovis, Verg.

increpitō, āre [*freq.* increpō]. **I.** *to call or cry out, to challenge* : Verg. **II.** *to chide, rebuke* : increpitare atque incusare reliquos Belgas, Caes.; cum verbis quoque increpitans, Liv.: aestatem seram, Verg.

in-crepō, āre, uī, itum (āvī, ātum, Pl., Suet.), *to make a noise, to rustle, rattle, clatter, etc.* **A.** Intrans. **1.** Lit.: discus, Cic.; corvorum exercitus alis, Verg.; Mavors clipeo, Verg.; arma, Liv. With *Intern.* Acc.: tuba terribilem sonitum, Verg. **2.** Transf. **a.** *to cry aloud, speak sharply or angrily* : Verg.; ad contionem, Liv. With *Intern.* Acc.: haec in regem, Liv. **b.** *to be noised abroad* : quidquid increpuerit, Catilinam timeri, Cic.; si quid increpuit terroris, Liv. **B.** Trans. **1.** Lit. *to cause to sound, rattle, clatter, etc.* : me Iuppiter (i.e. *thundered at me*), Pl.; increpuit unda latus (navis), Ov.; Iuppiter atras nubes, Ov.;

Sabella pectus increpare carmina, Hor. **2.** Transf. (most freq.) *to exclaim loudly against, to blame loudly, to chide, rebuke, reprove.* **a.** With Acc. of person : numquid increpavit filium ? Pl.; male dictis omnis bonos, Sall.; Liv.; cunctantis socios, Verg., and with GEN. of the charge : avaritiae, Suet. **b.** With abstr. Object : illis versibus eorum adrogantiam, Cic.; eorum mollitiem, Liv. **c.** With Acc. and *Inf.* : *to assert reprovingly* : Liv.

in-crēscō, crēscere, crēvī. **I.** *to grow in or upon.* **1.** Lit.: squamae cuti, Ov. **2.** Transf.: animis discordibus irae, Verg. **II.** *to increase, grow.* Transf.: certamen, audacia, Liv.

incrētus, a, um, *Part.* incernō.

in-cruentātus, a, um, *unstained with blood* : Ov.

in-cruentus, a, um, *bloodless, without bloodshed or loss* : victoria, Sall., Liv.; proelium, miles, Liv.; exercitus, Sall., Tac.; incruentam urbem intrare, Tac.

in-crūstō, āre, *to cover with a coat or rind, to encrust.* **1.** Lit.: ollam sapā et farre, Varr. **2.** Transf.: sincerum vas, Hor.

incubitō, āre [*freq.* incubō], *to lie in or upon* : Pl.

in-cubō, āre, uī, itum, *to lie in or upon ; to lean upon.* **1.** Lit. **a.** stramentis, Hor.; umero hasta, Ov.; caetris, Liv. **b.** In a temple for the cure of disease, or to receive communications from the deity : in Aesculapi fano, Pl. **2.** Transf. **a.** *to lie on, brood over* : ponto nox, Verg. **b.** *to brood over, to watch jealously* : pecuniae, Cic.; auro, Verg.; publicis thesauris, Liv. **c.** *to abide or dwell in* : rure in praefecturā meā, Pl.; Erymantho, Ov. **d.** *to weigh upon, press heavily on* : Italiae Hannibal, Hor.

in-culcō, āre [calcō], *to tread in, press down by treading.* Transf. **a.** *to cram, stuff, or foist in* : Graeca verba, Cic. **b.** *to press or force upon* : se inculcant auribus, Cic.; non modo oculis imagines sed etiam animis, Cic. With Acc. and *Inf.* : inculcatum est Metello se aratores evertisse, Cic.

in-culpātus, a, um, *blameless* : Ov.

in-cultē, *adv. in a rough, uncivilised manner ; uncouthly* : Cic. *Comp.* : Sall.

in-cultus, a, um, *untilled, uncultivated.* **1.** Lit.: ager, solum, Cic., Liv. *Comp.* : Cic. As Noun, **inculta**, ōrum, n. *pl. wilderness, desert* : Verg., Liv. **2.** Transf. *undressed, neglected.* **a.** Of dress, etc.: coma, genae, Ov.; homines intonsi et inculti, Liv. **b.** Of manners, etc.: *rough, unpolished, uneducated, uncivilised* : vita, Cic.

in-cultus, ūs, m. **I.** *want of attention to, neglect* : honores desertos per incultum, Liv.; Sall. **II.** *squalor, dirt* : incultu, tenebris, odore, foeda (Tulliani) facies est, Sall.

in-cumbō, cumbere, cubuī, cubitum [*cf.* cubō], *to lay oneself upon, to lean upon or against.* **1.** Lit. **a.** Prop. (mostly with *in* and Acc., or DAT.: toro, Verg.; Damon olivae, Verg.; equus eiecto (magistro), Verg.; sarcinis, Liv.; terrae, Tac.; alii in alios, Liv.; ad vos, Ov. **b.** *to fling one-*

self upon, *rush upon* : in gladium, Cic. ;
in hostem, Liv. ; sagittariis, Tac. **c.** *to
throw one's weight upon* : remis, Verg. So
of storms, etc. : silvis tempestas, Verg. ;
terris febrium cohors, Hor. ; aestus populo,
Lucr. **2.** T r a n s f. **A. a.** *to lean over* :
laurus arae, Verg. ; silex ad amnem, Verg.
b. *to lean towards, incline* : ut eos quocumque incubuerit possit impellere, Cic. ; Pl. ;
eodem municipia, Cic. **B.** *to fling oneself
upon, devote one's energy or attention to* :
et animo et opibus in bellum, Caes. ; in
causam, Cic. ; toto pectore ad laudem, Cic. ;
novae cogitationi, Tac. ; ad ulciscendas rei
publicae iniurias, Cic. With *ut* and *Subj.* :
Liv. With *Inf.* : Verg., Tac. **C.** *to lend
one's weight in support* : fato urguenti,
Verg. ; inclinatis rebus, Liv.
in-cūnābula, ōrum, *n. pl. cradle-clothes,
swaddling-clothes.* **1.** L i t. : Pl. **2.** T r a n s f.
a. *infancy, the 'cradle'* : ab incunabulis
imbutus odio tribunorum, Liv. ; Bacchi, Ov.
b. *a birthplace ; the cradle of a race* : in montis
patrios, et ad incunabula nostra, Poet. ap.
Cic. Ep. ; Iovis incunabula Creta, Ov. **c.**
source, origin : deorum, Caes. ; doctrinae,
Cic.
in-cūrātus, a, um, *neglected, uncured* :
ulcera, Hor.
incūria, ae, *f.* [cūra], *want of care, carelessness, negligence* : milites incuriā consumpti,
Cic. ; maculae quas incuria fudit, Hor. ;
magistratuum, Tac.
incūriōsē, *adv. carelessly, negligently* : Liv.
Comp. : Tac.
in-cūriōsus, a, um. **A.** A c t. *careless, unconcerned, regardless, indifferent.* With *in* :
in capite comendo, Suet. With GEN. :
famae, Tac. ; proximorum, Plin. Ep. ;
imperi proferendi, Tac. With ABL. : serendis frugibus, Tac. **B.** P a s s. *neglected,
not made* or *done with care* : finis, Tac. ;
historia, Suet.
in-currō, currere, currī (cucurrī), cursum,
to run into or *towards, to rush at, charge,
attack.* **1.** L i t. **A.** In gen. : desultorius
in quadrigarum curriculum, Cic. With
DAT. : alveo torrentes, Curt. **B.** M i l i t.
a. in hostis, Sall. ; Liv. With DAT. :
armentis, Ov. ; levi armaturae hostium,
Liv. ; Tac. With Acc. : novissimos, Tac.
b. *to invade* : in Macedoniam, Liv. **2.**
T r a n s f. **A.** *to run, extend into* : agri in
publicum Campanum, Cic. **B.** *to attack*
(with words) : in tribunos, Liv. **C.** Of
accidents, etc. **a.** *to run into* : amens in
columnas, Cic. ; ut in eum non invasisse
(intentionally) sed incucurrisse (accidentally) videamur, Cic. ; in oculos, Cic. Ep. ;
in morbos, in damna, Cic. ; in memoriam
notam, Tac. ; quaestus in odia hominum,
Cic. **b.** Of time-relation : *to fall on,
coincide with* : navigatio in ipsos etesias,
Cic. Ep. ; natalis plebeiis Circensibus,
Suet.
in-cursiō, ōnis, *f.* **1.** L i t. **a.** *a hostile
assault, onset* : armatorum, Cic. **b.** *an
invasion, raid* : hostiliter in finis incur-
sionem fecit, Liv. ; prohibere hostem ab
incursionibus, Caes. **c.** *a collision* : atomorum, Cic. **2.** T r a n s f. : incursio seditionis, Cic.

incursĭtō, āre [*freq.* inoursō], *to rush upon
violently.* T r a n s f. *to dash against, run
one's head against something* : totā vitā in-
cursitamus, Sen. Ep.
incursō, āre [*freq.* incurrō]. **1.** L i t. **a.**
to assault, attack vigorously. With *in* : in
agmen, Liv. ; Pl. With Acc. : aliquem
pugnis, Pl. ; aciem equitatus, Tac. ; Liv.
In *Pass.* : agmen incursatum ab equitibus
hostium, Liv. **b.** *to invade frequently* :
agros Romanos, Liv. **2.** T r a n s f. **a.** *to
dash against.* With DAT. : delphines altis
ramis, Ov. ; rupibus, Ov. **b.** *to fall upon,
strike* : in te dolor meus, Cic. Ep. ; laurus
in oculos, Cic. Ep. : ea oculis vel auribus,
Quint.
incursus, a, um, *Part.* incurrō.
incursus, ūs, *m.* [incurrō], *an assault, attack.*
1. L i t. : ceterorum incursūs refugit, Cic. ;
incursūs equitum sustinere, Caes. **2.**
T r a n s f. **a.** *invasion* or *assault* : undarum,
aquarum, Ov. ; tempestatum, Quint. **b.**
impulse : incursūs animus varios habet,
Ov.
in-curvēscō, ere [curvus], *to bend down* :
bacarum ubertate, Poet. ap. Cic.
in-curvō, āre, *to bend, curve in, crook.* **1.**
L i t. : flexos arcūs, Verg. ; bacillum, Cic.
2. T r a n s f. : aliquem querellā, Pers.
in-curvus, a, um, *bent* or *curved in, bowed,
crooked.* Of persons : incurvus, tremulus,
Ter. Of things : bacillum, Cic. ; aratrum,
Verg. ; carinae, Ov. ; litus (i.e. winding),
Lucr.
incūs, ūdis, *f.* [in cūdō], *an anvil.* **1.** L i t. :
Cic., Verg., Hor. **2.** T r a n s f. : Pl. ;
iuvenes, et in ipsā studiorum incude positi,
Tac. ; incudi reddere versūs (i.e. to recast),
Hor. P r o v. : incudem eandem tundere
(i.e. to labour always at the same thing),
Cic.
incūsātiō, ōnis, *f.* [incūsō], *a blaming, accusation* : Cic.
in-cūsō, āre [causa], *to bring into a charge ;
to accuse, to complain of, find fault with,
blame* (us. in extra-judicial sense : accuso,
to accuse in court) : eum ob defectionem,
Liv. ; eos quod putarent, etc., Caes. ; se
qui non acceperit Aenean, Verg. With
Acc. and *Inf.* : Liv. With Acc. of person
and GEN. of thing : alterum probri, Pl. ;
aliquem superbiae, Tac. With Acc. of
thing only : vestrum factum, Ov. ; iniurias Romanorum, Liv. ; duritiam operum,
Tac.
incussū, ABL. *sing. m.* [incutiō], *by the shock* :
armorum, Tac.
incussus, a, um, *Part.* incutiō.
in-custōditus, a, um. **A.** P a s s. **a.** *not
watched, unguarded* : ovile, Ov. ; incursare
incustoditus, Tac. **b.** *unconcealed* : amor,
Tac. **B.** A c t. *unguarded, imprudent* :
Plin. Ep.
in-cūsus, a, um [in cūdō], *forged with a hammer, fabricated* : lapis, Verg. ; incusa auro
dona, Pers.
in-cutiō, cutere, cussī, cussum [quatiō], *to
dash, strike upon* or *against.* **1.** L i t. **a.**
scipionem in caput alicuius, Liv. ; colaphum servo, Juv. **b.** *to dash, fling upon* :
tormentis faces et hastas, Tac. **2.** T r a n s f.
a. *to strike into, inspire with* : religionem

animo, Liv. ; alicui metum, Liv. ; desiderium urbis, Hor. ; vim ventis, Verg. Without Dat. : timor incutitur ex periculis, Cic. **b.** *to fling upon* : consuli foedum nuntium, Liv.

indăgătĭō, ōnis, *f.* [indăgō], *an investigation* : veri, Cic.

indăgātor, ōris, *m.* and **indăgātrix**, īcis, *f.* [indăgō], *an investigator, explorer* : celati, Pl. ; philosophia indagatrix virtutis, Cic.

indăgō, āre [ind-, agō]. Lit. *to drive into* (a net) ; hence *to track out* (as hounds). **1.** Lit. : canis natus ad indagandum, Cic. **2.** Transf. : rem, Pl. ; indicia communia exiti, Cic. ; de re publicā, Cic. Ep.

indăgō, ĭnis, *f.* [ind-, agō], *a hunting drive into.* **1.** Lit. **a.** velut indagine dissipatos Samnites agere, Liv. ; Hirt. ; indaginis modo silvas persultare, Tac. **b.** *a hunting encirclement* : saltūs indagine cingunt, Verg. ; Tib. **2.** Transf. : delatores in illā poenarum indagine inclusos, Plin. Pan.

indaudĭō, *v.* inaudiō.

inde, adv. [im, fr. is, and particle -de], *therefrom, thence.* **1.** Lit. Of place : Pl., Cic., etc. Often (in Eng. idiom), *on that side* : hinc militum, inde locorum asperitas, Tac. ; Liv. **2.** Transf. **A. a.** Of startingpoint : ut inde oratio mea proficiscatur, Cic. **b.** Of source, or origin : inde (ex audaciā) omnia scelera gignuntur, Cic. ; inde . . . quia (or quod), Liv. Also of persons : nati filii duo : inde ego hunc maiorem adoptavi mihi, Ter. **B.** Of time. **a.** *from that time forth, ever since* : inde usque repetens, Cic. ; iam inde ab incunabulis, Liv. **b.** *after that, next, then* : eodem impetu altera castra sunt adorti, inde tertia, deinceps reliqua, Caes. With Gen. : inde loci (transferred to time), *after that, thereupon*, Lucr. [Fr. pron. *en*, ' of it, from it.']

in-dēbĭtus, a, um, *not due* : regna, Verg. ; Ov.

in-dĕcēns, entis, adj. *unbecoming, unseemly, unsightly* : Quint., Mart., Suet.

in-dĕcenter, adv. *unbecomingly, indecently, disgracefully* : Quint. Comp. : Sen. Ep. Sup. : Quint.

in-dĕceō, ēre, *to be unbecoming to* (with Acc.) : Plin. Ep.

indēclīnābĭlis, e, adj. [dēclīnō], *inflexible, unchangeable* : Sen. Ep.

in-dēclīnātus, a, um, *unchanged, constant* : Ov.

in-dĕcor, oris, or **indĕcŏris**, e. adj. *without honour, inglorious, disgraceful* : Acc. ; nec genus indecores, Verg. ; regno indecores, Verg.

in-dĕcōrē, adv. *unbecomingly, indecently* : Cic., Tac.

in-dĕcŏrō, āre, *to disgrace, disfigure* : Acc. ; bene nata culpae, Hor.

in-dĕcŏrus, a, um, *unsightly, ungraceful.* **1.** Lit. : motus, Liv. ; gestus, Quint. ; forma, Tac. **2.** Transf. : *unbecoming* : *wanting in grace or propriety* : Cic. ; indecorum est, with *Inf.* : Liv., Tac.

indēfătīgābĭlis, e, adj. [dēfatīgō], *that cannot be wearied, untiring* : Sen.

in-dēfătīgātus, a, um [dēfatīgō], *unwearied* : Sen.

in-dēfensus, a, um, *unprotected, undefended* : Liv., Tac.

in-dēfessus, a, um, *unwearied, indefatigable* : Tac. ; dextra, Verg. ; agendo, Ov.

in-dēflētus, a, um, *unwept, unlamented* : animae, Ov.

in-dēiectus, a, um, *not thrown down* : Ov.

in-dēlēbĭlis, e, adj. *indestructible, imperishable* : nomen, Ov.

in-dēlībātus, a, um, *unimpaired* : opes, Ov.

in-demnātus, a, um [damnātus], *uncondemned* : Pl., Cic., etc.

indemnis, e, adj. [damnum], *unhurt* : Sen. Ep.

in-dēplōrātus, a, um, *unwept* : Ov.

in-dēprēnsus, a, um, *undetected* : error, Verg.

indeptus, a, um, *Part.* indipiscor.

in-dēsertus, a, um, *not deserted, unforsaken* : regna, Ov.

in-dēspectus, a, um, *unfathomable* : Tartara, Luc.

in-dēstrictus, a, um, *unscathed* : Ov.

in-dētōnsus, a, um, *unshorn* : Ov.

in-dēvītātus, a, um, *unavoided* : telum, Ov.

index, ĭcis, m. [in and weak form of root of dīcō], *the pointer.* **1.** Lit. **a.** *the forefinger* : Cic. Ep. ; indice monstraret digito, Hor. **b.** *an informer* : haec omnia indices detulerunt, Cic. ; Catilinam vallatum indicibus atque sicariis, Cic. ; index idem et testis, Tac. ; arcani, Tac. **2.** Transf. Of things : *that which discloses, betrays, reveals.* **a.** *indication* : vocem indicem stultitiae, Cic. ; auctoris anulus index, Ov. ; Ianum indicem pacis bellique fecit, Liv. **b.** *a test, touchstone* : silicem qui nunc quoque dicitur index, Ov. **c.** *a title, superscription* : librorum, Cic. ; orationis, Liv. ; tabula cum indice hoc posita, Liv. **d.** *a catalogue, index* : Quint., Plin. Ep.

Indī, ōrum, *m. pl. the people of India* ; **India**, ae, *f. their country* ; **Indus**, a, um ; **Indus**, ī, *m.* **a.** *an Indian* : Verg. Transf. *an Ethiopian* : Verg. **b.** *an elephant's driver, mahout* : Liv. ; **Indicus**, a, um ; **Indicum**, ī, *n. indigo.*

indĭcātĭō, ōnis, *f.* [indĭcō], *a valuation* : hence, *value, price* : Pl.

in-dĭcente, Abl. *sing., not speaking* : non me indicente haec fiunt, Ter. ; etiam me indicente, Liv.

indĭcĭum, ī, *n.* [index]. **I.** *information, disclosure.* **1.** Lit. **a.** In gen. : facite indicium si quis vidit, Pl. ; coniurationis, Cic. ; res est per indicium enuntiata, Caes. ; deferre ad aliquem, Tac. **b.** *evidence* (given before a court) : indicio legatorum convicti, Sall. ; indicium profiteri (Sall., Plin. Ep.) or offerre (Tac.), " to turn King's evidence." **2.** Transf. **a.** *permission to give evidence* : postulare, dare, Cic. **b.** *a reward for giving evidence* : edictum cum poenā atque indicio, Cic. **II.** *a sign, indication, proof* : certissima sceleris, Cic. ; indicio de se ipse erit, Ter. ; edere, Lucr.

indĭcō, āre (indicāsso, old *Fut.*, Pl. ; indicāssis, perh. old *Opt.*, Pl.) [index], *to point out, show, reveal, betray.* **1.** Lit. **a.** In gen. : Pl. ; rem dominae, Cic. ; rem patri, Ter. ; causam publicae pestis, Liv. ; tibi de epistulis, Cic. With *Indir. Quest.* : Quint. **b.** In court : *to depose or inform against,* *to give evidence :* Catilina non se purgavit, sed indicavit, Cic. ; de coniuratione, Sall. **c.** *to declare the price, put a price on :* Pl. ; fundum, Cic. **2.** Transf.: hoc res ipsa indicat, Ter. ; vultus indicat mores, Cic. ; lacrimis dolorem, Nep.

in-dīcō, dicere, dīxī, dictum (*Imper.* indice, Pl.), *to declare publicly, to proclaim, announce, ordain :* totius Galliae concilium Bibracte indicitur, Caes. ; exercitum in aliquem locum, Liv. ; bellum, forum, Verg. ; iter alicui, Verg. ; templis honorem, Verg. ; sibimet exsilium, Liv. ; tributum, Liv. ; pondus argenti senatoribus, Tac. ; funus, Suet. ; ex ante indicto, Liv.
(1) **indictus,** a, um, *Part.* indicō.
(2) **in-dictus,** a, um, *not said, unsaid :* quod dictum, indictum 'st, Ter. ; Liv. ; carminibus, Verg. ; indictā causā, *without a hearing, unheard,* Cic., Liv.

indidem, adv. [inde -dem], *from the same place.* **1.** Lit.: indidemne Ameriā, an ex urbe ? Cic. ; ex Aventino, Liv. ; Pl. **2.** Transf. *from the same matter or thing :* unde simile duci potest indidem verbum unum, Cic. ; Liv.

in-differēns, entis, adj. **I.** In ethics: *neither good nor bad :* Cic., Sen. Ep. **II.** Of persons : *indifferent, unconcerned :* circa victum indifferens, Suet. **III.** Of quantity of a syllable : *doubtful :* Quint.

indifferenter, adv. **I.** *without distinction :* Quint. **II.** *with unconcern :* Suet.

indigena, ae, adj. m. f. [indu- and root of gignō], *born within* (the district), *native, indigenous :* Verg., Liv. ; bos, Ov. As Noun, *a native :* Liv., Juv.

indigēns, entis. **I.** *Part.* indigeō. **II.** Adj. *in want of, needy, indigent.* With GEN.: illius, Cic. ; alienarum opum, Nep. As Noun, esp. in *pl.* : *a needy* or *indigent person :* Cic.

indigentia, ae, f. [indigēns]. **I.** *need, want :* ab indigentiā orta amicitia, Cic. **II.** *craving :* Cic.

ind-igeō, ēre, uī [ind- egeō]. **I.** *to need, want, to stand in need of, require.* With GEN.: ingeni et virtutis, Cic. Ep. ; alterius, Cic. With ABL.: bonā existimatione, Cic. ; iis rebus, Caes. ; constantia, Tac. ; pax et quies bonis artibus, Tac. **II.** *to crave, desire :* auri, Cic.

indiges, is, adj. [ind- egeō], *needy :* Pac.

indiges, etis, m. [perh. fr. ind- and agō], *native, indigenous :* of gods and heroes : Verg., Liv. ; in *pl.* : dii indigetes, Liv.

in-digestus, a, um, *unarranged, confused :* moles, Ov.

indignābundus, a, um [indignor], *enraged, indignant :* Liv., Suet.

indignandus, a, um [indignor], *to be scorned :* Ov.

indignāns, antis. **I.** *Part.* indignor. Adj.: *angry, impatient, chafing :* venti, Verg. ; verba, pectus, Ov.

indignātiō, ōnis, f. [indignor]. **I.** *angry displeasure, indignation :* Hor. ; movere, Liv. ; indignatio oborta (est), with ACC. and *Inf.* : Liv. In *pl.* : *expressions of indignation :* Liv. **II.** Rhet.: *an exciting of indignation :* Cic., Quint. **III.** *a cause of indignation :* Juv.

indignē, adv. **I.** *unworthily, undeservedly, dishonourably :* Pl., Ter., Caes. *Sup.* : Cic. **II.** *with indignation :* pati, Cic. ; ferre (with ACC. and *Inf.*) : Nep.

indignitās, ātis, f. [indignus]. **I.** *unworthiness, contemptible character.* **a.** Of men : hominis, Cic. ; accusatoris, Cic. **b.** Of things : *enormity, shamefulness :* rei, Caes. ; calamitatis, Cic. **II.** *degrading* or *insulting treatment, indignity :* alicuius adeundi, Cic. Ep. ; indignitates perferre, Caes. ; indignitatibus compulsus, Liv. **III.** *indignation* (at unworthy treatment), *sense of wrong :* indignitas atque ex eā ira animos cepit, Liv. ; Cic. Ep.

in-dignor, ārī [indignus], *to consider unworthy, undeserved, shameful ; to be angry* or *displeased at, to be indignant, chafe at, rebel against.* With ACC.: se ipsum, Lucr. ; aliquid, Cic. ; casum amici, Verg. ; suam vicem, Liv. ; pontem indignatus Araxes, Verg. With *quod-* clause : Caes., Verg. With *Inf.*: Ov., Liv., Quint. With ACC. and *Inf.* : Caes., Sall., Quint. *Absol.* : Quint. ; vita fugit indignata sub umbras, Verg.

in-dignus, a, um, *unworthy, undeserving.* **1.** Lit. Of persons. **a.** In relation to good things : divitias quivis, quamvis indignus, habere potest, Cic. With ABL.: honore, Cic. ; Quint., etc. With GEN. : magnorum avorum, Verg. With *rel.* : indigni, qui impetrarent, Cic. With *ut* and *Subj.* : Liv. *Sup.* : Cic. **b.** In relation to bad things : *undeserving, unoffending :* Pl., Lucr., Cic. ; iniuriā, Ter. ; morte, Quint. ; indignus quem mors tam saeva maneret, Juv. **2.** Transf. Of things. **a.** *unworthy, degrading, shameful :* dictum, Pl. ; vox populi maiestate indigna, Caes. ; lictoribus indignum in modum mulcatis, Liv. ; exempla, Ter. ; fortuna, Verg. *Comp.* : Cic. *Sup.* : Cic. ; aliquid pro indignissimo habere, Liv. *Neut.* indignum ! *shame !* Ov. **b.** *not worth :* with ABL.: relatu, Verg. ; Liv. With *Inf.* : fabula non indigna referri, Ov. ; Sall. **c.** *undeserved :* mors, Verg. ; Ov. *Neut. pl.* as Noun : indigna pati, Liv.

indigus, a, um [indigeō], *needing, in want.* With GEN.: nummorum, Pl. ; opis, Verg., Tac. ; rectoris, Tac. With ABL.: auxilio, Lucr.

in-dīligēns, entis, adj. *careless, slack :* Pl., Nep. *Comp.* : Caes.

indīligenter, adv. *carelessly, slackly :* Ter., Cic. Ep. *Comp.* : Caes.

in-dīligentia, ae, f. [indīligēns], *carelessness, slackness :* Pl. With *Subj.* GEN.: Aeduorum, Caes. With *Obj.* GEN.: litterarum missarum, Cic. Ep. ; veri, Tac.

ind-ipiscor, ipisci, eptus (and **indipiscō,** ere, Pl.) [ind- apiscor]. **I.** *to get, obtain, acquire :* mercedes, Pl. **II.** *to gain, reach :* hominem leti quies, Lucr. ; navem, Liv.

in-direptus, a, um *unplundered :* Capitolium, Tac.

in-discrētus, a, um. **I.** *unseparated, closely connected :* cum agri culturā, Varr. ; suum cuique sanguinem indiscretum, Tac. **II.** *without distinction, indiscriminate :* ineunt

locos, Tac. **III.** *indistinguishable :* proles,
Verg.

indisertē, *adv. ineloquently :* Cic. Ep.

in-disertus, a, um *ineloquent :* Academicus,
Cic. ; prudentia, Cic.

in-dispositus, a, um, *without order, confused :*
Tac.

in-dissolūbilis, e, *adj. that cannot be dissolved.* Transf. *imperishable :* Cic.

in-distīnctus, a, um. **I.** *confused, in a
tangle :* Cat., Quint. **II.** *indistinct, obscure :* defensio, Tac. **III.** *free from rhetorical display :* Quint.

inditus, a, um, *Part.* indō.

in-dīviduus, a, um, *indivisible.* **1.** Lit. :
Cic. As Noun, **individuum,** ī, *n. an atom :*
Cic. **2.** Transf. of friends : *inseparable :*
Tac. Transf. : comitatus virtutum, Sen.
Ep.

in-dīvīsus, a, um, *undivided.* **1.** Lit. :
ungulae equorum, Varr. **2.** Transf. *common :* as Noun in phr., pro indiviso, *in
common, indiscriminately,* Cato, Plin.

in-dō, dere, didī, ditum, *to put* or *place upon*
or *in.* **1.** Lit. : ignem in aram, Pl. ;
fenestras, Pl. ; custodes, Tac. ; effigiem in
statuā, Tac. With Dat. : compedis servis,
Pl. ; scintillam plumae, Liv. ; vinclo cervicem, Tac. **2.** Transf. **a.** *to introduce :*
novos ritūs, Tac. **b.** *to impart* or *give to :*
urbi nomen, Pl. ; alicui vocabulum, Tac. ;
puero ab inopiā Egerio nomen inditum, Liv. ;
pavorem suis, alacritatem hostibus, Tac.

in-docilis, e, *adj.* **I.** *difficult to teach* or *learn.*
1. Lit. **a.** Of persons : Cic. With Dat. :
quieti, Juv. With *Inf.* : pauperiem pati,
Hor. **b.** Of the thing : *hard to learn, severe :*
indocilem usūs disciplinam, Cic. **II.** *untaught.* **a.** Of persons : genus, Verg. **b.**
Of things, *untaught, rude :* numerus, Ov.

in-doctē, *adv. unlearnedly, unskilfully :* Pl.,
Cic.

in-doctus, a, um. **I.** *untaught, illiterate :*
Cic., Juv. **II.** *unschooled, untrained.* **a.**
Of persons. With *Inf.* : Hor. With Gen. :
pilae discive, Hor. **b.** Of things : moribus
indoctis, Pl. ; manus, Quint.

in-dolentia, ae, *f. freedom from pain :* Cic.,
Sen. Ep.

ind-olēs, is, *f.* [ind- and ol seen in adolēscō],
inborn character, native quality. **a.** in
savio, Pl. ; frugum, pecudum, Liv. **b.** Of
men : *natural abilities, talents, genius, disposition :* adulescentes bonā indole praediti, Cic. ; segnis, Tac. ; gener ob altam indolem ascitus, Liv. ; virtutis, Cic.

in-dolēscō, dolēscere, doluī [doleō], *to begin
to feel pain.* Transf. *to feel pain, be
grieved, sorry, indignant.* With Acc. (of
Neut. Pron.) : Ov. With Abl. : facto, Ov.
With *quod*-clause : Ov. With Acc. and
Inf. : Cic., Ov., Tac.

in-domābilis, e, *untameable :* Pl.

in-domitus, a, um, *untamed, wild.* **1.** Lit. :
boves, Varr., Liv. ; Hor. **2.** Transf.
unsubdued, untameable, ungovernable, wild :
mulier, Pl. ; pastores, Caes. ; gens, etc.,
Liv. ; nationes, Tac. Of things : oculi,
Pl. ; dextra, Ov. ; mors, Hor. ; animi cupiditates, Cic. ; Falernum, Pers.

in-dormiō, īre, *to sleep* or *fall asleep at, on,*
or *over.* **1.** Lit. : congestis saccis, Hor.

2. Transf. *to go to sleep over, to be careless*
or *remiss :* in isto homine colendo, Cic.
Ep. With Dat. : tantae causae, Cic. Ep. ;
longae desidiae, Plin. Ep.

in-dōtātus, a, um, *without dowry, portionless.*
1. Lit. : Ter., Hor. **2.** Transf. **a.**
without due funeral rites : corpora, Ov. **b.**
unadorned, poor : ars, Cic.

indu-, *v.* in ; **indugr-, indup-,** *v.* ingr-, imp-.

in-dubitābilis, e, *adj. that cannot be doubted :*
Quint.

in-dubitātus, a, um, *undoubted, sure :* Quint.

in-dubitō, āre, *to begin to distrust :* with
Dat. : viribus tuis, Verg.

in-dubius, a, um, *not doubtful, certain :* exempla, Quint. ; innocentia, Tac.

indūciae, *v.* indūtiae.

in-dūcō, dūcere, dūxī, ductum (indūxtī for
indūxistī, Ter.). **I.** *to lead* or *bring in.*
1. Lit. **a.** In gen. : turmas, Verg. ; eā
portā hastatos, Liv. With in and Acc. :
exercitum in Macedoniam, Liv. ; Sall.
With Dat. : fossā mare urbi, Suet. **b.** *to
exhibit, represent :* gladiatorum par nobilis-
simum inducitur, Cic. ; pater fabula quem
miserum vixisse inducit, Hor. **c.** *to bring into*
or *before a court:* aliquem in senatum, Plin.
Ep. ; reos in curiam, Suet. **d.** *to make an
entry* (in an account book), *to enter to
account :* pecuniam in rationes, Cic. ;
agrum alicui pecuniā ingenti, Cic. **2.**
Transf. **A.** *to bring in, introduce :* morem
hunc, Pl. ; seditionem in civitatem, Cic. ;
novum verbum in linguam Latinam, Cic.
So in speaking or writing : gravem personam, Cic. ; hinc illo Gyges inducitur a
Platone, Cic. ; hunc sermonem, Cic. Ep. ;
dubitationem, Tac. **B.** *to lead* or *draw on,
induce, persuade, seduce :* aliquem pretio,
spe, etc., Cic. ; aliquem in errorem, Cic. ;
ad misericordiam, ad pudendum, etc., Cic. ;
animum ad aliquid, Ter. With *ut* and
Subj. : Cic. With *Inf. :* Tac. Hence,
without definition : hic eos, quibus erat ig-
notus, decepit fefellit induxit, Cic. ; Tib.
C. Often with animum or in animum, *to
bring one's mind to* something. **a.** *to resolve, determine, decide.* With Acc. of *Neut.
Pron. :* Cic. Ep. With *Inf. :* Ter., Cic.,
etc. With *ut* or ne and *Subj. :* Pl., Cic.,
Liv. With *quo minus :* Plin. Ep. **b.**
With Acc. and *Inf. : to be convinced :* Pl.,
Ter., Liv. **II.** *to draw over* or on, *to overlay, spread over, drape, cover.* **1.** Lit. **a.**
In gen. : postis pice, Pl. ; scuta pellibus,
Caes. ; coria super lateres, Caes. ; vitibus
umbras, Verg. ; fontis umbrā, Verg. ; pulvis velut nube inductā omnia impleverat,
Liv. **b.** Of dress : tunicāque inducitur
artūs, Verg. ; manibus caestūs, Verg. ;
calceum, Suet. **c.** Of erasure : *to draw*
(the broad end of the stilus) *over : to
erase :* nomina, senatūs consultum, Cic. Ep.
2. Transf. *to cancel :* locationes, Liv.
[It. *indurre ;* Fr. *induire.*]

inductiō, ōnis, *f.* [indūcō], *a leading* or
bringing in. **1.** Lit. : aquarum, Cic. ;
horum (in circum), Liv. **2.** Transf. **a.**
a purpose, resolution, inclination, intention :
animi, Cic. **b.** erroris inductio : *a mis-
leading,* Cic. **c.** In logic : *induction :*
Cic., Quint.

inductor, ōris, *m. a persuader* (comic. for a whip) : Pl.

inductā, ABL. *sing. m.* [indūcŏ], *by inducing, persuasion :* huius persuasu et inductu, Cic. ap. Quint.

indūcula, ae, *f.* [indūŏ], *an under-garment worn by females :* Pl.

indulgēns, entis. I. *Part.* indulgeŏ. II. Adj. a. *indulgent, lenient :* Liv. With DAT. : obsequium peccatis, Cic. With *in* and ACC. : civitas minime in captivos indulgens, Liv. *Comp. :* nomen, Cic. b. *addicted to :* aleae, Suet.

indulgenter, *adv. indulgently, kindly :* Cic. *Comp.* and *Sup. :* Sen.

indulgentia, ae, *f.* [indulgēns], *indulgence, complaisance, lenience, tender love :* Cic. ; in (matris) sinu indulgentiăque educatus, Tac. With *in* and ACC. : Caesaris in se, Caes. With *Obj.* GEN. : corporis, Cic. ; indulgentiă filiarum commoveri, Cic.

indulgeŏ, dulgēre, dūlsī [perh. fr. root seen in Gk. δολιχός ; hence, *to be long over, be patient*]. A. I n t r a n s. *to be kind or indulgent, to show favour* or *complaisance, to give way.* 1. L i t. a. With DAT. of person : Caes., Liv. So, sibi imbecillitas, Cic. b. With DAT. of thing : militum ardori, Liv. ; irae vestrae, Liv. ; precibus, Plin. Ep. ; lacrimis, Ov. ; ordinibus (i.e. allow room for the rows), Verg. 2. T r a n s f. *to indulge in, be addicted :* novis amicitiis, Cic. ; vino, labori, hospitio, Verg. ; somno, Tac. *Impers. Pass. :* Liv. B. T r a n s. a. With ACC. of person : *to indulge, show favour to :* Ter. b. With ACC. and DAT. : *to concede, grant, permit something to somebody :* alicui usum pecuniae, Suet. ; ornamenta consularia procuratoribus, Suet. ; Tac. ; veniam pueris, Juv.

ind-uŏ, uere, uī, ūtum [ind. -uŏ, *cf.* exuŏ], *to put on,* esp. of dress. 1. L i t. : galeam, Caes. ; anulum, Cic. With ACC. of thing and DAT. of person : Herculi tunicam, Cic. ; alicui insignia Bacchi, Ov. In *Mid. :* with ACC. or ABL. : virgines longam indutae vestem, Liv. ; indutus galeā, Verg. ; soccis, Cic. 2. T r a n s f. a. *to put on, cover, drape :* dii indúti specie humanā, Cic. ; pomis se arbos, Verg. ; quos induerat Circe in vultūs ac terga ferarum, Verg. b. *to put on, assume :* personam iudicis, Cic. ; alicuius simulationem, Liv. ; sibi cognomen, Cic. ; magnum animum, Tac. ; falsos pavores, Tac. ; seditionem, societatem, Tac. ; proditorem (i.e. the character of a traitor), Tac. c. *to fall into* or *upon, to be entangled in :* se in laqueum, Pl. ; venti se in nubem, Cic. ; se vallis, Caes. ; sese mucroni, Verg. ; se hastis, Liv. d. *to entangle :* se in captiones, Cic. ; suā confessione indui, Cic.

in-dūrēscō, dūrēscere, dūruī, *to become hard, harden.* 1. L i t : corpus usu, Ov. 2. T r a n s f. : in pravum, Quint. ; miles induruerat pro Vitellio, Tac.

in-dūrŏ, āre, *to make hard, to harden.* 1. L i t. : nivem Boreas, Ov. 2. T r a n s f. : indurandus est animus, Sen. Ep. ; vultum, Tac.

indusārius, ī, *m.* [indusium], *a maker of women's under-garments :* Pl.

indusiātus, a, um [indusium], *wearing an under-garment :* Pl.

industria, ae, *f.* [industrius], *steady attention, diligence, determined effort :* navis summā industriā armaro, Caes. ; ingenium industriā alitur, Cic. ; in agendo, Cic. ; itineris, Suet. In *pl. :* Pl. P h r. : *on purpose, intentionally :* ex industriā, Liv. ; de industriā, Ter., Cic. ; industriā, Pl. ; ob industriam, Pl.

industriē (Cato, Caes., Quint.. etc.), and **industriōsē** (Suet., and *Sup. :* Cato), *adv. carefully, diligently.*

industrius, a, um [perh. fr. ind- struŏ], *diligent, attentive, painstaking :* Cic., Tac., Juv. *Comp. :* industrior : Pl.

indūtiae (-ciae), ārum, *f. pl. a temporary cessation of hostilities, a truce, armistice.* 1. L i t. : cum triginta dierum essent cum hoste pactae indutiae, Cic. ; facere, Cic. ; petere, conservare, Nep. ; agitare, *to keep,* Sall. ; per indutias, Liv. 2. T r a n s f. *a cessation, pause :* indutiae parumper fiant, si quid vis loqui, Pl. ; Ter.

indūtus, a, um, *Part.* induŏ.

indūtus, ūs, *m.* [induŏ], *a putting on, wearing :* vestis, quam indutui gerebat, Tac. ; Varr.

induviae, ārum, *f. pl.* [induŏ], *clothes, garments :* Pl.

in-ēbriŏ, āre (ēbrius), *to make drunk, intoxicate.* 1. L i t. : Sen. Ep. 2. T r a n s f. *to saturate :* aurem, Juv.

inedia, ae, *f.* [edŏ], *abstinence from food, starvation :* genua inediā succidunt, Pl. ; inediā necatus, Cic. ; Plin. Ep.

in-ēditus, a, um, *unpublished, unknown :* cura, Ov.

in-efficāx, ācis, *adj. ineffective, inefficient :* ratio, dii, Sen. With GEN. : vox verborum, Sen. *Comp. :* Plin.

in-ēlegāns, antis, *adj. not choice or tasteful :* orationis copia, Cic. ; deliciae, Cat.

inēleganter, *adv. without taste :* scribere, Cic.

in-ēluctābilis, e, *adj. whose grip one cannot break from :* fatum, tempus, Verg.

in-ēmendābilis, e, *adj. that cannot be corrected :* Sen., Quint.

in-ēmorior, *to die in or at ;* with DAT. : spectaculo, Hor.

in-emptus, a, um, *unbought, unpurchased :* dapes, Verg. ; Hor. ; Tac.

in-ēnārrābilis, e, *adj. indescribable :* labor, tabes, Liv. ; ratio, Quint.

in-ēnārrābiliter, *adv. in an indescribable manner :* Liv.

in-ēnōdābilis, e, *adj.* [ēnōdŏ], *that cannot be freed from knots, i.e. cannot be explained, inexplicable :* Acc. ; res, Cic.

in-eŏ, īre, iī, itum. A. I n t r a n s. *to go or come in, enter.* 1. L i t. : in urbem, Liv. ; ut ovans iniret, Plin. *Impers. Pass. :* Pl. 2. T r a n s f. Of time, *to begin :* ab ineunte adulescentiā, Cic. ; ineunte vere, Cic. ; ex ineunte aevo, Lucr. ; decus hoc aevi, te consule, inibit, Verg. B. T r a n s. *to go or come in, enter.* 1. L i t. : illius domum, Cic. ; urbem, Liv. ; Athenas, tecta, thalamos, Ov. *Pass. :* Hispania inita, Liv. ; Ov. 2. T r a n s f. : *to enter upon, begin.* a. In gen. : viam, iter, convivia, Cic. ; cursūs, Verg. ; proelium, Cic. ; pugnas

Verg.; bellum, Cic., Liv.; consilium, Caes., Cic., Ov.; societatem, Cic., Liv.; magistratum, Cic.; suffragium, Liv.; gratiam ab aliquo, Cic. Ep.; plures ineuntur gratiae, Cic.; apud regem initam gratiam volebant, Liv.; pro te tua munera inibo, Verg.; formam vitae, Tac. **b.** With rationem or numerum, *to enter on, make a calculation*: vix ratio iniri poterat, Caes.; initā subductāque ratione, Cic.; numerus interfectorum haud facile iniri potuit, Liv.; Caes. **c.** Of time (in *Pass.*): initā aestate, Caes.

ineptē, adv. *inappropriately, pointlessly, foolishly*: Pl., Cic., Hor. *Sup.*: Quint.

ineptia, ae, f. [ineptus], *silly behaviour*: Pl., Ter. In *pl.*: *nonsense, absurdities*: Cic.; sententiarum, Suet.

ineptiō, īre [ineptus], *to talk or act absurdly, to play the fool*: Ter., Cat.

in-eptus, a, um [aptus], *not fitted, useless.* **1.** Lit. *unfit for use*: chartae, Hor. **2.** Transf. **A.** *unsuitable, not pertinent, out of place.* **a.** Of things: causa, Ter.; negotium, sententia, ioca, Cic.; risu inepto res ineptior nulla est, Cat. *Sup.*: Quint. **b.** Of persons: *tasteless, tactless*: Ter., Cic., Hor. **B.** *foolish, absurd*: of things: Cic.

in-equitābilis, e, adj. *unfit for riding in*: campi, Curt.

in-ermis, e, and (Sall.) **inermus**, a, um [arma], *unarmed, defenceless.* **1.** Lit.: Caes., Cic., Verg., etc. Hence, *without an army, undefended*: ager, Liv.; legati, Tac. **2.** Transf. **a.** *unarmed, defenceless*: pedes, Sall.; in alterā philosophiae parte inermis est, Cic. **b.** *harmless*: carmen, Prop., Ov. **c.** *not using the sword*: iustitia, Juv.

in-errāns, antis, adj. *fixed*: stellae, Cic.

in-errō, āre, *to wander or ramble about in.* **1.** Lit.: montibus, Plin. Ep. **2.** Transf.: memoria imaginis oculis inerrabat, Plin. Ep.

in-ers, ertis, adj. [ars]. **I.** *without training, without skill, unskilful*: Cic. *Sup.*: Cic. **II.** *inactive, indolent, sluggish, inert.* **1.** Lit.: linguā factiosi, inertes operā, Pl.; senectus, otium, Cic.; aquae, Ov.; glaebae, Verg.; terra, Hor. *Sup.*: Cic. **2.** Transf. *numbing*: bruma, Hor.; frigus, Ov. **III.** *ineffective, uneventful, dull, insipid*: genus interrogationis, Cic.; querella, Liv.; somno et inertibus horis ducere oblivia, Hor.; vita, Tib.; versus, Hor.; caro, Hor. **IV.** *inert, timid, cowardly*: Cic., Hor., etc.; pecus, Verg. *Comp.*: Cic.

inertia, ae, f. [iners]. **I.** *lack of art or skill, unskilfulness*: Cic. **II.** *inactivity, idleness, laziness*: Cic., Hor.; laboris, Cic.; operis, Liv.

in-ēruditus, a, um, *uneducated, illiterate*: Cic., Quint.; voluptates, Quint.

in-ēscō, āre, *to draw to bait.* Transf. *to entice, deceive*: homines, Ter.; specie beneficii, Liv.; inescatam temeritatem, Liv.

in-ēvectus, a, um, *borne or mounted upon*: Verg.

in-ēvitābilis, e, adj. *unavoidable*: fulmen, Ov.; crimen, Tac.

in-excitus, a, um, *unmoved, calm*: Ausonia, Verg.

in-excūsābilis, e, adj. **I.** *without excuse or apology*: Hor. **II.** *that allows no excuse*: tempus, Ov.

in-exercitātus, a, um, *untrained*: miles, Cic.; ad dicendum, Cic.; eloquentia, Tac.

in-exhaustus, a, um, *unexhausted*: metalla, Verg.; pubertas, Tac.

in-exōrābilis, e, adj. *that cannot be moved by entreaty, inexorable*, Cic., Hor. With *in* or *adversus* and Acc.: in ceteros, Cic.; adversus te et rem tuam, Liv. With Dat.: delictis, Tac. Of things, *unswerving, strict*: fatum, Verg.; res, Liv.; odium, Ov.; disciplina, Tac.

in-experrēctus, a, um, *unawakened*: Ov.

in-expertus, a, um. **A.** Act. *inexperienced in, unaccustomed to*: Hor. With Abl.: exercitus bonis, Liv.; lasciviā, Tac. With *ad*: animus ad contumeliam, Liv. **B.** Pass. *untried, unproved*: ne quid inexpertum relinquat, Verg.; fides, potestas, Liv.; legiones, Tac.

in-expiābilis, e, adj. [expiō], *that cannot be atoned for, inexpiable.* **1.** Lit.: religio, Cic. **2.** Transf.: *implacable, irreconcilable*: bellum, odium, Liv.; invidia, Suet.

in-explēbilis, e, adj. [expleō], *that cannot be filled, insatiable.* **1.** Lit.: stomachus, Sen. Ep. **2.** Transf.: cupiditas, Cic.; vir inexplebilis virtutis, Liv.

in-explētus, a, um, *not filled, unsatisfied, unsated.* **1.** Lit.: alvus, Stat. **2.** Transf.: lumen, Ov.; inexpletus lacrimans, Verg.

in-explicābilis, e, adj. *that cannot be unfolded or loosened.* **1.** Lit.: vinculum, Curt. **2.** Transf. **a.** *impracticable*: continuis imbribus viae, Liv. **b.** *without result, endless*: facilitas, Liv.; bellum, Tac. **c.** *tangled, inexplicable*: res, Cic. Ep.

in-explōrātus, a, um, *unexplored, unknown*: vada, Liv. Abl. *sing.* n. **inexplōrātō**, as *Adv.*, *without reconnoitring*: Liv.

in-expugnābilis, e, adj. *that cannot be taken by assault, impregnable.* **1.** Lit.: arx, Liv. **2.** Transf.: homo, Cic.; gramen, Ov.

in-exspectātus, a, um, *unexpected.* Of persons: Ov. Of things: Cic., Sen. Ep., Quint.

in-exstinctus, a, um, *not extinguished, inextinguishable.* **1.** Lit.: ignis, Ov. **2.** Transf.: fames, nomen, libido, Ov.

in-exsuperābilis, e, adj. *that cannot be crossed, insurmountable.* **1.** Lit.: Alpes, Liv.; terrae, Liv. *Comp.*: Liv. **2.** Transf.: vis fati, Liv.; bonum, Sen. Ep. *Neut. pl.* as Noun: inexsuperabilibus vim adferre, Liv.

in-extricābilis, e, adj. [extricō], *that cannot be disentangled*: error (of the Labyrinth), Verg.

in-fabrē, adv. *unskilfully, rudely*: vasa non infabre facta, Liv.; Hor.

in-fabricātus, a, um, *unwrought, unfashioned*: robora, Verg.

infacētē (**infic-**), adv. *not brilliantly*: crudely: Suet. *Sup.*: Plin.

in-facētiae, ārum, f. pl. *crudity, silliness*: Cat.

in-facētus (**infic-**), a, um, *not brilliant, dull, crude, insipid*: homo, Pl., Cic.; saeclum, Cat.; mendacium, Cic. *Comp.*: Cat.

in-fācundus, a, um, *ineloquent* : Liv., Suet. Comp. : Liv.

infāmia, ae, *f.* [fāma], *ill fame, disrepute, dishonour, disgrace.* **1.** Lit. : Pl. ; in summā infamiā esse, Ter. ; rei, Caes. ; illa iudicia senatoria operta dedecore et infamiā, Cic. ; habere, sarcire, Caes. ; ferre, Cic. ; flagrare infamiā, Cic. Ep. ; inferre alicui, Cic. ; movere, Liv. ; trahere aliquid ad infamiam, Tac. In *pl.* : Pl., Tac. **2.** Transf. *that which brings into disrepute ; the disgrace :* Cacus Aventinae infamia silvae, Ov. ; saecli, Ov.

in-fāmis, e, *adj.* [fāma], *infamous, disreputable, notorious :* homines vitiis, Cic. ; Pl. ; Tac. ; vita, Cic. ; annus, Liv. ; sco puli, Hor.

in-fāmō, āre [fāma], *to bring into disrepute, to brand with infamy, to disgrace, to shame :* fidem, Quint. ; infamata dea, Ov. ; ut tua moderatio aliorum infamet iniuriam, Cic. Ep. With GEN. of charge : aliquem temeritatis, Sen. Ep.

in-fandus, a, um, *unutterable, monstrous, shocking :* res crudelis, infanda, Cic. ; epulae, Liv. ; amor, dolor, bellum, mors, etc., Verg. *Neut.*, as *interj.* : navibus (infandum !) amissis, *oh, woe unutterable !* Verg.

in-fāns, antis, *adj.* [in and *Pres. Part.* of fārī], *not speaking, unable to speak, speechless, mute.* **1.** Lit. : pueri, Cic. ; statua, Hor. ; pectora infantia (i.e. *of babes*), Ov. ; ossa, Ov. As Noun, *a little child, an infant :* Lucr., Caes., Verg., etc. **2.** Transf. **a.** *faltering, tongue-tied :* Cic. Comp. : Cic. Ep. Sup. : Cic. So, pudor, Hor. **b.** *young, fresh :* ova, Ov. **c.** *childish, silly :* illa Hortensiana, Cic. Ep. [It. *fante* ; Fr. *enfant.*]

infantia, ae, *f.* [Infāns], *inability to speak.* **1.** Lit. : linguae, Lucr. **2.** Transf. **a.** *want of eloquence :* Cic., Quint. **b.** *infancy, early childhood :* Quint. ; ab infantiā, Tac. **c.** *second childhood :* Juv.

infar-, v. Infer-.

in-fatuō, āre [fatuus], *to make a fool of :* Cic.

in-faustus, a, um. **I.** *disastrous :* auspicium, nomen, puppes, Verg. ; gradus, Ov. ; dies, amicitia, Tac. **II.** *unlucky :* bellis infaustus, Tac.

infector, ōris, *m.* [Inficiō], *a dyer :* Cic.

(1) infectus, a, um, *Part.* Inficiō.

(2) in-fectus, a, um [factus]. **I.** *not made or done, not accomplished :* ea, quae sunt facta, infecta refert, Pl. ; Liv. ; infectā pace, Ter. ; infectis iis quae agere destinaverat, Caes. ; re infectā abire, Liv. ; victoria, Liv. ; facta atque infecta, Verg. ; argentum, (i.e. not coined), Liv. ; aurum, Verg. ; pensa, Ov. ; infecta dona facere (i.e. *to revoke*), Pl. *Neut.* as Noun : omnia pro infecto sint, Liv. **II.** *not feasible, impossible :* rex nihil infectum Metello credens, Sall.

in-fēcunditās, ātis, *f.* *unfruitfulness :* terrarum, Tac.

in-fēcundus, a, um, *unfruitful :* ager arbore, Sall. ; arbusta, Verg.

in-fēlicitās, ātis, *f.* **I.** *ill-luck, misfortune :* Ter., Liv. **II.** *ill-success :* Cic. **III.** *unproductiveness* (in the arts) : Quint.

in-fēliciter, *adv.* **I.** *unhappily :* Ter. Comp. : Quint. **II.** *without success :* temptata res, Liv.

infēlicō, āre [Infēlix], *to make unhappy :* dii me et te infelicent, Pl.

in-fēlix, icis, *adj.* *unfruitful, not fertile.* **1.** Lit. : tellus frugibus, Verg. ; lolium, Verg. ; arbori infelici suspendito (i.e., on the gallows), Cic. **2.** Transf. **a.** *unfortunate, unhappy, miserable :* Cic., Verg. With GEN. : infelix animi, Verg. Comp. : Liv. Sup. : Cic., Quint. **b.** *causing misfortune, calamitous :* rei publicae, Cic. ; thalamus, Verg. ; erga plebem studium, Liv. ; opera, Quint. **c.** *foretelling calamity :* vates, Verg.

infēnsē, *adv.* *hostilely, bitterly :* Tac. Comp. : Cic., Liv.

in-fēnsō, āre [Infēnsus], *to make hostile or dangerous, fill with hostilities :* bello Armeniam, Tac. ; pabula, Tac. ; quasi infensantibus (sc. urbem) diis, Tac.

infēnsus, a, um [in and fēnsus, Part. of fendō seen in dēfendō, etc.], *striking at, attacking.* **1.** Lit. **a.** Of persons : Liv. **b.** Of things : *levelled to strike, aimed :* hasta, ignis, Verg. ; infensis hastis, Liv. **2.** Transf. *ready to attack, hostile, antagonistic, dangerous, offensive.* **a.** Of persons : with DAT. : Turno Drances, Verg. ; plebi, Liv. ; with *in* and ACC. : infensioribus in se iudicibus, Liv. **b.** Of things : animus, Cic. ; valetudo, servitium, Tac. ; principibus opes, Tac.

in-ferciō, īre [farciō], *to stuff in.* Transf. : verba, Cic.

inferī, ōrum, v. Inferus.

inferiae, ārum, *f. pl.* [Inferī], *rites and offerings to propitiate and honour the dead :* alicui inferias adferre, Cic. ; ferre, Verg. ; referre, Hor. ; dare, mittere, accipere, Ov. ; facere, Tac.

inferior, v. Inferus.

inferius, *adv.* v. Infrā.

inferne, *adv.* [for form, *cf.* superne], *below, beneath :* Lucr.

infernus, a, um [Inferus], *that which lies beneath, lower.* **a.** In gen. : stagna, Liv. ; mare, the Tuscan sea, Luc. **b.** *belonging to the lower or nether world :* dii, Liv. ; rex, Verg. ; Iuno, Verg. ; sedes, tenebrae, Verg. ; palus, Ov. ; ratis, rota, Prop. ; vim deum (GEN.) infernam, Verg. ; aspectus, Tac. ; infernas umbras carminibus elicere, Tac. As Noun, **infernī**, ōrum, *m. pl. the shades below :* Prop. **inferna**, ōrum, *n. pl. the underworld :* Tac. [Fr. *enfer.*]

in-ferō, inferre, intulī, inlātum, *to carry, bring in, on, or against.* **1.** Lit. **A.** In gen. : ne quis sepulcra deleat neve alienum inferat, Cic. With *in* or *ad* and ACC. : eum in equum, Caes. ; Scipionem lecticulā in aciem, Liv. ; aliquid in ignem, Caes. ; scalas ad moenia, Liv. With DAT. : templis ignis, Cic. ; semina arvis, Tac. **B.** In partic. **a.** Milit. (of taking the offensive) : conversa signa in hostis inferre, Caes. ; pedem, Liv. ; hostibus gradum, Liv. ; bellum contra patriam, Cic. ; bellum alicui, Cic. ; arma, Hor., Liv. **b.** Of offerings : spumantia cymbia lacte Verg. ;

honores Anchisae, Verg. **c.** With *Refl.
Pron.*, or in *Mid.*, or with pedem or gressūs :
to betake oneself to, repair to, rush or *throw
oneself into :* lucus, quo se Numa inferebat,
Liv. ; atque etiam se ipse inferebat, Cic. ;
se foribus, Verg. ; se in contionem, Liv. ;
in urbem inferri, Liv. ; pedem, Cic. ; gressūs, Verg. **2.** T r a n s f. **A.** In gen. : *to
bring upon, cause, introduce :* cunctationem,
Caes. ; spem alicui, Caes. ; moram alicui,
delicatum sermonem, Cic. ; mentionem,
Liv. **B.** In partic. **a.** Of violent action :
calamitatem, Caes. ; alicui iniuriam, Caes. ;
mortem alicui, vim et manūs alicui, Cic.,
Tac. ; iniurias in socios, Cic. ; pestilentiam
agris, Liv. ; crimen proditionis alicui, Cic. ;
litem in aliquem, Cic. **b.** Of accounts :
to enter : sumptum civibus, Cic. ; *also to
pay in :* pecuniam aerario, Plin. Ep. **c.**
In logic : *to conclude, draw an inference :*
Cic., Quint.

inferus, a, um, *below, underneath, lower* (opp.
superus). **A.** In gen. : limen, Pl. ; loca,
Cic. **B.** In partic. **a.** *lower, southern :*
mare inferum (i.e. the Tuscan Sea, opp.
mare superum, the Adriatic Sea) : Cic.
b. *belonging to the lower world :* di deaeque,
Pl., Cic., Liv. As Noun, **inferi**, ōrum, *m.
pl. the dwellers in the underworld, the dead :*
Cic., Liv. *Comp.* **inferior**, ius, *lower.*
1. L i t. : labrum, locus, pars, spatium,
Caes. ; ex inferiore loco dicere, Cic. Ep.
G e o g r. : Germania superior et inferior
(i.e. southern and northern), Tac. **2.**
T r a n s f. **a.** Of time : *subsequent, later :*
aetate inferiores, Cic. ; inferioris aetatis
esse, Cic. **b.** In quality, rank, or number :
lower, humbler, inferior : ex inferioribus ordinibus, Caes. ; inferioris iuris magistratus, Liv. With ABL. : fortunā, dignitate,
auctoritate, etc., Cic. ; animo, Caes. ;
navium numero, Caes. ; copiis, Nep. With
in and ABL. : in iure civili, Cic. As Noun :
inferiores extollere, Cic. ; non inferiora
secutus, Verg. *Sup.* **infimus** (earlier **infumus** ; *v.* also imus), *lowest.* **1.** L i t. :
ab infimis radicibus montis, Caes. ; cum
scripsissem haec infima, Cic. Ep. ; ab infimā arā, Cic. ; sub infimo colle, Caes.
Neut. as Noun, *the bottom :* ad infimum,
Caes. ; collis erat leniter ab infimo acclivis,
Caes. **2.** T r a n s f. (in quality or rank) :
lowest, meanest, basest : faex populi, Cic.
Ep. ; infimo loco natus, Cic. ; preces, Liv.
in-fervescō, fervēscere, ferbui, *to grow hot,
to boil :* Cato, Hor.

infestē, adv. *hostilely, violently :* Liv. *Comp. :*
Liv. *Sup. :* Cic.

infestō, āre [Infestus], *to make hostile* or
dangerous, to attack : Scylla latus dextrum,
laevum Charybdis infestant, Ov. ; Sen. Ep.

infestus, a, um [*cf.* Infēnsus]. **1.** L i t. :
made unsafe, infested ; unquiet, unsafe :
via excursionibus barbarorum infesta, Cic. ;
omnia serpentibus, Sall. ; infestum agrum
reddere, Liv. ; maro infestum habere, Cic. ;
infestissima pars Ciliciae, Cic. Ep. **2.**
T r a n s f. **a.** *endangered, insecure :* fili vita,
Cic. ; infestior salus, Cic. ; senectus,
regnum, Liv. **b.** *causing danger, dangerous,
threatening :* duae urbes huic imperio in-
festissimae, Cic. ; Sall. ; Gallia, Cic. ;

nautis Orion, Hor. ; pestis rei pūblicae,
Cic. ; virtutibus tempora, Tac. ; infestis
oculis conspici, Cic. ; animo infestissimo,
Cic. ; bellum, Liv. **c.** *aggressive, ready for
attack* or *battle, threatening :* infestis signis
impetum facere, Caes. ; infestis pilis procurrere, Caes. ; infesta tela ferre, Verg. ;
infesto spiculo aliquem petere, Liv. ; exercitu infesto in agrum Sabinum profecti, Liv.

inficēt-, *v.* Infacēt-.

in-ficiō, ficere, fēci, fectum [faciō]. L i t.
to make in, infuse in making ; hence,
A. Of colour : *to stain, dye, tinge.* **1.**
L i t. : suaso pallulam, Pl. ; se Britanni
vitro inficiunt, Caes. ; arma sanguine,
Verg. ; ora pallor, Hor. ; volumina fumi,
Ov. **2.** T r a n s f. *to steep, tinge :* aliquem
artibus, Cic. ; sapientia animum, Sen. Ep. ;
Juv. P o e t. : infectum eluitur scelus,
Verg. **B.** Of poison, etc. : *to poison, taint,
infect.* **1.** L i t. : pabula tabo, Verg. ;
dictamno amnem, Verg. **2.** T r a n s f. :
animum otio, Cic. ; cupiditatibus principum infici solet tota civitas, Cic. ; artibus
infectus, Tac.

in-fidēlis, e, *adj. faithless, disloyal :* Caes.,
Cic., Hor. *Comp. :* Pl. *Sup. :* Cic. Ep.

in-fidēlitās, ātis, *f. faithlessness, disloyalty :*
Caes., Cic. In *pl. :* Cic.

infidēliter, adv. *disloyally :* Cic.

in-fidus, a, um, *not to be trusted, faithless,
treacherous.* **1.** L i t. : Cic., Sall., Hor.
2. T r a n s f. (of things) : mare, Lucr. ; societas regni, Liv. ; pax, facinus, Liv. ; consilia, Tac.

in-figō, figere, fixi, fixum, *to fix, thrust, drive*
or *fasten in.* **1.** L i t. : gladium hosti in
pectus, Cic. ; ferreis hamis infixis, Caes. ;
infigitur sagitta arbore, Verg. ; (eum)
saxo infixit acuto, Verg. ; vulnus infixum,
Verg. **2.** T r a n s f. *to imprint, ingrain,
settle firmly* (esp. in *Part. Perf.*) : in hominum sensibus atque in ipsā naturā infixum,
Cic. ; religio infixa animo, Liv. ; Vologesi
penitus infixum erat arma Romana vitandi,
Tac.

infimātis, *v.* Infimātis.

infimus, a, um, *v.* Inferus.

in-findō, findere, fidi, fissum, *to cut into,
make by cutting into :* sulcos telluri, Verg. ;
sulcos (mari), Verg.

infinitās, ātis, *f.* [fīnis], *boundlessness, infinity :* locorum, Cic.

infinitē, adv. *without end :* Cic.

infinitiō, ōnis, *f.* [Infinitus], *boundlessness,
infinity :* Cic.

in-finitus, a, um, *unbounded, unlimited.* **1.**
L i t. Of space : aer, altitudo, Cic. ; imperium, Cic., Liv. Neut. as Noun : Lucr.
2. T r a n s f. *endless.* **a.** Of time : tempus,
Lucr., Cic. In time : caedes, Cic. **b.** Of
number or degree : magnitudo, Caes. ;
multitudo, Caes., Cic., Tac. ; spes, odium,
labor, Cic. As Noun : ad or in infinitum,
Plin. ; infinito plus *or* magis, Quint. **c.**
undefined, indefinite : infinitior distributio,
Cic. **d.** G r a m m. : verbum (i.e. the infinitive), Quint.

infirmātiō, ōnis, *f.* [infirmō], *a weakening,
invalidating.* **a.** In law : rerum iudica-
tarum (setting aside of precedents), Cic.
b. *a refuting, disproving :* Cic.

infirmē, adv. *not strongly; weakly, faintly.* **a.** Lit.: animatus, Cic. Ep. **b.** *Of speech: without vigour of expression :* Plin. Ep. **c.** *weakmindedly.* Comp. : Suet.

infirmitās, ātis, *f. want of strength, weakness, feebleness.* **1.** Lit. **a.** puerorum, Cic. ; oculorum, Plin. Ep. **b.** *infirmity, indisposition, sickness :* suspicionem infirmitatis dare, Suet. **2.** Transf. **a.** Concr.: *the weaker sex :* Liv. **b.** animi, Cic. **c.** *fickleness, inconstancy :* Gallorum, Caes.

infirmō, āre [Infirmus], *to deprive of strength, to weaken.* **1.** Lit.: legiones, Tac. **2.** Transf. **a.** *to invalidate, impair, refute :* fidem testis, Cic. ; res tam levis, Cic. **b.** *to annul, make void :* acta (Caesaris), Cic. ; legem, Liv.

in-firmus, a, um, *not strong; weak, feeble.* **1.** Lit. **a.** *Of health or physical strength :* infirmi ad resistendum, Caes. ; viribus infirmis, Cic. ; valetudo, Cic. ; pecus, Ov. Sup. : Cic. **b.** In gen. : civitas, Caes. ; classis, Cic. **2.** Transf. **a.** In mind or character : animus, Caes. ; Juv. ; quorum concursu terrentur infirmiores, Caes. ; Hor. **b.** Of things : *worthless, weak :* ad probandum utraque res infirma est, Cic. ; vinculum (amicitiae), Liv. ; senatūs consultum, Tac.

infit, *v. defect.* [fīō], *he* (or *she*), *begins :* with *Inf.* : Pl., Lucr., Verg. Hence, *he* (or *she*) *begins* (*to speak*): his vocibus, Verg. ; Liv. With Acc. and *Inf.* : Liv.

infitiās īre [in, *not,* and root of fateor]. Lit. *to go to denials ; to deny :* Pl., Ter. With Acc. : Pl., Nep. With Acc. and *Inf.* : Liv., Quint.

infitiālis, e, *adj.* [Infitiās], *negative, consisting in denial :* Cic., Quint.

infitiātiō, ōnis, *f.* [Infitior], *a denying :* Cic. Of a debt : Sen.

infitiātor, ōris, *m.* [Infitior], *a denier :* esp. *one who denies a debt* or *trust :* Cic.

infitior, ārī [*cf.* Infitiās īre], *to deny.* **a.** In gen. With Acc. of thing denied : omnia, Pl. ; verum, Cic. ; notitiam alicuius, Ov. ; progenies haud infitianda parenti, Ov. **b.** *to deny, repudiate a* debt, trust or promise : quid si infitiatur ? quid si omnino non debetur ? Cic. Ep. With Acc. : pretium, Ov. ; depositum, Juv.

infixus, a, um, *Part.* Infīgō.

inflammātiō, ōnis, *f.* [Inflammō], *a setting on fire.* Transf.: animorum (poëtarum), Cic.

in-flammō, āre [flamma], *to set on fire, kindle.* **1.** Lit. : taedas ignibus, Cic. ; classem, Cic. ; tecta, Liv. **2.** Transf. (of the mind) : contionibus et legibus invidiam senatūs, Cic. ; odio, furore, cupiditate, etc., inflammatus, Cic. ; a pueritiā inflammatus ad gloriam, Cic. ; aliquem amore, Verg. ; populum in improbos, Cic.

inflātiō, ōnis, *f.* [Inflō], *a blowing into* or *swelling up.* Of the body : *inflation, flatulence :* habet inflationem magnam cibus (faba), Cic. ; also *inflammation :* Suet.

inflātius, comp. adv. [Inflātus]. **I.** *too pompously :* aliquid perscribere, Caes. **II.** *with more exaggeration :* inflatius multo, quam res erat gesta, fama percrebuerat, Caes.

inflātus, a, um. **I.** Part, inflō. **II.** Adj. **a.** *blown up, swollen, puffed up, inflated :* bucca, Suet. ; serpens inflato collo, Cic. ; amnes, Liv. **b.** *puffed up, haughty :* animus, Cic. Comp. : iuvenis inflatior, Liv. **c.** Of style : *inflated, turgid :* of the author : Prop., Quint., Tac.

inflātus, ūs, *m.* [Inflō], *a blowing into, a blast.* **1.** Lit. : eae (tibiae) si inflatum non recipiunt, Cic. **2.** Transf. *inspiration :* divinus, Cic.

in-flectō, flectere, flexī, flexum, *to bend, bow, curve in* or *to.* **1.** Lit. : cum ferrum se inflexisset, Caes. ; bacillum, Cic. ; sinus ad urbem inflectitur, Cic. Hence, *to change, alter by bending* or *turning :* vestigium sui cursūs, Cic. **2.** Transf. **a.** Of the voice : *to modulate :* vocem ad sonum, Cic. ; voces cantu, Tib. *to change, alter :* orationem, Cic. ; ius civile gratiā, Cic. **c.** *to bend, sway, affect :* aliquem, Cic. ; solus hic inflexit sensūs, Verg.

in-flētus, a, um, *unwept :* Verg.

in-flexibilis, e, *adj. that cannot be bent, inflexible.* Transf. : iudicium, Sen. Ep. ; obstinatio, Plin. Ep.

in-flexiō, ōnis, *f.* [Inflectō], *a bending, swaying :* laterum, Cic.

inflexus, a, um, Part. Inflectō.

inflexus, ūs, *m.* [Inflectō], *a bending, curving :* vicorum, Juv. Transf. Of the voice : Sen.

inflictus, a, um, *Part.* Inflīgō.

in-flīgō, flīgere, flīxī, flīctum, *to strike, dash on* or *against.* **1.** Lit. : alicui securim, Cic. ; puppis inflicta vadis, Verg. Hence, *to cause by striking, inflict :* plagam, vulnera, Cic. **2.** Transf. : ex verbo adversari aliquid in ipsum infligitur, Cic. Hence, *to inflict :* alicui turpitudinem, Cic.

in-flō, āre, *to blow into.* **1.** Lit. **a.** tibicen tibias, Cic. ; calamos, Verg. ; tubam, Liv. **b.** *to blow into and so fill, to inflate :* buccas, Pl., Hor. ; inflatur carbasus Austro, Verg. **2.** Transf. **a.** *to inspire :* poetam quasi divino spiritu inflari, Cic. ; mendaciis regis spem, Liv. **b.** *to inflate, puff up, fill :* inflati laetitiā atque insolentiā, Cic. ; iactatione severitatis inflatus, Liv. ; aliquem vanā spe, Liv. ; animos ad superbiam, Liv. ; crescentem tumidis sermonibus utrem, Hor. Of speech and writing : Antipater paulo inflavit vehementius, Cic. [It. *en flare* ; Fr. *enfler*].

in-fluō, fluere, fluxī, *to flow in.* **1.** Lit. : Hypanis in Pontum, Cic. ; lacus in flumen Rhodanum, Caes. ; non longe a mari, quo Rhenus influit, Caes. ; Ov. **2.** Transf. **a.** *to flow, stream, pour in :* in Italiam Gallorum copiae, Cic. **b.** in universorum animos, Cic. ; oratio in sensūs eorum, Cic.

in-fodiō, fodere, fōdī, fōssum, *to dig in, to bury :* conchas, Verg. ; talens in terram, Caes. ; corpora terrae, Verg. ; infossus puer, Hor.

informātiō, ōnis, *f.* [Informō], *a shaping, sketch.* Transf. *an idea, conception :* dei, Cic.

informis, e, *adj.* [fōrma], *that has no form, unformed, unshapely, shapeless.* **1.** Lit. : cadaver, Verg. ; alveus, Liv. **2.** Transf. *hideous :* monstrum, Verg. ; letum, Verg. ;

color, Tib. ; hiemes, Hor. ; exitus, Tac. *Comp. :* Sen. Ep.

in-fōrmō, āre, *to give form to, shape.* **1.** Lit. : clipeum, Verg. **2.** Transf. **a.** Of the intellect : animus a naturā bene informatus, Cic. ; artes quibus aetas puerilis ad humanitatem informari solet, Cic. **b.** In the mind : deos coniecturā, Cic. ; in summo oratore fingendo talem informabo, Cic.

inforō, āre [forum], *to bring into court* (with pun on in and forō, cf. perforō) : Pl.

in-fortūnātus, a, um, *unfortunate :* Ter. *Comp. :* Cic.

infortūnium, I, n. [fortūna], *misfortune, punishment :* invenire, vitare, Pl. ; ferre, Ter. ; cavere infortunio, Pl. ; ni pareat patri, habiturum infortunium esse, Liv.

infossus, a, um, *Part.* infodiō.

infrā [inferā, Locat. Abl. of inferus], *adv.* and *prep.* **I.** Adv. : *on the under side, below, underneath.* **1.** Lit. **a.** infra nihil est nisi mortale, Cic. ; infra scripsi, Cic. Ep.; non seges est infra, Tib. With *quam :* quae sunt infra quam id, Cic. **b.** Geogr. *down south, down the coast :* onerariae paulo infra delatae sunt, Caes. ; mare quod alluit infra, Verg. *Comp.* **inferius :** *lower, farther down :* altius egressus caelestia tecta cremabis, inferius terras, Ov. **2.** Transf. *below, beneath.* **a.** In value or rank : descendere, Liv. ; liberos eius ut multum infra despectare, Tac. **b.** At table : Hor. *Comp.* **inferius :** *lower :* virtutem non flamma inferius adducet, Sen. Ep. **II.** Prep. with Acc. : *below, under.* **1.** Lit. (of place) : infra oppidum, Cic. ; infra caelum, Tac. **2.** Transf. **a.** Of time : *later than :* Cic. **b.** Of size : *smaller than :* uri sunt magnitudine paulo infra elephantos, Caes. **c.** In rank or esteem : quem infra esse infumos puto homines, Ter. ; res humanas despicere atque infra se positas arbitrari, Cic. ; infra Pallantis laudes iacebunt, Plin. Ep. **d.** At table : infra aliquem accumbere, Cic. Ep. ; Liv.

in-frāctio, ōnis, f. [infringō], *a breaking into.* Transf. *a weakening :* animi, Cic.

infrāctus, a, um. **I.** *Part.* infringō. **II.** Adj. : *broken into.* Transf. **a.** *impaired, weakened :* Latini, Verg. ; ad proelium vires, Verg. ; infractos animos gerere, Liv. ; fama, Verg. ; veritas, Tac. ; tributa, Tac. **b.** Of speech : *broken :* loquella, Lucr. ; so perh. oratio, Liv. *Neut. pl.* as Noun : infracta et amputata loqui, Cic.

in-fragilis, e, adj. *unbreakable.* Transf. *vigorous :* vox, Ov.

in-fremō, ere, ui, *to grunt :* (aper), Verg.

(1) in-frēnātus, a, um, *without a bridle :* equi, equites, Liv.

(2) infrēnātus, a, um, *Part.* infrēnō.

in-frendēns, entis, *gnashing :* dentibus infrendens gemitu, Verg.

infrēnis, e, and **infrēnus,** a, um [frēnum], *without a bridle, unbridled :* equus, Verg. ; Numidae, Verg.

in-frēnō, āre, *to bridle, rein in* (the team). **1.** Lit. : equos, Liv. ; currūs, Verg. **2.** Transf. : infrenatus conscientiā scelerum, Cic.

infrēnus, a, um, v. infrēnis.

in-frequēns, entis, adj. *not crowded.* **1.** Lit. **a.** Of persons : *not numerous, thinned in numbers :* copiae, Caes. ; senatus, Cic. Ep. ; et Romae et in praediis infrequens (i.e. with few servants), Cic. Ep. ; hostes, exercitus, Liv. *Comp. :* Caes. **b.** Of places and things : *thinly populated, poorly attended :* causa, Cic. ; signa, Liv. With Abl. : pars urbis aedificiis, Liv. ; armatis signa, Liv. Neut. as Noun : infrequentissima urbis, Liv. **2.** Transf. (of timerelation) *not constant, irregular :* deorum cultor, Hor.

in-frequentia, ae, f. [infrequēns], *a small number, thinness, scantiness.* **a.** Of persons : senatūs, Liv. ; legionum, Tac. **b.** Of places : *emptiness :* locorum, Tac.

in-fringō, fringere, frēgi, frāctum [frangō], *to break or break into.* **1.** Lit. : liminibus latus, Hor. ; infractis hastis, Liv. ; papavera liliaque, Ov. ; infractus remus (i.e. of appearance due to refraction), Cic. Comic. : alicui colaphum, Ter. **2.** Transf. *to break, break into, impair, affect :* linguam metu, Lucr. ; ut primus incursus et vis militum infringeretur, Caes. ; florem dignitatis, militum gloriam, spem, Cic. ; res Samnitium, animos hostium, Liv.

in-friō, āre, *to crumble into :* farinam in aquam, Cato.

in-frōns, ondis, adj. *without foliage :* Ov.

in-frūctuōsus, a, um, *unfruitful.* Transf. : militia, Tac. ; preces, Plin. Ep.

in-fūcātus, a, um, *painted in.* Transf. *showy :* vitia orationis, Cic.

infula, ae, f. *a band, bandage.* **1.** Lit. **a.** In gen. : Cic. **b.** *a white woollen fillet* (used for religious purposes, consisting of a long look of wool, knotted round at intervals with a riband), *a priest's fillet :* Cic., Verg. Also, *the fillet of the victim :* Lucr., Verg. *Of the fillet worn by a suppliant :* Caes., Liv., Tac. **2.** Transf. *an ornament, mark of distinction, badge of honour :* his infulis imperi venditis, Cic.

infulātus, a, um [infula], *adorned with the infula* (q.v.) : Suet.

in-fulciō, fulcīre, fulsī, fultum, *to cram in.* **1.** Lit. : alicui cibum, Suet. **2.** Transf. *to put in, foist in :* verbum, Sen. Ep., aliquid epistulae, Sen. Ep.

infumātis, is, m. [Infumus, v. Inferus], *formed to match summātēs], one of the lowest* (in rank) : Pl.

infumus, v. inferus.

infundibulum, I, n. [infundō], *a funnel :* Cato.

in-fundō, fundere, fūdī, fūsum, *to pour in or on.* **1.** Lit. **a.** Of liquids : aliquid, Hor. With *in* and Acc. : aliquid in vas, Cic. With Dat. : animas formatae terrae, Ov. **b.** Of non-liquids : *to pour on :* nimbum alicui, Verg. ; obruebatur navis infuso igni, Liv. ; umeris infusa capillos, Ov. ; sole infuso (terris), Verg. **c.** With Dat. of person *for whom : to pour into* (a cup, etc.), *administer :* alicui venenum, Cic. ; alicui poculum, Hor. **2.** Transf. **a.** *to pour or spread oneself* (in *Mid.* or *Pass.*) : coniugis infusus gremio, Verg. ; collo infusa mariti, Ov. ; circo infusum populum, Verg. :

deus infusus in mundo, Cic. ; cum homines in alienum infunderentur genus, Cic. **b.** In gen. : orationem in auris tuas, Cic. ; vitia in civitatem, Cic. ; infusa per artūs mens, Verg.

in-fuscō, āre [fuscus], *to make dark or dusky, to darken.* **1.** Lit. : vellera, Verg. ; harenam sanie, Verg. **2.** Transf. **a.** *to darken, spoil, tarnish :* eos barbaries, Cic. ; vicinitas non infuscata malevolentiā, Cic. **b.** *to obscure* (by diluting): vinum, Pl.

infūsus, a, um, *Part.* Infundō.

in-geminō, āre. **A.** Trans. *to redouble, repeat :* ictūs, voces, terrorem, Verg. ; me miserum ! ingeminat, Ov. **B.** Intrans. *to redouble :* Austri, curae, clamor, ignes, Verg. ; ingeminant plausu, Verg.

in-gemiscō (or **ingemēscō**), gemiscere, gemui, *to groan or sigh over a thing.* **1.** Lit. : Cic., Liv. With *in* and ABL. : in illā re civitas ingemuit, Cic. With DAT. : malo, Cic. ; condicioni suae, Liv. With ACC. : tuum interitum, Verg. With *ad :* Suet. With ACC. and *Inf. :* Cic. **2.** Transf. (of things) : ingemuere cavernae, Verg. ; limen, solum, Ov.

in-gemō, ere, *to groan or sigh over.* With DAT. : aratro, Verg. ; laboribus, Hor. ; agris, Tac.

in-generō, āre, *to implant, ingenerate :* natura amorem in eos, Cic. ; non ingenerantur hominibus mores, Cic. ; societatem natura, Liv.

ingeniātus, a, um [ingenium], *naturally constituted :* lepide ingeniatus, Pl.

ingeniōsē, adv. *cleverly, ingeniously :* Cic., Quint. *Comp. :* Plin.

ingeniōsus, a, um [ingenium]. **1.** Lit. Of mental qualities : *of good capacity, gifted with genius, of good natural talents* or *abilities, clever, ingenious :* Cic. ; dandis ingeniosa notis, Ov. ; ad aliquid, Ov. *Comp.* and *Sup. :* Cic. **2.** Transf. Of things. **a.** *requiring genius :* iocandi genus, Cic. ; res est ingeniosa dare, Ov. **b.** *possessed of natural qualities, naturally adapted :* vox mutandis sonis, Ov. ; ad segetes ager, Ov.

ingenitus, a, um. **I.** *Part. v.* ingenui. **II.** Adj. *inborn, native, natural :* terra ingenito umore egens, Liv. ; caritas liberum (GEN.), Liv. ; Tac. ; Suet.

ingenium, i, n. [gen. in gignō], *innate or natural quality, nature.* **1.** Prop. Of persons. **a.** *natural disposition, temper, mode of thinking, character, bent, inclination :* feci ego meum ingenium, Pl. ; ingenium hominum ab labore proclive ad lubidinem, Ter. ; redire ad ingenium, Ter. ; animi, Cic. ; Volscis suum rediit ingenium, Liv. ; ferox, mite, etc., Liv. ; procax, atrox, Tac. Of a number of persons : Neronianae aulae ingenium, Tac. **b.** Of the intellect : *natural capacity, talents, parts, abilities, genius :* singulare, acutum, acerrimum, tardum, etc., Cic. ; ingeni vis, acies, lumen, motūs, Cic. ; ingeni vena, Hor. ; vigor ingenii, Ov. ; fingere, Cic. ; ingenio abundare, Cic. Ep. ; aliere, acuere, Quint. ; imbuere artibus, Pl. ; omne ingenium contulit ad populi gloriam celebrandam, Cic. ; versabatur in hoc nostro studio cum ingenio,

Cic. ; extremi ingeni esse, Liv. **2.** Transf. (of things): *natural quality :* loci, Sall. ; arvorum, Verg. ; locorum, terrae, Liv. ; montis, Tac. **3.** Concr. **a.** Of persons : *a genius,* i.e. *a man of genius, a clever, ingenious person :* Cic., Liv. In *pl. :* Pl., Cic., Tac. **b.** Of things : *an invention, contrivance :* exquisita ingenia cenarum, Plin. Ep. ; Tac. [It. *ingegno* ; Fr. *engin.*]

ingēns, tis, adj. [perh. a fusion of in, "not" and root of gignō, i.e. "uncreated, unnatural," with in, "not" and root of gnōscō, i.e. "unknown"], *prodigious, monstrous, vast, huge.* **A.** Materially : praeda, pecunia, campus, Cic. ; acervus, cylindrus, Verg. ; aequor, Hor. ; aquae, Liv. In Verg. often with a suggestion of *uncouthness* or *mystery,* e.g. monstrum horrendum informe ingens ; perh. of *mystery :* pugnam imber ingentibus procellis effusus diremit, Liv. In Vergil, perh. also a sense of *native, inborn* [fr. in, *prep.* and root of gignō], e.g. sub ingenti matris umbrā ; ingens oleaster ; ingens Amiterna cohors ; stupet ipse Latinus ingentis, genitos diversis partibus orbis, inter se coiisse viros. **B.** Immaterially : famā ingens, Verg. ; Tac. ; ingens animi, Sall., Tac. ; gratiae, Ter. ; amor, Verg. ; virtus atque animus, Hor. ; ira, Ov. ; gloria, spiritus, Liv. *Comp. :* Verg.

ingenuē, adv. *in a manner befitting a person of free birth, liberally ; frankly :* Cic., Quint.

in-genui [v. gignō], *Perf. Indic.* I implanted, and **in-genitus** (q.v.), *Perf. Part. implanted.* **1.** Lit. : herbas tellus, Luc. **2.** Transf. : natura cupiditatem homini ingenuit, Cic.

ingenuitās, ātis, f. [ingenuus], *the position or characteristics of a free-born man or gentleman, good birth.* **a.** ornamenta ingenuitatis, Cic. ; Liv. ; Tac. **b.** *noble-mindedness, frankness, ingenuousness :* Cic.

ingenuus, a, um [gen. in gignō]. **1.** Lit. **a.** *inborn, innate, natural :* indoles, Pl. ; color, Prop. **b.** *native, not foreign :* fontes, Lucr. ; Juv. **2.** Transf. **a.** *free-born, born of free parents :* 'ingenuus homo' meant originally *one who had a certain father, one who could name or cite his father :* Liv. ; pueri, homo, Cic. ; parentes, Hor. As Noun : ingenuamne an libertinam, Pl. ; omnis ingenuorum adest multitudo, Cic. **b.** *worthy of a freeman, noble, upright, frank, candid, ingenuous :* animus, studia atque artes, dolor, fastidium, Cic. ; leo, Hor. ; amor, Hor. **c.** *delicate, tender* (as of one not used to roughness) : vires, Ov.

in-gerō, gerere, gessi, gestum, *to carry, throw, or heap in or on.* **1.** Lit. : aquam, Pl. ; ligna foco (DAT.), Tib. ; vinum oribus, Curt. Of weapons : *to hurl, thrust :* hastas in tergum fugientibus, Verg. ; saxa in sub-euntis, Liv. ; pugnos in ventrem, Ter. ; manūs capiti, Sen. Ep. **2.** Transf. **a.** Of language : *to fling or pile up :* convicia alicui, Hor. ; probra in eum, Liv. ; contumelias, Tac. **b.** *to obtrude, press upon :* ingerebat iste Artemidorum, Cic. ; nomen patris patriae a populo saepius ingestum repudiavit, Tac. ; nomina liberis, Tac.

inglōrius, a, um [gloria], *without glory or fame, inglorious :* vita, Cic. ; (rex apum), Verg. ;

imperium, Tac. With GEN.: militiae, Tac.

inglŭviēs, ēi, *f.* [fr. root seen in gluttiō], *the maw, crop,* of animals. **1.** Lit.: Verg. **2.** Transf. (of gluttony): stringere ingluvie rem, Hor.

ingrātē, *adv.* **I.** *unwillingly :* Ov. **II.** *ungratefully :* Cic. Ep., Tac.

ingrātĭficus, a, um [ingrātus faciō], *ungrateful :* Acc.

in-grātiis, and perh. **ingrātīs** [in, *not,* and grātiīs, *v.* grātia], *against one's will.* **a.** With *Possess. Pron.* or GEN.: tuis ingratiis, Pl. ; amborum ingratiis, Pl. **b.** Alone : Pl., Ter., Lucr., Cic.

in-grātus, a, um. **I.** *unpleasant, unwelcome, disagreeable.* **a.** Of things : Pl., Cic. Ep. ; oratio non ingrata Gallis, Caes. ; labor, Verg. ; otium, Hor. **b.** Of persons : exercitui non ingratus, Tac. **II.** *unthankful, ungrateful.* **1.** Lit. (of persons and their acts) : nihil cognovi ingratius, Cic. Ep. ; esse in aliquem, Cic., Liv. With GEN.: salutis, Verg. **2.** Transf. (of things). **i.** Act. *not thanking, ungrateful :* ingluvies, Hor. ; ager, Mart. **ii.** Pass. *receiving no thanks, thankless, unacknowledged :* donum, Pl. ; id erit tibi ingratum, Ter.

in-gravēscō, ere, *to grow heavy, become heavier.* **1.** Lit.: Plin. Poet. *to become pregnant :* Lucr. **2.** Transf. **a.** *to grow worse, more burdensome and oppressive :* annona, Caes. ; morbus, aetas, Cic. ; in dies malum, Cic. Ep. ; bellum, faenus, seditio, Liv. **b.** *to become weary :* corpora exercitationum, defetigatione, Cic.

in-gravō, āre, *to weigh down on.* **1.** Lit.: puppem, Stat. **2.** Transf. **a.** annis ingravantibus, Phaedr. **b.** *to render worse, to aggravate :* ingravat haec saevus Drances, Verg.

in-grĕdior, gredī, grēssus sum [gradior]. **I.** *to step or go into, to enter.* **1.** Lit. With ACC.: Cic., Liv., Quint., etc. With *in* and ACC.: Cic., Liv. With *intra :* Caes., Cic. With DAT.: Verg. **2.** Transf. **a.** *to enter upon, engage in, apply oneself to :* in sermonem, Caes. ; in vitam tamquam in viam ingressus, Cic. ; in causam, Cic. ; in bellum, Cic. ; vitam, pericula, Cic. ; magistratum, Sall. ; res antiquae laudis, Verg. ; ad discendum, Cic. With *Obj.* implied : Verg. **b.** With *Inf.: to begin :* Cic., Verg., etc. With dicere understood : sic contra est ingressa, Verg. **II.** *to step or proceed in* a place. **1.** Lit. **a.** tardius, Cic. ; Ov.; campo, solo, Verg. **b.** After being lame : incipiebat ingredi princeps, Phaedr. **2.** Transf.: vestigiis patris, Cic. With *Intern.* ACC.: vestigia patris, Liv. *Absol. :* nec tragoedia socco ingreditur, Quint.

ingrēssiō, ōnis, *f.* [ingredior]. **I.** *a going into, entering.* **1.** Lit.: fori, Cic. **2.** Transf. *a beginning :* Cic. **II.** *a stepping on, walking.* Hence, *gait, pace :* moderata, Cic.

ingrēssus, ūs, *m.* [ingredior]. **I.** *a going into, entering.* **1.** Lit.: Cic., Liv., Plin. Ep. Milit.: *a marching in, inroad :* ingressūs hostiles, Tac. **2.** Transf. *a*

beginning : in ingressu, Quint. ; ingressūs capere, Verg. **II.** *a stepping on, walking, gait :* Cic.; prohiberi ingressu, Caes. ; instabilem ingressum praebere, Liv.

in-gruō, uere, uī [*cf.* ἔχραον in Homer ; Lat. ruere], *to fall upon, rush upon, assail.* **1.** Lit.: Pl., Tac. ; in Italiam, Tac. ; Italis (DAT.), Verg. **2.** Transf.: bellum, Verg., Tac. ; ferreus imber, Verg. ; tela, nox, Tac. ; ingruere morbi in remiges coeperunt, Liv. ; umbra vitibus, Verg.

inguen, inis, *n.* **I.** *the groin :* Verg. In *pl. :* Liv. **II.** *the privy parts :* Hor., Ov.

ingurgitō, āre [gurges], *to pour in like a flood.* **1.** Lit.: ingurgitat merum in se, Pl. **2.** Transf. (with *Refl. Pron.*). **a.** *to swill oneself, gorge oneself :* crudique postridie se rursus ingurgitant, Cic. **b.** in alicuius copias se, Cic. ; se in flagitia, Cic.

in-gustātus, a, um, *untasted, not tasted before :* Hor.

in-hăbĭlis, e, *adj. awkward to handle, unmanageable, unwieldy.* **1.** Lit.: navis inhabilis prope magnitudinis, Liv. ; telum inhabile ad remittendum imperitis, Liv. ; Tac. **2.** Transf. *unfit, unapt :* studiis (DAT.), Sen. Ep. With *ad :* multitudo inhabilis ad consensum, Liv. ; ad parendum, Tac.

in-hăbĭtābĭlis, e, *adj. uninhabitable :* regiones, Cic.

inhăbĭtantēs, ium, *m. f. pl.* [inhabitō], *inhabitants :* Plin. Ep.

in-hăbĭtō, āre, *to dwell in, inhabit :* Ov., Sen. Ep.

in-haereō, haerēre, haesī, haesūrus, *to stick in, cling or cleave to.* **1.** Lit. With DAT.: animi corporibus, Cic. ; coniunx umeris abeuntis, Ov. With *ad :* ad saxa, Cic. With *in* and ABL.: in visceribus, Cic. *Absol. :* linguae, Cic. ; Ov. **2.** Transf.: in mentibus augurium, Cic. ; tibi suspicio, Cic. ; vultibus illa tuis, Ov. ; tergo fugientis, Liv. ; studiis, Ov.

in-haerēscō, haerēscere, haesī [inhaereō], *to get a hold on.* **1.** Lit.: ubi ignis hostium inhaeresceret, Caes. ; dextram amplexus inhaesit, Verg. **2.** Transf.: penitus in mentibus, Cic.

in-hālō, āre, *to breathe upon :* alicui popinam, Cic.

in-hĭbeō, ēre, uī, itum [habeō]. **I.** *to hold or keep in, restrain, curb, check.* **1.** Lit.: tela, Verg.; frenos, Liv.; equos, Ov.; inhibere remis (with or without navem), Liv., Curt., *or* inhibere retro navem, Liv., *or* inhibere alone, Cic. Ep., Liv., *to back water.* **2.** Transf.: impetum victoris, Liv. With *ab :* a turpi mentem probro, Cat. With ACC. of *Obj.,* and *Inf.:* Quint. **II.** *to set in operation, use, employ :* imperium, Pl. ; eadem supplicia nobis, Cic. ; imperium in deditos, Liv. ; coercitionem, Liv.

inhĭbĭtiō, ōnis, *f.* [inhibeō], *a restraining :* remigum, *backing water :* Cic. Ep.

in-hĭō, āre *to stand agape.* **1.** Lit.: ora luporum, Stat. **2.** Transf. *to stand agape* with wonder, desire, anxiety : in te, Lucr. ; Romulus uberibus lupinis, Cic. ; tenuit inhians Cerberus ora, Verg. ; attonitis inhians animis, Verg. ; pecudumque reclusis

pectoribus inhians, Verg. Occ. with Acc. :
hereditatem, aurum, etc., Pl. ; postia, Verg.
in-honestē, *adv. dishonourably, disgracefully* :
Ter., Cic. Ep.
inhonestō, āre [inhonestus], *to dishonour,
disgrace* : Ov.
in-honestus, a, um. **A.** Pass. *not regarded
with honour or respect.* **a.** *Because of
birth or conduct* : *unhonoured, inglorious,
degraded* : Pl., Hor., Tac. *Sup.* : Cic. ;
vita, Sall., Tac. ; mors, Liv. **b.** *ugly,
hideous* : homo, Ter. **B.** Act. **a.** *dis-
honouring, degrading* : cupiditas, Cic. Ep. ;
lubido, Sall. ; vulnera tergo, Ov. ; pax,
Tac. **b.** *disfiguring* : vulnus, Verg.
in-honōrātus, a, um. **I.** *unhonoured, dis-
regarded* : vita, Cic. ; dea, Ov. ; triumphus,
Liv. *Comp.* : Liv. **II.** *unrewarded* : aliquem dimittere, Liv. ; Ov. *Sup.* : Liv.
in-honōrus, a, um. **I.** *not respected* : Plin.
II. *stripped of ornaments, defaced* : signa,
Tac.
in-horreō, ēre, *to stand erect and bristling* :
haud secus quam vallo saepta inhorreret
acies (i.e. like chevaux de frise), Liv.
in-horrēscō, horrēscere, horruī. **1.** Lit.
a. *to send forth sharp points, to rise erect,
to bristle up* : spicea messis, Verg. With
Intern. Acc. : aper inhorruit armos, Verg.
b. *to be ruffled with a tremulous motion, to
quiver, vibrate, shudder* : pennis agitatus
aër, Ov. ; unda tenebris, Verg. ; veris adventus foliis, Hor. **2.** Transf. *to tremble,
shiver, shudder* : domus principis inhorruit,
Tac.
in-hospitālis, e, *adj. inhospitable* : Caucasus,
Hor.
in-hospitālitās, ātis, *f. inhospitality* : Cic.
in-hospitus, a, um, *inhospitable* : Syrtis,
Verg. ; tecta, Ov.
in-hūmānē, *adv. inhumanly, savagely* : Ter.,
Cic. *Comp.* : Cic.
in-hūmānitās, ātis, *f.* [inhūmānus]. **I.** *inhuman conduct, barbarity* : Cic. **II.** *want
of good breeding.* **a.** *incivility, discourtesy* :
Cic. **b.** *churlishness* : Cic. **c.** *niggardliness* : Cic.
in-hūmāniter, *adv.* [inhūmānus], *uncivilly,
discourteously* : Cic.
in-hūmānus, a, um. **I.** *inhuman, barbarous,
ruthless.* **a.** *Of persons* : Ter., Cic. **b.**
Of things : *cruel, brutal* : testamentum,
Cic. ; crudelitas, scelus, Liv. ; via, securi-
tas, Tac. **II.** *ill-bred, uncivil, discourteous* :
Cic. *Comp.* : Cic. *Sup.* : Ter. **III.** *uncultured* : aures, Cic.
in-humātus, a, um, *unburied* : Cic., Verg.
in-ibi, *adv. therein, there, in that place.* **1.**
Lit. (of place) : Cic. **2.** Transf. **a.**
Of time : *near at hand* : Pac. ; quod
sperare debemus aut inibi esse, aut iam confectum, Cic. **b.** *in that matter* : Pl.
ĭn-iciō, icere, iēcī, iectum [iaciō] (*Aor. Subj.*
iniexit, Pl.). **I.** *to cast, throw, fling in.*
1. Lit. : ignibus iniectis, Cic. ; se in ignem,
Ter. ; se in medios hostis, Cic. ; Verg. ;
milites in navis), Caes. With Dat. : sese
morti, Verg. **2.** Transf. **a.** *to inspire,
infuse, cause* : metum alicui in pectus, Pl. ;
tumultum civitati, Cic. ; alacritatem exercitui, Caes. ; eis iras, Verg. ; certamen
uxoribus, Liv. ; terrorem, religionem,

scrupulum, Cic. ; cunctationem, Liv. ;
periculum mortis, Tac. **b.** Of the mind :
to turn in reflexion : in quam se iniciens
animus, Cic. **c.** Of suggestion : *to throw
in a hint* or *mention* : Cic. With Acc. :
nomen, Cic. ; mentionem, Hor. **II.** *to
cast, throw, fling on* or *over.* **A.** In gen. :
pallium in me, Pl. With Dat. : ei pallium,
Cic. ; ignem castris, Liv. ; dextram foculo,
Liv. ; umeris ostrum, Verg. ; (flumini)
pontem, Liv. **B.** Of chains, etc. **1.** Lit. :
manicas alicui, Pl. ; alicui catenas, vincula, Cic. ; Turno catenas, Liv. ; vincula,
Verg. ; laqueum, Liv. **2.** Transf. : alicui tamquam frenos, Cic. ; frena licentiae,
Hor. **III.** Legal : manum alicui inicere.
A. *to take possession of* as one's property
(without a previous judicial decision). **1.**
Lit. : Liv. **2.** Transf. : (ei) manum
Parcae, Verg. ; quieti eius, Plin. Ep. **B.**
In summoning before a judge : Pl.
iniectiō, ōnis, *f.* [iniciō], *a laying on* : manūs,
(a form of taking possession without a
previous judicial decision) : Quint.
iniectus, a, um. *Part.* iniciō.
iniectus, ūs, *m.* [iniciō]. **I.** *a casting on* or
over : Tac. **II.** *a casting in.* Transf. :
animi in corpora, Lucr.
in-igō, igere, ēgī, āctum [agō]. **I.** *to drive
in* : Varr. **II.** *to incite* : feras ad nocendum, Sen. Ep.
inimīcē, *adv. in an unfriendly manner,
hostilely* : Cic. *Comp.* : Liv. *Sup.* : Cic.
inimīcitia, ae, *f.* [inimīcus], *unfriendliness,
enmity* : Pl., Cic. In *pl.* : *feuds, enmities* :
capere in aliquem, Ter. ; subire, exstinguere, Cic. ; habere conceptas, Caes. ;
habere, gerere cum aliquo, Cic. ; denuntiare alicui, Cic. ; fovere, ulcisci, Tac.
inimīcō, āre [inimīcus], *to make enemies* :
Hor.
in-imīcus, a, um [amīcus], *unfriendly, hostile.*
1. Lit. : Pl., Cic., Liv., etc. **2.** Transf.
a. Of things : *hurtful, injurious* : naves
accipiunt inimicum imbrem, Verg. ; odor
nervis, Hor. ; consilia cum patriae, tum
sibi, Nep. *Comp.* : nec quicquam inimi-
cius orationi versibus, Cic. *Sup.* : Plin.
b. For hostilis : nomina, castra, signa,
Verg. As Noun, **inimīcus**, ī, *m.* and **ini-
mīca**, ae, *f.* *a* (*personal*) *enemy* (dist. fr.
hostis, *a public enemy*) : Cic., Liv., etc.
Sup. : inimicissimus suus, *his bitterest
enemy*, Cic. [It. nemico ; Fr. ennemi.]
iniquē, *adv. unequally.* **1.** Lit. : Ter.
Comp. : Ter. *Sup.* : Cic. **2.** Transf.
a. *unjustly* : Pl., Cic., Hor., Liv. **b.** *not
patiently, indignantly.* *Sup.* : aliquid ferre,
Suet.
iniquitās, ātis, *f.* [iniquus]. **1.** Lit. Of
place : *unevenness, inequality* (mostly implying *disadvantage*) : loci, Caes. ; in talibus iniquitatibus locorum, Liv. **2.**
Transf. **a.** *unfavourableness, adverseness* :
rerum, Caes. ; temporum, Cic., Liv. **b.**
unfairness, injustice : Caes., Cic., Liv. In
pl. unjust demands (i.e. taxes) : Tac.
in-iquus, a, um [aequus], *unequal, uneven.*
1. Lit. **a.** Of ground : *not level, rising* :
dorsum, Verg. ; via, Ov. Milit. (mostly
implying *disadvantage*) : loco iniquo sub-
eundum erat ad hostis, Liv. **b.** In the

scales : *not of the right measure, too great* or
too small : iniquae heminae, Pers. **2.**
T r a n s f. **A.** *uneven, disadvantageous, adverse.* **a.** Of things : iniquissimo nostris
loco, Caes. ; iniquiorem hosti locum, Liv. ;
tributum iniquo tempore imperatum, Liv. ;
sors, Verg., Liv. ; palus iniqua nesciis, Tac. ;
pugnā congressus iniquā (*ill-matched*), Verg.
b. Of persons : *unfavourable, prejudiced* :
esse in aliquem, Ter. ; homines omnibus
iniqui, Cic. ; vultu iniquo spectare, Ov.
As Noun (in *pl.*) : Cic. ; also *Sup.* : Cic.
B. Of wrong measure. **a.** *excessive* : pondus, sol, Verg. **b.** *unfair, unjust, partial* :
iudices, causa, Ter. ; (pacis) condicio, Cic.
Ep. ; pax, Verg. ; Parcae, lex, Hor.
Comp. : Cic. **c.** *not calm, impatient, rebellious, unresigned* : iniquo animo pati,
Ter. ; iniquissimo animo mori, Cic. ; iniquae
mentis asellus, Hor. ; aliquid animo iniquo
ferre, Cic., Liv. ; so with iniquā mente, Ov.

initiāmenta, ōrum, *n. pl.* [initiō], *an initiation* into secret rites. T r a n s f. : sapientiae, Sen. Ep.

initiātiō, ōnis, *f.* [initiō], *an initiation* ; *a
participation* in sacred rites : Eleusiniorum
sacrorum, Suet.

initiō, āre [initium], *to initiate, consecrate,* or
admit. **1.** L i t. to secret religious rites, esp.
those of Ceres : Cic., Liv. Of other
mysteries : initiari Bacchicis, Liv. **2.**
T r a n s f. : studiis, Quint. ; litteris, Plin.
Ep.

initium, I, *n.* [*Part.* stem ito fr. eō, īre], *a
going* or *coming in, entrance* ; hence, *a beginning.* **1.** L i t. : bonis initiis orsus
tribunatus, Cic. ; initium capere, Caes. ;
sumere, facere ab aliquā re, Cic. ; transe-
undi, Caes. ; dicendi, Cic. The ABL. *sing.*
is used adverb., *in the beginning, at first* :
Cic., Nep. **2.** T r a n s f. (mostly in *pl.*).
a. *elements* : Cic. Hence, *first principles*
of a science : mathematicorum, Cic. **b.**
auspices, because with them everything was
begun ; hence, *the beginning of a reign* :
Curt., Tac. **c.** *sacred rites* or *mysteries,* to
which only the initiated were admitted :
Cic., Liv., etc. Also, *things used in celebrating these mysteries* : tympanum, tubam,
Cybele, tua, mater, initia, Cat.

initus, a, um, *Part.* ineō.

initus, ūs, *m.* [ineō]. **I.** *an entrance* : Lucr.
II. *a beginning* : movendi, Lucr.

iniūcunditās, ātis, *f. unpleasantness* : Cic.

iniūcundius, *comp. adv. rather unpleasantly* :
Cic. Ep.

in-iūcundus, a, um, *unpleasant* : labor, Cic. ;
adversus malos, Tac.

in-iūdicātus, a, um, *undecided* : id iniudica-
tum relinquo, Quint.

in-iungō, iungere, iūnxī, iūnctum. **1.** L i t.
a. *to join* or *fasten into* : tigno asseres,
Liv. **b.** *to join* or *attach to* : vineas moenibus, Liv. **2.** T r a n s f. *to lay on* : civitatibus servitutem, Caes. ; alicui laborem,
onus, leges, iniuriam, ignominiam, militiam,
etc., Liv. ; tributum, munera, Tac.

in-iūrātus, a, um, *unsworn* : Pl., Cic., Liv.

iniūria, ae, *f.* [in, and iūs], *wrong* ; *an
unjust* or *unfair act, an injustice, a wrong.*
1. L i t. : tibi a me nulla orta est iniuria,
Ter.; defendere, persequi, ulcisci, Caes. ;

alicui facere, imponere, inferre, Cic. ; propulsare, ab aliquo accipere, Cic. With
GEN. of person wronged : Pl., Caes., Liv.
With GEN. of definition : legatorum viola-
torum, Liv. The ABL. is used as *adv.* :
unjustly, undeservedly, without cause : Pl.,
Cic., etc. **2.** T r a n s f. **a.** *affront, slight,
indignity* : spretae iniuria formae, Verg. ;
iniuriarum multam dicere, Pl. ; actio iniuriarum, Cic. **b.** In *pl.* : *unjust severity,
harshness* : (filius) carens patriā ob meas
iniurias, Ter. **c.** *revenge* or *punishment for
wrong inflicted* : caedis nostrae, Verg. ; Liv.
d. *an unjust acquisition* : iniuriam obtinere, Liv. **e.** *damage, harm* : oblivionis,
Plin. Ep.

iniūriōsē, *adv. unjustly, wrongfully* : Cic.
Comp. : Cic.

iniūriōsus, a, um [iniūria], *acting unjustly,
wrongful.* **1.** L i t. : in proximos, Cic. ;
vita, Cic. **2.** T r a n s f. *hurtful, noxious* :
ventus, pes, Hor.

iniūrius, a, um [iūs], *wrongful, unjust* (esp.
in phr. iniurium est) : Pl., Cic., Liv.

iniūrus, a, um [iūs], *wrongful* : Pl.

in-iussū, ABL. *sing. m. without command* : in-
iussu suo et civitatis, Caes. ; Cic. ; Liv.

in-iussus, a, um, *unbidden, voluntary, of
one's own accord.* **1.** L i t. : Hor. **2.**
T r a n s f. Of things : virescunt gramina,
Verg.

iniustē, *adv. unjustly, wrongfully* : Pl., Cic.,
Nep. *Sup.* : Sall.

iniustitia, ae, *f.* [iniūstus]. **I.** *injustice* : Cic.
II. *severity* : Ter.

in-iūstus, a, um. **I.** *unjust, wrongful.* **1.**
L i t. (of persons) : Cic. **2.** T r a n s f. (of
things) : bellum, iracundia, Cic. ; arma,
Liv. ; iniusto carpere dente, Ov. As Noun,
iniūstum, ī, *n. injustice* : Hor. **II.** *unfair, tyrannical, severe.* **1.** L i t. (of persons) : Ter., Verg. **2.** T r a n s f. : onus,
Cic. ; fascis, Verg. ; faenus, Liv.

in-labefactus, a, um, *unshaken, unimpaired* :
vincula, concordia, Ov.

in-lābor, lābī, lāpsus, *to slip, glide, fall into*
or *on to.* **1.** L i t. : Cic., Hor. **2.**
T r a n s f. : pernicies in animos, Cic. ; da,
pater, augurium atque animis inlabere
nostris, Verg.

in-labōrātus, a, um, *not laboured, uncultivated, spontaneous* : terra, Sen. Ep. ; oratio,
fructus, Quint.

in-labōrō, āre, *to work upon, labour at* :
domibus, Tac.

in-lacessītus, a, um *unprovoked, unat-
tacked* : Tac.

in-lacrimābilis, e, *adj.* **I.** *unwept, unlamented* : Hor. **II.** *that is not* or *cannot
be moved by tears, inexorable* : Hor.

in-lacrimō, āre, and **inlacrimor**, ārī, *to
weep at* or *over, to bewail, lament* (perh. also
to burst into tears). **1.** L i t. : Cic., Hor.,
Liv., etc. With DAT. : alicuius morti, Cic. ;
errori, Liv. ; Ov. With ACC. and *Inf.* :
Tac. **2.** T r a n s f. Of things : *to weep*
(i.e. with moisture) : maestum templis ebur,
Verg.

in-laesus, a, um, *unhurt, unimpaired* : Sen.
Ep. ; corpus, Ov., Suet. ; valetudo, Suet.

in-laetābilis, e, *adj. cheerless, joyless* : ora,
murmur, Verg.

inlāpsus, a, um, *Part.* inlābor
in-lāqueo, āre, *to ensnare.* Transf. : Pac.; munera navium saevos duces, Hor.
inlātus, a, um, *Part.* inferō.
in-laudātus, a, um. I. *unpraised, without fame, obscure* : Plin. Ep. II. *unworthy of praise* : Busiris, Verg.
inlautus, *v.* inlōtus.
inlecebra, ae, *f.* [*cf.* inliciō], lit. *a drawing gently on* ; hence *an enticement, allurement, bait, lure.* 1. Lit. : Pl., Liv. In *pl.* : Cic., Hor., Liv. With *Obj.* GEN. : voluptatis, peccandi, etc., Cic. With *Subj.* GEN. : Cic. 2. Transf. (of a person) : *a decoy-bird* : Pl.
inlecebrōsē, *adv. alluringly, enticingly* : Pl.
inlecebrōsus, a, um [inlecebra], *attractive, seductive.* Comp. : Pl.
inlectus, a, um, *Part.* inliciō.
inlectus, ūs, *m.* [inliciō], *an allurement, enticement* : Pl.
in-lēctus, a, um [legō], *not read, unread* : Ov.
in-lepidē, *adv. impolitely, rudely, inelegantly* : Pl., Hor.
in-lepidus, a, um, *inelegant, unmannerly, churlish* : Pl., Cic.; deliciae, Cat.
inlex, icis, *m. f.* [inliciō], *a decoy, lure.* 1. Lit. : Pl. 2. Transf. (of a person) : Pl.
in-lēx, ēgis, *adj. lawless* : Pl.
in-lībātus, a, um [lībō], *undiminished, unimpaired* : divitiae, Cic.; vires, libertas, imperium, Liv.; gloria, Tac.
in-līberālis, e, *adj. unworthy of a freeman or gentleman, ungenerous, sordid.* A. In gen. : facinus, Ter.; quaestus, Cic.; mens, Quint. B. In partic. a. *disobliging* : in me, Ter., Cic. Ep. b. *stingy* : adiectio, Liv.
inlīberālitās, ātis, *f.* [inlīberālis], *conduct unworthy of a freeman, stinginess* : Cic.
inlīberāliter, *adv. ungenerously, meanly.* a. In gen. : Ter., Cic. b. *stingily* : Cic. Ep.
in-liciō, licere, lexi, lectum (*Inf. Perf. sync.* inlexe, Poet. ap. Cic.) [obsol. laciō, *cf.* adliciō], *to draw into* (a trap) or *towards* (an object); *to allure, entice, seduce, mislead, decoy* (us. in bad sense) : aliquem in fraudem, Pl. ; me ad illam, Pl. ; (eos) ad bellum spes rapinarum, Sall. ; lucro mercatorem ut sequatur agmen, Liv. ; inliciente Vitellio desererent regem, Tac. ; ab iisdem inlecti, Cic. Ep. ; cave ne iniciaris, Lucr.
in-licitātor, ōris, *m.* [licitō], *one who bids at an auction to make others bid higher, a sham bidder* : Cic.
in-licitus, a, um, *not allowed, unlawful* : Luc.; Sen. Ep.; amor, exactiones, Tac.
in-līdō, lidere, lisi, lisum [laedō], *to strike or dash against* or *upon* : caestus effracto inlisit in ossa cerebro, Verg. ; navis vadis, Verg. ; dentem fragili (corpori), Hor. ; fluctus se in litore, Quint.
in-ligō, āre, *to bind or tie on, to fasten, attach.* 1. Lit. : emblemata in poculis, Cic. ; litterae in iaculo inligatae, Caes. ; tigna, Caes. ; in currūs Mettium, Liv. ; manūs post tergum, Liv. 2. Transf. a. *to attach, connect closely* : sententiam verbis, Cic. ; in quo verborum inligantur lepores, Cic. ; multis pignoribus M. Lepidum res publica inligatum tenet, Cic. ; familiari

amicitia inligati Philippo, Liv. ; non iis condicionibus inligabitur pax, Liv. b. *to fetter, hamper* : inutilis inque ligatus cedebat, Verg. ; Romano bello, Liv. ; praedā, lento veneno, impeditis locis, conscientiā, Tac.
inlīmis, e, *adj.* [līmus], *without mud or slime* : fons, Ov.
in-linō, linere, lēvī, litum, *to smear over, besmear, bedaub.* 1. Lit. : collyria oculis, Hor. ; texta veneno, Ov. ; taedam pice, Liv. ; bruma nivis Albanis agris, Hor. ; aliquid chartis, Hor. 2. Transf. a. aurum vestibus, Hor. ; dona veneno, Liv. ; tela dolis, Luc. b. venustatis non fuco inlitus color, Cic.
in-liquefactus, a, um, *melted, liquefied, liquid.* Transf. : voluptates, Cic.
inlīsus, a, um, *Part.* inlīdō.
in-litterātus, a, um, *illiterate, uneducated.* 1. Lit. (of persons) : Cic., Quint. 2. Transf. (of things) : Cic. Ep. ; nervi, Hor. Sup. : litterae, Plin. Ep.
inlitus, a, um, *Part.* inlinō.
in-lōtus (inlūtus Pl.), a, um, *unwashed, uncleansed* : Pl., Cato, Verg., etc.
in-lūceō, ēre, *to be alight, ablaze on* : atra pix tuo capiti, Pl.
in-lūcēscō (-īscō), lūcēscere, lūxī. A. Intrans. : of the day or sun, *to grow light.* 1. Lit. : sol, Cic. ; alicui dies, Pl., Cic. ; dies, Cic., Ov. ; eā nocte, cui inluxit dies caedis, Suet. Without sol or dies : inluxit, *it grew light, day dawned* : Liv. 2. Transf. : populo Romano vox et auctoritas consulis in tantis tenebris, Cic. B. Trans. : *to shine upon* : sol, dies (etc.) aliquem, Pl.
in-lūdō, lūdere, lūsī, lūsum. A. Intrans. *to play upon, at, or with* : *to sport with, amuse oneself with.* a. In gen. : with DAT. : chartis, Hor. b. *to make sport or game of, to mock, or jeer at, to ridicule* : Cic. Ep. ; in aliquem, Ter., Cic. ; in aliquo, Ter. With DAT. : dignitati, Cic. ; capto, Verg. ; signis Romanis, Tac. ; Neroni fortuna, Tac. c. *to maltreat in sport or wantonly, do mischief to* (with DAT.) : frondi uri, Verg. ; matri eius, Tac. ; pecuniae, Tac. B. Trans. : *to play with.* a. In gen. : inlusas auro vestis (i.e. fancifully worked), Verg. b. *to scoff, mock, or jeer at* ; *to flout, ridicule* : aliquem, Ter., Cic. ; artem, Cic. ; Ov. ; virtutem, Verg. ; voces Neronis, quoties caneret, Tac. ; facetiis inlusus, Tac. c. *to maltreat in sport or wantonly, do mischief to* : vitam filiae, Ter. ; corpus alicuius, Tac.
in-lūmin̆ātē, *adv. clearly, luminously* : dicere, Cic.
in-lūminō, āre, *to bring into the light, to light up, illuminate.* 1. Lit. : luna inluminata a sole, Cic. 2. Transf. a. *to set in a clear light* : inluminata sapientia, Cic. b. *to embellish* : orationem sententiis, Cic. ; Quint.
inlūsiō, ōnis, *f.* [inlūdō], *a mocking, jeering, irony* : Cic.
inlūstris, e, *adj.* [in and root of lūstrō], *set in the light; lighted up, clear, bright.* 1. Lit. : locus, stella, etc., Cic. Comp. : solis candor inlustrior est quam ullius ignis, Cic. ; Pl. 2. Transf. a. *clear, distinct,*

plain, manifest : visus, oratio, rationes, factum, Cic.; exempla, Sen. Ep.; explanatio, Quint. *Comp. :* Cic. **b.** *distinguished, famous :* inlustribus in personis temporibusque, Cic.; adulescens, Caes.; feminae, Suet.; res, Caes.; Cic. *Sup. :* Varr.

inlūstrius, *comp. adv. more clearly, perspicuously :* Cic.

in-lūstrō, āre [in and obs. lūstrum, *lighting*], *to light up, make bright, illuminate.* **1.** Lit.: sol habitabilis oras, Hor. **2.** Transf. **a.** *to make clear, distinct, manifest :* consilia, quae clam essent inita contra salutem urbis, Cic.; . ius obscurum, Cic.; orationem, Quint.; philosophiam veterem Latinis litteris, Cic. **b.** *to make famous or distinguished :* familiam, Suet.; tuam amplitudinem hominum iniuria, Cic. Ep.; quid prius inlustrem satiris ? Hor.

inlūsus, a, um, *Part.* inlūdō.

inlŭtilis, e, *adj.* [inlūtus], *that cannot be washed out :* odor, Pl.

inlūtus, *v.* inlōtus.

inluviēs, ēi, *f.* **I.** [in, *not,* and lavō], *dirt, filth :* Ter., Verg., Tac. As a term of abuse : Pl. **II.** [in, *prep. cf.* adluviēs], *an inundation, floods* (due to overflowing) : Curt., Tac.

in-m-, *v.* imm-.

in-memorābilis, e, *adj.* **A.** Pass. **a.** *unworthy of mention :* Pl. **b.** *indescribable :* Lucr. **B.** Act. *that will not tell :* Pl.

inmoenis, e, *adj.* [moenus, old form of mūnus] *exempt from a public service.* **1.** Lit.: civis, Pl. **2.** Transf. *thankless :* facinus, Pl.

in-munditia, ae, *f.* [immundus], *uncleanness, filth :* Pl.

inmūtābilis, e, *adj.* [immūtō], *changed, altered :* vestitus, Pl.

in-nābilis, e, *adj. that cannot be swum in :* unda, Ov.

in-nāscor, nāsci, nātus, *to be born in, to grow or spring in.* **1.** Lit.: filix agris, Hor.; rupibus robora, Ov. **2.** Transf.: in hac elatione animi cupiditas principatūs, Cic.

in-natō, āre. **I.** *to swim or float in or on.* **1.** Lit. With DAT.: lactuca acri stomacho, Hor.; unda freto, Ov.; campis Tiberis, Plin. Ep. With Acc.: undam alnus, Verg. **2.** Transf.: innatans illa verborum facilitas (i.e. superficial), Quint. **II.** *to swim or float into :* pisciculi in concham, Cic.

in-nātus, a, um. **I.** *Part.* innāscor. **II.** Adj.; *inborn, natural :* cupiditas scientiae, Cic.; in nobis cognitionis amor, Cic. With DAT.: mihi avaritia, Pl.; Caes.; Cic.

in-nāvigābilis, e, *adj. unnavigable :* Tiberis, Liv.

in-nectō, nectere, nexui, nexum, *to entwine, twine in or among, bind or fasten about.* **1.** Lit.: inter se innexi rami, Liv.; palmas armis, colla auro, Verg.; tempora sertis, Ov.; crinem vittis innexa, Verg.; innecti cervicibus, Tac. **2.** Transf. **a.** alicui per adfinitatem innexus, Tac.; innexus conscientiae alicuius, Tac. **b.** *causas morandi,* Verg.; fraudem clienti, Verg.

in-nitor, nīti, nixus (nīsus, Tac.), *to lean or rest on, to support oneself on.* **1.** Lit. with DAT. or ABL.: scutis innixi, Caes.; hastā

innixus, Liv.; innitur hastae, Ov.; templa columnis, Ov. **2.** Transf.: haec innixa in omnium nostris umeris, Cic.; uni viro fortuna hostium, Liv.; alicui secreta imperatorum, Tac.; (urbs) eodem M. Furio, Liv.

in-nō, nāre, *to swim in.* **1.** Lit.: Cic., Verg. With Acc.: fluvium, Verg. With ABL.: marinā aquā, Suet. **2.** Transf. **a.** *to flow upon, to wash :* innantem Maricae litoribus Lirim, Hor. **b.** *to sail upon, navigate :* naviculae aquae, Liv.; levior classis vadoso mari, Tac. With Acc.: Stygios lacūs, Verg.

in-nocēns, entis, *adj. harmless.* **1.** Lit.: epistula, Cic. Ep.; innocentis pocula Lesbii, Hor.; loca, Tac. **2.** Transf. **a.** *blameless, guiltless, innocent :* Pl., Cic., Sall. With GEN.: factorum, Tac. *Masc.* as Noun : Cic., Sall., etc. **b.** *irreproachable, upright :* Cic., Suet. *Sup. :* Cic. **c.** *disinterested, unselfish* (opp. avarus) : nobilitas, Cic.

innocenter, *adv. blamelessly, unselfishly :* Quint., Tac. *Comp. :* Tac.

innocentia, ae, *f.* [innocēns], *harmlessness.* Transf. **a.** *innocence, guiltlessness :* Cic. Also concr. *the innocent :* innocentiam poenā liberare, Cic. **b.** *uprightness, integrity :* Cic., Liv. **c.** *disinterestedness, unselfishness* (opp. avaritia) : Caes., Cic.

innocuē, *adv.* **I.** *harmlessly :* Suet. **II.** *innocently :* vivere, Ov.

in-nocuus, a, um. **A.** Act. **1.** Lit. *harmless, innocuous :* litus, Verg.; iter, Ov. **2.** Transf. *innocent :* Ov.; agere causas innocuas, Ov. **B.** Pass. *unharmed :* sēdēre carinae, Verg.

in-nōtēscō, nōtēscere, nōtuī, *to become known or noted :* quod ubi intonuit, Liv.; carmina vulgo, Suet.; Tac. With ABL. of cause : fraude, Phaedr.

in-novō, āre, *to renew.* With *Refl. Pron. :* to return, start again : se ad suam intemperantiam, Cic.

in-noxius, a, um. **A.** Act. **1.** Lit. *harmless :* anguis, Verg. **2.** Transf. **a.** *safe :* iter, Tac. **b.** *not guilty, innocent :* servos, Pl.; paupertas, Tac.; Ov. With GEN.: criminum, Liv. With *ab :* Pl. **B.** Pass. *unharmed, unhurt :* Lucr., Sall., Tib., etc.

in-nūbilus, a, um, *unclouded, cloudless :* aether, Lucr.

innuba, ae, *f. adj.* [nūbō], *unmarried :* Sibylla, Ov. Of the laurel, because the maiden Daphne was changed into it : Ov.

in-nūbō, nūbere, nūpsī, *to marry into :* quo, Liv.; nostris thalamis, Ov.

in-numerābilis, e, *adj. countless, innumerable :* Cic., Hor., Quint.

innumerābilitās, ātis, *f.* [innumerābilis], *countless number :* Cic.

innumerābiliter, *adv. innumerably :* Lucr., Cic.

in-numerālis, e, *adj. numberless, innumerable :* numerus, Lucr.

in-numerus, a, um, *countless :* numerus, Lucr.; gentes populique, Verg.; miles, Ov.; pecunia, Tac.

in-nuō, nuere, nui, nūtum, *to give a nod (as a signal) :* ubi ego innuero vobis, Pl.; Ter.; Plin. Ep. Without DAT.: Ter., Liv., Juv.

in-nūpta, ae. **I.** *f. adj. unmarried :* puellae,

Verg. ; innuptae nuptiae, *a marriage that is no marriage.* Poet. ap. Cic. **II.** As Noun, *a maiden :* Cat., Verg., Prop.

in-nūtriō, īre, *to bring up in.* **1.** Lit. : mari innutritus, Plin. Ep. ; amplis opibus, Suet. **2.** Transf. : certis ingeniis, Sen. Ep. ; bellicis laudibus, Plin. Pan.

in-oblītus, a, um, *not forgetful :* Ov.

in-obrŭtus, a, um, *not overwhelmed :* Ov.

in-observābilis, e, *adj. unnoticed :* error, Cat.

in-observantia, ae, *f. inattention, negligence :* Quint., Suet.

in-observātus, a, um, *unobserved, unperceived :* sidera, Ov.

in-occĭduus, a, um, *never setting :* axis, Luc.

inocŭlātĭō, ōnis, *f.* [oculus], *a budding, grafting :* Cato.

in-odōrus, a, um, *without smell :* Pers.

in-offēnsus, a, um. **1.** Lit. **a.** Pass. : *not struck against :* meta, Luc. **b.** Act. *not striking against ; without breaking, without stumbling :* marc, Verg. ; inoffensum pedem referre, Tib. **2.** Transf. : *free from hindrance, uninterrupted :* vita, Ov. ; oratio, Sen. Ep. ; cursus honorum, Tac.

in-officiōsus, a, um. **I.** *careless of duties or obligations :* testamentum, Cic. **II.** *not obliging :* in aliquem, Cic. Ep.

in-olēns, entis, *adj. without smell :* olivum, Lucr.

in-olēsco, olēscere, olēvī, *to grow in.* **1.** Lit. : germen libro, Verg. **2.** Transf. : multa (mala), Verg.

in-ōminātus, a, um, *without omens, unhallowed :* cubilia, Hor.

inŏpĭa, ae, *f.* [inops], *want* (of means or resources). **1.** Lit. **a.** In gen. : *a state of want, need, poverty, indigence :* Pl., Caes., Cic., etc. Occ. *scanty supplies :* dispensatio inopiae, Liv. **b.** With defining Gen. : *want, dearth, scarcity, difficulty in obtaining :* argenti, Pl. ; frumenti, Caes., Sall. ; criminum, consili, Cic. ; loci, Liv. ; advocatorum, Tac. ; veri, Tac. ; frumentaria, Caes. **2.** Transf. **a.** Of a speaker : *poverty of ideas :* Cic. **b.** *want of protectors, helplessness :* Cic.

in-opīnāns, antis, *adj. not expecting, unaware :* Menapios oppresserunt, Caes. ; suis inopinantibus, Liv.

inopīnanter, *adv. unexpectedly :* Suet.

in-opīnātus, a, um. **A.** Pass. : *not expected, unexpected :* malum, Caes. ; tibi haec, Cic. ; Liv. ; as Noun in phr. **ex inopīnātō,** *unexpectedly :* Cic., Suet. ; **inopīnātō,** Abl. used as *Adv., unexpectedly :* Liv. **B.** Act. : *off one's guard, not expecting :* cum inopinatos invasissent, Liv.

in-opīnus, a, um, *unexpected :* quies, Verg. ; visus, Ov. ; Tac.

inopiōsus, a, um [inopia], *in want :* with Gen. : consili, Pl.

in-ops, opis, *adj. without means or resources.* **1.** Lit. **a.** In gen. : *destitute, needy, poor, indigent :* Hor., Ov. **b.** With defining Gen. : *wanting, lacking, in need of :* amicorum, amicitatis, Cic. ; animi, Verg. ; mentis, Ov. ; consili, Liv. ; senatus auxili humani, Liv. ; provinciae virorum, Tac. **c.** With Abl. : classem inopem milite,

Liv. ; Cic. **2.** Transf. **A.** Of persons. **a.** In language, ideas : *weak, poor :* verbis, Cic. ; ad ornandum, Cic. Of the language itself : Cic. **b.** *weak, helpless, forlorn, unprotected :* Cic., Verg., Liv. **B.** Of things. **a.** *poor, needy :* res, Pl. ; aerarium, Cic. With Gen. : terra pacis, Ov. **b.** *weak, helpless :* amor, Lucr. ; animus, cupido, Hor. ; causa, Cic. Ep.

in-ōrātus, a, um, *not pleaded :* legati Ameriam re inoratā reverterunt, Cic.

in-ōrdinātus, a, um, *not arranged, disordered :* milites, Liv. *Neut.* as Noun : idque ex inordinato (*out of disorder*) in ordinem duxit, Cic.

in-ōrnātus, a, um, *unadorned.* **1.** Lit. : mulieres, Cic. ; comae, Ov. **2.** Transf. **a.** Of an author's style : *plain :* Cic., Hor. **b.** *uncelebrated :* non ego te meis chartis inornatum silebo, Hor.

inpendiōsus, a, um [impendium], *spending much, extravagant :* Pl.

in-percō, ere [parcō], *to spare.* With Dat. : Pl.

inpluviātus, a, um [impluvium], *shaped like an impluvium :* vestis, Pl.

inpūrātus, a, um [impūrus], (morally) *defiled, vile :* Pl., Ter. *Sup. :* Pl.

inpūrĭtae, ārum, *f. pl.* [impūrus], (moral) *impurity :* Pl.

inp-, *v.* also imp-.

inquam, *Pres. Subj. let me say, I must say* (only in repeating one's own words with emphasis), *v.* inquit.

in-quĭēs, ētis, *adj. restless :* homo, ingenium, Sall. ; inquies Germanus spe, cupidine, Tac.

inquĭētō, āre [inquiētus], *to disquiet, unsettle.* **1.** Lit. : rumoribus inquietari, Plin. Ep. ; Suet. **2.** Transf. *to make difficult :* victoriam, Tac.

in-quĭētus, a, um, *restless, unsettled.* **1.** Lit. : lux, Liv. ; Hadria, Hor. **2.** Transf. : animus, ingenia, Liv. ; praecordia, Hor. ; urbs auctionibus, Tac. ; tempora, Tac. *Sup. :* Sen.

inquĭlīnus, I, *m.* [fr. root of colō, older quelō], *an inhabitant, tenant* (opp. to owner or native). **1.** Lit. : Sall., Cic., etc. **2.** Transf. : quos ego non discipulos philosophorum, sed inquilinos voco, Sen. Ep.

inquĭnātē, *adv. filthily :* loqui, Cic.

inquĭnātus, a, um. **I.** *Part.* inquinō. **II.** Adj. : *foul, filthy, polluted :* hominem ore, linguā, manu, vitā omni inquinatum, Cic. ; dextra inquinatior, Cat. ; Cic. ; sermo inquinatissimus, Cic.

inquĭnō, āre [*cf.* caenum], *to bedaub, befoul, stain, pollute.* **1.** Lit. : vestem, Pl. ; arma situs, Ov. ; aqua cadaveribus inquinata, Cic. **2.** Transf. : se vitiis, Cic. ; amicitiam nomine criminoso, Cic. ; famam alterius, Liv. ; Iuppiter aere tempus aureum, Hor.

in-quīrō, quīrere, quīsīvī, quīsītum [quaerō], *to search for among* (a number). **1.** Lit. : Flamini corpus magnā cum curā inquisitum non invenit, Liv. **2.** Transf. : *to institute an investigation.* **a.** *to examine, enquire into, pry into :* in ea quae etc. Cic. ; in se, Cic., Tac. ; patrios inquirit in annos, Ov. **b.** In law : *to search for grounds or proofs of a charge :* in competitores, Cic.

de iis quorum etc., Liv. **c.** *to search for:*
honestas quam natura maxime inquirit,
Cic. ; vitia alicuius, Hor. ; omnia ordine,
Liv. With *Indir. Quest.* ; Hor.

inquīsītiō, ōnis, *f.* [inquīrō]. **I.** *a searching
for* : militum, Curt. Concr.: *an object
of search* (or perh. *a cause of searching*) : in-
quisitioni mihi esse, Pl. **II.** *a searching
into, investigation.* **a.** In gen. : veri, Cic. ;
Quint. **b.** In law : *a searching for proofs
against* : candidati, Cic. ; postulare in aliquem, Plin. Ep. ; dare alicui, Plin. Ep.

inquīsītor, ōris, *m.* [inquīrō]. **I.** *a searcher :*
under the Empire, *a secret spy :* Suet. ;
algae, Juv. **II.** *an investigator ;* in law,
*one who searches for proofs to support an
accusation :* Cic., Tac., Plin. Ep.

(1) inquīsītus, a, um. *Part.* inquīrō.

(2) in-quīsītus, a, um [quaerō], *not searched
into :* res, Pl.

inquit, *v. def.* (the follg. forms were in use :
Pres. inquis, inquit, inquimus, inquiunt ;
Pres. Subj. inquam ; *Imperf.* inquībat or
inquiēbat : *Fut.* inquiēs, inquiet ; *Perf.*
inquii, inquīstī : *Imper.* inque, inquitō),
placed parenthetically after one or more
words of a quotation, like our *said I, said
he, etc.* **a.** In citing the words of a person :
qui ubi me viderunt, ' ubi sunt ' inquiunt,
' scyphi ?' Cic. ; Liv., etc. With DAT.
(rare) : tum Quintus, ' en,' inquit mihi,
' haec ego patior cottidie,' Cic. Ep. **b.** In
emphatic repetition : tuas, tuas, inquam,
suspiciones, Cic. ; Lucr. **c.** In stating objections to one's own arguments : ' quid ad
ineptias abis ?' inquies, Cic. **d.** Pleonastic : hoc adiunxit, ' pater,' inquit, ' meus
etc.,' Nep.

in-rādō, ere, *to scrape in :* silphium, Cato.

in-rāsus, a, um, *unshorn :* caput, Pl.

in-ratiōnālis, e, *adj.* **I.** *without reason,
irrational :* animal, Quint. ; Sen. Ep.
Neut. pl. as Noun : Quint. **II.** *without
exercising the reason, mechanical :* usus,
Quint.

in-raucēscō, raucēscere, rausī [raucus], *to
become hoarse :* Cic.

in-redivīvus, a, um, *irreparable, that cannot
be restored :* Cat.

in-redux, ucis, *adj. that does not bring back :*
via, Luc.

in-religātus, a, um, *not bound :* Ov.

in-religiōsē, *adv. impiously :* Tac.

in-religiōsus, a, um, *impious, irreligious :*
inreligiosum ratus sacerdotes pedibus ire,
Liv. ; inreligiosum est with *Inf.*), Plin. Ep.

in-remeābilis, e, *adj. not to be retraversed ;
from which there is no returning :* error,
Verg. ; unda (i.e. the Styx), Verg.

in-reparābilis, e, *adj. irrecoverable :* tempus,
Verg. ; vita, Sen. Ep.

in-repertus, a, um, *not found, undiscovered :*
aurum, Hor.

in-rēpō, rēpere, rēpsī, *to creep in.* **1.** Lit. :
draconem repente inrepsisse ad eam, Suet.
2. Transf. : *to creep or steal in unperceived, insinuate oneself :* eloquentia in sensūs, Cic. ; in testamenta locupletium, Cic. ;
penitus, Tac. With ACC. : militaris animos, Tac.

in-reprehēnsus, a, um, *blameless, without
blame :* probitas, Ov.

in-requiētus, a, um, *restless :* sors, Ov. ;
Charybdis, Ov.

in-resectus, a, um, *uncut, unpared :* pollex,
Hor.

in-resolūtus, a, um, *not loosened, not slack-
ened :* vincula, Ov.

in-rētiō, īre [rēte], *to catch in a net, to ensnare,
entangle.* Transf. : aliquem inlecebris,
Cic. ; loquacitas interrogationibus inretita,
Cic.

in-retortus, a, um, *not turned back :* oculo
inretorto, Hor.

in-reverēns, entis, *adj. disrespectful.* With
GEN. : operis, Plin. Ep.

in-reverenter, *adv. disrespectfully :* Plin. Ep.

in-reverentia, ae, *f. disrespect :* Tac. With
Obj. GEN. : studiorum, Plin. Ep.

in-revocābilis, e, *adj.* **I.** *irrevocable :* aetas
praeterita, Lucr. ; in casum inrevocabilem
se dare, Liv. ; verbum, Hor. **II.** *unchangeable, implacable :* Domitiani natura,
Tac. ; constantia, Plin. Ep. *Comp. :*
Tac.

in-revocātus, a, um, *not called back ; not
encored :* Hor.

in-rīdeō, rīdēre, rīsī, rīsum. **A.** Intrans.
to laugh at, to joke, jeer at : Ter., Cic., Tac.
With DAT. : mihi, Cic. Ep. **B.** Trans. *to
mock, ridicule, laugh to scorn :* aliquem, Pl.,
Cic., Hor., etc. ; res malas, Pl. ; Romam,
Cic. ; ratem, Verg. ; moram, Plin. Pan.

in-rīdiculē, *adv. without humour or wit :*
Caes.

in-rīdiculō, *Predic.* DAT. : inridiculo habere,
esse, *to make, be, a laughing-stock :* Pl.

inrigātiō, ōnis, *f. a watering, irrigating :*
agrorum, Cic. In *pl.* : Varr.

in-rigō, āre. **1.** Lit. **a.** *to lead or conduct
water or other fluids :* aquam in areas,
Cato ; imbris plantis, Verg. **b.** *to water,
irrigate :* Aegyptum Nilus, Cic. **c.** *to
overflow, inundate :* Circus Tiberi superfuso inrigatus, Liv. ; Pactolus culta auro,
Verg. **2.** Transf. **a.** *to pour in, diffuse :*
Venus Ascanio per membra quietem, Verg. ;
Lucr. **b.** *to flood, steep, bathe :* Democriti
fontibus Epicurus hortulos suos, Cic. ; sol
caelum candore, Lucr. ; sopor inrigat artūs,
Verg. ; Comic. : vino aetatem, Pl. ; aliquem plagis, Pl.

in-riguus, a, um. **A.** Pass. *watered, wet.*
1. Lit. : herba, Pl. ; hortus, Hor. ; stagna
aestibus maritimis, Liv. **2.** Transf.
soaked : corpus mero, Hor. **B.** Act.
watering, moistening. **1.** Lit. : fons, Verg. ;
aqua, Ov. **2.** Transf. : somnus, Pers.

inrīsiō, ōnis, *f.* [inrīdeō], *a scoffing, mockery :*
Cic.

inrīsor, ōris, *m.* [inrīdeō], *a mocker, scoffer :*
Cic.

inrīsus, a, um, *Part.* inrīdeō.

inrīsus, ūs, *m.* [inrīdeō], *a scoffing, mockery,
derision :* ab inrisu, Liv. With *Obj.* GEN. :
Tac. Also, *an object of derision, a laughing-
stock :* inrisui esse, Caes., Tac.

inrītābilis, e, *adj.* [inrītō], *easily excited or
enraged, sensitive :* animus, Cic. Ep. ; genus
vatum, Hor.

inrītāmen, inis, *n.* [inrītō], *an incitement, incentive :* amoris, Ov.

inrītāmentum i, *n.* [inrītō], *an incitement,
incentive* (mostly in *pl.*) : Liv. With

GEN.: gulae, Sall.; malorum, Ov.; certaminum, Liv.; pacis, invidiae, Tac.

inrītātĭō, ōnis, *f.* [inrītō], *an incitement.* **a.**
irritation to anger: animorum, Liv. **b.**
stimulans. With *Subj.* GEN.: conviviorum,
Tac. With *ad :* Sen. Ep.

inrītō, āre (*Aor. Opt.* or *Subj.* inrītāssīs, Pl.),
to enrage, incite, excite. **1.** Lit.: canem,
Pl.; aliquem, Pl., Ter.; vi virum, Cic.;
virum telis, Verg.; animos ad bellum, Liv.
2. Transf.: quietos amnīs, Hor.; flammas, amores, Ov.; sibi simultates, Liv.;
suspiciones, exitium, Tac.; delatores, Suet.

in-rĭtus, a, um [ratus]. **1.** Lit. **a.** *invalid,
null and void, futile :* quod modo erat ratum,
inritum est, Ter.; testamentum, Cic. **b.**
ineffective, useless, vain : Pl.; dona, tela,
Verg.; verba, moenia, Ov.; inceptum,
Liv.; remedium, Tac. *Neut.* as Noun:
spes ad inritum redacta, Liv.; Tac. **2.**
Transf. Of persons: *that undertakes in
vain* or *without effect :* legati remittuntur,
Tac.; Verg., etc. With GEN.: spei, Curt.;
legationis, Tac.

inrŏgātĭō, ōnis, *f.* [inrogō], *an imposing,
adjudicating* (of a penalty): multae, Cic.

in-rŏgō, āre (*Aor. Opt.* or *Sub.*, inrogāssit in
law in Cic.). **1.** Prop.: *to propose a
measure against :* leges privatis hominibus,
Cic.; privilegium, Cic. **2.** In gen.: *to
impose :* multam (alicui), Cic., Liv.;
poenam, Hor., Liv., Tac.

in-rŏrō, āre [rōs]. **1.** Lit. *to wet, moisten*
(with dew) : *to bedew ;* hence, crinem aquis,
Ov. With DAT.: extremo Aquarius anno,
Verg.; lacrimae foliis, Ov. **2.** Transf.
(of non-liquids). With ACC. and DAT.:
patinae piper, Pers.

in-rūctō, āre, *to belch on* or *at :* alicui in os,
Pl.

in-rumpō, rumpere, rūpī, ruptum, *to burst,
break,* or *rush in.* **1.** Lit.: Caes., Ov.,
etc.; huc intro, Ter.; Ov.; in castra,
Caes., Cic.; in medios hostis, Caes.; ad
aliquem, Sall. With ACC.: oppidum,
Caes.; portam, Sall.; limina, Verg.;
stationes, Tac. With DAT.: thalamo,
Verg. **2.** Transf. *to break in, intrude :*
in alicuius patrimonium, Cic.; luxuries in
domum, Cic.; calamitates ad me, Sen. Ep.;
adulatio, Tac.

in-rŭō, ruere, ruī. **A.** Trans. *to fling in :*
huc se, Ter. **B.** Intrans. *to rush in, force
one's way in.* **1.** Lit.: Ter., Verg.; in
aedīs, Ter.; in mediam aciem, Cic.; in
aliquem, Cic.; in forum, Liv. **2.** Transf.
a. in alienas possessiones, Cic.; in odium
alicuius, Cic.; cladibus, Luc. **b.** Of *blundering* in speaking : Cic.

inruptĭō, ōnis, *f.* [inrumpō], *a bursting* or
breaking in, an invasion : facere in popinam, Pl.; ferarum, Plin. Pan. Milit.:
facere, Cic.; in Chattos, Tac.

inruptus, a, um, *Part.* inrumpō.

in-ruptus, a, um, *unbroken, unsevered :*
copula, Hor.

in-salūbris, e, *adj. unhealthy, unwholesome :*
cibus, Curt.; Quint. *Sup. :* Plin.

in-salūtātus, a, um, *ungreeted, unsaluted :*
inque salutatam linquo, Verg.

in-sānābĭlis, e, *adj. incurable.* **1.** Lit.:
morbus, Cic., Liv.; caput, Hor. **2.**

Transf.: contumeliae, Cic.; ingenium,
Liv. *Comp. :* Liv.

īnsānē, *adv. madly, crazily :* amare, Pl.
Comp. : Hor.

īnsānĭa, ae, *f.* [īnsānus], *madness, frenzy,
folly.* **1.** Lit.: Ter., Cic., etc.; concupiscere aliquid ad insaniam, Cic.; belli, Verg.
2. Transf. **a.** Of poets: *rapture :* Hor.
b. *extravagant fancy* or *indulgence, mania :*
villarum, Cic. Ep.; libidinum, Cic.; ab
sano initio in hanc insaniam venire (of
expenditure), Liv.; orationis, Cic. **c.** In
pl. : mad whim or *acts :* Pl., Cic.

īnsānĭō, īre (*Imperf.* Insānībat, Ter.) [īn-
sānus], *to be unsound* (mentally), *mad, insane.* **1.** Lit.: Ter., Cic., Hor. **2.**
Transf. **a.** *to act like a madman, be mad,
crazy, frenzied :* ex amore, Pl.; ex iniuriā,
Liv.; insanire libet tibi, Verg. With
Intern. ACC.: errorem, stultitiam, sollemnia, Hor. With *in* and ACC.: in libertinas,
Hor. **b.** Of inspiration : Cic. **c.** Of the
sea : *to rage ;* Hor. **d.** Of style : Quint.

īnsānĭtās, ātis, *f. unsoundness, unhealthiness,
disease :* Cic.

īn-sānus, a, um, *unsound in mind, mad, insane.* **1.** Lit.: Cic., Juv. **2.** Transf.
a. Of persons and their acts or feelings :
acting like a madman, raving, frantic : ex
stultis insanos facere, Ter.; homo, contio,
cupiditas, Cic.; caedis cupido, Verg.;
amores, Hor.; trepidatio, Liv. *Comp. :*
Cic., Hor. *Sup. :* Cic. **b.** Of inspiration : vates, Verg. **c.** Of things : *raging,
furious, stormy :* fluctus, Verg.; Capreae
sidera, Hor.; vires Austri, Ov.; montes,
Liv.

in-satĭābĭlis, e, *adj.* [satiō]. **A.** Pass.:
that cannot be satisfied, insatiable : cupiditas, Cic.; humanus animus, Liv.; votum,
Juv. **B.** Act.: *that cannot cloy* or *sate :*
varietas, Cic. *Comp. :* Cic.

insatĭābĭlĭter, *adv. insatiably :* Lucr., Tac.,
Plin. Ep.

in-satĭĕtās, ātis, *f. insatiateness, insatiety :*
in *pl. :* Pl.

in-satŭrābĭlis, e, *adj. insatiable :* abdomen,
Cic.

insatŭrābĭlĭter, *adv. insatiably :* Cic.

in-scendō, scendere, scendī, scēnsum [scandō],
to climb in or *on, to climb up, mount, ascend.*
A. Intrans.: in arborem, Pl.; in rogum,
Cic. **B.** Trans.: quadrigas, Pl.; equum,
Suet.; inscendo (sc. navem), Pl.

inscēnsĭō, ōnis, *f.* [īnscendō], *a mounting,
embarking :* in navem, Pl.

inscēnsus, a, um, *Part.* inscendō.

in-sciēns, entis, *adj.* **I.** *not knowing, unaware :* Pl., Ter., Cic.; inscientibus
cunctis, Liv. **II.** *ignorant, stupid, silly :* Ter.

insciĕnter, *adv. without knowledge* or *skill :*
Cic., Liv.

in-sciĕntĭa, ae, *f.* **I.** *ignorance, inexperi-
ence :* Cic. With *Subj.* GEN.: Caes., Liv.
With *Obj.* GEN.: locorum, Caes.; dicendi,
Cic. **II.** *culpable ignorance :* Tac.

inscĭtē, *adv. unskilfully, clumsily :* Cic., Liv.

inscĭtĭa, ae, *f.* [Inscītus]. **I.** *culpable ignorance.* **a.** *folly :* Pl. **b.** *inexperience,
want of skill, neglect, inattention :* Liv.
With *Subj.* GEN.: Tac. With *Obj.* GEN.:
rerum, temporis, Cic.; veri, Hor.; artis

Suet.; aedificandi, Tac. **II.** *lack of knowledge, ignorance :* Tac. With *Subj.* GEN. : Tac. With *Obj.* GEN.: litterarum, Tac. With *erga :* erga domum suam, Tac.

in-scītus, a, um, *inexperienced, unskilful, stupid :* Pl. *Sup. :* Pl. Of things : somnium, Cic. *Comp. :* Cic.

in-scius, a, um, *not knowing, ignorant, unaware :* Caes., Cic. With GEN.: omnium rerum, Cic.; culpae, Verg.; of a colt, inscius aevi, Verg. With *de :* de verbis inscius, Pl. With Acc. and *Inf. :* Cic. With *Indir. Quest. :* Caes., Verg., Hor.

in-scrībō, scribere, scripsi, scriptum. **I.** *to write on, inscribe.* **1.** Lit.: aliquid in basi tropaeorum, Cic.; nomen suum monumentis, Cic.; in libellis nomen, Cic.; sit inscriptum in fronte unius cuiusque civis quid de re publicā sentiat, Cic.; inscripti nomina regum flores, Verg. O cc. *to address :* epistulam patri, Cic. **2.** T r a n s f. **a.** orationes in animo, Cic. **b.** *to trace lines, score :* pulvis inscribitur hastā, Verg. **II.** With *Predic. Adj. to entitle, proclaim by a notice.* **1.** Lit.: aedis venalis hasce inscribit litteris, Pl.; without venalis : aedis mercede, Ter.; eos libellos rhetoricos inscribunt, Cic. **2.** T r a n s f.: sibi nomen philosophi, Cic.; sua quemque deorum facies, Ov. O cc. *to ascribe as a cause :* deos sceleri, Cic.

inscriptiō, ōnis, *f. a writing upon, inscribing :* nominis, Cic.

(1) **inscriptus,** a, um, *Part.* Inscrībō.

(2) **in-scriptus,** a, um. **I.** *not marked, contraband :* Varr. **II.** *unwritten :* Quint.

in-sculpō, sculpere, sculpsi, sculptum. **1.** Lit.: *to cut or carve in or upon, to engrave :* sortis in robore, Cic.; summam patrimonii saxo, Hor.; columnā aeneā, Liv.; ara cum titulo insculpto, Liv. **2.** T r a n s f.: res in animo, Cic.; omnibus est in animo quasi insculptum esse deos, Cic.

insectātiō, ōnis, *f.* [Insector], *a vigorous pursuing, hot pursuit.* **1.** Lit.: hostis, Liv. **2.** T r a n s f. (with words) : principum, Liv.; studiorum et morum alicuius, Suet. In *pl. :* Tac.

insectātor, ōris, *m. a persecutor, censurer :* plebis, Liv.; vitiorum, Quint.

insector, ārī (and **insectō,** āre, Pl.) [*freq.* Insequor], *to pursue, attack furiously.* **1.** Lit.: impios furiae, Cic.; aliquem hastis, Pl.; verberibus, Tac. **2.** T r a n s f. **a.** adsiduis herbam rastris, Verg. **b.** With words : aliquem, Cic.; audaciam improborum, Cic.; damnum amissi corporis, Phaedr.

in-sectus, a, um, *cut in, notched :* dentes, Ov.

in-sēdābiliter, *adv. incessantly :* Lucr.

in-senēscō, senēscere, senui, *to grow old over :* with DAT.: libris et curis, Hor.; malis, Ov.; iisdem negotiis, Tac.

in-sēnsilis, e, *adj. that cannot be felt, imperceptible :* principia, Lucr.

in-sepultus, a, um, *unburied :* Cic., Hor., Liv.; sepultura (i.e. not deserving the name), Cic.

insequēns, entis. **I.** *Part.* Insequor. **II.** A d j. *the following, succeeding:* insequenti anno, anno insequente, Liv.; insequentibus consulibus, Liv.

in-sequor, sequi, secūtus. **1.** *to follow on or after.* **1.** Lit. (in space) : Verg. With Acc.: Orphea silvae, Hor.; fugientem lumine pinum, Ov. **2.** T r a n s f. (in time or order). **a.** *to come next, succeed :* stridor rudentum, Verg. With Acc.: hunc proximo saeculo Themistocles, Cic.; improborum facta suspicio, Cic. **b.** *to continue, proceed :* longius, Cic. With *Inf. :* Verg. **II.** *to follow after* or *up* (as an enemy), *to assail.* **1.** Lit.: agmen, Caes.; aliquem gladio, Cic.; hostem, Liv.; reliquias Troiae, Verg.; te bello, Verg. **2.** T r a n s f. **a.** iacto semine comminus arva, Verg. O cc. *to overtake :* mors Gracchum, Cic. **b.** With abuse, ridicule, etc. : clamore hominem, Cic.; aliquem inridendo, Cic.; turpitudinem vitae, Cic.

(1) **in-serō,** serere, sēvi, situm, *to graft.* **1.** Lit.: inseritur nucis arbutus horrida fetu, Verg.; Ov. **2.** T r a n s f.: *to implant :* num qua tibi vitiorum inseverit natura, Hor.; animos corporibus, Cic.

(2) **in-serō,** serere, serui, sertum, *to connect into a chain* or *series ; to mingle, blend, let in.* **1.** Lit.: inseritur radiis subtemen, Ov.; pellem auro, Verg.; gemmas soleis (DAT.), Curt.; insertas fenestras, Verg. **2.** T r a n s f. **A.** *to enrol, put among, unite :* se, Tac.; se turbae, se bellis, Ov.; concilio Iovis, Hor.; civium numero, Suet.; me lyricis vatibus, Hor.; ignobilitatem suam magnis nominibus, Tac.; nomen famae, Tac.; historiae iocos, Ov. **B.** *to attach, introduce, insert, put in.* **a.** falces longuriis, Caes.; collum in laqueum, Cic.; caput in tentoria, Liv. **b.** Of words, ideas, etc.: plura illi aetati, Cic.; adeo minimis etiam rebus prava religio inserit Deos, Liv.; querellas, Tac.

insertō, āre [*freq.* Inserō 2.], *to put in :* clipeo sinistram, Verg.

insertus, a, um, *Part,* inserō 2.

in-serviō, īre, *to be a slave, subject,* or *vassal.* **1.** Lit.: Tac. With Acc.: illum, Pl. **2.** T r a n s f.: *to serve, be devoted* or *attached to, be submissive to.* With DAT. **A.** Of person : Ter., Cic., Liv. **b.** Of things : honoribus, artibus, etc., Cic.; temporibus, Nep.; famae, Tac.

insessus, a, um, *Part.* Insīdō.

in-sibilō, āre, *to hiss in* or *among :* Eurus, Ov.

in-sideō, ēre (for insēdi, insēssum, *v.* insīdō) [sedeō], *to be seated, to sit in* or *on.* **1.** Lit. **a.** equo, Liv.; toro, Ov. **b.** With Acc. *to hold blocked, hold* (for attack, surprise, or ambush) : locum quem insideatis, Liv. **2.** T r a n s f. *to be fixed to.* **a.** capulo manus, Tac. **b.** Of abstracts : voluptas penitus in omni sensu implicata insidet, Cic.; in eius mente species eloquentiae, Cic.; in memoriā alicuius, Cic.; metus animis, Liv.

insidiae, ārum, *f. pl.* [Insīdō]. **1.** Lit. **a.** *an ambush.* Of the place : Pl.; signa in insidiis ponere, Cic.; milites in insidiis conlocare, Caes. **b.** Of the troops : donec insidiae coorirentur, Tac.; Hirt. **c.** Abstract : conlocare, Caes.; instruere, Cic.; componere, Tac. **2.** T r a n s f. *any trap, plot, snare,* or *artifice :* insidias dare alicui, Pl.; alicui parare, comparare, struere, conlocare, Cic.; ponere vitae alicuius, Cic.; avibus moliri,

Verg. ; noctis serenae, Verg. Phr.: insidiis (Cic. Ep.), per insidias (Caes., Cic.), ex insidiis (Cic., Sall.), *by artifice or stratagem.*

insidiātor, ōris, m. [Insidior]. 1. Lit.: *a soldier lying in ambush :* Hirt., Liv. 2. Transf. *one who lies in wait, a lurker, waylayer, plotter :* Liv. ; viae, Cic. ; imperi, Nep. ; libertatis, Liv.

insidior, ārī [Insidiae], *to lie in ambush, lie in wait.* 1. Lit.: with DAT.: Clodio in viā, Cic. ; hostibus, Ov. 2. Transf. a. *to plot :* Cic. With DAT.: mihi, Cic. b. *to watch for :* with DAT.: tempori, Liv. ; Cic.

insidiōsē, adv. *by underhand means, insidiously :* Cic. Sup. : Cic. Ep.

insidiōsus, a, um [Insidiae], *artful, deceptive, insidious :* Comp. : Cic. Of things : clementia, Cic. Ep. ; verba, pocula, Ov.

in-sīdō, sīdere, sēdī, sessum, *to settle in or on.* 1. Lit. A. In gen. (with DAT.) : apes floribus, Verg. ; credit digitos insidere membris, Ov. ; Apuliae vapor, Hor. ; inscia Dido, insidat quantus miserae deus, Verg. B. In partic. a. *to settle on :* Lydia gens iugis Etruscis, Verg. b. Milit. *to occupy* (for attack, surprise, ambush) : with Acc. : tumulos, viam, itinera, locum, Liv. ; arcem militibus, Liv. ; saltus insessus ab hoste, Liv. ; montes insessi, Tac. ; ea loca, Tac. So, insessum diris avibus Capitolium, Tac. With DAT. : silvis iniquis, Verg. 2. Transf. *to settle in, become fixed or rooted in :* tibi suspicio, Cic. ; in memoriā, Cic. ; in animo oratio, Cic. ; macula in nomine, Cic.

insigne, is, n. [insignis], *a conspicuous distinguishing mark or token.* 1. Lit. A. In gen.: navis Bruti ex insigni facile agnosci poterat, Caes. ; in praetoriā nave insigne nocturnum trium luminum fore, Liv. ; quod erat insigne cum ad arma concurri operteret (i.e. *the signal*), Caes. ; quod erat insigno eum facere civibus consili sui copiam (i.e. *an indication*), Cic. B. In partic. a. Milit. *badges of distinction* on shield or helmet ; or *decorations, medals :* Caes., Verg. b. *official or other distinctive badges :* imperatoris, Caes. ; insignia regia, Cic. ; sacerdotum, Liv. ; pontificalia, Liv. ; fortunae, Cic. 2. Transf. a. In *pl. : distinctions :* laudis, Cic. ; morbi, Hor. b. In speech : *gems* (in *pl.*) : orationis, verborum, sententiarum, Cic.

insigniō, īre [Insignis], *to make conspicuous, distinguish :* Pl. ; clipeum auro, Verg. ; cum omnis annus funoribus et cladibus insigniretur, Tac. ; aliquem, Plin. Ep.

insignis, e, adj. [signum], *marked, distinguished, conspicuous.* 1. Lit.: vestitus, Caes. ; vestis, Liv. ; (bos) maculis insignis, Verg. 2. Transf.: *marked, distinguished, prominent, eminent :* Ter. ; homo insignis notis turpitudinis, Cic. ; Hor. ; vir, Tac. ; calamitas, Caes. ; virtus, Cic. ; odium in aliquem, Cic. ; insignis ad invidiam fortuna, Liv. ; Cic. ; annus insignis incendio, Liv. ; magnificentia, Tac. Comp. : Liv. (v. also Insigne).

insignītē, adv. *markedly :* Pl., Cic. Comp. : Liv.

insigniter, adv. *markedly :* Cic., Plin. Ep , Suet. Comp. : Nep.

insignitus, a, um. I. Part. Insigniō. II. Adj. a. *marked, conspicuous, glaring :* Cato ; lacūs nomen, Liv. ; flagitium, infamia, Tac. Comp. : Liv. b. *clear, striking :* notae veritatis, Cic. ; imagines, Cic.

insilia, ium, n. *pl.* [Insiliō], *the treadle of a weaver's loom :* Lucr.

in-siliō, īre, uī [saliō], *to leap in or on.* 1. Lit.: e navi in scapham, Pl. ; in equum, Liv. ; in phalangas, Caes. With Acc.: undas, Ov. ; Aetnam, Hor. ; tauros, Suet. With DAT. : ramis, Ov. 2. Transf.: in malum cruciatum, Pl.

in-simul, adv. *at the same time :* Stat. [It. insieme ; Fr. ensemble.]

insimulātiō, ōnis, f. *a charge, an accusation :* Cic.

in-simulō, āre, *to allege something against a person.* a. *to accuse falsely :* insontem, Pl.; with Acc. and *Inf. :* Cic. With GEN. of charge : uxorem proditi, Pl. b. In gen. *to charge, accuse :* se peccati, Cic. ; se proditionis crimine insimulari, Liv. ; proditionis insimulatus, Caes. ; falso insimulare, Pl., Ov. ; falso crimine, Cic., Liv. With *Intern.* Acc. : id quod ego insimulo, Cic. ; Pl. ; Liv. With Acc. and *Inf. :* Ter., Cic., Liv. In *Pass.* with NOM. and *Inf. :* iuvisse eum insimulabantur, Liv.

in-sincērus, a, um, *not pure, adulterated :* cruor, Verg.

insinuātiō, ōnis, f. Rhet. *an ingratiating oneself into favour :* Cic.

in-sinuō, āre [sinus]. A. Trans. *to bring in, introduce by windings or turnings.* 1. Lit.: aestum per saepta domorum, Lucr. ; Romani quācumque data intervalla essent, insinuabant ordines suos, Liv. With *Refl. Pron. to wind or work one's way in, to wriggle or creep in :* se inter equitum turmas, Caes. ; se inter corpus armaque, Liv. ; se inter vallis flumen, Liv. Also with 2nd Acc. of place penetrated : lacunas se, Lucr. Without *Refl. Pron. :* caecas latebras, Lucr. 2. Transf. : se in antiquam philosophiam, Cic. ; se in familiarem usum, Liv. ; se in familiaritatem alicuius, Cic. ; Pl. ; se ad aliquem, Pl. B. Intrans. *to wind or steal into, work one's way in, penetrate.* Transf.: per pectora cunctis pavor, Verg. ; penitus in causam, Cic. ; in ipsius consuetudinem, Cic. Ep.

in-sipiēns, entis, adj. [sapiēns], *unwise, senseless, foolish :* Cic. Comp. : Pl., Cic. Sup. : Sen.

insipienter, adv. *unwisely, foolishly :* Pl., Cic.

insipientia, ae, f. [insipiēns], *want of wisdom, folly :* Pl., Cic.

in-sistō, sistere, stitī. I. *to set foot in or on, to step or tread on, take one's stand on.* 1. Lit. a. With DAT.: iacentibus, Caes. ; saxo, Ov. ; prope vestigiis abeuntium, Liv. With *in* and Acc. : in sinistrum pedem, Quint. With Acc. : plantam, Pl. ; limen, Verg. ; cineres, Hor. b. With *iter*, *viam*, etc., *to enter upon a route, road :* viam, Ter. ; vestigia certa viāī (of hounds), Lucr. ; iter, Pl., Liv. c. With DAT.: *to tread on the heels of ; to press closely upon :* effusis

hostibus, Liv.; fugientibus, Liv.; *Pass.*
Impers. : fracto iam Maroboduo, Tac. **2.**
T r a n s f. *to set about something, apply one-*
self to, press on with. With D a t. : vestigiis laudum suarum, Liv.; rebus magnis,
Tib.; perdomandae Campaniae, Tac.;
bellum moenibus, Liv. With *in* or *ad* and
Acc. : in bellum, Caes.; Pl.; ad spolia
legenda, Liv. With Acc. : rationem pugnae, Caes.; munus, Cic.; hoc negotium,
Pl.; viam domandi, Verg. With *Inf.* :
Cic. Ep., Liv.; sic institit ore (*sc.* loqui),
Verg. **II.** *to stand in* or *on.* **1.** L i t. **a.**
in iugo, Caes.; in manu Cereris simulacrum
victoriae, Cic. With D a t. : villae fluminis
margini, Plin. Ep. **b.** *to stand one's*
ground : Caes., Tac. **c.** *to come to a stand-*
still, halt : Cic.; stellarum motūs, Cic.
2. T r a n s f. **a.** *to remain, persist in :* in
tantā gloriā, Cic. With D a t. : spei,
crudelitati, caedibus, Tac. With *Inf.* : Pl.,
Nep. **b.** *to dwell upon* in words or thought :
singulis, Cic.; vitiis, Ov. **c.** *to come to a*
halt (in words) : Cic. **d.** *to pause* in doubt :
Cic.
insitiō, ōnis, *f.* [Inserō]. **I.** *grafting :* Cic.
II. *the time of grafting :* Ov.
insitīvus, a, um [Inserō]. **1.** L i t. *grafted :*
pira, Hor. **2.** T r a n s f. *substituted, spuri-*
ous : liberi, Phaedr.
insitor, ōris, *m.* [Inserō], *one who grafts :*
Prop.
insitus, a, um. **I.** *Part.* Inserō. **II.** A d j.
a. *implanted by nature, inborn, innate :*
notio in animis nostris, Cic.; menti cognitionis amor, Cic.; sapientia, Cic.; feritas,
Liv. **b.** *taken in, incorporated :* Cic., Tac.
in-sociābilis, e, *adj. with whom there can be*
no league or *partnership :* gens, Liv.;
regnum, Tac.; anus nurui, Tac.
in-sōlābiliter, *adv.* [sōlor], *inconsolably :*
dolere, Hor.
in-solēns, entis, *adj.* [From in, *not* and
soleō, i.e. *unaccustomed ;* also fr. in, *prep.*
and obs. soleō (*v.* insolēscō), i.e. *swelling*
with pride ; the two senses often combined],
contrary to custom, unaccustomed, unusual,
A. In relation to self : quid tu Athenas
insolens venisti ? Ter.; aspera aequora
emirabitur insolens, Hor. With G e n. :
belli, Caes., Tac.; infamiae, Cic. Ep.;
audiendi, Tac. With *in* and A b l. : in
dicendo, Cic. **B.** In relation to others.
a. *unusual, not in use :* verbum, Cic.,
Quint. *Sup.* : Quint. **b.** *immoderate, ex-*
cessive : alacritas, ostentatio, Cic.; laetitia, Hor. Also *extravagant :* insolens in
alienā re, Cic. **c.** *haughty, arrogant, in-*
solent : Cic. *Comp.* : Hirt. *Sup.* : Cael.
ap. Cic. Ep. Of things : nihil unquam insolens ex ore eius exstitit, Nep.; ludum
insolentem ludere, Hor.
insolenter, *adv.* **I.** *unusually, contrary to*
custom : Cic. **II.** *immoderately, exces-*
sively : Cic. *Comp.* : Cic. **III.** *arro-*
gantly, insolently : Caes., Cic. *Comp.* :
Caes.
insolentia, ae, *f.* [insolēns]. **I.** In relation
to self : *a want of custom* or *use, inexperi-*
ence : Liv. With G e n. : iudiciorum,
voluptatum, loci, Cic.; itineris, Sall. **II.**
In relation to others. **a.** R h e t. *novelty,*

strangeness : Cic. **b.** *excess, want of mod-*
eration : huius saeculi, Cic. **c.** *arrogance,*
insolence : Cic., Sall., Nep. In *pl.* :
Phaedr.
insolēscō, ere [obs. soleō, *cf.* Gk. σάλος, Eng.
swell], *to grow haughty* or *insolent, to be-*
come elated : ad superbiam, Cato; per
licentiam animus humanus, Sall.; rebus
secundis, Tac.
in-solidus, a, um, *not solid, soft :* herba, Ov.
in-solitus, a, um. **A.** A c t. *unaccustomed,*
inexperienced : Cic., Verg.; ad laborem,
Caes.; rerum bellicarum, Sall.; equi tumultūs, Liv. **B.** P a s s. *unusual, strange :*
mihi loquacitas, Cic.; verbum, Cic.; tumultus, Sall.; libertas, Liv.; as N o u n :
insolitum audere, Tac.
in-solūbilis, e, *adj. that cannot be loosed.*
T r a n s f. : *that cannot be refuted, incon-*
testable : signum, Quint.
insomnia, ae, *f.* [somnus], *sleeplessness, want*
of sleep : Ter., Suet. In *pl.* : Cic., Sall.
insomnis, e, *adj.* [somnus], *sleepless :* Verg.,
Tac., etc. Of things : nox, Verg.; cura,
Luc.
in-somnium, i, *n.* [fr. in somnis, but associated with insomnis], *a bad dream :*
Tac. In *pl.* : Verg., Tib.
in-sonō, āre, ui. **I.** *to make a noise in* or
at, to sound, resound : cavernae (i.e. *the*
hollows resounded within), Verg.; Boreae
spiritus alto Aegaeo, Verg. **II.** *to make a*
noise. With *Instr.* A b l. : flagello, Verg.;
pennis, calamis, Ov. With *Intern.* Acc. :
verbera insonuit, Verg. *Absol.* : Quint.
in-sōns, ontis, *adj. guiltless, innocent :* Pl.,
Sall., Verg., etc. With G e n. : fratern.
sanguinis, Ov.; publici consili, Liv. With
A b l. : crimine, Liv. In *pl.* as N o u n :
Sall., Liv. P o e t. *harmless :* Cerberus,
Hor.; casa, Ov.
in-sōpītus, a, um, *not lulled to sleep, sleepless :*
draco, Ov.
in-sopor, ōris, *adj. sleepless :* Ov.
inspectiō, ōnis, *f.* [Inspiciō]. **1.** L i t. *a*
looking into, scrutiny : tabularum, Quint. **2.**
T r a n s f. *consideration, investigation,* hence
theory : Quint.
in-spectō, āre, *to look at* or *on :* Pl.; ad-
stante et inspectante ipso, Caes.; Cic. Ep.;
with Acc. : Pl.
inspectus, a, um, *Part.* Inspiciō.
in-spērāns, antis, *adj.* (only in D a t. and A b l.)
not hoping, not expecting : insperante hoc,
Ter.; Cat.; insperanti mihi cecidit, Cic.
in-spērātus, a, um, *unhoped for, unexpected.*
a. Of persons : Pl. *Sup.* : Pl. **b.** Of
things : praesidium, Cic.; malum, Cic.;
lux, Verg.; pax, Liv. As Noun in adv.
phr., **ex insperātō** (Liv.), **insperātō** (Pl.),
unexpectedly.
in-spergō, spergere, spērsī, spērsum [spargō],
to sprinkle in or *on.* **1.** L i t. : molam et
vinum, Cic.; oleam sale, Cato. **2.**
T r a n s f. : inspersos corpore naevos, Hor.
in-spiciō, spicere, spexī, spectum [speciō].
I. *to look into.* **a.** In gen. : intro inspice,
Pl.; inspicere, tamquam in speculum, in
vitas omnium, Ter.; machina inspectura
domos, Verg. **b.** In partic. : leges, Cic.;
libros Sibyllinos, Liv.; carminis verba,
Ov.; exta, Tac. **II.** *to look at, examine,*

inspect. **1.** Lit. **a.** In gen.: has aedis, Pl.; candelabrum, Cic.; praedium, Cic. Ep. **b.** *to inspect, review :* arma militis, Cic.; arma, viros, equos, etc., Liv. **2.** Transf. *to consider, examine :* sententiam, Pl.; aliquem a puero, Cic.; res sociorum, aes alienum, Liv.; fidem, Ov.; rationes, Plin. Ep. With *Indir. Quest. :* Quint., Mart.

in-spīcō, āre, *to make pointed, to sharpen :* faces, Verg.

in-spīrō, āre, *to blow in* or *on.* **1.** Lit. (with Dat.): conchae, Ov.; ramis arborum aurae, Quint. **2.** Transf. *to breathe into, inspire :* occultum ignem, Verg.; fortitudinem, Curt.; iram, Quint.

in-spoliātus, a, um, *not plundered :* Verg., Quint.

in-spūtō, āre, *to spit on :* Pl.

in-stabilis, e, *adj. that does not stand firm, unstable, unsteady.* **1.** Lit. **a.** In gen.: cumbae, Verg.; pedes, ingressus, Liv.; gradus, Curt.; hostis, acies, Liv. **b.** *not firm, not giving a firm footing :* tellus, Ov.; locus ad gradum, Tac. **2.** Transf.: *unstable, inconstant :* maritimae res instabilem motum habent, Caes.; animus, Verg.; fortuna, fama, Tac.

instāns, antis. **I.** Part. Instō. **II.** Adj. **a.** *present :* bellum, Cic.; tempus, *present tense,* Quint. **b.** *pressing, threatening :* periculum, Nep.; tyrannus, Hor.; gestus, Quint. Comp. : species, Tac.

instanter, adv. *vehemently, pressingly :* Quint. Plin. Ep. Comp. : Tac.

instantia, ae, *f.* [Instō]. **I.** *a being present :* Cic. **II.** *perseverance, vehemence :* Plin. Ep.

instar, *n.* (only in Nom. and Acc.) [perh. fr. Instō; a rustic word for *scarecrow*], *image, likeness* (mostly on a large scale). Transf. **a.** In gen.: quantum instar (*sc.* est) in ipso ! Verg. **b.** In magnitude, size, measure : terra in medio posita quasi puncti instar obtinet, Cic.; navis maxima triremis instar, Cic.; (Neapolis et Tycha) instar urbium sunt, Liv.; instar montis equum, Verg. **c.** In number : cohortis quaedam quod instar legionis videretur (i.e. the equivalent of), Caes.; milites dati duarum instar legionum, Liv. **d.** In weight, importance : mihi unus instar est centum milium, Cic.; scelus hoc meriti pondus et instar habet, Ov. **e.** In character : *as good as, like :* ut instar muri hae saepes munimenta praeberent, Caes.; unus ille dies mihi instar immortalitatis fuit, Cic.; clientes appellari mortis instar putant, Cic.; instar veris vultus tuus adfulsit populo, Hor.; exhorruit aequoris instar, Ov.

instaurātiō, ōnis, *f.* [Instaurō], *a renewing, celebration :* sacrorum, Liv.

instaurātīvus, a, .um [Instaurō], *renewed, repeated :* ludi, Cic.

instaurō, āre [fr. root seen in Gk. σταυρός; lit. *to put on props*]. **I.** *to set up, establish, celebrate :* novam proscriptionem, Cic. Ep.; aras, Verg.; funus Polydoro, Verg.; epulas, sacrum diis, Tac. **II.** *to renew, restore.* **a.** In gen.: instaurare et renovare scelus pristinum, Cic.; novum de integro bellum, Liv.; instaurati animi, Verg.

Occ. *to start afresh :* ludos, Liv. **b.** Of annual rites : Latinas, Cic. Ep.; sacra, ludos, Liv. **c.** *to requite :* dii, talia Graiis instaurate, Verg.

in-sternō, sternere, strāvī, strātum, *to spread, strew* or *lay upon :* instrata cubilia fronde, Lucr.; instrati ostro alipedes (equi), Verg.; equus instratus speciosius, Liv.; modicis pulpita tignis, Hor.

instigātor, ōris, *m.* and **instigātrix,** īcis, *f. an instigator :* Tac.

instigō, āre [fr. root seen in Gk. στίγμα, στίζω], *to prick* or *goad on ;* hence, *to urge on, set on, incite :* conscientiā facinoris instigari, Caes.; instigante te, Cic.; Ter.; sequentem studiis, Verg.; agmen canum hortatibus, Ov.; Romanos in Hannibalem, Liv.

in-stillō, āre [stilla]. **I.** *to pour in by drops, to instil.* **1.** Lit.: lumini oleum, Cic.; oleum caulibus, Hor. **2.** Transf.: praeceptum auriculis, Hor. **II.** *to drop on* (with Acc.): guttae saxa, Poet. ap. Cic.

in-stimulātor, ōris, *m. an instigator :* seditionis, Cic.

in-stimulō, āre, *to urge on, incite :* aliquem, Ov.

instinctor, ōris, *m.* [Instinguō], *an instigator :* sceleris, Tac.

instinctū, Abl. *sing. m.* [Instinguō], *by instigation :* instinctu divino, Cic.; decurionum, Tac.

instinctus, a, um [for root *cf.* distinguō], *instigated, incited.* With Abl. *Instr. :* furore et audaciā, Cic.; his vocibus, furiis, Liv.; divino spiritu, Quint.

in-stipulor, āri, *to bargain, stipulate for :* Pl.

instita, ae, *f.* [Instō], *the stiff border* or *flounce of a Roman lady's tunic :* Hor., Ov.

institiō, ōnis, *f.* [Insistō], *a standing still :* errantium stellarum, Cic.

institor, ōris, *m.* [Insistō], *a hawker, pedlar.* **1.** Lit.: Hor.; mercis, Liv.; Juv. **2.** Transf.: eloquentiae, Quint.

institōrium, I, *n.* [Institor], *the trade of a hawker, etc. :* Suet.

in-stituō, uere, uī, ūtum [statuō], *to set in place.* **1.** Lit. **a.** *to fix, plant :* vestigia nuda pedis, Verg.; vineas, Cic.; arborem, Suet. **b.** *to set up ;* hence, *to build up, construct :* navis, turris, pontem, Caes.; officinam, Cic.; dapes, Verg. **2.** Transf. **A. a.** *to infix, implant :* argumenta in pectus, Pl.; (aliquid) in animo, Ter. **b.** *to arrange, marshal :* aciem, Caes.; tu actionem instituis, ille aciem instruit, Cic.; vitam sapienter, Ter.; civitates (*forms of constitution*), Cic.; formam civitatis, Tac. **c.** *to appoint :* me tutorem, me heredem, Cic. Ep.; aliquos sibi amicos, Cic.; magistratus Cn. Flavius institutus est, Cic. Ep. **B.** *to set up, establish, institute, ordain :* dilectum, sermonem, Caes.; mercatum, portorium vini, Cic.; sacros ludos, Ov.; Saturnalia, Liv. With *ut* and *Subj. :* Cic., Liv. **C.** *to build up, educate, train :* animum ad cogitandum, Ter.; aliquem ad dicendum, Cic.; adulescentis, Cic.; oratorem, Quint.; aliquem lyrā, disciplinis Graecis, Quint.; artibus, Juv. With *Inf. :* calamos cerā coniungere pluris, Verg.; amphora fumum bibere instituta,

Hor. **D.** *to settle on, resolve on, determine, undertake :* rationem operis, Caes. ; sibi certamen, Cic. ; negotium, Pl. ; iter, Hor. With *Inf. :* Caes., Cic. Ep., Liv.

institūtiŏ, ōnis, *f.* [Instituŏ]. **I.** *established custom :* conservare, Cic. Ep. **II.** *arrangement :* rerum, Cic. **III.** *education :* Cic. In *pl. principles of education :* Graecae, Cic.

institūtum, ĭ, *n.* [Instituŏ]. **I. a.** *established customs, laws* (in *sing.* and *pl.*) *:* Caes., Cic., Tac., etc. **b.** *a settlement, fixed terms :* militem ex instituto dare, Liv. **c.** *inculcated principles* (us. *pl.*) *:* philosophiae, Cic. **II.** *purpose, intention :* huius libri, Cic.

in-stŏ, stāre, stĭtī. **I.** *to stand in or on.* **I.** Lĭt. : iugis, Verg. ; in medio triclinio, Suet. **2.** Transf. : famae (i.e. keep up his reputation), Tac. With Acc. : rectam viam, Pl. **II.** *to be near or close.* **1.** Lĭt. : Caes. ; vestigiis, Liv. Hence, *to be on the heels of, press hard upon :* me, Pl. ; nostros, Caes. ; with Dat. : hosti, Liv. ; cedenti, Liv. ; Juv. *Impers. Pass. :* Liv., Tac. **2.** Transf. **a.** *to be at hand, approaching, to impend :* ludi, Cic. ; longinqua ab domo militia, Liv. ; quā re illud quod instet, agi oportere, Cic. ; poenae, Civ. ; illi iter, Cic. Ep. **b.** *to press on eagerly* (with an undertaking) : Cic. Ep. ; de indutiis, Caes. ; operi, Verg. ; solis aristis, Verg. With Acc. : Marti currum, Verg. **c.** *to press earnestly, urge, insist :* satis est, quod instat de Milone, Cic. Ep. ; te instante, Cic. Ep. With *Inf. :* Cic. With Dat. and *ut* and *Subj. :* Cic. With *ne* and *Subj. :* Pl.

instrātus, a, um, *Part.* Insternŏ.

in-strĕnuus -uos, a, um, *not brisk, spiritless :* homo, Pl. ; animus, Ter. ; dux, Suet.

in-strepŏ, ere, uĭ, itum, *to creak :* sub pondere faginus axis, Verg.

instructiŏ, ōnis, *f.* [Instruŏ]. **I.** *a constructing :* balinei, Trajan ap. Plin. Ep. **II.** *a setting in array :* signorum, Cic.

instructius, *comp. adv.* [Instructus], *with greater preparation ; in better style :* Liv.

instructor, ōris, *m.* [Instruŏ], *a preparer :* Cic.

instructus, a, um. **I.** *Part.* instruŏ. **II.** Adj. *supplied, equipped, stocked :* naves, domus, Cic. Of persons : in iure civili, Cic. ; artibus, Cic. ; vitiis instructior, Hor. ; ab historiā instructior, Cic. ; ad dicendum instructissimus, Cic.

instructus, ūs, *m.* [Instruŏ], *stock-in-trade* (of an orator) : Cic.

instrūmentum, ĭ, *n.* [Instruŏ], *equipment, outfit, furniture.* **1.** Lĭt. : hibernorum, Caes. ; belli, Cic. ; instrumenta belli, Liv. ; villae, Cic. ; militare, Caes. ; bellicum, nauticum, Liv. ; rusticum, Phaedr. ; venatorium, Plin. Ep. **2.** Transf. **A. a.** *instrument :* necis, Ov. **b.** *outfit, dress :* anilia, Ov. **c.** *dressing :* felicis ornent haec instrumenta libellos, Ov. **B.** *equipment, stock-in-trade, repertory.* **a.** Of an orator : Cic. **b.** *means for furthering or promoting* (esp. in *pl.*) *:* virtutis, Cic. ; luxuriae, Sall. ; imperi, Tac. ; instrumenta ad obtinendam sapientiam, Cic. **c.** *records,*

public documents : tribunatūs, Cic. , imperi, litis, Quint. ; instrumenti publici auctoritas, Suet.

in-struŏ, struere, struxī, structum. **I.** *to build on, set about building.* **1.** Lĭt. **a.** In gen. : tigna, Caes. ; contabulationem in parietes, Caes. **b.** *to build up, construct :* muros, Nep. ; aggerem, Tac. **2.** Transf. **A.** *to equip, stock, furnish.* **a.** Materially : navis, Caes. ; domicilia rebus omnibus, Cic. ; agrum, Liv. ; mensas epulis, Verg. ; socios armis, Verg. **b.** Immaterially : *to build up, equip, train :* disciplinae et artes, quibus instruimur, Cic. ; dolis instructus, Verg. **B.** *to furnish, provide, prepare.* **a.** convivium, orationem, accusationem, Cic. ; epulas, insidias, fraudem, Liv. ; dicta ad fallendum, Liv. ; locum insidiis, Liv. ; insidias mihi, Cat. ; consilia, Tac. ; se ad iudicium, Cic. **b.** Milit. *to marshal, form, array :* legiones, Pl. ; aciem, Caes., Cic. ; exercitum, Liv.

insuāsum, ĭ, *n. a kind of dark colour,* perh. *dark orange :* Pl.

in-suāvis, e, *adj. unpleasant* (to the taste), *disagreeable.* Transf. : littera, vita, Cic. *Sup. :* Cic. Of persons : *sour, harsh :* Hor.

in-sūdŏ, āre, *to sweat on :* (libellis) manus vulgi, Hor.

insuēfactus, a, um, *accustomed, trained* (to something) : Caes.

in-suēscŏ, suēscere, suēvī, suētum. **A.** Intrans. : *to become accustomed :* corpori, Tac. With *Inf. :* Ter., Sall., Liv. **B.** Trans. : *to accustom or habituate any one :* insuevit pater optimus hoc me, Hor. *Pass. :* ita se a pueris insuetos, Liv.

(1) insuētus, a, um, *Part.* Insuēscŏ.

(2) in-suētus, a, um. **I.** Of the person : *not accustomed to, unused to.* With Gen .: laboris, Caes. ; Cic. Ep. ; Liv. ; navigandi, Caes. ; Nep. With Dat. : moribus Romanis, Liv. ; operi manus, Tib. With *ad :* corpora ad onera portanda, Caes. ; Liv. ; ad tale spectaculum, Liv. With *Inf. :* Liv. **II.** Of the thing *to which one is not accustomed, unusual :* limen Olympi, Verg. ; solitudo, Liv. ; insueta civitati species, Liv. *Neut. pl.* as *Intern.* Acc. : insueta rudentem, Verg.

insula, ae, *f.* [perh. fr. in, *prep.* and root seen in Gk. ἅλος, *swelling water*], *an island.* **1.** Lĭt. **a.** In gon. : Cic. , Verg., etc. **b.** *the island-quarter at Syracuse :* Cic. **2.** Transf. *a detached house* or *block of houses* (let out in flats to poorer families) : Cic., Tac., Suet. [It. *isola ;* Fr. *île.*]

insulānus, ĭ, *m.* [Insula], *an islander :* Cic.

insulsē, *adv. tastelessly, insipidly :* dully *absurdly :* Cic.

insulsitās, ātis, *f.* [Insulsus], *tastelessness, insipidity ; dullness, absurdity :* Pl. ; Graecorum, Cic. ; orationis, Cic. ; villae, Cic. Ep.

in-sulsus, a, um [salsus], *unsalted, insipid.* Transf. **a.** *that longs for tasteless things :* gula, Cic. Ep. **b.** *tasteless, insipid, dull, absurd :* ingenium, Pl. ; adulescens, Cic. ; genus ridiculi, Cic. *Sup. :* Cat.

insultātiŏ, ōnis, *f.* [Insultŏ], *a taunting :* Quint.

insultŏ, āre [*freq.* Insiliŏ], *to spring, bound,*

gambol, prance on or *in.* **1.** L i t. : sonipes,
Verg. ; haedi floribus, Verg. ; busto Priami
armentum, Hor. ; fluctibus carinae, Ov. ;
Batavi aquis *(jump into)*, Tac. With Acc.
of extent : nemora matres, Verg. C o m i c. :
foris calcibus, Ter. **2.** T r a n s f. *to exult,
triumph over, taunt, treat highhandedly :*
Verg., Liv. With D a t. : tibi in calamitate, Cic. ; Liv. ; Ov. ; adversis rebus
eorum, Liv. With A c c. : aliquem, Sall. ;
segnitiam cuiuspiam, Tac. With *in* and
Acc. : in rem publicam, Cic. With A b l. :
morte meā, Prop.

insultūra, ae, *f.* [Insiliō], *a springing* or *leaping at* or *upon :* Pl.

in-sum, inesse, infuī, *to be in* or *on.* **1.**
L i t. : nummi in marsuppio, Pl. ; in hac
domo, Cic. With D a t. ; patri torulus,
Pl. ; fronti cornua, Ov. **2.** T r a n s f. *to be
contained* or *implied in, to belong (naturally)
to :* superstitio, in quā inest inanis timor
deorum, Cic. ; vitium aliquod in moribus,
Cic. With D a t. : cui virile ingenium
inest, Sall. ; quibus artibus prudentia
inest, Cic. ; rebus fides, Ov. ; with D a t.
understood : praecipue pedum pernicitas
inerat, Liv. ; Cic. ; Tac., etc.

in-sūmō, sūmere, sūmpsī, sūmptum, *to take
for some purpose ;* hence, *to apply to, expend upon :* operam frustra, Liv. ; sumptum in aliquam rem, Cic. With D a t. :
vitam veribus, Tac. ; paucos dies refici-
endae classi, Tac. With A b l. : non est
melius quo insumere possis, Hor. With
in and A b l. : nec in evolvendā antiquitate
satis operae insumitur, Tac.

in-suō, suere, suī, sūtum, *to sew in, to sew up
in :* plumbo insuto, Verg. ; aliquem in culleum, Cic. With D a t. : patrio femori (of
Dionysus), Ov. : vestibus aurum, Ov. ;
aliquem culleo, Suet.

in-super, *adv.* and *prep., over and above,
above and on.* **I.** A d v. : *on the top, above.*
1. L i t. : Caes., Verg., Liv., etc. **2.**
T r a n s f. *over and above, moreover, besides :*
si id parum est, insuper poenas expetite,
Liv. ; haec insuper addidit, Verg. ; Pl. ;
Ter. E l l i p t. : insuper quam, *besides*, Liv.
II. P r e p. **a.** With A c c. : *over, above,*
insuper arbores trabem planam imponito,
Cato. **b.** With A b l. : *besides :* insuper his,
Verg.

in-superābilis, e, *adj.* **I.** *insurmountable :*
via, Alpium transitus, Liv. **II.** *unconquerable :* genus bello, Verg. ; fatum, Ov. ;
valetudo, Plin. Ep.

in-sūrgō, sūrgere, surrēxī, insurrēctum. **I.**
to rise or *raise oneself on, stand up on :* ostendit dextram insurgens Entellus (on his
toes), Verg. ; remis (i.e. for the oar-stroke),
Verg. ; serpens arduus insurgens, Verg. ;
Tac. **II.** *to rise, swell, increase.* **1.** L i t.
(of things) : silex speluncae dorso, Verg. ;
colles, Liv. ; silva, Tac. ; tenebrae campis,
Verg. ; Aquilo, Hor. ; impetus undae, Ov.
2. T r a n s f. (of persons) : *to rise, grow.*
a. In political power : Tac. **b.** In literary
power : Horatius insurgit aliquando (i.e.
above mediocrity), Quint. **c.** In vigour :
Plin. Pan. **III.** *to rise against :* suis regnis,
Ov.

in-susurrō, āre, *to whisper in.* **1.** L i t. :

(alicui), ad aurem, Cic. ; in aurem, Cic.
With *Intern.* A c c. : mihi cantilenam, Cic.
Ep. ; vota diis, Sen. Ep. **2.** T r a n s f. :
Favonius ipse insusurrat, navigandi nobis
tempus esse, Cic.

in-tābēscō, tābēscere, tābuī, *to melt away by
degrees.* **1.** L i t. : igne cerae, Ov. ; matu-
tinae pruinae, Ov. **2.** T r a n s f. : pupulae,
Hor.

in-tāctilis, e, *adj. that cannot be touched, in-
tangible :* Lucr.

in-tāctus, a, um, *untouched, uninjured, intact.*
1. L i t. **a.** thesaurus, Hor. ; (iugo) cervix,
Verg. ; boves, Hor. ; ferro corpus, Liv. ;
exercitus, Liv. ; fines bellis, Liv. ; intactus
profugit, Sall. ; intactum aliquem dimittere,
Liv. **b.** *untouched, untried :* nihil intactum pati, Sall. ; bellum, Sall. ; carmen
Graecis, Hor. **2.** T r a n s f. **a.** *untouched,
untainted, unpolluted :* intactus infamiā,
Liv. ; vir haud intacti religione animi, Liv.
Of things : Dryadum silvas saltūsque intac-
tos (i.e. virgin), Verg. ; sacrilegas admovere
manūs intactis illis thesauris, Liv. **b.**
virgin, unmarried : Cat., Verg., Hor.

in-tāctus, ūs, *m. intangibility :* Lucr.

intāminātus, a, um [*cf.* contāminātus], *un-
sullied, undefiled :* honores, Hor.

(1) intēctus, a, um, *Part.* integō.

(2) in-tēctus, a, m, *uncovered.* **1.** L i t.
a. *unroofed :* domus, Sall. **b.** *unclothed :*
corpora, Sall. ; dux prope intectus, Tac. ;
pedes, Tac. **2.** T r a n s f. : *open, frank :*
aliquem sibi efficere, Tac.

integellus, a, um [*dim.* integer]. **I.** *fairly
pure :* Cat. **II.** *not seriously damaged,
practically whole* (comic.) : Cic. Ep.

in-teger, gra, grum [*tag* in tangō]. **I.** *untouched, intact.* **1.** L i t. **a.** then saurus, Pl. ;
sublicarum pars inferior integra remanebat,
Caes. ; litterae integris signis traduntur,
b. Of bodily health and vigour : *unimpaired, unexhausted, sound, fresh :* integris
viribus repugnare, Caes. ; florentes atque
integri, Cic. ; integer aevi, Verg. ; sanguis,
Pl., Quint. ; aetas, Ter. ; Suet. ; valetudo,
Cic., Suet. Of soldiers : cum integri de-
fessis succederent, Caes. ; integris turmis,
Tac. ; cohortes ab labore, Caes. ; gens a
cladibus belli, Liv. ; victor, Hor. Also
unwounded : Caes., Sall., Liv. **2.** T r a n s f.
intact, unimpaired, entire, complete : aestas,
annus, Cic. ; dies, Hor. ; opes, Hor. ;
fructus honorum, Cic. ; mens, Hor. ; fides,
Tac. Of persons : famā et fortunis integer, Sall. ; animi, mentis, Hor. Of land :
copiis integra regio, Sall. As Noun in
phr. : in integrum restituere, *to reinstate,
restore to a former condition :* Ter., Caes.,
Cic. **II.** *untouched, unaffected, untainted ;*
hence, *pure, clean, sound, fresh, chaste.*
1. L i t. : fontes, vinum, vini sapor, aper,
Hor. ; coniuges integras ab istius petulantiā conservare, Cic. ; virgines, Cat. ;
Pl. ; Ter. *Neut.* as Noun : anteponere integra contaminatis, Cic. **2.** T r a n s f. **a.**
Morally : vir, testes, vita, Cic. With
G e n. : integer vitae, Hor. **b.** Mentally :
unbiassed, unprejudiced, dispassionate : discipulus, Cic. ; se servare, Cic. Ep. ; bracchia
et vultum integer laudo (*heart-whole*), Hor.
c. Of things : *unaffected, unprejudiced, in*

entirety : rem integram ad reditum suum
iussit esse, Cic. ; Liv. ; ut quam integer-
rima ad pacem essent omnis, Caes. ;
iudicium a favore, Tac. ; integrum est mihi,
I have a free hand (occ. with *Inf.* or *ut* and
Subj.), Cic. **d.** *starting afresh, renewed :*
principium novi et integri laboris, Liv. ; ad
integrum bellum cuncta parare, Sall. ;
pugnam edere, Liv. P h r. : **ab integrō**
(Cato, Cic., Verg., etc.), **de integrō** (Cic.,
Liv.), **ex integrō** (Quint., Suet.), *afresh,
anew. Comp.* integrior : Cic., Liv. *Sup.*
integerrimus, Caes., Cic. [It. *intero ;*
Sp. *entero ;* Fr. *entier*.]

in-tegō, tegere, tēxī, tēctum, *to cover over.*
1. L i t. : villam, Pl. ; turris coriis, Caes. ;
tecta stramento, Liv. ; nebula saltum, Liv.
2. T r a n s f. *to protect :* loci altitudine (et)
vallo integi, Liv.

integrāscō, ere [integrō], *to begin afresh :*
Ter.

integrātiō, ōnis, *f.* [integrō], *a renewing,
restoring :* amoris, Ter.

integrē, *adv.* **I.** *wholly, entirely :* mutare,
Tac. **II.** *irreproachably, honestly :* Cic.
Comp. : integrius, Cic. *Sup.* integerrimē,
Plin. Ep., Suet. **III.** Of style : *purely,
correctly :* Cic.

integritās, ātis, *f.* [integer]. **I.** *unimpaired
condition, soundness.* **1.** L i t. : corporis,
valetudinis, Cic. **2.** T r a n s f. : nec mente
nec sensu, Cic. **II.** *purity.* **1.** L i t. (of
a woman) : Cic. **2.** T r a n s f. a. Morally :
Cic. ; vitae, Nep. **b.** Of style : Cic.

integrō, āre, *to make whole.* **1.** L i t. **a.** *to
renew, replenish :* amnes integrant mare,
Lucr. **b.** *to renew, heal, repair :* elapsos
in pravum artūs, Tac. **2.** T r a n s f. **a.**
to renew, start afresh : pugnam, lacrimas,
Liv. ; carmen, Verg. **b.** *to recreate, refresh :* animum, Cic.

in-tegumentum, i, n. *a covering, a protection.*
1. L i t. : corporis, Pl. ; consaepti, Liv.
2. T r a n s f. : dissimulationis, Cic.

intellēctus, a, um, *Part.* intellegō.

intellēctus, ūs, m. [intellegō]. **I.** *a perceiving, discerning by the senses :* saporum,
Plin. **II. a.** By the mind : *an understanding, comprehension :* with G e n. :
Quint., Tac. **III.** *the faculty of understanding, intellect :* Sen. Ep. **IV.** *meaning :* Quint. ; hiems et ver et aestas intellectum ac vocabula habent (i.e. are
understood), Tac.

intellegēns, entis. **I.** *Part.* intellegō. **II.**
A d j. **a.** *having understanding, intelligent,
acquainted with :* dicendi existimator, Cic.
iudicium, Cic. With G e n. : Cic. **b.** In
matters of taste : Cic.

intellegenter, *adv. intelligently :* Cic.

intellegentia, ae, *f.* [intellegō], *perception,
discernment.* **I.** By the senses : in gustu
et odoratu, Cic. **II.** By the mind : *understanding, knowledge :* Ter., Cic. With
G e n. : iuris, Cic. Occ. *taste, judgment :*
in rusticis rebus, Cic. **III.** *the faculty of
understanding, intelligence :* Cic.

intel-legō, legere, lēxī, lēctum [inter legō]
(intellēxtī for intellēxistī, Ter., Cic. Ep. ;
intellēxēs for intellēxissēs, Pl.), *to choose
between, to discern one thing from another,
to identify ;* hence, *to perceive, discern.* **I.**

By the senses : nullos ignis, Ov. With
Acc. and *Inf. :* Pl. **II.** By the mind :
to become aware, realise, recognise. With
Acc. and *Inf. :* Caes. With *Indir. Quest. :*
Cic. *Impers. Pass. :* ut intellectum est,
Caes. **III.** *to perceive* or *discern* by an
effort of the intellect, *to understand, comprehend.* **a.** magna ex parvis, Cic. ; linguam,
Graece scripta, Cic. With Acc. and *Inf. :*
Cic. With *Indir. Quest. :* Cic. *Impers.
Pass.* (with Acc. and *Inf.*) : Cic. In
answers, intellego, *I understand, I see,
very well :* Pl., Ter. **b.** *to have an accurate
knowledge of* or *skill in something, to be a
connoisseur :* non multum in istis rebus
intellego, Cic. ; Ter. **c.** Of persons : *to
understand, comprehend rightly :* Socrates
ab hominibus sui temporis parum intellege-
batur, Quint. ; Tac. ; Plin. Ep. **d.** *to
understand as the meaning, understand by :*
εὐταξία, in quā intellegitur ordinis conservatio, Cic. ; non habeo quod intellegam
bonum illud, Cic.

in-temerātus, a, um, *undefiled, spotless, pure.*
1. L i t. (of persons) : Verg., Ov., Tac. **2.**
T r a n s f. **a.** In gen. : fides, Verg. **b.** *unpolluted :* Tac. With D a t. of agent :
Tac. **c.** *pure, undiluted* (of libations) :
munera, Verg.

in-temperāns, antis, *adj. without self-
restraint, extravagant, intemperate.* **a.** In
gen. : intemperantis esse arbitror scribere,
quod occultari velit, Cic. ; in cupiditate,
Cic. Ep. ; in augendo, Liv. ; militaris gloria,
Cic. *Comp. :* Cic., Liv. **b.** *incontinent,
profligate :* Cic. ; adulescentia, Cic. *Sup. :*
Cic.

intemperanter, *adv. extravagantly, intemperately :* Cic., Plin. Ep. *Comp. :* Cic., Liv.,
Suet.

in-temperantia, ae, *f. want of self-restraint* or
moderation ; excess, extravagance. **a.** In
gen. : Cic. With defining G e n. : libidinum,
Cic. ; vini, Liv. ; litterarum, Sen. Ep. ;
linguae, Tac. **b.** *extravagant bearing :* Nep.

intemperātē, *adv. intemperately :* Cic.

in-temperātus, a, um, *immoderate :* benevolentia, Cic.

intemperiae, ārum, *f. pl. wild outbursts.* **1.**
L i t. Of weather : Cato. **2.** T r a n s f. Of
behaviour : *wildness, madness :* Pl.

in-temperiēs, ēi, *f.* [*in, not,* and *tempus ;* i.e.
missing the proper point or *moment*], *wildness, violence.* **1.** L i t. Of weather : caeli,
aquarum, Liv. **2.** T r a n s f. **a.** intem-
peries modo in nostram advenit domum,
Pl. **b.** Of behaviour : *wildness, outburst,
outrageous conduct :* amici, Cic. Ep. ; cohortium, Tac.

intempestivē, *adv. unseasonably, inoppor-
tunely :* Cic., Ov., etc.

in-tempestīvus, a, um, *untimely, unseason-
able :* postis intempestivos excisos credo,
Pl. ; imbres, Lucr. ; amicitia, Cic. ; cupido,
Ov. ; Minerva (spinning), Ov. ; honor, Tac.

in-tempestus, a, um [tempus]. **I.** *timeless,
unbroken :* nox (i.e. dead of night), Cic.,
Verg. Also of nox personified : Verg. **II.**
unhealthy : Graviscae, Verg.

in-temptātus, a, um, *untried, unattempted :*
miseri, quibus intemptata nites, Hor. ;
sors rerum, Verg. ; iter, Tac.

in-tendŏ, tendere, tendi, tentum (tēnsum, Sen.). **I.** *to stretch, strain tight.* **1.** Lit.: arcum, Verg.; vela Zephyri, Verg.; tabernacula carbaseis intenta velis, Cic.; duro bracchia tergo, Verg.; stuppea vincula collo, Verg. **2.** Transf. **a.** *to stretch, enlarge, spread :* se intendentibus tenebris, Liv.; socordiam, gloriam, vera, pretium, Tac. **b.** *to keep strained or at tension :* in eā re intentis animis, Caes. **c.** *to insist, maintain.* With Acc. and *Inf.* : Ter. In the courts : quo modo nunc intendit, Cic.; aliquid, Cic. Rhet. *to state* what is to be proved : Quint. **II.** *to strain, stretch, aim, direct towards or at.* **1.** Lit.: in hunc digitum, Pl.; dextram ad statuam, Cic.; aciem acrem in omnis partis, Cic.; auris ad verba, Ov.; bracchia remis, Verg. So too, digna res ubi nervos intendas, Ter. Hence, *to aim* a weapon : ballistam in me, Pl.; arcum in me, Cic.; tela in patriam, Cic.; tela iugulis civitatis, Cic.; sagittas, Verg. **2.** Transf. **a.** *to aim, direct against :* in senem fallaciam, Ter.; periculum in aliquem, Cic.; alicui actionem perduellionis, Cic.; crimen alicui *or* in aliquem, Liv.; probra et minas alicui, Tac. **b.** *to direct one's course* (esp. with iter) : quo nunc intendam ? Ter.; ut eo quo intendit perveniat, Cic.; iter in Italiam, Liv.; quonam iter intendissent, Liv.; a portā ad praetorem, Liv. **c.** Of the mind : *to direct one's thoughts or attention to :* oculi mentesque ad pugnam intentae, Caes.; ad bellum animum, Sall.; ad id omnis cogitationes, Liv.; curam ad apparatum belli, Liv.; animum ad virum liberandum, Cic.; Plin. Ep.; animum in aliquid, Cic.; Sall.; animum studiis, Hor.; omnium eo curae sunt intentae, Liv.; suos ad curam custodiae, Liv. With non-personal subject : eum ad cavendi omnia curam tot auditae proditiones, Liv. **d.** *to aim at, endeavour, intend :* Pl.; aliquid, Ter., Cic., Sall., etc. With *Inf.* : Sall., Liv.; also in Cic. with animo.

(1) intentātus, a, um, *Part.* intentō.

(2) in-tentātus, *v.* intemptātus.

intentē, adv. *strictly, earnestly, attentively :* audire, Quint.; pronuntiare, Plin. Ep. *Comp.* : dilectum habere, Liv.; se excusare, Tac.; premere obsessos, Tac.

intentiŏ, ōnis, *f.* [intendō]. **I.** *a stretching out, straining, tension.* **1.** Lit.: corporis, Cic.; vultūs, Tac. **2.** Transf. **a.** *increase :* doloris, Sen. Ep. **b.** Of the mind: *exertion, effort* (opp. remissio), Cic. **c.** *the major premiss of a syllogism :* Quint. **II.** *a directing.* Transf. **a.** *attention, application, care :* Sen. Ep. With *Obj.* Gen.: lusus, Liv.; rei familiaris, Plin. Ep. **b.** *attack, accusation :* Cic., Quint.

intentŏ, āre [*freq.* intendō], *to stretch out, hold out, aim at continually* (esp. threateningly). **1.** Lit.: sicam nobis, Cic.; in Appium manūs, Liv.; voces manūsque, Tac. **2.** Transf. **a.** *to hold out threateningly, threaten :* arma Latinis, Liv.; fulmen dictatorium, Liv.; probra, Tac.; viris omnia mortem, Verg.; terror omnibus intentabatur, Tac.; crimen, Quint. Without *Obj.* : quasi intentantis loco, Cic.

intentus, a, um. **I.** *Part.* intendō. **II.** Adj.: *strained, taut, tense.* **1.** Lit.: arcus, chordae, Cic.; oculi, Verg.; intenti exspectant signum, Verg. **2.** Transf. **a.** In mind or attention : Sall.; intenti pugnae proventum exspectabant, Caes. With Abl. :· aliquo ludo, Sall. With Dat.: recipiendo exercitui, Liv.; perh., ludo, Verg. With *Indir. Quest.* : Liv. **b.** Of speech : *earnest, vigorous :* Cic. **c.** *strict, rigid :* custodia, cura, conquisitio, Liv.; disciplina, Tac. *Comp.* : Liv., Tac. *Sup.* : Liv., Quint.

intentus, ūs, *m. a stretching out, extending :* palmarum, Cic.

in-tepeŏ, ēre, *to be lukewarm, to be warm :* lacus aestivis aquis, Prop.; Lernaea palus, Stat.

in-tepēscŏ, tepēscere, tepui, *to grow warm, be warmed :* mucro, Verg.; variae radiis comae, Ov.

inter, adv. and prep. [orig. comp. adv. fr. in ; *more inwardly*]. **I.** Adv.: only in compounds. **A.** Form: changed only in intellegere. **B.** Meaning. **a.** *in between :* intervenire, interfluere. **b.** *between* so as to break continuity, **i.** where a barrier results : intercludere. **ii.** where a gap or void results : interire, interficere. Often to be translated *out, off, up.* N.B. in Nouns the compound sometimes denotes the gap itself : intervallum, intercolumnium. **c.** *here and there ;* of time, *between whiles :* interrogare, intermittere. **d.** *among, amidst ;* of time, *during :* interesse, interdiu. **e.** *mutually, reciprocally, in combination :* intermiscere, interiungere. **II.** Prep. with Acc.: *between, betwixt, among, amidst.* **A.** In space (with verbs of rest or motion). **a.** Of two points : *between, betwixt :* (mons Iura) est inter Sequanos et Helvetios, Caes.; Liv. **b.** Of several : *among, amidst, between :* inter hostium tela versari, Cic.; inter patres lectus, Liv.; venisse inter falcarios in Laecae domum, Cic.; inter ferarum lustra, Verg.; inter medias stationes erupere, Liv. Phr.: inter manūs, *within reach :* Verg., Sen. Ep.; also *in or on the hands :* Cic., Liv.; inter viam (or vias), *on the way :* Pl., Ter., Cic. Ep. **B.** In time. **a.** Of two points : *between :* inter binos ludos, Cic.; inter horam tertiam et quartam, Liv. Prov.: inter caesa et porrecta, Cic. **b.** Of a period : *during, in the course of, within :* inter continuom triennium, Pl.; inter ipsum pugnae tempus, Liv.; inter tot annos, Cic.; inter noctem, Liv. With *Gerund :* Verg., Liv. With *Gerundive :* Pl., Liv., Suet. Phr.: inter haec, *meanwhile,* Liv. (freq.); also inter quae, Liv., Tac. **C.** Of other relations. **a.** Of discrimination, rivalry, etc.: *between :* discrimen inter gratiosos civis atque fortis, Cic.; hi omnes inter se differunt, Caes.; iudicium inter deas tris, Cic.; inter pugnae fugaeque consilium, Liv.; certamen inter primores civitatis, Liv.; trepidare inter scelus metumque, Tac. With *inter* repeated : Cic., Verg., Liv., etc. **b.** Of class or number : *among :* quantum inter omnis oratores unus excellat, Cic. Phr.: inter cuncta (i.e. before all), Hor.; inter cetera, *especially*, Liv.; inter sicarios (in the murder-court), Cic.; inter nos, *between ourselves, confidentially*, Cic. So with *Refl. Pron.*: *one with another, mutually, together*: inter se consultare, Cic.; inter se nondum satis noti, Liv.; illi inter se bracchia tollunt in numerum, Verg. [Fr. *entre*.]

inter-aestuō, āre, *to heave at intervals*: stomachus, Plin. Ep.

interāmenta, ōrum, *n. pl. the inner timbers and fittings of a ship*: navium, Liv.

inter-aptus, a, um, *joined together*: Lucr.

inter-ārēscō, ere, *to dry up, wither away*. Transf.: Cic.

interātim [inter; *cf.* paulātim], *meanwhile*: Pl.

inter-bibō, ere, *to drink up*: Pl.

inter-bītō, ere, *to perish, come to nought*: Pl.

intercalāris, e, *adj.* [intercalō], *inserted, intercalary*: Kalendae, *the first day of an intercalary month*, Cic., Liv.; Kalendae priores, *the first day of the first of two intercalary months*, Cic. Ep.

intercalārius, a, um [intercalāris], *intercalary*: mensis, Cic., Liv.

inter-calō, āre, *insert by proclamation, intercalate* a day or month: us. *Pass.* **1.** L i t.: ut pugnes ne intercaletur, Cic. Ep.; Cato; Suet. **2.** T r a n s f.: ut intercalatae poenae usuram habeant (i.e. *interest consisting of additional punishment*), Liv.

inter-capēdō, inis, *f.* [capiō], *an interruption, interval, pause*: scribendi, Cic. Ep.; molestiae, Cic.; Plin. Ep.

inter-cēdō, cēdere, cēssī, cēssum, *to go or come between*. **1.** L i t. **a.** In gen.: Pl.; inter legiones impedimenta, Caes. **b.** *to be, stand, or lie between*: palus, Caes. **2.** T r a n s f. **a.** Of time: *to intervene, pass*: annus, Cic.; pauci dies, Liv. **b.** *to occur, happen in the meantime*: saepe in bello parvis momentis magni casūs, Caes.; inter bellorum curas res parva, Liv. **c.** *to be or exist between* persons: ira inter eas, Ter.; inter nosmet ipsos vetus usus, Cic. Ep. **d.** *to come between* as surety: pro aliquo, Cic.; pro aliquo magnam pecuniam, Cic. Ep. **e.** *to interfere to prevent, protest against*. **i.** Of the tribunes: *to interpose a veto*: with DAT.: mihi, rogationi, Cic.; praetori, Cic. **ii.** In gen. *to interfere with, obstruct*: vestra auctoritas, Cic. Ep.; Suet. With DAT.: aegritudo gaudio, Ter.; imaginibus, consilio, Tac. With *quin* and *Subj.* (after negat.): Liv.

interceptiō, ōnis, *f.* [intercipiō], *a taking away between*: poculi, Cic.

interceptor, ōris, *m.* [intercipiō], *one who intercepts, an embezzler*: praedae, Liv.; donativi, Tac.

interceptus, a, um, *Part.* intercipiō.

intercēssiō, ōnis, *f.* [intercēdō], *a coming between*. **a.** In law: *an interposition, a becoming surety*: pecuniarum, Cic. **b.** Polit.: *an intervention* or *veto by a tribune of the people against a decree of the Senate*: Caes., Cic.; remittere, Liv.

intercēssor, ōris, *m.* [intercēdō]. **I.** In law: *a mediator* in money matters, *a surety*: Cic., Sen. Ep. **II. a.** Of a tribune: *one*

who interposes the veto: agrariae legi intercessorem fore professus est, Cic.; legis, Liv. **b.** In gen.: *an obstructor, preventer*: rei malae, Cic.

inter-cīdō, cīdere, cīdī [cadō]. **I.** *to fall between*. **1.** L i t. Of missiles: *to fall short*: ut vix ullum telum in mari vanum intercideret, Liv. **2.** T r a n s f. *to happen in the meantime*: si qua interciderunt, Cic. Ep. **II.** *to fall out, drop out, be lost*: nomen longis intercidit annis, Ov.; si interciderit tibi aliquid, Hor.; memoria, Liv.

inter-cīdō, cīdere, cīdī, cīsum [caedō], *to cut asunder, sever*. **1.** L i t.: interciso monte, Cic. Ep.; pontem, Liv.; venas, Tac.; commentarios (i.e. to falsify), Plin. Ep. **2.** T r a n s f. in *Perf. Part.*: *severed, broken*: iugum mediocri valle a castris intercisum, Hirt.; dies intercisi (on which no legal business was transacted either in the morning or evening), Varr.

inter-cinō, ere [canō], *to sing between*: medios actūs, Hor.

inter-cipiō, cipere, cēpī, ceptum [capiō]. **1.** L i t. *to take something away between* (i.e. while it is moving from one place to another); *to intercept*: me hostes, Cic.; magnum numerum iumentorum, Caes.; litteras, Cic.; commeatūs, Liv.; aliquem ab suis interceptum, Liv.; hostis discretos, Tac. O c c. *to receive what is meant for another*: venenum, Cic.; hastam, Verg. **2.** T r a n s f. **a.** *to appropriate, convert to one's own use, embezzle, purloin*: honorem, Cic.; agrum a populo Romano, Liv.; interceptae e publico pecuniae, Tac.; (aper) Cererem in spicis intercipit, Ov. **b.** Of untimely death: *to cut off*: interceptus veneno, Tac.; mortalitate interceptus, Plin. Ep. **c.** *to take up* (a position) *between*; hence *to obstruct, bar*: medio itinere intercepto, Liv.; loca inter consulum castra, Liv.; hostilis ingressūs, Tac.

intercīsē, *adv. piecemeal*: Cic.

intercīsus, a, um, *Part.* intercīdō.

inter-clūdō, clūdere, clūsī, clūsum [claudō], *to bar the way*; *to shut off, block up*. **1.** L i t. With Acc. of thing and DAT. of person: iter inimicis, Pl.; hisce aditūs ad Sullam, Cic.; exitum Romano, Liv. With Acc. alone: fugam, Caes., Cic. Ep., Liv.; exitum, viam, Liv.; animam (i.e. to suffocate), Liv. With Acc. of person and ABL. (with or without *ab*) of thing: reditu, itinere, re frumentariā intercludi, Caes.; adversarios ab oppido, Caes.; intercludi ab oppido, ab suis, a patriā, Liv. With Acc. of person alone: illos hiems, Verg. With *Instr.* ABL.: angustiis intercludi, Caes. **2.** T r a n s f.: aliquem in insidiis, Cic.; libertatem suis praesidiis interclusam tenere; Cic.; intercludor dolore quo minus etc., Cic. Ep.; consuli admiratio intercluserat vocem, Liv.; Cic.

interclūsiō, ōnis, *f.* [interclūdō]. **I.** *a stopping up*: animae, Cic. **II.** *a parenthesis*: Quint.

interclūsus, a, um, *Part.* interclūdō.

inter-columnium, ī, *n.* [columna], *the space between two columns*: Cic.

inter-currō, currere, cucurrī, cursum. **I.** *to run between*. Transf. **a.** *to intercede*:

Cic. **b.** *to run* between : quaedam distantia formis, Lucr. **c.** *to hasten in the meantime :* ipse interim Veios intercurrit, Liv. **II.** *to run among.* Transf. *to become intermingled with :* his laboriosis exercitationibus dolor, Cic.

intercursō, āre [*freq.* intercurrō]. **I.** *to run together frequently :* primordia principiorum motibus inter se, Lucr. **II.** *to make repeated attacks between the* lines : Liv.

inter-cursū, ABL. *sing. m. by running between, intervention :* fili, suorum, Liv.

inter-cus, utis, *adj.* [cutis], *between the skin* (and the flesh) : aqua (i.e. dropsy), Pl., Cic.

inter-dīcō, dīcere, dīxī, dictum. **I.** *to speak between, interpose, stop by speaking, forbid, prohibit, interdict.* **a.** In gen. With DAT. of pers. and ABL. of thing : omni Galliā Romanis, Caes. ; amoribus iuventuti, Cic. ; patribus commercio plebis, Liv. ; in *Pass.* : male rem gerentibus patribus bonis interdici solet, Cic. ; Liv. With DAT. of person and ACC. of thing : alicui admirationem, Sen. Ep. ; histrionibus scaenam, Suet. ; in *Pass.* : praemio interdicto, Cic. ; Suet. **b.** In law : alicui interdicere aquā et igni, *to forbid one the use of fire and water* (i.e. *to outlaw*), Caes., Cic. **II.** *to make a provisional order, to grant an injunction.* **1.** Lit. Of the praetor : de vi, de fossis, etc., Cic. With *ut* and *Subj.* : Cic. With *Subj.* alone : Hor. **2.** Transf. (nonlegal) : *to give an injunction or strong order.* With DAT. of pers. and *ut* and *Subj.* : Cic. ; also *Impers. Pass.* with DAT. of pers. and *ne* and *Subj.* : Ter. With *Subj.* alone : Pl.

interdictiō, ōnis, *f.* [interdīcō], *a prohibiting, outlawry :* tecti et aquae et ignis, Cic. ; finium, Liv.

interdictum, ī, *n.* [interdīcō]. **I.** *a prohibition :* Pl. ; deorum, Cic. **II.** In law : *a provisional injunction or award of* the praetor, esp. in suits respecting possession of disputed property : Cic.

interdictus, a, um, *Part.* interdīcō.

inter-diū (and **interdiūs**, Pl.), *adv.* [diū old LOCAT., diūs old GEN. of diēs], *during the day, by day* (opp. noctu or nocte) : Pl., Caes., Liv.

inter-dō, dare, datum. **I.** *to put, place between* (or *at intervals*) : nec requies interdatur ulla fluendi, Lucr. **II.** *to diffuse :* cibus interdatus, Lucr.

inter-ductus, ūs, *m. interpunctuation :* Cic.

inter-dum, *adv. between whiles, occasionally, now and then :* Pl., Cic., Tac., etc.

inter-duō [parallel form of interdō]. Opt. **interduim** : *to put between :* floccum non interduim, Pl.

inter-eā, *adv. during that* (or *this*) *time, meanwhile, in the meantime.* **1.** Lit. : Ter., Cic., Verg., etc. ; interea . . . dum, Caes. ; dum . . . interea, Cic. ; interea . . . cum, Cic. With loci (*Partit.* GEN.) : Pl., Ter. Transf. *perh. and yet :* cum interea nullus gemitus audiebatur, Cic. ; nunc tamen interea, Cat.

interemptor, ōris, *m.* [interimō], *a murderer :* eri, Sen. Ep.

interemptus, a, um, *Part.* interimō.

inter-eō, īre, iī, itum, *to go away from the midst, pass away, perish.* **1.** Lit. (esp. freq. in Caes.) : magnitudine maris stilla muriae, *becomes lost in it,* Cic. ; vectores mecum, Cic. ; Liv. ; segetes, Verg. ; pecunia, Nep. ; luna, Hor. With ABL. of cause : fame aut ferro, Caes. ; Liv. ; fraude, Liv. ; naves naufragio, Cic. ; omnia fato, Ov. As an exclamation : interii ! *I'm ruined :* interii, perii, Pl., Ter. ; inteream, *may I perish !* Hor. **2.** Transf. Of abstracts : salus urbis, Cic. ; cultus Cereris, Cic. ; nomen, regnum, Liv. ; ira morā, Ov.

inter-equitō, āre, *to ride among* (with or without ordines) : Liv.

inter-fārī (*Inf.*), fātus (*Pres. Indic.* interfātur), *to interrupt in speaking :* Verg., Liv., Plin. Ep.

interfātiō, ōnis, *f.* [interfārī], *an interrupting in speaking :* Cic., Quint.

interfectiō, ōnis, *f.* [interficiō], *a killing, slaying :* Brut. ap. Cic. Ep.

interfector, ōris, *m.* and **interfectrīx**, īcis, *f.* [interficiō], *a killer, murderer :* Cic., Liv., Tac. With GEN. : Cic., Tac.

interfectus, a, um, *Part.* interficiō.

inter-ficiō, ficere, fēcī, fectum [faciō], *to put out of the midst* (*cf.* intereō), *to destroy.* **a.** In gen. : usum, fructum, victum, Pl. ; herbas, Cic. ; messis, Verg. With ABL. (of separation) : aliquem et vitā et lumine, Pl. **b.** *to put to death, kill :* anum siti fameque atque algu, Pl. ; feras, Lucr. ; latrones, Caes.; se, Caes., Cic., Liv., etc.; aliquem per insidias, Cic. ; aliquem fame, Liv.

inter-fīō, fierī (used as *Pass.* of interficiō), *to pass away, be destroyed :* mores mali, Pl. ; fiammis, Lucr.

inter-fluō, fluere, fluxī, *to flow between :* Liv. With two ACC. : fretum, quod Naupactum et Patras interfluit, Liv. ; Tac.

inter-fodiō, fodere, fōdī, fossum, *to pierce bore into :* pupillas, Lucr.

interfossus, a, um, *Part.* interfodiō.

inter-fringō, fringere, frēgī, frāctum, *to break up :* Cato.

inter-fugiō, fugere, *to flee among :* Lucr.

inter-fulgeō, ēre, *to shine or glitter among :* Liv. (dub.).

inter-fūsus, a, um. **I.** *poured, spread, or flowing between :* novies Styx, Verg. ; interfusa aequora Cycladas, Hor. **II.** *spread here and there.* Transf. : maculis interfusa genas, Verg.

interfutūrus, v. intersum.

inter-iaceō, ēre, *to lie between :* campus, Liv. With two DAT. : campus Tiberi ac moenibus, Liv. Transf. (with DAT.) : Quint.

inter-iaciō, v. intericiō.

inter-ibi, *adv. in the meantime :* Pl.

inter-iciō, icere, iēcī, iectum [iaciō], *to throw or cast between or among ; to set, place between or among, to intermingle.* **1.** Lit. : trabes saxis interiectis continentur, Caes. ; sagittarios inter equites, Caes. With DAT. : nasus quasi murus oculis interiectus, Cic. **2.** Transf. : pleraque sermone Latino, Tac. ; moram, preces et minas, Tac. ; aliquot (paucis, Liv.) interiectis diebus, Caes. ; longo intervallo interiecto, Cic. ; penuria omnium rerum interiecta, Liv.

interiectiō, ōnis, *f.* [intericiō], *a throwing*

between. **a.** Gramm. *an interjection :*
Quint. **b.** Rhet. *a parenthesis :* Quint.
interiectus, a, um. I. *Part.* intericiō. **II.**
Adj. set between, lying between : mediocri
spatio interiecto, Caes. With inter : aer
inter mare et caelum, Cic. ; Liv. With two
Dat. : (montes) interiecti Macedoniae
Thessaliaeque, Liv.
interiectus, ūs, *m.* [intericiō], *a throwing
between, interposition.* **1.** Lit. : luna in-
teriectu terrae deficit, Cic. **2.** Transf.
lapse, interval : paucorum dierum, temporis, Tac.
interim, *adv.* [inter, and im, old Acc. *sing.*
of is]. **I.** *meanwhile, in the meantime :* Pl.,
Caes., Cic., etc. ; interim dum etc., Ter.,
Caes. **II.** *for the moment :* cum interim
Sulla solitudinem non quaereret, Cic. ;
interim legiones pro ripā locat, Tac. ; Suet.
III. *sometimes :* Quint. ; interim . .
mox, Tac. ; interim . . . interim, Quint.,
Plin. Ep. **IV.** perh. *and yet, however :*
interim velim mihi ignoscas, Cic. Ep. ;
Quint.
inter-imō, imere, ēmī, emptum [emō], *to
take from the midst ; to do away with, abolish,
destroy.* **1.** Lit. **a.** vitam, Pl. ; sensum,
Lucr. ; sacra, Cic. **b.** Of persons : *to kill :*
Pl., Cic., Verg., etc. **2.** Transf. : me
oratio, Pl. ; me hae voces Milonis, Cic.
interior, ius [a double *Comp. Adj.* with *Sup.*
intimus, fr. in, *cf.* exterior], *more inward,
inner, interior.* **1.** Lit. **a.** in interiore
(aedium) parte, Ter., Cic. ; domus, Verg. ;
secessit in partem interiorem, Liv. ; nationes, Cic. ; nota Falerni, Hor. As Noun :
in interiora regni se recepit, Liv. **b.** *on
the inner side ; nearer, near-side :* rota (i.e.
nearer to the turning-post), Ov. ; radit iter
laevum interior, Verg. ; naves ictibus (i.e.
within range), Liv. ; interior periculo vulneris (i.e. too near to be in danger), Liv.
2. Transf. **a.** *more hidden, secret, private :*
litterae, Cic. ; consilia, Nep. ; animi nota,
vita, aulici, Suet. **b.** *deeper, more intimate :*
societas, Cic. ; vicini, Cic. Ep. ; amicitia,
Liv. ; potentia, Tac.
interitiō, ōnis, *f.* [intereō], *destruction, ruin :*
aratorum, Cic.
interitus, ūs, *m.* [intereō], *removal, annihilation, ruin :* of things : Cic. ; of persons :
Cic., Verg.
inter-iungō, iungere, iūnxī, iūnctum. **I.**
to join together mutually, join, unite : dextrae interiunctae, Liv. **II.** *to unyoke :*
equos, Mart. ; Sen. Ep.
interius. I. *Adj. v.* interior. **II.** *Adv. inwardly.* **1.** Lit. : Verg., Ov. **2.** Transf.
a. *too short :* ne insistat interius (oratio),
Cic. **b.** *closely :* attendere, Juv.
inter-lābor, lābī, lāpsus, *to glide,* or *flow
between :* inter enim labentur aquae, Verg.
inter-legō, ere, *to pluck here and there :*
frondes, Verg.
inter-linō, linere, lēvī, litum, *to smear here
and there.* **1.** Lit. : caementa interlita
luto, Liv. **2.** Transf. *to erase here and
there :* tabulas, testamentum, Cic.
interlitus, a, um, *Part.* interlinō.
inter-loquor, loquī, locūtus, *to speak between,
interrupt in speaking :* Plin. Ep. With
Dat. : mihi, Ter.

inter-lūceō, lūcere, lūxī. **I.** *to shine out
clear* from its surroundings. **1.** Lit. :
duos soles noctu interluxisse, Liv. ; of flies
in amber : Tac. **2.** Transf. : quibus
inter gradūs dignitatis et fortunae aliquid
interlucet, Liv. **II.** *to show light here and
there* (i.e. to show gaps) : corona (militum),
Verg.
interlūnia, ōrum, *n. pl.* [lūna], *the inter-
lunary interval, new moon :* Hor.
inter-luō, ere. **I.** *to wash between.* With
Acc. : pontus arvaque et urbes interluit
aestu, Verg. ; Tac. **II.** *to wash* in the
intervals of doing something : manūs,
Cato.
intermēnstruus, a, um [mēnsis], *between
two months ; interlunar :* i.e. *at the time of
new moon :* tempus, Cic. *Neut.* as Noun,
the time of new moon : Cic.
(1) **in-terminātus,** a, um, *unbounded, endless :* Cic.
(2) **interminātus,** a, um, *Part.* interminor.
inter-minor, ārī. **I.** *to interpose threats.*
With Dat. of pers. threatened, foll. by Acc.
and *Inf. :* Pl. **II.** *to forbid with threats :*
aliquid alicui, Ter. With ne and *Subj. :*
Pl., Ter. *Part.* in *Pass.* sense : intermina-
tus cibus, Hor.
inter-misceō, miscēre, miscuī, mixtum, *to
mix among* or *together, to intermix :* turba-
bant equos pedites intermixti, Liv. With
Dat. : turbam indignorum dignis, Liv. ;
tibi undam, Verg.
intermissiō, ōnis, *f.* [intermittō], *interruption, temporary discontinuance :* forensis operae, Cic. ; per intermissiones has
intervallaque, Liv. ; intermissionem offici
facere, Cic. ; sine ullā intermissione, Cic.
inter-mittō, mittere, mīsī, missum, *to let go
here and there ;* hence, *to leave gaps in.*
A. Trans. **1.** Lit. Of space : *to break
off, interrupt :* mostly in *Perf. Part.* iso-
lated ; vallis, Caes. With Abl. of separation : custodiis loca, Liv. With ab : pars
oppida intermissa a flumine, Caes. With
Instr. Abl. : *separated, interrupted, broken :*
trabes paribus intermissae spatiis, Caes. ;
planities intermissa collibus, Caes. ; or
simply *breached :* intermissa moenia, Liv.
2. Transf. **a.** Of time : *to leave an interval, to let pass* or *elapse :* tempus a labore,
Caes. ; nulla pars nocturni temporis ad
laborem intermittitur, Caes. ; brevi tempore
intermisso, Caes. ; dies intermissus, Cic.
Ep. ; nunquam unum diem quin veniat,
Ter. ; Pl. ; Caes. **b.** Of other things :
to interrupt, discontinue : proelium, iter,
laborem, etc., Caes. ; studia, Cic. ; ludos,
Cic. ; curam rerum, Tac. ; vento intermisso, Caes. ; libertas intermissa, Cic. ;
bella, Hor. ; verba, Ov. With *Inf. :* Caes.,
Cic. **B.** Intrans. *to break off, cease,
pause.* **1.** Lit. Of space : quā flumen
intermittit, Caes. ; vidit hostis (non) a
fronte subeuntia intermittere, Caes. **2.**
Transf. : gallos sic adsidue canere coepisse ut nihil intermitterent, Cic.
intermixtus, a, um, *Part.* intermisceō.
inter-morior, morī, mortuus. **I.** *to die in
the midst* of business, etc. ; hence, *to die
suddenly* or *prematurely :* Cato ; civitas,
Liv. ; ignis, Curt. **II.** In *Perf. Part. :*

swooning, in a faint: Liv., Suet. Transf.:
half-dead: mores boni, Pl.; Catilinae reliquiae, Cic.; contiones, Cic.

inter-mundia, ōrum, *n. pl.* [mundus], *spaces between the worlds :* Cic.

inter-mūrālis, e. *adj.* [mūrus], *between two walls :* amnis, Liv.

inter-nātus, a, um, *growing between or among :* virgulta, Liv. With DAT.: herbae saxis, Tac.

internecīnus, a, um [interneciō], *exterminating ; of extermination :* bellum, Cic.

interneciō, ōnis, *f.* [internecō], *a massacre, general slaughter, extermination :* civium, Cic.; Lucerini ad internecionem caesi, Liv.; prope ad internecionem redigi, Caes.

internecīvus, a, um [internecō], *exterminating, of extermination :* bellum, Liv.

inter-necō, āre, *to kill off from the midst of others ; to exterminate :* Pl.

inter-nectō, ere, *to intertwine :* fibula crinem auro, Verg.

inter-niteō, ēre, *to shine among, shine forth :* sidera internitebant, Curt.

inter-nōdium, i, *n.* [nōdus], *the space between two knots or joints.* Of the leg : Ov.

inter-nōscō, nōscere, nōvī, nōtum, *to distinguish between :* geminos, Pl., Cic.; blandum amicum a vero, Cic.

internūntiō, āre, *to make use of* internuntii : Liv.

inter-nūntius, i, *m.* and **internūntia,** ae, *f.* (Pl., Cic.), *a messenger between :* Pl., Caes., Cic.; ad te ab libertinā esse, Pl. With *Obj.* GEN.: totius rei, Liv.; pacis, Curt. With *Subj.* GEN.: Iovis, Cic.

internus, a, um [intrā], *inward, internal.*
1. Lit.: arae, Ov. **2.** Transf. *internal, civil, domestic :* bellum, discordiae, Tac. *Neut. pl.* as Noun : si quando ad interna praeverterent, Tac.

in-terō, terere, trīvī, trītum, *to rub, pound, or crumble in :* catino, Cato ; panis intritus in aquam, Varr. ; in lacte, Varr. Prov.: tute hoc intristi ; tibi omne exedendum est, *you have made the mess and must eat it up,* Ter. [It. *intridere.*]

interpellātiō, ōnis, *f.* [interpellō], *an interruption in speaking.* **1.** Lit.: Pl., Cic., Quint. **2.** Transf.: *interruption, interference :* Cic. Ep.

interpellātor, ōris, *m.* [interpellō], *one who interrupts another in speaking.* **1.** Lit.: Quint., Suet. **2.** Transf. *a disturber :* se oblectare sine interpellatoribus, Cic.

inter-pellō, āre [*cf.* appellō], *to interrupt in speaking.* **1.** Lit. **a.** In gen.: Pl.; aliquem, Cic., Quint. **b.** *to break in on with* questions or demands : aliquem, Curt., Suet. **2.** Transf. *to interrupt, break off, obstruct, interfere with :* aliquem in iure suo, Caes.; partam iam victoriam, Caes.; poenam, Liv.; id Philippi interpellatum est, Liv.; me quo minus, etc., Cic. Ep.; tribunis interregem interpellantibus, ne senatūs consultum fieret, Liv. With *Inf.:* pransus non avide, quantum interpellet inani ventre diem durare, Hor.

interpolis, e, *adj.* [*cf.* poliō], *renewed here and there on the surface ;* hence, *painted, patched up :* istaec veteres quae se unguentis unctitant, interpoles, Pl.

interpolō, āre [*cf.* interpolis], colloq. *to spruce up.* **1.** Lit.: togam praetextam, Cic. Ep. Comic.: illic homo me interpolabit, meumque os finget denuo, Pl. **2.** Transf. (of the falsification of documents): Cic.

inter-pōnō, pōnere, posuī, positum, *to put, place between or among.* **1.** Lit.: pilae interponuntur ubi etc., Caes.; interpositi elephanti, Liv.; equitatui auxilia levis armaturae, Hirt. **2.** Transf. **a.** Of time : *to put in, insert :* nullam moram, Cic.; Caes.; spatium interponendum ad recreandos animos putabat, Caes.; spatio interposito, Cic., intercalariis mensibus interpositis, Liv. **b.** Of words, etc.: *to insert :* verbum, Cic.; Quint.; iudicium suum, Cic.; Quint.; quod neque conloquium interpositā causā tolli volebat, Caes. With *Indir. Quest. :* Nep. **c.** With *Refl. Pron. : to interfere or meddle with* (either to hinder or forward), *to mediate, mix oneself up with,* etc.; quid me interponerem audaciae tuae ? Cic.; semper se interposuit, Nep.; bello se, Liv.; se quo minus etc., Cic.; se in pacificationem, Cic. Ep. **d.** Also with such words as operam, studium, consilium, ius iurandum, religionem, decretum, etc., *to interpose* (in order to hinder or forward) : Caes., Cic., Liv.; in eam rem fidem suam, Caes., Cic.; fidem reliquis, Caes. **e.** *to interpolate, falsify :* rationes, Cic.

interpositiō, ōnis, *f.* [interpōnō]. **I.** *an insertion, introduction :* personarum, Cic.; of words in a MS., etc.: Cic. Ep. **II.** Rhet. *a parenthesis :* Quint.

interpositus, a, um, *Part.* interpōnō.

interpositū, ABL. *sing. m. by the interposition :* luna interpositu terrae deficit, Cic.

interpres, etis, *m.f.* [root seen in pretium], *an agent between the prices* (of buyer and seller). **1.** Lit. **a.** *a broker, negotiator :* Pl. With GEN.: corrumpendi iudici, Cic.; pacis, Liv.; divum (i.e. Mercury), Verg.; harum curarum, Verg. **b.** *an interpreter* (of language): Caes., Cic., Liv. **2.** Transf. **a.** *an explainer, expounder :* Cic., Liv. With GEN.: iuris, caeli, comitiorum, poetarum, Cic.; legum, Juv. Of things: mentis est oratio, Cic.; metu interprete, Liv. **b.** *a translator :* Cic.

interpretātiō, ōnis, *f.* [interpretor]. **I.** *an explanation, exposition :* Liv. With GEN.: iuris, Cic.; voluntatis, Liv. **II.** *the interpretation, meaning :* foederis, Cic. **III.** *a translation :* Quint.

interpretor, ārī [*cf.* interpres]. **I.** *to be an agent* (with DAT.) : memoriae alicuius, Pl. **II.** *to put a construction upon, take as the meaning, understand in a certain sense, explain :* ut ego interpretor, Cic.; sapienter, Cic.; recte an perperam, Liv.; aliquid mitiorem in partem, Cic.; ius, monstra, somnia, etc., Cic.; Lucr.; aenigmata, Quint.; grate beneficia, Plin. Ep. Occ. *to understand :* aliquem, Tac. With ACC. and *Inf. :* Cic., Liv., Suet. **III.** *to translate :* nec quicquam est philosophia, si interpretari velis, quam studium sapientiae, Cic. *Part.* in *Pass.* sense : haec ex Graeco carmine interpretata, Liv.

inter-prīmō, primere, pressī, pressum [premō], *to press, squeeze* (so as to stop up) ; alicui faucis, Pl.

interpūnctiō, ōnis, *f. punctuation :* verborum, Cic.

inter-pūnctus, a, um [pungō], *well-divided :* clausula, intervalla, Cic. ; narratio interpuncta sermonibus, Cic. *Neut. pl.* as Noun, *points, stops :* Cic.

inter-pungō, ere, *to put points between words, to punctuate :* Sen. Ep.

inter-putō, āre, *to prune here and there :* ficos, Cato ; Varr.

inter-quiēscō, quiēscere, quiēvī, *to rest between whiles.* **1.** Lit. : Cato, Cic. **2.** Transf. : dolor, Sen. Ep. ; lites, Plin. Ep.

inter-rēgnum, ī, *n.* **1.** Lit. *the time between the death of one king and the election of another, an interregnum :* Cic., Liv. **2.** Transf. : in the republic, of a similar interval between consuls : Cic. Ep. ; inire (i.e. to become interrex), Liv.

inter-rēx, rēgis, *m.* **1.** Lit. *one who acted as king during an interregnum : a regent, interrex :* Liv. **2.** Transf. in the republic, one who acted as chief magistrate in an interregnum : nominare, Liv. ; prodere, creare, Cic., Liv.

in-territus, a, um, *undaunted, undismayed :* Verg., Ov., Tac. ; classis, Verg. ; mens, Ov. With GEN. : mens leti, Ov.

inter-rogātiō, ōnis, *f.* **I.** *the insertion of a question.* With *Subj.* GEN. : tribuni, Liv. With *Indir. Quest.* : Cic. **II.** Gramm. *an interrogation :* Quint. **III.** In law : *cross-examination :* Quint. ; testium, Tac. **IV.** *a syllogism :* Cic., Sen. Ep.

interrogātiuncula, ae, *f.* [dim. interrogātiō], *a short argument or syllogism :* Cic., Sen. Ep.

interrogātum, ī, *n. an interposed question :* Cic.

inter-rogō, āre, *to question at intervals or to interpose a question.* **I.** *to ask, question :* hoc quod te interrogo, responde, Pl. ; aliquem de aliquā re, Cic. With *Indir. Quest.* : Cic. ; illud interrogo (with *Indir. Quest.*), Liv. ; sententiae interrogari coeptae, Liv. In *Pass.* (with retained Acc.) : ad haec, quae interrogatus es, responde, Liv. ; Suet. **II.** In law. **a.** *to cross-examine :* testem, Cic. ; testis in reos, Plin. Ep. **b.** *to bring to trial, indict, accuse :* legibus interrogari, Liv. ; me lege, Cic. ; consules legibus ambitūs interrogati, Sall. ; Tac. **III.** *to argue syllogistically :* Sen. Ep.

inter-rumpō, rumpere, rūpī, ruptum, *to break between, make a gap in, sever.* **1.** Lit. : pontem, agmen, Caes. ; aciem, Liv. ; ignis, Verg. ; itinera, venas, Tac. **2.** Transf. *to interrupt, break off :* sermonem, Pl., Tac. ; conloquia, orationem, Caes. ; iter amoris, Cic. ; querellas, Ov. ; rerum tenorem, Liv.

interruptē, *adv. interruptedly :* narrare, Cic.

interruptus, a, um, *Part.* interrumpō.

inter-saepiō, saepire, saepsī, saeptum, *to fence between ; to stop up, close, separate off by an obstacle.* **1.** Lit. : foramina, iter, Cic. ; itinera, Liv. ; quaedam operibus, Liv. ; legionem arbustis, Tac. ; vallo urbem ab arce, Liv. **2.** Transf. : Romanis conspectum exercitūs, Liv.

inter-scindō, scindere, scidī, scissum, *to cut* or *tear asunder.* **1.** Lit. : pontem, Caes., Cic. ; aggerem, Caes. ; venas, Tac. **2.** Transf. **a.** *to cut off, separate :* Chalcis arto interscinditur freto, Liv. **b.** *to interrupt :* laetitiam, Sen. Ep.

inter-scrībō, ere, *to insert in writing :* alia, Plin. Ep.

(1) inter-serō, serere, sēvī, situm, *to plant between :* pomis intersita, Lucr.

(2) inter-serō, serere, seruī, *to put* or *place between :* mediis oscula verbis, Ov. With Acc. only : causam, Nep.

inter-sistō, ere, *to pause in speaking :* Quint. ; oratio, Quint.

intersitus, a, um, *Part.* interserō (1).

inter-spīrātiō, ōnis, *f. a taking breath between :* Cic. In *pl.* : Cic.

inter-stīnctus, a, um [*cf.* distinctus], *pricked out here and there, spotted :* facies medicaminibus, Tac.

inter-stinguō, ere [*cf.* exstinguō], *to prick out of the midst :* hence, *to extinguish :* ignis, Lucr.

inter-stringō, ere, *to squeeze* (so as to stop up) : alicui gulam, Pl.

inter-sum, esse, fuī, futūrus. **I.** *to be* or *lie between.* **1.** Lit. in space : via perangusta, Liv. ; quas (segetes) inter et castra unus omnino collis intererat, Caes. ; Tiberis inter eos, Cic. **2.** Transf. **a.** In time : inter primum et sextum consulatum XLVI anni, Cic. ; Liv. **b.** *Impers.* (*v.* also IV) *there is a difference between* (with Acc. of extent) : inter hominem et beluam hoc maxime interest quod etc., Cic. ; ut inter eos ne minimum quidem intersit, Cic. ; tantum id interest veneritne eo itinere ad urbem an etc., Liv. **II.** *to be among, be present, take part, attend :* Cic., Suet. With DAT. : rebus divinis, proelio, Caes. ; senatui, Cic. ; consiliis, crudelitati, Cic. Ep. ; lacrimis patris, Verg. ; bello, spectaculo, Liv. ; velut si iam agendis quae audiebat interesset, Liv. ; Cic. ; Tragoedia Satyris, Hor. With *in* and ABL. : in convivio, Cic. ; in testamento faciendo, Cic. **III.** *to be apart from one another.* **1.** Lit. : clatros interesse oportet pede, Cato. **2.** Transf. *to be different, to differ :* hoc pater ac dominus interest, Ter. With *ab :* qui illa visa negant quicquam a falsis interesse, Cic. **IV.** **interest**, *there is a difference for, it makes a difference to, it is of importance to, it concerns* (for *Obj.* it takes GEN. of Nouns, or ABL. *fem.* of possessive Pronouns, meā, tuā, nostrā, vestrā ; for *Subject* an *Indir. Quest.,* or *Inf.,* or Acc. and *Inf.,* or *ut* (or *ne*) and *Subj.,* or a *Neut. Pron.*) : ad laudem civitatis, Cic. ; ad beate vivendum, Cic. With *Indir. Quest.* : quid interfuit utrum hoc decerneres an etc. ? Cic. ; nihil interest nunc an violaverim, Liv. With *Inf.* : quorum intersit id scire, Cic. With Acc. and *Inf.* : quanto opere rei publicae intersit manūs hostium distineri, Caes. ; Cic. ; Liv. With *ut* or *ne* and *Subj.* : quod ut facias tuā interesse arbitor, Cic. ; Caes. ; Liv. ; vestrā interest ne etc., Tac. With GEN of value or Acc. (used as *Adv.*) or *Adv.* : magni, permagni, tanti interest, Cic. Ep. ; multum, plurimum, quantum, Cic. ; nihil, Liv. ; quanto opero, Caes. ; maxime, vehementer, Cic. Ep. [It. *interesse* ; Fr. *intérêt*.]

inter-textus, a, um, *twined in among, interwoven* : flores hederis, Ov. ; chlamys auro intertexta, Verg. ; vestis intertexta notis, Quint.

inter-trahŏ, trahere, traxi, *to draw from the midst, to take away* : alicui animam, Pl.

inter-trimentum, i, n. [terō], *loss by wear, waste* (in working). **1.** Lit.: in auro, Liv. ; argenti, Liv. **2.** Transf.: sine ullo intertrimento, Cic. ; (non) sine magno intertrimento, Ter.

inter-turbātiŏ, ōnis, f. *disquietude, confusion* : animi, Liv.

inter-turbŏ, āre, *to confuse* or *put one out by interrupting* : Pl.

inter-vallum, i, n. Lit. *the space between two lines of stakes.* Transf. **a.** Of space in gen.: *space between, interval, distance* : trabes paribus intervallis in solo conlocantur, ea autem intervalla grandibus saxis efferciuntur, Caes. ; videt magnis intervallis sequentis, Liv. ; unius signi, Cic. ; in intervalla ordinum, Liv. ; mille passuum intervallo, Liv. : longo proximus intervallo, Verg. **b.** Of time : *intermission, pause* : Pl. ; annuum intervallum regni, Liv. ; sine intervallo loquacitas, Cic. ; per intervallum adventantes (i.e. in detachments), Tac. In music, *an interval* : Cic. In prosody : trochaeus temporibus et intervallis est par iambo, Cic. **c.** *difference, contrast* : inter maiorum consilia et istorum dementiam, Cic.

inter-vellŏ, vellere, vulsi (velli, Pl.), vulsum, *to pluck here and there* : alas (vocis), Pl. ; barbam, Sen. Ep. ; aliquid ex illis, Quint.

inter-veniŏ, venire, vēni, ventum, *to come between* or *among, to intrude, come on the scene* (mostly so as to interrupt, stop, or alter something). **1.** Lit.: Pl., Ter., Caes. With Dat. (of person): Cic. **2.** Transf. **A.** *to happen, occur* : casus mirificus quidam, Cic. Ep.; de caelo quod comitia turbaret intervenit, Liv. ; with Dat. of person : nulla mihi res tanta, Ter. ; exigua fortuna sapienti, Cic. *Impers. Pass.*: Ter., Cic. **B.** *to come in on* (and so *interrupt*). **a.** With Dat. of thing : querellis, Cic. Ep.; orationi, Liv. ; continuationi sermonis, Quint. ; nox proelio, Liv. ; Sabinum bellum coeptis, Liv. ; verbo omni plangor, Ov. ; hiems rebus gerendis, Liv. With Dat. implied : foedus intervenisse, Sall. ; neque senatu interveniente, Suet. **b.** With Acc.: *to delay, put off* : ludorum dies cognitionem, Tac. **c.** With *ne* and *Subj.* : Suet.

interventor, ōris, m. [interveniō], *an intruding visitor* : Cic.

interventus, ūs, m. *a coming on the scene, intrusion, intervention.* **a.** Of persons : Cic., Liv. **b.** Of things : proelium diremit nox interventu suo, Cic. ; noctis, Caes. ; malorum, Cic. **c.** *mediation* : principis, Plin. Ep.

inter-vertŏ (-vortŏ), vertere, verti, versum, *to intercept and divert, to embezzle.* **a.** Of material things : argentum, Pl. ; regale donum, Cic. ; vectigalia, Suet. ; inter-

sis patroni rebus, Tac. **b.** Of other things : promissum et receptum (consulatum), Cic. **c.** With Acc. of pers. and Abl. of thing : *to cheat, rob* : me muliere, Pl. With Abl. implied : quem intervortam ? Pl.

inter-visŏ, visere, visi, visum. **I.** *to go and look in on* or *at, to drop in on* : ipse crebro interviso, Cic. Ep.; domum, Pl. With *Indir. Quest.* : Pl. **II.** *to visit from time to time* : aliquem, Cic. Ep., Tac., Suet.

inter-volitŏ, āre, *to flit about between* or *among* : Liv.

inter-vomŏ, ere, ui, itum, *to throw up among* : aequor dulcis inter salsas undas, Lucr.

in-testābilis, e, adj. [testor], *unfit to give evidence.* Transf. *infamous, dishonoured.* **a.** Of persons : Sall., Hor., Tac. With Abl.: saevitiā, Tac. *Comp.* : Tac. **b.** Of things : periurium, Liv. **c.** In a pun (*cf.* intestatus 2.): Pl.

(1) in-testātus, a, um. **I.** *that has made no will, intestate* : Juv. Abl. *Neut.* as *Adv. without making a will* : Cic. **II.** *unconvicted by witnesses* : Pl.

(2) in-testātus, a, um [testis, *testicle*], *castrated* : Pl.

intestinus, a, um [intus], *inward, internal* : intestinum ac domesticum malum, Cic. ; bellum, Cic., Suet. ; incommodum, Liv. As Noun, **intestinum**, i, n. (Lucr., Juv.) and **intestina**, ōrum, pl. (Pl., Cic., Juv.), *intestines, entrails.*

in-texŏ, texere, texui, textum, *to weave in, inweave.* **1.** Lit. **a.** vestibus intexto auro, Ov. ; hence, intexti Britanni (i.e. in tapestry), Verg. **b.** *to twine, plait* : vimina, Caes. ; vaccinia casiā, Verg. ; vitibus ulmos, Verg. Also *to twine about* : hederae truncos, Ov. **2.** Transf.: te chartis, Verg. ; facta chartis, Tib. ; venae corpore intextae, Cic. ; tribus intextum tauris opus, Verg. ; ridicula intexta versibus, Liv.

intibum, i, n. [ἔντυβον], *endive* or *succory* : Verg., Ov. [It. *indivia* ; Sp. *endibia*.]

intimē, adv. **I.** *most intimately* : uti aliquo, Nep. **II.** *heartily, cordially* : commendari, Cic. Ep.

intimus (intumus), a, um, *Sup. Adj.* [fr. in ; *Comp.* interior], *most inward, inmost, innermost.* **1.** Lit.: traxit ex intumo ventre suspirium, Pl. ; in eo sacrario intimo, Cic. ; pectus, Cat. ; Tartara, Verg. **2.** Transf. *most secret, most profound, most intimate*, etc.: ex intimā philosophiā, Cic. ; consilia, sermo, artificium, animus, etc., Cic. ; amicitia, Nep. Of persons : *intimate* : Ter., Cic. Ep., Tac. As Noun. **a. intimus**, i, m. *a most intimate friend* : Pl., Cic. **b. intima**, ōrum, n. pl. *the inmost parts, the heart* : finium, Liv.

in-tingŏ or **in-tinguŏ**, tingere, tinxi, tinctum, *to soak in* : buccas rubricā, Pl. ; brassicam in acetum, Cato ; faces in fossā sanguinis, Ov. ; calamos, Quint.

in-tolerābilis, e, adj. *unbearable, insupportable* : sumptus, Pl. ; odoris foeditas, frigus, verba, etc., Cic. ; saevitia, regium nomen, vis Romanorum, Liv. *Comp.* : Cic. Ep., Juv., etc.

in-tolerandus, a, um, *insupportable, intolerable* : tyrannus, Cic. ; licentia rerum,

Cic. ; hiems, superbia, Liv. ; itineris labor, Tac. ; dominatio plebi, Tac.

in-tolerāns, antis, adj. **A.** A c t. *that cannot bear :* with GEN. : secundarum rerum, Liv. ; omnium, Tac. ; corpora laboris, Liv. *Comp. and Sup. :* Liv. **B. P a s s.** *insufferable, intolerable. Comp. :* subiectis intolerantior, Tac. ; servitus, Tac.

intoleranter, adv. *intolerably, immoderately, excessively :* Cic. *Comp. :* Caes., Cic. *Sup. :* Cic.

in-tolerantia, ae, f. *insufferable conduct, insolence :* Cic. ; morum, Suet.

in-tonō, āre, uī, ātus (Hor.), *to thunder.* **1.** Lit. **a.** pater omnipotens intonuit, Verg. ; Ov. ; intonuere poli, Verg. **b.** *Impers. :* intonuit laevum, Verg. ; Ov. **2.** T r a n s f. **a.** Of persons : intonuit vox tribuni, Cic. ; intonat ore, Verg. With Acc. : minas, Ov. ; cum haec intonuisset plenus irae, Liv. **b.** Of things : silvae, Verg. *Part.* in *Act.* sense : Eois intonata fluctibus hiems, Hor.

in-tōnsus, a, um, *unshorn, unshaven.* **1.** Lit. **a.** os, Verg. ; capilli, Hor. ; caput, Ov. ; mentum, Curt. **b.** Of persons : *bearded :* Cato, Hor. ; avi, Ov. But, Apollo (*long-haired*), Hor., Tib. **2.** T r a n s f. **a.** *unpolished, rude :* homines, Liv., Ov. **b.** Of woodland : *unshorn* (i.e. uncleared or unclipped) : montes, Verg. Of trees : Verg.

in-torqueō, torquēre, torsī, tortum. **I.** *to twist, screw, roll, wrap round :* procella nubibus sese, Lucr. ; mentum in dicendo, Cic. ; oculos, Verg. ; paludamentum circum bracchium, Liv. **II.** *to hurl against.* **1.** Lit. : tergo hastam, Verg. ; iaculum alicui, Verg. ; telum in hostem, Verg. ; Sen. Ep. **2.** T r a n s f. : contumelias, Cic.

intortus, a, um. **I.** *Part.* intorqueō. **II.** Adj. : *twisted.* **1.** Lit. : rudentes, Cat. ; funes, Ov. ; angues intorti capillis Eumenidum, Hor. **2.** T r a n s f. **a.** *tangled :* oratio, Pl. **b.** *crooked :* mores, Pers.

intrā, adv. and prep. [older intrād, Adv. ABL. of *Comp. Adj.* fr. in, lit. *by the inner way*]. **I.** Adv. **a.** *on the inside, within :* Quint., Suet. **b.** *towards the inside :* inferioribus (digitis) intra spectantibus, Quint. **II.** Prep. with Acc. *inside, within.* **a.** Of space : without motion : intra navim, Pl. ; intra parietes, Cic. ; intra Apenninum sese tenuere (i.e. *on their own side of*), Liv. ; **b.** With motion : intra portas compelluntur, Liv. ; qui intra finis suos Ariovistum recepissent, Caes. ; intra iactum teli progressus, Verg. **2.** T r a n s f. **a.** Of time : **i.** *within :* intra viginti dies, Pl. ; Liv., etc. ; intra decimum diem, quam Pheras venerat, Liv. **ii.** *during :* qui intra annos quattuordecim tectum non subiissent, Caes. ; intra iuventam, Tac. **b.** Of number : *within, under :* intra centum, Liv. **c.** Of other relations : epulari intra legem, Cic. Ep. ; intra finem iuris sui, Liv. ; intra famam sunt scripta, Quint. ; intra fortunam, Prop. **d.** intra se, *to one's self :* dicere, Quint. ; intra vos futura, Plin. Ep. [It. *tra.*]

intrābilis, e, adj. [intrō], *that can be entered :* os amnis, Liv.

in-tractābilis, e, adj. *not to be handled or*

meddled *with, formidable, dangerous.* **1.** Lit. Of persons : genus bello, Verg. **2.** Transf. : bruma (when no work is possible), Verg. ; aetas, Sen. Ep.

in-tractātus, a, um, *not handled, not broken in.* **1.** Lit. : equus, Cic. **2.** T r a n s f. *unessayed :* ne quid intractatum scelerisve dolive fuisset, Verg.

in-tremīscō, tremīscere tremuī, *to begin to shake, quiver :* mālus, undae, Verg. ; tellus, quercus, genua, Ov.

in-tremō, ere, *to shake, quake inwardly :* murmure Trinacria, Verg.

intrepidē, adv. *without disorder.* **1.** Lit. : Liv. **2.** T r a n s f. (mentally) : *calmly :* Liv.

in-trepidus, a, um, *not hustled* or *hurried, not in disorder, not excited, calm.* **1.** Lit. **a.** Milit. : *in good order :* Liv., Curt. **b.** In gen. of persons : intrepidus minantibus, Tac. **2.** T r a n s f. (of things) : vultus, Ov. ; hiems, Tac.

in-trīcō, āre [trīcae], *to entangle :* aliquem, Pl., Cic.

intrīn-secus, adv. [perh. fr. interim secus, cf. extrīnsecus]. **I.** *on the inside :* Lucr., Varr. **II.** *towards the inside, inwards :* Suet.

(1) intrītus, a, um, *Part.* interō.

(2) in-trītus, a, um, *not worn away.* T r a n s f. : *not worn out :* cohortes ab labore, Caes.

intrō, adv. of direction (cf. eō, quō) [fr. *Comp.* of in], *to the inner side, inwards, within, inside :* Pl., Caes., Cic., etc. In compounds, use. *into an enclosure, house, town.* [It. *entro*.]

intrō, āre (*Aor. Opt.* or *Subj.* intrāssis, Pl.) [cf. *penetrāre*], *to pass in, enter.* **A.** T r a n s. **1.** Lit. : limen, pomerium, etc., Cic. ; portas, saltūs, Liv. ; maria, Verg. ; silvae intratae, Liv. ; curia intratur, Tac. **2.** T r a n s f. : domum nec honor nec gratia, Liv. ; pavidos metus, Tac. ; animum cupido, Tac. **B.** I n t r a n s. **1.** Lit. : Pl. ; intra praesidia, Caes. ; in Capitolium, Cic. ; animus in corpus, Cic. ; in hortos, Ov. ; ad munimenta, Liv. *Impers. Pass. :* quo intrari possit, Caes. **2.** T r a n s f. : in rerum naturam, Cic. ; penitus in alicuius familiaritatem, Cic. Ep. ; in mentem iudicis, Cic. ; si intrarit dolor, Hor. [Fr. *entrer*.]

intrō-dūcō, dūcere, dūxī, ductum, *to lead or bring within.* **1.** Lit. **a.** Of troops : praesidium, cohortis, Caes. ; noctu milites, Sall. ; nacti portum eo navis introduxerunt, Caes. ; copias in finis hostium, Caes. ; Liv. **b.** *to usher in, present, introduce :* aliquem in senatum, Cic. ; legationes in senatum, Liv. ; ad senatum, Liv. **2.** T r a n s f. **a.** Of new things : *to introduce :* novum in re publicā exemplum, Caes. ; Liv. ; ambitionem in senatum, Cic. ; novas superstitiones, Quint. **b.** Of a character or subject : Catonem disputantem, Cic. ; sermones, Quint. **c.** Of an argument, etc. : deliberationem, Cic. With Acc. and *Inf.* : Cic.

intrōductiō, ōnis, f. *a bringing in :* adulescentulorum, Cic. Ep.

intro-eō, īre, iī, itum, *to go within, enter.* **A.** T r a n s. : domum, Pl., Cic. ; castra,

Sall. ; urbem, curiam, Suet. *Impers.*
Pass. : Syracusas introitum erat, Liv. ;
Cato ; Sall. **B.** Intrans. **1.** Lit. : Ter. ;
porta, Cic. ; in alienam domum, Pl. ; in
urbem, Cic. Ep., Liv. ; in domum, Cic. Ep. ;
ad aliquem, Ter., Cic. **2.** Transf. *to be
born* (opp. exire de vita) : Cic.

intrŏ-fĕrŏ, ferre, tuli, lātum, *to carry within* :
lectica in urbem introferri, Cic. ; Liv.

intrŏ-grĕdĭor, grĕdī, grĕssus, *to step within* :
Verg.

introĭtus, ūs, *m.* [introĕŏ], *an entering, entrance.* **1.** Lit. : primo introitu, Tac. ;
militum, Caes. ; navium in portum, Caes. ;
introitus Zmyrnam, Cic. ; in urbem, Cic.
2. Transf. **a.** *a (place of) entrance :*
omnes introitūs erant praeclusi, Caes. ;
Cic. ; Suet. **b.** Into a society, office, etc. :
certum aliquid pro introitu dare, Plin. Ep. ;
sacerdoti, Suet. **c.** *a beginning, prelude :*
defensionis, Cic.

intrŏlātus, a, um, *Part.* introfĕrŏ.

intrŏ-mittŏ, mittere, misi, missum, *to let
pass within, to admit within :* legiones (sc.
in oppidum), Caes. ; sex milia peditum
Nolam, Liv. ; ad Senecam aliquem, Tac.

intrŏrsum and **intrŏrsus**, *adv.* (contr. fr.
intrŏ-versum), *towards the inside, inwards,
into.* **1.** L i t. : Caes., Liv., Tac. **2.** Transf.
inwardly, inside within : Hor., Ov., Liv.

intrŏ-rumpŏ, rumpere, rūpī, ruptum, *to
burst within, force a way in :* Caes.

intrŏ-spectŏ, āre, *to look within :* Pl.

intrŏ-spĭcĭŏ, spicere, spexī, spectum [speciŏ],
to look within or *into.* **A.** Trans. **1.**
Lit. : casas, Cic. **2.** Transf. : ceterorum mentis, Cic. ; fortunam suam, Tac.
B. Intrans. Transf. *to look closely
into :* penitus in omnis rei publicae partis,
Cic.

intŭbum, I, *n. v.* intibum.

in-tŭĕor, tuĕrī, tuitus, *to look, gaze upon* or
towards. **A.** Trans. **1.** Lit. : Ter.,
Cic., Hor., etc. **2.** Transf. **a.** Mentally :
to contemplate, consider : veritatem, Cic. ;
tempestatem impendentem, Cic. ; causas
belli, Tac. **b.** cubiculum montes intuentur, Plin. Ep. **c.** *to look up to* (with
admiration or astonishment) : Cic., Liv.
B. Intrans. **1.** Lit. with *in* and Acc. :
Cic. **2.** Transf. (mentally) : in aliquod
malum, Cic. ; Plin. Pan. ; ad finiendum
bellum, Liv.

in-tŭmēscŏ, tumēscere, tumuī, *to begin to
swell up, rise.* **1.** Lit. : venter, genae,
Ov. **2.** Transf. **a.** *to increase, grow fuller :* vox, motus, Tac. **b.** *to become swollen* or *inflated :* iure potestatis, Quint. ;
superbia ferociaque, Tac. **c.** *to become
angry :* Ov.

in-tŭmŭlātus, a, um, *unburied :* Ov.

in-tŭor, tuī (old form for intueor), Pl., Ter.

in-turbĭdus, a, um, *undisturbed, quiet, calm :*
annus, vir, Tac.

intŭs, *adv.* [in ; *cf.* Gk. ἐντός], *inside.* **1.**
L i t. **a.** *within, at home :* Pl., Cic., Verg.,
etc. With *in* : in corpore, Cic. ; in cella
Fortis Fortunae, Liv. **b.** Of motion :
to the inside, within : Ov., Quint., Tac.
With *in* and Acc. : Lucr. **c.** *from within :*
Pl., Ter., Liv. **2.** Transf. Of character :
te intus et in cute novi, Pers. Prov. :

omnia intus canere (i e. to care for one's
self), Cic.

in-tūtus, a, um. **I.** *unguarded :* castra,
Liv. *Neut. pl.* as Noun : intuta moenium,
Tac. **II.** *unsafe :* latebrae, amicitia,
Tac.

ĭnŭla, ae, *f.* *elecampane,* a plant : Hor. [It.,
Sp. *enula* ; Fr. *aunée.*]

in-ultus, a, um. **I.** *unavenged.* **a.** Of persons : Cic., Verg., Liv., etc. **b.** Of things :
mors, Cic. ; dolores, Ov. ; preces, Hor.
II. *unpunished, with impunity.* **a.** Of persons : Pl., Cic., Ov., etc. **b.** Of things :
ferae, Hor. ; scelus, Sall. ; quidquid multis
pecca ur, inultum est, Luc. ; Ter.

in-umbrŏ, āre [umbra], *to bring shade on,
to shade.* **1.** Lit. : terra inumbratur,
Lucr. ; toros obtentu frondis, Verg. ; Curt.
Quint. **2.** Transf. **a.** inumbrante vesperā, Tac. **b.** *to cover :* ora coronis, Lucr.

inunctus, a, um, *Part.* inungŏ.

ĭnundātĭŏ, ōnis, *f.* [inundŏ], *a flowing upon*
or *over, inundation :* Plin., Suet. In *pl.* :
Suet.

in-undŏ, āre [unda], *to bring water on, to
flood.* **A.** Trans. **1.** Lit. : terram aqua,
Cic. ; Tiberis agros, Liv. ; campis inunda-
tis, Liv. ; sanguine Enna inundabitur, Liv. ;
Ciliciam cruore Persarum, Curt. **2.**
Transf. : multitudo campos, Curt. **B.**
Intrans. **1.** Lit. (of a river, etc.) : *to
overflow :* Liv. With *Instr.* Abl. : sanguine fossae, Verg. **2.** Transf. : densi in-
undant Troes, Verg.

in-ungŏ, ungere, ūnxī, ūnctum, *to anoint :*
Varr., Hor.

inurbānē, *adv.* *rudely, inelegantly, without
wit* or *humour :* Cic., Plin. Ep.

in-urbānus, a, um, *rustic, boorish, unpolished :*
habitus orationis, Cic. ; Hor. ; gestus,
Quint.

in-urgĕŏ, urgēre, ūrsī, *to push* or *thrust at :*
Lucr.

in-ūrŏ, ūrere, ūssī, ūstum, *to burn in* or *on,
to brand.* **1.** Lit. : notas et nomina gentis
(cattle), Verg. ; Curt. **2.** Transf. **a.** *to
brand :* with Acc. and Dat. : nomini notam
turpitudinis, Cic. ; genti maculam, Liv.
b. *to inflict :* mala rei publicae, Cic. ; alicui dolorem, Cic. **c.** Of style : *to crimp*
(like the hair) : aliquid calamistris, Cic.

inūsĭtātē, *adv.* *in an unusual manner :* Cic.
Comp. : Cic.

in-ūsĭtātus, a, um, *strange, unusual, extra-
ordinary :* belli ratio, Caes. ; magnitudo,
Cic. ; inusitatum est (with Acc. and *Inf.*) :
Cic. *Comp. :* Caes.

inūstus, a, um, *Part.* inūrŏ.

in-ūtĭlis, e, *adj.* *useless, unserviceable, unpro-
fitable.* **1.** L i t. **a.** Of persons : Cic., Verg.,
Liv. With *ad :* per aetatem ad pugnam,
Caes. ; ad rem gerendam, Caes. With
Dat. : aetate bello, Caes. ; sibi, Cic. ; rei
publicae, Liv. **b.** Of things : naves ad
navigandum, Caes. ; ferrum, Verg. ; alga,
Hor. ; impedimenta, Liv. **2.** Transf.
harmful, injurious : civis, Cic. ; oratio, Liv.
Comp. : Ov.

in-ūtĭlĭtās, ātis, *f.* **1.** L i t. *uselessness, un-
profitableness :* Lucr. **2.** Transf. *hurtful-
ness :* Cic.

inūtĭlĭter, *adv.* **1.** L i t. *uselessly, unprofit-*

ably : Liv. **2.** Transf. *hurtfully.* *Comp.:*
Varr.

in-vădō, vădere, văsī, văsum. **I.** *to go, come,*
make one's way in. **1.** Lit.: manus
Clodiana, Cic.; ignis quocumque invasit,
Cic. With Acc.: viam, portûs, Verg.;
urbem, Liv.; forum, Tac. **2.** Transf. *to*
enter upon, essay : aliquid magnum, Verg.;
Martem clipeis, Verg.; pugnam sagittis,
Curt. **II.** Of violent or hostile action : *to*
go against, to assail, fall upon, attack, invade.
1. Lit.: in oppidum, Pl.; Cic.; in collum
(mulieris), Cic.; in aliquem, Cic., Liv.; in
transversa latera, Liv.; in Galliam, Cic.
With *Obj.* implied : tria milia stadiorum
(in eum) invadit, Tac. With Acc.: agmen,
Caes.; urbem, medios, Verg.; aciem, castra,
Liv.; greges, Ov. In *Pass. :* Sall.
Impers. Pass. : Sall. **2.** Transf. **a.** *to fall*
upon, take violent possession of, usurp : in
multas pecunias, Cic.; in praedia alicuius,
Cic. With Acc.: imperium, Sall.; ius
praetoris, Tac. **b.** *to assail* (with words) :
Verg.; aliquem (foll. by *Indir. Quest.*),
Tac. **c.** Of disease, emotion, etc.: *to fall*
upon, attack : in genua flemina, Pl.; pestis
in vitam, Cic.; vis morbi in corpus, Liv.
With Acc.: eum morbus, Pl.; cupido
Marium, Sall.; with *Obj.* implied : tantus
repente terror, Caes.; Sall. With DAT.:
furor improbis, Cic. Ep.

in-valēscō, valēscere, valuī, *to become strong,*
grow stronger, more powerful. Transf. **a.**
opibus, Cic., Tac. **b.** consuetudo, Quint.,
Plin. Ep.; amor, Plin. Ep.

in-validus, a, um, *not strong, weak.* **1.**
Lit.: ad munera corporis senectâ invali-
dus, Liv.; Tac.; corpus, Ov.; Verg. **2.**
Transf.: *weak, inefficient, feeble :* stationes pro castris, Liv.; moenia adversus
inrumpentis, Tac.; ignes, Tac.

invāsus, a, um, *Part.* invādō.

invectiō, ōnis, *f.* [invehō]. **1.** Lit. *an im-*
porting of goods, importation : Cic. **2.**
Transf. *invective :* Cic.

invectus, a, um, *Part.* invehō.

in-vehō, vehere, vexī, vectum. **I.** *to carry*
or bring in (by horse, cart, boat, etc.). **1.**
Lit. **a.** In gen.: tantum in aerarium
pecuniae, Cic.; Ov. With DAT.: legiones
Oceano, Tac.; gazam urbi, Suet. **b.** With
Refl. Pron. or in *Mid.* or *Pass.:* *to ride,*
drive, sail in : beluis, Cic.; equo, Verg.,
Ov., Liv.; curru, Verg.; carpento, plaustro, Liv. With *in* and Acc.: in portum,
Cic.; (equites) in dissipatos, Liv. With
Acc.: moenia, undam, Verg.; urbem,
portum, Liv. **2.** Transf.: divitiae avaritiam, Liv.; Cic. **II.** *to carry against ;*
hence, with *Refl. Pron.* or in *Mid. : to ad-*
vance against. **1.** Lit.: Liv., Curt.; in
aciem, Liv.; in cornu, Curt. **2.** Transf.
to attack (with words): in aliquem, Cic.,
Liv., etc.; in eam artem, Quint.

in-vēndibilis, e, *unsaleable :* Pl.

in-veniō, venīre, vēnī, ventum. Lit. *to*
come upon. **1.** Lit. (by accident or by
search): *to find, meet with* (with Acc. of
thing or person): Pl., Caes., Verg., etc.
2. Transf. **a.** *to find out, discover :* ex
captivis (foll. by Acc. and *Inf.*), Caes.;
coniurationem, Cic.; apud auctores (foll.

by Acc. and *Inf.*), Liv. With *Praed.*
Noun : scis, Pamphilam meam inventam
civem ? Ter. **b.** *to find out, invent, devise :*
quandam fallaciam, Ter.; multa divinitus,
Cic.; auspicia, Cic.; artis, Verg.; verba,
Hor. With *Indir. Quest. :* Cic. With
Inf. : Verg. **c.** *to acquire, win :* laudem,
Ter.; cognomen ex aliquâ re, Cic.; fraude
culpam, Cic. **d.** With *Refl. Pron.* or in
Mid. : to find its way, show itself : se dolor,
Ov.; inveniebantur lacrimae, Ov.

inventiō, ōnis, *f.* [inveniō]. **I.** *an inventing,*
invention : Cic., Quint. **II.** *the faculty of*
invention : Cic., Quint.

inventor, ōris, *m.* and **inventrix,** īcis, *f.*
(Cic., Ov.) [inveniō], *a discoverer, author,*
inventor (with GEN.): Ter., Cic., Verg.,
etc.

inventus, a, um. **I.** *Part.* inveniō. **II.**
Noun, **inventum,** I, *n.* *an invention, dis-*
covery : Ter., Ov. In *pl. :* Cic., Quint.

in-venustus, a, um. **I.** *having no sex-*
appeal : Cat. **II.** *without charm, unat-*
tractive : actor, Cic. **III.** *unfavoured by*
Venus : Pl., Ter.

in-verēcundus, a, um, *shameless, immodest :*
Hor., Quint. *Sup. :* Pl.

in-vergō, ere, *to tilt on ;* hence, *to pour over :*
liquores in me, Pl.; fronti vina, Verg.

inversiō, ōnis, *f.* [invertō]. **I.** *transposition*
(of words): Quint. **II.** verborum, i.e.
irony : Cic. **III.** *an allegory :* Quint.

inversus, a, um. **I.** *Part.* invertō. **II.**
Adj. *turned upside down* or *inside out.* **1.**
Lit.: alvei navium, Sall.; vomer, Hor.;
pelles, Juv. **2.** Transf. *perverted :* verba,
Ter., Lucr.; mores, Hor.; consuetudo,
Quint.

in-vertō, vertere, vertī, versum, *to turn upon*
itself, turn upside down or *inside out, to turn*
about, invert. **1.** Lit.: pingue solum
tauri, Verg.; vinaria, Hor.; in locum
anulum, Cic.; nox caelum, Verg.; so,
annus inversus, Hor. **2.** Transf. *to alter*
(esp. for the worse): verba, Cic.; Tac.;
virtutes, Hor.

in-vesperāscit, ere, *evening is coming on :*
Liv.

investigātiō, ōnis, *f.* [investīgō], *a tracking*
out, research : veri, Cic.

investigātor, ōris, *m.* [investīgō], *a tracker,*
investigator : antiquitatis, Cic.

in-vestīgō, āre, *to follow the trail, track out.*
1. Lit.: illam, Pl.; latentis conscios,
Suet. Of hounds : Cic. **2.** Transf. *to*
track out, find out, discover : nihil investigo
quicquam de illâ muliere, Pl.; coniurationem, Cic. With *Indir. Quest. :* Pl., Cic.
Ep. Of a cipher : Suet.

in-veterāscō, veterāscere, veterāvī [invetě-
rātus], *to begin to grow old* (in service). **1.**
Lit.: exercitus in Galliâ, Caes.; equites
bellis, Caes. **2.** Transf. **a.** *to become*
chronic, become established : ulcus alendo,
Lucr.; consuetudo, Caes.; opinio, Cic.;
macula in populi nomine, Cic.; acs alienum, Nep. *Impers.* inveterascit (with *ut*
and *Subj.*): Cic. **b.** *to grow obsolete :*
Cic., Tac.

inveterātiō, ōnis, *f.* [inveterātus], *perma-*
nence (of a disease): Cic.

inveterātus, a, um [vetus], *ingrown by time,*

long established, of long standing : dolor,
malum, etc., Cic. ; licentia, Nep.
in-vicem, adv. [in vicem, i.e. to produce suc-
cession]. **I.** in turn, by turns, one after
another, alternately : Caes., Liv., etc. **II.**
among one another, mutually : Pl., Liv.,
Tac., etc.
in-victus, a, um, unconquered ; hence, in-
vincible. **1.** Lit.: se a labore praestare,
Cic. ; a civibus hostibusque animus, Liv. ;
a cupiditatibus animus, Liv. ; ad vulnera
corpus, Ov. ; adversum gratiam animus,
Tac. ; armis, Cic. ; bello, Verg. **2.**
Transf.: defensio, Cic.
invidēns, entis. **I.** Part. invideō. **II.** As
Noun : an envious person : Cic.
invidentia, ae, f. [invideō], an envious disposition : Cic.
in-videō, vidēre, vīdī, vīsum, to look upon
(with malice), cast an evil eye upon. **1.**
Lit.: Cat. With Acc.: florem liberum
(GEN.), Acc. ; id dei, Liv. **2.** Transf. to
envy, grudge, begrudge. With Acc. of per-
son envied : Pl., Cic., Ov., etc. ; Pass.
Impers.: Pl., Cic. With DAT. of thing envied :
Pl., Cic., Verg., etc. With DAT. of person and
Causal ABL., or in and ABL. : in hoc Crasso,
Cic. ; laude suā mulieribus, Liv. ; nobis
voluptate, Plin. Ep. ; with DAT. of person
implied : sepulturā, Tac. With DAT. of
person and Acc. of what is begrudged :
Verg., Liv., etc. With GEN. of thing :
Hor. Occ. in place of Acc. of thing. **a.**
Inf. : Hor., Luc. **b.** Acc. and Inf. : Pl.,
Hor., Ov. **c.** With ut or ne and Subj. :
Verg.
invidia, ae, f. [invidus]. **A.** Act. envy,
jealousy, ill-will : Cic., Verg., etc. With
Subj. GEN.: Nep., Liv. With Obj. GEN.:
laudis suae, Caes. ; divitiarum, Liv. Phr.:
sine invidiā, Ter., Mart. ; absit verbo invidia (of speaking without presumption),
Liv. **B.** Pass.: envy, odium, unpopu-
larity. **1.** Lit.: in invidiā esse, Cic. ;
lenire, Sall. ; habere, sedare, exstinguere,
Cic. ; conflare, Liv. ; pati, a se removere,
Ov. ; in invidiam adducere, Cic. Ep. ;
cumulare alicui, Suet. In pl. : Cic. **2.**
Transf. a. Personified : Verg., Hor., Ov.
b. a cause of ill-feeling : invidiae esse alicui, Cic. ; invidiae erat amissum praesidium,
Liv.
invidiōsē, adv. spitefully : Cic.
invidiōsus, a, um [invidia]. **A.** Act.:
envious, spiteful : formosis invidiosa Dea
est, Prop. ; vetustas, Ov. ; iocus, Suet.
B. Pass. **a.** In bad sense : envied, hateful,
odious : Cic. **b.** In good sense : envied :
Prop., Ov. **C.** Causative : exciting ill-
feeling, invidious : damnatio, Cic. ;
triumphus ad bonos, Cic. Ep. ; nomina,
Liv. ; continuatio honoris, Liv. ; invidio-
sum vobis est (with Acc. and Inf.), Liv. ;
id Othoni invidiosius, Tac. ; Ov. Subj. :
Cic.
invidus, a, um [invideō], envious, grudging,
jealous. **1.** Lit. (of persons) : Cic., Hor.,
Ov. With DAT. of person : aegris, Hor.
With GEN. of thing envied : laudis, Cic. As
Noun : Ter., Cic., Tac. **2.** Transf. (of
things) : nox coeptis invida nostris, Ov. ;
cura, dens, Hor.

in-vigilō, āre, to be awake over or on account
of (with DAT.). **1.** Lit.: rei publicae,
Cic. ; malis, Ov. **2.** Transf. to be watchful for, be intent upon : aliae victu (DAT.),
Verg. With pro : nostris pro casibus, Ov.
in-violābilis, e, adj. **I.** indestructible, in-
vulnerable : Lucr., Tac. **II.** inviolable :
pacis pignus, Verg. ; perfugium, Tac.
inviolātē, adv. inviolately : Cic.
in-violātus, a, um. **I.** unhurt, inviolate :
corpus, amicitia, Cic. **II.** inviolable : nomen,
Caes. ; tribunus plebis, Liv. ; fides, Sall.
in-visitātus, a, um. **I.** rarely seen : Galli
antea alienigenis, Liv. **II.** not seen before,
unfamiliar, strange : forma, Cic., Liv. ;
acies, Liv. ; avis invisitatā specie, Tac.
in-vīsō, vīsere, vīsī, vīsum. **I.** to go to see,
to visit : aliquem, Cic. Ep. ; ad me domum,
Pl. ; eum locum, Cic. ; domos castas, Cat. ;
Delum, Verg. **II.** to look after or into, to
inspect : res rusticas, Cic. ; urbes, Verg.
III. to look upon, descry : collis, Cat.
(1) invīsus, a, um. **I.** Part. invideō. **II.**
Adj. **A.** Pass.: hateful, detested, loathed,
odious : of persons or things : Ter., Cic.,
Verg., etc. With DAT. of person : Pl., Cic.,
Verg., etc. Comp. : Cic. Sup. : Plin. Ep.
B. Act. hostile, malicious : Verg., Luc.
(2) in-vīsus, a, um, unseen : maribus sacra,
Cic.
invītāmentum, ī, n. [invītō], an allurement,
attraction, inducement. With Subj. GEN.:
urbis et fori, Cic. With Obj. GEN. : temeritatis, Liv. With ad : ad luxuriam, Cic.
invītātiō, ōnis, f. [invītō]. **1.** Lit. an invitation : in Epirum, Cic. Ep. **b.** entertainment : hospitum liberalis, Cic. ; Liv.
2. Transf.: ad dolendum, Cic. With ut
and Subj. : Cic.
invītātū, ABL. sing. m. [invītō], by invitation :
tuo, Cic. Ep.
invītē, adv. against one's will, unwillingly :
Cic. Ep. Comp. : Cic.
invītō, āre (Aor. Subj. invītāssitis, Pl.), to
invite as a guest. **1.** Lit. **a.** aliquem ad
prandium, Cic. ; ad consulem, Liv. ; in
hospitium, Liv. ; domum suam, Cic. ; Liv.
With ut and Subj. : Cic. Ep. **b.** to entertain hospitably : Caes. ; aliquem tecto ac
domo, Cic. ; hospitaliter per domos, Liv. ;
aliquem epulis, Liv. ; liberaliter, Cic. ;
comiter, Liv. With Refl. Pron. : to treat or
regale oneself : sese in cenā plusculum, Pl. ;
se cibo, Sall. **2.** Transf. a. to invite,
summon : aliquem in legationem, Cic. Ep. ;
in deditionem, Hirt. ; ad audiendum,
Suet. **b.** to invite, attract, induce : in
vitatus praedā, Caes. ; praemiis, Cic. ;
somnos, Hor. ; hiems invitat, Verg. ; ad
agrum fruendum senectus, Cic. With ut
and Subj. : Pl., Caes. With Inf. : Verg.
invītus, a, um [fr. root seen in vīs, 2nd pers.
sing. of volō], against one's will, unwilling,
reluctant. **1.** Lit.: invitus me vides, Pl. ;
uti viatores etiam invitos consistere cogant,
Caes. ; invitus feci, Cic. ; Ov. Sup. : Cic.
Ep. Esp. freq. in ABL. Absol. : si se invito
transire conarentur, Caes. ; Cic. ; Verg.
Prov.: invitā Minervā (i.e. contrary to the
bent of one's genius), Cic., Hor. **2.**
Transf. (of things) : oratio, Cic. ; verba,
Hor. ; terra, Verg. ; ignes, Ov.

invius, a, um [via], *without a road, pathless, trackless, impassable.* **1.** Lit.: via, saxa, regna, lustra, saltus, Liv.; with DAT. of pers.; maria Teucris, Verg. *Neut. pl.* as Noun, *pathless places :* Liv. **2.** Transf.: nil virtuti invium, Tac.; Ov.

invocātiō, ōnis, *f. a calling upon, invocation :* deorum, Quint.

(1) **invocātus**, a, um, *Part.* invocō.

(2) **in-vocātus**, a, um, *unbidden, unsummoned.* **a.** In gen.: of persons : Cic. Ep.; of things : imagines rerum, Cic. **b.** As a guest : Pl., Ter., Nep.

in-vocō, āre. **I.** *to call in, summon to one, invoke.* **1.** Lit. (for aid) : deos, Pl., Liv., Tac.; Lucinam, Cic. With *Subj. :* Tac. **2.** Transf. *to appeal to :* leges, Tac.; fidem militum, Tac.; auxilia libertati, Tac. **II.** *to call, name, style :* aliquem mitissimum dominum, Curt.

involātū, ABL. *sing. m. from the flight* (of a bird) : Cic.

in-volgō, *v.* invulgō.

in-volitō, āre, *to float upon :* (comae) umeris, Hor.

in-volō, āre, *to fly, swoop, pounce upon.* **A.** Intrans. **1.** Lit.: equites ab dexterā, Pl.; in capillum, Ter.; in villam columbae, Varr. **2.** Transf.: in possessionem, Cic. **B.** Trans. **1.** Lit.: pallium, Cat.; castra, Tac. **2.** Transf.: animos cupido, Tac.

involūcre, is, *n.* [involvō], *a* (barber's) *wrap :* Pl.

involūcrum, ī, *n.* [involvō], *a wrap, covering.* **1.** Lit.: candelabri, clipei, Cic. **2.** Transf.: simulationum, Cic. Ep.

involūtus, a, um. **I.** *Part.* involvō. **II.** Adj.: *involved, complicated :* res, Cic. *Sup. :* Sen.

in-volvō, volvere, volvī, volūtum. **I.** *to roll in ;* hence, *to wrap up, envelop.* **1.** Lit.: caput, Cic.; se foliis, Lucr.; sinistras sagis, Caes.; involvi fumo, Ov.; nemus flammis, Verg.; Tac. **2.** Transf.: se litteris, Cic. Ep.; pacis nomine bellum, Cic.; obscuris vera, Verg.; se suā virtute, Hor.; aliquem fraudibus, Tac. **II.** *to roll on :* Ossae Olympum, Verg.; in caput, Verg.

involvolus, ī, *m.* [involvō], *a worm or caterpillar that wraps itself up in leaves :* Pl.

in-vulgō, āre [vulgus], *to give public information :* Cic. Ep.

in-vulnerātus, a, um, *unwounded :* Cic.

iŏ, *interj.* [= Gk. ἰώ ; monosyl. or disyl.]. **I.** Expressing joy, *ho! hurrah!* Pl., Tib., Hor., Plin. Ep. **II.** Expressing pain, *oh! ah!* Pl., Tib. **III.** In a sudden call: *hallo! ho there!* Verg., Ov.

Iŏ, ūs and **Iŏn**, ōnis, *f., d. of Inachus, king of Argos ; loved by Jupiter and changed by him into a cow through fear of Juno ; later worshipped as the Egyptian deity Isis.*

Iocasta, ae, and **Iocastē**, ēs, *f., w. of Laius and m. of Oedipus, whom she married unknowingly and by whom she had two sons, Eteocles and Polynices.*

iocin-, *v.* iecur.

iocor, ārī, and **iocō**, āre (Pl.) [iocus], *to jest, joke :* Pl., Ter., Cic.; in valetudinem oculorum, Liv. With *Intern.* ACC.: haec, Cic. Ep.; Cat.; Ov.; in faciem permulta iocatus, Hor.

iocōsē, *adv. jestingly, jocosely !* Ov[?]. Mp[?]. *Comp. :* Cic. Ep., Hor.

iocōsus, a, um [iocus], *full of jest, humorous, sportive.* **a.** Of persons : Varr., Hor., Ov. **b.** Of things : res, Cic.; lis, Ov.; furtum, imago, Ov.

ioculāris, e, *adj.* [ioculor], *laughable, sportive:* audacia, Ter.; ioculare istuc quidem, Cic. *Neut. pl.* as Noun, *jests, jokes :* Hor.; fundere, Liv.

ioculāriter, *adv. jestingly* or *in a comical manner :* Plin., Suet.

ioculārius, a, um [ioculus], *ludicrous, droll :* malum, Ter. [It. *giocolario.*]

ioculātor, ōris, *m.* [ioculor], *a jester, joker :* Cic. Ep. [It. *giocolatore.*]

ioculor, ārī [ioculus], *to jest, joke :* incondita quaedam, Liv.

ioculus, ī, *m.* [*dim.* iocus], *a little joke :* ioculo dicere aliquid, Pl.

iocus, ī, *m.* (in *pl.* **ioci**, *m.* and **ioca**, ōrum, *n.*), *a jest, joke.* **1.** Lit.: ioca atque seria cum aliquo agere, Sall.; seria ac iocos celebrare, Liv.; agitare iocos cum aliquo, Ov.; movere alicui iocum, Hor.; ioci causā, Cic.; ioco seriove, Liv.; extra iocum, remoto ioco (*joking apart*), Cic.; per iocum (*by way of joke, in jest*), Pl. **2.** Transf. **a.** Personified : Pl., Hor. **b.** *ludus et iocus, mere sport, child's play :* Liv. [It. *giuoco ;* Fr. *jeu.*]

Iolāus, ī, *m. s. of Iphiclus, and constant companion of his uncle Hercules.*

Iolē, ēs, *f. d. of Eurytus king of Oechalia ; married by Hercules to his son Hyllus after the destruction of Oechalia.*

Iŏnes, um, *m. pl. the Ionians, who inhabited a district on the W. coast of Asia Minor, having come there originally from Greece ;* **Iŏnia**, ae, *f. their country ;* **Iŏnius**, a, um, *Ionian ;* **Iŏnium**, ī, *n.* (*sc. mare*), *the sea to the West of Greece ;* **Iŏnicus**, a, um, *Ionian ;* **Iŏnica**, ōrum, *n. pl. the Ionic dance ;* **Iŏnicus**, ī, *m. an Ionic dancer ;* **Iŏnis**, idis, *f. an Ionian woman.*

iōta, *n. indecl.*, the name of the Greek letter ι (ἰῶτα) : Cic.

Iphianassa (for Iphigenia, q.v.) : Lucr.

Iphigenia, ae, (ACC. -īan, Ov.) *f. d. of Agamemnon and Clytemnestra ; she was to have been offered up in sacrifice at Aulis for the expiation of her father's guilt in killing a deer belonging to Diana, but was saved by the goddess, who conveyed her to the Tauric Chersonese, where she became priestess of Diana.*

Iphitus, ī, *m. s. of Eurytus and Antiope, one of the Argonauts ;* **Iphitidēs**, ae, *m. his son Coeranos.*

ipse (**ipsus**, Pl., Cato), ipsa (eapse, Pl.), ipsum [fr. is and -pse in sense of *self* or *own*] (ACC. and ABL. *m.* eumpse, eōpse, Pl.), *pron.* (used of all three persons with other *Pron.* and *Nouns* to distinguish emphatically that to which it is applied). **I.** In gen.: *self, very, mere, in person, for one's own part, on one's own initiative, unaided, etc.* **a.** With *Pron.* or alone : ego ipse cum eodem ipso non invitus erraverim, Cic.; agam per me ipse, Cic.; me ipse consolor, Cic.; tute ipse praescripsti, Ter.; lepide ipsi hi sunt capti, Pl.; eaque ipsa belli causa fuit,

Liv. ; Priscus se ipso interfecit, Tac. ; fratrem suum, dein se ipsum interfecit, Tac. With *et* : is, et ipse Alpinus amnis, Liv. ; qui et ipse crus effregerat, Suet. Also with *nec* : Liv. ; exurere classem Argivum atque ipsos potuit submergere ponto (i.e. the men, as dist. fr. the ships), Verg. In *Orat. Obliq.* ipse is used freq. of the subject of the verb of saying, to dist. him from a different subject in a subordinate clause : Caesar milites incusavit ; cur de suâ virtute aut de ipsius (i.e. Caesaris), diligentiâ desperarent ? Caes. **b.** With Noun : adest optume ipse frater, Ter. ; noctis vigilabat ad ipsum mane, Hor. ; valvae se ipsae aperuerunt, Cic. ; ipsae domum referent capellae ubera, Verg. ; ipso aevo, Verg. **II.** To define precisely number, time, or place : *just, exactly :* triginta dies ipsi, Cic. ; in tempore ipso advenis, Ter. ; Praeneste sub ipsa, Verg. With *adv.* : nunc ipsum, Cic. **III.** Of the master or mistress of the house : ego eo, quo me ipsa misit, Pl. ; Ter. Also of the head of a school of philosophy, etc., *the master* : ipse dixit, Cic. **IV.** Strengthened with -met : Pl., Cic. *Sup.* ipsissimus, *his own very self* : Pl.

ipsus, *v.* ipse.

ira (eira, Pl.**),** ae, *f. anger, wrath, frenzied impulse (cf.* iracundia). **1.** L i t. : facere aliquid per iram, Cic. ; acuere, attollere, Sall. ; ponere, Hor. ; irae moderari, Hor. ; irae indulgere, Liv. ; iram frangere, lenire, Quint. ; irâ commotus, Sall. ; ira defervescit, Cic. ; deflagrat, Liv. ; decedit, Ter. In *pl.* : iras excitare, exercere, Verg. ; gerere, Pl. ; mollire, Liv. With *Inf.* : Verg. With *Obj.* G E N. *(on account of)* : ereptae virginis irâ, Verg. ; ira interfecti domini, Liv. With *Prep.* : in *or* adversus Romanos, Liv. **2.** T r a n s f. **a.** Personified : in *pl.* : Verg. **b.** *an object or cause of wrath* : alicui esse irae, Verg. ; quae te mutaverit ira, Ov.

irācundē, *adv. passionately* : Cic. *Comp.* : Cic.

irācundia, ae, *f.* [īrācundus]. **I.** *a passionate nature, irascibility, hastiness of temper* : Cic., Suet. **II.** *a state of anger, wrath, rage, a feeling of resentment* : prae iracundiâ vix sum apud me, Ter. ; reprimere, omittere, Ter. ; remittere, Cic. ; suam rei publicae dimittere, Caes. ; iracundiâ ardere, Ter. ; iracundiâ efferri, inflammari, exardescere, Cic.

irācundus, a, um [īra], *irascible, passionate, choleric (denoting a disposition).* **1.** L i t. **a.** mens, Lucr. ; senes, Cic. ; leones, Ov. *Comp.* : Hor. *Sup.* : Sen. **b.** *nursing anger, resentful* : in aliquem, Cic. **2.** T r a n s f. : victoria, Cic. ; fulmina, Hor.

irāscor, ī [īra], *to grow angry* : Pl., Cic., Verg., etc. With DAT. (of person or thing) : Pl., Cic., Ov., etc. P o e t. : taurus irasci in cornua temptat. *to throw his rage into his horns,* Verg.

irātē, *adv. angrily* : Phaedr.

irātus, a, um. **I.** Used as *Part.* of irāscor. **II.** A d j. : *enraged, angry.* **1.** L i t. (of persons) : de iudicio, Cic. With DAT. of person : Pl., Cic., Ov. *Comp.* and *Sup.* :

Cic. **2.** T r a n s f. (of things) : mare, venter, preces (i.e. *imprecations*), Hor. ; sitis, Prop.

Iris, idis, *f.* (ACC. Īrim, Verg.), *d. of Thaumas and Electra ; the swift-footed messenger of the gods.*

irōnia, ae, *f.* [εἰρωνεία], *irony* : Cic.

ir-r-, *v.* in-r-.

Irus, ī, *m.* (ACC. -on, Ov.), *the name of a beggar in the house of Ulysses in Ithaca.*

is, ea, id (in Old Lat. ACC. *sing.* m. im ; DAT. *sing.* ēī for later eī ; DAT. and ABL. *pl.* ībus ; also *fem.* eābus) ; NOM. *pl.* m. iī in Ciceronian Latin ; DAT. and ABL. *pl.* iīs), *determ. pron.* (prop. used only with reference to something in the context, *the one, the said, the same, the aforesaid,* but it becomes *descriptive, v.* infra). **I.** In gen. **A.** For the 3rd *Person* : *he, she, it, they* ; and in GEN. *his, her, its, their* : venit mihi obviam tuus puer : is mihi litteras abs te reddidit, Cic. Ep. ; Myris ab eâ (i.e. Glycerio) egreditur, Ter. ; flumen est Arar ; id Helvetii transibant, Caes. ; eius consilio cognito, Caes. **B.** With a *Noun* : *this* or *that* : is locus, ea res, id flumen, Caes. **C.** With a *Relat.* **a.** Determinative : *the one who, the thing which* (put either before or after the Relat. clause ; the verb in the Relat. clause is in *Indic.*). Of *first* pers. : haec omnia is feci, qui sodalis Dolabellae eram, Cic. Ep. Of *third* pers. : ea quae ad effeminandos animos pertinent, Caes. ; eâ legione quam secum habebat, Caes. When *is* would be in the same case as the rel. it is us. omitted : partem tertiam incolunt qui . . . Celtae appellantur (i.e. ii qui), Caes. But when the rel. clause comes first, *is* is usually the first word after it, for the sake of clearness : quod virtute effici debet, id temptatur pecuniâ, Cic. **b.** Descriptive : *a person who, a thing which, such a one as* (the verb in the Relat. clause is in *Subj.*) : is sum qui istos plausūs semper contempserim, Cic. ; neque enim tu is es qui nescias, etc., Cic. Ep. ; also with *ut* and *Subj.* : is eram natus ut potuerim etc., Liv. **II.** In partic. **A.** With et, -que, nec : *and that too* (*not*), (when something striking is added) : merces nec ea parva, Cic. ; unâ legione eâque vacillante, Cic. **B.** With *quidem . . . sed : no doubt that was . . . but* : tuus dolor humanus is quidem sed etc., Cic. Ep. **C.** In agreement with Noun, instead of in GEN. defining it : neque servus quisquam ad quem ea suspicio pertineret, Cic. ; quae pars maior erit, eo stabitur consilio, Liv. **D.** Special uses of the *Neuter.* **a.** With *quod* (in appos. to a sentence or clause) : *a thing which, what* : si, id quod facile factu fuit, vi armisque superassem Cic. **b.** P h r. : ad id, *for that purpose or besides,* in id, *to that end,* Liv. ; id ad locorum, *hitherto, till now,* Liv. ; id aetatis, *at that age,* Cic. ; id, *therefore, on that account* : id ego gaudeo, doleo, etc., Cic. (this *Intern.* Acc. is often found with verbs which do not us. admit the ACC. of a Noun. *cf.* hoc, illud, etc.) ; in eo est, *it is gone so far* : cum iam in eo esset, ut in muros evaderet miles, Liv. ; in eo est, also means, *it consists in that, depends upon that* : totum in eo est, tectorium ut sit concinnum, Cic.; ex eō, *from that time*, Verg.; also, *from that, hence :* Cic.; cum eo ut etc., *with the condition that, etc.*, Liv. *v.* also eō and eā.

Isaeus, I, *m.* **I.** *a Greek orator, teacher of Demosthenes.* **II.** *a Greek orator, a contemporary of the younger Pliny.*

Ischomachē ēs, *f.* also called Hippodamia ; *at her wedding with Pirithous the conflict arose between the Lapithae and the Centaurs.*

Isis, is, and idis, *f.* (Acc. -in, Ov.) an Egyptian goddess (*v.* Io) ; **Isiacus**, a, um.

Ismarius, a, um, *of Mt. Ismarus in Thrace* ; hence, T*hracian :* Ov.

Isocratēs, is, *m.* a famous orator and teacher of rhetoric at Athens (ob. B.C. 338) ; **Isocratēus** (or **- īus**), a, um.

istāc, *adv.* [Abl. *fem.* of iste, with demonstr. -ce], *by that way :* Pl., Ter.

istāc-tenus, *adv. thus far :* Pl.

istaec, *v.* istic.

iste, a, ud (Gen. istīus ; poet. occ. istīus, Verg. ; old Gen. istī. Pl. ; Locat. istī, Verg. ; Dat. *f.* istae, Pl.), *demonstr. pron.* or *adj.* [is and -te seen in tūte], *this* or *that of yours, that near you.* **I.** In gen. : quae est ista praetura ? Cic. ; de istis rebus exspecto tuas litteras, Cic. Ep. ; adventu tuo ista subsellia vacuefacta sunt, Cic. **II.** In partic. **a.** *iste,* in a forensic speech, often means ' *your client* ' as opp. to *hic,* ' *my client* ' ; hence, either *prosecutor* or *defendant :* Cic. So also in disputations : tuus iste Stoicus sapiens, Cic. **b.** Though contempt is not contained in the actual meaning of *iste,* it is often implied by the context : animi est ista mollitia, non virtus, Caes. ; non erit ista amicitia, sed mercatura, Cic. ; de istis qui etc., Cic. **c.** With other *Pron.* : scio ista haec facta, Pl. ; istius ipsius in dicendo facultatis, Cic. **d.** *such, of such a kind :* homines istā auctoritate praediti, quā vos estis, Cic. **e.** Locat. **istī**, *there with you :* Pl., Verg.

Isthmus or **-os**, I, *m.* the *Isthmus of Corinth* ; **Isthmus**, a, um ; **Isthmia**, iōrum, *n. pl.* the *Isthmian games, held there every fifth year.*

istic, aec, oc and uc, *demonstr. pron.* or *pronom. adj.* [iste with the suffix -ce], *this* or *that of yours* : isne istic fuit, quem vendidisti ? Pl. ; quae istaec fabula est ? Pl. ; malum istoc, Pl. ; istuc est sapere, Ter. ; istaec loca, Cic. Ep. ; istuc considerabo, Cic. In form **isticine** in questions : istucine interminata sum hinc abiens tibi ? Ter.

istic, *adv.* [istī, Locat. of iste, with demonstr. suffix -ce], *there, in the place where you are.* **1.** Lit. : Pl., Cic. Ep., Liv. **2.** Transf. *therein, in that affair, on that occasion :* neque istic, neque alibi, Ter. ; istic sum, *I am with you, am attending,* Ter., Cic.

istim, *adv.* [iste ; *cf.* illim fr. ille], *from the place where you are :* Enn.

istimodi, *v.* istiusmodi.

istinc, *adv.* [istim with the suffix -ce], *from the place where you are, thence.* **1.** Lit. : Pl., Cic. Ep., Verg. **2.** Transf. **a.** istinc abstulit aetas, Hor. **b.** *thereof, of that thing :* memento dimidium istinc mihi de praedā dare, Pl.

istius-modi or **istimodi** (also separately **istius modi**, **isti modi**, Pl.), *of that kind, such :* istius modi amicos, Pl. ; istius modi ratio, Cic.

istō, *adv.* [*cf.* quō, eō], *to the place where you are.* **1.** Lit. : Pl., Cic. Ep. **2.** Transf. **a.** *thereto, into that thing :* Trebatium meum quod isto admisceas, nihil est, Cic. Ep. **b.** *therefore :* isto tu pauper es, Pl.

istōc, *adv.* [istō and suffix -ce], *thither :* accede illuc : nimium istoc abisti, Ter. [*v.* istūc.]

istōrsum, *adv.* [istō vorsum], *thitherwards :* Ter.

istūc, *adv.* [istō with the suffix -ce], *to the place where you are.* **1.** Lit. : Pl., Cic. Ep., Ov., etc. **2.** Transf. *thither, i.e. to that matter :* post istuc veniam, Ter.

istucine, *v.* istic.

ita, *adv.* [is], *in this* or *that manner, so, thus :* (it differs from *sic* as *is* differs from *hic*). **I.** Ref. to preceding context. **a.** In gen. : ita se res habet, Cic. ; quae cum ita sint, Cic. ; et hercule ita fecit, Cic. **b.** In questions (esp. in tone of surprise or ridicule) : (*really*) *so :* itan' credis ? Ter. ; itane est ? itane censes ? quid ita ? Cic. **c.** In answers : *yes, just so :* Menaechmum, opinor, te vocari dixeras ? *Men.* ita vero, Pl. ; Cic. **d.** In oaths, wishes, solemn assertions : *so :* ita ille faxit Iuppiter, Pl. ; ita me di ament, Ter. ; ita vivam, Cic. **e.** Stating a natural sequel : *thus, in these circumstances, consequently :* ita in Tiberim desilit, Liv. ; Cic. **f.** Of degree (mostly ellipt. esp. after negat.) : *so, thus, such a degree ;* (*not*) *so very,* (*not*) *particularly :* ita sunt omnia debilitata, Cic. Ep. ; non ita antiqua, Cic. ; haud ita multum frumenti, Liv. **II.** Ref. to what follows (either in order of words or logically). **a.** With a foll. non-dependent clause : *as follows :* haec ita digerunt, Cic. **b.** With a *depend.* clause in Acc. and *Inf.* : ita constitui : fortiter esse agendum, Cic. ; Liv. **c.** With a *comparative* clause : with *ut* (in the order ita . . . ut, or ut . . . ita), *quo modo, quem ad modum, so . . . as, just as ;* with *quasi, tamquam, just as if, just as though :* est, iudices, ita ut dicitur, Cic. ; faciam ita, ut vis, Pl. ; ut (Hercules) Eurysthei filios, ita suos configebat sagittis, Cic. ; ut quisque optime Graece sciret, ita esse nequissimum, Cic. ; castra incuriose ita posita tamquam procul abesset hostis, Liv. ; ut . . . ita may sometimes be translated, *although — yet :* ut a proeliis quietem habuerant, ita non nocte, non die unquam cessaverant ab opere, Liv. **d.** With a *consecutive* clause : *so* or *in such a way that :* ita se de populo meritos esse ut etc., Caes. ; inclusum in curiā senatum habuerunt ita multos dies ut interierint nonnulli fame, Cic. Ep. **e.** With a *limiting consecutive* clause. **i.** In sense of *thus far and no farther ; so, only so far :* sed ita triumpharunt, ut ille pulsus superaque regnaret, Cic. With *ut non,* it expresses avoidance, and the words can be translated *without :* ingenium eius ita laudo ut non pertimescam (*without being in awe of it*), Cic. **ii.** *on this one condition, on this understanding :* pacis ita aliqua spes est, si eam vos ut victi audiatis, Liv. ; non ita creditum, Hor. **f.** With a *purpose-clause* : librum peto a te ita corrigas ne mihi noceat, Cic. Ep.

Itali, ōrum, *m. pl.* (GEN. *pl.* Italum, Verg.), *the Italians ;* **Italia,** ae, *f. their country ;* **Italus, Italius, Italicus,** a. um ; **Italis,** idis, *f. adj.* ; **Italides,** um, *f. pl. Italian women :* Verg.

ita-que, *conj.* **I.** *and so, and thus ;* ita constitui, fortiter esse agendum, itaque feci, Cic. ; itaque rem suscipit et a Sequanis impetrat, Caes. **II.** In logical sense : *accordingly, therefore :* Cic., Hor., Liv. With ergo : itaque ergo perpaucis effugium patuit, Liv.

item, *adv.* [root of is and emphatic -em], *likewise, also.* **a.** Alone : Pl., Cic., Liv. **b.** In comparisons : item ut . . . sic, Cic. ; ut . . . sic item, Caes. ; item . . . quem ad modum, Caes. ; item . . . quasi, Liv. **c.** Like iterum, *again, a second time :* item . . . tertio, Varr. ; semel . . . item, Suet.

iter, itineris, *n.* (NOM. itiner, Pl. ; ABL. itere, Lucr.) [root of eō], *a going, a walk, way.* **1.** Lit. esp. in phr. in itinere, ex itinere, *on the way, en route :* ex itinere oppugnare conatus, Caes. ; ex itinere missa est epistula, Cic. ; Sall. ; ut in itinere copia frumenti suppeteret, Caes. ; in ipso itinere configere, Liv. ; iter habere, Pl., Cic. Ep. ; contendere iter, Cic. ; maturare, Caes. ; intendere, Liv. ; continuare die ac nocte, Caes. ; urgere, Ov. ; properare, Tac. ; aliquem itinere prohibere, Caes. **2.** Transf. **a.** *a journey, march :* facere, Caes., Cic., Liv. ; conficere, Liv. ; supprimere, Caes. ; flectere, peragere, Verg.; instituere, rumpere, Hor. ; convertere in aliquem locum, Caes. ; retro vertere, Liv. **b.** As a measure : *the distance travelled, a journey, a march :* iustum iter diei, Caes. ; magnis itineribus (*by forced marches*), Caes. **c.** *a route, way, road :* itineribus deviis proficisci in provinciam, Cic. ; erant omnino itinera duo, quibus itineribus domo exire possent, Caes. ; iter pedestre, Caes., Liv. ; terrestre, Liv., Tac. ; itineribus turbâ refertis, Liv. ; per medium mare, Verg. **d.** *a right of way :* alicui dare, Caes. ; sumere, Cic. **e.** Of any *passage :* vocis, Verg. **f.** *a way, course, method, path :* gloriae, Cic. ; honorum adipiscendorum, Cic. ; salutis, Verg. ; ad laudem, Cic., Plin. Ep.

iterātiō, ōnis, *f.* [iterō], *a repeating, repetition :* Cic., Quint. In *pl. :* Cic.

iterō, āre [iterum], *to do a second time, to renew.* **A.** In gen. : pugnam, Liv. ; ortûs (of the sun), Ov. ; cursûs relictos, aequor, Hor. ; tumulum, Tac. **B.** In partic. **a.** Of words : *to repeat :* Pl., Cic., Liv. Poet. : *to tell (again)* in poetry : Hor. **b.** *to plough again :* Cic.

iterum, *adv.* [fr. a comparat. formed fr. root of is], *a second time, anew.* **1.** Lit. : Pl., Cic., Hor., etc. ; primo (semel, Liv.) . . . iterum, Cic., Liv. ; aliquo consule iterum, Cic., Liv. **2.** Transf. *repeatedly :* in phr. iterum atque iterum, Verg., Hor.

Ithaca, ae (**Ithacē,** ēs). *f. an island in the Ionian Sea, kingdom of Ulysses ;* **Ithacēn-**

sis, e. adj. ; **Ithacus,** a. um : **Ithacus,** i, *m. Ulysses.*

itidem, *adv.* [ita and -dem, *cf.* idem], *in the same way, just (as), likewise :* Pl., Cic. With quasi : Pl. With ut (as) : Pl., Ter.

itiner, *v.* iter.

itiō, ōnis, *f.* [root of eō], *a going, walking, travelling :* Ter., Cic.

itō, āre [*freq.* eō]. *to go :* Ter., Cic. Ep.

itus, ûs, *m.* [eō], *a going.* **a.** *movement, tread :* Lucr. **b.** *going away, departure* (us. with reditus) : Cic. Ep., Suet.

Itylus, i, *m. s. of Zethus.*

Itys, yos, *m.* (ACC. -ym or -yn). **I.** *s. of Tereus and Procne :* he was killed by his mother and served up to his father for food, whereupon he was changed into a pheasant. **II.** *a Trojan* in Verg.

iuba, ae, *f. the (waving) mane of animals.* **1.** Lit. : equi, Caes., Cic., Verg. **2.** Transf. **a.** *the crest* or *plume of a helmet :* Verg. **b.** *the crest of a serpent :* Verg. **c.** *the beard* of mullets : Juv.

iubar, aris, *n.* [fr. root of iuba], *the radiance* (of heavenly bodies), *splendour, brightness.* **1.** Lit. : Ov. **2.** Transf. **a.** Of the sun itself, etc. : Lucr., Verg., Ov. **b.** Of the Emperor Domitian : fundens ab ore iubar, Mart.

iubātus, a. um [iuba], *crested :* anguis, Pl., Liv.

iubeō, iubēre, iûssī, iûssum (iûssō, *Fut. Indic.,* orig. *Aor. Subj.,* Verg. ; old *Perf. iousī* or *iûsī* ; iûstī for iûssistī, Ter. ; iûsse for iûssisse, Ter.) [fr. root seen in iuba and Gk. ὑσμίνη ; Lit. *to excite, arouse*], *to order bid, tell.* **I.** In gen. : Pl., Ter., Ov. Constr. us. with *Inf.,* or Acc. (of person ordered) and *Inf. :* lex recte facere iubet, Cic. ; eos suum adventum expectare iussit, Caes. ; Ter., Liv., etc. In *Pass. :* consules iubentur scribere exercitum, Liv. ; Caes. With *ut* or *ne* and *Subj. :* Pl., Cic., Hor., Liv., etc. With *Subj.* (without *ut*) : Ter., Ov., Liv. With Acc. of *thing ordered :* caedem fratris, Tac. ; Cic. Ep. With Acc. of thing and DAT. of pers. (like impero : q.v.) : *to impose :* tributum iis Drusus iusserat modicum, Tac. With Acc. of thing and *Pass. Inf. :* in *Pass. :* locus lautiaque legatis praeberi iussa, Liv. **II.** In partic. **a.** In sending greetings ; salvere iubere, *to bid one be safe and sound :* Cic. Ep. ; with salvere understood : iubeo Chremetem, Ter. **b.** Polit. *to ratify, approve :* senatus censuit populusque iussit, Cic. ; populus iussit de bello, Liv. ; legem populus R. iussit de civitate tribuendâ, Cic. ; ei provinciam Numidiam populus iussit, Sall. With *ut* or *ne* and *Subj.* : Cic., Liv. Freq. with *velle* in the formula velitis iubeatis (and *Oblique* vellent iuberent), Cic., Liv. ; Philippo regi bellum indici, Liv. ; with sciscō, dēcernō : Sall.

iūcundē, *adv. agreeably, pleasantly :* Cic., Suet. *Comp. and Sup. :* Cic.

iūcunditās, ātis, *f.* [iūcundus], *agreeableness, pleasantness, delight, enjoyment :* vitae, Cic. ; in homine, Cic. ; dare se iucunditati, Cic. ; iucunditate perfundi, Cic. In *pl. : good offices, favours :* Cic.

iūcundus, a. um [iuvō], *pleasing, agreeable, delightful :* voluntas, Cic. ; comes, Cic. ;

id militibus fuit iucundum, Caes. ; praemia, Hor. ; verba ad audiendum, Cic. *Comp.* : Cic. Ep., Juv. *Sup.* : Pl., Cic.

Iūdaea, ae, *f. the country of the Jews* ; **Iūdaeus, Iūdaicus,** a, um ; **Iūdaeus,** i, *m. a Jew.*

iūdex, icis, *m.f.* [iūs and root of dīcō], *one who hears and decides lawsuits, an arbitrator, umpire, judge.* **1.** L i t. : Cic., Hor. ; alicui iudicem dat (praetor), Cic., Plin. Ep. ; ferre (*to offer, propose*), Cic., Liv. ; dicere (this was done by the defendant), Liv. ; reicere, Cic. ; sedere iudicem in aliquem, Cic. In *pl.* : in public trials the *panel of jurors* presided over by a praetor : apud iudices causam agere, Cic. ; iudices petere, Plin. Ep. **2.** T r a n s f. *a judge, critic* : studiorum, Cic. ; sub iudice lis est, Hor. ; iudice te, Hor. [It. *giudice* ; Fr. *juge.*]

iūdicātiō, ōnis, *f.* [iūdicō]. **1.** L i t. *a judicial investigation* : Cic., Quint. **2.** T r a n s f. *a judgment, opinion* : Cic.

iūdicātum, i, *n.* [iūdicō], *a thing decided* : Cic.

iūdicātus, a, um, *Part.* iūdicō.

iūdicātus, ūs, *m.* [iūdicō], *the office of a judex* : Cic.

iūdiciālis, e, *adj.* [iūdicium], *of the courts of justice, judicial* : ius, Cic. ; annus (the year in which Pompey altered the composition of the panels of jurors), Cic.

iūdiciārius, a, um [iūdicium], *of the courts, judiciary* : lex, Cic., Suet. ; quaestus, Cic.

iūdicium, i, *n.* [iūdex], *a judicial investigation, trial* (esp. respecting *facts*). **1.** L i t. : de probro, Cic. ; inter sicarios (i.e. for murder), Cic. ; iudicium facere, Cic. ; vocare aliquem in iudicium, Cic. ; iudicio quempiam accessere, Cic. ; dare (said of the praetor who appointed the iudices) : in aliquem iudicium ex edicto dare, Cic. ; accipere, suscipere, Cic. **2.** T r a n s f. **A.** Public. **a.** *a court of justice* : Caes., Cic., etc. **b.** *the body of* iudices, *the court* : iudicium sortiri, Cic. **c.** *the sentence or decision of a court* : iudicium senatūs, Caes., Tac. **d.** *the right or power of exercising jurisdiction* : sub ius iudiciumque regis venisse, Liv. **B.** Non-public. **a.** *judgment, decision, opinion* : meum semper iudicium fuit, Cic. ; meo iudicio, Cic. ; de se facere, Caes. ; Cic. ; ex alicuius iudicio, Cic. **b.** *the faculty of judging, judgment, discernment* : studio optimo, iudicio minus firmo praeditus, Cic. ; acre, Lucr. ; subtile, Hor. Esp. *discretion, good judgment, taste or tact* : iudicio aliquid facere, Cic. ; Tac.

iūdicō, āre [iūdex], *to act as* iudex ; *to examine judicially, to judge.* **1.** L i t. a. Cic., Hor., etc. With Acc. : litem, Pl. ; res, causam, Cic. **b.** *to adjudge, decide* (with Acc. of offence and Dat. of person : or with Gen. of offence) : perduellionem Horatio, Liv. ; perduellionis Fulvio, Liv. With Acc. and *Inf.* : Sall. Oftener in *Perf. Part.* **i.** Of persons : *condemned, sentenced* : Pl., Cic., Liv. ; pecuniae, Liv. **ii.** Of things : *adjudicated* : res, Cic. **2.** T r a n s f. **a.** *to judge, form an opinion, be of opinion* : de itinere, Caes. ; sic statuo et iudico, Cic. ; aliquid oculorum fallacissimo sensu, Cic. **b.** With Predic. *Noun or Adj.* : *to declare,*

pronounce : aliquem hostem, Cic. ; Caes. [It. *giudicare* ; Fr. *juger.*]

ingālis, e, *adj.* [iugum], *yoked together.* **1.** Lit. : Curt. As Noun : **ingālēs,** *chariot-horses* : gemini, Verg. **2.** T r a n s f. **a.** *matrimonial, nuptial* : vinclum, Verg. ; dona, Ov. **b.** *fastened to the loom* : Cato.

ingārius vīcus [iugum], ' *yoke-makers' lane* ' off the Roman Forum : Liv.

ingātiō, ōnis, *f.* [iugō], *a binding* (e.g. of a vine) *to rails* : Varr., Cic.

iūgerum, i, *n.* (*pl.* mostly acc. to 3rd decl.) [fr. root of iungō]. Lit. *as much land as one yoke of oxen can plough in a day* ; hence, as a measure of land, about ⅔ of an English acre : Cic., Verg., etc.

iūgis, e, *adj.* [root of iungō], *continual, perennial* (esp. of *water*) : aqua, Sall. ; aquae fons, Hor. ; puteus, Cic. ; thensaurus, Pl.

iūglāns, andis, *f.* [Iovis glāns]. **I.** *a walnut* : Varr. **II.** *a walnut-tree* : Cic.

iugō, āre [iugum], *to couple.* T r a n s f. **a.** Of marriage : cui pater intactam dederat, primisque iugarat ominibus, Verg. **b.** In gen. : virtutes inter se nexae et iugatae sunt, Cic.

ingōsus, a, um [iugum], *mountainous* : silvae, Ov.

ingulae, ārum, *f. pl.* [*dim.* iugum], *Orion's belt* : Pl.

ingulō, āre [iugulum], *to cut the throat of.* **1.** Lit. Of animals or persons : Cic., Verg., Liv. C o m i c. : se fame, Pl. **2.** T r a n s f. : iugulari suo gladio, suoque telo, Ter. ; illum gladio plumbeo iugulatum iri, Cic. Ep. ; aliquem factis decretisque, Cic.

iugulum, i, *n.* and **iugulus,** i, *m.* (Juv.) [iungō], *the throat.* **1.** L i t. : demittere gladium in iugulum, Pl. ; iugulum dare, Cic. ; porrigere, Hor. ; resolvere, Ov. ; offerre, haurire, perfodere, Tac. ; iugulos aperire susurro, Juv. **2.** T r a n s f. (of an argument) : petere, Quint. ; iugulum causae premere, Plin. Ep.

ingum, i, *n.* [fr. root iungō]. **I.** *a yoke, collar for oxen, horses, etc.* **1.** L i t. : Cic., Verg., etc. **2.** T r a n s f. **a.** Of the animals yoked : *a yoke, pair* : of oxen : Cic. ; of horses : Verg. ; of the car itself : Verg., Juv. **b.** *a common bond, union* : ferre iugum pariter dolosi, Hor. ; pari iugo niti, Plin. Ep. **c.** *the yoke or bond of love, wedlock* : ferre iugum, Pl., Hor. ; Venus diductos iugo cogit aeneo, Hor. **d.** *the yoke of slavery or subjection* : a cervicibus iugum servile deiecerant, Cic. ; servitutis iugum depellere, Cic. ; exuere, Tac. ; excutere, Plin. Pan. **II.** *a cross-bar or other connecting link.* **a.** Milit. *the iugum* (consisting of a spear laid crosswise on two upright spears) : sub iugum (Caes., Cic., Liv.) or sub iugo (Liv.) mittere. **b.** *the cross-beam of a pair of scales* ; hence, the constellation Libra : Cic. ; of *a weaver's loom* : Ov. **c.** *a rower's bench* : Verg. **d.** *a ridge connecting two mountains* : Caes., Verg., Liv., etc. P o e t. (in *pl.*) the *heights* : Verg., Ov. [It. *giogo* ; Sp. *yugo* ; Fr. *joug.*]

Iugurtha, ae, *m. king of Numidia, conquered by Marius* , B.C. 106 ; **Iugurthinus** , a, um.

Iūlia, ae, *f.* **I.** *d. of Julius Caesar and w. of Cn. Pompeius.* **II.** *d. of Augustus and w. of Tiberius.*

Iūliānus, ī, *m. the 'Apostate,' Roman emperor*, A.D. 361–363.

Iūlius, a, *the name of a Roman gens, of which the Caesars were the most distinguished family ;* **Iūlius**, a, um ; **Iūlius**, ī, *m.* (*sc.* mensis), *July* (called after Julius Caesar ; earlier called Quinctilis) ; **Iūliānus**, a, um, *belonging to Julius Caesar :* **Iūliāni**, ōrum, *m. pl. Caesar's soldiers in the Civil War.*

Iūlus, ī, *m. s. of Ascanius and g.s. of Aeneas ; supposed ancestor of the gens Iulia ;* **Iūlēus**, u, um, *of Caesar or the family of the Caesars.*

iūmentum, ī, *n.* [fr. root of iungō], *a yoke-beast.* **a.** *a draught-animal* (us. mules) : Cic., Nep. **b.** *a beast of burden, pack-mule, pack-horse* (esp. in armies) : sarcinaria, Caes. ; Liv.

iunceus, a, um [iuncus]. **I.** *made of rushes, rush- :* vincula, Ov. **II.** *like a rush or reed :* puella, *a wisp of a girl*, Ter.

iuncōsus, a, um [iuncus], *full of rushes :* litora, Ov.

iūnctim, *adv. successively :* gerere duos consulatūs, Suet.

iūnctiō, ōnis, *f.* [iungō], *a joining, union :* Cic.

iūnctūra, ae, *f.* [iungō], *a joining.* Transf. **a.** Concr. *a juncture, joint :* genuum, Ov. ; laterum iuncturae (of a girdle), Verg. ; of a building (in *pl.*), Verg. **b.** *relationship :* generis, Ov. **c.** Rhet. : *combination, compounding :* verborum, Hor.

iūnctus, a, um. **I.** *Part.* iungō. **II.** Adj. **1.** Lit. : corpora inter se, Cic. ; equi (i.e. a chariot), Verg. ; ponto iunctior, Ov. **2.** Transf. **a.** By blood : Sup. : Tac. **b.** By friendship : iunctissimus illi comes, Ov. **c.** In gen. : causa cum exitu iunctior, Cic.

iuncus, ī, *m. a rush :* Pl., Ov.

iungō, iungere, iūnxi, iūnctum [*cf.* Gk. ζεύγνυμι], *to couple, bind together.* **I.** *to yoke, harness.* **1.** Lit. : iumenta, Nep. ; iuvencos, equos, leones, currūs, Verg. ; curru equos, Ov. ; raeda equis iuncta, Cic. Ep. ; iuncta vehicula, Liv. **2.** Transf. **a.** *to couple, mate* (in marriage) : aliquam alicui (conubio), Verg., Ov. ; aliquam secum matrimonio, Curt. ; cum pare, Ov. ; cum impari, Liv. Poet. : iuncta ulmus, Ov. **b.** *to bridge* a stream : flumen ponte or ratibus, Liv. Also iungere pontem, Verg., Tac. **c.** Of abstracts : *to mate, unite :* an virtus et voluptas inter se iungi possint, Cic. ; insignis improbitas et scelere iuncta, Cic. **II.** In gen. *to bind together, join, unite.* **1.** Lit. : tigna inter se, Caes. ; Cic. ; fenestras, Hor. ; oscula, Ov. ; ostia, Juv. With DAT. : ut hoc opus aedificio iungatur, Caes. ; mortua corpora vivis, Verg. ; Lucr. ; Hor. With *cum :* cum pede pes iunctus, Ov. **2.** Transf. **a.** amicos, Hor. ; sermonis et iuris societate iuncti, Cic. ; alicui foedere iungi, Liv. ; sanguine iunctus, Ov. ; se Romanis, Liv. ; Hasdrubal Hannibali iunctus, Liv. ; hospitio dextras, Verg. **b.** With abstract *Obj.* : amicitiam inter se, Pl. ; foedus, pacem, adfinitatem cum aliquo, Liv. : cum aliquo consuetudines, amicitias,

res rationesque, Cic. ; laborem (i.e. to keep uninterrupted), Plin. Ep. **c.** Geogr. : iuncta Aquilonibus Arctos, Hor. ; saltūs duo inter se iuncti, Liv. [It. *giugnere ;* Fr. *joindre.*]

iūnior, ōris, *comp. adj.* [perh. fr. iuvenior], *younger, comparatively young :* Cic., Hor. As Noun, **iūniōrēs**, um, *m. pl. men up to the age of 45 years, the younger members* of a centuria or of the senate : Cic., Liv.

iūniperus, ī, *f. the juniper :* Verg. [It. *ginepro ;* Sp. *enebro ;* Fr. *genièvre.*]

Iūnius, a, *the name of a Roman gens, of which Brutus was the most distinguished family ;* **Iūniānus**, a, um ; **Iūnius**, a, um, mensis, *June :* Cic. ; without mensis, **Iūnius**, ī, *m. :* Cic. Ep., Ov.

iūnix, īcis, *f.* [*cf.* iuvenca], *a young cow* or *heifer :* Pers.

Iūnō, ōnis, *f. the goddess Juno* (Greek Hera), *d. of Saturn, s. and w. of Jupiter, and the guardian-deity of women ;* **Iūnōnicola**, ae, *m.f. a worshipper of Juno :* **Iūnōnigena**, ae, *m. Juno-born,* i.e. *Vulcan ;* **Iūnōnius**, a, um, **Iūnōnālis**, e, *adj.*

Iuppiter (also **Diēspiter**), Iovis, *m.* [*cf.* Ζεύς, Διός, diēs, dīvus], *Jupiter* (Greek Zeus), *s. of Saturn, b.* and *h. of Juno ; the chief god of the Romans.* Transf. Iuppiter Stygius, i.e. *Pluto*, Verg. As the god of Heaven, Iuppiter is used by the poets fr. Enn. onwards for the *sky, heaven, open air.*

iūrātor, ōris, *m.* [iūrō], *a sworn judge :* Pl., Liv.

iūre cōnsultus, *v.* iūris cōnsultus.

iūre iūrō, āre [iūs iūrō], *to swear :* Liv.

iūre perītus, *v.* iūris perītus.

iūrgium, ī, *n.* [iūs agō], *brawling, squabbling, altercation :* Pl., Cic., Tac. ; iurgia iactare, Verg. ; nectere, Ov. ; per iurgia dicere, Ov.

iūrgō, āre [iūs agō], *to brawl, squabble, scold.* **A.** Intrans. : Ter., Cic., Hor. With Intern. Acc. : haec, Liv. **B.** Trans. : Trausius istis iurgatur verbis, Hor.

iūridiciālis, e, *adj.* [iūs dīcō], *relating to right* or *justice :* Cic.

iūris-cōnsultus or **iūre-cōnsultus** (also as separate words), *one learned in the law, a consulting barrister, lawyer :* Cic.

iūris-dictiō (also **iūris dictiō**), ōnis, *f. administration of justice.* **1.** Lit. : conficere, Cic. Ep. **2.** Transf. *a sphere of judicial administration, jurisdiction :* sub vestram iurisdictionem urbes subiungere, Cic. ; urbana et peregrina, Liv.

iūris-perītus or **iūre-perītus** (or as separate words), ī, *m. versed in* or *learned in the law :* Cic., Juv. Comp. and Sup. : Cic.

iūrō, āre [iūs. Lit. *to be at law*], *to swear, take an oath.* **1.** Lit. : Cic. ; vere, Cic. Ep. ; falsum, Cic. ; verissimum ius iurandum, Cic. ; in legem, Cic. With in verba, *to swear a prescribed form of oath :* Petreius in haec verba iurat, Caes. ; Liv. ; in verba magistri, Hor. ; in nomen alicuius (*to swear allegiance to someone*), Suet. ; apud aliquem, Tac. With Acc. and (*Fut.*) *Inf.* : Caes., Cic., Liv. **2.** Transf. **a.** *to conspire against :* in me somnus ventusque fidesque, Ov. **b.** *to swear by somebody :* per Iovem, Cic. ; Pl. ; Verg. With Acc. : Iovem lapidem, Cic. Ep. ; Terram, Mare, Sidera, Verg. ;

quaevis numina, Ov. In Pass.: iurata numina, Ov. c. *to renounce on oath, abjure*; calumniam, Liv. **iūrātus**, a, um, *Part.* in Act. sense: *having taken an oath* : Pl., Cic., Juv.; in verba alicuius, Liv.; in eadem arma, Ov. *Sup.*: Plin. Occ. *Pass.* : *what has been sworn* : Cic.

(1) **ius**, iūris, *n. broth, soup* : Pl., Cic., Hor., etc.; ius Verrinum (*hog-broth* and *Verres' administration* ; *v.* ius (2)), Cic.

(2) **ius**, iūris, *n. law as established by public authority* or *custom* (differs from lex, which is *statute law* and from fas, *divine law*). **1.** Lit.: Pl., Cic., etc. In *pl.* : legum atque iurum, Pl.; divina ac humana, Cic. Phr.: ius civile, *law as it affected* (*Roman*) *citizens*, Cic.; ius gentium (*the body of law of non-Romans* ; for its later identification with ius naturale, *v.* Maine's Ancient Law), Cic., Sall., Liv.; ius praetorium (*the principles of law embodied in a praetor's edict*), Cic.; ius publicum, *political* or *constitutional law*, Liv.; ius privatum, *the laws regulating the relations of private persons to one another*, Cic.; summum, *the strict letter of the law*, Cic.; ius dicere (Cic.), ius reddere (Liv.), iura dare (Verg.), *to give a judicial decision* or *administer justice* ; de iure respondere, *to give a legal opinion*, Cic. **2.** Transf. **a.** *a court of law* or *its proceedings* : in ius ambula, Pl., Ter.; ad praetorem in ius adire, Cic.; in ius procurrere, rapi, Hor. **b.** In gen.: *natural right* or *justice, justness* : absolverunt admiratione magis virtutis quam iure causae, Liv. Freq. in ABL. iure, *rightly, justly* : Cic., Juv.; so also, optimo iure, Cic.; Pl.; iusto iure, Liv. **c.** *administration of the law, jurisdiction* ; hence, *authority, sphere of administration* : ius Verrinum (*v.* ius (1)), Cic.; paucorum in ius dicionemque (omnia) concedere, Sall.; homines recipere in ius dicionemque, Liv.; sub ius iudiciumque regis venire, Liv.; sui iuris esse, *to be independent*, Cic. **d.** *right, rights* : de tergo ac vitā habere, Liv.; cum plebe agendi, Cic.; Liv.; tenere, retinere, Cic.; obtinere, Quint.; dictatorium, patrium, Liv.; communia iura, Cic.; muliebria, Ov.

ius iūrandum, I, *an oath* : iure iurando, ne quis . . ., inter se sanxerunt, Caes.; iure iurando civitatem obstringere, Caes.; accipere, Caes.; aliquem ius iurandum adigere, Caes.; dare, Pl.; conservare, violare, neglegere, Cic.; offerre, deferre, recipere, Quint.; ab aliquo exigere, Quint.; iure iurando teneri, Caes.; Cic.; provinciam in Pompei verba ius iurandum adigebat, Caes.; populum iure iurando adigere, Liv.; ad ius iurandum aliquem adigere, Sall.

iussū, ABL. *sing.* m. [iubeo], *by order* : vestro iussu, Cic.; Pl.; populi, Liv.; Neronis, Juv. Also, sine iussu alicuius, Sall.

iussus, a, um. **I.** *Part.* iubeo. **II.** *Neut.* as Noun (mostly in *pl.*), *an order.* **a.** In gen.: praetoris, senatūs, deorum, Cic.; Verg.; describere, Cic.; efficere, Sall.; capessere, facere, exsequi, etc., Verg.; spernere, detrectare, abnuere, patrare, etc., Tac. **b.** Of the people: iussa ac scita, Cic. **c.** *a* (*doctor's*) *prescription* : Ov.

iūstē, *adv. rightly, justly* : Cic., Ov. *Comp.* : Hor. *Sup.* : Quint.

iūstificus, a, um [iūstus faciō], *that acts justly* : Cat.

iūstitia, ae, *f.* [iūstus]. **I.** *just conduct, justice, fairness* : Ter., Caes., Cic. **II.** Abstract : Cic.

iūstitium, i, *n.* [iūs sistō], *a cessation from business in the courts of justice, a legal vacation* (on solemn or critical occasions). **1.** Lit.: edicere, Cic.; indicere, remittere, Liv.; sumere, Tac. **2.** Transf. *cessation, standstill* : omnium rerum, Liv.

iūstus, a, um [iūs]. **I.** *just, equitable, fair.* **1.** Lit. (of persons): Cic. With *in* and ACC.: in socios, Cic. *Comp.* : Cic. *Sup.* : Cic., Verg. **2.** Transf.: tellus (*fairly repaying*), Verg.; servitus, Ter.; iustis locis (opp. iniquis), *on fair ground*, Tac. **II.** *legal, lawful, legitimate.* **1.** Lit.: uxor, Cic., Liv.; hymenaei, Verg.; causa, Caes., Cic.; supplicia, Cic.; imperium, Caes., Cic. *Sup.*: Caes. **2.** Transf. **a.** *justified, deserved, well-founded* : triumphus, honores, odium, querimonia, Cic.; querella, fiducia, Ov. **b.** *regular, formal, in due order, of full measure*: bellum, Cic., Liv.; proelium, acies, exercitus, Liv.; iter, Caes.; victoria, Cic. Ep.; ad iusti cursum amnis, Liv.; iustos annos peragere, Ov.; vidulus, Pl.; altitudo, Caes.; statura, Suet. *Neut.* as Noun **iūstum**, i, *that which is right* or *just, justice.* **A.** In *sing.* : iustum ac ius colere, Cic.; plus iusto, *more than is right, too much*, Hor. **B.** In *pl.* **a.** *rights, privileges* : servis iusta praebere, Cic. **b.** *due ceremonies* or *formalities* : omnia iusta perficere, Liv.; iustis fungi, Liv. **c.** *funeral rites, obsequies* : (alicui) facere, Pl., Sall.; iustis funebribus confectis, Caes.; funeri solvere, Cic.; avis ferre, Ov.

Iūturna, ae, *f. a nymph, s.* of Turnus, king of the Rutuli.

iūtus, a, um, *Part.* iuvō.

iuvenālis, e, *adj.* [iuvenis], *youthful, juvenile* : Verg., Liv. Esp. **iuvenālēs lūdi** or **iuvenālia** (games introduced by Nero): Tac., Suet.

Iuvenālis, is, *m.* D. Iunius Iuvenalis, *a Roman satirist in the time of Domitian and Trajan.*

iuvencus, a, um [iuvenis], *young* : equus, Lucr. As Noun: **iuvencus**, i, *m.* **a.** (*sc.* bos), *a young bullock* : Varr., Verg., etc. **b.** (*sc.* vir), *a young man, youngster* : Hor. **iuvenca**, ae, *f.* **a.** (*sc.* bos), *a young cow, heifer* : Verg., Hor., Juv. **b.** (*sc.* femina), *a girl* : Ov.

iuvenēscō, iuvenēscere, iuvenui [iuvenis]. **I.** *to grow up* : Hor. **II.** *to grow young again* : Ov.

iuvenīlis, e, *adj.* [iuvenis], *youthful* : Cic., Verg., Ov. *Comp.* : Ov.

iuveniliter, *adv. youthfully, after the manner of youth* : Cic., Ov.

iuvenis, is, *adj. young, youthful* : maritus, Tib.; filius, Quint.; anni, Ov. As Noun: *one in the prime of life* (i.e. between 20 and 45 years of age), *a young man* or *woman* : Cic., Verg., etc. Occ. in *pl.* : *the young nobles* : Liv. *Comp.* : iuvenior, Plin. Ep.; but *v.* iūnior. [It. *giovins* or *giovane* ; Fr. *jeune.*]

iuvenor, āri (iuvenis]. *to act like a youth, to wanton :* versibus, Hor.

iuventa, ae, *f.* [iuvenis], *the season of youth, youth :* Verg., Ov., Liv. Personified : Ov.

iuventās, ātis, *f.* [iʳventa], *the season of youth, youth :* Lucr., Verg., Hor. Personified : Cic., Hor., Liv.

iuventūs, ūtis, *f.* [iuvenis], *the season of youth* (from the 20th to the 45th year), *youth ; the prime of life, manhood.* **1.** Lit. : Cic., Sall. **2.** Trans f. *the youth,* as collect. Noun for *young persons,* esp. *the men of military age :* Pl., Caes., Cic., Verg., etc. Hence, princeps iuventutis, in the time of the Republic, *the first among the knights,* Cic. ; under the Emperors, *a title of the imperial princes :* Tac.

Iūverna, *v.* Hibernia.

iuvō, iuvāre, iūvī, iūtum (iuvātūrus, Sall.), **I.** *to help, aid, assist :* aliquem, Cic., Verg., Ov. With *Instr.* Abl. : aliquem auxilio laboris, Cic. ; frumento, Caes. ; portu locoque, Ov. Of medical assistance : qui salutari iuvat arte fessos, Hor. Phr. : diis iuvantibus *or* deo iuvante, *with God's help :* Cic. With thing as *Subj.* or *Obj. :* facundia causam, Ov. ; imbres arva, Ov. ; beatae vitae (Gen.) disciplinam, Cic. In *Pass. :* Cic., Liv., Tac. *Impers. :* iuvat, *it is of use :* with *Inf. :* iuvat Ismara Baccho conserere, Verg. ; Ov. **II. a.** With Noun as *Subj. : to delight, gratify, please :* nec me vita iuvaret, Liv. ; multos castra, Hor. ; Verg. ; Pl. **b.** *Impers.* (with *Inf.* or Acc. and *Inf.*) : *it delights, pleases :* iuvat me nomina artiöcum concidisse, Cic. ; haec olim meminisse iuvabit, Verg.

iūxtā, *adv.* and *prep.* [fr. root seen in iungō]. **I.** Adv. (of place), *in close proximity, near by, by one's side.* **1.** Lit. : legio, quae iuxta constiterat, Caes. ; Verg., etc. With motion : accedere iuxta, Ov. **2.** Transf. *in like manner, equally, alike :* eorum ego vitam mortemque iuxta aestimo, Sall. ; iuxta insontes, Liv. With Dat. : rem parvam ac iuxta magnis difficilem, Liv. With *ac, atque, et, quam, cum : as well as, just the same as :* iuxta mecum omnes intellegitis, Sall. ; Pl. ; absentium bona iuxta atque interemptorum, Liv. ; iuxta ac si etc., Cic., Sall., Liv. ; iuxta quam cum viderent etc., Liv. **II.** Prep. with Acc. : *close to, near to.* **1.** Lit. (of place) : Caes., Tac., etc. Placed after the Noun : Verg., Tac. Transf. **a.** Of time : iuxta finem vitae, Tac. **b.** Of succession : *next to, immediately after :* iuxta divinas religiones humana fides colitur, Liv. ; Tac. **c.** *beside, along with :* periculosiores sunt inimicitiae iuxta libertatem, Tac. **d.** *near, approaching to, bordering upon :* iuxta seditionem esse, Sall. ; celeritas iuxta formidinem est, Tac. ; iuxta seditionem ventum est, Tac.

iūxtim, *adv.* [*cf.* iūxta], *close by.* **1.** Lit. **a.** *beside :* adsidebat iuxtim, Suet. **b.** *near :* Lucr. **2.** Transf. *alike, equally :* miscentes vulta parentum, Lucr.

Ixiōn, onis, *m. s. of Phlegyas, king of the Lapithae, and f. of Pirithous. For a sin against Juno, Jupiter hurled him into Tartarus, where he was bound to a perpetually*

revolving wheel ; **Ixioneus** (-ius), a, um. **Ixionidēs**, ae, *m. his son Pirithous ;* **Ixionidae**, ārum, *m. pl. his children, the Centaurs.*

J v. I

K

K, k, a guttural corresponding to l.E. *k,* Gk. κ.

Kaeso or **K.** a praenomen in the gentes Duilia, Fabia, Quinctia.

Kalendae (Cal-), ārum, *f. pl.* [calō, āre, *cf.* καλέω : the beginning of the month was proclaimed by the pontifices. Lit. proclamation day]. **1.** Lit. *the first day of the Roman month, the Kalends :* us. written Kal. (Cal.) : *e.g.* Kal. Ianuar., *the first of January,* Cic. (*v.* table at end of volume.) On the Kalends interest fell due : tristes Kalendae, Hor. ; celeres, Ov. This way of reckoning time was peculiar to the Romans ; hence, Prov. : ad Kalendas Graecas solvere (of postponing payment indefinitely), Suet. On the Kalends of March, married people celebrated the Matronalia, a festival in honour of Iuno Lucina ; Martiis caelebs quid agam Kalendis, Hor. **2.** Transf. *a month :* nec totidem veteres quot nunc habuere Kalendas, Ov.

Kalendārium, i, *n.* [Kalendae], *the accountbook of a moneylender* (*v.* Kalendae) : Sen.

kalō, *v.* calō.

koppa, *n. indecl.* [κόππα], orig. letter *q ;* later a Gk. numeral, 90 : Quint.

L

L, l, *indecl. n.* or (*sc.* littera), *f.* the eleventh letter of the Latin alphabet. **I.** Latin *l* represents. **a.** Orig. *l ;* also not infrequently *r.* **b.** Orig. *d* in some words becomes *l* in Latin ; thus *lingua* was orig. *dingua* (*cf.* Eng. *tongue*) ; and *lacrima* was *dacrima* (*cf.* Gk. δάκρυ). This happened gen. when the *d* was initial ; but is found also when it stood between two vowels : thus Gk. ὀδ-ωδ-α ; Lat. *odor,* but also *olere.* **c.** In many adjectives the termination is *-aris* or *-alis,* acc. as *l* is found, or *r,* in the preceding syllable ; thus *vulg-aris, popul-aris,* but *mort-alis, later-alis* **d.** In the composition and derivation of nouns and adjectives, *l* exercises an assimilating power over other consonants brought into contact or proximity with it : *libellus* from *liber ; ullus* from *unus ; labellum* from *labrum.* **II.** Changes of *l* in the Romance languages. **a.** In Ital. into *i : e.g.* Lat. *plus, flos, glacies ;* It. *più, fiore, ghiaccio.* **b.** In French into *r ; e.g.* Lat. *apostolus, capitulum, epistula ;* Fr. *apôtre, chapitre, épître.* Also in derivatives of Lat. *lusciniolus ;* It. *rossignuolo ;* Sp. *ruiseñor ;* Fr. *rossignol.* **c.** Iu a few words into *u : e.g.* Lat. *libella,* Fr. *niveau.* **d.** In a single case, into *d : e.g.* Lat. *amylum ;* It. *amido ;* Fr. *amidon.* **e.** Into *ll,* or *gl, ch,* or *lh : e.g.* Lat. *pilare,* Fr.

piller, It. *pigliare*. **f.** *ll* undergoes the same changes as those of the single consonant explained in *e*; in French, however, *ll* is seldom changed. **g.** When *ll* of the Latin word terminates the derived word, one *l* is, in French, usually omitted: e.g. Lat. *caballus*, Fr. *cheval*; Lat. *vallis*, *capillus*, *aucella*, *collum*; old Fr. *val*, *chevel*, *oisel*, *col*; mod. Fr. *cheveu*, *oiseau*, *cou*. **h.** The change of *l* into *u*, seen in the examples last given, often occurs in other combinations: e.g. Lat. *talpa*, *albus*, *delphinus*, *altus*, *alter*, *dulcis*; Fr. *taupe*, *aube*, *dauphin*, *haut*, *autre*, *doux*. **III.** As an abbreviation L. **a.** *us.* denotes the praenomen Lucius, though it also stands for libens and locus. **b.** As a numeral L stands for 50.

lăbāscō, ere [labō], *to be ready to fall, to totter, stagger, waver.* **1.** Lit.: Lucr. **2.** Transf.: Pl., Ter.

Labdacus, ī, *m. a king of Thebes, father of Laius*; **Labdacius**, a, um; **Labdacidēs**, ae, *m. a descendant of Labdacus; in pl. the Thebans.*

lăbēcula, ae, *f.* [dim. lăbēs], *a slight stain or disgrace*: Cic.

lăbe-făciō, facere, fēcī, factum (*Pass.* labefīō, fieri, factus) [lābor], *to cause to totter, to shake, loosen, to make ready to fall.* **1.** Lit.: dentis alicui, Ter.; partem muri, Caes.; membra vi voluptatis, Lucr.; iugera, ossa, Verg.; chartam a vinclis, Ov.; aedis, Tac. **2.** Transf. **a.** Polit.: res publica iam labefacta, Cic.; iura plebis, Liv.; hunc amicitia Seiani, Tac.; fidem (*credit*), Suet. **b.** Mental: quem nulla invidia labefecit, Cic.; animum labefactus amore, Verg.; primores classiariorum, Tac.

lăbefactō, āre [*freq.* labefaciō], *to cause to totter, to shake violently, to overthrow.* **1.** Lit.: signum vectibus, Cic.; horrea bellicis machinis, Suet. **2.** Transf. **a.** Polit.: rem publicam, consulatum, leges, iura, coniurationem, etc., Cic. **b.** Mental: *to break down, weaken*: aliquem, Pl., Ter., Cat., Cic.; animam, Lucr.; opinionem, Cic.; fidem, Cic.; Tac. **c.** In gen.: *to weaken, ruin, destroy*: sensūs, Lucr.; amicitiam, Cic.

lăbefactus, a, um, *Part.* labefaciō.

lăbefīō, *Pass.* of labefaciō.

(1) lăbellum, ī, n. [dim. labrum], *a little or dainty lip*: Pl., Cic., Verg.

(2) lăbellum, ī, n. [dim. lābrum], *a small washing vessel*: Cato, Cic.

Lăbērius, a, *the name of a Roman gens.* Esp. D. Laberius, *celebrated as a composer of mimes.*

(1) lābēs, is (ABL. lābī for lābe, Lucr.), *f.* [lābor], *a sinking, falling.* **1.** Lit.: agri, Cic.; terrae, Liv. **2.** Transf. **a.** *a fall, ruin, destruction*: innocentiae, Cic.; hinc mihi prima mali labes, Verg.; Pl. **b.** (*cause of*) *ruin*: (Verres) labes atque pernicies Siciliae, Cic.

(2) lābēs, is, *f.* [perh. *cf.* Gk. λώβη], *a spot, blot stain, blemish.* **1.** Lit.: Hor., Ov., Suet. **2.** Transf. **a.** Moral: animi, conscientiae, sceleris, Cic.; famae, Prop.; ignominiae, Tac.; vita sine labe peracta, Ov.; labem alicui inferre, Cic.; alicuius dignitati aspergere, Cic.; eximere, Verg.

b. Of persons: *a disgraceful, shameful fellow*: caenum illud ac labes, Cic.

labia, ae, *f.* (Pl., Ter.) and **labium**, ī, n. (Quint.) [lambō], *a lip.* Prov.: labiis ductare aliquem (like our ' *to lead anyone by the nose* '), Pl. Transf. of part of an oil-press: Cato.

lăbiōsus, a, um [labium], *having large lips*: Lucr.

labium, v. labia.

lăbō, āre [fr. same root as lābor], *to totter, be ready to fall, sink, or give way, to waver, wobble.* **1.** Lit. **a.** In gen.: signum labat, Cic.; ariete crebro ianua, Verg.; curvae naves, Ov. **b.** Of troops: *to waver, be unsteady*: sustinuit labantem aciem, Tac.; Liv. **c.** Of hand-writing: littera labat, Ov. **2.** Transf. **a.** Polit.: rei publicae partis labantis sanare, Cic.; labantem fortunam populi Romani, Liv.; disciplina gentis, Liv.; res Troiana, Ov.; labante iam Agrippinā, Tac. **b.** Mental: Cic.; animus, corda, Verg.; socii, fides sociorum, memoria, Liv.; mens, Ov. **c.** In gen.: res, Pl.; si unam litteram moveris, labent omnia, Cic.; si quid in moribus labaret, Tac.

lābor, lābī, lāpsus [*cf.* labō], *to slide, slip, or glide.* **A.** Of gentle unimpeded motion. **1.** Lit.: cupae involutae, Caes.; sidera, Cic.; columba aere lapsa quieto, Verg.; pennis lapsa per auras, Ov.; anguis per aras, Verg.; lapsa folia caducat, Verg.; ex oculis gutta, Ov.; uncta vadis abies, Verg. **2.** Transf.: res foras, Pl.; frigus per artūs, Verg.; fugaces anni, Hor.; occulte aetas, Ov. **B.** *to slip away and escape.* **1.** Lit.: custodiā, Tac. **2.** Transf.: pectore vultus, Verg. Of speech: *to fade away* (unheard): Cic. **C.** *to sink, glide, or slip down, to fall.* **1.** Lit.: per gradūs labi, Liv.; *labitur exsanguis, Verg.; temone, Verg.; equo, Hor.; ex equo, Liv.; ab arbore ramus, Ov.; lapsis saxis, Tac. **2.** Transf. *to fall, go to ruin, decline, be on the downgrade.* **a.** In gen.: labentem rem publicam fulcire, Cic.; disciplina, mores, etc., Liv.; acies, Prop. With ABL. of Separation: spe lapsi, Caes.; mente labi, Suet. **b.** Into faults, errors of judgment: labor eo ut adsentiar Epicuro, Cic.; in aliquā re, Cic.; in officio, Cic.; a verā ratione, Lucr.; verbo, Plin. Ep.; propter imprudentiam, Caes.; consilio, casu, Cic.; in vitium, Hor.; in errorem, Liv.

labor, ōris (NOM. **labōs**, Pl., Ter.), *m.* [*cf.* Gk. ἀλφάνω]. **I.** *labour, toil, effort, exertion* of body or mind. **1.** Lit.: Ter.; ex labore se reficere, Caes.; corporis, Cic.; nullo labore, Cic.; capere, suscipere, Cic.; alicui imponere, levare, Cic.; sibi sumere, Cic.; in rem insumere, Cic. **2.** Transf. **a.** *energy, industry*: Caes., Cic. **b.** *laborious effort, task, feat*: aspirat primo fortuna labori, Verg.; Herculeus, Hor.; perh. labores solis, Verg. **c.** *work done*: multorum mensium labor, Caes.; hominum boumque labores, Verg. **II.** *hardship, distress* (in *sing.* or *pl.*): Pl., Cic., Verg., etc. Poet.: lunae labores (*eclipses*), Verg. **III.** **Labōs** personified. Verg. [It. *lavoro*; Fr. *labeur*.]

lăbōrĭfer, a, um [labor ferō], *toil-enduring* : Hercules, Ov.

lăbōrĭōsē, *adv. wearisomely, with difficulty, laboriously* : Pl., Cat. *Comp. :* Cic. *Sup. :* Cic.

lăbōrĭōsus, a, um [labor]. **I.** Of things : *toilsome, wearisome, difficult, laborious :* deambulatio, Ter. *Comp. :* exercitationes, Cic. *Sup. :* opus, Liv. **II.** Of persons : *industrious :* Cic. **III.** *causing much trouble and hardship, harassing :* quid nobis laboriosius ? Cic.

lăbōrō, āre [labor]. **A.** Intrans. **a.** *to labour, take pains, exert oneself :* ne labora, Ter. ; sibi, Cic. ; in enodandis nominibus, Cic. ; circa memoriam, Quint. ; in spem, Ov. ; pro salute, Cic. With *Inf.: brevis esse* laboro, Hor. **b.** *to care or trouble oneself, to be solicitous, anxious :* animo laborabat, ut reliquas civitates adiungeret, Caes. ; Cic. ; Hor. ; in re familiari, Cic. Ep. ; tuā causā, Cic. Ep. ; de aliquā re, Cic. So, non laboro, nihil laboro, *I don't trouble myself about it, it concerns me not :* de iis, Cic. ; with *Indir. Quest. :* Cic. **c.** *to labour, to be hard-pressed, afflicted,* or *troubled ; to be in difficulty* or *danger.* **i.** Lit. : quos laborantis conspexerat, iis subsidia summittebat, Caes. ; Sall. ; ne quā populus laboret, Hor. Of illness : Cic. *Impers. Pass. :* maxime ad superiores munitiones laboratur, Caes. With *ex :* e dolore, Ter. ; ex intestinis, Cic. ; ex aere alieno, Caes. With *ab :* a re frumentariā, Caes. ; a pedite, Liv. ; ab avaritiā, Hor. With *Abl. :* domesticā crudelitate, Cic. ; quantā laborabas Charybdi, Hor. ; contemptu inter socios, Liv. ; obsidione, Suet. **ii.** Transf. Of inanim. and abstract subjects : ut utraeque triremes ex concursu laborarent, Caes. ; luna laborat (*suffers eclipse*), Cic. ; Aquilonibus querceta, Hor. ; veritatem laborare nimis saepe, aiunt, Liv. **B.** Trans. *to work out, elaborate ; to make, prepare with effort :* quale non perfectius meae laborarint manūs, Hor. ; vestis, Verg. ; frumenta ceterosque fructūs, Tac.

lăbōs, *v.* labor.

lăbrum, i, n. [*v.* labia]. **1.** Lit. *a lip :* Ter., Cic., Verg., etc. ; superius, Caes. Prov. : primis *or* primoribus labris gustare, *or* attingere aliquid (i.e. *to get a slight taste of, a superficial knowledge of*), Cic. **2.** Transf. *lip, edge, margin* (of a vessel, ditch, etc.) : Caes., Liv. [It. *labbro ;* Fr. *lèvre.*]

lābrum, i, n. [lavō], *a basin, tub.* **1.** Lit. : Cic. Ep., Verg., Liv. **2.** Transf. : *a bath, bathing-place :* Dianae, Ov.

lābrusca vītis *or* **ūva,** also alone **lābrusca,** ae, *f. the wild vine :* Verg. [Fr. *lambruche.*]

lābruscum, i, n. [lābrusca], *the wild grape :* Verg.

Lăbyrinthēus, a, um [Labyrinthus], *of the labyrinth :* flexus, Cat.

Lăbyrinthus, i, m. [Λαβύρινθος], *a labyrinth ;* esp. that built by Daedalus in Crete : Verg., Ov., Sen. Ep.

lac, lactis (Nom. lacte : Pl.), n. [*cf.* Gk. γάλα, γάλακτος], *milk.* **1.** Lit. : Cic., Verg., etc. Prov. : tam similem quam lacte lacti est, Pl. **2.** Transf. **a.** *the milky juice of plants :* Ov. **b.** *a milk-white*

---

colour : Ov. **c.** satiari velut quodam iucundioris disciplinae lacte, Quint. [Sp. *leche,* Fr. *lait.*]

Lăcaena, ae, *f. adj. Spartan ; as* Noun, *a Spartan woman.*

Lăcedaemōn (or -ō), onis (Acc. -ona, Abl. -one, Locat. -oni), *the city of Lacedaemon or Sparta ;* **Lăcedaemŏnĭus,** a, um ; **Lăcedaemŏniī,** ōrum, m. pl. *the Spartans.*

lăcer, era, erum [*cf.* Gk. λακίς], *mangled, lacerated, mutilated, torn to pieces.* **1.** Lit. : Lucr., Verg., Liv., etc. **2.** Transf. *rending, lacerating :* morsus, Ov.

lăcerātĭō, ōnis, *f.* [lacerō], *a mangling, tearing :* Cic., Liv. In *pl. :* Cic.

lăcerna, ae, *f. a cloak worn over the toga on journeys or in bad weather :* Cic., Ov., Suet.

lăcernātus, a, um [lacerna], *cloaked :* Juv.

lăcerō, āre [lacer], **1.** *to tear, to tear to pieces, to mangle, lacerate.* **1.** Lit. **a.** aliquem, Ter., Verg. ; loricam, Verg. ; corpus, Lucr. ; ora, comas, vestem, Ov. ; ferro, Hor. ; tergum virgis, Liv. **b.** *to break to pieces, shatter, wreck :* navem, Ov., Liv. ; pontem, Liv. **2.** Transf. **a.** *to pull to pieces* (of character), *calumniate, slander :* obtrectatione invidiaque plerosque, Cic. ; aliquem contumeliis, Cic. ; probris, Liv. ; famam sepulti, Liv. ; mea carmina, Ov. **b.** *to rend, torture :* dolore lacerari, Cic. ; me maeror, Cic. Ep. **c.** *to waste, squander, consume :* diem, Pl. ; pecuniam, Cic. ; patriam omni scelere, Cic. ; bona patria, Sall.

lăcerta, ae, *f.* (Hor., Ov., Juv.), and **lăcertus,** i, m. (Verg., Cic. Ep.). **I.** *a lizard.* Prov. : unius lacertae se dominum facere (i.e. *to get a place of one's own, however small*), Juv. **II.** *a sea-fish :* Cic. Ep.

lăcertōsus, a, um [lacertus], *muscular, brawny :* Cic., Ov.

(1) lăcertus, i, m. **1.** Lit. **a.** *the arm, from the shoulder to the elbow :* Lucr., Ov., Curt. **b.** *the arm :* Cic., Verg., Ov. Esp. in its muscular aspect : Cic. **2.** Transf. **a.** Of bees : Verg. **b.** In *pl. : muscle, vigour, power :* Cic., Hor.

(2) lăcertus, *v.* lacerta.

lăcessō, ere, īvi *or* ii, ītum [laciō]. **I.** *to incite, stir up, provoke, challenge.* **a.** With Acc. of person *or* thing stirred : te ad scribendum, Cic. Ep. ; hostis ad pugnam, Liv. ; manibus pectora, Verg. ; deos precibus, Hor. Poet. : corpora visum, Lucr. ; aera sole lacessita, Verg. ; pelagus carinā, Hor. **b.** With Acc. of thing produced : sermones, Cic. Ep. ; pugnam, Verg., Liv. ; bella, Verg. ; mentionem rei, Liv. **II.** *to incite, provoke, rouse to rage, exasperate :* aliquem ferro, Cic. ; proelio hostia, Caes. ; aliquem bello, Cic., Liv. ; Aeduos iniuriā, Caes. ; leonem, Hor. ; aliquem probris, Suet. ; aliquem capitaliter, Plin. Ep.

lăchănissō *or* **-nizō,** āre [λαχανίζω], *to be weak, languid :* Suet.

lăcĭna, ae, *f.* [*cf.* lacer], *the lappet or flap of a garment :* Pl. Suet. Prov. : aliquid obtinere laciniā (i.e. *barely, without a firm hold*), Cic.

Lăcĭnĭum, i, n. *a promontory in Bruttium with a temple of Juno ;* **Lăcĭnĭus,** a, um.

laciŏ, ere, *to draw gently.* [The verb itself is obsolete, but it has several compounds : e.g. *adliciŏ, ēliciŏ,* etc.]

Lăcŏ (**-ōn**), ŏnis, *m. a Laconian or Spartan* (also *a Spartan dog :* Hor.) ; **Lăcōnĭa**, ae, (or **-ĭcē, ēs**), *f. the country of which Sparta was the chief city :* **Lăcōnĭcus**, a, um ; **Lăcōnĭcum**, i, *n. a sweating-room, first used by the Spartans.* **Lăcōnĭs**, idis, *f. adj.*

lăcrĭma, ae, *f.* (older **lăcrŭma** and **dăcrŭma**) [*cf.* Gk. δάκρυ], *a tear.* **1.** Lit.: alicui exciere, elicere, Pl. ; cum lacrimis obsecrare, Caes. ; lacrimas effundere, Lucr., Cic. ; profundere, Cic. ; ciere, dare, Verg. ; fundere, demittere, Verg. ; effundi in lacrimas, Tac. ; commovere, Curt. ; pellere, Verg. ; mittere, Ter. ; tenere, Cic., Ov. ; cohibere, Plin. Ep.   Prov.: hinc illae lacrimae, Cic., Hor. **2.** Transf. *a tear,* or *gum-drop* of a plant : Narcissi, Verg. [It. *lagrima ;* Fr. *larme.*]

lăcrĭmābĭlis, e, *adj.* [lacrima], *worthy of tears :* Verg., Ov.

lăcrĭmābundus, a, um [lacrimō], *tearful, bursting into tears :* Liv.

lăcrĭmŏ (**lăcrŭmŏ**), āre [lacrima], *to shed tears, to weep.* **1.** Lit.: Pl., Cic., Verg. ; lacrumo gaudio, Ter. With Acc. of *Neut. Pron. :* num id lacrumat virgo ? Ter. **2.** Transf.: lacrimavit ebur, Ov. In *Perf. Part. : wept :* lacrimatas cortice myrrhas, Ov.

lăcrĭmōsus, a, um [lacrima]. **A.** *full of tears, tearful, weeping.* **1.** Lit.: lumina, Ov. ; voces, Verg. **2.** Transf.: electrum, Verg. **B.** *exciting* or *causing tears :* fumus, Hor., Ov. ; bellum, poemata, Hor.

lăcrĭmŭla, ae, *f.* [*dim.* lacrima], *a little tear ;* esp. *a sham tear :* Ter., Cic., Cat.

lăcrŭm-, *v.* lacrim-.

lactāns, antis, *adj.* [lac]. **I.** *giving milk :* ubera, Ov. **II.** *sucking :* vituli, Ov.

lactārĭus, a, um [lac], *giving milk :* Varr.

lactātĭŏ, ōnis, *f.* [lactō], *allurement :* Cic.

lactēns, entis, *adj.* [lac], *sucking milk, being a suckling.* **1.** Lit.: Cic., Ov. Poet.: viscera lactentia (i.e. sucking children), Ov. Of the spring : tener et lactens (annus), Ov. As Noun, *a suckling :* Liv. **2.** Transf. *milky, sappy, juicy :* frumenta, Verg. ; sata, Ov.

lacteŏlus, a, um [*dim.* lacteus], *white as milk :* puellae, Cat.

lactēs, ium, *f. the guts ;* esp. *the small intestines :* laxae lactes (i.e. *an empty stomach*), Pl. ; Pers.   Prov. of a useless attempt, adligare fugitivam canem agninis lactibus, Pl.

lactēscŏ, ere [lacteō], *to turn to* or *become milk :* Cic.

lactĕus, a, um [lac], *milky, full of milk.* **1.** Lit.: ubera, Verg. ; umor, Ov. **2.** Transf. **a.** *milk-coloured, milk-white :* colla, Verg. ; orbis (the Milky Way), Cic. ; via, Ov. **b.** Of style : Quint.

lactŏ, āre [*freq.* laciŏ], *to wheedle, dupe, cajole :* me amor lactat, Pl. ; animos, Ter.

lactūca, ae, *f. a lettuce :* Verg., Hor.

lactūcŭla, ae, *f.* [*dim.* lactūca], *a young lettuce :* Suet.

lăcūna, ae, *f.* [lacus], *a ditch, pit, hole ;* a *pool, pond.* **1.** Lit.: Lucr., Verg. Poet.:

salsae (i.e. *the sea*), Lucr. **2.** Transf. *a gap, deficiency :* rei familiaris, Cic. ; in auro, Cic. Ep. [It. *laguna ;* Fr. *lagune, lacune.*]

lăcūnar, āris, *n.* [lacūna], *a panel-ceiling* (so called from its sunken spaces) : Cic., Hor., Juv.

lăcūnŏ, āre [lacūna], *to panel like a fretted ceiling :* Ov.

lăcūnōsus, a, um, *full of hollows, sunken :* Cic.

lăcŭs, ūs, *m.* orig. *any hollow ;* hence, **a.** *a trough, vat.* Of *a wine-vat :* Cato, Verg., etc. ; transf.: oratio quasi de musto ac lacu fervida, Cic. Of *a smith's cooling-tank :* Verg., Ov. **b.** *a cistern, reservoir, tank, pool :* Hor., Ov., Liv.   Prov.: sicco vilior lacu, Prop. **c.** *a lake :* Lucr., Caes., Cic. Of *a deep pool in a river :* Verg. ; of the Styx : Verg. [It. *lago ;* Fr. *lac.*]

Lādās, ae, *m. a famous runner in the time of Alexander.*

laedŏ, laedere, laesi, laesum. **1.** Lit. **a.** *to knock, strike, dash :* aequora laedebant navis ad saxa, Lucr. **b.** *to hurt, gall, harm :* lora laedunt bracchia, Pl. ; ferro retunso semina, Verg. ; aliquem vulnere, Ov. ; frondes laedit hiems, Ov. **2.** Transf. **a.** *to strike, knock :* nulli os laedere (i.e. *to offend nobody*), Ter. **b.** *to hurt, gall, harm, wound.* With ABL. of means or manner : dicto, facto, Pl. ; aliquem periurio suo, Cic. ; versu scurram, Hor. Without ABL.: quia haesit prior, Ter. ; iniuste neminem, Cic. ; Pisonem, Cic. ; tua me infortunia laedent, Hor. **c.** *to violate a pledge or promise :* fidem, Caes., Cic., Hor. ; foedus, Verg. **d.** *to outrage dignity or honour :* numen, Verg., Hor. ; famam alicuius opprobrio, Suet.

Laelĭus, a, *the name of a Roman gens,* esp. C. Laelius. **I.** *a friend of Scipio Africanus.* **II.** *the Younger, a friend of Scipio Aemilianus.*

laena, ae, *f.* [Gk. χλαῖνα], *a lined upper garment, cloak, mantle,* worn by the flamens and by persons of distinction : Cic., Verg.

Lăērtēs, ae, *m.* (Acc. **-ēn**), *f. of Ulysses :* **Lăērtĭus**, a, um ; **Lăērtĭădēs**, ae, *m. s. of Laertes, Ulysses.*

laesĭŏ, ōnis, *f.* [laedŏ], *an attack.* Rhet. Cic.

Laestrȳgŏn, onis, *m.,* mostly in *pl.* **Laestrȳgones** (Acc. **-as**), *a mythical race of giants and cannibals in Italy, founders of Formiae ;* **Laestrȳgonius**, a, um, *of Formiae :* Hor.

laesus, a, um, *Part.* laedŏ.

laetābĭlis, e, *adj.* [laetor], *joyful, glad :* nihil, Cic. ; factum, Ov.

laetāns, antis. **I.** *Part.* laetor. **II.** *Adj.: joyful, glad :* Pl., Cic. ; loca, Lucr.

laetātĭŏ, ōnis, *f.* [laetor], *rejoicing, joy :* Caes.

laetē, *adv. joyfully, gladly :* Cic., Quint. *Comp. :* Liv., Tac., etc.

laetĭfĭcāns, antis. **I.** *Part.* laetificŏ. **II.** *Adj.: joyous :* Pl.

laetĭfĭcŏ, āre [laetificus]. **I.** *to fertilise :* Indus aquā agros, Cic. **II.** *to cheer, gladden, delight :* sol terram, Cic. In *Mid.: to rejoice, be glad :* laetificantur meo damno, Pl.

laetificus, a, um [laetus facio], *gladdening, glad, joyful :* fetus, Lucr. ; vites, Enn.

laetitia, ae, *f.* [laetus]. **I.** *fertility.* T r a n s f. (of speech) *richness, wealth or grace :* Tac. **II.** *exuberant joy, gladness :* Pl., Cic., Verg., etc. ; diem in laetitiā degere, Ter. ; maximā omnīs laetitiā adficere, Caes. ; alicui obicere, offerre, Ter. ; alicui dare, Cic. ; laetitiā perfrui, efferri, Cic. ; laetitiā exsultare, Cic. Ep. ; laetitiam percipere ex re, Cic.

laetor, āri [laetus], *to rejoice, be joyful or glad.* With ABL. : Ter., Cic., Juv. With *de* or *in* and ABL. : Cic. With ACC. of *Neut. Pron. :* Cic., Liv. With ACC. : Sall., Verg. With *quod-* clause : Hor. With ACC. and *Inf. :* Ter., Cic., Verg.

laetus, a, um. **1.** L i t. **a.** *sleek, fat :* boum armenta, Verg. ; glande sues laeti, Verg. **b.** *fertile, rich, luxuriant :* ager, Varr. ; flores, Cic. ; segetes, farra, Verg. With GEN. : frugum laetus ager, Sall. ; locus laetissimus umbrae, Verg. **2.** T r a n s f. **a.** Of style : *rich, copious :* Cic. ; of the author : Quint. **b.** Of appearance : *bright, sparkling, sprightly :* Verg., Ov. *Comp. :* Cic. **c.** To the mind : *pleasing, pleasant, cheering, welcome :* fructus, Cic. ; nuntii, Tac. ; laetam cognomine gentem, Verg. ; militibus nomen, Tac. *Comp.* and *Sup. :* Cic. **d.** *happy, fortunate, auspicious :* saecula, Verg. ; augurium, Tac. ; proeli finis laetior, Tac. **e.** *rejoicing, glad, cheerful, pleased :* laeti atque erecti, Cic. ; de amicā, Ter. ; laetus sum (with ACC. and *Inf.*), Ter. With ABL. : classis praedā, Liv. ; deum (GEN.) partu, Verg. ; Hor. With GEN. : laeta laborum, Verg. With *ob :* servatam ob navem, Verg. [It. *lieto ;* and Fr. *lie,* in *faire chère lie.*]

laeve, *adv. wrongly, awkwardly :* Hor.

laevus, a, um [*cf.* Gk. λαιός], *left, on the left side.* **1.** L i t. : manus, Cic. ; latus, Ov. ; iter, Verg. ; amnis, Tac. A d v. : ab laevā manu, *on the left,* Pl. ; laevum, *on the left,* Verg. ; in laevum, *to the left :* Ov. As Noun. **a. laeva**, ae, *f.* (*sc.* manus or pars), *the left hand, left side :* Pl., Cic., Verg., etc. ; ad laevam, Cic., Liv. ; laevā, *on the left,* Liv. **b. laeva**, ōrum, n. *pl. places lying on the left :* Verg., Ov. **2.** T r a n s f. **a.** *awkward, stupid :* Hor. ; mens, Verg. **b.** *ill-omened, pernicious :* lumen, Verg. ; tempus, picus, Hor. ; laevo monitu, Juv. **c.** In augury : *on the left,* corresponding to the Eastern quarter of the heaven (the augur facing S.) ; hence, *lucky, propitious :* numina, Verg. ; intonuit laevum, Verg. ; tonitru dedit omina laevo Iuppiter, Ov.

laganum, I, n. [λάγανον], *a kind of cake made of flour and oil :* Hor.

lageos, I, *f.* [λάγειος], *a Greek species of vine :* Verg.

lagoena (-**ōna**), ae, *f.* [λάγηνος], *a large earthenware vessel with a neck and handles ; a flagon :* Pl., Cic. Ep., Hor., etc.

lagois, idis, *f.* [λαγωΐς], *a bird,* perh. a kind of grouse : Hor.

laguncula, ae, *f.* [*dim.* lagoena], *a small flagon, flask :* Plin. Ep.

Lagus, I, m. *f.* of *Ptolemy I, king of Egypt ;* **Lageus**, a, um, *Egyptian.*

Laius, I, m. *s.* of *Labdacus and f. of Oedipus ;* **Laiades**, ae, m. *s.* of *Laius, Oedipus.*

lallo, āre, *to sing lullaby :* Pers.

lama, ae, *f. a bog, fen :* Hor.

lambero, āre, *to tear to pieces.* P r o v. : lepide me meo ludo lamberas (i.e. you beat me at my own game), Pl.

lambo, bere, bī [*cf.* Gk. λάπτω], *to lick, lap.* **1.** L i t. : Cic., Verg., Liv., etc. **2.** T r a n s f. Of a river : *to flow by, to wash :* quae loca fabulosus lambit Hydaspes, Hor. Of ivy : *to cling to, encircle :* Pers. Of fire : *to lick, reach up to, play about :* Aetna sidera, Verg. ; flamma comas, Verg. ; Hor.

lamenta, ōrum, n. *pl. wailing, moaning, weeping, lamentation :* Lucr., Cic., Verg., etc.

lamentabilis, e, *adj.* [lāmentor]. **I.** *deserving sorrow, pitiable :* regnum, Verg. **II.** *doleful, lamenting :* vox, Cic. ; comploratio, Liv. **III.** *mournful, attended with signs of woe :* funera, Cic.

lamentarius, a, um [lāmenta], *mournful, causing tears :* Pl.

lamentatio, ōnis, *f.* [lāmentor], *a wailing, weeping, lamenting :* Pl., Cic.

lamentor, āri [lāmenta], *to wail, moan, weep, lament :* Pl., Cic., Suet. With ACC. : *to weep over, to bewail :* Pl., Ter., Cic. With ACC. and *Inf. :* Pl., Hor.

lamia, ae, *f.* (λαμία), *a witch, a sorceress, enchantress :* Hor.

lamina, lammina, and **lamna** (Hor.), ae, *f. a thin piece of metal, wood, marble,* etc. ; *a plate, leaf.* **1.** L i t. : Caes., Cic., Tac., etc. ; laminae ardentes, *red-hot plates* (for torture), Cic. Also *a blade of a saw :* Verg. ; *of a sword :* Ov. **2.** T r a n s f. **a.** *coin :* Hor., Ov. **b.** *peel or shell* of an unripe nut : Ps.-Ov. [It. *lama ;* Fr. *lame.*]

lampas, adis, *f.* [λαμπάς], *a torch, link, flambeau.* **1.** L i t. : Pl., Lucr., Verg., etc. Of *a wedding-torch :* Ter., Cic. **2.** T r a n s f. **a.** From the Greek torch-race, in which one runner passed on the torch still burning to the next runner : quasi cursores vitāī lampada tradunt, Lucr. ; qui prior es, cur me in decursu lampada poscis ? Pers. **b.** *brightness :* mundi, solis, Lucr. ; Phoebea, Verg. Poet. like lumen, for *day :* nonā lampade, *on the ninth day,* Lucr. **c.** *a meteor resembling a torch :* Luc.

Lampetie, ēs, *f. d.* of *Phoebus and s. of Phaëthon.*

Lamus, I, m. **I.** *a mythical king of the Laestrygonians.* **II.** *s.* of *Hercules and Omphale.*

lana, ae, *f. wool.* **1.** L i t. : Cic., Verg., etc. ; lanam carere, *to card wool,* Pl. ; ducere, *to spin it,* Ov. **2.** T r a n s f. **a.** *a working in wool :* lanā et telā victum quaeritans, Ter. ; Lucretia lanae dedita, Liv. P r o v. : cogitare de lanā suā (i.e. to be unconcerned), Ov. Of things like wool : *soft hair or feathers, down :* nemora canentia lanā (i.e. cotton), Verg. Of *fleecy clouds,* " *cirri* " : vellera tenuia lanae, Verg. P r o v. : rixari de lanā caprinā (i.e. to dispute about trifles), Hor. [Fr. *laine.*]

lanarius, I, m. [lāna], *a worker in wool :* Pl.

lanatus, a, um [lāna], *woolly :* caprae, Liv. *Comp. :* Plin. As Noun, **lanatae**, ārum, *f. pl. sheep :* Juv.

lancea, ae, *f. a light spear, with a leathern thong fastened to it, a lance :* Sall., Verg., Tac.

lancinō, āre [lacer], *to tear to pieces.* T r a n s f. *to squander, waste :* bona, Cat. ; vitam, Sen. Ep.

lāneus, a, um [lāna], *woollen, of wool.* **1.** L i t. : Pl., Cic., Verg., etc. **2.** T r a n s f. *soft :* Cat., Mart. [Fr. *lange.*]

langue-faciō, facere, fēcī, factum, *to make faint, weary :* Cic.

languēns, entis. **I.** *Part.* langueō. **II.** A d j. : *drooping, weary, languid :* hyacinthus, Verg. ; incitare languentis, Cic. ; vox, Cic. ; cor, Cat. Of troops : languentes atque animo remissi, Caes. **III.** *Masc.* Noun : incitare languentis, Cic.

langueō, ēre [*cf.* Gk. λήγω, and laxus], *to be faint, weary, languid.* **1.** L i t. : de viā, Cic. ; corpora morbo, Verg. Of plants, etc. : *to droop, wither :* Verg., Prop. Of the sea or surf : *to be spent, retreat :* Verg. **2.** T r a n s f. *to be languid, inactive, listless :* languet iuventus, Cic. ; otio, Cic. ; amor, Ov.

languēscō, languēscere, languī [langueō], *to grow faint, weak, languid.* **1.** L i t. : corpore, Cic. Of disease : corpora, Ov. ; Suet. Of things : flos, Verg. ; Bacchus in amphorā, Hor. ; luna, Tac. ; a magno fluctus flatu, Ov. **2.** T r a n s f. *to grow languid, listless, spiritless :* Cic. ; mens, Quint. ; cupido, Plin. Ep.

languidē, *adv. faintly, feebly, without vigour.* *Comp.* : Caes., Cic.

languidulus, a, um [*dim.* languidus]. **I.** *sweetly languid :* somni, Cat. **II.** *drooping :* coronae, Cic.

languidus, a, um [langueō], *faint, weak, drooping, sluggish, languid.* **1.** L i t. : homines vino languidi, Cic. ; pecus, Cic. ; boves collo trahentes languido, Hor. ; flumen, Hor. ; vina (i.e. mellow), Hor. ; aqua, Liv. ; oculi, Quint. *Comp.* : Caes., Hor. **2.** T r a n s f. Of character : *feeble, listless, spiritless :* Cic. ; animus, Caes. ; studium, Cic. ; oratio, Quint. *Comp.* : Cic., Quint. **3.** A c t. : *enervating :* voluptates, Cic. ; quies, Verg.

languor, ōris, *m.* [langueō], *faintness, feebleness, weariness, languor, lassitude.* **1.** L i t. : Pl., Caes., Cic. In *pl.* : Cat. Esp. from disease : aquosus (i.e. dropsy), Hor. ; languor faucium, Suet. **2.** T r a n s f. of the mind : *dullness, sluggishness, listlessness :* Hor. ; languori se dedere, Cic. ; alicui adferre, Cic. ; in languorem vertere, Tac.

laniātus, ūs, *m.* [laniō], *a mangling, lacerating.* **1.** L i t. : ferarum, Cic. **2.** T r a n s f. (in *pl.*), *anguish of mind :* Tac.

laniēna, ae, *f.* [lanius], *a butcher's stall :* Liv.

lānificus, a, um [lāna faciō], *working in wool* (i.e. by spinning, weaving, etc.) : manus, Tib. ; ars, Ov. ; sorores (i.e. the Fates), Mart.

lāniger, a, um [lāna gerō], *wool-bearing, fleecy :* greges, Verg. As Noun. **a. lāniger**, erī, *m. a ram :* Ov. ; *a lamb :* Phaedr. **b. lānigera**, ae, *f. a sheep :* Lucr.

laniō, āre [lanius], *to tear to pieces, mangle, lacerate, rend.* **1.** L i t. : corpora, Cic. ; viscera, Liv. ; dentibus artūs, Verg. ;

digitis ora, Ov. ; crura, Tac. ; vestem, comas, Ov. **2.** T r a n s f. : sacrilegae carmina linguae, Ov. ; vitia cor laniant, Sen. Ep.

laniōnius, a, um [lanius], *of a butcher :* Suet.

lanista, ae, *m. a trainer of gladiators, fencing-master.* **1.** L i t. : Cic., Juv., Suet. **2.** T r a n s f. *a trainer in evil ; inciter to violence :* Cic., Liv.

lānitium, ī, n. [lāna], *the wool-crop :* Verg.

lanius, ī, *m.* [laniō], *a butcher.* **1.** L i t. : Pl., Cic., Liv., etc. **2.** T r a n s f. *an executioner :* Pl.

lanterna, ae, *f.* [λαμπτήρ], *a lantern, lamp :* Pl., Cic. Ep., Juv.

lanternārius, ī, *m.* [lanterna], *a link-boy, guide :* Cic.

lānūgō, inis, *f.* [lāna], *woolliness, down,* of plants : Lucr., Verg. ; of the cheeks : Verg., Ov., Suet.

lānx, lancis, *f.* [*cf.* λεκάνη]. **I.** *platter, dish :* Pl., Cic. Ep., Hor., Ov. Of freq. use in sacrifices : Verg. **II.** *the scale of a balance :* Cic., Verg.

Lāocoōn, ontis, *m. a Trojan, s. of Priam and Hecuba ; priest of Apollo ; with his two sons he was killed by two serpents from the sea.*

Lāodamīa, ae, *f. d. of Acastus and w. of Protesilaus.*

Lāomedōn, ontis, *m. f. of Priam, king of Troy ;* **Lāomedontēus (-ius)**, a, um ; **Lāomedontiadēs**, ae, *m. s. of Lāomedon ;* Priam ; in *pl. the Trojans.*

lapathum, ī, *n.* and **lapathus**, ī, *f.* (*m.* Lucil.) [λάπαθον or λάπαθος], *sorrel :* Hor.

lapicīda, ae, *m.* [lapis caedō], *a stonecutter, quarryman :* Liv.

lapicīdīnae, ārum, *f.* [lapis caedō], *stone-quarries :* Cic.

lapidārius, a, um [lapis], *of stone, stone-latomiae, stone-quarries,* Pl.

lapidātiō, ōnis, *f.* [lapidō], *a throwing of stones :* Cic. In *pl.* : Cic.

lapidātor, ōris, *m.* [lapidō], *a stone-thrower :* Cic.

lapideus, a, um [lapis], *of stone, consisting of stone.* **1.** L i t. : imber, Cic., Liv. ; murus, Liv. **2.** T r a n s f. *petrified :* lapideus sum, Pl.

lapidō, āre [lapis], *to pelt with stones :* templa, Suet. *Impers. :* lapidat, *it rains stones :* imbri lapidavit, Liv. ; de caelo lapidaverat, Liv. *Pass. Impers.* : quod de caelo lapidatum esset, Liv.

lapidōsus, a, um [lapis]. **I.** *full of stones, stony :* terra, Varr. ; montes, fluvius, Ov. **II.** *hard as stone, stony :* corna, Verg. ; panis (or perh. gritty), Hor. Of gout : *stony,* i.e. *producing chalk-stones in the joints :* Pers.

lapillus, ī, *m.* [*dim.* lapis], *a little stone, a pebble.* **1.** In gen. : Ov. Used for voting at trials : Ov. Lucky days were marked with white, unlucky ones with black stones : diem signare melioribus lapillis, Mart. **2.** In partic. **a.** *a precious stone, gem, jewel :* Hor., Ov. **b.** In *pl.* : *small pieces of stone,* esp. *of marble used in mosaic :* Libyci, Hor.

lapis, idis. *m.* [*cf.* Gk. λέπας], *a stone, stone.* **1.** L i t. : Pl., Lucr., Caes., Cic., etc. ;

lapidibus pluit, Liv. ; lapide candidiore diem notare (*cf.* lapillus), Cat. **2.** T r a n s f. **A.** For dullness, stupidity, want of feeling : quid stas, lapis ? Ter. ; Pl. ; Cic. ; Ov. P r o v.: **i.** lapidem ferre alterā manu, alterā panem ostentare (i.e. to flatter openly and injure secretly), Pl. **ii.** verberare lapidem, Pl. **iii.** lapides loqui (i.e. to speak hard words), Pl. **iv.** bis ad eundem (*sc.* lapidem offendere), Cic. Ep. **B.** E s p. **a.** Iuppiter lapis, *a Jupiter stone* ; prob. *a meteoric stone* used to swear by : Iovem lapidem iurare, Cic. **b.** *a milestone* : Varr., Ov., Liv., Tac. **c.** *an auctioneer's block* : Pl. Hence, of men bought like slaves : praetor duos de lapide emptos tribunos, Cic. **d.** *a landmark, boundary-stone* : Tib., Liv. **e.** *a tombstone* : Prop. **f.** *a precious stone* : Hor. **g.** *marble* : Verg., Hor. ; varii (in mosaic), Hor.

Lapithae, ārum (GEN. *pl.* Lapithum, Verg.), *m. pl. a mountain-tribe in Thessaly, who, at the marriage of their king Pirithŏus, engaged in a fierce conflict with the Centaurs ;* **Lapithaeus** and **Lapithēïus,** a, um.

lappa, ae, *f. a bur* : Verg., Ov.

lāpsïō, ōnis, *f.* [lābor], *a sliding.* T r a n s f. *propensity, tendency* : Cic.

lāpsō, āre [*freq.* lābor], *to slip repeatedly, stumble* : Verg., Tac.

lāpsus, a, um. **I.** *Part.* lābor. **II.** Adj.: *fallen, unfortunate* : Prop., Ov.

lāpsus, ūs, *m.* [lābor], *a slipping, gliding, steady motion, fall.* **1.** L i t.: celeri percurrunt fulmina, Lucr. ; volucrum lapsūs, Cic. ; horrifico lapsu Harpyiae, Verg. ; lapsu dracones effugiunt, Verg. ; stellae certo lapsu feruntur, Cic. ; Verg. ; fluminum, Hor. ; Cic. ; equi, Verg. ; terrae, Liv. Abstr. for concr.: rotarum lapsūs, Verg. **2.** T r a n s f. *a slip, error, fault* : Pl., Cic.

laqueāria, ium, *n. pl.* (Verg., Sen. Ep.), and Acc. *sing.* **laqueāre** (Verg.) [cogn. with lacūna], *a panelled ceiling.*

laqueātus, a, um [laqueāria], *having a panelled ceiling* : Cic., Hor., Liv.

laqueus, i, *m.* **1.** L i t. **a.** *a noose* : Pl., Caes., Sall. **b.** *a hangman's halter* : Cic., Liv., etc. **c.** *a snare* : Verg., Hor., Ov. **2.** T r a n s f. **a.** *a snare, trap* : iudici laqueos declinans, Cic. ; laquei Stoicorum. **b.** *fetters, hindrances* : Plin. Ep. [It. *laccio* ; Sp. *lazo* ; Fr. *lacs.*]

Lār, Laris, *m.* (GEN. *pl.* Larum, Cic. ; Larium, Liv.), mostly in *pl.* **Larēs** (older **Lasēs**), *tutelary deities, protectors of a locality.* **A.** P u b l i c : viales, Pl. ; praestites, Ov. ; agri custodes, Tib. ; permarini, Liv. ; compitales, Suet. **B.** P r i v a t e (most freq.), *household, domestic tutelary gods.* **1.** L i t.: familiares, Pl., Cic., Hor. In *sing.* : Pl. **2.** T r a n s f. *a hearth, dwelling, home* : Pl. ; relinquent larem familiarem suum ? Cic. ; paternus, Hor. ; deserere larem, Ov. ; lare recipere, Liv. In *pl.* : iussa pares mutare lares, Hor. P o e t. : of *a bird's nest* : Ov.

lārdum, *v.* lāridum.

Lārentia, ae, *f.* also **Acca Lārentia,** *w. of Faustulus, who suckled and reared the twins Romulus and Remus* ; **Lārentālia,** ium,

n. pl. a festival in her honour, celebrated on Dec. 23rd.

largē, *adv. plentifully, bountifully, liberally* : Pl., Cic., Tac. *Comp.* : Ter., Hor. *Sup.* : Cic.

largiflcus, a, um [largus faciō], *bountiful* : Lucr.

largifluus, a, um [largus fluō], *flowing copiously* : fons, Lucr.

largiloquus, a, om [largus loquor], *talking copiously, talkative* : Pl.

largior, īrī (*Imperf.* largībar, Prop.: *Fut.* largībere, Pl.) [largus], *to give bountifully, to bestow* or *impart freely* ; *to lavish.* **1.** L i t.: amico meā ex crumenā, Pl. ; qui eripiunt aliis, quod aliis largiantur, Cic. ; agros emeritis, Tac. ; pecuniam in aliquem, Tac. Of inanim. subjects : Gallis provinciae propinquitas multa ad copiam atque usūs largitur, Caes. O c c. with rhet. exaggeration : *to bestow, confer* : laetitiam alicui, Pl. ; solamen, Verg. ; nimium parcus in largiendā civitate, Cic. ; Hortensio summam copiam facultatemque dicendi natura largita est, Cic. Also of bribery : largiendo de alieno popularem fieri, Liv. ; Sall. ; Quint. **2.** T r a n s f. (*cf.* condono), *to condone, forgive* : id inertiae nostrae, Cic. ; rei publicae iniurias, Tac.

largitās, ātis, *f.* [largus], *abundance, bounty, liberality* : Ter. ; tui muneris, Cic. ; terra fruges cum maximā largitate fundit, Cic.

largiter, *adv. freely, largely, very much* : peccare, Pl. ; posse, *to be very powerful,* Caes.; distare, Lucr. ; auferre, Lucr.; Hor. With GEN. : auri et argenti (*plenty of*), Pl.

largitiō, ōnis, *f.* [largior]. **I.** *a giving freely, a bestowing* : aequitatis, civitatis, Cic. E s p. of money : Caes., Cic. In *pl.* : largitiones facere, Cic. P r o v.: largitio fundum non habet, Cic. **II.** *bribery, corruption,* esp. to obtain a public office : tribum turpi largitione corrumpere, Cic. ; profusissima, Suet.

largitor, ōris, *m.* [largior]. **I.** *a liberal giver, a bestower* : multarum rerum, pecuniae, Sall. ; praedae, Liv. In bad sense : *a squanderer,* Cic. **II.** *a briber* : Cic.

largus, a, um. **I.** Of things : *bountiful, copious, plentiful, ample* : imbres, undae, pabula, etc., Lucr. ; lux, Lucr., Cic. ; odores, Ov. *Comp.* : largior aether, Verg. ; ignis, Hor. ; largiore vino usus, Liv. ; stipendia, Tac. *Sup.* : munus largissimum edere, Suet. With GEN. : opum, Verg. ; Pl. **II.** Of persons : *bountiful, liberal, open-handed* : Pl., Cic., Tac. With ABL. : linguā, Pl. ; promissis, Tac. With *Inf.* : Hor. *Comp.* : Pl. *Sup.* : Cic.

lāridum, Pl., and **lārdum** (Hor., Ov., Juv.), I, *n.* (*cf.* Gk. λαρός, λαρινός), *the fat of* bacon. In *pl.* : Ov.

Lārissa (or **Lārīsa**), ae, *f. a city in Thessaly* ; **Lārissaeus,** a, um ; **Lārissēnsēs,** ium, *m. pl. its inhabitants.*

Lars, Lartis, *m. a praenomen or title of Etruscan origin, usually given to the eldest son.*

larva and **lārua,** ae, *f. a ghost, spectre.* **1.** L i t.: Pl. As a term of contempt, *bogy* : Pl. **2.** T r a n s f. *a mask* : larvae et tragici cothurni, Hor.

larvātus, a, um [larva], *bewitched* : Pl.

lasanum, I, n. [λάσανον], *a night-commode* : Hor.

lāsarpīcifer, era, erum [lāsarpīcium (v. lāserpīcium) ferō], *producing the plant lasarpicium, hence, producing asa foetida* : Cat.

lascivia, ae, f. [lascīvus], *sportiveness, playfulness, frolicsomeness*. **a.** In good sense : Pl., Lucr., Cic., Liv. Comic. : o virgarum lascivia, Pl. **b.** In bad sense : *petulance, impudence, wantonness* : Sall., Quint., Tac. Of style : Quint.

lascīvibundus, a, um [lascīviō], *sportive* : Pl.

lascīviō, īre [lascīvus], *to sport, frisk, frolic*. **a.** In good sense : Cic. ; agnus fugā, Ov. **b.** In bad sense : *to run wild, run riot, be wanton* : Liv., Tac. Transf. of style : Quint.

lascīvus, a, um [cf. Gk. λιλαίομαι, λῆμα]. **1.** Lit. **a.** In good sense : *playful, frolicsome, frisky* : nova proles (pecudum), Lucr. ; capella, Verg. ; pueri (*saucy*), Hor. ; verba, Hor. Comp. : Ov. **b.** In bad sense : *impudent, wanton, petulans* : puellae, femur, Ov. ; oscula, Tac. ; libelli, Mart. Sup. : picturae et figurae, Suet. **2.** Transf. (of growth), *unrestrained, wanton* : hederae, Hor.

lāserpicium, I, n. *the plant silphium*, which yielded asa foetida or lāser : Pl.

Lasēs, v. Larēs.

lassitūdō, inis, f. [lassus], *physical exhaustion, weariness, heaviness, lassitude* : Pl., Caes., Cic., Liv.

lassō, āre, *to weary, fatigue* : Prop., Ov., Curt.

lassulus, a, um [dim. lassus], *somewhat wearied* : Cat.

lassus, a, um, *weary, tired, exhausted*. **1.** Lit. : de viā, Pl. ; itinere atque opere castrorum et proelio fessi lassique, Sall. ; ab equo indomito, Hor. With Inf. : Prop. With Gen. : lassus maris et viarum, Ho. **2.** Transf. : collum, Verg. ; stomachus, aures, Hor. ; fructibus adsiduis humus, Ov.; natura, Plin. Ep.

lātē, adv. *broadly, widely, extensively*. **1.** Lit. : minus late vagari, Caes. ; Tac. ; populus late rex, Verg. ; Hor. ; often with longe, *far and wide* : late longeque diffusus, Cic. ; Caes. Comp. : Pl., Ov., Liv., etc. Sup. : Cic., Nep. **2.** Transf. *extensively, profusely* : ars late patet, Cic. ; Ov. Comp. : latius perscribere, Caes. ; loqui, Cic. ; opibus uti, Hor. Sup. : fidei bonae nomen latissime manat, Cic.

latebra, ae, f. [lateō], *a hiding-place, lurking-hole, retreat* (mostly in pl.). **1.** Lit. : Pl., Cic., Verg., etc. ; lunae (i.e. eclipses), Lucr. **2.** Transf. **a.** cum illa coniuratio ex latebris erupisset, Cic. ; Pl. ; Lucr. **b.** *a subterfuge, loophole* (only in sing.) : videant, ne quaeratur latebra periurio, Cic. ; latebram dare vitiis, Ov.

latebricola, ae, m.f. [latebra colō], *having low haunts* : Pl.

latebrōsē, adv. *in a hiding-place* : Pl.

latebrōsus, a, um [latebra], *full of lurking-holes* or *coverts*. **1.** Lit. : Pl., Cic., Verg., etc. **2.** Transf. *full of holes* : pumex, Verg.

latēns, entis. **I.** Part. lateō. **II.** Adj. :

Transf. : rem latentem explicare, Cic. ; causae, Verg. ; mandata, Ov.

latenter, adv. *in secret* : Cic., Ov.

lateō, ēre [cf. Gk. λανθάνω], *to lie hid or concealed, lurk*. **1.** Lit. : Pl., Cic., Verg., etc. Occ. *to skulk, keep out of sight*, in order not to appear in court : fraudationis causā, Cic. **2.** Transf. **a.** *to live retired* : crede mihi, bene qui latuit, bene vixit, Ov. **b.** *to lie safe, sheltered* : sub umbrā Romanae amicitiae, Liv. **c.** *to lurk* (in pretence) : sub nomine pacis bellum, Cic. **d.** (like Gk. λανθάνω), *to escape notice* : plurimarum rerum utilitas, Cic. With Acc. : nec latuere doli fratrem Iunonis, Verg. ; Ov. ; Varr. With Indir. Quest. : Nep.

later, eris, m. *a brick, tile* : Cic. Prov. : laterem lavare (i.e. to labour in vain), Ter.

laterāmen, inis, n. [later], *earthenware* : Lucr.

laterculus, I, m. [dim. later]. **1.** Lit. : *a small brick* or *tile* : Caes. **2.** Transf. : *a sort of cake* or *biscuit* : Pl., Cato.

latericius, a, um [later], *made of bricks* : turris, muri, Caes. ; urbs, Suet. Neut. as Noun : *brickwork* : Caes.

lātern-, v. lantern-.

latēscō, ere [lateō], *to hide oneself* : Cic.

latex, icis, m. *any liquid*, esp. *water* : Ov. ; in pl. : Lucr., Verg., Ov., Liv. Of *wine* : Lucr., Verg., Ov. Of other liquids : absinthi, Lucr. ; Palladii latices (i.e. oil), Ov.

latibulum, I, n. [lateō], *a hiding-place, lair*. **1.** Lit. (in pl.) : Cic., Cat. **2.** Transf. : doloris, Cic. Ep.

lāticlāvius, a, um [lātus clāvus], *having a broad purple stripe* (a mark of distinction worn by senators, military tribunes of the equestrian order, and the sons of distinguished families ; v. clavus) : Suet. As Noun, *one entitled to wear the latus clavus ; a senator, nobleman* : Suet.

Latīnē, adv. *in Latin* : Pl. ; loqui, Cic., Liv. ; scire, *to understand Latin*, Cic. ; reddere, *to translate into Latin*, Cic. ; formare, *to write* or *compose in Latin*, Suet. Occ. Latine loqui, *to speak plainly* (or *rightly*) : (gladiatorem) ut appellant ii, qui plane et Latine loquuntur, Cic.

Latīnitās, ātis, f. [Latīnus]. **I.** *pure Latin style, Latinity* : Cic. Ep. **II.** *the Latin rights and privileges*, also called ius Lati : Cic. Ep., Suet.

Latīnus, a, um [Latium], *Latin* : lingua, Cic. ; via (i.e. beginning at the Porta Latina), Cic., Liv. ; colonia (i.e. possessing the ius Lati), Cic. ; nomen (i.e. ius Lati), Cic., Sall.) ; feriae Latinae or simply Latinae, Liv.

Latīnus, i, m. *a king of the Laurentians, who gave his daughter Lavinia in marriage to Aeneas.*

lātiō, ōnis, f. [lātus : v. ferō], *a bearing, bringing*. Transf. : auxili, Liv. ; suffragi, Liv. ; legis (*a proposing of a law, a bill*), Cic. Ep.

latitō, āre [freq. lateō], *to be in the habit of concealing oneself, to keep in close hiding, to lurk* : Pl., Cic., Hor. Of things : *to be concealed* : invisa atque latitantibus rebus confidere, Caes. ; Lucr. Esp. *to keep out* *of the way*, in order not to appear before a court of justice : Cic.

lātitūdō, inis, *f.* [lātus], *breadth, width.* **1.** Lit. : Caes. In *pl.* : Cic. **2.** Transf. **a.** *extent* : possessionum, Cic. **b.** verb-orum, *a broad pronunciation*, Cic. **c.** *richness of expression* : Plin. Ep.

Latium, I, *n. the district in which Rome was situated, now the* Roman *Campagna* ; **iūs Latī** or simply **Latium**, *the political rights which belonged originally to the Latins, but were afterwards granted by the Romans to others.* Hence **Latius**, a, um, poet. for Roman ; **Latīnus**, a, um, q.v. ; **Latīnī**, ōrum, *m. pl. the Latins* ; **Latīnē**, *adv.* q.v. ; **Latiālis** (-iāris), e, *adj.* ; **Latiar**, āris, *n. the festival of* Iuppiter Latiaris ; **Latiniēnsis**, e, *adj.* ; **Latiniēnsēs**, ium, *m. pl. the Latins* ; **Latīnitās**, ātis, *f.* q.v.

lātom-, *v.* lautum-.

Lātōna, ae (**Lātō**, ūs), *f. d. of the Titan Coeus and Phoebe, and m. of Apollo and Diana, to whom she gave birth on the island of Delos* ; **Lātōnius**, a, um ; **Lātōnia**, ae, *f. Diana* ; **Lātōius** (**Lētō-**), a, um ; **Lātōius**, I, *m. Apollo* ; **Lātōus**, a, um ; **Lātōus**, I, *m. Apollo* ; **Lātōis** (**Lētō-**), idis or idos, *f. adj.* ; **Lātōis**, idis, *f. Diana* ; **Lātōnigena**, ae, *m.f. child of Latona* ; Latonigenae duo, i.e. *Apollo and Diana*, Ov.

lātor, ōris, *m.* [lātus : *v.* ferō], *a bringer or bearer.* Transf. *a mover or proposer of a law* : Caes. ; legis, Cic. ; rogationis, Liv.

lātrātor, ōris, *m.* [lātrō], *a barker.* **1.** Lit. : Anubis, Verg., Ov. **2.** Transf. *a brawler, blusterer* : Quint.

lātrātus, ūs, *m.* [lātrō], *a barking* : Verg. In *pl.* : Verg., Ov., Juv.

lātrīna, ae, *f.* [lavō]. **I.** *a bath* : Lucil. **II.** *a lavatory* : Pl., Suet.

lātrō, āre, *to bark.* **A. 1.** Lit. : canes, Cic., Lucr., Hor. *Impers. Pass.* : Ov. **2.** Transf. *to roar, rant, clamour.* **a.** Of speakers : Cic., Hor. **b.** Of things : undae, Verg. ; stomachus, Hor. **B.** With Acc. **1.** Lit. *to bark at* : senem canes, Hor. **2.** Transf. **a.** *to bark at, snarl at* (with abuse) : si quis opprobriis dignum latraverit, Hor. **b.** *to clamour for* : nil aliud sibi naturam latrare, Lucr. ; Hor.

latrō, ōnis, *m.* [*cf.* Gk. λατρεύω]. **I.** Lit. **a.** *a servant, hired servant* : Enn. **b.** *a mercenary soldier* : Pl. **2.** Transf. **a.** Of *disbanded mercenaries, freebooters* : Caes., Liv. **b.** *brigand, highwayman* : Caes., Cic., Juv. **c.** *a hunter* : Verg. ; of a wolf : Phaedr. **d.** = latrunculus : Ov. [It. *ladrone* ; Sp. *ladron* ; Fr. *larron.*]

latrōcinium, I, *n.* [latrōcinor]. **I.** *the military service of a mercenary* : in latrocinio fuisti, Pl. **II.** *freebooting, highway-robbery, brigandage, piracy* : Caes., Cic., Sall. ; latrocinii imago (*v.* latrunculus), Ov. In *pl.* : Caes., Cic., Liv. Transf. **a.** In gen. : quod putares hic latrocinium non iudicium futurum, Cic. **b.** *a band of brigands* (i.e. *scoundrels*) : si ex tanto latrocinio unus tolletur, Cic. [Fr. *larcin* ; Eng. *larceny.*]

latrōcinor, ārī [latrō]. **I.** *to serve as a mercenary, to be a hired soldier* : Pl. **II.** *to play the freebooter, highwayman*, or *pirate* : Cic.

latrunculus, I, *m.* [*dim.* latrō]. **I.** *a paltry freebooter, brigand* : Cic. **II.** *a piece* (' *man* ') *in a game* : Suet.

lātumiae, *v.* lautumiae.

(1) **lātus**, a, um [old Lat. stlātos], *broad, wide.* **1.** Lit. : Pl., Cic., Verg., Tac., etc. Comp. : Caes., Phaedr. Sup. : Caes. *Neut.* as Noun : crescere in latum, Ov. **2.** Transf. **a.** *extensive* : fines, Caes. ; Liv. ; Ov. ; quam latissimas solitudines habere, Caes. **b.** *wide-spread, extended* : gloria, Plin. Ep. **c.** *spread-out* (of a vainglorious person) : latus ut in Circo spatiere, Hor., Sen. Ep. **d.** Of pronunciation : *broad* : verba, Cic. **e.** Of style : *diffuse* : Liv. Quint., Tac. Comp. : Cic., Quint.

(2) **lātus**, eris, *n.* [perh. fr. same root as lātus 1.], *the side* or *flank of the body.* **1.** Lit. **a.** In gen. : Pl., Cic., Verg., etc. **b.** Phr. : tegere latus alicui (*to walk by the side of somebody*), Hor. ; nunquam discedere ab alicuius latere, Cic. ; addit eos ab latere tyranni, Liv. ; latus alicui cingere (*to cling to somebody*), Liv. ; latus dare or praebere (*to expose oneself in fencing*), Tib. ; alicuius lateri iungi, Liv. **c.** *the lungs* : lateris or laterum dolor : Cic., Hor. With ref. to oratory : voce magnā et bonis lateribus, Cic. ; nobilitatis ex lateribus et lacertis, Cic. ; Quint. **d.** = *corpus* : Hor., Ov. **2.** Transf. **a.** In gen. : *the side, flank, lateral surface* of any thing (opp. frons and tergum) : collis ex utrāque parte lateris deiectūs habebat, Caes. ; insulae, Caes., Cic. ; castrorum, Caes ; tum prora avertit et undis dat latus, Verg. ; domūs, mundi, Hor. Milit. of an army, *the flank* : ex itinere nostros latere aperto aggressi, Caes. Esp. **a** (ab) latere or a lateribus : *on the flank* or *flanks* (opp. a fronte, *and* a tergo) : Caes., Cic., Liv., etc. Also ex lateribus, Sall., Hirt., Liv. **b.** Phr. : lateri adhaerere gravem dominum (i.e. *threatens*), Liv. ; malo latus obdit apertum (*gives a handle to*), Hor. ; latere tecto abscedere (*to get off scot-free*), Ter. ; imperii nudare latus (*to leave the frontier exposed*), Luc.

latusculum, I, *n.* [*dim.* latus], *a little side* : Lucr., Cat.

laudābilis, e, *adj.* [laudō], *praiseworthy* : Cic., Ov., etc. Comp. : Cic., Liv.

laudābiliter, *adv.* *praiseworthily, laudably* : vivere, Cic.

laudātiō, ōnis, *f.* [laudō], *a praising, commendation* ; *a eulogy, panegyric.* **A.** In gen. : Cic. With *Subj.* Gen. : Cic. With *Obj.* Gen. : Cic., Quint. In *pl.* : Cic., Quint. **B.** In partic. **a.** *a funeral oration* or *panegyric* : funebris, Cic., Quint. With *Obj.* Gen. : Liv. **b.** *testimonial to character in a court of justice* : gravissima, Cic. ; iudicialis, Suet.

laudātīvus, a, um [laudō]. Rhet. : *laudatory* : Quint.

laudātor, ōris, *m.* and **laudātrix**, Icis, *f.* [laudō], *a praiser* ; *a eulogiser, panegyrist.* **A.** In gen. : voluptatis, Cic. ; temporis acti, Hor. ; Ov. **B.** In partic. **a.** *one who pronounces a funeral oration* : Liv., Plin. Ep. **b.** *one who bears testimony to character in a court of justice* : Cic.

laudātus, a, um. **I**. *Part.* laudŏ. **II**. Adj.: *praiseworthy, esteemed, excellent* : artes, Cic.; virgo laudatissima formae dote, Ov.

laudō, āre [laus], *to praise, commend, extol, eulogise, approve.* **A**. In gen.: bonos, Cic.; legem, Cic.; agricolam laudat iuris peritus, Hor.; Ov.; Tac., etc. *Pass.* with *Inf.*: exstinxisse nefas laudabor, Verg. **B**. In partic. **a**. *to pronounce a funeral oration or panegyric on* : quem cum supremo eius die Maximus laudaret, Cic. **b**. *to name, quote, cite* : Iovem supremum testem, Pl.; auctores, Cic. [It. *lodare* ; Sp. *loar* ; Fr. *louer*.]

laureātus, a, um [laurea], *crowned or decked with laurel* : imago, Cic.; litterae, a letter announcing a victory (because bound up with bay-leaves), Liv.; ne laureatis (*sc.* litteris) quidem gesta prosecutus est, Tac.

Laurentēs, um, *m. pl. the Laurentians, the people of Lavinium* ; in *sing*. **Laurēns**, entis, *adj.* ; **Laurentius, Laurentīnus**, a, um.

laureola, ae, *f.* [*dim.* laurea], *a little laurel-crown.* Transf. *a triumph* : Cic. Ep.

laureus, a, um [laurus], *of laurel, laurel-* : vectes, Cato; corona, Liv.; serta, Ov. As Noun, **laurea**, ae, *f.* **I**. (*sc.* arbor), *the laurel or bay-tree* : Hor., Liv. **II**. (*sc.* corona). **1**. Lit.: laureā donandus Apollinari, Hor.; decemviri laureā coronati, Liv.; Suet. **2**. Transf. *a triumph* : quam lauream cum tuā laudatione conferrem ? Cic. Ep.

lauricomus, a, um [laurus coma], *laurel-tressed* : montes, Lucr.

laurifer, era, erum [laurus ferŏ], *laurel-crowned* : Luc.

lauriger, era, erum [laurus gerŏ], *decked with laurel* : Phoebus, Ov.

laurus, i (ABL. laurū, Hor.; NOM. *pl.* laurūs, Verg., Tib.), *f. a bay-tree* (sacred to Apollo). **1**. Lit.: Pl., Cic., Verg., etc. **2**. Transf. *a laurel-crown* : triumphales, Ov.; hence, *a triumph* : incurrit haec nostra laurus in oculos, Cic. Ep.

laus, laudis, *f. praise, commendation, approval, glory, fame.* **1**. Lit.: in laude esse, Cic.; aliquem laude (*or* laudibus) ornare, onerare, cumulare, adficere, ad caelum efferre, Cic.; laudem alicui tribuere, Cic. Ep.; also *a cause of praise* : Fabio laudi datum est quod etc., Cic. With *Obj.* GEN.: Cic. Of *funeral orations* : Liv. **2**. Transf. *a praiseworthy deed, merit* : maximam putant esse laudem vacare agros, Caes.; bellicae laudes, Cic.; merui laude coronam, Verg.

Lausus, i, m. **I**. *s. of Numitor and b. of Rhea Silvia*. **II**. *s. of Mezentius, killed by Aeneas.*

lautē, adv. *elegantly, splendidly, sumptuously.* **1**. Lit.: Pl., Cic., etc. Comp.: Cic., Suet. **2**. Transf. *excellently, finely* : loqui, Pl.; munus administrasti tuom, Ter. Comp.: Plin. Ep.

lautia, ōrum, n. *pl. entertainment given at Rome to foreign ambassadors or distinguished guests at the expense of the State* : Liv.

lautitia, ae, *f.* [lautus], *elegance, splendour, sumptuousness of living* : Cic. Ep., Sen. Ep. In *pl.* : Suet.

lautumiae (lātomiae and **lātumiae)**, ārum,

f. pl. [Gk. λατομία], *a stone-quarry.* **1**. Lit.: Pl. Esp. the quarries at Syracuse, used as prisons : Cic. **2**. Transf. *a prison* at Rome (perh. the Tullianum) : Liv.

lautus, a, um. **I**. *Part.* lavŏ. **II**. Adj. **a**. Of things : *elegant, fine, neat, sumptuous* : supellex, Cic.; lautissima cena, Plin. Ep.; patrimonium, Cic.; civitas, Cic. Ep. **b**. Of persons : *refined, polished, fashionable, grand* : Pl., Cic. Comp. and Sup. : Cic.

lavābrum, i, n. [lavŏ], *a bath* : Lucr.

lavātiō, ōnis, *f.* [lavŏ], *a washing, bathing, bath.* **1**. Lit.: Pl. **2**. Transf. *bathing-apparatus* : Cic. Ep., Phaedr.

Laverna, ae, *f. the goddess of gain* (lawful or unlawful).

Lāvīnia, ae, *f. d. of Latinus and w. of Aeneas.*

Lāvīnium, i, n. *a city in Latium, founded by Aeneas in honour of his wife Lavinia* ; **Lāvīnus, Lāvīnius**, a, um ; **Lāviniēnsēs**, ium, *m. pl. its inhabitants.*

lavō, lavāre (lavere, Pl., Ter., Cato, Verg., etc.), lāvi, lautum (and lōtum or lavātum) [*cf.* λοέω]. **A**. Trans. **1**. Lit.: Pl., Cic., Verg., etc. In *Mid.* : lavantur in fluminibus, Caes.; Cic. **2**. Transf. **a**. *to wash, moisten, bedew* : salsi lautique domum redimus, Pl.; Lucr.; tabellas lacrimis, Pl.; corpora sanguis, Verg. **b**. Of the sea, of rivers, *to wash* (i.e. *to flow close by, to flow over*) : villam, Hor.; harenas, Ov.; Plin. Ep. **c**. *to wash away* : peccatum, Ter.; mala vino, Hor. **B**. Intrans. Pl., Ter., Liv.

laxāmentum, i, n. [laxŏ], *a loosening, widening.* Transf. *a relaxation, alleviation, respite* : si quid laxamenti a bello Samnitium esset, Liv.; dare laxamentum legi, Cic. ; ut minus laxamenti daretur iis ad auxilia Hannibali summittenda, Liv.

laxātus, a, um. **I**. *Part.* laxŏ. **II**. Adj.: *extended, loose* : ordines (aciei), Tac.

laxē, adv. *loosely, widely.* **1**. Lit.: manūs vincire, Liv. Sup. : Plin. Of troops: laxius stare (*in more open order*), Curt. **2**. Transf. **a**. Of time : laxius proferre diem, Cic. Ep. **b**. *unrestrictedly, freely* : in hostico laxius rapto sueti vivere, Liv.; Romanos, remoto metu, laxius licentiusque futuros, Sall.

laxitās, ātis, *f.* [laxus], *roominess, spaciousness, extent* : Cic.

laxō, āre [laxus]. **A**. Trans. *to make loose or wide.* **1**. Lit. **a**. *to expand, extend* : forum, Cic. Ep.; manipulos, Caes.; alveum Tiberis, Suet. **b**. *to open, undo, unloose* : vincula epistulae, Nep.; claustra, Verg.; via voci laxata dolore est, Verg. **c**. *to loosen, slacken, relax* : rudentis, Verg.; habenas, Curt.; arcum, Phaedr.; laxantur corpora rugis, Ov.; artūs (in sleep), Verg. **2**. Transf. **a**. *to set free, release, relieve* : laxatas sensit custodias, Liv. With ABL. of separation: libidinum vinculis laxatos esse, Cic.; corpore laxati, Cic. With *ab* : a contentione disputationis animos, Cic.; Liv. **b**. *to slacken, relax, abate, weaken* : sibi aliquid laboris, Liv.; laxatam pugnam vidit, Liv.; annonam, Liv. **c**. Of time : *to extend* : Quint. **B**. Intrans. *to slacken, fall off* : annona laxaverat, Liv. [It. *lasciare* ; Prov. *laissar* ; Fr. *laisser*.]

laxus, a. um [cf. langueō], *loose, slack, roomy, wide*. **1.** L i t. : laxius agmen, Sall. ; arcus, Verg., Hor. ; casses, Verg. ; funis, Hor. ; calceus, Hor. ; ianua, Ov. **2.** T r a n s f. **a.** Of time : *extended, prolonged* : diem, Cic. Ep. Comp. : tempus, Plin. Ep. **b.** In gen. : *slack, relaxed, free, not strict* : laxissimas habenas habere amicitiae, Cic. ; laxius imperium, Sall. ; annona (*cf.* Eng. " *market easy* "), Liv. ; neglegentiae laxior locus, Liv. [Sp. *lejos* ; Fr. *lâche.*]

lea, ae, *f.* [leō], *a lioness* : Lucr., Verg., Ov.

leaena, ae, *f.* [λέαινα], *a lioness* : Cat., Verg., Ov.

Leander, drī (Voc. -dre, Ov.), *m.* *a youth of Abydos, lover of Hero of Sestos, to whom he swam nightly across the Hellespont, until he was drowned in a storm.*

Learchus, ī, *m. s. of Athamas and Ino, killed by his father ;* **Learcheus**, a, um.

Lebedus, ī, *f. a town on the coast of Ionia, where theatrical games were held annually in honour of Bacchus.*

lebēs, ētis, *m.* [λέβης]. **I.** *a metal cooking-pan* or *cauldron :* Verg., Ov. **II.** *a wash-hand basin :* Ov.

lectica, ae, *f.* [*cf.* λέκτρον]. **I.** *a portable couch, a litter :* Cic., Hor., Tac., etc. **II.** *a bier* or *hearse :* Suet.

lecticārius, ī, *m.* [lectīca], *a litter-bearer :* Cic., Suet.

lecticula, ae, *f.* [*dim.* lectīca]. **I.** *a small litter :* Cic., Liv. **II.** *a small* or *humble bier :* Nep. **III.** *a small couch* or *settee :* Suet.

lēctiō, ōnis, *f.* [legō]. **I.** *a picking out, selecting :* iudicum, Cic. **II.** *a reading, perusal ; a reading aloud :* librorum, Cic., Quint. Hence, lectio senatūs, *a reading* or *calling over the roll of the senators* by the censor : Liv., Suet.

lectisterniātor, ōris, *m.* [lectisternium], *a slave who arranged the couches for reclining at table :* Pl.

lectisternium, ī, *n.* [lectus sternō], *a feast offered to the gods, in which their images were placed on couches* before tables covered with rich fare : Liv.

lēctitō, āre [*freq.* legō], *to read often* or *with eagerness :* Platonem, Cic. ; libros, Tac., Plin. Ep.

lēctiuncula, ae, *f.* [*dim.* lēctiō], *light reading :* Cic. Ep.

lēctor, ōris, *m.* [legō], *a reader :* Cic., Hor., Quint. Esp. *a slave who read aloud to his master :* Quint., Plin. Ep.

lectulus, ī, *m.* [*dim.* lectus]. **I.** *a humble bed :* Cic., Juv. **II.** *a couch for reclining on at meals :* Pl., Cic. **III.** *a funeral-bed :* Tac. **IV.** *a reading-couch, settee, sofa :* Cic., Ov., Plin. Ep.

lectus, ī [lectus, ūs, Pl.), *m.* [*cf.* λέχος]. **I.** *a couch, bed :* Pl. ; in lecto esse, Cic. ; lecto teneri, Cic. ; lecto surgere, Prop. ; lecto descendere, Tib. Esp. *a bridal-bed :* lectus genialis adversus (because it was opposite the door), Cic. ; iugalis, Verg. **II.** *a couch for reclining on at meals :* Cic., Hor., Liv. **III.** *a funeral couch, bier :* Tib., Quint. [It. *letto ;* Sp. *lecho ;* Fr. *lit.*]

lēctus, a, um. **I.** *Part.* legō. **II.** A d j. **a.** *picked, select :* pueri, Cic. ; equites, Verg. ;

virgines, Hor. **b.** *choice, excellent :* argenti lectae numeratae minae, Pl. ; Massicum, Hor. ; viri, verba, sententiae, Cic. Comp. and Sup. : Cic.

Lēda, ae, and **Lēdē**, ēs, *f. w. of Tyndarus, visited by Zeus in the form of a swan ; m. of Helen, Clytemnestra, Castor and Pollux ;* **Lēdaeus**, a, um.

lēgālis, e, *adj.* [lēx], *of* or *belonging to the law, legal :* Quint. [It. *leale ;* Sp. *leal ;* Fr. *loyal.*]

lēgātārius, ī, *m.* [lēgātum], *one to whom something is left by will, a legatee :* Suet.

lēgātiō, ōnis, *f.* [lēgō], *the office* or *post of a deputed representative.* **I.** Of a State or public body. **1.** L i t. **a.** *an embassy, a public commission* or *mission :* cum potestate aut legatione proficisci, Cic. ; is sibi legationem ad civitates suscepit, Caes. ; in legationem proficisci, Liv. **b.** libera legatio, *a free commission,* i.e. *a privilege granted to a senator* (nominally in an official capacity) to visit one or more provinces on his private affairs : Cic. Ep. Similarly, legatio votiva, *for paying a vow in a province :* Cic. Ep. **2.** T r a n s f. **a.** *the work* or *result of an embassy :* legationem renuntiare, Cic., Liv. ; ementiri, Cic. **b.** *the members of the mission :* Caes., Liv. **II.** *the office of a legatus,* i.e. *a deputy of a commander-in-chief :* legationem eius praeclaram cognoscite, Cic. ; Caes. Also *a nominal staff-appointment :* Cic. Ep. **III.** *the command of a legion :* Tac.

lēgātor, ōris, *m.* [lēgō], *one who leaves something by will, a testator :* Suet.

lēgātum, ī, *n.* [lēgō], *a bequest, legacy :* Cic. Ep., Quint., Juv.

lēgātus, ī, *m.* [lēgō], *a deputy, representative.* **I.** Of a State or public body : *an ambassador, envoy :* Caes., Cic., Liv., Ov., etc. **II.** *a deputy of a State official.* **a.** *the representative* (of a consul, proconsul, praetor), *second-in-command :* Caes., Cic., Liv. **b.** Under the Empire : *a deputy of the Emperor* in the imperial provinces, called legatus Augusti pro praetore : Tac., Suet. **III.** *the commander of a legion, as the deputy of the commander-in-chief :* Caes., Tac., Suet.

lēgifer, a, um [lēx ferō], *lawgiving :* Minos, Ov. ; Ceres (*creating social order*), Verg.

legiō, ōnis, *f.* [legō]. prop. *a selecting* (*cf.* dilectus), hence, *a* (*chosen*) *body of foot-soldiers.* **1.** L i t. **a.** *a Roman legion,* divided into 10 cohorts, the number of men varying between 4,200 and 6,000 : Caes., Cic., Liv., etc. **b.** Of the troops of other nations : *legions, soldiers :* Pl., Liv. **2.** T r a n s f. **a.** In g e n. *an army :* cetera legio, Verg. **b.** *forces, expedients :* sibi nunc uterque contra legiones parat, Pl.

legiōnārius, a, um [legiō], *of* or *belonging to a legion, legionary :* legionarii milites legionis decimae (i.e. as distinct from the cavalry), Caes. ; legionarii (opp. alarii) equites (the complement, us. about 300, of cavalry attached to a legion), Liv.

lēgirupa, ae, *m.* and **lēgirupiō**, ōnis, *m.* [lēx and *rup* seen in rumpō], *a law-breaker :* Pl.

lēgitimē, adv. *according to law, legally.* **1.** L i t. : Cic., Juv. **2.** T r a n s f. *duly, properly :* Tac., Juv.

lēgitimus (older **lēgitumus**), a, um [lex], fixed or allowed by some law. **1.** Lit.: legitimo tempore consulatūs, Caes.; si utar ad dicendum meo legitimo tempore, Cic.; controversiae legitimae et civiles, Cic.; potestas, imperium, etc., Cic.; aetas legitima ad petendam aedilitatem, Liv.; coniunx, Ov. As Noun, **lēgitima**, ōrum, n. pl. usages prescribed by law : legitimis quibusdam confectis, Nep. **2.** Transf. in gen. right, proper, regular : numerus, Cic.; poëma, Hor.; verba, Ov.

legiuncula, ae, f. [dim. legiō], a small or paltry legion : Liv.

lēgō, āre [lex], to ordain by law. **I.** to commission, depute, send on a public mission. **1.** Lit.: ut legati ex eius ordinis auctoritate legarentur, Cic.; Liv.; tres adulescentes in Africam legantur qui rem adeant, Sall. **2.** Transf. to commit : tibi negotium, Pl. **II.** to appoint or choose as deputy to a superior officer : ne legaretur Gabinius Pompeio expetenti, Cic.; Sall. **III.** In law : to appoint by will, to leave or bequeath as a legacy : usumfructum omnium bonorum Caesenniae legat, Cic.; Liv.; Quint. With a or ab and ABL. of the person who was to pay the legacy : uxori testamento legat grandem pecuniam a filio, si qui natus esset, Cic.; Quint.

legō, legere, lēgi, lēctum [cf. Gk. λέγω, ἐκ-λογή, ἐπι-λέγομαι], to gather, collect, pick. **1.** Lit. **A. a.** In gen.: oleam, Cato; nuces, Cic.; flores, māla, Verg.; flores in calathos, Ov.; spolia caesorum, Liv.; ossa, Ov. **b.** to pick up, wind up : of the Fates: fila alicui legere, Verg.; of Ariadne's clue: quae dedit ingrato fila legenda viro, Ov. **c.** Of sails: vela, Verg. **B.** to pick out, choose, single out : iudices, Cic.; de classe biremis, Verg.; civis in patres, Liv.; viros ad bella, Ov. Of a thief: to pick and steal, to purloin (cf. sacrilegus) : Hor. **C.** to make one's way through, to traverse (cf. Eng. to pick one's way) : vestigia retro observata legit, Verg.; Ov.; saltūs, Ov.; pontum, freta, Verg. Esp. to coast along, hug (the shore) : litora Epiri, Verg.; navibus oram Italiae, Liv. Hence, primi lege litoris oram in manibus terrae (i.e. skirt the fringe), Verg. **2.** Transf. **A.** to pick up news, gossip : alicuius sermonem, Pl. **B.** to traverse with the eyes, survey. **a.** to observe, scan : omnis longo ordine adversos, Verg. **b.** to read or peruse a writing : Cic., Ov., Liv., etc. With personal object: Ov., Quint. **c.** to read out or aloud, to recite : convocatis auditoribus volumen legere, Hor., etc. Hence, legere senatum, to read or call over the names of senators (v. lectio) : Liv. [It. leggere ; Sp. leer : Fr. lire.]

lēgulēius, I, m. [lex], a stickler for legal technicalities : Cic.

legulus, I, m. [legō], a gatherer or picker (of fruit) : Cato.

legūmen, inis, n. [legō], any leguminous plant (i.e. that has pods, e.g. the pea). **a.** pulse : Caes., Juv. **b.** the bean : Verg.

Leleges, um, m. pl. an ancient race that lived scattered over several parts of W. Asia Minor and Greece ; **Lelegēius**, a, um ; **Lelegēis**, idis, f. adj.

lembus, I, m. [λέμβος]. **I.** a ship's boat : Pl. **II.** a cutter, pinnace : Liv. **III.** an (ordinary) rowing-boat : Verg.

lēmma, atis, n. [λῆμμα]. **I.** a theme, matter, subject : Plin. Ep. **II.** the argument or title of an epigram : Mart. **III.** the epigram itself : Mart., Plin. Ep.

lēmniscātus, a, um [lēmniscus], adorned with pendent ribbons : palma, Cic.

lēmniscus, I, m. [λημνίσκος], a ribbon which hung down from a victor's wreath : Liv.

Lēmnos and **Lēmnus**, I, f. a large island in the Aegean Sea, the abode of Vulcan ; **Lēmnius**, a, um ; **Lēmniēnsis**, e, adj. ; **Lēmnias**, adis, f. a Lemnian woman ; **Lēmnicola**, ae, m. a dweller on Lemnos, i.e. Vulcan.

Lemūrēs, um, m. pl. ghosts, spectres : Hor.; **Lemūria**, ōrum, n. pl. a night-festival held on May 9th, 11th, 13th to drive ghosts from the house.

lēna, ae, f. [lēnō], a procuress, go-between. **1.** Lit.: Pl., Ov. **2.** Transf. a seductress : Cic., Ov.

Lēnaeus, a, um [ληνός, a wine-press], Lenaean, Bacchic : latices, i.e. wine, Verg.; **Lēnaeus**, I, m. Bacchus.

lēnīmen, inis, n. [lēniō], a soothing remedy ; an alleviation, solace : laborum, Hor.; senectae, Ov.

lēnīmentum, I, n. [lēniō], a soothing remedy ; an alleviation, sop : honestae missionis, Tac.

lēniō, īre (Imperf. lēnībat, Verg.; Fut. lēnībunt, Prop.) [lēnis]. **A.** Trans. to soften, alleviate, mitigate, assuage. **1.** Lit.: inopiam frumenti, Sall.; stomachum latrantem, Hor.; vulnera, Prop.; clamorem, Hor. **2.** Transf. to calm, pacify, soothe : aliquem, Pl.; iratum, Cic.; animum ferocem, Sall.; dolentem solando, Verg.; iras, seditionem, Liv. **B.** Intrans. to calm down : dum irae leniunt, Pl.

lēnis, e, adj. smooth, soft, mild, gentle. **1.** Lit.: opp. to asper, Ter., Cic.; vinum, Ter.; Hor.; venenum, Cic. Ep.; ventus, Cic. Ep.; tormentum, Hor.; volatus, Ov.; motus laterum, Quint. Comp. : Ter. Sup. : Cic. Ep. Neut. Acc. **lēne**, as Adv. : sonare, Ov. **2.** Transf. **a.** Of hills: gentle : iugum paulo leniore fastigio, Caes.; clivus, Liv. **b.** Of style : smooth : oratio, Cic. **c.** mild, moderate : servitutem lenem reddere, Pl.; sententia, Caes.; homo, ingenium, Cic.; populus R. in hostis, Cic.; consilium, Hor. Comp. : Pl., Caes. Sup. : Cic., Liv. With Inf. : Hor. **d.** calm, peaceful : somnus, Hor.

lēnitās, ātis, f. [lēnis], smoothness, softness, gentleness, mildness. **1.** Lit.: Arar in Rhodanum influit incredibili lenitate, Caes.; vocis, Cic. **2.** Transf. **a.** Of style : smoothness : Cic. **b.** clemency, gentleness, lenity : Cic.; legum, Cic.

lēniter, adv. **I.** softly, mildly, gently : adridens, Cic.; atterens caudam, Hor.; collis acclivis, Caes.; Liv. **II.** quietly, calmly, moderately : temptare, Pl.; dicere, sentire, Cic.; ferre aliquid, Ov. Comp. : Cic. Sup. : Cic. **III.** Of style : smoothly : dicere, Cic. **IV.** slackly, half-heartedly :

lenius agere, Caes. ; lenius proelio lacessere, Caes.

lēnĭtūdō, ĭnis, *f.* [lēnis]. **I.** *mildness, gentleness :* in istum, Cic. **II.** *smoothness :* orationis, Cic.

lēnō, ōnis, *m. a pimp, pander, procurer.* **1.** Lit. : Pl., Cic., Hor., etc. **2.** T r a n s f. *a go-between, an agent :* Cic., Ov.

lēnōcinium, ĭ, *n.* [lēnō], *the trade of a pander, pimping, pandering.* **1.** Lit. : facere, Pl. ; profiteri, Suet. **2.** T r a n s f. **a.** *the office of 'minister to pleasures' :* Cato ap. Cic. **b.** *an allurement, attraction :* se cupiditatium lenociniis dedere, Cic. **c.** *meretricious wheedling or seductive allurement.* Of dress : corporum, Cic. ; Suet. Of style : nec ullum orationi lenocinium addit, Tac. ; caret lenociniis expositio, Quint.

lēnōcinor, ārī [lēnōcinium]. Lit. *to play the pimp, to pander ;* hence, **a.** *to fawn on :* alicui, Cic. **b.** *to help on, promote :* insitae feritati, Tac. ; libro isti novitas, Plin. Ep.

lēnōnius, a, um [lēnō], *of pimping* or *of a pimp :* aedes, fides, genus, Pl.

lēns, lentis, *f. a lentil :* Cato, Verg.

lentē, adv. *slowly.* **1.** Lit. : Caes., Ov., Tac. Comp. : Caes. **2.** T r a n s f. **a.** *coolly, indifferently :* agere, Liv. ; respondere, Cic. Comp. : Cic., Quint. **b.** *leisurely ; with deliberate consideration :* aliquid probare, Cic. Ep.

lentēscō, ere [lentus]. **1.** Lit. **a.** *to become sticky :* sed picis in morem ad digitos lentescit habendo, Verg. **b.** *to become pliant :* Tac. **2.** T r a n s f. *to soften, weaken :* lentescunt tempore curae, Ov.

lentĭscĭfer, ēra, ērum [lentiscus ferō], *bearing mastic-trees :* Ov.

lentĭscus, ĭ, *f.* and **lentĭscum**, ĭ, *n. the mastic-tree.* **1.** Lit. : Poet. ap. Cic. **2.** T r a n s f. **a.** *mastic-oil :* Cato, Varr. **b.** *a mastic tooth-pick :* Mart.

lentĭtūdō, ĭnis, *f.* [lentus]. **I.** *slowness, hesitation :* coniuratorum, Tac. **II.** *dullness :* libros eiusdem lentitudinis ac toporis, Tac. **III.** *flabbiness, listlessness, apathy :* Cic.

lentō, āre [lentus], *to bend :* remum, Verg.

lentŭlus, a, um [dim. lentus], *rather slow :* Cic. Ep.

Lentŭlus, ĭ, *m. a cognomen of a distinguished family in the gens Cornelia.* Esp. **I.** P. Cornelius Lentulus Sura, *one of the Catilinarian conspirators.* **II.** P. C. L. Spinther, *father and son, friends of Cicero.* Hence, **Lentŭlĭtās**, ātis, *f. the name or nobility of a Lentulus :* Cic. Ep.

lentus, a, um. **1.** Lit. **a.** *clinging, tenacious, sticky :* vincla escaria, Pl. ; lentum convellere vimen, Verg. ; lentis adhaerens bracchiis, Hor. ; gluten visco lentius, Verg. Occ. *clogging :* harena, Juv. ; *sluggish :* in lento luctantur marmore tonsae, Verg. **b.** *tough, pliant, limber, supple :* vitis, Cat., Verg. ; rami, Verg. ; argentum (on greaves), Verg. ; lentior salicis virgis, Ov. **2.** T r a n s f. **a.** *long-lasting :* negotium, Cic. Ep. ; duellum, Hor. ; spes, Ov. ; tranquillitas lentissima, Sen. Ep. **b.** *slow, lingering :* in dicendo (i.e. drawling), Cic. ; inftiatores (i.e. procrastinating), Cic. ; mortis genus, Suet. ; venenum, Suet. **c.**

ut ease, at leisure, lazy : lentus in umbrā, Verg. **d.** *easy, indifferent, phlegmatic :* Pl., Cic., Liv. ; lentus in suo dolore, Tac. ; lentissima pectora, Ov.

lēnŭlus, ĭ, *m.* [dim. lēnō], *a little pimp :* Pl.

(1) lēnunculus, ĭ, *m.* [dim. lēnō], *a young pimp :* Pl.

(2) lēnunculus, ĭ, *m.* [a corruption of lembunculus, *dim.* lembus], *a small boat, a skiff :* Caes., Tac.

leō, ōnis, *m.* [*cf.* Gk. λέων], *a lion.* **1.** Lit. : Lucr., etc. **2.** T r a n s f. *the constellation* Leo : Hor.

lepas, adis, *f.* [λεπάς], *a limpet :* Pl.

lepĭdē, adv. *pleasantly, agreeably, charmingly, neatly.* **a.** Of appearance : ornata, Pl. **b.** Of speech : lepide in soceri mei personā lusit, Cic. ; Pl. ; Ter. **c.** As an affirmative answer : ego loquar ? *Bacch.* lepide licet, *by all means,* Pl. **d.** Of approval : euge, euge, lepide, Pl. Comp. and Sup. : Pl.

lepĭdus, a, um [v. lepōs], *pleasant, agreeable, charming, neat.* **a.** Of appearance : Pl., Ter. ; forma, Pl. **b.** Of manner, behaviour, etc. : Pl., Ter. ; mores, facinus, fama, Pl. Comp. : Pl. Sup. : Ter. In slighting sense : pueri, Cic. **c.** Of speech : versus, Cat. ; dictum, Hor.

lepōs (later **lepor**), ōris, *m.* [*cf.* Gk. λεπτός], *pleasantness, agreeableness, attractiveness, charm.* **a.** Of appearance : Pl., Lucr. **b.** Of manner, behaviour : Cic., Cat. **c.** Of speech : Pl., Cic. ; dicendi, Cic. ; sententiarum lepores, Cic. **d.** As a term of compliment : o mi lepos, Pl.

lepus, ŏris, *m. a hare.* **1.** Lit. : Verg., Hor., Ov. As a term of endearment : Pl. **2.** T r a n s f. *the constellation* Lepus : Cic. [It. *lepre* ; Fr. *lièvre.*]

lepusculus, ĭ, *m.* [dim. lepus], *a young hare, leveret :* Cic.

Lerna, ae, and **Lernē**, ēs, *f. a forest and marsh near Argos, through which flowed a stream of the same name ; the home of the Hydra, slain by Hercules, who then drained the marsh ;* **Lernaeus**, a, um.

Lesbos (-us), ĭ, *f. a large island in the Aegean Sea, birthplace of the lyric poets, Alcaeus and Sappho ;* **Lesbĭacus**, **Lesbōus**, a, um ; **Lesbĭas**, adis, and **Lesbis**, idis, *f. a Lesbian woman ;* **Lesbĭus**, a, um, *Lesbian ;* Lesbia vates, i.e. Sappho, Hor. ; vinum, Hor. ; alone, *Lesbian wine,* Hor. **Lesbĭa**, ae, *f., pseudonym of the mistress of Catullus ; prob. Clodia, s. of Clodius.*

lessum, Acc. *sing. m. a wailing cry :* Old law in Cic.

lētālis, e, *adj.* [lētum], *deadly, fatal, mortal :* vulnus, Verg. ; Suet. ; hiems, ensis, Ov.

lēthargĭcus, ĭ, *m.* [ληθαργικός], *a drowsy, lethargic person :* Hor.

lēthargus, ĭ, *m.* [λήθαργος], *drowsiness, lethargy :* Hor., Quint.

Lēthē, ēs, *f.* [λήθη], *forgetfulness; a river in the underworld, the water of which caused forgetfulness of the past ;* **Lēthaeus**, a, um. **1.** Lit. : Verg., Hor., etc. **2.** T r a n s f. *producing forgetfulness :* papavera, Verg.

lētĭfer, ēra, ērum [lētum ferō], *death-bringing, deadly.* **1.** Lit. : certamen, Cat. ; arcus, Verg. ; ictus, Ov. **2.** T r a n s f. *admitting death, mortal :* locus, Ov.

lētŏ, āre [lētum], *to kill, slay* : Paris hunc letat, Verg. ; Ov.

Lētōis, Lētōius, *v.* Lātōna.

lētum, i, *n. death.* **1.** Lit.: sibi consciscere, Pl. ; alicui ferre, parere manu, Verg. ; leto offerre caput, Lucr. ; leti potiri, Lucr. ; eodem leto perire, Cic. ; Pl. ; me pessimo leto adficere, Liv. ; novo genere leti mergi, Liv. ; leto se eripere, Verg. Old **phr.**: leto datus, *the dead, the slain* : Enn. ; Old law in Cic. ; aliquem leto dare, *to kill* : Verg., Ov. **2.** Transf. (of inanim. things), *ruin, destruction* : tenuis Teucrum res eripe leto, Verg.

leucaspis, idis, *f. adj.* [λεύκασπις], *having a white shield* : phalanx, Liv.

Leucippus, i, *m.* **I.** *f. of Phoebe and Hilaira who were carried off by Castor and Pollux.* **II.** *a philosopher, pupil of Zeno the Eleatic, and one of the founders of the atomic philosophy.*

Leucophryna, ae, *f.* (Lit. *of the white eyebrow*), *a cult-name of Diana at Magnesia.*

Leucothea, ae, and **Leucotheē**, ēs, *f. the name of Ino, d. of Cadmus, after she was made a sea-deity.*

Leuctra, ōrum, *n. pl. a small town in Boeotia where Epaminondas defeated the Spartans,* B.C. 371 ; **Leuctricus**, a, um.

levāmen, inis, *n.* [levō], *an alleviation, mitigation, solace.* **a.** Physical : Cat. **b.** Of debt : Liv. **c.** Mental : Cic. Ep., Verg.

levāmentum, i, *n.* [levō], *a lightening, an alleviation, mitigation, consolation* : tributi, Tac. ; miseriarum, Cic. ; doloris, Plin. Ep.

levātiō, ōnis, *f.* [levō], *a lightening* ; hence, **a.** *an alleviation, mitigation, relief* : dolorum, Cic. **b.** *a cause of relief* : alicui esse levationi, Cic. Ep. **c.** *a diminishing* : vitiorum, Cic.

leviculus, a, um [*dim.* levis], *somewhat light-headed, vain* : Cic.

levidēnsis, e, *adj.* [levis dēnsus], *slight, poor* : munusculum, Cic. Ep.

levi-fĭdus, a, um [levis], *of slight credit, untrustworthy* : Pl.

lēvigō, āre [lēvis], *to make smooth, to smooth* : parietes, Varr.

levi-pēs, pedis, *adj,* [levis pēs], *light-footed* : Varr.

levis, e, *adj.* [*cf.* Gk. ἐλαχύς], *light.* **1.** Lit. **a.** In weight (opp. gravis) : Pl., Lucr., Verg., etc. ; levis armaturae Numidae, Caes. (*v.* armatura) ; hence, of soldiers, *light-armed* : levis miles, Liv. ; nudi aut sagulo leves, Tac. Of soil : *light and poor* : Varr., Verg. Of the spirits of the dead: *unsubstantial* (or perh. *fleeting*) : turba, Hor. ; populi, Ov. **b.** In motion : *light, nimble, fleeting* : Parthi, cervi, Verg. ; ad motūs esse leviores, Nep. ; Nympharum chori, Hor. ; currus, venti, Ov. Of time : hora, Ov. **2.** Transf. **a.** Of food : *light, digestible* : Hor. **b.** Of rumour : *unfounded* : auditio, Caes. ; rumor, Cic. **c.** *light, unimportant, trivial, slight* : proelium, Caes., Liv. ; periculum, Caes. ; leviore de causā, Caes. ; nomen, dolor, etc., Cic. As Noun in phr. : in levi habitum, Tac. **d.** In character : *light-headed, unreliable, capricious, fickle, false* : homo levior quam pluma, Pl. ; Hor. ; iudices, Cic. ; Caes. ;

auctor, Liv. ; amicitiae, Cic. ; spes, Hor. , levissima fidei mutandae ingenia, Liv. **e.** In action : *easy-going, gentle, mild* : suis se concinnat levem, Pl. ; levior reprehensio, Cic. ; somni, Hor. Comp.: Pl., Lucr., Cic., etc. Sup. : Cic., Liv. [It. *lieve.*]

lēvis, *adj.* [*cf.* Gk. λεῖος], *smooth.* **1.** Lit. **a.** Cato ; corpora, Lucr. ; corpuscula, Cic. ; galeae, Hor. ; pocula, Verg. ; coma pectine levis, Ov. Comp. : Ov. Sup. : Lucr. Poet.: sanguis, *slippery*, Verg. **b.** *smooth, beardless, hairless* : iuventas, Hor. ; pectus, Verg. ; colla, Ov. Also *effeminate* : vir, Ov. **2.** Transf. of style : *smooth, flowing* : oratio, Cic. ; Quint.

levi-somnus, a, um [levis somnus], *lightly sleeping* : corda canum, Lucr.

levitās, ātis, *f.* [levis], *lightness* (opp. gravitas). **1.** Lit. **a.** plumarum, Lucr. ; armorum, Caes. **b.** Of movement : *nimbleness* : Lucr. **2.** Transf. **a.** *lightheartedness, fickleness, frivolity* : in populari ratione, Cic. ; animi, Caes. **b.** *shallowness, vainness* : opinionis, Cic.

lēvitās, ātis, *f.* [lēvis], *smoothness.* **1.** Lit.: speculorum, Cic. **2.** Transf. Of style : *smoothness, fluency* : Cic., Quint.

leviter, *adv. lightly.* **1.** Lit.: cadere, Caes. ; armati, Curt. **2.** Transf. **a.** *slightly, a little* : densae nubes, Lucr. ; inflexum bacillum, Cic. ; saucius, Cic. ; aegrotare, Cic. ; eruditus, Cic. Comp. : tanto levius miser, Hor. **b.** *mildly* : ut levissime dicam, Cic. **c.** *easily, with equanimity* : aliquid ferre, Liv. Comp. : Cic. Ep. Sup. : Cic.

levō, āre (*Aor. Subj.* levāssō, Enn.) [levis]. **I.** *to make light, lighten, to relieve, ease.* **1.** Lit.: hoc te fasce levabo, Verg. ; serpentum colla levavit, Ov. Similarly : alicui vincla, Verg. **2.** Transf. **a.** *to lighten, relieve, lessen* : morbum, egestatem, Pl. ; inopiam, Caes. ; annonam, Cic. ; faenus, Liv. ; sponsionis vinculum, Liv. ; sitim, Ov. ; vario viam sermone, Verg. ; ictum, Hor. ; pretia frugum, Tac. With ABL. of separation : civitatem hibernis, Caes. ; se aere alieno, Cic. Ep. ; aliquem supplicio, Cic. With (ablatival) GEN.: me laborum, Pl. **b.** Mentally : *to lighten, relieve, console* : angorem animi sermone, Cic. Ep. ; iniurias, Caes. ; calamitatem, luctum, curam, suspicionem, Cic. With ABL. of separation : aliquem miseriis, Cic. Ep. ; religione animos, Liv. ; aliquem metu, Liv. ; Tac. **c.** *to lessen, weaken, impair* : auctoritatem, Cic. ; regis facinus, Liv. ; omen, Verg. ; fidem, Hor. **II.** *to lift up, raise up* : se de caespite, Ov. ; se saxo, Ov. ; Verg. ; (navis) ipse tridenti, Verg. ; avis se alis, Liv.

lēvō, āre [lēvis], *to smooth, polish.* **1.** Lit.: tigna, Lucr. ; corpus, Cic. **2.** Transf.: aspera sano cultu, Hor.

lēvor, ōris, *m.* [lēvis], *smoothness.* **1.** Lit.: Lucr. **2.** Transf.: vocis, Lucr.

lēx, lēgis, *f.* [*cf.* legō]. **1.** Lit. **a.** *a contract, agreement, stipulation, condition* : Pl., Ter. ; dicere, Hor., Liv. ; in mancipi lege, Cic. Of conditions of peace : pacis, Verg. ; leges iungere, Verg. ; pax data Philippo in has leges est, Liv. **b.** *a proposal* or *motion* of law, *a bill* : legem ferre *and* rogare, *to propose*, Cic. ; iubere, *to sanction*, Cic. ; legem promulgavit pertulitque, *gave notice of, and carried*, Liv. ; antiquare, *to reject*, Cic. **c.** *a law, statute :* abrogare, *to repeal*, Cic. ; derogare, *to modify*, Cic. ; obrogare, *to invalidate by another law*, Cic. ; surrogare, *to supplement*, Cic. ; leges XII tabularum, Liv. ; constituere, imponere alicui, evertere, perfringere, perrumpere, etc., Cic. Roman laws were known by the gentile name of their proposers : e.g. Lex Porcia, Cornelia, etc. **Phr. a.** lege *and* legibus, *according to law, legally :* eius morte ca ad me lege redierunt bona, Ter. ; Nep. **b.** lege agere, *to proceed according to law :* **i.** of the lictor, *to execute a sentence :* Liv. ; **ii.** *to bring an action according to law :* lege egit in hereditatem paternam exheres filius, Cic. ; Pl. ; Ter. **c.** fraudem legi facere, *to evade a law*, Pl., Liv. **2.** T r a n s f. *an ordinance, law, rule, regulation :* amicitiae, Cic. ; veri rectique, Cic. ; historiae, Cic. ; sermonis, Quint. ; citharae, Tac. ; versibus est certa quaedam et definita lex, Cic. Of natural ' laws ' : homines eā lege natos esse, Cic. ; communis condicio lexque vitae, Cic. ; naturae, Sen. Ep. ; quā sidera lege mearent, Ov. Hence, sine lege, *without control* or *restraint :* iacent collo sparsi sine lege capilli, Ov. [It. *legge ;* Sp. *ley ;* Fr. *loi*.]

lexis, is, *f.* [λέξις], *a word :* Lucil.

lībāmen, inis, *n.* [lībō], *a taste* or *portion* (of food or drink) offered to the gods, *a libation.* **1.** L i t. : Verg., Ov. **2.** T r a n s f. : libamina famae, Ov.

lībāmentum, i, *n.* [lībō], *a taste* or *portion* (of food or drink) offered to the gods, *a libation.* **1.** L i t. : Cic. **2.** T r a n s f. : quasi libamenta praedarum, Cic.

lībātiō, ōnis, *f.* [lībō], *a libation :* Cic.

lībella, ae, *f.* [*dim.* lībra]. **I.** *a small silver-coin* (the tenth part of a denarius), *an* as. **1.** L i t. : Cat. Hence (the denarius being regarded as unity) heres ex libellā, *heir to one-tenth of the estate :* Cic. Ep. T r a n s f. *a very small sum :* Pl., Cic. ; ad libellam, *to a farthing, exactly :* Cic. **II.** *a level, water-level, plummet-line :* Lucr., Varr. [Sp. *nivel ;* Fr. *niveau*.]

libellus, i, *m.* [*dim.* liber]. **1.** L i t. *a small book, pamphlet :* Cic., Liv., Juv., etc. **b.** In *pl.*, perh. *a bookseller's shop :* te (quaesivimus) in omnibus libellis, Cat. ; Mart. **c.** *a memorandum-book, journal, diary :* si quid memoriae causā rettulit in libellum, Cic. **2.** T r a n s f. **a.** *a memorial :* in libellis laudationum decreta miserunt, Cic. **b.** *a petition :* Atticus libellum composuit, Cic. Ep. ; Juv., etc. **c.** *an answer to a petition, an (imperial) warrant :* in diplomatibus libellisque et epistulis signandis, Suet. **d.** *a notice, programme :* gladiatorum libellos, Cic. ; Tac. **e.** *a placard, hand-bill :* Cic., Juv. ; edere per libellos, Suet. **f.** *a letter :* Pl., Cic. Ep. **g.** *a lampoon, pasquinade :* famosi, Tac. ; libellos aut carmina ad infamiam cuiuspiam edere, Suet. **h.** *a deposition, a written accusation* or *complaint :* Juv. **i.** *a lawyer's brief :* Juv.

lībēns (older **lubēns**), entis [libet], *acting willingly* or *with readiness, willing, with good will, with pleasure.* **1.** L i t. : facio lubens, Pl. ; Ter. ; Cic. Freq. in A B L. : me lubente facies, Pl. ; Cic. ; fecit animo libentissimo populus Romanus, Cic. ; Caes. P h r. : libens *or* libens merito (abbreviated L. M.), a formula used in paying a vow : Iovi lubens meritoque vitulor, Pl. ; Inscr. **2.** T r a n s f. *glad, cheerful :* hilarum ac lubentem fac te in gnati nuptiis, Ter. ; Pl.

lībenter (older **lubenter**), *adv. willingly, gladly, with pleasure, readily :* Pl., Caes., Cic. *Comp. :* Cic., Quint., Juv. *Sup. :* Cic., Sen. Ep.

liber, bri, *m. the inner bark* or *rind* of a tree. **1.** L i t. : Cic., Verg., etc. **2.** T r a n s f. (fr. the use of this bark for writing on). **a.** *any writing material :* Pl. **b.** *a written work, book, treatise :* Cic., etc. ; scribere, edere, volvere, evolvere, etc., Cic. In partic. *a code of civil* or *religious laws :* in libris Etruscorum, Cic. ; caerimoniarum, Tac. In *pl.* esp. *the Sibylline books :* Cic., Liv. **c.** *a division of a work, a book :* tres libri de Naturā Deorum, Cic. ; Quint. With liber omitted : legi tuum nuper quartum de Finibus, Cic. ; Quint. **d.** *a list, catalogue, register :* Cic., Liv. **e.** *a letter, epistle :* Nep., Plin. Ep. **f.** *a rescript, decree :* Plin. Ep. [Fr. *livre*.]

Līber, erī, *m.* the old Italian god of growth and vegetation (later identified with Bacchus). **1.** L i t. : Pl., Cic., Verg., etc. Hence, **Līberālia,** ium, *n. pl. a festival in honour of Liber,* held on March 17th (at which young men received the toga virilis).

līber, era, erum [*cf.* ἐλεύθερος]. L i t. perh. *freely growing.* **I.** *free, unrestricted, unhampered, open, unoccupied.* **A.** In space : locus (free from intruders), Pl. ; lectulus (of a bachelor), Cic. Ep. ; campus, aedes, Liv. ; Ov. ; caelo liberiore frui, Ov. **B.** Of other things. **a.** lingua, cor, Pl. ; tempus, cogitationes, animus, etc., Cic. ; vox, Liv. ; verba, Juv. **b.** *uncontrolled :* faenus, custodia, Liv. ; pars quaestionum, Cic. ; disputatio, Quint. In bad sense : amores, Cic. ; consuetudo peccandi, Cic. **c.** *unconditioned :* legatio, amicitia, Cic. ; mandata, arbitrium, Liv. **d.** *unconstrained, unprejudiced, unbiased :* comitia, Caes. ; iudicium audientium relinquere integrum ac liberum, Cic. ; integro animo ac libero causam defendere, Cic. ; suffragia, Juv. **e.** *free-spoken, frank :* Hor., Quint. *Comp. :* Cic., Ov., Quint. *Sup. :* Hor., Quint. P h r. : liberum est (with *Inf.*), *it is open, permissible :* Quint., Plin. Ep. **C.** *free, exempt.* With A B L. (with or without *a* or *ab*) : ab omni sumptu, molestiā, munere, Cic. ; ab omni perturbatione animi, Cic. ; Sall. ; Ov. ; animo omni liber metu, Liv. ; equus carcere, Ov. With G E N. : laborum, Pl., Hor. ; fati, Verg. Without A B L. : agri immunes ac liberi, Cic. **II. a.** Socially : *free* (opp. to slave) : Pl., Cic., etc. Hence, toga libera (for toga virilis, q.v.), Ov. **b.** P o l i t. : *free* (of independent or democratic States) : Caes., Cic., Liv., etc. (*Sup.* līberrimus.)

Libera, ae, f. **I**. *Proserpina, d. of Ceres, and s. of Liber.* **II**. *Ariadne, w. of Bacchus.*

liberālis, e, *adj.* [liber]. **1**. Lit. **a**. *relating to freedom or to freeborn condition :* Pl.; *causa or* iudicium, *a suit concerning a person's freedom :* Pl., Ter., Quint.; coniugium (i.e. *between free persons*), Ter. **b**. *befitting a freeman* and esp. *one of gentle birth, gentlemanly, honourable :* ingenium, Pl.; artes, doctrinae, studia, Cic.; fortuna, Liv. *Comp.* : Liv. *Sup.* : Cic. **2**. Transf. **a**. *courteous, bountiful, generous :* Cic.; responsum, Cic. Ep.; epulae, Tac. With GEN.: pecuniae, Sall. With *in* and ACC.: in omne genus hominum liberalissimus, Suet. **b**. Of appearance : *handsome, comely :* Pl.

liberālitās, ātis, *f.* [liberālis], *a way of thinking or acting befitting a freeman or one of gentle birth.* **a**. *courteousness, kindness, affability :* Ter., Cic. **b**. *generosity, liberality :* Cic. **c**. Concr. *bounty, grant :* decima pars liberalitatis, Tac.; liberalitates, Suet.

liberāliter, *adv. in a manner befitting a freeman or one of gentle birth.* **1**. Lit. : educatus, Cic.; Caes. **2**. Transf. *courteously, affably, generously :* Caes., Cic. *Comp.* : Cic. Ep., Quint. *Sup.* : Cic. Ep.

liberātiō, ōnis, *f.* [līberō], *a setting free or becoming free, delivery.* **a**. In gen. : *with* GEN. of thing *from which :* molestiae, Cic.; Quint. **b**. In law, *a discharge :* Cic.

liberātor, ōris, *m.* [līberō], *a deliverer, liberator :* Pl., Liv. Esp. of Caesar's murderers : patriae liberatores, Cic.; nostri liberatores, Cic. Ep. As epithet of Jupiter : Tac. In appos. : liberator ille populi Romani animus, Liv.

liberē, *adv.* **I**. *freely, without let or hindrance :* Cic., Quint. *Comp.* : Ter. **II**. Of speech and action : *freely, frankly, outspokenly :* Cic., Liv., Quint. *Comp.* : Cic., Hor., Quint. **III**. *without stint or limit, ungrudgingly. Comp.* : Verg.

liberī, ōrum, *m. pl.* (*sing.* very rare : GEN. *pl.* līberum, Cic., Tac.) [līber], *children*. **1**. Lit. : Pl., Cic., Hor., etc.; ius trium liberorum, under the Emperors, *special privileges enjoyed by those who had three legitimate children*, Sen. **2**. Transf. of animals : Pl.

liberō, āre (*Aor. Subj.* līberāssō, Pl.) [līber], *to set free.* **A**. In gen. *to free, release, deliver* (mostly with ABL. of separation) : aliquem periculo, obsidione, Caes.; populum metu, Cic.; se aere alieno, Cic. Ep.; senatoris muneribus, Cic. With *ab* or *ex* : Cic., Nep. **B**. In law. : *to acquit, discharge, absolve :* aliquem crimine aliquo, Cic.; culpā liberatus, Cic. Ep. With GEN. : culpae eius regem, Liv.; voti liberari, Liv. **C**. With ACC. of thing removed (esp. of debts, promises, etc.) : *to free, get rid of, cancel :* fidem, promissa, Cic.; nomina (*debts*), Liv. So also, obsidionem urbis, Liv. **D**. Polit. and socially. **a**. *to set free, give freedom to, manumit :* servos, Caes.; Pl.; Cic. **b**. *to exempt* (a person or thing) *from taxes :* Cic., Liv.

liberta, ae, *v.* libertus.

libertās (old form, **loebertās**), ātis, *f.* [liber]. **I**. In gen. *the power of doing as one pleases,*

freedom from restraint, obligation : tabellā dat populo eam libertatem ut quod velint faciant, Cic. With GEN.: vitae, Caes.; vivendi, Cic.; omnium rerum, Liv.; caeli, Quint. With *Inf.* : Prop. **II**. *freedom of speech or thought, frankness, boldness, candour :* Ov., Quint.; libertas ingeni, Sall. **III**. Polit. and socially. **a**. *freedom, the condition of a freeman* (opp. to *slavery*) : Pl., Cic., etc.; aliquem in libertatem vindicare, Cic., Liv. **b**. *political freedom, liberty* of a people (opp. to *subjection*) : accipere, reciperare, Caes.; amittere, Liv.; in libertate permanere, Caes.; Aeduis libertatem eripere, Cic.; conditor libertatis, Liv.

libertīnus, a, um [libertus], *belonging to the class of a freedman* (opp. ingenuus) : homo, Cic.; mulier, Liv.; me libertino patre natum, Hor.; genus, Tac. As Noun, **libertīnus**, ī, *m.* and **libertīna**, ae, *f. a freedman, freedwoman* (with ref. to the class to which he or she belonged, whilst *libertus* and *liberta* are used with ref. to the *patronus*, the former master) : Pl., Cic., Hor., etc.

libertus, ī, *m.* and **liberta**, ae, *f.* [liber], *a manumitted slave, a freedman, freedwoman* (in relation to a manumitter) : Pl., Cic., etc.; regem (Polybius tradit) pilleatum, capite raso, obviam ire legatis solitum libertumque se populi R. ferre, Liv.

libet (older **lubet**), libēre, libuit and libitum est, *it pleases, is agreeable :* rogita quod lubet, Pl.; Cic. With DAT. of person : quod tibi lubet, idem mihi lubet, Pl.; sin tibi id minus libebit, non te urgebo, Cic. Pl. : quae cuique libuissent, Suet. With *Inf.* clause as subject : with or without DAT. : non libet mihi deplorare vitam, Cic.; Pl., etc. With ACC. and *Inf.* as Subject : Ter. Phr. : si lubet, *if you please ;* ut lubet, *as you please :* Pl., Ter.

libīdinor, āri [libīdō], *to indulge or gratify lust :* Mart., Suet.

libīdinōsē, *adv. wilfully, arbitrarily :* Cic., Liv.

libīdinōsus (older **lubīd-**), a, um [libīdō]. **I**. *wilful, self-willed, arbitrary, capricious :* Nep.; libidinosissimae liberationes, Cic. **II**. *licentious, sensual, lustful :* Cic.; caper, Hor. *Comp.* : Cic., Quint. *Sup.* : Cic.

libīdō (older **lubīdō**), inis, *f.* [libet]. **I**. *desire, inclination :* Pl.; tanta libido cum Mario eundi omnis invaserat, Sall.; Cic., Liv.; est lubido orationem audire, Pl. **II**. *will, wilfulness, arbitrariness, caprice, fancy :* instruitur acies ad libidinem militum, Liv.; Cic.; ex libidine magis quam ex vero, Sall. **III**. *inordinate desire, passion, lust :* Cic.; libidine accendi, Sall.; voluptatum libidine ferri, Cic.; more fully, mala libido, Liv. Of animals, *heat, rut :* Cic. With GEN. of Gerund. : Cic., Liv., etc. In *pl.* : Cic.

Libitīna, ae, *f. the goddess of the dead, in whose temple everything for funerals was sold.* Transf. **a**. perh. *the supplies in the temple of Libitina :* pestilentia tanta erat ut Libitina vix sufficeret, Liv. **b**. *a bier, a funeral pile :* Mart. **c**. *the grave, death :* multaque pars mei vitabit Libitinam, Hor.

libitum, *v.* libet; **libita,** ōrum, *n. pl. the pleasure, fancy, will* : ad libita Caesaris, Tac. ; sua libita exercere, Tac.

libō, āre [*cf.* Gk. λείβω], *to take a little from.* **1.** L i t. **a.** In gen. : *to take a taste of, to taste, to sip* : dapes, Verg. ; amnem, Verg. ; flumina summa (apes), Verg. ; iecur, Liv. ; pocula Bacchi, Verg. Hence, *to touch lightly* : cibos digitis, Ov. ; oscula natae, Verg. ; summam celeri pede harenam, Ov. **b.** *to give a taste of* the food and esp. of the drink to the gods ; *to make an offering or libation* : frugem Cereri, Ov. ; Cic. ; diis dapes, Liv. ; duo rite mero carchesia Baccho, Verg. ; in mensam laticum honorem, Verg. P o e t. : carmen aris, Prop. ; comas, Ov. ; Celso lacrimas adempto, Ov. **2.** T r a n s f. **a.** *to take a portion, cull, extract* : ex variis ingeniis excellentissima quaeque libavimus, Cic. Also, *omnis artis,* Tac. **b.** *to wear away, impair* : terra tibi libatur et aucta recrescit, Lucr. ; virginitatem, Ov. ; viris, Liv.

libra, ae, *f.* [perh. *cf.* λίτρα]. **I.** *a balance, pair of scales* : in alteram librae lancem animi bona imponebat, in alteram corporis, Cic. ; in navibus ad libram turris fecerat, Caes. ; librā et aere, i.e. by formal sale (*v.* mancipium), Liv. Hence *the constellation Libra* : Verg., Ov. **II.** *a water-level* : Vitr. **III.** *the Roman pound* of 12 ounces : Varr. ; corona libram pondo, Liv. ; Juv. Also *a measure for liquids* : Suet. [It. *livra, lira* ; Sp. *libra* ; Fr. *livre.*]

librāmentum, ī, *n.* [librō]. **I.** *a weight used to balance* or *give motive-power* : on a battering-ram, Liv. ; on a ballista, Liv., Tac. **II.** Of a spring of water : *fall, downward tendency* : Plin. Ep. **III.** *a level surface, horizontal plane* : Cic.

librāria, ae, *f.* [lībra], *a woman who weighs out the wool, a forewoman* (called also *lanipendia*) : Juv.

librāriolus, ī, *m.* [*dim.* librārius], *a transcriber's or bookseller's boy* : Cic.

librārius, a, um [liber], *of books* : taberna, Cic. ; scriptor, *a transcriber of books,* Hor. As Noun, **librārius,** ī, *m.* **a.** *a transcriber of books or documents, a copyist, scribe* : Cic., Liv. **b.** *a bookseller* : Sen.

librārium, ī, *n.,* *a place to keep books in, a bookcase, book-chest* : Cic.

librātus, a, um. **I.** *Part.* librō. **II.** A d j. : *swung, poised, hurled* : librato magis et certo ictu, Tac. *Comp.* : libratior ictus, Liv.

librīlis, e, *adj.* [lībra], *of a pound, weighing a pound* : fundis librilibus, or fundis, librilibus, *sc.* saxis, Caes.

librītor, ōris, *m.* [librō], *one who hurls* stones from an engine of war, *an artilleryman* : Tac.

librō, āre [lībra], *to balance* ; hence, **a.** *to keep balanced, hold in equilibrium* : terra librata ponderibus, Cic. ; Ov. ; his (lapillis) sese per nubila librant, Verg. **b.** *to cause to hang or swing evenly, keep in its place* : vela dubiā librantur ab aurā, Ov. **c.** *to swing, poise, level* a weapon : summā telum librabat ab aure, Verg. ; dextrā libratum fulmen ab aure, Ov. ; spiculum, Liv. Hence, *to swing, hurl* : Verg., Liv. **d.** *to make level* : Vitr.

Libs (Lips), Libis [λίψ]. *the W.S.W. wind.*

lībum, ī, *n. a cake, pancake* : Cato, Verg., Ov., etc. Often used in offerings to the gods, esp. on birthdays : Varr., Ov., etc.

Liburni, ōrum, *m. pl. a people of Illyria* ; **Liburnia,** ae, *f. their country* ; **Liburnus,** **Liburnicus,** a, um ; **Liburnus,** ī, *m. a Liburnian (slave)* : Juv. ; **Liburna (Liburnica,** Suet.), ae, *f. a light, fast-sailing vessel, a Liburnian galley* : Caes., Hor., etc.

Libyes, um, *m. pl. (sing.* **Libys,** yos), *the Libyans who lived in N. Africa* ; **Libya,** ae, and **Libyē,** ēs, *f. their country* ; also in gen., *Africa* ; **Libycus, Libyssus, Libystinus, Libyus,** a, um ; **Libystis,** idis, *f. adj.*

licēns, entis. **I.** *Part.* licet. **II.** A d j. : *free, unrestrained.* **a.** Of persons : Prop. **b.** In metre : *free from rule* : licentior dithyrambus, Cic. **c.** ioci, Stat.

licenter, *adv. freely, without restraint, lawlessly* : Cic., Liv., Quint. *Comp.* : Cic., Sall., Tac., etc.

licentia, ae, *f.* [licet], *freedom, absence of control.* **a.** In gen. : Pl. ; ludendi, Cic. ; Tac. ; iniuriae, Sall. **b.** *freedom of choice* (freq. of words), *uncontrolled power* : scribendi, dicendi, Cic. ; figurarum, Quint. ; nunquam ad unum (i.e. Caesarem) tanta pervenisset licentia, Cic. **c.** *freedom abused, lawlessness, license, dissoluteness* : Ter., Cic. ; habere, Cic. ; refrenare, Hor. ; coercere, Tac. ; gladiorum, Cic. Ep. ; ponti, Ov. ; cupiditatum, Cic.

licentiōsus, a, um [licentia], *capricious, arbitrary* : Quint.

liceō, ēre [licet]. **I.** *to offer to buy* : Pl. **II.** *to offer for sale* : quanti licuisse tu scribis (hortos), Cic. Ep. ; Hor., etc. (In Cic. and Hor. the meaning may be *to be valued.*)

liceor, ēri [*dep.* of liceō], *to bid at an auction* : Pl., Caes., Cic. ; digito liceri, Cic. With Acc. : *to bid for* : hortos liceri, Cic. Ep. ; Pers. ; Plin. Pan.

licet, licēre, licuit or licitum est [*cf.* liceō, liceor, polliceor] (*Aor. Subj.* or *Opt.* licēssit, Pl.), *it is allowed, permitted,* or *lawful.* **1.** L i t. : hoc feci dum licuit, Cic. ; per vos licet, Pl. ; Cic. With *Neut. Pron.* as Subject : illud non licet, Ter. ; Cic., etc. ; and with DAT. of person allowed : id ei licet, Cic. ; Verg. With *Inf.* as Subject (with or without DAT. of person) : introire in aedis numquam licitum est, Pl. ; Caes. ; Cic., etc. ; licet nemini contra patriam ducere exercitum, Cic. ; with *Pass. Inf.* : Caes., Cic., Liv. With a *Predic.* DAT. : tibi incenato esse hodie licet, Pl. ; Caes. ; Cic., etc. With Acc. and *Inf.* as Subject : licet me id scire, Pl. ; Cic., etc. N.B. the *Predic. Adj.* or Noun is often in the Acc. even when a DAT. accompanies licet : si civi Romano licet esse Gaditanum, Cic. ; Caes. ; Ov., etc. With *Subjunctive* clause as Subject : ludas licet, Ter. ; fremant omnes licet, Cic. ; Pl. ; Verg., etc. Occ. with *ut* and *Subj.* : Cic. P h r. : **i.** To express assent : *be it so, yes* : Pl. **ii.** To ask permission, esp. in legal formulas : e.g. in examining witnesses : licet rogare ? Cic. ; in asking the advice of a jurisconsult : licet consulere ?

Cic.; in summoning a witness: licet antestari? (v. antestor). **2.** From its use with *Subj.* comes its use as a conjunction: *granting that, although.* **a.** With *Subj.:* licet laudem Fortunam, tamen, ut ne Salutem culpem, Pl.; licet saepius tibi huius generis litteras mittam, sed tamen non parcam operae, Cic. Ep.; licet haec quivis arbitratu suo reprehendat, certe levior reprehensio est, Cic. **b.** Without a verb: is, licet caeli regione remotos, mente deos adiit, Ov.; Sen.

Lĭchās, ae, *m. an attendant of Hercules.*

lĭchēn, ēnis, *m.* [λειχήν]. **I.** *lichen :* Plin. **II.** *ringworm :* Plin., Mart.

Lĭcĭnĭus, a, *the name of a Roman gens ;* esp. **I.** L. Licinius Crassus, *the orator,* B.C. 140–91. **II.** M. Licinius Crassus, *consul with Pompey in* B.C. 70, *killed at Carrhae in Parthia,* B.C. 53.

lĭcĭtātĭō, ōnis, *f.* [licitor], *a bidding at sales :* Cic., Suet. In *pl. :* Cic.

lĭcĭtor, ārī [liceor], *to bid for :* Pl. With Acc.: Curt.

lĭcĭtus, a, um [licet], *permitted, allowed :* sermo, Verg. *Neut. pl.* as Noun, *things allowed* or *lawful :* per licita atque inlicita, Tac.

lĭcĭum, ī, *n.* [*cf.* obliquus], *the thrum* or *ends of a weaver's thread.* **1.** L i t. : licia telae addere, Verg. **2.** T r a n s f. **a.** *a thread* of anything woven. Often used in charms and spells : cantata licia, Ov.; Verg. **b.** Perh. also *woven fabrics :* Ov.

lĭctor, ōris, *m.* [ligō], *a lictor, an attendant on a Roman magistrate :* Pl., Cic., Liv., etc.

lĭcŭit, *v.* licet and liquet.

lĭēn, ēnis, *m. the milt* or *spleen :* quasi zonā, liene cinctus ambulo, Pl. In *pl. :* Cato.

lĭēnōsus, a, um [lien], *splenetic :* cor, Pl.

lĭgāmen, inis, *n.* [ligō], *a band, tie, bandage :* Prop., Ov. [It. *legame ;* Fr. *lien.*]

lĭgāmentum, ī, *n.* [ligō], *a band, bandage :* Tac.

lignārĭus, ī, *m.* [lignum], *a carpenter, joiner.* Hence, inter lignarios, a quarter in Rome, Liv.

lignātĭō, ōnis, *f.* [lignor], *a felling* or *procuring of wood :* Caes.

lignātor, ōris, *m.* [lignor], milit. *a woodcutter, a soldier sent to cut wood ;* us. *pl. :* Caes., Liv.

lignĕŏlus, a, um [*dim.* ligneus], *wooden,* of small objects : Lucil., Cic. Ep.

lignĕus, a, um [lignum], *of wood, wooden.* **1.** L i t. : ponticulus, Cic. ; turres, Caes. ; custodia (i.e. stocks), Pl. **2.** T r a n s f. *like wood, dry :* coniux, Cat.

lignor, ārī [lignum], *to fetch* or *procure wood :* esp. milit. : lignandi atque aquandi potestas, Caes. ; lignatum ire, Liv. ; Pl.

lignum, ī, *n.* [lego, *gather*], *wood,* freq. in *pl. fire-wood.* **1.** L i t. : Cato, Cic., Hor., etc. P r o v. : in silvam ligna ferre (*cf.* to carry coals to Newcastle), Hor. **2.** T r a n s f. **a.** (growing) *timber :* Verg., Hor. **b.** *timber* as material : Verg. **c.** *a writing-table :* Juv. [It. *legno, legna.*]

lĭgō, āre, *to tie, bind, bandage.* **1.** L i t. : manūs post terga, Ov.; crus fasciā, Phaedr.; dum mula ligatur, Hor. **2.** T r a n s f. **a.** By freezing : piscis in glacie ligatos, Ov. **b.** In union : dissociata locis concordi pace

ligavit, Ov. **c.** Of a bargain : *to bind fast, close :* pacta, Prop. [Fr. *lier.*]

lĭgō, ōnis, *m. a mattock.* **1.** L i t. : Hor., Ov. **2.** T r a n s f. *tillage :* Juv.

lĭgŭla and **lingŭla**, ae, *f.* [*dim.* fr. root seen in lingō ; but was perh. regarded as *dim.* of lingua], *a little tongue.* T r a n s f. **a.** *a tongue of land :* oppida posita in extremis lingulis promunturiisque, Caes. **b.** *a shoe-trap, shoe-latchet :* Juv. **c.** *a spoon :* Cato, etc.

Lĭgŭrēs, um, *m. pl. a people who lived along the coast of Italy from Etruria to the Gallic frontier ;* in *sing.* **Lĭgur** and **Lĭgus**, uris, *adj.* and *noun ;* **Lĭgŭria**, ae, *f. their country ;* **Lĭgusticus, Lĭgustīnus, Lĭguscus**, a, um.

lĭgŭrĭō and **lĭgurrĭō**, īre [lingō], *to lick, pick at* (food). **1.** L i t. **a.** Varr. ; semesos piscis tepidumque ius, Hor. **b.** *to pick at,* i.e. eat genteelly : Ter. **2.** T r a n s f. **a.** *to feed, prey upon :* Pl., Hor. **b.** *to long for, lust after :* improbissima lucra, Cic.

lĭgŭrītĭō (lĭgurr-), ōnis, *f.* [ligūriō], *lickerishness, daintiness :* Cic.

lĭgustrum, ī, *n. a plant ; privet,* or perh. *syringa :* Verg. ; candidior folio nivei, Galatea, ligustri, Ov.

lĭlĭum, ī, *n.* [*cf.* λείριον], *a lily.* **1.** L i t. : Varr. ; candida, Verg. ; breve, *short-lived,* Hor. **2.** T r a n s f. *spiked pits* (as defence-works) : Caes. [It. *giglio ;* Sp. *lirio ;* Fr. *lis.*]

līma, ae, *f.* [*cf.* λεῖος, lēvis], *a file.* **1.** L i t. : Pl., Plin., Phaedr., etc. **2.** T r a n s f. in literary work : limae labor, *file-work,* i.e. polishing, revision, Hor.

līmātĭus, *comp. adv. in a more polished manner, more elegantly :* scriptum, Cic.

līmātŭlus, a, um [*dim.* līmātus], *nicely discriminating :* iudicium, Cic. Ep.

līmātus, a, um. **I.** *Part.* līmō. **II.** *Adj.: polished, refined :* vir oratione maxime limatus, Cic.

līmāx, ācis, *m.f. a slug, snail :* Plin. T r a n s f. Pl.

limbōlārĭus, ī, *m.* [limbus], *a fringe-maker :* Pl.

limbus, ī, *m. a hem, fringe :* picto chlamydem circumdata limbo, Verg. ; Ov. T r a n s f. Varr.

līmen, inis, *n.* [perh. cf. līmus, *aslant*]. **1.** L i t. : *the lintel of a doorway* (limen superum), *the threshold, door-sill* (limen inferum) : Pl. But mostly *the threshold :* Pl., Caes., Verg., etc. **2.** T r a n s f. **a.** *doorway, door, entrance :* intra limen cohibere se, Pl. ; contineri limine, Liv. ; saxea, Verg. ; Cic. **b.** *the barrier* or *starting point in a race-course :* Verg. **c.** *house, home :* domos et dulcia limina mutant, Verg. ; sceleratum, Verg. **d.** *threshold, outset, beginning :* leti, Lucr. ; belli, Tac.

līmes, itis, *m.* [*cf.* līmen, līmus]. **1.** L i t. **a.** *a cross-path, balk between fields :* Varr. **b.** *a path in gen. :* transversi, Liv. ; latus, Verg. ; acclivis, Ov. ; eo limite signa extulerunt, Liv. Hence, si male dicetis, vostro gradiar limite, Pl. ; bene meritis de patriā quasi limes ad caeli aditum patet, Cic. **c.** *a boundary-path, a boundary :* partiri limite campum, Verg. ; saxum, līmes agro positus, Verg. **2. Transf. a.** *a fortified boundary-line, a frontier-line :* Tac. **b.** *a channel :* solito dum flumina currant limite, Ov. **c.** *the track or path of a comet, meteor, torch, etc. :* longo limite sulcus dat lucem, Verg.; *of the zodiac :* Ov. **d.** *course, way, manner :* eundem limitem agere, Ov. **e.** *line or margin of difference :* iudicium brevi limite falle tuum, Ov.; Quint.

Limnātis, idis, *f.* [Λιμνᾶτις, of marshes], *a cult-name of Diana.*

(1) līmō, āre [līma], *to file.* **1.** Lit.: Plin. **2. Transf. a.** *to rub.* Comic.: limare caput cum aliquo (i.e. *to kiss*), Pl. **b.** *to file, polish, finish :* quaedam institui, quae limantur a me politius, Cic.; *vir urbanitate* limatus, Cic. **c.** *to file down by investigation, to examine closely :* veritas ipsa limatur in disputatione, Cic.; Phaedr. **d.** *to file down, diminish :* tantum alteri adfinxit, de altero limavit, Cic.; mea commoda, Hor.

(2) līmō, āre [līmus, 1], *to bespatter with mud* (with pun on līmō (1) 2. a.): caput alicui, Pl.

līmōsus, a, um [līmus, 1]. **I.** *miry, muddy :* lacus, Verg.; ripa, Ov. **II.** *growing in mud :* iuncus, Verg.

limpidus, a, um, *clear, limpid:* lacus, Cat. [It. and Sp. *lindo.*]

līmulus, a, um [*dim.* limus, *adj.*], *slightly aslant, squinting :* oculi, Pl.

līmus, a, um [*cf.* ob-līquus], *sidelong, aslant:* limis oculis aspicere, Pl.; *without oculis,* Ter.; limis subrisit ocellis, Ov.; Quint.

(1) līmus, ī, *m.* [*cf.* λίμνη, λειμών], *slime, mud.* **1.** Lit.: Pl., Verg., Liv., etc. Occ. *dirt, grime of any kind :* gravis veteri craterae limus adhaesit, Hor. **2. Transf.:** malorum (*cf.* " Slough of Despond "), Ov.

(2) līmus, ī, *m.* [*cf.* līmus, *aslant* ; hence, *a cross-band*], *a girdle or apron trimmed with purple,* worn by the sacrificing priests : velati limo, Verg.

līnctus, a, um, *Part.* lingō.

līnea, ae, *f.* [līnum], *a linen thread, a string, line.* **1.** Lit. **a.** In gen.: Varr. **b.** *the string of a net or the net itself :* Plin. **c.** *a fishing-line :* Mart. Prov.: mittere lineam, *to cast a line, try to catch a person,* Pl. **d.** *a plumb-line* of masons and carpenters : Cic. Ep. Hence, ad lineam and rectā lineā, *in a straight line, vertically, perpendicularly :* Cic.; so, rectis lineis, Caes. **2. Transf. a.** In geom., *a line :* Quint. **b.** *a line* drawn : ducere, Plin. Prov. of " keeping one's hand in " : nulla dies sine lineā, Plin. Also *a line* ruled : Plin. **c.** In theatres : *a line* drawn to mark the seats : quid frustra refugis ? cogit nos linea iungi, Ov.; Quint. **d.** *an outline :* ducere, Quint. **e.** *a boundary-line, limit :* si quidem est peccare tamquam transire lineas, Cic.; mors ultima linea rerum est, Hor. Prov.: extremā lineā amare (i.e. *to love at a distance*), Ter. [Fr. *ligne.*]

līneāmentum (līniā-), ī, *n.* [līnea], *a line or stroke* made with a pen, etc. **1.** Lit. in geometry : Cic. **2. Transf. a.** In *pl. : features, lineaments :* oris, Cic., Liv.; hospitae, Cic.; corporis, Liv. **b.** In *pl. : outlines :* adumbratio deorum, Cic. **c.**

Mostly in *pl. : features of character :* animi, Cic.

līneāris, e, *adj.* [līnea], *of or by means of lines, linear :* Plin.

līneō, āre [līnea], *to fashion to a straight line, to make straight or perpendicular :* Pl., Cato.

līneus, a, um [līnum], *of flax, flaxen, linen:* vincula, Verg.; amictus, Tac. [Fr. *linge.*]

lingō, lingere, linxī, līnctum [*cf.* λείχω], *to lick up :* mel, Pl., Cat.

lingua (old form **dingua**), ae, *f. the tongue.* **1.** Lit.: Pl., Cic., Ov., etc. **2. Transf. a.** *speech, language :* Pl.; continere, Cic. Ep.; moderari, Sall.; tenere, Ov.; solvere, Ov.; linguā melior, Verg.; divite linguā, Hor.; Aetolorum linguas retundere, Liv. **b.** *the language of a people :* Gallicae linguae scientiam habere, Caes.; Latina, Graeca, Cic.; utraque lingua, i.e. *Greek and Latin,* Hor. Poet. *of the sounds made by animals :* volucrum, Verg.; *of land :* eminet in altum lingua, in quā urbs sita est, Liv.; Luc. [Fr. *langue.*]

lingula, *v.* ligula.

lingulāca, ae, *m.f.* [lingula], *a gossip, chatterbox :* Pl., Varr.

līniger, era, erum [līnum gerō], *linen-wearing, clothed in linen,* of Isis and her priests : turba, Ov.

līnō, linere, lēvī (and līvī), litum, *to daub, besmear.* **1.** Lit.: Cato; spiramenta cerā, Verg.; ferrum pice, Liv.; Sabinum (vinum), Hor. Occ. *to smear over writing* on wax-tablets; *to erase :* Ov. **2. Transf. a.** *to overlay, cover :* tecta auro, Ov. **b.** *to befoul :* splendida facta carmine foedo, Hor.

linquō, linquere, līquī [*cf.* Gk. λείπω]. **I.** *to leave, quit, forsake.* **a.** land, home, etc. : Pl., Cic., Verg., etc. **b.** life : linquere lumen, animam, vitam, Pl.; animas, Verg.; linqui animo, or linqui, *to faint, swoon :* Suet., Ov. **II.** *to leave or let alone, to abandon :* nil intemptatum nostri liquere poetae, Hor.; linquamus naturam artisque videamus, Cic. **III.** *to leave in any place or condition, to leave in the lurch :* erum in opsidione, Pl. **IV.** *Pass. Impers.* linquitur, *it is left, it remains* (with *ut* and *Subj.*): Lucr.

linteātus, a, um [linteum], *enrolled in a canvas-enclosure :* legio, cohortes, Liv.

linteō, ōnis, *m.* [linteum], *a linen-weaver :* Pl.

linteolum, ī, *n.* [*dim.* linteum], *a small linen cloth :* Pl.

linter, tris, *f.* (*m.* Tib.). **I.** *a trough, vat :* Cato, Verg., Tib. **II.** *a boat, skiff, wherry :* Caes., Cic., Liv. Transf.: naviget hinc aliā iam mihi linter aquā, Ov.; in liquidā nat tibi linter aquā, Tib.

linteus, a, um [līnum], *of linen :* vestis, Cic.; libri, Liv.; thorax, Liv. *Neut.* as Noun, *a linen cloth :* Pl. Transf. **a.** *canvas* (in *pl.*): Liv. **b.** *a sail :* dare lintea retro, Verg.; Hor.; Ov.

lintriculus, ī, *m.* [*dim.* linter], *a small boat :* Cic. Ep.

līnum, ī, *n.* [Gk. λίνον], *flax.* **1.** Lit.: Verg. **2. Transf. a.** *linen :* reticulum tenuissimo lino, Cic.; Massica integrum per-

dunt lino vitiata saporem, Hor. **b.** *a
thread.* Esp. *the thread with which letters
were bound* : Pl. ; linum incidimus, legimus,
Cic. **c.** *a fishing-line* : nunc in mole sedens
moderabar harundine linum, Ov. **d.** *a
rope, line* : subducere carbasa lino, Ov. **e.**
a hunter's or *fisher's net, casting-net* : Verg.,
Hor., Ov.

Linus (**-os**), i, *m. s. of Apollo, instructor of
Orpheus and Hercules ; he was killed by the
latter.*

Lipara, ae, and **Liparē**, ēs, *f. one of the
Aeolian Isles, north of Sicily, now Lipari* ;
in *pl.* **Liparae**, ārum, *f. the Aeolian islands.*
Liparaeus, a, um, and **Liparēnsis**, e ;
Liparēnsēs, ium, *m. pl. the inhabitants.*

lippiō, īre [lippus], *to have inflamed or watery
eyes, to be blear-eyed* : Cic. Ep. Comic. :
lippiunt fauces fame, Pl.

lippitūdō, inis, *f.* [lippus], *inflammation of
the eyes* : Pl., Cic.

lippus, a, um [*cf.* λίπος, ἀλείφω], *with inflamed eyes, blear-eyed.* **1.** Lit. : Pl., Hor. ;
oculus, Pl. Prov. : omnibus et lippis
notum et tonsoribus, Hor. **2.** Transf. **a.**
half-blinded : fuligine lippus, Juv. **b.** Of
an over-ripe fig : Mart. **c.** (*Mentally*)
blind : Hor.

lique-faciō, facere, fēcī, factum. Pass.
lique-fīō, fierī, factus, *to make liquid, to
melt, dissolve, liquefy.* **1.** Lit. : glacies
liquefacta, Cic. ; liquefactum plumbum,
Verg. ; margaritas aceto, Suet. **2.**
Transf. **a.** Of disease or death : *to decom-
pose* : liquefacta boum viscera, Verg. ; Ov.
b. *to waste, enervate* : quos laetitiae languidis
liquefaciunt voluptatibus, Cic. ; Ov.

liquēns, entis, *adj.* [liqueō, *cf.* liquet], *limpid,
clear, fluid* : vina, Verg. ; Varr. ; fluvius,
Verg. ; campi, Verg.

liquēns, entis. **I.** *Part.* liquor. **II.** Adj. :
flowing : mella, flumina, Verg.

liquēscō, liquēscere, licuī [liquet]. **I.** *to
become fluid* or *liquid, to melt.* **1.** Lit. :
Verg., Liv., etc. **2.** Transf. **a.** *to become decomposed* or *putrid* : (corpora) di-
lapsa liquescunt, Ov. **b.** *to grow soft,
effeminate* : quā (voluptate) liquescimus,
Cic. **c.** *to melt* or *waste away* : fortuna
liquescit, Ov. Of a person : Sen. Ep. **II.**
to become clear, clarify : aqua, Auct. B.
Alex.

liquet, liquēre, licuit, *it is clear, evident,
apparent* (used mostly in 3rd *pers. sing.*) :
quidquid incerti mi in animo fuit, nunc
liquet, Pl. ; Cic. With Acc. and *Inf.* :
Cic., Liv., etc. With *Indir. Quest.* : Liv.,
Plin. Ep. In *pl.* : ut liqueant omnia,
Pl. As a legal term : non liquet (abbrev.
N.L.), *it is not clear* (like the Scottish *not-
proven*) : non liquere dixerunt iudices,
Cic. ; Quint. So, on the contrary, liquet :
cum causam non audisset, dixit sibi
liquere, Cic.

liquidē, *adv. clearly, purely.* Transf. :
clearly, plainly : liquidius iudicare, Cic.

liquidiusculus, a, um [*dim.* of *comp.* of
liquidus], *rather more fluid* or *soft* : Pl.

liquidus, a, um (occ. līq- in Lucr.) [*v.* liquēns,
liquet]. **I.** *flowing, fluid, liquid.* **1.** Lit. :
Cato, Hor., etc. ; Nymphae, Ov. ; deus,
itor, Prop. As Noun, **liquidum**, i, *n. a*

liquid, water : Hor., Ov. In *pl.* : Lucr.
2. Transf. **a.** Of style : *flowing* : Cic.
b. *pure, unmixed* : voluptas, Lucr. ; Cic.
II. *clear, transparent, limpid, serene.* **1.**
Lit. : lumen, Lucr. ; caeli tempestas,
Lucr. ; fontes, ignis, aether, aer, iter, etc.,
Verg. ; color, Hor. **2.** Transf. **a.** Of
sound : *clear, liquid, pure* : voces (of
birds), Lucr. ; Verg. ; carmen citharae,
Lucr. ; vox, Hor. **b.** Mental : *clear, calm,
serene* : animo liquido et tranquillo es, Pl.
c. *clear, evident, certain* : auspicium, Pl.
As Noun, **liquidum**, *clearness, certainty* :
ad liquidum perducere aliquid, Quint.
ABL. **liquidō** as *Adv.*, *clearly, plainly* :
audire, confirmare, negare, Cic.

liquō, āre [liquēns, liquet]. **I.** *to melt, dissolve, liquefy* : vitrum, Plin. **II.** *to strain,
filter, clarify.* **1.** Lit. : vina, Hor. **2.**
Transf. of the florid language of youth :
defervisse tempore et annis liquata (dicta),
Quint.

liquor, līquī [*cf.* liquēns, liquet], *to flow.*
1. Lit. : toto corpore sudor, Verg. ; gelidus montibus umor, Verg. **2.** Transf. :
to melt or *waste away* : ilico res foras labitur,
liquitur, Pl. ; aetas, Lucr.

liquor, ōris, *m.* [*cf.* liquēns, liquet], *fluidity,
liquidity.* **1.** Lit. : liquor aquae, Cic. ;
Lucr. **2.** Transf. *a fluid, liquid* : liquo-
ris vitigeni latex, Lucr. ; liquores amnium,
Cic. ; Verg. ; Ov. Of *the sea* : quā medius
liquor secernit Europen ab Afro, Hor.

līrō, āre [līra, *ridge between two furrows*], *to
plough in the seed* : Varr.

līroe [λῆροι], *trifles* : Pl.

līs, lītis (old form **stlīs**, stlītis), *f.* **1.** Lit. **a.**
an action at law, a lawsuit : persequi lite
atque iudicio aliquid, Cic. ; iudicare, Pl.,
Cic. ; orare, contestari, obtinere, amittere,
Cic. ; alicui intendere, inferre, Cic. ; secare,
Hor. ; litem discerneret arvis, Verg. Phr. :
litem suam facere, of an advocate who
neglects the cause of his client and defends
himself, Cic. **b.** *the subject of an action at
law, the matter in dispute* : de totā lite
pactionem facere, Cic. ; litem aestimare, *to
assess damages*, Caes., Cic. ; litem in suam
rem vertere, Liv. **2.** Transf. *dispute,
wrangling* : contrahere, Pl. ; sub iudice lis
est, Hor. ; philosophi aetatem in litibus con-
terunt, Cic. ; litis sator, Liv. ; componere
litis, Verg. Of things : cum formā magnā
pudicitiae, Ov.

litātiō, ōnis, *f.* [litō], *a favourable sacrifice* :
Pl., Liv.

litātō, *adv.* [litō], *with favourable omens* :
Liv.

litera, *v.* littera.

litigātor, ōris, *m.* [lītigō], *a party to a lawsuit* :
Quint., Tac., etc.

litigiōsus, a, um [litigium], *contentious.* **1.**
Lit. **a.** disputatio, Cic. **b.** Of persons :
Cic. **2.** Transf. **a.** *disputed* : praediolum, Cic. **b.** *clamorous with wrangling* :
forum, Ov.

litigium, i, *n.* [lītigō], *a dispute, quarrel* : Pl.

litigō, āre [līs agō]. **I.** *to go to law* : Cic.
II. *to quarrel, squabble* : quā de re litigatis
inter vos ? Pl. ; cum aliquo, Cic. Ep.

litō, āre [*cf.* Gk. λιτή], *to offer acceptable
sacrifice* ; and so *to obtain favourable*

omens. **A.** Intrans. **1.** Lit.: Pl., Liv.,
Luc., etc. With DAT.: diis, Cic. With
ABL. of the victim: humanis hostiis, Tac.;
Cic.; Verg. **2.** Transf. *to propitiate,
appease:* litemus Lentulo, Cic.; publico
gaudio, Plin. Pan. **B.** Trans. *to offer
acceptably* or *duly:* sacra bove, Ov.;
sacris litatis, Verg.

litorālis, e, *adj.* [litus], *of the sea-shore:* dii,
Cat.

litoreus, a, um [litus], *of the sea-shore:* aves,
Verg.; harena, Ov.

littera, (old Lat. **litera, leitera**), ae, *f. a
letter* of the alphabet: Pl., Cic., etc. **Phr.**:
facere litteram or litteras, *to write,* Pl.;
litteras discere, *to learn to read and write,*
Cic. Comic.: Pl.; scire, *to know how
to read and write,* Pl.; so negatively, nescire
litteras, Sen., Suet.; litteram ex se longam
facere, *to make the letter I of oneself,* i.e.
hang one's self, Pl.; littera salutaris, i.e.
A. (absolvo) and tristis, i.e. **C.** (condemno),
which were used in voting: Cic.; homo
trium litterarum (i.e. fur, *a thief*), Pl. In
plural. **a.** *a letter, epistle:* resignare, Pl.;
signare, obsignare, Cic.; alicui dare ad
aliquem, ad aliquem mittere, Cic. In *sing.*:
Ov., Tib. **b.** *a public letter, dispatches:*
publicae, Nep.; Caes.; Cic. **c.** *public
documents* of various kinds: litterae publicae, Cic.; litteras revocavit, *cancelled his
commission,* Suet.; **d.** *an edict, ordinance:*
praetoris, Cic. **e.** *literature:* abest historia
litteris nostris, Cic.; Graecis litteris studere,
Cic.; Etruscae, Liv.; artem litteris sine
interprete percipere, Cic. Of *history:*
cupidissimus litterarum fuit, Nep.; Liv.
f. *literary composition, scholarship, belles
lettres* in gen.: homo sine litteris, Cic.;
litterarum cognitio, Cic.; orator tinctus
litteris, Cic. [It. *lettera;* Sp. *letra;* Fr.
lettre.]

litterārius, a, um [littera], *of the elements
of reading and writing:* ludus, Quint., Tac.,
etc.

litterātē, *adv.* **I.** *with plain letters, in a
clear hand:* Cic. **II.** *literally:* respondere, Cic. **III.** *learnedly, cleverly:* belle et
litterate dicta, Cic. *Comp.:* Latine loqui,
Cic.

litterātor, ōris, *m.* [littera], *an (inferior)
grammarian:* Cat.

litterātūra, ae, *f.* [littera]. **I.** *a writing
formed of letters, the letters,* or *alphabet:*
Graeca, Tac. **II.** *grammar:* Sen. Ep.,
Quint.

litterātus, a, um [littera], *lettered.* **I.** *marked
with letters, branded:* ensiculus, Pl. **II.**
learned. **a.** Of persons: *liberally educated,
scholarly:* Cic. Esp. of critics and ex-
pounders: quem litteratissimum fuisse
iudico, Cic. Ep. **b.** Of time: *devoted to
study:* otium, senectus, Cic.

litterula, ae, *f.* [*dim.* littera]. **I.** *a little
letter:* Cic. Ep. **II.** In *pl.* **a.** *a short
letter:* Cic. Ep. **b.** *poor literary efforts:*
Cic. Ep. **c.** *slight knowledge of literature:*
Hor.

littus, *v.* litus.

litūra, ae, *f.* [lino], *a smearing.* Esp. **a.**
a smearing of the wax on a writing tablet, in
order to erase something written; *an era-*

sure or *a passage erased:* unius nominis
litura, Cic.; carmen quod non multa litura
coercuit, Hor. **b.** *a blot, smear:* Prop.,
Ov. **c.** *a wrinkle:* Mart.

litus, a, um, *Part.* lino.

litus, oris, *n.* [*cf.* limus]. **I.** *Sing.* and *pl.:
the sea-shore, coast, beach, strand:* Cic.,
Verg., etc. Prov.: litus arare (of vain
labour), Cic.; in litus harenas fundere (of
foolish, unnecessary labour), Ov. **II.** *the
bank* of a lake or river: Cic., Cat., Verg.

lituus, i, *m.* [prob. an Etrusc. word; *crooked*].
I. *the curved staff borne by the augurs, an
augur's wand:* Cic., Verg., Liv. **II.** *a
curved trumpet, clarion* (used by the cavalry).
1. Lit.: Verg., Hor., etc. **2.** Transf. **a.**
a signal: Cic. Ep. **b.** *the starter:* meae
profectionis, Cic.

livēns, entis. **I.** *Part.* liveo. **II.** *Adj. black
and blue, bluish, livid:* plumbum, Verg.;
crura compedibus, Ov.

liveō, ēre, *to be black and blue, livid.* **1.** Lit.:
rubigine dentes, Ov.; catenis bracchia,
Prop. **2.** Transf.: *to be envious:* Mart.
With DAT. *to envy:* Mart., Tac.

livēscō, ere [liveo], *to turn black and blue,
become livid:* digiti in pedibus, Lucr.

Līvia, ae, *f.* **I.** *the second wife of Augustus.*
II. *wife of Caligula.*

lividulus, a, um [*dim.* lividus], *inclined to be
envious:* Juv.

lividus, a, um [liveo], *leaden in colour, blue.*
1. Lit. **a.** In gen.: vada, Verg.; racemi,
Hor. *Sup.:* Cat. **b.** *black and blue* from
bruises: ora, Ov.; bracchia, Hor. **2.**
Transf. *envious, spiteful:* Cic.; lingua,
Ov.; obliviones, Hor.

Līvius, a, *the name of a Roman gens.* Esp.
the freedman M. Livius Andronicus, *the
first Roman tragic poet* (ob. B.C. 204) and T.
Livius Patavinus, *the celebrated historian
who was born at Patavium* (B.C. 59–A.D. 17):
Līvius, Liviānus, a, um.

līvor, ōris, *m.* [liveo], *a bluish* or *leaden colour,
a black and blue spot.* **1.** Lit.: Pl., Tib.,
Quint., etc. **2.** Transf. *envy, spite:*
Brut. ap. Cic. Ep., Ov., Tac., etc.

lixa, ae, *m.* [perh. conn. with liceo, q.v.], *a
sutler.* **1.** Lit.: lixarum in modum ne-
gotiari, Liv.; Tac. **2.** Transf. (in *pl.*)
camp-followers, consisting of sutlers, cooks,
servants, etc.: Sall., Quint.

locātiō, ōnis, *f.* [loco], *a placing.* **A.** *an
arrangement:* verborum, Quint. **B.** (*cf.*
loco III). **a.** *a letting out, leasing:* praediorum rusticorum, Liv. **b.** *a building-lease*
or *contract:* Cic. Ep. **c.** *a contract of farming*
the taxes: Cic. Ep.

locātōrius, a, um [loco], *dealing with leases
and contracts:* provincia, Cic. Ep.

locātum, i, n. [loco], *a lease* or *contract;* or
perh. *a case* or *act of leasing:* iudicia quae
fiunt ex conducto aut locato, Cic.

locitō, āre [*freq.* loco], *to be in the habit of
hiring out:* Ter.

locō, āre (*Aor. Opt.* locāssim, Pl.; locāssint,
Cic.) [locus], *to place, put, lay, set.* **I.** In
gen. **1.** Lit.: cratis adversa locari iubet,
Caes.; milites in munimentis, Sall.; viros
sedili, Verg.; cohortis hibernaculis, Tac.;
fundamenta urbis, Verg.; vicos, Tac. **2.**
Transf.: alicui insidias, Pl.; vitam in

tam clarā luce, Lucr. ; aliquem in amplissimo gradu dignitatis, Cic. ; eo loco locati
sumus ut etc., Cic. **II.** locare in matrimonium *or* matrimonio, *or simply* locare, *to
give in marriage* : virginem locare alicui,
Pl. ; in matrimonium, Pl. ; nuptum virginem alicui, Tac. ; in matrimonio stabili et
certo, Cic. **III.** In business : *to put out
under contract.* **A.** *to let out on hire, to
lease, put out to interest, invest.* **1.** Lit. :
argentum, Pl. ; vectigalia, Cic. ; agrum
frumento, Liv. ; praedia nummo, Plin. Ep. ;
locare se *or* locare operam suam, *to hire oneself out, hire out one's services :* Pl. ; vocem
(to become a public crier), Juv. **2.**
Transf. : beneficia apud gratos, Liv. ;
Enn. **B.** *to give out a contract for, to contract for* (us. with *Gerundive*) : Pl. ; statuam
faciendam, Cic. ; Iunoni templum (*sc.* ex-
struendum), Liv. ; vestimenta exercitui,
Liv. [Fr. *louer.*]

loculus, i, *m.* [*dim.* locus]. **I.** *a little place :*
Pl. **II.** In *pl.*, *a small receptacle.* **a.** For
books : *a satchel :* Hor. **b.** For money :
Hor., Suet., etc.

locuplēs, ētis (GEN. *pl.* -tium, Cic., -tum,
Caes. ; ABL. *sing.* -ti *or* -te, Cic.), *adj.*
[locus and plēto-, particip. stem from ple-ō].
Lit. *full of landed property :* tum erat res
in pecore et locorum possessionibus ; ex
quo pecuniosi et locupletes vocabantur,
Cic. Hence, *rich, wealthy, opulent.* **1.**
Lit. : Pl., Cic., Juv., etc. ; praedā locuples,
Sall. ; Hor. *Comp. :* Quint. *Sup. :* Cic. ;
urbes, Caes. As Noun, *the rich :* Caes.,
Cic. **2.** Transf. **a.** Of language : oratione locuples, Cic. ; Latinam linguam
locupletiorem quam Graecam, Cic. **b.**
a 'good' surety, hence *reliable, trustworthy,
responsible :* testis, auctor, Cic. ; reus, Liv.,
Tac. ; tabellarius, Cic. Ep. *Comp. :* Cic.,
Tac.

locuplētō, āre [locuplēs], *to make rich, enrich.*
1. Lit. : homines fortunis, Cic. ; militem
praedā, Liv. **2.** Transf. : templum pic-
turis, Cic.

locus (old form stlocus like atlis for lis), i,
m. a place ; in *pl.* **loci,** *single places ;*
loca, *places connected with one another,
regions.* **1.** Lit. **A.** In gen. : Pl. ; quo
in loco Germani consederant, Caes. ; Galli
qui ea loca incolerent, Caes. ; locus editus,
Caes. ; locorum situm nosse, Liv. **Phr.** :
ex (*or* de) loco superiore agere *or* dicere
(from the bench *or* the rostra), ex inferiore
loco (from the body of the court), ex aequo
loco (on a level, as in the Senate *or* in conversation), Cic. **B.** Milit. *position, post :*
locum tenere, relinquere, Caes. ; se loco
tenere, Caes. ; loca iussa tenere, Verg. ;
locum dare *or* loco cedere, *to give way,* Sall. ;
in loco aequo (iniquo) pugnare, *to fight on
level (unlevel) ground ;* also *on fair (disadvantageous) ground or conditions ;* loca
superiora occupare, *to seize the higher
ground,* Caes., Liv. Transf. : loco cedere,
Nep. ; locum virtutis deseruit, Hor. **C.**
a place or seat in the theatre, circus, *or*
forum : Pl. ; locum ad spectandum dare,
Cic. ; in *pl.* loci *or* loca, Liv. Also *house-
room, lodging, quarters* (given to ambassadors) : Liv. **D.** *a place, site, spot, locality,*

district : Pl., Cic., Verg., etc. Sō illīc,
letifer locus (corporis), Ov. In *pl.* **a.** loca,
districts, regions : Pl., Cic., Verg., etc. **b.**
loci, *sites, single places, individual spots :*
Pl., Verg., Liv., etc. **2.** Of time. **a.** *a
space of time, period :* mostly in the phr. :
adhuc locorum, *hitherto,* Pl. ; ad id locorum,
till then, hitherto, Sall., Liv. ; post id locorum, *afterwards,* Pl. ; inde loci, *since then,*
Lucr. ; postea loci, *afterwards,* Sall. ; interea loci, *meanwhile,* Ter. ; ubicumque
locorum, *whenever,* Hor. **b.** *a point of
time, a (right) moment :* loco *or* in loco,
seasonably, opportunely, Cic. Ep., Hor. ;
neo vero hic locus est ut etc., Cic. ; locum
seditionis quaerere, Liv. ; et cognoscendi et
ignoscendi dabitur peccati locus, Ter. ;
Cic. **3.** Transf. **a.** *position, situation,
place, category :* si ego in istoc siem loco,
Pl. ; in liberum (GEN.) loco esse, Cic. ;
se eodem loco illos quo Helvetios habiturum,
Caes. ; parentis loco esse, Cic. ; hostium
loco esse, Liv. Of things : quo loco res
essent, Liv. ; Verg. ; criminis loco putant
esse quod vivam, Cic. ; *cf.* also eo loci, Cic.,
Tac. ; quo loci, Cic. **b.** *position, degree,
rank :* principem locum obtinere, Caes. ;
summus locus civitatis, Cic. ; huic Caesar
maiorum locum restituerat, Caes. So
esp. of *birth :* Tanaquil summo loco nata,
Liv. Of things : Socrates voluptatem
nullo loco numerat, Cic. **c.** *a passage* in a
book : *pl.* loci, Cic. ; loca, Hor. **d.** *a
topic* of discussion : Cic., Juv., etc. ; *pl.*
loci, Cic. **e.** *the ground* of argument :
Cic. ; esp. loci communes (*general grounds*),
Cic., Quint. **f.** *occasion, opportunity, cause,
place :* dare suspicioni locum, Cic. ; male
dicto nihil loci est, Cic. ; precibus relinquere
locum, Cic. Ep. ; quem locum habet fortitudo (apud eum) ? Cic. [It. *luogo ;* Sp.
lugar ; Fr. *lieu.*]

lōcusta, ae, *f. a locust :* Pl.

Lōcusta, ae, *f. a woman notorious for her
skill in poisons, in the time of Claudius and
Nero.*

locūtiō, ōnis, *f.* [loquor], *speech.* **I.** *style of
speech :* Cic. **II.** *pronunciation :* Cic.,
Quint.

locūtus, a, um, *Part.* loquor.

lōdicula, ae, *f.* [*dim.* lōdix], *a small coverlet,
blanket :* Suet.

lōdix, icis, *f. a blanket or counterpane :* Juv.

loeb-, *v.* lib-.

logicus, a, um [λογικός], *logical :* Cic. *Neut.
pl.* **logica,** ōrum, *logic :* Cic.

logos (-**us**), i, *m.* [λόγος], *a word.* **A.** In
gen. : Pl. **B.** In partic. **a.** *mere words,
empty talk :* dabuntur dotis tibi sescenti
logi, Pl. ; Ter. **b.** *a witty saying, bon-
mot, jest :* Pl., Cic.

lōlīg-, *v.* lollig-.

lolium, i, *n. darnel :* Verg. ; lolio victitare,
to live on darnel, and in consequence to have
bad eyes, Pl., Ov. [It. *gioglio, loglio ;*
Sp. *joyo.*]

lollīgō, inis, *f. a cuttle-fish.* **1.** Lit. : Cic.
2. Transf. : nigrae succus lolliginis (i.e.
calumny), Hor.

lollīguncula, ae, *f.* [*dim.* lollīgō], *a little
cuttle-fish :* Pl.

lōmentum, i, *n.* [lavō], *a face-cream* made of

bean meal and rice, **1.** Lit.: Mart. **2.**
Transf.: Cael. ap. Cic. Ep.
Londinium, i, n. *a city of Britain,* now
London.
longaevus, a, um [longus aevum], *of great
age, aged, ancient :* parens, Verg.; Ov.;
caput, Prop.
longē, adv. *far, far off, at a distance.* **1.** Lit.:
Pl.; Rhenum non longe a mari transire,
Caes.; ab eo oppido non longe fanum est
Iunonis, Cic.; longe lateque, Cic. Also
perh., longe gradientem, Verg. Comp. :
Caes., etc. **2.** Transf. **a.** Of time : longe
prospicere futuros casūs, Cic.; longius anno
permanere, Caes.; Varro vitam Naevi pro-
ducit longius, Cic.; Pl.; Hor., etc.; quoad
longissime potest mens mea respicere, Cic.
b. Of speech : only in Comp. : haec dixi
longius quam instituta ratio postulabat,
Cic. **c.** longe esse, abesse, with DAT. : *to
be far away* (i.e. to be of no assistance, of no
avail) : longe iis fraternum nomen populi
R. afuturum, Caes.; Verg., etc. **d.** *by
far, greatly, very much,* esp. with Comp. and
Sup. : errat longe, Ter.; longe dissimilis,
Cic.; longe aliud esse virgines rapere,
aliud pugnare cum viris, Liv.; longe ante
alias specie insignis, Liv.; longe melior,
Verg.; longe nobilissimus, Caes.; Cic.
[Fr. *loin.*]
longinquitās, ātis, f. [longinquus]. **1.** Lit.
Of space. **a.** *length, extent :* itineris, Tac.
b. *distance, remoteness :* Cic. Ep.; regionum, Tac. **2.** Transf. Of time : *long
continuance* or *duration :* Cic., Liv.;
aetatis, Ter.; temporum, morbi, Cic.;
bellorum, Liv.
longinquus, a, um [longus]. **1.** Lit. **a.**
long, extensive : linea, Plin. **b.** *far off,
remote, distant, at* or *from a distance :* hostis,
loca, Cic.; nationes, Caes.; cura, Liv.;
vulnera, Luc. Comp. : Caes. Neut. as
Noun : ex (e) longinquo, *from afar, from a
distance :* Liv., Tac.; longinqua imperi,
Tac. **c.** *living far off, foreign, strange :*
homo longinquus et alienigena, Cic.; Ov.
Masc. as Noun : Cic. **2.** Transf. Of
time. **a.** *long, of long duration* or *continuance, tedious :* vita, Pl.; oppugnatio, Caes.;
militia, Liv.; dolores, Cic. Comp. : Nep.
b. *long deferred, distant :* tempus, Cic.;
tempore longinqua victoria, Liv.; spes, Tac.
longiter, adv. *far :* Lucr.
longitūdō, inis, f. [longus]. **1.** Lit. in space :
length : pontis, Caes.; itineris, Cic.;
in longitudinem, *lengthways,* Caes., Cic. In
pl. : Cic. **2.** Transf. of time : *length,
long duration :* noctis, orationis, Cic.;
Quint. Also of sounds : Cic.
longiusculus, a, um [dim. of comp. of longus],
rather long : Cic.
longulē, adv., *rather far :* Pl., Ter.
longulus, a, um [dim. longus], *rather long :*
iter, Cic. Ep.
longurius, i, m. [longus], *a long pole :* Caes.
longus, a, um, long. **1.** Lit. **a.** intervallum,
Cic.; longissima epistula, Cic. Ep.; hastae,
Verg.; ferrum tris longum pedes, Liv.;
proficisci longissimo agmine, Caes. Phr. :
longa navis, *a war-ship,* Caes.; an nescis
longas regibus esse manūs, *far-reaching,*
Ov.; longus homo, *a tall fellow,* Cat.; so

in Comp.: Pl.; Neut. Intern. ACC.: longum
clamare, *so as to be heard afar off,* Hor. **b.**
vast, spacious : pontus, Hor.; Olympus,
Verg.; caelum, Ov. **2.** Transf. of time.
a. In gen. *long, of long duration* or *continuance :* horae quibus exspectabam, Cic.;
mora, Caes.; uno die longior mensis, Cic.;
longo post tempore, Verg. **b.** *long, protracted, drawn-out :* morbus, caedes, error,
Liv.; spes, Hor.; memoria alicuius, Sall.
As Noun : in longum dilata res est, Liv.;
nostros in longum ducis amores, Verg.;
Tac.; also, in longius, Tac.; also, ex longo,
Verg. In pronunciation : syllaba, Cic.,
Quint. **c.** *tedious.* Of persons : nolo esse
longus, Cic. Of things : oratio, Cic.
Comp. : Quint. Phr. longum est, *it would
be tedious* (alone or with Inf.) : Cic., Tac.;
ne longum faciam, *not to make a long story,*
Cic., Hor.; ne longum sit, Cic.
loquācitās, ātis, f. [loquāx], *talkativeness,
loquacity :* Cic., Liv., etc.
loquāciter, adv. *talkatively, loquaciously :*
Cic.; aliquid scribere, Hor.
loquāculus, a, um [dim. loquāx], *rather talkative :* Lucr.
loquāx, ācis, adj. [loquor], *talkative, chattering, loquacious.* **1.** Lit.: homo, senectus,
ars, Cic.; loquacem esse de aliquo, Prop.
Comp. and Sup. : Cic. **2.** Transf.:
ranae, stagna, nidus, Verg.; lymphae,
Hor.; oculi (i.e. expressive), Tib.; vultus,
fama, Ov. Comp. : Plin.
loquella (loquēla), ae, f. [loquor]. **1.** Lit.:
speech, discourse : Pl., Lucr., Verg. **2.**
Transf.: *a language :* Graia, Ov.
loquitor, āri [freq. loquor], *to speak often,
chatter :* Pl.
loquor, loqui, locūtus [cf. Gk. λακ- in λάσκω],
to speak, talk, say (colloquially ; opp. dicere,
orare, *to speak with ordered language*).
A. Intrans. **1.** Lit.: Pl.; male, Ter.;
bene et loqui et dicere, *to be both a good
talker and a good speaker,* Cic.; pure et
Latine, Cic.; male loqui alicui, Pl.; apud
aliquem loqui, Cic.; pro aliquo, Caes.;
adversom aliquem, Ter.; cum aliquo, Cic.
2. Transf. **a.** *to declare, clearly indicate :*
res loquitur ipsa, Cic.; oculi loquuntur,
Cic.; cum chartā dextra locuta est, Ov.
b. Of trees : Cat., Verg. **B.** Trans. **a.**
to say : non audis quae hic loquitur, Pl.;
quae de hominis ingenio locutus sum, Cic.;
haec locutus sublimis abiit, Liv. With
Acc. and Inf. : Cic. Ep., Verg., Liv. **b.**
to tell, mention, tell of : loquere tuom mihi
nomen, Pl.; ne singulas loquar urbes,
Liv.; proelia, Hor.; Ov., etc. **c.** *to talk
of, speak about :* Catilinam, Cic.; merum
bellum, Cic. Ep.
lōrārius, i, m. [lōrum], *a flogger :* Pl.
lōrātus, a, um [lōrum], *bound with thongs :*
iuga, Verg.
lōreus, a, um [lōrum], *of strips of leather :*
vostra faciam latera lorea, Pl.
lōrīca, ae, f. [lōrum]. **1.** Prop. *a leather
corselet* or *cuirass,* but also *of metal :* Pl.,
Cic., Verg., etc. **2.** Transf.: *a breast-
work, parapet :* pinnae loricaeque ex cratibus attexuntur, *mantlets,* Caes.; Tac.
lōrīcātus, a, um [lōrīca], *wearing a lorica,
mailed :* equites, statua, Liv.; Quint.

lōrīcula, ae, f. [dim. lōrīca], a small breast-work : Hirt.

lōrī-pēs, pedis, adj. [lōrum pēs], crook-footed, bandy-legged : Pl., Juv.

lōrum, i, n. [cf. Gk. εὔληρα], a (twisted) strip of leather, a thong. **1.** Lit. (mostly in pl.) : Pl. ; Hor. ; adducere, Liv. **2.** Transf. **a.** In pl. : a bridle, reins : loris ducere equos, Liv. ; lora dare, Verg. ; tendere, remittere, Ov. **b.** a whip, lash, scourge : Pl., Cic., Hor., etc. **c.** the leather bulla, worn by children of the poorer sort : Juv.

Lōtis, idis, and **Lōtos**, i, f. d. of Neptune, who was changed into a lotus-tree.

lōtium, i, n. [lavō], urine : Suet.

Lōtophagi, ōrum, m. pl. the Lotus-eaters ; a fabulous African people on the Lesser Syrtis.

lōtos and **lōtus**, i, f. [λωτός], the name of several trees and plants : Verg., Plin. Transf. **a.** the fruit of the edible lotus : Prop., Ov. **b.** a flute made of lotus-wood : Ov.

lōtus, i, v. lōtos.

lōtus, a, um, Part. lavō.

Lua, ae, f. a goddess who expiated blood shed in battle.

lubēns, lubenter, v. libēns, etc.

lubentia, ae, f. [libēns], delight, pleasure : Pl.

lubīdō, v. libīdō.

lūbrīcō, āre [lūbricus], to make smooth or slippery, to lubricate : Juv.

lūbricus, a, um [cf. Gk. ὀλιβρός], slippery, smooth. **1.** Lit. : loculi, Pl. ; glacies non vestigium recipiens, Liv. ; fastigium, Liv. Neut. as Noun : equi lubrico paludum lapsantes, Tac. ; per lubrica surgens, Verg. **2.** Transf. **a.** slippery, slimy, gliding in movement, easily moving : natura lubricos oculos fecit, Cic. ; anguis, Verg. ; amnis, Ov. **b.** gliding, fleeting : umbra, Ov. ; historia, Quint. ; annus, Ov. **c.** slippery, deceitful : patrias temptasti lubricus artis, Verg. **d.** slippery, uncertain, hazardous, critical : via vitae, Cic. ; cupiditas dominandi, Cic. ; vultus nimium lubricus aspici (i.e. dangerously attractive), Hor. ; principis aetas, Tac. Neut. as Noun with prep. : in lubrico versari, in a dangerous position, Cic. Later, even in Nom. : lubricum adulescentiae, the dangerous period of youth, Tac. ; lubricum aetatis, Plin. Ep.

Lūcāni, ōrum, m. pl. a people of S. Italy. **Lūcānus**, a, um ; **Lūcānia**, ae, f. their country, and **Lūcānicus**, a, um ; **Lūcānica**, ae, f. [Lūcānia], a kind of meat-sausage invented by the Lucanians : Cic. Ep., Mart. ; **Lūca bōs**, Lucanian cow for elephant (because the Romans first saw this animal in Lucania, in the army of Pyrrhus) : Enn., Luor.

Lūcānus, i, m. : M. Annaeus Lucanus, author of the poem entitled Pharsalia, put to death by Nero, A.D. 65.

lūcar, āris, n. [lūcus], a forest-tax for the payment of actors : Tac.

Lucceïus, i, m. : L. Lucceius, a friend of Cicero and Pompeius, author of a work on the Italian and Civil wars.

lucellum, i, n. [dim. lucrum], small or paltry gain, slight profit : Cic., Hor.

lūceō, lūcēre, lūxi [cf. Gk. λεῦκός, λευσσω], to be light, to shine. **1.** Lit. : (stella) luce lucebat alienā, Cic. ; globus lunae, Verg. ; igne rogus, Ov. ; via longo ordine flammarum, Verg. With Intern. Acc. : alicui lucere facem or cereum, to give one the light of a torch : Pl. Impers. : lucet, it is light, it is day : nondum lucebat, Cic. ; Pl. **2.** Transf. **a.** Of personal beauty : bombyce puella, Prop. **b.** virtus in tenebris, Cic. ; imperi nostri splendor, Cic. ; oratio, Quint. ; res ipsa tot tam claris argumentis, Cic. [Sp. lucir ; Fr. luire.]

Lūcerēs (Lūc-, Prop.), um, m. pl. one of the three tribes into which Romulus (or one of his successors) divided the Roman patricians : Cic., Liv., Ov., etc.

lucerna, ae, f. [cf. lūceō], a lamp, oil-lamp. **1.** Lit. : Cic., Hor., etc. ; exstinguere, Pl. ; accendere, Phaedr. **2.** Transf. ' midnight-oil ' : haec ego non credam Venusinā digna lucernā ? (i.e. of Horace), Juv.

lūcēscō and **lūciscō**, lūcēscere or lūciscere, lūxi [lūceō], to begin to shine : sol, Verg. ; Nonae, Ov. Mostly Impers. : lucescit or luciscit, day is breaking, it is dawn : Pl., Caes., etc.

lūci, old Locat. of lūx : Pl., Cic.

lūcidē, adv. clearly, distinctly : verbum definire, Cic. Comp. : Sen. Ep. Sup. : Quint.

lūcidus, a, um [lūx], containing light, clear, bright, shining. **1.** Lit. : aër, Lucr. ; sidera, Hor. ; gemma, Ov. Comp. : Ov. **2.** Transf. clear, lucid : ordo, Hor. ; narratio, ratio, auctor, etc., Quint. Comp. : Quint.

lūcifer, era, erum [lūx ferō], light-bringing. Lit. : pars Lunae, Lucr. ; equi, Ov. As Noun, **Lūcifer**, erī, m. **a.** the morning star, the planet Venus : Cic., Ov., etc. **b.** s. of Aurora and Cephalus : Ov. **c.** Transf. a day : paucis Luciferis, Prop. ; tres, Ov.

lūcifugus, a, um [lūx fugiō], light-shunning. **1.** Lit. : blattae, Verg. **2.** Transf. : homines, Cic.

Lūcilius, a, the name of a Roman gens. Esp. C. Lucilius, a native of the Campanian Suessa ; the father of Roman satire (ob. B.C. 103) : **Lūciliānus**, a, um.

Lūcīna, ae, f. [lūx], the goddess of childbirth. **1.** Lit. : Pl., Verg., etc. **2.** Transf. childbirth : Verg., Ov.

lūciscō, v. lūcēscō.

lucrātīvus, a, um [lucror], attended with gain, profitable, lucrative : Quint.

Lucrētius, a, the name of a Roman gens. Esp. **I.** Sp. Lucretius, f. of Lucretia, consul B.C. 508. **II.** Lucretia, d. of Sp. Lucretius, and w. of Collatinus, who, being dishonoured by Sex. Tarquinius, killed herself. **III.** T. Lucretius Carus, author of the poem De Rerum Naturā (ob. B.C. 55).

lucri-faciō, v. lucrum.

lucrificābilis, e, adj. and **lucrificus**, a, um [lucrum faciō], profitable : Pl.

lucri-fiō, v. lucrum.

lucrifuga, ae, m. [lucrum fugiō], a profit-shunner : Pl.

Lucrīnus, i, m. (alone, or with lacus), a small

lake on the coast of Campania, in the neighbourhood of Baiae, famous for its oysters: now *Lucrino;* **Lucrīnus,** a, um, and **Lucrinēnsis,** e.

lucrĭpeta, ae, *m.* [lucrum petō], *a profit-seeker :* Pl.

lucror, ārī [lucrum], *to gain, win.* **1.** Lit.: Tac. With Acc.: Cic., Hor. **2.** Transf.: indicia veteris infamiae, Cic.; domitā nomen ab Africā lucratus, Hor.

lucrōsus, a, um [lucrum], *profitable :* voluptas, Ov.

lucrum, ī, *n.* [*cf.* Gk. ἀπολαύω], *gain, profit.* **1.** Lit.: facere, Pl.; ex vectigalibus lucra facere, Cic.; ponere *or* deputare in lucro, Ter., in lucris, Cic., *to count as gain ;* lucro appone (lit. *enter to profits*), Hor.; lucro (Dat.) *or* in lucro est, *it is profitable ;* lucro esse alicui, Pl.; lucri facere, fieri, *to gain, be gained,* Pl., Cic.; *also to get the credit of :* Nep.; (alicui) de lucro vivere, *to live at the mercy of another,* Cic., Liv. **2.** Transf. **a.** *wealth, riches :* Pl.; omne lucrum tenebris alta premebat humus, Ov. **b.** *greed, avarice :* lucro aversa, Hor.; concidit domus ob lucrum, Hor. [Sp. *logro*].

luctāmen, inis, *n.* [luctor], *a wrestling ;* hence, *a struggling, effort :* remo ut luctamen abesset, Verg.

luctāns, antis. **I.** *Part.* luctor. **II.** Adj.: *reluctant :* luctantia oscula carpere, Ov.

luctātiō, ōnis, *f.* [luctor], *a wrestling.* **1.** Lit.: Cic. **2.** Transf. *a struggle, contest,* taetra ibi luctatio erat, Liv.; cum Academicis, Cic.

luctātor, ōris, *m.* [luctor], *a wrestler.* **1.** Lit.: Ov., Sen. Ep., etc. **2.** Transf.: (vinum) pedes captat primum, luctator dolosus est, Pl.

lūctĭfĭcābĭlis, e, *adj.* [lūctus faciō], *sorrowful, afflicted :* Pac.

lūctĭfĭcus, a, um [lūctus faciō], *causing sorrow or lamentation, woeful :* Allecto, Verg.

lūcti-sonus, a, um [lūctus sonō], *sad-sounding :* mugitus, Ov.

luctor, ārī, and **luctō,** āre (Pl., Ter.) [*cf.* λυγίζω], *to wrestle.* **1.** Lit.: Pl., Cic., Verg., etc. **2.** Transf. **a.** Of other physical struggles : in pestilenti atque arido solo, Liv.; inter se adversis cornibus haedi, Verg.; luctandum in turbā, Hor. With *Inf. :* Verg., Ov. Of things : in lento marmore (*sea*) tonsae, Verg.; luctantem Icariis fluctibus Africum, Hor. **b.** Of mental effort or of contention : cum aliquo, Cic. With *Inf. :* Ov. [It. *luttare,* Sp. *luchar,* Fr. *lutter.*]

lūctuōsius, *comp. adv. more lamentable :* perire, Liv.

lūctuōsus, a, um [lūctus]. **I.** *causing sorrow, sorrowful :* o diem rei publicae luctuosum, Cic.; exitium, Cic. *Comp.* and *Sup. :* Cic. **II.** *feeling sorrow, sorrowful :* Hesperia, Hor.

lūctus, ūs, *m.* [lūgeō], *sorrow, mourning, lamentation,* esp. over the loss of relatives. **1.** Lit.: Caes., Cic., etc. In *pl. :* Cic., Ov., etc. **2.** Transf. **a.** *mourning,* i.e. *mourning-dress or a period of mourning :* erat in luctu senatus, Cic.; senatūs consulto diebus XXX luctus est finitus, Liv.

lūcubrātiō, ōnis, *f.* [lūcubrō], *a working by lamp-light, night-work* or *study.* **1.** Lit.: Cato ; anicularum (i.e. evening-gossip), Cic. In *pl. :* Cic. **2.** Transf. Of the work thus done : perire lucubrationem meam nolui, Cic. Ep.

lūcubrātōrius, a, um [lūcubrō], *for night-studies :* lecticula, Suet.

lūcubrō, āre [lūcubrum, fr. root of lūceō], *to work by lamp-light, work at night :* Liv. In *Perf. Part.* composed *at night :* Cic.; also *spent in night-work :* nox, Mart. [Sp. *lobrecar.*]

lūculentē, *adv. brightly ;* hence, *brilliantly, splendidly, right smartly :* diem habere, Pl.; vendere, Pl.; aliquem calefacere (i.e. in chastising), Cic. Ep.; scribere, Cic.

lūculenter, *adv. brilliantly, smartly :* Cic.

lūculentus, a, um [lūx], *full of light, bright, brilliant.* **1.** Lit.: vestibulum, Pl.; caminus, Cic. Ep. **2.** Transf. *brilliant, splendid, smart, handsome,* etc.: femina, dies, divitiae, hereditas, facinus, Pl.; forma, Ter.; verba, scriptor, auctores, Cic. Ep.; patrimonium, Cic.; homo, Pl., Cic.

Lūcullus, ī, *m. a cognomen in the gens Licinia.* Esp. L. Licinius Lucullus *the conqueror of Mithridates, famous for his great wealth and luxury ;* **Lūcullēus, Lūculliānus,** a, um.

lūculus, ī, *m.* [*dim.* lūcus], *a small grove :* Suet.

Lucumō (Lucomō, and sync. **Lucmō),** ōnis, *m.* [an Etrusc. word, *inspired*], *an appellation of Etruscan princes and priests :* also as a Proper Name : Liv.

lūcus, ī, *m.* [lūceō ; hence, *a clearing*], *a sacred wood or grove.* **1.** Lit.: Pl., Cic., Verg., etc. **2.** Transf. in gen. *a wood :* aut quos Oceano propior gerit India lucos, Verg. Also *wood :* Pl.

lūdia, ae, *f.* [lūdius]. **I.** *an actress :* Mart. **II.** *a woman-gladiator :* Juv.

lūdibrium, ī, *n.* [lūdō]. **I.** *a mockery, derision :* ridicula ludibriaque, Lucr.; legati per ludibrium auditi dimissique, Liv. With *Obj.* Gen.: ludibrio fratris Remum novos transiluisse muros, Liv. With *Obj.* Gen. of a thing : oculorum, Liv., Curt.; corporum, Curt. **II.** *a subject of mockery, derision, or sport :* habere aliquem ludibrio, Pl., Lucr., Sall., Liv., etc.; esse ludibrio alicui, Cic., Sall., Liv., Tac., etc. **III.** **a.** Of a person, *a butt for ridicule :* is ludibrium verius quam comes, Liv. **b.** Of things : *the sport, plaything :* naves sunt ludibria ventis, Verg. Of abstracts : haec ludibria fortunae quae nos appellamus bona, Cic.; hoc quoque ludibrium casūs ediderit fortuna, Liv.

lūdibundus, a, um [lūdō], *playful, sportive, frolicsome.* **1.** Lit.: Pl.; milites ludibundi Beneventum rediere, Liv. **2.** Transf. *playing,* i.e. *at one's ease, free from danger :* Liv.

lūdicer (the Nom. *sing. m.* is not used), cra, crum [lūdus], *of sport, done in sport, sportive.* **A.** In gen. : exercitatio, Cic.; simulacrum pugnae, Liv. **B.** Esp. *of stage-plays or acting :* ars, Liv.; Tac.; ludicras partis sustinere, Suet. As Noun, **lūdicrum,** ī, *n.* **a.** *a show, public games :* Olympiorum sollemne ludicrum, Liv.; Suet., etc,

b. *a sport, plaything :* Cat. **c.** *a trifle :* versūs et cetera ludicra pono, Hor.

lūdificābilis, e, *adj.* [lūdificō], *used as means of ridiculing :* ludi, Pl.

lūdificātiō, ōnis, *f.* [lūdificō]. **I.** *a ridiculing, jeering :* With *Obj.* Gen.: veri, Liv. **II.** *a fooling, baffling :* exactā prope aestate per ludificationem hostia, Liv.

lūdificātor, ōris, *m.* [lūdificō], *one who makes game, a mocker :* Pl.

lūdificātui, *Predic.* Dat. *for (as) a subject of derision :* habere aliquem ludificatui, Pl.

lūdificō, āre (Pl., Lucr., Cic.) and **lūdificor,** ārī (Pl., Ter., Cic., Liv., Tac., etc.) [lūdus faciō], *to make sport of, to fool, delude.* **1.** Lit.: Cic. With Acc. of person : Pl., Liv., etc. With Acc. of thing : aliena mala, Plin. Ep.; in *Pass.* : ut puerorum aetas ludificetur, Lucr. With *Intern.* Acc. : nugas, Pl. **2.** Transf. *to thwart, baffle by tricks* or *contrivances :* locationem, Liv.; ea quae hostes agerent, Liv.; hostis Romanum, Tac.

lūdiō, ōnis, *m.* (Liv.), **lūdius,** ī, *m.* (Pl., Cic., Ov., etc.), *a stage-player, actor.*

lūdō, lūdere, lūsī, lūsum, *to play.* **1.** Lit. **a.** *to play at some game, to gamble.* With Abl. of the game : trocho, Hor. With Acc. of the game : par impar, Hor.; proelia latronum, Ov.; aleam, Troiam, Suet.; so in *Pass.* : alea luditur, Ov., Juv. With Abl. of the stakes : Suet. *Absol.* : Suet. **b.** *to play, sport, frolic, gambol :* inter nos, Pl.; sicco ludunt fuliçae, Verg.; ludunt iubae per colla, Verg.; exempla ludendi, Cic.; in numerum ludere (i.e. to dance), Verg.; cumba in lacu, Ov. **2.** Transf. **a.** *to sport* or *play with, to practise as a pastime, amuse oneself with :* ad ludendum arma sumere, Cic.; aliquid calamo, Verg.; carmina pastorum, Verg.; versibus, Verg. **b.** *to play amorously, dally :* Pl., Ov., Suet., etc. **c.** *to play a part, mimic, counterfeit :* civem bonum, Cael. ap. Cic. Ep.; opus, Hor. **d.** *to spend in play or amusement, to sport away :* otium, Mart. Hence, ludere operam (i.e. to throw away one's labour), Pl. **e.** *to make sport or game of.* **i.** *to ridicule, rally, banter :* Domitius in senatu lusit Appium conlegam, Cic. Ep.; in *Pass.* : Cic.; pericula, Mart. **ii.** *to delude, deceive :* ludere aliquem dolis, Ter.; me insania, Hor.; pedes glacies, Liv.

lūdus, ī, *m.* [lūdō], *play.* **1.** Lit. **a.** In gen. : *play, sport, game, diversion, pastime :* novum sibi aliquem excogitant in otio ludum, Cic.; Hor.; militaria, Liv. **b.** In *pl.* : *public games, plays, shows :* ludis Olympiae, Cic.; votivi, Cic.; magni, Liv.; ludi Consualia, Liv.; ludos facere, Cic., Liv.; apparare, Cic.; ludos in gramine Campi aspicere, Ov. Occ. for the stage-performances at the games : si examen apum ludis in scaenam venisset, Cic.; edidit etiam ludos regionatim urbe totā, Suet.; ineunt proscaenia ludi, Verg. **c.** *a place for exercise or training.* **i.** *a school for elementary instruction :* in ludum ire, Pl.; ludus litterarum, Liv.; Cic. **ii.** *a school for gladiators :* Caes., Hor. **2.** Transf. **a.** Of something easy or trifling :

more sport, child's play : illā perāusere ludus esset, Cic.; Graecis ius iurandum iocus est, testimonium ludus, Cic.; Liv. **b.** *amorous play, dalliance :* aetatis, Liv. In *pl.* : Cat. **c.** *sport, jest, joke, fun :* per ludum, *in sport,* Cic.; amoto ludo, Hor.; vertere seria ludo, Hor. Phr. : ludos facere aliquem *or* alicui, *to make game of, banter,* Pl.; si non te ludos pessumos dimisero (i.e. in scorn), Pl.; ludos praebere, *to afford fun,* Ter.; ludos alicui reddere, *to play a game on someone,* Ter.; nunc et operam ludos facit et retia (i.e. he labours in vain, loses his labour), Pl.; dare ludum alicui, *to give free play to someone* (i.e. to humour, indulge), Pl.; hence, amori dare ludum, Hor.

luella, ae, *f.* [luō], *an expiation, a punishment :* Lucr.

luēs, is, *f.* [cf. Gk. λύω, solvō], *a spreading or contagious disease, a plague, pestilence.* **1.** Lit.: Verg., Ov. **2.** Transf. **a.** *any spreading evil, general calamity or misfortune :* of war, Tac.; of an earthquake, Tac. **b.** *any corrupting or blighting influence :* Cic.

lūgeō, lūgēre, lūxī [cf. Gk. λυγρός, λευγαλέος], *to mourn.* **1.** Lit. **a.** Intrans. : Cic.; pro me, Cic. *Impers. Pass.* : Cat. **b.** Trans. : mortem Treboni, Cic.; orbum cubile, Cat. With Acc. and *Inf.* : Cic. In *Pass.* : lugebere nobis, Ov. **2.** Transf. : *to wear mourning.* **a.** Intrans. : Liv., Sen. Ep., Suet. **b.** Trans. : matronae annum, ut parentem, eum luxerunt, Liv.

lūgubris, e, *adj.* [lūgeō]. **I.** *of mourning, mourning :* vestis, Ter.; lamentatio, Cic.; cantus, Hor.; domus, Liv.; cultus, Tac. As Noun, **lūgubria,** ium, *n. pl. mourning-garments :* induere, Ov. *Neut. Intern.* Acc. : cometae sanguinei lugubre rubent, Verg. **II.** **a.** *fraught with sorrow, grievous, disastrous :* bellum, Hor., Liv.; Hispanis lugubre documentum Sagunti ruinae erunt, Liv. **b.** *doleful, plaintive :* vox, Lucr.; verba, Ov.

lumbifragium, ī, *n.* [lumbus frangō], *a breaking of the loins :* Pl.

lumbricus, ī, *m.* **I.** *an intestinal worm, maw-worm, stomach-worm :* Cato, Plin. **II.** *an earth-worm :* Pl. Transf. as term of contempt : Pl.

lumbus, ī, *m. the loin.* **1.** Lit. : Pl., Hor., Quint., etc. **2.** Transf. *the genital organs :* Pers., Juv. [It. *lombo* / Sp. *lomo.*]

lūmen, inis, *n.* [cf. lūceō], *light.* **1.** Lit.: Enn.; solis, Cic.; lumina solis, Lucr.; Verg.; solare, Ov. **2.** Transf. **A.** Of concrete things. **a.** *a light, a lamp, torch, etc.* : Cic. Liv., etc. **b.** *glow, gleam, brightness, sheen :* lumen iuventae purpureum, Verg.; ferri, Stat. **c.** *daylight, day :* se tollunt in luminis oras, Verg.; Enn.; Lucr.; lumine quarto, Verg.; Enn. **d.** *the light of life, life :* ipse Epicurus obit decurso lumine vitae, Lucr.; lumen linquere, Pl., Verg.; cassum lumine, Verg. **e.** *the light of the eye, the eye :* esp. in *pl.* (mostly poet.) : luminibus amissis, Cic.; adstantis lumine torvo Aetnaeos fratres, Verg.; lumina defixa tenere, Ov. **f.** *an opening for the light, a light :* Plin. Esp. *a window :* luminibus alicuius obstruere, Cic. Transf.:

Cic. **g.** the *light* in pictures (opp. shade): Plin. Ep. **B.** Abstract (but freq. of persons). **a.** *a shining light, glory, ornament :* civitatis, Cic. ; tot lumina ducum, Verg. ; orationis, Quint. : certa dicendi lumina, Cic. **b.** *a light* (i.e. a guide, helper) : hunc (puerum) lumen rebus nostris dubiis futurum, Liv. **c.** *light, clearness :* ordo est maxime, qui memoriae lumen adfert, Cic. [It. *lume ;* Sp. *lombre.*]

lūmĭnārĭa, ium, *n. pl.* [lūmen], *window-shutters, windows :* Cato, Cic. Ep.

lūmĭnōsus, a, um [lūmen], *full of light, luminous.* Transf. *bright, conspicuous :* partes orationis, Cic.

lūna, ae, *f.* [*cf.* lūceō], *the moon.* **1.** Lit. : plena, Caes. ; dimidiata, Cato ; extrema et prima, Varr. ; cum luna laboret, Cic. ; lunae defectus, Liv. ; lunae defectio, Quint.; aurea, Ov. **2.** Transf. **a.** *a month :* Ov. **b.** *a night :* roscida, Verg. ; Prop. **c.** *the figure of a crescent,* which the senators wore on their shoes : Juv.

lūnārĭs, e, *adj.* [lūna], *of the moon, lunar :* cursus, Cic. ; equi, Ov. ; cornua, Ov.

lūnātus, a, um [lūna], *shaped like the crescent moon ; crescent-shaped :* peltae, Verg. ; pellis (*v.* luna 2. c.), Mart.

lūnō, āre [formed from lūnātus], *to bend to the shape of a crescent :* acies geminos in arcūs, Prop. ; arcum, Ov.

lūnŭla, ae, *f.* [*dim.* lūna], *a little crescent,* as an ornament worn by women : Pl.

luō, luere, luī [*cf.* λύω, solvō], *to loose, get rid of :* hence, **a.** *to pay* a debt or penalty : aes alienum, Curt. ; luere poenas *or* poenam ; mei peccati luere poenas, Cic. Ep. ; rei publicae poenas luere, Cic. ; poenam pro caede, Ov. **b.** *to atone for, expiate :* stuprum voluntariā morte, Cic. ; noxam pecuniā, Liv. ; qui capite luerent, Liv. ; sanguine periuria, Verg. **c.** *to avert by expiation or punishment :* pericula publica, Liv.

lupa, ae, *f.* [lupus], *a she-wolf.* **1.** Lit. : Liv., Ov., etc. **2.** Transf. *a prostitute :* Pl., Cic., Liv., etc.

lŭpānar, āris, *n.* [lupa], *a disorderly house, a brothel :* Pl., Quint., Juv. As a term of abuse : Cat.

lŭpātus, a, um [lupus], *fitted with wolf's teeth,* i.e. iron jags like a wolf's teeth : lupatis frenis, Hor. As Noun, **lŭpāti,** ōrum, *m.* and **lŭpāta,** ōrum, *n. pl.* (*sc.* freni *or* frena), *a curb armed with sharp teeth :* duris parere lupatis, Verg.

Lŭpercus, ī, *m.* **I.** a Roman pastoral deity, identified with Pan. Hence, **Lŭpercal,** ālis, *n.* a grotto on the Palatine hill, sacred to him ; **Lŭpercālĭs,** e, *adj.* ; **Lŭpercālĭa,** ium and iōrum, *n. pl. a festival in his honour,* celebrated in February. **II.** a priest of Lupercus : Cic., Verg., Ov.

lŭpillus, ī, *m.* [*dim.* lupinus], *a small lupin :* Pl.

lŭpinus, ī, *m.,* and **lŭpinum,** ī, *n. a lupin.* **1.** Lit. : Cato, Verg. **2.** Transf. *stage-money, counters :* Hor.

lŭpinus, a, um [lupus], *of or belonging to a wolf, wolf's :* Pl.

lŭpus, ī, *m.* [*cf.* Gk. λύκος], *a wolf.* **1.** Lit. : Enn., Verg., Liv., etc. ; Martialis, *sacred to Mars,* Hor. ; vox quoque Moerim iam fugit ipsa : lupi Moerim videre priores (from the belief that, if a wolf saw a man before the latter saw the wolf, the man became dumb), Verg. Prov. **i.** lupus in fabulā *or* sermone (*cf.* "*talk of the devil*"), Pl., Ter., Cic. Ep. **ii.** lupum auribus tenere (*cf.* "*to catch a Tartar*"), Ter. **iii.** hac urget lupus, hac canis angit (*cf.* "*to be between two fires*"), Hor. **iv.** ovem lupo committere (*cf.* "*to set the fox to keep the geese*"), Ter. **v.** lupo agnum eripere (*cf.* "*to get the meat out of a dog's mouth*"), Pl. **vi.** ovis ultro fugiat lupus (of something unlikely), Verg. **vii.** tantum Boreae curamus frigora, quantum (ovium) numerum lupus (i.e. not at all), Verg. **2.** Transf. **a.** *a voracious fish, pike :* Hor., Mart. **b.** *a bit armed with points like wolves' teeth* (= frena lupata) : et placido duros (equus) accipit ore lupos, Ov. **c.** *a grapnel :* Liv. [Sp. *lobo ;* Fr. *loup.*]

lurco, ōnis, *m. a glutton :* Pl.

lūreō, ēre, *to be yellow* (perh. in Pl., Hor., Ov.).

lūrĭdus, a, um [lūreō], *pale yellow, sallow, wan, ghastly, lurid.* **1.** Lit. : maculae, Pl. ; Orcus, Hor. ; pallor, Ov. ; sol, Plin. Ep. **2.** Transf. *making pale or ghastly :* aconita, horror, Ov. [It. *lordo ;* Sp. *lerdo ;* Fr. *lourd.*]

lūror, ōris, *m. a yellowish colour, sallowness, paleness :* Lucr.

lūscĭnĭa, ae, *f.* (*masc.* **lūscĭnĭus,** ī, Sen. Ep., Phaedr.) [lūgeō canō], *the nightingale :* Hor.

lūscĭnĭŏla, ae, *f.* [*dim.* lūscinia], *the (little) nightingale :* Varr. ; *a pretty nightingale :* Pl. [It. *rossignuolo ;* Sp. *ruiseñor ;* Fr. *rossignol.*].

lūscĭnĭus, ī, *m. v.* lūscinia.

luscĭnus, a, um [luscus], *one-eyed :* Plin.

luscĭōsus and **luscĭtĭōsus,** a, um [luscus], *dim-sighted :* Pl., Varr.

luscus, a, um [perh. fr. root of lūceō], *one-eyed :* Pl., Cic., Juv. [Fr. *louche.*]

lūsĭo, ōnis, *f.* [lūdō], *play :* Cic. Ep. ; in *pl. games :* Cic.

Lūsĭtānĭa, ae, *f.* the W. part of Hispania, including the mod. Portugal ; **Lūsĭtāni,** ōrum, *m. pl.* the Lusitanians.

lūsĭtō, āre [*freq.* lūdō], *to play often :* Pl.

lūsor, ōris, *m.* [lūdō], *a player, gambler.* **1.** Lit. : Ov., Sen. **2.** Transf. **a.** *a playful writer :* tenerorum amorum, Ov. **b.** *a banterer, mocker :* Pl.

lūsōrĭus, a, um [lūsor]. **I.** *used by a player :* pila, Plin. **II.** *used for pleasure :* navis, Sen.

lūstrālĭs, e, *adj.* [lūstrum]. **I.** *of purification, lustral :* exta, Verg. ; aqua, Ov. ; sacrificium, Liv. **II.** *quinquennial* (*v.* lūstrum, 2.) : certamen, Tac.

lūstrātĭo, ōnis, *f.* [lūstrō], *a purification by sacrifice, a lustration.* **1.** Lit. : Liv. In *pl. :* Liv. **2.** Transf. (since the priest carried the lustral sacrifices round the person or thing to be purified) : *a going or wandering about :* municipiorum, Cic. In *pl.*

lūstrĭcus, a, um [lūstrum]. *of purification :* dies (the eighth or ninth day after a child's birth), Suet.

(1) lŭstrō, āre [lŭstrum], *to purify by means of a propitiatory offering.* **1.** Lit.: agrum, Cato; coloniam, Cic.; viros, Verg.; exercitum suovetaurilibus, Liv.; Ov. In *Mid.*: lustramur Iovi, *we purify ourselves in honour of,* Verg. **2.** Transf. (*v.* lustratio, 2): *to go round.* **a.** In gen. *to traverse*: Aegyptum, Cic.; pede barbaro lustrata Rhodope, Hor.; (sol lunaque) cursūs, Lucr.; navibus aequor, Verg.; montibus umbrae lustrabunt convexa, Verg. **b.** *to review, survey, observe, examine.* **i.** With the eyes: exercitum, Cic. Ep., Hirt.; animas ad lumen ituras, Verg. With *Indir. Quest.*: Verg. **ii.** With the mind: omnia ratione animoque, Cic.

(2) lŭstrō, āre [fr. lūceo, *cf.* inlūstris], *to light, illumine*: sol terras lumine lustrans, Lucr.; Cic. poet.; lampade terras Aurora, Verg.

lustror, ārī [lustrum], *to frequent brothels*: Pl., Lucil.

lustrum, ī, n. [lutum]. **1.** Lit. **a.** *a bog, morass*: Varr. **b.** In *pl.*: *wilds, forestland*: Verg.; hence, *haunts, lairs* (of wild animals): Verg. **2.** Transf. (in *pl.*) *brothels*: Pl., Cic. Hence, *debauchery, sensuality*: Pl., Cic., Hor., etc.

lŭstrum, ī, n. [lavō, luō], *a purificatory sacrifice, lustration.* **1.** Lit. **a.** Performed (exc. for some religious reason) by the censors every fifth year, after completing the census; in it a pig (or ram), a sheep, and a bull were offered (suovetaurilia): Liv.; condere lustrum, *to complete such a lustration,* Cic.; Liv. **b.** Of other purificatory sacrifices: Liv. **2.** Transf. **a.** *a period of five years, a lustrum*: Cic., Liv.; cuius octavum trepidavit aetas claudere lustrum, Hor.; mensibus egerunt lustra minora decem, Ov. **b.** In less exact sense, of *periods of years.* Of *four years* (of the Julian calendar): Ov.; ingens lustrum, *a hundred years,* at the end of which the ludi saeculares were celebrated, Mart. **c.** *the Capitoline games,* recurring every fifth year: Suet.

lūsus, a, um, *Part.* lūdō.

lūsus, ūs, *m.* [lūdō], *a playing, play, sport, amusement.* **1.** Lit.: per lusum atque lasciviam, Liv.; fraterno lusu, Liv.; calculorum, Plin. Ep.; aleae, Suet.; regnum lusu sortiri, Tac. Of hunting: Liv. In *pl.*: games: Ov., Liv. **2.** Transf. **a.** *anything done by way of sport or amusement; a joking*: facere de se, Quint. **b.** *dalliance*: apti lusibus anni, Ov.

lūteolus, a, um [*dim.* lūteus], *yellow* (of small things): caltha, Verg.

lūteus, a, um [lūtum], *of the colour of lūtum.* **1.** Lit. *golden-yellow, saffron-yellow, orange-yellow*: soccus (of a bride), Cat.; palla, Tib.; Aurora in roseis fulgebat lutea bigis, Verg.; Ov. **2.** Transf.: *sallow*: pallor, Hor.

luteus, a, um [lutum], *of mud or clay.* **1.** Lit.: Rheni caput, Hor.; opus, Ov. **2.** Transf. *grimy, dirty.* **a.** Physically: Volcanus, Juv. **b.** Morally: meretrix, Pl.; homo, negotium, Cic.

lutitō, āre [*freq.* lutō], *to bespatter with mud.* Transf.: Pl.

lutō, āre [lutum], *to bedaub with mud or clay*: granaria, Cato. Sarcastic: Mart.

lutulentus, a, um [lutum], *muddy, filthy.* **1.** Lit.: sus, Hor.; amnis, Ov. **2.** Transf. **a.** Of style: (Lucilius) cum flueret lutulentus, Hor. **b.** Of character: Pl., Cic.

lutum, ī, n. [*cf.* Gk. λῦμα, *offscourings*, luō], *mud, mire.* **1.** Lit.: Ter.; volutari in luto, Cic.; cratis luto contegere, Caes. Prov.: in luto esse *or* haerere: nunc homo in medio luto est; nomen nescit, Pl. As a term of abuse: Pl., Cic., Cat. **2.** Transf. *loam, clay, potter's earth*: pocula de facili luto componere, Tib.; homines compositi luto, Juv. [It. *loto*; Sp. *lodo*.]

lūtum, ī, n. [*cf.* lūreō], *a plant used in dyeing yellow, yellow-weed.* **1.** Lit.: Verg. **2.** Transf. *yellow*: Verg., Tib.

lūx, lūcis, *f.* (*m.*, Pl.) [*cf.* lūceō], *light.* **1.** Lit. **a.** In gen.: solis et lychnorum, Cic.; Verg. **b.** *light of day, daylight*: diurna, Lucr.; tum primum lucem aspicere visi sunt, Liv.; cum primo luci (ABL.), Pl., Ter.; ante lucem, Cic.; primā luce adesse, Caes. Hence, ABL. **lūce** (Cic., Verg., Liv.) and LOCAT. **lūci** (Pl., Cic.) *by daylight, in the daytime*: luci claro, Pl. **c.** *the reflected light, brightness* of polished bodies: luce coruscus aenā, Verg. Of the eye (*cf.* lumen): Ov. **2.** Transf. **a.** *a day*: centesima lux est ab interitu P. Clodi, Cic. Hence, lux aestiva, *summer,* Verg.; lux brumalis, *winter,* Ov. **b.** *the light of day,* i.e. *life*: eos luce privavit, Cic.; Ter.; corpora luce carentum, Verg. **c.** *the light of day,* i.e. *the public view, the public, the world*: nec vero ille in luce modo atque in oculis civium magnus, Cic.; familiam obscuram e tenebris in lucem vocare, Cic. **d.** *light, light of hope, encouragement*: civibus lucem ingeni et consili porrigere, Cic.; lucem adferre rei publicae, Cic.; lux adfulsit civitati, Liv.; o lux Dardaniae, Verg. **e.** *light, glory*: hanc urbem, lucem orbis terrarum, Cic. **f.** *light, illustration, elucidation*: historia lux veritatis, Cic.; sententiae auctoris lucem desiderant, Cic.

luxō, āre [luxus, *adj.*], *to put out of joint, to dislocate*: Cato, Plin., Sen. Ep.

luxor, ārī [luxus, 1], *to live riotously*: Pl.

luxuria, ae (Pl., Ter., Caes., Cic.) and **luxuriēs**, ēī (Cic., Verg.), *f.* [luxus], *rankness, exuberance, excess.* **1.** Lit. of growth: segetum, Verg.; Cic. **2.** Transf. *extravagance, excess.* **a.** Of mode of life: Pl., Cic., etc.; luxuriā diffluere, Ter., Cic. **b.** Of style: in oratione inest luxuries quae stilo depascenda est, Cic.

luxuriō, āre and **luxurior**, ārī (Quint.) [luxuria], *to be rank, luxuriant.* **1.** Lit. Of growth of vegetation: seges in pingui humo, Ov.; ager adsiduā aquā, Ov. **2.** Transf. **a.** Of the body: *to fill out, swell*: luxuriatque toris animosum pectus, Verg.; membra, Ov. **b.** *to show exuberance* of spirits, *to sport, frisk*: equus, Verg.; pecus, Ov. **c.** Of conduct: *to run to excess, run riot*: otio animi, Liv.; Capua felicitate, Liv. So also, ne haec laetitia luxuriet, Liv. **d.** Of style: in *Neut. pl.* of *Pres. Part.* used as Noun: luxuriantia compescet, Hor.; Quint.

luxuriōsē, *adv.* **1.** Of joy: *excessively*:

Cato. **II.** Of mode of living : *voluptuously* : Cic. *Comp.* : Nep.

luxuriōsus, a, um [luxuria], *rank, luxuriant, exuberant.* **1.** Lit. Of growth : frumenta, Cic. ; seges, Ov. **2.** Transf. **a.** Of feelings : laetitia nimis luxuriosa, Liv. **b.** Of mode of living : *extravagant, voluptuous* : homo, Cic. ; luxurioso otio esse, Sall. *Comp.* : Cic. As Noun : reprehendere luxuriosos, Cic.

(1) luxus, ūs, *m. excess, extravagance.* **a.** In living : luxu perditus, Ter. ; Sall. ; Verg. ; in vino ac luxu, Cic. ; per luxum aetatem agere, Sall. ; (Petronius) crudito luxu, Tac. **b.** In appearance : at domus interior regali splendida luxu instruitur, Verg. [It. *lusso* ; Sp. *lujo* ; Fr. *luxe*.]

(2) luxus, ūs, *m. a dislocation* : Cato.

luxus, a, um [*cf.* λοξός, luctor], *dislocated* : Cato.

Lyaeus, ī, *m. a surname of Bacchus* ; **Lyaeus,** a, um. Transf. *wine* : Hor., Ov.

Lycaeus, ī, *m. a mountain in Arcadia, where Jupiter and Pan were worshipped* ; **Lycaeus,** a, um, *Lycean* ; esp. as epithet of Pan.

Lycambēs, ae, *m. a Parian who promised his daughter to the poet Archilochus, and afterwards refused her ; for which he was pursued by the poet with such bitter lampoons that both he and his daughter hanged themselves* ; **Lycambēus,** a, um.

Lycāōn, onis, *m.* **I.** *king of Arcadia, f. of Callisto, whom Jupiter turned into a wolf* ; **Lycāonius,** a, um ; **Lycāonis,** idis, *f. his daughter Callisto.* **II.** *a grandson of the preceding, also called Arcas.*

Lycēum and **Lycīum,** ī, *n. a gymnasium at Athens, outside of the city, where Aristotle taught.*

Lycia, ae, *f. a mountainous country in S.W. Asia Minor* ; **Lycius,** a, um, *Lycian,* and **Lyciī,** ōrum, *m. the Lycians.*

Lycīdās, ae, *m.* **I.** *a centaur in Ov.* **II.** *a poetic pastoral name in* Verg.

lychnūchus, ī, *m.* [λυχνοῦχος], *a lamp-stand, candlestick* : Cic. Ep., Suet.

lychnus (lucinus, Enn. ; **lychinus,** perh. in Lucr.), ī, *m.* [λύχνος], *a light, a lamp* : Lucr., Cic., Verg.

Lycomēdēs, is, *m. a king of the isle of Scyros, with whom Achilles concealed himself disguised as a woman.*

Lyctus (-os), ī, *f. a city in Crete* ; **Lyctius,** a, um, *Lyctian or Cretan.*

Lycurgus, ī, *m.* **I.** *son of Dryas, king of the Edoni, who prohibited the worship of Bacchus, and was punished by him with madness and death.* **II.** *lawgiver of the Spartans* (date unknown). **III.** *an Athenian orator, the contemporary and friend of Demosthenes, noted for his inflexible integrity* ; **Lycurgēī,** ōrum, *m. pl. disciples of Lycurgus, i.e. severely upright.*

Lycus (-os), ī, *m. husband of Antiope, who divorced her and married Dirce.*

Lȳdē, ēs, *f.* **I.** *wife of the poet Antimachus of Claros.* **II.** *a female quack-doctor in* Juv.

Lȳdia, ae, *f. a country of Asia Minor, the capital of which was Sardis ; whence the Etruscans were said to have come* ; **Lȳdius,** a, um, *Lydian or Etruscan* : Lydius fluvius,

i.e. *the Tiber* (Verg.) ; **Lȳdus,** a, um ; **Lȳdī,** ōrum, *m. pl. the Lydians or the Etruscans.*

lympha, ae, *f. water ;* esp. *pure* or *spring water* : lymphae puteales, Lucr. ; fluvialis, Verg. Hence (thr. false conn. with Gk. νυμφή), *a water-nymph* : Hor.

lymphāticus, a, um [lympha ; perh. orig., *one attacked with hydrophobia*], *crazy, frantic* : pavor, Liv. ; metus, Sen. Ep. Comic. : nummi, *crazy to be spent,* Pl. As Noun, **lymphāticum,** ī, *n. craziness* : Pl.

lymphātus, a, um [lympha], *crazy, maddened* : furit lymphata per urbem, Verg. ; lymphati et attoniti, Liv. ; mentem lymphatam Mareotico, Hor. ; lymphatis caeco pavore animis, Tac. Hence, **lymphō,** āre, *to make mad* : Plin.

Lynceus (disyl.), Lynceī (or Lynceī, disyl.) (Acc. Lyncea, Ov.), *m.* **I.** *a Messenian, one of the Argonauts, famed for the keenness of his sight* ; **Lynceus,** a, um, *sharp-sighted* : Cic. Ep. **II.** *s. of Aegyptus and Hypermestra ; he was saved by his wife when his brothers were killed.*

Lyncus, ī, *m. a Scythian king, who was changed by Ceres into a lynx.*

lynx, lyncis, *m. f.* [λύγξ], *a lynx* : lynces Bacchi variae, Verg. ; Hor. ; Ov., etc.

lyra, ae, *f.* [λύρα], *a lute, lyre, a stringed instrument resembling the cithara.* **1.** Lit. : curva, Hor. ; Threicia, Ov. **2.** Transf. **a.** *lyric poetry, song* : imbellis lyra, Hor. ; Ov. **b.** *a constellation, the Lyre* of Orpheus : exoriente Lyrā, Ov.

lyricus, a, um [lyra], *of the lute* or *lyre, lyric* : lyrici soni, Ov. ; vates, Hor. As Noun. **a. lyrica,** ōrum, *n. pl. lyric poems* : Plin. Ep. **b. lyrici,** ōrum, *m. pl. lyric poets* : Quint.

lyristēs, ae, *m.* (Acc. -ēn) [λυριστής], *a lute-player, lyrist* : Plin. Ep.

Lyrnēsus (Lyrnēssus), ī, *f. a town in Troas, the birth-place of Briseis* ; **Lyrnēsius (Lyrnēssius),** a, um ; **Lyrnēsis (Lyrnēsis,** idis, *f. Briseis.*

Lysiās, ae, *m. a famous Athenian orator in the time of Socrates.*

Lȳsippus, ī, *m. a celebrated worker in brass and statuary of Sicyon, to whom alone Alexander the Great gave permission to cast a statue of him.*

Lysis, idis, *m. a Pythagorean of Tarentum, instructor of Epaminondas.*

M

M, m, the twelfth letter of the Latin alphabet. **I.** The Latin language, unlike the Greek, tolerated a final *m ;* but its sound was faint, and before an initial vowel, even in prose, was scarcely heard. Hence arose the rule of versification respecting the elision of final syllables terminating in *m.* To this also are owing the forms donec for donicum, veneo for venum eo, *etc.* The Latin termination *m* generally corresponds to the Greek final ν, in the inflexions both of nouns and verbs. **II.** *m* and *n* are interchanged in many instances in Latin for the sake of euphony : e.g. *eundem* for *eumdem ; quor-*

undam for *quorumdam* ; *imbellis* for *inbellis* ; *imprimis* for *in primis* ; *immanis* for *inmanis*, etc. *m* is substituted for *p* or *b* before a nasal suffix ; cf. *sop-or*, *som-nus* ; *scam-num*, *scabellum*. It is used to nasalise roots ending in *p* or *b*, as in *rumpo* (*rup*), *cumbo* (*cub*). **III.** The only change of *m* in the Romance languages is into *n* in a few words: e.g. Lat. *mespilum*, It. *nespolo*, Sp. *nespera*, Fr. *nèfle*. So with the omission of a vowel : e.g. Lat. *semita*, Sp. *senda*, Fr. *sentier* ; Lat. *comitem*, It. *conte*, Sp. *conde*. So when followed by *n* : e.g. Lat. *columna* ; It. *colonna* ; Fr. *colonne*. N.B. omission of *m* before *n* :` e.g. Lat. *domina*, *somnus* ; Sp. *doña*, *sueno* ; Port. *dona*, *sono*. **IV.** As an abbreviation. **a.** M. us. denotes the praenomen Marcus, and less freq. magister, monumentum, municipium ; M' denotes the praenomen Manius. **b.** As a numeral M, or CIƆ, denotes the number 1000.

Macareus (trisyl.), eī and eos, *m.* (Voc. Macareu), *son of Aeolus* ; **Macarēis**, idis (Acc. Macareïda, Ov.), *f. his daughter, Isse.*

maccis, is, *f. an imaginary spice* : Pl.

Macedō, onis, *m. a Macedonian* ; **Macedonia**, ae, *f. the country, situated between Thessaly and Thrace* ; **Macedonicus, Macedonius**, a, um ; also **Macedoniēnsis**, e.

macellārius, ī, *m.* [macellum], *a dealer in meat or other provisions* : Suet.

macellum, ī, *n.* [*cf.* Gk. μάκελλον and Sicil. μάκελλα], *a provision market* (where flesh, fish, and vegetables were sold): Pl., Cic., Hor., etc.

maceō, ēre [macer], *to be lean* : Pl.

macer, cra, crum [*cf.* Gk. μακρός, μακεδνός], *lean, skinny.* **1.** L i t. : taurus, Verg. ; boves, Varr. ; turdi, Hor. *Sup.* : corporis partes, Sen. Ep. **2.** T r a n s f. **a.** *thin, meagre* : solum, Cic. ; agellus, Hor. ; libellus, Mart. *Comp.* : Varr. **b.** si me palma negata macrum donata reducit opimum, Hor. [Fr. *maigre*.]

Macer, crī, *m.* : C. Licinius Macer, *a Roman historian, tribune of the plebs, B.C.* 73.

māceria, ae, *f.* [fr. root of Gk. μάσσω], *a wall* of brick or stone. **a.** In gen. : Cato, Caes., Liv. **b.** *a garden-wall* : Pl., Ter., Cic. Ep.

mācerō, āre [fr. root of Gk. μάσσω], *to make soft or tender, to knead, to soften by steeping.* **1.** L i t. : brassicam in aquam, Cato ; salsamenta, Ter. **2.** T r a n s f. **a.** Of the body : *to weaken, enervate* : multos iste morbus homines macerat, Pl. ; aliquem fame, Liv. ; lentis macerer ignibus, Hor. **b.** Of the mind : *to fret, worry, torment* : satis me lacrumis maceravi, Pl. ; Ter. ; quae vos macerent desiderio, Liv. ; Lucr. ; me macerat Phryne, Hor. In *Mid.* : Pl. ; maceror interdum, Ov. ; ex desiderio, Afran.

macēscō, ere [maceō], *to grow lean or thin* : Pl., Varr.

machaera, ae, *f.* [μάχαιρα], *a sword* : Pl., Suet.

machaerophorus, ī, *m.* [μαχαιροφόρος], *a sword-bearer, satellite* : Cic. Ep.

Machāōn, onis, *m. son of Aesculapius, a famous surgeon of the Greeks before Troy* ;

Machāonius, a, um [Machāōn], *surgical* : Ov.

māchina, ae, *f.* [μηχανή, Dor. μαχανά], *a machine, engine, any artificial contrivance for performing work.* **1.** L i t. **a.** *a crane, pulley* : Cic., Liv. **b.** *a windlass* : Hor. **c.** Esp. *of engines of war* : Sall., Verg. **2.** T r a n s f. **a.** *fabric* : moles et machina mundi, Lucr. **b.** *a device, stratagem* : quantas moveo machinas ! Pl. ; omnis adhibeam machinas ad tenendum adulescentem, Cic. ; omnes ad amplificandam orationem machinae, Cic.

māchināmentum, ī, *n.* [māchinor], *a machine, engine* : machinamenta quatiendis muris, Liv.

māchinātiō, ōnis, *f.* [māchinor], *an artificial contrivance, mechanism.* **1.** L i t. : machinatione quādam moveri, Cic. **2.** T r a n s f. **a.** Concr. *a machine* : Caes., Liv. In *pl.* : Caes. **b.** *a trick, device* : Cic.

māchinātor, ōris, *m.* [māchinor], *a machine-maker, engineer.* **1.** L i t. : bellicorum tormentorum (Archimedes), Liv. ; Tac. **2.** T r a n s f. *a contriver, inventor* : omnium architectus et machinator, Cic. ; Tac.

māchinor, ārī [māchina], *to engineer, devise, design* : incredibile est, quanta opera machinata natura sit, Cic. ; Lucr. E s p. in a bad sense : necem alicui, Liv. ; perniciem alicui, Sall. ; pestem in aliquem, Cic. *Perf. Part.* in *Pass.* sense : indicium a P. Antonio machinatum, Sall.

māchinōsus, a, um, *fitted with a mechanical contrivance* : navigium, Suet.

maciēs, ēī, *f.* [maceō, macer], *leanness, thinness.* **1.** L i t. Of the body : Cic., Hor., etc. ; equi macie corrupti, Caes. **2.** T r a n s f. **a.** Of soil, crops, etc. : *leanness, barrenness* : seges macie deficit, Ov. **b.** Of style : *meagreness, poverty* : qui haec ossa et hanc maciem probant, Tac.

macilentus, a, um [maciēs], *lean, skinny* : Pl.

macrēscō, ere [maceō], *to grow lean, thin.* T r a n s f. : invidus alterius macrescit rebus opimis, Hor.

macritūdō, inis, *f.* [macer], *leanness, skinniness* : Pl.

macrocollum, ī, *n.* [μακρόκωλον], *a large-sized sheet* (of paper) : Cic. Ep.

mactābilis, e, *adj.* [mactō, 2.], *deadly* : plaga, Lucr.

mactātū, ABL. *sing. m.* [mactō, 2.], *in or by sacrifice* (with *Subj.* GEN.) : mactatu parentis, Lucr.

macte, *v.* mactus.

mactea, *v.* mattea.

(1) mactō, āre [mactus, 1.], *to magnify.* **a.** In gen. *to extol, glorify, honour* : eos ferunt laudibus et mactant honoribus, Cic. ; Enn. **b.** Esp. *to glorify or worship* a deity : puerorum extis deos manis, Cic.

(2) mactō, mactāre, mactavi, mactātum and perh. mactum [perh. *cf.* Gk. μάχαιρα, *to smite, slay* (esp. in sacrifice). **1.** L i t. : Cato ; Lucr. ; lectas de more bidentis Cereri, Verg. ; se Orco, Liv. ; hostium legiones diis manibus, Tac. **2.** T r a n s f. **a.** aliquem morte, Cic. ; summo supplicio, Cic. ; hic mactat Ladona, Verg. **b.** aliquem malo, Pl., Enn. ; infortunio, Pl., Ter. ;

in Catilinae busto mactatus essem, Cic. ;
hostis patriae aeternis suppliciis vivos
mortuosque mactabis, Cic. ; perfidos et
ruptores pacis ultioni et gloriae mactandos,
Tac.

(1) **mactus**, a, um [perh. *cf.* Gk. μάκαρ],
magnified ; hence, *glorified, honoured,
adored* (perh. only in the *masc.* Voc.
macto). **1.** In addressing a deity to whom
a sacrifice is offered : macte hac dape esto,
Cato. **2.** T r a n s f. as an encouraging or
congratulatory exclamation addressed to
men : macte virtute (esto) ; L i t. *be blessed /
a blessing on you /* Lucil. ; tantumne est oti
tibi, ut etiam Oratorem legas ? macte virtute ! Cic. Ep. ; macte novā virtute, puer ; sic
itur ad astra, Verg. ; macte esto virtute, Hor. ;
macte hac gloriā, Plin. Ep. In *pl.* : macte
virtute milites Romani este, Liv. *Absol. :*
macte ! Cic. In *Orat. Obliq. :* iuberem (te)
macte virtute esse, Liv.

(2) **mactus**, a, um [perh. fr. old verb macō
or fr. mactō 2.], *hit, wounded :* boves Lucae,
ferro male mactae, Lucr.

macula, ae, *f. a spot.* **1.** L i t. **a.** In gen. :
bos maculis insignis et albo, Verg. ; in
ipsis quasi maculis (terrae), ubi habitatur,
Cic. **b.** *a spot, stain, blot, blemish :* corporis, Cic. ; Pl. ; maculas auferre de vestibus, Ov. **c.** *a mesh* in a net : reticulum
minutis maculis, Ov. **2.** T r a n s f. : Cic. ;
inest amoris macula huic homini in pectore,
Pl. ; est huius saeculi labes quaedam et
macula, virtuti invidere, Cic. ; Claudiae
genti eam inustam maculam, Liv. [It.
macchia, maglia ; Sp. *malla ;* Fr. *maille.*]

maculō, āre [macula], *to spot,* esp. *to stain.*
1. L i t. : corpus maculis luridis, Pl. ; solum
sanguine, Cat. ; terram tabo, Verg. ; can-
dorem corporum atro sanguine, Liv. **2.**
T r a n s f. : metus poenarum praemia vitae,
Lucr. ; rex ille optimi regis caede macu-
latus, Cic. ; crimine nomen, Verg. ; partūs
suos parricidio, Liv.

maculōsus, a, um [macula], *full of spots,
spotted, mottled.* **1.** L i t. **a.** In gen. :
corium, Pl. ; lynx, Verg. **b.** *spotted,
stained :* vestis, Cic. ; maculosae sanguine
harenae, Ov. **2.** T r a n s f. : senatores,
Cic. Ep. ; vir omni dedecore, Tac. ; nefas,
Hor.

made-faciō, facere, fēcī, factum ; *Pass.*
made-fīō, fieri, factus [madeō faciō], *to
make wet, to wet, moisten, soak, drench.* **1.**
L i t. : spongiam, Suet. ; imbuti sanguine
gladii, vel madefacti potius, Cic. ; herbas,
Verg. ; terram suo madefecit odore, Ov.
2. C o m i c. : with wine : Pl.

madēns, entis. **I.** *Part.* madeō. **II.** Adj. :
wet, moist. **a.** In gen. : umor sudoris,
Lucr. ; crinis, Verg. ; nix sole madens,
melting, Ov. ; campi, Tac. **b.** With wine :
mersus vino et madens, Sen. ; distentus ac
madens, Suet.

madeō, ēre [*cf.* Gk. μαδάω], *to be wet or
moist, stream, to be soaked or drenched.* **1.**
L i t. **a.** In gen. : natabant pavimenta
vino, madebant parietes, Cic. ; plurima tuso
sanguine terra madet, Verg. ; lacrimis genae
Ov. C o m i c. : metu, Pl. **b.** With wine :
membra vino madent, Pl. ; non festā luce
madere est rubor, Tib. **c.** In *Pass.* sense :

to be boiled, be softened by boiling : collyrae
facite ut madeant et colyphia, Pl. ; igni
exiguo properata maderent, Verg. **2.**
T r a n s f. **a.** fercula deliciis, Prop. **b.** *to
be steeped :* Socraticis madet sermonibus,
Hor.

madēscō, madēscere, maduī [madeō], *to
become moist* or *wet :* semiusta robora,
Verg. ; tellus nubibus adsiduis pluvioque
madescit ab austro, Ov. ; Quint.

madidē, adv. *in a soaked state* (with wine) :
non vides me ut madide madeam ? Pl.

madidus, a, um [madeō], *moist, wet, drenched.*
1. L i t. **a.** In gen. : fasciculus epistularum aquā madidus, Cic. Ep. ; genae, Ov. ;
alae (of Notus), Ov. ; capilli madidi
myrrhā, Ov. ; ver (i.e. rainy), Juv. **b.**
With wine : vino, Pl. ; Mart. ; dies, Mart.
c. *dyed :* vestis cocco, Mart. **d.** *boiled
soft :* Pl., Juv., etc. *Comp. :* Plin.
2. T r a n s f. *steeped :* Minervae artibus,
Mart. ; iocis libelli, Mart.

mador, ōris, *m.* [madeō], *moisture :* Sall.

madulsa, ae, *m.* [madeō], *a drunkard :* Pl.

Maeander (-dros, -drus), i, *m. a river in
Asia Minor, proverbial for its winding
course.* T r a n s f. *a winding.* **a.** *a winding border* (on a chlamys) : Verg. **b.** *a
devious course :* quos tu Maeandros quaesisti ! Cic.

Maecēnās, ātis, *m. an Etruscan name.* Esp.
C. Cilnius Maecenas, *a Roman eques, the
friend of Augustus, and the patron of Horace
and Vergil ;* **Maecēnātiānus**, a, um.

Maecia, ae, *f. a Roman tribe.*

Maelius, a, *the name of a Roman gens.* Esp.
Sp. Maelius, *who was suspected of aiming at
kingly power, and was killed by Ahala*
(B.C. 439) ; **Maeliānus**, a, um ; **Maeliāni**,
ōrum, *m. pl. his supporters.*

maena, ae, *f.* [μαίνη], *a kind of small sea-
fish,* eaten salted by the poor ; Cic., Ov.
As a term of abuse : Pl.

Maenas, adis, *f.* [μαινάς]. **I.** *a Bacchante ;*
us. *pl.* **Maenades**, um. **II.** *an inspired
prophetess :* Prop.

Maenius, a, *the name of a Roman gens ;*
Maenia Columna, *a pillar in the Forum, at
which thieves and refractory slaves were
scourged, and to which insolvent debtors were
summoned.*

Maenalus or **-os**, i, *m.* and **Maenala**, ōrum,
*n. pl. a range of mountains in Arcadia,
sacred to Pan ;* **Maenalius**, a, um : deus,
i.e. Pan, Ov. ; **Maenalis**, idis, *f. :* ursa,
i.e. Callisto, "The Great Bear," Ov.

Maeones, um, *m. pl. the Maeonians, an
ancient name of the Lydians ;* **Maeonia**, ae,
f. Maeonia, Lydia ; also *Etruria (because
the Etruscans were said to be descended from
the Lydians) ;* **Maeonidēs**, ae, *m. a native
of Maeonia ;* a poetical designation of
Homer, because believed to have been born in
Lydia. Also *an Etrurian* (Verg.) ; **Mae-
onis**, idis, *f. adj. a Lydian woman :* esp.
Arachne or Omphale (Ov.) ; **Maeonius**, a,
um, *Lydian,* also *Homeric* (Hor.) ; *Etruscan*
(Ov.).

Maeōtae, ārum, *m. pl. a Scythian people on
Lake Maeotis ;* **Maeōtis**, idis, *f. adj.
Scythian :* Maeotis palus *or* lacus, *the sea of
Azov ;* **Maeōtius**, a, um.

maereō, ēre [cf. maestus, miser]. **A.**
Intrans. *to be sad* or *mournful, to mourn,
grieve :* vos taciti maerebatis, Cic. ; dictis
maerentia pectora mulcet, Verg. ; fletus
maerens, Cic. With *Intern.* Acc.: talia,
Ov. ; illud, Cic. Ep. With Dat.: suo
incommodo, Cic. ; viro, Tib. **B.** Trans.:
to mourn : mortem civium, rei publicae
calamitatem, Cic. With Acc. and *Inf. :*
Cic.

maeror, ōris, m. [cf. maereō], *mourning,
sadness, grief :* maerore macerari, Pl. ; in
maerore esse, Ter. ; in maerore iacere,
Cic. Ep. ; maerore se conficere, Cic. ; maerorem atque luctum deponere, Cic. ; a
maerore recreari, Cic. Ep. ; cum maerore
et luctu vitam exigunt, Sall. With *Obj.*
Gen. : Cic. In *pl. :* Pl., Cic.

maestiter, *adv. like a mourner :* vestitae, Pl.

maestitia, ae, f. [maestus], *sadness, grief,
gloominess :* esse in maestitiā, Cic. ; mae-
stitiae resistere, Cic. ; theatris maestitiam
inferre, Cic. Of things : orationis, Cic.

maestitūdō, inis, f. [maestus], *sadness :* Pl.

maestus, a, um [cf. miser, maereō], *mourning,
sad, sorrowing* (mostly of feelings). **1.**
Lit.: quid vos maestos tam tristisque esse
conspicor ? Pl. ; maestus ac sordidatus
senex, Cic. ; maestissimus Hector, Verg.
Occ. *gloomy by nature :* oratores maesti et
inculti, Tac. **2.** Transf. **a.** Of things :
urbs, Juv. ; manus, Ov. ; timor, Verg. **b.**
connected with mourning, causing or *showing
sorrow* or *grief :* vestis, Prop. ; funera, Ov.
[It. *mesto.*]

Maevius, I, m. *a poet ridiculed by Vergil and
Horace.*

māgālia, ium, n. *pl.* [an African word], *huts,
kraals :* Cato, Sall., Verg.

mage, *adv.* [*neut. sing. fr.* magis], *more :* Pl.,
Lucr., Verg. (*v.* magis).

magicus, a, um [μαγικός], *magic, magical :*
artes, Verg. ; di, auxilia, Tib. ; arma, Ov. ;
superstitiones, Tac. ; chordae, Juv.

magis (and **mage**, Pl., Lucr., Verg.), *adv.*
[*Neut. comp. Adj.* fr. root of magnus], *more,
in a higher degree,* and occ. *rather.* **1.** Without a following *than-* clause. **A.** In gen.
a. With *Verbs :* plusque magisque viri
nunc gloria claret, Enn. ; tum magis id
diceres, Cic. ; Verg. **b.** With *Nouns* and
Pronouns : neminem hodie mage amat
corde, Pl. ; magis aedilis fieri non potuisset,
Cic. **c.** With *Adj.* or *Adv. :* quod est
magis veri simile, Caes. ; Pl. ; Ov., etc. ;
magis aperte, Ter. ; magis proprie, Cic.
Esp. with *Adj.* which have no proper
Comp. : magis necessarius, Cic. **d.** With
Comparatives : magis est dulcius, Pl.
B. Strengthened. **a.** By Abl. of Measure,
multo, tanto, quanto, eo, nihilo, *etc. ; the
more, so much the more :* ut quidque magis
contemplor tanto magis placet, Pl. ; cum
nihilo magis Vercingetorix in aequum
locum descenderet, Caes. ; Cic. **b.** By a
second magis ; magis magisque, magis et
magis, magis ac magis, and poet. also,
magis : cum cottidie magis magisque perditi
homines tectis ac templis urbis minarentur,
Cic. ; Verg., etc. **II.** With a following
than- clause. **A.** Mostly with *quam.* **a.**
With *Verbs :* magis honorem tribuere quam

salutem accipere, Caes. ; Pl. ; Cic., etc.
b. With *Nouns* and *Pronouns* or *Pronom.
Adj. :* quis homo sit magis meus quam tu
es ? Pl. ; magis ratione et consilio quam
virtute vicisse, Caes. ; Cic. ; Pl. ; (eam)
mage amo quam matrem meam, Pl. **c.**
With *Adj.* or *Adv. :* corpora magna magis
quam firma, Liv. ; Pl. ; Cic. **B.** With
atque : non Apollinis magis verum atque
hoc responsum est, Ter. **C.** With Abl.
of Comparison : quid philosophiā magis
colendum, Cic. ; Pl. ; Verg., etc. ; ab
secundis rebus magis etiam solito incauti,
Liv. **D.** Phr. **i.** magis est ut or quod, *there
is reason rather that :* magis est ut ipse moleste ferat errasse se quam ut etc., Cic. **ii.**
With negatives, often in special sense : *not so
much . . . as, just as much . . . as :* ad
casum ducis non perculsa magis quam in-
ritata est multitudo, Liv. ; non Hannibale
magis victo a se quam Q. Fabio, Liv. ; Cic.
[It. *mai ;* Sp. *mas ;* Fr. *mais ;* and from
iam magis, It. *giammai ;* Sp. *jamas ;*
Fr. *jamais.*]

magister, tri, m. [fr. root of old *comp.* of
magnus], *a superior, chief, master, director.*
1. Lit. **a.** In State affairs : curiae, Pl. ;
(sapiens) appellabitur magister populi (is
enim dictator est), Cic. ; Lartium modera-
torem et magistrum consulibus appositum
(i.e. dictator), Liv. ; dictator magistrum
equitum dicit L. Tarquitium, Liv. ; magister morum, *the censor,* Cic. ; magister sacrorum, *the chief priest,* Liv. ; vici, Suet. **b.**
In schools : *a master, teacher, trainer :* Cic.,
Liv. Hence, virtutis, Cic. ; artium libera-
lium, Cic. Of inanim. things : stilus optimus dicendi effector ac magister, Cic. ;
timor magister offici, Cic. ; Pl. ; rerum
omnium magister usus, Caes. **c.** In gen. :
societatis (a company), Cic. ; auctionis,
Cic. ; cenandi, Cic. ; convivi, Varr. ; pecoris, Varr. ; ovium, Verg. ; navium, elephanti, Liv. **2.** Transf. **a.** *an adviser,
guardian :* senes me filiis relinquont quasi
magistrum, Ter. **b.** *an adviser, instigator,
author :* magister ad despoliandum Dianae
templum, Cic. ; Ter. ; alicuius rei, Tac.
c. *an expert* (in apposition to another Noun) :
a tonsore magistro plecteris, Juv. [It.
and Sp. *maestro,* Fr. *maitre.*]

magisterium, i, n. [magister], *the office of a
magister, i.e. of a superior, chief, director,*
etc. ; *control.* **1.** Lit. **a.** In gen. : sacerdoti, Liv., Suet. ; equitum, Suet. ; morum,
the censorship, Cic. : me magisteria delectant a maioribus instituta (*sc.* conviviorum),
Cic. **b.** *the control* of a paedagogus : iam
excessit mihi aetas ex magisterio tuo, Pl.
2. Transf. *direction, advice :* virtute id
factum, et magisterio tuo, Pl. ; vana, Tib.

magistra, ae, f. [v. magister], *a superior,
director, mistress.* **1.** Lit. : ludo magistram
esse, Ter. **2.** Transf. : Pl. ; vita rustica
parsimoniae magistra est, Cic. ; arte
magistrā, Verg.

magistrātus, ūs, m. [magister], *the office* or
rank of a magister, *a magisterial office,
magistracy.* **1.** Lit. (mostly of civil offices) :
honores, magistratūs, imperia, potestates,
Cic. ; alicui dare, mandare, committere,
Cic. ; capere, inire, Cic. ; ingredi, Sall. ;

obtinere, Caes. ; habere, gerere, Cic. ; in
magistratu esse, manere, Liv. ; magistratum deponere, Caes. ; magistratu abire,
Cic. ; conlegae magistratum abrogare,
Cic. ; continuare, Sall., Liv. Occ. applied to *military commands* : in magistratu
esse, Nep. **2.** Transf. *a magistrate, State
official* : est proprium munus magistratūs,
intellegere se gerere personam civitatis,
Cic. ; seditiosi, Sall. ; creare, Liv.

magnanimitās, ātis, *f.* [magnanimus], *greatness of soul, magnanimity*, Cic. ; magnanimi-
tas est (with *Inf.*), Plin. Pan.

magnanimus, a, um [magnus animus],
great-souled, magnanimous : viri fortes,
magnanimi, Cic. ; heroës, Verg.

Magnēsia, ae, *f.* **I.** *a district of Thessaly,
on the Aegean Sea.* **II.** *a city in Caria,
near the Maeander.* **III.** *a city in Lydia, at
the foot of Mount Sipylus* ; **Magnēs**, ētis,
m. a Magnesian : also *Adj.*, Magnes
lapis, *the Magnesian stone, a magnet* ; **Mag-
nēsius**, a, um, **Magnēssa**, ae, *f. a Magnesian woman* : **Magnētis**, idis, *f. adj.*

magnidicus, a, um [magnus and dic, v.
dicō], *talking big, bragging* : homo, Pl.

magnificē, *adv.* **I.** *grandly, splendidly,
brilliantly* : Pl. ; laudare, Cic. ; vincere,
Cic. *Comp.* magnificentius, Cic. ; *Sup.*
magnificentissimē, Cic. Ep. **II.** In bad
sense : *grandly, pompously* : incedere, Liv.

magnificentia, ae, *f.* [magnificus], *grandeur.*
I. Of persons : *greatness* in feeling or action :
Cic. Of things : *grandeur, magnificence,
splendour* : epularum, Cic. ; publicorum
operum, Liv. **II.** *pompousness* : Ter. ;
verborum, Cic.

magnificō, āre [magnificus], *to make much of,
esteem highly* : aliquem, Pl., Ter., Plin. ;
aliquid, Plin.

magnificus, a, um [magnus faciō], *grand.*
I. a. Of persons : *great* in feeling or
action : vir factis magnificus, Liv. ; animus
excelsus magnificusque, Cic. ; civitas, Sall. ;
cives in suppliciis deorum, Sall. **b.** Of
things : *grand, splendid, on a large scale* :
ornatus, villae, Cic. ; funera, Caes. ; res
gestae, Liv. ; nomen, Tac. Of style :
dicendi genus, Cic. *Comp.* magnificentior,
and *Sup.* magnificentissimus, Cic. **II.**
pompous, bragging : miles, Pl. ; verba,
Ter. ; litterae, Suet.

magniloquentia, ae, *f.* [magniloquus], *grandeur* of language. **I.** *sublime* or *elevated
language* : Homeri, Cic. **II.** In bad sense :
pompous language, braggadocio : Liv.

magniloquus, a, um [magnus loquor],
speaking grandly. **I.** *sublime* : Homerus,
Stat. **II.** In bad sense : *pompous in
speech, vaunting* : Ov., Tac.

magnitūdō, inis, *f.* [magnus], *greatness.*
1. Lit. **a.** Of bulk, magnitude : mundi,
Cic. ; maris, Cic. ; aquarum, Liv. ; fluminis, Caes. ; corporum, Caes., Liv. In *pl.* :
magnitudines regionum, Cic. **b.** Of *number* and *quantity* : pecuniae, Cic. **2.**
Transf. **a.** Of abstract things : acerbitatis et odii, Cic. ; poenae, Caes. **b.** Of
persons : *rank, dignity* : imperatoris, Cic.

magnopere, more freq. **magnō opere**,
Comp. māiōre opere, Cato, but *v.* magis ;
Sup. maximō opere, Pl., Ter., Cic. Ep., but

v. maximē ; *very much, greatly, strongly*
(used as adv. of magnus) : edictum est
magno opere mihi ne etc., Pl. ; Diviciacum
magnopere cohortatus, Caes. ; magno opere
desiderare, mirari, providere, censere, etc.,
Cic. ; is magnopere censet ne etc., Liv. ;
negat Appius magno opere ad causam suam
pertinere, Liv. ; magnoque opere abs te
peto, Cic. Ep. ; occ. with *Nouns* : nulla
magno opere expectatio est, Cael. ap. Cic.
Ep. ; nullā magnopere clade acceptā, Liv. ;
maximo opere edicere, Ter. ; a te maximo
opere etiam atque etiam quaeso et peto,
Cic. Ep. ; rogare iussit te opere maximo,
Pl. ; Ter.

magnus, a, um. *Comp.* **māior** (earlier
māior), māius ; *Sup.* **maximus**, (earlier
maxumus), a, um, *great, large.* **1.** Lit.
(physical and material). **a.** Of size or
extent : Olympus, Enn. ; montes, Cat. ;
oppidum maximum, Caes. ; domus, Cic. ;
aquae, Liv. ; ossa lacertosque, Verg. ;
Lucil. ; homo. Lucil. ; sementis quam
maximas facere, Caes. ; magna itineribus,
Liv. **b.** In measure, weight, number :
copia pabuli, Caes. ; magna, maior, maxima
pars, Caes., Cic., Liv. ; maximum pondus
auri, magnum numerum frumenti, vim mellis maximam exportasse, Cic. ; caterva,
Verg. ; multitudo maior solitā, Liv. ;
maior quam pro numero iactura, Liv.
2. Transf. **A.** In time. **a.** *long, prolonged* (rare) : magnum sol circumvolvitur
annum (the cycle of 25,800 years), Verg. ;
Cic. **b.** Of age : magno natu, Nep., Liv. ;
homo magnus natu, Liv. Mostly in *Comp.*
or *Sup.* : *older, the elder* ; *oldest, the
eldest* : maior aetate, Liv. ; audivi ex
maioribus natu, Cic. ; Verg. ; annos natus
maior quadraginta, Cic. ; Liv. ; ex duobus
filiis maior, Caes. ; Ter. ; Liv. ; maxima
virgo, Ov. Esp. in *pl.* **māiōrēs**, um, *m.
ancestors, forefathers, fathers* ; *L.*
Philippus, vir patre, avo, maioribus suis
dignissimus, Cic. ; *more maiorum*, Cic.
B. Of mental, moral, and other qualities.
a. Of persons and things : *great, grand,
important, noble* : nemo igitur vir magnus
sine aliquo adflatu divino unquam fuit,
Cic. ; magnus hoc bello Themistocles fuit,
Nep. ; Magnus Alexander, Magnus Pompeius, Liv. ; Fabius Maximus, Liv. ; virtus,
alacritas, Caes. ; causa, opus, etc., Cic. ;
as *Noun* : magna di curant, parva negle-
gunt, Cic. ; magna loqui, Tib. **b.** maximus, *supreme, highest* : Iuppiter optimus
maximus, Liv. (*cf.* cum magnis dis, Enn.) ;
praetor maximus, Liv. **c.** *great, vehement,
violent, loud* : imber, Caes., Cic. ; incendium, Cic. ; magnā voce confiteri, Cic. ;
fletus, Caes. ; clamor, Caes., Cic., Liv. ;
stridor, murmur, Verg. ; hence, *Neut.*
Acc. **magnum** and **maximum** used as
Adv. : magnum clamat, Pl. ; exclamat
deropente maxumum, Pl. Of feeling :
studium, Caes., Cic. ; dolor, Caes. ; gaudium, spes, Nep. **d.** Of value or price in
Neut. **magni** and **magnō**, *at a higher
price* ; **māiōris**, *at a higher price* ; **maximi**, *at a very high price.* **i.** Lit. : magno
emere, vendere, Cic. ; magni aestimare,
Cic. ; multo maioris alapae mecum veneunt,

Phaedr. **ii. Transf.**: magno illi ea
cunctatio stetit, Liv.; magni facere,
pendere, Pl.; magni esse, Cic.; maxumi
facere, Ter.; maximi videri, Cic. Ep.
Simil.: **in māius,** to a higher degree : famā
incerta in maius vero ferri solent, Liv.;
extollere aliquid in maius (i.e. more highly
than it deserves), Tac.; so too, in maius
credere, accipere, celebrare, nuntiare, Tac.
For **magnō opere,** v. magnopere. [From
maior : It. maggiore ; Fr. maire ; Eng.
mayor, major.]

Māgō or **Māgōn,** ōnis, m. **I.** b. of Hannibal.
II. another Carthaginian, author of a work
on agriculture.

magus, i, m. [μάγος], a learned man among
the Persians. **1.** Lit.: Cic. **2. Transf.**
a magician, wizard : Ov.

magus, a, um [magus], magic : artes, manus,
Ov.

Māia (older **Maiia**), ae, f. d. of Atlas, and
Pleione, and m. of Mercury by Jupiter ;
Māius, a, um, of Maia ; mensis Maius,
the month of May, Cic., Ov.; also Maius
alone : Ov.; Kalendae Maiae, Cic. Ep., Ov.
[It. maggio, Sp. mayo, Fr. mai.]

māiālis, is, m. a gelded boar, a barrow hog :
Varr. As a term of abuse : Cic.

māiestās, ātis, f. [fr. mag- seen in magnus],
greatness, grandeur, dignity, majesty. **a.**
Of the gods : Cic., etc. Of men : Caes.,
Cic., Hor., Juv., etc. **b.** Of States, esp.
of Rome : Sall.; maiestatem populi
Romani defendere, Cic.; minuere, Cic.,
Tac.; laedere, Sen. **c.** Hence, maiestas
(sc. minuta or laesa), lèse-majesté, high-
treason : maiestatis crimen, iudicium, Cic.;
maiestatis damnari, condemnari, absolvi,
Cic.; legionem sollicitare, res est, quae lege
maiestatis tenetur, Cic. **d.** As a form of
address to a sovereign : Phaedr. [It.
maestà.]

māior, māiōrēs, v. magnus.

māius, v. magnus.

māiusculus, a, um [dim. of comp. of magnus].
I. somewhat greater : cura, Cic. Ep. **II.**
a little older : Pl.; Thaïs, quàm ego sum,
maiuscula est, Ter.

māla, ae, f. [prob. for maxla, cf. dim. maxilla],
the cheek-bone, jaw (prop. the upper or immoveable jaw), mostly in pl. **1.** Lit.:
Lucr., Verg., etc. **2. Transf.** the jaw,
cheek : Pl., Lucr., Verg., etc.

malacia, ae, f. [μαλακία], a calm at sea, dead
calm : Caes. **Transf.**: Sen. Ep.

malacissō, āre [μαλακίζω], to soften : Pl.

malacus, a, um [μαλακός]. **I.** soft : Pl.
II. delicate, luxurious : Pl.

male, adv. [malus], comp. **pēius** (earlier
peiius), sup. **pessimē** : badly, ill, wrongly,
etc. **a.** In gen.: male accipere aliquem,
Cic.; male vivere, Caes., Hor.; equitatu
agmen adversariorum male habere (to
harass), Caes.; hoc male habet virum,
Ter.; male se habere (i.e. to feel ill), Ter.;
male olere, Cic.; dum male optatos nondum premis inscius axīs, Ov.; male feriatos,
Hor.; male tum erratur, Verg. With
facere, dicere, velle, cogitare, etc. male is
equivalent to mala in sense : alicui male
facere, Pl., Cic. Ep.; male dicere alicui,
Pl., Cic., Hor.; male velle alicui, Pl.;

male cogitare, Cic.; male audire (to be
badly spoken of), Cic. Also with esse :
male est animo, Pl.; Antonio male sit si
etc., Cic. Ep. **b.** unsuccessfully : tuos
labores male cecidisse, Caes.; proelium
male pugnatum, Sall.; male sustinere
arma, Liv.; male emere, vendere, Cic. **c.**
With words having in themselves a bad
sense : badly, i.e. very much : male metuo,
Ter.; aliquem odisse, Caes. ap. Cic. Ep.;
rauci, Hor. **d.** When connected with an
adjective having a good sense, male sometimes means scarcely or not at all : civitas
male pacata, Cic.; scuta male tegebant
Gallos, Liv.; male viva, Ov.; male sanus,
Cic. Ep., Verg.; male gratus, Ov.; statio
male fida carinis, Verg. [Sp. Fr. mal.
From male aptus, Fr. malade.]

male-dicāx, ācis, adj. foul-mouthed, abusive :
Pl.

maledicē, adv. abusively : Cic., Liv.

maledicēns, entis. **I.** Part. male dicō. **II.**
Adj.: foul-mouthed, abusive, scurrilous :
homines, Pl. Comp. : maledicentior, Pl.
Sup. : in maledicentissimā civitate, Cic.

male-dicō, v. male. [Fr. maudire.]

maledictiō, ōnis, f. [male dicō], reviling,
abuse : Cic.

maledictitō or **male dictitō,** āre [freq. male
dicō], to curse, abuse often or much : Pl.

male-dictum or **male dictum,** i, n. a curse ;
abuse: male dicta in aliquem dicere, conferre, conicere, Cic.; male dictis figere aliquem, Cic.

maledicus, a, um [male and dic, v. dicō],
foul-mouthed, abusive, scurrilous : convicia-
tor, civitas, Cic.; esse in aliquem, Quint.
(for Comp. and Sup. v. maledicēns.]

malefactor, ōris, m. [malefaciō], an evil-
doer, malefactor : Pl.

male-factum (malfactum, Pl.) or **male
factum,** i, n. an evil deed, injury : Enn., Cic.

maleficē, adv. mischievously : Pl.

maleficentia, ae, f. [maleficus], evil-doing,
harm : Plin.

maleficium, i, n. [maleficus], a doing evil,
wrongdoing. **a.** Abstr.: ab iniuriā et
maleficio se prohibere, Caes.; malefici
occasione amissā, Liv. **b.** Concr. an
evil deed, wrong, harm, mischief : Pl.; admittere, committere, Cic.; sine ullo maleficio, Caes.; Liv.

maleficus, a, um [male faciō], evil-doing,
vicious, criminal : homo naturā maleficus,
Cic.; mores, Pl.; natura, Nep.; vita,
Tac. As Noun, **maleficus,** i, m. an evil-
doer, Pl. Esp. of the 'black arts,' magical :
carmina et devotiones aliaque malefica, Tac.
Sup. maleficentissimus, Suet.

male-suādus, a, um [male suādeō], ill-advis-
ing, seductive : fames, Verg.

male-volēns, entis, adj. ill-disposed, spiteful :
Pl.; ingenium, Pl. Sup. : malevolentis-
simae obtrectationes, Cic.

malevolentia, ae, f. [malevolēns], ill-will,
malice, spite : Cic., Sall.

malevolus, a, um [male volō], ill-disposed,
spiteful, malicious : omnibus est malevolus, Cic. Ep.; Cato in me fuit, Cic. Ep.
Of things : sermones, Cic. Ep. As Noun,
malevolus, i, m., Cic.; and **malevola,** ae,
f., Pl.

mālifer, a, um [mālum ferō], *apple-bearing* :
Verg.

malificus, v. maleficus.

malignē, *adv. ill-naturedly, spitefully, malign-antly.* **a.** In gen. : loqui, Liv. *Comp.* :
Curt. **b.** *stingily, grudgingly* : ager ma-
ligne plebi divisus, Liv. ; quippiam laudare
(i.e. "to damn with faint praise,"), Hor. ;
non mihi fuit tam maligne ut etc., Cat.
Comp. : Sen. Ep.

malignĭtās, ātis, *f.* [malignus], *ill-will, spite,
malice.* **a.** In gen. : Sen., Tac., Plin. Ep.
b. *stinginess, niggardliness* : Pl. ; maligni-
tatis auctores, Liv.

malignus, a, um [malus, *cf.* benĭgnus], *ill-
natured, ill-disposed, spiteful, malicious,
malignant.* **A.** In gen. **1.** Lit. Of persons : Hor., Juv. **2.** Transf. : mens,
votum, Cat. ; oculi, Verg. ; studia, leges,
Ov. *Sup.* : Sen. **B.** *stingy, niggardly.* **1.**
Lit. Of persons : Pl., Hor. **2.** Transf.
a. *niggardly in bearing* : colles, Verg.
Comp. : terra, Plin. Ep. **b.** *given with
niggardliness, stinted, niggardly* : aditus,
lux, Verg. ; fama, Ov. ; munus, Plin.

malitia, ae, *f.* [malus], *bad quality, badness,
vice.* **a.** In gen. : Sall. **b.** *roguery* : Pl.,
Cic., Quint. In *pl. roguish tricks* : Pl.
Also (in *sing.*) playfully : tamen a malitiā
non discedis, Cic. Ep.

malitiōsē, *adv. knavishly* : Cic. *Comp.* :
Cic.

malitiōsus, a, um [malitia], *full of evil,
knavish* : homo, Cic. ; iuris interpretatio,
Cic. As Name : silva Malitiosa, Liv.

maliv-, wrongly for malev-, q.v.

malleolus, i, *m.* [*dim.* malleus], *a small hammer* or *mallet.* Transf. *a kind of fire-
dart* used in sieges : Cic., Liv.

malleus, i, *m. a hammer, mallet, maul* : Pl.
Of the *maul* or *pole-axe* for felling animals :
Ov. [It. *maglio* ; Fr. *mail.*]

mālō, mālle, mālui (old forms : māvolō, Pl. ;
māvelim for mālim, etc., Pl.) [mage volō], *to
wish* or *choose rather, to prefer.* **A.** With
Acc. (mostly *Neut.*) : bonos et senatum,
Cael. ap. Cic. Ep. ; quod mallem, Ov. ;
ambigua, Tac. With double Acc. and
quam : fidem in bello quam praesentem
victoriam, Liv. ; Cic. ; Juv. With Acc.
and *Inf.* : principem se esse mavult quam
videri, Cic. ; Hor. With Nom. and *Inf.* :
esse quam videri bonus malebat, Sall. ; Juv.
With *Subj.* : mallem cognoscerem, Cic. Ep. ;
Cat. ; Liv. ; Juv. With Abl. of Comparison for quam : nullos his mallem ludos
spectasse, Hor. ; Tac. **B.** Strengthened,
a. by multo or haud paulo, *much* (*not a
little*), *rather* : Cic. **b.** by pleonastic
potius or *magis* : se ab omnibus desertos
potius quam abs te defensos esse malunt,
Cic. ; magis vere vincere quam diu imperare malit, Liv. **C.** With Dat. of person : *to be more favourable to* : in hac re
negotiatoribus, Cic. Ep.

malobathrum, i, *n.* [μαλόβαθρον], *an Indian*
or *Syrian plant, from which a costly ointment was prepared.* **1.** Lit. : Plin. **2.**
Transf. *the oil* or *unguent itself* : Hor.

mālum, i, *n.* [*cf.* Gk. μῆλον, Dor. μᾶλον], *an
apple.* **1.** Lit. : Verg. In pun with
mălum : Pl. Prov. : ab ovo usque ad

mala (from the Roman custom of beginning
dinner with eggs and ending with fruit),
Hor. **2.** Transf. Of other fruit : aurea
(*quinces*), Verg. ; felix (*citron*), Verg. ;
Verg. ; granatum or Punicum (*pomegranate*), Verg. [It. *melo.*]

(1) mālus, i, *f.* [μηλέα], *an apple-tree* : Varr.,
Verg.

(2) mālus, i, *m.* **I.** *a mast of a ship* : Cic.,
Verg., Hor. **II.** *a mast* or *pole*, to which
the awnings (at the theatre or circus), were
spread : Lucr., Liv. **III.** *an upright pole
at each corner of a building* : turrium mali,
Caes.

malus, a, um. *Comp.* **pēior** (older **peiior**),
pēius ; *Sup.* **pessimus**, a, um ; *bad* (either
physically or morally ; opp. bonus), *ill,
evil.* **A.** In gen. : malus et nequam homo,
Pl. ; philosophi minime mali illi quidem,
sed satis acuti, Cic. ; mores, Sall. ; consuetudo, Hor. ; libido, Liv. ; abi in malam
rem (i.e. *go to hell !*), Ter. Also *harmful,
noxious* : virus, gramina, Verg. ; cicuta,
Hor. *Neut.* as Noun, **malum**, i. **a.** *an
evil, ill* : alicui aliquid mali facere, Pl. ;
cavere malum, Cic. **b.** *harm, hurt* : clementiam illi malo fuisse, Cic. Ep. ; Pl.
Hence, *evil* inflicted ; *punishment* : malum
dare, Pl. ; malum minitari militibus, Liv. ;
vi malo plagis adductus, Cic. ; Sall. **c.**
wrongdoing : sperans famam exstingui veterum malorum, Verg. ; Sen. **d.** As a term
of abuse : quid tu, malum, me sequere ?
(*you pest*), Pl. ; Ter. ; Cic. **B.** In partic.
a. *adverse, unsuccessful* : pugna, Cic. ;
mala res, spes multo asperior, Sall. ; mala
avis (of ill omen), Hor. ; *Neut.* as Noun,
malum, i, *an adverse event, disaster* : hostes
inopinato malo turbati, Caes. ; Nep. Also
adversity, hardship : adsuetus malo, Verg.
b. Polit. : *unpatriotic* : cives, Nep. *Masc.*
as Noun : bonos et malos interfecit, Sall.
c. *ugly, ill-looking* : mulier, Pl. ; crus,
Hor. ; facies, Quint. **d.** *roguish* : pessi-
mae puellae, Cat. **e.** Of weight : *bad*, i.e.
light, poor : pondus, Pl. [Fr. *mal* in *malgré, malheur* = malum augurium.]

malva, ae, *f.* [*cf.* Gk. μαλάχη], *the mallow* :
Cic. Ep., Hor. [Fr. *mauve.*]

Māmers, ertis, *m.* the Oscan name for Mars :
Māmertīni, ōrum, *m. pl. a name assumed
by certain mercenary troops of Agathocles,
who after his death seized Messana* (c. 282
B.C.) ; **Māmertīnus**, a, um.

mamilla, ae, *f.* [*dim.* mamma], *a breast, teat* :
Juv.

mamma, ae, *f. a breast*, esp. of females : Pl.,
Lucr., Cic. Of animals : *teat, dug* : Cic.,
Liv. [Fr. *maman.*]

mammĕātus, a, um [mamma], *large-
breasted, full-bosomed* : Pl.

mammōsus, a, um [mamma], *large-breasted.*
1. Lit. : Laber. Of animals : canes
feminae, Varr. **2.** Transf. : pira, Plin.

mānābilis, e, *adj.* [mānō], *flowing* ; hence,
penetrating : frigus, Lucr.

manceps, cipis (earlier -cupis), *m.* [manus
capiō], *a purchaser, one who purchases* or
hires any thing from the State : or a 'praes'
(*surety*) as the agent purchasing for a
'societas' (*company*). **1.** Lit. **a.** *a purchaser* of this kind : societas coitur . . .

manceps fit Chrysogonus . . . tria praedia Capitoni propria traduntur, etc., Cic. ; nullius rei neque praes neque manceps, Nep. **b.** *a public contractor :* si res abiret ab eo mancipe, quem ipse apposuisset, Cic. ; itinera fraude mancipum et incuriā magistratuum interrupta, Tac. **c.** *a contractor* of people to applaud : Plin. Ep. ; of workmen (i.e. to let them out on hire) : operarum, Suet. **2.** T r a n s f. *a surety* (*cf.* praes) : Pl.

mancipium (older **mancupium**), i, *n.* [manceps], *a taking in hand ;* hence, **1.** Lit. *a formal taking possession, a formal sale or purchase* among the Romans by taking a thing in the hand and weighing out the money (per aes et libram) : minas quadraginta accepisti a Callicle et ille aedis mancupio aps te accepit, Pl. ; in mancipi lege (*in the contract of purchase*), Cic. ; hoc in mancipio non dixerat Marius (*at the time of the sale* or *purchase*), Cic. **2.** T r a n s f. **a.** In gen. : *a possession, property, right of ownership,* acquired by such purchase : mancipio (DAT.) dare, or accipere, *to give* or *take possession of : Ca.* memini et mancupio tibi dabo. *Cu.* egon' ab lenone quicquam mancupio accipiam ? Pl. ; Cic. In Roman law, property was classed as *res mancipi,* i.e. land, slaves, beasts of burden, and agricultural instruments (*v.* Maine's Ancient Law), and *res nec mancipi,* other property : in iis rebus repetendis, quae mancipi sunt, Cic. Hence : vita mancipio nulli datur, omnibus usu, Lucr. ; Sen. Ep. ; sui mancipi esse (to be one's own master), Brut. ap. Cic. Ep. **b.** *a slave :* Pl. ; mancipiis locuples rex, Hor. ; mancipia argento parata, Liv.

mancipō (older **mancupō**), āre [manceps], *to make over* or *deliver up as property* by a formal act of purchase (*v.* mancipium). **1.** Lit. *to transfer, sell :* alienos mancupatis, alienos manu mittitis, Pl. ; servos actori publico, Tac. ; agrum actori publico, Plin. Ep. Hence, quaedam, si credis consultis, mancipat usus (i.e. gives a legal title), Hor. **2.** T r a n s f. : luxu et saginae mancipatus, Tac.

mancus, a, um, *maimed, crippled.* **1.** Lit. : Pl., Cic., Ov., etc. *Masc.* as Noun : Liv. **2.** T r a n s f. : praetura, virtus, etc., Cic. ; fortuna, Hor. With ABL. : talibus officiis prope mancus, Hor. [Fr. *manchot.*]

mandātor, ōris, *m.* [mandō], *one who suborns accusers* or *informers :* Suet.

mandātū, ABL. *sing. m.* [mandō], *by command :* Sullae, Cic. ; meo, Cic. Ep.

mandātum, i, *n.* [mandō], *a charge, order, commission.* **a.** In gen. : procurare, Cic. Ep. More freq. in *pl. :* dare alicui ut etc., Cic. ; accipere ab aliquo, Cic. ; exponere, audire, Cic. ; deferre, Cic. Ep. ; facere, Pl. ; exsequi, Cic. ; perferre, persequi, Cic. Ep. ; efficere, Sall. ; perficere, Liv. ; neglegere, fallere, Ov. ; scripta, Liv. ; frangere (punningly), Hor. With *Inf. :* dabit et mandata reverti, Ov. **b.** In partic. : *an imperial command :* Plin. Ep. Esp. of the *secret orders* of the Emperor : Tac., Suet.

mandō, āre [manus dō], lit. *to put into one's hand ;* hence, *to commit to one's charge, entrust.* **1.** Lit. : filiam viro, Pl. ; tibi res

meas, Pl. ; alicui magistratum, Cic. ; honores, Cic. ; consulibus quaestionem de Bacchanalibus, Liv. ; aliquem alicui alendum, Verg. With *ut* or *ne, to commission, order :* Voluseno mandat ut ad se quam primum revertatur, Caes. ; without *ut :* huic mandat, Remos adeat, Caes. ; mandabat in urbem, nullum proeliorum finem expectarent, Tac. With *Inf. :* Tac. With ACC. and *Inf. :* Mart. **2.** T r a n s f. : aliquid alicuius fidei, Ter. ; se fugae, Caes. ; litteris, memoriae, historiae, scriptis, Cic. ; aliquem aeternis tenebris vinculisque, Cic. ; solitudini vitam, Cic. ; hordea sulcis, Verg. ; Ov. ; corpus humo, Verg.

mandō, mandere, mandī, mānsum [perh. *cf.* Gk. μασάομαι], *to chew, masticate.* **1.** Lit. : Cic. P o e t. : (equi) fulvum mandunt sub dentibus aurum, Verg. **2.** T r a n s f. *to eat, devour :* Enn. ; lora mandere, Liv. ; tristia vulnera saevo dente, Ov. P o e t. : mandere humum, like mordere humum (said of those who fall in battle), Verg.

mandra, ae, *f.* [μάνδρα], *a stall.* **1.** Lit. : mulorum, Mart. **2.** T r a n s f. **a.** *a drove* of cattle (i.e. the drovers), Juv. **b.** *a chequered gaming-board :* Mart.

mandūcō, āre [mandūcus], *to chew, masticate.* **1.** Lit. : Varr. **2.** T r a n s f. *to eat :* Aug. ap. Suet. [It. *mangiare ;* Fr. *manger.*]

mandūcus, i, *m.* [fr. root of mandō : *cf.* cadūcus]. **I.** *glutton :* Pompon. **II.** *a comic masked figure representing a person chewing,* used in processions, etc. : Pl.

māne, *neut. indecl.* **I.** Used as Noun in NOM., ACC., or ABL. (old LOCAT. **mānī** like lūcī, vesperī) *the morning, morn :* dum mane novum, Verg. ; vigilabat ad ipsum mane, Hor. ; multo mane (in the early morning), Cic. Ep. **II.** As *Adv.* [fr. old LOCAT. of mānus, *good ; cf.* Fr. de bonne *heure*], *early in the morning :* postridie eius diei, mane, Caes. ; hodie mane, Cic. ; cras mane, Ter. With other adverbs : tam mane, Ter. ; bene mane (very early in the morning), Cic. ; plane mane, Plin. Ep. [It. *mane* in *stamane* for *questa mane ; dimani, domani ;* Fr. *demain.*]

maneō, manēre, mānsī, mānsum [perh. *cf.* Gk. μένω]. **A.** I n t r a n s. *to stay, remain.* **1.** Lit. a. In gen. : Ter., Cic., Prop., etc. ; in loco, Caes. ; in patriā, Cic. *Impers. Pass. :* Caes., Cic. Ep. **b.** *to stay, stop, pass the night :* Ter. ; apud aliquem, Cic. Ep. ; eo die Venafri, Cic. Ep. ; sub Iove frigido, Hor. ; extra domum patris, Liv. **2.** T r a n s f. *to remain, endure, continue, abide by :* si in eo manerent, quod convenisset, Caes. ; in vitā, Cic. ; in veritate in pristinā mente, Cic. ; in officio, Hirt. ; in pactione, Nep. ; in condicione, Cic. ; in eā condicione, Liv. ; promissis, Verg. Of inanim. and abstr. subjects : munitiones integrae manebant, Caes. ; memoria, Cic. ; regna, Verg. With DAT. : manent ingenia senibus, Cic. ; Liv. **B.** T r a n s. **a.** In gen. : *to wait for, await :* Pl., Ter. ; hostium adventum mansit, Liv. **b.** Of fate : *to await :* quis me manet exitus ? Ov. ; quae (acerba) manent victos, Liv. Also, maneat nostros ea cura nepotes, Verg.

mānēs, ium, *m. pl.* [mānus ; lit. good, bene-
volent]. **1.** Lit. **a.** With or without dii,
*the deified souls of the dead, the beings of the
underworld* (as benevolent spirits, opp.
larvae and lemures) : manibus divis mactatus, Lucr. ; carmine di superi placantur,
carmine manes, Hor. ; deorum manium iura
sancta sunto, Cic. ; hostium legiones mac-
tandas dis manibus dabo, Liv. **b.** *the spirit
of the departed, ghost :* nec patris Anchisae
cinerem manīsve revelli, Verg. ; manes
Verginiae, Liv. **2.** Transf. **a.** *the lower
world :* manes profundi, Verg. ; fabulae
manes, Hor. **b.** *the last remains* (of the
body) : accipiet manis parvula testa meos,
Prop. ; sepulcra diruta esse, omnium nudatos manis, Liv.

mangō (**mangŏ**, Mart.), ōnis, *m.* [μάγγανον],
a (cajoling) salesman ; esp. *a slave-dealer :*
Hor., Quint.

mangōnicus, a, um [mangō], *of a salesman,*
esp. *of a slave-dealer :* quaestus, Suet.

māni, *v.* māne.

manicae, ārum, *f. pl.* [manus]. **I.** *hand-
cuffs, manacles :* Pl., Verg., Hor. Hence,
a grappling-iron : Luc. **II.** *the long sleeves
of a tunic,* reaching to the hand, and therefore serving as *gloves :* tunicae manicas
(habent), Verg. ; Tac. ; of a kind of *fur-
gloves, muff :* Cic. Worn by soldiers as a
protection : *an armlet, gauntlet :* Juv.
[It. *manica ;* Sp. *manga ;* Fr. *manche.*]

manicātus, a, um [manicae], *with long
sleeves :* tunica, Cic.

manicula, ae, *f.* [dim. manus], *a little
hand :* Pl.

manifestō, āre [manifestus], *to show plainly,
reveal :* aliquem latentem, Ov.

manifestus (earlier **manufestus**), a, um
[manus fendō, *cf.* infestus ; lit. "struck
with the hand"], *palpable, clear, plain.*
A. In gen. : manufesta res est, Pl. ; Cic. ;
Penates multo manifesti lumine, Verg.
With Gen. : doloris, Ov. ; vitae, Tac. **B.**
detected, caught, convicted. **a.** Of persons :
nec magis manufestum ego hominem um-
quam ullum teneri vidi, Pl. ; ut coniuratos
quam maxume manifestos habeant, Sall. ;
nocentes, Ov. ; rea, Ov. Comp. : Plin.
With Gen. : mendaci, Pl. ; rerum capitalium, Sall. ; ambitionis, Tac. With *Inf. :*
dissentire manifestus, Tac. **b.** Of things :
peccatum, Cic. *Neut.* as Noun : aliquid
pro manifesto habere, Liv. Abl. **manifestō** as *Adv. : plainly, evidently :* Pl. ;
freq. with prehendere and deprehendere,
Cic. ; Comp. manifestius, Verg., Tac.

manipl-, *v.* manipul-, *etc.*

manipulāris (**maniplāris**, Ov.), e, *adj.*
[manipulus], *of a maniple or company :*
miles, Ov. : iudices, Cic. As Noun, **manipulāris**, is, *m.* **a.** *a private, ranker :* Pl. ;
Cic. Ep. ; Rufus diu manipularis, dein
centurio, Tac. **b.** *a soldier of the same
company ; a comrade :* Pl. ; Fabius centurio, tris suos nactus manipularis, Caes.

manipulārius, a, um [manipulus], *of a
private (soldier) :* Suet.

manipulātim, *adv.* [manipulus]. **I.** *by
handfuls, in bundles :* Plin. **II.** *by maniples :* manipulatim structa acies, Liv.
Comic. : Pl.

manipulus (**maniplus** in poets), ī, *m.*
[manus and root of pleō], *a handful,* esp.
of hay, etc. **1.** Lit. : Varr., Verg. **2.**
Milit. (fr. the use of a bundle of hay on a
pole as a flag) : *a company, maniple of foot
soldiers* (one third of a cohort) : Pl., Caes.,
Ov., etc. ; laxare, Caes. ; ad signa manipulos continere, Caes. Also of non-
Roman troops : Liv. Comic. : *a gang :
furum,* Ter.

Manliūs, a, the name of a Roman gens ;
esp. **I.** M. Manlius Capitolinus (consul,
B.C. 392), *who saved the Capitol in the Gallic
invasion.* **II.** T. Manlius Torquatus (consul, B.C. 340), *famous for his strict military discipline ;* **Manliānus**, a, um.

mannulus, ī, *m.* [dim. mannus], *a little
(Gallic) pony :* Mart., Plin. Ep.

mannus, ī, *m.* [a Celtic word], *a small (Gallic)
horse, a cob :* Lucr., Hor., Ov., Sen. Ep.

Mannus, ī, *m. a god of the ancient Germans,
son of Tuisto.*

mānō, āre [perh. *cf.* madeō], *to trickle, drop,
flow.* **1.** Lit. : omni corpore sudor,
Enn. ; e toto corpore sudor, Lucr. ; toto
corpore sudor, Verg. ; tepidae manant ex
arbore guttae, Ov. ; lacrima, Hor. Of portents : simulacra multo sudore, Cic. ; signa
cruore, Liv. Of a weapon : cultrum man-
antem cruore, Liv. With *Intern.* Acc. :
lacrimas marmora, Ov. Poet. : poëtica
mella, Hor. **2.** Transf. **a.** Of non-liquid
substances : *to stream, spread :* sonitus per
auris, Lucr. ; aër, qui per maria manat,
Cic. ; alvei manantes per latera, Tac. **b.**
Of abstract things : *to spread :* malum
manaret in dies latius, Cic. , manat totā
urbe rumor, Liv. Esp. of origin : peccata
ex vitiis manant, Cic. ; ab Aristippo Cyrenaica philosophia manavit, Cic. Also (fr.
idea of an overflow) *to flow away* (and so
be forgotten) : omne supervacuum pleno
de pectore manat, Hor.

mānsiō, ōnis, *f.* [maneō], *a staying, remaining.* **1.** Lit. : Lemni, Ter. ; Formiis,
Cic. Ep. : in vitā, Cic. **2.** Transf. *a place
of abode :* pecorum, Plin. Esp. *a stopping-
place :* Suet. ; hence also *a day's journey :*
octo mansionibus distat, Plin. [It. *magi-
one ;* Fr. *maison.*]

mānsitō, āre [freq. maneō], *to stay, dwell
habitually :* sub eodem tecto, Tac.

mānsuē-faciō, facere, fēcī, factum. Pass.
mānsuēfīō, fieri, factus [mānsuēs faciō], *to
make tame, to tame.* **1.** Lit. : uri mansue-
fieri (non) possunt, Caes. **2.** Transf. :
a quibus (nos) mansuefacti et exculti, Cic. :
plebem, Liv. ; ferum ingenium, Suet.

mānsuēs, uis and uētis, *adj.* [manus, sueō
suēscō], *tame, mild, etc. :* Cato, Varr.
Transf. : Pl.

mānsuēscō, suēscere, suēvī, suētum [manus
suēscō ; lit. *to become accustomed to the
hand*]. **A.** Intrans. **1.** Lit. *to become
or grow tame :* ferae, Luc. **2.** Transf. :
to grow gentle, mild, soft : nesciaque humanis precibus mansuescere corda, Verg.
B. Trans. *to tame :* animalia, Varr. ;
fructūs feros, Lucr. (*v.* also mānsuētus.)

mānsuētē, *adv. gently, mildly :* Cic., Liv.

mānsuētus, a, um. **I.** *Part.* mānsuēscō
II. Adj. : *tame.* **1.** Lit. : Varr. ; sus

Liv. **2.** Transf. *tame, mild, gentle :* illud quaero, cur tam subito mansuetus in senatu fuerit, cum in edictis tam fuisset ferus, Cic. ; malum, Liv. ; amor, Prop. ; litora, Prop. *Comp. :* Musae, Cic. ; ira, Ov. *Sup. :* Cic.

mānsuētūdō, inis, *f.* [mānsuētus], *tameness.* Transf. *mildness, gentleness :* clementiā ac mansuetudine in aliquem uti, Caes. ; imperi, Cic.

mānsus, a, um, *Part.* mandō ; in *Neut.*, of maneō.

mantēle, is, *n.* [manus tergeō], *a towel, napkin :* tonsis mantelia villis, Verg.

mantēlum and **mantellum**, i, *n.* [*dim.* mantum, *a cloak*], *a cloak.* Transf. : nec subdolis mendaciis mihi usquam mantelum est meis, Pl. [Fr. *manteau.*]

mantica, ae, *f.* [mantum ; *v.* mantēlum], *a knapsack :* Hor. Prov. : sed non videmus, manticae quid in tergo est (i.e. our own failings), Cat.

manticinor, āre [μάντις, canō], *to play the diviner :* Pl.

mantō, āre [*freq.* maneō]. **A.** Intrans. *to stay, remain, wait :* Pl. **B.** Trans. *to wait for :* aliquem, Pl.

Mantō, ūs, *f.* **I.** *a prophetess, daughter of Tiresias.* **II.** *an Italian nymph who had the gift of prophecy, mother of Ocnus, the founder of Mantua.*

manuālis, e, *adj.* [manus], *that can be held in or that fills the hand :* saxa, Tac.

manubiae, ārum, *f. pl.* [perh. fr. manus and habeō], *money obtained from the sale of booty.* **1.** Lit. : Cic., Liv., etc. **2.** Transf. *proceeds of robbery :* Cic., Suet.

manubiālis, e, *adj.* [manubiae], *derived from the sale of booty :* Suet.

manubiārius, a, um [manubiae], *bringing in booty.* Transf. : amicus, Pl.

manūbrium, i, *n.* [manus], *a handle, hilt, haft :* Cic., Juv. Prov. : eximere alicui e manu manubrium, Pl.

manufestārius, a, um [manifestus], *plain, evident :* fur, Pl.

manulea, ae, *f.* (**manuleus**, i, *m.* Acc.) [manus], *a long sleeve reaching to the hand* = manica : Pl.

manuleārius, i, *m.* [manulea], *a maker of sleeves or muffs :* Pl.

manuleātus, a, um [manulea], *with long sleeves :* tunica, Pl. ; homo, Suet.

manūmissiō, ōnis, *f.* [manū mittō], *the freeing of a slave :* Cic., Plin. Ep.

manū-mittō (better as two words), mittere, misi, missum, lit. *to let go from the hand ;* hence, *to set at liberty, to emancipate, manumit a slave :* servos, Cic. ; manu vero cur miserit, Cic. ; Pl. ; Liv.

manu-pretium (later **manip-**), i, *n. a workman's* or *artist's pay, wages.* **1.** Lit. : Pl., Liv. **2.** Transf. *pay, reward :* manupretium perditae civitatis, Cic. In *pl.* : Sen. Ep.

manus, ūs, *f.* [*cf.* Gk. μάρη, εὐμαρής, Lat. ānsa], *a hand.* **1.** Lit. **a.** In gen. : Pl., Cic., Verg., etc. **b.** Of direction or nearness : est ad hanc manum sacellum, Ter. ; a laevā manu conspicienda, Ov. ; prae manu, *at hand*, Pl. ; ad manum esse, *to be at hand*, Liv. ; in manibus nostris hostes

videbantur, Caes. ; proelium in manus facere (i.e. at close quarters), Sall. **c.** Phr. (in Lit. or Transf. sense) : est in manibus oratio (i.e. still well known), Cic. ; in manu (or manibus) habere, *to have in hand* (i.e. to be occupied with), Cic. ; inter manūs aliquid habere, Plin. Ep. ; esse inter manūs (i.e. evident), Verg. ; manu tenere (i.e. to know for certain), Cic. ; manibus pedibusque aliquid facere (i.e. with might and main), Ter. ; per manūs tradere (i.e. to hand down from father to son), Liv. ; manūs dare, *to give way :* Caes. ; do manūs scientiae, Hor. ; aequis manibus or aequā manu (i.e. with equal advantage), Sall., Tac. ; manūs tollere, *to raise the hands in wonder*, Cic. ; alicui *or* ad aliquem tendere manūs (i.e. to offer assistance), Caes., Cic. **2.** Transf. **A.** Of force, effort, etc. **a.** In gen. : *main-force, prowess, vigour, effort :* ne usu manuque reliquorum opinionem fallerent, Caes. ; manu fortissimus, Liv. ; manu promptus, Sall. ; tela manu miseri iactabant invita Teucri, Verg. **b.** *force, violence, fighting, close combat :* res venit ad manūs atque ad pugnam, Cic. ; Liv. ; conserere manum, Cic., Liv. ; conferre manum, Verg., Liv. ; manum committere Teucris, Verg. ; manu capere urbes, Sall. ; per manūs libertatem retinere, Sall. **B.** *power* (physical or in gen.) : in manu esse mihi, Pl. ; suum familiarem ereptum e manibus hostium, Caes. ; emissus e manibus Hannibal, Liv. ; victoria in manu nobis est, Sall. ; haec non sunt in nostrā manu, Cic. ; neque mihi in manu, qualis Iugurtha foret, Sall. Esp. *the legal power of husband, master, etc.* : in manum venire, Cic. ; feminas in manu esse parentium, fratrum, virorum, Liv. ; servos manu mittere, Cic., Liv. **C.** *the work of the hand.* **a.** *work* (esp. artistic or artificial), *labour :* manus extrema *or* ultima (i.e. the finishing touch), Cic., Verg. ; oppidum et naturā loci et manu munitum, Caes. ; Cic. ; artificumque manūs inter se, Verg. ; manum non vertere (i.e. not to take the slightest pains), Cic. **b.** *labour*, i.e. workmen : nos aera, manūs, navalia demus, Verg. **c.** *handwriting :* manum suam cognovit, Cic. Perh. also in, servus a manu (i.e. amanuensis, secretary), Suet. **D.** *a body, company, corps, detachment.* **a.** Of soldiers : Caes., Liv., etc. **b.** Of others (mostly in a contemptuous sense) : coniuratorum, Cic. ; purpuratorum et satellitum, Liv. ; iuvenum, Verg. ; clientium, Suet. **E.** Applied to **a.** an elephant's *trunk :* Cic. **b.** *a grappling iron :* ferreae manūs, Caes., Liv. **c.** *a thrust or hit* in fencing : Quint. [It. Sp. *mano ;* Fr. *main.*]

mānus, old Lat. = *bonus.*

mapālia, ium, *n. pl.* [an African word]. **I.** *African huts, cottages :* Sall., Liv. **II.** *an African village, kraal :* Verg.

mappa, ae, *f.* [an African word], *a napkin, table-napkin.* **1.** Lit. : Hor., Juv. **2.** Transf. *a napkin or handkerchief* (used in starting races in the Circus) : Juv., Suet. [Fr. *nappe.*]

Marathōn, ōnis, *f. a village on the eastern coast of Attica, famed for the victory gained*

near it by Miltiades over the Persians,
B.C. 490 ; **Marathōnius,** a, um.

Marcellus, I, *m. a Roman cognomen in the plebeian gens Claudia.* Esp. **I.** M. Claudius Marcellus, *the first to gain an advantage over Hannibal, and the taker of Syracuse* (ob. B.C. 208) ; **Marcellia** (or **-ĕa**), ōrum, *n. pl., a festival in honour of the Marcelli in Syracuse.* **II.** M. Claudius Marcellus, *nephew of Augustus, whose early death is referred to in the Aeneid ;* **Marcelliānus,** a, um.

marceō, ēre, *to wither, droop, flag.* **1.** Lit.: annis corpus, Lucr. ; marcent luxuriā vino et epulis per totam hiemem confecti, Liv. **2.** Transf. **a,** *to slacken off, be slack* (of appetite) : marcentem (convivam) recreare, Hor. **b,** *enervating :* marcentem pacem nutrierunt, Tac.

marcēscō, ere [marceō], *to begin to wither, flag, droop.* Transf. *to grow enervated :* vino, Ov. ; desidiā, Liv. ; otia per somnos, Ov. ; otio civitas, Liv.

marcidus, a, um [marceō], *withered, flagging, drooping.* **1.** Lit.: lilia, Ov. **2.** Transf. *languid, enervated :* somno aut libidinosis vigiliis, Tac.

Marcius, a, *the name of a Roman gens.* Esp. Ancus Marcius, *the fourth king of Rome.* Hence, **Marcius,** a, um, and **Marciānus,** a, um.

marcor, ōris, *m.* [marceō], *a withering, rottenness.* **1.** Lit.: Sen., Plin. **2.** Transf.: Sen., Stat.

marculus, I, *m. a small hammer :* Plin., Mart.

mare, is, *n.* (ABL. *sing.* usually mari, but mare, Lucr., Ov., *etc.*) *the sea.* **1.** Lit. **a.** In gen.: infidum, Pl. ; ventosum, Hor. ; vastissimum, Cic. ; vastum atque apertum, Caes. ; terrā marique, Liv., etc. ; mari atque (ac, Liv. ; et, Nep.) terrā, Sall. In apposition with Oceanus : proximus mare Oceanum in Andibus hiemarat, Caes. Prov. : **i.** maria et montis polliceri (i.e. to make extravagant promises), Sall. **ii.** in mare fundere aquas, Ov. **iii.** mare caelo miscere (i.e. to make a great bluster), Juv. (taken fr. Verg.'s maria omnia caelo miscere). **iv.** terrā marique (i.e. at all hazards), Juv. **b.** Of some particular sea : mare nostrum, *the Mediterranean,* Caes. ; superum, *the Adriatic,* Cic. ; inferum, *the Tyrrhenian Sea,* Cic. **2.** Transf. **a.** *seawater, salt-water :* Chium maris expers, perh. *unmixed Chian wine,* Hor. (v. expers). **b.** Of the air : id omne aëris in magnum fertur mare, Lucr. [Fr. *mer.*]

Marea and **Mareōta,** ae, *f. a town and lake in Egypt, not far from Alexandria ;* **Mareōticus,** a, um, *Mareotic or Egyptian,* and **Mareōtis,** idis, *f. adj.*

margarīta, ae, *f.* and **margarītum,** I, *n.* (Tac.) [an Indian word borrowed through the Greek μαργαρίτης], *a pearl :* Cic.

marginō, āre [margō], *to provide with a border,* e.g. a kerbstone : vias, Liv.

margō, inis, *m.* and *f. an edge, brink, margin.* **1.** Lit.: flumen marginibus lapideis, Varr. ; terrarum, Ov. ; fontis, Ov. ; libri, Juv. **2.** Transf. *a boundary, frontier :* imperii, Ov. ; cenae (the side-dishes), Juv.

Marica, ae, *f. a Latin nymph, the mother of*

Latinus ; after whom the Lake of Minturnae was named Palus Maricae *or simply* Marica.

marīnus, a, um [mare], *of the sea, sea-, marine :* marini terrenique umores, Cic. ; fremitu marino, Verg. ; Venus, Nympha, Cat. ; Hor. *Neut.* as Noun : Quint.

marisca, ae, *f. an inferior kind of fig :* Cato, Mart. Transf. *the piles :* tumidae, Juv.

marītālis, e, *adj.* [maritus], *of married people, matrimonial, nuptial :* vestis, Ov. ; capistrum, Juv.

marītimus (older **-tumus**), a, um [mare]. **1.** Lit. **a.** *of the sea, sea- :* fluctus, Pl. ; **b.** *on the sea, seafaring, maritime :* ora, Caes., Cic., Liv. ; urbes, Cic. ; provincia, agri, Liv. ; cursus, Cic. ; vita, Pl. ; officium, Caes. ; homines maritimi, Cic. ; civitates, Caes. ; imperium, Cic. ; bellum, Sall. ; naves, Liv. *Neut. pl.* as Noun, **maritima,** ōrum, *the sea-coast :* Cic. Ep., Liv. **2.** Transf. *changeable, like the sea :* mores, Pl.

marītō, āre [maritus], *to marry ; give in marriage.* **1.** Lit.: lex de maritandis ordinibus (i.e. forcing the different orders to marry), Suet. ; filiam, Suet. ; maritandum principem suaderent, Tac. **2.** Transf. Of vines : *to wed* (i.e. *to fasten to another tree*) : adultā vitium propagine altas maritat populos, Hor. [Fr. *marier.*]

marītus, a, um, *of marriage, matrimonial, conjugal, nuptial.* **1.** Lit.: foedus, Ov. ; lex, Hor. ; vagabatur per maritas domos, Liv. **2.** Transf. Of plants : *wedded,* i.e. *trained to grow together :* arbores, Cato ; Cat. As Noun **A. maritus,** I, *m. a married man, husband.* **1.** Lit.: Pl., Cic., Verg., etc. **2.** Transf. **a.** *a lover, suitor :* aegram nulli quondam flexere mariti, Verg. ; Prop. **b.** Of animals : Verg., Hor. **B. marita,** ae, *f. a married woman, a wife :* Hor., Ov. Comic. of a dowry, *accompanied by a wife :* Pl. [Fr. *mari.*]

Marius, a, *the name of a Roman gens.* C. Marius, *conqueror of Jugurtha and of the Cimbri and Teutoni ;* **Marius,** a, um, **Mariānus,** a, um ; **Mariāni,** ōrum, *m. pl. his partisans.*

Marmaridēs, ae, *m. an African* (Ov.).

marmor, oris, *n.* [Gk. μάρμαρος], *marble.* **1.** Lit.: Cic., Verg., etc. In *pl. :* Hor., Quint., etc. **2.** Transf. **a.** *a piece of wrought marble ;* hoc tamen in tumuli marmore carmen erit, Ov. ; incisa notis marmora publicis, Hor. ; Sen. Ep., etc. **b.** *a marble pavement* (*in pl.*) *:* Mart., Juv. **c.** *stone* in gen.: Ov. **d.** *the bright smooth surface of the sea :* Enn., Lucr., Verg., [Fr. *marbre.*]

marmorārius, a, um [marmor], *of marble :* faber, Sen. Ep. *Masc.* as Noun, *a marble-mason :* Sen. Ep.

marmoreus, a, um [marmor], *made or consisting of marble, marble.* **1.** Lit.: signum, Cic. ; facere or ponere aliquem marmoreum, Verg., Hor. **2.** Transf. *like marble, marble :* pectus, Lucil. ; color, Lucr. ; cervix, Verg. ; pedes, Ov. ; aequor (the surface of the sea), Verg. ; gelu, Ov.

Marō, ōnis, *m. the cognomen of the poet Vergil ;* **Marōnēus, Marōniānus,** a, um.

Marōnēa or **Marōnia,** ae, *f. a town of Thrace, famous for its wine ;* **Marōnēus,** a, um.

Marpēsius (Marpēssius), a, um, *belonging to Marpessus* (a mountain in Paros, q.v.); *Marpessian, Parian.*

marra, ae, *f. a sort of hoe, a weeding-hook* : Juv.

Mārs, tis, *m.* [orig. Māvors, Osc. Māmers]. **1.** Lit. *the god of agriculture, pasture and of war ; as father of Romulus, he was progenitor of the Roman people* : Mars pater, Cato, Cic., Liv. In poetry he is mostly identified with Gk. Ares ; **Mārtius** (poet. also **Māvortius**), a, um, *of Mars:* campus, legio, Cic. ; with or without mensis, *the month of March* : Idūs Martiae, Cic. ; also **Mārtiālis**, e, *adj.* ; as Noun, *a priest of Mars* or *a soldier in the legio Martia.* **2.** Transf. **a.** *war, battle : the art of war* : Martem accendere cantu, Verg. ; apertus, Ov. ; equitem suo alienoque Marte pugnare, Liv. **b.** Mars forensis, Ov. Phr.: suo (nostro, vestro) Marte, *by one's own exertions:* rex ipse suo Marte res suas recuperavit, Cic. ; aequo Marte (on an equal footing) : parati prope aequo Marte ad dimicandum, Caes. ; aequato Marte, Liv. ; communis Mars belli, Cic. Ep., Liv. ; varia belli fortuna ancepsque Mars fuit, Liv. ; verso Marte, Liv. ; incerto Marte, Tac. **c.** *the planet Mars* : Cic. [From Martis dies, It. *martedì* ; Fr. *mardi*.]

Marsi, ōrum, *m. pl. the Marsians.* **I.** *an ancient and very warlike nation of central Italy ; the chief opponents of the Romans in the Social War* ; **Marsus, Marsicus**, a, um, *Marsian.* **II.** *a people of Germany.*

marsuppium, i, *n.* [μαρσύπιον], *a pouch, purse:* Pl.

Marsyās and Marsya, ae, *m.* **I.** *a satyr who challenged Apollo to a trial of skill on the flute ; he was vanquished and flayed alive.* There was a statue of Marsyas in the forum at Rome, near which business was transacted (Hor.). **II.** *a river in Phrygia.*

Mārtiālis, is, *m.* : M. Valerius, *a native of Bilbilis, in Spain, an epigrammatic poet under Domitian, Nerva, and Trajan ; his works are extant.*

Mārticola, ae, *m.* [Mārs colō], *a worshipper of Mars* : Ov.

Mārtigena, ae, *m.* [Mārs and gen in gignō], *begotten by Mars* : epith. of Romulus : Ov.

mās, maris, *m. a male* (opp. femina) : Cic., Hor., etc. As *Adj.* : *male.* **1.** Lit. : Pl., Cic., Hor. Of plants : ure maris olea, barren, Ov. **2.** Transf. *masculine, manly:* male mas, Cat. ; maribus Curiis, Hor. ; animi, Hor. ; marem strepitum fidis intendisse Latinae, Pers.

māsculīnus, a, um [māsculus], *male, masculine.* **1.** Lit. : sexus, Plin. ; membra, Phaedr. **2.** In gramm. : *masculine:* Quint.

māsculus, a, um [*dim.* mās], *male, masculine.* **1.** Lit. : genus, Phaedr. ; Mart. As Noun, *a male* : Pl., Liv. **2.** Transf. *manly, vigorous:* proles, Hor. ; Sappho, Hor. ; tura, Verg. [It. *maschio* ; Fr. *mâle.*]

massa, ae, *f.* [μᾶζα], *a lump, mass* : picis, Verg. ; lactis coacti, Ov. Esp. of metals : versantque tenaci forcipe massam, Verg. ; chalybis, Ov. Comic. of money : Pl.

Massicus, a, um [Massicus mons], *Massic :* vinum, Hor. ; Verg. Also without vinum : Hor.

Massȳlī, ōrum, *m. pl. a people of E. Numidia ;* **Massȳlus, Massȳlius**, a, um.

mastīgia, ae, *m.* [μαστιγίας], *a whip-needer, scoundrel* : Pl., Ter.

mastrūca, ae, *f.* [a Sardin. word], *a sheep-skin, a skin* : Cic. As a term of abuse : *sheepskin, ninny* : Pl.

mastrūcātus, a, um [mastrūca], *clothed in a sheepskin* : Cic.

matara, ae (Caes.), and **mataris**, is (Liv.), *f.* [a Celtic word], *a javelin or lance.*

matella, ae, *f.* [*cf.* matula], *a pot* : Pl., Cato, Mart.

matelliō, ōnis, *m.* [*dim.* matula], *a pot, vessel* : Corinthius, Cic.

māter, tris, *f.* [*cf.* Gk. μήτηρ, Dor. μάτηρ], *a mother.* **1.** Lit. : Pl., Cic., Ov., etc. Of animals : Varr., Verg., etc. Of trees : Verg. **2.** Transf. **a.** mater familias, *the mistress of a household* (v. familia) : also in *pl. mothers, matrons* : Verg., Liv., etc. **b.** Of goddesses : Magna Mater *or* Mater alone (also called Rhea or Cybele), Cic., Verg., Liv. ; Flora, Lucr. ; Vesta, Verg. ; Matuta, Liv. ; exercitum Diis Manibus Matrique Terrae deberi, Liv. **c.** As respectful address to priestesses or aged women : Pl. **d.** Of one's native-land : Verg., Liv. **e.** *a producing cause, origin, source*, etc. : mater omnium bonarum artium sapientia est, Cic. ; Hor. ; Quint. [It. and Sp. *madre*, Fr. *mère.*]

mātercula, ae, *f.* [*dim.* māter], *little mother, poor mother* : Pl., Cic., Hor.

māterfamiliās, v. familia.

māteria, ae, and less freq. **māteriēs**, ēi, *f.* [cogn. with Gk. δέμω]. **1.** Lit. **a.** *the materials, stuff, matter*, of which any thing is composed : Pl. ; materia rerum, ex quā et in quā sunt omnia, Cic. ; materiam superabat opus, Ov. **b.** *the wood of a tree, timber* for building : (freq. in Caes.) : in eam insulam materiam, calcem, etc. convexit, Cic. ; Caes. ; Liv. ; Tac. **2.** Transf. **a.** *subject-matter, subject, theme* : materiam artis eam dicimus in quā omnis ars versatur, Cic. ; crescit mihi materies, Cic. ; materia aequa viribus, Hor. ; Plin. Ep., etc. **b.** *a cause, occasion* : segetem ac materiem suae gloriae, Cic. ; Sall. ; Liv. ; criminandi, Liv. ; materiam praebere criminibus, Liv. ; Tac. **c.** *natural abilities, talent, disposition* : fac, fuisse in isto, C. Laeli, M. Catonis materiem atque indolem, Cic. ; non sum materiā digna perire tuā, Ov. [Fr. *matière* ; Port. *madera*, timber.]

māteriārius, a, um [māteria], *of timber :* fabrica, Plin. As Noun, **māteriārius**, i, *m. a timber-merchant* : Pl.

māteriātus, a, um [māteria], *timbered :* aedes male materiatae, Cic.

māteriēs, v. māteria.

māterior, āri [māteria], *to procure timber :* Caes.

materis, v. matara.

māternus, a, um [māter], *of a mother, a mother's, maternal* : animus, Ter. ; sanguis, Enn., Cic. ; tempora (i.e. time of pregnancy), Ov. ; Caesar ; cingens māternā

tempora myrto, Verg. ; materno veniens ab
avo Cyllenia proles, Verg.

mātertera, ae, *f.* [māter with comparative
suffix ; *a kind of mother*], *a mother's sister*,
an aunt on the mother's side : Pl., Cic., Ov.

mathēmaticus, a, um [μαθηματικός], *Masc.*
as Noun. **a.** *a mathematician :* Cic., Sen.
Ep. **b.** *an astrologer :* Tac., Juv. *Fem.* as
Noun. **a.** *mathematics :* Sen. Ep. **b.** *astrology :* Suet.

Matinus, i, *m. a mountain in Apulia, near
which Horace was born ; famous for honey ;*
Matinus, a, um.

Mātrālia, ium, *n. pl.* [māter], festa, Ov. ;
or simply Matralia, *the festival of Mater
Matuta* (on June 11th), Ov.

mātricīda, ae, *m.f.* [māter caedō], *a mother's
murderer, a matricide :* Cic. Ep., Suet.

mātricīdium, i, *n.* [mātricīda], *the murder of
one's mother, matricide :* Cic.

mātrimōnium, i, *n.* [māter], *wedlock, marriage, matrimony.* **1.** L i t. : ire in matrimonium, Pl. ; in matrimonium ducere aliquam, Cic. ; in matrimonium dare alicui
suam filiam, Caes. ; Pl. ; in matrimonium
conlocare, Cic. ; matrimonio uxorem exigere, Pl. ; matrimonio exturbare, Tac. ;
dimittere e matrimonio, Suet. **2.** T r a n s f.
in *pl. : wives :* matrimonia ac pecunias
hostium praedae destinare, Tac.

mātrimus, a, um [māter], *having a mother
still alive :* Liv., Tac.

mātrix, icis, *f.* [māter], *a female animal kept
for breeding.* **1.** L i t. : Varr. **2.** T r a n s f.
a. *the womb :* Sen. **b.** Of plants : *the
parent stem :* Suet.

mātrōna, ae, *f.* [māter], *a married woman,
wife, matron.* **1.** P r o p. : Pl., Verg., Liv.,
etc. **2.** Esp. *women of quality, ladies :*
Enn. ; ubi istas videas summo genere natas
summatis matronas, Pl. ; ut matrona
meretrici dispar erit, Hor. ; nec matronis
solum sed omnis ordinis feminis, Liv.,
Cic. ; matrona Iuno, Hor.

mātrōnālis, e, *adj.* [mātrōna], *of a married
woman or matron, womanly, matronly :*
oblitae decoris matronalis, Liv. ; genae,
Ov. As Noun, **Mātrōnālia**, ium, *n. pl.
a festival celebrated by matrons in honour of
Mars, on the first of March,* Ov.

matta, ae, *f. a mat made of rushes :* scirpea
matta, Ov. [Fr. *natte.*]

mattea or **mattya**, ae, *f.* [ματτύα], *a dainty
dish, dainty, delicacy :* Sen., Suet.

matula, ae, *f. a vessel, pot* for liquids : Pl.
As a term of abuse : Pl.

mātūrātē, *adv. betimes, quickly :* Pl.

mātūrē, *adv.* **I.** *seasonably, opportunely, at
the right time :* Pl., Caes., Cic. **II.** *betimes,
promptly, speedily :* Pl., Cic., Sall. *Comp. :*
Caes., Cic., Juv., etc. *Sup.* mātūrissimē,
Cato, Cic., and mātūrrimē : Caes., Sall.
III. *prematurely :* Pl., Nep.

mātūrescō, mātūrēscere, mātūruī [mātūrus],
to become ripe, ripen, mature. **1.** L i t. :
frumenta, Caes. ; partus, Cic. ; nubilibus
maturuit annis, Ov. **2.** T r a n s f. : virtutes alicuius, Plin. Ep.

mātūritās, ātis, *f.* [mātūrus], *ripeness,
maturity.* **1.** L i t. : frugum, Cic. ; neque
multum a maturitate aberant (frumenta),
Caes. **2.** T r a n s f. **a.** *the full* or *right time,*

perfection, ripeness, maturity : maturitates
gignendi, Cic. ; aetatis ad prudentiam, Cic.
Ep. ; maturitas Galli, Tac. In *pl. :* maturitates temporum, *the maturing of the
seasons,* Cic. **b.** *consummation, height :*
audaciae maturitas in nostri consulatūs
tempus erupit, Cic. ; si maturitas temporum exspectata foret, Liv. **c.** *promptness,
expedition :* poenae, Suet.

mātūrō, āre [mātūrus]. **A.** T r a n s : *to make
ripe, ripen, to bring to maturity.* **1.** L i t. :
uvas, Tib. ; omnia maturata, Cic. **2.**
T r a n s f. **a.** *to hasten, accelerate :* iter,
Caes. ; coepta, Liv. ; fugam, Verg. ; mortem
alicui, Cic. With *Inf. :* Pl., Caes, etc. **b.**
to do prematurely, to be too quick in doing :
ni Catilina maturasset signum dare, Sall.
B. I n t r a n s. (or *sc. Inf.*) *to make haste,
hasten :* iussis ceteris quantum possent
maturare sequi, Liv. ; successor tuus non
potest ita maturare ut etc., Cic. ; maturavit
Romanus ne etc., Liv. *Impers. Pass. :*
maturato opus esse, *that no time was to be
lost,* Liv. ; Sall.

mātūrus, a, um (*Sup.* usually mātūrissimus ;
less freq. mātūrrimus, Tac.) [fr. root of
mānus, *cf.* 'in good time'], *ripe, mature.*
1. L i t. **a.** poma, Cic. ; uva, Verg. ;
seges matura messi, Liv. **b.** Of living
beings : aetas, Verg. ; aevi maturus, Verg. ;
filia matura viro, Verg. ; progenies matura
militiae, Liv. ; Juv. **2.** T r a n s f. **a.** Of
morning-light : maturā iam luce, Verg.
b. *matured, mellow* (of the mind) : Thucydides si posterius fuisset, multo ma-
turior ac mitior fuisset, Cic. ; annis
gravis atque animi maturus Alotes, Verg.
c. *ripe,* i.e. *ready to be seized :* omnia
matura sunt : victoria, praeda, laus, Sall.
d. *seasonable, opportune, at the right time :*
maturam oppetere mortem, Cic. ; scribendi
tempus maturius, Cic. Ep. ; tempus anni
maturum ad navigandum, Liv. **e.** *early,
speedy, quick :* hiemos, Caes. ; iudicium,
Cic. **f.** perh. *ripening :* glaebasque iacentis
coquat maturis solibus aestas, Verg. [Sp.
maduro ; old Fr. *meür,* Fr. *mûr.*]

Mātūta, ae, *f.* **I.** *the goddess of the dawn.*
II. *a goddess, identified with Ino Leucothea.*

mātūtinus, a, um [*cf.* māne], *of the early
morning, morning- :* tempora, Cic. Ep. ;
frigora, Hor. ; equi, Ov. ; harena (i.e.
the morning-hunt in the circus), Ov. ;
pater (i.e. Janus), Hor. Equiv. to *adv.*
Aeneas se matutinus agebat, Verg. [It.
mattino and *mattinata ;* Sp. *mañana ;* Fr.
matin, matinée.]

Mauri, ōrum, *m. pl. the Moors, a people of
N.W. Africa ;* **Maurus**, a, um, *Moorish* or
African ; **Mauritānia (Maurētānia)**, ae,
f. their country ; **Maurūsiacus, Maurū-
sius**, a, um ; **Maurūsii**, ōrum, *m. pl. the
Mauretanians.*

Mausōlēus, a, um [Mausōlus], *of Mausolus,
Mausolean :* sepulcrum, or alone **Mausō-
lēum**, i, *n.* [Μαυσωλεῖον], *the magnificent
tomb erected in memory of Mausolus by his
wife Artemisia :* Plin. T r a n s f. in gen. *a
splendid sepulchre, mausoleum :* Caesarum,
Suet.

māvolō, *v.* **mālō**.

Māvors, Māvortius, *v.* **Mārs**.

maxilla, ae, f. [dim. māla], the jaw-bone, jaw (strictly, the lower jaw : cf. mala): Cic.; maxillae superiores, Plin. [It. mascella ; Sp. megilla ; Fr. mâchelière.]

maximē (older **maxumē**), adv. in the highest degree, most, very, extremely, very much, especially, particularly. **A.** Unstrengthened. **a.** With verbs : Pl., Caes., Cic., etc. **b.** With Adj. or Adv. (often giving a superlative force, esp. to those that have no regular Superlative) : loca maxime frumentaria, Caes. ; Cic. ; Quint., etc. Occ. with a Superlative : by far : quae maxime liberalissima, Cic. Ep. **c.** With Nouns and Pronouns : most, especially, particularly : supplementum maxime iaculatorum, Liv. ; quae ratio poetas, maximeque Homerum impulit ut etc., Cic. ; multa alia vidit sed illud maxime, Cic. In elliptical relative clause : tam enim sum amicus rei publicae quam qui maxime, Cic. Ep. ; grata ea res ut quae maxime senatui unquam fuit, Liv. **B.** Strengthened. **a.** With unus, unus omnium, omnium, multo, vel, and other particles : hoc uno praestamus vel maxime feris, Cic. **b.** With quam = as much as possible : ut dicatis quam maxime ad veritatem accommodate, Cic. **c.** With nunc, nuper, tum, cum : just, precisely, exactly : cum iis, quos nuper maxime liberaverat, Caes. ; haec cum maxime loqueretur, sex lictores eum circumsistunt valentissimi, Cic. ; (v. also cum) : consulem tum maxime res agentem a bello avocare, Liv. So in the phr. cum . . . tum maxime, but more especially : cum saepe, tum maxime bello Punico, Cic. ; Pl. ; Liv. **d.** In phr. of proportion : ut quisque maxime . . . ita maxime (or potissimum or minime) : ut quisque maxime ad suum commodum refert quaecumque agit, ita minime est vir bonus, Cic. **C.** Colloq. to denote emphatic assent : certainly, by all means, very well, yes : Ar. iace, pater, talos, ut porro nos iaciamus. De. maxume, Pl.

maximitās, ātis, f. [maximus], enormous greatness, magnitude : Lucr.

maxmopere, v. magnopere.

maximus (maxum-), a, um, v. magnus.

mazonomus, i, m. or **mazonomon**, i, n. [μαζονόμος (sc. κύκλος)], a dish, charger : Hor.

meāmet, ABL. sing. f. of meus, strengthened by -met, v. meus.

meāpte, ABL. sing. f. of meus, strengthened by -pte : causā, Ter.

meātus, ūs, m. [meō], a going, motion. **1.** Lit.: solis lunaeque meatus, Lucr. ; caeli, Verg. ; aquilae, Tac. ; animae, Plin. Ep. **2.** Transf. course, channel : of stars : Luc. ; of a river : Danuvius in Ponticum sex meatibus erumpit, Tac.

mecastor, v. ēcastor.

mēchanicus, i, m. [μηχανικός], a mechanic, engineer : Lucil., Suet.

mēd = mē : Pl.

meddix, v. medix.

Mēdēa, ae, f. d. of Aeetes, king of Colchis, who assisted Jason in obtaining the golden fleece, and accompanied him to Greece. When Jason afterwards repudiated her in order to marry Creüsa, she killed their children ;

Mōdōis, idis, f. adj. magical : herbae, Ov.

medēns, entis. **I.** Part. medeor. **II.** Noun, a physician, perh. only in pl. : Lucr., Ov.

medeor, ēri, to heal, cure. **1.** Lit. : aegrescit medendo, Verg. ; medendi ars, Ov. With DAT.: morbo, Cic. Prov.: cum capiti mederi debeam, reduviam curo, Cic. **2.** Transf.: adflictae rei publicae, Cic. ; inopiae rei frumentariae, Caes. ; Tac. With Acc.: cupiditates, Ter.

Mēdī, ōrum, m. pl. the Medes, a people of Asia ; poet. also for the Assyrians, Persians, and Parthians ; **Mēdus**, a, um ; **Mēdia**, ae, f. their country ; **Mēdicus**, a, um.

mediastīnus, i, m. [medius], a drudge : Cato, Cic., Hor.

mēdica, ae, f. [Μηδική], a kind of clover introduced from Media ; lucerne : Verg.

medicābilis, e, adj. [medicor], that can be healed, curable : Ov.

medicāmen, inis, n. [medicor], a drug, remedy, medicine. **1.** Lit. **a.** In gen. : Cic., Juv., Tac. **b.** Poisonous : infusum cibo venenum, nec vim medicaminis statim intellectam, Tac. **2.** Transf. **a.** a remedy : iratae medicamina fortia praebe, Ov. **b.** a tincture, dye : Plin. Esp. a paint, wash, cosmetic : Ov.

medicāmentum, i, n. [medicor], a drug, remedy, medicine. **1.** Lit. **a.** In gen. : medicamentum alicui dare ad aquam intercutem, Cic. ; medicamentis delibutus, Cic. ; salubria, Liv. **b.** Poisonous : Varr. ; coquere medicamenta, Liv. ; also a magic potion : Pl., Ov. ; amatorium, a love-potion, philtre, Suet. **2.** Transf. **a.** a relief, antidote : multorum medicamentum laborum, Cic. **b.** Rhet. an embellishment : medicamenta fucati candoris et ruboris, Cic.

medicātus, a, um. **I.** Part. medicō. **II.** Adj. of or for healing : medicinal : aquae, Sen. ; sapor aquae, Plin. Ep. Comp. and Sup. : Plin.

medicātus, ūs, m. [medicor], a magic charm : Ov.

medicīnus, a, um [medicus], of a medicus : ars, Varr. As Noun, **medicīna**, ae, f. **A.** (sc. domus or taberna) the shop of a physician or surgeon : Pl. **B.** (sc. ars) the healing or medical science, medicine, surgery : exercere, Cic. ; facere, Phaedr. **C.** (sc. res) a remedy, medicine. **1.** Lit. : adhibere, accipere, Cic. Ep. ; facere alicui, Cic. Ep. ; huic morbo facere, Pl. **2.** Transf.: singulis medicinam consili atque orationis meae adferam, Cic. ; sed non egeo medicinā ; me ipse consolor, Cic. ; With Obj. GEN.: doloris, periculorum, etc., Cic. ; furoris, Verg. ; malorum, Ov. In pl. : Cic.

medicō, āre [medicus], to cure, steep, medicate. **a.** semina, Verg. Esp. in magic : medicatus somnus (i.e. produced by a magic charm), Ov. **b.** to poison : boletum medicatum, Suet. **c.** to colour, dye : lana fuco, Hor.

medicor, āri [medicus], to heal, cure. **1.** Lit. With DAT. : senibus anhelis, Verg. With Acc. : cuspidis ictum, Verg. **2.** Transf. : in hac re mihi, Ter. ; metum, Pl.

medicus, a, um [medeor], *of healing, healing,*
curative, medical : medicas adhibere manūs
ad vulnera, Verg. ; ars, Ov. ; vis, usus,
Plin. As Noun, **medicus**, I, *m. a medical*
man, physician, surgeon : Pl., Cic., Suet.

mediē, *adj. moderately :* Tac.

medietās, ātis. *f.* [medius], *the mean* (a word
coined hesitatingly as philos. term in *pl.* by
Cic. [Fr. *moitié*].

medimnum, i, n. (Cic.) and **medimnus**, i,
m. (Nep.) GEN. *pl.* medimnum, Cic. [μέδιμ-
νος], *a Greek bushel* (containing 6 modii).

mediocris, e, *adj.* [medius], *middling,*
moderate, ordinary, average : spatium,
Caes. ; castellum, Sall. ; copiae, Caes. ;
amicitia, ingenium, eloquentia, Cic. ; orator,
Cic. ; copiae, Caes. ; multitudo, Liv. ;
poetae, Hor. Freq. with a neg. : *not common*
or *ordinary :* non mediocris hominis haec
sunt officia, Ter. ; non mediocrem sibi diligentiam adhibendam intellegebat, Caes.; Cic.

mediocritās, ātis, *f.* [mediocris], *a middle*
state between too much and too little, a
medium, mean ; moderation. **a.** mediocritatem illam tenere, quae est inter nimium
et parum, Cic. ; aurea, Hor. : in dicendo,
Cic. In *pl. :* mediocritates illi probabant,
moderate passions, Cic. **b.** *insignificance,*
mediocrity : ingeni, Cic. ; memoriae, Quint.

mediocriter, *adv.* **I.** *moderately, ordi-*
narily, not particularly : Cic. Mostly with
negat. : *in no slight degree,* i.e. *extraordi-*
narily, considerably : Pl., Caes., Cic. **II.**
with moderation, calmly, tranquilly : aliquid
ferre, Cic. *Comp. :* mediocrius, Cic.

medioxumus, a, um [medius], *in the middle,*
middlemost : ita me dii deaeque superi atque
inferi et medioxumi, Pl.

meditāmenta, ōrum, *n. pl.* [meditor].
practice, drill : belli, Tac.

meditātē, *adv. thoughtfully, purposely :*
illorum mores perquam meditate tenes
(i.e. thoroughly), Pl. ; Sen.

meditātiō, ōnis, *f.* [meditor]. **I.** *a thinking*
over, contemplating : futuri mali, Cic. **II.**
exercise, practice, preparation : campestris,
Plin. Pan. ; multa commentatio atque
meditatio, Cic. ; obeundi sui muneris,
Cic. ; mortis, Sen. ; dicendi, Quint.

mediterrāneus, a, um [medius terra], *mid-*
land, inland : in mediterraneis regionibus,
Caes. ; homines maxime mediterranei,
Cic. ; copiae, Plin. Ep.

meditor, āri [*freq. fr.* root seen in Gk. μήδο-
μαι, and Lat. mětior ; *cf. also* modus, Gk.
μέτρον]. **I.** *to reflect on, think over,*
ponder : mecum, Pl. ; de libertate, Caes. ;
nihil aliud cogitare meditari curare, Cic.
With *Indir. Deliberative :* Pl., Cic. **II.**
to turn over in the mind, meditate, contem-
plate : cursuram ad ludos Olympios, Pl. ;
fugam, Cic. Ep. ; fugam ad legiones, Suet. ;
furtivum amorem, Verg. With *Inf. :*
Cic., Nep. **III.** *to practise, exercise oneself*
in, study : nugas, Pl. ; Demosthenes per-
fecit meditando, ut nemo planius esse locutus putaretur, Cic. ; silvestrem Musam,
Verg. ; proelia, Juv. **IV.** *Passive* in *Part.*

meditātus, a, um, *thought over, premedi-*
tated, studied : doli, Pl. ; scelus, verbum,
commentationes, Cic. ; oratio. Liv. ; Ov.,
Tac., etc.

medius, a, um [*cf.* Gk. μέσσος, μέσος]. *mid,*
middle, in the middle. **1.** Lit. (in space).
a. media regio totius Galliae, Caes. ; Cic. ;
prima leo, postrema draco, media ipsa
Chimaera, Lucr. **b.** As *Predic. Adj. : in*
the middle (of), by the middle : in colle
medio, Caes. ; in mediā insulā, Cic. ; in
medio foro, Pl. ; Cic. Ep.; in solio medius
consedit, Ov. ; solio medius consedit,
Verg. ; per medios finis proficisci, Caes. ;
medium adripere aliquem, Ter. ; Liv. ;
se mediam locavit, Verg. ; discessere omnes
medii (*from the midst*) Verg. ; in medios
hostis me immittere, Liv. **2.** Transf.
A. In time : *middle, intervening, inter-*
mediate : ultimum, proximum, medium
tempus, Cic. ; medium fuit breve tempus,
Ov. ; mediis diebus, Liv. ; aetatis mediae
vir, Phaedr. ; Cic. As *Predic. Adj. : the*
middle (of) : mediā nocte, Caes. ; mediā
aestate, Cic. ; medio aestu, Verg. ; in
medios dormire dies, Hor. ; ad medium
conversa diem (i.e. the south), Verg. Hence,
in medio maerore, Cic. ; in medio ardore
belli, Liv. ; in medio ictu, Verg. ; medium
iter tenebat, Verg. **B.** Other relations.
a. *intermediate, indifferent :* ingenium, Liv. ;
cum inter bellum et pacem medium nihil
sit, Cic. ; Liv. ; media via consili, Liv. ;
pacis eras mediusque belli, Hor. : as Noun,
media sequi, Tac. In ethics : officium
medium quiddam esse quod neque in bonis
ponatur neque in contrariis, Cic. **b.** *midd-*
ling, common, ordinary : nihil medium
sed immensa omnia volvere animo, Liv. ;
bella, Liv. ; ingenium, Tac. **c.** *undecided,*
neutral : medios esse, Cic. Ep. ; medium se
gerere, Liv. **d.** *ambiguous :* responsum,
Liv. ; *Neut. pl.* as Noun : Tac. **e.** *medi-*
ating, as a mediator : medium sese offert,
Verg. ; Iuppiter medius fratris et sororis,
Ov. **f.** *intervening* (to give trouble) :
medius occurrere, Verg. ; quos inter medius
venit furor, Verg. **g.** *half :* media pars,
Ov. *Neut.* as Noun : **medium**, i, n. *the*
middle. **1.** Lit. : in medio aedium sedens,
Liv. ; medio stans hostia ad aras, Verg. ;
Liv. ; medio sextam legionem constituit,
Tac. ; medio viae ponere, Liv. ; in medium
sarcinas coniecerant, Liv. ; in media urbis
ac forum iretur, Liv. ; medio tutissimus
ibis, Ov. ; medii cuppedo, Lucr. ; medio
caeli terraeque volat (i.e. *midway between*),
Verg. ; medio montium et paludum, Tac.
Of time : diei, Liv. ; temporis, Tac. **2.**
Transf. **a.** *the general public, the com-*
munity, publicity : in medio omnibus palma
est posita, Ter. ; ponam in medio sententias
philosophorum, Cic. ; rem in medium proferre, rem in medium vocare, Cic. ; Cic. Ep.;
iacentia verba sustulimus e medio, Cic. ;
tollere hominem de medio, Cic. ; e medio
abire or excedere, Ter. Esp. in medium,
for or *on behalf of the public :* communia
utilitates in medium adferre, Cic. ; in
medium quaerebant, *for the common good,*
Verg. ; consulere in medium, Verg. ; conferre laudem, Liv. ; bona interfectorum in
medium cedant, Tac. **b.** in medio relinquere, *to leave undecided :* tantum in
medio relinquam, Cic. [It. *mezzo,* and (in
composition) Fr. *mi.*]

medius fidius (and as one word) [for mē dius fidius (*sc.* iuvet); fidius is adj. fr. root of fidēs; dius is old NOM. *cf.* deus, diēs], *by Heaven! most certainly!* unum medius fidius tecum diem libentius posuerim, Cic. Ep.; Pl., etc.

medix, *m. an Oscan magistrate* : with the epithet tuticus, Liv.

medulla, ae, *f.* **1.** Lit. **a.** *the middle* : ventris, Pl. **b.** *the marrow* : Hor.; in *pl.* : Cic., Ov., Juv. **c.** Of plants : Plin. **2.** Transf.: medullam mihi lassitudo perbibit, Pl.; Suadae medulla (of an orator), Enn.; in medullis populi Romani ac visceribus haerebant, Cic.; haec mihi semper erunt imis infixa medullis, Ov. [It. *midolla* ; Fr. *moëlle*.]

medullitus, *adv. from the very marrow.* Varr. Comic.: aliquem amare, Pl.

medullula, ae, *f.* [*dim.* medulla], *dainty marrow* : anseris, Cat.

Medūsa, ae, *f. d. of Phorcus, one of the Gorgons. Minerva turned her hair into serpents, and gave to her eyes the power of converting every thing they looked upon to stone. Perseus slew her, and carried off her head, while from the blood that dropped from it serpents sprang* ; **Medūsaeus**, a, um.

Megaera, ae, *f. one of the Furies.*

Megalē, ēs, *f. the Magna Mater (Cybele)* ; **Megalēnsis**, e ; **Megalēnsia** or **Megalēsia**, ium, *n. pl. a festival in honour of Cybele, celebrated on the 4th of April* ; **Megalēsiacus**, a, um.

Megara, ae, *f.* and **Megara**, ōrum (ABL. *pl.* in Plautus, Megaribus), *n. pl.* **I.** *the chief city of* **Megaris**, idis, *f. a country in Greece, lying between Phocis and Attica* ; **Megarēus**, i, *m. a Megarean* ; **Megaricus**, a, um ; **Megaricī**, ōrum, *m. pl. the followers of Euclid of Megara* ; **Megarus**, a, um. **II.** *a city of Sicily, also called* **Megaris**, *and formerly Hybla* ; **Megarēa**, ōrum, *n. pl. the country of Megara.*

Megareus (trisyl.), ei, *m. son of Neptune, and father of Hippomenes* ; **Megarēius**, a, um.

megistānes, um, *m. pl.* [μεγιστᾶνες], *the grandees in a king's suite* : Tac.

mehercle, **mehercule**, and **mehercules**, *v.* hercules.

mēiō, mēiere [*cf.* mingō], *to make water* : Cat., Hor., etc.

mel, mellis (ABL. *sing.* mellī, Pl.; GEN. and DAT. *pl.* not used), *n.* [*cf.* μέλι], *honey.* **1.** Lit. : Pl., Cic.; in *pl.* : Verg. **2.** Transf. : poëtica mella, Hor.; Homerici senis mella, Plin. Ep. Prov.: mel mihi videor lingere, Pl.; mella petere in medio flumine, Ov. As term of endearment : meum mel! Pl. [It. *miele* ; Fr. *miel*.]

Mela, ae, *m.* : Pomponius Mela, *geographer, a native of Spain, under the Emperor Claudius.*

Melampūs, podis, *m. a famous physician and soothsayer.*

melancholicus, a, um [μελαγχολικός], *having black bile, melancholy* : Cic.

melandryum, i, *n.* [μελάνδρυον], *' black heart of oak,' a piece of salted tunny-fish* : Mart.

Melanthius, i, *m. the goatherd of Ulysses.*

melanūrus, i, *m.* [μελάνουρος, *black-tail*], *a kind of sea-fish* : Ov.

meliculum, i, m. [Vㅌ. melenle, Pl.] *[dim.* mel]. A term of endearment, *little honey* : Pl.

melō, Gk. *pl.* of melos, *q.v.*

Meleager and **Meleagros (-agrus)**, grī, *m. son of the Calydonian king Oeneus, one of those engaged in the Calydonian boar-hunt* ; **Meleagrides**, um, *f. pl. the sisters of Meleager, changed into birds.*

mēlēs (mēlis), is, *f. a badger or marten* : Varr., Plin.

Melēs, ētis, *m. a river in Ionia, near Smyrna, on the banks of which, it is said, Homer was born, whence his name Melesigenes.* **Melētēus**, a, um, *Homeric* ; **Melētīnus**, a, um.

Meliboea, ae, *f. a maritime town of Thessaly, the birth-place of Philoctetes* ; **Meliboeus**, a, um, *Thessalian.*

Melicerta and **Melicertēs**, ae, *m. son of Ino and Athamas. His mother, being pursued by her mad husband, threw herself with Melicerta into the sea, whereupon he became a sea-god, called by the Greeks Palaemon, and by the Romans Portunus.*

melicus, a, um [μελικός]. **I.** *musical, melodious* : sonores, Lucr. **II.** *lyric, lyrical* : poëma, Cic.

melilōtos, i, *f.* [μελίλωτος], *a kind of clover melilot* : Ov.

melimēla, ōrum, *n. pl.* [μελίμηλα], *honeyapples, also called must-apple* (mustea mala) : Hor.

mēlīna, *v.* mellīna.

mēlinum, i, *n.* [μηλίνος], *quince-oil* or *quinceointment* : Plin.

Mēlinum, i, *n.* [Mēlos], *a pigment* ; *Melian white* : Pl.

melior, ius, *better* ; *comp.* of bonus, *q.v.* [fr. root seen in μάλα and Lat. multus]. [It. *migliore*, migliore ; Fr. *meilleur* ; from *adv.* melius, It. *meglio* ; Fr. *mieux*.]

melisphyllum and **melissophyllon**, i, *n.* [μελίφυλλον and μελισσόφυλλον (*honeyleaf, bee-leaf*)], *a herb of which bees are fond, balm, also called apiastrum* : Verg.

Melita, ae, or **Melitē**, ēs, *f.* **I.** *Malta* ; **Melitēnsis**, e, *adj.* ; **Melitēnsia**, ium, *n. pl.* (*sc.* vestimenta), *Maltese garments of fine linen* : Cic. **II.** *a sea-nymph.*

melius, *comp. adj.* and *adv. v.* bonus, bene, and melior.

meliusculē, *adv., rather better, pretty well* : cum meliuscule tibi esset (of a convalescent), Cic. Ep. Comic.: meliuscule quam satis fuerit biberis, Pl.

meliusculus, a, um [*dim.* melius], *rather better* : (of a convalescent), Ter. Of things : meliusculum est monere, Pl.; facies, Sen.

mella, ae, *f.* [mel], *mead* : Pl.

mellārius, a, um [mel], *of honey* : Plin. As Noun, **mellārius**, i, *m. a bee-keeper* : Varr.; **mellārium**, i, *n. an apiary* : Varr.

melliculus, a, um [*dim. adj.* fr. mel], *sweet as honey* : Pl.

mellifer, era, erum [mel ferō], *honey-producing, melliferous* : apes, Ov.

mellificium, i, *n.* [mel faciō], *honey-making* : Varr.

mellificō, āre [mel faciō], *to make honey* : Verg.

mellilla, ae, f. [dim. mel], a term of endearment, little honey : Pl. In pl. : endearments : Pl.

mellina, ae, f. [mel], sweetness, deliciousness, delight : Pl.

mellina, ae, f. [mēlēs] (sc. crumena), a pouch of badger-skin : Pl.

mellitus, a, um [mel], honeyed. **1.** Lit. **a.** filled with honey : favi, Varr. **b.** sweetened with honey : placenta, Hor. **2.** Transf.: mamillae, Pl.; oculi, Cat.; Cicero, Cic. Ep.

melos, ī, n. (Gk. pl. melē, Lucr.) [μέλος], a song, lay : Hor.

Melpomenē, ēs, f. the Muse of tragic poetry.

membrāna, ae, f. [membrum], a membrane, thin skin. **1.** Lit.: natura oculos membranis tenuissimis vestivit, Cic. Of the slough of snakes: Ov. **2.** Transf. **a.** the thin skin of plants and other things : Plin. **b.** a skin prepared for writing, parchment : Hor., Quint. **c.** a thin layer or film: coloris, Lucr. Transf.: dignitatis, Sen. Ep.

membrānula, ae, f. [dim. membrāna], a thin parchment : Cic. Ep.

membrātim, adv. limb by limb. **1.** Lit.: vitalem deperdere sensum, Lucr. **2.** Transf. **a.** In gen. piecemeal, singly, severally : Cic. **b.** Of style : in short sentences : dicere, Cic., Quint.

membrum, ī, n. [cf. Gk. μηρός], a limb, member of the body. **1.** Lit.: Pl., Cic., Verg., etc. Hence, Ponticus . . . Bassus . . . dulcia convictūs membra fuere mei, Ov. **2.** Transf. **a.** Of things : a part, portion, division : ratis, Ov.; omnes philosophiae partes atque omnia membra, Cic. Of a house : Lucr.; Cic. Ep.; dormitorium membrum, Plin. Ep. **b.** Of style : a member, clause : Cic.

mēmet, Acc. of ego with -met.

memini, isse [a reduplicated Perf. of the root men, but with Pres. sign. cf. μιμνήσκω, μέμνημαι]. to remember, recollect, to think of. **1.** Lit.: Pl., Cic., Ov. With GEN.: Lucr., Cic. With Acc.: Pl., Cic., Verg. With de : Pl., Cic. Ep., Juv. With Indir. Quest. : Ter., Cic., Liv. With Acc. and Inf.: Enn., Cic. With Acc. and Perf. Inf. (mostly when the subject was not present at the action): memineram divinum virum senile corpus paludibus occultasse demersum, Cic. With Inf.: memento dimidium mihi de praedā dare, Pl.; Cic. Ep.; scribas ad me velim, Varroni memineris excusare tarditatem, Cic. Ep.; (imperavit) uti meminisset arcem occupare, Liv. With cum (when) : memini cum haud audebat, Pl.; Cic. Ep. **2.** Transf. to make mention of, to mention : meministi ipse de exsulibus, Cic. With GEN.: Cic., Quint., Plin. Ep.

Memmius, a, the name of a Roman gens. Esp. C. Memmius, to whom Lucretius dedicated his poem on Nature .; **Memmiadēs**, ae, m. a (scion of the house of) Memmius, and **Memmiānus**, a, um.

Memnōn, onis, m. son of Tithonus and Aurora, king of the Ethiopians ; he went to the aid of the Trojans, and was slain by Achilles ; **Memnonius**, a, um, Mem-

nonian : also poet. Oriental, Moorish, black ; **Memnonides**, um, f. pl. (sc. aves), the birds that rose from his pyre : Ov.

memor, oris, adj. [cf. Gk. μέριμνα, μάρτυς], mindful of, remembering. **1.** Lit. **a.** In gen. : Cic. Ep., Verg., etc. With GEN.: Ter., Caes., Cic., Hor., etc. With Acc. and Inf. : Plin., Suet. With Indir. Quest. : Hor. **b.** Occ. with special sense given by the context : memor provisa repones (i.e. with forethought), Verg.; meritam gratiam memori mente persolvere (i.e. gratefully), Cic. **c.** possessed of a good memory : homo ingeniosus ac memor, Cic. Prov.: mendacem memorem esse oportet, Quint. **2.** Transf. Of things. **a.** remembering : ira, Verg., Liv.; lingua, pectus, cura, Ov. With GEN.: cadum Marsi memorem belli, Hor.; Liv. **b.** reminding : nota, Ov. With GEN.: nostri memorem sepulcro scalpe querellam, Hor.; erat in Anco ingenium et Numae et Romuli memor, Liv.

memorābilis, e, adj. [memorō], worthy to be mentioned, memorable, remarkable : Pl., Cic., Verg., etc. Comp. : Liv. Neut. pl. as Noun : Cic.

memorandus, a, um. **I.** Part. memorō. **II.** Adj.: worthy of mention, notable : Pl., Verg., Juv.

memorātus, ūs, m. [memorō], a mentioning, relating : istaec lepida sunt memoratui, Pl.; levia memoratu, Tac. ; Pl., etc.

memoria, ae, f. [memor]. **1.** Lit. **a.** the faculty of remembering, memory : optuma, inmortalis, Pl.; bona, Cic. Ep.; tenacissima, Quint. ; memoriā tenere, Caes., Cic.; memoriā comprehendere, custodire, Cic.; habere in memoriā, Ter.; in memoriam reducere, Cic. ; esse alicui in memoriā, Cic. ; deponere aliquid ex memoriā, Cic. ; excidere de memoriā, Cic. ; memoriā abire, cedere, Liv. **b.** (the exercise of the faculty) memory, remembrance : me fugiet memoria, Pl. ; Liv. ; ex memoriā exponere, Cic. ; rei memoriam deponere, Caes. ; alicuius memoriam amittere, Cic. ; memoriae prodere, Cic. ; traditur memoriae (foll. by Acc. and Inf.), Liv.; memoriam apud posteros adipisci, Tac. **2.** Transf. **a.** the time of remembrance, period of recollection, and in gen. time, lifetime : multi superiori memoriā se in alias civitates contulerunt, Cic. ; patrum nostrorum memoriā, Caes. ; paulo supra hanc memoriam, Caes. ; post hominum memoriam, Cic. ; princeps huius memoriae philosophorum, Cic. **b.** a memory, past event : veteris memoriae recordatio, Cic. **c.** Of something relatively future : a thought, design : ut belli inferendi memoria patribus aut plebi non esset, Liv. **d.** an historical account, relation, narration : liber, quo iste omnium rerum memoriam breviter complexus est, Cic. ; aliquid memoriā prodere, Cic. ; memoriam prodere, Caes. ; variat memoria actae rei, Liv. ; sine ullā pristini auctoris memoriā, Suet.

memoriālis, e, adj. [memoria], for memoranda : libellus, Suet.

memoriola, ae, f. [dim. memoria], a weak memory : memoriolā vacillare, Cic. Ep.

memoriter, *adv.* **I.** *from memory or recollection :* Cic., Suet. **II.** *with a good
memory, accurately :* Pl., Ter., Cic., etc.

memoro, āre [memor], *to mention, relate, tell.*
With *de :* Cic. With Acc. : Pl., Cic., Verg.,
etc. With Acc. and *Inf. :* Pl., Liv., Tac. ;
in *Pass. :* ubi ea quae dico gesta esse me-
morantur, Cic. ; Sall. With *Indir. Quest. :*
Hor. After quoted words : sic memorat,
Verg. [It. *membrare.*]

Memphis, is and idos, *f.* *a city of Middle
Egypt ;* **Memphītēs**, ae, *m. adj. Egyptian :*
bos (i.e. Apis), Tib. ; **Memphīticus**, a, um ;
Memphītis, idis, *f. adj. Egyptian :* vacca
(i.e. Io), Ov.

Menander or **Menandros** (**-us**), ī (also ŭ),
m. a famous Greek comic poet (c. B.C. 300)
imitated by Terence ; **Menandrēus**, a, um.

menda, ae, *f.* (*cf.* mendum), *a fault, blemish.*
1. Lit. Of the body : Ov. **2.** Transf.
a mistake, slip of the pen : Suet.

mendāciloquior, ius, *comp. adj.* [mendācium
loquor], *more lying :* Pl.

mendācium, ī, *n.* [mendāx], *a lie, falsehood.*
1. Lit. : Pl., Cic., Ov. **2.** Transf. Of
things : famae mendacia, Ov.

mendāciunculum, ī, *n.* [*dim.* mendācium],
a little lie, a fib : Cic.

mendāx, ācis, *adj.* [mentior], *given to lying,
false, mendacious.* **1.** Lit. Of persons :
Pl., Cic., Juv. *Comp. :* Hor. ; *Sup. :* Pl.
With Gen. : rei, Pl. As Noun in Prov. :
mendacem memorem esse oportet, Quint.
2. Transf. Of things (mostly poet.) :
mendacia visa, Cic. ; fundus, Hor. ; infamia, Hor. ; speculum, Ov.

mendābulum, ī, *n.* [mendīcō], *a beggar :*
Pl.

mendicitās, ātis, *f.* [mendīcus], *beggary :*
Pl. ; in summā mendicitate esse, Cic.

mendicō, āre and occ. **mendicor**, ārī
[mendīcus], *to beg, go a-begging :* Pl., Ov.,
Sen. With Acc. : frumentum ab Aetolis,
Liv. ; Pl. ; in *Pass. :* Juv. [Fr. *mendier,
mendiant.*]

mendiculus, a, um [mendīcus], *beggarly :* Pl.

mendicus, a, um, *reduced to beggary, poverty-
stricken.* **1.** Lit. : Cic. *Sup. :* Cic. As
Noun, **mendīcus**, ī, *m., a beggar :* Pl., Hor.
2. Transf. *beggarly, mean :* instrumentum,
Cic.

mendōsē, *adv. faultily :* Cic. Ep., Pers.
Sup. : scribere, Cic.

mendōsus, a, um [mendum]. **I.** *full of de-
fects.* **a.** Physically : Ov. **b.** In gen. :
full of faults, faulty : mendosum est (with
Inf.), Cic. ; exemplar testamenti, Plin. Ep. ;
mores, Ov. *Comp. :* historia, Cic. **II.**
committing faults, blundering : cur servus
in Verruci nomine mendosus fuerit, Cic.

mendum, ī, *n. a fault, defect.* **1.** Lit. **a.**
Physical : Ov. **b.** In writing : *a fault,
blunder :* quod mendum ista litura correxit : Cic. **2.** Transf. : Idūs Martiae
magnum mendum continent, Cic. Ep.

Menelāus, ī, *m. son of Atreus, brother of
Agamemnon, and husband of Helen ;* **Mene-
lāēus**, a, um.

Menēnius, a, *the name of a Roman gens.*
Esp. Menenius Agrippa, *who told the plebs
the fable of the belly and the limbs,* B.C. 494 ;
Menēniānus, **Menēnius**, a, um.

Menippus, ī, *m. a Cynic philosopher, famous
for his sarcasm, whence Varro gave to his
satires the name Menippeae.*

Menoeceus (trisyl.), eī and eos, *m. son of
the Theban king Creon, who sacrificed himself
for his country.*

Menoetius, ī, *m. father of Patroclus ;* **Menoe-
tiadēs**, ae, *m. Patroclus.*

mēns, mentis, *f.* [from the root seen in me-
minī], *the thoughts, mind, intellect, the intellectual faculties, the understanding, reason,
discernment, etc.* **I.** (sometimes found with
animus, as being only *a part,* or the more
active principle, of the soul) ; mens animi,
Pl., Lucr., Cat. ; mens cui regnum totius
animi tributum est, Cic. ; mente complecti
aliquid, Cic. ; deorum mente mundus regi-
tur, Cic. ; di vestris imperatoribus mentem
ademerunt, Liv. ; mente captus, Cic., Liv. ;
timor omnium mentis animosque perturba-
vit, Caes. ; huic ex tempore dicenti effluit
mens, Cic. ; sanum mentis esse, Pl. ; mentis suae esse, also, mentis compotem esse,
Cic. ; in mentem venire, Pl., Cic., Liv. ;
oft. *impers.* with Gen. : saepe ei venit in
mentem potestatis, Cic. ; with *ut* and *Subj. :*
Pl. ; with *Inf. :* Pl. **II.** With esp. ref.
to *certain faculties and functions of the mind,*
a. *the disposition, feelings :* mala mens,
malus animus, Ter. ; bona, Liv. ; inimica,
Nep. ; eorum mentis sensūsque vulneras,
Cic. ; sanguine inimici mentem satiare,
Cic. ; compesce mentis, Hor. **b.** *resolution, determination, courage :* Caes., Hor.,
Liv. ; demittunt mentis, Verg. **III.**
opinion, thoughts, idea : Verg. ; his ego
eorum hominum mentibus pauca respondebo, Cic. **IV.** *design, intention :* Dolabella
classem eā mente comparavit ut etc., Cic. ;
muta istam mentem, Cic. ; mens fuit (with
Inf.), Ov. **V.** Personified : Cic., Liv.

mēnsa, ae, *f.* [perh. fr. mētior]. **1.** Lit.
a measure, hence *an allowance* or *portion* of
food : Pl., Enn. ; parciore mensā uti, Tac. ;
secunda mensa, *the second course, the
dessert :* Cic. Ep., Nep. Perh. in, heus
etiam mensas edimus, Verg. **2.** Transf.
A. *a tray* or *table.* **a.** for food : cibos in
mensam alicui apponere, Pl. ; ad mensam
consistere, *to wait at table,* Cic. ; surgere a
mensā, Pl. **b.** *a sacrificial table :* Verg. **c.**
the guests at table : istorum conduxit mensa
choragum, Suet. **B.** Of other analogous
things. **a.** *a butcher's stall-block :* mensa
lanionia, Suet. **b.** *a money-changer's counter :* Pl., Cic., Hor.

mēnsārius, ī, *m.* [mēnsa], *a member of a
board of commissioners appointed to deal with
urgent financial questions :* Cic.,\Liv.

mēnsiō, ōnis, *f.* [*v.* mētior], *a measuring,
measure :* vocum, *metre* or *quantity :* Cic.

mēnsis, is, *m.* (Gen. *pl.* mēnsium or mensum,
occ. mēnsuum) [fr. root of mētior, *cf.* Gk.
μήν], *a month :* Pl., Cic., Hor., Liv., etc. ;
mense primo, *at the beginning of the month,*
Verg. In *pl.* of the *monthly periods* of
females : Varr., Plin. [It. *mese ;* Sp. *mes ;*
F. *mois.*]

mēnsor, ōris, *m.* [*v.* mētior], *a measurer.* **a.**
maris et terrae, i.e. *a mathematician,* Hor.
b. *a surveyor :* Ov. **c.** *an architect :* Plin.
Ep.

mĕnstruālis, e, *adj.* [mĕnstruus] **I.** *for a month :* epulae, Pl. **II.** *having monthly periods :* Plin.

mĕnstruus, a, um [mēnsis]. **I.** *of or for a month, monthly :* usura, Cic. Ep. As Noun, **mēnstrua**, ōrum, *n. pl. the monthly periods* of females : Plin. **II.** *lasting a month :* spatium, Cic. ; cibaria, Cic. As Noun, **mēnstruum**, ī, *n. a month's provisions :* Liv. ; *a month's term of office :* Plin. Ep.

mēnsula, ae, *f.* [dim. mēnsa], *a little table :* Pl.

mēnsūra, ae, *f.* [v. mētior], *a measuring, measurement.* **1.** L i t. : certis mensuris ex aquā (i.e. by means of the clepsydra, q.v.), Caes. ; mensuram facere alicuius, Ov. ; agere (i.e. to survey), Plin. Ep. **2.** T r a n s f. **A.** *a standard of measure, a measure.* **a.** Material : neque mensuras itineris noverunt, Caes. ; maiore mensurā reddere, Cic. ; mensurae et pondera, Plin. **b.** Of sound : quidquid sub aurium mensuram aliquam cadit, numerus vocatur, Cic. **c.** Immaterially : *an expected or required standard :* tanti nominis imples mensuram, Ov. ; legati, Tac. **B.** *a measure, amount, proportion, capacity, size.* **a.** Material : dare alicui mensuram bibendi, Ov. ; deerat pisci patinae mensura, Juv. **b.** Immaterial : mensura ficti crescit, Ov. ; buccae (i.e. of eloquence), Juv. ; summittere se ad mensuram discentis, Quint. [It. *misura ;* Fr. *mesure.*]

mēnsus, a, um, *Part.* mētiŏr.

menta (mentha), ae, *f.* [μίνθη], *mint :* Ov.

mentiēns, entis. **I.** *Part.* mentior. **II.** Noun, *a kind of fallacy, or sophism :* transl. of the Gk. ὁ ψευδόμενος (' the liar ') : Cic.

mentiō, ōnis, *f.* [from same root as mēns], *a calling to mind, a cursory speaking of, mention :* mentionem facere (with G E N. or *de*) : Pl., Caes., Cic., Liv., etc. ; movere, incohare, lacessere, habere, Liv. ; casu in eorum mentionem incidi, Cic. With *ut* and *Subj.* : mentione inlatā a tribunis, ut liceret, Liv. ; Pl. In *pl.* : secessionis mentiones ad vulgus serere, *to throw out hints,* Liv.

mentior, īrī [perh. fr. root of mēns] (old *Fut.* mentībitur, Pl.), *to invent in the mind, to lie.* **A.** I n t r a n s. *to speak falsely, to lie, act deceitfully.* **1.** L i t. : adversus or apud aliquem, Pl. ; alicui, Pl., Ter. ; de re aliquā, Cic. ; in re aliquā, Cic. Ep. **2.** T r a n s f. : frons, oculi, vultus persaepe mentiuntur, Cic. Ep. **B.** T r a n s. **a.** *to say falsely, to lie :* with Acc. and *Inf.* : Ov. **b.** *to invent, fabricate, etc.* : tantem rem, Sall. ; auspicium, Liv. ; gloriam, Ov. Of poetic invention : Hor. **c.** *to imitate, counterfeit :* nec varios discet mentiri lana colores, Verg. *Perf. Part. :* mentita fama (*lying* or *invented*), Ov. ; tela (*lying*), Verg. ; but *Pass.:* mentiti fictique terrores, Plin. Ep. ; Prop.

Mentor, oris, *m.* **I.** *friend of Ulysses.* **II.** *a famous artist in embossed metal work.* Transf. *a cup of his making :* Mart., Juv. ; **Mentoreus**, a, um.

mentum, ī, *n.* [fr. root seen in ē-mineŏ], *the chin of men and animals :* Cic. Poet. *pl.,* including *the beard :* incana, Verg.

meŏ, meāre, *to go, to pass :* quo simul mearis, Hor. ; in orientem meavisse, Tac. Of things : vapor per inane, Lucr. ; sidera, Ov. ; spiritus, Curt. ; sol, aura, Quint. ; triremes, Tac.

mephītis, is, *f. a noxious exhalation from the ground, malaria :* Verg.

mēpte, i.e. mē ipsum : Pl.

merāculus (merāclus), a, um [dim. merācus], *fairly pure :* Pl.

merācus, a, um [merus], *pure, undiluted, unmixed.* **1.** L i t. : esp. of wine : vinum meracius, Cic. Of other things : elleborum, Hor. **2.** T r a n s f. : nimis meraca libertas, Cic.

mercābilis, e, *adj.* [mercor], *that can be bought :* Ov.

mercāns, antis. **I.** *Part.* mercor. **II.** Noun, *a buyer, purchaser* (esp. in *pl.*) : Suet. [It. *mercante ;* Fr. *marchand.*]

mercātor, ōris, *m.* [mercor], *a trader, merchant,* esp. *a wholesale dealer* (opp. caupo) : Caes., Cic., Juv.

mercātōrius, a, um [mercātor], *for trading, mercantile :* navis, Pl.

mercātūra, ae, *f.* [mercor], *trading, trade.* **1.** L i t. : tenuis, magna, copiosa, Cic. ; mercaturas facere, Cic. **2.** T r a n s f. **a.** *purchase :* tamquam ad mercaturam bonarum artium, Cic. **b.** *goods, merchandise :* Pl.

mercātus, ūs, *m.* [mercor]. **1.** L i t. *trading, traffic* (esp. in bad sense) : instituere, Cic. **2.** T r a n s f. **a.** *a market, market-place :* Pl. **b.** *a fair* (esp. at the great games or at great religious festivals) : habere, Cic. ; Liv., Tac., etc. Hence, ad aedem Veneris mercatus meretricius, Pl. ; sarcastically of Verres' *sale of honours :* indicere, Cic. [Fr. *marché.*]

mercēdula, ae, *f.* [dim. mercēs]. **I.** *small wages, poor pay :* Cic. **II.** *small rent, income :* constituere mercedulas praediorum, Cic. Ep.

mercēnnārius, a, um [mercēs], *paid, hired, mercenary.* **1.** L i t. Of persons : Cic., Liv. As Noun, **mercēnnārius**, ī, *m. a hireling, hired servant, day-labourer :* Pl., Cic. **2.** T r a n s f. : liberalitas, Cic. ; vincla, Hor. ; arma, Liv.

(1) **mercēs**, ēdis, *f.* [merx]. **I.** *hire, pay, wages, salary, fee.* **1.** L i t. : operae, Cic. ; manuum, Sall. ; ne ars tanta abduceretur ad mercedem atque quaestum, Cic. ; uti Germani mercede accesserrentur, Caes. In *pl. :* Juv., Suet. Also of *a corrupt fee,* i.e. *a bribe :* Cic. ; magnā mercede pacisci cum aliquo, Cic. **2.** T r a n s f. *wages.* **a.** *recompense, reward :* mercedem alicuius rei constituere, Cic. ; exigere ab aliquo, Cic. ; alicui proponere, Cic. Ep. ; non aliā bibam mercede, Hor. ; appellare, solvere, Juv. ; alicui rei imponere, Juv. **b.** *cost, retribution :* temeritatis merces, Liv. ; non sine magnā mercede, Cic. ; Juv. **II.** *rent, income, interest :* (mostly in *pl.*) : Caes., Cic., Hor., etc. [It. *mercè ;* Fr. *merci.*]

(2) **mercēs**, v. merx.

mercimōnium, ī, *n.* [merx], *goods, wares, merchandise :* Pl., Tac.

mercor, ārī [merx]. **I.** *to trade, traffic :* Pl. **II.** *to buy, purchase.* **1.** L i t. : hortos

Hor. ; aliquid ab aliquo, Cic. ; fundum de pupillo, Cic. ; aliquid tanto pretio, Cic. ; quanti, Plin. **2.** Transf. : ego haec officia mercanda vitā puto, Cic. Ep. ; hoc magno, Verg. *Perf. Part. in Pass.* sense : Sall., Prop.

Mercurius, i, *m. the son of Jupiter and Maia, the messenger of the gods ; as a herald, the god of eloquence ; the god of traders and thieves ; the presider over roads ; conductor of departed souls to the Lower World ;* stella Mercuri, Cic. ; **Mercuriālis,** e, *adj.* : **Mercuriālēs,** ium. *m. pl. a corporation of traders at Rome.*

merda, ae, *f. dung, droppings :* Mart. In *pl.* : corvorum, Hor.

merenda, ae, *f.* [mereō], *a luncheon :* Pl.

mereō, ēre, and **mereor,** ērī [cf. Gk. μέρος, μείρομαι, μοῖρα], *to acquire, deserve, earn.* **1.** Lit. (us. in *Act.* form). **a.** In gen. : non amplius duodecim aeris, Cic. ; Pl., etc. ; hic meret aera liber Sosiis, Hor. **b.** *to acquire by purchase :* uxores vos dote meruerunt, Pl. ; Cic. ; Hor. **c.** Milit. : merere stipendia (or merere alone), *to earn pay, serve as a soldier :* stipendia in eo bello, Caes. ; compluris annos, Caes. ; adulescens patre suo imperatore meruit, Cic. ; triennio sub Hasdrubale, Liv. ; Romanis in castris, Tac. ; merere equo (i.e. in the cavalry), Cic. ; pedibus (i.e. in the infantry), Liv. In the *Mid.* form : Varr., Tac. **2.** Transf. *to win, acquire, earn, merit.* **A.** With Acc. or Obj. clause. **a.** In *Act.* form : praemia, Caes. ; fustuarium, Cic. ; scelus tantum, Verg. ; supplicium, Ov., Juv. ; nomen gloriamque, Tac. With *ut* and *Subj.* : Cic. With *Inf.* : Ov., Quint., Tac. **b.** In *Mid.* form : laudem, Caes., Cic. ; gratiam, poenam, Liv. ; honorem, Juv. ; indulgentiam, Tac. With *ne* and *Subj.* : Plin. With *Inf.* : Juv. **c.** *Perf. Part.* **meritus** in *Pass.* sense : Ter., Cic., Verg., Liv., etc. **B.** Used Intrans. **a.** In *Act.* form (mostly colloq.) : de aliquo, Pl. ; si quid bene de te merui, Verg. ; de re publicā optime, Cic. Ep. **b.** In *Mid.* form (most freq.) : *to be entitled, to deserve :* dignitatem meam, si mereor, tuearis, Cic. Ep. ; ut erga me merita est, Pl. Esp. with *de* and *bene, optime, male,* etc. : bene de re publicā, Caes., Cic. ; de mendico male, Pl. ; de me divinitus, Cic. ; socios bene merentis deserere, Caes.

meretriciē, *adv. after the manner of harlots :* Pl.

meretricius, a, um [meretrix], *of harlots :* ornamenta, Pl. ; domus, Ter. ; quaestus, Cic. As Noun, **meretricium,** i, *n. the trade of a harlot :* facere, Suet.

meretricula, ae, *f.* [dim. meretrix], *a pretty little courtesan :* Cic., Hor.

meretrix, icis, *f.* [mereō], *a harlot, courtesan :* Pl., Cic., Ov., etc.

mergae, ārum, *f. pl.* [cf. ἀμέργω], *a two-pronged pitchfork :* Pl.

merges, itis, *f.* [mergae], *a sheaf of corn :* Verg.

mergō, mergere, mērsī, mērsum, *to dip, plunge, immerse, sink.* **1.** Lit. : pullos in aquam, Cic. ; se in mari, Cic. ; me aequore, Verg. ; corpus sub aequora, Ov. In

Mid. : *to sink :* multae naves merguntur, Liv. **2.** Transf. **a.** Of a star, etc. : Bootes mergitur Oceano, Cat. **b.** *to plunge, thrust, bury :* mersis in effossam terram capitibus, Liv. ; canes mersis in corpore rostris dilacerant dominum, Ov. ; mersit suos in cortice vultūs, Ov. **c.** Morally or financially : *to sink, swamp, overwhelm :* mersus foro (i.e. bankrupt), Pl. ; Fortuna viros, Verg. ; me his malis, Verg. ; mergentibus sortem usuris, Liv. ; se in voluptates, Liv. ; vino somnoque mersus, Liv. ; Alexander mersus secundis rebus, Liv. ; mersis fer opem rebus, Ov.

mergus, i, *m.* [mergō], *a diver,* a kind of sea-bird : Verg., Hor., etc.

meridiānus, a, um [meridiēs], *of or at midday or noon.* **1.** Lit. : tempus, Cic. ; sol, Liv. ; somnus, Plin. Ep. ; hence, **meridiāni** (*sc.* gladiatores) : Suet. **2.** Transf. *southern, southerly :* caeli pars, Varr. ; regio, vallis, Liv. ; circulus, *the equator,* Sen.

meridiātiō, ōnis, *f.* [meridiō], *a siesta :* Cic.

meridiēs, ēī, *m.* [from medius diēs], *mid-day, noon.* **1.** Lit. : circiter meridiem, Pl. ; ante meridiem, post meridiem, Cic. **2.** Transf. *the south :* spectare ad meridiem, Caes. ; tum ad septemtriones, tum ad meridiem, Cic. ; a meridie Aegyptus obiacet, Tac.

meridiō, āre [meridiēs], *to take a siesta :* Cat., Suet.

Mēriōnēs, ae, *m. the charioteer and pilot of Idomeneus.*

meritō, āre [freq. mereō], *to earn regularly :* sestertia dena, Cic.

meritōrius, a, um [mereō], *on hire :* pueri, Cic. ; balinea, Plin. Ep. ; vehicula, Suet. As Noun, **meritōria,** ōrum, *n. pl. lodgings :* Juv.

meritus, a, um. **I.** *Part.* mereō. **II.** *Neut.* as Noun, **meritum,** i, *n. an act deserving* praise or blame. **1.** Lit. **a.** *a service, kindness, benefit :* propter militum divinum atque immortale meritum, Cic. ; Liv. ; Tac. Also in *Sup.* : meritissumo eius, Pl. **b.** *demerit, blame, fault :* Caesar a me nullo meo merito alienus esse debebat, Cic. ; nullo meo in se merito, Liv. ; quosdam punivit ex merito, Tac. ; Liv. **2.** Transf. *a good reason :* quo sit merito quaeque notata dies, Ov. ABL. **meritō** as *Adv.* : *deservedly :* Pl., Cic., Juv. Also *Sup.* meritissumō, Pl. ; meritissimō, Cic.

merobibus, a, um [merum bibō], *that drinks unmixed wine :* Pl.

Meropē, ēs, *f., d. of Atlas and Pleione,* one of the Pleiades ; her star is fainter than the rest because of her marriage to a mortal, Sisyphus.

Merops, opis, *m. king of Ethiopia, husband of Clymene, and the reputed father of Phaëthon.*

merops, opis, *f.* [μέροψ], *a bird that devours bees* (also called apiastra, *the bee-eater*) : Verg.

mersō, āre [freq. mergō], *to dip or plunge again and again.* **1.** Lit. : balantum gregem fluvio salubri, Verg. ; Tac. **2.** Transf. : (membra) rerum copia mersat, engulfs, Lucr. ; sitis corpora mersans, Lucr. ; mersor civilibus undis, *plunge into,* Hor.

mōrsus, a, um, *Part.* mergō.

merula, ae, *f.* **I.** *a blackbird :* Cic., Quint. **II.** *a kind of fish, the sea-carp :* Ov. [Fr. and Eng. *merle.*]

merus, a, um [*cf.* Gk. μαρμαίρω], *pure, unmixed, unadulterated.* **1.** L i t. : claror, Pl. ; argentum, Pl. ; undae, Ov. ; esp. of wine : *not mixed with water :* vina, Ov. ; Varr. *Neut.* as Noun, **merum,** ī (*sc.* vinum), *unmixed wine :* Pl., Hor., Quint., etc. **2.** T r a n s f. **a.** *undiluted :* amoris poculum meri, Pl. ; libertas, Liv. ; principes, Cic. ; virtus, Hor. **b.** *nothing but, only, mere :* nihil, nisi spem meram, Ter. ; mera monstra nuntiare, Cic. Ep. ; Pl.

merx (and **mers,** Pl.), cis, *f. goods, wares, merchandise.* **1.** L i t. : Pl., Quint., Plin. Ep. In *pl.* : Cic., Ov., Juv. **2.** T r a n s f. Of persons (*cf.* Eng. ' a bad lot '), mala merx haec, et callida est, Pl.

Messallina, ae, *f.* **I.** *w. of the Emperor Claudius.* **II.** *w. of the Emperor Nero.*

Messapia, ae, *f.* a town and district in S.E. Italy named after a mythical founder **Messapus,** ī, *m.* ; **Messapii,** ōrum, *m. pl. the people ;* **Messapius,** a, um, *Apulian.*

messis, is, *f.* (Acc. *sing.* messim, Pl.) [metō], *a reaping and gathering of the fruits of the earth, a harvest.* **1.** L i t. : Cic., Verg. ; seges matura messi, Liv. ; Cic. ; messem facere, Plin. P r o v. : adhuc tua messis in herbā est (*cf.* "don't count your chickens before they are hatched"), Ov. **2.** T r a n s f. **a.** Of the gathering of honey : Verg. **b.** *the time of harvest, harvest-time :* si frigus crit, si messis, Verg. **c.** *the crop harvested :* Verg. ; in *pl.* : Verg. **d.** *a harvest, a crop* (esp. of evil) : pro bene factis mali messem metere, Pl. ; Sullani temporis messem, Cic.

messor, ōris, *m.* [metō], *a reaper.* **1.** L i t. : Cic., Hor., Juv. **2.** T r a n s f. : scelerum, Pl.

messōrius, a, um [messor], *of a reaper :* corbis, Cic.

messus, a, um, *Part.* metō.

-met, a suffix attached to personal pronouns, and (less freq.) to pronom. adj. ; Eng. *self : v.* ego, tu, and meus.

mēta, ae, *f.* [*cf.* mētior], *a mark* (in the Circus Maximus a conical stone), *to measure* the distance in a race-course : the meta prima served as a turning-post, the meta secunda as a winning-post or a turning-post according to the length of the race. **1.** L i t. : Liv. ; as a *turning-post :* Verg., Hor., Ov., Suet. ; as a *winning-post* (only transf.) : Hor. **2.** T r a n s f. **a.** *anything of conical shape :* of a fountain, meta sudans, Sen. Ep. **b.** *the turning-point :* nox mediam caeli metam contigerat, Verg. ; metas lustrare Pachyni, Verg. ; hence, *a critical point or moment :* fama adulescentis haesit ad metas, Cic. ; inoffensam vitae tangere metam, Ov. **c.** *the finishing-post, the goal* of one's efforts : viarum, Verg. ; optatam contingere metam, Hor. ; Ov. ; of the end of life : ad metas aevi pervenire, Verg. Of the sun's goal : ut vices uno anno ad metam eandem solis unde orsi essent dies congruerent, Liv. **d.** Of both metae : sol ex aequo metā distabat utrāque, Ov. ; Lucr.

Metabus, ī, *m. a king of the Volscians, father of Camilla.*

metallum, ī, *n.* [μέταλλον]. **I.** *a metal :* auri, Verg. ; *potior metallis libertas,* Hor. **II.** Mostly in *pl. a mine, mines :* metalla vetera intermissa recoluit, Liv. ; Luc. ; damnare in metallum, Plin. Ep. ; condemnare aliquem ad metalla, Suet.

metamorphōsis, is, *f.* [μεταμόρφωσις], *a physical transformation :* in *pl.* **Metamorphōsēs,** -eōn, *the title of one of Ovid's poems :* Quint.

metaphora, ae, *f.* [μεταφορά], *a metaphor, a transferring of a word from its proper environment to another* (pure Lat. translatio, Cic.) : Quint.

mētātor, ōris, *m.* [mētor], *one who marks out or plans :* urbis, Cic.

Metaurus, ī, *m. a small river in Umbria, celebrated for the defeat of Hasdrubal on its banks,* B.C. 207 ; *now the Metauro ;* **Metaurus,** a, um.

Metellus, *a Roman cognomen in the gens Caecilia.* Esp. Q. Caecilius Metellus, *surnamed* Numidicus, *from his victories over Jugurtha.*

Mēthymna, ae, *f. a city in the island of Lesbos, the birth-place of the poet Arion ; also famed for its excellent wine ;* **Mēthymnaeus,** a, um ; **Mēthymnias,** adis, *f. adj.*

mētior, mētīrī, mēnsus [*cf.* Gk. μέτρον], *to measure* (lands, corn, etc.). **1.** L i t. **a.** In gen. : Cic., Hor., Liv. *Perf. Part.* sometimes in *Pass.* sense : mensa spatia conficere, Cic. **b.** With DAT. : *to measure out, distribute by measure :* frumentum militibus metiri, Caes. ; Hor. **2.** T r a n s f. **a.** *to measure by passing through, traverse :* aequor, Verg. ; aquas carinā, Ov. ; Luna iter annuom, Cat. Without Obj. : Pl. **b.** *to measure mentally, estimate, judge, consider :* mostly with ABL. of the standard of judgment: omnia quaestu, Cic. ; Hor. ; Liv., etc. With *ex* (rare) : Cic. With Acc. alone : Luc., Quint. [Sp. *medir.*]

metō, metere, messuī, messum [*cf.* Gk. ἀμάω], *to reap, mow, crop.* **1.** L i t. : Caes. With Acc. : pabula falce, Ov. ; hence, arva, Prop. P r o v. : **i.** ut sementem feceris, ita et metes, Cic. ; **ii.** mihi istic nec seritur, nec metitur (i.e. it does not concern me), Pl. ; **iii.** sibi quisque ruri metit (i.e. every one looks out for himself), Pl. **2.** T r a n s f. **a.** *to gather, cull :* uvas, Verg. Of bees : purpureosque metunt flores, Verg. **b.** *to mow down,* i.e. to cut down : virgā lilia summa metit, Ov. In battle : proxima quaeque metit gladio, Verg. So of death : metit Orcus grandia cum parvis, Hor. [It. *mietere.*]

Metōn, onis, *m. a celebrated Athenian astronomer, who discovered the cycle of nineteen years, which brings the sun and moon into nearly the same relative positions again.*

metōposcopus or **-os,** ī, *m.* [μετωποσκόπος], *one who tells fortunes by examining the forehead :* Suet.

mētor, ārī (also **mētō,** āre, Verg. App.) [*v.* mētior], *to measure off, to lay out by measure* (by surveying) : castra, Caes. ; agros, Verg ; agrum, Liv. *Perf. Part.* in *Pass.* sense : Hirt., Hor., Liv.

metrēta, ae, f. [μετρητής], an Athenian measure for liquids (about 9 gallons English) : navis metretas quae trecentas tolleret (of the tonnage of etc.), Pl. ; Cato ; Juv.

metricus, a, um [μετρικός], of measuring or measure. **a.** In gen. : leges, Plin. **b.** relating to metre, metrical : pedes, Quint.

metrum, ī, n. [μέτρον], a measure : esp. a poetical measure, metre : Quint.

metuculōsus, a, um [metus], full of fear. **a.** Subjective : fearful, timid : Pl. **b.** Objective : frightful : Pl.

metuēns, entis. **I.** Part. metuō. **II.** Adj. afraid, anxious : with GEN. : metuens futuri, Hor. Comp. : metuentior deorum, Ov. : metuentior in posterum, Tac.

metuō, uere, uī, ūtum [metus]. **A.** Trans. to fear, be afraid of, apprehend : miluos, Pl. ; deos, Pl., Ter. ; senem servi, Cic. ; bellum, Cic. ; supplicia a vobis, Cic. ; Pl. ; periculum ex illis, Sall. With Inf. : Pl., Liv., Hor., etc. With ne and Subj. : Pl., Ter., Cic. With ne non and Subj. : Pl., Ter. ; with ut for ne non : Pl., Ter., Cic., Hor. With quin and Subj. (after a negat.) : Pl. With Indir. Quest. : Pl., Ter. **B.** Intrans. to fear, be afraid, be apprehensive : Cic. With de : de suā vitā, Cic. Ep. With ab, to denote the source of fear : metuens ab Hannibale (i.e. of some movement on the part of Hannibal), Liv. With DAT. : pueris, Pl. ; senectae, Verg. ; moenibus patriae, Liv.

metus, ūs, m. (f. Enn.) fear, apprehension, dread, anxiety : in metu esse, Cic. ; metum accipere, Ter. ; habere, Cic. Ep. ; concipere, Ov. ; capere, Liv. ; alicui inicere, Caes. ; adferre, obicere, Cic. ; facere, Ov. ; inferre, Liv. ; intentare, Tac. ; alicui adimere, Ter. ; levare, deicere, Cic. ; removere, Liv. ; solvere, Verg. ; aliquem metu exonerare, Liv. With Obj. GEN. : Cic., Sall. With ab (denoting the quarter from which) : metus ab hoste, Liv. With Acc. and Inf. : senatum metus cepit resisti multitudini non posse, Liv. ; ut metum demeret periculi quicquam esse, Liv. Of religious awe : Verg., Hor. Personif. : Cic., Verg.

meus, a, um (Voc. meus for mī : Verg. ; GEN. pl. meum for meōrum, Pl.), pronom. adj. [mē], my, mine, belonging to me. **A.** Subjective : haec ero dicam meo, Pl. ; mei sunt ordines, mea discriptio, Cic. ; Ov. Impers. meum est, it is my part, duty, Cic. ; meā interest, it is of importance to me (v. interest). In appos. with GEN. : meum factum dictumve consulis, Liv. ; Cic. Phr. : meus est (i.e. I've got him) : meus hic est : hamum vorat, Pl. ; Ov. In Voc., mi, my dear ! my beloved ! o mi Aeschine, o mi germane ! Ter. As Noun, **mei**, ōrum, m. pl. my friends : Ter., Verg. ; **meum**, ī, n. what is mine : potat de meo (i.e. at my expense), Ter. Also strengthened with suffix -met or -pte. **B.** Objective : done to me, made against me : iniuria, Sall. ; crimina, Liv. [It. mio ; Fr. mon.]

Mezentius, ī, m. a tyrant of Caere or Agylla, slain by Aeneas.

mī. **I.** DAT. v. ego. **II.** VOC. v. meus. **III.** NOM. pl. of meus (for mei).

mica, ae, f. [cf. GR. ὀμικρός, μικρός], crumb, little bit, morsel : Lucr., Cat., Hor.

Micipsa, ae, m. son of Masinissa, and king of Numidia. In pl. poet. for Numidians, Africans (Juv.).

micō, āre, uī, to move quickly in a vibrating or quivering manner, to quiver, throb, flicker. **1.** Lit. **a.** In gen. : venae et arteriae, Cic. ; linguis micat ore trisulcis, Verg. ; semianimes oculi, Enn. ; semianimes digiti, equus, Verg. ; auribus, Verg. **b.** micare (sc. digitis), to raise the fingers suddenly (for another to guess the number held up), freq. done, like our toss, to decide some matter : micare, talos iacere, Cic. ; Suet. Prov. : dignus est quicum in tenebris mices (i.e. he is thoroughly honest), Cic. **2.** Transf. to flash, gleam, sparkle : ex oculis ardor, Lucr. ; oculis ignis, Verg. ; fulmina, Liv. ; gladii, Liv. ; micat inter omnis Iulium sidus, Hor. : stellae, Ov.

micturiō, īre [desider. mingō], to desire to make water : Juv.

Midās, ae, m. son of Gordius, and king of Phrygia. He requested and received from Bacchus the gift that everything he touched should be turned to gold. He was saved from starvation by bathing in the river Pactolus, whose sands from that time were golden. When, on the occasion of a musical contest between Apollo and Pan, Midas decided against the former, Apollo changed his ears into those of an ass.

migrātiō, ōnis, f. [migrō], a removal, a changing of one's habitation. **1.** Lit. : Cic., Liv. **2.** Transf. Of speech : a metaphorical use : migrationes in alienum multae, Cic.

migrātū, ABL. sing. m. [migrō], in the transporting : Liv.

migrō, āre [perh. cf. ἀμείβω]. **A.** Intrans. to change one's home, remove, migrate. **1.** Lit. : Cic., Juv. ; e fano foras, Pl. ; ex urbe rus, Ter. ; a Tarquiniis, Liv. ; ad generum, Cic. ; Veios, Liv. **2.** Transf. **a.** to go away, depart : ex hac vitā, Cic. ; de vitā, Cic. ; mens officio, Pl. ; lymphae ad severos, Cat. ; equitis migravit ab aure voluptas ad oculos, Hor. **b.** to change, pass into something else : omnia migrant, Lucr. **B.** Trans. to carry away, transport. **1.** Lit. : (v. migratu). **2.** Transf. to depart from, abandon : ius civile, Cic.

mihipte = mihi ipsi, v. ego.

Milaniōn, ōnis, m. the husband of Atalanta, whom he outran by means of the golden apples.

miles, itis, m.f. [perh. cogn. with ὅμιλος], a soldier. **1.** Lit. **a.** In gen. : milites scribere, Sall. ; deligere, ordinare, Liv. ; dimittere, Cic. Ep. **b.** a foot-soldier, infantryman : milites equitesque in expeditionem misit, Caes. **c.** a common soldier, private (opp. to an officer) : Cic., Sall., Liv. **2.** Transf. **a.** Collectively, soldiery, army : hic miles magis placuit, Liv. ; armato milite, Verg. ; etc. **b.** a retainer, follower : miles erat Phoebes, Ov. **c.** a man at backgammon : Ov.

Milētis, idis, f. Byblis, d. of Miletus.

Milētus, ī, f. one of the chief cities of Asia Minor ; **Milēsius**, a, um, Milesian, in the

Milesian manner, lascivious : **Milēsiī,** ōruш, *m. pl. its inhabitants ;* **Milētis,** idis, *f. adj. :* urbs, i.e. *Tomi, a colony of Miletus,* Ov.

milia, *v.* mille.

militāris, e, *adj.* [miles], *of soldiers, war, or military service, soldiers', military :* pueri, Pl. ; disciplina, Liv. ; signa, Caes. ; equus, funus, Nep. ; labor, Cic. ; aetas, *the age for bearing arms* (from the seventeenth to the forty-sixth year), Liv. ; via, *a military road,* Liv. ; Daunias (i.e. Apulia), *the land of soldiers,* Hor. ; cur neque militaris inter aequalis equitat ? *in military attire,* Hor. *Masc.* as Noun, *a military man :* Tac.

militāriter, *adv. in a soldierly or military manner :* Liv., Tac.

militārius, a, um [miles], *soldier-like, military :* gradus, Pl.

militia, ae, *f.* [miles], *military service, warfare, war.* **1.** L i t. : militiae disciplina, Cic. ; moenera militāī, Lucr. ; munus militiae sustinere, Caes. ; militiae vacatio, Caes. ; militiae scientia, Sall. ; militiam tolerare, Verg. In LOCAT. militiae, *in war, on service abroad* (us. opp. to domi) : quorum virtus fuerat domi militiaeque cognita, Cic. ; militiae domique, Liv. ; Ter. **2.** T r a n s f. **a.** *the body of soldiers, the military :* magister militiae, Liv. ; pars militiae, Ov. **b.** *a lover's service :* Pl. **c.** In civil life : *service* (with implied contrast to military service) : hanc urbanam militiam respondendi, scribendi, Cic. ; Ov.

militiola, ae, *f.* [dim. militia], *an insignificant term of military service :* semestris, Suet.

militō, āre [miles], *to be a soldier, to serve as a soldier.* **1.** L i t. : in cuius exercitu Catonis filius tiro militabat, Cic. ; sub signis alicuius, Liv. In P a s s. : omne militabitur bellum, Hor. **2.** T r a n s f. Of other service (esp. a lover's) : Pl., Hor., Ov.

milium, ī, *n.* [cf. μελίνη], *millet :* Verg.

mille, *noun or adj. ; pl.* **milia** (rarely **millia,** ium, *n. noun, a thousand, thousands.* **1.** L i t. In gen. : mille et quingentis passibus abesse, Cic. With GEN. : mille drachmarum, Pl. ; mille hominum, Cic. ; mille passuum, Caes., Liv. In *pl.* : sescenta milia mundorum, Cic. ; sagittarios tria milia (milia *here is in apposition*) numero habebat, Caes. ; Verg. Distributively : in milia aeris assis singulos, *on every thousand,* Liv. **b.** mille passuum or simply mille, *a thousand paces* (*v.* passus), i.e. *a Roman mile* (142 yards less than the English statute-mile) : Pl., Cic., Liv., etc. **2.** T r a n s f. *innumerable, countless :* Verg., Hor., Liv. [It. *mille, miglio :* Sp. *mil ;* Fr. *mille.*]

millesimus (-ēnsimus), a, um [mille], *the thousandth :* Cic. Ep., Ov., etc.

milliārium (mīli-), ī, *n.* [mille], *a milestone.* **1.** L i t. : Cic. Esp. : milliarium aureum, *a* (*gilded*) *milestone set up by Augustus in the forum, from which distances were reckoned,* Tac. **2.** T r a n s f. *a Roman mile :* Suet.

milliārius (mīli-), a, um, *containing or comprising a thousand :* decuriae, Varr. ; ala, Plin. Ep. ; porticus, Suet.

milliēns or **milliēs,** *adv. a thousand times.* T r a n s f. *innumerable times :* Ter., Cic.

(1) Milō and **Milōn,** ōnis, *m. a celebrated athlete of Crotona. He was caught in a tree which he tried to rend, and devoured by wild beasts.*

(2) Milō, ōnis, m. : T. Annius Milo, *a friend of Cicero and an enemy of Clodius ; he killed the latter in a skirmish at Bovillae, and, when tried for murder, was defended by Cicero ;* **Milōniānus,** a, um.

Miltiadēs, is, m. *the general who commanded the Athenians in the battle of Marathon,* B.C. 490.

miluīnus, a, um [miluus], *of the kite.* **1.** Lit. : plumae, Plin. **2.** T r a n s f. *kite-like ; rapacious, insatiable :* Pl., Cic. Ep. *Fem.* as Noun (sc. fames), *a kite's voracity :* Pl.

miluus (-uos), ī, *m. a bird of prey, a kite.* **1.** Lit. : Pl., Cic., Hor. **2.** T r a n s f. **a.** Of rapacious men : Pl. **b.** *a fish of prey; a gurnard :* Hor. **c.** *a constellation ; the Kite :* Ov.

mīma, ae, *f.* [mimus], *an actress in mime :* Cic., Hor.

Mimallones, um, *f. pl.* Bacchantes ; **Mimalloneus,** a, um ; **Mimallonis,** idis, *f. a Bacchante.*

Mimās, antis, m. **I.** *a promontory in Ionia, opposite Chios.* **II.** *one of the Giants.*

mīmicē, *adv. like a mime-actor :* Cat.

mīmicus, a, um [μιμικός], *suitable for mimes, farcical :* iocus, Cic. ; Plin. Ep.

Mimnermus, ī, m. *a Greek elegiac poet of Colophon* (c. B.C. 560).

mimographus, ī, m. [μιμογράφος], *a writer of mimes :* Suet.

mimula, ae, *f.* [dim. mīma], *a miserable little actress :* Cic.

mīmus, ī, m. [μῖμος]. **I.** *a mimic play, mime, farce.* **1.** L i t. : Cic., Ov., etc. **2.** T r a n s f. *anything farcical or unreal ; a farce :* e.g. *the sham triumph of Caligula,* Suet. **II.** *an actor in mime :* Cic., Ov., etc.

min', for mihine, *v.* ego.

mina, ae, *f. adj. smooth-bellied* (i.e. without wool) : ovis, Pl. ; Varr.

mina (mna, Plin.), ae, *f.* [μνᾶ]. **I.** *a Greek weight of a hundred Attic drachmas, a mina* (about 15·2 oz. troy). **II.** As an Attic *silver-weight* (its money-value being about £4 sterling) : argenti, Pl. ; or mina alone, Pl., Cic. **III.** *a gold-weight* (money-value about £20 sterling) : auri, Pl.

mināciae, ārum, *f. pl.* [mināx], *threats, menaces :* Pl. [It. *minaccia ;* Sp. *amenaza;* Fr. *menace.*]

māciter, *adv. threateningly, with threats :* Cic., Quint. Comp. : Cic.

minae, ārum, *f. pl.* [cf. minor]. **1.** L i t. *the projecting points or pinnacles of walls :* murorum, Verg. **2.** T r a n s f. **a.** Of persons : *threats, menaces :* Pl., Cic. ; intendere alicui, Tac. ; iactare, Cic. **b.** Of a snake : attollere minas, Verg. Of a bull : nullae in fronte minae : Ov. Of other things : hibernae, Tib. ; frigoris, Ov.

minanter, *adv. threateningly :* Ov.

minātiō, ōnis, *f.* [minor], *a threatening :* Pl. ; in *pl.* : Cic.

mināx, ācis, *adj.* [minor], *jutting out, projecting, overhanging.* **1.** L i t. : scopulus, Verg. ; Lucr. **2.** T r a n s f. *threatening, full of threats or menaces.* **a.** Of persons : Cic., Quint. ; adversus barbaros minacissimus, Suet. **b.** Of animals and things : vituli fronte, Ov. ; fluvii, Verg. ; aequor, Ov. ; litterae, Cic. Ep. ; vox, Hor. ; pestilentia minacior, Liv.

mineō, ēre [same root as minae and minor], *to jut, project :* Lucr.

Minerva, ae, *f.* [O. L. Menerva ; *cf.* mēns, memini], *the goddess of wisdom and of the arts and sciences,* identified with Greek Pallas Athene. T r a n s f. **a.** *genius, learning, skill, art :* crassā Minervā, Hor. ; invitā Minervā, *contrary to the bent of one's genius,* Cic. ; sus Minervam (*sc.* docet), Cic. **b.** *working in wool, spinning and weaving :* tolerare colo vitam tenuique Minervā, Verg. ; Ov., etc.

mingō, mingere, minxī, mictum [*cf.* mēiō], *to make water :* Hor.

miniānus, a, um [minium], *painted with vermilion :* Iuppiter, Cic.

miniātulus, a, um [*dim.* miniātus], cerula, Cic. Ep.

miniātus, a, um [minium], *coloured with red lead :* cerula, Cic. Ep. Hence, **miniō**, āre, Plin.

minimē (**minumē**), *sup. adv.* of parum, *in the smallest degree, least of all, very little ;* cum minime videbamur, tum maxime philosophabamur, Cic. ; Ter. With *Adj.* or *Adv.* (to make a negative superlative) : minime multi, Cic., Liv. ; minime arduus, Caes. ; minime densus, Liv. ; minime ad eos mercatores saepe commeant, Caes. Strengthened with *omnium* or *gentium :* ad te minime omnium pertinebat, Cic. ; minume gentium, Pl., Ter. With *quam : as little as possible :* quam minime dedecore facere possimus, Cic. In replies, as an emphatic negative, *by no means, not at all :* Pl., Ter., Cic. Strengthened with *gentium :* Ter.

minimus, a, um : *v.* parvus and minor.

miniō, āre, *v.* miniātus.

minister, trī, *m.* ; and **ministra**, ae, *f.* [minor ; *cf.* magister], *an inferior,* hence, *a server, servant, attendant, helper, agent.* **1.** L i t. **a.** In gen. : Falerni, Cat. ; Juv. ; centum aliae (famulae), totidemque pares aetate ministri, Verg. ; Ov. **b.** In religious rites : ministri publici Martis, Cic. ; Ov. **c.** Of public officers : ministros imperi tui, *under-officials,* Cic. Ep. ; pacis bellique ministras, Verg. **d.** In the law-courts : infimi homines ministros se praebent in iudiciis oratoribus (like our attorneys), Cic. **2.** T r a n s f. **a.** *agent, executor, tool, instrument :* legum ministri magistratūs (sunt), Cic. ; cupiditatum, Cic. ; scelerum, Lucr. ; minister fulminis ales (i.e. the eagle), Hor. ; sermonum, Tac. **b.** *help, support :* ministro baculo, Ov.

ministerium, ī, *n.* [minister], *the office or function of a minister ; service, ministry.* **1.** L i t. : Pl. ; ministerio fungi, Liv. ; aquila velut ministerio missa, Liv. ; diurna, Ov. ; triste, Verg. ; ministeria belli, Tac. **2.** T r a n s f. (in *pl.*) *a suite of attendants :* ministeria magistratibus conscribere, Tac. ;

varia harenae ministēriā, Suet. [Toi inii tiero ; Sp. *menester ;* Fr. *métier.*]

ministra, ae, *f. v.* minister.

ministrātor, ōris, *m.* and **ministrātrīx**, īcis, *f.* [ministrō], *an assistant, attendant, waiter, handmaid :* Cic., Sen. Ep. ; artes ministratrices oratoris, Cic.

ministrō, āre [minister], *to serve, attend, wait upon, serve, esp.* at table. **1.** L i t. : Pl., Cic. With A c c. : pocula, Cic. ; *in Pass. :* cena ministratur pueris tribus, Hor. ; with DAT. of person : Vinio ministrari iussit, Tac. **2.** T r a n s f. **a.** *to serve, supply, furnish,* with Acc. and DAT. : faces furiis Clodianis, Cic. ; populo R. adiumenta belli, Cic. ; viros et arma alicui, Tac. ; nova semina bello, Tac. ; prolem, Tib. ; umbram platanus, Verg. ; locus omnium rerum usūs humano generi, Liv. ; Furor arma, Verg. ; vinum verba, Hor. **b.** *to serve, manage :* navem velis, Verg., Tac. **c.** *to execute, carry out :* res timide, Hor. ; iussa, Ov.

minitābundus, a, um [minitor], *threatening :* Liv., Tac.

minitō, āre (Pl.) and **minitor**, ārī [*freq.* minor], *to threaten, menace :* Pl. With DAT. of person (if expressed) and Acc. of thing (Pl., Cic., Liv.), or ABL. (Enn., Cic., Sall.) or *Inf.* (Ter.), or Acc. and *Fut. Inf.* (Pl., Cic.).

minium, ī, *n.* [a Spanish word]. **I.** *native cinnabar, vermilion :* Prop. **II.** *red oxide of lead :* Verg., Suet.

minor, ārī [*cf.* mōns, mineō]. **1.** L i t. *to jut, project : in caelum scopuli,* Verg. **2.** T r a n s f. *to threaten, menace.* **a.** Of persons. With DAT. of person : Cic. ; and Acc. of thing : Cic. ; or ABL. : Sall., Verg. ; or Acc. and *Inf.* : Pl. (*Fut. Inf.,* Cic.). **b.** Of things : domus mea deflagrationem urbi minabatur, Cic. ; ornus, Verg. ; nec semper feriet quodcumque minabitur arcus, Hor. ; plaustra populo, Juv.

minor, us, *Comp.* of parvus. [It. *minore ;* Fr. *moindre.*]

Minōs, ōis (also -ōnis ; Acc. Minōem and Minōa), *m.* **I.** *s. of Zeus and Europa, b. of Rhadamanthus, king and lawgiver in Crete, and after death judge in the infernal regions.* **II.** *grandson of the former, likewise king in Crete; h. of Pasiphoë, f. of Ariadna ;* **Minōis**, idis, *f. Ariadna ;* **Minōius**, **Minōus**, a, um, *belonging to Minos,* also *Cretan.*

Minōtaurus, ī, *m. a monster with the head of a bull and the body of a man; slain by Theseus.*

minumē, *v.* minimē.

minumus [minus], *v.* parvus.

minuō, uere, uī, ūtum. **A.** T r a n s. *to make smaller.* **1.** L i t. **a.** *to break in pieces :* mullum in singula pulpamenta, Hor. ; ligna, Ov. **b.** *to lessen, reduce :* sumptūs civitatum, Cic. ; rem familiarem, Hor. ; minuuntur corporis artūs, Ov. **2.** T r a n s f. **a.** *to lessen, lower, impair, weaken :* matris inperium, Pl. ; auctoritatem, Caes. ; maiestatem populi R. per vim, Cic. ; magistratum, Liv. ; controversias, Caes. ; gloriam alicuius, Cic. ; spem, Caes. ; suspicionem, Cic. Ep. **b.** *to modify :* consilium, sententiam, Ter. ; opinionem, Cic. **B.** I n t r a n s. *to lessen, ebb :* minuente aestu, Caes.

minus, *n.* of minor, *nnun* and *adv. less.* **I.**
Noun (in Nom., Acc. and Gen.), *less, a less*
amount, a less degree : si minus de aliquo
dixero, Cic.; Pl.; consul minus est quam
privatus, Cic.; haud minus ac iussi faciunt,
Verg. Often with a Gen.: non minus
auctoritatis inerat in actione quam facultatis, Cic.; Caes., etc.; minus militum periit,
Liv.; accidere duo milia haud minus peditum, Liv.; in reverse order: ne minus
dimidium ad Trebonium pervenirent, Cic.
With Abl. of *Comparison :* Hamilcar cum
paulo minus duobus milibus militum traditur, Liv. As *Intern.* Acc. with *posse, valere :*
metūs ipsi per se minus valerent nisi etc.,
Cic. Gen. of Price: minoris emere, Cic.
II. *Adv.* (fr. *Neut.* Acc. used as *Intern.*
Acc.) *less, in a less degree.* **1.** Lit. **a.** With
Adj. or *Adv.* (to make a *negat. comp.*) :
minus multi, Pl.; imperium semper ad
optimum quemque a minus bono transfertur, Sall.; minus late, Caes. **b.** Phr.
With *quam :* respondebo tibi minus fortasse vehementer, quam abs te sum provoca-
tus, Cic. Without *quam :* madefactum iri
minus xxx. diebus Graeciam sanguine, Cic.
(*cf.* I). With Abl. of *Comparison :* nemo
fuit illo minus emax, Nep. N.B. haud (non)
minus quam (atque), *not less, no less, quite*
as much : non minus nobis iucundi sunt ii
dies, quibus conservamur quam illi quibus
nascimur, Cic.; Liv. With Abl. of *Measure,*
multo, nihilo (or nihil), quo, eo, etc. : puni-
endum certe nihilo minus, Cic.; Caes., etc.
Repeated, minus minusque, minus et (ac)
minus, *less and less :* mihi iam minus minusque optemperat, Ter. **2.** Often for *not at*
all, not : nonnunquam ea quae praedicta
sunt minus eveniunt, Cic.; Syracusis, si
minus supplicio adfici, at custodiri oportebat, Cic.; Ter.; Liv., etc.; sin minus,
if otherwise : quod si adsecutus sum gaudeo;
sin minus, hoc me tamen consolor, etc.,
Cic. Ep. For **quō minus**, *whereby not,*
v. quōminus. [It. *meno ;* Fr. *moins.*]

minusculus, a, um [*dim.* minor], *rather*
small : nomen, Pl.; villa, Cic. Ep.

minūtal, ālis, *n.* [minūtus], *a dish of minced*
meat : Juv.

minūtātim, *adv.* [minūtus], *piecemeal, in*
little bits. **1.** Lit.: Varr. **2.** Transf.
by bits, bit by bit : discere, Lucr.; interrogare, Cic.

minūtē, *adv. into small pieces.* Transf. **a.**
in a small hand. Sup.: scribere, Sen. Ep.
b. *in a petty, paltry manner :* res minutius
tractare, Cic. **c.** *minutely, closely :* minutius scrutantur omnia, Quint.

minūtia, ae, *f.* [minūtus], *smallness, fineness :*
ad minutiam redigere, Sen. Ep.

minūtulus, a, um [*dim.* minūtus], *tiny, wee :*
pueri, Pl.

minūtus, a, um. **I.** *Part.* minuō. **II.** Adj.
little, small, minute. **1.** Lit.: dii, Pl. Of
things: litterae, Pl.; opuscula, Cic.
Comp. : Lucr. **2.** Transf.: *petty, paltry:*
animus, Juv.; philosophi, Cic. *Sup. :*
Cic. [Fr. *menu.*]

Minyās, ae, *m. a mythical king of Thessaly ;*
Minyae, ārum, *m. pl. the Minyans, Argo-*
nauts, the companions of Jason ; **Minyēias**,
adis, *f. a daughter of Minyas ;* **Minyēides**,

um, *f. pl. the daughters of Minyas ,* **Min-**
yēius, a, um.

mirābilis, e, *adj.* [miror], *to be wondered at,*
wonderful, marvellous, extraordinary, admir-
able : candelabrum opere mirabili perfectum, Cic.; Pl.; hic tibi sit potius quam tu
mirabilis illi, Hor.; quod Regulus rediit
nobis nunc mirabile videtur, Cic.; mirabile
est (with Acc. and *Inf.*) : Ter., Liv.; (with
Indir. Quest.) : Cic. With Abl.: dictu,
Cic., Verg., Liv.; visu, Verg.; visu eventu-
que, Liv. *Comp. :* Cic. *Sup. :* Col. [It.
maraviglia ; Sp. *maravilla ;* Fr. *merveille.*]

mirābiliter, *adv. wonderfully, astonishingly :*
Cic. Ep., Nep. *Comp. :* Cic.

mirābundus, a, um [miror], *full of wonder or*
astonishment : with *Indir. Quest. :* Liv.

mirāculum, i, *n.* [miror]. **I.** *a wonderful or*
marvellous thing : a wonder, marvel : Cic.,
Verg., Liv., etc.; miraculum magnitudinis, Liv.; esse miraculo, Liv. **II.** *wonder,*
amazement, surprise : stupore ac miraculo
torpidos, Liv.; milites in itinere aggregan-
tur, alii conscientiā, plerique miraculo, Tac.
[It. *miracolo ;* Sp. *milagro.*]

mirandus, a, um [miror], *wonderful :* in mir-
andam altitudinem, Cic.; mirandum est
(with *Indir. Quest.*) : Juv.

mirātiō, ōnis, *f.* [miror], *wonder, admiration :*
facere, Cic.

mirātor, ōris, *m.* [miror], *an admirer :* Hor.,
Ov., Sen.

mirātrix, icis, *f. adj.* [miror], *admiring :*
vetustas sui, Luc.; turba, Juv.

mirē, *adv. wonderfully :* puero favent, Cic.
Ep.; laudare, Liv.; gratus, Liv.; mire
quam illius loci cogitatio delectat, Cic. Ep.

mirificē, *adv. wonderfully :* delectari, Cic.

mirificus, a, um [mirus faciō], *causing won-*
der or admiration, wonderful ; extraordi-
nary. Of persons : Cic. Ep. Of things :
Caes., Cic. *Sup. :* Ter.

mirimodis, *adv.* [mirus modus], *in a won-*
derful manner : Pl.

mirmillō, v. murmillō.

miror, āri [mirus], *to wonder or marvel at.* **I.**
to be astonished or amazed at. With Acc. :
Pl., Cic., Verg., etc. With Acc. and *Inf. :*
Cic. With *quod :* Cic. With *si :* Pl.,
Cic. With *Indir. Quest. :* Ter., Caes., Cic.
With *de :* Cic. **II.** *to look on with wonder,*
to admire : tabulas pictas, Sall. With
Causal Gen. : iustitiane prius mirer ? Verg.

mirus, a, um [*cf.* Gk. μειδάω], *wonderful,*
astonishing : Pl., Cic., etc.; miris modis,
wondrously, Pl., Ter., Verg.; mirum in
modum, *astonishingly,* Caes.; mirum est
(with Acc. and *Inf.*), Cic.; mirum videtur
(with *Indir. Quest.*), Caes.; mirum quam
or quantum, *it is wonderful how or how*
much, i.e. *extraordinarily:* mirum quantum
profuit ad concordiam, Liv.; Cic. Ep.;
mirum ni, nisi, or quin, *it would be wonder-*
ful, if not (i.e. I am very much mistaken,
if not, i.e. most probably) : mira sunt, nisi
invitavit sese in cenā plusculum, Pl.;
mirum, quin ab avo eius aut proavo acciperem, Pl.

miscellānea, ōrum, *n. pl.* [miscellus], *a*
hash of broken meat : Juv.

miscellus, a, um [misceō], *mixed :* uvae,
Cato; ludi, Suet.

misceō, miscēre, miscuī, mixtum [*cf.* Gk. μίγνυμι], *to mix, mingle, to intermingle, blend.* **I.** *to mix* (and so make a compound). **1.** L i t.: pix sulpure mixta, Verg.; cruor harēnā, Sall.; mella Falerno, Hor.; flumen Allia Tiberino amni, Liv.; fletum cruori, Ov. **2.** T r a n s f.: dulce amarumque mihi, Pl.; falsa veris, Cic.; tristia laetis, Ov.; gravitate leporem, Cic.; ex dissimillimis rebus misceri, Cic. **II.** *to make by mixing, brew.* **1.** L i t.: alteri mulsum, Cic.; pocula alicui, Ov.; aconita, Juv. **2.** T r a n s f.: animorum motūs dicendo, Cic.; proelia, Prop.; Verg.; certamina, Liv.; vulnera inter sese tauri, Verg.; ignes murmura, Verg. **III.** *to combine, associate, share, join together.* **1.** L i t.: cum meis lacrimis suas, Ov.; sanguinem et genus cum aliquo, Liv. **E s p.** *of sexual and social union*: corpus cum aliquā, Cic.; mulier mixta deo, Verg.; Teucri mixtique Sicani, Verg.; ipsa ad praetoria densae miscentur (i.e. gather in thick crowds), Verg.; se viris, Verg.; eos agmini suo, Liv. **2.** T r a n s f.: animum alicuius cum suo, Cic.; cum amico curas, Sen. Ep.; sortem omnem fortunae regnique sui cum rebus Romanis, Liv. **IV.** *to mix up, throw into confusion or disorder.* **1.** L i t.: sortis, *the lottery tickets*, Cic.; turbam cervorum, Verg.; maria caelo, Verg.; caelum terramque, Verg. **2.** T r a n s f.: omnia infima summis paria fecit, turbavit, miscuit, Cic.; rem publicam, Cic.; moenia miscentur luctu, Verg. P r o v.: caelum ac terras miscere, Liv.; caelum terris et mare caelo, Juv.

misellus, a, um [*dim.* miser], *wretched little* : homo, Cic. Ep.; passer, Cat.; pallium, Pl.; spes, Lucr.

miser, era, erum [*cf.* maestus], *wretched, unhappy, miserable* or (as regarded by others) *pitiful, pitiable.* **1.** L i t. Of persons. a. In gen.: Pl., Cic., etc. *Comp.* miserior and *Sup.* miserrimus, Cic. With G e n.: cultūs miser (*in dress*), Hor. Often inserted parenthetically or interjectionally: ossa atque pellis sum, misera, macritudine, Pl.; Lucr.; o me miserum, Cic., Ov.; miserum, Verg. **b.** In sickness, weariness, etc.: morbo, Pl.; *Sup.* Ter. **c.** *pitiful, sorry* (i.e. worthless): hominem perditum miserumque, Ter. **2.** T r a n s f. Of things. **a.** *pitiable, sad* : querella, Cic.; mors, Verg. **b.** *pitiful* (because excessive): amor, Verg.; ambitio, Hor. **c.** *pitiful, sorry* (i.e. worthless): praeda, Caes.; carmen, Verg.

miserābilis, e, *adj.* [miseror]. **I.** *to be pitied, pitiable*: Cic., Ov., Liv., etc. With A b l.: visu, Verg. *Comp.*: Liv. **II.** *moving pity, piteous* : voces, Liv., Cic.; elegi, Hor. *Neut.* Acc. as *Adv.*: Verg., Juv.

miserābiliter, *adv.* **I.** *pitiably* : emori, Cic. **II.** *piteously* : scripta epistula, Cic. Ep.; Liv.

miserandus, a, um [miseror], *pitiful, lamentable* : oratio, Cic.; Verg., etc.

miserātiō, ōnis, *f.* [miseror], *pity, compassion, commiseration.* **1.** L i t.: Cic., Quint. **2.** R h e t. *a pathetic appeal* : Quint.; in *pl.* : Cic.

miserē, *adv. wretchedly, miserably, unhappily.* **a.** In gen.: vivere, Cic. *Comp.* : Liv. **b.** *pitifully* (because excessively): amare, Pl.; invidere, Ter.; Hor.

misereō, ēre [miser]. **I.** *to pity, compassionate, commiserate, sympathise with* : with G e n.: hominum, Pl.; sui, Lucr. **II.** *Us. impers.* misereret, *it excites pity or compassion* : with A c c. of person who pities, and G e n. of the object of pity: miseret te aliorum, Pl.; eorum nos miseret, Cic. With vicem instead of simple G e n.: Menedemi vicem miseret me, Ter.

misereor, ēri [miser]. **I.** *to pity, compassionate.* With G e n.: sociorum, Cic.; nominis Romani, Liv.; Verg.; Ov. **II.** I m p e r s.: miseretur, miseritum est, etc., *it excites pity or compassion* : with A c c. of person who pities, and G e n. of the object of pity (*cf.* miseret): Pl., Cic. With G e n. only : supplicum, Cic.

miserēscō, ere [misereō]. **I.** *to turn to compassion, take pity* : his lacrimis vitam damus et miserescimus ultro, Verg. With G e n.: regis, Verg. **II.** I m p e r s.: (for constr. *v.* misereo): te miserescat mei, Ter.; Pl.

miseret, *v.* misereō.

miserētur, *v.* misereor.

miseria, ae, *f.* [miser], *wretchedness, unhappiness, misery.* **I.** In gen.: Pl.; in miseriā esse, Cic.; in miseriis versari, Cic. Ep.; in miserias incidere, Cic. **b.** *a cause of distress* : oneri miseriaeque esse, Sall. **c.** *distress due to anxiety, etc.*: miseriam capere, Ter.; omnia superstitiosā sollicitudine et miseriā credere, Cic. **d.** *distress due to poverty* : in urbe vis patrum in dies miseriaque plebis crescebant, Liv.

misericordia, ae, *f.* [misericors]. **I.** *pity, compassion, sympathy, mercy* : captare, commovere, concitare, implorare, exposcere, adhibere, tribuere, Cic.; misericordiā commoveri, capi, Cic.; misericordias habere, Pl.; ad misericordiam vocare, Cic.; omnibus vestram misericordiam patere, Liv. With *Obj.* G e n.: Caes., Cic. Ep. **II.** *appeals to pity* : haec magna cum misericordiā fletuque pronuntiantur, Caes.

misericors, rdis, *adj.* [misereō cor], *compassionate, sympathetic, merciful* : Pl., Cic.; in aliquem, Cic. *Comp.* : misericordior, Pl., Cic.

miseriter, *adv. sadly* : Cat.

miseror, āri [miser]. **I.** *to lament, bewail, deplore* : with A c c.: Pl., Cic. **II.** *to show pity on, commiserate* (of outward acts or words): aliquem, Sall., Liv.; ab humo miserans attollit amicum, Verg.; sortem animo iniquam, Verg.; animi iuvenem, Verg.; casum alicuius, Tac. (*v.* also miserandus).

missicius, a, um [mittō], *discharged from military service* : Suet.

missiculō, āre, *freq., to send often* : ad aliquem litteras, Pl.

missilis, e, *adj.* [mittō], *that may be thrown, for throwing* or *hurling, missile* : lapides, Liv.; ferrum, Verg.; sagittae, Hor. As Noun, **missilia**, ium, *n. pl.* **a.** *missiles* : missilibus Lacedaemonii pugnabant, Liv.; Verg.; in *sing.* : Luc. **b.** (also res mis-

siles) *presents thrown by the emperors* among
the people to be scrambled for : Suet.

missiō, ōnis, *f.* [mittō], *a letting go.* **a.** *a
release* from captivity : aliquid pro mis-
sione dare, Cic. **b.** *a discharge* from service (of soldiers, office-holders, gladiators),
a dismissal : praemium missionis ferre,
Caes. ; missionem negare, Liv. Of a
quaestor : Suet. **c.** Of gladiators in the
arena : *quarter* : Myrino peteretur missio
laeso, Mart. Hence, spectaculum sine mis-
sione, Liv. **d.** *a cessation, termination* :
ante ludorum missionem, Cic. Ep. **e.** *a
sending, despatching* : legatorum, Cic. ;
litterarum Cic. Ep.

missitō, āre [*freq.* mittō], *to send repeatedly* :
auxilia, Liv. ; Sall.

missus, a, um, *Part.* mittō.

missus, ūs, *m.* [mittō], *a letting go.* **A.** *a
throwing, hurling.* **1.** Lit.: vehementius
ictu missuque telum, Liv. **2.** Transf. *a
shot* (e.g. a bowshot): as measure of distance : vix absunt nobis missûs bis mille
sagittae, Lucr. **B.** *a sending* (with *Subj.*
Gen.): missu Caesaris, Caes. ; Verg.
C. *a start*, hence, *a course* or *heat* in the
games : spectaculum multiplicatis missibus
in serum produxit, Suet.

mitēscō, ere [mitis], *to become soft* or *mild.*
1. Lit. **a.** *to grow mellow, ripen* : uvae a
sole mitescunt, Cic. ; herbae, Ov. **b.** Of
weather : *to grow mild, calm, moderate* :
frigora, Hor. ; hiems, Liv. **2.** Transf.
a. Of animals : Liv. **b.** Of anger, etc.:
cor ferum, Acc. ; ira, Ov. ; discordiae,
Liv. ; seditio, Tac. Of persons : Hor.

Mithrās and **Mithrēs**, ae, *m. the sun-god* of
the Persians.

Mithridātēs, is, *m. the name of several kings
of Pontus :* esp. Mithridates VI. *surnamed
the Great, who waged war with the Romans ;
he was at last conquered by Pompey, and killed
himself* B.C. 63 ; **Mithridātēus, Mithri-
dāticus**, a, um.

mitigātiō, ōnis, *f.* [mitigō], *a soothing, calming* (of a violent emotion) : Cic.

mitigō, āre [mitis agō], *to make mild* or *soft.*
1. Lit. **a.** *to mellow, ripen* : Cic. **b.** *to
soften* : cibum, Cic. ; Indus agros, Cic. **2.**
Transf. (of emotions, etc.) *to soften, calm,
pacify, appease* : animum alicuius, Cic. ;
Gallorum animos a feritate insitâ, Liv. ;
tristitiam et severitatem, Cic. ; iras, Ov. ;
legis acerbitatem, Cic. ; aliquem pecuniâ,
Tac. ; valetudinem temperantia, Plin. Ep.

mitis, e, *adj. mild, mellow, soft.* **1.** Lit. **a.**
mellow, ripe : poma, Verg. ; Bacchus,
Verg. ; succi, Ov. **b.** *soft :* solum Tiburis,
Hor. Comic.: mitis sum fustibus, Pl.
c. *mild, placid :* caelum mitissimum (*mild
climate*), Liv. ; (fluvius) mitis in morem
stagni, Verg. **2.** Transf. **a.** *mild, gentle :*
homo, Pl., Cic. ; in aliquem, Cic. Ep., Liv. ;
adversus victos, Liv. ; paenitentiae mitior,
to the penitent, Tac. ; Ov. ; animus, doctrina,
Cic. ; consilium, Ov. ; responsum, Liv.
Comp. : Liv. *Sup.* : Cic., Liv. **b.** Of
style : *mellow* : Cic. *Comp.* and *Sup.* :
Cic. *Neut.* Acc. of *Comp.* **mitius**, as *Adv.* :
Ov ; also *Sup. Adv.* **mitissimē**, Caes.

mitra, ae, *f.* [μίτρα], *an Asiatic head-dress,
turban :* Cic., Verg., Juv.

mittō, mittere, misi, missum, *to let go, make to
go.* **I.** *to let go.* **A.** *to let fly, hurl, fling,
launch :* pila, Caes. ; hastam, Ov. ; ful-
mina, Hor. ; tela tormentis, Caes. ; fundâ
lapides, Liv. ; eum de ponte, Cat. ; puerum
ex arce praecipitem, Ov. ; talos in phimum,
Hor. ; pueros in aquam, Liv. ; sues saevos
in hostis, Lucr. With *Refl. Pron. :* se ab
aethere, Verg. ; se in rapidas aquas, Ov. ;
cf. animas in pericula, Verg. In *Mid. :*
sub tanta pericula missus, Verg. **B.** *to let
go forth, throw off* or *forth, emit, shed.* **a.**
In gen. : luna lucem in terras, Cic. ; magna
vis aquae caelo missa, Sall. ; membranas
de corpore, Lucr. ; fruges sanguinem, Liv. ;
mittere sanguinem provinciae (metaph. *to
bleed the province*), Cic. ; signum sanguinis,
Lucr. ; hence, signa timoris, Caes. **b.** Of
sounds : serpens horrenda sibila, Ov. Freq.
with vocem, *to utter :* vocem pro me nemo
mittit, Cic. ; Caes. ; Juv. ; vocem suppli-
cem, vocem liberam, Liv. **C.** *to let go one's
hold of, drop ; to let go from restraint.* **a.**
In gen. : mitte rudentem, sceleste, Pl. ;
arma, Caes. ; non missura cutem hirudo,
Hor. ; mittin' me intro, Pl. ; mitte me,
Ter. ; carcere equos, Ov. ; Hor. **b.** Of
prisoners and soldiers : *to release, free, discharge* (mostly in phr. missum facere):
nautas pretio certo missos facere, Cic. ;
Caes., etc. Of slaves (us. in phr. manu
mittere): Pl., Cic., Liv., etc. (*v.* manus).
Of meetings : *to dismiss :* senatum, Cic. ;
convivium, praetorium, Liv. **c.** *to let go,
give up, forgo :* missam iram facere, Ter.
(*cf.* C. b.); missos faciant honores, Cic. ;
timorem, certamen, Verg. ; spes, Hor. ;
odium, ambages, Liv. With *Inf.* : Pl.,
Cic., Hor., etc. **d.** *to let pass, to pass over
in silence :* Pl., Ter., Cic. ; ut haec missa
faciam, Cic. With *de :* Cic. With a
quod-clause : Cic. Ep. **II.** *to make to go ;
to send, despatch.* **A.** In gen. : huc missa
sum, Pl. ; legatos de deditione ad eum miserunt, Caes. ; filium suum foras, Cic. ; aliquem ad mortem, Cic. ; morti, Pl. ; damnatum in exsilium, Liv. ; pabulatum, Caes. ;
scitatum oracula, Verg. ; equitatum auxilio
Caesari, Caes. ; exercitum sub iugum (or
iugo) mittere, Caes., Liv. Occ. *to escort*
(=πέμπω) : (of Mercury) animas sub
Tartara, Verg. Also *to send for, invite :*
ad cenam, Cic. **B.** Esp. **a.** *to send news,
notify :* Deiotarus legatos ad me misit se
cum omnibus copiis esse venturum, Cic. ;
Liv. With *ut* and *Juss. Subj.* : Caes., Cic.
Ep., Liv. **b.** *to send as a gift, bestow, confer :*
sestertium centum milia, Nep. ; munera,
Hor. ; funera Teucris, Verg. ; hence, alicui mentem, Verg. ; salutem alicui, *greetings,*
Ov. Of a book : *to dedicate :* hunc librum
de Senectute ad te misimus, Cic. **c.** Of
produce : India mittit ebur, Verg. ; Ov.,
etc. [It. *mettere :* Sp. *meter :* Fr. *mettre.*]

mitulus or **mytulus** or **mūtulus**, i, *m.*
[μύτιλος], *a limpet :* Cato, Hor.

Mitylēnē, ēs, *v.* Mytilēnē.

mixtim, *adv.* [misceō], *mixedly :* Lucr.

mixtūra, ae, *f.* [misceō], *a mixing, blending.*
1. Lit.: rerum, Lucr. ; Varr. **2.** Transf.:
ex diversis, Quint. ; aliorum generum cum
aliis, Quint. ; vitiorum atque virtutum, Suet.

mna, v. mina.

Mnēmŏnĭdes, um. f. pl. the Muses.

Mnēmŏsўnē, ēs, f. [μνημοσύνη, remembrance], mother of the Muses.

mnēmŏsўnon, ī, n. [μνημόσυνον], a souvenir: Cat.

mōbĭlis, e, adj. [moveō], easy to move. **1.** Lit. **a.** moveable : turres, Curt. ; oculi, Cic. Comp. and Sup. : Cic. **b.** nimble, active, fleet : pedibus mobilis, Pl. ; venti, Ov. **2.** Transf. **a.** easily influenced ; pliant, excitable : aetas, Verg. ; populus mobilior ad cupiditatem agri, Liv. **b.** unsteady, changeable : nec in te animo fui mobili, Cic. Ep. ; Galli sunt in consiliis capiendis mobiles, Caes. ; gens ad omnem auram spei mobilis, Liv. ; natura malorum, Juv.

mōbĭlĭtās, ātis, f. [mōbilis], moveableness, mobility. **1.** Lit. : Cic. ; fulminis, Lucr. ; equitum, Caes. **2.** Transf. **a.** fluency : linguae, Cic. **b.** quickness, vivacity : animi, Quint. **c.** changeableness : Cic., Tac. ; ingeni, Sall.

mōbĭlĭter, adv. with rapid motion. **1.** Lit. : Lucr., Cic. Comp. : Lucr. **2.** Transf. : ad bellum mobiliter celeriterque excitari, Caes.

mōbĭlĭtō, āre [mōbilis], to make moveable or quick : Lucr.

mŏdĕrābĭlis, e, adj. [moderor], restrainable ; hence, restrained : Ov.

mŏdĕrāmen, ĭnis, n. [moderor], a means of controlling. **1.** Lit. **a.** navis (i.e. the rudder), Ov. **b.** control : equorum, Ov. **2.** Transf. government : rerum, Ov.

mŏdĕranter, adv. with control : Lucr.

mŏdĕrātē, adv. with moderation : Caes., Cic., Liv. Comp. and Sup. : Cic.

mŏdĕrātim, adv. in due measure, gradually : crescere, Lucr.

mŏdĕrātĭō, ōnis, f. [moderor], a limiting, restraining, controlling. **1.** Lit. **a.** divina in homines moderatio, Cic. ; mundi, Cic. ; effrenati populi, Cic. **b.** self-control, moderation : animi, Cic. ; in dicendo, Cic. **2.** Transf. **a.** regulation, rules : numerorum, Cic. **b.** observance of due measure : Cic. ; dicendi, Cic.

mŏdĕrātor, ōris, m. and **mŏdĕrātrix**, īcis, f. [moderor], a controller, governor, director : sibi, Pl. ; tanti operis, Cic. ; equorum, Ov. ; moderatrix offici curia, Cic.

mŏdĕrātus, a, um. **I.** Part. moderor. **II.** Adj. : restrained, controlled, orderly, well regulated : senes, Cic. Of things : ventus, Ov. ; mores, doctrina, oratio, otium, Cic. Comp. : Vell. ; Sup. Planc. ap. Cic. Ep.

mŏdĕror, ārī (and **mŏdĕrō**, āre, Pl.) [modus] to set bounds to ; to check, moderate, restrain. **1.** Lit. With Dat. : linguae, dictis, Pl. ; animo, Cic. ; uxoribus, Cic. ; irae, Hor. ; fortunae suae, Liv. With Acc. : gaudium, Tac. ; duritiam legum, Suet. **2.** Transf. to control, regulate, govern, direct : with Acc. : inmodestis te moribus, Pl. ; equos, Caes. ; habenas, Ov. ; res rusticas, Cic. ; linguam, Sall. ; fidem (i.e. the lyre), Hor. ; officio consilia, Cic. ; mens omnia, Cic. With Dat. : funiculo navi, Cic. ; ero, Pl. ; fortuna gentibus, Sall.

mŏdestē, adv. **I.** with moderation : Pl.,

Ĉĭc. Liv. Comp. : Quint. Sup. ; Vell. **II.** modestly, humbly : Ter., Cic.

mŏdestia, ae, f. [modestus], the keeping within due bounds, freedom from excess. **a.** In gen. : moderation, restraint, sober conduct : Cic. ; in omni vitā, in dicendo, Cic. **b.** absence of self-assertiveness, a sense of humility, a spirit of obedience : in milite desiderare, Caes. ; de suā modestiā diserebat, Tac. ; Pl. **c.** sense of propriety, correct behaviour : Cic. **d.** Of weather : moderate nature : hiemis, Tac.

mŏdestus, a, um [modus], keeping due measure or limits. **a.** moderate, restrained, sober : vir modestus et frugi, Cic. Ep. **b.** unassuming, hence, orderly, obedient : plebs, Cic. ; servitia, Tac. Sup. : Cic. **c.** wellbehaved, modest : mulier, Ter. ; adulescentulus, Cic. ; Pl. ; mores, pudor, Cic. ; lingua, oculi, Ov. Comp. : Cic. Ep. ; Sup. : Cic. Masc. as Noun : Cic.

mŏdiālis, e, adj. [modius], containing a modius or Roman peck : Pl.

mŏdĭcē, adv. with proper measure or restraint. **a.** moderately : dolorem ferre, Cic. **b.** in good order : se recipere, Liv. **c.** only slightly, not much : minae Clodi modice me tangunt, Cic. Ep. ; locuples, Liv. **d.** meanly : modice instratus torus, Suet.

mŏdĭcellus, a, um [dim. modicus], very moderate, very little : Suet.

mŏdĭcus, a, um [modus], observing a proper measure or limit, moderate. **a.** Of size : middling : modico gradu, Pl. ; potiones, Cic. ; acervus, Hor. ; amnis, Tac. **b.** moderate, not extravagant : convivia, severitas, Cic. ; domi modicus, Sall. ; supellex, Nep. **c.** middling, ordinary, mean, humble : genus dicendi modicum in delectando, Cic. ; canthari, Hor. ; tempus (i.e. short), Quint. ; amici, Juv. With Gen. : Sabinus modicus originis, Tac.

mŏdĭfĭcātus, a, um [modus faciō], measured : Rhet. : verba, membra, Cic.

mŏdĭus, ī, m. (Gen. pl. modium, Cic.) [perh. cf. modus], the Roman corn-measure, containing about 2 Eng. gallons. **a.** Prop. : tritici modius, Cic. **b.** Of other things besides corn : argenti, Pl. ; fabae, Hor. ; anulorum, Liv. Prov. : multos modios salis simul edendos esse ut amicitiae munus expletum sit, Cic. ; pleno modio, in full measure, abundantly, Cic. Ep. [Fr. muid.]

mŏdŏ, adv. (modŏ, Lucr.) [modus], lit. by measure, with a limit : hence to express restriction. **A.** Modal. **1.** In gen. **a.** only, but : semel modo, Pl. ; paulum modo, Cic. ; parvam modo causam timoris adferre, Caes. (For dum modo, solum modo, and tantum modo, v. dum, solum, and tantum.) **b.** non modo . . . sed (or verum) etiam (or et), or simply sed ; not only . . . but also : ut non modo secunda sperare debeas, sed etiam adversa fortissimo animo ferre, Cic. Also non modo non . . . sed (or verum) etiam or sed ne — quidem : hoc non modo non laudari sed ne concedi quidem potest, Cic. The second non is often absent : I do not say merely . . . but not even : talis vir non modo facere sed ne cogitare quidem quicquam audebit, Cic. ; cf. also, non modo ad expeditiones sed vix ad quietas stationes viribus sufficiebant. **2. a.** *in any way* or *degree, ut all, merely, even, only.* **i.** Alone: servus est nemo, qui modo tolerabili condicione sit servitutis, Cic. **ii.** So freq., si modo, *if only :* tute scis (si modo meministi), me tibi tum dixisse, Cic. **iii.** modo si for dum modo : *if only, provided that :* persequar inferius, modo si licet ordine ferri, Ov. **iv.** Also without *si* (*cf.* dum modo), with *Subj., if only, provided that :* quos, valetudo modo bona sit, tenuitas ipsa delectat, Cic.' So too, modo ne, *if only not, provided that not :* si quis est paulo ad voluptates propensior, modo ne sit ex pecudum genere, Cic. **b.** modo non, *all but, almost, nearly :* Fabi gloria modo non suä contumeliä splendet, Liv. ; Ter. **c.** Colloq. with imperatives, *just, now: sequere hac modo, Pl. ; vide modo, Cic. Indignantly : quin tu i modo, *you just be off !* Pl. **B.** Of time : *just now, just.* **a.** Alone. **i.** Of present time : advenis modo, Ter. **ii.** Of time just past : *just now, but this moment, a little while ago, lately :* Pl. ; sum illi villae amicior modo factus, Cic. Elliptically : superesse videt de tot modo milibus unum (i.e. lately existing), Ov. **iii.** Of time just to come : *immediately, directly. in a moment :* domum modo ibo, Ter. ; Cic. ; Liv. Hence = postmodo, Liv. **b.** modo . . . modo . . ., *now . . . now, at one moment . . . at another, sometimes . . . sometimes :* modo ait, modo negat, Ter. ; Cic. ; Liv. **c.** With another *adv. :* modo . . . nunc, Ov. ; modo . . . aliquando, Tac. ; also modo . . . tum (deinde, postea, saepe, interdum), *at first . . . then (etc.), at one time . . . at another (etc.) :* sol modo accedens, tum autem recedens, Cic. ; modo . . . interdum, Sall. ; modo . . . saepe . . . interdum, Hor. ; modo . . . modo . . . postremum, Tac. [It. *mo.*]

modulātē, *adv. measuredly, according to measure, in time :* canere, Cic.

modulātiō, ōnis, *f.* [modulor], *a regular measure.* In music or poetry : *a rhythmical measure :* Quint.

modulātor, ōris, *m.* [modulor], *one who measures rhythmically, a director of music, a musician :* Hor.

modulor, ārī [modulus], *to measure off properly, to regulate.* **A.** Of the voice. **a.** *to regulate the time of, to measure rhythmically, modulate :* ipsa natura quasi modularetur hominum orationem, in omni verbo posuit acutam vocem, Cic. ; virgines sonum vocis pulsu pedum modulantes, Liv. *Perf. Part. in Pass.* sense : ipso modulando dolore verba fundebat, Ov. **b.** *to regulate the time by some instrument, to sing to the accompaniment of :* carmina avenā, Verg. ; verba fidibus Latinis, Hor. **B.** *to attune, play or sing in tune :* lyram, Tib. ; carmina, Suet. *Pass. :* barbitos Lesbio modulatus civi, Hor.

modulus, ī, *m.* [*dim.* modus], *a small measure.* **1.** Lit.: Varr. ; ab imo ad summum moduli bipedalis, Hor. **2.** Transf.: metiri se suo modulo, Hor. [Fr. *moule.*]

modus, ī, *m.* [*cf.* meditor ; and perh. mōtior and Gk. μέδιμνος], *a standard of measurement, a measure.* **1.** Lit. **a.** In gen. :

modi, quibus metirentur rura, Varr. **b.** Of the voice and music : *measure, rhythmical movement, time :* vocum, Cic. ; saltare ad tibicinis modos, Liv. ; modum dare remis, Ov. ; lyrici, Ov. ; fidibus Latinis Thebanos aptare modos, Hor. **c.** *the measure or size of any thing :* filio agri reliquit non magnum modum, Pl. ; Caes. ; Cic. ; agrorum, Liv. ; hastae, Nep. **2.** Transf. **a.** *limit, boundary, bounds :* quis modus tibi exsilio eveniet ? Pl. ; imperi diuturnitati modum statuere, Cic. ; cupidinibus statuat natura modum, Hor. ; finem et modum transire, Cic. ; sine modo ac modestiā, Liv. ; Sall. ; ordine et modo, Cic. ; modum aliquem et finem orationi facere, Cic. ; imponere alicui, Liv. Also, imponere modum with *Indir. Quest. :* Liv. With *Gen.* of *Gerund :* modum ludendi retinere, Cic. **b.** *regulation, rule :* in modum venti nunc huc nunc illuc verso mari, Liv. ; modum belli et pacis facere, Liv. **c.** *a way, manner, mode :* nec semper (hae partes) tractantur uno modo, Cic. ; omnibus modis miser sum, Ter. With *Inf. :* modus inserere atque oculos imponere, Verg. Hence, modo, in modum, *or* ad modum, with *Gen. or Adj. : in the manner of, like :* servilem in modum cruciari, Cic. ; also, servorum modo, Liv. ; in nostrum modum, Tac. ; ad hunc modum distributis legionibus, Caes. Also eius (huius, cuius) modi, *of that or such (this, which) kind :* Caes., Cic., etc. **d.** In grammar : *the voice or mood of a verb :* in verbo fiunt soloecismi per genera, tempora, personas, modos, Quint.

moecha, ae, *f.* [μοιχή], *an adulteress :* Cat., Hor., etc.

moechissō, āre [μοιχίζω], *to ravish, debauch :* aliquam, Pl.

moechor, ārī [moechus], *to commit adultery :* Hor.

moechus, ī, *m.* [μοιχός], *a debaucher, adulterer* (pure Lat. adulter): Ter., Hor., Juv.

moenera = mūnera, *v.* mūnus.

moenia, ium, *n. pl.* [*cf.* mūniō, mūrus], *town-fortifications, ramparts.* **1.** Lit.: Enn., Caes., Cic., etc. ; moenia ac muros, Liv. ; Verg. **2.** Transf. **a.** *defences, bulwarks :* cum paene inaedificata in muris ab exercitu nostro moenia viderentur, Caes. ; theatri, mundi, Lucr. ; navis, Ov. ; caeli, Ov. ; Alpes moenia Italiae, Liv. **b.** *a fortified town :* Cic., Verg. **c.** *a stronghold, castle :* Ditis, Verg. ; intra moenia nostra, Ov.

moeniō, *v.* mūniō.

moerus and **moirus,** *v.* mūrus.

Moesi, ōrum, *m. pl. a people who lived between Thrace and the Danube ;* **Moesia,** ae, *f. their country, modern Bulgaria and S. Jugoslavia ;* **Moesiacus,** a, um.

mola, ae, *f.* [molō], *a mill-stone ;* esp. *the upper stone :* hence, us. in *pl., a mill.* **1.** Lit.: Pl. ; oleariae, Varr. ; trusatiles, hand-mill, Cato. ; pumiceae, Ov. Also sing.: Juv. **2.** Transf. *grits or grains of spelt coarsely ground and mixed with salt* (used at sacrifices and weddings): sparge molam, Verg. ; molam et vinum inspergere, Cic.

molāris, e, *adj.* [mola], *of a mill or grinding,*

mill- : lapis, *a mill-stone*, Plin. As Noun,
molāris, is, *m.* **a.** *a mill-stone* ; poet. for any large stone : Verg., Ov., Tac. **b.** (sc. dens), *a grinder, molar tooth* : Juv.
molārius, a, um [mola], *that turns a mill* : asinus, Cato, Varr.
mōlēs, is. *f.* [*cf.* Gk. μῶλος], *a shapeless, huge, heavy mass, mighty bulk.* **1. Lit. A.** In gen. : Chaos, rudis indigestaque moles, Ov. : vastā se mole moventem, Verg. ; clipei, Verg. ; urbem molibus oppugnare, Verg. ; vineis aliāque mole belli, Liv. **B.** Esp. **a.** *a mass of (natural) rock* : moles tenuis naturaliter objecta, Caes. ; in mole sedens, Ov. **b.** *Artificial : a huge, massive structure ; a dam, pier, mole ; a pile* (of a building) : moles oppositae fluctibus, Cic. ; Caes. ; insanae substructionum moles, Cic. ; regiae moles, Hor. ; Verg. **2. Transf. a.** *a mass* of people or things : tantae ad muros mole feruntur, Verg. ; tantae corporum moles in fugam consternati sunt, Liv. ; stetit aequore moles pinea (i.e. of ships), Prop. ; non alias maiore mole (belli) concursum, Tac. **b.** *greatness, might, weight* : molem invidiae sustinere, Cic. ; pugnae, Liv. ; vis consili expers mole ruit suā, Hor. **c.** *burden, difficulty, effort* : transveham navis haud magnā mole, Liv. ; tantae molis erat Romanam condere gentem, Verg. ; adversus ignaviam militum, Tac. **d.** *disturbance, calamity* : maior exorta domi moles, Liv. [It. *molo* ; Sp. *muelle* ; Fr. *môle.*]
molestē, adv. **I.** *with great annoyance* : moleste fero, Cic. Ep. Comp. and Sup. : Cic. Ep. **II.** *in a laboured manner, affectedly* : Cat.
molestia, ae, *f.* [molestus], *trouble, troublesomeness, annoyance* (coming fr. without). **1. Lit.** : liberi fuerunt ab omni sumptu, molestiā, munere, Cic. ; Pl. **2. Transf. a.** (Subjectively) : *vexation, annoyance, worry* : capere, Cic. ; habere, exhibere, Cic. Ep. ; alicui aspergere, adferre, Ter. ; demere, Cic. Ep. ; molestiis se laxare, Cic. Ep. ; navigandi, Suet. **b.** Of style : *stiffness, affectation* : diligens elegantia sine molestiā, Cic.
molestus, a, um [fr. root of mōlēs], *burdensome, troublesome, irksome.* **1. Lit.** : apecede hinc, molestus ne sis ! Pl. ; provincia, labor, Cic. **2. Transf. a.** *annoying, distressing* : adrogantia ingeni, Cic. ; otium, Cat. ; tunica, Juv. ; nisi molestum est, Cic. Sup.: Cic. **b.** Of style : *laboured, affected* : simplex in agendo veritas, non molesta, Cic. ; verba, Ov. ; Quint.
mōlīmen, inis, *n.* [mōlior], *a great exertion, effort.* **1. Lit.** : revellere pinum magno molimine, Ov. ; of the wind : Lucr. **2. Transf. a.** *laborious effort* : sceleris, Ov. ; hence, molimine vasto tabularia (*made by great effort*), Ov. **b.** *importance* : res suo ipsa molimine gravis, Liv. Of *self-importance* : Hor.
mōlimentum, i, *n.* [mōlior], *a great exertion, effort* : sine magno molimento, Caes. ; parvi molimenti adminiculis, Liv. ; eo minoris molimenti ea claustra esse, Liv.
mōlior, īri [mōlēs]. **A. Intrans.** *to exert oneself, make a great effort.* **a.** In gen. :

Pl. Tr... de occupando regnō, Cic. U.
Of preparations for a voyage : molientem hinc Hannibalem, Liv. ; naves a terrā, Liv. ; in insulam gladiatores navibus, Tac. **B. Trans.** *to set in motion, heave, hurl, wield, stir with effort.* **1. Lit. a.** In gen. : validam in vitis bipennem, Verg. ; ancoras, Liv. ; arva, Lucr. ; terram aratro, Verg. ; corpora ex somno, Liv. ; montis sede suā, Liv. **b.** *to labour at, construct with labour* : muros, Verg. ; classem, Verg. ; atrium, Hor. **c.** *to labour at destructively* : portas, Liv. ; foris, Tac. ; onera obiecta, Liv. **2. Transf.** of any undertaking, attempt, or design accompanied with labour and difficulty : aliquid calamitatis alicui, Cic. ; interitum urbis, Cic. ; fugam, moram, etc., Verg. ; imperium sibi, Liv., Tac. ; nuptias, Tac. ; crimina et accusatorem, Tac. ; fidem, *to undermine public credit*, Liv. With *Inf.* : Cic., Liv.
mōlītiō, ōnis, *f.* [mōlior], *a laborious effort or task.* **a.** In construction : Cic. **b.** In destruction : valli, Liv.
mōlītor, ōris, *m.* [mōlior], *a builder* (with effort). **1. Lit.** : mundi Deus, Cic. ; navis, Ov. **2. Transf.** : caedis, Tac. Also fem.
mōlītrix, īcis, *f.* novarum rerum, Suet.
molītus, a, um, *Part.* molō.
mōlītus, a, um, *Part.* mōlior.
mollēscō, ere [mollis], *to become soft.* **1. Lit.** : ebur, Ov. ; Cat. **2. Transf. a.** *to become gentle, mild, soft* : tum genus humanum primum mollescere coepit, Lucr. ; artibus pectora, Ov. **b.** *to become unmanly* : Ov.
molliculus, a, um [*dim.* mollis], *softish, tender, dainty.* **1. Lit.** : caseus, Pl. ; escae, Pl. **2. Transf.** *somewhat lascivious* : Cat.
molliō, īre [mollis], *to make soft, supple, or malleable.* **1. Lit.** : frigoribus durescit umor et idem mollitur tepefactus, Cic. ; agros Nilus, Cic. ; ferrum, Hor. ; ceram, Ov. ; humum foliis, Ov. ; artūs oleo, Liv. **2. Transf.** *to soften, mitigate, moderate.* **a.** In gen. : Hannibalem iuveniliter exsultantem patientia sua molliebat, Cic. ; animos, Verg. ; impetum, iras, Liv. ; fructūs feros colendo, Verg. ; verba usu, Cic. ; poenam, Ov. **b.** Of a hill-side : clivum, Caes., Liv. **c.** *to render effeminate* : legionem, Cic. ; animos, Cic. ; vocem, Quint. [Fr. *mouiller.*]
molli-pēs, pedis, *adj.* [mollis pēs], *softfooted* : boves, Cic. poet.
mollis, e, *adj.* [*cf.* Gk. μαλακός], *soft.* **1. Lit. a.** *soft to the touch* : cera, Cic. ; cutis, Liv. ; hyacinthus, castaneae, Verg. ; lana, capilli, Ov. **b.** *soft and yielding, springy* : harena, Ov. ; litus, Caes. ; prata, Verg. ; humus, Ov. ; feretrum, Verg. ; torus, Ov. **c.** *supple, pliant, flexible, malleable* : crura, Verg. ; bracchia, Ov. ; aurum, Verg. **d.** *soft, flabby* : arcus, Ov. **e.** *soft to the taste* : vina, Verg. ; Hor. ; Juv. **2. Transf. A.** Physically. **a.** Of weather, etc. : *mild, calm, soft* : aestas, Verg. ; Zephyri, Ov. ; Euphrates undis, Verg. **b.** Of hills, slopes, and routes : *easy, gentle* : fastigium, Caes. ; iugum montis, Tac. ; clivus, Verg. ; via, Quint. Comp. : ascensus, Liv. **B.** Of character, etc. **a.**

impressionable, sensitive : homo mollissimo animo, Cic.; mollibus annis, Ov.; mollis animus et ad accipiendam et ad deponendam offensionem, Cic. **b.** *ready to yield, soft, weak, effeminate :* corpus, Liv.; Gallorum mens, Caes.; in dolore, Cic.; **ad** taedium laboris, Liv.; in obsequium, Ov.; viri, Liv.; Verg.; sententia, disciplina, ratio, Cic.; querellae, Hor.; vita, Ov.; vox, Quint. **c.** *soft, mild, placid, gentle :* oratio, senectus, homo, Cic.; iussa, Verg.; molliora respondere, Liv., Tac. **d.** *tender, touching :* molli prece, Tib.; verba, Hor.; versus, Ov. **e.** *changeable :* nihil est tam molle quam voluntas erga nos civium, Cic. *Comp.* and *Sup. :* Cic., Verg., etc. [Fr. *mou, molle.*]

molliter, *adv. softly.* **1.** Lit. **a.** aves nidos mollissime substernunt, Cic.; Ov. **b.** Of movement : *with suppleness, softly :* incedere, Ov.; membra movere, Hor.; excudent alii spirantia mollius aera, Verg. **2.** Transf. **a.** *weakly, effeminately :* Cic., Sall. *Comp. :* Liv. **b.** *gently, softly, placidly :* aliquid ferre, Cic. *Comp. :* loqui, Verg.; abnuere, Liv.; interpretari mollius aliquid, Tac.

mollitia, ae, *f.,* and **mollitiēs,** ēī, *f.* [mollis], *softness.* **1.** Lit. **a.** To the touch : lanae, Plin. **b.** Of movement : *suppleness :* cervicum, Cic. **2.** Transf. **a.** *tenderness, sensitiveness :* naturae, Cic. Ep.; frontis, Plin. Ep. **b.** *weakness, irresolution :* animi est ista mollities inopiam pauliaper ferre non posse, Caes.; animi, Cic., Sall. **c.** *softness, effeminacy, enervation :* Liv.; civitatum mores lapsi ad mollitiam, Cic.; Tac. In *pl. :* Pl.

mollitūdō, inis, *f.* [mollis], *suppleness, flexibility, softness.* **1.** Lit. : Pac., Cic. **2.** Transf. *susceptibility :* humanitatis, Cic.

molo, ere, uī, itum [mola], *to grind in a mill :* Ter.; molita cibaria, Caes. *Neut.* of *Perf. Part.* as Noun : Pl. [Fr. *moudre.*]

molocinārius, ī, *m.* [Gk. μαλάχη, "a mallow"], *one who dyes with the colour of mallows :* Pl.

Molorchus, ī, *m. a poor vine-dresser near Nemea, who hospitably entertained Hercules ;* **Molorchaeus,** a, um.

Molossī, ōrum, *m. pl. the Molossians, a people in Epirus, who are said to have derived their name from Molossus, son of Pyrrhus, king of Epirus,* and *Andromache ;* **Molossus,** a, um ; **Molossus,** ī, *m. a Molossian hound :* Verg.; **Molossis,** idis, *f. the country of the Molossi.*

molossus, a, um, *Molossian.* In prosody, pes, *a metrical foot consisting of three long syllables :* Quint.

mōly, yos, ī, *m.* [μῶλυ], *a magic herb :* Ov.

mōmen, inis, *n.* [for movimen, from moveō], *movement, motion,* hence, **a.** *a heaving mass :* e salso consurgere momine ponti, Lucr. **b.** *impulse, momentum :* momine parvo moveri, Lucr.

mōmentum, ī, *n.* [contr. from movimentum, from moveō]. **I.** *a movement, motion.* **1.** Lit. : astra formā ipsā figurāque sua momenta sustentant, Cic.; Ov.; also of *violent movement :* Leonia, Hor. **2.** Transf. **a.** *change, alteration :* fortunae, Cic.; nullum

momentum annonae facere, Liv. **b.** Of time : *a turn, critical time,* hence, *a short time, brief space, moment :* parvo momento navis antecessit, Caes.; parvis momentis multa natura adfingit, Cic.; unius horae, temporis, occasionis, Liv.; horae, Hor. **II.** *a moving force, impulse.* **1.** Lit. : arbores levi momento impulsae occidunt, Liv. **2.** Transf. **a.** *an impulse, weight (*perh. mostly as metaph. fr. weight put into scales) : minimis momentis maximae inclinationes temporum fiunt, Cic.; parvae res magnum in utramque partem momentum habuerunt, Caes.; Ov.; ex momentis parvarum plerumque rerum summa belli pendet, Liv.; quorum adventus hoc momenti fecit ut etc., Liv. Hence, *importance, influence :* levi momento aestimare, Caes.; pari momenti sortis fuit quaestura, Cic.; id est maximi momenti, Cic.; consultatio levioris momenti, Liv.; perpendenti officiorum momenta, Cic. **b.** *motive :* momenta potentia, Ov.

Mona, ae, *f.* **I.** *the Isle of Man :* Caes. **II.** *the Isle of Anglesey :* Tac.

monēdula, ae, *f. a jackdaw, daw :* Cic., Ov. As a term of endearment : Pl.

moneō, ēre [*cf.* mēns, memini], *to call to mind, remind* or *advise ; to put in mind, point out* solemnly or in admonition. **A.** In gen. : Enn., Cic. With Acc. of person and *de* with ABL. of thing : Terentium de testamento, Cic. Ep.; or with GEN. : milites necessitatis, Tac.; or with *Intern.* (*Neut.*) Acc. : eos hoc, Cic.; Sall.; ut moneatur officium, Pl.; Cic.; or Acc. and *Inf. :* Caes.; or with *Indir. Quest. :* Ter., Liv.; or with *Jussive Subj.* (us. with *ut* or *ne*) : Caes., Cic., Hor., etc.; or with *Inf.* (instead of *Subj.*) : res monet cavere, Sall.; soror Turnum monet succurrere Lauso, Verg.; Tac. **B.** In partic. **a.** Of chastisement : puerili verbere moneri, Tac. **b.** Of instruction or prophetic warning : tu vatem, tu, diva, mone, Verg.; velut divinitus mente monitā, Liv.; vates multa horrenda, Verg.; amici somnio monitus, Suet.; sol caecos tumultūs, Verg.; ab ilice cornix, Verg.

monēris, is, *f.* [μονήρης (*sc.* ναῦς)], *a vessel with a single bank of oars, a galley :* Liv.

Monēta, ae, *f.* **I.** *mother of the Muses.* **II.** Moneta or Iuno Moneta, *in whose temple at Rome money was coined.* Transf. **a.** *the mint :* ad Philotimum scripsi de viatico, sive a monetā, sive ab Oppiis, Cic. Ep. **b.** *coin, money :* vietaque concedit prisca moneta novae, Ov. **c.** *a stamp* or *die for coining money :* a novā monetā, *of a new stamp,* Mart. Hence, communi feriat carmen triviale monetā, Juv. [Fr. *monnaie.*]

monētālis, e, *adj.* [monēta], *of the mint.* As Noun in jest, *the money-man :* Cic. Ep.

monīle, is, *n.* [*cf.* Gk. μάννος, μόννος], *a necklace, collar :* Cic., Verg., etc. Worn by boys : Ov.; by horses : Verg.

monim-, *v.* monum-.

monita, ōrum, *n. pl.* [moneō]. **I.** *warnings :* Cic. **II.** *prophecies :* Cic., Verg.

monitiō, ōnis, *f.* [moneō], *a reminding, warning :* Cic., Suet.

monitor, ōris, *m. a reminder, warner, counsellor.* **A.** In gen. : Ter. With *Obj.* GEN. :

offici, Sall. **B.** In partic. **a.** *a prompter*.
i. in points of law : Cic. **ii.** of people's
names (i.e. a nomenclator) : Cic. **b.** *a
teacher, tutor* : Cic., Hor.

monitus, ūs, *m.* [moneō], *a reminding,
warning, admonition (sing.* only in Abl. ;
pl. us. Nom. or Acc.). **a.** In gen. : monitu
nutricis, Ov. **b.** *a warning :* fortunae
monitu, Cic. ; revereri numinum monitūs,
Plin. Pan.

Monoecus, I, *m. a surname of Hercules ;*
Monoeci arx, *a promontory in Liguria* (now
Monaco).

monogrammus or **-os**, I, *m. adj.* [μονό-
γραμμος], lit. of pictures *that consist of
lines merely, an outline, sketch ;* hence
transf. *shadowy :* Epicurus monogrammos
deos commentus est, Cic. As Noun, *a
skeleton* or *shadow :* Lucil.

monopodium, I, *n.* [μονοπόδιον], *a table* or
stand with one foot : Liv.

monopōlium, I, *n.* [μονοπώλιον], *the exclusive
privilege of selling, a monopoly :* Suet.

monosyllabon, I, *n.* (*sc.* verbum) [μονο-
σύλλαβος], *a monosyllable :* Quint.

monotropus, I, *m. adj.* [μονότροπος], *single,
alone :* Pl.

mōns, montis, *m.* [*cf.* ēmineō], *a mountain,
range of mountains*. **1.** Lit. : Caes., Cic.,
Ov., etc. ; mons Cevenna, Caes. ; mons
Idaeus, Verg. Prov. : parturiunt montes,
nascetur ridiculus mus (' much ado about
nothing '), Hor. **2.** Transf. **a.** Of a large
mass or heap : Verg. ; argenti, Pl. ; hic
mons Tusculanus (ironically), Cic. ; aquae,
Verg. ; also, maeroris, Pl. Prov. : montis
auri polliceri (of extravagant promises),
Ter. ; maria montisque polliceri, Sall. **b.**
a huge mass (of rock) : fertur in abruptum
magno mons improbus actu, Verg.

mōnstrātiō, ōnis, *f.* [mōnstrō], *a pointing out*
(of the direction) : Ter.

mōnstrātor, ōris, *m.* [mōnstrō], *a pointer out*.
1. Lit. : hospiti, Tac. **2.** *a teacher, inventor :* aratri, i.e. Triptolemus, Verg.

mōnstrātus, a, um. **I.** *Part.* mōnstrō. **II.**
Adj. : *conspicuous, distinguished :* et hostibus simul suisque monstrati, Tac.

mōnstrō, āre [mōnstrum], *to point out*. **1.**
Lit. : viam erranti, Enn. ; iter, Curt. ;
palmam monstrant eandem, Cic. ; monstrari digito, Hor. ; quā semita monstrat,
Verg. **2.** Transf. **a.** *to point out, guide,
instruct :* alicui bene, Pl. ; Cic. Ep. ; Verg.
With *Indir. Quest.* : Pl., Hor. With *Inf.* :
Hor. With Acc. and *Inf.* : Liv., Juv. **b.**
to ordain, appoint, bid : monstratas excitat
aras, Verg. ; piacula, Verg. ; conferro
manum ira monstrat, Verg. **c.** *to denounce,
inform against :* alii ab amicis monstrabantur, Tac. **d.** *to reveal :* signum Iuno,
Verg. ; Vespasianus fatis monstratus, Tac.
[It. *mostrare* ; Fr. *montrer*.]

mōnstrōs-, v. mōnstruōs-.

mōnstrum, I, *n.* [moneō], *a warning ;* hence,
*any occurrence out of the usual course of
nature ; a sign, wonder, miracle, portent*.
1. Lit. : Enn., Cic. Esp. of something
foreboding evil: *an evil portent :* monstra
deum, Verg. ; signa dedit Tritonia monstris,
Verg. **2.** Transf. **A.** *any misshapen or
unnatural person or thing, a monster,* mon-

st ..rity a monstrum hominum, Ter. ; *aulla
iam pernicies a monstro* illo *atque pro-
digio comparabitur* (i.e. Catiline), Cic. ;
fatale (i.e. Cleopatra, Hor. **b.** Of beasts :
Verg. ; ferarum, Verg. **c.** Of things : of
the sea, Verg. ; of Argo : Cat. ; of the
Trojan horse : Verg. **B.** In gen. of any
unusual or extraordinary appearance or
thing : *a miracle, marvel :* monstra narrare,
Cic. ; Lucr.

mōnstruōsē, *adv. strangely, unnaturally :*
cogitare, Cic.

mōnstruōsus (**monstrōsus**, Luc.), a, um
[mōnstrum], *strange, unnatural, monstrous :*
monstruosissima bestia (viz. the ape), Cic. ;
libidines, Suet.

montānus, a, um [mōns]. **I.** *of a mountain,
mountain- :* flumen, Verg. ; homines, Caes. ;
Cic. ; Liv. As Noun, **montāni**, ōrum, *m.
pl. mountaineers :* Caes. **II.** *mountainous :*
Delmatia, Ov. ; loca, Liv. As Noun, **mon-
tāna**, ōrum, *n. pl. mountainous regions :*
inter montana, Liv.

monticola, ae, *m.f.* [mōns colō], *a dweller in
the mountains :* Silvani, Ov.

monti-vagus, a, um, *mountain-roaming :*
fera, Lucr. ; cursus, Cic.

montōsus (**montŏsus**, Verg.), a, um
[mōns], *mountainous :* regio, Cic.

monumentum (**monim-**), I, *n.* [moneō], *a
reminder ; a memorial, monument*. **a.** In
gen.: laudis, Cic. ; amoris, Verg. ; sibi,
Pl. ; monumenta quae ex fano Herculis
conlata erant, *votive offerings,* Caes. **b.** Of
statues, buildings, etc erected by or in
remembrance of a person : Pl. ; regis, Hor. ;
Mari (i.e. built by him), Cic. ; non meum
monumentum, monumentum vero senatūs
(the house of Cicero, built by order of the
Senate), Cic. ; monumenta Pompei, Tac. ;
sepultus in monumento avunculi, Nep.
c. *a record* (written or oral) of events :
monumenta rerum gestarum, Cic. ; Hor. ;
Liv. **d.** *a tok n* or *means of recognition :*
cistellam domo ecfer cum monumentis,
Pl. ; Pl.

Mopsopia, ae, *f. an old name of Attica and
Athens ;* **Mopsopius**, a, um: iuvenis, i.e.
Triptolemus, Ov. ; urbs, i.e. Athens, Ov.

(1) mora, ae, *f.* [*cf.* memor], *a delay, hindrance*. **1.** Lit. **a.** obicere, Pl. ; producere,
Ter. ; moram ad insequendum intulit,
Caes. ; alicui facere, Cic. ; facere dilectui,
Liv. ; adferre, interponere, Cic. ; nullā
morā interpositā, Caes. ; trahere, moliri,
Verg. ; removere, Pl. ; rumpere, Verg. ;
pellere, Ov. ; eximere, Liv. ; nec mora
ulla est, quin eam uxorem ducam, Ter. ;
so freq. in the poets : nec (haud) mora :
Verg., Ov. **b.** In speaking : *a pause :*
mora respirationeque, Cic. **2.** Transf.
a. *a cause of delay ; a hindrance :* resti-
tuendae Romanis Capuae mora atque impedimentum es, Liv. ; morae alicui esse,
Pl. ; morae esse nuptiis, Ter. ; Abas pugnae
nodusque moraque, Verg. **b.** *a space,
space of time :* dolor finitus est morā, Ov. ;
temporis, Liv. **c.** *a staying, sojourning :*
segnis mora, Liv.

(2) mora, ae, *f.* [μόρα], *a division of the
Spartan army, consisting of three, five,* or
seven hundred men ; a mora : Cic., Nep.

mōrālis, e, adj. [mōs], of morals, moral (a word coined and suggested by Cic.) : philosophia, Cic. ; Sen. ; Quint.

morātor, ōris, m. [moror], a delayer : publici commodi, Liv. Esp. an advocate who spoke only to gain time : Cic.

mōrātus, a, um, Part. moror.

mōrātus, a, um [mōs], mannered, with (good or bad) manners. **1.** Lit. **a.** viri bene morati, Cic. ; Pl. ; Liv., etc. **b.** adapted to the character of the person represented ; poēma, Cic. ; recte morata fabula, Hor. ; oratio, Quint. **2.** Transf. of a thing : charactered, natured : ita haec morata est ianua, Pl. ; male moratus venter, Ov.

morbidus, a, um [morbus]. **I.** sickly, diseased : apes, Varr. **II.** causing sickness, unwholesome : vis, Lucr.

morbus, i, m. a sickness, disease. **1.** Lit. (physical) : in morbum cadere, incidere, delabi, Cic. ; morbo languere, Lucr. ; morbo affici, adfligi, tabescere, urgeri, iactari, opprimi, Cic. ; in morbo esse, Cic. ; morbo aeger, Cic. ; morbo mori, Nep. ; absumi, Sall. ; levare, Pl. ; depellere, Cic. Ep. ; ex morbo convalescere, Cic. Ep. ; a morbo valere, Pl. ; morbus amplior fit, Ter. ; adgravescit, Ter. ; ingravescit, Cic. **2.** Transf. **a.** Mental : animi morbi sunt cupiditates, Cic. ; morbus et insania, Cic. ; ut, si qui aegrotet, quo morbo Barrus, Hor. **b.** distress, affliction : Pl. **c.** Personif. : Verg. [Fr. morve.]

mordācius, comp. adv. more bitingly : limā mordacius uti, Ov.

mordāx, ācis, adj. [mordeō], snapping. **1.** Lit. : canis, Pl. **2.** Transf. **a.** biting, stinging, sharp : urtica, Ov. ; mordaci ferro icta pinus, Hor. Comp. and Sup. : Plin. **b.** Of taste : pungent, tart : acetum, Pers. **c.** Of character : biting, snarling : Cynicus, Hor. Of things : carmen, Ov. Comp. : Quint. **d.** biting, carking : sollicitudines, Hor.

mordeō, mordēre, momordī (old form memordī], mōrsum [cf. Gk. σμερδνός, Eng. smart], to bite. **1.** Lit. **a.** In gen. : Cic., Mart. With Acc. : Enn. ; terram (i.e. in death-writhing) : procubuit moriens et humum semel ore momordit, Verg. ; Ov. **b.** to eat, devour : ostrea, Juv. **2.** Transf. **a.** to bite, grip : laterum iuncturas fibula, Verg. ; Ov. **b.** to bite into, gnaw : rura amnis, Hor. **c.** Of the action of cold, acid, etc. : to nip, bite, sting : matutina parum cautos frigora, Hor. ; Plin. ; Mart. **d.** to bite, sting, backbite : invidere omnes mihi, mordere clanculum, Ter. ; morderi dictis, Ov. ; Hor. ; livor iniquo dente momordit opus, Ov. **e.** to vex, mortify : Ter. ; valde me epistulae tuae, Cic. Ep. ; morderi quod etc., Cic. Ep.

mordicēs, um, m. pl. [mordeō], biting teeth, hence, bites : Pl.

mordicus, adv. by biting, with bites, with the teeth. **1.** Lit. : Pl., Cic. **2.** Transf. : verba tenent mordicus, Cic.

mōrē, adv. [mōrus], foolishly : Pl.

morētum, i, n. a country dish made with garlic, vinegar, oil, etc. ; a salad : Ov.

moribundus, a, um [morior]. **I.** dying, at the point of death : Pl., Cic., Liv. **II.** sub-

ject to death : membra, Verg. **III.** deathladen, deadly : moribundā a sede Pisauri, Cat.

mōrigeror, ārī [mōrigerō, āre, Pl.) [mōs gerō], to comply with, gratify, humour : adulescenti, Ter. ; voluptati aurium oratio, Cic.

mōrigerus, a, um [mōs gerō], complying, obsequious : patri, Pl. ; Lucr.

morior, morī (morīrī, Pl.), mortuus (Fut. Part. moritūrus, Cic., Verg. [cf. Gk. βροτός (for μβροτός)], to die. **1.** Lit. : Pl., Cic., Verg., etc. ; fame, Pl., Cic., Liv. ; desiderio, Cic. ; ex vulnere, Liv. ; amore, Ov. ; segetes in herbis, Ov. **2.** Transf. of things : to die away or out, pass away, fail, grow faint. **a.** unguenta, Plin. ; flammas et vidi nullo concutiente mori, Ov. **b.** Of abstracts : dies iam est dimidiatus mortuos, Pl. ; ne hominis memoria moreretur, Cic. ; gratia, Ov. ; Liv. [Fr. mourir.]

mormyr, ȳris, f. [μορμύρος], an unknown fish in Pontus : Ov.

mōrologus, a, um [μωρολόγος], foolish in words : sermones, Pl. As Noun, a fool : Pl.

mōror, ārī [μωρός], to be a fool : Suet.

moror, ārī [mora]. **A.** Intrans. to delay, linger, loiter. **a.** Lit. : auxilia, Caes. ; valde, Cic. Ep. ; haud multa moratus, Verg. In speech : quid moror ? Hor. ; quid multis moror ? Ter. ; ne multis morer, Cic. With Inf. : Caes. With quo minus or quin and Subj. (after a negat.) : Liv. **b.** to stay, stay on : quod adhuc Brundisi moratus es, Cic. Ep. ; Nep. ; rosa quo locorum sera moretur, Hor. **B.** Trans. to delay, retard. **1.** Lit. : aliquem, Pl., Cic. Ep. ; impetum hostium, Caes. ; ab itinere hostem, Liv. ; iter, Caes. **2.** Transf. **a.** to hold the attention of : morata recte fabula populum melius moratur, Hor. **b.** With negative, not to detain a person : Cic. Ep. **C.** Sempronium nihil moror (i.e. I withdraw the charge against S.), Liv. Also, not to heed, not to care for : nec me quaerentem vana moratur, Verg. ; vina nihil moror, Hor. ; alieno uti nihil moror, Pl. ; nil moror eum tibi esse amicum, Pl.

mōrōsē, adv. **I.** peevishly, morosely : Cic. **II.** scrupulously, punctiliously : Plin. Sup. : Suet.

mōrōsitās, ātis, f. [mōrōsus]. **I.** peevishness, fretfulness, moroseness : Cic. **II.** over-scrupulousness, pedantry : (stili), Suet.

mōrōsus, a, um [mōs], moody. **1.** Lit. **a.** peevish, fretful, morose : Cic. ; canities, Hor. **b.** over-nice or scrupulous, fastidious : circa corporis curam morosior, Suet. **2.** Transf. of things : ill-conditioned, stubborn : morbus, Ov.

Morpheus (disyl.), eos (Acc. -ea), m. the son of Sleep and god of dreams.

mors, mortis, f. [cf. morior], death. **1.** Lit. **a.** exsequi, Pl. ; sibi consciscere, Caes., Cic. ; obire, oppetere, Cic. ; occumbere, Cic., Liv. ; morti occumbere, Verg. ; aliquem ad mortem dare, Pl. ; morti dare, Hor. ; ad mortem duci, se offerre, Cic. ; aliquem morte multare, Cic. ; alicui mors appropinquat, Cic. In pl. when several persons are spoken of : praeclarae mortes sunt imperatorum, Cic. **b.** Of things : *destruction :* Lucr. **2.** T r a n s f. **a.** *a cause of death ;* cui legatio ipsa morti fuisset, Cic. **b.** *a dead body, corpse :* mortem eius lacerari, Cic. ; Cat. ; Liv. **c.** Like caedes ; *bloodshed :* Verg. **d.** P e r s o n i f.: Cic., Verg. [Sp. *muerte.*]

mōrsa, ōrum, *n. pl.* [mordeō], *bits, little pieces :* lanea, Cat.

mōrsiuncula, ae, *f.* [*dim.* mōrsus], *a little peck, a kiss :* Pl.

mōrsus, a, um, *Part.* mordeō.

mōrsus, ūs, *m.* [mordeō], *a biting, a bite.* **1.** L i t. **a.** contra avium minorum morsūs, Cic. ; canis vanos exercet in aera morsūs, Ov. ; morsu appetere, Tac. **b.** *eating :* mensarum morsūs, Verg. **2.** T r a n s f. **a.** *a biting, gripping ;* hence, *that which grips* (e.g. a prong, anchor) : discludere morsūs roboris, Verg. ; unco non adligat ancora morsu, Verg. **b.** *corrosion :* rubiginis, Luc. **c.** *pungency :* aceti, Mart. **d.** *a biting attack :* carmina venenare odio obscuro morsuque, Hor. **e.** *sting, gnawing pain, vexation :* doloris, Cic. ; curarum, Ov.

mortālis, e, *adj.* [mors], *subject to death, mortal.* **1.** L i t. : Cic. As Noun, *a mortal :* Liv.; and freq. *man, human being* (esp. in *pl.*) : Pl., Cic., Liv. **2.** T r a n s f. **a.** *mortal, perishable, transient :* inimicitiae, Cic. ; leges, Liv. **b.** *human, mortal, of human workmanship :* mucro, Verg. ; opera, Liv. *Neut. pl.* as Noun : Verg.

mortālitās, ātis, *f.* [mortālis], *the being subject to death, mortality.* **1.** L i t. : Cic. **2.** T r a n s f. **a.** *death :* explere, Tac. ; mortalitate interceptus, Plin. Ep. **b.** *mortals, mankind :* contra fortunam non satis cauta mortalitas est, Curt.

morticinus, a, um [mors] (only of animals), *that has died of itself, carrion :* Varr. As term of abuse : Pl.

mortifer or **mortiferus**, a, um [mors ferō], *death-bringing, death-dealing :* poculum, morbus, vulnus, Cic. ; bellum, Verg.

mortiferē, *adv. fatally :* aegrotare, Plin. Ep.

mortuālia, ium, *n. pl.* [mortuus] (*sc.* carmina), *funeral songs, dirges :* Pl.

mortuus (-uos), a, um. **I.** *Part.* morior. **II.** A d j.: *dead, deceased.* **1.** L i t. : mortuus concidit, Cic. P r o v.: mortuom esse alicui, *to be dead to one,* Pl. As Noun, **mortuus**, ī, *m. a corpse :* Cic. P r o v.: mortuo verba facere, *to talk to a corpse,* Pl. **2.** T r a n s f. of things. **a.** *decayed, withered, passed away :* lacerti, Cic. ; leges, Cic. ; plausus, Cic. Ep. **b.** *scared to death :* exsanguis et mortuus concidisti, Cic.

mōrulus, a, um [*dim. adj.* fr. mōrum], *blackberry-coloured :* Pl.

mōrum, ī, *n.* [μῶρον and μόρον]. **I.** *a blackberry :* Verg., Ov. **II.** *a mulberry :* Hor.

mōrus, ī, *f.* [mōrum], *a mulberry-tree :* Ov.

mōrus, a, um [μωρός], *foolish, silly :* amor mores hominum moros et morosos facit, Pl. As Noun, **mōrus**, ī, *m.* and **mōra**, ae, *f. a fool :* Pl.

mōs, mōris, *m.* [perh. *cf.* Gk. μαίομαι], *will, humour, caprice, mood.* **A.** In gen. **a.** opsequens mori atque inperiis patris, Pl. ; ex illius more vivere, Ter. ; more et ex-

emplo populi Romani, Caes. ; dominari pervincere mores, Prop. ; morem alicui gerere, *to humour anyone,* Pl., Ter., Cic. (*cf.* morigeror and gero). Of things : varium caeli morem, Verg. **b.** *custom, usage, fashion, practice.* Of persons : leges mori serviunt, Pl. ; legi morique parendum est, Cic. ; praeter civium morem, Ter. ; contra morem consuetudinemque civilem, Cic. ; more maiorum, Cic., Liv. ; more militari, Caes. ; sicut mens est mos, Hor. With *ut* and *Subj. :* virginibus Tyriis mos est ut etc., Verg. ; quod iam in morem venerat ut etc., Liv. With *prep. : according to custom :* de, ex more, Nep., Tac. Of things : more torrentis aquae, Verg. ; in morem fluminis, Verg. ; Hor. **B.** In partic. **a.** (*more*) *established practice, rule, law, ordinance :* moresque viris et moenia ponet, Verg. ; regere populos pacisque imponere morem, Verg. ; hence, tempestas sine more furit, Verg. Hence, *civilised life :* mos neque cultus erat, Verg. ; res eorum civibus moribus agris aucta est, Sall. **b.** In *pl. : conduct, behaviour, manners, morals, character :* Pl. ; iusti, Cic. ; totam vitam, naturam, moresque alicuius cognoscere, Cic. ; abire in avi mores, Liv. ; praefectura morum, Suet. [Fr. *moeurs.*]

Mōsēs (Juv.) and **Mōȳsēs** (Tac.), is, *m. Moses ; the famous Jewish lawgiver.*

mōtiō, ōnis, *f.* [moveō], *a moving, motion :* Cic.

mōtiuncula, ae, *f.* [*dim.* mōtiō], in medicine, *a slight attack of fever :* Suet.

mōtō, āre [*freq.* moveō], *to keep moving, move about :* Zephyris motantibus (umbras), Verg. ; lacertos, Ov.

mōtus, a, um, *Part.* moveō.

mōtus, ūs, *m.* [moveō], *a moving, motion.* **1.** L i t. **A.** In gen. : navium, remorum, siderum, Caes. ; orbes, qui versantur contrario motu, Cic. ; terrae, Cic. ; Verg. **B.** Esp. **a.** *artistic movement* of the body in dancing, exercise, acting : Cereri dare motūs, Verg. ; Liv. ; Ionici, Hor. ; palaestrici, Cic. **b.** Of the *gestures* of an orator : Cic. **c.** Of military or naval movements : Nep., Verg. **2.** T r a n s f. **A.** Of the mind. **a.** Of thought : *impulse, thought-process, inspiration :* motu mentis ac ratione uti, Cic. ; motūs animi celeres, Cic. ; Manto divino concita motu, Ov. **b.** Of the feelings or affections : *emotion, passion, agitation :* res quae dulcem motum sensibus adferunt, Cic. ; motūs animi turbati, Cic. ; vario misceri pectora motu, Verg. **B.** P o l i t. *a rising, tumult, commotion, rebellion, sedition :* omnis Catilinae motūs prohibere, Cic. ; Galliae, Caes. ; servilis, Liv. ; motum in re publicā impendere, Cic. ; civicus, Hor. **C.** R h e t. : *a figure of speech* (= figura, tropus) : Quint.

movēns, entis. **I.** *Part.* moveō. **II.** A d j.: *moveable :* res moventes, *moveable things* (as clothes, arms, furniture), Liv. **III.** Noun, **moventia**, *n. pl. motives :* Cic.

moveō, movēre, mōvī, mōtum [*cf.* Gk. ἀμεύσασθαι], *to move, stir, set in motion.* **1.** L i t. **a.** In gen. : se impigre, Cic. ; Ter. ; fila sonantia movit, Ov. In *Mid. :* priusquam moverentur Romani, Liv. ; agros,

tellurem moveri, Verg.; in *Act.* for *Mid.* :
terra movit, Liv. **b.** Of dancing, etc. :
histrio se movet, Cic.; ad certos modos
membra, Tib. In *Mid.* : Hor. **c.** From
a place (esp. milit.) : castra ex eo loco,
Caes.; signa e castris, Liv.; signum
movere loco, Cic. Esp. with *Pron. Reft.* or
in *Mid.* : *to change one's place or position, to
move* : praecepit iis ne se ex eo loco move-
rent, Liv. Also (*sc.* castra or signa) ;
Hannibal ex hibernis movit, Liv. ; Cic. Ep.
d. *to drive* (from a position), *dislodge, eject* :
hostem statu, Liv. ; aliquem possessione,
Cic. : de senatu, Cic. ; senatu, Sall. ; or
senatorio loco, Liv. **2.** Transf. **A.** Of
the mind. **a.** *to set in motion, stir, work
upon, excite, inspire* : multum consuetudine moveri, Caes. ; quae me causae
moverint, Cic. ; neutram in partem moveri,
Cic. ; movere ac moliri aliquid, Liv. ;
multa animo, Verg. ; animus illa movet,
Sall. Hence, *to set on foot, begin* : ego
istaec, Ter. ; bellum, Cic., Liv. ; mentionem cuiuspiam rei, Liv. ; cantūs, Verg.
b. Of emotions and feelings : *to affect, stir,
influence, excite, provoke* : moveri memoriā
amicitiae, Caes. ; populum gratiā, Cic. ;
specie movetur, Verg. ; aliquem ad bellum,
Liv. ; movet iuveni feroci animum comploratio sororis, Liv. With Acc. of feeling
excited or evoked : risum hominum, Cic. ;
fletum populo, Cic. ; odia, Verg. ; indig-
nationem, Liv. **c.** Of resolution : *to move,
shake, cause to waver* : alicuius sententiam,
Cic. Ep., Liv. ; misericordiā moveri, Caes. ;
plebem moverat oratio consulis, Liv. ;
nil moveor super imperio, Verg. **B.**
Polit. *to disturb, rouse* : quieta movere,
Sall. ; servitium in Siciliā movetur, Cic.
[It. *muovere* ; Fr. *mouvoir*.]

mox, *adv.* **I.** Of the future : *soon, immediately* : Pl., Cic., Verg., etc. ; mox ubi etc.,
Liv. With *quam* : exspecto quam mox
utatur, Cic. ; Pl. ; Liv. **II.** Of the past :
next in succession, *later, thereupon* : nam
extemplo fusi fugati ; mox intra vallum
compulsi, postremo exuuntur castris, Liv. ;
primum . . . deinde . . . mox . . . post,
Tac.

mū, *interj.* [μῦ], a sound made by just opening the lips : neque, ut aiunt, mu (or μῦ)
facere audent, Enn. Jestingly, *a trifle* : ne-
gato esse quod dem, nec mu nec mutuom, Pl.

mūceō, ēre [mūcus], *to be mouldy* : Cato.

mūcidus (mucc-), a, um [mūcus]. **I.**
snivelling, drivelling : homo, Pl. **II.**
mouldy, musty : panis frusta, Juv.

Mūcius, a, *the name of a Roman gens* ; esp.
I. C. Mucius Scaevola, *who attempted to
assassinate Porsenna and on being caught
burned off his right hand.* **II.** P. Mucius
Scaevola, *a friend of the Gracchi.* **III.**
Q. Mucius Scaevola, praetor in Asia, B.C.
121 ; **Mūcia,** ōrum, *n. pl.* (*sc.* festa), *a
festival held in his honour.*

mūcrō, ōnis, *m.* [perh. *cf.* ἀμύσσω], *a sharp
point or edge.* **1.** Lit. : ensis, Ov. ; coruscus, Verg. **2.** Transf. **a.** *a sword* : Cic.,
Verg., Liv. **b.** *edge, boundary* : Lucr.
c. *edge, keenness* : censori stili, Cic.

mūcus, i, *m.* [*cf.* Gk. μύξα, μυκτήρ, and Lat.
ēmungō], *snivel, mucus* of the nose : Cat.

mūgiēns, entis. **I.** *Part.* mūgiō. **II.** Noun
(in *pl.*) : *lowers, bellowers,* i.e. oxen, Hor.

mūgil and **mūgilis,** is, *m.* [*cf.* Gk. μυξῖνος], *a
sea-fish* ; *the mullet* : Plin., Juv. [It.
muggine ; Sp. *mujol* ; Fr. *muge.*]

mūginor, ārī, *to dally, trifle, hesitate* : Lucil.,
Cic. Ep.

mūgiō, īre [*cf.* μυκᾶσθαι], *to low, bellow.* **1.**
Lit. : boves, Cic. **2.** Transf. of loud
sounds : Tyrrhenusque tubae clangor, Verg. ;
Africis mālus procellis, Hor. ; cortina,
Verg. ; sub pedibus solum, Verg.

mūgītus, ūs, *m.* [mūgiō], *a lowing, bellowing.*
1. Lit. : boum, Verg. ; edere, dare, Ov. ;
tollere, Verg. **2.** Transf. of any loud
sound : terrae, Cic.

mūla, ae, *f.* [mūlus], *a she-mule* : Cic., Juv.
Prov. : cum mula peperit (i.e. never),
Suet.

mulceō, mulcēre, mulsī, mulsum. **1.** Lit.
a. *to stroke, caress* : manu mulcens barbam,
Ov. ; linguā pueros, Verg. ; caput, Quint.
b. *to touch lightly, stir gently, caress* : aëra
motu, Lucr. ; virgā capillos, Ov. ; Zephyri
flores, Ov. **2.** Transf. **a.** *to soothe, appease* : tigris, Verg. ; aliquem dictis, Verg. ;
Liv. ; iras, Verg. ; fluctūs, Verg. **b.** *to
soothe, alleviate* : variā vulnera ope, Ov.
c. *to gladden* : puellas carmine, Hor. ;
animos admiratione, Quint. [It. *molcere.*]

Mulciber, eris and erī, *m.* a name of Vulcan.
Transf. *fire* : Ov.

mulcō, āre [*cf.* Gk. βλάπτω] (Opt. mulcāssi-
tis, Pl.), *to beat, cudgel.* **1.** Lit. : aliquem,
Pl., Cic., Liv. ; usque ad mortem, Ter. **2.**
Transf. *to handle roughly.* **a.** *to damage* :
navis, Liv. **b.** scriptores male mulcatos,
Cic.

mulctra, ae, *f.* [mulgeō], *a milkpail* : Verg.

mulctrārium, ī, *n.* [mulgeō], *a milk-pail* :
Verg.

mulctrum, ī, *n.* [mulgeō], *a milk-pail* :
Hor.

mulgeō, mulgēre, mulsī [*cf.* ἀμέλγω], *to
milk* : ovis, Verg. Prov. : hircos, Verg.
[It. *mungere.*]

muliebris, e, *adj.* [mulier], *of a woman,
womanly, feminine.* **1.** Lit. : facinus, Pl. ;
comitatus, Cic. ; venustas, vox, Cic. ;
tutela, iura, Cic. ; Fortuna Muliebris, Liv.
Neut. pl. as Noun : Tac. **2.** Transf.
womanish, effeminate, unmanly : sententia,
Cic. ; luctus, Hor.

muliebriter, *adv. in a woman's way, like a
woman.* **1.** Lit. : Hor., Liv. **2.** Transf.
in an unmanly way : Cic.

mulier, eris, *f.* [perh. orig. a comparative
fr. root seen in mollis], *a woman.* **1.** Lit.
a. In gen. : Pl., Cic., etc. **b.** *a wife,*
opp. to a maiden, Cic., Hor., etc. **2.**
Transf. as a term of reproach, *a woman*
(i.e. no man), Pl. [It. *moglie* ; Sp. *mujer.*]

mulierārius, a, um [mulier], *of a woman* :
manus, Cic.

muliercula, ae, *f.* [*dim.* mulier]. **I.** *a weak
little woman* : Sulp. ap. Cic. Ep. **II.** *a
little hussy* : Cic., Hor.

mulierōsitās, ātis, *f.* [mulierōsus], *a fondness for women* : Cic.

mulierōsus, a, um [mulier], *fond of women* :
Pl., Cic.

mūlīnus, a, um [mūlus], *mulish* : cor, Juv.

mūliō, ōnis, *m.* [mūlus], *a mule-driver or -dealer* : Pl., Caes., Verg.

mūliōnius, a, um [mūliō], *of a mule-driver* : Cic.

mullulus, ī, *m.* [dim. mullus], *a little or pet mullet* : Cic.

mullus, ī, *m.* [μύλλος], *the red mullet* : Cic. Ep., Juv. [Fr. mulet.]

mulsa and **mulsum**, *v.* mulsus.

(1) **mulsus**, a, um, *Part.* mulceō.

(2) **mulsus**, a, um [cogn. with mel], *mixed with honey, sweet as honey.* **1.** Lit.: acetum. Cato. As Noun, **mulsum**, ī, *n.* (sc. vinum), *honey-wine, mead* : Cic.; given at triumphs: Pl., Liv. **2.** Transf.: dicta, Pl. As Noun, **mulsa**, ae, *f.* a term of endearment : *my honey* : Pl.

multa, ae, *f.* [fr. root of mulcō], *a fine, amercement, mulct.* **1.** Lit. **a.** In cattle: Cic. **b.** In money: multa praesens quingentum milium aeris, Liv.; multam alicui dicere, Cic.; certare (*to contest*), Liv. **2.** Transf. **a.** *a penalty* in gen.: haec ei multa esto; vino viginti dies ut careat, Pl.; ferre, Liv. **b.** *loss of money* : Cic. Ep.

multangulus, a, um [multus angulus], *having many angles* : Lucr.

multāticius, a, um [multō], *accruing from fines* : pecunia, Liv.

multātiō, ōnis, *f.* [multō], *a fining* : bonorum, Cic.

multēsimus, a, um [multus], *multesimal,* i.e. *very small, trifling* : pars, Lucr.

multibibus, a, um [multus bibō], *much-drinking* : lena, Pl.

multi-cavus, a, um [multus cavus], *many-holed* : pumex, Ov.

multicia, ōrum, *n. pl.* (sc. vestimenta), *soft, transparent garments* : Juv.

multifariam, *adv. on many sides, in many places* : Cato, Cic., Liv.

multifidus, a, um [multus findō], *much-cleft,* i.e. *divided into many parts* : faces, Ov.

multifōrmis, e, *adj.* [multus fōrma], *many-shaped, multiform* : qualitates, Cic. Transf.: Sen. Ep.

multiforus, a, um [multus foris], *having many holes* : buxus (i.e. a flute of boxwood), Ov.

multigeneris, e, (and **multigenus**, a, um, Lucr.), *adj.* [multus genus], *of many kinds* : Pl.

multiiugus, a, um (Liv.) and **multiiugis**, e (Cic. Ep.), *adj.* [multus iugum], *yoked many together.* **1.** Lit.: equi, Liv. **2.** Transf. *manifold, complex* : litterae, Cic. Ep.

multi-loquāx, ācis, *adj.* [multus loquāx], *talkative* : Pl.

multiloquium, ī, *n.* [multus loquor], *talkativeness* : Pl.

multiloquus, a, om [multus loquor], *talkative* : coquos, Pl.

multimodis, *adv. in many ways or modes, variously* : Pl., Ter., Lucr., Nep.

multiplex, icis, *adj.* [multus plicō], *that has many folds.* **1.** Lit.: alvus, Cic. **2.** Transf. **A.** Of material things. **a.** *that has many windings* : vitis serpens multiplici lapsu, Cic.; domus (the labyrinth), Ov. **b.** *that has many parts, manifold* : loci spatium, Lucr.; lorica, Verg.; fetus, Cic.

B. Of non-material things. **a.** *complin* Pl.; *genus orationis*, Cic. **b.** *many-sided, changeable* : natura, Cic. **c.** *many-sided, sly, cunning* (opp. to simplex): ingenium pueri, Cic. Ep. **d.** *many times as great ; far greater* : praeda, Liv.; multiplex quam pro numero damnum est, Liv.

multiplicābilis, e, *adj.* [multiplicō], *manifold* : Cic. poet.

multiplicātiō, ōnis, *f.* [multiplicō], *increasing, multiplying* : temporum, Sen. Ep.

multipliciter, *adv. in manifold or various ways* : Sall., Quint.

multiplicō, āre [multiplex], *to multiply, enlarge, increase greatly* : aes alienum, Caes.; domum, Cic.; multiplicatur gloria, Cic.; regnum, Liv.; flumina conlectis aquis, Ov.

multi-potēns, entis, *adj.* [multum potēns], *very powerful, very mighty* : Venus, pectus, Pl.

multitūdō, inis, *f.* [multus], *a great number, multitude.* **A.** Abstract: nationes, quae numero hominum ac multitudine ipsā poterant in provincias nostras redundare, Cic.; navium, Caes.; multitudine freti, Liv. **B.** Concrete. **a.** In gen.: *a great number of people together ; a crowd, multitude* : Caes., Cic., Liv., etc.; in *pl.* : Sall. **b.** *the populace* : ex errore imperitae multitudinis, Cic.; concitare, Cic.

multivolus, a, um [multus volō], *wishing or longing for much* : mulier, Cat.

multō, āre [multa], *to punish* : mostly of judicial punishment. With ABL. of the means or method: accusatorem multā et poenā multavit, Cic.; populos stipendio, Cic.; Pl.; Tac., etc. With DAT. of the person who received the fines : Veneri esse multatum, Cic.

multus (old form, **moltus**), a, um [*cf.* μάλα]. *Comp.* (**plūs**) **plūrēs**, **plūra** ; *Sup.* **plūrimus** (**-um-**), a, um ; in sing. *much ; great* ; in pl. *many.* **I.** In gen.: Pl., Cic., Verg., etc. In *pl.* when there is another *Adj.*, it is usual to have *et* : multi et varii timores, Liv.; except when i. the *Adj.* is a common one, or is essential element in the meaning: multi clari viri, Cic.; multa secunda proelia, Liv. **ii.** the *Adj.* is used as a *Noun* : multi nobiles, Cic.; multa falsa, Liv. **II.** Esp. **a.** *lengthy, copious, tedious* : homo, Pl.; multus in ro notā, Cic.; oratio, Cic. **b.** *with vigour, ardent* : Marius multus et ferox instare, Sall. **c.** The *sing.* is used poet. for the *pl.*, like our 'full many a . . .' : trudere multā cane apros in obstantia plagas, Hor.; multa victima, Verg. **d.** NOM. *pl.* **multi** as Noun (=οἱ πολλοί), *the many, the common mass* : numerarer in multis, Cic.; unus e or de multis, Cic. **e.** In *Neut. sing.* : multum est, *it is of importance* : Verg. As Noun with *Partit.* GEN.: iam multum diei processerat, Sall.; multum temporis, Cic. **multi** as GEN. of value: eam multi facere, Pl. **f.** *Neut. pl.* : multa, *many things ; much* : ne multa or ne multis, *not to be prolix ; to be brief,* Cic. Ep.; multa also as *Intern.* ACC.: multa luctari, Verg. (For multum and multo as *Adv. v.* infra). **III.** Of time : *far advanced* : ad multum

diem, *till late in the day*, Cic. ; multo denique die, Caes. ; multā nocte, Verg. **multum**, Acc. (of Extent : often too as *Intern.*
Acc.), *much, very much, greatly, very, often,
far :* salve multum, gnate mi, Pl. ; non
multum confidere, Caes. ; multum esse in
venationibus, Caes. ; longe omnis multumque superabit, Cic. With Adj. and *Part.* :
multum loquaces, Pl. ; multum iactatus in
alto, Verg. ; res multum et saepe quaesita,
Cic. With *Comp.* (for multo) : multum robus-
tior illo, Juv. ; Pl. With *post :* haud multum post mortem eius, Tac. With *infra :*
haud multum infra viam, Liv. **multō**,
Abl. (of Measure), *by much, much, a great
deal, by far.* **a.** Freq. with comparatives :
multo facilius iter, Caes. With verbs of
comparison : virtutem omnibus rebus multo
anteponentes, Cic. ; with malle, Pl. **b.**
With *Sup. :* multo maxima pars, Cic. ;
Pl. ; Hor. ; Liv. **c.** With particles denoting a difference : multo aliter, Ter. ;
non multo secus, Cic. Ep. **d.** In specifica-
tions of time, before *ante* and *post :* non
multo ante, Nep. ; multo ante, Cic. ; Liv.
Comp. **A.** In *sing.* **plūs**, plūris ; only as
Neut. Noun (or in Acc. as *Adv.*). **a.** Nom.
and Acc. : tantum et plus etiam ipse mihi
deberet, Cic. With Partitive Gen. : plus
honoris, Cic. ; plus hostium, Liv. With
quam : confiteor eos plus quam sicarios
esse, Cic. ; Pl. With Abl. : plus triginta
natus annis ego sum, Pl. ; plus aequo, Cic. ;
sescentis plus peditibus cecidit, Liv. ; de
paupertate tacentes plus poscente ferent,
Hor. With numbers mostly without *quam*
but keeping the case : plus dimidiati mensis cibaria, Cic. ; paulo plus ducentos passūs
a castris, Liv. ; Ter. **b.** Gen. of Value,
plūris, *of more value, of or at a higher price :*
esse, Pl. ; emere, vendere, aestimare, facere,
putare, habere, Cic. ; Hor. **B.** In *pl.*
plūrēs, plūra, Gen. plūrium, Dat. plūribus,
more, more numerous. **a.** As Adj. : with
quam : pluris esse intellego quam putaram,
Cic. ; Ter. ; Liv. **b.** As Adj. Of a great
number : *many, several :* Caes., Cic., Liv. **c.**
As Noun : *Masc. the populace :* Pl., Liv. ;
also (*cf.* oἱ πλείονες), *the majority ;* i.e.
the dead : quin prius me ad pluris pene-
travi ? Pl. *Neut.* in phr. : quid plura (*sc.*
dicam)? *why (should I say) more ?* Cic., Nep.
Sup. **plūrimus** (-**um**-), a, um, *most, very
much* or *many* (us. *pl.*). **a.** In gen. : simulacra, Caes. ; nos plurimis ignotissimi gentibus, Cic. In *sing. :* me plurumā praedā
onustum, Pl. Esp. in the standing form
of salutation at the beg. of letters : impertit
salutem plurimam ; and salutem plurimam
dicit (abbrev. S. P. D.). With *sing.* Noun
(*cf.* multus II. c.), *many a :* plurima mortis
imago, Verg. **b.** *very strong, vigorous, with
great energy, very ardent :* medio cum plurimus orbe sol erat, Ov. ; plurimus in Iunonis
honorem, Hor. ; labor, opera, Liv. ; Pl.
c. *Neut.* **plūrimum** as Noun. With
Partit. Gen. : sententiarum et gravitatis
plurimum, Cic. *Intern.* Acc. : qui apud
me dignitate plurimum possunt, Cic. Gen.
plūrimi (-**um**-) in statements of value, *of
the greatest value* or *importance ; at a very high
price :* pendere, Pl. ; facere, Nep. ; esse, Cic.

mūlus, I, *m. a mule :* Pl., Cic. As a term of
abuse : Cat.
Mulvius pōns, *a bridge across the Tiber ;*
Mulviānus, a, um.
Mummius, a, *the name of Roman gens.* Esp.
L. Mummius Achaicus, *the destroyer of
Corinth*, b.c. 146.
mundānus, I, *m.* [mundus], *a citizen of the
world, a cosmopolite :* Cic.
mundē and **munditer**, *adv. cleanly, neatly :* Pl.
munditia, ae (and later **munditiēs**, ēi), *f.*
[mundus]. **1.** Lit. **a.** *cleanness, cleanli-
ness :* Pl. ; munditias facere, *to do the
cleaning*, Pl., Cato. **b.** *neatness, elegance,
spruceness* (e.g. in dress, furniture) : Pl.,
Cic. In *pl. :* Pl., Hor., Ov., Liv., etc.
2. Transf. **a.** Of style : *neatness, terse-
ness :* Cic., Quint. **b.** Of manners :
politeness : urbanae, Sall.
mundulus, a, um [*dim.* mundus], *trim, spruce :*
Pl.
mundus, a, um, *clean, neat, elegant.* **1.** Lit. :
supellex, Hor. *Sup. :* Pl. **2.** Transf.
a. Of mode of living : *neat, elegant :* homines, Cic. ; cultus iusto mundior, Liv.
Neut. as Noun : in mundo, *in readiness :*
mihi in mundo sunt virgae, Pl. **b.** Of
style : *neat, fine, elegant :* verba, Ov.
mundus, I, *m.* **I.** *toilet-materials* (of a
woman) : Lucil., Liv. **II.** *the system of
the universe, the world, universe.* **1.** Lit.
(of the heavens) : Lucr., Cic., Verg., etc.
2. Transf. *the earth, mankind :* quicumque mundo terminus obstitit, Hor. [It.
mondo ; Fr. *monde.*]
mūnerārius, I, *m.* [mūnus], *an exhibitor of
gladiators :* Sen., Suet.
mūnerigerulus, I, *m.* [mūnus gerō], *a bearer
of presents :* Pl.
mūnerō, āre (Pl., Cic.), and **mūneror**, ārī
(Cic., Hor.) [mūnus], *to reward, make a
present to :* matrem, Pl. ; Cic. Ep. With
Acc. and Abl. : *to present with :* aliquem
aliquā re, Cic., Hor. With Acc. of thing
and Dat. of person : *to bestow on, present to :*
Pl., Cic.
mūnia, ōrum, *n. pl.* [*cf.* moenia, mūnus] (only
in Nom. and Acc.) *duties, functions ;* esp.
official or *professional duties :* candidatorum, Cic. ; belli pacisque munia facere,
Liv. ; munia consulatūs obire, Tac. ;
munia ducis implere, Tac. ; vitae servare
munia, Hor.
mūniceps, ipis, *m.f.* [mūnia capiō], *an inhabitant of a municipium* or *free town* or
borough ; a burgher, citizen. **1.** Lit. :
municeps Cosanus, Cic. **2.** Transf. *a
fellow-citizen, fellow-countryman :* municeps
noster, Cic., Caes. Of things : municipes
Iovis advexisse lagoenas (i.e. Cretan bottles),
Juv.
mūnicipālis, e, *adj.* [mūnicipium], *belonging
to a municipium :* Cic., Tac. As a term of
contempt, like our *provincial, country-* :
municipalis eques (of Cicero), Juv.
mūnicipātim, *adv. by* municipia : municipa-
tim dividendos censuit, Suet.
mūnicipium, I, *n.* [mūniceps], *a borough,
town* (esp. *in Italy*) *subject to Rome, but
governed by its own laws ; a free town :*
Caes., Cic., etc. Sometimes for colonia :
Lucense, Cic.

mūnĭfĭcē, adv. bountifully, generously : dare, Cic. ; adiuvare, Liv.

mūnĭfĭcentĭa, ae, f. [mūnĭficus], generosity, liberality : Sall., Liv.

mūnĭfĭcō, āre [mūnĭficō], to treat generously or liberally : aliquem aliquā re, Lucr.

mūnĭfĭcus, a, um [mūnus faciō], bountiful, generous, liberal. **1.** Lit. of persons : ut munifica sim bonis, Pl. ; in dando, Cic. Sup. : Cic. **2.** Transf. of things : splendid : opes, Ov. ; Mart.

mūnĭmen, inis, n. [mūniō], a defence : ad imbris, Verg.

mūnĭmentum, i, n. [mūniō], a defence, protection. **1.** Lit. : ut instar muri hae saepes munimenta praeberent, Caes. ; domūs munimentis saeptae, Tac. ; munimentis se defendere or tenere, Tac. ; fossa haud parvum munimentum, Liv. For the body : munimenta togae, Juv. **2.** Transf. : id munimentum (Horatium Coclitem) illo die fortuna urbis Romanae habuit, Liv. ; tribunicia potestas, munimentum libertati, Liv. ; rati noctem sibi munimento fore, Sall.

mūnĭō (older **moeniō**), īre [cf. moenia], to build (esp. a wall), to provide with a wall, to fortify. **1.** Lit. : locum, Caes. ; arcem, Nep. ; palatium, Liv. ; fessi muniendo, Liv. With Instr. Abl. : Alpibus Italiam munierat ante natura, Cic. ; castra vallo fossāque, Caes. : hence metaph. : magna moenia moenia, Pl. Occ. of roads : viam, Cic., Liv. ; iter, Nep. ; rupem, Liv. **2.** Transf. **a.** In gen. to defend, protect, shelter : spica contra avium morsūs munitur vallo aristarum, Cic. ; munio me ad haec tempora, Cic. ; se contra perfidiam, Cic. ; sese ab insidiis, Liv. ; adversus bella Romanum imperium, Liv. **b.** sibi viam ad stuprum, Cic.

mūnis, e, adj. [v. mūnia], ready to be of service, obliging : Pl.

mūnītĭō, ōnis, f. [mūniō], a building, constructing. **1.** Lit. **a.** a fortifying : milites munitione prohibere, Caes. **b.** Of roads : viarum, Cic. **c.** Of bridges : fluminum, Tac. **2.** Transf. **a.** Concr. : a fortification, defence-work, lines (mostly in pl.) : munitio ac moles lapidum, Cic. ; facere, Caes. ; munitiones et castella idoneis locis imposuit, Tac. ; Cic. ; Liv. **b.** a paving of the way : aditum ad causam et munitionem (sc. viae), Cic.

mūnītō, āre [freq. mūniō], to open up (a road). Transf. : viam, Cic.

mūnītor, ōris, m. [mūniō], a builder, engineer, sapper. Of walls or fortifications : Verg., Liv., Tac. Of an underground passage : Liv.

mūnītus, a, um. **I.** Part. mūniō. **II.** Adj. constructed. **1.** Lit. fortified. Sup. : Caes. Neut. pl. as Noun : munita viāī (i.e. of the teeth), Lucr. **2.** Transf. secured, protected : pudicitia contra tuam cupiditatem, Cic. ; se munitiorem ad tuendam vitam suam fore, Cic.

mūnus (older **moenus**), eris, n. [cf. mūnia], a service, office, function, duty. **1.** Lit. **a.** In gen. : curare, Pl. ; administrare, Ter. ; legationis, Caes. ; rei publicae munus explere, Cic. ; nullum vitae munus exsequi,

Cic. ; vigiliarum munus obire, Liv. ; interpretis munere fungi, Caes. ; Pl. ; inter se munera belli partiti sunt, Liv. ; moenera militiāī, Lucr. ; munere vacare, Caes. ; munus est alicuius (with Inf.), Cic. **b.** a public duty, service, charge, tax : detrectationem munerum militiae, Liv. ; iniuncta imperi munera impigre obeunt, Tac. ; imponere civitati, Cic. ; remittere, Caes. **2.** Transf. **a.** service, bounty ; a favour : totum muneris hoc tui est, Hor. ; Cic. Ep. **b.** Esp. a tribute to the dead : supremum mortis, Cat. ; suprema, Verg. ; fungi inani munere, Verg. **c.** Of a literary work (as a tribute) : solitudinis, Cic. **d.** a present, gift : deorum munere, Cic. ; munere aliquem donare, Verg. ; munera Liberi, Hor. **e.** a public function, show, exhibition, esp. a show of gladiators (as being provided as a bounty of magistrates or as a tribute to the dead, etc.) : functus est aedilicio maximo munere, Cic. ; praebere, Cic. ; alicui dare, i.e. in someone's honour, Cic. ; edere, Suet. **f.** a public building erected at the expense of an individual : Ov. ; transf. of the universe : moderator tanti operis et muneris, Cic.

mūnuscŭlum, i, n. [dim. mūnus], a small present : Cic. Ep., Verg., Juv.

mūraena, ae, f. [μύραινα], the murena, a kind of eel : Pl., Juv.

mūrālis, e, adj. [mūrus], of a wall, mural : pilum, used in fighting from walls, Caes. ; tormentum, for battering walls, Verg. ; falces, for pulling down walls, Caes. ; corona, a mural crown, given as a reward to the man who first scaled the enemy's walls, Liv. [It. muraglia ; Fr. muraille.]

Mūrcĭa, ae, f. the goddess of sloth.

mūrex, icis, m. the purple-fish, a kind of univalve mollusc, from which the Tyrian purple was obtained. **1.** Lit. : Enn., Hor. The shells were used for adorning grottoes : Ov. **2.** Transf. **a.** the purple dye, purple, made from the juice of this shell-fish : Verg. **b.** Of bodies shaped like the shell of the murex : **i.** a pointed rock or stone : Verg. **ii.** a caltrop : murices ferreos in terram defodisse Dareum, Curt.

mūrĭa, ae, f. [cf. πλημμυρίς], salt liquor, brine, pickle : Cato, Hor. Also **mūrĭēs**, ēī, f. Cato. [It. moia ; Sp. moje ; Fr. muire.]

mūrĭātĭcum, i, n. [muria], a pickled fish : Pl.

mūrĭcĭdus, i, m. [mūs caedō, mouse-killer], as a term of abuse, a coward : Pl.

murmillō, ōnis, m. [μόρμυρος], a gladiator who fought against a retiarius ; he wore a Gallic helmet with a metal fish as crest : Cic., Quint., etc.

murmur, uris, n. [cf. μορμύρω], a confused sound. **a.** Of living beings : a murmur, murmuring : strepit per agmina, Verg. ; populi, Liv. Of indistinct speech : Ov. Of the humming of bees : Verg. **b.** Of things : a murmur, roar, rushing, crashing, rumbling : fluctūs murmur dant, Lucr. ; maris, Cic. ; magno misceri murmure caelum, Verg. ; Juv. ; Of a volcanic mountain : Suet. Of wind-instruments : Hor., Ov. [It. mororio ; Fr. murmure.]

murmurillum, i, n. [dim. murmur], a low murmuring : Pl.

murmurō, āre [murmur], to murmur, mutter, grumble. **a.** Of persons : secum, Pl. **b.** Of things : to murmur, roar, rumble : intestina, Pl. ; mare, Cic. ; unda, Verg.

(1) **murra** (**myrrha**), ae, f. [μύρρα], a material of which costly vessels were made, perh. fluor spar : Plin.

(2) **murra** (**myrrha**), ae, f. [μύρρα], the myrrh-tree. **1.** Lit.: Ov. **2.** Transf. its gum, myrrh : Verg., Ov.

(1) **murreus** (**myrrheus**), a, um [murra]. made of murra : pocula, Prop., Sen. Ep.

(2) **murreus** (**myrrheus**), a, um [murra]. **I.** perfumed with myrrh : Hor. **II.** myrrh-coloured : onyx, Prop.

(1) **murrinus** (**myrrhinus**), a, um, made of murra : trulla, Plin. As Noun, **murrina**, ōrum, n. pl. (sc. vasa), vessels of murra, murrine vases : Plin.

(2) **murrinus** (**myrrhinus**), a, um [murra], of myrrh : odor, Pl. As Noun, **murrina**, ae, f. (sc. potio), a drink flavoured with myrrh : Pl.

mūrus (older **moerus**), i, m. [cf. moenia], a wall, esp. a town or city wall. **1.** Lit.: urbis, Cic. ; Caes. ; urbem muris saepire, Nep. ; muros ducere, Verg., Hor. ; the wall of a building : Cic. Ep. ; a dam or dike : a lacu milia passuum XIX perducit, Caes. **2.** Transf. **a.** the rim of a pot : Juv. **b.** defence, bulwark : lex Aelia et Fufia, propugnacula murique tranquillitatis, Cic. ; Graium (GEN.) murus Achilles, Ov.

mūs, mūris, m.f. [μῦς], a mouse or rat : Pl., Cic., Verg., etc. (The ancients included under this name the marten, sable, ermine.)

Mūsa, ae, f. [Μοῦσα], a Muse ; patron goddess of song, art and literature. (The Muses were nine in number.) Transf. **a.** genius, wit, talent, taste : crassiore musā, Quint. **b.** a song, a poem : silvestris, Verg. **c.** In pl., sciences, studies : agrestiores, Cic.

Mūsaeus, i, m. a mythical Greek poet in the time of Orpheus.

musca, ae, f. [cf. μυῖα], a fly. **1.** Lit.: Cic., Mart., etc. **2.** Transf. of prying, intrusive persons : Pl. [Fr. mouche.]

muscārium, i, n. [musca], a fly-flap, fly-brush, used also as a clothes-brush ; made of peacocks' tails : Mart.

muscipula, ae, f. and **muscipulum**, i, n. [mūs capiō], a mousetrap : Lucil., Phaedr., Sen. Ep.

muscōsus, a um [muscus], mossy : fontes, Verg. Comp. : Cic. Ep.

musculus, i, m. [dim. mūs], a little mouse, the common mouse. **1.** Lit.: Cic. **2.** Transf. **a.** a sea-mussel : Pl. **b.** a muscle of the body. Transf. of style : Plin. Ep. **c.** Milit.: a shed, mantlet : Caes.

muscus, i, m. moss : Hor., Ov. [Fr. mousse.]

Mūsēum, i, n. [Μουσεῖον], a seat of the Muses, a museum ; a library, academy, study : Varr., Suet.

Mūsēus (**-aeus**), a, um [Μουσεῖος], of the Muses, poetic, musical : mele, Lucr.

mūsicē, adv. pleasantly : agere aetatem (i.e. ' in clover '), Pl.

mūsicus, a, um [μουσικός]. **a.** of music, musical : leges, Cic ; sonus citharae, Phaedr. **b.** of poetry or culture in gen. : applicare se ad studium musicum, Ter. As Noun. **a.** **mūsicus**, i, m. a musician : Cic. **b.** **mūsica**, ōrum, n. pl. music : in musicis numeri, et voces, et modi, Cic. **c.** **mūsica**, ae, and **mūsicē**, ēs, f. (Quint.) [μουσική], the art of music, music ; also poetry, and every higher kind of artistic or scientific culture or pursuit : tractare, Cic. ; docere, Nep. Prov.: occultae musicae nullum esse respectum, Suet.

mussitō, āre [freq. mussō]. **A.** Intrans. **a.** to be silent : Pl. **b.** to speak in an undertone, to mutter, grumble : Liv. **B.** Trans. to bear in silence : haec mecum, Pl. ; iniuriam, Ter.

mussō, āre [perh. cf. μυάω and μύζω]. **I.** **a.** to bear in silence : id, Pl. **b.** to brood in silence : iuvencae, Verg. **c.** to brood over in silence, be undetermined : with Inf. : Verg. ; with Indir. Deliberative : Verg. Transf.: mussabat tacito medicina timore, Lucr. **II.** to speak in an undertone, to mutter, murmur : Verg., Liv. Of the murmuring of bees ; Verg.

mustāceus, i, m., and **mustāceum**, i, n. [mustum], a must-cake or laurel-cake, a kind of wedding-cake mixed with must and baked on bay-leaves : Cato, Juv. Prov.: laureolam in mustaceo quaerere, Cic. Ep.

mūstella (**-ēla**), ae, f. [mūs], a weasel : Pl., Hor.

mūstellīnus (**-ēlinus**), a, um [mūstella], of a weasel : color, Ter.

mustus, a, um, young, new, fresh : agna, vinum, Cato. As Noun, **mustum**, i, n. new or unfermented wine, must : Cato, Verg., Plin. Ep. In pl. : **musta**, ōrum, vintages, i.e. autumns : Ov. In simile : quasi de musto ac lacu fervidam orationem, Cic. [Fr. moût.]

Mūta, ae, f. a goddess (Lara or Larunda), struck dumb by Jupiter on account of her talkativeness.

mūtābilis, e, adj. [mūtō], changeable, mutable : corpus, Cic. ; femina, Verg. ; animus vulgi, Liv.

mūtābilitās, ātis, f. [mūtābilis], changeableness : mentis, Cic.

mūtātiō, ōnis, f. [mūtō], a changing, altering. **a.** a change, alteration : consili, Cic. ; cupido mutationis, Tac. **b.** an exchanging, interchange : vestis, Ter. ; officiorum, Cic.

mutilō, āre [mutilus], to cut or lop off, to crop, maim, mutilate. **1.** Lit.: naso auribusque mutilatis, Liv. ; caudam colubrae, Ov. **2.** Transf. to reduce, to diminish : aliquem (i.e. to rob), Ter. ; exercitum, Cic.

mutilus, a, um, maimed, defective. **1.** Lit.: alces mutilae sunt cornibus (i.e. hornless), Caes. **2.** Transf.: sic mutilus minitaris, Hor. As Noun : mutila et hiantia loqui, Cic.

mūtiō, v. muttiō.

mūtitiō, v. muttitiō.

mūtō, āre. **A.** Trans. to move about, shift ; to cause se luna quoquam mutat, Pl. ; ne quis invitus civitate mutetur, Cic. ; Liv. ; hinc dum muter, Ov. Hence (usual meaning), to shift, change. **1.** Lit.:

solum, Cic.; domos, Verg.; caelum non
animum, Hor.; patriam, Ov.; vestem,
Ter., Hor., Liv.; vestimenta, Cic.; croceo
vellera luto, Verg. Of exchange. **a.** *to
give in exchange* : pro Etruriā Tarentum,
Liv.; vestem cum aliquo, Ter. In trading :
to exchange, interchange, barter ; us. with
ABL. of instrument of exchange : pecoris et
mancipiorum praedas mutare cum mer-
catoribus vino advecticio, Sall. **b.** *to get
in exchange* (with ABL. of exchange) : uvam
furtivā strigili, Hor.; victoriae possessionem incertā pace, Liv.; pro Macedonibus Romanos dominos, Liv.; Sall. With
Acc. alone : Pl., Hor. **c.** Of giving and
receiving in exchange : res inter se, Sall.
2. T r a n s f. *to change, alter.* **a.** In gen. :
fidem, Pl., Ter.; consilium, Caes.; sententiam, Cic.; hostium consilia, Liv.; orationem, Cic.; tabulas (i.e. one's will), Juv.;
de uxore nihil, Ter.; de exercitu nihil, Liv.;
quantum mutatus ab illo Hectore, Verg.;
ex Graeco, Quint.; bona in peius, Quint.
b. *to change for the better* : Ter.; *for the
worse* : mutata est fortuna, Caes.; voluntas, Nep.; vinum, Hor. **c.** *to transform* :
Circe socios Ulixis, Ov.; in alitem, Hor.
d. Of allegiance : principem, Tac.; mutati
Laurentes, Verg. **B.** I n t r a n s. *to change,
alter* : aestus, Tac.; animi, Liv.; mores,
Liv. [Sp. *mudar* ; Fr. *muer*.]

muttiō, īre, *to mumble, mutter* : Pl., Ter.
Of things : Pl.

muttītiō, ōnis, *f.* [muttiō], *a mumbling, mut-
tering* : Pl.

mūtuātiō, ōnis, *f.* [mūtuor], *a borrowing* :
Cic. In *pl.* : Cic.

mūtuē, *adv. mutually, in return*: respondere,
Cic. Ep.

mūtuitō, āre [mūtuor], *to wish to borrow* : Pl.

mūtuor, ārī [mūtuus], *to borrow.* **1.** Lit. :
pecunias, Caes.; ab aliquo, Cic.; domum,
Tac.; auxilia ad bellum, Hirt. **2.** T r a n s f.
to take for one's use, to derive from : orator
subtilitatem ab Academiā, Cic.; verbum a
simili (*to speak metaphorically*), Cic.; consilium ab amore, Liv.; a viris virtus nomen,
Cic.

mūtus, a, um [*cf.* mūgiō, muttiō], *not articulate, speechless, dumb, mute.* **1.** L i t. :
Pl., Cic. As Noun : Pl., Juv. Of animals :
Cic., Hor. **2.** T r a n s f. Of things. **a.**
dumb, mute, silent : tintinnabulum, Pl.;
artes (the plastic arts, arts of design, opp.
to eloquence), Cic.; also, *the silent arts*
(such as medicine, i.e. which do not concern themselves with language), Verg.;
nunquam vox est de te mea muta, Ov.;
consonantes (*mutes, which cannot be sounded
by themselves*), Quint. **b.** Of places, *silent,
still* : mare, Pl.; forum, Cic. **c.** Of
times : *silent* : tempus mutum a litteris,
Cic. Ep.; silentia noctis, Ov. [Fr. *muet*.]

mūtuus, a, um [mūtō]. **I.** *interchangeable,
reciprocal, mutual* : funera, Verg.; officia,
Cic. Ep.; nox omnia erroris mutui implevit,
Liv.; odia, Tac. *Neut.* as Noun, **mūtuum**
(**-om**), i, *n. a like return* : facere (i.e. to return
like for like), Pl.; in amicitia facere, Cic.;
pedibus per mutua nexis (*one with another*),
Verg.; as *Intern.* Acc. : inter se mortales
mutua vivunt, Lucr. ABL. **mūtuō**, as

Adv., by turns, reciprocally, mutually : fun-
cere officia cum multis, Suet.; diligere,
Planc. ap. Cic. Ep. **II.** *borrowed, lent.* **1.**
Lit. : mutuom argentum rogare, quaerere,
dare, Pl.; mutuas pecunias sumere ab ali-
quo, Cic. **2.** T r a n s f. **mūtuum** (**-om**), i,
n. (*sc.* argentum), *a loan* : cum aliquo facere,
Pl.; si pudoris egeas, sumas mutuom,
Pl.; verbum aut translatum aut sumptum
aliunde, ut mutuo, Cic.

Mycēnae, ārum, or **Mycēnē**, ēs, *f. a very
ancient and celebrated city in Argolis, of
which Agamemnon was king* ; **Mycēnaeus**,
a, um, **Mycēnēnsis**, e, adj.; **Mycēnēnsēs**,
ium, *m. pl. the inhabitants* : **Mycēnis**, idis, *f.*
i.e. *Iphigenia, d. of Agamemnon.*

Mygdones, um, *m. pl. a people of Thrace, who
afterwards took possession of a part of
Phrygia* ; **Mygdonis**, idis, *f. adj. Mygdonian, Phrygian* ; also *Lydian* ; **Mygdo-
nius**, a, um, *Mygdonian, Phrygian.*

myoparō, ōnis, *m.* [μυοπάρων], *a kind of
light war-galley* : Cic.

myricē, ēs, or **myrica**, ae, *f.* [μυρίκη], *the
tamarisk* : Verg. Prov. : pinguia corticibus sudent electra myricae (of something
impossible), Verg.

Myrmidones, um, *m. pl. the Myrmidons* ;
*a people of Thessaly, under the sway of
Achilles.*

Myrōn, ōnis, *m. a celebrated Greek sculptor,
about 430 B.C.*

myropōla, ae, *m.* [μυροπώλης], *a dealer in
perfumes* : Pl.

myropōlium, i. *n.* [μυροπώλιον], *a perfumer's shop* : Pl.

myrrh–, v. murr–.

myrta and **murta**, ae, *f. v.* myrtus.

myrtētum (**murtētum**), i, *n.* [myrtus], *a
myrtle-grove* : Pl., Sall., Verg.

myrteus (**murteus**), a, um [myrtus], *of
myrtles, myrtle–.* **1.** Lit. : silva, Verg.
2. T r a n s f. *adorned with myrtle* : coma,
Tib.

Myrtōum mare, *the S.W. part of the Aegean
Sea, which takes its name from the island
of Myrtos.*

myrtum, i, *n.* [μύρτον], *a myrtle-berry* : Verg.

myrtus (also **myrta** or **murta**, ae), i, *f.* (*m.*
Cato) (GEN. myrtūs, Verg.) [μύρτος],
myrtle : viridi caput impedire myrto, Hor.
Poet. *a spear-shaft of myrtle* : Verg.

Mȳs, Myos, *m. a famous artist in metal work,
contemporary with Phidias.*

Mȳsi, ōrum, *m. pl. the Mysians* ; **Mȳsia**, ae,
f. their country in N.W. Asia Minor ;
Mȳsius, Mȳsus, a, um.

mysta or **mystēs**, ae, *m.* [μύστης], *a priest
of the mysteries of Ceres* : Ov.

mystagōgus, i, *m.* [μυσταγωγός], *one who
conducts through secret and sacred places as
a guide, a mystagogue* : Cic.

mystēria, ōrum, *n. pl.* [μυστήρια], *secret
rites, secret worship of a deity, divine mysteries.* **1.** Lit. : esp. of the mysteries of
Ceres, otherwise called sacra Eleusinia :
Cic.; mysteria facere, *to celebrate*, Nep.
Also of other festivals celebrated with
secret rites : Romana mysteria, *the mysteries or festival of the goddess* Bona Dea,
Cic. **2.** T r a n s f. in gen. : *a secret thing,
secret, mystery* : rhetorum mysteria, Cic.

mystēs, ae, v. mysta.

mysticus, a, um [μυστικός], *used in the mysteries :* vannus Iacchi, Verg.

Mytilēnē, ēs, f. or **Mytilēnae**, ārum, f. pl. *the chief town of Lesbos, birthplace of Sappho and Alcaeus ;* **Mytilēnaeus**, a, um ; **Mytilēnēnsis**, e.

N

N, n, the thirteenth letter of the Latin alphabet. **I.** For its assimilation to other consonants, v. in and con (cum). **II.** Changes of *n* in the Romance languages. Initial *n* undergoes no change. Medial *n* is changed, **i.** by dissimilation, into *l* : e.g. Lat. *venenum*, It. *veleno*. **ii.** It is omitted, often with some modification of the accompanying vowels : e.g. Lat. *diurnum*, *hibernum* ; Fr. *jour*, *hiver*. This takes place especially when *n* is followed by *s* : e.g. Lat. *constare*, It. *costare*, Fr. *coûter* : Lat. *mensis*, It. *mese*, Sp. *mes*, Fr. *mois*. **iii.** *nn* becomes *gn*, *ñ*, or *nh* : e.g. Lat. *grunnire*, It. *grugnire*, Fr. *grogner*, Sp. *gruñir*. **III.** As an abbreviation N usually stands for natus, nefastus dies, nepos, *etc.*, Ñ = natione, natus, nostri, nostro, *etc.*, numerus, numero, *etc.* N.D.N. = numini domini nostri. N.L. = non liquet (v. liqueo). N.M.V. = nobilis memoriae vir. NN. BB. = nobilissimi. NP. = nefastus prior. ℣M. = nummum (GEN. *pl.*).

Nabataeī, ōrum, m. pl. *a people of N. Arabia ;* **Nabataea**, ae, f. *their district ;* **Nabataeus**, a, um, *Nabataean or Arabian, Eastern.*

nablium, i, n. *a kind of harp :* Ov.

nactus, a, um, *Part.* nanciscor.

nae, v. nē.

naenia, v. nēnia.

Naevius, a, *the name of a Roman gens ;* esp. Cn. Naevius, *a Roman epic and dramatic poet who died c.* B.C. 201 ; **Naeviānus**, a, um.

naevus, i, m. *a mole on the body :* Cic., Hor., Ov.

Nāias, adis, and **Nāis**, idis and idos, f. [Ναϊάς and Ναΐς (floating, swimming, of the water)], *a water-nymph, Naiad.* **1.** Lit.: Verg. Adj.: puellae Naides, Verg. **2.** Transf. **a.** *a nymph* (hamadryad, nereid) : Ov. **b.** *water :* Tib.

nam, *conj.* used to confirm or give the ground of a statement or fact (in prose, always at the beginning of its clause), *for,* **A.** In good. of a simple explanation : percontatorem fugito ; nam garrulus idem est, Hor. ; Pl. ; Cic. ; etc. Poet. after another word : ego nam videor mihi sanus, Hor. **B.** To add a further fact : initium fugae factum est a Dumnorigis equitibus, nam equitatui Dumnorix praeerat, Caes. **C.** Very often it introduces the reason for an omission, where an objection is anticipated : nam quid ego de studiis dicam, [*I will not speak*] *for why need I speak of them,* Cic. ; Phoenices Hipponem . . . aliasque urbes in orā maritimā condidere . . . nam de Carthagine tacere melius puto, Sall. ; nam

quae sibi crimini obiciantur, deridiculum se reddere rationem, Liv. **D.** In citing examples or illustrations ; *for instance :* sed vivo Catone minores natu multi uno tempore oratores floruerunt ; nam et A. Albinus, etc., Cic. **E.** In emphatic interrogations. **a.** Giving a reason for surprise or some emotion : nam qui (*how*) perdidi ? Pl. ; nam quis te nostras iussit adire domos ? Verg. **b.** In good prose, as enclitic : esp. in such forms as quisnam, *who in the world ?* Cic., Pl. ; ubinam gentium sumus, *pray where in the world are we ?* Cic.

namque, *conj.* [nam que], an emphatic nam, *for indeed, for truly, for* (us. at the beginning of a sentence and only before a vowel) namque ita me di ament, Pl. ; Cic. ; Verg. etc. ; namque illud quare negasti ? Cic. After a word : mota namque omnia adventu Samnitium, Liv. ; Verg.

nanciscor, nanciscī, nactus or nanctus, *to obtain by accident* (esp. by good luck), *to meet with, light on, find :* anulum, Ter. ; nihil mali, Ter. ; quoniam nacti te sumus aliquando otiosum, Cic. ; nactus idoneam tempestatem, Caes. ; locum, Caes. ; morbum, Nep. ; quod hami nacti sunt, meum est, Pl. ; vitis claviculis suis quidquid est nacta complectitur, Cic.

nānus, i, m. [νάννος and νᾶνος], *a dwarf :* Prop., Juv., Suet. [Fr. *nain*.]

Napaeae, ārum, f. pl. [ναπαῖος], *the dell-nymphs :* Verg.

nāpus, i, m. *a kind of turnip :* Plin., Mart. [Fr. *navet* / Ital. *navone*.]

Narbō, ōnis, m. (also called Narbō Marcius), *a city in S. Gaul, from which Gallia Narbōnēnsis took its name ;* **Narbōnēnsis**, e, adj.

Narcissus, i, m. **I.** *s. of Cephisus and the nymph Liriope ; changed into the flower of the same name.* **II.** *a freedman and minister of the Emperor Claudius.*

nardus, i, f., and **nardum**, i, n. [νάρδος]. nard, spikenard. Transf. nard-balsam. nard-oil : Assyriāque nardo potamus uncti, Hor. ; Tib.

nāris, is, f. [v. nāsus], *a nostril,* us. pl. **nārēs**, ium, *the nostrils, the nose.* **1.** Lit.: Sing.: Ov. Pl. : Cic., Verg., Juv. **2.** Transf. *the nose,* as an organ expressive of sagacity, and also of scorn and anger : ne sordida mappa naris corrugat, Hor. ; Aesopus naris emunctae senex (*clean-nosed,* i.e. keen, acute), Phaedr. ; homo naris obesae (*dull-nosed,* i.e. slow of apprehension), Hor. ; naribus uti (i.e. to banter, ridicule), Hor.

nārrābilis, e, adj. [nārrō], *that can be narrated :* Ov.

nārrātiō, ōnis, f. [nārrō], *a relating, narrating, a narration, narrative :* narrationes credibiles, Cic. Rhet. : Cic., Quint., Tac.

nārrātiuncula, ae, f. [dim. nārrātiō], *a short narrative :* Quint., Plin. Ep.

nārrātor, ōris, m. [nārrō], *a relater, narrator :* Cic., Quint., Tac.

nārrātus, a, um. **I.** *Part.* nārrō. **II.** *Noun,* **nārrāta**, ōrum, n. pl. *that which is told :* Hor.

nārrātus, ūs, m. [nārrō], *a narration, narrative :* Ov.

nārrō, āre [gnārus], lit. *to make known,* hence, *to tell, relate, narrate.* **1.** Lit.:

with Acc.: Ter., Cic., Liv., etc. With
Acc. and *Inf.*: Cic. Ep. With *Indir.*
Quest.: Ter., Cic. Ep. With *de*: Cic.;
so, *male, bene narrare (de aliquo), to tell
bad or good news (about somebody),* Cic. Ep.
With things as Subject: Pl., Cic. Ep.
Impers. Pass. (with Acc. and *Inf.*): Tac.;
but the personal construction is commoner.
2. T r a n s f. *to say, tell, talk of:* Pl.
Hence, *narro tibi, I assure you* (a form of
asseveration): narro tibi, plane relegatus
mihi videor, Cic. Ep. With Acc.: Ter.
With *Indir. Quest.*: Ter., Hor. With
de: Prop.

narthēcium, ī, *n.* [ναρθήκιον (lit. a piece of
narthex-wood hollowed out to hold ointments and medicines)], *an ointment-box, a
medicine-chest*: Cic., Mart.

nārus, a, um, *v.* gnārus, *ad init.*

Nārycion, ī, *n.* and **Nāryx,** ycis, *f. a city of
the Opuntian Locrians, birthplace of Ajax
Oileus*; **Nārycius,** a, um: heros, i.e.
the son of Ajax Oileus, Ov.

nāscor, nāscī, nātus (and gnātus) [*cf.* gignō],
to be begotten, be born. **1.** L i t.: Cic. With
ex and ABL.: ex servā, Cic.; Ter., etc.;
ex improbo patre, Cic.; Liv., etc. With
ab: Verg., Tac. With *de*: Ov. With
ABL. alone: Enn., Cic., Verg., Liv., etc.
Very freq. in *Perf. Part.*: post homines
natos (i.e. since the beginning of the world),
Cic. See also nātus. **2.** T r a n s f. **a.** Of
plants, animals, and natural products:
to come into being, arise, to be native: As-
syrium vulgo nascetur amomum, Verg.;
nascitur ibi plumbum album, Caes. **b.** Of
stars: *to rise, wax*: Verg., Hor. **c.**
Of wind, water: *to rise*: Verg., Plin. **d.**
Of ground: *to rise*: ab eo flumine collis
nascebatur, Caes. **e.** Of abstract things:
to spring, arise, grow, be produced: initium
belli, Caes.; facinus a cupiditate, Cic.;
Caes.; querellae pectore ab imo, Cat.;
so *Impers.*: ex eo nascitur ut etc., Cic.,
Sen. Ep. [Sp. *nacer*; Fr. *naître*.]

nāsiterna, *v.* nassiterna.

Nāsō, ōnis, *m.* [nāsus], lit. 'bignose'; esp.
P. Ovidius Naso, the poet.

nassa, ae, *f. a wicker-basket with a narrow
neck for catching fish, a weel.* **1.** L i t.:
Plin. **2.** T r a n s f. of a dangerous place:
a snare, net: ex hac nassā exire constitui,
Cic. Ep.; Pl.; Juv.

nassiterna, ae, *f. a watering-pot*: Pl., Cato.

nāsturcium, ī, *n.* [nāsus torqueō], *a kind of
cress,* prob. the *garden cress*: Cic.; in *pl.*:
Verg. [It. *nasturcio*; Sp. *mastuerzo*.]

nāsus, ī, *m.* (**nāsum,** ī, *n.* Pl.), *a nose.* **1.**
L i t.: Pl., Cic., Hor. etc. **2.** T r a n s f. **a.**
the sense of smell (*cf.* naris): non quia nasus
illis nullus erat, Hor. **b.** As expressive **i.**
Of *sagacity, taste,* etc.: non cuicumque
datum est habere nasum, Mart. **ii.** Of
anger: disce ī sed ira cadat naso, rugosa
que sanna, Pers. **iii.** Of *scorn, derision,
satirical wit*: naso adunco aliquem suspendere, Hor. [It. *naso*; Fr. *nez.*]

nāsūtē, *adv. pertly, satirically, scornfully*:
Phaedr.

nāsūtus, a, um [nāsus], *big-nosed.* **1.** L i t.:
Hor. **2.** T r a n s f. *witty, satirical, cen-
sorious*: Mart. *Comp.*: Mart. *Sup.*: Sen.

nāta (**gnāta**), ae, *f.* [nātus], *a daughter*.
Pl., Verg., etc.

nātālicius, a, um [nātālis], *of the hour or day
of one's birth, natal*: Chaldaeorum natalicia praedicta, Cic. As Noun, **nātālicia,**
ae, *f. a birthday party*: nataliciam in
hortis dare, Cic.

nātālis, e, *adj.* [nātus, nāscor], *of birth, natal*:
dies, Pl., Cic.: hora, Hor.; tempus, lux,
Ov.; astrum, Hor. As Noun, **nātālis,**
is, *m.* (*sc.* dies), *a birth-day*: Cic. Ep.,
Verg., Hor., etc. In *pl.*: *birth, origin,
family*: claris natalibus, Tac.; natalibus
clarus, Plin. Ep.; Juv. [Fr. *noël.*]

natāns, antis. **I.** *Part.* natō. **II.** Noun, na-
tantēs, um, *f. pl. fishes*: Verg.

natātiō, ōnis, *f.* [natō], *swimming, floating*:
in *pl.*: Cic.

natātor, ōris, *m.* [natō], *a swimmer*: Ov.

natēs, ium, *v.* natis.

nātiō, ōnis, *f.* [nāscor], *a being born, birth.*
1. L i t.: Varr. Personif. *the goddess of
birth*: Cic. **2.** T r a n s f. **a.** *a race,
tribe, stock*: Caes., Cic., Tac. Often
opp. to organised or civilised peoples:
Cic. **b.** *tribe, class, breed* (mostly in playful or contemptuous sense): officiosissima
candidatorum, Cic.; fures maritimi,
famelica hominum natio, Pl.

natis, is, more freq. *pl.* **natēs,** ium, *f. the
rump, the buttocks. Sing.*: Hor. *Plur.*:
Pl., Juv.

nātīvus, a, um [nāscor], *that owes existence to
being born, born.* **1.** L i t.: nativos esse
deos, Cic. **2.** T r a n s f. **a.** *produced by
nature, not artificial, natural, native*:
mundus, animus, Lucr.; beluae nativis
testis inhaerentes, Cic.; coma, Ov.;
specus, Tac. **b.** *innate, inborn* (opp.
ascitus): sensus, Cic.; lepos, Nep. **c.**
Gramm.: *primitive*: verba, Cic. [Fr.
natif, naïf.]

natō, āre [*freq.* nō], *to swim, float.* **1.** L i t.:
studiosissimus homo natandi, Cic. Ep.;
aequore pisces, Ov.: uncta carina, Verg.;
naufragus natans, Cic. With Acc. of Extent: nocte natat caeca freta, Verg. Hence
Pass.: quot piscibus unda natatur, Ov.
2. T r a n s f. **a.** *to flow, stream*: quā Tiberinus campo liberiore natat, Ov. **b.** *to
swim, overflow*; *to be flooded*) with ABL.:
pavimenta vino, Cic.; plenis rura fossis,
Verg. **c.** Of the eyes: *to swim, to be feeble,
glassy*: vinis oculique animique natabant,
Ov.; Quint. **d.** *to move slackly or loosely*:
nec vagus in laxā pes tibi pelle (i.e. calceo)
natet, Ov. **e.** Of birds: *to float, fly*: Luc.
f. *to fluctuate, waver*: pars multa (hominum) natat, modo recta capessens, interdum
pravis obnoxia, Hor.; Cic.

natrix, īcis, *f.* (*m.* in Luc.) [nō], *a water-
snake.* **1.** L i t.: Cic. **2.** T r a n s f. **a.** Of
a dangerous person: Suet. **b.** *a scourge of
snake's skin*: Lucil.

nātū, ABL. *sing. m.* [nāscor], *by birth.* **1.**
L i t.: with tantus, grandis, maior, minor,
maximus, minimus, (i.e. *in age*): tantus
natu, Pl.; maior natu, Cic.; Liv., etc. Also,
homo magno natu, Liv. **2.** T r a n s f. *in
growth*: Plin.

nātūra, ae, *f.* [nāscor], *blood-relationship,
natural affinity.* **1.** L i t.: natūrā tu illi

pater es, Ter. ; naturā frater, adoptione
filius, Liv. **2**. T r a n s f. **a.** *the nature*, i.e.
the natural constitution or *features ; quality,
property, formation :* loci, montis, fluminis,
Caes. ; locus naturā et opere munitissimus,
Caes. ; animae, Cic. ; serpentium, Sall. ;
naturas apibus Iuppiter addidit, Verg.
b. Of character : *nature, natural disposition, bent, character :* Caes., Cic., Hor., etc. ;
societatem ingeneravit natura, Liv. **c.** *the
nature, course,* or *order of things :* naturae
fundamenta pervertere, Cic. ; naturae satis
facere (i.e. to die), Cic. ; also naturae concedere, Sall. ; in rerum naturā est, Cic. ;
Lucr. Often personified : Cic., Nep. **d.**
nature, i.e. *the world, the universe :* Cleanthes totius naturae menti atque animo hoc
nomen (dei) tribuit, Cic. ; rerum, Caes. **e.**
an element, thing, substance : Aristoteles
quintam quandam naturam censet esse, e
quā sit mens, Cic. **f.** *the organs of the body :*
Cic.

nātūrālis, e, *adj.* [nātūra], *natural.* **I.** *by
birth, one's own :* pater (opp. to adoptive
father), Cic. ; filius, Liv. **II.** *produced by*
or *agreeable to nature, natural :* lex, societas,
bonum, nitor, Cic. **III.** *relating to nature,
natural :* quaestiones, Cic. ; historia, Plin.

nātūrāliter, *adv. naturally, conformably to
nature, by nature :* Caes., Cic., etc.

nātus (gnātus), a, um. **I.** *Part.* nāscor.
II. Noun, **nātus (gnātus)**, ī, *m. a son*
(mostly poet.) : in *pl.* nati, *children :* Cic.,
Ov., etc. ; of animals : Verg. **III.** A d j.
a. *born, made, destined by nature.* With
DAT. : huic rei, Ter. ; sibi, Cic. ; gloriae,
Cic. With *ad* : ad haec tempora, Cic. ; ad
dicendum, Cic. ; ad sacra Cithaeron, Ov.
With *in* and ACC. : in usum laetitiae scyphi,
Hor. ; Ov. With *propter :* Juv. With
Inf. : Ov. **b.** *formed* or *constituted by
nature :* ita natus locus est, Liv. ; versūs
male nati, Hor. Hence, in p h r. pro or e
re natā, *in the (existing) circumstances, as
matters are :* ut in his pro re natā non in-
commode possint esse, Cic. Ep. ; Ter. **c.**
With annos : *so old, of the age of, etc. :*
eques Romanus annos prope XC natus,
Cic. Sometimes with maior or minor, without or with quam : homo annos natus
maior XL, *more than forty years old*, Cic. ;
cum liberis maioribus quam XV annos natis,
Liv. With *plus* or *minus :* plus XXX annis
natus sim, Pl. ; annos LX natus es aut plus,
Ter.

nātus, ūs, *m.* v. nātū.

nauarchus, ī, *m.* [ναύαρχος], *the captain of a
ship :* Cic., Tac.

nauci, *v.* naucum.

nauclēricus, a, um [ναυκληρικός], *of a ship-
owner* or *ship-master :* Pl.

nauclērus, ī, *m.* [ναύκληρος], *a ship-owner, a
ship-master, skipper :* Pl. [It. *nocchiere*
and Fr. *nocher*.]

naucum, ī, *n. something slight* or *trivial,
a trifle.* Mostly in GEN. of value with a
negative : non nauci (habere, facere, or
esse), *of no value, good for nothing :* homo
timidus nauci non erit, Pl. ; Cic.

naufragium, ī, *n.* [naufragus], *a shipwreck.*
1. L i t. : facere, to be ship-wrecked, Cic. Ep. ;
naufragio interire, Caes. P r o v. : naufragia

alicuius ex terrā intueri, Cic. Ep. ; tabula ex
naufragio (i.e. a means of deliverance, a
solace), Cic. Ep. **2**. T r a n s f. **a.** *a storm :*
naufragiis magnis multisque coörtis, Lucr.
b. *shipwreck, ruin, loss, destruction :* fortunarum, Cic. **c.** *shattered remains, wreck :*
conligere naufragium rei publicae, Cic. ;
Ov.

naufragus, a, um [navis and *frag* in frangō].
1. L i t. **a.** P a s s. : *shipwrecked, wrecked :*
Cic., Verg., etc. As Noun, *a shipwrecked
person :* Cic., Juv. **b.** A c t. : *wrecking :*
mare, Hor. **2.** T r a n s f. : *wrecked, ruined :*
as Noun : naufragorum eiecta ac debilitata
manus, Cic.

naulum, ī, *n.* [ναῦλον], *passage-money, fare :*
Juv. [It. *nolo, naulo.*]

naumachia, ae, *f.* [ναυμαχία], *a sea-fight* (as
a show). **1.** L i t. : naumachiam committere, exhibere, Suet. **2.** T r a n s f. *the
place where such exhibitions were given :*
Suet.

naumachiārius, a, um [naumachia], *a
(mock) sea-fight :* pons, Plin. As Noun, **naumachiārius**, ī, *m. a combatant in a (mock)
sea-fight :* Suet.

Nauplius, ī, *m. s. of Neptune and Amymone,
king of Euboea and f. of Palamedes ;* **Nau-
pliadēs**, ae, *m. Palamedes.*

nausea, ae, *f.* [ναυσία], *sea-sickness.* **1.** L i t. :
nauseae molestiam suscipere, Cic. Ep. **2.**
In gen. *sickness, vomiting :* Cato ; nauseam
fluentem coercere, Hor. ; Sen. Ep. [Fr.
noise.]

nauseō, āre [nausea], *to be sea-sick.* **1.** L i t. :
Hor. **2.** T r a n s f. **a.** *to be squeamish, to
vomit :* Cic. **b.** *to feel disgust* or *loathing :*
ista effutientem nauseare, atque tibi displicere, Cic. **c.** *to cause disgust :* Phaedr.

nauseola, ae, *f.* [dim. nausea], *a slight
squeamishness :* Cic. Ep.

Nausicaa, ae (and -**ē**, **ēs**), *f. d. of Alcinous,
king of the Phaeacians.*

nauta, ae, *m.* [ναύτης] (poet. and earlier Lat.
nāvita, Pl., Cato, Verg.), *a sailor, seaman,
mariner :* Caes., Hor. Of the captain of a
vessel : Cic. Of a merchant at sea : Hor.

nautea, ae, *f.* [ναυτία, another form of
vavoía], *nausea.* **1.** L i t. : facere, Pl.
2. T r a n s f. *a stinking liquid,* perh. *bilge-
water* or perh. *tanners' refuse :* hircus unctus
nauteā, Pl.

Nautēs, is, *m. a Trojan, mythical ancestor of
the Roman Nautii, hereditary guardians of the
rites of Minerva.*

nauticus, a, um [ναυτικός], *of ships* or *sailors,
nautical :* scientia nauticarum rerum, Caes. ;
exuviae, Cic. ; verbum, Cic. Ep. ; clamor,
Verg. As Noun, **nautici**, ōrum, *m. pl.
sailors, seamen :* Liv.

nautilus, ī, *m.* [ναυτίλος], *a shellfish that sails
like a ship :* Plin.

nāvālis, e, *adj.* [nāvis], *of ships, naval :* castra,
Caes. ; pugnae, bellum, disciplina, gloria,
Cic. ; acies, Liv. ; corona (given as reward
of a naval victory), Verg. ; navali surgentes
aere columnae, Verg. ; stagnum (for mock
sea-fights), Tac. ; navales socii, *sailors, seamen* (chosen from the colonists and allies),
Liv. As Noun, **nāvālia**, ium, *n. pl.* (poet.
also *sing.* **nāvāle**, is). **a.** *a dockyard, naval
arsenal ;* and in gen. *a dock :* Cic., Verg.,

Liv., etc. Esp. of the Roman docks: Liv. **b.** *materials for ship-building, tackling, rigging* : Verg., Liv.

nāvicula, ae, *f*. [*dim.* nāvis], *a small ship* : Caes., Cic.

nāviculārius, a, um [nāvicula], *of small ships* ; hence, **a. nāviculārius**, i, *m. a shipper* : Cic. **b. nāviculāria**, ae, *f.* (*sc.* res) *the shipping-business* (of goods and passengers) : facere, Cic.

nāvifragus, a, um, *adj.* [nāvis and *frag* in frangō], *causing shipwreck* : fretum, Ov. ; Verg.

nāvigābilis, e. *adj.* [nāvigō], *navigable* : amnis, mare, Liv. ; litora, Tac.

nāvigātiō, ōnis, *f.* [nāvigō], *a sailing, a voyage* : ex tuis litteris cognovi cursūs navigationum tuarum, Cic. Ep. ; Tac.

nāviger, era, erum [nāvis gerō], *ship-bearing, navigable* : mare, Lucr.

nāvigium, i, *n.* [nāvigō], *a vessel, a ship* : navigia facere, Cic. ; speculatoria navigia, Caes. ; Juv. Prov. : in eodem velut navigio participem esse periculi, Liv.

nāvigō, āre [nāvis agō], *to sail, put to sea.* **A.** Without Acc. **1.** Lit. : Caes., Cic., Hor. Of ships: Cic., Ov. Prov. : navigare in portu (i.e. to remain in safety), Ter. **2.** Transf. **a.** Of naval warfare : quam celeriter belli impetus navigavit, Cic. **b.** *to swim:* Ov. **B.** With Acc. **a.** Of Extent : *to sail over, navigate* : cum Xerxes maria ambulavisset, terramque navigasset, Cic. ; Tyrrhenum aequor, Verg. Hence, *Pass. :* laoūs classibus navigati, Tac. *Pass. Impers.* iis ventis istinc navigatur, Cic. **b.** Internal : *to gain by navigation* : quae homines arant, navigant, aedificant, Sall. [Fr. *nager.*]

nāvis, is, *f.* (Acc. nāvem, or nāvim ; the latter freq. in Cic. ; Abl. : nāvi or -e) [*cf.* Gk. vaῦs], *a ship.* **1.** Lit. : navis longa, *a ship of war,* Caes. ; oneraria or rotunda, *a transport* or *cargo-vessel,* Caes. ; mercatoria, Pl. ; praetoria, *the admiral's ship,* Liv. ; tecta, *decked,* Liv. ; aperta, *without a deck,* Liv. ; navis auri, *laden with gold,* Cic. ; deducere in aequam, *to launch,* Liv. ; or simply, deducere, Caes. ; deprimere, *to sink,* Caes., Tac. ; subducere, *to beach,* Caes. ; appellere, *to bring to land,* Caes., Cic. ; Liv. ; applicare terrae, Liv. ; solvere, *to set sail,* Pl., Caes. ; remis incitare, Caes. ; ornare, adornare, armare, Caes., Liv. ; navibus rem gerere, Hor. ; navium tutela, the image of the protecting deity, Ov. Prov. : **i.** navibus et quadrigis petere aliquid (i.e. with might and main), Hor. **ii.** navem perforare, quā ipse quis naviget (i.e. to injure oneself), Cic. **2.** Transf. **a.** Navis Argolica, or simply Navis, *the constellation* Argo : Cic. poet. **b.** una navis est iam bonorum omnium, Cic. Ep. [Fr. *nef.*]

nāvita, ae, *m. v.* nauta.

nāvitās (gnāv-), ātis, *f.* [nāvus], *promptness, energy* : Cic.

nāviter (gnāv-), *adv.* **I.** *energetically* : pugnare, Liv. ; Ter. **II.** *wholeheartedly, completely* : impudens, Cic. Ep. ; plenum, Lucr.

nāvō, āre [nāvus], *to do, conduct, or accomplish with vigour, energy,* or *diligence* : operam, Caes., Cic., Liv. ; operam alicui, Cic. Ep. ; bellum, Tac.

nāvus (gnāvus), a, um, *exertio, negotio vigorous !* homo, Cic.

Naxos, i, *f. the largest of the Cyclades, famous for its wines* ; **Naxius**, a, um.

(1) nē (not **nae**), *interj.* [vή, val], *truly, verily, indeed* (alw. with a personal or demonstr. pronoun). **a.** In gen. : ne ego homo infelix fui, Pl. ; Cic. ; Liv. **b.** Strengthened : edepol ne tu, Pl. ; ne tu hercle, Pl. ; ne ille medius fidius, Cic.

(2) nē (old form **nei**), *adv.* and *conj.* [the primitive Latin negative particle ; whereas nōn is a derivative, u. nōn, *ad init.*]. **I.** Adv. : *not.* **A.** To negative a word. **a.** In the early stage of the language : ne minores (verres) quam semestres, Varr. **b.** This adverbial use survived. **i.** In connexion with *quidem,* to negative emphatically the word or words placed between *ne* and *quidem, not even* : ne in oppidis quidem ; ne in fanis quidem, Cic. ; Verg., etc. **ii.** In composition, as an absolute negation (in form *nē* or contracted, or in form *nec* or *neg*) as in neque, nequicquam ; nescio, nefas, nequeo ; nemo (= ne homo), nihil, nullus, nunquam, etc. ; necopinans, neglego (= nec-lego), negotium (= nec otium). **B.** To negative a proposition (*cf.* Gk. use of μή). **a.** In prohibitions. With *Imperat.* : abi, ne iura, Pl. ; ne timete, milites, Liv. ; ne, pueri, ne tanta animis adsuescite bella, Verg. ; impius ne audeto, Cic. With *Subj.* : ne moveatis, Pl. ; ne repugnetis, Cic. ; ne pudori sit tibi, Hor. ; ne hoc feceris, Cic. ; ne transieris Hiberum, Liv. In *Orat. Obliq.* with *Imperf. Subj.* : ne aut suae magnopere virtuti tribueret, aut ipsos despiceret, Caes. **b.** Also (but more commonly *nedum,* q.v.) *let me not say, not to say, much less* : me vero nihil istorum ne iuvenem quidem movit unquam, ne nunc senem, Cic. ; Liv. **c.** In wishes and asseverations : ne id Iuppiter Opt. Max. sineret ! Liv. ; illud utinam ne vere scriberem ! Cic. ; ne vivam si scio, Cic. Ep. **d.** In concessive clauses : *granted that . . . not* : ne sit sane summum malum dolor ; malum certe est, Cic. ; ne sequaveritis Hannibali Philippum ; Pyrrho certe aequabitis, Liv. **e.** In provisional or restrictive clauses : *only let not, provided that . . . not* : sint sane liberales ex sociorum fortunis, ne illi sanguinem nostrum largiantur, Sall. More frequently, dum ne, dum modo ne, modo ne (*v.* dum and modo). **f.** In purpose-clauses. With *ut* (freq. in early Latin and Cic.) : vestem ut ne in quinet, Pl. ; ut lex Aelia ne valeret, Cic. With other relat. (rare) : qui (Abl.) ne, quo ne (and *quin* for qui ne) : ego id agam, mihi qui ne detur, Ter. ; quo ne per vacuum Romano incurreret hostis, Hor. **g.** With verbs of requesting and commanding, and impersonals like *oportet, licet* (where the clause with *ne* is semi-dependent) : moneo vos, ne refugiatis, Cic. ; Caesarem complexus obsecrare coepit, ne quid gravius in fratrem statueret, Caes. **II.** Conj. with *Subj.* **a.** In purpose-clauses : *lest, that not* : dolorem perpetiuntur ne in maiorem incidant, Cic. ; Verg., etc. Also in parenthetic purpose-clauses :

ne multa (or plura) dicam, Cic.; Liv., etc. **b.** After *facio, efficio, perficio*, to express a purpose or result : qui efficiant ne quid inter privatum et magistratum differat, Cic.; Verg.; Liv. **c.** After **v e r b s** and **n o u n s** denoting **f e a r** : *lest, that* : metuebat ne indicarent, Cic.; Pl.; Ov., etc.; pavor ceperat milites ne mortiferum esset vulnus, Liv. With another negative : vereor ne exercitum firmum habere non possit, Cic.; timere non debeo, ne non iste illā cruce dignus iudicetur, Cic. **d.** After some verbs of **h i n d e r i n g, r e f u s i n g**, etc., to denote a preventing cause : Deci corpus ne inveniretur nox quaerentis oppressit, Liv.; tu caves ne tui consultores, ille ne urbes capiantur, Cic.

-ne, *interrog. part.* (and apocopated **n'**) [a weakened form of **nē**], is enclitic, and is attached to the most important word in the question, making it emphatic. **A.** In *Direct Quest.* **a.** Occ. with full negative force retained : sumne infelix qui non curro domum ? Pl.; Cic. More rarely in sense of *surely not* (= num) : potestne virtus servire ? Cic.; tantaene animis caelestibus irae ? Verg. **b.** More commonly colourless, having no direct representative in English : tun' te audes Sosiam esse dicere ? Pl.; meministine me in senatu dicere ? Cic.; quiane auxilio iuvat ante levatos ? Verg. **c.** Sometimes affixed to an interrogative pronoun : quone malo mentem concussa ? timore deorum, Hor.; Pl. **d.** With an alternative : pacemne huc fortis an arma ? Verg.; Caes., etc. **B.** In *Indir. Quest.* **a.** interrogavit liceretne mittere, Caes.; Cic., etc. **b.** With an alternative (usually introduced by an, q.v.) *ne* is found in the second part with or without *utrum* in the first part : interrogatus est utrum pluris patrem matremne faceret, Nep.; ut in incerto fuerit, vicissent victine essent, Liv. Also *anne* : cum interrogetur tria pauca sint anne multa, Cic.; Pl. **c.** When the alternative is negatived, *necne* is usual : di utrum sint neone sint quaeritur, Cic.; Caes.

nebula, ae, *f.* [cf. Gk. νεφέλη], *mist, vapour, fog.* **1.** Lit. **a.** In gen. : Lucr., Verg., Liv. **b.** Of the clouds : Verg., Hor., Ov. **c.** Of smoke : Ov. **2.** T r a n s f. **a.** Of dust : pulveris, Lucr. **b.** Of something empty, worthless : nebulae cyathus, Pl.; Pers. **c.** Of the mind : erroris, Juv. [It. *nebbia*.]

nebulō, ōnis, *m.* [nebula], *a worthless fellow, humbug* : Ter., Cic., Hor.

nebulōsus, a, um [nebula], *misty, foggy* : ager, Cato ; caelum, Cic.

nec, *conj. v.* neque.

nec, an inseparable negative particle in compounds for *nē* : necopinans, necdum ; *v.* nē.

necdum and **neque dum**, *and not yet, nor yet* : si scis neque dum Romā es profectus, Cic. Ep.; Juv., etc.; necdum tamen ego Quintum conveneram, Cic. Ep.; Verg.

necessāriē, *adv.* (v. rare), *unavoidably, necessarily* : Cic.

necessārius, a, um [necesse]. **1.** L i t. **a.** *unavoidable, inevitable* (opp. to voluntarius) :

id quod imperator necessarium, Cic.; necessariā re coactus, Caes.; castra ponere necessarium visum est, Liv. **b.** *indispensable, needful, requisite* : omnia ad vitam necessaria, Cic.; res maxime necessaria, Cic. Ep.; Liv. *Neut. pl.* as Noun : Sall. **c.** Also of the absolutely indispensable *minimum* : *barest* : iumentorum acervi necessarium cubile dabant, Liv. **d.** *pressing, urgent* : tam necessario tempore, Caes.; causa necessaria ad proficiscendum, Caes. *Neut.* as Noun, *pressure of circumstances* : ABL. **necessāriō** used as *Adv.* : Caes., Cic., etc. **2.** T r a n s f. : *connected by blood* or *friendship, etc.* ; *related, closely connected, bound* : mors hominis necessari, *of an intimate friend*, Mat. ap. Cic. Ep.; homo, *a relation* (of a *father-in-law*), Nep. As Noun, **necessārius**, ī, *m.* and **necessāria**, ae, *f. a relative, kinsman* (kins-woman), *connexion, friend* (v. freq. in *pl.*) : Caes., Cic.

necesse, *indecl. adj. n.* (old form, **necessum**, Pl., Lucr., Liv.) **I.** *unavoidable, inevitable, necessary* ; only with esse and habere (*to regard as*) : nihil fit, quod necesse non fuerit, Cic.; Cato ; Caes.; eo minus habeo necesse scribere, Cic. Ep.; Ter.; Quint. With *Subj.* (with or without *ut*) : istum condemnetis necesse est, Cic.; hoc necesse est ut etc., Cic. **II.** *needful, requisite* : id quod tibi necesse minime fuit, facetus esse voluisti, Cic.

necessitās, ātis, *f.* [necesse]. **1.** L i t. **a.** *unavoidableness, inevitableness, necessity* : Pl.; necessitas mihi obvenit alicuius rei, Cic.; necessitatem alicui adferre, Cic.; tempori cedere, id est necessitati parere, Cic.; maiores necessitates, Liv.; nullo loco, nisi quantum necessitas cogeret, fortunae se commissurus, Liv.; mors est necessitas naturae, Cic.; leti, Hor.; extrema, suprema, ultima (i.e. death), Sall., Tac. Personified : Hor. **b.** In *pl.* : *wants, requirements* : vitae necessitatibus servire, Cic.; suarum necessitatum causā, Caes.; publicae necessitates, Liv. **c.** *privation, want* : famem et ceteras necessitates tolerabant, Suet. **d.** *urgency* : temporis, Caes.; expressit hoc patribus necessitas, Liv. **2.** T r a n s f. (like necessitudo) *connexion, relationship, friendship* : necessitatem familiaritatemque violare, Cic.; Caes.

necessitūdō, inis, *f.* [necesse]. **1.** L i t. **a.** *inevitableness, necessity* : Cic.; alicui facere, Tac.; neve eam necessitudinem imponatis ut etc., Sall. **b.** *need, want* : Sall. **2.** T r a n s f. **a.** *social connexion, relationship, clientship, friendship, intimacy* : necessitudo et adfinitas, Cic.; cum aliquo coniungere, Cic.; Sall.; in *pl.* : omnes amicitiae necessitudines, Cic. **b.** In *pl.* : *relatives, connexions, friends* : Curt., Tac., Suet.

necessum, *v.* necesse.

necne, *adv.* (v. nē) *or no, or not* : used in the second clause of a disjunctive question. **a.** Usually in an *Indir. Quest.* : quaero, potueritne Roscius ex societate partem suam petere, necne, Cic.; utrum proelium committi ex usu esset, necne, Caes.; Ter.; Hor. With the verb repeated : hoc doce, doleam necne doleam nihil interesse, Cic.

b. Rarely in a *Direct Quest.* (for annōn): sunt haec tua verba necne ? Cic.

necnōn, also **nec nōn** or **neque nōn** (and sometimes with words placed between the two negatives), *and also, moreover, v.* neque.

necō, āre [*cf.* Gk. νεκρός, νέκυς], *to kill, murder, do to death* (usually by violent means). **1.** Lit.: aliquem odore taetro, Lucr.; plebem fame, Cic.; aliquem igni, Caes.; aliquem ferro, Verg., Hor.; veneno, Suet. **2.** Transf. *to worry to death* (with talking): Pl.

nec-opīnāns, antis, adj. (v. nē), *not expecting, unaware :* Ariobarzanem necopinantem liberavi, Cic. Ep.; Phaedr.

nec-opīnātus (also separately **nec opīnātus**), a, um, *unexpected :* necopinata bona perspicere, Cic.; neo opinato adventu, Liv. *Neut.* as Noun : Cic.; hence, ex necopinato aversum hostem invadere, *unexpectedly,* Liv. ABL. **necopīnātō** as *Adv. unexpectedly :* Cic., Liv.

necopīnus, a, um [opīnor]. **A.** Pass. *unexpected :* mors, Ov. **B.** Act. *not expecting, unsuspecting, careless :* ipsum accipiter necopinum rapit, Phaedr.; Ov.

nectar, aris, n. [νέκταρ], *nectar, the drink of the gods.* **1.** Lit.: Cic., Ov., etc. **2.** Transf. **a.** Of delicious things : of honey : Verg.; of milk : Ov.; of wine : Verg., Ov.; of a pleasant smell : Lucr. **b.** Of poetry : Pers.

nectareus, a, um [nectar], *of nectar.* **1.** Lit.: aquae, Ov. **2.** Transf. *sweet or delicious as nectar :* Falernum, Mart.

nectō, nectere, nexui (or nexi), nexum, *to bind, tie, join together.* **1.** Lit. **a.** In gen. : necte tribus nodis ternos, Amarylli, colores, Verg.; flores, Hor.; talaria pedibus, Verg.; caput olivā, Verg.; bracchia, capillos, Ov.; nodum ab trabe, Verg. **b.** *to make by tying :* coronam, Hor.; catenas, Hor. **c.** *to bind, fetter, imprison,* esp. for debt : Cic., Liv. **2.** Transf. **a.** *to attach, connect, unite :* ut ex alio alia nectantur, Cic.; numeris verba, Ov. **b.** *to make a chain of, to weave,* i.e. devise : causas inanis, Verg.; dolum, Liv.; cum aliquo iurgia, Ov.; moras, Tac.

nē-cubi, adv. [cubi, v. ubi], *lest anywhere:* dispositis exploratoribus, necubi Romam copias traducerent, Caes.; Liv.; Luc.

nē-cunde, adv. [ounde, v. unde], *lest from any place:* circumspectans necunde impetus in frumentatores fieret, Liv.

nē-dum, conj. *not to say.* **A.** After an expressed or implied negative : *much less, still less :* ne voce quidem incommodā, nedum ut ulla vis fieret, Liv.; Ter.; Cic.; vix in ipsis tectis et oppidis frigus infirmā valetudine vitatur, nedum in mari, Cic. Ep.; Liv.; mortalia facta peribunt, nedum sermonum stet honos, Hor. **B.** After an affirmative : *not to say.* **a.** *much more :* adulationes etiam victis Macedonibus graves, nedum victoribus, Liv.; Quint. **b.** In the first clause : *not only :* nedum morbum removisti, sed etiam gravedinem, Cic. Ep.

nefandus, a, um [ne (v. nē) fāri, lit. ' not to be mentioned '], *abominable :* adulterium, Cic.; vehiculum, Liv.; fraus, Juv. Of persons : Quint. *Neut.* as Noun. *wrong :* sperate deos memores fandi atque nefandi, Verg.

nefāriē, adv. *impiously, execrably, heinously :* Cic.

nefārius, a, um [nefās], *impious, execrable, heinous :* homo, Cic.; Hor.; crudelitas, Caes.; audacia, facinus, Cic. *Neut.* as Noun : rem publicam nefario obstringere, Liv.

ne-fās, n. indecl., *that which is contrary to divine law, wrong, a crime, wickedness, abomination.* **1.** Lit.: quidquid non licet, nefas putare debemus, Cic.; quibus nefas est deserere patronos, Caes.; corpora viva nefas Stygiā vectare carinā, Verg.; fas et nefas, Verg.; per fas et nefas, Liv.; in omne nefas se parare, Ov.; belli, Luc. **2.** Transf. of persons or things : *an abomination :* exstinxisse nefas laudabor (i.e. Helen), Verg.

nefāstus, a, um [nefās], *forbidden, unlawful.* **1.** Lit. of days forbidden for public business : ille (Numa) nefastos dies fastosque fecit, Liv.; Ov. **2.** Transf. **a.** *irreligious, impious :* quae augur iniusta, nefasta dixerit, Law in Cic. **b.** *wicked, criminal :* Pl. *Neut.* as Noun : quid intactum nefasti liquimus ? Hor. **c.** *unlucky, inauspicious :* dies, Hor.; Tac.; ne qua terra sit nefasta victoriae suae, Liv.

negātiō, ōnis, f. [negō], *a denying, denial :* Cic.

negitō, āre [freq. negō], *to deny or refuse often or firmly :* Pl., Sall., Hor. With Acc. and Inf. : Pl., Lucr., Cic.

neglēctiō, ōnis, f. [neglegō], *a neglecting, neglect :* amicorum, Cic.

neglēctus, a, um, Part. neglegō.

neglēctus, ūs, m. [neglegō], *a neglecting, neglect :* Ter.

neglēgēns, entis. **I.** Part. neglegō. **II.** Adj. *heedless, careless, unconcerned :* Cic.; adulescentia, Liv.; in aliquem, Cic.; in deligendis amicis, Cic.; in sumptu, Cic.; circa deos, Suet. With Gen. : legum, offici, rei publicae, sociorum atque amicorum neglegentior, Cic.; Liv.; Tac. With Inf. : Pl. With ne and Subj. : neglegens ne quā populus laboret, Hor. Of things : sermo, amictus, Quint.

neglegenter, adv. *heedlessly, carelessly :* Cic., Quint., Tac. Comp. : Cic. Sup. : Sen. Ep.

neglegentia, ae, f. [neglegēns], *carelessness, heedlessness, neglect :* Cic.; in accusando, Cic.; tua, Ter.; caerimoniarum auspiciorumque, Liv.; sui, Tac.

neg-legō, legere, lēxi, lēctum [nec legō] (lit. *not to pick up*). **I.** *not to heed, not to trouble oneself about, to slight, neglect.* With Acc. : Cic., Hor., Liv. With Inf. : Pl., Cic. With de : de Theopompo, Cic. **II.** *to despise, disregard :* iram alicuius, Pl.; qui periculum capitis sui pro meā salute neglexit, Cic.; imperium alicuius, Caes. With Inf. : Cic., Hor. **III.** *to overlook, pass over :* iniuria alicuius, Caes.; pecuniam captam, Cic.

negō, āre [Aor. Opt. negāssim, Pl.] [nē agiō=āiō]. **I.** *to say ' no ' :* Diogenes ait, Antipater negat, Cic.; Pl.; Caes. **II.**

to say not, to deny : Cic. With Acc. and
Inf. : Caes., Cic., etc. *Pass. :* casta negor,
Ov. With *quin :* negare non posse quin
rectius sit, Liv. **III.** *to refuse, decline.* **1.**
Lit.: aliquid alicui, Enn., Cic., Ov., etc.
2. Transf. of things : segos negat victum,
Verg. ; poma regio, Ov. With *Inf. :* in
sua loca ire negant harenae, Verg. [It.
niegare ; Fr. *nier.*]

nĕgōtiālis, e, *adj.* [negōtium], *relating to*
affairs : Cic. Rhet. (=πραγματικός):
Quint.

nĕgōtiāns, antis. **I.** *Part.* negōtior. **II.**
Noun : *a business-man :* Cic. Ep., Suet.

nĕgōtiātiō, ōnis, *f.* [negōtior], *banking busi-*
ness : Cic. Ep., Liv. ; in *pl.:* Suet.

nĕgōtiātor, ōris, *m.* [negōtior], *a business-*
man. **a.** Usually *a money-lender, banker :*
Cic. **b.** In gen. *a trader, tradesman :* mercis
sordidae negotiator, Quint.

nĕgōtiolum, i, *n.* [*dim.* negōtium], *a trifling*
matter : Pl., Cic. Ep.

nĕgōtior, āri [negōtium], *to carry on business.*
a. Usually *to carry on a banking business*
(in the provinces) : Cic., Sall. **b.** In gen.
to trade, traffic : Liv.

nĕgōtiōsus, a, um [negōtium], *full of business,*
devoted to business, busy. Of persons : Pl.,
Sall. Of things : provincia, Cic. ; dies,
Tac. Comic. : tergum (on which business,
i.e. flogging, is performed), Pl. *Comp. :*
Sen.

nĕg-ōtium, i, *n.* [nec ōtium : *v.* nē ; lit. *want*
of leisure]. **1.** Lit. **A.** In gen. : *occupa-*
tion, business, work : negoti nunc sum plenus Pl. ; quid hic negoti esset tibi, Ter. ;
nihil habere negoti, Cic. ; quid in Galliā
Caesari negoti esset, Caes. **B.** Of a special
charge or *commission :* transigere, Cic. ;
datum negotium est consulibus ut etc.,
Liv. ; in ipso negotio, Caes. ; negotio desistere, Caes. ; mandare alicui, Cic. Ep. ;
infecto negotio, Sall. **C.** In partio. **a.**
Public business : forensia negotia, Cic. ;
negotium municipi administrare, Cic. Ep. ;
suscipere, procurare, Cic. ; publica, Pl., Cic.
b. Military : occasionem negoti bene gerendi, Caes. ; sibi cum viro forti esse negotium, Nep. **c.** Private or domestic : suum
negotium gerere, agere, Cic. **d.** Of money-
lending or banking in the provinces : gerere,
Cic. ; Trebonius ampla et expedita negotia
in tuā provinciā habet, Cic. Ep. ; Hor. ;
and of *trade in general,* maritima negotia,
Cic. **2.** Transf. **a.** *difficulty, pains,*
trouble, labour : alicui negotium exhibere,
Pl., Cic. ; facessere, Cic. Ep. ; facere,
Quint. ; dare, Pl. ; neque esse quicquam
negoti, Caes. ; Liv. ; nullo negotio, *without*
trouble, Caes. **b.** Like the Gk. πρᾶγμα, for
res, *a matter, thing :* quid est negoti ? Pl. ;
ineptum negotium et Graeculum, Cic. So
of persons : inhumanum, Cic.

Nēleus (disyl.), ei and eos, *m. s. of Neptune*
and the nymph Tyro, king of Pylos, and f.
of Nestor : **Nēlēius, Nēlēius,** a, um ;
Nēlīdēs, ae, *m. a male descendant of Neleus.*

Nemea, ae, and **Nemeē,** ēs, *f. a valley near*
Phlius in Argolis, where Hercules slew the
Nemean lion and founded the Nemean
festival ; **Nemeaeus,** a, um ; **Nemea,**
ōrum, *n. pl. the Nemean games.*

Nemesis, is and ios, *f. the goddess of justice,*
who punishes human pride and arrogance.

nēmō, *m.* and *f.* (Acc. nēminem, Gen. nūllīus,
Dat. nēminī, Abl. nūllō ; Gen. nēminis in
Pl., and Abl. nēmine in Pl., Tac.) [nē and
hemō, old form of homō], *no man, no one,*
nobody. **a.** In gen. : nemo me lacrumis
decoret, Enn. ; nemo ex tanto 'numero est
quin etc., Cic. ; nemo de iis qui etc., Cic. ;
nemo nostrum, Cic. ; omnium mortalium
nemo inimicior, Cic. **b.** Often with noun
in apposition : nemo civis, Enn. ; nemo
deus, civis, servus, Cic. ; vir nemo bonus,
Cic. ; nemo homo, Pl., Cic. **c.** Phr. :
nemo non, with a verb, *every one :* aperte
adulantem nemo non videt, Cic. ; non nemo,
some one : video de istis abesse non neminem, Cic. ; nomo unus, *no single person,*
Cic., Liv., Tac. ; nemo alius, *nobody else,*
Cic. ; nemo quisquam, *nobody at all,* Ter.

nĕmōrālis, e, *adj.* [nemus], *of groves or*
woods, sylvan : templum Dianae, Ov. ;
umbrae, Ov.

nĕmōrēnsis, e, *adj.* [nemus], *of a grove or*
wood. Esp. *of the grove of Diana, near*
Aricia : Ov. Hence, rex nemorensis, *the*
priest presiding over her sacrifices : Suet.

nĕmori-cultrix, icis, *f. dwelling in the woods:*
sua, Phaedr.

nĕmori-vagus, a, um, *roaming the woods :*
aper, Cat.

nĕmōrōsus, a, um [nemus]. **I.** *full of*
woods : Zacynthos, Verg. ; Atlas, Ov.
II. *full of foliage :* silvae, Ov.

nempe, *conj.* [=nam-pe : cf. quippe], *cer-*
tainly, truly, forsooth, to be sure (used to
confirm, explain, or ironically) : scio iam
quid velis : nempe hinc me abire vis, Pl. ;
unde iustitia, fides, aequitas ? nempe ab
his, Cic. Even at the beginning of a piece :
nempe dixi, Hor.

nĕmus, oris, *n.* [*cf.* Gk. νέμω, νομός], *a wood*
with open glades and grazing-land, a grove.
1. Lit.: Enn., Cic., Verg., etc. Esp.
a sacred grove : Cic., Verg. **2.** Transf.
a. *a wood :* Hor., Ov. **b.** *a plantation :*
Verg.

nēnia, ae, *f.* **1.** Lit. *a funeral dirge sung in*
praise of the dead : Cic., Hor., Suet. **2.**
Transf. **a.** *a doleful song, dirge* in gen. :
dixit neniam de bonis, Pl. ; Ceae retractes
munera neniae, Hor. **b.** *a magic song,*
incantation : Marsa, Hor. **c.** *a trifling*
song, a ditty : puerorum nenia, quae regnum recte facientibus offert, Hor. ; Phaedr.

nĕō, nēre, nēvi, nētum [*cf.* νέω], *to spin.* **1.**
Lit. : subtemen tenue, Pl. ; Ov. **2.**
Transf. *to weave, entwine :* tunicam auro,
Verg.

Neoclēs, is and i, *m., f. of Themistocles ;*
Neoclīdēs, ae, *m. son of Neocles, i.e.*
Themistocles.

Neoptolemus, i, *m., s. of Achilles, also called*
Pyrrhus.

nepa, ae, *f.* [an African word]. **I.** *a scor-*
pion : Cic. ; hence, *the constellation*
Scorpio : Enn., Cic. poet. **II.** *a crab :* Pl.

nēpenthes, *n. indecl.* [νηπενθές, *that drives*
away sadness], *a plant which, mingled with*
wine, had an exhilarating effect : Plin.

Nephelēis, idos, *f., d. of Nephelē (and*
Athamas), i.e. Helle.

nepōs, ōtis, *m.* [*cf.* ἀνεψιός, νέποδες], *a son's* or *daughter's son ; a grandson.* **1.** Lit.: Pl., Cic., Tac., etc. **2. Transf. a.** *a brother's* or *sister's son, a nephew :* Suet. **b.** *a descendant :* in this sense, mostly *pl.:* Cat. ; filius, anne aliquis magnā de stirpe nepotum ? Verg. ; in nepotum perniciem, Hor. **c.** *a spendthrift, prodigal :* quis ganeo, quis nepos, quis adulter, Cic. ; Hor. [Fr. *neveu.*]

Nepōs, ōtis, *m. a cognomen in the* gens Cornelia ; esp. Cornelius Nepos, *a Roman biographer, friend of Cicero.*

nepōtātus, ūs, *m.* [nepōs], *extravagance :* Suet.

nepōtinus, a, um [nepōs], *extravagant :* sumptus, Suet.

nepōtulus, ī, *m.* [*dim.* nepōs], *a little grandson :* Pl.

neptis, is, *f.* [*v.* nepōs], *a grand-daughter :* Cic., Tac. ; neptis Veneris (i.e. Ino), Ov. ; neptes Cybeles (i.e. the Muses), Ov. [Fr. *nièce.*]

Neptūnus, ī, *m. Neptune, b. of Jupiter and h. of Amphitrite ; the sea-god :* hence, *the sea :* Pl., Lucr., Verg., etc. **Neptūnius**, a, um, *of Neptune :* heros (i.e. his son Theseus), Ov. ; Troia (i.e. walled by Neptune), Verg. ; *also of the sea :* Pl., Verg. **Neptūninē**, ēs, *f. Neptune's grand-daughter :* Cat.

nēquam, *adj. indecl., worthless, good for nothing, bad.* **a.** In gen.: piscis nequam est nisi recens, Pl. **b.** Of character, *worthless, vile, bad :* Pl., Cic. *Comp.* nēquior, Pl., Cic. ; *Sup.* nēquissimus, Cic. As Noun, an *injury, harm :* alicui nequam dare, facere, Pl. ; nequam aps te habemus, Pl.

nē-quiquam, *adv. in no wise, by no means, not at all :* nequaquam comparandus, Cic. ; Pl. ; Hor. ; nequaquam idoneus locus ad egrediendum, Caes.

neque or **nec** (used indifferently before vowels and consonants), *adv.* and *conj.* [shortened form of nē and que]. **I. Adv.** In the earlier periods of the language neque and nec (esp. the latter) like nē = nōn, *not,* in which way they are occasionally used by later writers (*cf.* necopinatus): tu dis nec recte dicis, Pl. ; qui nec procul aberat, Liv. ; cui Parcae tribuere nec ullo vulnere laedi, Verg. Also in legal phrases. **II. Conj.:** *and not, also not.* **A.** In gen. **a.** Alone : multumque laborat nec respirandi fit copia, Enn. ; eos in fugam dederunt neque longius procedere potuerunt, Caes. With *ullus, quisquam, unquam,* etc. (for et nullus, et nemo, etc.) : Gorgias centum et septem annos complevit neque unquam in suo studio cessavit, Cic. Also in phr. like nec idcirco minus, Cic. ; nec eo minus *or* magis, Cic., Liv. **b.** Connected with *vero, enim, autem, tamen :* neque vero hoc solum dixit, sed ipse et sentit et fecit, *nor indeed,* Cic. ; neque enim beneficia faeneramur (in a parenthesis), Cic. ; nec tamen didici, etc., Cic. **B.** In partic. **a.** *but not, yet not :* oppida oppugnata nec obsessa, Liv. So for *et ne* or *sed ne :* nec quicquam raptim aut forte temere egeritis, Liv. **b.** nec . . . quidem for et ne . . . quidem : nec tunc quidem viris desidero adulescentis, Cic.

Also nec alant fra no quidem : Nahari bal nec ipse eruptionem cohortium sustinuit, Liv. **c.** Repeated, neque (nec) . . . neque (nec), *neither . . . nor :* virtus nec eripi nec surripi potest unquam ; neque naufragio neque incendio amittitur, Cic. With a preceding negative (which, however, does not lose its force) : neminem neque populum neque privatum fugio, Liv. **d.** neque (nec) . . . et (que) *and* et . . . neque (nec) ; *when one clause is affirmative :* on the one hand not . . . *and on the other hand ; not only not . . . but also ;* or the contrary ; on the one hand . . . *and on the other hand not ; not only . . . but also not :* **i.** nequo (nec) . . . et (que) : Canius nec infacetus et satis litteratus, Cic. **ii.** et . . . neque (nec) : patebat via et certa neque longa, Cic. **e.** neque (nec) non (also in one word, necnon). **i.** Emphatically affirmative, *and also, and besides, and indeed ;* neque meam mentem non domum saepe revocat exanimata uxor, Cic. **ii.** As a simple conjunction : *and likewise, and so too, also :* necnon et Tyrii per limina laeta frequentes convenere, Verg. **f.** neque (nec) dum, and in one word, needum, *and not yet, not yet :* illo autem quid agat, si scis neque dum Roma es profectus, scribas ad me velim, Cic. Ep. **C.** For et ne or neve in purpose-clauses : ut ea praetermittam neque eos appellem a quibus etc., Cic. For nec in prohibitions (for et ne or sed ne), *v.* B. a. [It. *nè ;* Fr. *ni ;* from Lat. nec ipse unus, It. *nessuno ;* from Lat. nec ens, It. *niente ;* Fr. *néant.*]

nequedum (**necdum**), *v.* necdum, neque.

ne-queō, quīre, quīvī (or quiī), quītum (*Fut.* nequibunt, Lucr. ; *Imperf.* nequibāt, Sall.), *not to be able, to be unable* (with *Inf.*) : Pl., Cic., Verg., etc. *Pass.* (followed by an *Inf. Pass.*) : quidquid sine sanguine civium ulcisci nequitur, iure factum sit, Sall. Rarely *impers.* : nequit, *it is impossible* (with *quin* and *Subj.*), Pl.

nē-quiquam (or **nē-quicquam**), *adv.* **I.** *in vain, to no purpose, fruitlessly :* Pl., Caes., Cic., Verg., etc. **II.** *without good reason :* ut non nequiquam tantae virtutis homines iudicari deberet ausos esse etc., Caes. ; Cat. **III.** *with impunity :* Pl.

nēquior, ius, *v.* nēquam.

nē-quis or **nē quis**, *v.* quis.

nēquissimus, a, um, *v.* nēquam.

nēquiter, *adv. worthlessly, vilely, wrongly,* etc. : Pl., Cato, Cic. *Comp.* nēquius, Liv., Mart. *Sup.* nēquissimē, Plin.

nēquitia, ae, and **nēquitiēs**, ēī, *f.* [nēquam], *worthlessness, badness.* **a.** Moral : me ipsum inertiae nequitiaeque condemno, Cic. **b.** By extravagance or excess : Pl. ; officina nequitiae, Cic. ; illum aut nequities expellet, Hor. ; tandem nequitiae pone modum tuae, Hor. ; Ov. ; in *pl.:* Mart.

Nēreus (disyl.), eī and eos, *m. s. of Oceanus and Tethys, a sea-god ; h. of Doris and f. of the Nereides.* T r a n s f. *the sea :* Tib., Ov. ; **Nērēis**, idis, *f. a daughter of Nereus, a sea-nymph, a Nereid ;* **Nērēius**, a, um ; **Nērīnē**, ēs, *f. a daughter of Nereus.*

Nēritos (**-us**), ī, *m. an island near Ithaca ;* **Nēritius**, a, um ; dux, i.e. Ulysses, Ov. ; ratis, i.e. *of Ulysses,* Ov.

Nĕrŏ, ōnis, m. *a cognomen in the* gens Claudia, esp. *the Emperor Nero* (A.D. 54–68) (*v. also* Claudius, Tiberius) ; **Nĕrōnĕus, Nĕrōnius, Nĕrōniānus**, a, um.

Nerthus, i, *a goddess of the Germani.*

Nerva, ae, m. : M. Cocceius Nerva, *Roman emperor*, A.D. 96–98 ; **Nervius**, a, um.

nervōsē, adv. *strongly, vigorously, energetically* : Planc. ap. Cic. Ep. Comp. : nervosius dicere, Cic.

nervōsus, a, um [nervus], *full of sinews, strong.* **1.** Lit. : dorcas, Lucr. ; poples, Ov. Comp. : Cat. **2.** Transf. of style : quis Aristotele nervosior ? Cic.

nervŭlus, i, m. [dim. nervus], *a little nerve, vigour :*. si tu nervulos tuos adhibueris, Cic. Ep.

nervus (-os), i, m. [cf. Gk. νεῦρον], *a sinew, tendon.* **1.** Lit. **A.** In gen.: Pl., Caes., Cic., Hor. **B.** In partic. **a.** *the string of a musical instrument :* Cic., Verg., Hor. **b.** *a bowstring :* Acc., Verg. **c.** *a thong with which a person was bound :* Pl. Hence, *a fetter :* Pl., Cato ; *a prison :* eximere de nervo aliquem, Liv. ; Pl. ; Ter. **d.** *the penis :* Hor., Juv. **e.** *the leather with which shields were covered :* Tac. **2.** Transf. in pl. **a.** *vigour, strength :* digna res est ubi tu nervos intendas tuos, Ter. ; opibus ac nervis uti, Caes. ; nervi belli pecunia (*sinews of war*), Cic. ; nervi coniurationis (*the leaders*), Liv. ; Lucil. Of style : *force, energy :* horum oratio neque nervos neque aculeos oratorios ac forensis habet, Cic. ; Hor. ; in dicendo, Cic. [It. *nervo* ; Fr. *nerf*.]

ne-sciŏ, īre, *not to know, to be ignorant of.* **A.** In gen. **a.** de illā amicā, Pl. ; nec me pudet fateri nescire, quod nesciam, Cic. ; quod scies (*or* scis), nescis (to warn to secrecy) : Pl., Ter. With Acc. and Inf. : Ter., Ov. With Indir. Quest. : Ter., Cic., Ov. Impers. Pass. : Cic. **b.** In the phrases, nescio quis, nescio quid, nescio quo modo, nescio quando, to denote uncertainty, real or pretended : *I know not who, what, how, when ; somebody, something, somehow, at some time or other :* prope me hic nescio quis loquitur, Pl. ; nisi me forte Paconi nescio cuius querellis moveri putes (in affected ignorance), Cic. Ep. ; pecunia nescio quo modo quaesita, Cic. Also nescio an, *I know not whether,* hence, *perhaps, probably, I feel sure* (cf. haud scio an) : ingens eo die res et nescio an maxima illo bello gesta sit, Liv. ; Cic. **B.** In partic. **a.** *not to know, to be unacquainted with* (with Acc. of direct obj.) : illa illum nescit, Pl. ; non nescire hiemem, Verg. ; Sen. **b.** *not to know how ; to be unable* (with Inf.) : Cic., Verg., etc.

nescius, a, um [nescio]. **A.** Act. **a.** *not knowing, ignorant, unaware.* With Gen. : nescia mens hominum fati, Verg. ; Plin. Ep. With de : Ov. With Acc. and Inf. : Cic. With Indir. Quest. : Ov. **b.** *not knowing how, unable, incapable* (with Inf.) : Verg., Hor., Ov. **B.** Pass. *not known, unknown :* locus, Pl. ; tributa, Tac. ; neque nescium habebat (with Acc. and Inf.), Tac.

Nessus, i, m. *a centaur who was slain by Hercules with a poisoned arrow ;* **Nessēus**, a, um.

Nestor, oris, m. *son of Neleus, and king of Pylos, famous among the heroes before Troy for his wisdom and eloquence. He is said to have lived through three generations of men ;* **Nestoreus**, a, um.

neu, adv. v. nēve.

neuter, tra, trum (Gen. neutrīus, Dat. neutri) [short form of nē and uter], *neither the one nor the other, neither of two.* **1.** Lit. : ut neutri illorum quisquam esset carior, Cic. ; Pl. ; Ov., etc. With pl. verb : neuter consulum potuerant bello abesse, Liv. ; Pl. In pl. to denote *neither of two different parties :* neutri alteros primo cernebant, Liv. ; Caes. ; Cic., etc. **2.** Transf. **a.** *of neither sex :* neuter anguis, Cic. ; Ov. **b.** Gramm. *of neither gender :* neutra nomina, or neutra, Cic.

ne-utiquam (**ne utiquam**, Pl., Ter.), adv. [short form of nē and utiquam], *in no wise, not on any account :* id ne utiquam mihi placet, Pl. ; neutiquam prohari potuit tam flagitiosa libido, Cic ; dictatori neutiquam placebat, Liv.

neutrō, adv. *to neither side :* neutro inclinatā spe, Liv. ; Tac.

neutrŭbi, adv. [neuter ubi], *in neither the one place nor the other :* Pl.

nē-ve and **neu**, adv. [nē ve], *or not, and not, nor,* or (esp. following ne or ut) : hoc te rogo, ne dimittas animum, neve te obrui magnitudine negoti sinas, Cic. ; Enn., etc. ; hortor ut maneas in sententiā neve vim pertimescas, Cic. ; Caes. ; Liv. After a simple Subj. : hic ames dici pater neu sinas Medos equitare inultos, Hor. After an Imperat. : agite, o agricolae, neu segnes iaceant terrae, Verg. Also in subdivision (like neque . . . neque) : ut eam ne quis nobis minuat, neve vivus, neve mortuus, neither . . . nor, Cic.

ne-volŏ, nevis, nevolt, etc., v. nōlō.

nex, necis, f. [v. necō], *death.* **1.** Lit. **a.** Mostly *violent death, murder, slaughter :* Enn. ; inferre alicui, Cic. ; sibi consciscere, Cic. ; aliquem neci dare, dedere, mittere, demittere, Verg. ; neci occumbere, Ov. ; vitae necisque in suos habet potestatem, Caes. With Obj. Gen. : multorum civium neces, Cic. With Subj. Gen. : venatorum, Phaedr. **b.** *natural death :* Suet. **2.** Transf. *the blood of the slain :* manūs neco Phrygiā imbutae, Ov.

nexĭlis, e, adj. [nectō], *tied* or *bound together :* vestis, Lucr. ; plagae, Ov.

nexum, i, v. nexus, ūs.

nexus, a, um. **I.** Part. nectō. **II.** Noun, **nexus**, i, m. *a free man who has pledged his person as security for a debt :* Liv.

nexus, ūs, m. [nectō], *a tying* or *binding together ; a grip.* **1.** Lit. : arto luctari nexu, Ov. ; bracchiorum nexibus elidere aliquem, Suet. **2.** Transf. **a.** *bond, restraint :* legis, Tac. ; causarum, Curt., Tac. **b.** In partic. **nexus**, ūs, m. and **nexum**, i, n. *the state* or *condition of a nexus, a personal obligation, a voluntary assignment of the person, slavery for debt :* se nexu obligare, Cic. ; nexum inire, Liv. ; mancipio et nexo, Cic. Ep. ; noxa civium liberare, tollere, Cic.

ni (older **nei**) and **nive**, adv. and conj., *not* and *or not* [identical with nē]. **I.** An absolute negative only in the interrogative form quidni ? (or separately, quid ni ?) *why not ?* quid ego ni ita censeam ? Pl. ; for the combination nimirum, *v.* nimirum. **II.** Like ne, with clauses. **a.** Of prohibition or purpose : *that not :* Pl. ; monent ni teneant cursūs, Verg. ; so nive for neve, Lucr. **b.** Much more freq. as negative in a conditional clause (*cf.* nisi, which is formed from it by the addition of si) : *if not, unless.* With *Indic. :* mirum, ni domi est, Ter. ; mirum ni puto, Cic. ; ni frustra augurium vani docuere parentes, Verg. With *Subj. :* quae ni fiant, nulla sit pacis condicio, Liv. ; ni ita se res haberet, Liv. ; ni faciat, Verg. ; Cic. Esp. in legal agreements, stipulations, *etc. :* cum is sponsionem fecisset, ni vir bonus esset, Cic. ; Pl. ; Liv. ; tum illud quod dicitur ' sive nive ' inrident, Cic.

nicētĕrium, I, *n.* [νικητήριον], *the prize of victory :* Juv.

nicŏ, nicere, nicī, *to beckon :* Pl.

nictŏ, āre [nicō], *to wink.* **1.** Lit. : neque illa ulli homini nutet, nictet, adnuat, Pl. **2.** Transf. of fire : nictantia fulgura fiammae, Lucr.

nidāmentum, I, *n.* [nidus], *material for a nest :* Pl.

nidor, ōris, *m.* [*cf.* Gk. κνῖσσα], *a vapour, reek, smell,* from anything burnt : Lucr., Cic., Verg., etc.

nidŭlus, I, *m.* [*dim.* nidus], *a little nest :* Ithacam illam in asperrimis saxulis, tamquam nidulum, adfixam, Cic.

nidus, I, *m.* *a nest.* **1.** Lit. : fingere et construere, Cic. ; facere, Ov. ; struere, Tac. ; tignis suspendere, Verg. **2.** Transf. (in *pl.* only). **a.** *nestlings, brood :* nidi loquaces, Verg. **b.** *abode, home :* tu nidum servas, Hor. **c.** *home, origin :* maiores pennas nido extendere, Hor. **d.** *a case for books, etc. :* Mart. [It. *nido ;* Fr. *nid.*]

niger, gra, grum, *black, sable, swarthy, dark, dusky* (contrast ater, *black, dismal*). **1.** Lit. (of persons and things) : Cic., Verg., etc. *Comp. :* Ov. As Noun, **nigrum,** I, *n. a black spot :* Ov. **2.** Transf. **a.** Of winds : *black, bringing darkness :* nigerrimus Auster, Verg. ; Hor. **b.** *of death ; dismal :* nigrorumque memor, dum licet, ignium, Hor. ; dies, Prop. **c.** *unlucky, ill-omened :* huncine solem tam nigrum surrexe mihi ? Hor. ; Prop. **d.** Of character, *black, bad, wicked :* Cic., Hor. [It. *nero ;* Sp. *negro ;* Fr. *noir.*]

nigrāns, antis. **I.** *Part.* nigrō. **II.** Adj. : *black, dusky :* color, Lucr. ; nigrantes terga iuvenci, Verg. ; Varr.

nigrēscō, nigrēscere, nigruī [niger], *to become black, grow dark :* latices nigrescere sacros, Verg. ; sanguine venae, Ov. [Fr. *noirtir.*]

nigrŏ, āre [niger], *to be black :* Lucr. Most freq. as *Adj.* (*v.* nigrans).

nigror, ōris, *m.* [niger], *blackness :* mortis, Lucr.

nihil [by apocope from nihilum, *i.e.* nē hilum : *cf.* nihilum], and **nil** (mostly poet.) *n.* (GEN. nullīus rei), *nothing.* With GEN. : nihil mali (*no evil*), Cic. With an *Adj. :* nihil exspectatione vestrā dignum dico, Cic. With ref. to persons : victor, quo nihil erat moderatius (i.e. than whose conduct), Cic.

Phrases. A. NOM. and ACC. **a.** *nothing, i.e. nothing useful, nothing to the point :* nihil agere, Pl., Cic., Hor. ; nihil adferre, *to advance arguments which are good for nothing,* Cic. ; *cf.* also nihil esse, *to be nothing* or *nobody, to be of no use :* in aliquā re, Cic. ; Ter. **b.** *nothing, i.e. no dealings :* nihil mihi cum illo est, Ter. ; Ov. **c.** With negatives, nihil, nec . . . nec (without destroying the negation) : nihil me nec subterfugere voluisse reticendo, nec obscurare dicendo, Cic. ; nihil non, *everything :* nihil non ad rationem derigebat, Cic. ; non nihil and haud nihil, *something, somewhat :* non nihil, ut in tantis malis, est profectum, Cic. ; nihil quicquam, *nothing whatever, nothing at all :* Cic. ; nihil nisi, nihil aliud nisi, nihil praeter (with ACC.), nihil praeterquam, *nothing else than, nothing but :* tu nihil nisi sapientia es, Ter. ; amare nihil aliud est, nisi eum ipsum diligere, quem ames, Cic ; nihil minus, *nothing less so,* i.e. *by no means, not at all,* Cic. With *quin* or *quo minus,* after a verb signifying *to omit, leave undone :* nihil praetermisi quin etc., Cic. ; nihil moror quo minus decemviratu abeam, Liv. With *Imperat.* or *Juss. Subj. :* nihil mihi rescribas, Ov. ; Cic. ; Hor. **e.** With *dum* (q.v.), *nothing as yet :* nihil dum audieramus, Cic. Ep. **f.** nihil est quod, cur *or* quam ob rem, *there is no reason why :* nihil est, quod adventum nostrum extimescas, Cic. ; nihil est in aliquo ut putes etc., *there is nothing in any one to justify the notion that etc.,* Cic. ; nihil est, *it is of no use, to no purpose, in vain :* Pl., Hor. ; nihil ad me (*sc.* pertinet) : recte an secus, nihil ad nos ; aut si ad nos, nihil ad hoc tempus, Cic. Also, nihil ad, *nothing in comparison with :* nihil ad Persium, Cic. **B.** ACC. **a.** Internal : nihil valere, *to have no weight, to be invalid :* Cic. ; Thebani nihil moti sunt, Liv. ; me nihil paenitet, Pl. ; beneficio isto legis nihil utitur, Cic. **b.** Adverbial : *in nothing, not at all :* nihil opus est, Ter., Cic.

nihilum (and **nilum,** Lucr., Hor.), I, *n.* [short form of nē and hilum], *nothing.* **A.** **nihilum** ACC. **a.** With preps. : ad nihilum recidit apparatus tuus, Cic. ; Lucr. ; in nihilum subito occidat, Cic. **b.** Intern. ACC. used as *Adv. :* nihilum metuenda timere, Hor. **B.** nihili, GEN. of Value : *of no value, worthless :* nihili est autem, suom qui officium facere inmemor est, Pl. Hence, nihili pendere *or* facere, Pl., Ter., Cic. **C.** nihilo ABL. **a.** With preps. : nihil ex nihilo fit, Lucr. ; Cic. ; aliquid pro nihilo putare, Cic. ; de nihilo, *for nothing, without cause or reason,* Pl., Liv. **b.** ABL. of Measure (with *Comp. Adj.* or *Adv.*), *by nothing :* nihilo pluris, Pl. ; nihilo tamen setius, Caes. ; nihilo benevolentior, Cic. Ep. ; nihilo segnius, Liv. So, nihilo minus, or, in one word, nihilo-minus, *no less, none the less, notwithstanding :* post eius mortem nihilo minus id facere conantur, Caes. ; Ter. ; Cic., etc. With minus omitted : nihilo ego quam tu nunc amata sum, Pl. So with setius, q.v. Similarly, nihilo aliter, *no otherwise :* Ter.

nil, nilum, nilŏ, *v.* nihil, nihilum, nihilō.

Nīlus, ī, *m. the river Nile*. Transf. a, *the god of the Nile:* Cic. b. *a canal, conduit:* Cic.; **Nīliacus**, a, um. a. *of the Nile.* b. *Egyptian:* Ov., etc.: **Nīlōticus**, a, um, *of the Nile;* **Nīlōtis**, idis, *f. adj.*

nimbātus, a, um [nimbus], perh. *light, trifling, frivolous:* Pl.

nimbifer, era, erum [nimbus ferō], *storm-bringing, stormy:* Ov.

nimbōsus, a, um [nimbus], *laden with storm-clouds, stormy:* Orion, Verg.; Ov.

nimbus, ī, m. [cf. νέφος, νεφέλη], *a cloud.* 1. Lit. a. *a black rain-cloud, storm-cloud, thunder-cloud:* Lucil., Cic.; involvere diem nimbi, Verg.; tempestas denso regem operuit nimbo, Liv. b. Of the cloud which enveloped the gods when they appeared on earth: nimbo succincta, Verg. 2.Transf. A. *a cloud of dust, smoke, sand:* Verg.; of other things: peditum, Verg.; velut nimbum sagittas ingerebant, Liv. B. *a storm of rain:* terrere animos fulminibus, tempestatibus, nimbis, nivibus, grandinibus, Cic.; Verg. Transf. of a sudden misfortune: hunc quidem nimbum cito transisse laetor, Cic. Ep.

nī-mīrum, *adv.* [nī and mirum, *strange if it were not so*], *without doubt, indisputably, certainly, surely, truly.* I. nimirum Themistocles est auctor adhibendus, Cic.; Ter.; Verg.; non omnia nimirum iidem dii dedere, Liv. II. Freq. in an ironical sense: *doubtless, to be sure, of course:* nimirum contra dici nihil potest, Cic.; Hor., etc.

nimis, *adv.* I. *not a little, very much, very, exceedingly:* nimis velim lapidem, Pl. So nimis quam, *very much:* nimis quam formido, Pl. With a negative: *not very, not particularly:* Caes., Cic., Liv. II. *too much, overmuch, excessively, beyond measure:* Ter., Cic., Hor., etc.; nimis multi pro inopiā commeatuum, Liv. With GEN.: nimis insidiarum, Cic.; nimis lucis, Ov.

nimius, a, um [v. nimis]. I. *very great, very much:* homo nimiā pulchritudine, Pl. *Neut.* **nimium** as Noun, *much, abundance:* nimium boni est quoi nihil est mali, Enn. So in ABL.: ne doleas plus nimio, Hor. As *Adv.* a. ACC. **nimium**, *very much, greatly, exceedingly:* o fortunatos nimium, sua si bona norint, agricolas! Verg.; felix, heu nimium felix, Verg.; nimium quantum, *as much as can be, very much indeed, exceedingly, very, ever so much:* differt inter honestum et turpe nimium quantum, Cic. Also, in same sense, nimium quam: nimium quam es barbarus, Pl.; non nimium, *not very much, not particularly,* Cic. b. ABL. of Measure, **nimiō**, *exceedingly, by far, much:* nimio mavolo, Pl.; nimio plus, Liv. II. *excessive.* a. *too great, too much:* nimia pertinacia atque adrogantia, Caes.; Cic.; Liv. b. *immoderate, intemperate:* rebus secundis nimii, Tac.; Hor. With LOCAT.GEN.: nimius animi, Liv.; imperi, Liv.; sermonis, Tac. *Neut.* **nimium** as Noun, *superabundance, excess:* mediocritatem illam tenebit, quae est inter nimium et parum, Cic. ACC. **nimium** as *Adv., too much:* Cic., Verg.

ningit and **ninguit** (Perf. ninxit, Acc.) [cf. nix], *impers. it snows.* 1. Lit.: Verg.

2. Transf. (with personal subject): *to shower down:* ningunt rosarum floribus, Lucr.

ninguēs, ium, *f. pl.* [ningō], *snow:* Lucr.

Ninus, ī, m. I. *s. of Belus, the first king of Assyria, husband of Semiramis, and builder of Nineveh.* II. *the city of Nineveh.*

Nioba, ae, and **Niobē**, ēs, *f. d. of Tantalus, and w. of Amphīon, king of Thebes, whose seven sons and seven daughters were slain by Apollo and Diana, and she herself was turned into a weeping rock:* **Niobēus**, a, um.

Nīreus (disyl.), eī and eos, *m. the handsomest man in the Greek host at Troy.*

nisi, *conj.* [nī sī], *if not, unless* (used with *Indic.* and *Subj.*, as in si-clauses). a. In gen.: desilite, commilitones, nisi vultis aquilam hostibus prodere, Caes.; nisi fallor, nisi me fallit animus, Cic.; quod nisi esset, certe postea non discessisset, Cic. b. After negatives, or interrogatives: *except, save only, only:* ne quis enuntiaret, nisi quibus mandatum esset, Caes.; negant enim quemquam esse virum bonum nisi sapientem, Cic.; quid est pietas, nisi voluntas grata in parentis? Cic. c. nisi si, *except if, unless:* nisi si quid in Caesare sit auxili, Caes.; Cic.; Liv. d. nisi ut, *except on condition that, unless:* neque convivia inire ausus est, nisi ut speculatores cum lanceis circumstarent, Suet.; also like Eng. *apart from, without:* quid ultra quam quod fecerit, nisi ut deleret Syracusas, facere hostiliter Marcellum potuisse? Liv. e. nisi quod, *except (the fact) that:* praedia me valde delectant, nisi quod me aere circumforaneo obruerunt, Cic. Ep.; Pl.; Tac., etc. f. nisi quia, *except because, i.e. until that:* at nescibam id dicere illam, nisi quia correxit miles, quod intellexi minus, Ter. g. nihil or nihil aliud nisi: erat historia nihil aliud nisi annalium confectio, Cic. Also non aliter (*on no other condition*) . . . nisi, Liv. h. nisi vero, nisi forte, nisi tamen: *unless indeed; unless perchance; unless however:* nisi forte volumus Epicureorum opinionem sequi, Cic.; Pl.

nīsus, a, um, *Part.* nītor.

nīsus and **nixus**, ūs, *m.* I. Lit. a. *a pressing or resting upon or against.* 1. Lit. a. *pressure, effort, firm posture:* sedato nisu, Pac.; astra se nixu suo conglobata continent, Cic.; nisu immotus eodem, Verg. Of childbirth; *labour:* fetūs nixibus edunt, Verg.; Ov. b. *soaring, climbing:* pinnarum nisus inanis, Lucr.; insolitos docuere nisūs, Hor.; uti prospectus nisusque per saxa facilius foret, Sall. 2. Transf.: ad summum non pervenit nisu, sed impetu, Quint.

Nīsus, ī, m. I. *king of Megara, father of Scylla, who cut off her father's purple hair, on which his life depended: Nisus was then changed into a sea-eagle:* **Nīsaeus**, a, um; **Nīsēis**, idis, *f. the daughter of Nisus;* **Nīsēius**, a, um; and **Nīsias**, adis, *f. adj. Megarian.* II. *friend of Euryalus in Verg.*

nītēdula, ae, *f. a kind of small mouse, a dor-mouse:* Cic.

nītēns, entis, *m.* I. *Part.* nīteō. II. Adj. *shining, gleaming, bright.* 1. Lit. a. oculi, Verg.; astra, Ov.; arma, Liv. b. *glowing with health or beauty:* Cat. *Comp.:*

Ov. **c.** *sleek :* taurus, Verg. **d.** *shining*
with pomade ; greasy : capilli malobathro,
Hor. **2.** Transf. **a.** Of plants, etc. :
culta, Verg. *Comp. :* Ov. **b.** Of speech :
oratio, Cic.

niteō, ēre, *to shine, beam, glisten.* **1.** Lit. **a.**
diffuso lumine caelum, Lucr. ; diversi nite-
ant cum mille colores, Ov. ; Hor. **b.** *to
glow* with health or beauty : miseri quibus
intemptata nites ! Hor. ; Mart. **c.** *to be
sleek :* oves, Pl. ; Phaedr. ; Juv. **d.** *to
shine* with ointment, *be greasy :* unguentis,
Cic. **2.** Transf. **a.** Of fields and plants :
campos nitentis desuper ostentat, Verg. **b.**
Of wealth : vectigal in pace niteat, Cic. ;
Hor. **c.** In gen. : recenti gloriā nitens,
Liv. ; Pl. ; Hor. **d.** Of speech : oratio,
Cic.

nitēscō, nitēscere, nitui [niteō], *to grow or
become bright and shiny.* **1.** Lit. **a.** caelum, Enn. ; exiguo stellarum nitore, Cic.
b. *to become aglow* with health or beauty :
Hor. **c.** *to grow sleek :* armenta, Plin. Ep.
d. *to shine* with ointment, etc. : iuventus
nudatos umeros oleo perfusa nitescit, Verg. ;
ex umero Pelopis ebur, Tib. **2.** Transf. :
eloquentiae gloriā nitescere, Tac.

nitidē, *adv. brightly, splendidly :* Pl.

nitidiusculē, *dim. adv. rather more finely,
sprucely :* Pl.

nitidiusculus, a, um [*dim. of comp.* of nitidus],
rather more shiny : caput, Pl.

nitidus, a, um [niteō], *shining, bright, glistening.* **1.** Lit. **a.** caput (solis), Verg. **b.**
glowing with health and beauty : nitidus
iuventā anguis, Verg. ; me pinguem et
nitidum bene curatā cute vises, Hor. **c.**
sleek : iumenta, Nep. **d.** *shining* with
ointment, oil, etc. : caesaries, Verg. ; ebur,
Ov. **2.** Transf. **a.** Of fields and plants,
luxuriant : fruges, Lucr. ; campi nitidissimi
viridissimique, Cic. Poet. : nitidissimus
annus, Ov. **b.** In gen. : *bright, smart,
trim, spruce, handsome :* aedes, femina,
Pl. ; villae, Hor. ; homines, Cic. As Noun :
ex nitido fit rusticus, Hor. **c.** *cultivated,
polished, refined :* nitidum quoddam genus
verborum, vox, oratio, orator, Quint. ;
Juv. *Comp. :* Cic.

nitor, ōris, m. [niteō], *brightness, sheen,
lustre.* **1.** Lit. **a.** nitor exoriens aurorae,
Lucr. ; argenti et auri, Ov. ; speculi, Plin.
b. *the glow* of health or beauty : corporis,
Ter. ; urit me Glycerae nitor, Hor. **c.** Of
colour : Lucr., Prop. **2.** Transf. **a.** Of
personal appearance : Cic., Juv. **b.** Of
family : generis, Ov. **c.** Of style : orationis, Cic. ; eloquii, Ov. ; descriptionum,
Tac.

nitor, nīti, nisus and nixus. **I.** *to support
oneself.* **1.** Lit. **a.** *to lean,* or *rest upon.*
With ABL. : stirpibus suis, Cic. ; hastili,
Cic. ; hastā, Verg. ; genibus, Pl., Liv. With
in and Acc. : in hastam, Verg. With *de*
and ABL. : de quā pariens arbore nixa dea
est, Ov. *Absol. :* partes (mundi) aequaliter
nituntur, Cic. ; in medium sunt omnia nixa,
Lucr. **b.** *to poise* or *balance oneself :* paribus Cyllenius alis, Verg. **c.** *to stand fast,
plant the foot firmly :* virtute nitebantur
atque omnia vulnera sustinebant, Caes. ;
anguem pressit humi nitens, Verg. **2.**

Transf. **a.** *to depend on, rest on* (with
ABL. or *in* and ABL.) : in vitā Pompei salus
civitatis, Cic. ; Nep. **b.** *to trust to, rely
upon.* With ABL. : auctoritate, virtute,
etc., Caes. ; spe, Cic. Ep. ; consilio atque
auctoritate alicuius, Cic. With *in* and ABL. :
in nomine inani, Lucr. With *ubi :* quo
confugies ? ubi nitere ? Cic. **II.** *to exert
oneself.* **1.** Lit. **a.** In childbirth : *to be in
labour :* Ov. **b.** *to make one's way with
an effort, to press forwards* or *upwards ; to
mount, climb :* corporibus, Sall. ; serpentes
simul ac primum niti possunt, Cic. ; per
ardua, Liv. ; gradibus, Verg. ; in aëra, Ov. ;
in adversum, Verg., Ov. **2.** Transf. of
mental effort : *to exert oneself, labour, endeavour :* modo tantum, quantum potest,
quisque nitatur, Cic. ; nihil contra se regem
nisurum existimabat, Caes. ; pro aliquo,
Liv. With *Inf. :* Sall., Ov. With *ad :*
ad sollicitandas civitates nituntur, Caes. ;
ad immortalitatem gloriae, Cic.

nitrum, ī, n. [νίτρον], also called sal nitrum,
native soda, natron. **1.** Lit. : Plin. **2.**
Transf. : *cleanser :* censuram lomentum
aut nitrum esse, Cael. ap. Cic. Ep.

nivālis, e, *adj.* [nix]. **1.** Lit. **a.** *snowy,
snow- :* dies, Liv. ; Hebrus nivali compede
vinctus, Hor. **b.** *covered with snow :* vertex Apennini, Verg. **2.** Transf. **a.** *wintry, cold :* dies, Sen. **b.** *chill, cold :* osculum, Mart. **c.** *snow-like, snowy :* equi
candore nivali, Verg.

nivātus, a, um [nix], *cooled with snow :* Suet.

nive, *v.* nēve and ni.

niveus, a, um [nix]. **1.** Lit. **a.** *of snow,
snowy :* aggeribus niveis informis, Verg.
b. *covered with snow :* mons, Cat. **c.**
cooled with snow : aqua, Mart. **2.** Transf.
snow-white, snowy : lacerti, Verg. ; lac,
Verg. ; color, Hor. ; vestis, Ov.

nivōsus, a, um [nix], *full of snow, snowy :*
hiems, Liv. ; Strymon, Ov.

nix, nivis, *f.* [cf. Gk. νίφα, νίφει], *snow.* **1.**
Lit. : Cic., Verg. In *pl., accumulated
snows :* miles nivibus pruinisque obrutus,
Liv. ; duratae solo nives, Hor. **2.** Transf.
of the hair : capitis nives, Hor. [It. *neve ;*
and, through nivea, Fr. *neige.*]

nixor, ārī [*freq.* nitor]. **I.** *to rest on.*
Transf. : fundamenta, quibus nixatur vita
salusque, Lucr. **II.** *to strive repeatedly,
struggle hard* or *often :* Lucr. ; pars vulnere clauda retentat nixantem (serpentem),
Verg. Of effort upwards : Lucr.

nixus, a, um, *Part.* nitor.

nixus, ūs, *m. v.* nisus.

nō, nāre [*cf.* Gk. νέω], *to swim, float.* **1.** Lit. :
Pl., Hor., Ov., etc. Prov. : nare sine
cortice, Hor. Of boats : Cat., Tib. **2.**
Transf. **a.** Of similar modes of motion :
to sail, flow, fly : iuventus per medium
classi navit Athon, Cat. ; nare per aetatem
liquidam, Verg. **b.** Of the eyes of drunken
persons : *to swim :* Lucr.

nōbilis, e (old form, **gnōbilis**), *adj.* [v. nōscō],
that can be or *is known.* **1.** Lit. **a.** *known :*
neque his nobilis fui, Pl. **b.** *noted, marked :*
addidit facinori fidem nobili gaudio, Tac.
c. *notable, well-known, famous :* dies, Pl. ;
magnus et nobilis rhetor Isocrates, Cic. ;
exemplum, Liv. With *Causal* ABL. : Corin-

thus acre, Ov.; nobilis clade Romană Claudina pax, Liv. With *Explanatory Inf.*: Hor. **d.** In bad sense, *notorious :* so scelere fieri nolunt nobiles, Pl.; Ter. **2.** Transf. **a.** *notable, of noble rank or birth, noble* (esp. of one who himself or the members of whose family had held a curule office) : nobili genere nati, Cic.; Clodia mulier non solum nobilis sed etiam nota, Cic.; Liv. In *pl.* as Noun, *the notables, nobles :* Liv. **b.** Of horses : *high-bred :* Ov., Juv. **c.** *excellent :* tres nobilissimi fundi, *very fine,* Cic.

nōbilitās, ātis, *f.* [nōbilis], *famousness, celebrity, renown.* **1.** Lit.: Pl., Cic., Liv. **2.** Transf. **a.** *high or noble rank or birth, nobility :* ad inlustrandam nobilitatem suam, Cic.; Ov.; Juv. **b.** Concr. *the nobility, the nobles :* coniurationem nobilitatis fecit, Caes.; nobilitas rem publicam deseruerat, Liv.; Luc. With plur. verb : coepere nobilitas dignitatem in dominationem vertere, Sall. In *pl. :* Tac. **c.** *excellence :* cum florere Isocratem nobilitate discipulorum videret, Cic.; eloquio tantum nobilitatis inest, Ov.; Tac.

nōbiliter, *adv. excellently :* Plin.

nōbilitō, āre [nōbilis], *to make known, to render famous or renowned :* poētae post mortem nobilitari volunt, Cic.; famam, Liv. Also in bad sense, *to render notorious :* aliquem flagitiis, Ter.; nobilitata crudelitas, Cic.

nocēns, entis. **I.** *Part.* noceō. **II.** Adj.: *hurtful, injurious, noxious.* **1.** Lit. (as Noun), a pestiforis et nocentibus refugere, Cic.; boletus, Juv. *Comp. :* cicutis ālium nocentius, Hor. **2.** Transf. (morally) : *criminal :* homines, Cic.; victoria, Cic.; mores, Quint. *Sup. :* Cic., Quint. As Noun : Cic., Ov., Liv.

noceō, ēre [fr. same root as necō], *to harm, hurt, injure :* arma alia ad tegendum, alia ad nocendum, Cic. With *Inten.* Acc.: noxam nocuerunt, Liv.; nihil nocet, Cic. Ep.; Juv. With Dat.: nemini, Pl.; alteri, Cic.; nihil iis nocituros hostis, Caes. *Pass. Impers. :* mihi nihil ab istis noceri potest, Cic.; ille respondit, ipsi nihil nocitum iri, Caes.; Pl. [It. *nuocere ;* Fr. *nuire.*]

nocivus, a, um [noceō], *hurtful, injurious, noxious :* Phaedr.

noctifer, erī, *m.* [nox ferō, *the night-bringer*], *the evening-star :* Cat.

noctilūca, ae, *f.* [nox lūceō], *that shines by night ;* hence, *the moon :* Hor.

nocti-vagus, a, um, *night-wandering :* faces caeli, Lucr.; currus (*sc.* Phoebus), Verg.

noctū, *f.* Abl. [nox, *cf.* diū fr. diēs], *by night, in the night-time :* Pl., Caes., Cic., Hor., etc.

noctua, ae, *f.* [nox], *the (short-eared) owl :* Pl., Verg.

noctuābundus, a, um [noctū], *travelling by night :* Cic. Ep.

noctuīnus, a, um [noctua], *of owls :* Pl.

nocturnus, a, um [nox], *of, at, or by night, nocturnal :* labores, Cic.; horae, Cic.; bella, Verg.; ora (i.e. dark), Pl. Sometimes used with force of *Adv. :* qui nocturnus sacra divum legerit, Hor.; Verg.

noctuvigilus, a, um [noctū, vigilō], *night-waking :* Venus, Pl.

nocuus, a, um [noceō], *hurtful, injurious, noxious :* Ov.

nōdō, āre [nōdus]. **I.** *to tie in a knot, to knot :* crines nodantur in aurum, Verg.; Cato; Ov. **II.** *to make knotty :* ferula nodata, Plin. [Fr. *nouer.*]

nōdōsus, a, um [nōdus], *full of knots, knotty.* **1.** Lit.: stipes, Ov.; plagae, Ov.; vitis, Juv. Of gout : Hor., Ov. **2.** Transf.: Cicuta (i.e. clever in tying legal knots), Hor.

nōdus, ī, *m. a knot.* **1.** Lit.: nodus vinculumque, Cic.; necte tribus nodis ternos, Amarylli, colores, Verg. **2.** Transf. **A.** *Material.* **a.** *a knot, knob, node* on an animal's joint : crura sine nodis, Caes.; Luc. **b.** *a knot or knob in wood or plants :* baculum sine nodo aduncum tenens, Liv.; Verg. *Prov. :* nodum in scirpo quaerere (i.e. to look for difficulties where there are none), Pl. **c.** Of clothing or hair : *a knot, bunch, knob :* nodo sinūs conlecta fluentis, Verg.; crinem nodo substringere, Tac. **d.** *a girdle :* Mart. Hence, nodus anni, *the equator,* Lucr. **e.** Of a wrestler : Cacum corripit in nodum complexus, Verg. **f.** Of a serpent's writhing : nixantem nodis, Verg. **B.** Abstract. **a.** *a band, bond :* amicitiae, Cic. **b.** *a bond, obligation :* exsolvere animos nodis religionum, Lucr.; Ov. **c.** *a knotty point, difficulty, impediment :* dum hic nodus expediatur, Cic.; exsolvere nodum erroris, Liv.; Abantem, pugnae nodumque moramque, Verg.; iuris, Juv. So of a complicated and critical situation in a drama : dignus vindice nodus, Hor. [Fr. *noeud.*]

noenum, noenu, *v.* nōn.

nōlo, nōlle, nōluī (old forms nevis, nevolt for non vis, nōn volt or vult, Pl.) [nē volō], *to wish not, to be unwilling, be loth, refuse.* **1.** Lit.: novi ingenium mulierum : nolunt, ubi velis, Ter.; Cic.; Luc. With Acc. of *Neut.* Pron.: idem velle, atque idem nolle, Sall.; Cic. Ep. With Acc. and *Inf. :* Caes., Cic., Hor. Esp. freq. in imperat. foll. by *Inf.,* as a polite imperative : noli irascier, Pl.; noli putare, Cic.; noli vexare, Juv. Sometimes even with velle : nolite velle, Cic. With *Perf. Part. :* nollem factum, *I could wish it had not been done,* Ter. **2.** Transf.: *to wish ill, to be spiteful :* cui qui nolunt, iidem tibi, quod eum ornasti, non sunt amici, Cic. Ep.

nomas, adis, *m. f.* [voμάς, *pasturing flocks*], *pl.* nomadēs, um, *nomads :* Plin. Esp. **a.** *a Numidian :* in pl.: Verg.; Nomas versuta, *a Numidian fortune-teller,* Prop. **b.** *Numidia :* Mart.

nōmen, inis, *n.* [*cf.* nōscō, cognōmen], *a name.* **1.** Lit. **A.** Simple sense. **a.** In gen.: quoi nomen est Phormio, Ter.; infaustum Allia nomen, Verg.; nomen dare, ponere, imponere alicui or alicui rei, Cic.; aliquem appellare nomine, Cic.; nomen ab aliquā re accipere, Caes.; ab aliquā re invenire, Cic.; ex aliquā re capere, Caes. With attracted Dat.: iis nomen histrionibus est datum, Liv.; Pl.; Cic.; Ov., etc. **b.** Phr.: nomen dare, edere, profiteri, ad nomen respondere, *to be enrolled as a soldier, to enlist ; to answer to one's name on the muster-roll :* Liv. Also, dare nomen in coniurationem, *to join a conspiracy,* Tac. **c.** *the gentile name,* e.g. Iulius, as distinct fr. the praenomen, e.g. Gaius, and the cognomen (=family name), e.g. Caesar : Quint. But occ. nomen is used for praenomen or cognomen, Cic. **d.** *a title :* imperatoris, Cic. **e.** Gramm. : *a noun :* Quint. **B.** In partic. **a.** In law. **i.** nomen alicuius deferre (*to hand in a man's name to the praetor,* i.e. to bring a charge against him), Cic. ; nomen recipere, (of the praetor) *to receive an accusation,* Cic. ; in aerarium alicuius nomen referre or deferre, *to report for some service* or *distinction,* Cic. ; nomen accipere (of the presiding magistrate at the Comitia Tributa), Liv. **ii.** *charge, heading, account :* nomine sceleris coniurationisque damnati, Cic. **b.** In trade : *the name (in which an account is entered).* **i.** Of the debtor : in tabulas referre, Cic. ; Pl. ; nomina sua exigere, *to call in one's debts,* Cic. ; nomen facere, *to enter or book the items of a debt,* Cic. **ii.** Of the guarantor : tibi certis nominibus grandem pecuniam debuit, Cic. **iii.** *the account of the debt :* solvere, dissolvere, expedire, Cic. ; in socios nomina transcribere, Liv. ; Juv. **c.** Polit. *a name ;* hence, *stock, race :* esp. in phr. nomen Latinum : concitatis sociis et nomine Latino, Cic. ; Liv. ; gens infestissima nomini Romano, Sall. ; Volscum nomen prope deletum est, Liv. **2.** Transf. **a.** *name, fame, reputation, renown :* huius magnum nomen fuit, Cic. ; officere nomini alicuius, Liv. ; nos aliquid nomenque decusque gessimus, Verg. Of things : nec Baccho genus aut pomis sua nomina servat, Verg. ; Cato. **b.** *account, heading ;* hence, *excuse, pretext, reason :* an alio nomine et aliā de causā abstulisse ? Cic. ; et gratias boni viri agebant ut tuo nomine gratulabantur, Cic. ; odisse etiam suo nomine Caesarem et Romanos, Caes. ; Tac. **c.** *a name,* as opposed to a reality : Campani magis nomen ad praesidium sociorum quam viris cum attulissent, Liv. ; nomen amicitia est, Ov. [It. *nome ;* Sp. *nombre ;* Fr. *nom.*]

nōmenclātor (**nōmenculātor**, Mart., Suet.), ōris, *m.* [nōmen calō], *a name-caller ;* i.e. *a slave who told his master the names of those whom they met* (esp. in canvassing) : Cic.

nōmenclātūra, ae, *f.* [nōmen calō], *a list of names :* Plin.

nōminātim, *adv. by name, expressly :* Pl., Caes., Cic.

nōminātiō, ōnis, *f.* [nōminō], *a nomination to an office :* Cic. ; consulum, Tac. ; facere, Liv.

nōminātīvus, a, um [nōmen], *nominative* (in Gramm.) : casus, Quint.

nōminātus, a, um. **I.** *Part.* nōminō. **II.** Adj. : *famed, renowned, celebrated :* Cic.

nōminitō, āre [freq. nōminō], *to name frequently* or *as a regular practice :* Lucr.

nōminō, āre [nōmen]. **1.** Lit. **a.** *to name, to call by name :* Enn. ; urbem a suo nomine Romam iussit nominari, Cic. **b.** *to mention by name :* Caes. ; esp. in phr. quem honoris causā nomino, *whom I mention with all*

respect, Cic. **2.** Transf. **a.** *to render famous :* nominari volunt omnes, Cic. **b.** *to nominate* or *appoint to an office :* patres interregem nominaverant, Liv. ; me augurem, Cic. ; Plin. Ep. **c.** *to name, denounce, arraign :* capita coniurationis apud dictatorem, Liv. ; inter socios Catilinae nominatus, Suet. ; Curt.

nomisma, atis, *n.* [νόμισμα], *a piece of money, a coin :* Hor., Mart.

nomos and **nomus**, i, *m.* [νομός]. **I.** *a district, province, nome :* Plin. **II.** In music : *a tune, air :* Suet.

nōn (old forms **noenum** and **noenu**), *adv.* [contr. from nē oenum (ūnum), *not one*], *not.* **A.** In gen. **a.** To negative a sentence or a single word : non respuit condicionem Caesar, Caes. ; hoc suo et non tuo impulsu fecit, Cic. **b.** Before another negative it often forms a weak affirmative : fortasse non nollem, si possem ad otium (*should not object*), Cic. ; so, non nemo=*some one ;* non nihil=*something ;* non nullus, a, um=*some.* **B.** After negatives. **a.** It forms a strong affirmative : nihil non, *everything,* nemo non, *everybody,* nullus non, *every,* Cic. **b.** Followed by nec . . . nec, it retains its negative force : non medius fidius prae lacrimis possum reliqua nec cogitare nec scribere, Cic. So also with ne . . . quidem : non fugio ne hos quidem mores, Cic. **C.** Other usages. For non modo (non) and non solum, *v.* modo, solum. For non quo, quod, quia, *v.* quo, quod, quia ; non nisi, *only ;* non ita, non tam, *not so very, not particularly :* simulacra non ita antiqua, Cic. ; non fere, *scarcely, hardly :* non fere quisquam, *hardly anyone,* Cic. **D.** Rare usages. **a.** In questions for nonne : quid haec amentia significat ? non vim ? non scelus ? non latrocinium ? Cic. ; Pl. **b.** With *Imperat.* or *Jussive Subj.,* instead of ne : Pl. ; non petito ut bene sit, Ov. ; non Teucros agat in Rutulos, Verg. ; Liv. ; non etiam sileas, Hor. ; Sen. In oblique : non ad unum omnia deferrent, Tac. **c.** Closely connected with and negativing a Noun : nec posse esse non corpus, *could be other than material,* Cic. ; Ov. **d.** In answers : *no :* aut idem aut non respondere, *to answer 'yes' or 'no,'* Cic.

Nōnacris, is, *f. a mountain and town in Arcadia ;* **Nōnacrīnus**, a, um, virgo (i.e. Callisto), Ov. ; **Nōnacrius**, a, um, heros (i.e. Euander), Ov. ; **Nōnacria**, ae, *f.* Atalanta, Ov.

Nōnae, ārum, *f. pl.* [nōnus], *the ninth day before the Ides, counting inclusively ; the fifth day in all the months, except March, May, July, and October, in which it was the seventh ; the nones :* Cic.

nōnāgēni, ae, a [nōnāgintā], *a group of ninety* or *ninety each :* Plin.

nōnāgēnsimus (**-ēsimus**, a, um [nōnāgintā], *ninetieth :* Cic.

nōnāgiēns (**-iēs**), *adv. ninety times :* nonagies sestertium, *nine million sesterces,* Cic.

nōnāgintā, *adj. indecl., ninety :* Cic.

nōnānus, a, um [nōna, *sc.* legiō], *belonging to the ninth* (*legion*) : miles nonanus, Tac. As Noun : **nōnānus**, i, *m. a soldier of the ninth* (*legion*) : Tac.

nōnāria, ae, *f.* [nōnārius, *of the ninth hour*], *a public prostitute :* Pers.

nōn-dum, *adv. not yet :* nondum centum et decem anni sunt, Cic. ; Pl. ; Verg.

nōngentī, ae, a, *nine hundred :* Cic.

nōn-ne, *adv. is it not ?* **a.** In direct questions : nonne meministi, *do you not remember ?* Cic. ; Caes. ; Pl. **b.** In indirect questions : *if . . . not, whether . . . , not ;* cum esset ex eo quaesitum, Archelaum Perdiccae filium nonne beatum putaret, Cic.

nōn-nēmō, inis, *m.* **I.** *some-one, many a one :* Cic. **II.** *some one, a certain person* or *persons :* Cic.

nōn-nihil, *v.* nihil.

nōn-nūllus, a, um, *some ;* in *pl. several :* nonnullā in re, Cic. ; esse nonnullo se Caesaris beneficio adfectum, Caes. ; Pl. Esp. freq. in *pl.:* nonnulli, *some persons,* Caes.

nōn-nunquam, *adv. sometimes :* nonnunquam interdiu, saepius noctu, Caes. ; Cic. With aliquando, Cic. Ep.

nōn-nūsquam, *adv. in some places :* Plin.

nōnus, a, um [novem], *ninth :* Cic., Hor. As Noun, **nōna,** ae, *f. (sc.* hora), *the ninth hour of the day :* post nonam venies, Hor.

nōnus-decimus, a, um, *nineteenth :* Tac.

Norīcum, i, *n. a mountainous country between the Danube and the Alps, famous for its steel ;* **Norīcus,** a, um.

nōrma, ae, *f. [cf.* γνωρίμη, γνώμων], *a square,* employed by carpenters and masons for making right angles. T r a n s f. *rule, standard :* vitam ad certam rationis normam derigere, Cic. ; musicorum acerrimā normā, Cic. ; loquendi, Hor. ; oratoris, Plin. Ep.

nōrmālis, e, *adj.* [nōrma], *made with a square :* angulus, Quint.

Nortia, ae, *f. a goddess of the Volsinii.*

nōs, Nom. and Acc., *we, us ;* noster, our, is used for the Possess. Gen., nostri and nostrum for the other Genitives (*v.* infra) ; nōbis, Dat. and Abl. [*cf.* νῶϊ]. **a.** Used in Nom. for emphasis only : nos, nos, consules desumus, Cic. **b.** Occ. like the Eng. royal or editorial ' we ' (instead of ego) : nos habemus, *I have,* Cic. ; and in the lang. of comedy, even with *sing.* concord : apsente nobis, Ter. **c.** nos, nobis often have the suffix *met :* noamet, nobismet. **d.** In the *Obj.* Gen. *towards us, for us,* the form nostri is usual : amor nostri, Cic. Ep. ; nil nostri miserere, Verg. **e.** In the *Partit.* Gen. the form nostrum is usual : uterque nostrum, Cic. In Pl. nostrorum ; nemo nostrorum, Pl. ; and nostrarum quisquam, Ter. [It. *noi ;* Fr. *nous.*]

nōscītō, āre [*freq.* nōscō]. **I.** *to try to track, examine closely :* vestigia, Pl. ; aedis, Pl. **II.** *to observe, look at :* circumspectare omnibus fori partibus senatorem raroque usquam noscitare, Liv. ; Pl. **III.** *to recognise, know :* Pl., Tac. ; aliquem facie, Liv.

nōscō, nōscere, nōvi, nōtum (old forms, **gnōscō,** gnōvi, gnōtum. The contracted forms in class. Lat. are, nōsti, nōram, nōrim, nōsse), [*cf.* γιγνώσκω], *to begin to know, to get knowledge of, become acquainted with, to learn.* **1.** Lit. **a.** In tenses of Present stem : deus ille, quem mente noscimus, Cic. ; Pl. ; Lucr., etc. With *Indir. Quest. :* Liv. Pass. : omnes philosophiae

partes tum facile noscuntur, Cic. ; noscere provinciam, nosci exercitui, Tac. ; nullique videnda, voce tamen noscar, Ov. ; Ter. **b.** In tenses of *Perf.* stem : *to have knowledge of, be acquainted with, to know :* si me novisti minus, Pl. ; qui non leges, non iura noritis, Cic. **2.** T r a n s f. **a.** *to examine, inquire into :* quae olim a praetoribus noscebantur, Tac. **b.** *to recognise, know again :* res suas, Liv. ; Ter. **c.** *to recognise, know, approve of :* hanc unam gratiam potentiamque noverunt, Caes. ; illam partem excusationis nec nosco, nec probo, Cic.

noster, stra, strum (Gen. *pl.* nostrum, Pl.) [nōs], *our, our own, ours.* **A.** S u b j e c t i v e (usual usage). **a.** nostris consiliis et laboribus, Cic. ; in wider sense, *belonging to our country (Rome) :* Rhodanus, qui provinciam nostram ab Helvetiis dividit, Caes. ; nostrum mare (i.e. the Mediterranean), Caes. Strengthened by suffix *-pte :* nostrāpte culpā, Ter. **b.** Like Eng. royal or editorial ' our ' (for ' my ') : nostri aequales, *my contemporaries,* Cic. **c.** In *masc.* as Noun : noster, *our friend ;* and *pl.* nostri, *our side, our men ;* impedimentis castrisque nostri potiti sunt, Caes. ; Ennius noster, Cic. **d.** In addresses : *my dear, good :* o Syre noster, salve, quid fit ? quid agitur ? Ter. **e.** *our own,* i.e. *favourable to us :* nostra loca, Liv. **B.** Objectively (rare) : amor noster, *love for us,* Cic. Ep. ; Liv. [It. *nostro ;* Sp. *nuestro ;* Fr. *notre.*]

nostrās, ātis, *adj. of our country, native :* verba nostratia, Cic. Ep. ; Cato ; nostrates philosophi, Cic.

nota, ae, *f.* [nōscō], l i t. *that by which a thing is known.* **I.** *a mark, sign, note.* **1.** L i t. : si signa et notas locorum ostenderem, Cic. ; clavum notam annorum numeri, Liv. ; caeruleae angui notae, Verg. ; Hor. **2.** T r a n s f. : notae ac vestigia suorum flagitiorum, Cic. ; ab urbe Numantinā ille notam traxit, Ov. **II.** *written characters, letters.* **A.** In gen. **1.** L i t. : qui primus sonos vocis paucis litterarum notis terminavit, Cic. **2.** T r a n s f. **a.** *a letter, epistle, writing :* inspicit acceptas hostis ab hoste notas, Ov. **b.** *notes, summaries :* argumentorum, Cic. **B.** *secret characters, secret writing, cipher :* foliis notas mandat, Verg. ; si qua occultius perferenda essent, per notas scripsit, Suet. T r a n s f. *a secret sign :* innuet ; acceptas tu quoque redde notas, Ov. **C.** *short-hand characters, stenographic signs :* Sen. Ep., Suet. **III.** *a critical mark,* made on the margin of a book : notam apponere ad malum versum, Cic. ; Sen. Ep. Also, *a mark of punctuation :* notae librariorum, Cic. **IV.** *a mark, brand.* **1.** L i t. **a.** On a wine-jar : Falerni, Hor. **b.** On cattle : Verg. **c.** Of tattoo-marks : Cic. **d.** On a bad slave : Suet. **2.** T r a n s f. **a.** *a brand,* i.e. *a particular kind :* meae notae (Falerni) sunt optimae, Cic. ; ex hac notā corporum est aër, Sen. **b.** *a distinctive mark or quality :* cuiusque generis dicendi nota, Cic. ; animi, Suet. **c.** *a stamp on a coin :* Suet. **d.** *a brand, stigma :* quae nota domesticae turpitudinis non inusta vitae tuae est ? Cic. ; Lucil. **V.** E s p. *the Censor's mark of disgrace,* placed against a

senator's or citizen's name. **1. Lit.:**
censoriae severitatis nota, Cic. ; ut censores
motis e senatu ascriberent notas, Liv.
2. Transf.: o turpem notam temporum
illorum I Cic. ; homo omnibus notis turpitudinis insignis, Cic. ; nota ignominiaque
Philippi, Liv.

nŏtābĭlis, e, adj. [notō], *noteworthy.* **a.** *remarkable, famous :* Cic. Ep., Juv., Tac.,
etc. *Comp. :* Quint. **b.** *notorious, infamous :* Quint. *Comp. :* Tac. **c.** *perceptible :* Sen.

nŏtābĭlĭter, adv. *in a marked manner, perceptibly :* expalluit, Plin. Ep. ; Suet.
Comp. : Tac.

nŏtārĭus, i, m. [nota]. **I.** *a short-hand
writer, stenographer :* Quint., Plin. Ep.
II. *a secretary :* Plin. Ep.

nŏtātĭō, ōnis, f. [notō], *a marking, noting.*
1. Lit. A. In gen. : tabellarum (i.e. *the
marking of the voting-tablets with wax of
different colours*), Cic. **B.** Esp. **a.** *the animadversion of a censor:* censoriae, Cic. **b.**
a designation, choice : iudicum, Cic. **2.**
Transf. **a.** *a noticing, observation :* naturae, temporum, Cic. **b.** *the analysis of a
word for the purpose of finding its precise
meaning :* Cic.

nŏtātus, a, um. **I.** *Part.* notō. **II.** Adj.:
marked, distinguished : homo omnium
scelerum libidinumque maculis notatissimus, Cic.

nŏtēsco, nŏtēscere, nŏtŭi [nŏtus], *to become
known :* Cat. ; malis facinoribus, Tac.

nŏthus, a, um [νόθος]. **1. Lit. a.** Of persons, *illegitimate, bastard.* As Noun : Verg.,
Quint. **b.** Of animals : *mongrel :* Verg.
2. Transf.: *not genuine, counterfeit :*
lumen (lunae), Lucr. ; Attis notha mulier,
Cat.

nŏtĭō, ōnis, f. [nōscō]. **1. Lit. a.** *a becoming
acquainted :* quid tibi hanc notio est
amicam meam ? Pl. **b.** *a taking cognisance of by a magistrate, an examination, investigation :* sine notione populi Romani,
Cic. ; ad censores, non ad senatum, notionem de eo pertinere, Liv. ; Tac. In *pl.* :
Cic. **2.** Transf.: *an idea, conception,
notion :* rerum, Cic. ; neque alia huic verbo
subiecta notio est, Cic. In *pl.* : Cic.

nŏtĭtĭa, ae (nŏtĭtĭēs, ēi, Lucr.), f. [nŏtus].
A. Pass. **1. Lit.** *a being known :* hi
propter notitiam sunt intromissi, Nep.
2. Transf. *fame :* Ov., Tac. **B.** Act.
a. *acquaintance with a person :* inter nos,
Ter ; in notitiam populi pervenire, Liv. ;
with *Obj.* Gen. : mulieris, Cic. ; notitiam
feminae habere, Caes. **b.** *a conception,
notion :* notitiam habere dei, Cic. ; natura
ingenuit sine doctrinā notitias parvas
rerum maximarum, Cic. ; praebero, Lucr.

nŏtō, āre [nota], *to mark.* **I.** *to distinguish
by a mark.* **1. Lit.:** tabellam cerā, Cic. ;
ungue genas, Ov. **2.** Transf. **a.** *to indicate, denote :* illa quae temporis naturam
notant, Cic. **b.** *to mark out :* notat et
designat oculis unum quemque nostrum ad
caedem, Cic. **c.** *to mark, note, observe :*
sidera, Cic. ; numerum in cadentibus
guttis, Cic. **II.** *to write.* **a.** In gen. :
litteram, chartam, nomina, Ov. ; hence,
to record (with *Indir. Quest.*) : Nep. **b.**

to write in cipher or in shorthand : note?
non perscripta erat summa, Suet. **III.**
to mark critically : scribit damnatque tabellas et notat et delet, Ov. **IV.** *to mark or
brand* (esp. of the Censors, v. nota). **1.**
Lit. : quos censores furti et captarum pecuniarum nomine notaverunt, Cic. **2.**
Transf. *to brand with infamy, stigmatise :*
aliquem ignominiā, Cic. ; stultus et improbus hic amor est dignusque notari, Hor. ;
ut tribunicia intercessio armis notaretur
atque opprimeretur, Caes.

nŏtus and **nŏtos,** i, m. [νότος], *the south wind.*
1. Lit.: violentus, Verg. ; udus, Hor. :
procellosus. Ov. But albus notus (=Gk.
λευκόνοτος), *fair, bringing fair weather,* Hor.
2. Transf. *wind in gen.:* tendunt vela
noti, Verg.

nŏtus, a, um. **I.** *Part.* nōscō. **II.** Adj.
A. Pass. **a.** *well-known :* res nota et
manifesta omnibus, Cic. *Comp. :* Caes.,
Cic. *Sup. :* Cic. With Causal Gen. :
notus in fratres animi paterni, Hor. As
Noun, **nŏti,** *acquaintances, friends :* Caes.,
Cic., Hor. **b.** *notorious :* Clodia, mulier
non solum nobilis sed etiam nota, Cic. ;
Ov. *Sup. :* Juv. **c.** *familiar, customary :*
nota sedes, Hor. **B.** Act. (as Noun) :
notis praedicas, *to those who know,* Pl.

nŏvācŭla, ae, f. *a sharp knife, a razor :* Cic.,
Liv., Mart. [Sp. *navaja.*]

nŏvālis, e, adj. [novus]. In agriculture. **I.**
that is ploughed afresh or for the first time.
1. Lit.: Varr. As Noun, **nŏvālis,** is, f.
(*sc.* terra), and **nŏvāle,** is, n. (*sc.* solum) :
a field ploughed for the first time : Plin.
2. Transf. **a.** *any cultivated field :* impius haec tam culta novalia miles habebit ?
Verg. **b.** *the crops :* Juv. **II.** As Noun,
fallow-land. **1. Lit.** : Verg. **2.** Transf.
unemployed land, meadow-land : Col.

nŏvātrix, īcis, f. [novō], *she who renews or
changes :* rerum, Ov.

nŏvē, adv. *newly, in a new or unusual manner :*
Pl., Sen. *Sup.* **nŏvissĭmē. a.** Of time :
recently, lately, a short time ago : Sall., Plin.
Ep. **b.** Of succession, *lastly, last of all,
finally :* Liv. ; dicam primum . . . deinde
. . . novissimo, Sen. ; Quint. ; novissime
cum etc. Hirt.

nŏvello, āre [novellus], *to till new fields, to set
out new vines :* Suet.

nŏvellus, a, um [*dim.* novus], *sweet young.* **1.**
Lit.: arbor et novella et vetula, Cic. ;
vites, Verg. ; turba, Tib. **2.** Transf. **a.**
recent, fresh : Cn. et L. Gavilii, novelli
Aquileienses, Liv. **b.** *new, i.e. unfamiliar :*
cum regerem tenerā frena novella manu, Ov.
[It. *novello ;* Fr. *nouveau, nouvelle.*]

nŏvem, *indecl. adj. nine :* Caes., Cic. [It.
nove, Fr. *neuf.*]

November and **Novembris,** is, adj. [novem],
of the ninth month of the old Roman year
(which began with March) : Kalendae,
Nonae Novembres, Cic. As *Masc.* Noun,
the month of November : Mart.

nŏven-decim and **novemdecim,** *indecl. adj.*
[novem decem], *nineteen :* Liv.

nŏvendĭālis (or **novem-**), e-, adj. [novem
diēs], *lasting nine days.* **a.** Esp. of rites
after misfortune or an omen of misfortune :
foriae, Cic. Ep. ; sacrum, sacrificium, Liv.

b. *that takes place on the ninth day ;* of offerings and feats for the dead : cena, Tac. ; pulveres (the ashes of the dead used in magic rites), Hor.

novēnsilēs (dīvī), ium, *m. pl.* [perh. from novus insidcŏ], *new gods* (those received from abroad) : Divi Novensiles, Di Indigetes, in a form of prayer, Liv.

novēni, ae, a [noveni]. **I.** *nine in a group* : ut virgines ter novenae per urbem euntes carmen canerent, Liv. **II.** Poet. *nine :* terga novena boum, Ov. In *sing. :* Stat.

noverca, ae, *f.* [novus], *a step-mother.* **1.** Lit. : Cic. ; iniusta, Verg. ; scelerata, Ov. Prov. : apud novercam queri (i.e. in vain), Pl. **2.** Transf. : rerum ipsa natura in eo non parens sed noverca fuerit, Quint.

novercālis, e, *adj.* [noverca], *of* or *like a step-mother :* odia, Tac. ; Juv.

novicius, a, um [novus]. **I.** *new, new-fangled :* quaestus, Pl. ; vinum, Plin. **II.** Often of slaves : *newly enslaved, raw :* Pl., Ter. As Noun : Cic. **III.** *newly arrived :* iam sedet in ripā taetrumque novicius horret porthmea, Juv.

noviēns (-iēs), *adv. nine times :* Varr., Verg.

novitās, ātis, *f.* [novus], *newness, novelty.* **a.** In gen. : rei, Cic. ; anni, Ov. In *pl. :* novitates non sunt repudiandae (i.e. new friendships), Cic. **b.** Polit. *the condition of a* novus homo, *newness of rank :* novitas mea, Cic. Ep. ; Sall. **c.** *strangeness, rareness :* perturbatis nostris novitate pugnae, Caes. ; rerum, Ov. ; sceleris a*t*que periculi novitas, Sall.

novŏ, āre [novus], *to make new, to renew, reno-vate.* **1.** Lit. : transtra, Verg. ; fessa membra, Ov. ; ardorem, Liv. ; ager novatus (i.e. ploughed again), Cic. **2.** Transf. **a.** *to change, alter :* nomen faciemque, Ov. ; Fortuna fidem novat, Verg. ; ne quid eo spatio novaretur, Sall. Esp. *to alter a constitution, to overthrow a government, make a revolution :* res, Liv. ; Tac. ; ubi primum dubiis rebus novandi spes oblata est, Sall. **b.** *to invent* or *new, devise :* verba, Cic. ; honores, Verg. ; opus, Ov.

novus -s, a, um [cf. Gk. νέϝος]. **A.** Positive. **a.** *new, fresh, recent,* etc. : civitates condere novas, Cic. ; novus veteri exercitus iungitur, Liv. ; miles, Sall. ; luna, Caes. ; dum mane novum, Verg. As Noun, **novum**, i, *n. news, a new thing :* Cic. **b.** *new, novel, strange, unusual, unheard of :* flagitia, Ter. ; ratio belli, Caes. ; crimen, Cic. ; Verg., etc. As Noun, **novum (-om)**, i, *n. a novelty :* Pl., Nep. **c.** *unaccustomed, not used, inexperienced :* equus, Cic. ; rudis ad partūs et nova miles eram, Ov. ; delictis novus, Tac. **d.** *new,* i.e. *a second, a modern :* Decius, Hor. ; Camillus, Liv. Also, *re-newed, revived :* serpens, Ov. ; positis novus exuviis, Verg. **e.** Phr. (mostly in sense of *changed*) : **Tabernae Novae** (opp. T. Veteres), *the new shops in the Forum,* Liv. ; **novae tabulae,** *new account-books* (i.e. the cancelling of debts) : Caes., Cic. ; **novus homŏ,** *a man newly ennobled by election to a* curule office, Cic. ; hic novus Arpinas, Juv. ; **novae rēs,** *political innovations, a revolu-tion :* Dumnorix cupidus rerum novarum, Caes. ; plebes novarum rerum cupida, Sall. ;

Cic. **B.** Superlative, **novissimus**, a, um, *last, latest.* **1.** Lit. **a.** In time : qui ex iis novissimus venit necatur, Caes. ; tempore, Nep. ; dixit novissima verba, Verg. **b.** In place : histriones, Cic. ; cauda (i.e. the end of the tail), Ov. Milit. novissimum ag-men, *the rear,* Caes. As Noun : novissimos adorti, Caes. **2.** Transf. *extreme, severest :* exempla, casus, Tac. *Neut. pl.* as Noun : Tac. [It. *nuovo ;* Sp. *nuevo ;* Fr. *neuf.*]

nox, noctis, *f.* [cf. νύξ], *night, a night.* **1.** Lit. : Enn. ; de nocte, *by night,* Cic. ; multā de nocte profectus est, *late at night,* Cic. Ep. ; nocte, *by night,* Cic. Ep., Liv., Juv. ; ad multam noctem pugnatum est, *till late at night,* Caes. ; Cic. ; sub noctem, *about nightfall,* Caes. ; concubiā nocte, *at dead of night,* Cic. ; mediā nocte, Cic. ; cibus die et nocte concoquatur, *in a day and a night,* Cic. ; noctis et dies urgeri, *night and day,* Cic. (*v.* also noctu). Personified : Cic., Verg., etc. **2.** Transf. **A.** Physical. **a.** *anything which is done at night, night-doings :* omnis et insanā semita nocte sonat, Prop. **b.** *sleep :* pectore noctem accipit, Verg. **c.** *companionship by night :* Pl., Cic. Ep., Ov., etc. **d.** *death :* una manet nox, Hor. ; in aeternam clauduntur lumina noctem, Verg. **e.** *darkness :* imbor noctem hiememque ferens, Verg. ; nim-borum, Lucr. ; quasi noctem rebus of-fundere, Cic. **f.** *blindness :* perpetuā tra-hens inopem sub nocte senectam Phineus, Ov. **B.** Abstract. **a.** *darkness, gloom :* do-leo me in hanc rei publicae noctem incidisse, Cic. ; nox ingens scelerum, Luc. **b.** *mental darkness, ignorance :* quantum mortalia pectora caecae noctis habent, Ov. **c.** *ob-scurity :* mei versūs aliquantum noctis habebunt, Ov. [It. *notte ;* Sp. *noche ;* Fr. *nuit.*]

noxa, ae, *f.* [noceŏ]. **1.** Lit. **a.** *hurt, harm, injury :* tristis noxas a foribus pollero, Ov. ; nihil eam rem noxae futuram, Liv. ; sine ullius noxā urbis, Liv. ; extra noxam conservari, Liv. **b.** *a cause of harm :* prava incepta consultoribus noxae esse, Sall. **c.** *a fault, offence, liability* (to punishment), *responsibility :* hisce (= hi) homines ob eam rem noxam nocuerunt, old form in Liv. ; noxae poenaeque, Liv. ; non noxae eximitur Q. Fabius sed noxae damna-tus, etc., Liv. ; noxā pecuniāque aliquem exsolvere, Liv. ; in eā noxā esse, Liv. ; graviorem noxam fateri, Ov. ; capitalis, Liv. ; ob noxam Aiacis, Verg. ; at quam ob noxam ? Liv. **2.** Transf. *punishment :* merere, Liv. ; nihil praeter tempus noxae lucrari, Liv. ; dedi noxae inimico, Liv.

noxia, ae, *f.* [noxius]. **I.** *wrong-doing, harm :* qui in latrocinio aut aliquā noxiā sint com-prehensi, Caes. ; noxiā carcre, Pl. ; in minimis noxiis, Cic. ; Liv. **II.** *guilt, blame, culpability :* manifesto teneo in noxiā ini-micos meos, Pl. ; in noxiā esse, Pl. ; ami-cum castigare ob meritam noxiam, Pl. ; remittere, Pl. ; metum et noxiam conscien-tiae pro foedere haberi, Tac. Hence, *a cause of blame :* desertori magis quam de-serto noxiae foro, Liv.

noxiōsus, a, um [noxia]. **I.** *hurtful, in-jurious :* res, Sen. **II.** *vicious :* animi, Sen.

noxius, a, um [noxa]. **I.** *hurtful, injurious, noxious* : noxium civem multā coerceto, Old Law in Cic.; aves, Mart.; crimina, Verg. **II.** *guilty, culpable* : Sall., Liv.; cords, Ov. With ABL.: eodem crimine, Liv. With GEN.: coniurationis, Tac. *Masc.* as Noun : Pl.

nūbēcula, ae, f. [*dim.* nūbēs], *a little cloud ; cloudy appearance*. Transf.: frontis tuae nubecula, Cic.

nūbēs, is, f. (**nūbis**, is, m. Pl.) [*cf.* νέφος, nebula], *a cloud.* **1.** Lit.: Cic., Verg., etc. **2.** Transf. **A.** Material: pulveris, Liv.; levium telorum, Liv.; volucrum, Verg.; locustarum, Liv. **B.** Abstract. **a.** *a phantom :* nubes et inania captare, Hor. **b.** *cloudiness, gloom :* deme supercilio nubem, Hor.; pars vitae tristi cetera nube vacet, Ov. **c.** *a veil* or *cloak ; means of concealment :* fraudibus obice nubem, Hor. **d.** *a threatening approach* (of war, etc.): belli, Verg. [Fr. *nue, nuage, nuer, nuance.*]

nūbifer, era, erum [nūbēs ferō], *cloud-bearing.* **a.** *cloud-capped :* Apenninus, Ov. **b.** *cloud-bringing :* Notus, Ov.

nūbigena, ae, m.f. [nūbēs and *gen* in gignō], *cloud-born :* amnes, Stat. *Of the Centaurs* (fabled to have been born of a cloud) : Ov.

nūbilis, e, *adj.* [nūbō], *marriageable :* filia, Cic.; Verg.; anni, Ov.

nūbilus, a, um [nūbēs], *cloudy, lowering.* **1.** Lit.: annus, Tib.; caelum, Plin. As Noun, **nūbilum**, i, n. (*sc.* caelum), *a cloudy sky, cloudy weather :* Plin. Ep., Suet. In *pl.* *the clouds :* Verg., Hor., Plin. Pan., etc. **2.** Transf. **A.** Material. **a.** *cloud-bringing, cloudy :* Auster, Ov. **b.** *dark, overshadowed :* via nubila taxo, Ov. **B.** Abstract. **a.** *beclouded, troubled :* ita nubilam mentem animi habeo, Pl. **b.** *gloomy, sad, melancholy :* toto nubila vultu, Ov.; Quint.; nubila nascenti seu mihi Parca fuit, Ov. [It. *nuvolo, nugolo.*]

nūbō, nūbere, nūpsi (nūpta sum, *Perf. Mid.*), nūptum [*cf.* νύμφη, νέφος, nūbēs], *to cover, veil.* Of women : *to be married to :* virgo nupsit ei, cui Caecilia nupta fuerat, Cic.; Ov., etc.; cum aliquo, Pl.; Cic. Ep.; in familiam clarissimam, Cic. In *Supine :* quo dedisti nuptum, abire nolumus, Pl.; nuptum locare virginem, Ter.; propinquas suas nuptum in alias civitates conlocasse, Caes. *Impers. Pass. :* Pl.

nucens, a, um [nux], *of a nut-tree :* Cato.

nucifrangibulum, i, n. [nux frangō], *a nut-cracker* (comically for *a tooth*) : Pl.

nucleus, i, m. [*dim.* nux]. **I.** *a nut* (i.e. as a fruit): amygdalae, Plin. Prov.: qui e nuce nucleum esse volt, frangit nucem, Pl.; nucleum amisi, retinui pignori putamina, Pl. **II.** *the kernel, the stone* of fruits : nuclei olivarum, Plin. [It. *nocchio.*]

nudius [contr. for nunc dius (diēs)], *it is now the . . . day since :* ego Lemno advenio Athenas nudius tertius (i.e. *the day before yesterday*), Pl.; nudius tertius dedi ad te epistulam longiorem, Cic. Ep.; recordamini, qui dies nudius tertiusdecimus fuerit, Cic.

nūdō, āre [nūdus], *to make naked* or *bare ; to strip, bare.* **1.** Lit.: corpora, Enn.; hominem, Cic.; caput, Verg. **2.** Transf.

A. Materially **a.** *to lay* [*bare, uncover*] : gladios, Liv.; viscera, Verg.; telum vaginā, Nep.; aedis culmen prope omni tecto nudatum, Liv. **b.** Milit. *to expose, leave uncovered* or *undefended :* latera sua, Liv.; murus nudatus defensoribus, Caes.; terga fugā nudant, Verg. **c.** *to strip, spoil :* spoliavit nudavitque omnia, Cic.; agros populando, Liv.; quem praeceps alea nudat, Hor. **B.** Abstractly. **a.** *to lay bare, expose, disclose :* te evolutum illis integumentis dissimulationis tuae nudatumque perspicio, Cic.; defectionem, Liv.; ingenium res adversae nudare solent, Hor. **b.** *to strip away, to divest of :* nudare omnibus rebus tribuniciam potestatem, Caes.

nūdus, a, um, *naked, bare, unclothed.* **1.** Lit.: Cic.; corpus, Caes.; membra, Lucr.; capite nudo, Sall.; nudis pedibus, Hor. Esp. *lightly clad* (i.e. in one's tunic) : nudus ara, sere nudus, Verg.; Cic. Prov.: vestimenta detrahere nudo, Pl. **2.** Transf. **A.** Materially. **a.** *bare, empty, uncovered :* subsellia, Cic.; silex, Verg.; collis, Liv. With GEN.: loca nuda gignentium, Sall. **b.** *unarmed, defenceless :* nudo corpore pugnare, Caes.; nudum et caecum corpus ad hostis vortere, Sall.; Liv. With ABL.: urbs nuda praesidio, Cic. Ep.; Liv. **c.** *stripped, spoiled, deprived,* or *destitute of.* With ABL.: nudus agris, nudus nummis, Hor. With *ab :* Messana ab his rebus sane vacua atque nuda est, Cic. **d.** *poor, needy, destitute, forlorn :* Cic.; senecta, Ov. **B.** Abstractly. **a.** *bare, mere :* nuda ista si ponas, iudicari non possunt, Cic.; nuda ira Caesaris, Ov.; rerum cognitio, Plin. Ep. **b.** *simple, unadorned :* commentarii (Caesaris), Cic.; Ov.; veritas, Hor. [Fr. *nu.*]

nūgae, ārum, f. pl. *idle speeches, trifles, nonsense.* **1.** Lit.: aufer nugas, Pl.; nugas agere, Pl.; and ellipt. without ago : quo illum sequar ? in Persas ? nugas, Pl.; nugis delectari, Cic. Of verse : nescio quid meditans nugarum, Hor. So of the *songs* of hired female mourners at a funeral : haec sunt non nugae : non enim mortualia, Pl. **2.** Transf.: *good-for-nothing fellows :* in comitatu nugarum nihil, Cic.

nūgātor, ōris, m. [nūgor], *a trifler ;* also, *a liar, a humbug :* Pl., Cic., Liv.

nūgātōrius, a, um [nūgātor], *trifling, frivolous, futile :* artes, Pl.; ad probandum res infirma nugatoriaque, Cic.

nūgāx, ācis, *adj.* [nūgor], *trifling, frivolous :* Varr., Cael. ap. Cic. Ep.

nūgigerulus, i, m. [nūgae gerō], *a dealer in women's finery :* Pl.

Nūgiepiloquidēs, is, m. [nūgae ἐπὶ loqui], *son of a nonsense-talker :* Pl.

nūgor, ārī [nūgae]. **I.** *to trifle, play the fool, talk nonsense :* Cic., Hor. **II.** *to trick, cheat :* Pl. With DAT.: Pl.

nūllus, a, um, GEN. nūllīus, DAT. nūllī, but GEN. m. nūllī, for nūllīus, Ter.; (GEN. f. nūllae, for nūllīus, Pl.; DAT. n. nūllō, Caes.) [nē ūllus], *not any, none, no.* **1.** Lit. **a.** nulla aptior persona, Cic.; nullo certo ordine, Caes.; nullis ille movetur fletibus, Verg. With *Partit.* GEN.: elephanto beluarum nulla prudentior, Cic. With *dum* : nulladum via, *no way as yet*, Liv. nullus non, *every* : nulla rerum suarum non relicta inter hostis, Liv. ; non nullus, *v.* nonnullus. **b.** Colloq. *not, not at all* : at tu edepol nullus creduas, Pl. ; Philotimus nullus venit, Cic. As Noun, *no one at all* : Pi. qui scire possum ? *Chry.* nullus plus, Pl. ; talem nulla pareret filium, Ter. ; Liv. For *no-one, none ;* esp. nullius (*m. f.* GEN.) and nullo (*m.* ABL.) for the GEN. and ABL. of nemo ; and the plural in gen. : sunt nulli, Cic. ; ab nullo defensus, Cic. ; nullo poscente, Verg. ; nullius consilio usus, Nep. *Neut.* = *nothing* (rare and not in NOM.) : Graii praeter laudem nullius avari, Hor. (*v.* also nihil.) **2.** T r a n s f. **a.** *non-existent, existing nowhere* or *in no way* : nolite arbitrari, me, cum a vobis discessero, nusquam aut nullum fore, Cic. ; proque viro, qui nullus erat, veniebat ad aras, Ov. **b.** *as good as non-existent, of no account* : ecce me nullum senem, Pl. ; ut sine his studiis vitam nullam esse ducamus, Cic. ; nullus repente fui, Liv. [Fr. *nul.*]

num, *adv.* **I.** Temporal [*cf.* νῦν], *now, v.* etiamnum. **II.** Interrogative. **A.** In *Direct Quest.* : *now, then, really, surely not, actually ?* (expecting the answer ' no '). **a.** num ista est nostra culpa ? Cic. ; Pl. ; num furis an ludis me ? Hor. ; Cic. **b.** Strengthened with -nam or -ne : eho numnam hic relictus custos ? Ter. ; deum ipsum numne vidisti ? Cic. ; Pl. **c.** With *Indef.* quis, quid, quando : num quis hic est ? nemo erat, Ter. ; num quae trepidatio ? num qui tumultus ? Cic. So in the polite form of leave-taking : num quid (aliud) vis ? (i.e. can I do anything (else) for you ?), Pl., Cic., Hor., etc. Also ellipt. num quid me ? Pl. **B.** In *Indir. Quest.* : *whether, if* : quaero num aliter ac nunc eveniunt evenirent, Cic. ; iusserunt speculari, num sollicitati animi sociorum essent, Liv. So also num quid and num quando : scire sane velim, num quid necesse sit comitiis esse Romae, Cic.

Numa, ae, *m.* : Numa Pompilius, *the second king of Rome.*

num-cubi, *interrog. adv.* [num cubi], *at any time ? ever ?* Ter.

numella, ae, *f. a kind of shackle* or *fetter*, for cattle and criminals : Pl.

nūmen, inis, *n.* [nuō], *a nodding with the head, a nod.* **1.** L i t. : Lucr. ; hence of swinging movement : (*cf.* nutus) in quem quaeque locum divorso numine tendunt, Lucr. **2.** T r a n s f. **A.** *a nod* as an indication of will or consent ; hence, **a.** *will, consent :* ad numen mentis movetur, Lucr. **b.** *the divine will, the will, behest,* or *favour of the gods :* deo, cuius numini parent omnia, Cic. ; Nox et Diana, nunc in hostilis domos iram atque numen vertite, Hor. ; ea numina divum, Verg. ; numine fatorum, Verg. ; regnator caelum ac terras qui numine torquet, Verg. **c.** Of human will or power : flectere tempta Caesareum numen numine, Bacche, tuo, Ov. ; adnuite, patres conscripti, nutum numenque Campanis, Liv. **B.** *divine power* or *majesty, divinity* : di immortales suo numine urbis tecta defend

unt, Cic. ; numen Iunonis adora, Verg. ; Liv. ; oft. in *pl.* : Dianae non movenda numina, Hor. ; numina Palladis, Verg. O c c. *a deity* : magna precati numina, Verg. ; numina montis, Ov. ; effigies numinum, Tac.

numĕrābĭlis, e, *adj.* [numerō]. **I.** *that can be counted* : calculus, Ov. **II.** *easily counted* : populus, Hor.

numĕrātĭō, ōnis, *f.* [numerō], *a counting out, paying* : Sen. Ep.

numĕrātus, a, um. **I.** *Part.* numerō. **II.** A d j. : *counted out* ; hence, *in ready money* : dos uxoris, Cic. ; Pl. As Noun, **numĕrātum**, I, *n. ready money* : Cic. Ep., Liv., Hor.

numĕrō, āre [numerus], *to count, reckon, number.* **1.** L i t. **a.** In gen. : si singulos numeremus in singulas (civitates), Cic. ; pecus, Verg. ; numerare per digitos, Ov. ; numera senatum (addressed to the Consul by a senator to see if there was a quorum present) : Cic. Ep. **b.** Of money, *to count out, pay* : pecuniam de suo, Cic. ; Caes. ; alicui pensionem, Liv. **2.** T r a n s f. **a.** *to reckon* as one's own (i.e. *to have, possess*) : donec eris felix multos numerabis amicos, Ov. ; Juv. **b.** *to reckon, consider* : Sulpicium accusatorem suum numerabat non competitorem, Cic. ; Thucydides nunquam est numeratus orator, Cic. ; aliquid in bonis, Cic. ; voluptatem nullo loco, Cic. ; aliquem inter suos, Cic. ; Liv. ; Ov., etc. ; aliquem post aliquem, Tac. **c.** *to enumerate, mention* : dies deficiat si velim numerare quibus bonis male evenerit, Cic. ; amores divum (GEN.), Verg. ; Tac.

numĕrōsē, *adv.* **I.** *numerously, multifariously.* Comp. : Plin. Sup. : Quint. **II.** *rhythmically, melodiously* : fidiculae numerose sonantes, Cic. ; dicere, Cic.

numĕrōsus, a, um [numerus]. **I.** *numerous, manifold* : civitas numerosissima provinciae totius, Tac. ; opus (i.e. of various contents), Quint. **II.** *measured, rhythmical, melodious* : oratio, Cic. ; Horatius, Cic. ; numerosa bracchia ducit, Ov. ; numerosior Asinius, Tac.

numĕrus, I, *m.* [*cf.* νέμω]. Lit. *distribution, apportioning* ; hence, **I.** *a number, tale.* **1.** L i t. **a.** *a fixed* or *required number* : obsides ad numerum (viz. XL) miserunt, Caes. ; si naves suum numerum haberent, Cic. ; numerumque referri iussit, Verg. ; supra numerum, Suet. **b.** *the total number* : haec in Aeduorum finibus recensebantur numerusque inibatur, Caes. ; Liv. ; clavum notam numeri annorum, Liv. ; siderum numerum subducat, Cat. ; Verg. Esp. in ABL. : totidem numero, Caes. ; classis mille numero navium, Cic. **c.** *a number, division, troop* (esp. milit.) : sparsi per provinciam numeri, Tac. ; nondum distributi in numeros erant, Plin. Ep. **d.** *a (great) number, numbers* : est in eādem provincia numerus civium Romanorum, Cic. ; auctoritate et hominum numero valere, Caes. ; illos defendit numerus, Juv. ; Verg. **2.** T r a n s f. **a.** Abstract : *a number, numbers* : duo hi numeri, Cic. ; numero deus impare gaudet, Verg. Hence, *a mere number, cipher* : nos numeri sumus, Hor. ; *the numbers* (i.e. dice) : seu ludet numeros que manu iactabit eburnos, Ov. Also *num-bers in science*, etc. : ut a sacerdotibus barbaris numeros et caelestia acciperet, *arithmetic and astronomy*, Cic. ; numeri Babylonii, *astrological calculations, horoscopes*, Hor. ; in grammar, *number* : Quint. **b.** *a class, category, list* : in eo numero esse, Caes., Cic., Liv. ; in deorum numero haberi, referre, reponere, Cic. ; ducere aliquem in numero hostium, Caes. ; in proscriptorum numerum relatus, Nep. ; carmina digerit in numerum, Verg. ; navita tum stellis numeros et nomina fecit. Verg. **c.** *rank, place, position* : missis legatorum numero centurionibus, Caes. ; parentis numero alicui esse, Cic. ; numero beatorum aliquem eximere, Hor. ; me ascribe in talem numerum, Cic. **d.** *estimation, regard* : in aliquo numero et honore esse, Caes. ; aliquo numero esse, Caes. ; Cic. ; homo nullo numero, Cic. ; numerum aliquem obtinere, Cic. **II.** *a portion, part assigned.* **A.** In gen. **1.** Lit. **a.** *quantity, measure* : magnus numerus frumenti, Cic. ; Caes. ; vini, Cic. (*cf.* **I.** l. d.) **b.** *a part of a whole, a member* : mundus perfectus expletusque omnibus suis numeris atque partibus, Cic. ; elegans omni numero poema, Cic. ; liber numeris omnibus absolutus, Plin. Ep. ; cum desit numeris ipsa iuventus suis, Ov. **2.** Transf. *a portion* (of work), *function, part* : Veneri numeros eripuisse suos, Ov. **B.** In music. **1.** Lit. *a measure, metre* : anapaestus procerior numerus, Cic. ; Pindarus numeris fertur lege solutus, Hor. ; impares (i.e. elegiac verses), Ov. Hence, *a measure, rhythm, time* : in musicis numeri et voces et modi, Cic. ; in numerum exsultant, Lucr. ; ad numerum motis pedibus, Verg. ; extra numerum si histrio paulum se movet, Cic. ; Lucr. ; in solutis etiam verbis inesse numeros, Cic. ; numeros memini, si verba tenerem, Verg. **2.** Transf.: verae numeros modosque ediscere vitae, Hor. ABL. **numerō** as *Adv.* **a.** *at the right time, just now* : numero mihi in mentem fuit, Pl. ; Varr. **b.** *too soon* : numero huc advenis ad prandium, Pl. [It. *numero, novero* ; Fr. *nombre.*]

Numida, ae, *m. a Numidian* ; *pl.* **Numidae,** ārum, *the Numidians, a people of N. Africa* ; **Numidia,** ae, *f. their country* ; **Numidicus,** a, um.

Numitor, ōris, *m. a king of Alba, brother of Amulius, father of Ilia, and grandfather of Romulus and Remus.*

nummārius, a, um [nummus]. *of* or *for money.* **1.** Lit. : theca, Cic. Ep. ; difficultas, lex, Cic. **2.** Transf. *mercenary, venal* : iudices, Cic.

nummātus, a, um [nummus], *moneyed* : homo bene nummatus, Cic., Hor.

Nummōsexpalpōnides, ae, *m.* [nummus expalpor], *son of a cash-wheedler* : Pl.

nummulārius, i, *m.* [nummulus], *a money-changer* : Mart., Suet.

nummulī, ōrum, *m. pl.* [*dim.* nummus], *petty cash, paltry cash* : Cic. Ep.

nummus, i, *m.* (GEN. *pl.* us. nummum) [perh. *cf.* νόμισμα], *currency.* **A.** In gen. *a piece of money, a coin* ; *money, cash* : Pl., Cic., Liv., etc. ; habere in nummis (*in ready*

money); Cic. ; [...] modo in aere alieno [...] sed in suis nummis multis esse, Cic. **B.** In partic. **a.** *the sesterce*, a small silver coin (called also nummus sestertius, Cic., Liv., or sestertius), in value about *twopence* : Pl., Cic., Hor., etc. Transf. any *small sum, a trifle, low price* : ad nummum convenit, Cic. Ep. ; sestertio addici alicui, Cic. ; Pl. **b.** As a Greek coin, *a di-drachma* (= two drachmas) : Pl.

num-nam and **num-ne,** *v.* num.

numquam, *v.* nunquam.

Numquamposteāēripides, ae, *m.* [numquam posteā ēripiō], *Son of Nevergetagain* : Pl.

num quandō, num quis, quid, *v.* num.

nunc (old form **nunce** seen in nunci-ne, Ter.). *adv.* [*cf.* νῦν], *now, at the present time.* **1.** Lit. **A.** In gen. **a.** Marcellus nunc aedilis curulis est, Cic. ; Pl. **b.** In contrast with past time : erat tunc excusatio oppressis, nunc nulla est, Cic. ; Pl. ; Verg. Occ. *in these days, to-day, nowadays* : haec studia tum vehementius colebantur quam nunc, Cic. **c.** In contrast with future time : deos nunc testis esse, mox fore ultores, Liv. ; Cic. ; Verg. **B.** Strengthened by demum, denique, primum, tandem : nunc demum intellego, Pl. ; nunc primum hoc aures tuae crimen accipiunt ? Cic. **C.** Phr. : ut nunc est (*as things now are*), Cic. Ep., Hor. ; iudiciis qui nunc sunt hominum (*of modern men*), Cic. Ep. ; Pl. ; nunc ipsum (*at this very moment*), Cic. Ep. **2.** Transf. **A.** Of past or future time imagined as present. **a.** Of past time : *now, at the time we are speaking of* : incerto nunc exitu victoriae signa intulerunt, Caes. ; Pl. ; Cic. ; Hor., etc. So occ. in *Orat. Obliq.* : dixit nunc demum se voti esse damnatum, Nep. ; Liv. ; Tac. **b.** Of future time : *from now on, henceforth* : quem nunc amabas ? Cat. **B.** Of the state of affairs. **a.** *now, in these circumstances, in view of this* : vera igitur illa sunt nunc omnia, Cic. ; Hor. ; Ov., etc. **b.** *but now, but as matters now stand, but as it is* : si haec non ad homines verum ad bestias conqueri vellem, . . . commoverentur ; nunc vero cum loquar ad senatores, etc., Cic. So occ. in *Orat. Obliq.* : Liv. **C.** nunc . . . nunc, *now* . . . *now, at one time* . . . *at another time* : tribuni plebis nunc fraudem, nunc neglegentiam consulum accusabant, Liv. ; Verg. ; nunc . . . modo, Liv., Ov. ; nunc . . . postremo, Liv.

nunci-ne, *v.* nunc.

nunc-iam, *v.* iam.

nun-cubi, *v.* numcubi.

nuncupātiō, ōnis, *f.* [nuncupō]. **I.** *a solemn and public pronouncing* (of vows) : votorum nuncupationes, Tac. **II.** *a naming* or *appointing as heir* : Suet. **III.** *the dedication of a book* : Plin.

nuncupō, āre [nōmen capiō]. **I.** *to announce* or *proclaim publicly* or *formally.* **a.** In gen.: cum ex *XII* tabulis satis esset ea praestari (vitia) quae essent linguā nuncupata, Cic. **b.** Of vows made by chief State officials : cum consul more maiorum secundum vota in Capitolio nuncupata, profectus ab urbe esset, Liv. Cic. With Acc. and Fut. *Inf.* : Liv. **c.** Of adoption : adoptionem, Tac. **d.** Of wills (announced before witnesses) : magnā **ex parte herodem** Caesarem, Tac. ; testamentum, Plin. Ep. **II.** *to call by name, to name :* illud quod erat a deo donatum nomine ipsius dei nuncupabant, Cic. ; eum Indigetem, Ov.

nŭndĭnae, ārum, *f. pl.* (*sc.* feriae) [novem diēs], *the ninth day,* i.e. *the market-day.* **1.** Lit.: Varr., Cic. Ep. **2.** Transf. **a.** *a market-place* or *town :* Cic., Liv. **b.** *trade, traffic :* totius rei publicae nundinae, Cic. ; vestigalium, Cic.

nŭndĭnālis, e, *adj.* [nŭndinae], *of the* nundinae *or markets :* coquos, Pl.

nŭndĭnātĭō, ōnis, *f.* [nŭndinor] (*corrupt*) *trading, trafficking :* Cic. ; iuris et fortunarum, Cic.

nŭndĭnor, ārī [nŭndinae], *to attend* or *hold a market ;* *to trade, traffic.* **1.** Lit.: in captivorum pretiis praedāque aliā, Liv. **2.** Transf. **a.** *to meet in large numbers :* in Solonio, ubi ad focum angues nundinari solent, Cic. **b.** *to get by trafficking ;* *to purchase, buy :* senatorium nomen, Cic. **c.** *to trade corruptly :* in cognitionibus patriis, Suet.

nŭndĭnum, ī, *n.* [novem diēs : cf. nŭndinae], *the market-time :* inter nundinum, *the time between two* nundinae : Lucil., Varr. ; trinum nundinum, *the time of three* nundinae, or at least 17 days : Cic. ; postquam comitia decemviris creandis in trinum nundinum indicta sunt, Liv.

nunquam (numquam), *adv.* [nē unquam], *at no time, never.* **a.** In gen.: Pl., Caes., Cic., etc. **b.** In prohibitions with *Subj.* : Pl. **c.** With a follg. negative : nunquam non ineptum (*always*), Cic. ; nunquam nisi honorificentissime, Cic. Ep. **d.** For an emphatic negative, *certainly not,* esp. with hodie : Pl. ; nunquam hodie effugies ! Verg.

nūntĭātĭō, ōnis, *f.* [nūntiō], (the augur's) *right of announcing :* Cic.

nūntĭō, āre [nūntius], *to announce, report.* **a.** In gen.: nuntium exoptabilem, Pl. ; vera, Cic. ; victoriam, Liv. ; horas, Mart. With Acc. and *Inf.* : Caes., Liv., etc. ; with litteras as Subject : Cic. Ep., Plin. Ep. *Pass.* : hoc adeo celeriter fecit, ut simul adesse et venire nuntiaretur, Caes., Liv. *Pass. Impers.,* with *de* and *Abl.* : Cic. ; with Acc. and *Inf.* : Caes., Cic., Liv. With Acc. of goal : Ameriam, Cic. ; domum, Romam, Liv. ; in Asiam, Cic. **b.** With *ut* or *ne* and *Subj.* : *to intimate authoritatively :* ne eum Lentulus aliique terrerent, Sall. ; Cic. ; Liv. ; Tac. With *Inf.* in this sense : nuntiat patri abicere spem, Tac.

nūntĭus, a, um [perh. from novus, veniō ; lit. *newly come* or *arrived*], *announcing, reporting :* nuntia littera venit, Ov. ; nuntia fibra deos, Tib. With Gen.: simulacra divinae nuntia formae, Lucr. ; habes animi nuntia verba mei, Ov. As Noun, **nūntĭus,** ī, *m.* (and **nūntĭa,** ae, *f.*) **a.** *a bearer of intelligence, news,* or *orders ; a messenger, courier :* Mercurius Iovis nuntius, Pl. ; litteras et nuntios mittere, Caes. ; nuntius expugnati oppidi, Caes. ; Cic. ; nuntius ibis Pelidae, Verg. ; nuntius adfert rem, Cic. ; historia nuntia vetustatis, Cic. **b.**

a message, news, tidings. **i.** In gen.: nuntium exoptabilem nuntiare, Pl. ; acerbum nuntium alicui perferre, Cic. ; alicui adferre, Cic. ; ferre ad aliquem, Liv. ; Cat. ; Verg. **ii.** *an authoritative notice ; an order, injunction :* quos senatus ad denuntiandum bellum miserat, nisi legatorum nuntio paruisset, Cic. ; nuntium uxori remittere or mittere (*a letter of divorce*), Cic. So of the rejection of the marriage contract by parents or guardians : Pl. **nūntĭum,** ī, *n. a message :* Varr. ; in *pl.* : ad auris nova nuntia referens, Cat.

nūper, *adv.* [noviper, from novus], *newly, lately, recently, not long ago.* **1.** Lit.: Ter., Cic., Hor. ; nunc nuper, *just now,* Pl., Ter. *Sup. :* nūperrimō, Cic. **2.** In wider sense : *in modern times :* neque ante philosophiam patefactam, quae nuper inventa est, Cic. ; Liv.

nūperus, a, um [nūper], *recent :* recens captum hominem nuperum et novicium te perdocere, Pl.

nūpta, ae, *f.* **I.** *Part.* nūbō. **II.** Adj. *married :* filia, Cic. **III.** Noun, *a bride :* Ter., Liv., Ov., etc. Comic. in *masc. :* novus nuptus, Pl.

nūptĭae, ārum, *f. pl.* [nūbō], *a marriage, wedding :* nuptias facere, adornare, Pl. ; alicui conficere, Ter. ; conciliare, Nep. ; in nuptias aliquem conicere, Ter. ; in nuptiis aliouius cenare, Cic. Ep. ; multarum nuptiarum (mulier), Cic. Ep. ; nuptiarum expers, Hor. [It. *nozze* / Fr. *noces*.]

nūptĭālis, e, *adj.* [nūptiae], *of marriage, nuptial :* ludi, Pl. ; dona, Cic. ; carmina, Cat. ; faces, Cic., Hor. ; pactio, Liv.

nūptus, *v.* nūpta.

nŭrus, ūs, *f.* [*cf.* νυός], *a daughter-in-law.* **1.** Lit.: Ter., Cic., Verg., etc. **2.** Transf. *a young woman, married woman :* Ov., Luc., Mart. [It. *nuora* / Sp. *nuera*.]

nūsquam, *adv.* [nē ūsquam], *nowhere, in no place.* **1.** Lit.: Pl., Cic., Verg., etc. With Gen.: nusquam gentium, *nowhere in the world,* Pl., Ter., Liv. **2.** Transf. **a.** *towards no place :* nusquam moturos, Liv. ; Pl. In a prohibition : nusquam te vestigio moveris, Liv. **b.** *on no occasion, in nothing :* praestabo sumptum nusquam melius poni posse, Cic. ; nusquam abero, Verg. ; nusquam minus quam in bello, Liv. **c.** *to* or *for nothing :* plebem nusquam alio natam, quam ad serviendum, Liv. **d.** nusquam esse, *not to exist :* Pl., Cic., Hor.

nūtō, āre [*freq. of* nuō seen in abnuō]. **1.** Lit. **a.** *to nod repeatedly :* neque illa ulli homini nutet, Pl. ; nutans, distorquens oculos, Hor. ; capite, Pl. ; capitis motu, Suet. (Ov. *to bid by a nod* (with *ne* and *Juss. Subj.*) : Pl. **b.** *to sway to and fro :* nutant circumspectantibus galeae, Liv. ; ornus, Verg. ; rami pondere, Ov. ; sedes terrae motu, Tac. **2.** Transf. *to totter, waver, falter.* **a.** In opinion : Democritus in naturā deorum, Cic. ; animus, Ov. **b.** In loyalty : Tac., Suet. **c.** In security or steadiness : tanto discrimine urbs, Tac. ; res publica, Suet. ; acies hostis, Tac. ; nutante mundi ruinā, Luc.

nūtrĭcātĭō, ōnis, *f.* [nūtrĭcō], *a nursing.* Transf. *rearing :* herbarum, Varr.

nūtrĭcātus, ūs, m. [nūtrĭcō], *a suckling, nursing*. **1.** Lit.: Pl., Varr. **2.** Transf. *rearing :* herbae, Varr.

nūtrĭcius, a, um [nūtrīx], *that suckles, nourishes ; nursing :* Varr. As Noun, **nūtrĭcius**, ī, m. *a bringer up, a tutor :* Caes.

nūtrĭcō, āre, and **nūtrĭcor**, ārī (Cic.) [nūtrīx], *to suckle, nourish, bring up, rear*. **1.** Lit.: pueros, Pl. ; porcos, Varr. **2.** Transf.: mundus omnia, sicut membra et partis suas, nutricatur, Cic. ; Pl.

nūtrĭcula, ae, f. [*dim.* nūtrīx], *a fond nurse.* **1.** Lit.: Hor., Quint., Suet. **2.** Transf.: nutriculae praediorum, Cic. ; causidicorum Africa, Juv.

nūtrīmen, inis, n. [nūtriō], *nourishment :* naturae, Ov. [Fr. *nourrain*.]

nūtrīmentum, ī, n. [nūtriō], *nourishment, nutriment* (esp. *in pl.*). **1.** Lit. **a.** In gen.: Suet. **b.** *rearing :* nutrimentorum eius locus ostenditur, Suet. **2.** Transf. **a.** Physically: suscepitque ignem foliis atque arida circum nutrimenta dedit, Verg. **b.** educata huius nutrimentis eloquentia, Cic.

nūtriō, īre (nūtrībam for nūtriēbam, Verg.) and **nūtrior**, īrī (Verg.), *to suckle, nourish, feed, foster, bring up, rear.* **1.** Lit.: quos lupa nutrit, Ov. ; nutritus lacte ferino, Ov. ; ilignā nutritus glande, Hor. **2.** Transf. **A.** Physically. **a.** Of plants : myrtos roscido umore, Cat. ; terra herbas nutrit, Ov. ; fruges humo nutriente, Curt. **b.** Of fire : ignis foliis et cortice sicco nutrit, Ov. **c.** Of the body, *to nurse, tend :* corpora, Liv. **B.** Mentally and morally: mens rite nutrita, Hor. ; amorem, Ov. ; damnum naturae (i.e. so as to cure it), Liv. ; simultates, Tac. ; marcentem pacem, Tac. [Fr. *nourrir*.]

nūtrītor, ōris, m. [nūtriō], *a bringer up, rearer, breeder :* Stat., Suet.

nūtrīx (older nōtrīx, acc. to Quint.), īcis, f. [nūtriō], *one who suckles: a wet-nurse, nurse.* **1.** Lit. (of persons and animals) : Pl., Cic., Verg., etc. **2.** Transf. **a.** In *pl.* the *breasts :* Cat. **b.** (agrum) nostram nutricem quae nos educat, Pl. ; Sicilia nutrix plebis Romanae, Cic. ; (Libya) leonum arida nutrix, Hor. **c.** For plants : *a nursery-bed :* Plin. **d.** est enim illa oratio quasi nutrix oratoris, Cic. [Fr. *nourrice*.]

nūtus, ūs, m. [nuō in abnuō], *a nodding, a nod.* **1.** Lit. **a.** In gen.: Verg., Ov. **b.** As an indication of will, consent, or command : monuit ad nutum omnes res ab iis administrarentur, Caes. ; Scipio nutu finire disceptationem potuisset, Liv. ; signaque dat nutu, Ov. **2.** Transf. **a.** *will, command, pleasure :* ad eorum arbitrium et nutum totos se fingunt, Cic. ; saevae nutu Iunonis eunt res, Verg. ; omnia deorum nutu atque potestate administrari, Cic. ; alterius sub nutu degitur aetas, Lucr. **b.** *a downward tendency or motion, gravity :* terrena suopte nutu et suo pondere in terram ferri, Cic. ; terra suā vi nutuque tenetur, Cic. ; in *pl.* : Cic.

nux, nucis, f. **a** *nut.* **1.** Lit.: Pl. ; nux iuglans, *a walnut*, Plin. ; sparge, marite, nuces (a custom at weddings), Verg. ; nux cassa (i.e. a thing of no value), Hor. Prov. :

nuces relinquere (i.e. to put away childish things), Pers. **2.** Transf. **a.** *any fruit with a hard shell or rind :* castaneae nuces, chestnuts, Verg. **b.** the tree itself ; e.g. *an almond-tree:* Verg. [It. *noce* ; Fr. *noix*.]

Nyctelius, a, um, *belonging to Bacchus, Bacchic* (Lit. *nocturnal ;* because *the mysteries of Bacchus were celebrated by night*).

Nycteus (disyl.), eī and eos, m. *father of Antiope :* **Nyctēis**, idis, f. *Antiope.*

Nyctimenē, ēs, f. *the daughter of Epopeus, king of Lesbos, changed by Minerva into a night-owl.*

nympha, ae, and **nymphē**, ēs, f. [νύμφη]. **1.** Lit. **a.** *a bride, a mistress :* Ov. **b.** Nymphae, *the spirits of fountains, rivers, the sea, woods, trees, and mountains ; nymphs:* Cic., Verg. ; vocalis Nymphe, i.e. *Echo*, Ov. **2.** Transf. *water* (*cf.* lympha): Prop. [It. and Sp. *ninfa*.]

Nysa (**Nyssa**), ae, f. *a city* (locality unknown), *where Bacchus was brought up :* **Nysaeus**, a, um ; **Nysēis**, idis, f. *adj.* ; **Nyseus** (disyl.), eī, m. *Bacchus :* **Nysias**, adis, f. *adj.* **Nysigena**, ae, m. *born at Nysa :* epith. of Bacchus ; and **Nysius**, a, um.

O

O, o, the *fourteenth* letter of the Latin alphabet. **I.** Relations of *o* with the other vowels. **a.** For those with *a, e,* and *i,* see those letters. **b.** With *u.* These two vowels are the most nearly allied, and their interchanges are very numerous. The oldest monuments of the Latin tongue frequently exhibit *o* where the classic language has *u.* So on the Column. rostr., exfociont, consol, primos (NOM. *sing.*), captom. And, on the contrary, *u* in the old forms, fruns, funtes, for the later frons, fontes. *o* and *u* both appear in connexion with consonantal *u :* e.g. avos and avus, servos and servus, though in these combinations *o* was preferred. **c.** *ŏ* is substituted for *au* (in popular pronunciation) in Clōdius, plōdo, plēstrum, sōdes, etc. **II.** Changes of *o* in the Romance languages : *ŏ* in Italian sometimes becomes *u, uo* ; e.g. Lat. *totus,* It. *tutto ;* in French it is most commonly changed to *ou, eu,* and *oeu :* e.g. Lat. *totus,* Fr. *tout ;* Lat. *hora,* Fr. *heure ;* Lat. *nodus,* Fr. *noeud.* Before *m* and *n* it sometimes remains unchanged, as Lat. *non,* Fr. *non ;* Lat. *pomum,* Fr. *pomme. ŏ* is generally changed, in It. into *uo ;* e.g. Lat. *bonus,* It. *buono ;* in Fr. into *eu* (*oeu*): Lat. *populus,* Fr. *peuple ;* Lat. *cor,* Fr. *coeur.* Before *l, m,* or *n,* it sometimes remains unchanged, as Lat. *schola,* Fr. *école ;* Lat. *homo,* Fr. *homme ;* Lat. *bonus,* Fr. *bon. ŏ* before a double consonant is sometimes changed in It. into *u ;* e.g. Lat. *ostium,* It. *uscio ;* in Fr. it almost always remains unchanged, as Lat. *fortis,* Fr. *fort ;* very rarely it becomes *ou* or *ui :* e.g. Lat. *cohors,* Fr. *cour ;* Lat. *post,* Fr. *puis.* **III.** As an abbreviation, O stands for omnis and optimus : I. O. M. Iovi Optimo Maximo.

ŏ, *interj.* expressing joy, astonishment, desire, grief, indignation, etc. ; *o! oh!* **a.** With Voc. in addressing a person : o mi Furni ! Cic. Ep. ; Enn. ; Verg. **b.** With Acc. or Nom. in exclaiming against or about something : o praeclarum custodem ovium, ut aiunt, lupum ! Cic. ; Ter. ; Lucr., etc. ; o vir fortis atque amicus ! Ter. ; Hor. ; Ov. **c.** to express a wish ; *O that !* with *utinam* : o utinam obrutus esset ! Ov. With *si* : quamquam, o, si solitae quicquam virtutis adesset ! Verg. **d.** With Gen. o nuntii beati, Cat. **e.** After a word : o lux Dardaniae, spes o fidissima Teucrum, Verg. It is us. long before another vowel : o ego laevus, Hor. ; though sometimes short : te Corydon, o Alexi ; trahit sua quemque voluptas, Verg.

Oariōn, ōnis, *m.* a poet. form for Orion, in Cat.

Oaxēs or **Oaxis**, is, *m. a river in Crete :* Verg.

ob (older **op-**), *adv.* and *prep.* [*cf.* ὀπι- ὀπίσσω ; akin to ἐπί]. **I.** Adv. (only in compounds). **A.** Form. **a.** Before vowels, ob remains unchanged, e.g. obambulo. **b.** Before *c, f, g, p,* the *b* is assimilated, e.g. occido, offero, oggero, oppeto. **c.** Before other consonants, ob remains unchanged except that **i.** the *b* is lost in omitto (*cf.* also operio). **ii.** ob was often pronounced and written op before *t* and *s*. **iii.** ob appears as os (for obs) in ostendo. **B.** Meaning. **a.** Of movement *towards* a meeting : obeo, occurro. **b.** Of pressure on a surface : offigo. **c.** Of covering a surface : obtego ; hence, **i.** of protecting : obduco, obtego, oppidum. **ii.** of overwhelming : opprimo. **d.** Of counterbalancing : oppignero, oppono. **e.** Where the new confronting occurrence or state affects the person implied or denoted by the Dative. **i.** In gen. : obsto, obicio, occino. **ii.** Where the person affected is an enemy and the direct object is protected from him : obtego, occulo. **iii.** Of a (pleasant) surprise : obvenio, offero, occasio. **f.** Where the new circumstance is directly or unexpectedly inflicted on a person denoted by the Accusative : occido, opprimo, obtestor ; of a pleasant effect : oblecto. **g.** Where the person affected by the new (unexpected) circumstance is the Subject of a (usually intransitive) verb : obstupesco, occido, obverto, omitto. **II.** Prep. with Acc. **a.** *in front of :* ob oculos, Pl., Cic., Liv. ; ob os, Cic. ; ob gulam, Pl. ; ob-viam (i.e. in face of the road one is taking, i.e. coming from the opposite direction so as to meet), Pl., Cic., etc. ; ob-iter, *by the way,* Sen., Juv. Also *towards :* ob Romam legiones ducere, Enn. **b.** *set against, balanced against, in return for :* ob asinos ferre argentum, Pl. ; Ter. ; pecuniam ob abolvendum accipere, Cic. ; pecuniam ob delicta dare, Tac. **c.** *to meet* a situation : ob rem (i.e. to the purpose, with advantage), Pl., Ter. ; aliquid ob rem facere, Sall. **d.** Hence, *on account of, à propos of, because of :* ob eam rem, Pl., Ter., Cic., etc. ; ob eam causam, Cic. ; ob eas causas, Caes. ; ob hanc causam, Cic. ; ob has causas, Caes. ; quam ob causam, Caes., Cic. ; quam ob rem, Cic. ; ob hoc, Cic., Liv. ; ob id, Cic.,

Liv., Tac. ; ob ea, Cic., Sall. ; ob haec, Liv. ; ob quae, Liv., Tac. ; ob stultitiam, Pl. ; ob illam iniuriam, Cic. ; ob iram, Verg., Liv. ; ob res gestas, Cic. ; ob rem iudicandum pecuniam accipere, Cic. ; ob consulatum obtinendum, Cic. ; ob industriam, *purposely,* Pl. **e.** Hence, *in the interest of, for the sake of :* mortem ob rem publicam obiisse, Tac.

ob-aerātus, a, um [ob aes], *overwhelmed by debt, in bondage on account of debt :* Suet. *Comp. :* Tac. As Noun, esp. in *pl., a debtor :* Caes., Cic., Liv., Tac.

ob-ambulō, āre, *to walk before* or *near, prowl about near :* Ov., Suet. With Dat. : muris, Liv. ; lupus gregibus, Verg. With Acc., *all over :* urbem, Pl. ; Cyclops Aetnam, Ov. With *prep. :* ante vallum, Liv. ; in herbis, Ov.

ob-armō, āre, *to arm against* someone : securi dextras, Hor.

ob-arō, āre, *to plough over* or *up :* Liv.

obba, ae, *f. a broad-bottomed cup, a noggin :* Varr.

ob-brūtēscō, ere, *to become dull* or *stupid* against ideas : anima, Lucr.

obc-, *v.* occ-.

ob-dō, dere, didi, ditum, *to put, place before* or *against.* **1.** Lit. : pessulum ostio, Ter. Hence *to close :* forem, Pl. ; foris, Ter., Ov., Tac. **2.** Transf. : rigidam vocibus obdere forem, Ov. Also *to expose :* hic nulli malo latus obdit apertum, Hor.

obdormiscō, dormiscere, dormivi [dormiō], *to fall fast asleep :* Pl., Cic., Suet.

ob-dūcō, dūcere, dūxi, ductum. **I.** With Acc. of thing placed : *to draw* or *place* something *as a protection* or *obstacle* (with or without Dat. of thing protected or obstructed). **1.** Lit. : vestem, Tac. ; ab utroque latere collis transversam fossam obduxit, Caes. ; seram, Prop. **2.** Transf. : obsidionem, Enn. ; ipse labor quasi callum quoddam obducit dolori, Cic. ; refricare obductum iam rei publicae cicatricem, Cic. ; obductā nocte, Nep. ; clarissimis rebus tenebras, Cic. **II.** With Acc. of person or thing brought : *to bring up against* or *in rivalry* (with Dat. or *ad* and Acc. of person affected) : eum putat uxor sibi obduxe scortum, Pl. ; ad vetus oppidum (i.e. senem) meum exeroitum, Pl. ; Curium competitorem, Cic. Ep. **III.** With Acc. of thing covered (with or without *Instr.* Abl. of the covering), *to cover* and so *hide* something by drawing another thing over it. **1.** Lit. : corpus operimento matris (i.e. terrae), Cic. ; vultūs, Ov. ; limosoque palus obducat pascua iunco, Verg. **2.** Transf. **a.** obductus dolor, Verg. ; Ov. ; obductā solvatur fronte senectus (*with clouded brow*), Hor. **b.** *to swallow :* venenum, Cic. ; potionem, Sen. **c.** Of time : *to cover, pass :* itaque obduxi posterum diem, Cic. Ep.

obductiō, ōnis, *f.* [obdūcō], *a veiling* of criminals before their execution : capitis, Cic.

obductō, āre [*freq.* obdūcō], *to bring as a rival :* Pl.

obductus, a, um, *Part.* obdūcō.

ob-dūrēscō, *to grow hard, to harden.* **1.** Lit. : Cato ; Gorgonis vultu, Prop. **2.** Transf. :

exspectando, Pl. ; consuetudine, Cic. ; contra fortunam, Cic. ; usu civitatis patientia, Cic. ; animus ad dolorem, Cic. Ep.

ob-dūrō, āre, *to be hard against.* T r a n s f. *to be firm against, to persist :* Pl., Cat., Hor. Impers. Pass. : Cic. Ep.

obeliscus, ī, m. [ὀβελίσκος, a small spit], *an obelisk :* Plin.

ob-eō, īre, iī (or īvī), itum. **A.** I n t r a n s. *to go towards, go to meet :* in infera loca, Cic. poet. ; ad omnis hostium conatūs, Liv. ; donec vis obiit, Lucr. **B.** T r a n s. **1.** L i t. *to go to visit, travel to or over :* tantas regiones peditus, Cic. ; villas, Cic. Ep. ; tantum telluris, Verg. ; nundinas, Liv. ; vigilias, Tac. **2.** T r a n s f. **a.** *to travel over, run over* with the eyes or in speaking : omnia visu, Verg. ; oculis exercitum, Plin. Ep. ; orationo omnis civitates, Cic. **b.** *to compass, encircle :* maria terras, Verg. ; equum leonis pellis, Verg. ; chlamydem limbus, Ov. **c.** Of duties, undertakings, business, etc. : *to enter upon, engage in, discharge :* negotium, hereditates, facinus, Cic. ; consularia munera, Liv. ; bella, sacra, Liv. ; pugnas, Verg. **d.** In law : *to meet :* vadimonium, diem (i.e. *to surrender to* one's bail), Cic. **e.** With diem or mortem, *to meet one's day, meet one's death :* diem suom, Pl. ; diem supremum, Nep. ; diem, Suet. ; mortem, Pl., Cic., Verg., Liv. ; in Pass. : morte obitā, Cic. Hence, perh. by ellipse of mortem (though *cf.* occidō) : malo cruciatu obire, Pl. ; tecum obeam libens, Hor. ; Liv. ; morbo, Tac. ; so too, voluntariā morte, Suet. Occ. of the heavenly bodies, *to set :* Lucr., Cic.

ob-equitō, āre, *to ride towards, ride up to :* with DAT. : castris, Liv. ; Curt.

ob-errō, āre, *to ramble about.* **1.** L i t. : tentoriis, Tac. ; crebris oberrantibus rivis, Curt. **2.** T r a n s f. **a.** periculi imago oculis, Curt. **b.** *to blunder at :* ut citharoedus ridetur, chordā qui semper oberrat eādem, Hor.

obēsitās, ātis, f. [obēsus], *fatness, corpulence :* Suet.

obēsus, a, um [edō], *fattened by eating ; fat, stout, plump.* **1.** L i t. : Verg., Hor. ; fauces (i.e. *swollen*), Verg. Sup. : Plin., Suet. **2.** T r a n s f. : *gross, coarse :* naris obesae (i.e. not nice or delicate), Hor.

obex, obicis, m. and f. [obiciō]. **1.** L i t. **a.** *a bar, bolt :* Verg., Liv., Tac., etc. **b.** *a barrier, barricade :* viarum, Liv. ; portarum, Tac. Of rocks on the sea-shore : Verg. **2.** T r a n s f. : nullae obices, nulli contumeliarum gradūs, Plin. Pan.

obf-, *v.* off-.

obg-, *v.* ogg-.

ob-haereō, ēre, *to stick fast ;* with DAT. : navis obhaerens vado, Suet.

ob-haerēscō, haerēscere, haesī, *to become fixed to ;* in Perf. tenses, *to stick or adhere to :* in medio flumine equus, Lucr. ; consurgenti ei lacinia obhaesit, Suet.

ob-iaceō, ēre, *to lie before or over against :* with DAT. : saxa pedibus, Liv. Absol. : obiacente sarcinarum cumulo, Liv. ; a meridie Aegyptus, Tac.

ob-iciō (poet. **obiciō**; older **obiciō**), icere, iēcī, iectum (Perf. Subj. obiexim, Pl.) [ob iaciō]. **I.** *to throw* or *fling something towards* or *before* a person or thing. **1.** L i t. : argentum, Ter. ; florem veteris vini naribus, Pl. ; tale visum obiectum est a deo dormienti, Cic. ; offam Cerbero, Verg. ; monstrum oculis, Verg. **2.** T r a n s f. : quoi homini di sunt propitii, lucrum ei obiciunt, Pl. ; moram alicui, Pl. ; alicui eam mentem ut patriam prodat, Liv. ; religione obiectā, Caes. ; obicitur animo metus, Cic. ; furorem alicui (i.e. *to inspire*), Cic. ; terrorem hosti, Liv. ; rabiem canibus, Verg. **II.** *to cast in the way, fling or set against* in opposition or as protection. **1.** L i t. : carros pro vallo, Caes. ; ericium portis, Caes. ; portas (i.e. *to bar*), Verg. ; foris, Liv. ; scutum, Liv. ; hastis prae se obiectis, Liv. ; clipeos ad tela, Verg. ; tela, Cic. ; so telis hostium, Cic. ; sese ad currum Turni, Verg. **2.** T r a n s f. **a.** In gen. : silvae obiectae, Caes. ; Alpium vallum contra ascensum transgressionemque Gallorum, Cic. ; glaucumam ob oculos (i.e. *dust* in his eyes), Pl. ; noctem peccatis, Hor. ; nubem oculis, Ov. **b.** Of abuse, reproaches, etc. : *to fling at, cast in one's teeth :* alicui facinora, Pl. ; alicui multa probra, Cic. ; ignobilitatem alicui, Cic. ; ista viris, Verg. ; crimen, Tac. ; interfectos amicos, Tac. ; de Cispio mihi, Cic. ; tibi quod Apollonium spoliasti, Cic. ; mihi (with Acc. and Inf.), Cic. Ep. **III.** *to throw, fling, expose* a person or thing *to* something. **1.** L i t. : corpus feris, Cic. ; exercitum tantae magnitudinis flumini, Caes. ; huic sicae vos, Cic. ; vivos homines laniandos, Suet. **2.** T r a n s f. : consulem morti, Cic. ; obicitur consulatus contionibus seditiosorum . . . ad omne donique periculum, Cic. ; me in tantas dimicationes, Cic. ; se adversus tribuniciam potestatem, Liv.

obiectāculum, ī, n. [obiectō], *a barrier, dam :* Varr.

obiectātiō, ōnis, f. [obiectō], *a hurling of reproaches :* ex aliorum obiectationibus, Caes.

obiectō, āre [freq. obiciō], *to throw repeatedly towards or against.* **1.** L i t. : (pelagi volucres) nunc caput obiectare fretis, nunc currere in undas, Verg. **2.** T r a n s f. **a.** *to expose, abandon :* eum periculis, Sall. ; animam pro aliquo, Verg. ; caput periclis, Verg. ; aliquem dolo, Tac. **b.** *to throw out a hint* to someone (with Acc. and Inf.) : Pl. **c.** Of abuse, reproaches, etc. : *to fling at, cast in one's teeth :* alicui inopiam, Pl. ; famem nostris, Caes. ; probrum alicui, Cic. ; vecordiam, Sall. ; natum (i.e. his death), Ov. ; veneficia in principem, Tac. With Inf. : mihi obiectant lenocinium facere, Pl. ; Liv.

obiectus, a, um. **I.** Part. obiciō. **II.** A d j. **a.** *lying in the way or before :* complures obiectae insulae existimantur (between Britain and Ireland), Caes. ; Verg. With DAT. : insula Alexandreae, Caes. **b.** *exposed.* T r a n s f. : obiectus fortunae, Cic. ; ad omnis casūs, Cic. Ep. **III.** Noun, **obiecta**, ōrum, n. pl. *charges, accusations :* Cic., Quint.

obiectus, ūs, m. [obiciō], *a throwing or putting against or in the way :* dare obiectum par-

māl, Lucr. ; plutei obiectu tectus, Caes. ;
insula portum efficit obiectu laterum, Verg.;
cum latera obiectu paludis tegerentur,
Tac. [It. *oggetto* ; Fr. *objet.*]

ob-igitō, āre [ob agitō], *to make a disturbance
against* : Enn.

ob-īrāscor, īrāscī, īrātus, *to grow angry at*
(with DAT.) : fortunae, Liv. ; fortunae
animus, Sen.

ob-iter, *adv. on the way, in going along.* **1.**
Lit. : obiter leget aut scribet, Juv. ; Plin.
2. Transf. *in passing, incidentally* : obiter dictum, Plin. ; Juv.

obitus, a, um, *Part.* obeō.

obitus, ūs, m. [obeō], *a going towards or to
meet, meeting.* **1.** Lit. : Ter. **2.** Transf.
(*cf.* obeo B. 2. e.) *death, last day* : post
eorum obitum, Caes. : Cic. ; longum mis-
erata dolorum difficilisque obitūs, Verg. ;
post obitum occasumque nostrum (i.e. my
exile), Cic. Of the heavenly bodies, *setting* :
Lucr., Cic., Verg.

obiūrgātiō, ōnis, *f.* [obiūrgō], *a reproving, rebuke* : Cic. With *Obj.* GEN. : Cic., Quint.
In *pl.* : Cic., Sen. Ep.

obiūrgātor, ōris, m. [obiūrgō], *a reprover* :
Cic., Sen. Ep.

obiūrgātōrius, a, um [obiūrgātor], *reproachful* : epistula, Cic. Ep.

obiūrgitō, āre [*freq.* obiūrgō], *to keep on reproving* : Pl.

ob-iūrgō, āre, *to scold, blame, rebuke, reprove.*
1. Lit. : aliquem, Pl., Cic. ; me plurumus
verbis malis, Pl. ; aliquem molli bracchio
de áliquā re, Cic. Ep. ; aliquem (with Acc.
and *Inf.*), Cic. Ep. ; canem venator,
Phaedr. ; meam in rogando verecundiam,
Cic. Ep. ; fatum, naturam, Sen. Ep. **2.**
Transf. **a.** *to deter by reproof* : me a peccatis, Pl. **b.** *to chastise, correct* : soleā
rubrā, Pers. ; flagris, Suet. ; sestertio centies, Son.

oblanguī, *Perf. to have become feeble, to have
languished* : litterulae meae oblanguerunt,
Cic.

ob-lātrātrix, īcis, *f.* [oblātrō], *a barker at*, i.e.
a railer : Pl.

ob-lātrō, āre, *to bark at.* Transf. : *to snap
or rail at* : alicui, Sen. With *Intern.* Acc. :
nescio quid, Suet.

oblātus, a, um, *Part.* offerō.

oblectāmentum, ī, n. [oblectō], *an attraction,
delight, amusement, pastime.* With *Obj.*
GEN. : requies oblectamentumque senectutis, Cic. ; oblectamenta puerorum, Cic. ;
with *Subj.* GEN. : rerum rusticarum oblectamenta, Cic., Liv. Without GEN. : Suet.

oblectāmina, um, n. *pl.* [oblectō], *delights* :
Ov.

oblectātiō, ōnis, *f.* [oblectō], *an attracting, delighting, amusing* : indagatio ipsa habet
oblectationem, Cic. ; animi, Cic. Also *a
charming away, diverting* : curarum, Cic.

ob-lectō, āre [*cf.* delectō], *to draw towards.*
1. Lit. **a.** *to attract* (the attention of),
keep amused : ego illum interea hic ob-
lectabo (i.e. delay), Pl. ; Ter. **b.** *to attract, delight, divert, amuse* : minime me
oblectavi, Cic. Ep. ; populum, Hor. With
Instr. ABL. : falso gaudio nos, Pl. ; se agri
cultione, Cic. ; Musae me carmine, Cat.
Ironically : vitam sordido pane, Pl. In

Mid. : ludis oblectamur, Cic. With *cum* :
cum his me oblecto, qui res gestas scrips-
erunt, Cic. With *in* : in eo me oblecto,
Ter. ; se in hortis. Cic. **2.** Transf. *to
make* (*time*) *pass pleasantly* : studio lacri-
mabile tempus, Ov. ; iners otium, Tac. ;
inter cenam otium temporis, Plin. Ep. ;
haec studia senectutem oblectant, Cic.

ob-lēniō, īre, *to soften, to soothe* : Sen.

ob-līdō, līdere, līsī, līsum [laedō], *to press
violently on, crush* : collum digitulis duobus, Cic. ; oblisis faucibus, Tac. ; oblisus
pondere, Plin. Ep.

obligātiō, ōnis, *f.* [obligō], *a binding.*
Transf. : *a pledging* : est gravior animi
et sententiae pro aliquo quam pecuniae
obligatio, Cic. Ep.

obligātus, a, um. **I.** *Part.* obligō. **II.** Adj. :
obliged, under an obligation : Cic. Ep.
Comp. : Plin. Ep.

ob-ligō, āre. **I.** *to bind over, tie up, bandage* :
crus fractum, Pl. ; epistulam, Pl. ; vulnus,
Cic. ; venas, Tac. **II.** *to bind, tie, or
fasten to.* **1.** Lit. : articulis muscus obligatus, Plin. **2.** Transf. **a.** In law and
religion : *to bind, make liable to* a person or
thing : se nexu, Cic. ; aliquem militiae
sacramento, Cic. ; voti sponsio, quā obli-
gamur deo, Cic. ; obligari foedere, Liv. ;
vadem tribus milibus aeris, Liv. ; hence,
Prometheus obligatus aliti (i.e. liable to the
bird as penalty), Hor. Of the thing
pledged : praedia, Cic. ; praedia fratri,
Suet. ; fidem suam, Cic. ; ergo obligatam
redde Iovi dapem, Hor. **b.** *to render liable
through guilt, to make guilty* : hence, *Pass.
to be guilty of* : populum scelere, Cic. ;
votis caput, Hor. ; est periculum, ne neg-
lectis iis impiā fraude obligemur. Cic. **c.**
to put under an obligation : aliquem sibi
liberalitate, Cic. Ep. ; obligabis me, Plin.
Ep. Mostly in *Pass.* : obligatus ei nihil
eram, Cic. Ep. ; obligor ipse, Ov. ; pro
amicis alicui obligari, Plin. Ep. **d.** In
Pass. to be hampered : iudicio destrictum
atque obligatum esse, Cic.

oblimō, āre [limus], *to cover with mud or
slime.* **1.** Lit. : mollitosque et oblimatos
ad serendum agros, Cic. ; sulcos, Verg. **2.**
Transf. : rem patris oblimare, Hor.

ob-linō, linere, lēvī, litum, *to daub or smear
over, to bedaub, besmear.* **1.** Lit. : cer-
ussā mālas, Pl. ; obliti unguentis, Cic. ;
caede, Ov. **2.** Transf. **a.** *to befoul, defile* : oblitus parricidio, Cic. ; aliquem
versibus atris, Hor. **b.** In *Perf. Part.* :
overloaded : oblitus peregrinis divitiis, Hor. ;
Sallusti scripta nimiā priscorum verborum
adfectatione oblita, Suet.

oblīquē, *adv. sideways, obliquely.* **1.** Lit. :
Caes., Cic. **2.** Transf. : *indirectly* : aliquem castigare, Tac.

oblīquō, āre [obliquus], *to turn, bend, or
twist aside or towards* : oculos, Cic. ; sinūs
(velorum) in ventum, Verg. ; crinem, Tac.

ob-līquus, a, um [ob and perh. *cf.* λοξός],
slanting, awry. **1.** Lit. : sublicae, Caes. ;
iter, Caes. ; motus corporis, Cic. ; verris
obliquum meditantis iotum, Hor. ; obliquo
claudicare pede, Ov. *Neut.* as Noun : ab
obliquo, *from the side*, Ov. ; per obliquum,
across, in a slanting direction, Hor. ; per

obliqua tendere, Liv. ; praevecti per obliqua campi, Liv. **2. Transf. a.** *sidelong, askance, envious* : obliquo oculo mea commoda limat, Hor. ; invidia, Verg. **b.** *indirect, covert* : verborum insectatio, Tac. ; obliquis orationibus carpere aliquem, Suet. In gramm. : obliquus casus, *an oblique case* (opp. to rectus, the NOM.), Varr. ; obliqua oratio, *indirect* (i.e. quoted) *speech* : Quint.

oblīsus, a, um, *Part.* oblīdō.

ob-lĭtēscō, litēscere, lituī [latēscō], *to hide or conceal oneself* : a nostro aspectu, Cic. ; Sen. Ep.

oblitterō, āre [littera], *to strike out (a letter), cancel.* **1.** Lit. of debts : nomina, Tac. **2. Transf. :** *to blot out* of remembrance : inimicitias, Acc. ; famam rei, Liv. ; Cic. ; memoriam, Liv. ; mandata aetas, Cat. ; ritūs sacrorum, Tac.

oblĭtus, a, um, *Part.* oblĭnō.

oblītus, a, um, *Part.* oblīviscor.

oblīviō, ōnis, f. [oblīviscor]. **A. Pass.** *a being forgotten, oblivion* : veteris belli, Cic. ; laudem alicuius ab oblivione vindicare, Cic. ; dare aliquid oblivioni, Liv. ; in oblivionem venire (with ACC. and *Inf.*), Liv. ; in oblivionem ire, Sen. *Plur.* : lividas obliviones, Hor. **B. Act. a.** *a forgetting* : capit me oblivio alicuius rei, Cic. ; in oblivionem negoti venire, Cic. **b.** *forgetfulness* : Tac., Suet.

oblīviōsus, a, um [oblīviō]. **I.** *forgetful, oblivious* : Cic. **II.** *that produces forgetfulness* : of wine, Hor.

oblīviscor, līviscī, lītus [perh. fr. root of līvor ; hence, *to have the mind darkened*], *to forget.* **1.** Lit. With GEN. of person or thing : Ter., Cic., Verg., etc. With ACC. (mostly of*things*) : Pl., Cic., Verg., Liv. With *Inf.* : Ter., Ov. With ACC. and *Inf.* : Cic. With *Indir. Quest.* : Cic. *Gerundive* in *Pass.* sense : oblitusque meorum, obliviscendus et illis, Hor. ; Pl. *Perf. Part.* in *Pass.* sense : Verg. **2. Transf. a.** *to be unmindful of, act inconsistently with one's character* : nec oblitus sui est Ithacus discrimine tanto, Verg. ; ut nostrae dignitatis simus obliti, Cic. ; Liv. Poet. : pomaque degenerant succos oblita priores, Verg. **b.** *to cause forgetfulness* : saecla, Cat.

oblīvium, ī, n. [oblīviscor] (poet. in *pl.* ; *sing.* once in Tac.) **A. Pass.** *a being forgotten, oblivion* : oblivia rerum, Lucr. ; sententiam oblivio transmittere, Tac. **B. Act. :** *a forgetting, forgetfulness, oblivion* : longa oblivia potant, Verg. ; succi qui patriae faciant oblivia, Ov. [Fr. *oubli.*]

oblocūtor, ōris, m. [obloquor], *a contradicter* : Pl.

ob-longus, a, um, *long towards the ends ; oblong* : scutula, Tac.

ob-loquor, loquī, locūtus, *to speak against.* **a.** *to interrupt* : mihi, Pl. **b.** *to answer in argument* : Cic. Ep. ; vestra exspectatio quae mihi obloqui videtur, Cic. **c.** *to contradict* : Liv. ; ferocissime, Curt. ; alicui, Liv. **d.** *to rail at, abuse* : Cat. **e.** In music : *to reply to, accompany* : Ov. With ACC. of *Direct Obj.* : obloquitur numeris septem discrimina vocum, Verg.

ob-luctor, ārī, *to strive or struggle against.* **1.** Lit. : genibusque adversae obluctor hare-

nae, Verg. ; flumini, Curt. **2. Transf. :** difficultatibus, Curt. ; morti, Luc.

ob-lūdo, ere, *to play off jokes against* : custodem, Pl.

ob-mōlior, īrī, *to push or throw up one thing before another* (as a defence or obstruction) : Liv. ; arborum truncos et saxa, Curt.

ob-murmurō, āre, *to roar against or in answer to* : with DAT. : precibusque meis obmurmurat ipse, Ov. ; Suet.

ob-mūtēscō, mūtēscere, mūtuī, *to become (suddenly) mute, silent.* **1.** Lit. : ipse obmutescam, Cic. ; aspectu, Verg. **2. Transf. :** *to be hushed ; to cease* : animi dolor, Cic.

ob-nātus, a, um, *growing on or about* : obnata ripis salicta, Liv.

obnīs-, *v.* obnīx- and obnītor.

ob-nītor, nītī, nīxus (not nīsus). **I.** *to plant oneself firmly* (by pressing against) ; hence, *to stand firm (against)* : stant obnixi Samnites, Liv. ; obnixos stabili gradu impetum hostium excipere, Liv. ; stant obnixa omnia contra, Verg. ; obnixo genu scuto, Nep. **II.** *to press against, strive or push hard against.* **1.** Lit. : taurus arboris obnixus trunco, Verg. ; versaque in obnixos urgentur cornua, Verg. ; toto corpore obnitendum, Quint. ; densis ales pinnis obnixa volabat vento, Enn. ; acuto in murice remi obnixi crepuere, Verg. ; navigia aplustria fractis obniter undae, Lucr. ; nec nos obniti contra (ventos) tantum suffoimus, Verg. **2. Transf. :** obnixus curam sub corde premebat ; nec omisit Seianus obniti, Tac. ; adversis, Tac. ; consilio hostium, Tac.

obnīxē, adv. *resolutely, strenuously* : Ter.

obnīxus, a, um. *Part.* obnītor.

obnoxiē, adv. I. *guiltily* : nihil obnoxie perire, Pl. **II.** *slavishly* : sententias dicere, Liv.

obnoxiōsius, comp. adv. *more slavishly* : Pl.

obnoxiōsus, a, um [obnoxius], *submissive* : alicui, Pl.

ob-noxius, a, um. 1. Lit. **a.** *liable to punishment, culpable* : ego tibi me obnoxium esse fateor culpae compotem, Pl. ; capita, Liv. With *Causal GEN.* : pecuniae debitae, Liv. **b.** *liable or addicted to, guilty of* (with DAT.) : animus lubidini obnoxius, Sall. ; communi culpae, Ov. **2. Transf. :** *liable to others.* **A.** *dependent, submissive.* **a.** In gen. : dum illos obnoxios fidosque sibi faceret, Sall. ; Liv. ; obnoxiam carnificis arbitrio animam, Liv. ; Latinos obnoxiā pace tenere, Liv. **b.** *slavish, abject* : si aut superbus aut obnoxius videar, Liv. ; alicui, Pl. ; emersisse civitatem ex obnoxiā pace, Liv. **B.** *indebted, obliged, under obligation* (with DAT.) : uxori, Ter. ; Crasso ex negotiis privatis, Sall. ; fratris radiis Luna, Verg. ; totam Graeciam beneficio libertatis obnoxiam Romanis esse, Liv. ; arva curae hominum, Verg. **C.** *liable, exposed, subject.* With DAT. : arbores frigoribus, Liv. ; Alexandrum multis casibus obnoxium, Liv. ; corpora hosti, Liv. ; terra nulli bello, Ov. ; infidis consiliis, Tac. ; urbs incendiis, Tac. With *ad* : terra solida ad talis casūs, Plin. Hence,

absol., exposed (i.e. to danger or misfortune) :
Sen. Ep.

ob-nūbilus, a, um, *overclouded, dark* : Enn.

ob-nūbō, nūbere, nūpsī, nūptum, *to veil,
cover* : lictor, conliga manūs, caput ob-
nubito, old formula in Cic., Liv. ; comas
amictu, Verg.

obnūntiātiō, ōnis, *f.* In augury, *an announcement of an adverse* or *evil omen* :
dirarum, Cic. Esp. *to stop public business* :
obnuntiationes interponere, Cic. Ep.

ob-nūntiō, āre. **1.** In augury, *to announce
an adverse* or *evil omen* (used both of the
augurs and of the magistrates) : augur
auguri, consul consuli obnuntiasti, Cic.
Pass. Impers. : Cic. Ep. **2.** T r a n s f. in
gen. *to announce bad news* : primus resoisco
omnia : primus porro obnuntio, Ter.

oboediēns, entis. **I.** *Part.* oboediō. **II.**
Adj. *obedient.* **1.** L i t. (with DAT.) : alicui,
Sall. ; natio huic imperio, Cic. ; imperiis
miles, Liv. With addition of dicto : magistro desinebat esse dicto oboediens, Liv.
With *ad* : ad nova consilia, Liv. *Comp.*
and *Sup.* : Liv. *Masc.* as Noun : Liv.
2. T r a n s f. : pecora ventri, Sall. ; omnia
secunda et oboedientia sunt, Sall.

oboedienter, *adv. obediently, readily* : Liv.
Comp. : Liv.

oboedientia, ae, *f.* [oboediēns], *obedience* :
Cic.

ob-oediō, īre [ob audiō]. **I.** *to give a hearing,
give ear* : alicui, Nep. **II.** *to obey, comply*
(with DAT.) **1.** L i t. : magistratibus, Cic. ;
legi, praecepto, voluntati, Cic. *Impers.
Pass.* : oboeditum dictatori est, Liv. **2.**
T r a n s f. : multorum tempori, Cic. ; libidines voluptatibus, Cic. [It. *ubbidire,
obbedire* ; Fr. *obéir.*]

ob-oleō, ēre, *to emit a smell towards, to smell
of.* **1.** L i t. : ālium, Pl., Suet. **2.** T r a n s f. :
to waft a smell to, hence, *to attract* : marsuppium huic oboluit, Pl.

ob-orior, orīrī, ortus, *to arise, appear,* or
spring up before one. **1.** L i t. : tenebrae,
Pl., Nep., Liv. ; lux, Liv. ; lacrimae,
Lucr., Verg., Liv., etc. **2.** T r a n s f. :
laetitia, Ter. ; bellum, tumultus, indignatio,
timor, Liv. ; vide, quanta lux liberalitatis
et sapientiae mihi oboriatur, Cic.

obp-, *v.* opp-.

ob-rēpō, rēpere, rēpsī, rēptum, *to creep up,
to steal upon.* **1.** L i t. : Tib. **2.** T r a n s f.
a. *to steal upon, come suddenly upon* : *to
take by surprise* : obrepsit dies, Cic. Ep. ;
senectus, Juv. With DAT. : adulescentiae
senectus, Cic. With ACC. : tacitum te
obrepet fames, Pl. ; torpedo animos, Sall.
With *ad* : ad honores, Cic. With *in* and
ACC. : imagines obrepunt in animos dormientium extrinsecus, Cic. **b.** *to 'steal a
march upon' : to deceive, cheat* : mihi
inprudenti, Pl.

obrēptō, āre [*freq.* obrēpō], *to steal on unawares* : ne quis obreptaverit, Pl.

obrētiō, īre [rēte], *to overwhelm in a net, to
entangle* : Lucr.

ob-rigēscō, rigēscere, riguī, *to become stiff,
to stiffen.* **1.** L i t. : pars frigore, Lucil. ;
pars terrae regionum nive pruināque, Cic.
Of persons : Cic. **2.** T r a n s f. : *to become hardened* : Sen. Ep.

ob-rōdō, ere, *to gnaw at* : Pl.

ob-rogō, āre, *to invalidate* an existing law by
introducing a new one (with DAT.) : ubi
duae contrariae leges sunt, semper antiquae obrogat nova, Liv. *Impers. Pass.* :
Cic.

ob-ruō, uere, uī, utum. **A.** T r a n s. : *to
cover by heaping something over ; to
whelm, bury.* **1.** L i t. **a.** oceanum rubra
aethra, Enn. ; thesaurum, Cic. ; sese
harenā, Cic. ; semina terrā, Ov. ; miles
nivibus obrutus, Liv. ; quod superest
Teucrum (GEN.) obrue, Verg. ; terram
nox obruit umbris, Lucr. **b.** Of the dead :
to bury, inter : cadaver, Suet. ; Tac. **c.**
With water : *to overwhelm, swamp* : sub-
mersas obrue puppis, Verg. ; Aegyptum
Nilus totā aestate obrutam oppletamque
(tenet), Cic. ; hence, se vino, Cic. **2.**
T r a n s f. **a.** *to overwhelm, destroy* : aliquid
vetustas, Cic. ; Marius talis viri interitu
sex suos obruit consulatūs, Cic. ; famam
alicuius, Tac. **b.** *to overwhelm, overpower* :
criminibus obrutus, Cic. ; faenore, Liv. ;
obruimur numero, Verg. **B.** I n t r a n s.
to fall to ruin : domus, Lucr.

obrussa, ae, *f.* [ὄβρυζον], *the testing of gold
by fire.* **1.** L i t. : Plin. ; aurum ad obrussam (i.e. refined gold), Suet. **2.** T r a n s f. :
a test : adhibenda tamquam obrussa ratio,
Cic. ; ad obrussam exigere, Sen.

obrutus, a, um, *Part.* obruō. *See* ob-ruō.

ob-saepiō (ops-), saepīre, saepsī, saeptum,
to hedge or *fence in* ; hence *to close up, render
impassable* or *inaccessible.* **1.** L i t. : saltum, Pl. ; obsaeptis itineribus, Liv. ; apertis (itineribus) quae vetustas obsaepserat,
Tac. **2.** T r a n s f. : haec omnia tibi accu-
sandi viam muniebant, adipiscendi obsae-
piebant, Cic. ; plebi iter ad curulis magistratūs obsaepsit, Liv.

ob-saturō (ops-), āre, *to choke with cramming.* Transf. (in *Pass.*) : *to have more
than enough* : istius, Ter.

obscaen-, *v.* obscēn-.

obscaevō (opsc-), āre [scaeva], *to give* or
bring a bad omen : Pl.

obscēnē (obscaenē), *adv. indecently, ob-
scenely* : Cic. *Comp.* : Cic.

obscēnitās (obscaen-), ātis, *f.* [obscēnus],
filthiness, indecency, obscenity : Cic. ; verborum, Cic. ; obscenitatis in feminas reus,
Suet.

obscēnus (obscaen-), a, um [perh. obs (ob)
and caenum]. **I.** *foul, filthy.* **1.** L i t. :
Allecto frontem obscaenam rugis arat, Verg. ;
cruor, Verg. **2.** T r a n s f. : *immodest, indecent, obscene* : iocandi genus, Cic. ; voluptates, Cic. ; dicta, Ov. ; gestus motusque,
Tac. *Comp.* : Cic. *Sup.* : Cic. Ep. **II.**
of adverse or *evil omen* : verba, Lucil. ;
omen, Cic. ; volucres, Verg. ; canes, Verg. ;
puppis (i.e. of Paris), Ov. ; anus, Hor. ;
fetus, Liv. [It. *osceno.*]

obscūrātiō, ōnis, *f.* [obscūrō]. **1.** L i t. : *a
covering, darkening* : solis, Cic. **2.**
T r a n s f. : *disappearance ; being lost sight
of* : Cic.

obscūrē, *adv. darkly, indistinctly.* **1.** L i t. :
cernere, Cic. **2.** T r a n s f. **a.** Of speech :
dicta, Quint. **b.** *covertly, secretly, imperceptibly* : Cic., Hirt. *Comp.* : Cic.

obscūritās, ātis, *f.* [obscūrus], *darkness, obscurity.* **1.** Lit. **a.** : latebrarum, Tac. **2.** Transf. **a.** Of something hard to understand : *obscurity* : Pythagorae, Cic. ; naturae, Cic. ; rerum, Cic. In *pl.* : obscuritates somniorum, Cic. **b.** Of birth or rank : *lowliness, meanness* : Cic., Tac.

obscūrō (ops-), āre [obscūrus], *to cover.* **1.** Lit. **a.** Of light : *to shade, darken* : obscuratur luce solis lumen lucernae, Cic. ; volucres aethera obscurant pennis, Verg. ; caelum nocte obscuratum, Sall. ; obscuratus sol, Cic. **b.** In gen. : *to cover, conceal* : caput obscurante lacernā, Hor. ; dolo ipsi atque signa militaria obscurati, Sall. ; nox coetūs nefarios, Cic. **2.** Transf. **a.** *to blind* the understanding : scio amorem tibi pectus opscurasse, Pl. **b.** Of speech, *to veil, obscure* : nihil dicendo, Cic. ; stilum adfectatione, Suet. **c.** Of articulation : littera m neque eximitur sed obscuratur, Quint. **d.** *to hide, suppress* : paupertas nomina, Enn. ; fortuna res cunctas lubidine celebrat obscuratque, Sall. ; laudes, Cic. ; magnitudo lucri obscurabat periculi magnitudinem, Cic. ; obscurata vocabula, Hor.

obscūrus (ops-), a, um [ob and root seen in scūtum, cutis], *covered, veiled.* **1.** Lit. **a.** *shaded, dark* : nox, Enn., Verg. ; coni acumen, Lucr. ; lumen, Sall. ; lucus, Verg. ; caelum, Hor. ; locus, Liv. ; iam obscurā luce, Liv. Of persons, *in the dark, darkling* : ibant obscuri solā sub nocte per umbram, Verg. *Neut.* as Noun, *darkness* : sub obscurum noctis, Verg. **b.** *concealed* : obscurus in ulvā delitui, Verg. ; taberna, Hor. ; antrum, Ov. **2.** Transf. **a.** *clouded, gloomy* : candidatorum vultūs obscuriores, Cic. **b.** Of language, feelings, etc. : *obscure, unintelligible* : Heraclitus clarus ob obscuram linguam, Lucr. ; brevis esse laboro, obscurus fio, Hor. ; res, Lucr. ; Heraclitus, Cic. ; spes, Cic. **c.** Rhet. *involved* : obscurum genus causae, Cic. **d.** *not known, unknown* : Caesaris in barbaria erat nomen obscurius, Caes. **e.** Socially : *obscure, low, mean* : Pompeius humili atque obscuro loco natus, Cic. ; obscuris orti maioribus, Cic. *Neut.* as Noun : in obscuro vitam habere, Sall. ; vitam per obscuram transmittere, Sen. Ep. **f.** Of character, *close, secret, reserved* : obscurus et astutus homo, Cic. ; adversus alios, Tac. ; natura obscurior, Tac. As Noun : plerumque modestus occupat obscuri speciem, Hor.

obsecrātiō, ōnis, *f.* [obsecrō], *a solemn appeal and entreaty.* **a.** *a public appeal* to the gods : Cic. ; indicere, Liv. ; habere, Suet. **b.** *an appeal* (with an invocation of the gods) to a jury or other audience : Cic., Quint.

ob-secrō (ops-), āre [sacrō], *to make a solemn appeal and entreaty to.* **a.** Prop. With Acc. of person : Pl., Cic. With Acc. of person and *ut* and *Subj.* : Pl., Cic. ; without *ut* : Plin. Ep. With Acc. of thing : vostram fidem, Pl. With Acc. of person and *Neut.* Acc. of thing : te hoc obsecrat ut etc., Cic. Occ. with *ab* : aps te, Pl. **b.** Colloq. to deprecate something, or as a mere expression of polite entreaty :

pray : quid illic, opsecro, tam diu restitisti ? Pl. ; Attica mea, obsecro te, quid agit ? Cic. Ep. ; Liv.

ob-secundō (ops-), āre, *to comply with, humour, fall in with, follow implicitly* : Ter., Liv. ; with Dat. : alicuius voluntatibus, Cic.

ob-sēp-, *v.* obsaep-.

obsequella (opsequēla), ae, *f.* [obsequor], *compliance, complaisance* : facere (alicui), Pl. ; Sall.

obsequēns (ops-), entis. **I.** *Part.* obsequor. **II.** Adj. **a.** In gen. : *compliant* : imperiis patris, Pl. ; patri, Ter. ; legiones nobis, Cic. Ep. *Comp.* : animus, Sen. Ep. ; Curt. *Sup.* : Quint. **b.** Of the gods : *indulgent, gracious* : Pl.

obsequenter, *adv. compliantly* : Liv., Plin. Ep. *Sup.* : Plin. Ep.

obsequentia, ae, *f.* [obsequēns], *complaisance* (with *Obj.* Gen.) : reliquorum, Caes.

obsequiōsus (ops-), a, um [opsequium], *complaisant* : alicui, Pl.

obsequium (ops-), i, *n.* [obsequor], *compliance, complaisance.* **1.** Lit. **a.** In gen. : Ter., Cic. **b.** *obedience, allegiance* : in populum Romanum, Liv. ; Tac. ; obsequium erga aliquem exuere, Tac. ; ad obsequium redigero, Suet. **2.** Transf. **a.** *indulgence* of desires : animo opsequium sumere, Pl. ; ventris, Hor. **b.** Of things : *yielding, pliancy* : Ov.

ob-sequor (opseq-), sequi, secūtus, *to accommodate oneself to the will of another* : *to comply with, yield to, submit to.* **1.** Lit. (with Dat.) : alicui, Cato, Cic. ; senatui, Liv. ; legibus patriae, Cic. ; imperio, Juv. ; with *Intern.* Acc. : ot id ego percupio opsequi meo, Pl. **2.** Transf. **a.** Of desires or feelings : *to yield to, give oneself up to, indulge* : amori, Pl. ; animo, Pl., Cic. ; cupiditati, Cic. ; studiis suis, Nep. **b.** Of other things : tempestati, Cic. Ep. ; fortunae, Caes. ap. Cic. Ep.

obserō (ops-), āre [sera], *to bolt, bar.* **1.** Lit. : ostium, Ter. ; aedificia, Liv. **2.** Transf. : palatum, Cat. ; auris, Hor.

ob-serō (ops-), serere, sēvī, situm. **I.** *to cover with seeds* or *plants, to sow* or *plant thickly.* **1.** Lit. : omnia arbustis obsita, Lucr. ; terram frugibus, Cic. ; loca obsita virgultis, Liv. **2.** Transf. : legati obsiti squalore et sordibus, Liv. ; terga (marinae beluae) obsita conchis, Ov. ; pannis annisque opsitus, Ter. ; montes nivibus, Curt. obsitus aevo, Verg. **II.** *to sow* or *plant thickly.* **1.** Lit. : frumentum, Pl. **2.** Transf. : pugnos, Pl. ; malos mores, Pl.

observābilis, e, *adj.* [observō], *easy to be observed and guarded against* : manus, Quint.

observāns, antis. **I.** *Part.* observō. **II.** Adj. **a.** *attentive, respectful* (with Gen.) : tui, Cic. *Sup.* : Cic. Ep. **b.** *watchful, attentive* (with Gen.) : *Sup.* : omnium officiorum, Plin. Ep.

observantia, ae, *f.* [observāns], *respectful attention* towards persons : *regard, respect* : Cic. ; in regem, Liv. With *Obj.* Gen. : tenuiorum, Cic.

observātiō (ops-), ōnis, *f.* [observō], *a close watching, observing, observation.* **1.** Lit. : opservationi operam dare, Pl. ; siderum,

Cic. **2.** Transf. **a.** *circumspection, care :* in bello movendo, Cic. **b.** In *pl. : observation, advice, remarks on :* coquendi, Plin. ; Suet.

observātor, ōris, *m.* [observō], *a watcher, observer :* Sen. Ep., Plin. Pan.

observĭtō, āre [*freq.* observō], *to watch or note carefully :* deorum voces, Cic.

ob-servō (ops-), āre, *to watch over, watch closely, watch for, take careful note of.* **1.** Lit. **a.** In gen. : ne me opservare possis, quid rorum geram, Pl. ; Verg. ; traiectiones motūsque stellarum, Cic. ; tempus epistulae alicui reddendae, Cic. Ep. ; occupationem alicuius, Cic. With *ut* and *Subj. :* Suet. **b.** *to watch, guard :* ianuam, Pl. ; greges, Ov. **2.** Transf. **a.** *to observe, keep, comply with :* leges, Cic. ; praeceptum diligentissime, Caes. ; ordines, Sall. ; diem concili, Liv. **b.** *to pay attention or respect to :* tribulis suos, Cic. ; regem, Verg.

obses, idis, *m.f.* [obsideō; lit. *one who remains with another,* i.e. *in his keeping*], *a hostage.* **1.** Lit. : obsides accipere, daro, Caes. ; Ov. ; inter se dare, Caes. ; obsides alicui imperare, Cic. **2.** Transf. : *surety, security, bail.* **a.** Of persons : accipere aliquem obsidem nuptiarum, Cic. ; Nep. ; Ov. **b.** Of things : habemus a C. Caesare sententiam tamquam obsidem perpetuae in rem publicam voluntatis, Cic. ; Liv.

obsessiō, ōnis, *f.* [obsideō], *a blockading :* militaris viae, Cic. ; omittere, Caes.

obsessor (ops-), ōris, *m.* [obsideō]. **I.** *a frequenter, haunter :* fori, Pl. ; aquarum (i.e. **a** water-snake), Ov. **II.** *a blockader :* Tac. ; curiae, Cic. ; urbis, Liv.

ob-sĭdeō (ops-), sidēre, sēdī, sēssum [sedeō]. **A.** Intrans. : *to be or stay seated by or near :* Pl., Ter. **B.** Trans. **1.** Lit. **a.** *to remain by or near, to haunt, frequent :* aram, Pl. ; Apollo umbilicum terrarum, Poet. ap. Cic. **b.** *to block by remaining near.* **i.** Milit. : *to blockade :* omnis aditūs armati, Cic. ; hostes vias, Caes. ; urbem, Caes., Liv. ; legio vallis obsessa, Verg. **ii.** In gen. : *to block, choke :* corporibus omnis obsidetur locus, Cic. ; palus obsessa salictis, Ov. **2.** Transf. **a.** *to keep blocked, to keep possession of :* totam Italiam opibus suis, Cic. ; cum obsideri auris a fratre cerneret, Liv. : meum tempus, Cic. **b.** *to lie in wait for :* stuprum, Cic. **c.** *to keep guard over :* curia rostra, Cic. ; ab oratoro iam obsessus est ac tenetur, Cic.

obsidĭālis, e, *adj.* [obsidium], corona graminea, given for *freeing* a camp, etc. *from a blockade :* Liv.

obsĭdĭō, ōnis, *f.* [obsideō], *a siege, blockade.* **1.** Lit. : obsidione urbes capere, Cic. ; also opp. to oppugnatio, Liv. ; hostis in obsidione habere, Caes. ; cingere urbem obsidiono, Verg. ; obsidionem tolerare, exsequi, Tac. ; liberare, solvere, *to raise the siege,* Liv., Tac. ; omittere, Tac. ; obsidione eximere, Liv. **2.** Transf. : *pressing danger :* obsidione rem publicam liberare, Cic.

(1) obsidium (ops-), i, n. [obsideō], *a siege, blockade.* **1.** Lit. : Enn. ; facere Ilio, Pl. ; urgero, liberare, Tac. ; obsidio circumdare, Tac. **2.** Transf. : *pressing danger :* tuo tergo opsidium adesse, Pl.

(2) obsidium, i, n. [obses], *the condition of a hostage :* Tac.

ob-sīdō, sidere, sēdī, sēssum, *to beset, invest, lay siege to :* vias oculorum aer, Lucr. ; pontem, Sall. ; milite campos, Verg. ; portas, Verg. ; obsidere et oppugnare, Liv. ; auriculum caries, Lucil.

obsignātor, ōris, *m.* [obsignō], *he that seals :* litterarum, Cic. Esp. of *the witnesses to a will :* Cic. ; testamenti, Cic. Ep.

ob-signō (ops-), āre, *to seal up, seal.* **1.** Lit. : cellas, Pl. ; epistulam, Cic. ; Pl. Esp. *to sign and seal,* as a witness : tabellas, testamentum, Cic. ; tabellis obsignatis agere cum aliquo (i.e. with the strictest formality), Cic. **2.** Transf. : *to stamp, impress :* formam verbis, Lucr.

ob-sĭpō, v. opsipō.

ob-sistō (ops-), sistere, stitī, stitum, *to place or post oneself in the way,* **1.** Lit. : Pl., Liv. ; alicui obviam, Pl. ; alicui abeunti, Liv. **2.** Transf. : omnibus eius consiliis, Cic. ; odiis, Cic. *Impers. Pass. :* Cic. With *ne* and *Subj. :* Cic., Nep. With *Inf. :* obstitit Oceanus in se inquiri, Tac.

obsĭtus, a, um, *Part.* obserō.

obsolēfacta, a, um, *Part.* obsolefīō.

obsolefīō, fierī, factus, *to become worn out, hence, to be spoilt, degraded :* dignitatis insignia, Cic. ; auctoritas, Sen. Ep.

ob-olēscō, olēscere, olēvī, olētum, *to grow out of use ; to grow old or out of date, grow shabby or worn out :* ista oratio, Cic. ; res per vetustatem, Cic. ; haec ne obsolescerent renovabam, cum licebat, legendo, Cic. ; laus, Tac.

obsolētus, comp. adv. *in an older or more worn out style, more shabbily :* Cic.

obsolētus, a, um. **I.** *Part.* obsolescō. **II.** Adj. **1.** Lit. **a.** *old, worn out, thrown off, tumble-down :* tectum, Hor. ; erat veste obsoletā, Liv. ; vestitu obsoletiore, Cic. Of persons, *shabbily dressed :* Cic. **b.** *out of date, out of use :* verba, Cic. **2.** Transf. : *worn threadbare,* oratio, Cic. ; crimina, Cic. ; gaudia, Liv. Of persons : paternis sordibus, Hor.

obsōnātor (ops-), ōris, *m.* [obsōnō], *a caterer, purveyor :* Pl., Sen. Ep.

obsōnātus, ūs, *v.* opsonātus.

obsōnium (ops-), i, n. [ὀψώνιον], *that which is eaten with bread ; viands,* esp. *fish :* Pl., Hor.

(1) obsōnō (ops-), āre, and **obsōnor (ops-),** ārī [ὀψωνέω]. **1.** Lit. **a.** *to cater, buy food :* Pl., Ter. ; opsonium, Pl. **b.** *to provide food or an entertainment :* de suo filiāī nuptiis, Pl. ; Ter. **2.** Transf. : obsonare ambulando famem, Cic.

(2) ob-sono (ops-), āre, *to interrupt by noise :* alicui sermone, Pl.

ob-sorbeō (ops-), ēre, *to gulp down, bolt.* **1.** Lit. : aquam, Pl. ; placentas, Hor. **2.** Transf. : fores, quae opsorbent quidquid venit intra pessulos, Pl.

obstāns, antis. **I.** *Part.* obstō. **II.** Noun, **obstantia,** n. *pl. hindrances, obstructions :* silvarum, Tac.

obstetrix (opst-), īcis, *f.* [ob stō, *to stand by, beside*], *a midwife :* Pl., Ter., Hor.

obstinātē (ops-), adv. *resolutely, firmly ; also stubbornly, obstinately :* Pl., Caes., Plin. Ep. Comp. and Sup. : Suet.

obstinātiō, ōnis, *f.* [obstino], *resolution, firmness, determination ; also stubbornness, obstinacy :* sententiae, Cic. ; taciturna, Nep. ; fidei, Tac.

obstinātus (ops-), a, um. **I.** *Part.* obstino. **II.** A d j. : *fixed, resolved, inflexible, resolute ;* also *stubborn, obstinate :* opstinato animo, Acc. ; aures, Hor. ; pudicitia, Liv. ; silentium, Liv. ; fides, Tac. ; ad decertandum obstinati animi, Liv. ; contra veritatem, Quint. ; in extrema, Tac. ; obstinatos animos pro Vitellio, Tac. With *Inf.* : iam obstinatis mori spes adfulsit, Liv. *Comp.* : voluntas obstinatior, Cic. ; adversus lacrimas, Liv. *Sup.* : Sen. Ep.

ob-stinō (ops-), āre [*cf.* dēstino], *to persist in, be resolved on :* adfinitatem hanc, Pl. With *Inf.* : obstinaverant animis aut vincere aut mori, Liv. With *ad :* ad obtinendas iniquitates, Tac.

obstipēscō, v. obstupēscō.

obstipus, a, um [*v.* stipō and stipēs]. **I.** *bent* or *inclined to one side* (opp. rectus) : Lucr. **II.** *bent* or *drawn back* (said of a proud person) : cervix rigida et obstipa, Suet. **III.** *bent forwards, bent* or *bowed towards the ground :* stes capite obstipo, Hor.

ob-stō (ops-), stāre, stitī, (obstātūrus, Quint.). **I.** *to stand over against :* soli luna, Enn. ; obviam, Pl. **II.** *to stand in the way, to withstand, thwart, hinder, oppose, obstruct :* Pl., Cic., Liv., etc. With DAT. : alicui, Pl. ; meis commodis, Cic. ; quae tardis mora noctibus obstet, Verg. With *ne, quo minus, quin,* or *cur non :* cum religio obstaret ne non posset nisi ab consule dici dictator, Liv. ; quid obstat, quo minus sit beatus ? Cic. ; Liv. ; quid obstat, cur non verae nuptiae fiant ? Ter. *Impers. Pass.* obstatur, *resistance is offered,* Cic. ; Ov.

ob-strepō (ops-), ĕre, uī, itum. **A.** I n t r a n s. **I.** L i t. **a.** *to make a noise at* or *against :* nihil sensere Poeni, obstrepente pluviā, Liv. ; fontesque lymphis obstrepunt manantibus, Hor. With DAT. : obstrepit Oceanus Britannis, Hor. **b.** *to interrupt* or *drown with clamour ; to shout down :* Quint. ; with DAT. : sibi ipsi, Cic. ; certatim alter alteri obstrepere, Liv. *Impers. Pass. :* Liv. **2.** T r a n s f. : *to cry down, overwhelm :* tibi litteris, Cic. Ep. **B.** T r a n s. (only in *Pass.*). **a.** *to be drowned in noise :* res tuae obstrepi clamore militum videntur, Cic. **b.** *to be filled with noise :* locus si non obstreperetur aquis, Ov.

obstrictus, a, um, *Part.* obstringō.

ob-stringō (ops-), stringere, strinxī, strictum **1.** L i t. **a.** *to bind to* or *about : to bind, tie* or *fasten up :* follem ob gulam, Pl. **b.** *to bind, bind up* or *fast :* laqueo collum, Pl. ; ventos, Hor. **2.** T r a n s f. **a.** *to bind, fetter :* civitatem iure iurando, Caes. ; donis, foedere, legibus, Cic. **b.** *to bind, to lay under obligation, oblige :* quam plurimas civitates suo sibi beneficio habere obstrictas, Caes. ; Cic. ; Tac. **c.** *to pledge :* fidem suam alicui, Plin. Ep. **d.** With *Refl. Pron.* or in *Mid. : to be bound* (i.e. liable) *for, to become guilty of :* qui se tot sceleribus obstrinxerit, Cic. ; se periurio, Liv.

ob-structiō, ōnis, *f.* [obstruo], *an obstruction, a barrier.* T r a n s f. : Cic.

obstructus, a, um, *Part.* obstruō.

obs-trūdō or **ob-trūdō (opt-)**, trūdere, trūsī, trūsum, *to thrust into* or *upon.* **a.** Of gulping down food : pernam, Pl. **b.** *to thrust* or *force on a person :* palpum alicui, Pl. ; Ter.

ob-struō (opstr-), struere, struxī, structum, *to pile before* or *against.* **1.** L i t. **a.** obstructae fenestrae (i.e. against the light), Varr. ; luminibus alicuius, Cic. ; saxa, Ov. ; validum pro diruto obstruentes murum, Liv. **b.** *to stop* or *block up, render impassable :* iter Poenis vel corporibus suis, Cic. ; portas, Caes. **2.** T r a n s f. : *to block, close against a person* or *thing :* viri deus obstruit auris, Verg. ; perfugia improborum, Cic. ; mentis, Tac.

obstrūsō, a, um, *Part.* obstrūdō.

ob-stupe-faciō (ops-), facere, fēcī, factum, *Pass.* **obstupefiō**, fieri, factus, *to render senseless, to paralyse, astound :* eum pudor, Ter. ; ipso miraculo audaciae obstupefecit hostis, Liv. ; obstupefactis hominibus, Cic.

ob-stupēscō or **obstipēscō (ops-)**, stupēscere, stupuī, *to become senseless, benumbed, paralysed.* **1.** L i t. : eius aspectu obstupuisset bubulcus, Cic. ; Verg. **2.** T r a n s f. (of astonishment) : Pl. ; ob haec beneficia, quibus illi obstupescunt, Cic.

ob-stupidus, v. opstupidus.

ob-sum (ops-), esse, fuī, (*Fut. Part.* -futūrus), *to be against, be prejudicial to :* Enn., Verg. ; with DAT. : Ty. nunc falsa prosunt. *Heg.* at tibi oberunt, Pl. ; pudor orationi, Cic. ; Ov. With *Inf.* : nihil obest dicere, *there is no harm in saying,* Cic. ; Ov.

ob-suō, suere, suī, sūtum. **I.** *to sew on :* obsutum caput, Ov. **II.** *to sew up, close by sewing.* T r a n s f. : spiritus oris obsuitur, Verg. ; obsuta lectica, Suet.

ob-surdēscō, surdēscere, surduī, *to become quite deaf.* **1.** L i t. : hoc sonitu completae aures obsurduerunt, Cic. **2.** T r a n s f. : *to turn a deaf ear :* Cic.

obtegēns, ntis. **I.** *Part.* obtegō. **II.** A d j. : *given to concealing :* with GEN. : animus sui obtegens, Tac.

ob-tegō (optigō, Pl.), tegere, tēxī, tēctum, *to cover over, cover up.* **I.** For protection. **1.** L i t. : Pl. ; aliquem armis, Caes. ; se servorum corporibus, Cic. **2.** T r a n s f. : obtectus meliorum precibus, Tac. **II.** For concealment. **1.** L i t. : domus arboribus obtecta, Verg. ; vehiculum pellibus, Curt. **2.** T r a n s f. : errata, Pl. ; vitia multis virtutibus, Cic. ; Tac.

obtemperātiō, ōnis, *f.* [obtemperō], *a complying with* or *submitting to ; submission, obedience* (with DAT.) : Cic.

ob-temperō (opt-), āre, *to comply with, attend to, conform to, submit to, obey :* with DAT. : non ego illi optempero quod loquitur, Pl. ; alicui, Cic. ; imperio populi R., Caes. ; voluntati alicuius, Caes. ; auctoritati senatūs, Caes. ; Cic. *Impers. Pass. :* Cic. With *ad :* ad id, quod ex verbis intellegi possit, obtemperare, Cic.

ob-tendō, tendere, tendī, tentum. **I.** *to stretch,* or *spread before.* **1.** L i t. **a.** For concealment : pro viro nebulam, Verg. ; sudarium ante faciem, Suet. **b.** With ACC. of thing concealed : diem nube atrā, Tac. In simile : quasi velis obtenditur unius cuiusque natura, Cic. **2.** T r a n s f. : *to plead as an excuse :* matris preces obtendens, Tac. ; rationem turpitudini, Plin. Ep. **II.** G e o g r. : *to stretch over against* (*in Mid.*) : Britannia Germaniae obtenditur, Tac.

(1) obtentus, a, um, *Part.* obtendō.

(2) obtentus, a, um, *Part.* obtineō.

obtentus, ūs, *m.* [obtendō], *a stretching or spreading out as a screen.* **1.** L i t. : frondis, Verg. **2.** T r a n s f. : *a screen, pretence, pretext :* obtentum habere, Tac. ; aliquid obtentui sumere, Tac. ; Sall.

ob-terō (opt-), terere, trīvī, trītum (*syncop. Pluperf. Subj.* obtrīsset for obtrīvisset, Liv.), *to bruise, crush by trampling.* **1.** L i t. : in angustiis portarum obtrītī sunt, Liv. ; Varr. ; ranas, Phaedr. **2.** T r a n s f. : *to crush.* **a.** By force : Samnites concurrunt ad Marcium consulem obterendum, Liv. ; Tac. **b.** laudem imperatoriam, Cic. ; Pl. ; calumniam, Cic. ; iura populi, Liv.

obtestātiō, ōnis, *f.* [obtestor], *an adjuring ; a taking of an obligation by calling the gods, etc. to witness.* **1.** L i t. : alicuius, Cic. **2.** T r a n s f. : *a solemn entreaty, supplication :* alicuius, Cic. Ep. In *pl.* : alicui, Tac.

ob-testor (opt-), ārī, *to call as a witness.* **1.** L i t. : de quo te, te, inquam, patria, obtestor, et vos, penates patrīque dī, Cic. ; deum hominumque fidem, Liv. ; Tac. **2.** T r a n s f. : *to adjure in God's name, solemnly entreat, supplicate :* per ego haec genua te, Pl. ; per omnis deos te, Cic. ; Verg. With *Intern.* Acc. : illud te pro Latio obtestor, Verg. With *ut* or *ne* and *Subj.* : Cic.

ob-texō, texere, texuī, *to weave to or over.* T r a n s f. : *to overspread :* caelum obtexitur umbrā, Verg.

ob-ticeō (opt-), ēre [taceō], *to be quite silent :* Ter.

obticēscō (opt-), ticescere, ticuī [obticeō], *to become* or *be struck dumb :* Pl., Hor., Ov.

ob-tineō (opt-), tinēre, tinuī, tentum [teneō]. **I.** T r a n s. **A.** *to keep firm hold of, possess.* **1.** L i t. **a.** In gen. : una pars Galliae quam Galli obtinent, Caes. ; suam quisque domum, Cic. **b.** M i l i t. : castra, vada custodiis, Caes. ; armis Galliam atque Italiam, Liv. **c.** P o l i t. : cum imperio Hispaniam citeriorem, Cic. Ep. ; provinciam Sardiniam, Nep. **2.** T r a n s f. **a.** In gen. : summum magistratum, Caes. ; auctoritatem, Cic. ; ius, Tac. ; fascis et imperium, Liv. ; firmitudinem animi, Pl. ; insitam pertinaciam, Liv. ; proverbi locum, Cic. ; quae fama plerosque obtinet, Sall. With *Inf.* : *to persist in :* Pl. **b.** Of opinions, etc. : *to hold, maintain :* causam suam apud eum, Caes. ; duas contrarias sententias, Cic. ; diu pugnare in iis, quae obtinere non possis, Quint. **B.** *to get a firm hold of, obtain and keep hold of.* **1.** L i t. : auris, Pl. **2.** T r a n s f. : instrumenta ad obtinendam adipiscendamque sapientiam, Cic. ; Romani si rem obtinuerint (i.e. the victory), Caes. With *ut* or *ne* and *Subj.* : Liv., Suet. With *quin* (after negat.) : Suet. **II.** I n t r a n s. : *to keep one's ground ; to hold, continue :* noctem insequentem eadem caligo obtinuit, Liv. ; quod et plures tradi-

dere auctores et fama obtinuit, Liv. ; pro vero obtinebat (foll. by *Inf.*), Sall.

ob-tingō (opt-), tingere, tigī [tangō]. **I.** *to fall to one's lot :* quod cuique obtigit, id quisque teneat, Cic. ; mihi optinget sors, Pl. With *ut* and *Subj.* : cum ei bellum ut cum rege Perse gereret obtigisset, Cic. **II.** Of events : *to happen, fall out :* exoptata optingent, Pl. ; istuc tibi ex sententiā tuā optigisse laetor, Ter. ; si quid obtigerit, aequo animo moriar, Cic.

ob-torpēscō, torpēscere, torpuī, *to become quite numb* or *stiff ; to be benumbed, lose feeling.* **1.** L i t. : manus metu, Cic. ; manūs prae metu, Liv. **2.** T r a n s f. : obtorpuerunt quodam modo animi, Liv.

ob-torqueō (opt-), torquēre, torsī, tortum. **I.** *to twist round to meet :* dextras in undas proram, Stat. ; Acc. **II.** *to twist about :* optorto collo, Pl ; Cic. ; obtortā gulā, Cic. ; circulus obtorti auri, Verg.

obtrectātiō, ōnis, *f.* [obtrectō], *detraction, disparagement :* Cic., Tac. ; adversus gloriam consulis, Liv. With *Obj.* G e n. : Caes., Liv. In *pl.* : Cic. Ep.

obtrectātor, ōris, *m.* [obtrectō], *a detractor, traducer, disparager :* Cic., Quint. With *Obj.* G e n. : Cic.

ob-trectō, āre [tractō], *to handle spitefully ; hence, to disparage, decry :* Cic., Suet. ; inter se, Nep. With D a t. : alicui, Cic. ; gloriae alicuius, Liv. ; *Impers. Pass.* : obtrectatum est Gabinio, Cic. ; laudibus ducis, Liv. With Acc. : si livor obtrectato curam voluerit, Phaedr. ; laudes alicuius, Liv. ; urbanas excubias, Tac.

obtritus, a, um, *Part.* obterō.

ob-trūdō, *v.* obstrūdō.

ob-truncō (opt-), āre, *to cut off* or *down.* **a.** Of animals : gallum, Pl. ; cervos ferro, Verg. **b.** Of persons (esp. in battle) : Pl., Sall., Liv., etc.

ob-tueor, ob-tuor, *v.* optueor.

ob-tundō (opt-), tundere, tudī, tūsum and tūnsum, *to beat* or *thump on.* **1.** L i t. **a.** os mihi, Pl. **b.** *to make blunt* or *dull by striking :* telum, Lucr. **2.** T r a n s f. **a.** *to pound away at* (i.e. deafen, stun, weary) : auris tuas, Pl. ; aliquem de aliquā re, Ter. ; rogitando, Ter. ; longitudo auris, Cic. **b.** *to blunt* (i.e. make dull, impair) : vocem, Lucr., Liv. ; mentem, ingenia, Cic.

obtūnsus, *v.* obtūsus.

ob-turbō (opt-), āre, *to throw into great disorder* or *confusion.* **1.** L i t. : hostis denso agmine, Tac. **2.** T r a n s f. : *to distract, trouble, bother :* Pl. ; Tac. ; solitudinem, Cic. Ep. ; me scriptio et litterae non leniunt sed obturbant, Cic. Ep. *Impers. Pass.* : Plin. Ep.

ob-turgēscō, ere, *to begin to swell up :* pes, Lucr.

obtūrō (opt-), āre, *to stop up, to close.* **1.** L i t. : gutturem, Pl. ; auris (i.e. to refuse to listen), Hor. ; obstructas eas partis et obturatas esse, Cic. **2.** T r a n s f. : amorem edendi, Lucr.

obtūsus and **obtūnsus,** a, um. **I.** *Part.* obtundō. **II.** A d j. : *blunt, dull.* **1.** L i t. : angulus, Lucr. ; pugio, Tac. ; vomer, Verg. **2.** T r a n s f. **a.** *dulled, blurred, thick :* vires, Lucr. ; stellis acies, Verg. ; vox, Quint.

b. Of the mind or feelings : *blunted, dulled* (i.e. not keen, not discriminating) : animi acies obtusior, Cic. ; adeo obtusa pectora, Verg. ; vigor animi, Liv. ; castrensis iuris dictio secura et obtusior, Tac.

obtūtus, ūs, *m.* [obtueor], *a fixed or close looking at, gaze.* **1.** Lit.: oculorum, Cic. ; dum stupet obtutuque haeret defixus in uno, Verg. ; obtutu tacito stetit, Verg. **2.** Transf.: in obtutu malorum, Ov.

ob-umbrō, āre, *to overshadow, to shade.* **1.** Lit. **a.** locus templum, Ov. ; obumbratus amnis, Curt. **b.** Of cover or concealment : aethera telis, Verg. ; coma umeros, Ov. ; gramineus caespes humum, Ov. **2.** Transf. **a.** *to cast into the shade :* nomina, Tac. **b.** *to cover, screen :* reginae nomen eum, Verg. ; crimen, Ov.

ob-uncus, a, um, *bent towards* the end, *bent in, hooked :* Verg., Ov.

obundāns, antis [unda], *overflowing.* Transf.: Enn.

ob-ūstus, a, um [ūrō], *burnt on the surface, partly burnt, hardened in the fire :* torris, sudes, Verg. Of the action of frost : glaeba canenti gelu, Ov.

ob-vāgiō, īre, *to whine* or *whimper about :* Pl.

ob-vāllō, āre, *to defend* or *fortify with a wall or rampart.* Transf.: locus omni ratione obvallatus (i.e. the consulate), Cic.

ob-veniō, venīre, vēnī, ventum, *to come before* or *in the way of, to meet.* **1.** Lit.: in tempore pugnae, Liv. **2.** Transf. **a.** *to come or fall to ; to fall to one's lot :* tibi iste labos, Pl. ; Syria Scipioni, Caes. ; Aemilio Etruria sorte obvenit, Liv. ; mihi hereditas, Plin. Ep. **b.** Of an event : *to happen, occur :* occasio, Pl. ; vitium (at the auspices), Cic. ; Suet.

ob-versor, ārī, *to move to and fro before ; to go about, show oneself before.* **1.** Lit.: Plin. Ep. ; palam Carthagini, Liv. ; limini, Plin. Ep. ; in urbe inter coetūs, Tac. **2.** Transf.: nomen dulce ad auris, Lucr. ; mihi ante oculos rei publicae dignitas, Cic. ; Caudinae cladis memoria non animis modo sed prope oculis, Liv.

obversus, a, um. **I.** *Part.* obvertō. **II.** Adj.: *turned* or *directed towards.* **1.** Lit.: faciemque obversus in agmen utrumque, Ov. ; ad matrem, Tac. **2.** Transf. **a.** *inclined to :* ad sanguinem ac caedis, Tac. ; militum studiis, Tac. **b.** As Noun in *pl.* **obversī**, *opponents, antagonists :* Tac.

ob-vertō (**-vortō**, Pl.), vertere, vertī, versum, *to turn towards* or *against :* mihi cornua, Pl. ; proras pelago, Verg. ; ordines ad clamorem, Liv. ; totam aciem in Samnites, Liv. ; signa in hostem, Liv. ; arcūs in aliquem, Ov. In *Mid.* : *to turn oneself, turn to :* obvertor ad undas, Ov.

ob-viam, *adv.* (also separately ob viam), lit. *in face of the way* someone is taking ; hence, with verbs of motion, *towards, against, to meet.* **1.** Lit.: qui obviam obsistat mihi, Pl. ; si quā ex parte obviam contra veniretur, Caes. ; proficisci, exire, Caes. ; alicui ire, prodire, procedere, Cic. ; mittere, Cic. Ep. ; progredi, effundi, Liv. ; fit obviam Clodio, Cic. ; obviam esse, Pl. ; de obviam itione ita faciam, Cic. Ep. **2.** Transf. **a.** Of facing, opposing, checking :

tibi nulla aegritudo est obviam animo, Pl. ; cupiditati hominum obviam ire, Cic. ; irae obviam ire, Liv. ; obviam ire periculis, Sall. **b.** Of meeting or remedying : ni Caesar obviam isset, tribuendo pecunias pro modo detrimenti, Tac. ; dedecori, timori, Tac.

obvigilātum, i, *n.* [*cf.* explorātum], obvigilato 'st opus, *there is need of vigilance,* Pl.

obvius, a, um [obviam], *in the way, so as to meet, meeting, to meet :* mostly with DAT. **1.** Lit. **a.** alicui obvium esse, Cic., Sall. ; cui mater mediā sese tulit obvia silvā, Verg. ; dare se obvium alicui, Liv. Of things : obvias mihi litteras mittas, Cic. Ep. ; simulacra nobis, Lucr. ; flamina, Ov. ; aquilones, Tac. *Neut.* as Noun : esse in obvio alicui, Liv. **b.** Of hostile movement : si ingredienti cum armatā manu obvius fueris, Cic. ; lugurthae obvius procedit, Sall. ; infesta subit obvius hastā, Verg. **2.** Transf. **a.** Of persons : *accessible :* Plin. Ep. **b.** Of things : *exposed :* rupes obvia ventorum furiis, Verg. **c.** Of abstr. things, *at hand, ready :* obvias opes deferre deos, Tac. ; Quint. ; Mart.

ob-volvō, volvere, volvī, volūtum, *to wrap round, muffle up, cover over.* **1.** Lit.: capite obvoluto, Pl., Cic., Liv. ; bracchium lanis fasciisque, Suet. **2.** Transf. **a.** fax obvoluta sanguine, Enn. **b.** verbis decoris vitium, Hor.

oc-caecō, āre, *to make blind, to blind.* **1.** Lit.: pulvere occaecatus, Liv. **2.** Transf. **a.** *to darken, obscure :* sol occaecatus, Pl. ; densa caligo occaecaverat diem, Liv. **b.** *to hide, conceal :* terra semen occaecatum cohibet, Cic. **c.** *to benumb :* timor occaecaverat artūs, Verg. **d.** Of the mind : occaecatus cupiditate, Cic. ; irā et pavore occaecatis animis, Liv. ; consilia, Liv. **e.** Of style, *to make dark, obscure :* obscura narratio totam occaecat orationem, Cic.

oc-callēscō, callēscere, calluī [calleō], *to grow thick-skinned, become hardened.* **1.** Lit.: qui latera occalluero plagis, Pl. ; os rostro, Ov. **2.** Transf.: *to become hard or callous :* iam prorsus occallui, Cic. Ep. ; longā patientiā, Plin. Ep.

oc-canō, canere, canuī, *to sound the attack :* cornicines occanuere, Sall. ; cornua, Tac.

occāsiō, ōnis, *f.* [occidō ; *lit.* a falling in the way of, a happening], *an accidental opportunity, fit time, convenient season :* ut primum occasio data est, Cic. ; Pl. ; occasione datā, Cic. ; in same sense, per occasionem, per occasiones, ex occasione, Liv. ; occasionem offerre, Cic., Suet. ; aperire ad invadendum, Liv. ; capere, Liv. ; nancisci, Cic. ; adripere, Liv. ; rapere, Hor. ; amplecti, Plin. Ep. ; praetermittere, Caes. ; amittere, Ter., Caes., Cic. ; occasione uti, occasioni deesse, Caes. ; opprimendi, Cic. ; ad occupandam Asiam, Cic. With *Inf :* Pl., Ter. With *ut* and *Subj.* : Pl., Quint. [It. *cagione.*]

occāsiuncula, ae, *f.* [*dim.* occāsiō], *a slight opportunity :* Pl.

occāsus, ūs, *m.* [occidō], *a setting,* of the heavenly bodies ; esp. of the sun. **1.** Lit.: solis, Caes., Liv. ; ante occasum Maiae, Verg. ; praecipiti in occasum die, Tac. Hence, *the quarter in which the sun sets, the* *west* : inter occasum solis et septentriones, Caes. **2**. T r a n s f. : *downfall, destruction* : post obitum occasumque nostrum, Cic. ; rei publicae, Cic. ; Troiae, Verg.

occātiō, ōnis, *f.* [occō], *harrowing* : Cic.

occātor, ōris, *m.* [occō], *a harrower* : Pl.

oc-cēdō, cēdere, cēssi, cēssum, *to go towards, go to, go up to* : in conspectum alicuius occedere, Pl. ; Varr.

oc-centō, āre [cantō]. **I.** *to sing at or before, to serenade* : Pl. ; with Acc. : senem, Pl. ; ostium, Pl. **II.** *to sing a satirical song or pasquinade* : Old Law in Cic.

occepsō, *v.* occipiō.

occeptō, āre (*Aor. Opt.* or *Subj.* occeptāssit, Pl.) [occipiō], *to begin* : Pl. ; with *Inf.* : Pl.

occĭdāns, entis. **I.** *Part.* occidō. **II.** Noun, *m.* (*sc.* sol) *the setting sun* ; hence, *the west* : ob oriente ad occidentem, Cic.

occīdiō, ōnis, *f.* [occidō], *a massacre, utter destruction, extermination* : orare ne in occidione victoriam poneret, Liv. Esp. in the phrase, occidione occidere or caedere : *to wipe out, annihilate* : Cic., Liv. So, occidione occumbere, Tac. ; equi, viri, cuncta viota occidioni dantur, Tac.

oc-cīdō, cidere, cidi, cisum [caedō], *to strike or cut down.* **1.** L i t. : aliquem pugnis, Ter. Esp. of killing : Enn. ; L. Verginius filiam suā manu occidit, Cic. ; fortissime pugnans occiditur, Caes. ; ad unum omnis, Liv. **2**. T r a n s f. : *to plague to death* : occidis me, quom istuc rogitas, Pl. ; occidis saepe rogando, Hor.

oc-cĭdō, cidere, cidi, cāsum [cadō], *to fall down, fall.* **1.** L i t. **a.** In gen. : alia signa de caelo ad terram occidunt, Pl. ; ut alii super alios occiderent, Liv. **b.** Of the heavenly bodies : *to set* : Pac., Cat. *Perf. Part.* occāsus, in *Act.* sense : ante solem occasum, *before sunset*, Pl. **c.** Of dying : extincto calore, occidimus ipsi, Cic. ; occiderit ferro Priamus ? Verg. **2**. T r a n s f. : *to be ruined, lost, undone* : plane occidimus, Cic. Esp. occidi, an exclamation of despair, *I am lost, ruined*, Pl., Ter. Of things : spes, dolus, Pl. ; lumen oculorum, Lucr. ; vita, Cic. ; una domus, Ov. ; vestra beneficia, Cic.

occĭduus, a, um [occidō], *going down, setting.* **1.** L i t. : sol, Ov. ; dies, Ov. **2**. T r a n s f. **a.** *western* : sol, Ov. **b.** *sinking, failing* : senecta, Ov.

occillō, āre [occō], *to break, smash* : mi os, Pl.

oc-cĭnō, cinere, cecini or cinui [canō], *to sing or sound against*, i.e. inauspiciously (in augury) : avis, Liv. ; corvus voce clarā, Liv.

oc-cĭpiō, cipere, cēpi, ceptum (old *Fut.* occepsō, Pl.) [capiō], *to begin.* **A.** T r a n s. : cantionem, Pl. ; magistratum, Liv., Tac. With *Inf.* : Pl., Liv., Tac. *Pass.* : Ter. **B.** I n t r a n s. : dolores, Ter. ; iuventus, Lucr. ; hiems, Tac.

occĭpĭtĭum, i, and **occĭput**, itis, *n.* (Pers.) [caput], *the back part of the head, the occiput* : Pl., Quint.

occīsiō, ōnis, *f.* [occidō], *a massacre, slaughter* : facere, Cic.

occīsor, ōris, *m.* [occidō], *a killer, murderer* : regum, Pl.

occīsus, a, um. **I.** *Part.* occidō. **II.** A d j. : *ruined* : occisa est haec res, Pl. *Sup.* : occisissumus sum omnium, qui vivont, Pl.

oc-clāmitō, āre, *to keep on bawling at* anyone : Pl.

oc-clūdō, clūdere, clūsi, clūsum (occlūsti for occlūsisti, Pl.) [claudō], *to shut or close up or against.* **1.** L i t. : ostium, aedis, Pl. ; tabernas, Cic. ; furax servus cui domi nihil sit occlusum, Cic. Of a person : me domi, Pl. **2**. T r a n s f. : linguam, Pl. ; lubidinem, Ter.

occlūsus, a, um. **I.** *Part.* occlūdō. **II.** A d j. : *shut or closed up* : qui occlusiorem habeant stultiloquentiam, Pl. ; ostium occlusissumum, Pl.

occō, āre, *to harrow* : Pl., Varr. ; segetem, Hor.

oc-cŭbō, āre, *to lie* (esp. in the grave) : ad tumulum, quo maximus occubat Hector, Verg. ; morte, Liv.

oc-culcō, āre [calcō], *to tread or trample down* : Cato, Liv.

occŭlō, culere, cului, cultum [*cf.* cēlō]. **I.** *to cover, cover over* : terra caput, Enn. ; virgula multā terrā, Verg. **II.** *to cover up, hide, conceal* : vitia corporis fuco, Pl. ; vulnera, Cic. Ep. ; se silvā, Liv. ; hastatos, Liv. ; classem sub rupe, Verg. T r a n s f. : vitia, Quint.

occultātiō, ōnis, *f.* [occultō], *a hiding, concealment.* **1.** L i t. : Cic. **2**. T r a n s f. : cuius rei nulla est occultatio, Caes.

occultātor, ōris, *m.* [occultō], *a hider, concealer* : in appos. : ille latronum occultator locus, Cic.

occultē, *adv. in concealment, in secret, secretly* : Ter., Caes., Cic., Ov. *Comp.* : Cic., Sall. *Sup.* : Caes., Sall., Liv.

occultō, āre (*Aor. Subj.* or *Opt.* occultāssis, Pl.) [*freq.* occulō], *to hide, conceal, secrete.* **1.** L i t. : legionem silvis, Caes. ; Ov. ; se latebris, Cic. ; Liv. ; se post montem, Caes. ; aliquid in terrā, Caes. ; se in hortis, Cic. Ep. ; me aps tuo conspectu, Pl. In *Mid.* : stellae occultantur, Cic. With *Inf.* : res est quaedam, quam occultabam tibi dicere (i.e. was refraining), Pl. **2**. T r a n s f. : fugam, Caes. ; gaudium, Cic.

occultus, a, um. **I.** *Part.* occulō. **II.** A d j. : *hidden, concealed, secret.* **1.** L i t. : in occultis locis, Pl. ; calles, Verg. ; exitus, Liv. *Neut.* as Noun : occulta saltuum scrutari, Tac. ; ex occulto, *from a place of concealment*, Ter., Sall., Liv. ; in occulto, Cic. **2**. T r a n s f. **a.** Of things : res, Lucr., Cic. ; cupiditas, Cic. ; sapor, Verg. ; crescit occulto aevo, Hor. *Neut.* as Noun : servi, quibus occulta creduntur, Cic. ; Juv. ; ox occulto, *secretly*, Cic., Liv. ; also, per occultum, Tac. **b.** Of persons : *close, reserved* : Cic. Ep., Liv., Tac. With *Gen.* : odi, Tac. Adverbially for occulte : itinera occultus insederat, Liv. ; Tac. *Comp.* and *Sup.* : Cic.

oc-cumbō, cumbere, cubui, cubitum [*v.* cubō], *to sink down.* Esp. with mortem or morto or morti, or similar words, *to fall to death* (or *in death*), *to fall dying* : letum, Enn. ; mortem, Cic., Liv. ; morte, Liv. ; morti obviam, Enn. ; certae morti, Verg. ; neci, Ov. So also alone : Enn., Cic. Ep., Ov., Suet.

occupātiō, ōnis, *f.* [occupō], *a taking possession of, a seizing.* **1.** Lit.: fori, Cic. **2.** Transf. **a.** Rhet.: ante occupatio, *an anticipation* of an opponent's objections, Cic. **b.** *business, employment, occupation* : maximis occupationibus impediri, Cic. ; relaxare se occupationes, Cic. Ep. With GEN.: neque has tantularum rerum occupationes sibi Britanniae anteponendas iudicabat, Caes.

occupātus, a, um. **I.** *Part.* occupō. **II.** Adj.: *taken up, occupied, employed, busied, engaged* : in opere, Caes. ; occupati profuimus aliquid civibus nostris, proximus etiam otiosi, Cic. ; in metendo, Caes. ; in patriā delendā, Cic. ; hostibus opere occupatis, Liv. Comp. : Cic. Ep. Sup. : Ci . Ep., Plin. Ep.

occupō, āre (*Aor. Opt.* occupāssit, Pl.) [capiō], *to seize in the face of or before some-one else.* **1.** Lit. **a.** Milit.: loca superiora, Caes. ; montem, Caes., Tac. ; urbem, Liv. ; urbem viribus, Verg. ; totam Italiam suis praesidiis, Cic. ; navis, Caes. **b.** Non-milit. : aditum, Verg. ; portum, Hor. ; Phaethon currum, Ov. **c.** *to occupy,* i.e. *to take up, fill with* : duas partis acies occupabant ; tertia vacabat, Caes. ; urbem aedificiis, Liv. ; caementis Tyrrhenum mare, Hor. ; atrā nube polum, Hor. **d.** *to get in the first blow at* ; *to strike first* : aliquem gladio, Verg. ; morsu, Ov. **e.** Without hostile sense ; *to drop upon, surprise* : Volteium mane Philippus occupat, et salvere iubet prior, Hor. **2.** Transf. **a.** *to seize, take possession of, get hold of* : familiam optumam, Pl. ; regnum, Caes., Cic. ; tyrannidem, Cic. **b.** With abstr. subject : timor exercitum, Caes. ; animos magnitudine rei, Cic. ; sopor artūs, Verg. ; fama auris, Verg. **c.** *to preoccupy,* i.e. *to take up, fill* : contio homines occupatos occupat, Pl. ; in funambulo animum, Ter. ; LXIII annos aeque multa volumina occupasse mihi, Liv. Of money : *to employ preferentially, invest, loan* : argentum, Pl. ; pecuniam apud populos, Cic. ; pecuniam dulescentulo grandi faenore, Cic. **d.** *to get . siart of, anticipate, do something first or before* another : occupat egressas quamlibet ante ratis, Ov. With *Inf.* as Object : Pl., Hor., Liv. Absol. : occupantes opp. to praeoccupati, Liv.

oc-currō, currere, currī (rarely cucurrī), cursum, *to run, hasten or go towards or to meet.* **1.** Lit. **A.** To persons. **a.** Intentionally : Pl. ; obviam alicui, Pl. ; alicui, Caes., Hor., Suet. Of hostile movement : legionibus, Caes. ; telis, Verg. **b.** Unintentionally : *to meet or fall in with, come across* : Hor. ; quibuscumque signis occurrerat, se aggregabat, Caes. **B.** To a place : *to hasten to* ; *to go to* : *to attend* : eo occurrere, Caes. ; in aliam civitatem, Cic. ; ad concilium, Liv. ; also, concilio, Liv. **C.** *to meet* by lying in the way : in asperis locis silex, Liv. **2.** Transf. **a.** *to meet, oppose, counteract* (by deeds or words) : eius consiliis, Cic. ; alicuius orationi, Tac. Impers. Pass. : occurritur nobis a doctis, Cic. **b.** *to meet, obviate* : venienti morbo, Pers. ; exspectationi, Cic. ; rei, Nep. **c.** Mentally : *to*

presens bodsJ, secur : quodcumque in mentem veniat aut quodcumque occurrat, Cic. ; Liv. ; Tac. ; ea animo, Liv. ; Cic.

occursātiō, ōnis, *f.* [occursō], *a running to meet* ; hence, *fussy attention* : Cic. In *pl.* : Cic.

occursō, āre [*freq.* occurrō], *to run, go, or come to meet, to meet.* **1.** Lit. **a.** In gen. : Sall. With DAT. : capro, Verg. ; fugientibus, Tac. Of hostile movement : Sall. ; gladio, Caes. **b.** To a place : *to hasten towards* : quid tu huc occursas ? Pl. **2.** Transf. **a.** *to forestall* : fortunae, Plin. Pan. **b.** Mentally : *to enter the thoughts, occur to* : verba, Plin. Ep. With DAT. : animo scripta, Plin. Ep. With ACC. : me occursant multae (mulieres), Pl.

occursus, ūs, *m.* [occurrō]. **I.** *a meeting, falling in with* : vacuis occursu hominum viis, Liv. ; occursum alicuius vitare, Tac. Of things : rota stipitis occursu fracta ac disiecta, Ov. **II.** *a hurried movement* : militum, Liv.

Ōceanus, ī, *m.* **I.** *the great sea that encompasses the land, the ocean* : Enn., Cic., Verg. **II.** *the part of the ocean-stream* determined by the context, the North Sea, the Atlantic, Indian Ocean. **III.** In myth, personified as *the son of Caelus (Heaven) and Terra (Earth)* ; *husband of Tethys, and father of the rivers and nymphs* ; **Ōceanitis**, idis, *f. a daughter of Ocean.*

ocellātum, ī, *n.* [ocellus], lit. *that which has little eyes* ; hence, *anything marked with small spots* (e.g. dice) : ocellatis ludere, Suet.

ocellus, ī, *m.* [*dim.* oculus], *a dear little eye* : Pl., Cat., Ov. As term of endearment : Pl., Cat. So of things : cur ocellos Italiae, villulas meas, non vides ? Cic. Ep. ; insularum, Cat.

ōcimum, ī, *n. basil* : Plin., Pers.

ōcior, ōcius, *comp. adj.* [*cf.* ὠκύς], *swifter, fleeter* : ocior ventis, Verg. ; Hor. Sup. ōcissimus : Plin.

ōciter, *adv. quickly, swiftly, speedily* : Enn. Comp. : idque ocius faciet, Cic. ; serius ocius sors exitura, Hor. Sometimes the Comp. is used in Posit. sense : *quickly, speedily* : Ter., Caes., Verg., etc. Sup. : quam ocissume ad provinciam accedat, Sall. ; Pl.

Ocnus or **-os**, *m. the founder of Mantua.*

ocrea, ae, *f. a greave* (protective armour for the shins) : Verg., Liv.

ocreātus, a, um [ocrea], *wearing greaves* : Hor.

Octāvius, a, *the name of a Roman gens* ; esp. C. Octavius, *the Emperor Augustus, who, as adopted son of C. Iulius Caesar, became C. Iulius Caesar Octavianus* ; **Octāvia**, ae, *f.* **I.** *sister of Augustus, wife of C. Marcellus and later of M. Antonius.* **II.** *d. of Claudius Caesar and wife of Nero* ; *murdered* A.D. 62.

octāvus, a, um [octō], *eighth* : pars, Cic. Ep. ; legio, Caes. ; ad octavum (*sc.* lapidem), Tac. ; marmor, Mart. As Noun, **octāva**, ae, *f.* (*sc.* hora) *the eighth hour of the day* : Juv. Neut. Acc. as *Adv.,* **octāvum**, *for the eighth time* : Liv. [It. *ottavo.*]

octāvus-decimus, a, um, *eighteenth* : Tac.

octiēns (**-iēs**), *eight times* : Cic.

octingentēsimus (**-ēnsimus**), a, um [octingentī], *eight hundredth* : annus, Cic.

octingentī, ae, a [octō centum], *eight hundred* : Cic., Liv.

octi-pēs, pedis, adj. [octō pēs], *eight-footed* : Prop., Ov.

octō, *indecl. adj.* [Gk. ὀκτώ], *eight* : Enn., Cic., etc. [It. *otto* ; Sp. *ocho* ; Fr. *huit*.]

Octōber, bris, [octō], *of the eighth month* of the Roman year, which originally began with March ; *of October* : Octobres Idūs, Mart. As Noun (*sc.* mensis) : *October* : Col.

octōgēnārius, a, um [octōgēnī], *of eighty* : Plin. Ep.

octōgēnī, ae, a, [octō], *a group of eighty* or *eighty each* : Liv.

octōgēnsimus (or **-gēsimus**), a, um [octōgintā], *eightieth* : Cic., Juv.

octōgiēns (**-iēs**), *adv. eighty times* : Cic.

octōgintā, *indecl. adj.* [octō], *eighty* : Cic. [It. *ottanta*.]

octō-iugis, e, *adj.* [iugum], *eight in a team, eight together* : transf. : nunc iam octoiugis ad imperia obtinenda ire, Liv.

octōnārius, a, um [octōnī], *consisting of a group of eight* : versus (an iambic verse of eight feet), Quint.

octōnī, ae, a [octō]. **I.** *a group* or *sum of eight* : octona milia, 8000, Caes., Liv. ; octonos (*sc.* asses) referentes Idibus aeris, Hor. ; octonis iterum natalibus actis, Ov. **II.** *eight each* : alii octonos lapides eofodiunt, Pl. ; huius generis octoni ordines ducti, Caes.

octōphoros, on, *adj.* [ὀκτώφορος], *carried by eight bearers* : lectica, Cic. As Noun : Cic. Ep., Mart., Suet.

octuplicātus, a, um [*cf.* duplicātus], *eightfold, multiplied by eight* : octuplicato censu, Liv.

octuplus, a, um [*cf.* duplus], *eight-fold* : pars, Cic. As Noun, **octuplum**, ī, n. *an eightfold penalty* : damnare aliquem octupli, Cic.

octussis, is, m. [octō assis (= as)], *a sum of eight asses* : Hor.

oculātus, a, um [oculus]. **I.** *having eyes, seeing* : testis, Pl. ; Clodius male oculatus, Suet. **II.** *that strikes the eye, exposed to view, conspicuous* : oculatissimus locus, S. C. ap. Plin. ; oculatā die vendere (i.e. for cash, opp. to caecā die), Pl.

oculeus, a, um [oculus], *sharp-sighted* : Argus, Pl.

oculicrepīda, ae, m. [oculus crepō], *Bangeyes* (comic. of a slave) : Pl.

oculissumus, a, um (comically-formed *Sup.* from oculus, *cf.* Eng. ' the apple of one's eye,' and Lat. ocellus) : oculissume homo, Pl.

oculitus, *adv. as one's eyes* (i.e. *most dearly*) : amare, Pl.

oculus, ī, m. [*cf.* ὄπωπα, ὄσσε, ὄσσομαι], *an eye*. **1.** L i t. : acuti, venusti, eminentes, Cic. ; maligni, Verg. ; nigri vegetique, Suet. ; oculis captus (i.e. blinded), Cic. ; altero oculo captus, Liv. ; oculos adicere ad aliquem (i.e. to glance at), Pl. ; oculos adicere alicui rei (i.e. to covet), Cic. ; oculos conicere in aliquem, Cic. ; Verg. ; de or ab aliquo deicere, Cic. ; in terram figere, Tac. ; demittere, Ov. ; attollere, premere, Verg. ; erigere, circumferre, Ov. ; auferre

spectanti (i.e. to cheat him before his eyes), Liv. ; in oculis esse (often mentally), Cic., Ov., Liv., etc. ; habere in oculis, Pl. ; ante oculos esse or habere, Cic., Liv. ; ante oculos ponere, Cic. ; sub oculis (alicuius) esse or habere, Caes., Liv., etc. ; traducti per hostium oculos, Liv. ; ab or ex oculis abire, Pl., Cic., Liv. ; concedere, Cic. ; elabi, Liv. ; auferri, Tac. As a term of endearment, *the apple of my eye* : Pl. **2.** T r a n s f. **a.** *the power of seeing, sight, vision* : oculum, oculos amittere, Cic. ; restituere alicui, Suet. **b.** Mental : mentis oculis videre aliquid, Cic. Also most of phrases under l. **c.** Of plants : *an eye, bud* : oculos imponere, Verg. Also *a knot* on roots, etc. : Cato, Varr. **d.** *a bright ornament* : hi duo illos oculos orae maritimae effoderunt (i.e. Corinth and Carthage), Cic. [It. *occhio* ; Fr. *oeil*.]

ōdēum, ī, n. [ᾠδεῖον], *a public building for musical performances* : Vitr., Suet.

ōdī, ōdisse, (*Perf.* ōsus sum, Pl. ; ōdīvit, Anton. in Cic. ; *Fut. Part.* ōsūrus, Cic.) a *Pres. Perf.* L i t. *to have taken a dislike, hence,* **a.** *to hate* : Acc., Cic., Ov., etc. With Acc. : Pl., Cic., Ov., etc. With *Inf.* : Pl., Hor. **b.** In less exact sense : *to dislike; to be displeased* or *disgusted at* : se odisse, Pl., Juv. ; Persicos apparatūs, Hor. ; odi cum cera vacat, Ov. For *Pass. v.* odium.

odiōsē, *adv. in a hateful manner, odiously* : Pl., Ter., Cic.

odiōsicus, a, um [odiōsus], *comically for* odiosus · Pl.

odiōsus, a, um [odium], *hateful, odious, annoying* : odiosus mihi es, Pl. ; genus hominum, Cic. ; Lucr. ; Ov. Of things : dona, Pl. ; motūs odiosiores, Cic. ; odiosissima natio, Phaedr.

odium, ī, n. [*cf.* ōdī], *dislike, ill-will, hatred, aversion.* **a.** In gen. : concitare, struere, Cic. ; movere, exercere, Ov. ; saturare, placare, restinguere, Cic. ; privato odio invisus, Liv. With *Subj.* G E N. : magnum odium Pompei suscepistis, Cic. Ep. ; odium alicuius subire, Cic. Ep. ; in alicuius odium inruere, Cic. With *Obj.* G E N. : magnum me cuiuspiam rei odium cepit, Cic. ; Nep. **b.** *an object of dislike* or *hatred* ; esp. in D A T. with esse, as *Pass.* of odi ; *to be an object of dislike* ; hence, *disliked* or *hated* : alicui esse odio, Pl., Cic., Verg., etc. **c.** In *pl.* : *feelings of dislike* : sibi conciliare odia, Caes. : omnium in se gentium odia convertisset, Cic.

odor (older **odōs**, like arbōs, labōs, *etc.* : Pl., Lucr.), ōris, m. [*cf.* Gk. ὄζω, ὀδμή], a *smell, scent, odour.* **1.** L i t. **A.** In gen. : taeter, Caes. ; gravis, Verg. ; foeditatis, Cic. **B.** When undefined. **a.** *a pleasant odour, perfume* : Hor. **b.** *a disagreeable smell ; a stench, stink* : Sall. **2.** T r a n s f. **a.** Mostly in *pl.* : *a perfume, aromatic substance* : fragrans Assyrio odore domus, Cat. ; ara fumat odore, Hor. ; perfusus liquidis odoribus, Hor. ; corpus differtum odoribus conditur, Tac. ; crocei, Verg. ; incendere odores, Pl., Cic. **b.** *a scent, inkling, suggestion* : hominum furta odore persequi, Cic. ; suspicionis, Cic.

odōrātiō, ōnis, *f.* [odōror], *a smelling*, *smell:* delectatio odorationum, Cic.

odōrātus, a, um. **I.** *Part.* odōrō. **II.** Adj.: *that has a smell;* esp. *sweet-smelling*, *fragrant:* Verg., Hor., Ov. *Comp.* and *Sup.:* Plin.

odōrātus, ūs, *m.* [odōror]. **I.** *the act of smelling:* pomorum, Cic. **II.** *the sense of smell:* Cic.

odōrifer, fera, ferum. **I.** *bringing odours*, *fragrant:* Prop. **II.** *producing perfumes or spices:* gens, Ov.

odōrō, āre [odor], *to give a fragrance to:* aëra fumis, Ov.

odōror, ārī [odor]. **1.** Lit. **a.** *to smell at*, *examine by smelling:* pallam, Pl. **b.** *to smell out*, *detect by the scent:* Pl.; cibum, Hor. **2.** Transf. **a.** *to snuff, to nose* (as a dog), i.e. *to seek for:* hunc decemviratum, Cic. **b.** *to search out, trace out, investigate:* Cic. With *Indir. Quest.:* Cic. **c.** *to get an inkling or smattering of:* philosophiam, Tac.

odōrus, a, um [odor]. **I.** *emitting a scent or odour, fragrant:* flos, Ov. **II.** *tracking by the smell, keen-scented:* odora canum vis, Verg.

odōs, *v.* odor, *ad init.*

Odrysae (-nsae), ārum, *m. pl. a people of Thrace*, *on the Hebrus;* **Odrysius**, a, um, *Thracian;* and **Odrysii**, ōrum, *m. pl. the Thracians.*

Odyssēa (-ia), ae, *f. the Odyssey; a poem of Homer; also a poem of Livius Andronicus.*

Oeager (-agrus), ī, *m. a king of Thrace, the father of Orpheus;* **Oeagrius**, a, um, *Thracian.*

Oebalus, ī, *m. king of Sparta, the father of Tyndareus and grandfather of Helen;* **Oebalidēs**, ae, *m. a male descendant of Oebalus;* in *pl.:* **Oebalidae**, ārum, *m.* i.e. *Castor and Pollux.* **Oebalis**, idis, *f. adj. Spartan.* **Oebalia**, ae, *f.* poet. for *Tarentum*, a colony of Sparta; hence, **Oebalius**, a, um, *Spartan*, and hence, **i.** *Tarentine:* Ov. **ii.** *Sabine;* because the Sabines were believed to be descended from the Spartans: Ov.

Oechalia, ae, *f. a town in Euboea;* **Oechalis**, idis, *f. a woman of Oechalia.*

Oeclidēs, ae, *m. son of Oecleus*, i.e. *Amphiaraus.*

oeconomia, ae, *f.* [οἰκονομία, *the management of household affairs*]. Rhet.: *the proper arrangement and division of a speech or play:* Quint.

oeconomicus, a, um [οἰκονομικός]. **I.** *of or on domestic economy:* in eo libro, qui *Oeconomicus* inscribitur, Cic. **II.** *orderly, methodical* (in arrangement): Quint.

Oedipūs, odis and ī, *m. king of Thebes, the son of Laius and Jocosta.* He solved the riddle of the Sphinx; in ignorance of his parentage he killed his father and married his mother. Oedipūs Colōnēus, *Oedipus at Colonus, the name of a tragedy of Sophocles, and of one by Caesar:* **Oedipodēs**, ae, *m. another form of Oedipus;* **Oedipodionius**, a, um.

Oeneus (disyl.), eī and eos, *m. king of Aetolia or (alydon, h. of Althaea, and f. of Meleager and Deianira;* **Oenēus** (trisyl.), a, um;

Oenīdēs, ae; *m. a male descendant of Oeneus*, i.e. *Meleager*, or *Diomedes, son of Tydeus.*

Oenomaus, ī, *m. king of Pisa in Elis, the father of Hippodamia.*

Oenōnē, ēs, *f. a Phrygian nymph, wife of Paris, but afterwards deserted by him.*

oenophorum, ī *n.* [οἰνοφόρον], *a wine-holder, wine-hamper:* Lucil., Hor., Juv., etc.

Oenopia, ae, *f. the ancient name of Aegina;* **Oenopius**, a, um.

oenopōlium, ī, *n.* [οἰνοπωλεῖον], *a wine-shop:* Pl.

Oenōtria, ae, *f. an old name of S.E. Italy*, and poet. for *Italy in general;* **Oenōtrius**, **Oenōtrus**, a, um, *Italian.*

oenus, a, um, an ancient form for ūnus, q.v.

oestrus, ī, *m.* [οἶστρος], *a stinging insect* (pure Lat. asilus). **1.** Lit. **a.** : Verg. **2.** Transf.: *frenzy, inspiration:* Juv. [It. Sp. *estro*.]

oesus, an ancient form for ūsus : Cic.

oesypum, ī, *n.* [οἴσυπος], *the greasy sweat and dirt of unwashed wool* (used as a cosmetic): Ov.

Oeta, ae, or **Oetē**, ēs, *f. a mountain range in the south of Thessaly, where Hercules ascended the funeral pile, now Katavóthra;* **Oetaeus**, a, um; **Oetaeus**, ī, *m. the Oetean god;* i.e. *Hercules.*

ofella, ae, *f.* [dim. offa], *a bit, morsel:* Juv.

offa, ae, *f. a little ball or pellet* made of flour. **1.** Lit.: Enn., Verg.; pultis, Cic. **2.** Transf. in gen.: *a lump, mass:* penita, Pl. Of *a swelling:* Juv. Of *a shapeless mass, abortion:* Juv.

offātim, adv. *in little lumps:* Pl.

offectus, a, um, *Part.* officiō.

of-fendō, fendere, fendī, fēnsum, *to strike or dash against.* **A.** Trans. **1.** Lit. **a.** With Acc. of part of body struck : latus, Cic.; pedem, Ov.; caput, Liv.; caput ad fornicem, Quint. **b.** With Acc. of person or thing struck against : aliquem cubito, Pl.; limen (*sc.* pede), Ov.; scutum, Liv. **2.** Transf. **a.** *to hit upon, light upon, meet with, find:* parata, Pl.; aliquem, Enn., Ter.; imparatum te offendam, Cic. Ep.; nondum perfectum templum, Cic. **b.** *to shock, offend, displease:* neminem unquam non re, non verbo, non vultu denique offendit, Cic.; exstinctum lumen recens offendit naris, Lucr.; si vultus eorum victorem offendisset, Liv. In *Pass.* (with Acc. and *Inf.*): Phaedr., Suet. **B.** Intrans. **1.** Lit. (with Dat. or in and Abl.): dens solido, Hor.; in scopulis puppis, Ov.; naves in redeundo (terrae) offenderunt, Caes. **2.** Transf. **a.** *to meet with a mishap or disaster, come to grief:* in periculo belli, Cic.; M. Atilius primo accessu ad Africam, Liv.; *Impers. Pass.:* Caes., Cic. Ep. Also in a law-suit: apud iudices offendere, Cic. **b.** *to stumble, blunder, make a mistake:* Cic., Nep. **c.** *to give offence, be offensive:* nihil tibi, Cic. Ep.; nomen consulare (*sc.* plebi), Liv. **d.** *to take offence:* in aliquem, Caes., Cic.

offensa, ae, *f.* [offendō], *a striking or grating against.* Transf. **a.** *displeasure:* magnā in offensā sum apud Pompeium, Cic. Ep.; offensam meruisse, Ov.; gravissimam contrahere, Suet. **b.** *an injury received ; an offence, affront :* offensas vindicet ense suas, Ov. ; Sen. Ep.

offensātiō, ōnis, *f.* [offēnsō]. **I.** Lit. : *a hitting* or *striking against :* Quint. **2.** Transf. *a stumbling, a blunder :* Sen.

offensiō, ōnis, *f.* [offendō], *a striking against, a stumbling.* **1.** Lit. : pedis, Cic. **2.** Transf. **a.** *a mishap, disaster :* Caes. ; offensionibus belli, Cic. In a law-suit : Cic. Of bodily ailments, esp. *a relapse :* Cic. **b.** In *pl.* : *acts giving offence :* iudiciorum, Cic. **c.** *offence received* or *felt ; displeasure, aversion :* suscipere apud aliquem, Cic. ; vitare, Cic. ; offensiones accendere, Tac. ; habere ac res aliquas offensionem atque fastidium, Cic.

offensiuncula, ae, *f.* [*dim.* offēnsiō]. **I.** *a slight displeasure :* Cic. Ep. **II.** *a slight check* or *mishap :* Cic.

offensō, āre [*freq.* offendō], *to strike* or *dash against repeatedly.* **1.** Lit. : Lucr., Liv. **2.** Transf. : *to stumble* in speaking : Quint.

offensus, a, um. **I.** *Part.* offendō. **II.** Adj. **a.** *brought into disfavour, offensive :* Cic. **b.** *offended, displeased, incensed :* Cic., Ov. ; animus, Cic. *Comp. :* Cic.

offensus, ūs, *m.* [offendō], *a striking against, a shock.* **1.** Lit. : Lucr. **2.** Transf. : *offence, dislike :* sin vita in offensu est, Lucr.

of-ferō, offerre, obtulī (optulī), oblātum, *to bring before* or *against ; to present, show.* **1.** Lit. : strictam aciem venientibus, Verg. ; dextram Philippo, Curt. Mostly *Refl. to present oneself* to a person ; *to meet, encounter :* se alicui, Ter., Cic., Verg. Of a hostile encounter : se hostibus, Caes., Verg. ; Liv. ; in *Pass. :* Alexandro cessisset in acie oblatus par Manlius Torquatus, Liv. **2.** Transf. **a.** *to present, show :* fors illis meum adventum, Ter. ; quam in partem fors eum obtulit, Caes. ; nulla mihi te fors obtulit, Hor. ; locum fors offert, Caes. More freq. in *Pass. :* occasione oblatā, Caes., etc. ; lex quaedam videbatur oblata, Cic. ; nova res oblata est, Verg. ; religio oblata est, Cic., Liv. **b.** *to present, expose :* meum caput vilitati, Pl. ; leto caput, Lucr. ; se morti, Caes. ; se periculis, Cic. ; se ad mortem, Cic. ; vitam in discrimen, Cic. **c.** *to offer, proffer, confer :* alicui optatissimum beneficium, Caes. ; Ter. ; Cic. ; in omnia ultro suam offerens operam, Liv. ; foedus, Verg. ; se medium paci, Verg. With Acc. and *Fut. Inf. :* Tac. **d.** *to offer (and do), cause, inflict :* alicui laetitiam, iniuriam, Ter. ; mortem patri, stuprum sorori, Cic.

offerūmenta, ae, *f.* [offerō], *a present :* comically for a stripe : Pl.

officina (older **opificina**), ae, *f.* [opifex], *a workshop, manufactory, shop.* **1.** Lit. : Pl., Cic., Hor. ; armorum, Caes. ; monetae, Liv. **2.** Transf. : falsorum chirographorum, Cic. ; sapientiae, Cic. ; corruptellarum, Liv.

of-ficiō, ficere, fēcī, fectum [faciō]. Lit. *to do* or *make against* or *in the way of, to get in the way of, obstruct, interfere with.* **A.** Trans. (only in *Puss.*): Lucr. **B.** Intrans. (with DAT.). **1.** Lit. : nunc quidem

paululum, inquit, a sole ; offecerat videlicet apricanti, Cic. ; ipsi sibi, Sall. ; hostium itineri, Sall. **2.** Transf. : *to oppose, obstruct, to be detrimental :* nec mentis quasi luminibus officit altitudo fortunae, Cic. ; meis commodis, Cic. ; consiliis alicuius, Sall. ; nomini, Liv. ; laetis frugibus herbae, Verg. With *quo minus* and *Sulj. :* Plin. Ep.

officiōsē, adv. *courteously, obligingly :* Cic. *Comp. :* Cic. Ep. *Sup. :* Plin. Ep.

officiōsus, a, um [officium]. **I.** *ready to serve, courteous, obliging :* homo, Cic. Ep. ; amicitia, Cic. ; sedulitas, Hor. *Comp.* and *Sup. :* Cic. **II.** *dutiful, in accordance with duty :* dolor, labores, Cic.

officium, i, *n.* [contr. of opificium], *a service of free-will.* **I.** Voluntary. **A.** In gen. : *a kind service, courtesy, attention :* Cic. **B.** In partic. **a.** *complimentary service, payment of respect, ceremonial :* facere, Hor. ; offici causā aliquem prosequi, Liv. ; ambitus officiorum, Tac. ; supremis in matrem officiis, Tac. ; triste, Ov. ; salutationis, Suet. With *Obj.* GEN. : novorum consulum, Suet. **b.** In love : Prop., Ov. **c.** *a readiness to do a service, obliging nature, sense of loyalty* or *duty :* Caes., Cic., Nep. ; in rem publicam, Cic. **II.** Obligatory (but done with freewill) : *duty* (social or public). **1.** Lit. **a.** In gen. : suom facere, Pl., Ter. ; exsequi, servare, deserere, Cic. ; rei publicae praestare, Caes. ; officio fungi, vacare, Cic. ; officio satis facere, deesse, Cic. ; ab officio discedere, Cic. **b.** Of subject nations, etc. : *submission, allegiance :* huic mandat, Remos in officio contineat, Caes. ; in officio manere, Nep. **2.** Transf. : *an (official) duty, office, function.* **a.** Of persons : toti officio maritimo M. Bibulus praepositus, Caes. ; legationis, Caes. ; censurae, Cic. In *pl.* : Caes. **b.** Of things : corporis, Lucr. ; Ter. **c.** CONCR. : *an office :* praetoris, Plin. Ep.

of-fīgō, fīgere, *to fasten down :* pedes, Pl. ; furcas, Cato ; ramos, Liv.

offirmātē, adv. *firmly, stubbornly :* resistere, Suet.

offirmātus, a, um. **I.** *Part.* offirmō. **II.** Adj. : *firm, resolute :* animus, Pl. *Comp. :* in hac iracundiā offirmatior, Cic. Ep.

of-firmō, āre. With or without *Refl. Pron. : to be determined, to persevere in :* certum offirmare est viam me quam decrevi persequi, Ter. With *Inf. :* Pl.

of-flectō, ere, *to turn about :* navem, Pl.

offōcō, āre [faucēs], *to strangle, choke :* Sen.

of-frēnātus, a, um, *curbed.* Transf. : Pl.

of-fringō, ere [frangō], *to break up by cross-ploughing :* Varr.

offūcia, ae, *f.* [fūcus], *a paint, wash for the face.* **1.** Lit. : Pl. **2.** Transf. : *a trick, delusion :* Pl.

offula (syncop., **offla**), ae, *f.* [*dim.* offa], *a little bit, a small piece :* Varr.

of-fulgeō, fulgēre, fūlsī, *to shine upon :* nova lux oculis, Verg.

of-fundō, fundere, fūdī, fūsum, *to pour before.* **1.** Lit. **a.** cibum (avibus), Pl. **b.** Mostly in *Mid. : to pour (itself) over ; to spread over :* nobis aër crassus offunditur, Cic. With NOM. of thing obscured : obscuratur et offunditur luce solis lumen lucernae, Cic. **2. Transf. a.** cum altitudo caliginem oculis offudisset, Liv. In *Mid.* : haec indoctorum animis offusa caligo est, Cic. ; omnium rerum terror oculis auribusque est offusus, Liv. **b.** With Acc. (or Nom. in *Mid.*) of person or thing covered : Marcellorum meum pectus memoria offudit, Cic. ; offusus pavore, Tac.

offūsus, a, um, *Part.* offundō.

og-gannĭō, īre, *to snarl at* : Pl. ; aliquid ad aurem, Ter.

og-gerō, ere, *to bring to, to proffer* : osculum alicui, Pl. : amor amarum oggerit, Pl.

Ōgўgēs, is, also **Ōgўgus**, i, *m. the mythic founder and king of Thebes in Boeotia, in whose reign a great deluge is said to have occurred ;* **Ōgўgius**, a, um, *Theban.*

oh, *interj.* an expression of various emotion : Pl., Ter. Repeated, oh, oh, oh, as an exclamation of lamentation : Pl. ; oh, oh, as an exclamation of exultation : Pl.

ōhē, *interj.* ho ! soho ! ho there ! ohe, iam satis est, Pl. ; Hor. ; Mart.

oi, *interj.* an exclamation of complaint or weeping : Ter.

Oīleus (trisyl.), ĕī and eos, *m. king of Locris, father of the lesser Ajax ;* **Oīlĭdēs**, ae, *m. Ajax son of Oileus.*

olea, ae, *m.f.* [ἐλαία], *an olive, an olive-berry.* **1.** Lit. : Cato, Hor. **2.** Transf. : *an olive-tree* : Pl., Cic., Verg., etc.

oleāgĭnus, a, um [olea and *gen* in gignō], *of the olive-tree* : radix, Verg.

oleārĭus, a, um [oleum], *of or for oil, oil-* : Cato, Cic. As Noun, **oleārĭus**, i, *m. an oil-seller* : Pl.

oleaster, strī, *m.* [olea], *the wild olive-tree, oleaster* : Verg., Ov.

Ōlĕnĭus, a, um, *of Olenus,* a town in Achaia and Aetolia ; hence, *Achaian* or *Aetolian* : Ov.

olēns, entis. **I.** *Part.* oleō. **II.** Adj. : *smelling, odorous ;* in good or bad sense. **1.** Lit. **a.** *sweet-smelling, fragrant, odoriferous* : Verg., Ov. **b.** *stinking, rank* : Pl., Verg., Hor., etc. **2.** Transf. : *musty* : Tac.

oleō, ēre (older **olō**, ere) [*cf.* odor], *to emit a smell, to smell* or *savour of.* **1.** Lit. : male, Pl. ; bene, Cic. Ep. With *Intern.* Acc. : nihil, Cic. Ep. ; unguenta, Pl., Ter. With Abl. : sulpure, Ov. ; Prop. **2.** Transf. : aurum huic olet, Pl. With *Intern.* Acc. : furtum, Pl. ; peregrinum, Cic. ; nihil ex Academiā, Cic. ; vina Camenae, Hor. ; verba alumnum, Quint. [It. *olire.*]

oleum, i, *n.* [ἔλαιον], *olive-oil, oil.* **1.** Lit. : Cato, Cic., Verg., etc. Prov. : oleum et operam perdere (i.e. to lose one's time and trouble), Pl. ; oleum addere camino (i.e. to pour oil on the fire), Hor. **2.** Transf. **a.** *the palaestra* (from the use of oil by the wrestlers) : Cat. **b.** *literary contests, rhetorical exercises* : Cic. [It. *olio* ; Fr. *huile.*]

ol-făcĭō, facere, fēcī, factum [oleō facĭō], *to smell, scent.* **1.** Lit. : aliquid, Cic. ; unguentum, Cat. **2.** Transf. : nummum, Cic. With *Indir. Quest.* : Ter.

olfactō, āre [*freq.* olfacĭō], *to smell at* : vestimentum, Pl.

olīdus, a, um [oleō], *smelling.* Of a bad smell, *rank* : capra, Hor. ; senex, Suet.

ōlim, *adv.* [ollus, the old form of ille], *at that time, at the time spoken of.* **A.** Followed by *cum* or *ubi* . saxum tunditur olim fluctibus condunt ubi sidera Cori, Verg. ; Pl. ; Lucr., etc. **B.** Of past time. **a.** *some time ago, once upon a time, formerly, in times past* : fuit olim senex, Pl. ; sic olim loquebantur, Cic. ; Hor., etc. ; olim . . . nuper, Cic. ; nunc . . . olim, Verg. ; olim . . . mox, Tac. ; olim . . . post . . . deinde . . . nunc, Sall. **b.** *now for a good while* : olim nescio quid sit otium, Plin. Ep. ; Juv. ; Tac. **C.** Of future time : *one day, on a future day, at a future time, in due time, hereafter* : utinam coram tecum olim, potius quam per epistulas ! Cic. Ep. ; forsan et haec olim meminisse iuvabit, Verg. ; Hor. **D.** *at any time, ever ;* also, denoting repetition or custom, *at times :* an quid est olim homini salute melius ? Pl. ; ut pueris olim dant crustula blandi doctores, Hor. ; Verg.

olit-, *v.* holit-.

olīva, ae, *f.* [ἐλαία], *an olive.* **1.** Lit. : Pl., Hor. **2.** Transf. **a.** *an olive-tree* : Cic., Verg., Hor. **b.** *an olive-wreath* : Verg., Hor. **c.** *a staff of olive-wood* : Verg., Ov.

olīvētum, i, *n.* [olīva], *an olive-grove* : Cic., Hor.

olīvĭfer, era, erum, *olive-bearing* : Mutuscae, Verg. ; arva, Ov.

olīvum, i, *n.* [ἔλαιον], *oil.* **1.** Lit. : Pl., Lucr., Verg., etc. **2.** Transf. **a.** *the palaestra* : our olivum vitat, Hor. **b.** *an unguent* : Syrio fragrans olivo, Cat. ; Prop.

olla (for aulula, q.v.), ae, *f. a pot* or *jar* : Cic. [Fr. *oille.*]

olle, ollus, *v.* ille, *ad init.*

olō, *v.* oleō.

olor, ōris, *m. a swan* : Verg., Hor., etc.

olōrīnus, a, um [olor], *of a swan* or *swans* : Verg., Ov.

olus, *v.* holus.

Olympia, ae, *f. a sacred region in Elis Pisatis, where the Olympian games were held ;* **Olympĭacus, Olympĭcus, Olympĭus**, a, um. **Olympĭum**, i, *n. the temple of the Olympic Jupiter* (Zeus).

Olympĭa, ōrum, *n. pl. the Olympic games held every four years at Olympia.*

(1) **Olympĭas**, adis, *f. an Olympiad (the period of four years between the Olympic games), which the Greeks usually employed in dating events. The first Olympiad is reckoned from* B.C. 776.

(2) **Olympĭas**, adis, *f. the wife of Philip, and mother of Alexander the Great.*

Olympĭonīcēs, ae, *m. a victor in the Olympian games* : Cic.

Olympus, i, *m. the name of several mountain ranges, the most celebrated of which is one on the boundary of Macedonia and Thessaly, regarded as the seat of the gods.* Transf. *the heavens :* Verg.

omāsum, i, *n.* [a Gallic word], *bullock's tripe.* **1.** Lit. : Hor. Transf. : *a paunch :* Hor.

ōmen, inis, *n.* **1.** Lit. : *a prognostic, sign, token, omen :* cum bonis ominibus incipere, Liv. ; i secundo omine, Hor. ; fati, Cic. ; triumphi, Juv. ; triste omen diem diffidit,

Liv.; avertere, Cic.; in alium vertere or convertere omen, Liv., Verg. N.B. that the derivation from os is implicit in many examples; i.e. *a chance-utterance* regarded as guidance from the gods: di te faxint cum istoc omine, Pl.; hominum voces quae vocant omina, Cic.; accipere, Cic., Liv.; exire malis ominibus, Cic. **2.** T r a n s f.: *of solemnities.* **a.** Of marriage: (virginem alicui) primis iugare ominibus, Verg. **b.** Of kingship: Verg. **c.** Of a promise: eâ lege atque omine, Ter. **d.** Of an escort's solemn good wishes: Cic.

ōmentum, I, *n. the fat-skin, adipose membrane.* **a.** In gen.: *fat:* Pers. **b.** *the membrane which includes the bowels, the caul:* hence, *the bowels:* Juv.

ōmĭnātor, ōris, *m.* [ōminor], *a diviner:* Pl.

ōmĭnor, ārī [ōmen], *to forebode, prognosticate, predict, prophesy:* aliquid rei publicae ominari, Cic.; felix faustumque imperium, Liv.; male ominatis parcite verbis, Hor. With Acc. and *Inf.:* Liv. With *Indir. Quest.:* Liv.

ōmĭnōsus, a, um [ōmen], *full of foreboding, ominous:* Plin. Ep.

ōmissus, a, um. **I.** *Part.* ōmittō. **II.** A d j.: *negligent, heedless, remiss:* animo esse omisso, Ter. *Comp.:* ab re omissior, Ter.

ō-mittō, mittere, mīsī, missum [ob mittō], *to let go, let loose, let fall suddenly.* **1.** L i t.: mulierem, Ter.; Pl.; pila, Caes.; arma, Liv.; animam (i.e. to die suddenly), Pl. **2.** T r a n s f. **a.** *to let go, abandon, give up:* tristitiam, Ter.; timorem, voluptates, Cic.; obsessionem nostrorum, Caes.; apparatum, Liv. With *Inf.:* Pl., Cic., Hor., etc. **b.** In speaking: *to pass over, say nothing of, omit:* ut alia omittam, Cic.; gratulationes, Cic.; Liv.; de reditu, Cic. **c.** *to disregard:* tempus, Caes.; hostem, Liv. **d.** Of faults: *to overlook:* unam hanc noxiam, Ter.; scelus impunitum, Sall.

omnĭfer, era, erum, *all-bearing, all-sustaining:* vultus (i.e. the surface of the earth), Ov.

omnĭgenus, a, um (GEN. *pl.* omnigenum, Verg.), *of all kinds:* Verg.

omnĭmŏdis (Lucr.) and **omnĭmŏdo** (and separately **omnī mŏdō**) (Sen.), *adv. by all means, wholly.*

omnīnō, *adv.* [omnis], *altogether, wholly, entirely.* **A.** Positively (or when the negative belongs to another word). **a.** With numerals, *in all:* diebus omnino decem et octo, Caes.; quinque omnino fuerunt, Cic. **b.** Of amount or measure: aut omnino aut magnâ ex parte, Cic.; sin omnino interierint omnia, Cic. Ep.; omnino quod cupis effugies, Cat. **c.** In general statements: *in general, universally:* de hominum genere, aut omnino de animalium loquor, Cic. So at the beginning of a general proposition: omnino fortis animus duabus rebus maxime cernitur, Cic. **d.** In concessions: *undoubtedly, no doubt, to be sure:* with *sed, tamen, autem:* pugnas omnino; sed cum adversariâ facili, Cic. **B.** With a negative: **a.** In order non (or haud) omnino: *not altogether, not entirely, not quite:* Pl., Cic., Verg., etc. Also, *absolutely not, not at all:*

ut non multum aut nihil omnino Graecis cederent, Cic.; ne faciam, inquis, omnino versûs, Hor. **b.** In order omnino non (or other negative): *altogether, absolutely not, not at all:* Cic.; omnino nullus, *absolutely none* or *non-existent,* Cic.; omnino nemo, *nobody at all,* Cic. **c.** non modo . . . sed omnino, to mark a climax: non modo imperator, sed liber habendus omnino non est, Cic. [It. *onninamente.*]

omni-părēns, entis, *adj. all-bearing, mother of all:* per terras omniparentis, Lucr.; terra, Verg.

omni-pŏtēns, entis, *adj. all-powerful, almighty:* Iuppiter, Enn., Cat.; fortuna, Verg.

omnis, e, *adj. all, every.* **a.** *all* (mostly in *pl.*): nemo omnium imperatorum qui vivunt, Liv.; Cic., etc.; praeda alia omnia militibus concessa est, Liv. Often without Noun, **omnēs,** *all men, all persons, everybody:* Ter., Cic. With *Partitive* GEN. (but mostly when omnes is qualified in some way): ut omnes Tarquiniae gentis exsules sunt, Liv.; praeter Verulanum omnes Hernici nominis, Liv. **omnia,** *all things, everything:* omnia quae sunt ad vivendum necessaria, Cic.; plebes omnia quam bellum malebat, Liv.; omnia facere: *to make every effort,* Cic.; esse omnia alicui, *to be one's all,* Ov., Liv. *Adv.* Acc.: omnia Mercurio similis, Verg. **b.** *every* (mostly in *sing.*): omni tempore, Caes.; omnis fraus, Cic.; militat omnis amans, Ov.; omnibus mensibus, Cic. **c.** *every kind of, all sorts of:* omnibus precibus petere contendit, Caes.; Cic.; omnis honestas, Cic.; Hor.; Liv. **d.** *the whole (cf.* tōtus*):* omnis insula est in circuitu viciens centena milia passuum, Caes.; caelum, Cic. *Neut.* as Noun, **omne,** *the universe:* Lucr. **e.** *general* (but only when it is a case of transferred epithet): omni defectione sociorum (= defectione omnium sociorum), Liv. **f.** Colloq. for ullus: *any:* sine omni periclo, Ter.; Pl.

omni-tŭēns, entis, *adj. all-seeing:* Lucr.

omni-văgus, a, um, *roving everywhere:* Diana, Cic.

omnĭvŏlus, a, um [volō], *willing every thing:* Cat.

Omphălē, ēs, *f. a queen of Lydia, whom Hercules served.*

onăger and **onăgrus,** I, *m.* [ὄναγρος], *a wild ass:* Varr., Verg.

onăgos, I, *m.* [ὀναγός], *an ass-driver:* Pl.

Onchēsmĭtēs, ae, *m.* [Ὀγχησμίτης], *a wind blowing from Onchesmus, a harbour of Epirus:* Cic. Ep.

Onchēstus, I, *f. a city of Boeotia;* **Onchēstius,** a, um.

onĕrārĭus, a, um [onus], *for carrying freight or burdens:* navis, Caes., Liv. Also without navis, Cic. Ep.; iumenta, Liv.

onĕro, āre [onus], *to load, burden, freight.* **1.** L i t.: navis, Caes.; iumenta, Sall.; aselli costas pomis, Verg. **2.** T r a n s f. **A.** umerum pallio, Ter.; vino et epulis onerati, Sall.; membra sepulcro, Verg.; mensas dapibus, Verg.; vina cadis, Verg. Comic.: aliquem pugnis, Pl. **B.** Abstractly. **a.** *to burden, overload, load:* aliquem mendaciis, Cic.; aliquem malis, Verg.; aethera votis,

Verg. ; aliquem laudibus, Liv. ; promissis, Sall. **b.** *to pile on, to aggravate :* iniuriam alicuius invidiā, Liv. ; pericula alicuius, Tac.

onerōsus, a, um [onus], *burdensome, heavy, oppressive.* **1.** L i t. : praeda, Verg. *Comp. :* Ov. **2.** T r a n s f. : onerosior altera sors est, Ov. ; damnatio, Plin. Ep.

onus, eris, n. (ABL. oneri, Pl.) *a load, burden, freight, cargo.* **1.** L i t. (on animals or ships) : Pl., Caes., Cic., Hor., etc. **2.** T r a n s f. **A.** Materially. **a.** Of the womb : gravidi ventris, Ov. **b.** In gen. : tanti oneris turris, Caes. ; tanta onera navium, Caes. ; ad minimum redigi onus, Ov. **B.** Abstractly. **a.** *a burden* (of taxes, expenses) : grave onus tributorum, Caes. ; civitatibus graviora onera iniungere, Caes. ; explicare, Cic. ; haec onera in dites a pauperibus inclinata, Liv. **b.** In gen. : Pl. ; onus offici suscipere, Cic. ; sustinere, adlevare, Cic. ; oneri esse alicui, Liv.

onustus, a, um [onus] *loaded, laden, burdened, freighted.* **1.** L i t. : asellus auro, Cic. Ep. ; naves frumento, Cic. With GEN. : cameli frumenti, Tac. **2.** T r a n s f. **A.** Materially. **a.** With food : cibo, Pl. ; corpus, Lucr. **b.** In gen. : *loaded, filled, full :* ager praedā, Sall. ; pharetra telis, Tac. ; pars vulneribus, Tac. Comic. : fustibus, Pl. With GEN. : auri, Pl. **B.** Abstractly : pectus laetitiā, Pl.

onyx, ychis, *m.* (also *f.*) [ὄνυξ, a finger-nail ; hence, from its colour], *a kind of yellowish marble, onyx,* of which vessels of many kinds were made ; it was also used for inlaying floors. **1.** L i t. : Plin., Mart. **2.** T r a n s f. : *a vessel of onyx, an onyx-box :* Hor. ; *fem. :* Mart. [It. *nichetto, niccolino.*]

opācitās, ātis, *f.* [opācus], *shadiness :* arborum, Tac.

opācō, āre [opācus], *to cover with shade, to shade :* platanus hunc locum, Cic. ; Verg.

opācus, a, um. **I.** *shady, in the shade :* ripa, Cic. ; nemus, Verg. ; frigus, Verg. *Comp. :* Plin. Ep. **II.** *darkened, dark, obscure :* nubes, Ov. ; mater (i.e. *the earth*), Ov. *Neut. pl.* as Noun : per opaca locorum, Verg.

ope, opēs, *v.* ops.

opella, ae, *f.* [dim. opera], *humble labour, service :* parva, Lucr. ; forensis, Hor.

opera, ae, *f.* [opus], *pains, exertion, labour, service.* **1.** L i t. **A.** In gen. : quam propter opera est mihi, Pl. ; res multae operae, Caes. ; dicare alicui, Ter. ; operam et laborem consumere in aliquā re, Cic. ; operam curamque in rebus honestis ponere, Cic. ; operam studiumque in res obscuras conferre, Cic. ; praebere amicis, Cic. ; tribuere rei publicae, Cic. ; exigere, interponere, impendere, perdere, Cic. ; insumere, alicui navare, Liv. **B.** *a service, rendering of service, assistance :* operas alicui dare, Pl. ; Cic. ; operam praestare in re militari, Caes. ; in omnibus bellis singulari eius operā fuerat usus, Caes. ; forensibus operis, Cic. ; in operis societatis, Cic. **2.** T r a n s f. **A.** *care, attention* bestowed on anything, esp. in phr. **a.** operam dare : alicui, Pl. ; amori, Ter. ; dare operam funeri (i.e. to attend), Cic. ; tonsori (i.e. to get shaved),

Suet. ; sermoni, Cic. ; bellis, Ov. ; dent operam consules ne quid res publica detrimenti capiat, Caes. **b.** est operae pretium, i.e. it is worth while (usually with *Inf.*), Enn., Cic., etc. ; and elliptically, est operae, Enn. ; operae pretium facere (i.e. to do what is worth the trouble), Liv. **c.** In ABL. operā meā, tuā, etc., *through me, you, etc. ; thanks to me, you, etc. :* meā operā, Q. Fabi, Tarentum recepisti, Cic. ; Pl. ; Caes., etc. **d.** unā or eādem operā, *in the same manner, at the same time :* unā operā mihi sunt sodales, quā iste, Pl. **e.** *practical experience ;* in ABL. : id operā expertus sum esse ita, Pl. **B.** *leisure, spare time :* operae ubi mihi erit, ad te venero, Pl. ; deest mihi opera, Cic. Ep. ; nec Hannibali operae esse legationes audire, Liv. **C.** Concr. **a.** *a day's work or labour* (mostly in *pl.*) : quaternis operis singula iugera confodere, Varr. **b.** *a day-labourer, journeyman ;* also, in gen. *a labourer, workman* (mostly in *pl.*) : Pl., Cic., Hor., Liv., etc. T r a n s f. in a bad sense, operae, *hired gangs of roughs, gangsters :* mercennariae, Cic. ; theatrales (claqueurs), Tac. **c.** *work done :* operae aranearum, Pl. ; Cic. Ep. [Fr. *oeuvre.*]

operārius, a, um [opera], *labouring :* homo, Cic. Ep. As Noun. **a. operārius,** i, *m. a labourer, workman :* Cato ; operarius linguā celeri et exercitatā, Cic. **b. operāria,** ae, *f. a work-woman* (with play on the word), Pl. [Fr. *ouvrier.*]

operculum, i, n. [operiō], *a cover, lid :* Cic.

operīmentum, i, *n.* [operiō], *a covering, cover, lid :* Cato, Cic., Sall.

o-periō, perīre, peruī, pertum [ob-par-i-ō, "to put on, over" ; *v.* aperiō], *to cover, cover over.* **1.** L i t. **a.** capita, Pl. ; capite operto esse, Cic. ; terras umbrā nox, Verg. Comic. : aliquem loris, Ter. **b.** *to cover and so overwhelm :* fons fluctu totus operiretur nisi etc., Cic. ; classem nimbo lapidum, Liv. **2.** T r a n s f. **A.** *to shut, close :* foris, Pl. ; ostium, Ter. ; oculos, Quint. **B.** Abstractly. **a.** *to overwhelm :* contumeliis opertus, Cic. ; infamiā, Tac. **b.** *to conceal :* quo pacto hoc operiam ? Ter. ; domestica mala, Tac. ; luctum, Plin. Ep.

operor, āri [opus], *to work, labour with great care, be busily occupied or engaged.* **a.** In gen. : in cute curandā, Hor. With DAT. : rei publicae, Liv. ; conubiis arvisque novis, Verg. ; ornandis capillis, Ov. ; studiis litterarum, Tac. **b.** On sacred rites (esp. in *Perf. Part.*) : sacra refer Cereri latis operatus in herbis, Verg. ; sacris, Hor. ; Liv. ; prodigiis procurandis, Liv. ; Vestae, Ov.

operōsē, *adv. with great labour or pains :* Cic., Ov. *Comp. :* Plin.

operōsus, a, um [opera]. **A.** A c t. : *active, busy, industrious.* **1.** L i t. : colonus, Ov. ; senectus, Cic. With GEN. : dierum, Ov. **2.** T r a n s f. of a medicine, *active, powerful :* herbae, Ov. **B.** P a s s. : *requiring much labour, made* (or *done*) *with much labour :* labor, Cic. ; artes, Cic. ; res, Liv. ; templa, Ov. ; carmina, Hor. *Comp. :* sepulcrum operosius, Cic. ; Hor.

opertus, a, um. **I.** *Part.* operiō. **II.** A d j. **a.** *covered, closed :* operto lectica latus est, Cic. **b.** *hidden, concealed :* Pl., Cic. *Neut.*

as Noun: Apollinis operta, *veiled oracles.*
Cic.; telluris operta, *hidden depths,* Verg.;
sacra in operto facere, Liv.

opēs, opum, *v.* ops.

Ophīonīdēs, ae, *m. s. of Ophīon,* i.e. *Amycus.*

ophītēs, ae, *m.* [ὀφίτης], *snake-stone, serpen-
tine* (a kind of marble): Luc., Mart.

Ophiūchus, ī, *m. the Serpent-holder, a constellation* (pure Latin Anguitenēns).

Ophiūsia, ae, *f. an old name of Cyprus :*
Ophiūsius, a, um, *Cyprian :* Ov.

ophthalmiās, ae, *m.* [ὀφθαλμίας], *a fish*
(in pure Lat. oculata): Pl.

opicus, a, um [another form of Opsus, Obscus
and Oscus, lit. *Oscan*]. Transf. *barbarous,
yokel :* Juv.

opifer, era, erum [ops ferō], *aid-bringing,
helping :* deus, Ov.

opifex, ficis, *m. f.* [opus faciō], *a maker,
framer, fabricator.* **1.** Lit. **a.** mundi deus,
Cic. **b.** *a handicraftsman, mechanic, arti-
san :* Cic., Sall. **2.** Transf. *: verborum,*
Cic. With *Inf. :* Pers.

opificīna, ae, *f.* [opifex], *a workshop :* Pl.

opificium, ī, *n.* [opifex], *a working, a work :*
Varr.

ŏpiliō, ōnis, *m.* [for *ovi-pil-iō,* from ovis; *cf.*
αἰ-πόλο-ς, βου-πόλο-ς], *a shepherd :* Pl.

opīmē, adv. *richly, splendidly :* Pl.

opīmitās, ātis, *f.* [opimus], *plentifulness,
abundance :* in *pl. :* Pl.

opīmus, a, um [perh. fr. ob and root seen in
pinguis], *fruitful, fertile, rich.* **1.** Lit. **a.**
In gen.: regio, Cic.; campus, Liv.; arva,
Verg. **b.** Of the body: *fat, plump :* boves,
Cic.; habitus corporis, Cic. **2.** Transf.
a. *enriched, rich :* opimus praedā, Cic.;
alterius macrescit rebus opimis, Hor.
Transf.: opus casibus, Tac. **b.** *enrich-
ing, lucrative :* accusatio, Cic. **c.** In gen.
abundant, copious, sumptuous, splendid :
divitiae, Pl.; praeda, Cic.; dapes, Verg.;
triumphus, Hor.; and esp. spolia opima,
the arms taken by one general from another,
Liv.; Verg.; and in gen. *the arms taken
from an enemy's general :* Liv. **d.** Rhet.:
gross, overloaded : dictionis genus, Cic.

opīnābilis, e, adj. [opīnor], *resting on mere
opinion or conjecture; conjectural, imaginary :* artes, Cic.

opīnātiō, ōnis, *f.* [opīnor], *conjecture, mere
opinion :* Cic.

opīnātor, ōris, *m.* [opīnor], *one who holds a
mere opinion* (opp. demonstrated truth), *a
supposer :* Cic.

opīnātus, a, um. **I.** *Part.* opīnor. **II.**
Adj. (in *Pass.* sense) *supposed, fancied :*
bona, mala, Cic. (*v.* also necopīnātus.)

opīnātus, ūs, *m.* [opīnor], *supposition, imagination :* in *pl. :* animi, Lucr.

opīniō, ōnis, *f.* [opīnor], *opinion, supposition,
conjecture.* **1.** In gen.: non re ductus sed
opinione, Cic.; fuisse in illā populari
opinione, Cic.; Liv.; habere opinionem
(with Acc. and *Inf.*), Cic.; ut opinio mea
est, Cic.; ut opinio mea fert, *as I incline to
believe,* Cic.; praebere opinionem timoris,
to convey the impression of fear, Caes.; adferre alicui, Cic.; in opinionem discedere,
Cic. Ep.; adducere aliquem in eam opinionem ut etc., Cic.; praeter opinionem, *contrary to expectation,* Nep.; dicere contra

opiniones omnium, Cic. So with *comp. :*
eo cum celerius omnium opinione venisset,
more quickly than had been expected, Caes.;
Pl. **2.** *general impression, estimation, repute.* **a.** About persons : opinione fortasse
nonnullā, quam de meis moribus habebat,
Cic.; equites, quorum inter Gallos virtutis
opinio est singularis, Caes. *Absol. : reputation :* Quint., Tac. Occ. *a bad reputation :* ingrati animi, Liv.; Tac. **b.** About
things: *general impression ; rumour :*
tanta huius belli ad barbaros opinio perlata
est, Caes.; opinio etiam sine auctore
exierat (with Acc. and *Inf.*), Liv.

opīniōsus, a, um [opīniō], *of fixed opinions.*
Sup. : Cic.

opīnor, ārī (**opīnō,** āre. Pl.) [opīnus], *to be of
opinion, to suppose, conjecture, imagine :*
male de Caesare, Suet.; Cic. With Acc.
and *Inf. :* Cic. Parenthetically : opinor *or*
ut opinor, Pl., Cic., Hor. Often of Stoic
ideals : sapiens nihil opinatur, Cic.

opīnus, a, um *v.* necopīnus and inopīnus.

opiparē, adv. *richly, splendidly, sumptuously :*
Pl., Cic.

opiparus, a, um [ops parō], *richly furnished,
splendid, sumptuous :* Athenae, Pl.; opsonia, Pl.

opisthographus, a, um [ὀπισθόγραφος],
written on the back : commentarii, Plin. Ep.

opitulor, ārī [ops and tul in tulī], *to bring aid ;
to help* (with Dat.): alicui, Pl., Cic.; urbibus sociis, Liv.; inopiae, Sall.

oportet, ēre, uit, *it is right and proper,* (one)
ought or should (in sense of *duty* or *obligation*) : alio tempore atque oportuerit, Caes.;
tamquam ita fieri non solum oporteret sed
etiam necesse esset, Cic. With Acc. and
Inf. : me tabulas tuas proferre oportebat,
Cic.; Pl.; Ter. With Acc. and *Pass.
Inf. :* pecuniam his oportuit civitatibus pro
frumento dari, Cic. With Acc. and *Perf.
Part.* (without esse) : signum ablatum non
oportuit, Cic.; Ter. With *Subj. :* Cato;
quae crimina diluas oportet, Cic.; valeat
possessor oportet, Hor.; Liv.

op-pango, pangere, pēgī, pāctum, *to fasten or
plant on :* savium, Pl.

op-pectō, ere, *to comb off.* Transf. *: to pick
off* (in eating): Pl.

op-pēdō, ere, *to break wind at.* Transf. :
of insulting : curtis Iudaeis, Hor.

op-perior, perīrī, pertus (peritus, Pl.) [*cf.*
experior]. **A.** Intrans. : *to wait :* Pl.,
Ter., Cic. Ep. **B.** Trans. : *to wait for,
await :* aliquem, Pl., Verg., Tac., etc.;
tempora sua, Liv. With *Indir. Quest. :
to wait and see :* Liv.

op-petō, petere, petīvī (or petiī), petītum,
to go to meet, to encounter (an evil): pestem,
Pl. Esp. with mortem, *to perish, die :*
Enn., Cic., Liv. Without mortem : Verg.,
Tac.

op-picō, āre, *to seal up with pitch :* corticem,
Cato.

oppidānus, a, um [oppidum], *of or in a town
other than Rome ; sometimes disparagingly, provincial :* genus dicendi, Cic.;
Tac. As Noun, **oppidānī,** ōrum, *m. pl. the
townsfolk :* Pl.

oppidātim, adv. [oppidum], *by towns, in the
towns :* Suet.

oppĭdō, *adv.* *quite, absolutely, exceedingly*
(colloq.) : oppido interii, Pl. ; ridiculus,
Cic. ; adulescens, Liv. ; oppido quam (in
same sense strengthened) : oppido quam
parva, Liv. As affirmative answer to a
question ; *quite, exactly* : Pl.

oppĭdulum, I, *n.* [*dim.* oppidum], *a small
town* : Cic. Ep., Hor.

oppĭdum, I, *n.* [perh. fr. ob and pedum (= Gk.
πέ-δον), i.e. a foundation to protect a plain],
a town (other than Rome, which was usually
called urbs). **1.** Lit. : Pl , Cic., Verg., etc.
2. T r a n s f. **a.** *a fortified wood* among the
Britons : Caes. **b.** Of an old man (in
metaphor) : Pl.

op-pignĕrō, āre, *to pledge, pawn.* **1.** Lit. :
libellos pro vino, Cic. ; Mart. **2.** T r a n s f. :
filiam, Ter. ; verbo se, Sen.

op-pīlō, āre, *to stop up, shut up* : metretam,
Cato ; ostia, Lucr. ; scalas, Cic.

op-pleō, ēre, ēvī, ētum, *to fill, block, choke up.*
1. Lit. : granaria, Pl. ; aedis spoliis, Pl. ;
Varr. ; nives iam omnia oppleverant, Liv. ;
oppletis non solum portibus, sed etiam litoribus, Caes. **2.** T r a n s f. : auris meas sua
vaniloquentia, Pl. ; mentes oppletae tenebris ac sordibus, Cic. ; haec opinio Graeciam,
Cic.

op-pōnō, pōnere, posuī (posīvī, Pl.), positum
(-postum, Lucr.). **I.** *to put, place or station
against or before.* **1.** Lit. (of defence or opposition) : se venientibus in itinere, Caes. ;
armatos homines ad omnis introitūs, Cic. ;
molis fluotibus, Cic. ; pro nudatā moenibus
patriā corpora, Liv. ; tibi foris, Ov. ; ante
oculos manūs, Ov. ; oculis manūs, Ov. Also,
se periculis, Cic. **2.** T r a n s f. a, *to interpose*
(as an obstruction) : auctoritatem suam,
Cic. **b.** Of arguments : *to set against* in
reply : quid opponas si negem ? Cic. ; ut
opponeret Stoicis (with Acc. and *Inf.*), Cic.
c. Geogr. (*v.* oppositus). **II.** *to set against
as a pledge, to pledge, mortgage.* **1.** Lit. :
anulum, Pl. ; ager oppositus est pignori ob
decem minas, Ter. In double sense : villula
nostra non ad Austri flatūs opposita est,
verum ad milia quindecim, Cat. **2.**
T r a n s f. : *to set off against*, by way of
balance or comparison : multis secundis
proeliis unum adversum, Caes. ; Cic. ; Juv.,
etc. **III.** *to offer, present* : auriculam, Hor.

opportūnē, *adv. fitly, seasonably, opportunely* :
Ter., Caes., Cic. *Comp.* : Liv. *Sup.* :
Caes., Liv.

opportūnĭtas, ātis, *f.* [opportūnus], *fitness,
convenience, suitableness.* **1.** Lit. : loci,
Caes. ; corporis, Cic. **2.** T r a n s f. a, *a
fit, opportune, or favourable time* : optimā
opportunitate venistis, Pl. ; temporis,
Caes., Cic. ; aetatis, Sall. **b.** *an advantage* :
opportunitate aliquā datā, Caes. In *pl.* :
Cic.

opportūnus, a, um [ob, portus, lit. *at or
before the port*], *fit, convenient, suitable.* **1.**
Lit. (of place) : locus, Cic. With *ad* :
locus ad insidias, Liv. ; amnis ad compor-
tanda quae usui sint, Liv. ; Caes. *Neut.
pl.* as Noun : locorum opportuna per-
munivit, Tac. **2.** T r a n s f. a. Of time :
tempus, Cic. ; opportuni venerunt, Liv.
Comp. and *Sup.* : Cic. Ep. **b.** Of persons :
suitable, adapted : ad omnia magis opportu-

nus, Ter. ; minime opportunus vir, Liv.
c. *advantageous, serviceable* : ceterae res
opportunae sunt singulae rebus singulis,
Cic. **d.** *suitable* for an enemy ; hence,
exposed, open : opportuniores quod intenti
operi erant, Liv. ; urbes ad occupandum,
Liv. ; Romanus opportunus huic eruptioni
fuit, Liv.

oppŏsĭtĭō, ōnis, *f.* [oppōnō], *opposition* (in
logic) : Cic.

oppŏsĭtus, a, um. **I.** *Part.* oppōnō. **II.**
A d j. *placed or standing against or oppo-
site* : soli luna, Cic. Geogr. . oppidum
Thessaliae, Caes. ; contra Zancleia saxa
Region, Ov.

oppŏsĭtus, ūs, *m.* [oppōnō]. **A.** A c t. : *a
placing against, an opposing* : laterum
nostrorum oppositūs et corporum pollice-
mur, Cic. **B.** P a s s. : solem lunae oppo-
situ deficere, Cic.

oppressĭō, ōnis, *f.* [opprimō], *a pressing
down* ; hence, **a.** *force, violence* : per op-
pressionem, Ter. **b.** *violent seizure* : curiae,
Cic. **c.** *violent interference with* ; *overthrow* : legum et libertatis, Cic.

oppressiuncula, ae, *f.* [*dim.* oppressĭō], *a
gentle pressure* : Pl.

oppressus, a, um, *Part.* opprimō.

oppressus, ūs, *m.* [opprimō], *a pressing
down, pressure* : Lucr.

op-prĭmō, primere, pressī, pressum [premō].
I. *to press upon, press or weigh down.* **1.**
Lit. : taleam pede, Cato · gravi armo-
rum onere oppressi, Caes. **2.** T r a n s f. :
opprimi onere offici, Cic. ; aere alieno, Cic. ;
onere faenoris, Sall. ; corpus doloribus,
Cic. **II.** *to press upon and crush, to overwhelm.* **1.** Lit. : opprimi ruinā conclavis,
Cic. ; classis a praedonibus oppressa, Cic. ;
senem iniectu vestis, Tac. C o m i c. : os
opprime, Pl. **2.** T r a n s f. : *to overwhelm,
suppress, subdue.* **a.** bello legionem, Caes. ;
reliquias huius belli, Cic. ; sine tumultu rem
omnem oppressere, Liv. ; Mithridatem,
Cic. ; aliquem falso crimine, Liv. ; Cic. ;
quaestionem, Liv. ; somno, timore oppressus, Caes. ; metu, Liv. ; flammam
aquā, Cic. ; orientem ignem, Liv. **b.** Of
abstracts : dolorem, libertatem, potentiam,
Cic. ; iram, Sall. **III.** *to catch and crush,
to surprise, take by surprise.* **1.** Lit. :
inprudentem, Ter. ; repentino adventu
incautos, Liv. ; Caes. **2.** T r a n s f. : Antonium mors oppressit, Cic. ; plenos crapu-
lae eos lux oppressit, Liv. ; instructos nox
oppressit, Liv. ; occasionem, Pl. ; rostra
(i.e. occupy), Cic.

opprŏbrāmentum, I, *n.* [opprobrō], *a reproach, disgrace* : Pl.

opprŏbrium, I, *n.* [probrum], *a reproach,
scandal, disgrace.* **1.** Lit. : opprobria culpae, Hor. **2.** T r a n s f. a, *a cause of disgrace, a disgrace* : vereor ne civitati meae
sit opprobrio si etc., Nep. Of persons :
opprobrium maiorum Mamercus, Tac. ;
Cat. ; Ov., etc. **b.** *a reproach, taunt* :
morderi opprobriis falsis, Hor. ; dicere,
Ov. ; fundere, Hor.

opprŏbrō, āre [probrum], *to taunt* : aliquid
alicui, Pl.

oppugnātĭō, ōnis, *f.* [oppugnō], *an assault* on a
town. **1.** Lit. : Liv. ; oppidorum, Cic.

sustinere, Caes. ; relinquere, Tac. In *pl.* :
Cic. **2.** T r a n s f. : *a verbal assault, attack* :
propulsare, Cic.

oppugnātor, ōris, *m.* [oppugnō], *an assailant,
attacker.* **1.** L i t. : Tac. **2.** T r a n s f. :
patriae, Cic. ; meae salutis, Cic.

op-pugnō, āre, *to attack, assault, attempt to
storm.* **1.** L i t. : Enn. ; oppidum, Cic. ;
castra, Caes. ; urbem, Liv. With play on
pugnus ; *to batter with the fists* : os, Pl.
2. T r a n s f. : nos clandestinis consiliis,
Cic. ; consilia alicuius, Pl. ; aequitatem
verbis, Cic.

ops, opis, *f.* (NOM. *sing.* only as a Proper
Name of the goddess of plenty, sister and
wife of Saturn and mother of Jupiter) [*cf.*
ἄφενος, cōpia], *power, might ; power to
help or aid.* ABL. *sing.* **ope** : summā ope
niti, *with one's utmost power*, Sall. ; omni
ope atque operā enitar, Cic. ; hinc ope bar-
baricā Antonius, Verg. ; Enn. ; sine ope
divinā, *without divine help*, Caes. GEN.
sing., **opis** : opis egens tuae, Enn. ; opis
indigere, Nep. ; aliquid opis rei publicae
tulissemus, Cic. Ep. ; gratis persolvere
dignas non opis est nostrae, Verg. ACC.
sing. **opem** : *help, aid* : ferre, Enn., Cic. ;
adripere ad hanc rem, Pl. ; adferre, admovere, Ov. ; ab aliquo petere, Cic. In
pl. **opēs** : *resources, means, wealth.* **a.** In
gen. : Pl., Cic., Verg., etc. **b.** *military or
political resources and power* : Caes., Nep.,
Verg. **c.** *personal power based on wealth* :
opes violentas concupiscere, Cic.

ops-, *v.* obs- (and ob.)

op-sipō, āre [ob and supō, *v.* dissipō], *to
sprinkle at or upon.* P r o v. : opsipat
aquolam (i.e. it refreshes, cheers me), Pl.

opsonātus, ūs, *m.* [obsonō], *a catering, mar-
keting* : Pl.

op-stupidus, a, um, *bewildered* : Pl.

opt-, *v.* obt-.

optābilis, e, *adj.* [optō], *desirable* : Cic., Ov.
Comp. : Cic.

optātiō, ōnis, *f.* [optō], *a wishing, a wish* :
in *pl.* : Cic. Rhet. : optatio atque exse-
cratio, Cic.

optātus, a. um. **I.** *Part.* optō. **II.** A d j. :
wished, desired, welcome : cives, Pl. ; rumores, Cic. Ep. *Comp.* and *Sup.* : Cic. Ep.
As Noun, **optātum**, ī, *n. a wish, desire* :
di tibi semper omnia optata offerant, Ter. ;
impetrare optatum, Cic. ; mihi in optatis
est, Cic. Ep. ; eveniunt optata deae, Ov.
ABL. *n.* **optātō**, as *Adv., according to one's
wish* : Pl., Cic. Ep., Verg.

op-tigō, *v.* obtegō.

optimās (optum-), ātis (GEN. *pl.*, optimā-
tum or optimātium) *adj.* [optimus], *belonging to the best men in political sense*, i.e.
to the aristocratic party ; aristocratic : Enn.,
Cic. Oftener as Noun in *pl.*, **optimātēs**,
the aristocratic party : Cic., Tac.

optimē, optimus, *v.* bene, bonus.

(1) **optiō**, ōnis, *f.* [optō], *choice, liberty to
choose, option* : Pl. ; optio vobis datur,
utrum velitis, Cic. ; facere alicui, ut eligat,
Cic. ; cui eligendi patroni optio datur,
Cic. ; extra sortem conlegae optionem dari
provinciae, Liv.

(2) **optiō**, ōnis, *m.* [optō], *a helper, an assistant.* **a.** In gen. : Pl. **b.** M i l i t. *an as-*

sistant (for private business) of a centurion
or decurion : Tac.

optīvus, a, um [opto], *chosen* : Hor.

optō, āre (optāssis, *Aor. Subj.* or *Opt.*, Pl.)
[*freq.* opiō ; perh. *cf.* Gk. ὄπωπα). **1.**
P r o p. : *to choose, select* : utrum vis opta
dum licet, Pl. ; locum tecto, Verg. ; ut
optet utrum malit, Cic. ; L. Furium, Liv. ;
sine sorte Macedoniam, Liv. **2.** T r a n s f. :
to wish for, desire (esp. with entreaty or
prayer) : tua vita optanda est, Ter. ; Juv. ;
nihil nisi quod honestum sit, Cic. ; aliquid
votis, Verg. With *ut* or *ne* and *Subj.* :
Cic., Liv., Ov. With *Subj.* alone : Verg.,
Ov. With *Inf.* : Ter., Liv., Tac., etc. With
Acc. and *Inf.* : Enn., Cic. Ep., Curt., etc.
With DAT. of person : *to wish* one something
in good or bad sense : tibi bona omnia, Pl. ;
eam rem publicam in quā etc., Cic. ; furorem alicui, Cic. ; mihi mortem, Liv.

op-tueor, tuērī, and **op-tuor**, tuī. **I.** *to
look at, gaze upon* : aliquem, Pl. **II.** *to
see clearly, closely* : Pl.

optumē, optumus, *v.* bene, bonus.

opulēns, entis, *v.* opulentus.

opulentē and **opulenter**, *adv. richly, sumptuously* : Sall. *Comp.* : Liv.

opulentia, ae, *f.* [opulēns]. **I.** *riches, wealth,
opulence* : Sall. In *pl.* : Pl. **II.** *resources
and power*, of a people : Nep., Verg., Tac.

opulentitās, ātis, *f.* [opulentus], *wealth,
power* : Pl.

opulentō, āre [opulentus], *to make rich, to
enrich* : erum bacis olivae, Hor.

opulentus, a, um (less freq. **opulēns**, entis)
[ops], *rich, wealthy, opulent.* **1.** L i t. **a.**
oppidum, Enn., Caes. ; civitas, Cic. ; aerarium, Liv. *Sup.* : Cic. With GEN. : provincia pecuniae, Ter. ; Hor. With ABL. :
auro, Pl. ; templum donis, Verg. ; pars
Numidiae agro virisque opulentior, Sall. ;
Sup. : Cic. **b.** *wealthy and powerful* :
reges, Sall. ; regnum, Cic. *Sup.* : Cic.
c. *powerful* (in resources) : agmen, factio,
Liv. *Comp.* : Liv. ; *Sup.* : viris armisque
gens opulentissima, Liv. **2.** T r a n s f. **a.**
rich, sumptuous : opsonium, Pl. ; dona, Suet.
b. *bringing riches* : stipendia, Liv.

opus, eris, *n. work, labour.* **1.** L i t. **A.** In
gen. : facere, Ter. ; mensis octo continuos
opus non defuit, Cic. ; res immensa operis,
Liv. ; omnibus una quies operum, Verg.
B. In partic. **a.** Agricultural : (in agro)
opus or opera facere, Ter., Cic. **b.** M i l i t. :
in opere occupatus, Caes. ; naturā et opere
munitus, Caes. ; in opere quis par Romano
miles ? Liv. ; grave Martis opus, Verg. ;
fatigatus miles operibus proeliisque, Liv.
c. Literary : Graeci opus quaerunt, Cic. ;
Liv. ; opus adgredior opimum casibus, Tac.
2. T r a n s f. : *work done.* **A.** M i l i t. **a.**
a defensive or offensive work in fortifying
or besieging ; *works, lines* : opere castrorum perfecto, Caes. ; tumulum operibus
magnis munire, Caes. ; Cic. **b.** *siege-
engines* : vineae aliaque opera, Liv. ; non
coronā sed operibus oppugnare urbem
adortus est, Liv. **B.** Of buildings, etc. :
aedium sacrarum publicorumque operum
depopulatio, Cic. ; Liv. ; urbis opus, Verg.
C. Artistic. **a.** *a work of art* : pocula,
opus Alcimedontis, Verg. ; marmoreum,

Ov. **b.** *workmanship* : bullarum non opere delectabatur sed pondere, Cic. ; haec omnia antiquo opere, Cic. **D.** Literary : habeo opus magnum in manibus, Cic. ; Quint. ; Tac. **E.** In gen. : *business, deed, action* : miserumst opus, Pl. ; operibus eum anteire, Caes. ; periculosae plenum opus aleae, Hor. ; his immortalibus editus operibus, Liv. **3.** Phrases : **magnō opere, tantō opere, quantō opere,** *v.* magnus, tantus, quantus.

opus est (sunt). A. *Lit. there is work for someone* (DAT.) *with something* (*Instr.* ABL.) ; *hence, there is need* (of) ; *the need is* (for) ; *one has need* (of). **a.** With *Instr.* ABL. : viro et gubernatore opus est, Liv. ; maiore pecuniā in stipendium opus erat, Liv. ; Cic. ; armis, Verg. ; with ABL. of *Perf. Part.* : properato, Cic. ; maturato, Liv. ; with ABL. of *Supine* or *Verbal Noun* : quod scitu opus est, Cic. ; Ter. **b.** With GEN. : ad consilium pensandum temporis opus esse, Liv. **c.** With NOUN as *Subject* : si quid ipsi a Caesare opus esset, Caes. ; dux et auctor nobis est, Cic. Ep. ; ubi ius, ubi iniuria opus sit, Liv. In *pl.* : maritumi milites opus sunt tibi, Pl. ; Cic. ; quae ad transitum Hellesponti opus essent, Liv. ; quae curando vulneri opus sunt, Liv. **d.** With Acc. : puero opus est cibum, Pl. ; Cato. **e.** With *Inf.* (*Act.* or *Pass.*): quid opus est plura (*sc.* proferre), Cic. ; Liv. ; taceri opus esse, Liv. **f.** With Acc. and *Inf.* (*Act.* or *Pass.*) : Pl., Cic. Ep., Liv. **g.** With *ut* and *Subj.* : Pl. With *Subj.* (without *ut*) : Plin. Ep. **B.** *it is useful, beneficial* : haud sciam an ne opus sit quidem nihil unquam omnino deesse amicis, Cic.

Opūs, ūntis, *f. a town of Locris in Greece* ; **Opūntius,** a, um ; **Opūntiī,** ōrum, *m. pl. the Opuntians.*

opusculum, ī, *n.* [*dim.* opus], *a little work* : Cic., Hor.

ōra, ae, *f.* **I.** *boundary-line, bound, border, edge* : ad carceris oras, Enn. ; oras pocula circum contingunt mellis liquore, Lucr. ; clipei, Verg. ; extrema ora mundi, Cic. ; silvae, Liv. ; regiones quarum nulla esset ora, nulla extremitas, Cic. **II.** *coastline, coast, seaboard* (mostly with maritima, unless the context is clear). **1.** Lit. : Caes., Cic. In *pl.* : Cic. **2.** Transf. : (*the inhabitants of*) *the coast* : ora maritima Cn. Pompeium requisivit, Cic. ; Campaniam oram descivisse, Tac. **III.** *expanse of country ; district, region.* **1.** Lit. : in gentium oras in quibus haec ne observantur quidem, CΙϽ. ; in eas oras nostrum exercitum esse adductum, Cic. ; Verg. ; luminis orae, Enn., Lucr., Verg. ; Acheruntis orae, Lucr. ; rex gelidae orae, Hor. **2.** Transf. **a.** (*the inhabitants of*) *a district* : vastationem sub Cimini montis radicibus iacens ora senserat, Liv. **b.** ingentis oras evolvite belli (i.e. *the vast expanse*), Verg. ; Enn. **IV.** *a shoreline, cable, hawser* : Liv. ; solvere, Quint. ; resolvere, Liv.

Ora (Hora), ae, *f. the name of Hersilia, as a goddess* : Ov.

ōrāculum (ōrāclum, Ov.), ī, *n.* [ōrō], *an utterance.* **1.** Lit. **A.** *a divine utterance,*

an oracle : edere, Cic. ; petere a Dodonā, Cic. ; quaerere, poscere, Verg. **B.** In gen. **a.** *any prophetic declaration, a prophecy* : somni et furoris oracula, Cic. **b.** *an oracular or authoritative saying* : physicorum oracula, Cic. **2.** Transf. : *the seat of oracles, an oracle.* **a.** illud oraculum Delphis tam celebre, Cic. ; sors oraculi, Liv. ; consulere, Ov. **b.** domus iure consulti, oraculum civitatis, Cic.

ōrārius, a, um [ōra], *coasting* : naves, Plin. Ep.

ōrāta, ōrum, *n. pl.* [ōrō], *requests, prayers* : Ter.

ōrātiō, ōnis, *f.* [ōrō], *a speaking.* **1.** Lit. **A.** In gen. **a.** (*the faculty of*) *speech* : ferae rationis et orationis expertes, Cic. **b.** *speech, language* (opp. to action) : Pl., Cic. **c.** *character* or *style* of speech : antiqua, Pl. ; tenuis, Ter. ; mollis, Cic. ; adstrictior et contractior, Cic. **d.** *language,* i.e. *the content of what is said* : captivorum oratio cum perfugis convenit, Caes. **e.** *a language* (e.g. Greek or Latin) : Cic. **B.** In partio. **a.** *formal language* (opp. sermo) : Cic. **b.** *a set speech* of an orator, *an harangue, oration* : habere, *to deliver,* Ter., Caes., Cic. ; facere et polire, Cic. ; angusta, concisa, concinna, cohaerens, volubilis, diffusa, etc., Cic. ; longa, acerba, Liv. **2.** Transf. **a.** *oratorical talent, eloquence* : satis in eo fuit orationis atque ingeni, Cic. **b.** *prose,* opp. to poetry : et in poëmatis et in oratione, Cic. **c.** Under the empire : *an imperial message, rescript* : Tac., Suet.

ōrātiuncula, ae, *f.* [*dim.* ōrātiō], *a little speech, brief oration* : Cic., Quint.

ōrātor, ōris, *m.* [ōrō]. **I.** *a spokesman, speaker* for a person or community : Pl., Cic., Verg., etc. ; pacis petendae, Liv. With *Obj.* GEN. : pacis (i.e. to sue for peace), Cic., Liv. **II.** *a speaker, orator* (very freq.) : Enn., Cic., etc. **III.** *a suppliant* : Pl.

ōrātōriē, *adv. oratorically* : dicere, Cic.

ōrātōrius, a, um [ōrātor], *of an orator, oratorical* : ornamenta, gestus, ingenium, Cic. As Noun, **ōrātōria,** ae, *f.* (*sc.* ars) *the oratorical art, oratory* : Quint.

ōrātrix, īcis, *f.* [ōrō], *a female suppliant* : Pl. ; pacis et foederis, Cic.

ōrātū, ABL. *sing. m.* [ōrō], *by praying, at or by request* : oratu tuo, Cic. ; Pl.

orbātor, ōris, *m.* [orbō], *a bereaver* : nostri orbator Achilles, Ov.

orbiculātus, a, um [orbiculus], *rounded, circular, round* : Varr., Plin.

Orbilius, ī, *m. a Roman grammarian, teacher of Horace.*

orbis, is, *m.* (ABL. orbī, Lucr.), *a circle* ; also, *anything circular,* as *a ring, disk, hoop, orbit,* etc. **1.** Lit. : in orbem torquere, Cic. ; iusto commodus orbe, Ov. ; ut (milites) in orbem consisterent, Caes. ; in orbem pugnare, Liv. ; facere, conligere, Liv. ; signifer (i.e. the Zodiac), Cic. ; lacteus (i.e. the Milky Way), Cic. Of a shield : Verg. Of a wheel : Verg. Of the eye : Verg. Of the eye-socket : Ov. Of a serpent, *the coils* : Verg. Of the orbit of a star : Verg. Of the sun or moon : Verg., Ov. Of a table : Mart., Juv. Esp. : orbis terrarum or terrae (i.e. the Earth, the world), Cic., Verg., Liv. Hence, also, *country, region* : Eoo dives ab orbe redit, Ov. **2**. T r a n s f. **a.** *a rotation, round, routine* : ut idem in singulos annos orbis volveretur, Liv. ; orbis hic in re publicā est conversus, Cic. Ep. ; in orbem (i.e. *in rotation*), Liv. **b.** *a routine* or *course of study* : Quint. **c.** Of style : *a rounding off, roundness, rotundity* : quasi orbem verborum conficere, Cic.

orbita, ae, *f.* [orbis], *a wheel-track, rut.* **1.** L i t. : Cic., Verg. **2.** T r a n s f. : *a rut, path* : Quint. ; veteris culpae, Juv.

orbitās, ātis, *f.* [orbus], *bereavement of parents* or *children, etc.* **1.** L i t. : *orphanage, widowhood* : Pl., Cic., Liv. In *pl.* : Cic. **2.** T r a n s f. : maximā orbitate rei publicae vivorum talium, Cic. Ep.

orbitōsus, a, um [orbita], *full of cart-ruts* : Verg.

orbō, āre [orbus], *to bereave of parents, children, etc.* ; *to make fatherless, motherless, childless, husbandless.* **1.** L i t. : patres, Ov. With ABL. of Separation : filio orbatus, Cic. ; Ov. **2.** T r a n s f. : me lumine, Enn. ; Italiam iuventute, Cic. ; forum voce eruditā, Cic.

Orbōna, ae, *f. the tutelary goddess of bereaved parents.*

orbus, a, um [*cf.* ὀρφανός], *bereaved, bereft* ; *parentless, fatherless, childless, husbandless.* **1.** L i t. : Cic. With GEN. : parens liberorum, Quint. ; Ov. With ABL. : liberis, Pl. With *ab* : a totidem natis, Ov. As Noun, **orbus**, ī, *m.* and **orba**, ae, *f. an orphan* : Ter., Liv., Quint. In *fem.* also *a widow* : Liv. **2.** T r a n s f. : plebs tribunis, Cic. ; forum litibus, Hor. ; res publica publico consilio, Liv. With GEN. : orbus auxili opumque, Pl. ; luminis, Ov.

orca, ae, *f. a large-bellied vessel, a butt, tun* : Hor., Pers.

Orcades, um, *f. pl., islands N. of Scotland* (now *the Orkneys*).

orchas, adis, *f. a kind of olive* : Verg.

orchēstra, ae, *f.* [ὀρχήστρα], orig. *the part of the theatre occupied by the chorus* (in Rome appropriated to *the senators*) ; *the orchestra* : Juv., Suet. Hence, *the Senate* : Juv.

Orcīnus, a, um [Orcus], *Plutonic* : senatores (i.e. who became members of the Senate by Caesar's will), Suet.

Orcus, ī, *m.* [*cf.* ἕρκος], *the underworld.* **1.** L i t. : Enn., Pl., Lucr., Verg. **2.** T r a n s f. **a.** *death* : Lucr., Varr., Hor. **b.** *the god of the underworld* : Pl., Cic., Verg. [Fr. *ogre.*]

orde-, *v.* horde-.

ōrdia prima, for prīmōrdia, q.v.

ōrdinārius, a, um [ōrdō], *according to the usual order, usual, regular* : consules (opp. to suffecti), Liv. ; consiliis ordinariis bellum gerere, Liv. ; oratio, philosophia, Sen. Ep.

ōrdinātim, *adv. in order.* **a.** *in regular succession* : honores petere, Sulp. ap. Cic. Ep. **b.** M i l i t. : *in good order* : ire, Brut. ap. Cic. Ep. **c.** *regularly, properly* : musculus ordinatim structus, Caes.

ōrdinātiō, ōnis, *f.* [ōrdinō]. **I.** *an orderly arrangement* : vitae, Plin. Ep. ; anni, Suet. Hence, *orderly government* : Plin. Ep. **II.** *an appointment to office, installation* : ordi-

natione proximā Aegypto praeficere Mettium Rufum, Suet.

ōrdinātus, a, um. **I.** *Part.* ōrdinō. **II.** A d j. : *well ordered, regular* : igneae formae cursūs ordinatos definiunt, Cic. ; disciplina, Liv. ; vita, vir, etc., Sen. *Comp.* : Sen.

ōrdinō, āre [ōrdō], *to order, set in order, arrange, regulate.* **1.** L i t. : copias, Nep. ; milites, aciem, Liv. ; agmina, Hor. ; arbusta, Hor. **2.** T r a n s f. **a.** partis orationis, Cic. ; publicas res, Hor. **b.** *to regulate, govern a country* : statum liberarum civitatum, Plin. Ep. ; provinciam, Suet. **c.** *to appoint to office* : magistratūs, Suet.

ōrdior, ōrdīri, ōrsus [perh. *cf.* ōrdō, prīmōrdia]. **1.** L i t. : *to begin a web, to lay the warp* : araneus telas, Plin. **2.** T r a n s f. in g e n. *to begin, undertake.* With Acc. : Cic. Ep., Verg., Liv. With *Inf.* : Cic., Verg., Ov. So (*sc.* loqui), sic orsus, Verg. With *ab* and ABL. of point *from which* : a principio, Cic. ; Nep. ; unde ordiri possumus ? Cic. [Fr. *ourdir.*]

ōrdō, inis, *m. a straight row* or *line, a regular series.* **1.** L i t. **A.** In farming : vitium, Cic., Verg. ; olearum, Cic. ; directōs in quincuncem ordines, Cic. ; pone ordine vitis, Verg. **B.** M i l i t. : *a line, file, rank of soldiers in formation* : ordines constituere, perturbare, Caes. ; servare, Caes., Liv. ; locare, Liv. ; signa atque ordines observare, Sall. ; signa et ordines confundere, Liv. ; restituere, Sall., Liv. ; ordine egredi, Caes., Sall., Liv. ; sine signis, sine ordinibus, Sall. Hence, **a.** *a company of soldiers*, esp. *a century* : Q. Lucanius eiusdem ordinis, Caes. ; in pluris ordines instruebantur, Liv. ; ducere, Caes., Cic., Liv. **b.** *the command of a company* : centuriones *ab inferioribus ordinibus in superiores traducti, Caes. ; alicui adsignare, Liv. **c.** *the officers in command of a company* : tribunis militum primisque ordinibus convocatis, Caes. ; Liv. **C.** In gen. : saxa quae rectis lineis suos ordines servant, Caes. ; obstructae portae singulis ordinibus caespitum, Caes. ; longus ordo flammarum, Verg. ; comitum, Juv. ; terno consurgunt ordine remi, Verg. In the theatre, *a row of seats* : Cic., Suet. **2.** T r a n s f. **A.** A b s t r a c t. **a.** In gen. : *methodical arrangement, order* : rei militaris ratio atque ordo, Caes. ; nullo ordine atque imperio, Caes. ; adhibere modum et ordinem rebus, Cic. ; in ordinem adducere, referre, Cic. ; decemviri querentes se in ordinem cogi (perh. a milit. metaphor), Liv. ; gula quasi in ordinem redigenda (est), Plin. Ep. ; ordinem conservare, tenere, sequi, immutare, perturbare, Cic. ; saeclorum nascitur ordo, Verg. **b.** A d v e r b. e x p r e s s i o n s. **i.** ordine, in ordinem, per ordinem, in ordine, ex ordine, *in order, in turn* : Pl., Cic., Verg., etc. **ii.** ordine, *regularly, properly* : Pl., Cic. **iii.** ex ordine, *in succession, without intermission* : Cic., Verg. **iv.** extra ordinem : *out of due course, in an exceptional manner* : Cic. Hence = *uncommonly, eminently, especially* : Cic. Ep. **B.** Of rank (political and social) : *a rank, order, class of citizens* : Pl. ; senatorius, equester, Cic., Liv. ; amplissimus (i.e. the senatorial), Cic. ; also, hic ordo, Cic. ; uterque ordo

(i.e. senatorial and equestrian), Suet.;
pedester, Liv.; aratorum, pecuariorum,
mercatorum, Cic.; libertini, Suet. [Sp.
órden ; Fr. *ordre*.]

Orêas, adis, *f.* ['Ορειάς], *a mountain-nymph,
Oread* : Verg., Ov.

Orestês, is and ae, *m.* (Voc. Oresta, Ov.),
*son of Agamemnon and Clytemnestra, who
avenged his father's death by killing his
mother* ; **Orestêus**, a, um.

organicus, i, *m.* [ὀργανικός], *a musician* :
Lucr.

organum, i, *n.* [ὄργανον], *an implement, instrument, engine.* **1.** Lit.: hydraulica, Suet.
Musical : Quint., Juv. **2.** Transf.: *an
instrument, means* : Quint. [Fr. *orgue.*]

orgia, ôrum, *n. pl.* [ὄργια], *a wild (nocturnal)
festival (in honour of Bacchus).* **1.** Lit.:
Verg., Ov. **2.** Transf. **a.** *mysteries* : Prop.
b. *frantic revels, orgies* : Juv.

orichalcum (**aurichalcum**, as if derived
from aurum), i, *n.* [ὀρείχαλκος], *yellow
copper ore*, also *the brass made from it* :
Pl., Cic., Verg., etc.

ôricilla, ae, *f.* [for auricilla, from auricula],
an ear-lap : Cat.

ôricula, *v.* auricula.

oriêns, entis. **I.** *Part.* orior. **II.** *Masc.
Noun.* **a.** *the sun-god, god of the morning* :
Verg. **b.** *the land of the rising sun, the
East* : Cic., Verg. **c.** *the morning* : Cic.,
Ov.

originâtio, ônis, *f.* [orïgō], *the derivation of
words, etymology* : Quint.

orïgô, inis, *f.* [orior], *the beginning, source,
origin.* **1.** Lit.: rerum, Lucr., Cic.;
omnium virtutum, Cic.; ab origine gentem
corripiunt morbi, Verg.; fontium qui celat
origines Nilus, Hor.; originem ducere ab
aliquo auctore, Hor.; clarus origine, Ov.;
modicus originis, Tac. In partic., Origines,
*the title of an historical work by Cato, the early
history of Italian towns* : Cic. **2.** Transf.:
ancestry, i.e. *a progenitor, founder* : eaeque
urbes brevi multum auctae, pars originibus
suis praesidio, Sall.; Liv.; *in sing.* : Liv.;
Aeneas Romanae stirpis origo, Verg.

oriola, *v.* horiola.

Orïôn, **Orïôn**, onis or ônis, *m.* ['Ωρίων], *a
handsome giant and hunter transformed into
the constellation Orion* : Verg., Hor., Ov.

orior, oriri, ortus (*Fut. Part.* oritûrus ; oreris,
orere, oritur in *Pres.* ; *Imperf. Subj.* sometimes orerêtur) [*cf.* Gk. ὄρ-νυμι], *to rise,
get up.* **1.** Lit. **a.** Of persons : Liv. **b.**
Of the heavenly bodies : Ov.; ad orientem
solem, ortâ luce, Caes.; orto sole, Hor.
So too, pulvis, Enn.; tempestas, ventus,
Nep. **2.** Transf. **a.** Of rivers, etc. : *to
rise* : Rhenus ex Lepontiis, Caes.; Liv.;
Rhenus Alpium vertice, Tac.; fons in
monte, Plin. Ep. **b.** Of persons (in respect
of origin) : a Germanis, Caes.; equestri
loco, Cic. **c.** In gen.: id facinus ex te,
Pl.; tibi a me nulla iniuria, Ter.; officia
a suo cuiusque genere virtutum, Cic.;
clamor, Caes.; bellum, controversia, Cic.;
caedes, Verg.; initium turbandi a feminâ,
Liv.

Orïthyïa (quadrisyl.), ae *f.* *daughter of
Erechtheus, and mother of Calaïs and Zetes
by Boreas.*

oriundus, a, um [orïor], *descended, sprung
from* (denoting *more remote origin* than
ortus): haud repudio Carthaginem; inde
sum oriundus, Pl.; Liv.; Albam, unde ipsi
oriundi erant, Liv.; Pl.; caelesti semine,
Lucr.; ab ingenuis, Cic.; a Zacyntho in-
sulâ, Liv.; ex Etruscis, Liv. Of things :
Albâ oriundum sacerdotium, Liv.

ornâmentum, i, *n.* [ornô], *equipment, ac-
coutrement, trappings, dress.* **1.** Lit. **a.**
In gen. : sine ornamentis mulierem vendidi,
Pl.; ornamenta a chorago stumpsit (i.e.
stage-dress), Pl.; ornamenta bubus instrata, Cato ; ceterae copiae, ornamenta,
praesidia, Cic. **b.** *ornament, decoration,
embellishment, trinket, etc.* : Pl.; pecuniam,
omniaque ornamenta in oppidum contulit,
Caes.; Cic. **c.** *a badge* (of office), *mark or
title of distinction* : ornamenta atque insignia honoris, Cic. Under the Empire, *the
outward distinctions and honours* (without
the duties) : ornamenta consularia, trium-
phalia, Suet. **2.** Transf. **a.** In *pl.* :
dressing up, trickery : Pl. **b.** *an ornament, a distinction* : decus atque ornamentum senectutis, Cic.; quae urbs ornamento
est civitati, Caes.; honoris, Cic. **c.** *rhetorical ornament* : dicendi, sententiarum,
Cic.

ornâtê, *adv. with full (rhetorical) equipment* :
dicere, Cic. *Comp.* : Cic. Ep. *Sup.* : Cic.

ornâtrix, icis, *f.* [ornô], *a woman hairdresser,
a tire-woman* : Ov., Suet.

ornâtulus, a, um [*dim.* ornâtus], *smartish* :
muliercula, Pl.

ornâtus, a, um. **I.** *Part.* ornô. **II.** Adj.
1. Lit. **a.** *fitted out, furnished, equipped,
dressed, harnessed, caparisoned* : fundus, Cic.;
scutis telisque ornati, Cic.; equus, Liv.;
naves omni genere armorum ornatissimae,
Caes. **b.** *well-dressed, adorned, embel-
lished* ; of persons : Pl.; of things : sepulcrum floribus, Cic. *Comp.* : Cic. **2.**
Transf.: ingenio bono, Pl.; sapiens
plurimis artibus, Cic.; lectissimus atque
ornatissimus adulescens, Cic.

ornâtus, ûs (GEN. ornâtî, Ter.), *m.* [ornô].
1. Lit. **a.** Abstr. : *a furnishing, providing* : Pl.; in aedibus nihil ornati, Ter.;
in ornatibus publicis, Varr. **b.** Concr.:
equipment, attire, dress : naulericus, Pl.;
regalis, militaris, Cic.; pulcher, turpis, Pl.;
pari fere ornatu, Liv.; ot a head-dress :
Verg.; Ov. **2.** Transf. **a.** *equipment* :
eloquentia quocumque ingreditur, eodem est
instructu ornatuque comitata, Cic. **b.**
decoration, embellishment : adferre ornatum
orationi, Cic.

ornô, âre, *to fit out, equip, furnish, dress.* **1.**
Lit. **a.** In gen.: aliquem, Pl.; prandium,
Pl.; convivium, Cic.; capillos, Ov.; decemviros appuritoribus, Cic.; aliquem armis,
Verg.; classem, Cic., Liv.; navis, Liv.
b. *to deck out, adorn, embellish* : Italiam
ornare quam domum suam maluit, Cic.;
scuta ad forum ornandum, Liv.; cornua
aertis, Verg. **2.** Transf.: *to set off,
adorn, decorate* (esp. by praise) : aliquid
magnificentius augere atque ornare, Cic.;
civitatem omnibus rebus, Caes.; hederâ
poetam, Verg.; candidatum suffragio,
Plin. Ep.

ornus, ī, *f. the mountain-ash* : Verg., Hor., etc.

ōrō, āre (ōrāssis, *Aor. Opt.* : Pl.) [ōs], *to speak*. **A.** In gen. : bonum aequomque oras, Pl. ; talibus orabat Iuno, Verg. **B.** Esp. **a.** *to plead a case* : causam capitis, Cic. ; litem, Cic. ; causam, Liv. ; causas, Verg. ; cum eo de salute suā orat, Caes. ; Ter. ; pro salute alicuius, Cic. ; pro se, Liv. **b.** *to pray, beg, beseech, entreat* : Caes. With double Acc. : multa deos orans, Verg. ; Cic. Ep. ; Suet. With Acc. of person : Enn., Cic., Ov., etc. With Acc. of thing asked for : Ter., Liv., Tac. With *ut* or *ne* and *Subj.* : Pl., Caes., Cic. With *Subj.* (without *ut*) : Pl., Verg., Ov. With *Inf.* : Verg., Tac. With Acc. and *Pass. Inf.* : Suet. In parenthesis : dic, oro te, clarius, Cic. Ep. ; ne illa quidem, oro vos, movent ? Liv.

Orontēs, is or ae (-ī, Verg.), *m. the chief river of Syria* ; **Orontēus**, a, um, *Syrian*.

Orpheus (disyl.), eī and eos (DAT. Orphēī, Orphī ; Acc. Orphea and Orphēā ; Voc. Orpheu), *m. a famous (mythical) master of music and song, the son of Oeagrus and Calliope, and husband of Eurydice* ; **Orphēus**, **Orphicus**, a, um, *Orphean, Orphic*.

ōrsus, a, um. **I.** *Part.* ōrdior. **II.** Noun : **ōrsa**, ōrum, *n. pl.* **a.** *beginnings, undertaking* : in melius tua orsa reflectas, Verg. ; tanti operis, Liv. **b.** Of words : sic orsa vicissim ore refert, Verg.

ōrsus, ūs, *m.* [ōrdior], *a beginning* : pectoris, Cic. poët. ; Verg.

orthographia, ae, *f.* [ὀρθογραφία], *orthography* : Suet.

ortus, a, um, *Part.* orior.

ortus, ūs, *m.* [orior]. **I.** *a rising* of the heavenly bodies : Cic., Verg. Hence, *the East* : sol ab ortu ad occasum commeans, Cic. ; Ov. **II.** Of persons : *origin, birth* : Cic., Ov. Of plants : Lucr. Of a river : *the source* : Ov. **III.** *the beginnings* : tribuniciae potestatis, Cic.

Ortygia, ae, or **Ortygiē**, ēs, *f.* Lit. *quail-island.* **I.** the old name of Delos ; **Ortygius**, a, um ; epith. of Apollo and Diana. **II.** *an island forming part of Syracuse* (called also **Nāsus** [νῆσος].)

ōrum, *v.* aurum, *ad init.*

oryx, ygis, *m.* [ὄρυξ], *a kind of wild goat or gazelle* : Juv.

oryza, ae, *f.* [ὄρυζα], *rice* : Hor. [It. *riso* ; Fr. *riz*.]

os, ossis, *n.* [*cf.* ὀστέον], *a bone*. **1.** Lit. **a.** In gen. : Cic., Verg., etc. **b.** From the funeral-pyre : Cic., Verg. Hence, cineres atque ossa, reliquiae Troiae, Verg. **2.** Transf. **a.** *the innermost parts, the very bones or marrow* : exarsit iuveni dolor ossibus, Verg. **b.** Of trees or fruits : arborum (*the heart*), Plin. ; olearum (*the stones*), Suet. **c.** Of style : ossa nudare (*to leave the bones bare*, i.e. *without adornment or beauty of expression*), Cic. ; Quint. [Sp. *hueso.*]

ōs, ōris (not used in GEN. *pl.*) *n.* **I.** Prop. : *the mouth.* **A.** Of men and animals. **1.** Lit. : Enn., Cic., Ov., etc. **2.** Transf. : of things. **a.** *the mouth, opening* : aedium, Pl. ; portūs, Cic. ; Ponti, Cic. ; ingentem

lato dedit ore fenestram, Verg. ; porta velut in ore urbis, Liv. ; specūs, Tac. ; in ore Tiberis, Liv. Of the *sources* of a stream : Verg. **b.** Of the *prow* of a ship : Hor. **B.** As the organ of speech. **1.** Lit. : quam tibi ex ore orationem duriter dictis dedit, Enn. ; consentiunt uno ore omnes, Cic. ; Ter. ; Verg. ; poscebatur ore vulgi dux Agricola, Tac. **Phr.** : *to be on people's lips, to be* (*become*) *talked about* : volito vivo' per ora virum (GEN.), Enn. ; Verg. ; in ora vulgi pervenire, Cat. ; in ora hominum abire, Liv. ; in ore vulgi or omnium esse, Cic. ; in ore esse, Cic., Liv. Also, habere aliquid in ore, *to be continually talking about something*, Cic. **2.** Transf. : of (*the character of*) *speech* : aliquid pleniore ore laudare, Cic. ; faciam uno ore Latinos, Verg. ; ruit profundo Pindarus ore, Hor. **II.** *the face, countenance.* **1.** Lit. **a.** ore rubicundo, Pl. ; figura oris, Ter. ; in os adversum, Caes. ; iratorum, Cic. ; sublime, Ov. Also, truncis arborum antefixa ora, Tac. Of animals : Verg. **b.** *the face*, i.e. *the sight or presence or person* : concedas hinc ab ore eorum, Ter. ; coram in os aliquem laudare, Ter. ; alicui laedere os, Ter. ; os praebere ad contumeliam, Liv. ; ora oculosque in aliquem convertere, Cic. ; in ore omnium versari, Cic. ; quae in ore atque in oculis provinciae gesta sunt, Cic. ; ante ora coniugum omnia pati, Liv. ; ante oculos atque ora parentum, Verg. ; traductos per ora hominum, Liv. **2.** Transf. **a.** With ref. to modesty or bashfulness : os durum ! (*brazen face !*), Ter. ; os durissimum, Cic. ; quo redibo ore ad eam quam contempserim ? Ter. ; molle (i.e. *bashfulness*), Sen. Ep. Without defining adj. : *effrontery, impudence* (*cf.* Eng. 'face') : nostis os hominis, nostis audaciam, Cic. **b.** *a represented head, a mask* : Gorgonis, Cic. ; ora corticibus cavatis, Verg.

oscen, inis, *m* [obs canō], *a foreboding bird.* In augury : *a bird from whose note auguries were taken* (e.g. the raven, crow, owl ; contrast praepes) : Cic. Ep., Hor.

Osci, ōrum, *m. pl. one of the most ancient tribes of Italy in Campania and Samnium ; akin to the Latins. In more remote times called* **Opici** *and* **Opsci** ; **Oscus**, a, um.

ōscillum, ī, *n.* [*dim.* ōs], *a little mask* : Verg.

ōscitāns, antis. **I.** *Part.* ōscitō. **II.** Adj. : *yawning* (i.e. *listless*). **1.** Lit. : iudex, Cic. **2.** Transf. : sapientia, Cic.

ōscitanter, *adv. listlessly* : Cic.

ōscitātiō, ōnis, *f.* [ōscitō], *a yawning, gaping.* **1.** Lit. : Mart. **2.** Transf. : *listlessness in speaking* : Quint.

ōscitō, āre (Enn., Lucr.) and **ōscitor**, ārī (Pl.) [ōs], *to open the mouth widely, to gape, yawn.* **1.** Lit. : Pl., Lucr. **2.** Transf. **a.** Of plants : Enn. **b.** *to yawn, be sleepy* (only in *Pres. Part.*) : Ter., Cic.

ōsculābundus, a, um [ōsculor], *kissing* : Suet.

ōsculātiō, ōnis, *f.* [ōsculor], *a kissing* : Cic., Cat.

ōsculor, ārī [ōsculum], *to kiss.* **1.** Lit. : aliquem, Pl., Cic. ; simulacrum, Cic. **2.** Transf. : *to caress, make much of* : inimicum meum, Cic. Ep. ; scientiam iuris tamquam filiolam, Cic.

ōsculum, ī, n. [*dim.* ōs], *a little mouth, sweet mouth.* **1.** Lit.: oscula libavit natae, Verg.; Ov. **2.** Transf. *a kiss* : Atticae, Cic. Ep.; oggerere, alicui ferre, Pl.; figere, Verg.; capere, sumere, carpere, accipere, dare, Ov.; iacere, Tac.; breve, Tac.

Osiris, is or idis, *m. an Egyptian deity, husband of Isis.*

ōsor, ōris, *m.* [ōdī], *a hater* : Pl.

Ossa, ae, *f.* (rarely *m.*), *a mountain range in N.E. Thessaly* ; **Ossaeus**, a, um.

osseus, a, um [os], *bony* : manus, Juv.

ossi-fragus, a, um [os and *frag* in frangō], *bone-breaking* : Sen. As Noun, **ossifragus**, ī, *m.* and **ossifraga**, ae, *f.* the lammergeyer, *or bearded vulture* : Lucr. [Fr. *orfraie.*]

os-tendō, tendere, tendī, tentum (and -tēnsum) [obs tendō], *to stretch out, hold forth.* **1.** Lit. **a.** manūs, Pl. Of soil : *to expose* : agrum soli, Cato; Aquiloni glaebas, Verg. **b.** *to exhibit, show, present* (esp. suddenly, vauntingly, etc.) : equites sese ostendunt, Caes.; Ter.; aciem, Liv.; umeros, Verg.; os suum populo Romano ostendere audet, Cic. **2.** Transf. **a.** *to hold forth, flourish* : quaedam mihi magnifica eius defensio ostenditur, Cic. **b.** *to hold forth to the mind, present* to the thoughts : spem, metum, Cic.; salutis viam, Verg.; victoriam, Liv. **c.** *to reveal, display* by acts : odium patris ex hoc ostenditur, Cic.; se alicui inimicum, Nep. Hence, illo dies cum gloriā maxumā sese nobis ostendit, Enn. **d.** *to make known, declare, set forth* in words : illi meum sensum, Pl.; sententiam, Ter. With Acc. and *Inf.* : Cic., Nep. With *Indir. Quest.* : Caes.

ostentātiō, ōnis, *f.* [ostentō]. **I.** *a frequent* or *impressive display* : saevitiae, Liv.; armorum, Plin. Pan. **II.** *a showing off, parade, advertisement, vain display, ostentation* : Cic.; (captivi) producti ostentationis causā, Cas.; ingeni, Cic. In *pl.* : Cic. Ep. **III.** *a mere show* ; *pretence* : consul veritate, non ostentatione popularis, Cic.; doloris, Sen. Ep.

ostentātor, ōris, *m.* [ostentō]. **I.** *one who holds out to view* : periculorum praemiorumque, Tac. **II.** *a vain parader* or *advertiser, vaunter* : Pl.; factorum, Liv.; Tac.

ostentō, āre [*freq.* ostendō], *to hold out, present, offer earnestly, impressively,* or *boastfully.* **1.** Lit. **a.** alicui iugula sua pro capite alicuius, Cic. Ep. **b.** *to present to view, show, exhibit* : passum capillum, Caes.; matres, Caes.; germanum ovantem, Verg.; equitatum iniciendi terroris causā, Caes.; cicatrices, Liv.; campos nitentis, Verg. **2.** Transf. **a.** *to hold up or point to as proof* or *example* : Ambiorigem fidei faciendae causā, Caes.; Tydiden nobis, Ov. **b.** *to hold out to the mind, present* or *suggest* to the thoughts : alterā manu fert apidem, panem ostentat alterā, Pl.; periculum capitis, Cic.; praemia, Sall.; minas Liv.; sociis spem pro re, Liv. **c.** *to display* (also *to show off*) by acts : tuam patientiam, Cic.; posteritati te, Cic.; se in aliis rebus, Cic.; triumphos suos. Sall. **d.** *to*

declare, set forth, parade in words : plūra dentiam, Cic. Ep.; me, Cic. Ep.; principem, Plin. Pan. With Acc. and *Inf.* : Cic. Ep. With *Indir. Quest.* : Suet.

ostentuī, DAT. *sing. m.* [ostendō], *for or as a show.* **1.** Lit. **a.** *as a public spectacle* : corpora extra vallum abiecta ostentui, Tac. **b.** So as *to mislead* : illa deditionis signa ostentui credere, Sall. **2.** Transf. **a.** *as a sign* or *proof* : ut Iugurthae scelerum ostentui essem, Sall. **b.** *for appearances* (so as *to deceive*) : nova iura Cappadociae dedit ostentui magis quam mansura, Tac.

ostentus, a, um. *I. Part.* ostendō. **II.** *Neut.* as Noun, *a prodigy, portent, miracle.* **1.** Lit.: Cic., Suet. **2.** Transf.: scis Appium ostenta facere, Cael. ap. Cic. Ep.

Ōstia, ae, *f.* and **Ōstia**, ōrum, *n. pl.* a port at the mouth of the River Tiber ; **Ōstiēnsis**, e, *adj.*

ōstiārium, ī, n. [ōstium], *a tax on doors, a door-tax* : Caes.

ōstiārius, ī, *m.* [ōstium], *a doorkeeper, porter* : Varr., Suet. [It. *usciere* ; Fr. *huissier* ; Eng. *usher.*]

ōstiātim, adv. *from door to door* : ostiatim oppidum compilare, Cic.; Quint.

ōstium, ī, n. [ōs], *a door.* **1.** Lit.: Pl., Cic.; opservare, Pl.; aperire, operire, Ter.; aperto ostio, Cic. **2.** Transf.: *any kind of entrance* or *exit* : Acheruntis, Pl.; Verg.; fluminis, Cic.; Caes.; Oceani (i.e. the Straits of Gibraltar), Cic.; portūs, Cic.; pleno subit ostia velo, Verg. [It. *uscio.*]

ostrea, ae, *f.* (Pl., Cic.) and **ostreum**, ī, *n.* (Lucil., Hor., Ov., Juv.) [ὄστρεον], *an oyster, mussel.* [Fr. *huitre.*]

ostreātus, a, um [ostrea], *covered with oyster-shells.* Transf.: *rough, scabby* : Pl.

ostreōsior, ius, *comp. adj.* [ostrea], *richer in oysters* : Cat.

ostrifer, fera, ferum, *abounding in oysters* : Verg., Luc.

ostrinus, a, um [ostrum], *purple* : Varr., Prop.

ostrum, ī, n. [ὄστρεον], *the colouring matter obtained from the sea-snail* ; *purple, v.* murex. **1.** Lit.: vestes ostro perfusae, Verg. **2.** Transf.: *a purple dress* or *covering* : stratoque super discumbitur ostro, Verg.; Lucr.; Hor.

ōsus and **ōsūrus**, a, um, *Part.* ōdī.

Othō, ōnis, *m.* a Roman cognomen ; *esp.* **I.** L. Roscius Otho, *a friend of Cicero, author of the law giving the ordo equester 14 rows of seats in the theatre.* **II.** M. Salvius Otho, *Roman emperor,* A.D. 69 ; **Othōniānus**, a, um.

Othryadēs, ae, *m.* **I.** *s.* of Othrys, i.e. Panthus, Verg. **II.** *a Spartan who in a battle with the Argives was the sole survivor.*

Othrys, yos, *m. a mountain in S. Thessaly.*

ōtiolum, ī, n. [*dim.* ōtium], *a little leisure* : Cael. ap. Cic. Ep.

ōtior, ārī [ōtium], *to be at leisure, to have leisure* : Cic., Hor.

ōtiōsē, adv. *at leisure, without occupation.* **1.** Lit.: Pl., Cic., Liv. **2.** Transf. **a.** *calmly, without haste* : Pl., Cic., Liv. **b.** *quietly, fearlessly* : Ter.

ōtiōsus, a, um [ōtium], *at leisure, unoccupied.* **1.** Lit. **a.** In gen.: cum essem otiosus domi, Cic.; Pl.; Ter. **b.** *without official employment, free from public affairs :* otioso vero et nihil agenti privato quando imperium senatus dedit ? Cic. *Sup. ;* Cic. As Noun : Cic. **2. Transf. A.** Of persons. **a.** *quiet, neutral :* Cic. As Noun : otiosis minabantur, Cic.; Tac. **b.** *quiet, calm, tranquil :* cum otiosus stilum prehenderat, Cic. With *ab :* otiosus ab animo, Ter. *Sup. ;* Cic. **B.** Of things. **a.** *free, unemployed, undisturbed* (opp. occupatus) : otium, Enn., Cic.; pecuniae, Plin. Ep. ; spatium ab hoste otiosum, Caes. ; provincia, Liv. *Comp. :* Sen. **b.** *idle, useless :* sententiae, Quint. ; otiosissimae occupationes, Plin. Ep. [Fr. *oiseux*.]

ōtium, ī, *n. leisure, vacant time, freedom from business.* **1.** L i t. **a.** In gen. : haut otium est, Pl. ; otium habere ad aliquid faciendum, Ter. ; auscultandi, Ter. ; in otio de negotiis cogitare, Cic. ; in otio vivere, Cic. ; otio languere, Cic. ; otia nostra, *my idle hours* (i.e. my poems), Ov. **b.** *freedom from public affairs, retirement, leisure-time* for writing and study : litteratum, Cic. ; studiosum, Plin. Ep. ; se in otium conferre, Cic. ; otium ad scribendum conferre, Cic. ; abundare otio et studio, Cic. **2. Transf. a.** *repose, peace* (opp. bellum) : Ter., Cic. ; multitudo insolens belli diuturnitate oti, Caes. ; res ad otium deducere, Caes. With *ab :* otium ab hoste fuit, Liv. ; ab seditionibus urbanis, Liv. ; otium bello rogare, Hor. ; mollia peragebant otia, Ov. **b.** Of *neutrality :* te in otium referres, Dolab. ap. Cic. Ep. **c.** A b l. adverbially : *at leisure, leisurely :* Phaedr. ; also, per otium, Liv.

Ovidius, a, *the name of a Roman gens ;* esp. P. Ovidius Nāsō, *a famous Latin poet in the time of Augustus ; born at Sulmo,* B.C. 43, *died at Tomi,* A.D. 17.

ovīlis, e, *adj.* [ovis], *of sheep :* stercus, Cato. *Neut.* as Noun, **ovīle, is,** *a sheepfold.* **1.** L i t. : Verg., Ov. Also, *a fold for goats :* Ov. **2.** T r a n s f. : *an enclosed space for voting in the Campus Martius :* Liv., Juv.

ovīllus, a, um [ovis], *of sheep :* caseus, Cato ; pecus, Varr. ; grex, Liv.

ovis, is (Acc. ovim, Pl.), *f.* [Gk. ὄϜις], *a sheep.* **1.** L i t. : Pl., Cic., Verg., etc. P r o v. : ovem lupo committere, Ter. **2.** T r a n s f. **a.** *wool :* Tib. **b.** *a simpleton, ninny :* Pl.

ovō, āre (in class. period, only in *Pres. Part.* ovāns), *to exult, rejoice.* **1.** L i t. **a.** In gen. : ovantes Horatium accipiunt, Liv. ; Verg. ; gutture corvi, Verg. **b.** Of the minor triumph (ovation) : ovans urbem ingrederetur, Liv. ; ovantem in Capitolium ascendere, Cic. **2.** T r a n s f. : currūs ovantes, Prop. ; patria, Juv. ; in *Pass.* : ovatum aurum (i.e. brought back in triumph), Pers.

ōvum, ī, *n.* [*cf.* ὠϜόν], *an egg.* **1.** L i t. : parere, Cic. ; facere, Varr. ; ponere, Ov. ; excudere, Cic., Varr. ; pullos ex ovis excudere, Cic. ; integram famem ad ovum adfero (i.e. to the beginning of the meal), Cic. Ep. ; ab ovo usque ad māla (i.e. from beginning to end), Hor. Also *the spawn of* fish : Cic. **2.** T r a n s f. (in *pl.*) : *wooden*

balls set up in a Circus, and removed one by one to mark the laps : Varr., Liv. [It. *uovo ;* Sp. *huevo ;* Fr. *œuf*.]

P

P, p, the fifteenth letter of the Latin alphabet. **I.** It almost always represents I. E. *p* and Gk. *π* in *lupus*, and perh. a few other words, it represents orig. *k*. Occ. in words borrowed from the Greek, Lat. *p* corresponds to Gk. φ as *Poenus*, Φοῖνιξ ; *purpura*, πορφύρα. In inscrs. and vulgar Latin *b* followed by *s* or *t* is often changed to *p*, as *opsides* for *obsides, apsens* for *absens, optinui* for *obtinui*, etc. **II.** Changes of *p* in the Romance languages. Into *b :* e.g. Lat. *apotheca ;* It. *bottega,* Fr. *boutique :* Lat. *apicula ;* Fr. *abeille.* Into *v :* e.g. Lat. *pauper, ripa ;* It. *povero, riva ;* Fr. *pauvre, rive :* Lat. *sapio, rapio, recipio ;* Fr. *savoir, ravir, recevoir.* Into *f :* e.g. Lat. *supplex ;* It. *soffice :* Lat. *caput :* Fr. *chef.* When *p* is doubled, one of the letters is often omitted, but not in Italian : e.g. Lat. *cippus, puppis ;* F. *cep, poupe.* *p* followed by *t* is frequently either changed into *t* or omitted : e.g. Lat. *aptus, captivus ;* It. *atto, cattivo ;* Fr. *chétif.* *ps* becomes *ss* or *s :* e.g. Lat. *capsa ;* It. *cassa,* Fr. *caisse,* etc. **III.** As an a b b r e v i a t i o n, P most frequently denotes the praenomen Publius ; P. C. usually stands for patres conscripti. P. M. for pontifex maximus, P. P. pater patriae, P. R. populus Romanus, P. S. pecuniā suā.

pābulātiō, ōnis, *f.* [pābulor], *pasture :* Varr. Milit. *a foraging :* pabulatione prohibere, intercludi, Caes. In *pl.* : Caes.

pābulātor, ōris, *m.* [pābulor]. Milit. *a forager :* Caes., Liv.

pābulor, ārī [pābulum], *to feed, graze,* hence, milit. *to forage :* angustius pabulantur, Caes. ; Liv. ; Tac. Comic. of making a living : of fishermen : ad mare huc prodimus pabulatum, Pl.

pābulum, ī, *n.* [*cf.* pā-scō], *food, nourishment.* **1.** L i t. **a.** Of men : pabula dura, Lucr. **b.** Of animals (also of birds), esp. those which graze : *fodder, food :* Pl., Sall., etc. ; secare, supportare, Caes. In *pl.* : Lucr. ; legere, Verg. ; decerpere, carpere, Ov. **2.** T r a n s f. : Acheruntia pabulum, Pl. ; amoris, Lucr. ; studi atque doctrinae, Cic. ; dederatque gravi nova pabula morbo, Ov.

pācālis, e, *adj.* [pāx], *of peace, peaceful :* olea, Ov.

pācātus, a, um. I. *Part.* pācō. **II.** A d j. : *peaceful, quiet, tranquil, undisturbed.* **1.** L i t. : civitates, Cic. ; (Galliae) pars, Caes. ; pacato agmine transire, Liv. ; mens, Lucr. ; vultus, Ov. ; mare, Hor., Liv. *Sup. :* Cic. In *Neut.* or with ager understood : vagi milites in pacato, Liv. ; ex pacatis praedas agere, Sall. **2.** T r a n s f. : nequitia, Cic. ; oratio pacatior, Cic. *Neut.* as Noun : nec diu in pacato mansit gens, Liv.

Pācideiānus, ī, *m. a famous gladiator, whose combat with Aeserninus the Samnite,* mentioned by Lucilius, became famous.

pācifer, era, erum [pāx ferō], *peace-bringing, peaceful* : oliva, Verg. ; Cyllenius, Ov.

pācificātiō, ōnis, *f.* [pācificō], *a peace-making, pacification* : Cic. Ep.

pācificātor, ōris, *m.* [pācificō], *a peace-maker, pacifier* : Cic. Ep., Liv. With *Obj.* GEN. : Cic. Ep.

pācificātōrius, a, um [pācificātor], *peace-making, pacificatory* : Cic.

pācificō, āre [pāx faciō], *to make* or *negotiate a peace.* **1.** Lit. : Sall., Liv. **2.** Transf. **a.** In *Mid.* : satin' tecum pacificatus sum ? Pl. **b.** In religion : *to appease :* hostia caelestis pacificasset heros, Cat.

pācificus, a, um [pāx faciō], *peacemaking, pacific* : Cic.

paciscor, paciscī, pepigī (*v.* pangō), pactus, *to fix, settle* ; hence, *to make a bargain or agreement* ; *to covenant, agree, contract.* **A.** Intrans. : cum illo paululā pecuniā, Pl. ; paciscitur magnā mercede cum Celtiberorum principibus ut etc., Liv. ; Ov. ; votis pacisci ne etc., Hor. **B.** Trans. **a.** *to stipulate for :* Pl. : Ciliciam sibi, Cic. ; ab aliquo vitam, Sall. Esp. of marriage contracts : ex quā pactus esset (*sc.* feminam) vir domo in matrimonium duceret, Liv. **b.** *to agree, pledge oneself* (with *Inf.*): Liv., Ov. **c.** *to barter, give up* in exchange : vitam pro laude, Verg. ; letum pro laude, Verg. *Perf. Part.* in *Pass.* sense. **a.** *stipulated :* pretium, dies, Cic. ; merces, Hor. In ABL. *Absol.* : pacto inter se ut . . ., Liv. **b.** *betrothed :* tibi Callicli filia, Pl. ; Cic. Ep. ; Verg. ; Liv. *Fem.* as Noun : Verg.

pācō, āre [pāx], *to bring into a state of peace* (by war) ; *to pacify.* **1.** Lit. : Allobroges, Caes. ; Amanum, Cic. Ep. ; Erymanthi nemora, Verg. ; mare a praedonibus, Aug. **2.** Transf. : incultae pacantur vomere silvae, Hor. [It. *pagare ;* Sp. *pagar ;* Fr. *payer.*]

pactiō, ōnis, *f.* [paciscor], *an agreeing, compact, contract, treaty.* **a.** In gen. : pactionem facere de aliquā re, Cic. ; cum aliquo conflare, Cic. ; cum aliquo facere ut etc., Cic. Ep. ; summā fide in pactione manere, Nep. In *pl.* : Cic. **b.** *a marriage-contract:* mecum adire ad pactionem, Pl. ; nuptialis, Liv. **c.** Made by the tax-farmers : pactiones cum aliquo conficere, Cic. Ep. **d.** *a secret* or *corrupt bargaining, collusion :* nonnullos pactionis suspicionem non vitasse, Cic. ; provinciae, Sall. **e.** *an agreement* to surrender : arma per pactionem tradere, Liv. **f.** pactio verborum, *a form of words :* Cic.

Pactōlus, ī, *m. a river in Lydia, said to bring down golden sands* ; **Pactōlis**, idis, *f. adj.*

pactor, ōris, *m.* [paciscor], *a contractor, negotiator :* Cic.

pactus, a, um. **I.** *Part.* paciscor. **II.** Noun, **pactum**, ī, *n. an agreement, covenant, contract, compact :* servare, Cic. ; manere in pacto, Cic. ; stare pacto, Liv. ; ex pacto, Cic. Ep. ; pactum et sponsalia, Juv. In ABL. *pactō, by or in* (some) *manner, way, means :* aliquo pacto, Pl., Ter. ; alio pacto, Pl., Ter., Cic. ; nescio quo pacto semper hoc fit, Cic. ; hoc pacto, Verg.

Pācuvius, ī, *m. a famous Roman tragic poet* (born B.C. 220), *a native of Brundisium,* nephew of Ennius ; **Pācuviānus**, a, um.

paeān, ānis, *m.* [Παιάν]. **I.** *an epithet of Apollo as the healing deity* ; **Paeānius**, a, um. **II.** *a festive hymn, hymn of triumph or praise, a paean* (orig. in honour of Apollo). **1.** Lit. : citare, Cic. ; conclamare, Verg. ; dicite io Paean, Ov. **2.** Transf. : *a paeon,* a metrical foot (*v.* paeon) : Cic.

paedagōgium, ī, *n. the place where boys of servile birth were trained as pages ; the pages' hall.* **1.** Lit. : Plin. Ep. **2.** Transf. : *the boys* in a paedagogium : Sen.

paedagōgus, ī, *m.* [παιδαγωγός], *a slave who had charge of the children.* **1.** Lit. : Pl., Cic., etc. **2.** Transf. : *a leader, guide, warden :* Sen. Ep., Suet. ; jestingly of a lover who accompanied his sweetheart to and from school : Ter.

paedor, ōris, *m. nastiness, filth :* Lucr., Tac. ; in *pl.* : Cic.

paegniārius, a, um [παίγνιον], *in jest :* gladiatores, Suet.

paelex, icis, *f.* [*cf.* παλλακίς], *a concubine, mistress* (usually of a married man). **1.** Lit.: Pl. Freq. with GEN. (or *Possessive Pronoun*) of the true wife : filiae, Cic. ; sororis meae, Ov. ; suas paelices nos esse aiunt, Pl. **2.** Transf. : *a mistress* (in gen.) : Curt.

paelicātus, ūs, *m.* [paelex], *concubinage :* Cic.

Paeligni, ōrum, *m. pl. a people of Central Italy, of Sabellian stock* ; **Paelignus**, a, um, Paeligni ruris alumnus, i.e. Ovid, Ov.

paene, *adv. nearly, almost :* foris paene effregisti, Pl. ; paene amicus, Cic. ; crescere paene opus, Liv. ; totidem paene genera, Cic. Comic *Sup.* ' quite almost ' : ita mea consilia perturbat paenissume, Pl.

paeninsula and **paene īnsula**, ae, *f. a peninsula :* Liv.

paenitendus, a, um [paeniteō], *to be regretted, far from satisfactory* (mostly with a negative) : sub haud paenitendo magistro, Liv. ; gens Flavia rei publicae non paenitenda, Suet.

paenitentia, ae, *f.* [paeniteō], *repentance, regret :* Liv., Tac. ; agere, i.e. to repent, Quint. With *Obj.* GEN. : Curt., Plin. Ep., etc.

paeniteō, ēre [*cf.* poena]. **I.** Personal. **A.** Trans. : *to cause to regret, to displease :* me haec condicio, Pl. **B.** Intrans. : *to be sorry, to regret* (with GEN., and only in *Inf., Part.,* and *Gerund*) : adsuefacere militem minus virtutis paenitere suae, Liv. ; paenitens consili, Sall. Without GEN. : optimus est portus paenitenti mutatio consili, Cic. ; tanta vis fuit paenitendi, Cic. **II.** Impersonal : *to cause to feel sorrow, regret,* or *dissatisfaction.* With ACC. of person, and GEN. of thing (cause), but both are not always expressed : num huiusce te gloriae paeniteat ? Cic. ; Pl., etc. ; paenitet et torqueor, Ov. ; or with *Inf.* as Subject : efficiunt, ut me non didicisse minus paeniteat, Cic. ; or with *quod*-clause : an paenitet vos quod exercitum traduxerim, Caes. ; Cic. Ep. ; or with *Indir. Quest.* : paenitetne quot ancillas alam ? Pl. ; quoad te quantum proficias non paenitebit, Cic. [It. *pentire, pentirsi.*]

paenŭla, ae, f. [φαινόλης], a cloak for journeys or rainy weather. **1.** Lit.: Lucil., Cic., Hor., etc. Prov.: paenulam alicui scindere (i.e. to press one to stay; opp. to, vix paenulam alicui attingere), Cic. Ep. **2.** Transf.: libertas paenula est tergo tuo, Pl.

paenŭlātus, a, um [paenula], wearing a paenula : Cic., Mart.

paeōn, ōnis, m. [παιών], a metrical foot of one long and three short syllables (which acc. to the position of the long syllable, is called primus, secundus, tertius, quartus) : Cic., Quint.

Paeŏnes, um, m. pl. a people of N. Macedonia; **Paeŏnia**, ae, f. their country; **Paeŏnis**, idis, f. adj.

Paestum, i, n. a town in Lucania, famous for its roses; **Paestānus**, a, um; **Paestāni**, ōrum, m. pl. its inhabitants.

paetŭlus, a, um [dim. paetus], having a slight cast in the eye : Cic.

paetus, a, um, adj. having a (slight) cast in the eyes, squinting : Hor., Ov.

pāgānus, a, um [pāgus], of a village or the country, rustic. **1.** Lit.: foci, Ov. As Noun, **pāgānus**, i, m. a peasant, villager, rustic : Cic. As term of contempt addressed to soldiers; bumpkins, yokels : Tac.; Juv.; Suet. **2.** Transf.: rustic, unlearned : cultus, Plin. Ep.

Pagāsa, ae, f. and **Pagāsae**, ārum, f. pl. a town on the coast of Thessaly, where the Argo was built; **Pagāsaeus**, a, um: puppis (i.e. Argo), Ov.; coniunx (i.e. Alcestis), Ov.; **Pagāsaeus**, i, m. Jason, Ov.

pāgātim, adv. [pāgus], by districts or villages, in every village : Liv.

pāgella, ae, f. [dim. pāgina], a little leaf of a book : Cic. Ep.

pāgina, ae, f. [fr. root of pangō], a written page or leaf of a body, letter, etc. **1.** Lit.: Cic., Juv. **2.** Transf.: the contents of a page : priore pāginā perturbatus, Cic. Ep.; Mart.

pāginŭla, ae, f. [dim. pāgina], a little leaf of a book : Cic. Ep.

pāgus, i, m. [fr. root of pangō], a country-district, a village. **1.** Lit. **a.** In gen.: Verg., Liv., Tac. **b.** a canton, province : omnis civitas Helvetia in quattuor pagos divisa est, Caes.; Tac. **2.** Transf. **a.** the country people : festus in pratis vacat otioso cum bove pagus, Hor.; Ov. **b.** (the people of) a canton : centum pagi consederunt, Caes. [Through low Lat. pāgēnsis, It. paese; Sp. pais; Fr. pays.]

pāla, ae, f. [pangō], **I.** a spade : Pl., Cato, Liv. **II.** the bezel of a ring (=funda) : Cic. [It. paletta; Fr. pelle.]

Palaemōn, ōnis, m. a sea-god, formerly called Melicerta.

palaestra, ae, f. [παλαίστρα], a wrestling-school, a place for physical exercises, palaestra (mostly public). **1.** Lit.: Pl., Cic., Verg., etc. **2.** Transf. **a.** Of a brothel : Pl., Ter. **b.** the exercise of wrestling, gymnastics : discere, nescire, Cic.; Ov.; exercere palaestras, Verg. **c.** training in rhetoric, philosophy, etc.; non tam armis institutus, quam palaestrā, Cic.; utemur eā palaestrā quam a te didicimus, Cic. Ep.

palaestricē, adv. after the manner of the palaestra : Cic.

palaestricus, a, um [παλαιστρικός], of or learnt in the palaestra : exercitus, Pl.; motus, Cic.; magister, Quint. As Noun, **palaestrica**, ae, f. the art of gymnastics : Quint.

palaestrīta, ae, m. [παλαιστρίτης], the director of a wrestling-school : Cic., Mart.

palam, adv. and prep. **I.** Adv. **a.** Of actions : openly, publicly : Pl., Cic., Verg., etc. **b.** Of words, etc., esp. with esse, ferre, facere : to be, make public : palam est res, facere : Pl.; Cic.; palam ferente Hannibale se ab Fabio victum, Liv.; celatā morte (Tarquini) opes suas firmavit; tum demum palam factum est, Liv.; Cic. Ep.; palam facere suis (with Indir. Quest.), Nep. **II.** As prep. (with Locat. Abl. (rare) : before, in the presence of : te palam, Hor.; rem creditori palam populo solvit, Liv.; Ov.

Palamēdēs, is, m. son of Nauplius, king of Euboea, who lost his life at Troy through the artifices of Ulysses.

Palātium, i, n. one of the seven hills of Rome, on which many famous Romans and most of the early Emperors had their residences; hence, in pl. a palace : Ov., Juv.; **Palātinus**, a, um, of the Palatium, Palatine; also of the imperial house, imperial : Ov., Juv., Suet. [It. palazzo; Fr. palais.]

palātum, i, n. and (rarely) **palātus**, i, m. the roof of the mouth, the palate. **1.** Lit. **a.** Vorg., Ov. **b.** As the organ of taste : Cic., Hor., Juv. **2.** Transf. **a.** taste, critical judgment : Cic. **b.** From the arched shape, a vault : caeli, Enn.

palea, ae, f. [cf. pollen, pulvis and Gk. παλύνω], chaff. **1.** Lit.: Varr.; in pl. : Verg. **2.** Transf. **a.** the dross of metal: Plin. **b.** the wattles of a cock : Varr. [It. paglia; Fr. paille.]

paleāria, ium, n. pl. [palea], the dewlap of an ox : Varr., Verg., Ov.

Palēs, is, f. the tutelary Italian goddess of shepherds and cattle; **Palīlis**, e, adj.; **Palīlia** (or **Parīlia**), ium, n. pl. the festival of Pales celebrated on April 21st.

Palīci, ōrum, m. pl. (sing. **Palīcus**, i, Verg., Ov.) twin sons of Jupiter and the nymph Thalia, worshipped at Palica in Sicily.

palimpsēstus, i, m. [παλίμψηστος], a parchment from which the old writing has been erased for the purpose of writing upon it again; a palimpsest : Cic. Ep., Cat.

Palinūrus, i, m. **I.** the pilot of Aeneas, drowned off Lucania. **II.** a promontory named after him.

paliūrus, i, m. [παλίουρος], a plant, Christ's thorn : Verg.

palla, ae, f. a long and wide upper garment. **1.** Lit. **a.** Of Roman ladies : Pl., Verg., Hor., etc. **b.** the mantle of a poet or tragic actor : Hor., Ov. **2.** Transf.: a curtain : Sen.

pallaca, ae, f. [παλλάκη], a concubine, mistress : Plin., Suet.

Pallantias, adis, and **Pallantis**, idos or idis, f. Aurora, descended from Hyperion, uncle of the giant Pallas.

Pallas, adis or ados, f. [Παλλάς], Athene, the deity of the Athenian Acropolis, identi-

fied with Minerva. Transf. **a.** *the Trojan image of Pallas, the Palladium :* Prop., Ov. **b.** *the olive :* Ov. ; *oil :* Ov. ; **Palladius,** a, um, *of Pallas :* arx (Troy), Prop. ; arces (Athens), Ov. ; with ref. to the olive : silva, Verg. ; latices, corona, Ov. ; **Palladium,** ī, n. *an image of Pallas Athene,* esp. *the one said to have fallen from heaven ; on it the safety of Troy (and later of Rome) depended :* Cic., Verg., Ov.

Pallās, antis (Voc. Pallā, Verg). m. **I.** *son of Pandion.* **II.** *a king of Arcadia, the great-grandfather of Euander.* **III.** *son of Euander ;* **Pallantēus,** a, um, *of Pallas, the ancestor of Euander ;* **Pallantēum,** ī, n. **i.** *a city in Arcadia, the residence of Pallas.* **ii.** *the city founded by Euander in Italy, where Rome afterwards stood.* **IV.** *a freed-man of the Emperor Claudius.*

pallēns, entis. **I.** Part. palleō. **II.** Adj.: *pale, sallow, wan.* **1.** Lit.: simulacra, Lucr.; umbrae Erebi, Verg.; terrore puellae, Ov.; Verg. **2.** Transf. **a.** *pale-coloured, grey-green, yellow-green :* olivae, Ov.; hedera, violae, Verg.; toga, Mart. Poet.: *that makes pale :* philtra, Ov.; curae, Mart. **b.** *sickly-coloured, drooping, weak:* fama, Tac.; mores (i.e. vicious), Pers.

palleō, ēre [*cf.* πολιός, pullus], *to be or look pale.* **1.** Lit.: Cic., Ov., etc. **2.** Transf. **a.** *to be or look yellow :* area nummis, Mart. **b.** *to lose the natural colour, to change colour, to fade :* Prop., Ov. **c.** *to be pale* (from emotion): ambitione malā, Hor.; ad omnia fulgura, Juv. With DAT.: *to show anxiety about :* pueris pater, Hor. Also of study : Quint.

pallēscō, pallēscere, palluī [palleō], *to grow or turn pale.* **1.** Lit.: nullā culpā, Hor.; umbraticā vitā, Quint. With Acc.: *to turn pale at the sight of :* scatentem beluis pontum, Hor. **2.** Transf. (of things). **a.** *to turn yellow :* saxum auro, Ov. **b.** *to fade :* frondes, Ov.

palliātus, a, um [*dim.* pallium]. *dressed in a pallium, cloaked* (mostly of Greeks): Pl., Cic. Hence, fabula palliata, *a play in which Greek characters were introduced,* Ter.

pallidulus, a, um [*dim.* pallidus], *palish :* Cat., Juv.

pallidus, a, um [palleō], *pale, sallow, grey-green, yellow-green.* **1.** Lit.: Hor., Ov., etc. Comp. : Cat., Ov. Esp. of the dead : Verg., Tib. ; of the underworld : Enn., Luc. **2.** Transf. **a.** *pale* from fright : nomine in Hectoreo, Ov. **b.** *pale, pining* from love : in lentā Naide, Ov. **c.** *pale, mouldy.* Comp. : vetustate ficus, Varr. **d.** *that makes pale :* mors, Hor.; vina, Prop.

palliolātim, adv. *in a mantle :* Pl.

palliolātus, a, um [palliolum], *wearing a cloak-cape or hood :* Mart., Suet.

palliolum, ī, n. [*dim.* pallium]. **I.** *a small or poor mantle or cloak :* Pl., Mart., Juv. **II.** *a covering for the head, a cape, hood :* Ov., Quint.

pallium, ī, n. [*cf.* palla]. **I.** *a coverlet, pall :* Ov., Suet., etc. **II.** *a Greek cloak or mantle :* Pl., Cic., Ov., etc. Prov. : **i.** manum intra pallium continere, i.e. *to speak calmly, without gesture,* Quint. **ii.** tunica propior pallio est, Pl.

pallor, ōris. m. [palleō], *pale colour, paleness, wanness.* **1.** Lit.: Cic., Verg., Hor., etc. In pl. : Tac. Of the Lower World : pallor hicmsque tenet late loca senta, Ov. **2.** Transf. **a.** *loss of natural hue or brightness, fading :* pallorem ducere, Ov. In pl.: Lucr. **b.** From love : Hor., Ov. **c.** From fear : palla pallorem incutit, Pl.

pallula, ae, f. [*dim.* palla], *a little cloak or mantle :* Pl.

palma, ae, f. [παλάμη]. **I.** *the palm of the hand.* **1.** Lit. **a.** Cic., Verg., etc. **b.** *the open hand :* passis palmis salutem petere, Caes. ; Verg. **c.** *the hand :* Pl., Cic., Verg. **2.** Transf.: *the broad end or blade of an oar :* Cat. **II.** *a palm-tree, a palm.* **1.** Lit.: Caes., Verg., etc. **2.** Transf. **a.** *the fruit of the palm-tree, a date :* Ov. **b.** *a broom made of palm-twigs :* Hor., Mart. **c.** *a palm-branch or palm-wreath,* as a token of victory ; hence, *the palm or prize :* eodem anno (461 A.U.C.) palmae primum victoribus datae, Liv. **d.** *victory, honour, glory, pre-eminence :* palmam possidet, Pl.; plurimarum palmarum gladiator, Cic.; alicuius rei palmam alicui deferre, Cic.; belli Punici, Liv. ; palmā donare aliquem. Ov.; Elea palma, Hor.; docto oratori palma danda est, Cic. ; huic equidem consilio palmam do, Ter. Poet. of the victor himself : post Helymus subit et iam tertia palma Diores, *the* (winner of the) *third prize,* Verg. **e.** *a branch* of any tree : cuiusque stipitis palma, Liv. ; of a vine : Varr.

palmāris, e, adj. [palma]. **I.** *of a hand's breadth :* Varr. **II.** *that merits the palm or prize,* hence, *excellent, admirable :* statua, Cic.

palmārius, a, um [palma], *of palms.* **1.** Lit.: Varr. **2.** Transf.: *deserving the prize.* Neut. as Noun, *a masterpiece :* Ter. [Fr. *palmier.*]

palmātus, a, um [palma], *worked or embroidered with palm-branches :* tunica (usually worn by generals in their triumphal processions), Liv. ; togao, Mart.

palmes, itis, m. [palma], *a young branch or shoot of a vine, a vine-sprout.* **1.** Lit.: Verg., Ov., etc. **2.** Transf.: in gen., *a bough, branch :* Curt., Luc.

palmētum, ī, n. [palma], *a palm-grove* (mostly in pl.): Hor., Tac.

palmifer, era, erum [palma ferō], *palm-bearing :* Prop., Ov.

palmōsus, a, um [palma], *abounding in palm-trees :* Verg.

palmula, ae, f. [*dim.* palma]. **I.** *the blade of an oar :* Verg. **II.** *the fruit of the palm-tree, a date :* Varr., Suet.

pālor, ārī [perh. *cf.* Gk. πλανᾶσθαι], *to wander hither and thither, wander about ; to be dispersed, to straggle.* **1.** Lit.: vagi per agros palantur, Liv. ; Sall. ; Tac. ; terga dabant palantia Teucri, Verg. ; palantia sidera, Lucr. ; Verg. Perf. Part. in Pres. sense : Liv. **2.** Transf.: errare atque viam pulantis quaerere vitae, Lucr. ; Ov.

palpātiō, ōnis, f. [palpō], *a stroking.* Transf. *a flattering* (in pl.) : Pl.

palpātor, ōris, m. [palpō] *one who strokes and caresses.* Transf.: *a wheedler, flatterer :* Pl.

palpebra, ae, f. [palpō], *an eyelid* (us. *pl.*) : Lucr., Cic. [Sp. *parpado* ; Fr. *paupière.*]

palpitō, āre [*freq.* palpō], *to throb, quiver* : Cic. ; lingua, Ov. Esp. of death-struggles : *to writhe, pant, gasp* : Ov., Suet.

palpō, āre (Cic. Ep., Juv.), and **palpor**, ārī (Pl., Hor.) [*cf.* ψάλλω], *to stroke, caress*. **1.** Lit.: pectora virginea manu, Ov. **2.** Transf.: *to coax, wheedle, flatter* : Pl. ; palpabo eoquonam modo possim, Cic. Ep. With DAT. : Pl., Hor. With ACC. : quem munere palpat Carus, Juv.

palpō, ōnis, m. [palpō], *a flatterer* : Pers.

palpus, ī, m. *the soft palm of the hand.* Transf. : *wheedling* : palpo percutere, Pl. ; alicui optrudere, Pl.

palūdāmentum, ī, n. *a military cloak.* **a.** *a soldier's cloak* (=sagum : *v.* rare) : Sall., Liv. **b.** *a general's cloak* : Sall., Liv., Tac.

palūdātus, a, um, *wearing a general's cloak* : Caes., Cic., Liv., Juv., etc.

palūdōsus, a, um [palūs], *fenny, boggy, marshy* : Prop., Ov.

palumbēs, is, m. and f. (**palumbus**, ī, m. Cato), *a wood-pigeon, ring-dove* : Varr., Verg., Hor. Prov. **i.** palumbem alicui ad aream adducere (i.e. to furnish a good opportunity to another), Pl. **ii.** duae unum expetitis palumbem (i.e. the same lover), Pl.

pālus, ī, m. [fr. root of pangō, πήγνυμι], *a stake, pale* : Pl., Tib., Ov. ; used for punishment : damnati ad palum adligati, Cic. ; Liv. ; for sword-exercise : Juv. ; transf. : exerceamur ad palum, Sen. Ep.

palūs (perh. palūs in Hor.), ūdis, f. (GEN. *pl.* palūdum, Caes. ; palūdium, Liv.) [perh. *cf.* πηλός], *marshy ground, a swamp, marsh, morass* : Caes., Cic., Liv., Verg., etc. ; of the Styx : Verg. Transf. : *sedge* : Mart.

palūster, tris, tre [palūs], *marshy, swampy, fenny.* **1.** Lit.: locus, Caes. ; ager, Liv. ; ulva, Verg. ; ranae, Hor. **2.** Transf.: *filthy, vicious* : lux, Pers.

Pammenēs, is, m. *a Greek rhetorician, instructor of Brutus* ; **Pammenia**, ōrum, n. *pl. the opinions* or *theories of Pammenes* : Cic. Ep.

pampineus, a, um [pampinus], *of, made of,* or *draped in vine tendrils* : umbrae, Verg. ; hasta·, Verg. ; uvae, Ov. ; odor, Prop. ; corona, Tac.

pampinus, ī, m. *a tendril* or *young shoot of a vine.* **1.** Lit.: Plin. Hence, *a vine-leaf, the foliage of a vine* : Pl., Verg., Hor. ; in *pl.* : Cic. **2.** Transf. *a clasper* or *tendril of any climbing plant* : Plin. [Fr. *pampre.*]

Pān, Pānos (Acc. Pāna), m. *the Greek god of flocks, woods, and shepherds* ; orig. *Arcadian, but identified largely with Italian Faunus* ; *inventor of the* σύριγξ (*Pan's pipes*) ; *represented with the legs of a goat* ; in *pl.* Pānes, *gods of the woods resembling Pan* : Ov.

panacēa, ae, f. and **panaces**, is, n. [πανάκεια, πάνακες], *a herb which was supposed to heal all diseases, heal-all, panacea* : Verg.

Panaetōlium, ī, n. *the general assembly of the Aetolians* ; **Panaetōlicus**, a, um, *of the whole of Aetolia* : concilium, Liv.

pānārium, ī, n. [pānis], *a bread-basket* : Varr., Stat., Plin. Ep. [It. *paniere* ; Fr. *panier.*]

Panathēnāicus, a, um, *of the Panathenaea, a festival of the Athenians* ; as Noun (*sc.* λόγος), *an oration of Isocrates delivered at the Panathenaea.*

Panchāia, ae, f. *a region in Arabia Felix, famous for its frankincense* ; **Panchaeus**, **Panchāicus**, a, um.

panchrēstus (panchristus), a, um [πάγχρηστος], *good* or *useful for everything* : suo illo panchresto medicamento, *by his sovereign remedy* (i.e. money), Cic.

pancraticē, adv. *like a competitor in the* pancratium, i.e. heartily, finely : valere, Pl.

pancratium or **-on**, ī, n. [παγκράτιον], *a contest which included both wrestling and boxing* : Prop., Plin., etc.

Pandarus, ī, m. **I.** *a distinguished Lycian archer in the Trojan army.* **II.** *s. of Alcanor, companion of Aeneas, killed by Turnus.*

pandiculor, ārī [pandō], *to stretch oneself* : Pl.

Pandiōn, onis, m. *king of Athens, father of Procne and Philomela* ; **Pandionius**, a, um.

pandō, āre [pandus], *to bend, bow, curve* : manum, Quint.

pandō, pandere, pandī, pānsum and pāssum. **I.** *to spread out, extend.* **1.** Lit.: palmas ante delubra, Lucr. ; Caes. ; capillo passo, Caes. ; Ter. ; Verg. ; crinibus passis, Liv. ; pennas ad solem, Verg. ; velo passo pervenire, Pl. ; velis passis pervehi, Cic. ; aciem Tac. ; racemi passi (i.e. spread out to dry), Verg. ; Pl. **2.** Transf.: vela orationis, Cic. With *Refl. Pron.* or in *Mid.* : tempora se veris florentia pandunt, Lucr. ; illa divina bona se pandunt, Cic. ; immensa panditur planities, Liv. **II.** *to fling wide, throw open, to open* or *open out.* **1.** Lit. **a.** ianuam Orci, Pl. ; limina, Verg. ; Helicona, Verg. ; dividimus muros et moenia pandimus urbis, Verg. **b.** *to open out and reveal* : agros pinguis, Lucr. ; tria guttura Cerberus, Verg. In *Mid.* : panduntur inter ordines viae, Lucr. **2.** Transf. **a.** *to lay open* (i.e. split) : rupem ferro, Liv. **b.** *to lay open, reveal, disclose* : spectacula caudā, Hor. ; viam fugae, viam salutis, viam alicui ad dominationem, Liv. ; rerum naturam dictis, Lucr. ; res altā terrā et caligine mersas, Verg. ; rem ordine, Verg. ; nomen, Ov.

pandus, a, um, *bent, crooked, curved* : carina, Enn., Verg. ; rami, Ov. ; asellus, Ov. Of persons : Quint.

panēgyricus, a, um [πανηγυρικός], *of a public assembly* or *festival* ; as Noun, **Panēgyricus**, ī, m. (*sc.* λόγος). **1.** Lit.: *the festival oration of Isocrates, in which he eulogised the Athenians* : Cic. **2.** Transf. *a eulogy, panegyric* : Quint.

Pangaeus, ī, m. and **Pangaea**, ōrum, n. *pl. a mountain-range in Thrace and Macedonia.*

pangō, pangere, pānxī, (pāctum) (*Perf.* -pēgī, -pāctus in compounds, and pepigī, pactus in sense 2. b.) [*cf.* πήγνυμι, paciscor], *to fasten, fix.* **1.** Lit.: clavum, Liv. Of planting : ramulum, Suet. **2.** Transf. **a.** Of literary composition : *to make, compose* : vostrum (GEN.) maxuma facta patrum, Enn. ; carmina, Lucr. ; aliquid Sophocleum, Cic. Ep. ; poemata, Hor. ; pangendi facultas, Tac. **b.** *to fix, settle, agree upon* (only in

Perf. forms ; *v.* also **paciscor**): dŭcentïs Philippïs rem pepïgī, Pl. ; pactam rem habēto, Pl. ; cum hoste indutïas, Cic. ; Liv. ; terminos, Cic. ; pacem nobïscum pepigistis ut etc., Li..; non fuit armillas tantï pepigisse Sabïnas, Ov. ; neque prima per artem temptamenta tui pepigī, perh. *sound you as to a compact,* Verg. With *ne* and *Subj. :* Cic., Tac. With *Inf. :* Tac. Freq. of a marriage contract : quod pepigere viri, pepigerunt ante parentes, Cat. ; pater hanc tibi, Ov.

pănĭceus, a, um [pānis], *made of bread.* Comic. : milites (*the Baker-street brigade*), Pl.

pănĭcŭla, ae, *f.* [*dim.* pānus], *a tuft* on plants : panicula tectoria, *tufts* of reeds used for thatching, Pl.

pănĭcum, ī, *n.* [pānus], *a kind of millet :* Caes.

pănĭfĭcium, ī, *n.* [pānis faciō], *the making of bread.* **1.** Lit. : Varr. **2.** Transf.: *any thing baked, as, bread, cakes :* Suet.

pānis, is, *m.* [fr. root of pāscō]. **I.** *bread :* Pl., Liv. ; cibarius (*coarse bread*), Cic. ; secundus, Hor. ; secundarius (*common household bread*), Suet. **II.** *a loaf of bread* (mostly *pl.*) : Pl., Caes., Suet. [Fr. *pain.*]

Pănĭscus, ī, *m. a little Pan :* Cic.

pannĭcŭlus, ī, *m.* [*dim.* pannus], *a small garment :* Juv.

Pannōnia, ae, *f. a country on the Danube, including parts of Hungary and Jugoslavia ;* **Pannonĭcus, Pannonĭus,** a, um ; **Pannonĭs,** idis, *f. adj.* **Pannonĭus,** ī, *m. a Pannonian.*

pannōsus, a, um [pannus], *ragged, tattered.* **1.** Lit. : homines, Cic. Ep. ; Juv. **2.** Transf. *tattered, wrinkled, mothery :* macies, Sen. ; mammae, Mart. ; faex aceti, Pers.

pannūceus and **pannūcius,** a, um, *ragged.* Transf. *wrinkled, shrivelled :* mâla, Plin. ; Baucis, Pers.

pannus, ī, *m. a piece of cloth.* **a.** As a garment : Hor., Juv., Plin. Ep. **b.** *a patch :* Hor. **c.** *rags, tatters :* pannis annisque opsitus, Ter. ; Lucr. ; Sen. ; Juv., etc.

Panomphaeus, ī, *m.* '*the author of all oracles,*' *an epithet of Jupiter.*

Panopē, ēs, and **Panopēa,** ae, *f.* **I.** *a sea-nymph.* **II.** *a town in Phocis.*

pānsa, ae, *adj. m. f.* [pandō], *broad-footed, splay-foot :* Pl.

pānsus, a, um, *Part,* pandō.

panthēra, ae, *f.* [πανθήρα], *a panther,* prob. also, *a leopard :* Cic. Ep., Ov.

panthērinus, a, um [panthēra], *of* or *like panthers.* Transf. *cunning :* pantherinum genus (hominum), (or perh. in allusion to the coat of the beast, *motley*), Pl.

Panthūs, ī, *m.* (Voc. Panthŭ), *a priest of Apollo at Troy, f. of Euphorbus ;* **Panthoïdēs,** ae, *m. s. of Panthus,* i.e. *Euphorbus ; and, by reincarnation, Pythagoras.*

pantĭcēs, um, *m. pl. the bowels :* Pl. Of sausages : Verg.

pantomīmĭcus, a, um [pantomīmus], *of* or *belonging to dumb show acting, pantomimic.* Sen. Ep.

pantomīmus, ī, *m.* and **pantomīma,** ae, *f.* (Sen.) [παντόμιμος], *an actor* (and *actress*) *in dumb show :* Sen. Ep., Suet.

pānus, ī, *m.* [πῆνος, Dor. πᾶνος], *the thread* wound upon the bobbin in a shuttle. **1.** Lit.: Lucil. **2.** Transf. **a.** *a tumour :* Plin. **b.** *an ear of millet :* Plin.

papae, *interj.* [παπαί], *wonderful !* how *strange ! indeed !* Pl., Ter.

păpas, ae and atis, *m.* [πάππας πάπας], *a tutor :* Juv.

păpāver, eris, *n.* (*m.*Pl.), *the poppy :* Pl.,Verg., Liv., etc.

păpāvereus, a, um [papāver], *of poppies :* comae, Ov.

Paphos (or -**us**), ī. **I.** *Masc. : s. of Pygmalion and founder of the city Paphos.* **II.** *Fem. : a city in Cyprus, sacred to Venus :* **Paphiē,** ēs, *f. Venus ;* **Paphius,** a, um ; **Paphii,** ōrum, *m. pl. the Paphians.*

păpĭlĭo, ōnis, *m.* [fr. root of πάλλω], *a butterfly :* Ov. [It. *padiglione.*]

papilla, ae, *f. a nipple, teat,* on the breast of men and animals. **1.** Lit. : Pl., Plin. Ep. **2.** Transf. *the breast :* Pl., Cat., Verg., Suet., etc.

pappō, āre, *to eat pap, to eat :* Pl., Pers.

pappus, ī, *m.* [πάππος], *an old man.* **1.** Lit. : Varr. **2.** Transf. *the woolly, hairy seed of certain plants* (cf. Eng. ' old man's beard ') : Lucr.

papula, ae, *f. a pustule, pimple :* Verg.

papȳrĭfer, a, um [papyrus ferō], *producing papyrus :* Nilus, Ov.

papȳrus, ī, *m.* and *f.* and **papȳrum,** ī, *n.* [πάπυρος], *the paper-reed, papyrus.* **1.** Lit.: Plin., Luc., Mart. **2.** Transf. **a.** *a garment made from the papyrus :* Juv. **b.** *the paper* made of papyrus : Cat., Mart., Juv. [Fr. *papier.*]

pār, paris. **I.** Noun. **A.** *Masc.* or *fem. : a match, peer.* **1.** Lit. : ei erat hospes, par illius, Pl. ; cuius paucos parïs haec civitas tulit, Cic. ; quibus ne di quidem immortales pares esse possint, Caes. ; Alexandro caesïsset in acie oblatus par Manlius Torquatus, Liv. ; Hor. ; quattuor carinae pares gravïbus remis, Verg. ; coeat par pari, Hor. ; nube pari, Ov. ; inter parïs aemulatio, Tac. Prov. : pares cum parïbus facillime congregantur, Cic. **2.** Transf. *a companion :* Pl., Cic., Ov. **B.** *Neut. : the like.* **1.** Lit. : par pari respondere, *like for like,* Pl., Cic. Ep. ; par pro pari referto, Ter. ; paria facere, *to make a settlement,* Sen. Ep. **2.** Transf. *a pair :* tria aut quattuor paria amicorum, Cic. ; par nobile fratrum, Hor. ; Ov., etc. ; ludere par impar (*even and odd*), Hor. **II.** Adj. : *equally matched, equal, like.* **A.** In gen. **a.** Of persons. With limiting ABL., *ad* and Acc., *in* and ABL., and poet. with *Inf. :* libertate parem cum ceteris, Cic. ; par ad virtutem, Liv. ; pares in amore, Cic. ; et cantare pares et respondere parati, Verg. The object of comparison is most freq. in the DAT. : quem ego parem summïs Peripateticis iudico, Cic. With *cum :* quem parem cum liberïs tuïs fecisti, Cat. With *inter :* sunt omnes pares inter se, Cic. **b.** Of things : pares eiusdem generis munitiones, Caes. ; pari intervallo, Caes. ; par certamen (i.e. with like weapons), Caes. ; par proelium, *a drawn battle,* Nep. ; aequo et pari iure cum civïbus vivere, Cic. ;

similia omnia magis visa hominibus quam paria, Liv. ; soli omnium opes atque inopiam pari adfectu concupiscunt, Tac. With *et, atque (ac)* : omnia fuisse in Themistocle paria et Coriolano, Cic. ; Sall. ; pari eum atque illos imperio esse iussit, Nep. ; Pl. ; Cic., etc. With *ac si* : Sall. **B.** Phr.: par est or videtur, *it is* or *seems fit, meet, suitable, proper, right.* With *Inf.* : Pl., Cic. With Acc. and *Inf.* : Pl., Cic. With *ut* and *Subj.* : Pl. Also, ut par est, in parenthesis : Cic. [It. *paio* ; Fr. *pair*, and, from it, Eng. *peer*.]

parābilis, e, *adj.* [parō], *easily acquired* : Cic., Hor., etc.

parabola, ae, and **parabolē**, ēs, *f.* [παραβολή], *a comparison* : Sen. Ep., Quint. [It. *parola;* Fr. *parole.*]

paraphrasis, is, *f.* [παράφρασις], *a paraphrase* : Quint.

parapsis, *v.* paropsis.

parārius, ī, *m.* [parō], *a go-between, agent:* Sen.

parasita, ae, *f.* [parasītus], *a female parasite* : Hor.

parasitaster, trī, *m.* [parasītus], *a mean parasite* : Ter.

parasitātiō, ōnis, *f.* [parasītus], *a playing the parasite, sponging:* Pl.

parasiticus, a, um [parasītus], *of a parasite, parasitical* : ars, Pl.

parasītor, ārī [parasītus], *to play the parasite, to sponge* : Pl.

parasītus, ī, *m.* [παράσιτος], lit. *one who eats with another.* **I.** *A guest,* pure Lat. conviva : Pl. ; parasiti Iovis, Varr. **II.** Mostly in bad sense, *a diner-out ; one who cringes or amuses to earn his dinner ; a sponger, toady, parasite* : Pl., Cic., Hor.

parātē, *adv.* **1.** Lit. : *preparedly, with preparation* : ad dicendum parate venire, Cic. paratius dicere, Cic. **2.** Transf. **a.** *carefully, vigilantly* : Pl. **b.** *readily, promptly:* paratius venire, Cic. ; *Sup.*: Plin. Ep.

parātiō, ōnis, *f.* [parō], *a preparing, striving to get* : regni, Sall.

paratragoedō, āre [παρατραγῳδέω], *to talk in a tragic, pompous style* : Pl.

parātus, a, um. **I.** *Part.* parō. **II.** Adj.: *prepared, ready.* **A.** In gen.: ex paratā re inparatam omnem facis, Pl. ; omnia ad bellum apta ac parata, Caes. ; sedes paratae, Verg. ; parata victoria, Liv. Of persons and their attitude. With *Inf.*: Caes., Cic. With Dat. : vel bello vel paci paratus, Liv. ; imperio, Liv. ; castris ponendis, Liv. ; veniae, Ov. ; animus sceleribus, Tac. ; also, ferri acies parata neci, Verg. With *ad* : animo ad dimicandum parati, Caes. ; Cic. ; ad omne facinus, Cic. ; Liv. ; Verg. **B.** In partic. **a.** *provided, furnished, equipped* : ad dicendum, Cic. ; quo paratior ad usum forensem esse possim, Cic. ; in omnis causas, Quint. ; with Abl. : scutis telisque parati ornatique, Cic. **b.** With *in* and Abl. : *well versed, skilled, experienced in* : in iure paratissimus, Cic. ; in agendo, Cic.

parātus, ūs, *m.* [parō], *preparation, provision, equipping* : vitae, Cic. ; militum et armorum, Sall. ; occulti sacri, Liv. ; proviso ante funebri paratu, Tac. In *pl.* : Ov., Tac. Of dress : Ov.

Parca, ae, *f. a goddess of Fate* ; in *pl. the Fates.*

parcē, *adv. sparingly, frugally, thriftily, penuriously.* **1.** Lit. : Pl., Caes., Cic. **2.** Transf. *sparingly, moderately, with restraint* : dicere, Cic., Quint. ; gaudere, Phaedr. *Comp.* : Cic., Verg., Hor. *Sup.* : Quint. ; civitatem Romanam parcissime dedit, Suet.

parceprōmus, ī, *m.* [parcē prōmō], *a niggard, curmudgeon* : Pl.

parcitās, ātis, *f.* [parcus], *sparingness, parsimony* : Sen.

parcō, parcere, peperci (parcī, Pl., and post-Aug.), parsum (*Fut. Part.* parsūrus, Liv., Suet.), *to act* or *use sparingly, be sparing, to spare, economise.* **1.** Lit. : se exigue dierum xxx habere frumentum, sed paulo etiam longius tolerare posse parcendo, Caes. With Dat. : nihil pretio parsit, Pl. ; sumptu, Cic. Ep. With Acc. : pecuniam, Pl. ; oleas, Cato ; fetūs, Luor. ; talenta natis tuis, Verg. **2.** Transf. **A.** Of effort, threats, etc. : *to spare, be sparing of, forbear to use, forgo, refrain from.* With Dat. : labori, Cato ; neque parcetur labori, Cic. Ep. ; nec impensae nec labori nec periculo, Liv. ; lamentis, Liv. ; bello, metu, Verg. ; flatibus Eurus, Verg. With *Inf.* : Ter., Verg. Liv., etc. With *ab* : precantes ut a caedibus parceretur, Liv. **B.** *to spare* (i.e. preserve by sparing). **a.** With Dat. of person : Ter., Cic., Verg., etc. **b.** With Dat. of thing : alicuius auribus (i.e. spare somebody's ears the sound of something unpleasant), Cic. ; oculis (i.e. spare the eyes the sight of something unpleasant), Prop. ; valetudini, Cic. Ep. ; amicitiis, Cic.

parcus, a, um [*v.* parcō], *sparing, thrifty, economical* ; also *niggardly.* **1.** Lit. : (of persons) : Cic., Ov. *Sup.* : Pl. With Gen. : veteris aceti, Hor. ; donandi, Hor. **2.** Transf. **a.** Of persons : *sparing, moderate, chary* : operā meā, Pl. ; in largiendā civitate, Cic. ; civium sanguinis, Tac. ; somni, Luc. ; deorum cultor, Hor. *Sup.* : Luc., Plin. Pan., Suet. **b.** Of things given or used : *niggardly, scanty, meagre* : parco sale contingere, Verg. ; lucerna, Prop. ; lintea, Ov. ; somnus, Plin. Pan. ; merito parcior ira meo, Ov.

pardalis, is, *f.* [πάρδαλις], *a female panther* : Curt.

pardus, ī, *m.* [πάρδος], *a panther* : Juv.

parēns, entis. **I.** *Part.* pāreō. **II.** Adj.: *obedient.* *Comp.* : exercitus, Cic. **III.** Noun : *a subject* (in *pl.*) : Sall.

parēns, entis, *m.* and *f.* (Gen. *pl.* parentum and parentium) [pariō], *a father* or *mother, a parent.* **1.** Lit. : Enn., Cic., Verg., etc. Occ. *of grand-parents, ancestors* : Cic., Verg., Liv. **2.** Transf. **a.** *relations, kinsfolk* (late and rare) : Curt. **b.** *a founder, inventor,* etc. : urbis, Cic. ; Mercurius curvae lyrae parens, Hor.

parentālis, e, *adj.* [parēns], *of parents and ancestors, parental* : umbrae, Ov. ; dies, *the day of the festival in honour of the dead,* Ov. As Noun, **parentālia**, ium, *n. pl. a festival in honour of dead ancestors and relations* : Cic.

parentō, āre [parēns], *to offer a solemn sacrifice in honour of deceased parents* or *relatives*. **1.** Lit.: alicui, Cic. Often Pass. Impers. : Cic., Sen. Ep. **2.** Transf. **a.** *to make an offering of* someone *to the manes of a near relative* or *fellow-countryman*: civibus Romanis, Caes. ; parentandum regi sanguine coniuratorum esse, Liv. ; Ov. **b.** *to propitiate*: internecione hostium iustae irae parentatum est, Curt.

pāreō, ēre [cogn. with parō], *to appear, be evident*. **1.** Lit. **A.** Impersonal: pāret, *it is clear* or *proved* (mostly in law): Cic. Often Acc. and Inf. : Cic. **B.** Personal. **a.** *to be clear, clearly known*: caeli cui sidera parent et linguae volucrum, Verg. **b.** *to appear* before the eyes or mind, *to present oneself*: illi Prochyta, Stat. ; immolanti iocinora replicata, Suet. ; diversa simul, Quint. **2.** Transf. (from sense of *appearing* as a servant), *to obey, be obedient to* (usual meaning). **a.** In gen.: dicto, Enn. ; imperio, Caes. ; praecepto, legibus, alicuius voluntati, Cic. Pass. Impers.: dicto paretur, Liv. ; Tac. Of things: freta ventis, Tib. ; Ov. ; gestus animo, Quint. **b.** *to obey, submit* (to some authority): nulla fuit civitas, quin Caesari pareret, Caes. ; auctoritati senatūs, Cic. ; necessitati, Cic. ; virtuti omnia, Sall. **c.** *to give way to, yield to* (feelings, etc.): cupiditatibus, Cic. ; et tempori et voluntati, Cic. ; Nep. **d.** *to comply with, make good*: promissis, Ov.

pāricida, *v.* parricida.

pariēs, etis, *m. a wall*, prop. *a wall* or *partition of a house* or *building*. **1.** Lit.: Pl., Cic., Ov. ; of a siege tower: Caes. ; of a labyrinth: Verg. Prov.: tua res agitur, paries cum proximus ardet, Hor. **2.** Transf.: neve inter vos significetis, ego ero paries, Pl.

parietīnae, ārum, *f. pl.* [paries], *old fallen-down walls*; *ruins*. **1.** Lit.: Corinthi, Cic. **2.** Transf.: rei publicae, Cic. Ep.

Parīlia, *v.* Palēs.

parīlis, e, *adj.* [păr], *equal*: aetas, Ov. ; noctes pariles diebus, Lucr.

pariō, parere, peperi, partum (*Fut. Part.* us. paritūrus), *to bring forth, to bear* (of animals, *to drop, lay, spawn*). **1.** Lit. **a.** Pl., Cic. **b.** In gen. *to breed, produce*: vermiculos, Lucr. ; fruges terra, Cic. **2.** Transf. *to produce, create, bring about, cause*: alicui aegritudinem, Pl. ; opsequium amicos, veritas odium parit, Ter. ; sibi salutem, Caes. ; dolorem, voluptatem, sibi laudem, Cic. ; sibi letum, Verg. ; amicos officio, Sall. ; gratiam apud aliquem, Liv.

Paris, idis (Voc. Pari), *m.* **I.** *s. of Priam and Hecuba, also called Alexandros. For his decision in the famous ' Judgment,' Venus gave him Helen; thus was caused the Trojan War, in which he was killed by Philoctetes.* **II.** *an actor, a freedman of Domitia.*

pariter, *adv.* [păr]. **I.** *equally, in an equal degree* or *measure*: caritate non pariter omnes egemus, Cic. ; Phaedr., etc. With *cum*: mecum pariter, Cic. ; Verg. With *ut, atque* (*ac*): filium pariter moratum ut pater fuit, Pl. ; pariter ac si hostis adesset, Sall. With DAT.: pariter ultimae (gentes) propinquis, Liv. **II.** *simultaneously, in*

concert, *at the same time, together*: plura castella Pompeius pariter, distinendae manūs causā, temptaverat, Caes. ; Verg. ; Liv. etc. With *cum*: pariter cum vitā sensus amittitur, Cic. ; pariter cum occasu solis, Sall. ; Liv. With *et, atque, que*: pariter sustulit clamorem acies et emissus eques in hostem invehitur, Liv. ; Quint. With double pariter: hanc pariter vidit, pariter Calydonius heros optavit, Ov. ; Plin. Ep.

paritō, āre [*freq.* parō], *to set about, busily prepare*. With *Inf.* : Pl. With *ut* and *Subj.* : Pl.

parma, ae, *f.* [πάρμη], *a small, round shield* or *buckler*, carried by light infantry and cavalry. **1.** Lit.: Enn., Prop., Liv. **2.** Transf. *any shield* : Lucr., Verg.

parmātus, a, um [parma], *armed with a buckler* : Liv. *Masc.* as Noun: Liv.

parmula, ae, *f.* [*dim.* parma], *a little round shield, a small buckler* : Hor.

parmulārius, i, *m.* [parmula], *a partisan of the gladiators called Threces, who were armed with the parmula* : Suet.

Parnāsus and **-os**, i, *m. a high mountain in Phocis with two peaks, sacred to Apollo and the Muses; on its slopes were the city of Delphi and the Castalian spring* ; **Parnāsis**, idis, *f. adj.* ; and **Parnāsius**, a, um.

parō, āre. **I.** *to set* or *put* (*cf.* com-parō) Transf.: eodem vos pono et paro ; parissumi estis hibus, Pl. **II.** *to get ready, prepare, furnish, provide.* **1.** Lit. Without Object: *to get ready, make preparations* or *arrangements*: Sall. ; ad iter, Liv. ; cum conlegā, Cic. Ep. ; cui fata parent, Verg. With *ut* or *ne* and *Subj.*: Pl., Ter. ; Pass. Impers.: Cic. With Acc.: prandium, Pl. ; falces testudinesque, Caes. ; convivium, ludos, navem, etc., Cic. ; incendia, Sall. ; ad integrum bellum cuncta, Sall. ; so ad proelium, Liv. **2.** Transf.: fugam, Ter., Verg. ; filio luctum, Ter. ; bellum, iter, Caes. ; proelium, Liv. ; se ad similem casum, Caes. ; se ad discendum, Cic. **III.** With *Inf.*: *to prepare, set about* : Enn., Caes., Verg., etc. **IV.** *to procure, get, acquire* : fidicinam, Pl. ; locum et sedes, Caes. ; Liv. ; amicos, Cic. ; regnum sibi, Sall. By purchase: piscatum mihi, Pl. ; iumenta, Caes. ; hortos, Cic. Ep. ; argento mancipia, Liv. (*v.* also paratus.)

parocha, ae, *f.* [παροχή], *a supplying of necessaries* (to State-officials when travelling), *purveyance* : Cic. Ep.

parochus, i, *m.* [πάροχος], *a purveyor* (*v.* parocha). **1.** Lit.: Cic. Ep., Hor. **2.** Transf. *a host* : Hor.

paropsis, idis, *f.* [παροψίς], *a dessert-dish* ; also, *a dish* in gen. : Juv., Suet.

Paros (**-us**), i, *f. one of the Cyclades, famous for its white marble* ; **Parius**, a, um ; **Parii**, orum, *m. pl. its inhabitants.*

parra, ae, *f. a bird of ill omen*, prob. *the common barn owl* : Pl., Hor.

Parrhasia, ae, *f. a district of Arcadia* ; **Parrhasis**, idis, *f. adj. Arcadian* : ursa, *the Great Bear* : Ov. ; **Parrhasis**, idis, *f. an Arcadian woman, Callisto*, Ov. **Parrhasius**, a, um, *Arcadian* : dea, i.e. *Carmenta, the mother of Euander*, Ov. ; virgo, i.e. *Callisto*, Ov.

Parrhasius, ī, *m. a celebrated Greek painter, a native of Ephesus* (c. B.C. 400).

parricida (older **pāricida**), ae, *m.f. the murderer of a parent or near relative.* **1.** L i t. : Cic., Hor., Liv., etc. **2.** T r a n s f. **a.** Of the murderers of Caesar (perh. as pater patriae) : Cic. ; *of fellow-citizens* : civium, Cic. **b.** *one guilty of high treason, a traitor* : rei publicae, Sall. ; Tac.

parricidium, ī, *n.* [parricīda], *the murder of a parent or near relative.* **1.** L i t. : Cic., Liv., Quint. **2.** T r a n s f. **a.** Of the murder of Caesar : Idūs Martias *parricidium* nominari (placuit), Suet. **b.** *an act of high treason* (against) : patriae, Cic. ; publicum, Liv.

pars, partis, *f.* (the old Acc. partim and ABL. parti are sometimes used) [*cf.* portiō, πέπρω-ται], *a part, portion, fraction, section, share.* **1.** L i t. **a.** In gen. : ne expers partis esset de nostris bonis, Ter. ; urbis, imperi, Cic. ; Gallia est omnis divisa in partis tris, Caes. In f r a c t i o n s (the proportion being indicated by the context) : dimidia pars, Caes. ; tertia, Caes. ; partes duae ($\frac{2}{3}$), Liv. ; tres partes ($\frac{3}{4}$), Caes. I n d e f. : magna pars in iis civitatibus, Cic. ; maxima pars hominum, Hor. ; pars maior ex acie Veios petierat, Liv. ; pars . . . pars ; pars . . . alii, *some* . . . *others* : pars circumvenire, pars . . . petere coepit, Caes. ; Liv. ; nos alii ibimus ad Afros, pars Scythiam veniemus, Verg. **b.** Of parts of the body : Ov., Juv., etc. **c.** Of place : *side, direction* : a sinistrā parte, Caes. ; continentur unā ex parte flumine Rheno, alterā ex parte monte Iurā, Caes. ; ex omnibus partibus advolare, Caes. ; in utramque partem, Cic. Also in *pl.* : *parts, divisions, regions* : civitates pagi omnes partes, Caes. ; ne ad Orientis partis, Cic. ; Ov. **d.** *a part* of a class or genus : Cic. **2.** T r a n s f. **A.** *a side, party, faction* : nullius partis esse, Cic. ; ut alius in aliam partem mente atque animo traheretur, Caes. In *pl.* : Cic., Sall., Tac. **B.** In *pl.* : *a part, rôle, function.* **a.** On the stage : primas partis agere, Ter. ; esse primarum secundarum aut tertiarum partium, Cic. **b.** In gen. : primas partis apud me habere, Ter. ; imperatoris sibi partis sumere, Caes. ; imperatoris partis suscipere, Cic. Ep. ; partis accusatoris obtinere, Cic. ; transactis iam meis partibus, Cic. ; fabulam compositam Volsci belli, Hernicos ad partis paratos, Liv. ; Ov. O c c. in *sing.* : plusquam pars virilis postulat, Cic. ; haec tibi reliqua pars est ut etc. ; Cic. ; pars consili pacisque, Tac. **C.** *portion, lot, fate* : hanc partem capio, Pl. **D.** P h r. **a.** Acc. : partim, *v.* partim ; magnam partem, *to a large extent, largely* : Cic., Liv. ; maximam partem lacto atque pecore vivunt, Caes. ; Liv. ; in (eam) partem, *in (that) direction, on (that) side* : in eam partem peccant quae cautior est, Cic. ; Ter. ; neque ego ullam in partem disputo, Cic. ; mitiorem in partem aliquid interpretari, Cic. ; in omnis partis, *in all directions, in every respect* : Cic. Ep. ; ad nullam partem, Liv. ; per partis (*in part, partly*) aliquid emendare, Plin. Ep. ; in partem, *to a share* : venire, Cic. ; vocare, Liv. **b.** ABL. : omni parte or ex (or ab)

omni parte, *on every side, in every respect, entirely* : gens omni parte pacata, Liv. ; omni ex parte perfectum, Cic. ; omnique a parte placebam, Ov. ; ex alterā parte, *on the other hand* : Cic., Liv. ; parte or ex parte, *in part, partly* : poma quae candida parte, parte rubent, Ov. ; ex parte gaudeo, Cic. Ep. ; Liv. ; aut omnino aut magnā ex parte, *to a large extent*, Cic. ; maximā parte inermes, Liv. ; in *pl.* : multis partibus plures, *by many parts, by a great deal*, Cic. Ep. ; Caes. ; pro (meā) parte, *for my part, to the best of (my) ability*, Cic. Ep. ; Ov. ; pro virili parte, *to the best of a man's ability*, Cic., Liv., Ov.

parsimōnia, ae, *f.* [parcō], *sparingness, frugality, thrift.* **1.** L i t. : Pl., Ter., Cic. ; supellectilis, Suet. In *pl.* : Pl. **2.** T r a n s f. (in *pl.*) of style : Cic.

Parthāōn, onis, *m. son of Agenor, king of Calydon, and father of Oeneus.*

parthenicē, ēs, *f.* [παρθενική], *an unknown plant* : Cat.

Parthenopaeus, ī, *m. son of Meleager and Atalanta, one of the Seven who fought against Thebes.*

Parthenopē, ēs, *f.* one of the Sirens, *from whom Neapolis derived its original name of Parthenope* ; **Parthenopēius**, a, um, *Neapolitan.*

Parthī, ōrum, *m. pl. the Parthians, a Scythian people, situated to the south-east of the Caspian, famed in antiquity as skilful archers* : *masters of the former Persian Empire from* B.C. 250–A.D. 226. **Parthus**, a, um ; **Parthia**, ae, *f. their country* ; **Parthicus**, a, um.

particeps, cipis, *adj.* [pars capiō], *taking a share, partaking.* **1.** L i t. With GEN. : Pl., Lucr., Cic., etc. As Noun, *a partner, confidant, confederate* : Pl., Ter. ; huius belli, Cic. Ep. ; Natalis particeps ad omne secretum Pisoni erat, Tac. **2.** T r a n s f. : *acquainted with, cognisant of* (with *Indir. Quest.*) : Pl.

participiālis, e, *adj.* [participium]. Gramm. : *of the nature of a participle* : verba, Quint.

participium, ī, *n.* [particeps]. Gramm. *a participle* : Quint.

participō, āre [particeps]. **I.** *to take a share in* : pestem parem, Enn. **II.** *to give a share of, to share* : homines inter se ius, Cic. ; suas laudes cum Caesonio, Liv. **III.** *to give a share to, make someone a sharer in* : aliquem sermone suo de amicā eri, Pl. ; servom sui consili, Pl. ; aliquem (with *Indir. Quest.*), Pl. In *Pass.* or *Mid.* : Pl. ; uti dentes sensu participentur, Lucr.

particula, ae, *f.* [dim. pars], *a small part, a little bit, a particle.* **a.** In gen. : Cic., Hor., Quint. **b.** R h e t. *a clause* of a sentence : Quint.

particulātim, *adv. part by part, piecemeal, singly* : Varr., Sen. Ep.

partim, old Acc. of pars, but mostly limited to special uses ; *to some extent, partly, in part.* **A.** When in some relation to the Subject or Object : *some.* With GEN. : partim eorum fuerunt qui etc., Cato ; Liv. With *ex* : partim ex illis dissipati iacent, Cic. Oftener partim . . . partim (=alii . . . alii), *one part* . . . *another part* :

some . . . others : eorum partim in pompā, partim in acie inlustres esse voluerunt, Cic. ; Caes. ; Verg. ; in *oppos. :* amici partim deseruerunt me, partim etiam prodiderunt, Cic. Ep. Also in conjunction with alii : bestiarum terrenae sunt aliae, partim aquatiles, aliae quasi ancipites, Cic. ; Sall. **B.** As pure *Adv.* **a.** *partly, in part :* partim uxoris misericordiā devinctus, partim victus huius iniuriis, Ter. ; partim quod . . . partim quod, Caes. ; Cic. **b.** *for the most part, mostly :* Pl., Cato.

partiō, ōnis, *f.* [pariō], *a bringing forth :* Pl.

partiō, īre, and **partior**, īrī (usual form in class. period) [pars], *to share, part : to divide, distribute.* **a.** In gen. : praedam, Pl. ; bona sua inter aliquos, Pl. ; pecunias, Cic. ; suum cum Scipione honorem, Caes. ; Cic. ; praedam in omnis, Verg. ; consules provincias inter se partiti, Liv. ; Sall. ; sol aetheris oras, Lucr. ; limite campum, Verg. ; *Perf. Part.* in *Pass. Sense :* Cic. ; partito exercitu, Caes. ; Liv. ; animi natura per artūs, Lucr. ; regionibus imperium, Liv. ; carcere partitos equos, Ov. **b.** Of logical division : genus universum in species, Cic. ; actio partienda est in gestum atque vocem, Cic.

partītē, *adv. with proper divisions, methodically :* dicere, Cic.

partītiō, ōnis, *f.* [partior], *a sharing, division, distribution.* **A.** In gen. : facere, Cic. ; praedae, aerari, Cic. **B.** In partic. **a.** *a logical division :* Cic., Quint. **b.** Rhet. *a rhetorical division :* Cic., Quint.

partītūdō, inis, *f.* [pariō], *a bearing, bringing forth young :* Pl.

parturiō, īre [pariō], *to desire to bring forth, to be in travail or labour.* **1.** Lit. : Ter., Ov. Prov. : parturiunt montes, nascetur ridiculus mus, Hor. **2.** Transf. **A.** *to be ready to produce, to teem with :* Germania horrida fetūs, Hor. ; nunc omnis parturit arbos, Verg. ; neque parturit imbris perpetuos (Notus), Hor. **B.** Mentally. **a.** Of meditated action : quod conceptum res publica periculum parturit, consilio discutiam, Cic. ; ira minas, Ov. **b.** *to be in labour with, i.e. to long to be delivered of* (by utterance) : ut aliquando dolor populi Romani pariat quod iam diu parturit, Cic. ; Liv.

partus, a, um, *Part.* pariō.

partus, ūs, *m.* [pariō], *a bearing, bringing forth, birth.* **1.** Lit. : Pac., Cic., Juv. In *pl. :* Hor. **2.** Transf. **a.** *the birth, i.e. the beginnings :* oratorum, Cic. **b.** *the young or offspring of any creature :* Cic., Verg., etc. In *pl. :* Hor.

parum, *orig. Noun fr.* parvus, *a little, too little.* **I.** Noun. **a.** magis offendit nimium quam parum, Cic. With GEN. : satis copiae, leporis parum, Cic. ; Sall. **b.** parum est, *it is not enough, not sufficient :* immo duas dabo, una si parum est, Pl. ; parumne est quod tantum homines fefellisti ? Cic. ; Ter. ; parum fuisse non laudari Africanum nisi etc. ; Liv. ; non nocuisse parum est, Ov. ; parum videtur (with Acc. and *Inf.*), Liv. ; parum habere (with *Inf.*), *to regard as insufficient :* Sall., Liv. **II.** Adverb : *little, too little,*

scarcely at all, insufficiently. With Verbs : Pl., Caes., Cic., etc. With Adjectives and Adverbs : Pl., Caes., Cic., Hor., etc. *Comp.* and *Sup.* minus and minimē, q.v.

parumper, *adv.* of time, *for a little while, just for a moment :* Pl., Cic., Verg., etc.

parvitās, ātis, *f.* [parvus], *smallness, littleness :* Cic.

parvulus (parvolus), a, um [*dim.* parvus], *very small, tiny, petty, slight.* **1.** Lit. **a.** In gen. : causa, Lucr. ; pecunia, impulsio, Cic. ; proelium, detrimentum, Caes. ; res, Hor. *Neut. pl.* as Noun : Hor. **b.** Of age : soror, Ter. ; a parvolo (*cf.* a puero, i.e. from infancy), Ter. ; ab parvulis, Caes. : Aeneas, Verg. Of animals : (uri) parvuli excepti, Caes. **2.** Transf. *too small, unequal :* quam illae rei ego sum parvolus ! Pl.

parvus (-os), a, um (-om) ; *Comp.* **minor**, us ; *Sup.* **minimus**, a, um (parvissimus, Lucr.) [*cf.* παῦρος], *small, little.* **1.** Lit. (of size, measure, number) : iumenta, Caes. ; pisciculi, liberi, terra, insula, Cic. ; Hibernia minor quam Britannia, Caes. ; minima tela, Liv. ; parvus, minimus cibus, Ov. *Neut.* as Noun, **parvum**, i, **minus** and **minimum** (only in NOM. and ACC.), *a little, small (smaller, smallest) measure or thing, a little :* parvo contentus esse possum, Cic. Ep. ; Hor., etc. ; si parva licet componere magnis, Verg. ; minus praedae quam speraverant fuit, Liv. ABL. (of *Measure*) : ut parvo admodum plures caperentur, Liv. **2.** Transf. **a.** In gen. : beneficium, Cic. ; commoda, Cic. Ep. ; minima licentia, Sall. ; vitia, Hor. *Neut.* as Noun : minimum firmitatis minimumque virium, Cic. ; minimum periculi erat, Liv. ACC. **minimum** as *Adv.* (orig. *Intern.* ACC.) : praemia apud me minimum valent, Cic. Ep. ; minimum credula, Hor. ; in quo non minimum Aetolorum operā regii fugati sunt, Liv. ; dormiebat minimum, Plin. Ep. (*v.* also minus.) **b.** Of time : *small, short, brief :* Ter., Caes., Cic., Ov., etc. *Comp. :* Ov., Juv. *Sup. :* Caes., Cic. **c.** Of age : *young :* Ter., Cic., Hor., etc. ; minor natu, Caes., Cic., etc. ; minimus or minimus natu, Cic., Sall. As Noun : **minōrēs**, um, *posterity :* Verg. **d.** Of worth, value or rank. **i.** parvae res magnum momentum habuerunt, Caes. ; meam erus esse operam deputat parvi preti, Ter. ; pretio parvo vendere, Cic. ; negotium minus, Cic. ; minimis momentis maximae inclinationes fiunt, Cic. Esp. in *Neut.* GEN. : parvi sunt foris arma nisi est consilium domi, Cic. ; parvi refert, Cic. Ep. ; parvi (minoris, minimi), facere, aestimare, ducere, pendere, *to esteem lightly, hold cheap, care little for,* Pl., Cic., etc. Occ. in ABL. : quanti emptus ? parvo, Hor. ; Cic. Ep. ; parvo stat magna potentia nobis, Ov. **ii.** Of persons : virtute et honore minores, Hor. ; minor capitis (= capite deminutus), Hor. ; sapiens uno minor est Iove, Hor. ; di minores, Ov. *Masc.* as Noun : Hor., Ov., Tac. **e.** Of quality : onus parvis animis maius, Hor. ; homo parvo ingenio, Plin. Ep. ; certare minor, Hor. ; vox, Ov.

pasceolus, I, *m.* [φάσκαλος, φάσκωλος], *a leather money-bag :* Pl.

păscō, păscere, pāvī, pāstum [cf. πατέομαι, pānis]. **A. Trans.** *to put to feed ; to feed, pasture.* **1.** Lit. **a.** cum sues puer pasceret, Cic. ; Verg. ; Ov. ; pecora pastum propellere, Liv. **b.** *to feed, keep :* iumenta, Caes. ; calones atque caballi pascendi, Hor. ; holusculis nos solos pascere, Cic. Ep. ; servos, Juv. With non-personal Subject : quos, dives Anagnia, pascis, Verg. ; me vulsis pascunt radicibus herbae, Verg. ; fundus erum, Hor. **c.** *to give as pasture :* horum (collium) asperrima, Verg. **d.** *to have as pasture, to graze, browse on :* Palatia vaccae, Tib. In *Mid. :* silvas, Verg. ; apes arbuta, Verg. **2.** Transf. **a.** *to feed, nourish, foster :* qui divus vestros campos pascit placide, Liv. ; ager filicem, Hor. ; polus sidera, Verg. ; sacrum crinem Baccho (i.e. let grow), Verg. ; barbam, Hor. ; Pergama flammas, Ov. ; nummos alienos (i.e. add to), Hor. Also, spes inanis, Verg. **b.** *to feed, feast,* i.e. *to gratify :* quos P. Clodi furor rapinis et incendiis pavit, Cic. ; eius cruciatu oculos, Cic. ; animum picturā inani, Verg. **B.** Intrans. *to graze, feed.* **1.** Lit. : Pl. ; capellae, Verg. ; saltibus in vacuis, Verg. In *Mid. :* armenta per herbas, Verg. ; pulli, Liv. ; with *Instr. ABL. :* frondibus, carice, etc., Verg. ; Ov. **2.** Transf. (in *Mid.* and with *Instr. ABL.*). **a.** *to feed, make a living :* qui maleficio pascuntur, Cic. **b.** *to feast :* discordiis civium et seditione, Cic. ; dolore alicuius, Cic.

păscuus, a, um [pāscō], *for pasture or grazing.* **1.** Lit. : ager, Pl., Cic. ; rura, Lucr. As Noun, **păscuum**, ī, *n. a pasture :* ab viridi pascuo, Varr. In *pl. :* Cic., Verg., Ov.

Păsiphaē, ēs, and **Păsiphaa**, ae, *f. d. of Helios, s. of Circe, w. of Minos, and m. of Androgeus, Phaedra, and Ariadna ; also of the Minotaur by a bull ;* **Păsiphaēius**, a, um ; **Păsiphaēia**, ae, *f. Phaedra :* Ov.

Păsithea, ae, and **Păsitheē**, ēs, *f. one of the three Graces.*

passer, eris, *m. a sparrow.* **1.** Lit. : Cic., Cat., Juv., etc. As term of endearment : Pl. **2.** Transf. **a.** passer marinus, *an ostrich* (marinus, because brought from a distance by sea), Pl. **b.** *a sea-fish, a plaice :* Hor., Ov.

passerculus, ī, *m.* [*dim.* passer], *a little sparrow :* Cic. As term of endearment : Pl.

passim, *adv.* [pāssus, pandō], *by spreading ;* hence, *here and there, hither and thither, in all directions.* **1.** Lit. : Lucr. ; fugere, Caes. ; volitare, Cic. ; Verg. ; Liv. **2.** Transf. : *indiscriminately, without distinction :* scribimus indocti doctique poëmata passim, Hor. ; Tib.

passivus, a, um [patior], *passive* (in gramm.) : Quint.

pāssum, ī, *n.* (*sc.* vinum) [pandō], *wine made from dried grapes, raisin-wine :* Verg., Plin.

pāssus, a. um. **I.** *Part.* pandō. **II.** Adj. : *spread out to dry, and hence dried, dry :* lac, (perh. *curdled*), Ov. *Neut.* as Noun : *wine made from dried grapes :* Pl., Varr., Verg.

pāssus, ūs, *m.* [pandō ; lit. *the extending or spreading of the legs in walking*], *a step, pace.* **1.** Lit. : Pl., Cic., Verg., etc. **2.** Transf. **a.** *a footstep, track, trace :* Ov.

b. As a measure of length (*a pace,* i.e. *five* Roman feet : 1000 passūs to the Roman mile) : Caes., Cic., etc. [Fr. *pas.*]

passus, a, um, *Part.* patior.

pastilus, ī, *m.* [perh. a dim. from Gk. πάστη], *a small lump of meal.* Transf. **a.** *a pill* or *lozenge :* Plin. **b.** *an aromatic lozenge* used to scent the breath : Hor.

pāstiō, ōnis, *f.* [pāscō], *a pasturing, grazing, feeding.* **1.** Lit. : in *pl. :* Varr. **2.** Transf. *a pasture :* Cic. ; in *pl. :* Varr.

pāstor, ōris, *m.* [pāscō] ; lit. *a feeder, a herdsman, esp. a shepherd :* Cato, Caes., Verg., etc. [Fr. *pâtre.*]

pāstōrālis, e, (Cic., Verg., Liv., etc.), **pāstōricius**, a, um (Cic.), **pāstōrius**, a, um (Ov.), [pāstor], *of a herdsman* or *shepherd, pastoral.*

pāstus, a, um, *Part.* pāscō.

pāstus, ūs, *m.* [pāscō], *pasture, feeding-ground.* **1.** Lit. : Cic., Verg. Of crows : Verg. **2.** Transf. **a.** *food* of men : Lucr. **b.** mendicitatis, Cic. ; animorum, Cic.

patagiārius, ī, *m.* [patagium, *a border on a Roman lady's tunic*], *a border-maker :* Pl.

patagiātus, a, um [patagium], *ornamented with a border :* tunica, Pl.

Patara, ae, *f. a sea-port town of Lycia, with a celebrated oracle of Apollo ;* **Patareus** (triayl.), eī and eos, *m. a surname of Apollo ;* **Pataraeus** (or **-rēus**), a, um ; **Patarāni**, ōrum, *m. pl. its inhabitants.*

Patavium, ī, *n. an important city of N. Italy, the birth-place of Livy,* now *Padua ;* **Patavīnus**, a, um ; and **Patavīnī**, ōrum, *m. pl. its inhabitants :* also, **Patavīnitās**, ātis, *f. Patavian provincialism* (ascribed to Livy by Pollio).

pate-faciō, facere, fēcī, factum and *Pass.* **pate-fīō**, fierī, (patēfēcit and patēfīet, Lucr.), [pateō], *to lay open, throw open.* **1.** Lit. **a.** ordines (aciei), Liv. ; portas, Liv. ; sulcum aratro, Ov. **b.** *to open up, make possible* or *accessible :* iter per Alpis, Caes. ; loca, Nep. ; vias discussā nive, Caes. ; Pontum legionibus, Cic. ; tellus in longas patefacta vias, Tib. Poet. : postera lux radiis latum patefecerat orbem, Ov. **2.** Transf. **a.** *to disclose, bring to light :* hoc, Ter. ; consilia, coniurationem, veritatem, verum, Cic. ; interiorem animi sui notam, Suet. With *Indir. Quest. :* Cic. Of a person : Lentulus patefactus indiciis, Cic. **b.** *to open,* i.e. make accessible : auris adsentatoribus, Cic.

patefactiō, ōnis, *f.* [patefaciō], *a disclosing, making known :* rerum, Cic.

patefīō, fierī, *v.* patefaciō.

patella, ae, *f.* [*dim.* patera], *a small pan* or *dish, a plate.* **1.** Lit. **a.** In gen. : Varr., Hor. **b.** In sacrifices : *an offering-dish :* Cic., Ov., Liv. [It. *padella ;* Sp. *padilla ;* Fr. *poêle.*]

patellārius, a, um [patella], patellarii diī, *platter-gods,* i.e. the Lares, Pl.

patena, *v.* patina.

patēns, entis. **I.** *Part.* pateō. **II.** Adj. **1.** Lit. **a.** *open, accessible, unobstructed, passable :* loca, Caes. ; caelum, Cic. ; pelagus, Verg. ; via, Liv. Comp. : Caes., Liv. *Neut.* as Noun : per patentia ruinis in urbem vadebant, Liv. **b.** *extensive :* campus, Liv. **2.** Transf. **a.** *open, ex-*

posed : domus patens atque adeo exposita cupiditati et voluptatibus, Cic. **b.** *evident, manifest :* causa, Ov.

patentius, *comp. adv. more openly* or *clearly :* Cic.

pateō, ēre [*cf.* πετάννυμι], *to stand* or *be wide open.* **1.** Lit. **a.** In gen. : aedes patent, Pl. ; portae, Cic., Liv. ; fenestrae, Plin. Ep. ; fores, Ov. ; in pectore vulnus, Verg. **b.** *to be open* or *accessible, passable :* aditus patet, Cic. ; semitae, Caes. ; fugae patebat locus, Liv. **c.** *to be exposed :* detecti patent nervi, Ov. ; vulneri equus, Liv. ; latus ictui, Tac. **d.** *to open out, stretch out, extend :* fines in longitudinem milia passuum cxl patebant, Caes. **2.** T r a n s f. **a.** *to be open, free, allowable, accessible, attainable :* cunctis undamque auramque patentem, Verg. ; reditus in amicitiam, Caes. ; si nobis is cursus pateret, Cic. Ep. ; aures querellis, Cic. ; commoda plebi nostra, Ov. **b.** *to be exposed, liable,* or *subject* (*to*)*:* Cic. ; occasioni fraudis, Liv. **c.** *to lie open to the view :* praestigiae, Pl. ; nulla coniuratio, Cic. With Acc. and *Inf.* as *Subject :* Cic. **d.** in quo vitio latissime patet avaritia, Cic.

pater, tris, *m.* [*cf.* πατήρ], *a father, sire.* **1.** Lit. : Pl., Cic., etc. In *pl.* only ; patres, oft. with conscripti (q.v.), *the senators :* Cic., Hor, etc. Of the patricians, opp. to plebeians : Liv. Of animals : gregis, Ov. **2.** T r a n s f. **a.** pater familiās or pater familiae, *v.* familia. **b.** In *pl. the generation before us :* Caes., Cic. Also, *forefathers :* Verg. **c.** Of the gods, esp. of Jupiter : Enn., Verg., Hor., Liv., etc. **d.** Of the founder of a race, school, etc. ; of Aeneas and Acestes, Verg. ; Zeno pater Stoicorum, Cic. ; Herodotus pater historiae, Isocrates pater eloquentiae, Cic. Also, *esuritionum,* Cat. **e.** Of a saviour of the nation : pater patriae, Cic. **f.** *the head, chief ;* perh. in pater patratus (*v.* patratus) ; pater cenae, Hor. ; pater senatūs, Tac. **g.** Of an old man, in respect : Pl., Verg. [It. and Sp. padre, Fr. père.]

patera, ae, *f.* [from root of pateō], *a broad flat dish* or *saucer, used esp. in offerings ; a libation-saucer* or *bowl :* Pl., Cic., Verg., etc.

paterfamiliās, *v.* familia.

paternus, a, um [pater], *of a father, paternal.* **1.** Lit. : Ter., Cic., Verg., etc. Objectively : iniuria, Ter. **2.** T r a n s f. *of one's fathers* or *forefathers :* flumen, Hor. ; terra, Ov.

patēscō, patēscere, patuī [pateō], *to be laid open, to open out to view.* **1.** Lit. **a.** atria longa, Verg. **b.** *to stretch out, extend :* latior patescit campus, Liv. ; neque poterat patescere acies, open out, be deployed, Tac. ; civitates in quas Germania patescit, Tac. **2.** T r a n s f. **a.** latius patescente imperio, Liv. **b.** *to be disclosed, to become manifest :* ratio, Lucr. ; Danaum insidiae, Verg. ; vera incessu patuit dea, Verg.

patibilis, e, *adj.* [patior]. **A.** P a s s. : *supportable, endurable :* dolores et labores, Cic. **B.** A c t. : *having sensation, sensitive :* natura, Cic.

patibulātus, a, um [patibulum], *fastened to the patibulum ; pilloried, gibbeted :* Pl.

patibulum. i, *n.* [pateō]. **I.** *a pillory, a fork-shaped yoke,* which was placed on the necks of criminals, and to which their hands were tied ; also, *a fork-shaped gibbet* (prob. like letter X, on which the victim was fastened like a 'spread eagle ') : Pl., Cic., Tac., etc. **II.** *a forked prop* for vines : Cato.

patiēns, entis. **I.** *Part.* patior. **II.** A d j. **A.** Physically : *experiencing, enduring, able to endure.* **1.** Lit. : patientissimus exercitus, Caes. With *Obj.* GEN. : corpus inediae, Sall. ; pulveris atque solis, Hor. ; longi laboris, Ov. ; liminis aut aquae caelestis, Hor. With *ad :* gens minime ad morae taedium ferendum patiens, Liv. **2.** T r a n s f. : aratrum, Ov. With *Obj.* GEN. : terra patiens vomeris, Verg. ; amnis navium (i.e. navigable), Liv., Tac. **B.** Mentally. **a.** *tolerant, patient :* Cic. ; aures, Cic. ; animus, Ov. *Comp. :* Cic. Ep. ; *Sup. :* Cic. **b.** *stubborn, unyielding. Comp. :* Prop.

patienter, *adv. patiently.* **a.** Physically : Caes., Cic. **b.** Mentally : Cic., Hor. *Comp. :* Cic. Ep.

patientia, ae, *f.* [patior], *experiencing, enduring, endurance.* **1.** Lit. (physically). **a.** In gen. : Cic. With *Obj.* GEN. : Cic., Liv. ; audiendi, Quint. **b.** *submission, pathicism :* Cic., Tac. **2.** T r a n s f. (mentally). **a.** *endurance, resignation, forbearance :* Cic., Hor. **b.** *compliance, want of spirit, tameness :* Tac., Plin. Ep. **c.** *submissiveness, subjection :* servilis, Tac. ; Britanniam veteri patientiae restituit, Tac.

patina, ae, *f.* [pateō]. *a flat dish, pan, stewpan :* Pl., Cic. Ep., Hor., etc.

patinārius, a, um [patina], *piscis* (cooked in a pan), Pl. ; strues (a pile of pans,) Pl.

patiō, old form for patior found in old legal formula in Cic.

patior, pati, passus [*cf.* πάσχω, παθεῖν], *to experience, undergo, suffer* (without or with idea of endurance). **1.** L i t. (physically). **a.** In gen. : fortiter malum, Pl. ; supplicium, Caes. ; hiemem et aestatem, Sall. ; dolores, Cic. ; graviora, Verg. ; Lucinam, Verg. ; mortem, Ov. ; damnum, Liv. P o e t. : in silvis, Verg. **b.** *to submit to* (as a pathic) : Pl. ; muliebria, Sall. **2.** T r a n s f. (non-physically). **a.** In gen. : extremam fortunam, Caes. ; servitutem, Cic., Tac. ; iniuriam, Cic. ; novem cornix saecula, Ov. **b.** *to submit to, put up with, allow, brook :* illorum delicta, Hor. ; ista ne pecudes quidem, Cic. ; neque dilationem pati tam vicinum bellum poterat, Liv. With Acc. of Object, and *Inf. :* Pl., Cic., Liv., etc. With *Inf. :* Verg., Hor. Often with adv. phr. : aequo animo pati, Pl. ; facile pati, Pl., Cic. ; indigne pati, Liv. ; periniquo animo pati, Cic. Ep. (most of these phrases are used with Acc. and *Inf.*) ; aegre pati (with Acc.), Liv. With *quin* or *ut* and *Subj. :* nullum patiebatur esse diem quin sic, Cic., Ter. ; neque suam neque populi R. consuetudinem pati uti socios desereret, Caes. **c.** In gramm. *to be passive, to have a passive sense :* Quint.

patrātor, ōris, *m.* [patrō], *an effecter, achiever, accomplisher :* necis, Tac.

patrātus [patrō], in phr. pater patratus (in *Act.* sense as if from *dep.* form), *the officiating father ;* i.e. the chief of the fetiales : Liv.

patria, ae, *v.* patrius.

patricē, *adv. paternally :* Pl.

patriciātus, ūs, *m.* [patricius], *the status of a patrician :* Suet.

patricius, a, um [patrēs], *of the status of the* patres ; *belonging to the patricians, patrician :* pueri, Pl. ; familia, Cic. ; gens, Juv. As Noun, **patricii**, ōrum, *m. pl. the. patricians* (opp. to plebeians, divided into patricii maiorum and minorum gentium (of the older and younger families) : Cic., Liv., Juv. ; exire e patriciis, i.e. into a plebeian family, Cic. In *sing. :* Cic.

patriē, *adv. like a father :* Quint.

patrimōnium, ī, *n.* [pater], *an estate inherited from a father, inheritance, patrimony.* **1.** Lit. : Cic., Juv. In *pl. :* Cic. **2.** Transf. : in populi Romani patrimonio, Cic. In *pl. :* Cic.

patrimus, a, um [pater], *that has a father living :* Cic., Liv., Tac.

patrissō, āre [πατρίζω], *to take after one's father :* Pl., Ter.

patritus, a, um [pater], *inherited from one's father :* philosophia, Cic.

patrius, a, um [pater], *of a father* (mostly as Subject but also as Object), *a father's* (paternus refers rather to his *property*). **1.** Lit. : Pl. ; animus, Ter., Cic., Liv. ; ius et potestas, Cic. ; amor, Cic., Verg. ; maeror, Cic. ; acerbitas, Liv. ; corpus, Pl. ; sepulcrum, Cic. ; pietas, Verg. **2.** Transf. *a. handed down from one's forefathers, inherited, hereditary :* mos, dii, Cic. ; praediscere patrios cultūsque habitūsque locorum, Verg. ; pedum dolor, Plin. Ep. **b.** *of one's fathers or forefathers, native :* sermo, ritus, Cic. ; Mycenae, Verg. As Noun, **patria**, ae, *f.* (*sc.* terra), *one's fatherland, native land.* **1.** Lit. : Pl., Cic., Verg., etc. **2.** Transf. *a dwelling place, home :* habuit alteram loci patriam, alteram iuris, Cic. Poet. : (Nilus) qui patriam tantae tam bene celat aquae, i.e. *the source,* Ov. ; **patrium**, ī, *n.* (*sc.* nomen), *a patronymic :* Quint.

patrō, āre [pater], *to father (cf.* patranti ocello, Pers.) ; hence, *to bring to pass, accomplish, complete :* sementim, Cato ; conata, Lucr. ; opera, Cic. ; bellum, Sall. ; pacem, Liv. ; ius iurandum, Liv. ; victoriam, remedium, mortis, Tac.

patrōcinium, ī, *m.* [patrōnus canō], '*playing the patronus.*' **1.** Lit. *the services of a patron :* cuius patrocinio civitas plurimum utebatur, Sall. ; patrocinium orbis terrae verius quam imperium poterat nominari, Cic. **2.** Transf. *the services of an advocate or defender.* **a.** In court : advocacy : Cic. ; faeneratorum, Liv. ; civilium controversiarum patrocinia suscipere, Cic. **b.** In gen. : *defence, advocacy :* voluptatis, Cic. ; mollitiae, Liv. ; in *pl. :* Quint. **c.** Concr. *clients :* Vatin. ap. Cic. Ep.

patrōcinor, ārī [patrōcinium], *to act as patronus or advocate* (with DAT. of person) : Ter., Tac., etc.

Patroclus, ī (**Patriclēs**, is, Enn.), *m. son of*

Menoetius, *the friend of Achilles, killed by Hector.*

patrōna, ae, *f.* [patrōnus], *a (legal) protectress, patroness.* **1.** Lit. (in relation to an ex-slave) : Plin. Ep. **2.** Transf. **a.** Of a goddess : mistress : Pl. **b.** *advocate :* te mihi patronam capio, Thais, Ter. **c.** *defender, safeguard :* lex ipsa sociorum patrona, Cic. ; provocatio, patrona illa civitatis, Cic.

patrōnus, ī, *m.* [pater], *a (legal) protector.* **1.** Lit. **a.** In relation to clients and dependants : Liv. **b.** In relation to exslaves : Pl., Cic. Ep., Tac. **c.** Of foreign communities : civitatum et nationum, Cic. ; coloniae, Cic., Liv. **2.** Transf. *a defender, advocate.* **a.** In court : *a counsel :* huic causae patronus exstiti, Cic. ; partis adversae, Quint. **b.** In gen., *a defender, advocate :* Ov. ; vestrorum commodorum, Cic. ; foederum ac foederatorum, Cic. Comic. : propter male facta es patronus parieti, Pl.

patruēlis, e, *adj.* [patruus], *of or descended from a father's brother :* Pl. ; origo, Ov. ; regna (of Danaus), Ov. As Noun : *a cousin* (of this descent). **1.** Lit. : Cic., Pers., etc. **2.** Transf. *a father's sister's son, a cousin :* Cic., Suet.

patruus, ī, *m.* [pater], *a father's brother, paternal uncle* (avunculus). **1.** Lit. : Cic., Hor. **2.** Transf. *a severe reprover :* Hor.

patruus, a, um [patruus], *of an uncle, an uncle's :* Hor., Ov. Comic. Sup. : patrue mi patruissume, *my best of uncles,* Pl.

patulus, a, um [pateō], *standing wide-open, open.* **1.** Lit. : pina, Cic. ; fenestrae, Ov. ; nares, Verg. ; aures, Hor. **2.** Transf. **a.** *spread out, spreading, broad :* mundus, Lucr. ; rami, Cic. ; plaustra, fagus, Verg. ; Iovis arbor, Ov. ; lacus, Ov. ; loca urbis, Tac. **b.** *open or common to all :* orbis, Hor.

pauciloquium, ī, *n.* [paucus loquor], *a speaking but little :* Pl.

paucitās, ātis, *f.* [paucus], *a small number, fewness, scarcity :* Caes., Cic., etc. With GEN. : militum, portuum, Caes. ; oratorum, Cic. ; suorum, Cic. ; loci, Liv.

pauculi, ae, a, *pl.* [dim. paucus], *very few, just a few :* Pl., Cic. Ep. *Neut. pl.* as Noun : paucula sciscitare, Pl. ; Ter.

paucus, a, um [*cf.* παῦρος], *few, little* (mostly *pl.*) : in diebus paucis Chrysis moritur, Ter. ; paucis diebus post mortem Africani, Cic. ; causae, homines, etc., Cic. *Comp. :* Sall. *Sing. :* tibia tenuis simplexque foramine pauco, Hor. Often as Noun, **pauci**, ōrum, *m. pl. few, a few :* ut metus ad omnis, poena ad paucos perveniret, Cic. Also, *the few, the select few :* paucorum iudicium, Cic. ; also in *Comp. :* Pl. In polit. sense, *the few* (*cf.* οἱ ὀλίγοι) : factio paucorum, Caes. ; paucorum potentia, Sall. Phr. : inter paucos (paucas, pauca), *especially* (also in paucis, Curt.) : inter paucos disertus, Quint. ; pugna inter paucas memorata, Liv. ; **pauca**, ōrum, *n. pl. a few words :* ausculta paucis, Ter. ; Pl. ; paucis docebo, Verg. ; Liv. ; pauca respondere, Hor. ; in *Sup. :* cetera quam paucissumis absolvam, Sall. [It. *poco ;* Fr. *peu.*]

paulātim (paullātim), *adv. by little and little, gradually :* labefacto paullatim, Pl. ; Germanos Rhenum transire, Caes. ; haec consuetudo prodire coepit, Cic. ; collis ad planitiem redibat, Caes. ; licentia crevit, Sall.

paulisper (paullisper), *adv. for a little while, for a short time :* Pl., Caes., Cic., Liv., etc.

paululus (paullulus), a, um [*dim.* paulus], *very little, very small, tiny :* pecunia, Pl. ; spatium, Ter. ; equi hominesque, Liv. ; via, Liv. As Noun, **paululum (paullu-lum)**, i, *n. a little bit, a trifle :* praedae, Pl. ; pecuniae, Ter. ; morae, Cic. *Intern.* Acc. as *Adv. :* apscede paullulum istuc, Pl. ; collis ex planitie editus, Caes. ; progredi, Caes. ; respirare, Cic. ABL. (of Price), *for a small sum ;* si nequeas paullulo, at quanti queas, Ter. ; ABL. (of Measure) with *Comp. by a little, somewhat :* paululo deterius, Lucc. ap. Cic. Ep.

paulus (paullus), a, um [*cf.* παῦρος], *little, slight, small :* paullo momento huc vel illuc impelli, Ter. As Noun, **paulum (paul-lum)**, i, *n. a little, a trifle :* de paullo paullu-lum hoc tibi dabo, Pl. ; Hor. ; paulum huic Cottae tribuit partium, Cic. ; laboris, Liv. Of time : post paulum, Caes. Acc. (*Intern.* or of Extent) as *Adv. :* paulum supra eum locum, Caes. ; commorari, Cic. ; epistulae me recreant, Cic. Ep. ; ABL. (of Measure), *by a little, a little :* paullo prius, Pl. ; paulo melior, Cic. ; paulo ante, Cic. ; post paullo, Sall., Liv. ; magnitudine paulo antecedunt, Caes. With non-comparative : paullo tolerabilis, Ter. ; Cic. Ep. ; aut nihil aut paulo concedere digna, Cat.

Paulus (Paullus), i, *m. a Roman cognomen in the gens Aemilia ;* esp. **I.** L. Aemilius Paulus, *who fell at the battle of Cannae,* B.C. 216. **II.** L. Aemilius Paulus, *son of the former, conqueror of Macedonia by the victory of Pydna,* B.C. 168

pauper, eris, *adj.* [perh. fr. root of paucus and parō], *of small means, poor* (but not destitute, egens). **a.** Of persons : Ter., Cic., Hor. With GEN. : pauperrimus bonorum, Hor. As Noun, *a poor man :* Hor. ; also in *Comp. :* pauperiorum turbae, Hor. ; in *Sup. :* sisne ex pauperrimo dives factus, Cic. **b.** Of things : *scanty, small, meagre, poor :* res, Pl. ; pauperis tuguri culmen, Verg. ; domus, Verg. ; carmen venā pauperiore fluit, Ov. ; eloquentia, Quint. [It. *povero ;* Sp. *pobre ;* Fr. *pauvre.*]

pauperculus, a, um [*dim.* pauper], *poor :* senex, Pl. ; mater, Hor. Of things : res nostrae, Pl.

pauperiēs, ēi, *f.* [pauper], *scanty, humble means :* Pl., Verg., Hor., Tac.

pauperō, āre [pauper], *to impoverish :* ali-quem, Pl. With ABL. of thing : *to rob :* dominum pretio, Pl. ; aliquem cassā nuce, Hor.

paupertās, ātis, *f.* [pauper], *small means, moderate circumstances, poverty* (but not destitution, egestas.) **1.** *Lit. :* Pl., Cic., Hor., etc. In *pl. :* Varr., Sen. Ep. 2. Transf. of language : sermonis, Quint. [Fr. *pauvreté.*]

pausa, ae, *f.* [παῦσις], *a stop, cessation :* facere, dare, Pl. ; dare conciliis, Lucr. ; vitāl, Lucr.

pausia, ae, *f. a thick-fleshed olive :* Cato, Verg., etc.

Pausiās, ae, *m. a famous painter, a native of Sicyon, contemporary with Apelles ;* **Pau-siacus**, a, um.

pausill-, *v.* pauxill-.

pauxillātim, *adv. little by little :* Pl.

pauxillisper, *adv. by little bits, by degrees :* Pl.

pauxillulus, a, um [*dim.* pauxillus], *very little, very small, tiny :* lembus, Pl. ; pisces, Pl. ; reliquom pauxillulum nummorum, Ter. *Neut.* as Noun : de tuis deliciis quid pauxil-lulum, Pl. *Intern.* Acc. as *Adv. :* hanc forem pauxillulum aperi, Pl.

pauxillus, a, um [*dim.* paucus], *very little, small :* res, Pl. ; Lucr. *Neut.* as Noun : ex pauxillo, *from a small stock,* Pl. Acc. as *Adv. :* Pl.

pavefactus, a, um [paveō faciō], *frightened, scared :* pectora, Ov. ; fumo ac murmure pavefactus, Suet.

paveō, pavēre, pāvī [*cf.* paviō]. **A.** Intrans.: *to quake, throb, tremble with fright, to be scared, to be in panic or terror :* intus paveo, Pl. ; sibi, Ter., Tac. ; ad omnia, Liv. ; Maurus incerto vultu pavens ad Sullam accurrit, Sall. ; admiratione, Liv. ; speque metuque, Ov. Also, (bal-sami) venae pavent, Tac. **B.** Trans. *to quake at, be scared at :* illud, Pl. ; omnia, Sall. ; Parthum, Hor. ; funera, Hor. ; ibin, Juv. ; tristiorem casum, Tac. With *Inf. :* Ov., Tac.

pavēscō, ere [paveō]. **A.** Intrans.: *to begin to quake, to become alarmed :* omni strepitu, Sall. **B.** Trans. *to begin to quake at or be scared of :* bellum, Tac.

pavidē, *adv. in a panic :* Lucr., Liv.

pavidus, a, um [paveō], *quaking, scared, in a panic, craven.* **1.** *Lit.* **a.** Of fear : Pl., Lucr. ; castris se pavidus tenebat, Liv. ; matres, Verg. ; lepus, Hor. ; miles, Tac. ; pavida ex somno mulier, Liv. ; ad omnis suspiciones, Tac. With GEN. : miles R. armis gravis et nandi pavidus, Tac. ; Luc. With *ne* and *Subj. :* Liv. *Comp. :* Plin. *Sup. :* Sen. *Neut.* Acc. as *Adv. :* pavi-dum blanditia, Ov. **b.** Of excitement : *with beating heart, nervous :* excipiunt plausu pavidos (pueros), Verg. **2.** Transf. **a.** Of feelings : metus, Ov. **b.** Of things : *causing alarm or anxiety, anxious :* murmur, Luc. ; quies pavida imaginibus, Suet.

pavimentō, āre [pavimentum], *to pave :* Cic.

pavimentum, i, *n.* [paviō], *a floor composed of small stones, earth, or lime, beaten down with a rammer ; a pavement ; hard floor,* Cato, Caes., Cic. Ep., Hor.

paviō, ire [*cf.* παίω], *to beat, strike.* **1.** *Lit. :* aequor harenam, Lucr. ; aliquid ex ore terram, Cic. **2.** Transf. *to beat, ram, or tread down :* aream esse oportet solidam, terrā pavitā, Varr.

pavitō, āre [*freq.* paveō]. **A.** Intrans. *to quake or tremble violently.* **a.** With fear : Verg. **b.** With ague : Ter. **B.** Trans. *to quake violently at :* Lucr.

păvŏ, ōnis (**păvus**, ī, Enn.), *m.* [*cf.* ταῶς], *a peacock :* sacred to Juno : Lucr., Cic. As a delicacy : Cic. Ep., Juv.

pavor, ōris, *m.* [paveō], *quaking, panic, terror, dismay.* **a.** Of fear : Enn., Cic. ; hic exsultat pavor, Lucr. ; terror pavorque omnīs occupavit, Liv. ; pavor ceperat milites ne etc., Liv. ; deponere, Ov. ; facere, alicui inicere, incutere, offundere, Liv. ; mortalia corda stravit pavor, Verg. In *pl. :* nocturni, Tac. ; Luc. **b.** Of excite-ment : cum spes adrectae iuvenum exsul-tantiaque haurit corda pavor pulsans, Verg. [It. *paura ;* Fr. *peur.*]

păx, pācis, *f.* [*cf.* paciscor], *a peace by mutual agreement, a state of peace,* as opp. to war. **1.** Lit. **a.** In gen. : pax Caudina, Liv. ; pax est vobis mecum, Pl. ; esse pacem alicui cum aliquo, Cic. ; habere, conciliare, Cic. Ep. ; conficere, coagmentare, servare, confirmare cum aliquo, Cic. ; petere, Caes. ; pangere cum aliquo, componere, parere, impetrare, alicui dare, Liv. ; agitare, Sall. ; rumpere, Verg. ; turbare, Tac. ; bello ac pace, Liv. ; Sall., etc. ; pax Romana, Plin., Sen. ; nostra, Tac. ; aliquem cum pace dimittere, Cic. ; in pace vivere, Cic. ; Hor. ; in mediā pace, Liv. ; mediā pace, Tac. In *pl. :* Pl., Sall., Hor. **Pax** personified as goddess : Nep., Hor., Ov., etc. **b.** In re-ligion : *right relations, grace and goodwill :* Iovis hostiis pacem expetere, Pl. ; divum (GEN.) pacem votis adit, Lucr. ; ab Iove Opt. Max. pacem ac veniam peto, Cic. ; exorat pacem divum, Verg. ; exposcere, Liv. **2.** Transf. **a.** In ABL. *without up-setting our peaceful relations, with (your) goodwill, with (your) good leave or permission :* pace quod fiat tuā, Ter. ; pace tuā dixerim, Cic. ; C. Claudi pace loquar, Liv. **b.** As an interj. : *peace / silence / enough /* pax ! abi, Pl. **c.** *peace, calmness, serenity, lull :* in animo, Cic. ; animi, Ov. ; flumen cum pace delabens, Hor. ; pacem vultus ha-bet, Ov. ; ventorum paces, Lucr. ; magna et aeterna pax, Sen. [Sp. *paz ;* Fr. *paix.*]

peccāns, antis. **I.** *Part.* peccō. **II.** Noun, *a sinner, offender :* Nep., Sen. Ep.

peccātum, ī, *n.* [peccō], *a fault, error, trans-gression :* corrigere, Ter. ; confiteri, Cic. ; in manifesto peccato teneri, Cic. ; in peccata incidere, Cic. ; luere, Verg. ; peccatis poenas aequas inrogare, Hor. ; peccatis veniam commodare, Tac. ; abstinere pec-catis, Plin. Ep. [Fr. *péché.*]

peccō, āre, *to make a mistake, go wrong, err, offend.* **1.** Lit. : Pl., Cic. With *Intern.* Acc. : unam syllabam, Pl. ; Empedocles multa alia peccat, Cic. ; talia, Ov. With *preps. :* erga te, Pl. ; in me, Cic. Ep. ; in Procillo (*in P's case*), Caes. ; in matronā, Hor. ; *Impers. Pass. :* in servo necando peccatur, Cic. ; in vitā et in oratione, Cic. With *ABL.* : ingenuo amore, Hor. ; mis-sione et pecuniā, Tac. **2.** Transf. of animals and inanimate things : *to fail, go wrong :* Hor., Mart. [Fr. *pécher.*]

pecorōsus, a, um [pecus], *rich in cattle :* Prop.

pecten, inis, *m.* [pectō], *a comb.* **1.** Lit. : Pl., Ov. **2.** Transf. of things like a comb.

a. *the reed* of a weaver's loom : Verg., Ov. **b.** *a comb* for carding wool : Juv. **c.** *a rake :* Ov. **d.** Of the form of the clasped hands : Ov. **e.** *a quill* (for striking the strings of the lyre) : Verg. Hence, *a poem* or *song :* dum canimus sacras alterno pectine Nonas, i.e. in elegiac verse, Ov. **f.** *a kind of shell-fish, a scallop :* Hor. [It. *pettine ;* Fr. *peigne.*]

pectinātim, *adv. in the form of a comb, like the teeth of a comb :* Plin.

pectō, pectere, pexī, pexum [*cf.* πέκω], *to comb.* **1.** Lit. : capillos, Ov. ; Verg. ; Hor., etc. **2.** Transf. **a.** *to comb* or *card* wool, flax, etc. : stuppam ferreis hamis, Plin. **b.** Comic. : pectere aliquem fusti or pugnis, Pl.

pectus, oris, *n. the breast.* **1.** Lit. : Pl., Cic., Verg., etc. In *pl. :* Verg., Ov. **2.** Transf. *the heart* as the seat. **a.** Of feel-ings and affection : somnum socordiamque ex pectore oculisque amovere, Pl. ; blan-dum per pectora amorem efficis, Lucr. ; in amicitiā apertum pectus, Cic. ; toto pectore amare, Cic. ; te vero iam pectore toto ac-cipio, Verg. ; mollities pectoris, Ov. ; metus insidens pectoribus, Liv. ; violenta pectora Turni, Verg. Of courage : te forti seque-mur pectore, Hor. ; Verg. **b.** Of the in-tellect : Pl., Liv. ; dignum pollenti pectore carmen condere, Lucr. ; nova pectore versat consilia, Verg. ; oculis pectoris aliquid haurire, Ov. ; rara occulti pectoris vox, Tac. ; pectore adripere artis, Tac. [It. *petto ;* Sp. *pecho ;* Fr. *pis.*]

pecū, *n. a flock of sheep.* **1.** Lit. : Pl. In *pl.* pecua, Pl., Cato, Liv., etc. Comic. of fish : squamosum pecu, Pl. **2.** Transf. **a.** In *pl. : pastures :* Cic. **b.** Comic. of money (in *pl.*) : Pl.

pecuārius, a, um [pecū], *of cattle* or *sheep :* res, live stock, Pl., Cic. ; greges, Varr. As Noun, **pecuārius**, ī, *m. a cattle-breeder, grazier :* Cic. Esp. *of those who pastured cattle on the public lands :* Liv. **pecuāria**, ae (*sc.* res), *f.* **i.** *a stock of cattle :* Varr. **ii.** *cattle-breeding :* Varr ; pecuariam facere, Suet. **pecuāria**, ōrum, *n. pl. herds of cattle* or *sheep :* Verg.

pecūlātor, ōris, *m.* [pecūlor] *an embezzler of public money :* Cic., Tac.

pecūlātus, ūs, *m.* [pecūlor], *an embezzlement of public money* or *property :* facere, Cic. ; Liv. Transf. : Pl., Liv.

pecūliāris, e, *adj.* [pecūlium], *as one's own private property, one's own.* **1.** Lit. : ovem tibi dabo peculiarem, Pl. ; Varr. ; Suet. **2.** Transf. *one's own, special :* peculiarem tuum testem, Cic. ; quam partem peculiarem rem publicam fecistis, Liv. ; me peculiaris impedit ratio, Plin. Ep. ; urbis vitia, Tac. ; meritum, Suet.

pecūliāriter, *adv. especially, particularly :* Plin., Quint.

pecūliātus, a, um [pecūlium], *provided with money :* Asin. Pollio ap. Cic. Ep.

pecūliō, āre [pecūlium], *to give as private property :* Pl.

pecūliolum, ī, *n.* [*dim.* pecūlium], *a nice little hoard, a nest egg :* Quint.

pecūliōsus, a, um [pecūlium], *having private property :* Pl.

pecūlium, ĭ, n. [dim. pecū; v. pecūnia], a small sum of money, small savings or gains (mostly belonging to slaves, but also of other members of the familia, and regarded as private property). **1**. Lit. **a**. Of slaves : Pl., Cic., Verg. **b**. Of a wife : Suet. **c**. Of a son (property earned by military service or bequeathed by his mother) : Liv. **d**. Contemptuously : paltry gain : cupiditate peculi, Cic. ; cura peculi, Hor. **2**. Transf. : sine ullo ad me peculio veniet (of a letter), Sen. Ep.

pecūnia, ae, f. [pecū], property, wealth. **a**. In gen. : Cic., Liv., Tac. ; facere, Cic. Personified : Hor. **b**. In partic. : money : praesenti pecuniā, with ready money, Pl. ; pecunia numerata, Cic. ; conlocatam habere (i.e. on mortgage), Cic. ; conficere, occupare, solvere, dissolvere, deferre, avertere, auferre, exigere, cogere, etc., Cic. In pl. : sums of money : pecunias exigere, capere, imperare, Cic. ; mutuas pecunias faenore quaerere, Liv.

pecūniārius, a, um [pecūnia], of money, pecuniary : rei pecuniariae socius, Cic. ; praemia rei pecuniariae magna, Caes. ; Tac. ; lis, Quint.

pecūniōsus, a, um [pecūnia], having much money, moneyed, rich, wealthy. **1**. Lit. : Cic. Comp. : Suet. Sup. : Cic. **2**. Transf. bringing in money : artes, Mart.

pecus, pecoris, n. [cf. pecū], cattle, as a collective, a herd or flock (opp. to pecus, pecudis). **1**. Lit. a. In gen. : Varr., Verg. b. In partic. : sheep : Cato ; magnus pecoris numerus, Caes. ; pecora et iumenta, Caes. ; balatus pecorum, Verg. ; pecora et armenta, Ov. **2**. Transf. a. Of other beasts : of pigs : Ov. ; of seals : Hor. ; of a single lion : Ov. Also of drone-bees : Verg. **b**. As a term of abuse (of persons) : Cat., Hor., Juv.

pecus, udis, f. [cf. pecū], a single head of cattle. **1**. Lit. a. In gen. : a beast, of domestic animals, wild beasts, fishes, etc. ; Pl., Cic., Verg., etc. **b**. a sheep : Lucr., Ov., etc. **2**. Transf. as a term of abuse : Cic., Tac.

pedālis, e, adj. [pēs], a foot long : sol mihi videtur quasi pedalis, Cic. ; transtra ex pedalibus in latitudinem trabibus, Caes.

pedāmentum, ĭ, n. [cf. pedātus], a stake or prop for vines and trees : Varr.

pedārius, m. adj. [pēs], of the foot, foot-. Transf. : pedarii senatores. inferior senators : Tac. ; also as Noun : Cic. Ep.

pedātū, Abl. sing. m. [pedō], tertio pedatu, at the third charge or assault : Pl., Cato.

pedātus, a, um [pēs], footed : male pedatus, ill set on his feet, Suet.

pedes, itis, m. adj. [pēs], on foot : si pedes incedat, Liv. ; Verg. ; Ov. As Noun a. a foot-soldier : Caes., Liv., etc. **b**. Collect. in sing., foot-soldiers, infantry : cum pedes concurrit, Liv. ; Tac. **c**. equites, pedites, as a general designation for the entire (Roman) people : Cic., Hor., Liv. ; in sing. : Pl.

pedester, tris, tre, adj. [pedes], on foot, pedestrian (opp. to equester). **1**. Lit. a. copiae, Caes. ; Tac. ; statua, Cic. **b**. of infantry : pugna, scutum, Liv. ; acies,

Liv., Tac. **c**. on land, by land : pedestres navalesque pugnae, Cic. ; itinera, Caes. **2**. Transf. of style (= πεζός). **a**. written in prose : oratio, Quint. ; historiae, Hor. **b**. plain, prosaic : sermo, Musa, Hor. [Fr. piètre.]

pedetemptim, adv. [pēs temptō], by feeling the way with the feet. **1**. Lit. : Pac. ; (elephanti) quaerendis pedetemptim vadis in terram evasere, Liv. **2**. Transf. : gradually, cautiously : Pl., Ter., Cic., etc.

pedica, ae, f. [pēs]. **I**. a fetter or chain for the feet : Pl. **II**. a springe, gin, snare : Verg., Ov., Liv. [Fr. piège.]

pediculōsus, a, um [pediculus], full of lice, lousy : Mart.

(1) pediculus, ĭ, m. [dim. pēs], a little foot : Plin.

(2) pediculus (pedŭculus), ĭ, m. [dim. pedis], a little louse : Plin. [It. pidocchio ; Fr. pou.]

pedis, is, m.f. [pēs], a louse : Pl., Varr.

pedisequus (-uos), ĭ, m. and **pedisequa**, ae, f. [pēs sequor], a male or female attendant; a footman, page, lackey ; a waiting-woman. **1**. Lit. : Pl., Cic. Ep., etc. **2**. Transf. : iuris scientiam eloquentiae tamquam ancillulam pedisequamque adiunxisti, Cic.

peditastellus, ĭ, m. dim., a miserable little infantryman : Pl.

peditātus, ūs, m. [pedes], foot-soldiers, foot, infantry (opp. to equitatus, cavalry) : Caes., Cic., etc.

pēditum, ĭ, n. [pēdō], a breaking wind : Cat.

pēdō, pēdere, pepēdī [cf. πέρδομαι], to break wind : Hor.

pedum, ĭ, n. [pēs], a shepherd's crook : Verg.

Pēgasus (-os), ĭ, m. a winged horse, which sprang from the blood of Medusa ; with a blow of his hoof he caused the fountain of the Muses (Hippocrene) to spring from Mount Helicon. Bellerophon mounted him, and with his aid destroyed the Chimaera ; **Pēgasēius, Pēgaseus**, a, um ; **Pēgasis**, idis, f. adj. As Noun, **Pēgasis**, idis, f. a fountain nymph ; **Pēgasides**, um, f. pl. the Muses.

pēgma, atis, n. [πῆγμα], a structure of boards. **a**. a bookcase : Cic. Ep. **b**. a stage or scaffolding, used in the Roman amphitheatres : Sen. Ep., Juv., Suet., etc. **c**. For the imagines in the atrium : Aus.

pēierō (peiierō, Pl., and **periūrō**), āre [per iūrō], to swear falsely, to forswear or perjure oneself : Pl., Cic., Juv., etc. ; per consulatum, Cat. ; also with Acc. of thing sworn by : Ov., Plin., Luc. ; ius peieratum, a false oath, Hor. Comic. for to lie : Pl.

peiierātiuncula, ae, f. dim. [pēierō], a petty perjury : Pl.

peiierōsus, a, um [peiierium=periūrium], perjured : Pl.

peiiūrium, v. periūrium.

pēior (peiior), us, v. malus.

pēius (peiius), adv. neuter : v. male. [Fr. pis.]

pelage, v. pelagus.

pelagius, a, um [πελάγιος] of the sea, sea- (pure Lat. marīnus) : Varr. ; cursus, Phaedr.

pelagus, ĭ, n. (Gk. pl. pelagē, Lucr.) [πέλαγος], the open sea, the main : Pac., Lucr., Verg., Tac., etc.

pēlamis, idis, and **pēlamys**, ydis, f. [πηλαμίς and πηλαμύς], a young tunny-fish : Plin., Juv.

Pelasgī, ōrum, m. pl. the most ancient inhabitants of Greece, who were spread also over a part of Asia Minor and other countries : often used by the poets for Greeks ; **Pelasgias**, adis, **Pelasgis**, idis, f. adj. and **Pelasgus**, a, um, poet. for Grecian.

Pelēthronius, a, um, belonging to Pelethronia, a region of Thessaly inhabited by the Lapithae.

Pēleus (disyl.) eī and eos (Acc. Pēlea ; Voc. Pēleu ; Abl. Pēleō), king of a district in Thessaly, s. of Aeacus, h. of Thetis, and f. of Achilles ; **Pēlīdēs**, ae, m. the son of Peleus, i.e. Achilles ; also the grandson of Peleus, i.e. Neoptolemus, son of Achilles.

Peliās, ae, m. king of Iolcos in Thessaly ; he induced his nephew Jason to make the Argonautic expedition. After Jason's return, Pelias was slain by his own daughters, by the craft of Medea ; **Peliades**, um, f. pl. his daughters.

Pēlion, ī, n. a lofty range of mountains in eastern Thessaly ; **Pēliacus**, a, um, **Pēlius**, a, um, and **Pēlias**, adis, f. adj.

Pella, ae, and **Pellē**, ēs, f. a city of remote antiquity in Macedonia, the birth-place of Alexander the Great ; **Pellaeus**, a, um : iuvenis, i.e. Alexander, Juv. Also Alexandrean : because Alexander founded Alexandrea : Luc. ; also Egyptian : Verg.

pellācia, ae, f. [pellāx], an allurement, charm : placidi ponti, Lucr.

pellāx, ācis, adj. [perliciō], seductive, deceitful, cajoling : Verg.

pellec-, pelleg-, v. perlec-, perleg-.

pellex, v. paelex.

pelliciō, v. perliciō.

pellicula, ae. f. [dim. pellis] a small skin or hide : haedina, Cic. ; furtivae aurum pelliculae, Juv. Prov.: pelliculam curare (i.e. to take care of one's skin, of oneself), Hor. ; pelliculam veterem retinere (i.e. to remain one's old self), Pers.

pelliō, ōnis, m. [pellis], a furrier : Pl.

pellis, is, f. [cf. πέλλα], a skin, hide (prop. of a beast). **1.** Lit.: Caes., Cic., Verg., etc. Used contemptuously of the human skin : ossa atque pellis tota est, Pl. ; frigida pellis duraque (in disease), Lucr. ; Juv. Prov. **a.** Of a fair exterior : speciosus pelle decorā, Hor. ; detrahere pellem, Hor. **b.** (=one's old self, cf. pellicula) quiescere in propriā pelle, Hor. **2.** Transf. **a.** In shoes, garments, etc. : dressed skin, leather, felt : ruptā calceus pelle patet, Juv. ; pes in pelle natat, Ov. ; nigrae pelles, Hor. ; pellibus tecta corpora, Ov. ; Hor. **b.** Milit. of huts covered with skins : sub pellibus hiemare, contineri, durare, Caes., Liv., Tac. Also of a shield-cover : Cic. **c.** a parchment cover : Mart. [Fr. peau.]

pellitus, a, um [pellis], clad in skins : testes (i.e. from Sardinia), Cic. ; Liv. ; oves, having their fleeces protected by leather jackets, Varr., Hor.

pellō, pellere, pepulī, pulsum [cf. πάλλω]. **I.** to set in motion by pushing, knocking, etc. **1.** Lit. **a.** vada remis, Cat. ; Enn. ; Cic. ; manu sagittam, Verg. ; navigia con-

tis, Curt. **b.** In music : to set the strings vibrating by striking : nervos, Cic. ; lyram manu, Ov. Also, classica pulsa, Tib. **c.** Milit. (but cf. II. 1. b.) to make an impression on, set moving : hostem pulsum exigite e campo, Liv. **2.** Transf. **a.** Mentally : to thrill, move, affect : species utilitatis pepulit eum, Cic. ; Liv. ; quod dictum cum animos hominum aurisque pepulisset, Cic. ; non mediocri curā Scipionis animum pepulit, Liv. Poet.: pulsusque resederat ardor, Ov. **b.** In musical metaphor and of sound-waves : ut nervi in fidibus, (omnes voces hominis) ita sonant ut a motu animi quoque sunt pulsae, Cic. ; longi sermonis initium pepulisti (the opening chord), Cic. ; ille canit, pulsae referunt ad sidera valles, Verg. **II.** to drive, thrust off, dislodge. **1.** Lit. **a.** In gen.: aliquem a foribus, Pl. ; istum ab Hispaniā, Cic. Ep. ; Ov. ; e foro, Cic. ; ex Galliae finibus, Caes. ; possessores suis sedibus, Cic. ; Liv. ; aliquem regno, Hor. ; exsules tyrannorum iniuriā pulsi, Liv. ; in exsilium pulsus, Cic. ; pudendis vulneribus pulsus, Verg. ; sol pepulit noctis umbras, Cat. ; Ov. **b.** Milit.: primo concursu hostes pelluntur, Caes. ; exeroitum, Caes., Cic. ; Liv. **2.** Transf.: procul a me dolorem, Pl. ; maestitiam ex animis, Cic. ; frigoris vim tectis, Cic. ; pulsus corde dolor, Verg. ; vino curas, Hor. ; sitim, Hor. ; glande famem, Ov. ; moram, Ov. Comic.: alicui pudicitiam, Pl. **III.** to beat on, buffet : foris, Ter. ; Tac. ; terram pede, Lucr., Hor. ; humum pedibus, Cat. ; pueros, Cic. ; arbor ventis pulsa, Lucr.

pellūc-, v. perlūc-.

Peloponnēsus, ī, f. the Peloponnesus (lit. island of Pelops) ; now Morea ; **Peloponnēnsis**, e, **Peloponnēsiacus, Peloponnēsius**, a, um.

Pelops, opis, m. s. of Tantalus, king of Phrygia, f. of Atreus and Thyestes, g.f. of Agamemnon and Menelaus. Being driven out of Phrygia, he went to Elis, and married Hippodamia, daughter of King Oenomaus, whom he succeeded on the throne ; **Pelopēias**, adis, and **Pelopēis**, idis, f. adj. Peloponnesian ; **Pelopēius, Pelopēus**, a, um, Pelopian or Mycenean, also Phrygian ; and **Pelopidae**, ārum, m. pl. the descendants of Pelops.

Pelōrus (-os), ī, m. the north-eastern promontory of Sicily, now Cape Faro : **Pelōrias**, adis, and **Pelōris**, idis, f. the Pelorian region.

pelōris, idis, f. [πελωρίς], a large shell-fish (perh. a mussel) : Hor.

pelta, ae, f. [πέλτη], a small, light shield of leather, used by Thracians, etc. : Verg., Liv., etc.

peltastēs or **-a**, ae, m. [πελταστής], a soldier armed with the pelta, a peltast : Liv.

peltātus, a, um [pelta], armed with the pelta : Ov.

Pēlūsium, ī, n. a city at the eastern mouth of the Nile ; **Pēlūsiacus, Pēlūsius**, a, um.

pelvis, is, f. [cf. πελλίς], a basin, laver : Caecil., Juv.

penārius, a, um [penus], of or for provisions : Cic.

Penātēs, ium, *m. pl.* [penus], *the Penates, old Latin guardian deities of the household-(and also the State-) stores ;* used with or without dii (or di). **1.** Lit.: Pl., Cic., Verg., etc. **2.** Transf. *dwelling, home :* a suis dis Penatibus praeceps eiectus, Cic. ; Verg. ; Liv. Poet. of bees: certi Penates, Verg.

penātiger, era, erum [Penātēs gerō], *carrying his household gods :* Ov.

pendeō, pendēre, pependī [*cf.* pendō]. **I.** *to hang* from, on, or by something, *to be hung, suspended.* **1.** Lit.: Pl., Ter., Hor. ; per pedes, Pl. ; in *or* ex arbore, Cic. ; sagittae ab umero, Cic. ; de viri collo dulce onus, Ov. ; tigridis exuviae per dorsum a vertice, Verg. ; e trabe triste onus, Ov. ; telum clipei umbone, Verg. ; sacra fistula pinu, Verg. ; Prop. Of names posted up : reos qui apud aerarium pependissent, Suet. ; Plin. Ep. So of debtors to the State, venalem pendere, Suet. Prov.: pendere filo *or* tenui filo (i.e. to be in great danger), Enn., Ov. **2.** Transf. **a.** *to hang on, depend on :* spes ex fortunā, Cic. ; salus nostra spe exiguā, Cic. ; tam levi momento mea apud vos fama, Liv. ; ex alterius vultu ac nutu, Liv. ; in sententiis omnium civium nostra fama, Cic. ; tyrannus, cum quo fatum pendebat amici, Juv. **b.** Of origin: hinc omnis Lucilius, Hor. **c.** *to hang* on attentively : Plin. Ep. ; narrantis ab ore, Verg., Ov. ; vultu, Quint. **II.** *to hang loose* or *free, be poised.* **1.** Lit. **a.** Of things overhanging, hovering, or floating : speluncas saxis pendentibus structas, Lucr. ; dum siccā tellure licet, dum nubila pendent, Verg. ; hi summo in fluctu pendent, Verg. ; circumfuso pendebat in aere tellus, Ov. ; nec litus opertum pendeat algā, Ov. **b.** Of flabby things : *to hang down :* fluidos pendere lacertos, Ov. ; pendentes genae, Juv. **2.** Transf. **a.** Of work in suspense : *to hang :* opera interrupta, Verg. Also of human idleness : nostroque in limine pendes, Verg. **b.** *to hang,* i.e. *be ready to fall :* nec amicum pendentem corruere patitur, Cic. **c.** Freq. *to hang in* doubt, uncertainty, etc., *to be in suspense :* animus tibi pendet, Ter. ; obscurā spe, Cic. ; pavidis mentibus, Lucr. ; pendebat adhuc belli fortuna, Ov. Esp. pendere animi, Ter., Cic., etc. ; so with *Indir. Quest. :* Pl., Cic. Ep. ; animus, Cic., Liv.

pendō, pendere, pependī, pēnsum [*cf.* pendeō]. **I.** Trans. *to make* or *cause to hang down,* esp. of scales ; hence, **A.** *to weigh, weigh out.* **1.** Lit.: huius domi aurum pendebatur, Cic. ; pensas examinat herbas, Ov. **2.** Transf. **a.** *to weigh* mentally, *ponder, consider :* verba, Cic. ; rem levi coniecturā, Cic. ; causam ex veritate, Cic. **b.** *to value, esteem* (with GEN. of valuo) : aliquem magni, Pl., Hor. ; aliquem parvi, minoris, nihili pendere, Pl. ; flocci, Ter. ; aliquid magni pendere, Lucr. **B.** *to pay by weight, pay out, pay* (because in the earliest times people paid by weight of metal). **1.** Lit.: ingentem pecuniam quotannis, Cic. ; vectigal populo Romano, Caes. ; Liv. ; tributum pro navibus, Tac. ; mercedem alicui,

Juv. **2.** Transf. *to pay* penalties : Syrus mihi tergo poenas pendet, Ter. ; maximas poenas pendo temeritatis meae, Cic. Ep. ; satis pro temeritate unius hominis suppliciorum pensum esse, Liv. ; capitis poenas, Ov. **II.** Intrans. *to weigh, have weight :* talentum ne minus pondo octoginta Romanis ponderibus pendat, Liv. ; Lucr.

pendulus, a, um [pendeō], *hanging, hanging down* or *free.* **1.** Lit.: collum, Hor. ; libra, Ov. Of places : *poised on high, lofty :* Mart. **2.** Transf. of suspense : dubiae spe pendulus horae, Hor.

Pēneleus, eī, *m. a son of Hippalmus and Asterope, one of Helen's suitors.*

Pēnelopē, ēs, and **Pēnelopa**, ae, *f. daughter of Icarius and Periboea, wife of Ulysses ;* **Pēnelopēus**, a, um.

penes, *prep.* [*cf.* penitus], lit. *within ;* hence, *in the house* (or *stores*) *of.* **1.** Lit. (with Acc.): thensaurum tuom me esse penes, Pl. ; hi servi centum dies penes accusatorem cum fuissent, Cic. ; Ter. ; Caes. **2.** Transf. **a.** In gen.: *in the possession* or *power of :* us. with Acc. of persons : quem penes est virtus, Pl. ; penes eos summam victoriae constare intellegebant, Caes. ; agrorum penes Cn. Pompeium potestas debet esse, Cic. ; culpam penes Maenium fore, Liv. ; penes quos sunt auspicia, Liv. ; me penes est custodia mundi, Ov. With Acc. of *Abstr.* Noun : penes usum arbitrium est et ius et norma loquendi, Hor. ; potissimam (causam) penes incuriam virorum feminarumque, Tac. **b.** With *Refl. Pron :* penes se esse (*cf.* apud se esse and ἐν ἑαυτῷ εἶναι), *to be in one's senses :* Hor.

penetrābilis, e, *adj.* [penetrō]. **A.** Act. *piercing, penetrating :* frigus, Verg. ; fulmen, Ov. **B.** Pass. *that can be pierced* or *penetrated, penetrable :* corpus nullo penetrabile telo, Ov. ; caput haud penetrabile Nili, Stat.

penetrālis, e, *adj.* [penetrō]. **I.** *piercing, penetrating :* frigus, ignis, Lucr. Comp.: Lucr. **II.** *inward, inner, internal :* di Penates etiam penetrales a poetis vocantur, Cic. ; foci, Cic. ; tecta, adyta, Verg. As Noun, **penetrāle**, is, *n.* and more freq. **penetrālia**, ium, *n. pl. the interior, an inner room.* **1.** Lit.: of a building : prytaneum, id est penetrale urbis, Liv. ; in penetralibus pontificum, Liv. ; Priami penetralia, Verg. Esp. of holy places or sanctuaries : Vestae, Apollinis, Verg. **2.** Transf. **a.** *the inmost parts, remotest parts :* in ipsis penetralibus Britanniae, Tac. **b.** Abstract: loci aperire penetralia (i.e. to go to the root of the matter), Quint. ; eloquentiae, Tac.

penetrō, āre [*cf.* penitus, penus]. **I.** Trans. **A.** *to put, place* or *set into.* **1.** Lit.: pedem intra aedis, Pl. ; ea intra pectus se penetravit potio, Pl. In *Mid.:* quae penetrata qucount sensum progignere acerbum, Lucr. ; se in fugam, Pl. ; se ad pluris, Pl. **B.** With Acc. of goal : *to make one's way into, to penetrate.* **1.** Lit.: Illyricos sinūs, Verg. ; iter L. Lucullo penetratum, Tac. ; vox auris, Lucr. **2.** Transf.: id Tiberi animum altius penetravit, Tac. ; penetrabat eos (with Acc. and *Inf.*), Lucr. **II.** In-

t r a n s. *to make one's way into, to penetrate
into.* **1.** L i t. : in palaestram, Pl. ; Liv. ;
ad urbis, Cic. ; per angustias, Cic. ; sub
terras, Cic. ; intra vallum, Liv. ; vox ad
auris, Ov. *Impers. Pass. :* Liv. **2.**
T r a n s f. : Romuli animus haec ipsa in
templa penetravit, Cic. ; res in animos,
Cic. ; quo non ars penetrat ? Ov.

Pēnēus, I, *m. the principal river of Thessaly,
which flows through the valley of Tempe ;
now the Salembria :* in mythology, *a river-
god, the father of Cyrene and Daphne ;* **Pē-
nēis,** idis, *f. adj. ;* **Pēnēius, Pēnēus,** a,
um.

pēnicillus, I, *m.* [*dim.* pēniculus], *a painter's
brush or pencil.* **1.** L i t. : Cic., Quint. **2.**
T r a n s f. : Britanniam pingam coloribus
tuis, penicillo meo, Cic. Ep. [*Fr.* pinceau.]

pēniculus, I, *m.* [*dim.* pēnis]. L i t. *a little
tail.* **a,** *a horse-tail as a brush*. for removing
dust : Pl. **b,** *a sponge :* Pl., Ter.

pēnis, is, *m.* [*cf.* πέος]. **I.** *a tail :* Cic. Ep.
II. *the membrum virile, penis.* **1.** L i t. :
Cic. Ep., Hor. **2.** T r a n s f. *lechery :* Sall.

penitē, *adv. inwardly :* Cat.

penitus, a, um, *inward, inner :* ex penitis
faucibus, Pl. *Sup. :* ex Arabiā penitissu-
mā, Pl.

penitus, *adv. inwardly, internally, in the inside.* **1.** L i t. **a,** *within :* penitusque deus,
non fronte notandus, Manil. **b,** *deeply, far
within, into the inmost or remotest part :*
saxum penitus excisum, Cic. ; Suevos penitus ad extremos finis sese recepisse, Caes. ;
penitus in Thraciam se abdidit, Nep. ; quos
turbo penitus alias avexerat oras, Verg. ;
penitus terrae defigitur arbos, Verg. **c,**
from deep within : penitus suspiria trahere,
Ov. **d,** *far, widely :* terrae penitus iacen-
tes, Ov. **2.** T r a n s f. **a,** *deeply, far within :*
periculum penitus in venis et visceribus rei
publicae, Cic. ; penitus sese dare in familiaritatem alicuius. Cic. ; opinio tam penitus
insita, Cic. **b,** *from deep within :* penitus
ex intimā philosophiā, Cic. **c,** *thoroughly,
wholly, utterly* (mostly with Verbs) : Cic.,
Verg., Hor. **d,** With *Comp. : far :* penitus crudelior, Prop.

penna, ae, *f.* [*cf.* πέτομαι], *a feather.* **1.**
Lit. : Pl., Ov. *Of a feather* on an arrow :
Ov. **2.** T r a n s f. **a,** In *pl. : wings :* Pl.,
Cic., Verg., etc. **b,** *a flying, flight :* Prop.
(*v.* also pinna.)

pennātus, a, um [penna], *feathered ;* hence,
winged : Zephyrus, Lucr. ; Fama, Hor. ;
serpentes, Ov.

penniger, era, erum [penna gerō], *feathered,
winged :* Cic.

penni-pēs, *v.* pinnipēs.

penni-potēns, entis, *adj. winged, able to fly :*
Lucr. As Noun : Lucr.

pennula, ae, *f.* [*dim.* penna], *a little wing :*
Lucr.

pēnsilis, e, *adj.* [pendeō], *hanging, pendent :*
restim volo mihi emere, qui me faciam
pensilem, Pl. ; uva, Hor. ; Varr. ; vehetur
pensilibus plumis, Juv. A r c h i t. : *hanging,
supported on arches :* Curt., Plin.

pēnsiō, ōnis, *f.* [pendō], *a weighing out :*
hence *a paying out, instalment.* **1.** L i t. :
nihil debetur ei, nisi ex tertiā pensione,
Cic. Ep. ; in pensiones aequas trienni solutio

aeris alieni dispensata est, Liv. ; discripta
pensionibus aequis, Liv. Of rent : aedium
pensio annua, Suet. **2.** T r a n s f. : ista
tua coniunx debet populo R. tertiam pensionem, Cic.

pēnsitō, āre [*freq.* pēnsō]. **I.** *to weigh,
weigh out very carefully.* T r a n s f. (mentally)
to weigh, ponder, estimate : rem, Liv. ; suas
et inimicorum viris, Suet. ; amicorum
iudicia, Suet. With *Indir. Deliberative :*
Plin. Ep. ; so too in ABL. *Absol. Impers. :*
Tiberius saepe apud se pensitato an etc.,
Tac. **II.** *to pay taxes :* vectigalia nobis,
Cic. Of property, *to be liable to pay rent :*
praedia quae pensitant, Cic.

pēnsō, āre [*freq.* pendō], *to weigh or weigh out
carefully.* **1.** L i t. : aurum, Liv. P r o v. :
pensare eādem trutinā (i.e. judge by the
same standard), Hor. **2.** T r a n s f. **a.**
Mentally : *to weigh, ponder, estimate carefully :* viris oculis, Lucr. ; ex factis, non
ex dictis amicos, Liv. ; consilium, Curt.
b. *to counterbalance :* adversa secundis,
Liv. ; Tac. ; transmarinae res quādam
vice pensatae, Liv. **c.** *to repay :* vulnus
vulnere, Ov. ; beneficia beneficiis, Sen. ;
Curt. **d.** *to atone or pay for :* nece pudorem, Ov. [It. *pensare ;* Fr. *penser,* also
peser.]

pēnsus, a, um. **I.** *Part.* pendō. **II.** Adj. :
weighed. **1.** L i t. : only Neut. as Noun,
pēnsum, I, *a portion weighed out* as a day's
work for spinners of wool ; hence, in gen.
a task, piece of work. **a.** Lit. : pensum
facere, Pl. ; nocturna carpentes pensa
puellae, Verg. **b.** T r a n s f. : *a task, duty,
office :* pensum meum lepide accurabo,
Pl. ; absolvere, Varr. ; me ad meum munus
pensumque revocabo, Cic. [It. *peso.*]
2. T r a n s f. : *valued, dear :* utra condicio
pensior, Pl. As Noun in *Neut.* GEN.,
in the category of the valued (with habere, esse or adesse) : nihil pensi habere,
to set no value on, have no regard for : Sall. ;
Tac. ; with *Inf.* or *Indir. Quest. :* Sall. ;
nec mihi adest tantillum pensi iam, quos
capiam calceos, Pl. ; illis neo quid dicerent
nec quid facerent quicquam unquam pensi
fuisse, Liv.

pentameter, tri, *m.* [πεντάμετρος (containing five metrical feet)], *a pentameter :*
Quint.

pentēris, is, *f.* [πεντήρης], *a quinquereme,
galley :* Auct. B. Alex.

Penthesilēa, ae, *f. queen of the Amazons,
who fought for Troy and was slain by Achilles.*

Pentheus (disyl.), eī and eos, *m. son of
Echion and Agaue, grandson of Cadmus and
king of Thebes. For rejecting the rites of
Bacchus he was torn in pieces by his mother
and her sisters when under Bacchus' influence.*

pēnula, *v.* paenula.

pēnūria, ae, *f.* [*cf.* πένης, πεῖνα], *dearth,
want, need :* cibi, Lucr. ; victūs, Hor. ;
edendi, Verg. ; frumenti, Liv. ; civium,
Ter. ; sapientium civium bonorumque,
Cic. ; mulierum, Liv. ; argenti, rerum
omnium, Liv.

penus, ūs and I, *m.* and *f.,* also **penum,** I,
and **penus,** oris, *n.* [*cf.* penitus], *store or
provision of food, provisions, victuals :*
Pl., Cic., Verg., etc.

peplum, i, *n.* and **peplus,** i, *m.* [πέπλον and πέπλος], *the robe of state of Athene at Athens, in which her statue was solemnly clothed in the Panathenaea :* Verg.

per, *adv.* and *prep.* [fr. same root as Gk. περί, παρά, πέρα, and Lat. porta, portō]. **I.** A d v e r b, only in Compounds. **a.** *through* so as to reach an end (of place, time, circumstance) : pervenire, perferre, permanere, perpeti ; so of degree, *thoroughly, to the end :* perficere, perlegere, perdomare, permagnus. **b.** *through* a place or series of things : percurrere, persalutare. **c.** *through* so as to break through an obstacle : perfringere, permittere. **d.** *through* in sense of *across the right line, hence* in *a wrong direction, fatally :* pervertere, perlicere, perdere, perire. **II.** P r e p. with Acc. of Extent. **A.** Of s p a c e : *through, through the midst of, throughout, over, all over :* per totam urbem, Pl. ; equites per oram disponere, Caes. ; so per munitiones deicere, Caes. ; per membrana oculorum cernere, Cic. ; per caelum, Verg. ; per agros vagari, Liv. ; per provincias pecuniam credere, Cic. Ep. ; per temonem percurrere, Caes. ; cervixque comaeque trahuntur per terram, Verg. Placed after its noun : viam per, Lucr. Often to be translated *from one to another :* per manūs tradere, Caes., Liv. ; per domos invitari, Liv. ; per aras pacem exquirunt, Verg. Also *before :* incedunt per ora vestra, Sall. ; Liv. ; traducti per hostium oculos, Liv. **B.** Of t i m e : **a.** *through, throughout, during :* per hiemem, Cato ; per triennium, Cic. ; per decem dies ludi facti sunt, Cic. **b.** *during, in a time of :* per idem tempus, Cic. ; per somnum imago visa, Verg. ; per indutias, per ludos, per otium, etc., Liv. ; per iram fecit, Cic. ; per furorem effata, Verg. **C.** Of other relations. **a.** I n s t r u m e n t a l : (i.) *through, by the agency of, by the aid of, by means of :* ea per Caeciliam geruntur, Cic. ; per exploratores cognovit, Caes. ; per se (per te, etc.), *through himself, of himself, of himself, etc. :* homo per se cognitus, Cic. ; satis per te tibi consulis, Hor. ; per se solus, Liv. ; ipse per se, Cic. (ii.) *by way of, with, by, in, on* (to indicate the manner) : per contumeliam, Caes. ; por cruciatum interfici, Caes. ; per ludum ac iocum, Cic. ; per vim, Sall. ; per artem, Verg. ; per commodum, Liv. (iii.) *by way of, under the name of* or *on the pretext of :* per causam exercendorum remigum, Caes. ; per speciem celebrandarum epularum, Liv. ; per simulationem offici, Tac. ; per fidem aliquem circumvenire, Caes. **b.** C a u s a l (i.) *through, for, by, by reason of, on account of, for the sake of :* per metum mussari, Pl. ; per aetatem ad pugnam inutiles, Caes. ; Cic. ; per causam equitatūs cogendi, Caes. ; per duces stetisse ne vincerent, Liv. ; per Afranium stare quo minus proelio dimicaretur, Caes. (ii.) *thanks to, by permission of, as far as concerns :* nihil quod per leges liceret, Cic. ; neque per senatum hoc efficere potuit, Nep. E s p. with pronouns : per me, per te, etc., *as far as concerns me, you, etc. :* per me vel stertas licet, Cic. ; si per te liceat, Caes. (iii.) In oaths,

entreaties, emphatic statements, *by :* per pol saepe peccas, Pl. ; per deos obtestabatur, Caes. ; per deos, Cic. Often with a word or words coming between *prep.* and Acc. : per ego te deos oro, Ter. ; per ego iura precor, Liv. ; per ego has lacrimas oro, Verg. [Fr. *par.*]

pĕra, ae, *f.* [πήρα], *a bag, wallet ;* Phaedr., Mart.

per-absurdus, a, um, *very absurd :* Cic.

per-accommodātus, a, um, *very convenient :* (in tmesi) Cic. Ep.

per-ācer, ācris, ācre, *very sharp.* T r a n s f. : iudicium, Cic. Ep.

per-acerbus, a, um, *very harsh to the taste :* uva gustatu, Cic. T r a n s f. : mihi peracerbum fuit quod etc., Plin. Ep.

per-acēscō, acēscere, acui, *to become thoroughly sour.* T r a n s f. : ita mihi pectus peracuit, Pl.

per-āctiō, ōnis, *f.* [peragō], *conclusion, last act :* fabulae ; hence, aetatis, Cic. **per-āctus,** a, um, *Part.* peragō.

peracūtē, *adv. very sharply, very acutely :* moveri, Cic.

per-acūtus, a, um, *very sharp.* **1.** L i t. : falx, Mart. **2.** T r a n s f. **a.** Of sound, *very clear or penetrating :* vox, Cic. **b.** Of the intellect, etc. : ad excogitandum, Cic. ; oratio, Cic.

per-adulēscēns, entis, *adj. very young :* homo, Cic.

per-adulēscentulus, i, *m. a very young man :* Nep.

per-aequē, *adv. quite equally* or *evenly, without distinction, uniformly :* Cic. ; Nep.

per-agitō, āre, *to drive* or *hunt about, to harass.* **1.** L i t. : vehementius peragitati ab equitatu, Caes. **2.** T r a n s f. : animos, Sen.

per-agō, agere, ēgi, āctum. **I.** *to carry through to the end, to accomplish, complete.* **a.** I n g e n. : carmen, Enn. ; fabulam aetatis, Cic. ; concilium, Caes. ; inceptum, Verg. ; sententiam, Liv. ; aetatem, vitam, Ov. ; partis suas, Plin. Ep. **b.** In law : *to prosecute to a conviction :* reum, Liv., Ov., etc. ; also, accusationem, Plin. Ep. **II.** *to keep moving about, to stir up, turn thoroughly.* **1.** Lit. : freta remo, Ov. ; humum, Ov. **2.** T r a n s f. **a.** animo omnia, Verg. **b.** *to harass :* totum Sempronium, Cael. ap. Cic. Ep. ; pecora asilus, Sen. Ep. **III.** With Acc. closely connected with per (ago being then *Intrans.*). **1.** Lit. **a.** In gen. *to pass through, traverse :* sol duodena signa, Ov. **b.** Of a thrust : latus ense, Ov. **2.** T r a n s f. **a.** Of time : salubrīs aestates, Hor. ; contentus perages (sc. aetatem), Pers. **b.** In words : *to go through, go over :* verbis auspicia, Liv. ; res pace belloque gestas, Liv. ; res tenuis tenui sermone, Hor.

peragrātiō, ōnis, *f.* [peragrō], *a traversing :* itineris, Cic.

peragrō, āre [ager]. **A.** T r a n s. : *to travel through, traverse.* **1.** L i t. : loca avia, Lucr. ; provincias, Cic. ; saltūs, Verg. **2.** T r a n s f. : omne immensum mente, Lucr. ; eloquentia omnīs peragravit insulas, Cic. **B.** I n t r a n s. (only transf.) : orator per animos hominum, Cic.

per-amāns, antis, *adj. very loving, very fond* : with GEN. : Cic. Ep.

peramanter, *adv. very lovingly* : Cic. Ep.

per-ambulō, āre, *to step or walk through ; to traverse.* **1.** Lit.: aedĭs, Pl.; multas terras, Varr.; rura, Hor. **2.** Transf.: frigus perambulat artūs, Ov.; recte necne crocum floresque perambulet Attae fabula, si dubitem, Hor.

per-amoenus, a, um, *very delightful* : Tac.

per-amplus, a, um, *very large* : Cic.

perangustē, *adv. very narrowly* : Cic.

per-angustus, a, um, *very narrow* : fretum, Cic.; aditus, Caes.; via, Liv.

perannō, āre [annus], *to live through a year:* Suet.

per-antiquus, a, um, *very ancient or old* : Cic.

per-appositus, a, um, *very suitable or apposite* : alicui, Cic.

per-arduus, a, um, *very difficult* : Cic.

per-ārēscō, ere, *to grow very dry* : Varr.

per-āridus, a, um, *very dry* : Cato.

per-argūtus, a, um. Transf.: *very acute, very witty* : homo, Cic.

per-armātus, a, um, *thoroughly armed* : Curt.

per-arō, āre, *to plough through.* Transf. **a.** *to furrow* : rugis ora, Ov. **b.** Of writing on a wax tablet. With ACC. of thing written : Ov. With ACC. of tablet used : Ov.

pērātim, *adv.* [pēra], *bag by bag* : peratim ductitare, Pl.

perattentē, *adv. very attentively* : Cic.

per-attentus, a, um, *very attentive* : Cic.

per-audiendus, a, um, *that must be heard to the end* : Pl.

per-bacchor, ārī, *to carouse or revel through* : multos dies, Cic.

per-beātus, a, um, *very happy* : Cic.

per-bellē, *adv. very prettily* : simulare, Cic. Ep.

per-bene, *adv. very well* : Pl., Cic., Liv.

per-benevolus, a, um, *very friendly* : alicui, Cic. Ep.

per-benignē, *adv. very kindly* : Ter.; *in tmesi* : Cic.

Perbibesia, ae, *f.* [perbibō], *Drink-hard-land* : Pl.

per-bibō, bibere, bibĭ, *to drink up, swallow up.* Transf. **a.** Of plants, i.e. be well watered : Cato. **b.** mihi medullam lassitudo perbibit, Pl. **c.** lacrimas, Ov.; lana colores, Sen. Ep. **d.** haec cum persuasi mihi et perbibi, Sen.

per-bĭtō, ere, *to go to ruin, perish* : fame, Enn.; Pl. Comic.: utinam malo cruciatu in Siciliam perbiteres, Pl.

per-blandus, a, um, *very charming, very attractive*: successor, Cic. Ep.; oratio, Liv.

per-bonus, a, um, *very good* : prandium, Pl.; ager, Cic.

per-brevis, e, *adj. very short, very brief* : orator, Cic.; perbrevi tempore, Cic.; *in tmesi* : altera pars per mihi brevis videtur, Cic. ABL. perbrevi, as *adv.*, *in a very short time* : Cic.

perbreviter, *adv. very briefly* : Cic.

perca, ae, *f.* [πέρκη], *a kind of fish, a perch* : Ov., Plin.

per-calefactus, a, um, *thoroughly warmed* : omnia motu, Lucr.; glaebae a sole, Varr.

per-calluī, *Perf. to have become very hardened, very callous.* Transf.: **a.** civitatis patientia percalluerat, Cic. **b.** *to have got a good knowledge of* (with ACC.): usum rerum, Cic.

per-caluī, *Perf. to have become very warm* : vis venti, Lucr.; umor ab igne solis, Ov.

per-cārus, a, um, *very dear, very costly.* **1.** Lit.: Ter. **2.** Transf. *very dear, very much beloved* : alicui, Cic.; Tac.

per-cautus, a, um, *very cautious* : Cic. Ep.

per-celebror, ārī, *to be talked of everywhere* : totā Siciliā percelebrantur versūs, Cic.; percelebrata sermonibus res est, Cic.

per-celer, eris, *adj. very quick* : interitus, Cic.

per-celeriter, *adv. very quickly* : Cic. Ep.

per-cellō, cellere, culī, culsum. **I.** *to strike down, beat down, knock down, overthrow.* **1.** Lit.: periĭ! perculit me prope, Pl.; eos Martis vis, Cic.; aliquem, Verg.; fulmina duo meam domum, Liv.; ventus plaustrum, Cato. Comic.: plaustrum perculi (*cf.* "I've upset the apple-cart"), Pl. **2.** Transf. **a.** *to overthrow, ruin* : adulescentiam, Cic.; rem publicam, Tac.; aliquem, Suet. **b.** *to scare to death, unnerve* : hostes perculsi, Caes.; haec te vox non perculit? Cic.; ad ducis casum perculsa multitudo, Liv.; is pavor perculit decemviros ut senatum consulerent, Liv.; civitates atrocibus edictis, Tac.; timore perculsi membra, Lucr. Also, *to drive in terror* : quos pavor perculerat in silvas, Liv. **II.** *to strike hard.* **1.** Lit.: legatum fetialem genu, Liv.; aliquem cuspide, Ov. **2.** Transf.: *to smite, thrill* : volucres perculsae corda tuā vi, Lucr.

per-cēnseō, ēre, uī, *to go through in counting, to count over, reckon up.* **1.** Lit.: inveniendi locos, Cic.; captivos, gentis, Liv.; numerum legionum, Tac. **2.** Transf. **a.** *to survey, review* : manipulos, Varr.; orationes, Liv. **b.** *to traverse, travel through* : Thessaliam, Liv.; of the sun, signa, Ov.

perceptiō, ōnis, *f.* [percipiō], *a gathering in, harvesting.* **1.** Lit.: frugum, Cic. **2.** Transf. *comprehension* : in *pl. concepts* : animi perceptiones, Cic.

perceptus, a, um. **I.** *Part.* percipiō. **II.** Noun, **percepta**, ōrum, *n. pl. doctrines, principles, rules* : Cic.

per-cīdō, cidere, cīdī, cīsum [caedō], *to beat or smash to pieces* : os alicui, Pl.

per-cieō, ciēre, and **per-ciō**, cīre, *to move greatly, to stir up, excite* : irā percitus, Pl.; Ter.; irāī fax subdita percit, Lucr.; verbum unum auris omnibus, Lucr. With abuse : istum inpudicum, Pl.

per-cipiō, cipere, cēpī, ceptum (percepset for percēpisset, Pac.) [capiō], *to take thoroughly or wholly, lay hold of.* **A.** Physically. **1.** Lit. **a.** *to get hold of, hold, catch, take in* : Icarus non ullas percipit auras, Ov.; colorem, Plin. **b.** *to gather in, harvest, reap* : fructūs, Cic. **2.** Transf. **a.** Of the senses : *to take in, feel* : sensus suam rem in se, Lucr.; corpore perceptarum voluptatum, Cic.; animus toto percepit pectore flammam, Verg.; rigorem, Ov.; ossibus aestum, Ov.; gaudia, Ov. **b.** Of the feeling as Subject : *to lay hold* *of, seize upon :* mihi horror membra percipit, Pl. ; medullam ventris fames, Pl. ; vitae percipit humanos odium, Lucr. **c.** Of hearing : ne, quod hic agimus, erus percipiat fieri, Pl. ; orationem, Caes. ; nunc querellae, nunc minae percipiebantur, Liv. ; quae dicam, Cic. ; aures sonum, Cic. **d.** *to gather in, harvest, reap :* fructum victoriae, Caes. ; praemia, Caes. ; vestri offici praemium, Cic. ; Nep. ; Suet. **B.** Mentally. **a.** *to take in by hearing, learn, know of :* fugam, Caes. ; omnium civium nomina, Cic. With *Indir. Quest. :* Verg. **b.** *to grasp with the mind, comprehend, understand :* usum eius generis proeliorum, Caes. ; aliquid animo, Cic. ; praecepta artis, Cic. ; virtutem et humanitatem, Cic.

percitus, a, um. **I.** *Part.* percieō. **II.** Adj. : *greatly roused or provoked.* **1.** Lit. : animo irato ac percito aliquid facere, Cic. **2.** Transf. : *excitable, impetuous :* corpore et linguā percitum, Sall. ; ingenium, Liv.

per-cīvīlis, e, adj. *very courteous :* sermo, Suet.

percoctus, a, um, *Part.* percoquō.

per-cognitus, a, um, *very well known :* Plin.

per-cōlō, āre, *to strain through, to filter :* vinum, Cato. In *Mid. :* umor per terras percolatur, Lucr.

per-cōlō, colere, colui, cultum. **I.** *to honour, revere, reverence greatly :* patrem, Pl. ; Tac. **II.** *to honour, embellish :* multos praefecturis, Tac. ; aliquid eloquentiā, Tac. **III.** *to crown, complete :* incohata, Plin. Ep.

per-cōmis, e, adj. *very friendly, very courteous :* Cic.

per-commodē, adv. *very conveniently, very well :* Cic.

per-commodus, a, um, *very suitable* (with Dat.) : castris, Liv.

percontātiō, ōnis, f. [percontor], *a searching inquiry :* Cic. ; derecta, Liv. ; ex captivis percontatio facta, Liv. ; percontationibus reperire, Caes.

percontātor, ōris, m. [percontor], *an inquisitive person :* Pl., Hor.

percontor, ārī [contus]. Lit. *to sound* (water) *with a pole ;* hence, *to question strictly, to inquire, investigate :* Cic. With Acc. of person : Pl. ; aliquem de aliquā re, Cic., Liv. With Acc. of person and *Indir. Quest. :* Pl., Cic., Liv., etc. With *si* and *Subj. :* Liv. With double Acc. : Pl., Hor., Liv. ; ex aliquo (with *Indir. Quest.*), Cic. ; ab aliquo, Cic., Curt. With *Indir. Quest.:* Pl. With *si* and *Subj. :* Liv.

per-contumāx, ācis, adj. *very obstinate :* Ter.

per-coquō, coquere, coxī, coctum, *to cook thoroughly.* **1.** Lit. : prandium, Pl. **2.** Transf. **a.** *to heat thoroughly :* terram, umorem, Lucr. **b.** *to ripen :* uvas, Ov. ; messem, Plin. Ep. **c.** *to scorch, to blacken by the heat of the sun :* nigra virum percocto saecla colore, Lucr.

per-crēbēscō, crēbēscere, crēbuī, and **per-crēbrēscō,** crēbrēscere, crēbruī, *to become very frequent or prevalent, to be spread abroad ;* esp.. *of reports :* omnium sermone, Cic. ;

cum fama per orbem terrarum percrebuisset (with Acc. and *Inf.*), Caes.

per-crepō, crepāre, crepuī, *to resound, ring :* lucus vocibus, Cic.

per-crucior, ārī, *Mid. to torment oneself :* Pl.

perculsus, a, um, *Part.* percellō.

percultus, a, um. **I.** *Part.* percolō. **II.** Adj. *highly adorned :* femina, Pl.

per-cupidus, a, um, *very fond of* (with Gen.) : Cic. Ep.

per-cupiō, cupere, *to wish or desire eagerly :* Ter. With *Inf. :* Pl.

per-cūriōsus, a, um, *very diligent or inquisitive :* Cic.

per-cūrō, āre, *to tend till cured, heal completely.* **1.** Lit. : percurato vulnere, Liv. **2.** Transf. : mentem aegram, Sen. Ep.

per-currō, currere, cucurrī or currī, cursum, *to run or hasten through or over ; to traverse.* **A.** With *ad* or *per* and Acc. **1.** Lit. : ad forum, Ter. ; per mare et terras, Lucr. ; per temonem, Caes. **2.** Transf. : per omnis civitates oratio mea, Cic. **B.** With Acc. (going closely with the *per*). **1.** Lit. : agrum Picenum, Caes. ; aristas, Ov. ; labro calamos, Lucr. ; pectine telas, Verg. ; luna fenestras, Prop. **2.** Transf. **a.** In speaking : partes, quas modo percucurri, Cic. ; multas res oratione, Cic. ; omnia poenarum nomina, Verg. ; modice beneficia, Tac. **b.** With the eye or mind : veloci oculo, Hor. ; paginas, Liv. ; multa animo et cogitatione, multa etiam legendo, Cic. *Impers. Pass. :* Cic. **c.** Of State-offices : amplissimos honores, Suet. ; Plin. Ep. **d.** Of feelings, emotions : pectora occulto metu percurrente, Curt.

percursātiō, ōnis, f. [percursō], *a travelling through :* Cic. ; Italiae, Cic.

percursiō, ōnis, f. [percurrō], *a running through or over.* Transf. **a.** With the mind : multarum rerum, Cic. **b.** Rhet. : *a hasty passing over a subject :* Cic.

percursō, āre [*freq.* percurrō], *to range or rove about.* With Locat. Abl. : finibus nostris, Liv. With Acc. : ripas, Plin. Pan.

percursus, a, um, *Part.* percurrō.

percussiō, ōnis, f. [percutiō], *a beating, striking.* **1.** Lit. : capitis, digitorum, Cic. **2.** Transf. in music, *a beating time ;* hence, *time :* in *pl. :* numerorum, Cic. ; Quint.

percussor, ōris, m. [percutiō], *a striker;* esp. of an assassin : Cic., Tac.

percussus, a, um, *Part.* percutiō.

percussus, ūs, m. [percutiō], *repeated beating :* Ov., Sen.

per-cutiō, cutere, cussī, cussum (*Perf.* percusti for percussisti, Hor.) (for the *Pres.* and *Imperf.* ferio is commonly used, q. v.) [quatiō]. **I.** *to strike through and through.* **1.** Lit. **a.** *to kill with a blow, wound sorely :* quo percusso atque exanimato, Caes. ; gladio percussus, Cic. ; Mamilio pectus, Liv. Esp. of beheading : securi percussus, Cic., Liv., Ov. **b.** *to cut through :* venam, Sen. Ep. **c.** *to make by cutting through :* fossam, Plin. Ep. **2.** Transf. **a.** Comic. of the effect of drink : meraclo se fiore Liberi, Pl. **b.** Of the feelings: calamitate, Cic. **c.** Colloq. of cheating: aliquem probe, Pl.; Cic.; hominem strategemate, Cic. Ep. **II.** *to strike or beat hard.* **A.** In gen. **1.** Lit.: lapidem lapis, Lucr.; tellurem tridenti, Verg.; ianuam manu, Tib.; aerem pennis, Ov.; lyram, Ov.; turres de caelo percussae, Cic.; luna solis radiis percussa, Lucr.; color percussus luce refulgit, Lucr. In *Mid.:* matres pectora percussae, Verg. **2.** Transf. of the mind and emotions: *to shock, make a deep impression upon, affect deeply:* aliquem inani cogitatione, Cic.; percussisti me de oratione prolatā, Cic. Ep.; laetitiā metuque percussus, Verg. **B.** Of money: *to strike, stamp, coin.* **1.** Lit.: nummum argenteum notā sideris capricorni, Suet. **2.** Transf.: ut omnia facta dictaque tua unā formā percussa sint, Sen. Ep.

per-decōrus, a, um, *very comely* or *pretty:* Plin. Ep.

per-dēlīrus, a, um, *very silly* or *foolish:* perdelirum esse videtur, Lucr.

per-depsō, ere, *to knead thoroughly.* Transf.: Cat.

per-difficilis, e, adj. *very difficult:* quaestio, Cic.; navigatio, Cic. Ep. *Sup.:* perdifficillimus aditus, Liv.

perdifficiliter, adv. *with great difficulty:* Cic.

per-dignus, a, um, *very worthy:* homo tuā amicitiā, Cic. Ep.

per-dīligēns, entis, adj. *very diligent:* Cic. Ep.

perdīligenter, adv. *very diligently:* Cic.

per-disco, discere, didicī, *to learn thoroughly, to get by heart:* omnia iura belli, Cic. With *Inf.:* Cic. With Acc. and *Inf.:* Pl.

per-disertē, adv. *very eloquently:* Cic.

perditē, adv. **I.** *in an abandoned manner:* se gerere, Cic. Ep. **II.** *desperately, excessively:* amare, Ter.; conari, Quint.

perditor, ōris, m. [perdō], *a ruiner, destroyer:* Cic.; rei publicae, Cic.

perditus, a, um. **I.** *Part.* perdō. **II.** Adj. **A.** In fortune, health, etc.: *ruined, desperate.* **a.** Of persons: Pl., Cic.; rebus omnibus, Cic. As Noun: valetudo, Cic.; amor, Cat. **B.** Morally: *abandoned, outcast, reckless, infamous.* **a.** Of persons: Cic. *Comp.:* Cic. Ep., Cat. *Sup.:* Cic. **b.** Of things: consilia, iudicia, vita, nequitia, Cic.

per-diū, adv. *for a great while, very long:* Cic.

per-diūturnus, a, um, *that lasts very long, protracted:* Cic.

per-dīves, itis, adj. *very rich:* Cic.

perdīx, īcis, m.f. [πέρδιξ], *a partridge:* Varr., Mart. [Fr. *perdrix.*]

per-dō, dere, didī, ditum (*Pres. Subj.* perduim, Pl., Ter.; also Cic. in phr. di te perduint'; for *Pass.*, exc. in *Part.*, pereō is usual), *to put through, do to pieces.* **1.** Lit.: *to make away with; to destroy, ruin:* aliquem, Pl., Cic.; perditus aere alieno, Cic.; Iuppiter fruges, Cic.; aliquem capitis (i.e. by a capital charge), Pl. Esp. in execrations: di te perduint, Pl., Ter., Cic. **2.** Transf. **a.** civitatem, Cic. Ep. **b.** Morally: adulescentem, Cic.; Sybarin

amando, Hor. **c.** *to waste, squander:* Pl., Ter.; tempus, operam, Cic.; Hor.; oleum et operam, Cic. Ep.; verba, Ov. **d.** *to lose utterly* or *irrevocably:* spem, Pl.; nomen, Ter.; memoriam, litem, causam, libertatem, Cic.; omnis fructūs industriae et fortunae, Cic. Ep.; liberos, Cic. Ep. Of a gambler: Ov.; with Acc.: Juv., Suet.

per-doceō, docēre, docuī, doctum, *to teach* or *instruct thoroughly:* aliquid mortalis ore, Ov.; multorum exitio perdocti, Lucr.; suam stultitiam, Quint.; res difficilis ad perdocendum, Cic. With Acc. (of Object) and *Inf.:* me coquitare, Pl.; Ov. With Acc. (of Object), and Acc. and *Inf.:* sol et luna perdocuere homines annorum tempora verti, Lucr.

perdoctē, adv. *very skilfully:* Pl.

perdoctus, a, um. **I.** *Part.* perdoceō. **II.** Adj.: *very learned, very skilful:* Pl., Ter., Cic.

per-dolēscō, dolēscere, doluī [doleō], *to become very indignant* or *pained, to take deeply to heart:* Ter. With Acc. and *Inf.:* Caes.

per-domō, āre, uī, itum, *to tame* or *subdue completely.* **1.** Lit.: Latium, Liv.; tauros furentis, Ov.; unum virum, Ov. **2.** Transf.: sulco solum, Plin. Ep.

per-dormiscō, ere, [dormiō], *to fall asleep and sleep on:* Pl.

per-dūcō, dūcere, dūxī, ductum, *to lead, bring, conduct through to a person* or *place.* **1.** Lit. **a.** In gen.: filium illuc, Ter.; omnis incolumis navis, Caes.; legiones ad aliquem, Cic. Ep.; legionem in Allobrogas, Caes.; bovem ad stabula, Verg.; in theatrum, Suet. **b.** Of walls, roads, water, etc.: a lacu ad montem murum, Caes.; porticum, Liv.; viam a Bononiā Aretium, Liv. **c.** *to spread over:* corpus odore ambrosiae, Verg. **2.** Transf. **a.** *to bring to a goal:* aliquem ex humili loco ad summam dignitatem, Caes.; aliquem ad amplissimos honores, Cic.; ad exitum, Cic. Ep.; aliquid ad finem, Lucr.; eo rem perduxit, Nep. **b.** *to draw* or *bring over, to persuade, induce to:* illam ad me suadelā meā, Pl.; Cic.; Hor.; aliquem ad (in, Caes.) suam sententiam, Cic. Ep.; aliquem ad se magnis pollicitationibus, Caes. With *ut* and *Subj.:* Pl. **c.** *to draw out, prolong, continue:* res disputatione ad mediam noctem perducitur, Caes.; Liv.; Cic. Ep. in noctem orationibus perductis, Liv.

perductō, āre [*freq.* perdūcō], *to lead, conduct to:* Pl.

perductor, ōris, m. [perdūcō], *a guide, conductor:* Pl.; esp. *a pimp, pander:* Cic.

per-dūdum, adv. *a very long time ago:* Pl.

perduelliō, ōnis, f. [perduellis], *hostile* or *traitorous conduct against one's country, treason:* alicui actionem perduellionis intendere, Cic.; duumviros qui Horatio perduellionem iudicent, Liv.

perduellis, is, m. [per-, duellis, i.e. bellum], *deadly enemy.* **I.** *a public* or *foreign enemy;* esp. in *pl., those engaged in war against one's country* (archaic for hostes): Pl., Cic., Liv. **II.** *a private enemy:* Pl.

per-dūrō, āre, *to last* or *hold out, to endure :* Ter., Ov., Suet.

Peredia, ae, *f.* [peredō], *Gobbledom, Eat-land* (*cf.* Perbibesia) : Pl.

per-edō, ēsse, ēdī, ēsum, *to eat up, consume :* **1.** Lit. : cibum, Pl. **2.** Transf. **a.** sale saxa peresa, Lucr. ; vellera morbo peresa, Verg. ; nec peredit impositam celer ignis Aetnam, Hor. **b.** languoribus peresus, Cat. ; quos durus amor crudeli tabe peredit, Verg.

per-egrē (per-egrī, Pl.), *adv.* [per ager]. **I.** *in a foreign place, abroad, away from home :* Pl. ; depugnare, Cic. ; habitare, Liv. Transf. : dum peregre est animus, Hor. **II.** *from foreign parts, from abroad :* venire, Pl. ; redire, Ter. ; in regnum Romam accitos, Liv. ; nuntiare, Liv. **III.** *to foreign parts, abroad :* abire, Pl., Plin. ; exire, Hor. ; proficisci, Suet.

peregrīnābundus, a, um [peregrīnor], *travelling about :* Liv.

peregrīnātiō, ōnis, *f.* [peregrīnor]. **I.** *a being* or *living abroad, travel :* Cic., Quint., etc. ; tempus in peregrinatione consumere, Cic. Ep. In *pl. :* Cic. **II.** Of animals : *a roaming, ranging :* Cic.

peregrīnātor, ōris, *m.* [peregrīnor], *one who travels about :* Cic. Ep.

peregrīnitās, ātis, *f.* [peregrīnus]. **I.** *the status of a* peregrinus *or foreigner :* Suet. **II.** *foreign habits* or *manners :* Cic. **III.** *a foreign tone* or *accent :* Quint.

peregrīnor, ārī [peregrīnus], *to be* or *live in foreign parts, to travel about.* **1.** Lit. : in alienā civitate, Cic. ; totā Asiā, Cic. **2.** Transf. **a.** haec studia nobiscum peregrinantur, Cic. ; animus late longeque, Cic. **b.** *to be a stranger :* philosophia Romae, Cic. ; vestrae aures, Cic.

peregrīnus, a, um [peregrē], *of foreigners* or *foreign places, foreign.* **1.** Lit. : navis, homo, facies, Pl. ; reges, Cic. ; mulier, Hor. ; amnes, caelum, fasti, Ov. ; labor (i.e. of travelling), Cat. ; terror (i.e. of a foreign enemy), Liv. ; urbe in ipsā velut peregrinum otium, Tac. ; of a praetor's jurisdiction : sors (the office of praetor peregrinus, who handled cases where a foreigner was concerned), Liv. As Noun, *m.* and *f.* *a foreigner, alien :* Pl., Ter., Cic. **2.** Transf. : *strange, inexperienced :* in agendo, Cic. [It. *pellegrino* ; Fr. *pèlerin* ; Eng. *pilgrim.*]

per-ēlegāns, antis, *adj.* *very fine* or *elegant :* genus, oratio, Cic.

perēleganter, *adv.* *very elegantly :* dicere, Cic.

per-ēloquēns, entis, *adj.* *very eloquent :* Cic.

peremnia, ium, *n. pl.* (*sc.* auspicia) [amnis], *the auspices taken on crossing a river* or *a spring :* Cic.

peremptus, a, um, *Part.* perimō.

perendiē, *adv.* [per, *cf.* πέραν and diēs], *on the day after to-morrow :* Pl., Cic. Ep.

perendinus, a, um [perendiē], *with dies* expressed or understood, (*the day*) *after to-morrow :* utrum diem tertium, an perendinum dici oporteret, Cic. ; perendino die, Caes. ; tu in perendinum paratus sis, Pl.

Perenna, *f. adj.* [per annus], *ever-circling,* an epithet of Anna, goddess of the moon : Ov.

perennis, e, *adj.* (ABL. *sing.* perenne, Ov.) [annus], *that lasts* or *continues the whole year through.* **1.** Lit. : militia, Liv. **2.** Transf. **a.** Of water : fons, Caes. ; aquae, Cic. ; amnis, Liv., Ov. ; puteus, Hor. **b.** In gen. : lucrum, Pl. ; fons gloriae, Cic. ; cursus stellarum, Cic. ; motio, Cic. ; maiorum virtus, Cic. ; loquacitas, Cic. ; animus in rem publicam, Cic. ; adamas, Ov. *Comp. :* monumentum aere perennius, Hor.

perenni-servos, ī, *m.* [perennis], *a perpetual slave :* Pl.

perennitās, ātis, *f.* [perennis], *lastingness, perpetual duration :* cibi, Pl. ; fontium perennitates, Cic.

perennō, āre [perennus, *cf.* Perenna], *to last for many years :* domus, Ov. ; arte amor, Ov.

pĕrenticida, ae, *m.* for pĕricīda [pēra caedō], *a cut-purse* (comically in allusion to parenticida) : Pl.

per-eō, īre, iī, itum (used as *Pass.* of perdō, q.v.), *to go through.* **1.** Lit. **a.** Of water : *to go to waste, perish :* imbres, Lucr. ; lymphae dolium pereuntis, Hor. ; vena aquae, Ov. **b.** *to go to waste, pass away, perish, be destroyed :* aedes cum fundamento, Pl. ; tantam pecuniam tam brevi tempore perire potuisse, Cic. ; Hor. ; urbes funditus, Hor. ; sole tepente nives, Ov. **c.** Of men : *to perish, lose one's life, die :* Caes., Cic., Hor., etc. ; naufragio, cruciatu, fame, Cic. ; hominum manibus, Verg. ; morbo, Hor. **2.** Transf. **a.** Of labour, lawsuits, etc. : *to be lost, wasted, spent in vain :* oleum et opera, Cic. Ep. ; actiones et res, Lucr. ; Liv. ; labor, Ov. ; minae, Ter. **b.** *to perish, be destroyed :* regna, Verg. **c.** Of a piece in a game : *to be slain,* i.e. taken : Ov. **d.** Of love : plurimum perire, Cat. ; indigno Gallus amore, Verg. ; quo beatus vulnere, quā pereat sagittā, Hor. With Acc. of the beloved : Pl. **e.** Morally : pudor, Pl. ; fides, Pl., Cic. ; virtus, Ov. **f.** In despair or tone of exaggeration : *to be lost, ruined, undone :* nisi illud perdo argentum, pereundum est mihi, Pl. ; perii animo, Pl. ; ingenio perii, Ov. ; quid fieri tum potuit ? iam pridem perieramus, Cic. Ep. Hence, perii, as an exclamation of despair, *I am lost, I'm undone :* perii, interii, occidi ! Pl. ; peristi, si intrassis intra limen, Pl. ; periimus, actum est, Ter. ; peream, si etc., Ov.

per-equitō, āre, *to ride through* or *about :* inter duas acies, Caes. ; longe ex viā, Liv. With Acc. (going closely with the *per*) : aciem, Cic.

per-errō, āre, *to wander, roam through* or *about.* **1.** Lit. : pontum, Verg. ; forum, Hor. ; freta, Ov. ; serpentis malum totam pererrat, Verg. In *Pass.,* Verg. **2.** Transf. **a.** Of a boxer trying to find an opening : omnem arte locum, Verg. **b.** With the eyes : totumque pererrat luminibus tacitis, Verg.

per-ērudītus, a, um, *very learned :* Cic. Ep.

perēsus, a, um, *Part.* perdō.

per-excelsus, a, um, *very high :* locus, Cic.

perexiguē, *adv.* *very meagrely :* Cic. Ep.

per-exiguus, a, um, *very small, tiny* (of size or amount): frumentum, Caes. ; semen, Cic. ; argentum, Liv. ; loci spatium, Caes. ; dies, Cic. ; bona corporis, Cic.

per-fabricō, āre, *to work over thoroughly.* Transf. *to take in, overreach* : aliquem, Pl.

per-facētē, adv. *very brilliantly* or *wittily* : Cic.

per-facētus, a, um, *very brilliant* (of persons or remarks) : Cic.

per-facilis, e, adj. **I.** *very easy* : disciplina cognitu perfacilis, Cic. ; Caes. *Neut.* Acc. as *Adv.* : Cic. **II.** *very courteous* : in audiendo, Cic. *Neut.* Acc. as *Adv.* : *very readily* or *willingly* : Pl.

per-familiāris, e, adj. *very intimate, very familiar* : alicui, Cic. Ep. As Noun, *a very intimate friend* : Epicuri, Cic.

perfectē, adv. *fully, completely, perfectly* : Cic.

perfectiō, ōnis, f. [perficiō], *a finishing.* **a.** *completion* : operum maximorum, Cic. **b.** *perfection* : hanc absolutionem perfectionemque in oratore desiderans, Cic.

perfector, ōris, m. [perficiō], *a finisher, perfecter* : voluptatum, Ter. ; stilus dicendi, Cic.

perfectus, a, um. **I.** *Part.* perficiō. **II.** Adj. : *finished, complete, perfect.* **a.** Of persons : orator, Cic. ; in dicendo, Cic. ; in geometriā, Cic. ; in arte, Ov. **b.** Of things : naturae, Cic. ; virtus, officium, ratio, Cic. *Comp.* : Cic., Hor. *Sup.* : Cic., Juv.

perferēns, entis. **I.** *Part.* perferō. **II.** Adj. : *very enduring* or *patient* : with Gen. : iniuriarum, Cic.

per-ferō, ferre, tulī, lātum, *to bear* or *carry through.* **1.** Lit. **a.** corpus Spartam, Nep. ; venti eum in ultimas terras, Cic. Also, pavor eos in silvas, Liv. ; Romanos ira eadem in castra, Liv. ; perfertur circa collem clamor, Liv. Poet. : lapis ictum, Verg. **b.** Of news, messages, etc. : mandata, Caes. ; ad aliquem litteras, alicui nuntium, Cic. Ep. ; epistulam, Nep. ; opinio perfertur, Caes. ; res secundae nuntiis ac litteris perferebantur, Caes. ; nuntius incensas perfert navis, Verg. ; cum ad eum fama tanti exercitūs perlata esset, Liv. **c.** Of a burden : *to carry to the end* or *successfully* : onus, Hor. ; gravissimae navium, Liv. ; partum, Plin. Poet. : intrepidos ad fata novissima vultūs, Ov. **2.** Transf. **a.** *to carry through, carry to a successful issue* : legem, Cic., Liv. ; rogationem, Cic. Ep., Liv. ; id quod suscepi, Cic. ; iussa omnia, Prop. ; mandata, Tac. **b.** *to bear, endure to the end, bear patiently* or *with courage* : omnis indignitates contumeliasque, Caes. ; militum conspectum, Caes. ; frigus, famem, sitim, crudelitatem, avaritiam, superbiam, etc., Cic. ; laborem, pauperiem, Verg. ; decem annorum poenam, Nep. With Acc. and *Inf.* : Prop., Tac.

perfica, ae, f. adj. [perficiō], *perfecting* : natura, Lucr.

per-ficiō, ficere, fēcī, fectum [faciō], *to do* or *make thoroughly* or *successfully, to complete, finish, accomplish.* **1.** Lit. : pontem,

munitiones, Caes. ; candelabrum e gemmis, Cic. ; murum, Liv. ; pocula argento, Verg. **2.** Transf. **a.** Of work begun, plans, etc. : comitia, Caes., Liv. ; bellum, dilectum, lustrum, censum, Liv. ; conata, Caes. ; cogitata, instituta, scelus, Cic. ; munus, Verg. So also, centum annos, Hor. **b.** *to make perfect, to perfect* : aliquem citharā, Ov. ; artem, Suet. **c.** *to bring about, to cause, effect* : with *ut* or *ne* and *Subj.* : Ter., Caes., Cic., etc.

per-fidēlis, e, adj. *very trusty, very faithful* : Cic. Ep.

perfidia, ae, f. [perfidus], *faithlessness, treachery, falsehood* : Caes., Cic., Tac., Juv., etc. In *pl.* : Pl.

perfidiōsē, adv. *faithlessly, treacherously* : Pl., Cic. *Comp.* : Suet.

perfidiōsus, a, um [perfidia], *faithless, treacherous.* **a.** Of persons : Cic., Tac. *Sup.* : Cic. **b.** Of things : amor, Pl. ; perfidiosum est (with *Inf.*) : Cic. *Comp.* : Cic. Ep.

perfidus, a, um [fidēs], *faithless, treacherous.* **a.** Of persons : Cic. As Noun : Juv. **b.** Of things : via, Prop. ; arma, verba, Ov. **c.** *Neut. Intern.* Acc. : perfidum ridens, Hor.

per-fīgō, fīgere, fīxī, fīxum, *to pierce through* : of a thunder-bolt : multaque perfigit, Lucr. ; gelidis telis perfixa pavoris, Lucr.

perflābilis, e, adj. [perflō], *that can be blown through* : Cic.

per-flāgitiōsus, a, um, *very shameful* : Cic.

per-flō, āre, *to blow through* or *over.* **I.** With Acc. going closely with the *per* : venti nubila, Lucr. ; venti terras turbine perflant, Verg. ; colles perflantur, Cic. **II.** With Acc. governed by *flo* : perflans murmura conchā, Luc.

per-fluctuō, āre, *to surge through* : Lucr.

per-fluō, fluere, fluxī, *to flow to waste, leak away.* **1.** Lit. : omnia pertusum congesta quasi in vas commoda perfluxere, Lucr. **2.** Transf. of inability to keep a secret : hac atque illāc perfluo, Ter.

per-fodiō, fodere, fōdī, fōssum. **I.** *to dig* or *pierce through, transfix* : parietes, Pl., Cic. ; montem, Varr. ; Cic. ; thorax perfossus, Verg. ; pectus, Plin. Ep. **II.** *to make by digging through, to excavate* : fretum, Liv.

per-forō, āre (in *tmesi,* perque forāre, Lucr.) **I.** *to bore, pierce through* : navem, Cic. ; ense latus, Ov. **II.** *to make by boring* : duo lumina, Cic. ; vias ad oculos a sede animae, Cic.

per-fortiter, adv. *very bravely* : Ter.

perfossor, ōris, m. [perfodiō], *a digger* or *breaker through* : parietum, Pl.

per-fōssus, a, um, *Part.* perfodiō.

perfrāctus, a, um, *Part.* perfringō.

per-fremō, ere, *to roar* or *snort along* : delphini, Acc. ap. Cic.

per-frequēns, entis, adj. *much frequented* : emporium, Liv.

per-fricō, fricāre, fricuī, frictum and fricātum, *to rub all over.* **1.** Lit. : caput unguento, Cic. ; caput sinistrā manu, Cic. ; dentis, Ov. **2.** Transf. : frontem, faciem, os (i.e. to cover up all appearance of shame, put on a bold face), Cic., Quint., Mart.

per-frigefaciō, facere, *to make quite cold, send a chill over*. T r a n s f. of fear: alicui cor, Pl.

per-frigēscō, frigēscere, frixī, *to catch a bad cold :* Varr., Juv.

per-frigidus, a, um, *very cold :* Cic.

per-fringō, fringere, frēgī, frāctum [frangō]. **I.** *to break through*. **1.** L i t.: munitiones, Caes.; phalangem pilis, Caes.; dextrā perfringere, Verg.; iumenta glaciem, Liv.; muros, domos, Tac. **2.** T r a n s f.: omnia repagula iuris, Cic.; conspirationem, Cic. Without Acc.: eloquentia, Cic. **II.** *to break to pieces, shatter, shiver*. **1.** L i t.: elephanto pugno bracchium, Pl.; perfracto saxo sortes erupere, Cic.; naves proras, Liv.; saxo caput, Liv.; Ov. **2.** T r a n s f.: decreta senatūs, Cic.; omnia cupiditate ac furore, Cic.

perfrūctus, a, um, *Part.* perfruor.

per-fruor, fruī, frūctus. **I.** *to experience the full benefit* or *enjoyment of :* ad perfruendas voluptates, Cic. With ABL.: laetitiā, Cic.; sapientiae laude, Cic.; otio, Cic. Ep. **II.** *to fulfil, perform* (with ABL.): mandatis patris, Ov.

perfuga, ae, m. [fugiō], *a deserter* to the enemy (strictly, *one who takes refuge with the enemy ;* dis . transfuga, *one who changes sides) :* Caes., Cic., Liv.

per-fugiō, fugere, fūgī, *to flee for refuge*. **a.** In gen.: ad Helvetios, Caes.; ad Porsennam, Liv.; ad tribunal, Tac.; in fidem Aetolorum, Liv. **b.** Of military desertion : a Pompeio ad Caesarem, Caes.; hostes ad nostros imperatores, Cic.

perfugium, i, n. [perfugiō], *a place of refuge, shelter*. **1.** L i t.: petere, pedibus parere, Pl.; paludes quo perfugio fuerant usi, Caes.; hiemis, Cic. **2.** T r a n s f.: perfugium unum, una spes reliqua est Roscio, Cic.; desperatissimum, Cic.; haec studia perfugium praebent, Cic.; perfugium omnium laborum somnus, Cic.

per-fūnctiō, ōnis, f. [perfungor], *a performing, discharging :* honorum, laborum, Cic.

perfūnctus, a, um, *Part.* perfungor.

per-fundō, fundere, fūdī, fūsum, *to pour over, bathe, drench*. **1.** L i t. **a.** In gen.: aliquem aquā ferventi, Cic.; fluviis pecus, Verg.; perfusus liquidis odoribus, Hor.; aliquem lacrimis, Ov.; artūs perfudit sudor, Verg. In *Mid.:* boves hic perfunduntur, Varr. **b.** Of dyeing : *to soak, steep :* ostro perfusae vestes, Verg. **2.** T r a n s f. **a.** Of non-liquids : sol perfundens omnia luce, Lucr.; cubiculum plurimo sole perfunditur, Plin. Ep.; omne genus perfusa coloribus, Lucr.; canitiem pulvere, Verg.; auro tecta, Sen. Ep. **b.** Of the senses and mind : *to steep, flood :* sensus iucunditate quādam perfunditur, Cic.; laetitiā, Cic.; gaudio, timore, Liv. E s p. of fear: qui me horror perfudit ! Cic. Ep.; nos iudicio perfundere, Cic. **c.** In *Mid.* or with *Refl. Pron. : to* have *a superficial sprinkling* or *smattering of :* studia, quibus perfundi satis est, Sen. Ep.

per-fungor, fungī, fūnctus, *to perform, discharge fully*. **1.** L i t. With ABL.: rei publicae muneribus, Cic.; honoribus et laboribus, Cic. Ep.; opere, militiā, Cic.

O c c. with idea of enjoyment: Ter.; omnibus bonis, Sulpic. ap. Cic. Ep.; epulis, Ov.; with Acc.: omnia vitāl praemia, Lucr. **2.** T r a n s f. *to go through, undergo :* Cic. With ABL.: periculis, Cic.; molestiā, Cic. Ep.; vitā (i.e. loss of life), Lucr.; fato, Liv. In *Pass.* sense : memoria perfuncti periculi, Cic.

per-furō, ere, *to rage wildly :* acri cum fremitu ventus, Lucr.; incensus et ipse perfurit, Verg.

perfūsōrius, a, um [perfundō], *superficial :* Sen. Ep.

perfūsus, a, um, *Part.* perfundō.

(1.) Pergamum, ī, n., and **Pergamus**, ī. f.: oftener **Pergama**, ōrum, n. pl. *the citadel of Troy*, poet. *Troy ;* **Pergameus**, a, um, *Trojan*.

(2.) Pergamum, ī, n. *a city in Mysia, on the Caicus, the capital of the kingdom of the Attalids, famous for its library and works of art ;* **Pergamēnus**, a, um; **Pergamēnī**, ōrum, m. pl., *its inhabitants*.

per-gaudeō, ēre, *to rejoice greatly* (with Acc. and *Inf.*) : Cic. Ep.

pergō, pergere, perrēxī, perrēctum [per regō]. **A.** T r a n s.: l i t. *to direct straight through ;* hence, *to go on uninterruptedly* or *undeviatingly with, to continue* or *proceed with to an end*. **1.** L i t.: iter, Ter., Sall., Tac., etc. With *Inf.:* Pl.; ire, Cic., Liv. **2.** T r a n s f. (with *Inf.*): pergin' (= pergisne), scelesta, perplexe loqui ? Ter.; animum exsolvere, Lucr.; istas partīs explicare, Cic. **B.** I n t r a n s.: *to go straight on, continue*. **1.** L i t.: opsonatum, Pl.; horsum pergunt, Ter.; eādem viā pergere, Cic.; in Macedoniam, ad Plancium, Cic.; ad castra, Caes.; Romam, Liv. **2.** T r a n s f.: *to pass on, proceed to :* pergamus ad reliqua, Cic. E s p. in speaking : *to go on, continue :* Cic., Liv.; sed perge de Caesare, Cic. Also of one who has not yet spoken : pergite, Pierides, Verg.

per-graecor, ārī, *to play the complete Greek* (i.e. *to carouse*): Pl.

per-grandis, e, *adj. very large*. **1.** L i t.: gemma, Cic. **2.** T r a n s f. **a.** lucrum, Pl.; vectigal, Cic. **b.** Of age : *very old :* pergrandis natu, Liv.

per-graphicus, a, um, *very skilful, very artful :* sycophanta, Pl.

per-grātus, a, um, *very agreeable, very pleasant :* litterae, Cic. *Neut.* as Noun : pergratum mihi feceris, Cic.; also *in tmesi :* Cic. Ep.

per-gravis, e, *adj. very weighty*. T r a n s f. *very important :* Ter.; testes, oratio, Cic.

per-graviter, *adv. very gravely, very seriously :* reprehendere aliquem, Cic.

pergula, ae, f. [pergō: cf. tegula, from tegō], *a projection ;* hence, *a roofed verandah, balcony*, or *loggia :* used as a painter's studio ; Plin.; as an astrologer's observatory : Suet. ; as a school : Suet. ; hence *the scholars :* Juv.; as a brothel : Pl., Prop. (pergula may perhaps have been *a room above a shop*, e.g. at Pompeii).

Pergus, ī, m. *a lake in Sicily, near Henna, where Pluto carried off Proserpina*.

per-hibeō, ēre [habeō]. **I.** *to hold, maintain, assert :* Electra, ut Graii perhibent, Atlantido arctus, Verg.; Pl.; bene qui coniciet, vatem hunc perhibebo optimum, Cic.; Enn. *Pass.:* montes, qui esse aurei perhibentur, Pl.; Cic.; Verg. **II.** *to produce* or *cite* as an instance or evidence : operam rei publicae fortem, Cato; quem Caecilius suo nomine perhiberet, Cic. Ep.; nec minus est Agesilaus ille perhibendus, Cic. Ep.; testimonium, Varr. **III.** *to bring, give :* alicui palmam, Plin.; hence *to attribute ;* magnam auctoritatem huic animali, Plin.

per-hīlum, *adv. very little :* Lucr.

perhonōrificē, *adv. very respectfully :* Cic.

per-honōrificus, a, um. **I.** *that does one much honour, very honourable :* discessus, Cic. **II.** *that shows much honour* or *respect, very respectful :* in me, Cic. Ep.

per-horrēscō, horrēscere, horruī, *to begin to tremble* or *shudder greatly :* toto corpore, Cic.; clamore Aetna, Ov. With Acc. of thing *at which :* hanc tantam religionem, Cic.; Bosporum, Hor.

per-horridus, a, um, *very frightful :* stagna perhorrida situ, Liv.

per-hūmāniter, *adv. very kindly, very politely :* Cic. Ep.

per-hūmānus, a, um, *very courteous, very polite :* sermo, epistula, Cic. Ep.

Periclēs, is and ī (Voc. Pericle), m. *a famous Athenian orator and statesman.*

periclitātiōne, ABL. *sing. f.* [periclitor], *by experiment* or *trial :* Cic.

periclitor, ārī [periculum]. **A.** T r a n s. **a.** *to put to the test, make a trial of :* pueros, belli fortunam, Cic. With *Indir. Quest. :* Caes. With Acc. and *Indir. Quest. :* animum tuom quid faceres, Pl. *Perf. Part.* in *Pass.* sense : periclitatis moribus amicorum, Cic. **b.** *to put in peril, to endanger :* non est saepius in uno homine salus summa periclitanda rei publicae, Cic. **B.** I n t r a n s. **a.** *to venture, to be bold* or *enterprising :* in iis exemplis, Cic.; proeliis et periclitando tuti sunt, Tac. **b.** *to be in danger, to incur* or *be exposed to danger :* Gallorum vita, Caes. T r a n s f.: verba, Quint. **c.** *to risk :* with ABL. or *Neut. Pron. :* quid aliud quam ingeni famā periclitarer ? Liv.; capite, Mart. With *Inf. :* Plin., Quint.

periculōsē, *adv. dangerously, hazardously, with danger, risk* or *peril :* aegrotans, Cic. Ep.; dico, Cic. *Comp. :* Auct. B. Alex. *Sup. :* Sen.

periculōsus, a, um [periculum], *dangerous, hazardous, perilous :* bellum, iter, curationes, Cic.; annus, Liv.; inimicitiae, Tac. With *in* and Acc.: in nosmet ipsos, Cic. Ep. With DAT.: populo Romano, Caes.; libertati, Liv. *Neut.* in ABL. *Absol. :* iuxta periculoso, ficta seu vera promeret, Tac. *Neut. pl.* as Noun : Sen. *Comp. :* Tac. *Sup. :* Cic., Liv.

periculum (contr. **periclum,** Pl., Ter., Lucr., Verg.), ī, n. [v. experior]. **I.** *a trial, experiment, attempt, proof.* **a.** In gen.: facere, Pl., Caes.; ex aliis facere (i.e. to use others' experience), Ter.; hostis, Caes.; utrimque periculum factum, Liv.; alicuius fidei periculum facere, Cic.; Stat. **b.** Of *an attempt* or *essay* in literary composition : Cic. **II.** (the most freq. sense),

risk, hazard, danger, peril : facere alicui, Pl.; Sall.; alicui intendere, conflare, comparare, facessere, moliri, etc., Cic.; in aliquem intendere, Cic.; in periculum vocare, arcessere, inferre, includere, Cic.; se committere in periculum, Cic.; adire, subire, ingredi, suscipere, Cic.; obire, Liv.; in periculo esse, Pl., Cic. Ep.; in periculo versari, Cic.; periculum depellere, subterfugere, etc., Cic.; ex periculis eripere, extrahere, Cic.; a periculo prohibere, Cic.; liberare periculis, Cic.; periculum est ne etc., Cic., Liv.; periculo meo, tuo, suo, *at my, your, his risk :* Pl., Cic. **III.** In partic., with ref. *to a trial, action, suit at law :* meus labor in privatorum periculis versatus, Cic.; Nep. Hence, *a legal record ;* esp. of *writs, sentences :* tabulae publicae periculaque magistratuum, Cic.; Nep.

per-idōneus, a, um, *very suitable, very well adapted :* consilia, Tac.; with DAT.: locus castris, Caes.; with *ad* and Acc.: Sall.

Perillus, ī, m. *a famous worker in metal, celebrated for the brazen bull which he made for the tyrant Phalaris ;* **Perillēus,** a, um.

per-illūstris (**perinl-**), e, *adj.* **I.** *very clear :* Nep. **II.** *greatly distinguished, highly honoured :* Cic. Ep.

per-imbēcillus, a, um, *very weak* or *feeble :* Cic. Ep.; Varr.

Perimēdēus, a, um, *belonging to the sorceress Perimede ; magical :* Prop.

Perimēlē, ēs, f. *a nymph, d. of Hippodamas, who was changed into an island.*

per-imō (or **peremō**), imere, ēmī, emptum [emō], *to take away entirely,* hence, **I.** *to annihilate, extinguish, destroy.* **1.** Lit.: sin autem (supremus ille dies) perimit ac delet omnino, Cic.; penitus materiem omnem, Lucr.; sensu perempto, Cic.; Troia perempta, Verg.; corpus macie, Liv. **2.** T r a n s f.: reditum, Cic.; causam publicam mea mors, Cic. **II.** *to cut off, slay :* Lucr.; indignā morte peremptus, Verg.; Ov.

per-impedītus, a, um, *very much obstructed:* locus, Auct. B. Afr.

per-incommodē, *adv. very inconveniently :* Cic. Ep.

per-incommodus, a, um, *very inconvenient :* alicui, Liv.

perinde, *adv. in the same manner, just as, equally.* **I.** vivendi artem tantam tamque operosam et perinde fructuosam relinquere, Cic.; ut culta ab incultis notaret et perinde dominos laudaret castigaretque, Liv.; Tac., etc. **II.** Esp. with such conjunctions as atque (ac), ut, quam : *just as, exactly as :* non perinde atque ego putaram, Cic. Ep.; perinde sunt ut aguntur, Cic.; nec perinde ut maluisset plebes, Liv.; Pl.; Cic.; nec perinde prosperis socius quam adversis abstractus, Tac. With *ac si* (also without si), quasi, tamquam, quam si, *just as if :* perinde aestimans ac si usus esset, Caes.; Cic.; Liv.; perinde ac satisfacere vellent, Caes.; perinde ac motus, Liv.; perinde valebit quasi armatissimi fuerint, Cic.; perinde hoc valet tamquam servum aliquis consulem futurum dicat, Liv.; ius iurandum perinde aestimandum, quam si Iovem fefellisset, Tac. Elliptically: si perinde cetera (sc. ac priora) processissent, Liv. ; Tac. ; Plin. Ep.

per-indignē, adv. very indignantly : ferre (with Acc. and Inf.) : Suet.

per-indulgēns, entis, adj. very indulgent, very tender : in patrem, Cic.

per-infāmis, e, adj. very infamous : Suet.

per-infirmus, a, um, very weak or feeble : Cic.

per-ingeniōsus, a, um, very clever : Cic.

per-iniquus, a, um. **I.** very unfair, very unjust : Cic. **II.** very unwilling, very discontented : periniquo animo pati (with Acc. and Inf.), Cic. Ep. ; aliquid periniquo animo ferre, Liv.

per-insignis, e, adj. very remarkable or conspicuous : Cic.

per-invītus, a, um, very unwilling : Liv.

periodus, ī, f. [περίοδος]. Rhet. a complete sentence, a period : Cic.

peripatēticus, a, um [περιπατητικός, Lit. "walking about"], of the peripatetic (i.e. Aristotelian) philosophy ; as Noun, **peripatētici**, ōrum, m. pl., philosophers of the peripatetic (Aristotelian) school, peripatetics : Cic., Varr.

peripetasmata, um, n. pl. [περιπετάσματα], curtains, draperies : Cic.

periphrasis, is, f. [περίφρασις], a roundabout way of saying a thing, a circumlocution : Suet.

per-īrātus, a, um, very angry : alicui, Pl., Cic. Ep.

periscelis, idis, f. [περισκελίς], a leg-band, anklet : Hor.

peristrōma, atis, n. [περίστρωμα], a coverlet : Pl., Cic.

peristylium, ī n. [περιστύλιον], a court surrounded with columns (on the inside) : Vitr., Plin. Ep., Suet.

peristylum, ī, n. [περίστυλον], a colonnade round a building, a peristyle : Cic., Varr., Suet.

peritē, adv. in an experienced manner, skilfully, expertly : Cic. Comp. : Sen. Ep. Sup. : Cic., Plin. Ep.

perītia, ae, f. [peritus], experience, knowledge gained by experience, practical knowledge, skill : Tac. With Obj. Gen. : locorum et militiae, Sall. ; legum, morum, Tac.

perītus, a, um [cf. experior, peri-culum], experienced, practised, skilful, expert : Pl. ; usu peritos, Cic. ; duces, Caes. ; Prop. With Gen. : multarum rerum, Cic. ; earum regionum, Caes. ; rei militaris, Liv. ; iuris, Juv. ; movendarum lacrimarum, Plin. Ep. With Abl. : iure, Lucil., Cic. With ad : ad usum et disciplinam, Cic. ; ad respondendum, Cic. With in and Abl. : in amore, Prop. With de : de agri cultura, Varr. With Inf. : Verg., Tac. Comp. : Cic., Liv. Sup. : Caes., Cic., etc. Masc. as Noun : Cic., Hor. ; also in Sup. : Cic.

periūcundē, adv. very agreeably, very pleasantly : Cic.

per-iūcundus, a, um, very agreeable, very pleasing : Cic. Also in tmesi : Cic.

periūriōsus, v. peiierōsus.

periūrium (peiiūrium, Pl.), ī, n. [periūrus], a false oath, perjury : Cic., Ov., etc. In pl. : Cic., Verg., etc.

per-iūrō, v. peiierō.

periūrus (peiierus, Pl.), a, um [per iūs], oath-breaking, perjured. **1.** Lit. : leno, Cic. ; Troia, Verg. ; fides, Hor. Sup. : Cic. Masc. as Noun : Cic. **2.** Transf. in gen. : false, lying : Pl. Comp. and Sup. : Pl.

per-lābor, lābī, lāpsus, to glide through or along. **a.** nulla perlabitur unda, Tib. ; aer per nostras acies, Lucr. With Acc. (going closely with the per) : summas perlabitur undas, Verg. ; luna umbras, Lucr. **b.** In gen. sense, to move or travel onwards, to make way imperceptibly : supra solis orbem, Lucr. ; ad nos, Cic. ; ad nos tenuis famae aura, Verg.

per-laetus, a, um, very joyful or glad : supplicatio, Liv.

perlāpsus, a, um, Part. perlābor.

per-lātē, adv. very widely or extensively : Cic.

per-lateō, ēre, to lie completely hid : Ov.

perlātus, a, um, Part. perferō.

perlēctiō, ōnis, f. [perlegō], a reading through, perusal : Cic. Ep.

per-legō (pellegō), legere, lēgī, lēctum. **I.** to review, scan, survey thoroughly : omnia oculis, Verg. ; Ov. **II.** to read through, read to the end : tabellas, Pl. ; litteras, Caes. ; librum, Cic. ; censores senatum (i.e. the list of names), Liv.

per-lepidē, adv. very pleasantly : Pl.

per-levis, e, adj. very light, very slight : momentum, Cic., Liv.

perleviter, adv. very lightly, very slightly : commoveri, Cic.

perlibēns (perlubēns), entis, adj. [perlibet], very willing, feeling much pleasure : Pl., Cic. Ep.

perlibenter (perlubenter), adv. very willingly, with great pleasure : Cic.

per-liberālis, e, adj. very well bred, very genteel : Ter.

perliberāliter, adv. very liberally : Cic.

per-libet (-lubet), libēre, it is very pleasing or agreeable (with Inf.) : Pl.

per-liciō (pelliciō), licere, lexī, lectum [cf. adliciō], to entice away (from the right place), inveigle, decoy. Transf.: Pl. ; senem per epistulas, Ter. ; mulierem ad se, Cic. ; animum adulescentis, Cic. ; populum in servitutem, Liv. ; ad vinum, Liv. ; accolas donis ad navis contrahendas, Liv. ; Chaucos ad deditionem, Tac. ; Numidam donis ut etc., Liv. ; Tac. ; maiorem partem sententiarum sale tuo et lepore pellexisti, Cic. ; with non-personal Subject : Lucr.

per-litō, āre, to sacrifice very auspiciously, with very favourable omens. With Dat. : saluti, Liv. With Instr. Abl. : bove, Liv. Pass. Impers. : Liv.

per-longē, adv. a very long way off, very far : Ter.

per-longinquos, a, om, very long, wearisome : Pl.

per-longus, a, um. **I.** very long : via, Cic. Ep. **II.** very tedious : Pl.

perlubēns, v. perlibēns.

per-lūceō (pellūceō), lūcēre, lūxī. **I.** Of light, to shine through, shine clearly, be clear and bright. **1.** Lit. : lux, Liv. **2.** Transf. **a.** to be clearly visible : ita is pellucet quasi lanterna Punica, Pl. ; fibrae in pectore, Ov. **b.** Of abstract things : mores dicentis ex oratione, Quint. ; Cic. **II.** *to let the light through, be transparent.* **1.** Lit. : aether, Cic. ; amictus, Ov. ; toga, Sen. Ep. ; hence, Cretice, perluces, Juv. **2.** Transf. : oratio (i.e. is clear, intelligible), Cic.

perlūcidulus, a, um [*dim.* perlūcidus], *sweetly transparent :* Cat.

perlūcidus (pellūcidus), a, um [perlūceō]. **I.** *shining through, very bright :* stella, Cic. **II.** *transparent, pellucid :* membrana, Cic. ; fons, Ov. ; fides perlucidior vitro, Hor.

per-lūctuōsus, a, um, *very mournful :* funus, Cic. Ep.

per-luō, luere, luī, lūtum, *to wash thoroughly :* manūs undā, Ov. In *Mid. :* in fluminibus perluuntur, Caes. ; gelidā undā, Hor. ; Ov.

per-lūstrō, āre. **I.** *to traverse completely :* hostium agros, Liv. **II.** *to review, survey.* **a.** With the eyes : omnia oculis, Liv. **b.** With the mind ; aliquid animo, Cic. ; mea dicta, Stat.

per-madefaciō, ere, *to wet through, to drench.* Transf. : amor cor meum, Pl.

per-madēscō, madēscere, maduī, *to become thoroughly wet.* Transf. : *to grow soft or effeminate :* deliciis, Sen. Ep.

per-magnus, a, um, *very great :* accessio, Cic. ; numerus, Caes. ; vis naturae, Cic. Of moral worth : homo, Cic. *Neut.* as Noun : permagnum aestimans trīs Olympionicas unā e domo prodire, Cic. ; permagni refert, Ter. ; permagni interest, Cic. ; decumas permagno vendere, Cic. Also *in tmesi :* Cic. Ep.

permānanter, *adv.* *by flowing through :* Lucr.

permānāscō, ere [permānō], *to begin to flow through.* Transf. : of a report : ad aliquem, Pl.

per-maneō, manēre, mānsī, mānsum, *to continue or persist in staying.* **1.** Lit. **a.** in eo loco, in armis, Caes. ; Liv. **b.** *to last on, endure :* cerā circumlita corpora, Cic. ; ad longinquum tempus, Cic. ; ad numerum, Cic. ; ad extremos rogos, Ov. ; in seros annos, Ov. **2.** Transf. **a.** in officio, Caes. ; in voluntate, in pristinā sententiā, Cic. Ep. ; in suscepto consilio, Cic. ; in fide, Liv. ; spe atque fiduciā, Caes. **b.** *to last on, endure :* ira tam diu, Ter. ; Athenis iam ille mos a Cecrope permansit, Cic.

per-mānō, āre, *to ooze, trickle, or flow through, penetrate.* **1.** Lit. : in saxis ac speluncis liquidus umor, Lucr. ; primordia per foramina, Lucr. ; succus in iecur, Cic. ; laticum venae in mare, Liv. With Acc. (going closely with the *per*) : calor argentum, Lucr. **2.** Transf. : amor usque in pectus, Pl. ; huc acre malum, Lucr. ; Pythagorae doctrina in hanc civitatem, Cic. ; macula ad animum, Cic. Of rumours : ne permanet palam haec nostra fallacia, Pl. ; hoc ad pluris, Caes. ; sermones hominum ad vestras auris, Cic.

permānsiō, ōnis, *f.* [permaneō], *a remaining, persisting :* in ratione bene consideratā, Cic.

per-marīnus, a, um, *that accompanies through the sea* as guardian : lares, Liv.

per-mātūrēscō, mātūrēscere, mātūruī, *to become quite ripe, to ripen fully :* Ov.

per-mediocris, e, *adj. very moderate :* Cic.

per-meditātus, a, um, *well-prepared, well-trained :* Pl.

permēnsus, a, um, *Part.* permētior.

per-meō, āre, *to go or pass through.* **1.** Lit. : hastae longius in hostis permeabant, Tac. With Acc. (going closely with the *per*) : littera nostra tot maria ac terras, Ov. ; Hister orbem, Luc. **2.** Transf. : intellegentia per omnia ea permeat, Cic.

Permēssus, ī, *m. a river in Boeotia sacred to Apollo and the Muses.*

per-mētior, mētīrī, mēnsus, *to measure through, measure out.* **1.** Lit. : solis magnitudinem, Cic. **2.** Transf. : *to travel through, traverse :* viam, Pl. ; aera multum camposque natantia, Lucr. ; classibus aequor, Verg. Also, saecula, Mart.

per-mingō, mingere, minxī, *to befoul with urine :* hence, *to pollute :* Hor.

per-mirus, a, um, *very wonderful :* Cic. ; *in tmesi :* Cic.

per-misceō, miscere, miscuī, mixtum, *to mix or mingle together.* **1.** Lit. : permixti cum suis fugientibus, Caes. ; Cic. ; Ov. With Abl. : permixti caede virorum equi, Verg. With Dat. : permixtum senatui populi concilium, Liv. ; Verg. **2.** Transf. **a.** tuas sordis cum clarissimorum virorum splendore, Cic. ; fructūs magnā acerbitate permixtos, Cic. **b.** Of throwing into confusion : divina humanaque iura, Caes. ; omnia, Cic. ; Graeciam, Cic. ; domum, Verg.

permissiō, ōnis, *f.* [permittō]. **I.** *a giving up, yielding ; an unconditional surrender :* Liv. **II.** *leave, permission :* mea permissio mansionis tuae, Cic. Ep.

permissū, *Abl. sing. m.* [permittō], *by leave or permission :* permissu tuo, Cic. ; Lentuli, Liv. ; legis, Cic.

permissus, a, um. **I.** *Part.* permittō. **II.** Noun, **permissum,** ī, *n. a permission :* Hor.

permitiālis, e, *adj. destructive :* discidium, Lucr. ; morbi, Liv.

permitiēs, ēī, *f.* [*cf.* μινύθω], *a complete wasting away :* Pl. ; hominum pecorumque Liv. Of a slave : erilis permities, Pl.

per-mittō, mittere, mīsī, missum, *to let go through, allow to pass through.* **1.** Lit. **a.** reliquerat intervalla per ordines peditum quā equi permitti possent, Liv. ; equos in hostem, Liv. In *Mid. :* odor permittitur longius, Lucr. **b.** *to let fly, cast, hurl :* longius tela, Hirt. ; saxum in hostem, Ov. **2.** Transf. **a.** *to let go :* habenas equo, Tib. ; hence, tribunatum (i.e. give the rein to), Liv. **b.** *to give up, leave, surrender :* alicui summam belli administrandi, Caes. ; permittitur infinita potestas, Cic. ; aliquem iudicum potestati, Cic. ; aliquem vitae, Luc. ; fortunas suas fidei alicuius, Caes. With *Refl. Pron. :* se suaque omnia in fidem atque potestatem populi R., Caes. ; se eorum potestati, Caes. ; Liv. ; se in deditionem consuli, Liv. **c.** *to concede, relinquish :* aliquid iracundiae, Cic. ; inimicitias temporibus rei publicae, Cic. **d.** *to* *give leave, allow, permit* : id lege permittitur, Cic. ; conatus est reficere pontis sed nec magnitudo fluminis permittebat nec etc., Caes. ; alicui permittere (with *Inf.*), Cic. ; alicui (with *ut* and *Subj.*), Cic., Liv. Often *Impers. Pass.* with *ut* and *Subj.*: Cic., Liv., etc. With *Indir. Deliberative* : senatus Fulvio quantum impenderet permisit, Liv. ; also in *Impers. Pass.* : Liv. With *Acc.* and *Inf.* : ille meas errare boves permisit, Verg.

permixtē, *adv. confusedly, promiscuously* : Cic.

permixtiō, ōnis, *f.* [permisceō]. **I.** Concr.: *a mixture* : Cic. **II.** *turmoil* : Sall.

permixtus, a, um. **I.** *Part.* permisceō. **II.** Adj.: *promiscuous, disordered*: caedes, mores, Lucr.

per-modestus, a, um, *very moderate, very modest* : homo, Cic. ; verba sensu permodesto, Tac.

per-modicus, a, um, *very moderate, small* : res familiaris, locus, Suet.

per-molestē, *adv. with much trouble or vexation* : ferre (with *Acc.* and *Inf.*) : Cic.

per-molestus, a, um, *very troublesome* : Cic. Ep.

per-mollis, e, *adj. very feeble or weak.* Transf.: Quint.

per-molō, ere, *to grind thoroughly.* Transf.: alienas uxores, Hor.

per-mōtiō, ōnis, *f.* [permoveō], *a moving, exciting.* Transf. of the mind (with or without mentis, animi) : *an emotion* : Cic. ; in *pl.* : Cic.

permōtus, a, um, *Part.* permoveō.

per-moveō, movēre, mōvī, mōtum, *to move* or *stir up thoroughly.* **1.** Lit.: mare permotum ventis, Lucr. **2.** Transf. of the mind. **a.** *to move deeply ; to influence, induce, prevail on* : conventum pollicitationibus, Caes. ; plebes dominandi studio permota, Sall. ; auctoritate Orgetorigis permoti, Caes. ; animos, Cic. ; mentem iudicum, Cic. **b.** *to stir, excite, deeply affect* : aliquem calamitates, Cic. ; milites gravius permoti, Caes. ; animo permotus, Caes. ; mente permotus, Cic. ; labore itineris, Caes. ; iracundiā, dolore, metu, Cic. Ep. ; ad miserationem, Tac. Of the feelings : invidiam, misericordiam, metum et iras, Tac.

per-mulceō, mulcēre, mulsī, mulsum, *to stroke all over, fondle, caress.* **1.** Lit.: aliquem manu, Ov. ; comas, Ov. ; barbam, Liv. **2.** Transf. **a.** *to soothe, lull, charm* : aram flatu permulcet spiritus austri, Cic. poet. ; sensum voluptate, Cic. ; verbis auris, Hor. ; Cic. ; medicatā lumina virgā, Ov. ; candida liquidis vestigia lymphis, Cat. **b.** *to soothe, appease* : animos, Lucr., Caes. ; senectutem, Cic. ; pectora dictis, Verg. ; plebem, Liv. ; iram, Liv. ; aliquem mitibus verbis, Tac. ; comitate militem, Tac.

permulsus, a, um, *Part.* permulceō.

per-multus, a, um. **I.** In *sing.* : *very much. Neut.* as Noun : permultum erit ex maerore tuo deminutum, Cic. ; Pl. *Intern. Acc.* : permultum interest, Cic. Also of Extent (of Time) : permultum ante, Cic. Ep. *Abl.* of Measure : *by far* : permulto

clariora, Cic. **II.** In *pl.* : *very many* : colles, Caes. ; imitatores, Cic. *Neut.* as Noun : Cic. Ep., Hor.

per-mūniō, īre. **I.** *to finish fortifying* : munimenta, Liv. **II.** *to fortify thoroughly*: castra, Liv. ; Tac.

per-mūtātiō, ōnis, *f.* [permūtō]. **I.** *a complete change* : magnā rerum permutatione impendente, Cic. ; defensionis, Quint. **II.** *an interchange, exchange* : partim emptiones, partim permutationes, Cic. ; captivorum, Liv. ; mercium, Tac. Of money : Cic. Ep.

per-mūtō, āre. **I.** *to alter or change completely* : ordinem, Lucr. ; sententiam, Cic. ; omnem rei publicae statum, Cic. **II.** *to interchange, exchange* one thing for another : nomina inter se, Pl. ; domum, Pl. ; galeam, Verg. ; captivos, Verg. With *Instr.* Abl. : valle Sabinā divitias, Hor. ; Plin. Esp. *to exchange* money ; *to remit by* or *negotiate* a *bill of exchange* : illud, quod tecum permutavi, Cic. Ep. *Impers. Pass.* : Cic. Ep.

perna, ae, *f.* [πέρνα], *a haunch* or *ham together with the leg* ; esp. *of pork, a ham* : Pl., Cato, Hor. Of men : Enn.

per-necessārius, a, um. **I.** *very necessary* : tempus, Cic. Ep. **II.** *very closely connected* with one : homo, Cic. As Noun : Cic. Ep.

per-necesse, indecl. *adj. indispensably necessary* : Cic.

per-negō, āre. **I.** *to deny altogether or flatly* : Pl., Cic. ; de aliquo alicui, Tib. ; with *Acc.* and *Inf.* : Cic. **II.** *to refuse or decline altogether* : Mart. ; Catoni populus R. praeturam negavit, consulatum pernegavit, Sen.

per-neō, nēre, nēvī, nētum, *to spin off to an end* : of the Fates : mihi supremos Lachesis annos, Mart.

perniciābilis, e, *adj.* [perniciēs], *destructive, ruinous* : Tac. (*v.* also pernitialis).

perniciēs, ēī, *f.* (Dat. pernicie, Liv. ; pernicii, Gen., Cic., Dat., Nep.) [*v.* necō], *destruction, ruin.* **1.** Lit.: Pl. ; perniciem rei publicae moliens, Cic. ; alicui machinari, Sall. ; alicui invenire, Tac. ; in apertam perniciem incurrere, Cic. ; incumbere ad perniciem alicuius, Cic. ; ad perniciem vocari, Cic. ; in nepotum perniciem, Hor. ; insanabilis, Liv. **2.** Transf. **a.** *a cause of ruin* : quae res contemnentibus pernicii fuit, Nep. ; **b.** Concr.: adulescentum, Pl. ; Ter. ; (Verres) pernicies provinciae Siciliae, Cic. ; lymphae, vini pernicies, Cat. ; macelli, Hor.

perniciōsē, *adv. destructively, ruinously* : Cic. *Comp.* : Cic.

perniciōsus, a, um, *adj.* [perniciēs], *destructive, ruinous* : leges, Caes. ; scripta auctori suo, Ov. *Neut. pl.* as Noun : Juv. *Comp.* : morbi perniciosiores, Cic. ; Sall. *Sup.* : Nep.

pernicitās, ātis, *f.* [pernix], *nimbleness, agility, swiftness* : Pl., Caes., Cic., etc. ; pedum, Liv.

perniciter, *adv. nimbly, quickly, swiftly* : Pl., Cat., Liv.

per-niger, gra, grum, *jet black* : oculi, Pl.

per-nimius, a, um, *much too great. Neut. Intern. Acc.* : pernimium interest, Ter.; in *tmesi* : Ter.

pernix, icis, adj. *nimble, brisk, active, agile.*
1. Lit.: pernix sum manibus, Pl.; alae, Verg.; Saturnus, Verg.; corpora, Liv.; genus, nuntii, Tac. With *Inf.*: Hor.
2. Transf.: temporis pernicissimi celeritas, Sen. Ep.

per-nōbilis, e, adj., *very famous:* epigramma, Cic.

per-noctō, āre, *to stay all night long, to pass the night.* **1.** Lit.: Pl., Cic.: extra moenia, Liv. **2.** Transf.: haec studia pernoctant nobiscum, Cic.

Pernōnidēs, ae, m. [perna]. Comic.: *Son of Ham, Hamson :* laridum Pernonidem, Pl.

per-nōscō, nōscere, nōvi, nōtum. **I.** *to examine thoroughly :* with *Indir. Quest.*: Ter. **II.** *to become thoroughly acquainted with, to get a correct knowledge of :* hominum mores ex corpore, oculis, vultu, Cic. In *Perf.*: *to know thoroughly :* facta probe, Pl.; ingenium hospitis, Pl.

per-nōtuit, uisse [pernōscō], *it has become everywhere or generally known :* with Acc. and *Inf.*: Tac.

pernōtus, a, um, *Part.* pernōscō.

per-nox, noctis, adj. *all-night :* luna pernox erat, Liv.; Ov.; iacet pernox, Verg.; luditur alea pernox, Juv.

per-numerō, āre, *to count out, reckon up piece by piece* (of money): Pl., Liv.

pērō, ōnis, m. *a kind of boot made of raw hide, a brogue,* worn by ploughmen and soldiers : Verg.; altus, Juv.

per-obscūrus, a, um, *very obscure :* quaestio, Cic.; fama, Liv.

per-odiōsus, a, um, *very troublesome, very annoying :* Cic. Ep.

per-officiōsē, adv. *very obligingly, very attentively :* Cic. Ep.

per-oleō, ēre, *to emit a penetrating odour :* Lucr.

pērōnātus, a, um [pērō], *wearing the pero :* Pers.

per-opportūnē, adv. *very conveniently, very opportunely :* Cic., Liv.

per-opportūnus, a, um, *very convenient or opportune :* deversorium, Cic.; victoria, Liv.; peropportuna mors Philippi fuit ad dilationem et ad viris bello subtrahendas, Liv.

per-optātō, Abl. *Neut.* as *Adv., very much to one's wish :* Cic.

per-opus, indecl. *noun, a very necessary thing :* peropus est (with Acc. and *Inf.*): Ter.

perōrātiō, ōnis, f. [perōrō], *the close or winding up of a speech, the peroration :* Cic.

per-ōrnātus, a, um, *very ornate :* Crassus in dicendo, Cic.

per-ōrnō, āre, *to adorn greatly or constantly :* senatum, Tac.

per-ōrō, āre. **I.** *to speak from beginning to end, to plead completely :* tribus horis, Cic.; ius perorandi in reum, Tac.; tantam causam, Cic. *Impers. Pass.* (with Acc. and *Inf.*): Liv. **II.** a. *to bring a speech to a close, to wind up :* Cic., Nep. **b.** Occ. *to bring proceedings in court to an end, to conclude, finish :* res illo die non peroratur, dimittitur iudicium, Cic.

per-ōsus, a, um [per and *Part.* of ōdi], *disliking strongly, detesting :* lucem, Verg.; genus omne femineum, Verg.; ignem, Achillem, etc., Ov.; plebs consulum nomen perosa erat, Liv.; Tac., etc.

per-pācō, āre, *to quiet completely, reduce to quietness :* urbem, Liv.

per-parcē, adv. *very parsimoniously :* Ter.

per-parvulus, a, um, *very little, very diminutive :* sigilla, Cic.

per-parvus, a, um, *very small :* semina, Lucr.; civitas, culpa, Cic.

per-pāstus, a, um, *well fed, in good condition :* canis, Phaedr.

per-paucī, ae, a, *very few :* homines, Ter.; Liv.; *in tmesi :* Ter. *Neut. pl.* as Noun: perpauca dicere, Cic.; Hor.

per-pauculi, m. *pl. adj. very few indeed :* perpauculis passibus, Cio.

per-paulum (-**paullum**), i, n. *a very little :* loci, Cic. *Intern.* Acc.: perpaulum declinare, Cic.

per-pauper, eris, adj. *very poor :* Cic. Ep.

per-pauxillum, i, n. *a very little :* Acc. as *Adv.:* Pl.

per-pavefaciō, facere, *to frighten very much :* Pl.

per-pellō, pellere, pulī, pulsum, *to push vigorously.* Transf. *to urge strongly, impel, induce, force :* animus hominem, homo animum, Pl.; ad deditionem, Liv.; Aulum spe pactionis perpulerat ut etc., Sall.; Liv.; cognitio Tiberium perpulit ut etc., Tac.; Antonium perpulerat ne contra rem publicam sentiret, Sall. Freq. in Liv. (and Tac.) with *ut* and *Subj.* (but without Acc. of person): perpellit ut legatos mittat, Liv. With Acc. (of Object) and *Inf.*: Tac.

perpendiculum, i, n. [perpendō], *a plummet, plumb-line :* ad perpendiculum columnas exigere, Cic.; ad perpendiculum, *perpendicularly,* Caes.

per-pendō, pendere, pendī, pēnsum, *to weigh carefully or exactly.* Transf.: aliquid acri iudicio, Lucr.; aliquid ad (*by the standard of*) disciplinae praecepta, Cic.; amicitia totā veritate perpenditur, Cic.; momenta officiorum, Cic.; vitia virtutesque, Suet.

perperam, adv. *wrongly, incorrectly, falsely :* loqui, insanire, Pl.; facere, iudicare, Cic.; interpretari, Liv.

perpes, etis, adj. [petō], *lasting throughout, continuous, uninterrupted.* Of time : noctem perpetem, Pl.

perpessiō, ōnis, f. [perpetior], *a bearing, suffering, enduring :* laborum, dolorum, Cic.

perpessū, Abl. *sing. m.* [perpotior], *in the enduring :* dolorem difficilem perpessu, Cic.

per-petior, peti, pessus [patior], *to bear with patience to the end, to endure :* Enn.; difficultates, Caes.; dolorem, etc., Cic.; Hor.; Ov. With *Inf.*: Ov. With Acc. and *Inf.*: *to endure, suffer, permit :* Pl., Verg., Ov.

per-petrō, āre [patrō], *to carry through, effect, accomplish :* opus, Pl.; caedem, facinus, sacrificium, sacrum, bellum, pacem, etc., Liv.; iudicium, promissa, etc., Tac. With *Inf.*: Pl. With *ut* or *ne* and *Subj.*: Tac.

perpetuitās, ātis, *f.* [perpetuus], *uninterrupted or continual duration or succession, continuity* : ad perpetuitatem, Cic. ; constare in vitae perpetuitate nobismet ipsis, Cic. ; in perpetuitate dicendi, Cic. ; perpetuitas verborum, Cic.

perpetuō, āre [perpetuus]. *to cause to continue uninterruptedly, to make perpetual, perpetuate* : data, Pl. ; potestatem, Cic.

perpetuus(-uos), a, um [petō], *going on or continuing throughout, unbroken, uninterrupted; in entirety.* **1.** L i t. **a.** non sarcire possum aedis meas quin totae perpetuae ruant, Pl. ; trabes perpetuae in longitudinem, Caes. ; agmen, Cic. ; munitiones, Caes. ; milites disponit perpetuis vigiliis stationibusque, Caes. ; mensae, Verg. ; perpetui tergo bovis, Verg. ; cum res a perpetuis orationibus in altercationem vertisset, Liv. *Neut.* as Noun : in perpetuum, *without break, continuously:* porticus in perpetuum suffulta columnis, Lucr. **b.** Of time : hunc diem perpetuom in laetitiā degere, Ter. ; Pl. ; possessio, Caes. ; stellarum cursus, Cic. ; ignis Vestae, Cic. ; lex, Cic. ; quaestiones, Cic. ; formido, Verg. ; sopor, Hor. Of a lover, *constant* : Telephus, Hor. *Neut.* as Noun : in perpetuum (*sc.* tempus), *for all time* : obtinere aliquid, Cic. ; Pl. ABL. as *Adv.* **perpetuō**, *constantly, uninterruptedly* : Pl., Cic., Ov., etc. **2.** T r a n s f. : *universal, general, that always holds good* : perpetui iuris et universi generis quaestio, Cic.

per-placeō, ēre, *to please greatly* : Pl. ; ea lex mihi perplacet, Cic. Ep. ; Pl.

perplexābilis, e, *adj.* [perplexor], *intricate, obscure* : verbum, Pl.

perplexābiliter, *adv. perplexing* : Pl.

perplexē (and **perplexim**), *adv. confusedly, obscurely* : loqui, Ter. ; defectionem haud perplexe indicavere, Liv.

perplexor, ārī (ārier, Pl.) [perplexus], *to cause perplexity* : Pl.

per-plexus, a, um, *entangled, intricate, confused.* **1.** L i t. : figurae, Lucr. ; iter silvae, Verg. **2.** T r a n s f. : *intricate, ambiguous, obscure* : sermones, responsum, Liv. *Neut.* as Noun : Liv. *Comp.* : Liv.

per-plicātus, a, um, *interlaced, entangled* : *in tmesi* : Lucr.

per-pluit, perpluere. **1.** L i t. **a.** *it rains through* : Cato. **b.** perpluit and perpluunt with a Subject : *it lets* (they let) *the rain through, it leaks* (they leak) : perpluont tigna, Pl. ; cum cenaculum perplueret, Quint. **2.** T r a n s f. **a.** ne bene facta perpluant, Pl. **b.** T r a n s. : tempestas, quam mihi amor in pectus perpluit meum, Pl.

per-poliō, īre, *to polish well.* T r a n s f. : perpolire atque conficere, Cic. ; opus, Cic. ; ea, quae habes instituta, perpolies, Cic. Ep.

perpolītus, a, um. **I.** *Part.* perpoliō. **II.** A d j. : *thoroughly polished or refined* : homines, Cic. ; litteris, Cic. ; vita humanitate, Cic.

per-populor, *to ravage, devastate thoroughly* : agrum, Liv. ; Tac. *Perf. Part.* in *Pass.* sense : Liv.

perpōtātiō, ōnis, *f.* [perpōtō], *a continued drinking, a drinking-bout* : *in pl.* : Cic.

per-pōtō, āre. **1.** [illegible] *stopping* : adsiduo, Pl. ; ad vesperum, Cic. ; totos dies, Cic. **II.** *to drink off* : amarum absinthi laticem, Lucr.

per-primō., ere [premō], *to press hard, to press perpetually* : cubilia, Hor. ; Sen. Ep.

per-propinquos, a, om, *very near* : commutatio rerum, Acc.

per-prosper, era, erum, *very favourable* : valetudo, Suet.

per-prūriscō, ere, *to begin to itch all over* : Pl.

per-pugnāx, ācis, *adj. very pugnacious* : in disputando, Cic.

per-pulcher, chra, chrum, *very beautiful* : dona, Ter.

per-pūrgō (**perpūrigō**, Pl.), āre, *to cleanse or purge thoroughly, to make quite clean.* **1.** L i t. : perpurgatis auribus, Pl. ; se, Cic. **2.** T r a n s f. : *to clear up, explain thoroughly* : locum orationis, Cic. ; de dote, Cic. Ep.

per-pusillus, a, um, *very small ; dwarfish* : Cic.

per-putō, āre, *to prune thoroughly.* T r a n s f. *to clear up, explain fully* : argumentum vobis, Pl.

perquam, *adv. extremely* : perquam indignis modis, Pl. ; perquam breviter, Cic. ; perquam pauci, Liv. ; *in tmesi* : Ter.

per-quīrō, quīrere, quīsīvī, quīsītum [quaerō]. **I.** *to ask or inquire carefully after, to make diligent search for* : vasa, Cic. ; aditūs viasque, Caes. With *Indir. Quest.* : Pl. *Impers. Pass.* : Cic. **II.** *to search through and through,* i.e. *to examine carefully.* T r a n s f. : cognitionem rei, Cic.

perquīsītius, *comp. adv. more exactly or accurately* : conscribere, Cic.

perquīsītor, ōris, *m.* [perquīrō]. *a seeker out, a hunter after* : auctionum, Pl.

per-rārus, a, um, *very uncommon, very rare* : Liv. ; perrarum est ut, etc., Plin. ABL. **perrārō** as *Adv., very seldom* : Cic., Hor.

per-reconditus, a, um, *very hidden or abstruse* : Cic.

perrēctus, a, um, *Part.* pērgō.

per-rēpō, rēpere, *to crawl through or over* : tellurem genibus, Tib.

perrēptō, āre [*freq.* perrēpō]. **I.** *to creep or crawl about* : omnibus latebris, Pl. **II.** With Acc. (going closely with the per) : *to creep or crawl through* : omne oppidum, Ter. ; Pl.

Perrhaebī, ōrum, *m. pl. a people of Thessaly* : **Perrhaebus**, a, um ; **Perrhaebia**, ae, *f. their country.*

perrīdiculē, *adv. very laughably* : Cic.

per-rīdiculus, a, um, *very laughable, very ridiculous* : Cic.

per-rogātiō, ōnis, *f. the passage of a law* : legis Maniliae, Cic.

per-rogō, āre, *to ask in succession, to ask one after another* : sententias, Liv., Tac.

per-rumpō, rumpere, rūpī, ruptum. **A.** Without Acc. : *to break or rush through, to force one's way through* : per medios hostis, Caes. ; in vestibulum templi, Liv. *Impers. Pass.* : Liv. **B.** With Acc. **a.** Going closely with the *per* : *to force one's way through* : paludem, Caes. ; Acheronta, Hor. ; perruptus hostis, Tac. **b.** *to break thoroughly or in two,* to *shatter* : ratis, Caes. ; perrumpitur concretus aer, Cic. ; bipenni limina, Verg. ; Ov. Transf.: leges, Cic. ; fastidia, Hor. ; perrumpi adfectu aliquo, Tac.

Persae, ārum, *m. pl. the Persians ;* (Sing. **Persa** or **Persēs**, ae). Transf. (poet.) *the Parthians ;* **Persis**, idis, *f.* and **Persia**, ae, *f. Persia ;* **Persis**, idis, also as *f. adj. Persian ;* **Persicus**, a, um, *Persian.* Transf. (poet.) *luxurious ;* **Persicum** ī, n. (*sc.* mālum), *a peach ;* **Persica**, ōrum, *n. pl. Persian history :* Dionis, Cic. ; **Persicē**, *adv., in Persian :* loqui, Quint.

per-saepe, *adv. very often :* Cic., Hor. ; *in tmesi*, Pl.

persalsē, *adv. very wittily :* Cic. Ep.

per-salsus, a, um, *very witty :* Cic.

persalūtātiō, ōnis, *f.* [persalūtō], *a saluting of all in turn :* Cic.

per-salūtō, āre, *to salute one after another :* omnis, Cic. ; Phaedr., etc.

per-sānctē, *adv. very sacredly* or *religiously :* deierare, Ter. ; Suet.

per-sapiēns, entis, *adj. very wise :* Cic.

persapienter, *adv. very wisely :* Cic.

Persē, ēs, or **Persa**, ae, or **Persēis**, idis, *f. d. of Oceanus, m. of Circe ;* **Persēis**, idis, *f. adj. magical.*

per-scienter, *adv. very discreetly :* Cic.

per-scindō, scindere, scidī, scissum, *to rend asunder* or *in pieces :* nubem, Lucr. ; omnia ventus, Liv.

per-scītus, a, um, *very clever ; in tmesi :* Ter., Cic.

per-scrībō, scrībere, scrīpsī, scrīptum. **I.** *to write in full* or *at length* (without abbreviation of the characters) : versum puris verbis, Hor. ; summam (i.e. not in figures, but in words), Suet. **II.** *to give a full statement, account* or *report of in writing :* rem gestam, Caes. ; orationem, Cic. ; unam ex tam multis orationem, Sall. ; res populi R. a primordio urbis, Liv. With *de :* Cic. Ep. With Acc. and *Inf. :* Caes. With *Indir. Quest. :* Cic. Ep. With *ut* and *Juss. Subj. :* hoc perscriptum in monumentis veteribus reperietis ut etc., Cic. **III.** *to enter, register :* senatūs consultum, Cic. ; aliquid in tabulas publicas, Cic. In an account-book : falsum nomen, Cic. ; Pl. **IV.** *to make over in writing, to assign :* argentum perscripsi illis, quibus debui, Ter. ; pecuniam, Cic. ; Liv.

perscriptiō, ōnis, *f.* [perscrībō]. **I.** *a writing down, an entry :* Cic. In *pl. :* Cic. **II.** *a making over in writing, an assignment :* Cic. Ep. In *pl. :* Cic. Ep.

perscriptor, ōris, *m. one who makes entries in books :* faenerationum, Cic.

perscriptus, a, um, *Part.* perscrībō.

per-scrūtō, āre (Pl.), and **per-scrūtor**, ārī (Cic.), *to search, examine thoroughly.* **1.** Lit.: aliquem, Pl. ; arculas, Cic. ; canes omnia, Cic. **2.** Transf.: sententiam scriptoris, Cic.

per-secō, secāre, secuī, sectum. **I.** *to cut into pieces, dissect.* Transf.: rerum naturas, Cic. **II.** *to cut through, destroy by cutting.* Transf.: vitium, Liv.

persector, ārī [*freq.* persequor], *to follow* or *pursue eagerly, to investigate :* primordia, Lucr. ; hoc (followed by *Indir. Quest.*), Pl.

persecūtiō, ōnis, *f.* [persequor], *a following after.* Transf.: *a prosecution, action, suit :* Cic.

persecūtus, a, um, *Part.* persequor.

per-sedeō (persideō), sedēre, sēdī, sēssum, *to remain sitting :* in equo dies noctisque, Liv. ; Curt., etc.

per-sēgnis, e, *adj. very sluggish* or *slack :* proelium, Liv.

per-senex, senis, *adj. very old :* Suet.

per-sentiō, sentīre, sēnsī. **I.** *to perceive plainly* (with Acc. and *Inf.*) : Verg. **II.** *to feel deeply :* pectore curas, Verg.

per-sentiscō, ere. **I.** *to begin to perceive clearly :* Pl., Ter. **II.** *to begin to feel deeply :* viscera persentiscunt, Lucr.

Persephonē, ēs, *f. the Greek name of Proserpina.*

persequēns, entis. **I.** *Part.* persequor. **II.** Adj.: *pursuing, given to the pursuit* or *practice of :* with GEN.: flagiti, Pl. *Sup. :* Auct. Her.

per-sequor, sequī, secūtus, *to follow persistently, continue to follow, follow to an end.* **1.** Lit. **A.** In gen.: servolum iubet illum persequi, Pl. ; me in Asiam, Ter. ; aliquem vestigiis, Pl., Cic. ; Verg. : alicuius vestigia, Cic. ; reliqui praefecti Cleomenem, Cic. **B.** In partic. **a.** Hostilely: *to pursue closely :* fugientis usque ad flumen, Caes. ; Medeam parens, Cic. ; feras, Ov. ; Curt. **b.** *to pursue in order to reach* or *obtain, to hunt for eagerly :* alios deos penatis, Pl. ; omnis solitudines, Cic. **c.** *to follow and overtake :* aliquem, Cic. ; mors et fugacem persequitur virum, Hor. **2.** Transf. **A.** *to follow persistently :* viam, Ter. ; Cic. Ep. ; eas artis, Cic. ; vitam inopem et vagam, Cic. **B.** *to follow word by word in writing :* celeritate scribendi quae dicerentur persequi, Cic. **C.** *to follow steadily, to imitate, copy :* Academiam veterem, Cic. **D.** Hostilely: *to proceed against, prosecute ; to take vengeance upon :* civitatem bello, Caes. ; hostem bello, Cic. ; aliquem iudicio, Cic. ; mortem alicuius, Caes., Cic., Liv. **E.** *to pursue, hunt for eagerly :* meum ius, Ter., Cic. ; hereditates, Ter., Cic. ; regnum, Pl. With *Inf. :* Pl., Hor. **F.** *to follow out, perform, accomplish.* **a.** In gen.: hoc, ut dico, factis persequar, Pl. ; inperium patris, Pl. ; mandata, Cic. Ep. ; si idem extrema persequitur qui incohavit, Cic. ; incepta, Liv. **b.** In speech or writing, *to set forth, describe, explain, etc. :* rationes, Lucr. ; aliquid voce, Cic. ; aliquid versibus, Cic. ; has res in eo libro, Cic. ; res Hannibalis, Cic.

Persēs, ae, and **Perseus** (disyl.), eī (GEN. rarely Persī ; DAT. Persī), *m. the last king of Macedonia, conquered by Aemilius Paulus,* B.C. 169 ; **Persicus**, a, um.

Perseus (disyl.), eī and eos (Acc. Persea), *m. son of Jupiter and Danae. He killed Medusa, and cut off her head, by means of which he turned into stone a sea-monster, and thus saved the life of Andromeda. whom he married ; after his death, he was placed among the constellations ;* **Perseus, Perseius**, a, um.

perseverāns, antis. **I.** *Part.* persevērō. **II.**

Adj.: *persistent, resolute. Comp.: Liv.* (dub.).

persevēranter, *adv. persistently ;* also *relentlessly :* coeptam rem tueri, Liv. ; diligere aliquem, Suet. *Comp. :* vereor ne perseverantius saeviant, Liv. *Sup. :* Plin. Ep.

persevērantia, ae, *f.* [persevērō], *persistence, resoluteness :* Cic. ; nautarum, Caes.

persevērō, āre [persevērus], *to continue resolutely* or *persistently, to persist.* **a.** in suā sententiā, Cic. ; in errore, Cic. ; in eo perseveravit, ius publicano non dicere, Cic. *Impers. Pass. :* perseveratum in irā est, Liv. ; Cic. ; in eo perseverandum putabat, Caes. **b.** With *Inf.* (expressed or understood): bello persequi, Caes. ; iniuriam facere, Cic. ; una navis (*sc.* navigare) perseveravit, Caes. ; cum Orestes perseveraret (*sc.* dicere) se esse Orestem, Cic. **c.** With Acc. of *Neut. Pron. :* quae te ipsum id perseverare potuisse, Cic. ; id constantius, Liv.

per-sevērus, a, um, *very strict :* imperium, Tac.

Persicus, a, um, *v.* Persae and Persēs.

per-sīdō, sīdere, sēdī, sessum, *to sink* or *settle deeply :* of moisture : umor aquāī (in vestis), Lucr. ; of disease : in fruges, Lucr. ; of cold : ad vivum, Verg.

per-signō, āre, *to mark* or *record in detail :* dona, Liv.

per-similis, e, *adj. very like* or *similar.* With GEN. : Cic. With DAT. : Hor.

per-simplex, icis, *adj. very plain* or *simple :* victus, Tac.

per-sistō, sistere, stitī, *to take up one's stand continually.* Transf.: *to continue steadfastly, to persist :* in eādem impudentiā, Liv. With *Inf.* : Cic., Tac.

Persius, ī, *m. a Roman name.* Esp. **I.** C. Persius, *an orator, contemporary of the Gracchi.* **II.** A. Persius Flaccus, *a celebrated satirist in the reign of Nero.*

persōlla, ae, *f.* [*dim.* persōna], *a little mask ;* hence, as a term of abuse : Pl.

per-sōlus, a, um, *quite alone :* oculum persolum mihi, Pl.

persolūtus, a, um, *Part.* persolvō.

per-solvō, solvere, solvī, solūtum, *to unloose* or *release completely.* Transf. **A.** *to unravel, solve, explain :* si hoc mihi ζήτημα persolveris, Cic. Ep. **B.** *to pay (in full).* **1.** Lit.: pecuniam ab aliquo (i.e. by a draft on some one), Cic. ; aes alienum, Sall. ; pecuniam alicui, Tac. **2.** Transf.: quod relicuom est, Pl. ; alicui laborum praemia, Cic. ; meritam diis gratiam, Cic. ; gratis, Verg. ; vota, Prop., Tac. ; honorem dis, Verg. ; poenas, Cic., Verg., etc. But also *of inflicting punishment :* poenae alicui ab omnibus persolutae, Cic. ; mortem alicui, Suet.

persōna, ae, *f.* [per sonō], *a mask* (esp. of actors), usually made of clay, but sometimes of wood or bark. **1.** Lit.: Lucr., Cic., Verg., Juv. **2.** Transf. **a.** *a rôle, part, character,* represented by an actor : parasiti, Ter. ; persona de mimo, Cic. **b.** In gen.: *the part* or *character* which any one sustains in the world or in a book : capere, adsumere, suscipere, appetere, sustinere, gerere, tenere,

deponere, abicere, Cic. ; dare ; sustinēre personam ferre, Liv. ; Inducere, agere, Sen. Ep. ; ecquae pacifica persona desideretur, Cic. Ep. ; induxi senem disputantem, quia nulla videbatur aptior persona, Cic. **c.** *a personage, individual, personality :* quid aptum sit personis, temporibus, aetatibus, Cic. ; Nep. **d.** *a mask, pretence :* Sen. Ep. [Fr. *personne*.]

persōnātus, a, um [persōna], *wearing a mask, masked.* **1.** Lit.: Roscius, Cic. ; pater, Hor. **2.** Transf. *in an assumed character, assumed :* cur personatus ambulem ? Cic. ; felicitas, Sen. Ep. ; fastūs, Mart.

per-sonō, sonāre, sonuī. **A.** Intrans. **a.** *to sound throughout, to resound, ring with :* domus cantu et cymbalis, Cic. ; domus Molossis canibus, Hor. **b.** id totis castris, Liv. With personal Subject : *to make a resounding noise* of any kind : citharā Iopas, Verg. ; incondita multitudo variis vocibus, Liv. ; Tac. **c.** With Acc. (going closely with the *per*) : *to sound through, to fill with sound* or *noise ; to make ring* or *resound :* regna latratu, Verg. ; aurīs vocibus, Cic. Ep. ; aurem, Hor. ; gemitu curiam, Curt. **B.** Trans. *to cry out aloud :* quas res isti in angulis personant, Cic. ; with Acc. and *Inf.* : Cic.

perspectē, *adv. with insight, intelligently :* ut docte et perspecte sapit ! Pl.

perspectō, āre [*freq.* perspiciō]. **I.** *to look through, look all about :* aedis, Pl. **II.** *to look at to the end :* certamen gymnicum, Suet.

perspectus, a, um. **I.** *Part.* perspiciō. **II.** Adj.: *clearly perceived, well-known :* Cic. *Sup. :* Cic. Ep.

per-speculor, ārī, *to examine* or *explore thoroughly :* de vallo, Auct. B. Afr. ; locorum situs, Suet.

per-spergō, ere [spargō], *to besprinkle, to wet.* **1.** Lit. : ligna, Cato ; aquā templum, Tac. **2.** Transf. : orationem tamquam sale, Cic.

perspicāx, ācis, *adj.* [perspiciō], *sharp-sighted.* Transf. (mentally) : Ter., Cic. ; ad aliquid, Ter.

perspicientia, ae, *f.* [perspiciō], *a full perception* or *knowledge :* veri, Cic.

per-spiciō, spicere, spexī, spectum [speciō], *to look* or *see through.* **1.** Lit. **a.** collis silvestris, ut non facile introrsus perspici posset, Caes. ; ut prae densitate arborum perspici caelum vix posset, Liv. **b.** *to look closely at, to take a close view of, to examine, inspect, observe :* villam, Cic. ; opus (of a camp), Caes. With *Indir. Quest. :* Pl. **2.** Transf. **a.** epistulas, Cic. Ep. **b.** res gestas, Lucr. ; cum se ipse perspexerit, Cic. ; virtutem, misericordiam, fidem alicuius, Cic. ; aliquid coniecturā (i.e. to guess), Cic. ; in sē fidem alicuius, Caes. With *Indir. Quest. :* Caes., Cic. With Acc. and *Inf.* : Pl., Cic. Ep.

perspicuē, *adv. transparently, clearly.* Transf. : Cic.

perspicuitās, ātis, *f.* [perspicuus], *transparency, clearness.* Transf. : in verbis, Quint. ; Cic.

perspicuus, a, um [perspiciō], *transparent, clear.* **1.** Lit. : aquae, Ov. **2.** Transf. :

quasi vero hoc perspicuum sit constetque inter omnis, Cic.

per-sternō, sternere, strāvī, strātum, *to pave all over* : viam silice, Liv.

per-stimulō, āre, *to incite* or *inflame violently* : tumidos spiritūs, Tac.

per-stō, stāre, stitī, stātum, *to stand firmly, continue standing*. **1.** Lit.: frenatis equis equites diem totum perstabant, Liv.; in limine, Tib. **2.** Transf. **a.** *to remain steadfast, to last, endure* : nihil est toto quod perstet in orbe, cuncta fluunt, Ov.; rabies, Luc. **b.** *to stand fast* or *firm, to hold out, continue, persevere, persist in* : Hor., Tac.; talia perstabat memorans, Verg.; mens eadem perstat mihi, Verg. With *in* and ABL.: in sententiā, Caes., Liv.; in impudentiā, Cic.; in pertinaci simulatione inopiae, Liv. *Pass. Impers.* : si perstaretur in bello, Tac.; optimates in Romanā societate perstandum censebant, Liv. With *Inf.* : Ov.

perstrātus, a, um, *Part.* persternō.

per-strepō, ere, *to make a great noise* : Ter.

perstrictus, a, um, *Part.* perstringō.

per-stringō, stringere, strīnxī, strictum. **I.** *to tie* or *press tightly*. **1.** Lit.: vitem, Cato. **2.** Transf. of the senses as objects : *to press upon, contract* ; hence *to blunt, deaden, dull* (i.e. dazzle, deafen, etc.): cum solis radii visūs perstrinxere, Plin.; minaci murmure cornuum auris, Hor. Also with personal object : horror ingens spectantis perstringit, Liv. **II.** *to press very closely*, hence *to graze, graze against*. **1.** Lit.: portam Capuae vomere, Cic.; solum aratro, Cic.; femur, Verg. **2.** Transf. (with words) **a.** *to glance at, censure* : alicuius voluntatem asperioribus facetiis, Cic.; aliquem oblique, Tac. **b.** *to touch lightly upon* : unam quamque rem, Cic.; celeriter reliquum vitae cursum, Cic.

perstudiōsē, *adv. very eagerly* : Cic.

per-studiōsus, a, um, *very eager* or *fond* (with GEN.) : Cic.

per-suādeō, suādēre, suāsī, suāsum, *to bring over by talking, to convince, persuade*. **A.** *to convince* a person of a fact : dicere ad persuadendum accommodate, Cic.; de paupertate, Cic. With ACC. of *Neut. Pron.* (followed by ACC. and *Inf.*): in primis hoc volunt persuadere, non interire animas, Enn. With DAT. of person : Caes. With DAT. of person and ACC. of *Neut. Pron.* : hoc mihi, Cic. Ep.; in *Pass.* : quod si tibi persuasum est, Cic. With DAT. of person and ACC. of *Neut. Pron.* (followed by ACC. and *Inf.*): Hor. With *Refl. Pron.* : *to satisfy oneself* ; *to be convinced, to have no doubt about* : velim tibi ita persuadeas (with ACC. and *Inf.*): Cic. Ep. So *Impers. Pass.* : mihi nunquam persuaderi potest (with ACC. and *Inf.*): Cic.; Caes.; sibi persuasum habebat (with ACC. and *Inf.*): Caes.; Plin. Ep.; ne hoc cuiquam persuadeatur (with *ut* and *Subj.*) : Cic. *Pers. Pass.* : si persuassus est, Caecina ap. Cic. Ep.; Ov. **B.** *to persuade* a person to do something. With DAT. of person, and *ut* and *Subj.*: Pl., Caes., Cic., etc.; also *Impers. Pass.* : Pl., Caes., Cic. With DAT. of person and *Inf.* :

Nep., Verg.; *Impers. Pass.* : ea loca provinciae adiungere sibi persuasum habebant, Caes. With *Inf.* alone : Tac.; *Impers. Pass.* : Pl. *Pers. Pass.* : Prop.

persuāsibilis, e, *adj.* [persuādeō], *convincing, persuasive* : Quint.

persuāsiō, ōnis, *f.* [persuādeō]. **I.** *a convincing, persuading* : Cic. **II.** *a conviction, persuasion, belief* : adrogans de se, Quint.; Suet.

persuāstrix, īcis, *f.* [persuādeō], *a female persuader* : Pl.

persuāsū, ABL. *sing. m.* [persuādeō], *by persuasion* : servi, Pl.; huius, Cic.

persuāsus, a, um. **I.** *Part.* persuādeō. **II.** *Adj.* : *that of which one is persuaded* or *convinced* : Cic. *Sup.* : Brut. ap. Cic. Ep. For phrase, persuasum habere (in *Sup.* persuasissimum habere, Suet.), *v.* persuadeo.

per-subtīlis, e, *adj. very fine*. **1.** Lit.: animus, Lucr.. **2.** Transf.: oratio, Cic.

per-sultō, āre [saltō], *to gambol, disport oneself about* (esp. of an exultant enemy): in agro, Liv.; ante vallum, Tac.; solo stabili, Liv.; Tac. With ACC. (going closely with the *per*): pecudes pabula, Lucr.; captam Italiam, Tac.; campos exercitu, Tac.

per-taedet, taedēre, taesum est, *to cause to feel complete disgust* or *weariness* (mostly *Impers.*) : usually with ACC. of person and GEN. of thing: me sermonis pertaesum est, Pl.; Lucr.; Cic. Ep., etc. In *Perf. Part.* : lentitudinis eorum pertaesa, Tac.; with ACC. : ignaviam suam, Suet.

per-tegō, tegere, tēxī, tēctum, *to cover all over*. **1.** Lit.: villam, Pl. **2.** Transf.: bene facta bene factis ne perpluant, Pl.

per-temptō, āre, *to probe, test thoroughly*. **1.** Lit.: utrumque pugionem, Tac. **2.** Transf. **a.** *to sound, test thoroughly* : aliquem. Ter.; adulescentium animos, Liv.; animum cohortis, Tac. **b.** *to probe, weigh carefully* in the mind: rem, Cic. Ep. **c.** *to probe, search, course through* : tremor terras, Lucr. Hence, tremor corpora, Verg.; gaudia pectus, Verg.; lues sensūs, Verg.

per-tendō, tendere, tendī, *to stretch on to some goal*. **A.** Intrans.: *to push on, go straight on*. **1.** Lit.: pars maxima Romam pertenderunt, Liv.; ad alteram ripam, Suet. **2.** Transf.: verum si incipies neque pertendes gnaviter, Ter.; Varr.; Prop. **B.** Trans.: *to push on with* : hoc, Ter.

per-tenuis, e, *adj. very thin, very small, fine* or *slender*. Transf.: argumentum, suspicio, ars, Cic.; spes, Cic. Ep.

per-terebrō, āre, *to bore through* : columnam, Cic.

per-tergeō, tergēre, tērsī, tērsum, *to wipe over*. **1.** Lit.: gausape mensam, Hor. **2.** Transf. of the air and light : *to brush lightly over* : aura (lux) oculos, Lucr.

perterre-faciō, facere [perterreō faciō], *to frighten* or *terrify thoroughly* : Davom, Ter.

per-terreō, ēre, *to frighten* or *terrify thoroughly*: hunc sacrilegum, Ter.; alios magnitudine poenarum, Caes.; metu perterriti, Cic.; a tuis aedibus vi atque armis perterritus (*away from*), Cic.

perterricrepus, a, um [perterreō crepō], *terrifyingly rattling* : sonitus, Lucr.

per-texō, texere, texuī, textum, *to weave to the end, weave off*. Transf. of bringing to an end : inceptum dictis, Lucr. ; pertexe quod exorsus es, Cic.

pertica, ae, *f. a pole, rod, a long staff*. **1.** Lit. : Pl., Ov., Plin. Esp. *a measuring-rod* (usually called decempeda) : Prop. **2.** Transf. *a measure*. Prov. : non unā perticā, quod dicitur, Plin. Ep. [Fr. *perche* ; Eng. *perch*.]

pertime-factus, a, um, *thoroughly frightened* : Brut. ap. Cic. Ep. ; pertimefactus animi maerore, Pac.

per-timēscō, timēscere, timuī, *to become very much frightened* : Pl. ; de suis periculis, Cic. With Acc. : famem, Caes. ; tantam religionem, Cic. With *ne* and *Subj.* : Cic.

pertinācia, ae, *f.* [pertināx], *obstinacy, stubbornness* : Caes., Cic., Tac. In good sense, *perseverance, constancy* : Liv., Suet. ; ad premendam obsidione Capuam, Liv.

pertināciter, adv. *very firmly, very tenaciously*. **1.** Lit. : haerere, Quint. ; Suet. Comp. and *Sup.* : Plin. **2.** Transf. : *constantly, steadily, perseveringly, stubbornly* : Varr., Suet. Comp. : Hirt., Liv. Sup. : Suet.

per-tināx, ācis, adj. [tenāx], *that holds fast, that clings firmly, very tenacious*. Transf. **a.** *very tight-fisted* : Pl. **b.** *steadfast, unyielding, resisting, stubborn* : Cic. ; in repugnando, Liv. ; ad obtinendam iniuriam, Liv. ; adversus impetūs, Liv. ; concertationes in disputando pertinaces, Cic. ; certamen, virtus, Liv. ; digito male pertinace, Hor. With *Inf.* : fortuna ludum insolentem ludere pertinax, Hor. Comp. : Liv. Sup. : Cic.

per-tineō, ēre, uī [teneō]. Lit. : *to hold through* ; hence, *to continue through or to, to reach*. **1.** Lit. : silva a flumine Rheno ad initium Remorum, Caes. ; aspera arteria ad pulmones usque pertinet, Cic. ; pertinens in omnia, Liv. **2.** Transf. **a.** *to reach, extend* : bonitas etiam ad multitudinem, Cic. ; ad posteritatis memoriam, Cic. ; caritas patriae per omnis ordines, Liv. **b.** *to tend or lead towards, to have as an object or result* : ad efferminandos animos, Caes. ; haec omnia eodem illo pertinere ut etc., Caes. ; illud quo pertineat, videte, Cic. ; quo pertinuit nudare corpus ? Tac. **c.** *to concern, relate to* : quid ista ad vidulum pertinent ? Pl. ; ad meum officium, Cic. Esp. in phrase quod pertinet ad, *as far as concerns, as regards* : ad indutias, Caes. ; ad nationes exteras, Quint. ; quantum ad decernentis pertinet, Plin. Ep. **d.** *to be applicable (to), apply (to)* : ad quem suspicio malefici pertineat, Cic. ; Pl. ; ad imperatorem prodigium, Liv. **e.** *to belong (to) as a right* : regnum ad se, Cic. ; ad quem iure regnum pertinet, Liv.

per-tingō, ere [tangō], *to reach (to), extend* : collis in immensum, Sall.

per-tolerō, āre, *to bear out, endure to the end* : tormenta aetatis, Lucr.

per-torqueō, ēre, *to twist awry, to distort* : ora foedo sapore, Lucr.

pertractāte, ṣṣṣ. [..][.] *wṣṣṣṣṣṣṣ ṃṣṣṇṇṣ :* nam pertractate facta est (fabula), Pl.

pertractātiō, ōnis, *f.* [pertractō], *a detailed or thorough handling*. Transf. : rerum publicarum, Cic. ; poetarum, Cic.

per-tractō, āre, *to feel, handle all over, fondle*. **1.** Lit. : papillam, Pl. ; mullos, Cic. **2.** Transf. : *to handle* or *treat carefully* or *systematically, to investigate, study* : mentem omni cogitatione, Cic. ; sensūs mentisque hominum, Cic. ; philosophiam, Cic. ; Plin. Ep.

pertractus, a, um, *Part.* pertrahō.

per-trahō, trahere, traxī, tractum. **I.** *to draw* or *drag through, to conduct forcibly to* : aliquem in castra, Liv. ; ratem ad alteram ripam, Liv. ; pertractus ad Vitellium, Tac. ; Phaedr. **II.** *to entice, allure to* : in locum iniquum pertractus, Liv. ; hostis sensim citra flumen, Liv.

pertrect-, *v.* pertract-.

per-tristis, e, adj. **I.** *very sad* or *mournful* : carmen, Cic. poet. **II.** *very morose* : patruus, Cic.

per-tritus, e, um [terō], *very hackneyed, very trite* : Sen.

per-tumultuōsē, adv. *in a very agitated manner* : aliquid nuntiare, Cic. Ep.

per-tundō, tundere, tudī, tūsum, *to punch* or *make a hole through, to perforate* : crumenam, Pl. ; calicem per fundum, Cato ; latus hasta, Enn. ; tigna, Lucr. ; guttae saxa, Lucr. ; tunicam, Cat.

perturbātē, adv. *confusedly, without order* : Cic.

perturbātiō, ōnis, *f.* [perturbō], *complete confusion, disorder, disturbance*. **1.** Lit. : magna totius exercitūs perturbatio facta est, Caes. ; caeli, Cic. **2.** Transf. **a.** Polit. : Cic. In *pl.* : Cic. ; comitiorum, Cic. **b.** Mental and Personal : animorum atque rerum, Cic. ; vitae, rationis, Cic. ; valetudinis, Cic. Ep. ; ipsorum perturbatio victoriam interpellavisset, Caes. **c.** Philos. : *an emotion, passion* : Cic. In *pl.* : Cic.

perturbātrix, īcis, *f.* [perturbō], *one that disquiets or disturbs* : Cic.

perturbātus, a, um. **I.** *Part.* perturbō. **II.** Adj. **a.** *troubled, disturbed, unquiet* : tempora, Cic. **b.** *alarmed, discomposed* : plebs, Liv. ; perturbatior metu, Cic. Ep.

per-turbō, āre, *to throw into confusion or disorder*. **1.** Lit. : reliquos (milites), Caes. ; aciem, Sall. ; ordines, Liv. **2.** Transf. **a.** Polit. and Civil : urbem, provinciam, Cic. ; pactiones bellicas periurio, Cic. **b.** Mental and Personal : mea consilia, Pl. ; magno animi motu perturbatus, Cic. Ep. ; animo, incommodo, Caes. ; de rei publicae salute, Cic. ; with *Indir. Quest.* : Caes. Esp. of fear : horum vocibus ac timore paulatim milites perturbabantur, Caes. ; clamore, Cic. ; mentis animosque timor, Caes.

per-turpis, e, adj. *very base* or *shameful* : Cic.

pertūsus, a, um. **I.** *Part.* pertundō. **II.** Adj. : *perforated, worn into holes* : sella, Cato ; laena, dolium, Liv. ; Juv. Prov. : congerere aliquid in pertusum dolium, Pl. ; Lucr. [It. *pertugiare* ; Fr. *pertuis*.]

pērula, ae, *f.* [*dim.* pēra], *a little wallet :* Sen.

per-ungŏ, ungere, ûnxi, ûnctum, *to besmear, anoint all over :* corpora oleo, Cic. ; nardo perunctus, Hor. ; faecibus ora peruncti, Hor. ; ora manu, Ov.

per-urbānus, a, um. **I.** *very polite, pleasant,* or *witty :* Cic. **II.** *over-fine.* *Masc.* as Noun (opp. rusticus) : Cic. Ep.

per-urgeŏ, urgēre, ûrsī, *to press* or *urge strongly :* aliquem ad capessendam rem publicam, Suet.

per-ûrō, ûrere, ûssī, ûstum, *to burn to the end, to burn up, consume.* **1.** Lit. **a.** ossa, Ov. ; agros, Liv. **b.** Of the effect of the sun (in *Part.*) : *burnt black :* Libyco sole perusta coma, Prop. ; perusta solibus uxor, Hor. **2.** Transf. **a.** sitis fatigatos et saucios, Curt. **b.** *to inflame, gall sorely :* Hibericis peruste funibus latus, Hor. ; oneri colla perusta, Ov. **c.** *to inflame, consume :* (me) iam hominem porustum, inani gloriā volunt incendere, Cic. Ep. ; valido aestu, Ov. ; intestina, Cat. **d.** Of the effect of cold : Cato ; terra perusta gelu, Ov.

Perusia, ae, *f.* *one of the twelve confederate towns of Etruria,* now *Perugia ;* **Perusīnus**, a, um ; **Perusīni**, ōrum, *m. pl. its inhabitants.*

perûstus, a, um, *Part.* perûrō.

per-ūtilis, e, *adj.* *very useful :* Cic. Ep.

per-vādō, vādere, vāsī, vāsum. **I.** *to go or come through, to pass* or *press through, to spread through.* **1.** Lit. : per omnis partis provinciae, Cic. ; incendium per agros pervasit, Cic. ; per aequa et iniqua loca pervadunt, Liv. With Acc. (going closely with the *per*) : Thessaliam cum exercitu, Liv. ; venenum cunctos eius artûs, Tac. **2.** Transf. : opinio per animos pervaserat, Cic. With Acc. : cum fama ea urbem atque forum pervasisset, Liv. ; murmur totam contionem, Liv. **II.** *to come through to a goal, penetrate, arrive at, reach.* **1.** Lit. : quas in oras, Cic. ; usque ad vallum, Liv. ; ad castra consulis, Liv. ; in naris, Cic. **2.** Transf. : pars belli in Italiam, Cic. ; quo non illius diei fama pervaserit, Cic. ; victoriae fama in Asiam, Liv. ; terror in totam aciem, Liv. ; ad summum aetatis finem, Lucr.

pervagātus, a, um. **I.** *Part.* pervagor. **II.** Adj. **a.** *wide-spread, well known :* sermo, gloria, verba, Cic. Sup. : Cic. **b.** *common, general :* pervagatior pars, Cic.

per-vagor, āri, *to wander* or *range through, to rove about.* **1.** Lit. : omnibus in locis, Caes. ; hic praedonum naviculae, Cic. With Acc. (going closely with the *per*) : domos, Liv. ; bello prope orbem terrarum, Liv. **2.** Transf. **a.** *to extend widely :* ne is honos nimium pervagetur, Cic. ; quod in exteris nationibus usque ad ultimas terras pervagatum est, Cic. **b.** With Acc. (going closely with the *per*) : *to spread through, pervade :* omnium mentis, Cic. ; dolor omnia membra, Plin. Ep.

per-vagus, a, um, *wandering* or *roaming about :* Ov.

per-variē, *adv.* *very variously :* Cic.

per-vastō, āre, *to lay waste, devastate thoroughly :* agros, finīs, Liv. ; Laevos, Liv. ; Italiam, Tac.

pervāsus, a, um, *Part.* pervādō.

pervectus, a, um, *Part.* pervehō.

per-vehō, vehere, vexī, vectum. **I.** *to bear, carry,* or *convey through :* commeatûs, Liv. In *Mid.* or *Pass.* : *to pass through, traverse :* freto Siciliae, Caes. ; with Acc. (going closely with the *per*) : Oceanum, Tac. **II.** *to carry, bring, convey through to a place :* virgines Caere pervexit, Liv. ; Suet. In *Mid.* or *Pass.* : *to ride, drive, sail through to a place :* in portum, Cic. Ep. ; pervectus Chalcidem, Liv. Transf. : *to attain to :* ad exitūs optatos, Cic.

per-vellō, vellere, vellī, *to pull, pluck* or *pinch hard.* **1.** Lit. : natīs, Pl. ; aurem, Phaedr. ; in sense, *to pull one's ear, i.e.* remind one, Sen. **2.** Transf. **a.** te dolor, Cic. ; fortuna te, Cic. **b.** With words : *to pull to pieces, abuse :* ius civile, Cic. **c.** *to stimulate :* stomachum, Hor.

per-veniō, venīre, vēnī, ventum (*Pres. Subj.,* pervenat, Pl.), *to come through to, arrive at, reach.* **1.** Lit. : nocte perveniunt, Liv. ; Sicuono huc, Pl. ; pauci per silvas ad T. Labienum in hiberna perveniunt, Caes. ; ad portam, Cic. ; in summum montis, Ov. ; eo, Caes. *Impers. Pass.* : Caes., Verg. **2.** Transf. **a.** *to reach* or *come to, to come to the knowledge* or *into the possession of* (mostly of things) : si ad erum haec res pervenerit, Cic. ; serrula ad Stratonem, Cic. ; in praedonum potestatem, Cic. ; res ad istius auris, Cic. With *Indir. Quest.* : necdum quae morae causa foret pervenerat ad duces, Liv. With Acc. : verba auris nostras, Ov. *Impers. Pass.* : quin erat dicturus, ad quem perventum non est, Cic. Ep. **b.** *to come to, arrive at ; to reach, attain to :* ad hunc locum, Caes. ; ad primos comoedos, Cic. ; in senatum, Cic. ; ad magnam partem laudis, Caes. ; ad desperationem, Caes. ; in magnum timorem ne etc., Caes. ; in odium civium, Nep. ; ad septuagesimum (*sc.* annum), Cic. Of prices : annona ad denarios L in singulos modios pervenerat, Caes. *Impers. Pass.* : pervenirier eo quo volumus, Ter. ; ad manûs pervenitur, Cic.

per-vēnor, ārī, *to hunt through :* urbem totam pervenarier, Pl.

perversē (**pervorsē**), *adv.* *awry, so as to face the wrong way.* **1.** Lit. : sella curulis in senatu perverse conlocata, Suet. **2.** Transf. : *perversely :* errare, interpretari, etc., Pl. ; dicere, Enn., Cic. ; uti deorum beneficio, Cic. ; imitari, Cic.

perversitās, ātis, *f.* [perversus], *distortion, perversity :* hominum, Cic. Ep. ; opinionum, Cic. ; morum, Suet.

perversus (**pervorsus**, Pl.), a, um. **I.** *Part.* pervertō. **II.** Adj. : *turned the wrong way, askew, awry.* **1.** Lit. : perversas induit comas, Ov. ; esse perversissimis oculis, Cic. **2.** Transf. : *askew, distorted, perverse :* dies, Pl. ; homo, sapientia, mos, Cic. ; Menalcas, Verg. ; ambitio, Quint.

per-vertō (earlier **per-vortō**), vertere, vertī, versum, *to turn the wrong way.* **1.** Lit. : *to overturn, upset, overthrow, throw down :* coqui aulas, Pl. ; turrim ballistā, Pl. ; arbusta, virgulta, tecta, Cic. ; aliquem,

Pl.; quippe ubi pedes instabilis vel au
inermi equite perverti posset, Liv. **2.**
Transf. **a.** *to overthrow, subvert :* hominem, Pl.; Cic.; aliquem amicitiā alicuius,
Tac.; amicitiam aut iustitiam, Cic.;
officium, Cic.; aliquos ambitio, Quint.
b. With words : *to put down, confute :*
aliquem, Cic.

per-vesperi, *adv. very late in the evening :*
Cic. Ep.

pervestīgātiō, ōnis, *f.* [pervestīgō], *a thorough
searching into, examining, investigation :*
scientiae, Cic.

per-vestīgō, āre, *to trace* or *search out
thoroughly* (like hounds). **1.** L i t. : omnia,
Cic. **2.** Transf.: sacrilegium, Liv.; Cic.
With *Indir. Quest. :* Pl.

per-vetus, eris, *adj. very old :* signum,
oppidum, Cic.; amicitia, Cic. Ep.

per-vetustus, a, um, *very old (and worn
out)* ; *antiquated :* verba, Cic.

perviam, *adv.* [per via], *accessible.*
Transf.: Pl.

pervicācia, ae, *f.* [pervicāx]. **I,** In good
sense : *persistence, doggedness :* in hostem,
Tac. **II.** In bad sense : *stubbornness,
obstinacy :* Cic., Liv.

pervicācius, *Comp. Adv. more stubbornly* or
obstinately : Liv., Tac.

pervicāx, ācis, *adj.* [vic in vincō]. **I.** In
good sense : *persistent, dogged, unyielding.*
With GEN.: recti, Tac. **II.** In bad
sense : *stubborn, obstinate, headstrong, wilful :*
Achilles, Musa, Hor.; adversus peritos,
Tac.; animus, Ter.; accusatio, Tac.;
mulierum iussa, Tac. *Comp. :* ira, Curt.

pervictus, a, um, *Part.* pervincō.

per-videō, vidēre, vidī, vīsum. **I,** *to look
over, survey.* **1.** L i t. : sol omnia, Ov.
2. Transf.: cum tua pervideas oculis
male lippus inunctis, Hor. With *Indir.
Quest. :* Lucr. **II.** *to see something through
something else, to discern clearly.* **1.** L i t. :
ita densos implicant ramos ut neque quae
cuiusque stipitis palma sit, pervideri possit,
Liv. **2.** Transf.: hoc, Cic.; infirmitatem
animorum, Cic. Ep.; satis, Liv.

per-vigeō, vigēre, viguī, *to continue to
flourish.* Transf.: honoribus, Tac.

per-vigil, ilis, *adj. ever wakeful, watchful :*
Ov., Plin. Pan.; custodia, Luc.; torus,
popinae, Juv.

pervigilātiō, ōnis, *f.* [pervigilō], *a religious
wakefulness, a vigil :* Cic.

pervigilium, I, *n.* [pervigil], *a keeping awake*
or *sitting up all night :* in *pl. :* Sen. Esp.
in religion : Lucr.; castra pervigilio neglecta, Liv.; celebrare, Tac.; indicere,
agere, Suet.

per-vigilō, āre, *to remain awake all night.*
1. L i t. : noctem, Cic.; Pl. ; ad luminis
ignis, Verg.; in armis, Liv. *Pass. Part. :*
nox pervigilata in mero, Ov. In religion :
to keep vigil : Veneri, Pl. **2.** Transf. :
tecum longos dies, Tib.

per-vilis, e, *adj. very cheap :* Liv.

per-vincō, vincere, vicī, victum, *to conquer* or
defeat completely. **1.** L i t. : pervicit Var-
danes, Tac.; ne nos perfidiā pervincamur,
Pl. **2.** Transf. **a.** dominae mores, Prop.
b. *to carry a point, maintain one's opinion :*
restitit ac pervicit Cato, Cic. Ep. **c.** *to*

sui pass; suade; *exceed :* pretiō suo (i.ur to
outbid), Pl. ; sonum, Hor. **d.** *to induce*
or *prevail upon with great effort, to effect with
labour :* hoc est tibi pervincendum, Cat. ;
neque pervincere potuit ut referrent consules, Liv.; multis rationibus pervicerat
Rhodios, ut Romanam societatem retine-
rent, Liv.; postquam ipsa virtus pervicerit
ne inhonorata esset, Liv.; illam non verbera
pervicere quin etc., Tac. **e.** *to prove,
demonstrate :* aliquid dictis, Lucr.

per-vivō, vīvere, vīxī, *to live on, survive to :*
usque ad summam aetatem, Pl.

pervius, a, um [via], *that may be passed
through* or *crossed, affording a passage,
passable.* **1.** L i t. : aedes, Ter.; transi-
tiones, Cic.; pervius usus tectorum inter
se, Verg.; saltus, Liv.; amnis, Tac.;
equo loca, Ov.; rima flatibus, Ov. *Neut.*
as Noun, **pervium,** I, *a thoroughfare,
passage :* Pl., Tac. **2.** Transf. **a.** *clear,
unobstructed :* cor mihi nunc pervium est,
Pl. **b.** *accessible :* nihil ambitioni, Tac.

pervolgō, *v.* pervulgō.

pervolitō, āre [*freq.* pervolō], *to fly* or *flit
about.* **1.** L i t. : of birds : Lucr.; with
Acc. (going closely with the *per*) : volucres
nemora avia, Lucr. **2.** Transf.: of sound :
per dissaepta domorum, Lucr.; of rays of
light : omnia loca, Verg.

per-volō, āre. **I.** *to fly through* or *about.*
1. L i t. : aedis, Verg. **2.** Transf. **a.**
hasta aerium iter, Ov. Of the sun's beams :
mare ac terras, Lucr. **b.** rumor agitatis
alis, Ov. **c.** LVI milia passuum cisiis,
Cic.; totam urbem, Juv. **II.** *to fly through
to, reach by flying.* Transf.: animus in
hanc sedem, Cic.

per-volō, velle, voluī, *to wish greatly.* With
Inf. : Cic., Liv.; *in tmesi :* Cic. Ep.
With Acc. and *Inf. :* Pl., Liv.

pervolūtō, āre [*freq.* pervolvō], *to turn over
often, to unroll :* libros, Cic.

pervolūtus, a, um, *Part.* pervolvō.

per-volvō, volvere, volvī, volūtum. **I.** *to
roll* or *tumble about.* **1.** L i t. : aliquem in
luto, Ter. **2.** Transf. (in *Mid.*) : *to be
very busy* or *much engaged :* ut in iis locis
pervolvatur animus, Cic. **II.** *to continue
to unroll* in reading : Zmyrnam, Cat.

pervor-, *v.* perver-.

pervulgātus (pervolg-), a, um. **I.** *Part.*
pervulgō. **II.** A d j. **a.** *very usual* or *common :* Pl.; consolatio, Cic. Ep. **b.** *well
known :* male dictis, Cic.

per-vulgō (-volgō), āre. **1.** L i t. **a.** *to
make publicly known, to publish, spread
abroad :* tabulas, Cic.; rem in vulgus, Cic.;
b. *to impart to the people, make common :*
quae causa deum per magnas numina gentis
pervulgarit, Lucr.; praemia virtutis in
mediocribus hominibus, Cic. **c.** *to prostitute :* Cic. **2.** Transf.: *to visit often, to
frequent, haunt :* solis fulgura caelum, Lucr.;
volucres nemora, Lucr.

pēs, pedis, *m.* [*cf.* πούς], *a foot of any animal.*
1. L i t. : Pl., Cic., Verg., etc.; altero
pede captus, Liv. Phr. (Lit. or Transf.)
a. In gen. : pede terram pulsare, *to dance,*
Hor.; pedem ferre, *to go* or *come,* Verg.;
pedem referre, *to go* or *come back, to return,*
Ov.; se in pedes conicere, *to take to one's*

heels, Ter.; pedes efferre (ecferre, Pl.), Cic.; pedibus, *on feet, afoot or by land*, Caes., Cic., Liv.; sub pedibus, *under one's feet* (i.e. *in one's power*, Verg.; (or *spurned*), Ov.; ante pedes esse *or* ante pedes positum esse (i.e. *to be evident*), Ter., Cic.; pes dexter, felix, secundus, i.e. *a happy or fortunate arrival* : Verg., Ov.; in sententiam alicuius pedibus ire, *to "divide" in favour of a resolution* in the senate, Cic., Liv. **b.** Milit.: ad pedes desilire, Caes.; descendere ad pedes, Liv.; pedibus merere, *to serve as a foot-soldier*, Liv.; pedem conferre, *to come in to close quarters*, Liv.; ad pedes pugna ierat, Liv. **2.** Transf. **a.** *a foot* of a table, stool : Ter., Ov., Sen., etc. **b.** *a rope attached to the bottom of a sail, a sheet* : Cat.; pede labitur aequo (cf. "*on an even keel*"), Ov.; pedibus aequis, Cic. Ep. Hence, facere pedem, *to veer out one sheet* : unā omnes fecere pedem ; pariterque sinistros, nunc dextros solvere sinūs, Verg. **c.** *a metrical foot* : Cic., Hor.; Musa per undenos emodulanda pedes, Ov. Hence, *a kind of verse, measure* : Lesbius, Hor. **d.** *a foot, as a measure of length* : fossa xv pedes lata, Caes.; pedem e villā egressi non sumus, Cic. Hence, pede suo se metiri, Hor. **e.** Of water : liquido pede detulit undas, Lucr.; retrahitque pedes unda relabens, Verg.; crepante lympha desilit pede, Hor. [It. *piede* ; Fr. *pied*.]

pessimē, *sup. adv. v.* male.

pessimus, a, um, *v.* malus.

Pessinūs, ūntis, *f. a very ancient town in Galatia, celebrated for its worship of Magna Mater* ; **Pessinūntius**, a, um.

pessulus, i, *m.* [πάσσαλος], *a bolt* of a door: Pl., Ter.

pessum, *adv.* [old Acc.; *cf.* infitiās ire], *to the ground, to the bottom, down* (esp. freq. with ire and dare). **1.** Lit.: ne pessum abeat ratis, Pl.; multae per mare pessum subsedere urbes, Lucr. **2.** Transf. **a.** pessum ire, pessum sidere, *to sink, perish* : Pl.; pessum ituros Italiae campos, Tac. **b.** pessum dare and, rarely, pessum premere, *to send to the bottom, to sink, ruin, destroy, put an end to* : me tuis blanditiis, Pl.; aliquem verbis, Cic.; civitates, Sall.; multos bonos, Tac.; aliquem pro suis factis pessumis pessum premere, Pl.

pestifer, era, erum [pestis ferō], *pestilential.* **1.** Lit.: odor, Liv. **2.** Transf.: *baneful, destructive, noxious* : res, Cic.; Antoni reditus, Cic.; bella, Cic.; fauces Averni, Verg.

pestiferē. *adv. balefully* : Cic.

pestilēns, entis, *adj.* [pestis] *pestilential, unhealthy, unwholesome, noxious.* **1.** Lit.: loci, opp. to salubres, Cic.; Africus, Hor. Comp. : annus, Liv. Sup. : annus, Cic. Ep. **2.** Transf.: munus, Liv. Comp. : homo, Cic. Ep.

pestilentia, ae, *f.* [pestilēns], *an unhealthy atmosphere or condition.* **1.** Lit.: autumni, Caes.; agrorum genus propter pestilentiam vastum atque desertum, Cic. **2.** Transf. **a.** pestilentiae possessores, Cic. **b.** *a plague, pest, pestilence* : Massilienses gravi pestilentiā conflictati, Caes.; Cic.; pestilentia gravis incidit in urbem,

Liv.; **o.** oratio plena veneni et pestilentiae, Cat.

pestilitās, ātis, *f. plague, pestilence* : Lucr.

pestis, is, *f. an infectious or contagious disease or sickness, a plague.* **1.** Lit.: Enn.; ibes avertunt pestem ab Aegypto (i.e. of serpents), Cic.; pecudum, Verg.; avertere a populo pestem, Liv.; alii aliā peste absumpti sunt, Liv. **2.** Transf. **a.** *bane, destruction, ruin* : Pl.; importare alicui, Cic.; sibi nefariam pestem machinari, Cic.; servatae a peste carinae, Verg.; Veienti populo pestem minitantes, Liv. **b.** Of a destructive person or thing : Pl.; illa furia ac pestis patriae (i.e. Clodius), Cic.; coluber, pestis boum, Verg.; variae pestes, Verg.; corporeae, Verg.

petasātus, a, um [petasus], *wearing a travelling-cap* : Cic. Ep., Suet.

petasiō and **petasō**, ōnis, *m.* [πετασών], *a leg or fore-quarter of pork* : Varr., Mart.

petasunculus, i, *m.* [*dim.* petasō], *a little leg or fore-quarter of pork* : Juv.

petasus, i, *m.* [πέτασος], *a travelling hat or cap, with a broad brim* (like a sombrero) ; Pl.

petaurum, i *n.* [πέταυρον], *a spring-board for acrobats* : Lucil., Juv., etc.

petessō and **petissō**, ere [*freq.* petō], *to strive for repeatedly or eagerly* : pugnam, auras, Lucr.; laudem, Cic.

petitiō, ōnis, *f.* [petō]. **I.** *an attack, a thrust,* pass. **1.** Lit.: in *pl.* : Cic. **2.** Transf. (of words) : petitiones rationesque dicendi, Cic. **II.** *a requesting, solicitation, application.* **A.** In gen.: indutiarum, Liv. **B.** For office : *candidature* : consulatūs, Caes.; pontificatūs, Sall.; petitioni se dare, Cic. Ep.; desistere de petitione, Liv.; abstinere petitione honorum, Tac. **C.** In court. **a.** *a suing, a suit,* in private or civil cases : integram petitionem relinquere, Cic.; pecuniae, Quint. **b.** *the right to sue for recovery or performance of contract* : Cic.

petitor, ōris, *m.* [petō]. **I.** *a striver for.* Transf.: famae, Luc. **II. a.** *an applicant* or *candidate* for an office : Hor., Suet. **b.** In law : *a claimant, plaintiff,* in a private or civil suit : Cic.

petitūriō, ire [*desid.* petō], *to long to become a candidate* : Cic. Ep.

petitus, a, um. **I.** *Part.* petō. **II.** Noun, **petitum**, i, *n. a request, desire* : Cat.

petitus, ūs, *m.* [petō], *a going towards* : terrae, Lucr.

petō, ere, īvī and iī, itum (*Perf.* petīt, Verg.; petīstī, Cic. *Pluperf. Subj.* petīssem, Cic., Liv.) [*cf.* Gk. πίπτω (=πι-πέτ-ω), πέτομαι, impetus]. **I.** *to direct one's course to, to make for.* **1.** Lit.: locum, continentem, Caes.; Dyrrachium, Cic.; navis, Nep.; cursu muros, Verg.; caelum pennis, Ov. With *Intern.* Acc.: aliam in partem fugam, Caes.; iter a Vibone Brundisium terrā, Cic.; alium cursum, Cic. Ep. Poet. of persons as Objects : ut te supplex peterem, Verg.; Ilionea dextrā, Verg. **2.** Transf.: navis portum, Cic.; campum amnis, Verg.; mons astra, Ov. **II.** Hostilely : *to make for,* i.e. *to attack, aim a blow at.* **1.** Lit.: caput et collum, Cic.; aliquem spiculo, Liv.;

mālo me Galatea (playfully), Verg. ; ungue genas, Ov. ; bello Ponatis, Verg. **2.** T r a n s f. **a.** eius latus mucro, Cio. **b.** aliquem epistulā, Cic. Ep. ; aliquem fraude et insidiis, Liv. ; aliquem falsis criminibus, Tac. **III.** *to go after, go in search of, seek out, seek.* **1.** L i t. : quadraginta minas a tarpezitā, Pl. ; aliud domicilium, Caes. ; grues loca calidiora, Cic. ; apibus stationem, Verg. **2.** T r a n s f. **a.** *to go after, strive after, seek to obtain :* eloquentiae principatum, Cic. ; fugā salutem, Nep. ; gloriam, Sall. ; praedam pedibus, Ov. With *Inf. :* Verg., Hor., Ov. With *ex* and ABL. : victoriam, imperium ex hostibus, Liv. **b.** *to endeavour to obtain, to solicit, court.* (i) Of canvassing for office : Cic. Ep. ; consulatum, Cic. ; praeturam, Cic., Liv. (ii.) Of courting in love : virginem, Liv. ; Ov. ; Sempronia viros, Sall. **c.** *to demand as a right.* (i.) In gen. : poenas ab aliquo, Cic. ; aliquem in vincula, Verg., Quint. ; aliquem ad supplicium, Quint. ; quantum res petit, Cic. (ii.) In law : *to bring an action of recovery, to sue for :* Ter. ; sibi soli, Cic. ; ab aliquo, Cic. ; calumnia litium alienos fundos, Cic. **d.** *to beg, beseech, entreat, ask :* vos peto atque opsecro, Pl. ; pacem ab aliquo, Caes. ; opem ab aliquo, Cic. ; a te pro Ligario, Cic. ; vitam nocenti, Tac. ; precibus per litteras ab aliquo ut etc., Cic. ; peto in benefici loco ut etc., Cic. ; ne conemini, Nep. With *Subj.* (without *ut*) : Caes. With Acc. and *Pass. Inf.* : Suet. **IV.** *to go after and fetch, to go to fetch.* **1.** L i t. : argentum, Pl. ; cibum e flammā, Ter. ; aggerem, Caes. ; aliquid ab impedimentis, Caes. **2.** T r a n s f. : aliquid a Graecis, Cic. ; a litteris doloris oblivionem, Cic. Ep. ; exemplum inde, Cic. ; exempla ex veteri memoriā, Tac. ; suspirium alte, Pl. ; gemitūs alto de corde, Ov. ; Hor.

petōritum or **petorritum**, i, *n. an open, four-wheeled Gallic carriage :* Hor.

Petosiris, idis, *m. an Egyptian mathematician and astrologer.* T r a n s f. : *any mathematician, astrologer :* Juv.

petra, ae, *f.* [πέτρα], *a rock, crag :* Enn., Curt., etc. [It. *pietra* ; Fr. *pierre*.]

petrō, ōnis, *m.* [petra], *an old wether :* Pl.

Petrōnius, a, *the name of a Roman gens.* Esp. Petronius Arbiter, *a Roman knight, a favourite of the emperor Nero* (*perh. the author of a Latin romance still extant*).

petulāns, antis, *adj.* [petō], *forward, pert, saucy, impudent :* homo, Cic. ; *genus dicendi*, Cic. ; iocus, Suet. In bad sense : *wanton, lascivious :* Cic.

petulanter, *adv. pertly, wantonly, impudently :* vivere, Cic. ; in aliquem invehi, Cic. *Comp. :* Cic. *Sup. :* Cic. Ep.

petulantia, ae, *f.* [petulāns]. **I.** *sauciness, freakishness, impudence :* adulescentium, Cic. ; linguae, Prop. **II.** *carelessness, heedlessness :* Pl. ; linguae, Suet.

petulcus, a, um [petō, *cf.* hiulcus from hiō], *butting, apt to butt :* agni, Lucr. ; haedi, Verg.

Peucetia, ae, *f. a region in Apulia :* **Peucetius**, a, um.

pexātus, a, um [pexus], *wearing a garment with the nap on it* (i.e. new) : Mart.

pexus, a, um, I. *Part. peotō.* II. *Adj.* ; *woolly, that still has the nap on, new :* tunica, Hor.

Phaeāces, um, *m. pl. a people described in the Odyssey as inhabiting the isle of Scheria :* poet. *in sing. :* **Phaeāx**, ācis, *noun and adj. ;* **Phaeācia**, ae, *f. their country ;* **Phaeācis**, idis, *f.* (*sc.* Musa), *a poem on the sojourn of Ulysses in Phaeacia ;* **Phaeācius, Phaeācus**, a, um.

Phaedra, ae, *f. daughter of Minos, and wife of Theseus.*

Phaedrus, i, *m.* **I.** *a pupil of Socrates ;* hence *the name of one of Plato's dialogues.* **II.** *an Epicurean philosopher of Athens, an instructor of Cicero.* **III.** *a freedman of Augustus, celebrated as a writer of fables.*

Phaestum, i, *n. a town of Crete ;* **Phaestias**, adis, *f. a female inhabitant of it ;* **Phaestius**, a, um.

Phaëthōn, ontis, *m.* **I.** *an epithet of the sun* (φαέθων, *shining*). **II.** *son of Helios* (*the Sun-god*) *and Clymene, who perished while trying to drive his father's chariot ;* **Phaëthonteus**, a, um ; **Phaëthontiades**, um, *f. pl. the sisters of Phaethon ;* **Phaëthūsa**, ae, *f. a sister of Phaethon.*

phala, ae, *v.* fala.

phalangae and **palangae**, ārum, *f. pl.* [φάλαγγες], *wooden rollers* (for moving ships and military machines) : Caes. [It. *spianga.*]

phalangitae, ārum, *m. pl.* [φαλαγγῖται], *soldiers belonging to a Macedonian phalanx :* Liv.

Phalantus, i, *m. a Spartan who emigrated to Italy and founded Tarentum.*

phalanx, angis, *f.* [φάλαγξ], *a band of soldiers, a host drawn up in close order.* **a.** In gen. : Verg., Juv. **b.** *a division of a Greek army drawn up in battle array, a phalanx :* Nep. E s p. *the Macedonian phalanx* (a compact parallelogram, usually of 50 men abreast and 16 deep) : Nep., Liv. Also of any similar formation : e.g. *an order of battle of the Gauls and Germans*, forming a parallelogram : Caes.

phalārica, *v.* falārica.

Phalaris, idis, *m. a tyrant of Agrigentum, for whom Perillus made a brazen bull, in which those condemned by him were to be roasted alive. Perillus was the first to suffer ; but Phalaris himself afterwards suffered the same fate.*

phalerae, ārum, *f. pl.* [τὰ φάλαρα], *metal plates or bosses.* **1.** L i t. **a.** worn by men as a military decoration : phaleris et torque aliquem donare, Cic. ; equites donati phaleris, Liv. ; phaleras deponere, Liv. ; Verg. **b.** *medallions for horses* (worn on forehead and breast) : equus phaleris insignis, Verg. ; Liv. **2.** T r a n s f. : *any external ornament or decoration :* ad populum phaleras ! Pers.

phalerātus, a, um [phalerae], *wearing phalerae.* **1.** L i t. : equi, Liv. Of men : Suet. **2.** T r a n s f. : *decorated, ornamented :* dicta, Ter.

Phalērum, i, *n. one of the harbours of Athens ;* **Phalēreus**, eī and eos, *m. adj. ;* **Phalērĭcus**, a, um.

Phanae, ārum, *f. pl. a promontory in Chios noted for its wine ;* **Phanaeus**, a, um.

phantasma, atis, n. [φάντασμα], an apparition, spectre : Plin. Ep. [Fr. fantôme.]
(1) **Phaön**, ōnis, m. a youth of Lesbos loved by Sappho.
(2) **Phaön**, ontis, m. a freedman of Nero.
pharetra, ae, f. [φαρέτρα], a quiver : Verg., Hor., Ov., etc.
pharetrātus, a, um [pharetra], wearing a quiver ; quivered : Camilla, Verg. ; Geloni, Hor. ; puer, i.e. Cupid, Ov. ; virgo, i.e. Diana, Ov.
pharmaceutria, ae, f. [φαρμακεύτρια], a sorceress : Verg.
pharmacopōla, ae, m. [φαρμακοπώλης], a vendor of medicines, a quack : Cic.
Pharsālos or **Pharsālus**, I, f. a town in Thessaly near which Caesar defeated Pompeius ; **Pharsālicus, Pharsālius**, a, um ; **Pharsālia**, ae, f. the territory of Pharsalus.
Pharus or **-os**, I, f. (rarely m.). 1. Lit.: an island near Alexandria, in Egypt, famous for its lighthouse ; **Pharius**, a, um, Pharian, Egyptian. 2. Transf.: a lighthouse : Caes.
phasēlus, I, m. and f. [φάσηλος], a kind of bean with an edible pod, French beans, kidney-beans. 1. Lit.: Verg. 2. Transf.: a light boat (of Egyptian origin) or pinnace, shaped like a kidney-bean : Cic. Ep., Cat., Hor., etc. [It. fagiuolo.]
Phāsis, idis or idos (Acc. also Phāsin, Voc. Phāsi), m. a river in Colchis, which flows into the Euxine Sea ; **Phāsis**, idis, adj. f. Colchian ; as Noun, the Colchian woman, i.e. Medea ; **Phāsiacus**, a, um, Colchian ; **Phāsiāna**, ae, f. and **Phāsiānus**, i, m. a pheasant ; **Phāsias**, adis, adj. f. Colchian.
phasma, atis, n. [φάσμα], an apparition, spectre : Ter.
Phēgeus (disyl.), eī, m., f. of Alphesiboea ; **Phēgēius**, a, um ; and **Phēgis**, idis, f. (Acc. Phēgida), d. of Phegeus, i.e. Alphesiboea, w. of Alcmaeon.
Pheneos, or **-us**, I, f. a town and lake of Arcadia ; **Pheneātae**, ārum, m. pl. its inhabitants.
phengītēs, ae, m. [φεγγίτης], phengite, selenite, or crystallised gypsum, used for window-panes : lapis, Suet.
Pherae, ārum, f. pl. a city of Thessaly, the residence of Admetus ; **Pheraeus**, a, um ; **Pheraei**, ōrum, m. pl. its inhabitants.
Phereclēus, a, um, belonging to Phereclus, who built the ships with which Paris carried off Helen.
Pherecȳdēs, is, m. I. a philosopher of Syros, an instructor of Pythagoras ; **Pherecȳdēus**, a, um. II. an Athenian chronicler, about B.C. 480.
phiala, ae, f. [φιάλη], a broad shallow drinking-vessel, a saucer : Mart., Juv.
Phidiās, ae (Acc. Phidian), m. a famous Athenian sculptor, contemporary with Pericles ; **Phidiacus**, a, um.
Phidippidēs, is, m. a famous Athenian courier.
phiditia, ōrum [φειδίτια], v. philitia.
Philaeni, ōrum (or Philaenōn), m. pl. [φίλαινοι, "lovers of praise"], two Carthaginian brothers, who, to extend the boundaries of their country, submitted to be buried alive. Philaenōn arae, "the altars of the Philaeni," a

place on the frontiers of Carthage and Cyrene, named after them.
Philammōn, ōnis, m. a son of Apollo, a celebrated singer.
philēma, atis, n. [φίλημα], a kiss : Lucr.
Philēmōn, onis, m. I. a rustic, the husband of Baucis. II. a Greek comic poet, a native of Soli in Cilicia, and a contemporary of Menander.
Philētās, ae, m. a Greek elegiac poet of Cos ; **Philētēus**, a, um.
Philippī, ōrum, m. pl. a city in Macedonia, on the borders of Thrace, celebrated for the battles in which Octavian and Antony defeated Cassius and Brutus, B.C. 42 ; **Philippēnsis**, e, and **Philippēus**, a, um.
Philippus, I, m. the name of several kings of Macedonia, the most celebrated of whom were (1) Philip II. the son of Amyntas, and father of Alexander the Great ; and (2) Philip V. contemporary with Hannibal. Transf.: as name of a gold coin (= 20 drachmae) : Pl., Hor. ; **Philippēus, Philippicus**, a, um ; **Philippica**, ae, f. a name for Cicero's speeches against Antony ; orig. of Demosthenes' speeches against Philip II.: Juv.
Philistus, i. m. an historian of Syracuse.
philitia, (also **phiditia**), ōrum, n. pl. [φιλίτια (φιδίτια)], the public meals of the Lacedaemonians : Cic.
Philō or **-ōn**, ōnis, m. an Academic philosopher, teacher of Cicero.
Philoctētēs, ae, m. son of Poeas of Thessaly, celebrated as an archer, a friend of Hercules, who gave him at his death the poisoned arrows without which Troy could not be taken ; **Philoctētaeus**, a, um.
philologia, ae, f. [φιλολογία], love of learning or letters. a. literary pursuits, the study of literature : nostra, Cic. Ep. b. explanation, interpretation of the writings of others : Sen. Ep.
philologus, a, um [φιλόλογος], learned, literary. As Noun, **philologus**, I, m. a. a man of letters, scholar : Cic. b. an interpreter of the writings of others : Sen. Ep.
Philomēla, ae, f. d. of Pandion, and s. of Procne ; changed into a nightingale. Transf.: the nightingale : Verg.
philosophē, adv. philosophically : Cic. Ironically in Pl.
philosophia, ae, f. [φιλοσοφία], philosophy. 1. Lit.: Cic., Sen. Ep. 2. Transf. a. a philosophical subject or question : Nep. b. In pl.: philosophical systems or sects : Cic.
philosophor, ārī [philosophus], to apply oneself to philosophy : Pl., Cic.
philosophus, a, um [φιλόσοφος], philosophical: scriptiones, Cic. As Noun, **philosophus**, I, m. a philosopher : Cic. ; **philosopha**, ae, f. Cic. Ep.
philtrum, I, n. [φίλτρον], a love-potion, philtre : in pl. : Ov., Juv.
phylira, ae, f. [φιλύρα], bast, the inner bark of the lime-tree, of which bands for chaplets were made : nexae philyris coronae, Hor. ; Ov.
Philyra, ae, f., d. of Oceanus, and m. of Chiron ; **Philyrēius**, a, um ; **Philyridēs**, ae, m. son of Philyra, i.e. Chiron.
phimus, I, m. [φιμός], a dice-box (= fritillus) : Hor.

Phīneus, (disyl.), eī and eos, m. *king of Salmydessus, in Thrace. He was tormented by the Harpies, from whom he was freed by the Argonauts ;* **Phīnēius, Phīnēus**, a, um ; **Phīnīdēs**, ae, m. *a male descendant of Phineus.*

Phlegethōn, ontis, m. [φλεγέθων, "*flaming*"], *a river in the Lower World ;* **Phlegethontis**, idis, f. *adj.*

Phlegra, ae, f. *a country of Macedonia, afterwards called Pallene, scene of the conflict of gods and giants ;* **Phlegraeus**, a, um.

Phlegyae, ārum, m. pl. *a Thracian or Thessalian people who destroyed the temple at Delphi.*

Phlegyās, ae, m. *king of the Lapithae, and father of Ixion.*

Phlīūs, ūntis, f. *a city of Peloponnesus, between Sicyon and Argolis.* Hence **Phlīāsius**, a, um ; *and* **Phlīāsiī**, ōrum, m. pl. *its inhabitants.*

phōca, ae, and **phōcē**, ēs, f. [φώκη], *a seal, sea-calf :* Verg., Ov.

Phōcaea, ae, f. *a coast town of Ionia, a colony from which founded Massilia in the sixth century,* B.C. ; **Phōcaeēnsēs**, ium, and **Phōcaeī**, ōrum. m. pl. *the Phocaeans ;* **Phōcaicus**, a, um, *Phocaean or Massilian.*

Phōcis, idis, f. *a country of Northern Greece, west of Boeotia.* **Phōcēnsēs**, ium, and **Phōciī**, ōrum, m. pl. *the Phocians ;* **Phōcēus**, a, um, *and* **Phōcaicus**, a, um.

Phoebē, ēs, f. *the moon-goddess, sister of Phoebus.* Transf. *night :* Ov.

Phoebus, I, m. *a name of Apollo, the sun-god.* Transf.: *the sun :* Hor., Ov. ; **Phoebigena**, ae, m. *his son Aesculapius ;* **Phoebēius, Phoebēus**, a, um ; **Phoebas**, adis, f. *a priestess of Apollo, a prophetess.*

Phoenīcē, ēs, f. *Phoenicia, i.e. the territory of Tyre, Sidon, etc. ; famed for its commerce ;* **Phoenīcēs**, um, m. pl. *the Phoenicians ;* **Phoenissa**, ae, f. *a Phoenician woman ;* esp. *Dido :* Verg.

phoenīcopterus, I, m. [φοινικόπτερος], *the flamingo :* Sen. Ep., Juv., etc.

phoenix, īcis, m. [φοίνιξ], *the phoenix (a fabulous Arabian bird, which was said to live 500 years, and end its life by placing itself on a burning pile, its ashes giving birth to a young phoenix) :* Ov., Tac., etc.

Phoenix, īcis, m. *son of Amyntor, the teacher and companion of Achilles.*

Pholoē, ēs, f. **I.** *a mountain in Arcadia, on the borders of Elis.* **II.** *a mountain in Thessaly, the abode of the Centaurs.*

phōnascus, I, m. [φωνασκός, *singing-master*], *a teacher of singing and declamation :* Varr., Quint., Suet.

Phorcus, I, m., s. *of Neptune, f. of Medusa and the other Gorgons ; who was changed after death into a sea-god ;* **Phorcis**, idos, f. *a female descendant of Phorcus, Medusa* (but *sorores* Phorcides, *the Graeae,* Ov.) ; **Phorcynis**, idos and idis, f. *Medusa.*

Phormiō, ōnis, m. *a peripatetic philosopher of Ephesus, who lectured before Hannibal on the art of war.* Transf. *a driveller :* Cic.

Phorōneus (trisyl.), eī and eos, m. *son of Inachus, and brother of Io ;* **Phorōnis**, idis, f. *Io.*

Phraātēs or **Phrahātēs**, ae, m. *the name of several kings of Parthia ;* esp. *Phraates IV, contemporary with Horace, expelled from his kingdom for his cruelty and restored by the Scythians.*

phrasis, is, f. [φράσις]. Rhet.: *diction* (pure Lat. *elocutio*) : Quint.

phrenēsis, is, f. [φρενῖτις], *madness, delirium, frenzy :* Sen., Juv. [Fr. *frénésie.*]

phrenēticus, a, um [φρενιτικός], *mad, delirious, frantic :* Cic.

Phrixus, I, m., s. *of Athamas and Nephele, and b. of Helle, with whom he fled to Colchis, mounted on a ram with a golden fleece ;* **Phrixēus**, a, um.

Phryges, um, m. pl. *the Phrygians, a people of Asia Minor ;* **Phrygia**, ae, f. *their country, divided into Great and Little Phrygia ;* **Phrygius**, a, um. a. *Phrygian :* *vestes* (i.e. embroidered), Verg. ; *modi* (a passionate kind of music), Ov. ; *mater* (i.e. Magna Mater), Verg. ; *maritus* (i.e. Pelops), Prop. b. *Trojan :* Verg., Ov. **Phryx**, ygis, adj. *Phrygian, Trojan.*

phrygiō, ōnis, m. *an embroiderer in gold, an embroiderer :* Pl.

Phrynē, ēs, f. *a celebrated hetaira at Athens in the time of Alexander.*

Phthīa, ae, f. *a city in Thessaly, the country of Achilles ;* **Phthias**, adis, f. *a woman of Phthia :* **Phthīōta**, ae, and **Phthīōtēs**, ae, m. *a Phthiote ;* **Phthīōtis**, idis, f. *the district of Phthia ;* **Phthīōticus, Phthīus**, a, um ; *Phthius rex* (i.e. Peleus), Ov.

phthisis, is, f. [φθίσις], *consumption, lung-disease :* Sen. Ep., Juv.

phy, interj. *pish / tush /* Ter.

phylaca, ae, f. [φυλακή], *a prison :* Pl.

Phylacē, ēs, f. *a small town of Thessaly, where Protesilaus reigned ;* **Phylacēis**, idis, f. *adj.* and **Phylacēius**, a, um : *coniunx* (i.e. Laodamia, wife of Protesilaus), Ov. ; **Phylacides**, ae, m. *Protesilaus.*

phylacista, ae, m. [φυλακιστής], *a gaoler.* Comic. *of a dunning creditor :* Pl.

phylarchus, I, m. [φύλαρχος], *the chief of a tribe, a prince, emir :* Cic. Ep.

Phyllis, idis and idos, f. *daughter of Sithon, a Thracian king, changed into an almond tree.*

Phyllodocē, ēs, f. *a sea-nymph, daughter of Nereus and Doris.*

Phyllēis, idis, f. *adj.* and **Phyllēius**, a, um, *of Phyllus, a city in Thessaly, Thessalian :* *iuvenis, i.e. Caeneus,* Ov.

physica, ae, and **physicē**, ēs, f. [φυσική], *natural science, natural philosophy, physics :* Cic.

physicē, adv. *in the manner of naturalists or scientists :* dicere, Cic.

physicus, a, um [φυσικός], *of or belonging to natural philosophy or physics, natural, physical :* Cic. As Noun, **physicus**, I, m. *a natural philosopher or scientist :* Cic., Varr. ; **physica**, ōrum, n. pl. *physics :* Cic.

physiognōmōn, ōnis, m. [φυσιογνώμων], *one who judges men's characters by their appearance ; a physiognomist :* Cic.

physiologia, ae, f. [φυσιολογία], *knowledge of nature, natural philosophy or science :* Cic.

piābilis, e, adj. [piō], *that may be expiated, expiable :* fulmen, Ov.

piăculāris, e, *adj.* [piāculum], *atoning, expiatory :* sacrificia, Liv. Without sacrificia : ut piacularia Iunoni fierent, Liv. Comic. transf. : Pl.

piăculum, ī, *n.* [piŏ], *a means of reconciling or appeasing a deity.* **1.** Lit. **a.** *the ceremony of reconciliation, propitiatory sacrifice :* pati, Cic. ; falsi mundi, Liv. In *pl.* : Hor., Ov. **b.** *a victim :* duc nigras pecudes, ea prima piacula sunto, Verg. **2.** Transf. **a.** *expiation of sacrilege :* dea a violatoribus (sui templi) gravia piacula exegit, Liv. **b.** *Of a guilty person :* ut luendis periculis publicis piacula simus, Liv. **c.** *Of remedial measures :* Hor. **d.** *Of an act requiring atonement :* Pl. ; rerum praetermissarum, Liv. ; piacula merituri, Liv. ; soluti piaculo, Tac.

piāmen, inis, *n.* [piŏ], *a means of expiation, an atonement :* Ov.

pīca, ae, *f. a jay or magpie :* Ov. [Fr. *pie.*]

pīcāria, ae, *f.* [pix], *a pitch-hut :* Cic.

pīcea, ae, *f.* [pix], *the spruce-fir :* Ov.

Pīcēnum, ī, *n. a district of Central Italy, bordering on the Adriatic :* **Pīcēns**, entis, *adj.;* **Pīcentēs**, ium, *m. pl. the inhabitants;* **Pīcēnus**, a, um.

pīceus, a, um [pix], *made of pitch.* **1.** Lit. : Luc. **2.** Transf. : *pitch-black :* caligo, Verg. ; nubes, Ov.

pīcō, āre [pix], *to bedaub with pitch.* **1.** Lit. : dolia, Cato, Suet. **2.** Transf. : picatum vinum, *tasting of pitch or resin,* Mart.

pictor, ōris, *m.* [pingŏ], *a painter :* Cic., Hor. [It. *pittore.*]

Pictor, ōris, *m. a cognomen in the gens Fabia.* Esp. Q. Fabius Pictor, *the earliest historian of Rome.*

pictūra, ae, *f.* [pingŏ], *painting.* **1.** Lit. **a.** In gen. : ars picturae, Cic. **b.** *a painting of the face* (for cosmetic purposes) : Pl. **2.** Transf. **A.** **a.** *a painting, picture :* Pl., Cic., Tac. **b.** *embroidery :* Lucr. **c.** *Of pictures in mosaic :* Verg. **B.** *a word-picture :* Cic.

pictūrātus, a, um [pictūra]. **I.** *painted :* Stat. **II.** *embroidered :* vestes, Verg.

pictus, a, um. **I.** *Part.* pingŏ. **II.** Adj.: *decorated, many-coloured, tattooed.* **1.** Lit.: Verg., Ov. **2.** Transf. **a.** *Of style : decorated, ornate :* orationis genus, Cic. Comp. : Cic. **b.** *painted, false :* metus, Prop.

pīcus, ī, *m.* **I.** *a woodpecker :* Pl. **II.** *a fabulous bird, the griffin :* Pl.

Pīcus, ī, *m. s. of Saturn, g. f. of Latinus ; changed by Circe into a woodpecker.*

piē, *adv. dutifully, affectionately :* Cic., Ov. Sup. piissimē, Cic.

Pīeria, ae, *f.* **I.** *a country of Macedonia, south of the Haliacmon.* **II.** *a country of Syria, between Cilicia and Phoenicia.*

Pīeros (-us), ī, *m. a king of Emathia, who gave to his daughters the names of the nine Muses.* Acc. to others, *a Macedonian, father of the nine Muses ;* **Pīeris**, idis *or* idos, *f. daughter of Pieros ; a Muse ;* **Pīerides**, um, *f. pl. the Muses;* **Pīerius**, a, um, *Pierian.* hence, *musical, poetic ;* **Pīeriae**, ārum, *f. pl. the Muses.*

piĕtās, ātis, *f.* [pius], *dutiful conduct towards* (and from) *gods, country, parents, brothers* and sisters, etc. **1.** Lit. **a.** *In respect* of the gods : Enn., Lucr. ; adversus deos, Cic. ; deos placatos pietas efficiet, Cic. ; si quid pietas antiqua labores respicit humanos, Verg. **b.** *In respect of country :* erga patriam, Cic. ; in patriam, Liv. *Of* colonies towards the mother-city : si ulla pietas antiquae urbis esset, Liv. **c.** *In respect of relatives :* Pl. ; in matrem, Cic. ; erga parentis aut alios sanguine coniunctos, Cic. ; felix nati pietate, Verg. ; sollemnia pietatis, Tac. *Of a wife :* Pl., Ov. **2.** Transf. : *fatherly kindness, tenderness, pity :* senatūs, Plin. Pan. ; so of the patres conscripti : Suet. [Fr. *piété* and *pitié.*]

piger, gra, grum [piget], *reluctant, unwilling, apathetic, slack, backward, slow, inert.* **1.** Lit. **a.** *Of persons :* in re militari, Cic. Ep. ; piger ad poenas princeps, ad praemia velox, Ov. ; pigriores ad facinus, Liv. ; ad cetera munia exsequenda, Curt. ; genus pigerrima ad militaria opera, Liv. With GEN. : militiae, Hor. With *Inf.* : Hor. **b.** *Of things :* taurus ipsā mole, Juv. ; serpens frigore, Ov. ; palus, Ov. ; mare, Tac. **2.** Transf. **a.** *slowly-moving, lingering :* annus, Hor. ; bellum, Liv. **b.** *reluctant or slow in bearing :* campus, Hor. **c.** *making slow or sluggish, benumbing :* brumae rigor, Lucr. ; sopor, Cat. ; frigora, senecta, Tib. **d.** *dull, dispirited :* Mart. ; vultus, Mart.

piget, pigēre, piguit and pigitum est [*cf.* πικρός]. *impers.* (*exc.* in oratione multitudo inducitur ad pigendum, Cic., *and* verba pigenda, Prop.) : (*it*) *causes a feeling of annoyance, vexation, dislike, or reluctance to a person.* **1.** Lit. With *Neut. Pron. or Inf.* as Subject : illud quod piget, Pl. ; recte facere, Sall. ; Juv. ; Suet. With a *quia*-clause : me, quia non accepi, piget, Pl. With GEN. of the cause of the feeling : me civitatis morum piget, Sall. ; Ter. **2.** Transf. **a.** For paenitet : (*it*) *causes regret to :* aliquid aliquem, Ter. **b.** For pudet : (*it*) *causes shame to* (with *Inf.* as Subject) : Liv.

pigmentārius, ī, *m.* [pigmentum], *a dealer in paints or unguents :* Cic. Ep.

pigmentum, ī, *n.* [pingŏ], *a material for colouring.* **1.** Lit. **a.** *a colour, paint, pigment :* Cic. Comic. of cudgelling : aliquem pingere pigmentis ulmeis, Pl. **b.** For cosmetics : Pl. **2.** Transf. of style : sententiae sine pigmentis fucoque puerili, Cic. [Sp. *pimiento.*]

pignerātor, ōris, *m.* [pigneror], *a mortgagee :* Cic.

pignerō, āre [pignus], *to pledge, pawn, mortgage.* **1.** Lit. : bona pigneranda poenae praebebant, Liv. ; alveolos, Juv. **2.** Transf. : velut obsidibus datis pigneratos habere animos, Liv.

pigneror, ārī [pignus], *to take as a pledge.* Transf. **a.** *to claim as one's due :* Mars ipse ex acie fortissimum quemque pigneratur solet, Cic. ; patria maximas nostri animi partis sibi, Cic. **b.** *to accept as a pledge :* quod des mihi, pigneror omen, Ov.

pignus, oris and eris, *n.* [cogn. with pangŏ], *any person or thing given as security ; a pledge, pawn, mortgage.* **1.** Lit. **a.** In gen. : se opponere pignori, Pl. ; ager oppositus est pignori, Ter. ; pignore animos centurionum devinxit, Caes. ; quos pignora pacis dederant, Liv. ; rem alicuius pignori accipere, Tac. ; faenus pignoribus positis, Juv. **b.** *security for a fine* (exacted by a consul for non-attendance of senators) : auferre, Cic. ; capere, Liv. ; senatores pignoribus cogere, Cic. **c.** *a bet, wager, stake :* dare, Pl. ; quovis pignore contendere, Cat. ; pignore certare cum aliquo, Verg. **2. Transf. a.** rei publicae datum, Cic. ; pignora voluntatis, Cic. ; fortunae, Liv. ; societatis, Tac. ; veri, Ov. ; mutuis pignoribus obligati, Liv. **b.** In *pl.* : *children* or *wives, etc.* : communia pignora natos, Prop. ; Ov. ; Tac. ; Plin. Ep. With defining GEN.: pignora coniugum ac liberorum, Liv.

pigrē, *adv. slowly, sluggishly :* Sen. *Comp. :* Liv., Luc.

pigritia, ae, and **pigritiēs**, ēi, *f.* [piger], *sluggishness, indolence, disinclination :* Cic. ; nox Romanis pigritiem ad sequendum ignotis locis fecit, Liv. ; Mart. [It. *pigrizia, pigrezza ;* Fr. *paresse.*]

pigrō, āre (Acc., Lucr.) and **pigror**, ārī (Cic. Ep.) [piger], *to be slow, slack, dilatory.*

(1) pīla, ae, *f.* [pīnsō], *a mortar :* Cato, Ov.

(2) pīla, ae, *f.* [fr. root of pangō], *a pillar.* **a.** In front of a shop : Cat., Hor. **b.** *a pier* or *mole :* saxea, Verg. ; pontis, Liv.

pila, ae (GEN. *sing.* pilāī, Lucr.), *f.* [*cf.* Gk. παλλω], *a ball, playing-ball.* **1. Lit. :** di nos quasi pilas homines habent, Pl. ; pilae studio teneri, Cic. ; pilā ludere, Hor. Prov.: mea pila est, *the ball is mine, I've won,* Pl. **2. Transf. a.** *a game of ball :* quantum alii tribuunt pilae, Cic. **b.** *a voting-ball* (of judges) : Prop. **c.** *a crystal* or *amber ball* used by Roman ladies to keep their hands cool : dura, Prop. **d.** In gen.: lanuginis, Plin. [It. *pillotta ;* Sp. *pelota ;* Fr. *pelote.*]

pilānus, ī, *m.* [pilum], *a triarius,* one of the soldiers forming the third rank in battle : Ov.

pilātus, a, um [pilum], *armed with a javelin :* agmen, Verg. (or perh. fr. pīla, "pillar" ; hence *in column*).

pilentum, ī, *n.* *an easy chariot* or *carriage* (used by Roman ladies at festivals) : Verg., Hor., Liv.

pilleātus (earlier **pīleātus**), a, um [pilleus], *wearing the felt-cap* (at Rome the emblem of liberty) : Liv., Mart., Suet., etc.

pilleolus, ī, *m.* [dim. pilleus], *a small felt cap, a skull-cap :* Hor.

pilleus (earlier **pīleus**), ī, *m.* and **pilleum**, ī, *n.* [*cf.* Gk. πῖλος], *a felt cap* or *hat* (made to fit close, and shaped like the half of an egg ; it was worn by the Romans at festivals, esp. at the Saturnalia, and was given to a slave at his enfranchisement, as a sign of freedom). **1. Lit. :** Pl., Liv. **2. Transf.:** *liberty, freedom :* servos ad pilleum vocare, Liv. ; Mart., etc.

pilōsus, a, um [pilus], *hairy, shaggy :* genae, Cic. ; Juv.

pilum, ī, *n.* [pīnsō], *a pestle.* **1. Lit. :** Cato. **2. Transf.:** *the heavy javelin of the Roman infantry :* Cic. ; mittere, Caes. ;

emittere, Liv. ; pilum haud paulo quam hasta vehementius ictu missuque telum, Liv. Prov.: pilum inicere alicui, Pl.

Pilumnus, ī, *m.* *the father of Daunus,* ancestor *of Turnus.*

pilus, ī, *m.* [pilum], *a division of the* triarii *in a Roman legion* (almost invariably in connexion with primus). **1. Lit. :** primus pilus, *the first century of the triarii :* P. Sextius Baculus, primi pili centurio, *the chief centurion* or *aquilifer,* Caes. ; ducere, Caes., Liv.; aliquem ad primum pilum traducere, *to promote to be chief centurion,* Caes. ; **primus pilus,** or in one word, **primipilus,** ī, *m. the chief centurion* of the triarii and therefore of the legion : Caes.

pilus, ī, *m. a hair.* **1. Lit.:** Cic., Hor., Ov. **2. Transf.:** *a hair, a trifle :* us. with a negative : ego ne pilo quidem minus me amabo, Cic. Ep. ; non facit pili cohortem, Cat. [It. *pelo ;* Fr. *poil.*]

Pimpla, ae, *f. a town in Pieria, sacred to the Muses ;* **Pimplēus (Pipl-)**, a, um ; **Pimplēa**, ae, *f. a Muse ;* also **Pimplēis**, idis, *f. a Muse.*

pinacothēca, ae, or -cē, cēs, *f.* [πινακοθήκη], *a picture-gallery :* Varr.

Pīnārius, a, *the name of a Roman sacerdotal family.*

Pindarus, ī, *m.* Pindar ; *a celebrated lyric poet of Thebes* (B.C. 522–442) ; **Pindaricus**, a, um.

Pindus or **-os**, ī, *m. a lofty mountain range separating Thessaly from Epirus.*

pinētum, ī, *n.* [pinus], *a pine-wood, pine-grove :* Ov.

pineus, a, um [pinus], *of the pine, pine-* : velamina, Lucr. ; claustra, Verg. ; ardor, Verg.

pingo, pingere, pinxī, pictum, *to draw, delineate, paint.* **1. Lit. a.** Alexander ab Apelle pingi volebat, Cic. ; hominis speciem, Cic. ; tabula picta, *a picture,* Cic. ; Ov. **b.** *to embroider :* stragulum magnificis operibus pictum, Cic. ; chlamys picto lembo circumdata, Verg. ; pingere acu, Ov. **2. Transf. a.** *to paint, stain, colour, set off* by contrasts of colour. (i.) pingi (paint one's face), Pl. ; frontem moris, Verg. ; vaccinia calthā, Verg. (ii.) herbas floribus, Lucr. **b.** *to adorn, decorate, embellish.* (i.) bibliothecam, Cic. (ii.) Of style : verba, Cic. ; Britanniam coloribus tuis penicillo meo, Cic. Ep. [It. *pignere ;* Fr. *peindre.*]

pinguēscō, ere [pinguis], *to become* or *grow fat.* Transf.: *to grow fertile* or *fat :* campi sanguine, Verg.

pinguis, e, *adj.* [*cf.* Gk. παχύς]. **1. Lit. a.** *fat :* pinguior agnus, Pl. ; Thebani, Cic. ; omasum, Hor. ; pinguissimus haedulus, Juv. As Noun, **pingue**, is, *n., fat :* denso pingui, Verg. **b.** *fat, oily :* oleum, olivum, caseus, Verg. ; pinguis unguine ceras, Verg. **2. Transf. a.** *fat, rich, fertile ;* also, *plump, in good condition :* sanguine pinguior campus, Hor. ; hortus, Verg. ; merum (*full-bodied*), Hor. ; taedae (*full of pitch*), Lucr. ; ficus (*plump, juicy*), Hor. ; lampades (*full of oil*), Ov. ; arae (*full of fat and blood*), Verg. ; mensa (*luxurious*), Cat. **b.** *fertilising :* pingui flumine Nilus, Verg. **c.**

bedaubed, besmeared: crura luto, Juv.; virga
(*limed*), Mart. **d.** *thick, dense :* caelum,
Cic.; toga, Suet. **e.** Of taste : *insipid :*
Plin. **f.** *dull, gross, heavy :* Cic.; ingenium,
Ov. **g.** *bold, strong :* verba, Quint. **h.** Of
pronunciation : *coarse, broad :* Lucil. **i.**
calm, quiet, comfortable, easy : pingui membra quiete levat, Ov.; otium, secessus,
vita, Plin. Ep. **j.** *sleek, spruce :* pexus
pinguisque doctor, Quint.

pinguitūdō, inis, *f.* [pinguis], *fatness.* **1.**
Lit.: Cato, Varr. **2.** Transf. of pronunciation : *coarseness, broadness :* Quint.

pinifer, era, erum [pinus ferō], *pine-bearing :*
Verg.

piniger, era, erum [pinus gerō], *pine-bearing :*
Ov.

pinna, ae, *f.* [another form of penna, q.v.],
a feather. **1.** Lit.: Enn., Cic., Lucr.,
etc. **2.** Transf. **a.** *a feathered arrow :*
Ov. **b.** *a wing* (mostly in *pl.*) : Cic., Verg.,
etc. Prov.: pinnas incidere alicui, Cic.
Ep.; decisis humilis pinnis, Hor.; maiores
pinnas extendere, Hor. **c.** *flight :* pinnā
veras dare notas, Ov. **d.** *the fin of a fish ;*
Plin. **e.** *a battlement, pinnacle :* Caes.,
Verg.

pinnātus, a, um [pinna], *feathered, winged :*
Cic.

pinniger, era, erum [pinna gerō], *winged.*
1. Lit.: Acc., Lucr. **2.** Transf.:
having fins, finny : piscis, Ov.

pinni-pēs, pedis [pinna pēs], *wing-footed :*
Cat.

pinni-potēns, v. pennipotēns.

pinnirapus, i, *m.* [pinna rapiō], *a crest-seizer,*
i.e. *a gladiator who fought with a Samnite
having a crest to his helmet :* Juv.

pinnula, ae, *f.* [dim. pinna], *a little wing :*
Pl.

pinotērēs, ae, *m.* [πινοτήρης], *the hermit-crab:*
Cic.

pinsō or **pisō,** pinsero, pinsi or pinsui,
pinsum, pinsitum, and pistum [cf. πτίσσω],
to beat, pound, bray, crush. **1.** Lit.: flagro,
Pl.; farinam, Varr. **2.** Transf.: o
Iane, a tergo quem nulla ciconia pinsit,
Pers. [It. *pigiare.*]

pinus, ūs and i, *f.* [cf. πίτυς], *a pine, pine-
tree* or *fir.* **1.** Lit. **a.** In gen.: Verg.,
Hor., Ov. **b.** *the stone-pine :* Verg. **2.**
Transf.: *anything made of pine.* **a.** *a
ship :* Verg., Hor., Ov. **b.** *a pine-torch :*
Verg. **c.** *a wreath of pine-leaves :* Ov. **d.**
an oar : Luc.

piō, āre [pius], *to reconcile* or *appease by
sacrifice, to propitiate.* **1.** Lit.: Silvanum
lacte, Hor. **2.** Transf. **a.** *to honour with
religious rites, to celebrate :* Pietatem, Pl.;
ossa, Verg.; aras ture, Prop.; busta, Ov.
b. *to purify with sacred rites :* Cic. Of
averting ill-omens : nefas triste, Verg.;
fulmen, Ov.; prodigia, Tac. Of guilt:
culpam morte, Verg.; mors morte pianda,
Ov.; Juv. Of madness : te piari iubes,
homo insanissume ? Pl.

piper, eris, *n.* [cf. πέπερι], *pepper :* Hor.,
Ov., Juv. [It. *pevere ;* Fr. *poivre.*]

pipilō, āre [pipō], *to chirp :* Cat.

pipō, āre, *to chirp :* Varr.

pipulum, i, *n.* and **pipulus,** i, *m.* [pipō], *a
squeaking ;* hence *an outcry, upbraiding :* Pl.

Pirāeeus (trisyl.) and **Pirāeus,** i, *m.* also
Pirāea, ōrum, *n. the principal harbour of
Athens, with which it was connected by long
walls ;* **Pirāeus,** a, um.

pirāta, ae, *m.* [πειρατής], *a corsair, pirate :*
Cic., Luc.

pirāticus, a, um [πειρατικός], *piratical :*
myoparo, Cic., Luc. As Noun, **pirātica,**
ae, *f. piracy :* piraticam facere, *to practise
piracy,* Cic.

Pirēne, ēs, *f. a fountain in the citadel of
Corinth, near which Bellerophon caught
Pegasus.* **Pirēnis,** idis, *f. adj. :* Pirenis
Ephyre (i.e. Corinth), Ov.

Pirithous, i, *m. son of Ixion, king of the
Lapithae, and friend of Theseus, with whom
he descended to the underworld.*

pirum, i, *n. a pear :* Cato, Verg., etc. [It.
pero ; Fr. *poire.*]

pirus, i, *f. a pear-tree :* Verg.

Pisa, ae, *f.* less frequently **Pisae,** ārum, *f.
pl. a city of Elis, on the Alpheus, near which
the Olympic games were celebrated ;* **Pisaeus,**
a, um ; **Pisaea,** ae, *f.= Hippodamia.*

Pisae, ārum, *f. pl. a very ancient city of
Etruria, a colony of Pisa in Elis, now Pisa ;*
Pisānus, a, um ; and **Pisāni,** ōrum, *m.
pl. its inhabitants.*

Pisander, drī, *m. a son of Polyctor, one of
Penelope's suitors.*

piscārius, a, um [piscis], *of fishing* or *fish,
fish-* : forum, Pl.

piscātor, ōris, *m.* [piscor]. **I.** *a fisherman,
fisher :* Pl., Cic., etc. **II.** *a fishmonger :*
Ter. [Fr. *pêcheur.*]

piscātōrius, a, um [piscātor], *of* or *belonging
to fishermen, fishing-* : naves, Caes.; Liv.

piscātus, ūs, *m.* [piscor], *a fishing, catching
of fish.* **1.** Lit.: Pl. **2.** Transf. **a.**
fishes, fish : parare piscatum, Pl.; Cic.
b. *a good haul, a catch* (i.e. of something
pleasant) : Pl.

pisciculus, i, *m.* [dim. piscis], *a little fish :*
Ter., Cic., etc.

piscina, ae, *f.* [piscis]. **1.** Lit.: *a fish-
pond :* Pl., Cic. **2.** Transf.: *a swimming-
pool :* Plin. Ep., Suet.

piscinārius, a, um [piscina], *of* or *belonging
to fish-ponds :* Varr. As Noun, **piscinārius,** i, *m. one fond of fish-ponds :* Cic.
Ep.

piscis, is, *m. a fish :* Pl., Cic., Hor., etc. As
a constellation : Verg.; Pisces, Ov.

piscor, ārī [piscis], *to fish :* Cic., Hor., etc.
Prov.: in aëre piscari, Pl.; piscari aureo
hamo, Suet. [Fr. *pêcher.*]

piscōsus, a, um [piscis] *full of fish :* scopuli,
Verg.; amnes, Ov.

pisculentus, a, um, *well-stocked with fish :*
loca, Pl.; Cato.

Pisistratus, i, *m. a celebrated tyrant of Athens*
(ob. B.C. 527); **Pisistratidae,** ārum, *m.
pl. his sons, Hippias and Hipparchus.*

Pisō, ōnis, *m. a Roman cognomen in the gens
Calpurnia ;* **Pisōniānus,** a, um.

pisō, v. pinsō.

pistillum, i, *n.* [pinsō], *a pestle :* Pl.

pistor, ōris, *m.* [pinsō]. **1.** Lit.: *a pounder ;
a miller :* Pl. **2.** Transf.: *a baker :*
Cic. Also of *pastry-cooks :* Mart.

pistrilla, ae, *f.* [dim. pistrina], *a little pounding-mill :* Ter.

pīstrīna, ae, *f.* [pīstor], *a bakehouse :* Lucil., Varr.

pīstrīnēnsis, e, *adj.* [pīstrīnum], *working a pounding-mill :* iumenta, Suet.

pīstrīnum, ī, *n.* [pīstor], *a place where corn is pounded, a pounding-mill.* **1.** Lit. : Pl., Ter., Cic. **2.** Transf. **a.** *a bakery :* Pl., Sen. Ep., Suet. **b.** *drudgery :* Cic.

pīstrīx, īcis, or **pīstris**, is, *f.* [πρίστις], *any sea-monster ; a whale, shark, saw-fish.* **1.** Lit. : Verg. **2.** Transf. **a.** As a constellation : *the Whale :* Cic. poet. **b.** As the name of a ship : Verg. **c.** *a species of swift-sailing ship :* Liv.

pīstus, a, um, *Part.* pīnsō.

pīthēcium, ī, *n.* [πιθήκιον], *a little ape :* Pl.

Pittacus or **-os**, ī, *m.* *one of the seven wise men of Greece, tyrant of Mitylene, in Lesbos* (c. B.C. 600).

Pittheus (disyl.), eī and eos, *m.* *king of Troezen, s. of Pelops, and f. of Aethra the mother of Theseus ;* **Pitthēus, Pitthēïus,** a, um ; also **Pitthēïs,** idos, *f., d. of Pittheus,* i.e. *Aethra.*

pītuīta, ae, *f.* (trisyl. : Hor., Pers.). **I.** *phlegm :* Cato, Cic. **II.** *rheum, catarrh, cold in the head :* Cat., Hor., Sen.

pītuītōsus, a, um [pītuīta], *full of phlegm, phlegmatic :* Cic.

pius, a, um (*Comp.* only magis pius. *Sup.* piissimus, used by Antonius, and condemned by Cicero ; but freq. afterwards ; Curt., Tac. ; etc.), *dutiful in relation to gods, country, parents, or near relatives.* **1.** Lit. **A.** In wide sense : Aeneas, Verg. **B.** In relation to the gods : *holy, righteous, godly :* Pl., Cic., Ov. As Noun, in *m. pl.* **a.** *the godly :* Cic., Verg. **b.** *Of the dead :* piorum sedes, Cic. ; arva piorum, Ov. **c.** *Of poets :* Cat., Verg. **d.** *Of the gods themselves :* Verg. **e.** *Of things connected with religion :* sacred, holy : far, Hor. ; luci, Hor. ; tura, Verg. **C.** *In relation to country :* bellum, Liv. **D.** *In relation to parents, etc. :* dutiful, affectionate, fatherly, brotherly, filial, etc. : uxor, Pl. ; Ov. ; in parentis, Cic. ; adversus sororem, Liv. ; impietate pia est (sisterly through want of maternal love), Ov. ; metus (of a wife), Ov. Of a wine-jar : testa (perh. *brotherly*), Hor. **2.** Transf. in gen. *honest, upright, conscientious :* quaestus, Cato ; dolor, pax, Cic. *Neut.* as Noun : Ov.

pix, picis, *f.* [*cf.* πίσσα], *pitch :* Pl., Caes., Ov., Liv., etc. In *pl. :* Verg. [It. *pece ;* Fr. *poix.*]

plācābilis, e, *adj.* [plācō]. **A.** Pass. : *easily pacified or appeased, placable :* animi, Cic. Ep. ; omnia aequiora et placabiliora, Cic. ; victorem placabiliorem fecit, Liv. ; placabile ad iustas preces ingenium, Liv. Poet. : ara Dianae, Verg. **B.** Act. : *pacifying, appeasing :* te ipsum purgare ipsis coram placabilius est, Ter.

plācābilitās, ātis, *f.* [plācābilis], *placable disposition :* Cic.

plācāmentum, ī, *n.* [plācō], *a means of pacifying or appeasing.* In *pl. :* deum (GEN.), Tac.

plācāmina, um, *n. pl.* [plācō], *means of pacifying or appeasing :* irae, Liv.

plācātē, *adv.* calmly, composedly ; *cf.* Cic. Ep. *Comp. :* Cic. Ep.

plācātiō, ōnis, *f.* [plācō], *an appeasing, propitiating :* deorum, Cic.

plācātus, a, um. **I.** *Part.* plācō. **II.** Adj. **1.** Lit. : *calmed, quiet :* maria, Verg. **2.** Transf. **a.** *appeased, pacified, reconciled :* exercitus duci placatior, Liv. **b.** *calm, tranquil :* animi status, Cic. ; vultu ac sermone in omnis placato, Liv. *Comp. :* placatiore animo aliquid facere, Liv. *Sup. :* quies placatissima, Cic.

placēns, entis. **I.** *Part.* placeō. **II.** Adj. : *pleasing :* aliquid, Cic. ; uxor, Hor.

placenta, ae, *f.* [*cf.* πλακοῦς], *a cake :* Cato, Hor., Juv.

placeō, ēre, uī and itus sum, itum [*cf.* plācō ; perh. lit. *to smooth*]. **I.** *to please, to be pleasing or agreeable, to give satisfaction, to satisfy :* Ter., Hor. With DAT. : non placet Antonio consulatus meus, Cic. ; Pl ; Hor. With DAT. of *Refl. Pron. : to be satisfied with oneself, to pride or plume oneself :* ego nunquam mihi minus quam hesterno die placui, Cic. ; Juv. **II.** *placet, it seems good, right, or proper; it is agreed upon, resolved.* **a,** In gen. : Locine placet ? Pl. ; si placet, Cic. ; si dis placet, Cic. ; Hor. Mostly with ACC. and *Inf.* , or *ut* and *Subj.* as Subject : Epicuro esse deos, Cic. ; Hor., Tac. ; placuit ei ut ad Ariovistum legatos mitteret, Caes. ; Cic. With *Inf. :* Caes., Hor. **b.** Esp. *of public decrees, etc. :* senatui placere, C. Cassium pro consule provinciam Syriam obtinere, Cic. ; Caes. ; Liv. ; senatui placere ut C. Pansa erat, Cic. ; Liv. [It. *piacere ;* Sp. *placer ;* Fr. *plaire* and *plaisir.*]

placidē, *adv.* calmly, peacefully, placidly, quietly, gently : forem aperire, Pl. ; progredi, Caes. ; ferre dolorem, Cic. ; loqui, Cic. ; campos pascere, Liv. ; acclivis, Liv. *Comp. :* Sall.

placidus, a, um [placeō], *calm, tranquil, quiet, gentle.* **a.** Of persons : Pl., Ter., Cic. **b.** Of things : pontus, Lucr. ; amnis, Ov. ; mare, dies, Plin. Ep. ; senectus, oratio, constantia, Cic. ; vita, Lucr. ; mors, Verg. *Comp. :* Liv. *Sup. :* pax, Cic.

placitō, āre [*freq.* placeō], *to be very pleasing :* neque placitant mores, Pl.

placitus, a, um. **I.** *Part.* placeō. **II.** Adj. **a.** *pleasing, agreeable, acceptable :* Verg., Ov., Tac., etc. **b.** *agreed upon, concluded :* locum ambobus placitum, Sall. ; foedus, Verg. **III.** Noun, **placitum,** ī, *n. that which is pleasing or agreeable.* **1.** Lit. : ultra placitum laudare, Verg. **2.** Transf. in *pl. : opinions, maxims, tenets :* Stoicorum, Tac. ; maiorum, Tac. ; Sen. Ep. [It. *piato.*]

plācō, āre [*cf.* placeō], *to quiet, calm.* **1.** Lit. : tumida aequora, Verg. ; Ov. ; ventos, Verg. **2.** Transf. **a.** *to calm, appease :* numen deorum immortalium, Caes. ; animos, Cic. ; aliquem beneficiis, Liv. ; iratum ventrem, Hor. ; invidiam, Hor. **b.** *to reconcile :* fac, illa ut placetur nobis, Ter. ; aliquem rei publicae, Cic. ; patrem sibi, Liv.

plāga, ae, *f.* [*cf.* πληγή, plangō], *a blow,*

stroke, stripe. **1.** L i t. **a.** Pl., Cic., Verg., etc.; plagas pati, Ter.; plagas perferre, accipere, Cic. **b.** *a wound :* plagam mortiferam infligere, Cic. **2.** T r a n s f. *a blow :* illa plaga est iniecta petitioni tuae maxima, Cic.; levior est plaga ab amico quam a debitore, Cic. Ep.; oratio plagam gravem facit, Cic.; hac ille perculsus plagā non succubuit, Nep. [Fr. *plaie.*]

(1) plaga, ae, *f.* [fr. root seen in Gk. πλακοῦς], *a flat surface, hence a region, tract.* **1.** L i t.: caeli rimari plagas, Lucr.; aetheria, Verg.; ponti, Verg.; plagae tellure premuntur, Ov.; quattuor plagae (the Zones), Verg.; ad orientis plagam, Curt. **2.** T r a n s f. (of the inhabitants of a district): Liv. [It. *piaggia, spiaggia ;* Fr. *plage.*]

(2) plaga, ae, *f.* [perh. fr. root of πλέκω]. **1.** L i t.: *the rope along the top and bottom of a hunting-net ;* hence **a.** *a rope or mesh of a net :* Verg., Hor. **b.** *a hunting-net, snare* (mostly in *pl.*): Pl., Cic., Ov., etc. **c.** *a curtain :* Varr. **2.** T r a n s f.: *a snare :* se impedire, conicere in plagas, Pl.; quas plagas ipsi contra se Stoici texuerunt, Cic.

plagiārius, ī, *m.* [plagium, *kidnapping*]. **1.** L i t.: *a plunderer :* Cic. Ep. **2.** T r a n s f.: *a literary thief, plagiarist :* Mart.

plăgiger, era, erum [plāga gero], *stripe-bearing :* Pl.

plăgi-gerulus, a, um [plāga gerulus], *stripe-bearing :* Pl.

plăgipatida, ae, *m.* [plāga patior], *a buffet-bearer :* Pl.

plăgōsus, a, um [plāga], *full of* (i.e. generous with) *stripes :* Hor.

plagula, ae, *f.* [dim. plaga], *woven hangings for a bed :* Liv.

plagūsia, ae, *f. a kind of fish :* Pl.

Plancius, a, *the name of a Roman gens.* Esp. Cn. Plancius, *whom Cicero defended against a charge of bribery.*

plānctus, ūs, *m.* [plangō], *a striking or beating accompanied with noise.* **a.** In gen.: planctus inlisae cautibus undae, Luc. **b.** In grief: Curt., Luc., Tac. [It. *pianto ;* Sp. *llanto.*]

plānē, *adv.* **I.** *clearly, distinctly, intelligibly :* videre, scribere, scire, Pl.; loqui, Pl., Cic. Comp. : Pl., Cic. Sup. : Cic. **II.** *wholly, entirely, completely, quite :* amare, Pl.; urbem exspoliare, Cic.; eruditus, Cic.; carere, Hor. **III.** In affirmative answers: *certainly, to be sure :* Pl.; plānissumē, Ter.

plangō, plangere, plānxi, plānctum [*cf.* root πλαγ of πλήσσω], *to strike, beat,* esp. so as to produce a noise. **1.** L i t. **a.** fluctūs plangentes saxa, Lucr.; tympana palmis, Cat.; moribundo vertice terram, Ov. **b.** *to beat the breast, head, etc.,* as a sign of grief: laniata pectora plangens, Ov. In *Mid.*: Ov. **2.** T r a n s f.: *to lament aloud, wring the hands :* Verg., Ov., Suet., etc. With Acc.: *to bewail :* Memphitem bovem (i.e. Apim), Tib. In *Pass.*: Tac., Juv. [It. *piangere ;* Fr. *plaindre.*]

plangor, ōris, *m.* [plangō]. **1.** L i t.: *a striking, beating,* accompanied with noise : Cat.; plangore ferire pectora, Ov. **2.** T r a n s f.: *a beating of the breast or face*

in token of grief ; *loud mourning :* plangore et lamentatione complere forum, Cic. ; Verg. ; dare, Ov.

plăniloquos, a, om [plānē loquor], *speaking clearly or intelligibly :* Pl.

plāni-pēs, pedis, *m.* [plānus pēs], *a kind of mime or ballet-dancer, who performed without the comic soccus or the tragic cothurnus :* Juv.

plānitās, ātis, *f.* [plānus], *distinctness, perspicuity :* sententiarum, Tac.

plānitiēs, ēī, *f.* (**plānitia,** ae, very rare) [plānus], *a flat or even surface, level ground, a plain :* Lucr., Caes., Cic., Liv., etc. [It. *pianezza.*]

planta, ae, *f.* **I.** *a shoot, sprig, scion ;* esp. *for propagating.* **1.** L i t.: Cic., Verg. **2.** T r a n s f.: *a plant :* Ov., Juv. **II.** *the sole of the foot :* Verg., Ov., Sen. Ep., etc.

plantāria, ium, *n. pl.* [planta], *sets, slips, or young trees.* **1.** L i t.: Verg., Juv. **2.** T r a n s f.: *the hair :* Pers.

plānus, a, um [fr. root seen in Gk. πλακοῦς], *level, flat, even.* **1.** L i t.: via, Pl.; litus, carina, Caes.; locus, Cic.; aditus, Liv. Comp. : Liv. Sup. : Cic. As Noun, **plānum,** ī, *n. level ground, a plain:* aciem in planum deducit, Sall.; urbs sita in plano, Liv. Phr. (lit. or transf.): per planum ire, Ov.; cadere in plano, Ov.; de plano (i.e. easily), Lucr.; e plano (i.e. out of court, extra-judicially), Suet. **2.** T r a n s f. **a.** omnia aequa et plana erunt Romana, Liv. **b.** *plain, clear, distinct, intelligible :* satin' haec sunt tibi plana et certa ? Pl.; narrationes, Cic.; planum facere, Lucr.; Cic. [It. *piano ;* Sp. *llano ;* Fr. *plain.*]

planus, ī, *m.* [πλάνος], *a vagabond ; an impostor :* Cic.

plasma, atis, *n.* [πλάσμα], *an affected modulation of the voice :* Pers., Quint.

Plataeae, ārum, *f. pl. Plataea ; a celebrated city in Boeotia, near which the Greeks defeated the Persians,* B.C. 479; **Plataeēnsēs,** ium, *m. pl. the Plataeans.*

platalea, ae, *f. the spoonbill :* Cic.

platanus, ī, (ūs, Verg. App.), *f.* [πλάτανος], *the (oriental) plane-tree :* Cic., Verg., Hor., etc.

platēa (platea, Cat., Hor.), ae, *f.* [πλατεῖα], *a street :* Pl., Caes., Hor., etc. [It. *piazza ;* Fr. *place.*]

Platō or Platōn, ōnis, *m. a celebrated Athenian philosopher, disciple of Socrates, and founder of the Academic philosophy* (B.C. 429–348); **Platōnicus,** a, um ; **Platōnici,** ōrum, *m. pl. the Platonists.*

plaudō (vulgar **plōdō,** Quint.), plaudere, plausī, plausum, *to clap, pat, flap.* **1.** L i t. **a.** With Acc. of Object and *Instr.* ABL. : pectora manu, Ov. ; perh. in, choreas pedibus, Verg. With Acc. alone (only in *Pass.*): plausae sonitus cervicis, Verg.; plausis alis, Ov. With ABL. alone: manibus, Pl.; alis, Verg.; rostro, pennis, Ov. **b.** (*sc.* manibus) *to clap in approval :* Pl., Hor., Quint.; manūs suas consumere in plaudendo, Cic. Ep. *Impers. Pass.* with DAT. of person applauded : Cic. Ep. **2.** T r a n s f. in gen.: *to express approbation, to approve, applaud :* Cic. Ep., Juv. With DAT. : mihi plaudo ipse, Hor. ; Plin. Ep.

plausibilis, e, *adj.* [plaudō], *deserving applause :* Cic., Sen. Ep., Quint.

plausor, ōris, *m.* [plaudō], *an applauder :* Hor.

plaustrum (vulgar **plōstrum**, Cato), i, *n. a waggon, cart :* Pl., Cic., Verg., etc. P r o v. : plaustrum perculi (*cf.* ' I've upset the applecart '), Pl. As a constellation, *Charles's Wain, the Great Bear :* Ov.

plausus, a, um, *Part.* plaudō.

plausus, ūs, *m.* [plaudō], *a clapping, flapping.* **1.** L i t. **a.** In gen. : Enn. ; plausum pennis dat, Verg. **b.** *a clapping of hands :* Cic. **2.** T r a n s f. : *applause, approbation :* Pl. ; dare, quaerere, captare, petere, Cic. ; tantis plausibus, Cic. Ep.

Plautus, i, *m. :* T. Maccius Plautus, *a celebrated Roman comic poet, a native of Sarsina in Umbria, born about 254 B.C. ;* **Plautīnus**, a, um.

plēbēcula, ae, *f.* [*dim.* plēbēs], *the rabble :* Cic. Ep., Hor., etc.

plēbēius, a, um [plēbēs], *of the plebs or the commons, plebeian.* **1.** L i t. : familia, Cic. ; consul, ludi, Pudicitia, Liv. ; Deciorum animae, Juv. **2.** T r a n s f. : *common, vulgar, mean, low :* plebeii et pauperes, Pl. ; Cic. ; purpura, Cic. ; sermo, Cic. Ep.

plēbēs, eī and ī, and **plēbs** (**plēps**), plēbis, *f.* [*cf.* πλῆθος], *the commons or commonalty, the plebeians.* **1.** L i t. : opp. to the patricians : Cic., Sall., Liv. ; to a king : Enn. Hence **plēbī** (**plēbis or plēbeī**) **scitum**, i, *n.* (ABL. plēbis scitū, Decree in Cic. Ep.) *a decree or ordinance of the commonalty :* Pl., Cic., Liv. **2.** T r a n s f. **a.** In less exact sense : *the populace, the lower class or order, the masses :* multitudo de plebe, Cic., Hor., Liv., etc. **b.** *Of the inferior deities :* Ov.

plēbicola, ae, *m. f.* [plēbēs colō], *one who courts the favour of the common people, a friend of the people :* Cic., Liv.

plēbs, v. plēbēs.

plectilis, e, *adj.* [plectō], *plaited :* corona, Pl.

plectō, v. plexus.

plēctor, ī [*cf.* πλήσσω], *to be beaten.* **1.** L i t. : Ter., Hor. **2.** T r a n s f. : *to be punished :* Cic., Hor., Ov. ; ut in iudiciis culpa plectatur, Cic.

plēctrum, i, *n.* [πλῆκτρον], *a little stick with which the player struck the chords of a stringed instrument, a quill, plectrum.* **1.** L i t. : Cic., Ov. **2.** T r a n s f. **a.** *a lyre or lute :* eburnum, Tib. ; aureum, Hor. **b.** *skill in lyric :* plectro graviore canere, Ov.

Plēias, adis, *f. ;* more freq. *pl.* **Plēiades** (**Pleiades**), um, *f. the seven daughters of Atlas and Pleione ; they were placed among the stars.*

Plēionē, ēs, *f., d. of Oceanus and Tethys, w. of Atlas, and m. of the Pleiades.*

plēnē, *adv. fully, completely :* perfectae munitiones, Caes. ; sapientes, Cic. ; aliquid perficere, Cic. Comp. : Ov., Quint. Sup. : Plin. Ep.

plēnus, a, um [v. pleō], *full, filled.* **1.** L i t. **A.** In gen. : poculum, Verg. ; auditorium, Quint. ; plenissimis velis navigare, Cic. With GEN. : rimarum, Ter. ; domus caelati argenti, Cic. ; bonarum rerum oppidum, Pl. ; Gallia civium Romanorum, Cic. With ABL. : domus ornamentis, Cic. ; urbs

bellico apparatu, Liv. *Neut.* as Noun : plenum et inane, Cic. ; ad plenum, *to repletion, copiously,* Verg. **B.** In partic. **a.** *stout, bulky, plump :* pleni enective simus, Cic. ; vulpecula pleno corpore, Hor. Comp. : Varr. **b.** *pregnant :* Pl., Cic., Ov. ; tellus, Ov. **2.** T r a n s f. **A.** Concr. **a.** *filled, satisfied, sated :* languet amator, Hor. ; plenus eras minimo, Ov. **b.** *full, packed, laden :* crura thymo plenae (apes), Verg. ; exercitus plenissimus praedā, Liv. ; vitis, Ov. **c.** *well-stocked, abundant :* non tam Siciliam, quam inanem offenderant, quam Verrem ipsum, qui plenus decesserat, Cic. ; urbes, Cic. ; domus, villa, Hor. ; mensa, Verg. ; pecunia, Cic. **B.** In number, measure, volume. **a.** *well-filled* with people : plenissimae viae, Caes. ; domus plena Caesarum, Tac. **b.** *full, complete, entire :* plenissima legio, Caes. ; numerus, Cic. ; annus, Cic. ; pleno gradu, Liv. ; nitendum vertice pleno est, Ov. ; luna, Ov. **c.** Of age : *full, mature :* plenis nubilis annis, Verg. ; plenus annis (i.e. old), Plin. Ep. **d.** Of the voice : *full, loud :* Verg. Comp. : Cic. Of pronunciation : *full, fully-sounded :* Cic. Sup. : Cic., Ov. **C.** Abstr. **a.** *full, filled, abounding in.* With GEN. : fraudis, sceleris, consilii, etc., Pl. ; negoti, ingeni, Cic. ; offici, Cic. Ep. ; irae, Liv. ; quae regio nostri non plena laboris ? Verg. With ABL. : laetitiā, Caes. ; exspectatione de Pompeio, Cic. Ep. ; Plin. Ep. **b.** Of style : *complete, copious :* oratio plenior, Cic. ; pleno ore laudare, Cic. *Neut. pl. comp.* as Noun : pleniora scribere, Caes. [Cit. pieno ; Sp. lleno ; Fr. plein.]

pleō, plēre [*cf.* πλέως, πιμπλημι], *to fill,* whence compleō, expleō, suppleō, etc.

plērus, a, um [fr. root seen in plēnus] (the old form of plērusque, plērique) : Old Law in Cic. ; Cato.

plērusque, aque, umque [plērus : *cf.* quisque from quis, etc.]. **A.** Sing. : *a very great part, the greater part, most :* iuventus pleraque Catilinae favebat, Sall. ; animos multiplex religio et pleraque externa invasit, Liv. *Neut.* as Noun, *the greatest part :* noctis, Sall. ; Europae, Liv. Acc. as *Adv.* **a.** *for the most part, mostly, generally, commonly :* Pl., Hor. ; plerumque . . . saepe, Cic. ; plerumque . . . interdum, Liv. **b.** *very often, frequently :* Tac. **B.** Plural. **a.** *the greater number, tae most :* habent hunc morem plerique argentarii, Pl. ; multi nihil prodesse philosophiam, plerique etiam obesse arbitrantur, Cic. ; plerique Belgae, Caes. ; Liv., etc. As Noun, with *ex* or GEN. : plerisque ex factione corruptis, Sall. ; plerique Poenorum, Cic. ; Liv. ; Tac., etc. **b.** *very many :* Nep., Tac. As Noun : Liv., Tac.

Pleurōn, ōnis, *f. a city in Aetolia ;* **Pleurōnius**, a, um.

plexus, a, um [*cf.* πλέκω, plicō], *interwoven, plaited :* coronae, Lucr. ; flores, Cat.

Plīas, v. Plēias.

plicātrīx, īcis, *f.* [plicō], *one who folds clothes :* Pl.

plicō, plicāre, plicāvī and plicuī, plicātum and plicitum, *to fold, to link together :* quasi anellis hamisque plicata quaedam, Lucr. ;

seque in sua membra plicantem (anguem), Vorg. [It. *piegare* ; Sp. *plegar* ; Fr. *plier* and *ployer*.]

Plīnius, a, *the name of a Roman gens.* Esp. **I.** *C.* Plinius Secundus, *author of a work on natural history ; perished in an eruption of Vesuvius*, A.D. 79. **II.** *His nephew*, C. Plinius Caecilius, (born A.D. *c.* 62), *author of Letters and a Panegyric on the Emperor Trajan ;* **Plīniānus**, a, um.

plōdŏ, *v.* plaudō.

plōrābilis, e, *adj.* [plōrō], *lamentable, deplorable :* Pers.

plōrātŏr, ōris, *m.* [plōrō] *a wailer, mourner :* Mart.

plōrātus, ūs, *m.* [plōrō], *a wailing, lamenting :* poet. In *pl. :* Liv.

plōrŏ, āre [perh. *cf.* pluō]. **A.** Intrans. : *to wail, lament, to weep aloud :* Pl., Cic. Ep., Hor., etc. ; *alicui*, Tib. **B.** Trans. : *to weep over, to lament :* turpe commissum, Hor. ; Juv. With *Inf. :* Pl. With Acc. and *Inf. :* Hor. [Fr. *pleurer*.]

plōs-, *v.* plaus-.

plōstellum, ī, *n.* [*dim.* plōstrum]. *a small waggon or cart, a toy-cart :* Varr., Hor.

ploxemum (ploxi-), ī, *n.* [a Gallic word], *a waggon-box :* Cat.

pluit, pluere, pluit (plūvit, Pl., Liv.) [fr. root seen in πλύνω], (*it*) *is raining.* **1.** Lit. : Pl., Cic., Juv. With *Intern.* Acc. : sanguinem, Cic. ; lapides, terram, Liv. With *Instr.* Abl. : lapidibus, lacte, Liv. **2.** Transf. : nec de concussā tantum pluit ilice glandis, Verg. [It. *piovere* ; Fr. *pleuvoir*.]

plūma, ae, *f. the downy part of a feather, a small, soft feather ;* freq. collect. *feathers, down.* **1.** Lit. : Pl., Cic., Verg., etc. In *pl. :* Cic., Ov., etc. **2.** Transf. : *of the first beard, down :* Hor.

plūmātile, is, *n.* (*sc.* vestimentum) [plūma], *a garment embroidered with feathers :* Pl.

plūmātus, a, um [plūma], *feathered.* **1.** Lit. : Cic. poet. **2.** Transf. : pars auro plumata, Luc.

plumbeus, a, um [plumbum], *made of lead, leaden.* **1.** Lit. : glans, Lucr. ; gladius, Cic. Ep. Of false coins : nummus, Pl. ; without nummus, Mart. **2.** Transf. **a.** *leaden,* i.e. *oppressive :* Auster, Hor. **b.** *heavy :* ira, Pl. **c.** *dull, stupid :* Ter. ; nisi plane in physicis plumbei sumus, Cic. **d.** *worthless :* vina, Mart.

plumbŏ, āre [plumbum], *to lead, to solder with lead :* Cato, Plin.

plumbum, ī, *n.* [*cf.* μόλυβδος], *lead.* **1.** Lit. : Cato ; plumbum album, *tin,* Lucr., Caes. **2.** Transf. **a.** *a leaden plate for ruling lines :* Cat. **b.** *a leaden bullet,* Verg., Ov. **c.** *a leaden pipe :* Hor. [It. *piombo* ; Fr. *plomb*.]

plūmeus, a, um [plūma], *downy, filled with down.* **1.** Lit. : culcita, Cic. ; torus, Ov. **2.** Transf. : *like feathers* (i.e. *light*) : pondera, Mart.

plūmi-pēs, pedis, *adj. feather-footed, with feathered feet :* Cat.

plūmōsus, a, um [plūma], *feathered.* **1.** Lit. : Prop. **2.** Transf. : *downy :* folia, Plin.

plūrālis, e, *adj.* [plūs]. In gramm. *of the*

plural number : Quint. *Neut. pl.* as Noun : Quint.

plūrāliter, *adv. in the plural :* Sen., Quint.

plūrēs, *v.* plūs, under multus.

plūrifāriam, *adv. in many parts or places :* Suet.

plūrimus (-umus), a, um, *v.* multus.

plūs, plūris, *v.* multus.

plūsculus, a, um [*dim.* plūs], *somewhat more, a little more :* plusculā supellectile opus est, Ter. *Neut.* as Noun : plusculum negoti, Cic. ; plusculum etiam, quam concedit veritas, amori nostro largiare, Cic. *Intern.* or *Adv.* Acc. : *somewhat more, rather more :* invitavit sese in cenā plusculum, Pl. ; laborare, Varr.

pluteus, ī, *m.*, less freq. **pluteum**, ī, *n.* *a shelter.* **1.** Lit. **a.** *a moveable penthouse, shed, or mantlet, made of hurdles covered with raw hides, to protect besiegers :* Caes., Liv. Comic. : ad aliquem vineas pluteosque agere, Pl. **b.** *a permanent breastwork, a parapet :* pluteos vallo addere, Caes. ; Liv. **2.** Transf. **a.** *the back of a settee or couch :* Suet. **b.** *a couch, dining-couch :* Prop., Mart. **c.** *a book-shelf, book-case :* Pers., Juv. **d.** *the board on which a corpse is laid out :* Mart.

Plūtŏ or **Plūtōn**, ōnis, *m. the king of the Lower World, h. of Proserpina,* and *b. of Jupiter and Neptune ;* **Plūtōnius**, a, um.

Plūtus, ī, *m.* [πλοῦτος], *the god of riches.*

pluviālis, e, *adj.* [pluvia]. **I.** *rain-bringing :* Auster, Verg. ; sidus, Ov. **II.** *produced by rain :* fungi, Ov. **III.** *of rain :* imbres, Tac.

pluvius, a, um [pluō]. **I.** *of rain, rain-:* tempestates, Cato ; aquae, Cic. ; arcus, Hor. ; aurum, Ov. As Noun, **pluvia**, ae, *f.* (*sc.* aqua) : Cic., Verg., etc. ; in *pl. :* Cic. Ep., Verg., etc. [It. *pioggia* ; Fr. *pluie.*] **II.** *rain-bringing, rain-causing, rain-:* Hyades, Verg. ; Iuppiter, Tib. ; venti, Hor.

po-, *v.* pollcō, polliceor, pōnō.

po', *a shortened form of* post ; as, po' meridiem : Quint.

pōcillum, ī, *n.* [*dim.* pōculum], *a little cup :* mulsi, Liv.

pōculum (pōclum), ī, *n.* [*cf.* pōtus], *a drinking vessel, a cup, goblet.* **1.** Lit. : Pl., Verg. ; exhaurire, Cic. ; ducere, Hor. **2.** Transf. : *a drink, draught, potion :* pocula sunt fontes liquidi, Verg. ; amoris poculum, Pl., Hor. ; (veneni), Cic. ; Ov. ; in tuis poculis, *over your cups :* Cic.

podagra, ae, *f.* [ποδάγρα], *gout :* Cic.

podagrōsus, a, um [podagra], *gouty :* Pl.

Podalīrius, ī, *m. son of Aesculapius, a celebrated physician.*

pōdex, icis, *m. the fundament, anus :* Hor.

podium, ī, *n.* [πόδιον], *a balcony.* **a.** In gen. : Plin. Ep. **b.** In the circus or amphitheatre, *a balcony next to the arena for the Emperor :* Juv., Suet. [It. *poggia.*]

Poeās, antis, *m. father of Philoctetes ;* **Poeantiadēs (Paeant-)**, ae, *m. son of Poeas,* i.e. *Philoctetes ;* **Poeantius**, a, um.

poēma, atis, *n.* (DAT. and ABL. *pl.* poēmatis, Cic.) [ποίημα], *a composition in verse, a poem :* facere, Cic. ; pangere, Hor.

poēmatium, ī, *n.* [ποιημάτιον], *a short poem :* Plin. Ep.

poena, ae, *f.* [*cf.* ποινή, pūniō], orig. *the payment made as an atonement* by a criminal ; *blood-money, compensation* ; hence, *penalty* (prop. of a fine). **1.** Lit. **a.** Phr. for *to pay the penalty* : poenam *or* poenas dare, Enn., Cic. ; pendere, Pl., Cic. Ep. ; dependere, Cic. ; solvere, Cic. ; persolvere, Verg. ; sufferre, Pl. ; suscipere, Cic. ; reddere, Liv. **b.** *to exact a penalty, demand satisfaction* : poenam *or* poenas ab aliquo petere, repetere, persequi, Cic. ; capere poenas de aliquo, Liv. ; quos illi poenas reposcent, Verg. ; aliquem poenā adficere, multare, Cic. ; inrogare peccatis, Hor. **c.** arbitros inter civitates dat qui litem aestiment poenamque constituant, Caes. ; poenas iustas et debitas, Cic. With defining GEN. : mortis, *capital punishment*, Cic. With *Obj.* GEN. : Cic., Verg. With *Subj.* GEN. : rei publicae, legum, Cic. **d.** Personified : Poena : Cic., Hor. **2.** Transf. **a.** *punishment, hardship* : paucorum poenā vos omnes salvi esse potestis, Cic. ; ire in poenas, Ov. Also in some of phrases in l. **a.** and **b. b.** In games : *loss, forfeit :* Ov. **c.** *hardship, pain* : frugalitatem exigit philosophia, non poenam, Sen. Ep. [It. *pena* ; Fr. *peine*.]

poenārius, a, um [poena], *penal* : Quint.

Poenī, ōrum, *m. pl.* *the Carthaginians*, so-called because descended from the Phoenicians ; **Poenus**, a, um : **Pūnicus, Pūnicānus, Poeniceus, Pūniceus**, a, um.

poeniō, *v.* pūniō.

poēsis, is, *f.* [ποίησις], *the art of composing poetry*. **1.** Lit. : Quint. **2.** In concr. sense ; *poetry, poems :* Anacreontis tota poesis, Cic. ; Hor.

poēta, ae, *m.* [ποιητής], *a maker, contriver*. **a.** In gen. : nec fallaciam astutiorem ullus fecit poeta, Pl. **b.** Of poetry : *a poet :* Enn., Cic., Hor., etc.

poēticē, *adv.* *after the manner of poets, poetically* : loqui, Cic. ; Plin, Ep.

poēticus, a, um [ποιητικός], *poetical* : verbum, Cic. ; mella, Hor. As Noun, **poētica**, ae (*sc.* ars) *or* **poēticē**, ēs (*sc.* τέχνη), *f.* *the art of poetry* : Cic., Hor., etc.

poētria, ae, *f.* [ποιήτρια], *a poetess* : Cic.

poētris, idis *or* idos, *f.* [ποιητρίς], *a poetess* : Pers.

pol, *interj.* [abbr. VOCAT. of Pollux] *by Pollux ! truly ! indeed !* pol me occidistis amici, Hor. With other asseverations : pol profecto, Pl. ; pol certe, Ter.

Polemōn, ōnis, *m.* *a Greek philosopher at Athens, a disciple of Xenocrates :* **Polemōnēus**, a, um.

polenta, ae, *f.* [perh. *cf.* pollen], *peeled barley, pearl barley :* Pl., Cato, Ov.

polentārius, a, um [polenta], *caused by* (*eating*) *pearl barley :* Pl.

poliō, īre (*Imperf.* polībant, Verg.), *to smooth, furbish, polish*. **1.** Lit. : daedala signa, Lucr. ; aegida, Verg. ; pumice frontis libelli, Ov. Of whitewashing : columnas albo, Liv. **2.** Transf. **a.** *to polish, improve :* agrum, Enn. ; cultura fundum, Varr. Of writings : orationem, Cic. ; carmina, Ov. ; verba, Quint. **b.** *to polish, order well :* aedificia, Varr. ; domus polita, Phaedr.

pollis, ... *in a polished manner; and feately elegantly :* Cic. Comp. : Cic.

politīa, ae, *f.* [πολιτεία], *the name of one of Plato's works :* Cic.

politicus, a, um [πολιτικός], *dealing with State-management, political :* philosophi, Cic.

politus, a, um. **I.** *Part.* poliō. **II.** Adj. : *polished.* Transf. : *accomplished, refined, cultivated :* doctrinā homines, Lucr. ; artibus, Cic. ; homo politus e scholā, Cic. ; oratio, humanitas, Cic. ; epistula, Plin. Ep. *Comp.* : Cic. ; Crassus (in dicendo) politior, Tac. *Sup.* : Cic. Ep.

pollen, inis, *n.* and **pollis**, inis, *m. f.* [*cf.* πάλη, palea], *fine flour, meal :* Ter., Cato.

pollēns, entis. **I.** *Part.* polleō. **II.** Adj. : *strong, powerful :* genus, Pl. ; Liv. ; animus, Sall. ; herbae, Ov. With ABL. : opibus, Lucr. ; Ov. With GEN. : vini pollens Liber, Pl. With *Inf.* : Luc.

pollentia, ae, *f.* [pollēns], *might, power :* Pl. Personified : Liv.

polleō, ēre, *to be of weight or powerful.* **1.** Lit. : Cic. ; potest polletque (populus), Liv. ; Pl. ; qui in re publicā tum plurimum pollebant, Caes. With *Inf.* as Subject : quantum in hac urbe polleat, multorum oboedire tempori, Cic. With ABL. : formā, Prop. ; armis, gratiā, nobilitate, etc., Tac. **2.** Transf. Of medicines : *to be potent* or *efficacious, to operate :* Plin.

pollex, icis, *m.* **I.** *the thumb :* Cic., Verg., etc. ; with digitus, Cato, Caes. To turn the thumb downwards (premere) was a sign of approbation : Hor. ; hence, in the amphitheatre, it was a signal that the people wished the life of a beaten gladiator to be spared : Plin. ; to turn it upwards towards the breast (vertere, convertere ; pollex infestus) was a sign of disapprobation, and of a wish that the gladiator should be killed : Juv. Poet. for the hand : virgineo demessum pollice florem, Verg. **II.** *the great toe :* Plin., Suet. [Fr. *pouce.*]

polliceor, ērī [por- for prō, liceor], *to make a bid or offer* (at a sale). **1.** Lit. : Pl. **2.** Transf. **a.** *to proffer, offer, promise :* hospitium et cenam, Pl. ; id tibi, Cic. ; alicui studium, Cic. Ep. ; liberaliter, Caes. ; benigne, Cic. Ep. With *Pres. Inf.* : Pl., Ter., Caes. With ACC. and *Fut. Inf.* : Caes., Cic. Prov. : montis auri, Ter. *Perf. Part.* in *Pass.* Sense : pollicita fides, Ov. **b.** Of an orator : *to make a promise* or *preliminary statement* at the beginning of a speech : docui quod primum pollicitus sum, Cic.

pollicitātiō, ōnis, *f.* [pollicitor], *a promising, a promise* (mostly in *pl.*) : Pl., Ter., Caes., etc.

pollicitor, ārī [*freq.* polliceor], *to promise freely ; make many promises :* Ter., Sall. ; operam suam alicui, Pl.

pollicitus, a, um. **I.** *Part.* polliceor. **II.** Noun, **pollicitum**, ī, *n.* *a promise :* Ov. In *pl.* : Ov.

pollinārius, a, um [pollen], *for fine flour, flour-, meal-* : cribrum, Pl.

pollinctor, ōris, *m.* [pollingō], *an undertaker's man who washed and prepared corpses :* Pl.

pollinctus, a, um, *Part.* pollingō.

pol-lingŏ, lingere, līnxī, līnctum [por for prŏ, lingŏ], *to lay out a corpse*, i.e. *to wash and prepare it.* **1.** Lit.: aliquem, Pl. **2.** Transf.: voluptas fucata aut medicamentis pollincta, Sen.

Polliŏ (Pōliŏ), ōnis, *m. a Roman surname.* Esp. C. Asinius Pollio, *a distinguished orator, poet and historian of the Augustan age.*

pollis, inis, *v.* pollen.

pollŭceŏ, lūcere, lūxī, lūctum, *to place upon an altar as a sacrifice, to offer, offer up :* decumam partem Herculi, Pl.; Cato. Comic. **a.** *to serve up as a dish :* non ego sum pollucta pago, Pl. **b.** *to entertain :* polluctus virgis servos, Pl.

pollŭcibiliter, *adv. sumptuously :* Pl.

pollŭctūra, ae, *f.* [pollūceō], *a sumptuous feast :* Pl.

pollŭctus, a, um. **I.** *Part.* pollūceō. **II.** Noun, **pollŭctum**, ī, *n. an offering, a sacrificial banquet :* Pl.

pol-luŏ, luere, luī, lūtum, *to soil, defile, pollute.* **1.** Lit.: dapes ore, Verg.; ora cruore, Ov.; cuncta sanie, Tac. **2.** Transf. (ceremonially or morally) : *to desecrate, defile, dishonour, violate :* sacra, Cic., Liv.; deorum hominumque iura, Cic.; Iovem hospitalem, Prop.; pacem, Verg.; rem publicam, Tac.; mentem suam et auris hominum nefariā voce, Tac.; fratris filiam incesto, Plin. Ep.; Juv.; Tac.

pollūtus, a, um. **I.** *Part.* polluŏ. **II.** Adj. **a.** *virgin no more :* Cat. **b.** *vicious, unchaste :* Liv., Tac.

Pollūx (rarely **Pollūcēs**, Pl.), ūcis (Voc. contr. Pol, *by* Pollux), *m. son of Tyndareus and Leda, and brother of Castor ; famous as a boxer.*

polus, ī, *m.* [πόλος], *the end of an axis, a pole.* **1.** Lit.: glacialis, *the north pole*, Ov.; also alone, *the north pole*, Ov.; australis, Ov. **2.** Transf. in *pl.* : Verg.; in *sing.* : Verg., Hor., Ov.

Polybius, ī, *m. a Greek historian, a native of Megalopolis, and friend of Scipio Aemilianus ; he wrote a history of the 2nd Punic War, etc., parts of which are extant.*

Polyclītus (-ētus), ī, *m. a celebrated Greek sculptor, contemporary with Pericles.*

Polydāmās (Pōl-, Ov.), antis, *m. son of Panthus and friend of Hector.*

Polydōrus, ī, *m. son of Priam and Hecuba ; murdered by Polymestor, king of Thrace ;* **Polydōrĕus**, a, um.

Polyhymnia, ae, *f. one of the Muses of lyric poetry.*

Polymēstŏr, oris, *m. king of the Thracian Chersonese, the husband of Ilione, daughter of Priam.*

Polynīcēs, is, *m. son of Oedipus and brother of Eteocles.*

polyphagus, ī, *m.* [πολυφάγος], *a glutton :* Suet.

Polyphēmus, ī, *m. son of Neptune, one of the Cyclopes in Sicily.*

pŏlypus, ī, *m.* [Dor. πώλυπος for πολύπους, *many-footed*], *a polypus.* **1.** Lit.: Pl., Lucil., Ov. **2.** Transf. **a.** Of rapacious men : Pl. **b.** *a polypus in the nose :* Hor.

Polyxena, ae, *f. daughter of Priam, whom*

Pyrrhus, *the son of Achilles, sacrificed at his father's grave ;* **Polyxenius**, a, um.

pōmārius, a, um [pōmum], *of fruit or fruit-trees, fruit- :* Cato. As Noun, **pōmārius**, ī, *m. a fruit-seller, fruiterer :* Hor.; **pō-mārium**, ī, *n.* **a.** *a fruit-garden, orchard :* Cic., Hor., Ov., etc. **b.** *a store-room for fruit :* Varr. [Fr. pommier.]

pōmeridiānus, *v.* postmeridiānus.

pōmērium or **pōmoerium**, ī, *n.* [post, and moerus for mūrus], *the space left free from buildings inside and outside the walls of a town.* **1.** Lit.: intrare, transire, Cic.; proferre, Liv. In *pl.* : Juv. **2.** Transf.: *bounds, limits :* qui minore pomerio finierunt, Varr.

Pōmētia, ae, *f.* or **Pōmētiī**, ōrum, *m. pl. a very old town of the Volsci, also called Suessa Pometia ;* **Pōmētīnus**, a, um.

pōmifer, era, erum [pōmum ferŏ], *fruit-bearing :* Hor.

Pōmōna, ae, *f.* [pōmum], *the goddess of fruit and fruit-trees.*

pōmōsus, a, um [pomum], *abounding in fruit :* Tib., Prop.

pompa, ae, *f.* [πομπή], *a solemn* or *religious procession.* **1.** Lit.: Cic.; ducere, Pl., Verg., Liv.; sollemnis pompas exsequi, Verg.; pompam funeris ire, Ov. **2.** Transf. **a.** *a train, retinue :* Pl.; lictorum, Cic. Ep.; Juv., etc. **b.** Of things : munera certā discurrunt pompā, Tib.; pecuniae, Sen. Ep. **c.** Of style : *display :* in dicendo adhibere quandam pompam, Cic.; rhetorum, Cic.

Pompēii, ōrum, *m. pl. a city on the coast of Campania, overwhelmed by an eruption of Vesuvius*, A.D. 79 ; **Pompēiānus**, a, um ; also **Pompēiāni**, ōrum, *m. pl. the inhabitants.*

Pompēius (trisyl.) or **Pompēius** (quadrisyl.), *a, the name of a Roman gens.* Esp. Cn. Pompeius Magnus (B.C. 106–48) ; **Pompēius**, **Pompēiānus**, a, um ; **Pompēiāni**, ōrum, *m. pl. the soldiers of Pompeius.*

Pompilius, a, *the name of a Roman gens.* Esp. Numa Pompilius, *the second king of Rome ;* **Pompilius**, a, um.

pompilus, ī, *m.* [πομπίλος], *a fish (that follows ships), the pilot-fish :* Ov.

Pompōnius, a, *the name of a Roman gens.* Esp. T. Pomponius Atticus, *a friend of Cicero ;* **Pompōniānus**, a, um.

Pomptīnus, a, um, *Pomptine ;* esp. **Pomptīnae palūdes**, *a marshy district in Latium near the sea coast, still called the Pomptine (Pontine) Marshes ;* in *sing.* : Juv.; **Pomptīnum**, ī, *n. the Pomptine district.*

pōmum, ī, *n. a fruit of any kind.* **1.** Lit. Varr., Cic.; in *pl.* : Verg., Ov. **2.** Transf. (for pomus): *a fruit-tree :* Cato, Verg., Plin. Ep. [It. pomo ; Fr. pomme.]

pōmus, ī, *f. a fruit-tree :* Tib.

pondĕrŏ, āre [pondus], *to weigh.* **1.** Lit.: pugnos, Pl.; amatorum sinūs, Prop. **2.** Transf.: *to weigh in the mind, to ponder, consider :* verborum delectum auribus iudicio, Cic.; non ex crimine sed ex moribus eius, Cic.; causas non ratione, sed verbis, Cic.

pondĕrōsus, a, um [pondus], *weighty, heavy.* **1.** Lit.: Pl., Varr. Comp. and *Sup.* : Plin. **2.** Transf.: epistula, Cic. Ep.

pondō [ABL. of an old form, pondus, pondī], *by weight, in weight :* neque piscium ullam unciam hodie pondo cepi, Pl. ; ut exercitus coronam auream dictatori libram pondo decreverit, Liv. As *indecl. Noun* (for libra pondo), *a pound :* auri quinque pondo abstulit, Cic. ; argenti pondo viginti milia, Caes. ; Pl. ; Liv.

pondus, eris, *n.* [pendō]. **1.** Lit. **a.** *a weight* used in a scale : paria pondera, Cic. ; iniqua, Liv. **b.** *weight :* magni ponderis saxa, Caes. ; hydria grandi pondere, Cic. ; utuntur taleis ferreis ad certum pondus examinatis pro nummo, Caes. ; moveri pondere, Cic. **2.** Transf. **A.** Material. **a.** In *pl. : balance of weight* producing equilibrium : Lucr. ; tellus ponderibus librata suis, Ov. ; et (terra) recipit prolapsa suas in pondera sedes, Lucr. ; quae ponderibus provoluta essent, Liv. In *sing. :* Manil., Plin. Pan. **b.** *a weight, mass :* in terram feruntur omnia suo nutu pondera, Cic. ; auri, Cic. ; argenti, Caes. ; baltei, Verg. **c.** Of the fruit of the womb : Ov. **B.** Abstract. **a.** *oppressive weight, burden* (poet. for onus) : rerum, Ov. ; senectae, Ov. ; Hor., etc. **b.** *weight, consequence, importance :* id est maximi momenti et ponderis, Cic. : testimoni, Cic. ; conscientiae, Cic. ; habet vim in ingenio et pondus in vitā, Cic. Of style : omnium verborum ponderibus est utendum, Cic. ; fabula sine pondere et arte, Hor. ; nugis addere pondus, Hor. **c.** *weight of character* (i.e. *stability*) : nulla diu femina pondus habet, Prop.

pōne, *adv.* and *prep.* **I.** A d v. : *after, behind :* (moveri) et ante et pone, ad laevam et ad dextram, Cic. ; Pl. ; Verg., etc. **II.** Prep. with Acc. : *behind :* pone quos aut ante labantur, Cic. ; pone castra, Liv. ; Pl. ; Tac.

pōnō, pōnere, posui (posīvī, Pl., Cat.), positum (postum, Lucr.) [po perh. for prō, and sinō]. **I.** *to lay aside, put aside, lay down.* **1.** L i t. : arma, Caes., Liv. ; tunicam, Cic. ; anulos, Liv. ; velamina de corpore, Ov. ; libros de manibus, Cic. Ep. **2.** Transf. : vitam, Pl. ; ambitum, vitia, dolorem, Cic. ; corda ferocia, Verg. ; animos ferocis, Liv. ; curas, Liv. ; metum, Plin. Ep. **II.** Of money, etc. : *to set aside, deposit* for safe-keeping, investing, storing, or as a prize or stake. **1.** Lit. **a.** In gen. : tabulas in aerario, Caes. ; Cic. ; Liv. ; in Prytaneum vasa aurea, Liv. ; pecuniam in praedio, Cic. ; in faenore nummos, Hor. ; praemia (as prizes), Verg., Liv. Hence of burial : corpus, Lucr. ; te patriā terrā, Verg. ; Ov. **b.** Of stakes, wagers (*cf.* depono) : pallium, Pl. ; pocula, Verg. Hence, caput periculo, Pl. **2.** Transf. **a.** *to lay out, employ, spend* (esp. of time or effort) : tempus in cogitatione, Cic. ; totum animum atque omnem curam in petitione, Cic. ; diem totum in consideratione causā, Cic. ; apud gratos homines beneficium, Cic. ; otia, Hor. ; rudimentum adulescentiae, Liv. **b.** *to stake* (i.e. make dependent upon) : salutis auxilium in celeritate, Caes. ; certamen in virtute, Caes. ; spem in vestris sententiis, Cic. ; haec in magno discrimine. Liv. ; in te positum est ut etc., Cic. Ep. **III.** *to set* or *put down, place, post, station.* **1.** L i t. **a.** In gen. : hastam pro aede, Cic. ; in foro sellam, Cic. ; oleas in solem, Cato ; omnia in ignis, Ov. ; sub quercu arma, Verg. ; simulacra castris, Verg. **b.** Of plants and trees : Verg., Hor. **c.** Of food and drink (*cf.* apponere) : Cato ; pavonem, Hor. ; merum in gemmā, Ov. ; cum cibo venenum, Liv. **d.** Of troops and camps : Caes., Cic. **e.** Of buildings and works of art : *to set up, erect, build, found :* templa, aras, moenia, Verg. ; opus, Ov. ; Byzantium, Tac. Hence of depicting, portraying : Orphea in medio, Verg. ; saxo, coloribus hominem, Hor. ; Venerem, Juv. **2.** T r a n s f. **a.** *to set, place :* ne istaec pollicitatio te in crimen populo ponat, Pl. ; pone ante oculos laetitiam senatūs, Cic. ; in laude positus, Cic. ; te apud eum in gratiā, Cic. Ep. ; se in gratiā reconciliatae pacis, Liv. **b.** *to put, place, reckon, regard as :* mortem in malis, Cic. ; in vitiis poni, Nep. **c.** *to lay down, assert, cite :* ut paulo ante posui, Cic. ; aliquid pro certo, Liv. ; exemplum, Cic. With Acc. and *Inf. :* Cic. Also *to put hypothetically, assume :* aliquid, Cic. With Acc. and *Inf. :* Ter., Cic. **d.** *to propose a theme* or *subject :* ponere iubebam de quo quis audire vellet, Cic. ; mihi quaestiunculam, Cic. ; pone Tigellinum, Juv. *Impers. Pass. :* Cic. **e.** *to lay down, appoint, ordain, establish :* leges, Cic. ; rebus novis nova nomina, Cic. ; Verg. ; Hor. ; his ego nec metas rerum nec tempora pono, Verg. ; festos laetosque ritūs, Tac. **IV.** *to lay, put, place.* **1.** L i t. : artūs in litore, Verg. ; collum in pulvere, Hor. ; se toro, Ov. ; somno positae, i.e. *lying asleep,* Verg. Also *to lay out* for burial : Verg., Ov. **2.** Transf. **a.** *to lay, smooth, calm :* freta, Hor. ; Prop. Of the winds (without Object) : *to abate :* Verg. **b.** *to compose, arrange, smooth :* comas, Ov. [It. *porre ;* Fr. *pondre.*]

pōns, pontis, *m.* [*cf.* πάτος], *a bridge.* **1.** Lit. : pontem in flumine facere, Caes. ; inicere, Liv. ; imponere flumini, Curt. ; pontem navibus efficere, Tac. ; flumen ponto iungere, Liv. ; ponto flumen transmittere, Plin. Ep. ; pontem interrumpere, Pl. ; interscindere, Cic. ; rescindere, Caes. ; dissolvere, Nep. ; vellere, Verg. ; rumpere, abrumpere, solvere, Tac. **2.** Transf. **a.** *the gangway* by which voters at the comitia passed into the enclosure : Cic. Ep., Ov. **b.** *a gangway* for embarking or disembarking : Verg., Liv. **c.** *a bridge* between two towers : Verg. **d.** *a drawbridge* between besiegers' towers and the walls of a town : Tac. **e.** *the deck of a ship :* Tac. [It. *ponte ;* Sp. *puente ;* Fr. *pont.*]

ponticulus, ī, *m.* [*dim.* pōns], *a little bridge :* Cic., Cat.

Ponticus, ī, *m.* a poet, contemporary with Propertius.

pontifex (also **pontufex**), icis, *m.* [pōns faciō], perh. orig. *bridge-maker* (with esp. ref. to the Pons Sublicius and to the propitiatory sacrifices to the river-god which the building of the bridge entailed) ; *a Roman* *high-priest*, *a pontiff*, *pontifex* : Cic., Liv., Ov., etc. The *chief pontiff* or *president* was called Pontifex Maximus : Caes., Cic. ; pontifices minores, Cic., Liv.

pontĭfĭcālis, e, *adj.* [pontifex] *of a pontifex, pontifical* : insignia, Liv. ; auctoritas, Cic.

pontĭfĭcātus, ūs, *m.* [pontifex], *the office of a pontifex* : Cic., Tac.

pontĭfĭcus, a, um [pontifex], *of a pontifex* : libri, Cic.

pontō, ōnis, *m.* [pōns], *a Gallic lighter* or *ferry-boat* : Caes.

pontus, ī, *m.* [πόντος], *the sea.* **1.** Lit. : Enn. ; aequora ponti, Lucr. ; freta ponti, Verg. **2.** T r a n s f. : *sea water* : ingens a vertice pontus in puppim ferit, Verg.

Pontus, ī, *m. the Euxine* or *Black Sea* ; in full, Pontus Euxinus. Hence **a.** *the region about the Black Sea.* **b.** *the kingdom of Mithridates between Bithynia and Armenia, afterwards a Roman province* ; **Pontĭcus**, a, um,

popa, ae, *m.* [perh. fr. root of πέπω], *a Roman priest's assistant* or *minister, who slew the victim* : Cic., Prop., Suet.

popanum, ī, *n.* [πόπανον], *a sacrificial cake* : Juv.

popellus, ī, *m.* [*dim.* populus], *the rabble, mob, populace* : Hor.

popīna, ae, *f.* [perh. *cf.* πέπω], *a cook-shop, eating-house.* **1.** Lit. : Pl., Cic., Hor., etc. **2.** T r a n s f. : *the food sold at a cook-shop* : Cic.

popīnō, ōnis, *m.* [popīna], *a frequenter of eating-houses* : Hor.

poples, itis, *m. the ham, the hough.* **1.** Lit. : Verg., Hor., Liv. **2.** T r a n s f. : *the knee* : Lucr. ; duplicato poplite, Verg. ; Hor. ; Curt.

Pōplĭcŏla, *v.* **Pūblĭcŏla.**

pōplus, *v.* populus.

poppysma, atis, *n.* [πόππυσμα], *a smacking* or *clucking with the tongue*, as a sign of approval : Juv.

populābĭlis, e, *adj.* [populor], *destructible* : Ov.

populābundus, a, um [populor], *laying waste, ravaging* : Liv.

populāris, e, *adj.* [populus]. **I.** *of the people, proceeding from* or *designed for the people.* **1.** L i t. **a.** In gen. : oratio, munus, honor, iracundia, leges, res publica, etc., Cic. ; ventus, Cic. ; aura, Hor. As Noun, **populāria**, ium, n. *pl.* (*sc.*subsellia), *the seats of the people in the theatre, the common seats* : Suet. **b.** *approved by the people, popular* : consul, pax, Cic. ; actio, Liv. *Comp.* : Liv. **c.** *favouring the people, democratic* ; *also in bad sense, demagogic* : sacerdos, Cic. ; vir, Liv. ; animus vere popularis, saluti populi consulens, Cic. ; ingenium, Liv. As Noun, **populārēs**, ium, *m. pl. the people's party, the democrats* (opp. optimates), Cic. **2.** T r a n s f. : *common, coarse* : sal, Cato. **II.** *of the same country, native.* **1.** L i t. : Geta, Ter. ; puellae, Hor. ; leaena, flumina, Ov. As Noun, **populāris**, is, *m. f. a fellow-countryman* : Pl., Cic., Liv., Ov. **2.** T r a n s f. : *one of the same party, associate, adherent* : as Noun : Liv. With GEN. : coniurationis, sceleris, Sall.

populārĭtās, ātis, *f.* [populāris]. **I.** *fellow-citizenship* : Pl. **II.** *a courting of popular favour, popular bearing* : Stat., Tac.

populārĭter, *adv.* **I.** *after the manner of the people* : loqui, Cic. **II.** *in a popular manner, like a demagogue* : agere, Cic. ; Juv.

populātĭō, ōnis, *f.* [populor], *a laying waste, ravaging, devastation, etc.* : facere, Liv. ; hostem rapinis pabulationibus populationibusque prohibere, Caes.

populātor, ōris, *m.* and **populātrīx**, īcis, *f.* [populor], *a devastator, ravager* : agrorum, Liv. ; Ov. ; populatrix Hymetti apis, Mart.

populātus, ūs, *m.* [populor], *a laying waste, devastation* : Luc.

pōpŭleus, a, um [pōpulus], *of poplars, poplar-* : frondes, Verg. ; Hor.

pōpŭlĭfer, era, erum [pōpulus ferō], *poplar-bearing* : Padus, Ov.

pōpŭlnus, a, um [pōpulus], *of poplars, poplar-* : sors, Pl.

populō, āre, and **populor**, ārī [populus ; l i t. *to overrun a place with people*], *to lay waste, ravage, devastate.* **1.** L i t. **a.** Form *populo* : litora vestra vi populat, Verg. *Pass.* : urbem Romanam morbo populari, Liv. **b.** Form *populor* : agros, Caes., Cic. ; Luc. ; Aequos, Liv. **2.** T r a n s f. : *to destroy, ruin, pillage.* **a.** Form *populo* : Pl. ; farris acervum curculio, Verg. ; capillos, Ov. ; populata provincia, Cic. ; populata tempora raptis auribus, Verg. **b.** Form *populor* : quisque suum iter, Verg. ; formam aetas, Ov.

populus (contr. **pōplus**, Pl.), ī, *m.* [*cf.* πλῆθος ; and Lat. plēnus), *a people, a political community, a nation.* **1.** L i t. : Thebanus, Pl. ; Romanus, Cic. ; hi populi, Atellani, Calatini, Liv. **2.** T r a n s f. **a.** Opp. to the senate : senatus populusque Romanus (abbreviated S. P. Q. R.) : patres in populi fore potestate, Liv. ; populus iussit, Cic. **b.** Opp. to the plebs (before the plebs obtained full citizenship) : non populi, sed plebis eum (tribunum) magistratum esse, Liv. Also in formal language : Cic. **c.** Opp. to the military : *civilians* : Nep. **2.** T r a n s f. **a.** *a region, district* : frequens cultoribus alius populus, Cic. **b.** *a multitude, crowd, throng* : concursus in forum populi, Liv. ; fratrum, Ov. **c.** *the public, the street* : coram populo, Hor. ; haec (i.e. frons Iani) populum spectat, at illa Larem, Ov. [It. *popolo* ; Sp. *pueblo* ; Fr. *peuple*.]

pōpŭlus, ī, *f. a poplar* : Verg., Ov. ; alba, *the silver-poplar*, Hor.

porca, ae, *f.* [porcus], *a sow* : Cato, Verg., Juv.

porcella, ae, *f.* [*dim.* porcula], *a little sow* : Pl.

porcellus, ī, *m.* [*dim.* porculus], *a little pig* : Varr., Phaedr., Suet. [Fr. *pourceau*.]

porcīnārĭus, ī, *m.* [porcīna], *a pork-seller* : Pl.

porcīnus, a, um [porcus], *of a hog, hog's, swine's* : polimenta, Pl. ; vox, Sen. As Noun, **porcīna**, ae, *f.* (*sc.* caro), *swine's flesh, pork* : Pl.

Porcĭus, a, *the name of a Roman gens* ; *esp.*

I, M. Porcius Cato, *the elder, called the Censor,* B.C. 235-149. **II.** *the younger, called Uticensis,* B.C. 95-46; **Porcius,** a, um.

porcula (or **porculēna**), ae, *f.* [*dim.* porca], *a little sow :* Pl.

porculus, I, m. [*dim.* porcus], *a young pig :* Pl.

porcus, i, m. [*cf.* πόρκος], *a domestic swine, a hog, pig.* **1.** Lit.: Pl.; villa abundat porco, agno, gallinā (collect.), Cic.; porcus femina, Cato, Cic. **2.** Transf.: Epicuri de grege porcus, Hor.; Cat.

pŏrgō, *v.* porrigo.

porphyrēticus, a, um [πορφύρα], *purple-red :* marmor, Suet.

Porphyriōn, ōnis, m. *one of the Giants.*

porrecta, ōrum, *n. pl.* [porriciō], *only in phr.* inter caesa et porrecta, *between the slaying and the offering.* Transf. (=at the last moment) : Cic. Ep.

porrēctiō, ōnis, *f.* [porrigō], *an extending :* digitorum, Cic.

porrēctus, a, um. **I.** *Part.* porrigō. **II.** Adj.: *extended, stretched out.* **1.** Lit.: Pl.; loca, Caes.; Hor.; senex (i.e. dead), Cat.; porrectior acies, Tac. **2.** Transf.: impori maiestas, Hor.; mora, *protracted,* Ov.; syllaba, *long,* Quint.; porrectior frons (i.e. less serious), Pl.

porriciō, ricere [prŏ iaciō], *a ritual word : to lay before, to offer :* exta, Pl.; exta in fluctūs, Verg.; cruda exta in mare porricit, Liv (*v.* also porrecta).

por-rigo, rigere, rēxī, rēctum (contr. form pōrgite, Verg.) [prŏ regō], *to reach out, stretch out, extend.* **1.** Lit. **a.** manum, Pl.; dexteram alicui, Cic.; membra, Cic.; crus, Liv.; bracchia caelo, Ov.; pocula, Hor. In voting by show of hands : manum, Cic. **b.** Of troops : aciem latius, Sall.; in longitudinem porrecta acies, Liv. **c.** Geogr. (in *Mid.*): Rhodope porrecta sub axem, Verg.; cuius (loci) pars in planitiem porrigebatur, Tac. **d.** On the ground : in spatium ingens ruentem porrexit hostem, Liv.; Ov. In *Mid.:* Tityos per tota novem cui iugera corpus porrigitur, Verg. **2.** Transf. **a.** ad pecora avaras manūs, Curt.; Sen. Ep. **b.** *to extend :* quis gradus ulterior, quo se tua porrigat ira, restat? Ov. **c.** *to offer, to grant :* praesidium clientibus, Cic.; Hor. **d.** *to lengthen :* syllabam, Quint.

porrigō, inis, *f. scurf, dandruff :* Hor. Of animals, perh. *mange :* Juv.

Porrima, ae, *f.* [porrō], *a cult-name of the birth-goddess Antevorta.*

porrō, *adv.* [πόρρω]. **1.** Lit. of space. **a.** Of motion : *forwards. farther on :* ire, Liv.; Ter.; Sall. **b.** Of rest : *far off, at a distance :* habitare, Pl.; inscius Aeneas, quae sint ea flumina porro, Verg.; Plin. Ep. **2.** Transf. **A.** Of time. **a.** *far, long ago :* Ov. **b.** *hereafter, in future :* Ter., Liv. **B.** Of sequence : *again, in turn :* dare aliquid porro, Pl.; saepe audivi a maioribus natu, qui se porro pueros a senibus audisse dicebant, Cic.; Verg.; Liv. **C.** In logic and rhetoric. **a.** *next, furthermore, moreover, besides :* Pl.; age porro, Cic.; sequitur porro, nihil deos ignorare, Cic.; civitati porro hanc fuisse

belli causam, Caes. **b.** *on the other hand :* porro erant qui censerent, Caes.

porrum, i, *n.,* and **porrus,** i, *m.* [πράσον], *a leek, chive :* Hor.

Porsenna, Porsena, Porsinna, ae, m. *king of Clusium in Etruria, who made war against Rome in the cause of the Tarquins.*

porta, ae, *f.* [*cf.* περάω, πόρος. Lit. *a passage, thoroughfare*]. **1.** Lit. **a.** *a city-gate, a gate :* Pl., Cic., Verg., etc. **b.** *the gate of a camp,* of which there were four; porta principalis (dextra and sinistra), porta praetoria, and porta decumana or quaestoria : Caes., Liv. **c.** *any avenue, entrance, passage, outlet, door :* venti velut agmine facto, quā data porta, ruunt, Verg. Of a cage : Pl. Of Hades : Verg., Hor. Also, belli, Enn., Verg. **d.** In *pl., a pass :* Nep., Plin. **2.** Transf. **a.** Of means of attack : et quibus e portis occurri cuique deceret, Lucr.; Pl. **b.** Of the body : iecoris, Cic.; patente portā, Cat. [Sp. *puerta.*]

portātiō, ōnis, *f.* [portō], *a carrying, carriage ;* in *pl.* : Sall.

por-tendō, tendere, tendī, tentum [prŏ tendō], *to point out, indicate, foretell, predict, presage :* malum tibi portentum est, Pl.; Sall.; pericula portenduntur, Liv.; libertas portenditur, Pl.; omnia laeta mihi, Liv. With Acc. and *Fut. Inf.* : Cic.

portentificus, a, um [portentum faciō], *marvellous, monstrous :* Ov.

portentōsus, a, um [portentum], *monstrous, unnatural :* aliqua portentosa nata dicuntur, Cic.; serpens portentosā magnitudine, Liv.; puer portentoso parvoque capite, Suet. *Comp. :* Sen. *Sup. :* portentosissima genera ciborum, Suet.

portentum, i, n. [portendō]. *a wonderful sign, an unnatural or supernatural thing or event, an omen, portent.* **1.** Lit.: Cic., Verg., etc. **2.** Transf. **a.** *a monster, monstrosity :* Lucr., Cic., Hor., etc. **b.** Of persons : P. Clodius, fatale portentum prodigiumque rei publicae, Cic.; Juv. **c.** Of stories : *a marvel :* poetarum et pictorum portenta, Cic.; Lucr.

porthmeus, (Acc. -ea), m. [πορθμεύς], *the ferryman,* i.e. Charon : Juv.

porticula, ae, *f.* [*dim.* porticus], *a small gallery or portico :* Cic. Ep.

porticus, ūs, *f.* [porta], *a walk covered by a roof supported on columns, a colonnade, portico.* **1.** Lit.: Pl., Cic., Verg., etc. **2.** Transf. **a.** *the entrance of a tent :* Acc. **b.** Milit. (in *pl.*) : *a system of galleries,* formed by placing vineae side by side : Caes. **c.** *the school* or *doctrines of the Stoics* (from στοά, a portico, the place where Zeno taught) : Chrysippus, qui fulcire putatur porticum Stoicorum, Cic.; Hor. [Fr. *porche.*]

portiō, ōnis, *f.* [akin to pars], *a portion, division, instalment :* id faer.. as quod superesset triennio aequis portionibus persolveretur, Liv.; vitae, Juv.; pro portione, *in proportion, proportionally :* Mamertinis pro portione imperaretur, Cic.; Liv.

portisculus, I, m. *a hammer with which the master of the rowers gave signals for the stroke.* **1.** Lit.: Enn., Cato. **2.** Transf.: ad loquendum atque ad tacendum, Pl.

(1) portitor, ōris, m. [portus], *a collector of harbour-dues, a customs-officer* : Pl., Cic. They also examined and forwarded letters : Pl., Ter. Hence of an inquisitive woman : Pl.

(2) portitor, ōris, m. [portō]. **I.** *a ferryman, boatman* : Sen. Of Charon : Verg. **II.** portitor Ursae, *the waggoner*, i.e. *the constellation Boōtes*, Stat.

portō, āre, *to carry* or *bear*. **1.** L i t. : Enn.; frumentum secum, Caes.; onera, Caes.; navis milites, Caes. ; Massilium in triumpho, Cic. ; eum equus, Verg. ; naves onerariae commeatum, Liv. **2.** T r a n s f. : *to bear, carry, bring* : alicui tantum boni, Pl. ; onustum pectus laetitiā, Pl. ; sociis auxilia, Sall. ; spes cogitationesque secum, Liv. ; bellum et pacem, Liv. ; ad coniuges nuntium, Liv. ; portantia verba salutem, Ov.

portōrium, ī, n. [portus], *harbour-dues, toll, import-* or *export-duty*. **1.** L i t : Pl., Caes., Cic., Liv. **2.** T r a n s f. : *a toll, tax* (on pedlars) : circumvectionis, Cic. Ep.

portula, ae, f. [dim. porta], *a small gate* : Liv.

Portūnus, ī, m. *the protecting god of harbours*, identified with Palaemon.

portuōsus, a, um [portus], *well-provided with harbours* : mare, Cic. ; pars Numidiae portuosior, Sall.

portus, ūs, m. [same root as porta], *a harbour, haven, port.* **1.** L i t. : Enn. ; portus Caietae, Cic. ; e portu proficisci, Caes. ; ex portu navis educere, Caes. ; e portu solvere, Cic. ; petere, Cic., Verg. ; capere, Caes. ; occupare, Hor. ; in portum venire, Cic. ; in portu operam dare, Cic. P r o v. : in portu navigare (i.e. to be out of all danger), Ter. P o e t. : *the mouth of a river* : Ov. **2.** T r a n s f. : *haven, a place of refuge* : corporis, Enn. ; tamquam portum aliquem exspecto illam solitudinem. Cic. ; populorum portus erat et refugium senatus, Cic. ; mihi parta quies, omnisque in limine portus, Verg. [Sp. *puerto*.]

pōsca, ae, f. [v. pōculum and pōtus], *a drink made of vinegar and water* : Pl., Plin.

pōscō, pōscere, popōsci, *to ask for urgently, to request* (usually implying more of a *petition* than a *demand of right*). **1.** L i t. **A.** In gen. With Acc. of thing asked for : Pl., Cic., Hor., etc. With ab and Abl. of person asked : Ter., Cic., etc. With Acc. of person and Acc. of thing : Cic., Hor., etc. Hence in Pass. with an Acc. of the thing asked for : posceris exta bovis, Ov. ; Palilia poscor, Ov. ; Hor. With ut and Subj. : poscimus ut cenes civiliter, Juv. ; Tac. With Inf., or Acc. and Inf. : Hor., Ov. **B.** E s p. **a.** *to demand for punishment, to require to be given up* : accusant ii, quos populus poscit, Cic. ; Liv. **b.** *to call, challenge* : clamore hominem posco, Pl. ; in proelia Turnum, Verg. **c.** *to call upon, invoke* : supplex tua numina posco, Verg. **d.** *to ask a price* : tanti quanti poscit vin' tanti illam emi ? Pl. ; Varr. **e.** *to offer a price* : agite licemini. qui cenā poscit ? ecqui poscit prandio ? Pl. **f.** *to ask, inquire* : causas veniendi, Verg. With Indir. Quest. : Verg.

2. T r a n s f. of inanimate and abstract Subjects : *to demand, require, need* : quod res poscere videbatur, Caes. ; Sall. ; Quint.

Posidōnius, ī, m. *a celebrated Stoic philosopher at Rhodes, an instructor of Cicero.*

positiō, ōnis, f. [pōnō], *a putting, placing, setting.* T r a n s f. **a.** *a position, posture* : corporis, Sen. **b.** *situation, climate* : caeli, Tac. **c.** Gramm. : *a form, termination* : Quint. **d.** R h e t. : *a proposition, theme* : Quint. ; also *a placing* or *use* of a word : Quint. ; also *affirmation* : Sen. Ep. **e.** *a state* of mind, *a mood* : mentis, Sen. Ep.

positor, ōris, m. [pōnō], *a builder, founder* : templorum, Ov.

positūra, ae, f. [pōnō]. **I.** *posture, situation* : corporum, Lucr. **II.** With Subj. Gen. : dei (i.e. the formation of the world by God), Prop.

positus, a, um. **I.** Part. pōnō. **II.** A d j. : of localities : *placed, situated, lying* : Roma in montibus posita, Cic. ; in valle, Caes. ; portus ex adverso urbi positus, Liv.

positus, ūs, m. [pōnō], *a position, arrangement* (mostly in Abl.) : insulae, Sall. ; regionis, Tac. ; positu variare capillos, Ov.

possessiō, ōnis, f. [possideō and possidō]. **1.** L i t. **a.** [possideō], *a possessing, possession, the exclusive use or enjoyment of a thing* (dist. from dominium, *ownership*) : tradere, Caes. ; possessionem bonorum dare alicui, Cic. Ep. ; tenere, Nep. ; esse in possessione bonorum, Cic. ; possessione deturbari, Cic. Ep. **b.** [possidō], *a getting possession, occupation* : bonorum emptio, possessio, Cic. ; regni, Liv. ; Monae insulae, Tac. ; in possessionem venire, proficisci, mittere, Cic. **2.** T r a n s f. **a.** *the thing possessed, a possession* : esp. *an estate* (us. pl.) : qui trans Rhodanum vicos possessionesque habebant, Caes. ; urbanae, Nep. ; Cic. **b.** Of immaterial things : prudentiae doctrinaeque, Cic.

possessiuncula, ae, f. [dim. possessiō], *a small estate* : Cic. Ep.

possessor, ōris, m. [possideō], *a possessor, occupier* : Cic., Hor., Liv., Luc. In law, *the possessor* of the thing claimed ; hence *the defendant* : Quint., Plin. Ep.

possessus, a, um, Part. possideō and possidō.

possibilis, e, adj. [possum], *that may exist or may be done, possible* : Quint.

pos-sideō, sidēre, sēdī, sessum [por perh. for prō, and sedeō], *to have the exclusive use and enjoyment of, to be the occupant of, possess.* **1.** L i t. : agros, fundum, bona, Cic. ; partem agri, Caes. ; solum bello captum, Liv. ; Juv. **2.** T r a n s f. **a.** *to abide in, dwell in* : Zephyri possidet aura nemus, Prop. ; Luc. **b.** *to possess, to have* : nomen, palmam, Pl. ; saecli mores in se, Pl. ; plus veritatis quam disciplinae possidet in se, Cic. ; magnam vim, magnam possidet religionem paternus maternusque sanguis, Cic.

pos-sidō, sidere, sēdī, sessum [por perh. for prō, and sidō], *to take possession of.* **1.** L i t. : bona alicuius sine testamento, Cic. ; medium thalamum, Ov. ; bona, Liv. With thing as subject : circumfluus umor ultima possedit, Ov. ; Lucr. **2.** T r a n s f. : totam eius praeturam, Cic.

pos-sum, posse, potuī (old forms, potis sum for possum, Pl. ; potis sunt for possunt, Pl. ; poti' or pote sim for possim, Pl. ; potesse for posse, very freq. : Pl., Lucr., etc. ; possiem, possiēs, etc., for possim, possīs, etc., Pl. Pass. : potestur, Enn., Lucr.) [for potis sum] to be able, have power ; I (thou, he, etc.) can. **A.** In gen. **a.** quantum valeam, quantumque possim, Cic. Ep. ; consilio, quantum potero, excubabo, Cic. ; potest fieri ut (it is possible that, possibly) fallar, Cic. Ep. ; potest (sc. fieri) ut alii ita arbitrarentur, Pl. ; non possum quin exclamem (I cannot but exclaim), Cic. ; ut nihil ad te dem litterarum, facere non possum (I cannot help writing to you), Cic. Ep. So, quantum or ut potest, as much or as far as possible : nos in senatu dignitatem nostram, ut potest in tantā hominum perfidiā, retinebimus, Cic. Ep. ; Pl. With Superlative : quam maximis potest itinerĭbus, Caes. ; re frumentariā quam celerrime potuit comparatā, Caes. ; Caesari te commendavi ut gravissime potui, Cic. Ep. **b.** Of moral ability, arising from disposition : sin possunt decedere solo, Verg. ; potuit rescindere, Verg. **c.** Of permission : to be allowed : esp. in urgent questions : possum scire, quo profectus, quoius sis, aut quid veneris ? Pl. **B.** In partic. : mostly with Intern. Acc., multum, plus, plurimum, nihil, etc. : to have power, influence, weight : plus potest qui plus valet, Pl. ; esse nonnullos qui privatim plus possint quam ipsi magistratūs, Caes. ; nihil equitatu, Caes. ; hoc pueri possunt, viri non poterunt ? Cic. ; multum potest fortuna, Caes. **C.** N.B. that in conditional sentences, when the verb in the Protasis is in the Subjunctive, the Indicative of possum is freq. used in the Apodosis : deleri totus exercitus potuit, si fugientis persecuti victores essent, Liv. [Through low Lat. potere for posse, It. potere ; Fr. pouvoir.]

post (older **poste**), adv. and prep. [cf. pōno, postrēmus.] **I.** Adv. **A.** Of space : behind, back, backwards : ante aut post, Liv. ; servi, qui post erant, Cic. ; ubi periculum advenit, invidia atque superbia post fuere, Sall. Also from behind : Juv. **b.** Of time : afterwards : initio . . . post autem, Cic. ; multis post annis, Cic. ; aliquanto post, Cic. ; post paulo, Caes. ; post tanto, Verg. **c.** further, next : poste nequiquam exornata est bene si morata est male, Pl. **II.** Prep. with Acc. **a.** Of place : behind : post nostra castra, Caes. ; post carecta, Verg. ; Pl. Transf. of rank : neque erat Lydia post Chloen, Hor. ; Sall. ; Sen. Ep. **b.** Of time, after, since : aliquot post mensīs, Cic. ; maxima post hominum memoriam classis, Nep. ; post urbem conditam, Cic. ; post Hectora, Ov. ; post id, Pl. With quam or quo : decessit post annum quartum quam expulsus fuerat, Nep. v. posteā, postquam. [It. poi ; Sp. pues ; Fr. puis.]

post-eā, adv. [cf. anteā], after this or that, hereafter, thereafter, afterwards. **1.** Lit. : postea in exercitu M. Crassi fuerat, Caes. ; non multo postea, Cic. With other adverbs : legati deinde postea missi ab

rege, Liv. ; postea deinceps Liv. With relat. adv. **posteā quam** (or as one word), after (cf. old Eng. after that) : postea vero quam equitatus in conspectum venit, Caes. ; Cato ; Cic. ; Liv. With loci : postea loci consul pervenit in oppidum, Sall. **2.** Transf. of succession : Pl. ; quid postea ? what next ? what further ? what then ? Ter. ; quid postea, si Romae adsiduus fui ? Cic. [It. poscia.]

poster, posteri, v. posterus.

posterĭtās, ātis, f. [posterus], future time, succeeding generations, posterity. **1.** Lit. : habeat rationem posteritatis et periculi sui, Caes. ; huius rei ne posteritatem quidem omnium saeculorum immemorem fore, Cic. ; sera, Ov. ; omnem spem posteritatis, Cic. ; posteritati servire, Cic. Adv. phr., in posteritatem, in the future (of an impending event), Cic. **2.** Transf. of animals : offspring : Juv.

posterus (poster), a, um [post]. **I.** Posit. : of time or succession : coming after, following, next, future : dies, Cic. ; postero die, Caes. ; lux, aetas, Hor. ; laus (of posterity), Hor. Without die or diem : quam minimum credula postero (to-morrow), Hor. ; in posterum oppugnationem differt, Caes. ; Liv. Also sc. tempus : multum in posterum providerunt, Cic. As Noun, **posteri,** ōrum, m. pl. future generations, descendants, posterity : Cic., Tac. **II.** Comp. **posterior,** ius : of both space and time : that comes or follows after ; next in order, time, or place : latter, later, posterior. **1.** Lit. : posteriores cogitationes, Cic. ; verbum, Hor. ; clades, Liv. ; Thucydides paulo aetate posterior, Cic. Neut. pl. as Noun : pars prior apparet, posteriora latent, Ov. Neut. Acc. posterius as Adv., later, afterwards : posterius dicere, Pl. ; posterius reverti, Cic. **2.** Transf. : inferior, of less account or value, worse : omnis res posteriores pono atque operam do tibi, Pl. ; non posteriores (sc. partis) feram, Ter. ; suam salutem posteriorem communi salute ducere, Cic. **III.** Sup. **A.** postrēmus, a, um [cf. extrēmus], hindmost, last. **1.** Lit. : alia prima ponet, alia postrema, Cic. ; acies (the rear), Sall. (also as Noun, postremi, the rearguard, Sall.) ; munus (i.e. the last service to the dead), Cat. ; cura (the last), Verg. ; postremā in comoediā (at the end of the comedy), Pl. Neut. pl. as Noun : non in postremis (i.e. in primis, especially), Cic. Adverbially. **a.** Abl. Neut., **postrēmō,** at last, finally : primum . . . deinde . . . postremo : denique . . . postremo, Cic. ; Hor. ; in primis . . . postremo, Caes. **b.** ad **postrēmum,** at last, finally, ultimately : sed ad postremum nihil apparet, Pl. ; Liv. **c. postrēmum,** for the last time : si id facis, hodie postremum me vides, Ter. ; Cic. **2.** Transf. : last, lowest, worst : homines, Cic. ; genus, Cic. **B. postumus,** a, um, the last (esp. of a child) : Silvius, tua postuma proles, Verg.

post-ferō, ferre, to put after, to esteem less : qui libertati plebis suas opes postferrent, Liv. ; Curt.

post-genitī, ōrum, m. pl. after-generations : Hor.

post-hăbĕō, ēre, uī, itum, *to place after, esteem less* : with ACC. and DAT. : seria ludo, Verg. ; Ter. Without DAT. : *to consider of secondary importance, to put aside, neglect, slight* : omnia reliqua, Caes. ; omnibus rebus posthabitis, Cic. ; posthăbĭtă Samo, Verg. ; posthabitam (filiam) dote solatus est, Tac.

post-hāc, *adv.* **I.** *hereafter, in future* : Pl., Cic., Cat. **II.** *later* : Cic.

post hinc, *hence* (i.e. from this place) *next* : Verg.

post hŏc or **posthŏc**, *adv. afterwards* : Hor.

post-ĭbi, *adv. hereupon, afterwards, then* : Pl.

postīculum, ī, *n.* [*dim.* postīcum], *a small back-building* : Pl.

postīcus, a, um [post ; like anticus from ante], *hind-, back-* : ostium, Pl. ; aedium partes, Liv. As Noun, **postīcum**, ī, *n. a back-door* : Pl., Hor.

postīdeā, *adv. afterwards* : Pl.

postīlēna, ae, *f.* [post], *a crupper* : Pl.

post-illā, *adv. afterwards* : Pl., Ter., Cat.

postis, is, *m.* (ABL. *sing.* postī, Ov.). *a doorpost.* **1.** Lit. : Cic., Hor., Liv., etc. **2.** Transf. (us. in *pl.*) **a.** *a door, double-doors* : Verg. In *sing.* : Luc. **b.** Of the eyes : videtur cernere res animus, sublatis postibus ipsis, Lucr.

post-līmĭnĭum, ī, *n.* [post līmen], *the civil right to return home and resume one's former rank and privileges, the right of recovery* : Cic. ABL. **postlīmĭnĭō**, *by the right of postliminium* : postliminio redeunt haec, homo, navis, equus, Cic. ; civi Romano licet esse Gaditanum, sive exsilio, sive postliminio, sive reiectione huius civitatis, Cic.

postmerīdĭānus (posm-), a, um, *in the afternoon* : tempus, sessio, Cic. ; dies, Sen. Ep.

post-modo (Ter., Hor., Ov., Liv.) and **post-modum** (Liv., Suet.), *adv. presently, shortly.*

post-partor, ōris, *m.* [parĭō], *a successor, heir* : Pl.

post-pōnō, pōnere, posuī, positum, *to put after, esteem less, consider of secondary importance, lay aside* (for something else) : ut omnia postponere videretur, Caes. ; Plin. Ep. With DAT. of thing preferred : scorto postponet honestum officium, Hor.

postpositus, a, um, *Part.* postpōnō.

post-principĭa, ōrum, *n. pl.* [principium], *continuance of a thing begun, sequel* : ut quisque rem accurat suam, sic ei procedunt postprincipia, Pl. ; Varr.

post-pŭtō, āre, *to consider of secondary importance* : omnīs res prae parente, Ter.

post quam or **postquam**, *conj. after-that, after, when.* **a.** Most freq. with *Perf. Indic.* (like *ut, simul ac, etc.*); also with *Histor. Pres.* : eo postquam Caesar pervenit, obsides, arma poposcit, Caes. ; Cic. ; Liv. ; postquam video nescio quid suspicarier, Ter. ; Pl. **b.** With *Imperf.* : postquam ad id parum potentes erant, in praesidia adversariorum patricii confugerunt, Liv. ; Caes. ; Sall. **c.** With *Pluperf.* (usually when a precise time is given) : undecimo die postquam a te discesseram, Cic. Ep. ; quartum post annum quam

redierat, Nep. ; postquam fetiales venerant res repetitum, temptationem aiebant esse etc., Liv. **d.** With *Subj.* (class. only in *Orat. Obliq.*) : et si nil habebam quod post accidisset, quam dedissem ad te liberto litteras, Cic.

postrēmō, postrēmus, *v.* posterus.

postrīdĭē, *adv.* [fr. LOCAT. of posterus and diēs ; *cf.* prīdĭē], *on the day after, on the following day* : Caes., Cic. With GEN. : postridie eius diei, Caes. With ACC. : postridie ludos Apollinaris, Cic. Ep. ; postridie Kalendas, Cic. Ep. ; Liv. With *quam* : Cic. Ep.

postrīdŭō, *adv.* [posterus diēs], *on the day after* : Pl.

post-scaenĭum, ī, *n.* [post scaena], *the part of the theatre behind the scenes.* Transf. : postscaenia vitae, Lucr.

post-scrībō, ere, *to write after* : Tiberi nomen suo, Tac.

postŭlāta, ōrum, *n. pl.* [postulō], *claims, demands* : Caes., Cic., Nep.

postŭlātĭō, ōnis, *f.* [postulō], *a claim, demand.* **A.** In gen. : aequa et honesta, Cic. ; postulationi alicuius concedere, resistere, Cic. **B.** In partic. **a.** *a complaint, expostulation* : Pl., Ter. **b.** In law : *an application to the praetor to allow the presentation of a complaint* : Cael. ap. Cic. Ep.

postŭlātor, ōris, *m.* [postulō], *a claimant, esp. a plaintiff* : Suet.

postŭlātus, ūs, *m.* [postulō], *a claim or demand in a court of justice, a suit* : only in ABL. : postulatu audito, Liv.

postŭlō, āre [*cf.* pōscō], *to claim, demand, require.* **1.** Lit. **a.** With ACC. of thing claimed : illinc partem, Pl. ; suom ius, Ter. ; num iniquom postulo ? Ter. ; auxilium, Caes. ; noctem sibi ad deliberandum, Cic. With *ab* of person from whom : quidvis ab amico, Cic. **b.** With *Inf.* : *to claim, expect* : Ter., Cic., Liv. With ACC. and *Pres. Inf.* : Pl., Cic. **c.** With *Subj.* : Caes., Liv., etc. With *ut* or *ne* and *Subj.* : Cic., Liv. ; aps te ut etc., Pl., Ter. **d.** With *de* (*concerning*) : a senatu de. foedere postulaverunt, Cic. ; Caes. **B.** In law. **a.** *to claim for trial, to arraign, impeach, prosecute* : Gabinium tres adhuc factiones postulant, Cic. ; Liv. ; aliquem de maiestate, Cic. Ep. ; de pecuniis repetundis, Cic. ; maiestatis, Tac. ; repetundis, Tac. ; aliquem impietatis reum, Plin. Ep. **b.** *to claim, demand* from the praetor (or other magistrate) *a writ or leave to prosecute* : in aliquem delationem nominis, Cic. ; quaestionem, Liv. **2.** Transf. of non-personal Subjects : ut loci natura necessitasque temporis postulat, Caes. ; causa postulat, Cic. ; veritas postulat, Cic.

postŭmus, *v.* posterus.

postus, a, um, *v.* pōnō.

pōtātĭō, ōnis, *f.* [pōtō], *a drinking, a drinking-bout* : Pl. ; quosdam hesternā ex potatione oscitantis, Cic. In *pl.* : Pl.

pōtātor, ōris, *m.* [pōtō], *a drinker, toper* : Pl.

pote, *adj. v.* potis.

pŏtēns, entis [possum]. **I.** *capable* (with GEN.) : regni, Liv. ; neque pugnae neque fugae, Liv. ; neque iubendi neque vetandi, Tac. **II.** *possessed of.* With GEN.: pacis, Pl. ; voti, Ov. With ABL.: praedā, Liv. **III.** *mighty, powerful.* **a.** civitates, Cic. ; familiae, Liv. ; ne quis ex plebe contra potentiorem auxili egeret, Caes. ; potentissimi reges, Cic. With *Instr.* (or *Defining*) ABL.: opibus, Ov. ; divitiis, virtute suā, tribus liberis, favore patrum, Liv. ; pecuniā et orbitate, Tac. **b.** With *Obj.* GEN.: *having power over, ruling over, master of* : dum mei potens sum, Liv. ; diva potens Cypri, Hor. ; potenti maris deo, Hor. ; rerum suarum urbisque, Liv. ; imperi, Liv. ; mentis, Ov. ; animal potens leti, Luc. **c.** Of things : *strong* (for some purpose), *powerful, efficacious* : herba ad opem, Ov. ; ad id parum potentes, Liv. ; fortuna in res bellicas potens, Liv. ; quaedam ad efficiendum potentiora, Quint. ; Ov. ; argumenta potentissima, Quint.

potentātus, ūs, *m.* [potēns], *political power, dominion* : Caes., Cic., Liv.

potenter, *adv.* **I.** *strongly, mightily, powerfully, effectually* : dicere, Quint. *Comp.* : perrumpere saxa, Hor. **II.** *according to one's ability* : rem legere, Hor.

potentia, ae, *f.* [potēns]. **A.** In gen. **a.** *force, power* : armorum tenendorum, Liv. **b.** *strength, force, efficacy* : solis, Verg. ; herbarum, Ov. ; morbi, Ov. ; occulti fati, Juv. **B.** In partic. : *political power,* esp. *unofficial* or *unconstitutional power* : erant in magnā potentiā, cui consulebantur, Cic. ; potentiam alicuius criminari, Cic.; singularis, Nep. ; divitias potentia sequebatur, Sall. In *pl.* : contra periculosissimas hominum potentias, Cic.

potērium, ī, *n.* [ποτήριον], *a drinking-vessel, goblet* : Pl.

potesse, *v.* possum, *ad init.*

potestās, ātis, *f.* [possum], *power, control.* **1.** Lit. **A.** In gen. of natural or legal power or control : habere potestatem vitae necisque in aliquem, Caes., Cic. ; in patriā potestate esse, Cic. ; habere familiam in potestate, Liv. ; in potestate suā esse, Cic., Liv. ; esse suae potestatis, Liv. ; ius potestatemque habere imperandi, Cic. **B.** In partic. **a.** Of the power of magistrates : praetoria, Cic. ; tribunicia, Caes. ; imperia, potestates (*military and civil offices*), Cic. ; gerere, Cic. ; in re publicā cum potestate versari, Cic. ; cum potestate in provinciam proficisci, Cic. Occ. : *an officer with power, a public officer, magistrate* : a magistratu aut ab aliquā potestate legitimā evocatus, Cic. ; hominum rerumque aeterna potestas, Verg. **b.** Of the *control* of one State by another, *dominion, sovereignty* : sese in eius fidem ac potestatem venire, Caes. ; tenere aliquem in suā potestate ac dicione, Cic. ; venire in arbitrium ac potestatem alicuius, Cic. ; in suam potestatem eos redigeret, Liv. **2.** Transf. **a.** *power, control* : vim tantam in se et potestatem habere tantae astutiae, Ter. ; exisse ex potestate dicimus eos qui e ffrenati feruntur aut libidine aut iracundiā, Cic. **b.** *power, opportunity, freedom of action* : ubi mihi potestas primum evenit, Pl. ; liberius vivendi, Ter. ; facere potesta-

tem (alicui), *to give an opportunity or permission* : pugnandi, Caes. ; conveniendi sui, Cic. ; potestatem sui facere (i.e. of fighting against oneself), Caes. ; vobis potestas fieret ostendendi, Liv. ; potestas (est), with *Inf.* : Verg., Luc. **c.** Of things : *power, properties, qualities* : potestates herbarum, Verg. ; plumbi, Lucr. [It. *podestà*.]

potestur, *v.* possum.

potin or **potin'** for potisne. **I.** potin es ? (i.e. potesne ?) *can you ? are you able ?* Ter. **II.** For potisne est (i.e. potestne ?): potin' ut taceas ? *can't you be silent ?* Pl. ; Ter.

pōtiō, ōnis, *f.* [*v.* pōtus], *a drinking.* **1.** Lit. : in mediā potione, Cic. **2.** Transf. : *a drink, draught.* **a.** In gen. : Cic., Varr. In *pl.* : Cic. **b.** *a poisonous draught* : Cic., Juv. **c.** *a draught of medicine* : dare potionis aliquid, Pl. **d.** *a magic potion, love-philtre* : Hor. [It. *pozione* ; Fr. *poison.*]

potiō, īre [potis], *to put into the power of, to subject to* : eum nunc potivit pater servitutis, Pl. ; potitu 'st hostium (*into the hands of the enemy*), Pl.

potior, īrī (potītur, Verg.) ; poterēmur, Ov.) [potis]. **I.** *to become master, to take possession, to get, acquire.* With *Acc.* : regnum, Pac. ; sceptra, Lucr. ; summum imperi, Nep. ; but usually only in *Gerundive* : spes urbis potiundae, Caes. ; Liv. With *Gen.* : regni, Cic. Ep. ; urbis, Sall. ; vexilli, Liv. With *Abl.* : muliere, Pl. ; impedimentis castrisque, Caes. ; imperio totius Galliae, Caes. ; victoriā, Caes. ; natura iis, Cic. ; sceptro, Ov. **II.** *to be master, to possess* : Cic. Ep. With *Acc.* : gaudia, Ter. ; Pl. With *Gen.* : civitas Atheniensium, dum ea rerum potita est, Cic. ; Tac. With *Abl.* : oppido, Liv. ; monte, Ov. ; iis voluptatibus senectus, Cic.

potior, *v.* potis.

potis, pote, *adj.* [*cf.* πόσις], *able, capable ; possible.* **I.** Posit. Mostly predic. with or without *esse* : *to be able* or *possible, may,* or *can* : aut quod non potis est, esse pudica velit, Cat. ; at ea supterfugere potis es pauca, Pl. ; non Euandrum potis est vis ulla tenere, Verg. ; nihil pote supra, Ter. ; Cat. ; nec devitari letum pote, Lucr. With *pl.* : duae plus satis dare potis sunt, Pl. **II.** Comp. **potior**, ius, *preferable, better.* **a.** Of persons : cives potiores quam peregrini, Cic. ; Pl. ; quibus tantam crederem rem, potiores habui, Liv. Of a lover : Tib. **b.** Of things : rem potiorem video, Pl. ; semper se rei publicae commoda privatis necessitatibus habuisse potiora, Caes. ; mors servitute potior, Cic. ; Sall. ; nihil mihi potius fuit quam ut etc., Cic. ; novistine locum potiorem rure beato ? Hor. *Neut. Acc.* **potius** as *Adv. rather, by preference, more* : in oratione non vis potius sed delectatio postulatur, Cic. ; Pl. With *quam* : Galliam potius esse Ariovisti quam populi R., Caes. ; Pl. ; haec patienda censeo potius quam trucidari corpora vestra, Liv. ; Caes. ; Cic. Sometimes the potius is omitted : Pl.,

Nep. With *quam ut* and *Subj.* : se milliens morituros potius quam ut tantum dedecoris admitti patiantur, Liv. With *quam* and *Subj.* : omnia patienda potius quam proderetur salus principum, Liv. ; Cic. Corrective: erravit aut potius insanivit Apronius ? Cic. **III.** *Superl.* **potissimus,** a, um, *chief, principal, most prominent, most important.* **a.** Of persons: Pl., Stat., Tac. ; Fabium potissimum auctorem habui, Liv. **b.** Of things : utrum potius, aut quid potissimum sit, quaeritur, Cic. ; primum ac potissimum omnium, Liv. ; cura, Stat. ; causa, Tac. *Neut.* Acc. **potissimum** (-umum) as *Adv., above all, especially :* tanta erat contentio qui potissimum ex magno numero conscenderent, Caes. ; Pl. ; Sall. ; Liv. ; id potissimum consecuti sumus, Cic.

potissimum, *v.* potis.

potis-sum, *v.* possum.

pōtitō, āre [*freq.* pōtō], *to drink often :* pocula, Pl.

pōtiuncula, ae, *f.* [*dim.* pōtiō], *a small draught or potion :* Suet.

potius, *v.* potis.

Potniae, ārum, *f. pl. a village in Boeotia, famous for its pastures and breed of horses ;* **Potnias,** adis, *f. adj.*

pōtō, āre (*Sup.* beside potātum, also pōtum) [*cf.* pōculum, πέπωκα], *to drink.* **1.** Lit. **a.** In gen.: Pl., Cic., Verg., etc. With Acc. : aquas, flumina, Ov. ; aquam, Suet. **b.** Of heavy drinking : Cic., Sall., Liv. With Acc. : crapulam, Pl. *Impers. Pass.* : Cic. **2.** Transf. of things : vestis sudorem, Lucr. ; vellera fucum, Hor.

pōtor, ōris, *m.* [*v.* pōtus], *a drinker.* **1.** Lit. : aquae, Hor. E s p. *a hard drinker, tippler :* Hor., Prop. **2.** Transf. : Rhodani (i.e. dweller by), Hor.

pōtrix, icis, *f.* [*v.* pōtus], *a (female) tippler :* Phaedr.

pōtulentus (**pōcul-**), a, um [pōtus]. **I.** *drinkable. Neut. pl.* as Noun : Cic. **II.** *in one's cups, intoxicated :* Suet.

pōtus, a, um. **I.** *Part.* (beside pōtātus) of pōtō : sanguine tauri poto, Cic. ; poti faece tenus cadi, Hor. **II.** A d j. : *drunken, intoxicated :* domum bene potus redire, Cic. ; anus, Hor.

pōtus, ūs, *m. a drinking, drink :* Cic., Tac., etc.

prae, *adv.* and *prep.* [LOCAT. of old noun (*cf.* Gk. παραι-)]. **I.** A d v.: *at the head, in the front, before.* **1.** Lit. : abi prae, iam ego sequar, Pl. ; Ter. **2.** Transf. with *ut* and *quam* (and in one word, **praeut** and **praequam**), *in comparison with, compared with, by the side of :* parum etiam, praeut futurum est, praedicas, Pl. ; Ter. ; parva res est voluptatum praequam quod molestum est, Pl. **3.** In Compounds. **A.** *in front* or *at the head,* **a.** praecedo, praefigo, praeceps. **b.** Of leading : praeduco, praeco, praetor. **c.** Of protecting : praesidium. **d.** Of blocking the way : praecludo, praemunio. **B.** Transf. of A. **a.** Of time. (i.) *beforehand :* praevideo, praefatio. (ii.) *prematurely :* praecerpo. **b.** Of rank : praesum, praeficio. **c.** Of degree : *surpassing, excessively :* praefulgeo,

praegravis. **d.** Of place, time or degree as *affecting some one's personal interest,* usually unfavourably : praetendo, praesumo, praevaricor, praeverto, praeiudicium, praesto (*excel*), praestringo (but *cf.* C.). The person unfavourably affected is in DATIVE (but contrast praeverto). **C.** *on the projecting* or *front portion, on the surface :* praeacutus, praeustus, praestringo. Hence with verbs of movement, *past, by :* praelabor, praevehor. **II.** P r e p. with ABL. : *in front, in advance, before.* **1.** Lit. (usually with *Refl. Pron.* in certain phrases) : ille stillantem prae se pugionem tulit, Cic. ; singulos prae se inermes mittebat, Sall. ; prae se armentum agens, Liv. ; (infantem) sinu prae se portans, Verg. **2.** Transf. **a.** In these or similar phrases : *openly, publicly, outright, plainly :* scelus prae se ferens (*admitting* or *boasting of*) et confitens, Cic. ; prae se declarant gaudia vultu, Cat. ; prae se iactare, Verg. **b.** prae manu, *at hand, to hand :* omne aurum, quod fuit prae manu, Pl. ; huic aliquid paulum prae manu dederis, Ter. **c.** *by the side of, compared with, in comparison with :* Gallis prae magnitudine corporum suorum brevitas nostra contemptui est, Caes. ; Pl. ; veros illos Atticos prae se paene agrestis putat, Cic. ; omnia prae divitiis humana, Liv. **d.** *by reason of, in consequence of* (in class. period mostly in negat. sentences) : prae laetitiā lacrumae praesiliunt mihi, Pl. ; prae gaudio ubi sim nescio, Ter. ; vivere non quit prae macie, Lucr. ; solem prae iaculorum multitudine non videbitis, Cic. ; prae clamore nulla adhortatio imperatoris audita est, Liv. ; prae indignatione rerum stupor patres defixit, Liv.

prae-acuō, uere, *to sharpen at one end or to a point :* Cato. Hence, **prae-acūtus,** a, um, *pointed :* surculus, Cato. ; sudes, Sall. ; tigna paulum ab imo praecuta, Caes. ; cuspis, Ov.

prae-altus, a, um. **I.** *very high :* rupes, Liv. **II.** *very deep :* Sall. ; flumen, Liv. ; paludes, Tac.

praebeō, ēre, uī, itum [for praehibeō, fr. prae, habeō], *to hold in front ;* hence **I.** *to offer, present.* **1.** Lit. : manūs verberibus, Ov. ; convivis aquam, Hor. ; collum cultris, Juv. **2.** Transf. : auris alicui or alicui rei, Cic., Ov., Liv. ; os ad contumeliam, Liv. **II.** *to offer, present, supply.* **1.** Lit. : aurum, vestem, Pl. ; panem, Nep. ; sponsalia, Cic. Ep. **2.** Transf. **a.** ludos, Ter. ; spectaculum, Sall. ; opinionem timoris, Caes. ; materiam seditionis, Liv. ; causam tollendi indutias, Liv. ; gaudium et metum, Liv. ; sonitum, Liv. ; operam rei publicae, Liv. ; materiam caussasque iocorum, Juv. **b.** *to represent, exhibit :* speciem atque opinionem pugnantium, Caes. ; exempla nequitiae, Cic. Mostly with *Refl. Pron.* (and *Predic. Adj.* or Noun), *to show oneself, behave :* in re misericordem se praebuit, Cic. ; Pompeius se auctorem meae salutis praebuit, Cic. ; in eos me severum, Cic. ; Also, pari se virtute, Nep. Also without *Pron.* : Phormio in hac re ut aliis strenuom hominem praebuit, Ter. With *Inf. Pass.* : praebuit ipsa rapi (i.e. suffered herself to be carried off), Ov. With *Gerundive :* conspiciendum se praebere, Plin. Ep. Hence, se legibus (to submit to the laws), Sen. Ep.

prae-bibō, bibere, bibī [*cf.* propīnō], *to drink before, to toast :* alicui venenum, Cic.

praebita, ōrum, *n. pl.* [praebeō], *provision, allowance :* annua, Suet.

praebitor, ōris, *m.* [praebeō], *a supplier, purveyor :* Cic.

prae-calidus, a, um, *very warm, hot :* Tac.

prae-calvus, a, um, *very bald :* caput, Suet.

praecantrix, īcis, *f.* [canō], *an enchantress, witch :* Pl.

prae-cānus, a, um, *grey before one's time :* Hor.

praecautus, a, um, *Part.* praecaveō.

prae-caveō, cavēre, cāvī, cautum, *to take care or heed in good time, to take precautions.* **a.** Pl., Cic.; sibi, Ter.; decemviris ab irā multitudinis, Liv.; ab insidiis, Liv. *Impers. Pass.* with *ne* and *Subj. :* Caes., Cic., Liv.; sed praecauto opust ne etc., Pl. **b.** With *Acc. :* illud, Pl.; peccata, Cic.; venena, Suet.

prae-cēdō, cēdere, cēssī, cēssum, *to go before, precede.* **A.** **Trans.** **1.** Lit.: agmen, Verg., Liv.; classem, Liv.; taurus armenta, Sen. Ep. **2.** **Transf.** **a.** Of time: quae venturas praecedet sexta Kalendas, Ov. **b.** *to surpass, excel :* Helvetii reliquos Gallos virtute praecedunt, Caes.; ego vestros honores rebus gerendis praecessi, Liv. **B.** **Intrans.** **1.** Lit.: ad confirmandam civitatem, Caes.; cum equite, Liv.; ex Paeoniā, Curt. **2.** **Transf.** **a.** Of things : fama praecessit ad auris, Ov. **b.** With DAT. : *to excel :* Pl.

praecellēns, entis. **I.** *Part.* praecellō. **II.** Adj.: *surpassing, pre-eminent :* vir et animo et virtute praecellens, Cic. *Comp. :* Plin. *Sup. :* Cic.

prae-cellō, ere [*cf.* antecellō]. **A.** **Intrans.** **a.** *to distinguish oneself, to excel :* ut quisque fortunā utitur, ita praecellet, Pl.; Liv.; mobilitate, Lucr.; per nobilitatem et eloquentiam, Tac. **b.** With DAT. : *to preside or rule over :* genti, Tac. **B.** **Trans.** *to surpass, excel :* aliquam fecunditate, Tac.

praecentiō, ōnis, *f.* [praecinō], *a singing before* a sacrifice *; a prelude :* Cic.

praeceps, cipitis (old form, **praecipes,** cipis, Pl.) [prae caput]. **I.** Adj.: *headforemost, headlong.* **A.** Of persons, etc. **1.** Lit.: praecipitem trahi, Pl.; se iacere praecipitem e vertice, Cat.; praeceps in vulnus abiit, Liv.; aliquem praecipitem deicere, Cic.; praeceps ad terram datus, Liv.; Hor.; proiecit in undas praecipitem (Palinurum), Verg. **2.** **Transf.** **a.** sol praecipitem lavit aequore currum, Verg.; praeceps in occasum sol erat, Liv.; praecipiti iam ad vesperum die, Liv.; senectus, Curt. **b.** praeceps in avaritiam animus, Liv.; praeceps ingenio in iram, Liv.; animus ad flagitia, Tac.; ad explendam cupidinem, Sall. **B.** Of places : *suddenly descending, downhill, steep, precipitous.* **1.** Lit.: via, Cic.; iter, Ov.; locus, Caes.; saxa, Liv.; fossae, Verg.; Anio (of the falls of Tivoli), Hor. **2.** **Transf.** *precipitous,* hence *dangerous :* iter

ad malum praeceps ac lubricum, Cic.; viā vitae, Cic.; praeceps periculo victoriā, Liv.; in tam praecipiti tempore, Ov.; alea, Hor. **C.** Of hurried movement : *headlong, hasty.* **1.** Lit.: praecipites fugae sese mandabant, Caes.; aliquem praecipitem agere, Caes., Cic.; praeceps amensque cucurri, Ov.; Hor.; nuntii, Tac. **2.** **Transf.** **a.** Of violent winds, rivers, etc. : amnis, Hor.; Boreas, Ov.; nox, Ov. **b.** remedium, Curt. **c.** Morally : agunt eum praecipitem poenae civium Romanorum, Cic.; ab inimicis praeceps agor, Sall.; in omnibus consiliis, Cic.; mens, Cic.; consilium, Suet. **II.** Noun, **praeceps,** cipitis, *n. a precipitous place, edge of cliff or abyss, verge.* **1.** Lit.: turrim in praecipiti stantem, Verg.; immane, Juv.; in praeceps deferri, Liv., in praeceps iacere, Tac.; per praecipitia deferri, Liv. **2.** **Transf.** : in praecipitia agebat consilia, Liv.; se et prope rem publicam in praeceps dederat, Liv.; Ov.; levare aegrum ex praecipiti, Hor.; debet orator erigi, attolli, ac saepe accedere ad praeceps (i.e. the sublime), Plin. Ep. **III.** Adv. **praeceps,** *headlong, into dire peril :* aliquem praeceps trahere, Tac.; eversio rei familiaris dignitatem ac famam praeceps dabat, Tac.

praeceptiō, ōnis, *f.* [praecipiō]. **I.** *a previous notion, preconception :* Cic. **II.** *a precept, injunction :* Cic. **III.** *the right of receiving in advance :* dare, Plin. Ep.

praeceptivus, a, um [praecipiō], *didactic :* Sen.

praeceptor, ōris, *m.* and **praeceptrix,** īcis, *f.* [praecipiō], *a teacher, instructor, preceptor :* Pl., Juv.; dicendi, Cic.; philosophiae, Nep.

praeceptum, ī, *n.* [praecipiō]. **I.** *a maxim, rule :* Cic. **II.** *an injunction, order :* Cic., Liv.; Tac.; observare, Caes. In *pl. :* Cic.; philosophiae, dicendi, Cic.; deum praecepta secuti, Verg.; dare, Cic., Verg.

prae-cerpō, cerpere, cerpsī, cerptum [carpō], *to pluck, gather before the time.* **1.** Lit.: messis, Ov. **2.** **Transf.** *to forestall, intercept:* fructum officii tui, Cic.; purpurae decus, Plin. Pan.

prae-cīdō, cīdere, cīdī, cīsum [caedō], *to cut off a projecting part, to cut short, lop off, mutilate.* **1.** Lit.: linguam alicui, Pl.; manum alicui, Cic.; manūs, Liv.; membra, capillos, Quint.; mediam canem, Liv.; ancoras, Cic.; Liv.; cotem novaculā, Cic.; navis, Cic. Ep. **2.** **Transf.** **a.** *to cut short, break off :* linguam oculi, Pl.; maximam partem defensionis, Cic.; praecide, inquit, Cic.; sibi reditum, Cic.; amicitias, Cic.; spem, Cic., Liv.; sibi licentiam libertatemque vivendi, Cic. **b.** Of a route : iter, Plin.; omnis sinūs maris, Sen. Ep.

prae-cingō, cingere, cīnxī, cinctum, *to gird in front.* **1.** Lit.: cincticulo praecinctus, Pl.; aliquem, Mart. In *Mid. :* praecingitur ense viator, Ov.; praecincti recte pueri, Hor.; altius praecinctis (for a journey), Hor. **2.** **Transf.** *to surround* (on the outside), *face with :* Brundisium praecinctum pulchro portu, Enn.; auro cervix, Ov.; lacus silvā, Ov.; fontem vallo, Prop.; parietes testaceo opere praecincti, Plin. Ep.

prae-cĭnō, cinere, cinuĭ, centum [canō].
A. I n t r a n s. **a.** *to play before :* sacrificiis, Liv. ; epulis magistratuum fides prae-
cinunt, Cic. **b.** Of uttering a spell : carmine cum magico praecinuisset anus, Tib.
B. T r a n s. *to predict :* magnum aliquid
deos praecinore, Cic. ; lucos praecinuisse
fugam, Tib.

prae-cĭpĭō, cipere, cēpĭ, ceptum [capĭō], *to
take or seize beforehand, to get or receive in
advance.* **1.** L i t. : aquam, Lucr. ; a
publicanis pecuniam insequentis anni mutuam, Caes. ; aliquantum viae (i.e. a considerable start), Liv. ; iter, Liv. ; litora,
Verg. ; si lac praeceperit aestus, Verg. ;
praecipitur seges, Ov. Also of time : aliquantum ad fugam temporis, Liv. In law :
to receive in advance : Plin. Ep. **2.**
T r a n s f. **a.** With the mind : *to grasp
beforehand, to anticipate :* animo victoriam,
Caes. ; haec usu ventura opinione, Caes. ;
consilia hostium, Cic. ; omnia praecepi,
Verg. ; spe hostem, Verg. ; spem, Liv. **b.**
to give rules or *precepts to, to admonish, warn,
direct :* omnia, Ter. ; officia, Cato ; alicui
aliquid, Pl., Cic. ; quidquid praecipies, esto
brevis, Hor. ; artem nandi, Ov. ; lugubris
cantûs, Hor. ; numerumque modumque
carinis, Verg. ; humanitatem, Plin. Ep. ;
de eloquentiâ, Cic. With *Inf. :* parcere
omnibus, Cic. With *Subj. :* Caes., Sall.,
Liv. With *ut* or *ne* and *Subj. :* Cic., Nep. ;
Impers. Pass. : erat ei praeceptum a
Caesare ne proelium committeret, Caes. ;
Cic.

praecipĭtanter, *adv. headlong :* agere man-
nos, Lucr.

praecipĭtium, ĭ, *n.* [praeceps], *a steep place,
a precipice :* Suet.

praecipĭtō, āre [praeceps]. **A.** T r a n s. **1.**
L i t. : *to throw* or *cast down headlong.* **a.**
Mostly with *Refl. Pron.: se* de montibus ad
terram, Lucr. ; se e Leucade, Cic. ; sese in
fossas, Caes. ; hac (*sc.* viâ) te praecipitato,
Ter. ; se de turri, Liv. ; se in Tiberim, Liv. ;
se praecipitare, Liv. ; Hor. In *Mid.:* cum
alii super vallum praecipitarentur, Sall. ;
super alium alii praecipitantur, Liv. ; in
insidias praecipitatur, Liv. ; iumenta multa
ex agmine praecipitata sunt, Liv. ; multi
in derupta praecipitati, Liv. ; Scorpios in
viridīs praecipitatur aquas, Ov. ; lux aquis,
Ov. **b.** Rarely with any other Acc. :
aliquem in flumen, Caes. ; exanimem equo,
Liv. ; currum scopulis, Ov. ; etiam pulcherrima, Juv. **2.** T r a n s f. **a.** praecipi-
tari ex altissimo dignitatis gradu, Cic. ; in
tanta mala praecipitatus ex patrio regno,
Sall. ; furor iraque mentem praecipitant,
Verg. ; spem festinando, Ov. *Pass.* or
Mid. : nox praecipitata, Ov. **b.** Of hurried action : consilia raptim praecipitata,
Liv. ; moras, Verg. ; cursum, Juv. With
Inf. : dare tempus praecipitant curae,
Verg. **B.** I n t r a n s. *to fall headlong, fall
suddenly.* **1.** L i t. : Cic. ; de montibus ad
terram, Lucr. ; Fibrenus in Lirem, Cic. ;
Nilus praecipitat ex montibus, Cic. ; in
fossam, Liv. ; in insidias, Liv. ; nimbi in
vada, Verg. ; nox caelo, Verg. **2.** T r a n s f.
a. hiems iam praecipitaverat, Caes. ; prae-
cipitante re publicâ, Cic. ; (eum) praecipi-

tantem impellamus, Cic. ; cum ad Cannas
praecipitasset Romana res, Liv. ; ad exitium,
Cic. Ep. **b.** Of hurried movement : Verg.
In words : Cic.

praecĭpŭē, *adv. especially, chiefly* (usually
with verbs) : Caes., Cic., Hor.

praecĭpŭus (**-uos**), a, um [praecipĭō], *taken
before other things.* **1.** L i t. **a.** *particular,
especial* (opp. communis and par) : Cic. ; sors
periculi, Liv. Used for praecipue : fratri
praecipuum decus di dederunt, Liv. **b.** In
law : *received beforehand :* peculium,
Ter. ; Pl. *Neut.* **praecipuum**, ĭ, as Noun, *a
legacy received before the general distribution :*
Suet. **2.** T r a n s f. *principal, distinguished,
extraordinary :* pietas, Pl. ; hic homost
hominum omnium praecipuos, Pl. ; Tac. ;
auctor, Suet. ; honor, Caes. ; amor, ius,
Cic. ; in eloquentiâ, Quint. With ABL. :
praecipuus scientiâ rei militaris, Tac. As
Noun, **praecipuum**, ĭ, *n. superiority, excellence :* Cic. **praecipua**, ōrum, *n. pl.* **a.**
matters of special importance : rerum, Tac.
b. *things of importance* (=προηγμένα of
Stoics ; i.e. things that come next to absolute good) : Cic.

praecīsē, *adv.* **I.** *in short, in few words,
briefly, concisely :* dicere (opp. plene et
perfecte), Cic. **II.** *absolutely :* negare, Cic.
Ep.

praecīsus, a, um. **I.** *Part.* praecīdō. **II.**
A d j. · *broken off, abrupt.* **1.** L i t. : acuta
silex praecisis undique saxis, Verg. ; iter,
Sall. ; rupes, Quint. **2.** T r a n s f. *shortened,
brief :* conclusio, Quint.

prae-clārē, *adv.* **I.** *very clearly, very plainly :*
aliquid explicare, Cic. ; intellego, memini,
Cic. Ep. ; invenire, Plin. Ep. **II.** *excellently, admirably :* facere, dicere, Cic. ;
Sup. : Cic. To express assent : *very good,
very well :* Cic.

prae-clārus, a, um, *very clear, very bright.*
1. L i t. : lux, Lucr. ; iaspis, Juv. **2.**
T r a n s f. **a.** *very beautiful* to the eye : vultus, Lucr. ; urbs situ praeclaro ad aspectum,
Cic. ; facies, Sall. *Comp.* · Acc. **b.** *very
beautiful* morally ; *very splendid, noble,
distinguished :* homo praeclarâ virtute et
formâ, Pl. ; multi praeclari in philosophiâ et
nobiles, Cic. ; gens bello praeclara, Verg. ;
res, Hor. ; o praeclarum diem ! Cic. With
GEN. : T. Livius eloquentiae ac fidei praeclarus, Tac. *Comp. :* Cic. *Sup. :* Nep.
In ironical sense : o praeclaram existimationem nostri ordinis ! Cic. **c.** In bad
sense : *notorious :* sceleribus suis praeclarus, Sall.

prae-clūdō, clūdere, clūsi, clūsum [claudō],
to shut in front ; hence, *to shut in one's
face, shut against, obstruct.* **1.** L i t. : portas
consuli, Caes. ; foris, Prop. ; viam, Suet.
2. T r a n s f. : omnem orbem terrarum
civibus Romanis, Cic. ; omnīs sibi aditûs
misericordiae iudicum, Cic. ; vocem alicui,
Liv. ; Phaedr. ; maritimos cursûs hiemis
magnitudo, Cic.

praecō, ōnis, *m.* [for *prae-vic-ō* from vocāre],
a crier. **1.** L i t. **a.** In the market : *an
auctioneer :* Pl., Hor. ; haec per praeconem
vendidit, Cic. ; subicere bona voci praeconis,
Cic. Ep. **b.** In the courts : *the person who
proclaimed silence* or *acted as clerk of the*

court : Enn., Cic. **c.** On the battlefield : Liv. **2.** T r a n s f. : *tuae* virtutis Homerum praeconem, Cic.

prae-cōgitō, āre, *to think upon beforehand, to premeditate* : facinus, Liv. ; Quint.

prae-cognitus, a, um, *foreknown, foreseen* : Planc. ap. Cic. Ep., Suet.

prae-colō, colere, cultum, *to cultivate prematurely.* T r a n s f. : animi habitūs quasi ad virtutem praeculti, Tac.

prae-compositus, a, um, *made up beforehand;* *studied* : os, Ov.

praecōnius, a, um [praecō], *of an auctioneer or public crier* : Pl. ; quaestus, Cic. As Noun, **praecōnium,** i, *n. the office of a public crier* : facere, Cic. Ep. T r a n s f. **a.** *a proclaiming, publishing* : domesticum, Cic. ; praeconia famae, Ov. **b.** *a celebrating, laudation* : mandare versibus laborum praeconium, Cic. ; formao praeconia, Ov. [Fr. *prône.*]

prae-cōnsūmō, sūmere, sūmptum, *to waste or spend beforehand* : Ov.

prae-contrectō, āre, *to handle beforehand (in thought)* : Ov.

praecordia, ōrum, *n. pl.* [cor], *the midriff, diaphragm.* **1.** L i t. : (Plato) cupiditatem subter praecordia locavit, Cic. ; Juv. **2.** T r a n s f. **A.** *the inside, the stomach* : Cic., Hor. **B.** *the breast, the heart.* **a.** In gen. : spiritu remanente in praecordiis, Liv. ; coit in praecordia sanguis, Verg. **b.** As the seat of the feelings and passions : redit in praecordia virtus, Verg. ; Hor. ; Juv. **c.** praecordia mentis, *the seat of the mind,* Ov. **C.** *the body* : in terrā ponunt praecordia, Ov.

prae-corrumpō, rumpere, ruptum, *to bribe beforehand* : Ov.

praecox, cocis, also **praecoquis,** e, [coquō], *ripe before its time, premature.* **1.** L i t. : Plin. **2.** T r a n s f. : *overhasty, premature* : pugna, Enn. ; fuga, Lucil. ; audacia, Sen. ; ingeniorum velut praecox genus, Quint.

praecultus, a, um. **I.** *Part.* praecolō. **II.** A d j. : *highly ornamented, bedecked.* **a.** auro, Stat. **b.** Of style : Quint.

prae-cupidus, a, um, *very desirous or fond* (with GEN.) : Suet.

praecurrentia, ium, *n. pl., things that go before, antecedents* : Cic.

prae-currō, currere, cucurri and curri, cursum. **A.** I n t r a n s. *to run on in advance, to precede.* **1.** L i t. : equites, Caes. ; huc, Pl. ; ante omnia, Caes. ; ad aliquem, Liv. **2.** T r a n s f. **a.** fama iam praecucurrerat, Caes. ; certis rebus signa, Cic. **b.** *to outdo* : celeritate, Caes. ; alicui studio, Cic. **B.** T r a n s. (only transf.). **a.** *to precede, anticipate* : illud, Lucr. ; amicitia iudicium, Cic. ; cogitatio aetatem studio, Cic. **b.** *to precede, surpass* : aliquem aetate, Cic. ; aliquem iudicio, Tac.

praecursiō, ōnis, *f.* [praecurrō]. **I.** *a previous occurrence* : visorum, Cic. **II.** Milit. *a preliminary combat, skirmish* : Plin. Ep. **III.** Rhet. *a preparation of the hearer* : Cic.

praecursor, ōris, m. [praecurrō]. **I.** *a forerunner* : Plin. Pan. **II.** Milit. *an advance·guard, vanguard* : Liv. **III.** *a scout, spy* : Cic.

praecursōrius, a, um [praecurrō], *sent in advance* : epistula, Plin. Ep.

prae-cutiō, cutere, cussi, cussum [quatiō], *to brandish before* : taedas, Ov.

praeda, ae, *f.* [*cf.* prehendō], *property taken in war, booty, spoil, plunder.* **1.** L i t. : capere de praedonibus, Pl. ; militibus donare, Caes. ; facere, Caes. ; praedas ac manubias in urbis ornamenta conferre, Cic. ; praedā spoliisque potiti, Verg. ; praedā onusti, Liv. ; ad praedam relinquere, Liv. *Predic.* DAT. : praedae esse, Cic., Liv. ; praedae dare, relinquere, Liv. Of animals : *prey* : Verg., Hor., etc. Of fishing : Pl., Ov. **2.** T r a n s f. of gains, profit : Pl. Hor. ; maximos quaestūs praedasque facere, Cic. [Fr. *proie.*]

praedābundus, a, um [praedor], *plundering* : Sall. ; exercitus, Liv.

prae-damnō, āre, *to condemn beforehand.* **1.** L i t. : conlegam, Liv. ; Suet. **2.** T r a n s f. : spem (i.e. to renounce), Liv.

praedātiō, ōnis, *f.* [praedor], *a taking of booty, plundering* (in *pl.*) : Tac.

praedātor, ōris, m. (and **praedātrix,** icis, *f.* Stat.) [praedor], *a plunderer, pillager.* **1.** L i t. : Cic. ; ex sociis, Sall. O c c. *a hunter* : Ov. **2.** T r a n s f. *a rapacious man* : Tib.

praedātōrius, a, um [praedātor], *plundering, marauding* : naves, Pl., Liv. ; manus (militum), Sall. ; classes, Liv.

prae-dēlassō, āre, *to weary out beforehand* : Ov.

prae-dēstinō, āre, *to determine beforehand* : triumphos, Liv.

praediātor, ōris, m. [praedium], *one who buys a landed estate* (mortgaged to the State) : Cic.

praediātōrius, a, um [praediātor], *relating to the sale of a praedium* : ius, Cic. ; lex, Suet.

praedicābilis, e, *adj.* [praedicō], *praiseworthy, laudable* : Cic.

praedicātiō, ōnis, *f.* [praedicō]. **I.** *a proclamation, publication* : Cic. ; temporis, societatis, Cic. **II.** *a praising, commendation* : Pl., Cic. Ep., Liv., etc.

praedicātor, ōris, m. [praedicō], *a praiser, eulogist* : benefici, Cic. ; Plin. Ep.

prae-dicō, āre, *to proclaim in public, make known by proclamation.* **1.** L i t. : Pl., Cic. ; auctionem, Pl. **2.** T r a n s f. **a.** In gen. : *to make publicly known, to assert, declare* : Ter. ; ut praedicas, Cic. ; vera, Pl. ; aliam mihi orationem, Pl. ; iniuriam, Caes. ; Cic. With Acc. and *Inf.* : Caes., Sall. **b.** *to praise, commend, boast, vaunt* : Pl. ; faciem alicuius, Ter. ; beatam vitam, Cic. ; Galli se omnis ab Dite patre prognatos praedicant, Caes. ; quae de illo viro Sulla praedicaverunt ! Cic. ; verecundia in praedicando, Tac. [Fr. *prêcher.*]

prae-dīcō, dīcere, dīxi, dictum. **I.** *to say or mention beforehand* : mihi, Ter. ; aliquid, Quint. ; illud tibi, Verg. ; Ter. Hence, *to name or fix beforehand, prearrange* : Naev. ; latebras, Liv. ; loco praedicto in quem convenirent, Liv. ; ad praedictum amnem convenere, Tac. ; ubi praetor reo atque accusatoribus diem praedixisset, Tac. **II.** *to foretell, predict, forecast* : futura, Cic. ; malum hoc, Verg. **III.** *to command, charge beforehand* (with *ut* or *ne* and *Subj.*) :

Pompeius suis praedixerat ut impetum exciperent, Caes. ; ei visam esse Iunonem praedicerⁿ ne id faceret, Cic. ; Liv. ; Tac. ; *Impers. Pass.* : praedicto ne in re publicā haberetur, Tac.

praedictiō, ōnis, *f.* [praedīcō]. **I.** Rhet. : *a premising* : Quint. **II.** *a foretelling* : mali, Cic. In *pl.* : Cic., Suet.

praedictum, ī, n. [praedīcō]. **I.** *a foretelling, prediction* : esp. in *pl.* : Chaldaeorum praedicta, Cic. ; Verg. **II.** *an order, command* (with *ne* and *Subj.*) : Liv. **III.** ex praedicto, *by prearrangement* : Liv.

praediolum, ī, n. [*dim.* praedium], *a small farm or estate* : Cic., Plin. Ep.

prae-discō, ere, *to learn beforehand* : aliquid, Cic., Verg.

prae-dispositus, a, um, *arranged in relays beforehand* : nuntii, Liv.

prae-ditus, a, um [datus, dō], *endowed, provided, supplied* (with ABL.) : armis, Pl. ; opibus ac facultatibus, Cic. ; tali ingenio, Ter. ; divino sensu, Lucr. ; spe, cupiditate, egestate, etc., Cic. ; mundus animo et sensibus, Cic.

praedium, ī, n. [praes], *a landed estate, farm* : Cato ; rustica, urbana, Cic. ; Hor.

prae-dives, itis, *adj. very rich* : Liv., Tac., Juv. ; cornu (Autumni), Ov.

prae-divinō, āre, *to have a presentiment of, to forebode* : Pl.

praedō, ōnis, m. [praeda], *a plunderer, robber* : Pl., Cic., Verg., etc. ; maritimus, Nep.

prae-doctus, a, um, *instructed beforehand* : a duce, Sall.

praedor, āri [praeda], *to make booty, to plunder.* **A.** Intrans. **1.** Lit. : Pl., Caes., Cic., Liv., etc. ; classis pluribus locis praedata, Tac. ; ex hereditate, Cic. ; Liv. ; de aratorum bonis, Cic. ; in re frumentariā, Cic. ; Liv. **2.** Transf. : ex alterius inscientiā, Cic. **B.** Trans. **1.** Lit. : socios, Tac. Also, piscis calamo, Prop. ; ovem, Ov. **2.** Transf. : amores alicuius, Ov. ; singula de nobis anni praedantur euntes, Hor.

prae-dūcō, dūcere, dūxī, ductum, *to draw in front* (for protection) : fossam et maceriam, Caes.

prae-dulcis, e, *adj. very sweet, luscious.* **1.** Lit. : mel, Plin. **2.** Transf. : decus, Verg. ; Quint.

prae-dūrus, a, um, *very tough.* **1.** Lit. : corium, Tac. **2.** Transf. **a.** homo praedurus viribus, Verg. **b.** *very impudent* : os, Quint. **c.** *very harsh* : verba, Quint.

prae-ēmineō, ēre, *to project forwards, be prominent.* **1.** Lit. : Sall. **2.** Transf. (with ACC.) *to surpass, excel* : ceteros peritiā legum, Tac.

prae-eō, īre, iī, itum, *to go before, lead the way, precede.* **1.** Lit. : Romam, Liv. ; praeeunte carinā, Verg. With DAT. : consulibus lictores, Cic. With ACC. : per avia ac derupta eum, Tac. **2.** Transf. (in words). **a.** *to go over before, to dictate a formula of* prayer, oath, etc. : alicui, Cic., Plin. Ep. ; de sc.ipto, l lin. Ep. ; praei verbis quid vis, Pl. ; praei verba, quibus me pro legionibus devoveam, Liv. ; carmen, Liv. ; sacramentum, Tac. **b.** *to dictate* (in gen.), *give the cue beforehand* : ut vobis voce praeirent

quid iudicaretis, Cic. ; Quint. **c.** *to ordain* : omnia uti decemviri praeierunt facta, Liv.

praefātiō, ōnis, *f.* [praefātur], *a saying beforehand.* **a.** *a form of words, formula* : donationis, Cic. ; sacrorum, Liv. **b.** *a foreword, preface, introduction* : to a book : Liv., Plin. ; to a speech : dicere, Quint., Plin. Ep. ; sine praefatione clementiae, Suet.

prae-fātur (3rd *sing.*), fārī, fātus sum. **I,** *to say* or *utter beforehand, to preface* : Liv. ; quae de deorum naturā praefati sumus, Cic. With ACC. and *Inf.* : Liv., Curt., etc. Phr. : praefari honorem, *to express respect before* speaking of something offensive : Cic. Ep. **II.** *to utter a preliminary prayer* : Cic.; Iovi, Cato ; pontifice maximo praefante carmen, Liv. ; carminibus, Liv. With ACC. *to invoke beforehand* : Cato, Verg. **III.** *to foretell* : talia felicia Pelei, Cat. ; cordi esse divis e carminibus praefantur, Liv.

praefectūra, ae, *f.* [praefectus], *the office of a* praefectus. **1.** Lit. **a.** *superintendence, prefecture* : villae, Varr. ; urbis, Plin. ; vigilum, annonae, praetori, Tac. ; domūs, Juv. ; morum (the duty of the censor), Suet. **b.** *the government of a district* or *town under* a proconsul or propraetor ; *a prefectship* : petere, sumere, Cic. Ep. ; accipere, Nep. Under the Empire : praefectura Aegypti, Suet. **2.** Transf. **a.** *an Italian city* or *town governed by a Roman* praefectus, *a prefecture* : Cic. ; earum regionum praefecturae, Caes. **b.** *the territory of a prefecture, a district* : Tac. Transf. : Pl.

praefectus, a, um. **I.** *Part.* praeficiō. **II.** Noun, **praefectus**, ī, m. *an overseer, superintendent, commander, prefect.* **a.** In gen. : with GEN. (but often with DAT. from its participial origin) : gymnasi, Pl. ; urbis or urbi, Liv. ; Tac. ; villae, Varr. ; praefecti Capuam creari coepti, Liv. ; praefectum ad iura reddenda ab Romā quotannis missuros, Liv. ; morum, Nep. ; moribus, Cic. ; annonae, Tac. ; aerari or aerario, Plin. Ep. ; castrorum or castris, Tac. ; classis, *an admiral*, Cic., Liv. ; fabrum, Caes. ; equitum, Hirt. ; and *absol.* praefectus, Caes. ; legionis, Tac. ; praetori or praetorio (*a commander of the imperial body-guard*), Tac. ; Aegypti, Suet. **b.** Of foreigners : *a satrap, governor, general* : totius Phrygiae, Nep. ; regis Darei, Nep. [Fr. *préfet.*]

prae-ferō, ferre, tulī, lātum. **I.** *to bear before, to carry in front.* **1.** Lit. **a.** In gen. : manūs, Ov. ; dextrā facem, Cic. ; in fascibus insignia laureae, Caes. ; fascis praetoribus, Cic. **b.** *to bear along at the head of* religious and triumphal processions : signa militaria, Liv. ; triumpho titulum, Suet. **2.** Transf. **a.** lumen menti, Cic. ; adulescentulo ad libidinem facem, Cic. **b.** *to place before, to prefer* : Gallorum quam Romanorum imperia, Caes. ; praelato invidit honori, Verg. ; aliquem alicui, Cic., Ov. ; pecuniam amicitiae, Cic. With *Inf.* : Hor. **c.** *to show, display, reveal* (= prae se ferre) : opinionem, Caes. ; avaritiam, Cic. ; amorem, Ov. ; sapientiae studium habitu corporis, Plin. Ep. **d.** *to anticipate* : diem triumphi, Liv. **II.** *to bear past* (= praeterferre). In *Mid.* : *to ride* or *march past, to* *outflank.* **1.** Lit.: praelatos hostis adoriri, Liv.; praelatus equo, Tac.; praeter castra praelati, Liv.; castra praelati. Liv. **2.** Transf. *to surpass:* (in Mid. or with Refl. Pron.): *virtute belli praeferri omnibus gentibus,* Caes.; se legionariis militibus, Caes.

prae-fĕrōx, ōcis, *adj. very defiant, impetuous:* Liv.; ingenio, Tac.

prae-ferrātus, a, um, *tipped with iron:* modius, Cato; pilum, Plin. Comic.: for *chained:* Pl.

prae-fervidus, a, um, *very hot.* **1.** Lit.: fulgor, Acc.; balneum, Tac. **2.** Transf.: ira, Liv.

prae-festīnō, āre. **I.** *to hasten before the time* (with *Inf.*): Pl., Liv. **II.** *to hasten past:* sinum, Tac.

praefĭca, ae, *f. a woman hired to lament at the head of a funeral procession:* Pl., Varr.

prae-fĭciō, ficere, fēcī, fectum [faciō], *to set over or at the head, to place in authority, appoint to the command.* **1.** Lit.: aliquem curatorem, qui statuis faciundis praesit, Cic.; in eo exercitu fratrem, Cic. With Dat.: te provinciae, Pl.; Tac.; legatos legionibus, Caes.; pontifices sacris, Cic.; imperatorem bello, Cic.; aliquem classi, Nep., Liv.; lucis Avernis, Verg.; libertos rationibus, Tac. **2.** Transf.: nec locus nec materia invenitur, cui divinationem praeficere possimus, Cic.

prae-fīdēns, entis, *over-confident:* sibi, Cic.

prae-fīgō, fīgere, fīxī, fīxum. **1.** Lit. **a.** *to fix, fasten, set up in front, to fix on the end or extremity:* ripa acutis sudibus praefixis munita, Caes. With Dat.: arma puppibus, Verg.; caput hastae, Suet. **b.** *to tip, head, point* (with Abl.): asseres cuspidibus praefixi, Caes.; iacula praefixa ferro, Liv.; Verg. **c.** *to pierce in front:* latus praefixa veru, Tib. **2.** Transf. *to fix or set up something in front* so as to block up: prospectūs omnis, Plin.

prae-fīnĭō, īre, *to determine, limit beforehand, to prescribe:* Lucr., Cic.; successori diem, Cic.; censum, Cic.

praefīnītō, *adv. in the prescribed manner:* loqui, Ter.

praefiscĭnē and **praefiscĭnī,** *adv.* [fascinum], *meaning no evil, without offence:* praefiscine hoc nunc dixerim, Pl.

praeflōrō, āre [flōs], *to deprive of its bloom.* Transf.: gloriam victoriae, Liv.

prae-flŭō, fluere, *to flow by or past:* infimā valle praefluit Tiberis, Liv.; Tac. With Acc.: Aufidus regna Dauni, Hor.; Noricam provinciam, Tac.

praefōcō, āre [faucēs], *to choke, strangle, suffocate:* animae viam, Ov.

prae-fodĭō, fodere, fōdī. **I.** *to dig before or in front of:* portas, Verg. **II.** *to dig or bury beforehand:* aurum, Ov.

prae-for, *v.* praefātur.

prae-fōrmō, āre, *to form beforehand:* infantibus litteras, Quint.

praefrāctē, *adv. resolutely, obstinately:* defendere, Cic.

praefrāctus, a, um. **I.** *Part.* praefringō. **II.** Adj. **a.** Rhet. *broken, abrupt. Comp.:* Cic. **b.** Of character: *stern, resolute:* Cic. *Comp.:* Val. Max.

prae-frīgĭdus, a, um, *very cold:* Auster, Ov.

prae-fringō, fringere, frēgī, frāctum [frango]. **I.** *to break off at the tip, end, etc.:* caulem, Cato; ligna, Lucr.; hastas, Liv.; cornu galeae, Liv.; praefracto rostro (triremis), Caes.

prae-fulciō, fulcīre, fulsī, fultum. **I.** *to support in front.* Transf.: illud praefulci atque praemuni ut etc., Cic. Ep.; miseriis praefulcior, Pl. **II.** *to place under as a stay.* Transf.: quin me suis negotiis praefulciat, Pl.

prae-fulgeō, fulgēre, fūlsī. **I.** *to gleam forth or conspicuously.* **1.** Lit.: pellis unguibus aureis, Verg. **2.** Transf.: Cassius atque Brutus, Tac.; consulari decore, Tac. **II.** *to shine beyond, outshine.* Transf.: huic triumpho triumphus recens, Liv.

prae-gelĭdus, a, um, *very cold:* loca, Liv.

prae-gestĭō, īre, *to be very eager* (with *Inf.*): Cic., Cat., Hor.

praegnāns, antis (**praegnās,** ātis, Pl.), *adj.* [prae and gnā in (g)nā-scor], *with child, pregnant.* **1.** Lit.: uxor, Cic.; Pl.; Juv.; sus, Varr. **2.** Transf.: *full of, swollen with:* succo herba, Plin.; stamine fusus, Juv. Comic.: plagae, Pl.

prae-gracĭlis, e, *adj. very slender, or lank:* proceritas, Tac.

prae-grandis, e, *adj. very large, huge.* **1.** Lit.: Pac., Plin., Suet. **2.** Transf.: *very great, powerful:* senex, Pers.

prae-gravis, e, *adj. very heavy.* **1.** Lit.: onus, Ov. **2.** Transf. **a.** *very heavy, unwieldy:* corpore, Liv. **b.** *very heavy, stupefied:* cibo vinoque praegraves, Tac. **c.** *very heavy, oppressive, burdensome:* servitium, Plin. **d.** *very wearisome:* delatores, Tac.

prae-gravō, āre, *to press heavily on, weigh down.* **1.** Lit.: praegravata telis scuta, Liv. **2.** Transf. **a.** *to outweigh* (i.e. eclipse): qui praegravat artis infra se positas, Hor.; Suet. **b.** *to weigh down, burden:* exonerare praegravante turbā regnum, Liv.; corpus animum, Hor.

prae-gredior, gredī, grēssus [gradior]. **I.** *to go before or in advance, to precede.* Lit.: Caes., Cic. With Dat.: gregi equus, Varr. With Acc.: agmen, Liv. **2.** Transf. *to outstrip:* non solum nuntios sed etiam famam adventūs sui, Liv. **II.** *to pass by, go past:* with Acc.: castra, Liv.; Tac.

praegrēssĭō, ōnis, *f.* [praegredior], *a going before.* **1.** Lit. (in *pl.*): stellarum, Cic. **2.** Transf.: causae, Cic.

praegustātor, ōris, *m.* [praegustō], *one who tastes* the meats and drinks *before they are served at table; a taster, cup-bearer.* **1.** Lit.: Suet. **2.** Transf.: libidinum, Cic.

prae-gustō, āre, *to taste beforehand:* cibos, Ov.; oleas mures, Liv.; pocula, Juv.

prae-hĭbeō, ēre [habeō], *to hold forth, offer.* **1.** Lit.: vestem, aurum, Pl.; alicui cibum, Pl. **2.** Transf.: alicui hospitium, Pl.; verba, Pl.

prae-iaceō, ēre, *to lie before, be situated in front of.* With Dat.: Plin. With Acc.: campus castra, Tac.

praeiūdĭcātus, a, um. **I.** *Part.* praeiūdicō. **II.** Adj.: *decided beforehand, prejudiced:*

opinio, Cic. ; praeiudicatum eventum belli habetis, Liv. **III.** N e u t. as Noun : ne quid praeiudicati adforatis, Cic. ; pro praeiudicato ferre, Liv.

prae-iūdicium, I, n. *a preliminary or previous judicial enquiry.* **1.** L i t. : facere, Cic., Plin. Ep. ; duobus praeiudiciis damnatus, Cic. ; Quint. **2.** T r a n s f. **a.** *prejudgment of a question :* rei tantae, Liv. **b.** *a precedent, example :* vestri facti praeiudicio demotus, Caes. ; aliquem praoiudicio iuvare, Plin. Ep.

prae-iūdicō, āre, *to decide beforehand, to prejudge.* **a.** In law : de maiore maleficio, Cic. **b.** In gon. : de iis censores, Cic.

prae-iuvō, iuvāre, iūvī, *to aid beforehand :* adfectam fidem, Tac.

prae-lābor, lābī, lāpsus, *to glide along, by or past :* piscis ante, Cic. poet. ; amnis, Luc. ; insula, in quam Germani nando praelabebantur, Tac. With Acc. : rotis flumina, Verg.

prae-lambō, ere, *to lick or taste beforehand :* (mus) omne, Hor.

prae-largus, a, um, *very ample :* Pers.

praelātus, a, um, *Part.* praeforō.

prae-lautus, a, um, *very elegant, sumptuous :* Suet.

prae-lēctiō, ōnis, *f.* [praelego], *a lecture :* Quint.

prae-legō, legere, lēgī, lēctum. **I.** *to read and explain to others, to lecture upon :* auctores, Quint. ; Suet. **II.** *to sail past, skirt :* Campaniam, Tac.

prae-ligō, āre, *to bind on in front.* **1.** L i t. : sarmenta cornibus (DAT.) boum, Liv. Also, coronam fasciā, Suet. ; and, *to bind up :* os, Cic. **2.** T r a n s f. : o praeligatum pectus ! (i.e. obdurate), Pl.

praelocūtus, a, um, *Part.* praeloquor.

prae-longus, a, um, *very long.* **1.** L i t. : gladii, Liv. ; hasta, Tac. ; homo, Quint. **2.** T r a n s f. : sermones, Quint.

prae-loquor, loquī, locūtus. **I.** *to speak before another, to forestall in speaking :* orationem, Pl. ; causam, Plin. Ep. **II.** *to say beforehand by way of preface :* Plin. Ep. ; epistulā, Plin. Ep. ; de aliquā re, Quint.

prae-lūceō, lūcēre, lūxī, *to shine or give light in front or before.* **1.** L i t. **a.** servus praelucens, Suet. ; alicui, Stat. **b.** Of the light itself : faces, Mart. ; ignis noster facinori, Phaedr. **2.** T r a n s f. **a.** amicitia bonam spem (*Intern.* Acc.) praelucet in posterum, Cic. **b.** *to outshine* (with DAT.) : nullus sinus Baiis, Hor.

prae-lūdō, lūdere, *to play beforehand by way of practice or prelude.* **1.** L i t. : Nero Pompeiano praeludit, Plin. **2.** T r a n s f. : aliquid operibus suis, Stat.

praelūsiō, ōnis, *f.* [praelūdō], *a prelude :* Plin. Ep.

praelūstris, e, *adj. very magnificent.* *Neut. pl.* as Noun : Ov.

praemandāta, ōrum, n. pl. *a warrant of arrest :* Cic.

prae-mandō, āre, *to order beforehand, to bespeak :* puerum aut puellam, Pl.

praemātūrē, adv. *prematurely :* Pl.

prae-mātūrus, a, um, *too early, untimely, premature :* denuntiatio, Planc. ap. Cic. Ep. ; cineres, Juv. ; honores, hiems, Tac.

prae-medicātus, a, um, *protected by drugs or charms :* Ov.

prae-meditātiō, ōnis, *f. a thinking or musing upon beforehand :* Cic. ; malorum, Cic.

prae-meditor, ārī, *to think over beforehand, to practise beforehand :* temptans citharam et praemeditans, Tac. With Acc. and *Inf.* : Cic. With *Indir.* *Deliberative :* Cic. Ep. *Perf. Part.* in *Pass.* sense : *previously thought out :* mala praemeditata, Cic. ; *Neut.* as Noun : Quint.

prae-mercor, ārī, *to buy before or beforehand :* ancillam, Pl.

praemetuēns, entis. **I.** *Part.* praemetuō. **II.** A d j. : *afraid or fearful beforehand :* with *Obj.* GEN. : ovis praemetuens doli, Phaedr.

praemetuenter, adv. *anxiously :* errorem vitare, Lucr.

prae-metuō, ere, *to be in fear beforehand :* mens, Lucr. ; praemetuens suis (*about his men*), Caes. With Acc. : deserti coniugis iras, Verg.

praemior, ārī [praemium], *to stipulate for a reward :* Suet.

prae-mittō, mittere, mīsī, missum, *to let go or send on in advance.* **1.** L i t. : a portu me praemisisti domum, Pl. ; legiones in Hispaniam, Caes. ; legatum ad flumen, Sall. ; Caes. ; edictum, Caes., Liv. ; litteras, Cic. Ep. **2.** T r a n s f. : postquam haec favorabili oratione praemisit, Tac. ; praemissā voce ' hoc age,' Suet.

praemium, I, n. [prae and emō], *what one takes or receives by prior right ; the pick of or a prize from the booty.* **1.** L i t. **a.** ecqua in istac pars inest praemi mihi ? Pl. ; praemia pugnae, Verg. ; spectat sua praemia raptor, Ov. ; Tib. ; praemia malle quam stipendia, Tac. **b.** Of game killed : quarry : Hor., Prop. P o e t. : raptae virginitatis, Ov. **2.** T r a n s f. **a.** *prerogative, due award :* honores et praemia, Caes. ; perfunctos vitā praemia, Lucr. ; legis, Cic. Ep. ; praemia donaque fortunae, Cic. ; frontis urbanae praemia, Tac. **b.** (In *pl.*) *special or choice gifts, guerdons :* vitae, Lucr. ; Veneris praemia (i.e. children), Verg. **c.** *recompense, reward :* Ter. ; proponere, consequi, Caes. ; persolvere, Cic. ; alicui pro aliquā re dare, Cic. ; reddere, Cat. ; aliquem praemio inducere, inlicere, Sall. ; so, invitare, Cic. ; elicere ad faciendum aliquid, Cic. ; adficere, Quint. ; augere, Tac. ; commoveri praemiis ad perdiscendum, Cic. ; persuadere alicui magnis praemiis, Caes. ; legibus praemia proposita sunt virtutibus, Cic. **d.** *an exploit* (worthy of reward) : Verg.

prae-molestia, ae, *f. trouble beforehand, presentiment of trouble :* Cic.

prae-mōlior, īrī, *to prepare thoroughly or elaborately beforehand :* res, Liv.

prae-moneō, ēre, *to forewarn, to advise or admonish beforehand.* **a.** In gen. : me praemonebat ut magnopere caverem, Cic. With *Subj.* alone : Plin. Ep. With *quod*-clause : Ov. With Acc. : conatūs hostium, Liv. With *Indir.* *Quest.* : Plin. Ep. **b.** Of prophecies : de periculis praemoneri, Cic. With Acc. : cornua caelo nefas, Ov. With Acc. and *Fut. Inf.* : Ov.

prae-monitus, ūs, m. *a forewarning :* Ov.

praemōnstrātor, ōris, *m.* [praemōnstrō], *a guide, director :* Ter.

prae-mōnstrō, āre, *to show beforehand, to point out the way, to guide, direct.* **a.** In gen.: currenti spatium, Lucr. ; praemonstro tibi, ut te aliorum miserescat, Pl. With *Indir. Quest. :* Pl. **b.** *to predict :* magnum aliquid populo R., Cic.

prae-mordeō, mordēre, (mōrsi, Pl.) and mordī, mōrsum, *to bite off the tip or end.* **1.** L i t. : linguam, Luc. ; Pl. ; Sen. **2.** T r a n s f. of pilfering : Juv.

prae-morior, morī, mortuus, *to die early, prematurely,* Ov. **1.** L i t. : Ov. **2.** T r a n s f. of the senses : Plin.

praemortuus, a, um. **I.** *Part.* praemorior. **II.** A d j. *prematurely dead.* **1.** L i t. : membra, Ov. **2.** T r a n s f. : pudor, Liv.

prae-mūniō, īre, *to fortify in front.* **1.** L i t. : aditūs magnis operibus, Caes. ; loca necessaria, Caes. ; fossā, Tac. **2.** T r a n s f. **a.** By antidotes : *to fortify, protect :* metu venenorum praemuniri medicamentis, Suet. **b.** Rhet. and in argument : quae praemuniuntur omnia reliquo sermoni, Cic.

praemūnītiō, ōnis, *f.* [praemūniō]. R h e t. : *preparation of the minds of hearers for what is to follow :* sine ullā praemunitione orationis, Cic. ; Quint.

prae-nārrō, āre, *to tell* or *relate beforehand :* rem, Ter.

prae-natō, āre, *to float* or *flow past.* T r a n s f. : domos amnis praenatat, Verg.

Praeneste, is, *n.* (*nom.* and *f.*) *an ancient town in Latium,* now *Palestrina ; situated on a lofty hill, famed for its temple of Fortune and the oracle connected with it ;* **Praenestīnus**, a, um ; **Praenestīni**, ōrum, *m. pl. the Praenestines.*

prae-niteō, ēre, *to outshine.* T r a n s f. (with DAT.) : tibi, Hor.

prae-nōmen, inis, *n. the fore-name, praenomen.* **a.** Prop. *the name* (e.g. Gaius, Marcus) *that stood before the gentile name* (e.g. Iulius, Tullius) : Cic. Ep., Hor., Liv. **b.** *a title placed before a person's name :* praenomen *Imperatoris,* Suet.

prae-nōscō, ere, *to learn beforehand :* futura, Cic. ; Ov.

praenōtiō, ōnis, *f.* [praenōscō] (a translation of the Epicurean πρόληψις), *an innate idea :* deorum, Cic.

prae-nūbilus, a, um, *very cloudy, very dark* or *gloomy :* lucus, Ov.

prae-nūntiō, āre, *to announce beforehand, to foretell :* futura, Cic. *Impers. Pass. :* de adventu alicuius, Nep.

prae-nūntius, a, um, *that foretells* or *forebodes :* verba, sibila, Ov. As Noun. **a.** *Masc.* and *Fem. : a foreteller, harbinger :* lucis praenuntius ales, Ov. ; Lucr. ; stellae calamitatum praenuntiae, Cic. ; Ov. ; Tac. **b.** *Neut.: an indication, token :* Sen., Plin.

praeoccupātiō, ōnis, *f.* [praeoccupō], *a seizing beforehand :* locorum, Nep.

prae-occupō, āre, *to seize upon* or *take possession of before* (another). **1.** L i t. : vias, iter, Caes. ; loca opportuna, Liv. **2.** T r a n s f. : animos timor, Caes. ; auris, Liv. ; praeoccupati beneficio animi, Liv. **b.** *to anticipate, prevent :* praeoccupari adventu Caesaris, Caes. ; alter alterum, Nep. With

[nf. : iugum praeoccupaverunt ferre (i.e. hastened to bring the bill quicker to the people), Liv.

prae-olō, ere [oleō], *to emit a smell beforehand.* T r a n s f. : ut praeolat mihi quod tu velis, Pl.

prae-optō, āre, *to choose before* or *in preference, to prefer.* With ACC. and DAT. : suas leges Romanae civitati, Liv. ; Nep. With *ut* and *Subj. :* Pl. With *Inf. :* Caes., Liv., Tac. ; meum potius caput periculo praeoptavisse quam is periret ponere, Pl. With ACC. and *Inf. :* ut puerum praeoptares perire potius quam esset cum illo nupta, Ter. With ACC. and *quam :* nemo non illos sibi quam vos dominos praeoptet, Liv.

prae-pandō, ere, *to open* or *spread before, to spread out, extend.* **1.** L i t. : cornua, Verg. **2.** T r a n s f. : lumina menti alicuius, Lucr.

praeparātiō, ōnis, *f.* [praeparō], *a preparation :* adhibere, Cic. R h e t. of the *preparation* of the minds of hearers : Quint.

praeparātus, a, um. **I.** *Part.* praeparō. **II.** Adverb. phr. : ex praeparato, *by previous arrangement,* Liv. ; *with preparation,* Sen. Ep. ; praeparato, *with preparation,* Quint.

prae-parō, āre, *to get* or *make ready beforehand, to prepare.* **1.** L i t. : commeatum, navis, Liv. ; locum domestici belli causā, Caes. ; frumentum in decem annos, Liv. ; praeparato ad talem casum perfugio, Liv. ; res necessarias ad vitam degendam, Cic. ; ova, Mart. **2.** T r a n s f. : animum, auris, Cic. ; orationem, animos, Liv. ; necem alicui, Tac. ; gratiam adversus publicum odium, Tac. ; bene praeparatum pectus, Hor.

praepedimentum, ī, *n.* [praepediō], *a hindrance :* Pl.

praepediō, īre [pēs, *cf.* impediō], *to shackle, tether, hobble.* **1.** L. t. : praepeditus latera ferro, Pl. ; praepeditis Numidarum equis, Tac. **2.** T r a n s f. a. sese praedā, Liv. **b.** timor dicta linguae, Pl. ; praepediuntur crura, Lucr. ; bonas artis avaritia, Sall. ; pudor, Liv. ; lassitudo fugam, Liv. ; singultu medios praepediente sonos, Ov. ; praepediri valetudine, Tac.

prae-pendeō, ēre, *to hang before, to hang down in front :* Caes., Prop.

praepes, etis, *adj.* [v. penna and petō]. **I.** In flight : *nimble, fleet :* avis, Enn. ; pennae, Verg. ; ferrum, Enn. **II.** *winged :* tela praepetis dei, Ov. As Noun, *m.f., a bird :* Iovis, Ov. Esp. in augury : *a bird of good omen :* Liv. As Adj. *lucky :* portus, Enn.

prae-pilātus, a, um [pila], *tipped with a ball* or *button :* missilia, Liv.

prae-pinguis, e, *adj. very fat.* **1.** L i t. : Galba, Suet. Of soil : *very rich :* solum, Verg. **2.** T r a n s f. *thick :* vox, Quint.

prae-polleō, ēre. **I.** *to be very powerful :* divitiis, virtute praepollens, Liv. **II.** *to surpass in power :* Phoenices mari, Tac. ; quibus additis praepollebat, Tac.

prae-ponderō, āre. **A.** T r a n s. *to outweigh.* T r a n s f. : neque ea (commoda) volunt praeponderari honestate, Cic. **B.** I n t r a n s. *to turn the scale.* T r a n s f. : in humaniorem partem, Sen. ; Varr. ; quaerere . . . quo praeponderet alea fati, Luc. ; Quint.

prae-pōnō, pōnere, posuī (posivī, Pl.), positum (*Sync. Part.* praepostus, Lucr.), *to put* or *set before, to place first*. **1.** Lit. **a.** praeponens ultima primis, Hor. ; fronti olivam, Hor. ; versūs in primā fronte libelli, Ov. **b.** *to place* or *set over in command* or *in charge* (with Acc. and Dat.) : sinistro cornu Antonium, Caes. ; aliquem provinciae, Cic. Ep. ; navibus, Cic. ; toti officio maritimo, Caes. ; vectigalibus, Tac. ; aliquem custodem loco, Ov. Also, ubi praepositus sum, Cic. **2.** Trans. *to set before, to prefer :* lucrum sopori, Pl. ; se alteri, Ter. ; salutem rei publicae vitae suae, Cic. ; urbem silvis, Hor.

prae-portō, āre, *to bear* or *carry before :* tela, Lucr. ; Cat.

praepositiō, ōnis, *f.* [praepōnō], *a putting before*. **a.** *a preferring, preference :* Cic. **b.** Gramm. *a preposition :* Cic.

praepositus, a, um. **I.** *Part.* praepōnō. **II.** Noun. **a.** **praepositus**, ī, *m. a chief, overseer, commander* (with Gen. or Dat.) : legatorum, Cic. ; Tac. ; cubiculo, *chamberlain*, Suet. **b.** **praeposita**, ōrum, *n. pl.* (= προηγμένα), with the Stoics, *preferable* or *advantageous things*, next after the absolutely good : Cic. *Sing. :* Cic. [Fr. *prévôt*.]

prae-possum, posse, potuī, *to get the upper hand :* postquam Macedones praepotuere, Tac.

praeposterē, *adv. in a reversed order, irregularly :* Cic., Plin. Ep.

prae-posterus, a, um, *having the last first, perverted*. **1.** Lit. : ordo, Lucr. ; verba, Cic. ; irigus (i.e. unseasonable), Sen. Ep. ; oratio, Plin. Ep. **2.** Transf. *wrong, perverted, perverse :* homines, Sall. ; Cic. Of things : consilia, Cic.

prae-potēns, entis, *adj. very powerful :* vir, Cic. ; Pl. ; terrā marique Carthago, Cic. With Gen. : rerum omnium, Cic. *Masc. pl.* as Noun : Cic.

prae-properanter (Lucr.) and **praeproperē** (Pl., Liv., etc.), *adv. very quickly, with over-haste.*

prae-properus, a, um, *very quick* or *hasty, over-hasty, precipitate :* festinatio, Cic. Ep. ; celeritas, ingenium, Liv.

prae-pūtium, ī, *n.* [prae πόσθιον], *the fore-skin, prepuce :* Juv.

prae-quam, *adv.* v. prae.

prae-questus, a, um [queror], *complaining beforehand* (with Acc.) : multa, Ov.

prae-radiō, āre, *to outshine :* signa minora, Ov.

praereptus, a, um, *Part.* praeripiō.

prae-riguisse, *Perf. Inf. to have become exceedingly stiff :* Tac.

prae-ripiō, ripere, ripuī, reptum [rapiō]. **I.** *to seize before another, to forestall* someone *in seizing* or *appropriating*. **1.** Lit. : sponsam meam, Pl. ; aliquem alicui, Ter. ; oscula, Lucr. ; arma Minervae, Ov. **2.** Transf. : aliis laudem, Cic. ; Plin. Ep. **II.** *to carry off hastily* or *prematurely :* populi beneficium, Caes. ; deorum beneficium festinatione, Cic. **III.** *to forestall, frustrate by forestalling :* consilia hostium, Cic.

prae-rōdō, rōdere, rōsum. **I.** *to gnaw at the*

end : digitos suos, Pl. **II.** *to gnaw off :* hamum (i.e. the bait), Hor.

prae-rogātīvus, a, um [prae rogō], *asked before others, voting before* or *first, prerogative :* centuria, Cic. Hence, omen praerogativum (' the omen of the first vote,' thought to indicate the result of the voting), Cic. As Noun. **A. praerogātīva**, ae, *f.* (*sc.* tribus or centuria), *the tribe* or *century which voted first in the Comitia*. **1.** Lit. : Cic. ; praerogativa Voturia iuniorum, Liv. **2.** Transf. **a.** *the vote of the century which voted first :* praerogativam referre, Cic. **b.** *a previous choice* or *election :* praerogativa militaris, Liv. ; equitum, Liv. **c.** *a sure sign, token, prognostic, omen :* dedit praerogativam suae voluntatis, Cic. **B. prae-rogātīva**, ōrum, *n. pl.* (*sc.* suffragia), praerogativa tribunum militum non petentem creant, Liv.

prae-rogō, āre, *to ask before* or *first :* sententias, Suet.

praerōsus, a, um, *Part.* praerōdō.

prae-rumpō, rumpere, rūpī, ruptum, *to break off before* or *in front :* funis, Caes. ; retinacula classis, Ov.

praeruptus, a, um. **I.** *Part.* praerumpō. **II.** Adj. : *broken off :* hence, of places : *broken, steep, abrupt*. **1.** Lit. : saxa, Cic. ; loca, Caes. ; nemus, Hor. ; descensus, Hirt. ; aquae mons, Verg. ; fossae, Tac. *Comp. :* Col. *Sup. :* Hirt. **2.** Transf. *headstrong, hasty, precipitate :* audacia, Cic. ; iuvenis animo praeruptus, Tac. ; dominatio (*headlong*, i.e. unmitigated), Tac.

praes, praedis, *m.* [prae and vas (vadis)], *one who stands bail for another, a surety*. **1.** Lit. : dare, Cic. ; praedem esse pro aliquo, Cic. Ep. ; praedes pecuniae publicae accipere, Cic. ; cavere populo praedibus ac praediis (i.e. obtain security for the nation), Cic. **2.** Transf. **a.** In simile : cum sex libris, tamquam praedibus, me ipsum obstrinxerim, Cic. **b.** *the property of a surety :* praedes vendere, Cic.

praes, *adv.* [prae], *at hand, now :* ibi tibi parata praes est, Pl.

praessep-, v. praesēp-.

prae-sāgiō, īre, and **praesāgior**, īrī (Pl.), *to feel beforehand, to have a presentiment* or *foreboding*. **1.** Lit. : Cic. ; animus plus mali, Pl. ; hoc ipsum praesagiens animo, Liv. ; Prop. With Acc. and *Inf.* : Pl., Liv. **2.** Transf. *to make one forebode :* exiguitas copiarum recessum, Cael. ap. Cic. Ep.

praesāgītiō, ōnis, *f.* [praesāgiō], *a presentiment, divining :* Cic.

praesāgium, ī, *n.* [praesāgio]. **I.** *a presentiment, foreboding :* mentis, Ov. With *Obj.* Gen. : malorum, Tac. **II.** *prognostic, prediction :* vatum, Ov. ; equorum, Tac.

prae-sāgus, a, um. **I.** *foreboding, foretelling, divining, prophetic :* mens praesaga mali, Verg. ; Ov. **II.** *prophetic, predicting :* verba, Ov. ; responsa, Tac. ; praesagi ignes fulminis, Verg.

prae-sciō, īre, *to know beforehand, to foreknow :* Ter., Suet.

prae-sciscō, ere, *to find out* or *learn beforehand :* Verg. With *Indir. Deliberative :* Liv.

prae-scius, a, um, *foreknowing, prescient :* corda, Verg. ; lingua, Ov. With *Obj.* GEN. : vates praescia venturi, Verg. ; (Messalinam) praesciam criminis facere, Tac.

prae-scrībō, scribere, scripsi, scriptum. **1.** Li t. *to write before* or *at the head :* sibi quae Vari praescripsit pagina nomen, Verg. ; monimentis nomina, Tac. ; diplomatibus principem, Tac. **2. Transf. a.** *to pre-ordain, appoint, prescribe :* finem rebus, Ter. ; iura civibus, Cic. ; imperandi modum, Cic. With *Indir. Quest. :* alicui quid fieri oporteret, Caes. With *Indir. Deliberative :* populo Romano quem ad modum suo iure uteretur, Caes. *Impers. Pass.* with *ne* and *Subj. :* Cic. Ep. With thing as Subject : ut maiorum iura moresque praescribunt, Cic. **b.** In law: *to bring an exception against :* ignominioso patri filius praescribit, Quint. **c.** *to dictate :* carmina, Tib. **d.** *to map out, outline :* formam futuri principatūs, Tac. **e.** *to plead as an excuse* or *in defence, to put forward* or *use as a pretext :* frustra Pulchram praescribi, Tac.

prae-scriptiō, ōnis, *f.* [praescrībō], *a writing before* or *at the head ;* hence *a heading, title, preface.* **1.** Li t. : legis, Cic. **2.** Transf. **a.** *a pretext, excuse :* Caes. ; tribuniciae potestatis praescriptione, Tac. **b.** *order, law :* naturae, rationis, Cic. ; Tac. **c.** In law : *an objection :* Quint. Transf. (in *pl.*) : Sen. Ep.

praescriptum, i, *n.* [praescrībō], *something written out first to be copied* or *learnt.* **1.** Li t. : Sen. Ep. **2.** Transf. : *an order, rule :* legum, Cic. ; ad praescriptum, Caes., Liv. ; ultra praescriptum, Suet. ; intra praescriptum, Hor.

prae-secō, secāre, secui, sectum, *to cut off the end* or *tip, to cut short :* praesectis mulierum crinibus, Caes. ; partem, Ov.

praesegmina, um, *n. pl.* [praesecō], *pieces cut off, parings* (as of the nails) : Pl.

praesēns, entis. **I.** *Part.* praesum. **II.** A d j. (ABL. *sing.* of persons, usually praesente ; of things, praesenti). **a.** *present* (now or at the time spoken of), *in sight* or *at hand, in person :* adsum praesens praesenti tibi, Pl. ; quo praesente, Cic. ; praesens tecum egi, Cic. Ep. ; praesenti bello, Nep. ; inopia praesentis temporis, Caes. ; fortuna viri, Liv. ; sermo, Cic. Ep. ; ora (deorum), Verg.; in praesens tempus, and more freq. in praesens, *for the present :* pleraque differat, et praesens in tempus omittat, Hor. ; Cic. ; si fortuna in praesens deseruit, Tac. ; Hor. So, ad praesens, *for the present :* munimentum ad praesens, in posterum ultionem, Tac. ; Suet. ; praesenti tempore and in praesenti, *at present, now ;* praesenti tempore, Ov. ; haec ad te in praesenti scripsi, ut speres, Cic. Ep. ; Liv. ; in rem praesentem venire, *to the very spot,* Cic. ; in rem praesentem perducere audientis, Quint. ; in re praesenti, *on the spot* or *at the immediate time,* Pl., Liv. *Comp. :* iam praesentior res erat, Liv. *Sup. :* Quint. As Noun, **praesentia**, ium, *n. pl., present circumstances, the present state of affairs :* praesentia sequi, Tac. ; Curt., etc. Phr. in praesentia (*sc.* tempora), *for the present, in the present state of affairs :* Ter., Cic.,

Tac., etc. **b.** *immediate, instant, prompt, ready :* pecunia, Pl., Cic. ; deditio, Caes. ; poena, Cic. ; diligentia, Sall. ; memoria, Liv. ; supplicium, Tac. ; fortuna laborum, Verg. **c.** *instant* (in operation), *prompt, efficacious, powerful :* auxilium, Cic. ; quo non praesentius ullum, Verg. With *Inf. :* Hor. **d.** Of character : *collected, resolute :* animo virili praesentique ut sis, para, Ter. ; Cic. ; non plures, sed etiam praesentioribus animis, Liv. **e.** (*cf.* adesse in legal sense) *present to help, propitious :* deus, Cic. ; divos, Verg. ; Hor. ; et sunt praesentes auxiliumque ferunt (*sc.* Lares), Ov.

praesēnsiō, ōnis, *f.* [praesentiō]. **I.** *a foreboding, presentiment :* Cic. **II.** *a pre-conception :* Cic.

praesēnsus, a, um, *Part.* praesentiō.

praesentāneus, a, um [praesēns], *immediate* (in operation), *effective :* remedium, Plin., Suet.

praesentārius, a, um [praesēns], *quickly at hand, ready :* malum est, Pl. ; argentum, Pl.

praesentia, ae, *f.* [praesēns], *presence.* **1.** Lit. : alicuius praesentiam vitare, Cic. ; urget praesentia Turni, Verg. **2.** Transf. **a.** praesentia animi, Caes., Cic. **b.** *effect, power :* veri, Ov. **c.** Of time : in praesentiā, *for the present :* Caes., Cic.

prae-sentiō, sentire, sēnsi, sēnsum, *to feel* or *perceive beforehand, to have a presentiment of, to divine :* haec canes, Pl. ; verum, Pl. ; animo providere et praesentire, Caes. ; Lucr. ; futura, Cic. ; dolos, Verg. ; Ov. With Acc. and *Inf. :* Ter., Cic. *Impers. Pass. :* Liv.

praesēpe (-**saepe**), is, *n.* and **praesēpis** (-**saepis**) or -**ēs**, is, *f.* [prae saepēs], *an enclosure.* **1.** Lit. **a.** *a stable, stall, pen :* Varr., Verg., Juv. **b.** *a crib, manger :* Cato, Varr., Ov. Comic. for a dinner-table : Hor. **2.** Transf. **a.** *a lodging, haunt :* Pl. ; in *pl.* : Pl. **b.** Of the hives of bees : Verg. **c.** Of a tavern : Cic.

prae-sēpiō (-**saepiō**), sēpīre, sēpsi, sēptum [saepiō], *to fence in front, to barricade :* aditus atque itinera trabibus, Caes.

praesertim, *adv.* [prae serō. Lit. ' foremost in a series '], *especially, particularly.* **A.** praesertim ut nunc sunt mores, Ter. ; praesertim homines tantulae staturae, Caes. ; Hor. **B. a.** With *cum :* praesertim cum de philosophiā scriberem, Cic. ; Ter. ; Caes., etc. : cum praesertim, Cic., Prop., Liv., etc. **b.** With *si :* Cic., Verg.

prae-serviō, ire, *to serve as a slave :* alicui, Pl.

praeses, idis, *adj.* [praesideō], li t. *sitting before as a guard ;* hence, *protecting, defending :* locus, Pl. ; praesides dii, Tac. As Noun. **a.** *a protector, guardian, defender :* Pl. ; senatus rei publicae custos, praeses, propugnator, Cic. ; exercitum satis firmum pacatae provinciae praesidem, Liv. **b.** *a leader, chief, ruler :* Liv. ; praeses belli, Verg. ; iuris consultos urbi ac foro praesides habendos esse, Liv. ; provinciarum, Suet.

praesidēns, entis. **I.** *Part.* praesideō. **II.** Noun, *a governor* (only in *pl.*) : superbia praesidentium, Tac.

prae-sĭdĕō, sĭdēre, sēdī [sedĕō], **I.** *to sit before* or *in front of :* pro aede, Suet. **II.** *to sit in front* or *at the head of.* **a.** In defence : hence *to watch over, guard, protect, defend :* Pl. With DAT. : tibi, Pl. ; urbi, Cic., Liv. ; Gallia huic imperio libertatique communi, Cic. With ACC. : socios, agros, Sall. ; proximum Galliae litus, Tac. **b.** *to preside over, direct, command.* With DAT. : urbanis rebus, Caes. ; armis, Ov. ; ludis, Suet. With *in* and ABL. : in agro Piceno, Sall. With ACC. : exercitum, Pannoniam, Tac.

praesĭdĭārĭus, a, um [praesidium], *on garrison-duty :* milites, Liv.

praesĭdĭum, I, n. [praeses], *defence, protection.* **1.** Lit. **a.** In gen. : apsque me foret et meo praesidio, Pl. ; in fugā sibi praesidium ponere, Caes. ; in tutelā ac praesidio bellicae virtutis, Cic. ; Veneris praesidio ferox, Hor. **b.** Milit. : legiones quae praesidio impedimentis erant, Caes. ; nocturnum praesidium Palati, Cic. **2.** Transf. **A.** Abstract : *safeguard, help, means of help :* Pl. ; praesidio litterarum, Caes. ; quod satis esset praesidi dedit, Nep. ; quaerere sibi praesidia periculis, Cic. ; magnum sibi praesidium ad beatam vitam comparare, Cic. ; rerum tuarum, Juv. **B.** Concrete. **a.** In gen. : *support, defence* (i.e. supporters) : armatorum, Cic. ; quantum praesidium pordis, Verg. ; insigne maestis praesidium rois, Hor. **b.** Milit. : *a protecting force, garrison, escort :* occupato oppido ibi praesidium conlocat, Caes. ; oppido imponere, Liv. ; ex oppido educere, Caes. ; dimittere, Cic. Ep. ; praesidia custodiasque disponere, Caes. ; locum praesidio tenere, Caes. ; Italiam praesidiis confirmare, Cic. ; Juv. ; praesidium dedit ut eo tuto perveniret, Nep. **c.** *a protected position,* (*military*) *post :* occupare et munire, Caes. ; communire, Liv. ; relinquere, Cic. ; milites in praesidiis disponere, Caes. ; in praesidiis esse, Cic. ; praesidio decedere, Liv. Transf. : de praesidio vitae decedere, Cic.

prae-signĭfĭcō, āre, *to show* or *signify beforehand* (with *Indir. Quest.*) : Cic.

praesignis, e, *adj.* [*cf.* insignis], *distinguished above others :* Ov.

prae-sŏnō, āre, *to sound before :* sollemni tibia cantu, Ov.

prae-spargō, ere, *to strew before :* Lucr.

praestābĭlis, e, *adj.* [praestō]. **I.** *eminent, distinguished, excellent* (mostly of things) : res magnitudine praestabiles, Cic. ; dignitas praestabilior, Cic. **II.** In *Comp. : preferable :* fuerat praestabilius ubivis gentium agere aetatem quam etc., Ter. ; nihil amicitiā, Cic. ; Sall.

praestāns, antis. **I.** *Part.* praestō. **II.** Adj. : *eminent, surpassing, extraordinary :* naturā excellens et praestans, Cic. ; praestans usu et sapientiā, Nep. ; praestanti corpore Nymphae, Verg. *Comp. :* virginibus praestantior omnibus, Ov. *Sup. :* in illis artibus praestantissimus, Cic. With GEN. : praestans animi iuvenis, Verg. ; praestantissimus sapientiae, Tac. With *Inf. :* Verg.

praestantĭa, ae, *f.* [praestāns], *superiority, excellence :* virtutis, fortunae (i.e. in virtue, etc.), Cic.

praestat, *v.* praestō.

prae-sternō, ere, *to strew* or *spread beforehand.* **1.** Lit. : folia farferi, Pl. Also, *to bestrew :* altaria, Stat. **2.** Transf. : tuis laudibus materiam, Plin. Pan.

praestes, itis, *m.f.* [praestō], *of deities, presiding, protecting :* Lares, Ov.

praestĭgĭae, ārum, *f. pl.* [praestringō], *a deception, illusion, juggler's trick :* patent praestigiae, Pl. ; verborum, Cic. ; per praestigias, Liv. In *sing. :* Quint. [Fr. *prestige.*]

praestĭgĭātor, ōris, *m.* and **praestĭgĭātrix**, icis, *f.* (Pl.) [praestigiae], *a juggler, impostor :* Pl., Sen.

prae-stĭnō, āre [*cf.* dēstĭnō], *to purchase :* Pl.

prae-stĭtŭō, uere, uī, ūtum [statuō], *to determine* or *appoint beforehand, to prescribe :* diem, Cic. ; Pl. With *Indir. Quest. :* Cic.

praestĭtus, a, um, *Part.* praestō.

praestō (earlier praestŭ), *adv.* [prae-situ], *at hand, ready, present.* **a.** In gen. : ipsum adeo praesto video, Ter. ; quod adest praesto, Lucr. Usually with *esse :* togulae lictoribus ad portam praesto fuerunt, Cic. ; tibi nulla fuit clementia praesto ? Cat. ; Pl. **b.** To help or benefit : ius civile didicit, praesto multis fuit, Cic. ; Pl. ; Tib. **c.** To oppose or resist : si quis mihi praesto fuerit cum armatis hominibus, Cic. [It. *presto :* Fr. *prêt.*]

prae-stō, stāre, stĭtī, stĭtum (*Fut. Part.* praestātūrus, Liv.). **I.** [prae stō] *to stand before* or *in front* (usually *Intrans.* with DAT.) **1.** Lit. : Luc. **2.** Transf. *to stand out, be superior, to distinguish oneself :* suos inter aequalia longe praestitit, Cic. ; petulantiā, Sall. With DAT. : ceteris Lucretia, Liv. ; cum virtute omnibus praestarent, Caes. : Lucr. ; Sall. ; quantum praestiterint nostri maiores prudentiā ceteris gentibus, Cic. ; Liv. With ACC. : belli gloriā Gallos, Hirt. ; Nep. ; Liv. **3.** *Impers.* with subject clause : *it is preferable* or *better.* With ACC. and *Pass. Inf. :* Pl. With *Inf. :* Caes., Cic. Ep., Verg. **II.** [praes stō] *to stand surety for, to guarantee, assume responsibility for, furnish an assurance of.* **1.** Prop. : id, Liv. ; impetūs populi, Cic. ; periculum iudici, Cic. ; invidiam, Cic. ; nepotibus aequor, Ov. ; mors omnia praestat (i.e. takes away nothing), Lucr. With *ab :* ego tibi a vi praestare nihil possum, Cic. Ep. With *de :* felicitatem de se ipso, Cic. With ACC. and *Inf. :* Cic. With ACC. and *Predic. Adj.* or *Part. :* socios salvos, Cic. ; invictum Romanum imperium, Liv. ; meliorem magistro discipulum, Juv. **2.** Transf. **a.** *to make good, fulfil, discharge :* Ov. ; suum munus, Cic. ; rei publicae atque imperatori officium, Caes. ; honorem debitum patri, Cic. ; fidem alicui, Cic., Liv. ; stipendium eius anni exercitui, Liv. ; tributa, Juv. In *Pass. :* victoribus senatūs fides praestabitur, Cic. ; Liv. **b.** *to show, exhibit, evince* (prop. what is expected or due) : virtutem, Caes. ; consilium suum fidemque, Cic. ; fratri pietatem, Cic. With *se :* victoria se praestet, Ov. With *Predic. Adj.* or *Part. :* se incolumem, Lucr. ; se invictum, Ov. ; te eum qui etc., Cic. Ep. ;

vel magnum praestet Achillem, Verg. **b.**
to present, supply, offer : alicui pecuniam,
Suet. ; caput fulminibus, Luc. ; nomen
terris, Luc. ; terga hosti, Tac. ; senatui
sententiam, Cic. In *Pass. :* Sen. Ep.,
Quint. [It. *prestare ;* Fr. *prêter.*]

praestōlor, ārī [perh. fr. praestō, *adv.*],
to stand ready for, to wait for, expect : Pl.
With DAT. : tibi ad forum Aurelium, Cic.
With ACC. : aliquem, Pl. ; Ter. ; huius
adventum ad Clupea, Caes.

prae-stringō, stringere, strīnxī, strictum,
to press in front, bind or tie up, squeeze. **1.**
Lit. : praestrictā fauce, Ov. ; pollices nodo,
Tac. ; tempora sertis, Stat. **2.** Transf.
to press in front ; hence *to blunt, dull.* **a.**
the edge of a weapon : Pl. **b.** the sight :
aciem oculorum, Pl., Liv. **c.** the mind :
aciem animi, mentis, ingeni, Cic. ; oculos
mentis, Cic. ; dignitas (eius) oculos Vatini,
Cic. ; Tac.

prae-struō, struere, struxī, structum. **I.** *to
build up in front, to block or stop up :* aditum
obice, Ov. **II.** *to build up beforehand.*
Transf. of preparing or contriving beforehand : fraus fidem in parvis sibi praestruit
ut etc., Liv. ; cum praestructum utrumque consulto esset, Suet.

praesul, ulis, *m.f.* (Cic.) [prae saliō] and
praesultātor, ōris, *m.* (Liv.) [praesultō],
*one who leaps or dances before others at the
games ; a public dancer.*

prae-sultō, āre [saltō], *to leap or dance
before :* hostium signis, Liv.

prae-sum, esse, fuī, *to be before ;* hence, *to be
set over, to preside, to have the charge or
command of.* **1.** Lit. : in provinciā, Cic.
With DAT. : omnibus Druidibus praeest
unus, Caes. ; classi, oppido, Caes. ; provinciae, Cic. ; Sall. ; vigiliis, Sall. ; statuis
faciendis, Cic. **2.** Transf. **a.** *to take the
lead :* non paruit ille Ti. Gracchi temeritati,
sed praefuit, Cic. **b.** *to preside over* (i.e.
protect) : Lares moenibus urbis, Ov.

prae-sūmō, sūmere, sūmpsī, sūmptum, *to
take before, take first to oneself.* **1.** Lit. :
domi dapes, Ov. ; remedia, Tac. **2.**
Transf. **A.** *to take in advance :* male
audiendi patientiam, Quint. **B.** *to forestall, anticipate.* **a.** In performing : heredum officia, Plin. **b.** In enjoying : fortunam principatūs inerti luxu, Tac. **c.** In
thought, hope, etc. : spe praesumito bellum,
Verg. ; hanc vitam, Plin. Ep. ; suspicionem,
Tac. ; praesumptum habere (i.e. *to take
for granted*), Tac.

praesūmptiō, ōnis, *f.* [praesūmō]. **I.** *a
forestalling or anticipation of enjoyment :*
bonae famae, Plin. Ep. **II.** Rhet. *an
anticipation of expected objections :* Quint.
III. *a preconception, supposition, presumption :* Sen. Ep.

prae-sūtus, a, um, *sewn over at the point.*
Transf. : hasta foliis praesuta, Ov.

prae-temptō, āre, *to feel, search, grope out
beforehand.* **1.** Lit. : pedibus iter, Tib. ;
baculo iter, Ov. ; pollice chordas, Ov. ;
sinum, Suet. **2.** Transf. *to test beforehand :* viris, Ov. ; iudicis misericordiam,
Quint.

prae-tendō, tendere, tendī, tentum, *to
stretch or hold before or in front.* **1.** Lit.

---

to hold out, present : nomen ulivae,
Verg. ; telā, Ov. Lit. *to hold or place before :* segeti saepem, Verg. ; morti muros,
Verg. ; vestem ocellis, Ov. ; quidquid
castrorum Armeniis praetenditur, Tac. Also,
decreto sermonem, Liv. **c.** In *Mid.* (of
places) : *to lie in front or before :* praetenta
Syrtibus arva, Verg. ; tenue litus praeten-
tum, Liv. ; gens nostris provinciis late
praetenta, Tac. **2.** Transf. *to hold out
as excuse or pretext :* hominis doctissimi
nomen immanibus et barbaris moribus,
Cic. ; coniugis taedas, Verg. ; decretum
calumniae, Liv. ; ignorantiam, Quint. With
ACC. and *Inf. :* Tac.

prae-tentō, *v.* praetemptō.

praetentus, a, um, *Part.* praetendō.

prae-tenuis, e, *adj.* **I.** *very thin or slender :*
folium pinūs, Plin. **II.** Of sound : *very
thin, shrill :* Quint.

prae-tepuī, *Perf. to have glowed before.*
Transf. : in quāvis amor, Ov.

praeter, *adv.* and *prep.* [prae, with the
suffix -ter, as in inter, subter, propter]. **I.**
Adverb. **A.** In Compounds. **1.** Lit.
along the front and past : praeterfero. Also
with further idea of *by or off :* praeterfluo.
2. Transf. **a.** Of neglect : praetermitto.
b. *past and beyond :* praetergredior. **c.**
in addition : praeterea, praeterhac. **B.**
passing by, except, save : cavendae sunt
quaedam familiaritates, praeter hominum
perpaucorum, Cic. ; Sall. ; Ov. ; inveniet-
que nil sibi legatum praeter plorare, Hor. ;
praeter si, Varr. (*v.* also praeterquam.)
II. Prep. (with ACC.). **1.** Lit. *past the
front of.* Of place : *past, by* (of motion) :
praeter castra Caesaris suas copias traduxit, Caes. ; servi eius praeter oculos Lolli
haec omnia ferebant, Cic. ; Pl. ; Lucr. ;
Ov., etc. **2.** Transf. **a.** *passing by, except, save :* nec nobis praeter me alius eat
servos, Pl. ; hoc nemini praeter me videtur,
Cic. ; Caes. **b.** Of surpassing or over-
stopping. **i.** *beyond, contrary to :* multa
praeter spem evenisse, Pl. ; praeter aetatem
stultus, Pl. ; nihil praeter rem loqui, Cic. ;
praeter naturam praeterque fatum, Cic. ;
cum lacus Albanus praeter modum crevisset,
Cic. **ii.** *beyond, more than :* illud praeter
alia mira miror, Pl. ; quae me igitur res
praeter ceteros impulit, Cic. ; Hor. **c.**
besides, in addition to : ut praeter se denos
ad conloquium adducerent, Caes. ; praeter
industriam fortuna quoque, Liv. ; praeter
haec, moreover, Ter.

praeter-agō, agere, *to drive by or past :* Hor.
praeter-bitō, ere, *to go by, to pass :* Pl.
With ACC. : Pl.

praeter-dūcō, ere, *to lead past or by :* pompam, Pl.

praeter-eā, *adv.* [*cf.* anteā]. **I.** *beyond this
or that, besides :* nihil, quod praeterea re-
quiratis, Cic. ; Pl. ; Verg. ; multisque
praeterea viris fortibus Narbone evocatis,
Caes. ; Verg. ; nihil praeterea cum consule
pacti quam quod etc., Liv. **II.** In enumerating : *besides, moreover, again :* multae
sunt causae . . . primum . . . praeterea,
Ter. ; nam et . . . et praeterea . . . praeterea, Cic. Ep. **III.** Of time : *hereafter ;
thereafter :* et quisquam numen Iunonis

adorat praeterea ? Verg. ; neque illum
praeterea vidit, Verg.
praeter-eō, ire, iĭ (and ivĭ), itum, *to go by or
past, to pass by*. **1.** L i t. **a.** In gen. : si
nemo hac praeteriit, Pl. ; praeteriens modo,
Ter. ; praeterit tempus, Ter. ; Cic. Ep. ;
Ov. With Acc. : erum, Pl. ; piątrinum,
Pl. ; hortos, Cic. ; hos cursu, Verg. ; Ov. ;
ripas flumina, Hor. **b.** Of avoiding or
escaping : nescis quid mali praeterieris, Ter.
2. T r a n s f. **A.** *to pass unnoticed, to escape
one's knowledge :* an quicquam Parmen-
onem praetereat ? Ter. With Acc. and
Inf. as Subject : non me praeterit me
longius prolapsum esse, Cic. ; Liv. With
Indir. Quest. as Subject : Cic. Ep. **B.**
*to pass by or over, leave out, omit, neglect,
forget.* **a.** aliquid silentio, Cic. ; quae nunc
ego omnia praetereo, Cic. ; tuum dedecus,
Ov. With *Inf.* : Pl. **b.** aliquem suffragiis, Cic. ; Philippus et Marcellus praetere-
untur, Caes. ; fratris filium praeteriit, Cic. ;
me quoque R. praeteriere patres, Ov. **C.**
to go beyond. **a.** *to surpass, excel :* virtus
alios tua praeterit omnis, Ov. ; Juv. ; hos
nobilitate, Varr. **b.** *to transgress :* iustum
praeterit ira modum, Ov.
praeter-equitāns, antis, *Part. riding by :*
Liv.
praeter-ferō, ferre, tulĭ, lātum, *to carry by*
or *past.* In *Mid.* or *Pass. :* latebras prae-
terlata acies est, Liv. ; pars vocum praeter-
lata, Lucr.
praeter-fluō, ere, *to flow by* or *past.* **1.**
L i t. : aqua, Varr. With Acc. : amnis moenia, Liv. ; Sall. **2.** T r a n s f. : voluptatem
praeterfluere sinit, Cic.
praeter-gredior, gredĭ, grēssus [gradior],
to march, go, or *pass by.* **1.** L i t. : castra,
Cic. Ep., Liv. ; primos suos, Sall. ; finis,
Tac. **2.** T r a n s f. *to surpass :* alios, Sall.
praeter-hāc, *adv. beyond this, in addition :*
praeterhac unum verbum, Pl.
praeteritus, a, um. **I.** *Part.* praetereō. **II.**
Adj. : *gone by, past, past and gone :* tempus,
Cic. ; anni, Verg. ; nox, viri, Prop. ; culpa, Ov.
Neut. as Noun in phr. de praeterito, *from the
past :* suspicari, Liv. ; ex praeterito, *from
the past :* Romae cum luctus ex praeterito,
tum timor in futurum erat, Liv. ; in praeteritum, *for the past :* Suet. In gramm. :
tempus praeteritum, *the past tense :* Quint.
III. Noun, **praeterita**, ōrum, *n. pl. :
things gone by, the past :* praeterita se fratri
condonare dicit, Caes. ; Cic.
praeter-lābor, lābĭ, lāpsus, *to glide, move
slowly and smoothly by.* **1.** L i t. : praeter-
labentia flumina, Quint. With Acc. : tumulum, Verg. ; hanc (tellurem), Verg.
2. T r a n s f. *to slip away :* (definitio) ante
praeterlabitur quam percepta est, Cic.
praeterlātus, a, um, *Part.* praeterferō.
praeter-meō, meāre, *to go by* or *past :* saepe
salutantum tactu praeterque meantum,
Lucr.
praetermissiō, ōnis, *f.* [praetermittō]. **I.** *a
leaving out, omission* (with GEN.) : Cic.
II. *a passing over, neglecting* (with GEN.) :
Cic.
praeter-mittō, mittere, mĭsĭ, missum. **I.**
to let go by, let pass : nullum diem, Cic. Ep. ;
occasionem navigandi, Caes. **II.** *to omit,*

neglect, leave undone : officium, Cic. Ep. ;
voluptates, Cic. With *Inf. :* Caes., Nep.
With *quin* (after negat.) : Cic. Ep. **III.**
In reading, writing, etc. : *to pass over,
leave out, make no mention of :* verba, Cic. ;
quod dignum memoriā visum, praeter-
mittendum non existimavimus, Caes. **IV.**
to pass by unnoticed : do, praetermitto, Ter. ;
Lucr. ; ius gentium violatum deorum neglegentiā praetermissum, Liv.
praeter-nāvigō, āre, *to sail by* or *past :*
Suet. With Acc. : Suet.
prae-terō, ere, *to wear down in front by rubbing :* anum limā, Pl.
praeter quam or **praeterquam**, *adv.* **I.**
further than, more than. **a.** *more than, beyond :* virgo praeter sapiet quam placet
parentibus, Pl. ; Ter. **b.** *more than, except* (after negat.) : si nullam praeterquam
vitae nostrae iacturam fieri viderem, Caes. ;
multitudo coalescere nullā re praeterquam
legibus poterat, Liv. ; Cic. ; Ov. With *relat.*
clause : sine ullis doloribus praeterquam
quos ex curatione capiebat, Nep. ; Ter. ;
Also, nec quod petamus quicquam est
praeterquam ut etc., Liv. **II.** With *quod :
beyond or apart from the fact that, except
that :* praeterquam quod ita Quinctio
placeret, et ipse existimabat, Liv. ; Ter. ;
Cic. ; praeter enim quam quod etc., Cic.
III. *Without quod :* malum praeterquam
atrox, etiam novum (i.e. not only . . . but
also), Liv.
praetervectiō, ōnis, *f.* [praetervehor], *a
place where people pass :* omnium, Cic.
praeter-vehor, vehĭ, vectus (*in tmesi*, praeter
erant vecti, Ov.), *to be carried past; to drive,
ride,* or *sail by.* **1.** L i t. : Cic. ; equo, Liv.
With Acc. : Apolloniam, Cic. ; Verg., etc.
2. T r a n s f. **a.** *to march by* (of foot soldiers) : forum, Tac. **b.** *to pass by :* locum
silentio, Cic. ; oratio scopulos, Cic. ; oratio
auris vestras, Cic.
praeter-volō, āre, *to fly by* or *past.* **1.** L i t. :
aquila, Suet. With Acc. : Cic. poet. **2.**
T r a n s f. *to slip by, escape :* occasionis opportunitas, Liv. ; Cic. With Acc. : sententiae hominum sensūs, Cic.
prae-texō, texere, texuĭ, textum, *to weave
before* or *in front, to edge, border.* **1.** L i t. :
amictūs, Ov. ; tunicam purpurā, Liv. **2.**
T r a n s f. **A.** *to fringe, border.* **a.** harundine ripas Mincius, Verg. ; litora puppes,
Verg. In *Mid.* : utraeque nationes Rheno
praetexuntur, Tac. **b.** *to adorn in front :*
Augusto praetextum nomine templum, Ov. ;
primis litteris sententiae carmen omne
praetexitur (like an acrostic), Cic. ; praetexta quercu domus, Ov. **B. a.** *to allege
as an excuse, to pretend :* cupiditatem triumphi, Cic. ; nomina speciosa, Tac. With
Acc. and *Inf. :* Tac. **b.** *to disguise,
screen :* hoc nomine culpam, Verg.
praetextātus, a, um [praetexta]. **1.** L i t.
a. In gen. : *wearing the toga praetexta :*
Clodius qui nunquam antea praetextatus
fuisset, Cic. **b.** Of boys : *before manhood,
under age :* decoxisse te praetextatum,
Cic. ; adulter, Juv. ; amicitia, Mart. **2.**
T r a n s f. *veiled, disguised* (i.e. *obscene,
unchaste*) : verba, Suet. ; mores, Juv.
praetextū, ABL. *sing. m.* [praetexō], *outward*

appearance, show, splendour. **1. Lit.:**
maiore praetextu, Tac.; senatūs, Tac.
2. Transf. *a pretext, pretence :* sub levi
verborum praetextu, Liv.

praetextum, i, n. [praetexō], *an ornament.*
1. Lit.: Sen. **2. Transf.** *a pretence,
pretext :* praetexto rei publicae, Tac.;
praetexto classem adloquendi, Tac.; ad
praetextum mutatae voluntatis, Suet.

praetextus, a, um. **I.** *Part.* praetexō. **II.**
Adj. *wearing the* toga praetexta *:* Prop.
III. Noun, **praetexta,** or **toga praetexta,**
ae, f. *the toga bordered with purple, worn by the
higher magistrates and by freeborn boys :*
Cic., Liv. Transf.: praetexta (sc.
fabula), a tragedy dealing with Roman (not
Greek) characters : Hor.

prae-timeō, ēre, *to fear beforehand :* Sen.
Ep.; sibi, Pl.

prae-tinctus, a, um, *dipped in beforehand :*
semina veneno, Ov.

praetor, ōris, m. [praeeō], *one who goes before
or first ;* hence, *a leader, chief, president.*
1. Lit. A. At Rome : orig. the name of
the chief magistrate of the Roman republic :
Cic.; of the Roman *consul* as chief judge :
Liv.; of the *dictator,* praetor maximus, Liv.;
aerari, *president of the treasury,* Tac. **B.**
In Italy. **a.** *the commander* of a contingent
of troops : Praenestinus, Liv. **b.** *the two
annual magistrates* of Capua as a colony : Cic.
C. Elsewhere. **a.** *the leader* of a league :
Liv. **b.** *the annual magistrates* in Greek
towns, e.g. Syracuse : Liv. **c.** the *sufetes* at
Carthage : Nep. **2. Transf. A.** *a praetor,* a
Roman magistrate chosen to assist the consul,
both in the administration of justice and in
the command of extra armies : praetor *or*
praetor urbis *or* praetor urbanus, *who tried
cases between Roman citizens* (B.C. 366), Pl.,
Cic., Liv.; peregrinus, *who tried those
between strangers* (B.C. 243), Cic., Liv.; for
Sardinia and Corsica (B.C. 227), Liv.; two
for the Spains (B.C. 221), Liv. The number
of praetors was raised to 8 by Sulla, to 16
by Caesar. **B.** For propraetor, *an officer
who, after the expiration of his praetorship,
was retained in office.* **a.** As commander of
an army : Liv. **b.** As governor of a
province : Cic.

praetōriānus, a, um [praetōrium], *of or
belonging to the Emperor's bodyguard, praetorian :* miles, Tac. As Noun, **prae-
tōriāni,** ōrum, m. pl. : Tac.

praetōricius, a, um [praetor], *received from
the praetor* (at the public games) : corona,
Mart.

praetōrius, a, um [praetor]. **I.** Adj. **A.**
of a commander-in-chief : cohors, Caes.
(hence scortatorum cohors praetoria, Cic.);
castra (*of the Emperor's bodyguard*), Plin.,
Tac., Suet.; navis (i.e. the flag-ship), Liv.;
imperium, Cic.; porta (in a camp, *the gate
nearest to headquarters*), Caes. **B.** *of a
praetor :* potestas, ius, turba, Cic.; comitia, Liv. **C.** *of a propraetor :* domus, Cic.
II. Noun. **A. praetōrius,** i, m. **a.** *an
ex-praetor :* Cic. Ep. **b.** *a man of praetorian rank :* Plin. Ep. **B. praetōrium,** i,
n. **1. Lit. a.** *the commander's quarters* in
camp, *headquarters :* Caes., Liv. Of bees :
Verg. **b.** *the official residence of the*

governor in a province ; Cic. **2. Transf.**
a. *a council of war :* mittere, dimittere,
Liv. **b.** *a palace :* Juv. **c.** *any magnificent building ;* an *imposing country-seat :*
Stat., Juv., Suet. **d.** *the Emperor's body-
guard :* Plin., Tac., Suet.

prae-torqueō, ēre, *to twist beforehand.*
Transf.: iniuriae collum, Pl.

prae-trepidāns, antis, *trembling greatly, very
impatient :* mens, Cat.

prae-trepidus, a, um. **I.** *palpitating :* cor,
Pers. **II.** *very disquieted :* Suet.

prae-truncō, āre, *to cut short or off, to maim :*
collos tergoribus, Pl.; linguam alicui, Pl.

praetūra, ae, f. [praetor], *the office of a praetor,
the praetorship :* praeturae iuris dictio,
Cic.; praetūrā se abdicare, Cic.; Tac.

prae-umbrāns, antis, *casting a shade.*
Transf. *obscuring :* Tac.

prae-ūstus, a, um. **I.** *burnt at the tip,
hardened at the end by fire :* sudes, Caes.,
Verg.; materia, Caes.; hasta, Liv. **II.**
frost-bitten : artūs, Liv.; nive membra, Plin.

prae-ut, v. prae.

praevalēns, entis. **I.** *Part.* praevaleō. **II.**
Adj.: *very strong, very powerful :* populus,
Liv.

prae-valeō, ēre, ui, *to be very or more able, to
have greater power or influence ; to have the
superiority, get the upper hand :* Plin. Ep.;
apud Neronem, Tac.; equestri pugnā,
Tac.; auctoritate, Suet.; auctoritas Cluvi
praevaluit ut etc., Tac.; sententia, Plin.
Ep. With ABL. of *Comp. :* virtute semper
praevalet sapientia, Phaedr.

prae-validus, a, um, *unusually strong.* **1.
Lit.:** iuvenis, Liv.; cohortes, Tac.;
manus, Ov. **2. Transf. a.** *very powerful, very important :* Blaesus, Tac.; urbes,
Liv.; nomina equitum, Tac. **b.** *too strong,
rank :* terra aristis, Verg.; vitia, Tac.

praevāricātiō, ōnis, f. [praevāricor], *collusion :* Cic., Plin. Ep.

praevāricātor, ōris, m. [praevāricor], *an
advocate guilty of collusion ; a sham accuser
or defender :* Cic. With GEN.: praevari-
cator Catilinae, Cic.

praevāricor, āri [vāricō], *to walk with the legs
apart or straddling.* Transf. of an advocate guilty of collusion : *to make a sham
accusation or defence, to play into the hands
of the opposite side :* Plin. Ep. With DAT.:
to favour collusively : Cic.

prae-vehor, vehī, vectus. **I.** *to be carried
in front, ride on in front.* **1. Lit.:** equo
nuntius, Verg.; equites, Liv.; ad exercitum, Tac. **2. Transf. a.** missilia hostium (fly in their faces), Tac. **b.** omnia
haec placent, cum impetu quodam et flumine
praevehuntur, Plin. Ep. **II.** *to flow along
past :* Rhenus Germaniam, Tac.

prae-vēlōx, ōcis, adj. *very swift.* **1. Lit.:**
Plin. **2. Transf.:** memoria, Quint.

prae-veniō, venīre, vēnī, ventum (in tmesi :
praeque diem veniēns, Verg.), *to come before,
get the start of :* Ov; hostis breviore viā
praeventurus erat, Liv. With ACC.: *to
forestall, anticipate :* talia agentem mors
praevenit, Suet.; desiderium plebis, Liv.
In *Pass.:* quae perfidiā clientis praeventa
(sunt), Sall.; Ov.; nisi praeveniretur
Agrippina, Tac.; Plin. Ep.

prae-verrō, ere, *to sweep before :* veste vias, Ov.

prae-vertō (older **-vortō**), vertere, vertī, versum, and **prae-vertor** (older **-vortor**), vertī, versus. A c t. *to turn* or *put in the first place.* *Mid.* and *Act. Intrans. to turn (oneself) first to.* **I.** In comparing the importance of two things. **A.** A c t. *to put first, take first* (in full with Acc. and Dat. or *prae* and Abl.) : uxorem prae re publicā, Pl. ; pietatem amori tuo, Pl. ; Cic. ; Liv. *Pass. :* ut bellum praeverti sinerent, Liv. In *Mid.* with Acc. : id serio, Pl. ; omnibus eam rem praeverti, Liv. ; id tempus eis rebus, Cic. ; aliud, Liv. **B.** M i d. and A c t. I n t r a n s. *to turn oneself to something first* (with Dat., or *ad* and Acc.) : ei rei primum praevorti volo, Pl. ; huic rei praevertendum existimavit, Caes. ; praeverti ad Armenios, Tac. ; ad interna praeverterent, Tac. ; illuc praevertamur, Hor. **II.** In comparing the time of the action of the verb and the time of some other intended action which is forestalled by it. **a.** *to head off, outstrip :* vestigia cervae, Cat. ; fugā praevertitur Eurum, Verg. ; equo praevertere ventos, Verg. **b.** *to forestall :* pulchre praevortar viros, Pl. ; neque praevorto poculum (take before my turn), Pl. ; praevertunt me fata, Ov. ; quorum usum forte oblata opportunitas praevertit, Liv. **c.** *to preoccupy, surprise :* vivo praevertere amore animos, Verg.

prae-videō, vidēre, vīdī, vīsum, *to see beforehand, to foresee.* **1.** L i t. : ictum venientem, Verg. ; praevisos in aquā timet hostia cultros, Ov. **2.** T r a n s f. : rem publicam in summis periculis, Cic. Ep. ; impetum hostium, Tac. ; periculum, Suet.

prae-vitiō, āre, *to taint beforehand :* gurgitem, Ov.

praevius, a, um [via], *going before, leading the way :* Ov. With Dat. : Ov.

prae-volō, āre, *to fly before* or *in advance :* Cic., Tac.

pragmaticus, a, um [πραγματικός], *skilled in civil business :* Cic. Ep. As Noun, **pragmaticus**, ī, m. *a law-expert* (who supplied orators and advocates with the principles on which they based their speeches) : Cic., Quint., Juv.

prandeō, prandēre, prandī (*Perf. Part.* prānsus in *Act.* sense) [prandium], *to take luncheon.* **1.** L i t. : Pl., Cic. ; pransus non avide, Hor. With *Intern.* Acc. : luscinias, Hor. ; Pl. **2.** T r a n s f. (in *Part.*) *well-fed :* exercitus, Cato ; dux, Cic. ; viri, Liv.

prandium, ī, n. [*cf.* πρώην], *a light meal* taken in the forenoon, *luncheon.* **1.** L i t. : opsonare, accurare, apparare, anteponere, comedere, etc., Pl. ; adducere aliquem ad prandium, Pl. ; invitare, vocare ad prandium, Cic. ; in prandio aliquem accipere apud se, Pl. **2.** T r a n s f. : *the morning feed* or *meal* of animals : Pl.

prānsitō, āre [*freq.* prandeō], *to eat habitually in the forenoon :* polentam, Pl.

prānsor, ōris, m. [prandeō], *a guest at luncheon :* Pl.

prānsus, a, um, *Part.* prandeō.

prasinus, a, um [πράσινος], *leek-green :*

color, Plin. ; factio (in the races of the Circus, ' the Greens '), Suet. ; Mart.

prātēnsis, e, adj. [prātum], *growing in meadows, meadow- :* fungi, Hor.

prātulum, ī, n. [*dim.* prātum], *a small meadow :* Cic.

prātum, ī, n. *a meadow.* **1.** L i t. : Cato, Cic., Verg. **2.** T r a n s f. **a.** *meadow-grass* (in *pl.*) : Pl., Ov. **b.** *a broad field, plain* (of the sea) : rostro Neptunia prata secare, Cic. poet. [Sp. *prado ;* Fr. *pré.*]

prāvē, adv. *crookedly.* T r a n s f. **a.** *amiss, ill, badly :* Ter., Cic., Hor. **b.** *badly, viciously :* Liv., Tac.

prāvitās, ātis, f. [prāvus], *crookedness, distortion.* **1.** L i t. : oris, membrorum, Cic. **2.** T r a n s f. *wrongness, gestures, etc.* : Cic. **b.** *perverseness :* quae ista est pravitas quaeve amentia ? Ter. ; conlegae, Liv. **c.** *viciousness, depravity :* mentis, Cic. ; morum, consili, Tac.

prāvus, a, um, *crooked, not straight, distorted.* **1.** L i t. : tecta, Lucr. ; membra, Cic. ; talus, Hor. *Neut.* as Noun : elapsi in pravum artūs, Tac. **2.** T r a n s f. **a.** *perverse :* adfectio, Cic. ; belua, Hor. ; ambitio, Tac. *Comp.* and *Sup. :* Cic. *Neut.* as Noun : in pravum induruerunt, Quint. **b.** *wrong, bad, vicious.* Of persons : Pl., Liv., Tac. *Neut. pl.* as Noun : Tac., Juv.

Prāxitelēs, is, m. *a celebrated Athenian sculptor in the 4th century* u.c. ; **Prāxitelīus**, a, um.

precārius, a, um [prex], *obtained by* or *dependent on entreaty.* **1.** L i t. : non orare solum precarium opem, sed pro debito petere, Liv. ; auxilium, Tac. *Neut.* Abl. **precāriō** as *Adv., by entreaty* or *request :* agere, Pl. ; nec vi nec clam nec precario possidere, Cic. ; praecesse (i.e. on sufferance), Tac. **2.** T r a n s f. *uncertain, precarious :* forma, Ov. ; precariam animam inter infensos trahere, Tac.

precātiō, ōnis, f. [precor], *a praying, prayer :* Cic. ; facere, Liv.

precātor, ōris, m. [precor], *one who prays, an intercessor :* Pl., Ter.

precēs, v. prex.

preciae, ārum, f. pl. *a kind of grape-vine :* Verg.

precor, ārī [prex], *to pray, beseech, entreat ; to pray to, supplicate.* **1.** L i t. : Verg., Liv., etc. With Acc. of person : Cic., Verg., etc. With Acc. of thing : haec, Cic. ; veniam, Verg. ; mortem, Ov. With double Acc. of person and thing : Cic. Ep., Liv. With *ab* and Abl. of person : a diis deabusque pacem, Liv. ; Cic. With *ut* or *ne* and *Subj.*, or *Subj.* alone : deos ut etc., Hor. ; Cic. ; Liv., etc. ; ab iis ut etc., Cic. ; hoc a diis ut etc., Nep. ; Cic. ; tandem venias precamur, Hor. ; Ov. ; ne iubeant, Ov. ; Curt. With Acc. and *Inf.* : Ov. With *pro* and Abl. of person *on whose behalf :* Ov. ; deos pro te, Plin. Ep. Rarely with *ad* and Acc. of deity addressed : di ad quos precentur, Liv. **2.** T r a n s f. : *to wish* (well or ill) : male, Pl. ; salutem, incolumitatem, reditum precari, Cic. ; tibi evenit ut omnes male precarentur, Cic. With Dat. of person *on whose behalf :* vobis mala, Cic. ; longum Augusto diem, Prop. ;

bona omnia Graccho, Liv.; mala multa Atridis, Hor.

prehendō, hendere, hendī, hēnsum, and **prendō,** prendere, prendī, prēnsum [prae; and *cf.* Gk. χανδάνω]. *to take hold of, to grasp, seize.* **1.** Lit. **A.** In gen.: te auriculis, Pl.; faucis alicui, Pl.; me pallio, Pl.; aliquem manu, Cic. **B.** In partic. **a.** *to catch hold of, to detain in order to speak to:* aliquem, Ter.; Cic. Ep.; aliquem dextrā, Verg. **b.** *to seize, arrest:* servum fugitivum, Cic.; quosdam, Liv.; prehendi in furto, Pl.; mendaci manufesto modo, Pl. **2.** Transf. **A.** In gen.: *to seize, occupy suddenly, hold:* Pharum, Caes.; arcem, Verg. **B.** In partic. **a.** *to grasp, make, reach:* Italiae oras, Verg.; quem prendere cursu non poterat, Verg. **b.** *to catch, surprise:* in patenti prensus Aegaeo, Hor. **c.** With the eyes: *to take in:* aliquid oculorum lumine, Lucr. **d.** Of the mind: *to seize, grasp:* Cic.

prehēnsō, and more freq. **prēnsō,** āre [freq. prehendō], *to make efforts to grasp, clutch at, grip.* **1.** Lit.: fastigia dextris, Verg.; Hor.; hostium tela, Tac.; exeuntium manūs, Liv. **2.** Transf. (in canvassing votes): circumire et prehensare patres, Liv.; prensat unus P. Galba (i.e. is a candidate), Cic. Ep.

prehēnsus, a, um, *Part.* prehendō.

prēlum, ī, n. [for *prem-lum,* from premō]. **I.** *a wine-* or *oil-press:* Cato, Verg. **II.** *a clothes-press:* Mart.

premō, premere, pressī, pressum, *to squeeze, press.* **I.** Simply. **1.** Lit. **a.** In gen.: pede pedem alicui, Pl.; matres ad pectora natos, Verg.; anguem, Verg.; mammas, Verg.; ubera, Ov.; ore grana, Ov. **b.** Of sitting or lying: sedilia, currum, Ov.; toros, cubilia, humum, frondes, Ov. **c.** *to press into shape, make by squeezing:* caseum, Verg.; pressum lac, Verg.; vina, oleum, mella, Hor. **2.** Transf. of moving or keeping close to: litus (*to hug*), Hor.; litora, Ov.; pressi forum, Cic.; vestigia alicuius, Tac.; amnis insulam, Ov. **II.** *to press upon heavily or hard.* **1.** Lit.: aliquid morsu, Lucr.; dente frena, Ov.; terga genu, Ov.; anguem pedibus, Juv.; trabes Hymettiae columnas, Hor.; gravi onere armorum pressi, Caes.; pressae carinae, Verg.; membra mero, Prop. **2.** Transf.: aut aere alieno aut magnitudine tributorum premuntur, Caes.; Cic.; re frumentariā, Caes.; invidiā, periculis, etc., Cic.; formidine, Verg.; iussa Fauni te premunt, Verg. **III.** *to press hard upon, press closely.* **1.** Lit. (of pursuit or attack): Pompeiani nostros, Caes.; novissimos, Caes.; Rutulus, Verg.; obsidione urbem, Caes.; Luceriam premendo obsidendoque, Liv.; spumantis apri cursum, Verg. **2.** Transf.: istum pessum, Pl.; necessitas eum tanta, Cic.; me verbo, Cic.; aerumnae me, Sall.; criminibus veris, Ov.; culpam poena comes, Hor.; reum voce, Tac.; argumentum, Cic. **IV.** *to press upon so as to cover or conceal.* **1.** Lit.: molli frondo crinem, Verg.; canitiem galeā, Verg.; aliquid terrā, Hor.; ossa male pressa, Ov.; omne lucrum humus, Ov.; arva pelago,

Hor. **2.** Transf.: dum nocte premuntur, Verg.; te nox, Hor.; curam sub corde, Verg.; odium, Plin. Pan.; iram, Tac. **V.** *to press together, to close.* **1.** Lit.: oculos, Verg.; alicui faucis, Ov.; laqueo collum, Hor.; presso gradu incedere, *in close ranks,* Liv. **2.** Transf.: haec quae dilatantur a nobis Zeno sic premebat, Cic. **VI.** *to repress, check, suppress.* **1.** Lit. **a.** *to curb, tighten:* habenas, Verg. **b.** *to check* growth (by pruning): falce umbras, Verg.; falce vitem, Hor.; luxuriem falce, Ov. **c.** *to check, stop:* vestigia, Verg.; sanguinem, Tac.; pressoque obmutuit ore, Verg.; lucem caligo, Liv. **2.** Transf. **a.** *to curb* by rule: dicione populos, Verg.; Mycenas servitio, Verg. **b.** *to check, stop:* vocem, gemitum, Verg.; sermones vulgi, Tac.; cursum ingeni tui premit haec clades civitatis, Cic. **VII.** *to press down, depress, let down, lower.* **1.** Lit. **a.** In gen.: aulaea, Hor.; mundus premitur Libyae devexus in Austros, Verg.; Ov.; presso sub vomere, Verg. **b.** *to make by pressing down, to make deep:* sulcum, Verg.; cavernae in altitudinem pressae, Curt. **2.** Transf. **a.** *to bring down, strike down:* armigerum, Verg.; paucos, Tac. **b.** *to lower, diminish, disparage:* humana omnia, Cic.; arma Latini, Verg.; superiores, Cic.; famam alicuius, Tac. Hence, *to outweigh, surpass:* facta annos, Ov. **VIII.** *to press or squeeze in or against.* **1.** Lit.: vestigio leviter presso, Cic.; vomer, Verg.; aratrum, Tib.; cubito remanete presso, Hor.; hastam sub mentum, Verg.; ferrum in guttura, Ov.; dentis in vite, Ov. **2.** Transf. **a.** Of stamping: rem notā, Ov. **b.** Of planting: virgulta per agros, Verg.

prendō, *v.* prehendō.

prēnsātiō, ōnis, f. [prēnsō], *a taking hold of.* Transf. *a canvassing* for an office: Cic. Ep.

prēnsō, *v.* prehēnsō.

prēnsus, a, um, *Part.* prehendō. [*Fr. pris.*]

pressē, *adv.* **I.** Of pronunciation: *with precise articulation, crisply, distinctly:* loqui, Cic. **II.** Of style. **a.** *concisely, not diffusely:* Cic. Comp.: Plin. Ep. **b.** *without ornament, simply:* dicere, Cic. Comp.: Plin. Ep. **c.** *exactly, accurately:* definiunt pressius, Cic.

pressiō, ōnis, f. [premō], *leverage; a fulcrum* or *jack:* Caes.

pressō, āre [freq. premō], *to press:* vomicam, Pl.; ubera, Verg.; uvam pede, Prop.; cineres ad pectora, Ov.

pressus, a, um. **I.** *Part.* premō. **II.** Adj. **A.** Rhet. *compressed, concise:* Thucydides verbis aptus et pressus, Cic.; in contionibus pressior, Plin. Ep. **B.** Of style. **a.** *compressed, plain:* Attici, Quint.; stilus, Plin. Ep. **b.** *quiet, subdued:* pressis et flebilibus modis, Cic. [It. *presso;* Fr. *près.*]

pressus, ūs, m. [premō], *a pressing, pressure.* With *Subj.* Gen.: Cic. With *Obj.* Gen.: ipso oris pressu, Cic.

prēstěr, ēris, m. [πρηστήρ]. **I.** *a fiery whirlwind; a waterspout:* Lucr., Plin. **II.** *a kind of serpent,* whose bite brings on burning thirst: Plin., Luc.

pretiōsē, *adv. in a costly manner* : vasa pretiose caelata, Cic. *Comp.* : Curt.
pretiōsus, a, um [pretium], *of great value, valuable.* **I. a.** equus, Cic. ; fulvo pretiosior aere, Ov. ; res pretiosissimae, Cic. With ABL. : loca metallo, Ov. **b.** *costly, expensive :* operaria, Pl. ; Prop. ; Sen. Ep., etc. **II.** In *Act.* sense ; *that gives a great price, extravagant :* emptor, Hor.
pretium, i, *n.* [cogn. with Gk. πέρ-νη-μι, πι-πρά-σκω], *price, worth, value.* **1.** L i t. : pretium statuere merci, Pl. ; pretium certum constituere, Cic. Ep. ; pacisci pro re aliquā, Cic. ; exsolvere, Pl. ; enumerare, Cic. ; parare sibi, vendere aliquid pretio, Pl. ; iacent pretia praediorum (i.e. are low), Cic. P h r. : magni, parvi preti esse, Pl., Cic., etc. ; pretium facere, *to set a price*, of the seller, Pl. ; of the buyer, Mart. ; pretium habere, *to be worth something*, Cato, Cic. ; but also, *to have a price, to be for sale*, Quint. ; in pretio esse, *to be prized* (i.e. to be in repute), Liv., Ov. ; in pretio pretium est (a play on words), *a man is worth what he is worth* (i.e. is esteemed according to the length of his purse), Ov. ; in pretio habere aliquid, *to regard as valuable*, Tac. **2.** T r a n s f. **A.** Freq. in phr. : pretium operae (or curae) esse, facere, *to be, make worth the service* or *trouble* (i.e. worth while) : operae pretium erat neglegentiam eius considerare, Cic. ; Enn. ; est pretium curae cognoscere, Juv. ; facturusne operae pretium sim . . . nec satis scio, Liv. Also, operae pretium habent libertatem, Liv. ; magna operae pretia mereri, Liv. Without operae : Germanico fuit pretium (with *Inf.*) : Tac. **B.** *price, reward, guerdon, meed :* pretium certaminis, Ov. ; palmae pretium certaminis, Ov. ; palmae pretium victoribus, Verg. ; pro cuiusque merito pretia poenasque exsolvere, Liv. ; debito beneficio addere, Liv. For misconduct (i.e. *punishment*) : pretia ignaviae, Pl. ; ferre, Ter. ; et peccare nefas, aut pretium emori, Hor. ; crucem pretium sceleris tulit, Juv. **C.** *fee* (of money). **a.** *expenditure :* nil pretio parsit, Pl. ; vectigalia parvo pretio redempta habere, Caes. ; urbem exiguam pretio posuit, Verg. **b.** *money as ransom :* captivis sine pretio dimissis, Liv. **c.** Of a bribe : pretio iudicem corrumpere, Cic. ; converso in pretium deo, Hor. [It. *pregio* ; Sp. *precio* ; Fr. *prix*.]
prex, ecis, *f.* (NOM. and GEN. *sing.* obsol. ; most freq. *pl.*) *a prayer, entreaty, intercession.* **1.** L i t. **A.** In gen. : te oro per precem, Pl. ; oro te prece, Hor. ; cum magnā prece ad aliquem scribere, Cic. Ep. ; omnibus precibus petere, adduci, Caes., Liv. ; precibus flecti, Verg. ; precibus moveri, vinci, Ov. ; fatigare aliquem precibus, Liv. **B.** E s p. **a.** *a prayer to a deity :* Cic., Ov. **b.** *a curse, imprecation :* omnibus precibus detestatus Ambiorigem, Caes. ; Hor. ; Ov. **2.** T r a n s f. : *a kindly wish :* tuis Kalendis damus alternas accipimusque preces, Ov.
Priamus, i, m., *s. of Laomedon, king of Troy, h. of Hecuba, and f. of Hector, Paris, Cassandra, etc. ; he was slain by Pyrrhus, the son of Achilles ;* **Priamēis**, idis, *f.* a

daughter of Priam, esp. Cassandra ; **Priamēïus**, a, um ; **Priamidēs**, ae, *m. a son of Priam.*
Priāpus, i, *m.* [Πρίαπος], *the god of gardens and vineyards.* **1.** L i t. : Verg., Hor., Ov. ; **Priāpēïus**, a, um. **2.** T r a n s f. **a.** Priapus vitreus, *a drinking-vessel of indecent shape*, Juv. **b.** *a lecherous person :* Cat., Ov.
prīdem, *adv. long ago, long since :* quam pridem sibi hereditas venisset, docet, Cic. ; Pl. ; Ter. ; haud ita pridem, Hor. ; Lucr. ; Cic.
prīdiānus, a, um [pridiē], *yesterday's :* Suet.
prī-diē, *adv.* [*cf.* postridiē], *on the day before :* Pl., Cic., Nep. With *quam* : pridie quam ego Athenas veni, Cic. Ep. ; Liv. ; with *Subj.* : Liv. With GEN. : pridie eius diei, Caes. ; Tac. With ACC. : pridie Idūs, Cic. Ep. ; Liv., etc.
prīmaevus, a, um [primus aevum], *in the first period of life, young, youthful :* Cat., Verg. ; flos, Verg.
prīmāni, ōrum, *m. pl.* [prima, *sc.* legiō], *soldiers of the first* (legion) : Tac.
prīmārius, a, um [primus], *of the first rank, principal :* vir, Pl., Cic. ; condicio, Pl. [It. *primiero* ; Fr. *premier*.]
prīmigenus, a, um [gen in gignō], *first produced, original :* dies primigenus maris, Lucr.
prīmipīlāris, is, *m.* [primipilus] (*sc.* centurio), *the chief centurion of a legion :* Sen., Tac. Of an *ex-primipilar :* Quint.
prīmipīlus, *v.* pilus.
prīmitiae, ārum, *f. pl.* [primus], *the first things of their kind, firstlings, first-fruits.* **1.** L i t. : Ov. ; metallorum, Tac. **2.** T r a n s f. : primitiae iuvenis miserae, Verg. [Fr. *prémices*.]
prīmitus, *adv. at first, originally, for the first time :* Lucil., Cat., Varr., Verg.
prīmordium, i, *n.* [ōrdior], *the beginning, origin.* **a.** In gen. : urbis, Liv. Mostly *pl.* (ordia prima, Lucr.) ; primordia rerum, Cic. ; mundi, Ov. ; eloquentiae, Tac. ; dicendi, Quint. **b.** *the beginning of a new reign :* Tac.
prīmōris, e, *adj.* [primus] (NOM. *sing.* not in use). **I.** *foremost, extreme, tip of :* sumere aliquid digitulis primoribus, Pl. ; Cato ; nasi primoris acumen, Lucr. ; versari (nomen) in labris primoribus, Pl. ; aliquid primoribus labris attingere, Cic. ; primori in acie versari, Tac. *Masc. pl.* as Noun : *the first, foremost :* provolat ad primoris, Liv. **II.** *first in rank or dignity, chief, principal :* Cat., Liv., Tac. *Masc. pl.* as Noun : *men of the first rank, chiefs, nobles :* Pl., Hor., Liv., etc.
prīmulus, a, um [*dim.* primus], *just the first :* primulo diluculo, Pl. *Neut.* ACC. as *Adv.* : *just at first, first :* Pl.
prīmum-dum, *v.* primus.
prīmus, a, um, *Sup. Adj.* [fr. root seen in priscus], *foremost.* **1.** L i t. (in position), *foremost, in front, in the front of, on the edge of, the tip of :* in primā parte aedium, Nep. ; primum agmen, Caes. ; equites in primo (*sc.* agmine) ire iubet, Sall. ; provolant in primum (*sc.* agmen), Liv. ; acies, signa, Liv. ; primis labris gustare, Cic. ; primus

digitus, Cat. ; in primā provinciā, Cic. Ep.
As Noun : recessum primis ultimi non
dabant, Caes. ; in primis pugnare, Sall.
2. Transf. **a.** In time : *foremost, first,
earliest, at the beginnning* : primus sol,
Verg. ; primis ab annis, Verg. ; primi consules sub iugum missi sunt (i.e. at the outset), Liv. ; primus in Thraciam introiit
(*was the first to*), Nep. ; leonem primus aut
in primis ferire (*Hist. Inf.*), Sall. ; primā
nocte (*at the beginning of the night*), Caes. ;
primo mense, Verg. ; primo tumultu, Liv.
With quisque, *the first possible, the very first* :
primo quoque die, Cic. ; primo quoque
tempore, Cic. Ep., Liv. *Neut.* as Noun :
a primo, *from the beginning, at first*, Pl.,
Cic. ; in primo, *at the beginning*, Cic., Liv. ;
si prima satis prospera fuissent (i.e. the
beginning), Liv. ; prima consiliorum, Tac.
b. In rank or station : *first, chief, principal,
most eminent* : homo, Cic. ; Ter., etc. ; sui
municipi facile primus, Cic. ; primas
partis or (simply) primas agere, *to play the
chief part* (orig. in acting), Ter., Cic. ; also
primas dare (alicui), Cic. As Noun :
iuvenum primi, Verg. ; Caes. ; prima
tenere, Verg. ; ad prima, Verg. ; in primis
(also imprimis) : oppidum in primis Siciliae
clarum, Cic. ; Nep. Also in same sense,
cum primis, Cic. *Neut. Acc.* **primum** as
Adv. **I.** *first, in the first place, in the
beginning.* In enumerations, with *deinde,
tum* : Caesar primum suo, deinde omnium
o conspectu remotis equis, Caes. ; primum
. . . deinde . . . tum . . . postremo, Cic. ;
primum . . . mox (postea), Hor., Liv. ;
iam primum . . . tum, Liv. With om-
nium : Pl., Cic. **II.** With *ut, ubi, simul ac,
cum : as soon as* : ubi primum potuit,
istum reliquit, Cic. **III.** *for the first time* :
ibique primum castra in conspectum hostibus data, Liv. Often with *Adv.* of time:
hodie, Pl. ; nunc primum, Ter. ; quo die
primum convocati sumus, Cic. **IV.** With
dum (*cf.* nondum) : primum dum or primumdum, *in the first place, first* : Pl.
Neut. Abl. **primo**, es *Adv.* **I.** *at first* :
primo non accredidit, Nep. ; Pl. ; Cic., etc.
II. With *dein, deinde, post, mox, denique,
nunc, etc.* : *at first, first* : primo pecuniae,
dein imperi crevit, Sall. ; primo . . .
postea . . . postremo, Liv. ; Ter. ; Caes. ;
Cic., etc. **III.** *firstly* (like primum) :
primo . . . iterum, Liv. ; Phaedr.

princeps, cipis, *adj.* [primus capiō], *first,
foremost, in front.* **1.** Lit. (in position) :
principem locum tenere, Caes. ; princeps
Horatius ibat, Liv. ; Cic. ; Verg., etc. **2.**
Transf. **a.** In time : princeps in proelium ibat (*was the first to*), Liv. ; Caes. ;
Cic. ; Hor., etc. ; dica imperi princeps, vitae
supremus, Tac. **b.** *foremost, chief, most
eminent* Eudoxus in astrologiā facile
princeps, Cic. ; Hor. ; Nep. As Noun,
princeps, cipis, *m. f. chief, leader.* **A.** In
gen. : coniurationis, sceleris, etc., Cic. ;
huius consili, Caes. ; belli inferendi, Caes. ;
Argonautarum, Stoicorum, Cic. ; genus a
quo principe nostrum, Verg. **B.** In public
life. **a.** Valerius princeps civitatis, Caes. ;
principes civitatis, Caes., Cic., Liv. ; legationis, Liv. ; princeps senatūs, Liv. ; sen-

tentiae princeps in senatu, Cic. ; trecenti
coniuravimus principes iuventutis Romanae
(i.e. of the patricians), Liv. ; princeps
iuventutis (i.e. one of the noblest of the
Roman knights), Cic. ; under the Empire,
it denoted *the presumptive heir to the throne:*
Tac. **b.** *the chief,* i.e. the Emperor (*sc.*
civitatis ; a title derived from the Republican period) : Hor., Ov., Tac., etc. **C.**
Milit. **a.** **principēs**, um, *m. pl. the second
line of soldiers between the* hastati *and*
triarii : Liv. **b.** In *sing.* **i.** *a maniple
or century of the* principes : Cic., Liv.
ii. *a centurion of the* principes : Caes., Liv.
iii. *the centurionship of the* principes : Liv.

principālis, e, *adj.* [princeps]. **I.** *foremost,
first.* **a.** *original, primitive* : Cic., Quint.
b. In rank or esteem : *chief, principal* :
Cic., Quint. **II.** *belonging to a prince* or
ruler : fortuna, Tac. ; curae, Plin. Pan. ;
maiestas, Suet. **III.** *of the chief street in a
camp* : via, porta, Liv.

principātus, ūs. *m.* [princeps]. **I.** *the first
place, pre-eminence.* **A.** In gen. : Gallia
huius belli sustinendi principatum tenet, Cic. ;
animi, Cic. **B.** Of political or military
rank. **a.** *the chief place, the post of commander-in-chief* : alicui tradere, Caes. ;
alicui dare, deferre, Cic. ; obtinere totius
Galliae, Caes. ; deici principatu, Caes. **b.**
Of the Emperor : *rule, sovereignty* : Tac..
etc. **II.** *a beginning, origin* : Cic.

principiālis, o, *adj.* [principium], *of the beginning* : caeli terraeque principiale tempus,
Lucr.

principium, I, *n.* [princeps]. **I.** *a beginning,
start, origin.* **1.** Lit. : nec principium nec
finem habere, Cic. ; Hor. ; a Iove principium, Verg. ; a sanguine Teucri ducere
principium, Ov. ; capessere, Tac. ; urbis,
criminis, bellorum, movendi, etc., Cic. ;
anni, Liv. ; pontis, Tac. Phr. : principio
(Pl., Cic., Verg. etc.), a principio (Cic.), in
principio (Cic.), *at* or *in the beginning, at
first.* **2.** Transf. **a.** *that makes a beginning, that votes first* (of the prerogative
tribe or curia) : Faucia curia fuit principium,
Liv. Also *the right of voting first* : eiusdem
curiae fuerat principium, Liv. **b.** *a beginner, originator* : Graecia principium
moris fuit, Ov. **c.** In *pl.* : *foundations,
principles* : Cic., Ov. ; iuris, naturae, Cic.
II. Milit. (in *pl.*). **a.** *the foremost ranks,
front line* : Ter., Sall., Liv., etc. **b.** *headquarters ; a large open space in a camp
containing the tents of the officers, standards,
etc.* : Nep., Liv., Tac.

prior, prius, ōris, *comp. adj.* [*cf.* primus].
1. Lit. (in position) : *fore, in front, the
first* : priores partes, Caes. ; pedes, Nep. ;
priore loco causam dicere, Cic. **2.** Transf.
a. In time : priore nocte, Cic. ; prioribus
comitiis, Cic. ; priore anno, Liv. ; prioris
anni consules, Liv. ; qui prior has angustias
occupaverat, Caes. ; Liv. ; Dionysius prior,
the elder, Nep. As Noun, **priōrēs**, um,
m. pl. forefathers, ancestors, the ancients :
Verg., Ov. ; nostri, Plin. Ep. **b.** In importance : ut nemo haberetur prior, Liv. ;
aetate et sapientiā, Sall. ; bellante prior,
Hor. Esp. with *potior* : res nulla prior
potiorque visa est, Liv. *Neut. Acc.* **prius**,

as *Adv.* **I.** *before, sooner, previously :*
prius exire de vitā, Cic. ; Liv. ; prius . . .
tum, Cato, Liv. ; prius . . . postea, Liv. ;
prius . . . nunc, Verg. With *quam* (often
as one word **priusquam**). **a.** *before (that),
before.* With *Indic.* : quod ego prius quam
loqui coepisti sensi, Cic. ; Pl., etc. ; prius
illi erimus quam tu, Pl. ; Caes. ; Cic., etc.
With *Subj.* (esp. to denote an action which
is forestalled or prevented) : prius quam
ea cura decederet patribus Romanis,
Etrusci belli fama exorta est, Liv. ; Ter. ;
Cic., etc. Also when there is no idea of
purpose : me vobis, prius quam provinciam
viderem, obligavit fortuna, Liv. With
Participles : arma deos prius quam homines
violatura, Liv. With ABL. *Absol.* : negant
se prius quam captā urbe hostium redituros
esse, Liv. With Acc. and *Inf.* following
preceding Acc. and *Inf.* : libertatem prius
reddendam esse quam arma danda, Liv.
b. *sooner, rather :* perdere prius quam
perire optantes, Liv. ; statuerat prius hos
iudicio populi debere restitui quam suo
beneficio videri receptos, Caes. ; Cic. Ep. ;
quidvis prius futurum esse quam ut etc.,
Cic. ; Aegyptii quamvis carnificinam prius
subierint quam ibin violent, Cic. **II.**
formerly, in former times : Cat., Prop.

priscē, *adv. in the old-fashioned manner,
strictly :* Cic.

priscus, a, um, *of or belonging to former
times.* **I.** *old, ancient, antique* (i.e. be-
longing to a bygone generation). **A.** Simply :
Cic., Ov. **B.** With the accessory idea. **a.**
old-time (i.e. venerable) : fides, Verg. ;
pudor, Hor. ; mos, Ov. ; sanctimonia, Tac.
b. *old-fashioned* (i.e. strict, severe) : severitas, Cic. ; prisci praecepta parentis, Cat. ;
Cato, Hor. **II.** (=pristinus), *former, previous :* Venus, Hor. ; nomen, Ov.

pristinus, a, um [*cf.* priscus, primus]. **I.**
former, earlier. **a.** consuetudo, Caes. ;
tua dignitas et gloria, Cic. ; Verg. ;
animum erga populum R. conservare,
Liv. ; coniunx, Verg. *Neut.* as Noun : aliquid in pristinum restituere, Nep. **b.** *just
past, previous :* diei pristini perfidia, Caes.
II. *old-fashioned, primitive :* mores, Pl.

prius..v. prior.

prīvātim, *adv.* **I.** *in private, privately* (opp.
publice, etc.) : Pl., Caes., Cic., etc. **II.**
at home : Pl., Liv.

prīvātiō, ōnis, *f.* [prīvō], *a taking away :*
doloris, Cic.

prīvātus, a, um. **I.** *Part.* prīvō. **II.** *Adj.*
(opp. *publicus*) *private, not public.* **1.** *Lit.*
a. Of things : *of a person in a private
capacity, private, personal :* ager, aedificia,
Caes. ; vita, Cic. ; census, Hor. ; vestem
mutare privato consensu, Cic. *Neut.* as
Noun : utatur privatis ut suis, Cic. ; in
privato, *in private,* ex privato, *from private
means* or *out of their homes,* in privatum,
for private use, Liv. **b.** Of persons : vir privatus or privatus (alone), *not official, a private
citizen :* Pl., Caes., Cic., etc. ; mulier (i.e.
no longer a queen), Hor. Also perh. *the
accused :* quoad capitis iudicasset privatos,
Liv. **c.** Under the Empire : *not imperial,
not belonging to the Emperor or his family :*
Tac., Plin. Ep. **2.** *Transf. ordinary, ex-*

pressed *in everyday language :* carmina,
Hor.

Prīvernum, I, *n. a very ancient town of
Latium,* now *Piperno ;* **Prīvernās,** ātis,
adj. ; **Prīvernātēs,** ium, *m. pl. its inhabitants.*

prīvigna, ae, *f.* [prīvignus], *a step-daughter :*
Cic. Ep.

prīvignus, I, *m.* [contr. from prīvigenus,
'born of one only (privus) of a married
pair'], *a step-son :* Cic., Hor., etc. **prī-
vigni,** ōrum, *m. pl. step-children :* Hor.

prīvilēgium, I, *n.* [prīvus lēx], *a bill* or *law
directed* **a.** *against an individual :* ferre,
inrogare, Cic. **b.** *in favour of an individual :*
habere, Plin. Ep. ; sacerdotum, Suet.

prīvō, āre [prīvus]. **I.** *to rob, strip :* erum
bonis, luce, honore, Pl. ; aliquem vitā, etc.,
Cic. ; se oculis, Cic. ; cibo, Lucr. ; lumine,
Ov. **II.** Occ. *to free, release, deliver from :*
aliquem iniuriā, exsilio, Cic. ; dolore, Lucr.,
Cic. ; formidine, Hor.

prīvus, a, um. **I.** *each single, every :* in dies
privos aborisci, Lucr. Hence, *one each :*
his discipulis privos custodes dabo, Pl. ;
Liv. **II.** *one's own :* Cato, Hor., Juv.
III. *deprived of :* militiae, Sall.

prō (**prōd** ; **prō-**, **pŏr-**), *adv.* and *prep.*
[old Directive or ABL. *forth, forth from, cf.*
Gk. πρό.] **I.** *Adv.* **A. a. prōquam,** *in
proportion as :* proquam largos exaestuat
aestūs, Lucr. **b. prout** or **prō ut,** *in proportion as, according as, just as :* prout
cuiusque natura ferebat, Caes. ; Cic. ;
Liv. (*cf.* pro eo quod, ut, quantum, II.
2. B and C.). **B.** In compounds. **a.**
forward : progredior, prodambulo, prospicio.
b. *forth and out :* prodeo, profundus.
Transf. *into publicity, publicly :* profero,
proclamo ; also proscribo, prodo. **c.** *forth
and off :* propello. Transf. of defence :
propugno. **d.** *forth and away :* profundo.
Transf. of wastefulness : prodigo, promis-
cuus. **e.** *forward and onward :* promoveo,
prosequor, proficiscor. Transf. of progress : proficio ; and of continuing by
procreation : procreo, produco. **f.** Of prolongation in time or of adjournment :
protraho, prodico. **g.** *forward and down,*
headlong : proicio, pronus. **h.** *instead of :*
proconsul. **II.** Prep. (alw. with ABL.
Locatival or of *Separation*). **1.** Lit. of
place. **a.** *before, in front of :* pro vallo
copias conlocare, Caes. ; sedere pro aede,
Cic. ; Liv. ; Caesar pro castris suas copias
produxit, Caes. **b.** *from the front of, on
the front of, on :* pro tribunali, Cic. ; Caes. ;
pro tectis aedificiorum, Sall. ; pro vallo,
Liv. **2.** Transf. **A.** *for, on behalf of.*
a. *on the side of, in the interest of :* Enn. ;
dimicare pro legibus, Cic. ; et locus pro
vobis et nox erit, Liv. ; pro patriā mori,
Hor. **b.** *for, in the name of :* pro conlegio
pronuntiare, Liv. **B.** *for, instead of, in
lieu of.* **a.** In gen. : ego ibo pro te, Pl. ;
Cic. ; Hor., etc. ; pro ope ferendā sociis
pergit ipse ire, Liv. **b.** *for, to serve as :*
pro vallo carros obiecerunt, Caes. ; cum
utrumque pro remedio petissent, Liv. N.B.
pro consule, pro praetore, pro quaestore
(later proconsul, propraetor, proquaestor) to
denote the substitution of a State appoint-

ment for the real thing by prolongation of the term of office : Cic., Liv., etc. **c.** *for, as good as, as being, just as :* pro occiso relictus, Cic. ; hunc amavi pro meo, Ter. ; pro victis Romanos habuisse, Liv. ; habere pro hostibus, Liv. ; pro mortuo esse, Cic. ; omnia pro infecto sint, Liv. ; pro viso renuntiare, Caes. ; pro certo ponere, Caes. ; pro certo scire, habere, Liv. ; **prō eō** with atque (ac), ac si, quasi *just the same as (if), even as (if), as though :* pro eo ac si concessum sit, Cic. **d.** *for, in return for, in payment for, in requital for :* pro frumento pecuniam solvere, Cic. ; Pl. ; Hor. ; gratiam referre pro meritis, Caes. ; ulcisci aliquem pro scelere, Caes. ; Liv. ; **prō eō quod,** *for the fact that, for the reason that :* pro eo quod pluribus verbis vos fatigavi, veniam a vobis velim, Liv. ; Cic. **C.** *for, according to.* **a.** *in proportion to, conformably with, according to :* tu pro oratione nec vir nec mulier mihi's, Pl. ; pro multitudine hominum, Caes. ; proelium atrociius quam pro numero pugnantium fuit, Liv. ; agere pro viribus, Cic. ; pro virili parte, *according to one's ability,* Cic. ; Ov. ; Liv. ; pro ratā parte *and* pro ratā, Caes. ; *and* pro portione, Liv., *in proportion, proportionately :* pro tempore et pro re, *according to the time and circumstances,* Caes. ; **prō eō quantum** or **ut,** *in proportion to or as, according to or as :* eaque pro eo quantum in quoque sit ponderis esse aestimanda, Cic. **b.** *by virtue of :* pro imperio, Ter., Liv. ; pro tuā prudentiā, Cic. Ep. ; pro tuo amore, Liv.

prō (not **prōh**), *interj.* expressing wonder or lamentation, *O ! ah ! alas !* With Nom. or Voc.: Ter., Cic., Hor., etc. With Acc.: Ter., Cic. ; elliptically, pro deum immortalium ! (*sc.* fidem), Ter. Also, tantum pro ! degeneramus a patribus, Liv. ; Ov.

proăgorus, i, m. [προήγορος], *the chief magistrate in some towns of Sicily :* Cic.

pro-auctor, ōris, m. *a remote ancestor, founder :* generis, Suet.

pro-avia, ae, f. *a great-grandmother :* Tac., Suet.

proavītus, a, um [proavus], *of a great-grandfather or one's ancestors :* Ov.

pro-avus, i, m. *a great-grandfather.* **1.** Lit.: Pl., Cic. **2.** Trans f. *a forefather, ancestor :* Cic. Ep., Hor., Ov.

probābilis, e, *adj.* [probō], *capable of being pronounced good.* **a.** *that may be approved ; commendable :* discipulus, Cic. ; genus orationis, Cic. ; ingenium, Cic. ; Liv. *Comp. :* Cic. **b.** *that may rightly be assumed or believed, likely, credible, probable :* causa, coniectura, etc., Cic. ; mendacium, Liv.

probābilitās, ātis, f. [probābilis], *probability, credibility :* Cic.

probābiliter, *adv. probably, credibly :* Cic., Liv. *Comp. :* Cic., Liv.

probātiō, ōnis, f. [probō]. **I.** *approval :* ob probationem pretium datum, Cic. **II.** *appraising* (by trial): athletarum, Cic. **III.** *demonstration, proof.* **a.** In gen.: Quint. **b.** *the third division of a discourse, the "proof" of statements made :* Quint.

probātor, ōris, m. [probō], *one who approves :* rationis, Cic. ; ingenii, Ov.

probātus, a, um. **1.** Part. prob. [ ] **Adj.: pronounced good, tested and found good. 1.** Lit. **a.** Of things : argentum, Pl. *Sup. :* Plin. **b.** Of persons : *of established reputation :* Caes., Cic. *Sup.:* Cic. **2.** Trans f. *esteemed, acceptable :* Cic. ; ut nemo probatior primoribus patrum esset, Liv. ; probatissimus alicui, Cic.

probē, *adv.* **I.** *properly, rightly, well :* milites armati atque animati, Pl. ; quem tu probe meministi, Cic. ; scire, Cic., Liv. As exclam. : *well done ! bravo ! fine !* unde agis te ? *Ca.* unde homo ebrius. *Philo.* probe, Pl. ; probissumē, Ter. **II.** Colloq. *properly, thoroughly :* appotus probe, Pl. ; Ter.

probĭtās, ātis, f. [probus], *uprightness, honesty :* Cic., Juv., Tac.

probō, āre [probus], *to make or pronounce serviceable or good.* **1.** Lit. **a.** In gen.: domum tuam, Cic. Ep. ; Pl. **b.** Of the censor : *to pronounce approval of public works :* opera quae locassent, Liv. ; villam publicam, Liv. **c.** Of a general : hunc cum reliquis rebus locum, Caes. **2.** Trans f. **a.** *to appraise, pronounce judgment on :* tuo ex ingenio mores alienos, Pl. ; amicitias utilitate, Ov. ; militem a viribus, Suet. **b.** *to consider serviceable or good, to approve of :* et causam et hominem, Caes. ; istam rationem, Cic. Ep. ; aliquem imperatorem, Caes. With *Inf. :* Caes. **c.** *to show to be serviceable or good, to make acceptable, to recommend :* suam operam, Caes. ; Cic. ; et civibus et sociis se probavit, Cic. ; libros tibi, Cic. Ep. With *de :* iis de meo reditu, Cic. Ep. **d.** *to make credible, to show, demonstrate, prove :* crimen, causam, etc., Cic. With Acc. and *Inf. :* Caes., Cic. In *Pass. :* patrio pater esse metu probor, Ov. [It. *provare ;* Fr. *prouver.*]

proboscis, idis, f. [προβοσκίς], *a trunk, proboscis, snout :* Varr. Of the *trunk* of an elephant : Plin.

probrĭlecebrae, ārum, f. *pl.* [probrum perliciō], *enticements to wrongdoing :* Pl.

probrōsus, a, um [probrum], *defaming, opprobrious, scandalous, abusive :* Pl. **1.** Lit.: sermones, carmina, Tac. ; probrosis altior Italiae ruinis, Hor. **2.** Trans f. of persons : vitā probrosus, Tac. ; Suet.

probrum, i, n. [prōferō, *cf.* Gk. προφέρω], *abuse, invective, aspersion, reproach, opprobrium.* **1.** Lit.: aliquem probris vexare, Cic. ; iactare in aliquem, Liv. ; ingerere, Liv. ; dicere alicui, Ov. ; iacere, cumulare, aggerare, Tac. ; increpare probris, Tac. **2.** Trans f. **a.** *a subject for reproach ; disgrace :* nemo id Alcumenae probro ducet, Pl. ; in probro esse, Ter. ; vita rustica, quam tu probro putas esse oportere, Cic. ; divitiae honori esse coeperunt, paupertas probro haberi, Sall. **b.** *a charge of infamous conduct :* probrum castis inferre, Cic. **c.** *a shameful action, infamy :* Pl., Cic., Ov., etc. Esp. *unchastity :* Pl., Cic., Ov., etc.

probus, a, um, *serviceable, excellent, good.* **1.** Lit. **a.** Of things : argentum, Pl., Liv. ; navigium, Cic. Prov. : proba merx facile emptorem reperit (*cf.* "good wine needs no bush"), Pl. **b.** Of persons : cantor, Pl. Colloq. *proper, thoroughgoing :*

lena, Pl. **2. Transf.** (morally) *upright,
honest, honourable, virtuous :* Pl., Ter., Cic.
Masc. as Noun : Cic.

procācitās, ātis, *f.* [procāx], *importunity,
boldness, impudence :* Cic.

procāciter, *adv. impudently, importunately :*
Curt. *Comp. :* Liv., Tac. *Sup. :* Curt.

Procās and Proca, ae, *m. king of Alba,
father of Numitor and Amulius.*

procāx, ācis, *adj.* [procō], *demanding pressingly, eagerly,* or *insistently.* **1. Lit.** of
persons : *insistent, forward, importunate,
impudent, insolent :* Pl., Cic. ; procax ore,
moribus, ingenio, Tac. *Comp. :* Pl. With
GEN. : procax oti (i.e. eager for peace),
Tac. **Poet. :** Auster, *blustering,* Verg. **2.
Transf.** of things (esp. of speech) : locutio, Cat. ; sermo, Sall. ; libertas, Phaedr. ;
nequitiae procaciores, Mart. ; procacissima
lixarum ingenia, Tac.

prō-cēdō, cēdere, cēssi, cēssum. **I.** *to go
forward, advance.* **1. Lit. a.** In gen. :
Ter., Hor. ; ad forum, Pl. ; illuc, Pl. ; a
portu, Cic. Ep. ; pedibus aequis, Ov. **b.**
Milit. : Caes., Liv. ; agmen, Cic. ; naves,
Caes. ; Verg. ; viam tridui, Caes. *Impers.
Pass. :* Caes., Liv. **2. Transf. a.** In
gen. : *to advance, make progress :* in philosophiā, Cic. ; honoribus longius, Cic. ; ad
virtutis aditum, Cic. ; eo vecordiae processit, Sall. ; eoque ira processit, Liv. ;
longius irae, Verg. ; ambitio et procedendi
libido, Plin. Ep. *Impers. Pass. :* Sall.
b. Of time : tempus, Caes. ; dies, Cic.,
Liv. ; plerumque noctis, Sall. ; maior pars
anni, Liv. ; aetate procedere, Cic. **II.** *to
go* or *come forth* or *out, come out in public.*
1. Lit. : foribus foras, Pl. ; castris, Verg. ;
extra munitiones, Caes. ; e tabernaculo in
solem, Cic. ; mediā ab aulā, Ov. ; in
medium, Cic. ; in contionem, Liv. ; obviam
alicui, Cic. ; Vesper Olympo, Verg. **2.
Transf. a.** Of words and behaviour :
voces contumaces, Tac. **b.** *to turn out,
result, succeed* (with or without bene, etc.).
i. parum procedere, Ter. ; non satis ex
sententiā, Cic. ; alicui pulcherrime, Cic. ;
alicui bene, Cic. **ii.** Without bene : si
processit, Cic. ; Pl. ; Liv. ; consilia alicui,
Liv. ; venenum, Tac. With *pers. subject :*
Ter. **Occ.** *to happen :* num quid processit
ad forum hodie novi ? Pl. **III.** *to go* or
come forth in succession. **1. Lit. :** cum
stationes procederent, Liv. **2. Transf.
a.** In gen. : altera iam pagella, Cic. Ep. ;
iis stipendia, Liv. **b.** In speech : *to go on,
continue :* ad dissuadendum, Liv. **c.** Of
time : iamque dies alterque dies processit,
Verg. ; magni menses, Verg. ; tempora
tarde, Ov.

procella, ae, *f.* **1. Lit.** *a violent wind, hurri-
cane, tempest :* Pl., Cic., Verg., etc. ; venti,
Lucr. **2. Transf. a.** In gen. (mostly
pl.) : tempestates et procellas in illis
fluctibus contionum, Cic. ; invidiarum,
Cic. ; seditionum, Liv. ; agitari tribuniciis
procellis, Liv. ; ferimur procellā, Verg.
b. Milit. *a violent charge, onset of cavalry :*
equestrem procellam, Tac. **c.** Of eloquence : eloquentiae procellam effundere,
Quint.

prō-cellō, ere, *to throw* or *cast forward :* Pl.

procellōsus, a, um [procella], *tempestuous,
boisterous :* ver, Liv. ; Noti, Ov.

procer, eris, *m.* (rare in *sing. :* old form
procus, I, q.v.), *a chief, noble :* agnosco pro-
cerem, Juv. Us. *pl.,* **procerēs,** um, *the
leading men, chiefs, nobles, princes :* Pl.,
Cic. Ep., Verg., Liv., etc.

prōcēritās, ātis, *f.* [prōcērus]. **1. Lit. a.**
height, tallness. Of persons : Cic., Tac. Of
plants : Tac. ; in *pl.,* proceritates arborum,
the different heights, Cic. **b.** *length :* cycni
adiuvantur proceritate collorum, Cic. **2.
Transf.** (in prosody) : pedum, Cic.

prōcērius, *comp. adv. to a greater length :* Cic.

prōcērus, a, um. **1. Lit. a.** *high, tall :*
pōpuli, Cic. ; Cat. ; Verg. ; Liv. ; habitu
procerus, Tac. ; homo procerae staturae,
Suet. ; (Galatea) longā procerior alno, Ov.
Sup. : Cic. **b.** *long, extended :* collum,
rostrum, Cic. ; passus, Lucr. **2. Transf.
a.** *upraised :* palmae, Cat. **b.** In prosody :
long : numerus, Cic.

prōcessiō, ōnis, *f.* [prōcēdō], *a marching onwards, an advance :* Cic.

prōcessus, ūs, *m.* [prōcēdō], *an advance,
progress :* dicendi, Cic. ; morbi, Verg. In
pl. : tantos processūs efficiebat, Cic. ; sic
tua processūs habeat fortuna perennis,
Ov.

Prochyta, ae, and **Prochytē,** ēs, *f. a small
island off the coast of Campania, now
Procida.*

prō-cidō, cidere, cidi [cadō], *to fall forwards,
to fall prostrate.* Of persons : Hor., Ov.,
Liv. Of things : cupressus, Hor. ; pars
muri, Liv.

prō-cinctū, ABL. *sing. m. a girding forth.*
Milit. in procinctu, *under arms, ready for
action :* in procinctu et castris habitos,
Tac. ; testamentum facere in procinctu, Cic.
Prov. : in procinctu habere aliquid, Sen.

prōclāmātor, ōris, *m.* [prōclāmō], *a bawler,*
said of a noisy advocate : Cic.

prō-clāmō, āre, *to cry* or *bawl out :* Cic.,
Verg., Liv. With ACC. and *Inf. :* Liv.

Proclēs, is or i, *m. twin-brother of Eurysthenes,
founder of one of the two royal houses of
Sparta.*

prō-clīnō, āre, *to make to slope forwards* or
down. **1. Lit. :** Nereus mare in litora,
Ov. **2. Transf. :** adiuvare rem proclina-
tam, *tottering,* Caes.

prōclīvis, e (**prōclīvus,** a, um, Pl., Lucr.),
[clīvus], *sloping forwards.* **1. Lit.** *steep,
going downwards :* solum, Varr. ; via, Liv.
As Noun, **prōclīve,** is, *n. a slope, descent,
declivity :* pelli per proclive, Liv. *Neut.*
Acc. **prōclīve** as *Adv. downwards :* Lucr.,
Cic. **2. Transf. a.** *downward :* proclivi cursu et facili delabi, Cic. **b.** *prone,
inclined* or *disposed to, liable* (mostly in a
bad sense) : ingenium ad lubidinem, Ter. ;
ad morbum proclivior, Cic. ; circa modestiam, Quint. **c.** *easy :* impetus, Lucr. ;
ratio, Cic. *Comp. :* Cic. *Neut.* as Noun :
proclivia anteponuntur laboriosis, Cic. ;
in proclivi esse, *to be easy,* Pl., Ter. *Neut.*
Acc. *Comp.* as *Adv.* **prōclīvius :** labi verba
proclivius, Cic. ; Lucr. **d.** *going downhill,
hence, insecure, difficult* (only in opp. to
planus) : faciam hanc rem planam ex proclivā
tibi, Pl.

prōclīvĭtās, ātis, *f.* [prōclīvis], *a steep descent.* **1.** Lit. : Auct. B. Afr. **2.** Transf. : *a tendency, proneness :* Cic.

prōclīvus, a, um, *v.* prōclīvis.

Procnē (Prognē), ēs, *f. daughter of Pandion and wife of Tereus ; changed into a swallow.* Transf. *a swallow :* Verg.

prŏcō, āre (**procor**, ārī, Sen.) [*cf.* precor], *to demand, require :* Cic. ; parere mihi mea vos maiestas procat, Liv. Andr.

prō-cōnsul (also **prō cōnsŭle**), ulis, *m.* one *who serves in the place of a consul* (usually by an extension in time of consular power). **a.** With military powers (during Hannibalic War) : Liv. **b.** As governor of a province : Caes., Cic., etc. **c.** Under the Empire : a governor of a senatorial province : Suet.

prōcōnsŭlāris, e, *adj.* [prōcōnsul]. **I.** *mock-consular :* imago, Liv. **II.** *belonging to a proconsul, proconsular :* ius, vir, Tac.

prōcōnsŭlātus, ūs, *m.* [prōcōnsul]. *the office of proconsul, a proconsulship :* Tac. Also *of the governorship of a propraetor :* Suet.

procor, *v.* procō.

prōcrāstĭnātĭō, ōnis, *f.* [prōcrāstinō], *a putting off from day to day, procrastination :* Cic.

prōcrāstĭnō, āre [crāstinus], *to put off the morrow,* i.e. *from day to day ; to defer, procrastinate :* rem, Cic.

prōcrĕātĭō, ōnis, *f.* [prōcreō], *a breeding, procreation :* Cic.

prōcrĕātor, ōris, *m.* [prōcreō], *a begetter.* **1.** Lit. (in *pl.*) : *parents :* Cic. **2.** Transf. : ille procreator mundi deus, Cic.

prōcrĕātrix, īcis, *fem.* of prōcreātor. Transf. : philosophia artium procreatrix, Cic.

prō-crĕō, āre, *to breed, beget, produce.* **1.** Lit. : liberos, Pl. ; liberos ex tribus uxoribus, Nep. ; de matre familias filios, Cic. ; fetūs, Cic. **2.** Transf. **a.** Of things : natura hinc sensūs animantum procreat omnis, Lucr. ; terra e seminibus truncos, Cic. **b.** tribunatus, cuius primum ortum inter arma civium procreatum videmus, Cic.

prō-crēscō, ere. **I.** *to be produced, to spring.* **1.** Lit. : quattuor ex rebus posse omnia procrescere, Lucr. **2.** Transf. : unde vis morbi procrescit, Lucr. **II.** *to continue to grow, to increase :* genitas procrescere posse, Lucr.

Procris, is and idis (Acc. Procrim, Verg.) *f.,* *d.* of Erechtheus, *and w.* of Cephalus, *who shot her in mistake for a wild beast.*

Procrūstēs, ae, *m. a noted robber in Attica ; said to have cruelly stretched his victims to the length of his bed, or mutilated them if too long. He was slain by Theseus.*

prō-cŭbō, āre, *to lie along the ground :* saxea umbra, Verg.

prō-cūdō, cūdere, cūdī, cūsum, *to beat out by hammering, to forge or re-sharpen.* **1.** Lit. : vomeris obtusi dentem, Verg. ; ensis, Hor. ; Lucr. **2.** Transf. **a.** dolos, Pl. ; voluptatem, Lucr. ; linguam, Cic. **b.** *to bring forth, produce :* ignem, Lucr. ; prolem propagando, Lucr.

procul, *adv.* [prōcellō]. **1.** Lit. **a.** *at a distance, in the distance, far* (not implying great remoteness) : Pl., Ciu. ; Verg ; ita *to a distance, far :* omnibus arbitris amotis, Sall. ; Ov. **c.** *from a distance, from afar :* vox sonat, Pl. ; tela conicere, Caes. ; procul e fluctu cernitur Aetna, Verg. Often (in any of these meanings) with hinc, inde, alicunde, longe, etc. : procul hinc, Pl., Ter. ; procul alicunde, Cic. ; procul inde, Ov. With *ab : at a distance from :* a terrā, Cic., Verg. ; a castris, Caes. ; Liv. With Abl. (without *ab*) : patriā, Enn. ; locus procul muro, Liv. ; urbe, Ov. **2.** Transf. : adsentatio vitiorum adiutrix procul amoveatur, Cic. ; Hor. ; homines procul errant, Sall. ; haud procul est (abest) quin etc., Liv. ; conscia mihi sum a me culpam hanc esse procul, Ter. ; ab omni metu, Cic. ; a litteris, Quint. ; negotiis, Hor. ; ambitione, Hor. ; plebem procul urbe haberi, Liv. ; voluptatibus aliquem habere, Tac. : dubio procul, Lucr. ; procul dubio, Liv., Quint.

prō-culcō, āre [calcō], *to tread down, trample upon.* **1.** Lit. : segetes, Ov. ; Curt. ; Tac. Of cavalry : sua subsidia territis equis, Liv. **2.** Transf. : senatum, Tac. ; rem publicam, Suet.

Procŭlēĭus, ī, *m. a Roman eques, friend of Augustus. He shared his fortune equally with his brothers, who had lost theirs in the civil wars.*

Proculus, ī, *m. a Roman cognomen.* Esp. Iulius Proculus, *a Roman senator, who asserted that Romulus had appeared to him after his death.*

prō-cumbō, cumbere, cubuī, cubitum [*cf.* incumbō, etc.]. **I.** *to lean or bend forward :* tigna secundum naturam fluminis, Caes. ; olli certamine summo procumbunt, Verg. **II.** *to sink to the ground, droop and fall.* **1.** Lit. : vulneribus confecti, Caes. ; humi bos, Verg. ; ad genua, Liv. ; genibus, Ov. ; frumenta imbribus, Caes. ; gravidis culmus aristis, Verg. ; agger in fossam, Liv. ; domus in domini caput, Ov. ; Quint. **2.** Transf. : *to fall or sink to ruin :* res meae, Ov.

prōcūrātĭō, ōnis, *f.* [prōcūrō], *management, control, superintendence.* **A.** Public. **a.** aedium sacrarum, annonae, negoti publici, Cic. ; regni, Sall. ; ministeri, Liv. **b.** Under the Empire : *the office of* procurator : Tac. **c.** Relig. : *attention to for purpose of expiating :* prodigi, Liv. ; incesti, Tac. ; sue facere, Cic. **B.** Private : mearum rerum, Cic. Ep.

prōcūrātor (**pro-**, Ov.), ōris, *m.* [prōcūrō], *one who is in charge.* **A.** Public. **a.** *an administrator, manager :* Cic. Ep. : peni, Pl. ; regni, Caes. ; alieni iuris vicarius, Cic. **b.** Under the Empire : *the* (Emperor's) *finance-agent, procurator :* Tac., Suet. ; sometimes in charge of a sub-province (e.g. of Judaea) : Tac., Suet. **B.** Private : *a manager* of an estate, *bailiff :* Cic.

prōcūrātrix, īcis, *f.* of prōcūrātor. Transf. : sapientiam hominis procuratricem esse, Cic.

prō-cūrō (**pro-**, Tib., Ov.), āre, *to hare or take charge of.* **A.** Public. **a.** pueros, Pl. ; perh., corpora, Verg. **b.** Under the Empire : *to be a* procurator : in Hispaniā, Plin. Ep. **c.** Relig. : sacrificia, Caes. ; sacra, Nep. Esp. *to give due attention to for* purpose of expiating or averting : monstra, Cic. ; Liv. ; Phaedr. With *ne* and *Subj.* : Tib. *Impers. Pass.* : Liv. **B.** Private. **a.** *to attend to, tend* : aliquem, Pl. ; arbores, Cato ; corpora, Verg. (but *v.* A. a.). **b.** *to administer, act as bailiff or attorney* : negotia Dionysi, Cic. Ep. ; hereditatem, Cic. Ep.

prō-currō, currere, cucurri and currī, cursum, *to run forwards.* **1.** Lit. : Caes., Verg., Liv. **2.** Transf. **a.** Of places : *to run or jut out* : saxa, Vorg. ; terra procurrit in aequor, Ov. ; Curt. ; Plin. Ep. **b.** Of money increasing : Sen. Ep.

prōcursātiō, ōnis, *f.* [prōcursō], *a skirmishing* : Liv. ; Numidarum, Liv.

prōcursātōrēs, um, *m. pl.* [prōcursō], *skirmishers* : Liv.

prō-cursō, āre, *to make frequent forward rushes, to skirmish. Impers. Pass.* : Liv.

prōcursus, ūs, *m.* [prōcurrō], *a running forwards, a charge* : Liv.

prō-curvus, a, um, *rounded forwards* : falx, Verg.

(1) procus, ī, (GEN. *pl.* procum), *a noble* : Cic. ; *v.* procer.

(2) procus, ī, *m.* [v. prex]. **I.** *a wooer, suitor* : Pl., Verg., Hor., etc. **II.** *a canvasser* : Cic.

Procyōn, onis, *m. a star that rises before the Dog-star* (pure Lat. Antecanis, is, m.).

prōdāctus, a, um, *Part.* prōdigō.

prō-deambulō, āre, *to take a walk abroad* (i.e. out-of-doors) : Ter.

prōd-eō, īre, iī, itum. **I.** *to go or come forwards, advance.* **1.** Lit. : Pl. ; longius, Caes. ; in proelium, Caes. ; in aciem, Cic. Ep. ; volando columbae, Verg. **2.** Transf. **a.** sumptu extra modum, Cic. ; Hor. **b.** *to project* : in mare rupes, Verg. ; immodico tubere, Ov. **II.** *to go or come forth, appear in public.* **1.** Lit. : foras, Pl., Cic. ; ad conloquium, Caes. ; ex portu, Caes. ; in publicum, Cic. Ep. ; obviam alicui, Cic. **2.** Transf. **a.** novae comoediae, Pl. ; ex iudice Dama, Hor. **b.** Of fashions, etc. : si haec consuetudo prodire coeperit, Cic. ; tot colores, Ov. **c.** Of plants : Varr., Ov.

prōdesse, *v.* prōsum.

prō-dīcō, dīcere, dīxī, dictum, *to name* (a day) *forward, to adjourn* : diem, Liv., Tac.

prō-dictātor, ōris, *m. a vice-dictator* : Liv.

Prodicus, ī, *m. a noted Greek sophist of Ceos, contemporary with Socrates* : **Prodicius**, a, um.

prōdigē, *adv. lavishly* : Cic., Sen. Ep.

prōdigentia, ae, *f.* [prōdigō], *profusion, extravagance* : opum, Tac. ; opp. to avaritia : Tac.

prōdigiālis, e, *adj.* [prōdigium], *that deals with unnatural things* : Iuppiter, Pl.

prōdigiāliter, *adv. unnaturally* : Hor.

prōdigiōsus, a, um [prōdigium], *unnatural, marvellous* : atria Circes, Ov. ; corpora, Quint. ; prodigiosum dictu ! Tac.

prōdigium, ī, *n.* [prō and root seen in Gk. δείκνυμι and Lat. dīcō], *a marvellous or wonderful sign, portent.* **1.** Lit. : Acc., Cic., Verg., etc. Esp. of evil significance : Sall., Verg. ; accipere aliquid in prodigium, Tac. **2.** Transf. **a.** Of deeds : *an un-*

natural crime : Cic. **b.** Of persons (in bad sense) : *a monster* : Cic.

prōd-igō, igere, ēgī, āctum [agō], *to drive forth.* **1.** Lit. : sues in lutosos limites, Varr. **2.** Transf. : *to squander, lavish* : opes, Suet. ; Pl. ; Sall. ; Tac.

prōdigus, a, um [prōdigō]. **I.** *lavish, wasteful.* **1.** Lit. : Cic., Juv. With GEN. : poculi sui, Pl. ; aeris, Hor. *Masc.* as Noun : Cic. **2.** Transf. (with GEN.) : arcani fides, Hor. **II.** *lavish, generous* (only transf.) : tellus, Ov. With GEN. : animae Paulus, Hor. ; locus herbae, Hor.

prōditiō, ōnis, *f.* [prōdō], *betrayal, treason* : amicitiarum proditiones, Cic.

prōditor, ōris, *m.* [prōdō], *a betrayer, traitor.* **a.** patriae, Cic. ; risus proditor latentis puellae, Hor. **b.** In ·appos. : exercitus proditor disciplinae, Liv.

prō-dō, dere, didī, ditum. **I.** *to put or bring forth.* **1.** Lit. : vina, Ov. ; suspiria, Ov. **2.** Transf. **a.** *to put forth, show, exhibit* : Caes. ; exemplum, Cic., Liv. ; crimen vultu, Ov. **b.** *to publish, make known, record* : decretum, Cic. ; ea quae scriptores prodiderunt, Cic. Esp. with memoriae *or* memoriā *or* litteris : Thucydides ossa eius clam ab amicis esse sepulta memoriae prodidit, Nep. ; quos natos in insulā ipsā, memoriā proditum dicunt, Caes. ; Cic. **c.** *to proclaim* on appointment to office : flaminem, Cic. ; interregem, Liv. **II.** *to forsake, abandon disloyally or treacherously, betray.* **1.** Lit. : Brutum, Cic. ; Caes. ; aquilam hostibus, Caes. ; classem praedonibus, Cic. ; aliquem ad mortem, Verg. ; in cruciatūs, Liv. **2.** Transf. : suam vitam, Ter. ; salutem meam, Cic. ; patriam, Cic. **III.** *to put forth* (to posterity), *to transmit, hand down* : regnum, Cic. ; ius ad memoriam, Cic. ; sacra posteris, Cic. ; genus, Verg. ; ut locus memoriam proderet, Caes. Hence, *to prolong* : vitam ad miseriam, Cic.

prō-doceō, ōre, *to preach or inculcate* (a doctrine) *publicly* : Hor.

prodromus, ī, *m.* [πρόδρομος], *a forerunner* : Cic.

prō-dūcō, dūcere, dūxī, ductum (prōdūxe for prōdūxisse, Ter.). **I.** *to draw or bring forward.* **1.** Lit. **a.** In gen. : fidicinam intus, Pl. ; copias pro castris, Caes. ; castris exercitum, Pl. ; milites centuriatim, Caes. **b.** *to bring on one's way, to conduct* : cum rus hinc, Ter. ; nec te mater produxi (i.e. to the grave), Verg. **c.** *to draw in front (of)* : scamnum lecto, Ov. **2.** Transf. **a.** *to bring forward, promote, advance* : aliquem ad dignitatem, Cic. ; aliquem omni genere honorum, Liv. **b.** *to bring on* in training, *to educate* : filiam, Pl. ; liberos, Tac. ; Juv. Also of plants : *to cultivate* : Hor. **c.** *to draw on, lead on, induce* : notitiā Septimi productus, Caes. ; quo discordia civis produxit, Verg. **II.** *to bring forth or out into public.* **1.** Lit. **a.** In gen. : aliquem foras ante aedis, Pl. ; aliquem in conspectum populi, Cic. ; aliquem in contionem, Cic., Liv. ; in iudicium, Cic. **b.** For sale : Ter., Suet. **2.** Transf. **a.** *to bring into the world, be the father of* : Pl., Sen. Ep., Juv. **b.** *to bring to light* : occulta ad patres crimina, Juv. **c.** Of an actor : *to bring on the stage, to perform* : nihil pravum, Cic. **d.** *to introduce, bring into fashion :* nova vocabula usus, Hor. **III.** *to bring forward, prolong, extend.* **1.** Lit.: aciem, Caes. ; ferrum incude, Juv. **2.** Transf. **A.** Of time. **a.** rem in hiemem, Caes. ; Cic. ; convivium ad multam noctem, Cic. ; cenam, Hor. **b.** *to prolong, spin out :* cyathos sorbillans diem, Ter. **c.** *to put off, adjourn :* diem in III. Id. Febr., Cic. With person as Object : *to put off :* aliquem falsā spe, Ter. ; Cic. **B.** In prosody : *to lengthen :* syllabam, Ov. ; Quint.

prōductē, *adv. in a lengthened manner, long :* dicere litteram, Cic.

prōductiō, ōnis, *f.* [prōdūcō], *a lengthening, prolonging.* **a.** temporis, Cic. **b.** In pronunciation : Cic.

prōductō, āre [*freq.* prōdūcō], *to draw out, spin out :* huic malo aliquam moram, Ter.

prōductus, a, um. **I.** *Part.* prōdūcō. **II.** Adj.: *lengthened, prolonged.* **1.** Lit.: productiore cornu, Tac. **2.** Transf. **a.** In time : commoditates tam productae temporibus, Cic. ; quinto productior actu fabula, Hor. **b.** In prosody : syllaba, Cic. **III.** Noun, **prōducta,** ōrum, *n. pl. preferable things* (= προηγμένα of the Stoics) : Cic.

proēgmenon, i, *n.* [προηγμένον], in the lang. of the Stoics, *that which is preferred :* Cic.

proeliāris, e, *adj.* [proelium], *of battle, battle- :* pugnae, Pl.

proeliātor, ōris, *m.* [proelior], *a fighter, combatant :* Tac.

proelior, āri [proelium], *to join battle, engage, fight.* **1.** Lit.: Caes., Cic. **2.** Transf. with words : Cic. Ep.

proelium, i, *n. a battle, combat.* **1.** Lit. **a.** Of men : committere, Caes., Cic., Liv. ; facere, Cic. ; inire, Liv. ; sumere, Tac. ; miscere, Prop. ; redintegrare, restituere, Caes. ; conficere, Hirt. ; obire, Lucr. ; proelio hostem lacessere, Caes. ; proelio dimicare, decertare, Cic. **b.** Of animals : Verg. ; proelia dant cervi, Verg. **c.** Of things : ventorum proelia, Verg. **2.** Transf. **a.** *contest, strife :* proelia te meā causā sustinere, Cic. Ep. ; Ov. Comic. : in eo uterque proelio potabimus, Pl. **b.** In *pl. : fighting-men :* Prop.

Proetus, i, *m. king of Tiryns ;* **Proetides,** um, *f. pl. his daughters.*

profānō, āre [profānus], *to make profanus ; to make ordinary, to desecrate.* **1.** Lit.: sacrum, Ov. ; dies festos, sacra, sacerdotes, Liv. **2.** Transf. *to pollute :* pudorem, Curt.

profānō, āre [fānum], *to offer before a shrine, to consecrate :* Cato.

profānus, a, um [fānum], *before,* i.e. *outside the sanctuary ; not sacred or dedicated, ordinary, common.* **1.** Lit. : opp. to sacrum, Pl. ; loci consecrati an profani, Cic. ; flamma, Ov. ; tegmina profana et usu polluta, Tac. Of persons : vulgus, Hor. As Noun : Verg. *Neut.* as Noun : in profano deseri placet sacra, Liv. **2.** Transf. **a.** *impious :* mens, Ov. *Neut. pl.* as Noun : Hor. **b.** *unconsecrated,* i.e. *ill-boding :* bubo, Ov.

prō-lātus (3rd *sing.*), fārī, fātus, *to speak forth, declare :* Lucr., Verg., Ov. With Acc.: nomen, Pac. ; plura, Hor.

profectiō, ōnis, *f.* [proficiscor], *a going forth, setting out.* **1.** Lit.: Pac., Caes., Cic., etc. **2.** Transf.: *source of origin :* pecuniae, Cic.

profectō, *adv.* [prō factō], *actually, really, assuredly :* Pl., Cic., Hor., etc.

profectus, a, um, *Part.* proficiscor.

profectus, a, um, *Part.* prōficiō.

prōfectus, ūs, *m.* [prōficiō], *progress, growth.* **a.** Plin. **b.** *profit, effect :* sine profectu, Ov. ; Varr. ; Quint. [It. *profitto ;* Fr. Eng. *profit.*]

prō-ferō, ferre, tulī, lātum. **I.** *to bring forward, advance.* **1.** Lit. **a.** gradum, Pl. ; passūs, Lucr. ; pedem, Hor., Quint. ; arma ex oppido, Caes. ; vineas, castra, Liv. ; ab urbe aliquid, Liv. ; signa, *to advance to battle,* Liv. **b.** *to bring forward, extend :* manum, linguam, Pl. ; digitum, Cic. **2.** Transf. *to carry forwards, impel :* pietas Caecilium, Cic. ; se ad civium caedīs, Plin. Ep. **II.** *to bring forth or out in public.* **1.** Lit. **a.** pateram, Pl. ; liberos in conspectum, Caes. ; nummos ex arcā, Cic. **b.** *to bring out and offer :* alicui minas viginti, Pl. ; Cic. **2.** Transf. **a.** *to produce in public, to publish :* orationem, Cic. Ep. ; artem, Suet. **b.** *to make known, reveal :* palam aliquid, Ter. ; aliquid foras, Cic. ; indicia exiti, Cic. ; ingenium, Tac. **c.** *to quote, mention :* libros, auctores, testīs, etc., Cic. ; progeniem suam usque ab avo, Ter. ; exempla, Cic. **d.** *to bring forth, produce :* caelum laurum, Plin. Ep. **e.** *to utter :* syllabas, Quint. **III.** *to carry forwards, extend, enlarge, expand.* **1.** Lit.: aggerem, castra, Caes. ; pomerium, terminos, Liv. ; imperium super Indos, Verg. **2.** Transf. **A.** finis officiorum, Cic. **B.** In time. **a.** beatam vitam usque ad rogum, Cic. ; fata parentis, Verg. ; diem, tempus, Liv. **b.** *to put off, defer :* auctionis diem, Cic. Ep. ; diem Ilio, Hor. ; rem in annum, Liv.

professiō, ōnis, *f.* [profiteor], *a public acknowledgment, declaration, profession.* **1.** Lit. **a.** In gen.: bene dicendi, Cic. ; flagitii, pietatis, Tac. **b.** *a public declaration of* one's name, property, business, etc. : Cic. ; in *pl. :* Liv. **2.** Transf. **a.** *a public register* of persons or property thus given in : Cic. **b.** *a business or profession :* Curt., Suet.

professor, ōris, *m.* [profiteor], *a recognised teacher or authority on a subject :* Quint., Suet. Esp. of rhetoric : Quint., Plin. Ep.

professōrius, a, um [professor], *of a professor : authoritative :* lingua, Tac.

professus, a, um, *Part.* profiteor.

pro-fēstus, a, um [*cf.* profānus], *not kept as a holiday, common :* dies, Pl., Hor., Liv.

prō-ficiō, ficere, fēcī, fectum [faciō], *to make* (way) *forward, advance.* **1.** Lit. : tridui viam a suis finibus, Caes. **2.** Transf. **a.** *to advance, make progress, gain advantage :* nihil in oppugnatione oppidi, Caes. ; in philosophiā aliquid profecimus, Cic. ; loci opportunitate, Caes. **b.** *to be useful, profitable, beneficial :* res ad dicendum proficit, Cic. ; parva certamina in summam totius spei, Liv. ; aliquid tua verba, Ov. ; radice vel herbā proficiente nihil, Hor.

proficiscō, for proficiscor : Pl.

proficiscor (prŏf-, Pl.), ficiscī, fectus [prŏ-ficiō], *to begin to go forward, to set out.* **1.** Lit. : in exercitum, Pl. ; hinc in pistrinum, Ter. ; ad bellum, Caes., Liv. ; ad eam domum, Cic. ; in pugnam, Caes. ; in Illyricum, Caes. ; Puteolos, Cic. ; domos, Liv. ; subsidio alicui, Nep. ; ab urbe, Caes. ; Liv. ; do Formiano, Cic. Ep. ; ex castris, Caes. ; domo, Sall., Liv. ; Athenis, Nep. **2.** Transf. **a.** ad somnum, Cic. ; ad dormiendum, Cic. **b.** *to go, proceed :* ad reliqua, Cic. **c.** *to set out, begin :* inde oratio mea, Cic. ; a philosophiā, Cic. **d.** *to come forth, proceed, originate from :* ex medicinā, Cic. ; genus a Pallante profectum, Verg. ; Tyriā de gente, Ov. ; omnes ab Aristotele profecti, Cic.

pro-fiteor, fitērī, fessus [fateor], *to declare publicly, acknowledge, avow frankly.* **I.** In gen. : Pl., Cic. With Acc. and Inf. : Cic. With *de* : Suet. *Perf. Part.* in *Pass.* sense : Ov. (hence, ex professo, *openly,* Sen. Ep.). **II.** In partic. **A.** *to make a declaration* or *return* of name, property, business, etc. **1.** Lit. : apud praetorem, Cic. ; aratores iugera sationum suarum, Cic. ; frumentum, Liv. With *Indir. Quest.* : Cic. **2.** Transf. : se grammaticum, Cic. With Acc. and *Inf.* : Cic. Also, philosophiam (i.e. the calling of a philosopher), Cic. ; ius, Ov. **B.** *to make a declaration* in general. **1.** Lit. : nomen (i.e. as candidate for election), Liv. ; so without nomen, Sall. ; indicium, Sall., Tac. **2.** Transf. : in his poeta nomen profitetur suom, Ter. **C.** *to offer freely, promise :* se ad eam rem adiutorem, Caes. ; in eam rem operam, Cic. ; meum studium in omni genere offici, Cic. Ep. ; magna, Hor. ; Ov. With Acc. and *Fut. Inf.* : Caes. *Absol. to volunteer :* Pl. **D.** *to be a professed teacher* or *authority:* Plin. Ep.

prōfligātor, ōris, *m.* [prōflīgō], *a spendthrift :* Tac.

prōfligātus, a, um. **I.** *Part.* prōflīgō. **II.** Adj. : *broken down in character, degraded :* Cic. *Sup.* : Cic., Suet.

prō-flīgō, āre, *to strike* or *dash to the ground ;* hence, *to overthrow.* **1.** Lit. : inimicos, Pl. ; copias hostium, Cic. ; Tac. ; classem hostium, Caes. **2.** Transf. **a.** *to shatter, destroy, break up :* rem publicam, Cic. ; opes, Nep. ; rem, Liv. **b.** *to bring nearly to an end* (*cf.* colloq. 'to break the back of') : bellum, Cic. Ep., Liv., Tac. **c.** Mentally or in spirit : Cic. *Morally : to debase, degrade :* senatoria iudicia, Cic.

prō-flō, āre, *to blow forth, breathe out.* **1.** Lit. : flammas, Ov. **2.** Transf. : toto pectore somnum, Verg.

prōfluēns, entis. **I.** *Part.* prōfluō. **II.** Adj. : *flowing onwards.* **1.** Lit. : aqua, Cic. Ep. ; also as Noun (*sc.* aqua) : Cic. **2.** Transf. of style : loquacitas, Cic. ; eloquentia, Tac.

prōfluenter, adv. *flowingly ;* i.e. *without checks, easily :* Cic.

prōfluentia, ae, *f.* [prōfluō], *fluency :* loquendi, Cic.

prō-fluō, fluere, fluxī, *to flow forth* or *onwards.* **1.** Lit. : gravedo, Pl. ; sanguis, Enn. ; umor, Verg. ; Mosa ex monte Vogeso, Caes. ; ad mare, Cic. **2.** Transf. : ab his fontibus profluxi ad hominum famam, Cic. ; ad incognitas libidines Messalina, Tac.

prōfluvium, ī, *n.* [prōfluō], *a flowing forth :* sanguinis, Lucr.

pro-for, *v.* profātur.

pro-fugiō, fugere, fūgī. **A.** Intrans. *to flee* or *fly forth and away, to escape.* **a.** domo, Pl., Cic., Liv. ; ex oppido, Caes. ; Sall. ; in Britanniam, Caes. ; pedibus Hadrumetum, Caes. **b.** *to take refuge :* ad Ciceronem, Caes. ; Cic. Ep. **B.** Trans. *to flee from :* agros, Hor. ; dominos, Curt.

profugus, a, um [profugiō], *in flight, fugitive.* **1.** Lit. **a.** profugus domo, Liv. ; ex urbe, Tac. ; Liv. ; e proelio, Tac. ; ad rebellis, Tac. ; boves, Prop. ; taurus altaribus, Tac. *Masc.* as Noun : *a fugitive :* Tiridates regni profugus, Tac. **b.** *banished, exiled :* Sall. ; patriā, Liv. ; fato profugus (i.e. by destiny), Verg. As Noun : *an exile :* Pl., Ov. **2.** Transf. *unsettled :* Scythae, Hor.

pro-fundō (prō-, Cat.), fundere, fūdī, fūsum, *to pour forth.* **1.** Lit. : aquam, vinum, Pl. ; sanguinem suum, Cic. ; lacrimas oculis, Verg. In *Mid.* or with *Refl. Pron.* : *to stream, burst* or *gush forth :* lacrimae se subito profuderunt, Cic. ; profusus e cervice cruor, Ov. **2.** Transf. **a.** puerum ex alvo matris natura, Lucr. With *Refl. Pron.* : multitudo sagittariorum se profudit, Caes. Of plants : Cic. **b.** vitam pro patriā, Cic. ; omnia ex ore, Lucr. ; pectore voces, Cat. ; odium in aliquem, Cic. ; in questūs sese, Liv. ; voluptates se, Cic. **c.** Of wastefulness : *to lavish, squander :* Ter. ; patrimonia, Cic. ; divitias in libidinum gurgitem, Cic ; ventis verba, Lucr. **d.** *to outstretch on the ground :* somnus membra, Lucr. In *Mid.* : profusae in terram, Lucr.

pro-fundus, a, um [fundus], *deep.* **1.** Lit. : Acheron, inane, Lucr. ; mare, Cic. ; Verg. ; Danuvius, Hor. **2.** Transf. **a.** Of vast height : caelum, Verg. ; altitudo, Liv. **b.** Of density : silvae, Lucr. ; Curt. ; umbras Erebi noctemque profundam, Verg. **c.** *boundless, insatiable :* libidines, Cic. ; avaritia, Sall. ; ruit profundo Pindarus ore, Hor. ; venter, Curt. **d.** *of the underworld :* manes, Verg. *Neut.* Noun, **profundum,** ī, *depth, the deep, an abyss.* **1.** Lit. : esse in profundo aquae, Cic. Esp. of the sea : Acc., Cic., Verg., etc. Comic. of the stomach : Pl. **2.** Transf. : natura in profundo veritatem abstruserit, Cic.

profūsē, adv. **I.** *in wild disorder :* consul obstitit profuse tendentibus suis in castra, Liv. **II.** *lavishly, extravagantly :* aedes exstructa, Suet. *Comp.* : Sall.

profūsiō, ōnis, *f.* [profundō], *profusion :* Plin. Ep., Suet.

profūsus, a, um. **I.** *Part.* profundō. **II.** Adj. **A.** *spread out, extended :* cauda, Varr. **B.** *lavish, extravagant.* **1.** Act. : nepos, Cic. With Gen. : alieni appetens sui profusus, Sall. **2.** Pass. **a.** profusis sumptibus vivere, Cic. ; convivia, Suet. **b.** hilaritas, Cic. ; cupido, Tac. *Sup.* : Suet.

prō-gener, erī, *m. a grand-daughter's husband :* Sen. Ep., Tac.

prō-generō, āre, *to beget, engender :* Hor.

prōgeniēs, ēī, *f.* [gen in gignō], *descent, line-age.* **a.** Abstract.: progeniem ab ali-quo proferre, Ter. ; divina, Cic. **b.** Concr.: *descendants, progeny :* se progeniem de-orum esse dicebant, Cic. ; Ov. ; Liv.; Sarpedon, mea progenies, Verg. ; progeni-em Troiano a sanguine duci, Verg. Of animals : Verg. Transf.: stirps haec progeniesque mea est (i.e. his poems), Ov.

prō-genitor, ōris, *m. the founder of a family, an ancestor :* Acc., Nep., Ov.

prōgenitus, a, um, *Part.* prōgignō.

prō-gignō, gignere, genui, genitum, *to beget, produce.* **1.** Lit.: Pl. ; illam terra parens, Verg. ; quae ex iis seminibus progignuntur, Cic. ; te ferae, Ov. **2.** Transf.: ex me morem malum, Pl. ; flumina myrtūs, Cat. ; sensum acerbum, Lucr.

prō-gnāriter, *adv. decisively, definitely :* indicare, Pl.

prō-gnātus, a, um, *born or descended from.* **1.** Lit.: a meo patre, Pl. Davo patre, Pl. ; Tantalo prognatus, Cic. Liv. ; Hor. ; ex Cimbris Teutonisque, Caes. As Noun, **prōgnātus**, ī, *m. a child, descendant :* Pl. **2.** Transf. of plants : Peliaco prognatae vertice pinūs, Cat.

Prognē, *v.* Procnē.

prognōsticon or **-um**, ī, *n.* [προγνωστικόν], *a sign or token* of the future, *a prognostic :* hence, **Prognōstica**, ōrum, *n. pl. the signs of the weather,* the title of Cicero's transla-tion of the Προγνωστικά of Aratus : Cic.

prō-gredior, gredī, grēssus [gradior]. **I.** *to step or march forwards, to advance.* **1.** Lit.: Pl., Cic. ; longius a castris, Caes.; in locum ini-quum, Caes. ; tridui viam, Caes. ; ante signa, Liv.: obviam alicui, Liv. Of ships: naves audacius progressae, Caes. **2.** Transf.: nunc ad reliqua progrediar, Cic. ; quo amentiae, Liv. ; absurdam in adulationem, Tac.; in virtute, Cic. ; progredientibus aetatibus, Cic. ; aetate progressus, Cic. **II.** *to go forth or out :* foras, Pl. ; ex domo, Cic.

prōgrēssiō, ōnis, *f.* [prōgredior]. **I.** *ad-vancement, progress, increase :* ad virtutem facere, Cic.; discendi, Cic. In *pl.* : Cic. **II.** Rhet.: *a progressive strengthening of expressions :* Cic.

prōgrēssus, a, um, *Part.* prōgredior.

prōgrēssus, ūs, *m.* [prōgredior], *a going for-wards, advance.* **1.** Lit.: Cic. In *pl.* : Cic. **2.** Transf. **a.** in studiis progressūs facere, Cic. ; Nep. ; aetatis, Cic. **b.** Of events : rerum progressūs, Cic.

prōh, *interj. v.* prō.

pro-hibeō, ēre (old forms, prohibēssit, Pl. ; proh̄bēssint, Cic. (law)) prōbeat = pro-hibeat, Lucr.) [habeō], *to hold or keep a per-son or thing off from or at a distance.* **1.** Lit.: illum ab illā, Pl. ; praedones prócul ab insulā, Cic. ; vim hostium ab oppidis, Caes. ; silva Suebos a Cheruscis prohibet, Caes. ; Germanos suis finibus, Caes. ; di malum, Ter. ; minas, Verg. With Dat.: aliquem alicui, Pl. **2.** Transf. **A.** *to hin-der. stop, prevent, interfere with.* **a.** With Acc. of person and Abl. (with or without

ab) of verbal noun : hostem a pugnā, Caes. ; Cic. ; itinere exercitum, Caes. Also, ali-quem a familiaritate, patrio iure, Cic. **b.** With Acc. of verbal noun : munitiones, Caes. ; Cic. ; loci natura aditum, Caes. ; aditum alicui, Auct. B. Afr. **c.** With Acc. of Object and *Inf.* : Cimbros intra finis suos ingredi, Caes. ; Pl. ; Çic. ; Verg., etc. ; ius de pecuniis dici, Liv. **d.** With *ne, quo minus,* and (after negat.) *quin* with *Subj.* : Pl., Cic. (rarely), Liv. ; also *quin* (without previous negat.): Tac. **B.** *to prevent,* i.e. *protect :* a periculo rem publicam, Cic. ; tenuiores iniuriā, Cic. ; Pl. ; populationibus Campaniam, Liv. With double Acc.: id te, Pl. **C.** *to prevent by words, forbid, not to permit :* Pl. ; lex contraria, Cic. With Acc. of Object and *Inf.* : Pl., Caes., Quint.

prohibitiō, ōnis, *f.* [prohibeō], *a forbidding, prohibition :* tollendi, Cic.

prō-iciō, icere, iēci, iectum [iaciō]. **I.** *to throw or fling forwards ;* and in *Mid.* or with *Refl. Pron., to rush forwards.* **1.** Lit.: aquilam intra vallum, Caes. ; glaebas in ignem, Caes. ; caestūs in medium, Verg. ; clipeum prae se, Liv. ; se ex navi, Caes. ; se in forum, Liv. **2.** Transf. of hasty action : proiectis ac proditis ad inconsultam pugnam legionibus, Caes. ; se in iudicium, Cic. ; epistulae tuae monent ne me proiciam, Cic. Ep. **II.** *to throw or fling forwards, on one's face, prostrate.* **1.** Lit.: se ad pedes alicui, Caes. ; se ad pedes alicuius, Cic. ; se ad genua alicuius, Liv. ; se super aliquem, Verg. ; effigiem, Tac. **2.** Transf.: in miserias proiectus sum, Sall. ; se in fletūs, Liv. ; senatūs auctoritatem, Tac. **III.** *to cast or put forward, make to project, extend.* **1.** Lit.: hastam, Nep. ; tectum, Cic. In *Mid.* : urbs proiecta in altum, Cic. **2.** Transf. (in time) *to put off :* qui ultra quinquennium proiciantur, Tac. **IV.** *to fling out in public, to expose.* **1.** Lit.: par-vam, Pl. ; se inhumatum, Cic. ; Liv. **2.** Transf. *to forsake, abandon :* aliquem, Caes. **V.** *to fling forth* (only transf. of words, with Acc. and *Inf.*), *to blurt out :* Liv. **VI.** *to fling forth and away, expel.* **1.** Lit.: arma, Caes. ; tantam pestem, Cic. ; aliquem ab urbe, Ov. ; Agrippam in insu-lam, Tac. **2.** Transf.: patriam virtutem, Caes. ; libertatem, Cic. ; pudorem, Ov. ; animas, Verg. ; spem salutis, Plin. Ep.

prōiecticius, a, um [prōiciō], *cast out, ex-posed :* puella, Pl.

prōiectiō, ōnis, *f.* [prōiciō], *a throwing for-wards :* bracchi, Cic.

prōiectō, āre [*freq.* prōiciō], *to reproach, assail :* aliquem probris, Pl.

prōiectū, Abl. *sing. m.* [prōiciō], *by a jutting out :* corporis, Lucr.

prōiectus, a, um. **I.** *Part.* prōiciō. **II.** **A.** *jutting out, projecting.* **1.** Lit.: saxa, Verg. ; ova, Liv. *Comp.* : venter, Suet. **2.** Transf.: audacia, Cic. **B.** *prostrate.* **1.** Lit. of persons : Caes., Cic. **2.** Transf. **a.** *abject, contemptible :* alga, Verg. ; consulare imperium, Liv. ; pati-entia, Tac. **b.** *downcast :* vultus, Tac. **c.** (excessively) *prone :* ad audendum, Cic. *Sup.* : Tac.

pro-inde and **proin** (monosyl. or disyl.), *onward from this point*, hence, *consequently, accordingly*. **a.** Alone (usually first word and with *Imperat.* or *Jussive Subj.*) : Pl., Cic., Verg., etc. **b.** With *ut* or *quam* : *accordingly as, exactly as, just as* : proinde ut quisque fortunā utitur, ita praecellet, Pl. ; Lucr. ; Liv. ; si proinde amentur mulieres diu quam lavant, Pl. **c.** With *quasi* or *atque (ac) si* and *Subj.* : *exactly as if* : Ter.. Caes., Cic. Ep., Liv. With *ac* for *ac si* : Lucr.

prō-lābor, lābi, lāpsus. **I.** *to glide, slip, or move gradually forwards*. **1.** Lit. : *Canis ad caudam serpens Argo, Cic. poet.* ; elephanti, Liv. **2.** Transf.: me longius prolapsum esse quam eto., Cic. ; ad istam orationem, Cic. ; ad seditiones, Tac. ; in misericordiam animus, Liv. ; Tac. **II.** *to fall forwards on one's face, headlong*, or *prostrate*. **1.** Lit.: ex equo, Liv. ; per caput equi, Liv. ; Hylas, Prop. Of things: Pergama, Verg. ; Laudicea tremore terrae, Tac. **2.** Transf.: huc mulieris libido est prolapsa ut eto., Cic. ; timore, Cic. ; cupiditate regni, Liv. ; studio magnificentiae, Tac. ; clade Romanum imperium, Liv. **III.** *to slip forth* or *out*. Transf. of words : ab aliquā cupiditate verbum, Cic.

prōlāpsiō, ōnis, *f.* [prōlābor], *a falling*. **1.** Lit.: in *pl.*: aedificiorum, Suet. **2.** Transf.: Cic.

prōlāpsus, a, um, *Part.* prōlābor.

prōlātiō, ōnis, *f.* [prōferō]. **I.** *a carrying forwards, enlargement* : finium, Liv. **II.** *a putting off, postponement* : Tac. ; diei, Caes. ; iudici, Cic. In *pl.* : Pl., Tac. **III.** *a citing* : exemplorum, Cic.

prōlātō, āre [*freq.* prōferō]. **I.** *to extend, enlarge*: effugium, Lucr. ; agros, Tac. ; vitam, Tac. **II.** Of time : *to put off, postpone* : Cic., Liv. ; diem ex die, Tac. ; dies, Sall. ; bellum, Sall., Tac.

prōlātus, a, um, *Part.* prōferō.

prōlectō, āre [*freq.* prōliciō], *to allure, entice, incite* : egentis spe largitionis, Cic. ; Pl. ; praeda animos, Ov.

prōlēs, is, *f.* [prō and *ol* in adolēsco, *etc.*], *offspring, progeny, scion*. **1.** Lit. **a.** In gen.: Lucr., Verg., Hor., Ov. Rarely in prose : Sall. **b.** Of partic. individuals: *offspring*, i.e. *child* or *descendant* : Verg., Hor., etc. **c.** *a race, stock* : Ausonia, Verg. ; aenea, argentea, Ov. Esp. of the *young manhood of the race* : law in Cic. ; Verg. **2.** Transf. of plants: olivae, Verg.

prōlētārius, ī, *m.* [prōlēs], us. *pl.*, proletarii, *the proletariat* (the lowest class in the Servian arrangement) : Enn., Cic., Liv. As Adj.: sermo, Pl.

prō-liciō, licere, lixī [laciō], *to entice forth, incite* : amos me huc, Pl. ; voluptatem, Ov. ; aliquem ad spem, Tac.

prōlixē, *adv.* **1.** Lit.: *widely-stretching* : capillus passus prolixe, Ter. **2.** Transf. *liberally, readily* and *willingly* : Cic. Comp.: Ter., Suet.

prō-lixus, a, um [laxus], *stretching forwards and far, widely-stretching, extended*. **1.** Lit.: barba, Verg. ; comae, Ov. ; caudae, arbores, Varr. ; ictus, Lucr. ; ramus, Suet. ;

prolixo corpore erat, Suet. *Comp.* : Varr. **2.** Transf. **a.** Of character : *liberal, generous, ready* and *willing* : animus, natura, Cic. Ep. ; in aliquem, Cic. Ep. *Comp.* : Cic. Ep. **b.** Of circumstances : *favourable* : Cato, Cic. Ep.

prōlocūtus, a, um, *Part.* prōloquor.

prōlogus, ī, *m.* [πρόλογος], *a preface to a play, a prologue*. **1.** Lit. : Ter., Quint. **2.** Transf. *the actor who speaks it* : Ter.

prō-loquor, loqui, locūtus, *to speak out* or *openly* : Pl., Prop. With Acc. : Pl., Enn. Rarely in prose : with Acc. and *Inf.* : Liv. ; with *Indir. Quest.* : Auct. B. Afr.

prōlubium, ī, *n.* [lubet], *fancy, inclination* : Ter.

prō-lūdō, ere, *to play beforehand, to spar, prelude*. **1.** Lit. : Ov. ; ad pugnam, Verg. **2.** Transf.: sententiis, Cic. ; iurgia, Juv.

prō-luō, luere, luī, lūtum, **I.** With Acc. of thing flushed : *to wash out, flush* : in vivo rore manūs, Ov. Poet. of drinking : leni praecordia mulso, Hor. ; Verg. Comic.: cloacam (i.e. ventrem), Pl. **II.** With Acc. of thing washed forth or away : *to wash* or *flood forth* or *away* : genus omne natantum litore in extremo fluctus proluit, Verg. ; tempestas ex montibus nivis, Caes. ; silvas Eridanus, Verg.

prōlūsiō, ōnis, *f.* [prōlūdō], *a prelude to a contest, preliminary sparring* : Cic.

prōluviēs, ēī, *f.* [prōluō]. **I.** *a flood* : Lucr., Cic. Ep. **II.** *offscourings, discharge* : alvi, Lucr. ; ventris, Verg.

prō-mercālis, e, *adj.* [merx], *that is bought and sold* : vestes, Suet.

prō-mereō, ēre, and **prōmereor**, ērī, *to deserve, merit* (either in good or bad sense). **a.** In gen.: aliquid, Pl. ; optume, Pl. ; reus levius punitus quam sit ille promeritus, Cic. ; poenam, Ov. With *ut* and *Subj.* : Pl. **b.** With *de* or *absol.*, *to deserve one's gratitude* (with or without *bene*) : Pl. ; bene de multis, Cic. ; ego te plurima nunquam negabo promeritam, Verg. **c.** With Acc. of person or his feelings : *to earn the goodwill of, to win over, gain* : socios, Suet. ; omnium voluntatem, Suet.

prōmeritum, ī, *n.* [prōmereor], *desert* (good or evil). **a.** *merit* : Lucr., Cic., Ov. **b.** *guilt* : Pl., Auct. B. Afr.

Promētheus (trisyl.), eī and eos, *m.*, *s.* of *Iapetus* and *Clymene*, *b.* of *Epimetheus*, and *f.* of *Deucalion*. *He taught mankind the use of fire, thereby incurring the anger of Jupiter* ; **Promēthēus**, a, um ; **Promēthīdēs** (or Promēthiadēs), ae, *m.* *son of Prometheus*, i.e. *Deucalion*.

prōminēns, entis. **I.** *Part.* prōmineō. **II.** Adj.: *projecting, prominent* : collis, Liv. **III.** Noun, **prōminēns**, entis, *n.*, *a projection, headland* : litoris, Tac.

prō-mineō, ēre, uī, *to jut forwards* or *out, hang forward, extend*. **1.** Lit.: matres de muro, Caes. ; Phaselis in altum, Liv. ; Ov. ; coma in vultūs, Ov. **2.** Transf.: iustitia foras, Cic. ; gloria in posteritatem, Liv.

prōmiscam (Pl.) and **prōmiscē** (Cic., Liv.) and **prōmiscuē** (Caes., Cic., Liv.), *adv. in common, indiscriminately*.

prōmiscuus (and **prōmiscus**, Liv.), a, um [misceō], *mixed, haphazard, common, indiscriminate, promiscuous.* **1.** Lit. **A.** In gen.: opera, Pl.; caedes, conubia, etc., Liv.; Sall.; multitudo, sepultura, etc., Tac. *Neut.* as Noun: in promiscuo. **a.** With habere: *to hold in common* : Liv. **b.** With spectare: *to have seats in common* (i.e. not reserved) *at shows* : Liv. **c.** With esse: *to be open to all and sundry* : dictatura, licentia, Liv.; arma, Tac. **B.** Gramm.: *common* : nomen, Quint. **2.** Transf. *common, ordinary.* As Noun: promiscua ac vilia mercari, Tac.

prōmissiō, ōnis, *f.* [prōmittō], *a promising, promise* : Cic.

prōmissor, ōris, *m.* [prōmittō], *a promiser* : Hor., Quint.

prōmissus, a, um. **I.** *Part.* prōmittō. **II.** Adj.: *that has been let grow,* hence, *hanging down, long* : capillus, Caes.; barba, Verg., Liv. **III.** Noun, **prōmissum**, i, *n*: *a promise* : facere, exigere, servare, Cic.; dare, Cat.; praestare, Liv.; absolvere, Varr.; promissis manere, Cic., Verg.

prō-mittō, mittere, mīsi, missum (prōmīstī for prōmisistī, Cat.; prōmisse for prōmīsisse, Cat.) **I.** *to let go forwards or forth, to let grow* : capillum ac barbam, Liv. **II.** *to put off* ; hence, *to promise.* **a.** Of payment, gifts, etc.: donum, Pl., Ov.; donum alicui, Cic.; auxilium alicui, Ov. With *Inf.* : Pl., Caes. **b.** *to promise, undertake, engage* or *pledge oneself* : me ultorem, Verg.; of dining engagements, etc.: ad fratrem, Cic.; ad cenam alicui, Phaedr. With Acc. and *Fut. Inf.* : Pl., Cic., Hor., etc. With Acc. and *Gerundive* : Liv. **c.** *to engage* (*oneself*), *answer for* : de alicuius voluntate, Cic. Ep.; Hor.

prōmō, prōmere, prōmpsi, prōmptum [prō emō], *to bring forth or out* from the stores. **1.** Lit.: illi vinum, Pl.; pecuniam ex aerario, Cic.; Liv.; vina dolio, Hor. **2.** Transf. **a.** tela e pharetrā, Ov; vaginā pugionem, Tac. With *Refl.* Pron. : cavo se robore promunt, Verg. **b.** *to bring* or *put forth* : argumenta, Cic.; vīris, Verg.; obscura, Hor.; in scaenam, Hor.; in publicum, Tac. **c.** *to bring to light, disclose* : percontanti omnia, Pl.; consilia, Cic. Ep.; quae acta essent, Liv.; clienti iura, Hor.

prōmontorium, *v.* prōmunturium.

prōmōta, ōrum, *n. pl.* [prōmoveō] (= the Stoic προηγμένα, *·cf.* producta): *things preferred, preferable things,* next after absolute good : Cic.

prō-moveō, movēre, mōvī, mōtum. **I.** *to move forwards, cause to advance.* **1.** Lit.: saxa vectibus, Caes.; castra ad Carthaginem, Liv.; legiones, Hirt.; unum pedem triclinio, Phaedr. **2.** Transf. **a.** *to advance* matters, *do some good* : nihil promoveris, Ter.; promoveo parum praesens, Ter. **b.** *to promote, advance* : ad amplissimas procurationes, Plin. Ep.; Curt. **II.** *to bring to light, reveal* : arcana loco, Hor. **III.** *to advance in extent, enlarge.* **1.** Lit.: imperium, Ov.; aggerem ad urbem, Liv. **2.** Transf. **a.** doctrina vim insitam, Hor. **b.** In time : *to put off, postpone* : nuptias, Ter.

prompte, *adv.* **1.** *readily, quickly* : Tac. Comp. : Tac. Sup. : Plin. Ep. **2.** *easily.* Comp. : Juv.

prōmptō, āre [*freq.* prōmō], *to give out, distribute* : thensauros Iovis, Pl.

prōmptū, ABL. *sing. m.* [prōmō], only in phr. in promptu. **a.** *in readiness, ready to hand* (lit. or transf.): omnia quae in promptu erant diripuerunt, Liv.; ea dicam quae mihi sunt in promptu, Cic. **b.** *in easiness, easy* : quadrupedes in promptu regere est, Ov.; Sall. **c.** *in evidence, manifest* : ut decorum sit in promptu, Cic.; in promptu est (with Acc. and *Inf.*), Lucr. With gerere, ponere, habere, etc. : *to show, display* : iram gerere, Pl.; aliquid ponere, Cic.; ingenium habere, Sall.; Ov.

prōmptuārius, a, um [prōmō], *distributing* : armarium, Cato. Comic. : cella (i.e. prison), Pl.

prōmptus, a, um. **I.** *Part.* prōmō. **II.** Adj.: *brought out* ; hence, **I.** *at hand, ready.* **1.** Lit.: sagittae, Ov.; Tac. **2.** Transf. **a.** *ready, prompt, resolute* : homo, fides, Cic.; eloquentia, Tac. With defining ABL.: ingenio, manu, Liv.; or Loc.: animi, Tac. With *ad* or *in* and Acc.: ad pericula, Cic.; ad lacessendum certamen, Liv.; ad bella suscipienda animus, Caes.; Cic. Ep.; in pavorem, in spem, Tac. With *in* and ABL.: celeritas in agendo, Cic.; Nep. With *pro* : pro patriā, Liv. With *adversus* : adversus insontis, Tac. With DAT.: libertati aut ad mortem animus, Tac.; veniae dandae, Liv. With *Inf.* : Luc. Comp. : Cic., Liv., etc. Sup.: Cic., Sall. *Masc.* as Noun : Caes. **b.** *easy, practicable* : defensio, Cic.; moenia oppugnanti, Liv.; mortis via, Tac. Sup.: Tac.; promptum est, with *Inf.* : Ov. **c.** *brought to light* ; *evident, manifest* : Enn., Cic., Sall. [It. *pronto*.]

prōmulgātiō, ōnis, *f.* [prōmulgō], *a making publicly known, a promulgation* : Cic.

prōmulgō, āre, *to put up public notice of* **a.** a bill or law, *to make known, publish* : rogationem, Cic.; legem, Liv. **b.** other things : proelia, Enn.; Cic.

prō-mulsis, idis, *f.* [mulsum], *a relish* of eggs, salt fish, mead, etc., served first at a Roman banquet : Cic. Ep.

prōmus, i, *m.* [prōmō], *a cellarer, steward, butler.* **1.** Lit.: Pl., Varr., Hor. **2.** Transf.: ego meo sum promus pectori, Pl.

prō-mūtuus, a, um, *advanced as a loan* : insequentis anni vectigal, Caes.

prōnē, *adv.* in *a sloping fashion* : Caes.

prō-nepōs, ōtis, *m. a great-grandson* : Cic., Ov.

prō-neptis, is, *f. a great-granddaughter* : Pers.

pronoea, ae, *f.* [πρόνοια], *providence* : pure Lat. providentia : Cic.

prō-nōmen, inis, *n. a pronoun* : Varr., Quint.

prōnuba, ae, *f.* [nubō]. **1.** Lit. **a.** *a matron who attended to the necessary arrangements of a wedding on the part of the bride* (*cf.* auspex) : Cat. **b.** Epithet of Juno, as goddess of marriage : Verg., Ov. **2.** Transf. **a.** Of Bellona as presiding over a marriage in which the bride is obtained by war: Verg. **b.** Of Tisiphone, where the marriage has proved unhappy: Ov. **c.** Of nox: Claud.

prōnūntiātiō, ōnis, *f.* [prōnūntiō], *a public declaration, proclamation.* **A.** In gen.: facere, Caes. Of the verdict of a court: Cic. **B. a.** Rhet.: *delivery, action :* Cic., Quint., etc. **b.** In logic: *a proposition :* Cic.

prōnūntiātor, ōris, *m.* [prōnūntiō], *a relater :* rerum gestarum, Cic.

prōnūntiātum, ī, *n.* [prōnūntiō]. In logic, *a proposition :* Cic.

prō-nūntiō, āre, *to make publicly known, to proclaim, announce.* **1.** Lit. **A.** In gen.: sententiam, leges, etc., Cic.; proelium in posterum diem, Liv. With Acc. and *Inf. :* Cic. With *ut* or *ne* and *Jussive Subj. :* Caes. **B.** In partic. **a.** Of an election: aliquem praetorem, Liv. **b.** *to put to the vote :* sententiam alicuius, Caes. **2.** Transf. **a.** *to recite, declaim :* versūs multos, Cic.; Quint.; Plin. Ep. **b.** *to declare:* aliquid, Caes., Cic. With Acc. and *Predic. Part. :* iam capta castra, Caes. With *Indir. Quest. :* Caes. **c.** *to announce* by way of prediction, promise, etc. : ut ipse pronuntiaverat, Caes.; pecuniam pro reo, Cic.; praemia militi, Liv.

prō-nurus, ūs, *f. a grandson's wife :* Ov.

prōnus, a, um [prō], *leaning, stooping, bending forwards.* **1.** Lit. **a.** pronus pendens in verbera, Verg.; Ov. **b.** *face-forwards* or *-downwards, headlong, downwards :* volvitur in caput, Verg.; ille iacens pronus matri dedit oscula Terrae, Ov.; prona et terram spectantia, Juv.; motus corporis, Cic. Of things: ilex paululum modo prona, dein flexa, Sall.; tigna, Caes.; urbs prona in paludes, Liv.; amnis, Verg.; via, Ov. Esp. of haste: *flying headlong :* currus, Ov.; leporem pronum catulo sectare, Ov. **c.** Of the setting of heavenly bodies: *sloping, sinking :* Orion, Hor.; Ov.; sidera, Prop. Also, annus, menses, Hor. **2.** Transf. **a.** *inclined, disposed :* anxitudo prona ad luctum, Cic.; boves ad domandum, Varr.; in obsequium, Hor.; deterioribus, Tac. *Comp. :* aures offensioni proniores, Tac. With GEN.: ruendi in ferrum mens, Luc. **b.** *inclined to favour :* misericordiā in Germanicum pronior, Tac.; Suet.; omnia victoribus, Tac.; pronis auribus accipere aliquid, Tac.; Luc. **c.** *easy, without difficulty :* omnia virtuti suae prona esse, Sall.; ad honores iter, Plin. Ep.; pronum est (with *Inf.*): Tac.; Luc. *Comp. :* id pronius ad fidem est, Liv.

prooemior, ārī [prooemium], *to make an introduction* or *preface :* Plin. Ep.

prooemium, ī, *n.* [προοίμιον]. **I.** *a prelude.* **1.** Lit.: citharoedi, Cic. **2.** Transf.: rixae, Juv. **II.** *a preface :* Cic., Quint.

propāgātiō, ōnis, *f.* [propāgō], *a spreading, propagation.* **1.** Lit. of plants: vitium, Cic. **2.** Transf. **a.** Of race: Cic.; nominis, Cic. **b.** Of territory: finium imperi, Cic. **c.** In time: *extension :* vitae, Cic.

propāgātor, ōris, *m.* [propāgō], *an enlarger :* provinciae, Cic. Ep.

propāgō, āre [prō and root of pangō]. **1.** Lit. of plants: *to spread, extend by slips* or *layers* which were fastened down : Cato, Plin. **2.** Transf. **a.** Of race: *to continue by generation, propagate :* stirpem, Cic.; prolem, Lucr. **b.** Of territory: *to extend :* finis imperi, Cic.; terminos urbis, Tac.; Liv. **c.** In time: *to extend, prolong :* vitam, Cic.; haec posteritati propagantur, Cic.; imperium consuli in annum, Liv.

propāgō (Verg. has prō- in sense of *a layer* or *set ;* and prō- in sense of *offspring, race*), inis, *f.* [*v.* propāgō above]. **1.** Lit. **a.** *a set, layer* of a plant: Cic. **b.** *a slip* or *shoot :* Verg., Hor. **2.** Transf.: *offspring, race, posterity :* Lucr.; de stirpe dei, Ov.; Romana, Verg.; clarorum virorum propagines, Nep.; catulorum, Lucr. [It. *propaggine ;* Fr. *provin.*]

prō-palam, *adv. openly, publicly :* Pl., Cic., Liv., Tac.

prō-patulus, a, um, *open to public view, clear.* **1.** Lit.: locus, Cic. As Noun, **prōpatulum**, ī, *n. an open space :* in propatulo aedium, Liv. **2.** Transf. (as Noun): pudicitiam in propatulo habere, Sall.; Tac.

prope, *adv.* and *prep.* (*Comp.* **propius** *; Sup.* **proximē**, older **proxumē**) [prō and suffix -pe seen in nempe]. **I.** Adv. **a.** Of place: *near, nigh, hard by :* Pl., Cic. With ABL. (with or without *ab*) *: bellum tam prope a Siciliā, Cic.; quam proxime castris, Caes.; Nep. With *ad :* prope ad portas sunt hostes, Liv. With verbs of motion: accessit propius, Caes.; Cic.; with *ad* or Acc.: prope ad aliquem adire, Pl.; propius muros accessit, Nep.; Pl.; Cic. Also *from near :* intueri aliquid, Cic. *Comp. :* Verg.; Hor. **b.** Of time: *near, not far off :* Pl., Ter., Liv. *Sup. :* Caes. **c.** Of abstract or gen. proximity: *nearly, almost ;* prope desperatis rebus, Cic.; prope funeratus arboris ictu, Hor.; iam prope erat, ut sinistrum cornu pelleretur, Liv.; Hannibalis vix senescebat et prope ad nihilum venerat in Liv. With *atque :* proxi me atque ille, Cic. Ep. **II.** Prep. with Acc. **a.** Of place: *near, hard by :* prope oppidum, Caes.; prope amnem, Verg. *Comp. :* Caes., Liv. *Sup. :* Sall., Liv. **b.** Of time: *nigh, towards, about :* prope maturitatem, Liv.; prope lucem, Suet. **c.** Of abstract proximity: *near to, not far from :* prope metum res fuerat, Liv.; prope seditionem ventum est, Tac.; propius est fidem, Liv.; Sall. *Sup. :* proxime morem Romanum, Liv.

propediem, *adv. at an early date, very soon, shortly :* Pl., Cic., Liv.

prō-pellō (propellat, Lucr.), pellere, puli, pulsum. **I.** *to drive, push,* or *urge forwards.* **1.** Lit.: aliquem praecipem, Pl.; navem remis, Cic.; in profundum e scopulo corpora, Ov.; pecora paputn, Liv.; aëra prae se, Lucr. **2.** Transf. *to impel :* corpus, Lucr.; terrore carceris ad voluntariam mortem, Tac. **II.** *to drive forth and away (from).* **1.** Lit.: hostis, Caes.; hostem a castris, Liv. **2.** Transf.: periculum vitae ab aliquo, Liv.

prope-modo (Pl., Liv.) and **prope-modum**, (Pl., Cic.), *adv. nearly, almost.*

prŏ-pendĕō, pendĕre, pendi, pēnsum, *to hang forth, hang down* (esp. of scales). **1.** Lit.: lanx, Cic. **2.** Transf. **a.** *to have the preponderance :* si bona propendent, Cic.; Pl. **b.** *to be inclined* or *disposed to :* Cic. Esp. favourably : in aliquem, Cic.

prŏpēnsē, *adv. willingly, readily :* Lentul. ap. Cic. Ep. *Comp. :* Liv.

prŏpēnsiō, ōnis, *f.* [prōpendĕō], *inclination, propensity :* ad summum bonum adipiscendum, Cic.

prŏpēnsus, a, um. **I.** *Part.* prōpendĕō. **II.** Adj. **a.** *weighty, important. Comp. :* Pl., Cic. **b.** *inclining towards. Comp. :* ad veritatis similitudinem, Cic. **c,** *inclined, disposed :* animus ad salutem alicuius, Cic.; ad bene merendum, Cic.; in alteram partem, Cic. *Comp. :* Cic. Esp. *favourably disposed :* propenso animo aliquid facere, Cic.; Liv.; Ov. *Sup. :* propensissimā civitatum voluntate, Auct. B. Alex.

properanter, *adv. hastily, speedily :* Lucr., Tac. *Comp. :* Sall., Ov.

properantia, ae, *f.* (Sall., Tac.) and **properātiō**, ōnis, *f.* (Cic. Ep., Sall.) [propĕrō], *haste.*

properātus, a, um. **I.** *Part.* properō. **II.** Adj.: *hastened, speedy :* mors, tabellae, Ov.; naves, tela, Tac. As Noun, **properātum**, ī, *n. haste :* properato opus est, Pl., Cic., Sall. **ABL. properātō** as *Adv. : in haste, speedily :* Tac.

propĕrē, *adv. hastily, in haste :* Pl., Sall., Hor., Liv.

properi-pēs, pedis, *adj. of speeding foot :* dux, Cat.

propĕrō, āre [properus]. **A.** Trans.: *to prepare with haste, hasten, accelerate :* opsonia, Pl.; iter, Sall., Tac.; fulmina, Verg.; pecuniam heredi, Hor.; mortem, Verg. **B.** Intrans.: *to make haste, to hasten :* Pl., Tac.; negoti causā properare, Sall.; ad praedam, ad gloriam, Caes.; in Italiam, Caes.; Romam, Cic.; sacris, Ov. With *Inf. :* Pl., Caes., Cic., Hor. *Pass. Impers. :* Cic., Verg.

Propertius, ī, *m. :* Sex. Aurelius Propertius, *a celebrated elegiac poet of the Augustan period.*

properus, a, um [root seen in parō], *speedy, hastening :* auriga, Verg.; Ov. With *Gen. :* oblatae occasionis, Tac. With *Inf. :* Tac.

prō-pexus, a, um, *combed forward :* barba, Verg.; ad pectora barba, Ov.

propīnātiō, ōnis, *f.* [propīnō], *a drinking to a person's health :* Sen. In *pl. : challenges to drink :* Sen.

propīnō (**prō-**, Pl., Ter., Mart.), āre [προπίνω], *to drink to a person's health, to give a toast.* **1.** Lit.: magnum poculum, Pl.; salutem, Pl.; propino hoc pulchro Critiae, Cic. **2.** Transf. **a.** *to give to drink :* conditum Sabinum, Mart. **b.** *to pass on* (like a cup), i.e. hand over to be finished : hunc vobis, Ter.

propinquē, *adv. near at hand :* Pl.

propinquĭtās, ātis, *f.* [propinquus], *nearness.* **1.** Lit. of place : Cic.; hostium, Caes.; silvarum ac fluminum propinquitates (i.e.

the near parts), Caes. ; ex propinquitate pugnare, Caes. **2.** Transf. **a.** *relationship :* si pietate propinquitas colitur, Cic.; nobilis, Nep.; arta, Plin. Ep. In *pl. :* Cic. **b.** *intimacy, friendship :* ad probos propinquitate se adiungere, Pl.

propinquō, āre [propinquus]. **A.** Intrans. *to draw near, approach.* **1.** Lit. of place : hostes, Liv. With *Dat. :* scopulo, Verg.; terrae classis, Liv.; domui ignis, Tac. With *Acc. :* amnem, Sall.; campos, Tac. **2.** Transf. of time : Parcarum dies, Verg. **B.** Trans. *to bring near, speed on :* augurium, Verg.

propinquus (**-uos**), a, um [prope]. **1.** Lit. of place, *near, neighbouring :* praedium, Cic.; Ter.; Hor., etc. With *Gen. :* ex propinquis itineris locis, Liv.; Nep. *Comp. :* exsilium paulo propinquius, Ov. *Neut.* as Noun : in (ex) propinquo, *in (from) a near position* or *the neighbourhood :* castra in p. sunt, Liv.; ex p. aspicere, cognoscere, etc., Liv. **2.** Transf. **A.** Of time : partitudo, Pl.; mors, Cic.; spes, Liv.; vespera, Tac. **B.** Of abstract relations. **a.** Of resemblance : motūs his animi perturbationibus, Cic. **b.** Of relationship : *near, related :* with *Dat. :* tibi genere, Sall.; Verg. As Noun, **propinquus**, ī, *m.*, esp. in *pl. relations, kinsmen :* Cic., Hor. Also *fem.* **propinqua**, ae, *a (female) relation :* Caes., Cic.

propior, ius, *Comp.*, and **proximus** (older **proxumus**), a, um, *Sup. adj.* [prope]. **I.** **propior. 1.** Lit. of place : *nearer :* Lucr., Sall., Verg., Liv. Prov.: tunica propior pallio est, Pl. With *Dat. :* Oceano India, Verg.; Ov. With *ab :* ab igne stetit, Sen. Ep. With *Acc. :* propior montem, Sall.; Hirt. *Neut. pl.* as Noun : propiora tenere, Verg.; propiora fluminis, Tac. **2.** Transf. **A.** Of time : *nearer,* i.e. more recent : epistula, Cic. Ep.; mors, Tib. With *Dat. :* funeri, Hor. *Neut. pl.* as Noun : Cic. **B.** Of abstract relations. **a.** Of relationship : gradu propior sanguinis, Ov.; Hor. With *Dat. :* alicui, Cic. **b.** Of resemblance : *more liable.* With *Dat. :* sceleri propiora quam religioni, Cic.; Verg.; Liv., etc. *Neut. pl.* as Noun : Hor. **c.** In gen.: *affecting* or *concerning more nearly, of greater import, more intimate :* societas, Cic.; cura, Ov.; sua sibi propiora pericula esse quam mea, Cic.; irae, timori, Tac. **II.** **proximus** (older **proxumus**), a, um [perh. for prop-i-simus], *nearest, next.* **1.** Lit. of place : vicinus, Pl.; paries, Hor.; oppida, Caes.; via, Lucr., Cic.; iter in Galliam, Caes. With *Dat. :* Germanis, Caes.; ponti villula, Hor. With *Acc. :* proximi Rhenum, Caes.; Pl.; Liv. With *ab :* dactylus proximus a postremo, Cic.; Liv.; Ov. *Neut.* as Noun, **proximum**, ī, *the neighbourhood :* Pl., Ter.; traicit in proxima continentis, Liv. **2.** Transf. **A.** Of time : *next (before or following) : previous, last, next :* quid proximā, quid superiore nocte egeris, Cic.; censor proximus ante me, Cic. ; se proximā nocte castra moturum, Caes; Cic.; proximis Nonis, cum venissemus, Cic. *Neut.* **ABL. proximō** as *Adv., very lately :* Cic. Ep.

B. Of other relations. **a.** Of order, rank, etc. : *next :* proximus huic insequitur Salius, Verg. ; Cic. ; proximos illi honores, Hor. ; proximum est ut etc., *the next point is e°c.,* Cic. **b.** Of resemblance : *most like :* ficta voluptatis causâ sint proxima veris, Hor. ; Cic. ; Verg., etc. **c.** Of relationship or connexion : *nearest, next of kin :* illi genere proxumus, Ter. ; cognatione, Cic. ; Nep, As Noun, **proximi,** ōrum, *m. pl. nearest relatives :* Cic., Phaedr. ; also, *intimate friends :* Cic. **d.** *nearest at hand,* i.e. most convenient : eamus ad me ; ibi proxumum est, ubi mutes, Ter.

propitiō, āre [propitius], *to render favourable, to appease :* Venerem, Pl. ; Tac. ; suum genium, Tac. ; manis, Suet.

propitius, a, um [prope], *favourable, gracious, well-disposed :* homini di sunt propitii, Pl. ; Cic. Of persons : Ter., Cic., Liv. Of things : propitio flumine, Liv. ; pax, Pl. ; voluntas, Nep.

propius, *comp. adv.* and *prep., v.* prope. [Fr, *proche.*]

propnigēum, i, n. [προπνίγειον], *the heating-room of a bath :* Plin. Ep.

Prōpoetides, um, *f. pl. Cyprian girls, who, having denied the divinity of Venus, were turned to stone.*

propōla, ae, *m.* [προπώλης], *a retailer, huckster :* Pl., Cic.

prō-polluō, ere, *to defile or pollute further :* Tac.

prō-pōnō, pōnere, posui, positum, *to put, place,* or *set forwards* or *forth to view, to display to view.* **1.** Lit. **a.** In gen. : vexillum, edictum, Caes. ; ediscendos fastos populo, Cic. ; legem in publicum, Cic. ; mensas palam, Cic. ; pugnae honorem, Verg. **b.** For sale : aliquid venale, Cic. ; haec aliquâ columnâ, Prop. **2.** Transf. **a.** *to set forwards, expose :* omnibus telis fortunae vitam, Cic. Ep. **b.** *to set forth* to the mind, *to publish :* rem gestam, Caes. ; Cic. ; in exemplum, Quint. With *Indir. Quest. :* Caes., Cic. With *de :* Caes. **c.** *to offer, hold forth* as promise or threat : praemium, Cic. ; Suet. ; improbis poenam, Cic. ; mortem sibi ante oculos, Liv. **d.** *to set forth* as a mental picture ; *to imagine :* eam vitam ante oculos vestros, Cic. ; spem, Cic. ; vim fortunae animo, Liv. ; sibi aliquem ad imitandum, Cic. **e.** *to lay before* oneself, *intend, purpose, design :* id quod animo proposuerat, Caes. ; Cic. Ep. With *Inf. :* proposituram est mihi hoc facere, Cic. With *ut* and *Subj. :* propositum est, ut eloquentiam meam perspicias, Cic. **f.** In logic : *to state the first premiss of a syllogism :* Cic.

Propontis, idos and idis, *f. the small sea between the Hellespont and the Thracian Bosporus, now the Sea of Marmora ;* **Propontiacus,** a, um.

prō-porrō, *adv.* **I.** *furthermore :* Lucr. **II.** *utterly, wholly :* Lucr.

prō-portiō, ōnis, *f. symmetry, analogy :* Cic., Quint.

prōpositiō, ōnis, *f.* [prōpōnō], *a placing before.* Transf. **a.** *an intention, purpose :* vitae, Cic. **b.** In logic : *the first premiss of a syllogism :* Cic. Hence **i.** *a theme :* Cic., Quint. **ii.** *a proposition* of any kind : Quint.

prōpositus, a, um. **I.** *Part.* prōpōnō. **II.** Noun, **prōpositum,** i, *n.* **a.** *a plan, intention, design, purpose :* habere, Caes. ; tenere, Caes., Liv. ; adsequi, Cic. ; iter a proposito diversum erat, Caes. ; tenax propositi, Hor. ; vitae, Phaedr. With *Obj. Gen. :* reprehendendi, Plin. Ep. **b.** *a theme :* a proposito aberrare, egredi, declinare, Cic. ; a proposito aversus, Liv. ; ad propositum redire, reverti, Cic. **c.** *the first premiss of a syllogism,* Cic.

prō praetōre or **prō-praetor,** ōris, *m.* **I.** *one who after his praetorship* had extension of office. **a.** With army (e.g. in Italy during Hannibalic War) : prorogatum Tubulo est ut pro praetore in Etruriam succederet Calpurnio, Liv. ; *cum bella* a propraetoribus administrantur, Cic. **b.** As governor of a province : M. Antonius Macedoniae propraetor, Cic. ; Caes. **II.** *one acting for the praetor* or *with praetorian rank ; a vice-praetor :* Labienus legatus pro praetore, Caes. ; Aulo fratre in castris pro praetore relictus, Sall. ; Liv.

propriē, *adv.* **I.** *in the proper* or *strict sense :* Cic., Liv. **II.** *strictly for oneself, all one's own :* Cic., Hor. **III.** *peculiarly, especially :* Quint.

proprietās, ātis, *f.* [proprius]. **I.** *a property, peculiarity.* **a.** In gen. : terrae caelique, Liv. ; frugum proprietates, Liv. ; Cic. **b.** Of words : *proper meaning :* Quint. **II.** *ownership :* iumenti, Suet.

propritim, *adv. properly, specifically :* Lucr.

proprius, a, um. **I.** Lit. **A.** *one's own, one's very own, peculiarly* or *exclusively one's own* (esp. with *Possess. Pron.*) : fines, Caes. ; libri, Hor. ; vires, Liv. ; tria praedia Capitoni propria traduntur, Cic. ; sua propria bona malaque, Liv. ; Caes. ; Cic. *Neut.* as Noun : Phaedr. **B.** *characteristic, peculiar, personal.* **a.** In gen. : libertatem propriam Romano generi, Cic. ; Tac. ; id non proprium senectutis est vitium sed commune valetudinis, Cic. ; contumelia, Liv. ; ira, Tac. *Neut.* as Noun : hoc proprium populi R. longe a domo bellare, Cic. ; Caes. **b.** Of words : certa ac propria vocabula, Cic. ; nomen, Cic. **2.** Transf. *lasting, permanent, continuous :* Pl., Cic., Verg., etc.

propter, *adv.* and *prep.* [prope]. **I.** Adv. : *near, hard by, at hand :* Ter., Lucr., Cic., etc. Also *from near* (transf.) : adulescentia voluptates propter intuens, Cic. **II.** Prep. with Acc. *near, close to.* **1.** Lit. of place : stat propter virum fortem, Pl. ; propter Platonis statuam, Cic. ; propter aquae rivum, Lucr. ; Verg. ; viam propter, Tac. **2.** Transf. **a.** *on account of, by reason of, because of :* parere legibus propter metum, Cic. ; Pl. ; propter frigora frumenta in agris matura non erant, Caes. ; quam (terram) propter tantos potui perferre labores, Verg. ; di numquam propter me de caelo descendent, Liv. ; Pl. **b.** *through, by means of :* propter quos vivit, Cic. ; Ter.

propter-eā, *adv. therefore, for that cause, on that account :* Pl., Cic. Freq. with *quod* or *quia :* Cic., etc. ; ergo propterea ne etc., Ter. Pleonastically : id propterea hunc sequor, Ter.

prŏpudiōsus, a, um [prŏpudium], *shameful, disgraceful :* Pl.

prŏpudium, ī, n. [pudet], *a shameful or infamous action.* **1.** Lit.: Pl. **2.** Transf. *a shameful person :* Pl., Cic.

prŏpugnāculum, ī, n. [prŏpugnō], *a bulwark, rampart.* **1.** Lit.: pontis et propugnacula iungunt, Verg. ; Tac. ; moenium, Tac. ; navium, Hor. ; Siciliae (i.e. the fleet), Cic. ; Cremona propugnaculum adversus Gallos, Tac. **2.** Transf. **a.** *a bulwark, safeguard :* lex Aelia et Fufia propugnacula tranquillitatis, Cic. **b.** *defence :* firmissimo propugnaculo uti, Liv.

prŏpugnātiō, ōnis, f. [prŏpugnō], *a defence, vindication :* Cic. ; dignitatis, Cic. Ep. ; pro ornamentis tuis, Cic. Ep.

prŏpugnātor, ōris, m. [prŏpugnō], *a defender.* **1.** Lit. (esp. milit. in pl.) : Caes., Cic., Tac. **2.** Transf.: senatūs, Cic.

prŏ-pugnō, āre. **I.** *to sally out and fight :* ex silvis, Caes. **II.** *to fight in defence.* **1.** Lit.: Caes. ; pro suo partu, Cic. **2.** Transf.: pro aequitate, Cic. With Acc.: absentiam suam, Suet. ; Tac.

prŏpulsātiō, ōnis, f. [prŏpulsō], *a warding off, a repulse.* Transf. : periculi, Cic.

prŏ-pulsō, āre, *to drive forth and away, to ward off, to repel.* **1.** Lit. : Sall. ; hostem, Caes. ; populum ab ingressione fori, Cic. **2.** Transf.: frigus, famem, Cic. ; periculum, Cic., Liv. ; suspicionem a se, Cic. ; bellum ab urbe, Liv.

prŏpulsus, a, um, Part. prōpellō.

Propylaea, ōrum, n. pl. [προπύλαια], *the famous entrance to the Acropolis of Athens :* Cic.

prŏ quaestōre, *a magistrate who, after his quaestorship at Rome, was associated with a proconsul in the administration of a province, a proquaestor :* Cic. In pl. : consul cum quaestoribus prove quaestoribus, Cic.

prŏquam, and, separate, **prŏ quam**, *according as :* v. prŏ.

prōra, ae, f. [πρῷρα], *the fore-part of a ship, the prow.* **1.** Lit.: Pl., Caes., Verg., etc. Prov.: mihi prora et puppis, *my whole design,* Cic. Ep. **2.** Transf. *a ship :* Verg., Ov. [Sp. proa : Fr. proue.]

prŏ-rēpō, rēpere, rēpsī, *to creep forth, crawl out :* (formica) non usquam prorepit, Hor. ; aegri ad conspectum tui, Plin. Pan. ; ad solarium, Suet.

prōrēta, ae, m. [πρῳρήτης], *the look-out at the prow, the under-pilot :* Pl.

prōreus (disyl.), ī, m. [πρῳρεύς], *the look-out at the prow :* Ov.

prŏ-ripiō, ripere, ripuī, reptum [rapiō], *to snatch, hurry, tear forth and away.* **1.** Lit.: hominem, Cic. ; nudos pedes, Ov. With Refl. Pron., *to hasten or hurry forth or away :* se ex curiā domum, Sall. ; Pl. ; Cic. ; se portā foras, Caes. ; se domo, Liv. ; se in publicum, Liv. Without the Pron. : quo proripis ? Verg. **2.** Transf.: libido se, Cic. ; virilis cultus in caedem Lycias catervas, Hor.

prŏ-rītō, āre [cf. inrītō], *to provoke, produce by irritation.* **1.** Lit.: Plin. **2.** Transf. *to incite :* aliquem spes, Sen. Ep.

prōrŏgātiō, ōnis, f. [prōrogō]. **I.** *a prolonging, extension of a term of office :*

imperi, Liv. **II.** *a putting off, deferring :* diei, Cic. Ep.

prŏ-rogō, āre. **I.** *to prolong, continue, protract :* vitam, Pl. ; vitae spatium, Tac. ; quinquenni imperium Caesari, Cic. ; imperium in insequentem annum, Liv. ; rem Romanam alterum in lustrum, Hor. ; ne quid temporis nobis prorogetur, Cic. Ep. ; memoriam alicuius, Plin. Ep. **II.** *to put off, defer :* spem militi in alium diem, Pl. ; dies ad solvendum, Cic.

prōrsum and **prōrsus**, adv. [contr. from prōvorsum (prōversum), prōvorsus (prōversus) = straightforwards, Pl. fr.] (old form, **prōsum** and **prōsus**, Pl.), *forwards.* **1.** Lit. **a.** prorsum Athenas abibo, Pl. ; cursari rursum prorsum, Ter. **b.** *straight on, right on :* ire prosum in navem, Pl. **2.** Transf. **a.** *wholly, absolutely :* prosum perit, Pl. ; prosus tacere nequeo, Ter. ; prorsum nihil intellego, Ter. ; nullo modo prorsus adsentior, Cic. ; ita prorsus existimo, Cic. ; hoc mihi prorsus valde placet, Cic. Ep. ; ea prorsus opportuna Catilinae, Sall. **b.** *in short, in a word* (summing up): prorsus in facie vultuque vecordia inerat, Sall.

prōrsus (**prōsus**), a, um [prō-versus], *straightforward.* Transf. of style : *in prose :* oratio, Quint. As Noun, **prōsa**, ae, f. (sc. oratio), *prose :* Quint.

prŏ-rumpō, rumpere, rūpī, ruptum. **A.** Trans. *to cause to burst forth, to fling forth :* atram ad aethera nubem, Verg. In Mid. : *to burst forth :* hinc prorumpitur in mare venti vis, Lucr. ; proruptus mare, Verg. ; proruptus corpore sudor, Verg. **B.** Intrans. *to burst, rush, or break forth or out.* **1.** Lit.: per medios, Caes. ; medios in hostis, Verg. ; (obsessi) omnibus portis prorumpunt, Tac. ; fluvius in mare, Verg. ; incendium, Tac. **2.** Transf.: illa pestis, Cic. ; vis morbi in unum intestinum, Nep. ; ad minas, Tac. ; in scelera, Tac. Into speech : Tac.

prŏ-ruō, ruere, ruī, rutum. **A.** Intrans. **a.** *to rush forth :* ex parte quā proruebat, Caes. ; in hostem, Curt. **b.** *to tumble down :* motu terrae oppidum, Tac. **B.** Trans. **a.** *to fling or rush headlong :* foras se, Ter. **b.** *to cause to fall forwards or down, to overthrow, demolish :* his (munitionibus) prorutis, Caes. ; columnam, Hor. ; Albam a fundamentis, Liv. ; vallum in fossas, Liv. ; terrae motibus prorutae domūs, Tac. ; hostem, Tac.

prōruptus, a, um. **I.** Part. prōrumpō. **II.** Adj.: *unrestrained :* Cic.

prōrutus, a, um, Part. prōruō.

prōsa, ae, f. v. prōrsus, a, um.

prōsāpia, ae, f. *a stock, race, lineage :* Pl., Sall., Cic. (who uses the word with an apology, as nearly obsolete).

proscaenium, ī, n. [προσκήνιον], *the part before the scene ; the proscenium, stage :* Pl., Liv. In pl. : Verg.

prō-scindō, scindere, scidī, scissum, *to tear or cleave open in front.* **1.** Lit. **a.** ferro quercum, Luc. **b.** Of the first ploughing : *to break or plough up :* Cato ; terram, Lucr., Verg. **2.** Transf. **a.** *to cleave, plough :* rostro aequor, Cat. **b.** *to satirise, de-*

fame : aliquem, Ov. ; aliquem convivio, Suet.

prōscissus, a, um, *Part.* prōscindō.

prō-scrībō, scribere, scripsi, scriptum. **I.** *to publish in writing, announce publicly* : legem, Cic. ; leges, Tac. With Acc. and *Inf.* : Cic. Ep. **II.** *to post up, advertise for sale, etc.* : Claudius proscripsit insulam, vendidit, Cic. ; tabulam proscripsit se familiam Catonianam venditurum, Cic. Ep. **III.** *to confiscate by public advertisement* : possessiones, Cic. ; Plin. Ep. With pers. object : Pompeium (i.e. his estate), Cic. **IV.** *to proscribe, outlaw* (by posting up the person's name in a public place) : Cic., Sall.

prōscriptiō, ōnis, *f.* [prōscrībō]. **I.** *a written public notice* of sale, *an advertisement* : facere, Cic. ; praediorum, Cic. In *pl.* : Cic. **II.** *notice of confiscation or outlawry, proscription* : de capite civis et de bonis proscriptionem ferre, Cic. ; capitis mei, Cic. Esp. of wholesale proscriptions (in *pl.*) : Cic.

prōscriptūriō, īre [*desider.* prōscrībō], *to be bent on a (general) proscription* : Cic. Ep.

prōscriptus, a, um. **I.** *Part.* prōscrībō. **II.** Noun, **prōscriptus**, ī, *m. a proscribed person, outlaw* : Cic., Sall.

prō-secō, secāre, secuī, sectum. **I.** *to break up with the plough* : solum, Plin. Ep. **II.** *to cut out the parts to be sacrificed* : hostiae exta, Liv. ; Pl. ; Cato.

prōsectum, ī, *n.* [prōsecō], *that which is cut out* (i.e. the entrails) : Ov.

prōsecūtus, a, um, *Part.* prōsequor.

prō-seda, ae, *f.* [sedeō], *a prostitute* : Pl.

prō-sēminō, āre, *to sow or scatter about.* **1.** Lit. : ostreas, Cic. **2.** Transf. *to propagate* : familiam, Cic.

prō-sentiō, sentīre, sēnsī, *to perceive beforehand* : Pl.

prō-sequor, sequī, secūtus, *to accompany a person on his way forth.* **1.** Lit. **a.** *to escort, attend* (out of respect or affection) : lacrimans, Verg. ; aliquem, Caes., Nep. ; maritum rus, Pl. ; Dianam ture, Cic. ; me lacrimis, Verg. ; defunctum questu, Tac. ; exsequias, Ov. ; oculis abeuntem udis, Ov. ; ventus euntis, Verg. ; naves eum, Liv. ; Tac. **b.** As an enemy : *to pursue* : fugientis, Caes. ; hostem, Caes. ; Liv. **2.** Transf. **a.** *to attend, honour, adorn* : aliquem beneficiis, benevolentiā, etc., Cic. ; aliquem laudibus, Liv. ; Remos liberaliter oratione, Caes. ; aliquem cum donis, favore, laudibus, Liv. ; virtutem alicuius gratā memoriā, Cic. ; Liv. ; eos honos, Cic. **b.** As an enemy : *to pursue* : aliquem contumeliosis vocibus, Caes. ; Cic. **c.** *to pursue, continue, proceed with* a narration, *etc.* : Verg. ; quod non prosequar longius, Cic. ; pascua versu, Verg. With *Indir. Quest.* : Quint. **d.** *to follow*, i.e. *to imitate* : antiquitatem, Cic. **e.** Of borders : *to march with* : Chattos saltus Hernycius, Tac.

Prōserpina, ae, *f. daughter of Ceres, and wife of Pluto.*

prō-serpō, ere, *to creep forwards or forth* : Pl.

prosuecha, ae, *f.* [προσευχή], *a place for prayer, an oratory* : Juv.

prō siliō, sĭlīre, sĭluī (silīvī or silīī, Sen.) [saliō], *to leap or spring forth, to spring up.* **1.** Lit. : Pl. ; repente, Cic. ; ex tabernaculo, Liv ; ab sede, Liv. ; de capitis paterni vertice (of Minerva), Ov. ; puppe, Luc. **2.** Transf. **a.** *to spring or burst forth, to spurt* : sanguis, scintilla, Ov. **b.** *to break or burst forth* : vaga prosiliet frenis natura remotis, Hor. ; ad arma dicenda, Hor. ; in contionem, Liv.

prō-socer, erī, *m. a wife's grandfather* : Ov., Plin. Ep.

prosōdia, ae, *f.* [προσῳδία], *the tone or accent of a syllable, prosody* : Varr.

prosōpopoeia, ae, *f.* [προσωποποιία]. **I.** *personification* : Quint. **II.** *dramatising* : in *pl.* : Quint.

prōspectō, āre [*freq.* prōspiciō], *to continue to look forth, look at a distant object ; to look at, view.* **1.** Lit. **a.** ex tectis fenestrisque, Liv. ; e terrā aliquem, Liv. ; Ov. ; turba euntem, Verg. ; carinam, Cat. ; avis mare, Cic. **b.** *to look about* : prospectare, ne uspiam insidiae sient, Pl. **c.** Of situation : *to look towards, command a view of* : locus late prospectans, Tac. ; villa subiectos sinūs, Tac. ; Tib. **2.** Transf. **a.** *to look forward to, to expect, await* : exsilium, Cic. With *Indir. Quest.* : Liv. **b.** Of destiny : *to await* : te fata paria, Verg.

prōspectus, a, um, *Part.* prōspiciō.

prōspectus, ūs, *m.* [prōspiciō], *a look-out, distant view, prospect.* **1.** Lit. **a.** sterilis, Pl. ; impedire, Caes. ; ex arce petere, Cat. ; Verg. ; eripere oculis, Verg. ; praebere, adimere, Liv. **b.** *full-view, sight, view* : aliquem in prospectum populi producere, Cic. ; cum iam extremi essent in prospectu, Caes. **2.** Transf. **a.** *gaze, eyesight* : late aequora prospectu metior, Ov. **b.** Of the thing seen : *a sight* : animum pascit prospectus, Verg. ; lugubris, Tac.

prō-speculor, ārī, *to look forward into the distance, look out* : de vallo, Auct. B. Afr. ; of reconnoitring : Liv. With Acc. : *to look out for* : e muris adventum imperatoris, Liv.

prosper, and more freq. **prosperus**, a, um [prō and root of spērō], lit. *according to one's hope ;* hence, *agreeable to one's wishes, favourable* : auspicium, Naev. ; fortuna, Cic. ; prosperae res, Cic. ; successus, Liv. *Comp.* : prosperior civium amor, Tac. ; Ov. *Sup.* : Plin. With GEN. : noctilucam, prosperam frugum, Hor. *Neut. pl.* as Noun : Luc., Tac.

prosperē, *adv. favourably, successfully* : Cic., Liv., Tac. *Sup.* : Vell., Suet.

prosperitās, ātis, *f.* [prosperus], *good fortune, success, prosperity* : vitae, Cic. ; valetudinis, Nep. In *pl.* : Cic.

prosperō, āre [prosperus], *to cause to succeed, to render fortunate or happy, to prosper* : ut (di) consilia sua prosperarent, Tac. ; Hor. ; hanc tibi veniam, Pl. With DAT. : amico meo, Pl.

prosperus, a, um, *v.* prosper.

prōspicientia, ae, *f.* [prōspiciō], *foresight, precaution* : Cic.

prō-spiciō, spicere, spexī, spectum [speciō]. **A.** Intrans. **1.** Lit. **a.** *to look forwards, look out* : ex superioribus locis in urbem,

Caes.; Hor.; procul, Verg.; per umbram, Verg. With *Intern.* Acc.: multum, Cic. Ep. **b.** *to be on the look-out :* Phaedr.; puer ab ianuâ, Nep. **2.** T r a n s f. *to look out, take care of, provide for* (esp. with DAT.): mihi, Ter.; rei frumentariae, Caes.; patriae, Cic. With *ut* or *ne* and *Subj.* : Cic.; so in *Impers. Pass.* : Caes. **B.** T r a n s. *to see afar off, to descry.* **1.** L i t. **a.** Italiam summâ ab undâ, Verg.; campos longe, Hor.; *ex edito* monte cuncta, Curt. **b.** *to be on the look-out for :* ex speculis adventantem hostium classem, Liv. **2.** T r a n s f. **a.** Of situations : *to command a view of :* domus agros, Hor.; Ov.; Plin. Ep. **b.** *to foresee :* futuros casûs rei publicae, Cic.; multum in posterum, Cic.; ex imbri soles, Verg. . **c.** *to look out for, provide :* aliquid, Ter.; ferramenta, Cic.; commeatûs prospectos in hiemem habere, Liv.; sedem senectuti, Liv.; maritum filiae, Plin. Ep.

prō-sternō, sternere, strāvī, strātum, *to throw to the ground, prostrate.* **1.** L i t. : ceteros, Ter.; pondere silvam, Ov.; se ad pedes alicuius, Cic.; se humi, Liv.; lapsu equi prostratus, Tac. **2.** T r a n s f. **a.** *to overthrow, destroy :* hostem, Cic. Of abstracts : virtutem, Cic.; carminum studium, Tac. **b.** *to debase :* se, Cic. Of prostitution : Suet.

prōstĭbĭlis, is, *f.* and **prōstĭbŭlum,** i, *n.* [prōstō], *a prostitute :* Pl.

prō-stĭtŭō, uere, uī, ūtum [statuō], *to expose for sale, to prostitute.* **1.** L i t. : populo vos, Pl.; sese toto corpore, Cat.; faciem suam lucro, Ov.; Suet. As Noun, **prōstĭtūta,** ae, *f. a harlot :* Plin., Suet. **2.** T r a n s f. **a.** *to sell dishonourably :* vocem ingrato foro, Ov. **b.** *to expose to dishonour :* tua famae peccata sinistrae, Ov.

prō-stō, stāre, stĭtī. **I.** *to stand forth, project :* angellis prostantibus, Lucr. **II.** *to stand forth in a public place.* **1.** L i t. **a.** Of a seller : Pl. **b.** Of wares : *to be set out for sale :* Hor. (but *cf. c.*). **c.** *to prostitute oneself :* Juv., Suet. **2.** T r a n s f. (of l. c.) : amicitiae numen, Ov.

prōstrātus, a, um, *Part.* prōsternō.

prō-sŭbĭgō, ere, *to root up :* terram pede, Verg.

prō-sum, prōdesse, prōfuī, *to be useful* or *of use, to do good, benefit, profit* (rare in 1st and 2nd persons) : Ter., Cic., Hor., etc.; tu corpore prodesse, nos animo, Ov. With *ad* or *in* and ACC. : quantum profuit ad concordiam, Liv.; in commune, Quint. With DAT. : sibi, Enn., Cic. With *Inf.* as Subject : Cic., Hor., Ov.

Prōtăgŏrās, ae, *m. a celebrated sophist of Abdera, an older contemporary of Socrates.*

prō-tĕgō, tegere, tēxī, tēctum. **1.** L i t. **a.** *to cover in front, to cover, protect :* aliquem scuto, Caes.; Verg.; Liv. **b.** *to cover with a projecting roof :* ratis cratibus, Caes.; aedis, Cic. **2.** T r a n s f. *to cover or shield from danger, to defend, protect :* aliquem, Cic., Liv., etc.; aliquem precibus, Tac.; aliquem adversus criminantis, Tac.; causam, Juv. Also, *to ward off :* hiemes, Stat.

prōtēlō, āre [perh. fr. prōtēlum], *to drive forwards and away.* T r a n s f. : aliquem saevidicis dictis, Ter.

prōtēlum, i, *n.* u [line of oxen harnessed] *together for draught, a team.* **1.** L i t. : Cato. **2.** T r a n s f. : protelo plagarum continuato, Lucr.

prō-tendō, tendere, tendī, tentum, *to stretch forth* or *out, to extend :* hastas, Verg., Tac.; cervicem fortiter, Tac.; aciem (oculorum) in aestûs pelagi, Cat.

prōtentus, a, um. **I.** *Part.* prōtendō. **II.** A d j. : *extended :* pedes temo protentus in octo, Verg.

prōtĕnus, adv. v. prōtinus.

prō-tĕrō, terere, trīvī, trītum, *to wear away by rubbing* or *trampling under foot, to trample down.* **1.** L i t. : aliquem pedibus, Pl.; equitatus aversos, Caes.; agmina curru, Verg. **2.** T r a n s f. **a.** ver proterit aestas, Hor. **b.** In gen. *to overthrow, crush :* Marte Poenos, Hor.: Tac.; aliquem proterere et conculcare, Cic.; umbram, Ov.

prō-terreō, ēre, *to frighten* or *scare away :* filium hinc, Ter.; Caes.; Verg.; a tuis aedibus proterritus, Cic.

prŏtervē, adv. **I.** *pertly, wantonly, impudently :* Pl., Ter., Cic. Comp. : Ov. **II.** In good sense : *pluckily :* Pl.

prŏtervĭtās, ātis, *f.* [protervus] *pertness, boldness, impudence :* Ter., Cic., Hor.

prŏtervus (-os), a, um [perh. *cf.* προπετής], *forward, bold, pert, impudent.* **1.** L i t. : animus, Pl.; homo, Cic.; dictum aut factum, Cic.; oculi, manus, etc., Ov. **2.** T r a n s f. : venti, Hor.; stella canis, Ov.

Prōtĕsĭlāus, i, *m. son of Iphiclus, the leader of the Thessalians against Troy, where he was the first man killed ;* **Prōtĕsĭlāĕus,** a, um.

Prōteus (disyl.), eĭ and eos (Acc. Prōtea), *m. a sea-god who had the power of assuming any form he pleased.* T r a n s f. *a fickle or cunning person :* Hor.

prŏthymē, adv. [προθύμως], *readily, willingly :* Pl.

prŏthymĭa, ae, *f.* [προθυμία], *readiness, willingness :* Pl.

prōtĭnam, adv. *forthwith, immediately :* Pl. Ter.

prō-tĭnus (prōtĕnus), adv. [tenus]. **A.** Of place : *straightforwards, forwards and onwards, right away.* **a.** me contuli in pedes, Pl.; Ter.; pergere, Cic.; ipse capellas protinus aeger ago, Verg. **b.** *continuously, uninterruptedly :* trans Lygios Gothones regnantur; protinus deinde ab Oceano Rugii et Lemovii, Tac.; protinus utraque tellus una, Verg. **B.** Of time or order : *straightway, directly, forthwith :* Caes., Cic., Hor. (but rare until post-Aug. period).

prō-tollō, ere, *to stretch forward.* **1.** L i t. : manum, Pl. **2.** T r a n s f. : *to prolong, put off :* vitam in crastinum, Pl.

prōtŏprāxĭa, ae, *f.* [πρωτοπραξία], *the (right of) preference* (over other creditors) *in exacting payment :* Plin. Ep.

prō-trahō, trahere, traxī, tractum. **I.** *to drag* or *draw forwards* or *onwards.* T r a n s f. ad paupertatem, Pl.; ad gestum pueros, Lucr. **II.** *to drag* or *draw forth.* **1.** L i t. : me capillo in viam, Pl.; aliquem hinc in convivium, Cic.; Calchanta in medium, Verg.; indicem ad indicium, Liv.; aliquem e tentorio, Tac. **2.** T r a n s f. *to bring to light, reveal, betray :* auctorem facinoris,

Liv.; verms latitantis, Ov. **III. a.** *to drag on, defer :* stipendia militum, Suet.; convivia in primam lucem, Suet. **b.** Of a dying man : *to drag on :* is quinque horas protraxit, Suet.

prōtrītus, a, um, *Part.* prōterō.

prō-trūdō, trūdere, trūsi, trūsum, *to thrust forwards, to thrust* or *push out.* **1.** L i t. : molem, Lucr.; cylindrum, Cic.; asellum in rupes, Hor. **2.** T r a n s f. (of time) : comitia in Ianuarium mensem, Cic. Ep.

prō-turbō, āre, *to hustle* or *drive off.* **1.** L i t. : his facile pulsis ac proturbatis, Caes.; Verg.; Liv., etc. **2.** T r a n s f. **a.** militum conviciis proturbatus, Tac. **b.** *to bear down, overthrow :* silvas, Ov.

pro-ut, *adv.* [prō ut ; more fully, prō eō ut], *accordingly as, in proportion as, just as, as :* prout res postulat, Cic.; Liv. With correl. ita : *according as* . . . *so* . . . : Cic.

prōvectus, a, um. **I.** *Part.* prōvehō. **II.** A d j. : *advanced* (of time) : provecta aetate mortua est, Cic.; provecta nox erat, Tac.

prō-vehō, vehere, vexi, vectum, *to carry forwards, to convey, transport.* **1.** L i t. : eam pol provexi ; avehere non quivi, Pl.; aer res, Lucr. Oftener in *Mid.* or *Pass. : to move, drive, ride,* or *sail forwards :* cum classe freto provehi, Caes.; provehimur portu, Verg.; provectus equo, Liv.; naves provectae in altum, Caes. **2.** T r a n s f. **a.** *to carry forwards* or *onwards :* haec spes provexit ut etc., Liv.; orationem, Cic.; vitam in altum, Lucr. In *Mid.* or *Pass. :* sentio me esse longius provectum quam proposita ratio postularet, Cic. **b.** *to advance, promote :* aliquem ad summos honores, Liv.; te virtus, Cic.; vim temperatam di quoque provehunt in maius, Hor. In *Mid.* or *Pass. :* longius in amicitiā provehi, Cic.; in male dicta, Liv.; ad continuas orationes, Tac.

prō-veniō, venire, vēnī, ventum. **I.** *to come* or *go forwards.* T r a n s f. **a.** *to go on, proceed :* decumae male, Lucil.; recte, nequiter, Pl. **b.** *to go on well, prosper, succeed :* sine malo, Pl.; consilia, Tac.; initia belli, Tac. **II.** *to come forth.* **1.** L i t. **a.** in scaenam, Pl. **b.** *to appear, arise, be produced, grow :* frumentum propter siccitatem angustius provenerat, Caes.; Liv.; *cf.* also, novā ubertate terra, Tac.; scriptorum magna ingenia, Sall.; lana, Ov.; qui mox provenere, Tac.; tanta pullorum suboles, Suet. **2.** T r a n s f. **a.** malum maxumum, si id provenit, Pl.; carmina, Ov.; ex studiis gaudium, Plin. Ep. **b.** *to come to pass, come about :* non haec humanis opibus, non arte magistra proveniunt, Verg.; ita tantum ea cura frumenti provenit ut etc., Liv.

prōventus, ūs, *m.* [prōveniō], *a coming forth, increase, crop.* **1.** L i t. : proventu oneret sulcos, Verg.; Suet. Of persons : poetarum, Plin. Ep.; Quint. **2.** T r a n s f. **a.** *an issue, result :* rerum, Caes. In *pl. :* Caes. **b.** *a fortunate issue, success :* superioris temporis, secundarum rerum, Liv.; orationis, Plin. Ep.

prōverbium, ī, *n.* [verbum], *an adage, proverb :* proverbii locum obtinere, Cic.; quod est Graecis hominibus in proverbio, Cic.;

quod proverbi loco dici solet, Cic.; illud in proverbium venit, Liv.

prōvidēns, entis. **I.** *Part.* prōvideō. **II.** A d j. : *provident, prudent :* Cic. *Comp. :* Cic. Ep. *Sup. :* Tac., Plin. Ep.

prōvidenter, *adv. providently, prudently :* Sall. *Comp.:* Quint. *Sup.:* Cic., Plin. Ep.

prōvidentia, ae, *f.* [prōvideō]. **I.** (Rarely) *foresight, foreknowledge :* Cic. **II.** *forethought, precaution, providence :* ex providentiā timorem adferre, Sall.; Plin. Ep. Esp. *of the wise ordering of the world by the gods :* divina or deorum providentia, Cic.; also personified, *Providence* (i.e. God) : Sen., Quint. With *Obj.* G E N. : neque feriendi neque declinandi, Tac.

prō-videō, vidēre, vidī, vīsum, *to see forward, to see in the distance* or *coming* or *in the darkness* or *in difficulties of some kind.* **1.** L i t. : erus est neque provideram, Ter.; non hercle te provideram, ita iracundia opstitit oculis, Pl.; aliquem, Hor.; in tenebris quid (missilibus) petatur procul provideri nequeat, Liv.; navem, Suet.; per imagines quidquid a tergo fieret, Suet. **2.** T r a n s f. **A.** Mentally. **a.** *to foresee.* With A c c. : Pac., Caes., Cic.; rem mens, Lucr. With *Indir. Quest. :* Cic. **b.** Without Object : *to act with foresight :* Cic. *Impers. Pass. :* Liv. **B.** *to foresee and provide for.* **a.** With A c c. of thing provided : rem frumentariam, Caes.; frumentum exercitui, Caes.; omnia, Sall., Verg.; providentia haec potissimum providet, Cic. Also *to foresee and provide against :* aliquid, Cic. Ep., Sall., Liv. **b.** Without Object : sibi, Pl.; rei frumentariae, Caes.; condicioni civium, Cic. *Impers. Pass. :* de re frumentariā, Caes. : de Brundisio, Cic. Ep.; with *ut* and *Subj. :* Cic. Ep.; with *ne* and *Subj. :* Ter., Caes., Cic.

prōvidus, a, um [prōvideō]. **I.** *foreseeing :* mens, Hor.; Tac. With G E N. : Cic., Ov., Liv. **II.** *cautious, circumspect, prudent :* homo, Cic., Hor. **III.** *providing, provident :* natura, Cic. With G E N. : natura utilitatum, Cic.; rerum vestrarum, Tac.; Ov.

prōvincia, ae, *f. charge, sphere of administration,* '*portfolio,*' *duty.* **1.** L i t. : classis provincia erat Lentulo, Liv.; Sicinio Volsci, Aquilio Hernici provincia evenit, Liv.; cum ambo consules Apuliam provinciam haberent, Liv. E s p. *of the praetor's* sphere of jurisdiction : praetoribus ut ius dicerent Romae provincia erat, Liv. Also of private life (mostly comic.) : parasitorum, Pl.; provinciam capere duram, Ter.; sibi provinciam depoposcit ut me in meo lectulo trucidaret, Cic. **2.** T r a n s f. (territorially) *a sphere of administration ; the part* of the Roman Empire *administered* or *governed, a province.* **a.** In gen. : consularis, praetoria, Cic.; alicui tradere, Cic. Ep.; aliquem provinciae praeficere, Cic. Ep.; in provinciam cum imperio proficisci, Cic. Ep.; provinciam consulari imperio obtinere, Cic.; administrare, Cic. Ep.; deponere, Cic.; de provinciā decedere, Cic. **b.** the first province in Transalpine Gaul (now *Provence*) : Caes.

prōvinciālis, e, *adj.* [prōvincia] *of or in a province, provincial :* administratio, Cic. Ep. ; abstinentia, edictum, etc., Cic. ; bellum, crimina, Tac. As Noun : *an inhabitant of a province, a provincial :* Cic. Ep., Plin. Ep. [Fr. provençal.]

prōvinciātim, *adv. by provinces, province by province :* Suet.

prōvīsiō, ōnis, *f.* [prōvideō], *foresight and forethought* (often with cautio) : aliquid longā animi provisione fugere, Cic. With *Obj.* GEN. (*against* something) : horum incommodorum una cautio est atque una provisio, Cic.

prō-vīsō, ere. **I.** *to go forth to see :* huc, Ter. With *Indir. Quest. :* Ter. **II.** [*freq.* prōvideō], *to be on the look-out for :* aliquem, Pl.

prōvīsor, ōris, *m.* [prōvideō], *a man of foresight or forethought.* With *Obj.* GEN. : *for* something : Hor. ; *against* something : Tac.

prōvīsū, ABL. *sing. m.* [prōvideō], *by looking forward.* **1.** Lit. : Tac. **2.** Transf. **a.** *by foreseeing :* periculi, Tac. **b.** *by or in the providing for, precaution, providence.* With *Subj.* GEN. : deum, Tac. With *Obj.* GEN. : rei frumentariae, Tac. ; civilium rerum, Tac.

prōvīsus, a, um, *Part.* prōvideō. ABL. *n.* **prōvīsō** as *Adv., with forethought :* Tac.

prō-vīxisse, *Perf. Inf.* [vīvō], *to have lived on :* Tac.

prōvŏcātiō, ōnis, *f.* [prōvocō]. **I.** *a citation before a higher tribunal, an appeal :* ad populum esto, Cic. ; provocatio, vindex libertatis, Liv. In *pl.* : Cic. **II.** *a challenging :* per provocationem, Liv.

prōvŏcātor, ōris, *m.* [prōvocātor], *a challenger ; a kind of gladiator :* Cic.

prō-vŏcō, āre, *to call forth, call out.* **1.** Lit. **a.** In gen. : aliquem, Pl. Poet. : rota Luciferi diem, Tib. ; Ov. **b.** *In invitation or challenge :* me in aleam, Pl. ; Pamphilam cantatum, Ter. ; aliquem ad pugnam, Cic. ; Liv. ; pedibus, Pl. ; equus cursibus auras, Verg. **c.** *In law : to summon or cite before a higher court, to appeal* (without Object) : Liv. ; ad populum, Cic., Liv. ; ab omni iudicio poenāque, Cic. ; a duumviris, Liv. **2.** Transf. **a.** *to challenge, incite, stir up :* aliquem sermonibus, Caes. ; aliquem beneficio, iniuriis, etc., Cic. ; minis, bello, etc., Tac. ; officia comitate, Tac. **b.** *to challenge,* i.e. *emulate :* aliquem virtute, Plin. Ep. ; Quint. **c.** *to call forth, occasion, cause :* bellum, Tac. **d.** *to appeal to as authority or proof, to cite :* ad Catonem, Cic. Ep.

prō-vŏlō, āre, *to fly forth.* Transf. : *to hurry forth, rush out :* Caes. ; in primum infestis hastis, Liv. ; sonitus provolat ictu, Lucr.

prōvŏlūtus, a, um, *Part.* prōvolvō.

prō-vŏlvō, volvere, volvi, volūtum. **I.** *to roll forwards or along :* aliquem in viam mediam, Ter. ; corpora, Lucr. ; truncum, Verg. ; congestas lapidum moles, Tac. ; glaebam e terrā, Lucr. ; cupas ardentis in opera, Hirt. **II.** In *Mid.* or with *Refl.* Pron. : *to prostrate oneself, wallow.* **1.** Lit. : se alicui ad pedes provolvere, Liv. ; ad genua alicuius provolvi, Liv. ; genibus eius, Tac. **2.** Transf. **a.** *to lower or*

humble oneself : usque ad nolta I allautu provoluta, Tac. **b.** In *Pass. : to be humbled or ruined :* fortunis, Tac.

prō-vŏmō, ere, *to vomit forth :* Lucr.

prō-vulgō, āre, *to make publicly known, to divulge :* Suet.

proximē, *v.* prope.

proximĭtās, ātis, *f.* [proximus], *nearness, proximity.* **1.** Lit. : Ov. **2.** Transf. **a.** *near-relationship :* Ov., Quint. **b.** *similarity, resemblance :* Ov.

proximus and **proxumus**, *v.* propior.

prūdēns, entis, *adj.* [contr. fr. prōvidēns]. **I.** Prop. **a.** *foreseeing, far-seeing :* Cic. **b.** *foreknowing, conscious, with eyes open :* ibis sub furcam prudens, Hor. ; Ov. ; prudens et sciens sum profectus, Cic. ; Ter. **II.** *circumspect, judicious, sensible, prudent :* Cic., Hor. ; ingenio, Cic. ; ad consilia, Cic. ; in disserendo, Cic. *Comp.* and *Sup. :* Cic. Of things : ratio, Cic. ; consilium, Nep. ; animi sententia, Ov. *Sup. :* Nep. ; animi sententia, Ov. **III.** *knowing, skilled, experienced.* With GEN. : ceterarum rerum, Cic. ; locorum, Liv. ; artis, Ov. ; animus rerum, Hor. *Sup. :* adulandi, Juv. With ABL. : iure, Cic. With *in* and ABL. : in iure, Cic. With *Inf. :* Hor. With Acc. and *Inf. :* Curt.

prūdenter, *adv.* **I.** *cautiously, prudently :* Cic. *Comp. :* Aug. ap. Suet. ; Quint. **II.** *skilfully, learnedly :* Cic. *Sup. :* Cic.

prūdentia, ae, *f.* [prūdēns]. **I.** *a foreseeing :* futurorum, Cic. **II.** *circumspection, good sense, sound judgment, discretion :* Cic., Verg., etc. ; civilis (i.e. statesmanship), Cic. **III.** *knowledge of :* iuris publici, Cic. ; Nep. ; cani rectoris, Juv.

pruīna, ae, *f.* [for provina, *cf.* Gk. πρωϜί], *hoar-frost, rime.* **1.** Lit. : Lucr., Cic. In *pl. :* Cic., Hor., Ov. **2.** Transf. **a.** In *pl. : a covering of frozen snow :* Verg. **b.** *winter :* Verg. [It. *brina.*]

pruīnōsus, a, um [pruīna], *frosty, rimy :* herbae, nox, Ov.

prūna, ae, *f.* [*cf.* Gk. πῦρ], *a live coal :* Verg., Hor.

prūnitius, a, um [prūnus], *of plum-tree wood :* torris, Ov.

prūnum, i, *n.* [prūnus], *a plum :* Verg., Ov.

prūnus, i, *f.* [προύμνη], *a plum-tree :* Verg.

prūrigō, inis, *f.* [prūriō], *an itching.* Transf. *lasciviousness :* Mart.

prūriō, ire, *to itch.* **1.** Lit. : Juv. **2.** Transf. **a.** For blows : Pl., Mart. **b.** For pleasure : Pl., Cat., Mart., Juv. [It. *prudere.*]

Prūsiās and **Prūsia**, ae, *m. king of Bithynia, who hospitably received Hannibal, but afterwards betrayed him to the Romans.*

prytanēum, i, *n.* [πρυτανεῖον], *a public building where the Prytanes assembled and dined :* Cic.

prytanis, is, *m.* (Acc. -in, Liv.) [πρύτανις], *a chief magistrate in some Greek cities :* Liv.

psallō, ere, i [ψάλλω], *to play upon a stringed instrument, esp. to play or sing to the cithara :* Sall., Hor., etc.

psaltērium, i, *n.* [ψαλτήριον], *a stringed instrument of the lute kind, a psaltery :* Cic., Verg., etc.

psaltēs, ae, *m.* (Quint.) [ψάλτης], and **psaltria**, ae, *f.* (Ter., Cic.) [ψάλτρια], *a player on the cithara.*

psecas, adis, *f.* [ψεκάς, *drizzle*], *a female slave who perfumed her mistress's hair* : Juv.

psēphisma, atis, *n.* [ψήφισμα], *a decree of the ecclesia* : Cic., Plin. Ep.

pseudo-catō, ōnis, *m. a sham Cato* : Cic. Ep.

pseudo-damasippus, i, *m. a sham Damasippus* : Cic. Ep.

Pseudolus, i, *m.* [ψευδής, *lying*], *the Liar*, the title of a comedy of Plautus : Cic.

pseudomenos or **-us**, i, *m.* [ψευδόμενος], in logic, *a sophistical syllogism* (pure Lat. mentiens) : Cic.

pseudothyrum, i, *n.* [ψευδόθυρον], *a back-door.* Transf.: nummi per pseudothyrum revertantur, Cic.

psilocitharista, ae, *m.* [ψιλοκιθαριστής], *one who plays on the cithara without singing to it* : Suet.

psithius, a, um [ψίθιος], *psithian*, the name of a species of vine : vitis, Verg. Also without vitis, Verg.

psittacus, i, *m.* [ψίττακος], *a parrot* : Ov., Pers.

Psŏphis, idis, *f. a city in Arcadia.*

Psychē, ēs, *f.* [ψυχή, 'soul'], *a maiden beloved by Cupid, and made immortal by Jupiter.*

psychomantium or **-ēum**, i, *n.* [ψυχομαντεῖον], *a place of necromancy* : Cic.

-pte, an emphatic suffix to personal pronouns and pronom. adjectives, esp. in the ablative ; *self, own* : meopte ingenio, Pl. ; suopte pondere, Cic. ; nostrāpte culpā, Ter. ; mepte fieri servom, Pl.

ptisana, ae, *f.* [πτισάνη], *barley-groats, pearl-barley.* Transf. *barley-water* : Varr., Plin. [It. *tisana* / Fr. *tisane.*]

ptisanārium, i, *n.* [ptisana], *a decoction of barley-groats.* Transf. *of rice* : Hor.

Ptolemaeus, i, *m. the name of a dynasty of kings of Egypt descended from Lagus, a general of Alexander the Great* ; **Ptolemaeëus, Ptolemaeŭs**, a, um.

Ptolemāis, idis, *f.* **I.** *a city in Egypt.* **II.** *a city in Phoenicia.* **III.** *Cleopatra.*

pūbens, entis, *adj.* [pūbēs], *arrived at the age of puberty.* Transf. of plants : *in full vigour, juicy* : herbae, Verg.

pūber, eris, *v.* pūbēs, *adj.*

pūbertās, ātis, *f.* [pūber], *marriageable age, puberty.* **1.** Lit. : ingredi, Tac. **2.** Transf. **a.** *manhood, virility* : inexhausta, Tac. **b.** *the signs of puberty, the first down or bloom* : Cic.

pūbes and **pūber**, eris, *adj.* [root pu- *to generate* : *cf.* puer], *that is grown up, of ripe age, adult.* **1.** Lit. : Cic., Nep. ; ad puberem aetatem, Liv. As Noun, **pūberēs**, um, *m. pl. grown-up persons, adults, men* : Caes., Sall., Tac. **2.** Transf. of plants : *downy* : folia, Verg.

pūbēs, is, *f.* [pūbēs, *adj.*], *the hair which appears on the body at the age of puberty.* **1.** Lit. : Caes. **2.** Transf. **a.** *the groin* : Verg., Ov. **b.** Collectively : *the youth, the manhood, grown-up males* : Pl., Cic., Cat., Verg., etc.

pūbēscō, pūbēscere, pūbui [pūbēs], *to reach the age of puberty, be grown to manhood.* **1.** Lit. : Lucr., Cic., Verg., etc. **2.** Transf. **a.** Of plants : *to grow up* : Cic. **b.** *to be covered* or *clothed* : vites pampinis, Enn. ; prata variorum flore colorum, Ov.

pūblicānus, a, um [pūblicus], *belonging to the public revenue* : Cic. Usually Noun, *a farmer of the Roman taxes* ; generally of the equestrian order : Cic., Liv.

pūblicātiō, ōnis, *f.* [pūblicō], *an adjudging to the public treasury, confiscation* : Cic.

pūblicē, *adv.* **I.** *at the cost, in behalf, in the name,* or *in charge of the State* : Ter., Caes., Cic., Liv., etc. **II.** *all together, as a body* : exulatum ire, Liv.

pūblicitus, *adv.* **I.** *at the public expense, by* or *for the State* : Ter. ; hospitio accipi (i.e. to be imprisoned), Pl. **II.** *before the people, in public, publicly* : Pl.

pūblicō, āre [pūblicus]. **I.** *to make public property, to seize for the use of the State, to confiscate* : regnum Iubae, Caes. ; privata, Cic. ; Liv. ; etc. **II.** *to exhibit to the people, throw open to the public* : bibliothecas, Suet. ; se (as an actor, etc.), Suet. ; oratiunculam (i.e. to publish), Plin. Ep. **III.** *to prostitute* : corpus, Pl.

Pūblicola or **Pŏplicola**, ae, *m.* '*friend of the people*,' a cognomen of P. Valerius (B.C. 509) *and of his descendants.*

pūblicus (also **pŏblicus** and **pōplicus**, Inscr.), a, um [contr. of populicus from populus], *of the people, State,* or *community* ; *that is done for the sake or at the expense of the State.* **1.** Lit. : tabulae, Cic. ; servus, Liv. ; res, Enn. ; magnificentia, Cic. ; sacrificia, Caes. ; iniuriae (i.e. done to the State), Caes. ; causa, *an affair of State,* Liv. ; also, *a criminal process* (as dist. from a *private suit*), Cic. : res publica, *the commonwealth, the State* ; *v.* res. As Noun. **a. pūblicus**, i, *m. a State official* : Pl., Caes. **b. pūblicum**, i, *n.* **i.** *the public purse, revenue* : bona alicuius vendere et in publicum redigere, Liv. ; in publicum referre, Nep. ; emere in publicum, Liv. ; de publico convivari, *at the public cost,* Cic. ; conducere publica, *to farm the public revenues,* Hor. ; also, habere publicum, Pl. ; frui publico, Cic. Transf. : consulere in publicum (i.e. for the public good), Plin. Ep. **ii.** *State possessions* : Campanum, Cic. **iii.** *a public place, public, street* (not in Nom.) : in publicum prodire, Cic. ; Tac. ; publicum aspicere, Liv. ; esse in publico, Cic. ; carere publico (i.e. to stay at home), Cic. ; abstinere publico, Tac. Transf. : epistulam in publico proponere, Cic. Ep. ; orationem in publicum dare, Plin. Ep. **2.** Transf. **a.** *general, public* : lex hominum, Pers. ; favor, Ov. Of a noted beauty : iuvenum publica cura, Hor. **b.** *common, ordinary, inferior* : structura carminis, Ov.

Publius, i, *m. a Roman praenomen, abbreviated* P.

pudendus, a, um. **I.** Gerundive of pudeo. **II.** Adj. : *of which one ought to be ashamed, shameful, scandalous* : Verg., Ov., Liv., etc. ; pudendum est (with *Inf.*), Cic. ; pudendum dictu, Tac.

pudēns, entis. **I.** Part. pudeō. **II.** Adj. : *shamefaced, bashful, modest* : Lucr., Cic., Hor. ; animus, Ter. Comp., Sup. : Cic.

pudenter, *adv. modestly, bashfully* : Cic., Hor. Comp., Sup. : Cic.

pudeō, ēre (*v.* rare exc. in 3rd sing.). **I.** *to be ashamed* : Pl. **II.** *to make ashamed.*

A. With Subject. **a.** non te haec pudent ?
Ter. **b.** Esp. 3rd *Sing.* **pudet** (*Inf.*
pudēre), puduit or puditum est ; with
Neut. Pron. (Pl., Ter.), *Inf.* (Ter., Cic.,
Hor.), or *quia- er quod-* clause (Pl.), as
Subject, and Acc. of person (if expressed)
as Object. **B.** **pudet**, etc. without Subject. **a.** With Acc. of person and Gen. of
origin of feeling : homines, quos infamiae
suae neque pudeat neque taedeat, Cic. ;
Pl. ; Hor., etc. ; pudet deorum hominumque (i.e. before gods and men), Liv. ; Pl.
b. With Abl. of Cause : te tui factis, Pl. ;
pudet dictu, Tac.

pudibundus, a, um [pudeō], *shamefaced,
bashful, modest* : Hor. ; ora, Ov.

pudicē, *adv. modestly, chastely, virtuously* :
Pl., Ter., Cat. *Comp. :* Pl., Plin. Ep.

pudicitia, ae, *f.* [pudicus], *chastity, modesty,
purity* (usually of body) : Pl. ; spoliare,
expugnare, Cic. ; alicui eripere, Cic. ;
amittere, Liv. ; prostituere, Suet. ; in
propatulo habere, Sall. Personified :
Liv.

pudicus, a, um [pudeō], *modest, pure, chaste,
virtuous* (usually of body). **1.** Lit. of
persons : Pl., Cic., Ov., etc. ; a turpi facto,
Hor. *Masc.* as Noun : Cic. *Comp. :* Ov.
Sup. : Plin. **2.** Transf. : nihil, Cic. ;
lectum, Prop. ; mores, fides, etc., Ov.

pudor, ōris, *m.* [pudeō], *shame, a sense of
shame* or *honour, shamefacedness, modesty*
in disposition or feeling. **1.** Lit. : Pl.,
Cic., Ov., etc. ; pudor est (with *Inf.*), Ov.
With Gen. of origin or cause of feeling :
famae, Cic. ; paupertatis, Hor. ; patris,
before a father, Ter. Occ. **a.** *sense of
honour* : pudore adducti, Caes. : Cic. **b.**
a woman's honour or *modesty* : deus pudorem rapuit, Ov. **2.** Transf. **a.** *shame,
ignominy, disgrace* : pro pudor ! *Oh shame*,
Hor. ; vulgare alicuius pudorem, Ov. **b.**
a cause of shame, disgrace : pudori esse
(alicui), Liv.

puella, ae, *f.* [*v.* puellus], *a girl-child, a girl,
lass, maiden*. **1.** Lit. : Pl., Cic., Verg.,
etc. **2.** Transf. **a.** *a young woman,
young wife* : Hor., Ov., Tac., etc. **b.** *a
beloved maiden, a sweetheart, mistress* : Hor.,
Ov. **c.** *a slave-girl* : Hor.

puellāris, e, *adj.* [puella], *of a girl* or *young
woman, girlish, maidenly* : anni, Tac. ;
animi, Ov. ; suavitas, Plin. Ep.

puellāriter, *adv. in a girlish manner, girl-
ishly* : Plin. Ep.

puellula, ae, *f.* [*dim.* puella], *a little* or *dear
little girl* : Ter., Cat.

puellus, ī, *m.* [*dim.* (contr. fr. puerulus) fr.
puer], *a little boy* : Pl.

puer, erī, *m.* (Voc. puere, Pl., as from puerus)
[root pu- *to beget*], orig. *a child*, whether
boy or girl. **1.** Lit. **a.** In gen. : sancta
puer Saturni filia, regina, Liv. Andr. In *pl.*
pueri, *children* (in general) : Pl., Cic., Hor.,
etc. **b.** *a male child, a boy, lad, young man*
(strictly till about the seventeenth year) :
Pl., Cic., Verg., etc. ; a puero, a pueris,
from a boy, from boyhood or *childhood* :
diligentiā matris a puero doctus, Cic. ; ex
pueris excedere, *to pass out of the age of
childhood*, Cic. **2.** Transf. **a.** *a boy in
waiting, a servant, slave, page* : Pl., Cic.,

Hor., etc. **b.** *an unmarried man, á
bachelor* : Ov. **c.** pueri deorum, *sons of
gods*, i.e. demigods, Hor. **d.** In familiar
address ; like "*my boy*" : promisti autem ?
de te largitor, puer, Ter.

puera, ae, *f.* [puer], *a girl, lass, maiden* : Liv.
Andr., Varr., Suet.

puerāscō, ere [puer], *to grow into the age of
boyhood* or *youth* : Suet.

puerīlis, e, *adj.* [puer], *childish, boyish, youthful*. **1.** Lit. : aetas, Cic. ; agmen, disciplina, species, etc., Verg. ; regnum, Liv.
2. Transf. *childish, puerile* : sententia,
Ter. ; consilium, Cic. ; vota, Ov.

puerīlitās, ātis, *f.* [puerīlis], *childishness,
puerility* : Sen. Ep.

puerīliter, *adv. like a child*. **1.** Lit. : Liv.,
Phaedr. **2.** Transf. *childishly*, i.e. foolishly : Pl., Cic., Tac.

pueritia (syncop. **puertia**, Hor.), ae, *f.*
[puer], *childhood, boyhood, youth* (usually
till the seventeenth year) : Ter., Cic., Sall.,
Tac.

puerperium, ī, *n.* [puerperus], *child-birth,
child-bed* : puerperio cubare, Pl. ; Tac.
In *pl.* : Tac.

puerperus, a, um [puer pariō], *of* or *helping
child-birth* : verba, Ov. As Noun, **puer-
pera**, ae, *f. a woman in labour* : Pl., Cat.,
Hor.

puertia, *v.* pueritia.

puerulus, ī, *m.* [*dim.* puer], *dainty boy-
slave* : Cic.

pūga, ae, *v.* pȳga.

pugil, ilis, *m.* [*cf.* pugnus], *a boxer, pugilist* :
Ter., Cic., Ov., etc.

pugilātiō, ōnis, *f.* (Cic.) and **pugilātus**, ūs,
m. (Pl.) [pugilor], *boxing with the caestus,
pugilism*.

pugilicē, *adv. like a boxer* : valere, Pl.

pugillāris, e, *adj.* [pugillus], *that can be held
in the hand* : Juv. As Noun, **pugillārēs**,
ium, *m. pl.* (*sc.* libelli), *writing tablets* :
Sen. Ep., Plin. Ep. Also, **pugillāria**, ium,
n. pl. : Cat.

pugillātōrius, a, um [pugillus], *struck with
the fist* : follis, Pl.

pugillus, ī, m. [*dim.* pugnus], *a fistful, handful* :
Cato, Plin.

pugiō, ōnis, *m.* [cogn. with pungō], *a dagger,
dirk, poniard* : Cic., Tac. ; to denote the
power of life and death : Tac., Suet. ; as
a military badge of distinction : Tac.
Transf. (of a futile argument) : a plum-
beum pugionem ! *O leaden dagger !* Cic.

pugiunculus, ī, *m.* [*dim.* pugiō], *a small
dagger, a stiletto* : Cic.

pugna, ae, *f.* [pugnus], orig. *a fight with fists,
a brawl*. **1.** Lit. : Verg. ; res ad pugnam
atque manūs vocabatur, Cic. ; pugna in
manūs venerat, Liv. **2.** Transf. **a.** In
gen. : *a fight, combat, battle* : dictator eam
pugnam laudibus tulit (of a single combat),
Liv. ; Caes. ; equestris, Cic. ; pedestris,
Verg. ; capessere, conserere, restituere, etc.,
Liv. ; adversus aliquem inire, Liv. ; ciere,
Liv. ; prospera, Suet. ; mala, Cic., Sall.
b. *battle-array, order of battle* : ordinata
per principes hastatosque ac triarios, Liv. ;
mutare, Curt. ; mediam pugnam tueri, Liv.
c. Of words, etc. : dare, Pl. ; alicui conserere, Pl. ; doctissimorum hominum, Cic.

pugnācitās, ātis. *f. fondness for fighting, combativeness* : Quint., Tac.

pugnāciter, *adv. contentiously, violently* : Cic. *Comp.* : Quint. *Sup.* : Cic.

pugnāculum, ī, *n.* [pugnō], *a fortress* : Pl.

pugnātor, ōris, *m.* [pugnō], *a fighter, combatant* : Liv., Suet.

pugnātōrius, a, um [pugnātor], *of a fighter* : arma (opp. to rudes), Suet.

pugnāx, ācis, *adj.* [pugnō], *fond of fighting, combative, warlike.* **1.** Lit.: Cic., Hor., Ov., etc. *Comp.* : Asin. Poll. ap. Cic. Ep. *Sup.* : Curt., Tac. **2.** Transf. **a.** Of things : oratio, Cic., Plin. Ep. ; hastae, Prop. With DAT.: ignis aquae, Ov. **b.** Of persons : *obstinate, pertinacious* : Cic.

pugneus, a, um [pugnus], *of the fist* : Pl.

pugnō, āre [pugna], *to fight.* **1.** Lit.: Caes., Cic., Liv., etc. ; ex equo, Cic. ; ex iniquiore loco, Hirt. ; de ponte, Hirt. ; Ter. ; comminus in acie, Cic. ; eminus lapidibus, Sall. ; cum hoste, Cic. ; Liv. ; in hostem, Sall., Liv. ; adversum multitudinem, Sall. ; adversus alios hostis, Liv. ; adversus *or* contra edictum, *in defiance of orders*, Liv. ; bene, prospere, male, Cic., etc. With ACC. : pugnam, Pl., Cic., Liv., etc. ; proelia, Sall., Hor. ; bella, Hor. *Impers. Pass.* : Caes. **2.** Transf. **a.** *to contend* with words, etc. Of persons : de dis immortalibus, Cic. With ACC. and *Inf.* : Cic. With *cum* : pugnant Stoici cum Peripateticis, Cic. With DAT.: alicui, Cat., Prop. ; placito amori, Verg. Of things : sententia secum, Hor. ; frigida calidis, Ov. **b.** *to struggle, strive.* With *ne* and *Subj.* : Cic., Ov. With *ut* : pugnarem conlegae ut etc., Liv. ; hoc pugnatur ut etc., Cic. With *Inf.* : Ov.

pugnus, ī, *m. a fist* : Pl., Cic., Hor., etc. [Fr. *poing.*]

pulchellus, a, um [*dim.* pulcher], *beautiful little* : Bacchae (i.e. Baccharum statuae), Cic. Ep.

pulcher, chra, chrum (less correctly **pulcer**, cra, crum), *beautiful, fair, handsome.* **1.** Lit. (physically) : virgo, Ter. ; puer, Cic., Hor. ; Verg. ; facies, Ter. ; color, Lucr. ; urbs, Cic., Liv. ; fluvius, Verg. ; panis, Hor. ; aspectu, Cic. *Neut.* as Noun : Hor. **2.** Transf. (morally) : fasces, Lucr. ; praetor, Cic. ; res publica, Sall. ; exemplum, Caes. ; poëmata, Hor. ; consilia, Verg. ; pulchrumque mori succurrit in armis, Verg. ; propino hoc pulchro Critiae, Cic. *Comp.* : Cic., Verg., etc. *Sup.* pulcherrimus, Cato, Cic., Hor., etc.

pulchrē (pulcrē), *adv. finely, beautifully* (usually colloq.) : Pl., Cic., etc. ; pulchre est mihi, *I am all right*, Cic., Hor. ; pulchre, as an exclamation of applause, *fine! well done!* Ter., Hor.

pulchritūdō, inis, *f.* [pulcher], *beauty, excellence.* **1.** Lit. (physically) : corporis, Cic. ; Liv. ; operis, Plin. Ep. **2.** Transf. (morally) : oratoris, virtutis, Cic. ; verborum, Quint.

pūlēium or **pūlegium**, ī, *n.* [pūlex], *pennyroyal.* **1.** Lit.: Cic., Mart. **2.** Transf. from its fragrance : ad cuius rutam pulegio mihi tui sermonis utendum, Cic. Ep.

pūlex, icis, *m. a flea* : Pl. [It. *pulce*; Fr. *puce*.]

pullārius, ī, *m.* [pullus], *the man who fed the sacred chickens, the chicken-keeper* : Cic., Liv.

pullātus, a, um [pullus, *adj.*], *clothed in soiled* or *black garments.* **a.** *in mourning* : Juv. **b.** Of the common people : Quint., Plin. Ep. As Noun, **pullāti**, ōrum, *m. pl. the common people* : Suet.

pullēiāceus, a, um [pullus, adj.], *black* : Aug. ap. Suet.

pullulō, āre [pullulus, *dim.* pullus, ī], *to sprout, spring forth.* **1.** Lit.: ab radice, Verg. ; of animals, *to bring forth young* : Verg. **2.** Transf.: luxuria, Nep. [It. *pollare.*]

pullus, ī, *m.* [root pu- *to beget*], *a young animal.* **1.** Lit. **a.** In gen. : columbini, Cic. Ep. : gallinacei, Liv. ; ranae, Hor. **b.** *a chicken* : Cato, Cic., Hor. **2.** Transf. of persons. **a.** A term of endearment : Pl., Hor., Suet. **b.** pullus miluinus, *young kite* (of an avaricious person), Cic. Ep. **c.** Of plants : *a young shoot* : Cato.

pullus, a, um [*cf.* πελλός], *dark-coloured, blackish-grey, dusky, blackish.* **1.** Lit.: Varr., Verg., etc. ; toga, tunica, *a dark-grey garment* (of undyed wool, the dress of mourners and of the lower orders), Cic. As Noun, **pullum**, ī, *n. a dark-grey garment* : Liv., Ov. **2.** Transf. *sad, mournful* : pulla stamina nere, Ov. ; Mart.

pulmentārium, ī, *n.* (Cato, Hor., Sen. Ep.) and **pulmentum**, ī, *n.* (Pl., Hor.) [puls], *anything eaten with bread, a relish* (fruit, salt, mustard, etc.). **1.** Lit.: Cato, Sen. Ep. **2.** Transf. *food, rations* : Pl. In *pl.* : Hor.

pulmō, ōnis, *m.* [πλεύμων, for πνεύμων]. **I.** *a lung* and *pl.* pulmones, *the lungs* : Pl., Cic., Ov., etc. **II.** *a marine animal, sea-lung* : Pl. [Fr. *poumon.*]

pulmōneus, a, um [pulmō], *of the lungs* : Pl.

pulpa, ae, *f. the fleshy portion of animal bodies.* **1.** Lit.: Cato, Mart. **2.** Transf.: scelerata pulpa, Pers.

pulpāmentum, ī, *n.* [pulpa], *the fleshy part of animals.* Transf. *food composed chiefly of bits of meat, tit-bits* : Pl., Cic. Prov.: lepus tute es et pulpamentum quaeris ? Ter.

pulpitum, ī, *n. a platform of boards* : grammatica, Hor. ; *esp. a stage* for actors : Hor., Juv., Plin. Ep. [Fr. *pupitre.*]

puls, pultis, *f. porridge made of meal, pulse,* etc. ; *the food of the Romans in early times* ; *also used* at sacrifices, and as food for the sacred chickens : Cato, Cic., Juv.

pulsātiō, ōnis, *f.* [pulsō], *a knocking, striking* : osti, Pl. ; scutorum, Liv. ; alicuius, Cic.

pulsō, āre [*freq.* pellō], *to batter, strike often* or *vigorously* or *violently.* **1.** Lit. **a.** ostium, Pl. ; ostia, Hor. ; aliquem, Cic., Verg. ; tellurem pede libero, Hor. ; muros ariete, Verg. **b.** *to strike, make to vibrate* the strings of a lyre or bow : Verg. **2.** Transf. of excitement : pavor pulsans, Verg. ; multa meum pectus pulsant, Pl. ; dormientium animos, Cic. ; te vecordia, Ov. [Fr. *pousser.*]

pulsus, a, um, *Part.* pellō.

pulsus, ūs, *m.* [pellō], *a beat, push, blow.* **1.** Lit.: pulsu externo agitari, Cic. ; remorum, Caes., Cic., Liv. ; pedum, Verg. ;

lyrae, Ov. **2.** T r a n s f. *impulse, influence :*
Cic. [Fr. *pouls.*]

pultātiō, ōnis, *f.* [pultō], *a beating, knocking*
at the door : Pl.

pultiphagōnidēs, ae, *m.* [pultiphagus], *pap-*
or porridge-eater, comically, for *an ancient*
Roman (*v.* puls) : Pl.

pultiphagus, ī, *m.* [puls φαγεῖν], *a pap-* or
porridge-eater : Pl.

pultō, āre [collat. form of pulsō], *to beat,*
strike, knock at : Pl. ; ostium, Ter. ; ianuam,
Pl. Also, pectus, Pl.

pulvereus, a, um [pulvis]. **I.** *of dust, dust-:*
nubes, Verg. **II.** *dusty :* solum, Ov. **III.**
fine as dust : farina, Ov. **IV.** *raising dust :*
Boreae palla, Ov.

pulverulentus, a, um [pulvis]. **1.** L i t. **a.**
dusty : via, Cic. Ep. ; Ceres, Lucr. ; femina,
Prop. Also, aestas, Verg. **b.** *raising dust :*
agmina cervorum, Verg. **2.** T r a n s f. :
militia, Ov.

pulvillus, i, *m.* [for pulvinulus, dim. pulvī-
nus], *a little cushion, small pillow :* Hor.

pulvinar (**polv-**), āris, *n.* [pulvīnus], *a cush-*
ioned couch. **A.** *a couch for the images*
of the gods in the temples and in the banquet
called lectisternium *:* Cic., Ov., Liv., etc.
B. *a State-couch.* **a.** In gen. : geniale
divae, Cat. ; Liviae, Ov. ; Messalinae, Juv.
b. Of the Emperor's seat in the circus :
Juv., Ov.

pulvīnārium, ī, *n.* [pulvīnar], *a dry-dock or*
anchorage : Pl.

pulvīnus, i, *m.* **I.** *a cushion, bolster, pillow :*
Pl., Cic., Sall. **II.** *a seat of honour :* Sen.,
Juv., Suet. **III.** In fields : *a raised*
border : Varr., Plin. Ep.

pulvis, eris, *m.* (*fem. :* Prop.) [*cf.* pollen],
powder. **1.** L i t. **a.** In gen. : Enn., Cic.,
Verg., etc. ; pulveris nebula, Lucr. ; nubes
pulveris, Liv. ; magna vis pulveris cernebatur, Caes. ; caeco pulvere miscetur campus,
Verg. P r o v. : in pulvere sulcos ducere
(i.e. to plough the sand), Juv. **b.** *the dust*
(*or sand*) *used by mathematicians for their*
figures : Liv. ; eruditus, Cic. **c.** Of the
race-course : pulverem Olympicum con-
legisse, Hor., Verg. **d.** Of dry soil :
Etrusca, Prop. ; hibernus (i.e. a dry winter),
Verg. **e.** Of the ashes of the dead : Hor.
2. T r a n s f. **a.** From the arena : *a place of*
contest, scene of action : doctrinam ex um-
braculis eruditorum in solem atque pulverem produxit, Cic. ; forensis, Quint. **b.**
exertion, toil, effort : cui sit condicio dulcis
sine pulvere palmae, Hor. ; pulvis belli,
Mart. [It. *polve, polvere ;* Fr. *poudre.*]

pulvisculus, ī, *m.* [dim. pulvis], *small dust,*
fine powder : cum pulvisculo (i.e. completely), Pl.

pūmex, icis, *m.* (*fem. :* Cat.) *pumice stone.*
1. L i t. : Plin. ; used for smoothing books :
Cat., Hor., Ov., etc. ; hence, p o e t. of
verses carefully polished : Prop. P r o v. :
aquam a pumice postulare (of trying to get
money), Pl. **2.** T r a n s f. : *soft stone,*
porous rock of any kind : Verg., Ov. In
pl. : Hor. [It. *pomice ;* Fr. *ponce,* Eng.
pounce.]

pūmiceus, a, um [pūmex], *of pumice-stone,*
or *of soft stone* in gen. : **1.** L i t. : molae,
Ov. **2.** T r a n s f. : oculi (i.e. dry), Pl.

pūmileō, ōnis *f.* [pūmex], *to smooth with pumice-*
stone : Lucil. ; pumicata frons, Mart. ;
Cat.

pūmiliō, ōnis, *m. f.* [pūmilus], *a dwarf, pygmy :*
Sen. Ep., Mart. Of women : Lucr.

pūmilus, ī, *m. a dwarf :* Stat., Suet.

pūnctim, *adv. with the point of the sword*
(opp. caesim, *with the edge*) : Liv.

pūnctiō, ōnis, *f.* [pungō], *a pricking,* hence,
a stitch in the side : Plin. [It. *punzone ;*
Fr. *poinçon.*]

pūnctus, a, um. **I.** *Part.* of pungō, *pricked*
in, like *a point ;* hence, of time : puncto
tempore, Lucr. **II.** Noun, **pūnctum**, i, *n.*
a prick, small hole, puncture. **1.** L i t. :
Mart. **2.** T r a n s f. **a.** *a point, small spot :*
ova punctis distincta, Plin. ; Plin. Ep. **b.**
a mathematical point : Cic. **c.** *a point* or
pip on dice : Suet. **d.** *a point or dot made*
on a wax tablet as the sign of a vote ; hence
a vote, ballot : quot in eā tribu puncta tulisti,
Cic. ; transf. : Hor. **e.** *the mark facing*
the tongue of a pair of scales, to show equilib-
rium : Pers. **f.** *a small point in space :*
Cic. ; in time, *a moment :* temporis, Ter.,
Caes. ; puncto temporis eodem, Cic. ;
nullo puncto temporis intermisso, Cic. ;
diei, Lucr. ; horae, Hor. In *pl.* : Cic.
g. In discourse : *a brief clause, short section :*
Cic. [It. *punto ;* Fr. *point.*]

pungō, pungere, pupugi, pūnctum, *to prick,*
puncture. **1.** L i t. : aliquem, Cic. Also
to make by pricking : vulnus acu, Cic. **2.**
T r a n s f. **a.** *to pierce into, penetrate :* corpus, Lucr. **b.** *to sting, bite :* pungunt
sensum, Lucr. **c.** *to prick, sting, vex,*
trouble : iam dudum meum ille pectus
pungit aculeus, Pl. ; scrupulus (animi) aliquem stimulat ac pungit, Cic. ; pungit me
quod scribis etc., Cic. Ep. ; suspiria somnos,
Prop.

Pūni, *v.* Poeni.

Pūnicē, *adv. in the Punic language :* loqui, Pl.

pūniceus, a, um [pūnicus], *reddish, rosy,*
purple-coloured : crocus, Ov. ; rotae (currūs
Aurorae), Verg. ; cruor, Ov. ; also, anima,
Verg. C o m i c. : corium (i.e. with weals),
Pl.

Pūnicus, a, um. **I.** [Poeni], *Punic, Cartha-*
ginian : Cic., Liv. ; mālum, or *absol., a*
pomegranate : Plin. **II.** *purple-coloured,*
purple-red [φοινίκεος] : sagum, Hor. ; of a
parrot's bill : Ov.

pūniō (older **poeniō**), īre (Cic., Liv., Ov.,
Quint.) and **pūnior,** īri (Cic., Quint.)
(*Imperf.* poenibat, Lucr.) [*cf.* poena]. **I.**
to punish : aliquem, Cic., etc. ; peccata,
Cic. In *Pass.* : capite puniri, Liv. ; Ov.
II. *to take vengeance for :* dolorem, Cic. ;
Graeciae fana, Cic. ; hominum necem, Cic.

pūnitor, ōris, *m.* [pūniō]. **I.** *a punisher :*
Suet. **II.** *an avenger :* doloris, Cic.

pūpa, ae, *f.* [pūpus], *a girl, damsel, lass.*
1. L i t. : Mart. **2.** T r a n s f. : *a doll,*
puppet : Varr., Pers.

pūpilla, ae, *f.* [dim. pūpula]. **I.** *an orphan*
girl, a ward, minor : Cic. **II.** *the pupil of*
the eye (*cf.* Gk. κόρη) : Lucr.

pūpillāris, e, *adj.* [pūpillus], *of an orphan*
or *ward :* pecunia, Liv. ; aetas, Suet.

pūpillus, i, *m.* [dim. pūpulus], *an orphan boy,*
an orphan ; also, *a ward :* Cic., Hor.

Pupīnia, ae, f. (sc. regio), a sterile tract of country near Rome ; also called **Pupīnius** and **Pupīniēnsis ager.**

puppis, is, f. (ABL. puppe, Ov. ; us. puppī), the hinder part of a ship, the stern. **1.** Lit. : Cic. Ep., Ov., etc. ; ventus surgens a puppi, from abaft, astern, Verg. **2.** Transf. **a.** a ship : Hor. **b.** A constellation, the Ship, us. called Argo : Cic. **c.** Comic. for the back : puppis pereunda est probe, Pl. [It. poppa ; Fr. poupe ; Eng. poop.]

pūpula, ae, f. [dim. pūpa], the pupil of the eye (cf. Gk. κόρη). **1.** Lit. : Cic., Cat., Hor. **2.** Transf. the eye : Cic, Ov..

pūpulus, i, m. [dim. pūpus], a little boy : Cat. Of an old man : Sen. Ep.

pūpus, i, m. [root pu- to beget], a boy, a child : Varr. As a term of endearment, puppet : Suet.

pūrē, adv. purely, cleanly, without spot or mixture. **1.** Lit. : eluere vasa, Pl. ; Liv. Comp. : splendens Pario marmore purius, Hor. **2.** Transf. **A.** clearly, plainly (i.e. without disguise, covering, etc.). **a.** res pure apparet, Hor. ; quid pure tranquillet (i.e. perfectly, fully), Hor. **b.** Of style : loqui, Cic. ; Pl. **B.** purely, chastely. **a.** Morally : agere aetatem, Cic. **b.** Religiously or ceremonially : deos venerari, Cic. ; Liv.

pūrgāmen, inis, n. [pūrgō], dirt, filth, sweepings. **1.** Lit. : Vestae, Ov. **2.** Transf. a means of purgation, purification : caedis, Ov.

pūrgāmentum, i, n. [pūrgō], sweepings, offscourings, refuse, filth, dirt : us. plur. : urbis, Liv. ; hortorum, Tac. As a term of abuse : Curt.

pūrgātiō, ōnis, f. [pūrgō], a cleansing, purging. **1.** Lit. : cloacarum, Traj. ap. Plin. Ep. ; with or without alvi, Cic. **2.** Transf. an apology, justification : Ter., Cic.

pūrgātus, a, um. **I.** Part. pūrgō. **II.** Adj. : cleansed, pure : auris, Hor. ; somnia pituitā purgatissima, Pers.

pūrgō (older **pūrigō**), āre [pūrum agō, cf. iūrgō]. **I.** to make clean, to cleanse, clear. **1.** Lit. : piscis, Ter. ; oleam a foliis et stercore, Cato ; falcibus locum, Cic. ; Ov. ; locum qui strage muri cumulatus erat, Liv. ; unguis cultello, Hor. With GEN. : morbi purgatum esse, Hor. **2.** Transf. **a.** Mentally : pectora, Lucr. **b.** to clear from accusation, to excuse, exculpate, justify : se alicui, Caes., Cic. ; Ter. ; aliquem crimine, Tac. ; aliquem alicuius rei, Liv. ; factum, Ov., Liv. ; innocentiam suam (i.e. to vindicate), Liv. With Acc. and Inf. : Liv. **c.** Relig. to cleanse, purify : urbem, Cic. ; populos, Ov. **d.** Commerc. to clear up, settle : rationes, Suet. **II.** to cleanse away, clear away. **1.** Lit. (medic.) to purge (by stool, vomiting, etc.) : purgor bilem, Hor. With GEN. : morbi purgari, Hor. **2.** Transf. **a.** se nubes in aethera, Verg. **b.** to clear away accusations, etc. : crimina, Cic., Liv. ; crimen gladio, Luc. ; probra, Tac. ; suspicionem, Liv. ; metum doloris, Quint. **c.** Relig. to cleanse away : nefas, Ov.

pūrificō, āre [pūrus faciō], to cleanse. **1.**

Lit. : luteos pedes aquā, Plin. **2.** Transf. (relig.) : Suet.

pūriter, adv. purely, cleanly. **1.** Lit. : Cato, Cat. Sup. : Cato. **2.** Transf. : agere vitam, Cat.

purpura, ae, f. [πορφύρα], the purple-fish. **1.** Lit. : Plin. **2.** Transf. **a.** purple colour, purple : Verg., Hor. Hence, grandeur, finery, rank : Pl., Lucr., Hor. **b.** the purple, i.e. purple cloth, a purple garment : Cic. ; regum, Verg. ; Ov. Hence, **c.** consular, imperial, or royal dignity : nova purpura, Ov. [Fr. pourpre.]

purpurātus, a, um [purpura], clad in purple : Pl., Liv. Masc. as Noun, a high officer at court ; a courtier : Cic., Liv.

purpureus, a, um [purpura]. **I.** purple-coloured, purple : including different shades of colour, as red, pink, violet. **a.** Of clothing, etc. : Cic., Verg., Hor. Transf. clothed in purple : Verg., Hor., etc. **b.** Of flowers : flos rosae, Hor. ; papavera, Prop. **c.** Of blood or flesh : Verg. ; rubor oris, Ov. **d.** Of hair : Verg. **e.** Of the sea : Cic., Prop. **f.** Of wine : Prop., Ov. **g.** Of the dawn : Ov. **II.** gleaming, flashing, lustrous : lumen iuventae, Verg. ; os, Hor. ; Amor, Ov. ; olores, Hor.

purpurissātus, a, um [purpurissum], painted, rouged : buccae, Pl.

purpurissum, i, n. [πορφυρίζον], a kind of dark purple colour, used for dyeing red and as a cosmetic : Pl.

pūrus, a, um [cf. putō], clear, clean, free from dirt or filth or admixture. **1.** Lit. **a.** In gen. : aer, Cic. ; argentum, Cic. ; aqua, amnis, Hor. ; unda, Verg. ; purissima mella, Verg. ; aëre purior ignis, Ov. ; sol, luna (i.e. unclouded), Hor. ; caelum, Tib. Neut. as Noun : purum liquidumque haurire, Cic. ; (sc. caelum), Verg., Hor. **b.** clean, cleansed, cleared : aedes, Pl. ; vestis, Verg. ; fictilia, Tib. ; terra (cleared of stones, timber, etc.), Cic. ; so, campus, Verg., Liv. ; purus ab arboribus campus, Ov. **c.** cleansing, purifying : sulfur, Tib. **2.** Transf. **A.** plain, unadorned, unwrought, unmixed, mere. **a.** Of concr. things : argentum (i.e. not chased), Cic. ; hasta (i.e. pointless), Prop. ; sensus (i.e. without bodily taint), Verg. **b.** Of style : oratio, Cic. ; sermo quam purissimus, Quint. **B.** Morally : pure, uncontaminated, undefiled, chaste : Cic. With GEN. : sceleris purus, Hor. Comp. : Cic. Of things : pectus, Enn., Hor. ; animus, anima, Cic. ; vita, Hor. ; noctes, Pl., Tib. ; gladius ab omni caede, Sen. Ep. ; forum caede purum, Cic. ; purum vitio pectus, Hor. **C.** Relig. : familia (i.e. that has duly performed funeral rites), Cic. ; domus, Cic. ; locus (i.e. not desecrated), Liv. ; dies (i.e. uncontaminated by death), Ov. **D.** In law : iudicium (i.e. unconditional, absolute), Cic. **E.** In business. Neut. as Noun : quid possit ad dominos puri ac reliqui provenire (i.e. clear profit and balance), Cic.

pūs, pūris, n. [cf. πύον, pūteō, etc.], the white viscous matter of a sore or wound. Transf. venom, malice : Hor.

pusillus, a, um, dim. adj. very little, petty, insignificant. **1.** Lit. : pueri, Cato ; mus,

Pl. ; testis, Cic. ; habuimus la Qumano quasi pusillam Romam, Cic. Ep. ; libelli, Cic. ; vox, Quint. **2.** T r a n s f. *petty, paltry :* animus, Cic. Ep. ; pusilli animi, Hor. ; causa, Ov. ; res, Quint.

pūsiō, ōnis, *m. a little boy :* Cic., Juv.

pūstula (**pūsula**), ae, *f.* [pūs], *a blister, pimple, pustule :* Sen. Ep., Mart.

pūstulātus (**pūsulātus**), a, um [pūstula], *blistered, i.e. refined, purified :* argentum, Suet. ; Mart.

puta, *Imperative* of putō, used adverbially : *suppose ; for example, for instance :* Hor., Sen., etc.

putāmen, inis, *n.,* [putō], *clippings ; shells, husks, etc.* (us. *pl.*) : iuglandium, Cic.

putātiō, ōnis, *f.* [putō], *a pruning* of trees : Cic.

putātor, ōris, *m.* [putō], *a pruner, dresser :* vitis, Ov. ; Varr.

puteal, ālis, *n.* [puteus], *a curb round the mouth of a well.* **1.** L i t. : Cic. Ep. **2.** T r a n s f. *a curb round a sacred spot :* puteal Libonis, in the Roman forum ; a favourite place for business-men to meet : Cic., Hor., Ov.

puteālis, e, *adj.* [puteus], *of a well, well-* : lymphae, Lucr. ; undae, Ov.

pūteō, ēre [*cf.* Gk. πύον], *to stink :* Hor. [Fr. *puer.*]

Puteolī, ōrum, *m. pl.* an important commercial *city on the coast of Campania, having mineral springs ;* now *Pozzuolo.* **Puteolānus,** a, um ; **Puteolānī**, ōrum, *m. pl. the inhabitants.*

puter and **putris**, tris, tre, *adj.* [*cf.* pūteō], *rotten, decaying.* **1.** L i t. : navis, Prop. ; fanum, Hor. ; poma, Ov. **2.** T r a n s f. *crumbling, friable, flabby :* glaeba, Verg. ; campus, Verg. ; lapis, Plin. Ep. ; mammae, *flabby,* Hor. ; oculi, *languishing,* Hor.

pūtēscō, pūtēscere, pūtuī [pūteō], *to become rotten :* Cato, Cic. ; (muriā) quā Byzantia putuit orca, Hor.

puteus, I, *m. a well.* **1.** L i t. : Pl., Cic., Hor., etc. **2.** T r a n s f. *a pit :* Verg. ; *for storing grain :* Varr. ; *a dungeon for slaves :* Pl. [It. *pozzo ;* Fr. *puits.*]

pūtidē, *adv. disgustingly, affectedly :* dicere, Cic. *Comp. :* Cic.

pūtidiusculus, a, um [*dim.* of *Comp.* of pūtidus], of discourse : *rather disgustingly tedious, going a little too far :* Cic. Ep.

pūtidus, a, um [pūteō], *rotten, decaying, stinking.* **1.** L i t. : caro, Cic. ; vinum, Pl. **2.** T r a n s f. **a.** As term of abuse : *old, half-rotten, withered :* femina, Hor. ; Pl. ; Cat. *Comp. :* putidius cerebrum (*more addled*), Hor. **b.** Of style : *unnatural, affected, disgusting :* etiam Demosthenes, Cic. ; vereor ne putidum sit scribere ad te, Cic. Ep. [It. *putto, puzzo.*]

putillus, a, um [*dim.* putus, I, *cf.* pusillus], *very little :* Pl.

putō, āre [root *pu ; cf.* pūrus, amputō], *to cleanse, clean, clear.* **1.** L i t. **a.** vellus, Varr. **b.** Of trees : *to trim, prune :* Cato ; vitem, Verg. **2.** T r a n s f. **A.** Of money-accounts : *to clear up, adjust, settle :* rationem (Pl., Cato) or rationes (Cic. Ep.) cum aliquo putare. Hence, **a.** with oneself, *to ponder, consider :* cam mecum rationem, Pl. ; haec (*cf.* roputo), Ter. ; illud, Cic. ;

multi suō suum sorde, Verg. **b.** cum aliquā rogumontis, to argue (*of dispute*), Pl. **B.** *to reckon, count, estimate, value.* **a.** numerus militum putatur, Tac. **b.** With phr. of value : tegulas pro binis, Cato ; aliquid denariis quadringentis, Cic. ; magni honores, Cic. ; parvi, Cat. ; tanti conubia nostra, Ov. ; aliquem nihilo, Cic. **c.** With *predic. adj.* or *phr.* : pro certo, Matius ap. Cic. Ep. ; pro nihilo, Cic. ; imperatorem aliquo in numero putare, Cic. ; id nil puto, Ter. ; hominem prae se neminem, Cic. ; turpem lituram, Hor. **d.** Most freq. *to conclude, think, deem :* recte putas, Pl. ; rem ipsam, Ter. With Acc. and *Inf.* : Ter., Cic., Ov., etc. ; illi etiam in iniquo loco dimicandum putant, Caes. ; Cic. Often parenthetically, puto or ut puto : Cic. Ep., Ov., etc. [It. *potare.*]

pūtor, ōris, *m.* [pūteō], *a foul smell, a stench :* Lucr.

putrefaciō, facere, fēcī, factum [puter faciō], *to make rotten.* **1.** L i t. : ligna putrefacta per imbris, Lucr. ; nudatum tectum patere imbribus putrefaciendum, Liv. **2.** T r a n s f. *to make to crumble :* glaebae per imbris putrefactae, Lucr. ; ardentia saxa infuso aceto putrefaciunt, Liv.

putrēscō, ere [putreō, from puter], *to grow rotten, to moulder :* ungulae, Varr. ; vestis, Hor.

putridus, a, um [putreō from puter], *rotten, corrupt, decayed.* **1.** L i t. : dentes, Cic. ; Luc. **2.** T r a n s f. *flabby :* pectora, Cat.

putris, e, *v.* puter.

putus, a, um (root *pu ; cf.* pūrus], *cleansed, perfectly pure, unmixed.* T r a n s f. : purus putus, sometimes purus ac putus : purus putus hic sycophanta est, Pl. ; purus putus est ipsus, *it's the real 'Simon Pure,'* Pl. ; Varr. ; meae putissimae orationes (humorously), Cic. Ep.

putus, I, *m.* [=pusus, Varr. fr. ; *cf.* puer], *a boy :* Verg.

pycta or **pyctēs,** ae, *m.* [πύκτης], *a boxer :* Phaedr., Sen.

Pydna, ae, *f. a city in Macedonia, near which was fought the battle in which Aemilius Paulus defeated Perseus,* B.C. 169 ; **Pydnaeī,** ōrum, *m. pl. its inhabitants.*

pyelus, I, *m.* [πύελος], *a bath :* Pl.

pȳga (**pūga**), ae, *f.* [πυγή], *the rump, buttocks* (Lat. nates) : Hor.

pȳgargus, I, *m.* [πύγαργος, *white-rump*], *a kind of antelope with white buttocks :* Juv.

Pygmaeī, ōrum, *m. pl.* [Πυγμαῖοι], *the Pygmies, a dwarfish race, especially in Africa ; said to have been constantly at war with the cranes, by which they were always defeated :* **Pygmaeus,** a, um.

Pygmalion, ōnis, *m.* **I.** *a king of Cyprus who became enamoured of a statue which he had made.* **II.** *son of Belus, king of Tyre, and brother of Dido, whose husband Sichaeus he murdered.*

Pyladēs, ae and is, *m. son of Strophius, celebrated as the friend of Orestes ;* **Pyladēus,** a, um.

Pylae, ārum, *f. pl.* [πύλαι, " *gates* "], *a narrow pass.* **a.** Tauri, *between Cappadocia and Cilicia.* **b.** *the pass of Thermopylae ;* **Pylaicus,** a, um : convontus, Liv.

Pylaemenēs, is, *m. king of the Paphlagonians, an ally of Priam.*

Pylus and **Pylos**, ī, *f. the name of cities of the Peloponnesus.* **a.** In Messenia, where Neleus reigned, now *Palaio Navarino.* **b.** In S. Elis, the abode of Nestor; **Pylius,** a, um; as Noun, *the Pylian, i.e. Nestor.*

pyra, ae, *f.* [πυρά], *a funeral pile, pyre* [Lat. rogus]: Verg.

pyramis, idis *f.* [πυραμίς, prop. an Egyptian word], *a pyramid.* **1.** Lit.: Prop., Tac. **2.** Transf. *a cone* (the geometrical figure): Cic.

Pyramus, ī, *m.* **I.** *the lover of Thisbe.* **II.** *a river in Cilicia.*

Pyrēnē (ȳ in Tib.), ēs, *f. a range of mountains in the north of Spain, the Pyrenees ;* **Pyrē-naeus** (ȳ in Lucan), a, um.

pyrethrum or **-on**, ī, *n.* [πύρεθρον], *a plant, Spanish chamomile, pellitory :* Ov. [It. *pilatro.*]

Pyrgi, ōrum, *m. pl. an ancient town in Etruria ;* **Pyrgēnsis**, e.

pyrōpus, ī, *m.* [πυρωπός, *fire-coloured*], *a metallic mixture, gold-bronze, bronze :* Lucr., Ov.

Pyrrha, ae, and **Pyrrhē**, ēs, *f. d. of Epimetheus, and w. of Deucalion.*

Pyrrhias, adis, *adj. of the city of Pyrrha in Lesbos, Pyrrhian.*

pyrrhicha, ae, and **pyrrhichē**, ēs, *f.* [πυρρίχη], *a dance in armour, the Pyrrhic dance :* Plin., Suet.

pyrrhichius, a, um [πυρρίχιος], in prosody: pes, or simply pyrrhichius, *a pyrrhic* (◡ ◡): Quint.

Pyrrhō, ōnis, *m. a philosopher of Elis, contemporary with Aristotle, and founder of the sceptical school of philosophy ;* **Pyrrhōnēi,** ōrum, *m. pl. his followers, the Pyrrhonists*

Pyrrhus, ī, *m.* **I.** *son of Achilles and Deidamia* (otherwise called Neoptolemus), *founder of a kingdom in Epirus ;* **Pyrrhidae,** ārum, *m. pl. the inhabitants of the said kingdom.* **II.** *a king of Epirus, who invaded Italy to assist the Tarentines against Rome.*

Pythagorās, ae, *m. a celebrated philosopher of Samos, about 540 B.C. He settled in Italy, and was the founder of the system of philosophy which received its name from him ;* **Pythago-rēus, Pythagoricus,** a, um; **Pythago-rēi,** ōrum, *m. pl. the Pythagoreans.*

Pythō, ūs, *f. an old name of Delphi ;* **Pythi-cus, Pythius,** a, um, *Pythian, Delphic:* Apollo, Liv.; oraculum, Cic.; **Pythia,** ae, *f. the priestess at Delphi, the Pythia;* **Py-thia,** ōrum, *n. pl. the Pythian games ;* celebrated every fourth year at Delphi in honour of Apollo.

Pythōn, ōnis, *m. the serpent slain near Delphi by Apollo.*

pytisma, atis, *n.* [πύτισμα], *that which is spit or spirted out* (in tasting wine, etc.): Juv.

pytissō, āre [πυτίζω], *to spit or spirt out wine in tasting :* Ter.

pyxis, idis, *f.* [πυξίς], *a small box, esp. for unguents, medicines, etc. Orig. of box-wood, but afterwards a box of any kind :* veneni, Cic.; aurea, Suet.

Q

Q, q, the sixteenth letter of the Latin alphabet. **I.** There was a manifest tendency in Latin to get rid of *q.* Thus in the oldest inscriptions the forms *pequdes, pequnia,* occur instead of *pecudes, pecunia.* So the original forms *quoius, quoi, quor* (quāre), became *cuius, cui, cur.* **II.** Relations of *q* with other letters. **1.** In Latin itself the only change is into *c,* of which examples are given above: in the composition and inflexion of words this change frequently occurs: e.g. *quatio, percutio ; sequor, secutus.* During the Republican period, *qu* does not occur before *u ;* either quom or cum is written, equos or ecus, etc. **2.** *qu* in Latin sometimes corresponds to π in Greek: e.g. *sequor,* ἕπομαι: also to τ ; e.g. *que, quattuor ;* τε, τέτταρες. **III.** Changes of *q* (or rather of *qu*) in the Romance languages. **1.** Into *c :* e.g. Lat. *quomodo ;* It. *come ;* Fr. *comme.* **2.** Into *g* (only in the middle of words): e.g. Lat. *aequalis ;* It. *eguale ;* Fr. *égal.* **3.** In Fr. *q* is sometimes omitted: e.g. Lat. *aqua, coquere, sequi ;* Fr. *eau, cuire, suivre.* **IV.** As an abbreviation, Q represents most freq. the praenomen Quintus, but also stands for quaestor, que, quinquennalis ; S. P. Q. R., senatus populusque Romanus.

qua, *v.* quis.

quā, ABL. *f.* of quī, quis. **I.** Relat.: *by which way* or *route, by the way by which, whereby, where.* **1.** Lit.: ad omnis introitūs quā adire poterat, Cic. ; Pl. ; quā te ducit via, dirige gressum, Verg. ; eādem quā ceteri fugere noluit, Cic. **2.** Transf. **a.** *whereby, by what means :* collis occupare quā despici posset, Caes. ; Cat. ; Verg., etc. **b.** *by what extent, as far as, as widely as :* vagari quā velit, Cic. ; Sall. ; Liv., etc. **c.** quā . . . quā, *as well . . . as, partly . . . partly :* omnium illo die quā plebis quā patrum eximia virtus fuit, Liv. ; Pl. ; Cic. **II.** Interrog. : *by what way ?* Transf. *by what means, whereby* (only in Indir. Quest.) : Ter., Cic., Verg. (*cf.* also nescio quā) **III.** Indef. : *by any way.* Transf. *in any way :* si quā fata sinant, Verg. (*cf.* also ne quā).

quā-cumque (later **-cunque**), as two words quā porro cumque, Lucr., quā se cumque, Verg., *adv., by whatever way, wherever.* **1.** Lit.: quācumque iter fecit, Caes. ; Cic. ; Liv. **2.** Transf. **a.** quācumque nos commovimus, ad Caesaris acta revocamur, Cic. Ep. **b.** *in what manner soever :* novas incidere litis, Verg.

quādam tenus, *adv. to a certain point, so far and no farther :* est quādam prodire tenus, si non datur ultra, Hor.

quadra, ae, *f.* **I.** *a square cake or piece of bread* on which food was set (also called mensa): Verg. **II.** *a square bit, morsel :* Hor. ; panis, Sen. ; casei, Mart. **III.** *a (square) dining-table :* Juv.

quadrāgēni, ae, a, (GEN.—ēnum, Caes.) [quadrāgintā], *forty in a group ;* hence, *forty each : sestertiis* quadragenis milibus, Cic. ; Caes. ; Liv.

quadrāgēsimus (-gēns-), a, um [quadrā-gintā], *fortieth* : Cato, Cic. As Noun, **quadrāgēsima**, ae, *f.* (sc. pars), *the fortieth part, a fortieth* : Suet. Esp. as a tax, 2½ *per cent. duty* : Tac. [Fr. *carême.*]

quadrāgiēns (-iēs), *adv.* [quadrāgintā], *forty times* : Cic., Liv.

quadrāgintā, *indecl. adj. forty* : Pl., Cic., Cat. [It. *quaranta* ; Sp. *cuarenta* ; Fr. *quarante.*]

quadrāns, antis, *m.* [quattuor], *a fourth part, a fourth, a quarter.* **a.** heres ex quadrante, *to the fourth part of an estate*, Suet. **b.** *a coin, the fourth part of an as* : Liv., Juv. As the price of a bath : Hor. **c.** As a weight : *the quarter of a pound* : Cato. **d.** As a liquid measure : *the quarter* of a sextarius : Varr., Mart. **e.** As a measure : *the quarter* of a foot : Cato.

quadrantal, ālis, *n.* [quadrāns], *a liquid measure (eight* congii) : Pl.

quadrantārius, a, um [quadrāns], *of a quarter.* **a.** tabulae (accounts of debts reduced to a fourth), Cic. **b.** mulier (i.e. Clodia, who sold herself for a bath ; *v.* quadrans b.), Cic.

quadrātus, a, um. **I.** *Part.* quadrō. **II.** Adj.: *squared, square* : saxum, Liv. ; statura, Suet. ; agmen (in regular order of battle), Cic., Tib., Liv., etc. ; quadrato agmine incedere, Sall. ; agmine quadrato amnem ingressus, Liv. **III.** Noun, **quadrātum**, i, *n.* **a.** *a square* : Cic., Hor. **b.** In astronom. : *quadrature* : Cic.

quadrīduum (quatr-), i, *n.* [quattuor diēs], *a space of four days* : in hoc quadriduo, Pl. ; quadridui sermo, Cic. ; iustitio quod quadriduum fuit, Liv. ; quadriduo quo haec gesta sunt, *four days after*, Cic.

quadriennium, i, *n.* [annus], *a space or period of four years* : Cic.

quadrifāriam, *adv. four-fold, in four parts* : coniurati quadrifariam se diviserunt, Liv.

quadrifidus, a, um [quattuor and *fid* in findō], *four-cleft, split into four parts* : sudes, Verg.

quadrigae, ārum, *f. pl.* (rare in *sing.*) [contr. from quadriiugae], *a team of four ; a chariot with four horses driven abreast.* **1.** Lit. : Cic., Verg., Liv., etc. Poet. of the chariot of the Sun : Pl. ; of Aurora : Verg. ; of Night : Tib. *Sing.* : Prop., Suet. **2.** Transf. : Pl. ; irarum effundere quadrigas, Enn. ; poēticae, Cic. ; navibus atque quadrigis petimus bene vivere, Hor.

quadrigārius, a, um [quadrigae], *of the driver of a* quadriga : habitus, Suet. As Noun, *the driver of a four-horse chariot* : Varr., Suet.

Quadrigārius, i, *m.* Q. Claudius, *a Roman historian* (1st cent. B.C.).

quadrigātus, a, um [quadrigae], *marked or stamped with the figure of a* quadriga : Liv.

quadrigulae, ārum, *f. pl.* [*dim.* quadrigae], *a little four-horse team* : Cic. In *sing.* : Plin.

quadriiugis, e. (Verg.) and **quadriiugus**, a. um (Enn., Verg., Ov.) [quattuor iugum], *of a team of four* : currus, Enn., Verg. ; equi, Verg., Ov. As Noun, **quadriiugi**, ōrum, *m. pl. a four-horse team* : Ov.

quadrilībris, e, *adj.* [quattuor libra], *that weighs four pounds* : Pl.

quadrimēstris, e, *adj.* [quattuor mēnsis]. **I.** *four months old* : Varr. **II.** *lasting four months* : Suet.

quadrimulus, a, um [*dim.* quadrimus], *only four years old* : parvolus, Pl.

quadrimus, a, um [quattuor, *cf.* bimus], *four years old* : Cic. Ep., Hor., Liv.

quadringēnārius, a, um [quadringēni], *consisting of four hundred men each ;* cohortes, Cic. Ep., Liv.

quadringēni, ae, a, [quadringenti], *a group of four hundred, hence four hundred each* : Liv., Suet.

quadringentēsimus (-ēns-), a, um [quadringenti], *the four hundredth* : annus, Liv.

quadringenti, ae, a [quattuor centum], *four hundred* : Cic., Juv.

quadringentiēs (-ēns-), *adv.* [quadringenti], *four hundred times* : Cic.

quadri-pertitus, a, um, *consisting of four parts, four-fold* : distributio accusationis, Cic. ; exercitus, Tac.

quadrirēmis, is, *f. adj.* [quattuor rēmus], *having four banks of oars* : navis, Liv. Also as Noun : *a quadrireme* : Caes., Cic., Liv.

quadrivium, i, *n.* [quattuor via], *a place where four ways meet, a cross-road* : Cat., Juv. [It. *carrobio.*]

quadrō, āre [quadrum]. **A.** Trans. *to make square.* Transf. **a.** *to square, complete* : acervum, Hor. **b.** *to join properly together* : orationem, Cic. **B.** Intrans. *to be square.* **1.** Lit. : in unguem secto via limite quadret, Verg. **2.** Transf. **a.** coniunctio, Cic. ; omnia in istam, Cic. ; tibi ita quadrat, *it suits* (i.e. pleases) *you*, Cic. **b.** Of accounts, *to square, agree* : quo modo sescenta eodem modo quadrarint, Cic. [Fr. *carrer.*]

quadrum, i, *n.* [quattuor], *a square.* Transf. : in quadrum redigere sententias, Cic.

quadrupedāns, tis, *adj.* [quadrupēs], *going on four feet, galloping*, canterius, Pl. ; Poet. : sonitus, Verg. ; as Noun in *pl.* : (*galloping*) *steeds* : Verg.

quadru-pēs, pedis, *adj.* [quattuor pēs], *four-footed, going on four feet* : ecus, Enn. ; transf. : Ov. Of men : quadrupedem constringito (i.e. hand and foot), Ter. ; of a person creeping *on all fours* : Ov., Suet. More freq. as Noun, *m. f. a four-footed animal, a quadruped* : Pl., Cic., Verg., etc.

quadruplātor, ōris, *m.* [quadruplus], *a multiplier by four ;* hence **a.** *a magnifier* : beneficiorum suorum, Sen. **b.** *a public informer* (perh. orig. against a person liable to a quadruplum, q.v.) : Pl., Cic. ; hence *of a base arbitrator* (who took for himself the disputed property) : Liv.

quadruplex, icis, *adj.* [quattuor plicō], *four-fold, quadruple* : pecunia, Pl. ; ordo, Liv. ; stellae (*four together*), Cic. poet.

quadruplicō, āre [quadruplex], *to make four-fold, multiply by four* : rem suam, Pl.

quadruplor, āri [quadruplus], *to be an informer* (*v.* quadruplator) : Pl.

quadruplus, a, um [quattuor ; *cf.* duplus], *four-fold, quadruple* : Suet. As Noun,

quadruplum, I, n. *a four-fold amount* (esp. *as penalty*), *four times as much :* faeneratorem condemnari quadrupli, Cato ; iudicium in aratorem in quadruplum dare, Cic.

quaeritō, āre [*freq.* quaerō], *to seek repeatedly or constantly.* **1.** L i t. **a.** In gen.: Pl. With Acc.: aliquem terrā marique, Pl. ; Ter. ; Cat. **b.** *to seek to obtain :* victum (i.e. to earn a living), Ter. ; hospitium ab aliquo, Pl. P r o v.: huius sermones cinerem haud quaeritant (i.e. need no polishing), Pl. **2.** T r a n s f. *to seek to know, keep on asking :* quid tu id quaeritas ? Pl. ; Ter.

quaerō (older **quaesō,** q.v.), quaerere, quaesivi *or* quaesii, quaesitum, *to look* or *search for.* **1.** L i t. **a.** In gen.: aliquem, Pl., Ter., Nep. ; liberos ad necem, Cic. ; portum, Caes. ; viam, Ov. ; herbas montibus, Verg. **b.** *to seek to obtain ; to get, procure :* rem honeste mercaturis faciendis, Cic. ; argentum, Hor. ; liberorum quaerundorum causā ei uxor data est, Pl. ; denique sit finis quaerendi (*sc.* pecuniam), Pl. **2.** T r a n s f. **a.** *to seek to find out, seek to obtain, seek :* laudem sibi, Ter. ; sibi remedium ad rem aliquam, Cic .; gloriam bello, Cic. ; occasionem fraudis, Caes. ; locum insidiis, Liv. With *Inf. :* Verg., Hor., Ov. **b.** Of things as Subject : *to demand, require :* bellum dictatoriam maiestatem, Liv. ; Cic. ; Ov. **c.** *to seek in vain, to miss :* Siciliam in uberrimā Siciliae parte, Cic. ; Hor. ; aliquem, Prop. **d.** *to seek to know, to ask, inquire.* With *ab* (Caes., Cic.), *de* (Cic., Ov., Liv.), *ex* (Caes., Cic. Ep.) of person *from whom* information is sought. With Acc. of thing sought : fidem imperatoris, Caes. With *Indir. Quest. :* Cic., Liv., etc. With *Indir. Deliberative :* Ter., Sall. With *de :* eorum de naturā Caesar quaerebat, Caes. P h r. (colloq.) si quaeris, si quaerimus, *if you, we ask* (for the facts), i.e. to tell the truth : Cic. ; noli quaerere *or* quid quaeris ? *in short, in one word :* Cic. Ep. **e.** *to examine* or *inquire into judicially :* rem, Ter., Cic. With *de :* de morte alicuius, Cic. ; de servo tormentis, Cic. ; de pecuniis repetundis, Cic. ; de servo in dominum, Cic. [It. *chiedere :* Fr. *quérir.*]

quaesitiō, ōnis, *f.* [quaerō], *a questioning* (by torture), *inquisition :* Tac.

quaesitor, ōris, *m.* [quaerō]. **I.** *the praetor* (*or other person*), *who presided in criminal trials :* Cic. Hence, of Minos : Verg.

quaesitus, a, um. **I.** *Part.* quaerō. **II.** Noun. **a. quaesitum,** i, n. *a question :* Ov. **b. quaesita,** ōrum, n. *pl. gains, money accumulated :* Verg., Hor. **III.** Adj. **a.** *sought out ; special :* leges quaesitiores (opp. to simplices), Tac. ; quaesitissimi honores, Tac. ; Sall. **b.** *far-fetched, studied :* comitas, Tac. Of style : Cic.

quaesō, ere [old form of quaerō]. **1.** L i t. *to seek :* Pl. **2.** T r a n s f. *to beg, pray.* **a.** Usually in parenthesis (= Eng. *please*) : ipsum decretum, quaeso, cognoscite, Cic. ; Pl. ; Ter. **b.** With Acc.: divum (GEN.) pacem prece, Lucr. **c.** With *ut* and *Subj.* : Ter., Cic., Liv. ; aliquem ut etc., Pl., Ter., Cato ; ab aliquo ut etc., Cic. With *Subj.* alone : Liv. With *ne* and *Subj.* : Cic., Liv.

quaesticulus, i, m. [*dim.* quaestus], *a small profit, slight gain :* Cic.

quaestiō, ōnis, *f.* [quaerō], *a seeking.* **1.** L i t.: tibi ne in quaestione essemus, Pl. **2.** T r a n s f. *an inquiry, investigation, research.* **a.** In gen.: res in quaestione versatur, Cic. ; res in quaestionem venit, Quint. ; rem in quaestionem vocare, Cic. ; instituere, solvere, Quint. ; facere de aliquā re, Juv. ; magna quaestio est (with *Indir. Quest.*), Cic. Also *a subject of investigation* or *research :* Cic., Quint., etc. **b.** In law : cum praetor quaestionem inter sicarios exercuisset, Cic.; Liv. ; quaestionem instituere (*or* habere) de morte alicuius, Cic. ; quaestionem de furto constituere, Cic. ; ferre in aliquem, Cic. ; quaestioni praeesse, Cic. ; quaestiones perpetuae (*standing courts*), Cic. ; quaestiones extraordinariae, Liv. With torture implied : quaestionem habere de servis, Cic. ; ex servis, Liv. ; servos in quaestionem dare, ferre, polliceri (i.e. *to offer them for examination under torture*), Cic. ; postulare servum in quaestionem, Cic. **c.** *a questioning* : rem quaestione captivorum explorare, Caes. With torture implied (*cf.* 2. b.) : de uxoribus in servilem modum habere, Caes.

quaestiuncula, ae, *f.* [*dim.* quaestiō], *a little* or *trifling question :* Cic., Quint.

quaestor, ōris, m. [contr. from quaesitor, from quaerō], *a quaestor ; a* Roman magistrate. **a.** *public prosecutors* or *judges* of criminal offences : Cic., Liv. **b.** *treasury-officials :* Pl., Cic., Liv., Tac. **c.** *financial officers* to consuls and praetors, proconsuls and propraetors : Caes., Cic., Liv., Tac.

quaestōrius, a, um [quaestor], *of a quaestor :* officium, Cic. Ep. ; scelus, Cic. ; porta (in a camp), Liv. As Noun. **a. quaestōrius,** i, m. *one who had been quaestor, an ex-quaestor :* Cic. **b. quaestōrium,** i, n. (*sc.* tentorium), *the quaestor's tent* in a camp : Liv. ; or *his residence* in a province : Cic.

quaestuōsus, a, um [quaestus]. **I.** *gainful, profitable :* ager, Cato ; mercatura, officina, edictum, annus, Cic. ; emporium, Liv. Comp., Sup.: Cic. **II.** *greedy for gain :* mulier, Pl. ; homo, Cic. **III.** *that has great gains, enriched :* Tac. ; spoliis, Curt.

quaestūra, ae, *f.* [quaestor], *the office of quaestor, the quaestorship.* **1.** L i t.: petere, Cic., Tac. ; gerere, Suet. ; ex quaesturā consulatum petere, Liv. **2.** T r a n s f. *public money :* Cic.

quaestus, ūs (GEN. quaestī, Pl., Ter.), m. [quaerō], *a gaining, acquiring ; gain, profit, advantage.* **1.** L i t.: Pl. ; cum quaestu dimittere, Cic. With *Obj.* GEN.: pecuniae, Caes. With *Subj.* GEN.: unius agri et unius anni, Cic. **2.** T r a n s f. **a.** *a source of gain :* quaestui habere rem publicam, Cic. ; Sall. T r a n s f.: ut quaestui habeant male loqui melioribus, Pl. **b.** *a way of making money, a business, occupation :* malus, Pl. ; quaestūs liberales, sordidi, Cic. ; meretricius, Cic. ; quaestum (corpore) facere (of a prostitute), Pl., Liv., Tac. **c.** *gain, advantage :* nullum in eo facio quaestum, Cic. Ep.

quā-libet (**quālubet**, *f.* ABL. of quilibet], *by any way you please, anywhere.* **1.** L i t.: quālubet perambula aedis, Pl. ; Tib.

Quint. **2.** Transf. *as you please, in any way* : quālubet esse notus optas, Cat.

quālis, e, *pron. adj.* [v. quī]. **I.** Interrog.: *of what sort, kind, or nature, what kind of* ? quali fide, quali pietate existimatis eos esse ? Cic.; Pl. In *Indir. Quest. :* Pl., Caes., Cic. **II.** Exclam.: hei mihi, qualis erat ! Verg. **III.** Relat.: as correlative to talis (*of such a sort*) *as :* ut qualem te iam antea populo R. praebuisti, talem et nobis impertias, Cic.; Verg., etc. Often the talis is omitted (translate *such as*) : in hoc bello, quale bellum nulla barbaria gessit, Cic.; Verg. Elliptically (translate by *in such wise* or *way, like as, as*) : qualis ubi fugit praesepia liber equus, Verg.; equitum acies qualis quae esse instructissima potest, Liv.; qualis exercet Diana choros, Verg.; Ov. **IV.** Indef.: *having some quality or other :* et ita effici quae appellant qualia, Cic.

quālis-cumque, quāle-cumque (or **-cun-que**) (*in tmesi*, quale id cumque est, Cic.), *adj.* [quālis]. **I.** Relat.: *of what quality soever, of whatever kind:* licet videre, qualescumque summi civitatis viri fuerunt, talem civitatem fuisse, Cic. With verb omitted: qualicumque urbis situ (*sc.* essent) sisti potuisse, Liv.; imperatores voto expetere, qualiscumque tolerare, Tac.; Ov. **II.** Indef.: *any whatever :* sin qualemcumque locum sequimur, quae est domestica sede iucundior ? Cic. Ep. [Fr. *quelconque.*]

quālis-libet, quāle-libet, *adj. of whatever sort or nature :* Cic.

quālitās, ātis, *f.* [quālis], *quality, property, nature* (a word coined by Cic. to translate ποιότης) : Quint. In *pl. :* Plin., Quint.

quāliter, *adv.* (*just*) *as :* lacrimae fluxere per ora, qualiter abiectā de nive manat aqua, Ov.

quālum, ī, *n.* (Cato), and **quālus**, ī, *m.* (Cato; perh. in Verg., Hor.), *a wicker basket.* **a.** For sowing : Cato. **b.** For straining wine : Verg. **c.** For wool: Hor.

quam, *adv.* [v. quī]. **I.** Interrog.: *to what extent* ! *how much* ! *how* ? : quam multis custodibus opus erit ? Cic. In *Indir. Quest.* : scio quam timida sit ambitio, Cic.; Sall.; Liv.; dici non potest quam sim disputatione tuā delectatus, Cic. **II.** Exclam.: quam cupiunt laudari, Cic. **III.** Relat. **A.** In gen. (*to such an extent*) *as.* **a.** As correl. to *tam :* quid tam populare quam libertas ? Cic.; Pl.; si tam cavere potuisset quam metuere solebat, Cic. **b.** As correl. to *sic :* Verg. **c.** Alone : quam celerrime potuit, Caes.; quam maximā voce possum dico, Cic. Without possum : sementia quam maximas facere, Caes.; quam primum, *as soon as possible,* Caes., Cic., Verg. **B.** In comparisons : (*in the way that*) . . . *as.* **a.** As correl. to *tam :* tam ego ante fui liber quam gnatus tuos, Pl.; Cic.; quam magis id reputo, tam magis uror, Pl.; Verg.; quam quisque pessume fecit, tam maxume tutus est, Sall. **b.** quam magis . . . tanto magis, Pl., Lucr. **c.** Alone : homo non quam isti sunt gloriosus, Liv.; quam magis . . . magis, Verg. **d.** After *Comparative Adj.* or *Adv.,* or *Verb* implying comparison

(translate *by than*) : qui plura militum eorum occidisset quam quod superaret, Liv.; Cic.; libentius quam verius, Cic.; esse quam videri bonus malebat, Sall.; Cic.; Liv., etc. **e.** After other particles and words : nihil aeque eos terruit quam robur ac color imperatoris, *so much as,* Liv.; contra faciunt quam professi sunt, *otherwise than,* Cic.; nil aliud quam, *nothing else than,* Liv.; aliter quam ego velim, *otherwise than,* Cic.; supra quam fieri possit, *more than,* Cic.; ultra quam satis est, *farther than,* Cic.; **f.** After *numerals of comparison :* dimidium tributi quam quod regibus ferre soliti erant, Liv. After words denoting succession of time, esp. *ante* and *post :* postero die quam illa erant acta, *the day after that,* Cic.; Liv. So, quinto die quam (i.e. *after*) ab senatu responsum accepissent, Liv. **IV.** Emphatically with adverbs : *exceedingly, very, quite, indeed :* quam familiariter, Ter.; nimis quam cupio, Pl.; mire quam, Cic. Ep.

quam diū or **quamdiū**, *adv.* **I.** Interrog.: *how long* ! Pl., Cic. **II.** Relat.: *as long as, until, during :* quam diu potuit, tacuit, Caes.; Cic.

quam dūdum, *v.* dudum.

quam-libet (-lubet), *adv.* (usually qualifying adjectives or adverbs) : *as much as you please :* quamlubet esto unica res, Lucr.; Quint.; Plin. Ep.; occupat egressas quamlibet ante ratis, *having had ever so much start,* Ov.

quam ob rem or **quamobrem**, *adv.* **I.** Interrog.: *for what reason* ! *on what account* ? Pl., Cic. In *Indir. Quest. :* Caes. **II.** Relat.: *for which reason, wherefore, why :* multae sunt causae, quam ob rem cupio abducere, Ter.; Cic. Ep.; verum illud est quam ob rem haec commemorarim, Cic.; Pl.

quam plūrēs, *cf.* quam, IV.

quam plūrimus, *v.* quam, III. A. c.

quam-quam (quanquam), *conj. though, although.* **A.** Most freq. with *Indic.* : Pl., Cic., Hor., Liv., etc. **B.** With *Subj.* : Nep., Liv. (in Cic., only if *potential, conditional,* etc). **C.** Ellipt. **a.** With *Part.* or *Adj.* : arma quamquam nobis invisa sumenda sunt, Sall.; Cic.; Liv., etc. **b.** At beg. of sentence : *and yet, however :* Cic., Verg.

quam-vis, *adv.* [vis from volō]. **A.** *Adv. :* *as much as you please, ever so.* **A.** With *Adj.* or *Adv. :* quamvis multos nominatim proferre, Cic.; Pl.; Caes., etc.; quamvis diu, Cic. **B.** As *Conj. : however much ;* hence, *although.* **a.** With *Subj. :* Cic., Verg. **b.** With *Indic. :* Nep., Verg., Liv., etc. **c.** Without verb : res bello gesserat, quamvis rei publicae calamitosas, at tamen magnas, Cic.; Tac.

quā-nam, *adv. by what way* or *route* (in *Indir. Quest.*) : Liv.

quandō, *adv.* [v. quī]. **I.** Interrog.: *at what time* ! *when* ? Ter., Cic., Hor., etc. In *Indir. Quest. :* Cic., etc. **II.** Indef.: *at any time, ever* (after *si, ne, num*) : ut, si quando auditum sit, prodigi simile numeretur, Cic.; Ov.; Liv. **III.** Relat. **a.** (*at the time*) *when :* quando esurio tum intestina crepant, Pl.; Cic.; Verg., etc.

b. Almost as *Conj.* : *when, since, because :* duo me ad eam, quando huc veni, Ter. ; Pl. ; Cic. ; Liv., etc. [Fr. *quand.*]

quandō-cumque or **-cunque** (separated): quando consumet cumque, Hor.), *adv.* **I.** Relat. : *at what time soever, whenever, as often as.* **a.** With *Indic.* : Cato, Hor., Liv., etc. **b.** With *Subj.* : Prop., Curt. **II.** Indef. : *at some time or other, in due time :* quandocumque mihi poenas dabis, Ov. ; Hor.

quandō-que, *adv.* **I.** Relat. **a.** *at what time soever, whenever, as often as :* Cic., Hor., Liv., etc. **b.** Almost as *Conj.* : *since :* Cic., Liv. **II.** Indef. : *at some time, at one time or other :* et tu, Galba, quandoque degustabis imperium, Tac. After *quoad :* Cic. Ep. After *ne :* Liv.

quandō-quidem (quandoq-, Verg.), *conj.* *since indeed, since, seeing that :* quandoquidem tu istos oratores tantopere laudas, Cic. ; Ter. ; Verg. ; Liv.

quan-quam, *v.* quamquam.

quantillus, a, um [*dim.* quantulus]. **I.** Interrog. : *how much?* (with an implication of smallness), *how little?* Pl. **II.** Exclam. : Pl. **III.** Relat. : *the little which :* Pl.

quantitās, ātis, *f.* [quantus], *greatness, extent, quantity :* umoris, Plin. ; vocis, modi, numeri, Quint.

quantō opere and **quant-opere**, *adv.* **I.** Interrog. *with what pains or care?* hence, *how greatly?* (in *Indir. Quest.*) : Caes., Cic. ; video quanto se opere custodiant bestiae, Cic. **II.** Relat. *(with such care, hence so greatly) . . . as :* neque enim tanto opere hanc a Crasso disputationem desiderabam, quanto opere eius in causis oratione delector, Cic.

quantulus, a, um [*dim.* quantus], *how great or much* (but with an implication of smallness) ; *how little, how small, how trifling.* **I.** Interrog. : Cic. In *Indir. Quest. :* Pl., Lucr., Juv. **II.** Exclam. : Cic. **III.** Relat. : quantulum visum est, Cic. ; Hor.

quantulus-cumque, acumque, umcumque, *relat. adj. however small, however unimportant :* Cic., Juv. *Neut.* as Noun : quantulumcumque dicebamus, Cic.

quantus, a, um [*v.* quī], *how great.* **I.** Interrog. : Iovem quanto honore esse arbitramini ? Cic. In *Indir. Quest.* : Cic., etc. *Neut.* as Noun, **quantum**, **I**, *how much?* : quantum dedit ? Cic. **quanti** (GEN. or LOCAT. of Value or Price) : quanti emi potest ? Pl. ; ede mihi scriptum quanti emeris, Cic. **quantō** (ABL. of Measure) : videtote quanto secus ego fecerim, Cato ; Cic. **II.** Exclam. : Cic. *Neut.* as Noun, **quantum**, **I**, *how much :* quantum terroris iniecit! Cic. ; quantum (*Intern.* ACC.) mutatus ! Verg. **quanti** (GEN. or LOCAT. of Value or Price) : quanti est sapere ! Ter. ; quanti est ista hominum gloria, Cic. **quantō** (ABL. of Measure) : quanto sapientius maiores nostri fecerunt ! Cic. **III.** Relat. (freq. as correl. to tantus) : *(so great) . . . as :* cum tantis copiis quantas nemo habuit, Nep. ; tanta est inter eos quanta maxima esse potest morum studiorumque distantia, Cic. Without tantus :

quantus non umquam antea exercitus venit, Liv. ; Pl. ; Caes. ; Verg., etc. ; quantā maximā poterat vi perculit, Liv. (*v.* also quantus quantus). *Neut.* as Noun, **quantum**, **I** : quantum est frumenti exaraverunt, Cic. ; Caes. ; in quantum, *to whatever extent, as far as :* in quantum satis erat, Tac. ; Ov. ; in quantum maxime potest, Quint. So ACC. (*Intern.* or of Extent) : domum me rusum quantum potero tantum recipiam, Pl. ; Liv. ; quantum iuniores patrum plebi se magis insinuabant, eo acrius contra tribuni tenebant, Liv. Without correl. : Liv. **quantī** (GEN. or LOCAT. of Value or Price) : quanti aestimabat tanti vendidit, Cic. **quantō** (ABL. of Measure) : quanto diutius abest, magis cupio tanto, Ter. ; Caes. ; tanto acceptius in vulgum quanto modicus privatis aedificationibus, Tac.

quantus-cumque, acumque, umcumque, *relat. adj., however great :* quantuscumque sum ad iudicandum, Cic. Also implying smallness : *however small :* Liv. *Neut.* as Noun : **quantumcumque** (ACC. of Extent) : quantumcumque possum, Cic.

quanticumque (GEN. or LOCAT. of Value or Price) : Sen. Ep.

quantus-libet, alibet, umlibet, *adj. as great as you please :* quantolibet ordine dignus, Ov. ; Tac. *Neut.* ACC. of Extent, **quantum-libet**, *as much as you please :* Liv., Quint.

quantus quantus, a, um, *however great, however much :* quanta quanta haec mea paupertas est, tamen etc., Ter. ; Pl. ; tu quantus quantus nihil nisi sapientia es, Ter. **quanti quanti** (GEN. or LOCAT. of Price) : Cic. Ep.

quantus-vis, avis, umvis, *adj. as much or as great as you please, however great :* quantasvis magnas copias sustineri posse, Caes. ; Liv. *Neut.* as Noun, **quantum-vis** : Pl., Hor. ACC. of Extent : quantumvis licet excellas, Cic. ; ille catus, quantumvis rusticus, Hor.

quā-propter (*in tmesi :* quā me propter adduxit, Ter.), *adv.* [*cf.* proptereā], *for what, wherefore, why.* **I.** Interrog. : Pl., Ter. **II.** Relat. : quid est quāpropter nobis vos malum minitamini ? Pl., Ter. Resumptive : *wherefore, (and) therefore, (and) on that account :* quapropter hoc dicam, Cic. ; Ter.

quā-quā, *adv. by whatever way or route :* quāquā incedit, Pl.

quā-quam, *adv. by any way :* Lucr.

quā rē or **quā-rē**, *adv.* **I.** Interrog. **a.** *by what means? how?* : Pl., Ter. **b.** *from what cause? wherefore? why?* : Cic., Hor., etc. In *Indir. Quest. :* Cic. **II.** Relat. **a.** *by which means, whereby :* Cic., Nep. **b.** *from which cause, wherefore, why :* quaeramus quae tanta vitia fuerint in unico filio quā re is patri displiceret, Cic. Resumptive : *for which reason, wherefore :* quare pro certo habetote, Sall. ; Cic. Ep. [Fr. *car.*]

quarta-decimāni, ōrum, *m. pl.* [quarta decima, *sc.* legiō], *soldiers of the fourteenth* (*legion*) *:* Tac.

quartānus, a, um [quartus]. **I.** *recurring every fourth day :* febris, Cic. As Noun,

quartāna, ae, *f.* (*sc.* febris), *a quartan ague :* frigida, Hor. **II. quartāni**, ōrum, *m. pl. the soldiers of the fourth* (*legion*): Tac.

quartārius, ī, *m.* [quartus], *a fourth part, quarter ;* esp. of a sextarius, *a quartern, gill :* vini, Liv.

quartus, a, um [quattuor], *fourth :* pars, Caes. ; quartus ab Arcesilā, Cic. ; Pl. ; Verg. **quartum**, Acc. *n. for the fourth time :* eo quartum consule, Cic. ; Enn. ; Liv. **quartō**, ABL. *n. for the fourth time :* Ov., Auct. B. Hisp.

quartus-decimus, a, um, *the fourteenth :* Cic., Tac.

quasi, *adv. as if, just as.* **a.** With *Indic. :* quasi poma ex arboribus, cruda si sunt, vix avelluntur, sic . . ., Cic. Strengthened with *item, perinde, proinde : exactly as :* Pl., Cic. **b.** With *Subj. : as* (*would be* or *would have been the case*) *if :* homines corrupti superbiā ita aetatem agunt quasi vestros honores contemnant, Sall. ; Cic. Strengthened with *item, perinde, proinde :* Pl., Cic. With added *si :* quasi si esset ex se nata, Pl. **c.** With *Part. : as* (*would be* or *would have been the case*) *if :* hostes insecuti quasi partā victoriā, Caes. ; Cic. **d.** With *Adj.* or *Adv. : as it were, so to speak :* volunt probabile aliquid esse et quasi veri simile, Cic. ; quasi in extremā paginā, Cic. **e.** With numerals : *about, nearly, almost :* quasi talenta ad quindecim, Ter. ; Pl. ; Cic.

quasillum, ī, *n.* and **quasillus**, ī, *m.* [*dim.* quālus], *a small basket :* Cato, Cic., Tib.

quassātiō, ōnis, *f.* [quassō], *a shaking :* capitum, Liv.

quassō, āre [*freq.* quatiō], *to shake* or *toss repeatedly* or *violently.* **A.** Trans. **1.** Lit. **a.** caput, Pl., Verg. ; hastam, Verg. ; ramum Lethaeo rore madentem super utraque quassat tempora, Verg. **b.** *to shatter :* vasa, Lucr. ; quassata ventis classis, Verg. Neut. *pl. Part.* as Noun : quassata muri reficere, Liv. **2.** Transf. : quassatā re publicā, Cic. **B.** Intrans. : caput, Pl. ; siliquā quassante, Verg. [Fr. *casser*.]

quassus, a, um. **I.** *Part.* quatiō. **II.** Adj. *shattered, broken.* **1.** Lit. **a.** Pl., Hor., Ov., Liv., etc. **b.** *made by breaking :* faces, Ov. **2.** Transf. : quassā voce, Curt.

quassus, ūs, *m.* [quatiō], *a shaking :* Pac.

quate-faciō, facere, fēci [quatiō faciō], *to shake.* Transf. *to weaken :* quatefeci Antonium, Cic. Ep.

quā-tenus, *adv. how far.* **I.** Interrog. (only transf. in *Indir. Quest.*). : quātenus sint ridicula tractanda oratori, Cic. **II.** Relat. : *as far as :* ut quātenus tuto possent ire, spectatum irent, Liv. **III.** Transf. **a.** Of time : *how long ?* quibus auspiciis istos fascia acciperem ? quātenus haberem ? Cic. **b.** *in so far as, inasmuch as, seeing that, since, as :* quātenus innocentiae meae nusquam locus est, Tac. ; Hor. ; Ov.

quater, *adv.* [quattuor], *four times :* Varr., Verg. ; quater quini, Pl. ; Ov. ; ter et quater, ter aut quater, or terque quaterque (i.e. *over and over again*), Verg., Hor.

quater deciēns (**-iēs**), *adv. fourteen times :* Cic.

quaternī, ae, a (GEN. -um, Liv.). **I.** *a group of four, four together :* primam aciem quaternae cohortes ex quintā legione tenebant, Caes. ; Hor. **II.** *four in each lot, four each :* quaternos denarios in singulas vini amphoras exegisse, Cic. ; Liv. [Fr. *cahier.*]

quatiō, quatere, (no *Perf.*), quassum, *to shake, cause to vibrate* or *tremble.* **1.** Lit. **a.** alas, Verg. ; telum manu, Verg. ; scuta, Tac. ; caput, Ov. ; equus magnā vi caput, Liv. ; ungula campum, Verg. ; pede terram, Hor. ; quatitur terrae motibus Ide, Ov. Also, horror membra, Verg. ; populum risu, Hor. **b.** *to shatter, beat, strike :* hominem cum dono foras, Ter. ; fenestras, Hor. ; scutum hastā, Liv. ; muros arietibus, Liv. ; Verg. ; sontis flagello, Verg. **2.** Transf. : aegritudine animum, Cic. ; Hor. ; ingenium, Tac. ; cursu equum, Verg. ; oppida bello, Verg.

quatriduum, *v.* quadriduum.

quattuor, *indecl. adj.* [*cf.* Gk. τέτταρες], *four :* Enn., Cic., Verg., etc.

quattuor-decim, *indecl. adj. fourteen :* Cic., Liv., etc. [Fr. *quatorze*.]

quattuorvirātus, ūs, *m.* [quattuorviri], *the office of the* quattuorviri : Asin. Poll. ap. Cic. Ep.

quattuor-virī, ōrum, *m. pl. a board of four officials,* esp. in the municipia or colonies : Cic.

-que, *conj.* [*cf.* Gk. καί and τε], an enclitic copulative particle : *and* (usually implying some natural relation between the things connected ; or serving to complete the sense). **I.** Singly. **A.** To co-ordinate words. **a.** Of clearly connected meaning : fuga pavorque, Liv. ; Pl. ; Cic. ; Verg., etc. **b.** Of contrasted meaning : ultro citroque, Cic. ; pace belloque, Liv. ; Pl. ; Hor., etc. **B.** Adding or explaining : fratres consanguineosque, Caes. ; Liv., etc. ; ad tempus non venit, metusque rem impediebat, Sall. ; Liv., etc. **C.** Completing : *and lastly :* pacem tranquillitatem otium concordiamque adferat, Cic. **II.** Repeated : *both . . . and, as well . . . as :* Verg. ; noctesque diesque, Cic. ; Hor., etc. ; quique in urbe erant quosque acciverant, Liv. ; Pl. **III.** Followed by other conjunctions : -que . . . et (not in Caes., Cic.) : signaque et ordines, Liv. ; Pl. ; Sall. ; -que . . . ac, Verg., Liv., etc. ; -que . . . et . . . ac, Liv. **IV.** Equivalent to *sed,* when preceded by a negation, *but :* ut neque bonus quisquam intereat paucorumque poenā vos omnes salvi esse possitis, Cic. ; Ov. ; Liv. **V.** N.B. -que is usually placed after the first word of the connexion, but **a.** It is rarely attached to monosyllables, hence, e.g. sub occasumque solis, Caes. ; de provinciāque, Cic. (Contrast exque eo tempore, Cic. ; haec de se deque provinciā, Liv.) **b.** In the poets it is often placed after several words : Messallam terrā dum sequiturque mari, Tib.

quei, queis, *v.* qui.

quem ad modum or **quemadmodum**, *adv. in* or *after what manner, how.* **I.** Interrog. : Pl., Cic., etc. In *Indir. Quest.* : Caes., Cic., etc. In *Indir. Deliberative* :

Caes. **II.** Relat.: ius esse belli ut qui vicissent iis quos vicissent quem ad modum vellent imperarent, Caes. With *sic, ita,* etc.; *just as, as :* quem ad modum soles de ceteris rebus, sic de amicitiā disputaris, Cic.; Liv.

queō, quire, quivi or quii, quitum (*Imp.* quibam, Pl.), *to be able.* With *Inf. :* Pl., Cic., Verg., etc. *Pass.* (with an *Inf. Pass.*): forma nosci non quita est, Ter.; Pl.; Lucr.

quercētum, i, *n.* [quercus], *an oak-forest :* Varr., Hor.

querceus, a, um [quercus], *of oak-leaves :* Tac.

quercus, ūs, *f.* an oak (used of several species, esp. *the Italian* or *esculent oak.* **1.** Lit.: Enn., Lucr., Cic., Verg., etc. **2.** Transf. **a.** *a garland of oak-leaves:* Capitolina, Juv.; (given to one who had saved a citizen in battle): Ov.; civilis, Verg. **b.** *acorns :* Juv.

querella (querēla), ae, *f.* [queror], *a complaining, complaint.* **1.** Lit.: Cic.; querellam habere (with *quod*-clause), Liv.; est querella (with Acc. and *Inf.*), Quint. **2.** Transf. **a.** Of the plaintive sounds of animals: Lucr., Verg. **b.** Of the tibia: Lucr. **c.** pulmonis, i.e. *a lung-complaint*, Traj. ap. Plin. Ep.

queribundus, a, um [queror], *complaining :* vox, Cic.

querimōnia, ae, *f.* [queror], *a complaint :* esp. of a formal statement of grievances: sociorum querimonias deferre ad aliquem, Cic.; Hor.; Liv.; querimoniae de iniuriis, Cic.

queritor, āri [*freq.* queror], *to complain repeatedly* or *strongly :* Tac.

querneus, a, um [v. quornus], *of oak, oak- :* frons, Cato; corona, Suet.

quernus, a, um [=querc-nus, from quercus], *of oak, oak- :* glandes, Verg.; corona, Ov. [Fr. *chéne.*]

queror, queri, questus, *to complain, lament, bewail ;* and formally *to lay a complaint.* **1.** Lit.: Cic. With Acc. of Object : suum fatum, Caes.; Pl.; Cic.; Ov., etc. With Acc. and *Inf. :* Cic., Ov., Liv., etc. With *quod*-clause : Caes., Cic., Nep., etc. With *cum* (Cic., Liv.), *apud* (Pl., Cic. Ep.), or Dat. (Juv.) of person to whom complaint is made). **2.** Transf. of animals : bubo, Verg.; dulce queruntur aves, Ov.; Hor.; amissos queritur philomela fetūs, Verg. Of apes : Ov. Of a musical instrument: flebile nescio quid (*Intern.* Acc.) queritur lyra, Ov.

querquetulānus, a, um [from querquētum, for quercētum], *of little oak-woods :* an earlier name of the Mons Caelius at Rome, Tac.

querulus, a, um [queror], *full of complaints, complaining.* **1.** Lit.: senex, Hor.; Plin. Pan.; vox, dolor, etc., Ov.; libelli, Plin. Ep. **2.** Transf. of animals and things: cicadae, Verg.; tibia, Hor.; tuba, Prop.

ques, *v.* qui, *ad init.*

questus, a, um, *Part.* queror.

questus, ūs, *m.* [queror], *a complaining, complaint, lamentation.* **1.** Lit.: Cic.; rumpebat poctoro questūs, Verg.; effundere in aëra, Ov.; edere, Ov.; in questūs effundi, Tac. **2.** Transf.: of the nightingale : Verg.

qui, quae, quod (old forms, Nom. quei, Gen. quōius, Dat. quoi ; Abl. qui, e.g. in quicum *with whom, with which ; pl.* quēs or queis, *fem.* quai, *neut.* qua ; Dat. and Abl. queis and quis). **I.** Interrog.: *what ?* (adjectively ; while quis, quid, aro used as Noun *who ? what ?*) : quis fuit igitur ? iste Chaerea. qui Chaerea ? Ter.; Cic., etc. ; quod mare ? Hor. ; Cic., etc. In *Indir. Quest. :* Cic., Verg., etc. **II.** Relat. *who, which, what, that.* **A.** In gen.: summo magistratu praeerat, quem Vergobretum appellant, Caes.; Cic.; coloniam, quam Fregellas appellant, Liv.; ab Ocelo, quod est citerioris provinciae extremum, Caes. The Relat. often agrees in gender. **a.** With the complementary Nom. or Acc. in its own clause : est locus in carcere, quod Tullianum appellatur, Sall.; Cic. **b.** With the *real* rather than the *formal* antecedent : illa furia (i.e. Clodius) qui eto., Cic. It is sometimes attracted to the *case* of its antecedent : circiter sescentas eius generis, cuius supra demonstravimus, navis, Caes. The antecedent is sometimes repeated after the relative (esp. in Caes.): erant itinera duo, quibus itineribus domo exire possent. **B.** With *Subj.* **a.** Of Cause (translate by *as, because*) : maluimus iter facere pedibus, qui incommodissime navigassemus, Cic. Ep. **b.** Of Result (translate by *such as to, to*) : dignus est, qui imperet, Cic. **c.** Of Purpose (translate by *in order to, to*) : equitatum qui sustineret hostium impetum misit, Caes. **d.** Of Concession (translate by *although*) : qui egentissimus fuisset erat insolens, Cic. **C.** For is, ea, id, with a conjunction : res loquitur ipsa, quae semper valet plurimum, *and this*, Cic. (N.B. that in such instances the *Inf.* is used in *Orat. Obliqua.*) **D.** For *qualis* or *talis* (esp. in *Orat. Obliqua*), *what sort of, what a, such :* qui vir, et quantus ! Cic.; quae tua natura est, *such is your disposition*, Cic. Ep. **E.** Acc. *sing. n.* **quod** (*Intern.* or of Extent). **a.** *as much as, as far as :* adiutabo quod potero, Ter.; quod ad me attinet, Cic.; quod sciam, *as far as I know*, Pl., Cic., Liv. **b.** *to what extent, as to what ; wherein :* si quid erat, quod mea opera opus sit vobis, Ter. **F.** Abl. *sing. n.* **quō** (of Measure) with Comparatives : quo . . . eo, quo . . . hoc, *by how much . . . by that*, hence *the (more) . . . the (more) :* quo difficilius, hoc praeclarius, Cic. (*v.* also quo.) **III.** Indef. qui, qua (quae rare), quod, *any one, any* (with *si, nisi, ne, num*): si qui graviore vulnere accepto equo deciderat, Caes.; Cic.; Liv. [It. *chi, che ;* Sp. Fr. *qui, que.*]

qui, Abl. of qui. **I.** Interrog.: *whereby ? wherewith ? by what means ? how ? why ?* Pl., Ter., Hor., Liv. Esp. with possum in Cic. Also of price : *at what price ?* Pl. In *Indir. Quest. :* Pl., Cic., Liv. **II.** Exclam. in curses : qui te di omnes perdant ! Pl.; Ter.; Cic. Ep. **III.** Relat.: *by which, with which :* mihi dari vehicula qui vehar, Pl.; Ter.; Cic.; Nep. **IV.** Indef.: *in some way, somehow :* Pl., Ter.

quia (and Interrog. **quianam**). **I.** Interrog.: *wherefore :* only **a.** With -ne: quiane auxilio iuvat ante levatos ? Verg. ; Pl. **b.** quianam : *why in fact ! why pray !:* Pl., Verg. **II.** Relat.: *wherefore, because :* urbs, quae quia postrema aedificata est, Neapolis nominatur, Cic. ; Pl. ; Hor., etc. (Occ. made more precise by *eo*, *ideo*, *idcirco* as antecedent.)

quicquam, *v.* quisquam.

quicque, *v.* quisque.

quicquid, *v.* quisquis.

quicum [old ABL. of qui with cum], *with whom, with which* : Pl., Cic., etc.

qui-cumque, quaecumque, quodcumque (or **-cunque** ; and separately : quam se cumque in partem, Cic.). **I.** Relat.: *whoever, whatever, whosoever, whatsoever, everyone who, everything that, all that.* **a.** In gen.: petere fortunam quaecumque accidat, Caes. ; ut quodcumque vellet, liceret facere, Nep. With *Partit.* GEN. : quodcumque hoc regni, Verg. ; Cic. Ep. **b.** For qualiscumque : *of whatever kind :* quaecumque mens illa fuit, Gabini fuit, Cic. **II.** Indef.: *any whatsoever, any possible, every possible :* quae sanari poterunt, quācumque ratione sanabo, Cic. ; quocumque modo, Prop. ; Caes. ; Liv.

quid, *v.* quis.

quidam, quaedam, quoddam, and (as Noun) quiddam, *a certain* (not mentioned by name) *person* or *thing, somebody, something.* **a.** In gen.: quidam ex advocatis, Cic. ; quodam tempore, Cic. ; quidam Gallus, Caes. ; excesserunt urbe quidam, alii mortem sibi consciverunt, Liv. With GEN.: quidam bonorum caesi, Tac. ; Liv. ; quiddam, *something :* quiddam divinum, Cic. With *Partit.* GEN. : quiddam mali, Cic. **b.** To soften an expression : *a kind of, what one might call :* timiditate quādam ingenuā, Cic.

quidem, *adv.* (almost invariably placed after the emphatic word in positive sentences), *indeed, certainly, in truth.* **A.** Emphasising. **a.** In gen.: sibi quidem persuaderi, Caes. ; Ter. ; Cic., etc. **b.** et quidem (emphasising an added phrase) : in his locis post solstitium Canicula oritur, et quidem aliquot diebus, Cic. **c.** ne (the old negative, *v.* nē) ... **quidem** (the word emphasised is placed betw. ne and quidem) *not even :* sine quā ne intellegi quidem ulla virtus potest, Cic. So, nec (neque) ... quidem (not et ne ... quidem) : nec te quidem recusare censeam, Liv. ; Cic. **B.** Qualifying or Limiting : *certainly, at least, at any rate :* ex me quidem nihil audire potuisses, Cic. ; Pl., etc. **C.** Concessive : *that is so I admit* (with *but* following) : est istuc quidem honestum, verum hoc expedit, Cic. **D.** *for example, in fact :* Dicaearchus quidem et Aristoxenus ... dixerunt, Cic. ; Nep.

quid-, *v.* quis-.

quiēs, ētis, *f.* [*cf.* Gk. κεῖμαι], *rest (from labour).* **I.** Lit. **a.** In gen.: Cic. ; capere, Caes. ; pati, Sall. ; a proeliis quietem habere, Liv. ; ex diutino labore quieti se dare, Caes. ; laborum, Cic. In *pl.* : Cic. **b.** *a period of quiet, a calm, lull* (of things) :

Verg. Also opp. [...] [...]; Tac [...] *peace :* Sall., Ov., Tac. Of *neutrality* betw. warring political parties : Nep., Tac. **d.** *sleep :* Pl. ; alta, Verg. ; capere, Ov. ; ire ad quietem, Cic. ; quieti se tradere, Cic. In *pl.* : Sall. **e.** *the repose of death :* Verg., Prop. **2.** Transf. **a.** *a dream :* Stat. ; dira, Tac. **b.** *a resting-place, lair* of a wild beast (only in *pl.*) : Lucr. **c.** Personified : Liv., Stat.

quiēscō, quiēscere, quiēvī, quiētum (*Perf. Sync.* quiērunt, quiēsse, *Plup. Indic.* and *Subj. sync.* quiērant, quiēssem) [quiēs], *to come to rest, to rest, keep quiet.* **1.** Lit. **a.** In gen.: Pl., Cic., Verg., etc. Of things : arma, silvae, aequora, flamma, Verg. ; ossa, Verg., Ov. ; voces, Ov. **b.** *to enjoy a period of rest, calm*, or *peace* (after war or civil disturbance) : Verg., Liv. Of neutrality : Cic. Ep. **c.** *to sleep :* Pl., Cic., Nep. **2.** Transf. **a.** *to suffer* or *allow quietly* (colloq.) : quiescere rem adduci ad interregnum, Cic. Ep. **b.** *to cease, leave off, desist* (with *Inf.*) : Pl., Hor. **c.** *to rest, be free :* civitas nostra a suppliciis, Liv.

quiētē, *adv. calmly, quietly :* Cic. *Comp.* : Liv. *Sup.* : Caes.

quiētus, a, um [quiēscō], *at rest, resting.* **1.** Lit. **a.** In gen.: Ter., Cic., Verg. ; aetas, Cic. *Sup.* : Cic. **b.** Of things : *at rest, peaceful, calm* : statio (*anchorage*), Caes. ; aer, Verg. ; salis fluctus, Verg. ; amnes, Hor. *Comp.* : Hor. Of style : *calm ; sermo, Cic. With ref. to war or polit. strife : *peaceful, at peace, undisturbed :* Cic., Sall., Verg. ; provincia a bello, Liv. ; vita, Cic. *Comp.* : Caes., Liv. **c.** *sleeping :* Tac. **2.** Transf. Of the mind or character : *calm, tranquil, untroubled :* Plin. Ep. ; de istoc, Pl. ; animus, Caes., Cic., Verg. *Sup.* : Plin. Ep. [It. *cheto* ; Fr. *quitte*.]

qui-libet, quaelibet, quodlibet and (as Noun) quidlibet, *indef. pron., anyone you please, anyone, no matter who* or *what :* quaelibet minima res, Cic. ; Pl. ; Hor., etc. ; sollertius quam quilibet unus ex his, Liv. ; quidlibet audere, Hor.

quin. I. Interrog. [quī ABL., and nē= nōn], *why not ! how not !* **A.** Direct. **a.** With *Indic.* : quin conscendimus equos ! Liv. ; Pl. ; Cic. ; Verg. **b.** With *Imperative :* quin sic attendite, iudices, Cic. ; Pl. Hence, **c.** With *Indic.* (with negat. and interrog. force lost) : *nay rather, nay but, yea indeed :* hercle quin tu recte dicis, Pl. ; Ter. ; Cic. Ep. Strengthened by *et, etiam, potius*, etc. : quin etiam necesse erit cupere et optare, Cic. ; Verg. ; quin et, Hor. ; quin potius, Liv. **B.** Indirect (with *Subj.*). **a.** In *Orat. Obliq.* : Liv. **b.** With *negat.* or *interrog.* (of a negat. kind) verbs or phrases expressing mental hesitation or doubt, etc. : *why not, how not, but that :* non dubitari debet quin fuerint ante Homerum poetae, Cic. ; haud dubium est quin etc., Ter., Caes., etc. ; quis ignorat quin etc. ? Cic. ; neque abest suspicio quin ipse mortem consciverit, Caes. ; neque Caesarem fefellit quin etc., Caes. ; quī (ABL.) recusare Philippus potest quin et socii sibi consulant ? Liv. **II.** Relat. **A.** [quī NOM., and nō=nōn], *who not,* *but that* (always dependent on negat. or virtually negat. sentence). With *Subj.* (Generic or Consecutive). **a.** Strictly : nemo est curiosus quin sit malevolus, Pl. ; Caes. ; Cic. **b.** In other *genders :* **i.** *Fem. sing. :* nulla est civitas quin ad id tempus partem senatūs Cordubam mitteret, Caes. ; Cic. **ii.** *Neut. sing. :* horum autem nihil est quin intereat, Cic. ; Ter. **c.** In other *cases :* nego ullam picturam esse quin inspexerit, Cic. **B.** [quī ABL., and nē= nōn], *whereby not, how not, but that* (with *Subj.* of Purpose or Result). **a.** After negat. verbs or phrases of *opposing, refraining, etc. :* Pl. ; milites aegre sunt retenti quin oppidum inruerent, Caes. ; per eum non stetit quin fides praestaretur, Liv. **b.** After various negat. phrases : facere non possum quin ad te mittam, Cic. Ep. ; non enim possum quin revortar, Pl. ; nihil praetermisi quin, Cic. ; Liv. ; non multum afuit quin, Cic., Liv., etc. ; quid est causae quin coloniam in Ianiculam possint deducere ? Cic. ; Pl.

qui-nam, quaenam, quodnam, *interrog. adj. which, what, pray ?* Ter., Caes., Cic. In *Indir. Quest.* (=uter) : controversias habebant quinam anteferretur, Caes.

Quinctīlis, is, *adj.* [quintus], *of the fifth* month : Liv. With or without mensis, *the fifth month* (i.e. July) of the old Roman year : Cic. Ep., Suet.

Quinctīlius (Quint-), a, *the name of a Roman gens.* Esp. **I.** Quinctilius Varus, *proconsul of Syria, afterwards commander of the Romans in Germany, defeated by Arminius* about A.D. 9. **II.** *a poet of Cremona, a friend of Horace, and kinsman of Vergil.*

Quinctius (Quint-), a, *the name of a Roman* gens. Esp. **I.** L. Quinctius Cincinnatus : *v.* Cincinnatus. **Quinctiānus,** a, um. **II.** T. Quinctius Flamininus, *victor over the* Macedonians at Cynoscephalae (B.C. 197).

quincūnx, ūncis, *m.* [quīnque ūncia], *the fraction five-twelfths.* **1.** L i t. : Hor., Mart., Plin. Ep. Of interest, *five per cent. :* Pers. **2.** T r a n s f. *the figure five* (as arranged on cards or dice *******) : directi in quincuncem ordines, Cic. ; Caes.

quindeciēns (-iēs), *adv. fifteen times :* Cic., Mart.

quindecim, *indecl. adj.* [quīnque decem], *fifteen :* Pl., Caes., Hor. [Fr. *quinze.*]

quindecim-primī, ōrum, *m. pl. the board of fifteen chief magistrates* in a municipium : Caes.

quindecimvir, *v.* quīndecimvirī.

quindecimvīrālis, e, *adj.* [quīndecimvirī], *of the* quindecimviri *or council of fifteen :* Tac.

quindecim-virī, ōrum, *m. pl.* (separated, quindecim Diana preces virorum, Hor. ; GEN. *pl.* : -virum, Tac.), *a board of fifteen men :* quindecimviri Sibyllini *or* sacris faciundis, Tac.

quindēnī, *v.* quīnī dēnī.

quingēnārius, a, um [quingēnī], *consisting of five hundred each :* cohortes, Curt.

quingēnī, ae, a [quingentī], *a group of five hundred :* hence, *five hundred each :* Cic. Ep., Suet.

quingentēsimus (-ēns-), a, um, *the five hundredth :* Cic.

quingentī, ae, a [quīnque centum], *five hundred :* Pl., Cic., Hor., etc. Of any very large number : Pl., Cat.

quingentiēs (-ēns), *adv. five hundred times :* Cic.

quīnī, ae, a [quīnque], *five in a group :* nomina, Liv., Verg. Hence, *five each :* quini in lectulis, Cic. ; Caes. ; Liv.

quīnī dēnī or **quīn-dēnī,** ae, a, *fifteen in a group :* perh. in Pl. Hence, *fifteen each :* Liv., Suet.

quīnī vicēnī, or **quīnivicēnī,** ae, a, *twenty-five each :* Liv.

quīnquāgēnī, ae, a [quīnquāgintā], *fifty in a group :* Mart. ; hence, *fifty each :* Cic.

quīnquāgēsiēns, *adv. fifty times :* Pl.

quīnquāgēsimus (-ēs-), a, um [quīnquāgintā], *fiftieth :* Cic. As Noun, **quīnquāgēsima,** ae, *f.* (*sc.* pars), *a fiftieth part, 2 per cent.,* as a tax : Cic.

quīnquāgiēns (-iēs), *adv. fifty times :* Plin.

quīnquāgintā, *indecl. adj. fifty :* Pl., Cic., Verg.

quīnquātrūs, uum, *f. pl.* and **quīnquātria,** ōrum and ium, *n. pl.* [quīnque, as falling on the fifth day after the Ides], *a festival of Minerva,* of which two were celebrated at Rome : the greater on the 19th of March ; and the lesser on the 13th of June : Cic. Ep., Ov., Liv.

quīnque, *indecl. adj. five :* Cic. [It. *cinque* ; Sp. *cinco* ; Fr. *cinq.*]

quīn-que, for et quīn : Pl.

quīnquennālis, e, *adj.* [quīnquennis]. **I.** *that takes place every fifth year, quinquennial :* Cic., Liv., etc. **II.** *lasting five years :* censura, Liv.

quīnquennis, e, *adj.* [quīnque annus]. **I.** *of five years, five years old :* Pl., Hor., Ov., Liv. **II.** *Neut. pl.* as Noun : *games celebrated every fifth year :* Stat.

quīnquennium, i, *n.* [quīnquennis], *a period of five years, five years :* Lex ap. Cic., Ov.

quīnque-partītus (quīnquepert-), a, um, *divided into five parts, five-fold :* argumentatio, Cic.

quīnque-primī (and separ. **quīnque primī),** ōrum, *m. pl. the five leading men* in a municipium : Cic.

quīnquerēmis, e, *adj.* [quīnque rēmus], *having five banks of oars :* navis, Liv. As Noun, *f.* (*sc.* navis), *a quinquereme :* Cic., Liv.

quīnquevir, *v.* quīnquevirī.

quīnquevirātus, ūs, *m.* [quīnquevirī], *the office of a quinquevir :* Cic.

quīnque-virī, ōrum, *m. pl. a board of five men :* Cic., Liv., etc. In *sing.* : *a member of the board :* Cic., Liv.

quīnquiēns (-iēs), *adv. five times :* Cato, Cic.

quīnquiplicō, āre [quīnque plicō], *to multiply five-fold :* Tac.

quīntadecimānī, ōrum, *m. pl. the soldiers of the fifteenth* (legion) : Tac.

quīntānus, a, um [quīntus], *of the fifth :* Nonae (*falling on the* 5th), Varr. As Noun. **A. quīntāna,** ae, *f.* (*sc.* via), *a street in a camp* (of two legions), *running between the* 5th *and* 6th *maniple and the* 5th *and* 6th *turma* of *cavalry.* **1.** L i t. : Liv. (as tho

market in the camp.). **2.** T r a n s f .: *a
market* : Suet. **B. quintāni**, ōrum, *m. pl.
the soldiers of the fifth (legion)* : Tac.
Quintiliānus (Quinct-), I, *m. a Roman cognomen.* Esp. M. Fabius Quintilianus, *a
celebrated rhetorician, native of Calagurris in
Spain, whose rhetorical work,* De Institu-
tione Oratoriā, *is still extant.*
Quintīlis, *v.* Quinctilis.
quintus (quinctus, Pl.), a, um, *fifth* : Pl.,
Cic., Hor., etc. *Neut.* Acc. **quintum** and
ABL. **quintō**, *for the fifth time* : Liv.
Quintus, *a Roman praenomen, abbreviated*
Q.
quintus decimus, a, um *fifteenth* : Cic., Liv.
quippe, *adv.* and *conj.* [quid (or perh. ABL.
qui), with -pe ; cf. nempe], a corroborating
particle : *certainly, to be sure, by all means,
indeed, in fact.* **A.** In gen. : recte igitur
diceres te restituisse ? quippe : quid enim
facilius ? Cic. Ironically : movet me quippe
lumen curiae, Cic. ; quippe vetor fatis,
Verg. **B.** Introducing an explanation :
in fact. **a.** Alone : Ter., Verg., Liv., etc.
b. Strengthened with *etiam* or *et* : quippe
etiam festis quaedam exercere diebus fas
et iura sinunt, Verg. ; Prop. **c.** quippe
qui (*who*), and quippe cum. **i.** With Indic. :
occ. in Pl., Cic. Ep., Sall., Liv. Also quippe
ubi : Lucr. ; quippe quando : Pl. **ii.** With
Subj. (when required by the meaning ; *v.*
qui and cum) : Cic., Nep. Also quippe
ubi : Liv.
quippiam, *v.* quispiam.
quippi-ni, *adv. why not ?* or *certainly, to be
sure* : Pl.
Quirinus, I, *m. the name given to Romulus
on his deification.* Hence, **Quirinus**, a,
um ; **Quirinālis**, e, *adj. belonging to
Quirinus* collis, *the Quirinal Hill, one of
the seven hills of Rome* ; **Quirinālia**, ium,
*n. the festival in honour of Romulus cele-
brated annually on the* 17th *of February.
The name* Quirinus *is used* **i.** *of* gemini
Quirini, i.e. *Romulus and Remus* (Juv.) ;
ii. *of* Janus ; **iii.** *of Augustus* ; **iv.** *of*
Antony.
quiris or **curis** [a Sabine word], *a spear* : Ov.
Quiris, itis, *m.* (Curēs], *an inhabitant of the
Sabine town* Cures : Verg., Liv. After the
union of the Sabines and Romans, the latter
also called themselves, in a civil capacity,
Quirites. They were styled on all solemn
occasions Populus Romanus Quirites (-que),
Liv. ; which in later times was distorted
into Populus Romanus Quiritium, Liv. ;
rarely with the copula : devovisse eos se pro
patriā Quiritibusque Romanis, Liv. It was
a reproach for soldiers to be addressed as
Quirites instead of milites : Tac., Suet.
Sing. : *a Roman citizen* : Hor., Ov.
Transf. *of bees* : regem parvosque
Quirites, *citizens,* Verg.
quiritātiō, ōnis, *f.* (Liv.) and **quiritātus**,
ūs, *m.* (Plin. Ep.) [quiritō], *a plaintive cry,
a scream, shriek.*
Quirites, *v.* Quiris.
quiritō, āre, *to raise a plaintive cry, to wail.*
1. Lit : Lucil., Liv. Hence, *to exclaim
in distress* : Asin. ap. Cic. Ep. **2.** T r a n s f .
of an orator, *to scream* : Quint. [It.
gridare ; Sp. gritar ; Fr. crier.]

quis (*m. f.*), quid (OLD NOM. pli quia), *pron.*
I. I n t e r r o g . *who ? which ? what ?* **A.**
quis. **1.** S u b s t a n t i v a l : **a.** Of males :
Pl., Cic., etc. In *Indir. Quest.* : Cic.,
Liv., etc. **b.** Of females : Pl., Enn. **2.**
A d j e c t i v a l (for *qui*) : *what ? what sort
of a person ?* **a.** Mostly of male persons :
Cic., Hor., etc. In *Indir. Quest.* : Liv.
b. In gen. : quis color ? Verg. ; Cic. ; Tac.
In *Indir. Quest.* : Liv. **B.** quid (Substantival), *what ?* **a.** In gen. : quid dicam
de moribus ? Cic. ; Pl., etc. In *Indir.
Quest.* : Cic., etc. **b.** With GEN. : *what
kind of ? what in the way of ?* quid mulieris
uxorem habes ? Pl. ; quid pictarum tabularum ? Cic. In *Indir. Quest.* : Cic.
c. Idiomatic : quid ? tu me hoc tibi man-
dasse existimas, Cic. Ep. ; quid ita ? *why
so ?* Cic. ; quid ni, also in one word,
quidni ? *why not ?* Ter. ; quid si ? Cic. ;
quid tum ? Cic., Verg. ; quid enim ? Cic.,
Liv. In introducing a fresh instance or
particular, mostly with something of
climax : quid ? *what shall be said to this ?*
and then ; furthermore : quid iuris consulti, quid pontifices, quid augures, etc. ?
Cic. Esp. foll. by quod (lit. *what of the
fact that . . . ?*) : quid quod sapientissimus
quisque aequissimo animo moritur, then
there is this further consideration, that . . .
Cic. **d.** Acc. quid as *Adv.* : *how ? why ?*
quid plura disputo ? Cic. ; Pl. ; Liv. ;
quid plura ? *why (do I say) more ?* i.e.
in short, Cic. **II.** I n d e f . : *any one, anybody, anything ; some one, somebody, something* : simplicior quis et est ? Hor. ; Pl. ;
Cic. But in prose usually after *si, nisi,
num, ne, cum* : Caes., Cic., Liv., etc.
quis (= quibus), *v.* qui.
quis-nam (or **quis nam**), quaenam, quidnam,
pron. interrog. who, which, what in fact or
pray ? quisnam igitur tuebitur P. Scipionis
memoriam mortui ? Cic. With *num* :
num quidnam amplius tibi cum illā fuit ?
Ter. ; in aedibus quid tibi meis nam erat
negoti ? Pl. ; nam quis te nostras iussit
adire domos ? Verg. In *Indir. Quest.* :
Ter., Nep., etc.
quispiam, quaepiam, quodpiam and (as
Noun) quidpiam or quippiam, *pron. indefin., some one, something* : cum quaepiam
cohors ex orbe excesserat, Caes. ; Ter. ;
si cuipiam pecuniam fortuna ademit, Cic.
Neut. Acc. as *Adv., in some respect, somewhat* : si grando quippiam nocuit, Cic. ; Pl.
quis-quam, quaequam, quicquam or quid-
quam, *pron. indefin. any, anyone* or *anything at all* (usually Substantival and in
negative or virtually negative sentences) :
Pl. ; estne quisquam omnium mortalium,
de quo melius existimes tu ? Cic. ; nec quisquam ex agmine tanto audet adire virum,
Verg. With *unus* : quia nondum in
quemquam unum saeviebatur, Liv. After
Comparatives : taetrior quam quisquam
superiorum, Cic. With *si* : si quicquam
sperent, Caes. ; Cic. quisquam, like quis,
is sometimes *fem.* in early writers : anum
quemquam, Pl. ; Ter.
quis-que, quaeque, quodque and (as Noun)
quidque, *pron. indefin., whoever* or *whatever* ;
hence, *each, every one, every thing* taken

separately. **A.** In gen.: ut in quo quisque artificio excelleret, is in suo genere Roscius diceretur, Cic.; quod cuique obtigit, id quisque teneat, Cic. But oftener unus quisque, *v.* unus. The *sing. pron.* found with a *pl. verb*: ubi quisque vident, eunt obviam, Pl.; Verg. N.B. that in conjunction with *se* or *suus*, it almost always stands next after the *Refl. Pron.*: pro se quisque ad populum loquebatur, Cic.; consules in suas quisque proficiscerentur, Liv.; Pl. **B.** In partic. **a.** Like quis, quisque is sometimes *fem.* in early writers: omnis meretrices, ubi quisque habitant, invenit, Pl.; Ter. **b.** With *Partit. Gen.*: tuorum quisque necessariorum, Cic. **c.** With *Sup.* to express universality: optimum quidque rarissimum est (i.e. *everything is rare in proportion to its excellence*), Cic.; doctissimus quisque, *all the most learned men*, Cic.; Caes.; Liv., etc. In *pl.*: Pl., Cic., Liv. **d.** With *primus*: *the first possible*: primo quoque tempore, Cic.; Liv. With any ordinal numeral: quinto quoque anno, *every fifth year, every five years*, Cic.; Pl. **e.** Rarely for uterque, *each of two, both*: oscula quisque suae matri properata tulerunt, Ov.; Liv. **f.** For quisquis or quicumque: Pl., Sall. **g.** In Lucr. quisquis often stands for quisque.

quisquiliae, ārum, *f. pl. refuse, sweepings.* Transf. of vile persons or things: *refuse, dregs*: Cic.

quis-quis, quaequae, quodquod and (as Noun) quidquid (or quicquid), *pron.* **I.** Relat. *whoever, whosoever, whatever, whatsoever*: quisquis ille est, Pl.; Cic.; Tib.; quoquo consilio fecit, Cic. With *Partit. Gen.*: deorum quisquis amicior, Hor.; quidquid navium habebat, Caes.; quidquid sceleris erit, Cic. N.B. quisquis is occ. *fem.* in Pl. Acc. **quidquid** as *Adv.*: *however far, however much*: ride quidquid amas Catullum, Cat.; Liv. **II.** Indef. *anyone, anything whatsoever*: liberos suos quibusquibus Romanis mancipio dabant, Liv.; Ter. Also standing for quisque in Lucr.

qui-vis, quaevis, quodvis and (as Noun) quidvis, *pron. indefin. who* or *what you please, any whatever, anyone, anything*: ad quemvis numerum ephippiatorum equitum quamvis pauci adire audent, Pl.; Cic.; Hor., etc. With unus, *any one person*: si tu solus, aut quivis unus, Cic.; Ter.

quivis-cumque, quaeviscumque, quodviscumque, *pron., whosoever, whatsoever.* **I.** Relat.: Mart. **II.** Indef.: Lucr.

(1) **quō** (old Directive or Dat. of quis, qui). **I.** Interrog. *to what place?* or *to whom?* **1.** Lit.: quo, quo, sceleste, ruitis? Hor.; quo illae nubent? Pl.; with Gen.; quo gentium? Pl. In *Indir. Quest.*: Cic., with Gen.: quo terrarum possent abire, Liv. **2.** Transf. *to what end or purpose? wherefore? why?* quo tantam pecuniam? Cic.; Hor. In *Indir. Quest.*: Cic., Hor. **II.** Indef. *to any place, anywhither, anywhere* (after *si, nisi, ne*): si quo tu me ire vis, Pl.; Caes.; si quando Romam aliove quo mitterent legatos, Liv. **III.**

Relat. *to which place, whither.* **1.** Lit.: locus quo exercitui aditus non erat, Caes.; Cato; non longius hostes aberant quam quo telum adici potest, Caes. Of persons: *to whom*: homo apud eos, quo se contulit, gratiosus, Cic.; Pl. **2.** Transf. *to the end that* (with *Subj.*): *in order that* (with *Subj.*): eo scripsi quo plus auctoritatis habeam, Cic. Ep.; sese idcirco ab suis discedere noluisse quo etc., Caes. Without eo or idcirco: Pl., Ov.

(2) **quō** (Locat. of quis), *where?* (in *Indir. Quest.* and with *Partit.* Gen. loci or locorum): Cic., Hor.

(3) **quō** (*Instr.* Abl. of qui relat.). **I.** *by which means, whereby*: quo factum est ut etc., Nep. Esp. with *Subj.* of purpose or Result. **a.** Mostly with *Comp. Adj.* or *Adv.*: castella communit quo facilius prohibere possit, Caes.; Cic.; Liv. (*v.* also quo minus). **b.** Without *Comp.*: haec faciunt quo Chremetem apsterreant, Ter.; Verg.; Liv. **II.** *by reason of which, wherefore, because*: quo aequior sum Pamphilo, Ter.; Cic.; non quo libenter male audiam sed quia etc., Cic.; Pl.; Ter. **III.** Abl. of Measure with *Comp.*: quo plures erant, maior caedes, *by what the more . . . the greater, i.e. the more . . . the greater*, Liv.; quo plura . . . eo ampliora, Cic.

quo-ad, *adv.* (prob. alw. monosyl. in verse). **I.** Interrog. **A.** Of place: *how far?* (in *Indir. Quest.*): videte nunc quoad fecerit iter apertius, etc., Cic. **B.** Of time: *how long?* senem quoad exspectatis? Ter. **II.** Relat. **A.** Of place: *as far as*: in aquam progressi quoad capitibus exstare possunt, Liv.; quoad insequi potuit, Liv. **B.** Of time. **a.** *as long as*: quoad vixit, Cic. **b.** *until*. With *Indic.*: Cic., etc. With *Subj.* (only in formal or virtual *Orat. Obliq.*): ipse interea quoad legiones conlocasset in Galliā morari constituit, Caes.; Liv. **C.** Of other relations: *as far as*: ius civile eātenus exercuerunt quoad populum praestare voluerunt, Cic. With *eius* in the phr.: quoad eius (facere) possum, *as far as* (i.e. *as well as*) *I can*: Cic., Liv.

quō-circā (separated: quō, bone, circā, Hor.), *adv. for which reason, wherefore*: Cic., Verg.

quō-cumque (separated: quo nos cumque feret, Hor.), *relat. adv. to whatever place, whithersoever*: Cic., Verg., Hor.

quod, *relat. conj.* [Acc. *Neut.* of qui]. **I.** (*at, as for,* or *in the fact*) *that, in that, the fact that, because* (often with *eo, idcirco, propterea*): eo deceptum quod etc., Caes.; Liv.; Tac.; mirari Cato se aiebat quod non rideret haruspex, Cic.; praetereo quod illam sibi domum delegit, Cic.; adde quod pubes tibi crescit omnis, Hor.; id quoque accesserat quod etc., Liv.; propterea quod, Ter.; propter hanc causam quod, Cic.; quod improviso tantum pagum adortus esset, *as for his having surprised* etc., Caes. (N.B. that the *Subj.* is used only in formal or virtual *Orat. Obliq.*) **II.** *in that, on the ground that, for that, because* (very freq.): tibi agam gratias quod me vivere coegisti, Cic. Ep. ; noctu ambulabat Themistocles quod somnum capere non posset, Cic. ; non quod doleant sed quia etc., Cic. **III.** *for the fact that, wherefore, why :* hoc est quod ad vos venio, Pl. ; Hor. ; in viam quod te das hoc tempore, nihil est, Cic. ; ne causae quid sit quod te quisquam quaeritet, Pl. ; quid est quod etc. ? Cic. **IV.** Special usages. **a.** *in that (cf.* I. ; and, quod scribis ad me venturum, ego vero volo, *as for your writing etc.,* Cic. Ep.) ; with *Subj. in so far as, as for* (your saying) *that, though :* quod enim te liberatum iam existimationis metu cogites, mihi crede, etc., Cic. ; Pl. ; Ter. ; also with *Indic.* in this sense : Prop., Ov. **b.** *as far as :* adiutabo quod potero, Ter. ; Cic. ; quod sine iactura rei publicae fieri posset, Liv. (*v.* qui, II. E.) **c.** *since that, since :* iam diu est quod victum non datis, Pl. ; de pactione statim quod audieram etc., *immediately on hearing of the agreement, etc.,* Cic. ; tertius dies est quod non audivi, Plin. Ep. **d.** With *si, nisi, cum, quia, ubi,* etc., to connect sentences : *and therefore, but (therefore) :* quod si quid ei a Caesare gravius accidisset, Caes. ; quod utinam minus vitae cupidi fuissemus ! Cic. Without another conjunction : quod te per superos oro, Verg.

quōdam-modo or **quōdam modō,** *adv. in a certain manner, in a measure :* Cic., Nep.

quoi for cui, **quŏius** for cūius, *v.* qui.

quoi, *v.* qui, *init.*

quŏiās or **quŏiātis,** e, for cūiās or cūiātis : Pl.

quō-libet, *adv. whither it pleases, to any place whatever :* Lucr., Ov., Liv.

quom, *v.* cum.

quō-minus, *conj. v.* impediō, obstō, etc.

quō modō or **quō-modo,** *adv.* **I.** Interrog.: *in what manner ? in what way ? how ?* Maecenas quomodo tecum ? Hor. ; Pl. ; Cic. In *Indir. Quest.*: Cic. **II.** Exclam.: quo modo se venditabat Caesari ! Cic. **III.** Relat.: *in the (same) way that, just as :* quo modo hoc est consequens illi, sic illud huic, Cic. ; Liv. [It, *come ;* Sp. *como ;* Fr. *comme.*]

quōmodo-cumque, *adv.* **I.** Relat.: *in whatever manner, howsoever :* Cic. **II.** Indef.: *in some way or another :* Pl.

quōmodo-nam, *adv. in what manner pray ? how ? :* Cic. Ep.

quō-nam, *adv. whither pray ?* **1.** Lit.: Pl., Caes., Cic. **2.** Transf.: quonam haec omnia nisi ad suam perniciem pertinere ? Caes.

quondam, *adv. for* quomdam. **I.** *at a certain time, at one time, once formerly :* quum illa quondam socrus, paulo ante uxor fuisset, Cic. ; Pl. ; Ov., etc. **II.** Of the future: *one day, some day, ever :* Verg., Tib., Hor. **III.** *at times, sometimes :* quondam citharā tacentem suscitat Musam Apollo, Hor. ; Cic. ; Verg., etc.

quoniam, *adv.* [quom iam], *seeing that, whereas, since, because.* Usually with *Indic.:* Pl., Cic., Verg., etc. With *Subj.* in formal or virtual *Orat. Obliq. :* de suis privatim rebus ab eo petere coeperunt, quoniam civitati consulere non possent, Caes.

quōpiam, *adv. to any place, whither [?]:* Pl., Ter., Liv.

quŏquam, *adv. to any place, whithersoever :* Pl., Lucr., Cic., etc.

quoque, *adv. also, too* (placed after the emphasised word) : quā de causā Helvetii quoque reliquos Gallos virtute praecedunt, Caes. ; quis exsul se quoque fugit ? Hor. Pleonast. with *et, etiam :* quin mihi quoque etiam est ad portum negotium, Pl. ; Lucr.

quō-quō or **quō quō,** *adv. to whatever place, whithersoever, whichever way.* **1.** Lit.: Pl. With gentium : quoquo hinc abducta est gentium, Pl. ; quoquo terrarum, Ter. **2.** Transf.: quoquo sese verterint Stoici, Cic.

quŏquō-modo, or **quŏquō modō,** *adv. in whatever way, howsoever :* Cic.

quŏquō-versus (-um) or **quŏquōvorsum,** *in every direction, every way :* legatos quoquoversus dimittere, Caes. ; Cato ; Cic.

quŏrsum and **quŏrsus,** *adv.* [for quōversum or -us], *in what direction ? whither ?* **1.** Lit.: nescio hercle, neque unde eam, neque quorsum eam, Ter. **2.** Transf. **a.** sed quorsum haec pertinent ? Cic. ; Pl. **b.** *to what purpose ? to what end ? for what ?* quorsum haec disputo ? Cic. ; Hor.

quot, *adj. indecl.* [*v.* quī]. **I.** Interrog.: *how many ?* quot sunt ? Pl. In *Indir. Quest.:* Cic. **II.** Exclam.: quot calamitates ! Cic. **III.** Relat.: *as many as :* quot homines, tot causae, Cic. ; Pl. ; Ov., etc. Hence, quot mensibus, *every month,* Cato ; quot Kalendis, Pl. ; quot annis (or quotannis), *every year,* Caes., Cic., Verg.

quotannis, *adv. v.* quot, *fin.*

quot-cumque, *adv. however many, as many as* (rare) : Cic.

quotēni, ae, a [quot], *how many each :* Cic.

quotid-, *v.* cottid-.

quotiēns (-iēs), *adv.* **I.** Interrog.: *how many times ?* Cic. **II.** Exclam.: Verg. **III.** Relat.: *as many times as :* Cic., Verg., Hor.

quotiens-cumque (-cunque), *adv. as often soever as, however often :* Cic., Nep.

quot-quot, *adj. indecl. as many soever as, however many :* Cic., Cat., Hor.

quotumus, a, um [quotus], *which number in the series ?* Pl.

quotus, a, um [quot], *what number in the series ?* quotus erit iste denarius, qui non sit ferendus ? Cic. ; hora quota est ? Hor. ; tu quotus esse velis (i.e. how many besides yourself), Hor. ; quota pars laudis (i.e. how small), Ov. With *quisque* (or in one word, quotusquisque), to denote a small number, *how few ?* quotus enim quisque philosophorum invenitur, qui sit ita moratus, ut ratio postulat ? Cic. ; Ov. ; Tac.

quotus-cumque, acumque, umcumque (-cunque), *whatsoever in number :* pars quotacumque, *the smallest fraction possible,* Tib.

quotus-quisque, *v.* quotus.

quō ūsque or **quō-ūsque,** *adv.* **I.** Of place: *how far ?* Liv. **II.** Of time: *until what time, till when, how long ?* Pl., Cic. ; quo usque tandem abutere patientiā nostrā ? Cic.

quō-vis, *adv. to any place whatever :* Pl. With gentium : Ter.

quum, wrongly for cum.

R

R, r, the seventeenth letter of the Latin alphabet. **I.** It corresponds in general to Indo-European *r* (which however is sometimes represented in Latin by *l*), and to Greek ρ. **II. 1.** In many Latin words an original *s*, standing between two vowels, has been changed to *r* ; e.g. asa, lases, meliosem, have become ara, lares, meliorem. So also dirimo is formed from dis-emo. In neuter nouns of the type of *genus*, the oblique cases, generis, etc., were originally *genes-is*, etc. This change, however, is not uniformly found ; *s* in many words has remained unaltered between vowels ; quaeso maintains itself beside quaero, and nasus beside naris. A similar change to that above mentioned sometimes takes place in *final s* ; arbos, colos, labos, have become arbor, color, labor. **2.** In meridies, *r* has been substituted for *d* through the influence of dissimilation. **3.** *r* is elided for euphony in crebesco, etc. **III.** Changes of *r* in the Romance languages. **1.** Into *l* : this is the most frequent change : e.g. Lat. arbor, It. albero ; Lat. fragrare, peregrinus ; Fr. *flairer*, *pèlerin*. **2.** Into *d* : Lat. quaerere, rarus ; It. *chiedere*, *rado*. **3.** *rs* into *ss* ; Lat. *dorsum* ; It. *dosso*. **4.** *r* often changes its place : Lat. *vervex*, *temperare*, Fr. *brebis*, *tremper*. **5.** When, by the disappearance of a vowel of a Latin word, the combination *mr* is formed, in French it is changed to *mbr* ; Lat. num(e)-*rus*, cam(e)ra ; Fr. *nombre*, *chambre* ; also in Sp. *hombro* from Lat. hum(e)rus. So *nr* in French becomes *ndr* ; Lat. gen(e)r, pon(e)re ; Fr. *gendre*, *pondre* : and *lr* becomes *ldre*, further changing to *udre* by vocalisation of *l* ; Lat. mol(e)re, sol(ve)re, Fr. *moudre*, *soudre*. **IV.** As an abbreviation, R. signifies Romanus, also Rufus, recte, reficiendum, regnum, ripa, etc. ; R. P. res publica ; R. R. rationes relatae.

rabidē, adv. *ravingly*, *rabidly* : Cic.

rabidus, a, um [rabiēs], *raving*, *furious*, *enraged*, *mad* : canes, Lucr., Plin., etc. ; tigres, Verg. ; leones, Hor. Of persons : Cat., Sen. Of things : furor animi, Cat. ; lingua, Prop. ; mores, Ov.

rabiēs, em, ē (GEN. rabiēs, Lucr.), *f.* [rabiō], *rage*, *madness*. **1.** Lit. : esp. of dogs : Verg., Plin. Of men : Pl., Liv. **2.** Transf. *rage*, *frenzy* (of passion) : Cic., Hor., Tac. ; civica, Hor. ; hostilis, Liv. With *Obj.* GEN. : edendi, Verg. Of love : Ter., Lucr., Hor. Of inspiration : Verg. Of things : ventris, Verg. ; caeli marisque, Verg. ; ventorum, Ov. ; rabies fatalis temporis, Liv. [It. *rabbia* ; Fr. *rage*.]

rabiō, rabere, *to rave*, *be mad* : Caecil., Varr., Sen. Ep.

rabiōsē, adv. *ravingly*, *furiously* : Cic.

rabiōsulus, a, um [*dim.* rabiōsus], *rather rabid* : litterae, Cic. Ep.

rabiōsus, a, um [rabiēs], *raving*, *fierce*, *mad*, *rabid* : homo, Pl. ; canis, Hor. ; fortitudo, Cic.

rabula, ae, *m.* [rabiō], *a brawling*, *noisy advocate* : Cic., Quint.

racēmifer, era, erum [racēmus ferō], *cluster-bearing*, *clustering* : uvae, Ov. ; Bacchus, Ov.

racēmus, i, *m.* [ῥάξ, ῥαγός], *a bunch* or *cluster of grapes and similar fruits.* **1.** Lit. : Verg., Hor., Ov. **2.** Transf. *wine* : Ov. [Fr. *raisin.*]

radiātus, a, um [radius]. **I.** *having spokes*, *spoked* : rota, Varr. **II.** *having rays*, *irradiated* : sol, Cic. ; Acc. ; Lucr., etc. : caput (attribute of a divine personage), Plin. Pan.

rādicitus, adv. [rādix], *by* or *with the roots.* **1.** Lit. : Cato, Varr., Cat., etc. **2.** Transf. *utterly* : radicitus tollere atque extrahere cupiditatem, Cic. ; Pl.

rādicula, ae, *f.* [*dim.* rādix], *a small root* : Cic.

radiō, āre and **radior,** āri [radius], *to emit beams*, *to beam*, *glitter*, *radiate* : miles in armis, Prop. ; galeae gemmis radiantur et auro, Ov. Esp. **radiāns,** antis : sidera, Lucr. ; lumina solis, Ov. ; luna, Verg. See also radiatus. [Fr. *rayer.*]

radiōsus, a, um [radius], *having many beams*, *radiant* : sol, Pl.

radius, i, *m.* [perh. *cf.* rādix, rāmus]. **1.** Lit. **a.** *a stake* : Liv. **b.** *a spoke of a wheel* : Verg., Ov., Curt. **c.** Math. **i.** *a staff*, rod for measuring : Cic., Verg. **ii.** *a semi-diameter*, *radius* of a circle : Cic. **d.** In weaving : *a shuttle* : Lucr., Verg., Ov. **e.** In botany, *a kind of long olive* : Cato, Verg. **2.** Transf. *a beam* or *ray* of any shining object ; esp. of the sun : Pl., Lucr., Cic., Verg. ; of lightning : Verg. ; of the halo round the heads of divine or deified personages : aurati, Verg. [It. *raggio*, *razzo* ; Fr. *raie.*]

rādix, īcis, *f.* [*cf.* ῥίζα], *a root* of a plant (us. pl.). **1.** Lit. **a.** radices capere, *to take root*, Cato ; radices agere, *to strike root*, Varr. ; arbores ab radicibus subruere, Caes. ; radicibus eruta pinus, Verg. ; Ov. **b.** *an edible root* : Caes. ; esp. *a radish* : Hor. **2.** Transf. **a.** *the lower part of an object*, *the foot* of a hill, mountain, etc. : sub ipsis radicibus montis, Caes. ; a Palati radice, Cic. **b.** *the root*, *base*, *foundation* : saxi, Lucr. ; linguae, Ov. **c.** *a root*, basis, *foundation*, *origin* (us. pl.) : vera gloria radices agit atque etiam propagatur, Cic. ; Pompeius eo robore vir, iis radicibus, Cic. ; virtus altissimis defixa radicibus, Cic. ; patientiae, Cic. ; a radicibus evertere domum, Phaedr.

rādō, rādere, rāsī, rāsum, *to scrape*, *scratch*, *smooth.* **1.** Lit. **a.** In gen. : mulieres genas ne radunto (in mourning), XII. Tab. ap. Cic. ; terram pedibus corvōs, Pl. ; tigna, Lucr. ; virgas, Verg. **b.** *to shave* : caput et supercilia, Cic. ; Juv. ; caput (as a mark of slavery), Liv. ; barbam, Suet. ; aliquem, Cic. **c.** *to scratch out* or *smooth over* ; *to erase* : nomen fastis, Tac. ; Ov. **2.** Transf. **a.** *to graze*, *touch in passing* : ripas flumina, Lucr. ; Ov. ; saxa Pachyni radimus, Verg. ; traiectos surculus, Suet. **b.** *to scour* : arva imbribus Eurus, Hor. **c.** *to strip off* : damnosa canicula quantum raderet, Pers. **d.** *to grate upon*, *hurt*, *offend* : auris delicatas, Quint. **e.** Of satirising : mores, Pers.

raeda, ae, *f.* [a Celtic word], *a four-wheeled travelling-carriage* : Caes., Hor., etc.

raedārius, a, um [raeda], *of a* raeda : mulae, Varr. *Masc.* as Noun, *a coachman* : Cic.

Raeti, ōrum, *m. pl. a Celtic people between the Rhine and the Inn* ; **Raetia**, ae, *f. their country* ; **Raeticus, Raetius, Raetus**, a, um.

rāllus, a, um [*dim.* for rārulus, from rārus], *thin* : tunica, Pl.

rāmālia, ium, *n. pl.* [rāmus], *twigs, sticks, brushwood* : Ov., Tac. In *sing.* : Pers.

rāmentum, ī, *n.* (**rāmenta**, ae, *f.* Pl.) ; us. *pl.* **rāmenta**, ōrum [rādō], *scrapings, shavings, chips*. **1.** Lit. : ferri, Lucr. ; auri, ligni, Plin. **2.** Transf. : patri omne (aurum) cum ramento reddidi, Pl.

rāmeus, a, um [rāmus], *of boughs* or *branches* : fragmenta, Verg.

rāmex, icis, *m.* [rāmus]. **I.** *a blood-vessel of the lungs* : Pl., Varr. **II.** *a rupture* : Juv.

Ramnēs and **Ramnēnsēs**, ium, *m. pl.* **I.** *a Latin race ; one of the three original Roman tribes* : Liv. **II.** Usually Ramnenses : *the stock of the* Ramnes ; *one of the three centuries of* equites : Cic., Liv. Poet. for *nobles of the olden time* : Hor.

rāmōsus, a, um [rāmus], *having many branches, branching*. **1.** Lit. : arbor, Lucr. ; Ov. *Comp.* : Plin. **2.** Transf. **a.** cornua cervi, Verg. Of the clouds, *forked* : Lucr. Of the hydra : Ov. *Comp.* and *Sup.* : Plin. **b.** compita, Pers.

rāmulus, ī, *m.* [*dim.* rāmus], *a twig, sprig* : Cato, Cic.

rāmus, ī, *m.* [perh. for *rad-mus*, *cf.* rādix], *a branch, bough, twig*. **1.** Lit. : Enn., Cic., Verg., etc. **2.** Transf. **a.** For *a tree* : Verg. **b.** *a branch of a stag's antlers* : Caes. **c.** *a club* : Prop. **d.** *a branch* or *arm of the Greek letter* Y, used by Pythagoras as a symbol of the two paths of life ; hence called, Samii rami, Pers. **e.** Abstract : ramos amputare miseriarum, Cic. **f.** Of relationship : Pers.

rāna, ae, *f. a frog*. **1.** Lit. : Cic. Ep., Verg., etc. The entrails of frogs were used for charms : Juv. **2.** Transf. : rana marina, *a sea-fish, the frog-fish, fishing frog, angler* : Cic.

rancēns, entis, *adj. stinking, putrid* : viscera cadaverum, Lucr.

rancidulus, a, um [*dim.* rancidus], *tainted*. **1.** Lit. : opsonia, Juv. **2.** Transf. *disgusting* : Pers.

rancidus, a, um, *stinking, rank, rancid*. **1.** Lit. : cadavera, Lucr. ; aper, Hor. **2.** Transf. *disgusting, loathsome* : Plin. *Comp.* : Juv.

rānunculus, ī, *m.* [*dim.* rāna], *a little frog, tadpole* : Cic. Comic. of the inhabitants of Ulubrae (as residing near marshes) : Cic. Ep. [It. *ranocchia* ; Fr. *grenouille*.]

rapācida, ae, *m.* [rapāx], *Snatch-son* : Pl.

rapācitās, ātis, *f.* [rapāx], *greediness, rapacity* : Cic., Mart.

rapāx, ācis, *adj.* [rapiō], *grasping, greedy of plunder, rapacious*. **1.** Lit. **a.** Of persons and animals : Pl., Cic., Hor., etc. *Sup.* : Suet. **b.** Of things : falces, amnes, Lucr. ; mors, Tib. ; ventus, ignis, Ov. *Sup.* : Plin. **2.** Transf. : nihil est rapacius quam fluvius, Cic. With GEN. : rapacia virtutis ingenia, [illegible] *Sup.* : Plin.

rapidē, *adv. impetuously, rapidly*. **1.** Lit. : dilapsus (fluvius), Cic. *Comp.* : Tac. **2.** Transf. : Cic.

rapiditās, ātis, *f.* [rapidus], *impetuous swiftness, rapidity* : fluminis, Caes.

rapidus, a, um [rapiō], *tearing, hurrying and carrying away, impetuous*. **1.** Lit. **a.** Of rivers : Pl., Lucr., Verg., Quint., etc. *Sup.* : Caes. **b.** Of winds : Lucr., Verg., etc. **c.** Of flames and heat : Verg., Ov., etc. ; sol, Verg. **d.** Of animals : *tearing away, snatching, seizing* : Ov. Of hunting-dogs : agmen, Ov. **2.** Transf. **a.** Of speed : *tearing, impetuous, whirling* : currus, cursus, manūs, Verg. ; volucris, axis, Ov. ; agmen, Verg., Tac. *Sup.* : Ov. **b.** Of speech or action : *impetuous* : oratio, Cic. ; rapidus in consiliis, Liv. ; rapidus in urbem vectus, Tac. **c.** Of *quick-working* poison : Tac.

rapīna, ae, *f.* [rapiō], *plundering, pillage* (mostly in *pl.*). **1.** Lit. : Cic., Sall., Hor., etc. ; hostem rapinis prohibere, Caes. In *sing.* : Ov., Liv. **2.** Concr. : *plunder, booty* : abstractaeque boves abiurataeque rapinae, Verg.

rapiō, rapere, rapui, raptum (old *Aor. Subj.* rapsit, Cic.) [*cf.* ἁρπάζω], *to seize and carry off, to snatch, tear, wrench off*. **1.** Lit. **A.** In gen. **a.** quo rapitis me ? Pl. ; Verg. ; hostis vivos ex acie, Pl. ; ab aede funale, Ov. ; repagula de posti, Ov. Esp. of *seizing and hurrying off* to punishment, judgment, etc. : aliquem ad carnuficem, Pl. ; in ius, Pl. ; in ius ad regem, Liv. ; ad supplicium ob facinus, Cic. ; ad mortem, Cic. ; virginem ad virum, Cat. ; matres, virgines, pueros ad stuprum, Liv. **b.** Of rivers, winds, etc. : lembum in praeceps alveus, Verg. ; Saturnia rapit per aequora navem, Verg. ; (frondes) arbore ventus, Verg. **B.** *to carry off as plunder, to snatch, seize*. **a.** In gen. : Pl., Cic. ; aliquid, Pl. ; praedas, Verg. ; aliquem, Cic. ; virgines, Sall, Liv., Ov. ; oscula, Hor. Of death : improvisa leti vis rapuit gentis, Hor. ; ab ubere raptos, Verg. ; Suet. **b.** *to seize and plunder, to pillage, ravish* : Pergama, Verg. ; castra primo impetu, Liv. ; Armeniam, Tac. ; gratus raptae raptor, Ov. **C.** *to hurry off, quickly seize* : Turnus totam aciem in Teucros, Verg. ; quattuor hinc rapimur raedis, Hor. ; legiones, Plin. Pan. ; arma manu (i.e. seize in haste), Verg. ; Ov. ; commeatum in navis, Liv. Poet. : flammam in fomite, Verg. ; comae nigrum colorem, Ov. Esp. with *Refl. Pron.* : se ad caedem alicuius, Cic. ; ocius hinc te ni rapis, Hor. **2.** Transf. **a.** *to carry away, snatch* : cum fertur quasi torrens oratio, quamvis multa cuiusque modi rapiat, Cic. ; me fortuna periclo, Prop. ; tecum solatia, Verg. ; almum hora diem, Hor. Esp. of passions, desires, etc. : cupiditas aliquem, Cic. ; animus cupidine caecus ad inceptum scelus rapiebat, Sall. ; Hor. ; ea (cupiditas) ad oppugnandam Capuam rapit, Liv. In good sense : rapi ad opes augendas generis humani, Cic. **b.** *to wrest, wrench, twist, pervert* : aliquem in deterio-

rem viam, Pl.; comoodiam in peiiorem
partem, Pl.; aliquem in invidiam, Cic.; si
quis in adversum rapiat casusve deusve,
Verg.; victoriae gloriam in se, Liv.; commoda ad se, Cic. **c.** *to snatch, seize hastily :*
Venerem, Verg., Hor.; occasionem de die,
Hor.; viam, Ov.; raptae inter arma nuptiae, Liv.; inlicitas voluptates, Tac.

raptim, adv. [rapiō], *impetuously, violently,*
hurriedly : Lucr., Caes., Verg., Liv., etc.

raptiō, ōnis, f. [rapiō], *a carrying off, abduc-*
tion : Ter.

raptō, āre [*freq.* rapiō]. **1.** Lit. **a.** *to seize*
and carry off, to drag or hurry away : ali-
quem, Pl., Cic.; Hector raptatus bigis,
Verg.; Enn.; viscera viri per silvas, Verg.;
Lucr.; membra de iuvenco, Cat.; arbitrio
volucrum raptatur equorum, Ov.; Lucr.;
vexilla huc vel illuc, Tac.; signa turbine
atque undā raptabantur, Tac. **b.** *to rav-*
age, plunder : adhuc raptabat Africam Tac-
farinas, Tac. **2.** Transf. **a.** In gen. :
quid raptem in crimina divos? Prop. **b.**
Of passion : *to agitate :* me amor, Pl.

raptor, ōris, m. [rapiō], *a robber, plunderer,*
ravisher. **1.** Lit. : Pl., Hor., Ov., Tac.,
etc.; lupi raptores, Verg. With GEN. :
panis et peni, Pl.; orbis, filiae, Tac. **2.**
Transf. : alieni honoris, Ov.

raptus, a, um. **I.** Part. rapiō. **II.** Noun,
raptum, ī, n. *plunder :* vivere rapto, Verg.,
Liv.; ex rapto vivere, Ov.; rapto potiri,
Verg.

raptus, ūs, m. [rapiō]. **I.** *a violent snatching*
or dragging away : Inoo lacerata est altera
raptu, Ov. **II.** *a carrying off, depredation :*
ad praedam et raptūs congregare, Tac.;
raptūs exercere, Tac. **III.** *abduction, rape :*
Tac.; alicuius, Cic., Ov.

rāpulum, ī, n. [*dim.* rāpum,] *a little turnip :*
Hor.

rāpum, ī, n. [*cf.* ῥάφη], *a turnip :* Varr.
Transf. of tree-roots : Sen. Ep.

rārē, adv. *rarely, seldom :* Pl.

rārē-faciō, facere, fēcī, factum [rārus], *to*
rarefy : rareque facit, Lucr. *Inf. Pass.*
rārĕfĭerī, Lucr.

rārēscō, ĕscere [rārus]. **1.** Lit. **a.** *to grow*
thin, lose density, to become rarefied : nubila
caeli, Lucr.; umor aquāī ab aestu, Lucr.;
tellus in aquas, Ov. **b.** *to grow wider*
apart, widen out : angusti claustra Pelori,
Verg.; colles paulatim, Tac. **2.** Transf. :
sonitus, Prop.

rāritās, ātis, f. [rārus]. **I.** *looseness of tex-*
ture, distance apart (opp. densitas) : Cic.,
Quint. **II.** *thinness, fewness.* **a.** capillorum, Suet.; stellarum (opp. multitudo),
Plin. **b.** dictorum, Cic.; Quint.; lavandi, Suet.

rārus, a, um. **1.** Lit. **a.** *not close or thick,*
thin, loose in texture (opp. to densus) : tex-
tura, corpus, aer, Lucr.; vestis, Cat.;
retia, Verg.; cribrum, Ov.; rariores silvae.
Tac.; terra rarissima, Verg.? **b.** *far apart,*
scattered, thin, scanty : raris ac prope nullis
portibus, Caes.; vides habitari in terrā
raris et angustis in locis, Cic.; rarum holus,
Verg.; raris vocibus hisco, Verg.; apparent
rari, Verg.; manat rara meas lacrima per
genas, Hor.; ignes, Liv. Milit. : *in*
loose or open order : accedebat huc, ut nun-

quam conferti, sed rari magnisque intervallis proeliarentur, Caes.; Liv.; ordines,
Liv.; acies, Verg.; rarior acies, Curt.,
Tac. **2.** Transf. **a.** *few, rare, infrequent :*
optimum quidque rarissimum, Cic.; vitio
parentum rara iuventus, Hor.; Verg.;
litterae, Liv.; lites, infelicitas, Quint.;
Oceanus raris navibus aditur, Tac.; rarum
est (with *ut* and *Subj.*), Quint. Adverbially for raro : nec Iliacos coetūs nisi rarus
adibat, Ov.; Tac. ABL. **rārō** as *Adv., seldom,*
rarely : Pl., Cic., Ov., etc.; *Comp.* rārĭus :
Cic. Ep.; *Sup.* rārissimō : Suet. **b.** *un-*
common, scarce, rare : rara puella fuit,
Prop.; avis (*sc.* pavo), Hor.; rara Fides,
Hor. *Comp.* : Ov. *Sup.* : Ov., Sen. [It.
rado.]

rāsĭlis, e, adj. [rādō], *smoothed by scraping or*
shaving : foris, Cat.; torno rasile buxum,
Verg.; fibula, Ov.

rāsĭtō, āre [*freq.* rādō], *to shave often :* Suet.

rāstellus, ī, m. [*dim.* rāstrum,] *a small hoe,*
rake : Varr., Suet. [Fr. *râteau.*]

rāstrum, ī, n. (in *pl. us.* rāstrī, ōrum, m. :
Pl., Cato, Verg., etc.) [rādō], *an instru-*
ment for scraping, hence *a toothed hoe, a*
mattock : rastris glaebas frangit, Verg.;
Ov. Comic. as the comb of Polyphemus,
along with the sickle as his razor : Ov.

rāsus, a, um, Part. rādō. [Fr. *ras.*]

ratĭō, ōnis, f. [*cf.* reor, ratus], *a reckoning,*
account, calculation, computation. **I.** Of
business. **1.** Abstract : rationem reddere, tenere, computare, Pl.; ducere, *to*
make a calculation, Cic.; also, habere,
Caes., Cic.; inire, *to cast an account,* Caes.
In *pl.* : rationes cum publicanis putare,
Cic.; Cato; conferre, referre, deferre, Cic.
Ep.; falsas rationes inferre, Cic. **2.** Concrete : *accounts.* **a.** bene ratio accepti
atque expensi inter nos convenit, Pl.; auri
ratio constat, Cic.; ut par sit ratio acceptorum et datorum, Cic.; repetere de
pecuniis repetundis, Cic.; rationes a colono
accepit, Cic. **b.** *a business, matter, affair :*
ratio domestica, bellica, Cic.; aeraria,
Cic.; re ac ratione cum aliquo coniunctus,
Cic. Esp. in *pl.* : *affairs, interests :* res
rationesque Ballionis curo, Pl.; si meas
rationes vestrae saluti anteposuissem, Cic.;
Sall.; rationes familiaris componere, Tac.
II. Transf. **A.** From business. **1.** Abstract : *reckoning, calculation :* eam mecum rationem puto, Pl.; mecum has
rationes puto, Ter.; initā subductāque
ratione nefaria scelera meditantes, Cic. **2.**
Concrete. **a.** *account :* census quom
sum, iuratori recte rationem dedi, Pl.;
abs te rationem reposcent, Caes.; Cic.;
rationem vitae suae reddere, Cic.; eam
condicionem esse imperandi ut non aliter
ratio constet quam si uni reddatur, Tac.
b. *the sum total :* lenonum, Pl. **c.** *a list,*
register : omnium proeliorum, Caes.; cedo
rationem carceris, Cic.; totius imperi,
Suet. **d.** *a transaction : business : affairs :*
fori iudicium rationem suscepit, Cic.; cum
in reliquis fere rebus, publicis privatisque
rationibus; Graecis utantur litteris, Caes.
B. In gen. **1.** Abstract. **a.** *considera-*
tion, account, regard, respect : alicuius
rationem habere, Caes., Cic., Liv.; ali-

cuius salutis rationem habere, Caes.; so
with frumentandi, Caes.; dignitatis vel
commodi, Cic.; omnis hac in re habenda
ratio et diligentia est ut etc., Cic.; habere
rationem (with *Indir. Quest.*), Cic.; pro
ratione pecuniae liberalius est tractatus,
Cic. Ep. **b.** *considerations* leading to
action; *grounds* or *reasons* of action or
thought: rationem mei consili accipite,
Caes.; totius rei consilium his rationibus
explicavit ut etc., Caes.; ut ipsi Catoni
rationem facti probem, Cic.; nihil rationis
adfert quam ob rem etc., Cic., non ratio est
or nulla ratio est, *it is unreasonable* (with
Inf.), Cic.; ratio est (with DAT. of person
and *Inf.*), Liv., Tac. **c.** In logic and
rhet. **i.** *a* ground or *reason* adduced:
conquirere, adferre, subicere (often with
quod-clause or *Indir. Quest.*), Cic.; nostra
confirmare argumentis ac rationibus, Cic.
ii. *a reasoning, argument, proof :* Cic.,
Quint. **2.** Concrete. **a.** *a thought-out
plan, scheme, system, method, procedure :*
ratio ordoque agminis aliter se habebat,
Caes.; equestris proeli, Caes.; civitatis,
Cic.; novae rationes bellandi, Caes.;
totam Gallici belli rationem prope iam ex-
plicatam perturbare, Cic.; mea ratio in
dicendo haec esse solet ut etc., Cic.;
rationem instituere, Pl., Caes.; inire (with
Indir. Deliberative), Caes.; (with *ut* and
Subj.), Cic.; (with GEN.), Liv.; vitae
rationes suscipere, comparare, Cic.; res
ratione modoque tractari non vult, Hor.;
ab nostris eâdem ratione quâ pridie resistitur, Caes.; quid refert quâ me ratione
cogatis? Cic. **b.** *reasoned theory ; science,
knowledge :* ratio atque usus belli, Caes.;
navigi, Lucr.; ratio civilia, ratio vivendi,
ratio vitae, Cic.; magis ratione et consilio
quam virtute. vicisse, Caes. **c.** *a theory,
doctrine, system :* Stoicorum, Cic. **C.**
reason as a mental faculty: Cic., Verg.,
etc.; quantum ratione provideri poterat,
Caes.; quantum in ratione esset exploratum habuit, Hirt. [It. *ragione ;* Fr.
raison.]

ratiōcinātiō, ōnis, *f.* [ratiōcinor]. **I.** R h e t.
*an exercise of the reasoning powers, reason-
ing :* Cic. **II.** *a set form of reasoning, a
syllogism :* Cic., Quint.

ratiōcinātīvus, a, um [ratiōcinor]. R h e t.
of reasoning, syllogistic : Cic., Quint.

ratiōcinātor, ōris, *m.* [ratiōcinor], *a reckoner,
accountant.* **1.** L i t. : Cic. Ep. **2.**
T r a n s f. : Cic.

ratiōcinor, ārī [ratiō], *to reckon, compute,
calculate.* **1.** L i t. : de pecuniâ, Cic. **2.**
T r a n s f. **a.** *to consider, deliberate :* id
ratiocinor (with *Indir. Deliberative*), Pl.
b. *to reason, argue ; to conclude :* sic
ratiocinabantur (with Acc. and *Inf.*), Cic.
With *Indir. Quest. :* Cic.

ratiōnābilis, e, *adj.* [ratiō], *possessing reason,
rational :* natura, Sen.

ratiōnālis, e, *adj.* [ratiō]. **I.** *possessing
reason, rational :* animal, Quint. *Neut.* as
Noun (*sc.* animal): Quint. **II.** *concerned
with reason, rational :* philosophia, Sen. Ep.;
Quint. **III.** *syllogistic :* Quint.

ratiōnāliter, *adv. reasonably, rationally :*
Sen. Ep.

ratiōnārium, i, *n.* [ratiō], *a statistical table,
schedule :* imperi, Suet.

ratis, is, *f.* [*cf.* ἐρέσσω, rēmus]. **1.** L i t.
a. *a raft :* Caes., Cic. In *pl.* : *pontoons :*
ratibus quibus iunxerat flumen, Liv. **b.**
a float (for learning to swim): Pl. **2.**
T r a n s f. **a.** P r o v. : servavisti omnem
ratem, Pl. **b.** *a bark, boat :* Enn., Cat.,
Verg.

ratiuncula, ae, *f.* [*dim.* ratiō], *a small reckoning, a little account.* **1.** L i t. : subduxi
ratiunculam, quantum aeris mihi sit, Pl.;
Ter. **2.** T r a n s f. **a.** *a slight ground* or
reason : leves, Cic. **b.** *a trifling syllogism :*
concludunt ratiunculas Stoici, Cic.

ratus, a, um. **I.** *Part.* reor. **II.** A d j. :
*reckoned, calculated, fixed by calculation ;
hence, settled, established, sure, certain,
unalterable :* Ter.; motūs (stellarum) con-
stantes et rati, Cic.; testamenta, decretum,
tempus, etc., Cic.; vita, Verg.; dicta, Ov.;
amicitia, Tac. *Sup.* : Cato. P h r. **a.**
pro ratâ parte (portione), secundum ratam
partem, and *absol.* pro ratâ, *in a certain* or
fixed ratio, proportionally : utinam ex
omni senatu pro ratâ parte esset! Cic.;
tantum pediti daturum fuisse credunt, et
pro ratâ aliis, Liv. **b.** ratum aliquid
facere (efficere, Ov.), habere, ducere, *to
make* or *consider fixed* or *valid ; to confirm,
ratify, approve :* quid augur (habet), cur a
dextrâ corvus, a sinistrâ cornix faciat
ratum? (i.e. *a favourable augury*), Cic.;
qui non duxerint societatem ratam, Liv.;
also, ratum servare, Plin. Ep.; also,
ratum alicui esse, *to be confirmed :* ista
ipsa, quae te emisse scribis, non solum rata
erunt, sed etiam grata (i.e. *I accept the*
bargain), Cic.

rauci-sonus, a, um, *hoarse-sounding :* cantus
cornicum, Lucr.; Cat.

raucus, a, um [*cf.* rāvim], *hoarse.* **1.** L i t.
a. Of persons and animals: Pl., Cic.,
Verg., etc.; fauces, Lucr.; guttur, vox,
Ov. **b.** Of inanimate things: hoarse, hollow or deep sounding, harsh : cornu, Prop.;
aes (i.e. *tuba*), Verg.; Hadria, Hor. **2.**
T r a n s f. : te vero nolo, nisi ipse rumor iam
raucus erit factus, ad Baias venire, Cic. Ep.

raudus (also **rōdus** and **rūdus**), eris, *n.* a
rude mass ; esp. a piece of copper used as
a coin : cum rudera milites iacerent, Liv.

rausculum (**rōd-** and **rūd-**), i, *n.* [*dim.*
raudus], *a small sum of money :* Cic. Ep.

rāvim, Acc. *sing. f.* [*cf.* raucus], *hoarseness :*
Pl.

rāviō, īre [rāvim], *to talk oneself hoarse :*
Pl.

rāvus, a, um [*cf.* grāvastellus : γῆρας, γραῦς],
greyish or *tawny :* mare, Cic.; lupa, Hor.

re or **red,** *an inseparable particle.* **I.** F o r m :
red is used before vowels and *h ;* also in reddo, and perh. with the connecting vowel *i*
in red-i-vivus, q.v. In later Latin words
only, *re* is sometimes found before vowels
and *h ; e.g.* reaedifico, reexinanio, reinvito,
etc. The orthography and quantity of
words compounded with *re* are in general
somewhat arbitrary, especially in the ante-
and post-class. poets. **II.** M e a n i n g. **a.**
back or *backward* (of rest or motion) : redire,
revertere. **b.** Of restoration to a previous

or normal state, *back*, *again* : reficio, repono.
c. *resting behind*, *in reserve* : retinere,
relegare. **d.** *in return or response* : reddo,
rependo. **e.** *in opposition or resistance to* :
repugnare. **f.** *back to the beginning or to
the roots* : restinguere, resecare, **g.** Of
reversing an action, *un-* : recludo. **h.**
looking backwards, *on second thoughts* :
respicere, recognoscere, reputare. **i.** Of
repetition, *again*, *repeatedly* : recinere.

rea, ae, *v.* reus.

reapse, *adv.* [contr. from rē eāpse=rē ipsā],
in fact, *in reality*, *actually*, *really* : Pl., Cic.

Reāte, is, *n.* *an ancient Sabine town*, now
Rieti ; **Reātīnus**, a, um ; **Reātīnī**, ōrum,
m. pl. its inhabitants.

rebellātiō, ōnis, *f.* [rebellō], *a renewal of
hostilities*, *revolt* : Tac.

rebellātrix, īcis, *f. adj.* [rebellō], *revolted*,
rebellious : Germania, Ov. ; Liv.

rebelliō, ōnis, *f.* [rebellō], *a renewal of war
(by a conquered people)* ; *a revolt* : Liv. ;
facere, Caes. ; coeptare, parare, comprimere, Tac. In *pl.* : Cic.

rebellis, e, *adj.* [rebellō], *that renews war*,
insurgent. **1.** Lit. : Verg., Curt., Tac.
As Noun, **rebellēs**, ium, *m. pl. rebels* :
Tac. **2.** Transf. : amor, Ov.

rebellium, ī, *n.* [rebellō], *a renewal of war*,
rebellion : Liv.

re-bellō, āre, *to break out into war again* (said
of the conquered) ; *to revolt.* **1.** Lit. :
Liv. Poet. : tauro mutatus membra re-
bello, Ov. **2.** Transf. : pudor rebellat,
Sen. Trag. ; Plin.

re-bītō, ere, *to go back*, *return* : Pl.

re-boō, āre. **I.** *to give back a sound*, *to
re-echo* : tympana, Cat. ; silvae, Verg.
II. With Acc. : *to make to resound* : citharae tecta, Lucr.

re-calcitrō, āre, *to kick back* (of horses).
Transf. of rejected addresses : Hor.

re-caleō, ēre, *to be warm again* : recalent
nostro Tiberina fluenta sanguine, Verg.

re-calēscō, ere, *to become warm again*, *to grow
warm.* **1.** Lit. : Cic. **2.** Transf. : mens,
Ov. ; in scribendo, Plin. Ep.

re-calfaciō, facere, fēcī, *to make warm again.*
1. Lit. : calidum priori caede telum, Ov.
2. Transf. : tepidam montem, Ov.

re-calvos, a, om, *bald in front* : Pl.

re-candēscō, candēscere, canduī. **I.** *to grow
white in response* (to the beat of the oars) :
percussa unda, Ov. **II.** *to grow hot*, *to glow
in response* (to the sun). **1.** Lit. : tellus
solibus aetheriis, Ov. **2.** Transf. : ira, Ov.

re-cantō, āre. **I.** *to recant* : recantatis
opprobriis, Hor. **II.** *to charm back*, *charm
away* : curas, Ov. **III.** Without Obj. :
to sound back, *re-echo* : Mart.

re-cēdō, cēdere, cēssī, cēssum, *to go back or
away*, *to retire*, *withdraw*, *retreat.* **1.** Lit.
A. Of living beings : aps te procul, Pl. ;
a Mutinā, Cic. ; Liv. ; a stabulis longius
apes, Verg. ; centuriones ex eo loco, Caes. ;
de medio, Cic. ; loco, Pl. Of *retiring to
rest* : Ov. **B.** Of things : **a.** ut illae undae
ad alios accedant, ab aliis autem recedant,
Cic. ; anni, Hor. ; voces illae, Plin. Pan.
b. Of situation : *to stand back*, *recede* (i.e.
to be distant, retired) : Anchisae domus,
Verg. ; Plin. Ep. Of apparent retirement :

provehimur portu, terraeque urbesque rece-
dunt, Verg. ; Ov. **c.** *to be severed* : caput
e cervice, Ov. ; caput cervice, Ov. **2.**
Transf. **a.** Of living beings : ab officio, ab
armis, a vitā, etc., Cic. ; ab oppugnatione,
Hirt. ; in otia, Hor. **b.** Of things : ira,
Ov. ; labor ille a vobis, Cato ; res a consuetudine, Cic. ; vita patrio corpore, Pl. ;
in ventos vita, Verg.

re-cellō, ere, *to spring back*, *recoil* : Lucr. :
gravi libramento plumbi recellente ad
solum, Liv.

recēns, entis (ABL. *sing.* us. **-ī** ; in the poets
sometimes **-e** : Cat., Ov. ; GEN. *pl.* recentum, Hor.). **1.** Lit. **a.** *fresh*, *young*,
recent (opp. vetus) : piscis nequam est, nisi
recens, Pl. ; caespites, Caes. ; sanguis,
Cat. ; flores, Hor. ; prata, Verg. **b.** *fresh
in strength* (opp. defetigatus) : Caes., Liv.,
Ov. ; animus, Liv. *Masc.* as Noun :
Caes. **2.** Transf. **a.** Of what has recently happened : *fresh*, *recent* : re recenti,
Pl., Cic. ; recenti negotio, Cic. ; recentium
iniuriarum memoriam, Caes. ; proelium,
victoria, Caes. ; Liv. ; epistula, Cic. Ep.
Comp. and *Sup.* : Cic. **b.** Of persons :
newly come, *just arrived* : Senones recentis-
simi advenarum, Liv. ; (as Noun, recen-
tiores, *modern writers*, Cic.). With ABL. :
Regini quidam Romā recentes, Cic. ; praeturā, caede, Tac. With *preps.* : e provinciā, Cic. ; Homerus, qui recens ab
illorum aetate fuit, Cic. ; recens ab illorum
aetate fuit, Cic. ; recens a vulnere Dido,
Verg. ; ab excidio urbis, Liv. ; recentes in
dolore, Tac. ; recentissimum ad laborem
militem, Liv.

recēns, *adv. lately*, *just*, *recently*, *etc.* : Pl.,
Lucr., Sall., Liv., etc. *Sup.* : Plin.

re-cēnseō, cēnsēre, cēnsuī, cēnsum, *to count
over again.* **1.** Lit. **a.** *to make a regular
list of*, *to muster* (for inspection), *review* :
haec in Aeduorum finibus recensebantur numerusque inibatur, Caes. ; omnem suorum
numerum, Verg. ; exercitum, legiones,
Liv. ; recensuit captivos, quot cuiusque
populi essent, Liv. Poet. : signa recen-
suerat bis sol sua, Ov. **b.** Of the censors :
equites, Liv. **2.** Transf. of *reviewing*
events : fata fortunasque virum (GEN.),
Verg. ; biduo acceptam cladem, Liv. ; Ov.

recēnsiō, ōnis, *f.* [recēnseō], *a revision of a
list* : Cic., Suet.

recēnsus, a, um, *Part.* recēnseō.

recēnsus, ūs, *m.* [recēnseō], *a review* :
populi, Suet.

receptāculum, ī, *n.* [receptō]. **I.** *a reservoir*,
magazine, *receptacle* : cibi alvus, Cic. ;
cloaca maxima, receptaculum omnium pur-
gamentorum urbis, Liv. ; Nili, Tac. **II.**
a place of refuge, *a lurking-place*, *shelter*, *retreat* : pro receptaculo turrim facere,
Caes. ; castra sunt victori receptaculum,
victo perfugium, Liv. ; Cic. With GEN. :
Capua receptaculum aratorum, Cic. ; Caes. ;
illud tibi oppidum receptaculum praedae
fuit, Cic. ; receptaculum adversae pugnae,
Liv. ; mors aeternum nihil sentiendi receptaculum, Cic.

receptiō, ōnis, *f.* [recipiō], *a receiving*, *reception* : with *Obj.* Acc. : quid tibi huc
receptio ad te est meum virum ? Pl.

receptō, āre [freq. recipiō]. **I.** to take to one-self or to take back repeatedly : placido natura receptat cuncta sinu, Lucr. ; Enn. **II.** to receive to one's home often, to harbour habitually : meum filium ad te, Ter. ; mercatores, Liv. ; Saturni sese quo stella receptet, Verg. **III.** to strive hard to recover, to tug at to regain : hastam receptat ossibus haerentem, Verg.

receptor, ōris, m. and **receptrix**, īcis, f. [recipiō], a receiver, shelterer ; in bad sense, a harbourer, concealer : ipse ille latronum occultator et receptor locus, Cic. ; Tac. ; Messana, praedarum ac furtorum receptrix, Cic.

receptus, a, um. **I.** Part. recipiō. **II.** Noun, **receptum**, ī, n. an engagement, obligation : Cic.

receptus, ūs, m. [recipiō]. **I.** a drawing back, drawing in again. **1.** Lit. : spiritus in receptu difficilis, Quint. **2.** Transf. withdrawal : sententiae, Liv. **II.** a drawing or falling back, a retiring, retreat. **1.** Lit. **a.** Milit. : ut expeditum ad suos receptum habeant, Caes. ; signum receptui canere, Liv. ; Cic. ; receptum alicui dare, Caes. In metaph. : canere receptui a miseriis contemplandis, Cic. **b.** Non-milit. : cum receptus primis non esset (from a fire), Liv. In pl. : (bucina) cecinit iussos inflata receptūs, Ov. **2.** Transf. **a.** In pl. : place of retreat, refuge : tuti receptūs, Verg. **b.** a return : receptus ad Caesaris gratiam atque amicitiam, Caes. ; ad paenitendum, Liv. ; a malis consiliis, Liv.

recessim, adv. backwards : Pl.

recessus, ūs, m. [recēdō], a going back, receding, retiring, retreat. **1.** Lit. : accessus ad res salutaris, a pestiferis recessus, Cic. ; recessum primis ultimi non dabant, Caes. Of the tide : Cic. **2.** Transf. **a.** Concr. : a retired or secret spot, a nook, retreat, recess : mihi solitudo et recessus provincia est, Cic. ; hic spelunca fuit, vasto summota recessu, Verg. ; Liv., etc. In pl. : Verg., Liv., etc. Transf. : in animis hominum tantae latebrae sunt et tanti recessūs, Cic. **b.** tum accessus a te ad causam facti, tum recessus, Cic. Ep.

recharmidō, āre [Charmidēs], to 'uncharmidise' oneself (a burlesquely-formed word), Pl.

recidīvus, a, um [recidō]. **I.** restored after a fall : Pergama, Verg. **II.** recurring, returning : nummus, Liv.

re-cidō (poet. also **rē-**), recidere, reccidī, recāsurus [cadō], to fall back to a former position. **1.** Lit. : quia et recidant omnia in terras et oriantur e terris, Cic. ; Lucr. ; Ov. ; ramulum in oculum suum recidisse, Cic. ; etiam si recta recciderat navis, Liv. **2.** Transf. **a.** post interitum Tati cum ad Romulum potentatus omnis recidisset, Cic. ; Syracusae in antiquam servitutem, Liv. ; in graviorem morbum, Liv. ; contentio nimia vocis, Cic. **b.** to recoil on the author : in te istaec contumeliae, Pl. ; hunc casum ad ipsos recidere posse, Caes. ; suspicio in vosmet ipsos, Cic. ; Ov. ; consilia in ipsorum caput, Liv. **c.** With the idea of cado predominating : to fall low (deserv-

adj, is repeatedly) : to descend, of reduced ars musica ad paucos, Ter. ; tantus apparatus ad nihilum, Cic. ; Lucr. ; ex laetitia et voluptate ad luctum et lacrimas, Cic. ; rex in eam fortunam, Liv. ; Cic. ; hucine tandem omnia recciderunt ut etc. ? Cic. ; ex quantis opibus quo reccidissent Carthaginiensium res, Liv.

re-cīdō, cīdere, cīdī, cīsum [caedō], to cut back (to the stem or trunk), to lop. **1.** Lit. : vepres, Cato ; sceptrum imo de stirpe, Verg. ; hirsutam barbam falce, Ov. ; pollicem alicui, Quint. ; capillos, Plin. Ep. Also, ceras inanis, Verg. ; columnas, Hor. **2.** Transf. : nationes partim recisas partim repressas, Cic. ; ambitiosa ornamenta, Hor. ; aliquid priscum ad morem, Tac.

re-cingō, cingere, cīnctum, to ungird, unloose : tunicas, Ov. ; Verg. In Mid. : recingitur anguem, Ov.

re-cinō, cinere [canō]. **I.** to sound again and again, re-echo, resound, repeat : in vocibus nostrorum oratorum quiddam urbanius, Cic. With Acc. : nomen imago, Hor. ; haec recinunt iuvenes dictata senesque, Hor. **II.** to sound against, give warning notes : parrae recinentis omen, Hor.

reciper-, v. recuper-.

re-cipiō, cipere, cēpī, ceptum (old Fut. recepsō, Cat.) [capiō]. **I.** to hold back (in sales), to keep in reserve, retain : posticulum hoc recepit quom aedis vendidit, Pl. ; Cic. **II.** to take back, withdraw. **1.** Lit. **a.** ensem multā morte recepit, Verg. ; ad limina gressum, Verg. ; milites defessos, Caes. ; suos omnis incolumis (ex oppido in castra), Caes. ; Liv. **b.** With Refl. Pron. : to draw back, withdraw ; and milit. to retreat : se ex eo loco, Pl. ; Cic. ; se ex fugā, Caes. ; se ad dominum, Pl. ; se ad suos, Caes. ; se ad ordines suos, Caes. ; se in castra, Caes., Liv. ; se intra munitiones, Caes. ; se domum, Pl. ; se Larisam, Caes. ; se eo, Caes. Also without Refl. Pron. : Pl., Caes. ; signum recipiendi, Cic. **2.** Transf. : se ad reliquam cogitationem belli, Caes. ; Pl. ; Cic. ; se a voluptatibus in otium, Plin. Pan. **III.** to take back, regain, recover. **1.** Lit. **a.** argentum, Pl. ; si velit suos recipere, obsides sibi remittat, Caes. ; Tarentum, Cic. ; suas res amissas, Liv. Hence, pecuniam ex novis vectigalibus, Cic. **b.** Of rescuing : illum medio ex hoste, Verg. ; civis qui in potestate hostium fuerant, Liv. ; fruges (ex undis) receptae, Verg. **2.** Transf. **a.** anhelitum, Pl. ; animam, Ter. ; spiritum, Quint. ; mentem, Hor. ; animum vultumque, Ov. ; a (e) pavore animum (animos), Liv. ; antiquam frequentiam urbs, Liv. **b.** With Refl. Pron. : se ex timore, Caes. ; se (ex stupore), Cic. ; totā se mente, Ov. **IV.** to admit, receive to oneself, take on oneself, suffer, etc. **1.** Lit. **a.** In gen. : a latere tela, Caes. ; num ut gladiatoribus imperari solet, ferrum non recipit ? Cic. ; equus frenum, Hor. **b.** to admit to one's house, hospitality, friendship, etc. : excludor, ille recipitur, Ter. ; munitio perterritos, Caes. ; aliquem, Cic. ; fluvium mare, Pl. ; aliquem domum ad se hospitio, Caes. ; Pl. ; Cic. ; exercitum tectis ac aedibus suis, Cic. ; aliquem finibus

suis, Caes. ; Hor., etc. ; aliquem ad epulas,
Cic. ; me in tectum, Pl. ; aliquem in
civitatem, Cic., Hor., Liv. ; aliquem in
amicitiam, Sall. ; aliquem in caelum, Cic. ;
aliquem . in fidem, Pl. ; aliquem in loco,
Pl. ; Ov. Also, to citizenship, surrender,
etc. : aliquem in civitatem, Cic. ; aliquem
in deditionem, Caes., Liv. ; aliquem in
ius dicionemque, Liv. ; aliquem in fidem,
Caes., Cic., Liv. **c.** O c c. for the usual
capio : oppidum, civitatem, Siciliam, etc.,
Caes. ; Liv. ; rem publicam armis, Sall. ;
phalerae multo sudore receptae, Verg.
2. T r a n s f. **A.** In gen. : *to admit, take on
oneself, suffer.* **a.** tua dicta in auris
recipio, Pl. ; recepi causam Siciliae, Cic. ;
mandatum, officium, Cic. ; antiquitas
recepit fabulas, haec aetas autem respuit,
Cic. ; poenas ab aliquo, Verg. ; in semet
ipsum religionem, Liv. **b.** nec incon-
stantiam virtus recipit, Cic. ; Caes. ; re
iam non ultra recipiente cunctationem,
Liv. **B.** In law. **a.** Of the praetor : *to
receive* notice of a prosecution : recipere
nomen, Cic. ; recipere reum *or* aliquem
inter reos, Tac. **b.** Of a surety, pledge,
etc. : *to guarantee, undertake, promise* :
dico et recipio ad me, Pl. ; promitto in
meque recipio, Cic. Ep. ; de aestate, Cic.
Ep. ; Liv. ; ea quae tibi promitto ac
recipio, Cic. Ep. ; Caes. With Acc. and
Fut. Inf. : Caes., Cic. ; so with hoc : Liv.
With Acc. and *Pres. Inf.* : Cic. Ep. [It.
recevere ; Fr. *recevoir.*]

reciprocō, āre [reciprocus], *to move backwards, or backwards and forwards.* **A.**
T r a n s. **1.** L i t. : rursus prorsus fluctus
feram, Enn. ; (ventus) cum iam spiritum
includeret nec reciprocare animam sineret,
Liv. In *Mid.* : quinqueremem in adversum aestum reciprocari non posse, *to tack
about,* Liv. ; of the tide : Curt. **2.**
T r a n s f. *to reverse, convert* a proposition :
Cic. **B.** I n t r a n s. (Of the ebb and flow
of the tide) : Cic., Liv., etc.

reciprocus, a, um, *going backwards or forwards, ebbing and flowing.* **1.** P r o p. :
reciproca tendens nervo equino concita
tela, Acc. ; aestus maris paribus intervallis
reciproci, Plin. **2.** *ebbing, receding* : va-
dosum ac reciprocum mare, Plin., Tac.

recisus, a, um, *Part.* recīdō.

recitātiō, ōnis, *f.* [recitō], *a reading aloud.*
a. Of documents in judicial proceedings :
Cic., Suet. **b.** Of a new literary work,
by the author : Tac., Plin. Ep., Suet. In
pl. : Tac., Plin. Ep.

recitātor, ōris, *m.* [recitō], *a reader.* **a.** Of
documents in judicial proceedings : Cic.
b. Of literature : Hor., Sen. Ep., Plin. Ep.

re-citō, āre, *to read out, recite.* **a.** Esp. a
document, statement, report, in public or
legal proceedings : testimonium, edictum,
orationem, etc., Cic. ; Caes., etc. ; responsum ex scripto, Liv. ; elogium de testamento, Cic. With personal *Obj.* : *to read
out the name of an individual* in a will, etc. :
testamento si recitatus heres esset pupillus
Cornelius, Cic. ; senatum, *read the roll,* Cic.,
Liv. **b.** I n g e n. *to read out, recite* anything : scripta in medio foro, Hor. ; Ov. ;
Plin. Ep., etc. ; sacramentum, Tac.

reclāmātiō, ōnis, *f.* [reclāmō], *a cry of opposition or disapproval* : Cic.

reclāmitō, āre [*freq.* reclāmō], *to cry out
strongly against.* T r a n s f. : istius modi
suspicionibus ipsa natura, Cic.

re-clāmō [rēclāmat, Lucr. 1. 623], āre. **I.**
to cry out against, to contradict loudly. **1.**
L i t. : si paulum modo offensum est, theatra
tota reclamant, Cic. ; Hor. ; Liv. With
DAT. : promissis, Cic. ; alicui, Plin. Ep. ;
aliquid alicui, Quint. With *Juss. Subj.* :
unā voce omnis iudices, ne is iuraret, recla-
masse, Cic. With Acc. and *Inf.* : Suet.
Impers. Pass. : Cic., Suet. **2.** T r a n s f. :
quod ratio reclamat vera, Lucr. **II.** *to
reverberate, resound* : scopulis inlisa reclamant aequora, Verg.

reclīnis, e, *adj.* [reclīnō], *leaning back* : in
sinu, Ov. ; super pedes cubitantis, Tac. ;
cubili, Tac.

re-clīnō, āre [*cf.* acclīnō], *to bend or lean back,
recline.* **1.** L i t. : scuta, Verg. In *Mid.* :
te in remoto gramine reclinatum, Hor. ;
Caes. With *Refl. Pron.* : alces huc se
reclinaverunt, Caes. **2.** T r a n s f. : nullum
ab labore me reclinat otium, Hor. ; ad
aliquem onus imperi, Sen.

re-clūdō, clūdere, clūsi, clūsum [claudō].
I. *to open* what had been closed, *to unclose.*
1. L i t. : portas, Verg. ; Pl. ; Lucr. ;
Tac., etc. ; (poet. : fata, i.e. the gates of
death, Hor.) ; armarium, Pl. ; adyta,
Verg. ; caelum alicui, Verg. ; viam arcis,
Ov. ; tellurem, Verg. ; humum, Tac. ;
pectora pecudum (in augury), Verg. **2.**
T r a n s f. *to lay open, disclose.* **a.** ensem,
Verg. ; pectus mucrone, Verg. ; Hor. ; ora
fontana, Ov. ; Verg. ; thesauros tellure,
Verg. ; (sol) caelum aestivā luce, Verg. **b.**
Of secrets : ebrietas operta recludit, Hor. ;
si recludantur tyrannorum mentes, Tac.
II. *to shut up* : speculum, Stat.

recoctus, a, um, *Part.* recoquō.

re-cōgitō, āre, *to think over, reconsider* :
aliquid, Sen. With *de* : Cic. With *Indir.
Quest.* : Pl.

recognitiō, ōnis, *f.* [recognōscō], *a reviewing,
re-investigation* : per recognitionem alicuius,
Cic. With *Obj.* GEN. : sui, Sen. ; equitum,
Suet.

re-cognōscō, gnōscere, gnōvī, gnitum. **I.**
to learn or call to mind again, to review :
se non tum illa discere, sed reminiscendo
recognoscere, Cic. ; sacra eruta annalibus,
Ov. ; Tac. ; aliquem, Cic. With *Indir.
Quest.* : Liv. **II.** *to look over again, to
re-examine, re-inspect, review* : leges, Cic. ;
socios navalis, agros, Liv. ; dona populorum, Verg. ; res ad recognoscendas
biduum dominis datum est (i.e. to claim
their property), Liv. **III.** *to re-examine* a
writing in respect of its genuineness and
value : decretum, Cic.

re-colligō, *v.* re-conligō.

re-colō, colere, coluī, cultum. **I.** *to till or
cultivate again.* **1.** L i t. : desertam terram,
Liv. ; Ov. Also, metalla intermissa, Liv.
2. T r a n s f. **a.** *to cultivate again,* i.e. to
resume : eas artis quibus a pueris dediti
fuimus, Cic. ; Pl. ; ingenia nostra medita-
tione, Plin. Ep. **b.** *to honour again* :
Galbae imagines, Tac. **c.** *to think over*

again, recall to mind, reflect upon : haec illeo animo, Pl. ; Cat. ; quae si tecum ipse recolis, Cic. ; inclusas animas lustrabat studio recolens, Verg. **II.** *to inhabit again, revisit :* locum, Phaedr.

re-comminiscor, I, *to recall to mind, recollect* (with Acc. and *Inf.*) : Pl.

re-compōnō, pōnere, positum, *to put together again.* **1.** L i t. : comas, Ov. **2.** T r a n s f. (of persons), *to smooth down again :* Plin. Ep.

reconciliātiō, ōnis, *f.* [reconciliō], *a winning back again, re-establishing :* concordiae, Cic. ; gratiae, i.e. *reconciliation,* Cic. ; also in this sense without gratiae : Cic., Liv. In *pl. :* Suet.

reconciliātor, ōris, *m.* [reconciliō], *a restorer :* pacis, Liv.

re-conciliō, āre (old *Fut.* reconciliāssō, Pl.), *to bring back.* **1.** L i t. *to restore :* aliquem domum, Pl. ; aliquem in libertatem, Pl. ; apes, Varr. **2.** T r a n s f. *to win back again, restore, regain.* **a.** With person or his feelings as Object : aliquem alicui, Cic. ; inimicos in gratiam, Cic. ; Liv. ; militum animos imperatori, Liv. ; Cic. Ep. ; gratiam, Cic. ; gratiam cum aliquo, Liv. *Absol. :* Plin. Ep. **b.** With thing as Object : diuturni laboris detrimentum, Caes. ; pacem, Nep., Liv. ; concordiam, Liv. ; existimationem iudiciorum amissam, Cic. ; oratione Parum insulam, Nep.

re-concinnō, āre, *to set right again, repair :* pallam, Pl. ; tribus locis aedifico, reliqua reconcinno, Cic. Ep.

reconditus, a, um. **I.** *Part.* recondō. **II.** A d j. : *put out of the way, hidden, concealed.* **1.** L i t. : venae auri argenticae, Cic. ; saltus, Cat. As Noun, **recondita**, ōrum, *n. pl. remote, sequestered places :* templi, Caes. **2.** T r a n s f. *out of the common way.* **a.** *profound, abstruse, recondite :* litterae, res, Cic. ; Tac. *Comp. :* Cic. **b.** *reserved :* Quinctius naturā tristi ac reconditā fuit, Cic.

re-condō, condere, condidī, conditum. **1.** L i t. **a.** *to put back again (into storage) :* Caecubum, Hor. So too, gladium in vaginam, Cic. **b.** *to put into due or requisite store, to stow away :* Cic., Liv. ; opes aerario, Quint. ; Pl. ; in tabulis tamquam in vaginā reconditum, Cic. **2.** T r a n s f. **a.** P o e t. : Triton ore aquam, Ov. ; ensem in pulmone, Verg. ; gladium lateri, Ov. ; oculos (i.e. close again), Ov. **b.** mens alia recondit, e quibus memoria oritur, Cic. ; Venerem interius, Verg. ; verba, vultūs in crimen detorquens recondebat, Tac.

re-cōnflō, āre, *to blow up again, rekindle.* T r a n s f. : Lucr.

re-coquō, coquere, coxi, coctum, *to cook, boil, bake again.* **1.** L i t. **a.** lana recocta (in dyeing), Sen. Ep. ; Peliam (i.e. to restore his youth by the magic cauldron), Cic. ; hence, seni recocto, Cat. ; Hor. **b.** *to recast, remould :* patrios ensis, Verg. **2.** T r a n s f. : (Cicero se) Moloni velut recoquendum dedit, Quint.

recordātiō, ōnis, *f.* [recordor], *a calling back to mind, recollection, remembrance :* Cic., Plin. Ep. With *Obj.* G E N. : Cic., Quint. With Acc. and *Inf.* (subiit recordaiio) : Plin. Ep. In *pl. :* Cic., Tac.

recordor, ārī [cor], *to bring back to mind, recall, recollect, remember.* **a.** P r o p r i i Cic With Acc. : Pl., Caes., Cic., Verg., etc. With Acc. and *Inf.* : Caes., Cic., Ov. With *Indir. Quest. :* Pl., Caes., Cic. With *quod-* clause : Suet. With *de :* Cic. With G E N. (very rare) : Cic. **b.** Of the future : *to think over, dwell on :* nunc ego non tantum, quae sum passura, recordor, Ov.

re-creō, āre, *to make or create anew, to reproduce, restore.* **1.** L i t. : sol lumen, Lucr. ; res fluentis, Lucr. **2.** T r a n s f. : *to restore to a good condition, to revive, re-invigorate.* **a.** Physically : homines, Pl. ; viris, Lucr. ; voculam, Cic. Ep. ; ex gravi morbo, Cic. ; ex vulnere, Cic., Liv. ; arbor aestivā recreatur aurā, Hor. ; umerum leni vento, Hor. **b.** Mentally : mentem, civitatem, populum, hominem, etc., Cic. ; spatium interponendum ad recreandos animos, Caes.; se ex magno timore, Cic. ; animus se conlegit atque recreavit, Cic.

re-crepō, ere, *to sound back in response, resound :* cymbala, Cat. With Acc. : lapis murmura pulsus, Verg.

re-crēscō, crēscere, crēvī, *to grow again, be renewed :* terra, Lucr. ; luna, Ov. ; suboli Scipionum accisis recrescenti stirpibus, Liv.

re-crūdēscō, crūdēscere, crūduī, *to become raw again :* of wounds, *to open afresh.* T r a n s f. : Cic. Ep. ; pugna, seditio, Liv.

rēctā, *adv. v.* rēctus, l. a.

rēctē, *adv. in a straight line* (perpendicularly or horizontally). **1.** L i t. : Cato ; quae (atomi) recte, quae oblique ferantur, Cic. **2.** T r a n s f. **a.** *rightly, correctly, properly, suitably, well :* recte et sapienter facit, Pl. ; recte et bene, vere et recte, Pl. ; recte atque ordine, Cic., Liv., etc. ; recte ac merito, Cic. ; recte factum, opp. to turpiter, Caes. ; Hor. ; cum fuit cui recte ad te litteras darem, Cic. Ep. ; recte cavere, Pl. ; recte vendere (opp. to male), Cic. ; ludi recte facti, Liv. Of health : recte valere, vivere, Pl. ; recte esse, Cic. Ep., Hor. *Comp. :* rectius bella gerere, Liv. ; Pl. *Sup. :* rectissime iudicas, Cic. **b.** With adjectives, like our *right well, quite :* salvos sum recte, Pl. ; Cato. **c.** E l l i p t. esp. in answers, *good, very good : quite right, excellent :* Pl., Ter., Quint. **d.** As a courteously evasive answer, like benigne and the Gk. καλῶς, or κάλλιστα ἔχει, *it's all right ;* or, in politely declining an offer, *no, thank you :* Pl., Ter., Hor.

rēctiō, ōnis, *f.* [regō], *a guiding, controlling, direction :* rerum publicarum, Cic.

rēctor, ōris, *m.* (and **rēctrix**, īcis, *f.* Sen. Ep.) [regō], *a guider, controller.* **1.** L i t. Of a helmsman : Cic., Verg., Ov. Of a horseman : Ov., Tac. Of an elephant-driver : Liv. Of a herdsman : Plin. Ep. **2.** T r a n s f. : civitatis, Cic. ; caelestum, Cat. ; Verg. : Dolopum, pelagi, Ov. ; (exercitūs) rectores destinati, Tac. ; of a *tutor :* Sen. Ep., Tac., etc. ; animus incorruptus, aeternus, rector humani generis, Sall.

rēctus, a, um. **I.** *Part.* regō. **II.** A d j. *kept or drawn in a straight line* (horizontal or vertical). **1.** L i t. **a.** rectis lineis in caelestem locum subvolare, Cic. ; Caes. ; pars remorum, Lucr. ; velut rectae acies con-

currissent, Liv. Of roads: via, Pl., Quint.;
recto in Hiberum itinere, Caes.; rectā
regione iter instituere, Liv.; Lucr.; ne qua
forent pedibus vestigia rectis, Verg. Also,
recto flumine ducam, Verg. *Sup.* : Quint.
ABL. *f.* **rēctā** as *Adv.* (*sc.* viā), *straight
forward, right on*: Pl.; a subselliis in
rostra rectā, Cic. Hor. **b.** *upright, erect.*
Of persons: Cat., Hor.; senectus, Juv.
Of things: *straight, steep*: saxa, rupes,
Liv.; truncus, Ov.; crus, Hor. *Comp.*:
Hor., Ov., Sen. Ep. **c.** Of the eyes:
not lowered, unflinching: rectis oculis
hanc urbem intueri, Cic.; Sen. Ep.;
acies, Ov. **2.** T r a n s f. **a.** *right, correct,
appropriate, befitting*: in rectam redire
semitam, Pl.; rectā viā depelli, Quint.;
recto ac iusto proelio dimicare, Liv.; nominibus rectis expendere nummos (i.e. on good
securities), Hor.; cena, Mart.; so, recta
(*sc.* cena), Mart., Suet.; si quid novisti
rectius istis, Hor.; rectissima ratio, Quint.
Neut. as Noun, **rēctum**, I, *right* : Cic.
b. *direct, straightforward, unaffected, plain*
(of movement, dress, language, etc.): quae
sunt recta (in gestibus) laudantur, Cic.;
commentarii Caesaris, Cic.; sermo rectus
et secundum naturam enuntiatus, Cic.;
figura, Prop.; domus, Sen. Ep. *Neut. pl.*
as Noun : recta et vera loquere, Pl. **c.**
Morally : *right, correct, virtuous, good* : Ter.,
Cic.; iudex, Quint.; consilia, Liv.; animus
secundis temporibus dubiisque rectus, Hor.
Sup.: Cic. *Neut.* as Noun. **rēctum**, I,
uprightness, virtue : Cic., Verg., etc. **d.**
Gramm. : rectus casus, *the nominative case*,
opp. to obliqui casūs : Quint.
re-cŭbō, āre, *to lie back (and rest)* : Lucr.,
Cic.; toro, Tib.; solo, Verg.; sub tegmine
fagi, Verg.
rēcŭla, ae, *f.* [*dim.* rēa], *a little thing* : Pl.
recultus, a, um, *Part.* recolō.
re-cumbō, cumbere, cubuī. **I.** *to lay oneself
back.* **1.** L i t. **a.** Lucr.; in cubioulo, in
herbā, Cic.; spondā, Ov. **b.** Of taking
one's place at table : Phaedr.; in triclinio,
Cic.; lectis, Hor. **2.** T r a n s f. *to fall or
sink back or down* : pons in palude, Cat.;
nebulae campo, Verg.; in umeros cervix,
Verg.; cervix umero, Ov.; minax ponto
unda, Hor. **II.** perh. *to lie down again* :
Cic.
recŭperātiō, ōnis, *f.* [recuperō], *a getting
back, recovery* : libertatis, Cic.
recŭperātor (**recip-**), ōris, *m.* [recuperō],
one that regains or *recovers.* **a.** In gen. :
urbis, Tac. **b.** In law, recuperatores *were
arbiters, at least two, sometimes three in number, originally instituted for the decision of
suits between Romans and peregrini, but subsequently employed in any cases requiring
a speedy decision* : Pl., Cic., Liv., etc.
recŭperātōrius, a, um [recuperātor], *of the
recuperatores* : iudicium, Cic.; Plin. Ep.
recŭperō (**recipĕrō**), āre, *to get or obtain
again* ; *to regain, recover, etc.* : eropta, Cic.;
amissa, Caes.; pecuniam depositam, Cic.;
arma, Liv.; civitates, Caes.; rem publicam,
Cic.; provinciam, Tac. With abstract Obj. :
veterem belli gloriam libertatemque, Caes.;
voluntatem eius, Cic.; gratiam, Tac. With
personal Obj. : obsides, Caes.; captivos nos-

tros a Carthaginiensibus, Cic. T r a n s f. :
adulescentulos, Nep.; se quiete, Varr.; si
me ipsum recuperaro, Cic. Ep. [It. *ri-
coverare.*]
re-cŭrō, āre, *to restore* (to health, etc.) *by
treatment* : me otio et urticā, Cat.; chartam, Plin.
re-currō, currere, currī, *to run* or *hasten
back.* **1.** L i t. : Pl.; ad aliquem, Pl., Cic.
Ep.; ad raedam, Cic.; in arcem, Liv.;
rure, Hor.; in suos fontis versa aqua, Ov.
2. T r a n s f. **a.** Of the *revolution* of the
sun : Verg.; and of the year : Hor. **b.**
to come back, return, recur : mox bruma re-
currit iners, Hor.; Ov.; naturam expellas
furcā, tamen usque recurret, Hor.; Plin.
Pan. **c.** *to come back, revert* : ad easdem
condiciones deditionis, Caes.; ad eam rationem, Quint.
recursō, āre [*freq.* recurrō], *to keep running
back* ; *to continue to return* : **1.** L i t. :
Lucr.; huc, Pl. **2.** T r a n s f. : curae,
Verg.; animo vetera omina, Tac.
recursus, ūs, *m.* [recurrō], *a running* or
hurrying back, return, retreat : inde alios
ineunt cursūs aliosque recursūs, Verg.;
Ov.; ut recursus pateret, Liv.
re-curvō, āre, *to curve* or *bend backwards* :
colla equi, Ov.; recurvatae undae (Mae-
andri), Ov.
re-curvus, a, um, *curving back, crooked* :
cornu, Verg.; puppis, tectum, tergum, etc.,
Ov.
recūsātiō, ōnis, *f.* [recūsō]. **I.** *a declining,
refusal* : disputationis, Cic.; *sine recusa-
tione, Cic.; Caes. **II.** In law. **a.** *an
objection, protest* : poena violatae religionis
iustam recusationem non habet, Cic. **b.**
a counter-plea ; opp. to petitio : Cic.,
Quint.
re-cūsō, āre [causa], *to plead against, to make
objections, to be reluctant, to refuse.* **1.** L i t.
a. In gen. : Caes., Cic., Verg. With *de* :
Caes., Cic. With Acc. : uxorem, Ter.;
populum Romanum disceptatorem, Cic.;
populi R. amicitiam, Caes.; nullum periculum, laborem, etc., Caes.; Verg. With
Inf. : Caes., Verg., Liv., etc. With Acc.
and *Inf.* : Plin., Tac. With *ne* and *Subj.* :
Caes., Cic., Liv. With *quo minus* or *quin*
(after a negat.) : Caes., Cic., Liv. **b.** *to
object, take exception, plead in defence* : Cic.;
numquid recusas contra me ? Pl. With
Acc. and *Inf.* : Cic. **2.** T r a n s f. : vincla
leones, Verg.; genua cursum, Verg.; ignis
alimenta, Ov.
recussus, a, um [*Part.* as fr. recutiō, re and
quatiō], *rebounding from a blow, reverberating* : uteroque recusso insonuere cavae
cavernae, Verg.
recŭtītus, a, um [cutis], *with skin* (out)
back, i.e. circumcised. **1.** L i t. : Iudaei,
Mart. **2.** T r a n s f. *Jewish* : sabbata, Pers.
redāctus, a, um, *Part.* redigō.
red-ambŭlō, āre, *to walk back* : Pl.
red-amō, āre, *to love in return* : Cic.
red-arguō, arguere, arguī, *to disprove, refute,
contradict* : Cic., Quint.; aliquem, Cic.,
Quint.; orationem, Cic.; crimen, Quint.
Of abstract Subjects : improborum pros-
peritates redarguunt vim omnem deorum,
Cic.; Verg.

red-auspicō, āre, *to take the return-auspices ;* comic. for *to return :* Pl.

redditus, a, um, *Part.* reddō.

red-dō, dere, didi, ditum (old *Fut.* reddĭbō, reddĭbitur.) **I.** *to put* or *give back, replace, restore.* **1.** Lit. **a.** In gen.: mihi pallam, Pl. ; argentum aut virginem, Pl. ; captivos, Caes., Liv. ; equos, Cic. ; hereditatem alicui, Cic. ; corpora mortuorum, Verg. With *abstract Obj. :* salutem, Pl. ; his libertatem, Pl., Nep. ; patriam, Liv. ; ereptum honorem, Verg. **b.** With *Refl. Pron.* or in *Mid.* (or *Pass.*) *: to return :* se convivio, Liv. ; se in arma, Verg. ; lux terris se reddit, Verg. ; redditus terris Daedalus, Verg. ; Hor. **2.** Transf. **a.** Of reflexions, etc. ; *to reflect, represent, reproduce, imitate :* hominum facies, Lucr. ; faciem locorum, Ov. ; te nomine Silvius Aeneas, Verg. ; patris ingeni virtutisque effigiem, Liv. ; paternam elegantiam in loquendo, Quint. **b.** Of words *: to repeat, recite :* dictata, Hor. ; Cic. ; Lucr. ; Ov., etc. **II.** *to place* or *give in return* or *in reply.* **1.** Lit.: alias tegulas, Pl. ; paria paribus, Cic. ; responsum, Verg., Liv. ; veras audire ac reddere voces, Verg. ; cithara sonum, Hor. ; animam excipere eandemque reddere, Cic. ; Verg. ; fructum praedia, Ter. **2.** Transf. **a.** *to give* or *pay in return :* pretium alicui pro bene factis eius, Pl. ; pro meritis iura legesque, Caes. ; vitam pro vitā, Caes. ; pro carmine dona, Verg. ; accepta ad Cannas redderetur hosti clades, Liv. **b.** Of translation *: to render :* ea Latine, Cic. ; verbum pro verbo, Cic. ; verbo verbum, Hor. **c.** With *Predic. Adj.* or *phr. : to render, make :* te ex ferā mansuetem, Pl. ; Cic. ; aliquem placidum mollemque, Cic. ; Verg., etc. With *ut* and *Subj. :* Ter. **III.** *to give up as due* or *expected, to render, pay, deliver.* **1.** Lit.: alicui litteras, Caes., Cic. Ep. ; caprum quem merui, Verg. ; vota nymphis, Verg. ; liba deae, Ov. **2.** Transf.: tibi rationem, Pl. ; praemia debita, Verg. ; gratiam alicui, Sall. ; debita naturae, Cic. ; poenas, Sall. ; dierum XX supplicationes, Caes. ; Hernici suae leges redditae, Liv. ; neque iis petentibus ius redditur, Caes. ; peccatis veniam, Hor. ; iudicium (a date for a trial), Ter., Cic. ; conubia, Liv. [It. *rendere ;* Fr. *rendre.*]

redemptiō, ōnis, *f.* [redimō]. **I.** *a buying back ; a ransoming :* Liv. ; ducis, Quint. **II.** *a buying up.* **a.** *bribing :* iudici, Cic. In *pl. :* Cic. **b.** *a farming* of the revenue : Cic. [Fr. *rançon.*]

redemptō, āre [*freq.* redimō], *to buy back* or *ransom repeatedly :* Tac.

redemptor, ōris, *m.* [redimō], *a contractor ; farmer* of revenues, etc. : Cato, Cic., Hor., etc.

redemptūra, ae, *f.* [redimō], *a contracting, farming* (in *pl.*) *:* Liv.

redemptus, a, um, *Part.* redimō.

red-eō, īre, iī, itum. **I.** *to go* or *come back, to return.* **1.** Lit. **a.** Of living beings : Pl., Cic., Liv., etc. **a.** a foro domum, Pl. ; a Caesare, Cic. Ep. ; Verg. ; ab Africā, Hor. ; e provinciā, Cic. ; Pl., etc. ; rure, Pl., Ter. ; Ov. ; exsilio, Pl. ; ad navem, Pl. ; ad

aliquem, Pl., Caes. ; in urbem, Pl., Liv. ; in proelium, Liv. ; in caelum, Hor. ; Cic. ; Verg., etc. ; domum, Pl., Hor., Liv., etc. ; Romam, Cic. With *Inf. :* Verg. *Impers. Pass. :* Pl., Caes., Liv. **b.** Of things : astra ad idem unde profecta sunt, Cic. ; collis ad planitiem, Caes. ; flumen in eandem partem, Cic. ; Ov. ; gramina campis, Hor. ; Ov. **2.** Transf. **a.** In gen. : animus, Pl. ; mens et color, Ov. ; ingenium, Liv. ; memoria, Quint. ; in pristinum statum, Caes. ; in statum antiquum res, Liv. ; cum suis inimicissimis in gratiam, Cic. ; in amicitiam (fidem) alicuius, Liv. ; in memoriam mortuorum, Cic. ; Pl. ; ad ingenium, Ter. ; ad se (i.e. to recover one's senses), Ter., Lucr., Liv., etc. ; in iuvenem, Ov. ; calor ossibus, Verg. ; agricolis labor, Verg. **b.** Of a speaker *: to return, revert to* a former subject : ad rem, Ter. ; ad illa prima, Cic. ; ad Scipionem, Cic. ; illuc unde abii, Hor. Of the subject itself : haec oratio, Ter. ; res, Cic. **II.** *to return, be returned ; to come in, be yielded* as income. **1.** Lit.: tribus tantis illi minus redit, Pl. ; pecunia publica ex metallis, Nep. ; Mart. **2.** Transf.: ex otio bellum, Liv. **III.** *to fall back on, have recourse to, be brought to* or *be reduced to :* pilis omissis ad gladios redierunt, Caes. ; Caesar opinione trium legionum deiectus ad duas redierat, Caes. ; res ad interregnum, Liv. ; in eum res rediit locum ut etc., Ter. ; incommoditas huc, Ter. ; haec bona in tabulas publicas, Cic. Of inheritances, power, etc. : *to revert (to), devolve (upon) :* ad hos lege hereditas, Ter. ; regnum ad aliquem, Pl. ; res ad patres, Liv. ; quorum ad arbitrium summa omnium rerum redeat, Caes.

red-hālō, āre, *to breathe forth again, exhale :* Lucr.

red-hibeō, hibēre, (hibui) hibitum [habeō], *to take back* (esp. of the seller of a defective article): mancipium iure civili, Cic. ; Pl. Also of the buyer : Pl.

red-igō, igere, ēgi, āctum [agō]. **I.** *to drive, lead,* or *bring back.* **1.** Lit.: (Sol) disiectos redegit equos, Lucr. ; oppidani (hostem) fusum fugatumque in castra redigunt, Liv. ; in sua rura boves, Ov. **2.** Transf.: aliquem in concordiam, Pl. ; rem ad pristinam belli rationem redegit, Caes. ; disciplinam militarem ad priscos mores, Liv. ; in memoriam (with *Acc.* and *Inf.*), Cic. **II.** Of money or property, *to get back, call in :* argentum tibi, Pl. ; pecuniam ex vectigalibus, Cic. ; pars maxima (praedae) ad quaestorem, Liv. ; quidquid captum ex hostibus est vendidit consul ac redegit in publicum, Liv. ; praedam in fiscum, Tac. ; pecuniam, Cic., Hor. **III.** *to bring* or *reduce* to a required or expected condition. **a.** Of persons or countries, etc.: viros in servitutem, Pl. ; Caes. ; Arvernos in provinciam, Caes. ; Tac. ; prope ad internecionem gentem, Caes. ; genus ad interitum, Lucr. ; rem publicam in tranquillum, Liv. ; eo redigis me ut etc., Ter. With *sub* or *in* and *Acc.* : *to reduce* or *bring under the power of :* civitatem in dicionem potestatemque populi R., Caes. ; Cic. ; Liv. ; Galliam sub populi R. im-

perium, Caes. ; barbaros sub ius dicionemque, Liv. **P o e t.** : mentem in veros
timores, Hor. **b.** Of things : *to make,
render :* victoriam ad vanum et inritum,
Liv. ; aliquid ante dubium ad certum, Liv. ;
quae facilia ex difficillimis animi magnitudo
redegerat, Caes. Of persons : Ubios Suebi
multo inferiores redegerunt, Caes. **c.**
Of number or quantity, *to reduce :* ex
hominum milibus LX vix ad D sese redactos
esse dixerunt, Caes. ; familiam ad paucos,
Cic. ; quod si comminuas, vilem redigatur
ad assem, Hor.

redimiculum, i, n. [redimiŏ], *a band, fillet,
chaplet, frontlet.* **1.** L i t. : Cic., Verg., etc.
2. T r a n s f. *a bond, fetter :* Pl.

redimiŏ, īre, iī, ītum (old *Imperf.* redimībat,
Verg.) *to bind* or *wreathe round, to crown.*
1. L i t. : caput et umeros coronis, Lucr. ;
Verg. ; Ov. ; sertis redimiti, Cic. ; domus
corollis redimita, Cat. **2.** T r a n s f. : loca
silvis redimita, Cat. ; lauro tabellas, Ov.

red-imŏ, imere, ēmī, emptum. **I.** *to buy
back, repurchase.* **1.** L i t. **a.** Pl. ; eam
(domum) non minoris, quam emit Antonius,
redimet, Cic. **b.** *to buy back, ransom, redeem* a prisoner, slave, *etc. :* Pl. ; captos ab
hoste, Cic. ; captos a servitute, Cic. ; aliquem pretio, Verg. ; servi in publicum
redempti ac manu missi, Liv. **2.** T r a n s f.
to buy off, rescue by payment. **a.** pecuniā
se a iudicibus, Cic. ; Liv. ; fratrem Pollux
alternā morte, Verg. ; redimite armis
civitatem quam auro maiores vestri red-
emerunt, Liv. So, *to buy up, buy in :* libros
suppressos, Suet. **b.** uno quaestu decuma-
rum omnia sua pericula, Cic. ; quam (acerbitatem) a re publicā meis privatis incommodis redemissem, Cic. **c.** *to redeem* or
make amends for past conduct : flagitium,
Sall. ; vitium, Ov. **d.** *to redeem, keep
one's word* : verba sua, Sen. **II.** *to take
or undertake by contract ; to hire, farm, etc. :*
1. L i t. : omnia Aeduorum vectigalia parvo
pretio, Caes. ; piscarias de censoribus,
Cic. ; istum eripiendum, Cic. **2.** T r a n s f. :
ego vitam omnium civium quinque homi-
num perditorum poenā redemi, Cic. ; pacem
Ariovisti ne obsidibus quidem datis, Caes. ;
militum voluntates largitione, Caes.

red-integrŏ, āre, *to make whole again; to
restore, renew :* ut deminutae copiae red-
integrarentur, Caes. ; virīs, animum, spem,
Caes. ; proelium, Caes., Liv. ; memoriam,
Cic., Liv. ; clamorem, luctum, Liv.

red-ipiscor, ī [apiscor], *to get back :* Pl.

reditiŏ, ōnis, f. [redeŏ], *a returning, return :*
Cic. ; huc, Pl. ; domum, Caes.

reditus, ūs, m. [redeŏ]. **I.** *a coming back,
returning.* **1.** L i t. : Cic., Verg., etc. ;
aliquem reditu intercludere (arcere, Cic. ;
excludere, Nep.), Caes. ; in Italiam, Caes. ;
Cic. ; in nemora, Cat. ; Verg. ; in patriam
ad parentis, Liv. ; ad vada, Cat. ; Romam,
domum, Cic. In *pl. :* Verg., Hor., Ov.
2. T r a n s f. : in gratiam cum inimicis,
Cic. ; in amicitiam, Caes. ; ad rem, ad
propositum, Cic. **II.** Of money : *a return,
revenue, proceeds :* pecuniae, Nep. ; in
reditu esse (i.e. to make returns), Plin. Ep.
In *pl. :* Ov. ; metallorum, Liv.

redivia, v. reduv-.

redi-vivus, a, um, *renewed, renovated,* of old
building materials used as new : lapis, Cic.
Neut. as Noun : Cic.

red-oleŏ, olēre, oluī, *to emit an odour ; to
smell (of).* **1.** L i t. : Lucr., Ov. With
ABL. : thymo mella, Verg. ; Ov. With
GEN. : Mart. With *Internal* ACC. : vinum,
Cic. ; Ov. ; Quint. **2.** T r a n s f. : ex
illius orationibus ipsae Athenae, Cic. With
Internal ACC. : orationes antiquitatem, Cic.

re-domitus, a, um, *retamed, broken in again :*
improbi cives, Cic.

re-dŏnŏ, āre. **I.** *to give back again, restore :*
te dis patriis, Hor. **II.** *to give up :* iras
et invisum nepotem Marti, Hor.

re-dormiŏ, īre, *to go to sleep again :* Plin.
Ep.

re-dūcŏ (rē-, Lucr.), dūcere, dūxī, ductum.
I. *to draw back.* **1.** L i t. : falces tormentis,
Caes. ; in iaculando bracchia, Quint. ; Verg. ;
ad pectora remos, Ov. ; auras naribus,
Lucr. **2.** T r a n s f. : socios a morte, Verg. ;
me a contemplatu mali, Ov. **II.** *to lead* or
bring back. **1.** L i t. **a.** hunc ex Alide
huc, Pl. ; aliquem de exsilio, Cic. ; ab exsilio, Quint. ; a pastu vitulos ad tecta,
Verg. ; Silenium ad parentis, Pl. ; Caes. ;
Cic. ; exercitum in castra, Caes. ; regem,
Cic. **b.** *to conduct* or *accompany back* as
a mark of respect : aliquem domum, Pl.,
Cic., etc. Hence, quos Elea domum reducit palma, Hor. **c.** Of marrying again
(after a separation) : uxorem, Ter., Nep.
2. T r a n s f. **a.** P o e t. : solem, diem, noctem, etc., Verg. ; hiemes, somnum, febrim,
Hor. **b.** In gen. : ad divitias, Pl. ; aliquem ad officium sanitatemque, Cic. ;
legiones veterem ad morem, Tac. ; animum
aegrotum ad misericordiam, Ter. ; aliquem
in gratiam, Ter., Cic. ; in gratiam cum
aliquo, Cic., Liv. ; in memoriam (with
Indir. Quest.), Cic. ; spem mentibus anxiis,
Hor. ; eius modi exemplum, Plin. Ep. **III.**
to bring to a due or *normal condition, to
restore :* (catulum) lambendo in formam,
Ov. ; cicatrices ad colorem, Plin.

reductiŏ, ōnis, f. [redūcŏ], *a restoration :* regis,
Cic. Ep.

reductor, ōris, m. [redūcŏ], *a restorer.* **1.**
L i t. : plebis Romanae in urbem, Liv. **2.**
T r a n s f. : litterarum iam senescentium,
Plin. Ep.

reductus, a, um. **I.** *Part.* redūcŏ. **II.**
A d j. : drawn back. **a.** Of place : *retired,
remote :* vallis, Verg., Hor. **b.** *aloof, removed :* virtus est medium vitiorum et
utrimque reductum, Hor. **c.** In painting :
alia eminentiora, alia reductiora fecerunt,
Quint. **d.** P h i l o s. : producta et reducta
(bona) = Stoic προηγμένα καὶ ἀποπροηγμένα,
Cic.

red-uncus, a, um, *curved* or *bent backwards :*
rostrum, Ov. ; cornua, Plin.

redundantia, ae, f. [redundŏ], *an overflowing,
excess.* T r a n s f. (of style), *redundancy :*
Cic.

red-undŏ, āre, *to stream back, overflow.* **1.**
L i t. : mare, lacus, Cic. ; Nilus campis,
Lucr. ; Ov. ; pituita, Cic. **Poet.** re-
dundatus for redundans : (Boreae vis)
redundatas flumine cogit aquas, Ov. **2.**
T r a n s f. **A.** *to overflow, be soaked :* san-

guine hostium Africa, Cic. ; Luc. **B.** Of
excess or abundance. **a.** *to be in excess
or abundance :* aurum, Lucil. ; multitudo,
Cic., Tac. Of style : hic ornatus orationis
in Crasso, Cic. ; Asiatici oratores, Cic. ;
Quint. **b.** With ABL. : *to abound* or *over-
abound in :* luctu victoria, Cic. ; Curiana
defensio hilaritate quādam et ioco, Cic. ;
clientelis exterarum nationum, Cic. ; armis,
Tac. Of style : iuvenili quādam dicendi
licentiā, Cic. **C.** Of the results of excess
or abundance. **a.** With *de* or *ex : to overflow* or *stream from, to be over from :* si quid
redundabit de vestro frumentario quaestu,
Cic. ; ex rerum cognitione oratio, Cic. ;
hinc illae extraordinariae pecuniae, Cic.
b. With *ad* or *in* and ACC. : *to overflow* or
stream into or *on :* ad amicos infamia
(vitiorum), Cic. ; Plin. Ep. ; nationes
numero hominum ac multitudine ipsā
poterant in provincias nostras redundare,
Cic. ; in me periculum, Cic. [Fr. *rédonder*.]
reduvia, ae, *f. a hang-nail, whitlow.* Prov. :
cum capiti mederi debeam, reduviam curo,
Cic.
redux (**rĕ-,** Pl.), ucis, *adj.* (ABL. reduce,
Lucr. ; -uci, Ov.) (re dūcō.) **A.** Act. :
that leads or *brings back :* Iuppiter, Ov. ;
Curt. **B.** Pass. : *brought back, recovered :*
Pl., Cic., Verg., etc. ; reduces in patriam
ad parentis facere, Liv. ; Pl.
refectiō, ōnis, *f.* [reficiō], *a restoring, repair-
ing.* **1.** Lit. : Capitoli, Suet. **2.**
Transf. (of the body and plants) : Plin.,
Quint., Plin. Pan. In *pl.* : Plin. Pan.
refector, ōris, *m.* [reficiō], *a restorer :* Colossi,
Suet.
refectus, a, um, *Part.* reficiō.
re-fellō, fellere, felli [fallō], *to confute, rebut :*
Ter. ; aliquem, Cic., Quint. ; sensūs,
Lucr. ; mendacium, Cic. ; dicta, Verg. ;
orationem vitā, Cic. ; crimen ferro, Verg.
re-ferciō, fercire, fersi, fertum [farciō], *to
stuff far back ;* to *stuff, cram, choke.* **1.**
Lit. : horrea, Plin. ; meministis corporibus
civium cloacas referciri, Cic. **2.** Transf. :
libros fabulis, Cic. ; auris sermonibus, Cic. ;
hominum vitam superstitione omni, Cic.
re-feriō, ire, *to strike back* or *in return.* **1.**
Lit. : Ter., Sen. ; aliquem, Pl. **2.**
Transf. : speculi referitur imagine Phoebus, Ov.
re-ferō, referre, rettuli, relātum (rĕlātum,
Lucr.). **I.** *to carry* or *bring back.* **1.** Lit.
a. In gen. : vasa domum, Pl. ; Verg. ;
signa ad Caesarem, Caes. ; Pl. ; digitos
ad frontem, Ov. ; Quint. ; pecunias in templum, Caes. ; intro pedem, Pl. ; ad me
pedem, Pl. ; pedes in Tusculanum, Cic. Ep. ;
caelo pedem, Ov. With *Refl. Pron.* :
sese in castra, Caes. ; se huc, Caes. ; se
Romam, Cic. ; sese ab Argis, Verg. : se
sol, Cic. **b.** Of things borrowed, stolen,
etc. : Pl., Cic., Hor. ac. Milit. (with
pedem *or* gradum) : vulneribus defessi
pedem referre coeperunt, Caes. ; Cic. ;
Liv. Also, ad Tuneta castra, Liv. In
Mid. : a prinā acie ad triarios sensim
referebantur, Liv. **2.** Transf. : ni quid
tibi hinc in spem referas, Pl. ; ad equestrem
ordinem iudicia, Cic. ; oculos animumque
ad aliquem, Cic. ; animum ad veritatem,

Cic. ; Tac. ; se ad philosophiam, Cic. ; In
suam domum calamitatem, Cic. ; e cursu
populari aspectum in curiam, Cic. ; multa
dies in melius, Verg. ; o mihi praeteritos
referat si Iuppiter annos ! Verg. ; Hor.
II. *to carry back, to give back in answer.*
1. Lit. : saxum voces, Acc. ; ex locis
inclusis soni referuntur ampliores, Cic. ;
nostra theatra, Hor. ; "coeamus" rettulit
Echo, Ov. **2.** Transf. : *to say in answer,
to reply :* Cic., Verg. ; alicui, Cic. ; id
illorum defensioni, Cic. ; talia voce, Verg. ;
pectore voces, Verg. **III.** *to bring back,
bring up for reconsideration ; to reproduce,
repeat.* **1.** Lit. : Hecyram iterum referre,
Ter. ; Hor. ; rem iudicatam, Cic. ; consuetudo longo intervallo relata, Cic. ; hunc
morem, Verg. ; caerimonias ex magno
intervallo, Liv. ; Dictaeos Curetas (i.e.
in play), Lucr. **2.** Transf. : *to reproduce, recall* a likeness, etc. : maiorum
vultūs vocesque, Lucr. ; parentis sui
speciem, Liv. ; Plin. Ep. ; parvulus qui te
ore referret, Verg. ; sermone vultuque Suebos, Tac. ; amissos colores lana, Hor. **IV.**
to bring or *pay what is due* or *expected,*
etc. ; *to repay.* **1.** Lit. **a.** mercedem, Pl. ;
octonos Idibus aeris, Hor. **b.** nobis nisi
Caesaris capite relato pax esse nulla potest,
Caes. ; tabulas ad Caesarem, Caes. ; cornua
in publicum, Caes. ; spolia, Verg., Ov.
2. Transf. **a.** Of gratitude, moral debts,
etc. : gratiam alicui referre, Pl., Cic., etc. ;
alicui pro eius meritis, Caes. ; Cic. ; Verg. ;
gratiam factis, Ov. ; par pari referto, Ter.
b. Of reports, news, etc. : *to bring* (*news*),
to report : hominum sermones ad me, Cic.
Ep. ; responsa, mandata ad aliquem,
Caes. ; factum dictumve, Liv. ; sermones
deorum, Hor. ; pugnam, Ov. With Acc.
and *Inf.* : Hor., Liv., etc. Poet. (with
Nom. and *Inf.* as in Greek) : rettulit Aiax
esse Iovis pronepos, Ov. With *ut* (*how*)
and *Subj.* : Hor. **c.** Of official or formal
reports to the senate : *to bring* or *lay before
the senate* (often for the purpose of consultation) : de pace Caudinā consules rettulerunt, Liv. ; Caes. ; Cic. ; de eius honore ad
senatum, Cic. ; de legibus abrogandis ad
senatum, Cic. ; rem ad senatum, Liv. ;
Impers. Pass. : Sall. With *Indir. Quest.* :
Sall. Sometimes of other public bodies :
id ad populum (perh. *to refer back from the
senate*), Cic. ; eam rem ad consilium, Liv. ;
de signo dedicando ad pontificum conlegium, Cic. Also of oracles, *to consult :*
de rebus et obscuris et incertis ad Apollinem censeo referendum, Cic. **d.** *to put
on record* (in publio or mercantile matters),
to enter, list, register, set down (actually or
mentally) : indicium in tabulas publicas,
Cic. ; aliquid in annalis, Liv. ; in aes, Liv. ;
absentem in reos, Cic. ; in deorum numero,
Cic. ; hi inter Germanos referuntur, Tac. ;
diem inter festos, Tac. Esp. of *presenting
an account :* rationes (ad aerarium), Cic. ;
relatis ad Caesarem publicis cum fide rationibus, Caes. ; pecuniam in aerarium, Liv. ;
pecuniam populo, Cic. ; pecuniam operi
publico (i.e. *to charge to*), Cic. For acceptum *or* in acceptum referre, *v.* accipio
and acceptus. **e.** *to ascribe, assign, refer,*

give the responsibility or *credit of :* ad voluptatem omnia, Cic. ; hinc omne principium, huc refer exitum, Hor. ; causam ad matrem, Tac. ; cuius adversa pravitati ipsius, prospera ad fortunam referebat, Tac. ; aliquid in claritatem eius, Tac. ; tuum est, Caesar, quid mihi nunc animi sit, ad te ipsum referre, Cic.

rĕ-fert, ferre, tulit, *impers.*, *it concerns, is of consequence* or *importance to.* **A.** With meā, tuā, nostrā, vestrā, suā, of the person concerned (if expressed). **a.** With *Neut. Pron.* as Subject : tuā istuc refert maxume, Pl. ; Ter. ; Cic. ; id tuā refert nihil, Pl. ; Cic. Ep. With GEN. of Value : nihilo pluris tuā hoc quam quanti illud refert meā, Ter. ; Cic. ; Lucr. **b.** With *Inf. :* parvi retulit non suscepisse, Ter. ; Pl. ; neque refert videre, etc., Cic. ; Verg. With Acc. and *Inf. :* Pl. ; primum illud parvi refert nos publicanis amissis vectigalia postea victoriā recuperare, Cic. **c.** *Indir. Quest. :* quid refert utrum voluerim fieri an gaudeam factum ? Cic. ; Pl. ; Hor. ; ne illud quidem refert consul an dictator spoponderit, Liv. **d.** With *si :* quid refert, si hoc ipsum salsum illi videbatur ? Cic. ; Pl. **e.** Rarely with Noun as Subject : adeo magni refert studium atque voluptas, Lucr. ; Plin. **B.** With GEN. of person concerned : praefatus ipsorum referre si etc., Liv. ; Sall. ; Juv. ; with *Indir. Quest. :* Juv., Tac. **C.** With *ad* and Acc., or DAT. of person concerned : quid id ad me aut ad meam rem refert (with *Indir. Quest.*), Pl. ; Varr. ; dic quid referat intra naturae finis viventi (with *Indir. Quest.*), Hor. ; non referre dedecori si citharoedus demoveretur, Tac.

refertus, a, um. **I.** *Part.* referciō. **II.** Adj.: *crammed, packed, stuffed, well-filled.* **1.** Lit.: urbs, domus, aerarium, Cic. ; agri, Tac. *Comp.:* Cic. With ABL. (mostly of things ; rarely of persons): loca referta praedā, Liv. ; Caes. ; Cic. ; Ov. ; domus aleatoribus, Cic. *Sup. :* Cic. Ep. With GEN. (mostly of persons ; rarely of things) : refertam urbem fanorum, Cic. ; Gallia negotiatorum, Cic. ; mare praedonum, Cic. **2.** Transf. **a.** Of persons : refertus honestis studiis, Cic. **b.** Of things : vita bonis, Cic. ; litterae omni officio, Cic. Ep. ; carmina contumeliis, Tac. With *de:* de nugis libri, Cic.

re-ferveō, ēre, *to boil* or *bubble over.* Transf.: falsum crimen in purissimam vitam, Cic.

refervēscō, ere [referveō], *to begin to bubble over :* sanguis, Cic.

re-ficiō, ficere, fēci, fectum [faciō]. **I.** *to make again* or *afresh, to restore, repair.* **1.** Lit.: aggerem, portas, classem, etc., Caes. ; Cic. ; Hor. ; Liv. ; ea quae sunt amissa, Caes. ; copias ex dilectibus, Caes. ; ordines, exercitūs, Liv. ; aliud ex alio natura, Lucr. ; flammam, Ov. **2.** Transf. **A.** *to restore, revive :* salutem communem, Cic. ; spem, Liv. ; fidem, Tac. **B.** *to reinvigorate, restore, refresh.* **a.** Of the body : exercitum ex labore atque inopiā, Caes. ; militem (or *ab*) iactatione maritimā, Liv. ; ex vulnere, Tac. ; saucios cum curā, Sall. ; viris cibo, Liv. ; aliquem, Cic. Ep. ; equos, Caes.: boves quiete,

Liv. ; saltūs roscida luna, Verg. **b.** Of the mind : animum ex forensi strepitu, Cic. ; militum animos, Liv. ; me Pompei consilium, Cic. **II.** Of money, etc. : *to get back again, get in return :* nemo sanus debet velle impensam facere in culturam si videt non posse refici, Varr. ; plus sibi mercedis ex fundo, Cic. ; Liv. **III.** Of magistrates : *to remake, reappoint, re-elect :* consulem, Liv. ; tribunos, Cic., Liv.

re-figō, figere, fīxī, fixum, *to unfix, unfasten.* **1.** Lit.: tabulas, Cic. ; clipeum de poste, Verg. ; signa templis, Hor. ; caelo refixa sidera, Verg. **2.** Transf.: *to take down* the tables of the laws, i.e. *to annul :* leges, Cic., Verg.

re-fingō, ere, *to fashion* or *mould anew :* Pac. ; cerea regna, Verg.

refixus, a, um, *Part.* refīgō.

re-flāgitō, āre, *to demand again, demand back urgently :* Cat.

reflātū, ABL. *sing. m.* [reflō], *by blowing against :* Plin. Concr. *by a contrary wind* Cic. Ep.

re-flectō, flectere, flexī, flexum. **A.** Trans.: *to bend* or *turn back* or *backwards, to turn.* **1.** Lit.: caput leviter, Cat. ; colla, Verg. ; oculos, Ov. ; longos reflectitur unguis, i.e. his nails are made into long hooked claws, Ov. **2.** Transf. *to turn* or *bring back :* aliquem ius iurandum, Ter. ; pedem inde sospes, Cat. ; animum incitatum, Cic. ; animum, Verg. ; in melius tua orsa, Verg. **B.** Intrans. : *to turn back, give way :* morbi causa, Lucr.

reflexus, a, um, *Part.* reflectō.

re-flō, āre. **A.** Intrans. *to blow back, blow contrary :* reflantibus ventis, Cic. Transf.: fortuna, Cic. **B.** Trans. *to blow back from oneself, to breathe out again :* (aer) cum ducitur atque reflatur, Lucr.

re-fluō, ere. **I.** *to flow* or *run back :* Maeandros ambiguo lapsu refluitque fluitque, Ov. **II.** *to flow back, overflow :* Nilus refluit campis, Verg. ; Plin.

refluus, a, um [refluō], *flowing back, ebbing :* mare, Ov. ; Plin.

re-focillō, āre, *to rewarm.* Transf.: *to revive :* Plin. Ep.

refōrmātor, ōris, *m.* [reformō], *a reshaper, reviver :* litterarum senescentium, Plin. Ep.

reformīdātiō, ōnis, *f.* [reformīdō], *a great fear* or *dread :* Cic.

re-formīdō, āre, *to start back in dread ;* hence, *to shun through dread.* **1.** Lit.: Cic. ; Hor. : bellum, dolorem, homines, etc., Cic. ; Tac. etc. With *Inf. :* Cic., Liv. With *Indir. Quest. :* Cic. With *quod*-clause : Caes. **2.** Transf.: bracchia (vitium) reformidant ferrum, Verg. ; lumina solem, Ov. ; diligentia (mea) speculatorem, Cic.

re-fōrmō, āre, *to shape back again* to original form), *to reshape, remould.* **1.** Lit.: sed preme, quidquid erit, dum quod fuit ante reformet, Ov. **2.** Transf.: mores depravatos, Plin. Pan. Of persons : Sen. Ep.

refōtus, a, um, *Part.* refoveō.

re-foveō, fovēre, fōvī, fōtum, *to warm* or *fondle again ; to refresh, restore, revive,* etc. **1. Lit.**: corpus refoventque fovent-que, Ov. ; artūs admoto igne, Curt. ; ignis tepidos, Ov. ; viris mollitiā caeli,' Tac. **2. Transf.**: longa pax cuncta, Curt. ; studia prope exstincta, Plin. Ep. ; provincias internis certaminibus fessas, Tac.

refrāctāriolus, a, um [dim. refrāctārius from refrāctus], rather stubborn (i.e. in regard to literary treatment): dicendi genus, Cic. Ep.

refrāctus, a, um, Part. refringō.

refrāgor, ārī [cf. suffrāgor], to thwart, gainsay. **1. Lit.** (with DAT.) : petenti, Cic. ; alicuius honori, Liv. **2. Transf.**: lex petitioni tuae, Cic. ; tacita quaedam cogitatio his omnibus, Quint. ; materia, Plin. Ep.

re-frēnō, āre, to rein back, curb, restrain. **1. Lit.**: equos, Curt. **2. Transf. a.** fluvios, Lucr. ; aquas, Ov. **b.** iuventutem, Cic. ; libidinem, Cic. ; Hor. ; adulescentis a gloriā, Cic. ; religione refrenari, Lucr.

re-fricō, āre, uī, ātum, to rub or scratch open again. **1. Lit.** of a wound : to re-open, to irritate or inflame again : Cato ; vulnus, Cic. ; obductam iam cicatricem, Cic. Without Object : lippitudo, Cic. Ep. **2. Transf.**: memoriam pulcherrimi facti, Cic. ; dolorem orationie, Cic. ; Ov. ; animum memoria, Cic.

refrigerātiō, ōnis, f. [refrigerō], a cooling, coolness : Cic.

re-frigerō, āre, to cool again, cool off. **1. Lit.**: frumentum, Cato ; calorem, ignem, Cic. ; membra unda, Ov. ; potest illa aetas umbris aquisve refrigerari, Cic. **2. Transf.**: to cool off ; mostly in Pass., to grow cool or languid : defessā ac refrigeratā accusatione, Cic.

re-frigēscō, frīgēscere, frīxī, to grow cold or cool again. **1. Lit.**: vinum, Cato ; plaga per auras, Lucr.; cor vulnere laesum refrixit, Ov. **2. Transf.** to cool down, grow stale or slack ; to flag, fall flat : illud crimen de nummis caluit re recenti, nunc refrixit, Cic. ; quod de Pompeio Caninius agit, sane quam refrixit, Cic. Ep. ; belli apparatus, Cic. ; Romae a iudiciis forum, Cic. Ep. ; oratio, Quint.

re-fringō, fringere, frēgī, frāctum [frangō], to break back. **1. Lit. a.** to break open : cellas, Pl. ; portas, Caes. ; claustra, Cic. ; carcerem, Liv. **b.** to break off short : virgulta, Cat. ; ramum, Verg. ; mucronem, Plin. ; quae demersa liquore obeunt, refracta videntur, Lucr. **2. Transf.** to break and fling back : vim fluminis, Caes. ; Liv. ; Achivos, Hor. ; impotentem dominationem, Nep. ; ingeniorum impetūs, Plin. Ep.

re-fugiō, fugere, fūgī. **A. Intrans.**: to flee back, run back, shrink from. **1. Lit.**: Caes., Verg., Liv. ; ex castris in montem, Caes. ; ex cursu ad Philippum, Liv. ; acie, Caes. ; in portum, Caes. ; in silvam, Verg. ; intra tecta, Verg. ; Syracusas, Cic. Of things : vites a caulibus brassicaque refugere dicuntur, Cic. ; sol medio orbe, Verg.; timido sanguen, Enn. **2. Transf. a.** a dicendo, Cic. ; a consiliis fortibus, Cic. ; animus luctu, Verg. ; animus, Cic. ; possum multa tibi veterum praecepta referre ni refugis, Verg. **b.** Of situation : ab

litore templum, Verg. ; ex oculis humus, Ov. **B. Trans.**: to run away from ; to avoid, shun. **1. Lit.**: impetum, Cic. ; iudicem, Cic. ; anguem, Verg. **2. Transf.**: foeda ministeria, Verg. ; Hor. ; Ov. ; Quint. With Inf. : Hor.

refugium, I, n. [refugiō], a place of refuge. **1. Lit.**: silvae tutius dedere refugium, Liv. **2. Transf.**: populorum refugium senatus, Cic.

refugus, a, um [refugiō], retiring, receding : unda, Ov. ; equites, Tac. Masc. pl. as Noun : Tac.

re-fulgeō, fulgēre, fūlsī, to flash or gleam back, to reflect a light. **1. Lit.**: obliquā percuassus luce refulget, Lucr. ; Verg. ; Venus roseā cervice, Verg. ; Aeneas clarā in luce, Verg. ; nautis stella, Hor. ; sol a liquidā aquā, Ov. ; arma, Liv. ; corpus versicolori veste, Liv. **2. Transf.**: splendida a docto aevo fama, Prop. ; Hor.

re-fundō, fundere, fūdī, fūsum, to pour back ; to cause to overflow. **1. Lit.**: Cic. ; aequor in aequor, Ov. In Mid. or Pass. : imis stagna refusa vadis, Verg. ; ponto refuso, Verg. ; Tiberis refusus, Tac. **2. Transf.**: refunditur alga, Verg. ; tot spoliatis, tot trucidatis sanguinem et bona, Plin. Pan.

refūsus, a, um, Part. refundō.

refūtātiō, ōnis, f. [refūtō]. **Rhet.**: a refutation : Cic., Quint.

refūtātū, ABL. sing. m. [refūtō], by a refutation . Lucr.

re-fūtō, āre [cf. cōnfūtō], to check, drive back, repress. **1. Lit.** (rare) : nationes bello, Cic. **2. Transf. a.** virtutem, libidinem, clamorem, etc., Cic. ; temporis munera, Quint. ; fors dicta refutet I Verg. **b.** to repel, rebut by words, etc. ; to confute, refute, disprove : testis, Cic. ; periuria testimoniis, Cic. ; tribunos oratione feroci, Liv. ; res refutat id, Lucr. With Acc. and Inf. : Lucr.

rēgāliolus, ī, m. [dim. rēgālis], a small bird, perh. the golden-crested wren : Suet.

rēgālis, e, adj. [rēx], kingly, regal (whereas regius is us. simply of a king): genus civitatis, Cic. ; sceptrum, Ov. ; purpura, Cic. ; luxus, Verg. ; situs pyramidum, Hor. Rarely (like regius), of a king, royal : nomen, Cic. ; comae, Verg. ; carmen, Ov. Comp. : Pl. [It. reale ; Fr. royal ; Sp. real.]

rēgāliter, adv. royally, in royal style (in good or bad sense) : Liv., Ov.

re-gelō, āre. **I.** to restore to coolness ; to cool off, air : granaria, Varr. **II.** to unfreeze, thaw, warm. **1. Lit.**: Mart. **2. Transf.**: aetas mea vix mediā regelatur aestate, Sen. Ep.

re-gerō, gerere, gessī, gestum, to bear, carry, or throw back. **1. Lit.**: terram e fossā, Liv. ; tellurem, Ov. ; faces in obsessos iaculantur, obsessi regerunt, Tac. **2. Transf. a.** convicia, Hor. ; invidiam in aliquem, Quint. ; Tac. ; culpam in aliquem, Plin. Ep. **b.** Of records : aliquid in commentarios, Quint.

rēgia, ae, f. v. rēgius.

rēgiē, adv. royally (in good or bad sense) : Pl., Cic., Varr.

rēgĭfĭcus, a, um [rēx facĭo], *kingly, royal, magnificent :* Verg.

re-gignō, ere, *to reproduce :* Lucr.

rēgillus, a, um [*dim.* rēgius], *royal, magnificent :* inducula, Pl. ; Varr.

Rēgillus, I, and **Rēgilli**, ōrum, *m.* **I.** *a town of the Sabines ;* **Rēgillānus**, a, um ; **Rēgillēnsis**, e. **II.** *a lake in Latium, celebrated for the victory over the Latins gained on its banks by the Romans under the dictator Postumius*, B.C. 496 ; **Rēgillēnsis**, *cognomen of the Postumii*. **III.** *a Roman cognomen in the gens Aemilia*.

regimen, inis, *n.* [regō], *a controlling, guiding, steering*. **1.** Lit. **a.** fluctūs regimen navis impediunt, Tac. ; regimen equorum exercere, Tac. ; Plin. ; Concr.: *the steering*, i.e. the rudder : Ov. **2.** Transf. **a.** regimen totius magistratūs penes Appium erat, Liv. ; summae rei, Tac. ; cohortium, Tac. ; in omnia, Tac. ; tenere, Tac. **b.** *the direction of State affairs, rule, government:* regimen suscipere, Tac. ; Stat. **c.** Concr.: *a ruler, governor :* regimen rerum, Liv. [Fr. *régime*.]

rēgĭna, ae, *f.* [rēx], *a queen*. **1.** Lit. **a.** In gen.: Pl., Cic., Verg., etc. **b.** Of goddesses : Pl., Cic., Verg., etc. **2.** Transf. **a.** *a daughter of a king, a princess :* Verg., Ov., Curt. **b.** *a noble woman, woman of rank:* Pl., Ter. **c.** Of abstracts : (iustitia) omnium est domina et regina virtutum, Cic. ; Pac. ; Hor. [It. *reina ;* Sp. *reyna ;* Fr. *reine*.]

regĭō, ōnis, *f.* [regō]. **I.** *a (drawn) straight line*. **1.** Lit. **A.** nullā regione viāi declinare, Lucr. ; notā excedo regione viarum, Verg. ; oppidi murus ab planitie rectā regione MCC passūs aberat, Caes. ; non rectā regione iter instituit, sed ad laevam flexit, Liv. ; ubi primos superare regionem castrorum animum adverterunt, Caes. **B.** e regione, adverbially. **a.** *in a straight line, directly :* ut cadat e regione loci, Lucr. ; ferri, petere, moveri, Cic. **b.** *in a parallel line, over against, exactly opposite :* acie e regione instructā, Nep. With GEN. or DAT.: erat e regione oppidi collis, Caes. ; fere e regione castris castra posuit, Caes. ; Cic. **C.** *a boundary-line, boundary :* finis imperi non terrae sed caeli regionibus terminat, Cic. Esp. in augury : lituo Romulus regiones derexit, Cic. ; regionibus ratis, Cic. **2.** Transf.: de rectā viā deflecto, Cic. ; argumenti regiones determinabo, Pl. ; quibus regionibus vitae spatium circumscriptum est, Cic. **II.** *the space between lines* or *boundaries (cf.* fīnēs*) ; a quarter, region, tract*. **1.** Lit. **A.** Indefinite. In astronomy: exoriens mediā ab regione diei, Lucr. ; regio lunae, quae tum est aquilonaris, tum australis, Cic. ; caeli in regione serenā, Verg. ; regione occidentis, Liv. **b.** Geogr.: in hac regione, Pl. ; agri fertilissima regio, Caes. ; pestilens, Cic. ; deserta siti regio, Verg. ; eā regione quā Sergius erat, Liv. In *pl. :* Pl., Cic. **B.** More definite. **a.** *a province, district (of a country :* Caes., Cic., Liv., Hor., etc. **b.** *a quarter, ward* of Rome : Plin., Tac. **2.** Transf.: *province, department, sphere :* dum in regionem astutiarum

mearum te induco, Pl. ; consilium situm mediā regione in pectore haeret, Lucr. ; bene dicere non habet definitam aliquam regionem, Cic.

regĭōnātim, *adv. by districts* or *wards :* Liv.

Rēgĭum (Rhēg-), I, *n.,* **I.** *a town in Gallia Cisalpina ;* **Rēgĭēnsēs**, ium, *m. pl., its inhabitants.* **II.** *a city in S. Calabria on the Strait of Messina ;* **Rēgĭnus**, a, um ; **Rēgĭni**, ōrum, *m. pl., its inhabitants.*

rēgĭus, a, um [rēx], *belonging to a king, of a king, royal ; with* or *against the king, etc.* **I.** Lit.: genus, Cic. ; exercitus, Caes. ; anni, Cic. ; scelus, Liv. ; ales, Ov. ; bellum, Cic. ; sponsus, Hor. ; puer, Verg. As Noun, **rēgĭa**, ae, *f.* **A.** (*sc.* domus) *a royal abode, palace.* **1.** Lit. **a.** In gen. : Caes., Cic., Cat., Ov., etc. **b.** *the regia* (orig. Numa's), used as the residence of the Pontifex Maximus : Cic., Ov., etc. **c.** *the royal tent* in a camp : Liv., Curt. **2.** Transf.: *the court*, i.e. the royal family and the courtiers : Liv., Tac. **B.** (*sc.* urbs) *a royal city, capital :* Verg., Hor. **C.** For Gk. basilica, *a colonnade, portico ; a hall :* Aug. ap. Suet. **II.** Transf. *royal, princely, splendid, magnificent (cf.* regalis) : forma, Pl. ; charta, Cat. ; moles, Hor. ; regia res est succurrere lapsis, Ov.

re-glūtĭnō, āre, *to unglue, to unstick :* Cat.

rēgnātor, ōris, *m.* [rēgnō], *a ruler, sovereign :* deorum, Pl., Tac. ; summi Olympi, Verg.

rēgnātrix, ĭcis, *adj. f.* [rēgnō], *ruling, imperial :* in domo regnatrice, Tac.

rēgnō, āre [rēgnum], *to have royal power, to be king, to reign.* **1.** Lit. **a.** Pl., Cic., etc. ; Albae, Liv. ; Amyclis, Verg. ; Latio, Verg. ; in nos, Tac. With GEN. (Gk. constr.) : Hor. Impers. Pass. : Verg., Liv. **b.** In *Pass. : to be under kings, be ruled over :* terra regnata Lycurgo, Verg. ; Hor. ; Ov. ; exceptis iis gentibus quae regnantur, Tac. **2.** Transf. **a.** *to be supreme, hold sway :* in equitum centuriis, Cic. Ep. ; in iudiciis, Quint. Of the gods : Hor., Ov. **b.** Esp. of one exercising unconstitutional power in a free State : *to domineer, tyrannise :* Cic., Liv. **c.** Of things : unor in arvis, Lucr. ; ignis per ramos victor regnat, Verg. ; ebrietas, Ov. ; hic eloquentia, Quint.

rēgnum, I, *n.* [rēx]. **I.** Abstract: *kingly government.* **1.** Lit.: *kingship, royal power, monarchy :* Cic., Liv. ; regi regnum stabilire, Pl. ; stabat regno incolumis, Verg. ; obtinere, Caes. ; in suā civitate occupare, Caes. ; labefactare, Cic. ; regem regno spoliare, Cic. **2.** Transf. **a.** *supremacy, control, sovereignty, direction :* possidere regna, Ter. ; nationes quae in populi R. regno ac dicione sunt, Cic. ; regnum civitatis alicui deferre, Caes. ; regnum alicui permittere, Hor. ; adoptione in regnum pervenire, Sall. ; te in meum regnum accepi, Sall. ; regnum sine vi tenere, Ov. ; regna vini sortiere, Hor. **b.** Of unconstitutional power : *absolute power, despotism, power :* appetere, occupare, Cic. ; damnatus crimine regni, Ov. ; quod tribuni militum in plebe Romanā regnum exercerent, Liv. Hence, regnum iudiciorum, Cic. **c.** Of things, *rule :* voluptatis, Cic. ; Ov. **II.** Concrete : *a realm, kingdom.* **1.** Lit. : Caes., Cic., Liv., Hor., etc. Of bees : cerea regna, Verg. **2.** Transf. : *an estate, realm :* Cic. In *pl. :* Verg.

regō, regere, rēxī, rēctum, *to keep or lead in a straight line or in the proper course ; to guide, conduct, direct.* **1.** Lit. **a.** manus una navem, Lucr. ; deus id corpus, Cic. ; regi velis (of ships), Caes. ; vela, Prop. ; arte ratem, Ov. ; equum, Liv., Ov. ; frena, Ov. ; currūs, Ov., Curt. ; tela per auras, Verg. ; tenui vestigia filo, Cat. ; Verg. **b.** In law : regere finīs, *to mark out the limits :* Cic., Tib. **2.** Transf. **a.** *to guide, direct :* alicuius animum, Pl., Hor. ; animum dictis, Verg. ; rem consilio, Ter. ; bella, Caes. ; Lucr. ; errantem, Caes. ; iuvenem, Cic. Ep. ; mores, Cic. ; studia vestra consiliīs, Cic. ; consilia senatūs, Quint. ; valetudines principis, Tac. **b.** *to control, govern, rule, command, have supremacy over :* civitates, rem publicam, Cic. ; populos imperio, Verg. ; diva Antium, Hor. ; Frisios, Tac. ; legiones, Tac. Without Object : Verg., Tac.

re-gredior, gredī, grēssus [gradior], *to step back, to go or come back ; to return.* **1.** Lit. **a.** In gen. : Cic. ; illuc ab ostio, Pl. ; ex itinere in castra, Liv. ; Tarraconem, Liv. ; ad Hiberum, Liv. **b.** Milit. *to retire, retreat :* Caes. ; in collis, Sall. **2.** Transf. in memoriam (with *Acc.* and *Inf.*), Pl. : in illum annum, Cic. ; ad formandos animos, Quint. ; eodem regressus, Sall.

regrēssus, a, um. *Part.* regredior.

regrēssus, ūs, *m.* [regredior], *a going back, return.* **1.** Lit. **a.** In gen. : Verg. In *pl. :* Cic., Ov. **b.** Milit. : *a retreat :* Liv., Tac. **2.** Transf. **a.** neque locus paenitendi aut regressūs ab irā relictus est, Liv. ; nullo ad paenitendum regressu, Tac. **b.** *recourse :* ad principem, Tac.

rēgula, ae, *f.* [regō], *a straight edge or strip.* **1.** Lit. **a.** *a rule, ruler :* Cic. ; materiam ad regulam exigere, Plin. **b.** Of boards : Caes. **2.** Transf. : *a rule, standard, pattern, model, example :* regula, quā vera et falsa iudicarentur, Cic. ; nos studia nostra nostrae naturae regulā metiamur, Cic. ; regula, ad quam eorum deriguntur orationes, Cic. ; locuti sunt ad hanc regulam, Quint. ; loquendi, Quint. ; adsit regula, peccatis quae poenas inroget aequas, Hor.

rēgulus, ī, *m.* [*dim.* rēx]. **1.** Lit. *a petty king, prince, chieftain :* Sall., Liv., Tac. **2.** Transf. *a king's son, a prince :* Sall., Liv.

Rēgulus, ī, *m. a Roman cognomen* esp. *of the consul,* M. Atilius Regulus, *who was taken prisoner by the Carthaginians in the first Punic war.*

re-gustō, āre, *to taste again or repeatedly.* **1.** Lit. : Sen., Pers. **2.** Transf. : litteras, Cic. Ep.

re-iciō (poet. rēiciō, but rēice, Verg.), icere, iēcī, iectum. **I.** *to throw, cast or fling back or backwards.* **1.** Lit. **a.** *to fling over one's shoulder or behind one ; to fling back off one :* paenulam, Cic. ; vestem, Cat. ; amictum ex umeris, Verg. ; togam ab

umerō, Liv. ; umerīs ..., Ov. ; de corpore vestem, Ov. ; capillum circum caput neglegenter, Ter. ; scutum, Cic. ; Verg. Occ. *to fling away from one :* pila, Caes. ; librum e gremio suo, Ov. ; sanguinem, Plin. Ep. ; vinum, Suet. **b.** With *Refl. Pron. : to throw or cast oneself back :* se in eum, Ter. ; se in gremium tuom, Lucr. ; *cf.* fatigata membra, Curt. **c.** *to fling back, repel* living beings : aliquem, Pl. ; in bubile boves, Pl. ; a flumine capellas, Verg. ; Alcides a se mea pectora (in wrestling), Ov. ; in postremam aciem, Liv. E sp. milit. : eos, qui eruptionem fecerant, in urbem reiciebant, Caes. ; ab Antiocheā hostem, Cic. Ep. ; Tusci reiecti armis, Verg. ; reiectae Hannibalis minae, Hor. **d.** Nautical (in *Pass.*), *to be driven back :* Caes., Cic., Liv. **2.** Transf. **a.** *to fling or cast back or off one :* aps te socordiam, Pl. ; ferrum et audaciam, Cic. ; hanc proscriptionem a vobis, Cic. ; Lucr. P o e t. : pars vocum solidis locis reiecta, Lucr. ; oculos Rutulorum arvis, Verg. **b.** *to cast off* with contempt, *to reject, scorn :* aliquem, Ter., Hor., Ov. ; istam disputationem, Cic. ; praedam, Hor. ; relationem, Liv. **c.** *to set aside, challenge, reject* members of the board of iudices : Cic. **d.** With *ad* and *Acc.* : *to refer to, make over to :* rem ad senatum, populum, magistratūs, pontifices, Hannibalem, etc., Liv. ; Caes. ; legati ab senatu reiecti ad populum, Liv. ; in hunc gregem Sullam, Cic. ; ad ipsam te epistulam, Cic. Ep. **e.** *to put off, defer, postpone :* a Kal. Febr. legationes in Idūs Febr., Cic. Ep. **II.** *to fling in return :* telum in hostis, Caes.

reiectāneus, a, um [reiciō]. Philos. *that which is to be rejected* (= Gk. ἀποπροηγμένος): Cic.

reiectiō, ōnis, *f.* [reiciō], *a throwing back.* **1.** Lit. : sanguinis, Plin. **2.** Transf. **a.** *a rejecting, rejection :* reiectione huius civitatis, Cic. **b.** In law, *a challenging, rejection* of a iudex : iudicum, Cic. ; reiectione interpositā, Cic.

rēiectō, āre [*freq.* reiciō], *to throw or cast back :* Lucr.

reiectus, a, um. **I.** *Part.* reiciō. **II.** Noun. **reiecta** or **reicienda**, ōrum, *n. pl., things to be rejected* (= reiectaneus, q.v.) : Cic.

reiciō, reiciō, etc., *v.* reiciō.

re-lābor, lābī, lāpsus, *to slide or glide back ; to sink or fall back.* **1.** Lit. : vix oculos tollens iterumque relabens, Ov. ; in sinūs nostros, Ov. ; unda, Verg. ; Tiberis, aestus, Tac. ; rivi montibus, Hor. **2.** Transf. : in Aristippi furtim praecepta relabor, Hor.

re-languēscō, languēscere, languī, *to sink back fainting.* **1.** Lit. : (soror) imposito fratri moribunda relanguit ore, Ov. **2.** Transf. *to faint, grow feeble :* iis rebus animi eorum, Caes. ; Cic. Ep. ; animo ardor, Ov. ; taedio impetus regis, Liv. ; indignatio, Tac.

relātiō, ōnis, *f.* [referō], *a carrying back, bringing back.* **1.** Lit. : Quint. **2.** Transf. **A.** P o l i t. : *a report made by a magistrate to the senate or emperor :* Cic. ; approbare, Liv. ; incipere, mutare, egredi, etc., Tac. Of *a report in gen. :* Quint.

B. In law: *a retorting*: criminis, Cic.
C. Rhet. and Gramm. **a.** *repetition,
reiteration*: Cic. **b.** *reference, relation*:
ad aliquid, Quint. **D.** *a returning*: gratiae, Sen.

relātor, ōris, *m.* [referō], *one who makes a
relatio or report*: Balb. ap. Cic. Ep.

relātus, a, um, *Part.* referō.

relātus, ūs, *m.* [referō]. **I.** *an official report*: abnuentibus consulibus eā de re
relatum, Tac. **II.** *a narration, recital*:
virtutum, Tac.

relaxātiō, ōnis, *f.* [relaxō], *a slackening of
tension, an easing*. Transf. **a.** animi
(opp. contentio), Cic. **b.** doloris, Cic.

re-laxō, āre, *to unloose again, to expand or
widen again*. **1.** Lit.: vincla, nodos,
Lucr.; alvus relaxatur, Cic.; densa
relaxare, Verg.; vias et caeca spiramenta,
Verg.; tunicarum vincula, Ov.; glaebas,
Varr. **2.** Transf. **A.** Of style: constructio verborum dissolutionibus relaxetur,
Cic. **B.** Of the mind. **a.** *to release, set
free*: (animi) cum se plane corporis
vinculis relaxaverint, Cic.; se occupationibus, Cic. Ep.; se a nimiā necessitate, Cic.
b. *to relax (the tension of), to unbend, ease*:
animum, Cic.; animos doctrinā, Cic.;
risus tristitiam, Cic. In *Mid.*: homines
interdum animis relaxantur. *Absol.*:
dolor relaxat, Cic.

relēctus, a, um, *Part.* relegō.

relēgātiō, ōnis, *f.* [relēgō], *a sending into
retirement, banishment*: Cic., Liv.

re-lēgō, āre, *to remove to a distance, send into
retirement*. **1.** Lit. **a.** In gen.: relegati
longe ab ceteris, Caes.; Cic.; Liv.:
filium in praedia rustica, Cic.; tauros in
sola pascua, Verg.; exercitum in aliā
insulā, Tac. With DAT. of recipient:
Verg. **b.** Of a milder form of banishment
than exsilium or deportatio, from Rome or
Italy, and usually for a limited time, without capitis deminutio: Cic., Liv., Tac.;
aliquem in exsilium, Liv.; in insulam,
Tac.; ultra Carthaginem, Liv.; exercitus
(Cannensis) relegatur in Siciliam, Liv.;
in decem annos, Tac. **2.** Transf. **a.** *to
put aside, reject*: dona, Cic.; ambitionem,
Hor.; verba alicuius, Ov. **b.** *to refer,
impute*: culpam in hominem, Quint.;
orationem ad philosophos, Quint.; causas
alicui, Tib.

re-legō, legere, lēgī, lēctum, *to gather up or
collect again*. **1.** Lit. **a.** a coactore pecuniam, Cato; ianua difficilis filo est inventa
relecto, Ov. **b.** Of a coasting voyage:
to pick up or travel over or through again:
litora, Verg.; Ov.; Asiam, Tac. Also of
other movement: caelum luna, Stat.
2. Transf. *to go over, review*. **a.** In
thought: Cic. **b.** In speech: suos sermone labores, Ov.; Quint. **c.** In reading:
scriptorem, Hor.; scripta, Ov.

re-lentēscō, ere, *to grow slack again, to
slacken*. Transf.: amor, Ov.

re-levō, āre, *to restore to lightness, to lighten
again*. **1.** Lit. **a.** *to lift up or raise again*:
corpus e terrā, Ov.; in cubitum membra,
Ov. **b.** *to make light, lighten*: vimina
favi, Ov.; minimo ut relevere labore utque
marem parias, Ov. Comic.: epistulam

graviorem perlectione, Cic. Ep. **2.**
Transf.: *to relieve, alleviate*: animum,
Ter.; curā et metu relevati, Cic.; (morbo)
relevari, Cic.; animum molestiis, Cic.:
aegrum, Ov.; membra sedili, Ov.; mens
a curā relevata, Ov.; famem, Ov.; publi-
canos tertiā mercedum parte, Suet.

relictiō, ōnis, *f.* [relinquō], *a leaving behind,
abandoning*: consulis sui, Cic.

relictus, a, um, *Part.* relinquō.

relicuos and **relicus**, a, um, *v.* reliquus.

religātiō, ōnis, *f.* [religō], *a binding back,
tying up*: vitium, Cic.

religiō (poet. also **rēligiō** or **relligiō**), ōnis,
f. [religō]. **I.** Subjectively.: *scrupu-
lousness*. **1.** Prop. in religion: *a religious
scruple, pious misgivings*. **A.** In gen.:
cum summā religione, tum summo metu
legum teneri, Cic.; religio eius rei tenet
senatum, Liv.; obstrinxisti religione populum Romanum, Cic.; obicere religionem,
Pl.; inicere alicui, Cic.; non recordabantur
quam parvulae causae vel terroris repentini
vel obiectae religionis magna detrimenta
intulissent, Caes.; liber erat religione
animus, Liv.; animos religione solvere *or*
levare, Liv.; mentis religione liberare,
Liv.; augures eam religionem eximerent,
Liv.; se domumque religione exsolvere,
Liv.; templum religione liberare (perh.
from the feeling that it was tainted by blood),
Liv.; in religionem ea res versa est, Liv.
In *pl.*: plerique novas sibi ex loco religiones
fingunt, Caes.; Cic.; Liv. **B.** Special
phrases. **a.** With *Inf.* or GEN. or DAT. of
Gerund.: aliquem religio capit, vetat, etc.;
religio *or* religioni est, *there are scruples*
(about doing something); religionem facere,
religioni habere, *to regard* (something) *as a
matter involving religious scruples* *or
objections*: quosdam religio ceperit ulterius
quicquam eo die conandi, Liv.; rivos
deducere nulla religio vetuit, Verg.; ut velut
numine aliquo defensa castra oppugnare
religio fuerit, Liv. (With ACC. and *Inf.*:
conlegam suffici censori religio erat, Liv.);
dictu mirabile et quod dimovendis statu
suo sacris religionem facere posset, Liv.
(With ACC.: nec eam rem habuit religioni,
Cic.) **b.** With *ne* or *quo minus* and *Subj.*:
ne confestim bellum indiceretur religio
obstitit, Liv. (Also with obiecta *or*
oblata *or* iniecta est.) **C.** In bad sense:
superstition (freq. in the Epicurean poet
Lucretius): oppressa gravi sub religione
vita, Lucr.; refrenatus religione, Lucr.;
tantum religio potuit suadere malorum,
Lucr.; (perh. in) natio est omnium Gallorum admodum dedita religionibus, Caes.;
animos externa religio incessit, Liv.;
prava, Liv. **2.** Transf. in morals:
*scruples, sense of obligation, conscientious-
ness*: religio fuit, denegare nolui, Pl.;
nihil esse mihi religio'st dicere, Ter.;
in consilio dando, Cic. Ep.; ut quae religio
C. Mario non fuerat quo minus praetorem
occideret eā nos religione in privato
puniendo liberaremur, Cic.; iuris iurandi,
Caes., Cic.; testimoniorum, offici, Cic.;
vitae, Cic.; iudicis, Cic.; iudicum religiones,
Cic.; mendaci, Caes.; nulla mihi religio
est, Hor. **II.** Objectively. **1.** Lit.

(abstract). **a.** *sanctity, sacredness inherent* in a religious object : funi, signi, sacrari, Cic. ; loci, Verg. ; in sacerdotibus tantā offusā oculis animoque religione motus, Liv. **b.** Of violated sanctity : *taint, pollution :* templum religione liberare, Liv. (but *cf.* I. 1. A.) ; expiatis religionibus, Liv. **2.** T r a n s f. (concr.) *an object of veneration :* Agrigentini signum Apollinis, religionem domesticam, ornamentum urbis requirebant, Cic. ; praedo religionum, Cic. ; religiones maximas violavit, Cic. ; quae roligio aut quae machina belli, Verg. **III.** (*strictness in regard to*) *ceremonial observances; cult-observance.* **a.** In gen. : religio est quae superioris cuiusdam naturae curam caerimoniamque adfert, Cic. ; silva religione patrum sacra, Verg. ; deorum immortalium, Cic. ; Druides religiones interpretantur, Caes. ; ceterae nationes pro religionibus suis bella suscipiunt, istae contra omnium religiones, Cic. ; de religionibus hi magistratūs consuluere, Liv. More abstract : *piety, reverence :* aliquem a pietate, religione deducere, Cic. **b.** Of some deity or numen : sacra Cereris summā maiores nostri religione confici caerimoniāque voluerunt, Cic. ; mira quaedam totā Siciliā privatim ac publice religio est Cereris Hennensis, Cic.

religiōsē, *adv.* **I.** *scrupulously, conscientiously :* Cic., Nep. *Comp. :* Col. *Sup. :* Plin. Ep. **II.** *piously, reverently :* Comp. : Liv., Plin. Ep. *Sup. :* Cic.

religiōsus (poet. also **rēlig-** or **rellig-**), a, um [religiō]. **I.** S u b j e c t i v e l y : *scrupulous.* **1.** P r o p. in religion. **A.** *involving scruples* or *religious difficulty :* quem campi fructum religiosum erat consumere, Liv. ; religiosum fuit (with Acc. and *Pass. Inf.*), Liv. ; illum diem religiosum Carthaginiensibus ad agendum quicquam rei seriae esse, Liv. **B.** Of persons. **a.** *scrupulous :* Liv. ; civitas religiosa (with *ne* and *Subj.*), Liv. **b.** In bad sense : *superstitious :* Ter. **2.** T r a n s f. in morals : *scrupulous, conscientious :* testis, Cic. ; iudex, Quint. ; in testimoniis (dicendis), Cic. Also, ad Atticorum auris teretis et religiosas se accommodant, Cic. *Sup. :* Cic. **II.** O b j e c t i v e l y : of religious objects, *sacred, venerated, holy :* templum, signum, etc., Cic. ; deorum limina, Verg. *Sup. :* Cic. **III.** *concerned with* or *attentive to ceremonial observances* or *cult-observance.* **a.** Of things : mortuis religiosa iura tribuere, Cic. ; mores, Cic. ; Quint. **b.** Of persons : *pious, reverent :* Pl., Cic. *Sup. :* Sall.

re-ligō, āre, *to bind, tie, fasten,* or *tether back* or *behind.* **1.** L i t. : trabis axibus, Caes. ; Hectorem ad currum, Cic. ; Liv. ; Cybele iuga, Cat. ; equos, Verg. ; comam, Hor. ; Tac. ; religata comas in nodum, Hor. Of ships : navis ad terram, Caes. ; funem in Cretam, Cat. ; ab aggere classem, Verg. ; litore classem, Ov. **2.** T r a n s f. : prudentia, si extrinsecus religata pendeat, Cic.

re-linō, linere, lēvi, *to take out the resin from a jar,* to *uncork :* dolia, Ter. P o e t. : servata mella thesauris, Verg.

re-linquō, linquere, līqui, lictum. **I.** *to leave behind.* **A.** In gen. **1.** L i t. : puerum apud matrem domi, Pl. ; post tergum hostem, Caes. ; aliquem in Galliā, Caes. ; greges sub opacā valle, Ov. ; longius delatus aestu sub sinistrā Britanniam relictam conspexit, Caes. With *Predic. Adj.* or *Part.* or phrase : cum Plautus locum reliquit integrum, Ter. ; Morini, quos Caesar pacatos reliquerat, Caes. ; Cic. ; Verg., etc. ; aliquid incohatum, Cic. ; copias sine imperio, Caes. **2.** T r a n s f. : hanc excusationem, Cic. Ep. ; aculeos in animis, Cic. ; aetatem, Ov. **B.** By death : *to leave, bequeath.* **1.** L i t. : alicui agrum, Pl. ; Cic. ; Ov., etc. **2.** T r a n s f. : sibi hanc laudem, Ter. ; rem publicam nobis, Cic. ; memoriam brevem, Cic. ; monumentum audaciae suae noternum, Cic. ; Hor. ; scripta posteris, Quint. ; Cic. ; Ov. **II.** *to leave behind* as a representative, substitute, or in reserve, etc.. : me pro atriensi in sedibus, Pl. ; me filiis quasi magistrum, Ter. ; me servom pro te, Pl. ; Fabium legatum cum legionibus duabus castris praesidio relinquit, Caes. ; in provinciā alterum mo, Cic. Ep. ; eā causā miles hic reliquit symbolum, Pl. Of an heir : hunc testamento, Cic. ; Ter. **III.** *to let remain, leave free ; not to take away, remove,* or *alter* (and in *Pass.* to remain). **1.** L i t. : nihil in aedibus, Ter. ; nihil de tanto patrimonio, Cic. ; equitatūs partem illi attribuit, partem sibi reliquit, Caes. ; Hor. ; Ov. ; ne palene quidem ex omni fructu relinquerentur, Cic. **2.** T r a n s f. : Aedui nullum sibi ad cognoscendum spatium relinquunt, Caes. ; facultatem sui colligendi, Caes. ; Pl. ; mihi consilium, Tac. ; Cic. ; vita turpis ne morti quidem honestae locum relinquit, Cic. ; quod munitioni castrorum tempus relinqui volebat, Caes. ; ut vobis ne libertatis quidem recuperandae spes relinquatur, Cic. ; Ov., etc. With Acc. and *Inf.* : Lucr., Ov. With *Inf.* as Object : Hor. ; vestro iudicio relinquimus (with *Indir. Quest.*), Liv. Impers. *Pass.* with *ut* and *Subj.* : Caes., Cic. **IV.** *to leave behind, desert, forsake, abandon.* **A.** In gen. **1.** L i t. : te hic, Pl. ; domum propinquosque, Caes. ; dominos, Cat. ; limen, mensas, Verg. ; moenia, Hor. ; volucres ova, Lucr. **2.** T r a n s f. : aliquem animus, Pl., Caes., Ov. ; aliquem vita, Lucr., Ov. ; vitam, Verg. ; Tac. ; ab omni honestate relictus, Cic. **B.** In partic. : *to leave in the lurch, forsake, abandon.* **1.** L i t. : reliquit deseruitque me, Pl. ; o desertum hominem, desperatum, relictum, Cic. ; medio in opere aratra, Verg. ; signa, Liv. ; parmulam, Hor. ; urbem direptioni et incendiis, Cic. ; aliquem poenae, Ov., Plin. Ep. **2.** T r a n s f. : alias res, Pl. ; relictis rebus (omnibus), Pl., Lucr., Caes., Cic., etc. ; et agrorum et armorum cultum, Cic. ; Hor. ; caedis relinquo, libidines praetereo (i.e. *leave unmentioned*), Cic. ; Hor. With *Inf.* as Object : Lucr.

reliquiae (poet. also **rēliq-** or **relliq-**), ārum, *f. pl.* [relinquō], *leavings, remains, remnant.* **1.** L i t. **A.** In gen. : de bonis

quod restat roliquiarum, Pl. ; gladiatoriae
familiae, Caes. ; cibi, Cic. With *Subj.*
Gen. : belli, Sall., Liv. ; pugnae, Liv. ;
Danaum, Verg. **B.** In partic. **a.** Of a
meal : Pl., Phaedr., Suet. (*cf.* in double
sense : vellem Idibus Martiis me ad cenam
invitasses ; reliquiarum nihil fuisset, Cic.
Ep.). **b.** Of a body that has been burned :
Cic., Verg., Tac., etc. **c.** Of a sacrifice :
Suet. **2.** T r a n s f. : vitae, Lucr. ; pristinae fortunae, Cic. With *Subj.* Gen. : ut
avi reliquias persequare, Cic.

reliquus (relicus ; earlier **relicuos** ; Abl.
rĕlĭcuŏ, Lucr.), a, um [relinquŏ], *that which
is left behind* or *over ; the remaining.* **1.**
L i t. **A.** In gen. : si qua reliqua spes est,
Cic. ; Ter. With Dat. of person : erant
oppida mihi complura reliqua, Cic. ; Ter. ;
Sall. **B.** In partic. **a.** Of time : *remaining, subsequent, future :* spe reliquae tranquillitatis, Cic. ; monet ut in reliquum
tempus omnis suspiciones vitet, Caes. ;
Cic. **b.** Of debts : *remaining, outstanding :*
Pl., Cato, Cic. Ep. **C.** More freq. as Noun,
reliquum, ī, n. (and occ. **reliqua,** orum,
n. *pl.*), *the remainder, what remains :* Pl. ;
quid est huic reliqui ? Cic. ; Liv. ; quid
reliqui habemus praeter etc. ? Sall. ; quae
reliqui summa fuit, Cic. ; illud breve vitae
reliquum, Cic. ; quod belli reliquum erat,
Liv. ; reliqua belli perfecta, Liv. ; Tac.
Of debts (mostly in *pl.*) : Cic. Ep., Plin.
Ep. ; in pun, D. Special phrases.
a. reliquum est, *it remains.* With *ut* and
Subj. : Cic., Nep., Quint. With *Inf. :*
Sall. **b.** reliquum aliquem *or* aliquid facere,
aliquid reliqui facere, *to leave behind, leave
remaining* or *over :* quos belli calamitas
reliquos fecerat, Cic. ; quos reliquos fortuna
ex caede fecerat, Liv. ; quae reliqua iis
bellum fecerat, Liv. Esp. negatively :
nihil de fructu suis reliqui fecit, Cic. ;
Sall. ; Liv. ; ne hoc quidem sibi reliquit
ut etc., Cic. Also, *to leave undone, to omit,
neglect* (only negatively) : nihil ad celeritatem sibi reliqui fecerunt, Caes. ; Nep. ;
nihil reliqui faciunt (with *quo minus* and
Subj.), Tac. **c.** in reliquum, *for the future,
in future :* Cic., Sall., Liv. **2.** T r a n s f.
that which remains after a part just mentioned, *the remaining, the rest, the remainder :*
Servilius consul reliquique magistratūs,
Caes. ; Cic. ; reliquam partem exercitūs
non putat exspectandam, Caes. ; Cic. ;
Lucr. As Noun : de reliquo quid tibi ego
dicam ? Cic. Ep. ; Pl. ; magnam partem
eorum concidit ; reliqui sese fugae man-
darunt, Caes. ; Cic. ; audi reliqua, Pl. ;
Cic.

rellig-, relliq-, *v.* relig-, reliq-.

re-lūceō, lūcēre, lūxī, *to give back* or *reflect
light :* stella, Cic. poet. ; flamma, Verg. ;
fiamma ex capite, Liv. ; e Vesuvio flammae,
Plin. Ep. ; igni freta, Verg. ; Ov.

re-lūcēscō, lūcescere, lūxī [relūceō], *to grow
bright again :* solis imago, Ov. ; dies, Tac.
Impers. : Plin. Ep.

re-luctor, ārī, *to struggle against, resist.* **1.**
L i t. : hostis, Ov., Curt. ; coniunx, Tax. ;
vitulus, Verg. ; dracones, Hor. **2.** T r a n s f.
a. luna, Ov. ; aquae, Quint. **b.** Of reluctance in persons : Curt., Quint.

re-macrēscō, macrēscere, macruī, *to grow
very lean* or *thin :* Suet.

re-maledicō, ere, *to abuse* or *revile in return :*
Vesp. ap. Suet.

re-mandō, ere, *to chew over again :* Plin. ;
cibum, Quint.

re-maneō, manēre, mānsī, *to stay* or *remain
behind.* **1.** L i t. **a.** In gen. : Caes., Cic. ;
in castris, Caes. ; Cic. ; Romae, Caes. ; ad
urbem cum imperio, Caes. ; apud aliquem,
Caes. ; ferrum ex hastili in corpore, Nep.
b. *to remain, continue :* equos eodem
vestigio remanere adsuefaciunt, Caes. ;
animi post mortem, Cic. ; Lucr. **2.**
T r a n s f. **a.** In gen. : vestigia antiqui
offici, Cic. ; usque ad nostram memoriam
disciplina navalis, Cic. ; vobis aeterna
sollicitudo, Sall. ; ne quid ex contagione
noxae remaneret penes nos, Liv. ; in duris
rebus amicus, Ov. **b.** With *Predic. Adj. :*
to remain, continue in a certain state :
potentia senatūs gravis et magna remanebat, Cic. ; Caes. ; Ov.

re-mānō, āre, *to flow back :* Lucr.

remānsiō, ōnis, f. [remaneō], *a staying* or
remaining behind in one's place : Cic.

remedium, ī, n. [medeor], *that which heals
again ; a cure, remedy, medicine, antidote.*
1. L i t. : Lucr., Cic. **2.** T r a n s f. : veneficiis remedia invenire, Cic. ; Ter. ; quibus
rebus nostri haec reperiebant remedia,
Caes. ; id remedium timori fuit, Liv. ;
acrioribus saluti suae remediis subvenire,
Cic. ; ad moram quaerere, Cic. ; ad magnitudinem frigorum comparare, Cic. ; sibi
comparare ad tolerandum dolorem, Cic. ;
in ceteros, Tac. ; adversus reliqua uti
remediis, Quint. With *Obj.* Gen. : Ter.,
Cic., Quint., etc.

re-mēnsus, a, um, *Part.* remētior.

re-meō, āre, *to go* or *come back, to return.*
1. L i t. : intro, Pl. ; in patriam, Ov. ;
Tac. ; ad se (legati), Liv. ; ex Campaniā,
Verg. ; Aegypto, Tac. ; victor ad Argos,
Verg. ; victor domito ab hoste, Ov. With
Acc. : patrias urbes, Verg. Of inanimate
subjects : aer, Cic. ; naves mari, Tac. ;
flumen, Tac. **2.** T r a n s f. : dies, Tib.
With Acc. : aevum remeare peractum,
Hor.

re-mētior, mētīrī, mēnsus, *to measure back,
retrace.* **1.** L i t. : si modo rite memor
servata remetior astra, Verg. *Perf. Part.*
in *Pass.* sense : pelago remenso, Verg.
2. T r a n s f. **a.** *to void* or *discharge again :*
vinum vomitu, Sen. **b.** *to reflect upon :*
totum diem facta ac dicta mea remetior,
Cic. **c.** *to pass over again : transmissum discrimen convalescendo* (i.e. *be continually
making progress in recovery*), Plin. Ep.

rēmex, igis, m. [rēmus agō], *a rower, oarsman :*
Pl., Cic., Hor. *Sing.* collect. for remiges :
Verg., Ov., Liv., Tac.

rēmigātiō, ōnis, f. [rēmigō], *a rowing :* Cic.
Ep.

rēmigium, ī, n. [rēmex], *a rowing.* **1.** L i t. :
homines remigio sequi, Pl. ; Verg. **2.**
T r a n s f. **a.** *Concr. the oarage, oars :*
Cat., Verg., Hor., Tac. Of wings : remigio
alarum, Verg. **b.** *oarsmen, rowers :* Cic.

rēmigō, āre [rēmex], *to row :* Caes., Cic.,
Tac.

re-migrō, āre, *to move back* (home). **1.** Lit.: domum, Pl.; in locum, Lucr.; in domum veterem e novā, Cic.; trans Rhenum in suos vicos, Caes. **2.** Transf.: ad iustitiam, Cic.; Pl.; animus mihi, Pl.

re-miniscor, minīscī [v. meminī and mēns], *to recall to mind, recollect, remember* : Cic. With GEN.: Caes., Nep., Ov. With ACC.: Nep., Verg., Ov. With ACC. and *Inf.* : Lucr., Ov. With *Indir. Quest.*: Nep., Liv.

re-misceō, miscēre, mixtum, *to mix over and over again.* **1.** Lit.: venenum cibo, Sen. **2.** Transf.: veris falsa, Hor.; Sen. Ep.

remissē, *adv. gently, mildly* : Cic., Quint. *Comp.* : Cic., Quint.

remissiō, ōnis, *f.* [remittō], *a letting go back.* **1.** Lit. **a.** *a releasing* or *letting go home* : captivorum, Liv. **b.** (opp. contentio or contractio), *a relaxing, slackening* (e.g. of the muscles): Cic.; superciliorum, Cic.; vocis, Cic., Quint. In *pl.*: Cic. **2.** Transf. **A.** *a remission, abatement* : poenae, Cic.; tributi, Tac.; post magnas remissiones (of rent), Plin. Ep. **B.** Mental. **a.** *relaxation, recreation* : Cic., Quint.; animi, Cic. In *pl.* : Quint., Tac., Plin. Ep. **b.** *slackness* : in acerbissimā iniuriā remissio animi, Cic. Ep. **c.** *mildness, leniency* : Cic. **C.** Intrans. (*cf.* the use of remitto in *Mid.*), *an abatement* : morbi, Cic. Ep.; febris, Suet.

remissus, a, um. **I.** *Part.* remittō. **II.** Adj.: *relaxed, slack, loose.* **1.** Lit.: ut onera contentis corporibus facilius feruntur, remissis opprimunt, Cic.; arcus, Hor.; vox remissior, Quint. **2.** Transf. **A.** Of the weather : *mild, gentle* : remissior ventus, Caes.; remissiora frigora, Caes. **B.** genus dicendi, Cic.; cantūs remissiores, Cic. **C.** Of character or behaviour. **a.** *mild, gentle, indulgent, unbending* : magistratūs, Cic.; Tac.; animus, Cic. *Comp.* : in ulciscendo, Cic.; in eo sermone, Cic.; amicitia, Cic.; ioci, Ov.; sermones, Suet. *Sup.* : Suet. *Masc.* as Noun : Cic. **b.** *slack, negligent, remiss* : Caes.; remissior in petendo, Cic.; esse remisso animo, Caes. *Masc.* as Noun : Hor. *Neut.* as Noun : Sall.

re-mittō, mittere, mīsī, missum. **I.** *to let go back.* **A.** *to send back* : a legione omnes remissi sunt domum, Pl.; aliquem domum, Caes.; mulieres Romam, Cic. Ep.; obsides alicui, Caes.; aliquem ad aliquem, Pl.; paucos in regnum, Caes.; argentum huc, Pl.; navis ad aliquem, Caes.; scripta ad eum mandata, Caes.; litteras Caesari, Caes.; Cic. Ep.; tigna umor aquae, Lucr. **B.** *to let go back* (from tension), *to slacken, relax.* **1.** Lit.: habenas, Cic.; bracchia, Verg.; frena, lora, digitos, vincla, Ov. Of *thawing* or *melting* : mella calor liquefacta remittit, Verg.; se purpureo vere humus, Tib. **2.** Transf. **a.** Intrans. **i.** ventus, Caes.; imbres, pestilentia, Liv.; dolores pedum, Cic.; Ter. **ii.** remittentibus tribunis plebis (i.e. from their opposition), Liv.; de maritimis custodiis, Caes.; de tributo, Liv. With *Intern. Acc.* : aliquid ex pristinā virtute, Caes.; aliquid de severitate, Cic.; de voluntate nihil, Cic.; Tac.; nihil ex adrogantiā, Tac.

b. Trans. **i.** Of the mind : imminui temporis contentionem, Caes.; curam et diligentiam, Caes.; curam animi, Cic.; ea studia, Cic.; animos a contentione pugnae, a certamine, a religione, Liv.; animos per festos dies licentius, Liv. In *Mid.*: cum remittor, lego, Plin. Ep. **ii.** In gen.: pugnam, Sall.; bellum, belli opera, Liv.; aliquid laboris, Liv.; aliquid iracundiae, Cic. **iii.** With *Inf.* : *to forbear, desist* : Ter., Sall., Hor. **II.** *to let go from oneself, give forth, yield, produce.* **1.** Lit.: umorem ex se, Verg.; sanguinem e pulmone, Ov.; quod baca remisit olivae, Hor. **2.** Transf. **A.** *to cast off, dismiss* : aliquid ex animo, Lucr.; opinionem animo, Cic. **B.** Of yielding to a request, etc. **a.** *to resign, concede, surrender, etc.* : Gallis imperium, Caes.; vestrum vobis beneficium, Caes.; Cic.; utramque provinciam, Cic.; veniam, Verg.; contionem (i.e. his intention of haranguing), Liv.; memoriam simultatium patriae (DAT.), Liv.; privata odia publicis utilitatibus, Tac.; integram causam ad senatum, Tac. **b.** *to let off, remit, forgive* : alicui noxiam, Pl.; iniuriam, Sall.; multam, Cic.; poenam alicui, Liv.; Ov. Of actual debts or obligations : aedis venditas tibi, Pl.; pecunias, Caes., Liv.; stipendium, Caes.; (navem ex foedere) remisisti in triennium, Cic. **III.** *to let go from oneself* or *send back in return* or *response.* **1.** Lit.: pila intercepta, Caes.; tractum de corpore telum, Ov. **2.** Transf.: specula simulacra, Lucr.; vocem nemora alta, Verg.; chorda sonum, Hor.

remixtus, a, um, *Part.* remisceō.

re-mōlior, īrī, *to heave back* : pondera terrae, Ov.; Sen.

re-mollēscō, ere, *to become soft again.* **1.** Lit.: sole unda, sole cera, Ov. **2.** Transf. **a.** ad laborem ferendum, Caes. **b.** precibus, Ov.

re-molliō, īre, *to make soft again.* Transf. **a.** Physically : *to weaken* : artūs, Ov. **b.** Of the feelings : eo se inhibitum ac remollitum, Suet.

re-mora, ae, *f. delay, hindrance* : quae remoram faciunt rei privatae et publicae, Pl.

remorāmina, um, *n. pl.* [remoror], *delays, hindrances* : Ov.

re-mordeō, mordēre, mōrsum. **I.** *to bite back* or *in return.* Transf.: aliquem, Hor. **II.** *to gnaw repeatedly, worry, fret.* Transf.: animus se, Lucr.; te cura, Verg.; libertatis desiderium animos, Liv.

re-moror, ārī. **A.** Intrans. *to stay behind, linger, loiter* : Cat., Lucr., Ov.; intus, Pl.; ibi, Lucr.; in Italiā, Liv. **B.** Trans. *to keep back, hinder, delay* : aliquem, Pl., Ov.; eae res, quae ceteros remorari solent, non retardarunt, Cic.; ab negotiis nunquam voluptas remorata, Sall.; nox atque praeda castrorum hostis quo minus victoriā uterentur remorata sunt, Sall.; Prop.; iter, Sall., Ov.; alicuius commodum, Ter.; meas spes, Cic. Ep. *Perf. Part.* in *Pass.* sense: Pl., Ov.

remōtē, *adv. at a distance, afar off.* *Comp.* : Cic.

remōtiō, ōnis, f. [removeō], *a putting away, removing.* Transf.: criminis, Cic.

remōtus, a, um. **I.** *Part.* removeō. **II.** Adj. **1.** Lit. **a.** *out of the way, retired, sequestered :* silvestribus ac remotis locis, Caes. ; pars domūs, i.e. penetralia, Ov. ; ab arbitris remoto loco, Cic. ; remoti ab oculis populi, Cic. *Comp. :* Ov. **b.** *distant, remote :* Gades, Hor. ; sedes remotas a Germanis, Caes. **2.** Transf. **a.** *far removed, separate, free from :* natura deorum sensibus ab nostris, Lucr. ; a Tib. Gracchi aequitate longissime remotus, Cic. ; sermo a forensi strepitu remotissimus, Cic. ; a vulgo longe lateque, Hor. **III.** *Neut. pl.* as Noun (philos. = reiectanea, q.v.) : Cic.

re-moveō, movēre, mōvi, mōtum (*Perf.* remōrunt, Ov. ; *Perf. Inf.* remōsse, Lucr. ; *Pluperf.* remōrant, Hor.), *to move or draw back ; to withdraw, put away or out of sight.* **1.** Lit.: pernam, Pl. ; dapes, mensam, Ov. ; tegimen, Ov. ; bracchia a latere, Quint. ; Ov. ; plura de medio, Cic. ; aliquem, Cic., Hor. ; pecora, Caes. ; equos ex conspectu, Caes. ; se a vulgo, Hor. ; navis longas ab onerariis navibus, Caes. Also, oculos, Cic. ; arcanis oculos profanos, Ov. **2.** Transf.: moram, Pl. ; sumptum, Cic. ; subtilitatem disputandi, Cic. ; metum, Sall., Tac. ; remoto ioco, Cic. Ep. ; aliquem a studio, Ter. ; aliquem ab re publicā, Caes., Liv. ; aliquem a vitā, Lucr. ; illam suspicionem a se, Cic. ; Ov. ; omnis tribu, Liv. ; ordine, Tac. ; pudorem thalamis, Ov. With *Refl. Pron. : to withdraw :* se a negotiis publicis, Cic. ; Ov. ; se a suspicione, Cic. ; se ab amicitia alicuius, Cic.

re-mūgiō, ire, *to bellow back or in reply :* ad mea verba, Ov. ; tympanum, Cat. ; Sibylla antro, Verg. ; gemitu nemus, Verg. ; mons, Hor.

re-mulceō, mulcēre, mulsi, *to stroke back :* caudam (i.e. droop), Verg.

remulcum, i, n. [perh. *cf.* Gk. ῥυμουλκέω), a *tow-rope or any other contrivance for towing :* Caes., Liv.

remūnerātiō, ōnis, f. [remūneror], *a repaying, recompense :* Cic. ; benevolentiae, Cic.

re-mūneror, āri (post-Aug. **remūnerō**, āre), *to repay, recompense :* Cic. ; aliquem munere, Cic. ; aliquem magno praemio, Caes. ; te his suppliciis, Cat. ; quibus officiis T. Anni beneficia remunerabor ? Cic. ; meritum, Liv.

re-murmurō, āre, *to murmur back in reply :* unda, Verg. ; pinus, Stat.

rēmus, i, m. [*cf.* Gk. ἐρετμός], *an oar.* **1.** Lit.: Pl., Cic., Verg., etc. ; remis navem incitare, Caes. ; remis contendere, Caes. ; remis insurgere, incumbere, Verg. *Prov. :* remis velisque, velis remisque, ventis remis, i.e. with all one's might, with all possible speed ; etc., Cic. **2.** Transf. **a.** Of the wings of birds : alarum, Ov. **b.** Of the hands and feet of a swimmer : Ov. **c.** orationem dialecticorum remis propellere (opp. to vela orationis pandere), i.e. to be content with argument without eloquence, Cic. [Fr. rame.]

Remus, i, m. *the brother of Romulus ; killed by him.*

re-nārrō, āre, *to tell over again :* facta, Ov. ; fata divum, Verg.

re-nāscor, nāsci, nātus, *to be born again ; to grow, rise, or spring up again.* **1.** Lit.: de nilo, Lucr. ; fibrae, Verg. ; corpore de patrio parvus phoenix, Ov. ; Pythagorae arcana renati, Hor. Comic.: (mosae) pinnae, Cic. Ep. **2.** Transf.: velut ab stirpibus laetius feraciusque renatae urbis, Liv. ; (fluvius) alio orbe, Ov. ; bellum, Cic. Ep., Liv., Tac. ; principium exstinctum non ipsum ab alio renascetur, Cic. ; Troiae renascens fortuna, Hor. ; vocabula, Hor.

renātus, a, um, *Part.* renāscor.

re-nāvigō, āre, *to sail back :* Cic. Ep.

re-neō, nēre, *to unspin, unravel :* fila (of destiny), Ov.

rēnēs, renum, m. pl. *the kidneys :* Pl., Cic., Hor.

renīdeō, ēre, *to shine back, reflect light, be resplendent.* **1.** Lit.: domus argento fulgenti, Lucr. ; fluctuat aere renidenti tellus, Verg. ; Lares, Hor. ; non ebur meā in domo, Hor. **2.** Transf. **a.** *to beam with joy :* puer, Ov. ; ore renidenti, Ov. Also, hilarior oratio, Quint. With *Acc.* and *Inf. :* Hor. **b.** *to smile, laugh :* Cat. ; renidens ait, Liv. With *Intern. Acc. :* falsum renidens vultu, Tac.

renīdēscō, ere [renīdeō], *to begin to shine back or reflect light :* aere tellus, Lucr.

re-nītor, nīti, *to strive or struggle against, to withstand.* **1.** Lit.: alter alteri, Plin. **2.** Transf.: cum illi renitentes pactos dicerent sese, Liv.

re-nō, nāre, *to swim or float back :* imis saxa vadis levata, Hor.

rēnō or **rhēnō**, ōnis, m. [a Celtic word], *fur, a fur-garment :* Caes., Sall.

re-nōdō, āre. **I.** *to tie back in a knot :* comam, Hor. **II.** *to untie :* Val. Fl.

renovāmen, inis, n. [renovō], *a renewal, new condition :* Ov.

renovātiō, ōnis, f. [renovō]. **I.** *a renewing, renewal.* **1.** Lit.: mundi, Cic. **2.** Transf.: doctrinae, Cic. ; auspiciorum, Liv. **II.** *compound interest :* centesimis sexenni ductis cum renovatione singulorum annorum, Cic.

re-novō, āre, *to make new again ; to restore, renovate, repair.* **1.** Lit. **a.** mare fontes, Lucr. ; templum, Cic. ; durum arvum (by ploughing) ; also, by leaving fallow), Ov. ; veteres colonias, Cic. **b.** *to take compound interest :* renovato in singulos annos faenore, Cic. Ep. **2.** Transf. **a.** *to renew, restore, revive :* scelus, institutum, vetus exemplum, Cic. ; veterem iram, Tac. ; bellum, Caes., Cic., Liv. ; proelium, Caes., Sall., Ov. ; omnis casūs, Verg. ; sacra rite, Liv. ; memoriam prope intermortuam, Cic. ; Liv. ; foedus, Liv. ; dextras, Tac. ; florem aetatis ex morbo, Liv. ; annos, Ov. ; senectutem, Ov. **b.** *to repeat, reaffirm :* de lege renovabo ea quae dicta sunt, Cic. With *ut* and *Jussive Subj. :* Liv. **c.** *to refresh, revive :* quies renovavit corpora animosque ad omnia patienda, Liv. ; Cic. ; se novis opibus copiisque, Cic. ; virtus animum a satietate, Quint.

re-numerō, āre, *to count over again.* Of money : *to pay back :* aurum alicui, Pl. ; dotem huc, Ter.

renūntiātiō, ōnis, *f.* [renūntiō], *a formal report* or *return.* **a.** In gen. : cognoscite renuntiationem ex litteris publicis, Cic. **b.** *a return* made by the presiding official at elections : Cic. ; suffragiorum, Cic.

re-nūntiō, āre. **I.** *to bring back word, to report.* **A.** In gen. : Pl., Ter. ; hoc mihi, Pl. ; nihil, Suet. ; meae uxori de pallā, Pl. ; istaec tibi renuntiantur (with Acc. and *Inf.*), Pl. ; Ter. With *Indir. Quest.* : Ter. *Impers. Pass.* : Pl. ; (with Acc. and *Inf.*), Cic. Ep. **B.** Of official reports. **a.** Cic. ; postulata Caesaris, Caes. ; legationem, Cic., Liv. ; Volusenus revertitur quaeque ibi perspexisset renuntiat, Caes. ; haec dicta legatis renuntiataque in consilium, Liv. ; acta tua domum ad senatum suum renuntiaverunt, Cic. With (or without) DAT. of person, and Acc. and *Inf.* : Caes., Cic., Liv. **b.** Of election-returns : *to return, declare elected* : aliquem consulem, Cic., Liv. ; ter praetor primus centuriis cunctis renuntiatus sum, Cic. **II.** *to retract a promise, etc.* ; *to renounce, revoke, call off* : Cic. Ep. ; hospitium alicui, Cic. ; societatem et amicitiam alicui, Liv. ; Tac. ; alicui prandium, Sen. (*cf.* iube domi, cenam coqui atque ad illum renuntiari, Pl.) With DAT. : ne Stoicis renuntiaretur, Cic. ; civilibus officiis, Quint. ; vitae, Suet.

re-nūntius, ī, *m.* *one who brings back news* : Pl.

re-nuō, nuere, nuī, *to deny by a motion of the head, to deny, refuse* : Hor., Tac. ; renuente deo, Ov. ; Tib. With DAT. : crimini, Cic. ; alicui, Tac. With Acc. : convivium, Cic. ; Hor.

renūtō, āre [*freq.* renuō], *to refuse repeatedly* or *positively* (with *Inf.*) : Lucr.

reor, (rērī), ratus [*cf.* ratiō], *to reckon, calculate.* Transf. *to think, suppose, deem* : quos quidem pluris quam rebar esse cognovi, Cic. ; Pl. In parenthesis : reor *or* ut reor, Cic. ; ut rebatur, Liv. ; ut rebare, Verg. With Acc. and *Inf.* : Pl., Cic., Verg., etc. With Acc. and *Predic. Adj.* : omnia potiora fide Iugurthae rebatur, Sall. ; Italiam tu iam rere propinquam, Verg.

repāgula, ōrum, *n. pl.* [re and pag- in pangō], *bolts, bars* of a door. **1.** L i t. : Pl., Cic., Ov. **2.** T r a n s f. : omnia repagula iuris perfringere, Cic.

re-pandus, a, um, *bent* or *curved backwards* or *upwards* : Lucil. ; calceoli, Cic.

reparābilis, e, *adj.* [reparō], *that may be repaired, retrievable* : damnum, Ov. ; Sen.

re-parcō, *v.* repercō.

re-parō, āre. **I.** *to get* or *acquire again.* **A.** *to recover, make good, retrieve.* **1.** L i t. : amissas res, Hor. ; id eodem ex agro, Cic. **2.** T r a n s f. : damna, Hor. ; exercitum (*to recruit*), Liv. ; Tac. ; corpora fessa labori, Ov. ; animos, Liv. **B.** *to restore, repair, renew.* **1.** L i t. : tecta Troiae, Hor. ; sublapsa aedificia, Plin. Ep. **2.** T r a n s f. : tribuniciam potestatem, Liv. ; bellum, Liv. ; populos artibus, Ov. **II.** *to get in return* or *exchange.* **1.** L i t. : vina merce, Hor. **2.** T r a n s f. : latentia classe citā oras, Hor.

repastinātiō, ōnis, *f.* [repastinō], *a digging up again* (in *pl.*) : agri, Cic.

re-pascuo, āre, *to dig up again ; to stock, Varr.*

re-pectō, pectere, pexum, *to comb back* or *again* : comam, Ov.

re-pedō, āre, [pēs], *to step back* : Lucil.

re-pellō, repellere, reppulī, repulsum, *to drive* or *push back, repulse, repel.* **1.** L i t. : homines inermos armis, Cic. ; eum his foribus, Pl. ; Hor. ; Ov. ; Liv. ; nostros ab castris, Caes. ; Cic. ; Liv. ; hostis in silvas, Caes. ; mihi manum, Pl. ; telum aere repulsum, Verg. ; mensas, Ov. P o e t. : iuvenis pedibus tellure repulsā arduus in nubes abiit, Ov. ; Verg. **2.** T r a n s f. : aliquem a consulatu, Cic. ; Liv. ; a cognitione legum, Cic. ; ab hac spe repulsi, Caes. ; procos, Ov. ; Prop. ; ictūs, Caes. ; cute ictūs, Ov. ; furores Clodi a cervicibus vestris, Cic. ; vim, pericula, Cic. ; conubia nostra, Verg. ; fraudem, Ov.

re-pendō, pendere, pondī, pēnsum. **1.** L i t. **a.** *to weigh in return, return by weight* : pensa erae, Ov. ; Prop. **b.** *to return in payment (by weight)* : cui (Septumuleio) pro C. Gracchi capite erat aurum repensum, Cic. **2.** T r a n s f. **a.** *to pay in return, repay* : magna, Verg. ; pretium vitae, Prop. ; gratiam facto, Ov. ; suum decus cuique (posteritas), Tac. **b.** *to pay for in return* : hac vitam servatae dote rependis ? Ov. ; Plin. Pan. **c.** *to counterbalance, compensate* : fatis contraria fata rependens, Verg. ; damna formae ingenio, Ov.

repēns, entis, *Part.* rēpō.

repēns, entis, *adj.* *sudden, hasty, unexpected* (mostly in NOM. *sing.*). **1.** L i t. : Cic., Verg., Ov., Liv. Instead of *Adv.* : (Ianus) bina repens oculis obtulit ora meis, Ov. **2.** T r a n s f. (for recens), *new, recent* : Tac.

repēnsō, āre [*freq.* rependō], *to recompense* : merita meritis, Sen.

repēnsus, a, um, *Part.* rependō.

repente, *adv.* [repēns], *suddenly, unexpectedly* : Pl., Caes., Cic., Verg., etc.

repentinus, a, um [repēns], *sudden, hasty, unexpected* : bonum, Ter. ; consilia, defectio, coniuratio, Caes. ; mors, amor, edictum, Cic. ; periculum, Caes., Cic. ; nobilitas, Liv. ; repentinus et tumultuarius exercitus, Liv. ; venenum, Tac. ; ignoti homines et repentini, i.e. upstarts, Cic. ABL. *n.* **repentinō** as *Adv., suddenly, unexpectedly* : Pl., Caes., Cic.

re-percō (-parcō), percere, persī or pepercī [parcō], *to be sparing* with anything. With DAT. : Pl. With Acc. of *Neut. Pron.* : Lucr.

repercussus, a, um, *Part.* repercutiō.

repercussus, ūs, *m.* [repercutiō], *a rebounding, repercussion,* of light, sound, wind, etc. : solis, Plin. Ep. ; vocis, Tac.

re-percutiō, cutere, cussī, cussum, *to make to rebound, reverberate, re-echo from a hard blow* : (mostly, until Quint., in *Perf. Part.* **repercussus**, *rebounding, reverberating, re-echoing*). **1.** L i t. : discus repercussus in aëra, Ov. ; clamores augebant nemora repercussae valles, Liv. ; montis anfractu repercussae voces, Tac. **2.** T r a n s f. **a.** Of light : *reflected* : lumen, Verg. ; Ov. ; of water :

quod huius fontis excursum repercutiat, Plin. Ep. **b.** *to beat back, repel* by retort : aliena, Quint. ; orationes dicto, Plin.

re-perĭō, reperīre, repperī, repertum [parĭō], *to produce again ; * hence, *to find* what is lost or that for which one is searching ; *to find out.* **1.** Lit. : aliquem, Pl., Ter., Cic. ; aliquid, Pl., Caes., Verg. **2.** Transf. **a.** *to find, get, obtain : * propter paupertatem nomen, Pl. ; occasionem, Pl. ; gloriam armis, Ter. ; sibi salutem, Caes. ; veras amicitias, Cic. ; rem omnem ex tuo magistro, Pl. **b.** *to find, find out, ascertain, learn.* With *Predic. Adj.* or *Part.,* etc. : omnis inimicos mihi istoc facto repperi, Pl. ; hoc si secus reperies, Pl. (In *Pass.* : ingratus repertus est, Pl. ; Cic.) With Acc. and *Inf. : * Pl., Caes., Cic., etc. (in *Pass.* with Nom. and *Inf. : * in eas Italiae partis Pythagoras venisse dicitur, Cic. ; Lucr.). With *Indir. Quest. : * Caes. **c.** *to find out something new ; to invent, devise : * sibi aliquam astutiam, Pl. ; nihil novi, Cic. ; serrae repperit usum, Ov. ; ipse vias sibi repperit usus, Verg. ; ludus scaenicus repertus, Hor. ; Quint.

repertor, ōris, *m.* [reperĭō], *a discoverer : * vitis, Varr. ; mellis, Ov. ; medicinae, Verg. ; doctrinarum, Lucr. ; novi iuris, Tac. ; facinorum omnium, Tac.

repertus, a, um. **I.** *Part.* reperĭō. **II.** Noun, **reperta,** ōrum, *n. pl. discoveries, inventions : * Lucr.

repetitiō, ōnis, *f.* [repetō]. **I.** *a repeating, repetition : * eiusdem nominis, Quint. **II.** Rhet. : *a repetition of the same word at the beginning of several sentences* (ἀναφορά): Cic., Quint.

repetitor, ōris, *m.* [repetō], *one who demands back, a reclaimer : * nuptae ademptae, Ov.

re-petō, petere, petīvī or petii, petītum, *to make for back again, to try to reach again, to return to ; to aim at again.* **1.** Lit. **a.** In gen. : urbem, Verg. ; Macedoniam, Nep. ; Penatis ab orā Hispanā, Hor. ; castra, Liv. ; retro Apuliam, Liv. ; fratresque virumque, Ov. Rarely, viam quā venisset (for locum quā viā venisset), Liv. **b.** *to return for and fetch back : * filium istinc, Pl. ; sarcinas relictas, Caes. ; aliquem, Cic. ; alios elephantos, Liv. ; aurum ab Theotimo domum, Pl. **c.** *to make for again* as an enemy, *to attack again : * Quint. ; regem saepius, Liv. ; Nolam armis, Liv. ; quater exegit repetita per ilia ferrum, Ov. Hence in law, *to prosecute again : * aliquem, Suet. **2.** Transf. **A.** *to return to, resume, renew, repeat : * eadem vetera consilia, Cic. ; longo intervallo haec studia, Cic. ; relicta, Hor. ; pauca supra, Sall. ; verba, Ov. ; auspicia de integro, Liv. ; pugnam, Liv. ; iter, Ov. ; sollemnia, Tac. With *Inf. : * Lucr. With Acc. and *Inf. : * Quint. **B.** *to go back to* the beginning or source ; *to derive or trace : * populi originem, Cic. ; populum a stirpe, Cic. ; aliquid a Platonis auctoritate, Cic. ; ab ultimā antiquitate, Cic. ; verba ex ultimis tenebris, ex vetustate, Quint. ; Cic. ; alte repetita oratio, Cic. ; altius repetita atque enumeratis diebus, Caes. **C.** Esp. with memoriā, memoriam, *to*

*return to in memory, return to the recollection of ; to recall, recollect : * mihi memoriā vetera repetenti, Cic. ; temporis illius memoriam, Cic. ; memoriam ex annalibus, Liv. Without memoriā or memoriam : Cic., Sall., Verg. ; animo exempla, Verg. ; tuos fastūs, Prop. ; noctem, Ov. With Acc. and *Predic. Part. : * repeto me correptum ab eo, etc., Plin. Ep. Abl. *n.* of *Perf. Part.* (with Acc. and *Inf.*): Tac. **D.** *to demand back* (in restitution or satisfaction), *to claim back.* **a.** In gen. : mutuom, Pl. ; bona sua, Cic. ; ereptas pecunias, Cic. ; obsides, Caes. ; ab aliquo pecuniam, Cic. ; urbes bello superatas in antiquum ius, Liv. ; repetita Proserpina, Verg. ; eam dignitatem, Cic. ; poenas ab aliquo, Cic. ; beneficia ab aliquo, Sall. ; pro eo beneficio gratiam, Liv. ; libertatem, Cic., Liv., Tac. ; civitatem in libertatem, Liv. *Impers. Pass.* with *ut* and *Subj.* : Liv. **b.** Of a public demand by the fetiales : repetere res, Cic., Sall., Liv. **c.** In law, res repetere, *to claim one's property* before a court : Cic.

repetundae, ārum, *f. pl.* (with or without pecuniae), *money, etc.* (extorted, etc. by any State official) *of which the return is required ; * hence *the offence of extortion in government : * L. Piso de pecuniis repetundis legem primus tulit, Cic. ; accusare aliquem de pecuniis repetundis, Cic. ; pecuniarum repetundarum reus, Sall. ; repetundarum teneri, argui, damnari, absolvi, Tac.

repexus, a, um, *Part.* repectō.

re-pleō, plēre, plēvī, plētum. **I.** *to fill again, fill up, replenish, restore to fulness.* **1.** Lit. : exhaustas domos, Cic. ; repleto his rebus exercitu, Caes. ; exercitum, Liv. ; scrobes terrā, Verg. ; haustum cratera, Ov. **2.** Transf. : quod voci deerat plangore replebam, Ov. ; Quint. **II.** *to fill to overflowing (cf.* refercio). **1.** Lit. : terras, Enn. ; templa, Cic. ; delubra corporibus, Lucr. ; campos strage hominum, Liv. ; sanguine venas, Ov. ; repleti amnes, Verg. ; foramen auris, Lucr. With Gen. : repletae semitae puerorum et mulierum, Liv. **2.** Transf. : auris, Pl. ; nemora gemitu, Lucr. ; Verg. ; populus sermone, Verg. ; pontum rumore, Ov. ; vias oculorum luce, Lucr. ; numerum, Lucr. ; (terra) trepido terrore repleta, Lucr. ; vi morbi repletos, Liv. ; eruditione variā repletus, Suet.

replicātiō, ōnis, *f.* [replicō], *a folding or rolling back.* Transf. : ut replicatione quādam mundi motum regat, Cic.

re-plicō, āre, *to fold back, unfold, turn back.* **1.** Lit. : surculos ad vitis caput, Cato ; labra, Quint. **2.** Transf. : memoriam temporum, annalium memoriam, Cic.

rēpō, rēpere, rēpsī [cf. ἕρπω, serpō], *to creep, crawl.* **1.** Lit. : repens animans, Lucr. ; cochleae inter saxa, Sall. ; quā unus homo vix poterat repere, Nep. **2.** Transf. **a.** Of any slow motion : milia tum pransi tria repimus, Hor. Of boats : Enn. Of clouds : Lucr. Of a snare : Stat. **b.** sermones repentes per humum, Hor.

re-pōnō, pōnere, posui (posīvī, Pl.), positum (*Perf. Part.* repostus, poet.). **I.** *to lay backwards, lay (or bend) back : * cervicem,

Lucr., Quint. ; pullus mollia crura, Verg. ;
Enn. **II.** *to put, place,* or *lay back ;* *to
replace.* **1.** Lit. **a.** insigne regium quod
abiecerat, Cic. ; pilleum apte, Liv. ; humum, Verg. ; lapidem suo loco, Cic. ;
pecuniam in thesauris, Liv. ; se in oubitum,
Hor. ; togam, Quint. **b.** *to replace* with
a substitute ; *to restore :* nummos, Pl. ;
flammis ambesa robora navigiis, Verg. ;
ruptos vetustate pontis, Tac. ; amissa
urbi, Tac. ; ligna super foco, Hor. ; plena
pocula, Verg. ; epulas, Verg. ; cibos,
Quint. ; vina mensis, Verg. ; donata, Hor.
2. Transf. **a.** *to replace, restore :* nos in
sceptra, Verg. ; Quint. **b.** *to substitute :*
Aristophanem pro Eupoli, Cic. Ep. ; nec
vera virtus, cum semel excidit, curat reponi
deterioribus, Hor. **c.** *to repay, return like
for like :* Juv. ; tibi idem, Cic. Ep. ; iniuriam, Sen. **III.** *to place, put, lay in the
due, right, natural,* or *expected place.* **1.**
Lit. : grues in tergo praevolantium colla
et capita, Cic. ; litteras in gremio, Liv. ;
membra toro, Verg. ; nidum ante foris
sacras, Ov. **2.** Transf. **a.** *to place, rest*
(hopes, etc.) *in reliance on :* spem omnem
in virtute, Caes. ; Liv. ; in se omnem spem,
Cic. ; in vestra mansuetudine causam
totam, Cic. ; plus in duce quam in exercitu,
Tac. ; Liv. ; fiduciam in re, Plin. Ep. **b.**
to place, reckon among : sidera in deorum
numero, Cic. ; homines morte deletos in
deos, Cic. ; aliquid in fabularum numerum,
Cic. **IV.** *to put away* or *aside, lay up in
reserve, put on the shelf, store up.* **1.** Lit. :
remum, Pl. ; arma, Caes. ; onus, Cat. ;
telasque infectaque pensa, Ov. ; fructus,
Cic. ; caseum hiemi, Verg. ; alimenta in
hiemem, Quint. ; Caecubum ad festas dapes,
Hor. ; farris acervum tecto, Verg. Poet. :
falcem arbusta reponunt, Verg. ; eadem
(gratia) sequitur tellure repostos (laid in
their graves), Verg. ; Hor. ; Prop. **2.**
Transf. : manet alta mente repostum
iudicium Paridis, Verg. ; aliquid scriptis,
Quint. ; odium, Tac.

re-portō, are, *to carry* or *bring back.* **1.** Lit.
a. In gen. : aurum ab Theotimo domum,
Pl. ; candelabrum secum in Syriam, Cic. ;
massam picis urbe, Verg. ; naves, quibus
(milites) reportari possent, Caes. ; Tac. ;
exercitum duobus commeatibus, Caes. ;
legiones, Liv. ; ducem, Hor. Poet. :
reportare pedem, Verg. ; quos variae viae
reportant, Cat. **b.** Of spoils, etc. : nihil
ex praeda domum suam, Cic. ; a rege
insignia victoriae, non victoriam, Cic. ;
Also, gloriam ex proconsulatu, Plin. Ep.
2. Transf. **a.** In gen. : spem bonam
certamque domum reporto, Hor. ; (Echo)
audita verba reportat, Ov. **b.** Of a
report : adytis haec tristia dicta reportat,
Verg. ; Prop. With Acc. and *Inf. :* Verg.

re-pōscō, ere, *to demand back.* **1.** Lit. :
Cic. ; virginem, Pl. ; pecuniam, Tac. ;
Pl. ; ab hac puerum, Pl. With double
Acc. : Parthos signa, Verg. ; Pl. : Cic.
2. Transf. *to demand back* or *as due, to
claim :* attentas auris, Lucr. ; vitam mea
fata, Prop. ; foedus flammis, Verg. ; pretium libelli, Plin. Ep. ; aliquem ad poenas,
Verg. ; poenas ab aliquo, Cat. ; ab altero

rationem vitae, Cic. ; rationem reposcere
(with *Indir. Quest.*), Liv. ; similitudo
periculi datum auxilium, Liv.

repositōrium, I, *n.* [repōnō], *a stand, tray,
waiter, etc. :* Plin., Sen. Ep.

repositus (repostus), a, um. **I.** *Part.*
repōnō. **II.** Adj. *remote, distant :* Mas-
sylum gentes, Verg.

repostor, ōris, *m.* [repōnō], *a restorer :* templorum, Ov.

repostus, a, um, *v.* repositus.

repōtia, ōrum, *n. pl.* [pōtō], *a* (second)
drinking or *carousing on the day after an
entertainment :* Hor.

repraesentātiō, ōnis, *f.* [repraesentō]. **I.**
Rhet. *a bringing before one, vividness of
presentation :* Quint. **II.** Mercant. *a
cash-payment :* Cic. Ep.

repraesentō, āre [praesēns], *to make present
again, to bring back actually* or *vividly,
to reproduce.* **1.** Lit. : si repraesentari
morte mea libertas civitatis potest, Cic. ;
virtutem moresque Catonis, Hor. ; templum repraesentabat memoriam consulatus
mei, Cic. ; memorias vis aliquid, Quint. ;
adfectum patris amissi, Plin. Ep. ; cum
iras caelestis repraesentatas casibus suis
exposuisset, Liv. **2.** Transf. *to do on the
spot* or *at once.* **a.** *to execute immediately*
or *without delay ;* hence, *to hasten ;* aliquid,
Caes. ; temporis medicinam, Cic. Ep. ;
poenam, Phaedr. ; tormenta poenasque,
Suet. **b.** Commerc. : *to pay* (spot) *cash :*
pecuniam, Cic. Ep. ; Suet.

re-prehendō (-prendō), endere, endi, ēnsum. **I.** *to lay hold of for the purpose of
pulling back ;* hence, *to hold back.* **1.**
Lit. : aliquem pallio, Pl. ; quosdam manu,
Liv. **2.** Transf. **a.** *to hold back, restrain,
check :* reprendi me ne etc., Ter. ; res ab
exitio euntis, Lucr. ; virtus reprehendit
manu, Cic. **b.** *to hold fast, retain :* aliquid
memori mente, Lucr. **c.** *to blame, censure,
reprove :* Cic. ; aliquem, Ter., Cic., etc. ;
aliquem communi vituperatione, Cic. ;
temeritatem cupiditatemque militum, Caes. ;
Cic. ; aliquid in eo, Cic. ; Caes. ; nihil
in Homero, Hor. ; ea res communi iudicio
reprehendebatur, Caes. **d.** Rhet. *to refute :*
Cic. **II.** *to lay hold of again, return to :*
quod erat imprudentia praetermissum, Cic. ;
Ter.

reprehēnsiō, ōnis, *f.* [reprehendō], *a holding
back.* Transf. **a.** *a checking, check,* in
speaking : Cic. **b.** *blame, censure, reprimand, reproof :* iusta reprehensione carere,
Cic. ; sine reprehensione, Quint., Tac. ;
citra reprehensionem, Quint. ; capere,
Quint. With *Obj.* Gen. : culpae, etc.,
Cic. ; Quint. With *Subj.* Gen. : doctorum,
Cic. In *pl. :* Cic., Quint. **c.** *the fault
blamed :* Quint. ; emacitatis, Plin. Ep.
d. Rhet. : *refutation :* Cic., Quint.

reprehēnsō, āre [freq. reprehendō], *to hold
back repeatedly* or *eagerly* or *strongly :* singulos, Liv.

reprehēnsor, ōris, *m.* [reprehendō]. **I.** *a
censurer, reprehender :* Cic. ; delicti, Ov.
II. *one who is entitled to revise* or *modify :*
comitiorum, Cic.

repressor, ōris, *m.* [reprimō], *a restrainer :*
Cic.

re-prīmō, primere, pressī, pressum [premō], *to press* or *keep back ; to check, curb, restrain.* **1.** Lit.: labra, Pl.; dextram, Verg.; retro pedem, Verg.; cursum, fugam, Caes.; lacum Albanum, Cic.; currentia vina, Verg.; aliquem, Caes., Cic. **2.** Transf.: iracundiam, Ter.; conatūs alicuius, Cic.; alacritatem, Caes.; ferocitatem, fletum, etc., Cic.; gemitum, Ov.; odium suum a corpore alicuius, Cic.; memoria repressa vetustate, Cic.; me horum aspectus in ipso cursu orationis, Cic.; Ter.; me reprimam ne etc., Ter. In *Mid.* : vix reprimor quin etc., Pl.

reprōmissiō, ōnis, *f.* [reprōmittō], *a counterpromise :* Cic.

re-prōmittō, mittere, mīsī, missum. **I.** *to promise in return, to engage* or *bind oneself.* **1.** Lit. (commerc.): aliquid alioui, Pl., Cic. **2.** Transf.: tibi istuc, Cic.; ad hunc gustum totum librum, Plin. Ep. **II.** *to promise again :* Suet.

rēptō, āre [*freq.* rēpō], *to creep, crawl about.* **1.** Lit.: Plin. **2.** Transf. (of walking slowly or lazily): Pl., Lucr., Hor., Plin. Ep.

repudiātiō, ōnis, *f.* [repudiō], *a rejection, refusal:* Cic. Ep.; supplicum, Cic.

repudiō, āre [repudium], *to reject, refuse; to scorn, repudiate.* **a.** In gen.: condicionem, Pl.; consilium, Ter.; gratiam populi, Caes.; eius vota a vestris mentibus, Cic.; legem, Cic.; aliquem, Pl., Caes., Cic. **b.** Of a betrothed or wife : *to put away, cast off, divorce :* Pl., Ter., Quint., Suet.

repudiōsus, a, um [repudium], *that ought to be rejected, offensive :* nuptiae, Pl.

repudium, ī, *n. a putting away, a separation, divorce, repudiation :* prop. of a betrothed, but also of a wife: renuntiare repudium sponsae, Pl.; remittere uxori, Pl., Suet.; dicere, Tac.

re-puerāscō, ere, *to become a child again.* **1.** Lit.: Cic. **2.** Transf. *to play* or *frolic like a child :* Pl., Cic.

repugnāns, antis. **I.** *Part.* repugnō. **II.** Noun, **repugnantia**, ium, *n. pl.* Rhet.: *contradictions :* Cic.; Quint.

repugnanter, *adv. reluctantly :* Cic.

repugnantia, ae, *f.* [repugnō], *resistance.* Hence, *antagonism, incompatibility :* rerum, Cic.; inter honesta et utilia, Cic.; inducere, Cic.

re-pugnō, āre, *to fight against, oppose, resist.* **1.** Lit.: nostri primo integris viribus fortiter repugnare, Caes.; Verg.; Liv. **2.** Transf. **a.** *to oppose, offer opposition :* Catone acerrime repugnante, Caes.; Cic.; de praedā volucres, Lucr.; natura, Cic. With *Dat.* : fortunae, Cic.; dictis, amori, Ov.; historiae, Quint.; alicui, Cic. Ep., Plin. Ep.; his omnibus rebus unum repugnabat quod etc., Caes. With *contra :* contra veritatem, Cic. With *ne* and *Subj.* : Ov.; also, when negatived, with *quo minus* and *Subj.* : Cic. With *Inf.* : Ov. **b.** *to oppose from natural incongruity, to disagree with, be inconsistent, incompatible :* haec inter se, Cic.; simulatio amicitiae, Cic.; illud repugnat (with Acc. and *Inf.*), Cic.

repulsa, ae, *f.* [repellō], *a rejection, repulse.* **a.** In candidature for an office : Caes.,

Cic., Hor.; ferre (i.e. *miss being elected*), Cic.; solari, Tac.; omnis magistratūs sine repulsā adsequi, Cic.; cum repulsā, Cic.; consulatūs, Cic. **b.** In gen.: *a refusal, denial :* fatigatos tot repulsis Aetolos, Liv.; amor crescit dolore repulsae, Ov.; pati, Ov.

re-pulsāns, antis, *throbbing in return.* Transf. of re-echoing: *throbbing with :* colles verba repulsantes, Luor.; pectus dicta, Lucr.

repulsū, *Abl. m. sing.* [repellō], *by* or *with repulsion* (i.e. reflexion, reverberation): effigies crebro repulsu reiectae, Lucr.; scopulorum, Cic. poet.

repulsus, a, um, *Part.* repellō.

re-pungō, ere, *to prick* or *goad again.* Transf.: illorum animos, Cic. Ep.

re-pūrgō, āre, *to restore to a normal* (or *required*) *clean* or *clear state ; to clean* or *clear again.* **1.** Lit.: iter (of obstacles), Liv.; caelum (of clouds), Ov.; alveum Tiberis, Suet. **2.** Transf. (of purging away): Ov., Plin.

reputātiō, ōnis, *f.* [reputō], *a reviewing in thought :* veterum novorumque morum, Tac.

re-putō, āre. **I.** *to calculate back in the past :* solis defectiones, Cic.; tempora, Tac. **II.** *to review in thought, to think over, reflect upon :* Tac.; haec mecum, Ter.; Sall.; Tac.; cum animo facinus suum, Sall.; hoc animo reputet (with Acc. and *Inf.*), Liv.; haec, Cic.; Pl.; scelera sua, Tac. With Acc. and *Inf.* : Cic. Ep., Tac. With *Indir. Quest.* : Pl., Cic. Ep., Sall.

re-quiēs, ētis, *f.* (Acc. requiētem and requiem, Cic.; Voc. requiēs, Lucr. Abl. requiēte, Cic. poet., requiē, Ov.; the other cases are not found), *repose* from labour, trouble, etc.; *rest, relaxation, recreation :* Lucr., Cic., Verg., Tac., etc.; laborum, Verg.; curarum, Cic. With *Subj.* Gen.: pedum, Hor.

re-quiēscō, quiēscere, quiēvī, quiētum (*sync.* requiērunt, Verg.; requiērant, Cat.; requiēsset, Cat.; requiēsse, Liv.). **A.** Intrans.: *to become at rest again* or *after labour.* **1.** Lit. **a.** *to rest, repose :* Pl.; legiones, Caes.; in nostris sedibus, Cat.; in sellā, Cic.; lecto, Prop.; sub umbrā, Verg.; somno molli, Cat.; a rei publicae muneribus, Cic.; Ov. **b.** Of the dead: in sepulcro, Cic.; in urnā, Ov. **2.** Transf. **a.** Of things: *to find rest :* luce sacrā humus, Tib.; aures a strepitu, Liv.; Cat.; vitis in ulmo, Ov. Also, *to cease :* amor, Tib.; labor, Quint. **b.** *to repose, find rest :* in spe alicuius, Cic.; Quint.; animus ex multis miseriis, Sall. **B.** Trans.: *to put* or *lay at rest again, to rest again :* (perh. in) requierunt flumina cursūs, Verg. In *Pass. Part.* : paululum requietis militibus, Sall.; militem requietum, integrum, Liv.; ager, Ov.

requīritō, āre [*freq.* requīrō], *to keep on asking after :* res novas, Pl.

re-quīrō, quīrere, quīsīvī or quīsītum, *to search for somebody* or *something missing* or *lost.* **1.** Lit. **a.** In gen.: aliquem, Pl., Caes., Cic.; iuvenem oculīsque animoque,

Ov. ; ossa, Ov. ; extractum anulum, Suet. ;
portūs Velinos, Verg. ; arma toro tectisque,
Verg. **b.** *to seek* (for the satisfaction of
some want) : libros, Cic. ; vinum genero-
sum, Hor. **2.** T r a n s f. **a.** *to seek to
know, to inquire after* : Cic., Ov., Quint. ;
rationes rerum, Cic. ; vera, Lucr. ; causani,
Ov. With *Indir. Quest.* : Pl., Cic., Verg.,
etc. *Impers. Pass.* : Cic. **b.** With *prep.*
and ABL. of person, *to inquire of, to question* :
nihil ex te, Cic. ; aliquid de antiquitate
ab aliquo, Nep. ; Cic. ; ex aliquo (with
Indir. Quest.), Cic., Tac. **c.** *to ask for
something needed* ; *to need, want, require* :
quid requirat, ut sit beatior, Cic. ; magnam
res diligentiam requirebat, Caes. ; in hoc
bello virtutes animi magnae et multae
requiruntur, Cic. ; divitias, Tib. **d.** *to
perceive to be wanting, to look in vain for,
to miss* : pristinum morem iudiciorum, Cic. ;
Caesaris in se indulgentiam requirunt,
Caes. ; aliquem, Ov.

requisītus, a, um, *Part.* requīrō.

rēs, reī, *f.* (rēī, GEN. and DAT., Lucr. ; also
rēī, Lucr., etc.) [perh. *cf.* reor, ratus].
I. In gen. : *a thing, matter, affair, circumstance, occurrence, etc.* : de Alcumenā ut
rem teneatis rectius, Pl. ; de rerum naturā,
Lucr. ; divinarum humanarumque rerum,
Cic. ; si res postulavit, Cic. ; rerum scriptor,
Liv. ; sunt lacrimae rerum, Verg. ; bellicam rem, Cic. ; iudiciaria, militaria, navalis,
rustica, uxoria, etc., *trials, war, nautical
affairs, husbandry, matrimony, etc.* ; res
mala, Sall. ; res bonae, secundae, prosperae,
adversae, dubiae, Pl., Cic., Hor., Liv., etc.
Emphatically with *Sup.* : scilicet rerum
facta est pulcherrima Roma, Verg. ; quid
agis dulcissime rerum? Hor. A d v e r b i a l
p h r a s e s : pro re, *according to circumstances* : ipse pro re atque loco paulatim
procedere, Sall. ; Caes. ; Verg., etc. ; pro
re natā, *as matters stand*, Cic. Ep. ; e re,
Ter., Cat. **II.** In partic. **1.** *reality* as
opp. to appearance, opinion, talk, etc. ;
an actual thing, the thing itself, fact, truth :
re experior quanti facias uxorem, Pl. ;
rem opinor spectari oportere, non verba,
Cic. ; qui hos deos non re sed opinione esse
dicunt, Cic. ; vides quantum distet argumentatio tua ab re ipsā atque a veritate,
Cic. ; nihil est aliud in re, Liv. Hence in
ABL. *sing.*, re *or* in verā, *in reality*, Cic.,
Lucr., Liv., etc. **2.** *effects, substance,
property, possessions* : Pl., Cic., Hor., etc. ;
rem facere, *to get rich*, Cic. Ep. ; esp. with
familiaris : suam rem familiarem auxisse,
Caes. In *pl.* : Enn. ; privatae res, Cic. ;
res repetere, Cic. **3.** *benefit, advantage,
interest* : haec tuā re feceris, Pl. ; melius
illi consulas quam rei tuae, Pl. With *in,
ex, ob (advantageous)* : mihi quid magis
in rem est ? Pl. ; imperat quae in rem sunt,
Liv. ; in rem est (with Acc. and *Inf.*),
Pl., Ter., Liv. ; ex tuā re non est ut etc.,
Pl. ; e re publicā esse *or* videri, Cic. ; aliquid
ob rem facere, i.e. with advantage, Sall.
With *ab (disadvantageous ; contrary to the
interest)* : ab re consulit, Pl. ; haec haud
ab re duxi referre, Liv. ; haud id eat ab re
aucupis, Pl. ; Liv. **4.** *cause, reason,
ground, account* : only in ABL., or in ACC.

with *ob* : *therefore, on that account* : ob eam
rem se ex civitate profugisse, Caes. ; Pl. ;
illud eā re a se esse concessum quod, etc.,
Cic. ; Cato ; Lucr. (*v.* also quā re and quam
ob rem). **5.** *a matter of business, an affair,
transaction* : rem habere cum aliquo, Pl. ;
rem cum aliquo transigere, Cic. ; rem
suscipit, Caes. ; res alicui est cum aliquo,
Cic. **6.** In law, *a cause, suit* : tot homines
statuere non potuisse, utrum rem an litem
dici oporteret, Cic. ; Liv. ; iudicare, Cic. ;
res certabitur, Hor. **7.** In literature,
subject, matter : cui lecta potenter erit res,
Hor. **8.** *military operations* : esp. in phr.
rem (res) gerere, Ter., Caes., Liv., Hor.,
etc. ; rem agere, Hor. ; ante rem, Liv. ;
cum Thebanis sibi rem esse existimant,
Nep. **9.** *historical events* : res populi
Romani perscribere, Liv. ; agitur res in
scaenis, Hor. **10.** res publica, *the common
weal, a commonwealth, state, republic* ; also
*political affairs, administration, government,
etc.* : dum modo ista privata sit calamitas
et a rei publicae periculis seiungatur, Cic. ;
Pl., etc. And sometimes simply res :
cunctando restituit rem, Enn. ; Romana,
Verg., Liv., etc. In *pl.* : custode rerum
Caesare, Hor. ; Verg. ; rerum potiri, Cic.
11. P h r. : res novae, *political changes, a
revolution* : cupiditate regni adductus novis
rebus studebat, Caes. ; Cic. ; plebes novarum rerum cupida, Sall. [Fr. *rien*.]

re-sacrō, *v.* resecrō.

rē-saeviō, īre, *to rage again* : Ov.

resalūtātiō, ōnis, *f.* [resalūtō], *a greeting in
return* : Suet.

re-salūtō, āre, *to greet in return* : Cic.

re-sānēscō, sānēscere, sānuī, *to grow sound
again, to heal again*. T r a n s f. : error
animi, Ov.

re-sarciō, sarcīre, sartum, *to patch* or *mend
again* ; *to repair*. **1.** L i t. : vestem, Ter. ;
Tib. ; tecta, Liv. **2.** T r a n s f. : detrimentum in bello acceptum, Caes. ; damnum
liberalitate, Suet.

re-scindō, scindere, scidī, scissum, *to tear* or
cut back ; *to cut* or *break down* ; *to tear open.*
1. L i t. : pontem, Caes., Liv. ; vallum
falcibus, Caes. ; vestem e membris, Tib. ;
ense teli latebram penitus, Verg. ; vulnera,
Ov., Plin. Ep. **2.** T r a n s f. **a.** *to tear* or
force open : vias nostris sensibus, Lucr. ;
locum praesidiis firmatum, Cic. ; latentia
vitia, Quint. **b.** Of an old wound :
obductos annis luctūs, Ov. ; Hor. **c.** *to
annul, repeal, rescind* a law, agreement,
etc. : acta alicuius, Cic. ; testamenta mortuorum, Cic. ; res iudicatas, Cic. ; Ter. ;
Ov., etc. ; aevi leges validas, Lucr.

re-sciscō, sciscere, scii (*or* scivi), scitum, *to
learn, find out, ascertain* (what has been
concealed) : omnia, Ter. ; Pl. ; quod ubi
Caesar resciit, Caes. ; Cic. ; Ov., etc.

rescissus, a, um, *Part.* rescindō.

re-scrībō, scrībere, scrīpsī, scrīptum. **I.** *to
write back* or *in reply*. **A.** In gen. : ad
litteras, Cic. Ep. ; tibi ad ea quae requisieras,
Cic. Ep. ; ad aliquem, Cic. Ep. ; tuis litteris,
Cic. Ep. ; orationibus, Quint. ; nil mihi,
Ov. ; orationem, Tac. With Acc. and *Inf.* :
Caes. ; hoc (with *Indir. Quest.*), Hor. **B.**
Polit. and legal : *to answer in writing a*

petition or legal question ; *to give a rescript*
or *a judicial decision :* Tiberio Augustus
(with Acc. and *Inf.*), Suet. **C**. Of money :
to write back or off, i.e. *pay to one's credit.*
1. Lit. : illud argentum mihi, Ter. ;
Cic. **2**. Transf.: Hor. **II**. *to write over
again.* **A**. *to rewrite, revise :* Caesaris
commentarios, Suet. ; actiones, Plin. Ep.
B. Milit. **a**. *to enrol again, re-enlist :*
rescriptae ex eodem milite novae legiones.
Liv. **b**. *to transfer :* decimam legionem ad
equum (i.e. make into a cavalry squadron),
Caes.

rescriptus, a, um. **I**. *Part.* rescrībō. **II**.
Noun, **rescriptum**, i, n. *an imperial
rescript :* Tac.

re-secō, secāre, secuī, sectum, *to cut back* (or
off), *cut short.* **1**. Lit. : linguas scalpello,
Cic. ; palpebras, Cic. ; enodis truncos,
Verg. ; radices, capillos, etc., Ov. ; de
tergore exiguam partem, Ov. **2**. Transf.:
nimia, Cic. ; libidinem, Cic. ; spem longam, Hor. ; haec (dicta), Plin. Ep. Phr.:
ad vivum aliquid resecare, *to the very quick*
(i.e. to be very precise and strict about a
matter), Cic. ; de vivo aliquid resecare (of
merciless extortion), Cic.

re-secrō (**resacrō**, Nep.), āre. **I**. *to
pray or beseech again or repeatedly :* Pl.
II. *to uncurse,* i.e. *to free from a curse :* Nep.

resectus, a, um, *Part.* resecō.

re-secūtus sum, *Perf., followed* (Act.) *in
reply :* Arachne talibus resecuta est Pal-
lada dictis, Ov.

re-sēminō, āre, *to sow again :* poet. *to beget
or produce again :* se phoenix, Ov.

reserō, āre [sera], *to unbolt, unlock.* **1**. Lit. :
foris, Tib. ; limina, Verg. ; ianuam, etc.,
Ov. **2**. Transf. **a**. Italiam exteris gentibus, Cic. ; rem familiarem, Cic. ; reserata
viget genitabilis aura Favoni, Lucr. ; pectus
(i.e. tear open), Ov. ; auris, Liv. ; longum
annum, Ov. ; Plin. Pan. **b**. *to disclose,
reveal :* oracula mentis, Ov.

re-servō, āre, *to keep back, lay up, reserve, to
keep for some purpose.* **a**. In gen. : ad eius
periculum legiones, Caes. ; Cic. ; Verg. ;
commeatūs ad obsidionem urbis, Caes. ;
Cic. ; aliquos in unum pugnae laborem,
Liv. ; Cato ; Cic., etc. With Dat. or
Directive Adv. : praedam illis reservari,
Caes. ; Cic. ; Ov., etc. ; cui te exitio
fortuna reservat ? Verg. ; Lucr. ; quo
civem importunum reserves ? *to what
end ?* Cic. **b**. *to spare, preserve :* reserva-
tis Aeduis atque Arvernis, Caes. ; Tac. ;
incolumem Pallanta mihi fata, Verg. **c**. *to
hold fast to :* quaesita, Ov.

reses, residis [resideō], *that remains seated.* adj.
[*resideō*], *that remains seated.* Hence **a**.
motionless, inactive, idle, sluggish : aqua,
Varr. ; plebs in urbe, Liv. ; Ov. **b**. *unmoved, calm :* viri, Verg. ; animi, Verg.

re-sideō, sidēre, sēdī, *to remain seated,
remain behind.* **1**. Lit. : tergo aselli,
Ov. ; corvus arbore, Phaedr. ; in villā,
Cic. ; Ov. ; in patriis terris, Tac. ; per
artūs (anima), Lucr. **2**. Transf. **a**. *to
remain idle or listless :* Plin. With Intern.
Acc. : venter gutturque resident esurialis
ferias, Pl. **b**. *to remain behind :* in vobis
mores pristini, Pl. ; Cic. ; in corpore sensus,

Cic. ; in (eorum) consilio pristinae virtutis
memoria, Caes. ; Cic. ; horum tectis bellum,
Cic. ; apud me plus offici, Cic. Ep. ; si qua
(ira) ex certamine residet, Liv. **c**. *to rest,
dwell :* in nutu eorum auctoritas, Cic. ;
huius incommodi culpa ubi resideat, Cic.
Ep.

re-sīdō, sidere, sēdī (-sīdī, doubtful). **1**.
Lit. **a**. *to resume one's seat, sit down or
settle again :* Cic. **b**. *to sit back, sit down* or
settle for some time ; *to sink down :* mediis
aedibus (for a talk), Verg. ; medio rex ipse
agmine, Ov. For a long rest : fessus valle,
Verg. ; lassus in humo, Ov. ; saxo pastor,
Ov. Of permanent settlement : Siculis
arvis, Verg. In death : Ov. **2**. Transf.
a. *to sink* or *settle down* to the normal or
desired state ; *to abate, grow calm, subside :*
(ventorum) flatus, Verg. ; Plin. Ep. ; flammae, Tac. ; tumor animi, Cic. ; Verg. ;
impetus animorum ardorque, Liv. ; Ov. ;
mentes ab superiore bello, Caes. ; bellum,
Hor. ; Verg. ; poema apte et varie, Plin.
Ep. **b**. Of the ground, etc., *to sink down,
settle, subside :* montes, Cic. ; maria in se,
Verg. **c**. Of permanent settlement : cruri-
bus asperae pelles, Hor.

residuus (-uos), a, um [resideō], *that is left
behind, that remains over and above, remain-
ing.* **a**. Of unpleasant things : odium, Cic.
Ep. ; simultas, Liv. ; pecuniae (*arrears*), Cic.,
Liv. ; also (*sc.* pecuniae), Suet. *Neut.* as
Noun : in calamitate quid potest esse
residui ? Cic. **b**. In gen. : Plin. Ep., Suet.
Masc. as Noun : residui nobilium, Tac.
Neut. as Noun : residuum cibariorum,
Suet. ; residua diurni actūs, Suet.

re-signō, āre, *to unseal, open.* **1**. Lit.:
litteras, Pl., Cic. Ep. ; testamenta, Hor. ;
lumina morte, Verg. **2**. Transf. **a**. *to
disclose, reveal :* venientia fata, Ov. **b**. *to
annul, cancel :* tabularum fidem, Cic. **c**.
to cancel by repayment, *to repay :* quae
(Fortuna) dedit, Hor. (or as metaph. from
transferring in an account, *cf.* rescribo).

re-siliō, silire, siluī [saliō], *to leap or spring
back.* **1**. Lit. **a**. Of persons : a taetro
veneno, Lucr. ; in gelidos lacūs, Ov. ;
velites ad manipulos, Liv. **b**. Of things :
to rebound, recoil : Lucr. ; tecti a culmine
grando, Ov. ; Plin. Also *to shrink, contract :* in spatium resilire manūs breve
vidit, Ov. **2**. Transf. : ab hoc crimen,
Cic. ; Quint.

re-simus, a, um, *bent back, turned up :* labra
canis, Varr. ; nares, Ov.

rēsina, ae, f. [ῥητίνη], *resin :* Cato, Plin.,
Mart.

rēsinātus, a, um [rēsina], *resined.* **a**.
flavoured with resin : vinum, Plin., Mart.
b. *smeared with resin* (to make the skin
smooth) : iuventus, Juv.

re-sipiō, sipere [sapiō], *to savour, taste,* or
smack of through contact. **1**. Lit. : poem
uva, Plin. ; Varr. **2**. Transf. : Epicurus
minime patriam, Cic.

resipiscō, sipiscere, sipīvī or sipiī (resipuī,
Cic. Ep. ; resipīstī, Pl. ; resipīsset, Cic.)
[re-sapiō], *to recover one's senses.* **1**.
Lit. : Pl., Plin., Suet. Humorously :
Prop. **2**. Transf.: Ter., Cic., Liv.,
etc.

re-sistō, sistere, stiti. **I.** *to stop behind, to come to a standstill, halt, stop short.* **1.** Lit.: Pl., Caes., Cic., Ov., etc.; in occulto, Caes.; cum aliquo (*to stop* to talk), Cic. Ep.; ad omnis municipiorum amoenitates, Tac. **2.** Transf. **a.** vita extra limen carceris, Cic. **b.** *to stop short, pause* in speaking: in hoc, Cic.; mediā in voce, Verg.; verba, Ov.; oratio, Quint. **II.** *to stand against, to withstand, oppose, resist.* **1.** Lit. **a.** Milit.: fortiter, acerrime, aegre, etc., Caes.; Sall.; caeco Marte resistunt, Verg. With Dat.: legiones hostibus, Caes.; Liv.; eruptionibus, Caes. *Impers. Pass.*: Caes. **b.** In gen.: resistentibus conlegis, Sall.; Caes., Liv.; mollis ac minime resistens ad calamitates perferendas, Caes. With Dat.: alicui pro re publicā, Cic.; Sall.; iniuriis, Cic. Ep.; Ov. *Impers. Pass.*: his sententiis resistitur, Caes.; Cic.; Ov., etc. With *quin* and *Subj.* (after a negat.): vix deorum opibus (*Instr.* Abl.), quin obruatur Romana res, resisti posse, Liv. **2.** Transf. of things: vis humana, Lucr.; prominentia montium, Tac. With Dat.: vis tribunicia libidini consulari, Cic.; Symplegades ventis, Ov. With *adversus*: Varr. **III.** *to regain one's footing.* Transf.: ex fluvio fortuna, Enn.; nihil est iam, unde nos reficiamus, aut ubi lapsi resistamus, Cic.

re-solvō, solvere, solvī, solūtum, *to loosen or release again; to untie, unbind, unfasten; to open.* **1.** Lit. **a.** claustra, Lucr.; fila, Ov.; equos, Ov.; litteras, Liv.; oras (*shore-cables*), Liv.; iugulum mucrone, Ov.; venas, Tac.; satis ora, Verg.; Ov.; iuncta iuga leonibus, Cat.; virginem catenis, Ov. Occ. *to melt, thaw*: ignis aurum, Lucr.; nivem, Ov.; resolutus repente Rhenus, Suet. Hence, *to dissolve*: nebulas ventis ac sole, Ov.; tenebras, Verg. Also, Zephyrro se glaeba, Verg. **b.** Of limbs, etc.: *to relax*: nexos artūs, membra ad mollis choros, Ov.; corpus somno, Ov.; fatigatione resolutus, Curt. **2.** Transf. **A.** *to loosen again, gain release from.* **a.** In gen.: dolos tecti ambagesque, Verg. **b.** Of the discharging or payment of debts: minas, argentum, Pl.; pro vecturā, Cato. **B.** *to grant release from.* **a.** In gen.: *to release, dispel, annul*: curas, Verg.; iura pudoris, Verg.; litem lite, Hor.; vectigal et onera commerciorum, Tac. **b.** Of disentangling difficulties by argument. With *Indir. Quest.*: Lucr. **C.** With Acc. of person: *to release*: teque piacula nulla resolvent, Hor. In *Pass.*: amore resolutus, Tib. **D.** *to relax, enfeeble*: felicitas hos totos resolvit, Sen. Ep.; iudices, Quint.: disciplinam militarem, Tac. [Fr. *résoudre*.]

resonābilis, e, *adj.* [resonō] *resounding*: Echo, Ov.

re-sonō, āre. **A.** Intrans.: *to sound or ring in answer; to resound, re-echo.* **1.** Lit.: clupei, Enn.; poculum, theatrum, Cic.; aera, Ov.; e sacrā quercu examina, Verg. With Abl.: plangoribus aedes, Verg.; Hor.; Ov.; arbusta cicadis, Verg. With *ad* (*in answer to*): ad nervos resonant in cantibus, Cic. With Dat.: suave locus voci resonat conclusus, Hor. With *Intern.*

Acc.: litora alcyonem Verg.; [*frangunt* Amaryllida,' Verg.; Prop. *Impers. Pass.*: in fidibus testudine resonatur aut cornu, Cic. **2.** Transf. **a.** in vocibus nostrorum oratorum recinit quiddam et resonat urbanius, Cic. **b.** gloria virtuti resonat tamquam imago, Cic. **B.** Trans.: *to make to resound*: lucos adsiduo resonat cantu, Verg.

resonus, a, um [resonō] *resounding, re-echoing*: voces, Ov.; valles, Luc.

re-sorbeō, ēre, *to suck back, swallow again*: saxa (pontus), Verg.; Ov.; mare in se resorberi videbamus, Plin. Ep.; Tac.; spiritum, Quint. Of a magnet: Lucr.

respectō, āre [*freq.* respiciō], *to look back or behind repeatedly or intently; to look or gaze about.* **1.** Lit.: Pl., Verg., Liv.; leti ianua, Lucr. With Acc.: funera, Lucr.; arcem Romanam, Liv. For support, etc.: alium alius, Tac. **2.** Transf. *to have regard to, have a thought for*: Lucr., Cic. With Acc.: meum amorem, Cat.; par ab iis munus, Cic.; pios numina, Verg.

respectus, ūs, m. [respiciō], *a looking back (at), a backward-look.* **1.** Lit.: sine respectu fugit, Liv.; Verg.; castrorum, Liv.; Cic. For help or protection: ad Romanos, Liv. Hence, *something to look back to or fall back on*: illis timidis, qui respectum habent, Liv.; pulcherrimum respectum rei publicae adimere, Cic. **2.** Transf.: *respect, regard, consideration*: respectum ad senatum non habere, Cic.; respectum amicitiae habere, Liv.; Cic.; factione respectuque rerum privatarum Appius vicit, Liv.; Ov.; sine respectu humanitatis, Liv.; Tac. [It. *rispitto*; Fr. *répit*; Eng. *respite.*]

re-spergō, spergere, spersī, spersum [spargō], *to sprinkle or splash (back or in return).* **1.** Lit.: pelagus, Acc.; praetoris oculos praedonum remi, Cic.; vitulus ictus multos cruore, Liv.; Cat.: caede fraternā respersus, Cat.; Cic.; Ov.; Aurora lumine terras, Lucr. **2.** Transf.: servili probro respersus, Tac.

respersiō, ōnis, f. [respergō], *a sprinkling or splashing*: pigmentorum, Cic.

respersus, a, um, *Part.* respergō.

re-spiciō, spicere, spexi, spectum (old *Aor. Subj.* respexis, Pl.) [speciō], *to look back or behind one.* **1.** Lit.: Pl., Cic., Verg., etc.; ad me, Pl.; ad laevam, Pl.; ad oppidum, Cic.; Ov.; huc, Pl.; longe retro, Cic. With Acc.: *to look back at, to see behind one*: aliquem, Pl., Caes., Verg., Ov.; signa, Caes.; versas ad litora puppis, Verg.; litora, Liv. With Acc. and *Inf.*: Verg. **2.** Transf. **a.** *to look to, have regard to*: M. Bibulus cuncta administrabat: ad hunc summa imperi respiciebat, Caes.; Quint. With Acc.: spatium praeteriti temporis, Cic.; Lucr.; Galliam finitimam, Caes. For help, guidance, etc.: spem ab Romanis, Liv.; exempla vitae, Hor. **b.** *to have regard or consideration for, be mindful of*: ad utilitatem alicuius, Quint. With Acc.: deus nos, Pl.; Cic. Ep.; Verg.; idem deus rem publicam, Cic. Ep.; Caesarem, Caes.; miseros aratores, Cic.; Pylium Nestora, Hor.; se, Pl., Ter., Cic.; uetatem tuam,

Ter. ; rem publicam, Cic. ; populi R. commoda. Cic. ; mala sua, Lucr. ; pietas antiqua labores humanos, Verg. With Acc. and *Inf. :* Pl. **c.** *to look back :* ad curam rerum ab elocutione. Quint.

respīrāmen, inis, *n.* [respīrō]. *the windpipe :* Ov. In *pl. :* Ov.

respīrātiō, ōnis, *f.* [respīrō]. **I.** *a breathing back, respiration.* **1.** Lit. : Cic., Quint. **2.** Trans f. *exhalation (from) :* aquarum, Cic. **II.** *a taking breath, a pause to take breath :* sine respiratione ac respectu pugnare, Liv. ; morae respirationesque, Cic. ; Quint.

respīrātus, ūs, *m.* [respīrō]. *a drawing breath, respiration :* Cic.

re-spīrō, āre. **I.** *to blow* or *breathe back :* venti, Lucr. ; animam a pulmonibus, Cic. **II.** *to take breath (again), to recover one's breath.* **1.** Lit. : Pl., Ter., Cic., Quint. **2.** Trans f. **a.** Of recovery from alarm, etc. : *to breathe again :* Cic., Verg., Liv. With *ab :* a metu, Cic. ; ab eorum minis, Liv. ; a continuis cladibus, Liv. *Impers. Pass. :* Liv. **b.** Of things, *to abate, slacken :* oppugnatio, avaritia, Cic.

re-splendeō, ēre, *to flash back light, gleam back :* fulvā fragmina harenā, Verg.

re-spondeō, spondēre, spondī, spōnsum. Lit. *to pledge in return* (as in the phrase : par pari respondere.) **I.** *to match, balance, return, correspond.* **a.** In argument : par pari respondere dicto (ABL.), *to return tit for tat with your reply,* Pl. ; paria paribus, Cic. Ep. **b.** Of friendship, etc. : amori amore, Cic. Ep. ; fratris liberalitati subsidiis amicorum, Cic. Ep. : coniunx illi curis, Verg. **c.** Of reflexions or resemblance : sidera in aquā, Lucr. ; res simili formā atque colore, Lucr. ; ad parentum speciem, Varr. : Lucullus patri (in education), Cic. **d.** Of other things : porticus Palatio, Cic. ; contra (i.e. to Athens) Gnosia tellus, Verg. ; verba verbis quasi demensa et paria, Cic. Also, *to match,* i.e. *to answer* or *come up to expectations :* fortuna meis optatis, Cic. Ep. ; seges votis, Verg. ; favor meritis, Hor. : Papirio ad spem eventus, Liv. ; metalla plenius fodienti, Sen. Ep. **II.** In law (with or without *ad nomen*) : *to answer to a pledge* or *to bail* ; *to appear* (in court). **1.** Lit. : Cic., Hor., Liv., etc. ; qui ad nomina non respondissent, Liv. **2.** Trans f. : ipsi (*sc.* pes paeon et herous) se offerent et respondebunt non vocati, Cic. ; verba, Quint. **III.** *to answer, reply, respond.* **1.** Lit. **A.** In gen. : Pl., Caes., Cic., etc. ; alicui, Enn., Cic., etc. (*Impers. Pass. :* mihi responsum est, Pl.) ; epistulae, orationi, criminibus, etc., Cic. ; ad ea quae quaesita erant, Cic. ; adversus aliquem, Liv. (Rarely with *Neut.* Acc. : illud respondere cogam cur etc., *to that,* Cic.) With *Direct Object.* **a.** In *Neut.* Acc. : aliud tibi, Pl. ; plerique ad voluntatem eorum ficta respondent, Caes. ; tibi de versibus plura, Cic. ; multa contra patronos, Quint. (Hence in *Pass. :* quid nunc renuntiem aps te responsum ? Ter.) **b.** In Acc. and *Inf. :* Pl., Caes., etc. **c.** In *Indir. Quest. :* Cic. **d.** In quoted words : Cic. **B.** Of lawyers, priests, oracles, etc. :

to give an opinion, response, decision, advice : de iure consulentibus respondere, Cic. Also, ius, Cic., Plin. Ep. ; civica iura, Hor. ; quae consuluntur, minimo periculo respondentur, Cic. ; ex prodigiis haruspices, Sall. ; haruspices responderunt (with Acc. and *Fut. Inf.*), Cic. ; deliberantibus Pythia respondit (with *ut* and *Juss. Subj.*), Nep. ; possumus seniores amici quiete respondere, Tac. **2.** Trans f. of echoes : saxa et solitudines voci, Cic. ; respondent flebilo (*Intern.* Acc.) ripae, Ov. Also of amoebaean verse (in music and song) : Verg.

respōnsiō, ōnis, *f.* [respondeō], *an answer, reply.* **a.** *a refutation :* Cic. In *pl. :* Pl. **b.** Rhet. : sibi ipsi responsio, *a replying to one's own argument,* Cic., Quint.

respōnsitō, āre [*double freq.* respondeō], of lawyers, *to be in the habit of giving an opinion* or *advice :* Cic.

respōnsō, āre [*freq.* respondeō]. **1.** Lit. **a.** *to be in the habit of replying* or *answering back :* num ancillae tibi responsant ? Pl. **b.** Of answering the door : Pl. **2.** Trans f. **a.** exoritur clamor ripaeque lacūsque responsant circa, Verg. **b.** *to defy :* cupidinibus, Hor. ; ne gallina malum responset dura palato, Hor.

respōnsor, ōris, *m.* [respondeō], *one who answers* or *replies :* Pl.

respōnsū, ABL. *sing. m.* [respondeō], *in replying :* quam brevia responsu, Cic.

respōnsus, a, um. **I.** *Part.* respondeō. **II.** Noun, **respōnsum**, *i, n. an answer, reply.* **A.** In gen. : suis postulatis responsa exspectare, Caes. ; responsum senatūs, Liv. ; dare, reddere, Cic., Liv. ; ferro ab aliquo, *to receive,* Caes. ; Cic. ; referre, *to deliver,* Cic. Ep., Liv. ; auferre ab aliquo, Cic. ; accipere, Liv. ; petere, Hor. ; elicere, Quint. : sine responso legatos dimisit, Liv. ; triste, mitius, ferox, Liv. ; mollius, Tac. **B.** In partic. **a.** Of lawyers : Cic. **b.** Of priests, oracles, etc. : Pl., Cic., Verg., etc.

rēs pūblica, *v.* rēs.

re-spuō, spuere, spui, *to spit back, reject.* **1.** Lit. : gustatus quod valde dulce est respuit, Cic. **2.** Trans f. **a.** lumen per cornu transit, imber repuitur, Lucr. ; invisum cadaver humus, Ov. **b.** Of contemptuous rejection : aliquid ex animo, Lucr. ; orationem, Cic. ; condicionem, Caes. ; Caesaris interdicta respuuntur, Cic. ; Liv. **c.** quis te tum audiret illorum ? respuerent aures, Cic. ; ratio iuris hanc defensionem, Cic.

re-stagnō, āre, *to run over, overflow.* **1.** Lit. : Liv. **2.** Trans f. : *to be inundated :* late is locus, Caes.

restaurō, āre, [*v.* instaurō,] *to restore, rebuild :* theatrum, Tac.

resticula, ae, *f.* [*dim.* restis], *a small rope, a cord :* Cato, Cic.

restīnctiō, ōnis, *f.* [restinguō], *a quenching* (of thirst) : Cic.

re-stinguō, stinguere, stīnxī, stīnctum [*cf.* exstinguō], *to put out again* or *completely, to quench, extinguish.* **1.** Lit. : Caes., Hor., Liv. ; ignem aquā, Pl. ; ignem, Cic. ; Verg. ; flammam, Lucr., Cic., Liv. ; incendium, Liv. ; aggerem, Caes. ; solem, Lucr. **2.**

Transf. a. sitim, Cic., Verg.; ardentis Falerni pocula lymphā, Hor. **b.** Pl.; mentis inflammatas, Cic.; animorum incendia, Cic.; cupiditates eloquentiā, Cic.; studia, Cic., Liv.; animos hominum morte, Cic.

restĭō, ōnis, *m.* [restis], *a rope-maker, rope-seller.* **1.** Lit.: Suet. **2.** Transf. *a roper,* i.e. *one who is scourged with ropes :* Pl.

restĭpŭlātĭō, ōnis, *f.* [restipulor], *a counter-engagement* or *obligation :* Cic.

re-stĭpŭlor, ārī, *to obtain a promise* or *undertaking in return :* Cic.

restis, is, *f.* (Acc. restim or restem ; ABL. us. reste) *a rope, cord :* Pl., Varr., Liv., etc. Prov.: ad restim res rediit (i.e. *to hanging oneself*), Ter.

restĭtō, āre [*freq.* restō], *to hang back in hesitation :* Pl., Ter., Liv.

restĭtrix, īcis, *f.* [resistō], *she that stays behind :* Pl.

re-stĭtŭō, stĭtuere, stĭtuī, stĭtūtum [statuō], *to set up again.* **I.** *to restore* a thing *to its place, to put* or *set back again.* **1.** Lit.: Minervam quam turbo deieccrat, Cic.; arborem quo modo steterit, Verg.; turbatas comas, Ov.; ordines, Sall.; aciem, Liv. **2.** Transf. **a.** *to restore, re-establish, reinstate :* te pietas, Hor.; te in gaudia, Pl.; aliquem in gratiam, Ter.; aliquem a limine mortis, Cat.; fratrem in antiquum locum gratiae et honoris, Caes.; te in eundem locum, Cic.; civis ex servitute in libertatem, Liv.; libertatem in eundem locum, Pl.; Siciliam in antiquum statum, Cic.; consilia in integrum, Liv. **b.** In law and politics : *to replace* ono *in his former* or *proper position ; to reinstate :* Licinium de aleā condemnatum, Cic.; tribunos plebis in suam dignitatem, Caes.; Liv.; Acarnanas in antiquam formulam iurisque ac dicionis eorum, Liv.; Britanniam patientiac veteri, Tac.; nonnullos ambitūs Pompeiā lege damnatos in integrum restituit, Caes.; Cic. **c.** Occ. *to quash, cancel :* iudicia, Cic. **II.** *to re-erect, replace, restore* what has been damaged, etc. **1.** Lit.: foris effractas, Ter.; oppida, Caes.; Nep. **2.** Transf.: cunctando rem, Enn., Verg.; rem, Liv.; rem prolapsam, Liv.; res perditas, Liv.; Ter.; veteres clientelas, Caes.; tribuniciam potestatem, Cic.; veterem prudentiam, Cic.; damna, Liv.; proelium, Caes., Liv.; aciem, Liv. Also of reforming : adulescentem corruptum, Pl. **III.** *to restore, give back to* the rightful owner. **1.** Lit. **a.** Of things: filio paterna bona, Pl.; bona iis, Caes.; agrum Veientibus, Liv.; amissa, fraudata, Cic. **b.** Of persons: alicui filium, Ter.; Caes.; captum victori, Liv.; Ov.; Cloelia sospites omnis Romam ac propinquos, Liv.; sospites in patriam ad parentis, Liv. **2.** Transf.: meam vocem et auctoritatem vobis, Cic.; his animos, Liv.

restĭtūtĭō, ōnis, *f.* [restituō], *a restoration.* **1.** Lit.: domūs, Suet. **2.** Transf. **a.** omnis pristinae fortunae, Suet. **b.** *a reinstating :* damnatorum, Cic.; Quint.

restĭtūtor, ōris, *m.* [restituō], *a restorer.* **1.** Lit.: templorum, Liv. **2.** Transf.: salutis meae, Cic.

re-stō, stāre, stĭtī (*Perf. Subj.* resurrexit Prop.). **I.** *to stand one's ground (against),* *resist firmly.* **1.** Lit.: Pl., Lucr., Ov. Esp. milit.: Enn., Sall., Prop., Liv. (*Impers. Pass.* perh. in Liv.) With DAT.: Liv. **2.** Transf.: aera claustris, Lucr.; restantibus laminis adversum pila et gladios, Tac. **II.** *to stay behind* or *in reserve, to remain* or *be left behind.* **1.** Lit. **a.** In gen.: pugnandi causā nemo restitit, Caes.; Liv.; ad urbis incendium Romae restiterunt, Liv. **b.** In life : Ter., Cic., Hor.; superstes restarem ut genitor, Verg.; de viginti solus, Ov.; e nobis aliquid, Ov. Also, de bonis quod restat reliquiarum, Pl.; duae noctes de mense secundo, Ov. With DAT.: dona pelago et flammis restantia Troiac, Verg. **2.** Transf.: iam duo fata, Pl.; quao studia sola ei in malis restiterunt, Cic.; unam sibi spem reliquam in Etruscis rostare, Liv. *Impers.* restat: with *ut* and *Subj. :* Cic., Hor.; with *Inf. :* Ter., Liv., Ov. **III.** Of the future : *to await hereafter :* placet (vobis) socios sic tractari quod restat ut etc., (i.e. *during the time* to come), Cic.; hoc Latio (DAT.) restare canunt, Verg.; Lucr.

restrictē, *adv.* **I.** *closely, sparingly :* facere, Cic. *Sup. :* Plin. Ep. **II.** *strictly, exactly :* observare ne etc., Cic.

restrictus, a, um. **I.** *Part.* restringō. **II.** *Adj.* = *bound back, tight, confined.* **1.** Lit.: togae, Suet.; restrictiores digiti (pedum), i.e. *shorter,* Suet. **2.** Transf. **a.** *tight-fisted, niggardly :* in aliquo, Cic. *Comp. :* Cic. Ep. **b.** *moderate, modest.* *Comp. :* Plin. Ep. **c.** *strict, stern, rigorous :* imperium, Tac.

re-stringō, stringere, strīnxī, strīctum, *to draw back tightly ; to bind back, bind fast, tighten.* **1.** Lit.: Prometheus silici restrictus membra catenā, Cat.; lacertos, Hor.; laevam, Quint.; restringitur vinculis, Tac. **2.** Transf. **a.** Of dogs : *to draw back* (and show) the teeth : dentis, Pl.; rabio restrictā minari, Lucr. **b.** natura homines ad custodiam pecuniae restrinxit (i.e. *made them tight-fisted*), Plin. Ep.; sumptūs (i.e. *to restrict*), Plin. Ep.; animum maestitiā, Tac. [Fr. *restreindre.*]

re-sūdō, āre, *to sweat back* or *out, to exude :* umor solo, Curt.

resultō, āre [*freq.* resiliō], *to rebound.* **1.** Lit.: corpora conflicta, Lucr.; tela inrita galeā clipeoque, Verg.; aqua obiectu lapillorum, Quint. **2.** Transf. **a.** Of sound : offensa resultat imago, Verg. Of echoing places : pulsati colles clamore resultant, Verg.; Tac. **b.** Of style : *to produce a jumping* or *jerky effect :* (verba) brevium (syllabarum) contextu, Quint.; barbara nomina Graecis versibus, Plin. Ep.

re-sūmō, sūmere, sūmpsī, sūmptum, *to take up again, resume.* **1.** Lit.: terra gentis, Enn.; positas (tabellas), Ov.; arma, Tac.; elapsum baculum, Suet. **2.** Transf.: viris, Ov.; pugnam, militiam, sacramentum, voluptates, etc., Tac.; interruptum somnum, Suet.

re-supīnō, āre, *to throw* or *fling one on his*

back : adsurgentem ibi regem umbone re-
supinat, Liv. ; Ter. ; Juv.

re-supīnus, a, um, *lying back face-upwards,
bending backwards.* **1.** Lit.: resupinum
in caelo contueri, Acc. ; Lucr. ; Verg. ;
Ov. Of a proud gait : (Niobe) mediam
tulerat gressūs resupina per urbem, Ov. ;
Quint., etc. **2.** Transf.: *lazy, negligent :*
voluptas, Quint.

re-sūrgo, sūrgere, surrēxi, surrēctum, *to
rise* or *raise oneself up again.* **1.** Lit.:
Hor., Ov., Tac. Of convalescence : Ov.
Of things : herbae, Ov. ; arbor, urbs,
Tac. ; cumba de mediis aquis, Ov. **2.**
Transf.: regna Troiae, Verg. ; Ov. ;
amor, Verg. ; cum res Romana velut
resurgeret, Liv. ; bellum, rabies, Tac. ;
legiones in ultionem, Tac.

re-suscitō, āre, *to rouse again.* Transf.:
positam iram, Ov.

re-sūtus, a, um, *unstitched ;* hence, *ripped
open :* tunica, Suet.

retardātiō, ōnis, *f.* [retardō], *a hindering,
delaying :* Cic.

re-tardō, āre, *to make slow again, check.*
1. Lit.: *to make slow again, retard, impede :* (stellarum vagarum) motūs tum
retardantur, Cic. ; aliquem in viā, Cic. ;
flumina equos, Verg. **2.** Transf.: Tigra-
nem Asiae minitantem, Cic. ; celeritatem
persequendi, Cic. ; illius animos atque
impetūs, Cic. ; aliquem a scribendo, Cic.
Ep. ; aliquem ab alicuius commodo, Cic. ;
te mea fortuna, Ov. ; consuetudinem, loquacitatem, Cic.

re-taxō, āre, *to rebuke :* Suet.

rēte, is, *n.* (ABL. usually rēte ; rōtī, Pl.)
[serō], *a net.* **1.** Lit.: iaculum, *a casting-
net,* Pl. ; araneolae quasi rete texunt, Cic. ;
retia ponere cervis Verg. ; ducere in retia
piscis, Ov. ; Pl. **2.** Transf. of a snare :
Pl. ; retibus amoris exire, Lucr. ; tendis
iners docto retia nota mihi, Prop. [It.
rezza ; Sp. *red.*]

re-tegō, tegere, tēxī, tēctum, *to uncover, lay
bare, open.* **1.** Lit.: thecam nummariam,
Cic. Ep. ; sacra, Prop. ; iugulum simul
pectusque, Ov. ; homo retectus (i.e deprived of his shield), Verg. **2.** Transf.
a. Titan radiis orbem, Verg. ; diem Lucifer,
Ov. **b.** caecum scelus, Verg. ; arcanum
consilium, Hor. ; occulta coniurationis, Tac.

re-temptō, āre, *to try, test,* or *attempt again :*
verba intermissa, Ov. ; fila lyrae, Ov. ;
viam leti, Ov. ; memoriam meam, Sen.
Ep. With *Inf. :* Ov.

re-tendō, tendere, tendi, tentum or tēnsum,
to release from tension, unbend, slacken. **1.**
Lit.: arcum, Ov., Phaedr. **2.** Transf.:
Quint.

retēnsus, a, um, *Part.* retendō.

retentiō, ōnis, *f.* [retineō], *a keeping back.*
1. Lit. (with *Subj.* GEN.): aurigae, Cic.
Ep. **2.** Transf. (with *Obj.* GEN.): ad-
sensionis, Cic.

(1) retentō, āre [*freq.* retineō], *to continue to
keep back,* to *hold fast.* **1.** Lit.: our me
retentas ? Pl. ; agmen, Liv. ; frena, Ov. ;
puppis, Pl. ; fugientis, Tac. ; caelum a
terris, Lucr. ; (mens divina) penitus sensūs
hominum vitasque retentat (i.e. from destruction), Cic.

(2) re-tentō, *v.* retemptō.

(1) retentus, a, um, *Part.* retineō.

(2) retentus, a, um, *Part.* retendō.

re-texō, texere, texuī, textum, *to unweave,
unravel.* **1.** Lit.: telam, Cic., Ov. **2.**
Transf. **a.** nec corpora possunt retexi,
Lucr. ; luna plenum orbem, Ov. **b.** Of
reversing : quinque orbis explent cursu
totidemque retexunt huc illuc, Verg. ; Ov. ;
properata retexite fata, Ov. **c.** *to break
up, cancel, annul :* istius praeturam, Cic. ;
orationem meam, Cic. ; scriptorum quaeque (of revision), Hor. ; Ov.

rētiārius, ī, *m.* [rēte], *a net-fighter* (a kind of
gladiator, who tried to entangle his adver-
sary in a net) : Mart., Quint., Suet.

reticentia, ae, *f.* [reticeō], *a keeping silent.*
a. In gen. : Pl., Cic. **b.** Rhet.: *a pause
in the middle of a speech :* Cic., Quint.

re-ticeō, ēre, *to keep silent, refrain from
answering :* Ter., Cic., Sall. ; de adversis,
Tac. ; Cic. With DAT. of person : Liv.,
Ov., Tac. With Acc. (usually *Neut.*) of
thing about which one keeps silent : nihil
reticebo, quod sciam, Pl. ; ea quae etc.,
Cic. Ep. ; Sall. ; vestros dolores, Prop.
In *Pass. :* reticetur formula pacti, Ov.

rēticulātus, a, um [rēticulum], *made like a
net :* fenestra, Varr.

rēticulum, ī, *n.* [*dim.* rēte]. **I.** *a little
fishing-net :* Pl. **II.** *a net-work bag, a
reticule :* Cic., Hor., Ov., Juv. **III.** *a hair-
net :* Juv.

retinācula, ōrum, *n. pl.* [retineō], *a tether,
halter, hawser.* **1.** Lit.: Cato, Verg., Liv.,
etc. **2.** Transf.: vita abrupit, Plin. Ep.

retinēns, entis. **I.** *Part.* retineō. **II.** Adj.
tenacious, observant (with GEN.): libertatis,
Cic. ; avitao nobilitatis, Tac.

retinentia, ae, *f.* [retinēns], *a retaining in the
memory, recollection* (with GEN.) : Lucr.

re-tineō, tinēre, tinuī, tentum [teneō]. **I.** *to
hold* or *keep back ;* to *detain, restrain.* **1.**
Lit.: aliquem (manu), Pl. ; concilium
dimittit, Liscum retinet, Caes. ; Cic. ;
biduum tempestate retentus, Caes. ; Pl. ;
milites in loco, Caes. ; legiones ad urbem,
Caes. ; aegre sunt retenti quin oppidum
irrumperent, Caes. ; aliquem vinclis, Ov. ;
morbo retineri, Liv. ; arcum manu, Cic. ;
Prop. ; lacrimas, Ov. **2.** Transf.: liberos, Ter. ; aliquem in officio, Cic. ; animos
sociorum in fide, Liv. ; gaudia, rabiem, Ov. ;
linguam metu, Ov. ; retineri nequeo quin
dicam ea, Pl. **II.** *to hold back in reserve,
keep one's hold of, keep, maintain.* **1.**
Lit.: armorum tertiam partem in oppido,
Caes. ; navis pro bonis Tarquiniorum (i.e.
as security), Liv. **2.** Transf.: fidem,
Pl., Cic. ; pristinam virtutem, Caes. ;
hunc morem, Cic. ; officium, ius, caritatem,
iustitiam, etc., Cic. ; memoriam pristinae
virtutis, Caes. ; aliquid memoriā, Cic. ;
commissa aures, Hor. With *ne* and
Subj. : Cic. **III.** *to hold against somebody,
keep safe :* provinciam vi militum, Cat. ;
oppidum, Caes. ; arces, Cat. ; summos
cum infimis pari iure, Cic. ; amicos obser-
vantiā, Cic. ; Hor.

re-tinniō, īre, *to ring back, resound :* Varr.;
in vocibus nostrorum oratorum quiddam
urbanius, Cic.

re-tonō, āre, *to thunder back, resound :* loca fremitu, Cat.

re-torqueō, torquēre, torsī, tortum, *to twist or bend back.* **1.** L i t. : agmen ad dextram, Caes. ; caput in sua terga, Ov. ; cervices, Plin. Pan. ; tergo bracchia, Hor. ; amictum, Verg. ; oculos ad hanc urbem, Cic. ; Ov. ; omnium oculos in se, Quint. ; litore undas, Hor. Of hurling : missilia in hostem, Curt. **2.** T r a n s f. : mentem, Verg. ; animum ad praeterita, Sen.

re-torridus, a, um, *parched, burned,* or *dried up.* **1.** L i t. : prata, Varr. ; fructus, Plin. **2.** T r a n s f. : mus, *wizened* (i.e. old and shrewd), Phaedr.

retortus, a, um, *Part.* retorqueō.

retractātiō, ōnis, *f.* [retractō]. **I.** *a rehandling, reconsideration :* eorum qui fuerunt, Sen. Ep. **II.** *a holding back. hesitation* (only in A B L. with *sine*) : Cic., Liv.

re-tractō (**retrectō**), āre. **I.** *to rehandle, take in the hand again.* **1.** L i t. : ferrum, Verg. ; arma, Liv. ; vulnera, Ov. ; Venerem, Lucr. **2.** T r a n s f. : locus orationis a me retractandus, Cic. ; Ceae munera neniae, Hor. ; dolorem, Cic. Ep. ; vulnera cruda, Ov. ; gaudium, Plin. Ep. **II.** *to draw back, refuse, be reluctant :* Cic., Verg., Liv. With A c c. : *to withdraw :* dicta, Verg. ; largitiones, Trajan ap. Plin. Ep.

retractus, a, um. **I.** *Part.* retrahō. **II.** A d j. *withdrawn, remote :* emporium in intimo sinu Corinthiaco, Liv. C o m p. : retractior a mari murus, Liv. ; cubiculum, Plin. Ep.

re-trahō, t.ahere, traxī, tractum, *to draw or drag back.* **1.** L i t. a. aliquem, Pl., Cic., Liv. ; aliquem in urbem, Caes. ; Hannibalem in Africam, Liv. ; castra intra penitus, Liv. ; manum, Cic. ; pedem, Verg. ; quo fata (nos) retrahant, Verg. ; se, Cic. ; se ab ictu, Ov. ; pecuniam, Liv. **b.** aliquem ex fugā, Sall. ; Caes. ; Cic. ; Liv. ; aliquem ad eosdem cruciatūs, Tac. **2.** T r a n s f. **a.** poetam ab studio, Ter. ; aliquem a re publicā, Cic. ; Thebas ab interitu, Nep. ; imaginem nocturnae quietis ad spem haud dubiam, Tac. ; oblitterata aerari monimenta, Tac. **b.** Treviros in arma, Tac. ; Antistium absolutum adulterii ad dicendam maiestatis causam, Tac.

retrectō, *v.* retractō.

re-tribuō, uere, uī, ūtum, *to give back* as due : corpora rebus, Lucr. ; fructum quem meruerunt, Cic. ; populo pecuniam acceptam, Liv.

retrō, *adv.* [from re and the suffix -trō ; cf. citrō, ultrō, intrō, *etc.*], *backwards, back, behind.* **1.** L i t. (in space). **a.** Of motion : Lucr., Verg., Liv., etc. **b.** Of rest : Ter., Cic., Tac. **2.** T r a n s f. **a.** In time : *backwards* or *back in the past :* et deinceps retro usque ad Romulum, Cic. ; quodcumque retro est, *is past,* Hor. **b.** Of other relations, *back :* ut omnia, quae sine eā (honestate) sint, longe et retro ponenda censeat, Cic. ; Verg. ; retro vivere, Sen. Ep.

retro-agō, agere, ēgī, āctum, *to move or push back.* **1.** L i t. : capillos a fronte, Quint. **2.** T r a n s f. : iram, Sen. ; ordinem (i.e. reverse), Quint.

retrōrsum, *adv.* [retrō versum], *back, backwards, behind.* **1.** L i t. : vela dare, Hor. **2.** T r a n s f. *back, in reversed order :* Cic., Quint. [It. *ritroso.*]

re-trūdō, trūdere, trūsum, *to thrust back.* **1.** L i t. : me invitum, Pl. ; simulacra, Cic. **2.** T r a n s f. : haec penitus in philosophiā retrusa, Cic.

re-tundō, tundere, tudī (rettudī, Phaedr.), tūnsum (older) and tūsum, *to hammer back ;* hence, *to blunt, dull.* **1.** L i t. : tela, Ov. **2.** T r a n s f. **a.** gladios in rem publicam destrictos, Cic. ; Hor. ; coniurationis tela, Cic. ; censori stili mucronem, Cic. ; mucronem ingeni, Quint. **b.** impetum erumpentium, Liv. ; Aetolorum linguas, Liv. **c.** Of weakening or checking : animum qui lasciviā diffluit, Ter. ; superbiam, Phaedr. ; conlegam, Tac.

retūnsus or **retūsus**, a, um. **I.** *Part.* retundō. **II.** A d j. *blunt, dull.* **1.** L i t. : Pl., Lucr., Verg., Ov. **2.** T r a n s f. : cor, Pl. ; ingenia, Cic.

reus, ī, *m.,* and **rea**, ae, *f.* [rēs]. In law. orig. *a party to an action* (rēs), *a plaintiff* or *defendant.* **I.** In orig. wide sense. **1.** L i t. : Cic. **2.** T r a n s f. : iudexque sim reusque ad eam rem, Pl. **II.** In narrower sense. **A.** *one who is answerable* or *bound for anything* (with G E N.). T r a n s f. : ut suae quisque partis tutandae reus sit, Liv. ; voti reus (his prayer being granted), Verg. ; ignominiosae pacis, Liv. Also, sponsores nos sumus rei satis locupletes in corpora nostra, Liv. **B.** *one accused* or *arraigned, a defendant ;* also, *one condemned, a criminal.* **1.** L i t. : Cic., Liv. ; citare, Cic., Liv. ; reum peragere, Liv. ; postulare aliquem reum, Plin. ; aliquem in reos referre, Cic. With G E N. : facti, Pl. ; aliquem rei capitalis reum facere, Cic. ; parricidi, peculatūs, etc., Cic. ; capitis, Quint. With *de :* de vi, de ambitu, Cic. With A B L. : eodem crimine, Cic. **2.** T r a n s f. : reus agor, Ov. ; facinoris, Tac.

re-valēscō, valēscere, valuī, *to regain one's former strength* or *condition.* **1.** L i t. : Ov. **2.** T r a n s f. : Laudicea (tremore terrae prolapsa), Tac. ; diplomata Othonis, Tac.

re-vehō, vehere, vexī, vectum, *to carry back.* **1.** L i t. : aliquem domum, Pl. ; Diana Segestani Carthagine revecta, Cic. ; tela ad Graios, Ov. ; praedam inde, Liv. In *Mid.* or *Pass.* : equo citato ad urbem revectus, Liv. ; inde ad proelium, Liv. ; non satis est Ithacam revehi ? Hor. **2.** T r a n s f. : famam optimam ex Bithyniā, Plin. Ep. ; ad paulo superiorem aetatem revecti sumus, Cic.

re-vellō, vellere, vellī, vulsum (earlier volsum), *to pull* or *tear back* or *away.* **1.** L i t. : claustra, crucem, Cic. ; Liv. ; tela de corpore, Cic. ; Verg. ; caput a cervice, Verg. ; Ov. ; saxum e monte, Ov. ; scuta manibus, Caes. ; herbas radice, Ov. ; aliquem, Ov. ; aliquem urbe, Verg. **2.** T r a n s f. : totum consulatum ex omni monumentorum memoriā, Cic. ; Pers.

re-vēlō, āre, *to unveil, uncover :* os, Ov. ; frontem, Tac. ; caput, Suet.

re-veniō, venīre, vēnī, ventum, *to come again, come back, return.* **1.** L i t. : Pl.,

Tac. ; huc, Pl. ; domum, Pl., Cic. : domum de hippodromo, Pl. ; in urbem, Tac. ; ex longinquo, Tac. **2.** T r a n s f. : cum aliquo ex inimicitia in gratiam, Pl. ; in eum haec revenit res locum ut etc., Pl. *Impers. Pass.* : Pl.

rĕ vĕrā, *v.* rēs.

rĕ-verberŏ, āre, *to beat or cast back, to repel.* **1.** L i t. : saxa, Son. ; Curt. **2.** T r a n s f. : iram Fortunae, Sen.

reverendus, a, um. **I.** *Gerund.* revereor. **II.** A d j. *inspiring awe, venerable :* nox, Ov. ; facies, Juv.

reverēns, entis. **I.** *Part.* revereor. **II.** A d j. *respectful, reverent :* sermo erga patrem imperatoremque reverens, Tac. *Comp.* : erga senatum, Suet. ; Plin. Ep. ; Tac. *Sup.* (with *Obj.* Gen.) : Plin. Ep.

reverenter, adv. *respectfully :* Plin. Ep. *Comp.* : Tac. *Sup.* : Plin. Ep., Suet.

reverentia, ae, *f.* [revereor], *fear, awe, respect, reverence :* adversus homines, et optimi cuiusque et reliquorum, Cic. ; famae, Ov. ; legum, Juv. ; superiorum, Tac. ; sacramenti, imperi, Tac. ; poscendi, Prop. ; praestare alicui, Plin. Ep.

re-vereor, verēri, veritus, *to stand in awe or fear of ; to respect, honour, revere :* eius opulentitatem, Pl. ; fulgorem ab auro, Lucr. ; adsentandi suspicionem, Cic. ; multa adversa reverens, Cic. ; Liv. Rarely of persons : aliquem, Pl., Cic., Tac.

re-verrŏ, *v.* revorrŏ.

reversiŏ (revors-), ōnis, *f.* [revertŏ]. *a turning back* before reaching one's destination. **a.** Of persons : Cic. ; revorsionem ad aliquem facere, Pl. **b.** Of things, *a return :* febrium, Cic. **c.** R h e t. : *inversion :* Quint.

re-vertor (older **re-vortor** ; also **re-vertŏ**, ere, Lucr.), verti, *Perf.* verti (or versus sum), *to turn oneself back, to come back, return.* **1.** L i t. : Pl., Caes., Cic., etc. ; ex itinere, Cic. ; a foro, Pl. ; Hor. ; a bello, Cic. ; ab exsilio, Tac. ; silvā, Ov. ; Epheso, Cic. Ep. ; huc, Pl. ; Cic. ; domum, Pl., Cic., Hor. With *ad* and Acc. : Pl., Caes., etc. With *in* and Acc. : Cic., Sall., etc. Of things : sol a terrā, Lucr. ; sub terras, Lucr. ; Tiberis, Hor. **2.** T r a n s f. **a.** In gen. : leti limine ab ipso ad vitam, Lucr. ; ad sanitatem, Caes. ; Cic. ; poena in caput tuum, Ov. ; Tac. ; nescit vox missa reverti, Hor. **b.** *to return* from a digression, *revert (to) :* ad propositum, Cic. ; Pl. ; illuc, Nep.

revictus, a, um, *Part.* revincŏ.

re-video, ēre, *to go back to see, to visit again :* ad eram, Pl.

re-vinciŏ, vincīre, vīnxī, vīnctum, *to bind back, fasten (back).* **1.** L i t. : terra caelo revincta, Lucr. ; ancorae pro funibus ferreis catenis revinctae, Caes. ; aliquem ad saxa, Ov. ; zonam de poste, Ov. ; errantem (insulam) o Mycono, Verg. ; manūs iuvenem post terga devinctum, Verg. P o e t. : latus ense, Prop. Also, *to entwine fast :* templum fronde, Verg. **2.** T r a n s f. : mentem amore, Cat.

re-vincŏ, vincere, vici, victum, *to beat back, crush, repress.* **1.** L i t. : victrices catervae consiliis iuvenis revictae, Hor. ; con-

iurationem, Tac. ; primordia rerum, Lucr. **2.** T r a n s f. : *to refute, disprove :* Lucr. ; aliquem, Cic., Tac. ; crimina rebus revicta, Liv.

re-vinctus, a, um, *Part.* revinciŏ.

re-virēscŏ, virēscere, viruī, *to become or grow green again.* **1.** L i t. : laesae silvae, Ov. ; arbor in novos fetūs, Tac. **2.** **b.** *to grow strong again ; to reflourish, revive :* ad renovandum bellum, Cic. ; domus Germanici, Tac. ; partes, Tac.

re-visŏ, ere. **A.** T r a n s. *to go or come to see again ; to visit again.* **1.** L i t. : aliquem, Cic. Ep., Hor. ; urbem, Lucr. ; Cic. ; Verg. **2.** T r a n s f. **a.** longos obitūs sidera, Lucr. **b.** multos aeterna Fortuna, Verg. **B.** I n t r a n s. *to go or come back* (to a person or thing) *to see, to revisit.* **1.** L i t. : ad me, Pl. ; ad stabulum, Lucr. **2.** T r a n s f. : signa ad lunam, Lucr. ; rabies eadem, Lucr.

re-vivescŏ (-vivēscŏ), vivescere, vixi, *to come to life again, to revive.* **1.** L i t. : Ter., Cic., Liv. **2.** T r a n s f. : res publica, iustitia, etc., Cic.

revocābilis, e, *adj.* [revocŏ], *that may be recalled or revoked, revocable* (us. with neg.) : poenae, Sen. ; cum iam revocabile telum non fuit, Ov.

revocāmen, inis, *n.* [revocŏ], *a calling back, recall :* Ov. In *pl.* : Ov.

revocātiŏ, ōnis, *f.* [revocŏ], *a calling back or away, a recalling.* **1.** L i t. : a bello, Cic. **2.** T r a n s f. **a.** ad contemplandas voluptates, Cic. **b.** R h e t. *a withdrawing, revoking :* verbi, Cic.

re-vocŏ, āre. **I.** *to call back, recall.* **1.** L i t. **A.** In gen. : Pl., Hor., Liv., etc. ; aliquem, Pl. ; aliquem ex itinere, Cic. ; aliquem de exsilio, Liv. ; Caesar in Italiam revocabatur, Caes. Also, a morte aliquem, Verg. ; spes Campanae defectionis Samnites rursus ad Caudium revocavit, Liv. **B.** M i l i t. **a.** From the march or battle, etc. : legiones, Caes. ; Cic. ; Liv. ; Verg. ; milites ab opere, Caes. ; navis, Caes. **b.** Back from furlough to the colours : milites, Cic. ; veteranos, Tac. **C.** Of an actor or scene, etc. in a play : *to call back, to encore :* Plin. Ep. ; Archiam, Cic. ; Liv. ; primos trīs versūs, Cic. *Impers. Pass.* : Cic. **D.** Polit. and legal (rare) : *to recall* for trial or voting : hominem populus, Cic. Ep. ; tribuni easdem tribūs, Liv. **2.** T r a n s f. **a.** pedem ab alto, Verg. ; gradum, Verg. ; cupidas manūs, Ov. ; oculos, Ov. ; capillum a vertice, Suet. **b.** *to recall* to the old, normal, or required state ; *to resume, regain, recover :* viris et corpus, Cic. Ep. ; gelidos artūs in vivum calorem, Ov. ; studia longo intervallo intermissa, Cic. ; priscos mores, Liv. ; Hor. ; Tac. ; se interdum, Cic. ; se industriam, Cic. ; eos ab illā consuetudine, Cic. ; ad humanitatem animos hominum, Cic. ; eos spes praedandi ab agri culturā revocabat, Caes. ; disceptationem ab rege ad Romanos, Liv. ; illa revocatur (with *Inf.*), Prop. **c.** *to apply duly, to refer to* a standard : rationem ad veritatem, Cic. ; omnia ad artem, Cic. **d.** *to recall, revoke, retract :* facta, Ov. ;

promissum, Sen.; libertatem, Ia0. ■;
to invite in return : Cic.; vulpem ciconia,
Phaedr.

re-volō, āre, *to fly back* : grus, Cic.; mergi,
Verg.; Daedalus alis, Ov.; telum, Ov.

revols-, *v.* revuls-.

revolūbilis, e, *adj.* [revolvō], *that may be
rolled back.* **1.** Lit.: Ov. **2.** Transf.:
fatorum nulli revolubile carmen, Prop.

revolūtus, a, um, *Part.* revolvō.

re-volvō, volvere, volvi, volūtum. **I.** *to
(make to) roll back or backwards.* **1.** Lit.:
pontus aestu revoluta resorbens saxa, Verg.;
auster fluctûs, Tac.; molis obiectu revolu-
tus amnis, Tac. With *Refl. Pron.* or in
Mid. : *to roll back* : Draco se, Cic. poet.;
ter sese attollens cubitoque adnixa levavit,
ter revoluta toro est, Verg.; revoluta rursus
eodem est, Ov. **2.** Transf. (in *Mid.*).
a. Of other motion : *to roll back, return in
due course* : itaque revolvor identidem in
Tusculanum, Cic. Ep. Of the cycle of
time : dies, Verg. **b.** *to roll back, return in
due course, come back or round* : in eandem
vitam, Ter.; in veterem fato figuram,
Verg.; animus in sollicitudinem, Curt.;
ad patris sententiam, Cic.; ad dispensa-
tionem annonae, Liv.; Tac.; eo quo
minime vult, Cic.; eo revolvi rem ut etc.,
Liv. Also in *Act.* : iterum revolvere casûs
Iliacos, Verg. **II.** *to roll back, unroll* (a
book). **1.** Lit.: scripta et lecta, Quint.;
Hor.; tuas adversus te Origines, Liv. **2.**
Transf. **a.** quid ego haec ingrata revolvo? Verg.; saecula, Ov.; dicta factaque eius secum, Tac. **b.** rursus perplexum
iter omne revolvens (*cf.* retexo), Verg.

re-vomō, vomere, vomul, *to vomit forth
again, disgorge* : salsos pectore fluctûs,
Verg.; umor aquae tigna, Lucr.; Ov.

re-vorrō, ere, *to sweep back, scatter again* :
hoc quod convorri, Pl.

revors-, revort-, *v.* revers-, revert-.

rēx, rēgis, *m.* [regō], *a director, ruler of a
country* ; *a king, monarch.* **1.** Lit. **A.**
At Rome. **a.** Orig. without odious sense :
regem deligere, creare, constituere, Cic.;
Hor.; Liv., etc. This survived in title
rex sacrorum, rex sacrificiorum, rex sacrificulus, Liv.; rex sacrificus. **b.** With odious
sense (under the Republic) : *an unconstitutional ruler, a despot, usurper* : Caes.,
Cic., Hor., etc. **B.** Elsewhere : *of the
King of Persia*, Ter., Nep., etc.; *king of
the Tuscans*, Verg.; *of one of the sufetes at
Carthage*, Nep. **2.** Transf. **a.** Of the
gods in their realms : divum pater atque
hominum rex, Verg.; Cic.; Hor.; aquarum, Ov.; umbrarum, Ov.; rex infernus,
Verg. **b.** Of a nation : populum late
regem, Verg. **c.** In gen. : *of Aeneas*,
Verg.; *lions*, Phaedr.; *the queen-bee*,
Verg.; *the Eridanus*, as the chief river of
Italy, Verg. **d.** *the leader, king* in children's games : Hor. **e.** *a patron* : Pl.,
Hor., Juv., etc. **f.** *a rich and prosperous
man* (mostly in *pl.*) : Pl., Hor. **g.** Of
royal persons in gen. : *a king's son*, Verg.
In *pl.* *the king and queen*, Liv.; also, *the
royal family*, Liv. **h.** Of the feelings of a
king : rex patrem (i.e. paternum animum)
vicit, Ov. [It. *re* ; Sp. *rey* ; Fr. *roi*.].

Rhadamanthus, i, m. *of Jupiter by*
Minos, a judge in the underworld.

Rhaetī, ōrum, *v.* Raetī.

Rhamnūs, ūntis, *f. a town in Attica, famous
for a statue of Nemesis* ; **Rhamnūsius**, a,
um ; **Rhamnūsia**, ae, and **Rhamnūsis**,
idis, *f.* Nemesis.

rhapsōdia, ae, *f.* [ῥαψῳδία], *a rhapsody*
(i.e. an episode from Homer for recitation) :
Nep.

Rhea Silvia, *d. of Nunitor, and m. of Romulus
and Remus.*

Rhea, ae, *f. another name for Cybele.*

rhēda, rhēdārius, *v.* raeda, raedārius.

Rhēgium, *v.* Rēgium.

rhēnō, ōnis, *v.* rēnō.

Rhēnus, i, *m. the Rhine* ; **Rhēnānus**, a, um.

Rhēsus, i, *m. a Thracian prince who came to
the assistance of Troy. where he was killed
by Diomedes and Ulysses.*

rhētor, oris, *m.* [ῥήτωρ]. **I.** *a teacher of
rhetoric, a rhetorician* : Cic., Mart., Tac.
II. *an orator* : Nep.

rhētoricē, *adv. in an oratorical* or *rhetorical
manner, rhetorically* : Cic.

rhētoricus, a, um [ῥητορικός], *of a rhetorician, rhetorical* : ars, *a treatise on rhetoric*,
Cic.; doctores, Cic. As Noun, **rhētorica**,
ae -and **-ē, ēs**, Quint.), *f. the fine art of
oratory* : Cic.; exercore, Quint. **rhētorici**,
ōrum, *m. pl. teachers of rhetoric* : Cic.; also
books on rhetoric : Quint. **rhētorica**,
ōrum, *n. pl. a treatise on rhetoric* : Cic.

rhinocerōs, ōtis, *m.* [ῥινόκερως], *a rhinoceros.* **1.** Lit.: Curt., Mart., Suet. **2.**
Transf. *a vessel made of the rhinoceros's
horn* : Juv.

rhō, *indecl.* [ῥῶ], *the Greek name of the letter
r* : Cic.

Rhodanus, i, *m. the Rhone.*

Rhodopē, ēs, *f. a lofty mountain range in
Thrace, now Despoto Dagh* ; **Rhodopēius**,
a, um, *Thracian* : vates, i.e. Orpheus (Ov.).

Rhodos (rarely **Rhodus**), i, *f.* **I.** *an island
on the south coast of Asia Minor, celebrated
for its Colossus, and for the skill of its people
in navigation, now Rhodes* ; **Rhodius**, a,
um, *and* **Rhodiēnsis**, e ; **Rhodii**, ōrum,
m. pl. the Rhodians. **II.** *the nymph of the
island of Rhodes.*

Rhoetēum, i, *n. a promontory of the Troad,
on the Hellespont* ; **Rhoetēus**, a, um.
Poet.: *Trojan* : ductor, i.e. Aeneas, Verg.
As Noun, **Rhoetēum**, i, *n. the sea about the
promontory of Rhoeteum* (Ov.).

rhombus, i, *m.* [ῥόμβος]. **I.** *a magician's
circle* : Prop., Ov. **II.** *a kind of fish, the
turbot* : Hor., etc.

rhomphaea, *v.* rumpia.

rhythmicus, i, *m.* [ῥυθμικός], *one who pays
attention to* or *teaches the art of preserving
rhythm* (in style) : Cic., Quint.

rhythmos or **-us**, i, *m.* [ῥυθμός], *symmetry,
harmony, rhythm* in music or speech :
Quint.

rhytium, i, *n.* [ῥύτιον], *a horn-shaped drinking vessel* : Mart.

rica, ae, *f. a veil* (worn over the head by
Roman women at a sacrifice) : Pl.

ricinum, i, *n.* [rīca], *a small mantle with a
cowl,* worn esp. by women and mourners :
Lucil., Cic.

rictus, ūs, *m.* (**rictum**, ī, *n.* : Cic. ; *pl.* : riota, Lucr.) [ringor], *the opened mouth* (esp. in laughing) : Lucil., Lucr., Cic., etc. ; in *pl.* : Ov. Of animals and serpents : Ov., Juv. ; in *pl.* : Lucr., Ov.

rideō, rīdēre, rīsī, rīsum. **A.** Intrans. **1.** Lit. **a.** *to laugh* : Pl., Cic., Hor. With *Intern.* Acc. : multum, Pl. ; Cic. Ep. **b.** *to laugh pleasantly, to smile* : Enn., Ov. ; parenti, Verg. With *Intern.* Acc. : dulce, Hor. ; dulce ad patrem, Cat. **2.** Transf. of things : sedes diffuso lumine, Lucr. ; argento domus, Hor. ; Ov. ; tempestas, Lucr. ; acanthus, Verg. With Dat. : tibi aequora ponti, Lucr. ; Cat. ; Hor. **B.** Trans. **a.** *to laugh at, laugh over* : aliquem, Pl., Hor., etc. ; ioca tua, Cic. Ep. ; vitia, Tac. ; Tib. ; Ov. In *Pass.* : natura ridetur, Cic. ; Hor. ; Ov. **b.** *to smile upon* : aliquem, Pl. **c.** *to ridicule, jeer at* : aliquem, Cic. Ep., Quint. ; nostram amentiam, Cic. ; praesaga verba, Ov. ; Hor. In *Pass.* : Cic., Hor., etc. [Fr. *rire.*]

ridibundus, a, um [rideō], *laughing* : Pl.

ridica, ae, *f. a vine-prop* : Cato, Varr.

ridiculārius, a, um [rīdiculus], *laughable, droll.* *Neut. pl.* as Noun : Pl., Cato.

ridicule, *adv.* **I.** *jokingly* : Pl., Cic. **II.** *ridiculously, absurdly* : Cic.

ridiculōsus, a, um [rīdiculus], *laughable, amusing, droll* : parasitus ridiculosissumus, Pl.

ridiculus, a, um [rideō], *that makes one laugh.* **a.** *laughable, amusing, droll* (of persons or things) : Pl., Cic., Hor., etc. With *Inf.* : ridiculus totas absorbere placentas, Hor. ; ridiculum est (with Acc. and *Inf.*) : Ter. *Masc.* as Noun, **ridiculus**, ī, *a jester, buffoon* : Pl., Ter. *Neut.* as Noun, **ridiculum**, ī, *a laughing matter, jest, joke* : ridiculi causā, Pl. ; mihi solae ridiculo fuit, Ter. ; iacere, mittere, Cic. ; per ridiculum dicere, Cic. ; ridicula facere, dicere, Quint. **b.** *laughable, silly, ridiculous, absurd* (of persons or things) : Lucr., Cic., Hor., Quint. ; ridiculum est (with *Inf.*, or Acc. and *Inf.*), Cic.

rigeō, ēre [*cf.* ῥιγέω, frīgeō], *to be stiff.* **1.** Lit. (with cold) : frigore, Lucr. ; partes terrae frigore, Cic. ; animalia gelu, Liv. ; prata, Hor. **2.** Transf. **a.** gelido comae terrore rigebant, Ov. **b.** ora indurata, Ov. ; signa, Lucr. ; vestes auroque ostroque, Verg. ; sine frondibus arbos, Ov. ; Tmolus, Ov. ; lorica ex aere, Verg. ; caput, Quint.

rigescō, rigēscere, riguī [rigeō], *to grow stiff.* **1.** Lit. (with cold) : vestes, Verg. **2.** Transf. **a.** sensi metu riguisse capillos, Ov. **b.** Gorgone corpora visā, Ov.

rigidē, *adv.* **I.** *stiffly* : Sen. **II.** *rigorously, severely* : Ov.

rigidus, a, um [rigeō], *stiff, hard.* **1.** Lit. (with cold) : pruinae, Lucr. ; tellus, Verg. ; Niphates, Hor. ; aqua, Ov. ; artūs morte, Lucr. **2.** Transf. **a.** *stiff* in gen. : crura, Cic. ; cervix, Liv. ; quercus, Verg. ; rostrum saetae, ensis, mons, etc., Ov. **b.** *making stiff* : frigus, mors, Lucr. **c.** *hard, inflexible, stern, strict* : Sabini, Hor. ; Ov. ; censor, parens, Ov. ; Tac. ; mens, vultus, mores, Ov. ; Cato rigidae innocentiae, Liv. ; vox, Quint. *Comp.* : Cic.

rigō, āre [*cf.* βρέχω], *to wet, moisten, water, bedew.* **A.** In gen. **1.** Lit. : imbres terras, Lucr. ; Nilus Aegyptum, Lucr. ; Hor. ; lucum perenni aquā fons, Liv. ; lacrimis ora, Verg. ; Ov. Without Object : Lucr., Curt. **2.** Transf. : natos vitali rore, Cic. poet. ; ora nostra Phileteā aquā, Prop. ; lux terras, Lucr. **B.** (*cf.* inrigo) *to convey water, etc.* **1.** Lit. : squam Albanam emissam per agros, Liv. **2.** Transf. : hinc motūs per membra rigantur, Lucr.

rigor, ōris, *m.* [rigeō], *stiffness.* **1.** Lit. (of cold) : coldness, numbness : Lucr., Ov., Liv., Tac. **2.** Transf. **a.** *stiffness* or *hardness* in gen. : auri, Lucr. ; ferri, Verg. ; Ov. ; cervicis, Plin. **b.** *hardness, severity, sternness, strictness* : Ov., Tac. ; animi, disciplinae, Tac. Of the voice : Quint.

riguus, a, um [rigō]. **A.** Act. *watering.* rigui in vallibus amnes, Verg. **B.** Pass. *watered* : hortus, Ov.

rima, ae, *f.* [fr. root of ringor], *a cleft, crack, chink, fissure,* Hor. ; Ov. ; naves rimis fatiscunt, Verg. ; Liv. ; rimas facere, Ov. ; rimas agere, *to be cracked,* Cic. Ep., Ov. ; explere, Cic. Poet. : ignea rima micans, Verg. Comic. : plenus rimarum sum, Ter. ; Pl.

rimor, ārī [rima], *to lay open, cleave.* **1.** Lit. : rastris terram, Verg. **2.** Transf. *to lay open in searching, to probe.* **a.** vultura viscera epulis, Verg. ; haruspex pectora pullorum matur, Juv. ; humum pilis et lanceis, Tac. **b.** secreta, Tac. ; Cic. With *Indir. Quest.* : Cic.

rimōsus, a, um [rima], *full of cracks or chinks, leaky.* **1.** Lit. : fores, Prop. : cumba, Verg. **2.** Transf. : auris, Hor.

ringor, ī, *to open the mouth wide, to show the teeth.* Transf. *to snarl, be angry* : Ter., Hor., Sen. Ep.

ripa, ae, *f. the bank of a stream.* **1.** Lit. : Enn., Cic., Verg., etc. Often in *plural* of several places along the bank : Liv., etc. **2.** Transf. **a.** Of the sea-shore : Hor. **b.** Comic. : ripis superat mihi atque abundat pectus laetitiā meum, Pl. [It. *riva* : Fr. *rive.*]

Riphaei montēs, *a mountain-range in Northern Scythia.*

ripula, ae, *f.* [*dim.* ripa], *a little bank* : Cic. Ep.

riscus, ī, *m.* [ῥίσκος], *a trunk, chest* : Ter.

risiōnēs, um, *f. pl.* [rideō], *laughs, laughter* : quot risiones ! Pl.

risor, ōris, *m.* [rideō], *a laugher, banterer* : Hor.

risus, ūs, *m.* [rideō], *a laugh or smile, laughter* : risu emoriri, Ter. ; risum continere, Pl. ; alicui risum movere, Cic. Ep. ; risūs captare, edere, Cic. ; risu cognoscere matrem, Verg. Also, *an object of laughter* : deus omnibus risus erat, Ov. ; risui sorori fuit, Liv. [It. *riso* : Fr. *ris.*]

rite, *adv.* [perh. Abl. of an obsolete *ritis* = rītus], *with due observances or rules, according to religious usage.* **1.** Lit. : Cic., Verg., Liv., etc. **2.** Transf. **a.** In gen. : *duly, rightly, fitly, justly* : Cic., Verg., etc. **b.** *according to custom or usage* : Lucr., Verg., Hor. **c.** *fortunately, successfully* : Pl., Verg., Hor.

ritus, ūs, *m. a religious usage or observance,*
ritual. **1.** Lit.: sacra diis aliis Albano
ritu facit, Liv. ; tempestates quae populi
Romani ritibus consecratae sunt, Cic. ;
morem ritūsque sacrorum, Verg. ; profanos
ritūs exuere, Tac. **2.** Transf. **a.** *a cus-*
tom, usage : cognosse Sabinae gentis ritūs,
Ov. ; in alienos ritūs mores legesque verti,
Liv. ; Suet. **b.** More freq. in ABL. *sing. :*
after the usage, manner, or fashion (of) :
pecudum ritu, Cic. ; Liv. ; fluminis, Hor. ;
Ov., etc. ; cantherino ritu astans, Pl. ; suo
ritu res quaeque procedit, Lucr. ; novo
sublime ritu moliar atrium, Hor.

rivālis, is, *m.* [rīvus], *one who uses the same*
stream, a neighbour. Transf. *one who has*
the same mistress ; a rival : Pl., Cat.,
Ov., Suet. Prov.: so amare sine rivali,
Cic., Hor.

rivālitās, ātis, *f.* [rīvālis], *rivalry in love :*
Cic.

rivulus (**rivolus**). i, *m.* [dim. rīvus], *a small*
brook, rivulet. Transf.: rivulos consec-
tari, fontis rerum non videre, Cic.

rivus, ī, *m. a small stream.* **1.** Lit. **a.** Of
water : *a brook :* Lucr., Caes., Cic., Verg.,
etc. Prov.: e rivo flumina magna
facere, Ov. **b.** Of other liquids : lactis,
Hor. ; sanguinis, Verg. ; auri, Lucr. ;
lacrimarum, Ov. ; sudor fluit undique rivis,
Verg. **2.** Transf.: liquidus fortunae rivus,
Hor. [It. *rio* ; O. Fr. *rui.*]

rixa, ae, *f. a brawl, fight ; fisticuffs.* **1.** Lit.:
Cic., Hor. ; rixa ac prope proelium fuit,
Liv. ; iurgia primum, mox rixa, Tac. ; in
rixam ire, Quint. ; in rixā esse, Liv. ; rixam
sedare, Liv. ; crebrae ut inter vinolentos,
Tac. ; Centaurea cum Lapithis, Hor. **2.**
Transf. **a.** Academiae nostrae cum Ze-
none 'magna rixa est, Cic. **b.** Of beasts :
Ov.

rixor, āri [rixa], *to brawl, come to blows.* **1.**
Lit.: Lucr. ; cum aliquo de aliquā re.
Cic. **2.** Transf. **a.** *to be ready to quarrel*
to blows, to quarrel, squabble : Quint. ; de
lanā caprinā, Hor. **b.** *to clash, disagree :*
inter se cupiditas et timor, Sen. Ep. ; cum
theatro saeculoque, Mart.

rōbiginōsus (**rūbīg-**), a, um [rōbīgŏ], *rusty.*
1. Lit.: strigilis, Pl. **2.** Transf. *blight-*
ing (i.e. envious), Mart.

rōbigō (**rūbīgō**), inis, *f.* [robus=ruber]. *rust*
of metals. **1.** Lit.: Pl., Verg., Plin.
2. Transf. **a.** *rust* on plants ; *blight, mil-*
dew : Varr., Verg. Person.: Ov. **b.**
film on the teeth : Ov. **c.** ingenium longā
rubigine laesum torpet, Ov. ; Sen. Ep.
[Fr. *rogne.*]

rōboreus, a, um [rōbur], *oaken, of oak :* pons,
Ov.

rōborō, āre [rōbur], *to make strong ; to*
strengthen. **1.** Lit.: artūs, Lucr. ; Plin.
2. Transf.: gravitatem perpetuā constantiā, Cic. ; recti cultūs pectora roborant,
Hor.

rōbur (older **rōbus**), oris, *n.* [*cf.* ῥώννυμι,
ῥώμη], *hard wood,* esp. *oak.* **1.** Lit.:
naves totae factae ex robore, Caes. ; Cic. ;
in robore accumbere, Cic. ; antiquo robore
quercus, Verg. ; Ov. ; solido de robore
myrtūs, Verg. Of an *oak-tree :* Ov. **2.**
Transf. **A.** Of things made of hard wood :

a lance, Verg. ; *a bolt,* Ov. **B.** *the lower*
dungeon of the prison at Rome, called
Tullianum : Lucr., Hor., Liv., Tac. **C.**
hardness, strength, vigour. **a.** Of things :
robora ferri, Lucr., Verg. ; saxi, Lucr. ;
navium, Liv. **b.** Of physical powers :
satis aetatis atque roboris habere, Cic. ;
Verg. ; imperatoris, Liv. Of an army, etc. :
neque his ipsis tantum virium aut roboris
fuit, Liv. **c.** Of mental or moral qualities :
animi, Cic., Liv. ; Hor. ; Ov. ; aliquid
roboris petitioni adferre, Cic. In *pl. :*
Ov. **d.** *the élite, pick, flower, pith, kernel :*
versaris in optimorum civium vel flore vel
robore, Cic. ; senatūs, Liv. ; caesum in
acie quod roboris fuit, Liv. ; Caes. ; robora
pubis, Verg. ; Liv. **e.** Of a place : *a*
stronghold : coloniam robur ac sedem
bello legere, Tac. [It. *rovere ;* Fr. *rouvre.*]

rōbustus, a, um [rōbus : *v.* rōbur], *of oak*
or *other hard wood.* **1.** Lit.: Cato, Hor.,
Liv. **2.** Transf. **A.** carcer (*v.* robur, 2.
B.), Pl. **B.** *hard, strong, firm, robust.* **a.**
Physically : Lucr., Cic., Hor., etc. Comp. :
Cic. Sup. : Suet. Of things : Plin. **b.**
res publica, Cic. ; animus, fortitudo, etc. ;
annus, Ov. Comp. : Cic.

rōdō, rōdere, rōsī, rōsum, *to gnaw.* **1.**
Lit.: clipeos mures, Cic. ; pollicem dente,
Hor. ; Ov. **2.** Transf. **a.** *to eat away,*
corrode : ferrum (rubigo), Ov. **b.** *to back-*
bite, disparage : in conviviis, Cic. ; absentem amicum, Hor.

rogālis, e, *adj.* [rogus], *of a funeral pile :*
flammae, Ov.

rogātiō, ōnis, *f.* [rogō]. **I.** *a proposal to the*
people for passing a law or decree, a pro-
posed law or decree, a bill : ferre de aliquo *or*
de aliquā re, Cic., Liv. ; in aliquem, Cic. ;
ad populum, Caes. ; ad plebem, Liv. ;
promulgare, Cic. ; suadere, Cic. ; accipere,
Cic. Ep. ; perferre, Cic. Ep., Liv. ; iubere,
antiquare, Liv. ; rogationi intercedere,
Cic. **II.** In gen. **a.** Rhet. *a question :*
Cic., Quint. **b.** *an asking, request :* Cic.

rogātiuncula, ae, *f.* [dim. rogātiō]. **I.** *an*
unimportant bill or proposed law : Cic.
II. *a little question :* Chrysippi, Cic.

rogātor, ōris, *m.* [rogō]. **I.** *one who pro-*
poses a law to the people : Lucil. Transf.:
haec epistula non suasoris est sed rogatoris.
Cic. Ep. **II.** *an officer who took the votes*
in the comitia, a polling clerk : Cic. **III.**
a beggar : Mart.

rogātū, ABL. *sing. m.* [rogō], *by or at the re-*
quest : alicnius, Cic.

rogātiō, ōnis, *f.* [rogitō], *a (? frequently)*
proposed law : Pl.

rogitō, āre [*freq.* rogō], *to ask or inquire*
frequently or eagerly : Pl., Ter. ; aliquem
aliquid, Pl., Ter. ; aliquem (with *Indir.*
Quest.), Pl. ; piscis, *to ask for fish,* Pl. ;
multa super Priamo, Verg.

rogō, āre (rogāssit, old *Fut.*, Cic.) *to ask for*
information, to question. **1.** Lit. **A.** In
gen. : Pl., Ter., Cic. ; aliquem, Pl., Ter.,
Cic. ; aliquid, Pl., Ter., etc. ; aliquem aliquid, Pl., Ter., Cic. ; aliquem de aliquo *or*
de aliquā re, Pl., Ter., Cic. ; aliquem (with
Indir. Quest.), Pl., Cic., Hor., etc. **B.** In
public affairs. **a.** rogare aliquem sententiam, Cic. ; primus rogatus sententiam, Sall.,

Liv. **b.** rogare populum *or* legem, *to ask the people about a proposal,* hence, *to propose a law, introduce a bill :* Cic., Liv. *Impers. Pass. :* nunc rogari ut populus consules creet, Liv. **c.** *to propose or offer for election :* consules, Cic., Liv. ; qui plebem R. tribunos plebi rogaret, Liv. **C.** In law : *to ask a person for a promise ; to propose a stipulation :* Pl. **D.** Milit. : rogare milites sacramento, *to administer the oath to the troops,* Caes., Liv. **2.** Transf. *to ask a favour, beg, request :* aliquem, Caes., Cic. (esp. in *Pass.* rogatus, *when asked*) ; aliquid, Pl., Caes., Cic., etc. ; aliquem aliquid, Pl., Cic., Hor., etc. ; aliquid de (*from*) aliquo, Pl. ; aliquid ab aliquo, Sall. ; aliquem (with *ut* or *ne* and *Jussive Subj.*), Pl., Cic., Hor., etc. ; with *Jussive Subj.,* without *ut* or *ne :* Caes., Ov., Plin. Ep. Prov. : malo emere quam rogare, Cic.

rogus, i, *m. a funeral-pile.* **1.** Lit. : Pl., Cic., Verg. **2.** Transf. (in *pl.*). **a.** Of destruction : Ov. **b.** Of the grave : Prop.

Rōma, ae, *f. Rome ;* **Rōmānus,** a, um ; **Rōmānicus,** a, um and **Rōmānĭēnsis,** e, Cato **Rōmāni,** ōrum. *m. pl.*

Rōmulus, i, *m. the founder and first king of Rome, worshipped after his death as* Quirinus ; **Rōmuleus, Rōmulus,** a, um ; and **Rōmulĭdae,** ārum, *m. pl. the descendants of Romulus, the Romans.*

rōrārii, ōrum, *m. pl.* [rōs], *skirmishers,* a kind of light-armed Roman troops, who usually made the first attack and then retired : Pl., Liv.

rōridus, a, um [rōs], *bedewed :* terga iugi, Prop.

rōrifer, era, erum [rōs ferō], *dew-bringing :* umbrae, Lucr.

rōrō, āre [rōs], *to drop or distil dew* (only in 3rd pers.). **1.** Lit. : (Aurora) toto rorat in orbe, Ov. More often, rorat (*impers.*), *dew falls :* Varr., Suet. *Perf. Part. : fallen as dew :* aquae, Ov. ; *also bedewed :* tellus rorata pruinā, Ov. **2.** Transf. **a.** Intrans. : *to drop, trickle :* pocula rorantia, *pouring drop by drop,* Cic. ; pennae, Ov. ; sanguine vepres, Verg. ; Quint. **b.** Trans. : *to bedew, moisten :* circumstant, lacrimis rorantes ora genasque, Lucr.

rōs, rōris, *m.* [perh. *cf.* ἔρση]. **I.** *dew.* **1.** Lit. : Pl., Lucr., Caes., Verg., etc. **2.** Transf. *moisture :* lympharum, Lucr. ; ros salis, *sea-water,* Lucr. ; ros, *water,* Verg., Hor., Ov. ; lacrimarum, Ov. ; Syrius (*perfume*), Tib. In *pl.* : Verg. **II.** rōs, rōris, *m.* (Verg.) or **rōs marīnus** (Hor.), or **rōsmarīnum,** n. (Plin.), *rosemary.*

rosa, ae, *f.* [*cf.* ῥόδον], *a rose.* **1.** Lit. : Cic., Hor., etc. **2.** Transf. **a.** As a term of endearment : Pl. **b.** *a rose-tree :* Lucr., Verg., Hor. **c.** Collect. : *roses, beds or wreaths of roses :* Cic., Hor.

rosārium, i, *n.* [rosa], *a rose-garden* (mostly in *pl.*) : Verg., Prop., Ov.

rōscidus, a, um [rōs], *wet with dew, dewy.* **1.** Lit. : herba, Varr. ; māla, Verg. ; dea. i.o. *Aurora,* Ov. **2.** Transf. **a.** *dropped like dew :* mella, Verg. **b.** *bedewed, moistened :* roscida rivis saxa, Verg.

Roscius, a, *the name of a Roman gens.* Esp. **I.** L. Roscius Otho, *a friend of Cicero, tribune of the plebs,* B.C. 67. **II.** Q.

Roscius, *a celebrated actor, the intimate friend of Cicero, and defended by him in an extant oration ;* **Rosciānus,** a, um. **III.** Sex. Roscius, *of Ameria, defended by Cicero, in an extant oration, on a charge of murder.*

Rōsea or **Rōsia,** ae, *f. a fertile district near Reate ;* **Rōseus (Rōsius),** a, um.

rosētum, i, *n.* [rosa], *a garden or bed of roses :* Varr., Verg.

roseus, a, um [rosa]. **I.** *of roses, rose-vinculum,* Sen. ; Verg. **II.** *rose-coloured, rosy :* roseā sol alto lampade lucens, Lucr. ; Phoebus, Verg. ; labella, Cat. ; os (Veneris), Verg.

rōs marīnus and **rōs-marīnum,** *v.* rōs.

rōstrātus, a, um [rōstrum], *beaked, curved :* navis, Cic. ; ora navium rostrata, Hor. ; corona rostrata *or* corona navalis, *a crown given to the man who first boarded an enemy's vessel,* Plin. ; *cf.* (Agrippae) tempora navali fulgent rostrata coronā, Verg. ; columna rostrata, *a column adorned with the beaks of conquered vessels, erected to commemorate a naval victory,* Liv.

rōstrum, i, *n.* [rōdō], *the bill or beak of a bird ; the snout or muzzle of an animal.* **1.** Lit. : Cic., Ov., Liv., etc. Contemptuously *of human beings, beak, snout :* Pl. **2.** Transf. *of similarly shaped objects.* **a.** Of hammers, ploughs, etc. : Plin. **b.** *the curved end of a ship's prow, a ship's beak :* Caes., Verg., Liv., etc. **rōstra,** ōrum, *n. pl. 'the beaks,'* i.e. the place adorned with beaks of ships (taken from Antium, B.C. 338) ; a raised platform for speakers, orig. betw. the comitium and forum, later in front of the temple of Caesar : in rostra escendere, Cic., Liv. ; descendere de rostris, Cic. ; aliquem deducere de rostris, Caes. ; rem a subselliis ad rostra detulit, Cic. ; ut in rostris prius quam in senatu litterae recitarentur, Liv. ; aliquem defunctum laudare e more pro rostris, Suet. ; Sen. ; Tac. In *sing.* : Luc.

rōsus, a, um, *Part.* rōdō.

rota, ae, *f. a wheel.* **1.** Lit. **a.** In gen. : Pl., Cato, Lucr., Verg., Hor., etc. **b.** *a potter's wheel :* Hor., Tib., Sen. Ep. **c.** *a wheel for torture :* in rotam escendere, Cic. ; Sen. Ep. Comic. : crucior in amoris rotā, Pl. **2.** Transf. **a.** *a car, chariot :* Prop., Ov. **b.** *a disk :* solis, Lucr. ; Enn. **c.** fortunae rotam pertimescere, Cic. ; Tib. etc. **d.** Of elegiac verse : imparibus vecta Thalia rotis, Ov. [Fr. *roue.*]

rotō, āre [rota], *to turn (a thing) round like a wheel ; to whirl round about.* **1.** Lit. : flammam venti, Lucr. ; Learchum bis terquo per auras more rotat fundae, Ov. ; ensem fulmineum, Verg. ; telum, Liv. ; fumum (flammae), Hor. In *Mid.* : *to roll round, to revolve :* circum caput igno rotato, Ov. ; saxa rotantia lato impulerat torrens, Verg. **2.** Transf. : aut curtum sermone rotato torqueat enthymema, Juv.

rotula, ae, *f.* [dim. rota], *a little wheel :* Pl., Plin. [Fr. *rôle.*]

rotundē, *adv. smoothly, elegantly :* Cic.

rotundō, āre [rotundus], *to make round, to round off.* **1.** Lit. : aliquid ad volubilitatem, Cic. **2.** Transf. of a round sum of money : mille talenta rotundentur, Hor.

rotundus, a, um [rota], *round, circular*, also *spherical*. **1.** Lit.: Lucr., Cic. *Comp.* : Cic., Hor. *Neut.* as Noun : Cic., Hor. **2.** Transf. of sphere-like perfection. **a.** Of the Stoic 'wise man' : in se ipso totus teres atque rotundus, Hor. **b.** Of style : verborum quasi rotunda constructio, Cic. ; Graiis dedit ore rotundo Musa loqui, Hor. Of the author himself : Cic. [It. *rotondo* ; Fr. *rond*.]

rube-facĭō, facere, fēcī, factum, *to make red or ruddy, to redden* : sanguine saetas, Ov.

rubellus, a, um [*dim.* ruber], *reddish* : vinum, Mart. ; Pers.

rubēns, entis. **I.** *Part.* rubeō. **II.** Adj. **a.** *red, crimson* : Lucr., Verg., Hor., Suet. **b.** *red with blushing* : os, Tib.

rubeō, ēre [v. ruber], *to be red or ruddy.* **a.** In gen .: ocelli fiendo rubent, Cat. ; aviaria sanguineis bacis, Verg. ; Ov. **b.** *to blush* : Cic., Hor.

ruber, bra, brum [*cf.* Gk. ἐρυθρός], *red, ruddy.* **1.** Lit.: Lucr., Verg., Hor., etc. Mare Rubrum, *the Arabian and Persian Gulfs,* Cic., Verg., Liv. ; Oceanus, *the Indian ocean,* Hor. *Comp.* : Plin. **2.** Transf. leges maiorum (because their titles were written in red letters), Juv.

rubēsco, rubēscere, rubuī [rubeō], *to grow red, to redden* : Aurora, Verg. ; tempora matutina, Ov. ; saxa sanguine, Ov. ; Verg. Of blushing : Ov., Sen. Ep.

rubēta, ae, f. [rubus], *a kind of toad living among bramble-bushes,* prob. *the common toad* : Prop., Juv.

(1) rubeus, a, um [rubus], *of bramble, bramble-* : virga, Verg.

(2) rubeus (robeus), a, um [*cf.* ruber], *red* : color, Varr.

Rubicō, ōnis, m. *a small stream which formed the boundary between Italy and Cisalpine Gaul* ; now *the Pisatello.*

rubicundulus, a, um [*dim.* rubicundus], *somewhat red, reddish* : Juv.

rubicundus, a, um [rubeō], *red, ruddy* : os, Pl. ; corna, Hor. ; Ceres, Verg. *Comp.* : Varr.

rubidus, a, um [rubeō], *red, reddish* : ampulla, Pl.

rūbig-, *v.* rōbig-.

rubor, ōris, m. [rubeō], *redness* (of all shades). **1.** Lit. **a.** In gen.: Cic., Verg., Tac. In *pl.* : Verg. **b.** *a blush* : Cic., Ov. ; Masinissae rubor suffusus, Liv. **2.** Transf. **a.** *bashfulness, sense of shame* : Cic. ; ruborem incutere, Liv. ; adferre, Tac. **b.** *shame, disgrace* : censoris iudicium nihil fere damnato nisi ruborem adfert, Cic. ; rubori esse alicui, Liv. ; (with *Inf.*), Ov.; nec rubor est, Liv., Ov., Tac.

rubrica, ae, f. [ruber] (*sc.* terra), *red earth.* **1.** Lit. *red earth for colouring, red ochre, red chalk* : Pl., Hor. **2.** Transf. *a law* (because the title was written in red) : Pers., Quint.

rubus, i, m. [*cf.* ruber], *a bramble-bush, blackberry-bush.* **1.** Lit.: Caes., Verg., etc. **2.** Transf. *a blackberry* : Prop.

rūctō, āre, and **rūctor**, ārī (Varr., Hor.) [*cf.* Gk. ἐρεύγω], *to belch.* **1.** Lit.: Pl.,

Cic., Juv.   With Acc.: Varr., Mart., Juv. **2.** Transf.: versūs, Hor. [Fr. *roter*.]

rūctus, ūs, m. [*cf.* rūctō], *a belching* : Pl., Cic. Ep.

rūdectus, a, um [rūdus], *full of stones or rubbish* ; hence, *poor* : terra, Cato.

rūdēns, entis [rudō], lit. *creaking, rattling,* hence (*sc.* funis), m. (*f.* Pl.), *a halyard, sheet, etc.* **a.** In *sing.* : Pl. **b.** In *pl.* : *the rigging* : Pl., Cic., Verg., etc. Transf.: rudentibus apta fortuna, Cic.

Rudiae, ārum, f. *pl. a town in Calabria, the birth-place of Ennius* ; **Rudīnus**, a, um.

rudiārius, ī, m. [rudis], *a gladiator presented with the* rudis (q.v.), *i.e. discharged* : Suet.

rudimentum, ī, n. [rudis, adj.], *a first attempt, a beginning.* **a.** In gen.: rudimentum primum puerilis regni, Liv. ; civilium officiorum rudimenta, Suet. **b.** Milit.: militare, Liv. ; dura rudimenta belli, Verg. ; adulescentiae ponere, *to complete one's noviciate,* Liv. ; prima rudimenta castrorum duci approbavit, Tac.

rudis, e, *adj. in the natural state, not improved by art* ; hence, *unwrought, untilled.* **1.** Lit.: terra, Varr. ; campus, Verg. ; humus, Ov. ; moles (*Chaos*), Ov. ; aes (opp. to signatum), Plin. ; marmor, Quint. ; lana, Ov. **2.** Transf. **a.** Of artificial things, *ill-made, rudely finished, coarse* : hasta, Verg. ; textum, Ov. **b.** *new, untried* : illa (carina, *sc.* Argo) rudem cursu prima imbuit Amphitriten, Cat. ; agna, Mart. **c.** *rude, unpolished, uncultured, unskilled, ignorant, awkward, clumsy* : consilium, Pl. ; forma ingeni impolita et plane rudis, Cic. ; ingenium, Hor. ; rude in Graecis intactum carmen, Hor. ; rudis adhuc aetas, Tac. ; vox, stilus, Quint. With *in* and ABL.: rudis in re publicā, Cic. ; in disserendo, Cic. ; sermo nullā in re, Cic. With ABL.: Ennius ingenio maximus, arte rudis, Ov. With GEN.: Graecarum litterarum, Cic. ; civilis belli, Hor. ; artium, Liv. ; dicendi, Tac. With *ad* : ad spectacula, Liv. ; gens ad oppugnandarum urbium artis rudis, Liv. ; ad mala, Ov. [It. *rozzo, rude.*]

rudis, is, f. *a slender stick or rod.* **a.** *a stirring-stick, spatula* : ferrea, Plin. **b.** *a foil used in practice-exercises by soldiers and gladiators* : Liv., Ov., Suet. Also *a foil presented to a gladiator on his discharge* : Cic., Juv. Transf.: spectatum satis et donatum iam rude, Hor. ; Ov.

rudō (rūdō, Pers.), rudere, rudīvī, ruditum [*cf.* Gk. ὠρύω], *to bray, bellow, roar* : intempestivo rudit ille (asellus) sono, Ov. ; gemitus leonum rudentum, Verg. Of wild men : (Cacum) insueta (*Intern.* ACC.) rudentem, Verg. Of things : *to strain and creak* : prora, Verg.

rūdus, eris, n. **I.** *stones broken small and mixed with lime* for plastering walls, etc.; *rough-cast* : Plin. Also *old rubbish* of decayed buildings : Tac. **II.** *a piece of brass* : v. raudus.

rūdus, rūdusculum, I. v. raudusculum.

rūfulus, a, um [*dim.* rūfus], *reddish, rather red* : Pl.

Rūfuli, ōrum, m. *pl.* [derived fr. Rutilius Rūfus], *the military tribunes chosen by the*

general *himself*, opp. to the comitiati, who
were chosen by the people : Liv.

rūfus, a, um [*cf.* ruber], *red, reddish :* rufus
quidam (*red-headed*), Pl. ; Ter. ; vestes,
Mart. Comp. : Plin.

rūga, ae, *f. a wrinkle* (us. *pl.*) : Cic., Verg., Ov.,
etc. In *sing.* : Prop., Ov., Juv.

rūgō, āre [rūga], *to become wrinkled* or
creased : vide palliolum ut rugat, Pl.

rūgōsus, a, um [rūga], *wrinkled, shrivelled.*
1. Lit. : pellis, Hor. ; genae, Ov. Comp. :
Mart. **2.** Transf. **a.** senecta, Tib. **b.**
frigore pagus, Hor. **c.** *creased, corrugated :*
cortex pōpuli, Ov.

ruina, ae, *f.* [ruō], *a tumbling down.* **1.** Lit.
a. *a falling down, fall :* grandinis, Lucr. ;
iumentorum sarcinarumque, Liv. ; caeli,
Verg. ; primique ruinam dant (*cause*)
sonitu ingenti, Verg. ; Liv. **b.** Of buildings : *a tumbling* or *falling down, ruin :*
turris repentinā ruinā concidit, Caes. ; tecta
Penthei disiecta non leni ruinā, Hor. ; Cic. ;
ruinam dare, *to come tumbling down*, Verg. ;
also trahere, Verg. ; aedificiorum, Suet. In
pl. : Pl., Lucr., Hor., Suet. **2.** Transf.
a. Concr. : *the debris, ruins* (mostly in
pl.) of falling or fallen buildings : Verg.,
Liv., Ov. **b.** *a castastrophe, overthrow,
destruction :* incendium meum ruinā re-
stinguam, Sall. ; Cic. ; ut communi ruinā
patriae opprimerentur, Liv. ; in hac ruinā
rerum, Liv. ; ille dies utramque ducet
ruinam, Hor. In *pl.* : praetermitto ruinas
fortunarum tuarum, Cic. ; Lucr. ; Hor.
c. Of a person : illa ruina rei publicae,
demolisher, Cic.

ruinōsus, a, um [ruina], *going to ruin.* **1.**
Lit. : aedes, Cic. **2.** Transf. *fallen,
ruined :* domus, Ov.

rumex, icis, *f. sorrel :* Pl., Verg.

rūmificō, āre [rūmor faciō], *to report :* aliquam probam, Pl.

Rūmina, ae, *f. a Roman goddess, who was
worshipped in a separate temple near the
fig-tree under which Romulus and Remus had
sucked the breast* (rumis) *of the she-wolf ;*
Rūminālis, e, *adj. :* ficus, *the fig-tree of
Romulus and Remus* (Liv.) : called also
Rumina ficus (Ov.).

rūminātiō, ōnis, *f.* [rūminō], *a chewing over
again, chewing the cud, rumination.* **1.**
Lit. : Plin. **2.** Transf. **a.** *a doubling ;
a repetition, return :* corticis, Plin. **b.**
a thinking over in the mind, ruminating : Cic.
Ep.

rūminō, āre [rūmen, *the throat ; cf.* rūctō],
to chew over again, chew the cud : bos, Plin.
With Acc. ; bos herbas, Verg. ; revocatas
herbas, Ov.

rūmor, ōris, *m.* [*cf.* Gk. ὡρύω, Lat. raucus,
rudō]. **I.** *shouting, cheering* (in ABL. with
secundo). **1.** Lit. : Enn., Verg. **2.**
Transf. : aliquid accipere secundo rumore,
Tac. ; Hor. **II.** *common talk, hearsay,
rumour :* multa rumor fingebat, Caes. ;
manat per compita rumor, Hor. ; rumores
Africanos excipere, Cic. ; Ov. With Acc.
and *Inf.* : Pl. ; rumor venit datum iri
gladiatores, Ter. ; meum gnatum rumor
est amare, Ter. ; Cic. Ep. ; rumores ad-
ferebantur Belgas contra populum R.
coniurare, Caes. With quoted words :

Cic. With *de :* Caes., Cic., Liv. With
tamquam and *Subj.* or *Fut. Part. :*
Tac. With GEN. : belli civilis rumores,
Tac. **III.** *common* or *general opinion,
the popular voice, reputation* (good or
bad) : rumori servire, Pl. ; rumorem
quendam et plausum popularem esse quaesitum, Cic. ; adversus famam rumoresque
hominum firmus, Liv. ; adverso rumore
esse, Liv. ; Hor. ; Tac.

rumpia (**rhomphaea**), ae, *f.* [ρομφαία], *a
long javelin of* certain barbarous nations :
Liv.

rumpō, rumpere, rūpī, ruptum. **I.** *to break :*
membrum, XII. Tab. ; Decree in Liv. **II.**
to break, burst open or *asunder, break down.*
1. Lit. : ramices, Pl. (also, me rupi cur-
rendo, Pl.) : ilia, Cat. ; vesiculas, Cic. ;
vincula, Lucr., Cic., Verg., etc. ; claustra,
Hor. ; pontem, Liv. ; vestis, Ov. ; montem
aceto, Juv. ; guttura cultro, Ov. ; Verg. ;
pectora fremitu leones, Lucr. ; nubem vis
venti, Lucr. ; horrea messes, Verg. ; frigore
saxa hiems, Verg. **2.** Transf. **a.** Ingen. :
frena pudoris, Prop. ; licentiā audacium
rumpebar, Cic. Ep. ; Verg. **b.** *to break,
burst through* (mostly milit.) : media agmina, Verg. ; proelia misso equo, Prop. ;
mediam aciem, ordines, Liv. **c.** With
Proleptic Acc. : viam, iter, *to burst* or *force
a way* for oneself, Verg., Liv., etc. **d.** With
Refl. Pron. or in *Mid.* : *to force a way,
burst forth :* se nubibus imber ruperat,
Verg. ; amnes rumpuntur fontibus, Verg. ;
rupto turbine, Verg. **e.** Causative : *to
make to burst forth :* vocem, questūs pectore,
Verg. ; Tac. ; fontem ungula, Ov. **f.** *to
break down, destroy :* alicui reditum, Hor.
g. *to break, violate, annul :* rogationes,
Pl. ; foedera, Lucr., Cic., etc. ; testamentum, Cic. ; fidem indutiarum, Liv. ; Verg. ;
sacramenti religionem, Liv. ; Tac. ; ius
gentium, Liv. ; amores, Verg. ; nuptias,
Hor. ; fata aspera, Verg. **h.** *to break off
suddenly, cut short :* silentia, Lucr., Verg.,
etc. ; taciturnitatem, Tac. ; moras, otia,
Verg., etc. ; visum, Cic. ; somnum, Verg. ;
sacra, amores (but with suggestion of sense
g.), Verg. [It. *rompere ;* Fr. *rompre.*]

rūmusculi, ōrum, *m. pl.* [*dim.* rūmor], *idle
gossip :* Cic.

rūna, ae, *f. a kind of dart :* Cic.

runcō, āre [*cf.* runcina, *a plane*], *to weed out.*
1. Lit. : spinas, Cato ; segetes, Varr. **2.**
Transf. (of hair) : Pers.

ruō, ruere, ruī, rutum (but *cf.* rūta caesa ;
Fut. Part. ruitūrus, Ov., etc.), *to tumble
down.* **I.** Intrans. **A.** *to fall with violence, fall down, come to ruin.* **1.** Lit. :
parietes, aedes, etc., Pl. ; Lucr. ; Hor. ;
Liv., etc. ; alto a culmine Troia, Verg. ;
Lucr. Of persons : Verg. **2.** Transf.
a. caeli templa, Lucr. ; arduus aether,
Verg. ; caelum in se, Liv. ; turbidus imber
aquā, Verg. ; tempestas, Tac. ; de montibus amnes, Verg. ; flumina per campos,
Ov. ; in Galliam Rhenus, Tac. ; imbriferum
ver (i.e. to its close), Verg. Prov. : caelum ruit, Ter. ; res publica, Cic. ; ratio,
Lucr. ; omnia circum eum Liv. ; Vitellium
ruentibus rebus debilitatum, Tac. **B.** *to
rush headlong* or *hurriedly.* **1.** Lit. : Cic.,

Tac.; eques portis, Liv.; in castra, in vulnera ao tela, Liv.; in ferrum, Verg.; per proelia, Verg.; ad urbem, Liv.; Tac. **2.** Transf. **a.** Mostly of persons: Cic., Tac.; ad interitum, Cic.; ad seditiones, Tac.; in crudelitatem, Liv.; Cic.; in exitium, Tac.; omnia fatis in peius, Verg.; quo ruis? Verg.; Hor. With *Inf.* : Prop. **b.** venti ruunt, Verg.; revoluta dies, Verg.; Oceano (*from Ocean*) nox, Verg.; (*ex antro*) voces, responsa Sibyllae, Verg. **II.** Trans. **A.** *to cast down with violence, to dash or hurl to the ground :* imbres antemnas, Pl.; navis vis venti, Lucr.; cumulos harenae, Verg. Of persons: ceteros, Ter. **B.** *to throw up, rake up :* mare harenam, Lucr.; totum mare a sedibus imis venti, Verg.; divitias aerisque acervos, Hor.

rūpēs, is, *f.* [rumpō], *a rock, cliff :* Caes., Verg., Liv., etc.

ruptor, ōris, *m.* [rumpō], *a breaker.* Transf. : foederis, Liv.; pacis, Tac.

ruptus, a, um, *Part.* rumpō.

rūricola, ae, *adj. m.f. n.* [rūs colō], *tilling the ground ;* hence, *rural, rustic :* boves, Ov.; Ceres, Ov.; aratrum, Ov. *Masc.* as Noun, *an ox :* Ov.

rūrigena, ae, *m.* [rūs and *gen* in gignō], *born in the country ; a countryman, rustic :* Ov.

rūrō, āre (Pl.) and **rūror**, ārī (Varr.) [rūs], *to live in the country.*

rūrsus or less freq. **rūrsum (rūsum**, Pl.), *adv.* [contr. from reversus or revorsum, from revertō; *cf.* prōrsus and sūrsum], *backwards, back.* **1.** Lit. (of motion): Pl., Ter., Varr. **2.** Transf. **a.** *on the contrary, in return, again :* capiunt voluptates, capiunt rusum miserias, Pl.; hi rursus in vicem anno post in armis sunt, Caes.; Cic.; aequum est peccatis veniam poscentem reddere rursus, Hor.; clamore sublato excipit rursus ex vallo clamor, Caes.; Sall. **b.** *again, anew, afresh :* Pl., Lucr., Caes., Cic., etc.

rūs, rūris (*pl.* only in Nom. and Acc.), *n. the country,* as opp. to the town: *lands, fields; a country-seat, farm, estate.* **1.** Lit.: Cic., Ov. In *pl.* : Lucr., Verg., Ov. Acc. **rūs**, *to the country :* Pl., Ter. Locat. **rūri** (or **rūre**, *in the country :* Pl., Cic., Liv., Ov., etc. With *Adj.* : rure paterno, Hor.; Ov. Abl. **rūre**, *from the country :* Pl., Ter. **2.** Transf. *rusticity :* idem infaceto est infacetior rure, Cat.; manent vestigia ruris, Hor.

rūscum, ī, *n. butcher's broom :* Verg.

russus, a, um [*cf.* ἐρυθρός], *red :* Lucr., Cat. [It. *rosso ;* Fr. *roux.*]

rūsticānus, a, um [rūsticus], *of or in the country, rustic, country :* municipia, homines, Cic.; relegatio, Cic.

rūsticātiō, ōnis, *f.* [rūsticor], *a living in the country, country life :* Cic.

rūsticē, *adv. in a countrified manner, clownishly :* loqui, Cic. *Comp.* : rusticius toga defluit, Hor.

rūsticitās, ātis, *f.* [rūsticus], *the manners of country people, rustic behaviour, rusticity.* **a.** In good sense: Plin., Plin. Ep. **b.** In bad sense: Ov., Quint., Suet.

rūsticor, ārī [rūsticus], *to live in the country,*

nobiscum, peregrinantur, rusticantur, Cic.

rūsticulus, a, um [*dim.* rūsticus], *rather rustic or coarse :* libellus, Mart. *Masc.* as Noun: Cic.

rūsticus, a, um [rūs ; *cf.* silvāticus], *of or in the country, rural, rustic, country-.* **1.** Lit.: opus, Ter.; vita, praedia, res, homo, Cic.; mus, Hor.; numina, Ov. As Noun, **rūsticus**, ī, *m. a countryman. rustic, peasant :* Pl., Cic., Hor., Ov. ; **rūstica**, ae, *f. a country-girl :* Ov. **2.** Transf. *country-like, countrified,* in good sense, i.e. *plain, simple, uncorrupted :* mores, Cic.; or (*more* freq.) in bad sense, i.e. *boorish, clownish :* Pl., Verg.; vox, Cic.; convicia, Ov. *Masc.* as Noun : Pl., Verg., Ov. *Fem.* as Noun : Pl., Ov.

rūsum, *v.* rūrsus.

rūta caesa, or **rūta et caesa** [ruō, caedō]. In law, *every thing dug up and cut down on an estate without being wrought,* and which is reserved by the owner at a sale: *the minerals and timber :* Cic.

rūta, ae, *f.* [ῥυτή], *a bitter herb, rue.* **1.** Lit.: Cic. Ep., Ov., etc. **2.** Transf. *bitterness, unpleasantness :* cras exspecto Leptam, ad cuius rutam pulegio mihi tui sermonis utendum est, Cic. Ep.

rutābulum, ī, *n.* [ruō], *a fire-shovel, oven-rake :* Cato, Suet.

rutilō, āre [rutilus]. **A.** Transf. : *to make or colour red :* comas, Liv.; Tac. **B.** Intrans. : *to have a reddish glow :* aurora, Acc.; rutilantia arma, Verg.

rutilus, a, um [*cf.* Gk. ἐρυθρός], *red* (inclining to golden yellow): caput, Pl.; of the hair, Ov., Tac.; fulgor rutilus quem Martium dicitis, Cic.; ignis, Verg.

rutrum, ī, *n.* [ruō], *a spade :* Cato, Liv., Ov.

rūtula, ae, *f.* [*dim.* rūta], *a little bit of rue :* Cic. Ep.

Rutulī, ōrum, *m. pl. an ancient people of Latium, whose capital was Ardea ;* **Rutulus**, a, um.

Rutupiae, ārum, *f. pl. a town in the S.E. of Britain ; now Richborough ;* **Rutupīnus**, a, um.

rutus, a, um, *Part.* ruō.

S

S, s, indecl. *n.* or (agreeing with littera), *f.* **I. a.** Latin *s* in the middle of words corresponds to Greek σ. Initial *s* has as its regular representative in Greek the rough breathing ; thus we have *sal*=ἅλς ; *sedeo* =ἕζομαι ; *semi*=ἡμι- ; *septem*=ἑπτά ; *sequor*=ἕπομαι ; *serpo*=ἕρπω. **b.** In the earlier periods of the Latin language, before *z* came back into use, ζ in words borrowed from the Greek was represented by *ss*; thus μᾶζα became *massa*, Ἀττικίζω *atticisso*, κωμάζω *comissor.* Original initial *s* before a consonant has been lost in many Latin words: as *fallo, pituita, tego,* etc. **II.** *s* had, as in English, two different sounds, a *sharp* and a *flat* (or *weak*). It had the sharp sound at the beginning of words, as also in the middle of words before and after other consonants. But between vowels it had the weaker sound, which was like that of English *z*, or of *s* in Fr. and Eng. *rose*. Hence in this position it was often changed to *r* (see article on letter R). Final *s* had the weak sound. Its weakness led to its frequent disappearance, as in such nominatives as *nauta* (ναύτης), *poeta*, and in *ille, iste*, etc. Its loss took place especially in the popular Latin of the oldest, and again of the most recent, period. Hence in the anteclassical poets down to the time of Cicero, final *s* was often dropped before words beginning with a consonant, as Fulviu' Nobilior, vivo' per, gravi'terra, Hyperioni' cursum. Hence also arose the secondary forms of the second person sing. of pass. and dep. verbs, as *patere* for *pateris, amabere* for *amaberis*, etc. Hence, too, such forms as *ain', satin', scin', viden'* for *aisne, satisne, scisne, videsne;* also perh. *mage* for *magis* and the like. **III.** Changes of *s* within the Latin language. **1.** As we have seen, between vowels it very commonly becomes *r*. **2.** It is assimilated before *f* in the compounds of *dis* : e.g. *differo, difficilis, diffluo*. **3.** With the gutturals it combines to form *x* ; o.g. *rex*=*reg-s, pax*=*pac-s* ; so the perfects *rexi, duxi, vexi*, from *rego, duco, veho*. **IV.** In the Romance languages initial *s* commonly remains unchanged ; sometimes in Ital. it becomes *z* ; e.g. Lat. *sapphirus*, It. *zaffiro, zoccolo*. When followed by *p, c,* or *t,* it frequently has a prefixed *e,* and in French is often omitted ; e.g. Lat. *species, spiritus,* Fr. *espèce, esprit* (Sp. *espiritu*) ; Lat. *scribere, scala, stabulum* ; Fr. *écrire* (Sp. *escribir*), *échelle, étable*. Medial *s* is often lost before a consonant in French, the omission (which did not take place in old Fr.) being indicated by a circumflex over the preceding vowel ; e.g. Lat. *asinus, bestia, pascere, crescere ;* Fr. *âne, bête, paître, croître,* etc. Sometimes medial *s* becomes *sc* (It.) or *ss* (Fr.) ; e.g. Lat. *vesica,* It. *vescica,* Fr. *vessie ;* Lat. *designare,* Fr. *dessiner ;* very rarely it is changed to *r,* as in *orfraie* from Lat. *ossifraga, Marseille* from *Massilia*. When medial *s* becomes final in French, it is sometimes changed to *z,* as in *nez* from *nasus, chez* from *casa ;* or to *x* as in *roux* from *russus, toux* from *tussis ;* the suffix -*osus* regularly becomes -*eux*. **V.** As an abbreviation, S denotes *sacrum, semis, sibi, suis,* etc. S. AS. D., sub asciâ dedicavit. S. C., senatûs consultum. S. P., suâ pecuniâ. S. P. Q. R., Senatus Populusque Romanus.

Saba, ae, *f. a town in Arabia Felix, celebrated for its frankincense.* **Sabaeus,** a, um, *Sabaean ;* **Sabaei,** ōrum, *m. pl. the Sabaeans :* **Sabaea,** ae, *f. the country.*

Sabāzius, i, *m. a surname of Bacchus ;* **Sabāzia,** ōrum, *n. pl. a festival in honour of Bacchus.*

sabbata, orum, *n. pl.* [σάββατα, a Hebrew word], *the day of rest among the Jews, the Sabbath.* **1.** Lit.: Plin., Suet. **2.** Transf. *of other Jewish holidays :* Hor., Ov., etc.

sabbatārii, ōrum, *m. pl. Sabbath-keepers :* Mart.

Sabelli, ōrum, *m. pl.* [dim. Sabini], a name for the Sabines ; **Sabellus, Sabellicus,** a, um ; **Sabellus,** i, *m. the Sabellian* or *Sabine,* i.o. *Horace :* Hor.

Sabini, ōrum, *m. pl. an ancient people of Central Italy, N. of Latium ;* **Sabinus,** a, um, *Sabine :* herba, *a kind of juniper, the savin,* Cato, Ov., etc.; **Sabina,** ae. *f. a Sabine woman ;* **Sabinum,** i, *n. Sabine wine ; also, in sing. or pl., Horace's Sabine estate.*

Sabrina, ae, *f. the R. Severn.*

sabulō, ōnis, *m. coarse sand, ballast :* Varr.

sabulōsus, a, um [sabulō], *full of sand, sandy, gravelly :* terra, Plin.

sabulum, i, *n. coarse sand, gravel :* Varr., Curt.

saburra, ae, *f.* [sabulō], *sand for ballast :* Varr., Liv. [It. *zavorra*.]

saburrō, āre [saburra], *to fill with ballast, to ballast.* **1.** Lit.: Plin. **2.** Transf.: ubi saburratae sumus (comically for saturatae), Pl.

Sacae, ārum, *m. pl. a Scythian tribe.*

saccipērium, i, *n.* [saccus pēra], *a pocket for a purse :* Pl.

saccō, āre [saccus], *to strain through a bag, to strain, filter.* **1.** Lit.: Caecuba, Mart. ; saccata aqua, Sen. Ep. **2.** Transf.: saccatus umor corporis, Lucr.

sacculus, i, *m.* [dim. saccus], *a little bag,* esp. *for money, a purse :* sacculus plenus aranearum, Cat. ; Juv. ; *for filtering :* Lucil.

saccus, i, *m.* [σάκκος], *a sack, bag :* Cic., Phaedr. ; nummorum, Hor. *Of a beggar's wallet :* ad saccum ire, Pl. *Of a filtering bag :* Plin., Mart.

sacellum, i, *n.* [dim. sacrum], *a small unroofed sanctuary ; a chapel :* Ter., Cic., Verg., etc.

sacer, sacra, sacrum (*pl.* sacrēs, Pl.), *consecrated to a deity.* **1.** Lit. **a.** *consecrated, sacred, holy* (opp. profanus): Pl., Cic., Verg., etc. Occ. of the deity: Vesta, Prop. With GEN.: urna Veneris, Pl. ; Cat. ; Cic. ; Hor. With DAT.: Iovi quercus, Ov. ; Verg. ; Tac. Sacer Mons, a hill about 3 miles from Rome, beyond the Anio, to which the Roman plebs retired (B.C. 494), Liv. ; Sacra Via, or (poet.) Sacer Clivus, a Roman street, leading from the Forum to the Capitol, Cic., Hor., Mart. **b.** *devoted to a deity for destruction, forfeited, accursed :* XII Tab., Hor., Liv. With DAT.: caput Iovi, Old Law in Liv. **2.** Transf. **a.** *sacred, venerable (and mysterious) :* silentium, Hor. ; amantes, Prop. ; patris memoria, Quint. Of diseases : sacer ignis, Verg. Of some Emperors : sacrā Caesaris aure frui, Mart. ; occupationes, Suet. **b.** *accursed, execrable, detestable.* Of persons : Pl., Lucil. ; *Sup.* sacerrimus, Pl. Of things : libellus, Cat. ; auri fames, Verg. With DAT. : Remi sacer nepotibus cruor, Hor. *Neut.* as Noun. **A.** *Sing.,* **sacrum,** i, *a holy or sacred thing.* **a.** *In gen. :* omne sacrum rapiente dextrā, Hor. ; Pl. **b.** *an offering, victim for sacrifice :* sacrum id Volcano cremavit, Liv. ; Ov. *Prov.* **b.** inter sacrum saxumque stare, Pl. **c.** *a sacred rite, a sacrifice :* bove sacrum Herculi factum est, Liv. ; Cic. ; Prop. **d.** *a holy place, shrine* : Pl., Quint. **B.** *Plur.,* **sacra,** ōrum. **a.** *holy things, sacred objects or utensils, etc.* : Cic., Verg., etc. **b.** *sacred rites, ritual, divine worship, or religion in gen.* : Romulus Sabinos in civitatem ascivit, sacris communicatis, Cic. ; qui (Mercurius) sacris anniversariis coleretur, Cic. ; sacra Cereris conficere, Cic. ; sacra Iovi Stygio perficere, Verg. ; sacra Iovi facere, Ov. ; Liv. ; sacra obire, Liv. Sometimes of the *rites* of a gens, family, etc. : gentilicia, Liv. ; iisdem uti sacris, Cic. ; nuptialia, Quint. ; iugalia, Ov. **Prov.** : hereditas sine sacris, *an inheritance without responsibilities,* i.e. a rose without a thorn, Pl. **Transf.** : sacra tori, Ov. ; sacra tradentium artis, Quint. ; litterarum colere, Quint. ; studiorum profanare, Tac. **c.** *holy places* : Ov. **d.** *poems* (as sacred to the Muses) : Ov., Quint., etc.

sacerdōs, ōtis, *m. f.* [sacer], *a priest ; a priestess* : Pl., Cic., Verg., etc. In apposition : regina, i.e. Rhea Silvia, Verg. ; Pl. ; Quint. Sarcastically : ille popularis sacerdos, i.e. Clodius, Cic. ; also, stuprorum sacerdos, Cic.

sacerdōtālis, e, *adj.* [sacerdōs], *given by priests* : ludi, Plin. Ep.

sacerdōtium, ī, n. [sacerdōs], *the priesthood* : Cic., Liv. In *pl.* : Caes., Cic.

sacrāmentum, ī, n. [sacrō]. **I.** In law : *the sum of money which the parties to a suit deposited,* orig. with the tresviri capitales, *later with the praetor ; a guarantee, deposit.* **1.** Lit. : de multae sacramento consules comitiis centuriatis tulerunt, Cic. **2.** Transf. **a.** Prop. : *a civil suit :* sacramentum iustum iudicaverunt, Cic. **b.** *a dispute, contention* in gen. : iusto sacramento contendere, Cic. **II.** Milit. *a preliminary engagement* entered upon by newly enlisted soldiers (afterwards completed by the formal oath, *ius iurandum*). **1.** Lit. : Liv. **2.** Transf. **a.** For ius iurandum, *the military oath of allegiance* (to the general and later to the Emperor) : milites Domitianos sacramentum apud se dicere iubet (i.e. they replied " idem in me " to the words dictated), Caes. ; sacramentum dicere, Caes. ; so, with alicui, Tac. ; sacramento (ABL.) dicere *or* dicere alicui, Liv. ; adigere (*or* rogare) sacramento aliquos, Liv., Tac. ; sacramento aliquem tenere, Caes. ; aliquem obligare militiae sacramento, Cic. ; alicuius sacramentum exuere, Tac. ; mutare, Suet. **b.** *any oath, solemn obligation or engagement* : Cic. Ep. ; non ego perfidum dixi sacramentum, Hor. ; se sacramento obstringere ne etc., Plin. Ep. [Fr. *serment.*]

Sacrānus, a, um, *of the Sacrani, an ancient people of Latium.*

sacrārium, ī, n. [sacra, v. sacer]. **1.** Lit. **a.** *a place for keeping sacred things, a sacristy* : Cic., Liv. **b.** *a holy place, shrine, chapel* : Cic. ; sacraria Ditis, Verg. ; Liv., etc. **2.** Transf. : scelerum, Cic. ; Sen.

sacrātus, a, um. I. Part. sacrō. **II.** Adj. *hallowed, consecrated, holy, sacred* : Verg., Ov. Comp. : Mart. Sup. : Plin. [Fr. *sacré.*]

sacres, v. sacer.

sacricola, ae, *m. f.* [sacra colō], *a sacrificing priest* or *priestess* : Tac., Suet.

sacrifer, era, erum [sacra ferō], *bearing sacred things* : rates Aeneae, Ov.

sacrificālis, e, *adj.* [sacrificus], *sacrificial* : apparatus, Tac.

sacrificātiō, ōnis, *f.* [sacrificō], *a sacrificing, sacrifice* : Cic.

sacrificium, ī, n. [sacra faciō], *a sacrifice* : Druides sacrificia publica ac privata procurant, Caes. ; sacrificium *or* sacrificia facere, Cic. ; sacrificium (alicui) facere, parare, perpetrare, Liv. ; sacrificiis studere, Cic. ; aliquem sacrificiis interdicere, Caes. ; anniversaria, sollemnia, Cic., Liv.

sacrificō (sacruficō), āre [sacra faciō], *to make* or *offer a sacrifice, to sacrifice* : Pl., Cic., Ov., Liv., etc. (*Impers. Pass.* : Liv.). With DAT. of deity : Pl., Curt. With *Instr.* ABL. : Iovi argento, Pl. ; Iunoni hostiis, Liv. With ACC. of thing sacrificed : Pl., Ov., Liv.

sacrificulus, ī, *m.* [sacrificus], *a sacrificer, sacrificing priest* : Liv., Suet. Esp. in phr. : rex sacrificulus : Liv. (*v.* rex).

sacrificus, a, um [sacra faciō], *sacrificial* : securis, Ov. ; os, Ov.

sacrilegium, ī, n. [sacrilegus], *temple-robbing, sacrilege.* **a.** Prop. : Liv., Phaedr., etc. In *pl.* : Suet. **b.** *violation or profanation of sacred rites* : Nep., Sen.

sacrilegus, a, um [sacra legō], *temple-robbing, sacrilegious.* **1.** Lit. : bellum, Cic. ; sacrilegas admovere manūs, Liv. Mostly as Noun, **sacrilegus,** ī, *m.* : Cic., Quint. **2.** Transf. in gen., *that violates or profanes sacred things, sacrilegious, impious, profane* : Ter., Cic., Ov., etc. ; dextra, Ov. ; Hor. *Sup.* : Pl. As Noun, **sacrilegus,** ī, *m.* (Pl., Ter., Sall., Ov.), and **sacrilega,** ae, *f.* (Ter., Ov.).

sacrō, āre [sacer], *to set apart as sacred.* **I.** *to consecrate* or *devote to a divinity.* **1.** Lit. **a.** aurum, Cic. ; rite pecudes, Verg. ; praedam, Liv. ; agrum Veneri, Ov. ; laurum Phoebo, Verg. ; aras Iovi, Liv. **b.** *to devote to destruction, to declare accursed* : de sacrando cum bonis capite leges, Liv. ; caput Iovi, Liv. **2.** Transf. **a.** *to set apart, devote, give* : alicui honorem, Verg. ; Ov. **b.** *to doom* : Parcae telis sacrarunt Euandri (Halaesum), Verg. **II.** *to hallow, consecrate, canonise, declare inviolable.* **1.** Lit. : foedus, quod in Capitolio sacratum fuisset, Liv. ; Cic. ; sacrata lex, Cic., Liv. ; ossa, Ov. Of a deity : sacrata Vesta, Ov. ; te patrem deum hominumque hac sede, Liv. **2.** Transf. : aliquem Lesbio plectro, Hor. ; Catonis eloquentia sacrata scriptis omnis generis, Liv. ; Ov.

sacrō-sānctus, a, um [sacrum sanciō], lit. *consecrated by a religious act* or *by a religious penalty* (of outlawry against any one guilty of violence to the person, etc., that was sacrosanctus), *sacred, inviolable, sacrosanct.* **1.** Lit. : tribuni, Liv. ; accusator, Tac. ; possessiones, Cic. ; vacatio, Liv. **2.** Transf. *sacred, revered* : Rufi mihi memoria, Plin. Ep.

Sacrovir, i, *m.* Iulius Sacrovir, *a nobleman of the Aedui in Gaul* ; **Sacrovuriānus**, a, um.

sacrufĭcō, *v.* sacrifico.

sacrum, ī, *n. v.* sacer.

saeculāris, e, *adj.* [saeculum], *of a period of 100 years* : ludi, Plin., Tac., Suet. ; carmen, a hymn for these games, Hor., Suet.

saeculum (poet. **saeclum**), i, *n.* **I.** *the period of one generation* (i.e. 33⅓ years), *a generation.* **1.** L i t. **a.** P r o p. : Cic., Verg., Liv., etc. **b.** More vaguely : aureum, Cic. ; Pyrrhae, Hor. **2.** T r a n s f. **a.** *the people living at a particular time, a generation* : Pl., Lucr., Cic., Verg., etc. **b.** In *pl.* : *successive generations, races* : Lucr. **c.** *the spirit of the age, the times* : nec corrumpere et corrumpi saeculum vocatur, Tac. **II.** *the full period of a man's life, a period of a hundred years, a century.* **a.** P r o p. : Varr., Cic., Hor. **b.** More vaguely : *an age* : Cic. [It. *secolo* ; Fr. *siècle*.]

saepe, *adv.* [perh. *cf.* συχνός]. **I.** *often, frequently, ofttimes* : Pl., Cic., Hor., etc. ; minime saepe, Caes. *Comp.* : Pl., Cic., etc. *Sup.* : Pl., Cic. **II.** With -**numerō**, *again and again, very frequently* : Caes., Cic., Sall.

saepēs, is, *f. a hedge, fence.* **1.** L i t. : Pac., Caes., Verg., etc. **2.** T r a n s f. (of any enclosure) : portarum, Ov.

saepimentum, ī, *n.* [saepiō], *a hedge, enclosure* : Cic., Varr.

saepĭō, saepīre, saepsī, saeptum [saepēs], *to surround with a hedge, to fence in.* **1.** L i t. : vepribus sepulcrum, Cic. ; Liv. **2.** T r a n s f. (of enclosing in gen.). **a.** fori aditūs, Cic. ; saltum plagis, Lucr. ; feram venantum coronā, Verg. ; urbem moenibus, Cic. ; castra tectis parietum pro muro, Liv. ; se tectis, Verg. ; aliquem veste, Pl. ; omnia complexu cetera saepsit aether, Lucr. ; obscuro gradientis aëre, Verg. **b.** locum omnem cogitatione, Cic. ; inventa memoriā, Cic. ; saeptus legibus, Cic. ; omnia pudore, Liv. ; mulieres saeptae pudicitiā, Tac.

saeta, ae, *f. a thick, coarse,* or *stiff hair of an animal, a bristle* (mostly in *pl.*). **1.** L i t.: Pl., Lucr., Verg., etc. In *sing.* (esp. collect.) : Cic., Verg. **2.** T r a n s f. **a.** Of stiff, coarse human hair : Verg., Ov., Juv. **b.** Of anything made of bristles : a casting-line, Ov., Mart. ; a brush, Plin.

Saetabis, is, *f. a town in Hispania Tarraconensis, famous for its flax* ; **Saetabus**, a, um.

saetĭger, era, erum [saeta gerō], *bristly* : sus, Lucr., Verg., Ov. *Masc.* as Noun, *the bristly one* (i.e. the boar) : Ov., Mart.

saetōsus, a, um [saeta], *bristly* : aper, Verg. ; frons, Hor. ; verbera, Prop.

saevē, *adv. fiercely, ferociously, barbarously* : Luc., Suet. *Comp.* : Hor., Ov. *Sup.* : Plin.

saevĭdĭcus, a, um [saevus dīcō], *spoken furiously* or *angrily* : dicta, Ter.

saevĭō, īre, iī, ītum (*Imperf.* saevībat, Lucr.) [saevus], *to be fierce* or *furious, to vent one's rage.* **1.** L i t. (of animals) : Lucr., Verg. ; lupus rabieque fameque, Ov. ; aper in

pecudes, Ov. **2.** T r a n s f. **a.** Of persons : *to be brutal, furious, violent, angry* : Pl., Verg., Liv., etc. ; seditionibus saevire, Liv. ; in obsides innoxios, Liv. ; Ov. ; Tac. ; flagellis in aliquem, Juv. ; in tergum et in cervices, Liv. With DAT. : alicui, Ov. With *Inf.* : Ov. *Impers. Pass.* : Liv., Tac. **b.** Of things : ventus, Lucr., Caes. ; mare ventis, Sall. ; Hor. ; Tac. ; amor, Hor. ; amor ferri, Verg. ; ira in aliquem, Ov.

saevĭter, *adv. ferociously, cruelly* : Pl.

saevĭtia, ae, *f.* [saevus], *a raging, ferocity.* **1.** L i t. (of animals) : Plin., Quint. **2.** T r a n s f. **a.** Of persons : *brutality, savageness, barbarity, severity* : Ter., Cic., Prop., Liv., etc. ; in aliquem, Cic. In *pl.* : Sall. **b.** Of things : undae, Ov. ; temporis, Sall. ; caeli, Curt. ; annonae, Tac.

saevus (-**os**), a, um, *roused to fierceness, raging, furious, ferocious, cruel.* **1.** L i t. (of animals) : Lucr., Verg., Ov., etc. *Comp.* : Verg. **2.** T r a n s f. **a.** Of persons : *brutal, cruel, barbarous, violent, severe, etc.* : Pl., Verg., Hor., etc. ; ex amore, Pl. ; metu, Suet. With DAT. : alicui, Verg. With ABL. : accusandis reis, Tac. With *Inf.* : Hor. *Comp.* : Suet. *Sup.* : cum tyranno saevissimo et violentissimo in suos, Liv. ; Suet. (saevus in Verg. and perh. other poets often seems to mean *terrible to foes, relentless* : e.g. Iuno, Hector, in armis Aeneas, etc.). **b.** Of things : fluctus, Pl. ; mare, Sall. ; Ov. ; procellae, Lucr. ; ventus, Cic. Ep., Liv. ; hiems, Liv. ; minae, Prop. ; verba, militia. etc., Hor. ; amor, Enn., Verg. ; dolores, Verg.

sāga, ae, *f.* [sāgus], *a wise-woman, fortune-teller* : Cic., Hor., Ov., etc.

sāgācĭtās, ātis, *f.* [sagāx], *keenness, acuteness.* **1.** L i t. (of the senses). Esp. of dogs : canum ad investigandum sagacitas narium, Cic. **2.** T r a n s f. (of the intellect) : Cic., Nep.

sāgācĭter, *adv. keenly, with quickness of scent.* **1.** L i t. (of the senses). *Comp.* : Cic. Ep., Hor. *Sup.* : Cic. **2.** T r a n s f. (of the intellect), *acutely, sagaciously* : Cic., Liv., etc.

Sagaris, is (**Sangarius**, ī), *m. a river of Asia Minor, falling into the Euxine* ; now *the Sakaria* ; **Sagaritis**, idis, *f. adj.* ; **Sangarius**, a, um.

sāgātus, a, um [sagum], *wearing a sagum* : Cic., Mart.

sāgāx, ācis, *adj.* [sāgĭō], *keen, acute.* **1.** L i t. (of the senses). Esp. of dogs : Pl., Cic., Ov. *Comp.* : Ov. *Sup.* : Plin. **2.** T r a n s f. (of the intellect) : Cic., Hor., etc. ; mens, Lucr., Cic. ; animus, ratio, Lucr. With *ad* : ad suspicandum sagacissimus, Cic. With GEN. : utilium rerum, Hor. With ABL. : civitas rimandis offensis, Tac. With *Inf.* : Ov.

sāgīna, ae, *f.* [*cf.* σάττω], *a stuffing, cramming, fattening.* **1.** L i t. : in saginam se conicere, Pl. ; multitudinem non auctoritate sed saginā tenebat, Cic. ; anserum, Varr. **2.** T r a n s f. **a.** *food, rations* : gladiatoria, Tac. ; Prop. ; Juv. **b.** *a fatted animal* : Pl. **c.** *fatness* produced by overeating. T r a n s f. of style : Quint.

saginō, āre [sagīna], *to fatten animals*. **1.** Lit.: boves ad sacrificia, Varr.; porcum, Prop. **2.** Transf. **a.** saginatus nuptialibus conis, Liv.; terra copiā rerum omnium illos Gallos, Liv. **b.** rei publicae sanguine saginari, Cic.; Tac.

sāgiō, īre, *to perceive quickly or keenly by the senses or by the intellect*: Cic.

sagitta, ae, *f. an arrow*: Pl., Cic., Verg., etc. Astron. *a constellation, the Arrow*: Cic. poet. [It. *saetta*.]

sagittārius, a, um [sagitta], *of or for an arrow, arrow-*: calamus, Plin. As Noun, **sagittārius**, ī, *m. an archer, bowman* (mostly in *pl.*): Caes., Cic., etc. Sing. collectively: levis armatura cum equite sagittario, Tac. Astron. *the constellation of the Archer or Sagittarius*: Cic. poet.

sagittifer, era, erum [sagitta ferō], *arrow-bearing*: Parthi, Cat.; Geloni, Verg.; pharetra, Ov.

sagitti-potēns, entis, *m.* for Sagittarius, *the constellation of the Archer*: Cic. poet.

sagittō, āre [sagitta], *to shoot arrows*. **1.** Lit.: Curt. **2.** Transf.: saviis sagittatis percussus, Pl.

sagmen, inis, *n. a tuft of sacred herbs* plucked in the Capitol by the consul or praetor, and carried by the fetiales to mark their inviolability: Liv.

sagulātus, a, um [sagulum], *wearing a sagulum*: Suet.

sagulum, ī, *n.* [dim. sagum], *a small military cloak*; esp. *the purple cloak of general officers* (=paludamentum): Caes., Cic., Verg., etc.

sagum, ī, *n.* [perh. a Celtic word], *a coarse woollen mantle*. **a.** Of servants: Cato. **b.** Of the Germans: Tac. **c.** Of soldiers, *a military cloak* (opp. to toga, *civilian dress*): Caes., Hor., Liv.; sagum (*or* saga) sumere, ad saga ire, said esp. of the civilian population, *to get into uniform, prepare to take the field*, Cic.; in sagis esse, Cic.

Saguntum, ī, *n.*, and **Saguntus (-os)**, ī, *f. a city on the east coast of Spain, the taking of which by Hannibal occasioned the second Punic war*; now *Murviedro*; **Saguntinus**, a, um; **Saguntini**, ōrum, *m. pl. the Saguntines*.

sāgus, a, um [prob. cogn. with sāgiō, sagāx], *presaging, prophetic*: aves, Stat.

Saïtae, ārum, *m. pl. the inhabitants of Saïs, in Lower Egypt*.

sāl, salis, *m.* [*cf.* Gk. ἅλς], *salt*. **1.** Lit.: Pl., Cic., Verg., etc. In *pl.*: Varr., Ov. **2.** Transf. **A.** *the brine, sea-water, the sea*: Lucr., Verg., Ov. **B.** *seasoning, flavour*. **a.** In words: *pungency, shrewdness*; hence, *wit, humour* (often with lepos and facetiae): Ter., Cat., Cic., Hor., etc. In *pl.*: Cic., Hor., etc. **b.** *good taste, elegance*: tectum plus salis quam sumptūs habebat, Nep. [Fr. *sel*.]

salacō, ōnis, *m.* [σαλάκων], *a swaggerer, braggart*: Cic. Ep.

salamandra, ae, *f.* [σαλαμάνδρα], *a salamander*: Plin., Mart.

Salamis, īnis (Acc. Salamīna; Abl. Salamīne), *f.* **I.** *an island in the Saronic gulf, opposite Eleusis*; now *Koluri*. **Salamīnius**, a, um; also **Salamīnii**, ōrum, *m. pl.*, *its*

inhabitants. **II.** *a city in Cyprus, founded by Teucer*; **Salamīnius**, a, um; **Salamīnii**, ōrum, *m. pl., its inhabitants*.

salapūtium, ī, *n. a tiny man, a manikin*: Cat. [Etym. unknown.]

salārius, a, um [sāl], *of salt, salt-*: annona, *the yearly revenue from the sale of salt*, Liv. Via Salaria *or* Salaria alone, *the Salt Road* (from the Porta Collina to the Sabine country), Cic., Liv. As Noun, **salārius**, ī, *m.*, *a salt-fish dealer*: Mart. **salārium**, ī, *n.*, orig. *the money given to soldiers for salt*; hence, *an allowance, stipend*: Plin., Tac., Juv., etc. Transf. *a meal*: Mart.

salāx, ācis, *adj.* [saliō], *lustful, lecherous*. **1.** Lit.: Varr., Hor., Ov. **2.** Transf. *that provokes desire, salacious*: erucae, Ov.; Mart.

salebra, ae, *f.* [saliō], *a jolting*. Hence, *a rut or uneven place in a road*. **1.** Lit.: Prop., Hor., Mart. **2.** Transf. of style: haeret in salebrā, Cic.; Herodotus sine ullis salebris fluit, Cic.; Mart.

Sālentini (Sall-), ōrum, *m. pl., a people who occupied the south-eastern extremity of Italy*; **Sallentinus**, a, um.

Saliāris, e, *adj.* [Salii], *of the Salii (q.v.), Salian*. **1.** Lit.: carmen Numae, Hor.; saltus, Sen. Ep. **2.** Transf. of banquets (*sumptuous*): cum epulati essemus Saliarem in modum, Cic. Ep.; dapes, Hor.

Saliātus, ūs, *m.* [Salii], *the office or dignity of a Salius*: Cic.

salictum, ī, *n.* [contr. from salicētum, from salix], *a plantation or thicket of willows*: Pl., Cic., Verg., etc. [It. *salceto*: Fr. *saussaie*.]

salientēs, ium, *f. pl.* (*sc.* aquae) [saliō], *springs, fountains*: Cic. Ep.

salignus, a, um [salix], *of willow or willow-wood, willow-*: Cato, Verg., etc.

Salii, ōrum, *m. pl.* [saliō; hence, prop. *the Leapers*], *a college of 12 priests dedicated to the service of Mars Gradivus, who, armed and bearing the ancilia, made solemn processions, with songs and dances, through Rome on the Kalends of March*: Cic., Verg., etc.

salilum, ī, *n.* [dim. for salinulum, from salinum], *a little salt-cellar*: Cat. Comic.: animae, Pl.

salinae, ārum, *f. pl.* (*sc.* fodinae) [sāl], *salt-works, salt-pits*: Caes., Cic., Liv. Esp. Salinae (Romanae) near Ostia, Liv.

salinum, ī, *n.* (*sc.* vas) [sāl], *a salt-cellar*: Pl., Hor., Liv.

saliō, salīre, saluī (*or* salii), saltum [*cf.* Gk. ἅλλομαι], *to leap, spring, bound, jump*. **1.** Lit. **a.** In gen.: Pl., Hor., Ov.; saxo, Pl.; de muro, Liv.; per praecipitia, Liv.; per utres, Verg.; super vallum, Liv.; in gurgite ranae, Ov. **b.** Of the sex-act of animals (with Acc., or in *Pass.*): Lucr., Varr., Ov. **2.** Transf. **a.** Of things: cor, Pl.; pectora trepido motu, Ov.; aqua, Varr.; rivus, Verg.; in tectis grando, Verg.; in culleum de dolio vinum, Cato; farre pio placant et saliente sale, Tib.; Hor. **b.** Mentally: aliena negotia centum per caput et circa saliunt latus, Hor. [Fr. *saillir*.]

Sali-potēns, *v.* Salipotēns.

Salisuhsnl (--al), ulls, *m.* [Salii subsilió], *a cognomen of Mars or a priest of Mars :* Cat.

saliunca, ae, *f. the wild nard :* Verg.

saliva, ae, *f.* [*cf.* Gk. σίαλον], *spittle, saliva.* **1.** Lit.: Cat., Sen., Juv. In *pl.* : Lucr. **2.** Transf. *taste, appetite :* Methymnaei Graia saliva meri, Prop. ; Aetna tibi salivam movet, Sen. Ep.

salix, icis, *f. a willow-tree, willow :* Cato, Lucr., Verg.

Sallustius, ï, *m.* : **I.** C. Salluatius Crispus, *a Roman historian ;* **Sallustiānus**, a, um. **II.** Crispus Sallustius, *grand-nephew of the historian, famed for his great wealth. The* Sallustiani horti *were named after him.*

salmacidus, a, um [salgama (pickles preserved in brine) and acidus], of water, *having a salt and sour taste, brackish :* aquae, Plin.

Salmacis, idis (Voc. Salmaci, Ov.), *f. a fountain in Caria, fabled to render soft and effeminate all who drank of it.* Hence personified, *the nymph of the fountain :* Ov. Also *a weak effeminate person :* Enn.

Salmōneus (trisyl.), ëos, *m. s. of Acolus, b. of Sisyphus, who imitated lightning, and was on that account hurled into Tartarus by Jupiter ;* **Salmōnis**, idis, *f. his daughter Tyro.*

salō, salere, salsum, *or* **saliō**, ire, ltum [sāl], *to salt, salt down :* pernas, oleas, Cato ; Sall. (*v.* also salsus).

salsāmentārius, ï, *m.* [salsamentum], *a salt-fish dealer :* Suet.

salsāmentum, ï, *n.* [salsus]. **I.** *salted* or *pickled fish* (mostly in *pl.*): Ter., Varr. **II.** *brine, fish-pickle :* Cic.

salsē, *adv. wittily, facetiously :* Cic., Quint. *Sup. :* Cic.

Salsi-potēns, entis, *adj. that rules the salt sea :* frater Iovis, *Neptune,* Pl.

salsūra, ae, *f.* [salsus]. **I.** *a salting, pickling.* Transf. *sourness,* i.e. *ill-humour :* ita meae animae salsura evenit, Pl. **II.** *brine, pickle :* Varr.

salsus, a, um. **I.** *Part.* salō (or fr. sāl): *salted, flavoured with salt :* hoc salsumst, hoc adustumst, Ter. ; fruges, Verg. **II.** Adj. *salt, briny.* **1.** Lit. : gurges, Pl. ; aequor, Lucr. ; Verg. ; sputa, lacrimae, Lucr. ; sudor, robigo, Verg. As Noun, **salsa**, ōrum, *n. pl. salted food :* Pl. **2.** Transf. **a.** *flavoured* as with salt : Pl. **b.** Of speech : *sharp, witty :* sermo, Hor. ; Cic. ; Quint. ; *Neut. pl.* as Noun : Cic. Of persons : Cic., Cat. [Fr. *sauce.*]

saltātiō, ōnis, *f.* [saltō], *a dancing, a dance :* Cic., Quint. In *pl.* : Pl.

saltātor, ōris, *m.* [saltō], *a dancer :* Cic., Quint.

saltātōrius, a, um [saltātor], *of* or *for dancing :* orbis, Cic.

saltātrix, icis, *f.* [saltō], *a female dancer, dancing-girl :* Cic.

saltātus, ūs, *m.* [saltō], *a (religious) dance :* Liv. In *pl.* : Ov.

saltem (saltim), *adv. at least. at the least, at all events.* **I.** Affirmatively, with the *preferable* alternative stated : si illud non licet, saltem hoc licebit, Ter. ; cum

defondere aut sequi saltem, Caes. ; Cic.. etc. Often with alternative omitted : istuc sapienter saltem fecit filius, Pl. ; Cic. ; Hor., etc. **II.** Interrogatively : quis ego sum saltem, si non sum Sosia ? Pl. **III.** Negatively, with non, nequo, *not even, nor even* (elliptical usage): non deorum saltem, si non hominum, memores, instruunt aciem, *not even heeding the gods* (*as they might at least have done*), Liv. ; Tac., etc.

saltō, āre [*freq.* saliō], *to dance* (including pantomime and gesticulation). **1.** Lit. : Pl., Cic., Ov., etc. ; nemo saltat sobrius nisi forte insanit, Cic. ; ad tibicinis modos, Liv. With *Intern.* Acc. : *to represent by dancing and gesticulation, to dance :* Cyclopa, Hor. ; tragoediam, Suet. ; saltata poemata, Ov. **2.** Transf. of an orator speaking in disconnected sentences : Cic. [Fr. *sauter.*]

saltuōsus, a, um [saltus], *wooded :* loca, Sall., Liv., Tac.

1. saltus, ūs, *m.* [saliō], *a leaping, leap, spring, bound :* saltu uti, Cic. ; praeceps saltu sese in fluvium dedit, Verg. ; Lucr. ; saltum dare, Ov. In *pl.* : Ov.

2. saltus, ūs, *m. an upland, wooded pasture.* **1.** Lit. **a.** In gen. : Lucr., Caes., Cic., Verg., etc. **b.** *a pass* or *passage through mountains* or *forests :* Caes., Verg., Liv. **2.** Transf. **a.** Coarsely, of the female pudenda : Pl. **b.** Of a "tight corner": saltus damni, Pl.

salūber, *m.*, **salūbris**, *m. f.*, **salūbre**, *n.* [salūs], *promoting health, healthful, healthy, wholesome.* **1.** Lit. **a.** Of localities, climate, water, breezes, etc. : Cic., Verg., etc. *Comp. :* Varr. *Sup. :* Caes. **b.** Of herbs, medicine, etc. : Cato, Cic. ; somnus, Verg. With *Dat.* : gravi corpori malvae, Hor. ; Cato. With *ad :* lotium ad omnis res salubre est, Cato. *Sup. :* Plin. **c.** Of persons : Phoebe saluber, ades, Ov. *Comp. :* Pl. **2.** Transf. **a.** In gen. : quidquid est salubre in oratione, Cic. ; iustitia legesque, Hor. ; mendacium, sententiae, Liv. ; consilia, Cic. Ep., Tac. With *Dat.* : rem salubriorem inopi quam potenti, Liv. ; sententiam rei publicae saluberrimam, Cic. **b.** Of the body : *healthy, sound :* Sall., Liv., Mart., Tac. *Comp. :* Liv. *Sup. :* Tac.

salūbritās, ātis, *f.* [salūbris]. **I.** *wholesomeness, healthiness.* **1.** Lit. **a.** Of localities, climate, water : Cic., Liv., Tac. **b.** Of wine : Plin. **2.** Transf. *a means of safety :* Cic. **II.** Of the body : *healthiness, good health.* **1.** Lit. : Cic., Tac. **2.** Transf. : Atticae dictionis, Cic.

salūbriter, *adv. healthfully, healthily.* **1.** Lit. : Cic. *Comp.* and *Sup. :* Plin. **2.** Transf. *beneficially :* bellum trahi, Liv. ; emere, i.e. *cheaply,* Plin. Ep. *Sup.* salūberrimē, Plin. Ep.

salum, ï, *n.* [*cf.* Gk. σάλος], *the sea-swell, the high-sea.* **1.** Lit. **a.** Prop. : Cat. ; tirones salo nauseāque confecti, Caes. ; in salum navo evectus, Liv. ; Cic. ; in salo in ancoris stare, Liv. **b.** *the sea* in gen. : Verg., Hor., Ov., etc. **c.** Of a river : Stat. **2.** Transf. (of the mind) : aerumnoso navigare salo, "*a sea of troubles,*" Cic. poet.

salūs, ūtis, *f.* [*cf.* salvus and Gk. ὅλος], a *sound* or *whole condition, health.* **1.** Lit. (of the body). **a.** In gen.: quod cum salute eius fiat, Ter.; mater redit suā salute ac familiae maxumā, Pl.; aegrorum, Cic.; firmā potiri salute, Ov. **b.** Personified: Pl., Cic., Liv., etc. **2.** Personi-fied: Pl., Cic., Liv., etc. **2.** Transf. **a.** *well-being, welfare* in gen.; *life, safety:* Pl.; dare, alicui ferre, Cic.; amittere, Pl.; suae saluti diffidere, consulere, Caes.; in aliquo *or* in aliquā re salus (alicuius) posita est, nititur, consistit, Cic.; Liv.; (una salus victis) nullam sperare salutem, Verg.; Ov. As term of endearment: Pl. **b.** *a means* or *hope of safety:* haud tibi est in me salus, Pl.; saluti esse alicui, Pl., Cic.; una salus victis (nullam sperare salutem), Verg.; Ter. **c.** *a wish for one's welfare, a greeting:* alicui dare, nuntiare, Pl.; accipere, Pl.; Terentia impertit tibi multam salutem, Cic. Ep.; dicere alicui, Pl., Cic. So at the beginning of a letter, salutem dicit alicui (usually abbreviated S. D.) *or* with multam (S. D. M.) *or* with plurimam (S. D. P.), Pl., Cic. Ep.; *without* dicit: Cic.; mittere per aliquem, Cic. Ep.; Ov.; reddere, Pl., Liv. Tac.; salute datā redditāque, Liv. Rarely of a farewell greeting: multam salutem foro dicam, Cic. Ep.

salūtāris, e, *adj.* [salūs], *of health.* **1.** Lit. **a.** *healthful, wholesome, health-giving, healthy:* Cic., Ov., etc.; ars salutaris (of healing), Hor. With Dat. of person: hominum generi cultura agrorum est salutaris, Cic.; Pl. *Comp.:* Cic. With *ad:* decoctum ad dentium dolorem, Plin. With *contra:* Plin. *Neut. pl.* as Noun: Cic. **b.** As epithet of Iuppiter: Cic. **c.** Collis Salutaris, part of Quirinal, so-called from the temple of Salus which stood on it, Varr. **2.** Transf. **a.** *beneficial to well-being* in gen.: Cic.; oratio, Liv.; littera (i.e. A for absolvo on the voting tablet for acquittal), Cic. With *ad:* stella Iovis aut Veneris coniuncta cum Lunā ad ortūs puerorum salutaris sit, Cic. *Neut. pl.* as Noun: Cic., Tac. Of persons: civis, Cic. **b.** *used in greeting:* digitus, Suet.

salūtātiō, ōnis, *f.* [salūtō], *a greeting, saluting, salutation.* **A.** In gen.: Cic.; facere, Liv.; reddere, Tac. Rarely of a written greeting: Cic. **B.** In partic. **a.** *a cere-monial visit, morning call, levée:* Sen. Under the Empire, of *paying respects by attending a levée:* Suet. In *pl.:* Suet. **b.** Collect.: *the callers themselves:* ubi salutatio defluxit, Cic. Ep.

salūtātor, ōris, *m.* and **salūtātrix**, īcis, *f.* as Adj. with *fem.* Noun [salūtō], *one who gives greeting.* **a.** In gen.: regum, Stat.; pica, Mart. **b.** *one who makes complimentary morning calls* or *attends a levée:* Suet.; turba, Juv.

salūtifer, era, erum [salūs ferō], *health-bringing:* anguis urbi, Ov.

salūtigerulus, a, um [salūs gerō], *greeting-carrying:* pueri, Pl.

salūtō, āre [salūs]. **I.** *to keep in safety:* Plin. **II.** *to wish health to, to greet* (either on arrival or departure). **1.** Lit. **a.** In gen.: aliquem, Pl., Cic. **b.** *to greet by*

name *or title : quom quidam eum Caesarem salutabant, Cic. Ep.; Tac.,* etc. Of a *successful general:* aliquem impera-torem, Tac.; Caes. **c.** *to send a greeting to, deliver a message of greeting to :* Diony-sius te omnisque vos salutat, Cic. Ep.; Ov. **2.** Transf. **a.** Of paying reverence to a deity, etc.; Pl., Cic., etc.; augurium clamore, Verg.; to a place: Italiam laeto clamore, Verg. **b.** *to pay respects to, pay a morning-call on :* Cic. Ep., Sall., Hor. Under the Empire, *to attend the levée :* Tac., Suet. **c.** *to receive one's·visitors :* Cic. Ep.

salvē, *adv.* [salvus], *well, in good health, in good circumstances :* Pl. Esp. in phr. satine salve (*sc.* agis *or* agit *or* agitur) ? Pl., Ter., Liv.

salvē, *imper.* of salveō.

salveō, ēre [salvus], *to be well* or *in good health* (very rare exc. in *Imper.* and *Inf.*). Usually in greeting: salvē, salvētō, salvēte, *hail! good morning! good day!* and (ali-quem) salvēre iubeō, Pl., Cic., Liv., etc. In *Fut. :* salvebis a meo Cicerone, *my son begs to be remembered to you,* Cic. Ep. In addressing a deity or any revered object: salve, vera Iovis proles (*sc.* Hercules), Verg.; Hor.; Ov. Rarely with notion of favour shown to the invoker : mihi salve rite vocanti, Hor.; and with vale, in taking leave, *farewell, good-bye :* vale, salve, Cic. Ep.; Pl. Hence also in bidding farewell to the dead : salve aeternum mihi, maxime Palla, aeternumque vale, Verg.

salvus (**salvos**), a, um, *safe, alive, sound.* **1.** Lit. **a.** Of persons : Pl.; salvum atque incolumem exercitum, Caes.; Cic.; Hor., etc. **b.** Of things : navis, Pl.; res, Pl., Ter. Esp. in Abl. *Absol., without violation of, saving :* salvo officio, Cic.; salvā fide, Cic.; Pl.; Ov., etc. **2.** Transf. **a.** *well-circumstanced, free from difficulties* (with esse): salvos sum, salva spes est, ut verba audio, Pl.; ne sim salvus, si . . ., Cic. Ep.; Pl.; Ter.; salvos sis, for salve, *good day to you!* Pl. **b.** *chaste :* Penelope, Prop. [Fr. *sauf.*]

sambūca, ae, *f.* [σαμβύκη], *a triangular stringed instrument of a very shrill tone :* Pl., Pers.

sambūcina, ae, *f.* [sambūca canō], *a woman-sambuca-player :* Pl.

sambūcistria, ae, *f.* [σαμβυκίστρια], *a woman sambuca-player :* Pl.

Samē, ēs, *f.* less freq. **Samos**, ī, *f.* (Ov.), *the ancient name of the island of Cephallenia.* Also, *the capital of the island.* **Samaei**, ōrum. *m. pl. its inhabitants.*

Samnium, ī, *n. a country of central Italy, whose inhabitants were an offshoot from the Sabines ;* **Samnis**, ītis, *adj. Samnite,* also as Noun, *a kind of gladiator armed with Samnite weapons :* Cic.; **Samnītēs**, ium (Gen. rarely Samnitum; Gk. Acc. Sam-nitas), *m. pl. the Samnites ;* **Samnīticus**, a, um.

Samos (**Samus**), ī, *f.* **I.** *an island off the W. coast of Asia Minor, famous as the birth-place of Pythagoras, and for the worship of Juno (Hera) ; its chief city had the same name, now Samo ;* **Samius** (also *dim.*

Samiolus, Pl.), a, um,; **Samil,** ōrum, *m. pl. its inhabitants ;* **Samia,** ōrum, *n. pl. Samian pottery* (which was very fragile). **II.** *v.* Samē.

Samothrācia, ae, *f.,* **Samothrācē,** ēs, *f.* and **Samothrāca,** ae, *f. an island in the northern Aegean, the chief seat of the mystic worship of the Cabiri, now Samothraki ;* **Samothrācius,** a, um ; **Samothrāces,** um, *m. pl. the inhabitants of Samothrace.*

sānābilis, e, *adj.* [sānō], *that can be healed, curable.* **1.** Lit.: vulnus, Ov. Comp. : Cels. **2.** Transf. of the mind : Cic.

sānātiō, ōnis, *f.* [sānō], *a healing, curing :* corporum, Cic.

sanciō, sancīre, sānxī, sānctum (sancītum, Lucr.) [*cf.* sacer], *to consecrate, hallow, to make sacred and inviolable, to confirm or ratify solemnly* (mostly of laws and public proceedings). **1.** Lit. **A.** With person as Subject. **a.** legibus quas senatus de ambitu sancire voluerit, Cic. ; Hor. ; Liv. ; sanciendo novam legem ne quis etc., Liv. ; tabulas bis quinque viri, Hor. ; iura nobis, Cic. ; foedus, Cic., Liv. With *Instr.* ABL.: foedera sanguine, Cic. ; foedera fulmine, Verg. (*cf.* morte tuā consulum imperia, Liv.). **b.** With Acc. and *Inf.* as *Obj.* : fide sanxerunt liberos Tarentinos leges suaque omnia habituros, Liv. ; Suet. **c.** With the thing decreed in Acc., or *de* and ABL., or *Subj.,* and the law, etc. in *Instr.* ABL. (esp. after *Impers. Pass.*): alia moribus confirmarunt, sanxerunt autem alia legibus, Cic. ; de iure praediorum sanctum est iure civili ut etc., Cic. ; Liv. ; iure iurando sancitur ne etc., Caes. ; habeat legibus sanctum si quis . . . uti etc., Caes. ; Flaccus sanxit edicto ne etc., Cic. Also without *Instr.* ABL.: Cic. **d.** With *Indir. Quest.* : Lucr. **B.** With the law, etc., as Subject : hoc Corneliae leges non sanciunt, Cic. ; consularis lex sanxit ne etc., Cic. **2.** Transf. **a.** *to forbid under pain of punishment, to enact a penalty against:* Solon capite sanxit, si qui in seditione non alterius utrius partis fuisset, Cic. Ep. ; incestum pontifices supplicio sanciunto, Cic. **b.** *to consecrate, dedicate :* alicui carmina, Stat.

sānctē, *adv.* **I.** *solemnly, religiously :* Pl., Ter., Cic., Liv. **II.** *scrupulously, conscientiously :* Cic. Comp. : Cic. Sup. : Cic. Ep., Quint. **III.** *chastely, purely :* Curt. Of style : Quint.

sānctimōnia, ae, *f.* [sānctus]. **I.** *sacredness, sanctity :* Cic., Tac. **II.** *moral purity, chastity :* Cic., Tac.

sānctiō, ōnis, *f.* [sanciō], *that part of a law, etc., which deals with the penalties* attaching to a violation of its terms : Cic. ; iacere inritas sanctiones, Liv. Perh. *the enactment itself* in, sanctiones sacrandae sunt poenā, Cic.

sānctitās, ātis, *f.* [sānctus]. **I.** *sacredness, sanctity, inviolability :* tribunatūs, Cic. ; templi, Liv. ; templo attribuere, Tac. In *pl. :* Cic. **II.** *moral purity, holiness, chastity, integrity :* Cic. ; exemplum veteris sanctitatis, Cic. ; matronarum, Cic. ; Tac. ; sanctitatem feminarum abrogare, Liv. In *pl. :* Cic.

sānctitūdō, inis, *f.* [sānctus], *sacredness, sanctity :* Iovis, Acc. ; sepulturae, Cic. In *pl. :* Acc.

sānctor, ōris, *m.* [sanciō], *an enacter :* legum, Tac.

sānctus, a, um. **I.** *Part.* sanciō. **II.** Adj. *consecrated, hallowed, made sacred and inviolable.* **1.** Lit.: tribuni, societas, campus, ius, etc., Cic. ; hospites, Caes. ; fides indutiarum, Liv. ; aerarium sanctius (a reserve-fund of the State), Caes., Cic. Ep., Liv. Of the gods : Enn., Lucr. Of the dead : Sall., Verg. ; *Sup.* : Cic., Verg. Of poets : Enn., Cic. After Augustus, a title of the Emperors : Ov. **2.** Transf. **a.** *venerable, sacred, holy :* fana, Lucr. ; Cic. ; fons, Cic. ; ignes, Verg. ; sanctior dies, Hor. ; amicitiae nomen, Ov. ; libertas, Liv. **b.** *morally pure, saintly, virtuous, chaste :* Cic., Hor., etc. ; vir in publicis religionibus sanctus, Cic. ; sententia, Lucr. ; consilium, Liv. ; pudor, Tib. ; mores, Juv. ; oratio, Quint. ; eloquentia, Tac. Comp. : Cic., Liv., etc. Sup. : Cic. [It. Sp. *santo* ; Fr. *saint.*]

Sancus, I, *m. a deity of the Sabines, also worshipped at Rome* ; perh. the same as Dius Fidius.

sandaliārius, a, um [sandalium], *of sandals* or *sandal-making :* Apollo Sandaliarius (i.e. of Shoemakers' Street), Suet.

sandaligerulae, ārum, *f. pl.* [sandalium gerō], *maids who carried their mistresses' slippers :* Pl.

sandalium, ī, n. [σανδάλιον], *a slipper, sandal :* Ter.

sandapila, ae, *f. a common kind of bier* for people of the lower classes : Mart., Juv., Suet.

sandyx, ȳcis, *f.* [σάνδυξ], *a colour like vermilion,* perh. *scarlet :* Verg., Prop.

sānē, *adv.* **I.** *sensibly, reasonably, discreetly :* Pl. Comp. : Hor. **II.** (*cf.* valde). **A.** In gen. : *truly, indeed, right, very :* odiosum sane genus hominum officia exprobrantium, Cic. ; oratio sane longa, Cic. ; Pl. ; Hor., etc. **B.** In partic. **a.** In *answers : of course, to be sure :* Pl., Ter., Cic. **b.** Ironically : *indeed, to be sure :* beneficium magnum sane ! Phaedr. ; Pl. **c.** *sane quam, how very,* i.e. *very much indeed, exceedingly* (*cf.* admodum quam, valde quam) : conclusa est a te tam magna lex sane quam brevi, Cic. **d.** With negatives : *really, at all :* haud sane diu est, Pl. ; nihil sane esset, Cic. ; Hor., etc. **e.** In restrictive concessions : *then, I admit, of course :* haec si vobis non probamus, sint falsa sane, Cic. ; Ov. ; Quint., etc. **f.** With imperatives : *pray then, if you will :* abi sane, Pl. ; Ter. ; Liv.

sanguen, inis, *n.* v. sanguis.

sanguināns, antis [sanguis], *bleeding.* Transf. *blood-thirsty :* eloquentia, Tac.

sanguinārius, a, um [sanguis]. **I.** *for blood ;* hence, herba (i.e. that stanches a flow of blood), Plin. **II.** *blood-thirsty, sanguinary, savage :* iuventus, Cic. Ep. ; Suet. ; sententiae, Plin. Ep.

sanguineus, a, um [sanguis], *of blood, bloody, blood-stained.* **1.** Lit.: imber, Cic. ; guttae, Ov. ; Mavors, Verg. ; rixae, Hor. **2.**

Transf. *blood-coloured, blood-red :* iuba (anguis), Verg. ; Luna, Ov. ; Liv. [It. *sanguigno.*]

sanguinolentus, a, um [sanguis], *blood-stained, bloody.* **1.** L i t. : soror, Tib. ; pectora, Ov. ; seditiones, Varr. **2.** **Transf.** **a.** *blood-red :* color, Ov. **b.** *bloody, sanguinary :* littera, Ov.

sanguis (sanguis, Ov. M. XII. 127), sanguinis, *m.,* and **sanguen,** inis, *n.* (Enn., Cato, Lucr.), *blood.* **1.** L i t. : Pl., Lucr., Cic., etc. ; pugnatum plurimo sanguine, Liv. ; sanguinem haurire, *to shed freely another's blood,* Cic., Liv. ; dare, *to shed one's own blood,* Liv. ; effundere, profundere, *to bleed freely,* Cic. ; mittere, *to bleed surgically,* Cic. Ep. ; demere e capite, Varr. ; cohibere, sistere, Plin. **2.** **Transf.** **a.** *blood,* i.e. *consanguinity, descent, stock :* sanguine coniuncti, Cic. ; alicui materno a sanguine iungi, Ov. ; progeniem Troiano a sanguine duci, Verg. **b.** *a descendant, offspring :* o sanguen dis oriundum, Enn. ; reges, deorum sanguinem, Hor. ; sanguis meus, Verg. ; in suum sanguinem saevire, Liv. ; Tac. **c.** *life-blood :* Pl. ; quae cum do sanguine detraxisset aerari (i.e. had let the blood of), Cic. ; missus est sanguis invidiae, Cic. Ep. ; rei publicae, Cic. ; integer aevi sanguis, Verg. Of style : Cic., Quint.

saniēs, em, ē, *f. corrupted blood, bloody matter.* **1.** L i t. : Enn., Cato, Verg., Tac., etc. **2.** **Transf.** : *venom, slaver :* of serpents, Verg., Ov. ; of Cerberus, Hor. Of various liquids : Plin.

sānitās, ātis, *f.* [sānus], *soundness of body, health.* **1.** L i t. : Pl., Cic., Phaedr., etc. **2.** **Transf.** **a.** *soundness of mind, good sense, discretion, sanity, etc. :* animi, Cic. ; ad sanitatem reverti, Caes. ; ad sanitatem redire, se convertere, Cic. ; ad sanitatem aliquem reducere, Cic. ; sanitatem animis adferre, Liv. ; Phaedr. **b.** Of style : *healthy tone, correctness, purity :* orationis, oratoris, Cic. ; eloquentiae, Tac. **c.** *solidity, permanence :* victoriae, Tac. [Fr. *santé.*]

sanna, ae, *f.* [σάννας], *a mimicking grimace, a mocking :* Pers., Juv.

sanniō, ōnis, *m.* [sanna], *one who makes mimicking grimaces, a buffoon :* Cic. [It. *zanni ;* Eng. *zany.*]

sānō, āre [sānus], *to make sound or healthy, to heal, cure.* **1.** L i t. : aliquem, Cic., Ov., etc. ; vulnera, Cic., Ov. etc. ; dolores medicina, Prop. **2.** **Transf.** : mentem, Lucr. ; Caes. ; voluntates consceleratas, Cic. ; incommodum commodis, Caes. ; curas, Tib. ; domestica mala, Liv.

Sanquālis (Sanguāl-), e, *adj.* [Sancus], *of Sancus :* avis, *the young of the osprey,* Liv.

sānus, a, um [*cf.* Gk. σάος], *physically sound, whole, healthy.* **1.** L i t. : Pl., Cic., Hor., etc. *Neut.* as Noun : Prop. *Comp.* : Pl. **2.** **Transf.** **a.** In gen. *safe, sound :* Pl. ; res publica, Cic. Ep. ; civitas, Liv. **b.** *sound in mind, rational, sane :* Pl., Ter., Cic. ; sanus mentis, Pl. ; vix sanae montis estis, Liv. ; Hor., etc. ; sensus, Verg. ; animi, Liv. ; male sani poetae, Hor. ; male sana Dido, Verg. ; Cic. Ep. With *ab :* ego sanus ab illis (vitiis), Hor. *Comp.* :

Hor. *Sup.* : Cic. *Masc.* as Noun : Cic. ; pro sano loqui, Pl. ; Caes. ; ut vix pro sano nuntius audiretur, Liv. **c.** Of style : *sound, correct :* oratores, Cic., Plin. Ep. *Comp.* : Cic. [Fr. *sain.*]

sapa, ae, *f. must or new wine boiled thick :* Varr., Ov. [Fr. *sève.*]

sāperda, ae, *m.* [σαπέρδης], *an inferior kind of salt fish from the Euxine :* Varr., Pers.

sapiēns, entis. **I.** *Part.* sapiō. **II.** Adj. *wise, sensible, judicious.* **a.** Of persons : Pl., Cic., Ov., etc. *Comp.* : Pl. *Sup.* : Pl., Cic. **b.** Of their acts, etc. : opera, Pl. ; mores, Pl. ; excusatio, Cic. Ep. ; temperatio, Cic. ; consilium, Ov. **III.** Noun. **a.** *a wise man ; a sage, a philosopher :* Pl., Cic., Hor. **b.** *a man of nice or discriminating taste :* Pl., Hor.

sapienter, *adv. sensibly, judiciously, wisely :* Pl., Cic., Ov., etc. *Comp.* : Pl., Cic. *Sup.* : Cic.

sapientia, ae, *f.* [sapiēns], *good sense, discernment, prudence, wisdom.* **A.** In gen. : Pl., Cic., Hor., etc. **B.** In partic. **a.** *wisdom* (i.e. a deeper insight into the nature of things, got by learning and meditation), *philosophy :* Pl., Cic., Tac. **b.** *knowledge* of methods, principles, etc., *science :* Lucr., Cic. ; ceterarum rerum, Cic. Of jurisprudence : Scaevolarum, Cic. Of oratory : Cic. Of statesmanship : constituendae civitatis, Cic. Of mathematics : Suet.

sapiō, sapere, sapivi *or* sapii [*cf.* Gk. ὀπός, σαφής and σοφός], *to have a flavour.* **1.** L i t. : oleum male sapiet, Cato. With *Intern.* Acc. : *to taste, savour, or smack of :* piscis mare ipsum, Sen. ; Plin. ; Juv. Rarely *to smell of :* unguenta crocum, Cic. ; Pl. **b.** *to have a sense of taste :* (nec sequitur ut, cui cor sapiat) ei non sapiat palatus, Cic. **2.** **Transf. a.** patruos, Pers. **b.** *to have sense or discernment ; to be sensible, discreet, judicious, wise :* Pl., Cic., Ov., etc. ; ad aliquid, Pl., Ter. ; animus sibi per se sapit, Lucr. ; cui cor sapiat, Cic. With *Intern.* Acc. : *to have knowledge or understanding of :* nullam rem, Pl. ; nihil, aliquid, Cic. ; nihil parvum, Hor. ; quantum ego sapio, Plin. Ep. [It. *sapere,* savere ; Fr. *savoir.*]

sāpō, ōnis, *m.* [a Germ. word], *soap :* Plin. [Fr. *savon.*]

sapor, ōris, *m.* [sapiō], *a taste, relish, flavour.* **1.** L i t. : Lucr., Cic. ; dulcis, Cic., Hor. ; salsus, Lucr. ; asper in ore, Verg. ; tristis, Ov. In *pl.* : Lucr., Hor., Plin. **2.** **Transf. A. a.** Of style : vernaculus, Cic. ; Atticus, Quint. **b.** Of conduct : homo sine sapore, Cic. **B. a.** *a sense of taste, a taste :* seorsus sapor oris habet vim, Lucr. **b.** *a flavour* (i.e. juice) : tunsum gallae saporem, Verg. Mostly in *pl.* : Verg., Tib., Plin. [Fr. *saveur.*]

Sapphō, ūs (Acc. Sapphō), *f.* a celebrated Greek lyric poetess, born at Mytilene in the island of Lesbos, who is said to have thrown herself from the Leucadian rock into the sea ; **Sapphicus,** a, um, Musa, i.e. Sappho (as a tenth Muse), Cat.

sarcina, ae, *f.* [sarciō], *a package, bundle, pack* of a soldier. **1.** L i t. : Pl., Hor. (*cf.* essem militiae sarcina fida tuae, Prop.).

In *pl.* : Caes., Liv., Tac., etc. ; impeditos in agmine et sub sarcinis adoriri, Caes. Hence before a battle : sarcinas (in unum locum) conferre, Caes. ; in medium conicere, Liv. ; conligere, Sall. **2.** T r a n s f. *load, burden.* **a.** Of the womb : Ov. **b.** Of cares or griefs : Ov.

sarcinārius, a, um [sarcina], *of or belonging to baggage, pack-* : iumenta, Caes.

sarcinātor, ōris, *m.* [sarciō], *a patcher, botcher of old garments* : Pl.

sarcinātus, a, um [sarcina], *laden, burdened* : homines, Pl.

sarcinulae, ārum, *f. pl.* [*dim.* sarcinae, v. sarcina], *a little pack* : Cat. ; adligare, Plin. Ep. Of a woman's trousseau : Juv.

sarciō, sarcīre, sarsī, sartum, *to patch, mend, repair.* **1.** L i t. : funis, centones, etc., Cato ; aedis, Pl. P o e t : lapsas ruinas generis (apum), Verg. **2.** T r a n s f. : detrimentum in bello acceptum, Caes. ; damna, Cic. Ep., Liv. ; infamiam, Caes. ; iniuriam, Cic. ; male sarta gratia, Hor.

sarcophagus, a, um [σαρκοφάγος], *flesh-devouring* : lapis, a kind of limestone used for coffins, Plin. As Noun, **sarcophagus**, ī, *m. a grave, sepulchre* : Juv.

sarculum, ī, *n.* [sariō], *a light hoe* : Cato, Hor., Ov.

Sardanapālus, ī, *m. the last king of the Assyrian empire of Nineveh.*

Sardēs (**Sardis**), ium, *f. pl. Sardis : the capital of Lydia, on the Pactolus ;* **Sardiānus**, a, um ; **Sardiāni**, ōrum, *m. pl. the inhabitants.*

Sardī, ōrum, *m. pl. the inhabitants of Sardinia ;* **Sardus**, **Sardōus**, a, um, *Sardinian ;* **Sardinia**, ae, *f. Sardinia ;* and **Sardiniēnsis**, e.

sardonyx, ychis, *m.* (Mart., Juv.), *f.* (Pers., Juv.) [σαρδόνυξ], *a precious stone, sardonyx* : Juv.

sargus, ī, *m.* [σαργός], *a kind of sea-fish* : Enn., Ov.

sariō, īre, īvī or uī, *to hoe, weed* : Pl., Cato, Varr.

sarisa, ae, *f.* [σάρισα], *a long Macedonian lance* : Liv., Ov., Curt.

sarisophoros, ī, *m.* [σαρισοφόρος], *a Macedonian lancer* : Liv., Curt.

saritor (**sartor**, Pl.), ōris, *m.* [sariō], *a hoer, weeder.* **1.** L i t. : Varr. **2.** T r a n s f. (comic.) : sator sartorque scelerum et messor, Pl.

Sarmatae (**Sauromatae**), ārum, *m. pl. the Sarmatians ; a barbarous people, who occupied the eastern parts of Europe ;* esp. *portions of S.E. Russia ;* **Sarmatia**, ae, *f. their country ;* **Sarmaticus**, a, um, and **Sarmatis**, idis, *f. adj. Sarmatian.*

sarmentum, ī, *n.* (and **sarmen**, inis, *n.* Pl.) [sarpō, *to trim, prune*]. **I.** *twigs, brushwood* : Varr., Liv. In *pl.* : Caes., Cic. **II.** In *pl. : twigs or shoots* (esp. on vines) *that need pruning* : Cic.

Sarnus, ī, *m. a river in Campania.*

Sarpēdōn, onis, *m.* **I.** *son of Jupiter and Europa, king of Lycia.* **II.** *his grandson, killed before Troy by Patroclus.*

Sarra (**Sara**), ae, *f.* (=Hebr. *Zor*). *another name for the city of Tyre ;* **Sarrānus**, a, um, *Tyrian :* ostrum, Verg.

sarrācum, ī, *n.*, *v.* serrācum.

Sarrastēs, um, *m. pl. a people of Campania, near the Sarnus.*

sarriō, sarritor, *v.* sariō, saritor.

Sarsina, ae, *f. a town in Umbria, the birthplace of Plautus.*

sartāgō, inis, *f. a frying-pan.* **1.** L i t. : Plin., Juv. **2.** T r a n s f. : sartago loquendi, *a hotch-potch, medley,* Pers.

sartor, *v.* saritor.

sartus, a, um. **I.** *Part.* sarciō. **II.** A d j. *mended, repaired, put in order, only in phrase* sartus tectus, *in good repair.* **1.** L i t. : aedem Castoris sartam tectam tradere, Cic. ; omnia (*sc.* aedificia) sarta tecta exigere, Cic. ; Liv. **2.** T r a n s f. : sarta tecta tua praecepta usque habui meā modestiā, Pl. ; aliquem sartum et tectum conservare, Cic. Ep.

sat, satag-, *v.* satis.

satagius, a, um [satagō], *over-anxious* : Sen. Ep.

satelles, itis, *m. f. an attendant, a member of a bodyguard or retinue.* **1.** L i t. : Pl., Cic., Ov., Liv., etc. **2.** T r a n s f. **a.** P o e t. Of storms : Neptuni, Pl. Of the eagle : Iovis, Cic. poet. Of Charon : Orci, Hor. **b.** Of *political partisans* : Hannibalis, Liv. **c.** *a minister, abettor* : scelerum, audaciae, etc., Cic. ; sensūs hominis satellites, Cic.

satiās, ātis, *f.* (**satiēs**, em, ē, Plin.) [satis], *a sufficiency, abundance, plentifulness.* **A.** P r o p. : Pl. ; cibi, Lucr. ; frumenti, Sall. ; fessus satiate videndi, Lucr. **B.** *overabundance, satiety.* **1.** L i t. : Tac. ; vini, Liv. **2.** T r a n s f. : studiorum, Ter. ; amoris, Liv. ; satias capit aliquem, Ter., Liv., Tac.

Saticula, ae, *f. a town of Samnium, near Campania ;* **Saticulānus**, a, um ; **Saticulāni**, ōrum, *m. pl. the inhabitants ;* **Saticulus**, ī, *m. a native of Saticula* : Verg.

satietās, ātis, *f.* [satis], *a sufficiency, abundance, plentifulness.* **A.** P r o p. : ornandi, Pl. **B.** *overabundance, satiety.* **1.** L i t. : cibi, Cic. ; ad satietatem, Pl., Liv. **2.** T r a n s f. : capere, Pl. ; satietatem amoris sumere, Ter. ; mei, Cic. ; dominationis, Sall. ; studiorum omnium satietas vitae facit satietatem, Cic. ; vincere aurium satietatem, Cic. ; inimicos satietas poenarum suarum cepisset, Liv. In *pl.* : Cic.

satin and **satine** for satis-ne.

satiō, āre [satis], *to satisfy, fill, glut.* **1.** L i t. **a.** Of the appetite : satiati agni ludunt, Lucr. ; canes satiatae sanguine, Ov. ; desideria naturae, Cic. ; famem, Ov. ; sitim, Mart. **b.** Of things : *to fill sufficiently, to saturate* : fretum aquis, Ov. ; odoribus ignis, Ov. ; lumine, Mart. **2.** T r a n s f. **a.** In gen. : libidines, Cic. ; Cat. ; aviditatem legendi, Cic. ; in eius corpore lacerando animum, Cic. ; iram, Ov. ; populum libertate, Cic. ; Lucr. ; oculos amore, Prop. ; satiatus somno, suppliciis, poenā, Liv. With GEN. : dextera caedis, Ov. **b.** *to overfill, cloy* : satiari fastidio similitudinis, Cic. ; agricola assiduo satiatus aratro, Tib. ; prosperis adversisque satiatus, Tac.

satiō, ōnis, *f.* [serō], *a sowing, planting* : Cic., Verg., Liv. In *pl., sown fields* : Cic.

satira, v. satur.

satis and **sat**, *indecl. adj. or noun, and adv.* [*cf.* Gk. ἅδην]. **I.** As Adj. or Noun : *enough, sufficient.* **A.** P o s i t i v e. **a.** As Noun : sat *or* satis habeo, Pl., Ter. ; satis superque habere dicit ; plus quam satis doleo, Cic. ; non satis efficit oratio, Quint. Often with GEN.: ea amicitia non satis habet firmitatis, Cic. ; Pl. ; Hor., etc. ; satis superque vitae est, Liv. **b.** As Adj. or Noun in Predic. : ad eas res biennium sibi satis esse duxerunt, Caes. ; si ad arcendum Italiā bellum consul alter satis esset, Liv. ; novum militem ne temptando quidem satis certamini fore, Liv. ; semel fugiendi si data est occasio, satis est, Pl. ; Cic. ; Hor. With *Inf.* as Subject : satis erat respondere, Cic. ; perdere posse sat est, Ov. ; Ter. ; nunc satis est dixisse, Hor. ; vos satis habebatis animam retinere, Sall. With Acc. and *Inf.*: libertatem repeti satis est, Liv. ; Tac. With *quod*-clause : Liv. With *ut* and *Subj.* : Fabio satis visum ut ovans urbem iniret, Liv. **B.** C o m p a r a - t i v e, **satius**, prop. *more satisfying* ; hence *better, preferable* : satius est (with *Inf.*), Pl., Cic., Verg., etc. ; (with Acc. and *Inf.*), Pl., Liv., etc. ; satius visum est (with *Inf.*), Pl., Liv. **II.** As Adv.: *enough, sufficiently* ; often *fairly, moderately, tolerably* ; (colloq.) *pretty, quite.* **a.** With verbs : Pl., Cic., Verg., etc. *Comp.* satius : Varr. **b.** With adjectives : Pl., Cic., Verg., etc. **c.** With adverbs or adv. phrases : Pl., Caes., Cic., etc. **III.** P h r a s e s. **a.** **sat agitō** (or **satagitō**), *to have enough to do, to have one's hands full* (with GEN.) : suarum rerum, Pl. **b.** **satis agō** or **sat agō** (or **satagō**). **i.** *to satisfy, pay a creditor* : Pl. **ii.** *to have enough to do, to have one's hands full* : Pl., Ter. *Impers. Pass.* : Cic. Ep. **iii.** *to bustle about, make a fuss* : Quint. **c.** **satis dō (accipiō)**, *to give or offer (take) sufficient bail or security*, Pl., Cic. ; satis acceptum habere, Pl. ; satisdato, *by giving bail*, Cic. Ep. **d.** **satis faciō** (or **satisfaciō**), *to give satisfaction, to satisfy, content.* **i.** In gen. : Cic. With DAT.: illis ex disciplinā, Pl. ; Siculis, Cic. ; alicui petenti, Cic. ; officio meo, illorum voluntati, Cic. ; ut omnium vel suspicioni vel crudelitati satis fiat, Cic. With *in* and ABL.: in iure civili, Cic. ; histriones in dissimillimis personis, Cic. **ii.** In business, *to satisfy, pay, or secure* a creditor : alicui, Caes., Cic. **iii.** *to give satisfaction* (by word or deed), *to make amends or apology* : Caes. ; mihi, Pl. ; Caesari, Caes. ; de iniuriis, Caes. ; Aeduis de iniuriis, Caes. In *Pass.* : ut mihi satis fieri paterer a te, Cic. **iv.** With DAT. of person, and Acc. and *Inf.* : *to satisfy some one by proof, to demonstrate sufficiently* : Cic., Nep. [From ad satis, It. *assai* ; Fr. *assez* ; from satis facere, It. *soddisfare* ; Fr. *satisfaire*.]

satisdatiō, ōnis, *f.* [satis dō, v. satis III. c.], *a giving of bail or security* : Cic. Ep.

satisfactiō, ōnis, *f.* [satis faciō, v. satis III. d.], *amends, reparation, apology* : Caesar Ubiorum satisfactionem accepit, Caes. ; Cic. Ep. ; recipere, Tac. ; satisfactionem de culpā proponere, Sall.

sator, ōris, *m.* [serō], *a sower, planter.* **1.** Lit. : Lucr., Cic. **2.** T r a n s f. **a.** *a begetter, father, creator* : hominum atque deorum, Verg. **b.** *a promoter, author* : sator scelerum et messor, Pl. ; litis, Liv.

satrapēa or **satrapīa**, ae, *f.* [σατραπεία], *the office or province of a satrap, a satrapy* : Curt.

satrapēs, is, *m.* [a Pers. word], *a governor of a province of the Persian empire, a viceroy, a satrap* : NOM. satrapēs, Ter. ; GEN. satrapīs, Nep. ; ACC. satrapēn, Nep. ; satrapam, Curt. ; *pl.* NOM. satrapae, Nep.

satur, ura, urum [v. satis], *full of food, full-fed, sated.* **1.** Lit. : Pl., Lucr., Cic., Verg., etc. (Comic. of a pregnant woman : Pl.) With ABL. : nepos anseris extis, Pers. ; Pl. ; Ov. With GEN.: omnium rerum, Ter. ; Lucr. ; Hor. **2.** T r a n s f. **A.** Of things : *well-filled, rich* : Tarentum, Verg. **B.** Of colour : *full, rich* : color, Verg., Plin. **C.** Of game : *fatted, plump* : Mart. **D.** Of matter for oratory : *rich, fruitful.* *Neut. pl.* as Noun : Cic. **E. satura**, ae, *f.* (*sc.* lanx), orig. *a dish filled with various kinds of fruits or food composed of various ingredients, a medley, olio.* T r a n s f. **a.** lex satura, *a law containing provisions relating to matters essentially different.* Hence, per saturam, *in the gross or lump ; without order, confusedly* : quasi per saturam exquisitis sententiis, Sall. **b. satura** or **satira**, *a satire, a species of literary composition dealing with a medley of topics* : Hor., Liv., Juv. ; satura tota nostra est, Quint.

Saturae palūs, *a marsh in Latium*, perh. *a part of the Pomptine Marshes.*

saturēia, ōrum, *n. pl.* (**-a**, ae, *f.* Plin.), *the pot-herb* cunila, *savory* : Ov.

Saturēiānus, a, um, *Satureian* ; prob. = *Apulian.*

saturitās, ātis, *f.* [satur], *fulness, repletion, satiety.* **1.** Lit. : Pl. ; ad saturitatem, Pl. **2.** T r a n s f. **a.** *fulness, plenty, abundance* : Cic. **b.** Of colour : *fulness, richness* : Plin.

Sāturnīnus, ī, *m. a Roman surname.* Esp. L. Appuleius Saturninus, *tribune of the plebs,* B.C. 102.

Sāturnus, ī, *m.* **I.** *a mythical king of Latium, who came to Italy in the reign of Janus ; afterwards honoured as the god of agriculture and of civilisation in general ; hence early identified with the* Κρόνος *of the Greeks, and regarded as the father of Jupiter, Pluto, Neptune, and Juno :* **Sāturnius**, a, um : numerus, *Saturnian metre :* Hor. ; **Sāturnius**, ī, *m. Jupiter ;* also *Pluto :* **Sāturnia**, ae, *f. Juno ;* also *a town on the Capitoline Hill, the fabled beginning of Rome ;* **Sāturnālis**, e : **Sāturnālia**, ium and iōrum, *n. pl. the Saturnalia ; a festival in honour of Saturn, beginning on Dec. 17th and lasting several days.* **II.** *the planet Saturn* : Hor.

saturō, āre [satur], *to fill, glut, cloy, satiate.* **1.** Lit. : cytiso apes, Verg. ; Cic. ; Ov. **2.** T r a n s f. **A.** Of inanimate things : fimo pingui sola, Verg. ; pallam murice, Ov. **B.** Of the mind. **a.** mens saturata bonarum cogitationum epulis, Cic. ; se sanguine civium, Cic. ; lumina nati cara saturata figura, Cat. ; crudelitatem, Cic. **b.** *to disgust* : hae res vitae me saturant, Pl.

satus, a, um. **I.** *Part.* sero. **II.** Noun. **a. satus,** i, m. *a son* (lit. *begotten of*) ; **sata,** ae, *f. a daughter* (both with ABL.) : satus Anchisa, i.e. Aeneas, Verg. ; satae Pelia, *the daughters of Pelias,* Ov. **b. sata,** orum, *n. pl. crops* : Verg., Ov.

satus, us, m. [sero], *a sowing, planting.* **1.** Lit. : Cato, Cic. In *pl.* : Cic. **2.** Transf. **a.** *a begetting* : Acc., Lucr., Cic. **b.** philosophia praeparat animos ad satus accipiendos, Cic.

satyriscus, i, m. [σατυρίσκος], *a little Satyr* : Cic.

satyrus, i, m. [σάτυρος], *a kind of sylvan deity resembling an ape, with a horse's tail* (later the Satyr was given two goat's feet). **a.** Prop. : Lucr., Cic., Hor., Ov. **b.** *a kind of Greek drama in which Satyrs often formed the Chorus* : Hor. **c.** *a kind of ape,* perh. *the Chimpanzee* : Plin.

sauciatio, onis, f. [saucio], *a wounding* : Cic.

saucio, are [saucius], *to wound, hurt.* **1.** Lit. : aliquem, Cic. ; aliquem virgis, Pl. ; Sall. ; genas ungue, Ov. **2.** Transf. **a.** Of the *breaking up* of the ground : vomer humum, Ov. **b.** famam, Pl. ; cor odio, Pl.

saucius, a, um, *wounded, hurt.* **1.** Lit. : Caes., Verg., etc. ; saucius ense latus, Prop. *Masc.* as Noun : Caes., Cic., etc. **2.** Transf. **A.** *stricken, smitten.* **a.** Of persons : gladiator ille (i.e. Catiline), Cic. ; fato saucia, Prop. **b.** Of things : malus Africo, Hor. ; ianua rixis, Prop. ; (tellus) saucia vomeribus, Ov. ; glacies sole, *stricken, melting,* Ov. **B.** *wounded* (mentally). **a.** (suspicionibus) animus, Cic. Ep. **b.** With love : in Veneris proelio, Pl. ; mens amore, Lucr. ; regina gravi saucia cura, Verg. ; ipse a nostro igne, Ov.

Sauromatae, v. Sarmatae.

saviatio (**suav-**), onis, f. [savior], *a kissing* : Pl.

saviolum (**suav-**), i, n. [dim. savium], *a sweet kiss* : Cat.

savior (**suav-**), ari [savium], *to kiss* : aliquem, Cic. ; os oculosque, Cat.

savium (**suav-**), i, n. [suavis]. **I.** *a mouth or lips* puckered up to kiss : Pl. **II.** *a kiss* : Pl., Cic.

saxatilis, e, adj. [saxum], *that dwells among rocks* : columbae, Varr. As Noun, **saxatilis,** *a rock-fish* : Ov.

saxetum, i, n. [saxum], *a rocky place* : Cic.

saxeus, a, um [saxum], *of rock, rocky, stony.* **1.** Lit. : Acc., Lucr., Cic., Verg., etc. ; umbra, Verg. **2.** Transf. of persons : Plin. Ep.

saxificus, a, um [saxum facio], *that makes into stone, petrifying* : vultus Medusae, Ov.

saxifragus, a, um [saxum frango], *stone-breaking* : undae maris, Enn.

saxosus, a, um [saxum], *full of rocks or stones, rocky, stony* : montes, Verg. As Noun, **saxosa,** orum, n. pl. *rocky or stony places* : Plin., Quint.

saxulum, i, n. [dim. saxum], *a little crag or rock* : Cic.

saxum, i, n. [cf. secare], *any large, rough stone* ; *a detached fragment of rock* ; *a rock.* **a.** In gen. : Pl., Cic., Verg., etc. ; e saxo sculptus, Cic. Prov. : satis diu hoc iam saxum volvo (alluding to the story of Sisyphus in Hades), Ter. ; inter sacrum saxumque stare ; v. sacrum. **b.** *the Tarpeian rock* : Pl., Lucr., Cic. Ep., etc. [It. *sasso.*]

scabellum, v. scabillum.

scaber, bra, brum [scabo], *mangy, itchy.* **1.** Lit. : oves, Pl., Cato. **2.** Transf. *rough* (esp. from dirt), *scurfy, fretted* : pectus inluvie scabrum, poet. ap. Cic. ; scaber intonsusque homo, Hor. ; manus, Ov. ; rubigine dentes, Ov. ; robigo (pilorum), Verg. Of porous stone : Verg. Of bark : Plin.

scabies, em, e, f. [scabo]. **1.** Lit. : *mange, itch* : Cato, Verg., Juv., etc. **2.** Transf. **a.** *roughness* (esp. fr. dirt or rust), *scurf* : Verg., Juv. **b.** *an itching, pruriency* : Cic. ; lucri, Hor.

scabillum, i, n. [dim. scamnum], *a low stool, foot-stool.* **1.** Lit. : Cato, Varr. **2.** Transf. *an instrument of the castanet kind, worked with the foot,* esp. used in dramatic representations : Cic. [It. *sgabello* ; Fr. *escabeau.*]

scabiosus, a, um [scabies], *mangy, itchy.* Transf. **a.** *rough* : curalium, Plin. **b.** *mouldy* : far, Pers.

scabo, scabere, scabi [cf. Gk. σκάπτω], *to scratch, to scrape* : caput, Lucil., Hor.

Scaea porta (or in *pl.*), *the western gate of Troy.*

scaena (**scena**), ae, f. [σκηνή, " a booth " used as stage dressing-room]. **I.** *the background* (of the stage), *scene presented.* Transf. : silvis scaena coruscis, Verg. In *pl.* : Verg. **II.** *the proscenium, the stage.* **1.** Lit. : Lucr., Cic., Verg., etc. ; dum histrio in scaena siet, Pl. ; Cic. ; scaenis agitatus Orestes, Verg. ; agitur res in scaenis, Hor. ; extra scaenam fiunt proelia, Pl. ; ad ostentationem scaenao gaudentis miraculis, Liv. **2.** Transf. **a.** *the stage of the world, the public eye* : scaenae servire, Cic. Ep. ; si minus in scaena sunt, Cic. ; se a vulgo et scaena in secreta removant, Hor. **b.** *the scene* ; *outward show, pretext* : scaenam criminis parat, Tac. **c.** Of the schools of rhetoric : Tac.

scaenalis (**scen-**), e, adj. [scaena], *scenic, theatrical* : species, Lucr.

scaenicus (**scen-**), a, um [scaena], *of the stage, scenic, theatrical* : artifices, Cic. ; ludi, Liv., etc. ; gestus, venustas, Cic. ; decor quidam, Quint. ; dicacitas, Quint. ; adultera (i.e. represented on the stage), Ov. ; scaenicum est (with *Inf.*), Quint. *Masc.* as Noun, *a player, actor* : Cic., Suet., etc. ; applied to Nero, *a* (*would-be*) *stage-hero,* Tac.

Scaevola, ae, m. [scaevus ; hence *left-handed*], *a cognomen in the gens Mucia* ; orig. *of* C. Mucius, *who made his way into the camp of Porsenna to kill him, and on being discovered burned off his own right hand.*

scaevus, a, um [cf. Gk. σκαιός], *left, on the left.* **1.** Lit. As Noun, **scaeva,** ae, f. *a sign* or omen *observed on the left-hand side* :

bona scaeva est mihi, Pl.; căninii, 11.
2. Transf. *perverse, awkward* : Romulus,
Sall.

scălae, ārum, *f. pl.* [scandō], *a flight of steps, a
ladder or ladders* : Cic. ; scalas dare alicui
utendas, Pl. ; admovere, ponere, Caes. ;
murum scalis adgredi, Sall. ; scalis ascendere muros, Verg. ; Hor. [Fr. *échelle.*]

scalmus, ī, *m.* [σκαλμός], *a peg to which an
oar was strapped ; a thole-pin, rowlock* :
Cic. [Fr. *échome.*]

scalpellum, ī, *n.* [*dim.* scalprum], *a small
surgical knife, a scalpel, lancet* : Cic. [It.
scarpello.]

scalpō, scalpere, scalpsī, scalptum [perh. *cf.*
Gk. γλύφω], *to carve.* **1.** Lit. : Cic. ; marmora, Plin. ; sepulcro querellam, Hor.
2. Transf. **a.** *to scratch* : terram unguibus, Hor. ; verrucam, Suet. ; caput uno
digito, Juv. **b.** *to tickle, titillate* : tremulo
intima versu, Pers.

scalprum, ī, *n.* [scalpō], *a cutting instrument* ;
a chisel, Liv. ; *a knife,* Hor. ; *a pen-knife,*
Tac.

scalptor, ōris, *m.* [scalpō], *a cutter, graver*
(us. of gems) : Plin.

scalptūra, ae, *f.* [scalpō], *the act of cutting,
carving,* or *graving* in stone. **1.** Lit. :
Plin. **2.** Transf. *a graved figure, a carving,
sculpture* : Suet.

scalpurriō, īro [scalpō], *to scratch* : Pl.

Scamander, drī, *m. a river at Troy, called
also Xanthus from its red colour.*

scambus, a, um [σκαμβός], *bow-legged* (pure
Latin, varus) : Suet.

scammōnea, ae, *f.* (**scammōneum**, ī, *n.*
Cato ; **scammōnium**, ī, *n.* and **scammō-
nia**, ae, *f.* Plin.) [σκαμμωνία], the plant
scammony : Cic.

scamnum, ī, *n.* [*cf.* σκήπτω, scīpiō], *a bench,
stool.* **1.** Lit. : Ov., Mart. Of a throne :
Enn. **2.** Transf. *a bank* or *ridge* left in
ploughing : Plin.

scandō, scandere, scandī, scānsum, *to climb,
clamber, mount.* **1.** Lit. : Lucr., Quint. ;
in aggerem, Liv. ; Ov. ; per coniuncta
aedificia, Tac. ; super testudinem, Tac.
With Acc. : Pl. ; mālos, Cic. ; muros,
Liv. ; in curru Capitolium, Liv. ; equum,
Verg. ; cumbam, cubile, Prop. ; fatalis
machina muros, Verg. **2.** Transf. **a.**
to mount : timor et minae eodem quo dominus, Hor. ; supra principem, Tac. With
Acc. : scandit aeratas vitiosa navis cura,
Hor. **b.** *to rise* : gradus aetatis adultae,
Lucr.

scandula (later **scindula**), ae, *f.* [scandō], *a
shingle* for roofing : Hirt., Plin.

scapha, ae, *f.* [σκάφη], *a light boat, a skiff* :
Pl., Caes., Cic., etc. ; biremis, Hor.

scaphium, ī, *n.* [σκάφιον], *a concave vessel* or
basin. **I.** *a drinking-bowl* : Pl., Lucr.,
Cic. **II.** *a chamber-pot* : Mart., Juv.

scapulae, ārum, *f. pl.* the *shoulder-blades,* in
men and animals. **1.** Lit. : Varr., Ov. **2.**
Transf. *the shoulders, back,* in gen. : Pl.,
Sen.

scāpus, ī, *m.* [*v.* scamnum], *a shaft, stalk,
trunk, etc.* : Varr., Plin., Sen. Ep. Of a
weaver's yarn-beam : Lucr.

scarĭfō, āro [σκαρφάομαι], *to scratch open,
scarify* : gingivas, Plin. ; Mart.

scăn uuj i, m [προον] *a kind of sea-fish* :
Hor., Ov., etc.

scatebra, ae, *f.* [scateō], *a bubbling* or *gushing
up* of water : Plin. In *pl.* : Verg.

scateō, ēre, and **scatō**, ere (Enn., Lucr.), *to
bubble, gush.* **1.** Lit. **a.** Of the liquid :
Enn., Lucr. **b.** Of the place (with ABL.) :
arx fontibus, Liv. ; Pl. **2.** Transf. *to
gush, teem, abound.* **a.** cuniculi in Hispaniā,
Plin. **b.** Of the place. With ABL. : beluis pontus, Hor. ; Hispania metallis,
Plin. With GEN. : terra ferarum, Lucr.
Comic. With *Intern.* Acc. : amas pol,
misera ; id tuos scatet animus, Pl.

scaturrigēs (Varr.) or **scaturriginēs** (Liv.),
um, *f. pl.* [scaturriō], *springs.*

scaturriō, īre [scatuō], *to gush* or *flow.*
Of the place. **1.** Lit. : solum fontibus,
Col. **2.** Transf. : Curio totus hoc sca-
turrit, Cael. ap. Cic. Ep.

scaurus, a, um [σκαῦρος], *with large* or
projecting ankles : Hor.

scăzon, ontis, *m.* [σκάζων, *limping*], *an iambic
trimeter, with a spondee* or *trochee in the last
foot, giving the effect of a limp* : Mart.,
Plin. Ep.

scelerātē, adv. *wickedly, criminally* : Cic.
Sup. : Cic.

scelerātus, a, um. **I.** *Part.* scelerō (or fr.
scelus). **II.** Adj. *polluted, profaned, desc-
crated* or *accursed by crime* (or *misfortune*).
1. Lit. **a.** Of places : terra, Verg., Ov. ;
limen, Verg. ; Sceleratus Vicus, Liv., Ov. ;
Campus, Liv. ; Castra, Suet. **b.** Of persons : *accursed, banned, outlawed* : Caes.,
Cic., Liv., Ov. As Noun : Caes. **2.**
Transf. **A.** *villainous, criminal, scoundrelly, infamous.* **a.** Of persons : Cic.,
Ov., etc. Comp. : Ov. Sup. : Cic.,
Sall., Liv. As Noun, *villain, scoundrel,
rascal* : Pl., Cic., etc. **b.** preces, Cic. ;
contra patriam scelerata arma capere, Cic. ;
insania belli, Verg. ; coniuratio, Liv.
Comp. : Cic. Sup. : Quint. **B.** *wicked,
plaguy, plaguesome, malicious* : sinapis,
Pl. ; frigus, Vorg. ; lues, poemata, Mart.

scelerō, āro [scelus], *to pollute, desecrate* :
divos parentis, Cat. ; manūs, Verg. ; san-
guino dextram, Stat.

scelerōsus, a, um [scelus], *full of wickedness,
accursed, scoundrelly* : ille, Ter. ; facta,
Lucr.

scelestē, adv. *wickedly, criminally* : Pl., Liv.
Comic. *roguishly* : Cic. Ep.

scelestus, a, um [scelus]. **I.** *criminal,
wicked, villainous, infamous.* **a.** Of persons : Pl., Sall., Hor., etc. Comp. and
Sup. : Pl. As Noun, *rogue, scoundrel* :
Pl., Ter. **b.** facinus, Pl., Cic., Liv. ; aedes,
cena, servitus, Pl. ; nuptiae, Sall. ; sermo,
Liv. Comp. : Pl., Liv. **II.** Comic. :
villainous, i.e. *unlucky,* etc. : annus, Pl. ;
ego, Pl. Comp. : Pl.

scelus, eris, *n. a wicked* or *impious action* ;
an evil deed, a crime. **1.** Lit. : facinus
est vincire civem R., scelus verberare,
Cic. In contrast to flagitium, Cic., Tac.
With perfidia, Cic., Liv. With audacia,
furor, avaritia, Cic. Opp. to pietas, Cic. ;
concipere in se, fingere, excogitare, moliri,
admittere, facere, perficere, edere (in aliquem), anhelare, suscipere, Cic. ; scelere

adstringi, obstringi, se adligare, Cic. ;
scelere obrui, Liv. With GEN.: scelus
legatorum contra ius gentium interfectorum,
Liv. **2.** T r a n s f. **a.** *a misfortune, cala-*
mity : Pl., Ter., Mart. **b.** As a term of
reproach : *scoundrel, rascal ;* and of
women, *baggage :* Pl., Ter. **c.** *a fault*
(of nature): scelera naturae, Plin. ; bestiarum, Plin.

scēn-, *v.* scaen-.

Scĕpsis, is, *f. a town in Mysia :* **Scĕpsius**,
a, um ; *Masc.* as Noun, *Metrodorus of*
Scepsis.

scēptrĭfer, era, erum [scēptrum ferō], *sceptre-*
bearing : Ov.

scēptrum, I, *n.* [σκῆπτρον], *a regal staff,*
a sceptre. **1.** L i t. : Cic., Verg., etc.
P o e t. in *pl. :* Verg., Ov. **2.** T r a n s f. **a.**
C o m i c. : ferulae tristes, sceptra paeda-
gogorum, Mart. **b.** In *pl. : kingdom,*
dominion, authority : sic nos in sceptra
reponis, Verg. ; sceptra Asiae tenere, Ov. ;
Heliconiadum comites, quorum unus Homerus sceptra potitus, Lucr.

scēptūchus, I, *m.* [σκηπτοῦχος], *a sceptre-*
bearer, a high officer of state in the East :
Tac.

scheda (scida, Cic.), ae, *f.* [σχέδη], *a strip*
of papyrus bark : Plin. ; *a leaf of paper :*
Cic. Ep., Mart., Quint.

schēma, ae, *f.* and atis, *n.* [σχῆμα], *a figure,*
form, style. **a.** In gen. : servilis, Pl. ;
exemplar imperatae schemae, Suet. ; anti-
quom, Lucil. **b.** R h e t. *a figure of speech,*
rhetorical figure ; puro Latin, figura :
Quint.

Schoeneus (disyl.), eī, *m. king in Boeotia,*
father of Atalanta : **Schoenēis**, idis, *f.*
Atalanta ; **Schoenēius**, a, um : virgo,
i.e. *Atalanta,* Ov. ; **Schoenēïa**, ae, *f.*
Atalanta.

schoenobatēs, ae, *m.* [σχοινοβάτης], *a rope-*
dancer : Juv.

schoenus, i, m. [σχοῖνος]. **I.** *a reed or grass*
of an aromatic kind : Cato, Pl. **II.** *a*
measure of distance among the Persians :
Plin.

schola, ae, *f.* [σχολή, *leisure*], *leisure devoted*
to learning ; a learned conversation or debate,
a lecture, dissertation. **1.** L i t. : Cic.,
Quint. ; certae scholae sunt do exsilio,
de interitu patriae, etc., Cic. **2.** T r a n s f.
a. *a place for learned conversation or*
instruction, a school : in scholā adsidere,
Cic. ; politus e scholā, Cic. ; e philosophorum scholis tales fere evadunt, Cic. ;
Quint. ; Plin. Ep. **b.** *the pupils or dis-*
ciples of a teacher, a school, sect : Cic., Plin.
Ep. [It. *scuola* ; Sp. *escuela;* Fr. *école.*]

scholasticus, a, um [σχολαστικός], *of a school,*
scholastic : controversiae, Quint. ; Tac. ;
litterae, Plin. Ep. As Noun, **scholastica**,
ōrum, *n. pl. School exercises :* Quint. ; **scho-**
lasticus, i, *m. one who teaches* or *studies*
rhetoric : Quint., Tac., etc. Of a grammarian : Verg., Tac.

Sciathos (-us), i, *f. an island in the Aegean*
Sea, now *Skopelo.*

scida, ae, *v.* scheda.

sciēns, entis. **I.** *Part.* sciō. **II.** A d j. **a.**
knowing, having knowledge ; hence *know-*
ingly, intentionally, with one's eyes open :

prudens, sciens, vivus vidensque pereo,
Ter. ; Pl. ; habebit igitur te sciente et vi-
dente curia senatorem, Cic. **b.** *knowing,*
understanding, acquainted with, skilled or
expert in : Pl. ; *Comp. :* Hor. ; *Sup. :*
quae (navis) scientissimo gubernatore
utitur, Cic. With GEN.: locorum, Sall. ;
pugnae, citharae, Hor. ; iuris, Latinae
linguae, Tac. With *Inf. :* Hor.

scienter, *adv. wisely, skilfully, expertly, etc.* :
Caes., Cic. *Comp. :* Caes., Cic. *Sup. :* Cic.

scientia, ae, *f.* [sciēns], *a knowing or being*
skilled in, knowledge, skill, expertness :
scientia atque usus militum, Caes. ; Cic.
With *Obj.* GEN.: linguae Gallicae, Caes. ;
oppugnationis, Caes. ; iuris, rei militaris,
regionum terrestrium, Cic. ; verborum
deligendorum, Cic. With *in* or *de* and ABL.:
in legibus interpretandis, Cic. ; de omnibus, Cic.

scilicet, *adv.* [scire licet, " *one may know* " ;
cf. vidē-licet and I-licet], *it is evident, clear,*
plain, or *manifest ; of course, evidently,*
certainly. **1.** L i t. **a.** With ACC. and *Inf. :*
Pl., Ter., Lucr., Sall. **b.** As simple *Adv. :*
Pl., Cic., Hor., etc. Often followed by
sed, tamen, sed tamen ; *certainly, no doubt,*
. . . *but still, etc. :* Cic. **c.** Elliptically
esp. in answers : *Le.* abi ad meam sororem.
St. ibitur. *Le.* et gratulator meae sorori.
St. scilicet, Pl. ; Ter. ; Lucr. **d.** I r o n i-
c a l l y : *of course, to be sure, doubtless, for-*
sooth : Ter., Cic., Verg., etc. **2.** T r a n s f.
as an explanatory particle : *namely, that is*
to say : sub nomine alieno, nepotum scilicet
et uxoris sororisque, Suet. ; Nep.

scilla (**squilla**), ae, *f.* [σκίλλα]. **I.** *a sea-*
onion, sea-leek, squill : Varr., Plin. **II.** *a*
small fish of the lobster kind (*v.* pinoteres),
prob. *a prawn* or *shrimp ;* in this sense more
usually written squilla : Lucil., Cic., Hor.

scin' for **scisne.**

scindō, scindere, scidī, scissum [*cf.* Gk.
σχίζω], *to cut, rend, split, cleave,* or *tear*
asunder. **1.** L i t. : vela, Pl. ; limen por-
tae, Pl. ; epistulam, Cic. Ep. ; vallum,
Caes., Liv. ; cuneis lignum, Verg. ; capillos,
Ov. ; vestem, Liv. ; vestem tibi de corpore,
Prop. ; pontem, Tac. ; agmen, Tac. ;
ferro aequor, Verg. ; vomere terram, Ov.
P r o v. : paenulam alicui (i.e. to press one
to stay), Cic. Ep. With *Refl. Pron.* or in
Mid. : so nubes, Verg. ; Cato ; scinditur
in geminas partis circumfluus amnis, Ov. ;
Lucr. **2.** T r a n s f. : dolorem meum, Cic.
Ep. ; aliquem quāvis cuppedine curae,
Lucr. ; verba fletu, Ov. ; genus amborum
scindit se sanguine ab uno, Verg. ; scinditur
incertum studia in contraria vulgus, Verg. ;
Tac.

scindula, *v.* scandula.

scintilla, ae, *f. dim.* [*cf.* Gk. σπινθήρ], *a*
spark. **1.** L i t. : Lucr., Verg., Liv., etc.
2. T r a n s f. : Pl. ; ingeni, Cic. ; belli,
Cic. Ep. [Fr. *étincelle.*]

scintillō, āre [scintilla], *to sparkle, gleam,*
flash : oculi, Pl. ; templa caeli, Lucr. ;
oleum testā ardente, Verg. ; carbunculi
contra radios solis, Plin.

scintillula, ae, *f.* [*dim.* scintilla], *a little*
spark : (perh.) animae, Pl. ; in pueris
virtutum, Cic.

scĭō, scīre, scīvī (perh. not in Livy, who uses scīvī only as the *Perf.* of scīscō) or scĭī, scītum (old *Imperf.* scībam, Cat.; *Fut.* scībō, Ter. *Pass.* : scībitur, Pl. *Perf.* sync. scīstī, Ov.; so regularly *Inf.* scīsse, Cic.), *to know, to understand, perceive*; *to have a knowledge of* or *skill in* : Pl.; quem, ut scītis, unice dilexi, Cic.; quod sciam, *for aught I know* or *as far as I know*, Pl., Cic. With *Acc.* of thing known or understood : Pl., Cic., Hor., etc.; aliquid ex aliquo, Pl., Cic. Ep.; aliquid de (*from*) aliquo, Cic. Ep.; in *Pass.* : Pl., Cic. With *Acc.* and *Inf.* : Pl., Cic., Hor., etc. *Impers. Pass.* : Cic. With *Indir. Quest.* : Pl., Cic., Hor., etc. (For haud scio an, *v. an.*) With *de* : de legibus instituendis, de bello ac pace, Cic. With *Inf.* : *to know how* (*to*) : Cic., Hor., Liv. (The negative of scīo is usually nescĭō, *q.v.*)

scīpĭō, ōnis, *m.* [*cf.* scēptrum], *a staff* (carried by persons of rank or station) : Pl., Cat.; eburneus (carried by the viri triumphales), Liv.; given as a present from the Roman nation to friendly princes : Liv.

Scīpĭō, ōnis, *a celebrated family in the gens* Cornelia, the most famous members of which were the two conquerors of the Carthaginians, P. Cornelius Scipio Africanus maior, in the 2nd, and P. Cornelius Scipio Aemilianus Africanus minor, in the 3rd Punic war; hence **Scīpĭădēs**, ae (*Acc. sing.* Scīpiadem; *Acc. pl.* Scīpiadas), *m.* one of the Scipio family, a Scipio (a patronymic form coined for use in hexam. verse : Lucr., Verg.).

Scīrŏn, ōnis, *m.* **I.** *a noted robber, killed by Theseus.* **II.** *an Epicurean philosopher in the time of Cicero.*

scirpeus (**sirp-**), a, um [scirpus], *of rushes, rush-* : simulacra, Ov. As Noun, **scirpea** (**sirp-**), ae, *f.* *a basket-work of rushes to form the body of a waggon* (esp. for carrying manure) : Cato, Varr., Ov.

scirpĭcŭlus (**sirp-** and **surp-**), a, um [scirpus], *of* or *for rushes* : falces, Cato. As Noun, **scirpicŭlus**, ī, *m.* and **scirpicula**, ae, *f.* *a basket made of rushes, a rush-basket* : Pl., Varr., Prop.

scirpus (**sirpus**), ī, *m.* [cogn. with γρῖπος], *a rush,* or *reed-grass* : Pl. *Prov.* : nodum in scirpo quaerere (to find a difficulty where there is none), Pl., Ter.

sciscĭtor, ārī, and **sciscĭtō**, āre (Pl.) [*freq.* sciscō], *to seek information repeatedly* or *earnestly* ; *to ask, inquire, question repeatedly* or *earnestly* : Liv., Quint. With *Acc.* of thing asked about, and *ex* or *ab* with *Abl.* of person (if expressed) : Pl., Cic., Liv., Tac. With *Indir. Quest.* : Ter., Cic., Liv., etc. With *de* : de victoriā, Cic.; de Domitio ubi sit, Cic. Ep. With *Acc.* of person, *to consult* : deos, Liv.; singulos (with *Indir. Quest.*), Suet.

sciscō, sciscere, scīvī, scītum [sciō]. **1.** Lit. **a.** *to seek to know* ; *to search, inquire* (with *Indir. Quest.*) : Pl. **b.** *to learn, ascertain* : id factum, Pl. **2.** Transf. **A.** Of public procedure : *to assent to* or *approve after examination, to vote for, enact, ordain* : rogationes plurumas populus, Pl.; rogationem de Liguribus plebes scivit iussitque,

populus iuberet, Cic.; de aliquō ut etc., Cic. In *Pass.* : Cic. **B.** In gen. of an individual : primus scivit legem de publicanis, Cic. Also, quod ipsa natura sciscat, Cic.

scissūra, ae, *f.* [scindō], *a rending, dividing* ; *a rent, cleft* : Sen., Plin.

scissus, a, um. **I.** *Part.* scindō. **II.** Adj. *split, cleft.* **1.** Lit. : aures, Plin. **2.** Transf. : genus vocum, Cic.

scītāmenta, ōrum, *n. pl.* [scītus], *delicate food, dainties* : Pl.

scītē, *adv.* *expertly, skilfully, tastefully* : Pl., Cic., Liv. *Sup.* : Pl.

scītor, ārī [*freq.* sciō], *to seek to know* ; *to ask, inquire* : scitari et quaere.e causas, Verg.; Ov.; aliquid ex aliquo, Pl., Hor.; ab aliquo, Ov. With *Indir. Quest.* : Ov. With *Acc.* of person or thing consulted : oracula Phoebi, Verg.

scītŭ, Abl. *sing. m.* [scīscō]. **I.** *by an enacting* : neque populi iussu neque plebi scitu, Decr. ap. Cic. **II.** *an enactment* or *decree of the plebs* : comitia de senatūs sententiā plebique scitu sunt habita, Liv.

scītŭlus, a, um [*dim.* scītus], *neat, trim, elegant* : facies, Pl.

scītum, ī, *n.* [scīscō], *an ordinance, statute, decree.* **a.** With plebis, plebi, or plebei, *an ordinance* or *decree of the people, a plebiscite* (opp. to senatūs consultum, *a decree of the Senate*) : Pl.; quae (lex) postea plebei scito Canuleio abrogata est, Cic.; de altero aedile scitum plebi est factum rogantibus tribunis, Liv. Without plebis : scita ac iussa nostra, Cic. **b.** With populi, of the decrees of other nations : Cic., Liv. Also of Rome : Tac. **c.** Rarely of other public or official ordinances : Pontificis, Liv.; decemvirorum, Liv.

scītus, a, um. **I.** *Part.* sciō and scīscō. **II.** Adj. *knowing, shrewd, experienced, skilful, etc.* **1.** Lit. **a.** Of persons : Pl., Ter., Liv.; *Comp.* : Pl. With *Gen.* : vadorum, lyrae, Ov.; pugnandi, Quint. **b.** Of things : *suitable, proper, judicious, sensible, witty, etc.* : syngraphum, oratio, Pl.; sermo, Cic.; Tac. *Sup.* : Pl. Phr.: scitum est, *it is a shrewd saying* or *plan* : vetus illud Catonis admodum scitum est, Cic.; hoc scitum est, periculum ex aliis facere, tibi quod ex usu siet, Ter.; Cic. **2.** Transf. *smart, fine, etc.* (colloq.): puer, Ter.; nox scitast exercendo scorto, Pl.

sciūrus, ī, *m.* [σκίουρος, *shadow-tail*], *a squirrel* : Plin., Mart.

scobis, is, *f.* [scabō], *powder* or *dust produced by sawing, rasping, etc.; sawdust, scrapings, filings, etc.* : Hor., Juv.

scomber, brī, *m.* [σκόμβρος], *a mackerel* : Pl., Cat., etc.

scōpae, ārum, *f. pl.* [cogn. with scāpus], *thin branches, twigs, shoots.* **1.** Lit. : Cato. **2.** Transf. *a broom, besom* : Pl., Hor. *Prov.* : scopas dissolvere (i.e. to throw anything into confusion), Cic.

Scōpās, ae, *m.* **I.** *a famous Greek sculptor of Paros.* **II.** *a Thessalian despot, the grudging patron of Simonides of Ceos.*

scopos, ī, m. [σκοπός], *a mark, aim :* Suet.

scopulōsus, a, um [scopulus], *full of rocks, rocky, craggy.* **1.** Lit.: mare, Cic. ; rupes, Luc. **2.** Transf.: intellego quam scopuloso difficilique in loco verser, Cic.

scopulus, ī, m. [σκόπελος]. *a projecting point of rock ; a rock, cliff, crag,* esp. *a rock or ledge* in the sea. **1.** Lit.: Caes., Verg., Ov. Of *a promontory :* Hor., Ov. On land : Verg., Ov. With ref. to the hardness of a rock : natus es e scopulis, Ov. ; scopulis surdior, Hor. **2.** Transf. of a danger, harm, etc. (freq. in Cic.) : qui te ad scopulum e tranquillo inferat, Ter. ; (Piso et Gabinius) geminae voragines scopulique rei publicae, Cic. [It. *scoglio* ; Fr. *écueil.*]

scorpiō, ōnis (**scorpios** and **-us**, iī ; Ov., and Cic. poet.), m. [σκορπίων], *a scorpion.* **1.** Lit.: Pl., Ov. **2.** Transf. **a.** *a military engine for throwing darts, stones, and other missiles, a scorpion :* Caes., Liv. **b.** *a kind of sea-fish :* Ov. **c.** *the Scorpion,* one of the signs of the Zodiac : Cic. poet., Ov.

scortātor, ōris, m. [scortor], *a fornicator :* Pl., Hor.

scorteus, a, um [scortum], *made of hides or leather- :* Ov. *Fem.* as Noun (sc. vestis) : Sen., Mart.

scortor, ārī [scortum], *to associate with prostitutes :* Pl., Ter., Varr.

scortum, ī, n. [*cf.* corium for scorium], *a skin, hide.* **1.** Lit.: Varr. **2.** Transf. *a harlot, prostitute ; a lewd person of either sex :* Pl., Ter., Cic., Hor.

screātor, ōris, m. [screō], *a hawker, hemmer :* Pl.

screātus, ūs, m. [screō], *a hawking, hemming :* Ter.

screō, āre, *to clear the throat noisily, to hawk, hem :* Pl.

scriba, ae, m. [scrībō], *a government clerk, secretary,* or *notary :* Cic., Hor., Liv., etc.

scriblīta (**scribilīta**), ae, f. *a kind of tart :* Pl., Cato, Mart.

scrībō, scrībere, scrīpsī, scrīptum (*Perf. syncop.* scrīpstī, Pl.) [*cf.* γράφω, scrobis, scrōfa], prop. *to scratch* or *grave* with a sharp point ; hence, *to write, draw, grave, make lines* or *letters,* etc. **I.** In gen. **1.** Lit. **a.** With Acc. of letters, etc.: in libro calamo litteras, Pl. ; suā manu, Liv. ; Cic. ; carmen columnā, Prop. ; scribitur Cynthia corticibus, Prop. ; lineam, Cic. ; formam porticūs, Plin. Ep. ; Cat. ; fugitivo stigmata, Quint. **b.** With Acc. of thing marked : tabellas, Pl. ; lapidem his notis, Tib. ; aurum, Juv. **2.** Transf.: illa dicta in animo, Ter. ; in vento et rapidā aquā, Cat. **II.** With the idea of intellectual action, *to compose, describe ; to draw up, communicate in writing.* **a.** In gen. : Pl., Cic., Ov., etc. ; fabulam, Pl. ; versūs, Lucr. ; de publicā multa, Cic. ; bellum, Liv. ; formam et situm agri, Hor. ; carmina, epistulam, litteras, Cic., etc. ; salutem, Pl. Of letters : usually with *ad* and Acc. of pers. (rarely DAT.), and *de* with ABL. of thing : scriberem ad te de hoc plura, Cic. Ep. With Acc. and *Inf.* : in litteris scribit se celeriter adfore, Caes. ; Pl. ; Cic. ; Hor. With *Indir. Quest.* or *Deliberative :*

Cic. Ep. A request or command is expressed by *Subj.*, with or without *ut* or *ne* expressed : Scipioni scribendum, ne bellum remitteret, Liv. ; scribit Labieno, ne veniat, Caes. Also with *Inf.* : Tac. **b.** *to draw up* a law, decree, treaty, etc. : leges, Cic. ; amicitiae foedus, Liv. ; senatūs consultum, Cic. Ep. **c.** Milit. *to enrol, enlist, levy :* milites, legiones, etc., Sall. ; Liv. ; supplementum legionibus, Cic. Ep. Transf. : scribe tui gregis hunc, Hor. **d.** In law : dicam scribere (alicui), like δίκην γράφειν τινί, *to bring an action against* (v. dica) : testamentum, Cic. With personal object and *Predic.* Noun, *to appoint* or *designate any one :* aliquem heredem, Cic. ; Caes. : Hor., etc. ; aliquem tutorem liberis, Cic. Of contracts, notes, drafts, etc.: pulchre scripsti ; soitum syngraphum ! Pl. ; nummos, usuras, Pl. ; tabulas, Hor. [It. *scrivere* ; Sp. *escribir* ; Fr. *écrire.*]

scrīnium, ī, n. [perh. fr. scrībō], *a case* or *box for keeping books, papers, letters, etc. ; an escritoire, portfolio.* **1.** Lit.: Sall., Cat., Hor., Ov., etc. **2.** Transf. *a case* or *casket* in gen. : Plin. [It. *scrigno* ; Fr. *écrin.*]

scrīptiō, ōnis, f. [scrībō]. **I.** *the act of writing :* Cic. Ep. **II.** *a composing in writing, composition :* Cic. In *pl.* : Cic. **III.** *the written wording, text of a law,* etc.: ex scriptione interpretari, Cic.

scrīptitō, āre [*freq.* scrībō], *to write regularly* or *often.* **I.** in palmarum foliis, Plin. **II.** **a.** Of letter-writing: aliquid, Cic. Ep. ; ad aliquem media, Tac. ; alicui, Tac. **b.** *to write* or *compose in writing habitually :* accurate, Cic. ; multum, Cic.

scrīptor, ōris, m. [scrībō], *a writer.* **I.** In gen. : *a scribe, secretary :* Cic. ; scriptor librarius, Hor. **II. a.** *one who composes in writing ; a writer, composer, author, etc. :* Cic., Hor., etc. ; rerum scriptor, Cic., Liv. ; artium, Cic. ; Satyrorum, Hor. ; Troiani belli, Hor. ; carminum, tragoediarum, etc., Quint. **b.** In law : *a drawer-up, compiler :* Quint. ; legum Numa, Cic. ; testamenti, Suet.

scrīptula, ōrum, n. *pl.* [*dim.* scriptum], *the lines on the board in the game of* duodecim scripta : Ov.

scrīptūra, ae, f. [scrībō]. **I.** Abstract. **a.** *a writing :* mendum scripturae, Caecin. ap. Cic. Ep. ; Mart., etc. **b.** *a writing, composing :* Ter., Cic., Liv., etc. **II.** Concrete. **A.** *something written, a writing :* Ter. ; diurna actorum, Tac. **B.** In law. **a.** *a tax paid on public pastures :* Pl., Cic. **b.** *a written law :* Suet. **c.** *a testamentary provision :* Cic.

scrīptus, a, um. **I.** *Part.* scrībō. **II.** Noun, **scrīptum**, ī, n. *something written* or *drawn.* **I.** In gen. *a line :* duodecim scripta, *a game played on a board divided into squares by twelve lines :* duodecim scriptis ludere, Cic. **II. a.** *a written composition.* **a.** *a treatise, book, work, etc. :* Cic., Ov. ; de (*from*) scripto dicere, Cic. ; Hortensius ea sine scripto verbis iisdem redderet, Cic. In *pl.* : Cic., Hor., etc. **b.** scriptum legis, and simply, scriptum, *a written ordinance, law :* Cic. [Fr. *écrit.*]

scripulum (or **scrŭpulum** or **scriptulum**), i, n. [scrūpulus], a *small weight* or *measure* : Cic. Ep., Ov.

scrobis, is, m., less freq. f. [v. scrĭbō]. **I.** a *ditch, dike, trench* : Pl., Cic., Ov., etc. **II.** a *grave* : Mart., Tac.

scrōfa, ae, f. [cf. scrĭbō], a *breeding-sow* : Varr., Juv.

scrōfĭpascus, i, m. [scrōfa pascō], a *swine-keeper, swine-breeder* : Pl.

scrūpeus, a, um [scrūpus], *of sharp* or *pointed stones; rugged, stony* : saxum, Enn.; speluncs, Verg.

scrūpōsus, a, um [scrūpus], *full of sharp* or *rough stones, jagged, rugged.* **1.** Lit.: via, Pl. **2.** Transf.: ratio, Lucr.

scrupulōsē, adv. *precisely, carefully* : Quint. Comp.: Plin., Quint.

scrūpulōsus, a, um [scrūpulus], *full of small sharp* or *pointed stones; rough, rugged, jagged.* **1.** Lit.: Pac., Plin. **2.** Transf. **a.** In simile : tamquam e scrupulosis cotibus enavigavit oratio, Cic. **b.** *very nice, precise, careful* : disputatio, Quint. ; Plin. Ep.

scrūpulum, i, v. scripulum.

scrūpulus, i, m. [dim. scrūpus], a *small sharp* or *rough pebble.* Transf. *an uneasy feeling, a doubt, hesitation, scruple* : alicui inicere, Ter., Cic.; alicui ex animo evellere, Cic.; alicui eximere, Plin. Ep.

scrūpus, i, m. a *rough* or *sharp stone.* Transf. *uneasiness* of mind : Cic.

scrūta, ōrum, n. pl. [cogn. with γρύτη; v. scrĭbō], *old* or *broken stuff, trash, frippery* : Lucil., Hor.

scrūtātor, ōris, m. [scrūtor], a *searcher, examiner.* **1.** Lit.: Suet. Poet. of a fisherman : profundi, Stat. **2.** Transf.: fati, Luc.

scrūtor, ārī [scrūta ; perh. lit. "to rummage among rubbish heaps"], *to pry into, probe; to search carefully, examine thoroughly.* **1.** Lit. Of persons : Pl.; aliquem, Cic., Tac. Of things : terrāī abdita ferro, Lucr.; loca abdita, Sall.; Tac.; domos, navis, Cic.; mare, Tac. **2.** Transf. *to probe* or *search into* with a view to finding out something, *to scrutinise.* **a.** In gen.: caeli plagas, Enn.; ea quae sunt inania, Cic.; omnis sordis, Cic. Ep.; reconditas littoras, Cic.; nomina ac vultūs alacritatem tristitiamque coeuntium, Tac.; animos ceterorum secretis sermonibus, Tac. **b.** Of secrets : arcanum illius, Hor.; fibras inspiciunt, mentis deum (GEN.) scrutantur in illis, Ov.; sua Caesarisque fata, Tac.

sculpō, sculpere, sculpsi, sculptum [v. scalpō], *to carve, grave, chisel* in stone, bronze, wood, etc.; *to form by carving, graving, etc.* **1.** Lit.: ebur, Ov.; Hor.; e saxo sculptus, Cic. **2.** Transf. (in words): Quint.

sculpōneae, ārum, f. pl. an *inferior kind of wooden shoe, sabots, clogs* : Pl.

sculptilis, e, adj. [sculpō], *graved, carved* : opus dentis Numidae, Ov.

sculptor, ōris, m. [sculpō], *one who works in marble, wood, etc.; a sculptor* : Plin., Plin. Ep.

sculptūra, ae, f. [sculpō]. **I.** Abstr. a *carving* in stone, wood, etc.: Quint.;

gemmae, Quint. **II.** Concr. an pl. *works of plastic art* : Plin.

scurra, ae, m. **I.** a *buffoon, jester,* esp. a *professional jester* : Pl., Cic., Hor., etc.; scurra Atticus, i.e. Socrates, Cic. **II.** a *town-wit, man-about-town* : Pl., Cat., Cic.

scurrīlis, e, adj. [scurra], *jeering, scurrilous* : iocus, Cic.; dicacitas, Quint.

scurrīlĭtas, ātis, f. [scurrilis], *buffoonery, scurrility* : Quint., Tac.

scurrīlĭter, adv. *jeeringly, like a buffoon* : Plin. Ep.

scurror, ārī [scurra], *to play the buffoon* : Hor.

scŭtāle, is, n. [scūtum], *the thong of a sling* : Liv.

scŭtārius, i, m. [scūtum], a *shield-maker* : Pl.

scŭtātus, a, um [scūtum], *armed with a* scutum or *oblong shield* : Caes., Verg., Liv. Masc. pl. as Noun: *troops armed with shields* : Liv.

scutella, ae, f. [dim. scutra], a *saucer* or *flat bowl; a cup* : dulciculae potionis, Cic. [Fr. écuelle.]

scŭtica, ae, f. [Σκυθική], a *Scythian whip, knout* : Hor., Ov., Juv.

scŭtĭgerulus, i, m. [scūtum gerō], a *shield-bearer* : Pl.

scutra, ae, f. a *flat dish* or *pan* (to heat things in): Pl., Cato.

(1) **scutula**, ae, f. [dim. scutra], a *little dish* or *platter* of a nearly square form : Cato, Mart., Tac. Of a *patch* on the eye : Pl.

(2) **scutula** (**scytala** or **scytalē**), ae, f. **I.** a *wooden roller* : biremis subiectis scutulis in interiorem partem traduxit, Caes. **II.** a *small roller* used by the Spartans for sending secret dispatches : Nep. **III.** a *kind of snake* : Plin., Luc.

scutulātus, a, um [scutula], *diamond-* or *lozenge-shaped* : Plin. Of cloths : *checked,* Neut. pl. as Noun: a *checked garment* : Juv.

scŭtulum, i, n. [dim. scūtum], a *small shield* : Cic.

scŭtum, i, n. [cf. σκῦτος], an *oblong shield,* made of wood covered with leather ; a *buckler* (clipeus, a round shield of metal). **1.** Lit.: Caes., Cic., Verg., Liv., etc. **2.** Transf. for a *protection, defence,* etc.; scuto vobis magis quam gladio opus est, Liv.; Cic. [It. scudo; Sp. escudo; Fr. écu.]

Scylacēum (**Scylacium**), i, n. a *town on the coast of Bruttium,* now *Squillace* ; **Scylacēus**, a, um.

Scylla, ae, f. **I.** a *celebrated rock between Italy and Sicily, opposite to Charybdis.* Personified as the *daughter of Phorcus,* transformed by Circe into a sea-monster, with dogs about her haunches ; **Scyllaeus**, a, um. **II.** daughter of Nisus ; v. Nisus.

scymnus, i, m. [σκύμνος], a *cub, whelp* : leonum, Lucr.

scyphus, i, m. [σκύφος], a *cup, goblet* : Pl.; Cic., Verg., etc.

Scyros or **Scyrus**, i, f. one of the Sporades near Euboea, now Skyros; **Scyrius**, a, um, and **Scyrias**, adis, f. adj. : puella, i.e. Deidamia, Ov.

scytala and **scytalē**, ēs, v. scutula (2).

Scytha and **Scythēs**, ae, *m. a Scythian* ; **Scythae**, ārum, *m. pl. the Scythians*, a general name for the nomadic tribes of the centre and north of Europe and Asia, beyond the Black Sea ; **Scythia**, ae, *f. their country* ; **Scythicus**, a, um, *Scythian* : amnis, i.e. *the Tanais*, Hor. : **Scythissa**, ae, and **Scythis**, idis. *f. a Scythian woman.*

sē or **sēsē** (ACC.), **sui** (GEN.), **sibi** or **sibi** (DAT.), **sē** or **sēsē** (ABL.), *refl. pron.* of 3rd *pers. sing.* and *pl.* (old forms : sēd, ACC. and ABL. ; sibei or sibe, DAT.) ; sometimes strengthened : sēpse (i.e. sē ipse), Cic. ; sēmet, Hor., Liv. [*cf.* Gk. ἕ, σφέ], *himself, themselves, one another.* **I.** Prop. as *Refl. Pron.* **A.** Referring to the *Grammatical Subject* : statim homo se erexit, Cic. ; exercitum ante se mittit, Caes. ; ut sit similis sui, Pl. ; habetis ducem memorem vestri, oblitum sui, Cic. ; is sibi legationem suscepit, Caes. ; segregat ab se omnis, Pl. ; praedam prae se agentes, Liv. ; Veientes pro se quisque fremunt, Liv. **B.** Referring to the *Logical Subject* or other marked word in a sentence, when there is no ambiguity, and often when the *Refl. Pron.* is an integral part of a phrase, like se recipere) : deforme est de se ipsum praedicare, Cic. ; neque praeter se umquam ei servos fuit, Pl. ; neque sui colligendi hostibus facultatem relinquunt, Caes. ; haec cum apud timentis sibimet ipsos increpuissent, Liv. **C.** In *Oblique* clauses (formal or virtual), the *Refl. Pron.* regularly refers to the *Subject of the principal sentence:* conclamavit quid ad se venirent, Caes. ; qui dixisse fertur a se visum esse Romulum, Cic. ; Postumius mihi nuntiavit se a Marcello ad me missum esse, Cic. Ep. (Also ref. to the *Subject of a subordinate clause*, when there is no ambiguity : Caesar milites incusavit ; cur de suā virtute aut de ipsius (i.e. Caesaris) diligentiā desperarent ? Caes.) Also in *non-Oblique* clauses : Metellus in iis urbibus quae ad se defecerant praesidia imponit, Sall. ; Caes. ; Cic. ; Hor., etc. **D.** Phrases : ad se, apud se, *at* or *to one's house*, Pl., Cic., etc. ; apud se also *in one's senses*, Ter. ; sibi velle, *to mean* : quid ergo sibi vult pars altera orationis ? Liv. ; quidnam sibi repentinus clamor vellet, Liv. ; Ter. With *cum* always as one word, sēcum. **II.** As *Reciprocal Pronoun* : patres ac plebem in semet ipsos versos, Liv. Usually in phr. inter se, *one another, mutually* : video eos inter se amare, Ter. ; ut inter se contingant trabes, Caes. ; inter se aspicere, Cic. ; inter se nondum satis noti, Liv. ; Verg.

sē or **sēd** or **sēt**, *v.* sēd.

sē- in compounds, *v.* sēmi- and sē- sēs- for sex-.

Sēbēthos, I, *m. a small stream in Campania;* **Sēbēthis**, idis, *f. adj.*

sēbum, I, *n. tallow, suet, grease* : Pl. [It. *sevo, sego* : Fr. *suif*.]

sē-cēdō, cēdere, cēssi, cēssum, *to go apart* or *aside, to withdraw.* **1.** Lit. **a.** In gen. : Cic., Ov. ; de viā, Pl. ; a vestro lusu, Prop. ; de coetu, Ov. ; corpore nostro, Ov. ; huc, Pl. ; in abditam partem aedium, Sall. ; ad deliberandum, Liv. **b.** Polit. :

Cic. ; plebes a patribus, Sall. ; in Sacrum Montem, Liv. **c.** Of retiring from public life : Plin. Ep., Suet. **2.** Transf. **a,** Of things : (luna) quantum solis secedit ab orbe, Lucr. ; ab imis terrā, Ov. ; villa xvii milibus passuum ab urbe secessit, Plin. Ep. ; a fesso corpore sensus, Cat. **b.** Mentally : secedere et aliā parte considere, Sen. Ep. ; ad stilum, Quint.

sē-cernō, cernere, crēvi, crētum, *to sift apart* ; hence, *to put* or *set apart, to sunder, separate.* **1.** Lit. : seorsum utramque partem, Lucr. ; sparsos flores, Ov. ; nihil praedae in publicum, Liv. ; illa litora genti, Hor. ; a terris caelum, Lucr. ; Ov. ; inermis ab armatis, Liv. ; se a bonis, Cic. ; se e grege imperatorum, Liv. **2.** Transf. **a.** *to separate, dissociate* : hosce ego homines excipio et secerno, Cic. ; sua a publicis consiliis, Liv. ; Cic. With ABL. of Separation : me Nympharum chori populo, Hor. **b.** *to separate, distinguish* in thought : blandum amicum a vero, Cic. With ABL. of Separation : turpi honestum, Hor. **c.** *to reject, set aside* : Cic. Ep. ; minus idoneos senatores, Suet.

secespita, ae, *f.* [secō], *a long iron sacrificial knife* : Suet.

sēcēssiō, ōnis, *f.* [sēcēdō], *a going aside.* **a.** *withdrawal* : subscriptorum, Cic. Milit. : facere, Caes., Liv. **b.** Polit. *a secession* : Cic. ; plebis, Cic., Liv. ; per secessionem Aventinum occupavere, Sall. ; secessio ab decemviris facta est, Liv. ; in Aventinum montem secessionem factam esse, Liv.

sēcēssus, ūs, *m.* [sēcēdō], *a going apart* or *away.* **1.** Lit. **a.** In gen. : avium, Plin. **b.** *retirement, solitude* : Ov., Quint., Tac., etc. In *pl.* : Quint. **2.** Transf. **a.** Concr. *a retreat, recess* : est in secessu longo locus, Verg. ; Sen. ; Suet. In *pl.* : Tac., Suet. **b.** Of the *by-paths* of study : Quint.

secius, *adv. v.* secus.

sē-clūdō, clūdere, clūsi, clūsum [claudō]. **I.** *to shut off apart, shut in a separate place* ; *to bar off, seclude.* **1.** Lit. : aquulam, Cic. ; carmina antro, Verg. ; munitione flumen a monte, Caes. **2.** Transf. : supplicium a libero spiritu atque a communi luce, Cic. **II.** *to sunder, shut out* or *off.* **1.** Lit. : cur luna queat terram secludere solis lumine, Lucr. ; dextrum cornu a sinistro secludum, Caes. ; Liv. **2.** Transf. : corpore vitam, Pl. ; (corde) curas, Verg.

sēclum, *v.* saeculum.

sēclūsus, a, um. **I.** *Part.* sēclūdō. **II.** *Adj. secluded* : nemus, Verg. *Neut.* as Noun : in secluso, Varr.

secō, secāre, secui, sectum [*cf.* κείω, σχίζω], *to cut.* **1.** Lit. **a.** In gen. : digitum, Pl. ; pabulum, Caes. ; herbam, Hor. ; animal, Cic. ; tergora in frusta, Verg. ; marmora, Hor. ; secto elephanto, Verg. **b.** In surgery : Liv. ; vomicam, Pl. ; varices Mario, Cic. **c.** Of castration : Mart. **2.** Transf. **A.** Of any kind of physical wounding : postis tarmes, Pl. ; corpora vepres, Verg. ; Ov. ; acuto ne secer ungui, Hor. ; verbere terga, Tib. **B.** Of pain : si quem podagra

secat, Cat. ; Mart. **C.** to divide, separate :
populos secans interluit Allia, Verg. ; Plin.
Ep. ; sectus orbis, Hor. ; in longas vias
orbem, Ov. Esp. of motion through or
between, to cleave, part : pontum, Verg. ;
aequor puppe, Ov. ; avis aëra pennis,
Cic. poet., Verg. **D.** to make (a way, etc.)
by parting, to mark out : viam ad navis,
Verg. ; Quint. ; sub nubibus arcum Iris,
Verg. Transf. : spem, Verg. **E.** In
words or thought. **a.** to cut up, satirise :
Lucilius urbem, Pers. **b.** to divide : causas
in plura genera, Cic. ; Quint. **c.** Of disputes, to decide (cf. causa) : litis, Hor.
[It. segare ; Fr. scier.]

sĕcordia, v. sōcordia.

sĕcrētĭō, ōnis, f. [sēcernō], a dividing, separating : Cic.

sĕcrētus a, um. **I.** Part. sēcernō. **II.**
Adj. **A.** separate, apart : imperium, Liv.
Of a person : vacuis porticibus secretus
agitat, Tac. Instead of Adv. : tu secreta
pyram tecto interiore erige, Verg. Neut.
ABL. as Adv. **sēcrētō,** apart, separately,
by oneself : secreto te huc foras seduxi,
Pl. ; facere, Pl. ; secreto in occulto cum
aliquo agere, Caes. ; secreto hoc audi,
Cic. Ep. ; Hor. ; consilia secreto ab aliis
coquere, Liv. **B. a.** Of places : retired,
solitary, deserted : Hor., Ov., Quint., Tac.
(cf. secretae Troades in actà flebant, for
secretà in actà, Verg.). **b.** Of persons and
their actions : private, secret : Quint., Plin.
Ep. Sup. : Sen. Ep. Neut. as Noun, **sēcrētum,** i, solitude, secrecy and concr. a retreat,
solitude : in secretum viro abducto, Liv. ;
tempus in secreto terere, Liv. ; secreti
longi causà, Ov. ; secreto suo satiatus,
Tac. In pl. : horrendae secreta Sibyllae,
Verg. ; Hor. ; Ov. ; Tac. Also in comp. :
the more remote parts : in secretiora Germaniae, Tac. **C.** hidden, secret : artes,
Ov. ; libidines, Tac. ; aliquid secretum ab
aliquo habere, Liv. Comp. : libertus ex
secretioribus ministeriis, Tac. Neut. as
Noun, **sēcrētum,** i, a secret, mystery :
(Minervae) secreta, Ov. ; omnium secreta
rimari, Tac. ; oratio animi secreta detegit,
Quint. Of a secret conversation or interview :
Plin. Ep. **D.** uncommon, rare : Quint.
E. parted from, deprived of, wanting (with
ABL. or GEN.) : cibo, Lucr. ; frigoris,
Lucr. [It. segreto.]

secta, ae, f. a path ; hence a way, course,
method, mode, manner (mostly with sequi).
a. In gen. : omnis natura habet sectam
quam sequatur, Cic. ; hanc sectam rationem-
que vitae secuti sumus, Cic. ; Quint. ; diviti-
oris sectam sequuntur, Lucr. ; exsequi, Cat. ;
persequi, Cic. ; eidem incumbere sectae,
Juv. **b.** Polit. : alicuius sectam sequi,
i.e. to be a member of somebody's party,
Cic., Liv. **c.** Philos. : a philosophical
method or school of thought : eorum philosophorum sectam secutus es, Cic. ; Cynicam
sectam profiteri, Tac. ; adsumptà Stoicorum adrogantià sectàque, Tac. In pl. :
Quint.

sectārius, a, um [secō], cut, gelded : vervex,
Pl. (or perh. fr. secta, hence, one that leads
the way).

sectātor, ōris, m. [sector], a follower, atten-

dant, member of a retinue. **a.** In gen. :
Cic., Tac. **b.** Philos. a follower, adherent
of a philosophical method or school : Tac.,
Suet.

sectilis, e, adj. [secō]. **I.** that can be cut :
Plin., Juv. **II.** cut, cleft, divided : Ov.,
Plin., Suet.

sectĭō, ōnis, f. [secō], a cutting. **1.** Lit. :
Plin. **2.** Transf. (in law), a buying in
lots at an auction of State-property : ad
scelus sectionis accedere, Cic. ; sectiones
exercere, Tac. Also of the things so sold,
lots : sectionem oppidi vendidit, Caes. ;
Cic.

sector, ōris, m. [secō], a cutter. **1.** Lit. :
zonarius, Pl. ; collorum, Cic. **2.** Transf.
(in law), a buyer at a sale of State-property :
Cic., Tac. ; bonorum, Cic. ; Pompei, Cic.

sector, ārī [freq. sequor], to follow continually
or eagerly (in a good or bad sense). **1.**
Lit. **a.** to run after, chase : gallinam, Pl. ;
aliquam, Pl., Cic. ; apros, Verg. ; leporem,
Hor. ; mulieres, Pl. ; Hor. **b.** to follow,
attend : aliquem, Pl. ; Chrysogonum servi,
Cic. ; candidatum conducti, Cic. ; Hor. ;
agnos, aratrum, Tib. **2.** Transf. **a.** facinora, Pl. ; praedam, Caes., Tac. ; nomina
tironum, Hor. ; gymnasia, Plin. Ep. ;
omnis dicendi Veneres, Quint. ; eminentia
virtutes, Tac. With Indir. Quest. : Hor.
With ut and Final Subj. : Quint. **b.** With
a view to imitating : habitum vultumque,
Tac.

sectūra, ae, f. [secō], a cutting. **1.** Lit. :
Varr. **2.** Transf. (in pl.), diggings, mines :
Caes.

sectus, a, um, Part. secō.

sēcubĭtus, ūs, m. [sēcubō], a lying or sleeping
alone : Cat., Ov. In pl. : Ov.

sē-cubō, cubāre, cubuī, to lie alone, sleep by
oneself. **1.** Lit. : Cat., Tib., Ov., Liv.
2. Transf. to live alone or in solitude :
Prop.

sēcŭl-, v. saecul-.

sē-cum, v. sē.

secundānī, ōrum, m. pl. [secunda, sc. legiō],
soldiers of the second (legion) : Liv., Tac.

secundārĭus, a, um [secundus], second-rate,
inferior. **a.** panis, Plin., Suet. **b.** Of
abstract things : status (rei publicae),
Cic.

secundō, āre [secundus], to direct favourably,
to further : di nostra incepta, Verg. ; rite
visūs, Verg. ; nautis aura iter, Prop. ;
Ov. ; secundante vento, Tac.

secundum, adv. and prep. [sequor]. **I.**
Adv. after, behind : iro, Pl. **II.** Prep.
with Acc. **A.** Of space. **a.** following
after, behind : ire secundum aliquem, Pl.
b. following along, along, by : legiones
secundum flumen duxit, Caes. ; Pl. ; Cic.
Ep. **c.** Transf. of addition, following
upon, besides : secundum ea multae res
eum hortabantur, Caes. ; Cic. **B.** Of
time. **a.** immediately after, next to : ludos,
Pl. ; hunc diem, Cic. ; Liv. **b.** during :
quietem, Cic. **C.** Of rank or quality, next
to : secundum deos homines hominibus
maxime utiles esse possunt, Cic. ; Pl. ;
Liv. **D.** agreeably to. **a.** in compliance or
accordance with : tigna prona et fastigata
ut secundum naturam fluminis procum-

berent, Caes. ; secundum naturam vivere,
Cic. ; secundum legem, Liv. **b.** *in favour
of, to the advantage of :* de absente secundum
praesentem iudicare, Cic. ; Tac. ; secundum
eam partem litem iudices dare, Liv.

secundus, a, um [sequor], *following.* **I.
1. Lit.**: in time or order, *next, second :*
secundo anno Olympiadis septimae, Cic. ;
Enn. ; secunda vigilia, Caes. ; mensa, Cic.
Ep., Verg. ; prioribus equitum partibus
secundis additis, Cic. ; haec erit a mensis
fine secunda dies, Ov. **Abl.** *neut.* **secundō**
as Adv. *secondly :* primum . . . secundo
. . . tertium, Cic. ; primo . . . secundo,
Phaedr. **2. Transf.** in rank, value, etc.
a. quorum ordo proxime accedit ut secundus
sit ad regium principatum, Cic. ; Aiax
heros ab Achille secundus, Hor. ; Liv. ;
tu secundo Caesare regnes, Hor. ; nulli
Campanorum secundus, Liv. **b.** With idea
of inferiority : haud ulli veterum virtute
secundus, Verg. ; panis, Hor. ; persona,
Nep. ; partes (i.e. in a drama), Hor. Hence
as Noun, **secundae**, ārum, *f. pl.* (*sc.*
partes), *the second* or *inferior part* in dramas :
Plin. Transf.: qui fuit M. Crassi quasi
secundarum, Cic. ; ferre, Hor. ; agere,
Sen. ; deferre alicui, Quint. **II.** *following*
(opp. adversus). **1. Lit.**: of wind or
water : secundo flumine iter facere (i.e.
down stream), Caes. ; Verg. ; Liv. ; totā
rate in secundam aquam labente, Liv. ;
et ventum et aestum nactus secundum,
Caes. ; vento secundo, Pl. ; Cic. ; Hor.,
etc. Poet.: Neptunus curru (Dat.) dat
lora secundo, Verg. Also, navigatio, Tac.
Sup. : ventus, Cic. **2. Transf.** *supporting, favourable, propitious :* secundo populo
aliquid facere, Cic. ; rumor, Enn., Hor. ;
clamore secundo exit, Verg. ; Cic. Ep. ;
proelium, consilia, Caes. ; auspicia, Cic. ;
haruspex, Verg. ; aures, Liv. ; Iuno,
Verg. ; verba secunda irae, Liv. **rēs
secundae** (Enn., Cic., Verg., etc.), or
secunda, ōrum, *n. pl.* (Ter., Hor., Liv.,
Tac.), *prosperity, success. Comp. :* proelium nostris, Caes. *Sup. :* proelia, Caes. ;
leges plebei, Liv.

sēcūrē, *adv.* **I.** *fearlessly, unconcernedly :*
Plin. Ep., Suet. *Comp. :* Sen. Ep. **II.**
safely : Plin. Ep.

sēcūricula, ae, *f.* [*dim.* secūris], *a little axe, a
hatchet :* Pl.

sēcūrifer, era, erum [secūris ferō], *axe-
bearing :* Ov.

sēcūriger, era, erum [secūris gerō], *axe-
bearing :* Ov.

sēcūris, is, *f.* (Acc. -im or -em ; Abl. -ī or
-e) [secō], *an axe, hatchet, chopper.* **1. Lit.**
For domestic uses : Pl., Cato, Cat., Verg.
For sacrificing : Verg., Hor., Ov. Of *a
battle-axe :* Verg., Ov. Of *an executioner's
axe* (carried by the lictors with the fasces) :
Cic., Verg. ; aliquem securi ferire, Cic.,
Liv. ; securi percutere, Cic. ; securi necare,
Liv. ; securibus cervices subicere, Cic.
2. Transf. a. *a mortal blow :* graviorem
rei publicae infligere securim, Cic. **b.**
power of life and death ; (Roman) *supreme
authority* or *sovereignty* (from the axe in
the fasces), us. *pl. :* Caes., Hor., Tac.
[It. *scure.*]

sēcūritās, ātis, *f.* [secūrus]. **1. Lit. a.**
freedom from care, unconcern, composure :
Cic., Liv., Tac., etc. ; animi, Cic. ; vocis ac
vultūs, Tac. **b.** *a feeling of security,* i.e.
false confidence of safety ; carelessness :
Quint., Tac. ; scribendi, Quint. **2.**
Transf.: objectively, *freedom from danger ; safety, security :* itinerum, Plin. ;
annonae, Tac. ; securitati ante quam vindictae consulere, Tac.

sēcūrus, a, um [cūra], *free from care* or
anxiety ; untroubled, fearless, composed.
I. Prop. 1. Lit. of persons : ut, meis
ab tergo tutis, securus bellum Nabidi in-
feram, Liv. ; Cic. ; Cores natā secura re-
ceptā, Ov. ; de bello Romano, Liv. ; Cic.
Ep. ; ab hac parte, Curt. ; securior ab
Samnitibus agere, Liv. ; pro me securior,
Tac. With Gen. : Verg., Hor., Tac., etc.
With *Indir. Quest. :* Hor. With *ne* and
Final Subj. : Liv. **2. Transf.** of things.
A. Objectively, *free from danger, safe,
secure :* hostis nullum locum quietum aut
securum esse sineret, Liv. With Gen. :
loca secura eius modi casuum, Tac. *Comp. :*
Tac. **B. a.** *tranquil, cheerful :* quies leti,
Lucr. ; otia, Verg. ; dies, Tib. ; vox securae
claritatis, Quint. ; tempus securius, Quint. ;
securior materia, Tac. **b.** *care-dispelling :*
latices, Verg. **II.** *careless, negligent.* **a.**
Of persons : reus, Quint. **b.** Of things :
castrensis iuris dictio, *careless* (of legal
subtleties), *off-hand*, Tac. [Fr. *sûr.*]

secus, *indecl. n.* (*v.* sexus) [secō], lit. *a
division ;* hence *sex.* **a.** Mostly as limiting
Acc. with virile or muliebre : concurrentium undique virile et muliebre secus,
Sall. ; Pl. ; Liv., etc. **b.** Rarely Nom. :
adfluxere avidi talium virile ac muliebre
secus, omnis aetas, Tac.

secus, *adv.* and *prep.* **I.** Adv. **A.** Positive : *otherwise, differently.* **a.** id
secus est, Cic. ; Pl. ; pro bono aut secus
consulto, Liv. With *quam* or *atque :* no
quid fiat secus quam volumus, Cic. Ep. ;
Ter. ; eadem membra paulo secus a me
atque ab illo partita, Cic. **b.** With negat. :
not otherwise, i.e. *even so, just so :* bibitur
quasi in popinā, haud secus, Pl. ; Verg. ;
fit obviam Clodio horā fere undecimā aut
non multo secus, Cic. ; Hor. ; Tac. With
Gen. : neque multo secus in iis virium,
Tac. With *ac* or *quam :* cuius salutem
non secus ac meam tueri debeo, Cic. ; Ov. ;
non secus quam, Ov. ; nec secus quam,
Pl. ; haud secus quam, Pl., Liv., Ov. ;
haud secus ac, Sall., Verg. (esp. to introduce
a comparison). **c.** Elliptically, *otherwise
than rightly* or than *what is desired,* i.e.
ill, badly : si secus acciderit, Cic. Ep. ;
bellum secus cessarat, Sall. ; existimare de
aliquo, Cic. ; scribere de aliquo, Liv. ;
cadere, Tac. **B.** Comparative, **sequius**
or **sētius** (not secius), *otherwise, differently*
(usually with negat.) : invitus, quod sequius
sit, de meis civibus loquor, Liv. ; nihilo
setius Caesar, ut ante constituerat, iussit,
Caes. ; Pl. ; instat non setius, Verg. **II.**
Prep. **a.** With Acc. : *by, beside, along, on :*
Enn., Cato. **b.** Affixed to a pronoun it
signifies *side :* e.g. altrinsecus, *on the other
side,* utrinsecus, *on both sides.*

secŭtor (sequŭtor), ōris, *m.* [sequor]. *one that follows another, a pursuer, a gladiator who fought with a retiarius :* Juv., Suet.

sēd, sē. sed, set [orig. ABL. of *Refl. Pron.* sē ; *by oneself, by itself, apart*]. **I.** As Adv. only in compounds : secludo, secerno, etc. **II.** As Prep. in old Latin for sine, q.v., *without :* se fraude esto, Old law in Cic. **III.** As Conjunct. (in form **sed**), *apart from, setting aside, except, only ;* usually *but, yet.* **A.** Adversative (after a previous negat.) : *but, on the contrary :* non ego erus tibi sed servos sum, Pl. ; non eros nec dominos appellat eos, sed patriae custodes, sed patres et deos, Cic. ; Verg. In a climax, non modo (solum) . . . sed *or* sed potius *or* sed etiam (et, quoque), *not only, but also :* Caes., Cic.. etc. ; non modo (solum) non . . . sed, sed etiam, sed ne . . . quidem, *not only not . . . but, but even, but indeed, but not even :* iudicetur non modo non consul, sed etiam hostis Antonius, Cic. Also (when the sense is sufficiently obvious), without the second non in the first clause, and with ne . . . quidem in the second, doubly negative : quod mihi non modo irasci, . . ., sed ne dolere quidem impune licet. *not only* not *to be angry, but not even,* Cic. **B.** Corrective after a previous affirmative. **a.** Limiting : C. Memmius perfectus litteris sed Graecis, Cic. ; Pl., etc. Strengthened, sed autem, *but then ;* sed enim, *but indeed, but in fact,* Pl., Cic., Verg. **b.** Adding or in climax : ego to hodio reddam madidum, sed vino, probe, Pl. Usually with *etiam* (or *et*) : hic mihi primum meum consilium defuit, sed etiam obfuit, Cic. Ep. **C.** Resumptive or in transition or in breaking off a subject. **a.** sed ad instituta redeamus, Cic. **b.** sed, si placet, in hunc diem hactenus, Cic. ; Pl. ; Verg.

sēdātē, *adv. calmly, tranquilly, sedately :* Pl., Cic.

sēdātĭo, ōnis, *f.* [sēdō], *an allaying, calming :* animi, Cic. ; maerendi, Cic. ; aegritudinis, Cic.

sēdātus, a, um. **I.** *Part.* sēdō. **II.** Adj. *composed, calm, quiet :* in ipsis numeris sedatior, Cic. ; amnis, Cic., Hor. ; animus, Cic. Ep. ; cor, Verg. ; gradus, Liv. ; tempus, Cic.

sēdecim, *indecl. adj.* [sex decem], *sixteen :* Pl., Caes., Liv. [Fr. *seize*].

sēdĕcŭla, ae, *f.* [*dim.* sēdēs], *a little seat, a low stool :* Cic. Ep.

sedentārĭus, a, um [sedeō], *sitting, sedentary :* sutores, Pl.

sedeō, sedēre, sēdi, sessum [*cf.* Gk. ἕζομαι, *to be seated, to sit, remain sitting.* **1.** Lit. **A.** In gen.: Pl., Cic., Prop. With *in* and ABL. of the seat : Pl., Cic., Ov.. etc. With ABL. alone : Verg., Liv., Ov. With other prepositions and adverbs : inter ancillas, Pl. ; ante foris, Ov. ; sub arbore, Ov. ; apud quem, Cic. ; istic, Pl. **B.** Of magistrates, etc. : *to sit in council, in court, on the bench :* Cic., Liv., Ov., etc. **C.** *to continue sitting ;* hence **a.** *to be inactive ; to linger, loiter* (often of culpable inactivity) : Pl., Cic., Verg. ; sedemus desides domi, Liv. Prov.: compressis, quod aiunt,

manibus sedēre, Liv. **b.** In war, either *to remain encamped, or to sit down before a town* in blockade : dum apud hostis sedimus, Pl. ; sedendo bellum gerere, Liv. ; ad Suessulam, Liv. ; Verg. ; sedendo expugnare urbem, Liv. **2.** Transf. **a.** Of clothes, *to sit ;* sodet melius pars togae, Quint. ; toga umero, Quint. Hence, bene umeris tuis imperium, Plin. Pan. **b.** *to be fixed, lie still :* neque tam fuerunt gravia ut depressa sederent, Lucr. ; Tib. ; esca simplex tibi, Hor. **c.** Geogr. *to lie low :* convallibus arva, Luc. **d.** *to remain fixed or fast, to stick fast :* in liquido ossa cerebro, Ov. ; librata glans, Liv. ; plaga, Ov. ; alta sedent vulnera, Luc. **e.** Of fixed resolution : si mihi non animo fixum immotumque soderet no etc., Verg. ; id sedet Aeneae, Verg.

sēdēs, is (GEN. *pl.* sēdum), *f.* [sedeō], *a seat, chair, throne.* **1.** Lit.: Cic., Ov. ; in iis sedibus quae erant sub platano, Cic. ; curulis, Cic. ; sedes honoris, Cic. ; sedes honoris sui, Liv. ; regia, Liv. **2.** Transf. **a.** *fixed abode, settled home :* eam sibi domum sedemque delegit, Cic. ; nisi fata locum sedemque dedissent, Verg. ; sedem quaerero, Liv. ; sedes habere in Gallia, Caes. ; ut aliud domicilium alias sedes potant, Caes. ; deos ipsos convulsos ex sedibus suis, Liv. ; Cic. ; Lucr., etc. Of the dead : Tac. ; in *pl.*, Verg. **b.** Of things : *fixed place, situation, foundation :* nunquam haec urbs summo imperio domicilium ac sedem praebuisset, Cic. ; patriam pulsam sede suā, Liv. ; voluptas mentem e suā sede demovet, Cic. ; montis moliri sede suā, Ov. ; neque verba sedem habere possunt si rem subtraxeris, Cic. ; Veios an Fidenas sedem belli caperent (i.e. seat of the war or headquarters), Liv. ; Tac. ; ipsa Roma propo convulsa sedibus suis visa est, Cic., Verg. ; maro a sedibus imis ruere, Verg. **c.** In rank : at priores tenet sedes Homerus, Hor. [It. *seggia* ; Fr. *siège* ; Eng. *see* of a bishop.]

sedile, is, *n.* [sedeō], *a seat, bench, stool, chair :* Verg., Ov., Sen. Ep. In *pl.: seats in the theatre,* Hor. ; *rowers' benches,* Verg. ; of other seats, Varr., Ov., etc.

sēdĭtĭo, ōnis, *f.* [sēd itĭo], *a going apart,* hence *an insurrectionary separation, civil discord, mutiny.* **1.** Lit.: ne qua seditio oriretur, Caes. ; Liv. ; coorta, Verg. ; facere, Caes., Cic. ; concitare, commovere, Cic. ; coeptare, Tac. ; sedare, Cic. ; componere, Tac. In *pl.* : Cic., Hor., Liv., etc. **2.** Transf. **a.** Of things : seditionem facit lien, occupat praecordia, Pl. ; intestina corporis, Liv. **b.** Of quarrels : domestica, Liv. ; Ov. ; adulescentulo filiam dare in seditionem, Ter. ; pantomimorum, Suet.

sēdĭtĭōsē, *adv. seditiously :* Cic., Liv., Tac. Comp. : Tac. Sup. : Cic. Ep.

sēdĭtĭōsus, a, um [sēditĭo], *factious, turbulent, mutinous, seditious.* **1.** Lit.: tribuni plebis, Cic. ; oratio, Caes. ; contiones, Cic. ; voces, Liv. Sup. : Cic., Tac. **2.** Transf. **a.** *quarrelsome :* Cic. Ep. **b.** *troublous, disturbed :* vita, Cic.

sēdō, āre [fr. same root as sedeō], *to settle, still, lay, allay, calm.* **1.** Lit.: mare, flammam, Cic. ; incendium, Liv. ; ventos, Ov. ; vela, Prop. ; pulverem, Phaedr. In *Mid.* : tempestas **sedatur**, Cic. **2.** Transf. **a.** sitim, Lucr., etc. ; carno ieiunia, Ov. ; cupidinem, iram, Pl. ; appetitūs, Cic. ; rabiem, Hor. ; pavorem, Liv. **b.** tumultum, Caes., Liv. ; seditionem, bellum, pugnam, discordias, invidiam, etc., Cic. ; proelium, contentionem, pestilentiam, Liv. Rarely with a personal object : ut vix a magistratibus iuventus sedaretur, Liv. ; Pl.

sē-dūcō, dūcere, dūxī, ductum, *to lead aside or apart, to withdraw.* **1.** Lit.: aliquem seorsum ab aedibus, Pl. ; aliquem a debitā peste, Cic. ; singulos separatim, Liv. ; aliquem blandā manu, Ov. ; aliquem in secretum, Phaedr. **2.** Transf. **a.** *to withdraw :* ocellos, Prop. **b.** *to separate :* seducit terras unda duas, Ov. ; mors animā seduxerit artūs, Verg.

sēductiō, ōnis, *f.* [sēdūcō], *a leading aside* (in *pl.*) : testium, Cic.

sēductus, a, um. **I.** *Part.* sēdūcō. **II.** Adj. **1.** Lit. *distant :* ex alto seductas aethero longe despectat terras, Ov. **2.** Transf. *withdrawn :* consilia seducta a plurium conscientiā, Liv.

sēdulitās, ātis, *f.* [sēdulus]. **I.** *assiduity, application :* Cic., Ov., etc. **II.** *officiousness :* Hor.

sēdulus, a, um [perh. fr. root of sedeō]. **I.** *diligent, industrious :* Cic., Hor., Ov., etc. ABL. *n.* **sēdulō** as *Adv., diligently :* Pl., Ter., Cato, Cic. With added notion of *purposely, intentionally :* Pl., Ter., Liv. **II.** *officious :* Tib., Hor., Ov.

seges, etis, *f. a corn-field.* **A.** Prop. **1.** Lit.: Cato ; in proximas segetes, Caes. ; uberes, Cic. ; laetae, Verg. ; occaro, Hor. **2.** Transf. **a.** ubi prima paretur arboribus seges, Verg. **b.** segetom ac materiem suae gloriae, Cic. **B.** *standing-corn, a crop.* **1.** Lit.: matura, Caes. ; Ov. In *pl.* : segetes collibus et campis habere, Lucr. With GEN.: seges farris, Liv. ; Verg. **2.** Transf. **a.** seges clipeata virorum, Ov. **b.** Of things thickly crowded together : ferrea telorum seges, Verg. **c.** Of profit : quae inde seges, Juv. ; Ov.

Segesta, ae, *f. a city on N.W. coast of Sicily ;* **Segestānus**, a, um ; **Segestānī**, ōrum, *m. pl. its inhabitants ;* **Segestānum**, ī, *n. the territory of Segesta.*

segestre, is, *n. a covering, wrapper, wrap of* straw or hides : Lucil., Varr., Suet.

segmentātus, a, um [segmentum], *ornamented with strips of tinsel, etc. : flounced, purfled :* cunae, Juv.

segmentum, ī, *n.* [secō], *a cutting, a piece cut off, a slice.* **1.** Lit.: Plin. In *pl.* : *strips of tinsel, brocade, etc. : trimmings, flounces,* or perh. *an ornamental patch of* purple or gold thread at the top of a woman's dress : Ov., Juv. **2.** Transf. *a zone or segment* of the earth : Plin.

sēgni-pēs, pedis, *m.* [sēgnis], *slow-foot,* poet. of a jaded horse : Juv.

sēgnis, e, adj. *slow, lingering, sluggish, inactive.* **1.** Lit.: Cic. Ep., Tac. ; quia tardius irent propter onus segnes, Hor. ; obsidio, oppugnatio, bellum, pugna, militia,

navigatio, mora, terror, Liv. ; pes, Hor. ; voluptas, Ov. ; otium, ingenium, indoles, Tac. ; aquae, Curt. *Comp.* : videor segnior fuisse, Cic. Ep. ; Sall. ; Tib. ; equus segnior annis, Verg. ; mors, Liv. *Masc.* as Noun (in *Posit.* or *Comp.*) : Caes., etc. With *ad :* segniores ad imperandum, Cic. ; ad credendum, Liv. ; ad laetitiam, Ov. ; ad pericula, Tac. With *in* and ACC. : in Venerem, Verg. With *in* and ABL. : in oxsequendis conatibus, Suet. With GEN.: occasionum haud segnis, Tac. With *Inf.* : Hor., Ov. ACC. *n.* **sēgne** as *Adv.* : Liv. (for *Comp. Adv. v.* sēgniter). **2.** Transf. **a.** Of land : *sluggish, left fallow :* campus, Verg. **b.** *barren :* carduus, Verg.

sēgniter, *adv. sluggishly, slowly, without energy :* Liv., Stat., Tac. *Comp.* **sēgnius**, Cato, Hor., Liv., Ov., etc. ; nihilo segnius, Sall. Liv.

sēgnitia, ae (Ter., Cic., Liv., Tac.) and **sēgnitiēs**, em, ē (Pl., Cic., Verg., Liv.), *f.* [sēgnis], *sluggishness, slowness, inactivity, dilatoriness.*

Segontiacī, ōrum, *m. pl. a tribe of S. Britain, in modern Hampshire.*

sē-gregō, āre (*in tmes.*), sēque gregāri, Lucr.), [grex], *to separate from the flock.* **1.** Lit.: ovis, Phaedr. **2.** Transf. *to set apart, to separate* from others. **a.** aliquem ab aliquo, Pl. ; a numero civium, Cic. ; aliquem a senatu, Pl. ; captivos, Liv. **b.** (Transf. of a.) spes opes auxiliaque ab aliquo, Pl. ; suspicionem ab so, Pl. ; virtutem a summo bono, Cic. ; publicam causam a privatorum culpā, Liv. ; pugnam, Liv.

sē-iugātus, a, um, *disjoined, separated :* animi partem non ab actiono corporis seiugatam, Cic.

sēiugis, is, *m.* (*sc.* currus) [sex iugum], *with a team of six horses, a chariot drawn by six horses :* Liv.

sēiunctim, *adv. separately :* Tib.

sēiunctiō, ōnis, *f.* [sēiungō], *a separation, division :* Cic., Quint.

sēiunctus, a, um, *Part.* sēiungō.

sē-iungō, iungere, iūnxī, iūnctum, *to disunite, disjoin, separate.* **1.** Lit. : omnia a principiis, Lucr. ; Alpos Italiam a Galliā, Nep. ; aliquem ex fortissimorum civium numero, Cic. **2.** Transf.: defensio seiuncta a voluntate ac sententiā legis, Cic. ; Lucr. ; se a verborum libertate, Cic. ; istam calamitatem a rei publicae periculis, Cic. With ABL. : corpore seiunctus dolor, Lucr.

Sēius, I, *m. a Roman name.* Hence **Sēiānus** ; esp. L. Aelius Seianus, *the powerful Praefectus Praetori of Tiberius.*

sēlēctiō, ōnis, *f.* [sēligō], *a choosing out, choice, selection :* Cic. ; vitiorum, Cic.

sēlēctus, a, um, *Part.* sēligō.

Seleucus, I, *m. the name of several kings of Syria ; their ancestor, Seleucus Nicator, a general of Alexander the Great, after the death of the latter, founded the kingdom of the Seleucidae.*

sē-libra, ae, *f.* [sēmi], *a half-pound :* Cato, Liv.

sē-ligō, ligere, lēgī, lēctum, *to pick out apart* or *from others, to choose out.* **a.** In gen.:

exempla, Cic. ; aliquem socium, Ov. **b.**
iudices selecti, *the judges in criminal suits
selected by the praetor* : Cic., Hor., Ov.
Selīnūs, ūntis, *f*. **I.** *a town on the south-west
coast of Sicily.* **II.** *a town on the coast of
Cilicia.*
sella, ae, *f.* [*dim.* for sed-la, from root of
sedeō], *a seat, chair, stool :* Pl., Cic. ; *a
mechanic's work-stool,* Cic. ; *a teacher's
chair,* Cic. Ep. ; *a portable chair or sedan,*
Mart., Juv., Plin. Ep., Tac. (also called sella
gestatoria, Suet.) ; *a magistrate's seat or
chair,* Caes., Cic., Hor., Liv. ; sella curulis,
v. curulis.
sellāriolus, a, um [sellāria], *of or for sitting
or lounging :* popinae, Mart.
sellārius, a, um [sella], *of seats or settles.
Masc. pl.* as Noun : Tac. *Fem. sing.*
sellāria, ae (*sc.* camera), *a room furnished
with seats ; a drawing-room :* Plin., Suet.
sellisternia, ōrum, *n. pl.* [sella sternō ; *cf.*
lectisternium], *religious banquets offered
to female deities :* Tac.
sellula, ae, *f.* [*dim.* sella], *a little seat or stool ;
also, a sedan :* Tac.
sellulārius, a, um [sellula], *using a chair.
Masc.* as Noun, *a mechanic :* Liv.
sēmanimis, *v.* sēmianimis.
semel, *adv.* [*cf.* simplex, singulus], *once, a
single time.* **1.** Lit. : non semel sed
centiens, Pl. ; non semel sed saepe (or
saepius), Cic. ; semel in vitā, Cic. ; semel
atque iterum, i.e. more than once, Caes.,
Cic. **2.** Transf. **a.** *but once, once for all :*
aut vitam semel aut ignominiam finire,
Liv. ; Cic. ; Verg., etc. **b.** *Of succession, the first time, first :* bis in potestatem pervenisse Caesaris, semel ad Corfinium, iterum in Hispaniā, Caes. ; Liv.
Without iterum, etc. : cum ad idem, unde
semel profecta sunt, cuncta astra redierint
(i.e. originally), Cic. **c.** In gen., to
denote simple antecedence ; *once, ever, at
some time, at any time :* freq. with ut, ubi,
quando, cum, si, etc. : quod semel dixi,
haud mutabo, Pl. ; proclivius ad perniciem, cum semel coepit, labitur, Cic. ;
Hor. With participles : ut incitato semel
militi adderent impetum, Liv.
Semelē, ēs or **Semela**, ae, *f. d. of Cadmus,
and m. of Bacchus by Jupiter ;* **Semelēius**,
a, um : proles, i.e. Bacchus, Ov.
sēmen, inis, *n.* [*cf.* serō], *that which is sown or
planted ; seed, germ.* **1.** Lit. **a.** Of plants
and animals : Pl., Lucr., Cic., Ov., etc.
b. *a seedling, young plant, young shoot,
set* (for propagating) : Varr., Verg. Poet.
child, offspring : Ov. **2.** Transf. **A.**
seeds (i.e. elements) *of other bodies* (e.g.
fire, water, etc.) : Lucr., Verg., Cic. **B.**
stock, race : Cic., Liv. **C.** *seed* (i.e. origin,
promoter, etc.). **a.** Of persons : sceleris,
Pl. ; malorum omnium, Cic. ; huius belli,
Cic. ; tribunos plebis, semina discordiarum,
Liv. **b.** Of things : semina discordiae,
Tac. ; Cic. ; Liv.
sēmentifer, era, erum [sēmentis ferō], *seed-
bearing, fruitful :* Verg.
sēmentis, is (Acc. -em or -im ; Abl. usually
-e, rarely -i) *f.* [sēmen], *a sowing or planting.*
1. Lit. : facere, Cato, Liv., etc. ; per
sementem (*seed-time*), Cato. In *pl.* :

facere, Caes. Prov. : ut sementem feceris,
ita metes, Cic. **2.** Transf. **a.** Comic. :
hisce ego sementem in ore faciam pugnosque
opseram, Pl. **b.** In *pl., the growing crops,
young corn :* Ov. [Fr. *semence.*]
sēmentīvus, a, um [sēmentis], *of sowing or
at seed-time :* feriae, Varr. ; called, also,
sementiva dies, Ov.
sēmermis, *v.* sēmiermis.
sēmēstris (**sēmēnstris**), e, *adj.* [sex mēnsis],
lasting six months, half-yearly : regnum,
Cic. ; imperium, Caes. ; dux, Liv. ; tribunatus militaris, Plin. Ep. ; Juv. ; annua
et semestria censura, Liv.
sēmēsus, a, um [sēmi edō], *half-eaten, half-
consumed :* Verg., Hor., Ov., Suet.
sē-met, *v.* sē.
sēmi- (sometimes written and pronounced
sēm- before vowels ; **sē-** before libra,
mēstris (from mēnsis), and modius), an
inseparable particle employed as a prefix,
denoting *half-, demi-, semi-* [*cf.* Gk. ἡμι-].
sēmi-adapertus (quinquesyl.), a, um, *half-
opened :* ianua, Ov.
sēmi-ambūstus, a, um, *half-burned :* cadaver, Suet.
sēmi-animis (quadrisyl. in verse), e, *adj.*
(Enn., Verg., Liv., etc.) and **sēmi-animus**
or **sēmanimus**, a, um (Lucr., Sall., Liv.,
etc.) [anima], *half-alive, half-dead.*
sēmi-apertus, a, um, *half-open :* fores
portarum, Liv.
sēmi-barbarus, a, um, *semi-barbarous :*
Galli, Suet.
sēmi-bōs, bovis, *m. adj. half-ox :* vir, Ov.
sēmi-caper, pri, *m. half-goat :* Ov.
sēmi-cremātus and **sēmicremus**, a, um
[cremō], *half-burnt :* Ov.
sēmi-crūdus, a, um. **I.** *half-raw :* exta,
Suet. **II.** *that has only half digested :*
Stat.
sēmi-cubitālis, e, *adj. a half-cubit long :*
hastile, Liv.
sēmi-deus, a, um, *half-divine :* Dryades,
Ov. ; canes, Luc. *Masc.* as Noun, *a demi-
god :* Ov.
sēmi-doctus, a, um, *half-taught :* Pl., Cic.
sēmi-ermis (**sēmermis**), e, *adj.* (Liv.),
and **sēmiermus**, a, um (Tac.) [arma],
half-armed.
sēmi-ēsus, a, um, *v.* sēmēsus.
sēmi-factus, a, um, *half-made, half-finished :*
opera, Tac.
sēmi-fer, era, erum [ferus], *half-beast.*
1. Lit. : caput Panis, Lucr. ; pectus
Tritonis, Verg. As Noun : *of the Centaurs :*
Ov. **2.** Transf. *half-savage :* Cacus,
Verg. ; Plin.
sēmi-fultus, a, um [fulciō], *half-propped :*
Mart.
sēmi-germānus, a, um, *half-German :*
gentes, Liv.
sēmi-graecus, a, um, *half-Greek :* Suet.
sēmi-gravis, e, *adj. half-overcome :* vino,
Liv.
sē-migrō, āre, *to go apart or away :* a patre,
Cic.
sēmi-hiāns, antis, *adj. half-open :* labellum,
Cat.
sēmi-homo, inis, *m. a half-man.* **1.** Lit. :
Centauri, Ov. **2.** Transf. *half-human :*
Cacus, Verg.

sēmi-hōra, ae, f. half an hour : Cic.

sēmi-lacer, era, erum, half-mangled : Ov.

sēmi-lautus, a, um, half-washed : crura, Cat.

sēmi-līber, era, um, half-free : Cic. Ep.

sēmi-lixa, ae, m. half-sutler : Liv.

sēmi-marīnus, a, um, half in the sea : corpora, Lucr.

sēmi-mās, maris, m. a half-male, hermaphrodite. 1. Lit.: Ov., Liv. 2. Transf. gelded, castrated : ovis, Ov. ; Varr.

sēmi-mortuus (-os), a, um, half-dead : Cat.

sēmĭnārium, ī, n. [sēmen], a nursery-garden, seed-plot. 1. Lit.: Cato. 2. Transf.: seminarium rei publicae, Cic. ; Catilinarium, Cic. ; senatūs, Liv.

sēmĭnātor, ōris, m. [sēmĭnō], an originator, author. a. Cic. b. omnium malorum, Cic.

sēmi-necis (Nom. does not occur), adj. [nex], half-killed : alicui semineci rapere arma, Verg. ; seminecem eum in acervo caesorum corporum inventum, Liv. ; Ov. ; Tac.

sēmĭnĭum, ī, n. [sēmen], a procreation. 1. Lit.: Pl., Varr. 2. Transf. stock, breed : leonum, Lucr. ; Varr.

sēmĭnō, āre [sēmen], to sow, plant. a. Of trees, to propagate, produce : viscum quod non sua seminat arbos, Verg. b. Of animals and human beings, to beget, procreate : Pl. [Fr. semer.]

sēmi-nūdus, a, um. I. half-stripped : consules, Liv. II. half-unarmed : pedes prope seminudus genere armorum, Liv.

sēmi-pāgānus, ī, m. half-rustic : Pers.

sēmi-perfectus, a, um, half-finished : opera, Suet.

sēmi-pēs, pedis, m. half a foot : Cato, Varr.

sēmi-placentīnus, ī, m. a half-Placentine : Cic.

sēmi-plēnus, a, um, half-full, half-manned : naves, Cic. ; stationes, Liv.

sēmi-putātus, a, um, half-pruned : vitis, Verg.

Semiramis, is or idis (Acc. Semiramin ; Abl. Semiramī and Semiramide), f. a celebrated queen of Assyria, consort and successor of Ninus ; Semiramius, a, um.

sēmi-rāsus, a, um, half-shaven : Cat.

sēmi-reductus, a, um, half-bent back : Ov.

sēmi-refectus, a, um, half-repaired : classis, Ov.

sēmi-rutus, a, um, half-demolished, half-ruined : murus, Liv. ; vallum, Tac. Neut. pl. as Noun : Liv.

sēmis, issis, m. [sēmi as], half a unit. A. In gen.: a half : Africae, Plin. ; e bonis, Suet. B. In partic. a. As a coin, half an as : Cic., Hor. Hence, worthless : non semissis homo, Vatin. ap. Cic. Ep. b. As a rate of interest, one half per cent. a month, or, six per cent. per annum (cf. bes, triens, etc.) : semissibus magna copia (pecuniae) est, Cic. Ep. c. As a measure of dimension : half a iuger of land : bina iugera et semisses agri adsignati, Liv. ; Plin. Also, half a foot : Plin.

sēmi-senex, senis, m. an elderly man : Pl.

sēmi-sepultus, a, um, half-buried : ossa, Ov.

sēmi-somnus, a, um, and sēmi-somnis, e, adj. half-asleep : Pl., Cic. Ep., Liv., etc. ; cor, Phaedr.

sēmi-supīnus, a, um, half on one's back : Ov., Mart.

sēmita, ae, f. a narrow way, foot-path, lane. 1. Lit.: Pl., Caes., Cic., Verg., etc. Of ants : opere (formicarum) omnis semita fervet, Verg. 2. Transf. : Cic. ; fallentis vitae, Hor. ; tranquillae vitae, Juv.

sēmĭtālis, e, adj. [semita], of foot-paths or by-ways : dei, Verg.

sēmĭtārius, a, um [sēmita], of or frequenting foot-paths or by-ways : moechi, Cat.

sēmi-ūstilātus (-ūstulātus), a, um, half-burnt : Cic. ; facibus semiustilatus, Cic. Also. sēmūstulandus, a, um, Suet.

sēmi-ūstus (sēmūstus), a, um, half-burned, charred. 1. Lit.: fulmine corpus, Verg. ; tectorum vestigia, Tac. 2. Transf.: se populare incendium priore consulatu semiustum effugisse, Liv.

sēmi-vir, virī, m. adj. half-man. 1. Lit. Of a Centaur, the Minotaur, or a hermaphrodite : Ov. 2. Transf., as Adj. a. unmanned : of a priest of Cybele : Juv. b. unmanly, effeminate : Verg., Liv.

sēmi-vivus, a, um, half-alive, half or almost dead. 1. Lit.: ibi hominem fumo excruciatum, semivivum reliquit, Cic. ; Nep. 2. Transf.: semivivis vocibus, Cic.

sēmi-vocālis, is, f. (sc. littera), a semivowel (acc. to the old grammarians, seven : f, l, m, n, r, s, x) : Quint.

Sēmō, ōnis, m. and Sēmō Sancus, an ancient god who presided over crops.

sē-modius, ī, m. a half-modius : Cato, Juv.

sēmōtus, a, um. I. Part. sēmoveō. II. Adj. remote, distant. 1. Lit.: conloquium petunt semoto a militibus loco, Caes. ; terris semota, Hor. Neut. pl. as Noun : Lucr. 2. Transf.: omnis divum natura semota a nostris rebus, Lucr. ; curā semotus metuque, Lucr. ; verba, Cic. ; Tac.

sē-moveō, movēre, mōvī, mōtum, to move or put aside. 1. Lit.: aliquem, Ter. ; aliquem ab aliquo, Cic. 2. Transf.: te a curis, Lucr. ; voluptatem, Cic. ; Strato ab eā disciplinā omnino semovendus est, Cic.

semper, adv. [root seen in semel, and -per as in nūper, etc.], in unbroken sequence ; ever, always. A. In gen. a. With Verbs : Pl., Cic., Verg., etc. b. With Adjectives and Nouns : Ter., Cic., Verg., etc. ; Hasdrubal pacis semper auctor, Liv. c. Strengthening Adjectives and Adverbs, e.g. cottidie, adsiduo, perennis, Pl., Ter. ; adsiduus, Cic. ; omnis, Cat. B. Distributively. a. With Comp. : candidior semper candidiorque veni, Cat. ; Hor. b. In gen. : always, regularly, on each occasion : Pl., Caes., Cic., etc.

sempiternus, a, um [semper], everlasting. a. Prop.: memoria, Pl. ; deorum vita, Ter. ; aevo sempiterno frui, Cic. ; potentia, Tac. b. lasting for life, life-long : gratias agere sempiternas, Pl. ; amicus, Ter. ; verae amicitiae, Cic. Neut. Acc. sempiternum (Pl.), and Aut. sempiternō (Cato) as Adv.

Semprōnius, a, *name of a Roman gens.*
Esp. Ti. and C. Sempronius Gracchus :
v. Gracchus ; **Semprōniānus**, a, um.

sēm-ūncia, ae, *f. a half-ounce, the twenty-fourth part of an as.* **a.** As a weight : auri,
Cic., Liv. **b.** As a measure of capacity :
Cato. **c.** Of any unit : *a twenty-fourth part :* facit heredem ex deunce et semunciā
Caecinam, Cic. Hence, *a trifle :* semuncia
recti, Pers.

sēmūnciārius, a, um [sēmūncia], *amounting to one twenty-fourth of an as or of any unit :*
faenus, *interest at the rate of one twenty-fourth of the capital,* i.e. about four per
cent. per annum, Liv.

sēmūstus, a, um, *v.* sēmiūstus.

senāculum, i, *n.* [*cf.* senātus], *an open place in the Forum, used for meetings of the Senate :*
Liv.

sēnāriolus, i, *m.* [sēnārius], *a little, insignificant verse of six feet :* Cic.

sēnārius, a, um [sēni], *consisting of six each.*
Esp.: versus, *a verse consisting of six feet*
(usually iambic), Quint. ; and as Noun
(*sc.* versus) : Cic., Quint.

senātor, ōris, *m.* [*v.* senex], *a member of a senate, a senator :* Caes., Cic., Liv., etc.

senātōrius, a, um [senātor], *of a senator, in a senate, senatorial :* gradus, Cic. ; ordo,
Caes. ; litterae, Cic.

senātus, ūs, *m.* (GEN. senātī, Pl., Sall.,
and occ. in Cic.) [senex], *the council of the elders, the Senate at Rome or elsewhere.*
1. Lit.: senatus populusque Romanus,
Cic. ; Aeduorum, Caes. ; cum potestas
in populo, auctoritas in senatu sit, Cic. ;
princeps senatūs, Liv. ; senatum convocare,
cogere, Cic. ; vocare, Liv. ; habere, Cic.
Ep. ; legatis dare (i.e. an audience), Cic.,
Liv. ; dimittere, Cic. ; mittere, Cic. Ep. ;
in senatum venire, Cic. ; senatum cooptare,
Cic. ; aliquem de senatu movere, Cic. ;
senatu movere, Sall. ; senatu emovere,
Liv. ; ex *or* de senatu eicere, Cic., Liv.
For **senātūs** (**senātī**) **cōnsultum**, *v.*
cōnsultum ; *v.* also auctoritās. **2.** Transf.
a council, committee : de re argentariā
consiliarius, Pl.

Seneca, ae, *m.* **I.** M. Annaeus Seneca,
a native of Corduba (Cordova, in Spain),
a celebrated rhetorician in the time of Augustus
and Tiberius. **II.** *his son,* L. Annaeus
Seneca, *the Stoic philosopher, instructor of*
Nero.

senectus, a, um [senex], *aged, old :* aetas,
Pl., Lucr. ; membra, Lucr. ; corpus, Sall.
As Noun, **senecta**, ae, *f. old age, senility :*
Pl., Lucr., Verg., Tac., etc.

senectūs, ūtis, *f.* [senex], *old age.* **1.** Lit. :
Pl., Cic., Verg., etc. **2.** Transf. **a.**
Concr. : *old men :* Cic., Juv. **b.** Of
signs of age : of hoary hair, Verg. ; of
gloominess, Hor. **c.** Of the slough of
serpents, etc. : Plin. **d.** Of full maturity
of style : Cic. **e.** Of things (for vetustas) :
vini, Juv. ; vos (tabellas) cariosa senectus
rodat, Ov.

seneō, ēre [*v.* senex], *to be old :* Pac., Cat.

senēscō, senēscere, senuī [seneō], *to grow old,*
become aged. **1.** Lit. : avus, Suet. ; equus,
Hor. ; tacitis senescimus annis, Ov. ;
aetas, Cic. **2.** Transf. **a.** *to decline,*

become *feeble;* diminish *etc. :* amore hui
bendi, Hor. ; otio, Liv. ; Hannibal famu
et viribus, Liv. ; dis hominibusque accusandis, Liv. **b.** Of things : *to wane, to draw to*
a close or *to weaken :* hiems, luna, morbus,
Cic. ; monumenta virum (GEN.), Lucr. ;
vires, bellum, pugna, fama, invidia, consilia, etc., Liv. ; Tac. ; continuā messe
ager, Ov.

senex, senis (old GEN. senicis, Pl.), *adj.* and
noun *m.* (rarely *f.*) [*cf.* Gk. ἕνος, ἔνη], *old,*
aged, advanced in years. **I.** Adj.: Cato,
Cic., Ov., etc. ; saecla, Verg. *Comp.*
senior : Lucr., Cic. ; anni, Ov. ; oratio
(i.e. more mature), Cic. **II.** Noun, *an*
old man : Pl., Cic., Hor., etc. ; *an old*
woman : Tib., Stat. *Comp.* **senior**, *an elderly*
person, an elder. **a.** In gen. : Caes.,
Verg., Hor., Ov. **b.** Esp. with reference
to the classification of citizens as seniors
(over 45) and juniors : (Servius Tullius)
seniores a iunioribus divisit, Cic. ; centuriae iuniorum seniorumque, Liv. [From
senior come It. *signore* ; Sp. *señor* ; Fr.
seigneur, sire ; Eng. *sir.*]

sēni, ae, a, *adj.* [for sex-ni ; for loss of *x,*
cf. sēmēstris]. **I.** *a group of six, six at a*
time, half a dozen : aspice bis senos cyenos,
Verg. ; Ov. **II.** *six in a group, six each :*
senum pedum crassitudo, Caes. ; Liv. So,
sēni dēni, Cic., Liv., Tac.

senīlis, e, *adj.* [senex], *of old people, aged,*
senile : prudentia, stultitia, Cic. ; animus,
Liv. ; anni, Ov. ; artus, Ov. ; guttur,
Hor. ; statua incurva, *of an old man,* Cic.

sēniō, ōnis, *m.* [sēni], *a group of six, a six*
on dice : Pers., Suet.

senior, ōris, *v.* senex.

senium, i, *n.* [*v.* senex], *the feebleness of age,*
decline, decay. **1.** Lit. : senio confectus,
Enn., Suet. ; senio debilis, Phaedr. ;
fessus senio, Tac. ; Galbae, Tac. **2.**
Transf. **a.** Of things : (mundum) omni
morbo seniove carere, Cic. ; lentae velut
tabis senio, Liv. **b.** *affliction, grief :* hae
res mihi senio sunt, Pl. ; tota civitas confecta senio est, Cic. ; senio et maerore
consumptus, Liv. **c.** *moroseness, peevish-*
ness : inhumanae Camenae, Hor. **d.**
Concr. : *old creature :* Ter.

sēnsibilis, e, *adj.* [sēnsus], *perceptible by the*
senses, sensible : Sen. Ep.

sēnsiculus, i, *m.* [*dim.* sēnsus], *a little sen-*
tence : Quint.

sēnsifer, era, erum [sēnsus ferō], *producing*
sensation : Lucr.

sēnsilis, e, *adj.* [sentiō], *capable of sensation,*
sensitive : Lucr.

sēnsim, *adv.* [sentiō], *feeling one's way,*
tentatively : hence, *carefully, gently, gradu-*
ally : Pl., Cic., Liv., Ov., etc. With
pedetemptim, leniter, and moderate : Cic.

sēnsus, a, um. **I.** *Part.* sentiō. **II.** Noun,
sēnsa, ōrum, *n. pl. sentiments, thoughts :*
Cic., Quint.

sēnsus, ūs, *m.* [sentiō]. **I.** Physical :
sensation, sense, the faculty of sense, capacity
for feeling : si quis est sensus in morte, Cic.;
Ov. ; aurium, oculorum, Cic. ; Lucr. ;
audiendi, videndi, Cic. ; moriendi sensum
celeritas abstulit, Cic. **II.** Moral. **a.**
feeling, sentiment, emotion : sensibus per-

moveri, Cic.; humanitatis, amoris. Cic.; diligendi, amandi, Cic. Esp. in phr. communis sensus (hominum), *feeling* (of all kinds) *common to all mankind*, Cic., Hor., Sen., Juv.; in *pl.*, Cic. **b.** *attitude. disposition, frame of mind, view* (but *cf.* III. b.): vestri sensūs ignarus sum, Cic. Of political attitude: valdo mihi placebat sensus eius de re publicā, Cic. Ep.; erat eodem quo Alcibiades sensu, Nep. **III.** Intellectual. **a.** *understanding, intelligence. judgment :* in his rebus aliquem sensum habet, Cic.: misero quod omnis eripit sensūs mihi, Cat.; Ov.; purumque relinquit aetherium sensum (i.e. the highest reason or speculative intellect), Verg. **b.** *intellectual attitude* (*cf.* II. b.), *intent, meaning :* dissidenti sensūs suos aperire, Nep.; Cic.; Plin. Ep. **c.** Of language: *meaning, purport, intent, signification, sense :* verbi, Ov.; Hor.; Quint.; testamenti sensum conligere, Phaedr.; salvo poetae sensu, Quint. **d.** Concr. *a sentence :* Quint., Tac. Hence, communes sensūs, *commonplaces*, Tac.

sententia, ae, *f.* [sentiō], *a way of thinking, opinion, judgment ; wishes, purpose, decision.* **1.** Lit. **A.** In gen.: eā omnes stant sententiā, Pl.; in sententiā manero, permanere, perstare, Cic.; aliquem do sententiā deducere, deicere, deterrere, Cic.; aliquem sententiā depellere, Cic.; de sententiā decedere, desistere, Cic.; de (*about*) diis habero stabilem certamque sententiam, Cic. Phrases: sententia est (with *Inf.*), *it is my purpose*, Cic.; also. stat sententia, Ov.; de sententiā alicuius (*in accordance with some one's wish*) aliquid facere, gerere, scribere, Pl., Cic., Liv.; meā sententiā, *in my opinion*, Pl., Cic.; ex (meā) sententiā, *to* (*my*) *mind or liking*, Pl., Cic., etc. Prov.: quot homines, tot sententiae, Ter., Cic. **B.** *official opinion.* **a.** In tho Senate: sententiam dicere, Cic.; dare, Liv.; peragere, Liv.; in sententiam alicuius pedibus iro (i.e. in a "division" on a motion, or perh. to cross the floor of the house to support a speaker), Liv. Of the presiding official: rogare aliquem primum sententiam, Cic. Ep.; loco sententiae (i.e. when one's turn to vote or speak came round), Cic., etc.; ex senatūs sententiā (*decision*) aedificata est domus, Cic. **b.** Of the people in tho comitia: de singulis magistratibus sententiam ferro (i.e. vote), Cic. **c.** In the courts, *decision, verdict, sentence.* vote; sententiam pronuntiare, Caes.; dicere, Cic.; per tabellas ferre, Cic.; condemnatur perpaucis sententiis, Cic. Phrase: ex animi (mei) sententiā (in an oath), *to the best of* (*my*) *meaning and belief ;* iurare, Cic. **d.** In gen.: variis dictis sententiis quarum pars censebant etc., Caes. **2.** Transf. **A.** Of discourse, *meaning, signification, sense :* verborum, Lucr.; legis, Cic.; cognoscere, Cic. **B.** Concr. **a.** *a sentence, period :* Cic., Hor., Quint. **b.** *an aphorism, maxim :* Cic., Quint.

sententiola, ae, *f.* [dim. sententia], *a little sentence or aphorism :* Cic., Quint.

sententiōsē, *adv. sententiously :* Cic.

sententiōsus, a, um [sententia], *full of meaning, pithy, sententious :* genus dictionis, Cic.

senticētum, i, *n.* [sentis], *a thorn-brake:* Pl.

sentina, ae, *f. the lowest part in the hold of a ship ; also the bilge-water.* **1.** Lit.: Caes., Cic. In simile: ii Romam. sicuti in sentinam, confluxerant, Sall. **2.** Transf. **a.** Of a low position: sedebamus in puppi; nunc vix est in sentinā locus, Cic. Ep. **b.** Of the populace, *refuse, scum :* sentina rei publicae, Cic.; Liv.

sentiō, sentīre, sēnsī, sēnsum (*Perf. sync.* sēnstī, Ter.), *to discern by the senses ; to feel, hear, see, etc.* **I.** Physical. **a.** Pl., Lucr., Cic.; sonitum, Pl.; calorem et frigus, Lucr.; suavitatem cibi, Cic.; colores, odores, Lucr.; famem, Liv. With *Inf.* or Acc. and *Inf. :* aporiri foris, Pl.; Lucr. **b.** *to experience, undergo :* quid ipso ad Avaricum sensisset, Caes.; tecum Philippos et celerem fugam sensi, Hor.; damna, Cic.; cladem belli, famem, inopiam rerum omnium, Liv. Of things as Subjects: Pl.; alnos fluvii cavatas, Verg.; transitum exercitūs (agor), Liv.; pestilentem sentiet Africum fecunda vitis, Hor. **II.** Mental. **a.** In gen.: *to feel, perceive, observe, notice :* id iam pridem sensi, Pl.; Cic.; praesentia numina, Hor. With (Acc. and) *Inf. :* Pl., Cic., Hor., etc. With *Indir. Quest. :* Pl., Cic., Hor. With *de :* ox fremitu do profectione, Caes. In Gk. construction with Nom. of *Part. :* sensit medios delapsus in hostis, Verg. **b.** *to experience, feel :* voluptatem et dolorem, Cic.; victoriae tantae gaudium, Liv. **III.** *to think, deem, judge, suppose.* **a.** In gen.: aps te seorsum sentio, Pl.; cum aliquo sentire, Pl., Cic.; humiliter demisseque, Cic.; iocansne an ita sentiens, Cic.; aliud, Liv.; quid gravius de vobis sentire possunt? Caes.; qui omnia de re publicā praeclara atque egregia sentirent, Cic. With *Predic. phr. :* aliquem bonum civem, Cic. With Acc. and *Inf.:* Ter., Cic. **b.** In law and jurisprudence, *to vote, declare, decide :* lenissime, Cic. Ep.; quae vult Hortensius omnia dicat et sentiat, Cic.

sentis, is, *m.* (*fem.* Ov.), *a thorn, brier, bramble* (us. *pl.*). **1.** Lit.: Pl., Lucr., Caes., Verg. **2.** Transf. of thievish hands: Pl.

sentiscō, ero [sentiō], *to begin to perceive, observe :* Lucr.

sentus, a, um, *rough, foul, uncared for :* homo, Ter.; loca senta situ, Verg.; Ov.

seorsus, a, um [se-vorsus fr. se- and vortō (vertō)], *sundered, apart, separate :* Cato. As *Adv.* **sēvorsus** (old Latin) and **seorsum** (also in poets disyl. **sōrsus, sōrsum**), *asunder, separately, apart :* in custodiā habitus, Liv.; Pl.; Lucr., etc. With *ab :* seorsum ab rege exercitum ductare, Sall.; Pl. With ABL.: seorsum corpore, *apart from*, Lucr.

sēparābilis, e, *adj.* .[sēparō], *that may be separated, separable :* a corpore, Cic.

sēparātim, *adv. asunder, apart, separately :* separatim singularum civitatium copias conlocare, Caes.; unā in re elaborare, Cic.; with singuli, Liv.; with quisque, Caes., etc.

sēparātiō, ōnis, *f.* [sēparō], *a severing, separation* : Cic., Tac.

sēparātius, *comp. adv. less closely* : Cic.

sēparātus, a, um. **I.** *Part.* sōparō. **II.** A d j. *separate, distinct, particular, different* : privati ac separati agri apud eos nihil est, Caes.; volumen, Cic.; tu (Bacchus) separatis uvidus in iugis, Hor.; separatae singulis aedes, Tac. With *ab* : quaestiones a complexu rerum, Quint.

sē-parō, āre, *to put apart, to separate.* **1.** L i t. : nos mare separat, Ov.; omnem equitatum, Liv.; Cic. With *ab* : senatoria subsellia a populari consessu, Cic.; Ov. With ABL. : Seston Abydenā urbe fretum, Ov. **2.** T r a n s f. (in thought or feeling) : officium, Quint.; Cic. With *ab* : suum consilium ab reliquis, Caes.; Cic.; Liv. [It. *sceverare* ; Fr. *sevrer*.]

sepelībilis, e, *adj.* [sepeliō], *that may be buried.* T r a n s f. : stultitia, Pl.

sepeliō, sepelīre, sepelīvi (*or* -ii), sepultum, *to bury.* **1.** L i t. : aliquem, Cato, Cic.; corpora, Liv.; ossa, Ov. **2.** T r a n s f. **a.** Of suppressing, ending, etc. : somnum, Pl.; dolorem, bellum, patriam, etc., Cic.; salutem in aeternum, Lucr.; meam famam, Ov. **b.** somno sepultus, Verg.; without somno, Lucr., Verg.

sēpēs, *v.* saepēs.

sēpia, ae, *f.* [σηπία], *the cuttle-fish.* **1.** L i t. : Pl., Cic. **2.** T r a n s f. of its discharge used as ink : Pers. [It. *seppia* ; Fr. *seiche.*]

sēpim-, **sēpiō**, *v.* saepim-, saepiō.

sēpiola, ae, *f.* [*dim.* sōpia], *a little cuttle-fish* : Pl.

Sēplasia, ae, *f. a street in Capua, where perfumes were sold.*

sē-pōnō, pōnere, posui, positum, *to put or place apart or aside ; to reserve.* **1.** L i t. **a.** In gen. : ornamenta, Cic.; prīmitias magno Iovi, Ov.; se et pecuniam et frumentum in decem annos, Liv.; pecuniam in aedificationem templi, Liv.; de mille sagittis unam, Ov.; aliquem, Tac., Plin. Ep. **b.** Of banishment : aliquem a domo, Tac.; aliquem in provinciam specie legationis, Tac.; Suet. **2.** T r a n s f. **a.** *to set apart, reserve* : sibi ad eam rem tempus, Cic.; materiam senectuti, Tac.; Aegyptum, Tac. **b.** *to lay aside, banish* : curas, Ov. **c.** *to separate* : a ceteris dicendi eam partem dicendi, Cic. With ABL. : inurbanum lepido dicto, Hor.

sēpositus, a, um. **I.** *Part.* sēpōnō. **II.** A d j. **a.** *distant, remote* : fons, Prop. **b.** *select, choice* : vestis, Tib. **c.** *distinct, private* : gloria, Ov.

sēps, sēpis, *m. f.* [σήψ], *a poisonous snake* : Plin., Luc.

sēpse, *pron. refl.* [*v.* ipse], *oneself* : Cic.

septem, *indecl. adj.* [*cf.* Gk. ἑπτά], *seven* : Pl., Cic., Hor., etc. As *indecl. Noun, the seven sages of Greece* : Cic. [It. *sette* ; Sp. *siete* ; Fr. *sept.*]

September, bris, *adj.* [septem], *of or belonging to the seventh month* (of the old Roman year), *of September* : mense Septembri, Cic.; Idibus Septembribus, Liv.; Septembribus horis, Hor.

septemdecim, *v.* septendecim.

septemflŭus, a, um [fluo], *seven-fold flowing from* : Nilus, i.e. flowing from its mouths, Ov.

septem-geminus, a, um, *seven-fold* : Nilus (as having seven mouths), Cat.; Verg.; Roma (i.e. of the seven hills), Stat.

septem-pedālis, e, *adj. of seven feet, seven feet high* : Pl.

septemplex, icis, *adj.* [plicō], *seven-fold* : clipeus (of oxhides in seven layers), Verg.; Nilus (as having seven mouths), Ov.

septemtriōnālis, e, *adj.* [septemtriōnēs], *of the north, northern* : circulus, Varr.; oceanus, Plin. As Noun, **septemtriōnālia**, ium, *n. pl. the northern regions* : Britanniae, Tac.

septem-triōnēs (and **septentriōnēs**), um, *m. pl.* [prop. the seven ploughing oxen, *v.* triōnēs], *seven stars near the North Pole,* belonging to the constellation called *the Wain* or *the Great Bear ; also, the seven stars of the Little Bear.* **1.** L i t. : Pl., Cic., Ov. **2.** T r a n s f. **a.** In *sing.* : *either of the two constellations* above named : maior or minor, Cic., Vitr. **b.** *the northern regions, the north.* In *sing.* : spectant in septentrionem, Caes.; Liv.; Tac. Separated : Hyperboreo septem subiecta trioni gens, Verg. In *pl.* : omnis Gallia ad septentriones vergit, Caes.; Cic. **c.** *the north-wind.* In *sing.* : Liv. In *pl.* : Cic. Ep.

septemvir, *v.* septemviri.

septemvirālis, e, *adj.* [septemviri], *of the septemvirs, septemviral* : auctoritas, Cic. As Noun, **septemvirālēs**, ium, *m. pl. the septemvirs* : Cic.

septemvirātus, ūs, *m.* [septemviri], *the office of the septemvirs, the septemvirate* : Cic., Plin. Ep.

septem-viri, ōrum, *m. pl., a board or college of seven men, the septemvirs.* **a.** *the epulones* (*v.* epulo, 2). : Tac. **b.** For dividing lands : Cic. *Sing.* : Cic.

septēnārius, a, um [septēni], *consisting of seven, septenary* : numerus, *the number seven,* Pl.; cum tam bonos septenarios (*sc.* versūs) fundat ad tibiam, *heptameters,* Cic.

septendecim (less correctly, **septemdecim**), *adj.* [septem decem], *seventeen* : Cic., Liv. (Also septem decem, decem septem, etc.)

septēni, ae, a [septem]. **I.** *a group of seven, seven in a group* : fila lyrae, Ov.; Prop. In *sing.* : *seven-fold* (of the Nile), Luc.; (of the Danube), Stat. **II.** *seven in a group, seven each* : duo fasces septenos habuere libros, Liv.; Prop. So, **septēni dēni**, Cic.

septentr-, *v.* septemtri-.

septiēns (**-iēs**), *adv.* [septem], *seven times* : Cic., Liv.

septimānus, a, um [septimus], *of or on the seventh* : Nonae (of March, May, July, and October) : Varr. As Noun, **septimāni**, ōrum, *m. pl.* [septima], *soldiers of the seventh legion* : Tac. [It. *settimana* : Fr. *semaine.*]

septimontiālis, e, *adj.* [septem mōns], *of the feast* (Septimontium) *of the Seven Hills* : sacrum, Suet.

septimus (**septumus**), a, um [septem], *seventh* : Pl., Cic., Ov. P h r. : die septimi (Locutivo), *on the seventh day,* Pl. Acc. *sing. n.* **septimum** as *Adv., for the seventh* *time :* Marius tam feliciter septimum consul, Cic.

septimus-decimus, a, um, *seventeenth :* Cic.

septingentēsimus (earlier **-ēnsimus**), a, um [septingenti], *seven hundredth :* Liv.

septingenti, ae, a, [septem centum], *seven hundred :* Pl., Cic., Liv.

septirēmis, is, *adj.* [septem rēmus], *having seven banks of oars :* Curt.

septizōnium, I, n. *a building in Rome :* Suet.

septuāgēnsimus (-ēsimus), a, um [septuāgintā], *seventieth :* Cic., Liv.

septuāgintā, *indecl. adj. seventy :* Cic., Liv. [It. *settanta.*]

septuennis, e, *adj.* [septem annus], *of seven years, seven years old :* Pl.

sēptum, v. saeptum.

septunx, ūncis, m. [septem ūncia], *seven ounces* or *seven-twelfths of an as or of any unit.* **1.** Lit.: auri, Liv.; terna iugera et septunces viritim, Liv. **2.** Transf. *a seven(-cup-)name* (i.e. demanding as many cups as letters in the name): Mart.

sēptus, v. saeptus.

sepulcrālis, e, *adj.* [sepulcrum], *of a tomb :* fax, arae, Ov.

sepulcrētum, I, n. [sepulcrum], *a burial-place :* Cat.

sepulcrum, I, n. [sepeliō], *a grave, tomb.* **1.** Lit. **a.** Pl., Cic., Verg., etc. **b.** Of the place of burning and burial : Ter., Verg. **2.** Transf. **a.** Of a vulture's maw : Enn. Of the ruins of Troy : commune sepulcrum Europae Asiaeque, Cat. **b.** Of a cenotaph : Verg., Tac. **c.** In *pl.,* for the dead : Cat. **d.** Comic. of an old man : Pl.

sepultūra, ae, f. [sepeliō], *burial, interment, sepulture :* corpus ad sepulturam dare, Cic.; aliquem sepulturā adficere, Cic.; honore sepulturae carere, Cic. In *pl.:* Cic. Occ. of the rites of burning and burial : in foro qui locus sepulturae destinabatur, Tac.

sepultus, a, um, *Part.* sepeliō.

sequāx, ācis, *adj.* [sequor], *following, pursuing, clinging.* **1.** Lit.: (Arcadas) Latio dare terga sequaci, Verg.; curae sequaces, Lucr.; flammae, capreae, fumus, Verg. *Comp. :* Plin. **2.** Transf.: naturas hominum varias moresque sequaciš, Lucr.

sequēns, entis. **I.** *Part.* sequor. **II.** Adj. *next in order of time, following :* sequenti die, Liv.; sequens aetas, Tac. **III.** Noun, *an epithet :* Quint.

sequester, trī or tris, m. In law, *a depositary* or *trustee,* in whose hands the thing in dispute was placed. **1.** Lit.: Pl. Neut. **sequestrum,** I, *a deposit* or *security :* sequestro ponitur, Pl. **2.** Transf. **a.** In cases of bribery : *an agent with whom the money was deposited :* Cic., Quint. **b.** *a mediator :* Menenius Agrippa, qui inter patres et plebem publicae gratiae sequester fuit, Sen.; Luc. *Fem.* **sequestra,** ae, as Noun in apposition : pace sequestrā, Verg.

sequius, v. secus.

sequor, sequī, secūtus [*cf.* Gk. ἕπομαι]. **1.** *to attend, escort, accompany, follow.* **1.** Lit.: Pl.; Caes., Hor., etc.; intro, Pl.; curriculo, Pl. With Acc.: ex urbe amicitiae causā Caesarem Caes.;

Pl.; Cic.; Hor. Of thing as Subject : magna multitudo carrorum Gallos, Hirt.; neque ulla arbor brevom dominum sequetur, Hor.; de cortice sanguis, Verg. Of thing as Object, *to follow :* vestigia alicuius, Ov.; viam, Ov.; vallem, Liv.; signa (militaria), Sall., Liv.; victricia arma, Verg. **2.** Transf. *to accompany, to go along with* or *after, to follow.* **a.** Of inheritances, etc.: heredem sacra non sequuntur, Cato; heredes monumentum, Hor.; Liv.; belli praeda Romanos, Liv. **b.** *to follow* some leadership, authority, guidance, party, etc.: naturam ducem, Cic.; Polybium, Cic.; amicum vel bellum patriae inferentem, Cic.; sectam, Cic., Liv.; auctoritatem, Caes., Cic. Ep.; sententiam Scipionis, Caes.; novum consilium, Cic. Of a course of action or "plan of campaign" : Caesar hanc in re publicā viam quae popularis habetur secutus est, Cic.; haec qui dicunt, quam rationem sequantur vides, Cic. **c.** *to follow* or *come of itself* or *easily* or *readily :* volens facilisque ramus, Verg.; Varr.; manum nullo cogente sagitta, Verg.; telum, Liv.; oratio, verba, numerus, Cic.; Verg.; Ov.; verba provisam rem, Hor. **d.** *to follow* in order of time or as a natural sequel (consequence sometimes implied, *cf.* e.): aestatem autumnus, Enn.; sequitur hiems, tempestas, Caes.; secutum est bellum Africanum, Cic.; sequitur hunc annum nobilis clade Romanā Caudina pax, Liv.; sequitur clamor, Verg.; tonitrum nimbi, Ov.; lacrimae verba, Verg. **e.** *to follow* as a consequence : damnatum poenam sequi oportebat, Caes.; gloria virtutem tamquam umbra, Cic.; Sall. With *preps. :* post gloriam invidia, Sall.; Cic. Ep.; mediocre discrimen opinionis ex hac re, Liv. Hence in logical conclusions, sequitur with Acc. and *Inf.,* or with *ut* and *Subj. :* Cic. **II.** *to go after, follow in pursuit.* **1.** Lit.: moechas, Hor. Usually as an enemy : Caes.; hostis, Caes.; Ov.; hostem pilo, Tac.; fugacem, Hor.; feras, Ov. **2.** Transf. **a.** Of an end or object : matris commodum, Ter.; gratiam Caesaris, Caes.; utilitatem, iustitiam, otium ac tranquillitatem vitae, etc., Cic.; mercedes, Hor.; linguam et nomen, Liv.; ferro extrema, Verg.; spem vanam, Ov. **b.** Of a place : *to (make an effort to) reach :* Formias, Cic. Ep.; loca demissa, Caes.; Italiam, Verg.; Italiam fugientem, Verg.; pennis astra, Verg. **c.** Of a hearer : *to (make an effort to) follow :* aliquos apud iudicem fabulantis, Tac. [It. *seguire* ; Fr. *suivre.*]

sequo- and **sequū-,** v. secū- and sequor.

sera, ae, f. [serō, 1], *a moveable bolt* or *bar for fastening doors :* Ov.

Serāpis, is and idis, m. *an important Egyptian divinity.*

serēnitās, ātis, f. [serēnus], *fair weather.* **1.** Lit.: tranquilla, Liv.; mira serenitas cum tranquillitate, Liv.; caeli, Liv. **2.** Transf.: praesentis fortunae, Liv.

serēnō, āre [serēnus], *to make clear, fair,* or *serene, to clear up.* **1.** Lit.: caelum tempestatesque (Iuppiter), Verg.; luce serenanti, Cic. poet. **2.** Transf.: Verg.

serēnus, a, um [cf. Gk. σειρός, θελάς], *clear, bright, cloudless, fair.* **1.** Lit.: tempestas, Enn.; caelum, Lucr., Cic. Ep., Verg., etc.; lumen solis, Lucr.; lux, Verg., Liv.; sidera, Lucr.; nox, Lucr., Cic., Verg.; ver, aestas, Verg. Also, of Favonius, Pl.; unde serenas ventus agat nubes, Verg. *Comp.*: Mart. As Noun, **serēnum**, i, n. *a clear or cloudless sky, fair weather*: in sereno noctu, Cato; Priverni sereno per diem totum rubrum solem fuisse, Liv.; Luc. In *pl.*: soles et aperta serena, Verg.; Lucr. **2.** Transf.: aevum, Lucr.; vultus, Lucr., Cat., etc.; frons, Cic.; animus, Ov. [Fr. *serein.*]

Sēres, um, *m. pl.* (Acc. Sēras, Hor.) *a people of E. Asia, the Chinese*, famous for their silken fabrics; **Sēricus**, a, um, *Seric*; also *silken*: Prop., Hor., Quint., Tac.; **Sērica**, ōrum, *n. pl. silks*: Prop.

serēscō, ere [cf. serēnus], *to grow dry*: vestes serescunt, Lucr.

Sergius, a, *the name of a Roman gens.* Esp. L. Sergius Catilina; *v.* Catilina.

sēria, ae, f. *a long jar* for preserving liquids, fruit, salted provisions, etc.: Pl., Ter., Liv., etc.

sēricātus, a, um [Sēricus, v. Sēres], *dressed in silk*: Suet.

Sēriēs, v. Sēres.

seriēs, em, ē, f. [serō, 1], *a chain, row, succession.* **1.** Lit.: vinculorum, Curt.; iuvenum (in dancing), Tib. **2.** Transf.: cetera series deinde sequitur, Cic.; rerum, disputationum, sententiarum, Cic.; Verg.; fati, Ov.; laborum, Ov.; annorum, Hor.; temporis, Ov.; saeculorum, Tac.; loquendi, Quint. Of lineage: Prop., Ov.

sēriola, ae, f. [dim. sēria], *a small jar*: Pers.

Sēriphus or **-os**, i, f. *a small and unimportant island, one of the Cyclades, now Serphos*; **Sēriphius**, a, um; **Sēriphius**, i, m. *a Seriphian.*

sērius, a, um [cf. sevērus], *grave, earnest, serious*: res, Pl., Cic., etc.; verba, Tib.; verba seria dictu, Hor.; tempus, Plin. Ep.; quaestiones, Suet. As Noun, **sērium**, i, n. and more freq. **sēria**, ōrum, n. pl.: aliquid in serium convertere, Pl.; ioca, seria (cum aliquo agere), Cic.; cum his seria ac iocos celebrare, Liv.; sed tamen amoto quaeramus seria ludo, Hor.; per seria per iocos, Tac. Abl. sing. n. **sēriō** as *Adv. in earnest, seriously*: nec ioco nec serio, Pl.; Ter.; Liv., etc.

sermō, ōnis, m. [serō, 1], lit. perh. *connected speech*; hence, *a conversation, a talking with, a talk, dialogue.* **1.** Lit. **a.** In gen.: Pl.; multa inter sese vario sermone serebant, Verg.; sermonem cum aliquo conferre, Cic.; instituere, Caes.; sermonis aditum cum aliquo habere, Caes.; fit sermo inter eos, Cic.; erat in ore, in sermone omnium, Cic.; referre sermones deorum, Hor. **B.** In partic. **a.** *learned talk, literary conversation, discourse,* or *discussion*: Laeli de amicitia, Cic.; Socratici sermones, Hor.; habere, Cic.; in sermonem ingredi, Cic. **b.** *common talk, gossip*: in sermonem hominum venire, Cic.; vix feram sermones hominum, Cic.; sermones lacessere, reprimere, Cic. Ep.;

diffugere, Cic.; persolvenda... res, Cic.; materiam sermonibus praebere, Tac.; per urbem solus sermo est omnibus (with Acc. and *Inf.*), Pl.; sermo est totā Asiā dissipatus (with Acc. and *Inf.*), Cic. **c.** *talks in everyday language* (e.g. of Horace's satires and epistles): Hor. **2.** Transf. **A.** *a topic of conversation*: filius meus per urbem sermo est omnibus, Pl.; Cic. Ep.; Prop.; alicui dare, Cic. Ep. **B.** *language, diction.* **a.** elegantia sermonis, Cic. Ep.; Quint.; rusticus, urbanus, Liv. **b.** *everyday language, prose*: sermonis plenus orator, Cic.; scribere sermoni propiora, Hor.; Quint.; pedester, Hor. **c.** *language of a nation*: Latinus, Cic.; Persarum, Nep. Perh. *vocabulary* or *power of expression in*, patrii sermonis egestas, Lucr.; Hor.

sermōcinātiō, ōnis, f. [sermōcinor], *a conversation, discussion*: Auct. Her., Quint.

sermōcinor, ārī [sermō], *to talk with, to converse, discourse.* **a.** In gen.: cum aliquo, Cic. **b.** Of literary or philosophical discussion: Suet.

sermunculus, i, m. [dim. sermō], *paltry gossip, tittle-tattle*: Cic. Ep., Plin. Ep. In pl.: Cic., Plin. Ep.

1. serō, serere, seruī, sertum [cf. Gk. εἴρω, *to put in a row, to connect*; hence *to link up, entwine.* **1.** Lit. (only in *Perf. Part.*): loricae, Nep.; sertas nardo florente coronas, Luc. (v. also serta, under sertus). **2.** Transf.: mihi sermonem, Pl.; multa inter sese vario sermone, Verg.; aliquid sermonibus occultis, Liv.; secreta conloquia cum eo, Liv.; bella ex bellis, Sall., Liv.; certamina cum patribus, Liv.; crebra proelia, Tac.; crimina belli, Verg.

2. serō, serere, sēvī, satum, *to sow, plant.* **1.** Lit. **a.** With Acc. (of *seed* or *plant*, or *of land sown*): oleam et vitem, Cic.; frumenta, Caes.; satae messes, Verg.; iugera, Cic.; sulcos, Tib. **b.** Of living beings (esp. in *Perf. Part.* satus): non temere sati et creati sumus, Cic.; de Numitore, Ov.; and with *ab*, Ov.; most freq. with simple *Abl.*: satus Anchisā, Verg.; sato sanguine divum, Verg.; stirpe divinā satus, Liv.; Ov. **2.** Transf.: aere vulnera, Lucr.; leges, instituta, rem publicam, Cic.; civilis discordias, Liv.; invidiam in alios, Tac.; rumores, Verg.; ex aeternitate causa causam serens, Cic.

serpēns, entis, m. f. [serpō], *a creeping thing,* esp. *a snake, serpent.* Masc.: Lucr., Sall., Verg., Hor., Ov. Fem.: Lucr., Cic., Hor., Ov. Astron.: *the Serpent,* a constellation: Ov.

serpentigena, ae, m. [serpēns and gen in gignō], *sprung from a serpent*: Ov.

serpenti-pēs, pedis, m. [serpēns pēs], *serpent-footed*: Ov.

serperastra (serpir-), ōrum, n. pl. *knee-splints* or *bandages* for straightening the crooked legs of children: Varr. Humorously of officers, who hold the soldiers in check: Cic. Ep.

serpillum, v. serpyllum.

serpō, serpere, serpsī, serptum [cf. Gk. ἕρπω, ῥέπω], *to creep, crawl.* **1.** Lit. (only of animals): Lucr., Cic., Ov. **2.** Transf.

a. Of material things: sol, Lucr.; Hister in mare, Ov.; aestus aetheris, Lucr.; fiamma per continua, Liv.; vitis serpens multiplici lapsu et erratico, Cic.; contagia per vulgus, Verg. **b.** neque serpit, sed volat in optimum statum res publica, Cic.; ne latius serperet res, Liv.; Cic.; serpit nescio quo modo per omnium vitas amicitia, Cic.; hic rumor, Cic.; per agmina murmur, Verg.; quies, Verg. Of a grovelling style: serpit humi tutus, Hor.

serpyllum (-ullum or -illum), I, n. [ἑρπυλλον], thyme, wild thyme: Cato, Varr., Verg. In pl.: Verg.

serra, ae, f. [perh. = sec-ra, from secō], a saw: Lucr., Cic., Verg., etc. [Sp. sierra.]

serrātus, a, um [serra], saw-edged, serrated: dentes, Plin.; nummi, Tac.

serrula, ae, f. [dim. sorra], a small saw: Cic.

Sertōrius (Q.), I, m.: a general of Marius, who held out in Spain against the partisans of Sulla, until he was assassinated by Perperna; **Sertōriānus**, a, um; **Sertōriāni**, ōrum, m. pl. the partisans of Sertorius.

sertus, a, um. **I.** Part. serō, l. **II.** Noun, **serta**, ōrum, m. pl. wreaths of flowers, festoons: Pl., Cic., Verg., etc. Also, **serta**, ae, f.: Prop.

serum, I, n. [cf. Gk. ὁρός], the watery part of curdled milk, whey. **1.** Lit.: Verg., Ov. **2.** Transf. of other things: Cat., Plin.

sērus, a, um. **I.** late: sero a vespere, Ov.; serā nocte, Prop., Liv.; dies, Tac.; hiems magis sera, Liv.; anni, Ov.; gratulatio, Cic. Comp. (rare): (bellum) spe omnium serius, Liv. Poet. after: nepotes, Ov.; serior aetas, Ov. Predic.: serus in caelum redeas, Hor.; (me) arguit incepto serum accessisse labori, Ov. With GEN.: o seri studiorum, Hor. Neut. as Noun, **sērum**, I, a late hour: serum erat diei, Liv.; sero diei, Tac.; in serum noctis convivium productum, Liv.; in serum rem trahere, Liv.; Suet. Acc. sing. n. **sērum** and Acc. pl. n. **sēra** as Adv.: Verg. ABL. sing. n. **sērō** as Adv.: Cato, Cic.; Comp. **sērius**: Cic., Ov., Liv., etc.; serius setius, Hor.; Ov.; Sup. sērissimē, Caes. **II.** too late: Kalendae, Cic.; condiciones pacis, Suet.; Liv. Prodic.: ud possessu venis praeceptaquo gaudia serus, Ov.; Verg. ABL. sing. n. **sērō** as Adv.: Pl., Cic., Liv. Comp. **sērius**: Caes., Cic. [Fr. soir.]

serva, ae, f. [servus], a female slave: Pl., Hor., Liv.

servābilis, e, adj. [servō], that can be saved or rescued: Ov.

servāns, antis. **I.** Part. servō. **II.** Adj. keeping, observant of: with GEN.: Rhipheus servantissimus aequi, Verg.

servātor, ōris, m. and **servātrix**, icis, f. [servō], one who attends to. **a.** a preserver, deliverer, saviour. rei publicae (opp. perditor), Cic.; servatorem liberatoremque acclamantibus, Liv.; arcis (anser), Lucr.; Ov. Fem.: Ter., Cic., Ov. **b.** a watcher, observer: Olympi, Luc.

servilis, e, adj. [servus], of a slave or slaves, servile. **1.** Lit.: nuptiae, Pl.; vestis, Cic.; in servilem modum de uxoribus

quaestionem habent, Caes.; tumultus, a slave-war, Caes.; terror, of an insurrection of slaves, Liv.; manus, Hor. **2.** Transf.: iugum, Cic.; indoles, Liv.

serviliter, adv. slavishly, servilely: Cic., Tac.

Servīlius, a, the name of a Roman gens. Esp. C. Servilius Ahala: v. Ahala. There were many consuls, praetors, etc., from this gens; **Servīlius, Serviliānus**, a, um.

serviō, īre (Imperf. servībās, Pl.; Fut. servībō, Pl.) [servus], to be a servant or slave. **1.** Lit. **a.** Prop.: Pl., Cic., Hor., etc. With DAT. of person: Pl., Cic., etc. With apud: to be a slave in anyone's house: apud aliquem, Pl., Cic., Liv. With Intern. Acc.: servitutem servire, Pl., Cic., Liv. **b.** Polit., etc.: to be subject, be obedient: Cic., Liv. With DAT.: regi, populo R., Cic.; Nep.; Ov.; marito, Verg. **2.** Transf. **a.** In gen.: alicui, Pl.; sibi, Cic.; populo, Cic.; rumori, Pl., Caes.; bello, Caes.; compendio suo privato, Caes.; rei publicae commodis, Cic.; auribus alicuius, Caes.; incertis rumoribus, Caes.; cupiditati, amori, iracundiae, dignitati, existimationi, gloriae, posteritati, tempori, pecuniae, etc., Cic. Impers. Pass.: Cic. **b.** In law, of buildings, lands: to be subject to certain burdens or services; to be mortgaged: Cic. [From Part. serviēns. It. sergente; Fr. sergent; Eng. sergeant.]

servitium, I, n. [serviō], the condition of a slave or servant, slavery, servitude. **1.** Lit. **a.** Prop.: Ter., Sall.; aliquem in servitium abstrahere, ducere, Liv.; servitio exire, Verg.; aliquem servitio levare, Hor. **b.** Polit., etc.: civitatem nostram a servitio abstrahere, Brut. ap. Cic. Ep.; domus Assaraci Phthiam servitio premet, Verg. **2.** Transf. **a.** animi imperio, corporis servitio magis utimur, Sall.; Tac.; servitium amoris ferro, Ov.; boum, Verg. **b.** Concr. (a body of) slaves: Pl., Cic. Tac. In pl.: Cic., Sall.

servitrītius, a, um [servus tritus], slavery-galled, as a term of abuse: Pl.

servitūdō, inis, f. [servus], slavery, servitude: Liv. (dub.).

servitūs, ūtis, f. [servus], the condition of a slave; slavery, serfdom. **1.** Lit. **a.** Prop.: Pl., Cic.; aliquem in servitutem abstrahere (Caes.), abducere, adiudicare (Cic.), addicere (Caes., Liv.), adserere (Liv.). With DAT.: alicui, Pl. As Intern. Acc.: servitutem servire, Pl. **b.** Polit., etc.: in servitute atque in dicione Germanorum teneri, Caes.; liberum populum servituto adficere, Cic.; servituto Graeciam liberaro, Cic.; nunquam exuitur servitus muliebris, Liv. **2.** Transf. **a.** In gen.: huius tanti offici, Cic.; iuris, Quint. **b.** In law, liability (of lands, houses, etc.) to certain burdens, payments, or services: Cic. Ep. **c.** slaves, servants (collectively): adde quod servitus crescit nova (of lovers), Hor.

Servius, a, a Roman proper name, esp. in the gens Sulpicia; abbreviated Ser.

Servius Tullius, I, m. the sixth king of Rome.

servō, āre (old Fut. servāssō, Pl.), to attend to, watch over. **1.** Lit. **a.** In gen.: serva !

Pl.. Hor. ; vestimenta sua, Pl. ; scelesta me, Pl. ; iter alicuius, Caes. ; sidera, Verg. ; haedos, Verg. Esp. in augury : caelum servare, Lucr. ; de caelo servare, Cic. **b.** *to watch over, keep unharmed, protect, preserve, retain :* ita me servet Iuppiter, Ter. ; Pl. ; aliquem, Cic. ; Hor. ; impedimenta cohortisque, Caes. ; urbem insulamque Caesari, Caes. ; rem suam, Hor. With *Predic. Adj. :* urbem et civis integros incolumisque, Cic. With *cæ* or *ab :* aliquem ex periculo, Caes. ; ex iudicio, Cic. ; carinas a peste, Verg. **c.** *to keep in store, to store, reserve :* vinum in vetustatem, Cato ; Massicum, Hor. ; sub imagine falcem, Verg. **2.** Transf. **a.** *to keep to a place, to continue to dwell in :* domum, limen, silvas, Verg. ; atria, nidum, Hor. **b.** *to keep, retain, observe:* inperium probe, Pl. ; promissum, Pl., Cic. ; fidem cum aliquo, Pl., Cic. ; ordines, Caes. ; ordinem laboris quietisque, Liv. ; iura indutiarum, Caes. ; praesidia indiligentius, Caes. ; custodias, Liv. ; iustitiam, aequitatem, dignitatem, consuetudinem, amicitiam, etc., Cic. ; amorem, Verg. ; aequam mentem, Hor. With *Predic. Adj. :* se castos, Cic. ; also with *ab :* pudicitiam liberorum ab eorum libidine tutam, Cic. With *ut* or *ne* and *Subj. :* cum decemviri servassent ut unus fascis haberet, Liv. With *Indir. Quest. :* Pl. **c.** *to keep in store, to reserve :* so temporibus aliis, Cic. ; se ad maiora vindicem, Liv. ; in aliquod tempus quam integerrimas viris militi servare, Liv. ; res iudicio voluntatique multitudinis, Cic. ; voismet rebus secundis, Verg. [It. *serbare.*]

servolicola, ae, *f.* [servolus colo], *she who waits upon slaves :* Pl.

servolus, i, *m.* and **servola,** ae, *f.* (Cic. Ep.) [*dim.* servus *and* serva], *a young slave, servant-lad, servant-girl :* Pl., Cic., etc.

servus (-os), i, *m.* and **servus (-os),** a, um, *adj. a slave, servant.* **1.** Lit. **a.** Prop.: Pl., Cic., Ov., etc. As *Adj. :* homo servos, Pl. ; capita, Liv. ; opera, Pl. **b.** Polit. (only as *Adj.*) : Graeciae urbes servae et vectigales, Liv. ; Sall. **2.** Transf. **a.** libidinum, Cic., Plin. Ep. As *Adj. :* o imitatores, servum pecus, Hor. **b.** In law, of buildings, lands, etc.: *liable to certain burdens* or *services* (only as *Adj.*) : praedia, Cic.

sescēnāris, e, *adj.* [perh. fr. sēsqui annus], *a year and a half old :* bos, Liv.

sescēnārius, a, um [sēscēni], *consisting of six hundred :* cohortes, Caes.

sescēni (sēscentēni, Suet.) ae, a [sēscenti], *six hundred in a group* or *six hundred each :* Cic.

sescentēsimus (older **-tēns-**), a, um [sēscenti], *six hundredth :* Cic.

sescenti, ae, a [sex centum], *six hundred.* **1.** Lit. : Pl., Cic. **2.** Transf. of an indefinitely large number : Pl., Ter., Cic. *Neut. pl.* as Noun : Pl., Cic.

sescentiēs (older **-iēns**), *adv.* [sēscenti], *six hundred times :* Cic. Ep., Plin. Ep.

Sēscentōplāgus, i, *m.* [plāga], *Six-hundred-blow-man :* Pl.

sēscūncia, ae, *f.* [sēsqui ūncia], *one and a half* urciuc, i.e. *a twelfth and a half of a twelfth,*

one *eighth of a unit :* Plin. **As** *Adj. :* pulae sesciunciae, *an inch and a half thick,* Pl.

seselis, is, *f.* [σέσελις], a plant, *hartwort, seseli :* Cic.

Sesōstris, is, or **Sesōsis,** idis, *m. a celebrated king of Egypt, belonging to the 12th Dynasty, who effected great conquests.*

sēsqui, *adv.* [perh. fr. sēmis que, "*and a half*"], *one half more, more by a half :* aut altero tanto aut sesqui maiorem, Cic.

sēsqui-alter, era, erum, *one and a half :* Cic.

sēsqui-hōra, ae, *f. an hour and a half :* Plin. Ep.

sēsqui-lībra, ae, *f. a pound and a half :* Cato.

sēsqui-modius, i, *m. a peck and a half :* Cic.

sēsqui-octāvus, a, um, *containing one and an eighth, nine-eighths ; bearing the ratio of nine to eight :* intervallum, Cic.

sēsqui-opus, operis, *n. the work of a day and a half :* Pl.

sēsqui-pedālis, e, *adj. of a foot and a half ; one foot and a half* in length, breadth, or diameter : Cato, Caes. Comic.: dentes, Cat. ; verba, Hor.

sēsqui-pēs, pedis, *m. a foot and a half* (in length, breadth, etc.) *:* Pl., Varr.

sēsqui-plāga, ae, *f. a blow and a half :* sesquiplagā interfectum (sc.), Tac.

sēsqui-plex, icis, *adj.* [plicō], *one and a half times as much :* sesquiplex aut duplex, Cic.

sēsqui-tertius, a, um, *containing one and a third, four-thirds ; bearing the ratio of four to three :* intervallum, Cic.

sēssibulum, i, *n.* [sedeō], *a seat, chair:* Pl.

sēssilis, e, *adj.* [sedeō], *fit for sitting on :* **1.** Lit. (*Pass.*) : tergum (equi), Ov. **2.** Transf. (*Act.*) : of plants, *growing close to the ground, dwarf :* lactuca, Mart.

sēssiō, ōnis, *f.* [sedeō], *a sitting.* **1.** Lit. **a.** In gen.: Cic. In *pl. :* Cic. **b.** *a sitting idly, a loitering, tarrying :* Cic. Ep. **c.** *a sitting* or *session* for discussion : postmeridiana, Cic. **2.** Transf. *a seat, sitting-place :* sessiones gymnasiorum, Cic.

sēssitō, āre [*freq.* sedeō], *to sit much* or *long :* Cic.

sēssiuncula, ae, *f.* [*dim.* sēssiō], *a little meeting* or *company for conversation,* etc. (in *pl.*) : Cic.

sēssor, ōris, *m.* [sedeō], *one who sits, a sitter.* **1.** Lit. : in the theatre, Hor. ; on a horse, Suet. **2.** Transf. *a resident :* sessores veteres urbis, Nep.

sēstertium, Gen. *pl.* of sēstertius (q.v.); used also as *Neut.* Noun in Nom. *pl.* 1000 *sesterces :* sescenta sestertia, 600,000 *sesterces,* Cic. Esp. with *Adv.,* e.g. deciens sestertia, i.e. deciens centena milia sestertium (*v.* sestertius). For *sing.* sestertium declined (*v.* sestertius).

sēstertius, a, um [contr. fr. sēmis tertius], *consisting of a third half,* i.e. *of two and a half asses* (librae) or *any units :* only with nummus or milia : (bona C. Rabiri Postumi) nummo sestertio addicuntur, Cic. ; ut asinus venierit sestertiis milibus LX,

Varr. As Noun, **sēstertius**, I, *m.* (GEN.
pl. usually sēstertium), written often HS,
i.e. II et Semis, *a sesterce*, a small silver
coin, equal to two and a half asses, or one
fourth of a denarius (i.e. a little over 2d.).
The sestortius was the ordinary Roman unit
in accounting. **a.** Sums below 2000 sesterces are expressed by a cardinal numeral,
o.g. centum sestertii. **b.** Sums from 2000
upwards are expressed by milia sestertium
or sestertia (*v.* sestertium) with the group-
number (bina, centena, etc.) or the cardinal
number (duo, centum, etc.). **c.** Sums of
1,000,000 and upwards are expressed by
the numeral adverb in -iens (-ies) with
sestertium (as GEN. pl.) declined as *sing.*
Neut. Noun) deciens (*sc.* centena milia)
sestertium, *one million sesterces* (in figures
HS |X̄|) : Cic. ; accepto quinquagiens
sestertio, Tac. ; syngrapha sesterti centies
per legatos facta, Cic.
Sēstius, a, *the name of a Roman gens* ; esp.
P. Sestius, whom Cicero defended ; **Sēstius**,
Sēstiānus, a, um, *of a Sestius.*
Sēstos (-**us**), ī, *f. a city on the Hellespont,
the home of Hero* ; **Sēstus**, a, um, puellā,
i.e. *Hero*, Ov. ; **Sēstiānus**, **Sēstiacus**, a,
um.
sēt-, *v.* saet-.
sētanium, ī, *n. a kind of bread* : Pl.
Sētia, ae, *f. a town in Latium, celebrated
for its excellent wine, now Sesse or Sezze* ;
Sētinus, a, um ; **Sētinī**, ōrum, *m. pl. the
inhabitants.*
sētius, *v.* secus.
seu, *adv.*, *v.* sīve.
sevērē, *adv. gravely, seriously, austerely,
rigidly, severely* : Cic., Sall., etc. *Comp.* :
Caes., Cic. Ep. *Sup.* : Cic.
sevēritās, ātis, *f.* [sevērus], *gravity, sternness,
strictness, severity either in good or in bad
sense* : Ter., Cic., Sall. ; imperi, Caes. ;
iudiciorum, Cic. ; disciplinae, Quint. ;
orationis, Plin. Ep.
sevēritūdō, inis, *f.* [sevērus], *gravity, aus-
terity* : Pl.
sevērus, a, um, *serious, grave, strict, austere,
stern.* **A.** Of persons in aspect, demeanour,
conduct, etc. **a.** Pl., Lucr., Cic., Verg.,
etc. ; vitā severus, Cic. ; iudex in aliquem
severus, Cic. ; ad iudicandum, Cic. *Comp.* :
Cat. ; *Sup.* : Cic., etc. *Masc.* as Noun :
Cat., Hor., Plin. **b.** In bad sense : *harsh,
rough* : Pl., Prop. ; in aliquem, Cic., Liv.
Comp. : Liv. **B.** Of things. **a.** severā
fronte, Pl. ; Ov. ; iudicia, sententiae, etc.,
Cic. ; tragoedia, Hor. ; fidibus voces cre-
vere soveris, Hor. ; Falernum (i.e. in
flavour), Hor. *Neut. pl.* as Noun : Hor.
Comp. : vultus, imperia, Cic. ; poena,
Sall. *Sup.* : imperium, Liv. **b.** In bad
sense : *ruthless, grim* : Pl. ; silentia noctis,
Lucr. ; amnem severum Cocyti, Verg. ;
uncus, Hor. ; hiems, Quint.
Sevērus, I, *m. a Roman name.* Esp. **I.**
Cornelius Severus, *a poet in the Augustan
age.* **II.** Septimius Severus, *Roman emperor*, A.D. 193. **III.** Alexander Soverus,
Roman emperor, A.D. 222.
Sevērus Mōns, *a mountain in the country of
the Sabines.*
sē-vocō, āre. *to call apart or aside. to call away*

to. **1.** Lit. : aliquem, Pl., Cic., Ov., etc. ;
plebem in Aventinum, Cic. Comic. :
se e senatu, Pl. **2.** Transf. *to withdraw,
remove* : cura me sevocat a doctis virginibus (i.e. Musis), Cat. ; animum a negotio,
Cic. ; mentem a sensibus, Cic. ; de communi quidquid poterat ad se in privatam
domum, Cic.
sēvum, *v.* sōbum.
sex, *indecl. adj.* [*cf.* Gk. ἕξ], *six* : Pl., Cic.,
Verg., etc. [It. *sei* ; Sp. *seis.*]
sexāgēnārius, a, um [sexāgēnī], *of or containing sixty* ; mostly of age, *sixty years
old* ; and as Noun, *a man of sixty* : Quint.
sexāgēnī, ae, a [sexāgintā]. **I.** *sixty in a
group* : milia, Cic. **II.** *sixty each* : Liv.
sexāgēnsimus (-**ēs-**), a, um [sexāgintā],
sixtieth : Ter., Cic., Mart.
sexāgiēns (-**iēs-**), *adv.* [sexāgintā], *sixty
times* : Caes., Cic.
sexāgintā, *indecl. adj.* [sex], *sixty* : Pl.,
Cic., Liv., etc. [It. *sessanta* ; Fr. *soixante.*]
sex-angulus, a, um, *hexagonal* : Ov., Plin.
sexcen-, *v.* sēscen-.
sexdecim, *v.* sēdecim.
sexennis, e, *adj.* [sex annus], *six years old* :
Pl. ; sexenni die, *in a period of six years,*
Caes.
sexennium, ī, *n.* [sexennis]. *a period of six
years* : Pl., Cic.
sexiēns (-**iēs-**), *adv.* [sex], *six times* : Liv.
sex-primī (also **sex primī**), ōrum, *m. pl.
a board of six leading men in provincial
towns* : Cic.
sexta-decimāni, ōrum, *m. pl. the soldiers of
the sixteenth (legion)* : Tac.
sextāns, antis, *m.* [sex], *a sixth part of an
as, or of any unit.* **a.** In gen. : heredes in
sextante (i.e. of the inheritance), Cic. Ep.
b. As a coin ; *the sixth part of an as* : Liv.
c. Of weight : Ov., Plin. **d.** As a land-
measure, *the sixth part of a iuger* : Varr.
e. As a liquid measure, *the sixth part of a
sextarius, or two cyathi* : Mart., Suet.
sextārius, ī, *m.* [sextus], *the sixth part of a
measure, weight*, etc. **a.** In gen. : Plin.
b. As a liquid measure, *the sixth part of a
congius, about a pint* : Cato, Cic., Hor.
[It. *sestiere* ; Fr. *setier.*]
Sextīlis, e, *adj.* [sextus], *of or belonging to
the sixth month of the old Roman year* (which
began with March) : Sextili mense, Hor. ;
Kalendae, Liv. *Masc.* as Noun (*sc.* mensis),
afterwards called Augustus, *in honour of
the emperor Augustus* : Cic.
sextula, ae, *f.* (*sc.* pars) [*dim.* sextus], *the
paltry sixth part of an uncia* : Cic.
sextus, a, um [sex], *the sixth* : Pl., Cic., Ov.,
etc. Acc. *Neut.* **sextum** as *Adv., for the
sixth time* : sextum consul, Cic.
sextus-decimus, a, um, *sixteenth* : Cic.
sex-ungula, ae, *f. six-claws* ; of a rapacious
woman : Pl.
sexus, ūs, *m.* (**secus**, *indecl. n.* q.v.) [fr.
root of secō], *sex* : Pac., Cic., Liv., etc.
sī (older **sei**), *conj.* [pronh. *cf.* Gk. εἰ, and Lat.
sīc], *assuming or supposing that, in case* ;
if ever, whenever, when (the negative of *si* is
usually *nisi*). **I.** With various tenses of
Indic. : quid est, Catilina, quod iam
amplius exspectes, si nec privata domus
continere voces coniurationis tuae potest ?

Cic. ; Pl., etc. ; de us tō, si qui illе forte locus admonuerit, commonebo, Cic. ; nec mirum eos si orationes turbaverant, Liv. ; quos (tyrannos) si (*whenever*) boni oppresserunt, civitas recreatur, Cic. ; si quando (*whenever*) nostri navem religaverant, hostes succurrebant, Caes. With *quidem*. **a.** *if indeed :* Ter., Cic., etc. **b.** *since indeed :* Pl., Cic., etc. With *quod : and if, but if :* quod si in philosophiā tantum intereat, quid tandem in causis existimandum est ? Cic. With verb omitted : aut nemo, aut, si quisquam, ille sapiens fuit, Cic. **II.** With *Subj. :* abire hinc nullo pacto possim si velim, Pl. ; Cic., etc. ; si id fecisses, melius famae consuluisses, Cic. With *ac* or *perinde ac, perinde quam* in comparisons : *just as if :* perinde aestimans ac si usus esset, Caes. ; Cic. ; Liv., etc. To express a wish : si nunc se nobis ille aureus arbore ramus ostendat ! Verg. Often with *o :* o mihi praeteritos referat si Iuppiter annos ! Verg. **III.** Elliptically : *in the hope that, to see if, to try if* (with *Subj.*) : circumfunduntur hostes si quem aditum reperire possent, Caes. ; paludem si nostri transirent, hostes exspectabant, Caes. ; Pl. ; Cic. ; Verg., etc. **IV.** In *Indir. Quest.* (much less freq. than *num*) : Pl., Cic., Verg., etc.

sibīlō, āre [sibilus]. **A.** Intrans.: *to hiss, to whistle :* serpens, Verg. ; ferrum igne rubens, Ov. Comic. of gossips : Pl. **B.** Trans.: *to hiss at, hiss down :* aliquem, Cic. Ep., Hor. [Fr. *siffler*.]

sibilus, ī, m. (*pl.* in poets, **sībīla**, ōrum, *n.*), *a hissing, whistling*. **a.** In gen. : Lucr., Verg., Liv., etc. As *Adj. :* colla colubrae, Verg. **b.** To show contempt : sibilum metuis ? Cic. Mostly in *pl. :* e scaenā sibilis explodi, Cic.

Sibylla (**Sibulla**, Tac.), ae, *f.* [σίβυλλα], *a prophetess, Sibyl :* Pl., Cic., Verg., etc. ; **Sibyllīnus**, a, um, *of a Sibyl :* libri, Cic., Liv. ; versus, Cic., Hor.

sic (older **seic** ; and **sīce**, Pl.) and *interrog.* **sīcine**, *demonstr. adv.* [si, LOCAT. fr. pron. stem seen in Gk. ὅ, ἥ, and -ce as in hīce, etc.], *thus, so, in this way ; in such a way.* **1.** Lit. **A.** Deictic (often with suitable gesture, tone, or action) : amictus sic hac ludibundus incessi, Pl. ; sic deinde quicumque alius transiliet moenia mea, Liv. ; sic furi datur, Pl. Also, like our " *so so* " : *Da.* quid rei geri ? *Ge.* sic tenuiter, Pl. Also as said with an imaginary gesture : non sic nudos in flumen deicere voluerunt, Cic. ; Hor. **B.** Ref. to an action just mentioned or about to be mentioned : *thus, in this or the following way, in these circumstances.* **a.** sic deinceps omne opus contexitur, Caes. ; ingressus est sic loqui, Cic. Occ. predicatively with *est* (in sense of talis) : sic vita hominum est, Cic. **b.** With correlative, usually *ut,* in comparison or contrast : ut tu nunc de Coriolano, sic Clitarchus de Themistocle finxit, Cic. With *quem ad modum, sicut, tamquam, quasi :* Cic., etc. With *velut :* Verg., Liv. With *ceu :* Verg. **c.** In assent (often with verb omitted) : *just so, yes :* Ter., Cic., etc. **2.** Transf. **a.** With a result-clause (*cf.*

---

itu[tam] adsa); *l...... ...... l .... ;* sic accidit ut ex tanto navium numero nulla omnino navis desideraretur, Caes. ; eius responso iudices sic oxarserunt ut condemnarent, Cic. **b.** Conditionally, as the equivalent of a protasis : *in this case, on these* or *such conditions :* decreverunt ut id sic ratum esset si patres auctores fuissent, Liv. ; reliquas illius anni pestis recordamini ; sic enim facillime perspicietis, Cic. ; sic demum lucos Stygios aspicies, Verg. ; sic te diva potens Cypri regat, Hor.

sica, ae, *f.* [*cf.* secō], *a dagger, poniard :* Enn., Cic., etc.

Sicambrī, v. Sigambrī.

Sicāni, ōrum, *m. pl. a very ancient people of Italy, a portion of whom migrated to Sicily :* **Sicānus** (Sicānus, Aus.), a, um ; **Sicanius**, a, um, *Sicilian :* **Sicania**, ae, *f. the island of Sicily ;* and **Sicanis**, idis, *f. adj. Sicilian.*

sicārius, ī, m. [sica], *an assassin, murderer :* Cic., Hor., etc. ; aliquem inter sicarios accusare, defendere, Cic.

siccē, *adv. dryly, without damp.* Transf. *firmly, solidly :* dicere, Cic.

siccine (**sicine**), v. sic.

siccitās, ātis, *f.* [siccus], *dryness.* **1.** Lit. **a.** In gen. (of places, etc.): Pl., Caes., Cic. **b.** Of the weather, *dryness, drought :* Cic. Ep., Liv. In *pl. :* Caes. **2.** Transf. **a.** Of the human body, *freedom from gross humours* or *from flabbiness :* Cic. **b.** Of speech, *dryness,* i.e. want of ornament : orationis, Cic.

siccō, āre [siccus], *to dry, dry up, drain.* **a.** In gen.: paludes, Cic. ; Lucr. ; infirma urbis loca, Liv. ; vellera, Verg. ; amnis, herbas, Ov. ; iocis lacrimas, Quint. Poet : ovis ubera, Verg. ; calices, Hor. **b.** Of wounds, humours, etc. : *to stanch, heal :* vulnera lymphis, Verg. ; Plin. [Fr. *sécher.*]

siccoculus, a, um [siccus oculus], *dry-eyed :* Pl.

siccus, a, um, *dry.* **1.** Lit. **a.** In gen. : harena, Verg. ; glaebae, Hor. ; solum, Quint. ; lacus, Prop. ; carinae, Hor. ; lumina, oculi, Hor., Prop., Quint., etc. ; genae, Prop. ; of constellations that do not dip below the horizon, Ov. ; vox, Ov. ; panis, Sen. Ep. As Noun, **siccum**, ī, n. (Verg., Prop., Liv.) and **sicca**, ōrum, n. *pl.* (Plin., Quint.), *dry land, a dry place.* **b.** Of weather, *dry, without rain :* Canis, Tib. ; dies, Hor. ; fervores, Ov. ; caelum, ver, etc., Plin. **2.** Transf. **A.** Of the body, *dry, firm, not flabby* (opp. to rheumy, catarrhal, etc.) : Pl., Cat. *Comp. :* Cat., Plin. **B.** *dry, thirsty :* nimis dii sicci sumus, Pl. ; Verg. ; Hor. Hence, *abstemious, sober :* (opp. vinolentus), Cic. ; Pl. ; Hor. *Masc. pl.* as Noun : Hor. **C.** Of oratory. **a.** *firm, solid* in argument : Cic. **b.** *dry, insipid :* Tac. [It *secco :* Fr. *sec.*]

Sicilia, v. Siculī.

sicilicissitō, āre [Siculī], *to imitate the Sicilian fashion :* Pl.

sicilicula, ae, *f.* [*dim.* sicilis, *a sickle ; cf.* sica], *a small sickle :* Pl.

Siciliēnsis, v. Siculī.

sicine, v. sic.

si-cubi, *adv.* [si and cubi=ubi, q.v.], *if in some place, if anywhere, wheresoever*

sicubi nactus eris, Cic. ; Ter. ; Verg. ; Liv., etc.

sicula, ae, *f.* [*dim.* sica], *a little dagger.* Transf.: Cat.

Siculi, ōrum, *m. pl. an ancient Italian people, a portion of whom migrated to the island of Sicily, which derived its name from them ;* **Siculus,** a, um, *Sicilian ;* **Sicilia,** ae, *f. Sicily ;* **Siciliēnsis,** e, *adj. Sicilian,* and **Sicelis,** idis, *adj. f. :* Sicelides Musae, *Sicilian, with special reference to Theocritus, who was a native of Syracuse.* As Noun, *a Sicilian woman.*

si-cunde, *adv.* [sī and cunde=unde], *if from some place* (rare) : Cic. Ep., Liv.

sic-ut and **sic-uti,** *adv. so as, just as, as.* **1.** Lit. **a.** sicut dixi, faciam, Pl. ; Lucr. ; Cic., etc. (Sometimes the verb in the sicut clause is omitted : Pl., Cic., Hor., etc.) **b.** Correl. to *ita, itidem, sic* : itidem, sic : sicut tuom vis gnatum tuae superesse vitae, ita te optestor, Pl. ; Caes. ; Cic., etc. ; sicut . . . ita (like ut . . . ita) can often be translated *although . . . yet.* **c.** To confirm a statement (most freq.), with esse, *as indeed it is (was), as it really is (was)* ; ait ista res magna, sicut est, Cic. ; Caes. : Ov., etc. ; quod fore, sicut accidit, videbat, Caes. **2.** Transf. **a.** To introduce a comparison : *as it were :* ut sese splendore animi et vitae suae sicut speculum praebeat civibus, Cic. ; Enn., etc. **b.** To introduce an example : *as, as for instance :* quibus in causis omnibus, sicut in ipsā M'. Curi, fuit summa de iure dissensio, Cic. ; Enn., etc. **c.** *just as, exactly as,* us. with esso : sicut eram fugio, Ov. ; Tib. ; Liv., etc. **d.** *as if, just as if (cf.* quasi) : sicuti iurgio lacessitus foret, in senatum venit, Sall.

Sicyōn, ōnis, *f. the capital of Sicyonia, in N.E. Peloponnesus, famous for its school of art ;* **Sicyōnius,** a, um ; **Sicyōnii,** ōrum, *m. pl. its inhabitants.*

sidereus, a, um [sīdus], *of or containing constellations or stars.* **1.** Lit. : aethra, Verg. ; caelum, Ov. ; sedes, Verg. ; dea (i.e Nox), Prop. ; ignes, Ov. **2.** Transf. *heavenly, divine :* (Aeneas) sidereo flagrans clipeo et caelestibus armis (but perh. *starry, star-spangled*), Verg.

Sidicīni, ōrum, *m. pl. a people of Campania whose chief town was* Teanum ; **Sidicinus,** a, um.

sidō, sidere, sidi or sēdi, sessum [*cf.* Gk. ἵζω, and sedeō], *to seat oneself, to settle, alight* **1.** Lit. : viridi solo, Verg. ; quaesitis terris, ubi sidere detur, Ov. ; columbae super arbore, Verg. **2.** Transf. **a.** Of things : *to sink down, settle, subside :* sidebant campi, Lucr. ; sederunt medio terra fretumque solo, Ov. ; nebula campo, Liv. ; in toto pallia lecto, Prop. ; montes, Tac. **b.** *to stick fast :* csca tibi, Hor. ; glans librata, Liv. Of ships : cumbae, Liv. ; Tac. ; vadis navis, Prop. **c.** *to sink down, to sink out of sight :* non flebo in cineres arcem sedisse paternos Cadmi, Prop. **d.** sidento paulatim metu, Tac.

Sidōn, ōnis, *f. an ancient and celebrated Phoenician city ;* **Sidōnius,** a, um, *Sidonian ;* also *Phoenician ;* also (because

Thebes in Boeotia was said to have been founded by Cadmus), *Theban ;* **Sidōnii,** iōrum, *m. pl. the Sidonians ;* **Sidōnicus,** a, um ; **Sidōnis,** idis, *f. adj.*

sīdus, eris, *n. a group of stars, a constellation.* **1.** Lit. **A.** Prop. : Lucr., Caes., Cic., Verg., etc. In *pl.* of a single constellation : Arcturi sidera, Verg. **B.** *a heavenly body* in gen. : Cic., Ov., etc. **C.** In partic. **a.** To denote time or season : quo sidere terram vertere conveniat, Verg. ; hiberno sidere, Verg. ; Ov. ; aequinocti, Tac. **b.** Of weather : triste Minervae, Verg. ; grave sidus et imbrem vitare, Ov. ; patrium, Plin. Pan. **c.** In relation to a sea-voyage : tot sidera emensae, Verg. **d.** In astrology : sidera natalicia, Cic. ; adveniet fausto cum sidere coniunx, Cat. ; vivere duro sidere, Prop. ; pestifero sidere icti, Liv. ; grave, Ov. **2.** Transf. **A.** In *pl.* **a.** *the sky, the heavens :* (Hercules) flammis ad sidera missus, Juv. ; evertunt actas ad sidera pinos, Verg. ; Prop. ; Curt. **b.** Of fame or fortune : tuum nomen cantantes sublime ferent ad sidera cycni, Verg. ; Hor. ; Ov. **B.** Of any beautiful or glorious thing : sidere pulchrior ille, Hor. ; o sidus Fabiae, Maxime, gentis ades, Ov. ; Curt. As term of endearment : Hor., Suet.

siem, siēs, etc., *v.* sum.

Sigambri (Sicambri, Sygambri, and **Sugambri),** ōrum, *m. pl. a powerful people of Germany ;* **Sigamber,** bra, brum ; **Sigambra,** ae, *f. a Sigambrian woman.*

Sigēum, ī, *n. a promontory in Troas, and a town of the same name, where Achilles was buried, now* Yenishehr ; **Sigēus,** a, um, *Sigean.*

sigilla, ōrum, *n. pl.* [*dim.* signum]. *little figures or images :* Cic., Hor., Ov. Of the impression made by a seal-ring, *a seal :* Cic., Hor. [Fr. *sceau* fr. sing. form sigillum.]

sigillātus, a, um [sigilla]. *adorned with little images or figures :* acyphi, Cic.

signātor, ōris, *m.* [signō]. *a sealer, signer.* **I.** *a witness to a will :* falsus, Sall., Juv. **II.** *a witness to a marriage-contract :* Juv.

signātus, a, um. **I.** *Part.* signō. **II.** Adj. *sealed, secured :* Varr., Prop.

Signia, ae, *f. a town in Latium, now Segni ;* **Signīnus,** a, um ; **Signīnī,** ōrum, *m. pl. its inhabitants.*

signifer, era, erum [signum ferō]. **I.** *bearing signs, figures, or images :* puppis, Luc. **II.** *bearing the heavenly signs or constellations, starry :* aether, Lucr. ; orbis, Cic. **III.** *Masc.* as Noun. **1.** Lit. : *a standard-bearer, ensign :* Caes., Cic., Liv., Ov. **2.** Transf. : nostrae causae, Cic. ; coniurationis, Suet.

significāns, antis. **I.** *Part.* significō. **II.** Adj. : of style, *expressive, graphic, distinct, clear :* Quint. Of orators : Quint. *Comp. :* Quint.

significanter, *adv. clearly, graphically :* Quint. *Comp. :* Cic. Ep., Quint.

significātiō, ōnis, *f.* [significō], *an indicating by a sign ; a signal.* **A.** In gen. : ignibus significatio factā, Caes. ; gestus sententiam non demonstratione sed significatione

declarans, Cic. ; clamore victoriae fit significatio, Caes. ; voluntatis, Cic. ; in *pl.* : Cic.
With *Subj.* GEN. : ex significatione Gallorum. Caes. ; litterarum, Cic. With ACC.
and *Inf.* : Cic. **B.** In partic. **a.** *a sign or
token* of assent or approval : ut ex ipsā
significatione potuit cognosci, Caes. ; populi iudiciis atque omni significatione
florere, Cic. In *pl.* : Liv. **b.** Rhet. :
significance, emphasis : Cic., Quint. **c.**
Gramm. : *meaning, signification* : Cic.,
Quint.

significō, āre [signum faciō], *to make signs ;
to show, indicate, make known by signs.* **A.**
In gen. : significare inter sese coeperunt,
Cic. ; Pl. ; ut fumo significabatur, Caes. ;
de fugā Romanis, Caes. ; aliquid alicui,
Pl., Cic. ; deditionem, Caes. ; stultitiam,
Cic. ; timorem fremitu, Caes. ; aliquid per
gestum, Ov. With ACC. and *Inf.* : Caes.,
Cic. With *Indir. Quest.* : Cic. Ep., Ov.
With *ut* and *Juss. Subj.* : Caes. **B.** In
partic. **a.** *to betoken, foreshow, portend* :
futura, Cic. ; quid haec tanta celeritas
significat ? Cic. ; quid sibi significent,
trepidantia consulit exta, Ov. ; Tac.
b. *to mean, signify* : verba aliud, Varr. ;
Cic. Of a fable : Phaedr.

signō, āre [signum], *to mark, incise, inscribe,
imprint, stamp.* **1.** Lit. **A.** In gen. **a.**
With ACC. of thing marked and usually
Instr. ABL. : cubitum longis litteris, Pl. ;
limite campum, Verg. ; moenia aratro,
Ov. ; plumam sanguine, Ov. ; carmine
saxum, Ov. ; locum ubi cistella excidit,
Pl. Also, cruor signaverat herbam, Ov.
b. With ACC. of mark and ABL. of place
(with or without *in*) : caeli regionem in
cortice, Verg. ; summo vestigia pulvere,
Verg. ; nomina saxo, Ov. Hence of things :
(aliquid) quasi signabit in animo suam
speciem, Cic. **B.** In partic. **a.** *to mark
with a seal ; to seal, seal up* : libellum, Cic.
Ep. ; tabellas, Tib., Ov. ; epistulam,
Nep. ; volumina, Hor. ; testamentum,
Plin. Ep. **b.** *to mark with a stamp ;* hence,
to stamp, coin : aes argentum aurumve,
Cic. ; pecunia signata Illyriorum signo,
Liv. ; cur navalis in aere altera (forma)
signata est, Ov. **2.** Transf. **a.** *to stamp,
impress* : memori pectore nomen, Ov. ;
fama signata loco est, Ov. ; nomen (Caieta)
ossa signat, Verg. ; pater ipse suo superum
(GEN.) iam signat honore, Verg. ; vocis
infinitos sonos paucis notis, Cic. **b.** *to
mark, note, observe :* aliquem oculis, Verg. ;
ora sono discordia, Verg. ; Ov. **c.** *to seal,
attest :* iura, Prop. ; vota, Plin. Ep. **d.** *to
seal* and so end : Mart.

signum, I, *n.* **I.** In gen. : *a mark, sign,
token, indication :* signa ostendam haec
(crepundia), Ter. ; signa et notas locorum,
Cic. ; pecori signum impressit, Verg. ;
oculis mihi signum dedit ne sciret, Pl. ;
dicere deos gallis signum dedisse cantandi,
Cic. ; metam constituit signum nautis
unde reverti scirent, Verg. With GEN. :
pudoris, Ter. ; mortis, Lucr. ; timoris,
Caes. ; doloris, Cic. ; servitii, Ov. ; signa
sequendi, Verg. **II.** In partic. **A.** Milit.
a. *a standard, ensign* (esp. of the cohorts
and maniples) : Caes., Cic., Liv., etc. ;

militaria, Caes., Hor., Liv., etc. Phrases
(in which signa can often be translated by
troops, men, ranks, etc.) : signa subsequi,
to keep in order of battle, Caes. ; sequi,
Sall., Liv. ; observare, Sall. ; servare,
Liv. ; ab signis discedere, *to leave the ranks,*
Caes., Liv. ; signa relinquere, Sall., Liv. ;
deserere, Liv. ; signa ferre, *to break up
camp,* Caes., Liv. ; ferte signa in hostem,
advance to the attack, Liv. ; movere, Verg.,
Liv. ; convellere, Liv. ; Verg., Liv. ;
signa inferre, *to advance to the attack,* Caes.,
Cic., Liv. ; proferre, Liv. ; signa convertere, *to wheel or face about,* Caes., Liv. ;
in hostem obvertere, Liv. ; signa conferre
(cum aliquo), *to engage or begin a battle,* Pl.,
Cic., Liv., etc. ; but also, *to bring the standards together, to concentrate troops,* Caes.,
Liv. ; constituere, *to halt,* Caes. ; statuere,
to post troops, Liv. ; signa transferre, *to
desert,* Caes. ; signa hostium turbare, Liv. ;
sub signis ducere legiones, ire, esse, *in
regular order,* Pl., Liv., etc. ; ante signa,
in front of the army, Liv. ; post signa, Liv.
b. *a watchword, password :* Tac., Suet.
B. *a signal* given by a flag, trumpet, etc.
a. Milit. : proeli signum exposcere, Caes. ;
signum tubā dare, Caes. ; proeli committendi dare, Caes. ; recipiendi dare, Caes. ;
receptui dare, Liv. ; signum dare ut etc.,
Liv. ; concinere, Caes., Liv. ; canere,
Sall., Liv. **b.** In gen. : for a chariot-race
to begin : Enn., Liv. ; for rites to begin :
Verg. **C.** Of a *prognostic* or other *warning
or symptom :* equus concidit ; nec eam
rem habuit religioni, obiecto signo, ne committeret proelium, Cic. ; morborum, Verg. ;
prospera, Ov. **D.** *an image, figure, statue,
picture, engraving, design.* **a.** In gen. :
Pl., Lucr., Cic., Verg., etc. **b.** On a signet-
ring ; hence *a seal :* Pl., Cic., Hor., etc.
E. Of the heavenly signs or bodies, *a
constellation :* Lucr., Cic., Verg., etc.
[It. *segno.*]

Sila, ae, *f.* *an extensive forest-range in the
country of the Bruttii.*

silānus, I, *m.* [σιληνός, Dor. σιλανός], *a
fountain or jet of water* (usually gushing
from a head of Silenus) : Lucr.

Silarus, I, *m.* *a river forming the boundary
between Lucania and Campania, now the
Sele.*

silēns, entis. **I.** Part. sileō. **II.** Adj. *still,
calm, silent :* nox, Verg., Liv., etc. ;
agmen, Liv. ; lucus, Verg. ; umbrae, i.e.
the dead, Verg. **III.** silentēs, um, *m. f.
pl.* the dead : Ov. ; also of the Pythagoreans,
Ov.

silentium, I, *n.* [sileō], *a being still or silent,
stillness, silence.* **1.** Lit. **a.** In gen. :
taciturna silentia, Lucr. ; huic facietis
fabulae silentium, *keep silence,* Pl. ; nec
longa silentia feci, Ov. ; silentium habere,
Sall. ; tenere, obtinere, Liv. ; Ov. ; tenere
se intra silentium, Plin. Ep. ; cum silentio
animadvertere, Ter. ; cum silentio audire,
Liv. ; silentio audire, Caes. ; audire magno
silentio, Cic. Ep. ; silentio praeterire, Cic. ;
Tac., etc. ; agere per silentium, Ter. ;
silentium significare, *to call for silence,*
Cic. ; silentium facere, *to make or obtain
silence,* Cic., Liv. ; ipse conticuit et ceteris

silentium fuit, Cic. ; alta silentia rumpere,
Verg. ; furto silentia demere, Ov. **b.**
During the taking of auspices, etc. : Cic.
In *pl.* : Verg. **2.** Transf. **a.** Of Nature :
stillness : Enn. ; in silentio noctis, Caes. ;
silentio noctis, Caes., Liv. ; per silentium
noctis, Liv. ; silentia noctis, Lucr. ; silentia
ruris, Ov. ; lunae, Verg. **b.** *tranquillity,
inactivity* : iudiciorum ac fori, Cic. ; inter
armatos, Liv. **c.** Perh. *obscurity* (i.e. from
not being spoken about) or *freedom from
notoriety* : vitam silentio transire, Sall. ;
praeturae, Tac.

Silēnus, i, *m.* **I.** *the tutor and constant
attendant of Bacchus, represented as old and
bald-headed, with short horns and a flat nose,
mounted on an ass and usually drunk.*
II. *a Greek historian of Sicilian and Roman
affairs.*

sileō, ēre, ui, *to be still or silent, to keep silence*
(implying a cessation of all noise). **1.**
Lit. : Pl., Liv., Ov. ; de nobis, Cic. ;
(*Impers. Pass.* : de iurgio silotur, Ter. ;
Cic.). With Acc. : haec omnia, Cic. ; te,
Hor. ; fortia facta, Ov. ; in *Pass.* : ea
res siletur, Cic. ; Liv. ; Ov., etc. ; silenda
(*Neut. pl.* of Ger. Adj. as Noun), *things
not to be spoken of*, i.e. mysteries, Liv.
With *Indir. Quest.* : Ov., Liv. **2.** Transf.
a. Of Nature : *to be hushed or still* : in-
tempesta nox, Verg. ; aequor, Verg. ;
late loca, Verg. ; immotae frondes, Ov.
b. *to be hushed, to remain inactive, to rest,
cease* : legos inter arma, Cic. ; ambitus,
Cic. ; ceterae nationes, Tac. **c.** With
Acc. : *to leave unmentioned or unnoticed* :
te, Verg. ; si chartae sileant quod bene
feceris, Hor. In *Pass.* : Cic.

siler, eris, *n. a kind of brook-willow, an osier* :
Verg.

silēscō, ere [sileō], *to become hushed and still* :
hae turbae, Ter. ; caeli furor, Cat. ; Verg. ;
venti, Ov.

silex, icis, *m.* (*f.* : Verg., Ov., etc.) *a pebble-
stone, a flint, flint-stone.* **1.** Lit. : Cic.,
Verg., Liv., etc. With lapis : Pl., Liv.,
etc. With saxum : Liv. **2.** Transf. **a.**
a rock, crag, cliff : Lucr., Verg., etc. **b.** Of
hard-heartedness : non silice nati sumus,
Cic. ; Tib. ; Ov.

silicernium, i, *n. a funeral feast.* Transf.
of an old dry-bones : Ter.

silīgō, inis, *f. a kind of very white wheat, winter-
wheat.* **1.** Lit. : Cato, Varr. **2.** Transf.
fine wheaten flour : Juv.

siliqua, ae, *f. a pod or husk of leguminous
plants.* **1.** Lit. : Varr., Verg. **2.**
Transf. (in *pl.*) : *pulse* : Hor., etc.

Silius, a, *the name of a Roman gens* ; **Siliānus**
a, um. Esp. C. Silius Italicus, *epic poet,
author of a poem called* Punica, *the subject of
which is the Second Punic War* : 1st cent. A.D.

silō, ōnis, *m.* [silus], *one who has a snub-
nose* : Pl.

silphium, i, *n.* [σίλφιον], *the plant laser-
picium* : Cato.

Silūres, um, *m. pl. a warlike British people
in South Wales.*

silūrus, i, *m.* [σίλουρος], *a river-fish, prob. the
sheat-fish* : Plin., Juv.

silus, a, um, *having a broad, turned-up nose,
snub-nosed* : Cic.

silva (poet. **silua** as trisyl.), ae, *f.* [*cf.* ὕλη].
1. Lit. **a.** *a wood, woodland, the bush* (in
sing. and *pl.*) : Enn., Lucr., Cic., Verg.,
etc. **b.** *a tree* (mostly in *pl.*) : Verg.,
Prop., etc. **2.** Transf. **A.** *a shrubbery*,
a. Of wild tangled growth : Verg., etc.
b. Of a cultivated garden : Cic., Nep.,
Hor. **B.** Of any crowded mass, *a forest,
crop, growth.* **a.** Of darts in a shield :
Verg. Of hair : Juv. **b.** Abstract : silvae
satis ad rem, Pl. ; ubertas et quasi silva
dicendi, Cic. ; virtutum et vitiorum, Cic.
c. As the title of a book : Quint. [It.
selva.]

Silvānus, i, *m.* [silva], *the god of woods and
plantations.* In *pl.*, *the gods of the woodlands.*

silvāticus, a, um [silva]. **I.** *used for*
(lopping) *trees* : falces, Cato, Varr. **II.**
growing or running wild : pirus, Cato,
Varr. ; sus, Varr. [Fr. *sauvage.*]

silvēscō, ere [silva]. Of the vine, *to run to
wood* : Cic.

silvestris, e, *adj.* [silva], *overgrown with
woods, wooded* : *living in woods, woodland-.*
1. Lit. : collis, Caes. ; locus, Cic., etc. ;
antra, Ov. ; homines, Hor. ; belua, Cic. ;
Lucr. ; virgulta, Verg. ; bellum, Lucr.
Neut. pl. as Noun, *woodlands* : Liv. **2.**
Transf. **a.** Of plants and animals, *growing
wild, wild* : arbor, Verg. ; corna, Hor. ;
oliva, Ov. ; tauri, Plin. *Comp.* : Plin.
b. For agrestis, *sylvan, rural, pastoral* :
Lucr., Verg.

silvicola, ae, *m. f.* [silva colō], *inhabiting
woods, sylvan* : Faunus, Verg. ; Pales, Ov.

silvi-cultrix, icis, *f. adj.* [silva colō], *living
in the woods* : cerva, Cat.

silvifragus, a, um [silva frangō], *breaking
the forest or trees* : fiabra venti, Lucr.

Silvius, i, *m. the name of several kings of* Alba
Longa.

silvōsus, a, um [silva], *wooded* : sa tus,
Liv.

simia, ae, *f.* [prob. from simus], *an ape.*
1. Lit. : Pl., Cic., etc. **2.** As a term of
abuse : vide, ut fastidit simia ! Pl. ; Plin.
Ep. [It. *scimmia* ; Fr. *singe.*]

similis, e, *adj.* [*cf.* ἅμα, simul], *like, resembling, similar* : Pl., Cic., Verg., etc. With
Gen. (most freq.) : Pl., Lucr., Cic., etc. ;
narrationem veri similem, *probable*, Cic.
With Dat. : Pl., Cic., Ov., etc. With
inter : homines inter se cum formā tum
moribus similes, Cic. ; Ov. With *atque*
(ac), *et* or *ut si, tamquam si* : ut simili
ratione atque ipse fecerit suas iniurias
persequantur, Caes. ; Cic. ; nec similem
habeat vultum et si ampullam perdidisset,
Cic. *Comp.* : Pl., Cic., etc. *Sup.* similli-
mus, Pl., Cic., Ov., etc. *Neut.* **simile**, is,
as Noun. **a.** *a likeness, comparison, parallel
case* : Cic., Quint. **b.** *resemblance* : Quint.

similiter, *adv. in like manner, similarly* :
Pl., Cic. *Comp.* : Phaedr. *Sup.* : simil-
limē, Cic. With *atque* (ac), *ut si* : similiter
ut si dicat, Cic. ; simillime atque ut illā
lege, Cic. With Dat. : Liv.

similitūdō, inis, *f.* [similis], *likeness, resemblance.* **A.** In gen. **a.** Cic., Liv., etc. ;
in *pl.* : Cic. With *cum* : est homini cum
deo similitudo, Cic. With Gen. : id ex

similitudine floris lilium appellabant, Caes. ; Cic., etc. With *inter :* in his inter ipsos, Cic. **b.** *imitation :* Cic., Tac. **B.** In partic. **a.** Of style : *sameness, monotony :* Cic. **b.** Rhet. *analogy :* Cic. **c.** Rhet. *a comparison, simile :* Cic., Quint.

similō, v. simulō.

simiolus, ī, m. [*dim.* simius], *a little ape,* as a term of abuse : Cic. Ep.

simitu, adv. [old form, *cf.* simul], *together, at the same time :* Pl. With *cum :* cum eo simitu mitti, Pl.

simius, ī, m. [*cf.* simia], *an ape.* Transf. of an imitator : Hor.

Simoīs, oentis, m. *a small river in Troas, which falls into the Scamander.*

Simōnidēs, is, m. **I.** *a celebrated lyric poet of Ceos,* about B.C. 500. **II.** Simonides of Amorgos, *an iambic poet, who lived in the seventh century,* B.C.

simplex, icis (ABL. us. simplicī ; simplice, Lucr.), adj. ["*one-fold,*" for sem-plex (v. semel), from plicō], *single, simple, uncompounded, unmixed.* **1.** Lit. **a.** In gen.: argumentum, Ter. ; aut simplex est natura animantis aut concreta ex pluribus naturis, Cic. ; res aperta et simplex, Cic. ; officium, Cic. ; via mortis, Verg. ; aqua, Ov. ; verba, Quint. *Comp. and Sup.* : Quint. **b.** *in single file :* decem lembi simplici ordine intrarunt urbem, Liv. ; Tac. **2.** Transf. **a.** *plain, ordinary, natural, without elaboration :* esca, myrtus, ius, Hor. ; simplex munditiis, Hor. ; genus mortis (i.e. without torture), Liv. **b.** In moral sense : *single-minded, artless, open, frank, ingenuous :* vir apertus et simplex, Cic. ; Ov., etc. Of things : regio, Cic. ; animal, Ov. ; cogitationes, Tac. *Comp.* : Hor. *Sup.* : Sen.

simplicitās, ātis, f. [simplex], *simpleness, simplicity.* **1.** Lit. : Lucr., Plin. **2.** Transf. *plainness, frankness, candour :* Liv., Ov., etc.

simpliciter, adv. *simply, plainly.* **1.** Lit. : Cic. ; quidam ludere eum simpliciter, quidam haud dubie insanire aiebant, Liv. *Comp. :* Plin. **2.** Transf. **a.** *simply, without art or elaboration, straightforwardly :* dicere, Cic. ; frondes positae, Ov. **b.** *artlessly, openly, frankly, candidly :* Cael. ap. Cic. Ep. ; Plin. Ep., etc. *Comp. :* Quint., Tac., etc. *Sup. :* Tac.

simplus, a, um [v. simplex and duplus], *simple.* As Noun, **simplum,** ī, n. *the simple sum or number :* solvere, Pl. ; duplum simplum, Cic. ; imperare, Liv. **simpla,** ae, f. (sc. pecunia), *the simple purchase-money :* Varr.

simpulum, ī, n. *a small ladle* (for libations). Prov. : excitare fluctūs in simpulo (*cf.* "to make a storm in a teacup"), Cic.

simpuvium, ī, n. *a bowl* for libations : Cic., Juv.

simul, adv. [v. similis], *at once, together, at the same time.* **A.** In gen.: ambo in saxo simul sedent, Pl. ; Zmyrnae cum simul ossemus, Cic. ; tres simul soles effulserunt, Liv. Strengthened with *unā* : i mecum unā simul, Pl. With *cum :* quas ·(res) tecum simul didici, Cic. ; Pl. ; Hor., etc. With simple ABL. : simul nobis habitat,

Ov. ; Hor. ; Tac. With *et, ut, si* etc. : ut crosceret simul et neglegentia cum audaciā hosti, Liv. ; Sall., etc. ; militibus simul et de navibus desiliendum, et in fluctibus consistendum, et cum hostibus erat pugnandum, Caes. ; Liv., etc. Also to introduce an independent sentence : alterum ipse efficiam ut attente audiatis ; simul illud oro, etc., Cic. ; Pl. ; Caes., etc. ; also more freq. simul et, Pl., Caes., Cic., Liv., etc. **B.** In partic. **a.** simul . . . simul, *as well . . . as, both . . . and :* ad eum in castra venerunt, simul sui purgandi causā, simul ut de indutiis impetrarent, Caes. ; Verg. ; Liv. **b.** **simul āc** or **atque** ; also (rarely) **simul ut** (and perh. **simul et**), and **simul** (alone), with *Perf.* or *Fut. Perf., as soon as :* Pl., Caes., Cic., Liv., Verg., etc.

simulācrum, ī, n. [simulō], *a likeness, image, form, representation.* **1.** Lit. **a.** In art : deorum, Caes., Cic., Verg., etc. ; Herculis, Liv. ; oppidorum, Cic. ; pugnarum, Liv. ; montium, fluviorum, Tac. Of the Trojan horse : Verg. **b.** *a copy* (e.g. a sham-fight) : belli simulacra cientes, Lucr. ; Verg. ; in portu simulacrum navalis pugnae edit, Liv. ; vindemiae, Tac. **2.** Transf. **a.** *a dream-figure ; a form of the living or the dead ; an apparition, phantom :* Lucr., Verg., Ov. **b.** *the form of an object as presented to the mind, a conception :* Lucr. **c.** *a sign, type, emblem :* ut simulacris pro litteris uteremur, Cic. **d.** *a portraiture of character :* Liv. **e.** *a likeness or similitude :* Pl. **f.** Of things : *a mere ghost or shadow of its former self :* simulacrum aliquod ac vestigium civitatis, Cic. Ep. ; simulacra virtutis, Cic. ; libertatis, Tac.

simulāmen, inis, n. [simulō], *a copy, imitation :* Ov.

simulāns, antis. **I.** *Part.* simulō. **II.** Adj. *imitating, imitative. Comp.* with GEN. : Ov.

simulātē, adv. *feignedly, pretendedly :* Cic.

simulātiō, ōnis, f. [simulō], *a false show,· a pretence, hypocrisy :* Ter., Cic., etc. ; in *pl.* : Tac. With GEN. : insaniae, Cic. ; rei frumentariae, Caes. ; cum simulatione timoris agere, Caes. ; muliones equitum specie ac simulatione collibus circumvehi iubet, Caes. ; Cic. ; Tac. ; per simulationem amicitiae me prodiderunt, Cic.

simulātor, ōris, m. [simulō]. **I.** *a copier, imitator :* figurae, Ov. **II.** *a pretender, counterfeiter :* Tac. ; in omni oratione simulatorem Socratem accepimus, i.e. *fond of irony,* Cic. With GEN. : animus cuius roi libet simulator ac dissimulator, Sall. ; Luc. ; Tac.

simulō, āre [similis], *to make like (to).* **A.** In gen. : *to copy, imitate, represent :* nimbos et fulmen, Verg. ; cupressum, Hor. ; aera Alexandri vultum simulantia, Hor. ; corpora igni simulata, Lucr. ; Verg. With *Acc.* and *Inf.* : Pallas simulat terram edere fetum olivae, Ov. **B.** *to take or put on the appearance of :* Pallas anum, Ov. ; aegrum Hannibal, Liv. ; sanum, Ov. In *Pass. Part., made like, in the likeness of :* Homeri illa Minerva simulata Mentori, Cic. Ep. **C.** *to counterfeit, feign, pretend*

a thing to be what it is not : Ter., Cic. Ep.,
Sall., etc. ; experiar quid simules, Pl. ;
pacem, Cic., Sall. ; deditionem, Sall. ;
obsequium, constantiam, Tac. ; non simu-
latur amor, Ov. ; simulatā amicitiā, Caes. ;
officio simulato, Cic. ; simulatā mente,
Verg. With Acc. and *Inf.* : Pl., Cic., Ov.,
etc. With *quasi* : Pl., Curt. [It. *sem-
brare* ; Fr. *sembler.*]

simultās, ātis, *f.* (GEN. *pl.* simultātium, freq.
in Liv.) [simul, and therefore orig. *a coming
together, an encounter*], *a hostile encounter,
dissension, rivalry, feud* : Pl. ; sibi privatam
simultatem cum Campanis nullam esse,
Liv. ; Cic. ; cum aliquo in simultate esse,
Nep. ; simultatem deponere, Cic. Ep.
Mostly in *pl.* : Caes., Ov. ; simultates
cum aliquo habere, exercere, Cic. ; Liv. ;
suscipere, Cic. ; provocare, gerere, Quint. ;
facere, nutrire, Tac. ; finire, dirimere,
oblitterare, Liv.

simulus, a, um [*dim.* simus], *rather flat-
nosed* or *pug-nosed* : Lucr.

simus, a, um [*cf.* σιμός], *flat-nosed, snub-
nosed* : capellae, Verg. ; Plin.

sin, *conj.* [sī nē], *if however, if on the contrary,
but if.* **A.** After *si, nisi, quando, dum* :
si domi sum, foris est animus ; sin foris
sum, animus domi est, Pl. ; si ita est,
faciat, sin aliter, respondeat mi, Ter. ;
accusator illum defendet, si poterit ; sin
minus poterit, negabit, Cic. Strengthened
with *autem*, or *vero* : Pl., Cic., etc. After
nisi, quando, and *dum* : Pl. **B.** Without
a preceding *si*-clause : orat ac postulat
rem publicam suscipiant. sin timor ede-
fugiant, etc., Caes. Strengthened with
autem (or *vero*) : Caes., Cic.

sināpi, is, *n.* (**sināpis**, *f.* Pl.) (σίναπι,
mustard : Plin. [Fr. *sénevé.*]

sincērē, *adv. honestly, frankly* : dicere, Ter. ;
loqui, Cat. ; Caes.

sincēritās, ātis, *f.* [sincērus], *cleanness,
soundness.* **1.** Lit. : olei, Plin. **2.**
Transf. : Sen., Phaedr.

sincērus, a, um, *clean, sound, untainted,
pure, uninjured, whole, real, genuine.* **1.**
Lit. : porci sacres, Pl. ; tergum (i.e. free
from weals), Pl. ; membra, Lucr. ; corpus
(sine vulnere), Ov. ; vas, Hor. ; gens,
populus, Tac. *Neut. pl.* as Noun : omnia
fucata et simulata a sinceris atquo veris
(internoscere), Cic. **2.** Transf. : iudicium, Cic. ; Minerva, Ov. ; nobilitas, Liv. ;
fides, gaudium, Liv. ; concordia, Tac. ;
equestre proelium, Liv. ; vir, Sen. Ep.

sinciput, pitis, *n.* (and **sincipitāmentum**,
i, *n.* Pl.) [sēmi caput], *half a head.* **1.**
Lit. of the smoked *cheek* or *chap* of a hog :
Pers., Juv. **2.** Transf. *the brain* : Pl.

sindōn, onis, *f.* [σινδών], *a fine fabric of cotton*
or *linen, muslin* : Mart.

sine, *prep.* with ABL. *without* : tu sine pennis
vola, Pl. ; non sine magnā spe, Caes. ; ut
urbs sino regibus sit, Cic. ; Verg., etc. ;
sine impensā operā, Liv. After its case :
flammā sine turo liquescere, Hor. [It.
senza ; Fr. *sans.*]

singillātim, *adv.* [obsol. singillus from sin-
gulus], *one by one, singly* : singillatim
potius quam generatim atquo universe
loqui, Cic. ; Ter. ; Lucr., etc.

singlāriter, *adv., v.* singulāriter.

singulāris, e, *adj.* [singulus], *alone, one at a
time, single.* **1.** Lit. **a.** In gen. : non
singulare nec solivagum genus (sc. homines),
Cic. ; ubi aliquos singularis ex navi egredientis conspexerant, Caes. ; potentia, i.o.
absolute power, Nep. ; imperium, Cic. **b.**
Gramm. *of the singular number* : casus,
Varr. ; numerus, Quint. **c.** As Noun.
singulārēs, ium, *m. pl. a special kind of
troops*, perh. *a select body-guard* : Tac.
2. Transf. *unique, unparalleled* : Aristoteles in philosophiā, Cic. ; virtutis opinio
singularis, Caes. ; virtus, innocentia, etc.,
Cic. In a bad sense : nequitia ac turpitudo, Cic. [Fr. *sanglier.*]

singulāriter, *adv.* (contr. **singlāriter**, Lucr.).
1. Lit. **a.** *singly, separately* : Lucr. **b.**
Gramm. *in the singular number* : Quint.
2. Transf. *particularly, exceedingly* : aliquem diligere, Cic. ; Plin. Ep.

singulārius, a, um [singulāris], *single,
separate* : catenae, Pl.

singultim, *adv.* [singultus], *with sobs* or
gasping. Transf. : loqui, i.e. falteringly,
Hor.

singultiō, īre [singultus], *to sob* or *gasp
spasmodically.* Transf. *to throb* with
pleasure : vena, Pers.

singultō, āre [singultus]. **A.** Intrans. *to
sob* or *gasp spasmodically, to gurgle.* **1.**
Lit. **a.** Of speakers : Quint. **b.** Of per-
sons in their death-agony : Verg. **2.**
Transf. : truncus sanguine, Verg. **B.**
Trans. *to sob* or *gasp out* : animam, Ov.

singultus, ūs, *m. a sobbing* or *spasmodic
gasping* or *gurgling.* **a.** Of speech interrupted by sobs : Lucr., Cic., Ov., etc. In
pl. : Cat., Hor., Ov. **b.** Of persons in
their death-agony : Verg. **c.** Of water :
Plin. Ep. [It. *singhiozzo* ; Fr. *sanglot.*]

singulus, a, um [for *sen-culu-s* : *v.* semel],
one by itself or *separately, single, one at a
time, one by one.* **a.** In gen. : singulum
video vestigium, Pl. ; Varr. Usually in
pl. : honestius eum agrum vos universi
quam singuli possideretis, Cic. ; Pl. **b.**
one each, one apiece : duodena in singulos
homines iugera, Cic. ; filiae singulos filios
parvos habentes, Liv. ; in dies singulos,
every day, daily (with *Comp.,* or words
denoting increase or decrease) : crescit in
dies singulos hostium numerus, Cic.

Sinis, is, *m. a cruel robber on the Isthmus of
Corinth, who was said to have killed his
victims by fastening them to two trees bent
down and then left to recover their position ;
he was killed by Theseus.*

sinister, tra, trum (*Comp.* sinisterior). *on
the left hand* or *side.* **1.** Lit. : cornu, Ter.,
Caes. ; pars, Caes. ; manus, Nep. ; ripa,
Hor. ; pes, bracchium, etc., Quint. *Comp.* :
Ov., Suet. As Noun. **sinistrī**, ōrum, *m.
pl.* (sc. milites) : Liv. **sinistrum**, i, *n.*
(sc. latus), *the left side* : reicere a sinistro
togam, Quint. **sinistra**, ae, *f.* **a.** (sc.
manus) *the left hand* : sinistrā impedita
satis commode pugnare non poterant,
Caes. ; Ov. etc. **b.** (sc. pars) *the left side,
the left* : aspice nunc ad sinistram, Pl. ;
sub sinistrā Britanniam relictam conspexit,
Caes. ; cur a dextrā corvus, a sinistrā

cornix faciat ratum? Cic. **2.** T r a n s f. **A.** *wrong, perverse* : liberalitas, Cat. ; mores, Verg. ; Tac. **B.** *unfavourable, injurious* : arboribus satisque Notus pecorique sinister, Verg. ; interpretatio, Tac. ; fama *or* sermones de aliquo, Tac. ; Ov. *Neut.* **sinistrum** as Noun : Ov. **C.** In augury. **a.** *auspicious, lucky* (because the Romans in taking the auspices turned the face towards the south, and so had the eastern or fortunate side on the left): sinistra cornix, Verg. ; tonitrus, Ov. ; Cic. **b.** Sometimes (following Greek custom) *inauspicious* : approbatio, Cat. ; omen, Ov. Perh. also, fulmen, Cic.

sinisteritās, ātis, *f.* [sinister], *awkwardness, perversity* : Plin. Ep.

sinistrē, *adv. badly, unfairly, wrongly, perversely* : Hor., Tac.

sinistrōrsus (Caes.) and **sinistrōrsum** (Hor.), *adv.* [contr. from sinistrŏvorsus, from sinister versus (*v.* vertŏ)], *towards the left side, to the left.*

sinō, sinere, sīvi (siī, Ter.), situm (Syncop. *Perf.* sīstī, Pl. ; *Perf. Subj.* sīris, sirit, etc., Pl., Liv. ; *Plup. Subj.* sisset, Cic., Liv.) [*cf.* pōnŏ], *to set down, leave, let.* **1.** L i t. **a.** In gen. : neu propius tectis taxum sine, Verg. ; sinite arma viris et cedite ferro, Verg. (*v.* also situs). **b.** *to found, build* (only in *Perf. Part.*) *:* urbem a Philippo sitam, Tac. **2.** T r a n s f. **A.** In gen. : *to leave, let, allow, permit, suffer* : Pl., Cic., Ov. With Acc. : id nos non sinemus, Ter. ; Ov. With Acc. of Object and *Inf.* : sine loqui me, Pl. ; Cic. ; Verg., etc. ; vinum ad se importari, Caes. ; latrocinium in Syriam penetrare, Cic. ; in *Pass.* : accusare eum moderate non est situs, Cic. With *Predic. Adj.* : morem inultum sinere, Liv. With *Juss. Subj.* : sine sciam, Liv. ; Pl. ; Verg., etc. **B.** In partic. **a.** Colloq. *let it be, let:* pulchre ludificor, sine, Pl. ; sine veniat, Ter. ; insani feriant sine litora fluctūs, Verg. **b.** sine modo, *only let,* i.e. *if only* (with *Subj.*): Pl. **c.** ne di sirint (sinant), ne Iuppiter sirit, *God forbid, Heaven forefend!* Pl. ; ne istuc Iuppiter sirit, Liv. ; Plin. Ep.

Sinōn, ōnis, *m. s. of Aesimus, through whose treachery the Trojans were induced to take the wooden horse inside Troy.*

Sinōpē, ēs (**-a,** ae), *f. a famous Greek colony on the S. coast of the Euxine, birthplace of Diogenes the Cynic, and residence of Mithridates ;* **Sinōpēnsēs,** ium, *m. pl. its inhabitants;* **Sinōpeus,** a, um, *of Sinope* : Pl. ; Cynicus, i.e. *Diogenes,* Ov.

Sinuessa, ae, *f. a border city of Latium, on the confines of Campania ;* **Sinuessānus,** a, um.

sinum, *v.* sīnus, ī, *m.*

sinuō, sinuāre [sinus], *to wind, curve, bend, arch :* angues volumine terga, Verg. ; anguis corpus in orbis, Ov. ; equus alterna volumina crurum, Verg. ; arcum, Ov. ; muri introrsus sinuati, Tac. ; donec Chaucorum gens in Chattos usque sinuetur, Tac.

sinuōsus, a, um [sinus], *full of windings, curves,* or *folds :* winding, sinuous. **1.** L i t. : Verg., Ov., Plin., etc. **2.** T r a n s f. *roundabout, intricate :* Quint.

sinus, ūs, *m. a curved or bent surface, a curve, fold.* **I.** In gen. : draco conficiens sinūs e corpore flexos, Cic. poet. ; Ov. ; sinu ex togā facto, Liv. Of a net : Pl. ; *a seine-net,* Juv. Of a bellying sail : Verg., Ov., Quint., etc. Of hair, *a curl, ringlet :* Ov. **II.** In partic. **A.** *the hanging fold of the upper part of the toga, the bosom* of a garment used as a pocket. **1.** L i t. : Cic., Verg., etc. P r o v. : sinu laxo ferre aliquid (i.e. to be careless about a thing), Hor. **2.** T r a n s f. **a.** *the bosom* or *lap* of a person : Ter., Liv., Ov., etc. **b.** *Abstractly, the bosom,* i.e. *loving care, protection :* Ter. ; in sinu et complexu alicuius esse, aliquem habere, Cic. ; suo sinu complexuque aliquem recipere, Cic. ; negotium sibi in sinum delatum esse dicebat, Cic. ; falsa in sinu avi perdidicerat, Tac. **c.** *the inmost part :* intra moenia atque in sinu urbis sunt hostes, Sall. ; Tac. **d.** Of a secret place or hiding-place : ut in sinu gaudeam, Cic. ; in tacito cohibe gaudia clausa sinu, Prop. ; abditis pecuniis per occultum aut ambitiosos sinūs, Tac. **e.** *a purse* (which was carried in the bosom of the toga): Prop., Ov., Sen., etc. **f.** Also of any flowing garment : Tib., Ov. **B.** *a bay, bight, gulf.* **1.** L i t. : Caes., Cic., Verg., etc. **2.** T r a n s f. of the land forming a gulf ; *a bend or curve of coast :* Liv., Tac. **C.** *a curve in land, a hollow :* Arpini terra in ingentem sinum consedit, Liv. ; montium, Curt. [It. *seno ;* Fr. *sein.*]

sinus, ī, *m.* (**sinum,** ī, *n.*), *a large round drinking-vessel :* Pl., Verg.

siparium, ī, *n.* [cogn. with supparum, σίπαρος, orig. *a little sail*]. **I.** *the smaller curtain in a theatre, the "act-drop"* (drawn up between the scenes of a comedy : *v.* aulaeum). **1.** L i t. : Cic., Juv. **2.** T r a n s f. *comedy :* Sen. **II.** *a curtain or screen over judges' seats :* Quint.

siphō (**sīfō**), ōnis, *m.* [σίφων, *a small pipe*]. **I.** *a siphon,* called also diabetes : Lucil., Sen., Juv., etc. **II.** *a fire-engine :* Plin. Ep.

siphunculus, ī, *m.* [dim. sīphō], *a small pipe of a fountain* : Plin. Ep.

Sipylus, ī, *m. a mountain in Lydia, on which Niobe was changed into stone.*

si quandō (**sīquandō**) and **si quidem** (**sīquidem** ; siquidem, Ov.), *v.* sī.

siqui, siquis, *v.* quī, quis.

siremps and **sirempse,** *adj.* [from sī (*cf.* sīc) rem ipsam], *like, the same :* sirempse legem iussit esse Iuppiter, Pl. ; Sen. Ep.

Sirēnes, um, *f. pl. the Sirens,* or *sea-nymphs who had the power of charming by their songs all who heard them ; they lived off the S.W. coast of Italy.* T r a n s f. (in *sing.*) : improba Siren desidia, Hor.

siris, sirit, etc., *v.* sīnō.

Sīrius, ī, *m.* [σείριος], *the dog-star, Sirius :* Verg., Tib. As *Adj.* : ardor, Verg.

sirpe, is, *n.* [σίλφιον], *a plant* (also called silphium, laser: Pl.)

sīrus, ī, *m.* [σιρός], *a pit for corn, an underground granary :* Curt.

sīs. I. *Subj.* of sum. **II.** Colloq. contr. of sī vīs, *if you please, v.* volŏ. **III.** Old form of suīs, *v.* suus.

Sisenna, ae, *m.* **I.** L. Cornelius, *a Roman annalist, born about* B.C. 118. **II.** *a notorious slanderer in Rome :* Hor.

sistō, sistere, stitī, statum [fr. root *sta*, with reduplication ; *cf.* ἵστημι]. **I.** T r a n s. **A.** In gen. : *to cause to stand, to set, put, place :* monstrum sacratā arce, Verg. ; me in vallibus Haemi, Verg. ; eum in Syriā, Tac. ; suem ad aram, Verg. ; victima sistitur ante aras, Ov. ; huc sororem, Verg. Of an army : Verg., Tac. With *Refl. Pron. :* hic dea se primum rapido nisu sistit, Verg. ; Cic. Ep. With *Predic. Adj. :* ego vos salvos sistam, Pl. ; Cat. ; Verg. ; Liv. **B.** As law-court term : *to produce in court ;* and in *Pass.* (or *Mid.*), or with *Refl. Pron., to present oneself, appear.* **1.** L i t. : Cic., Liv., etc. ; vadimonium sistere, *to make good one's recognisances,* Cic., Nep. **2.** T r a n s f. : Cic. ; of a lover's appointment : Pl. ; of an appointment with the hangman : Pl. **C.** *to stay, stop* a moving object. **1.** L i t. : aquam fluviis, Verg. ; equos, Verg. ; invehentem se iam Samnitem, Liv. ; gradum, Verg., Curt., etc. ; iter, Tac. ; sanguinem, Tac. ; se ab effuso cursu, Liv. **2.** T r a n s f. : lacrimas, querellas, labores, etc., Ov. ; ruinas, Plin. Pan. ; pretia (i.e. increasing prices), Tac. **D.** *to set up, set firmly, make fast.* **1.** L i t. : effigiem, Tac. **2.** T r a n s f. : rem Romanam, Verg. With *Predic. Adj. :* servitio vacuum me, Prop. ; Pl. **E.** (Only in *Perf. Part.*) *to establish, fix definitely :* status dies, Pl. ; stato loco statisque diebus, Liv. ; Tac., etc. ; statum sacrificium, Cic., Liv. ; stata sacra, Ov. **II.** I n t r a n s. **A.** *to set oneself, to stand, rest :* Verg. ; capite, Pl. ; in terrā terra, Lucr. **B.** In law : *to present oneself* in court, *to appear :* Cic. **C.** *to stop, stay :* Verg., Tac. **D.** *to stand fast, to last, endure :* res publica, Cic. ; Lucr. Also *to stand firm* against attack : sistere contra, Verg. With *Dat. :* inruenti turbae, Tac. E s p. *Impers. Pass.* (freq. in Liv.) : plebem aere alieno demersam esse nec sisti posse nisi etc., Liv. ; Pl. ; Tac.

sistrātus, a, um [sistrum], *bearing a sistrum :* Mart.

sistrum, ī, *n.* [σεῖστρον], *a metallic rattle* used by the Egyptians in the rites of Isis, etc. ; perh. *a tambourine* or *timbrel.* **a.** In gen. : Ov., Juv., etc. **b.** In war : Verg., Prop.

Sisyphus, ī, *m. s.* of Aeolus, *king of Corinth, notorious for his robberies and cunning. He was killed by Theseus ; and his punishment in Hades was to roll to the top of a hill a stone which constantly rolled back again ;* **Sisyphius**, a, um ; **Sisyphidēs**, ae, *m. a male descendant of Sisyphus, i.e. Ulysses.*

sitella, ae, *f.* [dim. situla], *a kind of urn used in drawing lots* when partly filled with water : Pl., Cic., Liv.

Sithonii, iōrum, *m. pl. a Thracian tribe;* hence in gen. *the Thracians ;* **Sithonius**, a, um ; **Sithōn**, onis, *adj. Thracian ;* **Sithonis**, idis, *f. adj. ;* also as Noun, *a Thracian woman.*

siticulōsus, a, um [sitis]. **I.** *thirsty, dry :* Apulia, Hor. **II.** *thirst-producing :* Plin.

sitiēns, entis. **I.** *Part.* sitiō. **II.** Adj. *thirsting, thirsty.* **1.** L i t. : Cic., Hor., Ov., etc. **2.** T r a n s f. **a.** Of places, plants, etc. : *dry, parched, arid :* Ov., Plin. Also, Afri, Verg. **b.** *parching :* Canicula, Ov. **c.** Of capacity : modice sitiens laguena. Pers. **d.** *athirst,* i.e. *eager :* Cic., Ov. With GEN. : virtutis, Cic.

sitienter, *adv. thirstily,* i.e. *eagerly :* Cic.

sitiō, īre [sitis]. **A.** I n t r a n s. *to thirst, be thirsty.* **1.** L i t. : Pl., Lucr., Suet. P r o v. : sitire mediis in undis, Ov. **2.** T r a n s f. of dry or parched land and plants : Cic., Verg., etc. **B.** T r a n s. *to thirst for* or *after.* **1.** L i t. : patrium Salonem, Mart. In *Pass. :* Ov., Plin. **2.** T r a n s f. of eager desire : sanguinem nostrum, Cic. ; libertatem, Cic.

sitis, is, *f. thirst.* **1.** L i t. : Pl., Verg., etc. ; sitim potione depellere, Cic. ; sitim explere, Cic., Ov. ; sedare, Lucr., Ov., Plin., etc. ; restinguere, Verg. ; exstinguere, Ov. ; pellere, finire, Hor. ; levare, relevare, compescere, Ov. ; stimulare. facere, accendere, adferre, Plin. ; sitis guttur urit, Ov. **2.** T r a n s f. **a.** Of dry or parched land and plants : deserta siti regio, Verg. ; Tib. **b.** Of eager desire (with *Obj.* GEN.) : libertatis, Cic. ; argenti, Hor. ; cruoris, Ov. ; audiendi, Quint.

sititor, ōris, *m.* [sitiō], *a thirster for* or *after :* aquae, Mart.

sittybus, ī, *m. a strip of parchment, attached to a roll or book, bearing the title and the author's name :* Cic. Ep.

situla, ae, *f.* (**situlus**, ī, *m.* Cato), *a bucket :* Pl. Used for drawing lots (*cf.* sitella) : Pl.

situs, a, um. **I.** *Part.* sinō. **II.** Adj. (from sense " *allowed to lie,*" as in aqua sita siet horam unam, Cato), *lying, situated,* **1.** L i t. **a.** In gen. : aurum in latebris, Pl. ; Romuli lituus in curiā Saliorum, Cic. Rarely of living persons : amicos procul iuxtaque sitos, Sall. ; nobilissimi Britanniae in ipsis penetralibus siti, Tac. More freq. of the dead : C. Mari sitae reliquiae, Cic. ; Aeneas super Numicium flumen, Liv. E s p. on epitaphs : hic situs est, Tib. **b.** Of geographical situation : locus in mediā insulā situs, Cic. ; Liv. **c.** *founded, built* (*v.* sino). **2.** T r a n s f. **a.** In gen. : *placed, lying :* in melle sunt linguae vostrae, Pl. ; quae ceteris in artibus sita sunt, Cic. ; voluptates in medio, Cic. **b.** *resting, dependent* (on) : huiusce rei potestas omnis in vobis sita est, Cic. ; Pl. ; qui spes omnis in fugā sita erat, Sall. ; Archiae, quantum est situm in nobis, opem forre debemus, Cic. ; est situm in nobis ut etc., Cic. : in officio colendo sita vitae est honestas, Cic.; laus in medio, Tac.

situs, ūs, *m.* [sinō]. **I.** In geography and topography : *lie, position, situation.* **1.** L i t. **a.** In gen. : urbis, Caes., Cic., Liv. ; terrae, Cic. ; Africae, Sall. ; agri, Hor. ; urbes naturali situ inexpugnabiles, Liv. In *pl.* : Caes., Cic., etc. **b.** Of the body, etc. : figura situsque membrorum, Cic. ; revocare situs foliorum, Verg. **2.** T r a n s f. **a.** *structure :* pyramidum, Hor. **b.** *a region :* meridianus, Plin. **II.** *a lying* *neglected, neglect, filth* or *mould arising from neglect.* **1.** Lit.: corrumpor situ, Pl. ; araneosus, Cat. ; loca senta situ, Verg. ; immundus, Prop., Ov. ; en ego victa situ, Verg. ; et segnem patiere situ durescere campum, Verg. ; arma squalere situ, Quint. **2.** Transf. of the mind : *neglect, want of use, etc.* : senectus victa situ, Verg. ; marcescere otio situque civitatem, Liv. ; Ov. Also, verborum, Sen. Ep. ; Hor.

sive (older **seive**), and **seu**. *conj.* [si ve], *or if.* **A.** Introducing an alternative condition. **a.** With a preceding *si :* si ego volo seu nolo, Pl. ; si omnes atomi declinabunt, sive aliae declinabunt, Cic. ; si arborum trunci sive naves essent a barbaris missae, Caes. **b.** Without a preceding *si :* bis denas Italo texamus robore navis, seu pluris complere valent, Verg. ; Ter. ; Quint., etc. **B.** Disjunctive. **a.** With alternative in repeated *sive* (or *seu*) clause : sive (seu) . . . sive (seu) *be it that . . . or that, whether . . . or :* sive timore perterriti, sive spe salutis inducti, Caes. ; Pl., etc. ; sive deae seu sint dirae volucres, Verg. ; Cimmeriis aspectum solis sive deus aliquis, sive natura ademerat, sive loci situs, Cic. **b.** With a corresp. *si :* sive immolaris, sive avem aspexeris ; si Chaldaeum si haruspicem videris, si fulserit, Cic. **c.** With another particle (*aut, vel, ne,* or *an*) : (saxum) seu turbidus imber proluit, aut annis solvit sublapsa vetustas, Verg. ; Tac. **d.** So, seu . . . seu without real conditional sense : hic mos seu consulto seu temere vulgatae opinioni fidem apud quosdam fecit, etc., Liv. **e.** Alone, *or :* flagitia Democriti seu etiam Leucippi, Cic. ; Liv. ; miracula visa sive ex metu credita, Tac.

smaragdus, *v.* zmaragdus.

smaris, idis, *f.* [σμαρίς], *a small sea-fish of inferior quality :* Ov., Plin.

smilax, acis, *f.* [σμῖλαξ], *bind-weed, a kind of convolvulus :* Plin. Personified, *a maiden changed into the convolvulus :* Ov.

Smintheus (disyl.), eī (Acc. Sminthea, Ov.), *m. an epithet of Apollo.*

Smyrna (Zm-), ae, *f. a town in Asia Minor.*

sobol-, *v.* subol-.

sōbriē, *adv. moderately, temperately.* **1.** Lit.: vivere, Cic. **2.** Transf. *sensibly, sanely :* Pl.

sōbriĕtās, ātis, *f.* [sōbrius], *temperance* in drinking : Sen.

sōbrīnus, ī, *m.* and **sōbrīna**, ae, *f.* [contr. for sororīnus from soror], *a cousin* by the mother's side : Pl., Cic., Tac.

sōbrius, a, um [perh. connected with ēbrius]. **1.** Lit.: *not drunk, sober :* Pl., Cic., Hor., etc. **2.** Transf. **a.** Of things : *without wine ; without excess of wine-drinking :* pocula, Tib. ; nox, Prop. ; convictus, Tac. ; rura, Stat. **b.** *sober, temperate, continent :* parcus ac sobrius, Ter. ; homines frugi ac sobrii, Cic. ; Hor. **c.** Of the mind : *sensible, sane, reasonable :* satin' sanus es aut sobrius ? Ter. ; vigilantes homines, sobrii, industrii, Cic. ; Ov.

socculus, ī, *m.* [dim. soccus], *a small soccus :* Sen., Suet. Worn by a comic actor : Quint., Plin. Ep.

soccus, ī, m. = *a kind of low-heeled, light shoe* worn by the Greeks ; *a slipper.* **a.** In gen.: Pl., Cic., Cat. ; worn by effeminate Romans : Suet. **b.** *the low shoe worn by comic actors :* Ov. Hence, *comedy :* Hor., etc.

socer (NOM. **socerus**, Pl.), erī, *m.* [*cf.* ἑκυρός], *a father-in-law.* **1.** Lit.: Pl., Cic., Ov., etc. In *pl.*, soceri, *parents-in-law :* Verg., Ov. **2.** Transf.: *a son's father-in-law :* Ter.

sociābilis, e, *adj.* [sociō], *capable of union, compatible :* consortio inter reges, Liv.

sociālis, e, *adj.* [socius], *of partners* or *allies.* **a.** Of States or peoples : lex, Cic. ; foedus, exercitus, etc., Liv. ; equitatus, Tac. ; bellum, Juv. **b.** Of man and wife : amor, iura, sacra, etc., Ov. **c.** *sociable :* homo sociale animal, Sen.

sociāliter, *adv. in a sociable way :* Hor.

sociennus, ī, *m.* [socius], *a fellow, comrade :* Pl.

sociĕtās, ātis, *f.* [socius], *companionship, partnership, association, alliance.* **a.** In trade or business : gerere, Cic. ; quae pecunia tibi ex societate debeatur, Cic. ; rerum, quae in Galliā comparabantur, Cic. For farming the taxes : nulla Romae vectigalium, Cic. ; provinciarum, Caes. ; in *pl.* : Cic. **b.** Of States : cum rege facere, Caes. ; Ambiorigem sibi societate adiungere, Caes. ; in societate manere, Nep. ; societatem alicuius induere, Tac. ; belli, Sall. **c.** In gen. : Enn. ; generis humani, Cic. ; cum aliquo inire, coire, dirimere, Cic. ; conflare, confirmare, Cic. With *Obj.* GEN.: consiliorum omnium, Cic. ; beate vivendi, Cic.

sociō, āre [socius], *to join together* or *unite, to associate :* coetūs hominum iure sociati, Cic. ; omne genus hominum sociatum inter so, Cic. ; periculum vitae tuae mecum, Cic. ; Tib. ; quae nos domo socias, Verg. ; se alicui vinclo iugali, Verg. ; Liv. ; verba chordis, Hor. ; Ov. ; sociati parte laboris functus, Ov. In *Mid.* : sociari facinoribus, Liv.

sociofraudus, ī, *m.* [socius fraudō], *a comrade-deceiver :* Pl.

socius, a, um [fr. root of sequor], *accompanying.* **I.** *acting in union, joint, allied, leagued, confederate :* reges, Cic. ; agmina, Verg. ; urbs, Liv. ; classis, Ov. ; cohortes, Tac. As Noun, **socius**, ī, *m.* and **socia**, ae, *f. a companion, partner, ally.* **a.** In trade or business : Cic. Of the *company* of tax-farmers : Cic. Ep. **b.** Polit. Of States, peoples, etc. : *an ally, confederate :* Pl., Cic., Liv., etc. ; Boios receptos ad se socios sibi asciscunt, Caes. E sp. *the Italian allies :* socii et Latini or socii et nomen Latinum, Cic., Liv., etc. ; socii navales, Liv. But, socii Latini nominis, *the Latin allies,* Liv. **c.** In gen. : Cic., Verg., etc. ; socium ad malam rem quaerere, Pl. ; tuorum consiliorum, Pl. ; Cic. ; Hor. ; tori, generis, sanguinis, Ov. ; alicui socius, Pl. ; hos castris adhibe socios, Verg. ; Romuli socius in Sabino proelio, Cic. **II.** *held in union, held in common, joint, common :* consilia, Cic. ; regnum, lectus, templum, sepulcrum, etc., Ov.

sŏcordia (sēcordia), ae, *f.* [sōcors]. **I.**
weakmindedness, silliness, folly, stupidity :
Suet. **II.** *apathy, indolence, inactivity* :
Pl., Sall., Liv., Tac.

sŏcordius, *comp. adv.*, *more or too apatheti-
cally* : Sall., Liv., Tac.

sŏcors, ordis, *adj.* [sŏ cor]. **I.** Intellectually : *weak-minded, senseless, stupid* :
Cic., Liv. ; animus, ingenium, Tac. **II.**
apathetic, inactive, indolent : Pl., Sall., Tac.
With GEN. : ceterarum rerum, Ter. ;
futuri, Tac.

Sŏcrătēs, is, *m.* *a celebrated Athenian philosopher, put to death* B.C. 399 ; **Sŏcrăticus**,
a, um ; **Sŏcrătici**, ōrum, *m. pl.* *the Socra-
tics, or disciples of Socrates.*

socrus, ūs, *f.* [v. socer], *a mother-in-law* :
Ter., Cic., Ov., etc.

sodālicium, ĭ, *n.* [sodālis], *fellowship, intimacy, companionship.* **1.** L i t. : Cat.
2. Concr. *an association, society* (esp.
unlawful) : Cic.

sodālicius, a, um [sodālicium], *of fellowship
or companionship* : iure sodalicio mihi
functus, Ov.

sodālis, is, *m. f.* [perh. fr. root of Gk. ἔθος],
a mate, fellow, intimate, comrade. **a.** In
gen. : Pl., Cic., Ov., etc. As *Adj.* : turba,
Ov. ; Hebrus, Hor. **b.** *a member of a
society, priestly college, etc.* : sodales in
Lupercis, Cic. ; sodales Augustales, Tac.
c. *a member of an unlawful association* :
Pl., Cic. **d.** *a gallant* : Mart.

sodālitās, ātis, *f.* [sodālis], *fellowship, companionship, brotherhood.* **1.** L i t. : Cic.,
Tac. **2.** Concr. **a.** *a society, club* : Pl.
In *pl.* : Cic. **b.** *a society, association*,
esp. for relig. purposes : Lupercorum, Cic.
c. *an unlawful association or society* : Cic.

sodālitium, sodālitius, v. sodālic-.

sōdēs [contr. from sī audēs = avidēs], *if you
will, please, with your leave* (colloq. and
mostly with *Imperat.*) : dic sodes mihi,
bellan' videtur specie mulier ? Pl. ; iube
sodes nummos curare, Cic. ; vescere sodes,
Hor.

sōl, sōlis, *m.* [cf. Gk. σέλας], *the sun.* **1.**
L i t. **a.** In gen. : Pl., Lucr., Cic., Verg.,
etc. ; surgente a sole, Hor. ; oriente sole,
Caes. ; solis occasu, Caes., Liv. ; ad
(sub) solis occasum, Caes. ; sole orto, Liv.
b. Geogr. oriens sol (or solis ortus),
the east ; occidens sol (or solis occasus),
the west : Caes., Cic., Liv., etc. **2.**
T r a n s f. **a.** *sunlight, sunshine, warmth of
the sun, a sunny place* : sol semper hic
est a mani ad vesperum, Pl. ; in sole
ambulare, Cic. ; iter in calescente sole
factum erat, Liv ; patiens pulveris atque
solis, Hor. ; Ov. In *pl.* : Lucr., Verg.,
Plin., etc. T r a n s f. : in solem ac pulverem procedere (opp. to umbra eruditorum), Cic. ; cedat stilus gladio, umbra
soli, Cic. **b.** *a day* : Lucr., Verg., etc.
c. Of a great man : Cic. **d.** Personified, *the Sun* (*-God*) : Pl., Cic., Ov., etc.

sŏlăciolum, ĭ, *n.* [dim. solācium], *a little
comfort or solace* : doloris, Cat.

sŏlācium, ĭ, *n.* [sōlor], *a soothing, assuaging ;
a comfort, solace, relief* : haec sunt solacia,
haec fomenta summorum dolorum, Cic. ;
Verg. ; hoc sibi solaci proponebant, Caes. ;

alicui dare, adferre, praebere, Cic. ; surdae
adhibere menti, Ov. ; suae morti invenire,
Liv. ; aliquem adficere solacio, Tac. ; id
solacio est, Pl., Caes. ; aves, solacia ruris,
Ov. ; annonae, Cic.

sŏlāmen, inis, *n.* [sōlor], *a comfort, solace* :
mali, Verg.

sōlāris, e, *adj.* [sōl], *of the sun ;* lumen, Ov.

sōlārium, ĭ, *n.* [sōl]. **I.** *a sun-dial.* **1.**
Lit. : Pl., Varr. Hence of the place in
the Forum where the sun-dial stood : ad
solarium, Cic. **2.** T r a n s f. *a clock* in gen. :
Cic. **II.** perh. *a sunny spot, terrace,
balcony* : Pl., Suet.

sōlāt-, v. sōlāc-.

sōlātor, ōris, *m.* [sōlor], *a comforter, consoler* :
Tib. ; lugentum, Stat.

soldūrii, ōrum, *m. pl.* [a Celtic word],
retainers of a chieftain : Caes.

soldus, a, um, v. solidus.

solea, ae, *f.* [solum], *a covering for the soles
of the feet, a sole or sandal* (worn by men
in the house only and taken off at meals).
1. L i t. : demere, Pl. ; deponere, Mart. ;
cēdo soleas mihi ; auferte mensam, Pl. ;
poscere, Hor. ; festinare, Sall. **2.** T r a n s f.
a. *a kind of fetter* : ligneae, Cic. **b.** *a
kind of* (removeable) *shoe* for animals : Cat.,
Suet. **c.** *a flat fish, a sole* : Ov., Plin. In
pun : Pl.

soleārius, ĭ, *m.* [solea], *a sandal-maker* :
Pl.

soleātus, ĭ, *m.* [solea], *wearing sandals* :
Cic., Mart.

sōlemni-, v. sollemni-.

sŏleō, sŏlēre, sŏlitus, *to be accustomed, be in
the habit.* **a.** In gen. : artior quam solebat
somnus amplexus est, Cic. ; sic soleo, Ter. ;
Pl. ; quod plerumque in atroci negotio
solet, Sall. ; cum quaedam in collibus, ut
solet, controversia pastorum esset orta,
Cic. ; Pl. *Pres. Part.* freq. in Plautus with
sum : mala femina es. solens sum ; ea est
disciplina, Pl. With *Inf. :* Pl., Cic.,
Verg., etc. **b.** *to have carnal intercourse
with :* cum viris, Pl., Cat. ; Maeciliam,
Cat.

sōler-, sōlic-, v. soller-, sollic-.

sŏlidē, *adv.* *firmly, securely.* T r a n s f. :
id scire, Pl., Ter.

sŏliditās, ātis, *f.* [solidus], *solidity* : corporum, Cic.

sŏlidō, āre [solidus], *to make firm, compact,
or dense :* area cretā solidanda, Verg. ;
aedificia, Tac. [Fr. *souder*.]

sŏlidus (soldus), a, um [cf. Gk. ὅλος], *firm,
dense, compact, solid.* **1.** L i t. : Ter., Cic.,
Ov., etc. ; crateres auro solidi, Verg.
Sup. : Lucr., Ov. *Neut.* as Noun, *a solid
substance, solid ground, etc. :* Cic., Verg.,
Liv., etc. **2.** T r a n s f. **a.** *whole, complete,
entire :* stipendium, Liv. ; solida taurorum
viscera, Verg. ; vires, Verg. ; dies, Hor. ;
annus, Liv. *Neut.* as Noun, *the whole sum :*
ita bona veneant, ut solidum suum cuique
solvatur, Cic. ; Hor., etc. **b.** *firmly-
grounded, sound, firm, genuine, real :*
solida et perpetua fides, Pl. ; Tac. ; solida
et robusta frequentia, Cic. ; iudicia solida
et expressa, Cic. ; solida veraque laus,
Cic. ; suavitas austera et solida, Cic. ;
mens, Hor. ; libertas, Liv. ; gratia, Pl.,

Ov. *Neut.* as Noun ! quidus ex rebus mini
est, quod solidum tenere possis, Cic. ; in
solido, *in safety*, Verg.

sōliferreum, i, *n.* [sōlus ferrum], *a missile
made entirely of iron :* Liv.

sōlistimus, a, um [sōlus stō], *full, complete*
(only with tripudium, q.v.) : Cic., Liv.

sōlitārius, a, um [sōlus], *alone, lonely,
solitary :* natura solitarium nihil amat,
Cic. ; solitarius homo atque in agro vitam
agens, Cic. ; vita, Quint.

sōlitūdō, inis, *f.* [sōlus], *loneliness, solitari-
ness.* **a.** Of persons : Ter., Cic., Sall.
b. Of places : Caes., Cic., Liv., Tac. ; in
pl. : Caes., Cic. With GEN.: in hac omnis
humani cultūs solitudine, Curt. **c.** *a being
left alone, a state of want, deprivation :* Cic. ;
huius (orbae) : Ter. ; liberorum, Cic. ;
magistratuum, Liv.

solitus, a, um. **I.** *Part.* soleō. **II.** Adj.
accustomed, wonted, usual, habitual : torus,
Tib. ; virtus, Verg. ; opus, locus, artes,
etc., Ov. ; honores, Tac. With DAT. :
armamenta Liburnicis, Tac. *Neut.* as
Noun : solitum quicquam liberae civitatis,
Liv. ; praeter solitum, Verg., Hor. ; ultra
solitum, Tac. ; esp. in ABL. with comparatives : solito formosior Aesone natus,
Ov. ; plus solito, Liv., Ov. ; magis solito,
Liv.

solium, i, *n.* [from root of sedeō ; *v.* solum].
I. *a seat ;* esp. *a seat* or *chair of state,
throne.* **1.** Lit. : Cic., Verg., Liv., etc.
2. Transf. *throne, i.e. rule, dominion :*
Lucr., Hor., Ov. ; in paterno solio, Liv. ;
Tac. **II.** *a tub,* esp. for bathing : Cato,
Lucr., Liv., etc. **III.** *a stone coffin, sarco-
phagus :* Suet. [It. *soglio.*]

sōlivagus, a, um [sōlus vagor], *roving alone.*
1. Lit. : bestiae, Cic. **2.** Transf. *single,
solitary :* cognitio, Cic.

sollemnis, e, adj. [O. Lat. sollus, q.v.,
annus], *annual, recurring, periodic.* **1.**
Lit. : sacra, Cato ; sacrificia, Cic., Liv. ;
dapes, Verg. ; statum iam ac prope sollemne in singulos annos bellum, Liv. **2.**
Transf. *established, stated.* **a.** In religion : *ceremonious, religious, solemn :*
sacra, Lucr., Sall. ; epulae, Cic., Tac. ;
ludi, Cic., Ov. ; iter ad flaminem, precatio
comitiorum, etc., Cic. ; vota, dona, arae,
etc. ; fax, vox, etc., Ov. ; habitus, Liv.
As Noun, **sollemne**, is, *n. a religious* or
solemn rite, feast, sacrifice : Liv. ; clavi
figendi, Liv. ; funeris, Tac. ; celebrare,
Tac. ; tumulo sollemnia mittere, Verg. ;
sollemnia eius sacri, Liv. ; nuptiarum,
Tac. **b.** Of recurrence only : *usual, wonted :* imperium, Verg. ; lascivia, Liv. ;
Romanis sollemne viris opus (venatio),
Hor. ; gloria, Phaedr. As Noun, **sollemne**,
is, *n. practice, usage :* nostrum illud sollemne servemus ut etc., Cic. Ep. ; mos
traditus ab antiquis inter cetera sollemnia
manet, Liv. ; Tac. As *Intern.* Acc. :
insanire putas sollemnia me, Hor.

sollemniter, adv. *in a religious* or *solemn
manner :* Liv.

sollers, ertis, adj. [O. Lat. sollus, q.v., and
root of ars, *cf.* iners], *skilled, skilful, clever,
expert.* **1.** Lit. (of persons) : Ter., Nep.,
Ov. ; in omni vel officio vel sermone, Cic.

Comp. : Cic. *Sup.* . Dalli Masti Pr. :
with *Inf. :* Hor., Ov. With Gen. : Muse
lyrae sollers, Hor. **2.** Transf. (of things) :
natura, descriptio, Cic. ; cor, Cat. ; custodia, Verg. ; animus, Liv. ; ingenium,
Ov. *Comp. :* Lucr., Cic. *Sup. :* Cato.

sollerter, adv. *skilfully, shrewdly, cleverly :*
Cic., Tac. *Comp. :* Cic., Ov. *Sup. :*
Cic.

sollertia, ae, *f.* [sollers]. *skill, shrewdness,
ingenuity :* Caes., Cic., Tib. ; ingeni, Sall. ;
of an *ingenious plan :* placuit sollertia,
Tac. With *Obj.* GEN. : agendi cogitandi-
que, Cic.

sollicitātiō, ōnis, *f.* [sollicitō], *an inciting,
tampering with* (the loyalty of) : Allo-
brogum, Cic.

sollicitē, adv. **I.** *with concern* or *solicitude :*
Sen. Ep. **II.** *carefully, diligently :* se cus-
todire, Sen. ; recitare, Plin. Ep. *Comp. :*
Plin. Ep. *Sup. :* Suet.

sollicitō, āre [sollicitus], *to stir thoroughly,
to shake, agitate, displace, disturb.* **1.** Lit. :
tela manu, Enn. ; mundum suis ex sedi-
bus, Lucr. ; tellurem, Verg. ; nequiquam
spicula dextrā sollicitat, Verg. ; Ov. ; Sen. ;
feras, Ov. **2.** Transf. *to rouse, excite,
disquiet, molest.* **a.** In gen. : erile scelus
me sollicitat, Pl. ; istuc facinus tuum animum, Pl. ; haec cura me, Cic. ; Verg. ;
de posteris sollicitor, Cic. ; rebellando nos
sollicitant, Liv. ; pacem, Liv. ; magnum
bello Iovem, Ov. ; cupidinem, Hor. ;
aliquem ad hoc opus, Quint. ; aliquem ad
emendum (signum), Plin. Ep. ; maritum
precibus ne etc., Ov. With *Inf. :* Lucr. ;
in *Pass.* : sollicitor putare, etc., Ov.
Rarely of the body : mala copia quando
aegrum sollicitat stomachum, Hor. **b.** Of
exciting to war, rebellion, etc. : *to incite,
tamper with :* civitates, Caes. ; aliquos,
Caes., Cic., etc. ; servum verbis, Cic. ;
Ov. ; pretio animos egentium, Cic. ; Liv. ;
pudicam fidem donis, Ov. ; opifices et
servitia ad Lentulum eripiendum, Sall. ;
Cic. ; ad transeundum hostia, Liv. With
ut and *Subj.* : civitates sollicitant ut in
libertate permanere vellent, Caes. ; Cic.
Ep. ; Liv. [Fr. *soucier.*]

sollicitūdō, inis, *f.* [sollicitus], *disquiet, care,
anxiety :* Pl., Cic., Hor., etc. ; aliquem
sollicitudine adficere, Ter. ; sollicitudinem
alicui adferre, struere, Cic. Ep. ; sustinere,
Cic. Ep. ; aliquem adficit, vexat sollicitudo,
Cic. ; in *pl. :* Ter., Cic., Hor. With *pro :*
Liv. With *Obj.* GEN. : nuptiarum, Ter.
With Acc. and *Inf. :* Liv. Also *a cause
of anxiety :* istaec mihi res sollicitudini 'st,
Ter. ; Pl.

sollicitus, a, um [sollus, q.v., and cieō],
wholly, i.e. violently or *continually moved,
stirred up, tossed.* **1.** Lit. : (aëris) motus,
Lucr. ; mare, Verg. ; rates, Ov. **2.**
Transf. **a.** Mentally : Pl., Cic., Verg.,
etc. ; initia belli sollicitam Italiam habebant,
Caes. ; Pl. ; Cic., etc. ; animus, Cic.,
Liv., Hor. ; mentes, pectus, Ov. With
ABL. : sollicitam civitatem suspicione,
Cic. ; Pl. ; Hor. With *de :* Cic. Ep.,
Liv. With *pro :* Cic., Tac. With *propter :*
Liv. With *ex :* Ter., Curt. With
vicem (q.v.) : Liv. With *ne* and *Subj. :*

Cic., Liv. With *Indir. Quest. :* Cic. Ep.,
Liv. *Comp. :* Sen., Tac. **b.** Of things :
cupiditas, amor, custodia, Cic. ; frons,
vita, etc., Hor. ; manus, senecta, fuga,
etc., Ov. ; animal (canis) ad nocturnos
strepitūs, Liv. ; Ov. *Comp. :* Sen., Quint.
Sup. : Sen. **c.** Occ. *disquieting :* Cic.,
Hor., Ov.

sollif-, sollist-, *v.* sōlif-, sōlist-.

sollus, a, um, an Oscan and old Lat. word
= totus, *whole :* Fest.

sōlō, āre [sōlus], *to make lonely ; to lay waste :*
urbes populis, Stat.

soloecismus, ī, *m.* [σολοικισμός], *a grammatical fault, a solecism:* Sen., Quint., Juv.

Solōn, ōnis, *m.* a *famous legislator of the
Athenians, one of the seven sages of Greece,
born about* 638 B.C.

sōlor, ārī [perh., through the notion of healing,
akin to salvus]. **I.** With person as
Object : *to comfort, console, solace :* aliquem, Cat., Verg., etc. ; diffidentem verbis
suis, Pl. ; Verg. ; posthabitam dote, Tac. ;
solantia verba, Ov. **II.** With thing as
Object : *to relieve, mitigate :* curas, metum,
Verg. ; Ov. ; cladem, Tac. ; laborem cantu,
Verg. ; fluviis aestum, Hor. ; Plin. Ep.

sōlstitiālis, e, *adj.* [sōlstitium], *of the summer-
solstice.* **1.** Lit. : metae, Lucr. ; dies,
orbis, Cic. ; tempus, nox, Ov. **2.** Transf.
a. *of midsummer or summer-heat :* herba,
morbus, Pl. ; tempus, Liv. **b.** *solar :*
annus, qui solstitiali circumagitur orbe,
Liv.

sōlstitium, ī, *n.* [sōl sistō], *the time when the
sun seems to stand still,* either in Cancer or
in Capricorn, *the* (summer- or winter-)
solstice. **1.** Lit. : Plin. Esp. of the
summer-solstice : Cato, Cic., etc. **2.**
Transf. *summer-time, the heat of summer :*
Verg., Hor., Ov., Sen.

solum, ī, *n.* [perh. *cf.* οὖδας], *bottom, ground,
floor.* **A.** In gen. **1.** Lit. : fossae, Caes. ;
(villarum) sola marmorea, Cic. ; Ov. ;
imum stagni, Ov. ; tremefacta solo tellus,
Verg. ; solo aequata omnia, Liv. ; clivus
Publicius ad solum exustus est, Liv. ;
Cereale solum (i.e. wheaten platter), Verg.
P o e t. *floor* of sea or heaven : tremit ictibus
aerea puppis, subtrahiturque solum, Ov. ;
astra tenent caeleste solum, Ov. **2.**
Transf. : regni, Enn. ; solum quoddam
atque fundamentum, Cic. ; solo aequandae
sunt dictaturae, Liv. **B.** *the sole* of the
foot or of a shoe : Pl., Lucr., Cic. **C.** Of
the earth (esp. as tilled) : *the surface,
soil.* **1.** Lit. : solum proscindere terrae,
Lucr. ; agri, Caes. ; terrae sola sanguine
maculans, Cat. ; solum exile et macrum,
Cic. ; incultum et derelictum, Cic. ; pingue,
putre, viride, Verg. ; fecundum, vivax,
etc., Ov. ; solum exercere sub vomere,
Verg. ; solo recubans, Verg. ; sola terrarum ultimarum, Cic. **2.** Transf. **a.**
one's country : solum, in quo tu ortus et
procreatus, Cic. ; Liv. ; patriae, Cic. ;
patrium, Liv. ; natale, Ov. ; solum vertere,
to leave one's country (of an exile), Cic. ;
Liv. **b.** In law : res soli, *land,* and all
that stands upon it, *real estate* (opp. to
res mobiles) : Sen., Plin. Ep. ; duas patrimoni partis in solo conlocare, Suet.

sōlus, a, um (GEN. regular. sōlīus ; DAT.
sōlī ; DAT. *f.* sōlae, Pl., Ter.), [*cf.* sollus],
alone, only, single, sole. **1.** Lit. **A.** In
gen. : cum omnibus potius quam soli
perire voluerunt, Cic. ; Pl. ; Ov., etc. ;
cognitionem sine consiliis per se solus
exercebat, Liv. ; ego meorum solus sum
meus, Ter. With numerals : te unum
solum venisse, Cic. ; Pl. ; cum solā decimā
legione iturum, Caes. *Neut.* Acc. **sōlum**
as *Adv. alone, only, merely, barely.* **a.**
Affirmatively : nos nuntiationem solum habemus ; consules etiam spectionem,
Cic. **b.** Negatively : non solum, nec
(neque) solum . . . sed (verum) etiam
(et), *not only . . . but also :* Cic., Hor.,
etc. ; non solum . . . sed paene, Caes. ;
non solum . . . sed ne quidem, Cic. (concerning the omission of negative in former
clause, *v.* non). **B.** *lonely, solitary, for-
saken :* sola sum ; habeo hic neminem.
Ter. ; Sall. ; Prop. **2.** Transf. of places,
etc. : *lonely, solitary :* Pl., Lucr., Cic.,
Verg., etc. [Fr. *seul.*]

solūtē, *adv.* [solūtus], *loosely.* **1.** Lit. :
corpora diffusa solute, Lucr. **2.** Transf.
freely, without hindrance, negligently : so-
lūte moveri ac libere, Cic. ; Liv. ; solutius
lascivire, Tac. ; solute dicere, Cic. ; Tac.

solūtilis, e, *adj.* [solvō], *that is easily loosed*
or *taken apart :* navis, Suet.

solūtiō, ōnis, *f.* [solvō]. **1.** Lit. **a.** *a
loosening, unloosing :* linguae, Cic. **b.** *payment :* iusti crediti, Liv. ; Cic. ; solutione
impeditā, Cic. In *pl.:* Caes. **2.** Transf.
a solution, explanation : Sen.

solūtus, a, um. **I.** *Part.* solvō. **II.** Adj.
unbound, loose. **1.** Lit. **a.** cum eos vin-
ciret, te solutum Romam mittebat ? Cic. ;
Pl. ; Liv. Also, *unbandaged :* Cic. **b.** Of
soil : *loose, friable :* Plin. *Comp. :* Sen.
Ep. **2.** Transf. **A.** *free* from obligations.
cares, etc. : Cic. ; omni faenore, Hor. ;
cā religione, Liv. ; ab omni sumptu, Cic. ;
animus, Cic. *Comp. :* Cic. With GEN. :
operum, Hor. **B.** *free* from punishment,
etc. : omne illud tempus habeat per me
solutum ac liberum, Cic. With *Inf. :*
maxime solutum fuit prodero etc., Tac.
C. *free* from restraint, *etc.* : homines,
Cic. ; Tac. ; civitatis voluntas, Cic. Ep. ;
iudicium senatūs, Cic. ; ab omni imperio
externo, Liv. ; orator in gestu, Cic. ;
risus, Verg. ; dicta factaque solutiora, Tac. ;
Sup. : Cic. In bad sense : populi, Cic. ;
P. Clodi praetura, Cic. ; licentia, amores,
Cic. ; libido solutior, Liv. **D.** *lax, negligent, weak :* Quint., Tac. *Comp. :* lenitas,
Cic. ; cura, Liv. **E.** Of style. **a.** *fluent :*
ad dicendum, Cic. **b.** *free* from rules of
composition : oratio, Quint. **c.** verba soluta *or* oratio soluta, *prose :* Cic. ; also,
verba soluta modis, Ov. **d.** *unrhythmical :*
Cic. **III.** *Neut.* as Noun, **solūtum,** ī,
a. *a state of looseness :* Sen. Ep. **b.** *a
discharged debt :* Sen.

solvō, solvere, solvī (solui, trisyl., Cat.,
Tib.), solūtum [sē luō], *to unloose, loosen,
untie, unbind, free, release.* **I.** With Acc.
of the thing fastened. **1.** Lit. (of persons
or material things). **a.** In gen. : aliquem,
Pl., Cic., Vorg., etc. ; opistulam, Nep.,

Ov.; vela, Verg.; ŏquum, Hor.; ʌɪrʌm; Verg., etc.; texta, Prop.; togam, Quint.; terrae solutae (i.e. from frost), Hor.; de rupe Promethei bracchia, Prop.; canem catenā, Phaedr. **Esp.** of ships: navim, Pl.; navis, Caes., Liv.; classem, Liv.; Prop.; navis a terrā, Caes.; Liv.; Luc.; navim e portu, Pl. Without navem or navis: Caes.; Cic. Ep.; a Brundisio, Liv. (v. also II. 1.). **b.** to dissolve, break up: membra ratis, Ov.; navis, Curt.; pontem, Curt., Tac. Of the action of Nature: tabes corpora, Lucr.; senectus omnia, Liv.; vitam, Prop., Sen. Ep. **Esp.** in Pass.: rigor auri solvitur aestu, Lucr.; viscera, Verg.; cerao igne, Ov.; (pluviā) nives, Ov.; herba, Plin.; terra in tabem, Sen. **2.** Transf. **a.** In gen.: to free from any restraint, obligation, care, etc.: te corpore, Verg.; corpore animam, Quint.; aliquem scelere, Cic.; Ov.; religione civitatem, Cic.; Hor.; me debito, Sen. Ep.; militiā, sacramento, Tac.; Iliensis publico munere, Tac.; eos curā, Cic.; Ter.; pectus curā, Lucr.; soluti metu, Liv.; formidine terras, Verg.; urbem obsidione, Liv.; me dementiā, Hor.; somno solutus, Cic.; in otia solvi, Prop.; animum, Hor., Sen.; tristis adfectūs, Quint.; frontem, Mart. With Inf.: ut manero solveretur, Tac. **b.** Of debt: rem solvere, to free one's estate, i.e. make payment: pro vecturā, Pl.; creditori, Liv. With Instr. Abl.: tergo, pugnis, Pl. With rem omitted: Liv.; pro vecturā solvere, Cic. Ep.; populo, Cic.; solvendo non erat, he was insolvent, Cic., etc.; Impers. Pass.: Pl., Cic. **c.** Of exemption from laws by privilege: legibus solvi, Cic., Liv., etc. Also, leti lege solutas, Lucr.; Verg.; Sen.; numeris lege solutis, Hor. Also, testamentis solvi, Cic. **d.** to dissolve, break up, separate, weaken, etc.: ordines, Liv., etc.; agmina diductis choris, Verg.; commissas acies, Prop.; convivium, Liv.; coetum, Ov.; urbem, Cic.; solutus luxu, Quint., Tac.; soluti in luxum, in lasciviam, Tac. Of sleep, sickness, etc. (esp. with Instr. Abl.): languentia membra, Lucr.; somno vinoque soluti, Verg.; Ov.; solvitur in somnos, Verg.; solvuntur frigore membra, Verg.; membra solvit sopor, Verg.; Ov.; segnitia oratorio animos (i.e. wearies), Quint. Of style: versum, etc., Quint. Of logical refutation: argumentum, Quint.; Cic. **II.** With Acc. of that which binds or ties. **1.** Lit. (of material things): zonam, cistulam, Pl.; vittas, Verg.; catenas, Ov.; fasciculum, Cic. Ep.; animāi nodos a corpore, Lucr.; bracchia a corpore, Ov.; corollas de fronte, Prop.; redimicula collo, Ov. Of ships: retinacula, Ov. With navis as Subject: naves ex superiore portu solverunt, Caes. **2.** Transf. **A.** In gen.: to discharge, get rid of, cancel by payment, pay, fulfil. **a.** Of debts: pecunias creditas, Caes., Cic.; pecuniam, Cic., Liv., etc.; pro frumento pecuniam (pretium), Cic., Liv.; stipendium, Liv.; dona, Ov.; aliquid praesens, to pay cash, Cic. Ep.; alicui pecuniam debitam, Cic.; Liv. Of moral debts:

cum patriae quod debui solvisse [illegible]; Liv. **b.** Of other obligations: omnia paterno funeri iusta, Cic.; iusta Remo, Ov.; exsequias, Verg.; suprema militibus, Tac.; vota, Cic., Ov., etc.; Voneri votum, Pl.; Ov.; Sen.; fidem, Ter., Ov.; iustas et debitas poenas, Cic.; Lucr.; capite poenas, Sall.; iniuriam, Ter.; nefas, culpam, Ov. **B.** to get rid of, remove, break down, weaken, etc. **a.** Of feelings, passions, etc.: animi curas e pectore, Lucr.; iram, pudorem, Verg.; corde metum, Verg. With Instr. Abl.: curam Lyaeo, Hor. Also of sleep: clamore soporem, Ov. **b.** Of restraints, obstacles, etc.: vim plebis, Sall.; imperium, Sall.; obsidionem, Liv., etc.; morem, Liv.; luxuriā disciplinam militarem, Liv. **c.** Of friendships, etc.: nodum amicitiae, Hor.; amores, Tib., Ov. Also, amicos, Prop. **d.** Of unravelling and solving difficulties: carmina non intellecta, Ov.; nodos iuris, Juv.; quaestiones, aenigmata, etc., Quint. [Fr. soudre.]

Solyma, v. Hierosolyma.

Solymus, i, m. a Trojan, the mythical founder of Sulmo.

somniculōsē, adv. sleepily: Pl.

somniculōsus, a, um [dim. somniculus, fr. somnus], drowsy, sleepy, sluggish: senectus, Cic.; glires, Mart.

somnifer, era, erum [somnus ferō], sleep-bringing, soporific. **1.** Lit.: Ov., Plin. **2.** Transf.: benumbing, deadly: venenum, Ov.; Luc.

somniō, iāre [somnium], to dream; to dream of or see in a dream. **1.** Lit.: Cic.; somnium, Pl., Cic.; ovum, Cic. With Acc. and Inf.: Pl., Cic. With de: Cic. **2.** Transf. to think idly, to talk foolishly: Pl., Cic.; aliquid, Pl., Cic.

somnium, i, n. [somnus], a dream. **1.** Lit.: Pl., Lucr., Cic., Verg., etc. **2.** Transf. **a.** Personified (in pl.): Cic., Ov. **b.** Of any whim, fancy, or nonsense: Ter. In pl.: Ter., Lucr., Cic., Hor. [It. sogno; Sp. sueño; Fr. songe.]

somnus, i, m. [for sopnus, v. sopor], sleep. **1.** Lit.: petere, Ov.; parere, conciliare, adferre, etc., Plin.; somnos invitare, Hor.; somnum capere, Pl.; videre, Ter., Cic.; somno se dare, Cic.; me artior somnus complexus est, Cic.; somno sepulti, Enn., Lucr.; somno oppressus, Caes.; somno vinctus, Liv., Ov.; somnum tenere, Cic.; somnos ducere, Verg.; in somnis (per somnum) aliquid videre, Pl., Cic., Verg., etc.; aliquem e (ex) somno excitare, suscitare, Cic.; somno solutus, Cic.; somnum adimere, avertere, Hor.; porturbare, Quint.; altus, Hor.; gravior, Plin.; intermissus, Quint. **2.** Transf. **a.** sloth, indolence: Cic., Sall., Tac. **b.** night: Verg. **c.** With longus, niger, frigidus, etc., of the sleep of death: Hor. **d.** Of the calmness of the sea: Stat. **e.** Personified: Verg., Ov. [It. sonno.]

sonābilis, e, adj. [sonō], sounding, noisy: sistrum, Ov.

soni-pēs, pedis, adj. [sonus], with sounding-feet, noisy-footed. As Noun, of a horse: Cat., Verg.

sonĭtus, ūs, *m.* [sonō], *a noise, sound, din :*
ungularum, Pl. ; armorum, ventorum,
Lucr. ; remorum, Caes. ; verborum, Cic. ;
vocis, tubarum, etc., Verg. In *pl. :* Cic.
Ep., Stat.

sonĭvĭus, a, um [sonus], *noisy ;* only with
tripudium, Cic. Ep.

sonō, sonāre (sonere, Enn., Lucr.), sonuī,
sonĭtum (*Fut. Part.* sonātūrus, Hor.)[sonus].
to make a noise, to sound, ring, resound.
1. Lit. : vox, mare, Pl. ; tympana, Caes. ;
extrema graviter, acute, Cic. ; classica,
Verg. ; silvae Aquilone, Hor. ; omnia
mulierum ploratibus, Liv. ; clamore viri,
stridore rudentes, Ov. ; dicta non sonant
(i.e. ring like coins), Pl. With *Intern.*
Acc. : quiddam confusum sonantes, Cic. ;
mortale, Verg. ; nec vox hominem sonat,
Verg. ; furem sonuere iuvenci, i.e. betrayed
by their lowing, Prop. ; sonante mixtum
tibiis carmen lyrā, Hor. **2.** Transf. :
quid sonet vox voluptatis, Cic. ; te carmina
nostra, Ov. ; lyrā sonari, Hor.

sonor, ōris, *m.* [sonō], *a noise, sound, clang,
din :* Lucr., Verg., Tac.

sonōrus, a, um [sonor]. *noisy, clanging,
resounding :* cithara, Tib. ; tempestates,
flumina, Verg.

sōns, sontis, *adj. guilty, criminal :* reos, Pl. ;
anima, Verg. ; Ov. As Noun (mostly in
pl.) : Pl., Cic., Liv., Ov.

sontĭcus, a, um [sōns], *critical :* morbus
(exempting from public duty), XII Tab.,
Plin. Hence, in gen., *serious, weighty,
important:* Cato ; Tib.

sonus, ī, *m. a noise, sound.* **1.** Lit. : Enn.,
Cic., Ov., etc. ; tubae, Caes. ; tibiarum,
Cic. ; urbis, Verg. ; fluminis, Liv. **2.**
Transf. (of style) : *tone, character :* Cic.,
Quint. [It. *suono :* Sp. Fr. *son.*]

sŏphĭa, ae, *f.* [σοφία], *wisdom :* Enn., Mart.

sŏphisma, atis, *n.* [σόφισμα], *a false conclusion, fallacy :* Sen.

sŏphistēs, ae, *m.* [σοφιστής], *a sophist :*
Cic.

Sŏphoclēs, is and ī (Voc. Sophoclē), *m. the
second in order of time of the three great
Athenian tragic poets ;* **Sŏphoclēus**, a,
um.

sŏphos or **sŏphus**, ī, *m.* [σοφός], *a wise
man, sage:* Mart. As *Adj.:* gubernator,
Phaedr.

sŏphōs, *adv.* [σοφῶς], *an exclamation of
applause ; well done!* Mart.

Sŏphus, ī, *m.* [σοφός, "the wise"], *a surname
of P. Sempronius, the consul.*

sōpĭo, īre [v. sopor], *to put or lull to sleep,*
hence, *to stun.* **1.** Lit. **a.** In gen. : vino
oneratos sopire, Liv. ; impactus ita est
saxo, ut sopiretur, Liv. ; Ov. Most freq.
in *Perf. Part.* : ut sopito corpore ipse
(animus) vigilet, Cic. ; Lucr. ; Ov. ; sensus, Verg. ; sopitae quietis tempus, Liv.
b. Of the sleep of death : Homerus sceptra
potitus eādem aliis sopitu' quiete est,
Lucr. **2.** Transf. of things : draconis
impetum, Enn. ; sopitos suscitat ignis,
Verg. ; moenera militāī, Lucr. ; sopita
virtus, Cic.

sopor, ōris, *m.* [cf. ὕπνος, somnus], *a deep*
or *heavy sleep* (poet. also for *sleep* in gen.).
1. Lit. **a.** In gen. : Pl., Lucr., Coculos

sopor operit, Cat. ; fessos sopor inrigat
artūs, Verg. ; placidum soporem petere,
carpere, Verg. **b.** Of death : Pl., Lucr..
Hor. **2.** Transf. **a.** *stupefaction, stupor :*
Cael. ap. Quint. **b.** *laziness, indifference :*
sopor et ignavia, Tac. ; Mart. **c.** *a sleep-
ing-draught, sleeping-potion :* Nep., Sen.
Ep. Hence in partic., *poppy-juice, opium :*
Plin. **d.** Of the temple of the head :
Stat.

sopōrātus, a, um [sopor], *sleep-drugged :*
hostes, Ov. ; dolor, Curt. ; ramus vi
Stygiā, Verg. Hence, **sopōrō**, āre : Plin.

sopōrĭfer, era, erum [sopor ferō], *sleep-
bringing :* papaver, Verg. ; Lethe, Ov.

sopōrus, a, um [sopor]. **I.** *sleep-bringing :*
Nox, Verg. **II.** *drowsy :* Val. Fl.

Sōracte, is, *n. a mountain in Etruria 26 miles
N. of Rome ;* now *Monte di S. Oreste.*

sōracum, ī, *n.* [σώρακος], *a pannier, hamper :*
Pl.

sorbeō, ēre, uī [cf. Gk. ῥοφέω], *to suck in,
drink down, swallow.* **1.** Lit. : sanguinem,
Pl. ; Charybdis fluctūs, Verg. ; flumina
terra, Ov. ; margaritas aceto liquefactas,
Suet. **2.** Transf. : aliquid animo, Cic. ;
odia, Cic. Ep.

sorbĭllō, āre [sorbeō], *to sip :* cyathos,
Ter.

sorbĭlō, *adv.* [sorbeō], *by sipping.* Transf.
drop by drop, bit by bit : vicitare, Pl.

sorbĭtĭo, ōnis, *f.* [sorbeō], *a drink, draught,
broth, etc. :* Pl., Cato, Pers., etc.

sorbum, ī, *n. a sorb-apple, service-berry* (or
perh. *cider* made from the *service berry,*
sorbus, ī, *f.*) : Cato, Verg., etc.

sordeō, ēre [sordes], *to be dirty, filthy, unwashed, unkempt, shabby.* **1.** Lit. : Pl.,
Sen. Ep. ; fumo, Stat. **2.** Transf. *to
seem shabby, mean,* or *paltry :* alicui,
Liv. ; sordent tibi munera nostra, Verg. ;
pretium aetas altera sordet, Hor. ; cuncta
prae campo, Hor.

sordēs, is, *f. dirt, filth, shabbiness, meanness.*
1. Lit. **a.** In gen. : Pl., Lucr., Hor. In
pl. : Pl., Cic., Hor., Ov. **b.** In *pl. : a
shabby* or *mean garment* as sign of mourning
or humility : Cic., Liv., etc. ; iacere in
lacrimis et sordibus, Cic. ; sordis suscipere,
Tac. **2.** Transf. **a.** Of rank : *meanness,
baseness :* obscuritas et sordes tuae, Cic. ;
fortunae et vitae, Cic. ; in infamiā relinqui
et sordibus, Cic. Ep. ; Liv. ; sordes verborum, *low, vulgar expressions,* Tac.
Concr. *the rabble :* apud sordem urbis
et faecem, Cic. Ep. ; Tac. **b.** Of
behaviour, etc. : *shabbiness, meanness :*
Cic. ; sordes et avaritia, Tac. In *pl. :*
(populus Romanus) non amat profusas
opulas, sordis et inhumanitatem multo
minus, Cic. ; Hor. ; Quint. ; minimas
ediscere sordis, Juv.

sordēscō, sordēscere, sorduī [sordeō], *to
become dirty :* Hor., Plin.

sordĭdātus, a, um [sordidus], *in dirty,
shabby,* or *mean clothes :* Pl., Ter., Cic.
Esp. as sign of mourning : Cic., Liv.,
Suet.

sordĭdē, *adv.* **I.** *meanly, basely, vulgarly :*
loqui, Pl. ; dicere, Cic. ; sordidius nati,
Tac. **II.** *meanly, penuriously :* facere aliquid, Suet. ; Plin. Ep.

sordidulus, a, um [dim. sordidus], rather soiled or shabby. **1.** Lit.: toga, Juv. **2.** Transf.: low, mean : servoli, Pl.

sordidus, a, um [sordeō], dirty, filthy, shabby, mean. **1.** Lit. **a.** In gen.: vestis, Enn. ; servolicolae, Pl. ; amictus, Verg. ; mappa, fumus, nati, Hor. ; sordidior toga, Mart. Poet.: autumnus calcatis sordidus uvis, stained, Ov. ; terga suis, smoked, Ov. **b.** Of mourners: clad in mourning : Cic. **2.** Transf. **a.** Of rank or position: low, mean, base ; and rarely, humble : causam commisisse homini egenti sordido, sine horrore, sine censu, Cic. ; Hor. ; loco non humili solum sed etiam sordido natus, Liv. ; panis, Pl. ; villula, Cic. Ep. ; rura, Verg. Sup. : Liv. **b.** Of character or behaviour : shabby, mean, low, vile : Cic., Hor., etc. ; iste omnium turpissimus et sordidissimus, Cic. ; ratio, Cic. ; virtus repulsae nescia sordidae, Hor. ; cupido, Hor. ; adulterium, Liv. ; qui pecuniam praeferre amicitiae sordidum existiment, Cic.

sorditūdō, inis, f. [sordēs], dirt, filth : Pl.

sōrex, icis, m. [cf. Gk. ὕραξ], a shrew-mouse : Ter., Varr. [It. sorcio ; Fr. souris.]

sōricinus, a, um [sōrex], of the shrew-mouse : nenia, Pl.

sōrītēs, ae (DAT. sōritī, Cic.), m. [σωρείτης], a logical conclusion drawn from an accumulation of arguments, a sorites : Cic.

soror, ōris, f. a sister. **1.** Lit.: Pl., Cic., Verg., etc. ; germana, Pl., Cic. Of the Fates : tristes, Tib. ; tres, Cat., Hor., etc. Of the Muses : Prop. ; doctae, Tib. ; novem, Ov. **2.** Transf. **a.** a cousin : Ov. **b.** a playmate, companion : Verg., Tib. **c.** Of things in pairs or similar : dextera sororque laeva, Pl. ; Cat. ; Verg. [Fr. soeur.]

sorōricida, ae, m. [soror caedō], a murderer of a sister : Cic.

sorōrius, a, um [soror], of or in honour of a sister : cena, Pl. ; stuprum, Cic. ; moenia, oscula, Ov. ; tigillum, Liv.

sors, tis, f. (NOM. sortis, Pl. ; ABL. sortī, Pl., Liv.) [serō], a lot ; i.e. a small ticket or billet, for casting into the bag or urn. **1.** Lit.: coniciam sortis in sitellam, Pl. ; conicere in hydriam, Cic. ; ponere in sitellam, Liv. ; deicere, Caes. ; in id (for that) deicere, Cic. ; sortis miscere, Cic. ; ducere, Cic. ; sortes extenuatae, attenuatae, Liv. ; ut cuiusque sors exciderat, Liv. ; cum mea prima sors exisset, Cic. **2.** Transf. **a.** a casting of lots, decision by lot, lot : Pl., Caes., Cic. ; ei sorte provincia Sicilia obvenit, Cic. ; cui Sicilia provincia sorte evenisset, Liv. ; Q. Caecilio sorte evenit ut etc., Liv. **b.** Of the praetor's allotted duties : Cic. ; urbana, peregrina, Liv. ; comitia suae sortis esse, Liv. **c.** an oracular response, a prophecy : Cic., Verg., etc. ; responsa sortium, Liv. **d.** one's lot in life ; fate, destiny, etc. : nescia mens hominum fati sortisque futurae, Verg. ; iniqua, Verg., Liv. ; alteram sortem, Hor. ; non tuae sortis iuvenem, Hor. ; aliena, Liv. ; ferrea sors vitae, Ov. ; Saturni sors ego prima fui (i.e. child), Ov. With GEN. : portion, share : puer in nullam

sortem bonorum natus, Liv. ; Hor. ; Ov. **e.** Mercant.: capital bearing interest, principal : et sors et faenus, Pl. ; Ter. ; Cic. Ep. ; Liv. [It. sorte ; Sp. suerte ; Fr. sort.]

sorticula, ae, f. [dim. sors], a small tablet or ticket : Suet.

sortilegus, a, um [sors legō], foretelling, prophetic : Delphi, Hor. Masc. as Noun, a fortune-teller, soothsayer : Cic., Luc.

sortior, ītī (sortītō, īre, Pl., Varr.) [sors], to cast or draw lots. **1.** Lit. **A.** Intrans.: Pl. ; praetores designati, Cic. ; consules, Liv. ; tibi, Pl. ; legiones de ordine agminis, Tac. **B.** Trans. to draw or cast lots for, to assign, or appoint by lot, to allot ; also in the Perfect tenses, to obtain or receive by lot : iudices, tribūs, Cic. ; regna vini talis, Hor. ; necessitas sortitur insignis et imos, Hor. ; consules inter se provincias, Liv. ; aliquos ad ignominiam, Cic. With Indir. Quest. or Deliberative : Cic., Liv. Perf. Part. in Pass. sense : Cic. Ep., Prop. **2.** Transf. **a.** to share, divide, distribute : pariter laborem sortiti, Verg. **b.** to choose, select : subolem armento, Verg. **c.** In gen.: to obtain, receive : mediterranea Asiae, Liv. ; amicum, Hor. ; Ov., etc. [Fr. sortir.]

sortis, is, v. sors.

sortītiō, ōnis, f. [sortior], a casting or drawing of lots, a choosing or determining by lot : Pl. ; aedilicia, praerogativa, Cic. ; provinciarum, Cic. In pl. : Suet.

sortītus, a, um. **I.** Part. sortiō and sortior. **II.** sortītō, ABL. sing. n. as Adv., by lot. **1.** Lit.: Cic., Suet. **2.** Transf. by destiny : Pl., Hor.

sortītus, ūs, m. [sortior], a casting or drawing of lots : specula in sortitu 'st (al. sorti 'st) mihi, Pl. ; pluribus de rebus uno sortitu rettulisti, Cic. ; quae sortitūs non pertulit ullos, Verg.

sōs, archaic for eōs and suōs.

Sosius, a, the name of a Roman gens. Esp. the Sosii, two brothers, famous booksellers at Rome in the time of Horace.

sōspes, itis, adj. [cf. Gk. σόος, σῶς]. **I.** safe and sound, unhurt, unharmed : Pl., Hor., Liv., etc. ; navis ab ignibus, Hor. ; Ov. **II.** auspicious : diem sospitem rebus meis agundis, Pl.

sōspita, ae, f. [sōspes], the Saver, Preserver ; an epithet of Juno : Cic., Ov.

sōspitālis, e, adj. [sōspes], giving health or safety, salutary : Pl.

sōspitō, āre [sōspes], to save, preserve, prosper : regnum, Enn. ; Pl. ; Cat. ; progeniem, Liv.

sōtēr, ēris, m. [σωτήρ], a saviour, a giver of health or safety : Cic.

sōtēria, ōrum, n. pl. [σωτήρια], a congratulatory feast or presents given on a person's recovery from sickness : Mart.

spādix, icis, m. f. [σπάδιξ], date-brown, nut-brown : (equi) spadices glaucique, Verg. Also, a stringed instrument : Quint.

spadō, ōnis, m. [σπάδων], a eunuch : Hor., Liv., etc.

spargō, spargere, spārsī, spārsum [cf. σπείρω], to throw here and there, to strew, scatter, sprinkle. **I.** With ACC. of thing thrown.

1, Lit. **a.** In gen.: hastas, Enn.; tela, Verg.; semina, Cic.; humi, per humum, in agros semina, Ov.; nummos populo de rostris, Cic.; nuces, flores, Verg.; Hor.; harenam pedibus, Verg. **b.** Of liquids: cruorem, Lucr.; umorem toto terrarum in orbe. Lucr.; per totam domum aquas, Hor. **2.** Transf. **a.** *to strew, scatter, spread abroad :* animos in corpora humana, Cic.; omnia quae gerebam in orbis terrae memoriam sempiternam, Cic.; voces in vulgum, Verg.; nomen fama per urbes, Ov.; suspiciones, Quint. *Impers. Pass.* spargebatur (with Acc. and *Inf.*): Tac. **b,** *to scatter, disperse :* Enn.; corpora, Lucr.; aper canis, Ov.; per vias speculatores, Liv.; exercitum per provincias, Tac.; sparsam *tempestate* classem, Liv.; se in fugam, Liv.; Lucr. Of squandering: tua prodigus, Hor. **II.** With Acc. of thing besprinkled, and *Instr.* ABL.: saxa sanguine, Enn.; aras sanguine, Lucr.; aram immolato agno, Hor.; corpus lymphā, Verg.; genas lacrimis, Lucr.; virgulta fimo, Verg.; molā caput, Hor.; umerum capillis, Hor.; anguis aureis maculis sparsus, Liv.; Verg.

spārsiō, ōnis, *f.* [spargō], *a sprinkling, scattering.* **a.** Of perfumes: Sen. **b.** Of presents in the theatre: Stat.

spārsus, a, um. **I.** *Part.* spargō. **II.** Adj. **a.** *freckled, spotty :* sparso ore, Ter. **b.** *spread out.* Comp. : Plin.

Sparta, ae, and (poet.) **Spartē,** ēs, *f.* (Acc. -ēn, Ov.) *the capital of Laconia, also called* Lacedaemon; **Spartānus,** a, um; **Spartānus,** i, *m. a Spartan :* Pl., Nep., Tac.; **Spartiātēs,** ae, *m. a Spartan :* Pl., Cic.; **Spartiāticus, Sparticus,** a, um.

Spartacus, i, *m. a Thracian gladiator who led the gladiators in their war against Rome* (B.C. 73–71). Transf. of Antony: Cic.

sparteus, a, um [spartum], *made of Spanish broom :* funes, amphorae, Cic.

spartum, i, *n.* [σπάρτον], *Spanish broom* (used in making ropes, mats, nets, etc.) : Varr., Liv. [Sp. *esparto.*]

sparulus, i, *m.* [*dim.* sparus, a kind of fish], *bream :* Ov., Mart.

sparus, i, *m. a small missile weapon with a curved blade, a hunting-spear :* Sall., Verg., Liv.

spatha, ae, *f.* [σπάθη]. **I.** *a broad, flat wooden instrument for stirring liquids, a spatula :* Plin. **II.** *a batten* used by weavers to drive home the threads of the woof: Sen. Ep. **III,** *a broad two-edged sword without a point:* Tac [It. *spada;* Fr. *épee.*]

spatior, iāri [spatium], *to walk* (as in an open space), *to walk* or *stride with measured steps* or *majestically, to promenade.* **1.** Lit.: Cic.; pompa, Prop.; in xysto, Cic.; Hor.; Pompeiā in umbrā (i.e. porticu), Prop.; sub umbrā, Ov.; cornix in harenā, Verg.; late arvo, Ov.; summā harenā, Ov.; Dido ante ora deum (GEN.) ad aras, Verg. **2.** Transf. *to spread out :* alae, bracchia, Ov.; radices in summā tellure, Plin.; morbi vires, Sen.

spatiōsē, *adv. widely, greatly.* **1.** Lit.: Plin. Comp.: Ov., Plin. Ep. **2.** Transf. of time: Prop.

spatiōsus, a, um [spatium], *roomy, spacious, ample ;* and poet. *broad, large.* **1.** Lit.: insula, Plin.; loca, Quint.; taurus, corpus, etc., Ov. Comp. : Ov. Sup. : Plin. Pan. **2.** Transf. of time : *long-continuing, prolonged :* nox, tempus, senectus, Ov.

spatium, i, *n.* [perh. *cf.* Gk. σπάω]. **1.** Lit. (of space). **A.** In gen.: *room, space, expanse, extent :* locus ac spatium quod inane vocamus, Lucr.; caeli, Lucr., Verg.; reliquum spatium quā flumen intermittit, Caes.; castrorum, Caes.; quod spatium non esset agitandi equos, Nep.; spatiis locorum animadversis, Caes. Hence of dimension, bulk, etc.: serpentis, Ov.; oris et colli, Ov.; rhombi, Juv.; itineris, Caes.; viae, Ov. **B.** More concr. **a.** *an open space, public place :* urbs delubris distincta spatiisque communibus, Cic.; Stat.; silvestria, Cic.; illi medio in spatio chorus occurrit, Verg.; locus planis porrectus spatiis, Hor. **b.** *distance, interval* betw. two points: hic locus aequo fero spatio ab castris utrisque aberat, Caes.; inter duas acies tantum erat relictum spati ut etc., Caes.; magnum spatium abesse, Caes.; magno spatio confecto, Caes.; Ov. In *pl.* : Cic. **C.** *a limited* or *defined space.* **a.** *(the length of) a walk, promenade :* uno basilicae spatio, Cic.; duobus spatiis factis, Cic.; orator ex Academiae spatiis, Cic. **b.** *a race-course, the lists, a lap* in the course, etc.: equōs spatio supremo vicit Olympo, Enn.; decurso spatio, Cic.; addunt in spatia, Verg.; sou septem spatiis Circo meruere coronam, Ov. Transf.: decurso aetatis spatio, Pl.; deflexit de spatio consuetudo, Cic.; vitae spatio decurrere, Ov. **2.** Transf. (of time). **A.** In gen.: *a space of time, interval, period :* breve, Ter., Lucr., Hor.; parvum, Prop.; longum, Cic.; diei. Caes.; dierum triginta, Cic.; praeteriti temporis, Cic.; spatia omnis temporis, Caes.; Prop. **B.** *time, leisure, opportunity :* dare, Cic.; irae suae dare, Liv.; spatium dare (with *ut* and *Subj.*), Ter.; petere furori, Verg.; breve spatium 'st perferundi quae minitas mihi, Pl.; Liv.; spatium Vitellianis datum refugiendi, Tac.; dare alicui spatium ad aliquid faciendum, Caes., Cic., Ov.; so with sumere and habere, Cic.; postulare, Caes.; nec fuit spatium ad contrahenda castra, Caes.; spatium apparandis nuptiis (DAT.) dabitur, Tor. **C.** *metrical time, measure, quantity :* trochaeus qui est eodem spatio quo choreus, Cic.; Quint. [It. *spazio;* Fr. *espace.*]

speciālis, a, *adj.* [speciēs], *individual, particular, special :* Sen. Ep., Quint.

speciāliter, *adv. particularly, specially :* Quint.

speciēs, ēi, *f.* (GEN. and DAT. *pl.* not used) [speciō], *a seeing, sight* (*Act.* or more freq. *Pass.*). **I.** In gen. **1.** Lit.: speciem quo vertimus, Lucr.; doloris speciem ferre non possunt, Cic.; Caes.; non tulit hanc speciem, Verg. **2.** Transf. (mentally), *a notion, idea :* insidebat in eius mente species eloquentiae, Cic.; Hor.; viri boni, Cic.; vera species senatūs Romani, Liv. **II.** *that which is seen, the*

outward appearance, shape, outline : Pl.,
Lucr., Cic. ; urbis, Pl. ; navium, Caes. ;
oppidi, agri, hominis, populi, etc., Cic.
III. *a fine appearance, splendour, beauty.*
1. Lit.: mulieris, Pl. ; corporis, Curt. ;
iuvenis, Juv.; species et gratia, Hor.;
caeli, Cic.; triumpho praebere, Liv.;
addere, Liv. **2.** Transf.: adhibero in
dicendo, Cic. ; populi Romani, Cic. **IV.**
an unreal or *deceptive appearance, semblance,
show.* **1.** Lit.: in montis speciem cur-
vari, Ov.; paucis ad speciem tabernaculis
relictis, Caes. Hence, *a vision, apparition* :
Lucr. ; consuli visa species viri, Liv. ;
Ov. Also, *a likeness, image* : species ex
aere vetus, Cic. poet. **2.** Transf.: secu-
ritas specie quidem blanda sed roapse etc.,
Cic.; specie . . . re verā, Liv.; cuius
rei species erat accepto frumenti, Sall. ;
fraudi imponere aliquam speciem iuris,
Liv.; per speciem celebrandarum cantu
epularum, Liv.; sub specie infidae pacis,
Liv.; Curt.; dilatā in speciem actione, re
verā etc., Liv. **V.** *a particular kind* or
sort, a species : Cic., Quint., etc. [It.
spezie ; Fr. *espèce* and *épice.*]

specillum, i, *n.* [speciō], *a surgical instrument, a probe* : Cic.

specimen, inis, *n.* [speciō], *visible evidence ;
an example, proof.* **1.** Lit.: Pl. ; specimen dare in aliquā re, Cic. ; ingeni, etc.,
Cic.; consili, virtutis, Liv. ; Solis avi,
Verg. With *Indir. Quest.* : Pl., Lucr.
2. Transf. *a pattern, model, ideal* : ceteris
esse, Cic. ; humanitatis, suavitatis, innocentiae, etc., Cic. ; antiquitatis, Tac.

speciō (spiciō), specere, spexi [*cf.* Gk. σκέπτο-
μαι], *to look, look at, behold* : Pl. ; specimen,
Pl.

speciōsē, *adv. showily, handsomely, beauti-
fully.* **1.** Lit.: Plin. *Comp.* : Hor., Liv.
Sup. : Quint. **2.** Transf.: dictum,
Quint. *Sup.* : Quint.

speciōsus, a, um [speciēs], *showy, handsome,
beautiful.* **1.** Lit.: femina, corpora,
Quint.; hunc speciosum pelle decorā,
Hor. *Comp.* : Sen. Ep. *Sup.* : Quint.
2. Transf. **a.** miracula, Hor.; vocabula
rerum, Hor.; Quint.; damnum, Ov.
b. *specious, plausible* : causa, Cic. Ep. ;
titulus, ministerium, Liv. ; speciosa nomina culpae imponere, Ov. *Comp.* and
Sup. : Quint.

spectābilis, e, *adj.* [spectō]. **I.** *that can be
seen, visible* : Cic., Ov. **II.** *worth seeing,
notable, admirable, remarkable* : Niobe
vestibus intexto Phrygiis spectabilis auro,
Ov.; Plin.; victoria, Tac.

spectāculum (spectāclum, Prop.), i, *n.*
[spectō], *a show, sight, spectacle.* **1.** Lit.
a. In gen.: Pl., Cic., Verg., etc. ; supera-
rum rerum atquo caelestium, Cic. ; Liv.,
Ov., etc.; praebere, Cic., Liv., Ov.; alicui
spectaculo esse, Liv. **b.** *a public show,
a stage-play, spectacle* : Cic. ; gladiatorium,
Liv.; gladiatorum, circi, Liv. ; scaenae,
Ov.; dare, Cic.; committere, Liv. ; spectaculo interesse, Liv. **2.** Transf. (in
pl.) *seats* at a show, in the theatre, etc. :
Pl., Cic., Liv., Ov., etc.

spectāmen, inis, *n.* [spectō], *a mark, sign,
proof* : Pl.

sight, contemplation. **a.** In gen.: Pl., Pl. ;
apparatūs, Cic. Ep. **b.** *an examining,
testing* of money : Cic.

spectātor, ōris, *m.* (and **spectātrix,** īcis, *f.*
Pl., Ov.) [spectō], *a looker-on, beholder,
observer.* **1.** Lit.: Cic.; rerum caelestium, Cic.; certaminis, Liv.; Mart.
Esp. *a spectator* in a theatre, at games,
etc.: Pl., Cic. **2.** Transf. *a judge, critic* :
elegans formarum, Ter. ; Liv.

spectātus, a, um. **I.** *Part.* spectō. **II.**
Adj. **a.** *tried, tested, proved* : mores, Pl. ;
homo, fides, virtus, etc., Cic. ; Liv.; homo
in rebus iudicandis, Cic. ; rebus iuventus,
Verg.; pietas per ignis, Ov.; mihi satis
spectatum est (with Acc. and *Inf.*), Sall. ;
id cuique spectatissimum sit, Liv. **b.** *looked
up to, respected, esteemed* : vir, Pl., Cic. ;
castitas, Liv. *Sup.* : Cic.

spectiō, ōnis, *f.* [speciō]. In augury, *an
observing of the auspices* ; also, *the right
of observing them* : Cic.

spectō, āre [*freq.* speciō], *to look at, behold
intently ; to gaze at, watch, observe.* **1.**
Lit. **a.** In gen.: Pl., Hor.; alte, Cic.
With Acc.: Pl., Cic., Ov., etc. With *ad*
and Acc.: Pl. With *in* and Acc.: Cic.
With *Indir. Quest.* : Pl., Ov. *Impers.*
Pass. with ne and *Subj.* : Pl. **b.** *to look
at* as a spectator: fabulam, Pl. ; ludos,
Hor.; Cic. **c.** *to look at* with a view to
testing: argentum, Pl.; Cic.; aurum in
ignibus, Ov. **d.** Of places, *to look, face
towards* : ad orientem solem, Caes. ; Cic. ;
munitiones in urbem spectantes, Liv. ;
Belgae in septentriones, Caes. ; Aquitania
spectat inter occasum solis et septentriones,
Caes. ; Acarnania solem occidentem, Liv. ;
Sall.; eo, Pl.; vestigia retrorsum, Hor.
2. Transf. **a.** *to look at, consider* : audaciam alicuius, Ter. ; Pl. ; signorum
ordinem, Cic. **b.** *to look for, seek* : quem
locum probandae virtutis tuae spectas ?
Caes. **c.** Most freq. *to have in view, bear
in mind, have regard to* : aliquid, Lucr.,
Cic., etc.; deos, Curt.; ad aliquid, Cic.,
Verg., etc. ; in nos (i.e. rely on), Cic.
With *Indir. Quest.* : Cic. Ep. With *ut*
and *Subj.* : Cic. Ep. **d.** *to look to, contemplate, meditate, tend towards* : arma et
bellum, Liv. ; ad defectionem, Liv. Of
impersonal Subjects: res ad arma, Cic. Ep. ;
ad perniciem patriae res, Cic. ; Liv. ; ad
te unum oratio, Cic. ; in unum exitum,
Cic.; quorsum spectat oratio ? Cic. ;
hoc eo spectabat ut etc., Cic. **e.** *to look
at, examine* with a view to testing : aliquem,
Pl.; hominem in periclis, Lucr. ; illum
ex trunco corporis, Cic. ; philosophos non
ex singulis vocibus sed ex perpetuitate
atque constantiā, Cic. ; Ter.

spectrum, i, *n.* [speciō], *an apparition,
spectre* : Cic.

specula, ae, *f.* [speciō], *a look-out, watch-
tower.* **1.** Lit.: Pl. ; Cic., Verg., Liv. **2.**
Transf. **a.** nunc homines in speculis sunt,
observant, Cic. ; Liv. ; Ov. **b.** *a height*
(of a mountain or wall) : Verg.

specula, ae, *f.* [*dim.* spēs], *a slight hope, a
gleam of hope* : Pl., Cic.

speculābundus, a, um [speculor], *on the*

look-out, on the watch : Tac. With Acc. : **signa,** Suet.

speculāris, e, *adj.* [speculum]. **I.** *like a mirror :* Sen. **II.** *transparent :* lapis, perh. *mica,* Plin. Hence, **speculāria,** iōrum, *n. pl. window-panes, a window :* Sen., Mart., Juv., Plin. Ep.

speculātor, ōris, *m.* [speculor]. M i l i t. *a spy, scout.* **1.** L i t. : Caes., Cic., Liv., etc. Under the emperors they were employed as special adjutants, messengers, and body-guards of a general : Sen., Tac., Suet. **2.** T r a n s f. *an explorer, investigator* in gen. : naturae, Cic. ; Prop.

speculātōrius, a, um [speculātor], *of spies* or *scouts :* navigia, Caes. ; naves, Liv. ; caliga, Suet. As Noun, **speculātōria,** ae, *f. (sc.* navis), *a spy-boat :* Liv.

speculātrix, īcis, *f.* [speculor], *a* (female) *watcher over.* **1.** L i t. : Furiae, Cic. **2.** T r a n s f. (with G E N.) : speculatrix villa profundi, Stat.

speculor, ārī [specula], *to act as scout ; to spy out, watch, observe :* Caes. ; in omnis partis, Ov. With Acc. : loca, Pl. ; Veag. ; rostra, Cic. ; avem, Verg. ; consilia, Sall., Tac. ; opportunitatem (i.e. watch for), Tac. With *Indir. Quest. :* Pl., Liv. With *ne* and *Subj. :* Pl. With non-personal Subject : te multorum oculi et aures, Cic.

speculum, ī, *n.* [speciō], *a looking-glass, mirror* (made of polished metal). **1.** L i t. : Pl., Lucr., Cic., Ov., etc. **2.** T r a n s f. **a.** lympharum, Phaedr. **b.** futuri temporis, Lucr. ; naturae, Cic. [It. *specchio.*]

specus, ūs (ī, Cato), *m.* (Enn., Cic. Ep. Cat., Liv., Ov., etc.), *f.* (Enn.), *n.* (Verg.) [*cf.* Gk. σπέος], *a cavity, grotto, cavern, etc.* **1.** L i t. : Enn., Cic. Ep., Verg., Liv., etc. **2.** T r a n s f. : vulneris, Verg. ; Phaedr.

spēlaeum, ī, *n.* [σπήλαιον], *a cave, den :* Verg.

spēlunca, ae, *f.* [σπήλυγξ], *a cave, den :* Cic., Verg., etc.

spērābilis, e, *adj.* [spērō], *that can be hoped for :* Pl.

spērātus, a, um. **I.** *Part.* spērō. **II.** Adj. *hoped or longed for :* Cic. **III.** Noun, *m.* and *f. : a betrothed, bride :* Pl.

Sperchēos or **Sperchīus,** ī, *m. a river of southern Thessaly :* **Sperchēis,** ĭdis, *f. adj. :* **Sperchiōnidēs,** ae, *m. a dweller by the Sphercheos.*

spernō, spernere, sprēvī, sprētum. **1.** L i t. *to put far off, remove :* opes auxiliaque a me spernunt se, Pl. **2.** T r a n s f. *to reject, scorn, spurn :* aliquem, Enn., Cic., Verg., etc. ; meam speciem, Pl. ; spretao iniuria formae, Verg. ; aliorum iudicia, Cic. ; voluptates, Hor. ; consilium, Ov. ; con-sulis imperium, Liv. ; doctrina deos sper-nens, Liv. With G E N. (of cause) : morum spernendus, Tac. With *Inf. :* Hor., Ov.

spērō, āre [spēs], *to look for, expect,* us. of *something desirable ; to hope, to promise* or *flatter oneself.* **a.** In gen. : Pl., Cic., etc. With *de :* Cic. With Acc. : aliquid, Pl., Cic., Hor., etc. ; aliquid sibi, Cic. ; victoriam ab aliquo, Caes. ; Cic. Ep. ; omnia ex victoriā, Caes. ; hoc sperans ut etc., Caes. With Acc. and *Fut. Inf.*

(most freq.) : Pl., Cic., etc. With Acc. and *Pres.* or *Perf. Inf. :* Pl., Cic., Verg., etc. With *ut* and *Subj. :* Liv. **b.** *to put trust in, to trust, believe :* deos, Pl. With Acc. and *Inf. :* Cic. **c.** Of something un-desirable, *to anticipate, apprehend :* tan-tum dolorem, Verg. ; Ter. ; Cat. ; Quint. With a negative particle : sin a vobis, id quod non spero, deserar, Cic. ; Pl. [Fr. *espérer.*]

spēs, speī, *f.* (N O M. and Acc. *pl.* usually **spēs,** but **spērēs,** Enn.), *a looking for, expecting.* **I. A.** A b s t r. : *hope, expectation.* **a.** In gen. : aliquem in spem adducere, Cic. Ep. ; spem alicui inicere, Ter. ; spem sibi pro-ponere, Cic. ; concipere, Ov., Plin. Ep. ; in aliquā re ponere, Cic., Verg. ; in aliquā re deponere, Curt. ; in aliquā re habere, Cic. ; omnia in spe habere, Sall. ; spe adduci, duci, Cic. ; spem alere, augere, Cic. ; de spe decidere, Ter. ; a spe decidere, Liv. ; hac spe lapsus, deiectus, Caes. ; ab hac spe repulsi, Caes. ; de spe depulsus, Cic. ; spe depulsus, Liv. ; (a) spe destitu-tus, Curt. ; spei finem imponere, Liv. ; alicui spem praecidere, Cic. ; alicui minuere, Caes. ; spes ad inritum redacta, Liv. ; aliquem spes fallit, Cic., etc. ; omnis Cati-linae spes atque opes concidisse, Cic. ; praeter spem, Pl., Ter., Cic. Ep. ; contra spem, Liv. With *Obj.* G E N. : Ter., Cic., Ov., etc. ; templi capiendi, Liv. ; Cic. P h r a s e s with Acc. and *Fut.* or *Pres. Inf. :* spe, Liv. ; spes est etc., Pl. ; magna me spes tenet etc., Cic. ; in spem maximam adducti etc., Cic. ; magnam in spem venie-bat etc., Caes. ; Cic. Ep. ; spe duci, Cic. ; spem habere, Caes. P h r a s e s with *ut* and *Subj. :* quae te ratio in istam spem induxit etc. ? Cic. ; spem adferro ut etc., Cic. ; inritā spe agitari ut etc., Tac. With *de :* de argento, Pl. ; de flumine transeundo, Caes. With *ad* and *Gerund. :* Cic., Liv. **b.** *the hope of being heir :* Hor. ; in spem secundam adsumebantur, Tac. **B.** C o n c r. *an object of hope :* puppes, spes vestri reditūs, Ov. ; vestras spes uritis, Verg. Esp. of children, young animals, or the fruits of the earth : per spes surgentis Iuli, Verg. ; Quint. ; spem gregis, Verg. As a term of endearment : spes mea, Pl. ; Cic. Ep. **II.** *an anticipation* or *appre-hension* of evil : Cic. ; Sall. ; id (bellum) quidem spe omnium serius fuit, Liv. ; in spe Hannibali fuit defectio Tarentinorum, Liv. ; Luc. **III.** P e r s o n i f i e d : Pl., Cic., Ov., etc.

Speusippus, ī, *m. nephew of Plato, and his successor in the Academy.*

sphaera, ae, *f.* [σφαῖρα], *a ball, globe, sphere* (pure Lat. globus, Cic.). **a.** In gen. : Cato, Cic. **b.** *a globe* or *sphere* made to represent the motions of the heavenly bodies : Cic.

sphaeristērium, ī, *n.* [σφαιριστήριον], *a place for playing ball, a tennis-court :* Plin. Ep., Suet.

Sphinx, ingis, *f.* [σφίγξ], *the Sphinx, a fabulous monster which dwelt on a rock near Thebes :* overcome by Oedipus : Pl., Plin., Suet., etc.

spica, ae, *f.* (**spicum,** ī, *n.* Cic. poet.) [*cf.*

σπίλος, spina]. **1.** Lit. *a point ;* hence, of grain, *an ear, spike :* Cic., Cat., Ov., etc. **2.** Transf. **a.** *a top, tuft, head* of other plants : Cato, Prop., Ov. **b.** *the brightest star in the constellation Virgo :* Cic. poet., Plin. [Fr. *épi.*]

spiceus, a, um [spica], *of or made of ears of corn :* corona, Tib. ; serta, Ov. ; messis, Verg.

spicilegium, ī, *n.* [spica legō], *a gleaning of corn-ears :* Varr.

spicō, āre [spica], *to put forth ears :* Plin.

spiculum, ī, *n.* [*dim.* spicum ; *v.* spica], *a little sharp point or sting.* **1.** Lit. : of bees : Verg. ; of a scorpion : Ov. ; of a hornet : Ov. Of *the point* of a missile weapon : Cic., Liv., Ov., etc. **2.** Transf. *a dart, arrow :* Cic., Verg., etc. [Fr. *épieu.*]

spīnă, ae, *f.* [*cf.* spica], *a thorn.* **1.** Lit. : Lucr., Verg., Tac., etc. **2.** Transf. **a.** *a thorn-bush :* Ov., Plin. **b.** Of animals : *a prickle* of a hedgehog : Cic. ; *a fish-bone :* Ov. ; *the backbone, spine :* Varr., Verg., etc. Hence, *the back :* Ov. **c.** In *pl., subtleties, perplexities :* disserendi spinae, Cic. ; also *cares, anxieties,* and *failings :* Hor. [Fr. *épine.*]

spinetum, ī, *n.* [spina], *a thorn-hedge, a thicket of thorns :* Verg., Plin.

spineus, a, um [spina], *made of thorns :* vincula, Ov.

spinifer, era, erum [spina ferō], *thorn-bearing, prickly :* Cic. poet.

spinōsus, a, um [spina], *full of thorns or prickles, thorny, prickly.* **1.** Lit. : loca, Varr. ; herbae, Ov. *Comp. :* Plin. **2.** Transf. **a.** *stinging, galling :* curae, Cat. **b.** Of style : *thorny, crabbed, obscure :* Stoicorum disserendi genus, Cic. *Comp. :* Cic.

spinter (spinthēr), ēris, *n.* [prob. from σφιγκτήρ], *a kind of bracelet* which kept its place on the arm by its elasticity : Pl.

spinturnicium, ī, *n.* [*dim.* spinturnix ; *cf.* Gk. σπινθαρίς], *a little bird of ill omen :* Pl.

spinus, ī, *f.* [spina], *a blackthorn, sloe-tree :* Verg.

Spiō, ūs, *f. a sea-nymph, daughter of Nereus and Doris.*

spira, ae, *f.* [σπεῖρα]. **I.** *a coil, fold, spire* (of a serpent) : Verg., Ov. **II.** Of things having a spiral form : *the base of a column :* Plin. ; *a kind of twisted cake :* Cato ; *a braid of hair :* Plin. ; *a twisted tie* for fastening the hat under the chin : Juv. **III.** Transf. (in *pl.*) of a crowd of men : Enn.

spīrābilis, e, *adj.* [spirō]. **A.** Pass. *that can be breathed, good to breathe, breathed :* Cic. ; caeli spirabile lumen, Verg. **B.** Act. *that can breathe :* viscera, Plin.

spīrāculum, ī, *n.* [spirō], *an air-hole, vent :* Lucr., Verg., Plin.

spīrāmen, inis, *n.* [spirō]. **I.** *a breathing-hole, air-hole, vent :* Enn., Luc. **II.** *a blowing, puff :* Luc. ; fessi ignis, Stat.

spīrāmentum, ī, *n.* [spirō], *a breathing-hole, air-hole, vent, pore.* **1.** Lit. : animae (i.e. the lungs), Verg. ; caeca spiramenta relaxat, Verg. **2.** Transf. *a breathing-space,* i.e. *a brief pause or interval :* intervalla ac spiramenta temporum, Tac.

spiritus, ūs, *m.* [spirō], *a breathing* of *gentle blowing, a breath of air, breeze.* **1.** Lit. **a.** In gen. : Austri, Enn., Cic. poet. : Boreae, Verg. ; caeli, Cic. **b.** *the air :* Enn., Cic. **c.** *an exhalation, perfumed breath :* unguenti, Lucr. **d.** *breathed air, a breath :* Pl., Lucr., Cic. ; tranquillum spiritum ducere, Cic. ; filiorum postremum spiritum ore excipere, Cic. ; attractus ab alto spiritus, Verg. **e.** *a breathing, respiration :* aer spiritu ductus, Cic. ; quas ducat spiritus auras, Ov. ; intercludere, includere, Liv. Of a sigh : potitus imo spiritu, Hor. ; Prop. **2.** Transf. **A.** *the breath of life, life :* alicui auferre, Cic. ; extremum spiritum effundere, Cic. ; Tac. ; dum spiritus hos regit artūs, Verg. ; Ov. **B.** *inbreathing, inspiration :* poetam quasi divino quodam spiritu inflari, Cic. ; spiritu divino tactus, Liv. **C.** *spirit, disposition, character, etc.* **a.** Of the poetic disposition, etc. : Pindaricus, Prop. ; spiritum Phoebus mihi, Phoebus artem carminis dedit, Hor. **b.** In gen. : regius, Cic. ; muliebris, patricius, Liv. ; avidus, Hor. ; fiducia ac spiritus, Caes. ; Verg. ; Hor., etc. In *pl.* : tribunicii, Cic. ; tanti, Caes. ; feroces, Liv. ; in re militari sumere, Caes. ; Liv. ; hostilis spiritūs gerere, remittere, Cic. ; frangere, Liv. ; cohibere, Tac. [*Sp. espiritu ;* Fr. *esprit.*]

spīrō, āre, *to breathe, blow.* **A.** Intrans. **1.** Lit. **a.** In gen. : flabra, Lucr. ; Verg. ; Ov. **b.** Of smell : graviter spirantis thymbrae, Verg. **c.** Of flames or boiling water : e pectore flamma, Ov. ; freta, Verg. **d.** *to breathe, draw breath, respire :* Cic. Most freq. in *Pres. Part. :* Cic., Sall. ; corpus, Curt. ; Luc. ; exta, Verg. ; margarita viva ac spirantia, Tac. **2.** Transf. **a.** *to breathe auspiciously* (like a breeze), *be favourable :* Cynthia nobis, Prop. ; di spirate secundi, Verg. **b.** *to be animated, live, be alive :* Laeli mens etiam in scriptis, Cic. ; spirante etiam re publicā, Cic. ; amor, Hor. Of paintings, sculpture : excudent alii spirantia mollius aera, Verg. **c.** *to have poetic spirit or inspiration :* Hor. With *Intern.* Acc. **1.** Lit. **a.** In gen. : Zephyros secundos, Verg. ; venti frigora, Verg. **b.** Of smell : ambrosiae comae divinum vertice odorem, Verg. ; Juv. **c.** Of flames, etc. : equi spirantes naribus ignem, Lucr. ; flammas boves, Liv. **2.** Transf. *to breathe out* (i.e. be full of, express) : amores, Hor. ; inquietum hominem et tribunatum etiam nunc spirantem, Liv. ; Lucr. ; Prop. ; immane, Verg. ; tragicum satis, Hor. ; maiora, Curt.

spissē, *adv. thickly, closely.* **1.** Lit. : Plin. *Comp. :* Plin. **2.** Transf. *slowly :* Cic. *Comp. :* Varr.

spissesco, ere [spissus], *to become thick, to condense :* Lucr.

spissi-gradus, a, um [spissus gradus], *slow-paced :* Pl.

spissō, āre [spissus], *to thicken, make thick, condense :* ignis densum spissatus in aera, Ov. ; Plin.

spissus, a, um, *thick, close, compact, dense.* **1.** Lit. : tunica, Pl. ; corpus, Lucr. ;

vimen, Verg. ; harena, Verg. ; non tam
spissa viris, Verg. ; theatra, Hor. ; coma,
Hor. ; ramis laurea, Hor. ; liquor, aer,
nubes, Ov. ; noctis umbrae, Verg. ; caligo,
Ov. *Comp.* : Luc. *Sup.* : Plin. **2.**
T r a n s f. **a.** Of time : *slow, tardy, late* :
Pl., Cic. **b.** *hard, difficult* : spissum opus
et operosum, Cic. Ep. *Comp.* : Cic. [It.
spesso : Sp. *cespeso* ; Fr. *épais.*]

splēn, ēnis, *m.* [σπλήν], *the milt* or *spleen* :
Plin., Pers.

splendeō, ēre, *to be clear and bright, to gleam
with pure light, to be spotlessly* or *transparently bright.* **1.** L i t. : oculi, Pl. ;
stella candida, Pl. ; hastis campus, Enn. ;
sedes fulgenti auro, Cat. ; Lucr. ; labra,
Verg. ; tremulo sub lumine pontus, Verg. ;
focus, Glycera, Hor. ; cubiculum marmore,
Plin. Ep. **2.** T r a n s f. : virtus per sese
semper, Cic. ; alienā invidiā, Liv.

splendēscō, ere [splendeō], *to become clear
and bright, be burnished.* **1.** L i t. : vomer,
Verg. ; Aetnaeā caelum fiammā, Ov. **2.**
T r a n s f. : oratione, Cic. ; canorum illud
in voce, Cic. ; opus limā, Plin. Ep.

splendĭdē, *adv., brightly, brilliantly.* **1.** L i t. :
ornare convivium, Cic. **2.** T r a n s f. : acta
aetas, Cic. ; loqui, facere, Cic. ; splendide
mendax, Hor. ; splendidissime natus,
Sen. Ep.

splendĭdus, a, um [splendeō], *clear and bright,
spotlessly* or *transparently brilliant, gleaming,
glistening, etc.* **1.** L i t. : stellae, Enn. ;
Lucr. ; lumina solis, Lucr. ; Ov. ; fons
splendidior vitro, Hor. ; Galatea, Ov. ;
splendidissimus candor, Cic. **2.** T r a n s f.
a. Of tone, *clear* : vox, Cic. **b.** Of moral
character, *spotless, untarnished* : arbitria,
Hor. **c.** Of style of dress, rank, etc. :
Cic. ; domus, Cat. ; Verg. ; cultus, Quint. ;
secundas res splendidiores facit amicitia,
Cic. ; vir splendidissimus civitatis suae,
Cic. ; Plin. Ep. Also, oratio, verba, causa,
Cic. ; facta, Hor. **d.** *showy, fine, specious* :
nomen, Cic. ; verba, Ov.

splendor, ōris, *m.* [splendeō], *clearness and
brightness, brilliance, lustre, sheen.* **1.** L i t. :
Pl., Lucr. ; ex gemmis, Cic. ; flammae, Ov. ;
argenti, Hor. **2.** T r a n s f. **a.** Of tone,
clearness : vocis, Cic. **b.** Of character,
spotlessness : vitae, Cic., Liv. ; animi et
vitae, Cic. **c.** In gen. : *brilliance, lustre* :
Cic. ; equester, Cic. ; imperi, Cic. ; verborum Graecorum, Cic. ; suae dignitatis,
Cic.

splēniātus, a, um [splēnium], *having a plaster*
or *patch on* : mentum, Mart.

splēnium, I, *n. a plaster* or *patch* (for the face) :
Plin., Mart., Plin. Ep.

spoliārium, i, *n.* [spolium], *a place in the
amphitheatre where the clothes were stripped
from the slain gladiators* : Sen.

spoliātiō, ōnis, *f.* [spoliō], *a stripping,
pillaging.* **1.** L i t. : omnium rerum, Cic. ;
Liv. In *pl.* : Cic. **2.** T r a n s f. : consulatūs, dignitatis, Cic.

spoliātor, ōris, *m.* (Cic., Liv., Juv.) and
spoliātrix, īcis, *f.* (Cic., Mart.) [spoliō],
a stripper, pillager : monumentorum, Cic. ;
templi, Liv. ; pupilli, Juv.

spoliātus, a, um. **I.** *Part.* spoliō. **II.** A d j.
stripped : nihil illo regno spoliatius, Cic. Ep.

spoliō, āre [spolium], *tn strip, to deprive of
clothing.* **1.** L i t. : aliquem, Liv., Luc. ;
aliquem vestitu, Cic. ; Nep. ; corpus uno
torque, Liv. **2.** T r a n s f. *to rob, pillage,
plunder* in gen. : aliquem, Pl. ; fana sociorum,
Cic. ; Verg., etc. ; aliquem argento, Cic. ;
spoliari fortunis, Cic. ; ut Gallia omni
nobilitate spoliaretur, Caes. ; Liv. ; aliquem vitā, Verg. ; aliquem dignitate, Cic. ;
te coniuge, Ov. [It. *spogliare.*]

spolium, i, *n.* [*cf.* σκύλον; *v.* spūma], *the
skin* or *hide* of an animal stripped off.
1. L i t. (mostly in *pl.*) : pelles et spolia
ferarum, Lucr. ; leonis, Ov. **2.** T r a n s f.
a. *arms and clothing,* and esp. *the armour
stripped from a slain enemy* (usually in
pl.) : Cic., Verg., Liv., etc. In *sing.* :
Verg. **b.** In partic. spolia opima (*v.*
opimus). **c.** *spoils, booty* in war (in *pl.*) :
Caes., Verg., etc. ; nautica, Cic. ; exercitūs
iacentis, Liv. ; agrorum, Liv. **d.** *pillage*
of other things : aliorum spoliis nostras
facultates augere, Cic. ; fert secum spolium
sceleris, Ov. [It. *spoglia.*]

sponda, ae, *f. the frame* of a bedstead or sofa.
1. L i t. : Ov. **2.** T r a n s f. *a bed, couch,
sofa* : Verg., Suet., etc.

spondālium or **spondaulium**, i, *n. a sacrificial hymn, accompanied by the flute* :
Cic.

spondeō, spondēre, spopondī, spōnsum.
1. L i t. **a.** In law and public affairs :
to promise solemnly, to bind, engage, or
pledge oneself : Pl., Cic. ; aliquid, Cic. ;
ego meā fide spondeo futurum ut etc.,
Plin. Ep. ; *Ly.* filiam tuam sponden' mihi
uxorem dari ? *Ch.* spondeo, Pl. Esp. of
going bail for another : Cic., Liv., Hor. ;
pro multis, Cic. ; Liv. ; spoponderunt
consules, legati, quaestores, Liv. ; nihil
hosti, Liv. ; pacem, Liv. **b.** In gen. :
to promise sacredly, to vow. With Acc.
and *Fut. Inf.* : Cic., Liv. With Acc.
and *Pres. Inf.* : Cic. Ep. With Acc. :
hoc de me tibi, Cic. Ep. ; honores et
praemia, Cic. ; fidom, Ov. ; (hoc) mihi,
Verg. ; officium Amori, Ov. **2.** T r a n s f.
of non-personal Subjects : spondet fortuna
salutem, Verg. ; Liv. ; spondentia sidera,
Ov.

spondēus, i, *m.* [σπονδεῖος], *a spondee* (a
metrical foot, consisting of two long
syllables) : Cic., Hor. etc.

spondylus, i, *m.* [σφόνδυλος], *a kind of shell-
fish* : perh. *a mussel* : Plin., Mart.

spongia, ae, *f.* [σπογγιά], *a sponge.* **1.** L i t. :
Lucr., Cic., etc. **2.** T r a n s f. **a.** *an open-
worked coat of mail* : Liv. **b.** Of other
sponge-like things : Plin., Mart. [Fr.
éponge.]

spōnsa, ae, *v.* spōnsus.

spōnsālis, e, *adj.* [spōnsus], *of betrothal* :
Varr. As Noun, **spōnsālia,** ium (GEN.
spōnsāliōrum, Suet.), *n. pl.* **a.** *a betrothal,
espousal* : facere, Cic. Ep., Liv., Ov. ;
parare, Ov. **b.** *a betrothal feast* : a. d.
VIII Id. Apr. sponsalia Crassipedi praebui,
Cic. Ep. [It. *sponsalizia* ; Fr. *épousailles.*]

spōnsiō, ōnis, *f.* [spondeō], *a solemn promise*
or *engagement; a guarantee.* **a.** In gen. :
Cic. ; non foedere pax Caudina sed per
sponsionem facta est, Liv. ; spunsionem

interponere, repudiare, Liv. ; sponsione se obstringere, Liv. ; sponsionem faciunt uti etc., Sall. ; Ocriculani sponsione in amicitiam accepti, Liv. **b.** In civil suits : *an agreement between two parties that the loser should pay a certain sum to the other :* sponsionem facere, Cic. ; sponsione se defendere, Liv. ; aliquem sponsione lacessere, vincere, Cic. Hence, in gen. : *a bet, wager :* Juv.

spōnsor, ōris, *m.* [spondeō], *a bondsman, surety :* sponsor es pro Pompeio, Cic. Ep. ; alicuius, Cic. In gen. sense : promissorum alicuius, Cic. ; coniugii, Ov. ; illi do meā voluntato, Cic.

spōnsū, ABL. *sing. m.* [spondeō], *(by) engagement* or *contract :* Cic. Ep.

spōnsus, a, um. **I.** *Part.* spondeō. **II.** Noun, **spōnsus**, ī, *m.*, and **spōnsa**, ae, *f. a betrothed ; a bridegroom, a bride :* Pl., Cic., Liv., Hor. Poet. of Penelope's suitors : Hor. ; **spōnsum**, ī, *n. a covenant, agreement, engagement :* negare, Hor. ; ex sponso egit, Cic. [It. *sposo ;* Sp. *esposo ;* Fr. *époux.*]

sponte, ABL. (and **spontis**, GEN. in phr. suae spontis esse, *to be one's own master,* Varr.) [spondeō]. **I.** Of persons. **a.** *of one's own accord, voluntarily* (mostly with meā, tuā, suā) : si hic non insanit satis suā sponte, instiga, Ter. ; Caes. ; Cic. ; Verg. ; Liv., etc. Without *Possess.* Pron. : Italiam non sponte sequor, Verg. ; Ov. ; Quint. ; Tac. With *Possess.* GEN. of Noun : deorum, Luc. ; naturae, Plin. ; principis, Tac. **b.** *of* or *by oneself, unaided :* nequeo pedibus meā sponte ambulare, Pl. ; cum Poenis suo nomine ac suā sponte bellare, Cic. ; Caes. ; neo suā spontc sed eorum auxilio, Cic. Ep. **II.** Of things. **a.** *of itself, spontaneously :* ardor non alieno impulsu sed suā sponte movetur, Cic. ; Lucr. ; Verg. ; clamor suā sponte ortus, Liv. ; te sponte suā probitas iuvat, Ov. Without *Possess.* Pron. : ut numeri sponte fluxisse videantur, Quint. With quādam : Quint. **b.** *on its own account, for its own sake :* sapientem suā sponte ac per se bonitas et iustitia delectat, Cic.

Sporades, um, *f. pl. islands in the Aegean Sea, between the Cyclades and Crete.*

sporta, ae, *f.* [cogn. with Gk. σπυρίς], *a plaited basket* or *hamper :* Cato. Used as a sieve : Plin., Mart.

sportella, ae, *f.* [dim. sporta], *a little basket, a fruit-basket :* Cic. Ep., Suet.

sportula, ae, *f.* [dim. sporta], *a little basket.* **1.** Lit. : Pl. **2.** Transf. *of a distribution or gift of food or money to clients :* Mart., Juv., Suet. Of a present in gen. : Plin. Ep.

sprētiō, ōnis, *f.* [spernō], *disdain, scorn, contempt :* Romanorum, Liv.

sprētor, ōris, *m.* [spernō], *a despiser, scorner :* deorum, Ov.

sprētus, a, um, *Part.* spernō.

spūma, ae, *f.* [spuō], *foam, froth, scum.* **a.** In gen. : cum spumas agerot in ore, Cic. ; Enn. ; Lucr. ; per armos spuma (apri) fluit, Ov. ; spumas salis aere ruebant, Verg. **b.** caustica spuma, *a kind of plant :* a preparation used by the Teutons for reddening the hair : Mart.

spūmatū, ABL. *sing.* = [spūmō], *foam, slaver* of a serpent : Stat.

spūmātus, a, um [spūma], *covered with foam :* saxa salis niveo liquore, Cic. poet.

spūmēscō, ere [spūma], *to grow foamy* or *frothy :* aequora remo, Ov.

spūmeus, a, um [spūma], *foaming, frothy :* Nereus, Verg. ; torrens, Ov.

spūmifer, era, erum [spūma ferō], *foambearing, foaming :* amnis, Ov.

spūmiger, era, erum [spūma gerō], *foaming :* sus, Lucr.

spūmō, āre [spūma], *to foam, froth.* **1.** Lit. : spumans aper, Verg. ; fluctu caorula, Verg. ; Enn. ; Lucr. ; pocula lacte, Verg. Of an angry person : spumantibus ardens visceribus, Juv. **2.** Transf. (with *Intern.* ACC.) : spumans ex ore scelus, Auct. Her.

spūmōsus, a, um [spūma], *full of foam, foaming.* **1.** Lit. : litora, Cat. ; undae, Ov. ; Verg. **2.** Transf. *frothy, bombastic :* carmen, Pers.

spuō, uere, uī, ūtum (*cf.* Gk. πτύω], *to spit :* Plin. With ACC. : terram ore, Verg.

spurcātus, a, um. **I.** *Part.* spurcō. **II.** Adj. *filthy, foul.* Sup. : Cic.

spurcē, *adv. filthily.* Transf. : qui in illam miseram tam spurce, tam impie dixeris, Cic. Comp. : Cato. Sup. : perscribere, Cic. Ep.

spurcidicus, a, um [spurcus dicō], *using filthy language, smutty, obscene :* versus, Pl.

spurcificus, a, um [spurcus faciō], *making filthy, smutty, obscene :* Pl.

spurcitia, ae, *f.* (Varr., Plin.) and **spurcitiēs**, ēī, *f.* (Lucr.) [spurcus], *filth, dirt, smut.* In *pl.* : Varr., Plin.

spurcō, āre [spurcus], *to make filthy, to befoul, defile.* **1.** Lit. : spurcatur nasum odore inlutili, Pl. **2.** Transf. : senectus spurcata impuris moribus, Cat.

spurcus, a, um, *filthy, dirty, nasty, unclean, impure.* **1.** Lit. : Lucil., Lucr., Cat. Sup. : tempestas, Cic., Suet. **2.** Transf. **a.** noctes, Pl. ; lupae, Mart. **b.** Of character or condition : homo, Lucil., Varr. ; Dama, Hor. Comp. : Mart. Sup. : Cic. **c.** mors, Sen. Ep.

Spurinna, ae, *m. the haruspex who warned Caesar to beware of the Ides of March.*

spūtātilicus, a, um [spūtō], *that deserves to be spit at, loathsome :* crimina, Sisenn. ap. Cic.

spūtātor, ōris, *m.* [spūtō], *a spitter :* Pl.

spūtō, āre [freq. spuō], *to spit, spit out.* **1.** Lit. : sanguinem, Pl. ; Ov. **2.** Transf. *to avert by spitting* (as a charm) : morbus, qui sputatur, Pl.

spūtum, ī, *n.* [spuō], *spit, spittle :* Plin. In *pl.* : Lucr., Prop., ete.

squāleō, ēre, *to be rough, scaly, furred, wrinkled, etc. ; to be coated, clotted, stiff.* **1.** Lit. : squalentis conchas, Verg. ; picti squalentia terga lacerti, Verg. ; squalentia tela venenis, Ov. ; tunicam squalentem auro, Verg. **2.** Transf. **a.** *to be overgrown, to be covered with filth* or *weeds* from neglect : supellex atque aedes meae, Pl. ; barba, Verg. ; coma, Ov. ; squalent abductis arva colonis, Verg. ; squalens litus,

Tac. ; arma situ, Quint. **b.** In mourning :
squalebat civitas publico consilio mutatā
veste, Cic. **c.** *cracked and parched :* pulvere fauces, Luc.
squālidē, *adv. without ornament, rudely.*
Comp.: dicere, Cic.
squālidus, a, um [squāleō], *rough, scaly,*
stiff. **1.** L i t. : corpora, Lucr. ; rubigo,
Cat. Of serpents : Acc. **2.** T r a n s f.
a. *unkempt, neglected :* homo, Pl., Ter. ;
corpora, Liv. ; carcer, humus, Ov. **b.** In
mourning : reus, Ov. ; Quint. ; tristi
morā, Tac. **c.** *cracked and parched :*
siccitate regio, Curt. **d.** Of speech : *rough,*
without ornament. Comp. : Cic.
squālor, ōris, m. [squāleō], *roughness, stiffness.*
1. L i t. : Lucr. **2.** T r a n s f. **a.** *filth* from
neglect : Pl., Cic., Tac. ; obsita erat
squaloro vestis, Liv. ; inluvie, squalore
enecti, Liv. ; locorum, Curt. **b.** In mourning : aspicite, iudices, squalorem sordisque
sociorum, Cic. ; Liv. ; Tac. **c.** Of speech :
roughness : Quint.
squālus, a, um, *filthy :* vestis, Enn.
squalus, i, m. *a kind of sea-fish,* belonging
to the shark or dog-fish group : Varr., Ov.
squāma, ae, f. *a scale* (of a fish, serpent, etc.).
1. L i t. : Cic., Verg., Ov. **2.** T r a n s f.
a. *scale-armour :* Verg. **b.** *a fish :* Juv.
c. Of other scale-like things : Plin.
squāmeus, a, um [squāma], *scaly :* anguis,
Verg. ; Ov.
squāmifer (Cic. poet.) [squāma ferō] and
squāmiger, era, erum [squāma gerō],
scale-bearing, scaly : pisces, Cic. poet. ;
cervices (anguis), Ov. As Noun, **squāmi-**
gerī, ōrum, m. pl. *fishes :* Lucr., Plin.
squāmōsus, a, um [squāma], *covered with*
scales, scaly : pecus (i.e. pisces), Pl. ;
draco, Verg. ; Ov.
squilla, v. scilla.
st, *interj. hist! hush!* Pl., Cic. Ep.
'st, abbrev. for est, r. sum.
stabilīmen, inis, n. [stabiliō], *a stay, support :*
regni, Acc.
stabilīmentum, i, n. [stabiliō], *a stay,*
support : ventris, Pl. ; favorum, Plin.
stabiliō, ire [stabilis], *to make firm,* or *stable :*
to establish. **1.** L i t. : Enn., Lucr., Caes.
2. T r a n s f. : regnum, Pl. ; rem publicam,
Cic. ; res Capuae stabilitas Romanā disciplinā, Liv.
stabilis, e, adj. [stō], *firm, steady, stable.*
1. L i t. : domus, Pl., Cic. ; via plana et
stabilis, Cic. ; locus ad insistendum, Liv. ;
elephanti pondere ipso, Liv. ; medio sedet
insula ponto, Ov. ; gradus, pugna, acies,
Liv. ; Tac. ; stabilior Romanus erat,
Liv. **2.** T r a n s f. **a.** fundamentum, Lucr. ;
amici, matrimonium, possessio, sententia,
oratio, etc., Cic. ; animus stabilis amicis,
Cic. ; virtus maneat stabili pede, Ov. ;
spondei, Hor. ; pedes, syllabae, etc., Quint.
Comp. : imperium stabilius, Tor. *Sup. :*
Cato. **b.** stabile est, with Acc. and *Inf. :*
it is settled : Pl.
stabilitās, ātis, f. [stabilis], *steadiness,*
firmness, durability. **1.** L i t. : Cic. ; peditum, Caes. **2.** T r a n s f. : Cic. ; fortunae,
amicitiae, Cic.
stabiliter, adv. *firmly, durably :* Vitr.
Comp. : Suet.

stabulō, āre [stabulum], **A.** T r a n s. *to*
stable or *house cattle, etc.* : pecus in fundo,
Varr. In *Mid.* or *Pass. :* Varr., Ov.
B. I n t r a n s. *to stable, have their stall :*
centauri in foribus stabulant, Verg.
stabulum, i, n. [stō], *a standing-place,*
steading, quarters, abode. **1.** L i t. **a.** In
gen. : Pl. ; pastorum, Cic. ; Verg. ; Liv. ;
ovium, Varr. ; Verg. ; taurorum, apium,
ferarum, Verg. **b.** Of low haunts, taverns,
brothels, etc. : Pl., Cic., Mart., Plin. Ep.
2. T r a n s f. **a.** confidentiae, Pl. **b.** As
term of abuse : stabulum nequitiae, Pl.
[Fr. *étable.*]
stacta, ae (Pl., Lucr., Plin.) and **stactē,** ēs
(Pl., Plin.), f. [στακτή], *myrrh-oil.*
stadium, i, n. [στάδιον], *a stade.* **1.** L i t.
a. Prop. as measure of length, about a
furlong : Cic., Sall. **b.** *a race-course for*
foot-racing (among the Greeks) : qui
stadium currit, Cic. **2.** T r a n s f. : in
stadium artis rhetoricae prodire, Auct.
Her.
Stagīra, ōrum, n. pl. *a town in Macedonia,*
the birth-place of Aristotle ; **Stagīrītēs,**
ae, m. *a native of Stagira ;* esp. *Aristotle.*
stagnō, āre [stagnum], **A.** I n t r a n s. *to*
form a pool of standing water, to stagnate.
1. L i t. : Nilus, Verg. ; Indus, Curt. **2.**
T r a n s f. *to be overflowed* or *inundated :*
paludibus orbis, Ov. ; Sall. **B.** T r a n s.
to make stagnant. **1.** L i t. : Cecropio
stagnata luto, Stat. **2.** T r a n s f. *to over-*
flow, inundate : (loca) stagnata paludibus
umont, Ov. ; Tiberis plana urbis stagna-
verat, Tac.
stagnum, i, n. [sta, root of stō], *a piece of*
standing water, a pool, swamp, lagoon, etc.
(mostly in *pl.*). **1.** L i t. : Enn., Verg.,
Liv., etc. **2.** T r a n s f. **a.** *still* or *enclosed*
waters : Baiarum, Prop. ; navale, Tac.
b. *narrow waters, straits :* Euripi, Cic. ;
imis stagna refusa vadis, Verg. [Fr. *étang.*]
stalagmium, i, n. [σταλάγμιον], *an ear-*
drop, pendant : Pl.
stāmen, inis, n. [sta, root of stō ; cf. Gk.
στή-μων], *the warp in the upright loom of*
the ancients. **1.** L i t. : Varr., Tib., Ov.
2. T r a n s f. **a.** *a thread hanging from the*
distaff : aut ducunt lanas aut stamina
pollice versant, Tib., Ov. Of *the threads*
of the Parcae : Tib., Ov., Juv. **b.** *threads*
of other sorts : of the spider, Ov., Plin. ;
the *strings* of an instrument, Ov. ; of the
fibres of wood, of a nct, etc., Plin. **c.** *a*
cloth which is made of threads ; *the fillets*
of priests : Prop. [Fr. *étamine.*]
stāmineus, a, um [stāmen], *consisting of*
threads, full of threads, thready : rota
rhombi, Prop. ; vena ligni, *fibrous,* Plin.
stannum, i, n. **I.** *an alloy of silver and lead :*
Plin., Suet. **II.** Later, *tin.* [From form
stagnum, It. *stagno ;* Fr. *étain.*]
stata, f. adj. : only in phr. stata mater
(perh. Vesta) : Cic.
statārius, a, um [stō], *standing, standing*
firm, stationary, steady : miles, hostis, Liv.
Of an orator : *calm :* Cic. As Noun,
statāria (sc. comoedia), *so called from the*
quiet acting of the performers, Ter. ; **sta-**
tāriī, ōrum, m. pl. *the actors in the* comoedia
stataria, Cic.

statēra, ae, *f.* [στατήρ], *a steelyard* or *scales.* **1.** Lit.: aurificis, Cic.; Stat.; Suet. **2.** Transf. *the yoke-bar* of a waggon, etc. : Stat.

staticulum, i, *n.* [*dim.* statua], *a statuette* : Plin.

staticulus, i, *m.* [stō], *a kind of gentle dance* : Pl., Cato.

statim, *adv.* [stō], *steadfastly* or *where one stands* or *without giving ground.* **1.** Lit.: nemo recedit loco quin statim rem gerat, Pl.; Enn.; statim stant signa, Pl. **2.** Transf. **a.** *steadily* (i.e. regularly): ex his praediis talenta argenti bina statim capiebat, Ter. **b.** *on the spot, straightway, at once, immediately, instantly* : Pl., Caes., Cic., Lucr., etc. Followed by various conjunctions and preps.: statim ut, Cic.; statim post, Suet. With ABL. *Absol.* : Cic., Nep.

statiō, ōnis, *f.* [stō], *a standing, a standing still.* **1.** Lit.: mostly in phr. in statione, *without moving, in a firm posture* : Lucr., Ov.; stationem facere, *to stand still,* Plin.; stationes matutinas facere, Plin. **2.** Transf. (concr.) *a station, fixed place.* **A.** In gen. *a post, abode, residence* : Cic. Ep.; quā positus fueris in statione, mane, Ov.; apricis statio gratissima mergis, Verg.; plerique in stationibus sedent, Plin. Ep.; pone recompositas in statione comas, Ov. **B.** Milit. **a.** *a post, station* : in stationem succedere, Caes.; stationem inire, Tac.; in statione, in stationibus esse, Caes.; in statione manere, Ov.; stationem habere, Liv.; cohortes ex statione emissae, Caes.; stationem relinquere, Verg.; deserere, Suet. Transf.: de praesidio et statione vitae decedere, Cic. **b.** *a picket* ; esp. in *pl., sentries, sentinels* : ut stationes dispositas haberent, Caes.; Liv. **C.** Nautical, *an anchorage, roadstead* : quieta, Caes.; male fida, Verg.; Liv. [It. *stagione* ; Sp. *estacion.*]

Stātius, i, *m.* **I.** Caecilius Statius, *a comic poet* : v. Caecilius. **II.** P. Papinius Statius, *a poet of the time of Domitian, author of the* Thebais, Silvae, *etc.*

stativus, a, um [status], *standing still, stationary.* **a.** In gen.: aquae, Varr. **b.** Milit.: castra, Caes., Cic., etc.; praesidium, *appointed* or *fixed post,* Cic., Liv. As Noun, **stativa**, ōrum, *n. pl.* (*sc.* castra): Liv., Tac.

stator, ōris, *m.* [stō], *a magistrate's attendant* : Cic. Ep.

Stator, ōris, *m.* [sistō], *the Stayer* (from flight), epithet of Jupiter : Cic., Liv., Ov.

statua, ae, *f.* [status, from stō], *an image, statue.* **1.** Lit.: Pl., Cic., Cat., Hor., etc.; ex auro, Pl.; equestris, Cic. **2.** Transf. of a silent, stolid person : Pl.

statuārius, a, um [statua], *of or relating to statues* : ars, Plin. As Noun, **statuāria**, ae, *f.* (*sc.* ars) *the art of sculpture* : Plin.; **statuārius**, i, *m. a maker of statues, a statuary* : Quint.

statūmen, inis, *n.* [statuō], *a support, stay. prop:* Plin.; *a rib of a boat,* Caes.

statuō, uere, uī, ūtum [status, from stō]. **1.** Lit. **A.** *to cause to stand, to set up, place in position.* **a.** In gen.: aquilam,

Pl.; signum, Liv.; mē lūctālem Pl.; tabernacula, Caes.; tabernaculum in medium, Liv.; tabernacula in foro, Liv.; crateras, Verg.; aliquem in convivio, Cic.; captivos in medio, Liv.; bovem ad fanum Dianae et ante aram, Liv.; Verg.; aliquem ante oculos, Cic. Of planting a tree : agro meo triste lignum, Hor.; Plin. **b.** Of more permanent constructions : *to build, found* : aram et statuam, Pl.; monumentum, Cic.; statuam in rostris, Cic.; templum, Ov., Tac.; urbem, Verg.; carceres in circo, Liv.; aliquem statuere (=alicui statuam statuere), Ov., etc. **B.** *to cause to stand still* or *rest* : navem, Pl.; fessos boves, Prop. **2.** Transf. **A.** *to establish, set up* a precedent, principle, etc.: exemplum alicui, Pl.; in aliquo exemplum huius modi, Cic.; documentum, Liv., Tac.; ius, iura, Cic., Liv.; Numa omnis partis religionis, Cic.; hoc iudicium unae rei, Cic.; vectigal novum ex salariā annonā, Liv. **B.** Of appointments to a position: arbitrum me huius rei, Cic. Ep. **C.** *to set, fix, determine* limits, conditions, price, time : diuturnitati imperi modum, Cic.; modum orationi, Cic.; Ter.; felicitati modum, Liv.; cupidinibus modum, Hor.; novos finis, Liv.; inimicitiarum modum, Cic.; hanc condicionem Gaditanis, Cic.; eam sibi legem ut etc., Cic.; pretium alicui rei, Pl.; Ter.; Tac.; pretium (vecturae et sali), Liv.; diem, Mart.; diem insidiis, Sall.; diem comitiis, Liv.; multitudini diem statuit ante quam sine fraude liceret etc., Sall.; diem patrando facinori, Liv.; Tac.; statuto tempore, Plin., Curt. **D.** *to settle, fix, decide* disputes, etc. **a.** Between others : conlegae de religione, Liv.; Cic.; de aliquo (i.e. esp. with ref. to punishment) Caes., Sall., Tac.; super tantā re, Tac. With Acc. of *Neut. Pron.* : Caes., Tac., etc. With *Indir. Quest.* or *Deliberative* : Cic., Liv., Tac., etc. *Impers. Pass.* : Liv.; non ex rumore statuendum, Tac. **b.** With ref. to the Subject's own mind : *to decide, make up one's mind.* With *Indir. Quest.* or *Deliberative* : Cic., Liv., etc.; statuerent apud animos quid vellent, Liv. **E.** *to decide, decree, arrange.* **a.** In regard to others : sic, Ov.; poenam, Cic., Tac., etc.; triste aliquid, Ov.; aliquid gravius in aliquem, Caes., Cic.; in Pompeiam Sabinam exsilium statuitur, Tac.; remedium, Tac.; Vestalibus stipendium, Liv.; Tac.; alicui (with *Indir. Deliberative*), Cic.; Liv. With *ut* or *ne* and *Jussive Subj.* : Caes., Cic., Liv., Ov. **b.** With reference to the Subject's own acts (alw. with *Inf.*): Caes., Cic., Liv., Tac., etc. **F.** *to hold, judge* as a decided opinion or conviction : hoc, Cic. With Acc. and *Inf.* : Cic., Cat., Ov., etc. With *Gerund.* clause : Caesar statuit exspectandam classem, Caes.; Cic.; Sall. With *Predic. Adj., Noun,* or *Inf.* : voluptatem summum bonum statuens, Cic.; si rectum statuerimus concedere amicis quidquid velint, Cic.; Tac.

statūra, ae, *f.* [stō], prop. *an upright posture* ; hence, *height* or *size* of the body, *stature* : Pl., Caes., Cic.

status, a, um. **I.** *Part* sistŏ. **II.** Adj. *set,
fixed, appointed, due :* sacrificium, Cic.,
Liv. ; sacra, Ov. ; dies, locus, Liv.;
tempus, Tac. Also, forms (mulieris), Enn.
status, ūs, *m.* [stŏ], *a standing, mode of
standing, position, posture.* **1.** Lit.
(physically). **a.** In gen. : Cic., Ov. ;
hominis, Pl. ; stat in statu ut etc., Pl. ;
in gestu status (oratoris) erectus, Cic. ;
rectus, indecorus, Quint. ; crebro conmutat
statūs, Pl. Of statues, dreams, etc. :
Lucr., Cic., Nep., etc. Of external appearance, dress, etc. : Pl., Suet. **b.** Milit.
a position : statu movere hostem, Liv.
2. Transf. **A.** *posture, position, situation,
state.* **a.** Of public affairs : rei publicae,
civitatis, suarum rerum, etc., Caes., Cic.,
Liv., Ov. ; in eo statu civitas est ut etc.,
Cic. ; eo statu res erat ut etc., Caes. ;
Latio is status erat rerum ut etc., Liv. ;
Siciliam in antiquum statum restituere,
Cic. ; in pristinum statum venire, Caes. ;
urbanae res in commodiorem statum perveniunt, Caes. ; statum rei publicae labefactare, convellere, commutare, Cic. ; so,
firmare, sollicitare, Liv. ; ordinare, turbare,
evertere, restituere, Suet. ; ad visendum
statum regionis, Liv. (In these phrases,
status rei publicae or civitatis often means
"*form of constitution.*") **b.** Of private
affairs, civil position, social or professional
standing, etc. : Pl., Cic., Hor., etc. ; bonorum, Cic. ; hunc vitae statum usque ad
senectutem obtinere, Cic. ; statu periclitari,
Quint. ; vitae statum commutare, Nep. ;
me de vitae meae statu deducere, Cic. ;
multorum excisi status, Tac. **c.** Of Nature :
ex alio terram status excipit alter, Lucr. ;
aëris, Lucr. ; huius totius mundi atque
naturae, Cic. ; statum caeli notare, Liv.
d. Rhet. : refutatio accusationis appellatur Latine status, Cic. Also, *the essential
point :* Quint. **e.** Gramm. *the mood of
a verb :* Quint. **B.** *position* (*cf.* 1. b.):
adversarios de statu omni deiecimus, Cic. ;
ea vis formidine animum perterritum loco
et certo de statu demovet, Cic. ; de meo
statu declinare, Cic. [Sp. *estado ;* Fr. *état.*]
statūtus, a, um. **I.** *Part.* statuŏ. **II.** Adj. :
tall : Pl.
stega, ae, *f.* [στέγη], *the deck* of a ship : Pl.
stēlla, ae, *f.* [For sterula ; *cf.* Gk. ἀστήρ],
a star. **1.** Lit. : Enn., Lucr., Cic., Verg.,
etc. ; diurna, *Lucifer,* Pl. ; stella comans,
a comet, Ov. ; crinita, Suet. Poet. :
perhaps for sidus, *a constellation :* Verg.,
Hor., Ov. Of *the sun :* stella serena, Ov.
2. Transf. *a figure of a star :* chlamys
distincta aureis stellis, Suet. ; Plin. [Fr.
étoile.]
stēllāns, antis, *adj.* [stēlla], *starry.* **1.** Lit. :
caelum, Lucr., Verg. ; ora Tauri, Ov. **2.**
Transf. : gemmis caudam (pavonis)
stellantibus implet, Ov. ; Plin.
stēllātus, a, um [stēlla]. **I.** *set with stars,
starry.* Transf. : Argus, Ov. ; ensis
iaspide fulvā, Verg. ; Plin. **II.** *made into
a star :* Cepheus, Cic.
stēllifer, era, erum [stēlla ferŏ], *star-bearing,
starry :* Cic.
stēlliger, era, .erum [stēlla gerŏ], *star-
bearing, starry :* orbes, Cic. poet. ; Varr.

stēllŏ, ōnis, *m.* [stēlla], *a kind of lizard*
(having star-like spots on its back). **1.**
Lit. : Verg. **2.** Transf. of a crafty
person : Plin.
stēllŏ, are [stēllātus], *to set* or *cover with stars :*
(in *Pass.*) : Plin.
stemma, atis, *n.* [στέμμα]. **1.** Lit. *a garland* or *wreath* hung upon an ancestral
image : Plin., Sen. **2.** Transf. **a.** *a pedigree, genealogical tree :* Pers., Sen. Ep.,
Juv., etc. **b.** In *pl. : antiquity, history :*
Mart.
stercoreus, a, um [stercus], *dungy, foul :*
as a term of abuse, Pl.
stercorŏ, āre [stercus], *to dung, manure :*
agrum, Cic.
sterculīnium, I, *v.* sterquilīnium.
stercus, oris, *n. dung, ordure :* Cic., Hor.,
etc. As a vulgar term of abuse : *stercus
curiae* dici, Cic.
sterilis, e (*Neut. pl.* sterila, Lucr.), *adj.*
[*cf.* Gk. στείρα], *unfruitful, barren.* **1.**
Lit. of plants, animals, or soil : Lucr.,
Cat., Verg., Curt., etc. **2.** Transf. **a.**
causing barrenness, blighting : robigo,
Hor. ; hiems, Mart. **b.** *barren, bare,
empty :* manus, Pl. ; amicus, Juv. ; epistulae, Plin. Ep. Also, prospectus, Pl.;
corpora sonitu, Lucr. ; domus, Prop.
c. *unproductive, fruitless, vain :* Februa-
rius, Cic. Ep. ; amor, Ov. ; pax, Tac.
With GEN. : virtutum saeculum, Tac. ;
Pers.
sterilitās, ātis, *f.* [sterilis], *unfruitfulness.
barrenness.* **1.** Lit. of soils, plants, and
animals : Cic., Plin. In *pl.:* Suet., Plin.
Ep. **2.** Transf. : in sterilitatem emar-
cuit auctoritas, Plin. ; fortunae, Plin.
sternāx, ācis, *adj.* [sternŏ], *that throws to
the ground :* equus, Verg.
sternŏ, sternere, strāvi, strātum [*cf.* Gk.
στορέννυμι]. **I.** *to strew, bestrew, spread*
a bed, etc., with a coverlet, etc. **1.** Lit.
a. lectum, etc., Pl., Cic. (*Impers. Pass. :*
Plin. Ep.); equos (*sc.* sellis), Liv. With
Instr. ABL. : cubilia herbis, Lucr. ; pelli-
culis lectulos, Cic. ; Juv. **b.** Of paving
roads, etc. : locum, Cic. Ep. ; aspreta
saxis, Liv. ; vias silice, Liv. **2.** Transf.
a. *to bestrew :* solum telis, Verg. ; foliis
nemus, Hor. ; ante aras terram caesi
stravere iuvenci, Verg. **b.** *to pave, level :*
viam per mare Xerxes, Lucr. ; aequora
venti placidi, Verg. ; argento iter omne
viarum, Lucr. **c.** *to smooth :* odia militum,
Tac. **II.** *to strew, spread, extend* something
on the ground, etc. **A.** In gen. : poma
passim, Verg. ; harenam, herbas, Ov. ;
vestis, Ov. ; in solo vellus, Ov. ; fessi
sternunt corpora, Liv. ; se somno in litore,
Verg. In *Mid. :* humi stratus, Cic.:
membra sub arbuto stratus, Hor. ; sterni-
mur optatae gremio telluris, Verg. ; somno
strati, Liv. **B.** *to stretch out* on the
ground ; *to prostrate, overthrow.* **1.** Lit. :
caede viros, Verg. ; Liv. ; aliquem leto,
morte, Verg., Liv. ; sternitur vulnere,
Verg. ; Gallorum catervas, Liv. ; adversos
duces, Tib. ; aliquem morti, Verg. ; humi
bovem, Verg. ; ferro pecus, Hor. ; primos
et extremos humum, Hor. ; torrens agros,
Verg. ; moenia, Ov. ; a culmine Troiam,

Verg. ; arieto muros, Liv. **2.** T r a n s f. : adflictos se et stratos esse fatentur, Cic. ; mortalia corda pavor, Verg. ; virtus populi R. haec omnia strata humi erexit, Liv.

sternūmentum (sternūtāmentum, Sen.), I, *n.* [sternuō], *a sneezing.* **1.** L i t. : Cic., Plin. **2.** T r a n s f. *a sneezing powder* (to cause sneezing) : Plin.

sternuō, uere, uî [*cf.* Gk. πτάρνυμαι], *to sneeze.* **1.** L i t. : Plin. With *Intern.* Acc. : approbationem, Cat. ; omen, Prop. **2.** T r a n s f. : lumen sternuit, et nobis prospera signa dedit, Ov.

Steropē, ēs, *f. one of the Pleiades.*

Steropēs, is, *m. one of Vulcan's Cyclopes.*

sterquilīnium (stercul-), and **sterquilīnum** (Phaedr.), I, *n.* [stercus], *a dung-heap* : Cato, Varr. As term of abuse : Pl., Ter.

Stertinius, I, *m. a Stoic philosopher, ridiculed by Horace* ; **Stertinius**, a, um.

stertō, ere, *to snore* : Pl., Lucr., Cic., etc.

Stēsichorus, I, *m. a Greek lyric poet of Himera.*

Sthenelus, I, *m.* **I.** *king of Mycenae* ; *s. of Perseus and f. of Eurystheus* ; **Sthenelēius**, a, um, hostis, i.e. *Eurystheus,* Ov. **II.** *king of the Ligurians* ; *f. of Cycnus who was changed into a swan* ; **Sthenelēius**, a, um ; **Sthenelēis**, idis, *f. adj.* volucris, i.e. *Cycnus,* Ov. **III.** *one of the Epigoni, charioteer of Diomede at Troy, and one of those shut up in the wooden horse.* **IV.** *a Rutulian, killed by Pallas* : Verg.

stibadium, I, *n.* [στιβάδιον], *a semi-circular couch* or *seat* : Mart., Plin. Ep.

stibium, I, *n.* [στίβι], *antimony,* used to colour the eye-brows : Plin.

stigma, atis, *n.* [στίγμα], *a brand* stamped on slaves or others, as a mark of disgrace. **1.** L i t. : Sen., Quint., Juv., etc. **2.** T r a n s f. **a.** *a mark of disgrace, a stigma* : Mart., Suet. **b.** *a cut* (made by a clumsy barber) : Mart.

stigmatiās, ae, *m.* [στιγματίας], *one who is branded,* of a slave : Cic.

stigmōsus, a, um [stigma], *branded* : Plin. Ep.

stilla, ae, *f.* [*dim.* stiria], *a drop.* **1.** L i t. : muriae, Cic. **2.** T r a n s f. *a mere drop* : olei, Mart.

stillicidium, I, *n.* [stilla cadō], *a liquid falling drop by drop* : Lucr., Sen. E s p. of *rain-water falling from the eaves of houses* : iura stillicidiorum, Cic.

stillō, āre [stilla]. **A.** I n t r a n s. **1.** L i t. **a.** Of the liquid : *to drop, drip, trickle* : aqua, Varr. ; cera tabescens, Lucr. ; unguenta e capillo, Tib. ; mella de viridi ilice, Ov. **b.** Of the substance : umida saxa, Lucr. ; pugio, Cic. ; saxa guttis, Lucr. ; sanguine sidera, Ov. ; paenula multo nimbo, Juv. **2.** T r a n s f. : oratio, Sen. Ep. **B.** T r a n s. *to cause to drop, let fall in drops, distil.* **1.** L i t. : ex oculis rorem, Hor. ; stillata de ramis electra, Ov. **2.** T r a n s f. of calumny : in aurem alicuius exiguum de veneno, Juv.

stilus, I, *m.* [for stiglus ; *cf.* στίζω, στίγμα]. **I.** *a stake, pale* : Auct. B. Afr. **II.** *a pointed instrument* for writing on wax-tablets ; *a stile* or *style* : Pl., Cic., Hor. ;

stilum vertere, *to reverse the stile* (i.e. use the blunt end for erasing), Cic., Hor. T r a n s f. **a.** (*practice in*) *writing* : stilus optimus dicendi effector ac magister, Cic. ; multus stilus et adsidua lectio, Quint. ; stilo incumbere, Plin. Ep. **b.** *a manner of writing, mode of expression, style* : artifex, Cic. ; tardus, neglegens, rudis, confusus, fidelis, Quint. Also of speech : diligentis stili anxietas, Tac. ; pressus demissusque, Plin. Ep. ; pugnax, laetior, Plin. Ep.

stimulātiō, ōnis, *f.* [stimulō], *an incitement* : Plin., Tac.

stimulātrix, icis, *f.* [stimulō], *an inciter* : Pl.

stimuleus, a, um [stimulus], *consisting of prickles* or *goads* : supplicium, Pl.

stimulō, āre [stimulus], *to prick with a goad, to prick* or *urge on.* T r a n s f. **a.** *to goad, torment, trouble* : larvae virum, Pl. ; stimulatus furenti rabie, Cat. ; scrupulus, qui aliquem dies noctisque stimulat, Cic. ; consulem cura de minore filio stimulabat, Liv. **b.** *to spur on, incite, excite* : stimulante fame, Ov. ; Curt. ; aliquem, Liv. ; stimulata paelicis irā, Ov. ; irā stimulanto animos, Liv. ; Lucr. ; ad alicuius salutem defendendam stimulari, Cic. ; Sall. ; ad arma, Liv. ; ad iram, Tac. ; iniuriae dolor in Tarquinium eos stimulabat, Liv. ; in formidinem, Tac. ; nostra simultas antea stimulabat me ut caverem, Cic. Ep. With *ne* : Tac. With *Inf.* : Verg., Luc.

stimulus, I, *m.* (**stimulum**, I, *n.* Pl.) [for stig-mulus, *v.* stilus and īnstigō], *a goad* for driving cattle, slaves (usually in *pl.*). **1.** L i t. : Pl., Tib., Ov. **2.** T r a n s f. **a.** M i l i t. *a pointed stake concealed below the ground* : Caes. **b.** *a spur* (i.o. an incentive) : aliquem fodere stimulis (stimulo, Pl.), Cic. ; alicui admovere, Cic. ; stimulos sub pectore vertit Apollo, Verg. ; subdere animo, Liv. ; gloriae, industriae, Cic. ; amoris, Liv. ; Ov. ; defendendi Vatini, Cic. Ep. ; agrariae legis tribuniciis stimulis plebs furebat, Liv. ; ad dicendum pudor stimulos habet, Quint. ; in aliquem stimulis accendi, Tac. **c.** *a goad* (i.e. a sting or torment) : Pl., Lucr. ; doloris, Cic. ; res malae stimulos admovent, Cic. ; stimulos in pectore caecos condidit, Ov. P r o v. : advorsum stimulum calcare, Ter.

stinguō, ere, *to quench, extinguish* : Lucr.

stīpātiō, ōnis, *m.* [stīpō], *a thronging crowd, retinue* : hominum perditorum, Cic. ; Plin. Ep.

stīpātor, ōris, *m.* [stīpō], *an attendant* : in *pl., suite, retinue* : Cic., Sall., Hor. ; corporis, Cic.

stīpendiārius, a, um [stipendium]. **I.** *liable to impost* or *tax* (in fixed sums of money), *tributary* : civitas, Caes. ; Italiam vectigalem et stipendiariam facere, Liv. Also, vectigal, Cic. As Noun, **stīpendiāriī**, ōrum, *m. pl. tributaries* : socii stipendiariique populi Romani, Cic. ; Caes. ; Liv. **II.** M i l i t. *receiving pay* : Liv.

stīpendium, I, *n.* (contr. of stipipendium, from stips pendō]. **I.** *a tax, impost, tribute* (payable in money). **1.** L i t. : imponere victis, Caes. ; pendere, Enn., Caes., Liv., etc. ; conferre, solvere, Liv. ;

capero, Caes. ; stipendio eos liberare, Caes.
2. Transf. a. pauperes satis stipendi
pendere si liberos educent, Liv. **b.** Of
penalties : ferens stipendia tauro, Cat. ;
quod me manet stipendium ? Hor. **c.** Of
the income or allowances of priests : Liv.
II. Milit. *pay, soldiers' wages.* **1.** Lit. :
militare (adj.), Liv. ; flagitare, Caes. ; dare,
Liv. ; numerare militibus, Cic. ; persolvere,
Cic. Ep. ; dare pecuniam in stipendium,
Caes. ; stipendio exercitum adficere, Cic. ;
augere, fraudare, Caes. Phr. : merere or
mereri stipendia, lit. *to earn a soldier's
pay :* hence, *to perform military service,
to serve :* Cic. ; stipendia emereri, *to serve
out one's time,* Cic., Sall., Liv. **2. Transf.
a.** *military service* (usually in *pl.*) : facere,
Sall., Liv. ; milites stipendiis confecti,
Cic. ; stipendiis exhausti, Liv. In *sing.* :
homo nullius stipendi, Sall. ; sextus decimus
stipendi annus, Tac. **b.** *a year's service, a
campaign :* qui eorum minime multa stipendia haberet, Liv. ; Pl. ; Tac. **c.** In
gen. : libidinis, Cic. ; humanae vitae,
Sen. Ep.

stipes, itis, *m.* [same root as stipo], *a log,
trunk of a tree, etc.* **1.** Lit. : Caes., Cat.,
Verg., Liv., etc. **2. Transf. a.** As term
of contempt : Ter. **b.** *a tree :* Ov. **c.** *a
branch :* Luc., Mart.

stipo, āre [*cf.* Gk. στέφω]. **I.** *to crowd or
press together :* materies stipata, Lucr. ;
ingens argentum, Verg. ; apes mella,
Verg. ; Graeci stipati, quini in lectulis,
saepe plures, Cic. ; stipata cohors, Verg. ;
Liv. ; arto stipata theatro Roma, Hor. ;
in arto stipatae erant naves, Liv. **II. A.**
to crowd or *throng* a place, etc. : curia
patribus stipata, Ov. ; tribunal, Plin. Ep. ;
pontis calonibus et impedimentis stipatos,
Suet. **B.** *to crowd* or *throng around* a
person, *to close round.* **1.** Lit. : senatum
armatis, Cic. ; Catilina stipatus choro
iuventutis, Cic. ; Ov. ; telis stipati, Cic.
2. Transf. : senectus stipata studiis
iuventutis, Cic.

stips, stipis, *f.* *a small coin* (esp. used in
offerings and gifts and fees) : Cic., Liv.,
Ov., etc.

stipula, ae, *f.* [perh. *cf.* stipes], *a stalk, blade,
halm.* **1.** Lit. Of grain : Verg., Plin.
Of the stalks left after reaping, *stubble :*
Ter., Varr., Verg., Ov. Of hay : Varr.
Of bean-stalks : Ov. **2. Transf.** *a reed-
pipe :* Verg.

stipulātio, ōnis, *f.* [stipulor]. In law, *a
formal promise,* and in gen. *an agreement,
bargain, covenant :* aliquem stipulatione
adligare, Cic. ; ut ea pecunia ex stipulatione
debeatur, Cic.

stipulātiuncula, ae, *f.* [*dim.* stipulātio],
a little, insignificant promise or *stipulation :*
Cic.

stipulātor, ōris, *m.* [stipulor]. In law,
one who demands a formal promise or *covenant ; a bargainer, stipulator :* Suet.

stipulor, ārī. In law, *to demand a formal
promise ; to bargain, covenant, stipulate :*
Pl., Varr., Cic. In *Pass.* sense : haec
pecunia . . . stipulata sit, Cic.

stiria, ae, *f.* *a frozen drop ; an icicle :* Verg.,
Plin., Mart.

stirpes, *v.* stirps.

stirpitus, *adv. by the roots.* Transf. : errorem extrahere, Cic.

stirps (stirpis and **stirpēs,** Liv.), stirpis,
f. (*m.* : Enn., Cato, Verg.) *the lower part
of the trunk* of plants, including the roots ;
a stock, stem ; a root. **1.** Lit. : Cic.,
Verg., etc. **2. Transf. A.** *the roots* of
other things : Carthago ab stirpe interiit,
Sall. ; velut ab stirpibus renata urbs,
Liv. ; gens ab stirpe exstincta est, Liv. ;
omnis intra annum cum stirpe exstinctos,
Liv. **B.** *a plant, shrub* (mostly in *pl.*) :
Cic., Luc., Tac. **C.** *a shoot, sprout, sucker :*
Cato, Lucr. **D.** Of men. **a.** *stock, lineage :*
Cic. ; a stirpe supremo, Enn. ; divina,
Verg. ; antiquissima. Cic. ; hominum
sceleratorum, Caes. ; Herculis stirpo geno-
ratus, Cic. ; Priami de stirpe, Verg. ;
unum relictum, stirpem genti Fabiae
futurum, Liv. **b.** *progeny :* Verg. ; ex
sese, Liv. ; virilis, Liv. ; liberum (GEN.),
Enn., Liv. **E.** Of abstracts : *the root*
(i.o. the origin or cause) : si exquiratur
usque ab stirpe auctoritas, Pl. ; populum
a stirpe repetere, Cic. ; stirpes stultitiae,
Cic. ; superstitionis, Cic.

stiva, ae, *f.* *a plough-handle :* Varr., Verg.

stlātārius (stlattārius), n, um [stlāta, *a*
kind of ship so named from its breadth ;
stlātus the orig. form of lātus, q.v.], *of a
ship.* **1.** Lit. : Enn. **2.** Transf. *brought
by sea :* purpura, Juv.

stloppus, ī, *m.* *a slap* (the sound produced by
striking upon the inflated cheek) : Pers.
[It. *schioppo,* "a gun," *scoppio,* "noise "]

sto, stāre, stetī, statum (*Perf.* stĕtērunt,
Verg.) [*cf.* Gk. ἕστην fr. ἵστημι], *to stand,
stand still, remain standing.* **1.** Lit. **A.**
Of persons. **a.** In gen. : Pl., Cic., etc. ;
ante ostium, Ter. ; Pl. ; ante oculos, Ov. ;
ad ianuam, Cic. ; Verg. ; proptor in
occulto, Cic. ; pede in uno, Hor. *Impers.
Pass. :* Pl., Ter. **b.** Milit. : *to stand,
be placed :* ut quisquo steterat, iacet
optinetque ordinem, Pl. ; centuriones ex
eo loco quo stabant recesserunt, Caes. ;
in Asiā totius Asiae vires, Liv. ; ordine
certo acies, Luc. Also, *to stand firm, stand
one's ground :* comminus, Caes. ; in acie,
Liv. **c.** *to remain :* aut stantem aut
fugientem, Cic. ; in illo gaearum tuarum
nidore atque fumo, Cic. ; Hor. ; cum gladiis
in conspectu senatūs, Cic. ; ad curiam, Cic.
B. Of material things. **a.** *to stand, stand
upright, be set up :* signa, Pl. ; columna.
Hor. ; statuae in rostris, Cic. ; signa ad
impluvium, Cic. ; acuta silex, Verg. ;
moenia iam stabant, Ov. ; Hor. ; Liv.
b. *to stand firm :* arae domi, Enn. ; domus,
urbs, Cic. ; muri, Liv. ; stat glacies iners,
Hor. ; hasta toro, Ov. Also, facies, Luc.
c. Of ships, *to lie* or *ride at anchor :* litore
puppes, Verg. ; classis instructa in portu,
Liv. ; ante hostium portūs in salo stare,
Liv. **d.** *to stand up* or *out, to be fixed,
stiffened, etc. :* papillae, Lucil. ; comae,
Verg. ; saetae, oculi, etc., Ov. ; in vertice
cristae, Ov. With *Instr.* ABL. : pulvere
campi, Enn. ; pulvere caelum, Verg. ;
lumina flammā, Verg. ; nive Soracte, Hor.
2. Transf. a. *to stand :* mentes rectae

stare solebant, Enn.; in fastigio eloquentiae,
Quint. **b.** *to stand, be, continue,* or *remain*
in a position or state : tantā stat praedita
culpā natura, Lucr.; neque aliter stare
possemus, Cic.; Gabinium sine provinciā
stare non posse, Cic.; cum placidum ventis
staret mare, Verg.; diu pugna neutro
inclinata stetit, Liv. So, stat sententia,
it is resolved : Ter.; with *Inf. :* Liv., Ov.
Also, stat (without sententia), Cic. Ep.,
Nep., Verg. **c.** Of plays : *to stand, to
keep a place on the stage, to succeed :*
Ter., Hor. **d.** *to stand firm or unshaken,
to persist, be maintained :* res publica,
urbs, civitas, curia, etc., Cic.; regnum,
Ov.; sermonum honos, Hor. With LOCAT.
ABL. (with or without *in*) : in fide, Cic.;
in sententiā, Liv.; eā sententiā, Pl.;
decreto, Caes.; censoris opinione, Cic.;
conventis, Cic.; *Impers. Pass. :* stabitur
consilio, Liv.; legibus, pacto, foedere,
Liv.; famā rerum, Liv. With *Instr.*
ABL. : res publica stetit virtute tuā, Liv.;
Enn.; Cic.; Tac. **e.** *to rest* (on), *be
centred* (on) *:* omnia in Ascanio stat cura
parentis, Verg. **f.** With *ab, cum,* and
(less freq.) *pro : to stand by, be on the side
of :* a senatu et a bonorum causā constantius, Cic.; di cum Hannibale, Liv.; nobiscum adversus barbaros, Nep.; cum eo
senatūs maiestas, Liv.; pro vobis adversus
reges, Liv.; pro iure gentium, Liv.; Ov.;
pro meā patriā ista virtus, Liv. Also,
hinc stas, illinc causam dicis, Pl.; Iuppiter
hac stat, Enn., Verg. **g.** With *per :* per
aliquem (rarely aliquid) stat, *it was owing
to some one, it was some one's fault, some one
was responsible, etc. :* per me stetisse ut
credat, Ter.; per ignorantiam stetit ut
tibi obligarer, Plin. Ep.; per utros stetisset
quo minus discederetur ab armis, Liv.;
Ter.; Caes.; ne praestaremus per vos
stetit, Liv.; Suet.; quoniam per eum non
stetisset quin praestaretur, Liv. **h.** Of
price: *to stand* a person (DAT.) at such a
price, i.e. *to cost :* centum talentis ea res
Achaiis, Liv.; Cic.; Verg.; multo sanguine ea Poenis victoria stetit, Liv.; Ov.;
periclum vitae meae tuo stat periculo,
Pl. [Sp. *estar.*]

Stŏīcē, *adv. like a Stoic :* agere austere et
Stoice, Cic.

Stŏīcus, a, um [στωϊκός], *of the Stoic philosophy* or *the Stoics,* Stoic : schola, Cic. Ep.;
libelli, Hor.; secta, sententia, Sen. Ep.
As Noun, **Stŏīcus,** i, m. *a Stoic philosopher, a Stoic :* Cic., Hor.; **Stŏīca,** ōrum,
n. pl. *the Stoic philosophy :* Cic.

stŏla, ae, f. [στολή], *a long upper garment.*
1. L i t. **a.** In gen. : Enn., Varr. **b.** Esp.
of a dress worn by the Roman matrons, and
reaching from the neck to the ankles :
Cic., Hor., Ov., etc. Of the ceremonial
dress of musicians : Varr., Ov. Of the
dress of a voluptuary : Hor. **2.** T r a n s f.
a noble dame or *matron :* Plin., Stat.
[Fr. *étole.*]

stŏlātus, a, un [stola], *wearing a* stola;
in woman's dress. **1.** L i t. : Ulixes sto-
latus, a nickname of Livia, Calig. ap. Suet.
2. T r a n s f. *proper to a matron :* pudor,
Mart.

stolidē, ..., Sall. Liv. Tac.

stŏlidus, a, um, *dull, doltish, obtuse, stupid.*
1. L i t. : Pl., Ter., Hor. *Comp. :* Sall.
Sup. : Liv., Ov. *Masc.* as Noun : Pl.,
Liv., etc. **2.** T r a n s f. of things : aures
Midae, Ov.; vires, Liv.; causae, Cic.;
postulatio, superbia, fiducia, Liv.; pro-
cacitas, Mart.; audacia, Tac. *Comp. :*
Pl.

stŏmachor, āri [stomachus], *to be irritated,
vexed ; to fume :* Cic. With *ob* and ACC. :
Hor. With *Causal* ABL. : Cic. Ep. With
quod- clause : Cic. Ep. With *si-* clause :
Cic. With *cum* and ABL. : cum aliquo,
Cic. With *Neut.* ACC. : stomachor omnia,
Cic. Ep.; Ter.

stŏmachōsius, *comp. adv. rather angrily :*
Cic. Ep.

stŏmachōsus, a, um [stomachus], *angry,
irritable, choleric :* Hor.; genus acuminis,
Cic. *Comp. :* Cic. Ep.

stŏmachus, i, m. [στόμαχος], *the gullet,
oesophagus.* **1.** L i t. : Cic. **2.** T r a n s f.
a. *the stomach :* Lucr., Cic., Hor., etc.
Hence **b.** *taste, liking, appetite :* ludi non
tui stomachi, Cic. Ep.; in hoc agello stomachum multa sollicitant, Plin. Ep. **c.**
With bonus, *good digestion ;* hence *good-
humour, patience :* Quint., Mart. **d.** *displeasure, irritation, chagrin :* Pl.; homo
exarsit iracundiā ac stomacho, Cic.; stomachum movere alicui, Cic.; alicui facere,
Cic. Ep.; epistula plena stomachi et
querellarum, Cic.; Hor. [Fr. *estomac.*]

stŏrea (stŏria), ae, f. [fr. the root of sternō],
a straw-mat, rush-mat, rope-mat : Caes.,
Liv. [It. *stoia ;* Fr. *store.*]

străbō, ōnis, m. [στραβών], *a squinter :*
Cic., Hor. Of jealous persons : Lucil.,
Varr.

strāgēs, is, f. [sternō], *a throwing to the
ground, laying low ; a throwing into a confused heap ;* and perh. concr., *confused
debris, etc.* **1.** L i t. **a.** In gen. : ruinarum,
Liv.; strage armorum saepta via est,
Liv.; aedificiorum et hominum, Tac.;
Liv.; Ov.; (nimbus) dabit stragem satis,
Verg.; atrox tempestas stragem fecit,
Liv. **b.** Of a general massacre : *carnage,
havoc :* Cic. poet., Tac.; ciere, Verg.;
confusae stragis acervus, Verg.; complere
strage campos, Liv. In *pl. :* facere, Cic.;
edere, Cic., Verg. **2.** T r a n s f. : quas ego
pugnas et quantas strages edidi ! Cic.
Ep.

străgulus, a, um [fr. root of sternō], *that serves
for spreading over* or *covering :* vestis,
Cic., Hor., Liv. As Noun, **străgulum,** i,
n. *a covering, rug, carpet :* Varr., Sen. Ep.;
a bed-covering : Cic.; *a covering for a corpse :*
Suet.; *a horse-cloth :* Mart.

strāmen, inis, n. [sternō], *straw, litter :*
tecta stramine casa, Ov.; Verg.; Plin.
In *pl. :* Ov.

strāmentum, i, n. [sternō], *straw, litter.*
1. L i t. : Cato; Liv.; casae stramentis
tectae, Caes.; Liv. Of a *straw-bed :*
agreste, Verg.; Varr.; in *pl. :* Pl., Hor.
2. T r a n s f. *a covering, saddle-cloth :* mulorum, Caes.

strāmineus, a, um [strāmen], *made of straw,
straw- :* Quirites, Ov.; casae, Prop.

strangŭlō, āre, *to throttle, choke, stifle.* **1.**
Lit.: aliquem, Cic. Ep.; Plin. Ep.; stran-
gulata laqueo, Tac.; piro, Suet. **2.**
Transf.: fauces tumentes vocem, Quint.;
strangulat inclusus dolor, Ov.; Sen. Ep.;
aliquem congesta pecunia, Juv.; arca
divitias, Stat.

strangūria, ae, *f.* [στραγγουρία], *difficult
and painful discharge of urine, strangury :*
Cato, Cic., Plin.

stratēgēma, atis, *n.* [στρατήγημα], *a piece
of generalship, a stratagem.* **1.** Lit.:
Cic. **2.** Transf. *any stratagem or trick :*
Cic. Ep.

stratēgus, I, *m.* [στρατηγός], *a military leader,
general, commander.* **1.** Lit.: Pl. **2.**
Transf. *the president* at a banquet : Pl.

stratiōticus, a, um [στρατιωτικός], *of a
soldier, soldier-like :* homo, mores, Pl.

strātūra, ae, *f.* [sternō], *a paving, pavement :*
viarum, Suet.

strātus, a, um. **I.** *Part.* sternō. **II.** Noun,
strātum, I, *n.* **A.** *a bed-covering, coverlet,
quilt, blanket.* **1.** Lit.: lecti mollia strata,
Lucr.; Ov.; Suet. **2.** Transf. *a bed, couch :*
quies molli strato arcessita, Liv.; strato
surgit Palinurus, Verg.; Nep. In *pl. :*
Ov. **B.** *a horse-cloth, pack-saddle :* Ov.,
Liv., etc. **C.** *a pavement :* saxea strata
viarum, Lucr.

strēna, ae, *f.* [a Sabine word], *an omen of
good luck.* **1.** Lit.: Pl. **2.** Transf. *a
new-year's present:* Suet. [Fr. *étrennes.*]

strēnuē, *adv. briskly, vigorously :* Pl., Ter.,
Cic.

strēnuitās, ātis, *f.* [strēnuus], *briskness :*
Ov.

strēnuō, uāre [strēnuus], *to be brisk :* Pl.

strēnuus (-uos), a, um [*cf.* Gk. στρηνής,
στερεός], *brisk, active, vigorous.* **1.** Lit.:
mercator, Cato; homo, Ter.; Pl.; Cic.;
Hor.; Liv., etc.; imperator in proeliis,
Quint.; manu fortis et bello strenuus, Nep.;
gens linguā magis strenuā quam factis, Liv.
With GEN.: strenuus militiae, Tac.
Comp. : Pl.; *Sup. :* Cato. In bad sense:
multi mali et strenui, *restless*, Tac.; in
perfidiā, Tac. **2.** Transf.: adulescens
strenuā facie, Pl.; navis, Ov.; strenua
nos exercet inertia, Hor.; saltus, remedium,
mors, Curt.

strepitō, āre [*freq.* strepō], *to make a continued rustling, clattering :* alae, Tib.;
corvi, Verg.; arma, Tib.

strepitus, ūs, *m.* [strepō], *a noise, din, clatter;
a clashing, crashing, clanking, rumbling,
rustling, etc.* **a.** In gen.: Pl., Cic., Ov., etc.;
fluminum, Cic.; rotarum, Caes.; valvarum,
Hor.; fori, Cic.; Romae, Hor.; prae
strepitu et clamore, Liv. In *pl. :* Liv.
b. Of musical sounds : testudinis aureae
dulcem strepitum, Hor.; citharae, tibi-
cinae, Hor.

strepō, ere, uī, itum, *to make a noise ; to
clatter, clang, rattle, rustle, rumble, roar. etc.*
1. Lit.: Achivi inter se, Cic. poet.; vocibus
truculentis, Tac.; rauco cornua cantu,
Verg.; lituï, Hor.; fluvii, Hor.; galea,
Verg. Of the place or thing which rings,
rattles, roars, etc. with the din : murmure
campus, Verg.; omnia terrore ac tumultu,
Liv.; urbs apparatu belli, Liv.; Tac.; aures

clamoribus plorantium, Liv.; placidum
aequor remis, Tac. With *Intern.* Acc.:
milites haec, Liv. **2.** Transf.: intra
Albanam arcem sententia Messalini, Tac.

stria, ae, *f. a furrow, groove :* Varr., Plin.

striātus, a, um [stria], *grooved, fluted :* Plin.
As Noun, **striāta**, ae, *f.* (perh. *sc.* concha),
a scallop : Pl.

strictim, *adv.* [stringō], *so as to graze.* **1.**
Lit.: attondere, Pl. **2.** Transf. **a.**
superficially : aspicere, Cic. **b.** *cursorily :*
dicere, Cic.; Quint.

strictūra, ae, *f.* [stringō], lit. *a tightening ;*
hence *a hardening* of metal. Concr. *a
mass of (molten) iron :* Verg.

strictus, a, um. **I.** *Part.* stringō. **II.** Adj.
drawn together, close, close-knit, tight, narrow.
1. Lit.: nodus, Liv.; artūs, Tac. *Sup. :*
ianua, Ov. **2.** Transf. **a.** lex, Stat.
b. Of style : Quint. *Comp. :* Quint.
[It. *stretto ;* Fr. *étroit ;* Eng. *strait.*]

strīdeō, strīdēre, strīdī, and **strīdō**, stridere.
strīdī, *to make a grating* or *hissing noise;
to creak, hiss, whizz, whistle, shriek, etc.*
Of metals : Enn., Lucr., Verg. Of molten
metal : Lucr., Verg. Of seething water :
mare undis, Verg. Of missiles, arrows,
wings : Enn., .Verg. Of snakes : Tib.,
Verg. Of harsh notes : barbara horribili
tibia cantu, Cat.; striges, Ov. Of other
things : plaustra, apes, Verg.; susurri,
Hor.; rudentes Aquilone, Ov. Of persons :
Acc., Stat.

stridor, ōris, *m.* [strīdeō], *a grating, creaking,
hissing, shrieking, etc. :* serrae, Cic.;
ianuae, Ov.; maris, Verg.; pinnarum,
Plin.; serpentis, Ov.; simiae, suis, apium,
Ov.; elephantorum, Liv.; Aquilonis,
Acc.; procellae, Prop.; rudentum, Verg.;
tribuni plebis, Cic. In *pl. :* Plin.

strīdulus, a, um [strīdeō], *creaking, hissing,
etc. :* cornus (i.e. hasta), Verg.; plaustra,
fax, Ov.; vox, Sen. Ep. [It. *strillo.*]

strigilis, is, *f.* [stringō], *a scraper* (of horn or
metal) used by athletes at the bath : Pl.,
Cic., Hor., etc. [It. *stregghia, striglia :*
Fr. *étrille.*]

strigō, āre [strix, *a furrow,* or striga, *a swath*],
to stop in ploughing. **1.** Lit.: Plin. **2.**
Transf. **a.** In gen.: Sen. Ep. **b.** Of a
mule, perh. *to jib :* Verg.

strigōsus, a, um [stringō], *lean, lank.* **1.**
Lit.: Lucil. *Comp. :* Liv. **2.** Transf.
of an orator : *meagre :* Cic.

stringō, stringere, strīnxī, strictum. **I.** [*cf.*
Gk. στλεγγίς], *to strip, clip, prune.* **1.** Lit.
a. oleam, Cato ; bacam, Varr.; frondes,
etc., Verg.; folia ex arboribus, Caes., Liv.
With *Proleptic Obj. :* remos (i.e. stripped
and made oars), Verg. **b.** Of swords, etc.
(*sc.* e vaginā), *to unsheathe, draw :* gladios,
Caes., Verg., etc.; ensem, Verg., Ov.;
ferrum, cultrum, Liv. Poet.: manum,
Ov. **2.** Transf. **a.** rem ingluvie, Hor.
b. in hostis stringatur iambus, Ov. **II.**
[*cf.* strangulō], *to press close.* **A.** *to draw
tight, to bind* or *tie tight :* te ad carnarium,
Pl.; vitta comas, Luc.; habenam, Stat.;
ferrum, Plin. Ep.; stricta matutino frigore
vulnera, Liv. **B.** *to graze, touch slightly.*
1. Lit.: laevas cautis, Verg.; latus,
Prop.; summas ales undas, Ov.; metas

interiore rotā, Ov.; tĕllī ꝏlꝑuoo, ꝗ | coluber dento pedem, Ov. **2.** Transf. **a.** Of speech: narrationis loco rem stringat, Quint. **b.** *to touch, wound :* animum patrino strinxit pietatis imago, Verg.; Ov.; nomen alicuius, Ov.

stringor, ōris, *m.* [stringō], *a shock or twinge from touching :* gelidāī aquāī, Lucr.

strix, strigis, *f.* [στρίγξ], *an owl,* prob. *a screech-owl :* Pl., Tib., Ov., Plin.

stropha, ae, *f.* [στροφή, lit. *a turning*], *a trick, artifice :* Mart., Plin. Ep. In *pl. :* Sen. Ep., Phaedr.

Strophades, um, *f. pl. two islands off Messenia, the home of the Harpies.*

strophiārius, ī, *m.* [strophium], *a stay-maker :* Pl.

strophium, ī, *n.* [στρόφιον]. **I.** *a band, stay, stomacher,* worn by women under the breasts : Pl., Cic., Cat. **II.** *a head-band, chaplet :* Verg.

Strophius, ī, *m. a king of Phocis, father of Pylades.*

structilis, e, *adj.* [struō], *of or for building :* caementum, Mart.

structor, ōris, *m.* [struō]. **I.** *a builder, mason, carpenter :* Cic. Ep. **II.** *a server at table, a carver :* Mart., Juv.

structūra, ae, *f.* [struō], *a mode of building, construction :* **1.** Lit. : parietum, Caes.; antiqua, Liv. In *pl. :* Quint. **2.** Transf. **a.** Concr. *a structure :* Plin. **b.** Of style : verborum, Cic.; carminis, Ov.; Quint.; Tac.

structus, a, um. **I.** *Part.* struō. **II.** Noun, **structa**, ōrum, *n. pl. buildings :* saxorum structa, Lucr.

strues, is, *f.* [struō], *a heap, pile :* Ov.; laterum, Cic. Ep.; corporum, Liv.; rogi, Tac.; confusā strue implicantur, Liv. Of little offering-cakes : Cato, Ov.

struix, īcis, *f.* [struō], *a heap, pile :* Pl.

strūma, ae, *f.* [perh. fr. struō], *a scrofulous tumour, wen :* Plin. In simile : qui exsecant pestem aliquam, tamquam strumam civitatis, Cic.

strūmōsus, a, um [strūma], *scrofulous :* Juv.

struō, struere, struxī, structum [*cf.* στρώννυμι, sternō], *to pile up, arrange in layers or rows.* **1.** Lit. **a.** In gen. : ordinatim trabes, Caes.; ad sidera montis, Ov.; frugem ordine, Cic.; penum ordine longo, Verg.; acervum, Hor.; arbores in pyram, Ov. Also, convivia, Tac. Poet. : altaria donis, Verg. **b.** *to build, erect :* fornacem lateribus, Cato; speluncas saxis structas, Lucr.; templa saxo structa, Verg.; Ov.; pyras, Verg.; domos, Hor. **c.** *to set or arrange in proper order, to dispose :* copias ante frontem castrorum, Caes.; aciem, Verg., Liv.; armatos in campo, Liv. **2.** Transf. **a.** Of words, *to join together,* i.e. compound : Quint. **b.** *to prepare something detrimental ; to cause, devise, contrive, plot :* sycophantias, Pl.; aliquid calamitatis, Cic.; hoc ipsum, Verg.; consilia, Liv.; causas, Tac.; crimina et accusatores, Tac.; odium in alios, Cic.; sollicitudinem sibi, Cic. Ep.; insidias alicui, mortem alicui, Tac.; periculosas libertati opes, Liv. **c.** *to order, arrange, dispose,*

rɑꝗꝗꝇꝗꝇ ꝇꝏꝟꝓ Ꝁꝟꝇꝗꝇꝇ · ꝟꝯꝯꝑꝯ, Cic.; oratiōnem, Quint.

strūtheus (**strūthius**), a, um [στρούθειος] *of sparrows, sparrow- :* māla, Pl., Cato.

strūthiocamēlus, ī, *m. an ostrich :* Plin.

Strȳmōn (**Strȳmō**), onis, *m.* (Acc. -ona, Nep., -onem, Liv.), *a river forming the boundary betw. Thrace and Macedonia ;* **Strȳmonius**, a, um ; **Strȳmonia**, ae, *f. adj. Thracian.*

studeō, ēre, uī [*cf.* Gk. σπεύδω], *to be eager, keen, or zealous, to take pains (with), to busy oneself (with), apply oneself (to).* **a.** In gen. : Ter. ; in eā re, Cato. With *Neut.* Acc. (and rarely of a Noun) : id ut etc., Pl., Ter. : id ne etc., Liv. ; eadem, Ter. ; illud, Cic. ; hoc unum, Hor. ; has res, Pl. With *Inf. :* Pl., Cic., Nep., etc. With Acc. and *Inf. :* Pl., Lucr., Caes., Cic., etc. Most freq. with DAT. ; somno, Pl. ; huic rei ut etc., Caes. ; agri culturae, Caes. ; novis rebus, Caes., Cic. ; praeturae, pecuniae, gloriae, virtuti, dignitati, etc., Cic. ; commodis communibus, Plin. Ep. ; patrimonio augendo, Cic. ; Pl. **b.** *to favour* a person or a cause ; *to be a partisan (of) :* Sall. With DAT. : Catilinae, Cic. ; Ov. ; rebus Atheniensium, Nep. ; petitioni alicuius, Quint. **c.** *to apply oneself to learning, to study :* littoris, arti, etc., Cic. Without DAT. : Quint., Plin. Ep. ; apud aliquem, Sen., Quint., Suet. ; inter Menenios et Appios, Tac. Hence, **studēns**, entis, *m. a keen student :* Plin. Ep.

studiōsē, *adv. eagerly, keenly, carefully, diligently :* Ter., Cic., Tac. *Comp. :* Cic. Ep., Nep., Ov., etc. *Sup. :* Cic., Plin. Ep., etc.

studiōsus, a, um [studium], *eager, keen, enthusiastic, zealous, anxious, devoted.* **a.** In gen. : homo, Cic. ; animus, Plin. Ep. With GEN. : venandi aut pilae, Cic. ; eloquentiae, Cic. ; dicendi, Cic. ; florum, Hor. ; Ov. ; culinae aut Veneris, Hor. With DAT. : Pl. With *ad :* ad opus, Varr. *Comp. :* Cic. Ep., Varr. *Sup. :* Suet. *Masc.* as Noun : Cic. **b.** *favouring, partial to* a person or cause (with GEN.) : alicuius, Cic. ; nobilitatis, Cic. ; existimationis meae, Cic. ; alterius partis, Suet. *Comp. :* Cic. Ep., Suet. *Sup. :* Cic., Suet. **c.** *devoted to learning, studious, learned :* litterarum, doctrinarum, etc., Cic. Without GEN. : Hor., Quint., Plin. Ep. Also, disputatio, Quint. ; otium, Plin. Ep. *Masc. pl.* as Noun : Cic., Quint., Plin. Ep.

studium, ī, *n.* [studeō] *a busying oneself (with) or application (to) ; eagerness, keenness, enthusiasm, zeal, fondness.* **a.** In gen. : aliquid curare studio maxumo, Pl. ; aliquem retrahere ab studio, Ter. ; alacritate ac studio uti, Caes. ; studio incendi, duci, Cic. ; in *pl. :* Cic., Hor. With GEN. : studium itineris reprimere, Acc. ; pugnae, Lucr. ; Carthaginienses ad studium fallendi studio quaestūs vocabantur, Cic. ; efferor studio patres vestros videndi, Cic. ; pugnandi, Caes. ; dicendi, Cic. ; scribendi, Cic., Plin. Ep. ; visendi, Verg. ; nandi, Tac. ; in *pl. :* Cic. **b.** *keenness or zeal for a person or cause ; devotion, good-will, party-spirit :*

Cic., Liv. ; Diviciaci in populum R., Caes. ; Tac. ; in rem publicam, Sall. ; in aliquem habere, Cic. ; erga aliquem, Cic. Ep. ; erga populum R., Liv. ; erga meam dignitatem, Cic. ; studiis odiisque carens, Luc. ; aliquid studio partium facere, Cic. ; studia vulgi amittere, Sall. ; contraria studia, Verg. ; ultio senatum in studia diduxerat, Tac. **c.** *application* to learning ; *study* ; esp. in *pl.*, *learned studies* : Cic. ; studia oxercere, Cic. Ep. ; se studiis illis dedisse, Cic. ; studiis se relinquere, Plin. Ep. ; animum studiis intendere, Hor. With GEN. : doctrinae, Cic. Rarely, *the results of study* : ut omnia sua studia publicaret, Tac. [Fr. *étude*.]

stultē, *adv. foolishly, sillily* : Pl. *Comp.* : Cic., Liv. *Sup.* : Cic.

stultiloquentia, ae, *f.* and **stultiloquium**, i, *n.* [stultus loquor], *silly talk, babbling* : Pl.

stultiloquos, a, om [stultus loquor], *talking foolishly, babbling* : Pl.

stultitia, ae, *f.* [stultus], *folly, foolishness, silliness* : Pl., Caes., Cic., Hor., etc. In *pl.* : Cic.

stultividus, a, um [stultus video], *that sees things in a foolish light* : Pl.

stultus, a, um [*cf.* stolidus], *foolish, silly, stupid.* **1.** Lit. of persons : Pl., Cic., etc. *Comp.* and *Sup.* : Pl. *Masc.* as Noun : Pl., Cic., Ov., etc. **2.** Transf. of things : adrogantia, Caes. ; civitas, Cic. ; laetitia, Sall. ; dies, Tib. ; ignes, Ov. ; stultum est (with *Inf.*), Ter. ; quid autem stultius quam etc. ? Cic. ; consilium stultissimum, Liv.

stūpa, *v.* stuppa.

stupe-faciō, facere, fēcī, factum, and *Pass.* **stupe-fīō**, fieri [stupeō], *to make senseless, to benumb, stun, deaden* : privatos luctūs stupefecit publicus pavor, Liv. ; ut nostro stupefiat Cynthia versu, Prop. ; quem stupefacti dicentem intuentur, Cic. ; Ov. ; ingenti motu stupefactus aquarum, Verg.

stupeō, ēre, uī. **A.** Intrans. *to be struck senseless, to be benumbed, stunned, bewildered, astounded.* **1.** Lit. : animus, Ter. ; semisomnus, Cic. ; quae cum intuerer stupens, Cic. ; Verg. With GEN. (or LOCAT.) : tribuni capti et stupentes animi, Liv. With ABL. : exspectatione, Liv. ; carminibus, Hor. With *in* and ABL. : in Turno, Verg. ; Hor. With *ad* : ad auditas voces, Ov. ; Sen. Ep. **2.** Transf. of things : ad frigus vinum, Plin. ; pigro unda lacu, Mart. ; stupente ita seditione, Liv. **B.** Trans. *to be amazed at* : donum Minervae, Verg. ; Mart.

stupēscō, stupēscere, stupuī [stupeō], *to become numbed, bewildered,* or *amazed.* **1.** Lit. (of persons) : Cic. **2.** Transf. : Ixionis orbis, Ov. ; ignava verba palato, Ov.

stūpeus, *v* stuppeus.

stupiditās, ātis, *f.* [stupidus], *senselessness, dullness* : Acc., Cic.

stupidus, a, um [stupeō], *struck senseless, astounded, amazed.* **1.** Lit. : Pl. ; Echionis tabula te stupidum detinet, Cic. **2.** Transf. *dull, doltish, stupid* : Cic., Mart., Juv. *Sup.* : Varr.

stupor, ōris, *m.* [stupeō], *numbness insensibility, bewilderment.* **1.** Lit. : in corpore, Cic. ; sensūs, cordis, linguae, Cic. ; oculos stupor urget, Verg. ; Ov. ; stupor omnium animos tenet, Liv. ; tantus te stupor oppressit, Cic. ; cum stupor silentiumque ceteros defixisset, Liv. **2.** Transf. : *dullness, stupidity* : Cic., Ov. ; talis iste meus stupor nil videt, nil audit, Cat.

stuppa (earlier **stūpa**), ae, *f.* [στύππη (στύπη)], *the coarse part of flax, tow* : Lucr., Caes., Verg., Liv.

stuppeus, a, um [stuppa], *of tow* or *made of tow* : vincula, Verg. ; Ov. ; flamma, Verg.

stuprātor, ōris, *m.* [stuprō], *a defiler, debaucher, ravisher* : Quint., Suet.

stuprō, āre [stuprum], *to debauch, ravish.* **1.** Lit. : feminam, Pl., Cic., Liv. **2.** Transf. : *to defile, pollute* : pulvinar, Cic.

stuprum, i, *n.* *dishonour, disgrace* (caused or suffered) ; esp. fr. *unchastity* ; *dishonour, unchastity, debauchery* : Pl., Cic., Ov., etc. ; stuprum reginae intulit, Cic. ; cum sorore facere, Cic. ; rapere ad stuprum virgines matronasque, Sall. ; matronas ad populum stupri damnatas, Liv. ; filiae stupro violatae, Tac. ; corporis, Sall. In *pl.* : Cic., Hor.

sturnus, i, *m. a starling* : Plin., Stat.

Stygiālis, Stygius, *v.* Styx.

stylobatēs, is, and **stylobata**, ae, *m.* [στυλο-βάτης], *the pedestal of a column* or *row of columns* ; *a stylobate* : Varr.

stylus, *v.* stilus.

Stymphalus, ī, *m.* or **Stymphalum**, ī, *n. a district in Arcadia, with a town, mountain, and lake of the same name, the haunt of odious birds of prey, which were destroyed by Hercules* ; **Stymphalicus, Stymphalius**, a, um ; **Stymphalis**, idis, *f. adj.*

Styx, ygis and ygos, *f.* [Στύξ, *the loathly*]. **I.** *a river in Arcadia.* **II.** *the chief river in the underworld, by which the gods swore* : **Stygius**, a, um, *Stygian, infernal* ; also, *deadly* : Verg., Ov. ; **Stygiālis**, e, *adj.*

suādēla, ae, *f.* [suādeō], *persuasion* : Pl. Personified : Hor.

suādeō, suādēre, suāsī, suāsum [*cf.* suāvis], *to recommend as pleasant* or *agreeable* ; hence, *to recommend, advise, urge.* **1.** Lit. **a.** In gen. : Pl., Ter., Cic. ; male, Pl. ; recte, pulchre, Ter. ; bene, Cic. ; de pace, Quint. With DAT. of person : Cic. With Acc. of thing : Pl. ; pacem, Cic. Ep. ; legem, rogationem, Cic., Liv. ; digito silentia, Ov. ; quietem, Suet. ; multa multis, Pl. ; Cic. Ep. ; Hor. ; in *Pass.* : Pl. With *Inf.* : Cic., Quint. ; in *Pass.* : a sorore suasus ducere uxorem, Pl. With Acc. and *Inf.* : suadebant amici nullam esse rationem, Cic. ; Iuturnam succurrere fratri suasi, Verg. With *ut* or *ne* and *Juss. Subj.* : Pl., Cic., Tac., etc. ; without *ut* : Pl., Nep. **b.** With DAT. of *Refl.* Pron., *to satisfy oneself, arrive at a definite conviction* (with Acc. and *Inf.*) : Cic. **2.** Transf. of things : autumno suadente, Lucr. ; fames, Verg. ; ita suadentibus annis, Plin. Ep. With Acc. of thing : tantum religio potuit suadere malorum, Lucr. ; cadentia

sidera somnos, Verg. With Inf.: Verg.:
so with Acc. of person : me pietas matris
commodum suadet sequi, Ter. ; Lucr.
With Dat. of person and ut and Subj. :
Enn.

suādus, a, um [suādeō], *persuasive :* cruor,
Stat. Personified as Noun, **Suāda**,
ae, f. *persuasion :* Suadae medulla, Enn.,
Cic.

suāsiō, ōnis, f. [suādeō], *a recommending.*
a. In gen.: *advice :* Sen. Ep. **b.** *advocacy* of a proposed law: legis, Cic. **c.**
Rhet. *eloquence of the persuasive kind :*
Cic. In pl. : Cic.

suāsor, ōris, m. [suādeō], *a recommender,
adviser.* **a.** In gen.: Pl. ; profectionis,
Cic. Ep. ; armorum abiciendorum, Cic. ;
pacis, Ov. **b.** Of a proposed law : legis, Liv.

suāsum, I, n. *the name of a dye :* Pl.

suāsus, a, um, *Part.* suādeō.

suāsus, ūs, m. [suādeō], *an advising :* ob
meum suasum, Ter.

suāve-olēns, entis, adj. [suāvis oleō], *sweet-
smelling, fragrant :* Cat.

suāviātiō, v. sāviātiō.

suāvidicus, a, um [suāvis dīcō], *sweet-
spoken :* Lucr.

suāvi-loquēns, entis, adj. [suāvis loquor].
I. *sweet-speaking :* os, Enn. **II.** *sweet-
spoken :* carmen, Lucr.

suāviloquentia, ae, f. [suāviloquēns], *sweetness of speech :* Cic.

suāviolum, suāvior, v. sāv-

suāvis, e, adj. [cf. ἡδύς], *sweet, pleasant.*
1. Lit. (to the senses): Pl., Lucr., Cic.,
etc. *Comp. :* Pl., Plin. *Sup. :* Plin.
Neut. Intern. Acc. suave : suave rubens
hyacinthus, Verg. ; suave locus resonat,
Hor. **2.** Transf. (to the mind or feelings).
a. Of things : dies, Pl. ; amicitia, Lucr. ;
Cic. Ep. ; suave est (with *Inf.*), Pl., Lucr. ;
so, suavissimum est, Cael. ap. Cic. Ep.
Sup. : amor, Pl. **b.** Of persons : Pl.,
Ter., Cic. [It. *soave ;* Fr. *suave.*]

suāvitās, ātis, f. [suāvis], *sweetness, pleasantness.* **1.** Lit. (to the senses) : Pl., Cic. ;
piscium, cibi, Cic. ; odorum, Cic. ; coloris,
Cic. ; oris et vocis, Nep. In *pl. :* Cic.
2. Transf. (to the mind or feelings) :
hominis, Cic. ; sermonum atque morum,
Cic. ; in cognoscendo, Cic. ; propter multas
suavitates ingeni, offici, humanitatis tuae,
Cic. Ep.

suāviter, adv. *sweetly, pleasantly.* **1.** Lit.
(to the senses) : loqui, Cic. ; suavissime
legero, Plin. Ep. **2.** Transf. (to the
mind) : mominisse, Cic. ; epistula scripta,
Cic. Ep. ; Hor. *Sup. :* Cic. Ep.

suāvitūdō, inis, f. [suāvis], *sweetness, pleasantness,* as term of endearment : Pl.

suāvium, v. sāvium.

sub, adv. and prep. [cf. Gk. ὑπό]. **I.** Adv.
(only in compounds). **A.** Form. sub
remains unchanged before vowels and
b, d, l, n, s, t, v, and consonantal i. Before
m and r it is frequently, and before c, f, g, p
regularly assimilated. A form sus (or su-)
from subs is found regularly in usage,
suscitaro, suspendo, suspicio, suspicor,
sustineo, sustendo, sustollo, sustuli ; rather
uncertain in suscenseo and succenseo,
suscipio and succipio. **B.** Meaning. **a.**

up from under, up [cf. below] *upwards,*
succrescere, succedere, suscipere
many vague, incorrect (in geogr.) usages
under this heading, cf. Eng. "up to Town,"
" up to Oxford," " up the deck," etc.)
b. *up towards, close up to ;* also, *just after :*
subsequi, succedere, subnectere, succinere.
c. *to help, in assistance :* subvenire,
succurrere. **d.** *slightly :* subaccusare, sub-
irasci. **e.** *in substitution :* sufficere, sub-
rogare. **f.** *under* (i.) of rest : subesse,
subiacere. (ii.) of motion : subicere,
substernere. **g.** *secretly :* subducere, sur-
ripere. **II.** Prep. with Acc. or Abl.
1. Lit. in space. **A.** With Acc. **a.** *up
to from below or beneath, up towards, close
up to :* hostes sub primam nostram aciem
successerunt, Caes. ; missi sub muros, Liv. ;
oculos sub astra tenebat, Verg. ; sub ictum
venire, Liv. **b.** *to under, along under :*
manum sub vestimenta deferre, Pl. ; exercitum sub iugum mittere, Caes., Sall., Liv. ;
sub terras ire, Verg. ; sub divum rapere,
Hor. Transf. : sub iudicium sapientis
cadunt, Cic. **B.** With Abl. **a.** *at the foot
of, close under, under :* est ager sub urbe,
Pl. ; sub monte considere, Caes. ; sub ipsis
moenibus, Cic. ; sub oculis esse, Liv. ;
sub ictu esse, Liv. ; quo sub ipso volat
Diores (i.o. close on his heels), Verg. **b.**
under (simply) : sub terrā semper habitare,
Cic. ; sub hoc iugo Aequos misit, Liv. ;
vitam sub divo agit, Hor. ; esse *or* vivere
etc. sub armis, Enn., Caes. ; sub signis,
Pl. ; sub sarcinia, sub pollibus, Caes.
2. Transf. **A.** In time. **a.** With Acc. :
*approaching, close upon, about, just before
or just after :* sub noctem, sub lucem,
Caes., Verg. ; sub vesperum, Caes. ; sub
idem tempus, Liv. ; sub galli cantum,
Hor. ; sub haec dicta, Liv. ; sub adventum
praetoris, Liv. ; quod bellum fuit sub
recentem pacem, Liv. **b.** With Abl.
(less freq.) : *contemporaneously* or *simultaneously with, at :* uno fieri sub tempore
multa, Lucr. ; ne sub ipsā profectione
milites oppidum inrumperent, Caes. ; sub
luce, Hor., Ov., Liv. ; sub eodem tempore,
Ov. **B.** Of other relations. **a.** With Acc. :
to under : hoc succedit sub manūs negotium,
Pl. ; sub legum potestatem cadere, Cic. ; sub
populi R. imperium dicionemque cadere,
Cic. ; Liv. **b.** With Abl. : *under :* sub
Veneris regno vapulo, Pl. ; sub regno
esse, Cic. ; sub Romanorum dicione esse,
Caes., etc. ; sub rege, Cic., Hor. ; adhuc
sub iudice lis est, Hor. ; sub nomine pacis
bellum latet, Cic. ; *sub* specie pacis leges
servitutis inponere, Liv. ; falsā sub
proditione, Verg. ; sub condicione, sub
condicionibus, Liv.

subabsurdē, adv. *rather absurdly :* Cic.

sub-absurdus, a, um, *rather absurd :* Cic.
Neut. pl. as Noun : dicere, Cic.

sub-accūsō, āre, *to blame or accuse somewhat :* Cic.

subāctiō, ōnis, f. [subigō], *a working up.*
Transf. : subactio est usus, auditio,
lectio, litterae, Cic.

subāctus, a, um, *Part.* subigō.

sub-adroganter, adv. *rather proudly* or
arrogantly : Cic.

sub-aerātus, a, um, *having bronze under-neath :* aurum, Pers.

sub-agrestis, e. *adj. somewhat rustic, rather boorish :* consilium, Cic.

sub-ālāris, e, *adj. placed* or *carried under the arms :* telum, Nep.

sub-albus, a, um, *rather white :* Varr.

sub-amārus, a, um, *rather bitter :* Cic.

sub-aquilus, a, um, *rather dusky, brownish :* corpus, Pl.

sub-auscultō, āre, *to listen secretly :* Cic. With Acc. : Cic. Ep. With *Indir. Quest. :* Pl.

sub-basilicānus, ī, m. [basilica], *one who lounges about near the basilicas, a lounger :* Pl.

sub-bibō, bibere, bibī, *to drink a little, to tipple :* Suet.

sub-blandior, īrī (*Fut.* subblandībitur, Pl.), *to caress* or *fondle a little :* Pl. ; alicui, Pl.

subc-, *v.* succ-.

sub-dēbilis, e, *adj. somewhat crippled :* femur, Suet.

sub-dēficiō, dēficere, *to fail somewhat* (in strength) : Curt.

sub-difficilis, e, *adj. rather difficult :* quaestio, Cic.

sub-diffīdō, ere, *to be rather distrustful :* Cic. Ep.

subditīcius, a, um [subdō], *substituted, suppositicious, counterfeit :* servos, Pl.

subditīvus, a, um [subditus], *substituted, spurious, counterfeit.* Of persons : Pl., Cic.

subditus, a, um, *Part.* subdō.

sub-diū, *adv., by day :* Pl.

sub-dō, dere, didī, ditum. **I.** *to put* or *apply under.* **1.** Lit. : ignem, Cato, Cic., Liv. ; faces, Lucr. With Dat. of *Indirect Obj.* : manum oculo, Lucr. ; calcaria equo, Liv. ; furcas vitibus, Plin. ; se aquis, Ov. ; tauros aratro, Tac. **2.** Transf. **a.** stimulum timoris, Lucr. ; inritatis militum animis ignem, Liv. ; ingenio stimulos, Ov. **b.** *to subdue, subject :* Plutonis subdita regno magna deum proles, Tib. **II.** *to put in the place of, to substitute :* quos in eorum locum subditos domi suae reservavit ? Cic. Esp. of false substitution : subditum se suspicatur, Ter. ; me subditum et paelice genitum appellant, Liv. ; aliquem reum, Tac.

sub-doceō, ēre, *to teach as an assistant :* aliquem, Cic. Ep.

subdolē, *adv. rather craftily, cunningly :* Cic.

sub-dolus, a, um, *secretly crafty* or *deceitful, underhand in sly cunning.* **1.** Lit. : Pl. ; alicui esse, Pl. ; advorsus senem, Pl. ; fingendis virtutibus, Tac. ; Iugurtha, cognitā vanitate legati, subdolus eius augere amentiam, Sall. **2.** Transf. of things : mendacia, Pl. ; oratio, Caes. ; pellacia ponti, Lucr. ; animus, Sall. ; lingua, Ov. ; modestia, Tac. ; ea loci forma incertis vadis subdola, Tac.

sub-domō, āre, *to tame to submission :* Pl.

sub-dubitō, āre, *to be rather undecided :* Cic. Ep.

sub-dūcō, dūcere, dūxī, ductum. (*Perf.* subdūxtī for subdūxistī, Ter.) **I.** *to draw up from under* or *from below ;* hence, *to draw* or *pull up, to raise, to pull up and remove, take away.* **1.** Lit. **a,** In gen.: susum animam, Cato ; cataractam funibus (*Instr.* Abl.), Liv. ; tunicas usque ad inguen, Hor. With *inde* or *ex* and Abl. of place *from which :* inde cenam corbulis (*Instr.* Abl.), Pl. ; lapides ex illā turri, Caes. So, with Dat. : subduc cibum unum diem athletae, Cic. **b.** Of ships, *to draw* or *haul up :* navis, Caes., Liv. ; navim in pulvinarium, Pl. ; navis in aridum, Caes. ; navis subducta in terrā, Pl. ; Liv. ; classis ad Gytheum subducta, Cic. ; classis Corcyrae subducta, Liv. **c.** Milit. *to draw off, withdraw* from one position to another : copias in proximum collem, Caes. ; Sall. ; agmen in aequiorem locum, Liv. ; evocatos in primam aciem, Sall. ; triarios ex postremā acie, Liv. ; Caes. ; ordines, Liv. **2.** Transf. **a.** In gen. : terra se pedibus, Lucr. ; rerum fundamenta, Cic. ; quā se subducere colles incipiunt, Verg. **b.** Of accounts : *to draw up, to balance* (by subtracting debit side from credit or reversely) : ratiunculam (with *Indir. Quest.*), Pl. ; summam, Cic. Ep. Transf. : bene subductā ratione, Ter. ; Medea et Atreus initā subductāque ratione nefaria scelera meditantes, Cic. ; rationibus subductis summam feci cogitationem mearum, Cic. Ep. **II.** *to withdraw (from under) by stealth* or *secretly :* viatica, Hor. ; obsides furto, Liv. ; se clam, Nep. With Dat., or *de,* or *ab* and Abl., or Abl. alone of person or thing *from which :* alicui anulum, Pl. ; te mihi, Ter. ; lac subducitur agnis, Verg. ; pugnae Turnum, Verg. ; de circulo se, Cic. Ep. ; se ab ipso vulnere, Ov. ; ignem aethereā domo, Hor.

subductiō, ōnis, f. [subdūcō], *a drawing up.* **1.** Lit. *a hauling up* of ships : in *pl.*, Caes. **2.** Transf. *a reckoning, calculation :* Cic.

sub-edō, ēsse, ēdī, *to eat from below.* Transf. : scopulum unda, Ov.

sub-eō, īre, iī (īvī, Ov.), itum. **I.** *to come* or *go up from under* or *from a* (real or implied) *lower level, to come* or *go up (to), to mount, climb.* **1.** Lit. **a.** Of persons : Ov. ; testudine factā subeunt, Caes. ; Liv. ; ex inferiore loco, Caes. With simple Acc., or *sub, ad,* or *in* and Acc. : iniquissimum locum, Caes. ; collem, Hirt. ; impositum saxis Anxur, Hor. ; muros, Liv. ; adverso amne Babylona, Curt. ; Aeneae mucronem, Verg. ; aliquem (i.e. to assail), Verg. ; (in *Pass.* : Juv.) ; sub falas, Pl. ; ad tecta, Verg. ; ad urbem, ad hostis, etc., Liv. ; in adversos montis, Liv. ; in adversum, Liv. With Dat. : muro, Verg. **b.** Of things : herbae, Verg. ; barba, Mart. With Acc., or *in* and Acc. : lacus Trasumennus montis, Liv. ; aqua in caelum, Plin. **2.** Transf. **a.** morbi tristisque senectus, Verg. ; incommoda, Quint. With Acc. : nox orbem medium, Verg. ; umbra terras, Ov. **b.** *to come up* into the mind : sententiae verbaque, Cic. ; genitoris imago, Verg. With Acc. : spes, cogitatio animum (with Acc. and *Inf.*), Liv. ; animos patrum memoria beneficiorum, Liv. ; subit animum (with *Indir. Quest.* or ACC. and *Inf.* as *Subject*), Liv., Ov.; so, subit alone (with *Indir. Quest.*), Ov.; (with *Inf.*), Plin.; me recordantem miseratio, Plin. Ep.; audita nobis, Ov.; animo Latmia saxa, Ov. **II.** *to come* (to a position) *under.* **1.** L i t. **a.** *to come to rest under, to come for shelter or cover :* Caes., Verg., Ov.; limina, Verg.; telluris operta, Verg.; macra cavum, Hor.; paludem, Ov.; in nemoris latebras, Ov. **b.** *to come under and so support :* umeris (*Instr.* ABL.) parentem, Verg.; asellus dorso onus, Hor.; currum iuncti leones, Verg.; ingenti feretro, Verg. **2.** T r a n s f. *to undergo, submit to :* crimen, condicionem, deditionem, Caes.; labores, pericula, poenam, vim atque iniuriam, legis vim, iudicium multitudinis imperitae, aliquid invidiae aut criminis, etc., Cic.; Plin. Ep. With *Inf.* : *to attempt :* Stat. **III.** *to come close after.* **1.** L i t. : pone coniunx, Verg.; iniquo spatio Serestus, Verg. **2.** T r a n s f. (in succession): argentea proles, Ov.; Latinum Epytus, Ov. **IV.** *to come to the assistance of :* dexterae alae sinistra subiit, Liv. **V.** *to come up in place* or *substitution of.* **1.** L i t. : Ov.; alii aliis in custodiam, Liv.; furcas columnae, Ov. **2.** T r a n s f. : in quorum subiere locum fraudesque dolique, Ov. **VI.** *to come to* or *approach stealthily* or *secretly.* **1.** L i t. : multi nomine divorum thalamos subiere pudicos, Ov. **2.** T r a n s f. : furtim lumina fessa sopor, Ov.; amor, Ov.; fallendus est iudex et variis artibus subeundus, Quint.

sūber, eris, *n. a cork-tree.* **1.** L i t. : Verg., Plin. **2.** T r a n s f. *cork :* Verg. [It. *sughero.*]

subi-, subg-, *v.* suff-, sugg-.

sub-horridus, a, um, *rather rough* or *uncouth :* Cic.

sub-iaceō, ēre, uī, *to lie under* or *close to* (mostly with DAT.). **1.** L i t. : Plin., Curt.; fenestris vestibulum villae, Plin. Ep.; monti, Plin. Ep. **2.** T r a n s f. *to be under, be connected with :* causa, cui plurimae subiacent lites, Quint.; utilitati illa defensio, Quint.

sub-iciō (first syllable scanned as long until post-Aug. period), icere, iēcī, iectum [iaciō]. **I.** *to throw, fling,* or *shoot up from below.* **1.** L i t. **a.** In gen.: inter carros rotasque mataras ac tragulas, Caes.; terram ferro subicere (*or* subigere), Cic.; corpora saltu in equos, Verg.; aliquem in equum, Liv.; se laurus, Verg.; flamma subiecta, Verg. **b.** *to throw up, bring up close under, to expose* to troops on higher ground : exspectans si iniquis locis Caesar se subiceret, Caes.; paene castris Pompei legiones, Caes. **2.** T r a n s f. *to cast* or *bring into* the mind, *to suggest, prompt :* aliquid, Ter.; subiciens quid dicerem (*Indir. Deliberative*), Cic.; quae dolor querentibus subicit, Liv.; Prop. With ACC. and *Inf.* : Liv. **II.** *to throw, lay, place under.* **1.** L i t. **a.** biremis subiectis scutulis subduxit, Caes.; ignem circum, Cic.; Ov.; faces, Cic. With DAT., *or* (less freq.) with *sub* and ACC.: ignis tectis, Cic.; cervices securi, Cic.; aliquid oculis, Cic.; bracchia

---

mollia, Ov.; agmina ... (*metuit*) muniam, Varr.; se luna sub sphere solis, Cic.; res sub oculos, Quint. **2.** T r a n s f. **a.** *Of subjecting* to authority, risk, etc.: se imperio alicuius, Cic.; populi R. imperio subiectos, Caes.; gentis servitio, Liv.; gentem dicioni nostrae, Tac.; Galliam securibus, Caes.; deos penatis libidini tribunorum, Cic.; bona civium voci praeconis, Cic.; domum periculo, Quint.; hiemi navigationem, Caes.; scelus nocentis odio civium, Cic.; aliquid calumniae, Liv.; virtutem sub varios incertosque casūs, Cic. **b.** *Under a heading : to range under a general head, to subordinate, treat of under :* formarum certus est numerus quae cuique generi subiciantur, Cic.; Quint.; sub metum subiecta sunt pigritia, pudor, terror, etc., Cic.; Quint. **c.** *to place under* or *after, to add, append, reply :* cur sic opinetur, rationem subicit, Cic.; quod subicit (with ACC. and *Inf.*), Cic.; Liv.; narrationem prooemio, Quint.; pauca furenti, Verg. **d.** *to bring under* one's notice, *to submit* to one's judgment, etc.: ea quae sub sensūs subiecta sunt, Cic.; res sonsibus, Cic.; cogitationi aliquid, Cic.; cum Sullae libellum malus poeta subiecisset, Cic. **III.** *to set on surreptitiously, to suborn :* aliquem, Caes.; testis adversarius, Quint. **IV.** *to substitute.* **1.** L i t. **a.** copias integras vulneratis defessisque, Auct. B. Alex. **b.** *to forge :* testamenta, Cic.; Quint. **2.** T r a n s f. : pro verbo proprio aliud, Cic.

subiectiō, ōnis, *f.* [subiciō]. **I.** *a laying* or *placing under.* T r a n s f. **a.** rerum sub aspectum, Cic.; Quint. **b.** R h e t. *the suggestion of an answer to a question.* **II.** *a substituting, forging :* testamentorum, Liv.

subiectissimē, *sup. adv. most humbly* or *submissively :* haec exponere, Caes.

subiectō, āre [*freq* subiciō]. **I.** *to toss up from below :* saxa, Lucr.; harenam, Verg.; grana e terrā, Varr. **II.** *to apply keenly from below upwards :* manūs, Ov.; lasso stimulos, Hor.

subiector, ōris, *m.* [subiciō], *a forger :* testamentorum, Cic.

subiectus, a, um. **I.** *Part.* subiciō. **II.** *Adj.* **1.** L i t. *lying under* or *near, bordering on* (with DAT.): Heraclea Candaviae, Caes.; rivus castris, Caes.; Aquiloni, Caes.; septem subiecta trioni gens, Verg.; viae campus, Liv. **2.** T r a n s f. *subjected, subject :* Ov.; subiectior in diem et horam invidiae, Hor. **III.** *Noun* (in *pl.*), *a subject :* parcere subiectis, Verg.

subigitātiō, ōnis, *f.* [subigitō], *lewd incitement :* Pl.

subigitātrix, īcis, *f.* [subigitō], *a lewd inciter :* Pl.

sub-igitō, āre [agitō], *to excite* or *handle lewdly :* aliquam, Pl.

sub-igō, igere, ēgī, āctum [agō]. **I.** *to move* or *work up from below* (from a real or implied lower level). **1.** L i t. **a.** *Of ploughing :* terram, Cato; glaebas, Cic.; terram ferro (but perh. subicere), Cic.; segetes aratris, Cic.; arva, Verg.; vomere terram,

Ov. **b.** Of pounding up or kneading : corium pilis, Cato ; aliquid oleo, Plin. ; panem, Plin. **c.** Of working a boat : adverso flumine lembum remigiis, Verg. ; ratem conto, Verg. ; navis ad castellum, Liv. **d.** In gen. : sues in umbrosum locum, Varr. **2.** T r a n s f. **a.** digitis opus (of spinning), Ov. ; in cote securis (i.e. work up, whet), Verg. **b.** Of the mind, *to discipline, train :* ingenium, Cic. ; subacti atque durati bellis, Liv. **II.** *to move* or *drive* (to a position) *under*. T r a n s f. *to tame, break in, subdue, constrain* to one's will. **a.** Of animals : beluam, Cic. **b.** Of peoples or countries : Paphlagonas subegit solus, Pl. ; eos armis, Cic. ; urbes atque nationes, Sall. ; Galliam, Hirt. ; tertiam partem orbis terrarum, Cic. ; ad deditionem Volscos, Liv. ; Tac. ; nos in deditionem, Curt. ; metu (fame, Curt.) in dicionem, Liv. **c.** In gen. *to constrain, force.* With Acc. of person, and *ut* and *Subj. :* Pl. ; and *Inf. :* aliquem metu subegerat frumentum exercitui praebere, Liv. ; Verg. T r a n s f. : vis subegit verum fateri, Pl. ; iniuria te subegit decernere etc., Sall.

sub-impudēns, entis, *adj. rather impudent :* Cic. Ep.

sub-inānis, e, *adj. rather empty :* Cic. Ep.

sub-inde, *adv.* **I.** Of time in gen. : *immediately afterwards, just after :* Hor., Liv., Tac., etc. **II.** Of repeated actions : *from time to time, repeatedly :* Mart., Plin. Ep., etc. [It. *sovente* ; Fr. *souvent*.]

sub-insulsus, a, um, *rather tasteless* or *insipid.* T r a n s f. : Cic.

sub-invideō, ēre, *to envy a little* (with DAT. of person, and Acc. and *Inf.*) : Cic. Ep.

sub-invisus, a, um, *rather odious :* Cic.

sub-invitō, āre, *to invite slightly :* me ut ad te scriberem, Cic. Ep.

sub-īrāscor, īrāsci, īrātus, *to be rather angry :* Cic. With DAT. : brevitati litterarum, Cic. Ep. With *quod*-clause : Cic. Ep.

subitārius, a, um [subitus], *raised in haste* or *to meet an emergency.* **1.** L i t. (milit.) : milites, exercitus, Liv. ; Pl. **2.** T r a n s f. : aedificia, Tac.

subitus, a, um [subeō], *sudden.* **1.** L i t. **A.** A c t. : *coming up* or *upon one suddenly* or *by surprise :* Pl. ; imbres, Lucr. ; maris tempestas, Cic. ; rei subitae admiratio, Liv. ; bellum, Caes. ; formido, Cic. Predicatively : subitae adsunt Harpyiae, Verg. ; Tac. ; Plin. Ep. *Neut.* as Noun, **subitum,** I, *a sudden occurrence* or *resolution, a sudden emergency :* Pl. ; subitum est alicui (with *Inf.*), Cic. Ep. In *pl. :* ad subita belli, ad subita rerum, Liv. ; etiam fortis viros subitis terreri, Tac. ABL. *sing. n.* **subitō** as *Adv. suddenly :* Pl., Cic., Verg., etc. **B.** P a s s. : *entered upon* on the spur of the moment or in emergency : consilia, Caes. ; ministeria belli, Liv. **2.** T r a n s f. : miles (*cf.* subitarius), Tac. ; homo (i.e. rash), Cic.

sub-iungō, iungere, iūnxi, iūnctum, *to yoke* or *harness under.* **1.** L i t. : curru (DAT.) tigris, Verg. **2.** T r a n s f. **A.** *to join* or *add to.* **a.** Aeneia puppis rostro Phrygios subiuncta leones, Verg. **b.** omnis artis oratori, Cic. ; Calliope haec percussis

subiungit carmina nervis, Ov. **c.** Of speech : verbo idem verbum, Quint. With *Indir. Quest. :* Quint. **B.** *to bring under, subdue, subjugate :* urbes sub imperium populi R., Cic. ; tantam gentem, Verg. ; mihi res, Hor. **C.** *to lay under :* fundamenta rebus, Lucr.

sub-lābor, lābi, lāpsus. **I.** *to fall* or *sink from below.* **1.** L i t. : aedificia vetustate sublapsa, Plin. Ep. **2.** T r a n s f. : retro sublapsa referri spes, Verg. **II.** *to glide up to imperceptibly :* annis sublapsa vetustas, Verg. ; lues udo sublapsa veneno pertemptat sensūs, Verg.

sublāpsus, a, um, *Part.* sublābor.

sublātē, *adv. highly, loftily.* T r a n s f. : dicere, Cic. *Comp. :* de se dicere, Cic.

sublātiō, ōnis, *f.* [*v.* tollō], *a lifting up raising, elevation.* T r a n s f. **a.** In rhythm : Quint. **b.** animi, Cic. **c.** *an annulling :* iudici, Quint.

sublātus, a, um. **I.** *Part. v.* tollō. **II.** A d j. *uplifted, elated :* fidens magis et sublatior ardet, Ov.

sublectō, āre [lactō], *to wheedle, cajole :* os, Pl.

sublēctus, a, um, *Part.* sublegō.

sub-legō, legere, lēgi, lēctum. **I.** *to gather up, pick up :* (puer) sublegit quodcumque iaceret inutile, Hor. **II.** *to pick up secretly* or *by stealth.* **1.** L i t. : liberos (i.e. to kidnap), Pl. **2.** T r a n s f. : clam aliquius sermonem, Pl. ; carmina, Verg. **III.** *to choose in the place of, to substitute :* in demortuorum locum, Liv. ; Tac.

sublestus, a, um, *slight, trifling, weak :* fides, Pl.

sublevātiō, ōnis, *f.* [sublevō], *a lightening, alleviation :* Cic.

sub-levō, āre, *to lift up from beneath, to raise up, support.* **1.** L i t. : aliquem ad pedes stratum, Cic. Ep. ; iubis equorum sublevati, Caes. ; terrā sublevat ipsum, Verg. ; alterni innixi sublevantesque invicem, Liv. **2.** T r a n s f. of (moral) support. **a.** By encouragement : aratores, Cic. ; aliquem necessario tempore, Caes. ; oppidanos re frumentariā, Caes. **b.** By lightening or alleviating : militum laborem, Caes. ; hominum pericula, calamitates, res adversas, vitia, Cic. ; fortunam industriā, Caes. ; fugam pecuniā, Nep.

sublica, ae, *f. a stake* or *pile :* Caes., Liv. Esp. of *piles for a bridge :* Caes., Liv.

sublicius, a, um [sublica], *resting upon piles :* pons (a wooden bridge across the Tiber, built by Ancus Marcius), Liv., Tac.

subligāculum, i, n. (Cic.) and **subligar,** āris, *n.* (Plin., Mart., Juv.) [subligō], *a short garment covering the loins, an apron, kilt, etc.*

sub-ligō, āre, *to bind* or *tie below :* vitis, Cato ; ensem lateri atque umeris, Verg.

sublimen (for sublime or sublimem), (dub.) : Pl., Ter., etc.

sublimis, e (and **sublimus,** a, um, Enn., Lucr.), *raised aloft, uplifted.* **1.** L i t. **a.** P r o p. : rapite sublimem foras, Pl. ; sublimem raptum (esse) procellā, Liv. ; sublimis in aëre Nisus, Verg. ; ipsa Paphum sublimis abit, Verg. ; Liv. **b.** *standing* *high, placed* or *raised high* in gen. : tenuem texens sublimis aranea telam, Cat. ; iuvenem sublimem stramine ponunt, Verg. ; sedens solio sublimis, Ov. ; in equis, Verg. ; curru, Liv. ; sublimis versus ructatur, Hor. ; os, Ov. ; vertex, Verg. ; atrium, Hor. ; columna, Ov. *Comp.* : Juv. *Neut.* as Noun : in sublime, Plin., Suet. ; per sublime, in sublimi, ex sublimi, Plin. ; sublima caeli, Lucr. Acc. *sing. n.* **sublīme** as *Adv.*, *aloft* (with verbs of motion or rest) : Lucr., Cic., Verg., Liv. **2.** T r a n s f. **a.** Mentally or morally : viri, Varr. ; mens, Ov. ; sublimis, cupidusque et amata relinquere pernix, Hor. *Comp.* : Plin., Juv. **b.** Of style or language : *lofty, elevated* : naturā sublimis et acer, Hor. ; Aeschylus, Quint. ; genus dicendi, verbum, oratio, Quint. : carmina, Juv. *Comp.* : Quint. Acc. *sing. n. comp.* **sublīmius** as *Adv.* : Quint.

sublīmitās, ātis, *f.* [sublīmis], *loftiness, height.* **1.** L i t. : corporis, Quint. In *pl.* : lunae, Plin. **2.** T r a n s f. **a.** animi, Plin. ; in picturā, Plin. **b.** Of style : Quint. ; heroici carminis, Quint. ; narrandi, Plin. Ep. ; Platonica illa, Plin. Ep.

sublingiō, ōnis, *m.* [lingō], *an under-licker, a lick-dish* (i.e. scullion) : coqui, Pl.

sub-linō, linere, lēvī, litum. **I.** *to smear secretly* the face (os) of a sleeper. T r a n s f. *to bamboozle, cheat* : os alicui, Pl. **II.** *to smear underneath, to underlay* : maceriam calce, Cato ; Plin.

sublitus, a, um, *Part.* sublinō.

sub-lūceō, ēre *to shine out faintly, to glimmer* : crepuscula sublucent, Ov. ; violae sublucet purpura nigrae, Verg. ; Plin.

sub-luō, luere, lūtum, *to wash underneath.* **1.** L i t. : inguina, Mart. **2.** T r a n s f. : montem flumen subluebat, Caes. In *Pass.* : Curt.

sublūstris, e, *adj.* [v. inlūstris], *having a faint light, glimmering* : nox, Hor., Liv. ; umbra (noctis), Verg.

sublūtus, a, um, *Part.* subluō.

subm-, v. summ-.

sub-nāscor, nāscī, nātus. **I.** *to grow up under* : herbae, Ov. **II.** *to grow in succession* : poma, folia, plumae, etc., Plin.

sub-nectō, nectere, nexuī, nexum, *to bind* or *tie under* or *beneath.* **1.** L i t. : cingula mammae, Verg. ; antemnis velum, Ov. ; fibula vestem, Verg. **2.** T r a n s f. : inventioni iudicium, Quint.

sub-negō, āre, *to half-deny* or *-refuse* : aliquid alicui, Cic. Ep.

sub-niger, nigra, nigrum, *rather black, blackish* : Pl., Varr.

subnimia, ae, *f.* *a kind of garment for women* : Pl.

sub-nixus (-nīsus), a, um, *supporting oneself* or *supported from beneath, propped up on, resting* or *leaning on.* **1.** L i t. : subnixis alis me inferam, Pl. ; duos circulos caeli verticibus ipsis subnixos vides, Cic. ; solio subnixa resedit, Verg. ; Petelia muro, Verg. **2.** T r a n s f. : subnixus et fidens innocentiae animus, Liv. ; victoriis divitiisque subnixus, Cic. ; adrogantiā, Cic. ; Hannibal victoriā Cannensi, Liv. ; robore

mentis, Mart. ; civitas tot inlustribus viris, Tac.

sub-notō, āre. **I.** *to note down* or *at the foot of the page, to record, register.* **a.** libellos, Plin. Ep. **b.** nomina palam, Suet. **II.** *to note* or *observe secretly* : verba, Mart. ; aliquem vultu digitoque, Mart.

subnuba, ae, *f.* [nubō], *a rival* : lecti nostri, Ov.

sub-nūbilus, a, um, *somewhat cloudy, overcast* : nox, Caes.

subō, āre, *to be in heat* : Lucr., Hor., Plin.

sub-obscēnus, a, um, *rather obscene* : ridiculum, Cic.

sub-obscūrus, a, um, *rather obscure.* T r a n s f. of style : Cic.

sub-odiōsus, a, um, *rather vexatious* or *odious* : Cic. Ep.

sub-offendō, ere, *to give some offence* : apud faecem populi, Cic. Ep.

sub-olet (*Pres. Subj.* subolat, Ter.), ēre, *to give out a slight smell.* T r a n s f. with D a t. of person : (*I*) *get a faint scent of* (i.e. an inkling of), Pl. ; also without D a t. of person : Pl.

subolēs, is, *f.* [v. alō ; and *cf.* prōlēs]. **1.** L i t. *that which grows up (from below)*, a *sprout, off-shoot* : Plin. **2.** T r a n s f. of men and animals : Pl., Cic., Verg., etc. ; iuventutis, Cic. ; deum (GEN.), Verg. ; fortunati patris matura suboles, Liv. ; gregis, Hor.

sub-olēscō, ere, *to grow up* : iuventus subolescens, Liv.

sub-orior, orīrī, *to rise up, spring up in succession* (so as to make up for wastage) : Lucr.

sub-ornō, āre. **I.** *to fit out, furnish* (so as to help). **1.** L i t. : aliquem pecuniā, Anton. ap. Cic. **2.** T r a n s f. : a naturā subornatus, Cic. ; nullis praeceptis contra dolorem subornatus, Sen. Ep. **II.** *to equip* or *prime secretly, to suborn* : fictus testis subornari solet, Cic. ; (homines) ad caedem regis, Liv. ; medicum indicem subornabit, Cic. ; militem ut perferret nuntium, Liv.

subortus, ūs, *m.* [suborior], *a rising* or *springing up in succession* : Lucr.

subp-, v. supp-.

sub-rancidus, a, um *slightly tainted* : Cic.

sub-rāsus, a, um, *scraped below* : fici, Cato.

sub-raucus, a, um, *rather hoarse* : vox, Cic.

subrēctus (surr-), a, um, *Part.* sūrgō.

sub-rēmigō (surr-), āre, *to paddle under* (water) : laevā tacitis subremigat undis, Verg.

sub-rēpō (surr-), rēpere, rēpsī (*Sync. Perf.* surrēpsti, Cat.), *to creep* or *steal up to.* **1.** L i t. : sub tabulas, Cic. ; mediis vinea muris, Luc. With Acc. : moenia, Hor. **2.** T r a n s f. : iners aetas, Tib. ; dissimulata actio, Quint. With D a t. : alicui, Cat. ; quies ocellis, Ov. ; insinuatio animis, Quint. *Impers. Pass.* : Quint.

subrepticius, subreptus, v. surr-.

sub-rīdeō, rīdēre, rīsī, *to smile* : Cic., Verg., etc. [Fr. *sourire.*]

sub-rīdiculē, *adv.* *rather laughably* or *humorously* : Cic.

sub-rigō, v. sūrgō, surrigō.

sub-ringor, ringī, *to make rather a wry face, to be a little vexed* : Cic. Ep.

sub-ripiō, v. surripiō.

sub-rogō, āre, *to propose as a substitute :* alios decemviros, Cic. ; magistratūs, Liv. ; conlegam in locum Bruti, Liv. ; conlegam sibi, Liv.

sub-rōstrāni, ōrum, *m. pl.* [rōstra], *loungers about near the* Rostra : Cael. ap. Cic. Ep.

sub-rubeō, ēre, *to blush slightly :* puella, Ov. ; uva purpureo mero, Ov.

sub-rubicundus, a, um, *somewhat ruddy, reddish :* vultus, Sen.

sub-rūfus, a, um, *rather red :* Pl.

sub-ruō, ruere, ruī, rutum, *to tumble from* or *at the base, etc., to tear down below, to undermine, to dig under.* **1.** L i t. : arbores, Caes. ; Ov. ; turrim, murum, Caes. ; Liv. ; Ov. ; moenia cuniculo, Liv. ; muri partem ariete incusso, Liv. ; speluncas aetas, Lucr. **2.** T r a n s f. : omnem naturam, Lucr. ; libertatem, Liv. ; animum laudis avarum, Hor ; animos militum variis artibus, Tac.

sub-rūsticus, a, um, *rather clownish* or *rustic :* Cic.

sub-rutilus, a, um, *reddish :* Plin.

subrutus, a, um, *Part.* subruō.

subs-, for words not found here, v. sus-.

sub-scrībō (sups-), scrībere, scripsī, scrīptum, *to write underneath.* **A.** statuis subscripsit, reges ab se in gratiam esse reductos, Cic. ; litterarum exemplum subscripsi, Balb. ap. Cic. Ep. ; si quaeret " Pater Urbium " subscribi statuis, Hor. **B.** *to attach something in writing to* (at the foot of) an indictment ; viz. either the charge or the name of the accuser or his supporter : homini dicam, Pl. ; in L. Popillium subscripsit L. Gellius quod is pecuniam accepisset, Cic. ; quia causa parricidi subscripta esset, Cic. T r a n s f. *to assent* or *agree to :* odiis accusationibusque Hannibalis, Liv. ; Caesaris irae, Ov. **C.** Of the censor, *to set down* (under a man's name) the reason of his censure : causam, Cic. ; haec de iudicio corrupto, Cic. **D.** *to sign* any formal document : de supplicio ex more subscribere, Suet. **E.** *to note down, register, record :* numerum aratorum, Cic. ; suspiria nostra, Tac.

subscriptiō, ōnis, *f.* [subscribō], *anything written underneath* or *at the foot.* **A.** Serapionis, Cic. Ep. **B.** In law : *a subscription* or *joint subscription* to an accusation : Cic. **C.** Of the censor : *a noting down* of the offence censured : censoria, Cic. **D.** *a signing, signature* (of or to a document) : litteras publicas sine subscriptione dare, Suet. **E.** *a register, record :* iugerum, Cic.

subscriptor, ōris, *m.* [subscribō], *a signer* or *joint-signer* of an accusation : Cic.

subscriptus, a, um, *Part.* subscribō.

subscūs (sups-), ūdis, *f.* [sub cūdō], *the tongue* or *tenon of a dovetail :* Pl., Cato.

subsecivus, v. subsicivus.

sub-secō, secare, secuī, sectum, *to cut under, cut away below ; to clip, pare :* manipulum falce, Varr. ; unguis ferro, Ov. ; papaveris ungue comas, Ov.

subsellium (sups-), i, n. [sella], *a bench,* or *seat below* (i.e. below the tribunal or stage, etc., or for humble people). **1.** L i t. In the curia : Cic. In the courts : Cic.,

Quint. In the theatre : Pl., Cic., Suet. In the house : Pl. **2.** T r a n s f. **a.** vir imi subselli, Pl. **b.** *the occupants of a bench :* Mart. **c.** *a law-court :* Cic. Ep. In *pl.* : Cic.

sub-sēnsi (sups-) *Perf.* [sentiō], *I perceived secretly, had an inkling of :* id (with Acc. and *Inf.*) : Ter.

sub-sequor (sups-, Pl.), sequī, secūtus, *to follow close after.* **1.** L i t. : Pl., Caes., Liv., Ov. With Acc. : te, Pl. ; has cohortis, Caes. ; signa, Caes. ; senem, Ov. **2.** T r a n s f. **A.** *to follow close upon ; to back up, support.* **a.** With personal Subject : ipse suo sermone subsecutus est humanitatem litterarum tuarum, Cic. Ep. ; tribuni inclinatam rem in preces subsecuti, Liv. **b.** With inanimate or abstract Subject : (Hesperus) tum antecedens, tum subsequens, Cic. ; totidem libri, Cic. With Acc. : hos motūs gestus, Cic. ; si ducis consilia favor subsecutus militum foret, Liv. **B.** *to follow, conform to, imitate :* Speusippus Platonem avunculum subsequens, Cic.

sub-serviō (sups-), īre, *to be a slave under, to be subject.* **1.** L i t. (with D a t.) : Pl. **2.** T r a n s f. : orationi, Ter.

subsicivus, a, um [sub secō]. In surveying : *that is cut off and left remaining.* **1.** L i t. Neut. as Noun, *a remainder* or *small patch of land, etc.* : Varr., Suet. **2.** T r a n s f. *over-, odd, extra :* tempora, Cic. ; tempus, Plin. Ep. ; opera, Lucil. ; operae, Cic.

subsidiārius, a, um [subsidium]. M i l i t. *in reserve, subsidiary :* cohortes, Caes., Liv., Tac. As Noun, **subsidiāriī**, ōrum, *m. pl. the reserve, body of reserve :* Liv.

subsidium (sups-), i, n. [sub and root seen in sedeō, sīdō]. M i l i t. **1.** L i t. **A.** Concr. **a.** *the reserve-ranks, triarii :* subsidia et secundam aciem adortus, Liv. ; locare, Liv. **b.** In gen. *a body of reserve :* (nullum) esse subsidium quod summitti posset, Caes. ; subsidia magna, Lucr. ; conlocare, Caes. ; ceterum exercitum in subsidiis locare, Sall. **B.** Abstract : *military support, relief, aid* (often in Predic. D a t.) : funditores subsidio oppidanis mittit, Caes. ; Italiae subsidio proficisci, Caes. ; cum alius alii subsidium ferrent, Caes. ; missi in subsidium equites, Tac. **2.** T r a n s f. in gen. *support, aid :* Pl. ; subsidium bellissimum existimo senectuti otium, Cic. ; sine talium virorum subsidio, Cic. ; his difficultatibus duae res erant subsidio, Caes. ; Ov. With *Obj.* G e n. : fidissimum annonae subsidium, Liv. In *pl.* : industriae subsidia, Cic. ; ad omnis casūs subsidia comparabat, Caes. ; mare circa Capreas importuosum et vix modicis navigiis pauca subsidia, Tac.

sub-sīdō (sups-, Pl.), sīdere, sēdī, sessum, *to settle down.* **A.** In gen. **1.** L i t. **a.** Of men and animals : *to crouch down :* Pl. ; adversus emissa tela ab hoste, Liv. ; poplite, Verg. ; elephanti clunibus, Liv. **b.** Of things : *to settle, sink, subside :* saxa, Lucr. ; pariter cum civibus urbes (in an earthquake), Lucr. ; valles, Ov. ; undae, Verg. **2.** T r a n s f. **a.** Of female animals, *to crouch under* : maribus pecudes et equae, Lucr. ; Hor. **b.** galeā imā subsedit Acestes, Verg. ; venti, Prop. **c.** in controversiis impetus dicendi, Quint. **B.** *to settle down* in a place, in quarters, etc., *to stay, stop* : Verg. ; multitudo calonum in castris, Caes. ; in Siciliā, Cic. Ep. ; Suet. **C.** *to crouch down* or *to take up a position in ambush* : eo in loco, Cic. ; in insidiis, Liv. With Acc. ; *to lie in wait for* or *to await in reserve* (*cf.* the ἐφέδρος who fought the winner of a previous contest) : devictam Asiam subsedit adulter, Verg.

subsignānus, a, um [signum], *that is under the standard* : milites (special soldiers of the reserve), Tac.

sub-signō, āre. **I.** *to add one's seal* or *signature underneath, to endorse* or *subscribe to* an opinion, etc. : Ciceronis sententiam ipsius verbis, Cic. Of endorsing an agreement : *to guarantee* : aliquid apud aliquem, Plin. Ep. **II.** *to enter under* a heading, *to register, record* : apud aerarium praedia, Cic.

sub-siliō (**sups-**, Pl.), silīre. siluī (saliī), *to leap up* : Pl., Varr., Prop. ; ignes ad tecta, Lucr.

sub-sistō (**sups-**, Pl.), sistere, stitī, *to stand up*. **1.** Lit. **a.** *to take a firm stand, make a stand* : Pl., Caes., Verg. ; of ships : neque ancorae funesque subsistebant, Caes. With Dat., *to stand up against, withstand* : Hannibali eiusque armis, Liv. ; Verg. With Acc. : Romanum, Liv. ; feras, Liv. **b.** *to come to a standstill, to halt, stop* : in itinere, Caes. ; in aliquo flexu viae occultus, Liv. ; ad muros, Verg. **c.** *to stay, remain behind* : ipse Arimini, Caes. ; intra tecta, Plin. Ep. **2.** Transf. **a.** *to withstand, meet, support* : sumptui, Brut. ap. Cic. Ep. **b.** *to come to a standstill* or *halt, to stop* : Thybris undā, Verg. ; lingua timore, Ov. ; clamor, Ov. Also, ingeniumque meis substitit omne malis, Ov. **c.** *to remain* : intrā priorem paupertatem, Tac. ; (in dicendo), Quint.

sub-sortior, īrī. In law, *to substitute by lot* : in M. Metelli locum, Cic. With Acc. : iudicem, Cic. *Perf. Part.* in *Pass. sense* : Cic.

subsortītiō, ōnis, f. [subsortior], *a substituting by lot* of other judges for those rejected : Cic. ; of citizens in allotting corn-doles : Suet.

substantia, ae, f. [sub stō], *the underlying* or *fundamental essence, substance.* **a.** hominis, rerum, rhetorices, Quint. In *pl.* : Sen. Ep. **b.** Of property (perh. orig. *real property*) : sine substantiā facultatum, Tac.

sub-sternō, (**sups-**), sternere, strāvī, strātum, *to strew* or *spread under.* **1.** Lit. **a.** segetem ovibus, Cato ; verbenas, Ter. ; Ov. ; Plin. **b.** Of a bed, etc. : solum paleis, Varr. ; gallinae nidos mollissime, Cic. **2.** Transf. **a.** Of the sea : pelage late substrata, Lucr. With sense of *paving under* : natura pontum avaris, Prop. **b.** *to spread out freely, lay at one's service* : delicias, Lucr. ; rem publicam libidini suae, Cic. ; pudicitiam alicui, Suet.

sub-stituō, uere, uī, ūtum [statuō], **I.** *to set* or *place next* : post elephantos armaturas

levīs, Auct. B. Afr. **II.** *to place under.* Transf. **a.** Under the eyes or mind : funera fratrum oculis tuis, Ov. ; animo speciem corporis amplam, Liv. **b.** Under a charge : crimini, Plin. Ep. **III.** *to put instead* or *in the place of, to substitute.* **a,** In gen. : in eorum locum civis Romanos, Cic. ; pro te Verrem alterum civitati, Cic. ; equites Siculis, Liv. ; Quint. **b.** substituere heredem (alicui), *to make next* or *second heir* : heredes invicem, Suet.

sub-stō (**sups-**), stāre, *to stand up to, to stand firm, hold out* : metuo, ut substet hospes, Ter.

substrātus, a, um, *Part.* substernō.

substrictus, a, um. **I.** *Part.* substringō. **II.** Adj. *drawn close, contracted* ; hence, *small, narrow, tight* : ilia, crura, Ov. ; Plin.

sub-stringō, stringere, strīnxī, strictum. **I.** *to press close up to* : aurem loquaci, Hor. **II.** *to bind, tie,* or *draw up.* **1.** Lit. : caput equī loro, Nep. ; crinem nodo, Tac. ; Luc. **2.** Transf. of checking or restraining : bilem, Juv. ; effusa, Quint.

substructiō, ōnis, f. [substruō], *a substructure, foundation* : Caes., Cic., Liv.

sub-struō (**sups-**), struere, strūxī, structum, *to build beneath, to lay a foundation* : fundamentum, Pl. ; Capitolium saxo quadrato, Liv. ; vias glareā, Liv.

subsultim, adv. [subsiliō], *by leaps and bounds* : decurrere, Suet.

subsultō (**sups-**), āre [*freq.* subsiliō], *to spring up energetically.* **1.** Lit. : Pl. **2.** Transf. of jerky style : sermo imparibus spatiis, Quint.

sub-sum, esse. **I.** *to be close up to, to be near* or *at hand.* **1.** Lit. of place : mons, vallis, Caes. ; Liv. ; vicina taberna, Hor. With Dat. : templa mari, Ov. **2.** Transf. of time : nox, hiems, Caes. ; dies comitiorum, Cic. **II.** *to be under.* **1.** Lit. : subucula tunicae, Hor. ; nigra lingua palato, Verg. ; cum Sol Oceano subest, Hor. **2.** Transf. : eadem causa, Cic. ; in quā re nulla subesset suspicio, Cic. With Dat. : his vitiis ratio, Cic. ; silentio facinus, Curt. Poet. : amica suberit notitiae tuae, Ov.

sub-sūtus, a, um [suō], *fringed at the bottom* : vestis, Hor.

subtēmen, inis, n. [contr. from subtexmen, from texō], *the thread running under the warp, the woof* : Pl., Verg., Ov., Plin. Of the *threads* of the Fates : Cat., Hor.

subter (**supter**), *adv.* and *prep.* [sub]. **I.** Adv. *below, beneath, underneath* : omnia haec, quae supra et subter, unum esse, Cic. ; aliam naturam subter habere, Lucr. In compounds : *beneath, underneath* : e.g. subterlabor. **b.** *secretly, privately* : e.g. subterfugio. **II.** Prep. *beneath, underneath.* With Acc. **a.** *underneath, along beneath, to beneath* : cupiditatem subter praecordia locavit, Cic. ; manu subter togam exsertā, Liv. ; agere vias subter mare, Verg. ; subter fastigia tecti Aenean duxit, Verg. **b.** *up to* or *close* (*to*) *beneath* : subter murum advehitur, Liv. With Abl. : subter litore, Cat. ; subter densā testudine, Verg.

subter-dūcō (supter-), dūcere, dūxī, *to draw off secretly.* With *Refl. Pron.* : ne tibi clam so supterducat istinc, Pl.

subter-fugiō (supter-), fugere, fūgī. **A. Intrans.** *to flee secretly or by stealth, to get off* : supterfugisse sic mihi hodie Chrysalum, Pl. **B. Trans.** *to evade, avoid* : mare, Pl. ; poenam, calamitatem, vim criminum, Cic. ; tempestatem belli, Liv. With *Inf.* : Quint.

subter-lābor, lābī, *to glide or flow under.* **1.** Lit. : fluctūs, Verg. ; muros, Verg. **2.** **Transf.** *to slip away, escape* : subterlabens celeritate, Liv.

sub-terō (sup-), terere, trīvī, trītum, *to wear away underneath* : ungulas, Pl. ; Cato, etc.

sub-terrāneus, a, um [terra], *underground, subterranean* : specus, Cic. Ep. ; Juv. ; Tac., etc.

sub-texō, texere, texuī, textum, *to weave under or weave into the fabric as an addition.* **Transf. a.** With DAT. (of the fabric) : inceptis chartis carmina de te, Tib. ; subtexit fabulae huic (with Acc. and *Inf.*), Liv. ; huic volumini familiarum originem, Nep. ; lunam alutae, Juv. **Poet.** : patrio capiti (i.e. soli) nubes, Ov. **b.** With Acc. (of fabric) : nubila caelum, Lucr. ; with Instr. ABL. : caerula nimbis, Lucr. ; caelum fumo, Verg.

subtīlis, e, *adj.* [for *subtēlis* ; *v.* tēla], *woven fine, of fine texture.* **1.** Lit. : mitra, Cat. **2.** **Transf. A.** *fine, slender* : ventus subtili corpore tenuis, Lucr. ; subtili praedita filo, Lucr. ; acies gladi, Sen. ; farina, Plin. **B.** *fine, nice, discriminating, delicate.* **a.** Of the senses : palatum, Hor. **b.** Of the intellect or judgment : iudicium, Cic. Ep. ; iudex, Hor. ; definitio, Cic. *Comp.* : Cic. Ep. *Sup.* : Plin. **C.** Of style : *simple, unadorned* : genus dicendi, Cic. ; oratio, Cic. ; oratione limatus atque subtilis, Cic. ; quis illo (Catone) in docendo edisserendoque subtilior ? Cic. [It. *sottile* ; Fr. *subtil.*]

subtīlitās, ātis, *f.* [subtīlis], *fineness, slenderness, minuteness.* **a.** linearum, Plin. **b.** Of the intellect or judgment : *keenness, acuteness, refinement* : sententiarum, sermonis, Cic. ; disputandi, Cic. ; credunt plerique militaribus ingeniis subtilitatem deesse, Tac. **c.** Of style : *plainness, simplicity* : Cic.

subtīliter, *adv. finely.* **a.** Materially : conexae res (i.e. closely), Lucr. ; Plin. **b.** Of the intellect or judgment : *finely, acutely, discriminatingly, accurately* : iudicare, Cic. ; exsequi numerum, Liv. *Comp.* : Cic. **c.** Rhet. *plainly, simply, without ornament* : privatas causas agere subtilius (opp. to ornatius), Cic. ; Quint. *Comp.* : Cic. Ep.

sub-timeō, ēre, *to be rather afraid* : num quid subtimes ? Cic.

subtractus, a, um, *Part.* subtrahō.

sub-trahō (supt-), trahere, traxī, tractum. **I.** *to draw or drag up from beneath.* **1.** Lit. : subtrahitur solum Oceani, Verg. ; Tac. With DAT. : pedibus raptim tellus subtracta, Lucr. ; Numidam superincubanti Romano, Liv. ; colla iugo, Ov. **2.** **Transf.** neque verba sedem habere possunt, si rem subtraxeris, Cic. **II.** *to draw away underneath or secretly or unnoticed.* **1.** Lit. : aggerem cuniculis (*Instr.* ABL.), Caes. ; dediticios, Cic. ; hastatos ex acie, Liv. ; se a curiā, Cic. Ep. ; te aspectu nostro, Verg. ; se, Liv. ; without se, Suet. Also, oculos, Tac. With DAT. : viro peculium, Pl. ; Cic. **2.** **Transf.** : nomina candidatorum, Tac. ; Quint. With DAT. : cui iudicio eum mors subtraxit, Liv. ; se legum actionibus, Quint.

sub-tristis (supt-), e, *adj. rather sad* : Ter.

subtrītus, a, um, *Part.* subterō.

sub-turpiculus, a, um, *rather inclined to be disgraceful* : Cic. Ep.

sub-turpis, e, *adj. rather disgraceful* : Cic.

subtus (suptus), *adv.* [sub ; like intus, from in], *below, beneath, underneath* : Pl. ; ambulare, Cato ; subtus Macedones cuniculis oppugnabant, Liv. [It. *sotto* ; Fr. *sous.*]

sub-tūsus, a, um [tundō], *rather bruised* : Tib.

subūcula, ae, *f. a man's under-garment, a shirt* : Varr., Hor., Suet.

sūbula, ae, *f.* [suō], *an awl* : Sen. Ep., Mart.

subulcus, ī. *m.* [sūs ; on false analogy of bubulcus], *a swineherd* : Varr., Mart.

Subūra, ae, *f. a district in Rome, N.E. of the Forum and under the Esquiline and Quirinal hills* : **Subūrānus,** a, um.

suburbānitās, ātis, *f.* [suburbānus], *nearness to Rome* : provinciae, Cic.

sub-urbānus, a, um, *situated near Rome, suburban* : rus, Cic. ; caulis, Hor. ; peregrinatio, Tac. As Noun, **suburbānum,** ī, *n.* (*sc.* praedium), *an estate near Rome, a suburban villa* : Cic., etc. ; **suburbānī,** ōrum, *m. pl. the inhabitants of the towns near Rome* : Ov.

suburbium, ī, *n.* [urbs], *a suburb* : Cic.

sub-urgeō, ēre, *to drive or urge close to* : proram ad saxa, Verg.

sub-ūrō, ūrere, *to burn slightly, to singe, scorch* : crura nuce ardenti, Suet.

subvectiō, ōnis, *f.* [subvehō], *a carrying up, supplying, conveyance* : frumenti, Liv. ; Tac. In *pl.* : Caes.

subvectō, āre [*freq.* subvehō], *to carry or bring up frequently or regularly* : asini rure virgas ulmeas, Pl. ; saxa umeris, Verg. ; frumentum Tiberi, Tac.

subvectus, a, um, *Part.* subvehō.

subvectus, ūs, *m.* [subvehō], *a carrying up, conveyance* : commeatuum, Tac.

sub-vehō, vehere, vexī, vectum, *to carry, bring, convey up by boat, cart, etc.* : Lucr. ; frumentum flumine navibus, Caes. ; Philippus lembis flumine adverso subvectus, Liv. ; Verg. ; Tac. ; per vias commeatus ex Samnio, Liv. ; ad Palladis arces subvehitur regina, Verg.

sub-veniō, venire, vēnī, ventum (*Fut.* subvenībō, Pl.), *to come up to aid, to reinforce, relieve* : Pl., Cic., Ov., etc. With DAT. : alicui, Pl., Caes., Cic., etc. ; civitati, Caes. ; patriae, Cic. ; his tam periculosis rebus, Cic. ; vitae alicuius, Caes. ; saluti suae, Cic. *Impers. Pass.* : Cic., Liv., etc. [Fr. *souvenir.*]

subventō, āre [*freq.* subveniō], *to speed to the aid of :* Pl.

sub-vereor, ērī, *to be rather afraid* (with *ne* and *Subj.*) : Cic. Ep.

subversō (**subvorsō**), āre [*freq.* subvertō], *to ruin completely :* Pl.

subversor, ōris, *m.* [subvertō], *an overthrower, repealer :* legum, Tac.

subversus, a, um, *Part.* subvertō.

sub-vertō (**-vortō**), vertere, vertī, versum, *to turn downside up* and so *upside down ; to upset, overthrow.* **1.** L i t. : subversi montes, Sall. ; te calceus, Hor. ; tantas operum moles, Ov. ; mensam, Suet. **2.** T r a n s f. : aliquem, Ter., Tac. ; maiestatem soliorum, Lucr. ; leges et libertatem, Sall. ; Tac. ; imperium, Sall. ; avaritia fidem, Sall. ; subversa Crassorum domus, Tac.

sub-vexus, a, um [sub vehō], *sloping upwards from below :* Liv.

sub-volō, āre, *to fly upwards :* sursum in caelestem locum, Cic. ; avia, Ov.

sub-volvō, ere, *to roll up :* manibus saxa, Verg.

subvor-, *v.* subver-.

sub-vulturius (**-vol-**), a, um, *rather vulture-like :* corpus, Pl.

suc-cavus (**subc-**), a, um, *hollow underneath :* areae, Cato ; loca terrae, Lucr.

succēdāneus or **succidāneus**, a, um [succēdō], *substituted :* ut meum tergum stultitiae tuae subdas succedaneum, Pl.

suc-cēdō, cēdere, cēssī, cēssum. **I.** *to go up from under* or *from a lower level.* **1.** L i t. : sub montem, Caes. ; sub primam aciem, Caes. ; sub vallum, Liv. ; ad urbem Liv. ; in arduum, Liv. P o e t. : in montem succedere silvas cogunt, Lucr. With A c c. : portas, Caes. ; murum, Liv. With Directive (quo, eo, etc.) : Caes. With D a t. : alto caelo, Verg. ; munimentis, Liv. **2.** T r a n s f. **a.** *ad* or *in* summum honorem, Lucr. ; ad superos famā, Verg. **b.** G e o g r. : ad alteram partem succedunt Ubii, Caes. **II.** *to follow in succession, to come after.* **1.** L i t. (perh. here belong the examples given under III. 1). **2.** T r a n s f. **a.** In time : cottidie melius tempus, Caes. ; post illas aenea proles, Ov. With D a t. : horum aetati Isocrates, Cic. ; consules maiori gloriae rerum gestarum, Liv. *Impers. Pass.* : Liv. **b.** Of an issue or result : *to go on* (to an issue), *to turn out* (successfully), with res, negotium, inceptum, etc. (expressed or understood) : lepide hoc succedit sub manūs negotium, Pl. ; hoc bene successit, Ter. ; res nulla successerat, Caes. ; inceptum non succedebat, Liv. ; si ex sententiā successerit, Cic. Ep. ; Ter. With D a t. : coeptis, inceptis, fraudi, facinori, Liv. ; Minervae, Ov. *Impers. Pass.* : Liv. **c.** Of belonging to a class or type : haec comparativo generi, Quint. **III.** *to come up into the place of* or *as substitute for* or *in relief.* **1.** L i t. : in stationem, Caes. ; in pugnam, Liv. With D a t. : integri defetigatis, Caes. ; integri fessis, Liv. **2.** T r a n s f. **a.** in eorum locum Remi, Caes. ; in Pompei locum heres, Cic. ; Liv. With D a t. : ego vicarius tuo muneri, Cic. **b.** Of things : in teretis lignum suras, Ov. ;

go under or below. **1.** L i t. (with D a t.) : tecto imbris vitandi causā, Cic. ; Verg. ; tumulo terrae, Verg. **2.** T r a n s f. : sententiae verbaque sub acumen stili, Cic. With D a t. : oneri, Verg. ; operi, Plin.

suc-cendō, cendere, cendī, cēnsum [candō], *to set on fire* or *kindle up from below.* **1.** L i t. : aggerem cuniculo, Caes. ; rogum, etc., Liv. ; Ov. ; succensis ignibus, Cic. **2.** T r a n s f. **a.** rubor igneus ora, Luc. **b.** Castora Phoebe, Prop. ; Deucalion Pyrrhae succensus amore, Ov. ; dulcedine famae succensus, Juv.

succēnseō, *v.* suscēnseō.

suc-centuriō, āre, *to receive as a substitute into* a centuria. T r a n s f. : Ter.

suc-centuriō, ōnis, *m.* *an assistant to* or *substitute for a centurion :* Liv.

suc-cernō, cernere, crēvī, crētum, *to sift up* (by draining away the liquid). **1.** L i t. : vinaceos, Cato. **2.** T r a n s f. : gradum cribro pollinario, Pl.

successiō, ōnis, *f.* [succēdō], *a following in succession* (or *as substitute*) in office, possession, etc. **1.** L i t. : in Antoni locum successio, Brut. ap. Cic. Ep. ; ad spem successionis admoveri, Suet. ; Neronis principis, Plin. ; Tac. ; iura successionum, Tac. **2.** T r a n s f. : doloris amotio successionem adficit voluptatis, Cic.

successor, ōris, *m.* [succēdō]. **I.** *an approach* or *advance up a hill :* Caes., Verg. **II.** Only t r a n s f. *a* (happy) *issue, success :* successu exsultans, Verg. ; Ov. ; elatus successu, Liv. ; contentus fortuito successu, Liv. ; multo successu Fabiis audaciam crescere, Liv. ; successu rerum ferocior, Tac. ; petitionum, artis, etc., Plin. In *pl.* : Ov.

succidāneus, *v.* succēdāneus.

succīdia, ae, *f.* [succīdō], *a leg* or *side of meat*, esp. of pork ; *a flitch of bacon.* **1.** L i t. : Varr. **2.** T r a n s f. : iam hortum ipsi agricolae succidiam alteram appellant (an addition to their income), Cic.

suc-cīdō, cīdere, cīdī, cīsum [caedō], *to cut from below :* pernas, Enn. ; vivos succisis feminibus poplitibusque invenerunt, Liv. ; arbores, Caes. ; florem aratro, Verg.

suc-cīdō, cīdere, cīdī [cadō]. **I.** *to fall under :* Varr. **II.** *to sink under* (oneself), *give way :* genua inediā, Pl. ; Curt. ; artūs, Lucr. ; terra, Lucr. ; in mediis conatibus aegri succidimus, Verg.

succidus (**sūcidus**), a, um [succus], *sappy, fresh :* lana, Varr., Mart., Juv. C o m i c. : puella (i.e. plump), Pl.

succiduus, a, um [succidō], *sinking under, failing :* genu, Ov.

succīnctus, a, um. **I.** *Part.* succingō. **II.** A d j. **a.** Of trees, *with the foliage at the top ; having the trunk bare :* succinctiores arbores, Plin. **b.** *short, concise, succinct :* libellus, Mart.

suc-cingō, cingere, cīnxī, cīnctum, *to gird* or *tuck up.* **1.** L i t. (mostly in *Mid.*) : sic succincta, Pl. ; Scylla canibus succincta, Verg. ; Lucr. ; Scylla canibus succingitur alvum, Ov. ; pallā succincta, Verg. ; vestem succincta, Ov. ; succincta Diana, Ov. **2.** T r a n s f. **a.** succincta comas pinus (i.e.

with bare trunk), Ov. **b.** *to gird* (i.e. equip) : succinoti gladiis, Enn. ; succincta pharetrā, Verg. ; cultro succinctus, Liv. **c.** se canibus, Cic. ; succinctus armis legionibusque, Liv. ; Carthago succincta portibus, Cic. **d.** se terrore, Plin. Pan.

succingulum, ī, *n.* [succingō], *a girdle* : Pl.

suc-cinō, ere [canō], *to sing or play second to* or *after* another, *to accompany.* T r a n s f. **a.** *to chime in after* another (with quoted words) : Hor. **b.** agri cultura pastorali, Varr.

succin-, *v.* sūcin-.

succipiō, *v.* suscipiō.

succisīvus, *v.* subsicīvus.

succīsus, a, um, *Part.* succīdō.

succlāmātiōnēs, um, *f. pl.* [succlāmō], *calling out* or *shouting after* or *in reply* : Liv., Suet.

suc-clāmō, āre, *to call out* or *shout after* or *in reply* : alicui, Liv. With quoted words : Liv. With Acc. and *Inf.* : Liv. With *Indir. Quest.* : Liv. With *Jussive Subj.* : Liv. *Impers. Pass.* : Brut. ap. Cic. Ep. ; Liv.

succollō, āre [collum], *to take upon the neck, to shoulder* : apes fessum regem, Varr. ; lecticam, Suet.

suc-contumēliōsē, *adv. rather insolently* : tractari, Cic.

suc-crēscō, crēscere, crēvī, *to grow up from under.* **1.** L i t. : ab imo cortex, Ov. **2.** T r a n s f. **a.** mores mali, quasi herba inrigua, succreverunt uberrume, Pl. ; per se vina, Ov. **b.** With D a t. : *to grow up to* in magnitude : non ille mediocris orator vestrae quasi succrescit aetati, Cic. ; gloriae seniorum, Liv.

succrētus, a, um, *Part.* succernō.

suc-crispus, a, um, *rather curled* or *crisped* : Cic.

suc-cumbō, cumbere, cubuī, cubitum, *to lay oneself* or *fall* or *sink under.* **1.** L i t. **a.** In gen. : victima ferro, Cat. **b.** Of a woman : alicui, Varr., Cat., Ov. **c.** In sickness : Suet. **2.** T r a n s f. *to yield, surrender, succumb* : hac ille perculsus plagā non succubuit, Nep. With D a t. : labori, Caes. ; nulli neque homini neque perturbationi animi nec fortunae, Cic. ; senectuti, doloribus, Cic. ; so, non esse viri (*sc.* dolori) succumbere, Cic. ; culpae, Verg. ; malis, Ov. ; oneri, tempori, pugnae, etc., Liv. ; oculi (*sc.* somno), Ov.

suc-currō, currere, currī, cursum. **I.** *to run* (or *move hastily*) *up from below.* **1.** L i t. : aliud nequeat succurrere lunae corpus, Lucr. **2.** T r a n s f. **a.** To the mind : ut quidque succurrit, libet scribere, Cic. Ep. ; legentibus, Liv. With *Inf.* as Subject : Plin. With *Indir. Quest.* as Subject : Curt. **b.** Of facing dangers or threats : Cic. **II.** *to hasten to the aid of ; to help, succour.* **1.** L i t. (with D a t.) : laborantibus, Caes., Cic. ; domino, Cic. ; suis cedentibus auxilio (*Predic.* D a t.), Caes. *Impers. Pass.* : Caes. **2.** T r a n s f. tantis malis, Caes. ; saluti fortunisque communibus, Cic. *Impers. Pass.* : Ter. ; adversae fortunae, Liv.

succus (**sūcus**), ī, *m. juice, sap.* **1.** L i t.

(of plants, fruits, animal bodies, etc.) : Pl., Cic., Verg., etc. Of medicinal liquids : Tib., Ov. **2.** T r a n s f. **a.** *flavour, taste* : (cibi) succum sentimus in ore, Lucr. ; ova succi melioris, Hor. ; Ov. **b.** *sap* (i.e. life-blood, strength, etc.) : succus ac sanguis (civitatis), Cic. Ep. ; ornatur oratio succo suo, Cic. ; omnes etiam tum retinebant illum Pericli succum, Cic. ; ingeni, Quint.

succussō, āre [*freq.* succutiō], *to shake hard* or *frequently, to jolt* : Acc.

succussus, ūs, *m.* [succutiō], *a shaking, jolting* : Pac.

suc-custōs, ōdis, *m. an assistant-* or *under-keeper* : Pl.

suc-cutiō, cutere, cussī, cussum [quatiō], *to fling up from below* : rotarum orbis, Lucr. ; currum, Ov. ; mare, Sen.

sūcidus, *v.* succidus.

sūcinum, ī, *n. amber* : Plin., Mart., Juv.

sūcinus, a, um [sūcinum], of *amber* : Plin., Mart.

sūcō, ōnis, *m.* [*v.* sūgō]. *a sucker ;* of a usurer : Acc.

sūctus, a, um, *Part.* sūgō.

(1) sūcula, ae, *f.* [dim. sūs], prop. *a little sow* or *pig* : Pl. (*cf.* 2.). In *pl.* suculae as mistranslation of Hyades (from ὕειν, *to rain*, not from ὗς, *a pig*) : Cic., Plin.

(2) sūcula, ae, *f.* [perh. fr. root of Gk. σεύω], *a winch, windlass* : Pl., Cato. Of a wine- or oil-press : Cato.

sūcus, *v.* succus.

sūdārium, ī, *n.* [sūdō], *a handkerchief, towel* : Cat., Quint., Suet.

sūdātiō, ōnis, *f.* [sūdō], *a sweating, perspiration* : Sen. Ep.

sūdātōrius, a, um [sūdō], *belonging to* or *serving for sweating, sudatory* : unctiones, Pl. As Noun, **sūdātōrium**, ī, *n. a sweating-room* : Sen. Ep.

sūdātrix, īcis, *f. adj.* [sūdō], *that causes sweating* : toga, Mart.

sūdiculum, *v.* sūduculum.

sūdis, is, *f. a stake, pile.* **1.** L i t. (mostly in *pl.*) : Caes., Verg., Ov. As a weapon : Liv. **2.** T r a n s f. of the dorsal fin of a fish : Juv.

sūdō, āre [*cf.* Gk. ἱδρώς], *to sweat, perspire.* **A.** I n t r a n s. **1.** L i t. **a.** In gen. : Pl., Cic., Hor., Ov. **b.** Of miracles : deorum simulacra, Cic. ; Verg. With A b l. : scuta sanguine, Liv. **2.** T r a n s f. **a.** Of natural objects : *to sweat, drip, etc.* With A b l. of moisture : Enn., Lucr., Verg. With A b l. of Separation, and N o m. of moisture : ligno balsama, Verg. **b.** From mental exertion : Ter., Lucr. ; sudandum est his pro communibus commodis, Cic. P o e t. : has meus ad metas equus, Prop. With *Inf.* : Stat. **B.** T r a n s. **1.** L i t. **a.** *to sweat out, exude* : quercūs mella, Verg. ; sudata ligno tura, Ov. ; nemora ubi tura et balsama sudantur, Tac. **b.** *to soak with sweat* : vestes sudatae, Quint. **2.** T r a n s f. *to sweat over* or *at* : deunces, Pers. ; laborem, Stat. [Fr. *suer.*]

sūdor, ōris, *m.* [sūdō], *sweat, perspiration.* **1.** L i t. : Pl., Cic., Verg., etc. In *pl.* : Lucr., Plin., etc. **2.** T r a n s f. **a.** *moisture* in gen. : maris, Lucr. veneni, Ov. ; picis,

Plin. **b.** Of *toil* of any kind: exercitūs, qui suo sudore ac sanguine inde Samnites depulisset, Liv.; multo sudore ac labore, Cic.; Pl.; Verg.; stilus ille tuus multi sudoris est, Cic. [Fr. *sueur*.]

sūdŭcŭlum, i, *n.* [sūdor], *sweat-maker* (i.e. a whip): Pl.

sūdus, a, um [sē ūdus], *without moisture, dry :* ventorum flamina, Lucil.; Varr. Of the weather, *dry, clear, cloudless :* ver, Verg. *Neut.* as Noun: cum sudum est, Pl.; Cic. Ep.; arma per sudum rutilare vident, Verg.

suēmus (trisyl. or disyl.) [as if fr. sueō, suēre, *v.* suēscō], *we are accustomed* (with *Inf.*): Lucr.

suēscō, suēscere, suēvī, suētum (us. disyl.; sync. forms, suēstī, suērunt, suēsse, etc.) [*cf.* Gk. ἔθος, ἦθος]. **A.** Intrans. *to become accustomed ;* in *Perf. tenses, to be wont* or *accustomed.* **a.** With DAT. or ABL.; also Acc. of *Neut. Pron. :* militiae, Tac.; a te id, quod suesti, peto, Cic. Ep. **b.** With *Inf. :* Lucr., Prop. **B.** Trans. *to accustom :* viros disciplinā et imperiis, Tac. *Perf. Part.* **suētus. a.** With DAT.: armis, Verg.; Tac.; coniugiis suscipiendis, Tac. **b.** With *Inf. :* Lucr., Sall., Verg., Liv., etc.

Suētōnius, a, *the name of a Roman gens.* Esp. C. Suetonius Tranquillus, *a contemporary of Pliny the Younger, and author of biographies of the first twelve Roman Emperors.*

suētus, a, um. **I.** *Part.* suēscō. **II.** Adj.: of things: *customary, familiar, usual :* Cheruscis sueta apud paludes proelia, Tac.; sueto militum contubernio gaudere, Tac.

sūfes (**suffes**), etis, *m.* [a Phoen. word, " *a judge* "], *the chief magistrate of the Carthaginians :* Liv.

suf-farcĭnō, āre, *to stuff full up, to cram :* suffarcinati cum libris, Pl.; vidi Cantharam suffarcinatam, Ter.

suffectus, a, um, *Part.* sufficio.

suf-fĕrō, sufferre, *to bear up* (*under*), *to support.* **a.** Physically: plagas, laborem, solem, sitim, Pl.; vulnera, Lucr.; labores, Varr.; pro alicuius peccatis supplicium, Ter.; alicui poenas (*cf.* poenas dare), Pl.; nec claustra (vim Pyrrhi) sufferre valent, Verg.; vix suffero, Ter. **b.** Non-physically: sumptus, Ter.; poenam sui sceleris, Cic.; multam, Cic. (*v.* also tollo). [Fr. *souffrir*.]

suffertus, a, um [farciō], *crammed full up :* Lucil. *Neut.* as Noun: aliquid se sufferti tinniturum, Suet.

suffes, *v.* sūfes.

suf-fĭcĭō, ficere, fēcī, fectum [faciō]. **I.** Trans. **A.** *to put under.* **a.** Of a colour (*cf.* inficio), *to underlay,* i.e. *to stain, steep, dye :* lanam medicamentis, Cic.; (angues) ardentia oculos suffecti sanguine et igni, Verg. Transf.: (perh.) milites excursionibus, Liv. **b.** *to supply, furnish :* cibus aliam naturam ex se, Lucr.; tellus umorem, Verg.; salices pecori frondem, Verg. Transf.: Danais animos, Verg. **B.** *to put in place of, to make up a deficiency, to substitute :* aliam ex aliā generando prolem, Verg. Esp. polit. *to elect in the*

Liv.; consul in sufficiendo collega consuli tus, Cic.; conlegam suffici censori religio erat, Liv.; Tac.; sperante heredem suffici se proximum, Phaedr. **II.** Intrans. *to make up* (*enough*) *;* hence, *to be adequate* or *sufficient, to suffice :* quoad sufficere remiges potuerunt, Liv.; Cic.; Verg.; nec iam vīris sufficere cuiusquam, Caes. With DAT.: Volscis milites, Liv.; vires oneri, Plin.; Plin. Ep.; umbo ictibus, Verg. With *prep. :* terra ingenito umore egens vix ad perennis suffecit amnis, Liv.; oppidani ad omnia tuenda non sufficiebant, Liv.; nec locus in tumulos nec sufficit arbor in ignis, Ov. With *adversus :* Liv. With *Inf. :* nec nos obniti contra sufficimus, Verg. With *Inf.* as Subject: Quint., Mart., Suet. With *ut* or *ne* and *Subj.-*clause as Subject: Plin. Ep. *Impers.* with *si-*clause: Plin. Ep.

suf-fīgō, figere, fīxī, fīxum, *to fasten* or *fix up :* columnam mento suo, Pl.; ianua suffixa tigillo, Cat.; cruci suffixus, Cic.; aliquem in cruce, Hor.; caput hastā suffixum, Suet.

suffĭmentum, i, *n.* (Cic.) and **suffīmen**, inis, *n.* (Ov.) [suffiō], *fumigation, incense.*

suffĭō, fīre [*cf.* Gk. θύος and fūmus], *to fumigate, perfume :* locum, Prop.; testam sertā, Cato; Lucr.; thymo, Verg. Poet.: ignibus aetheriis terras, Lucr.

suffixus, a, um, *Part.* suffīgō.

sufflāmen, inis, *n.* a *brake, drag-chain.* **1.** Lit.: rotam adstringit multo sufflamine, Juv. **2.** Transf. of any *clog* or *hindrance :* nec res atteritur longo sufflamine litis, Juv.

sufflātus, a, um. **I.** *Part.* sufflō. **II.** Adj. *puffed up, bloated.* **1.** Lit.: corpus, Varr. **2.** Transf. (with anger): Pl.

suf-flāvus, a, um, *yellowish, blond :* capillus, Suet.

suf-flō, āre. **A.** Trans. *to blow up from below, to inflate.* **1.** Lit.: buccas, Pl.; venae sufflatae ex cibo, Cato; ignis, Plin. **2.** Transf. (in rage): with *Refl. Pron.* and *Intern.* Acc.: nescio quid se sufflavit uxori meae, Pl. **B.** Intrans. *to blow, puff.* **1.** Lit.: Plin.; buccis suis, Mart. **2.** Transf. (with pride): Pers. [It. *soffiare ;* Fr. *souffler*.]

suf-fōcō, āre [faucēs], *to draw the throat close ;* hence, *to choke, strangle.* **1.** Lit.: patrem, Cic.; Lucr. **2.** Transf. **a.** vox suffocatur, Quint. **b.** urbem et Italiam fame, Cic. Ep.

suf-fŏdĭō, fodere, fōdī, fōssum, *to stab, pierce,* or *dig underneath* or (*up*) *from below :* equos, Caes.; Verg.; ilia equis, Liv.; sacella, Cic.; muros, Tac.

suffossus, a, um, *Part.* suffodiō.

suffrāgātĭō, ōnis, *f.* [suffrāgor], *a voting in any one's favour, support :* Cic., Liv.; in *pl.*, Cic. With *Obj.* GEN.: suffragatio consulatūs, Cic.; Sall.

suffrāgātor, ōris, *m.* [suffrāgor], *one who votes for another, a supporter.* **1.** Lit.: Cic., Plin. Ep.; quaesturae, Sen. **2.** Transf.: Pl., Varr., Plin. Ep.

suffrāgātōrius, a, um [suffrāgātor], *belonging to the support of a candidate:* amicitia, Q. Cic.

suffrăgium, ĭ, n. [suffrāgor], a voting-tablet, a ballot ; and in gen. a vote, suffrage. **1.** Lit. : sine suffragio populi aedilitatem gerere, Pl. ; equitum centuriae cum sex suffragiis, Cic. ; centurias in suffragium mittere, Liv. ; suffragium inire, Liv. ; suffragium ferre (in illā lege or de aliquā re), Cic. ; suffragi latio, Cic., Liv. ; suffragiorum confusionem, aequationem, Cic. ; suffragia diribere, Varr. ; nisi duo confecerint legitima suffragia, Liv. ; libera, Juv. ; tacita, Plin. Ep. **2.** Transf. **a.** right of voting : (alicui) dare, impertire, Liv. ; suffragio privari, Cic. **b.** a decision, judgment ; also, a favourable decision, approval : rhetor suffragio tuo et compotorum tuorum, Cic. ; ventosae plebis suffragia, Hor. ; Plin. Ep.

suffrāgo, inis, f. the upper part of a quadruped's hind leg, the ham : Plin.

suffrāgor, āri, to register one's vote in support, to support with one's vote. **1.** Lit. : Cic., Liv. **2.** Transf. in gen. : to favour, recommend : suffragante Theramene, Nep. ; fortunā suffragante, Cic. Ep. ; memoria, cogitatio, tempus, Quint. With DAT. : tibi Hortensius, Cic. ; domus domino, Cic. ; huic consilio suffragabatur etiam illa res, Caes.

suf-fringo, ere [frango], to break below : talos alicui, Pl. ; canibus crura, Cic.

suf-fŭgĭo, fugere, fūgi. **I.** to flee under for shelter : in tecta, Liv. **II.** to avoid, elude : manuum tactum, Lucr. ; aliquem, Suet.

suffŭgium, ĭ, n. [suffugiō], a shelter, covert. **1.** Lit. : Ov. ; ferarum imbriumque, Tac. ; Plin. Ep. ; subterranei specūs suffugium hiemi, Tac. ; adversus perpetuum caeli rigorem, Sen. **2.** Transf. : infirmitatis, Quint. ; urgentium malorum, Tac.

suf-fulcĭo, fulcīre, fulsi, fultum, to prop up from beneath, to underprop, underpin. **1.** Lit. : se, Pl. ; porticus paribus suffulta columnis, Lucr. **2.** Transf. : propterea capitur cibus ut suffulciat artūs, Lucr.

suf-fundo, fundere, fūdī, fūsum, to pour or send a stream up to or over. **1.** Lit. **a.** In gen. : aquolam, Pl. ; Neptunus mare vinis, Pl. ; animum esse cordi suffusum sanguinem, Cic. ; intumuit suffusā venter ab undā (of dropsy), Ov. **b.** Of tears, blood (in blushing), etc. (often in Mid. or Pass.) : lacrimis oculos suffusa, Verg. ; tepido suffundit lumina rore, Ov. ; suffusi cruore oculi, Plin. ; Luna virgineum ore ruborem, Verg. ; Masinissae (DAT.) rubor suffusus, Liv. ; suffunditur ora rubore, Ov. **2.** Transf. **a.** Of other material things, to stain, overspread : nebulae suffundunt suā caelum caligine, Lucr. ; calore suffusus aether, Cic. ; agricola minio suffusus, Tib. ; lingua suffusa veneno, Ov. **b.** aquam frigidam suffundere (i.e. to slander, calumniate), Pl. **c.** metus omnia suffundens mortis nigrore, Lucr. ; animus malevolentiā suffusus, Cic. Ep. ; sales suffusi felle, Ov.

suf-fūror, āri, to filch : Pl.

suf-fuscus, a, um, rather brown, dusky : margarita, Tac.

suffūsus, a, um, Part. suffundō.

sug-gĕrö, gerere, gessi, gestum, to bring close up to, to supply or add (what is needed or lacking). **1.** Lit. : tela mihi, Verg. ; miluinam (cibo), Pl. ; flammam costia aëni, Verg. ; divitias alimentaque tellus, Ov. ; cibum animalibus, Tac. ; suggestā humo (but this may mean heaped up, raised), Prop. **2.** Transf. **a.** In gen. : verba quae desunt, Cic. ; damna aleatoria (so as to complete the list of misdeeds), Cic. ; invidiae flammam ac materiam criminibus suis, Liv. ; quidam annales nihil praeter nomina consulum, Liv. ; Bruto statim Horatium (to place next to in the records), Liv. **b.** Of supplying expected arguments : huic sententiae ratiunculas, Cic.

suggestĭo, ōnis, f. [suggerō]. Rhet. a figure in which the orator puts a question and answers it himself : Quint.

suggestum, ĭ, n. (Varr., Cic.) and (more freq.) **suggestus**, ūs, m. [suggerō], a raised place, a platform, stage. **a.** In gen. : Cato, Varr., Plin. Poet. : comae, Stat. **b.** Of a platform from which the people, troops, etc., were addressed : Caes., Cic., Liv., Tac.

suggestus, a, um, Part. suggerō.

sug-grandis, e, adj. rather large : Cic. Ep.

sug-gredior, gredi, grēssus, to go or come close up to, to approach : propius, Tac. Hostilely (with Acc.) : eos acie, Tac. ; Sall.

sūgillātĭo, ōnis, f. [sūgillō], a livid mark, bruise. **1.** Lit. : Plin. **2.** Transf. an affronting : consulum, Liv. ; maiestatis, Plin.

sūgillō, āre, to beat black and blue. **1.** Lit. : oculos patri, Varr. ; athletam, Sen. Ep. **2.** Transf. to affront, taunt, revile : aliquem, Liv.

sūgō, sūgere, sūxi, sūctum, to suck. **1.** Lit. : Cic. ; agni matris mammam, Varr. **2.** Transf. : cum lacte nutricis errorem, Cic.

suī, v. sŭo.

suillus, a, um [sūs], of swine : pecus, caro, Varr. ; grex, Liv.

sulcātor, ōris, m. [sulcō], a furrower, plougher. Transf. : harenae, Luc. ; Averni (i.e. Charon), Stat.

sulcō, āre [sulcus], to furrow, plough. **1.** Lit. : agros, Tib. ; vomere humum, Ov. **2.** Transf. : fossas, Varr. ; anguis harenam, Ov. ; vada carinā, Verg. ; rate undas, Ov. ; maria arbore, Plin. ; cutem rugis, Ov.

sulcus, ī, m. [cf. Gk. ὁλκός], a furrow. **1.** Lit. : Varr., Verg., etc. ; altius imprimere, Cic. ; ducere sarculo, Plin. ; patefacere aratro, Ov. ; telluri infindere sulcos, Verg. ; sulco vario arare, Cato ; Plin. **2.** Transf. **a.** a ditch made with a plough (to mark out a town) : locum concludere sulco, Verg. ; designat moenia sulco, Ov. **b.** a trench for plants : Cato, Verg., etc. **c.** a track of a vessel or meteor : Verg. **d.** a wrinkle in the skin : Mart. **e.** Of the female pudenda : Lucr., Verg. **f.** a ploughing : Plin., Plin. Ep. [It. solco ; Sp. surco.]

sulfur, v. sulpur.

Sulla, ae, m. *a Roman surname, esp. of L.* Cornelius Sulla Felix, *the famous Roman dictator* (ob. B.C. 78); **Sullānus**, a, um; **Sullāni**, ōrum, m. pl. *his supporters.*

sullāturiō, īre, [Sulla], *to long to be a Sulla or to play the part of Sulla* : animus, Cic. Ep.

Sulmō, ōnis, m. *a town of the Paeligni, near* Corfinium ; *the birth-place of Ovid* ; **Sulmōnēnsis**, e ; and **Sulmōnēnsēs**, ium, m. pl. *its inhabitants.*

Sulpicius, a, *the name of a Roman gens* ; **Sulpicius, Sulpiciānus**, a, um.

sulpur (sulfur), uris, n. *brimstone, sulphur.* **1.** Lit.: Cato, Lucr., Liv., Ov., etc. In pl. . Verg., Ov., Quint. **2.** Transf. of lightning : Pers., Luc. [It. *solfo, zolfo* ; Fr. *soufre.*]

sulpurātus, a, um [sulpur], *impregnated with sulphur* : Plin., Mart. *Neut. pl.* as Noun, *sulphur-matches* : Mart.

sulpureus, a, um [sulpur], *of or like sulphur, sulphurous* : aqua, Verg. ; fornaces, Ov. ; color, odor, Plin.

sultis = si vultis ; v. volō.

sum, esse, fuī (fūī, occ. in Pl.), futūrus (*Fut. Inf.* fore for futūrum esse very freq. (v. also III. c. infra) ; hence *Imperf. Subj.* forem for essem, very freq., exc. in Cic. Old forms : *Indic. Pres.* esum for sum, acc. to Varr. ; *Fut.* escit for erit, Lucr. ; *Perf.* fūvimus for fuimus, Enn. ; *Subj. Pres.* siem, siēs, siet, etc.. freq., esp. in Pl ; fuam, Pl. ; fuat, Pl., Lucr., Verg.) [fr. roots seen in Gk. εἰμί and φύω]. **I.** To denote simple existence : *to be, exist, to happen, take place* : nolite existimare me nusquam aut nullum fore, Cic. ; illa (defectio solis) quae fuit regnante Romulo, Cic. Particular usages. **a.** sunt quae praeterii, *there are some facts*, Cic. ; fuere complures, qui ad Catilinam initio profecti sunt, Sall. With *Subj.* : erat nemo in quem suspicio conveniret, Cic. **b.** With DAT. : est mihi, *I have* (in my possession) : privatus illis census erat brevis, Hor. ; Pl. ; Cic., etc. Hence phr. : tecum nihil rei nobis est, *I have nothing to do with you*, Ter. **c.** In *Perf.* tense (euphem.), *to be no more, be over and gone* : fuimus Troes, Verg. ; so of the Catilinarian conspirators who had been executed,—fuere ! Cic. **d.** Before a Noun-sentence with *ut, ubi*, etc. ; *it is possible, it may be (that)* : non est igitur ut mirandum sit, Cic. ; non est ut copia maior ab Iove donari possit tibi, Hor. ; futurum esse ut omnes pellerentur, Caes. Also with *Inf.* : unde plus haurire est, Hor. **e.** *to be present, to have arrived* : ecquid in mentem est tibi ? Pl. ; portūs in praedonum fuisse potestatem sciatis, Cic. ; qui neque in provinciam cum imperio fuerunt, Cic. Ep. **II.** Forming a Predicate with other words : the complement being a Noun, an *Adj.*, or less freq. an *Adv.* or Phrase with *Prep.* **a.** *to be* : e.g. sum homo, sum bonus ; ita res est, etc. ; frustra id inceptum Volscis fuit, Liv. ; cum est in sagis civitas, Cic. (For such Phr. as ab aliquo esse, pro aliquo esse, v. ab, pro ; and for in eo esse, v. is.) **b.** *to be valued*

us : dum...etc. nd erph., *cold at one-sixth of* um eng Li. (For [............] [............] v. tantus, etc.) **c.** With GEN., to bel. to, *it is the duty or part of* ; *it is the characteristic of* : est adulescentis maiores natu vereri, Cic. **d.** With GEN. or ABL. of Quality or Description ; *to be characterised by, possessed of* : magni iudici esse, Cic. ; somni brevissimi erat, Suet. ; tenuissimā valetudine esse, Caes. **e.** With DAT. denoting end, purpose, etc. : oneri ferendo esse, *to be equal to bearing a burden*, Liv. ; non solvendo esse, *you were insolvent*, Cic. ; cui bono fuerit, *for whose advantage it was*, Cic. **f.** esse ad aliquid, *to be useful or of service for* : taedā et pice quae sunt ad incendia, Caes. **III.** As an auxiliary verb. **a.** With *Perf. Part.*, sum, eram, ero, sim, essem (or forem), esse, to form the *Perf.*, etc. Also, fuī, etc., esp. in Sall. **b.** With *Fut. Part.* or *Gerundive* any tense of sum is possible. **c.** fore (i) as alternative to futūrus (esse). (ii) with *Perf. Part.* to form a *Fut. Perf. Inf. Pass.* or *Dep.* : debellatum fore, Liv. ; dico me satis adeptum fore, Cic.

sūmen, inis, n. [contr. of sūgmen, from sūgō], *a breast, teat, udder.* **1.** Lit.: Lucil. Esp. *a sow's udder* : Pl., Mart. **2.** Transf. *a breeding sow* : Juv.

summa, v. summus.

sum-mānō (subm-), āre, *to trickle a little* (with Acc. of Extent) : vestimenta, Pl.

Summānus, ī, m. *a Roman deity to whom nocturnal lightnings were ascribed.*

summārium, ī, n. [summa, v. summus], *a summary, abstract* : Sen. Ep.

summās, ātis, m. f. [summus], *high-born, eminent, noble* : Pl.

summātim, adv. *on the top or surface, slightly.* Transf. of composition, etc. : *giving only the heads, summarily in summary* : Lucil., Cic. Ep., Lucr., Liv., Quint., etc.

summātus, ūs, m. [summus], *supremacy, sovereignty* : Lucr.

summē, adv. *in the highest degree, exceedingly* : cupere, Caes., Cic. ; officiosi, Cic. ; munitus, Hor.

sum-mergō (subm-), mergere, mērsī, mērsum, *to dip or plunge under, to sink* : navis summersa, Caes. ; Verg. ; Tac. ; summersus equus voraginibus, Cic. ; ipsos ponto, Verg. ; ferrum in undā, Ov. ; aliquot procellis summersi paene sumus, Liv.

sum-merus, a, um, *pretty pure* : vinum, Pl.

summinia, v. subnimia.

sum-ministrō (subm-), āre, *to supply in support or so as to help.* **1.** Lit.: frumentum, Caes. ; auxilia hostibus nostris, Caes. ; pecuniam alicui, Cic. **2.** Transf.: arti adiumenta atque ornamenta, Cic. ; materiam eloquentiae, Tac. ; occasiones alicui, Suet.

summissē (subm-) and **summissim** (Suet.), adv. **I.** Of speech : *in a low voice, softly* : dicere, Cic. Comp. : Cic. **II.** Of character : *humbly, modestly* : alicui supplicare, Cic. ; Ov. ; Tac. Comp. : Cic.

summissiō (subm-), ōnis, f. [summittō], *a lowering, dropping.* Transf. : vocis, orationis, Cic.

summissus (subm-), a, um. **I.** *Part.* summittō. **II.** Adj. **A.** *let down, lowered, stooping.* **1.** Lit.: scutis super capita densatis, stantibus primis, secundis summissioribus, Liv. **2.** Transf. **a.** Of the voice or of speech: vox, Cic., Ov.; oratio, Caes., Cic.; orator, Cic., Quint. *Comp.:* Quint. *Neut. pl.* as Noun: Quint. **b.** Of character or disposition: *humble, submissive.* In good sense: Verg.; causae reorum, Quint.; civitates calamitate summissiores, Hirt. In bad sense: *too submissive; grovelling, abject :* Cic.; adulatio, Quint. **B.** *let grow :* capillo summissiore, Suet.

sum-mittō (subm-), mittere, misi, missum. **I.** *to let go or send up from below, to cause or allow to spring up, to raise.* **1.** Lit. **a.** Of the earth : tellus flores, Lucr.; colores humus, Prop.; monstrum, Hor. **b.** Of the farmer raising crops, stock, etc.: prata in faenum, Cato; Varr.; arietes, Varr.; tauros, vitulos, Verg. Also, vinea capreas non semper edulis, Hor. **2.** Transf.: crinem barbamque (i.e. let grow), Tac.; capillum, Plin. Ep. **II.** *to send up* in support or as reinforcements : cohortis equitibus praesidio, Caes.; auxilium laborantibus, Caes.; subsidium, Caes. **III.** *to send as substitute :* (aliquem) alicui, Cic. **IV.** *to let go or put under.* **1.** Lit. **a.** singulos agnos binis nutricibus, Col. **b.** *to cast down, to lower :* se ad pedes, Liv.; se patri ad genua, Suet.; latus, caput in herbā, Ov.; summisso vertice, Ov.; fascis, Liv.; oculos, Ov.; faciem, Suet. In *Mid. :* Tiberis aestate summittitur, Plin. Ep. **2.** Transf. **A.** With *se* or *animum, to lower oneself, condescend, submit (to), yield :* se in amicitiā, Cic.; se in privatum fastigium, Liv.; se culpae, Ov.; se temporibus, Sen.; ad calamitates animos, Liv.; animos amori, Verg.; animum saevienti fortunae, Tac. Also, imperium (suum) Camillo (i.e. Camilli imperio), Liv. **B.** *to lower, moderate.* **a.** Of tone in speaking : Cic.; vocem, Quint. **b.** Of restraint in style : verba, Sen.; orationem, Plin. Ep. **c.** In gen. : furorem, Verg. **V.** *to send or despatch secretly :* ad pupillae matrem, Cic.; summittebat Timarchidem qui moneret eos etc., Cic.; Suet.

summolestē (subm-), adv. *with some feeling of annoyance :* aliquid ferre, Cic. Ep.

sum-molestus (subm-), a, um, *rather troublesome or annoying :* illud est mihi submolestum quod etc., Cic. Ep.

sum-moneō (subm-), ēre, ui, *to give a hint to or remind privately :* Suet.; aliquem quod etc., Ter.

summopere, v. summus.

sum-mōrōsus (subm-), a, um, *rather moody or peevish :* ridicula, Cic.

summōtus (subm-), a, um, *Part.* summoveō.

sum-moveō (subm-), movēre, mōvi, mōtum. **I.** *to move up :* cohortis sub murum, Caes. **II.** *to move off or away* so as to make room, *to make room, to clear* (e.g. the court), and milit. *to drive off, dislodge.* **1.** Lit.

a. In gen. : Gallos, Liv.; summotā contione, Cic.; summoto populo stabant accusator et reus, Liv.; recusantis advocatos, Cic.; arbitros, Liv.; in castra hostium equitatum, Liv.; hostis a portā, Caes.; hostis ex muro, Caes.; hostis ex agro Romano trans Anienem, Liv.; hostium lembos statione, Caes.; alios longe summotos arcet harena, Verg. **b.** Of a lictor : i, lictor, summove turbam, Liv. Without Acc. : Liv. *Impers. Pass. :* summoveri (or *sc.* populum) iussit, Liv.; summoto (or *sc.* populo) incesserunt, Liv. **c.** *to expel, banish :* patriā, Ov.; Suet.; ad Histrum, Ov. **2.** Transf. **a.** aliquem a re publicā, Cic.; aliquem a maleficio, Cic.; reges a bello, Liv.; aliquem administratione rei publicae, Suet. **b.** spelunca fuit vasto summota (ex oculis) recessu, Verg.; silva Phoebeos ictūs, Ov.; Alpes Germaniam ab Italiā, Plin. **c.** summotus pudor, Hor.; neque consularis lictor summovet tumultūs mentis, Hor.; vitia, Sen. Ep.; sermonem a procoemio, Quint.

summus, a, um [for sub-mus, *cf.* ὕπατος fr. ὑπό], *uppermost, highest, topmost, at the highest or uppermost part, on or at the top or surface of, at the highest.* **1.** Lit. of place : vestimentum, Pl.; iugum montis, Caes.; Hor.; in summā Sacrā Viā, Cic.; in aquā summā, Pl.; per summa aequora, Verg. Of position at table : Hor. As Noun, **summus,** i, m. *the (one who sits at) head of the table :* Pl., Cic. **summum,** i, n. *the top, surface* (mostly with *preps.*) : Caes., Cic.; also *the highest place, the head* of the table : igitur discubuere . . . in summo Antonius, Sall. **2.** Transf. **a.** Of the voice : summā voce, Pl., Cic., etc. **b.** Of time or succession, *last, latest, final, the end of :* haec est praestituta summa argento dies, Pl.; venit summa dies, Verg.; vix ad summam senectutem, Cic.; summo carmine, Hor. **c.** Of degree, rank, etc. : *extreme, utmost ; highest, greatest, best, most distinguished or noble ; most important, weighty* (mostly of mental or moral qualities) : summā vi, summā industriā, Enn.; non agam summo iure tecum, Cic.; fides, constantia, iustitia, turpitudo, etc., Cic.; summi viri, Pl., Cic.; also, summi alone, Cic.; amicus, Ter.; imperator, Cic.; also in *neut. pl.* summa ducum Atrides, Ov.; scelus, Sall.; res publica (i.e. the highest welfare or interests of the State), Cic.; also, res summa (i.e. the general cause), Verg.; in summo et periculosissimo rei publicae tempore, Cic.; aestas, *the height of summer*, Cic.; hiems, *the depths of winter*, Caes. *Neut.* Acc. **summum** as *Adv., at the utmost or furthest or* perh. *at the latest :* triduo aut summum quadriduo, Cic.; uno aut summum altero proelio, Liv. Also **summō opere (summopere),** *very much, exceedingly :* Lucr., Cic., Liv. As Noun, **summa,** ne, *f.* (*sc.* res), *that which is at the top or on the surface.* **I.** *the main thing, chief point, main issue, gist, summary ; the main body ; the chief power ; perfection :* lectis rerum summis, Liv.; in hoc summa iudici causaque tota consistit, Cic.; haec summa est,

Verg.; universi belli (i.e. the *whole force* of the war as a whole), Liv.; totius belli summa (i.e. the chief direction of the whole war), Caes.; summa rei bellicae (i.e. the highest influence in military matters), Liv.; imperi, Caes., Cic.; summam rerum administrare, Cic.; penes unum est omnium summa rerum, Cic.; solus summam habet hic apud nos, Pl.; remittendo de summā quisque iuris, Liv. **II.** Of numbers: *the amount, the sum, sum total.* **1.** Lit.: de summā nihil decedet, Ter.; Cic.; Liv., etc.; facere, Cic.; pecuniae, Liv.; Hor. **2.** Transf.: macrorum, Pl.; de summā mali detrahere, Cic.; vitae summa brevis, Hor.; summarum summa est aeterna (i.e. the entire universe), Lucr.; Pl.; Sen. Ep.; ad discrimen summam rerum adducere (i.e. their all), Liv.; ad summam rerum consulere, Caes. [Fr. *somme.*]

sūmō, sūmere, sūmpsī, sūmptum [sub emō]. *to take up.* **1.** Lit. **a.** In gen.: fustem, Pl.; legem in manūs, Cic.; pecuniam mutuam, Cic.; cyathos, Hor.; ferrum, Ov.; arma, Quint.; a me argentum, Ter.; pomum de lance, Ov. **b.** Of dress, etc. *to put on, assume:* virilem togam, Cic.; regium ornatum nomenque, Nep.; alas pedibus, Ov. **2.** Transf. **a.** perventum est eo quo sumpta navis est, Cic. **b.** Of time: diem ad deliberandum, Caes.; Liv.; tempus cibi quietisque, Liv. **c.** Of a penalty, *to exact, inflict :* satis supplici, Pl.; more maiorum supplicium, Caes.; poenas, Verg.; de aliquo supplicium, Cic., Liv.; so, ex aliquo, Liv.; pro maleficio poenam, Cic. **d.** Of mental attitude: opsequium animo, Pl.; calorem animo, Lucr.; sibi tantam adrogantiam, Caes.; animum, Ov.; animos, Liv., Ov.; spiritūs, Liv. **e.** Of action, line of conduct, etc.: *to take up, undertake, etc. :* frustra operam, Ter.; laborem, Caes.; bellum, Sall., Liv.; bellum cum aliquo, Liv.; proelia, Suet.; vocis temptamina, Ov. **f.** *to take* (by choice): philosophiae studium, Cic.; Hor.; Ov.; Miltiadem sibi imperatorem, Nep.; Sall.; disceptatorem, Liv. With *Inf. :* Hor. **g.** *to take as one's own, to appropriate, arrogate* (mostly with mihi, tibi, etc.): sibi imperatorias partis, Caes.; Cic.; mores antiquos, Liv.; vultūs acerbos (but perh. cf. l. b.), Ov.; laudem a crimine, Ov. **h.** *to take for granted, to assume, suppose:* aliquid pro certo, Cic.; Lucr.; ea ad concludendum, Cic. With Acc. and *Inf. :* Cic., Liv. **i.** *to bring up* or *forward* as a proof, example, etc.: exempla, Cic.; homines notos, Cic.; quid quisquam potest ex omni memoriā sumere inlustrius ? Cic. **j.** *to take* at a price, *to buy, purchase :* Cic., Hor.

sūmptiō, ōnis, f. [sūmō]. In logic : *a premiss taken for granted, an assumption :* Cic.

sūmptuārius, a, um [sūmptus], *relating to expense, sumptuary :* rationes nostrae, Cic. Ep.; lex, Cic. Ep.

sūmptuōsē, adv. *expensively :* Cat., Suet. *Comp. :* Cic., Plin. Ep.

sūmptuōsus, a, um [sūmptus], *expensive,*

costly, **a.** Of things : ludi, Cic.; cena, Hor.; Liv., etc.; Comp.; ludi sumptuosiores, Cic. Ep. *Sup. :* Suet. **b.** Of persons : *lavish, wasteful, extravagant :* Pl., Ter., Cic., etc.

sūmptus, a, um, *Part.* sūmō.

sūmptus, ūs (sūmptī, Pl.), m. [sūmō], *expense, cost, charge :* sumptui esse alicui, Pl., Cic. Ep.; magnum numerum equitatūs suo sumptu alere, Caes.; sine sumptu tuo, Ter.; publico sumptu, Hor., Liv.; dare, Cic.; in aliquid facere, insumere, Cic., Liv.; sumptum melius ponere, Cic. Ep.; sumptum suom exercere (i.e. to earn one's keep), Ter.; aedilitatis, Cic.; perpetuos sumptūs suppeditare, Cic.; minuere, Cic.; in eos sumptūs pecuniam erogare, Liv.

suō, suere, suī, sūtum, *to sew* or *stitch, to sew, join,* or *tack together.* **1.** Lit. : tegimenta corporum, Cic.; corticibus suta cavatis alvearia, Verg. **2.** Transf. : metuo lenonem, ne quid suo suat capiti, Ter.

suōmet and **suōpte,** v. suus.

suovetaurīlia, ium, n. pl. (sc. sacra) [sūs ovis taurus], *a sacrifice consisting of a swine, a sheep, and a bull,* offered esp. at lustrations (v. Smith's Ant. 356) : Liv., Tac. (Form **sōlitaurīlia** [sōlus (=sollus), taurus] : Quint.

supellex, lectilis, f. [super legō], *household utensils, furniture,* or *goods* (only in *sing.*). **1.** Lit. : Pl., Cic., Hor., etc. **2.** Transf. : amicos parare, optimam et pulcherrimam vitae, ut ita dicam, supellectilem, Cic.; tecum habita, et noris quam sit tibi curta supellex, Pers.; copiosa verborum supellex, Quint.; oratoria, Cic.

super, adj. v. superus.

super, adv. and prep. [*cf.* Gk. ὑπέρ]. **I.** Adv. : *above, on the top.* **1.** Lit. of place : eo super tigna bipedalia iniciunt, Caes.; haec super e vallo prospectant, Verg. **2.** Transf. of number and quantity. **a.** *over, moreover, besides :* satis superque esse sibi suarum cuique rerum, Cic.; super quam quod etc. (*besides that etc.*), Liv.; incipio super his, Verg.; his accensa super, Verg. **b.** *over, left, remaining :* super tibi erunt, qui dicere laudes tuas cupiant, Verg.; Nep.; Liv.; sola super imago, Verg. **3.** In compounds, super denotes *over, above.* **A.** Lit. of place : supergredior. **B.** Transf. **a.** Of quantity, degree, etc. : superaddo. **b.** Of a surplus or remainder : supersum. **II.** Prep. with Acc. or Abl. **A.** With Acc. **1.** Lit. **a.** Of place or situation : *over, above, upon, on :* super terrae tumulum aliquid statuere, Cic.; cum alii super aliorum capita ruerent, Liv. **b.** Of order or arrangement : *above, higher, beyond :* Nomentanus erat super ipsum, Porcius infra, Hor.; Curt. Geogr. : super Numidiam Gaetulos accepimus, Sall.; Verg. **2.** Transf. **a.** Of time : *over* (i.e. *during*) : super vinum et epulas, Curt.; Plin. Ep. **b.** Of number or quantity, *over, above, besides :* super LX milia, Tac.; alii super alios, Liv.; dare savia super savia, Pl.; super modum, Quint.; Punicum exercitum super morbum etiam fames adfecit, Liv. **c.** Of rank or worth,

only in the phr., **super omnia**, *above all,
before all :* talia carminibus celebrant ;
super omnia Caci speluncam adiciunt,
Verg. ; Liv. Of an official charge : super
armamentarium positus, Curt. **B.** With
ABL. **1.** Lit. of place or situation (rare) :
over, above, upon : districtus ensis cui super
impiâ cervice pendet, Hor. ; ligna super
foco large reponens, Hor. ; Caes. ; Verg.
2. Transf. **a.** Of time : *on, at :* nocte
super mediâ, Verg. ; super mero, Hor.
b. Of abstract relation (for *de*) : *upon,
concerning :* hac super re scribam ad te,
Cic. Ep. ; Pl. ; super suâ laude, Verg. ;
cura super tantâ re, Liv. ; super tali causâ
missi, Nep. **c.** *over and above, besides :*
modus agri . . . hortus . . . fons . . . et
paulum silvae super his, Hor. [Fr. *sur.*]

superä, *v.* suprā.

superābilis, e, *adj.* [superō], *that may be
got over or surmounted.* **1.** Lit. : murus,
Liv. **2.** Transf.: nullis casibus Romani,
Tac. ; non est per vim superabilis ulli, Ov.

super-addō, addere, additum, *to put on or
besides :* tumulo carmina, Verg. ; laurum
busto, Prop.

super-adstō (**-astō**), āre, *to stand over :*
Sall.

superāns, antis. **I.** *Part.* superō. **II.** Adj.
prevailing, predominant : superantior ignis,
Lucr.

superātor, ōris, *m.* [superō], *a conqueror :*
populi Etrusci, Ov. ; Gorgonis, Ov.

superbē, *adv. haughtily, arrogantly, tyrannically :* Pl., Caes., Liv. *Comp. :* Cic.,
Tac. *Sup. :* Cic.

superbia, ae, *f.* **I.** Usually in bad sense :
*overbearingness, haughtiness, tyrannical
bearing, cruel arrogance :* Pl., Cic., Verg.,
etc. In *pl. :* Pl. **II.** In good sense,
lofty spirit, honourable pride : sume superbiam quaesitam meritis, Hor. ; Tac.

superbiloquentia, ae, *f.* [superbus loquor],
arrogant discourse : Poet. ap. Cic.

superbiō, īre [superbus], *to be exalted.* **a.** *to
be proud or arrogant :* patriis actis, Ov. ;
Prop. ; miles, Tac. **b.** *to be superb, magnificent :* quae sub Tyriâ concha superbit
aquâ, Prop. ; Plin.

superbus, a, um [super], *exalted, uplifted
in mind ; hence,* **A.** *overbearing, haughty,
arrogant, tyrannical, despotic.* **1.** Lit. of
persons : Pl., Cic. Ep., Verg., Liv., etc. ;
in fortunâ, Cic. Ep. ; opibus, Verg. ; Pl.
Comp. : Cic. Ep., Ov. *Sup. :* Sall. **2.**
Transf. of things. **a.** sceptra, Liv. ;
victoria, responsa, decreta, etc., Cic. ; iura,
lex, pax, Liv. ; vita, Prop. ; superbum est
(with *Inf.*), Cic., Ov. *Sup. :* Cic., Liv.
Neut. pl. as Noun : superba loqui, Cic.
b. *disdainful, fastidious :* dens, Hor. ;
aures, Liv. ; aurium iudicium, Cic. ; oculi,
Ov. *Sup. :* Cic. **B.** In good sense, *splendid, magnificent, superb :* populum late
regem belloque superbum, Verg. ; triumphus, Hor. ; Cat. ; Sen. Ep.

super-cilium, ī, *n. an eye-brow.* **1.** Lit. :
Pl., Cic., Verg., etc. ; torta, Pl. ; constricta,
Quint. ; coniuncta, Suet. **2.** Transf. **a.**
beck (i.e. *will*) : cuncta supercilio movens
Iuppiter, Hor. **b.** *a brow, summit :* cli-
vosi tramitis, Verg. ; tumuli, Liv. **c.**

arrogance, superciliousness : supercilium
ac regius spiritus, Cic. ; Ov., etc. [Fr.
sourcil.]

super-ēmineō, ēre, *to overtop, rise above :*
viros omnis, Verg. ; umero undas, Ov.

super-ficiēs, ēī, *f.* [faciēs], *the upper side,
the top, surface.* **a.** In gen. : testudinum,
Plin. **b.** In law, *anything placed upon
the ground so as to become attached to it,* us.
a building erected on another man's land :
Cic. Ep., Liv.

super-fiō, fieri, *to be over and above, to be left
over :* locus, Pl.

super-fixus, a, um, *fixed on the top :* capita
hostium, Liv.

super-fluō, fluere, *to overflow.* **1.** Lit. :
Plin., Tac. **2.** Transf. **a.** populus, pe-
cunia, Sen. **b.** Of style : iuvenili quâdam
dicendi impunitate et licentiâ superfluens,
Cic. ; nihil neque desit neque superfluat,
Quint. ; orator superfluens, Tac.

superfluus, a, um [superfluō], *running over,
overflowing.* **1.** Lit. : flumina campis,
Plin. Pan. **2.** Transf. *superfluous, unnecessary :* Sen. Ep.

super-fundō, fundere, fūdi, fūsum, *to pour
over or upon.* **1.** Lit. **a.** Of liquids : *to
overflow, flood* (esp. in *Mid.* or with *Refl.
Pron.*) : Circus Tiberi superfuso inrigatus,
Liv. ; Tiberis ripis superfunditur, Plin. Ep. ;
nuda gentis tingamus corpora lymphis,
Ov. **b.** Of weapons, etc. : magnam vim
telorum, Tac. ; iacentem hostes superfusi
oppresserunt, Liv. **2.** Transf. *super-
fundenti* se laetitiae, Liv. ; Macedonum
fama superfudit se in Asiam, Liv. ; nondum
fortuna se animo eius superfuderat, Curt.
With Acc. governed by *super,* and with
Instr. ABL. : sedecim alarum coniuncta
signa nube ipsâ superfundent equites
equosque, Tac.

super-gredior, gredi, grëssus [gradior], *to
step, walk, or go over.* **1.** Lit. : Plin.
2. Transf. : feminas pulchritudine, Tac. ;
omnem laudem, Quint.

super-iaciō, iacere, iēci, iectum or iactum,
to cast or throw over or upon. **1.** Lit. :
membra superiectâ cum veste, Ov. ; aggerem, Suet. ; superiecto natarunt aequore
damae, Hor. With *Instr.* ABL., and ACC.
going closely with the *super :* pontus
scopulos superiacit undâ, Verg. ; Plin.
2. Transf. *to overshoot :* superiecere quidam augendo fidem, Liv.

superiectus, a, um, *Part.* superiaciō.

super-immineō, ēre, *to hang over, overhang :*
Verg., Sen.

super-impendēns, entis, *overhanging :* silvae, Cat.

super-impositus, a, um [*v.* impōnō], *put
or placed upon :* saxum, statua, Liv. ;
Stat., etc.

super-incidēns, entis, *falling on the top of :*
tela, Liv.

super-incubāns, antis, *Part. lying over or
upon :* Liv.

super-incumbō, cumbere, cubui, *to fling
oneself down upon :* Ov.

super-indūcō, dūcere, dūxi, ductum, *to
draw or cover over :* corpus, Quint.

super-induō, duere, *to put on over :* paenulam, Suet.

super-ingerō, gerĕre, gestum, to heap upon : acervos, Plin. ; montem, Stat.

super-iiiciō, īnĭcere, iniēci, iniectum, to throw or cast over or upon : raras frondes, Verg. ; Ov. ; Plin.

super-insternō, sternere, strāvi, to spread or lay over : tabulas, Liv.

superior, v. superus.

superius, adv., v. superus and suprā.

super-iūmentārius, i, m. a superintendent of the drivers of beasts of burden : Suet.

superlātiō, ōnis, f. [super ferō]. Rhet. : an exaggerating, hyperbole : veritatis, Cic. ; Quint.

super-lātus, a, um, extravagant, exaggerated : verba, Cic. ; Quint.

super-mittō, mittere, mīsi, to put in afterwards, add, etc. : Curt.

supernās, ātis, adj. [supernus], upper or northern ; on or from the Adriatic (mare superum) : Plin.

superne, adv. above, from above : desinat in piscem mulier formosa superne, Hor. ; gladium superne iugulo defigit, Liv.

supernus, a, um [super], lying above, upper ; celestial : Lucr. ; Tusculum, Hor. ; Plin. ; numen, Ov.

superō, āre [superus]. **A.** Intrans. to go or pass over or above, to overtop. **1.** Lit. : sol ex mari, Pl. ; iugo, Verg. With Instr. ABL. : capite, Verg. **2.** Transf. **a.** to have the upper hand, to be superior : nostra manus, Pl. ; Liv. ; sententiā Sabini, Caes. ; morbus, Plin. Ep. With Instr. ABL. : numero hostis, virtute Romanus, Liv. ; Caes. ; animis, Verg. **b.** to exceed, be superfluous : pecunia, Cic. ; alicui, Cic. ; illis divitiae, Sall. **c.** to be abundant : tibi superbia, Pl. ; gentis tibi laudes, Tib. ; Verg. ; otium, Liv. **d.** Of things or persons : to be left over, to remain, survive : Pl., Caes., Cic., Hor. ; vitā, Caes. ; nihil ex raptis commeatibus, Liv. With DAT. : captae urbi, Verg. **B.** Trans. to go or pass over, rise above : to surmount, overtop. **1.** Lit. **a.** temo stellas, Enn. ; tempestas summas ripas fluminis, Caes. ; munitiones, Liv. ; montis, Verg. ; superat (Parnasus) cacumine nubes, Ov. ; tantum itineris, Tac. **b.** to go past or beyond : regionem castrorum, Caes. ; Liv. **c.** Nautical : to sail past, to double : promunturium, Liv. **2.** Transf. **a.** to surpass, outstrip : quaestum sumptus, Pl. ; Varr. ; aliquem virtute laude, dignitate, Cic ; Pl. ; Ov. ; Phoebum canendo, Verg. ; vel cursu canem vel viribus aprum, Hor. ; omnis in ceteris artibus, Nep. **b.** Milit. to overcome, vanquish : Massilienses bis proelio navali superati, Caes. ; Pl. ; Verg. Transf. : casūs omnis, Verg. ; meam spem vis improborum, Cic.

super-obruō, ere, to overwhelm : Tarpeiam armis, Prop.

super-pendēns, entis, overhanging : saxa, Liv.

super-pōnō, pōnere, posui, positum (mostly in Perf. Part.), to put or place over or upon. **1.** Lit. : capiti decus, Liv. ; aegra superpositā membra fovere manu, Ov. ; villam colli, Suet. **2.** Transf. **a.** Perperna in maritimam regionem superpositus, Liv.

super-... [to place above], ... sen. Hpt **a.** to place beyond, pone (with ACC. and DAT.) : Quint.

super-scandō, ere, to climb or step over : corpora, Liv.

super-scriptus, a, um, written over (as a correction in a MS.) : Suet.

super-sedeō, sedēre, sēdi, sēsum, to sit upon or above. **1.** Lit. (with DAT.) : elephanto, Suet. **2.** Transf. **A.** to preside over : vilicus litibus familae, Cato. **B.** to sit above or aloof (from), to forbear, to refrain or desist (from). **a.** Usually with ABL. : istis rebus, Pl. ; labore itineris, Cic. Ep. ; proelio, Caes. Impers. Pass. : Cic., Liv. **b.** With Inf. : Liv., Tac., etc.

super-stagnō, āre, to overflow and so form a lake : amnis, Tac.

superstes, itis, adj. [superstō]. **I.** standing over as witness. **1.** Lit. : Pl. ; Old legal formula in Cic. **2.** Transf. : unde velut victrix despicit undas, Ov. **II.** standing or existing beyond (in time) ; hence, outliving, surviving. **a.** Of persons : Ter., Liv., Suet. With DAT. : alicui, Pl., Cic., Ov., etc. ; tuae vitae, Pl. ; rei publicae, Cic. Ep. ; Hor. ; gloriae suae, Liv. With GEN. : alicuius, Liv., Tac., etc. ; non solum vitae sed etiam dignitatis meae, Cic. Ep. ; bellorum, Tac. **b.** Of things : fama, Hor., Ov. ; post mea fata opus, Ov. With DAT. : cenis tribus perna, Mart.

superstitiō, ōnis, f. [superstes], unreasonable or excessive belief or fear ; superstition (partic. of belief in magic, etc., or in foreign ideas) : superstitio, in quā inest timor inanis deorum, Cic. ; also dist. fr. religio and deorum cultus pius, Cic. ; superstitiones aniles, Cic. ; sagarum, Cic. ; tristis, Hor. ; magicae, Tac. ; captus quādam superstitione animus, Liv. ; Verg. ; barbara, contaminata, Cic. ; victi superstitione (from Etruria), Liv. ; exitialis (of the Christians), Tac. ; novas superstitiones introducere, Quint.

superstitiōsē, adv. **I.** superstitiously : Cic. **II.** too scrupulously : Quint.

superstitiōsus, a, um [superstitiō], full of superstition. **a.** Of persons who are thought to possess occult gifts : Pl. Also, hariolationes, Enn. **b.** Of persons who themselves hold false beliefs : Cic., Liv. Also, sollicitudo, Cic.

superstitō, āre [superstes]. **A.** Intrans. to be over or remaining : Pl. **B.** Trans. to keep alive, preserve : regnum, Enn.

super-stō, āre, to stand upon or over : Verg., Liv. With DAT. : corporibus hostium, Liv. ; signa cum columnis, quibus superstabant, Liv. With ACC. : Ov.

super-strātus, a, um, strewn (as a covering) above : Liv.

super-struō, struere, struxi, structum, to build upon : ligneam compagem, Tac. ; aliquid his fundamentis, Quint.

super-sum, esse, fui, futūrus (in tmesi : super unus eram, Verg.), to be over and above. **A.** As a remainder. **a.** Of persons or things : to be left, to remain, to exist still : Enn., Cic. ; ex eo proelio circiter milia hominum cxxx superfuerunt, Caes. ; quod superest (as to what remains, i.e. for the rest), Cic. Ep., Verg. ; superest dicere, Ov. ; superest (with *ut* and *Subj.*), Plin. Ep. With DAT. : quantum satietati superfuit, Cic. ; deos Ambraciensibus non superesse, Liv. ; fessis tantum maris, Verg. **b.** *to outlive, survive :* Suet. ; alicui, Liv. ; tuae vitae, Pl. ; fugae, Liv. ; dolori, Ov. **B. a.** *to be in abundance, to abound :* vita, Verg. ; vereor ne iam superesse mihi verba putes, Cic. Ep. ; Ter. ; animi ad sustinendam invidiam, Liv. ; labori, Verg. **b.** *to be in excess, to be superfluous :* ut neque absit quicquam neque supersit, Cic.

super-tĕgō, ere, *to cover above* (only *in tmesi*) : ossa favilla, Tib.

super-urgĕns, entis, *pressing above :* fluctu superurgente, Tac.

supĕrus, a, um : *Comp.* **supĕrior**, ius; *Sup.* **suprēmus**, a, um (v. also **summus**) [super]. **A.** P o s i t i v e : *that is above.* **a.** In gen. : di superi atque inferi, Pl. ; omnia supera, infera, media, Cic. ; Verg., etc. ; mare (*Adriatic Sea :* mare inferum, the *Tyrrhene Sea*), Pl., Cic., etc. *Masc. pl.* as Noun, **supĕri**, ōrum, *the gods above :* Verg., Hor., Ov. *Neut.* as Noun. **i.** In *sing.* in phrases, de supero, *from above*, Pl. ; ex supero, Lucr. **ii.** In *pl.* **supĕra**, ōrum, *the heavenly bodies :* Enn., Cic. ; also, *higher places :* Cic. **b.** *of the upper regions* or *upper world*, opp. to the lower regions : superas evadere ad auras, Verg. ; Lucr. ; Ov. Neut. *pl.* **supĕra** as Noun : Verg. **B.** *Comp.* **supĕrior**, ius, *higher, upper.* **1.** L i t. of place : Pl., Caes., Cic., etc. ; superior accumbere (i.e. at table, *cf.* summus), Pl. **2.** T r a n s f. **a.** Of time and succession, *former, previous ;* of age, *older :* quid proxima, quid superiore nocte egeris, Cic. ; milites superioribus proeliis exercitati, Caes. ; tempus, annus, Cic. ; superior Africanus, Cic. ; aetate superiores, Varr. **b.** Of quality, condition, number, etc. : *higher, greater, superior :* Cic., Liv. With ABL. of point *in which :* pecuniis, famā, fortunā, etc., Cic. ; hostes equitatu, Caes. M i l i t. : ita ut nostri omnibus partibus superiores fuerint, Caes. ; semper discessit superior, Nep. **C.** *Sup.* **suprēmus**, a, um. **1.** L i t. of place : *highest* or *very high :* Lucr., Verg., Hor. **2.** T r a n s f. **a.** Of time or succession, *last, latest, extreme, final :* supremo te sole domi manebo, Hor. ; supremam bellis imposuisse manum, Ov. ; spes, Verg. **suprēmum** (*Neut.* as *Intern.* Acc.), *for the last time :* quae tunc est conspecta supremum, Ov. E s p. of the close of life, *last, closing, dying :* dies, Cic. ; (also of *the day of burial*, Cic., Liv.) ; tempus, Hor. ; sociamque tori vocat ore supremo, Ov. ; honor, Verg. ; officia, Tac. ; funera, oscula, ignes, etc., Ov. **suprēmum** (*Neut.* as *Intern.* Acc.), *for a last farewell :* animam sepulcro condimus et magnā supremum voce ciemus, Verg. ; Ov. ; Tac. As Noun, **suprēma**, ōrum, *n. pl.* (**i.**) *the last moments, death :* Plin., Tac. (**ii.**) *funeral rites :* Verg., Plin., Tac. (**iii.**) *a last will and testament :* Tac. **suprēmum**, I, *n. the last moment, end :* ventum ad supremum est, Verg. **b.** Of degree, *highest, greatest :* supplicium,

Cic. ; macies, Verg. **c.** Of rank, *most exalted :* Iuppiter supreme, Pl. ; comes, Pl.

supervacāneus, a, um [vacŏ], *over and above what is strictly necessary, superfluous :* vasa, Cato ; opus (i.e. done in leisure hours), Cic. ; oratio, Liv. ; de timore supervacaneum est disserere, Sall. *Masc.* as Noun : Liv.

super-vacuus, a, um, *superfluous, useless, needless :* metus, Ov. ; littera, labor, Quint. ; supervacuum habeo (with *Inf.*), Plin. ; mihi Baias Musa supervacuas Antonius facit, Hor. *Neut.* as Noun : res ad praecavendum vel ex supervacuo movit, Liv. *Neut.* ABL. as *Adv.* : Plin.

super-vādō, ere, *to go* or *climb over, to surmount :* munimenta, Liv. ; Sall.

super-vehor, vehī, *to sail, drive, etc. beyond* or *past :* montem, Cat. ; promunturium, Liv.

super-venio, venīre, vēnī, ventum. **I.** With Acc. (going closely with the *super*) : *to come upon* or *on the top of.* **1.** L i t. : unda undam, Hor. ; crura terra, Ov. ; aliquem, Curt. **2.** T r a n s f. *to surpass, excel :* Stat. **II.** *to come upon the scene, to arrive suddenly.* **1.** L i t. Liv., Curt., Tac. ; ab Romā, Liv. With DAT. : alicui, Verg., Liv. ; huic laetitiae, Liv. **2.** T r a n s f. : hora, Hor.

superventus, ūs, *m.* [superveniō], *a coming up, an* (*unexpected*) *arrival :* Tac.

super-vivo, ere, *to outlive, survive* (with DAT.) : gloriae suae triginta annis, Plin. Ep. [Fr. *survivre.*]

super-volito, āre, *to hover over :* sua tecta alis, Verg. ; Tac.

super-volō, āre, *to fly over :* hasta, Verg. ; Plin. With Acc. : totum orbem, Ov.

supīnō, āre, *to put* or *throw face upwards,* i.e. *on the back* ; *to upturn :* manus modice supinata, Quint. ; glaebas, Verg. In *Mid.* : nasum nidore supinor, Hor.

supīnus, a, um [from sub : *cf.* ὕπτιος, from ὑπό], *face-upwards ; lying, turned, etc. upwards.* **1.** L i t. (mostly of animals and parts of the body) : Pl., Lucr., Cic., etc. Often of attitude in prayer : tendoque supinas ad caelum manūs, Verg. ; Ov. ; Liv., etc. Also, iactus (telorum), Liv. **2.** T r a n s f. **a.** Of land : *upturned* (towards the sun), also *sloping upwards :* Verg., Hor., Liv., etc. **b.** Of streams : *flowing upwards* to their source : Ov. T r a n s f. of verses that can be read backwards : Mart. **c.** Mentally : *on one's back, lazy, indolent, careless :* Quint., Juv. ; animus, Cat. Also, auris, Mart. ; compositio, Quint. *Comp.* : Mart.

suppāctus, a, um, *Part.* suppingŏ.

sup-paenitet, ēre, *to cause* (*someone*) *some slight regret* (with Acc. of person and GEN. of thing regretted) : Cic. Ep.

sup-palpor, ārī, *to fondle* or *wheedle a little :* alicui vino, Pl.

sup-pār, aris, *adj. nearly equal :* Cic.

sup-parasitor, ārī, *to act the parasite a little :* alicui, Pl.

supparum (v. siparium), I, *n.*, and **supparus**, ī, *m.* [an Oscan word, orig. perh. *linen stuff* in gen.], *a linen garment worn by women :* Pl.

suppeditătiō, ōnis, *f.* [suppeditŏ], *abundance*: bonorum, Cic.

suppedito, āre. **A.** Intrans. *to stand by or in support* ; *to support, to be ready* ; (of things) *to be ready* or *be supplied.* **1.** Lit.: adempta est suppeditandi facultas, Cic. ; flumina, Lucr. ; multitudo, tela, Liv. ; his rebus omnibus, Cic. With DAT. (mostly of person) : alicui sumptibus, Ter. ; charta tibi, Cic. Ep. With *ad* or *in* and Acc. (*sufficiently for*) : parare ea quae suppeditent et ad cultum et ad victum, Cic. ; manubiae vix in fundamentum suppeditavere, Liv. Also, multitudo armatorum facile suppeditabat (with *ut* and *Subj.*), Liv. *Impers. Pass.* : Cic. Ep. **2.** Transf.: omnis apparatus ornatusque dicendi, Cic. ; consilium, oratio, Liv. ; tuo amori, Ter. ; labori, Pl. ; gaudiis gaudium (i.e. follows in support), Pl. ; alicui vita, Cic. With *Inf.* as Subject : dicero suppeditat, Lucr. **B.** Trans. (with Acc. of thing given as supply) : *to give in support, to supply.* **1.** Lit.: luxuriae sumptūs, Pl. ; sumptum, cibos, frumentum, etc., Cic. ; omnium rerum abundantiam, Cic. ; rem frumentariam alicui, Cic. Ep. ; Nep. ; aquam templis, Cic. **2.** Transf.: praecepta nobis (patria), Lucr. ; oratoribus mirabilem copiam dicendi, Cic. : voluptatem, Cic. ; multa ad luxuriam invitamenta, Cic.

sup-pēdō, ere, *to break wind quietly* : Cic. Ep.

suppetiae, ārum, *f. pl.* (only used in NOM. and ACC.) [suppetŏ], *aid, assistance, succour* : auxilia mihi et suppetiae sunt domi, Pl. ; Suet. In ACC. with verbs of motion (in sense of ad suppetias) : ne tibi suppetias tempore adveni modo, Pl. ; venire, ire, occurrere, Auct. B. Afr.

suppetior, iārī [suppetiae], *to come to the aid (of), to assist* : mihi, Cic. Ep.

sup-petō, petere, petīi or petīvī, petītum, *to be forthcoming for one's use, to be at hand* or *in store.* **1.** Lit.: frumentum copiaeque, Liv. ; Caes. ; alicui (aliquid), Pl., Cic. With personal Subject : Pl. **2.** Transf. **a.** In gen.: vita, Cic., Plin. Ep. ; vita longior, Liv. ; mihi crimina, Cic. ; Liv. With *Indir. Deliberative* as Subject : neque quo manūs porrigeret suppetebat, Nep. **b.** *to suffice, be equal to* : plagae, Lucr. ; amori, ambitioni, sumptibus copiae, Cic. ; quibuscumque vires suppetebant ad arma ferenda, Liv. ; alicui rerum usus, Hor. ; rudis lingua libertati, Liv. With personal Subject : novis doloribus, Hor.

sup-pīlō, āre, *to pillage secretly, to filch* : Pl. ; mihi pallam ex arcis, Pl. With *Personal Object* : clam domi uxorem tuam, Pl.

sup-pingō, pingere, pāctum [pangŏ], *to fasten underneath, to clout* : fulmentas soccis, Pl.

supplantō, āre [planta], *to put the foot under* and so *trip up.* **1.** Lit.: aliquem, Cic. **2.** Transf.: vitis in terram, Plin. ; tenero supplantat verba palato, Pers.

supplēmentum, ī, *n.* [suppleŏ], *that with which any gap* or *want is filled* (mostly milit.). **a.** *a filling up to the proper* number : in supplementum classis Latinorum armaque data, Liv. ; servos ad supplementum remigum dedit, Liv. ; legiones veteres eodem supplemento explere, Liv. **b.** Concr. *reinforcements* : per causam supplementi cogendi, Caes. ; aliquos supplementi nomine in legiones distribuerat, Caes. ; distribuere, Curt.

sup-pleō, ēre, ēvī, ētum, *to fill up to a desired or requisite fulness* ; *to make good losses, damage*, etc. **a.** In gen.: fiscellam, Cato ; summam, Lucr. ; bibliothecam, Cic. Ep. ; referendis praeteritis verbis id scriptum, Cic. ; feturā gregem, Verg. ; vulnera lacrimis, Ov. ; damna incendiorum, Suet. **b.** Milit.: remigium, Verg. ; legiones subito dilectu, Tac. ; navis remigio, Liv. ; exercitūs damna, Tac.

supplex, icis, *adj.* [sub plicŏ], *kneeling* ; hence, *in supplication, in humble entreaty.* **1.** Lit. of persons : Pl., Cic., Verg., etc. ; pro aliquo, Cic. With DAT.: alicui, Pl., Cic., Ov., etc. ; plurimis pro te, Cic. ; alicui ut etc., Cic. *Masc.* as Noun : Caes., Cic. ; with *Pron. Adj.* or *Obj.* GEN.: vester, Cic. ; Hor. ; dei, Nep. ; vestrae misericordiae, Cic. **2.** Transf. of things : manus, Cic., Ov. ; verba, Cic. Ep. ; vox, Sall. ; dona, vota, Verg. ; querellae, Tib. ; vitta, Hor. [It. *soffice*/ Fr. *souple*.]

supplicātiō, ōnis, *f.* [supplicŏ], *a public kneeling* in thanksgiving or entreaty ; oftener *a thanksgiving for success in war* (hence, as a special honour to the general) : supplicatio diis immortalibus pro singulari eorum merito meo nomine decreta est, Cic. ; Caes. ; constituere, Cic. ; in quadriduum supplicationes decernere, Liv. ; indicere, Liv. ; habere, Liv.

suppliciter, *adv. humbly, suppliantly* : Caes., Cic., Verg., etc.

supplicium, ī, *n.* [supplicŏ], *an act of kneeling.* **A.** In entreaty ; hence, *supplication, prayer* (rare in this sense and usually in *pl.*). **a.** To the gods : Pl. ; suppliciis votisque fatigare deos, Liv. ; votis muliebribusque suppliciis, Sall. **b.** In gen.: Vagenses fatigati regia suppliciis, Sall. ; legatos ad consulem cum suppliciis mittit, Sall. **B.** To receive *punishment* (esp. beheading, scourging) ; hence, *punishment*, esp. *capital punishment, execution* : dabitur supplicium mihi de tergo vostro, Pl. ; sumere (de aliquo), Pl., Caes., Cic., etc. ; aliquem alicui ad supplicium dedere, Caes. ; ad supplicium tradi (rapi, Cic.), Tac. ; supplicio adfici, Caes. ; supplicio perire, Tac. ; suā manu supplicium persolvere, Tac. ; supplicia haurire, Verg. ; suppliciis delicta coercere, Hor. ; ad innocentum supplicia descendunt, Caes. ; Cic. [Fr. *supplice*.]

sup-plicō, āre (old *Aor. Subj.* supplicāssis, Pl.), *to fold* or *bend under* ; hence, *to kneel* or *humble oneself, to entreat, pray*, or *beg humbly.* **a.** In gen.: Pl., Cic., etc. With DAT.: alicui, Pl., Cic., Ov. ; Caesari pro te, Cic. Ep. Transf.: tot res vestris animis, Cic. **b.** To the gods : Pl., Liv. ; in fano, Pl. ; circa fana deorum, Liv. With DAT.: Lari familiari pro copiā, Cato ; per hostias diis, Sall. [Fr. *supplier*.]

sup-plōdō, plōdere, plōsi [plaudō], *to stamp the foot :* pedem, Cic.

supplōsiō, ōnis, *f.* [supplōdō], *a stamping the foot :* pedis, Cic.

sup-pōnō, pōnere, posuī, positum (*Perf.* supposīvī, Pl. *Part. sync.* supposta, Verg.). **I.** *to put, place, or set under* (with DAT. of *Indir. Obj.*). **1.** Lit. : has res, Lucr. ; anatum ova gallinis, Cic. ; cervicem polo (of Atlas), Ov. ; caput fontibus, Hor. ; falcem aristis, Verg. ; per ignis suppositos cineri doloso, Hor.; agresti fano pecus, Ov. Also, aliquem sub cratim, Pl. **2.** Transf. *to make subject :* aethera ingenio suo, Ov. **II.** *to put in the place of, to substitute.* **a.** In gen. : meliorem, quam ego sum, suppono tibi, Pl. ; aliquem in alicuius locum, Cic. Transf. : operae nostrae vicaria fides amicorum supponitur, Cic. **b.** Of false substitution : (puella) erae meao supposita est parva, Pl. ; Liv. ; Verg. ; qui supposità personâ falsum testamentum obsignandum curaverit, Cic. ; testamenta falsa, Cic. **III.** *to put next to or next under, to add, subjoin :* exemplum epistulae, Cic. Ep. ; huic generi partis quattuor, Cic.

sup-portō, āre, *to carry, bring,* or *convey up to :* frumentum ex Sequanis, Caes. ; commeatūs terrestri itinere, Liv. ; frumentum exercitui navibus, Caes. ; omnia hinc in castra, Liv.

supposīticius, a, um [suppōnō], *put in the place of, substituted.* **a.** In gen. : Hermes sibi ipsi, Mart. **b.** Falsely : *spurious :* Pl.

suppositiō, ōnis, *f.* [suppōnō], *a putting in the place of, substitution :* pueri, puellae, Pl. ; facere, Cic.

suppositus, a, um, *Part.* suppōnō.

suppostrix, īcis, *f.* [suppōnō], *a fraudulent substituter :* puerorum, Pl.

suppressiō, ōnis, *f.* [supprimō], *a keeping back of money, embezzlement :* praedae ac suppressiones iudiciales, Cic.

suppressus, a, um. **I.** *Part.* supprimō. **II.** *Adj.* **a.** *short :* meritum, Varr. **b.** Of the voice, *subdued, low :* suppressâ voce dicere, Cic. *Comp. :* Cic.

sup-primō, primere, pressi, pressum [premō], *to press down* or *under.* **1.** Lit. **a.** *to sink* (a ship) : quattuor naves suppressae, Liv. **b.** *to press* or *hold down, to repress, check, put a stop to :* hostem nostros insequentem, Caes. ; iter, Caes. ; habenas aerii cursūs, Ov. ; fugam, Ov. **2.** Transf. **a.** *stultiloquium,* Pl. ; aegritudinem, Cic. ; impetum militum, Liv. ; iram, Liv. ; querellas, Ov. **b.** *to keep secret, suppress :* pecuniam, Cic. ; senatūs consulta, Liv. Transf. : decreti famam, Liv. ; indicium coniurationis, Curt. ; Tac.

sup-prōmus, ī, *m. an assistant-* or *under-butler :* Pl.

sup-pudet, ēre, *to cause some slight feeling of shame* (with ACC. of Person and GEN. of Cause) : eorum me suppudet, Cic. Ep.

suppūrātiō, ōnis, *f.* [suppūrō], *a purulent gathering, suppuration :* Plin., Sen. Ep.

suppūrō, āre [pūs], *to gather matter under the skin, to fester, suppurate.* **1.** Lit. : cancer sub carne, Cato ; Plin. *Perf. Part.*

neut. *pl.* **suppūrāta**, as Noun, *pus :* Plin. **2.** Transf.: voluptates angusto corpori ingestae, Sen. Ep.

suppus, a, um, *head-downwards :* Lucr.

sup-putō, āre, *to prune upwards :* to trim up, clear up. **1.** Lit. : oleas teneras, Cato. **2.** Transf. *to count up, compute :* sollicitis supputat articulis, Ov. ; numeros, Sen. Ep.

suprā (orig. form, **superā**, Lucr.), *adv.* and *prep.* [superus]. **I.** Adv. *on the upper side, on the top, above.* **1.** Lit. of place : Caes., Cic., Ov. ; quae supra et subter (sunt), Cic. ; Cato ; toto vertice supra est, Verg. **2.** Transf. **a.** Of time, *above,* i.e. *earlier :* uti supra demonstravimus, Caes. ; ut supra dixi, Cic. ; supra repetere, Sall. *Comp. :* dixi superius, Phaedr. **b.** Of number or measure : *beyond, over, more :* supra adiecit Aeschrio, Cic. ; nihil supra deos lacesso, Hor. ; Ter. ; tricena aut supra stipendia, Tac. With *quam : beyond (what), more than :* supra quam fieri possit, Cic. ; Sall. ; so without *quam :* caesa (sunt) supra milia viginti, Liv. **II.** Prep. with Acc. **1.** Lit. of place, *above, over :* eum locum, Caes. ; Cic. ; Pl. ; accubueram horâ nonâ, et quidem supra me Atticus, infra Verrius, Cic. Ep. ; saltu supra venabula fertur, Verg. *Phr. :* supra caput esse, *to be imminent, threatening,* Sall., Verg., Liv., etc. ; also, supra capita, Liv. Geogr. *above, beyond :* supra Suessulam, Liv. ; Enn. **2.** Transf. **a.** Of time, *beyond,* i.e. *before :* paulo supra hanc memoriam, Caes. ; Liv. **b.** Of number or quantity, *over, above, beyond :* supra tris cyathos, Hor. ; hominis fortunam, Cic. ; viris, Hor. ; morem, Verg. ; modum, Liv. ; hominem, Cic. **c.** Of office, *in charge of :* quos supra somnum habebat, Curt. [It. *sopra;* Sp. *sobre.*]

suprā-scandō, ere, *to climb* or *pass over, surmount :* finīs, Liv.

suprēmō (Plin.), **suprēmum**, and **suprēmus**, *v.* superus.

sūra, ae, *f. the calf of the leg :* Pl., Verg., Plin., etc.

sūrculus, ī, *m.* [*dim.* sūrus, *a branch, shoot :* Fest.]. **I.** *a young twig* or *branch, a shoot, sprout, twig :* Cic., Verg. **II.** *a scion, graft, sucker, slip for propagation :* Cic.

surdaster, tra, trum [surdus], *rather deaf :* Cic.

surditās, ātis, *f.* [surdus], *deafness :* Cic.

surdus, a, um, *deaf.* **1.** Lit. : Cic. *Masc.* as Noun : Pl., Lucr. *Phr.* surdo narrare, canere, etc. (i.e. *to preach to deaf ears,* talk to the wind) : so, non canimus surdis, Verg. ; Ter., etc. Also, quae vereor ne vana surdis auribus cecinerim, Liv. **2.** Transf. **a.** *deaf,* i.e. *unheeding, regardless,* etc. : Pl. ; iudex, Cic. ; ad mea munera surdus, Ov. ; ad omnia solacio aures, Liv. ; surdos in tua vota deos, Liv. ; mens, Ov. ; leges rem surdam, inexorabilem esse, Liv. ; in alicuius sermone, Cic. ; tuis lacrimis, Mart. *Comp. :* Hor., Ov. **b.** *yielding a dull, indistinct sound :* theatrum, Varr. ; vox, Quint. **c.** Objectively, *noiseless, silent, mute :* lyra, Prop. ; non erit officii gratia surda tui, Ov. ; ictus, Plin. ; surdo verbere, Juv. **d.** Of smell, appearance, meaning, etc. : *faint, dim, dull, indistinct :* spirant cinnama surdum (*Neut. Intern.* Acc.), Pers. ; colos, Plin. ; materia, Plin. ; res surdae ac sensu carentes, Plin. [It. Sp. *sordo* ; Fr. *sourd*.]

suréna, ae, *m.* among the Parthians, *the grand vizier :* Tac.

súrgō, súrgere, surrěxī, surrēctum (for un-contr. forms, surrigit, etc., *v.* surrigō ; syncop.: surrēxtī, Mart. ; surrēxe, Hor.) [contr. from surrigō, from sub regō], *to rise, arise, to get* or *stand up.* **1.** Lit. **a.** In gen. : a mensā, Plin. ; a cenā, Plin. Ep. ; e lectulo, Cic. ; de sellā, Cic. ; solio, Ov. ; ab umbris ad lumina vitae, Verg. Of an orator : Cic. ; ad dicendum, Cic. ; ad hos, Ov. Of hostile movement : in Teucros ab Arpis, Verg. Of things : undae, aequora, Verg. ; fontes, Quint. ; umeri, Verg. ; in cornua cervus, Verg. ; ventus, Verg. ; dies, luna, Verg. ; sol, Hor. ; aquis nox ab isdem, Ov. ; ignis ab arā, Ov. **b.** *to get up* from bed, from sleep : Cic., Hor., Ov. **c.** Of growth, *to spring up, grow up :* Ceres ut culmo surgeret alto, Hor. ; arx, Verg. ; Plin. Ep. ; Ascanius, Verg. **2.** Transf. : pugna, discordia, Verg. ; honor, Ov. ; rumor, Tac. ; animo sententia, Verg. ; sex mihi surgat opus numeris (of the rise of a verse), Ov. ; supra prosam orationem, Quint. [Fr. *sourdre*.]

súrp-, *v.* surripiō.

surpiculus, *v.* scirpiculus.

surr-, for all words not found here, see subr-.

surreptícius, a, um, *stolen.* **1.** Lit. : puer, Pl. **2.** Transf. *stolen,* i.e. *secret :* amor, Pl.

surreptus, a, um, *Part.* surripiō.

surrēptus, a, um, *Part.* surrēpō.

sur-rígō (subrígō), rigere, rēxī, rēctum [sub regō ; *cf.* sūrgō], *to lift* or *raise up, to erect, elevate :* auris, Verg., Plin. ; mucrone subrecto, Liv. ; turres subrectae, Sen. Ep.

sur-ripiō, ripere, ripuī (rupuī, Pl.), reptum (syncop. forms, sūrpite, Hor. ; sūrpere, Lucr. ; sūrpuerat, Hor. ; sūrpuit, Pl. ; sūrpuerit, Pl. *Aor. Subj.* surrepsit, Pl.), [rapiō], *to snatch secretly, to withdraw privily, to filch, pilfer, purloin.* **1.** Lit. **a.** puerum, Pl. ; librum, Cic. Ep. ; filium ex patriā, Pl. ; vasa ex privato sacra, Cic. ; de mille fabae modiis unum, Hor. With DAT. (*from which* or *whom*) : me morti, Hor. ; mappam praetori, Mart. With *Refl. Pron.* : surripuisti te mihi dudum de foro, Pl. ; Hor. **b.** Of literary plagiarism : a Naevio multa, Cic. ; aliquid Ennio Vergilius, Sen. Ep. **2.** Transf. : motūs quoque surpere debent, Lucr. ; virtus, quae nec eripi nec surripi potest, Cic. ; crimina oculis patris, Ov.

sur-rogō, *v.* subrogō.

sūrsum (sūsum, Pl., Cato ; **sūrsus,** Lucr.), *adv.* [contr. fr. subvorsum], *upwards, on high.* **a.** With words denoting motion : Pl., Lucr., Quint., etc. With *versus* (*versum, vorsum*) : Pl., Lucr., Cic. With *deorsum :* Pl., Lucr., Cic. With *deorsum : up and down, to and fro :* Ter., Cic. **b.** With words denoting rest (rare) : Ter., Cic., Varr. [Fr. *sus.*]

sūs, suis (DAT. *pl.* sūbus, Lucr.), *m. f.* [*cf.* Gk. ὗς]. **I.** *a swine, hog, pig, boar, sow :* Cic., Hor., Ov. Prov.: sus Minervam, ut aiunt, docet, Cic. **II.** *a kind of fish :* Ov.

Sūsa, ōrum, *n. pl.* the ancient capital of Persia.

sus-cēnseō (succ-), ēre, uī, perh. *to underestimate,* hence, *to be angry, have a grudge* (*against*) : Pl., Liv. ; propter aliquid, Suet. With DAT. of person : Pl., Ter., Cic. ; non esse aut ipsi aut militibus suscensendum, Caes. With Acc. and *Inf.* : Liv.

susceptiō, ōnis, *f.* [suscipiō], *a taking in hand, undertaking :* Cic. ; causae, Cic.

susceptus, a, um, *Part.* suscipiō.

sus-cipiō (perh. also **succipiō**), cipere, cēpī, ceptum [sus for subs (*v.* sub) and capiō] **I.** *to catch a thing up* or *underneath* (*i.e. before it falls*), *to support :* sol aeternam lampada mundi, Lucr. ; cruorem pateris, Verg. ; dominam ruentem, Verg. ; labentem domum, Sen. ; theatrum futuris ac substructionibus, Plin. Ep. **2.** Transf. **a.** nocentis reos, Quint. ; famam defuncti, Plin. Ep. **b.** Of an unfinished argument, talk, etc. : *to pick up, take up, resume :* sermonem, Quint. With quoted words : Varr., Verg. **II.** *to take up from below* or *from the ground, to raise up :* cava suscepto flumine palma sat est, Prop. Esp. of taking up a new-born child in recognition of fatherhood and of the consequent responsibility of rearing it. **1.** Lit. : puerum, Ter., Cic. **2.** Transf. **a.** In gen. : *to get, beget,* or *bear children :* filia, quam ex te suscepi, Pl. ; liberos ex libertini filiā, Cic. ; de te subolem, Verg. **b.** *to accept, receive,* as a citizen, under one's protection, as a pupil, etc. : aliquem in civitatem, Cic. ; discipulos, Quint. ; aliquos erudiendos, Quint. **c.** Of a duty, task, etc. : *to take on oneself, undertake :* votum, Pl. ; inimicitias, Ter., Cic. ; bellum, laborem, negotium, actionem, disputationem, etc., Cic. ; rei publicae partem, Cic. ; invidiam, Cic. ; dolorem gemitumque, Cic. ; personam viri boni, Cic. ; pulvinar, Liv. ; morbos, Lucr. ; in se scelus, Cic. ; legationem ad civitates sibi, Caes. ; sibi auctoritatem, Cic. ; susceperat rem militarem impediendam, Liv. With Acc. and *Inf.* : *to undertake* (*to prove*) *that :* Cic. With *ut* and *Subj.* : *to take on oneself* (*and allow*) : suscepit vita hominum ut etc., Cic.

sus-citō, āre [sus for subs and citō], *to stir up.* **1.** Lit. **a.** In gen. : vulturium a capite, Cat. ; terga aratro, Verg. ; lintea aura, Ov. **b.** Of buildings, *to raise :* delubra, Lucr. **c.** From sleep : *to rouse up, awaken :* me somno, Pl. ; aliquem e somno, Cic. ; aliquem e molli quiete, Cat. **2.** Transf. **a.** Of persons and their feelings : se ad suom officium, Pl. ; te ab tuis subselliis contra te testem, Cic. ; tacentem Musam, Hor. ; in arma viros, Verg. **b.** Of things : sopitos ignis, Verg. ; Ov. ; of the flames of love : Ov. ; crepitum, Prop. ; bellum civile, Brut. et Cass. ap. Cic. Ep. ; clamores, Phaedr. Also, fictas sententias, Enn.

suspectŏ, āre [freq. suspiciŏ]. **I.** to continue to look up at, to gaze up at : Plin. ; tabulam pictam, Ter. **II.** to distrust, suspect : Agrippinam magis magisque, Tac. With Acc. and Inf. : Tac.
suspectus, a, um. **I.** Part. suspiciŏ. **II.** Adj. mistrusted, suspected : habere aliquem suspectum, Pl., Caes. ; super tali scelere suspectum se habere, Sall. ; in morte matris, Suet. ; Quint. ; Tac. ; Comp. : Cic. With Gen. : suspecti capitalium criminum, Tac. With Perf. Inf. : Tac. With Dat. of person by whom : meis civibus suspectus, Cic. ; Ter. Of things : nomen infame, suspectum, Cic. ; locus, Liv. ; Hor. ; Ov. With Dat. of person : Cic. ; suspectum (est), with Inf. : Ov. Comp. : Quint.
suspectus, ūs, m. [suspiciŏ], a looking up or upwards. **1.** Lit. : ad aetherium caeli suspectus Olympum, Verg. ; turris vasto suspectu, Verg. **2.** Transf. a looking up to with esteem : honorum, Ov. ; sui, Sen.
suspendium, i, n. [suspendŏ], a hanging of oneself, a hanging : Pl., Cic. In pl. : Ov.
sus-pendŏ, pendere, pendi, pēnsum, to hang up. **1.** Lit. **a.** pernas in fumo, Cato ; in litore vestis, Lucr. ; oscilla ex altā pinu, Verg. ; columbam mālo ab alto, Verg. ; arcum umeris, Verg. ; reste suspensus, Liv. In Mid. : laevo suspensi loculos lacerto, Hor. **b.** to hang, i.e. kill by hanging : se, Pl. ; aliquem in oleastro, Cic. ; aliquem de ficu, Cic. ; se e ficu, Quint. **c.** Of votive offerings : votas vestis, Verg. ; vestimenta deo, Hor. ; Verg. **d.** Of buildings : to support, prop up : tignis contignationem, Caes. ; murum furculis, Liv. (cf. nidum tignis hirundo, Verg.). **e.** Of ploughing : tellurem tenui sulco, Verg. **f.** In walking : pes summis digitis suspenditur, Quint (v. also suspensus). **2.** Transf. **a.** to hang up, keep in suspense, keep unsettled : medio responso rem, Liv. ; animos fictā gravitate, Ov. ; aliquem exspectatione, Plin. Ep. ; iudicium animos, Quint. ; exspectationem, Curt. **b.** to stay, check temporarily : fletum, Ov. ; spiritum, sermonem, Quint. **c.** In Pass., to depend, rest upon : extrinsecus bene vivendi rationes, Cic. Ep. ; ex quo (genere) ceterae species suspensae sunt, Sen. Ep. **d.** to hang or fix upon : pictā vultum mentemque tabellā, Hor. **e.** Of sneering : naso suspendis adunco ignotos, Hor.
suspēnsus, a, um. **I.** Part. suspendŏ. **II.** Adj. raised, elevated, hanging, balanced. **1.** Lit. **a.** Roma conaculis sublata atque suspensa, Cic. ; saxis suspensam rupem, Verg. **b.** Of stepping, etc. : suspenso gradu ire, Ter. ; Ov. ; fluctu suspensa tumenti ferret iter, Verg. ; aura suspensa levisque, Lucr. ; aquila suspensis alis, Liv. ; catuli suspensis dentibus, Lucr. Also, suspensā manu commendare (i.e. slightly), Plin. Ep. **2.** Transf. **a.** uncertain, hesitating : suspensam et incertam plebem, Cic. ; civitas suspensa metu, Cic. ; multo suspensum numine, Verg. ; tot populos inter spem metumque suspensos animi habetis, Liv. ; pro aliquo, Plin. Ep. ;

animus, Cic. ; timor, Ov. ; verba, Tac. ; dimissis suspensā re legatis, Liv. ; Comp. : Auct. B. Afr. Neut. as Noun : rem totam in suspenso reliqui, Plin. Ep. ; Sen. Ep. ; ipse in suspenso tenuit, Tac. **b.** dependent : suspensa ex fortunā fides, Liv.
suspĭcāx, ācis, adj. [suspicor]. **A.** Act. apt to suspect, suspicious : Nep., Liv. ; animus, Tac. **B.** Pass. or Causative, mistrusted or causing mistrust, suspicious : silentium, Tac.
su-spĭciŏ, spicere, spexi, spectum [sub specio]. **I.** to look up or upwards, to look up at. **1.** Lit. : Cic. ; caelum, Cic. ; ramos, Ov. ; in caelum, Cic. **2.** Transf. with the mind, esp. in admiration or respect, etc. : nihil magnificum ac divinum, Cic. ; viros, Cic. ; eloquentiam, naturam, Cic. ; argentum et marmor vetus aeraque et artis, Hor. **II.** to look at furtively or askance ; hence, to mistrust, suspect (us. in Perf. Part.) : Bomilcar suspectus regi et ipse eum suspiciens, Sall. (v. suspectus).
suspĭciŏ, ōnis, f. [suspicor], mistrust, distrust, suspicion. **1.** Lit. : Pl., Cic. ; suspicio de me incidit, Ter. ; movere, Cic. ; in suspicionem alicui venire or cadere, Cic. ; aliquem suspicione exsolvere, Ter. ; a se removere, Cic. ; multae causae suspicionum dantur, Cic. ; suspicio est (alicui), with Acc. and Inf. : Pl., Cic., etc. With Obj. Gen. : in suspicione poni stupri, Pl. ; alicui suspicionem reconciliatae gratiae dare, Cic. Ep. ; in suspicionem coniurationis (regni appetendi, etc.) vocari, venire, incidere, Cic. ; belli suspicione interpositā, Caes. **2.** Transf. an ill-defined, imperfect notion : deorum, Cic. [Fr. soupçon.]
suspĭciōsē, adv. in a way to raise suspicion, suspiciously : Cic. Comp. : Cic.
suspĭciōsus, a, um [suspiciŏ]. **A.** Act. mistrustful, ready to suspect, suspicious : Ter., Cic. ; in aliquem, Cic. ; vita, Sen. **B.** Causative : that excites mistrust or suspicion, suspicious : Cato ; crimen, Cic. ; Sen. Ep. Sup. : Cic.
suspĭcor, āri (and **suspĭcŏ**, āre, Pl.), to mistrust, suspect. **1.** Lit. : aliquid, Pl., Cic. ; aliquid de aliquo, Ter., Cic. Ep. ; aliquem, Pl. With Acc. and Inf. : Pl., Caes., Ov., etc. **2.** Transf. to suspect, surmise, suppose, believe : Pl. ; aliquid, Pl., Cic. ; aliquid de aliquo, Cic. ; aliquem, Pl., Ter. With Acc. and Inf. : Cic., Ov. With Indir. Quest. : Cic.
suspīrātĭŏ, ōnis, f. (Plin., Quint.) and **suspīrātus**, ūs, m. (in pl. : Ov.) [suspīrō], a fetching a deep breath, a sighing, sigh.
suspīritus, ūs, m. [suspīrō], a breathing deeply or with difficulty, a deep breath, a sigh : Pl., Cic. Ep., Liv.
suspīrium, i, n. [suspīrō], a deep breath, a sighing, sigh : alte petere, Pl. ; trahere ex intimo ventre, Pl. ; sino suspirio, Cic. In pl. : repetere, Tib. ; ducere ab imo pectore, Ov.
su-spīrŏ, āre [sub spīrō], to breathe up, to heave a sigh, to sigh : Cic. Ep., Ov. ; ab imis pectoribus, Ov. ; puella in flavo hospite, Cat. ; Ov. Poet. : curae suspirantes, Enn. With Acc. and Inf. : Lucr. With ne and Subj. : Hor. Occ.

to sigh for (in longing): Chloen, Hor. ; amores, Tib. [Fr. *soupirer*.]

susque dēque, *adv.* [sus=subs], *up and down* (usually with fero or habeo), to express indifference : de Octavio susque deque, Cic. Ep. ; Pl.

sustentāculum, ī, *n.* [sustentō], *a prop, stay, support :* Tac.

sustentātiō, ōnis, *f.* [sustentō], *forbearance :* habere, Cic.

sustentō, āre [*freq.* sustineō], *to hold up or upright, to uphold, support.* **1.** Lit. : sustentata moles et machina mundi, Lucr. ; fratrem ruentem, Verg. ; se et arma, Curt. **2.** Transf. **a.** iacentem (civitatem), Cic. ; amicos suos fide, Cic. ; Venus Troianas opes, Verg. ; aciem, Tac. ; manu, voce pugnam, Tac. ; spes inopiam, Caes. ; Cic. **b.** By food, money, etc. : familiam, Ter. ; beluae sustentatus uberibus, Cic. ; frumento plebem, Liv. ; se subsidiis patrimoni, Cic. ; saucios largitione et curā, Tac. ; pecore extremam famem, Caes. ; parsimoniam patrum suis sumptibus, Cic. ; aer animantis, Cic. In *Mid.* : mutando sordidas merces sustentabatur, Tac. Also in *Act.* without Object : Pl. **c.** Of trouble, grief, etc. : miserias plurumas, Pl. ; maerorem doloremque, Cic. Without Object : Caes., Liv., etc. *Impers. Pass.* : Caes. **d.** *to hold up or back, put off, delay* : rem, Cic. Ep. ; Ov. **e.** *to hold up or back, keep in check* : milites, Sall. ; hostem, Tac.

sus-tineō, tinēre, tinuī, tentum [sus for subs, and teneō], *to hold up, support.* **1.** Lit. **a.** onus alicui, Pl. ; umeris bovem vivum, Cic. ; baculo artūs, Ov. ; arma membraque, Liv. ; furcis spectacula, Liv. ; lapis albus pocula cum cyatho duo sustinet, Hor. ; se, Caes. ; se alis, Ov. ; se a lapsu, Liv. **b.** *to hold up or back, to keep in, check :* currum equosque, Lucil., Caes., Cic. ; perterritum exercitum, Caes. ; Liv. ; gradum, Ov. ; manum, Ov. ; a iugulo dextram, Verg. ; flumina lyrā, Prop. **2.** Transf. **a.** With food, money, etc. : veterem amicum labentem re, fortunā, fide, Cic. ; hinc patriam parvosque nepotes, Verg. ; alicuius munificentiā sustineri, Liv. ; necessitates aliorum, Liv. **b.** Of any burden, duty, responsibility, etc. : historiam veterem haec mea senectus, Pl. ; causam publicam, Cic. ; dignitatem civitatis, Cic. ; gravitatis personam, Cic. ; exspectationem, Cic. **c.** Of trouble, etc. : malas res, Pl. ; labores, Cic. ; alicuius imperia, Caes. ; oppugnationem, vulnera, Caes. ; certamen, Liv. ; poenam, Cic., Liv. ; preces alicuius, Cic. ; senatus eos querentis non sustinuit, Liv. ; Ov. ; vultum Hannibalis, Liv. With *Inf.* : me ferire, Liv. ; Ov. With Acc. and *Inf.* (mostly with negat.) : Cic., Ov., etc. **d.** Of holding up, putting off, deferring : oppugnationem ad noctem, Caes. ; rem in noctem, Liv. **e.** Of holding up, checking, restraining, etc. : impetum hostis, Caes. (Transf. impetum benevolentiae, Cic.) ; bellum consilio, Liv. ; iram, Liv. ; se a respondendo, Cic.

sus-tollō, ere [sus for subs and tollō], *to lift or take up, to raise up, raise.* **a.** amiculum, Pl. ; vela, Cat. ; navem levi nisu, Lucr. ;

ad aethera vultūs, Ov. **b.** Rarely (*cf.* tollo) of destroying : has aedis totas, Pl. ; erilem filiam, Pl.

susurrātor, ōris, *m.* [susurrō], *a mutterer, whisperer :* Cael. ap. Cic. Ep.

susurrō, āre [susurrus], *to murmur.* **1.** Lit. : apes, ventus, lympha, Verg. ; aut ego cum carā de te nutrice susurro, Ov. With Acc. : pars, quid velit, aure susurrat, Ov. *Impers. Pass.* (with Acc. and *Inf.*) : Ter.

susurrus, ī, *m. a low, gentle noise, a murmuring, whispering, etc.* : Pl., Cic. ; apum, Verg. In *pl.* : Prop., Hor., Plin. Pan. Personified : *the Whispers ; the attendants of Fame :* Ov.

susurrus, a, um [susurrus], *murmuring, whispering* : lingua, Ov.

sūtēlae, ārum, *f. pl.* [suō], *sewings together,* or *things sewn together.* Transf. *artifices, tricks :* Pl.

sūtilis, e, *adj.* [suō], *sewn together, bound or fastened together, sutured* : balteus, Verg. ; cumba, Verg. ; Plin. ; coronae, Ov.

sūtor, ōris, *m.* [suō], *a shoemaker, cobbler* : Pl., Varr. Of the lower class in gen. : id sutores et zonarii conclamarunt, Cic., Juv. Prov. : sutor ne supra crepidam (iudicaret), *cf.* " let the cobbler stick to his last," Plin.

sūtōrius, a, um [sūtor], *of a shoemaker or cobbler* : atramentum, Cic. ; Turpio sutorius, *an ex-shoemaker*, Cic. Ep.

sūtrīnus, a, um [contr. of sūtōrīnus, fr. sūtor], *of a shoemaker or cobbler, shoemaker's-* : taberna, Tac. As Noun, **sūtrīna**, a, um, *a shoemaker's shop*, Plin. ; also, *the shoemaker's trade*, Varr. ; **sūtrīnum**, ī, *n. the shoemaker's trade*, Sen. Ep.

sūtūra, ae, *f.* [suō], *a sewing together, a seam, suture :* in *pl.* : Liv.

sūtus, a, um. **I.** *Part.* suō. **II.** Noun, **sūta**, ōrum, *n. pl. joints* : per aerea suta, Verg.

suus (suos), a, um (suom), *possess. pron. refl.* of 3rd pers. [*cf.* Gk. ὅφε, ἕ, ἑός, and Lat. sē], *his (own), her (own), one's (own), its (own), their (own).* **I.** Ordinary use. **A.** Ref. to the *Grammatical Subject* of the clause (usually *Subjective* and *Possessive*, though occ. *Objective* for sui). **a.** Simply : nunc facere volt era officium suom, Pl. ; Caesar copias suas divisit, Caes. ; naves 'n portu expugnatae sunt cum suis oneribus, Liv. With quisque (in prose, regularly in the order suus quisque) : suus cuique erat locus, Caes. ; quod suos quisque servos in tali re facere voluisset, Cic. **b.** Strengthened. With sibi or proprius : serviat suo sibi patri, Pl. ; in suo proprio eum proelio equites Volscorum tenuissent, Liv. With suffix -pte or -met : suopte nutu et suo pondere, Cic. ; suomet ipsi more praecipites eant, Sall. **B.** **a.** Ref. to another word (Acc., Gen., Dat., or Abl.) in the clause, usually when the word precedes and there is no ambiguity : hunc sui cives eiecerunt, Cic. ; eosdem ad commilitonum suorum pericula impulistis, Cic. ; Siculis ereptae sunt suae leges, Cic. **b.** With *Impers.* verbs : si Caesarem benefici sui paeniteret, Cic. **c.** In generalisations, *one's (own)* : atrocius est patriae parentem quam suum occidere, Cic. **C.** In Oblique clauses (formal or " virtual" *Orat. Obliq.*), suus regularly refers to the Subject of the main verb as part of his words, thought, etc. (but *v.* also ipse) : Clodius Caesaris potentiam suam potentiam esse dicebat, Cic. ; quae gens ad Caesarem legatos miserat ut suis omnibus facultatibus uteretur, Caes. ; Paetus libros quos frater suus reliquisset mihi donavit, Cic. Ep. **II.** In partic. **a.** *proper, appointed, due :* cessit e vitā suo magis quam suorum civium tempore, Cic. **b.** As Noun, *his, her, their, one's own people, troops, property, etc. :* Octavius, quem quidem sui Caesarem salutabant, Cic. Ep. ; Caesar suos a proelio continebat, Caes. ; meum mihi placebat, illi suum, Cic. ; se suaque defendere, Caes. **c.** *one's own master, at one's own disposal, free, independent :* ancilla, mea quae fuit hodie, sua nunc est, Pl. But oftener expressed by sui iuris esse, suo iure uti, etc. : Puteolos, qui nunc in suā potestate sunt, suo iure, libertate aequā utuntur, totos occupabunt, Cic. For suā sponto, suo Marte, *v.* sponte, Mars. **d.** *inclined or devoted to, favourable, friendly :* Alphenus utebatur populo sane suo, Cic. ; perh. also, suo loco pugnam facere, Sall.

Sybaris, is, *f. a town and river in Magna Graecia* (*S. Italy*), *noted for the luxuriousness, effeminacy, and debauchery of its inhabitants ;* **Sybarita,** ae, *m. a Sybarite ;* **Sybaritānus, Sybariticus,** a, um ; **Sybaritis,** idis, *f. the name of a lascivious poem.*

Sȳchaeus (Sich-), i, *m. husband of Dido ;* **Sychaeus,** a, um.

sȳcophanta, ae, *m.* [συκοφάντης, perh. *a fig-shower,* i.e. one who (by threat of accusation) blackmailed rich men, or one who actually was an informer ; *v.* Aristophanes passim], *a false accuser ;* also *a slanderer ; a trickster, cheat :* Pl., Ter. Esp. of a cunning parasite : Pl.

sȳcophantia, ae, *f.* [συκοφαντία], *craft, cunning, deceit :* Pl. In *pl. :* Pl.

sȳcophantiōsē, adv. *knavishly, deceitfully :* Pl.

sȳcophantor, ārī [sȳcophanta], *to play the rogue ;* alicui, Pl. ; hoc, Pl.

Syēnē, ēs, *f. a town at the southern extremity of Upper Egypt,* now *Assouan ;* **Syēnītēs,** ae, *m. adj.*

syllaba, ae, *f.* [συλλαβή], *a syllable :* **1.** Lit. : Pl., Cic., Ov., etc. ; auceps syllabarum, *a word-catcher,* Cic. **2.** Transf. in *pl. : verses* (of Catullus) : Mart.

syllabātim, adv. *syllable by syllable :* Cic.

syllogismus or **-os,** i, *m.* [συλλογισμός], *a form of reasoning in which a conclusion is drawn from two premises, a syllogism :* Sen. Ep., Quint.

syllogisticus, a, um [συλλογιστικός], *of a syllogism, syllogistic :* Quint.

Symaethus, i, *m. a river, the southern boundary of Aetna, and a town situated upon it ;* **Symaethius** (ȳ in Verg.), a, um, **Symaethēus,** a, um ; **Symaethis,** idis, *f. adj.*

symbola, ae, *f.* [συμβολή], *a contribution of*

money to a feast, *a share of* a reckoning. **1.** Lit. : Pl., Ter. **2.** Transf. of blows : Pl.

symbolus, i, *m.* (**symbolum,** i, *n.* Pl.) [σύμβολος or *-ον*], *a sign or mark, a token, symbol :* Pl.

symmetria, ae, *f.* [συμμετρία], *proportion, symmetry :* Plin.

symphōnia, ae, *f.* [συμφωνία], *an agreement of sounds, concord, symphony :* Cic., Hor., Liv. In *pl. :* Cic. [It. *zampogna*.]

symphōniacus, a, um [συμφωνιακός], *of or belonging to concerts or to music :* pueri, Cic.

Symplēgades, um, *f. pl.* [Συμπληγάδες, *striking together*], *two rocky islands in the Euxine which* (acc. *to fable*) *floated about dashing against each other until they were fixed by the passage of the Argo.*

symplegma, atis, *n.* [σύμπλεγμα], *a group of persons wrestling or embracing :* Plin., Mart.

symposium, i, *n.* [συμπόσιον], *the Banquet,* the title of one of Plato's dialogues : Nep.

synedrus, i, *m.* [σύνεδρος], *a councillor, senator,* among the Macedonians : Liv.

Synephēbi, ōrum, *m. pl.* [συνέφηβοι], *the Fellow-young-men* (of 18 yrs.), the title of a comedy by Statius Caecilius : Cic.

syngrapha, ae, *f.* [συγγραφή], *a written agreement to pay, a promissory note, bond :* Cic. ; ex syngraphā agere, Cic.

syngraphus, i, *m.* [σύγγραφος]. **I.** *a written contract :* Pl. **II.** *a passport, pass :* Pl.

Synnada, ōrum, *n. pl. a town in Phrygia, famous for its marble ;* **Synnadēnsis,** e.

synodūs, ontis, *m.* [συνόδους], *a kind of fish,* perh. *a bream :* Ov., Plin.

synthesinus, a, um [συνθέσινος], *of or belonging to a dressing-gown :* vestis, Suet.

synthesis, is, *f.* [σύνθεσις]. **I.** *a dinner service :* Mart., Stat. **II.** *a suit of clothes :* Mart. **III.** *a loose, easy garment worn at table :* Mart.

Syphāx, ācis, *m. a king of Numidia at the time of the second Punic war.*

Syrācūsae, ārum, *f. pl. the chief city in Sicily, on the east coast ;* **Syrācūsānus, Syrācūsius, Syrācosius,** a, um ; **Syrācūsāni,** ōrum, and **Syrācosii,** ōrum, *m. pl. the Syracusans.*

Syria, ae, *f. a country in Asia, on the Mediterranean Sea, between Asia Minor and Egypt ;* **Syrius, Syrus, Syriacus, Syriscus,** a, um, **Syrii,** ōrum, and more freq. **Syri,** ōrum, *m. pl. the Syrians.*

Sȳrinx, ingis, *f. a nymph changed into a reed* in Ov.

syrma, ae, *f.* [σύρμα], *a robe with a train :* Sen. ; worn esp. by tragic actors : Juv. Transf. *tragedy :* Mart., Juv.

Syrophoenix, icis, *m. a Syrophoenician.*

Sȳros, i, *f. one of the Cyclades,* now *Syra.*

syrtis, is, *f. a sand-bank in the sea ; a quicksand :* Verg. Esp. as the name, **1.** Lit. of two gulfs in the N. of Africa : Sall., Verg., Liv., etc. ; **Syrticus,** a, um ; **Syrtis,** idis, *f. adj.* **2.** Transf. of the lands near them : Hor.

T

T, t, *indecl. n.* or (*sc.* littera) *f.* **I.** Latin *t* corresponds to Skr. *t* (and sometimes *th*) and to Gk. τ. In accordance with Grimm's law, in Gothic (and low-German generally, including English) *th* regularly answers to it, and in O.H.G. (with which modern German commonly agrees) *d.* Lat. *tres* ; Gk. τρεῖς τ; (Eng. *three*) ; O.H.G. *dri* (Germ. *drei*). **II.** In the Romance languages *t* initial us. remains unchanged, in the middle of words it sometimes becomes *d* ; thus Lat. *litus*, It. *lido* ; Lat. *lutum*, Sp. *lodo* ; Lat. *adiutare*, Fr. *aider*. This change also often happens when *t* has become final by omission of a suffix, as in Fr. *plaid* from Lat. *placitum*. *Aigu, vertu*, etc., were *aigud, vertud* in an earlier stage of the French language. In Spanish the change of Lat. *t* to *d* is particularly frequent ; thus it is regularly seen in past participles, as *hablado* from Lat. *fabulatum*. The termination *-aticus*, which is frequent in low Lat., regularly becomes *-aggio* in It. and *-age* in Sp. and Fr. ; thus Lat. *silvaticus*, It. *selvaggio*, Fr. *sauvage* ; Lat. *viaticum*, It. *viaggio*, Sp. *viage*, Fr. *voyage*. When *te* or *ti* in Latin is followed by a vowel the *e* or *i* in the derived French word commonly disappears, and the *t* becomes *c, ç, s* or *ss* ; thus Lat. *platea*, Fr. *place* ; Lat. *adnuntiare*, Fr. *annoncer* ; Lat. *redemptio*, Fr. *rançon* ; Lat. *ratio*, Fr. *raison* ; Lat. *nutritio*, Fr. *nourrisson*. In Italian, the Lat. *ti* followed by a vowel becomes *gi* ; thus Lat. *ratio, statio* ; It. *ragione, stagione* ; or, more commonly, *zi*, as in *navigazione* from Lat. *navigatio*. In Sp. the same Lat. combination becomes *z*, as in *razon* from Lat. *ratio* ; or *ci*, as in Sp. *nacion* from Lat. *natio, oracion* from Lat. *oratio*. Lat. *tr* in the middle of a word in Italian and Spanish remains unchanged or becomes *dr* ; in French, *rr* or *r* ; thus Lat. *latro*, It. *ladrone*, Sp. *ladron*, Fr. *larron* ; Lat. *vitrum*, It. *vetro*, Sp. *vidrio*, Fr. *verre* ; Lat. *petra*, It. *pietra*, Sp. *piedra*, Fr. *pierre* ; Lat. *pater* (*patrem*), It. Sp. *padre*, Fr. *père*. Lat. *st* in the middle of a word sometimes becomes in It. *sc*, in Fr. *ss* ; as in Lat. *angustia*, It. *angoscia*, Fr. *angoisse* ; Lat. *ostiarius*, It. *usciere*, Fr. *huissier*. **III.** As an abbreviation, T. stands for Titus, Ti. for Tiberius ; Tr. tribunus ; T. F. testamenti formula ; T. F. C. titulum faciendum curavit ; T. P. tribunicia potestas.

tabānus, i, *m. a horse-fly* : Varr., Plin.

tabella, ae, *f.* [*dim.* tabula], *a small board.* **A.** In gen. : liminis, *the door-sill*, Cat. ; parva tabella capit ternos utrimque lapillos, *small gaming-board*, Ov. Of the "ark" in which Romulus and Remus were set adrift : Ov. **B.** *a writing-tablet* : Ov., Quint. Also *a tablet and its contents*, e.g. a letter, contract, will, records, etc. (mostly in *pl.*) : Pl., Cic., Liv., Juv., etc. **C.** *a voting-tablet* used in the election of magistrates and in voting on proposed measures : populo dare, Cic. ; tabellā

aliquem consulem declarare, Cic. ; as aliquo tabellas dirimere, Cic. Also used in giving a verdict in the courts : tabellam iudicibus (de aliquo) dare, committere, Cic. ; Caes. ; Prop. **D.** *a painted tablet, a small picture* or *painting* : Cic. Ep., Hor., Ov., etc. **E.** *a votive tablet* hung up in a temple in acknowledgment of the succour or beneficence of a deity : votiva, Hor. ; memores, Ov.

tabellārius, a, um [tabella], **I.** *letter-* or *mail-carrying* : naves, Sen. Ep. As Noun, **tabellārius,** i, *m. a letter-carrier, courier* : Cic., Liv. **II.** *relating to votive-tablets* : lex, Cic. ; Plin. Ep.

tābeō, ēre [tābum]. **I.** *to waste away.* **1.** Lit. : corpora, Ov. ; Lucr. **2.** Transf.: seditio, Enn. **II.** *to be in a liquid state, to stream, run* : genae, Verg. ; sale artūs, Verg.

taberna, ae, *f. a wooden-booth* ; hence **a.** *a hut, hovel, cottage* : Hor. **b.** perh. *blocks of seats* or "*stalls*" in the Circus : Cic. **c.** *a booth, shop, stall* : Cic., Hor. ; libraria, Cic. ; vinaria, cretaria, etc., Varr. ; argentaria, Liv. ; sutrina, Tac. ; veteres, novae (in the Forum), Liv. **d.** *a hostel, inn* : Cic. ; deversoria, Pl. ; Hadriae, Cat. [Fr. *taverne*.]

tabernāculum, i, *n.* [taberna], *a tent.* **a.** In gen. : Caes., Cic., Liv., etc. **b.** In augury, tabernaculum capere, *to choose a place for a tent* (outside the city), in which to observe the auspices previously to holding the comitia, Cic., Liv.

tabernārii, ōrum, *m. pl.* [taberna], *shop-keepers* : Cic.

tabernula, ae, *f.* [*dim.* taberna], *a small booth* or *shop, a little tavern* : Suet.

tābēs, is, *f.* [*cf.* Gk. τήκω, and the earlier form tābum], *a decaying, melting, wasting, dwindling.* **1.** Lit. **a.** Abstr.: Cic., Liv., Ov., etc. From hunger : Plin. **b.** Concr. *the moisture of a melting* or *decaying substance, corruption* : Lucr., Liv., Ov., etc. **2.** Transf. *a wasting disease, pestilence* : Sall., Liv. Transf.: quos durus amor crudeli tabe peredit, Verg. ; infecit ea tabes legionum motas iam mentis, Tac.; aegritudo habet tabem, cruciatum, etc., Cic. ; crescentis faenoris, Liv.

tābescō, tābēscere, tābui [tābeō], *to melt gradually, to begin to waste away* or *decay.* **1.** Lit.: Cato ; Ov. ; calore umor, Cic. ; nives radiis solis, Lucr. Of weeping : adsiduo lumina fletu, Cat. **2.** Transf.: maerore, Pl. ; Lucr. ; Cic. ; amore, Ov. ; crescere itemque dies licet et tabescere noctis, Lucr. ; quodque aliena capella gerat distentius uber, tabescat, Hor.

tābidulus, a, um [tābidus], *wasting, consuming* : mors, Verg.

tābidus, a, um [tābeō]. *melting* or *wasting away, decaying.* **A.** Pass.: nix, Liv. ; corpus, Suet. Transf.: mens, Ov. **B.** Act. or Causative : *corrupting, infectious* : lues, Verg. ; vetustas, Ov. ; venenum, Tac. ; pestis, Mart.

tābificus, a, um [tābēs faciō], *melting, wasting.* **1.** Lit.: radii (solis), Lucr. ; venenum, Suet. **2.** Transf.: mentis perturbationes, Cic.

Tab 739 Tae

tabula, ae, *f. a board, plank.* **A.** In gen.: Cic., Verg., Ov., etc. **B.** *a writing-tablet (and its contents,* e.g. a letter, etc.): Pl., Caes., Hor. In *pl.* : *account-books, registers, etc. (and their contents)* : Pl.; aliquid in tabulas referre, Cic.; tabulas conficere, Cic.; testamenti, Caes.; Ov.; Plin. Ep.; in tabulis deberi, Cic.; tabulae novae (i.e. abolition of the old accounts and recorded debts), Caes., Cic.; publicae, Cic.; tabularum cura (i.e. the censor's lists), Liv.; tabula praerogativae, *a list of votes,* Cic.; xii tabulae, *the Twelve Tables of laws,* Cic.; tabula Sullae, *the list of proscribed persons,* Juv. **C.** *a bill advertising an auction ;* hence, *an auction* : adest ad tabulam; licetur Aebutius, Cic. **D.** *a painted tablet* or *panel, a painting, picture* : tabula picta, Pl.; Cic.; Prop., etc. Prov.: manum de tabulā (from a remark of Apelles; i.e. " enough, no more work on the picture "), Cic. Ep. **E.** *a map* : Cic. Ep. **F.** *a votive-tablet* : Hor.

tabulārium, i, *n.* [tabulae] *a record-office ; archives* : Cic., Verg., Ov., Liv., etc.

tabulārius, i, *m.* [tabulae], *a keeper of archives* : Sen. Ep.

tabulātiō, ōnis, *f.* [tabula], *a planking* or *flooring, a floor* or *story* : Caes.

tabulātus, a, um [tabula], *boarded, floored* : transitus, Plin. Ep. As Noun, **tabulātum**, i, *n. a flooring, floor, storey.* **1.** Lit.: Enn., Cato, Caes., Verg., Liv. **2.** Transf. *a layer, row* : tabulata sequi, Verg.

tābum (only in Nom., Acc., and Abl. *sing.*), *n. [cf.* Gk. τήκω, and **tābes**], *corrupt moisture, matter.* **1.** Lit.: Enn., Verg., Tac., etc. **2.** Transf. *an infectious disease, a plague, pestilence* : Verg., Liv., Ov.

Taburnus, i, *m. a small mountain chain between Samnium and Campania.*

taceō, ēre, ui, itum, *to be silent, refrain from speaking, hold one's peace* or *tongue.* **A.** Without Object. **1.** Lit.: Pl., Cic., Liv., etc.; de aliquā re, Cic. Impers. Pass. : Ter., Cic. **2.** Transf. for silere, of animals and things, *to be still, noiseless, quiet* : nox, Cat.; omnis ager pecudes pictaeque volucres, Verg.; Ov.; loci, Tac. Transf.: indoles illa Romana, Liv.; blanditiae, Ov. **B.** With Acc. (mostly of *Neut. Pronouns* and 'the like), *to be silent about, refrain from mentioning, pass over in silence* : hoc, Pl.; Cic.; commissa, Hor.; cladis, Liv.; aliquem, Verg., Ov. In *Pass.* : Ter., Liv., Ov. Gerundive : tacenda dicenda, Hor.

tacitē, *adv. silently, secretly* : Pl., Cic., Liv., Ov., etc.

taciturnitās, ātis, *f.* [taciturnus], *habitual silence, taciturnity* : Ter., Cic., Hor., etc.

taciturnus, a, um [tacitus], *remaining silent (Act.* or *Pass.).* **a.** Of persons : *not fond of talking* : Cic. **b.** Of things : *noiseless, quiet* : silentia, Lucr.; amnis, ripa; Hor.; vestigia, Ov.; obstinatio, Nep. Comp. : Hor. Sup. : Pl.

tacitus, a, um. **I.** *Part.* taceō. **II.** *Adj.* **A.** Act. *not speaking, mute, silent.* **a.** Of persons : Pl., Cic., Hor. Used instead of *Adv.* : voluntatem tacitorum perspicis, Cic.; Pl.; si mori tacitum oportet, Liv. **b.** Of

things : *mute, still :* nemus, unda, caelum, limen, Verg.; corvus, lyra, Hor.; nox, Ov.; totum pererrat luminibus tacitis, *with silent glances,* Verg. *Neut.* as Noun : septem surgens sedatis amnibus altus per tacitum Ganges *(in silence),* Verg. **B.** Pass. *passed over in silence, kept secret, unmentioned.* **1.** Lit.: Pl., Cic., Verg., etc.; aliquid tacitum relinquere, tenere, ferre, pati, Cic., Liv. **2.** Transf. **a.** In law: *silently agreed upon, assumed, implied* : Cic., Liv. **b.** *secret, hidden :* aures ipsae tacito eum modum sensu sine arte definiunt, Cic.; tacitum vivit sub pectore vulnus, Verg.; ira, pudor, Ov.

Tacitus, i, *m. :* C. Cornelius, *a celebrated Roman historian, born about* A.D. 55.

tāctilis, e, *adj.* [tangō], *that may be touched, tangible :* Lucr.

tāctiō, ōnis, *f.* [tangō], *a touching, touch.* **1.** Lit. as verbal noun with Acc. : quid tibi hanc digito tactio est ? Pl. **2.** Transf. *the sense of touch, feeling :* in *pl.* : Cic.

tāctus, a, um, *Part.* tangō.

tāctus, ūs, *m.* [tangō], *a touching, touch, handling.* **1.** Lit.: Lucr., Cic., Verg., etc. **2.** Transf. **a.** *the sense of touch :* Lucr., Cic. **b.** *influence, effect :* solis, Cic.; caeli, Verg.

taeda, ae, *f. resinous fir-* or *pine-wood, pitch-pine.* **1.** Lit.: Caes. In *pl.* : Verg., Hor. **2.** Transf. **a.** Of a torch : Enn., Cic., Ov., etc. Used in torture : Lucr., Juv. Of a wedding-torch : Verg., Ov.; hence, *a wedding :* Verg., Ov., etc. **b.** *a pine-board, plank :* Juv.

taedet, taedēre, taeduit or taesum est, *it causes a feeling of weariness (to) :* with Acc. of person and Gen. of the cause : quos libidinis infamiaeque suae neque pudeat neque taedeat, Cic.; Pl.; Sall. Less freq. with *Inf.* as Subject : Ter., Verg.

taedifer, era, erum [taeda ferō], *torch-bearing :* dea, Ov.

taedium, i, *n.* [taedet], *weariness, irksomeness :* cum oppugnatio obsidentibus taedium adferat, Liv.; facere, Plin.; parere, Quint.; taedio aliquem adficere, Tac.; ne te capiant taedia, Tib. With *Obj.* Gen.: rerum adversarum, Sall.; belli, Liv.; taedium movere sui, Tac.; educationis taedium suscipere, Plin. Ep.; in *pl.* : Verg., Ov. Also, *a cause of weariness :* esse taedio alicui, Plin. Ep.

taenia, ae, *f.* [ταινία], *a band, ribbon for the head.* **1.** Lit.: Enn., Verg. **2.** Transf. of a tape-worm : Cato.

Taenarus (-os), i, *m. f.* and **Taenarum (-on)**, i, *n.* **I.** *the most southerly point of the Peloponnesus, on which stood a celebrated temple of Neptune ;* now *C. Matapan.* Also, *a town of the same name on the promontory :* **Taenarius**, a, um, *Taenarian, Spartan :* Eurotas, Ov. **Taenaridēs**, ae, *m. a son of Taenarus,* i.e. *a Spartan ;* **Taenaris**, idis, *f. adj. Taenarian* or *Spartan.* **II.** *the infernal regions, the entrance to which was said to be near Taenarus* (Hor.) :

Taenarius, a, um : fauces, Verg.

taesum, est, *v.* taedet.

taeter (**tĕter**), tra, trum, *foul, noisome, revolting, offensive* (esp. of smell). **1.** L i t. : Lucr., Caes., Cic., Verg., etc. ; quam taeter incedebat, quam truculentus, Cic. ; *Comp.* : Lucr. ; *Sup.* taeterrimus, Cael. ap. Cic. Ep., Juv. *Neut.* as Noun, **taetrum**, ĭ, Cic. **2.** T r a n s f. (morally). **a.** Of persons : Cic. Ep. *Comp.* : Cic. *Sup.* : Pl. ; immanitate taeterrimus, Cic. **b.** discordia, Enn. ; facinus, Cic. ; libido, Hor. ; prodigia, Liv. *Comp.* : Cic. *Sup.* : bellum, Cic. Ep.

taetricus, *v.* tētricus.

tagax, ācis, *adj.* [tangŏ], *light-fingered, thievish* : Cic. ; manus, Lucil.

Tages, is, *m. an Etrurian deity, grandson of Jupiter ; he taught the Etrurians the art of divination.*

tālāris, e, *adj.* [tālus], *of or reaching to the ankles* : tunica, Cic. As Noun, **tālāria**, ium, *n. pl.* **a.** *the parts about the ankles* : Sen. **b.** (*sc.* calceamenta) *winged sandals fastened to the ankles* : Cic. ; of Mercury : Verg. P r o v. : talaria videamus (i.e. let us think of flight, let us flee), Cic. Ep. **c.** (*sc.* vestimenta) *a long garment reaching down to the ankles* : Ov.

tālārius, a, um [tālĭ, *dice*], *of dice* : ludus, Cic. Ep., Quint.

talāsiō (**talassiō**), ōnis, *or* **talassius**, ĭ, *m. a (very ancient) wedding-cry* : Cat., Liv.

Talaus, ī, *m. one of the Argonauts* ; **Talaïonidēs**, ae, *m.*, i.e. *Adrastus.*

tālea, ae, *f.* [tālus], *a heel-piece* ; hence, *a cutting, set, layer.* **1.** L i t. : Cato, Varr. **2.** T r a n s f. *a stake, bar, rod* : ferreae, Caes. [It. *taglia* ; Fr. *taille.*]

talentum, ī, *n.* [τάλαντον], *a talent.* **I.** *a (Greek) weight,* varying in different States, but usually about half a hundred weight : auri eborisque talenta, Verg. ; Plin. **II.** *a sum of money.* **a.** *the Attic talent, of sixty minae* (or £243 15s.) sometimes called magnum : Pl., Cic., Verg., etc. **b.** *another talent of eighty minae* : Liv.

tāliō, ōnis, *f.* [tālis]. In law, *a punishment of the same kind as the injury done* (*cf.* "an eye for an eye") : Cato, Cic. ; sine talione, Mart.

tālis, e, *adj.* [fr. root seen in tam and tantus], *of that kind, of such kind, such.* **A.** In gen. **a.** Ref. to something previously expressed : Pl., Cic., Liv., etc. **b.** Ref. to something following : Enn., Nep., Verg., etc. **c.** With corresponding *qualis, atque* (rare), *ut or qui* : ut facillime, quales simus, tales esse videamur, Cic. ; Verg., etc. ; faxo tali eum mactatum, atque hic est, infortunio, Ter. ; Cic. ; talis nos esse putamus, ut iuro laudemur, Cic. ; talem te esse oportet, qui te ab impiorum civium societate seiungas, Cic. Ep. ; Prop. **B.** E m p h a t i c, *of a peculiar kind or nature* (in both a good and a bad sense), *so distinguished, great, excellent, such* : talem, tali ingenio atque animo natum ex tantā familiā, Ter. ; quibus rebus tantis, talibus gestis, Cic. ; tali tempore, Verg. ; pro tali facinore, Caes. [It. *tale* ; Fr. *tel.*]

tālitrum, ī, *n. a rap or flick with the knuckles* : Suet.

talpa, ae, *f.* (*masc.* : Verg.) *a mole* (animal) : Cic. [Fr. *taupe.*]

Talthybius, ī, *m. the herald of Agamemnon.*

talus, ī, ꜜ.. *the ankle, ankle-bone ; of animals, the pastern-bone,* dᴇᴇ-ᴅᴏᴍᴇ. **1.** L i t. : Ov., Plin. ; extorquere, Sen. ; expellere, Mart. **2.** T r a n s f. in gen. **a.** *the foot, the heel* : Cic., Hor., Ov. P o e t. : securus cadat an recto stet fabula talo, Hor. **b.** *an oblong die* (orig. made from the *pastern-bone* of certain animals), *or knuckle-bone* (used in dicing, but marked on four sides only ; while the *tesserae* were cubes, and marked on all six sides) : se ad talos conferre, Cic. ; Pl. ; Hor. [It. *tallone* ; Sp. Fr. *talon.*]

tam, *adv.* [orig. an ACC. *or* LOCAT. fr. root seen in tālis, tantus, etc.], *to that extent, to such an extent, so, so very.* **A.** In gen. **a.** Alone (with *Adj. or Adv.*) : tam necessario tempore, tam propinquis hostibus, Caes. ; Pl. ; Cic. ; Lucr., etc. ; cum tam procul a finibus Macedoniae absint, Liv. ; Pl. ; Cic. ; Lucr., etc. Rarely with verbs : Pl., Ter., Cic. Ep. **b.** With *quam, atque, quasi, ut, qui,* or *quin* : tam ego fui ante liber, quam gnatus tuos, Pl. ; tam enim sum amicus rei publicae, quam qui maxime, Cic. ; tam facile, quam tu arbitraris, Cic. (less freq. with verbs : tam hoc scit me habere quam egomet, Pl.) ; tam consimil'est atque ego, Pl. ; non se esse tam barbarum, ut non sciret, Caes. ; quis est tam lynceus, qui in tantis tenebris nihil offendat ? Cic. ; nec quisquam est tam ingenio duro quin sibi faciat bene, Pl. ; ut nullus dies tam magnā tempestate fuerit quin solem homines viderint, Cic. **B.** P h r a s e s. **a.** With Superlatives : *so much the, all the, the* (rare) : quam quisque pessume fecit, tam maxumo tutus est, Sall. ; Pl. ; Cato. **b.** non tam . . . quam, *not so much . . . as, less . . . than* (very freq.) : utinam non tam fratri pietatem quam patriae praestare voluisset ! Cic. With *Comp. Adj.* instead of *Positive* : non tam in bellis et proeliis quam in promissis et fide firmior, Cic. ; Pl. ; Verg.

tamarix, ĭcis, *f.* (and **tamaricē**, ēs, *f.* Plin.), *a tamarisk* : Lucr.

tam diū or **tamdiū**, *adv. so long* : Pl., Cic. Ep. With corresponding *quam diu, quam, dum,* or (rarely) *quoad* : *as long as* : tam diu requiesco, quam diu ad te scribo, Cic. Ep. ; vixit tam diu, quam licuit bene vivere, Cic. ; tam diu laudabitur, dum memoria rerum Romanarum manebit, Cic. ; tam diu velle debebis quoad te non paenitebit, Cic.

tamen, *conj.* [tam, *so,* and en, on, *onwards*], *in the same way straight onwards* ; hence, *all the same* (even *after that*), *none the less, nevertheless.* **a.** retraham ad me illud argentum tamen, Ter. ; semper Aiax fortis, fortissimus tamen in furore, Cic. ; Liv., etc. **b.** With corresponding "*although*" clause : etsi sine ullo periculo proelium fore videbat, tamen committendum non putabat, Caes. ; Cic., etc. I n p a r t i c. : difficile factu est, sed conabor tamen, Cic. ; nil mihi rescribas, at tamen veni, Ov. ; quantus iste est hominum error ! ac tamen facile patior, Cic.

Tamesis, is, *m. a river in Britain, now the Thames ; also* **Tamesa**, ae (Tac.).

tam-etsi, *conj. in that way even if, just the same although, even though, although.* **A. a.** Usually with *Indic. :* Pl., Ter., Cic., etc. **b.** With *Subj.* (very rare): Pl., Ter. **B.** With a corresponding *tamen:* quae tam-etsi Caesar intellegebat, tamen legatos appellat, Caes. ; Cic.

tam-quam (tanquam) [tam quam, q.v.], *so as, just as, as much as.* **A.** In gen. : repente te tamquam serpens e latibulis intulisti, Cic. ; Pl., etc. With *sic* or *ita :* ex vitā ita discedo tamquam ex hospitio, non tamquam e domo, Cic. ; Ter. **B.** With *si,* in suppositions with *Subj.* (*v.* si) : *just as if, as if.* **a.** ut istum tamquam si esset consul, salutarent, Cic. ; Pl. ; Liv., etc. **b.** Sometimes *si* is omitted : tamquam de regno dimicaretur, ita concurrerunt, Liv. ; Cic., etc.

Tanager, grī, *m. a river in Lucania.*

Tanais, is, *m. a river of Sarmatia, now the Don.*

Tanaquil, ilis, *f. the wife of the elder Tarquin.*

tandem, *adv.* [tam and the suffix -dem (*cf.* prī-dem). *"in that very way," "while this continued"*]. *at length, at last, in the end, finally.* **1.** Lit. **a.** Alone : Pl., Lucr., Caes., Ov., etc. **b.** Strengthened with *iam, aliquando :* iam tandem Italico fugientis prendimus oras, Verg. ; Pl. ; Cic. ; tandem aliquando L. Catilinam ex urbe eiecimus, Cic. **2.** Transf. in urgent interrogations : *pray now, pr ay :* quanto tandem illum maerore adf'ictum esse putatis ? Cic. ; Pl. ; Hor., etc.

tangō, tangere, tetigi, tāctum {old *Aor. Subj.* tagam, Pac.) [*cf.* Gk. τεταγών], *to touch.* **1.** Lit. **A.** In gen. : utramvis digitulo, Pl. ; genu terram, Cic. ; Ov. ; tangere et tangi, nisi corpus, nulla potest res, Lucr. **B.** *to touch,* i.e. *to meddle with, handle* (and so *take away* or *pollute*): aliquid, Pl. ; do praedā meā teruncium, Cic. Ep. ; ea in templa tacta ac violata elataque inde sunt, Liv. ; virginem, Ter. **C.** *to touch* food and drink, *to taste :* aliquid, Pl., Ov. ; singula dente superbo, Hor. ; saporem, Ov. **D.** Of places. **a.** *to reach, come to :* provinciam, Cic. ; portūs, Verg. ; Ov., etc. **b.** *to border on :* haec civitas Rhenum, Caes. ; villa viam, Cic. **E.** *to touch* forcibly, i.e. *to strike, hit, beat :* chordas, Ov. ; flagello Chloen, Hor. **Esp.** de caelo tactus (i.e. by lightning), Cic., Verg., Liv. ; ulmus fulmine tacta, Ov. **F.** Like tingo, *to touch, besprinkle, wash, anoint :* corpus aquā, Ov., Plin., etc. Also of dyeing : supercilium madidā fuligine, Juv. **2.** Transf. **A.** Of the intellect and feelings, *to touch, affect, etc. :* minae Clodi modice me tangunt, Cic. Ep. ; mentem mortalia, Verg. ; cor spectantis, Hor. ; Numitori animum memoria nepotum, Liv. ; religione tactus, Liv. Also perh. in *Pass., to be convinced* (with *Acc.* and *Inf.*): Ov. **B.** (*cf.* I. E.) *"to touch up"* (colloq.) : *to gall, nettle :* Rhodium in convivio, Ter. **b.** *to take in, dupe :* patrem, Pl. ; aliquem triginta minis, Pl. **C.** *to touch upon* in words, *to mention :* leviter unum quidque, Cic. ; Ter. **D.** *to take in hand, undertake :* carmina, Ov.

E. Of relationship, *to touch* (i.e. *to bo connected with*) : ortus ab Aeneā tangit cognata sacerdos numina, Ov.

tanquam, *v.* tamquam.

Tantalus, I, *m. son of Jupiter, and father of Pelops and Niobe. Having offended Jupiter by divulging the secrets of his table, to which he had been admitted, he was punished in the infernal regions by continued hunger and thirst, food and drink being apparently within his reach, but always eluding his grasp :* **Tantalens,** a, um ; **Tantalidēs,** ae, *m. a male descendant of Tantalus ;* **Tantalis,** idis, *f. a female descendant of Tantalus.*

tantillus, a, um [*dim.* tantulus], *so little, so small :* donum, Pl. ; quem ego modo puerum tantillum in manibus gestavi meis, Ter. *Neut.* as Noun, **tantillum,** I, Pl. ; with *Partit.* GEN.: loci, Pl. *Intern.* ACC.: tantillum peccare, Pl. ABL. of amount of difference : tantillo minus, Pl.

tantisper, *adv.* [tantus: *cf.* paulisper], *just so long* (and no longer) ; *just for a moment :* Pl., Cic., Liv. With *dum :* ut ibi esset tantisper, dum culleus compararetur, Cic. ; Pl. ; Ter.

tantō opere (tantopere), *v.* tantus.

tantulus, a, um [*dim.* tantus], *so little, so small :* tempus, Pl. ; vim, quae ex fici tantulo grano tantos truncos procreet, Cic. ; homines tantulae staturae, Caes. *Neut.* as Noun, **tantulum,** I, Cic., Hor. With *Partit.* GEN.: morae, Cic. *Intern.* ACC.: tantulum commoveri, Cic. ABL. of price : cur tantulo venierint, Cic.

tantum, tantummodo, *v.* tantus.

tantundem, *v.* tantusdem.

tantus, a, um [tam], *of such size or measure, so great* (occ. *so little*) in amount, extent, value, degree. **A.** Alone : Pl. ; ne tantao nationes coniungantur, Caes. ; tantas et tam infinitas pecunias, Cic. ; tantorum ingentia septem terga boum, Verg. ; sescenta tanta reddam, *six hundred times as much,* Pl. ; **tantō opere** or **tantopere** as *Adv., so much, with so much effort* or *effect :* Pl., Cic., etc. **B.** With corresponding *quantus, ut, qui ;* rarely *quam : so great as :* nullam (contionem) unquam vidi tantam quanta nunc vestra est, Cic.; tanta erat operis firmitudo ut etc., Caes.; (ceterarum provinciarum vectigalia tanta sunt ut etc., *so little,* Cic.) ; nulla est tanta vis, quae non frangi possit, Cic. ; quae (litterae) non tantum gaudium ab recenti metu attulerunt, quam a vetere famā, Liv. As Noun, **tantum,** I, *n. so much, so many :* argenti tantum, Pl. ; habero tantum molestiae quantum gloriae, Cic. ; tantum hostium, Liv. ; (praesidi tantum, *so little,* Caes. ; tantum navium, *so few,* Caes.). Colloq. tantum est, *that is all, nothing more :* Pl., Ter. **tanti,** GEN. *of price* or *value.* **1.** Lit.: frumentum tanti fuit, quanti iste aestimavit, Cic. ; Pl. **2.** Transf.: tanti eius apud se gratiam esse ostendit, Caes. ; dicere, nihil esse tanti, Cic. Ep. ; est mihi tanti (with *Inf.* as Subject), Cic. **tantō,** ABL. of measure, *by so much, so much the* (*more* or *less*), usually with comparatives : quanto erat in dies gravior oppugnatio, tantô crebriorum litterae etc., Caes.; bis tanto amici sunt inter se quam prius, Pl.; si Cleomenes non tanto ante fugisset, Cic. Colloq. tanto melior I Pl.; tanto hercle melior, Ter. So, tanto nequior I Ter. **in tantum,** *so far, so much, to such a degree :* in tantum suam felicitatem virtutemque enituisse, Liv. **tantum,** Acc., as *Intern.* Acc., or Acc. of Extent or *Adv., so much, so greatly ; also, so little ; to such a degree, so.* **a.** tantum quantum quis fuge, Pl.; tantum progressus a castris ut dimicaturum appareret, Liv.; id tantum abest ab officio ut etc., Cic. (*v.* also absum); tantum ibi moratus (i.e. *so long*), Liv. (tantum . . . quantum often means, *just so much,* i.e. *so little* . . . *as ; only so far as :* tantum monet quantum intellegit, Cic.; Caes.) With *Adj.*: Verg., Hor. **b.** (Perh. orig. Nom. fr. phr. tantum est etc., *it is just so much* or *so little), only, merely, but :* tantum de vitâ quaerere, Cic.; Hor., etc. Esp. with *unum :* unum flumen tantum intererat, Caes.; Cic.; Liv. Strengthened **tantum modo** or **tantummodo,** *only just so much, only just :* pedites tantum modo umeris exstare, Caes.; ut tantum modo, Hor. **Phrases:** tantum non (*cf.* Gk. μόνον οὐ), *almost, all but, very nearly :* Liv., Suet.; tantum quod (of time), *only just, scarcely :* tantum quod ex Arpinati veneram cum eto., Cic. Ep.; Suet.; tantum quod non, *only that not, nothing is wanting but :* tantum quod hominem non nominat, causam quidem totam perscribit, Cic. [Fr. *tant.*]

tantus-dem, tantadem, tantundem [tantus, *cf.* idem fr. is], *just so great* or *large, so great :* Pl., Liv. As Noun, **tantundem,** tantidem, *n.* **a.** hinc tantundem accipies, Pl.; ex parvo tantundem haurire, Hor.; Liv. With *Partit.* Gen.: Cic., Liv., Quint. As *Intern.* Acc.: valere, Quint. **b.** With corresponding *quantum :* magistratibus tantundem detur in cellam quantum semper datum est, Cic.; Pl.; Liv. With *Partit.* Gen.: tantundem argenti quantum debuit dedit illi, Pl.; Caes.; Liv.; Tac. **c.** **tantidem,** Gen. of price, *for just so much* (and no more): Pl., Ter., Cic.

tapēta, ae, *m.* (Verg.), **tapēta,** ōrum, and **tapētia,** ium, *n. pl.* (Pl., Verg., Liv., etc.) [*cf.* Gk. τάπης, ητος], *a carpet, tapestry, hangings, coverlet.* [It. *tappeto ;* Fr. *tapis.*]

Taprobanē, ēs, *f. an island in the Indian Ocean, now Ceylon.*

tardē, adv. *slowly, tardily :* Pl., Cic., Verg. *Comp. :* Caes., Cic. *Sup. :* Cic.

tardēscō, ere [tardus], *to become slow, to falter :* lingua, Lucr.; Tib.

tardi-gradus, a, um [tardus gradus], *slow-paced :* quadrupes, Pac.

tardi-pēs, pedis, *adj.* [tardus], *slow-footed, limping :* deus (i.e. *Vulcan*), Cat.

tarditās, ātis, *f.* [tardus], *slowness, tardiness.* **1.** Lit.: Cic.; in rebus gerendis, Cic.; pedum, Cic.; navium, Caes.; veneni, Tac. In *pl.* : Cic. **2.** Transf. **a.** aurium, Plin.; occasionis, Cic. **b.** *dullness, heaviness, stupidity :* ingeni, Cic.; hominum, Cic.

tardissimě, ... iñís, ... [...], ... *tardiness :* Pl.

tardiusculus, a, um [*dim.* of *comp.* of tardus], *rather slow, slowish :* Ter.

tardō, āre [tardus]. **A.** Trans. *to make slow, to hinder, delay.* **1.** Lit.: cursum, Cic.; profectionem, Cic. Ep.; impetum hostium, Caes.; alas, Hor.; palus Romanos ad insequendum tardabat, Caes.; pedes alta harena, Ov. In *Pass.* (with *Inf.*): Caes. **2.** Transf. : studia alicuius, Cic.; ne exercitûs nostri tardentur animis, Cic. **B.** Intrans. *"to go slow," tarry, delay :* Plin. *Impers. Pass. :* Cic. Ep.

tardus, a, um, *slow* (in movement and action), *sluggish, tardy.* **1.** Lit. **a.** Of living creatures : Pl., Cic., Verg., etc. *Comp.* : aetate tardiores, Pl.; ad iniuriam, Cic.; ad deponendum imperium, Cic. *Sup.* : Pl. **b.** Of things : frumenti tarda subvectio, Liv.; noctes, Verg.; podagra (i.e. *causative, crippling*), Hor.; sapor, *lingering,* Verg. *Comp. :* tibicinis modi, Cic.; poena, Cic.; fata, Hor. **2.** Transf. **a.** (Mentally) *slow :* Pl., Cic.; tardo ingenio esse, Cic.; mentes, Cic.; sensûs hebetes et tardi, Cic. *Comp.* : Cic. **b.** Of speech or of a speaker : *slow, measured, deliberate :* in cogitando, Cic.; sententiis, Cic. *Comp. :* pronuntiatio, Quint.

Tarentum, i, *n. an important Greek city, situated on the west coast of Calabria, now Taranto ;* **Tarentīnus,** a, um ; **Tarentīni,** ōrum, *m. pl. the Tarentines.*

tarmes, itis, *m. a worm that eats wood, a wood-worm :* Pl.

Tarpēius, a, *a Roman proper name.* Esp. **Tarpēia,** ae, *f. a Roman maiden, who treacherously opened the citadel to the Sabines ;* **Tarpēius,** a, um : esp. mons Tarpeius, *the Tarpeian rock on the Capitoline Hill, from which criminals were thrown headlong.*

tarpezīta (trapezīta), ae, *m.* [τραπεζίτης], *a money-changer, banker :* Pl.

Tarquinii, ōrum, *m. pl. a very ancient and important town of Etruria, near Corneto ;* **Tarquinius,** a, um ; **Tarquinius,** i, *m. the fifth king of Rome, surnamed Priscus ; also the last king of Rome, surnamed Superbus ;* **Tarquiniēnsis,** e, *adj. ;* **Tarquiniēnsēs,** ium, *m. pl. its inhabitants.*

Tartarus or **-os,** i, *m.* ; in *pl.* **Tartara,** ōrum, *n.* [Τάρταρος, *pl.* Τάρταρα], *the infernal regions ;* esp. *the abode of the guilty, Tartarus :* Lucr., Verg., etc. ; **Tartareus,** a, um, *custos,* i.e. *Cerberus,* Verg. ; *sorores,* i.e. *the Furies,* Verg.

tat and **tatae,** exclamations of surprise : Pl.

tata, ae, *m.* colloq. like our "*daddy*" : Varr., Mart.

Tatius, i, *m.* : T. Tatius, *a king of the Sabines, who afterwards reigned jointly with Romulus ;* **Tatius,** a, um ; **Tatiēnsēs,** ium, *m. pl. one of the three original Roman tribes.*

Taum, i, *m. an arm of the sea in N. Britain, now the Firth of Tay.*

taureus, a, um [taurus], *of a bull* or *of bull's hide :* vincla (i.e. *glue*), Lucr.; terga, Verg.; also for *a drum :* Ov. As Noun, **taurea,** ae, *f. a whip of bull's hide :* Juv.

Tauri, ōrum, *m. pl. a barbarous people, living in the peninsula now called the Crimea* (Chersonesus Taurica), *who sacrificed foreigners to Diana :* **Tauricus**, a, um.

taurifer, fera, ferum [taurus ferō], *bullbearing :* campi, Luc.

tauriförmis, e, *adj.* [taurus förma], *bullshaped,* epithet of the River Aufidus : Hor. ; *cf.* taurinus.

Taurii lüdi, *games at Rome in the Circus Flaminius, held in honour of the gods of the lower world :* Liv.

taurinus, a, um [taurus]. **I.** *of or made from bulls, bull's :* gluten, Lucr. ; tergum, Verg. ; sanguis, Plin. **II.** *bull-like :* vultus (Eridani), Verg. ; frons, Ov.

taurus, ī, *m. a bull.* **1.** L i t.: Pl., Cic., Verg., etc. **2.** T r a n s f. **a.** Of the bronze bull of Phalaris (q.v.) : Cic., Ov. **b.** A s t r o n. a constellation, *the Bull :* Verg., Plin.

tax, *v.* tuxtax.

taxātiō, ōnis, *f.* [taxō], *a rating, valuing :* eius rei, Cic.

taxillus, ī, *m.* [*dim. v.* tālus], *a small die* (for dicing) : Cic.

taxō, āre [*freq.* tangō], *to touch repeatedly, to handle.* T r a n s f. *to appraise by handling ;* hence, **a.** *to appraise, rate, value, estimate* the worth of : senatorum censum duodeciens HS. taxavit, Suet. ; Plin. **b.** In gen. *to estimate, judge of, etc. :* timorem tuum taxa, Sen. Ep. ; quanti illud taxavimus, Sen. **c.** *to reproach, charge, or tax* with a fault ; divortium suum cum uxore, Suet. ; quādam epistulā sic taxat Augustum (with quoted words), Suet.

taxus, ī, *f. a yew, yew-tree :* Caes., Verg. Considered, from its poisonous properties, as a tree of the infernal regions : Ov.

Täÿgetē, ēs, *f. daughter of Atlas and Pleione, one of the Pleiades.*

Täÿgetus, ī, *m.* and **Täÿgeta**, ōrum, *n. pl. a lofty range of mountains in Laconia.*

tē, *v.* tū.

-te, a pronominal suffix, e.g. tūte, tēte : *v.* tū.

Tecmēssa, ae, *f. daughter of Teuthras, and wife of Ajax the son of Telamon.*

techna (and **techina**), ae, *f.* [τέχνη], *a wile, trick, artifice :* Pl., Ter.

tēctē, *adv. covertly, cautiously :* Cic. Ep. Comp., : Cic., Ov.

tēctor, ōris, *m.* [tegō], *a plasterer :* Varr., Cic.

tēctōriolum, ī, *n.* [*dim.* tēctōrium], *a little plaster-work :* Cic. Ep.

tēctōrius, a, um [tēctum and tēctor]. **I.** *for roofing :* paniculum, Pl. (but *v.* II.). **II.** *of a plasterer, stucco-worker, painter :* opus, Cic. ; atramentum, Plin. ; penicilli, Plin. ; and perh. peniculum (instead of paniculum in I.), Pl. As Noun, **tēctōrium**, ī, *n. plaster, stucco, fresco-painting, a wash* for walls. **1.** L i t.: Cic., etc. **2.** T r a n s f. **a.** For the complexion : *a beauty-plaster* or *-wash :* Juv. **b.** Of hypocritical speech : pictae tectoria linguae, Pers.

tēctus, a, um. **I.** *Part.* tegō. **II.** A d j. *hidden, concealed.* **1.** L i t.: cuniculi, Hirt. **2.** T r a n s f. *not frank or plain ; concealed, disguised :* verba, Cic. Ep. ; tectior cupi-

ditas, Cic. ; amor, Ov. Of persons : Cic., Verg. Comp. and Sup. : Cic. **III.** Nouu, **tēctum**, ī, *n.* **1.** L i t. **a.** *a roof :* Pl., Lucr., Cic. Ep., Verg., etc. **b.** *a ceiling :* caelata, laqueata, Enn., Hor. ; aurata, Cic. **c.** *a canopy :* Hor. **2.** T r a n s f. *a cover, shelter, house, dwelling :* Pl. ; exercitūs tectis ac sedibus suis recipere, Cic. ; Verg. ; qui inter annos xiv tectum non subissent, Caes. ; solidis clauditur in tectis, Ov. [It. *tetto ;* Fr. *toit.*]

tēda, tēdifer, *v.* taeda, taedifer.

Tēdigniloquidēs, is, *m.* [tē digna loquēns|, a comio patronymic : Pl.

Tegea, ae, *f. a very ancient town in Arcadia ;* **Tegeaeus**, a, um, [Tegeа], *Arcadian ;* **Tegeaeus**, ī, *m. the Tegean (god), Pan ;* **Tegeaea**, ae, *f. the Arcadian maiden,* i.e. *Atalanta* (Ov.) ; **Tegeātae**, ārum, *m. pl. the Tegeans.*

teges, etis, *f.* [tegō], *a mat :* Varr., Juv.

tegillum, ī, *n.* [*dim.* tegulum, *a covering,* from tegō], *a small covering, a hood* or *cowl :* Pl., Varr.

tegimen (older **tegumen** and sync. **tegmen**), inis, *n.* [tegō], *a covering, cover :* textile, Lucr. ; Scythicum, Cic. ; aeneum, Liv. ; Verg. ; Tac. ; sub caeli tegmine, Lucr. ; sub tegmine fagi, Verg.

tegimentum (older **tegumentum** and sync. **tegmentum**), ī, *n.* [tegō], *a covering, cover :* Caes., Cic., Liv., etc. ; tegimenta corporum vel texta vel suta, Cic.

tegō, tegere, tēxī, tēctum [*cf.* Gk. στέγω], *to cover.* **1.** L i t. **a.** In gen. : tegillo tectus, Pl. ; res corio aut callo aut cortice tectae, Lucr. ; casae stramentis tectae, Caes. ; corpus pallio, Cic. ; Hor. ; caput galea, Prop. ; ensis vaginā tectus, Hor. ; naves tectae (i.e. decked), Caes., Liv. **b.** *to cover* (and so conceal) : insignia militum, Caes. ; fugientem silvae, Caes. ; Ov. ; ferae latibulis se tegunt, Cic. ; dira supplicia (manibus), Verg. ; nebula inceptum, Liv. **c.** *to cover* (and so' protect), *to shelter, defend :* aliquem, Cic. ; portus ab Africo tegebatur, Caes. ; spurco Damae latus (from jostling), Hor. ; Suet. In *Mid.* : tegi magis quam pugnare, Liv. Of attendants : omnis eum stipata tegebat turba ducum, Verg. **d.** *to cover* (and so bury) : ossa humus, Ov. ; harenā tegi, Mart. **2.** T r a n s f. **a.** In gen. : modestiā tectus, Pl. **b.** Of concealing : triumphi nomine cupiditatem suam, Cic. ; aliquid mendacio, Cic. ; turpia facta oratione, Sall. ; exercitūs incommodā, Caes. ; nostram sententiam, Cic. ; causam doloris, Ov. **c.** Of protecting or defending : aliquid excusatione amicitiae, Cic. ; innocentiā tectus, Cic. ; libertatem armis, Sall. ; legatos ab irā impetuque hominum, Liv.

tēgula, ae, *f.* [tegō], *a tile :* Cic. Ep., Ov., Liv., Juv. More freq. *pl. : tiles, roof-tiles, a tiled roof :* Pl., Cic., Liv. [It. *tegola ;* Fr. *tuile.*]

tegumen, *v.* tegimen.

tegumentum, *v.* tegimentum.

tēla, ae, *f.* [for *tex-la*, from texō ; *cf.* subtēmen], *any woven stuff.* **1.** L i t. **a.** Prop. *a web :* Ter., Cic., Verg., etc. Of a *spider's web :* Pl., Cat., Juv. **b.** *the threads that*

run lengthwise in the loom, the warp : Verg.,
Ov. **2.** T r a n s f. **a.** *a weaver's beam,
yarn-beam ;* also, *a loom :* Cato ; Ov. **b.**
a web, i.e. a plan, design : texere, Cic. ;
detexere, Pl. [It. *tela ;* Fr. *toile.*]

Telamōn, ōnis, *m. an Argonaut, son of
Aeacus, brother of Peleus, king of Salamis,
and father of Ajax and Teucer ;* **Tela-
mōnius**, ī, *m.* and **Telamōniadēs**, ae, *m.
a son of Telamon, i.o. Ajax.*

Telchīnes, um, *m. pl. a mythical family in
Crete, Cyprus, and Rhodes, famous for their
skill in metallurgy and magic arts.*

Tēleboae, ārum, *m. pl. a people of Acarnania ;
also a colony of them in Capreae.*

Tēlegonus, ī, *m. son of Ulysses and Circe,
who killed his father without knowing him ;
the reputed founder of Tusculum.*

Tēlemachus, ī, *m., s. of Ulysses and Penelope.*

Tēlephus, ī, *m. king of Mysia, s. of Hercules
and Auge. He was wounded by the spear
of Achilles, but was afterwards cured by
its rust.*

Telethūsa, ae, *f. the wife of Lygdus, and
mother of Iphis.*

tellūs, ūris, *f. the earth.* **1.** L i t. **a.** Opp.
to other planets, *the globe :* Cic., Verg.,
Ov. **b.** Opp. to sea and air, *earth, land :*
Verg., Hor., Ov. **c.** P e r s o n i f i e d : Tellus mater, Liv. ; Cic. ; Hor. **2.** T r a n s f.
a. *a land, country, district :* Aegyptia,
Ov. ; Verg. ; nova, Hor. **b.** As property :
pecore et multā dives tellure, Hor.

tēlum, ī, *n. a missile of any kind* (e.g. an
arrow, dart, javelin). **1.** L i t. : tela manu
iacere, Enn. ; iacere volatile telum, Lucr. ;
iacere, depellere, Cic. ; conicere, mittere,
vitare, Caes. ; in medios torquere, Verg. ;
tela derigere arcu, Hor. ; telis repulsi,
Caes. ; ad coniectum teli venire, Liv. ;
tempestas telorum, Verg. ; nubes telorum,
Liv. ; ferrea telorum seges, Verg. **2.**
T r a n s f. **a.** *an offensive weapon* of any
kind : esse cum telo, Cic. ; strictis agmina
telis, Ov. ; ut pereat positum robigine
telum, Hor. Of the caestus : Verg. **b.** *a
shaft* of light. Of a sunbeam : lucida tela
diei, Lucr. Of lightning : arbitrium est
in sua tela Iovi, Ov. **c.** Abstract :
hunc telo suo, malitiā pollere, Pl. ; telis
perfixa pavoris, Lucr. ; tela fortunae,
Cic. Ep. ; de corpore rei publicae tuorum
scelerum tela revellere, Cic. ; necessitas,
quae ultimum ac maximum telum est,
Liv. ; linguae tela subire tuae, Ov.

temerārius, a, um [temere]. **I.** *accidental,
casual :* Pl. **II.** *heedless, thoughtless.* **a.**
Of persons : Ter., Caes., Ov. **b.** Of things :
thoughtless, ill-considered : caeca ac teme-
raria dominatrix animi cupiditas, Cic. ;
vox, Liv. ; impetus sequentium, Liv. ;
virtus, bella, error, etc., Ov. ; temerarium
est (with *Inf.*), Plin. Ep.

temere, *adv. in the dark, blindly ;* hence,
A. Mostly with *forte, casu, fortuito :* by
chance, at random, idly, without cause :
Ter., Cic., Liv., etc. ; temere . . . de
industriā, Liv. ; non temere est quod
etc., *it is not mere chance that etc.,* Pl. ;
haud temere est visum, Verg. ; Liv. **B.**
without thought or consideration, heedlessly,

at random : Caes., Cic.;
Hor., Ov., etc. ; non temere, *not lightly,*
or *easily :* qui hoc non temere nisi libertis
suis deferebant, Cic. ; nullus dies temere
intercessit, quo non ad eum scriberet
(i.e. *hardly a day passed but etc.*), Nep.;
non temere, *hardly ever,* Liv. **b.** Of things :
numquam temere tinniit tintinnabulum,
Pl. ; saxa iacentia, Liv.

temeritās, ātis, *f.* [temere]. **I.** *chance,
accident :* opp. to ordo, Cic. ; also to ratio
and consilium, Cic. **II.** *heedlessness, foolhardiness, rashness :* Caes., Cic., Liv. In
pl. : acts of foolhardiness : Cic.

temerō, āre [fr. root seen in temere], *to
darken, blacken ;* hence *to violate, defile,
disgrace :* templa Minervae, Verg. ; aras,
sepulcra, etc., Liv. ; fluvios venenis, Ov. ;
castra infausta temerataque, Tac. ; thalamos pudicos, Ov. ; maritam, Ov. ; sacra
deae, Tib. ; hospitii sacra, Ov. ; puram
fidem, Ov.

Temesē, ēs, and **Tempsa**, ae, *f. a town in
Bruttium,* perh. now *Torre del Piano del
Casale ;* **Temesaeus**, a, um, and **Temp-
sānus**, a, um.

tēmētum, ī, *n.* [*cf.* tēmulentus, abstēmius],
any intoxicating drink, mead, wine, etc. :
Pl., Cato, Cic., Hor.

temnō, temnere, tempsī, temptum [*cf.* Gk.
τέμνω, *to cut*], *to slight, disdain, despise :*
praesentia, Lucr. ; divos, Verg. ; vulgaria,
Hor. ; haud temnendae manūs ductor,
Tac.

tēmō, ōnis, *m.* [fr. root tek- seen in texō,
etc.], *a beam, pole, tongue* of a carriage,
cart, etc. **1.** L i t. : Caes., Verg., Ov.
2. T r a n s f. *a waggon :* Juv. Of the
constellation, *Charles' Wain* (or the Great
Bear) : Enn., Ov. [Fr. *timon.*]

Tempē, *n. pl. indecl., a beautiful valley in
Thessaly, through which ran the river Peneus,
between Olympus and Ossa.* T r a n s f. of
any such valley : Verg., Ov.

temperāmentum, ī, *n.* [temperō], *a mixing
in due proportion ;* hence, *a due measure,
moderation :* inventum est temperamen-
tum, quo tenuiores cum principibus aequari
se putarunt, Cic. ; die senatūs Caesar
orationem habuit meditato temperamento,
Tac. ; fortitudinis, Tac.

temperāns, antis. **I.** *Part.* temperō. **II.**
A d j. *observing moderation, self-restrained,
moderate, temperate :* Cic. Comp. : principes temperantiores a cupidine imperi,
Liv. Sup. : Cic. With *Obj.* G e n. : famae temperans, Ter. ; potestatis temperan-
tior, Tac.

temperanter, adv. *with moderation, moderately :* Tac. Comp. : Cic. Ep.

temperantia, ae, *f.* [temperāns], *self-control,
moderation, discreetness :* in widest sense :
Caes., Cic. ; dicacitatis, Cic. ; in victu,
Cic. ; adversus sitim, Tac.

temperātē, adv. *in due proportion, moderately.*
1. L i t. : tepebit, Cato. **2.** T r a n s f. :
agere, Cic. Ep. Comp. : scribere, Cic. Ep.

temperātiō, ōnis, *f.* [temperō], *a due mingling*
or *tempering* of ingredients, hence **I.** *the
composition* of a thing, *the due mixture*
in a thing. **1.** L i t. : corporum, aëris,
caeli, etc., Cic. **2.** T r a n s f. : rei publicae,

civitatis, Cic. ; ordinum, Liv. **II.** *the
controlling power :* mens mundi et temperatio, Cic.

temperător, ōris, *m.* [temperō], *one who
exercises due control :* huius varietatis,
Cic. Poet.: armorum flumen (i.e. that
duly tempers arms), Mart.

temperātus, a, um. **I.** *Part.* temperō.
II. Adj. *kept within due measure, rightly
tempered.* **1.** Lit.: escae, Cic. *Comp.:*
loca temperatiora, Caes. *Sup.:* anni
tempus, Varr. **2.** Transf. (of morals),
self-controlled, temperate : Cic.; mores,
Cic. ; mens in bonis ab insolenti temperata
laetitiā, Hor. ; animus virtutibus, Liv. ;
oratio, Cic. *Comp.* and *Sup. :* Cic.

temperi, temperius, *v.* tempus.

temperies, ēi, *f.* [temperō], *a due mingling,
temperature.* **a.** ubi temperiem sumpsere
umorque calorque, Ov. ; caeli, Ov., Curt.,
Plin. Ep. ; temperie blandarum captus
aquarum, Ov. **b.** Of climate, *moderate
temperature, mildness :* Hor. ; caeli, Curt.,
Plin. Ep.

temperō, āre [tempus]. **A.** Trans. *to
combine, compound,* or *keep in due proportion, to blend, temper.* **1.** Lit.: ea cum
tria sumpsisset, unam in speciem tempera-
vit, Cic. ; acuta cum gravibus, Cic. ;
scatebris arentia arva, Verg. ; Etesiarum
flatu nimii temperantur calores, Cic. ;
aquam ignibus, Hor. ; pocula, Hor. ;
herbas, Ov. ; venenum, Suet. ; colores,
Plin. ; aes, ferrum, Plin. **2.** Transf.
a. cuius acerbitas morum ne vino quidem
permixta temperari solet, Cic. ; in perpetuā oratione hi numeri sunt inter se
miscendi et temperandi, Cic. ; amara lento
risu, Hor. ; non modice temperatam sed
nimis meracam libertatem, Cic. **b.** *to
regulate, moderate, tone, tune :* victoriam,
Cic. ; iras, Verg. ; sumptūs, Ov. ; annonam
macelli, Suet. Also, citharam nervis,
Ov. **c.** *to regulate, govern, control* (of a
ruler, etc.): civitates, Cic. ; rem publicam
institutis et legibus, Cic. ; aequor, Verg. ;
Iuppiter res hominum ac deorum, mare ac
terras, Hor. ; orbem, undas, ratem, etc.,
Ov. ; ora frenis, Hor. Also, (Musa)
testudinis aureae strepitum, Hor. **B.**
Intrans. *to observe due measure ; to be
moderate, temperate, restrained.* **a.** In gen. :
in amore, Pl. ; in multā, Liv. ; Sall. With
DAT. of thing restrained : linguae, Pl.,
Liv. ; manibus, oculis, irae, Liv. ; victoriae,
Sall. ; lacrimis, Curt. ; gulae, Plin. Ep.
With DAT. of person spared : alicui (in
aliquā re), Cic. ; Hor. ; Liv. ; of thing
spared : templis deum (GEN.) temperatum
est, Liv. **b.** *to show* or *exercise forbearance,
to abstain.* With *ab* and ABL., or ABL.
alone : ab iniuriā et maleficio, Caes. ;
a lacrimis, Verg. ; ab oppugnatione urbium
temperatum, Liv. ; ab excidio civitatis,
Tac. ; (rarely with *ab* and ABL. of persons :
ab sociis, Liv.) ; lacrimis, risu (but these
may be DAT.), *cf.* B. a.), Liv. With *Inf.:*
Pl. With *ne* and *Subj. :* Pl. With *quin*
(after a negat.) and (rarely) *quo minus :*
(i.) With DAT. of *Refl. Pron.* or *animis, to
restrain oneself from, etc. :* Caes., Liv., etc.
(ii.) Alone : Sen., Tac. *Impers. Pass. :*

aegre temperatum est quin etc., Liv. [Fr.
tremper.]

tempestās, ātis, *f.* [tempus], *a portion,
point,* or *space of time.* **I.** *a time, season,
period* (in this sense, somewhat archaic
for tempus): quā tempestate Poenus in
Italiam venit, Cic. ; illā tempestate, Liv. ;
Pl. ; Ov., etc. In *pl. :* Sulla sollertissimo
omnium in paucis tempestatibus factus est,
Sall. ; Euander multis ante temporibus
ea tenuerat loca, Liv. **II.** *time,* with
respect to its physical qualities, *weather.*
1. Lit. **a.** In gen. : liquida, Pl. ; liqui-
dissima caeli tempestas, Lucr. ; cum tempestas adridet, Lucr. ; clara, Verg. ; secunda, Tac. ; nactus idoneam ad navigandum tempestatem, Caes. ; turbida,
saeva, Pl., Lucr. ; perfrigida, Cic. ; foeda,
Verg., Liv. In *pl. :* Enn., Lucr., Cic. Ep.
b. *stormy weather ; a storm, tempest :*
Pl., Caes., Cic., Verg., etc. **c.** Personified : Cic., Hor., Ov. **2.** Transf. :
Cic., Verg. ; qui in hac tempestate populi
iactemur et fluctibus, Cic. ; periculi,
Gallici adventūs, comitiorum, etc., Cic. ;
invidiae, Cic., Liv. ; telorum, Verg. ;
Punici belli, Liv. [Fr. *tempête.*]

tempestīvē, adv. *seasonably, fitly :* Cato,
Cic., Ov. *Comp. :* Hor.

tempestīvitās, ātis, *f.* [tempestīvus], *a
right* or *proper time, seasonableness :* Cic.

tempestīvus (-os), a, um [tempestās], *happening at the right time, timely, seasonable, fit.*
a. In gen. : ad navigandum mare, Cic. ;
venti, Cic. ; oratio, Liv. ; tempora, Liv. ;
multa mihi ad mortem tempestiva fuerunt,
Cic. ; tempestivo pueris ludus, Hor.
b. *full-grown, ripe :* maturitas, Cic. ; pinus,
Verg. ; Cato ; Lucr. Of persons : tempestiva viro, Hor. ; caelo heros, Ov. **c.** *in
good time, betimes, early.* Of early risers :
Plin. Of early banquets : Cic., Tac.,
etc.

templum, i, *n.* [prob. for tem-lum, *cf.* Gk.
τέμενος, fr. τέμνω], *a space cut off.* **1.**
Lit. in augury, *an open place for observation* (in heavens or on earth), *marked off*
by the augur. **a.** In gen. (on the ground) :
Liv. **b.** Esp. *a place set apart and consecrated* by the augurs for public functions
(opp. to aedes, *a consecrated dwelling* of a
god) : in rostris, in illo, inquam, inaugu-
rato templo ac loco, Cic. ; Liv. ; templum
ordini ab se aucto curiam fecit, Liv. ;
sub tutelā inviolati templi (of Romulus'
" sanctuary of refuge "), Liv. **2.** Transf.
a. *any open space, quarter* (perh. as being
thought holy). Of the heavens : in caerula
caeli templa, Enn. ; Lucr. ; Iovis, Enn. ;
dei hoc templum est omne quod conspicis,
Cic. ; mundi magnum et versatile templum,
Lucr. Of the underworld : Acherusia
templa Orci, Enn. Of *the open spaces* of
the sea : loca Neptunia templaque tur-
bulenta, Pl. Of the *space inside the mouth* :
Lucr. **b.** *a dedicated shrine* or *temple :*
deorum, Hor. ; Iunonis Sospitae, Cic. ;
Verg. ; Herculis, Cic. ; Sychaei, Verg. ;
Virtutis, Concordiae, etc., Cic. **c.** Transf.
shrine, sanctuary : (curia) templum sanctitatis, consili publici, Cic. ; pectus templaque
mentis, Lucr.

temporālis, e, adj. [tempus], *lasting only for a time, temporary* : causa, Sen. ; laudes, Tac.

temporārius, a, um [tempus]. **I.** *depending on* or *according to the time* : liberalitas, Nep. **II.** *lasting only for a time, ephemeral, changeable* : amicitiae, Sen. Ep. ; ingenia, Curt. ; gravitas, Plin. Ep.

tempori, *v.* tempus.

temptābundus, a, um [temptō], *trying again and again* : miles, Liv.

temptāmentum, ī, *n.* [temptō], *a proof, attempt, essay* (usually in *pl.*) : Ov. ; tui, Verg. ; fide (GEN.), Ov. ; civilium bellorum, Tac.

temptāmina, um, *n. pl.* [temptō], *trials, essays, attempts :* Ov. ; vocis, Ov.

temptātiō, ōnis, *f.* [temptō]. **I.** *a trial, proof :* perseverantiae, Liv. **II.** *an attack* of sickness (in *pl.*) : Cic. Ep.

temptātor, ōris, *m.* [temptō], *an assailant :* integrae Dianae Orion, Hor.

temptō, āre, *to probe, feel, test by probing or feeling.* **1.** Lit. **A.** In gen. : corvus ficum rostro, Ov. ; manibus pectora, Ov. ; flumen pede, Cic. ; quadratum, Lucr. ; invisos amictūs, Verg. ; venas, Quint. ; aciem pugionum, Suet. **B.** *to test* or *prove the strength of a thing ; to assail, make an attempt upon.* **a.** Milit. : scalis et classe moenia oppidi, Caes. ; urbem, munitiones, Liv. ; Achaiam, Caes. **b.** Of disease, etc. : morbo corpora temptari possunt, Cic. ; Hor. ; gravis autumnus omnem exercitum valetudine temptaverat, Caes. ; ovis scabies, Verg. ; vina pedes, Verg. ; frigore corpus, Hor. **2.** Transf. **A.** **a.** In gen. *to test, make trial of :* Thetim ratibus, Verg. ; Oceanum, Tac. ; alicuius scientiam, Cic. ; regis prudentiam, Cic. ; belli fortunam, Caes. ; patientiam vestram, Cic. ; spem pacis, Liv. ; libertatem, Liv. With *Indir. Quest. :* Pl., Cic., Verg. **b.** *to make trial of, attempt, essay :* Pl., Hirt. ; culturam agelli, Lucr. ; iter per provinciam per vim, Caes. ; viam, Verg. ; rem frustra, Caes. ; quaestionem, Cic. ; intercessionem, etc., Liv. ; crimina, Hor. With *Inf. :* Lucr., Hirt., Liv., Verg., Ov. With *ut* and *Subj. :* Cic., Suet. ; *Impers. Pass. :* Liv. **B.** *to assail, tamper with, make an attempt upon* (loyalty, virtue, etc.) : nationes lacessere bello et temptare, Cic. ; rem publicam, Cic. ; iudicium pecuniā, Cic. ; Iunonem Ixion, Tib. ; alicuius fidem per promissa, Tac. **C.** *to tamper with, attempt to influence, to try to induce :* aliquem, Caes., Cic. ; aliquem promissis ac minis, Tac. ; animos servorum spe et metu, Cic. ; animum precando, Verg. ; animos popularium, Sall. ; deos multā caede bidentium, Hor. [Fr. *tenter*.]

tempus, ŏris, *n.* (LOCAT. temperī, Pl. ; see below) [*cf.* templum], *a portion cut off* or *marked out* (of space or time). **I.** Of space, only of the *temples* of the head (perh. regarded as holy or mysterious). **1.** Lit. (mostly in *pl.*) : Lucr., Verg., Ov., etc. ; temporibus canebat senectus, Verg. **2.** Transf. of *the head :* Cat. In *pl.* : Verg., Prop., Hor. **II.** Of time : *a portion* or *period of time.* **1.** Lit. **a.**

With defining *Noun* in *Adj.*, etc. : *tempus* diei, Ter. ; tempus anni, Caes., Cic. ; extremum diei tempus, Cic. ; tempus duorum mensium petere ad dilectūs habendos, Liv. ; tantulum, Pl. ; matutina tempora, Cic. ; anni tempora, Lucr. ; hoc, eo, illo tempore, Cic., etc. ; brevi tempore, Cic., etc. ; longo post tempore, Verg. ; longis temporibus ante, Cic. ; id temporis, *at that time*, Cic., etc. ; per idem tempus, Cic. **b.** Not *fitting* or *appointed time* in gen. : hos siderum errores id ipsum esse quod rite dicitur tempus, Cic. ; neque, ut celari posset, tempus spatium ullum dabat, Ter. ; tempus pacis an belli, Cic. ; tempus committendi proeli, Caes. ; Cic. ; Hor. ; ad consultandum alicui dare, Cic. ; ut tempora belli postulabant, Liv. ; id certis temporibus futurum, Cic. **2.** Transf. **a.** *the due* or *fixed period* or *time*, e.g. of office : Cic. **b.** *the fitting* or *appointed time, proper period, opportunity* (*cf.* Gk. καιρός) : tempus maximum est ut etc., Pl. ; tempus habes tale quale nemo habuit unquam, Cic. ; suo tempore, Cic. ; an consurgendi iam triariis tempus esset, Liv. ; Cic. ; tempus est, with *Inf. :* Cic., Verg., Liv. ; tibi abire, Hor. ; with Acc. and *Inf. :* Cic., Verg. Also in many adverbial phrases (see below). **c.** *time* in poetry and rhetoric, i.e. *measure, quantity* (mostly in *pl.*) : Cic., Hor., Quint. **d.** Gramm. *tense* of a verb : Varr., Quint. **e.** *the state of the times, condition, circumstances ;* esp. of dangerous or distressing circumstances, hence, *dangers, troubles, crisis :* tempori meo defuerunt, Cic. ; tempore summo rei publicae, Cic. ; tempori cedere, id est necessitati parere, Cic. Ep. ; mecum tempus in ultimum deducto, Hor. ; indignatus dici ea in tali tempore audirique, Liv. ; Lucr. In *pl. :* very freq. in Cic. **3.** Adverbial phrases. **a.** **temperī** (with *Comp.* **temperius**), **-orī**, and **tempore**. (i.) *at the right* or *fitting time, at the appointed time, in time, seasonably :* ut cenam coqueret temperi, Pl. ; ego renovabo commendationem sed tempore, Cic. Ep. ; Ov. *Comp. :* Cic. Ep., Ov. (ii.) *by time* or *in the course of time* (only in form **tempore**) *:* tempore patiens fit taurus aratri, Ov. **b.** **ad tempus**. (i.) *at the right* or *appointed time :* Cic., Liv. (ii.) *for the moment, for the occasion :* Cic., Liv., Tac. **c.** **ante** or **post tempus**, *before* or *after the due time :* Pl., Cic., Sall. **d.** **ex tempore**. (i.) *on the spur of the moment :* Cic., Quint. (ii.) *according to circumstances :* consilium capere, Cic. **e.** **in tempore**, *at the right moment, (just) in time :* Ter., Liv., Tac. ; in ipso tempore, *in the very nick of time*, Ter. **f.** **in tempus**, *for the occasion :* Tac. ; in omne tempus, Cic. Ep. **g.** **per tempus**, *at the right time, (just) in time :* Pl. **h.** **prō tempore**, *according to the occasion* or *circumstances :* consilium pro tempore et pro re capere, Caes. ; Sall. ; Verg. ; Ov. [It. *tempo ;* Sp. *tiempo ;* Fr. *temps*.]

tēmulentus, a, um [fr. root of tēmētum], *drunken, intoxicated :* Ter., Cic., Liv., etc.

tenācĭtās, ātis, *f.* [tenāx], *a holding fast, tenacity.* **a.** In gen.: unguium, Cic. **b.** Of money : Liv.

tenācĭter, *adv. firmly, tightly, tenaciously.* **1.** Lit.: Ov. **2.** Transf.: urgere, Ov.

tenāx, ācis, *adj.* [teneō], *holding fast, griping, gripping, clinging, sticky.* **1.** Lit.: hedera, Cat. ; forceps, Verg. ; dens (ancorae), Verg. ; cerae, Verg. ; loca limosa tenacia gravi caeno, Tac. ; gramen, Hor. ; complexus, Ov. *Comp.*: pondere tenacior navis, Liv. *Sup.*: glaebis tenacissimum solum, Plin. Ep. **2.** Transf. **A.** *holding on to* a purpose, etc. **a.** In good sense: *firm* (mostly with GEN.): propositi, Hor. ; Quint. ; ficti pravique (Fama), Verg. ; iustitiae, Juv. ; memoria tenacissima, Quint. ; disciplinae tenacissimus, Plin. Ep. **b.** In bad sense: *obstinate*: equus, Liv. ; Pl. ; equus contra sua vincla, Ov. ; ira Caesaris, Ov. **B.** *holding fast to wealth, power,* etc. ; *niggardly, stingy* : Pl., Cic. With GEN.: quaesiti, Ov.

tendĭcŭlae, ārum, *f. pl.* [tendō], *little stretchers.* **1.** Lit. (for clothes): Sen. **2.** Transf. *little snares :* litterarum, Cic.

tendō, tendere, tetendī, tentum (tēnsum) [*cf.* Gk. τείνω], *to stretch, stretch out, spread, hold out, strain.* **I.** Trans. **1.** Lit. **a.** In gen.: plagam, Pac. ; Cic. ; rete accipitri, Ter. ; retia (alicui), Prop. ; Hor. ; Ov. ; chordam, Pl. ; barbiton, Hor. ; arcum, Verg. ; sagittas arcu, Hor. ; spicula cornu, Verg. ; pariterque oculos telumque, Verg. ; lora manu, Ov. ; vela Noti, Verg. ; praetorium, Caes. ; cubilia, Hor. **b.** Of the hands, etc.: manūs, Verg. ; manūs ad caeli caerula templa, Enn. ; manūs ad caelum, Caes., Verg. ; bracchia ad caelum, Ov. ; ad legatos supplices manūs, Caes. ; Ov. ; manūs alicui, Caes., Ov. ; manūs supplices dis immortalibus, Cic. ; patri Iulum, Verg. ; munera, Ov. **2.** Transf. **a.** insidias alicui, Cic., Sall. ; in saturā ultra legem tendere opus, Hor. ; cursum (i.e. to direct), Lucr. ; cursum unde et quo, Liv. ; iter ad navis, Verg. ; iter pennis, Verg. ; iter in Hispaniam, Auct. B. Afr. **b.** civibus lucem ingeni et consili sui, Cic. **II.** Intrans. **A.** Of encamping (= tentoria tendere): sub vallo, Caes. ; in arvis, Verg. ; iisdem castris, Liv. ; Tac. ; hic, Verg. ; Lugduni, Tac. **B.** *to direct one's course, go, aim* (*for*), *tend.* **1.** Lit. **a.** Of persons: Venusiam, Cic. Ep. ; ad castra, Liv. ; Verg., etc. ; in castra, Liv. ; huc, Ov. ; quo tendis ? Hor. ; Verg. ; Nep. **b.** Of things : in quem locum quaeque (imago) tendat, Lucr. ; via sub moenia, Verg. ; aethera, Luc. ; quā tendit Ionia, Prop. **2.** Transf. *to aim, strive, be directed* or *inclined.* **a.** Towards something : ad reliqua alacri animo, Cic. ; ad suum, Liv. ; ad Carthaginiensis, Liv. ; ad eloquium, Ov. ; alii alio, Liv. ; tenes quorsum haec tendant, Pl. ; Hor. With *Inf.* : Verg., Hor., Liv., etc. With *ut* and *Subj.* : Liv. With *Intern.* Acc.: quid tendit ? Cic. **b.** Against something : magnā vi, Sall. ; summā vi, Liv. ; contra, Verg., Liv. ; adversus, Liv. ; contra (with *ut* and *Subj.*),

Liv. With *ne* and *Subj.* : Liv. With *Intern.* Acc.: nihil contra, Verg. ; Cic.

tenebrae, ārum, *f. pl. darkness.* **1.** Lit. **a.** In gen. : in tenebris, Lucr. ; cum obscurato sole tenebrae factae essent repente, Cic. ; in scalarum tenebris se abdidit, Cic. ; obtentā densantur nocte tenebrae, Verg. **b.** Of night : redire luce, non tenebris, Cic. ; Ov. ; primis tenebris (classem) movit, Liv. ; tenebris obortis, Nep. ; pulsis tenebris, Ov. **c.** Of a swoon : tenebrae oboriuntur, Pl. ; tenebris nigrescunt omnia circum, Verg. ; Ov. **d.** Of death : Prop. ; ante tenebras (i.e. night) tenebras (i.e. death) persequi, Pl. **e.** Of blindness : Lucr., Ov. **2.** Transf. **a.** *a dark, gloomy place :* clausi in tenebris, Sall. ; robur et tenebrae, Liv. ; quanti tenebras unum conducis in annum ? Juv. ; ubi sint tuae tenebrae, Cat. ; infernae, Verg. ; Hor. ; Ov. **b.** Of mind, fortune, social position, etc. : quas tu mihi tenebras cudis ? Pl. ; quae iacerent omnia in tenebris nisi lumen litterarum accederet, Cic. ; calumniae, Phaedr. ; vitae, Lucr. ; in illis rei publicae tenebris, Cic. ; si quid tenebrarum offudit exsilium, Cic. ; vestram familiam e tenebris in lucem evocavit, Cic. [Sp. *tinieblas* ; Fr. *ténèbres.*]

tenĕbrĭcōsus, a, um [tenebricus], *full of* or *shrouded in darkness, gloomy.* **1.** Lit.: popina, Cic. ; iter, Cat. **2.** Transf.: sensūs, libidines, Cic. *Sup.*: tempus, Cic.

tenĕbrĭcus, a, um [tenebrae], *dark, gloomy.* **1.** Lit.: Cic. poet. **2.** Transf.: fames, Pac.

tenĕbrōsus, a, um [tenebrae], *dark, gloomy* : Verg., Ov., etc.

Tenĕdos or **-us**, ī, *f. an island in the Aegean Sea, off the coast of Troas,* still called *Tenedos* ; **Tenĕdĭus**, a um ; **Tenĕdiī**, ōrum, *m. pl. the inhabitants.*

tenellŭlus, a, um [*dim.* tenellus], *tender little, delicate* or *dainty little :* puella tenellulo delicatior haedo, Cat.

tenellus, a, um [*dim.* tener], *dainty :* Casina, Pl. ; ungulae pullorum equorum, Varr. ; vultus, Stat.

tĕneō, tenēre, tenuī, (tentum) [perh. fr. root seen in Gk. τείνω and Lat. tendō], *to hold, hold fast, keep.* **I.** Trans. **A.** In gen. **1.** Lit.: aliquid, Pl., Verg., Liv., etc. ; aliquid in manu, Cic. ; aliquid manu, Ov., Hor., Quint. ; radicem ore, Cic. ; aliquem sinu *or* in sinu, Ov. ; colla lacertis, Ov. ; aliquem nodo, Hor. **2.** Transf. **a.** Of the mind, *to hold, comprehend, grasp :* alicuius reconditos sensūs, Cic. ; Pl. ; quo pacto cuncta tenerem, Hor. With *Indir. Quest.* : Pl., Ter., Cic. **b.** *to comprise :* haec formula reges, Hor. ; id quod (genus officiorum) teneatur hominum societate, Cic. **B.** With added idea of possession, mastery, occupation, retention, etc. **1.** Lit.: multa hereditatibus, multa emptionibus, multa dotibus tenebantur, Cic. ; quae tenuit dives Achaemenes, Hor. ; montis, Caes. ; Verg. ; colles ab exercitu tenebantur, Caes. ; collis praesidiis, Caes. ; alterum cornu, Nep. ; ea loca, Liv. ; rem

publicam, Cic.; tenente Caesare terras,
Hor.; summam imperi, Caes.; te sub
custode, Hor. Colloq. teneo te, *I have
you, I've got you,* or *I have you once again,*
Pl., Cic., Verg., etc. **2. Transf. a.** Of
the passions and desires: *to hold in bondage,
dominate* : magna me spes tenet, Cic.;
te tanta pravitas mentis, Cic.; aliquem
perniciosior libido, Sall.; dum me Galatea
tenebat, Verg.; neque irā neque gratiā
teneri, Cic.; Verg. **b.** *to hold fast, keep,
maintain* : *to hold, defend* : foedus, leges,
ordinem, statum, ius suum, consuetudinem,
etc., Cic.; morem, Cic., Verg.; tenebat
non modo auctoritatem sed etiam imperium
in suos, Cic.; causam apud centumviros,
Cic.; propositum, Caes.; silentium, Liv.;
naves cursum, Caes.; Cic.; quo iter,
Verg.; Plin. Ep. **c.** With or without
memoriā, *to remember* : eas res memoriā,
Caes.; Cic.; memoriā tenere (with Acc.
and *Inf.*), Cic.; numeros memini si verba
tenerem, Verg.; Pl.; Hor.; Quint. **C.**
Of reaching a place or attaining an objective. **1. Lit.** : montis petebant Sabini,
et pauci tenuere, Liv.; Hesperiam, Ov.;
cum navibus insulam, Tac. **2. Transf.** :
per cursum rectum regnum tenere, Cic.;
virtute regnum tenuisse, Liv. **D.** Of holding in check, restraint, etc. **1. Lit.** :
naves vento tenebantur, Caes.; aliquem,
Cic.; castris sese, Caes.; exercitum in
stativis, Liv.; se procul ab hoste intervallo, Liv.; pecus, Verg.; a te manūs,
Ov.; lacrimas, Caes.; Cic.; se intra silentium, Plin. Ep. **2. Transf.** : iracundiam,
cupiditates, somnum, Cic.; risum, Cic.,
Hor.; nec se tenuit quin etc., Cic.; se
ab accusando, Cic. Ep. Esp. by laws,
oaths, etc.: leges eum non tenent, Cic.;
Liv.; interdicto non teneri, Cic.; poenā,
Cic.; iuro iurando, Caes.; foederibus,
Liv.; in manifesto peccato teneri, Cic.
With Gen. of charge: caedis teneri,
Quint.; teneri repetundarum, Tac. **II.
Intrans.** *to hold, keep on, persist.* **1.
Lit. a.** Of a milit. position : tenent Danai
quā deficit ignis, Verg.; Cic.; Liv. **b.** Of
a course (at sea) : ab Siciliā classe ad
Laurentem agrum, Liv.; Diam, Ov.;
medio tutissimus ibis . . . inter utrumque
tene, Ov. **2. Transf.** : imber per noctem
totam tenuit, Liv.; per aliquot dies ea
consultatio tenuit, Liv.; fama tenuit
(with Acc. and *Inf.*), Liv.; nomen illud
tenet, Liv.; Ov. With *ut* or *ne* and *Subj.* :
tenuere patres ut Fabius consul crearetur,
Liv.; plebs tenuit ne consules crearentur,
Liv.

tener, era, erum. **1. Lit. a.** *soft, tender,
delicate* : terra (from being well pounded),
Cato; corpus, Lucr.; arbores, radices,
Caes.; Cic.; lanugo, Verg.; gramen,
plantae, etc., Verg.; rami, uvae, Ov.;
gallina, Hor.; virgines, Hor.; aer (perh.
yielding, or possibly as equivalent of
tenuis), Lucr., Verg. Sup. tenerrimus,
Cato; Ov. **b.** *youthful, young* (some of the
examples in l. a. may belong here): tener
et rudis, Cic.; Lucil.; equus, Cic.; vitulus,
Hor.; tener in cunis puer, Prop.; a
teneris unguiculis (i.e. from early childhood),

Cic.; so, de tenero ungui, Hor. As Noun
in phr. in teneris (i.e. in early youth),
Verg.; a tenero, Quint. **2. Transf. a.**
impressionable ; *tender, weak* : pueri animus, Cic.; mentes, Hor., Quint.; anni,
Quint., etc.; virtus in amicitiā, Cic.;
oratio, Cic.; versus, Hor.; carmen, Ov.;
pudor, Ov. Comp. : Cic. Ep., Quint.,
etc. **b.** *weak* (and *voluptuous* or *effeminate*). Of elegiac poets : Cat., Ov. Of
dancers : Cic. Of the voice : Quint.
[Fr. *tendre.*]

tenerēscō (tenerĕscō, Plin.), ere [tener],
to grow weak : in corpore tenero mens,
Lucr.

tenerē, adv. *softly* : dicere, Tac. Sup. :
Plin.

teneritās, ātis, *f.* (and **teneritūdō**, inis, *f.*
Varr., Suet.) [tener], *softness, tenderness.*
a. In gen. : brassicae, uvarum, Plin.
b. Of the *weakness* of early years : Cic.

tēnesmos, I (Acc. -on), *m.* [τεινεσμός],
a straining at stool : Nep.

tenor, ōris, *m.* [teneō], *a holding on* ; hence,
an uninterrupted course. **1. Lit.** : hasta
servat tenorem, Verg.; aulaea placido
educta tenore, Ov. **2. Transf.** : interrumpere tenorem rerum, Liv.; pugnae,
Liv.; tenore iuris nunquam intermisso,
Liv.; tenorem servant in narrationibus,
Quint.; in clementiae tenore permanere,
Suet. **Phrases** : uno tenore (i.e. uninterruptedly), Cic., Liv.; eodem tenore
(i.e. uniformly), Liv.

tēnsa, ae, *f.* the car on which the images of the
gods were carried in the Circensian games :
Cic., Liv., Suet.

tentā-, wrongly for **temptā-**.

tentīgō, inis, *f.* [tendō], *lust* : Hor., Mart.,
Juv.

tentō, wrongly for **temptō**.

tentōrium, I, *n.* [tendō], *a tent* : Hirt.,
Verg., Ov., etc.

tentus (tēnsus, Lucr., Luc., Quint.), a, um.
I. Part. tendō. **II.** Adj. *stretched out,
drawn tight, distended* : tympana, frons,
Lucr.; ubera, Hor.; collum, Quint.;
lacerti, Luc. Comp. : vox tensior, Quint.

tenuiculus, a, um [dim. tenuis], *slight, poor* :
apparatus, Cic. Ep.

tenuis (in poetry sometimes disyl.), e, *adj.*
[fr. root seen in τείνω, tendō, etc.], *thin,
fine.* **1. Lit. a.** Of texture : subtemen,
Pl.; vestes, Tib., Ov.; natura oculos
membranis tenuissimis vestivit, Cic.; toga
filo tenuissima, Ov. **b.** Of substance :
aer, caelum (opp. to crassus), Cic.; aethe-
reus locus tenuissimus est, Cic.; animae,
Ov.; pluviae, Verg.; aqua, Ov.; cauda,
Ov.; nitedula, Hor.; comae, Tib.; capilli,
Ov.; agmen, Liv.; acies, Tac. Also,
shallow : sulcus, Verg.; rima, Ov.; aqua,
Liv.; frons, Hor. **2. Transf. A.** *fine*
in technique : *delicate, refined, elaborated* :
argumentandi filum tenue, Cic.; tenui
deducta poemata filo, Hor.; oratio teres
et tenuis, Cic.; orator, Cic.; in verbis
tenuis cautusque serendis, Hor.; nec sua
plus debet tenui Verona Catullo, Mart.;
aures, Lucr.; Athenae, Mart. Also, *refined, elaborate, precise* : cura, Ov.; res
tenui sermone peractae, Hor. **B.** In

quality : *slight, trifling, poor, mean :*
oppidum, murus, victus, opes, Cic. ; praeda,
Caes. ; mensa, census, Hor. ; sermo, Cic. ;
artificium, Cic. ; gloria, Verg. ; damnum,
Tac. ; tenuissimarum rerum iura, Cic.
C. Of persons. **a.** Physically : tenuissimā
valetudine esse, Caes. **b.** Mentally : animus, Caes. ; ingenium, Quint. ; spes,
suspicio, Cic. **c.** In means or rank : Cic.,
Liv. ; adulescentes loco tenui orti, Liv. ;
mihi parva rura et spiritum Graiae tenuem
Camenae Parca dedit, Hor. *Masc. pl.*
of *Comp.* as Noun : Cic. *Sup.* : Cic.
tenuĭtās, ātis, *f.* [tenuis], *thinness, slightness.*
1. Lit. : animi, Cic. ; crurum, Phaedr. ;
caudae, sanguinis, Plin. **2.** T r a n s f. **a.**
fineness, elaborate minuteness in language
or treatment : limata tenuitas et rerum et
verborum, Cic. ; alicuius, Cic. ; Boiorum, Caes.
aerari, Cic. ; alicuius, Cic. ; Boiorum, Caes.
tenŭĭter, *adv. thinly, slightly.* **1.** Lit. **a.**
aluta confecta, Caes. **b.** *indifferently,*
poorly : Da. quid rei gerit ? Ge. sic,
tenuiter, Ter. **2.** T r a n s f. **a.** *finely,*
exactly : disserere, Cic. ; scribere, Plin. Ep.
b. *slightly, superficially :* Cic. *Sup.* : Cic.
tenŭō, āre [tenuis], *to make thin or slender ;*
to dissolve, contract. **1.** Lit. (often in *Mid.*
in poets) : adsiduo vomer tenuatur ab usu,
Ov. ; tenuatum corpus, Hor., Tac. ; artūs
in undas, Ov. ; viam vocis, Ov. ; tenuata
luna, Ov. **2.** T r a n s f. *to make small or*
trifling, to lessen, lower, etc. : iram, Ov. ;
meae culpae famam oblivia, Ov. ; magna
modis tenuare parvis, Hor.
tenus, oris, *n.* [fr. root of tendō ; *cf.* tendi-
culae], *a cord-snare, springe :* Pl.
tenus [fr. root of tendō], orig. Acc. of direction, and hence joined with GEN. ; afterwards *prep. with* ABL. : *reaching to, as far*
as, up or *down to* (always placed *after* its
case). **1.** Lit. **a.** With GEN. : labrorum
tenus, Lucr. ; crurum tenus, Verg. ; Liv. ;
urbium Corcyrae tenus, Liv. **b.** Most
freq. with ABL. : Tauro tenus, Cic. ; pectoribus tenus, Liv. ; Verg. ; Ov. ; poti faece
tenus cadi, Hor. **2.** T r a n s f. : vere
tenus, or nomine tenus *as far as the meaning*
of the word extends, in name, nominally :
veteres verbo tenus de re publicā disserē-
bant, Cic. ; Liv. ; Tac.
Teos (Teus), I, *f. a town in Ionia, birthplace*
of Anacreon ; **Tēĭus,** a, um ; **Tēĭī,** ōrum,
m. pl. its inhabitants.
tepe-făcĭō (tepĕ-, Cat.), facere, fēcī, factum,
to make moderately warm, to warm : solum,
Cic. ; flumina caede, Cat. ; ferrum acutum
in matris iugulo, Hor. In *Perf. Part.* :
Lucr., Cic., Verg.
tepĕō, ēre, *to be moderately warm.* **1.** Lit. :
dolium, Cato ; tepentes aurae, Verg. ;
ubi plus tepeant hiemes, Hor. ; sole tepente, Ov. **2.** T r a n s f. **a.** *to be warm*
or to glow (with love) : corde tepente,
Ov. With ABL. of person loved *: to be*
enamoured of : Hor. **b.** *to be lukewarm* (in
love) : Ov. Also, adfectus, Quint.
tepēscō, tepēscere, tepuī [tepeō], *to become*
moderately warm, to grow warm. **1.** Lit. :
maria agitata ventis, Cic. ; ferrum in pulmone, Verg. **2.** T r a n s f. (of emotion) *to*
grow lukewarm, cool down : mentes, Luc.

tepĭdĭus, *comp. adv. rather tepidly :* Plin. Ep.
tepĭdus, a, um [tepeō], *moderately warm,*
lukewarm, tepid. **1.** Lit. : vapor, Lucr. ;
cruor, Verg. ; ius, sol, Hor. ; lac, focus, etc.,
Ov. *Comp.* : fastigia, dies, Varr. *Sup.* :
cubiculum, Plin. Ep. **2.** T r a n s f. : tepidam recalescere mentem, Ov. ; ignes (of
love), Ov. [Fr. *tiède.*]
tepor, ōris, *m.* [tepeō], *a gentle warmth.* **1.**
Lit. **a.** Cic. ; uvae, Cic. ; solis, Liv. ;
calor ac frigus, mediique tepores, Lucr.;
Cat. **b.** *coolness, want of heat* of a bath :
Tac. **2.** T r a n s f. *coldness* of language :
Tac.
ter, *adv.* [v. trēs], *three times, thrice.* **1.**
Lit. : ter in anno, Pl., Cic. ; ter nocte,
Hor. In multiplying : ter quattuor, Enn. ;
ter centum, Verg. ; terni ter, Hor. ; Varr.
2. T r a n s f. of an indefinite number : terque quaterque, Verg. ; ter et quater, Hor.
With *Adj.* : ter felix, Ov. ; terque quaterque beati, Verg. ; ter tanto peiior, Pl.
ter-decĭēns (-ĭēs), *adv. thirteen times :* Juv. ;
HS. terdeciens, Cic.
terebinthus, ī, *f.* [τερέβινθος]. *the terebinth*
or *turpentine tree :* Verg., Plin.
terebra, ae, *f.* [v. terō], *a borer, a gimlet :*
Cato, Plin.
terebrō, āre [terebra], *to bore, bore out.* **1.**
Lit. : Cato ; telo lumen acuto, Verg. ;
buxum per rara foramina, Ov. **2.** T r a n s f.
(of wheedling) : Pl.
terēdō, inis, *f.* [v. terō], *boring-larva* or *-worm :*
Ov., Plin.
Terentĭus, a, *the name of a Roman* gens.
Esp. **I.** M. Terentius Afer, *the celebrated*
comic poet, Terence : 2nd *century,* B.C.
II. M. Terentius Varro, *a celebrated scholar,*
the contemporary of Cicero. **III.** C. Terentius Varro, *Roman consul at the battle of*
Cannae. **IV.** In *fem.* Terentia, *the wife of*
Cicero. **Terentĭānus,** a, um.
Terentus (Tar-) or **-os,** ī, *f. a place in the*
Campus Martius, *where the ludi saeculares*
were held : **Terentīnus,** a, um.
teres, etis, *adj.* [terō], *rounded off, well-*
turned, smooth. **1.** Lit. : stipites, Caes. ;
trunci arborum, Verg. ; virga, Ov. ; hastile,
Liv. ; lapillus, Ov. **2.** T r a n s f. **a.** *smooth*
and round, smoothed, polished, shapely :
cervices, Lucr. ; Verg. ; bracchiolum, Cat. ;
surae, Hor. ; membra, Suet. ; puer, Hor. ;
strophium, Cat. ; plagae, Hor. ; zona,
Ov. ; gemma, Verg. **b.** *finished off to*
perfection : oratio, Cic. ; sapiens, Hor.
c. Of taste, *polished :* Atticorum aures,
Cic. **d.** Of the voice, *smooth :* Quint.
Tēreus, eī or eos, *m. king of Thrace, husband*
of Procne, sister of Philomela ; **Tēreĭdēs,**
ae, *m. his son Itys.*
ter-gemĭnus, a, um, *v.* trigeminus.
tergĕō, tergēre (less freq. **tergō,** tergere),
tērsī, tērsum [*cf.* stringō], *to scour, scrape*
or *wipe off, wipe dry, clean, cleanse.* **1.** Lit. :
aliquid, Pl. ; fossas, Cato ; mantelio
manūs, Varr. ; manu lacrimantia lumina,
Ov. ; mensam mentae, Ov. Of burnishing
metal : arma, Liv. ; argentum, Juv. ;
with *Predic. Adj.* : levis clipeos et spicula
lucida, Verg. **2.** T r a n s f. : auris sonus
(i.e. grates upon), Lucr. ; palatum (i.e. to
smooth or " sleek down "), Hor.

terginum, I, n. [tergum], *a hide, raw-hide*, as a scourge : Pl.

tergiversātiō, ōnis, f. [tergiversor], *a declining ; a subterfuge, evasion* : Cic.

tergi-versor, ārī [tergum], *to (continually) turn one's back ;* hence, *to be shifty, to shuffle, seek an evasion* : Cic., Liv.

tergō, v. tergeō.

tergum, I **(tergus**, oris, poet. and post-Aug. prose ; tegoribus, Pl.), n. *the back* of men or animals. **1.** Lit. **a.** In gen.: Pl., Cic., Ov., etc. **b.** Phrases: terga vertere (i.e. to take to flight), Caes. ; so, terga dare, Liv., Ov. ; (transf.: iam felicior aetas terga dedit, Ov.) ; terga fugae praebere, Ov. ; terga praestare (fugae), Tac. Of position (with verbs of rest or motion) : a or ab tergo, *on* (or *in) the rear*, Caes., Cic., Liv. ; in tergo, Liv. ; post tergum (hostium), Caes. ; (transf.: omnia, quae post tergum erant, strata, Curt. ; qui iam post terga reliquit sexaginta annos, Juv.). Also, terga, *the rear* (i.e. the troops in the rear) : terga caedere, Liv. **2.** Transf. **A.** *the back* of things. **a.** Of the rear : terga collis, Liv. ; margine libri scriptus et in tergo Orestes, Juv. **b.** *a ridge :* proscisso quae suscitat aequore terga, Verg. ; Ov. **B.** For the whole body. **a.** serpens convolvens sublato pectore terga, Verg. ; horrentia centum terga suum, Verg. **b.** Of the carcase, *the chine :* perpetui tergo bovis, Verg. ; resecat de tergore (suis) partem, Ov. **C.** *the (stripped) back* or *body, the hide.* **a.** Verg., Ov., Plin. **b.** Of things made of hide or leather : venti bovis tergo inclusi (i.e. a bull's hide bag), Ov. ; duroque intendere bracchia tergo (i.e. hide boxing-gloves), Verg. ; taurea terga (i.e. a tambourine), Ov. Also of a hide-layer of a shield, Ov.

termes, itis, m. *a bough of the olive-tree :* Hor.

Terminālia, ium and iōrum, n. pl. [Terminus] *the festival of Terminus (the god of boundaries), held on the 23rd of Feb. :* Cic. Ep., Hor., Ov., Liv.

terminātiō, ōnis, f. [terminō], *a fixing of bounds.* Transf. **a.** *the decision.* With *Subj.* Gen. : aurium, Cic. With *Obj.* Gen. : Cic. **b.** *the conclusion, clausula :* Cic.

terminō, āre [terminus], *to set bounds to, mark off by boundaries, to bound, limit.* **1.** Lit.: mare terras terminat, Lucr. ; finis imperi caeli regionibus, Cic. ; fana, Liv. ; agrum publicum a privato, Liv. ; imperium Oceano, famam astris, Verg. *Impers. Pass.* (with *Indir. Quest.*) : Liv. **2.** Transf. **a.** In gen.: iisdem finibus gloriam quibus vitam, Cic. ; spem possessionum Ianiculo et Alpibus, Cic. ; sonos vocis paucis litterarum notis, Liv. ; lingua vocem, Cic. **b.** Philos. *to fix, determine, define :* summam voluptatem omnis privatione doloris, Cic. **c.** Rhet. *to end, close :* sententiam numerose, Cic. ; clausulas longā syllabā, Cic.

terminus, I, m. [cf. Gk. τέρμα], *a boundary-line, boundary, bound, limit.* **1.** Lit.: Cic. ; possessionum, Cic. ; Hor. ; templi,

Liv. ; urbis, Tac. **2.** Transf. **a.** termini egestatis, Pl. ; qui sint in amicitiā quasi termini diligendi, Cic. ; senectutis nullus est certus terminus, Cic. : (sibi) terminos constituere, pangere, Cic. ; dignitati statuere, Plin. Ep. ; nullis terminis circumscribere ius suum, Cic. **b.** Personified : **Terminus**, the god of boundaries : Hor., Liv.

terni, ae, a [v. trēs]. **I.** *a group of three, three in a group, a triad :* quid ternas litteras ? Pl. ; tres equitum turmae ternique ductores, Verg. ; milia terna, Hor. ; terni ter cyathi, Hor. In *sing. :* terno consurgunt ordine remi, Verg. **II.** *three apiece, three each :* in iugera singula ternis medimnis decidere, Cic. ; Caes. ; Verg., etc.

terō, terere, trīvī, trītum [cf. Gk. τείρω, τρίβω], *to rub, crush, wear out.* **I.** Lit. **a.** lapis lapidem, Pl. ; Plin. ; oculos, Ter. ; lumina manu, Cat. ; labellum calamo, Verg. ; unguibus herbas, Ov. **b.** Of grinding corn, crushing berries, etc.: frumentum, Varr. ; area culmos, Verg. ; Hor. ; aliquid in farinam, Plin. ; bacas trapetis, Verg. **c.** Of polishing, smoothing, whetting : oculos, Pl. ; pumice crura, Ov. ; hinc radios trivere rotis, Verg. ; dentibus (apri) in querno stipite tritis, Ov. ; vitrum torno, Plin. **d.** *to rub away, wear away by use, wear out :* navem saepe tritam, Pl. ; (tempus) rigidas silices terit, Ov. ; mucronem robigine silicem liquore, Prop. ; Hor. ; vestem, Hor. Of a road or path : angustum formica terens iter, Verg. ; Appiam (viam), Hor. ; Lucr., etc. **2.** Transf. *to use up, spend, waste.* **a.** Of time : teritur dies, Pl. ; Liv. ; tempus, Cic., Liv. ; tempus in convivio, Liv. ; omne aevum ferro, Verg. **b.** Of strength, etc.: in opere sese, Liv. ; in armis plebem, Liv. **c.** Of language : hoc verbum sermone, Cic. ; quae nomina nunc consuetudo diurna trivit (i.e. has rendered commonplace or trite), Cic. (v. also tritus).

Terpsichorē, ēs, f. (Acc. -ēn, Juv.), *the Muse of dancing ;* hence for *Muse, poetry :* Juv.

terra, ae (Gen. terrāī, Lucr.), f. [cf. torris, torreō], prop. *dry land ;* hence, *the earth, land.* **A.** As opp. to air and sea : Pl. ; terrae motūs, Cic. ; res invectae ex terrā, Cic. ; aditum habere a terrā, Caes. ; vitam in terris agere, Verg. ; sub terris, Prop. ; mei sub terras ibit imago, Verg. ; Cic. ; terrā marique, et terrā et mari, terrā ac mari, terrā mari, etc., Pl., Cic., etc. ; iter terrā petere, Cic. ; Liv. Personified : Cic., Ov., etc. **B.** *the ground, earth, soil :* Pl., Cic., Verg., etc. ; ratis terrā et aggere integere, Caes. ; terrae glaeba, Liv. ; aquam terramque petere, Liv. ; Samia terra (for pottery), Plin. ; terrā orti, Quint. ; terrae filius, Cic. Ep. **C.** *the earth,* as opp. to the rest of the universe : Cic. ; perh. occ. in phr. orbis terrae, Cic. ; orbis terrarum, Liv. (but see D.). **D.** *a land, country, region, territory :* Ter. ; terra Gallia, Caes. ; terra Italia, Liv. ; in quascumque terras, Cic. ; orbis terrarum gentiumque omnium, (v. orbis), Cic. ; Liv. ; also, orbis terrae (esp. of the Roman Empire, but see C.), Cic. ; ubi terrarum, Ter., Cic.

terrăneola, ae, *f. a crested lark :* Phaedr.

terrēnus, a, um [terra]. **I.** *earthly, terrestrial ; corpora*, Cic. ; *bestiarum terrenae sunt aliae, partim aquatiles*, Cic. **Poet.**: *eques Bellerophon*, Hor. ; *numina*, Ov. **II.** *made of earth, earthen ; tumulus*, Caes. ; *agger*, Verg., Suet. ; *colles*, Liv. **As Noun**, **terrēnum**, i, *n. land, ground :* Liv. [Fr. *terrain*.]

terreō, ēre, ui, itum [*cf.* Gk. τρέω], *to frighten, terrify, affright*. **1.** L i t. : Liv. ; *aliquem*, Caes., Cic., etc. ; *eum hominem istis exsili minis*, Cic. ; Liv. ; *territus hoste novo*, Ov. ; *aliquem ne etc.*, Hor., Liv. ; *territus animi*, Sall., Liv. **2.** T r a n s f. **a.** *to drive away by terror, to scare away :* profugam per totum terruit orbem, Ov. ; *volucris*, Hor. ; *avaras spes*, Hor. **b.** *to deter, prevent by frightening :* ut, quo minus libere hostes insequerentur, terreret, Caes. ; *ne rem committerent*, Liv. ; *aliquem metu gravioris serviti a repetendā libertate*, Sall.

terrestris, e, *adj.* [terra], *of or on the earth or land ; earth-, land- :* *pecudes*, Pl. ; *rerum caelestium atque terrestrium*, Cic. ; *archipirata*, Cic. ; *proelia, exercitus*, Nep. ; *iter*, Liv., Plin.

terreus, a, um [terra]. **I.** *of earth, earthen :* *agger*, Varr. **II.** *sprung from earth :* *progenies*, Verg.

terribilis, e, *adj.* [terreō], *frightful, dreadful :* *sonitus*, Enn., Lucr. ; *clamor*, Liv. ; *terribilis aspectu*, Cic. ; *noverca*, Ov. ; *ipsi urbi*, Liv. *Comp.* : Cic., Liv.

terricula, ōrum, *n. pl.* [terreō], *a means of frightening, a scarecrow :* Acc. ; *nullis minis, nullis terriculis se motos*, Liv. ; *sine tribuniciae potestatis terriculis*, Liv.

terrificō, āre [terrificus], *to make afraid, to terrify :* Lucr. ; *animos*, Verg.

terrificus, a, um [terreō faciō], *causing terror or awe :* *cristae*, Lucr. ; Ov. ; *vates*, Verg. ; *vaticinationes*, Plin. Ep.

terrigena, ae, *m. f.* [terra and gen in gignō], *earth-born. Of the first men :* Lucr. *Of the men who sprang from the dragon's teeth which had been sown :* Ov. *Of Typhoeus :* Ov.

terriloquus, a, um [terreō loquor], *terror-speaking :* dicta vatum, Lucr.

territō, āre [*freq.* terreō], *to frighten frequently or greatly ; to intimidate :* *aliquem verbis*, Pl. ; *aliquem metu*, Caes. ; *alias (civitates) territando, alias cohortando*, Caes. ; *urbes*, Verg. ; Liv.

territōrium, i, *n.* [terra], *the land round a town, a domain, territory :* coloniae, Cic.

terror, ōris, *m.* [terreō], *great fear, fright, dread, alarm, terror*. **1.** L i t. : Pl. ; *(alicui) terrorem iniicere, inferre, adferre, offerre, incutere*, Caes., Cic., Liv. ; *facere*, Liv. ; *aliquem in terrorem conicere*, Liv. ; *tantus terror incidit exercitui ut etc.*, Caes. ; *tantus repente terror invasit ut etc.*, Liv. ; *tantus habet pectora terror*, Verg. ; *mortis*, Cic. ; *servilis (from slaves)*, Liv. ; *externus, peregrinus*, Liv. ; *arcanus*, Tac. **2.** T r a n s f. *an object or cause of fear or dread, a terror :* esse terrori alicui, Caes. ; Liv. ; *duobus huius urbis terroribus depulsis*, Cic. ; *in omnem terrorem vultum componens*, Suet.

terrūncius, *v.* terūncius.

tersus, a, um. **I.** *Part.* tergeō. **II.** A d j. **1.** L i t. *clean, neat :* *mulier*, Pl. ; Varr. ; *plantae*, Ov. **2.** T r a n s f. *cleaned up ; hence, neat, terse :* *iudicium, auctor*, Quint. ; *opus, praefationes*, Plin. Ep. *Comp.* : Quint. *Sup.* : Stat.

tertia-decimānī, ōrum, *m. pl. (sc. milites)* [tertia decima, *sc.* legiō], *soldiers of the thirteenth (legion) :* Tac.

tertiānus, a, um [tertius], *of the third*. **A.** *recurring every second day, tertian :* febris, Cic. **As Noun**, **tertiāna**, ae, *f. (sc. febris), the tertian ague :* Plin. **B. tertiānī**, ōrum, *m. pl. (sc. milites), soldiers of the third (legion) :* Tac.

tertius, a, um [*v.* trēs], *third :* Pl., Cic., etc. ; *ab Iove tertius*, Ov. **Poet.** : *tertia regna* (i.e. the underworld), Ov. ; *so, numina*, Ov. Acc. *n.* **tertium** *as Adv. for the third time :* Cato, Cic., Liv. Abl. *n.* **tertiō**, *as Adv.* **a.** *(for) the third time :* Ter., Cic., Liv. **b.** *in the third place, thirdly :* Caes. [It. *terzo ;* Fr. *tiers*.]

tertius-decimus (-umus), a, um, *thirteenth :* Tac.

ter-ūncius (terr-), i, *m. (sc. nummus)* [ūncia]. **I.** *three-twelfths of an as, a quarter-as.* **1.** L i t. : Varr. **2.** T r a n s f. *a mere trifle :* sic in provinciā nos gerimus, ut nullus teruncius insumatur in quemquam, Cic. Ep. ; neque ridiculos terrunci (Gen. of value) faciunt, Pl. **II.** *Of inheritances, the fourth part :* heres ex teruncio, Cic. Ep.

ter-venēficus, i, *m. thrice poisoner, as a term of abuse :* Pl.

tesqua (tesca), ōrum, *n. pl. rough or wild regions, wastes, deserts :* Acc., Hor.

tessella, ae, *f.* [*dim.* tessera], *a small cube of stone :* for mosaic pavements, tables, etc. : Sen., Juv.

tessellātus, a, um [tessella], *mosaic, tessellated :* pavimenta, Suet.

tessera, ae, *f.* [perh. fr. Gk. τέσσαρες, *a, four*], *a square, square piece, cube of stone, wood, etc., for various purposes.* **a.** *a die for playing, numbered on all the six sides (cf.* talus*) :* ludere tesseris, Ter. ; se aut ad talos aut ad tesseras conferunt, Cic. ; tesseras iacere, Cic. ; mittere, Ov. ; in tesserarum prospero iactu, Liv. **b.** Milit. *a square tablet on which the watchword was written, a watchword, countersign :* tessera per castra ab Livio consule data erat, Liv. ; Verg. **c.** tessera hospitalis, *a tally, token, which was divided between two persons for mutual recognition between themselves or their descendants :* Pl. **d.** *a token, ticket, for the distribution of corn or money :* frumentariae, Suet. ; frumenti, Juv. ; nummariae, Suet. **e.** *a square block or cube, for pavements, etc. :* Plin.

tesserārius, i, *m.* [tessera], *the officer of the watch-word :* Tac.

tesserula, ae, *f.* [*dim.* tessera]. **I.** *a small square bit or cube of stone, for paving or mosaic work :* Lucil. **II.** *a voting-tablet :* Varr. **III.** *a small tally or ticket, for the distribution of corn :* Pers.

testa, ae, *f.* [fr. root seen in torreō, tostus],

a *piece of burned clay*. **1.** Lit. **a.** *a brick, tile* : Cato, Cic. **b.** *earthenware of any kind*, e.g. a pot, pitcher, lamp : Verg., Hor., Plin., etc. **c.** *a broken piece of pottery, potsherd, crock* : Ov., Plin., etc. Used by Athenians in voting : Nep. ; by the Romans in applauding : Juv. **2.** T r a n s f. **a.** *the shell* of shell-fish or of testaceous animals : Cic. Hence, *the shell-fish* : Hor. **b.** *a shell or covering*, in gen. : lubricaque immotas testa premebat aquas, Ov. **c.** Of the *skull* : Aus. **d.** *a sort of clapping* with the flat of the hands (as if with two crocks, see l. c.), in token of applause, invented by Nero : Suet. [It. *testa* ; Fr. *tête*.]

testāmentārius, a, um [testāmentum], *concerned with wills* : lex, Cic. As Noun : **testāmentārius**, I, m. *a will-forger* : Cic.

testāmentum, I, n. [testor], prop. *the declaration of one's last will* ; hence, *a will, testament* : testamentum facere, conscribere, legere, mutare, obsignare, rumpere, supponere, subicere, Cic., etc. ; inritum facere, Cic. ; resignare, Hor. ; aliquid ex testamento relinquere, Cic. ; testamento venerat (hereditas), Cic. ; testamento aliquem adoptare, Nep. ; testamento legare pecuniam, Cic.

testātiō, ōnis, f. [testor]. **I.** *a calling to witness* (usually the gods) : foederum ruptorum, Liv. **II.** *a giving evidence* : Quint.

testātor, ōris, m. [testor], *a testator* (of a will) : Suet.

testātus, a, um. **I.** P a r t. testor. **II.** A d j. in Pass. sense : *attested, published, public* : ut res quam maxime clara ac testata esse posset, Cic. ; testatum est (with *Indir. Quest.*), Cic. Ep. Comp. : ut res multorum oculis esset testatior, Cic. ; Nep.

testiculus, I, m. [dim. testis, 2], *a testicle.* **1.** Lit. : Mart., Juv. **2.** T r a n s f. *virility, manly vigour* : Pers.

testificātiō, ōnis, f. [testificor], *a giving evidence.* **1.** Lit. : eius rei, Cic. In pl. : Cic. **2.** T r a n s f. *evidence, proof* : repudiatae legationis, Cic.

testificor, ārl (*Perf. Part.* in Pass. sense : Cic., Ov.) [testis faciō], *to bear witness, give evidence, attest, vouch for.* **1.** Lit. : Cic. ; haec, Cic. With Acc. and *Inf.* : Cic., Ov. With *Indir. Quest.* : Cic. **2.** T r a n s f. **a.** In gen. *to show, publish, bring to light*, etc. : sententiam meam, Cic. Ep. ; amorem meum, Cic. Ep. ; antiquas opes, Ov. ; auctam lenitatem suam, Tac. With Acc. and *Inf.* : Tac. **b.** *to call to witness* : deos hominesque amicitiamque (with Acc. and *Inf.*), Cael. ap. Cic. Ep. ; numen Stygiae aquae, Ov.

testimōnium, I, n. [testis], *evidence, testimony, witness, deposition* (oral or written). **1.** Lit. : falsa, Pl., Liv. ; Ciceronis, Caes. ; dicere aliquid pro testimonio, Pl., Cic. ; dicere in aliquem, contra aliquem, de aliquā re, Cic. ; vocare aliquem ad testimonium, Varr. ; legite testimonia testium vestrorum, Cic. **2.** T r a n s f. *evidence, proof* : laboris sui periculique adferre, Caes. ; dare sui iudici, Cic. ; eius rei testimonium est quod etc., Caes. ; testimonio

sunt clarissimi poetae, Quint. ; Cic. [Fr. *témoin.*]

(1) testis, is, m. f. n. *a witness* (orally or in writing). **1.** Lit. : pluris est oculatus testis unus quam auriti decem, Pl. ; apud me argumenta plus quam testes valent, Cic. ; eius rei populum R. esse testem, Caes. ; vosque, dii, testis facio, Liv. ; (alicui) dare testis (in aliquam rem), Cic. ; testis citare, proferre, adhibere, producere, Cic. ; testibus uti, Caes., Cic. ; so with Acc. and *Inf.* : Caes. ; inducere testem in senatu, Suet. Of things : testis est Sicilia, Cic. ; quid debeas, o Roma, Neronibus, testis Metaurum flumen, Hor. ; Ter. ; Prop. **2.** T r a n s f. *an eye-witness, spectator* : Messana libidinum, Cic. ; vulnera, Ov. ; lunā testo moventur, Juv.

(2) testis, is, m. *a testicle* : Pl., Hor., Plin.

testor, ārl [testis]. **I.** *to be a witness, to testify, depose.* **1.** Lit. : Ov., Quint. *Perf. Part.* in Pass. sense : nomen testatas intulit in tabulas, Cat. ; testata est voce praeconis libertas Argivorum, Liv. **2.** T r a n s f. **a.** In gen. *to make known, show, prove, vouch for* : auctoritatem huius indici monumentis publicis, Cic. ; suos gemitu dolores, Ov. (With things as Subject : campus sepulcris proelia, Mor. ; verba nos gratos, Ov. ; in *Pass.* : Catonis oratione testatum est, Quint.) With Acc. and *Inf.* : Cic. With *Indir. Quest.* : Liv. **b.** *to make a will* : Liv., Quint. With Acc. and *Inf.* : Quint. **II.** *to invoke as witness* : Venus, testem te testor mihi, Pl. ; vos, dii patrii ac penates, testor (with Acc. and *Inf.*), Cic. ; vos, aeterni ignes et non violabile vestrum testor numen, Verg. ; id testor Deos, Ter. ; Cic. ; alicuius indulgentiam, Cic.

testū, ABL. n. (Cato, Ov.), also **testō** (Cato, Verg., Plin.), and Acc. **testum** (Cato) [cf. testa], *an earthenware lid or pot with a lid.*

testūdineus, a, um [testūdō]. **I.** *of a tortoise* : gradus, Pl. **II.** *made of tortoise-shell* : lyra, Prop. ; conopeum, Juv.

testūdō, inis, f. [testa], *a tortoise.* **1.** Lit. : Pac., Cic., Liv. **2.** T r a n s f. **A.** *tortoise-shell* : Cic., Verg., Ov. **B.** Of things arched like a tortoise-shell. **a.** *a lyre, lute, cithern* : Verg., Hor. **b.** *an arch, vault* in buildings : Cic., Varr., Verg. **c.** M i l i t. *a covering, shed for besiegers* : Caes. Also formed by interlocked shields : Caes., Verg., Liv., Tac. **d.** *the armour-spines* of a hedgehog : Mart.

testula, ae, f. [dim. testa], *a voting-sherd* (ὄστρακον), used at Athens : Nep.

testum, v. testū.

tēte, v. tū.

tēter, v. taeter.

Tēthys, yos, f. *a sea-goddess, wife of Oceanus, and mother of the sea-nymphs and river-gods.* Transf. *the sea* : Ov.

tetradrachmum (tetrachmum, Liv.), I, n. [τετράδραχμον], *a silver coin of four drachmas* among the Greeks : Cass. ap. Cic. Ep.

tetraō, ōnis, m. [τετράων], *a black-cock, grouse*, or perh. *capercailzie* : Plin., Suet.

tetrarchēs, ae, m. [τετράρχης], *a ruler of the fourth part of a country, a tetrarch* ; in gen. *a petty prince* : Cic., Caes., Hor., etc.

tetrarchia, ae, f. [τετραρχία], *the dominions of a tetrarch ; a tetrarchy :* Cic.

tētrē, v. taetrē.

Tetrica, ae, f. *a rocky mountain in the Sabine territory.*

tetricus, a, um [perh. fr. Tetrica], *forbidding, gloomy, sour :* puella, Ov. ; Sabinae, Ov. ; tetrica ac tristis disciplina Sabinorum, Liv.

tetulī, v. ferō.

Teucer (**Teucrus**), crī, m. **I.** *son of Telamon, king of Salamis, and brother of Ajax.* **II.** *son of Scamander of Crete, son-in-law of Dardanus, and afterwards king of Troy ;* **Teucrus**, a, um ; **Teucri**, ōrum, m. *pl. the Trojans ;* **Teucria**, ae, f. *the Trojan country, Troy.*

Teuthrās, antis, m. *an ancient king of Mysia, father of Thespius ;* **Teuthrantēus**, a, um, *Mysian ;* **Teuthrantius**, a, um : turba, *the fifty daughters of Thespius,* Ov.

Teutoni, ōrum (**Teutonēs**, um), m. *pl. the Teutons, a German race ;* **Teutonicus**, a, um.

texō, texore, texui, textum, *to weave.* **1.** Lit. **a.** telam, Ter. ; tegimenta corporum vel texta vel suta, Cic. ; vestis, Tib. ; aranea telam, Cat. **b.** Of basket-work, etc.: *to plait* (mostly *to make by plaiting*) : rubeā texatur fiscina virgā, Verg. ; cratis, Hor. ; parietem lento vimine, Ov. ; texendae saepes, Verg. ; harundine hibernacula, Liv. ; varios flores, Ov. **2.** Transf. **a.** *to fabricate, build* (*in layers or checkerfashion*) : basilicam columnis, Cic. Ep. ; robore navis, Verg. **b.** *to weave, compose, devise :* sermones longos, Pl. ; epistulas cottidianis verbis, Cic. Ep. ; (opus) quod tua texuerunt scripta, Ov. [Fr. *tisser.*]

textilis, e, adj. [texō], *woven, wrought :* tegmen, picturae, Lucr. ; stragulum, Cic. ; dona, Verg. As Noun, **textile**, is, n. (*sc.* opus), *a woven fabric :* Cic., Liv.

textor, ōris, m. [texō], *a weaver :* Pl., Hor., etc.

textrinum, ī, n. (*sc.* opus) [textor], *weaving :* Cic.

textrix, īcis, f. [texō], *a* (*female*) *weaver :* Tib., Mart.

textūra, ae, f. [texō], *a web, texture.* **1.** Lit.: aranearum, Pl. ; Minervae, Prop. **2.** Transf. of any fabric : (naturae animi), Lucr. ; laterum, Luc.

textus, a, um. **I.** Part. texō. **II.** Noun, **textum**, ī, n. *woven cloth, a web.* **1.** Lit.: pretiosa texta, Ov. **2.** Transf. of any fabric made in layers or plaited : pinea texta carinae, Cat. ; Ov. ; non enarrabile clipei textum, Verg. ; forrea, Lucr.

textus, ūs, m. [texō], *texture, tissue.* **1.** Lit.: haec sunt tenuia textu, Lucr. ; Plin. **2.** Transf. of language : Quint.

Thāis, idis, f. *a celebrated courtesan of Athens.*

thalamēgus, ī, f. [θαλαμηγός], *a statebarge fitted up with cabins :* Suet.

thalamus, ī, m. [θάλαμος]. **1.** Lit. **a.** *woman's room :* Verg., Ov. **b.** *a sleepingroom of a woman or of husband and wife :* Verg., Ov. **2.** Transf. **a.** *marriage-bed :* Prop. **b.** *marriage, wedlock :* Verg., Ov. In *pl.* : Verg., Hor., Ov.

thalassicus, a, um [θαλασσικός], *sea-green :* colos, Pl.

thalassinus, a, um [θαλάσσινος], *sea-green :* vestis, Lucr.

Thalēs, is and ētis (Acc. Thalem, Thalēn, and Thalētem), m. *a celebrated Greek philosopher of Miletus, one of the Seven Sages, born about 610 B.C.*

Thalia, ae, f. **I.** *the Muse of Comedy.* **II.** *a sea-nymph.*

thallus, ī, m. [θαλλός], *a green stalk, green bough :* Verg.

Thamyrās, ae, and **Thamyris**, idis, m. *a Thracian poet who entered into a contest with the Muses, and, being vanquished, was deprived of his sight.*

Thapsus or **-os**, ī, f. **I.** *a city in Sicily.* **II.** *a city in Africa, where Caesar defeated the Pompeians,* B.C. 46; **Thapsitāni**, ōrum, m. *pl. the inhabitants.*

Thasus, or **-os**, ī, f. *an island in the Aegean Sea, off the coast of Thrace, now Thaso ;* **Thasius**, a, um.

Thaumās, antis, m., f. of Iris ; **Thaumantēus**, a, um, **Thaumantias**, adis, f. ; **Thaumantis**, idis, f. *Iris.*

theātrālis, e, adj. [theātrum], *of or in a theatre, theatrical :* theatrales gladiatoriique consessūs, Cic. ; operae, Tac. ; lascivia, Tac. Transf.: humanitas (i.e. makebelieve), Quint.

theātrum, ī, n. [θέατρον], *a place for seeing a show or public spectacle of any kind, a play-house, theatre.* **1.** Lit.: Verg. Usually of a built theatre : Caes., Cic., Verg., Hor., etc. Of the Greek theatre, used for public meetings : Cic., Liv., Tac. **2.** Transf. **a.** *a theatrical audience :* Cic., Quint. In *pl.* : Cic., Hor., Quint. **b.** *a field, theatre for any public act or display :* nullum theatrum virtuti conscientiā maius est, Cic. ; quasi in aliquo terrarum orbis theatro versari, Cic. ; Curt.

Thēbae, ārum (**Thēbē**, ēs), f. *pl. Thebes.* **I.** *a very ancient and celebrated city in Upper Egypt ;* **Thēbaeus**, a, um, and **Thēbaei**, ōrum, m. *pl. its inhabitants.* **II.** *the capital of Boeotia, one of the most ancient cities in Greece, founded by Cadmus ;* **Thēbānus**, a, um. **Thēbāni**, ōrum, m. *pl. the Thebans ;* **Thēbais**, idis, f. adj. : *pl.* **Thēbaides**, *the women of Thebes.* **III.** *a city in Mysia, destroyed by Achilles ;* **Thēbāna**, ae, f. *Andromache, the daughter of Eetion, king of Thebes in Mysia.*

thēca, ae, f. [θήκη], *a thing or place for putting or storing, a case, envelope :* vasorum, Cic. ; calamaria, Suet. ; Mart.

thema, atis, n. [θέμα], **I.** *a subject or topic treated of, a theme :* Sen., Quint. **II.** *the position of the celestial signs at one's birth, a nativity, horoscope :* Suet.

Themis, idis, f. *the goddess of justice and of prophecy.*

Themistoclēs, ī and is, m. *a celebrated Athenian statesman and general ;* **Themistoclēus**, a, um.

thēsaurārius, a, um [thēsaurus, v. thēsaurus], *of treasure :* fures, Pl.

Thēsaurochrȳsonicochrȳsidēs, ae, m. *a comic patronymic :* Pl.

thēsaurus, v. thēsaurus.

Theocritus, ĭ, m. *the founder of Greek pastoral poetry* (3rd cent. B.C.); *born at Syracuse.*

theologus, ĭ, m. [θεολόγος], *one who treats of the Deity and of divine things, a theologian :* Cic.

Theon, ŏnis, m. *a notoriously sarcastic person referred to by Horace ;* **Theoninus**, a, um.

Theopompus, ĭ, m. *a Greek historian and orator, pupil of Isocrates ;* **Theopompēus** or **-ĭnus**, a, um.

Therapnae, ārum, f. pl. *a town in Laconia, the birthplace of Helen ;* **Therapnaeus**, a, um, *Spartan.*

thermae, ārum, f. pl. (sc. aquae)[θερμὰ ὕδατα], *warm springs, warm baths* (natural or artificial) : Plin., Mart., etc.

Thermōdōn, ontis, m. *a small river of Pontus, on which dwelt the Amazons ;* **Thermōdontēus, Thermōdontiacus**, a, um, *Amazonian.*

thermopōlium, ĭ, n. [θερμοπώλιον], *a place where warm drinks were sold :* Pl.

thermopōtō, āre [Gk. θερμοποτεῖν], *to flush with warm drink :* gutturem, Pl.

Thermopylae, ārum, f. pl. *a famous pass between Mt. Oeta and the sea, defended by Leonidas,* B.C. 490.

thermulae, ārum, f. [dim. thermae], *a little warm bath :* Mart.

Thērodamās, antis, m. *a Scythian king, who fed lions with human flesh ;* **Thērodamantēus**, a, um.

Thersītēs, ae, m. *a Greek before Troy, distinguished for ugliness and scurrility.*

thēsaurārius, v. thēns-.

Thēsaurochrȳsonicochrȳsidēs, v. Thēns-.

thēsaurus (older **thēnsaurus**), ĭ, m. [θησαυρός]. **I.** *a store-house.* **1.** Lit.: Liv. Of the cells of bees : Verg. **2.** Transf.: Pl. ; rerum omnium memoria, Cic. : Quint. **II.** *a store, hoard, treasure.* **1.** Lit.: Pl., Cic., Hor., etc. **2.** Transf.: thensaurus mali, Pl. [It. Sp. *tesoro;* Fr. *trésor.*]

Thēseus (disyl.), eī and eos, m. *king of Athens, s. of Aegeus and Aethra ; h. of Ariadna* (whom he abandoned), *and afterwards of Phaedra ; f. of Hippolytus, friend of Pirithous ; conqueror of the Minotaur ;* **Thēsēus**, a, um, **Thēsēius**, a, um ; **Thēsīdēs**, ae, m. *a male descendant of Theseus, esp. Hippolytus ;* **Thēsīdae**, ārum, m. pl. *the Athenians.*

thesis, is, f. [θέσις]. Rhet. *a proposition, thesis* (pure Latin, propositum) : Quint.

Thespiae, ārum, f. pl. *an ancient town in Boeotia ;* **Thespius**, a, um ; **Thespiēnsēs**, ium, m. pl. *its inhabitants ;* **Thespias**, adis, f. adj. *Thespian ;* **Thespiades**, um, f. pl. *the Muses* (Thespiae being situated at the foot of Helicon).

Thespis, is, m. *the founder of Greek tragedy,* 6th cent. B.C.

Thessalia, ae, f. *the most northerly district of Greece ;* **Thessalicus, Thessalus**, a, um ; **Thessalis**, idis, f. adj. ; **Thessalī**, ōrum, m. pl. *the Thessalians.*

Thestius, ĭ, m. *king of Aetolia, f. of Leda and Althaea ;* **Thestiadēs**, ae, m. *a male descendant of Thestius ;* **Thestias**, adis, f., d. of Thestias, i.e. Althaea.

Thestor, oris, m. f. of Calchas ; **Thestoridēs**, ae, m. Calchas.

Thetis, idis or idos (Abl. Thetide and Thetī) f. *a sea-nymph, d. of Nereus and Doris, w. of Peleus, and m. of Achilles.*

Thia, ae, f. w. of Hyperion, und m. of Sol.

thiasus, ĭ, m. [θίασος], *a Bacchic troop :* Cat., Verg.

Thisbē, ēs, f. **I.** *a small town of Boeotia ;* **Thisbaeus**, a, um. **II.** *a maiden of Babylon, loved by Pyramus.*

Thoās, antis, m. **I.** *king of Tauris, slain by Orestes ;* **Thoantēus**, a, um. **II.** *a king of Lemnos, father of Hypsipyle ;* **Thoantias**, adis, f. Hypsipyle.

tholus, ĭ, m. [θόλος], *a round building with a dome or cupola* (esp. as part of a temple) : Varr., Verg., Ov.

thōrāx, ācis, m. [θώραξ], *a breast-plate, cuirass :* Verg., Liv., etc.

Thrāca, ae, **Thrācē**, ēs, and **Thrācia**, ae, f. *an extensive country to the N. of the Aegean ;* **Thrācius**, a, um, **Thrēicius**, a, um, **Thrāx**, ācis, m., and **Thrēissa** or **Thrēssa**, ae, f. *Thracian ;* **Thrāx** and **Thrēx**, also, *a kind of gladiator, so called from his Thracian equipment;* **Thrēcidicus**, a, um ; **Thrēcidica**, ōrum, n. pl. *arms of a Threx.*

Thrasea, ae, m. : P. Thrasea Paetus, *a distinguished Roman senator and Stoic philosopher, put to death by Nero.*

Thrasymachus, ĭ, m. *a celebrated Greek sophist of Chalcedon.*

thronus, ĭ, m. [θρόνος], *an elevated seat, a throne :* Iovis, Plin.

Thūcȳdidēs, is, m. *the celebrated Greek historian ;* **Thūcȳdidīus**, a, um ; **Thūcȳdidiī**, ōrum, m. pl. *Thucydideans, imitators of Thucydides.*

Thūlē (or **Thȳlē**), ēs, f. *an island in the extreme north of Europe* (Iceland, or one of the Shetland Islands).

thunnus, v. thynnus.

Thūriī, ōrum, m. pl. *a city of Lucania, on the Tarentine Gulf, near the site of Sybaris ;* **Thūrīnus**, a, um ; **Thūrīnī**, ōrum, m. pl. *the Thurians.*

thūs, thūr-, v. tūs, tūr-.

thȳa or **thȳia**, ae, f. [θύα or θυία], *the citrus-tree :* Plin.

Thȳēnē, ēs, f. *a nymph who nursed Jupiter and Bacchus.*

Thyestēs, ae, m., s. of Pelops, b. of Atreus, *who set before him for food the flesh of his own son ; father of Aegisthus ;* **Thyestēus**, a, um ; **Thyestiadēs**, ae, m. Aegisthus.

Thȳias (disyl.) or **Thȳas**, adis, f. *a Bacchante.*

Thymbra, ae, or **Thymbrē**, ēs, f. *a city in Troas, with a temple of Apollo ;* **Thymbraeus**, ĭ, m. *epithet of Apollo.*

thymbra, ae, f. [θύμβρα], *a plant, savory :* Verg.

thymum, ĭ, n. [θύμον], *thyme :* Verg., Hor., Ov., Plin. In pl. : Ov., Mart.

Thȳnī, ōrum, m. pl. *a Thracian people, who emigrated to Bithynia ;* **Thȳnus**, a, um, *Bithynian* (Hor.) ; **Thȳnia**, ae, f. *their country ;* **Thȳniacus**, a, um ; **Thȳnias**, adis, f. adj. *Bithynian.*

thynnus, ĭ, m. [θύννος], *the tunny-fish :* Hor., Ov., Plin.

Thyŏnē, ēs, *f.*, *m. of the fifth Bacchus ;* **Thyōneus** (trisyl.), eī, *m. Bacchus.* Transf. *wine :* Cat.

Thyrē, ēs, *f. a town in the Peloponnesus, the possession of which was contested by the Argives and the Lacedemonians ;* **Thyreātis**, idis, *f. adj.*

Thyrsis, idis, *m. the name of a shepherd in* Verg.

thyrsus, ī, *m.* [θύρσος], *a stalk, stem of a plant.* **A.** In gen. : Plin., Suet. **B.** *a Bacchic wand or staff twined round with tendrils of vine and ivy and surmounted with a fir-cone.* **1.** Lit. : Hor., Ov. **2.** Transf. *an incitement, goad :* Lucr., Ov.

tiāra, ae, *f.*, or **tiārās**, ae, *m.* [τιάρα or τιάρας], *the head-dress of Orientals, a turban, tiara :* Pl., Verg., Ov., Sen.

Tiberis, is, also contr. **Tibris (Thybris)**, is or idis (Acc. Tiberim, Tibrim and -in) *m. the Tiber ;* **Tiberīnus**, a, um ; **Tiberinus**, ī, *m. the river-god of the Tiber ;* **Tiberinis**, idis, *f. adj.*

Tiberius, ī, *m. a Roman praenomen* (abbrev. Ti.). Esp. *the Emperor Tiberius,* Tiberius Claudius Nero Caesar ; **Tiberius**, **Tiberiānus**, a, um.

tibia, ae, *f. the shin-bone, tibia.* **1.** Lit. : Phaedr., Plin. Ep. **2.** Transf. *a pipe, flute* (orig. made of bone) : Pl., Lucr., Cic., Verg., etc.

tibiālis, e, *adj.* [tibia]. **I.** *of the shin-bone.* As Noun, **tibiāle**, is, *n. a stocking or legging :* Suet. **II.** *used for flutes :* harundo tibialis calami, Plin.

tibicen, inis, *m.* and **tibīcina**, ae, *f.* : Pl., Hor., Ov., etc.) [tibia canō], *a flute-player.* **1.** Lit. : Pl., Cic., Hor. etc. **2.** Transf. *a kind of pillar or prop of a building :* Cat., Ov., Juv.

Tibullus, ī, *m.* : Albius, *a celebrated Roman elegiac poet, born about* B.C. 65, *a contemporary and friend of Ovid and Horace.*

Tibur, uris, *n. an ancient town of Latium on the Anio, now Tivoli, founded by a colony from Argos under Tiburtus ;* **Tiburs**, urtis, *adj.,* also *n. noun* (ABL. Tiburti or Tiburte) *the Tiburtine territory ;* **Tiburtēs**, um, *m. the Tiburtines ;* **Tiburtīnus**, **Tiburnus**, a, um ; **Tiburnus**, ī, *m. an inhabitant of Tibur* (Stat.) ; also = Tiburtus, *founder of Tibur.*

Tigellīnus, ī, *m. the most hated of Nero's favourites.*

Tigellius, ī, *m.* : Hermogenes, *a censurer of Horace.*

tigillum, ī, *n.* [*dim.* tignum], *a little beam or log of wood :* Pl., Cat., Tib., Liv.

tignārius, a, um [tignum], *working on beams :* faber, Cic.

tignum, ī, *n.* [*cf.* τέκτων *and* texō], *building-stuff ;* hence, *a piece of timber, a trunk of a tree, a log, beam :* Pl., Lucr., Caes., Ov., etc.

tigris, is or idis, *f.* (occ. *m.* in prose) [τίγρις (in Persian, *an arrow* : Varr.)]. **1.** Lit. : *a tiger, tigress :* Varr., Verg., Hor., Ov., etc. **2.** Transf. *a tiger-skin as a horse's trappings :* Stat.

Tigris, is or idis, *m. a large river of western Asia, east of the Euphrates, which joins it.*

tilia, ae, *f. the linden or lime-tree :* Verg., Ov.

Timaeus, ī, *m.* **I.** *a Greek historian of Sicily, under Agathocles.* **II.** *a Pythagorean philosopher, a contemporary of Plato ; whence the name of one of Plato's dialogues.*

Timāgenēs, is, *m. a learned rhetorician in the time of Augustus.*

Timāvus, ī, *m. a river in Histria.*

timefactus, a, um [timeō faciō], *frightened, alarmed :* religiones, Lucr. ; libertas, Cic.

timēns, entis. **I.** Part. timeō. **II.** Adj. *fearful* (with GEN.) : mortis, Lucr. **III.** *Masc. pl.* as Noun : Caes.

timeō, ēre, uī, *to fear, be afraid, to dread :* Pl., Caes., Cic., etc. With *de* (*about, concerning*) : Cic. ; so, with *Intern.* Acc. : de suo periculo nihil, Caes. ; Liv. With *pro* : Ov., Curt., Plin. Ep. ; so, with *Intern.* Acc. : plus pro te, Sen. ; Cic. Ep. With DAT. of the person or thing *for whom* or *for which* : Ter., Caes., Verg., Hor. ; so, *Impers. Pass.* : Luc. With Acc. of the source of fear) : Pl., Caes., Cic., Hor., Ov., etc. With *Inf.* : Caes., Hor., Ov., etc. With Acc. and *Inf.* : Liv. With *Indir. Quest.* : Pl., Ter., Cic., Liv. With *ne* or *ne non* (less freq. *ut*) : timeo ne hoc propalam fiat, Pl. ; Caes., Cic. ; timuit ne non succederet, Hor. ; Curt. ; ut supportari posset (res frumentaria) timere dicebant, Caes. [It. *temere ;* Sp. *temer.*]

timidē, *adv. fearfully, timidly :* Caes., Cic., Hor., Ov. Comp. : Caes., Cic. Sup. : Quint.

timiditās, ātis, *f.* [timidus], *fearfulness, cowardice, timidity :* Pac., Cic., Suet. In *pl.* : Cic.

timidus, a, um [timeō], *fearful, faint-hearted, cowardly :* Cic. ; in labore militari, Cic. Ep. ; ad mortem, Cic. With GEN. : procellae, Hor. ; deorum, Ov. ; Sen. With *Inf.* : Hor. Of *Impers.* Subject : metus, Enn. ; animus, Cic. ; spes, amor, fides, cursus, preces, navis, Ov. Comp. : Cic. Ep., Varr. Sup. : Ov.

timor, ōris, *m.* [timeō], *fear, dread, alarm.* **1.** Lit. : timor praepedit dicta linguae, Pl. ; timor omnem exercitum occupavit, Caes. ; prae timore concidere, Pl. ; timore de aliquo adfici, Cic. Ep. ; res quae mihi facit terrorem, Cic. Ep. ; timore perterritus, Cic. ; aliquem in timorem dare, Pl. ; (alicui) timorem inicere, incutere, Cic. ; in timore esse, Liv. ; alicui timorem eripere, deicere, Cic. ; timorem omittere, Cic. ; abicere, Cic. Ep. ; timore sublato, Caes. ; so ex timore conligere, Caes. With *ab* (of source of fear) : Liv. With *ne* and *Subj.* : Verg., Liv. With Acc. and *Inf.* : Cic., Liv. With *Obj.* GEN. : Caes., Cic., Lucr., Ov. In *pl.* : Lucr., Cat., Cic., Hor. **2.** Transf. *an object that excites fear, a terror* : Cacus Aventinae timor silvae, Ov. ; Hor., etc. **b.** Personified, *Fear* : Verg., Hor. In *pl.* : Ov.

tinctilis, e, *adj.* [tingō], *in which something is dipped :* virus, Ov.

tinctus, a, um. **I.** Part. tingō. **II.** Noun, **tincta**, ōrum, *n. pl.* dyed or coloured stuffs : Cic.

tinea, ae, *f. a grub or gnawing worm* of any kind: agrestes, Ov. Of the *larva* or "*moth*" in clothes: Cato, Hor., Ov. In books: Hor. In beehives: Verg. In the human body: Plin.

tingō, tingere, tinxĭ, tinctum [*cf.* Gk. τέγγω], *to wet, dip, soak.* **1.** L i t. **a.** In gen.: tunicam sanguine, Cic.; aera lacu, Verg.; pavimentum mero, Hor.; gemmam lacrimis, Ov.; in amne comas, Prop.; Ov.; pedes, Plin.; Ov. **b.** Of dyeing: lanas murice, Hor., Ov.; ora cruore, Ov. **2.** T r a n s f. **a.** Of the moon: globus candenti lumine tinctus, Lucr. **b.** orator tinctus litteris, Cic.; sales lepore Attico tincti, Mart.; verba sensu tincta, Quint. [It. *tingere*; Fr. *teindre.*]

tinnimentum, ĭ, *n.* [tinniō], *a tinkling:* Pl.

tinniō, īre, *to ring, tinkle.* **1.** L i t.: hastilibus umbo, Enn.; tintinnabulum, Pl. With Acc.: aes, Varr.; exspecto maxime, ecquid Dolabella tinniat (i.e. is inclined to pay), Cic. Ep. **2.** T r a n s f. of a shrill voice: nimium tinnis, Pl.; canorā voce, Pl.; aliquid (i.e. trill, sing), Suet.

tinnītus, ūs, *m.* [tinniō], *a ringing, jingling, tinkling* of metals, etc. **1.** L i t. (often in *pl.*): Verg., Ov., Sen., etc. **2.** T r a n s f. of language: Gallionis, Tac.

tinnŭlus, a, um [tinniō], *ringing, tinkling, shrill-sounding.* **1.** L i t.: sistra, Ov.; vox, Cat. **2.** T r a n s f. of speakers: *jingling, full of empty phrases:* Quint.

tintinnābŭlum, ĭ, *n.* [tintinnō], *a bell;* e.g. a door-bell, call-bell, cattle-bell: Pl., Plin., Juv., etc.

tintinnāculus, a, um [tintinnō], *jingling. Masc.* as Noun: educi ad tintinnaculos (i.e. either the chain-gang or the fasteners of the chains), Pl.

tintinō (tintinnō), āre [tinniō], *to ring:* compedes, Naev.; sonitu suopte tintinant aures, Cat.

tīnus, ĭ, *f. the laurustinus:* Ov., Plin.

Tīphys, yos (Voc. Tiphy), *m. the pilot of the Argo.*

tippŭla, ae, *f. a water-fly, water-spider:* Pl., Varr.

Tīrĕsiās, ae, *m. a celebrated blind soothsayer of Thebes.*

Tīridātēs, ae, *m. the name of several kings of Armenia.*

Tīrō, ōnis, *m. a learned slave and afterwards freedman of Cicero;* **Tīrōniānus,** a, um.

tīrō, ōnis, *m. a young soldier, recruit.* **1.** L i t.: Caes., Cic., etc. In apposition: tirones milites, Cic.; exercitus, Cic. Ep., Liv. **2.** T r a n s f. of any beginner: usu forensi atque exercitatione tiro, Cic.; in foro, Quint.; deductus in forum tiro, Suet.; bos, Varr.

tīrōcĭnium, ĭ, *n.* [tirō], *the first military service, inexperience in soldiering.* **1.** L i t.: Liv. **2.** T r a n s f. **a.** Collectively: *a body of young troops, raw recruits:* Liv. **b.** *a beginning, a first trial:* in L. Paulo accusando tirocinium ponere, Liv.; malo tirocinio imbuere Samnitem, Liv.; tirocinii metum transire, Quint.; dies tirocinii, Suet.

tīrunculus, ĭ, *m.* [*dim.* tirō], *a young beginner:* Sen. Ep., Juv., Plin. Ep. In apposition: miles, Suet.

Tīryns, Tirynthis or os, *f. a town in Argos,* one of the most ancient in Greece, where Hercules was brought up; **Tīrynthius,** a, um, esp. as epithet of Hercules.

tis, old GEN. of tū: Pl.

Tīsamĕnus, ĭ, *m. son of Orestes and king of Argos.*

Tīsĭphonē, ēs, *f. the Avenger of Blood; one of the Furies;* **Tīsĭphonēus,** a, um.

Tītānes, um or **Tītāni,** ōrum, *m. pl.* (in *sing.* **Tītān,** ānis, or **Tītānus,** ĭ), *the sons of Uranus (Heaven) and Ge (Earth); they rebelled against and dethroned their father and put Cronus on the throne of heaven. Their names were Oceanus, Coeus, Creius, Hyperion, Iapetus,* and *Cronus. Also of anyone of Titanian race,* e.g. *Prometheus* and *the old Sun-god (Helios or Sol);* **Tītānis,** a, um; **Tītānis,** ae, *f.:* (i.) *Latona,* as daughter of the Titan Coeus. (ii.) *Pyrrha,* as descendant of Prometheus. (iii.) *Diana,* as sister of Sol. (iv.) *Circe,* as daughter of Sol. **Tītāniacus,** a, um; **Tītānis,** idis or idos, *adj. f.;* **Tītānis,** idis, *f. a female Titan, Titaness:* e.g. *Circe* or *Tethys,* as sister of Sol.

Tīthōnus, ĭ, *m. son of Laomedon, consort of Aurora; endowed with immortality, but changed after reaching a decrepit old age into a grasshopper;* **Tīthōnius,** a, um; **Tīthōnia,** ae, *f. Aurora.*

Tĭtĭēs, ium, and **Tĭtĭēnsēs,** ium, *m. one of the three original Roman tribes:* see also **Tatius.**

tĭtillātĭō, ōnis, *f.* [titillō], *a tickling:* non est voluptatum quasi titillatio in senibus, Cic.

tĭtillō, āre, *to tickle, titillate.* **1.** L i t.: sensūs, Lucr.; sensūs quasi titillare, Cic. **2.** T r a n s f.: ne vos titillet gloria, Hor.; macrorem, Sen. Ep. In *Mid.,* or *Act. Intrans. to amuse oneself:* Sen. Ep.

tĭtĭvillĭtĭum, ĭ, *n. a very small trifle, a bagatelle:* Pl.

tĭtŭbanter, *adv. falteringly:* Cic.

tĭtŭbantia, ae, *f.* [titubō], *a staggering, faltering.* T r a n s f.: linguae (i.e. stammering), Suet.

tĭtŭbātĭō, ōnis, *f.* [titubō], *a staggering.* **1.** L i t.: Sen. Ep. **2.** T r a n s f.: Cic.

tĭtŭbō, āre, *to stagger, totter, reel.* **1.** L i t.: titubans annis meroque, Ov.; pes, Phaedr. *Perf. Part.* in *Act.* sense: vestigia titubata, Verg. **2.** T r a n s f. **a.** Of speech: lingua, Ov. **b.** *to falter, waver:* Pl., Nep., Hor.; verbo, Cic.; animus, Pl. With *Intern.* Acc.: ne quid titubet, Pl.; nihil, Cic. Ep. Hence, in *Pass.:* si quid forte titubatum est, Cic. Ep.; Pl. *Impers. Pass.:* Cic.

tĭtŭlus, ĭ, *m. a superscription, inscription, label, notice, advertisement* or *bill of sale,* etc. **1.** L i t.: aram condidit dedicavitque cum ingenti rerum ab se gestarum titulo, Liv.; ascribere humatis titulum, Liv.; sepulcri, Juv.; Plin. Ep.; titulum inscribere (with Acc. and *Inf.*), Liv.; quorum titulus per barbara colla pependit, Prop.; sub titulum nostros misit avara lares, Ov.; Plin. Ep.; libelli, Ov.; Quint.; cumque ducum titulus oppida capta legat, Ov. **2.** T r a n s f. **a.** *an honourable appellation, title of honour:* sustinere titulum consulatūs, Cic.; stupet in titulis et imaginibus, Hor.; Ov. **b.** *repute, renown* : par titulo tantae gloriae fuit, Liv.; Stat.; prioris perpetrati belli, Liv. **c.** *a cause or reason alleged, a pretext* : praetendere titulum belli, Liv.; sub titulo aequandarum legum, Liv.; aliquid accipere foedissimo titulo, Plin. Ep. [It. *titolo* ; Fr. *titre*.]

Tityos, yĭ, *m. a giant, slain by Apollo for insulting Latona, and cast into Tartarus.*

Tityrus, ĭ, *m. the name of a shepherd in Vergil's Eclogues* ; *sometimes identified with Vergil himself.*

Tlēpolemus, ĭ, *m.*, *s. of Hercules.*

Tmaros or **-us**, ĭ, *m. a mountain in Epirus.*

Tmōlus, and poet. **Timōlus**, ĭ, *m. a mountain of Lydia in which the Pactolus rises, producing excellent wines* ; **Tmōlius**, a, um ; **Tmōlitēs**, is, *m. adj.*

tocullō, ōnis, *m.* [τόκος, *usury*], *a usurer* : Cic. Ep.

tōfīnus, a, um [tōfus], *of tufa* : metae (circi), Suet.

tōfus (**tōphus**), ĭ, *m. tufa* or *tuff-stone* (a variety of volcanic rock of an earthy texture): Verg., Ov., Plin. [It. *tufo*; Fr. *tuf*.]

toga, ae, *f.* [tegō], *a covering, garment.* **1.** Lit. **a.** In gen. : Varr., Mart. **b.** *the outer garment of a Roman citizen in time of peace* : Cic., Hor., etc. ; toga praetexta, *the toga of magistrates and freeborn children, bordered with purple* (v. praetextus), Cic. ; pura or virilis, *the plain toga of youth who had laid aside the* praetexta, Cic., Liv., etc. ; so, libera, Prop. ; picta, *the embroidered toga of a* triumphator, Liv. ; candida, *the toga worn by candidates for office, with the wool artificially whitened,* Liv. ; pulla, *the dark-grey toga of mourners,* Cic. **2.** Transf. **a.** For peace : cedant arma togae, Cic. poet. **b.** For Roman nationality : et nominis et togae oblitus, Hor. **c.** For a scortum : Tib.

togātārius, ĭ, *m.* [togātus], *an actor in the* fabula togata : Suet.

togātus, a, um [toga], *wearing a toga.* **A.** In gen. : Cic., Verg., Liv., etc. As Noun, **togātī**, ōrum, *m. pl. Roman citizens* : Cic., Liv. **togāta**, ae, *f.* **a.** (*sc.* fabula), *the national* (*Roman*) *drama* (treating of Roman subjects): Cic., Hor., etc. **b.** *a prostitute* (as *wearing the* toga): Hor. **B.** *in a civil* (opp. to *a military*) *office* ; cui non togato supplicationem (senatus) decreverit, Cic. **C.** Contemptuously of the *clientes* at Rome : turba, Juv. ; opera, Mart. As Noun, **togātus**, ĭ, *m. a humble client* : Juv.

togula, ae, *f.* [dim. toga], *a little toga* : Cic., Mart.

tolerābilis, e, *adj.* [tolerō]. **A.** Pass. *bearable, endurable* : condicio servitutis, Cic. ; oratores, Cic. ; non tolerabile numen, Verg. ; Minucius vix tolerabilis, Liv. Comp. : Cic. ; tolerabilius est (with *Inf.*), Liv. **B.** Act. *readily endurant, patient* : Ter.

tolerābilius, comp. adv. *more* or *fairly patiently* : dolores tolerabilius pati, Cic.

tolerāns, antis. **I.** Part. tolerō. **II.** Adj. *bearing, enduring* (with Gen.): corpus laborum, Tac.

toleranter, *adv. patiently* : Cic.

tolerantia, ae, *f.* [tolerō], *a bearing, endurance* (with *Obj.* Gen.): Cic., Tac., etc.

tolerātiō, ōnis, *f.* [tolerō], *a bearing, endurance* : dolorum, Cic.

tolerātū, Abl. *sing. m.* [tolerō], *in the enduring* : difficile toleratu, Cic.

tolerātus, a, um. **I.** *Part.* tolerō. **II.** Adj. *endurable, tolerable.* Comp. : Tac.

tolerō, āre [*cf.* Gk. τλῆναι and tollō], *to bear, support, endure.* **1.** Lit. : pondus, Plin. **2.** Transf. **a.** *to support, maintain by food, money, etc.* : his rationibus equitatum, Caes. ; equos, Caes. ; Tac. ; vitam, Caes., Verg. ; aevum, Lucr. ; egestatem, Pl. ; famem, Caes. ; inopiam, Sall. Also, erum servos ne pessum abeat, Pl. **b.** *to hold out* (*against*), *to endure* : Caes. ; hiemem, Cic. ; labores, pericula, etc., Sall. ; aequo animo servitutem, Sall. ; sitim aestumque, Tac. ; vaporis vim, Ov. ; Ter. ; *Impers. Pass.* : Tac. With *Inf.* : Tac. With Acc. and *Inf.* : Enn., Sall.

tollēnō, ōnis, *m.* [tollō], *a swing-beam, a swipe* or *" shadoof,"* e.g. to raise a water-bucket from a well, or to raise great weights like *a crane* : Pl., Liv.

tollō, tollere, sustulī, sublātum [forms from sufferō], *to lift up, raise up, etc.* **1.** Lit. **A.** In gen. : me iacentem, Pl. ; Cic. ; te in collum, Pl. ; aliquem in equum, in crucem, in caelum, Cic. ; in arduos tollor (*Mid.*) Sabinos, Hor. ; caput, gradum, Pl. ; manūs, Cic. ; pectus coluber, Verg. ; fulgor ad caelum se, Lucr. ; aquila in sublime sustulit testudinem, Phaedr. ; se tollere a terrā, Cic. ; de terrā, Cic. ; terrā, Ov. **B.** *to take up,* i.e. *to accept, acknowledge,* and so, *to bring up, educate* as one's own (*cf.* suscipio) : puellam, Ter. Also of the mother : si quod peperissem, id educarem ac tollerem, Pl. Hence in gen. *to have* a child : qui ex Fadiā sustulerit liberos, Cic. **C.** Nautical. *to* tollere ancoras, *to weigh anchor* : Caes., Liv. **b.** *to take on board, carry* : navis metretas trecentas, Pl. ; navis ducentos ex legione, Caes. ; tollite me, Teucri, Verg. ; se in lembum, Liv. Also on to a carriage : me raedā, Hor. ; te in currūs, Ov. **2.** Transf. **A.** In gen. : tollitur in caelum clamor, Enn., Verg. ; clamor tollitur, Cic. ; clamor se tollit ad auras, Verg. ; risum, Hor. ; animos, Pl., Ter., Liv. ; animos alicui (i.e. *to animate*), Liv. ; amicum (i.e. *to cheer up*), Hor. ; aliquem laudibus ad caelum, Cic. ; Verg. ; supra modum se tollens oratio, Quint. **B.** *to take up* a thing from its place, *to take away, remove* : praedam, Caes. ; mensam, Cic. ; pocula, Verg. ; frumentum de areā, Cic. ; pecunias e fano, Caes. ; Cic. ; me per hostīs, Hor. Milit. : signa (i.e. *to move camp*), Caes. **C.** *to take up* or *away* (and so destroy), *to remove, do away with.* **a.** aliquem de medio, Cic. ; aliquem e medio, Liv. ; aliquem ferro, veneno, Cic. ; Titanas fulmino, Hor. ; Carthaginem funditus, Cic. **b.** *to abolish, cancel, etc.* : leges, metum, deos, etc., Cic. ; rei memoriam, Cic. ; querellas,

Hor.; dictaturam funditus ex re publică, Cic.

tolūtim, *adv.* [fr. root of tollō; prop. *lifting up the feet*], *at a trot, full trot* : Pl., Varr.

tomāculum, or contr., **tomāclum**, i. *n.* [Gk. τομή], *a kind of sausage* : Mart., Juv.

tōmentum, i, *n. a stuffing* for cushions (e.g. of wool, feathers, etc.) : Varr., Tac.

Tomi, ōrum, *m. pl.* and **Tomis**, is, *f. a town of Moesia, on the Euxine, to which Ovid was banished* ; **Tomitae**, ōrum, *m. pl. its inhabitants* ; **Tomītānus**, a, um.

Tomyris, is, *f. a Scythian Queen, by whom the elder Cyrus was defeated.*

tonāns, antis. **I.** *Part.* tonō. **II.** Noun, *the thunderer* (an epithet of several deities, esp. of Jupiter) : Ov., Mart.

tondeō, tondēre, totondi, tōnsum [*cf.* τέμνω], *to clip, shear, shave, etc.* **A.** Of hair and wool. **1.** Lit.: Cic. ; barbam et capillum, Cic. ; Pl. ; Verg., etc. ; lanam, Hor. ; ovem, Pl., Verg., etc. ; os, Cat. ; cutem, Hor. **2.** Transf. *to fleece* (i.e. to plunder) ; aliquem auro usque ad cutem, Pl. ; Prop. **B.** Of trees, *to clip, prune* : bracchia (vineti), Verg. ; ilicem bipennibus, Hor. ; myrtos, Quint. **C.** Of meadows and fields. **a.** *to mow, reap* : arida prata, Verg. ; tonsas novalis, Verg. ; segetem, Tib. Of flowers : comam hyacinthi, Verg. **b.** *to browse* or *graze* or *to crop* : gramina (pecudes), Lucr. ; dumeta (iuvenci), Verg.

tonitrālis, e, *adj.* [tonitrus], *thunderous* : templa caeli, Lucr.

tonitrus, ūs, *m.* (Lucr., Verg., Plin. ; and in *pl.* : Liv., Ov., etc.) and **tonitruum**, i, *n.* (Plin. ; and in *pl.* : Cic., Ov., Plin.) [tonō], *thunder.* In *pl.* : *claps of thunder.* [Fr. *tonnerre.*]

tonō, āre, ui, itum, *to thunder.* **1.** Lit. (mostly *Impers.* or with Iuppiter, caelum, etc., as Subject) : Pl., Cic., Verg., etc. **2.** Transf. **a.** Of any loud noise : tympana tenta tonant, Lucr. ; Aetna ruinis, Verg. ; Pericles fulgere, tonare, dictus est, Cic. **b.** With Acc. of the thing uttered : verba foro, Prop. ; ter centum tonat ore deos (i.e. in invoking), Verg. [Fr. *tonner.*]

tōnsilis, e. *adj.* [tondeō]. **I.** *that can be clipped* or *shorn* : villus, Plin. **II.** *clipped, cut* : buxetum, Mart. ; Plin.

tōnsillae, arum, *f. pl. the tonsils* in the throat : Cic.

tōnsitō, āre [*freq.* tondeō], *to repeat the shearing of* : ter in anno ovis, Pl.

tōnsor, ōris, *m.* [tondeō], *a shearer, barber, shaver* : Pl., Cic., Hor., etc.

tōnsōrius, a, um [tōnsor], *used in shearing* or *shaving* : culter, Cic. ; Mart.

tōnstricula, ae, *f.* [*dim.* tōnstrix], *a little female hair-cutter* or *barber* : Cic.

tōnstrina, ae, *f.* [tondeō], *a barber's shop* : Pl., Plin.

tōnstrix, icis, *f.* [tondeō], *a female hair-cutter* or *barber* : Pl., Mart.

tōnsūra, ae, *f.* [tondeō], *a shearing, clipping* : capillorum, Ov. ; vitis, Plin. In *pl.* : Varr.

tōnsus, a, um. **I.** *Part.* tondeō. **II.** Noun, **tōnsa**, ae, *f. an oar-blade* : Enn. In *pl.* : Enn., Lucr., Verg.

tōnsus, ūs, *m.* [tondeō], *the cut or mode of dressing the hair, coiffure* : Pl.

tonus, i, *m.* [τόνος], *the sound, tone* of an instrument. Transf. of colour, *tone* : Plin.

tōph-, *v.* tōf-.

topiārius, a, um [τόπος], *of* or *belonging to* (ornamental) *gardening* : opus, Plin. As Noun, **topiārius**, i, *m. an ornamental gardener* : Cic. Ep., Plin. Ep. **topiāria**, ae, *f.* (*sc.* ars), *ornamental gardening* : Cic. Ep.

topica, ōrum, *n. pl.* [τοπικά], *the title of a work of Aristotle, of which Cicero made an abridgment* : Cic. Ep.

topicē, ēs, *f.* [τοπική], *the art of finding topics* : Cic.

topper, *adv.* [tōtō opere], *with all diligence, speedily* : Enn., Acc.

toral, ālis, *n.* [torus], *a valance of a couch* : Hor.

torcular, āris, *n.* [torqueō]. **I.** *a* (*wine- or oil-*) *press* : Plin. **II.** *an oil-cellar* : Plin.

torculārius, a, um [torcular], *of a press* : vasa, Varr. As Noun, **torculārium**, i, *n. a press* : Cato ; Plin.

torculus, a, um [*cf.* torcular], *of a press* : vasa, funis, Cato. As Noun, **torculum**, i, *n. a press* : Varr., Plin., Plin. Ep.

toreuma, atis, *n.* [τόρευμα], *work executed in relief, embossed work* : Cic., Sall., Mart.

tormentum, i, *n.* [torqueō]. **A.** In gen.: Caes. **B.** *a windlass* specially equipped for hurling missiles ; in *pl. a siege-train* (including catapulta, scorpio, and bullista). **1.** Lit.: tormentis missa tela, Hirt. ; Caes. ; telorum, Cic. ; bellica, Liv. **2.** Transf. **a.** cum omnibus machinis ac tormentis oppugnari (i.e. politically), Cic. **b.** *a bolt* or *shot* from the tormentum : tormenta mittere, Caes. ; e navibus excutere, Curt. **c.** Comic. (for a chain) : ferreum, Pl. **C.** *a rack for torture* ; and *torture* in gen. **1.** Lit.: omnibus tormentis excruciatas interficiunt, Caes. ; verberibus ac tormentis quaestionem habere, Cic. **2.** Transf. (mentally). **a.** Of an inducement : lene tormentum ingenio admovere, Hor. **b.** *torture, pangs* : tormenta fortunae, Cic. ; invidiā non maius tormentum, Hor. ; tormentis gaudet amantis, Juv. ; cruciatūs et tormenta pati, Plin. Ep.

tormina, um, *n. pl.* [torqueō], *a griping of the bowels, colic* : Cato ; Cic.

torminōsus, a, um [tormina], *subject to colic* : Cic.

tornō, āre [tornus], *to turn in a lathe, to round off.* **1.** Lit.: sphaeram, Cic. **2.** Transf.: male tornati versūs, Hor. [Fr. *tourner.*]

tornus, i, *m.* [τόρνος]. **I.** *a turner's wheel, lathe.* **1.** Lit.: Lucr., Verg., Plin. **2.** Transf.: angusto versūs includere torno, Prop. **II.** *a burin, a graving-tool* : Verg.

torōsus, a, um [torus], *muscular, brawny* : colla boum, Ov.

torpēdō, inis, *f.* [torpeō]. **I.** *numbness, sluggishness, lethargy* : Cato ; occupavit vos torpedo, Sall. ; animos obrepsit, Sall. ; torpedo invaserat animum,

Tac. **II.** *the torpedo, cramp-fish,* or *electric ray :* Cic.

torpeō, ēre, *to be numb* or *benumbed, inactive, sluggish.* **1.** Lit. : torpentes gelu, Liv. ; torpent infractae ad proelia vires, Verg. ; oculi, Quint. ; vox spiritusque, Liv. ; amnis torpens, Stat. ; lacus, Stat. ; palatum, Juv. **2.** T r a n s f. **a.** Mentally : timore, Pl. ; metu, Liv. ; desperatione, Curt. ; Pausiacā torpes tabellā (i.e. of admiration), Hor. ; cessatione, Cic. **b.** Of things : consilia re subitā, Liv. ; regna gravi veterno, Verg.

torpēscō, torpēscere, torpuī, [torpeō], *to grow numb* or *listless.* **1.** Lit. : dextrae, Liv. ; lingua retenta metu, Ov. **2.** Transf. : ne per otium torpescerent manūs aut animus, Sall. ; deliciis et desidiā, Tac.

torpidus, a, um [torpeō], *benumbed, stupefied :* somno, Liv.

torpor, ōris, *m.* [torpeō], *numbness, sluggishness.* **1.** Lit. : Cic., Verg., Ov. **2.** Transf. (mental) : Sen. Ep., Luc., Tac.

torquātus, a, um [torquis], *adorned with a neck-chain* or *collar :* Allecto torquata colubris, Ov. ; palumbus, Mart.

Torquātus, ī, *m. :* T. Manlius, *so called from the chain-collar which he took from a Gaul whom he slew ; a surname in the gens Manlia.*

torqueō, torquēre, torsī, tortum, *to turn, twist, wind, wrench.* **A.** In gen. **1.** Lit. : terra circum axem se torquet, Cic. ; serpens squamosos orbis, Ov. ; cervices oculosque, Cic. ; ora, Cic., Verg. ; oculos ad moenia, Verg. ; ab obscenis sermonibus aurem, Hor. ; capillos ferro (i.e. to crimp or wave), Ov. ; taxos in arcūs, Verg. ; remis aquas, Ov. ; spumas, Verg. **2.** T r a n s f. : suam naturam (sententias, Tac.) huc et illuc torquere, Cic. ; cuncta tuo qui bella, pater, sub numine torques, Verg. ; omnia ad suae causae commodum, Cic. **B.** Of javelins, etc. : *to whirl, hurl, fling with force.* **1.** Lit. : verbera fundae, Verg. ; lapidem machina, Hor. ; amentatas hastas lacertis, Cic. ; tela manu, Ov. ; iaculum in hostem, Verg. ; fulmina Iuppiter, Verg. **2.** T r a n s f. : curvum sermone rotato enthymema, Juv. **C.** Of torturing on the rack, etc. : *to rack, wrench.* **1.** Lit. : eculeo torqueri, Cic. ; Pl. ; aliquem servilem in modum, Suet. **2.** T r a n s f. **a.** Of moral torture (*cf.* tormentum) : aliquem mero, Hor. **b.** Mentally : tuae libidines te torquent, Cic. ; malorum memoriā torqueri, Cic. ; invidiā vel amore vigil torquebere, Hor. ; torqueor (with *ne* and *Subj.*), Hor. [Fr. *tordre.*]

torquis or **torquēs,** is, *m.* and *f.* [torqueō], *a twisted neck-chain, necklace, collar.* **1.** Lit. : Cic., Hor., Liv., Ov. **2.** T r a n s f. **a.** *a coupling-collar* for oxen : Verg. **b.** *a festoon :* Verg., Plin.

torrēns, entis *f.* **I.** *Part.* torreō. **II.** Adj. *burning.* **1.** Lit. : pice torrentis ripas, Verg. ; flammis ambit torrentibus amnis, Verg. *Sup.* : Stat. **2.** T r a n s f. *seething.* **a.** Of streams : Varr., Verg., etc. *Comp. :* Plin. *Sup. :* Stat. **b.** T r a n s f. of speech : oratio, Quint. ; copia dicendi, Juv. ;

Demosthenes, Juv. *Comp. :* Juv. **III.** Noun, **torrēns,** entis, *m. a seething stream, a torrent.* **1.** Lit. : Cic., Verg., etc. **2.** T r a n s f. : se inani verborum torrenti dare, Quint. ; Tac.

torreō, torrēre, torruī, tostum, *to parch, roast, scorch, burn, etc.* **1.** Lit. : me pro pane, Pl. ; cum undique flammā torrerentur, Caes. ; fruges flammis, Verg. ; in Phalaridis tauro inclusus torreri, Cic. ; Gallorum corpora sol, Caes. ; torrentia agros sidera, Hor. ; exta in veribus, Verg. **2.** T r a n s f. **a.** Of fever-heat : at mihi, vae miserae, torrentur febribus artūs, Ov. ; Sen. Ep. **b.** Of love : si torrere iecur quaeris idoneum (Venus), Hor. ; me amor Glycerae, Hor. ; Ov. **c.** Of cold : frigore, Varr.

torrēscō, ere [torreō], *to become parched* or *burned :* flammis, Lucr.

torridus, a, um [torreō], *parched, baked, dried up.* **1.** Lit. : tellus, Lucr. ; campi siccitate, Liv. ; farra, Ov. ; fontes, Liv. ; aer, Prop. ; zona ab igni, Verg. ; homo macie torridus, Cic. P o e t. : aestas (perh. causatively, *parching*), Verg. **2.** T r a n s f. of cold : iumenta torrida frigore, Liv.

torris, is, *m.* [torreō], *a brand, fire-brand :* Verg., Ov.

tortē, *adv. crookedly, awry :* Lucr.

tortilis, e, *adj.* [torqueō], *twisted, winding, spiral :* aurum, Verg. ; bucina, Ov. ; pampinus, Plin.

tortō, āre [*freq.* torqueō]. In *Pass. to writhe in torture :* vulnere, Lucr.

tortor, ōris, *m.* [torqueō]. **I.** *torturer :* Cic., Hor., etc. **II.** *a wielder.* **1.** Lit. : habenae, Luc. **2.** T r a n s f. : occultum quatiente animo tortore flagellum, Juv.

tortuōsus, a, um [tortus], *full of crooks* or *turns, winding.* **1.** Lit. : alvus, loca, serrula, Cic. ; amnis, Liv. *Comp. :* Plin. **2.** T r a n s f. *tortuous, involved :* ingenium, Cic. ; genus disputandi, Cic.

tortus, a, um. **I.** *Part.* torqueō. **II.** Adj. *twisted, crooked.* **1.** Lit. : quercus, Verg. ; via (Labyrinthi), Prop. **2.** T r a n s f. *complicated* (or *dubious*) : condiciones, Pl. [Fr. *tort.*]

tortus, ūs, *m.* [torqueō], *a twisting.* **a.** *writhing :* serpens longos fugiens dat corpore tortūs, Verg. ; Cic. poet. **b.** *a twirling, whirling* of a sling : Stat.

torulus, ī, *m.* [*dim.* torus], *a tuft* of hair : Pl., Varr.

torus, ī, *m.* prop. *any protuberance.* **I.** *a knot, bulge :* (funis), Cato. **II.** *the muscular* or *fleshy part, the muscle, brawn* of animal bodies (mostly in *pl.*) : Cic. poet., Verg., Ov., Plin. **III.** *a raised ornament, a boss, knot,* on a garland. T r a n s f. of language : Cic. **IV.** *a mattress ; a bed, couch* of any kind : Verg., Ov., Plin., Tac. **V.** *a knoll, mound* of earth : riparum toros, Verg. ; pulvinorum, Plin.

torvitās, ātis, *f.* [torvus], *grimness, savageness :* Plin. ; vultūs, Tac.

torvus (-os), a, um, orig. of the look : *fierce, grim, savage :* oculi, Ov. ; lumine torvo Aetnaeos fratres, Verg. ; vultus, Hor., Sen. ; frons, Verg. ; Medusa, Ov. ; leaena, Verg. ; taurus, Ov. Also, proelia, Cat. *Neut.*

Intern. Acc.: torva tuens, Verg.; torvum clamat, Verg.

tostus, a, um, *Part.* torreō.

tot, *indecl. adj.* [from I. E. pronoun-stem ta], *so many.* **a.** Simply: tot civitatum coniuratio, Caes.; Pl.; Cic.; Ov., etc.; tot et tantae et tam graves civitates, Cic. Rarely as Noun: Cic., Ov. **b.** With a corresponding *quot* or (less freq.) *quotiens* (*-ies*), or *ut :* quot homines, tot causae, Cic.; Ov., etc.; tot . . . quotiens, Cic.; tot vestigiis impressa ut (with *Subj.*), Cic. Ep.

totidem, *indecl. adj.* [tot and -dem seen in idem, etc.], *just so many, just as many.* **a.** Simply: equitum milia erant sex, totidem numero pedites, Caes.; Cic.; Ov., etc. Rarely as Noun: Hor. **b.** With corresponding *quot :* quot orationum genera esse diximus, totidem oratorum reperiuntur, Cic.; Pl., etc.

totiēns or **totiēs**, *adv.* [tot], *so many times, so often.* **a.** Simply: Cic., Verg., etc.; ter die claro totiensque gratā nocto, Hor. **b.** With corresponding *quotiens* (*-ies*) or *quot :* totiens quotiens praescribitur Pacu-nem citare, Cic.; quotienscumque dico totiens mihi videor etc., Cic.; moverat eum subeunda dimicatio totiens quot coniurati superessent, Liv.

tōtus, a, um (GEN. tōtius, but tōtius, Lucr.; DAT. tōti; but *m.* tōtō exercitui, Caes.; tōtō orbi, Prop.; *f.* tōtae familiae, Pl.), *the whole, entire.* **A.** In gen.: pervigilat totas noctis, Pl.; unum opus, totum atque perfectum, Cic.; totum corpus rei publicae, Cic.; totā nocte continenter ierunt, Caes.; urbe totā, totā Italiā, Cic.; toto in orbe terrarum, Liv.; qui esset totus ex fraude factus, Cic. **B.** Of persons: *wholly taken up with* or *devoted to :* nescio quid meditans nugarum, totus in illis, Hor.; Pl.; totus et monte et animo in bellum insistit, Caes.; Philippus totus in Persea versus, Liv. **C.** *Neut., the whole matter, all :* totum in eo est, tectorium ut concinnum sit, Cic. Ep. **D.** Adv. phr.: **ex tōtō**, *wholly, totally:* Ov., Sen., etc. **in tōtō**, *upon the whole, in general :* Cic. Ep. **in tōtum**, *wholly, totally :* Plin., Sen., etc. [It. *tutto ;* Sp. *todo ;* Fr. *tout.*]

toxicum, i, *n.* [τοξικόν], orig. *a poison in which arrows were dipped :* Ov. Hence, in gen. *poison :* Pl., Hor., Suet. In *pl. :* Prop., Ov.

trabālis, e, *adj.* [trabs]. **I.** *of* or *for beams, beam- :* clavus, Cic., Hor. **II.** Poet.: trabale telum, *stout as a beam*, Enn., Verg.

trabea, ae, *f. a robe of state* of augurs, kings, knights, etc. **1.** Lit.: Verg., Ov., Suet. **2.** Transf. *the equestrian order :* Stat., Mart.

trabeātus, a, um [trabea], *wearing a trabea :* Quirinus, Ov.; equites, Tac. As Noun, **trabeāta** (*sc.* fabula), *a drama with exalted characters :* Suet.

trabs (**trabēs**, Enn.), trabis, *f. a beam, a timber.* **1.** Lit.: Lucr., Caes., Ov. **2.** Transf. **A.** (growing) *timber, a tree :* Ov. In *pl. :* fraxineae, Verg.; silva frequens trabibus, Ov. **B.** *Anything made of beams* or *timbers.* **a.** Of a ship: abiegna,

Enn.; Hor.; mare turbari trabibus vide-bis, Verg. **b.** *a roof :* sub trabe citreā, Hor. In *pl. :* Hor. **c.** *a battering-ram :* Val. Fl. **d.** *a shaft of a spear :* Stat. **e.** *a cudgel, club :* Stat. **f.** *a table :* Mart.

Trāchās, antis, *f. another name of the town usually called Tarracina, near the Pomptine Marshes.*

Trāchin, inis, or **Trāchyn**, ȳnos, *f. a town of Thessaly on Mount Oeta, where Hercules burned himself :* **Trāchinius**, a, um ; **Trāchinis**, i, *m. Ceyx, king of Trachin ;* **Trāchiniae**, ārum, *f. pl. the Trachinian Women, a tragedy of Sophocles.*

tractābilis, e, *adj.* [tractō], *that can be touched* or *handled, manageable, tractable.* **1.** Lit.: Cic., Stat.; mare nondum tract-abile nanti, Ov.; non tractabile caelum (i.e. stormy), Verg.; vox, Quint. **2.** Transf.: virtus in amicitiā, Cic.; (nec) voces ullas tractabilis audit, Verg.; animus arte, Ov. *Comp. :* Cic. Ep., Suet.

tractātiō, ōnis, *f.* [tractō], *a handling, management, treatment.* **1.** Lit.: armorum, tibiarum, beluarum, Cic. **2.** Transf. **a.** litterarum, philosophiae, Cic.; usus et tractatio dicendi, Cic. **b.** *Of the treatment of a person :* mala, Quint. **c.** Rhet. *a special usage* of a word : Cic.

tractātus, ūs, *m.* [tractō], *a touching, handling, management.* **1.** Lit.: nucum, Plin. **2.** Transf. **a.** artium, Cic.; trop-orum, Quint. In *pl. :* legales, Quint. **b.** *a treatise :* Plin.

tractim, *adv.* [tractus], *by drawing along,* i.e. *little by little, slowly :* Pl.; ire, Lucr.; susurrare, Verg.; dicere, Sen. Ep.

tractō, āre [*freq.* trahō]. **I.** *to drag about* or *with violence, to maul :* Hectorem sic, Enn.; malis morsuque ferarum, Lucr.; comis antistitam Phoebi, Ov. **II.** *to handle, wield, deal with, work up, manage.* **1.** Lit.: aliquid manibus, Pl.; gubernacula, Cic.; pellem, Verg.; ceram pollice, Ov.; unotis calicem manibus, Hor.; consona fila lyrae, Ov.; tela, Liv.; res igni, Lucr.; solum terrae aere, Lucr.; bibliothecen, Cic. Ep.; pecuniam publicam, Cic. **2.** Transf. **a.** rem suam, Pl.; causas amico-rum, Cic.; condiciones, Caes., Liv.; bellum, Liv.; proeliorum vias, Tac.; consilia de libertate, Liv.; personam in scaenā, Cic.; partis secundas, Hor.; vitam more ferarum, Lucr. With *de :* de con-dicionibus, Nep.; *Impers. Pass. :* do religionibus tractabatur, Tac. With *Indir. Quest. :* Quint., Tac.; *Impers. Pass. :* Quint. **b.** *Of persons : to treat, deal with* or *conduct oneself towards :* pater parum pie tractatus a filio, Cic.; pauloque benig-nius ipsum se tractare voles, Hor.; Pl. [Fr. *traiter.*]

tractus, a, um. **I.** *Part.* trahō. **II.** Adj. *proceeding continuously, flowing, fluent,* of language : Cic. **III.** Noun, **tractum**, i, *n.* **a.** *a long piece of dough :* Cato. **b.** *a flock of wool drawn out for spinning :* Tib.

tractus, ūs, *m.* [trahō], *a drawing, dragging.* **I.** Abstract (mostly in ABL.). **1.** Lit.: harenam fluctus trahunt; Syrtos ab tractu nominatae, Sall.; tractu gementem rotam, Verg.; in spiram tractu se conligit anguis, Verg. Of *drawing* a letter: Prop. **2.** T r a n s f. *a drawing out, extension :* verborum, Cic.; belli, Tac.; illa (historia) tractu placet, Plin. Ep. **II. C o n c r e t e. A.** Of a line: *a trail, track, course.* **1.** L i t.: vides longos flammarum ducere tractūs, Lucr.; Verg.; (Phaëthon) longo per aëra tractu fertur, Ov.; of the moon, Cic.; arborum, Nep. **2.** T r a n s f.: aevi, Lucr.; orationis, Cic. **B.** Of a space. **a.** *extent, tract, distance :* urbis, Cic.; castrorum, Liv.; immensis tractibus Alpes, Luc. **b.** *district, region :* oppidi, Caes.; Venafranus, Cic.; Verg.; Hor.; corruptus caeli tractus, Verg. [Fr. *trait.*]

trădĭtĭō, ōnis, *f.* [trādō], *a handing over, surrender.* **1.** L i t.: urbis, Liv. **2.** T r a n s f. **a.** Of instruction: Quint. **b.** Of a record or account: supremorum, Tac. [Fr. *trahison.*]

trădĭtor, ōris, *m.* [trādō] (for the more usual proditor), *a betrayer, traitor :* Tac. [Fr. *traître.*]

trā-dō (**trānsdo** sometimes in Caes.), dere, didī, ditum [trāns dō], *to put or hand over, to convey, deliver, surrender.* **1.** L i t. **a.** In gen.: aliquid in manum, Pl.; mihi istuc argentum, Pl.; poculum alicui, Cic.; equum comiti, Verg.; testamentum tibi legendum, Hor.; arma per manūs, Caes.; arma, Caes.; urbem, Liv.; Capuam in manum hostibus, Liv.; se hostibus, Caes.; se in omnis cruciatūs, Liv. **b.** For shelter, protection, marriage, imprisonment, etc.: in tuam custodiam meque et meas spes, Pl.; sic ei te commendavi et tradidi, Cic. Ep.; Hor.; hos (obsides) Aeduis custodiendos tradit, Caes.; Liv.; filiam alicui, Tac.; hunc ad carnuficem, Pl.; aliquem in custodiam vel in pistrinum, Cic. Ep.; aliquem supplicio, Suet. **c.** Treacherously: *to betray* (less freq. than prodo): aliquem, Cic.; penatīs, Ov.; causam advorsariis, Ter. **2.** T r a n s f. **a.** In gen.: meam partem loquendi tibi, Pl.; summam imperi Aulerco, Caes.; liberam possessionem Galliae sibi, Caes.; aliquid memoriae, Cic. With Acc. of Object and *Inf.* : tristitiam portare ventis, Hor. **b.** With *Refl. Pron.* : se quieti, Cic.; Plin. Ep.; se totos voluptatibus, Cic. **c.** As an inheritance, record, memory, etc.: regnum alicui, Pl.; consuetudo a maioribus tradita, Cic.; traditum inde feritur ut eto., Liv.; pugnae memoriam posteris, Liv.; Socratis ingenium immortalitati scriptis suis Plato tradidit, Cic. With Acc. and *Inf.* : ipsum regem tradunt operatum his sacris se abdidisse, Liv.; so, traditur memoriae, Liv.; so, traditur, Cic. Also personally in *Pass.* with Nom. and *Inf.* : Aristides unus omnium iustissimus fuisse traditur, Cic. **d.** By teaching: multa de sideribus disputant et iuventuti transdunt, Caes.; praecepta dicendi, Cic.; Caes.; virtutem hominibus, Cic. [Fr. *trahir.*]

trā-dūcō (**trānsdūcō**), dūcere, dūxī, ductum (*Imperat.* trādūce, Ter.) [trāns dūcō], *to lead, bring across or over, to transfer.* **1.** L i t. **A.** In gen.:. huc ad nos uxorem

tuam, Pl.; cohortis ad se in castra, Caes.; exercitum ex Galliā in Ligures, Liv.; hominum multitudinem trans Rhenum in Galliam, Caes.; regem Antiochum in Europam, Liv.; per finis Sequanorum copias, Caes. With Abl. of the route: legiones Alpibus, Tac.; Hirt. F r e q. with double Acc., or in *Pass.* with one Acc.: copias flumen, Caes.; Liv.; traductus exercitus silvam Ciminiam, Liv. **B.** *to parade* in public. **a.** traducere equum (of a knight who passed muster at the inspection by the censor), Cic.; victimas in triumpho, Liv. **b.** In disgrace: traducti sub iugum et per hostium oculos, Liv.; vestros liberos traductos per ora hominum, Liv.; delatores flagellis caesi ac traducti per amphitheatri harenam, Suet. **2.** T r a n s f. **A.** In gen.: centuriones ex inferioribus ordinibus in superiores ordines, Caes.; ad plebem P. Clodium, Cic. Ep.; hominem ad optimatis, Cic. Ep.; me ad suam sententiam, Cic.; animos iudicum a severitate ad hilaritatem, Cic. **B.** *to parade, display* in public. **a.** se Ulixem ancipitem, Juv. **b.** In disgrace: libidinem, Sen. Ep.; Juv.; rideris multoque magis traduceris, Mart. **C.** Of time, *to pass, lead :* adulescentiam eleganter, Cic.; leniter aevum, Hor.; otiosam aetatem et quietam sine ullo labore et contentione, Cic.; noctem his sermonibus, Liv. Hence of discharging duties: munus summā modestiā, Cic. Ep. [Fr. *traduire.*]

trăductĭō, ōnis, *f.* [trādūcō]. **A.** *a transferring.* **a.** From one rank to another: traductio ad plebem hominis perditi, Cic. **b.** R h e t.: Cic. **B.** *a parading* in public, *public disgrace :* Sen. **C.** Of time, *passage, course :* temporis, Cic.

trăductor, ōris, *m.* [trādūcō], *the conveyor, transferrer :* (of Pompey, who allowed Clodius to be transferred to a plebeian gens), Cic. Ep.

trăductus, a, um, *Part.* trādūcō.

trădux, ducis, *m.* [trādūcō], *a vine-branch, vine-layer* trained for propagation : Varr., Tac.

tragĭcē, *adv. in a tragic manner, tragically :* Cic., Sen. Ep.

tragĭcŏcōmoedĭa, ae, *f.* [τραγικοκωμῳδία], *a drama with a mixture of tragedy and comedy, tragi-comedy :* Pl.

tragĭcus, a, um [τραγικός], *of tragedy, tragic.* **1.** L i t.: carmen, cothurnus, ars, Hor.; actor, Liv.; tragicus Orestes, Cic. As Noun, **tragĭcus**, i, *m. a tragic poet, writer of tragedy :* Cic., Quint. **2.** T r a n s f. **a.** *in the tragic style, lofty, sublime :* orator, Cic.; color, Hor. *Neut. Intern.* Acc. spirat tragicum satis, Hor. **b.** *of a tragic nature; tragic, horrible:* sceleris tragici exemplum, Liv.; ignes (i.e. amor), Ov.; Juv.

tragoedĭa, ae, *f.* [τραγῳδία], *a tragedy.* **1.** L i t.: facere, Pl., Cic.; scribere, Tac. **2.** T r a n s f. **a.** *the art of tragedy* or (personified) *Tragedy :* Hor., Ov. **b.** *high-flown, pompous talk :* neque istis tragoediis tuis perturbor, Cic. **c.** *a great commotion or disturbance :* eius Appiae nomen quantas tragoedias excitat, Cic.; tragoedias in nugis agere, Cic.

tragoedus, I, *m.* [τραγῳδός], *a tragic actor, tragedian :* Pl., Cic., Hor.

trāgula, ae, *f.* [fr. root of trahō], *a kind of javelin* or *dart.* **1.** L i t. : Lucil., Caes., Liv. **2.** T r a n s f. : tragulam in aliquem inicere, Pl.

tragus, I, *m.* [τράγος (*a goat*)]. **I.** *an unknown kind of fish :* Ov. **II.** =hircus, *the rank (goatish) smell of the armpits :* Mart.

trahāx, ācis, *adj.* [trahō], *greedy, covetous :* procax, rapax, trahax, Pl.

trahea, ae, *f.* [trahō], *a drag, sledge :* Verg.

trahō, trahere, traxī, tractum (*Perf. Inf. sync.* trāxe, Verg.). **I.** *to draw, trail.* **1.** L i t. **a.** In gen. : (amiculum) sine trahi, quom egomet trahor, Pl. ; vestem per pulpita, Hor. ; Iris mille varios colores, Verg. ; vapor aëra secum, Lucr. ; limum harenamque fluctūs, Sall. ; Scylla navis in saxa, Verg. ; plaustra per altos montis boves, Verg. ; machinae carinas, Hor. ; genua aegra, Verg. **b.** Of persons : *to take with one* or *in one's train :* natum conventūs in medios, Verg. ; Astyanacte avo, Verg. ; Scipio gravem spoliis exercitum, Liv. **c.** *to draw in* or *up* (water, air, etc.) : ex puteis aquam, Cic. ; pocula arente fauce, Hor. ; Servilius animam, Liv. ; auras ore, Ov. ; odorem navibus, Phaedr. Also, penitus suspiria, Ov. ; vocem imo a pectore, Verg. **d.** *to draw, pull out :* e corpore ferrum, Ov. ; de corpore telum, Ov. ; viscere tela, Ov. ; vellera digitis, Ov. ; manibus lanam, Varr. ; lanam mollire trahendo, Ov. Also, *to lengthen :* pedum digitos, Ov. ; Apollo auris Midae, Ov. **e.** *to draw in* or *together, to contract :* coria et carnem in unum, Lucr. ; vultum rugasque, Ov. **2.** T r a n s f. **a.** In gen. *to draw :* trahimur omnes studio laudis, Cic. ; trahit sua quemque voluptas, Verg. ; omnes trahimur ad scientiae cupiditatem, Cic. ; aliquem in aliam partem, Cic. Ep. ; Caes. ; Drusum in partis, Tac. ; aliquem in suam sententiam, Liv. ; civitatem ad regem, Liv. ; rem ad Poenos, Liv. ; ea res longius nos ab incepto, Sall. **b.** *to take with one* or *in one's train :* pluris secum in animam calamitatem, Cic. ; Lucanos ad defectionem, Liv. ; quo fata trahunt sequamur, Verg. ; turris ruinam trahit, Vorg. **c.** *to draw up* or *out* (as from a source), *to derive :* maiorem ex pernicie rei publicae molestiam, Cic. Ep. ; cognomen ex contumeliā, Cic. ; nomen ab illis, Ov. ; ab isto initio sermonem, Cic. ; facetiae multum ex vero, Tac. **d.** Of things, *to draw* or *take to itself, to take on :* squamam cutis durata, Ov. ; colorem, calorem, Ov. ; faciem virorum, Ov. ; robiginem, Plin. **e.** *to draw over* or *to, to ascribe, attribute, refer, etc.* : egomet me adeo cum illis unā ibidem traho, Pl. ; captae decus Nolae ad consulem, Liv. ; in se crimen, Ov. ; omnia non bene consulta in virtutem, Sall. ; Tac. ; aliquid in religionem, Liv. ; spinas in exemplum, Ov. ; cuncta in deterius, Tac. ; fortuita ad culpam, Tac. ; varie trahebant (with *Indir. Quest.*), Tac. **f.** *to draw out, spin out :*

vitam in luctu tenebrisque, Verg. ; noctem sermone, Verg. ; iurgiis tempus, Liv. ; sera crepuscula noctem, Ov. ; bellum, Cic. Ep., Liv. ; pugnam aliquamdiu, Liv. ; rem de industriā in serum, Liv. Also, of spinning out in the mind : belli atque pacis rationem, Sall. ; trahere cum animo suo (with *Indirect Deliberative*), Sall. **II.** *to drag, hale.* **A.** In gen. **1.** L i t. : Amphitruonem collo, Pl. ; cum a custodibus trinis catenis vinctus traheretur, Caes. ; corpus tractum et laniatum, Cic. ; trahebatur crinibus a templo Cassandra, Verg. **2.** T r a n s f. (mentally) : quae meum animum divorse trahunt, Ter. ; Vologeses diversas ad curas trahebatur, Tac. **B.** Of plundering. **1.** L i t. : cetera rape, trahe, Pl. ; Sall. ; de aliquo spolia, Cic. ; praedam ex agris, Liv. **2.** T r a n s f. of squandering money : omnibus modis pecuniam, Sall. [Fr. *traire.*]

Trāiānus, I, *m.* : M. Ulpius, *Roman emperor,* A.D. 98–117.

trā-iciō or **trāns-iciō** (sometimes in Caes.), icere, iēcī, iectum [iaciō], *to throw, cast, shoot, etc. over* or *across.* **I.** With Acc. going closely with the verbal element. **1.** L i t. **a.** In gen. : telum, Caes. ; funem, Verg. ; rudentem, Ov. ; vexillum trans vallum hostium, Liv. ; malis antemnisque de nave in navem traiectis, Liv. ; super acervos pedes, Prop. **b.** *to transport, transfer* from one place to another : alterno leve pondus equo, Prop. E s p. of *throwing* troops *across* water, etc. : suo ponte Afranius legiones quattuor, Caes. ; huc legionem, Caes. ; omnis suos trans Rhodanum, Liv. ; legiones in Siciliam, Liv. With *Refl. Pron.* : ad Achillam sese ex regiā, Caes. ; dux Romanus sese in Africam, Liv. In *Mid.* or *Pass.* : Marius traiectus in Africam, Cic. ; Liv. ; Tac. ; exercitus Pado traiectus Cremonam, Liv. Without expressed Object : ad Aethaliam insulam, Liv. ; classis ex Africā, Liv. ; veteres Hiberi, Tac. **2.** T r a n s f. **a.** *to cast :* quocumque oculos traiecimus, Lucr. **b.** *to transfer :* ex illius invidiā deonerare aliquid et in te traicere, Cic. ; Quint. ; arbitrium litis in omnis, Ov. ; in *Mid.* : in cor traiecto lateris capitisque dolore, Hor. Also, verba, Cic. ; verba in clausulas, Quint. **II.** With double Acc. **a.** M i l i t. *to throw troops across :* equitum magnam partem flumen traiecit, Caes. ; se Alpis, Cic. Ep. **b.** *to pass* something *through :* traiectus lora per pedes tumentis, Verg. **III.** With Acc. going closely with the *trans.* **A.** *to cross* a river, etc. **1.** L i t. : flumen, amnem, Trebiam, mare, Liv. ; Tac. (in *Pass.* : postquam cernant Rhodanum traiectum, Liv.) ; utribus amnem, Curt. ; flumina nando, Suet. ; Aurora medium aetherio cursu axem, Verg. **2.** T r a n s f. : fati litora magnus amor, Prop. **B.** *to pass through, pierce.* **a.** Of troops : pars magna equitum mediam aciem, Liv. Also, si Hannibal ad portas venisset murumque iaculo traiecisset, Cic. **b.** With a weapon : aliquem pilis, scorpione, Caes. ; femur tragulā, Caes. ; Verg. ; Liv. ; se uno ictu, Suet. ; serpentem cuspide, Ov.

trāiectiō, ōnis, *f.* [trāiciō]. **I.** *a trans-ferring.* Transf. **A.** In gen.: in alium, Cic. **B.** Rhet. **a.** *a transposition* of words : Cic. **b.** *exaggeration, hyperbole :* Cic. **II.** *a crossing* or *passing over, passage :* (maris), Cic. Ep. With *Subj.* GEN.: traiectiones stellarum, Cic.

trāiectus (trānsiectus), a, um, *Part.* trāiciō.

trāiectus, ūs, *m.* [trāiciō], *a crossing* or *passing over, passage :* in Britanniam, Caes. ; in traiectu Albulae amnis, Liv. Concr.: Plin. [Fr. *trajet.*]

trālāt-, *v.* trānslāt- and trānsferō.

trā-loquor, loqui, *to talk over, recount :* inpuritias tuas, Pl.

trā-lūceō, *v.* trānslūceō.

trāma, ae, *f.* [fr. root of trāns], *the woof, weft,* or *filling* of a web. **1.** Lit.: Varr., Sen. Ep. **2.** Transf.: putidae, Pl. ; figu-rae, Pers.

trā-meō, *v.* trānsmeō.

trāmes, itis, *m.* [fr. root seen in trāns], *a cross-way, side-way, by-path, foot-path.* **1.** Lit.: Pl., Cic. ; in Apennini tramitibus, Cic. ; silvae, Verg. ; transversis tramitibus transgressus, Liv. **2.** Transf. **a.** *a path* of any kind : Verg., Hor., Ov., Sen. Ep. **b.** Of *a track* marked out by philosophy : Lucr.

trā-mi-, *v.* trānsmi-.

trā-natō, *v.* trānsnatō.

trā-nō (trānsnō), nāre, *to swim over* or *across.* **I.** Without Acc.: Caes. ; ad suos, Caes. ; Lethaeas per undas, Verg. **II.** With Acc. going closely with the *trans.* **1.** Lit.: flumen, Caes., Verg. ; Gangem, Cic. ; paludem, Curt. Poet. in *Pass. :* obsequio tranantur aquae, Ov. ; Verg. **2.** Transf.: auras, foramina, Lucr. ; omnia, Cic. ; nubila, Verg.

tranquillē, *adv. calmly, quietly :* Pl., Cic. *Comp. :* Sen. Ep. *Sup. :* Suet.

tranquillitās, ātis, *f.* [tranquillus], *quiet-ness, stillness, calmness, tranquillity.* **1.** Lit. of wind or weather : Caes., Cic., Liv. ; maris, Cic. In *pl. :* Cic. Ep. **2.** Transf. of mind or affairs : Cic., Liv., Tac. ; animi, Cic. ; pacis et oti, Cic. ; otium et tran-quillitatem vitae sequi, Cic.

tranquillō, āre [tranquillus], *to calm, still.* **1.** Lit.: mare oleo, Plin. **2.** Transf. **a.** voltum, Pl. **b.** Hor. ; animos, Cic. ; res Romanas, Nep.

tranquillus, a, um, *quiet, calm, still, tranquil.* **1.** Lit.: mare, Cic., Liv. ; aquae, Ov. ; caelum, dies, Plin. ; serenitas, Liv. As Noun, **tranquillum**, i, *n. a calm :* Pl. ; in tranquillo tempestatem adversam optare dementis est, Cic. ; tranquillo navigare, Liv. ; tranquillo pervectus Chalcidem, Liv. **2.** Transf. **a.** frons, Cic. ; vultus, Suet. **b.** illum tranquillum facere ex irato, Pl. ; appetitūs, animus, vita, Cic. ; pectus, Lucr. ; senectus, Hor. ; pacatae tranquillae-que civitates, Cic. ; tutae tranquillaeque res, Sall. ; Liv. With *ab :* ab hostili metu agmen, Liv. *Comp. :* hanc canem faciam tibi oleo tranquilliorem, Pl. ; tran-quilliorem plebem fecerunt, Liv. Of an orator : in transferendis faciendisque verbis tranquillior, Cic. *Sup. :* tranquillissima res, Ter. ; tempus, Cic. ; otium, Plin. Ep.

As Noun, **tranquillum**, i, *n. calmness, etc. :* seditionem in tranquillum conferre, Pl. ; vitam in tam tranquillo locare, Lucr. ; in urbe ex tranquillo neoopinata moles discordiarum exorta est, Liv. ; re publicā in tranquillum redactā, Liv.

trāns, *adv.* and *prep.* **I.** Adv., only in compounds. **A.** The form varies between trā and trāns : trado and transdo, traduco and transduco. The *s* of trans usually disappears before a following *s :* transilio, transcendo. **B.** Meaning. **1.** Lit. *across, over, beyond, through :* traicio, transeo, transfigo ; Transalpinus. **2.** Transf. **a.** Of transference or change : trado, transcribo. **b.** Of thoroughness or completeness : transigo, translego. **II.** Prep. with Acc.: *across, over, beyond, on the farther side of.* **a.** With verbs of motion : Pl. ; qui trans mare currunt, Hor. ; trans Rhenum in Galliam tra-ducere, Caes. ; trans Alpis transferri, Cic. **b.** With verbs of rest : Germani trans Rhenum incolunt, Caes. ; eo tempore trans mare fui, Cic. [Fr. *très.*]

trāns-abeō, īre, iī. **I.** *to go beyond, pass by :* aliquem fugā, Stat. **II.** Of a weapon, *to go through :* ensis costas, Verg.

trānsāctor, ōris, *m.* [trānsigō], *a manager :* rerum, Cic.

trānsāctus, a, um, *Part.* trānsigō.

trānsadāctus, a, um, *Part.* trānsadigō.

trāns-adigō, igere, ēgī, āctum, *to drive* or *thrust home through.* With Double Acc.: costas ensem, Vegr. With one Acc. (going closely with the *trans*), *to pierce through :* hasta costas, Verg. ; aliquem ferro, Stat.

Trāns-alpīnus, a, um, *that is* or *lies beyond the Alps, Transalpine :* Gallia, Caes. ; nationes, Cic. Ep. ; bella, Cic. As Noun, **Trānsalpīnī**, ōrum, *m. pl. the nations beyond the Alps, Transalpine nations :* Suet.

trānscendō or **trāns-scendō**, scendere, scendī, scēnsum [scandō], *to climb* or *step over, to overstep, surmount.* **1.** Lit.: ab asinis ad boves, Pl. ; in hostium navis, Caes. ; in Italiam, in Campaniam, Liv. With Acc.: fossam, Caes. ; muros scalis, Liv. ; Caucasum, Cic. ; Liv.; flumen, Tac. **2.** Transf.: ūnīs iuris, Lucr. ; ordinem naturae, Liv. ; prohibita impune, Tac.

trāns-cīdō, cīdere, cīdī, [caedō], *to flog soundly :* loris omnis, Pl.

trānscrībō or **trāns-scrībō**, scribere, scripsi, scriptum, *to transfer in writing* (from one book to another), *to copy off.* **1.** Lit.: testamentum in alias tabulas, Cic. ; eun-dem librum in exemplaria mille, Plin. Ep. **2.** Transf. **a.** In law, *to transfer, convey :* in socios nomina, Liv. **b.** In gen. *to transfer, remove :* tua sceptra colonis, Verg. ; urbi matres, Verg.

trāns-currō, currere, currī or (in later authors) cucurrī, cursum, *to run* or *hasten over* or *across* or *through, to run by* or *past.* **1.** Lit.: curriculo ad nos, Pl. ; hin? ad forum, Ter. ; per spatium, Lucr. ; praeter oculos, Ov. ; remos transcurrentis detergere, Caes. ; *Impers. Pass. :* in altera transcursum castra ab Romanis est, Liv. With Acc.:

Hellespontum, Nep.; Campaniam, Suet.; caelum nimbus, Verg. **2. T r a n s f.**: hic tamen ad melius poterit transcurrere quondam, Hor. Of time: aestas, Plin. Ep. With Acc.: suum cursum, Cic.; narrationem, Sen.; Quint.

trānscursus, ūs, *m.* [trānscurrō], *a running, darting,* or *flying through.* **1. L i t.**: beluarum, Liv.; avium per aera, Sen.; fulguris, Suet. **2. T r a n s f.** of speech: *a running through, cursory mention :* in transcursu, Plin.

trāns-d-, *v.* trād-.

trānsenna, ae, *f.* [perh. fr. root of trāns; lit. *cross-work*]. **I.** *a fowler's net.* **1. L i t.**: Pl., Sall. **2. T r a n s f.**: hominem in transonnam doctis ducam dolis, Pl. **II.** *a grating, lattice-* or *trellis-work ; a lattice-window :* Cic.

trāns-eō, īre, iī, itum, *to go over or across, to cross over, pass over.* **1. L i t. a,** In gen.: per hortum ad amicam, Pl.; per media castra, Sall.; Ov.; o suis finibus in Helvetiorum finis, Caes.; in Britanniam, Caes.; ad Messanam, Cic.; Mosa in Rhenum, Caes. With Acc.: omnis mensas, Pl.; Rhenum, Caes.; Cic.; maria, Cic.; Hor.; campos pedibus, Lucr.; Apenninum, Cic. Ep., Liv.; serpentem rotā, Verg. In *Pass. :* Rhodanus vado transitur, Caes.; Liv. **b.** Of desertion: *to go over, desert :* nec manere nec transire aperte ausus, Liv.; Tac.; ad hostis, Pl.; Cic.; ad Pompeium, Caes.; a patribus ad plebem, Liv. **c.** Of parading: *to pass along the streets* (in a triumph): Liv. **d.** In a race: *to pass, outstrip :* Verg. With Acc.: equum cursu, Verg. **2. T r a n s f. A.** *to go* or *pass over into anything by transformation* : in humum saxumque, Ov.; aqua mulsa in vinum, Plin.; frequens imitatio in mores, Quint. **B.** *to go* or *pass over.* **a.** To another opinion : in sententiam alicuius, Liv.; senatus frequens in alia omnia, Hirt. **b.** To another emotion : in iram, Ov. **c.** To another subject : ad partitionem, Cic.; proximus liber ad rhetoris officia, Quint. *Impers. Pass. :* transeatur ad alteram contionem, Liv. **C.** *to pass over.* **a.** *to make no mention of :* aliquid silentio, Cic. Ep.; lacrimas alicuius, Stat.; hoc, Quint.; Neronem, Plin. Ep. With *Indir. Quest. :* Quint. **b.** *to go quickly over* or *through, to deal cursorily with* a subject : leviter, Cic.; ea, Cic. Ep.; brevi auditu quamvis magna transibat, Tac. **D.** Of time, *to pass by, pass :* multi menses, Caes.; Phaedr.; legis dies, Cic. Ep.; aetas, Tib. (O c c. *to pass* to the end, *pass away :* Plin.; imperium, Tac.; fortuna imperi, Tac.). With Acc.: vitam silentio, Sall.; tribunatūs annum quiete et otio, Tac. **E.** *to run through, pervade :* intellegentia per omnia ea, Cic. **F.** *to pass beyond, overstep* (with Acc.). **a.** finem et modum, Cic.; finem aequitatis et legis in iudicando, Cic. In time: spatium iuventae, Ov. **b.** *to surpass, excel :* Pompeium, Luc. Without Acc. expressed : Quint.

trāns-ferō, ferre, tulī, lātum (also trālātum),

side. **1. L i t. a.** In gen.: ... King a me huc, Pl.; hoc (simulacrum Dianae) Carthaginem, Cic.; castra trans Peneum, Liv.; signa ex statione, Caes. Of personal Objects: illinc huc virginem, Ter.; in Galliam Naevius, et trans Alpis usque transfertur, Cic.; o Venus, te Glycerae transfer in aedem, Hor. **b.** *to transfer by writing, to copy :* litteras de tabulis in libros, Cic.; versūs, Suet. **c.** Of parading : in eo triumpho XLIX coronae aureae translatae sunt, Liv.; Quint. **2. T r a n s f. A.** *to transfer :* amorem huc, Ter.; alio amores, Hor.; sermonem alio, Cic.; in Celtiberiam bellum, Caes.; ad se bellum, Caes.; in ius Lati nationes Alpium, Tac.; animum ad accusandum, Cic.; hoc in magistratūs, Cic.; culpam in alios, Cic.; invidiam criminis, Tac. With *Refl. Pron. :* se ad artis componendas, Cic.; se ad genus dicendi, Tac. **B,** *to transform :* omnia in species novas, Ov.; civitas se, Tac. **C.** *to put off, postpone, defer :* sese in proximum annum transtulit, Cic. **D.** Of language, *to translate :* istum ego locum totidem verbis a Dicaearcho transtuli, Ep.; locos quosdam, Cic.; haec ex Graeco, Quint.; in linguam Latinam, Plin.; Latine ad verbum, Quint. **E.** R h e t. **a.** *to transfer* a word from the literal sense to a metaphorical or figurative signification; *to use figuratively :* verbum, Cic. **b.** translatum exordium (*not pertinent*), Cic.

trāns-fīgō, fīgere, fīxī, fīxum. **I.** *to thrust* or *pierce* a *person through :* sagittā Cupido cor meum, Pl.; hastā transfixus, Caes.; Cic.; Q. Fabium gladio per pectus, Liv.; transfixo pectore, Verg. In *Mid.* or *Pass.* with retained Acc.: hastis corpus transfigi solent, Pl.; Luc. **II.** *to drive* or *thrust* a weapon *through :* hasta duplicat virum transfixa dolore, Verg., Luc.

trāns-fīgūrō, āre, *to change in shape, to transform.* **1. L i t.**: corpora, Stat.; puerum in muliebrem naturam, Suet.; Plin. **2. T r a n s f.**: non emendari tantum sed transfigurari, Sen. Ep.; iudicum animos in eum quem volumus habitum, Quint.

trānsfīxus, a, um, *Part.* trānsfīgō.

trāns-fodiō, fodere, fōdī, fōssum, *to thrust* or *stab through :* in scrobis delapsi transfodiebantur, Caes.; fugienti latus, Liv.; oculum, Tac. In *Pass.* with retained Acc.: pectora duro transfossi ligno, Verg.

trānsfōrmis, e, *adj.* [fōrma], *changed in shape, transformed :* corpora, Ov.

trāns-fōrmō, āre, *to change in shape.* **1. L i t.**: in vultūs sese anilis, Verg.; gemmas in ignis, Ov. **2. T r a n s f.**: animum ad naturam eorum de quibus loquimur, Quint.

trāns-forō, āre, *to pierce through :* gladius, Sen.

trānsfōssus, a, um, *Part.* trānsfodiō.

trānsfretō, āre [fretum], *to cross a strait, pass over the sea :* Suet.

trānsfuga, ae, *m. f.* [trānsfugiō], *a deserter* (*cf.* perfuga). **1. L i t.**: Cic., Tac. **2. T r a n s f.**: transfuga divitum partis linquere gestio, Hor.; Plin.; Plin. Ep.

trāns-fŭgĭō, fugere, fūgī, *to flee over to the other side, go over to the enemy, desert.* **1.** Lit.: ad Romanos, Liv.; Nep.; Tac. **2.** Transf.: illius oculi atque aures atque opinio ad nos, Pl.; ab adflictā amicitiā, Cic.

trānsfŭgĭum, ĭ, n. [trānsfugiō], *a going over to the enemy, desertion :* Tac. In pl. : Liv., Tac.

trāns-fundō, fundere, fūdī, fūsum, *to pour from one vessel into another, to decant, transfuse.* **1.** Lit.: Plin.; aliquem mortuum in urnam, Luc. **2.** Transf.: omnem amorem in hanc, Cic.; suas laudes ad aliquem, Cic. Ep.; divinum spiritum in effigies mutas, Tac.

trānsfūsĭō, ōnis, f. [trānsfundō], *a pouring from one vessel into another.* **1.** Lit.: aquae, Plin. **2.** Transf. *a transmigration* of a people : Cic.

trānsfūsus, a, um, *Part.* trānsfundō.

trāns-grĕdĭor, gredī, grēssus [gradior], *to step, go,* or *pass across* or *over* or *through.* **1.** Lit. **a.** In gen. : Sall., Tac.; in Italiam, Liv.; Suet.; Rheno, Tac. With Acc.: flumen, Caes.; Liv.; Araxem ponte, Tac.; pomerium, Cic.; munitiones, Caes.; Taurum, Cic. Ep.; colonias, Tac. **b.** *to go over* to another party: ad vos, Tac.; in partīs Vespasiani, Tac. **2.** Transf. **a.** *to pass on* to another subject : ab indecoris ad infesta, Tac. **b.** With Acc., *to exceed :* mensuram, Plin.

trānsgrĕssĭō, ōnis, f. [trānsgredior], *a going across, passage.* **1.** Lit.: Gallorum, Cic. **2.** Rhet. **a.** *transposition :* verborum, Cic. **b.** *a transition :* Quint.

trānsgrĕssus, a, um, *Part.* trānsgredior.

trānsgrĕssus, ūs, m. [trānsgredior], *a passing over:* in transgressu amnis, Tac.; Sall.

trāns-ĭcĭō, trānsĭect-, v. trāicĭō, trāiect-.

trāns-ĭgō, igere, ēgī, āctum [agō], *to drive, carry,* or *thrust through.* **1.** Lit. *to pierce through* with a weapon : gladio pectus, Phaedr.; so ipsum gladio, Tac. **2.** Transf. **a.** *to carry through* to the end ; *to finish, settle :* fabulam, Pl.; negotium, res, meas partīs, Cic.; aliquid·per aliquem, Cic.; pleraque per se, Liv.; aliquid cum aliquo, Sall.; de praetoribus transacta res, quae transigi sorte poterat, Liv.; certamen cum aliquo, Liv.; bella, Tac.; rixam caede, Tac. With *cum :* cum expeditionibus, Tac. *Impers. Pass. :* Cic. Ep.; so of negotiations : de pace transigi potuisse, Liv. **b.** *to bring to an end, to pass, spend :* placidas sine suspirio noctis, Sen. Ep.; tempus per ostentationem, Tac.; diem sermonibus, Plin. Ep.; adulescentiam, Suet. **c.** *to settle* a difference or controversy, *to come to an agreement* or *understanding :* inter se transigant ipsi, Ter.; cum reo, Cic.; rem cum aliquo, Cic. *Impers. Pass. :* cum aliquo minore pecuniā, Cic. Ep.

trānsĭlĭō or **trāns-sĭlĭō**, silīre, silui [saliō], *to leap, jump,* or *spring across* or *over.* **1.** Lit.: per hortum ad nos, Pl.; ex humilioribus in altiorem navem, Liv. With Acc. going closely with the *trans :* novos muros, Liv.; rates vada, Hor.; positas flammas, Ov. **2.** Transf. (with

Acc.). **a.** *to overstep , exceed :* modici munera Liberi, Hor. **b.** *to skip over, *pass over* or *by :* ne rem unam transiliat oratio, Cic.; ante pedes posita, Cic.; proxima pars vitae transilienda meae, Ov.

trānsĭtāns, antis, *Part.* [trānsitō, freq. of trānseō], *going* or *passing through :* Cic. Ep.

trānsĭtĭō, ōnis, f. [trānseō], *a going across* or *over, a passing over, passage.* **1.** Lit. **a.** visionum, Cic. **b.** From one party to another ; ad plebem, Cic.; sociorum, Liv.; Numidas ad transitionem perlicere, Liv. In pl. : Cic., Liv. **c.** Concr. (in pl.), *passages :* Cic. **2.** Transf : *infection, contagion :* Ov.

trānsĭtōrĭus, a, um [trānsitus], *having a passage-way :* domus, Suet.

trānsĭtus, a, um, *Part.* trānseō.

trānsĭtus, ūs, m. [trānseō], *a going across* or *over, a passing over, passage.* **1.** Lit. **a.** difficili transitu flumen, Caes.; nostros transitu prohibere, Caes.; Batavos transitu arcere, Tac.; per agros transitum dare, Liv. Also, *a passing by, passing :* capta in transitu urbs, Tac. **b.** *a passing over* to another side, *desertion :* ad Vitellium, Tac. **c.** Concr.: fossae, Cic. **2.** Transf. **a.** Of time : tempestatis, Cic. Ep. **b.** Of circumstances : *change, period of change :* in illo a pueritiā ad adulescentiam transitu, Quint.; transitūs rerum, Tac. **c.** Of the *fading* of colours : Ov., Plin. **d.** Rhet.: *a transition :* Quint. Also, in transitu aliquid tractare, *in passing,* Quint.

trānslātĭcius (**trālātĭcius**), a, um [trānsferō], *transmitted, according to precedent, customary.* **1.** Lit.: edictum, Cic.; ius, Suet. **2.** Transf. *usual, common :* mos, Phaedr.; officia, Plin. Ep.; funus, Suet.; hoc tralaticium est, Cic. Ep.

trānslātĭō or **trālātĭō**, ōnis, f. [trānsferō], *a carrying* or *removing from one place to another, a transferring.* **1.** Lit. **a.** pecuniarum a iustis dominis ad alienos, Cic.; domicili, Suet. **b.** Of plants : *a transplanting, ingrafting :* Varr., Plin. **2.** Transf. **A.** In gen.: criminis, Cic.; Quint. **B.** Of language. **a.** *a version, translation :* Quint. **b.** *a metaphor, figure :* Cic., Quint.

trānslātīvus, a, um [trānslātiō], *transferable :* constitutio, Cic.; Quint.

trānslātor, ōris, m. [trānsferō], *one who carries* or *hands over, a transferrer :* Verres, translator quaesturae, aversor pecuniae publicae, Cic.

trānslātus, a, um, *Part.* trānsferō.

trāns-lĕgō, ere, *to read through* (aloud): Pl.

trāns-lūcĕō or **trālūcĕō**, ēre. **I.** *to shine across, be reflected* (from one to another): e speculo in speculum imago, Lucr. **II.** *to shine through :* in liquidis aquis, Ov.; Plin.

trāns-marīnus, a, um, *beyond* or *from beyond sea, transmarine :* hospes, Pl.; gentes, legationes, Liv.; vectigalia, res, doctrina, Cic.; peregrinatio, Quint.

trāns-mĕō or **trāmĕō**, meāre, *to go over* or *across, to pass* (over) : Plin.; terrā marique, Tac.

trāns-migrō, āre *to move* from one place to another, *to migrate :* urbem quaesituri sumus, quo transmigremus, Liv. ; Veios, Liv. ; e Carinis Esquilias, Suet.

trānsmissiō, ōnis, *f.* [trānsmittō], *a sending across ; a passing over :* ab eā urbe in Graeciam, Cic.

trānsmissus, a, um, *Part.* trānsmittō.

trānsmissus, ūs, *m.* [trānsmittō], *a passing over, passage :* ex Galliā in Britanniam, Caes.

trāns-mittō or **trāmittō**, mittere, mīsī, missum. **I.** With -mitto used transitively : *to let go, put, carry, convey* or *send across* or *over.* **1.** Lit. **a.** mihi illam, Pl. ; exercitum equitatumque, Caes. ; auxilia in Italiam, Liv. ; Tac. ; magnam classem in Siciliam, Liv. ; pontem, Suet. Also, *to put through :* per viscera elephanto bracchium, Pl. ; per medium amnem equum, Liv. **b.** *to let pass through :* exercitum per finis suos, Liv. ; Favonios, Plin. Ep. ; venenum (through the bowels), Tac. **2.** Transf. **a.** *to hand* or *make over, to transfer, entrust, etc. :* bellum in Italiam, Liv. ; huic hoc tantum bellum, Cic. ; me famulo famulamque Heleno habendam, Verg. ; (so, with *Inf. :* longo transmisit habere nepoti, Stat.) ; omne meum tempus amicorum temporibus, Cic. ; eandem vim in me (i.e. to apply), Tac. **b.** *to let go over* or *by, to pass over, neglect, resign, etc. :* Iunium mensem, Tac. ; Gangen amnem et quae ultra essent, Curt. ; munia imperi, Tac. **II.** With -mitto used intransitively, *to go* or *cross over, to cross, pass* from one place to another. **1.** Lit. : Cic. ; a Brundisio, Cic. ; ab Lilybaeo Uticam, Liv. ; ex Corsicā in Sardiniam, Liv. ; naves in Africam, Liv. ; *Impers. Pass. :* Liv. With Acc. going closely with the trāns : tot maria, Cic. ; Hiberum, Liv. ; equites campos, Lucr. ; cursu campos, Verg. ; in *Pass. :* transmissus amnis, Tac. ; Cic. Ep. ; flumen ponte transmittitur, Plin. Ep. **2.** Transf. (with Acc.). **a.** *to pass over, leave unmentioned :* sententiam silentio, Tac. **b.** Of time, *to pass, spend :* vitam per obscurum, Sen. Ep. ; sterilis annos, Stat. ; tempus quiete, Plin. Ep. **c.** *to pass through, endure :* febrium ardorem, Plin. Ep.

trāns-montāni, ōrum, *m. pl. the people beyond the mountains :* Liv.

trāns-moveō, movēre, mōtum, *to remove* from one place to another. **1.** Lit. : Syriā legiones, Tac. **2.** Transf. : gloriam in se, Ter.

trāns-mūtō, āre, *to change, shift :* fortuna transmutat incertos honores, Hor.

trāns-natō or **trānatō**, āre, *to swim over, across,* or *through.* **1.** Lit. : Caes., Tac. **2.** Transf. : tuum nomen Gangem, Cic.

trāns-nō, *v.* trānō.

trāns-nōminō, āre, *to change a name :* Septembrem mensem et Octobrem ex appellationibus suis Germanicum Domitianumque transnominavit, Suet.

Trāns-padānus, a, um, *beyond the R. Po ; Transpadane ;* **Trānspadāni**, ōrum, *m. pl. the nations beyond the R. Po.*

trānspectus, ūs, *m.* [trānspiciō], *a seeing through, a view, prospect :* apertus, Lucr.

trānspiciō or **trāns-spiciō**, spicuiō [ūpīsītī] *to look* or *see through :* Lucr.

trāns-pōnō, pōnere, posuī, positum, *to remove, transfer :* militem, Tac. ; advecta onera in flumen, Plin. Ep.

trāns-portō, āre, *to convey from one place to another ; to remove, transport :* duas legiones, Caes. ; onera et multitudinem iumentorum, Caes. ; exercitum in Hispaniam, Liv. ; Caes. ; Cic. With Acc. going closely with *trans :* milites his navibus flumen transportat, Caes. ; ripas horrendas et rauca fluenta (*sc.* the unburied), Verg.

trānspositus, a, um, *Part.* trānspōnō.

Trāns-rhēnānus, a, um, *beyond the Rhine. Transrhenish ;* **Trānsrhēnāni**, ōrum, *m. pl. the people beyond the Rhine.*

Trāns-tiberīnus, a, um, *beyond the Tiber ; Transtiberine ;* **Trānstiberīni**, ōrum, *m. pl., the people beyond the Tiber.*

trāns-tineō, ēre [teneō], *to go through, pass through :* commeatus trans parietem, Pl.

trānstrum, i, *n.* [trāns], *a cross-timber or beam in a vessel from side to side, hence a bench for rowers, a thwart :* Caes., Cic., Verg., Ov.

trānsultō or **trāns-sultō**, āre [*freq.* transiliō], *to leap over* or *across habitually* or *regularly :* in recentem equum ex fesso, Liv.

trānsūmō or **trāns-sūmō**, ere, *to take from one to another, to adopt, assume.* **1.** Lit. : hastam laevā, Stat. **2.** Transf. : mutatos cultūs, Stat.

trānsuō or **trāns-suō**, suere, *to sew* or *stitch through ;* hence, *to pierce through :* exta veribus, Ov.

trānsvectiō or **trāvectiō**, ōnis, *f.* [trānsvehō], *a carrying* or *transporting across* or *past.* **a.** Acherontis, Cic. **b.** *a riding past* or *parade of the Roman knights before the censor, a review :* Suet.

trāns-vehō or **trāvehō**, vehere, vexī, vectum, *to carry, conduct,* or *convey across* or *over ; to transport.* **1.** Lit. **a.** milites, Caes. ; copias ponte, Plin. ; exercitum in Britanniam, Suet. ; Hispanos inflati utres, Liv. In *Mid., to travel, ride,* or *sail across* or *over :* Medi navibus in Africam transvecti, Sall. ; Liv. ; transvectae a fronte pugnantium alae, Tac. **b.** Of parading : *to carry, lead,* or *conduct along* in triumph : arma spoliaque multa carpentis, Liv. In *Mid.* of the Roman knights, *to ride past* or *parade before the censor :* Liv., Suet. **2.** Transf. (in *Mid.*) of time : *to pass, elapse :* transvectum est tempus, Tac.

trāns-verberō, āre, *to strike* or *thrust through, transfix :* bestiam venabulo, Cic. Ep. ; pectus abiete, Verg. ; in utrumque latus transverberatus, Tac.

trānsversārius, a, um [trānsversus], *lying across, cross, transverse :* tigna, Caes.

trānsversus or **trāversus** (older **-vorsus**), a, um, *going* or *lying across, athwart, crosswise.* **1.** Lit. : Lucr. ; fossa, tigna, Caes. ; viae, Cic. ; tramites, Liv. ; transverso ambulare foro, Cic. ; transverum unguem discedere, etc., *a nail's breadth* (mostly transf.), Cic., Pl. ; (versibus) adlinet atrum transverso calamo signum,

Hor. *Neut.* as Noun. **a.** In *Adv.* phrases: ex transvorso cedit, quasi cancer solet, Pl.; Lucr.; Liv.; in *and* per traversum, Plin. **b.** *Intern.* Acc.: (venti) mutati transversa fremunt, Verg. **2.** Transf.: transversa incurrit misera fortuna rei publicae, Cic.; transversum iudicem ferre, Quint. *Neut.* as Noun in *Adv.* phr.: de transverso L. Caesar . . . rogat, etc. (i.e. contrary to expectation), Cic. Ep. [Fr. *travers.*]

trāns-volĭtō, āre, *to flit through :* clausa domorum, Lucr.

trāns-volō or **trăvolō**, āre, *to fly over or across.* **1.** Lit.: Pontum (grues), Plin. **2.** Transf. **a.** Of any rapid motion: foraminibus liquidus ignis, Lucr.; eques inde in partem alteram, Liv. Also, arma in hostis, Pl. With Acc.: Alpis, Asin. ap. Cic. Ep.; vox auras, Lucr. **b.** *to fly past :* importunus (Cupido) transvolat aridas quercūs, Hor.; transvolat in medio posita illa Sallustiana brevitas audientem, Quint.

trānsvorsus, *v.* trānsversus.

trapētus, ī, *m.* (Cato, Verg.) [τραπητός] and **trapētes**, um, *m. pl.* (Cato, Varr.) [τράπητες], *an olive-mill, oil-mill.*

trapezīta, *v.* tarpezīta.

Trapezūs, ūntis, *f. a city in Pontus,* now *Trebizond.*

Trasimennus (Trasu-, Trasy-) lacus, or simply **Trasimēnus**, ī, *m. a lake in Etruria,* now *Perugia, on the shores of which Hannibal gained a great victory over the Romans,* B.C. 217.

trā-v-, *v.* trānsv-.

trecēnī, ae, a [trēs centum], *three hundred in a group or three hundred each :* treceni equites in singulis legionibus, Liv.; treceni tauri quotquot eunt dies, Hor.

trecentēsimus (-ēns-), a, um [trecentī], *three-hundredth :* Cic.

trecentī, ae, a [trēs centum], *three hundred :* Pl., Cic., Verg. To denote an indefinitely large number: Hor.

trecentiēs (-ēns), [trecentī], *three hundred times :* Cat.

trechedipnum, ī, *n.* (*sc.* vestimentum) [τρεχέδειπνον (*running to a banquet*)], *a light garment worn at table by parasites :* Juv.

tredeciēns (-iēs), *v.* terdeciēns.

tredecim, *indecl. adj.* [trēs decem], *thirteen :* Liv. [Fr. *treize.*]

treis or **tris**, *v.* trēs.

tremebundus, a, um [tremō], *trembling, quivering :* Iphianassa, Lucr.; manus, Cic.; membra, Ov.

tremefaciō, facere, fēcī, factum [tremō faciō], *to cause to shake, quake :* nutu Olympum, Verg.; se tellus, Cic. poet. Esp. in *Perf. Part. :* tremefacta tellus, Verg.; folia tremefacta Noto, Prop.; Ov.

tremendus, a, um. **I.** *Gerund.* tremō. **II.** Adj. *dreadful, terrible, tremendous :* regem tremendum, Verg.; Chimaera, Alpes, tumultus, Hor.; oculi, Ov.; monita Carmentis, Verg.

tremēscō (-īscō), ere [tremō], *to begin to shake or tremble, to tremble for fear, to tremble (at) :* plaustri concussa tectu,

Lucr.; montes, Ov.; tonitru ardua terrarum, Verg. With Acc.: sonitumque pedum vocemque tremesco, Verg. With Acc. and *Inf. :* Verg.

tremō, ere, uī [*cf.* Gk. τρέω], *to quake, quiver, tremble, etc.* **a.** In gen.: Pl., Cic.; toto pectore, Cic.; corde et genibus, Hor. With Acc. of Extent: tremit artūs, Lucr.; tremis ossa pavore, Hor. Of things: membra, Pl.; artūs, umeri, Verg.; os, Hor., Ov.; genua, Sen. Ep.; vela, Lucr.; frusta, hasta, Verg.; ilices, Hor.; verbere ripae, Hor.; aequor, Ov. **b.** With Acc. *to quake or tremble at :* virgas ac securis dictatoris, Liv.; offensam Iunonem, Ov.; Hor.; te Stygii lacūs, Verg. [Fr. *craindre.*]

tremor, ōris, *m.* [tremō], *a sha..ing, quaking, trembling.* **1.** Lit. **a.** In gen.: omnia corusca prae tremore fabulor, Pl.; Cic.; gelidusque per ima cucurrit ossa tremor, Verg. Of things: dum tremor (ignium) est clarus, Lucr. **b.** Of the earth: tremor terras graviter pertemptat, Lucr. In *pl. :* Lucr., Ov., Plin. **2.** Transf. (concr.) *an (object of) dread :* silvarum tremor (Cacus), Mart.

tremulus, a, um [tremō], *shaking, quaking, quivering, trembling.* **1.** Lit.: anus, Pl.; artūs, Lucr.; manus, Plin.; manūs anxiusque metuque, Ov.; harundo, Ov.; iubar ignis, Lucr.; lumen, Verg.; motus, Lucr. **2.** Transf. *that causes to shake or shiver :* frigus, Cic. poet.

trepidanter, *adv. tremblingly, in an excited, hurried,* or *agitated manner :* Suet. *Comp. :* Caes.

trepidātiō, ōnis, *f.* [trepidō], *a state of confused hurry, agitation :* Cic.; nec opinata res plus trepidationis fecit, Liv.; inicere, Liv.; hostium, Liv.; inter primam trepidationem, Liv.; per trepidationem, Tac.; ut ex trepidatione concurrentium turba constitit, Liv.; nervorum, Sen.

trepidē, *adv. hastily, in a state of confusion :* Liv., Phaedr., Suet.

trepidō, āre [trepidus], *to hurry* or *bustle about anxiously, be in a state of agitation.* **A.** Of persons: Pl., Caes., Verg., etc.; ad arma, Liv.; dum in sua quisque ministeria discursu trepidat ad prima signa, Liv.; tota civitas ad excipiendum Poenum, Liv.; ancipiti trepidant terrore per urbes, Lucr.; Ov.; in dubiis periclis, Lucr.; inter scelus metumque, Tac.; trepidas in usum poscentis aevi pauca, Hor.; multa (*Intern.* Acc.) manu medicā trepidat, Verg.; *Impers. Pass. :* Ter., Lucr.; totis trepidatur castris, Caes. With *Inf. :* Verg. With *ne* and *Subj. :* Juv. With Acc. *to shudder* or *start at :* harundinis umbram, Juv. **B.** Of things, *to move irregularly, to quiver, hurry :* Lucr.; flammae, Hor.; penna, exta, Ov.; aqua per pronum trepidat cum murmure rivum, Hor.; mens metu, Hor. With *Inf. :* octavum trepidavit aetas claudere lustrum, Hor.

trepidus, a, um, *agitated, anxious, hurried.* **A.** Of persons, etc.: trepidae inter se coeunt pennisque coruscant (apes), Verg.; curia trepida ancipiti metu, Liv.; Sall.; Verg. With GEN.: trepidi rerum suarum, Liv.; Verg.; admirationis ac metūs, Tac. **B.**

Of things: undam trepidi aeni, Verg.; unda, Ov.; venae, Ov.; cursus, Verg.; pes, vultus, Ov.; motus, Ov.; tumultus belli, Lucr.; certamen, Hor.; terror, Lucr.; Ov.; consul perculsis omnibus ipse satis, ut in re trepidā, impavidus turbatos ordines instruit, Liv.; in trepidis rebus, Liv.; Hor., etc.; incerta et trepida vita, Tac.

trēs (**treis** and **tris**; Acc. tris or trēs), tria, adj. [cf. Gk. τρεῖς, τρία], three: Pl., Lucr., Cic., etc. To denote a small number: tribus verbis, Pl., Cic. Ep., Ov., etc.; tribus chartis, Cat. [It. tre; Sp. tres; Fr. trois.]

trēssis, is, m. [trēs as] three asses (us. quadrans). **a.** Prop.: Varr. **b.** a mere trifle: non tressis agaso, Pers.

trēs-virī, ōrum, m. pl. a board of three commissioners more freq. triumviri (q.v.). As overseers of prisons and punishments (capitales): Pl. As superintendents of sacrifices and religious feasts: epulones, Cic. As commissioners to distribute land among colonists: Liv.

triangulus, a, um [trēs angulus], three-cornered, triangular: Cic. As Noun, **triangulum**, i, n. a triangle: Cic., Quint.

triāriī, ōrum, m. pl. [trēs], the veteran Roman soldiers who formed the third line, the triarii, the reserve: Liv.; rem ad triarios rediisse (prov. of a critical case), Liv.

tribrachys, yos, m. [τρίβραχυς], a poetical foot consisting of three short syllables, a tribrach: Quint.

tribuārius, a, um [tribus], of a tribe or tribes: Cic.

tribūlis, is, m. [tribus]. **I.** a fellow-tribesman: Ter., Cic., Hor., Liv. **II.** one of the lower classes of the people: Mart.

tribulum, ī, n. [terō, cf. Gk. τρίβω], a threshing-sledge (a wooden platform with sharp pieces of flint or with iron teeth underneath): Varr., Verg. [It. trebbia.]

tribulus, ī, m. [τρίβολος], a caltrop, a kind of thorn: Verg., Ov., Plin.

tribūnal, ālis, n. [tribūnus], a raised platform. **a.** Of the platform on which the seats of magistrates were placed; a judgment-seat, tribunal: Caes., Cic., Liv., Mart., etc. **b.** Of the elevation in camps from which generals addressed their soldiers or administered justice: Liv., Tac. **c.** the seat of the praetor in the theatre: Suet. **d.** a monumental mound, cenotaph: Tac. **e.** Of any mound: Plin.

tribūnātus, ūs, m. [tribūnus]. **I.** the office of tribune of the people: Cic., Liv. **II.** the office of military tribune: Cic., Liv.

tribūnīcius, a, um [tribūnus]. **I.** of a tribune of the plebs: potestas, Cic.; vis, Caes.; procellae, Liv.; comitia, Cic. Ep. As Noun, **tribūnīcius**, ī, m. an ex-tribune: Cic., Liv. **II.** of a military tribune: honos, Caes.

tribūnus, ī, m. [tribus; prop. officer of a tribe], a tribune. **I.** tribuni plebis, and more freq. simply tribuni, tribunes of the people, whose office it was to defend the rights and interests of the Roman plebeians: Cic., Liv. **II.** tribuni militum consulari potestate, military tribunes with consular power; appointed during the struggle between the patricians and plebeians, B.C. 444–366. They were chosen from the patrician and plebeian orders, and were at first three, then four, and finally six in number: Liv. **III.** tribuni militares or militum, tribunes of the soldiers, military tribunes: these were officers of the army (ranking after the consul and the two legati), six to each legion; they commanded in turn, each two months at a time: Caes., Cic., etc. Also of others with honorary rank (esp. towards the end of the Republican period and under the Empire). **IV.** tribuni aerarii, perh. paymasters; by the Lex Aurelia the tribuni aerarii were made iudices: Cato; Cic. **V.** tribunus Celerum, captain or commander of the Celeres (in the kingly period), Liv.

tribuō, uere, uī, ūtum [tribus]. **1.** Lit. **a.** to classify, divide: rem universam in partis, Cic. **b.** to assign, apportion, allot (us. implying that that which is given is due): ei plurimum, Cic.; suum cuique, Cic.; praemia bene meritis, Caes.; eius sceloribus tanta praemia, Sall.; sumptis paucis, paucisque tributis, Lucr. **2.** Transf. **a.** Of time: tempus conviviis, Cic.; comitiis omnibus perficiundis XI dies, Caes. **b.** to allow, concede: aliquid voluptati, Cic.; aliquid amicitiae, Caes.; hoc matris precibus, Ov.; mihi omnia, Cic. **c.** to assign, ascribe: aliquid iuri potius quam suae culpae, Caes.; aliquid ignaviae, Cic. Without Acc.: magno opere virtuti, Caes. **d.** to grant, bestow: tantum dignitati civitati, Caes.; mulieri honorem, Cic.; Ov.; inventoribus gratiam, Cic.; misericordiam alicui, Cic.; silentium orationi alicuius, Cic.; veniam alicui, Tac.; pacem terris, Ov.; vocabula monti, Ov.

tribus, ūs, f. [fr. root of trēs], orig. a third part of the Roman people (the number of tribes finally increased to 35, of which 31 were rusticae tribūs and 4 urbanae tribūs). **1.** Lit.: Cic., Liv., etc. **2.** Transf. **a.** grammaticas ambire tribūs, Hor. **b.** the poor folk, the masses: Mart.

tribūtārius, a, um [tribūtum], paying tribute or money: Suet.; tabellae (i.e. letters of credit), Cic.

tribūtim, adv. [tribus], tribe by tribe, by tribes: Cic., Hor., Liv.

tribūtiō, ōnis, f. [tribuō], a dividing, distributing: Cic.

(1) tribūtus, a, um. **I.** Part. tribuō. **II.** **tribūtum**, ī, n. (**tribūtus**, ī, m.: Pl.) an assigned or allotted payment, a contribution, tribute; esp. a kind of income tax levied on all citizens. **1.** Lit.: in singula capita tributum imponere, Caes.; tributa pendere, Caes.; ex censu conferre, Cic.; civitates tributis liberare, Cic. Ep.; populo indicere, imperare, Liv.; Tac. **2.** Transf. **a.** Of fruit yielded to the proprietor by a tree: Ov. **b.** Of a gift or present (from a dependant): Stat., Juv.

(2) tribūtus, a, um [tribus], formed or arranged into tribes: comitia, Liv.

tricae, ārum, f. pl. [acc. to Plin. fr. Trica, ae, f., the name of a small, unimportant town in Apulia], trifles, toys, stuff, nonsense. **1.** Lit.: Pl., Mart. **2.** Transf. (cf.

intricō) : *hindrances, subterfuges, tricks* :
Pl., Cic. Ep.

tricēni, ae, a [trigintā], *thirty in a group or
thirty each* : Cic., Plin., Mart.

triceps, cipitis. *adj.* [trēs caput], *three-
headed* : Cerberus, Cic. ; Hecate (who
was also Luna and Diana), Cic.

tricēnsimus (-ēs-) and **trigēsimus** (Mart.),
a, um [trigintā], *thirtieth* : Cic., Hor., etc.

trichila, ae, *f. a bower, arbour, summer-
house* : Caes., Verg. [Fr. *treille.*]

triciēns (-iēs), *adv.* [trigintā], *thirty times* :
triciens (*sc.* centena milia) aeris habere
(i.e. three millions), Cic.

triclīnium, ī, *n.* [τρικλίνιον], *a couch for
reclining on at meals, running round three
sides of a table, an eating-couch, table-couch.*
1. Lit. : Cic., Mart., etc. **2.** T r a n s f. *a
dining-room, supper-room* : Cic., Phaedr.

tricō, ōnis, *m.* [tricae], *a plotter, trickster* :
Pl.

tricor, ārī [tricae], *to make or start difficulties* ;
to trifle, shuffle, play tricks : Cic. Ep.

tricorpor, oris, *adj.* [trēs corpus], *three-
bodied* : umbra, Verg.

tri-cuspis, idis, *adj. three-pointed* : telum,
Ov.

tri-dēns, entis, *adj. three-pronged* : rostra,
Verg. As *Masc.* Noun, *a trident* : as an
attribute of Neptune, Verg., Ov. ; as
a weapon of the net-fighters (retiarii),
Juv. ; *used to spear large fish*, Plin.

tridentifer (and **-ger**), erī, *m.* [tridēns and
ferō or gerō], *the trident-bearer*, an epithet
of Neptune : Ov.

triduum (older **triduom**), ī, *n.* [trēs diēs],
the space of three days, three days : hoc
triduom solum, Pl. ; decrevit habendas
triduum ferias, Cic. ; triduo intermisso,
Caes. ; cum tridui viam processaisset,
Caes.

triennia, ium, *n. pl.* (strictly, *n. pl.* of *adj.*
triennis, e, *sc.* sacra), *a festival celebrated
every three years, a triennial festival* : Ov.

triennium, ī, *n.* (*sc.* spatium) [trēs annus],
the space of three years, three years : Pl.,
Caes., etc.

triēns, entis, *m.* [trēs, *a third part, a third*.
A. In gen. : Cic. Ep., Plin. Of inheritances : heres ex triente, *heir to one-third of
a property*, Suet. **B.** In partic. **a.** *the
third part of an as* : Varr., Hor. **b.** *a
third of a sextarius* ; Prop.

trientābulum, ī, *n.* [triēns], *land given by
the State as an equivalent for one-third of the
sum which the State owed* : Liv.

trientius, a, um [triēns], *sold for a third* :
ager, Liv.

triērarchus, ī, *m.* [τριήραρχος], *the captain
of a trireme, a trierarch* : Cic., Tac.

triēris, e, *adj.* [τριήρης], *having three banks
of oars* : navis, Auct. B. Afr. As Noun,
triēris, is, *f. a trireme* : Nep.

trietēricus, a, um [τριετηρικός], *recurring
every three years, triennial* : sacra, Ov.
As Noun, **trietērica**, ōrum, *n. pl. the
festival of Bacchus* : Ov.

trietēris, idis, *f.* [τριετηρίς], *a space of three
years.* **1.** Lit. : Stat., Mart. **2.** T r a n s f.
a triennial festival. Of the festival of
Bacchus : Cic.

trifāriam, *adv. in three parts or places* :

distrahere exercitum, Liv. ; adoriri castra,
Liv. ; munire, Liv. ; epulas dispertire,
Suet.

trifaux, faucis, *adj.* [trēs faucēs], *triple-
throated* : latratus (Cerberi), Verg.

trifidus, a, um [trēs *and* fid in findō], *cleft
or cloven into three parts, three-forked* :
flamma, Ov.

trifilis, e, *adj.* [trēs filum], *having three
threads or hairs* : calva, Mart.

triformis, e, *adj.* [trēs fōrma], *having three
forms, shapes, or natures* ; *three-fold* :
Chimaera, Hor. ; diva (i.e. *Diana*, who
was also Luna and Hecate), Hor. ; Ov. ;
mundus, Ov.

tri-fūr, fūris, *m. a triple-thief* : non fur,
sed trifur, Pl.

tri-furcifer, erī, *m. a triple-gallowsbird* :
Pl.

tri-geminus (tergeminus), a, um [trēs
geminus], *three born at a birth* : Pl., Liv.
(*Masc.* as Noun : Liv.) Also, *of three
born together* : spolia, Liv. T r a n s f. in
gen. : *three-fold, triple* : Hecate (because
she was also Luna and Diana), Verg. ;
of Cerberus, Ov. ; of Geryon, Lucr. ;
honores, Hor. ; tergemina dextra (of the
three Graces), Stat. ; trigeminae victoriae
triplicem triumphum egistis, Liv.

trigintā, *indecl. adj.* [*cf.* Gk. τριάκοντα],
thirty : Pl., Cic., Verg. [It. *trenta* ; Fr.
trente.]

trigōn, ōnis, *m.* [τρίγων *or* τρίγωνον], *a
kind of ball for playing with*, esp. in the
baths : Hor., Mart.

trilibris, e, *adj.* [trēs lībra], *of three pounds
weight* : mullus, Hor.

trilinguis, e, *adj.* [trēs lingua], *triple-tongued* :
os (Cerberi), Hor.

trilix, īcis, *adj.* [trēs līcium], *woven with
three sets of leashes, triple-twilled* : lorica
auro trilix, Verg.

trimēstris, e, *adj.* [trēs mēnsis], *of three
months* : haedi, *three months old*, Varr. ;
consul, Suet.

trimetros *or* **-trus**, tra, trum [τρίμετρος], in
prosody, *containing three metres or double-
feet, trimeter* : versus, Quint. As Noun,
trimetrus, ī, *m. a trimeter* : Hor., Quint.

trimodia, ae, *f.* (**trimodium**, ī, *n.* Pl.) [trēs
modius], *a vessel that contains three modii* :
Varr.

trimulus, a, um [*dim.* trimus], *only three
years old* : Suet.

trimus, a, um [trēs : *v.* bimus], *three years
old* : Pl., Varr., Hor.

Trinacria, ae, *f.* [Τρινακρία] and **Trinacris**,
idos (Ov.), *f. the island of Sicily* ; **Trina-
crius**, a, um ; **Trinacris**, idis, *f. adj.
Sicilian.*

trini, ae, a, and **trinus**, a, um, *grouped as
three, or three in a group, triple* : castra,
Caes., Liv. ; ludi, Cic. ; annales, Liv. ;
trinis catenis vinctus, Caes. ; cantus trino
conficitur versu, Plin. ; forum, Stat.

Trinobantēs, um, *m. pl. a people in the
eastern part of Britain, in Essex and Middle-
sex.*

trinoctiālis, e, *adj. for (the space of) three
nights* : Mart.

trinōdis, e, *adj.* [trēs nōdus], *three-knotted,
knotty* : clava, Ov.

trinūndinum, ī, *n. v.* nūndinum.

triōbolus, ī, *m.* [τριώβολος], *a piece of three oboli, a half-drachma* : Pl.

triōnēs, um, *m. pl.* orig. *the ploughing-oxen ;* hence, *the constellations of the Greater and Lesser Bear* (*cf.* septemtriones) : Verg., Ov.

Triopās, ae, *m.*, *f. of Erysichthon ;* **Triopēius**, ī, *m. Erysichthon ;* **Triopēis**, idis, *f. a grand-daughter of Triopas*, i.e. *Mestra.*

tri-parcus, a, um, *thrice* (i.e. *very*) *sparing, miserly, niggardly* : homines, Pl.

tripart-, *v.* tripert-.

tripectorus, a, um [trēs pectus], *triple-breasted* : vis Geryonāī, Lucr.

tri-pedālis, e, *adj. of three feet* in measure : parma, Liv. ; Varr.

tri-pertītus (**tripart-**), a, um, *divided* or *divisible into three parts* : Cic., Tac. **ABL.** *n.* **tripertītō** (**tripart-**) as *Adv. in* or *into three parts* : adgredi urbem, Liv. ; Caes. : bona dividere, Cic. ; Caes.

tri-pēs, pedis, *adj. having three feet, three-footed* or *-legged* : mensa, Hor.

triplex, icis, *adj.* [ter plicō], *three-fold, triple* : doli, Pl. ; acies, Caes. ; animus, Cic. ; murus, Verg. ; aes, Verg., Hor. ; cuspis, mundus, regnum, Ov. ; gens, Verg. ; vultus Dianae (who was also Luna and Hecate), Ov. ; deae (i.e. the Fates), Ov. ; poenarum deae (i.e. the Furies), Ov. As Noun. **a. triplex**, icis, *n. three times as much, a three-fold portion* : Hor., Liv. **b. triplicēs**, um, *m. pl.* (*sc.* codicilli), *a writing-tablet with three leaves* : Cic. Ep., Mart.

triplus, a, um [*cf.* duplus], *three-fold, triple* : pars, Cic. **Neut. ABL.** as Noun : triplo plus scortorum, *three times as many*, Pl.

Triptolemus, ī, *m. son of Celeus, king of Eleusis ; he was a favourite of Ceres, and the inventor of agriculture : he became a judge in the infernal regions.*

tripudiō, āre [tripudium], in relig. lang. *to beat the ground with the feet, to leap, dance* as a religious act. **1.** Lit. : Inscr. **2.** Transf. **a.** Of a war-dance : tripudiantes more suo, Liv. **b.** In gen. *to leap, dance, caper* : Cic.

tripudium, ī, *n.* **I.** *a measured stamping, leaping, dancing* in relig. solemnities, *a solemn religious dance* (usually in *pl.*). **1.** Lit. : Salios ancilla ferre ac per urbem ire canentis carmina cum tripudiis sollemnique saltatu iussit, Liv. **2.** Transf. **a.** *war-dances :* cum sui moris tripudiis arma (quisque) capiebat, Liv. **b.** *dances in* gen. : Cat. **II.** *a kind of favourable omen, when the sacred chickens ate so greedily that the food dropped from their mouths to the ground* : Cic., Liv., Suet.

tripūs, podis, *m.* [τρίπους], *a three-footed seat, a tripod.* **1.** Lit. : Verg., Hor. Esp. *the tripod of the priestess at Delphi* : Cic., Verg., Ov. **2.** Transf. **a.** *the oracle at Delphi* : Ov. **b.** *an oracle* in gen. : Stat.

triquetrus, a, um, *three-cornered, triangular.* **a.** *Sicilian :* orae, Lucr. ; tellus, Hor. **b.** Of Britain : insula, Caes.

tri-rēmis, e, *adj.* [rēmus], *having three banks of oars* : naves, Caes. As Noun, **trirēmis**, is, *f. a vessel with three banks of oars, a trireme* : Cic., Hor., Liv.

tris, *v.* trēs.

triscurria, ōrum, *n. pl.* [root of trēs, with scurra], *gross buffooneries* : Juv.

tristiculus, a, um [*dim.* tristis], *rather glum* or *sombre* : Cic. Ep.

tristificus, a, um [tristis faciō], *making gloomy, ill-boding* : voces, Cic. poet.

tristis, e, *adj. gloomy, dismal, sombre, forbidding, harsh, severe, stern.* **A.** Of character in gen. **a.** Of persons and their appearance, manner, habits, etc. : truculentis oculis, tristi fronte, Pl. ; supercilium, Plin. Pan. ; tristis severitas inest in voltu, Ter. ; vultus severior et tristior, Cic. ; iudex tristis et integer, Cic. ; navita (i.e. Charon), Verg. ; Erinys, Verg. ; vita, sors, Cic. ; tetrica et tristis disciplina veterum Sabinorum, Liv. ; in iudiciis tristem et impexam antiquitatem, Tac. ; dicta, Verg., Tac. ; sententia, Liv., Ov. ; senatūs consultum, Liv. **Masc.** as Noun : Cic., Hor. **b.** Of things : Tartara, Verg. ; tristi palus inamabilis undā, Verg. ; Kalendae, Hyades, bella, Hor. ; funera, ministerium, Verg. ; ius sepulcri, Ov. ; trunci, Sen. Ep. Of taste, *harsh, bitter :* Lucr., Verg., Liv., etc. Of smell : Ov. As Noun, **triste**, is, *n. : triste lupus stabulis, maturis frugibus imbres, Verg. ; mitibus mutare tristia, Hor. ; Ov. ; Tristia, " dismal surroundings," Ov. **B.** Of a particular mood, etc. **a.** *gloomy, sad, mournful, dejected, sad.* (i.) Of persons and their appearance, etc. : Pl., Caes., Cic., Hor., etc. ; dii, Hor. ; voltus, Pl. **Comp.** : Pl. **Sup.** ; cum tuum laetissimum diem cum tristissimo meo conferam, Cic. ; exsilium, Liv. (ii.) Of things : morbus, Verg. ; clades, Hor. ; eventus Alexandri, Liv. **Sup.** : exta (i.e. ill-boding), Cic. **b.** Of temper, humour, etc. : *glum, ill-tempered, morose :* alicui esse, Pl., Prop.

tristitia, ae, *f.* and **tristitiēs**, ēī, *f.* (Pac., Tac.) [tristis], *gloominess, harshness, severity, sternness.* **A.** Of character in gen. : Cic., Prop., Ov. Esp. of some philosophers : Plin. Ep. Of things : lenitate verbi rei tristitiam mitigare, Cic. ; caeli, Plin. **B.** Of a particular mood, etc. : *glumness, dejection, sadness :* in eādem tristitiā permanere, Caes. ; ad tristitiam contorqueri, Cic. ; omnis tristitia invasit, Sall. ; haec tristitia temporum, Cic. Ep.

tri-sulcus, a, um [trēs sulcus], *having three furrows ;* hence, *three-cleft, three-forked :* lingua (serpentis), Verg. ; telum Iovis, Ov. ; Varr.

tritavus, ī, *m.* [tritus (= tertius) avus], *the father of an atavus* or *atavia ; great-great-great-grandfather :* Pl. Of a remote ancestor : Varr.

triticeus (**tritīcēius**, Pl.), a, um [triticum], *of wheat, wheaten :* paleae, Cato ; furfures, Varr. ; messis, Verg. ; Ov.

triticum, ī, *n.* [Varr. derives it from tritus, terō], *wheat :* Pl., Caes., Cic. [Sp. *trigo.*]

Trītōn, ōnis or ōnos, *m.* **I.** *a sea-god, son of Neptune, who blows through a shell to calm the sea.* **II.** *a river and lake in Africa, near the Lesser Syrtis, where, according to some authorities, Minerva was born ;*

Trĭtōnĭus, a, um; **Trĭtōnĭa**, ae, f. *Minerva :* **Trĭtōnĭăcus**, a, um; and **Trĭtōnis**, idis or idos, *Minerva ; as adj. Palladian :* arx, *the citadel of Pallas or Minerva,* i.e. *Athens,* Ov.

trītor, ōris, m. [terō], *a rubber, grinder :* colorum, Plin. C o m i c. : compedium, stimulorum, Pl.

trītŭ, ABL. *sing. m. by* or *in rubbing :* lapidum, Cic.

trītūra, ae, f. [terō], *a threshing* of grain : Varr., Verg.

trītus, a, um. **I.** *Part.* terō. **II.** A d j. **1.** L i t. *worn, beaten, frequented :* iter, via, Cic. ; Ov. ; subucula, Hor. *Sup. :* Sen. **2.** T r a n s f. **a.** *practised, expert :* tritas auris habere, Cic. **b.** Of language, *used often, common, commonplace, trite :* tritum sermone proverbium, Cic. *Comp. :* Cic.

trĭumphālis, e, adj. [triumphus], *of* or *connected with a triumph, triumphal :* provincia, Cic. ; porta, Cic., Suet. ; ornamenta (usually a wreath of gold, embroidered toga (toga picta) and tunic (tunica palmata), ivory staff, etc.), Cic. ; insignia, Tac. ; imagines, Hor. ; status, Plin. Ep. ; senex, Hor. As Noun, **trĭumphālis**, is, m. *one who has had the honours of a triumph :* Suet. **trĭumphālĭa**, ium, n. pl. (sc. insignia), *the distinctions of a triumph without the actual triumph :* Tac.

trĭumphō, āre [triumphus]. **1.** L i t. *to make a triumphal procession, to celebrate a triumph, to triumph :* Cic., Liv. ; ex praeturā, Cic. ; de Numantinis, Cic. ; Liv. *Impers. Pass. :* Cic., Liv. **2.** T r a n s f. **a.** Pl. ; de me Amor, Prop. ; Ov. **b.** Of exultant joy : Ter. ; gaudio, Cic. ; in omnium gemitu, Cic. **3.** In *Pass.* **a.** *to be triumphed over* (usually in *Perf. Part.*) : triumphatas gentis, Verg. ; Hor. ; Tac. ; ne triumpharetur Mithridates, Tac. **b.** In *Perf. Part. : won by victory :* bos, Ov.

trĭumphus (old form **trĭumpus**), i, m. [cf. θρίαμβος, *a procession in honour of Bacchus*]. **1.** L i t. **a.** triumpe, *a cry raised at the festival of Mars held by the Arval Brothers :* Inscr. **b.** *a triumphal procession after an important victory, a triumph :* Cic., Liv. ; Verg. ; nomine ciere, Liv. ; deportare, Cic. ; de aliquo agere, Cic., Liv. ; ex Etruriā agere, Liv. ; Pharsalicae pugnae agere, Cic. ; Boiorum, Liv. ; in triumpho duci, Cic. ; aliquem per triumphum ducere, Cic. ; triumpho clarissimo urbem est invectus, Liv. ; io triumphe (the shout of the soldiers and spectators during the procession), Hor. **2.** T r a n s f. *a triumph, victory :* ut repulsam tuam triumphum suum duxerint, Cic. [It. *trionfo.*]

trĭumvir, v. triumviri.

trĭumvĭrālis, e, adj. [triumviri], *of the triumvirs, triumviral :* flagella, Hor. ; supplicium, Tac.

trĭumvĭrātus, ūs, m. [triumviri], *the office of a triumvir, a triumvirate :* triumviratus (coloniae deducendae), Cic., Liv. ; rei publicae constituendae, Suet.

trĭum-vĭri (and **trēs-vĭri**, q.v.), ōrum or um, m. pl. [três vir ; Lit. in *sing.* "one man of three " ; cf. duumviri], *three men holding*

an office conjointly, a commission of three ; in *sing.* **trĭumvir**, *a member of such a commission.* **a.** coloniae deducendae or agro dando, Liv. In *sing. :* Cic., Sall., Liv. **b.** capitales, *police-magistrates, superintendents of public prisons and executions,* Pl., Cic., Liv. **c.** epulones : v. tresviri. **d.** rei publicae constituendae ; in the case of Antony, Octavian, and Lepidus, Suet. *Sing. :* Nep. **e.** For various other purposes : Liv. **f.** Of the chief magistrates of a municipium. In *sing. :* Cic.

trĭvĕnēfĭca, ae, f. [root of três, with venēfica], *a "triple-dyed" poison-mixer, an absolute witch :* Pl.

trĭvĭālis, e, adj. [trivium], *of the cross-roads.* T r a n s f. : *found everywhere, commonplace, ordinary :* scientia, Quint. ; carmen, Juv. ; verba, Suet.

trĭvĭum, i, n. [três via], *a place where three roads meet, a cross-road.* **1.** L i t. : Cic., Verg. **2.** T r a n s f. *a public street, highway :* Cic., Lucr., Hor., etc. ; adripere male dictum ex trivio, Cic.

trĭvĭus, a, um [trivium], *of the crossways* or *crossroads ; worshipped at the crossroads :* virgo (i.e. Diana or Hecate), Lucr. ; dea, Prop. As Noun, **Trĭvĭa**, ae, f. *Diana* or *Hecate :* Enn., Cat., Verg., Ov.

Trōas, adis, v. Trōs.

trochaeus, i, m. [τροχαῖος]. **I.** *a metrical foot of two syllables, a long and a short* (— ⌣), *a trochee :* Cic. **II.** *another name for the tribrachys, a metrical foot of three short syllables* (⌣ ⌣ ⌣), *a tribrach :* Cic.

trochaïcus, a, um [τροχαϊκός], *consisting of trochees, trochaic :* Quint.

trochlĕa, ae, f. [τροχαλία], *a case* or *sheaf containing one* or *more pulleys, a block.* **1.** L i t. : Cato, Lucr. **2.** T r a n s f. : trochleis pituitam adducere, Quint.

trochus, i, m. [τροχός], *a hoop, a trundling-hoop for children :* Hor., Ov., etc.

Troezēn, ēnis, f. *a very ancient city of Argolis where Theseus was born ;* **Troezēnĭus**, a, um.

Trōĭa, Trōĭus, v. Trōs.

Trōïlus, i, m., s. of Priam, *slain by Achilles.*

Trōĭugĕna, ae, m. f. *Troy-born, born in Troy, of Trojan descent, Trojan :* gentes, Lucr. As Noun, *a Trojan :* Cat., Verg. ; also, *a Roman :* Juv.

tropaeum, i, n. [τρόπαιον], *a sign and memorial of victory, a trophy* (orig. of captured arms, etc., attached to a tree-trunk and dedicated). **1.** L i t. : Cic., Verg., etc. **2.** T r a n s f. **a.** *a victory :* nova cantemus Augusti tropaea Caesaris, Hor. ; Nep. ; Ov. T r a n s f. : Cic. **b.** *a mark, token, sign, memorial, monument :* necessitudinis atque hospiti, Cic. ; Prop.

Trophōnĭus, i, m. *a brother of Agamedes, in conjunction with whom he built the temple of Apollo at Delphi ; after his death he had a celebrated oracle ;* **Trophōnĭānus**, a, um.

Trōs, ōis, m. *a king of Phrygia, after whom Troy was named ;* **Trōïa** or **Trōĭa**, ae, f. *Troy ; a city of Asia Minor, famous for its ten years' siege by the Greeks.* (Also of a sort of sham fight on horse-back : Verg.

Tac.) ; **Trŏius** (**Trōus**), a, um, **Trŏiānus**, a, um, and **Trōiāni**, ōrum, *m. pl. the Trojans ;* **Trōs**, Trōis, *m. a Trojan ;* **Trōicus**, a, um ; **Trōas**, ădis or ădos, *f. adj. ; as Noun, a Trojan woman, also the region about Troy, the Troad ;* **Trōiugena**, ae, *m. a Trojan, also a Roman.*

trucīdātiō, ōnis, *f.* [trucīdō], *a slaughtering, massacring, butchery :* civium, Cic. ; pecorum, Liv. In *pl. :* Cato.

trucīdō, āre [trunc̄us caedō], *to slaughter, butcher, massacre.* **1.** Lit. : sicut pecora trucidari, Sall. ; civis Romanos trucidandos curavit, Cic. ; Liv., etc. Comic. : seu piscis seu porrum et caepe trucidas (a hit at the Pythagoreans), Hor. **2.** Transf. : ignem, Lucr. ; plebem faenore, Liv. ; Cic.

truculentia, ae, *f.* [truculentus], *savageness, harshness :* tua, Pl. ; caeli, Tac.

truculentius, *comp. adv. more savagely or ferociously :* Cic. *Sup. :* Quint.

truculentus, a, um [trux], *savage, ferocious, grim, harsh, etc.* **a.** Of persons and their appearance, etc. : Pl., Cic., Ov., etc. ; oculi, Pl. ; voces, Tac. *Comp. :* Ov., Tac. *Neut. Intern. Acc. :* truculenta loquens, Ov. **b.** Of things : aequor, Cat. *Neut. pl.* as Noun : truculenta pelagi tulistis, Cat. ; caeli, Tac.

trudis, is, *f.* [trūdō], *a pointed pole, a pike :* Verg.

trūdō, trūdere, trūsi, trūsum, *to thrust, push, shove, drive, impel.* **1.** Lit. : Lucr. ; haec, Pl. ; adverso monte saxum, Lucr. ; pectore montem (*sc.* nivis), Verg. ; glaciem flumina, Verg. ; Cherusci trudunt adversos, Tac. ; apros in plagas, Hor. Of buds : pampinus gemmas, Verg. ; se de cortice gemmae, Verg. **2.** Transf. : ad mortem trudi, Cic. ; semet in arma, Tac. ; Cic. ; fallacia alia aliam trudit, Ter. ; truditur dies die, Hor.

trulla, ae, *f.* [dim. trua, *a ladle ; cf.* Gk. τορ-ύνη], *a small ladle, dipper, or scoop* (esp. for wine). **1.** Lit. : Cato, Cic., Hor., etc. **2.** Transf. **a.** *a scoop-shaped fire-pan, a cresset :* Liv. **b.** *a wash-basin :* Juv.

trulleum (**-ium**), i, *n.* [trulla], *a basin, wash-basin :* Cato ; Varr.

truncō, āre [truncus], *to maim, mutilate, or lop :* holus foliis, Ov. ; arbores, Suet. ; simulacra deum, statuas regis, Liv. ; truncato ex vulneribus corpore, Tac.

truncus, a, um. **1.** Lit. **a.** *lopped, stripped* of branches and leaves : pinus, Verg. **b.** *maimed, mutilated :* nares (inhonesto vulnere), Verg. ; corpus, Curt. ; frons Acheloi, Ov. ; vultus naribus auribusque, Mart. ; tela, Verg. **2.** Transf. **a.** *imperfect, undeveloped, wanting some of its natural parts :* corpus, Liv. ; ranae pĕdibus truncae, Ov. ; manus, Prop. With Gen. : animalia trunca pedum, Verg. **b.** *maimed, dismembered, lacking some essential feature :* urbs, sine senatu, sine plebe, sine magistratibus, Liv. As Noun, **truncus**, i, *m.* **1.** Lit. **a.** *the lopped tree, the stock, bole, or trunk of a tree :* Lucr., Caes., Cic., Verg., etc. **b.** Of the human body, *the trunk, body :* Lucr., Cic.,

Verg. **2.** Transf. **a.** *a piece* of flesh *cut off* (to be smoked) : Verg. **b.** *a stock, blockhead, dolt :* Cic. **c.** ipso trunco aegritudinis everso, Cic.

trūsitō, āre [*freq.* trūdō], *to push or thrust often :* mulum, Phaedr.

trūsus, a, um, *Part.* trūdō.

trutīna, ae, *f.* [τρυτάνη], *a balance, pair of scales.* **1.** Lit. : Varr. **2.** Transf. : quādam populari trutinā examinantur, Cic. ; pensantur eādem scriptores trutinā, Hor. ; Juv.

trutīnor, āri [trutina], *to weigh, balance.* Transf. : verba, Pers.

trux, ucis, *adj. savage, ferocious, grim.* **a.** Of living beings and their appearance, manner, etc. : tribunus plebis, Cic. ; Liv. ; vultus, Hor., Ov., Liv. ; oculi, Luc., Tac. ; animus, Ov. ; sententia, Liv. ; eloquentia, oratio, Tac. ; arietes, Pl. ; aper, taurus, Ov. **b.** Of things : pelagus, Hor. ; Eurus, Ov. ; venti, Plin. ; classicum, Hor. ; sonor, Tac.

tryblium, i, *n.* [τρύβλιον], *a plate, salver :* Pl.

trygōnus, i, *m.* (Pl.) and **trygōn**, ōnis, *m.* (Plin.) *a sting-ray.*

tū and *pl.* **vōs** (Acc. *sing.* tēd, Pl., Gen. *sing.* tis, Pl. Gen. *pl. :* vostrōrum, Pl. ; *fem.* vostrārum, Ter.), *pron. pers. of 2nd pers.* [*cf.* Attic σύ, Doric τύ], *thou, you* (for *pl. v.* vos) : ego tu sum, tu es ego : uni animi sumus, Pl. ; Cic. ; Verg., etc. With the emphatic suffix -te or -met or temet : tute, Pl., Cic. ; tutemet mirabere, Ter. ; ita vosmet aiiebatis, Pl. ; vosmet ipsi, Liv. *tu* is often used of a typical or imaginary person (as *you* in English). *vos* is sometimes used with a collective or representative noun in *sing. :* vos, o Calliope, precor aspirate canenti, Verg. ; Cic. ; Liv. [It. Sp. Fr. *tu* ; It. *voi* ; Sp. *vos* ; Fr. *vous.*]

tuātim, *adv.* [tuus], *after your manner :* iam tuatim facis, Pl.

tuba, ae, *f.* [same root as tubus], *a trumpet,* esp. *a war-trumpet.* **1.** Lit. : Pl., Cic., Verg., etc. ; signum tubā dare, Caes., Liv. It was used also at religious festivals, games, funerals : Verg., Hor., Ov., etc. **2.** Transf. : tuba belli civilis, Cic.

tūber, eris, *n.* [fr. root seen in tumeō], *a hump, bump, swelling.* **1.** Lit. : Ter. ; cameli, Plin. **2.** Transf. **a.** Of great moral failings : qui ne tuberibus propriis offendat amicum postulat, ignoscet verrucis illius, Hor. **b.** *a truffle :* Plin., Mart., Juv.

tuber, eris, *f.* a kind of *apple-tree.* **1.** Lit. Plin. **2.** Transf. (*masc.*) of its fruit : Plin., Mart., Suet.

tubicen, inis, *m.* [tuba canō], *a trumpeter :* esp. in war : Liv., Ov. Also, sacrorum, Varr.

tubilūstrium, i, *n.* [tuba lūstrō], *a ritual cleansing of the sacred trumpets,* a festival held on March 23rd and May 23rd : Varr. In *pl. :* Ov.

tuburcinor, āri, *to eat greedily, gobble up, devour :* de suo, Pl.

tubus, i, *m. a pipe, tube :* Plin.

tuccētum or **tūcētum**, i, *n. a kind of sausage* or *haggis :* Pers.

tuditāns, antis [v. tundō], *striking* or *beating often* : corpora rem, Lucr. T r a n s f. : Enn.

tueor (older **tuor** and **tueō**), tuērī, tūtus or tuitus, *to look* or *gaze at, behold, watch, observe.* **A.** In gen. : Verg. With Acc. of Object : Tac., Lucr., Verg. With *Intern.* Acc. : acerba, Lucr. ; aversa, transversa, torva, Verg. With Acc. and *Inf.* : Lucr. **B.** Of guarding, protecting, defending, maintaining. **1.** L i t. : castra, Caes. ; oppidum unius legionis praesidio, Caes. ; se, vitam corpusque, Cic. ; Liv. ; sex legiones re suā, Cic. ; finis suos ab excursionibus, Cic. ; Phaedr. ; (eos) contra illius audaciam, Cic. ; Tac. ; se adversus Romanos, Liv. ; Tac. **2.** T r a n s f. : mores et instituta vitae, Cic. ; dignitatem, Cic. ; concordiam, auctoritatem, Cic. Ep. ; personam in re publicā, Cic. ; libertatem, Tac.

tugurium, I, *n.* [tegō], *a hut, cot, hovel, cottage* of shepherds, peasants, etc. : Cic., Verg.

Tuiscō, ōnis, *m. the progenitor of the Germans, honoured by them as a god.*

tuitiō, ōnis, *f.* [tueor], *a looking after, guarding ; defence :* sui, Cic.

tuli, *v.* ferō.

Tulliola, ae, *f. dim. an affectionate name for* Tullia, *the daughter of Cicero.*

Tullius, a, *the name of a Roman gens.* Esp. Servius Tullius, *the sixth king of Rome ;* and M. Tullius Cicero, *the renowned statesman and orator : killed* B.C. 43 B.C. **Tulliānus**, a, um ; **Tulliānum**, I, *n. the dungeon of the State-prison in Rome, built by Servius Tullius.*

tum, *adv.* [from the I.E. pronoun-stem *ta-*, Gk. το-, Latin *to-*]. **I.** As A d v. **1.** L i t. of past time : *at that time, then.* **a.** Simply : vastae tum in his locis solitudines erant, Liv. ; Pl. ; Cic. ; Verg., etc. **b.** With corresponding *cum* (quom), *postquam, ubi, etc.* : Hercules tum dolore frangebatur cum immortalitatem ipsā morte quaerebat, Cic. ; Pl. ; Ov., etc. ; postquam rem publica adolevit, tum lex Porcia aliaeque paratae, Sall. ; Cic., etc. ; ubi eorum dolorem cognovi, tum eos hortatus sum, Cic. ; Pl. ; Liv., etc. **c.** Strengthened with *demum* (*then and not till then*), *denique* (*then at last*), *maxime* (*then especially*), *vero* (*then indeed* or *then more than ever*) : morte eius nuntiatā tum denique bellum confectum arbitratus est, Cic. ; Caes. ; Lucr., etc. ; confecto proelio tum vero cerneres, etc., Sall. ; Cic. ; Ov., etc. **2.** T r a n s f. **A.** Of succession of events (mostly in past time, but occ. of present or future) : *then, next, thereupon.* **a.** Simply : quid tum ? Pl., Ter., Cic., etc. ; tum Piso exorsus est, Cic. ; Pl. ; primum colonos Romanos expulit, inde Lavinium recepit, tum deinceps etc., Liv. **b.** With corresponding *cum* (quom), *etc.* : tum cum tu es iratus permittis iracundiae dominatum animi tui, Cic. ; Pl., etc. **c.** Strengthened as in I. c. : talibus incensus dictis tum vero in curas animum diducitur, Verg. ; Cic., etc. **B.** Of enumeration of facts or arguments : *then, again, moreover, in the next place.* **a.** Simply : gigni autem terram, aquam,

ignem, tum ex illis omnia, Cic. ; Pl. ; Liv., etc. **b.** Strengthened as in I. c. : tum primum, Caes., Lucr., Cic. ; tum etiam, Ter., Caes., Cic. **II.** A d v e r b i a l c o n j u n c t i o n, always either repeated or connected with *cum* (quom). **a.** tum ... tum, *first* ... *then* ; *at one time* ... *at another time* ; *now* ... *now, as well* ... *as, both* ... *and, partly* ... *partly,* Pl., Cic., etc. **b.** cum (quom) ... tum, *both* ... *and especially, not only* ... *but also, if* ... *then surely* : quae virtus cum in paucis est, tum in paucis iudicatur et cernitur, Cic. ; fortuna quae plurimum potest cum in reliquis rebus tum praecipue in bello, Caes. ; cum .. tum etiam, Caes. (N.B. that the verb in the *cum* clause is sometimes *Subj.* : cum in omnibus causis gravioribus commoveri soleam vehementius, tum in hac causā me multa perturbant, Cic.)

tume-faciō, facere, fēcī, factum, *to cause to swell.* **1.** L i t. : vis fera ventorum caecis inclusa cavernis extentam tumefecit humum, Ov. **2.** T r a n s f. (with joy, pride, etc.) : laetitiā tumefactus inani, Prop. ; Mart.

tumeō, ēre, *to swell, be bloated, swollen* or *puffed out.* **1.** L i t. : Pl. ; pedes, Verg. ; nares ac pectus, Quint. ; corpus veneno, Ov. ; Lucr. ; Achelous imbre, Ov. ; a vento unda, Ov. **2.** T r a n s f. **a.** With anger : Cic. ; irā, Liv. With D a t. of person *against whom :* Stat. **b.** With any passionate excitement, pride, etc. : rabie corda tument, Verg. ; laudis amore, Hor. ; tument negotia, Cic. Ep. ; bella, Ov. ; Galliae, Tac. **c.** Of speech : Quint., Mart., Tac.

tumēscō, tumēscere, tumuī [tumeō], *to begin to swell, to swell up.* **1.** L i t. : mare, Cic. poet. ; vi maria, Verg. ; colla, Ov. ; vulnera, Tac. **2.** T r a n s f. (with anger, passionate excitement, pride, etc.) : ora mihi cum mente, Ov. ; operta bella, Verg. ; mens inani persuasione, Quint.

tumidus, a, um [tumeō], *swollen, rising high, puffed out.* **1.** L i t. : membrum, Cic. ; Python, Ov. ; mare, Auster, Verg. ; Nilus, Hor. **2.** T r a n s f. **a.** With anger, passionate excitement, pride, etc. : tumida ex irā corda residunt, Verg. ; cor, minae, Hor. ; institor eloquentiae, Quint. ; *Sup.* : Sen. T r a n s f. : honos, Prop. **b.** Of speech : Quint., Plin. Ep. Of the orator himself : Quint. *Comp.* : tumidior sermo, Liv. ; Plin. Ep.

tumor, ōris, *m.* [tumeō], *a swelling, bulging, protuberance.* **1.** L i t. : oculorum, Cic. ; Prop. ; tumor ille loci permansit et alti collis habet speciem, Ov. **2.** T r a n s f. **A.** Of the mind. **a.** From anger : cum tumor animi resedisset, Cic. ; erat in tumore animus, Cic. ; tumor et irae, Verg. **b.** From pride : Quint. In *pl.* : Luc. **B.** Of any passionate excitement : rerum, Cic. Ep. **C.** Of turgid or bombastic speech : Sen., Quint. [Fr. *tumeur.*]

tumulō, āre [tumulus], *to cover with a mound, to bury* : Cat., Ov.

tumulōsus, a, um [tumulus], *full of hills, hilly :* locus, Sall.

tumultuārius, a, um [tumultus]. Milit. of troops *brought hurriedly together, raised to meet an emergency.* **1**. Lit.: exercitus, milites, Liv. **2**. Transf. *that is done or happens in a hurry, hurried, extemporised, irregular :* pugna (opp. to iusta acies), Liv.; opus, castra, dux, Liv.

tumultuātiō, ōnis, *f.* [tumultuor], *a bustling, confusion :* Liv.

tumultuō, āre and **tumultuor**, ārī [tumultus] *to make a bustle* or *disturbance, to be in great agitation* or *confusion, to be in uproar.* **A**. Form tumultuo : Pl. *Impers. Pass. :* Caes., Liv. **B**. Form tumultuor : Pl., Cic.; Galliae, Suet. Of orators and oratory : Quint.

tumultuōsē, *adv. with bustle* or *confusion :* Liv. *Comp. :* Caes., Liv. *Sup. :* Cic.

tumultuōsus, a, um [tumultus], *full of bustle, confusion,* or *tumult : boisterous, disquieting, alarming :* sonitus, Pl.; vita, Cic.; contiones, Cic. Ep.; turba, multitudo, genus pugnae, proelia, nuntius, Liv.; mare, Hor. *Comp. :* iter, Liv.; litterae, Suet.; Cic. Ep. *Sup. :* quod tumultuosissimum pugnae erat, Liv.

tumultus, ūs (GEN. tumultī, Pl., Ter., Sall.) *m. [cf.* tumeō], *a rising, disturbance, uproar, violent commotion, tumult.* **1**. Lit. **a**. In gen.: magno cum strepitu ac tumultu castris egressi, Caes.; Pl.; ars inter tumultum capta est, Liv.; with trepidatio, Cic., Liv.; with formido, Sall.; with turba, terror, Liv.; armorum et cantuum, Tac.; caecos tumultūs instare, Verg.; Hor. **b**. Of the elements: tremendo Iuppiter ruens tumultu, Hor.; vides quanto trepidet tumultu Orion, Hor.; pelagi caelique, Luc. **c**. *a sudden rising* or *outbreak of war, insurrection, rebellion, civil war :* servilis, Caes.; hostilis, Tac. In Sardinia, Histria : Liv. Esp. of the Gauls in N. Italy : Cic., Liv.; Gallicus, Cic., Liv. **2**. Transf. of the mind or feelings : mentis, Hor.; sceleris, Hor.

tumulus, ī, *m. [cf.* tumeō], *a mound, rising* or *raised ground.* **a**. In gen.: terrenus, Caes.; ignis e speculā sublatus aut tumulo, Cic.; Verg. Of the *hills* of Rome : Liv. **b**. *a sepulchral mound, barrow :* Achillis, Cic.; hostilis, Verg.; statuere, facere, Verg.; struere, Tac.; inanis, Verg.; honorarius, Suet.

tunc, *adv.* [tum with demonstr. suffix -ce]. **1**. Lit. of past time : *at that very time, then, immediately.* **a**. Simply : tunc duces Nerviorum conloqui sese velle dicunt, Caes.; Enn.; Ov., etc.; nunc aiunt quod tunc negabant, Cic. In *Orat. Obliqua* (for *nunc* of *Orat. Recta*) : tunc ita habeant (senatum) ut de re publicā loqui prohibeant, Liv. **b**. With corresponding *cum* (quom), *etc. :* eo damnato tunc cum iudicia fiebant, Cic.; Pl.; Verg., etc. **c**. Strengthened with *demum, denique, primum, etc.* (*cf.* tum for the meaning) : tunc demum missus est nuntius, Liv.; Sall.; Ov., etc. **2**. Transf. **A**. Of succession of events (mostly of past time, but occ. of present or future) : *then, next, thereupon.* **a**. Simply : is finis pugnae equestris fuit ; tunc adorti peditum aciem, Liv.; Cic.;

Tac. **b**. With corresponding *cum* (quom) : tunc cum omnia dicta sunt testes dantur, Cic.; Cat., etc. **c**. Strengthened with *demum, vero, etc. :* in turbatos iam hostis equos immittunt : tunc vero Celtiberi omnes in fugam effunduntur, Liv. **B**. Of enumeration of facts or arguments : *then, again, moreover, in the next place ;* ante omnia . . . deinde . . . tunc, Suet.

tundō, tundere, tutudī, tūnsum or tūsum, *to beat, strike, thump, buffet with repeated strokes.* **1**. Lit. **a**. In gen.: lapidem digito, Lucr.; oculos bacillo, Cic.; Pl.; pectora manu, Ov.; Verg.; pede terram, Hor.; cymbala, Prop.; litus undā, Cat.; saxa alto salo, Hor.; Verg. In *Mid. :* tunsae pectora palmis, Verg. Prov.: eandem incudem diem noctemque tundere (*cf.* "harp on the same string"), Cic. **b**. Of grain, etc.: *to pound, bruise, bray :* tunsum gallae saporem, Verg.; fruges, Verg.; in farinam, Plin. **2**. Transf. of importunity, etc.: tundendo atque odio denique effecit senex, Ter.; auris, Pl.; adsiduis vocibus heros tunditur, Verg.

Tūnēs, ētis, *f.* (Acc. -ēta or -ētem), *a maritime town of Africa, now Tunis.*

tunica, ae, *f. the ordinary sleeved garment* worn at Rome by both sexes, *a tunic.* **1**. Lit.: Pl., Cic., Hor., etc. Prov.: tunica propior pallio est, Pl. (A tunic with long sleeves was thought effeminate : Pl., Cic., Verg.) **2**. Transf. *a jacket, skin, membrane, husk, etc. :* (gemmarum) tunicae, Verg.; boletorum, Plin.; teretis ponunt tunicas aestate cicadae, Lucr.

tunicātus, a, um [tunica], *wearing a tunic.* **1**. Lit.: Cic.; quies, Mart. Esp. of the common people, who wore the tunic only : Pl., Cic., Hor., Tac. **2**. Transf. (*cf.* tunica, 2.), *coated :* caepe, Pers.

tunicula, ae, *f. [dim.* tunica], *a little tunic.* **1**. Lit.: Pl., Varr. **2**. Transf. *a thin skin* or *coating :* oculorum, Plin.

tūnsus, a, um, *Part.* tundō.

tuor, *v.* tueor.

turba, ae, *f.* [*cf.* τύρβη], *an uproar, disorder, turmoil, riot.* **1**. Lit. **a**. Prop. (caused by several people) : Pl., Cic., Sall., Ov. In *pl.* : efficere turbas, Cic.; populares, Quint. **b**. (caused by one person), *a brawl, row, disturbance :* Pl., Ter.; turba atque rixa, Cic.; uxori turbas conciet, Pl. **2**. Transf. *a mob, throng, troop, rabble, rout.* **a**. Of persons : in foro turbāque, Cic.; cum ex hac turbā et conluvione discedam, Cic.; forensis, Liv.; militaris, Liv.; conferta, Liv.; patronorum, Cic.; ducum, Verg.; clientium, poetarum, Hor.; omnis Circi, Quint. **b**. Of things : ferarum, Ov.; Lucr.; pecorum, Liv.; materiāl, Lucr.; rotarum, Ov. Also, castrensium negotiorum, Plin. Ep. **c**. Of a speech : Cic.; inanium verborum, Quint. [Fr. *tourbe*.]

turbāmenta, ōrum, *n. pl.* [turbo], *means of disturbance :* rei publicae, Sall.; vulgi, Tac.

turbātē, *adv. confusedly, with disorder :* Caes.

turbātiō, ōnis, *f.* [turbo], *confusion, disorder :* rerum, Liv.

turbātor, ōris, m. [turbō], *a troubler, disturber :* vulgi, belli, Liv. ; plebis, Germaniae, Tac.

turbātus, a, um. **I.** *Part.* turbō. **II.** Adj. **A.** *disorderly, confused.* **1.** L i t. : turbatius mare, Suet. ; caelum, Suet. **2.** T r a n s f. : placare voluntates turbatas, Cic. **B.** *exasperated :* Pallas, Verg.

turbellae, ārum, *f. pl.* [*dim.* turba], *a bustle, stir, row :* facere, Pl.

turben, v. turbō.

turbidē, adv. *in disorder, confusedly :* Cic., Tac.

turbidus, a, um, *in wild confusion, boisterous, confused, disordered.* **1.** L i t. **a.** In gen. : tempestas, Pl., Lucr., Caes. ; tempestas telorum, Verg. ; Auster, Hor. ; aequora ponti, Lucr. ; ventis freta, Ov. ; imber, nubila, Verg. ; caelum, Plin. Ep. ; scaturrigines, Liv. **b.** Of fluids, *thick, muddy, turbid :* aqua, Cic. ; gurges caeno, Verg. ; auro Hermus, Verg. **2.** T r a n s f. : mores, Pl. ; turbidi concitatique motūs animorum, Cic. ; esse in turbidis rebus, Cic. ; hoc tam turbido tempore, Nep. ; reduxit in hiberna turbidos et nihil ausos, Tac. ; ex oculis se turbidus abstulit Arruns, Verg. ; puella, Ov. ; *Comp.* : pectora sunt ipso turbidiora mari, Ov. ; *Quint. Sup.* : turbidissimus quisque, Tac. *Neut.* as Noun : si turbidissima sapienter ferebas, Cic. Ep. ; in turbido, Liv., Tac. ; mens turbidum (*Intern.* Acc.) laetatur, Hor.

turbineus, a, um, [turbō], *top-shaped, cone-shaped :* vertex, Ov.

turbō, inis, m. (turben, inis, n. Tib.) [*cf.* turba], *any strong circular motion ; a whirl, swirl, eddy, twirl ; a coiling* or *spiral motion.* **1.** L i t. **a.** In gen. : cum caeli turbine ferri, Lucr. ; lunae, Lucr. ; immani turbine (i.e. fulminis), Verg. ; quo turbine torqueat hastam, Verg. ; turbine saxi, Verg. ; turbine crescit (bucina) ab imo, Ov. **b.** Of wind : Enn., Lucr., Cic., Verg., etc. In apposition : exoritur ventus turbo, Pl. **2.** T r a n s f. **A.** in turbinibus ac fluctibus rei publicae, Cic. ; ego te in medio versantem turbine leti eripui, Cat. ; cum illi soli essent duo rei publicae turbines, Cic. ; miserae mentis, Ov. **B.** Of things that have a spiral shape or whirling motion. **a.** *a spinning-top :* Verg., Tib. **b.** *a reel, whorl, spindle :* Cic., Cat., Hor., Ov.

turbō, āre [turba], *to throw into disorder* or *confusion, to disturb, confuse, etc.* **1.** L i t. **a.** In gen. : Liv., Ov. ; magno turbante tumultu, Verg. ; ventorum vi agitari atque turbari mare, Cic. ; Lucr. ; Ov. ; equitatus turbaverat ordines, Liv. ; capillos, Ov. ; Quint. *Impers. Pass.* : Liv. **b.** Of water, *to make thick* or *turbid :* aquam limo, Hor. ; aquas lacrimis, Ov. **2.** T r a n s f. : Ter. ; Fortuna, civitas, Tac. ; quantas res turbo ! Pl. ; qui omnia infima summis paria fecit, turbavit, miscuit, Cic. ; ne incerta prole auspicia turbarentur, Liv. ; milites nihil in commune turbantes, Tac. ; oculis simul ac mente turbatus, Liv. *Impers. Pass.* : Ter., Cic., Verg.

turbulentē (turbulenter, Cic. Ep.), *adv. in wild confusion, tumultuously, boisterously :* Cic. *Comp.* : Cic.

turbulentus, a, um [turba]. **A.** P a s s. *in wild confusion, wild, boisterous, agitated.* **1.** L i t. of weather, wind, water, etc. : tempestas, Pl., Cic. ; loci Neptunii, Pl. ; aqua, Phaedr. ; atomorum concursio, Cic. **2.** T r a n s f. : res, praeda, Pl. ; res publica, Cic. Ep. ; errores, animi, contio, Cic. *Comp.* : annus, Liv. *Sup.* : tempus, Cic. **B.** A c t. *wild, turbulent, factious :* civis, Cic. ; tribuni, Tac. ; consilia Antoni, Cic. Ep. ; minae, Quint. *Sup.* : tribuni plebis, Caes.

turdus, i, m. (**turda,** ae, *f.* Pers.) *a thrush* (prob. includes also *other species of* turdus) : Varr., Hor., etc. Also of a kind of fish : Plin. [It. *tordo.*]

tūreus, a, um [tūs], *of frankincense :* virga, Verg. ; grana, Ov.

turgeō, turgēre, tursi [*cf.* Gk. σπαργάω, σφριγάω], *to swell out, be swollen.* **1.** L i t. : lienes, Cato ; gemmae, frumenta, Verg. ; lumina gemitu, Prop. ; ora (ab ictu), Ov. ; uva mero, Mart. **2.** T r a n s f. **a.** With anger : uxor mihi, Pl. **b.** Of bombastic speech : professus grandia turget, Hor. ; oratio, Auct. Her.

turgēscō, ere [turgeō], *to begin to swell, to swell up, swell.* **1.** L i t. : semen in agris, Ov. ; Varr. **2.** T r a n s f. **a.** With anger : sapientis animus nunquam turgescit, Cic. ; bilis, Pers. **b.** Of bombastic speech : Quint.

turgidulus, a, um [*dim.* turgidus], *poor swollen little :* ocelli flendo, Cat.

turgidus, a, um [turgeō], *swollen, inflated.* **1.** L i t. : oculi, Pl. ; membrum, Cic. ; mare, Hor. ; loca semine, Lucr. ; vela vento, Hor. ; (haedi) frons cornibus, Hor. **2.** T r a n s f. of bombastic speech or writer : Hor.

tūribulum, i, n. [tūs], *a censer :* Cic.

tūricremus, a, um [tūs cremō], *incense-burning :* arae, Lucr., Verg. ; foci, Ov.

tūrifer, era, erum [tūs ferō], *producing incense :* Indus, Ov. ; Plin.

tūrilegus, a, um [tūs legō], *incense-gathering :* Arabes, Ov.

turma, ae, *f.* [fr. same root as turba], *a troop, squadron of horse* (a division of Roman cavalry, the tenth part of an ala, consisting of thirty men). **1.** L i t. : Caes., Cic. Ep., Hor. **2.** Transf. of any troop or crowd : equestrium (statuarum), Cic. Ep. ; immanis Titanum, Hor. ; feminea, Ov.

turmālis, e, *adj.* [turma], *of a troop* or *squadron.* **1.** L i t. (as Noun) : cum suis turmalibus evasit, Liv. **2.** T r a n s f. *of the equestrian order, equestrian :* Stat. In a pun, *equestrian* and *in troops :* statuae, Cic.

turmātim, adv. [turma], *by troops* or *squadrons.* **1.** L i t. : Caes., Liv. **2.** T r a n s f. : Lucr.

Turnus, i, m. *a king of the Rutuli, killed by Aeneas.*

turpiculus, a, um [*dim.* turpis], *dainty little ugly* or *misshapen.* **1.** L i t. : nasus, Cat. **2.** T r a n s f. *rather indecent :* res turpiculae et quasi deformes.

turpificātus, a, um [turpis faciō], *debased, corrupted.* Transf. : animus, Cic.

turpilucricupidus, i, *adf. m.* [turpis lucrum cupidus], *covetous of dishonest gain :* Pl.

turpis, e. adj. *ugly, unsightly, deformed, foul, filthy* in appearance. **1.** Lit.: Pl., Cic., Verg., etc. **2.** Transf. (morally): mores, Pl.; verbum, Ter.; causa, Caes.; vita, adulescentia, fuga, Cic.; Hor.; luxuria omni aetati turpis est, Cic.; formido, Cic., Verg.; fama, Tac.; turpe est (with *Inf.* or Acc. and *Inf.* as *Subject*), Cic., Ov. *Comp.*: Caes., Cic. *Sup.*: turpissima fuga, Caes.; homo, Cic. *Neut.* **turpe** as Noun: Cic., Ov. *Intern.* Acc.: turpe incedere, Cat.

turpiter, adv. *in an ugly or unsightly manner.* **1.** Lit.: Hor., Ov. **2.** Transf. of any ugly or dishonourable action : Ter., Caes., Cic., Ov., etc. *Comp.* : Ov. *Sup.* : Cic.

turpitūdō, inis, *f.* [turpis], *ugliness, unsightliness, foulness, deformity.* **1.** Lit.: Cic. **2.** Transf. (morally): fugae, Caes.; verborum, Cic.; ut nulla turpitudo ab accusatore obiceretur, Cic.; (divitiis) abuti per turpitudinem, Sall.

turpō, āre [turpis], *to make ugly or unsightly, to defile, disfigure.* **1.** Lit.: aram sanguine, Enn.; capillos sanguine, Verg.; frontem (cicatrix), Hor.; ipsos (scabies), Tac. **2.** Transf. (morally): ornamenta, Cic.; avos, Stat.

turriger, era, erum [turris gerō], *turret-bearing, turreted :* urbes, Verg.; umeri elephantorum, Plin. As epithet of the Magna Mater (Cybele), Ov.

turris, is (Acc. -im and -em ; Abl. -e and -i, *f.* [τύραις, τύρρις], *a tower.* **1.** Lit. **a.** In gen.: Pl., Cic., Hor., Ov. **b.** For the defence of a camp or the walls of a city : Caes., Cic., Verg. **c.** For attack in a siege : Caes., Liv. **d.** *a howdah* on an elephant : Liv. **e.** On a ship : Liv. **2.** Transf.: pauperum tabernas regumque turris, Hor.; regia, Ov.; Suet. Of a dove-cote : Varr., Ov. [It. *torre* ; Fr. *tour*.]

turritus, a, um [turris], *turreted, castellated, embattled.* **1.** Lit.: boves Lucas turrito corpore taetros (*cf.* turris l. d.), Lucr.; puppes, Verg.; moenia, Cic.; corona (of the Magna Mater or Cybele), Ov.; also as epithet of the Magna Mater herself, Ov. **2.** Transf.: scopuli, Verg.

turtur, uris, *m. a turtle-dove :* Pl., Varr., Verg., etc.

tūs, tūris, *n.* [*cf.* Gk. θύος], *incense, frankincense:* Pl., Cic., Verg., etc. In pl.: Verg., Ov.

Tuscī, ōrum, *m. pl. another name for Etrusci, v.* Etruria : **Tuscus**, a, um.

Tusculum, i, *n. a very ancient town of Latium, about ten miles from Rome ;* near the modern *Frascati :* **Tusculānus**, a, um, **Tusculānēnsis**, e, and **Tusculus**, a, um : **Tusculāni**, ōrum, *m. pl. its inhabitants.*

tūsculum, i, *n* [*dim.* tūs], *a little frankincense :* Pl.

tussicula, ae, *f.* [*dim.* tussis], *a slight cough :* Plin. Ep.

tussiō, īre [tussis], *to cough, to have a cough :* Pl., Hor., Quint.

tussis, is, *f. a cough :* Ter., Cat., Verg., Plin., etc. [Fr. *toux*.]

tūsus, a, um, *Part.* tundō.

tūtāmen, inis, *n.* (Verg.) and **tūtāmentum**, i, *n.* (Liv.) [tūtor], *a means of defence, protection.*

tūtē, pron. *v.* tū.

tūtē, adv. *safely :* Pl., Auct. Her.

tūtēla (**tūtella**), ae, *f.* [tūtus], *a watching, charge, safeguard, protection.* **1.** Lit.: **a.** tutelam gerere, Pl.; Apollo cuius in tutelā Athenae erant, Cic.; Liv.; sub tutelā, Liv.; dii quorum tutelae ea loca essent, Liv.; subicere aliquid tutelae alicuius, Cic.; tutela ac praesidium bellicae virtutis, Cic.; ut dicar tutelā pulsa Minervae, Ov. With *Obj.* Gen.: ianuae, Pl.; tenuiorum, Suet.; generis humani tutela saluti tuae innisa est, Plin. Ep. **b.** In law : *guardianship, wardship* of minors, insane persons, etc.: fraudare pupillum qui in tutelam pervenit, Cic.; in suam tutelam venire (i.e. to come of age), Cic.; legitima, Cic.; ad sanos abeat tutela propinquos, Hor. Hence, filios suos parvos tutelae populi commendare, Cic. **2.** Transf. (concr.). **a.** *keeper, guardian :* (Philemon et Baucis) templi tutela fuere, Ov.; o tutela praesens Italiae, Hor.; rerum mearum, Hor. Of an image : navis tutela ebore caelata est, Sen. Ep. **b.** Pass.: *an* (*object of*) *charge, care :* virginum primae puerique claris patribus orti, Deliae tutela deae, Hor.; Lanuvium annosi vetus est tutela draconis, Prop.; Ov.

tūtemet, *v.* tū.

tūtor, ārī (also **tūtō**, āre, Pl.; and in *Pass.* : Cic.) [*freq.* tueor and tueō] *to watch, guard, protect continually.* **1.** Lit.: domum, Pl.; provincias, rem publicam, Cic.; muris urbem, Liv.; res Italas armis, Hor.; ab irā Romanorum vestra, Liv.; adversus multitudinem hostium, Liv.; contra regis copias, Tac.; spes virtute et innocentiā, Sall.; genae ab inferiore parte tutantur (oculos), Cic. **2.** Transf. *to guard against* an evil: inopiam, Caes.; pericula, Sall.

tūtor, ōris, *m.* [tueor], *a watcher, protector.* **1.** Lit. **a.** pater Silvane, tutor finium, Hor.; tutorem imperi agere, Suet. **b.** In law : *a guardian* of minors, women, insane persons, etc.: Pl., Cic., Liv. **2.** Transf.: orbae eloquentiae quasi tutores relicti sumus, Cic.; Ov.

tūtus, a, um. **I.** *Part.* tueō. **II.** Adj. *safe, secure, out of danger.* **1.** Lit. **a.** In gen.: Lucr.; mare tutum praestare, Cic.; tutissimus portus, Caes.; nemus, Hor.; via fugae, Cic.; perfugium, Cic.; tutior receptus, Caes.; iter, Hor.; tutissima custodia, Liv.; vita, Cic.; regnum et diadema tutum deferens uni, Hor.; male tutae mentis Orestes, Hor. With *ab :* a periculo, Caes.; Hor.; provinciam tutam servare a periculis, Cic.; ab hoste, Ov. With *ad :* ad omnis casūs, Caes.; ad omnis ictūs, Liv. With *adversus :* Curt., Sen. Also, tutum est (with *Inf.* as Subject), Prop., Quint.; so, tutius est, Caes. **b.** *cautious, prudent :* serpit humi tutus nimium timidusque procellae, Hor.; consilia, Liv. *Comp.* : Liv. **III.** Noun, **tūtum**, i, *n. a safe place, etc., safety* (mostly with *prep.*): tuta et parvula laudo, Hor.; Ov.; in tutum receptus est, Liv.; Pl.; esse in tuto, Ter., Cic. Ep., Liv.; also, esse tuto, Cic. Ep. (and *Sup.* tutissimo

esse, Cic. Ep.) ; ex tuto, *from a safe place
or in safety, safely*, Liv. ABL. **tŭtō** as
Adv. safely : Pl., Lucr., Caes. *Comp.* :
tūtius, Caes., Sall.

tuus (tuos), a, um (tuom) [tū], *thy, thine,
your, yours* (of the singular *your*). **A.**
Mostly Subjectively. **a.** tuos est servos,
Pl. ; Cic., etc. ; tuom est (with *Inf.* as
Subject), Pl., Ter. As Noun: de tuis
unus est, Cic. Ep. Strengthened by suffix
-pte : tuopte ingenio, Pl. **b.** *proper,
suitable,* or *right for you* : tempore tuo
pugnasti, Liv. ; Mart. **B.** For *Obj.* GEN. :
for or *of you* : desiderio tuo, Ter. ; Planc.
ap. Cic. Ep.

tuxtax, a word intended to imitate the
sound of blows : *whacks* : Pl.

Tyana, ōrum, n. *pl. a city in Cappadocia,
the birthplace of the philosopher Apollonius* ;
Tyanēius, a, um.

Tychius, I, *m. a famous shoemaker of Boeotia.*

Tydeus (disyl.), eī and eos, *m. son of Oeneus
and father of Diomedes* ; **Tydīdēs**, ae, *m.
Diomedes.*

tympanizāns, antis [τυμπανίζω], *playing
on a drum or timbrel* : Suet.

tympanotriba (typan-), ae, *m.* [τυμπανοτρί-
βης], *a laborer, a timbrel-player* (alluding
to the priests of the Magna Mater) : Pl.

tympanum (typ- Cat.), ī, *n.* [τύμπανον], *a
drum, timbrel, tambour, tambourine,* esp.
as beaten by the priests of the Magna
Mater. **1.** Lit. : Pl., Lucr., Caes., Verg.
etc. **2.** Transf. **a,** Of something effeminate : Sen. ; tympana eloquentiae, Quint.
b. *a drum* or *wheel,* in machines for raising
weights, in water-organs, etc. : Lucr., Verg.,
Plin.

Tyndareus (trisyl.), eī, and **Tyndarus**, ī,
m. king of Sparta, and h. of Leda ; *f. of
Castor and Clytemnestra, and reputed father
of Pollux and Helen* ; **Tyndarius**, a, um ;
Tyndaridēs, ae, *m. a male descendant of
Tyndareus* ; **Tyndaris**, idis, *f. a female
descendant of Tyndareus.*

Typhoeus (trisyl.), eī or eos (also **Typhōn**,
ōnis), *m. a giant, struck with lightning by
Jupiter, and buried under Mount Etna* ;
Typhōius, a, um, and **Typhōis**, idis,
f. adj.

typus, ī, *m.* [τύπος], *a figure, image,* on a
wall : Cic. Ep.

tyrannicē, *adv. tyrannically* : Cic.

tyrannicida, ae, *m.* [tyrannus caedō], *a
killer of a tyrant, a tyrannicide* : Sen.,
Tac., etc.

tyrannicīdium, ī, *n.* [tyrannus caedō],
the killing of a tyrant, tyrannicide : Sen.,
Quint.

tyrannicus, a, um [τυραννικός], *tyrannous,
tyrannical* : leges, Cic.

tyrannis, idis (Acc. -idem or -ida), *f.*
[τυραννίς], *the sway of a tyrant, arbitrary*
or *despotic rule* : Ov., Juv. ; adfectare,
occupare, delere, Cic. ; destruere, Quint.

tyrannoctonus, ī, *m.* [τυραννοκτόνος], *the
killer of a tyrant* : Cic. Ep.

tyrannus, ī, *m.* [τύραννος], *a despotic ruler.*
1. Lit. **a.** In gen. of the *holder of sovereign
power in a State* : Naev., Nep., Verg., Ov.
Of gods : Ov. Of the constellation Capricorn : Hor. **b.** *a usurper* of sovereign

power, *an unconstitutional monarch* : Syra-
cusanorum, Cic. ; Liv. Of Caesar : Cic.
c. With idea of cruelty or oppression :
Cic., Liv. **2.** Transf. **a,** Of any person :
nos tyrannos vocas, Cic. Of Verres and
Clodius : Cic. **b,** animus noster modo rex
est, modo tyrannus, Sen. Ep.

Tyrās, ae, *m. a river in Sarmatia,* now *the
Dniester.*

tyrianthina, ōrum, n. *pl.* [τυριάνθινα], *purple-
violet coloured garments* : Mart.

Tyrō, ūs, *f. daughter of Salmoneus.*

tyrotarichos, ī, *m.* [τυροτάριχος], *a dish
of salt-fish prepared with cheese* : Cic. Ep.

Tyrrhēni, ōrum, *m. pl. a Pelasgian people
who migrated to Italy and formed the parent
stock of the Etrurians* ; **Tyrrhēnus**, a, um ;
Tyrrhēnia, ae. *f. Etruria* ; **Tyrrhēnicus**,
a, um.

Tyrrheus (disyl.), eī, *m. the shepherd of King
Latinus* ; **Tyrrhidae**, ārum, *m. pl. his
sons.*

Tyrtaeus, I, *m. an Athenian poet* (7th cent.
B.C.), *who roused the courage of the Spartans against the Messenians.*

Tyrus or **-os**, ī, *f. a famous maritime and
commercial city of the Phoenicians* (now the
ruins of *Sur*) ; **Tyrius**, a, um, *Tyrian,*
and poet. *Theban* (with a ref. to the
Phoenician colony of Cadmus), or *Carthaginian* (Carthage being a colony from
Tyre) ; and **Tyrii**, ōrum, *m. pl. the Tyrians,*
or *the Carthaginians.*

U

U, u (orig. V, which character arose from the
Greek *Y*). **I.** It did not correspond
phonetically to Greek *v*, which, at least
in the mature period of the Greek language,
was pronounced like French *u* or German
ü ; *ov* is more commonly put for it by the
Greeks in transliterating Roman names
or other Latin words. (In this volume,
the letter *v* is used to represent consonantal
u.) **II.** Etymologically it answers to
I.-E. *u,* and therefore to Gk. *v* ; thus Lat.
sus, Gk. (σ)ῦς ; though it has often arisen
from a modification of another vowel, as in
ursus, cf. ἄρκτος ; *ulcus, cf.* ἕλκος ; *humus,
cf.* χαμαί. The diphthong *oe* (orig. *oi*) is
closely akin to *u* ; *cf.* munio, *moenia* ;
punio, *poena*. **III.** Unaccented *u* almost
always becomes in French either *o* or *ou* ;
thus Lat. voluntatem, Fr. volonté ; Lat.
gubernare, nutrire, sufflare ; Fr. gouverner,
nourrir, souffler. Accented *u,* if long by
nature, remains unchanged ; thus Lat.
nudus, murus, luna, Fr. nu, mur, lune ;
if in long syllable, it remains unchanged,
as in *pulpe* from pulpa, or becomes *o,* as in
monde, onde, from mundus, unda, or *ou,*
as in bouche, sourd, from bucca, surdus ;
if short, it almost always becomes *ou,* as in
joug, loup, où, from iugum, lupus, ubi ; in
a few words, however, it changes to *eu,*
as in fleuve, jeune, gueule, from fluvius,
iuvenis, gula. In Italian, long *u* is generally
unchanged, as in duro, luna, from durus,
luna ; but short *u* often changes to *o,* as in

golu, omero, goccia, from *gula, umerus, gutta.* **IV.** As an abbreviation, V (for U) stands for uti ; so V.V., uti voverant.

(1) über, eris, n. [*cf.* Gk. οὖθαρ], *a teat, udder, a breast that gives suck.* **1.** Lit.: Enn., Lucr., Verg., Ov., Suet. In *pl.:* Lucr., Cic., Verg., Tac., etc. **2.** Transf. *richness, fertility :* fertilis ubere campus, Verg. ; glaebae, Verg.

(2) über, eris, *adj.* [prob. ident. with über, *udder*], *rich, fruitful, fertile, plentiful.* **1.** Lit.: messis, Pl. ; seges spicis uberibus, Cic. ; Ov.; fruges, Hor. ; ager, Liv.; onus, Pl. ; imber, Lucr. ; aqua, Cic. Ep. ; aquae, Ov. *Comp. :* Pl., Cic., Ov. *Sup. :* Ter., Cic., Ov. **2.** Transf. of style, language, etc. : orator, Cic. ; animi motūs ad explicandum ornandumque uberes, Cic. *Comp. :* spes uberior, Cic. ; haec pleniora etiam atque uberiora Romam ad suos perscribunt, Caes. ; in dicendo, Cic. ; Tac. ; tuasque ingenio laudes uberiore canunt, Ov. *Sup. :* uberrima supplicationibus triumphisque provincia, Cic. ; artes, Cic. ; oratorum eā aetate uberrimus erat, Tac.

überius (*Neut. Intern.* Acc. and *comp. adv.*) (also *Sup.* **überrimē**), *more* (*most*) *fruitfully, luxuriantly.* **1.** Lit.: Cic., Ov. *Sup. :* Pl. **2.** Transf. of style, speech, etc. : Cic., Plin. Ep. *Sup. :* Cic.

übertās, ātis, *f.* [über], *richness, fruitfulness, productiveness.* **1.** Lit.: mammarum, agrorum, frugum, etc., Cic. ; vini, Suet. ; in percipiendis fructibus, Cic. **2.** Transf.: ingeni, Cic. ; ubertates et copiae virtutis, Cic. ; in dicendo, Cic. ; oratoris, Plin. Ep. ; verborum, Quint. ; illa Livi lactea ubertas, Quint.

übertim, *adv.* [über], *plentifully :* Cat., Suet.

ubi and **ubi,** *adv.* **I.** Interrogative : *in what place ? where ?* **A.** In *Direct Quest. :* Pl., Cic., Ov., etc. Strengthened with *gentium* (*where in the world ?*): Pl. ; ubinam gentium? Pl., Cic. **B.** In *Indir. Quest. :* Cic. ; ubinam (*where in fact*), Cic. ; ubi terrarum, Pl., Cic. Ep., Liv. **II.** Relativo : *in which place, where.* **1.** Lit.: in eam partem ituros atque ibi futuros, ubi eos constituissent, Caes. ; agros, ubi hodie est haec urbs, Cic. ; (occ. of persons: neque nobis praetor to quisquam fuit ubi nostrum ius obtineremus, i.e. *with whom,* Cic. ; Pl. ; Ter. ; Ov.) Repeated, **ubi ubi** (or **ubiubi**), *wherever, wheresoever :* sperantes facile, ubi ubi essent, se conversuros aciem, Liv. ; Ter. With *gentium :* ubi ubi est gentium, Pl. **2.** Transf. of time: *at which* or *what time, when :* ubi friget, huc evasit, Ter. ; Pl. ; Verg., etc. ; ubi primum nostros equites conspexerunt, Caes. ; Cic. ; ubi semel quis pcieraverit, ei credi postea non oportet, Cic. With *Subj. :* Hor.

ubi-cumque (-quomque, Pl.; and **-cunque)** and **ubicumque** (Ov.), *adv.* **I.** Relative: *wherever, wheresoever :* etsi, ubicumque es, in eādem es navi, Cic. Ep. ; Pl. ; Hor. ; Ov. With *terrarum, locorum, gentium :* qui ubicumque terrarum sunt, etc., Cic. ; ubicumque locorum vivitis,

Hor. With *Subj. :* Ter. **II.** Indefinito: *wherever it may be, anywhere, everywhere :* te, dea, munificam gentes ubicumque loquuntur, Ov. ; Hor. ; Quint.

ubinam, *v.* ubi.

ubi-que, *adv. everywhere, anywhere:* Pl., Cic., Verg., etc. Esp. in the phrase, omnes qui ubique sunt, Cic. ; and without omnes : qui ubique sunt propugnatores huius imperi, Cic.

ubiubi, *v.* ubi.

ubi-vis, *adv. anywhere* or *everywhere you wish:* nemo sit, quin ubivis, quam ibi, ubi est, esse malit, Cic. ; ubivis facilius passus sim, quam in hac re, me deludier (i.e. in anything you please), Ter. With *gentium :* ubivis gentium agere aetatem, Ter.

Ucalegōn, ontis, *m. a Trojan, mentioned by* Verg.

ūdus, a, um [*cf.* ūvidus], *wet, moist, damp :* paludes, Ov. ; litus, Hor. ; apium, Hor. ; pomaria rivis, Hor. ; vere udo terrae, Verg. ; oculi, Ov. ; tempora Lyaeo (i.e. with wine), Hor. ; so, aleator, Mart. ; gaudium (i.e. with tears), Mart.

Ufens, entis, *m. a small river in Latium,* now *Uffente ;* **Ufentinus,** a, um.

ulcerō, āre [ulcus], *to make sore, cause to ulcerate.* **1.** Lit.: ulcerato serpentis morsu Philocteta, Cic. ; Hor. **2.** Transf. (with love) : tuum iecur, Hor.

ulcerōsus, a, um [ulcus], *full of sores, ulcerous.* **1.** Lit.: facies, Tac. **2.** Transf. (with love) : iecur, Hor.

ulciscor, ulciscī, ultus, *to avenge oneself on, take vengeance on.* **1.** Lit. *to punish.* **a.** With personal Object: aliquem, Pl., Cic., Hor. ; aliquem pro scelere, Caes. ; illum ulciscentur mores sui, Cic. ; illum siti, Pl. ; victos acerbius, Sall. **b.** With non-personal Object: senis iracundiam, Ter. ; iniurias, Caes., Cic., etc. ; iniurias rei publicae, Cic. ; iniurias bello, Cic. ; offensas tuas, Ov. ; regum libidines, Hor. In *Pass.* sense: quidquid sine sanguine civium ulcisci nequitur, Sall. ; ob iras graviter ultas, Liv. **2.** Transf. *to take vengeance for ;* *to avenge :* patrem, Cic. ; se, Cic. ; caesos fratres, Ov. ; cadentem patriam, Verg. In *Pass.* sense : ulta ossa patris, Ov. ; Liv.

ulcus, eris, n. [*cf.* Gk. ἕλκος], *a sore, ulcer.* **1.** Lit.: Lucr., Verg., Hor. Prov.: ulcus tangere (i.e. to touch on a delicate subject), Ter. **2.** Transf.: ulcus (i.e. amor) vivescit et intumerascit alendo, Lucr. ; quidquid horum attigeris, ulcus est, Cic.

ūlīgō, inis, *f.* [contr. of ūvīligō, fr. ūveō], *moisture, swampiness* (of earth): Varr., Verg., Tac.

Ulixēs, is or ĕī, or ĕī, *m. Ulysses, a king of Ithaca, famed among the Grecian heroes of the Trojan war for his craft and eloquence ; s. of Laertes, h. of Penelope, and f. of Telemachus and Telegonus.*

ūllus, a, um (GEN. *sing.* ūllī, Pl.), [contr. of ūnulus, fr. ūnus], *any, any at all.* **A.** Usually in negat. sentences. **a.** As *Adj. :* neque praeter to in Alide ullus servos istoc nomine est, Pl. ; sine ullo domino esse, Cic. ; Caes. In a "virtually" negat. sentence : ultra quam ullus spiritus durare possit, Quint. ; Pl. **b.** As Noun : Pl., Caes., Cic., etc. **B.** In interrogative (direct or indirect) sentences : eat ergo ulla res tanti, ut . . . ? Cic. ; Pl. **C.** In hypothetical clauses (of a negat. or despairing tone) : si ulla mea apud te commendatio valuit, Cic. Ep. ; Pl., etc. **D.** In affirmative clauses : dum amnes ulli rumpuntur fontibus, Verg.

ulmeus, a, um [ulmus], *made of elm, elm-: virgae,* Pl. ; cena, Juv.

ulmitriba, ae, *m.* [ulmus τρίβω, terö]. *a wearer-out of elm-rods* (in being flogged) : Pl.

ulmus, i, *f. an elm, elm-tree.* **1.** L i t. : Verg., Hor., Ov., Plin. **2.** T r a n s f. *elm-rods :* ulmorum Acheruns, Pl. [It. *olmo.*]

ulna, ae, *f.* [cf. Gk. ωλένη], *the elbow.* **1.** L i t. : Plin. **2.** T r a n s f. **A.** *the arm :* Cat., Prop., Ov. **B.** As a measure of length. **a.** *an ell :* Verg., Hor., Ov. **b.** the length of both arms outstretched, *a fathom :* Plin.

ulpicum, i, *n. a kind of leek :* Pl., Cato.

Ulpius, *v.* Trāiānus.

ulterior, ius, *comp. adj.* [fr. the obsolete ulter in which ul=ol in ol-le (ille) and ol-im], *farther, on the farther side, that is beyond.* **1.** L i t. of space : Ter. ; Gallia (opp. to citerior), Cic. ; pars urbis, Liv. ; ripa, Verg. As Noun : ab proximis (*sc.* Germanis) impetrare non possent, ulteriores temptant, Caes. ; Liv. ; Tac. ; pons qui ulteriora coloniae adnectit, Tac. *Neut. Intern.* Acc. : ulterius abire, Ov. **2.** T r a n s f. in gen. : *beyond, further, later, etc. :* quo quid ulterius privato timendum foret ? Liv. As Noun : Ov. *Neut. Intern.* Acc. : ulterius ne tende odiis, Ov. ; ulterius iusto, Ov. *Sup.* **ultimus,** a, um, *farthest, most distant, uttermost, extreme, at the end.* **1.** L i t. of space : campi, Pl. ; partes, Cic. ; in ultimas maris terrarumque oras, Liv. ; (luna) ultima a caelo, citima terris luce lucebat alienā, Cic. Also, *the farthest part of :* in ultimis aedibus, Ter. ; Pl. As Noun : recessum primis ultimi non dabant, Caes. ; caelum quod extremum atque ultimum mundi est, Cic. ; ultima signant, Verg. **2.** T r a n s f. **A.** Of time or order of succession, *remotest, earliest ; also, last, latest. final :* ultimi et proximi temporis recordatio, Cic. ; principium, Cic. ; auctor sanguinis, Verg. ; dies, Ov. ; lapis, Prop. ; cerae, Mart. As Noun : perferto et ultima exspectato, Cic. A d v e r b i a l l y : ad ultimum, *to the last,* Liv. ; ultimum, *for the last time,* Liv. **B.** Of degree or rank. **a.** *utmost, greatest, most extreme :* summum bonum, quod ultimum appello, Cic. ; supplicium, Caes. ; crudelitas, Liv. ; necessitas, inopia, etc., Liv. ; desperatio, Tac. *Neut.* as Noun, *the worst :* ultima audere, Liv. ; omnia ultima pati, Liv. ; ultima cernunt, Verg. ; ad ultimum inopiae adducere, Liv. ; consilium sceleratum, sed non ad ultimum demens, Liv. **b.** *lowest, meanest :* laus, Hor. As Noun : ut vigiliis et labore cum ultimis militum certaret (consul), Liv.

ultimus, *v.* ulterior.

ultiō, ōnis, *f.* [ulcīscor]. *a taking vengeance,*

avenging, revenge : petere, Liv. ; ex aliquo petere, Tac. ; se ultione explere, Tac. ; Juv. With *Subj.* GRN. : irae, Liv.

ultor, ōris, *m.* [ulcīscor], *a punisher, avenger revenger :* Verg. ; coniurationis, Cic. In apposition : ultores ignes, Prop. ; ultores dii, Tac. As epithet of Mars : Ov., Tac.

ultrā, *adv.* and *prep.* [v. ulterior, and *cf.* intrā, ci-trā]. **I.** A d v. : *beyond, farther, besides.* **1.** L i t. : eatne aliquid ultra, quo progredi crudelitas possit ? Cic. ; Sall. ; Verg., etc. **2.** T r a n s f. **a.** Of time : quod ultra est, Hor. ; nec ultra bellum Latinum dilatum, Liv. **b.** Of measure : negavit ultra plebem decipi, Liv. Often followed by *quam :* ultra quam satis est, Cic. ; quid ultra fieri potuit quam quod nos fecimus ? Liv. ; nec ultra moratus quam etc., Tac. **II.** P r e p. with Acc. : *on the farther side of, beyond, past.* **1.** L i t. of space : ultra montem castra fecit, Caes. ; Hor. ; cis Padum ultraque, Liv. Placed after the noun : Euphratem ultra, Tac. **2.** T r a n s f. **a.** Of time : ultra mediam noctem, Liv. ; (Gorgias) ultra Socratem usque duravit, Quint. ; ultra puerilis annos, Quint. **b.** Of number, measure, degree : *beyond, over, more than :* modum quem ultra progredi non oporteat, Cic. ; ultra pignus, Cic. ; ultra placitum, Verg. ; viris ultra sortemque senectae, Verg. ; ultra fas, Hor. [Fr. *outre.*]

ultrix, īcis, *adj.* [ulcīscor], *avenging, vengeful :* Dirae, Curae, Verg.

ultrō, (*directive*) *adv.* [v. ulterior], *to the farther side, beyond.* **1.** L i t. : ultro istum a me, Pl. Mostly with *citro, on that side and on this :* ultro citroque, Caes., Cic. ; ultro et citro, Cic. ; ultro citro, Cic., Suet. **2.** T r a n s f. **a.** *beyond, besides, moreover, too :* celavit suos civis ultroque iis sumptum intulit, Cic. ; Pl. ; Verg., etc. **b.** *of one's own accord, without being asked or spoken to :* cum id, quod antea petenti denegasset, ultro polliceretur, Caes. ; Pl. ; Cic., etc. ; ultro adfata, Verg. ; se ultro obtulerat, Verg. ; ultro bello venturam, Verg. **c.** P h r. : **ultrō tribūta** (and as one word, **ultrōtribūta**), *expenditure incurred by the State for public works :* Liv.

ultus, a, um, *Part.* ulcīscor.

Ulubrae, ārum, *f. pl. a small town of Latium, near the Pomptine Marshes ;* **Ulubrānus,** a, um.

ulula, ae, *f.* [cogn. with ululō], *a screech-owl :* Varr., Verg.

ululātus, ūs, *m.* [ululō], *an excited shouting or crying.* **a.** Of Maenads, etc. : Cat., Ov. **b.** Of the wild yells or war-cries of the Gauls : Caes. **c.** Of the wailing of mourners : Verg., Ov., Curt.

ululō, āre [cf. Gk. ὀλολύζω], *to utter excited cries.* **1.** L i t. (orig. of excited joy) : Cat., Verg., etc. ; ululanti voce canere, Cic. ; canis, Enn., Verg. ; lupi, Verg. With *Intern.* Acc. : quem sectus ululat Gallus, Mart. ; hence, in *Pass. :* Hecate ululata per urbem, Verg. **2.** T r a n s f. of places : *to ring* or *resound with excited cries :* plangoribus aedes femineis ululant, Verg. [It. *urlare ;* Fr. *hurler.*]

ulva, ae, f. sedge : Cato, Verg., etc.

umbella, ae, f. [dim. umbra], a little shadow. Transf. a sun-shade, parasol : Juv.

umbilicus, i, m. [cf. Gk. ὀμφαλός], the navel. **1.** Lit. : Liv. **2.** Transf. **a.** the middle, centre : dies ad umbilicum est dimidiatus mortuos, Pl. ; of Delphi : umbilicus orbis terrarum, Liv. ; qui locus umbilicus Siciliae nominatur, Cic. **b.** a projecting end of cylinders on which books were rolled : Cat. ; iambos ad umbilicum adducere, Hor. **c.** a kind of sea-snail, sea-cockle : Cic.

umbō, ōnis, m. [cf. Gk. ὀμφαλός], a convex elevation ; hence, a boss of a shield. **1.** Lit. : Verg., Liv. **2.** Transf. **a.** a shield : Verg., Liv., Juv. **b.** the elbow : Mart. **c.** a projection of the dress ; hence, umbo candidus (i.e. a toga), Pers.

umbra, ae, f. shade, darkness (caused by shade), a shadow (cast by an object). **1.** Lit. : Pl., Cic., Verg. Prov.: umbras timere, Cic. **2.** Transf. **A.** the shadow as opp. to the reality. **a.** the phantom, shade, ghost of a dead person : Lucr., Verg., Suet., etc. **b.** an uninvited guest brought by an invited one : Pl., Hor. **c.** a ghostlike fish, perh. a grayling : Ov. **d.** a shadow of its former self, imperfect copy : amantum, Pl. ; equitis Romani, Cic. ; civitatis, Cic. ; foederis, Liv. ; pietatis, Ov. ; umbras falsao gloriae consectari, Cic. **B.** shade as opp. to sunlight. **a.** In painting : of light and shade : Cic. **b.** Of a place : shade, shaded place : vacuā tonsoris in umbrā, Hor. ; studia in umbrā educata, Tac. **c.** =shelter, cover : umbra et recessus, Cic. ; vestri auxili, Liv. ; magni nominis, Quint. **d.** = leisure, idleness : ignavā cessamus in umbrā, Ov. |It. ombra ; Fr. ombre.]

umbrāculum, i, n. [umbra], anything that gives shade. **1.** a bower, arbour. **1.** Lit.: Cic., Verg. **2.** Transf. : = a school : Cic. **II.** a sun-shade, parasol : Tib., Ov.

umbrāticola, ae, m. [umbrātus colō], one who is fond of the shade, a lounger : Pl.

umbrāticus, a, um [umbra], too fond of the shade (i.e. of idleness) : Pl.

umbrātilis, e, adj. [umbra], remaining in the shade, private, retired : vita, Cic. ; oratio philosophorum, Cic.

Umbri, ōrum, m. pl. an ancient people of Central Italy, akin to the Latins ; **Umber**, bra, brum ; **Umbria**, ae, f. their country.

umbrifer, era, erum [umbra ferō], shade-bringing. **a.** shady : nemus, Verg. ; rupes, Varr. **b.** bearing the ghosts of the dead : unda, Stat.

umbrō, āre [umbra], to shade, cover. **1.** Lit.: tempora quercu, Verg. **2.** Transf.: (with a beard) : umbratus genas, Stat.

umbrōsus, a, um [umbra], shady : locus umbrosior, Cic. Ep. ; vallis, Verg. ; nemus, Ov. Sup. : Plin.

ūmectō, āre [ūmectus], to moisten, wet : lacrimis genas, Lucr. ; Verg. ; Ov. ; flaventia culta, Verg.

ūmectus, a, um [ūmeō], moist, damp : Cato, Varr., Lucr.

ūmeō, ēre [ūmor], to be moist, damp, wet :

locus aquā, Ov. In Pres. Part. : litora, umbra, Verg. ; oculi, Ov. ; spongia, Suet.

umerus, i, m. [cf. Gk. ὦμος], the upper part of the arm or the shoulder. **1.** Lit.: Pl., Cic., Ov., etc. **2.** Transf.: rem publicam umeris sustinere, Cic. ; quid valeant umeri, Hor.

ūmēscō, ere [ūmeō], to grow or become moist or wet : oqui spumis, Verg. ; oculi, Plin. Pan.

ūmidē, adv. from damp: tigna putrent, Pl.

ūmidulus, a, um [dim. ūmidus], dampish : Ov.

ūmidus, a, um [ūmeō], moist, damp, wet : tellus, saxa, Lucr. ; of timber, unseasoned : Caes., Cic. ; nox, Verg. ; dies, Ov., Quint. ; regna, solstitia, Verg. ; lumina, Ov. Neut. as Noun, a wet place : Curt., Tac.

ūmor, ōris, m. [fr. root seen in Gk. ὑγρός], moisture, fluid : fusus in corpore, Cic. ; marinis terrenisque umoribus, Cic. ; pluvius, lactis, aquā, Lucr. ; roscidus, Cat. ; Massicus Bacchi, Verg. ; umor in genas labitur, Hor. ; linguam defecerat umor, Ov.

umquam, v. unquam.

ūnā, adv. by one (and the same) way, in company, together : unā venire, Cic. ; Verg. ; unā cum iis proficisci, Caes. ; Pl. ; Cic. ; aliquid unā cum praetextā togā ponere, Cic.

ūnanimāns, antis, adj. [ūnus animus], of one mind, of one accord : Pl.

ūnanimitās, ātis, f. [ūnanimus], unanimity, concord : Liv.

ūnanimus, a, um [ūnus animus], of one mind, heart, or will ; of one accord, harmonious, unanimous : Pl. ; sodales, Cat. ; soror, Verg. As Noun : distinere unanimos, Liv.

ūncia, ae, f. [ūnus], a twelfth part, a twelfth. **a.** Of inheritances : Cic. Ep. **b.** Of weight, the twelfth part of a pound (as or libra), an ounce : esp. with pondo : auri pondo uncia, Pl. ; Juv. [Fr. once ; Eng. ounce, inch.]

ūnciārius, a, um [ūncia], of a twelfth part, containing a twelfth : faenus (i.e. 8¼ per cent. per annum), Liv., Tac.

ūnciātim, adv. [ūncia], by twelfths. Transf. little by little : Ter.

uncīnātus, a, um [uncīnus, App.], hooked, barbed : Cic.

ūnciola, ae, f. [dim. ūncia], a paltry twelfth : Juv.

ūnctiō, ōnis, f. [ungō], a besmearing, anointing : sudatoria, Pl. ; Cic.

ūnctitō, āre [2nd freq. ungō], to besmear often : se unguentis, Pl.

ūnctiusculus, a, um [dim. of comp. of ūnctus], rather too unctuous : Pl.

ūnctor, ōris, m. [ungō], an anointer : Pl., Cic. Ep., Quint.

ūnctūra, ae, f. [ungō], an anointing of the dead : Cic.

ūnctus, a, um. **I.** Part. ungō. **II.** Adj. **1.** Lit. **a.** Cic., Hor., Sen. Ep. ; caput, Cat. **b.** greasy : manus, aqua, Hor. **c.** resinous : taeda, Ov. **2.** Transf. rich, luxurious, sumptuous : ita palaestritas defendebat, ut ab illis ipse unctior abiret, Cic. ; Hor. ; Corinthus, Juv. ; cena,

Mart. *Neut.* as Noun. **a.** *a rich banquet, sumptuous feast :* Hor., Pers. **b.** *ointment.* T r a n s f. : Cic. Ep.

uncus, I, *m.* [*cf.* Gk. ἀγκών, Lat. ancus], *a hook, clamp, grappling-iron.* **a.** In gen. : Cato, Hor., Liv. **b.** *a hook by which the bodies of executed criminals were dragged to the Tiber :* Cic., Ov., Juv.

uncus, a, um [*cf.* uncus, I], *hooked, crooked, barbed :* vomer aratri, Lucr. ; Verg. ; labrum, ungues, Lucr. ; pedes, manus, Verg. ; hamus, Ov. ; unco non adligat ancora morsu, Verg.

unda, ae, *f.* [*cf.* Gk. ὕδωρ], *water.* **1.** L i t. **a.** In gen. : unda cum est pulsa remis purpurascit, Cic. ; prora remissa navem undae adfligebat, Liv. ; unda Trinacria, Verg. ; Sicula, Hor. ; Acherontis ad undas, Verg. ; Lucr. ; Ov. ; fontis, Ov. **b.** Of water disturbed by wind, etc., *a wave, billow :* magno vento mare plenum undarum, Pl. ; unda dehiscens terram aperit, Verg. ; Hor. ; spumosis volvitur undis, Cic. **2.** T r a n s f. **a.** Of any *liquid* or *fluid* (esp. in motion): preli, Plin. ; aëriae undae, Lucr. ; quā plurimus undam fumus agit, Verg. **b.** Of other wavy or rippling things : of a lion's mane, Mart. **c.** *a stream* or *billowing surge* of persons : illae undae comitiorum, Cic. ; salutantum unda, Verg. **d.** Of abstract things : *a stream* or *surge :* curarum, Cat. ; mersor civilibus undis, Hor. [It. Sp. *onda ;* Fr. *onde.*]

unde, adv. [*v.* ubi], *from which* or *what place, from where, whence.* **I.** I n t e r r o g a t i v e. **a.** In *Direct Quest. :* unde deiectus est Cinna ? ex urbe, Cic. ; Pl. ; unde domo ? Verg. ; (occ. of persons : unde haec patera est ? *from whom ?* Pl.). With *gentium, from where in the world ?* Pl. **b.** In *Indir. Quest. :* Caes., Cic., Prop., Liv. ; unde domo, Hor. (occ. of persons : quaerere unde hunc anulum habuerit, *from whom,* Ter.). **II.** R e l a t i v e. **1.** L i t. of place : te redigam eodem unde orta es, Pl. ; Caes. ; eos in finis suos unde erant profecti reverti iussit, Caes. ; Cic. ; Verg. ; regna unde genus ducis, Verg. ; ibi . . . unde, inde . . . unde, Cic. **2.** T r a n s f. of persons, etc. : qui eum necasset unde ipse natus esset, *from whom,* Cic. ; Ter., etc. ; unde petitur (i.e. the defendant), Cic. ; eventus belli . . . unde ius stabat, ei victoriam dedit (i.e. *on which side*), Liv. ; unde agger comportari posset, nihil erat reliquum, *from which,* Caes. **III.** I n d e f i n i t e, only in repeated **unde unde** or **undeunde,** *from some* (*source*) *or other, somehow or other, by hook or by crook :* nisi mercedem aut nummos unde unde extricat, Hor. ; Cat. [It. *onde.*]

ūndeciēns (**-iēs**), adv. [ūnus deciēns], *eleven times :* Mart.

ūndecim, indecl. adj. [ūnus decem], *eleven :* Cic. Ep., Mart. [Fr. *onze.*]

ūndecimus, a, um [ūnus decimus], *eleventh :* Verg., Liv.

unde-cumque (**undecunque ;** in *tmesi :* unde vacefit cumque locus, Lucr.), *adv. from whatsoever place :* Quint., Plin. Ep.

ūn-dēnī, ae, a [ūnus], *eleven in a group, a group of eleven :* Musa per undenos emodulanda pedes, Hor.

ūndēnōnāgintā, indecl. adj. [ūnus dē nōnāgintā], *eighty-nine :* Liv.

ūndeoctōgintā, indecl. adj. [ūnus dē octōgintā], *seventy-nine :* Hor.

ūndēquadrāgintā, indecl. adj. [ūnus dē quadrāgintā], *thirty-nine :* Cic.

ūndēquinquāgēnsimus (**-ēs-**), a, um [ūndēquinquāgintā], *forty-ninth :* Cic.

ūndēquinquāgintā, indecl. adj. [ūnus dē quinquāgintā], *forty-nine :* Liv.

ūndēsexāgintā, indecl. adj. [ūnus dē sexāgintā], *fifty-nine :* Liv.

ūndētricēnsimus (**-ēs-**), a, um [ūndētrigintā], *twenty-ninth :* Liv.

unde-unde, *v.* unde.

ūndēvicēnsimus (**-ēs-**), a, um [ūndēvigintī], *nineteenth :* Cic.

ūndēvigintī, indecl. adj. [ūnus dē vigintī], *nineteen :* Cic., Liv.

undique, adv. [unde que ; *cf.* quisque]. **I.** *from any and every place* or *side, from all parts* or *sides, on all sides, everywhere :* Caes., Cic., Hor., Liv. **II.** *in all respects, utterly :* Cic., Quint.

undi-sonus, a, um [unda sonus], *sounding* or *roaring with the waves :* dei, Prop. ; rupes, Stat.

undō, āre [unda]. **A.** I n t r a n s. *to move* or *rise in waves, to swell,* as the sea. **1.** L i t. : Enn. **2.** T r a n s f. **a.** *to move like waves, to roll in eddies, to wave :* chlamys, Pl. ; ad caelum undabat vertex, Verg. ; undantem ruptis fornacibus Aetnam, Verg. undantes habenae, Verg. **b.** Of the mind, *to waver, be agitated :* curis, Val. Fl. **c.** *to overflow, abound with :* vultus sanguine, Stat. ; regio equis, Val. Fl. **B.** T r a n s. *to fill with water* or *waves.* T r a n s f. : sanguine campos, Stat.

undōsus, a, um [unda], *full of waves, billowy :* Verg.

ūnetvicēnsimāni (**-ēs-**), ōrum, *m. pl.* [ūnetvicēnsima, *sc.* legiō], *soldiers of the twenty-first* (legion) : Tac.

ūnetvicēnsimus (**-ēs-**), a, um [ūnus et vicēnsimus], *twenty-first :* Tac.

ungō (**unguō**), ungere, ūnxī, ūnctum, *to smear, besmear with oil, tar, resin,* etc. : aliquam unguentis, Pl. ; Cic. ; corpus, Varr. ; globos melle, Cato ; caulis oleo, Hor. ; natat uncta carina, Verg. ; Enn. ; arma uncta cruoribus, Hor. [It. *ugnere ;* Fr. *oindre.*]

unguen, inis, *n.* [ungō], *a fatty substance, fat ; an ointment :* Cato ; Verg.

unguentārius, a, um [unguentum], *dealing in ointments, unguents, perfumes :* taberna, Varr., Suet. As Noun. **unguentārius,** I, *m. a dealer in unguents, a perfumer :* Cic., Hor. **unguentāria,** ae, *f.* **a.** *a female perfumer :* Plin. **b.** (*sc.* ars) *the art of making perfumes :* Pl. **unguentārium,** I, *n. money for* (*buying*) *perfumes :* Plin. Ep.

unguentātus, a, um [unguentum], *anointed, perfumed :* Pl., Cat.

unguentum, I (GEN. *pl.* unguentum, Pl.), *n.* [ungō], *an ointment, unguent, perfume :* Pl., Cic., Hor., Ov., etc.

unguiculus, I, *m.* [*dim.* unguis], *a small nail of the finger or toe* : Pl., Cic. ; perpruriscere ex unguiculis (i.e. all over), Pl. Prov. : a teneris unguiculis (i.e. from earliest infancy), Cic. Ep.

unguis, is, *m.* [*cf.* Gk. ὄνυξ], *a nail* of a human finger or toe ; of animals, *a claw, talon* or *hoof* : Hor., Ov., Plin., Mart. Proverbial phrases : (i) ab imis unguibus usque ad verticem summum, *from top to toe*, Cic. (ii) non transversum unguem discedere, *not to depart a nail's breadth from*, Cic. Ep. ; excedere, Pl. (iii) cum medium ostenderet unguem (i.e. showed contempt by pointing), Juv. (iv) de tenero ungui (i.e. from childhood), Hor. (v) ad *or* in unguem (i.e. to a hair, to a nicety, exactly), ad unguem factus homo, Hor.

ungula, ae, *f.* [unguis], *a claw, talon, hoof.* **1.** Lit. Of a horse : Enn., Cic., Verg. Of swine : Cato. Of hens : Pl. Of kites and eagles : Pl. Prov. : toto corpore atque omnibus ungulis (i.e. with tooth and nail), Cic. **2.** Transf. *a horse* : rapit ungula currūs, Hor. [It. *unghia* ; Fr. *ongle.*]

unguō, *v.* ungō.

ūnicē, *adv. solely, singularly, in an extraordinary degree* : aliquem unice diligere, Cic. ; quid Tiridatem terreat, unice securus, Hor. With unus : Pl.

ūni-color, ōris, *adj. of one (and the same) colour* : Ov.

ūnicornis, e, *adj.* [ūnus cornū], *one-horned, having a single horn* : Plin. [It. *licorno* and, from it, Fr. *licorne.*]

ūnicus, a, um [ūnus], *one and no more, only, single.* **1.** Lit. : gnatus, Pl. ; filia, Ter. ; Cic. ; Verg., etc. With unus : Cat. **2.** Transf. *alone of its kind, unparalleled, unique* : Pl. ; eximius imperator, unicus dux, Liv. ; maritus, Hor. ; liberalitas, Cic. With solus : quamlubet esto unica res quaedam nativo corpore sola, Lucr.

ūni-fōrmis, e, *adj.* [ūnus fōrma], *having only one shape or form, uniform* : Tac.

ūnigena, ae, *adj.* [ūnus and gen in gignō]. **I.** *only-begotten, only* : Cic. **II.** *of one (and the same) parentage* : te, Phoebe, relinquens unigenamque simul, Cat.

ūni-manus, a, um, *one-handed* : puer, Liv.

ūniō, ōnis, *m.* [ūnus], *a single large pearl* : Sen., Plin., Mart.

ūnitās, ātis, *f.* [ūnus], *oneness, uniformity* : Sen., Plin.

ūniter, *adv. together in one, conjointly* : Lucr.

ūniversālis, e, *adj.* [ūniversus], *of or belonging to the whole, universal* : praecepta, Quint. ; Plin. Ep.

ūniversē, *adv. in general, generally* : singillatim potius quam generatim atque universe loqui, Cic.

ūniversitās, ātis, *f.* [ūniversus]. **I.** *the whole* : generis humani, Cic. ; Plin. Ep. **II.** *the whole world, the universe* : universitatis corpus, Cic.

ūniversus (**-vorsus**), a, um (**ūnōrsum**, Lucr.), [ūnus versus ; *cf.* dī-versus], *all together, all taken collectively, the whole* : terra, provincia, familia, vita, odium, etc., Cic. ; triduom, Ter. ; bellum, Liv. ; gregem univorsum totum, Pl. ; de universis

generibus rerum dicere, Cic. ; in illum universi tela coniciunt, Caes. ; omnibus univorsis, Pl. As Noun, **ūniversi**, ōrum, *m. pl. the whole body* of citizens : Cic.

ūniversum, I, *n. the whole (world), the universe* : Cic. Adv. phr. : in universum, *in general, generally* : non nominatim, sed in universum, Liv. ; Tac.

ūnoculus, a, um [ūnus oculus], *one-eyed* : Cyclops, Acc. As Noun, **ūnoculus**, I, *m. a one-eyed person* : Pl.

ūnomammia, ae, *f.* [ūnus mamma], "*one-breasted land*" (i.e. the country of the Amazons) : Pl.

unquam (**umquam**), *adv.* of time, *at any time, ever.* **I.** In negative sentences : quod (principium) si nunquam oritur, ne occidit quidem unquam, Cic. ; Pl. ; Verg., etc. With a negat. implied : cave posthac, si me amas, umquam istuc verbum ex te audiam, Ter. ; raro unquam, Quint. **II.** In interrogations : *Le.* sed tu, en umquam cum quiquam viro consuevisti ? *Si.* nisi quidem cum Alcesimarcho nemine, Pl. **III.** In conditional clauses : si unquam in dicendo fuimus aliquid, Cic. Ep. ; Pl. ; si quando unquam etc., Liv. **IV.** In affirmative sentences (usually in comparison, so *cf.* II.) : plus amat quam te umquam amavit, Pl. ; si Isocrates reliquis praestet omnibus qui unquam orationes attigerunt, Cic. ; tyranno qui unquam fuit saevissimo, Liv. ; Ov. [It. *unque* ; Fr. *onc.*]

ūnus, a, um, *adj.* and *noun* (GEN. *sing.* usually ūnīus, but sometimes ūnius in poets ; DAT. ūnī), *one, a single one, one alone.* **1.** Lit. **A.** In gen. *one* : divisit unum populum in duas partīs, Cic. ; Pl., etc. ; unus et alter (*one or two*), Cic., Hor., Liv., Ov. ; omnes ad unum, *all to a man*, i.e. every single one, Caes., Cic., Liv., etc. ; Verg. ; in unum (*Neut.* Noun), *into one place, together*, Cic., Verg., etc. In pl. : decumae, tabellae, Cic. ; excidia, Verg. ; Ter. **B.** Emphatically : *one alone, a single one, one only*, and in *pl. alone, only* : erat omnino in Galliā ulteriore legio una, Caes. ; Pl. ; Cic., etc. ; ille unus ex omnibus intactus profugit, Sall. ; Cic. ; ille unus ordinis nostri exsultavit etc., Cic. ; Liv. ; unus est solus inventus etc., Cic. ; Hor. ; unum flumen tantum intererat, Caes. ; Liv. ; unus modo, Cic., Liv., etc. ; nemo unus, Cic., Liv. ; sequere me trīs unos passūs, Pl. ; Ubii qui ex . . . uni legatos miserant, Caes. **C.** Of pre-eminence, *the one supremely, absolutely the one.* **a.** With *Adj.* (esp. *Sup.*) : virum unum totius Graeciae doctissimum Platonem accepimus, Cic. ; Pl. ; unus iustissimus qui fuit in Teucris, Verg. ; felix una, Verg. **b.** Without *Adj.* : inter mulieres unam aspicio adulescentulam, Ter. ; Cic. **D.** *one and the same* (sometimes with *idem*) : omnibus erit unus honos, Verg. ; Pl. ; uno tempore, Caes. ; uno ore, Cic., Verg. ; unis moribus vivunt, Cic. ; exitus quidem omnium unus et idem fuit, Cic. ; Hor. **2.** Transf. : indefinitely, *a or an, one, some, some one, any one, a mere individual.* **a.** sicut unus pater familias, Cic. ; Pl. ; unus e togatis, Cic. ; unus de multis, Cic. ; in turbă togatorum unus privatus, Liv. ; consul velut unus turbae militaris erat, Liv. ; transfugam nihil aliud quam unum vile atque infame corpus esse ratus, Liv. **b.** With a *Pronoun :* ad unum aliquem confugere, Cic. ; unus Quiritium quilibet, Liv. **c. ūnus quisque** (older **ūnus quisquis**, Pl., Lucr.), *every one individually :* pono ante oculos unum quemque regum, Cic. ; unus quisque opiniones fingebat, Caes. (*v.* also **ūnā.**) [It. Sp. *uno ;* Fr. *un.*]

ūpĭlĭŏ (ōpĭlĭŏ), ōnis, *m.* [*v.* ōpĭlĭŏ], *a shepherd :* Verg.

ŭpŭpa, ae, *f. a hoopoe.* **1.** Lit. : Plin. **2.** Transf. *a hoe or mattock :* Pl.

Ŭrānĭa, ae, or **Ŭrănĭē, ēs,** *f. the Muse of Astronomy.*

urbānē, *adv.* **I.** *courteously, politely :* agere, Cic. Comp. : Cic. **II.** Of speech, *wittily, elegantly, happily :* Cic., Quint.

urbānĭtās, ātis, *f.* [urbānus], *a living in a city, city-life.* **1.** Lit. : Cic. Ep. **2.** Transf. **a.** Of manners or speech : *elegance, refinement, politeness :* Cic. **b.** *wit, pleasantry, raillery :* Cic. Of a mischievous kind : Tac.

urbānus, a, um [urbs], *of the city or town, city-, town-.* **1.** Lit. : civis, scurra, leges, Pl. ; tribus, Cic. : praetor, Caes. ; administratio rei publicae, Cic. ; exercitus, Liv. As Noun, **urbānus, i,** *m. an inhabitant of a city, a city-man :* Pl., Cic., Liv. **2.** Transf. **a.** In manners or speech : *elegant, polished, courteous :* Cic. ; artes, Liv. ; genus dicendi, Cic. Comp. : Cic., Tac. **b.** *witty, humorous, facetious :* Cic., Hor. Sup. : Cic. In bad sense : *forward, impudent :* audacia, Cic. ; frons, Hor.

urbĭcapus, i, *m.* [urbs capiŏ], *a taker of cities :* Pl.

urbĭcus, a, um [urbs], *of or belonging to the city, civic :* Suet.

urbs, urbis, *f.* [perh. *cf.* orbis], *a walled town, a city.* **1.** Lit. **a.** In gen. : Enn., Cic., Verg., etc. Defined : urbs Patavi, Buthrotum (here the meaning may be "*ringwall*"), Verg. **b.** Esp. *the city of Rome, the capital :* Enn., Caes., Cic., Ov., etc. ; ad urbem esse, *to stop at or near Rome :* Cic., Caes., Sall. **2.** Transf. **a.** *the city, for the citizens :* urbem somno vinoque sepultam, Verg. **b.** urbem philosophiae prodita, dum castella defenditis, Cic.

urceolus, i, *m.* [dim. urceus], *a little pitcher or water-pot :* Juv.

urceus, i, *m.* (Pl., Hor., Plin.), and **urceum,** *n.* (Cato) [*cf.* Gk. ὕρχα], *a water-pot, pitcher, ewer.*

ūrēdŏ, inis, *f.* [ūrŏ], *a blast, blight* of plants : Cic.

urgeō, urgēre, ūrsi, *to press, press hard on, press onward, push on or forward.* **1.** Lit. **a.** onus urget, Pl. ; hinc Pallas instat et urget, Verg. ; Hor. ; urget ab alto Notus, Verg. With Acc. : qui insistunt adversa nobis vestigia urgent, Cic. ; legionem urgeri ab hoste, Caes. ; iusto proelio Romanos, Liv. ; navis in syrtis, Verg. ; ruiturum saxum (Sisyphus), Ov. **b.** *to press close, crowd ;* ab tergo Alpes, Liv. With Acc. : urbem hanc urbe aliā, Cic. ;

vallem densis frondibus atrum urget utrimque latus, Verg. **2.** Transf. **a.** In gen. : onus urgentis senectutis, Cic. ; nihil urget, Cic. Ep. ; malum, Cic ; urgenti fato incumbere, Verg. ; urgente fato, Liv. With Acc. : te scelus, Pl. ; aliquem morbus, Hor. ; fames exercitum, Liv. ; populus militiā atque inopiā urgebatur, Sall. In *Pass.* with GEN. of charge : urgeri criminum, Tac. **b.** With arguments, etc. : etiam atque etiam insto atque urgeo, Cic. ; Hor. ; ut interrogando urgeat, Cic. With Acc. : Arcesilas Zenonem, Cic. ; me meis versibus, Cic. With Acc. and *Inf.* : Cic. **c.** *to push forward* or *press on with* any work, etc. ; *to ply hard, press home,* etc. : eundem locum diutius, Cic. ; opus, Tib. ; vestem, Verg. ; iter, Ov. ; propositum, Hor. ; ius, aequitatem, Cic.

ūrīna, ae, *f.* [*cf.* Gk. οὖρον], *urine.* **1.** Lit. : Cic., Juv. In *pl.* : Plin., Suet. **2.** Transf. *semen :* Juv. ; genitalis, Plin.

ūrīnātor, ōris, *m.* [ūrīnor], *a diver :* Liv.

ūrīnor, ārī and **ūrīnō, āre** [ūrīna], *to plunge under water, to dive :* Cic., Varr.

urna, ae, *f.* [*cf.* urceus], *a water-pot, water-jar.* **1.** Lit. : Pl., Hor., Ov., etc. **2.** Transf. **a.** *a voting-urn :* Cic., Verg., etc. Hence, *the urn of fate :* omnium versatur urnā serius ocius sors exitura, Hor. ; Verg. ; Liv. **b.** *a cinerary urn :* Ov., Suet. **c.** *a money-pot, money-jar :* Hor. **d.** A liquid measure containing half an amphora : Cato, Plin., Pers. ; also of a measure in gen. : Cato, Juv.

ūrŏ, ūrere, ūssi, ūstum [*cf.* Gk. εὕω, αὕω]. **1.** Lit **a.** In gen. *to burn, burn up* : picem et ceras, Ov. ; homines in usum nocturni luminis, Tac. ; hominem mortuum, XII Tab. ; Lucr. ; stipulam flammis, Verg. **b.** Of hostile ravaging : Carthaginis arces, Hor. ; agros, Liv. ; urbes hostium, Tac. **c.** Of encaustic painting, *to burn in :* picta coloribus ustis puppis, Ov. **d.** In surgery, *to cauterise :* Cic. **2.** Transf. **A.** Physically. **a.** *to scorch, parch, dry up :* Pl. ; partes terrarum uruntur calore, Cic. ; campum (seges), Verg. ; faucis sitis, Hor. ; pestilentia urbem atque agros, Liv. **b.** *to gall, chafe :* calceus si (pede) minor uret, Hor. ; uri virgis, Hor. ; Ov. **c.** With cold, *to sting, pinch, nip :* montibus uri, Cic. ; Ov. **B.** Transf. (mentally). **a.** With love or other passion : me amor, Verg. ; Hor. ; uritur infelix Dido, Verg. ; meum iecur bilis, Hor. ; ira utrumque, Hor. **b.** *to gall, harass :* uro hominem, Ter. ; eos bellum Romanum, Liv. ; captos legibus tuis, Ov.

ursus, i, *m.* [*cf.* Gk. ἄρκτος], *a bear :* Hor., Ov., Sen., etc. and **ursa, ae,** *f. a she-bear :* Ov., Mart. Prov. : fumantem nasum vivi temptaveris ursi, Mart. Fem. a constellation, either Ursa Maior, *the Greater Bear,* or Ursa Minor, *the Lesser Bear :* Ov., Suet. [It. *orso ;* Fr. *ours.*]

urtīca, ae, *f. a nettle, stinging-nettle.* **1.** Lit. : Cat., Hor., Plin. **2.** Transf. **a.** *a sea-nettle :* Plin. ; marina, Pl. **b.** *desire, pruriency :* Juv. [Fr. *ortie.*]

ūrus, i, *m.* [a Celtic word], *a kind of wild ox,* or *aurochs :* Caes., Verg.

ūsĭtātē, *adv. in the usual manner* : Cic.

ūsĭtātus, a, um [ūtor], *usual, customary, familiar* : Caes., Cic., etc. ; usitatum est (with Acc. and *Inf.*), Quint. *Comp.* and *Sup.* : Cic., Quint.

ūspiam, *adv.* [*v.* ūsquam], *at or in any place, anywhere, somewhere*. **1.** L i t. : Pl., Cic. **2.** T r a n s f. *in any matter* : Pl.

ūsquam, *adv.* [ubs fr. ubi, and -quam], *at or in any place, anywhere* (usually with negatives). **1.** L i t. **a.** nullus usquam consistendi locus, Cic. ; Pl., in questions of a negat. tone : num eius color pudoris signum usquam indicat ? Ter. Also in conditional clauses : si quid usquam iustitia est, Verg. ; Quint. **b.** Rarely affirmatively : unde quod est usquam inspicitur; Ov. ; Cic. ; Verg. **2.** T r a n s f. **a.** *in any way* : neque esset usquam auctoritati locus, Cic. ; quasi iam usquam tibi sint viginti minae, Ter. **b.** With verbs of motion, *to any place, anywhere* : Pl., Hor.

ūsque, *adv.* [ubs fr. ubi and -quam], *all the way, right on, continuously*. **1.** L i t. o f s p a c e : Pl. ; usque a mari supero Romam proficisci, Cic. ; usque ex ultimā Syriā navigare, Cic. ; usque ad castra hostium, Caes. ; Cic. ; trans Alpis usque transfertur, Cic. ; quod eos usque istinc exauditos putem, Cic. With quāque, *everywhere*, Pl., Cic. **2.** T r a n s f. **a.** Of time : opinio iam usque ab heroicis ducta temporibus, Cic. ; deinceps retro usque ad Romulum Cic. ; usque a mani ad vesperum, Pl. ; iam inde usque a pueritiā, Ter. ; inde usque repetens, Cic. ; usque antehac, Ter. ; usque eo se tenuit quoad etc., Cic. With quāque, *every moment, continually* : Pl., Cat., Cic., etc. ; usque . . . dum, Pl., Cic. Ep., Hor. **b.** Of other relations : usque ad ravim poscam, Pl. ; hoc malum usque ad bestias perveniat, Cic. ; familiaris est factus usque eo ut etc., Cic. ; usque adeo, Verg. With quāque, *in everything, on all occasions* : Cic.

ūstor, ōris, m. [ūrō], *a burner of dead bodies, a corpse-burner* : Cic., Cat., etc.

ūstŭlō, āre [*dim.* ūrō]. **I.** *to burn a little, to scorch, singe* : palos, Vitr. **II.** *to burn up, consume by fire* : scripta lignis, Cat.

ūstus, a, um, *Part.* ūrō.

ūsū capĭō or **ūsū-capĭō**, capere, cēpī, captum. In law, *to acquire ownership of a thing by long use, to acquire by prescription* : hereditatem, Cic. Ep. ; quod Hannibal iam velut usu cepisset Italiam, Liv.

ūsū-capĭō, ōnis, f. In law, *the acquisition of ownership by long use or possession* : Cic.

ūsūra, ae, f. [ūtor], *a using, use or enjoyment*. **1.** L i t. **a.** In gen. : lucis, Cic. ; Pl. Of money lent : ab aliquo pecuniam pro usurā auferre, Cic. **2.** T r a n s f. **a.** *interest paid for the use of money, usury* (reckoned by the month among the Romans) : alicui usuram pendere, Cic. Ep. ; perscribere, Cic. Ep. ; minuere, Plin. Ep. ; plurium annorum, Plin. Ep. ; ut sine usuris creditae pecuniae solvantur, Caes. ; aes alienum multiplicandis usuris crescere, Nep. ; Liv. ; faenus agitare et in usuras extendere,

Tac. **b.** T r a n s f. : terra nunquam sine usurā reddit quod accepit, Cic. ; intercalatae poenae usuram habere, Liv. ; has usuras voluptatium pendimus, Sen. Ep.

ūsūrārius, a, um [ūsūra]. **I.** *that of which one has the use or enjoyment* : Pl. **II.** *that pays interest* : aera, Pl.

ūsurpātĭō, ōnis, f. [ūsurpō], *a making use of* : doctrinae, Cic. ; vocis, Liv. ; insoliti itineris, Liv.

ūsurpō, āre [perh. for ūsū (DAT.) rapiō], *to take into use ; to make use of ; to employ, practise, etc.* **a.** In gen. : inter novam rem verbum vetus, Pl. ; hoc genus poenae in improbos civis, Cic. ; nomen tantum virtutis, Cic. ; consolationes, Cic. ; alicuius memoriam, Cic. ; ius, Liv. ; otium post labores, Tac. ; comitatem et temperantiam, Tac. **b.** Of the senses : *to experience, observe* : aliquid sensibus, Lucr. ; aures sonitum, Pl. **c.** In law, *to enter upon possession of* : amissam possessionem, Cic. ; hereditatem, Tac. Wrongfully : alienam possessionem, Liv. ; Tac. Also, civitatem Romanam, Suet. **d.** *to make use of a name or term* : Graecum verbum, Cic. ; alicuius vocem, Liv. Hence, *to call* : is, qui Sapiens usurpatur, Cic. ; haec eadem usurpare corpora prima, Lucr.

ūsus, a, um, *Part.* ūtor.

ūsus, ūs, m. [ūtor], *a using or making use of*. **1.** L i t. **a.** lini, Caes. ; in usu habere, Caes., Plin. Ep. ; multa ad suum usum reservabat, Cic. ; membrorum, Cic. ; pervius usus tectorum inter se, Verg. ; huius nominis, Ov. ; plures quam quot in usum erant ignes, Liv. ; aurum cogere in humanos usūs, Hor. Also of excessive use : adsiduo consumitur anulus usu, Ov. **b.** *using, use, exercise, practice* : tantum usu cottidiano et exercitatione efficiunt uti etc., Caes. ; usus forensis, Cic. ; rerum magnarum, Cic. ; usus est magister optimus, Cic. **c.** *use, experience, skill* : Ter., Cic. ; magnum in re militari usum habere, Caes. ; in re publicā, Cic. ; militaris, Cic. ; rei militaris, Caes. ; nauticarum rerum, Caes. ; belli, Sall. ; seris venit usus ab annis, Ov. **d.** *use, usage, habit, custom* : communis, Cic. ; agrestis, Verg. ; quem usum belli haberent, Caes. ; loquendi, Cic. **e.** In law, **ūsus et frūctus** and more freq. **ūsusfrūctus**, *the use and enjoyment of property belonging to another, usufruct* : omnium bonorum, Cic. (*v.* also usucapio). **f.** Of persons, *familiarity, intimacy* : domesticus usus et consuetudo, Cic. ; familiaris, Liv. ; Ov. **2.** T r a n s f. **A.** *use, usefulness, utility, profit* : Cic. ; naves factae ex umidā materiā non eundem usum celeritatis habebant, Caes. ; nescis quem praebeat usum (nummus) ? Hor. ; (arborum) consectio magnos usūs adfert ad navigia facienda, Cic. Phr. **ūsui** or **ex ūsū esse**, *to be of use, to be useful, serviceable*, or *profitable* : bono usui esse, Pl. ; ea quae sunt usui ad armandas navis, Caes. ; Liv. ; magno usui rei publicae esse, Cic. ; utrum proelium committi ex usu esset necne, Caes. ; Liv. **B.** *use, need, necessity* : usum provinciae supplere, Cic. ; quae belli usūs poscunt suppeditare

Liv. Esp. in phr. **a. ūsus est** and **ūsus venit**, *there is need of :* fero quod usus est, Pl. ; si quando usus esset, Cic. ; si usus veniat, Caes. ; Pl. ; Ter. With ABL. : curatore usus est, Cic. ; Pl. ; Verg., etc. ; ubi usus veniat consertā manu, Pl. **b. ūsus est, adest**, etc., *there comes a fit occasion* or *opportunity :* si usus fuerit, Cic. ; Caes. **c. ūsū venit**, *it happens, occurs :* Caesar haec de Vercingetorige usu ventura opinione perceperat, Caes. ; Cic.

ūsusfrūctus, v. ūsus, 1., e.

ut or **utī**, *adv.* **I.** Non-dependent (exc. in Oblique clauses). **A.** Interrogative: *how ? in what manner ?* **a.** Direct: ut sese in Samnio res habent ? Liv. ; Pl. ; Hor. **b.** Indirect: edoce eum ut res se habet, Pl. ; nonne vides ut India mittit ebur, Verg. ; Cat. With *Subj. :* Pl., Caes., Cic., Verg., etc. **B.** Exclamatory: *how.* **a.** Direct: ut se ipse sustentat ! Cic. ; Pl. ; Verg., etc. **b.** Indirect (as A. b.). **c.** In wishes: ut illum di deaeque perdant ! Ter. ; Verg. **d.** In concessions: *let, granted that, although* (with *Subj.*) : ut omnia contra opinionem acciderent, tamen se plurimum navibus posse, Caes. ; Ov. **II.** Relative: *how, in the manner that, as.* **A.** With Indic. **1.** Lit. **a.** Simply: Labienus, ut erat ei praeceptum, proelio abstinebat, Caes. ; Pl. ; Cic., etc. Often the verb of the *ut* -clause is omitted: multi ut ad ludos convenerant, Pl. ; canem et felem ut deos colunt, Cic. ; Liv., etc. **b.** Repeated ut ut, *howsoever :* ut ut res se habet, pergam, Pl. ; Ter. **c.** With corresponding *sic, ita.* (i) In gen. : Pomponium Atticum sic amo ut alterum fratrem, Cic. Ep. ; Pl., etc. ; ut sementem feceris, ita metes, Cic. ; Pl. ; Liv., etc. (ii) ut . . . sic or ita, *though . . . yet :* Saguntini, ut a proeliis quietem habuerant per aliquot dies, ita non cessaverant ab opere, Liv. ; Tac. (iii) in *proportion as, according as . . . so* (esp. with quisque) : ut quisque est vir optimus, ita difficillime esse alios improbos suspicatur, Cic. ; ut quisque gradu proximus erat, ita ignominiae obiectus, Liv. **2.** Transf. **a.** Of time. (i) Of an occurrence immediately preceding : *as, when, as soon as :* principio ut illo advenimus, continuo Amphitruo delegit viros, Pl. ; Cic. ; Liv. (ii) Rarely of the same or a subsequent time : *while, since :* ut numerabatur argentum, intervenit homo de improviso, Ter. ; ut Brundisio profectus es, nullae mihi abs te sunt redditae litterae, Cic. Ep. But freq. of repeated actions (mostly with quisque) : ut quaeque pars castrorum premi videbatur, eo auxilium ferre, Caes. ; ut quisque me viderat, narrabat, Cic. ; Liv., etc. **b.** Rarely of place : *where :* Indos, litus ut tunditur undā, Cat. ; Pl. ; labitur . . . ut forte, Verg. **B.** With Subjunctive. **1.** Expressing result or consequence (negat. ut non). **a.** In gen. (often corresp. to a demonstrative word, e.g. *sic, ita, tam, adeo; talis, tantus, is,* etc.) : *(so) that, as that, that, as to,* etc. : Tarquinius sic Servium diligebat ut is eius filius

haberetur, Cic. ; Pl. ; Caes., etc. **b.** After verbs of *happening, coming about* or *bringing about :* sol efficit ut omnia floreant, Cic. ; accidit ut unā nocte omnes Hermae deicerentur, Nep. **c.** After impersonal phrases, e.g. mos est, necesse est, sequitur, (tantum) abest, etc. : mos est hominum ut nolint eundem pluribus rebus excellere, Cic. **d.** Also the explanatory use of ut, *to the effect that, to wit that :* vetus est lex amicitiae ut idem amici semper velint, Cic. ; non haec dederas promissa parenti, cautius ut velles, Verg. **e.** ut non after a preceding non can often be translated by *without :* non possunt unā in civitate multi rem ac fortunam amittere ut non pluris secum in eandem trahant calamitatem, Cic. **2.** Expressing purpose, intention, etc. (negat. *ne* or *ut ne*) : *to the end that, in order that, that :* constituerunt sementis quam maximas facere, ut in itinere copia frumenti suppeteret, Caes. ; Pl. ; Cic., etc. **3.** After verbs of *wishing* (cf. I. B. c.), *asking, advising, urging, commanding, striving,* etc. : Phaethon ut in currum patris tolleretur optavit (or with *Inf.*), Cic. ; petebant uti equites praemitterent, Caes. ; Pompeium monebat ut meam domum metueret, Cic. ; consul edicere est ausus ut senatus ad vestitum rediret, Cic. ; auctor sum ut etc., *I recommend that* etc., Cic. ; cura ut valeas, Cic. Ep. **4.** After verbs of fearing (for the more usual *ne non*) : timeo ut sustineas labores, Cic. ; veretur Hiempsal ut foedus satis firmum sit, Cic. ; Caes. **5.** For concessive use, v. I. B. d.

ut-cumque (-quomque, Pl., and **-cunque**) *adv. in whatever way, howsoever, however.* **1.** Lit. **a.** Relative : Pl., Cic., Verg., etc. **b.** Indefinite : ea quoque temptata utoumque, Liv. **2.** Transf. *at whatever time, whenever :* Hor., Liv.

ūtēns, entis. **I.** *Part.* ūtor. **II.** *Adj. possessing :* utentior sane sit, Cic.

ūtēnsilis, e, *adj.* [ūtor], *useful :* Varr. As Noun, **ūtēnsilia**, ium, *n. pl. things for use, utensils, materials :* exutus omnibus utensilibus miles, Liv. ; Tac.

ūter, ūtris, *m.* [*cf.* uterus], *a bag* or *bottle made of skin, a skin for wine, oil,* etc. **1.** Lit. : Pl., Verg., Curt., etc. Often inflated and used for crossing streams : Caes., Liv. **2.** Transf. of conceit : crescentem tumidis inflat sermonibus utrem, Hor.

uter, utra, utrum (GEN. utrius ; occ. utrius in poets), *pron.* and *adj.* **I.** Interrog. : *which of the two ?* **a.** Direct: uter nostrum popularis est ? Cic. ; Pl. ; Hor. Rarely with plural verb: uter meruistis culpam ? Pl. (In *pl.* only of two sets of people.) **b.** Indirect : ignoratis rege uter esset Orestes, Cic. ; Pl. ; Hor., etc. ; quaerere uter utri insidias fecerit, Cic. ; videte utrum sit aequius hominem dedi inimicissimis nationibus an reddi amicis, Cic. **II.** Relat. *which of the two, the one that :* utram harum vis condicionem accipe, Pl. ; Cic. ; Hor., etc. **III.** Indef. *either of the two :* si uter velit, Cic.

uter-cumque (-cunq-), utracumque, utrumcumque, *pron.* and *adj.* **I.** R e l a t. *which-ever of the two* : Cic. **II.** I n d e f. *either of two* : Quint.

uter-libet, utralibet, utrumlibet, *pron.* and *adj. which of the two you please, whichsoever of the two, either of the two* : utrumlibet elige, Cic. ; eos consules esse, quorum utrolibet duce bellum . . . geri recte possit, Liv.

uter-que, utraque, utrumque (GEN. utrīusque, but occ. utriusque in poets), *pron.* and *adj.* [for the indef. -que, *cf.* quisque], *both the one and the other, both, each of two* (severally) : uterque (appellatus est sapiens) alio modo, Cic. ; sermones utriusque linguae, Hor. ; parens, Ov. ; sententia in utramque partem tuta, Caes. With *pl.* predicate : uterque insaniunt, Pl. ; uterque ambigui, Tac. In *pl.*, usually *each party, each lot* : utrique Socratici et Platonici volumus esse, Cic. ; Pl. ; Caes., etc. ; of two individuals : Pl., Caes., Cic., Verg., etc.

uterus, i, m. **(uterum,** i, n. Pl.) [*cf.* Gk. ὑστέρα], *the womb, matrix.* **1.** L i t. : Pl., Cic., Verg., etc. **2.** T r a n s f. **a,** Of the cavities of the earth : Lucr. **b.** Of the belly of the Trojan horse : Verg. **c.** Of the unborn child : Tac. **d.** *belly, paunch* of a man : Juv.

uter-vis, utravis, utrumvis, *pron. which* or *either of the two you will* : at minus habeo virium quam vestrum utervis, Cic. P r o v. : in aurem utramvis otiose dormire (i.e. to be free from anxiety), Ter.

uti, *v.* ut ; **ūti,** v. ūtor.

ūtibilis, e, *adj.* [ūtor]. *useful, fit, serviceable* : locus, Pl. ; ad rem, Pl.

Utica, ae, f. *a very ancient city in Africa Propria, N.W. of Carthage, where the younger Cato committed suicide* ; **Uticēnsis,** e ; also **Uticēnsēs,** ium, m. *pl. the inhabitants of Utica.*

ūtilis, e, *adj.* [ūtor]. *useful, serviceable, profitable, expedient.* **a.** In gen. : Cato, Cic., Hor. ; utile est (with *Inf.*), Pl., Cic., Hor. ; so, utilissimum est, Nep. With DAT. of person or thing benefited : Pl., Cic., Verg., etc. With *ad* and ACC. of the purpose : homo ad nullam rem utilis, Cic. ; Pl. ; res utiles ad rem tutandam, Ter. With *Inf.* : Hor. With *Instr.* ABL. : pomis arbor, Verg. ; Ov. *Comp.* : Cic. *Neut.* as Noun, *what is useful or expedient* : Hor. ; in *pl.* : Hor., Quint. **b.** *adapted, fit* : lignum navigiis, Verg. ; bello equi, Ov. ; ventri lactuca movendo, Mart. With GEN. : radix medendi, Ov.

ūtilitās, ātis, f. [ūtilis], *usefulness, expediency, advantage* : Pl., Cic., Hor. In *pl.* : utilitates ex amicitiā maximae capientur, Cic.

ūtiliter, *adv. usefully, profitably* : Cic., Hor., Liv. *Comp.* : Ov. *Sup.* : Quint.

uti-nam, *adv.* [uti], *oh that!* *I wish that!* *would that!* : utinam mihi ore uti liceret alieno ! Cic. ; Pl. ; Hor., etc. Negatively, utinam ne and utinam non, Ter., Cic. Ep., Curt.

uti-que, *adv.* [for the indef. *que, cf.* quisque], *anyhow ; in any case, at any rate, at least or especially.* **a.** velim Varronis et Lolli mittas laudationem, Lolli utique, Cic. Ep. ; Liv. ;

hoc tibi mando, ut pugnes, ne intercaletur ; annum quidem utique teneto, Cic. ; at (haec) in Graeciā, utique olim, magnae laudi erant, Nep. **b.** With n e g a t i v e s : monentes (eum), ne utique vellet, Liv. ; Quint.

ūtor (older **oetor**), ūti, ūsus (and **ūtō,** ūtere, Cato), *to use, make use of* (mostly with ABL.). **1.** L i t. (of material things). **a.** In gen. : oculis, Pl. ; sensibus, Lucr. ; armis, equis, Cic. ; navium materiā atque aere ad reliquas reficiendas, Caes. ; eā paterā ad res divinas, Cic. ; eis turribus propugnaculis, Liv. ; taleis ferreis pro nummo, Caes. With ACC. : cetera, Pl. ; Cato ; Varr. ; hence, quae utenda vasa semper vicini rogant, Pl. ; quae bona Heraclio omnia utenda ac possidenda tradiderat, Cic. ; Ov. **b.** Of food, clothing, possessions, etc. : *to have, possess, enjoy* : quaerere et uti, Hor. ; parvis tegimentis, Caes. ; suis bonis, Cic. ; cibo, Nep. ; lacte et herbis, Ov. Of persons : facili me patre, Ter. ; bonis iustisque regibus, Cic. ; Hor. **2.** T r a n s f. **a.** *to make use of, enjoy, practise, etc.* : ad eam rem tuā operā, Pl. ; fide lenoniā, Pl. ; sermonibus morologis, Pl. ; inprobi viri officio, Pl. ; eā condicione, Caes. ; valetudine non bonā, Caes. ; tuo iudicio, Cic. ; argumentis in re eius modi, Cic. ; praeposteris consiliis, Cic. ; patientiā, ratione, clementiā, Cic. ; vestrā benignitate, Cic. ; viribus per clivos, Hor. With ACC. : operam meam, Pl. **b.** Of friendship, intimacy, etc. (usually with *Adv.* and ABL. of person) : *to enjoy (the friendship of)* : his Fabriciis semper est usus Oppianicus familiarissime, Cic. ; regibus, Hor. ; me quasi magistro, Plin. Ep. With ACC. : Cato.

ut-pote, *adv.* [lit. *as is* (or *was*) *possible*], *as being, as, inasmuch as.* **a.** Usually with *Relat. Pron.* : satis nequam sum, utpote qui hodie inceperim amare, Pl. ; Cat. ; Cic. **b.** With *Participles* : inde Rubos fessi pervenimus, utpote longum carpentes iter, Hor. ; Nep. **c.** With *Adj.* : quo sane populus numerabilis, utpote parvus coibat, Hor.

ūtrārius, i, m. [ūter], *one who brings water in skins, a water-carrier* : Liv.

ūtriculārius, i, m. [ūtriculus, *a small skin*], *a bagpiper* : Suet.

utrimque (utrinque), *adv.* [uterque], *from or on both sides or parts* : magnae utrimque copiae, Cic. ; acriter utrimque pugnatum est, Caes. ; Pl. ; Hor., etc. ; utrimque constitit fides, Liv. ; Piso M. Crasso et Scriboniā genitus nobilis utrimque, Tac. ; With *secus* : *along both sides* : quā re utrimque secus cum corpus vapulet, Lucr.

utrō, (*directive*) *adv. to which of the two places or sides?* : nescit utro potius ruat, Ov.

utrobi-, *v.* utrubi-.

utrōlibet, (*directive*) *adv. to either of two sides, to either side* : Quint.

utrōque, (*directive*) *adv. to both places or sides, in both directions.* **1.** L i t. : utroque versis signis, Liv. ; Cic. ; Verg. **2.** T r a n s f. : auctores utroque trahunt, Liv. ; moderatum utroque consilium, Liv. With *vorsum* (*versum*) : Pl.

utrŭbi, *adv.* [utro- with suffix *-bi* ; *cf.* -ibi], *at* or *on which of two places, or sides* (interrog. or relat.) : *St.* utrubi accumbo ? *Sa.* utrubi tu vis, Pl.

utrŭbĭque, *adv.* [utrubi and indef. suffix *-que*], *on both parts* or *sides* : Cic. ; ut utrubique res publica prospere gereretur, Liv. ; utrubique Eumenes plus valebat, Nep. ; pavor est utrubique molestus, Hor.

utrum, *interrog. adv.* [*Neut.* of uter], introducing alternative questions (*cf.* old Eng. *whether ?*). **I.** In gen. **a.** Direct : utrum ea vestra an nostra culpa est ? Cic. ; Pl., etc. Strengthened by *-ne* : utrum taceamne an praedicem ? Ter. ; Cic., etc. With more than two alternatives : utrum hostem an vos an fortunam utriusque populi ignoratis ? Liv. ; Cic. With negat., *an non* (or *annon*), in alternative : Cic. **b.** Indirect : multum interest utrum laus imminuatur, an salus deseratur, Cic. ; Pl., etc. Strengthened by *-ne* : ea res nunc in discrimine versatur, utrum possitne se defendere an etc., Cic. ; Pl., etc. With the particle *-nam* (*in fact*) : cum percontatus esset, utrumnam Patris universa classis in portu stare posset, Liv. With negat. (usually) *necne*, in alternative : Caes., Cic., Liv. **II.** Sometimes without a second clause. **a.** Direct : utrum in clarissimis est civibus is, quem iudicatum hic duxit Hermippus ? Cic. ; Liv. **b.** Indirect : cum nuntios misisset consultum, utrum . . . veniret, Nep. ; Pl. ; Cic.

utut, *v.* ut, II. 1. b.

ūva, ae, *f. a grape* ; usually collect. *a bunch* or *cluster of grapes.* **1.** Lit. : Cato, Cic., Verg., etc. **2.** Transf. **a.** *a vine* : Verg. **b.** *a bunch* or *cluster of any fruit* : amomi, Plin. **c.** *a cluster* of bees swarming : Verg., Plin.

ūvens, entis [*v.* ūvēscō], *moist, wet* : scopuli, Stat.

ūvēscō, ere [*cf.* Gk. *ὑγρός*, ūmor], *to grow* or *become moist.* **1.** Lit. : Lucr. **2.** Transf. of drinking : modicis poculis, Hor.

ūvĭdŭlus, a, um [dim. ūvidus], *wet* (of dainty things) : a fletu, Cat.

ūvĭdus, a, um [*v.* ūvēscō], *moist, wet, damp.* **1.** Lit. : Pl., Hor., Ov., etc. ; rura adsiduis aquis, Ov. ; Menalcas (i.e. wet with dew), Verg. ; Iuppiter (i.e. rainy), Verg. **2.** Transf. (internally, from drinking) : Bacchus, Hor.

uxor, ōris, *f. a wife.* **1.** Lit. : ducere, Pl., Cic., etc. ; adiungere, Cic. **2.** Transf. **a.** Of animals : olentis uxores mariti, Hor. **b.** Comic. a poor man's cloak : Mart.

uxorcŭla, ae, *f.* [*dim.* uxor], *a dear little wife* : Pl., Varr.

uxōrĭus, a, um [uxor]. **I.** *of a wife* : dos, Ov. ; abhorrens ab re uxoriā (i.e. marriage), Ter. ; levamentum, Tac. **II.** *excessively fond of one's wife, uxorious* : Verg. ; amnis (Tiberis), Hor.

V

V, v, is in this volume used to represent consonantal *u*. **I.** Latin (consonantal) *u*

corresponds to Greek digamma. It occurs in many Latin words, whose Greek cognates contain no corresponding sound ; but those cognates originally had a *ϝ*, which in the course of time was lost : *cf.* ver (= *vever*), *ἔ(σ)αρ*, *ἦρ* ; vestis, *ἐσθής* ; vicus, *οἶκος* ; vinum, *οἶνος* ; viola, *ἴον* ; veho, *ὄχος* ; ovis, *ὄις* ; silva, *ὕλη* (= *συλϝα*), etc. **II.** In the Romance languages, Lat. consonantal *u* normally becomes *v*. In a few instances it becomes *b*, as in It. *berbice*, Fr. *brebis*, from Lat. *vervex* ; Fr. *berger*, from Low Lat. *vervicarius* ; *courbe*, from Lat. *curvus* ; this change had probably shown itself in popular Latin at an early period. In a certain number of Italian and French words *v* has, through a Germanic corruption of the consonant, been changed to *gu* or *g* ; thus Lat. *vespa*, Fr. *guêpe* ; Lat. *viscum*, Fr. *gui* ; Lat. *vadum*, It. *guado*, Fr. *gué* ; Lat. *vastare*, It. *guastare*, Fr. *gâter*. Medial (consonantal) *u* is frequently omitted in the Romance languages, as in It. *rio*, from *rivus* ; Fr. *paon*, *peur*, from *pavo*, *pavor*. As a final, in French it becomes *f* ; thus *cerf*, *bref*, *neuf*, *boeuf*, from *cervus*, *brevis*, *novus*, *bovem*. **III.** As an abbreviation V. stands for vir, vivus, vixit, voto, vale, verba, etc. ; V.C., vir clarissimus ; V.C.P., voti compos posuit ; V.V., virgo Vestalis. **IV.** As a numeral, V. stands for *five*, being in this case perhaps half of the X or cross, which was the symbol of *ten*.

văcātĭō, ōnis, *f.* [vacō], *a being free* from a duty, service, etc. ; *a freeing, exempting ; freedom, exemption.* **1.** Lit. : Cic. With *ab* : ab belli administrationе, Liv. ; Cic. With *Obj.* Gen. : militiae, Caes., Liv. ; (so, without militiae, Cic., Liv., Tac.) ; omnium munerum, Cic. ; laboris, militiae, rerum denique omnium, Cic. With *Subj.* Gen. : adulescentiae, Cic. ; aetatis, Nep. **2.** Transf. *a sum paid for exemption from military service* : vacationes annuas exsolvere, Tac.

vacca, ae, *f. a cow* : Cic., Verg., etc. [Fr. *vache*.]

vaccĭnĭum, I, *n. the whortle-berry* ; acc. to others, *a hyacinth* : Verg., Ov., Plin.

vaccŭla, ae, *f.* [*dim.* vacca], *a little cow* or *heifer* : Cat.

văcĕ-fīō, fieri [vacuus], *to become* or *be made empty* : multusque vacefit in medio locus, Lucr.

văcerrōsus, a, um [vacerra, *a log, stock*], *wooden-headed* : Aug. ap. Suet.

văcillātĭō, ōnis, *f.* [vacillō], *a rocking to and fro, a reeling motion* : in dextrum ac laevum latus, Quint. ; Suet.

văcillō (**văcĭllō**, Lucr.), āre, *to sway to and fro* ; *to stagger, reel, totter.* **1.** Lit. : arbor ventis pulsa vacillans aestuat, Lucr. ; ex vino, Cic. ; in utramque partem toto corpore vacillans, Cic. ; accepi tuam epistulam vacillantibus litterulis, Cic. Ep. **2.** Transf. *to waver, vacillate* : aegrotat fama vacillans, Lucr. ; tota res vacillat et claudicat, Cic. ; in vetere aere alieno, Cic.

văcĭvē, *adv. at leisure, leisurely* : libellum perlegere, Phaedr.

văcĭvĭtās, ātis, *f.* [vacivus], *emptiness, want* : cibi, Pl.

vacīvus (**vocīvos**, Pl., Ter.), a, um [vacō], *empty, void* : aedis facere alicui, Pl. With GEN. : valens adflictet me vocivom virium, Pl. ; tempus laboris, Ter.

vacō (perh. also **vocō** in Pl.), āre, *to be empty, void*. **1**. L i t. **a**. In gen. : aedes, Pl. ; spatium, Lucr. ; triclinium, Cic. Ep. ; agri, Caes. ; saltūs, Verg. With ABL. : umore, Cic. ; hoste vacare domos, Verg. ; milite et pecuniā, Liv. ; custode, Ov. With *ab* : a custodiis classium haec loca, Caes. **b**. Of possessions : cum agri Ligustini aliquantum vacaret, Liv. *Neut. pl.* of *Part.* as Noun : ut populus vacantia teneret, Tac. **2**. T r a n s f. **a**. Of persons, etc. *to be void, free,* or *aloof* (esp. fr. labour, business, etc.) : si vacabis, Cic. Ep. ; festus in pratis vacat otioso cum bove pagus, Hor. With ABL. : curā et negotio, officio, studiis, vitio, Cic. ; metu ac periculis, Liv. With *ab* : ab opere milites, Caes. ; a publico officio et munere, Cic. ; nullum tempus illi vacabat a forensi dictione aut a scribendo, Cic. **b**. With DAT. : *to be free* (*for*), *to have leisure* or *time* (*for*) : philosophiae, Cic. ; Tac. ; paulum (*Intern. Acc.*) palaestricis, Quint. ; discendo iuri, Quint. With *in* or *ad* and ACC. : in grande opus, Ov. ; ad istas ineptias, Sen. Ep. With *Inf.* : Stat. Alone : dum perago tecum pauca, vaca, Ov. **c**. I m p e r s. *there is time, room,* or *leisure* (*for*) : dum vacat, Ov. ; si vacat, Juv. Usually with *Inf.* : si vacet annalis nostrorum audire laborum, Verg. ; Quint. With DAT. of person : non vacat exiguis rebus adesse Iovi, Ov. ; Quint. ; Plin. Ep.

vacŭĕ-faciō, facere, fēcī, factum [vacuus]. *to empty, clear, free* : subsellia vacuefacta sunt, Cic. ; Nep.

vacŭĭtās, ātis, *f.* [vacuus], *a freedom, exemption* : molestiae, Cic. ; ab angoribus, Cic. Of a vacancy in an office : Brut. ap. Cic. Ep.

Vacūna, ae, *f. the goddess of rural leisure, particularly honoured by the Sabines ;* **Vacūnālis**, e.

vacŭō, uāre [vacuus], *to empty, clear, free ;* locus inanitus ac vacuatus, Lucr.

vacuus (**vacuos**), a, um [vacō], *empty, clear, void, wanting, without*. **1**. L i t. **a**. In gen. : spatium, Lucr. ; castra, Caes. ; caelum, agri, Verg. ; locus, Liv. ; manus, Quint. (As Noun, **vacuum**, i, *n. an empty space, a void* : Lucr. ; in vacuum poterunt se extendere rami, Verg. ; ne per vacuum incurreret hostis, Hor.) With ABL. : moenia defensoribus, Liv. ; Cic. ; Ov. With *ab* : oppidum ab defensoribus, Caes. ; Liv. With GEN. : ager frugum, Sall. **b**. Of possessions, *vacant, without an occupant* or *master* : praedia, Cic. ; vacuam possessionem regni sperans, Caes. ; res publica, Sall., Liv. ; sacerdotia, Tac. *Neut.* as Noun : si quis casus puerum egerit Oreo, in vacuum venias, Hor. **c**. With DAT. : *free* (*for*) : Romanis vatibus aedem, Hor. Also, domus scelestis nuptiis, Sall. ; Suet. **d**. *empty, worthless, useless* : si res publica et senatus vacua nomina sunt, Tac. ; vacuos exercet in aëra morsūs, Ov. ; tollens vacuum plus nimio gloria verticem,

Hor. **2**. T r a n s f. **a**. Of persons : *free, void, devoid* (esp. fr. labour, business, etc.) ; quoniam vacui sumus, dicam, Cic. ; si quid vacui sub umbrā lusimus, Hor. ; animus, Cic. ; mentes, Verg. ; aures, Hor., Quint. ; civitas, Liv. ; Rutilius animo vacuus, Sall. ; te semper vacuam sperat, Hor. ; nec rursus iubeo, dum sit vacuissima, quaeras, Ov. With ABL. : animus per somnum sensibus ac curis, Cic. ; cupiditate et timore, Cic. ; negotiis, Cic. ; laboribus vita, Ov. ; tali culpā, Tac. ; nullum tempus beneficio, Plin. Pan. With *ab* : ab omni sumptu, molestiā, munere, Cic. ; domus a suspicione, Cic. ; ab odio, amicitiā, irā atque misericordiā, Sall. ; censores ab operum locandorum curā, Liv. With GEN. : operum, Hor. ; Ov. Also of places : Tibur, Hor. **b**. Of women : *free, unmarried* : Tac. ; also, *widowed* : Ov. **c**. Of time : dies, Cic. ; nox, Liv.

vadĭmōnĭum, i, *n.* [vas, vadis]. In law, *a promise* (to appear in court) *secured by the offer of sureties* (vades) or *bail ; bail, security, recognisance* : facere, Pl. ; promittere, Cic. ; constituere, Cic. ; concipere, *to draw up a form of recognisance,* Cic. ; vadimonium est mihi cum aliquo, Cic. ; sistere, *to keep one's recognisance,* Cato, Cic. ; obire, Cic. ; ad vadimonium venire ; ad vadimonium currere, Prop. ; so, with occurrere, Suet. ; non venire ad vadimonium, Cic. ; vadimonium deserere, Cic. ; missum facere, *to release one's bail,* Cic.

vādō, ere, *to go*. **1**. L i t. : Enn. ; pede vago, Cat. ; ad eum postridie mane vadebam, Cic. Ep. E s p. *to make one's way :* Verg. ; in hostem, Liv. ; per hostis, Tac. ; in mortem, Verg. ; ad amnem, Ov. **2**. T r a n s f. : ardua per praeceps gloria vadit iter, Ov. [It. *vado, vo ;* Fr. *vais, vas, va*.]

vador, ārī [vas, vadis]. In law, *to bind* (anyone) *over by bail* (vades) *to appear in court :* Cic., Ov. ; aliquem, Pl., Cic. ; tot vadibus reum, Liv. ; respondere vadato, Hor. *Perf. Part.* in *Pass.* sense (transf.) : me vadatum amore vinctumque attines, Pl.

vadōsus, a, um [vadum], *full of shallows, shallow :* mare, Caes. ; Syrtes, Sall. ; ostium portūs, Liv. ; amnis, Verg.

vadum, i, *n.* (**vadus**, i, *m.* Sall.) [*cf.* vadō]. **1**. L i t. **a**. *a shallow, shoal, ford :* Rhodanus nonnullis locis vado transitur, Caes. ; vado superari amnis non poterat, Liv. ; amnis incerto vado, Tac. **b**. In *pl. shallow waters of a river or in the sea or by the shore :* Lucr., Caes., Liv., Ov. ; brevia, caeca, Verg. **2**. T r a n s f. **A**. *the waters* of the sea or a river (perh. regarded as a highway) : longā sulcant vada salsa carinā, Cat. ; Hor. **B**. *the bottom of the sea,* etc. : imis saxa vadis levata, Hor. ; Ov. ; Plin. ; of a well : Phaedr. ; Plin. **C**. T r a n s f. **a**. With ref. to safety : omnis res iam est in vado, Ter. ; Pl. **b**. With ref. to danger : emersisse iam e vadis et scopulos praetervecta videtur oratio mea, Cic. [It. *guado ;* Fr. *gué*.]

vae, *interj.* [*cf.* Gk. οὐαί], *ah ! oh ! woe ! alas !* Mantua vae, miserae nimium

vicina Cremonae, Verg. ; Pl. ; Hor. With
D A T. : vae misero mihi, Ter. ; vae victis,
Liv. With Acc. : vae te ! Pl. ; Cat.

vaen-, *v.* vēn-.

vafer, fra, frum, *sly, crafty, subtle* : in dis-
putando, Cic. ; Hor. ; Ov. ; ius, Hor.
Sup. : somniorum vaferrimus interpres,
Cic. ; interrogationes, Sen. Ep.

vafrē, *adv. slyly, artfully :* Cic.

vagax, ācis, *adj. roaming :* (perh. in) Hor.

vagē, *adv. far and wide, dispersedly :* Liv.

vāgīna, ae, *f. a scabbard, sheath.* **1.** Lit. :
Caes., Cic., Verg., etc. **2.** Transf. **a.**
the sheath of an ear of grain, etc., *the hull,
husk :* Cic. **b.** In anatomy, *the vagina :*
Pl., Juv. [It. *guaina ;* Fr. *gaine.*]

vāgiō, īre. Of children, *to cry, squall :* Ter.,
Cic., Ov. Of swine : Mart. Also, clamor
ad caelum per aethera vagit, Enn. [It.
guaire.]

vāgītus, ūs, *m.* [vāgiō], *a crying, squalling*
of children : Verg. ; Lucr. ; dare, Ov. ;
edere, Quint. Of the *bleating* of kids :
Ov. Of a *crying* from pain : (in *pl.*),
Lucr.

vāgor, ōris, *m.* [vāgiō], *the cry or wail* of an
infant : Enn., Lucr.

vagor, ārī (and **vagō,** āre, Pl.) [vagus], *to
range, wander, roam, rove.* **1.** Lit. : boves,
Pl. ; in agris homines passim more bestiarum vagabantur, Cic. ; Liv. ; volucres
huc illuc, Cic. ; canes circum tecta, Verg. ;
toto foro, Cic. ; totā urbe, Verg. Of
military raids : Germani latius iam
vagabantur, Caes. ; qui populabundi in
finibus Romanorum vagabantur, Liv. **2.**
Transf. : nostrum nomen latissime, Cic. ;
fama, Verg. ; oratio, Cic. ; animus errore,
Cic. ; idcircone vager scribamque licenter ?
Hor.

vagus, a, um, *ranging, roving, wandering.*
1. Lit. : pecus, aves, pisces, Hor. ; vagi
per silvas ritu ferarum, Quint. ; motūs
bestiarum, Cic. ; Hercules, Pl. ; vagus
et exsul, Cic. ; mercator, Hor. ; pes, Cat. ;
pedes, Ov. ; errores, Ov. ; stellae, Cic. ;
sol, Cat. ; luna, Hor. ; flumina, venti,
flamma, Hor. ; fulmina, crines, Ov. **2.**
Transf. of inconstancy, hesitation, and
vagueness : sententia, fortuna, Cic. ; supplicatio, Liv. ; puellae, Prop. ; vagus animi,
Cat.

vah (fuller form, **vaha,** Pl.), *interj.* [ovā], *ah,
oh !* Pl., Ter.

valdē, *adv.* [contr. from validē], *strongly,
intensely, greatly.* **a.** With verbs (*cf.* valide) : Pl., Cic., Cat. *Comp. :* Hor.
Sup. : Sen. **b.** As *Adv.* of degree, with
Adj. and *Adv. : exceedingly, very :* Cic.,
Cat. **c.** As a strongly confirmative reply ;
yes, certainly ; to be sure : Pl.

valē, *v.* valeō.

vale-dīcō, ere, *to say farewell, bid adieu :*
Sen.

valēns, entis. **I.** *Part.* valeō. **II.** Adj.
A. *strong, stout, vigorous.* **1.** Lit. : Pl.,
Cic. ; satellites, Cic. ; membris valens,
Verg., Ov. ; tunicae, Ov. *Sup. :* Cic.
2. Transf. **a.** Of medicines : Plin. **b.**
Milit. and morally : civitas, Cic. ; (Caesari)
tam valenti resistere, Cic. Ep. ; ad letum
causae satis valentes, Ov. *Comp. :* Cic.,

Ov. ; deus morbo omni valentior, Stat.
Sup. : oppida, Nep. **B.** *well* in health,
healthy, hale, hearty : Pl., Cic., Prop.
Masc. pl. as Noun : Cic.

valenter, *adv. strongly.* **1.** Lit. : Ov. **2.**
Transf. *forcibly, energetically :* dicere,
Sen.

valentulus, a, um [*dim.* valēns], *a strong
little :* ut valentula est ! Pl.

valeō, ēre, *to be strong.* **I.** In gen. *to be
strong, vigorous.* **1.** Lit. : puer ille multum (*Intern.* Acc.) valet, Pl. ; pugnis
plus valet, Pl. ; vites novella, Cato. With
ad : velocitate ad cursum, viribus ad
luctandum valere, Cic. With *Inf. :* Lucr.,
Hor., Ov., Suet. **2.** Transf. **a.** Of medicine (with *ad* or *contra*) : Plin. **b.** Of
sounds : Quint. **c.** Milit. and morally :
to be strong, powerful, valid, etc. : arma,
lex, auctoritas, verba, opinio, etc., Cic. ;
ius gentium, Liv. ; terror, Liv. ; preces,
Ov. ; id responsum quo (*Directive*) valeat,
nemo intellegebat, Nep. ; Cic. With *ad :*
ad leges evertendas, Cic. ; Caes. ; ista
quaestura ad eam rem valet ut etc., Cic. ;
Liv. With *Inf. :* religionibus obsistere,
Lucr. ; nec continere suos ab direptione
castrorum valuit, Liv. ; Hor. ; Tib. ;
ergo fungar vice cotis, acutum reddere
quae ferrum valet, Hor. With Abl. of
the thing *in which* or *by which :* hoc pectus
perfidiā, Pl. ; pedestribus copiis, Caes. ;
multum (*Intern.* Acc.) Caesar equitatu
valebat, Caes. ; qui plus (*Intern.* Acc.)
opibus, armis, potentiā valent, Cic. ; omnia
magistratuum auctoritate, Cic. ; gratiā
aut misericordiis, Caes. ; pedum cursu,
Verg. ; dicendo, Nep. ; Ov. With *in*
and Abl. : in populari genere dicendi,
Cic. ; Quint. With *in* and Acc. (mostly
of validity or applicability) : num in deos
immortalis inauspicatam legem valuisse ?
Liv. ; Cic. With *contra :* hoc contra te,
Cic. ; aliquid contra caput alicuius aut
existimationem, Cic. With *pro* and Abl. :
Cic., Liv., Ov., etc. With *apud* or *ad* and
Acc. of the person influenced : apud te,
Ter. ; apud te veritas, Cic. ; Caes. ; apud
magnam partem senatūs valebat gratiā,
Liv. ; ad populum dicendo, Cic. ; metus
ad omnis, Liv. **d.** Of money value :
to be of the value of, to be worth : pro argen-
teis decem aureus unus, Liv. Hence, *to
be equivalent to, have the force of :* vana pro
veris, Liv. ; epitheton pro nomine, Quint.
e. Of words (*cf.* Gk. δύνασθαι), *to mean,
signify :* quaerimus verbum Latinum par
Graeco et quod idem valeat, Cic. ; Quint.
II. In health : *to be well, healthy, etc.*
A. In gen. : Pl., Ter. ; recte, Pl., Cato,
Cic. Ep. ; optime, Cic. ; corpore, Cic.,
Ov. ; pedibus, Nep. ; stomacho, Juv. ;
a morbo, Pl. Comic. : haud a pecuniā
perbene, Pl. *Impers. Pass. :* Pl. Esp.
at the beginning of letters : si vales, bene
est (S. V. B. E.), Cic. Ep. **B.** In leave-
taking, *farewell, adieu.* **1.** Lit. : bene
vale, Pl. ; vos valete et plaudite, Ter. ;
vive valeque, Hor. ; Verg. *Oblique* with
iubes, dico : illum salutavi ; post etiam
iussi valere, Cic. Ep. ; Suet. At the end
of letters : vale, bene vale, *or* cura ut valeas,

Cic. Ep. In bidding farewell to the dead:
in perpetuom, frater, ave atque vale,
Cat.; salve aeternum mihi, maxime Palla,
aeternumque vale, Verg.; supremumque
vale, Ov. **2.** T r a n s f. as an expression of
dismissal, refusal, or scorn: *be off! begone!* valeas, tibi habeas res tuas, reddas
meas, Pl.; si talis est deus, ut nullā hominum caritate teneatur, valeat, Cic.; castra
peto, valeant puellae, Tib.; Hor., etc.
[Fr. *valoir*.]
valēscō, ere [valeō], *to grow strong, acquire
strength.* **1.** L i t : ut puerorum aetas
recreata valescat, Lucr. **2.** T r a n s f.: superstitiones, Tac.; scelera impetu, bona
consilia morā, Tac.
valētūdinārius, a, um [valētūdō], *sickly,
infirm* : Varr. *Masc.* as Noun, *an invalid,
valetudinarian* : Sen.
valētūdō, inis, *f.* [valeō], *state of health.*
A. In gen. **1.** L i t : bona, Lucr., Cic.,
etc.; optima valetudine uti, Caes.; valetudine minus commodā uti, Caes.; integra,
confirmata, Cic.; infirma, aegra, Cic.;
dura, Hor. In *pl.* : Cic. **2.** T r a n s f.
a. Of the mind: mala valetudo animi,
Cic.; bona valetudo mentis, Sen. Ep.;
qui valetudinis vitio fuererent, Cic. **b.** Of
style : Cic. **B.** *good-health :* Pl., Cic.,
Hor. **C.** *ill-health :* adfectus valetudine,
Caes.; gravis autumnus omnem exercitum
valetudine temptaverat, Caes.; curatio
valetudinis, Cic.; oculorum, Cic. Ep.;
novissimā valetudine conflictabatur, Plin.
Ep. In *pl.* : Plin., Tac., Suet.
valgus, a, um, *bow-legged.* **1.** L i t : Pl.
2. T r a n s f.: savia, Pl.
validē, *adv. strongly, mightily, vehemently,
etc.* **1.** L i t : ut valide tonuit ! Pl.
Comp. : validius clamare, Phaedr.; *Sup.
Sup.* : validissime alicui favere, Cael. ap.
Cic. Ep.; cupere, Plin. Ep. **2.** T r a n s f.
(in a reply) : *certainly, to be sure :* Pl.
validus, a, um [valeō], *strong, stout, powerful,
able.* **A.** In gen. **1.** L i t : homines, Pl.;
tauri, legiones, lacerti, pontes, fulmen,
venti, aestus, etc., Lucr.; Cic.; vires,
Verg.; urbs muris, Liv.; validiores munitiones, Liv.; validissima forma, Quint.
With *ad* : nequaquam satis valido ad
lacessendum hostem equitatu, Liv. **2.**
T r a n s f. **a.** Of drugs : Ov., Tac. *Sup.*
(with *contra*) : Plin. **b.** Morally: Iuppiter, Pl.; aevi leges, Lucr.; urbs, Cic.;
mente minus validi quam corpore toto,
Hor.; opibus, ingenio validus, Tac.;
ingenium sapientiā, Sall.; Tiberius spernendis rumoribus validus, Tac.; ad Caesaris
amicitiam, Tac.; contra consentientis,
Liv. With Gen. : colonia virium et opum,
Tac.; orandi, Tac. **B.** In health : Pl.,
Cic. Ep., Hor.; necdum ex morbo satis
validus, Liv.
vallāris, e, *adj.* [vallum], *given for valour
at the enemy's rampart :* corona, Liv.;
Suet.
vallēs (Caes., Verg.) and **vallis**, is, *f.* [*cf.*
Gk. ἔλος], *f. a valley, vale.* **1.** L i t :
Caes., Cat., Verg., Liv., etc. **2.** T r a n s f.
a hollow : valle sub alarum, Cat.
vallō, āre [vallum], *to palisade, entrench.*
1. L i t : Tac.; castra, Liv., Tac. **2.**

T r a n s f.: hydra venenatis vallata colubris,
Lucr.; Prop.; Pontus et regiis opibus et
ipsā naturā regionis vallatus, Cic.; ius
legatorum divino iure vallatum, Cic. In
Mid. : sol radiis frontem vallatus acutis,
Ov.
vallum, i, *n.* [vallus]. **1.** L i t. **a.** *(stakes
for) palisading :* petere, Liv. Also, perh.
caedere et parare, ferre, Liv. **b.** *a pali-
saded rampart, entrenchment :* castra vallo
fossāque munire, Caes.; Liv. In circumvallation of a town : oppidum vallo et
fossā circumdare, Cic. Ep., Verg., Liv.,
etc. **2.** T r a n s f.: India vallo munitur
eburno, Lucr.; Alpium, Cic.; munitae
sunt palpebrae tamquam vallo pilorum,
Cic.
vallus, i, *m.* [*cf.* Gk. ἧλος], *a stake, pale.*
1. L i t. **a.** For supporting vines : Verg.
b. M i l i t. : Caes.; caedere, Liv. (*v.* also
vallum). Also c o l l e c t. : *palisading ; a
rampart of palisades :* Caes., Tib. **2.**
T r a n s f.: pectinis, Ov.
valvae, ārum, *f. pl. the folds* or *valves of a
door, folding-doors :* Caes., Cic., Hor., Ov.,
etc.
vānēscō, ere [vānus], *to pass away, disappear.*
1. L i t.: nubes, Ov.; nubes in latitudinem, Plin. Ep.; in auras, Ov.; cuncta
in cinerem, Tac. **2.** T r a n s f.: luctus,
Cat.; dicta per auras, Ov.; ira plebis,
Tac.; inanis credulitas, Tac.
vānidicus, a, um [vānus dīcō], *false-speaking.*
As Noun, *a liar* : Pl.
vāniloquentia, ae, *f.* [vāniloquus], *empty* or
idle talk, prating : Pl., Liv., Tac.
vāniloquidōrus, i, *m.* [vānus loquor δῶρον],
gabble-giver of *a liar*) : Pl.
vāniloquus (-**quos**), a, um [vānus loquor],
talking emptily, **a.** *lying* : Pl. **b.** *boastful, bragging, vaunting* : Liv.
vānitās, ātis, *f.* [vānus], *emptiness.* **a.** *uselessness, worthlessness, frivolity, untrust-
worthiness, etc.* : Ter., Cic.; opinionum,
Cic.; itineris, Liv.; populi, Liv. In *pl.* :
Liv. **b.** *vainglory, vanity, conceit* : Sall.,
Tac., etc.; qui se per vanitatem iactassent
tamquam amicos Persei, Liv.
vānitūdō, inis, *f.* [vānus], *emptiness, lying
talk :* vera vanitudine convincere, Pl.
vannus, i, *f. a fan for winnowing grain :*
mystica vannus Iacchi, Verg.
vānus, a, um [for vac-nus, from the root of
vacuus, vacō], *empty, void, vacant.* **1.**
L i t.: aristae, Verg.; ne vana urbis
magnitudo esset, Liv.; imago (of the dead),
Hor.; vanior acies, Liv. **2.** T r a n s f.
a. *empty* as to purport or result, *idle,
groundless, useless :* falsum aut vanum
aut fictum, Ter.; error, Lucr.; oratio,
Cic.; fides, Verg.; omen, spes, verba,
Ov.; pila omnia, ictus, agitatio armorum,
Liv.; promissa, Tac.; vaniore dicendi
genere, Quint.; equestris pugna effectu
quam conatibus vanior, Liv. With Gen. :
aut ego (Iuno) veri vana feror, Verg. As
Noun, **vānum**, i, *n. emptiness, baselessness,
uselessness :* ex vano criminatio, Liv.;
ad vanum et inritum redacta victoria,
Liv.; haud vana attulere, Liv.; Cic.
Intern. Acc.: laetantem animis, ac vana
tumentem, Verg. With Gen. : corruptus

vanis rerum, Hor. **b.** Of persons, *false, deceptive, void of truth* : auctor, Liv. ; vanus et perfidiosus et impius, Cic. ; vanus mendaxque. Verg. ; ingenium dictatoris, Liv. **c.** *vainglorious, vain, conceited* : ingenio vanus, Liv. *Comp.* : Sall. [Fr. *vain.*]

vapidē, *adv. poorly, ill* : se habere, for malo se habere, a favourite expression of Augustus, Suet.

vapidus, a, um [*v.* vapor], *that has emitted steam* (i.e. that has lost its spirit) ; *flat, rapid,* T r a n s f. **a,** *spoiled, bad* : pix, Pers. **b.** Morally, *corrupt* : astutam vapido servas sub pectore vulpem, Pers. [Fr. *fade.*]

vapor (vapōs, Lucr.), ōris, *m. steam, exhalation, vapour.* **a.** In gen.: Verg.; aquarum Cic.; Lucr. In *pl.* : Cic., Hor. **b.** *a warm exhalation, warmth heat* : Lucr. ; terrae, Cic. ; solis, Lucr. ; siderum, Hor. : finditque vaporibus arva (Phoebus), Ov. ; locus vaporis plenus, Liv. [Fr. *vapeur.*]

vapōrārium, i, *n.* [vapor], *a steam-pipe in the Roman baths, which conveyed the heat to the sweating-room* : Cic. Ep.

vapōrifer, era, erum [vapor ferō], *that gives off steam, vaporous* : Stat.

vapōrō, āre [vapor]. **A.** T r a n s. *to wrap in steam or vapour.* **1.** L i t. : templum ture, Verg. ; lacvum decedens (sol) curru fugiente vaporet, Hor. ; Plin. **2.** T r a n s f. : inde vaporatā lector mihi ferveat aure, Pers. **B.** I n t r a n s. *to emit steam, vapour, or smoke.* **1.** L i t. : Plin. **2.** T r a n s f. : invidiā, ceu fulmine, summa vaporant, Lucr.

vappa, ae, *f.* [vapor], *flat, rapid wine.* **1.** L i t. : Hor., Plin. **2.** T r a n s f. *a roué* : Cat., Hor.

vāpulāris, e, *adj.* [vāpulō], *that gets a flogging* : tribunus, Pl.

vāpulō, āre, *to wriggle, squirm under blows : to be flogged or beaten.* **1.** L i t. : Pl., Lucr., Prop. ; ab aliquo fustibus vapulare, Quint. **2.** T r a n s f. (colloq.) **a.** Of troops : septima legio, Cael. ap. Cic. Ep. **b.** Of property *dissipated* : peculium. Pl. ; Sen. **c.** Of things : olea, Varr. **d.** In gen. : sub Veneris regno, Pl. ; omnium sermonibus, Cic. Ep.

variantia, ae, *f.* [variō], *a difference, diversity* : rerum, Lucr.

variātiō, ōnis, *f.* [variō], *a difference, variation* : Liv.

vāricō, āre [vāricus], *to straddle* : Quint. [It. *varcare.*]

vāricōsus, a, um [varix], *with dilated veins, varicose* : Pers. Juv.

vāricus, a, um [vārus], *straddling* : Ov.

variē, *adv. with diverse colours, in a variegated manner.* **1.** L i t. : Plin. **2.** T r a n s f. *diversely, with changing fortune* : moveri, Cic. ; bellare, Liv. ; disserere, Tac.

varietās, ātis, *f.* [varius], *difference, diversity, vicissitudes* : fructuum, Cic. ; bellum in multā varietate versatum, Cic. ; caeli, Cic. ; sententiarum, Cic. ; esse in varietate ne dissensione, Cic. ; varietates vocum, utilitatis, etc., Cic. ; varietates nonnunc. Liv.

variō, āre [varius]. **A.** T r a n s. **1.** L i t.

---

of colour, light and shade : *to diversify, fleck, variegate* : aliquem virgis et loris, Pl. ; colores, Lucr. ; vestis variata figuris, Cat. ; ortum maculis (of the sun), Verg. ; corpora caeruleis guttis, Ov. **2.** T r a n s f. : orationem, vocem, Cic. ; sententias, Liv. ; variatis hominum sententiis, Cic. ; voluptatem, Cic. ; vicis, Verg. ; variabant secundae adversaeque res non fortunam magis quam animos hominum, Liv. ; laborem otio, otium labore, Plin. Ep. In *Mid.* : formas variatus in omnis, Ov. *Impers. Pass.* : Cic. ; cum sententiis variaretur, Liv. **B.** I n t r a n s. **1.** L i t. *to change colour, to be diversified, variegated* : liventibus uva racemis, *turns colour,* Prop. ; Plin. **2.** T r a n s f. (of any diversity or change): inter se figurae, Lucr. ; fama, Liv. ; timores, Ov. ; lex nec causis nec personis, Liv. With *Intern.* Acc. : si fortuna aliquid variaverit, Liv. *Impers.* : ibi si variaret (i.e. if there were a difference of opinion), Liv.

varius, a, um, *parti-coloured, spotted, striped, variegated.* **1.** L i t. : lutea loris varia, Pl. ; uvae, Cato ; lynces, Verg. ; flores, Tib. ; serpens, colores, Ov. ; testudine postes, Verg. **2.** T r a n s f. of anything checkered, varied, diverse, or changeable in its nature : poema, oratio, sermones, mores, fortuna, voluptas, jus, etc., Cic. ; eventus varij fortunae, Caes. ; victoria, Sall., Liv. ; animus, Sall. ; varius incertusque agitabat, Sall. ; vultu et oculis pariter atque animo varius, Sall. ; varium est (with *Indir. Quest.*), i.e. *there are different opinions,* Cic. *Neut.* as Noun : varium et mutabile semper femina, Verg.

Varius, a, *the name of a Roman gens.* Esp. L. Varius, *a distinguished epic poet of the time of Vergil and Horace.*

varix, icis, *m. f. a dilated vein, varix* : Cic., Quint.

Varrō, ōnis, *m. a surname in the gens Terentia* : *v.* Terentius ; **Varrōniānus**, a, um.

Vārus, i, *m. a surname, esp. in the gens Quinctilia.* Esp. P. Quinctilius Varus, *defeated and slain by Arminius* (A.D. 9) ; **Vāriānus**, a, um.

vārus, a, um [perh. *cf.* curvus], *knock-kneed.* **1.** L i t. : Pl., Varr., Hor. **2.** T r a n s f. **a.** In gen. *bent, crooked* : manus, cornua, Ov. **b.** *contrary, opposed* : alterum (genus) huic varum, Hor.

vas, vadis, *m. a surety* (i.e. *a person who goes bail for another* ; praes, "*security*"). **1.** L i t. : vas factus est alter eius sistendi, Cic. ; so dare vadem pro amico, Cic. ; vades poscere, Cic. ; vades deserere, Liv. ; Hor. **2.** T r a n s f. : vestram virtutem rerum quas gesturus sum vadem praedemque habeo, Curt.

vās, vāsis (**vāsum**, Nom. *sing.*, Pl. ; and *pl.* regularly, **vāsa**, ōrum), *n. a vessel, dish* ; also, *a utensil, implement* of any kind : Pl., Lucr., Cic., Hor., etc. Milit. (in *pl.*), *camp-utensils, packs, baggage* : ille ex Siciliā inm castra commoverat et vasa conlegerat, Cic. ; Liv. ; vasa conclamare, Caes.

vāsārium, i, *n.* [vās]. **I.** *an allowance for the hire of an oil-mill* : Cato. **II.** *allow-*

ance for utensils (including furniture), given to a governor of a province : Cic.

vāsculārius, ī, *m.* [vāsculum], *one who makes vessels of metal, a metal-worker* : Cic.

vāsculum, ī, *n.* [dim. vās], *a small vessel* : Pl., Cato, Juv.

vastātiō, ōnis, *f.* [vastō], *a laying waste, ravaging* : omnium, Cic. ; agri, Liv. In *pl.* : Cic., Liv., Tac.

vastātor, ōris, *m.* [vastō], *a ravager* : gentium Alexander, Son. ; forarum Amycus, Verg. ; Arcadiae (aper), Ov.

vastē, *adv.* **I.** *coarsely, uncouthly* : loqui, Cic. *Comp.* : Cic. **II.** *widely, hugely* : vastius insurgens impetus undao, Ov.

vastificus, a, um [vastus faciō], *laying waste, devastating* : belua, Cic. poet.

vastitās, ātis, *f.* [vastus], *a state of desolation, a waste, desert, emptiness.* **1.** Lit.: Cic., Tac. ; iudiciorum et fori, Cic. **2.** Transf. **a.** *an act (or scene) of desolation* : officere, Cic. ; reddere, facere, Liv. ; vastitatem ac templis, urbe, Italiā depellebam, Cic. ; inferre tectis atquo agris, Cic. ; Italiam totam ad vastitatem vocas, Cic. **b.** *immensity, vastness* : Plin. **c.** Concr. of persons : has duplices pestis sociorum, publicanorum ruinas, provinciarum vastitates, Cic.

vastitiēs, ēi, *f.* [vastus], *ruin, destruction* : voluptatem omnium, Pl.

vastō, āre [vastus], *to make empty or vacant, to leave untenanted or uninhabited.* **1.** Lit. **a.** forum, Cic. ; vastati agri sunt, Liv. ; pati terram stirpium asperitate vastari, Cic. With ABL. : cultoribus agros, Verg. **b.** Milit. *to lay waste, ravage* : agros, Cic., Caes., Cat. ; Italiam, Cic. ; partem provinciae incursionibus, Caes. ; omnia ferro ignique vastata, Liv. ; direpti vastatique classe, Tac. ; omnia late vastant, Verg. ; fana tumultu, Hor. **2.** Transf. : ita conscientia mentem excitam vastabat, Sall. [It. *guastare;* Sp. *gustar;* Fr. *gâter.*]

vastus, a, um [parh. *cf.* vacuus], *empty, waste, desert, desolate.* **1.** Lit. **a.** In gen.: urbs, Liv.; (with ABL.), incendiis ruinisque, Liv.; dies per silentium vastus, Tac. Also, viduae et vastae virgines, Enn. **b.** Milit. *laid waste, ravaged* : Pl. ; haec ego vasta dabo, Verg. **2.** Transf. **a.** *uncultivated, rude, clumsy, uncouth* : vultu motuque corporis vasti atquo agrestes, Cic. ; vastus homo atquo foedus, Cic. ; Liv. ; littera vastior (i.e. *too rough in sound*), Cic. **b.** *vast, immense, enormous* : pulvis, Enn. ; belua, Cic. ; fossa, Cic. ; mare, Caes. ; antrum, campi, Verg. ; iter, Ov. ; arma, clamor, certamen, Verg. ; impetus, Hor. ; potentia, Ov. ; silentium, Liv., Tac. *Comp.* : Cic. *Sup.* : Caes., Cic. **c.** *vast, insatiable* : animus, Sall.

vāsum, *v.* vās.

vātēs, is (Gen. *pl.* us. vātum), *m. f. a foreteller, soothsayer* (whose utterances were made in verse). **1.** Lit.: Pl., Cic., Verg., etc. With Obj. GEN.: Liv. **2.** Transf. *a poet or bard* : Enn., Verg., Hor., Tac.

Vāticānus mōns *or* collis, *a hill in Rome, on the right bank of the Tiber.*

vāticinātiō, ōnis, *f.* [vāticinor], *a foretelling, a prediction* : Caes., Cic.

vāticinātor, ōris, *m.* [vāticinor], *a soothsayer, prophet* : Ov.

vāticinium, ī, *n.* [vāticinus], *a prediction, prophecy* : Plin.

vāticinor, ārī [vātēs canō], *to foretell, prophesy.* **1.** Lit.: per furorem, Cic. ; vaticinantis in modum cecinit, Liv. ; Ov. ; furor vera, Cic. With Acc. and *Fut. Inf.* : Ov. **2.** Transf. **a.** *to utter as a prophet or poet* (with Acc. and *Inf.*) : Cic. **b.** *to keep on chanting or harping on* : vetera, Pl. **c.** *to rave, talk wildly* : Cic.

vāticinus, a, um [vātēs canō], *prophetic* : libri, Liv. ; furor, Ov.

vatillum, ī, *n. v.* batillum.

vatīniānī, ōrum, *m. pl.* [Vatinius], *cups and tumblers made by Vatinius* : Mart.

-ve, *enclitic conj.* [vel apocopated], *or* (leaving the choice free) : telum tormentumve, Caes. ; libidines iracundiaeve, Cic. ; Ter., etc.

vē- (sometimes also **vae-**), an inseparable particle, which **a.** negatives, e.g. ve-grandis, *small.* **b.** emphasises a negative idea, e.g. ve-pallidus, *very pale.*

vēcordia, ae, *f.* [vēcors], *want of reason, senselessness ; madness* : Ter., Ov., Sall.

vē-cors, cordis, *adj.* [cor] : Cic., Liv., Ov. ; scelere et metu vecordes, Tac. ; mons, Cic., impetus, Liv. *Sup.* : Cic.

vectātiō, ōnis, *f.* [vectō], *a carrying or being carried, a riding* : Sen. ; equi, Suet.

vectīgal, ālis, *n.* [vectigālis]. **1.** Lit. **a.** *a toll, tax, impost paid to the State* : Caes., Cic. ; imponere agris, Cic. ; pensitare, Cic. ; levare agrum voctigali, Cic. **b.** *a contribution or honorarium paid to a magistrate* : praetorium, Cic. Ep. **2.** Transf. of private persons, *revenue, rents, income, etc.* : Cic., Hor., Plin. Ep. Prov.: magnum vectigal est parsimonia, Cic.

vectīgālis, e, *adj.* [vectus]. **I.** *paying tribute, productive of revenue, taxed* : hos voctigalis sibi fecerunt, Caes. ; agri, civitas, Cic. ; equi, Cic. **II.** *paid as tribute* : pecunia, Cic.

vectiō, ōnis, *f.* [vehō], *a carrying, conveyance* : in *pl.* : quadrupedum, Cic.

vectis, is, *m.* [vehō]. **I.** *a lever or crowbar* : Ter., Caes., Cic., Hor., Ov. **II.** *a bar, bolt* : Cic., Verg.

Vectis, is, *or* **Vecta**, ae, *f. the Isle of Wight.*

vectō, āre [freq. vehō], *to carry about* (often) : corpora Stygiā carinā, Verg. ; vectari equis, Ov. ; Curt.

vector, ōris, *m.* [vehō]. **A.** Act. : *a bearer, carrier* : Lucil. ; Sileni (asellus), Ov. **B.** Pass. : *a passenger, rider.* On a ship : Cic., Verg., Ov. On a horse : Prop., Ov.

vectōrius, a, um [vehō], *engaged in transport, transport-* : navigia, Caes.

vectūra, ae, *f.* [vehō], *a bearing, conveying, transportation by carriage, horse, or ship ; carriage.* **1.** Lit.: equi idonei ad vecturam, Varr. ; pro vecturā solvere, Cic. Ep.; sine vecturae periculo, Cic. Ep. In *pl.*, *transport, conveyances* : remiges, arma, tormenta, vecturae imperabantur, Caes. **2.** Transf.: *carriage-money, freightage, carriage* : Pl., Sen. [It. *vettura;* Fr. *voiture.*]

vectus, a, um, *Part.* vehō.

vegeō, ēre, *to move, quicken, arouse* : Enn.

vegetus, a, um [vegeŏ], *lively, animated, vigorous*. **1.** Lit.: Cic. Ep., Hor.; oculi, Suet. *Masc.* as noun: fessi cum recentibus ac vegetis pugnabant, Liv. **2.** Transf.: mens, Cic.; ingenium, Liv.

vē-grandis, e, *adj. not large ; small :* gradus, Pl.; oves, Varr.; farra, Ov.

vehemēns (scanned as vēmēns, Ter., Lucr., Cat., Hor.), entis, *adj. violent, furious, impetuous, ardent.* **1.** Lit.: in agendo, Cic.; in alios, Cic. With ferox, acer, severus, inexorabilis, Cic.; lupus, Hor.; fuga, Hirt. **2.** Transf. **a.** Of inanimate things : *forcible, powerful :* ictus, Lucr.; pilum vehementius ictu missuque telum, Liv.; vehemens violentia vini, Lucr.; brassica tenui succo vehementissima, Cato. **b.** Of abstract things : causa ad obiurgandum, Ter.; incitatio, Cic.; quaestio, Quint.; argumentum vehementius, Quint.; vis in oratione vehementissima, Quint.

vehementer, adv. **I.** *impetuously, violently :* irata, Pl.; eos incusavit, Caes.; commotus, Caes.; se agere, Cic. *Comp.:* insectari aliquem vehementius, Cic.; Caes. *Sup.:* vehementissime contendere, Caes. **II.** *strongly, forcibly, powerfully :* adstringere manūs, Pl.; id retinebatur, Cic.; displicere, Cic. Ep.; Cic.; quod vehementer ad has res attinet, Lucr. *Comp.:* Cic. *Sup.:* Cic.

vehementia, ae, *f.* [vehemens]. **I.** *eagerness, fervency :* Plin. **II.** *strength :* vini, odoris, Plin.

vehiculum, i, *n.* [vehŏ], *a carriage, conveyance :* Pl., Cic., Liv., Tac. *Of a ship :* furtorum vehiculum, Cic.

vehŏ, vehere, vexi, vectum, *to carry, convey by carriage, horse, ship, etc. :* reticulum panis onusto umero, Hor.; ille taurus, qui vexit Europam, Cic.; cum triumphantem (Camillum) albi per urbem vexerant equi, Liv.; uxorem plaustro, Tib.; Troica sacra ratibus, Tib.; Ov. *Pass.* or *Mid.* **vehor**, vehi, vectus, *to ride, sail, travel, etc. :* ut animal sex motibus veheretur, Cic.; in equo, Cic.; Ov.; in essedo, Cic.; curru, Cic.; Ov.; in navibus, Cic.; navi, Pl.; puppe, Ov.; apes liquidum trans aethera vectae, Verg.; per medias laudes quasi quadrigis vehens, Cic.; cui lectica per urbem vehendi ius tribuit, Suet.

Veii, ōrum, *m. pl. a very ancient city in Etruria about twelve miles from Rome, taken by Camillus 396 B.C.;* **Vēiens**, entis, **Vēientānus** a, um, and **Vēius** (disyl. or trisyl.), a, um; also **Vēientēs**, ium, *m. pl. the inhabitants of Veii.*

Vēiovis or **Vēdiovis**, is, *m. an Etruscan divinity, a god of the under-world (anti-Jove).*

vel, *conj.* and *adv.* [imperat. of volŏ, and therefore, lit. *choose, take your choice].* **I.** Conj. **A.** Singly. **a.** In gen.: *or if you wish :* eius modi coniunctionem tectorum oppidum vel urbem appellaverunt, Cic.; Pl., etc. **b.** Corrective, *or rather :* clariore vel plane perspicuā, Cic.; Liv.; sed stuporem hominis vel dicam pecudis attendite, Cic. With *potius :* tu certe nunquam in hoc ordine vel potius nunquam in hac urbe mansisses, Cic. With *etiam :* *or even :* laudanda est vel etiam aman-

da vicinitas, Cic. **B.** Repeated: *either . . . or ; be it . . . or :* vel tu me vende, vel face quod tibi lubet, Pl.; Caes.; Cic., etc.; vel vi, vel clam, vel precario, Ter.; quae vel ad usum vitae vel etiam ad ipsam rem publicam conferre possumus, Cic.; haec vel ad odium, vel ad misericordiam, vel omnino ad animos iudicum movendos sumentur, *or in general*, Cic. In the poets and post-Aug. prose-writers sometimes, aut . . . vel or vel . . . aut, for vel . . . vel. **II.** Adv. *if you like, even* (perh. prop. an elliptical expression, the less emphatic alternative being understood). **A.** se vel principes eius consili fore profiterentur, Caes.; Pl.; Verg., etc.; per me vel stertas licet, Cic.; hoc ascensu vel tres armati quamlibet multitudinem arcuerint, Liv.; Pl. **B.** with superlatives. **a.** To denote the highest possible degree : cuius vel maxima apud regem auctoritas erat, Liv.; Cic. **b.** *perhaps :* domus vel optima Messanae, notissima quidem certe, Cic. **C.** Giving an instance, where others might equally well be given ; *for instance, in particular :* cuius innumerabilia sunt exempla, vel Appi maioris illius qui etc., Cic.; Ter.

Vēlābrum, I, *n. a district in Rome near the Palatine, where provision dealers dwelt.*

vēlāmen, inis, *n.* [vēlŏ], *a draping, covering, garment :* Verg., Ov., Tac.

vēlāmentum, I, *n.* [vēlŏ], *a draping.* **A.** *a veil, curtain.* **1.** Lit.: Sen. **2.** Transf.: quaerentis libidinibus suis velamentum, Sen. **B.** In *pl.* olive-branches draped with woollen fillets, or rods wound about in like manner, which suppliants bore before them : Liv., Ov., Tac.

vēlārium, I, *n.* [vēlum], *a covering, screen, awning over the theatre :* Juv.

vēlāti, ōrum, *m. pl.* [vēlŏ; *soldiers covered with a cloak only], supernumerary troops ;* always in the phrase, accensi velati (i.e. accensi et velati), Cic.

vēles, itis, *m.* (mostly in *pl.*) [perh. *cf.* vēlōx], *a kind of light-armed soldier, a skirmisher* (before the general engagement). **1.** Lit.: Lucil., Liv., Ov. **2.** Transf.: ut scurram velitem, Cic. Ep.

Velia, ae, *f.* **I.** *an elevated portion of the Palatine Hill at Rome.* **II.** *a town on the coast of Lucania. a colony of the Phocaeans, afterwards called Elea ;* **Veliēnsis**, e, and **Velinus**, a, um ; **Veliēnsēs**, ium, *m. pl. the inhabitants.*

vēlifer, era, erum [vēlum ferŏ], *sail-bearing :* carina, Prop.; Ov.

vēlificātiŏ, ōnis, *f.* [vēlificŏ], *a making sail, sailing :* mutare, Cic. Ep.

vēlificor, āri (Cic., Prop.) and **vēlificŏ**, āre (Prop., Plin.) [vēlum faciŏ], *to make sail, to sail.* **1.** Lit.: nauta per urbanas velificabat aquas, Prop.; Plin.; (ratia) ad infernos velificata lacūs, Prop. *Perf. Part.* in *Pass.* sense, *sailed through :* velificatus Athos, Juv. **2.** Transf. of an effort to achieve or effect (with DAT.): honori suo, Cic.

Velinus, I, *m a river in the Sabine territory,* now *Velino, which forms several lakes, the largest of which is called* lacus Velinus.

vēlitāris, e, *adj.* [vēles], *of the* velites : arma, Sall. ; hastae, Liv.

vēlitātiō, ōnis, *f.* [vēlitor], *a skirmishing.* Transf. : vorbis velitationem fieri, Pl.

vēlitēs, um, *v.* vēles.

vēlitor, āri [vēles], *to fight like the* velites *or light troops, to skirmish.* Transf. (in words) : nescio quid vos velitati estis inter vos duos, Pl.

vēlivolus, a, um (**vēlivolāns**, antis, Poët. ap. Cic.) [vēlum volō], *sail-flying, winged with sails* : naves, Enn. ; Lucr. ; Ov. Of the sea : Verg., Ov.

Vellēius, a, *the name of a Roman gens.* Esp. C. Velleius Paterculus, *a historian under Augustus and Tiberius.*

vellicō, āre [vellō], *to pluck, twitch, pinch, nip.* **1.** Lit. : cornix volturios, Pl. ; Quint. **2.** Transf. **a.** Of taunting or railing at : Pl., Cic. ; aliquem, Hor. **b.** Of rousing : excitandus e somno et vellicandus est animus admonendusque, Sen. Ep.

vellō, vellere, velli (volsi, vulsi), vulsum (volsum), *to pluck, pull ; to pluck out.* **1.** Lit. **a.** ovis, lanam, Varr. ; caudae pilos equinae, Hor. ; tot spicula, Verg. ; albos a stirpe capillos, Prop. ; Plin. ; hastam de caespite, Verg. ; signa, Verg. ; Liv. **b.** to *pull* or *twitch* : aurem, Verg. ; bracchia, Hor. ; latus digitis, Ov. **c.** *to pull* or *pick* : poma manu, Tib. **2.** Transf. *to tear* or *pull down* : postis a cardine, Verg. ; vallum, munimenta, Liv.

vellus, eris, *n.* wool shorn off, *a fleece.* **1.** Lit. : Lucr., Varr., Hor., Ov. **2.** Transf. **a.** *the skin of a sheep with the wool on it, the fell* or *pelt entire* : Verg., Ov. **b.** *the skin of any other animal with the fur* : Ov. **c.** *any wool-like substance* (in *pl.*). Of silk : Verg. Of clouds : Verg. Of snow : Mart. **d.** Of woollen bands or fillets : Stat.

vēlō, āre [vēlum], *to cover, drape, wrap up, envelop, veil.* **1.** Lit. : capite velato, Cic. ; velatus togā, Liv. ; Hor. ; Ov. ; velatae antemnae, Verg. ; delubra fronde, Verg. ; velatis manibus orant (*v.* velamentum, B.), Pl. ; velati ramis oleae, Verg. ; velatas comas, Verg. ; tempora vittis, Ov. **2.** Transf. : odium fallacibus blanditiis, Tac.

vēlōcitās, ātis, *f.* [vēlōx], *swiftness, rapidity.* **1.** Lit. : Caes., Cic. ; corporis, Cic. In *pl.* : Cic. **2.** Transf. : cogitationum, Plin. ; animi, Quint. ; mali, Tac. Of style : Sallusti, Quint.

vēlōciter, *adv.* *swiftly, speedily* : Ov., Quint. Comp. : Cic. Sup. : Caes., Cic.

vēlōx, ōcis, *adj.* [*cf.* volō], *swift, quick, fleet.* **1.** Lit. : Hor., Liv. ; pedites velocissimi, Caes. ; cervi, Verg. ; pes, Ov. ; flamma, Lucr. ; iaculum, Verg. ; procella, Hor. ; victoria, toxicum, Hor. ; navigatio, Quint. With *ad* : ad praemia, Ov. With *Inf.* : Stat. Adverbially : ille velox desilit in latices, Ov. **2.** Transf. : nihil est animo velocius, Cic. ; Hor. ; ingenium, Quint. ; velox ingenio, Tac. ; materiam decurrere stilo quam velocissimo, Quint.

vēlum, i, n. **1.** Lit. **a.** *a sail, sail-cloth* (mostly in *pl.*). vela dare, Cic., Hor., Liv. ; ad id unde aliquis flatus ostenditur

vela do, Cic. ; in altum vela dare, Verg. ; facere, Cic., Verg. ; pandere, Quint. ; solvere, Verg. ; derigere ad castra Corneliana, Caes. ; tendunt vela Noti, Verg. ; ventis implero, Verg. ; contrahere, Cic. Ep. ; logere, Verg. ; subducere, Auct. B. Alex. **b.** *a covering, awning* : Cic., Plin. Ep. Of *chamber-curtains, hangings* : Juv., Suet. ; adlevare, Sen. Ep. Of the *awnings* stretched over the theatre and other public places : Lucr., Prop., Ov. **2.** Transf. : vela pennarum, Lucr. ; pandere vela orationis, Cic. ; dare vela Famae (DAT.), Mart. ; dare vela irae (DAT.), Plin. Ep. Prov. phr. : remigio veloque (Pl.), remis velisque (Cic.), i.e. with might and main. So too, non agimur tumidis velis, Hor. ; plenissimis velis navigare, Cic. [Fr. *voile.*]

vel-ut or **vel-uti**, *adv.* *even as, just as, like as.* **a.** studeo hunc perdere, velut meum corum macerat, Pl. ; ne vitam silentio transeant veluti pecora, Sall. ; Verg. ; Liv. Rarely with corresp. *sic* or *ita* : *just as . . . so* : velut in cantu et fidibus, sic ex corporis totius naturā et figurā varios motūs ciere, Cic. ; Liv. **b.** *as, for instance, for example* : nunquam tam male est Siculis, quin aliquid facete et commode dicant : veluti in hac re aiebant, etc., Cic. ; Pl., etc. **c.** To introduce a rhetorical or poetical simile : *as, like as, as it were* : concurrunt veluti venti, Enn. ; frena dabat Sipylus, veluti cum rector carbasa deducit, Ov. ; Verg. ; Liv. **d.** To introduce a hypothetical comparison : velut si or velut, *just as if, just as though, as if, as though* : absentis Ariovisti crudelitatem, velut si coram adessent, horrerent, Caes. ; Liv. ; Ov. ; velut ea res nihil ad religionem pertinuisset, Liv. ; Ov.

vēna, ae, *f.* *a blood-vessel, vein.* **1.** Lit. : incidere, Cic. ; ferire, Verg. ; abrumpere, abscindere, interscindere, exsolvere, Tac. Also of *an artery* : Cic. ; venas temptare, *to feel the pulse*, Suet. ; so, tangere, Pers. **2.** Transf. **A. a.** *a water-course* : Hirt., Ov. **b.** *a vein of metal* : Cic., Juv. **c.** *a vein* in wood or stone : Plin., Stat. **d.** *the penis* : Mart. **B.** Of the interior, intimate or natural quality of a thing : periculum inclusum penitus in venis et visceribus rei publicae, Cic. **C.** Of natural bent, disposition : benigna ingenii, Hor. ; tenuis et angusta ingeni, Quint. **D.** Of strength : vino fulcire venas cadentis, Sen. Ep.

vēnābulum, i, n. [vēnor], *a hunting-spear* : Cic. Ep., Verg., Ov.

Venāfrum, i, n. *a very ancient town of the Samnites, celebrated for its olive-oil* ; now *Venafro* : **Venāfrānus**, a, um.

vēnālicius, a, um [vēnālis], (*exposed*) *for sale* : familiae, Suet. ; Plin. As Noun, **vēnālicius**, i, m. *a slave-dealer* : Cic.

vēnālis, e, *adj.* [vēnum], *to be sold, for sale.* **1.** Lit. : aedes, Pl. ; horti, Cic. ; urbs, Sall. ; familia, Quint. As Noun, **vēnālis**, is, m. *a slave offered for sale* : Pl., Cic. Also in gen. sense, venales=servi, Hor. **2.** Transf. *open to bribes* : multitudo pretio, Liv. ; amicae ad munus, Prop. ; fides, ius iurandum, veritas, officium, etc., Cic.

vēnāticus, a, um [vēnātus], *for hunting, hunting-*. **1.** Lit.: canis, Pl., Cic.; catulus, Hor. **2.** Transf.: prolatis rebus parasiti venatici sumus (i.e. gaunt as hounds), Pl.

vēnātiō, ōnis, *f.* [vēnor], *hunting, the chase.* **1.** Lit. **a.** In gen.: Cic. In *pl.* : Caes. **b.** *a hunting-spectacle, hunt, battue ;* also, *a combat of wild beasts :* Cic., Suet. **2.** Transf. *game :* Varr., Liv., Plin. Ep. [Fr. *venaison.*]

vēnātor, ōris, *m.* [vēnor], *a hunter.* **1.** Lit.: Pl., Caes., Cic., Hor. In apposition: venator canis, Verg. **2.** Transf. *a tracker:* physicus, id est, speculator venatorque naturae, Cic.

vēnātōrius, a, um [vēnātor], *of a hunter, hunter's, hunting-:* galea, Nep.; instrumentum, Plin. Ep.

vēnātrix, īcis, *f.* [vēnor], *a huntress :* Verg. In apposition: dea, i.e. Diana, Ov.; canis, Mart.

vēnātūra, ae, *f.* [vēnor], *hunting, the chase.* Transf.: oculis facere, Pl.

vēnātus, ūs, *m.* [vēnor], *hunting, the chase.* **1.** Lit.: Cic., Verg., Ov. In *pl.* : Ov. **2.** Transf. of fishing : Pl.

vēndibilis, e, adj. [vēndō], *saleable.* **1.** Lit.: Cic., Hor. *Comp.* : Varr. **2.** Transf. *much sought after, popular :* orator, oratio, Cic.; puella, Ov. *Comp.* : Cic.

vēnditātiō, ōnis, *f.* [vēnditō ; lit. *an offering for sale*], *an advertising, blazoning, vaunting :* Cic.

vēnditātor, ōris, *m.* [vēnditō], *a self-advertiser :* famae nec incuriosus nec venditator, Tac.

vēnditiō, ōnis, *f.* [vēndō], *a selling, sale.* **1.** Lit.: bonorum, Cic. In *pl.* : Cic. **2.** Transf. (in *pl.*), *goods sold :* Plin. Ep.

vēnditō, āre [*freq.* vēndō], *to try to sell, to hawk.* **1.** Lit.: sese, Pl.; Tusculanum, Cic. Ep.; agellum, Plin. Ep.; mutationes stativorum, Tac. **2.** Transf. *to cry up, puff, advertise :* te, Cic. Ep.; pacem pretio, Liv.; operam suam, Liv.; Tac.; se plebi, Liv.; Cic. Ep.; se existimationi hominum, Cic.

vēnditor, ōris, *m.* [vēndō], *a seller, vendor.* **1.** Lit.: Cic. **2.** Transf. of one who receives a bribe : Cic.

vēndō, vēndere, vēndidī, vēnditum [contr. fr. vēnum dō], *to put up for sale, to sell, vend.* **1.** Lit.: aliquid, Pl., Caes., Cic.; quam optime, Cic.; male, Cic.; fanum pecuniā grandi, Cic.; pluris, minoris, Pl., Cic. **2.** Transf. **a.** *to sell, betray :* cum te trecentis talentis regi Cotto vendidisses, Cic.; suffragia, Juv.; auro patriam, Verg. **b.** *to cry up, puff, advertise :* Ligarianam, Cic. Ep.; poema, Hor.; te peregrinis muneribus, Prop. [The classical *Pass.* of vēndō is usually vēneō, q.v.]

venēficium, ī, *n.* [venēficus]. **1.** *a drug-making :* in *pl.*, Cic., Ov. **2.** *a poisoning* (freq. in *pl.*): veneficiis remedia invenire, Cic.; Liv.; de veneficiis accusare, Cic.; venefici damnari, Tac.

venēficus, a, um [venēnum faciō], *drug-making, magical, poisonous :* verba, Ov.; artes, Plin. As Noun, **venēficus**, ī, *m.* and

venēfica, ae, *f.* *a poisoner, sorcerer, sorceress :* Cic., Hor., Ov., etc. *Fem.* as term of abuse ; *witch, hag :* Pl., Ter.

venēnārius, ī, *m.* [venēnum], *a poisoner :* Suet.

venēnātus, a, um. **I.** *Part.* venēnō. **II.** Adj. : *drug-steeped.* **1.** Lit. **a.** *magic, enchanting :* virga Circes, Ov. **b.** *envenomed, poisonous :* colubrae, Lucr.; dentes, Ov.; morsus, Plin. **2.** Transf. : nulla venenato littera mixta loco, Ov.

venēnifer, era, erum [venēnum ferō], *poisonous, venomous :* palatum, Ov.

venēnō, āre [venēnum], *to drug, poison.* **1.** Lit.: spatium caeli, Lucr.; carnem, Cic.; sagittas, Hor. **2.** Transf. of calumny, etc.: non odio obscuro morsuque venenat, Hor.

venēnum, ī, *n.* *a drug, juice.* **I.** *a magical drug, a love-potion.* **1.** Lit.: Pl., Cic., Hor., Ov. **2.** Transf. *charm, attraction :* occultum inspirae ignem fallasque veneno (i.e. amoris), Verg.; Prop. **II.** *a drug, dye :* Verg., Hor., Ov. **III.** *a harmful drug, poison* (orig. venenum malum). **1.** Lit.: Cic., Lucr., Verg., etc.; dare, Cic., Liv.; veneno aliquem occidere, Cic.; sumere, Nep., Liv. **2.** Transf. **a.** *poison, bane, curse :* discordia ordinum est venenum urbis huius, Liv.; crudele venenum vitae, Cat. **b.** Of speech, *virulence :* orationem plenam veneni et pestilentiae, Cat.; Rupili pus atque venenum, Hor.; lingua suffusa veneno, Ov. [It. *veleno ;* Fr. *venin.*]

vēneō, īre, iī, (itum) [vēnum eō], *to go for sale,* i.e. *to be sold* (as *Pass.* of vendo): Pl.; sub coronā veniere, Liv.; cogis eos plus lucri addere, quam quanti venierant, cum magno venissent, Cic.; quia veneat auro rara avis, Hor.

venerābilis, e, adj. [veneror], *worthy of honour, respect,* or *reverence, venerable :* dives, Hor.; donum, Verg.; venerabilis vir miraculo litterarum, venerabilior divinitate creditā matris, Liv.; partes eloquentiae, Tac.

venerābundus, a, um [veneror], *worshipping, reverential :* venerabundi templum iniere, Liv.; Suet.

venerātiō, ōnis, *f.* [veneror], *the highest honour* or *respect, reverence :* Cic., Tac. ; orga reges, Curt.

venerātor, ōris, *m.* [veneror], *a reverencer :* domūs vestrae, Ov.

venereus (-ius), v. venus.

veneror, ārī (**venerō**, āre, Pl.) [*cf.* venia], *to ask reverently (for), to pray to (for), beseech (for).* **1.** Lit. With Acc. of person and Acc. (or *ut* or *ne* and *Subj.*) of thing asked for: quisquis est deus veneror ut etc., Pl.; saluto te, Apollo, veneroque te ne etc., Pl.; multa deos, Caecina ap. Cic. Ep. With Acc. of person only : deos, Cic.; Nymphas, Verg.; Larem farre pio, Verg.; Perf. Part. in Pass. sense : Sibylla, Verg.; Ceres, Hor. With Acc. of thing only, *to pray for :* nihil horum, Hor.; also, supplicibus me tabellis, Prop. **2.** Transf. *to revere, honour, worship :* deos, Cic.; eos in deorum numero, Cic.; Epicurum ut deum, Cic.; lapidem e sepulcro pro deo,

Cic.; templa dei, Verg.; secundum deos nomen Romanum, Liv.; Augustum, Hor.; amicos, Ov.; se, Hor.

Venetī (Henetī), ōrum, *m. pl.* **I.** *a people in N.E. Italy, in the region about modern Venice :* **Venetia**, ae, *f. their country ;* **Venetus**, um, *Venetian :* also, *bluish :* Juv.; factio, *the party* (in the Circus) *dressed in blue*, Suet.; hence, **Venetus**, i, *m. one of the Blues :* Mart. **II.** *a people in N.W. Gaul ;* **Venetia**, ae, *f. their country ;* **Veneticus**, a, um.

venia, ae, *f.* [cf. veneror], *goodwill, favour, grace, indulgence.* **A.** *Of the gods :* ab Iove pacem ac veniam peto precorque ut etc., Cic. **B.** In gen. **a.** veniam mihi pater dedit de Chrysalo, Pl.; precor hanc veniam supplici des ut etc., Liv.; datur petentibus venia, Caes.; extremam hanc oro veniam, Verg.; vos oro, iudices, ut attente bonāque cum veniā verba mea audiatis, Cic.; Liv. **b.** *indulgence,* i.e. permission to do anything: petere veniam legatis mittendis, Liv.; veniam dicendi ante alios exposcere, Tac.; datā veniā, Liv. Esp. in phr. bonā veniā : bonā hoc tuā veniā dixerim, Cic.; bonā veniā vestrā liceat etc., Liv.; Ter. **c.** *indulgence, grace* (in forgiving), *pardon :* pacem veniamque impetrare a victoribus, Liv.; errati veniam impetrare, Cic.; veniam dat Aeduis, Caes.; veniam et impunitatem dare, Cic.; veniam tuis dictis supplice voce roga, Ov.; aliquem veniā donare in praeteritum, Suet.

veniō, venīre, vēnī, ventum, *to come.* **A.** Simply. **1.** Lit. **a.** In gen. : Pl., Cic., etc.; ad urbem, Cic. Ep.; Pl., etc.; ad aliquem, Pl., Cic., etc.; in Cariam ex Indiā, Pl.; in Sabinos, Cic.; Delum Athenis, Cic. Ep.; Lavinia litora, Verg.; in conspectu, Caes.; in conspectum, Hirt.; sub aspectum, Cic.; vox mihi ad auris, Pl. *Impers. Pass. :* dum ad flumen veniatur, Caes.; ventum in insulam est, Cic.; Lilybaeum venitur, Cic.; ubi eo ventum est, Caes. **b.** *to come* for a purpose : ad te ad cenam, Pl.; huc ad ludos, Pl.; ad conloquium, Caes.; ad se oppugnandum, Caes.; ad causam dicendam, Liv.; auxilio, subsidio, etc., Caes.; pabulatum, Caes. **2.** Transf. **a.** Of or in time : ea dies venit, Caes.; tempus victoriae, Caes.; veniens annus, Cic. Ep.; Ov.; ventura bella, Verg.; nepotes venturi, Verg., Ov.; quod hodie venit, Tac. **b.** Of things in gen. : hereditas uni cuique nostrum, Cic.; pulchro veniens in corpore virtus, Verg.; quod in buccam venerit, scribito, Cic. Ep.; si quid in mentem veniet, Cic. Ep.; venit mihi in mentem oris tui (i.e. the thought of), Cic.; ad aliquem dolor, Cic.; clades, Liv.; gloria mihi, Ov.; ex otio meo commodum rei publicae, Sall. **c.** Of crops : arbores sponte suā, Verg.; felicius uvae, Verg. **d.** Of descent : Amyci de gente, Verg. **B.** *to come, arrive, reach.* **1.** Lit. : sagitta, Verg.; per ilia harundo, Verg.; in tergum, Verg. **2.** Transf. (esp. with *in* and Acc.), *of reaching a state* or condition, etc. : in calamitatem, Cic.; in odium, Cic.; in consuetudinem, Caes., Cic.; in periculum, Caes.; in spem, Caes.;

summum in cruciatum, Caes.; alicui in amicitiam, Caes.; alicui in contemptionem, Caes.; in alicuius fidem ac potestatem, Caes.; res venit prope secessionem, Liv.; speramus eo rem venturam ut etc., Hor. In speaking or writing : a fabulis ad facta, Cic.; ad istius morbum et insaniam, Cic.

vēnor, ārī, *to hunt, chase.* **1.** Lit. : Pl., Cic.; venatum in nemus ire parant, Verg.; Pl. With Acc. : leporem, Pl.; canibus leporem, Verg. **2.** Transf. : suffragia plebis, Hor.; viduas avaras frustis et pomis, Hor.

vēnōsus, a, um [vēna], *full of veins, venous.* **1.** Lit. : Plin. **2.** Transf. : liber Acci, Pers.

venter, tris, *m. the belly.* **1.** Lit. **a.** Cic., Liv., etc.; in *pl.* : Plin., Mart. **b.** Of gluttony : ventri operam dare, Pl.; quidquid quaesierat, ventri donabat, Hor.; Juv. **2.** Transf. **a.** *the womb :* Juv. **b.** *the fetus, child unborn :* Varr., Liv., Hor., Ov. **c.** *Of any thing that swells* or *bellies out :* tumidoque cucurbita ventre, Prop.; Verg.; lagoenae, Juv.

ventilō, āre [dim. fr. ventus], *to fan, brandish in the air, wave.* **1.** Lit. **a.** In gen. : populeas ventilat aura comas, Ov.; facem, Prop.; cubitum utrumque in diversum latus, Quint.; aestivum aurum, Juv.; frigus (i.e. by fanning), Mart. In Mid. : alio atque alio positu ventilari, Sen. **b.** Of winnowing : Varr. **2.** Transf. : linguā quasi flabello seditionis contionem, Cic.

ventiō, ōnis, *f.* [veniō], *a coming :* quid tibi huc ventio est ? Pl.

ventitō, āre [freq. veniō], *to come often, keep coming, resort :* mercatores ad Ubios, Caes.; Cic.; in castra, Caes.; domum, Cic. Ep.; quo puella ducebat, Cat.

ventōsus, a, um [ventus]. **1.** Lit. **a.** *full of wind, windy :* loca, Lucr.; folles, aequora, Verg.; Hor.; Ov.; hiems, Plin.; dies, Quint. *Comp. :* Germania, Tac. *Sup. :* regio, Liv. **b.** *of the wind :* murmur, Verg. **c.** *wind-like, wind-swift :* equi, Ov. Also, mens cervorum, Lucr. **2.** Transf. **a.** *puffed up* (i.e. vain, conceited) : lingua, gloria, Verg.; natio, Plin. Pan.; Sen. **b.** *changeable, fickle :* plebs, Hor.; ingenium, Liv.; extraordinarium imperium, Cic.

ventriculus, ī, *m.* [dim. venter], *the belly.* **1.** Lit. : Juv. **2.** Transf. *a ventricle :* cordis, Cic.

ventriōsus, a, um [venter], *big-bellied, pot-bellied :* Pl.

ventulus, ī, *m.* [dim. ventus], *a slight wind, breeze :* Ter.

ventus, ī, *m.* [cf. Gk. ἄημι and Lat. aura], *wind.* **1.** Lit. : Pl., Lucr., Cic., etc.; remissior, Caes.; secundus, adversus, Cic.; prosper, Liv. In apposition : ventus turbo, Pl.; Corus ventus, Caes.; Cic. Prov. (i.) in vento et rapidā aquā scribere, Cat. (ii.) profundere verba ventis, Lucr. (iii.) verba ventis dare (of breaking a promise), Ov. (iv.) ventis remis : *v.* remus. **2.** Transf. *the wind* as a symbol of fortune, fame, applause, etc. : cuius (Caesaris) nunc venti valde sunt secundi, Cic.

Ep. ; Hor. ; rumorum et contionum ventos conligere, Cic. Of an unfavourable wind : vento aliquo in optimum quemque excitato, Cic.

vēnūcula (vennuncula), ae, *f. a kind of grape fit for preserving* : Hor.

vēnula, ae, *f.* [*dim.* vēna], *a small vein.* Transf. : Quint.

vēnum (Acc.) and **vēnō** (Dat.), *n.*, *for sale* or *to be sold :* dare aliquem venum, (esp. of captives or slaves), Sall., Liv. ; venum ire, Sen. ; tradere venum, Luc. ; posita veno inritamenta luxūs, Tac. (*v.* also **vēnumdō**.)

vēnum-dō (vēnundō), dare, dedī, datum [vēnum dō], *to offer for sale* (mostly of captives or slaves). **1.** Lit. : imbelle vulgus sub coronā venundatum, Tac. ; captivos, Suet. ; Minoä venumdata Scylla figurā, etc., *sold for,* i.e. bribed by, Prop. **2.** Transf. : quaesturam, sententiam, Tac.

venus, veneris, *f. grace, charm, the qualities that excite love.* **1.** Lit. : amoenitates omnium venerum atque venustatum adfero, Pl. ; bene nummatum decorat suadela venusque, Hor. Also, fabula nullius veneris, Hor. ; quod cum gratiā quādam et venere dicatur, Quint. ; Isocrates omnis dicendi veneres sectatus est, Quint. **2.** Transf. **A.** Personified. *Venus.* **a.** Orig. a Latin goddess of the spring : Cic. **b.** Identified with Aphrodite, the goddess of love (esp. of sensual love), mother of Erōs (*Cupid*) and Aeneas : Lucr., Cic., Verg., etc. **Venereus (-ius),** a, um, *of Venus :* sacerdos, Pl. ; servi (i.e. of a temple of Venus), Cic. **B.** *the pleasures of love, sexual love* or *indulgence, mating :* Ter. ; Ov. ; frigida in venerem senior, Verg. ; sunt ante omnis barbaros Numidae effusi in venerem, Liv. ; iuvenum sera venus, Tac. Hence, **venereus,** a, um, *of sexual love :* res, voluptates, Cic. **C.** *a beloved object, beloved, love :* mea venus, Verg. ; Hor. ; nec veneres nostras hoc fallit, Lucr. **D.** *the planet Venus :* Cic. **E.** *the Venus* (or *highest*) *throw* at dice : Hor., Prop.

Venusia, ae, *f. a town on the borders of Lucania and Apulia, the birthplace of the poet Horace, now Venosa ;* **Venusinus,** a, um ; and **Venusini,** ōrum, *m. pl. the inhabitants.*

venustās, ātis, *f.* [venus], *charm, grace, beauty.* **1.** Lit. : corporis, Cic. ; muliebris, Cic. ; signa eximiā venustate, Cic. **2.** Transf. **a.** Mental : Pl. ; homo adfluens omni lepore et venustate, Cic. In *pl.* : Pl. **b.** Of style or manner : (oratoris est) agere cum dignitate ac venustate, Cic.

venustē, adv. *charmingly, gracefully :* dicere, Quint. ; scribere mimiambos, Plin. Ep. *Comp. :* Sen. *Sup. :* Cael. ap. Cic. Ep.

venustulus, a, um [*dim.* venustus], *a charming little :* oratio, Pl.

venustus, a, um [venus], *lovely, charming, winning, graceful.* **1.** Lit. : species, Pl. ; voltus, Ter. ; soror, Cat. ; gestus et motus corporis, Cic. ; diva venustissima Venus, Pl. ; forma, Suet. ; Sirmio, Cat. ; sphaera, Cic. ; hortuli, Phaedr. **2.** Transf. **a.**

Mentally : Graecus facilis et valde venustus, Cic. ; Plin. Ep. *Comp. :* Cat. **b.** In style or manner : sententiae, Cic. ; antiqua comoedia, Quint. *Comp.* and *Sup. :* Quint.

vē-pallidus, a, um, *very pale :* mulier, Hor.

veprēcula, ae, *f.* [*dim.* veprēs], *a little thorn-* or *brier-bush :* in *pl.*, Cic.'

veprēs, is, and more usually *pl.* **veprēs,** um, *m.* (occ. *f.*), *a thorn-bush :* Cato, Lucr., Cic., Verg., etc.

vēr, vēris, *n.* [*cf.* Gk. ἔαρ, ϝῆρ], *the season of spring, the spring.* **1.** Lit. : Pl., Cic., Verg., etc. **2.** Transf. **a.** *the productions of spring :* ver populantur apes, Mart. Phr. : ver sacrum (i.e. *an offering from the firstlings of spring*) : ver sacrum vovendum, si bellatum prospere esset, Liv. **b.** *the spring-time of life, youth :* iucundum cum aetas florida ver ageret, Cat. ; Ov. [It. Sp. *primavera.*]

vērātrum, ī, *n. hellebore :* Lucr., Plin.

vērāx, ācis, *adj.* [vērus], *truthful :* Pl., Tib., Hor. ; oraculum, Cic. ; signa, Tib. *Comp. :* Cic. [Fr. *vrai.*]

verbēna, ae, *f.* and more freq. **verbēnae,** ārum, *f. sacred herbs* or *boughs* carried by the fetiales : Liv. ; also by priests suing for protection, Cic. ; and used in sacrifices and other religious acts, Pl., Verg., Hor., Ov.

verbēnātus, a, um [verbēnae], *crowned with a sacred wreath :* Suet.

(verber), only in Gen. and Abl. *sing.* **verberis, verbere ;** and in *pl.* **verbera,** um, *n.* [*cf.* Gk. ῥάβδος], *a scourge, rod.* **1.** Lit. : verbere torto, Verg. ; verberibus caedere, Pl. ; verbera movere, Prop. ; Liv. **2.** Transf. **a.** *a thong of a sling and other similar missile weapons :* Verg. **b.** *a scourging, flogging,* etc. : Ov. In *pl.* : Pl., Cic., Hor., Ov., etc. **c.** Of any blow : remorum, Ov. ; Hor. ; caudae, Hor. ; ventorum, Lucr. **d.** Abstract : contumeliarum, Cic. ; linguae, Hor. Of conscience : surdo verbere caedit, Juv.

verberābilissumus, a, um [verberō], *very worthy of a flogging :* Pl.

verberātiō, ōnis, *f.* [verberō], *a flogging :* Q. Cic. ap. Cic. Ep.

verbereus, a, um [verber], *worthy of a flogging :* Pl.

verberō, āre [verber], *to scourge, flog, beat.* **1.** Lit. : aliquem, Pl., Cic. ; oculos virgis, Cic. ; laterum contsa ense, Ov. **2.** Transf. **a.** *to batter, flog, beat* in gen. : tormentis Mutinam, Cic. ; aquila aethera alis, Verg. ; (Charybdis) sidera verberat undā, Verg. ; fundā amnem, Verg. ; navem Auster, Hor. **b.** With words : aliquem verbis, Pl. ; senatūs convicio verberari, Cic. ; auris sermonibus, Tac.

verberō, ōnis, *m.* [verber], *one worthy of stripes, a scoundrel, rascal :* Pl., Ter., Cic. Ep.

verbōsē, adv. *with many words, verbosely :* Cic. *Comp. :* Cic. Ep., Quint.

verbōsus, a, um [verbum], *full of words, wordy, prolix :* simulatio prudentiae, Cic. ; T. Livius in historiā, Suet. *Comp. :* epistula, Cic. Ep. ; Quint. *Sup. :* Quint.

verbum, ī, *n.* [*cf.* Gk. ἐρῶ, εἴρω]. (Gen. *pl.* verbum, Pl.), *a word.* **A.** In gen. : ver-

bum nullum fecit, Pl., Cic. ; verbum usita-
tius et tritius, Cic. ; verbum voluptatis,
Cic. In *pl.* : Pl. ; verba rebus impressit,
Cic. ; verba facere (i.e. to speak), Caes. ;
with ref. to the praetor's court, tria verba
(*do, dico, addico*), Ov. ; contumelia verborum, Caes. P r o v. : verba facit emor-
tuo (i.e. in vain), Pl. A d v e r b i a l
p h r a s e s : (i.) ad verbum, *word for word,
exactly, literally* : Ter., Cic. Also, verbum
e (de or pro) verbo exprimere, Cic. ; verbum
verbo reddere, Hor. (ii.) verbi causā or
gratiā, *for example, for instance* : Cic.
(iii.) uno verbo, *in one word, briefly* : Ter.,
Cic. ; so, tribus verbis, Pl. Also, verbo,
Sall., Liv. (iv.) meis, tuis, suis verbis,
*in the words I etc. should use; for me, you,
or him* : gratum mihi feceris, si uxori
tuae meis verbis eris gratulatus, Cic. Ep. ;
denuntiatum Fabio senatūs verbis, Liv.
B. In partic. **a.** *a saying, expression,
phrase, sentence* : Pl., Ter., Sall. Also, *a
proverb* : verum est verbum, quod memora-
tur : ubi amici, ibidem opus, Pl. ; Ter.
b. Of words in a formula of dedication :
praeire verba, Liv. **c.** *mere talk, mere
words,* opp. to deed, fact, reality : verbo
sunt liberi omnes, Cic. ; verborum sonitus
inanis, Cic. Hence, verba dare (alicui),
to give one empty words, to deceive, cheat :
cui verba dare difficile est, Ter. ; Cic. Ep. ;
dare verba curis, Ov. **d.** Gramm. *a
verb* : Cic.
Vercingetorix, igis, *m. the celebrated leader
of the Arverni in the Gallic war.*
vērculum, i, *n.* [dim. vēr], *little spring,* as a
term of endearment : meum, Pl.
vērē, *adv. truly, really, properly, rightly* :
Ter., Cic., Verg., etc. *Comp.* : Cic., Liv.
Sup. : Cic. [Fr. *voire.*]
verēcundē, *adv. bashfully, shyly, modestly* :
Cic., Liv. *Comp.* : Cic., Quint.
verēcundia, ae, *f.* [verēcundus]. **I.** *bashfulness, shyness, reserve, modesty* : Cic.,
Liv., etc. ; in rogando, Cic. Ep. **II.** With
Obj. GEN. : *dread, awe, respect, reverence* :
turpitudinis, Cic. ; legum, Liv. ; negandi,
Cic. ; parentis, deorum, Liv. Also, apud
or adversus aliquem, Cic. **III.** *shame,
(feeling of) disgrace* : verecundia Romanos
cepit (with *Acc.* and *Inf.*), Liv. **IV.** *over-
shyness, timidity* : Quint. [It. *vergogna* ;
Sp. *vergüenza* ; Fr. *vergogne.*]
verēcundor, āri [verēcundus], *to feel bashful
or ashamed, to be shy or diffident.* **1.** L i t. :
Pl., Cic. With *Inf.* : Cic. **2.** T r a n s f.
of things, to express shame : manūs, Quint.
verēcundus, a, um [vereor], *bashful, shy,
reserved, modest, diffident* : Pl., Cic., Hor. ;
pudor, vita, vultus, Ov. ; color, Hor. ;
rubor, Ov. ; translatio, Cic. ; oratio,
Quint. *Comp.* : verecundior in postu-
lando, Cic. *Sup.* : Vell.
verēdus, i, *m. a swift hunting-horse* : Mart.
verendus, a, um. **I.** *Gerund.* vereor. **II.**
A d j. *inspiring respect, venerable* : maiestas,
Ov. ; patres, Ov. **III.** Noun, **verenda,**
ōrum, *n. pl. the private parts* : Plin., Plin.
Ep.
vereor, ēri, itus. **I.** *to be uneasy in mind,
to be apprehensive, afraid, anxious, hesitating,
shy* : Pl. With DAT. : eo minus (*Intern.*

Acc.) veritus navibus, Caes. With *de* : Cic.
With ACC. : Pl., Caes., Cic., Hor., etc.
With GEN. : Ter., Cic. Ep. With *Inf.* :
Pl., Caes., Cic., Hor., etc. *Impers.* : Cy-
renaici, quos non est veritum in voluptate
summum bonum ponere, Cic. With Acc.
and *Inf.* : Pl., Ov. With *ne* (and sometimes
ut for *ne non*) and *Subj.* : Caes., Cic., Hor.,
etc. With *Indir. Quest.* : Ter., Cic. Ep.
II. *to have a sense of shame or modesty* :
hic vereri perdidit, Pl. **III.** With Acc.
of person, *to have respect, regard, or reverence
for* : Pl., Cic., Nep., Liv.
veretrum, i, *n. the private parts* : Phaedr.,
Suet.
Vergiliae, ārum, *f. pl. the Pleiades* : Cic.
poet.
Vergilius (Virg-), i, *m.* P. Vergilius Maro.
a famous epic poet in the time of Augustus,
Vergil.
Verginius (Virg-), a, *the name of a Roman
gens.* Esp L. Verginius, *f. of Verginia,
whom he killed to save her from the decemvir
Appius Claudius.*
vergō, vergere, (vērsī, *Perf.* dub., Ov.), *to
turn, incline.* **A.** T r a n s. : alicui venenum,
Lucr. ; in gelidos amoma sinūs, Ov. In
Mid. : in terras igitur solis quoque vergitur
ardor, Lucr. **B.** I n t r a n s. **1.** L i t. of
places : Galliae pars ad septentriones,
Caes. ; collis ad flumen, Caes. ; portus
in meridiem, Liv. ; omnes partes in medium,
Cic. **2.** T r a n s f. : Bruti auxilium ad
Italiam vergere, Cic. ; nox ad lucem, Curt. ;
suam aetatem vergere, Tac. ; femina ver-
gens annis, Tac. ; illuc (i.e. in Tiberium)
omnia, Tac.
Vergobretus, i, *m. the title of the chief magistrate among the Aedui.*
vēridicus, a, um [vērus dīcō]. **A.** A c t.
speaking the truth : Liv. ; os, Lucr. ; voces,
Cic. **B.** P a s s. *truly spoken ; true* : usus,
Plin.
vēri-similis, vēri-similitūdō, *v.* vērus and
similis, similitūdō.
vēritās, ātis, *f.* [vērus], *truth, truthfulness.*
1. L i t. **a.** veritas odium parit, Ter. ; veritatis cultor, Cic. **b.** *the truth, the real
facts* : veritatem patefacere, Cic. ; plus
quam res et veritas concedat, Cic. **2.**
T r a n s f. **a.** In art, etc. *reality, real life* :
veritatem imitari, Cic. ; ex veritate, in
accordance with truth, Sall. ; oratores sunt
veritatis ipsius actores, Cic. **b.** Gramm.
or in etymology : *correctness* : Cic. **c.**
Of character : *rectitude* : tristis veritas
inest in voltu atque in verbis fides, Ter. ;
Cic. ; iudiciorum religionem veritatemque
perfringere, Cic. [It. *veritā* ; Sp. *verdad* ;
Fr. *vérité.*]
vēriverbium, i, *n.* [vērus verbum], *a telling
the truth, truthfulness* : Pl.
vermiculātus, a, um. **I.** *Part.* vermiculor.
II. A d j. *inlaid so as to resemble the tracks
of worms, vermiculated* : Lucil., Plin.
vermiculor, āri [vermiculus], *to be worm-
eaten* (of trees) : Plin.
vermiculus, i, *m.* [dim. vermis], *a little worm,
grub, in decaying things* : Lucr., Plin.
[It. *vermiglio* ; Fr. *vermeil.*]
vermina, um, *n. pl.* [cf. vermis], *gripings,
writhings with pain* : Lucr.

vermis, is, *m. a worm :* Lucr., Plin.

verna, ae, *m. f.* [fr. root seen in Gk. ἄστυ], *a slave born in his master's house, a home-born slave.* **1.** Lit.: Pl., Cael. ap. Cic. Ep., Hor. As a term of abuse: Pl. **2.** Transf. *a native :* Mart. In apposition: apri, lupi, liber, Mart.

vernāculus, a, um [verna], *of home-born slaves.* **1.** Lit.: multitudo, Tac. As Noun, **vernāculi**, ōrum, *m. pl. buffoons, jesters* (home-born slaves being often treated as such): Mart., Suet. **2.** Transf. *native, domestic :* volucres, Varr.; consilium, Pl.; festivitas, Cic. Ep.; crimen domesticum ac vernaculum, Cic.

vernīlis, e, *adj.* [verna], *slavish, fawning.* **1.** Lit.: blanditiae, Tac. **2.** Transf. *jesting, pert, waggish :* dictum, Tac.

vernīlitās, ātis, *f.* [vernīlis]. **I.** *fawning subservience :* Sen. Ep. **II.** *pertness, sauciness :* Pl., Quint.

vernīliter, *adv.* **I.** *slavishly, servilely :* fungi officiis, Hor. **II.** *jestingly :* Sen.

vernō, āre [vēr], *to show signs of spring.* **1.** Lit.: humus, Ov.; avis, Ov.; arbores, Plin. **2.** Transf.: dum vernat sanguis, Prop.; dubiā lanugine malae, Mart.

vernula, ae *m. f.* [*dim.* verna], *a little or young home-born slave.* **1.** Lit.: Sen., Plin., Juv. **2.** Transf. *native :* Tiberinus et ipse vernula riparum, Tac. In apposition: libelli, Mart.

vernus, a, um [vēr], *of the spring, spring- :* tempus, Lucr., Ov.; aequinoctium, Liv.; venti, Hor.; frigus, Ov.; flores, Hor. ABL. *sing.* as **vernō**, *in the spring :* Cato.

vērō, *adv.* [ABL. *sing. n.* of vērum, *v.* vērus], *in truth, in fact, certainly, assuredly.* **1.** Lit. **a.** eho, mavis vituperari falso, quam vero extolli ? Pl.; ego vero cupio te ad me venire, Cic. Ep.; Liv. Ironically: Ter., Cic., Verg., Liv. **b.** In corroborative replies: *M.* fuisti saepe, credo, in scholis philosophorum. *A.* vero, ac libenter quidem, Cic.; Ter. With immo; sed da mihi nunc, satisne probas ? immo vero, Cic.; Ter. With minime: *S.* quid ? totam domum num quis alter, praeter te, regit ? *L.* minime vero, *certainly not*, Cic. **c.** In urgent or encouraging expostulation: minue vero iram, Ter.; Pl. **d.** To indicate a climax, *even, indeed ;* esp. with tum : tum vero ardemus, freq. in Verg.; Cic. **e.** In transitions: nec vero tibi de versibus respondebo, Cic. **2.** Transf. as a strongly corroborative adversative particle, *but in fact, but indeed, however* (always placed after a word): dixisti non auxilium mihi, sed me auxilio defuisse. ego vero fateor, hercule, quod etc., Cic.; Caes., etc.

Vērōna, ae, *f. a city in Northern Italy, the birth-place of Catullus, and of Pliny the Elder ;* **Vērōnēnsis**, e, and **Vērōnēnsēs**, ium, *m. pl. its inhabitants.*

verpa, ae, *f. the penis :* Cat., Mart.

verpus, ī, *m. a circumcised man :* Cat., Juv.

verrēs, is, *m. a male swine, boar-pig.* **1.** Lit.: Varr., Hor. **2.** Transf.: contemptuously of a man : Pl.

Verrēs, is, *m. the surname of the praetor C. Cornelius, notorious for his bad govern-*

ment of Sicily ; **Verrius**, a, um, and **Verrīnus**, a, um.

verrīnus, a, um [verrēs], *of a boar-pig, boar-, hog-, pork- :* iecur, Plin. In a pun: ius verrinum (Verrinum), Cic.

verrō, verrere, verrī, versum [perh. *cf.* ἐρύω and ἐverriculum, *a dragnet*], *to pull, drag.* **1.** Lit. **a.** *to drag, to drag away, carry off :* domi quidquid habet verritur ἔξω, Pl.; Mart.; canitiem longa per aequora, Ov. **b.** *to scour, sweep, brush :* Cic. With Acc. *of thing swept away :* favillas, Ov.; quidquid de Libycis verritur areis, Hor. With Acc. *of thing scoured :* aedis, Pl.; matres crinibus templa, Liv.; aequora caudis (delphines), Verg.; pavimentum, Juv.; vias, Suet. **2.** Transf. *to drag or sweep* (*along*) : verrunt venti nubila, Lucr.; aequora, Cat., Verg.; remis vada, Verg.; maria ac terras (venti) verrant per auras, Verg.

verrūca, ae, *f. a wart* on the human body. **1.** Lit.: Plin. **2.** Transf. *a slight blemish, small failing :* Hor. [Fr. *verrue.*]

verrūcōsus, a, um [verrūca], *full of warts, warty.* Transf. *of style ;* prob. *rough, rugged :* Antiopa (a tragedy), Pers.

verruncō, āre [vertō], *to turn about ;* hence, in relig. lang. *to turn out well, have a fortunate issue :* Acc., Liv.

versābilis, e, *adj.* [versō], *moveable, shifting.* **1.** Lit.: aer, Sen.; acies, Curt. **2.** Transf.: fortuna, Curt.

versābundus, a, um [versō], *turning around, revolving :* Lucr.

versātilis, e, *adj.* [versō], *capable of turning, revolving, moveable.* **1.** Lit.: mundi templum, Lucr.; tabulae, Suet.; Sen. Ep. **2.** Transf.: ingenium ad omnia, Liv.

versicolor, ōris, *adj.* [vertō color], *changing colour, of various colours.* **1.** Lit.: plumae, Cic.; arma, Verg.; vestis, Liv. **2.** Transf.: elocutio, Quint.

versiculus, ī, *m.* [*dim.* versus]. **I.** *a short or single line of* prose or verse: Cic.; epistulae, Cic. Ep.; Hor. **II.** *poor little verses, humble lines :* versiculi mei, Cat., Verg.

versificātiō, ōnis, *f.* [versificō], *verse-making, versifying :* Quint.

versificātor, ōris, *m.* [versificō], *a verse-maker, versifier :* Quint.

versificō, āre [versus faciō], *to put into verse, write in verse, versify :* Lucil., Quint.

versipellis (**vors-**), e, *adj.* [vertō pellis], *that changes shape or appearance.* **1.** Lit.: (Iuppiter) vorsipellem se facit, Pl.; capillus fit vorsipellis (i.e. turns grey), Pl. **2.** Transf. *skilled in dissimulation, sly :* Pl., Lucil.

versō (older **vorsō**), āre [*freq.* vertō], *to turn often or violently ; to twist, twirl or whirl about.* **1.** Lit.: qui caelum vorsat, Enn.; turbinem puer, Tib.; turdos in igne, Hor.; manum, Ov.; currum in gramine, Verg.; sortem urnā, Hor.; desectum gramen, Ov.; pecunias, Suet. With *Refl. Pron.* or in *Mid.* : versabat se in utramque partem, non solum mente, verum etiam corpore, Cic.; mundum versari circum axem caeli, Cic. **2.** Transf. **a.** *to be continually* or *habitually turning* or *bending :* ad omnem malitiam et fraudem mentem suam, Cic.; fors omnia versat, Verg.; versatur celeri fors levis orbe rotae, Tib.; verba, Cic.; se ad omnis cogitationes, Curt. **b.** *to keep turning* or *on the move ; to agitate, work on, overturn :* vorsabo ego illum hodie, si vivo, probe, Pl.; haerere, versari, rubere, Cic.; sic fortuna in certamine utrumque versavit ut etc., Caes.; Liv.; odiis domos, Verg. **c.** *to turn over* a thing in the mind, *to reflect upon :* multas res in meo corde, Pl.; dolos dirumque nefas in pectore, Verg.; Quint.; versate diu, quid ferre recusent, quid valeant umeri, Hor.

versor (older **vorsor**), ārī [*freq.* vertor], *to turn oneself constantly, to be (about) constantly* or *frequently, to dwell, stay.* **1.** Lit.: domi, Pl.; in castris, Caes.; in fundo, in conviviis, Cic.; intra vallum, Caes.; inter aciem, Caes.; inter eos, Cic. Ep.; nobiscum, Cic.; apud aliquem, Nep. **2.** Transf. **a.** in malis, Ter.; in simili culpā, Caes.; in pace, in laude, etc., Cic.; in medio turbine leti, Cat. Of abstract Subjects: mors, exsilium mihi ob oculos versabantur, Cic.; aliquid in dubitatione, Cic.; Mithridaticum bellum in multā varietate versatum, Cic. **b.** *to be busy, to be engaged in* anything: in sordidā arte, Cic.; in re publicā atque in his vitae periculis laboribusque, Cic.; circa mensuras, Quint. Of abstract Subjects: eius omnis oratio versata est in eo ut etc., Cic.; dicendi omnis ratio in hominum more et sermone versatur, Cic.; haec pars (tragoedia) circa iram, odium, metum, miserationem fere tota versatur, Quint.

versōria, *v.* vorsōria.

versum (**vorsum**), *adv.* [*cf.* versus], *turned :* us. after other *Adv.* of direction: rusum vorsum, *backwards,* Pl.; susum vorsum, *upwards,* Cato; ad se vorsum, Sall.

versūra (**vors-**), ae, *f.* [vertō], *a turning around, rotating.* **1.** Lit.: foliorum, Varr. **2.** Transf. **a.** *the borrowing of money to pay a debt :* (ab aliquo) facere, Cic.; Tac. Transf.: vorsurā solvere (i.e. to get out of one difficulty by getting into another), Ter. **b.** *a loan* of any kind: versuram (ab aliquo) facere, Cic.; Nep.

versus (**vors-**), a, um, *Part.* vertō.

versus (**vors-**), ūs, *m. a turning ;* hence, **a.** In agriculture, *a furrow :* Plin. **b.** *a row, line :* in versum distulit ulmos, Verg. **c.** *a line* of writing; and in poetry, *a line, verse :* Caes., Cic., Liv., Verg., etc. **d.** *a land-measure :* Varr. **e.** *a kind of dance ;* or *a turn, step, pas,* in a dance : Pl.

versus (**vors-**), *adv., turned (towards) :* usually after a word denoting place : ad Oceanum versus, Caes.; in forum versus, Cic.; sursum versus, *upwards,* Cic.; Cato. With Acc. of place-names : Massiliam versus, Caes.; Cic.

versūtē, *adv. craftily :* Cic.

versūtiae, ārum, *f. pl.* [versūtus], *cunning tricks :* Liv.

versūtiloquus (**-uos**), a, um [versūtus loquor], *crafty-speaking, sly :* Poët. ap. Cic.

versūtus (**vors-**), a, um [vertō, versus], *adroit, dexterous.* **a.** In good sense: *shrewd, clever, ingenious :* Pl., Cic.; animus, Cic. *Sup. :* Cic. **b.** In bad sense, *crafty, cunning, wily, deceitful :* Pl., Cic., Ov. *Comp. :* Pl. *Sup. :* Vell.

vertebra, ae, *f.* [vertō], *a joint :* Sen.

vertex (older **vortex**), icis, *m.* [vertō]. **I.** *an eddy.* **1.** Lit. **a.** Of water: *a whirl, eddy, strong current :* torto vertice torrens, Verg.; Hor.; Liv., etc. **b.** Of wind or flame : *a tornado, whirlwind, spire of flame:* Lucr., Verg., Liv. **2.** Transf.: amoris, Cat.; officiorum, Sen. Ep. **II.** *the pole* (as being the pivot) of the heavens : Cic. poet., Verg. **III.** *the crown* or *top* of the head. **1.** Lit.: Cic., Hor., Ov. Hence in gen., *the head :* Cat., Verg., Ov. **2.** Transf. **a.** *the top, summit* of a mountain, tree, house, etc.: Lucr., Cic., Verg., Ov., etc.; a vertice (*from aloft*), Verg. **b.** *the highest, uppermost, chief :* dolorum anxiferi vertices, Cic. poet.

verticōsus (**vort-**), a, um [vertex], *eddying, swirling :* mare, Sall.; amnis, Liv.

vertīgō, inis, *f.* [vertō], *a turning* or *whirling around.* **1.** Lit.: caeli, Ov.; venti, Sen.; alicuius, Plin. **2.** Transf. *giddiness, dizziness :* Liv. Of persons intoxicated : Juv.

vertō (older **vortō**), vertere, vertī, versum, *to turn, to turn round* or *about.* **A.** Trans. **1.** Lit. **a.** In gen.: vorte hac te, Pl.; verti me a Minturnis Arpinum versus, Cic. Ep.; se, Plin. Ep.; ora huc et huc, Hor.; terga, pedem, gradum, Ov.; fenestrae in viam versae, Liv. In *Mid.* : magnus caeli si vertitur orbis, Lucr.; Verg.; ad caedem, Liv. Also, *to upturn, invert, tilt :* ferro terram, Verg.; glaebas aratra, Ov.; agros bove, Prop.; freta lacertis (in rowing), Verg.; hastam, Verg.; cadum, Hor.; also perh., ab imo moenia Troiae (i.e. to overthrow), Verg. Also, ex illā pecuniā magnam partem ad se vertit, Cic. **b.** Milit.: se verterunt et loco cesserunt, Caes.; terga vertere, Caes., Liv.; hostem in fugam, Liv.; iter retro, Liv. In *Mid.* : versi in fugam hostes, Tac.; Liv. **c.** Of revolving periods of time (in *Mid.*) : septima iam vertitur aestas, Verg.; hunc mensem vortentem, *in the course of this month,* Pl.; anno vertente, *in the course of a year,* Cic.; annus vertens, *a great cycle* (25,800 years), Cic. **2.** Transf. **a.** In gen.: perii ! quid agam ? quo me vortam ? Ter.; Cic.; stimulos sub pectore Apollo, Verg.; ne ea in suam contumeliam vertat, Caes.; in suam rem litem, Liv.; in religionem comitia biennio habita, Liv.; di vortant bene quod agas, Ter.; in melius somnia, Tib.; bellum eo, Liv. In *Mid.* : Philippus totus in Persea versus, Liv.; toti in impetum atque iram versi, Liv. **b.** *to ascribe, impute :* (aliquid) alicui vitio, Cic.; alia in deum (GEN.) iras velut ultima malorum, Liv.; cum omnium secundorum adversorumque in deos verterent, Liv. **c.** *to turn,* i.e. *to change, alter, transform :* Iuppiter in Amphitruonis vortit sese imaginem, Pl.; natura cibos in corpora viva vertit, Lucr.; Verg.; omnia in peiorem partem, Cic.; Auster in Africum se vertit, Caes. ; (in *Mid.* : ventus in Africum versus, Liv.) ; Ilion in pulverem, Hor. ; in deum ex bove, Ov. ; civitatis statum, Tac. P r o v. : in fumum et cinerem vertere, Hor. In *Mid.* : omnia vertuntur, Prop. ; Hor. **d.** *to exchange :* gladios, Pl. ; triumphos funeribus, Hor. ; solum (i.e. to emigrate or go into exile), Cic., Liv. **e.** *to translate* : Philemo scripsit, Plautus vortit barbare, Pl. ; sic Platonem, Cic. ; multa de Graecis, Cic. ; annalis Acilianos ex Graeco in Latinum sermonem, Liv. **f.** *to overthrow, destroy :* ad extremum omnia, Cic. ; fluxas Phrygiae res fundo, Verg. ; Cycnum vi multā, Ov. ; cuncta, Tac. **g.** In *Mid.* (*cf.* versor), *to be engaged in, to be in* a place or condition : in mercaturā, Pl. ; catervis in mediis, Verg. ; res in maiore discrimine, Liv. ; Pl. **h.** In *Mid.* : *to depend upon* or *centre in* a thing or person : omnia in unius potestate, Cic. ; spes civitatis in dictatore, Liv. ; circa hanc consultationem disceptatio omnis, Liv. ; puncto temporis maximarum rerum momenta, Liv. ; hic victoria, Verg. *Impers.* with *Indir. Quest.* : Liv. **B.** I n t r a n s. *to turn (oneself).* **1.** L i t. : alio, Tac. ; mea vocula dominae in auriculas, Prop. **2.** T r a n s f. **a.** In gen. : talia incepta in (*against*) consultorem, Sall. ; exemplum in eos, Liv. ; pernicies in accusatorem, Tac. **b.** *to turn out :* res tibi male, Ter. ; Pl. ; quod bene vertat, Liv. ; Verg. **c.** *to turn, change :* fortuna, Liv. ; in glaciem lacunae, Verg. ; libertatem aliorum in suam vertisse servitutem conquerebantur, Liv.

Vertumnus (Vort-), ī, *m. the god of the changing year, i.e. of the seasons and their productions.*

verū, ūs (Nom. *sing.* verum, Pl.), n. **I.** *a spit, esp. for roasting :* Varr., Verg., Ov. **II.** *a dart, javelin :* Verg., Tib.

veruīna, ae, *f.* [verū], *a small javelin :* Pl.

Verulāmium, ī, *n. a town in Britain, now St. Albans.*

verum, ī, *v.* verū.

vērum, ī, *v.* vērus.

vērum, *adv.* [orig. *neut.*, Nom. ' it is true '], *true /* **1.** L i t. *just so, yes :* Pl., Ter. **2.** T r a n s f. **a.** *true but ; but in truth, but notwithstanding, but yet ;* and after negative clauses, *but even, but ;* standing at the beginning of its clause, like *sed* : Pl., Cic., Verg., etc. E s p. in the construction, *non modo* (solum, tantum) . . . *verum etiam* (quoque), *not only, . . . but also,* Cic., Hor., etc. **b.** In making a transition to another subject, *but, yet, still :* verum veniat sane, Cic. ; Pl., etc. Strengthened with enim, vero, and enimvero, *but truly, but indeed :* Pl., Ter., Cic., etc. In breaking off discourse : verum quidem haec hactenus, Cic. Also **vērum tamen** (or **vērumtamen**), *but yet, notwithstanding, nevertheless :* consilium stultum, verum tamen clemens, Cic. ; Pl., etc. Sometimes, in resuming after a parenthesis : cum essem in Tusculano (erit hoc tibi pro illo tuo *cum essem in Ceramico*), verum tamen cum ibi essem, Cic. Ep.

vērus, a, um, *true, real, actual, genuine.* **1.** L i t. **a.** via, Pl. ; res, amicus, Cic. ; vera, gravis, solida gloria, Cic. ; virtus, dolores, Hor. *Comp.* and *Sup.* : Cic. As Noun, **vērum,** ī, *n. what is true* or *real, the truth, reality, the fact :* verum dicere, Pl. ; si verum scire vis, Cic. ; nec procul a vero est, Ov. ; recta et vera loquere, Pl. ; Cic. ; Hor. E s p. **vērī similis,** *probable,* and **vērī similitūdō,** *probability :* narrationem iubent veri similem esse, Cic. ; Caes. ; Liv. ; veri simillimum, Cic. ; veri similitudinem sequi, Cic. **b.** *speaking* or *containing the truth, true, veracious :* sum verus? Ter. ; vates, Ov. *Comp.* and *Sup.* : Plin. Ep. **2.** T r a n s f. *fair, reasonable, just :* lex, Cic. ; Ter. ; verum est (with *Inf.,* or Acc. and *Inf.*), Caes., Cic., Liv., Hor. ; and in *Comp.* : Verg., Liv. ; (with *ut* and *Subj.*), Cic., Nep. As Noun, **vērum,** ī, *n. what is right ; honour, duty :* nil Grosphus nisi verum orabit et aequum, Hor. ; vero pretium anteferre, Sall. ; in *pl.* : Sall.

verūtum, ī, *n.* [verū], *a dart, javelin :* Enn., Lucr., Caes., Liv.

verūtus, a, um [verū], *armed with a dart* or *javelin :* Verg.

vervēx, ēcis, *m. a wether.* **1.** L i t. : Pl., Cic. **2.** T r a n s f. as a term of abuse, ' *mutton-head* :' Pl., Juv. [Fr. *brebis.*]

vēsānia, ae, *f.* [vēsānus], *madness, insanity :* Hor., Plin.

vēsāniēns, entis, *adj.* [vēsānus], *raging, furious :* ventus, Cat.

vē-sānus, a, um, *not of sound mind, mad, insane.* **1.** L i t. : Cic., Hor. **2.** T r a n s f. of things, *savage, furious, raging :* vultus, impetus, Liv. ; fames, Verg. ; flamma, Cat. ; pontus, Prop.

vescor, vesci [*cf.* edō, esca], *to feed, eat.* **1.** L i t. : Cic., Sall., Hor., Tac. With Abl. : Cic., Sall., Hor. With Acc. : Acc., Sall., Tib., Tac. **2.** T r a n s f. : vitalibus auris, Lucr. ; aurā aetheriā, Verg. ; praemiis patris, Acc. ; paratissimis voluptatibus, Cic.

vescus, a, um [vē esca]. **I.** *nibbled off ;* hence, *meagre, feeble :* vescaeque parva vocant (farra), Ov. ; papaver, Verg. ; vescas salicum frondes, Verg. ; vires, Afran. ; corpus, Plin. **II.** *nibbling at ;* hence, *consuming, corroding :* vesco sale saxa peresa, Lucr.

vēsica (vēnsica), ae, *f. the bladder* in the body of animals, *the urinary bladder.* **1.** L i t. Pl., Cic., Hor. Hence of the pudendum muliebre : Juv. **2.** T r a n s f. **a.** *anything made of bladder,* e.g. *a purse, cap, lantern, football,* etc. : Varr., Ov., Plin., etc. **b.** *bombast :* Mart. [Fr. *vessie.*]

vēsicula, ae, *f.* [*dim.* vēsica], *a little bladder* or *bag,* containing air : Lucr. ; containing seeds : Cic.

vespa, ae, *f.* [*cf.* Gk. σφήξ]. *a wasp :* Varr., Phaedr., etc. [Fr. *guêpe.*]

Vespasiānus, ī, *m.* : T. Flavius Sabinus, *Roman emperor,* A.D. 70.

vesper, eris and erī (in class. prose Acc. usually vesperum, Abl. vespere ; Locat. vesperi), *m.* [*cf.* Gk. Ϝέσπερος, Ϝεσπέρα], *the evening.* **1.** L i t. : iam diei vesper erat,

Nall.; ad vesperum, Caes., Cic.; sub vesperum, Caes.; primo vespere, Caes., Cic. Ep.; vesperi, *in the evening*, Pl., Ter., Caes., Cic. P r o v.: cum quid vesper ferat incertum sit, Liv. **2.** T r a n s f. **a.** *the eveningmeal :* de suo (*or* de alicuius) vesperi cenare, i.e. to sup at one's own (somebody else's) expense, Pl. **b.** *the evening-star :* Verg., Hor., Plin. **c.** *the west :* Verg., Ov. [Fr. *vêpres*.]

vespera, ae, *f.* [Ϝεσπέρα], *the evening :* prima vespera, Pl.; prima vesperā, Liv.; vesperā, Plin.; ad vesperam, Cic.; a mane usque ad vesperam, Suet.; inumbrante vesperā, Tac.

vesperāscō, ăre [vespera], *to become evening, grow towards evening :* vesperascente caelo, Nep.; vesperascente die, Tac. *Impers. :* vesperascit, Ter.

vespertīliō, ōnis, *m.* [vesper], *a bat :* Plin.

vespertīnus, a, um [vesper], *of or in the evening, evening-.* **1.** L i t.: tempora, Cic. Adverbially : si vespertinus subito te oppresserit hospes, Hor. **2.** T r a n s f. *western :* regio, Hor.

vesperūgo, inis, *f.* [vesper], *the evening-star :* Pl.

vespillō, ōnis, *m.* [*cf.* vesper], *a corpse-bearer,* who carried out the bodies of the poor at night : Mart., Suet.

Vesta, ae, *f. goddess of the fire burning on the hearth and of domestic life.*

Vestālis, e, *adj.* [Vesta], *of Vesta, Vestal:* sacra, Ov.; virgines, *her priestesses, Vestals,* Cic., Liv. As N o u n, **Vestālis**, is, *f.* (*sc.* virgo), *a Vestal :* Liv., Ov. A d j.: Vestales oculi, *of the Vestals,* Ov.

vester (older **voster**), tra, trum [vōs], *your* (in addressing more than one person) : Pl., Cic., etc. For the *Obj.* G e n. of vos: odio vestro, *towards you,* Liv. As Noun : ibi voster cenat, *your master,* Pl.; quid ego vos de vestro impendatis hortor ? *your own stock,* Liv. G e n. *pl.* as equivalent of G e n . *pl.* of vos : Pl.

vestibulum, i, *n. the (enclosed) space between the entrance of a house and the street, a forecourt, entrance-court.* **1.** L i t.: Pl., Cic., Ov., etc. **2.** T r a n s f. **a.** sepulcri, Siciliae, Cic.; castrorum, urbis, Liv. **b.** *an opening, beginning :* vestibulum modo artis alicuius ingredi, Quint. In *pl. :* Cic.

vestigium, i, *n.* [vestigo], *a footstep, step ; footprint, foot-track, track.* **1.** L i t.: socci, Pl.; ponere vestigia, Cic.; in foro vestigium facere, Cic.; vestigiis persequi (sequi, Liv.) aliquem, Cic.; quod (litus solidum) nec vestigia servet, Ov.; eodem romanero vestigio, Caes.; in suo vestigio mori quam fugere, Liv.; vestigium abscedi ab Hannibale, Liv. **2.** T r a n s f. **A.** *a trace* of any kind. **a.** *Material :* earum ferarum, Caes.; Cic.; in vestigiis huius urbis, Cic. **b.** Of manners, character, etc.: a pueritiā vestigiis ingressus patris, Cic.; patris vestigia premere, Tac.; amoris vestigia, Quint. **B.** *the foot* (in *pl.*): Cic., Cat., Verg. **C.** Of time (only with *in* or *ex or* ABL. alone : *on the spot, i.e. at that very moment, instantly :* in illo vestigio temporis, Caes.; repente e vestigio, Cic.; Caes.; eodem vestigio, Caes.; vestigio temporis, Caes.; eodem et loci vestigio et temporis, Cic.

vestīgō, āre, *to track, trace.* **1.** L i t.: te, Enn.; feras, Sen. Trag.; tigris odore raptorem, Plin. **2.** T r a n s f. *to find out by tracing, to trace out.* **a.** perfugas inquirendo, Liv.; ramum oculis, Verg. **b.** Of facts, etc.: causas rerum, Cic.; Liv.; ratione omnis illorum conatūs, Cic.

vestīmentum, i, *n.* [vestiō], *a garment,* (oft. *pl., clothes)* : Ter., Cic., Hor., etc. P r o v.: nudo detrahere vestimenta, Pl.

vestiō, īre. (*Imperf.* vestībat, Verg.) [vestis], *to dress, clothe.* **1.** L i t.: candide vestitus, Pl.; homines male vestiti, Cic.; te lanae, Hor. In *Mid. :* Cato; pellibus sunt vestiti, Caes. Of animals : aliae villis vestitae, Cic.; sandyx agnos, Verg. **2.** T r a n s f. **a.** Of inanimate things, *to clothe, cover :* trabes multo aggere, Caes.; oculos membranis, Cic.; montis silvis, Liv.; messibus agros, Ov.; genas flore, Verg.; se gramine terra, Verg.; aether campos lumine, Verg. **b.** sententias mollis et perlucens vestiebat oratio, Cic.; gloriā aliquem, Hor. [Fr. *vêtir*.]

vestiplica, ae, *f.* [vestis plicō], *a clothes-folder, laundress :* Pl.

vestis, is, *f.* [*cf.* Gk. ἐσθής, ἔννυμι], *a garment, clothing.* **1.** L i t.: Pl., Cic., Hor., etc.; mutare vestem, *to put on mourning garments,* Cic., Liv.; (also in gen. of changing one's clothes : Ter., Liv., etc.); vestis mutatio, Ter., Cic. **2.** T r a n s f. **a.** *a blanket, coverlet, hangings, tapestry* (in *sing.* and *pl.*): Cic., Verg., Hor., Liv., etc. **b.** Of a serpent's skin *or* slough : Lucr. **c.** Of the beard : Lucr. **d.** Of a spider's web : Lucr. **e.** Of a veil : Stat.

vestispica (*al.* vestiplica, q.v.), ae, *f.* [vestis speciō], *a wardrobe-woman :* Pl.

vestītus, ūs, *m.* [vestiō], *clothing, clothes, dress.* **1.** L i t.: Pl., Caes., Cic., Liv., etc.; mutare vestitum, *to put on mourning garments,* Cic.; redire ad suum vestitum, *to go out of mourning,* Cic. **2.** T r a n s f. **a.** Of inanimate things : vestitūs densissimos montium, Cic. **b.** orationis, Cic.

veterāmentārius, a, um [vetus], *of old things,* sutor, Suet.

veterānus, a, um [vetus], *old, veteran :* hostis, Liv.; milites, *or* veterani alone, Caes., Cic., Liv.

veterāscō, veterāscere, veterāvī [vetus], *to grow old :* ad gloriam, Cic.

veterātor, ōris, *m.* [vetus], *one who has grown old or skilled in anything, ' an old hand' :* in causis privatis, Cic.; in cunning, *a sly old fox :* Pl., Ter., Cic.

veterātōriē, *adv. craftily :* Cic.

veterātōrius, a, um [veterātor], *crafty, cunning, sly :* Cic.; ratio dicendi, Cic.

veterīnus, a, um [prob. contr. fr. vehiterinus, fr. vehō], *of burden or draught :* bestia, Cato; equi, Lucr. As Noun, **veterīnae**, ārum, *f. pl.* and **veterīna**, ōrum, *n. pl. draught-cattle, beasts of burden :* Varr., Plin.

veternōsus, a, um [veternus], *lethargic.* **1.** L i t.: Cato; Plin. **2.** T r a n s f. **a.** *sleepy, drowsy :* homo, Ter. **b.** *languid, spiritless :* animus, Sen. *Sup. :* Sen. Ep.

veternus, i, *m.* [vetus]. **I.** *old age, lethargy, sleepiness* (of old people) : Pl. **II.** *drowsi-*

ness, sluggishness, sloth : Cael. ap. Cic. Ep., Cat., Verg., Hor.

vetĭtus, a, um. **I.** *Part.* vetŏ. **II.** Noun. **vetĭtum,** i, n. *a prohibited thing* or *a prohibition :* Cic., Verg., Ov., Tac.

vetō (votō, Pl.), āre, uī (āvī, Pers.), ĭtum, *to forbid, prohibit.* **A.** In gen. : Pl. ; vetant leges Iovis, Hor. ; res ipsa, Ov. ; lex, Quint. With Acc. (of Direct Object) and *Inf.* : ab opere legatos Caesar discedere vetuerat, Caes. ; lex peregrinum vetat in murum ascendere, Cic. ; hos vetuit me numerare timor, Prop. ; Verg., etc. ; so, Nom. and *Inf.* in *Pass. :* Nolani muros adire vetiti, Liv. ; Cic. With *Inf.* alone : Hor., Ov. With *ut* or *ne* and *Subj. :* Hor. With *Subj.* alone : Tib. With *quin* (after a negat.) : Pl., Sen. With Acc. alone. **a.** Of the thing : bella, Verg. ; Ov. ; in *Pass. :* vetiti Hymenaei, Verg. ; vetĭtā legibus aleā, Hor. ; factum vetitum, Plin. Ep. **b.** Of the person : Hor. ; in *Pass. :* vetamur vetere proverbio, Cic. ; vetor fatis, Verg. ; (mathematici) genus hominum quod in civitate nostrā vetabitur, Tac. **B.** veto, *I forbid it, I protest.* **a.** In the formal intercessio of the tribunes of the people, Liv., Suet. **b.** In the protest of the praetor against an unlawful measure : Cic. **c.** Of the augurs or augural signs : Ter., Cic., Ov.

vetŭlus, a, um [*dim.* vetus], *wretchedly* or *pitiably old :* Pl., Cic., Cat., Hor., etc. As Noun, *masc.* and *fem. :* Pl., Cic. Ep., Juv.

vetus (veter, Enn.), veteris (ABL. usually vetere, but veterī, Juv.), *adj.* [fr. root seen in Gk. ϝέτος], *old, long-standing, aged* (of persons or things) : maceria, Pl. ; senex, Pl. ; Sall. ; Liv. ; amicus, Pl. ; Cic. ; invidia, Cic. ; contumelia, Caes. ; consuetudo, nobilitas, Sall. ; naves, copiae, Caes. ; exercitus, Caes., Liv. ; miles, Cic. ; milites, Caes., Liv. ; legiones, centuriones, Liv. ; provinciae, Liv. ; veterrima amicitia, Cic. With GEN. : militiae, laboris, regnandi, etc., Tac. As Noun, **veterēs,** um, **a.** *m. pl. the ancients, ancient authors, etc. :* Ter., Cic., Quint. **b.** *f. pl.* (*sc.* tabernae), *the old booths* or *shops* on the S. side of the Forum Romanum : Pl., Liv. **vetera,** um, *n. pl. old things, traditions, antiquity :* Pl., Cic., Sall., Tac.

vetustās, ātis, *f.* [vetus]. **I.** *age, long existence :* possessionis, Cic. ; aevi, Verg. **II.** *antiquity, ancient times :* contra omnia vetustatis exempla, Caes. ; Cic. ; Liv. **III.** With ref. to the future (rare) ; *long duration, great age :* quae mihi videntur habitura etiam vetustatem, Cic. Ep. ; Ov., etc. Hence of the remote future : de me semper omnes gentes loquentur, nulla unquam obmutescet vetustas, Cic. ; Verg.

vetustus, a, um [vetus], *that has existed a long time ; ancient, of old standing* (stronger than vetus : in *posit.* mostly poet. and almost exclusively of things). **1.** Lit. : vinum, Pl. ; templum Cereris, Verg. ; opinio, Cic. ; amicitia, Ov. ; cornicum saecla vetusta, Lucr. Of persons : Hor. ; gens, Verg. *Comp. :* Plin. *Sup. :* foedera, tempora, Quint. ; instrumentum imperi,

Suet. ; sepulcra, Suet. Of persons : qui vetustissimus ex iis, qui viverent, censoriis esset, Liv. ; Tac. **2.** Transf. *old-fashioned, antiquated :* Laelius vetustior et horridior quam Scipio, Cic.

vexāmen, inis, n. [vexō], *a shaking, quaking :* mundi, Lucr.

vexātĭō, ōnis, *f.* [vexō], *a jolting, jostling, shaking, tossing* (and the pain, etc., so caused). **1.** Lit. **a.** Prop. : vexationem vulneris in viā iactanti, Liv. **b.** corporis, Cic. ; cum omni genere vexationis processerunt, Liv. ; partūs, Plin. **2.** Transf. of ill-treatment or abuse : ut virgines Vestalis ex acerbissimā vexatione eriperem, Cic. ; vexatio direptioque sociorum, Cic. ; per vexationem et contumelias, Liv.

vexātor, ōris, m. *a jostler, hustler, vexer :* urbis, aetatulae suae, furoris (i.e. Clodi), Cic.

vexillārĭus, i, m. [vexillum]. **I.** *a standard-bearer, ensign :* Liv., Tac. **II. vexillāriī,** ōrum, *m. pl.* under the Emperors, *soldiers who had served for sixteen years,* and, *for their remaining four years of service, formed a special reserve* (sub vexillo) : Tac.

vexillātĭō, ōnis, *f.* [vexillum], *a body of* vexillarii, *esp.* to others, *any body of soldiers united under one flag, a corps, battalion :* Suet.

vexillum, i, n. [*dim.* vēlum], *a military ensign, standard, flag.* **1.** Lit. : Caes., Cic. Esp. *a red flag* hoisted on the general's tent, as a signal for battle : proponere, Caes. ; vexillo signum dare, Caes. **2.** Transf. *the troops belonging to a vexillum, a company, troop :* Liv., Tac., Stat.

vexō, āre [*freq.* vehō], *to jolt, jostle, shake, toss violently.* **1.** Lit. **a.** Prop. : rector per confragosa vexabitur, Cic. ; navigia in summum veniant vexata periclum, Lucr. ; Verg. **b.** In gen. : venti vis montis supremos silvifragis vexat flabris, Lucr. ; venti nubila, Ov. **2.** Transf. *to distress, harass, trouble, maltreat.* **a.** Physically : (milites) locorum asperitas hostiliter vexavit, Liv. ; vexati difficultate viae, Liv. ; comas (i.e. in curling), Ov. ; faucis (tussis), Mart. Of hostile action : agros, hostis, omnem Galliam, Caes. ; Cic. **b.** Mentally : aliquem probris, contumeliis, etc., Cic. ; sollicitudo vexat impios, Cic. ; conscientia mentem, Sall. ; mentem mariti philtris, Juv.

via (vea, Varr.), ae, *f.* (GEN. *sing.* viāī, Lucr.) [fr. root seen in vehō], *a way, highway, road, highroad, street.* **1.** Lit. : Pl., Caes., Cic., Liv., etc. ; de viā in semitam degredi, Pl. ; aestuosa et pulverulenta, Cic. Ep. ; militaris, Liv. ; munire, *to build, make,* Cic. ; silice sternere, Liv. ; strata viarum, Verg. ; via Appia, Cic. ; via Sacra, Hor. ; in viam se dare, Cic. Ep. **2.** Transf. **a.** *the road,* i.e. *a march, journey :* cum de viā languerem, Cic. ; tridui via, Caes. ; longitudo viae, Liv. ; flecte viam velis, Verg. ; feci per freta puppe vias, Ov. ; ne inter vias praeterbitamus, *on the road,* Pl. **b.** Of any passage. In the theatre : Mart. Of the veins : Cic. Of the windpipe : Ov. Of the track of an arrow : Verg. Of a cleft : Verg. Of a

stripe in a parti-coloured fabric : Tib.
c. *a way, method, mode :* rectam vitae
viam sequi, Cic. ; Hor. ; vivendi, Cic. ;
laudis, gloriae, Cic. ; defensionis ratio
viaque, Cic. ; mortis, Tac. ; optimarum
artium vias tradere, Cic. ; ad gloriam,
Cic. ; ad salutem, Liv. Also, *the right
way, the true method :* Pl., Cic. ; viā et
arte dicere, Cic. ; Ter. [Fr. *voie.*]

viālis, e, *adj.* [via], *of the roads :* Lares,
Pl.

viārius, a, um [via], *concerning roads :* lex,
Cael. ap. Cic. Ep. [Fr. *voyer.*]

viāticātus, a, um [viaticum], *provided with
travelling-money :* Pl.

viāticus, a, um [via], *relating to a journey :*
cena (i.e. before setting out), Pl. As
Noun, **viāticum,** i, *n. travelling-money,
provision for a journey.* **1.** Lit. : Pl.,
Cic., Hor., Liv., etc. **2.** Transf. *allowances or savings of soldiers on service :* Hor.,
Tac., Suet. [It. *viaggio ;* Fr. *voyage.*]

viātor, ōris, m. [via]. **I.** *a wayfarer, traveller :*
Caes., Cic., Verg., Hor., etc. **II.** *a sum-
moner, apparitor,* whose duty was to summon persons before the magistrates : Cic.,
Liv.

vibix, icis, *f. a weal* (from a blow): Pl.,
Cato, Pers.

vibrō, āre. **A.** Trans. *to set in tremulous
motion, to make to quiver, to brandish, shake.*
1. Lit. **a.** hastas ante pugnam, Cic. ;
vibrabant flamina vestis, Ov. ; viscera
vibrantur (equitando), Tac. In *Mid.* :
mea vibrari membra videres, Ov. **b.** Of
hurling : iaculum, Ov. ; tela, Curt. ; fulmina (Iuppiter), Ov. ; vibratus ab aethere
fulgor, Verg. **2.** Transf. **a.** crines ferro
vibrati (i.e. curled), Verg. **b.** Of language,
to fling : trucis iambos, Cat. **B.** Intrans.
to be in tremulous motion, to quiver, vibrate ;
esp. of dancing, flickering, shimmering,
sparkling light. **1.** Lit. : linguā vibrante
(serpentis), Lucr. ; mare, quā a sole con-
lucet, albescit et vibrat, Cic. ; gladius,
Verg. ; ictus, Ov. Of sound : Plin.,
Sen. **2.** Transf. of language : oratio
incitata et vibrans, Cic. ; sententiae,
Quint. ; fulmina (Demosthenis), Cic.

viburnum, i, *n. the wayfaring-tree :* Verg.
[Fr. *viorne.*]

vicānus, a, um [vicus], *dwelling in a village :*
Cic. ; haruspices (perh. *touring the villages*),
Enn. As Noun, **vicāni,** ōrum, *m. pl.
villagers :* Liv.

Vica Pota, ae, *f. Victress and Possessor,
goddess of Victory.*

vicārius, a, um [vicis], *taking the place of
a person or thing, substituted :* fides amicorum, Cic. As Noun, **vicārius,** i, *m.*
a. In gen. *a substitute, deputy, proxy :*
Cic., Hor., Liv. **b.** *an under-servant, under-
slave,* kept by another slave : Pl., Cic.,
Hor. [Fr. *viguier.*]

vicātim, *adv.* [vicus]. **I.** *from street to street :*
Hor., Tac. **II.** *from village to village ;
in hamlets :* habitare, Liv.

vicēnārius, a, um [vicēni], *of the number
twenty :* lex ne perdit quina vicenaria
(by which young people under five-and-
twenty were incapable of making contracts),
Pl.

vicēni, ae, a [viginti], *twenty in a group* or
twenty each : Caes., Liv., Mart.

vicēsima, ae, v. vicēnsimus.

vicēnsimāni (**-ēs-**), ōrum, m. pl. [vicēnsima],
soldiers of the twentieth (legion) : Tac.

vicēnsimārius (**-ēs-**), a, um [vicēnsima],
derived from the vicensima : aurum, Liv.

vicēnsimus (**-ēs-**), or **vigēnsimus** (**-ēs-**),
a, um [viginti], *twentieth :* Pl., Cic., etc.
As Noun, **vicēnsima** (**-ēs-**), ae, *f.* **a.** (*sc.*
legio) : v. vicensimani. **b.** (*sc.* pars),
the twentieth part, as a tax : *the twentieth
part* or *5 per cent. of the value* of a slave
manumitted : Cic. Ep., Liv. As an ad
valorem duty on exports : portori, Cic.
As a tax on inheritances : Plin. Ep.

vicia, ae, *f. a vetch :* Cato, Varr., Verg., Ov.
[It. *veccia ;* Fr. *vesce.*]

viciens (**-iēs**), *adv.* [viginti], *twenty times :*
Caes., Cic. HS. viciens (*sc.* centena milia),
two millions, Cic. Ep.

vicinālis, e, *adj.* [vicinus], *neighbouring,
near :* usus, Liv.

vicinia, ae, *f.* [vicinus], *neighbourhood, near
ness.* **1.** Lit. : hic viciniae, Ter. ; hic
proxumae viciniae, Pl. ; in viciniā nostrā
Averni lacūs, Cic. ; Verg., etc. **2.** Transf.
a. Concr. *the neighbourhood,* i.e. neighbours : Hor., Ov., Liv., etc. **b.** *near
likeness :* diversarum rerum, Quint.

vicinitās, ātis, *f.* [vicinus], *neighbourhood,
proximity.* **1.** Lit. : Ter., Cic., Liv. In
pl. : Cic. **2.** Transf. **A.** Concr. **a.**
neighbourhood, i.e. region : Cic. **b.** *the
neighbourhood,* i.e. the neighbours : Cato,
Caes., Cic., etc. In *pl.* : Cic. **B.** *near
likeness :* Plin., Quint.

vicinus, a, um [vicus], *near, neighbouring.*
1. Lit. : taberna, Hor. ; Verg. ; bellum,
Liv. ; iurgia, Hor. With Dat. : vicina
astris sedes, Verg. As Noun, **vicinus,**
i, *m.,* and **vicina,** ae, *f. a neighbour :* Pl.,
Cic., Verg., etc. **vicinum,** i, *n. a neighbouring place, the neighbourhood :* stellae in
vicino terrae, Plin. In *pl.* : Ov., Plin.
2. Transf. (in nature or quality), *like,
kindred, allied :* virtutibus vitia, Quint. ;
Cic. ; Liv. [Sp. *vecino ;* Fr. *voisin.*]

vicis (Gen. ; the Nom. *sing.* does not occur),
vicem, vice ; Nom. *pl.* vicēs, Acc. vicis
or vicēs, Dat. and Abl. vicibus), *f. change,
interchange, alternation, succession.* **1.** Lit.
a. In gen. : alternā vice, Enn. ; commoti
vice fortunarum humanarum, Liv. ; hac
vice sermonum, Verg. ; Ov. ; mutat terra
vicis, Hor. ; cur vicibus factis convivia
ineant, Ov. ; nec tela nec ullas vitavisse
vicis Danaum, Verg. ; vices loquendi,
Quint. Adverbially : **in vicem** (and
invicem) (Caes., Verg., Liv., etc.) and
vicem (Liv.) and **in vicis** (Ov., Tac.), *by
turns, in their turn, alternately, mutually.*
b. *return, requital, recompense, retaliation :*
vicem offici praesentis, Cic. ; redde vicem
meritis, Ov. ; beneficio vicem exsolvere,
Tac. ; sequenti redde vicis, Ov. **c.** *the
changes of fate, fate, condition, fortune, misfortune :* et meam et aliorum vicem pertimescere, Cic. ; Liv. ; convertere huma-
nam vicem, Hor. ; fors et debita iura
viceaque superbae te maneant ipsum, Hor.
2. Transf. *the position, stead, office, duty*

(obtained by succession): per speciem
alienae fungendae vicis opes suas firmavit,
Liv.; ad vicem alicuius accedere, Cic.;
succedens in vicem imperi tui, Liv. More
generally, *office, function* : sortiti vicis,
Verg.; fungar vice cotis, Hor.; vestram-
que meamque vicem explete, Tac. A d v e r-
b i a l l y : **vicem** with G e n . or *Possess.
Pron.* **a.** *instead of :* eri vicem meamque,
Pl.; Liv., etc. **b.** *on account of :* tuam
vicem saepe doleo, *on your account,* Cic.
Ep.; Liv.; Tac. **c.** *after the manner of,
like :* Sardanapali vicem in suo lectulo
mori, Cic. Ep.; Sall. **vice. a.** *on account
of :* exanimes vice unius, Liv. **b.** *after
the manner of :* quaeque dixerat oracli
vice accipiens, Tac.; Plin.; Quint. **in
vicem** (or **invicem**), *instead of, in place
of :* missis in vicem earum legionum quinque milibus sociorum, Liv.; defetigatis
in vicem integri succedunt, Caes. [Sp.
vez ; Fr. *fois.*]

vicissim (Pl., Cic., Verg., etc.) and **vicissā-
tim** (Pl.) [vicis], *in turn, again.*

vicissitūdō, inis, *f.* [vicis], *change, interchange, alternation :* omnium rerum, Ter.;
studiorum officiorumque, Cic.; ex alio in
aliud, Cic. In *pl. :* dierum noctiumque,
Cic.; fortunae, Cic. Ep.

victima, ae, *f. a beast for sacrifice, a sacrifice,
victim.* **1.** L i t . : Pl., Caes., Verg., Liv.,
etc. **2.** T r a n s f . : so victimam rei publicae praebere, Cic.; Ov.

victimārius, a, um [victima], *of (sacrificial)
victims :* Plin. As Noun, **victimārius,**
i, *m. an assistant at sacrifices :* Liv.

victitō, āre [*freq.* vivō], *to live, support oneself, subsist on :* ficis aridis, Pl.; parce, Pl.;
bene lubenter, Ter.

victor, ōris, *m.* [vincō], *a conqueror, vanquisher.*
1. L i t . : Caes.; belli, Pl., Cic., Liv.;
trium bellorum, Liv.; maximarum gentium, Caes.; Cic. With A b l . : civili
bello victor, Cic., Tac. In apposition:
exercitus, Caes.; Graii, Ov.; galli, Cic.;
equus, Verg.; currus, Ov. **2.** T r a n s f . :
animus libidinis et divitiarum victor, Sall.;
propositi, Hor.

victōria, ae, *f.* [victor], *victory.* **a.** In war :
Enn.; ab aliquo reportare, Cic.; con-
clamare, Caes.; victoriae eorum bellorum,
Cic.; certaminis, Liv.; de Hannibale
Poenisque, Liv.; ex Campanis victoriam
peperunt, Liv.; ex Etruscā civitate victoriam tulit, Liv. **b.** In civil life : ex
conlegā quaerere, Liv.; victoria penes
patres fuit, Liv. **c.** Personified : Pl.,
Cic., Ov.

victōriātus, i, *m.* (*sc.* nummus) [victōria],
*a silver coin stamped with the image of
Victory,* in Varro's time worth half a
denarius : Cato, Cic., Liv.

Victōriola, ae, *f.* [*dim.* Victōria], *a little statue
of Victory :* Cic.

victrix, īcis, *f.* and *n.* [vincō], *a conqueror.*
1. L i t . : erat res publica, Cic. Ep. In
apposition : Athenae, Cic.; litterae, Cic. Ep.;
classis, Liv.; dextra, Ov.; arma, Verg.
2. T r a n s f . : mater victrix filiae, non
libidinis, Cic.

victus, a, um, *Part.* vincō.

victus, ūs (G e n . *sing.* victi, Pl.), *m.* [vīvō],

living. **I.** *means of living, sustenance :*
Caes., Verg., etc.; tenuis, Cic. In *pl. :*
Pl., Cic., Ov. **II.** *a way of life :* consuetudo
victūs, Caes.; Hor.; omni vitā atque
victu excultus, Cic.; splendidus non minus
in vitā quam victu, Nep.

viculus, i, *m.* [*dim.* vīcus], *a little village,
hamlet :* Cic., Liv.

vīcus, i, *m.* [*cf.* Gk. ϝοῖκος]. **1.** L i t . **a.**
a farm-house (and the cottages built alongside it) : Cic. Ep., Hor. **b.** *a village,
hamlet :* Caes., Cic., Liv. **2.** T r a n s f . *a
quarter* or *ward in a town,* or *a street, lane*
through it : Caes., Cic., Liv., Hor., Ov.

vidēlicet, *adv.* [vidēre licet ; *cf.* I-licet and
scī-licet], *it is easy to see, clearly, evidently,
etc.* **1.** L i t . **A.** With A c c . and *Inf. :*
Pl., Lucr. **B.** As *Adv.* **a.** *evidently, undoubtedly :* quae videlicet ille non ex agri
consiturā, sed ex doctrinae indiciis inter-
pretabatur, Cic.; Pl., etc. **b.** In ironical
sense (when the contrary is intended), *of
course, forsooth :* tuus videlicet salutaris
consulatus, perniciosus meus, Cic.; Sall.,
etc. **2.** T r a n s f . as a complementary
or explanatory particle, *to wit, namely :*
caste iubet lex adire ad deos, animo videlicet,
Cic.

video, vidēre, vidi, visum (viden', for vidēsne,
Pl., Verg.) [*cf.* ϝεῖδον], *to see.* **I.** In gen.
1. L i t . **a.** Cic., Verg. ; aliquid *or* aliquem,
Pl., Cic., Hor., etc. ; iuvat ovis videre
properantis domum, Hor. With A c c . and
Inf. : Hor. With *ut (how)* and *Ind.*
or *Subj. :* viden', ut geminae stant vertice
cristae ! Verg. ; vides ut altā stet nive
candidum Soracte, Hor. ; Verg. In *Pass.*
(contrast II.) : in aperto loco stationes
equitum videbantur, Caes. ; Verg. ; Liv.,
Ov., etc. **b.** *to see on purpose, to look at :*
vide me, Pl. ; quin tu me vides ? Cic.
With *Indir. Quest. :* Pl. With a following
si- clause : Ter. **c.** C o l l o q . *to go to see,
to visit :* aliquem, Cic. Ep., Plin. Ep.
2. T r a n s f . **a.** Of things as Subjects:
casūs marinos abies, Verg. ; triclinium
hortum, Plin. Ep. **b.** By other senses,
to perceive, be aware of : naso plus quam
oculis, Pl. With A c c . and *Inf. :* mugire
videbis sub pedibus terram, Verg. ; Hor. ;
Prop. **c.** With the mind : aliquid in
somnis, Cic. ; exitum animo, Cic. ; video
meliora proboque, Ov. ; in futurum, Liv.
Often with a *Comp. Adv. :* aliena melius
videre et diiudicare, Ter. ; acutius atque
acrius, Cic. ; plus in re publicā videre,
to have a deeper political insight, Cic. With
ut (how) and *Indic. :* Verg. **d.** *to look at,
think* or *reflect upon ; to see to, care for :*
vinum, Ter. ; prandium nobis, Cic. Ep. ;
sodem sibi, Cic. ; sibi aliud consilium, Cic.
With *Indir. Quest. :* quid agas, Cic. With
ut or *ne* and *Subj. :* Cic., Liv. ; *Impers.*
Pass. : Cic. **e.** *to live to see* a period or
event : utinam eum diem videam cum
etc., Cic. Ep. ; Ter. ; Cic. ; Liv. **II.** In
Mid. or *Pass.* (as dist. fr. the *Pass.* of
I. *to be seen, be in sight*). **A.** P e r s o n a l :
to present oneself, to be regarded ; hence,
to appear, seem : ut imbelles timidique
videamur, Cic. ; quae Aristoni omnino
visa sunt pro nihilo, Cic. ; rem iniquiorem

visum iri intellegebant, Cic. With *Inf.*: ut beate vixisse **videar**, Cic. ; Verg., etc. Esp. in official decisions: consul adiecit senatūs consultum, Ambraciam non videri vi captam esse, Liv., Caes. ; Cic. **B.** With Acc. and *Inf.* clause as Subject : non mihi **videtur**, ad beate vivendum satis posse virtutem, Cic. ; Liv. **C.** Impers. *to seem proper, right or good* ; ut consul, quem **videretur** ei, cum imperio mitteret, Liv. ; ubi visum est, sub vesperum dispersi discedunt, Caes. ; ut videtur, si videtur, Cic., etc. [It. *vedere* ; Sp. *ver* ; Fr. *voir*.]

viduĭtās, ātis, *f.* [viduus], *bereavement.* **a.** *want* : opum, Pl. **b.** *widowhood* : Cic., Liv.

vidŭlus, ī, *m. a leather travelling-trunk, portmanteau, knapsack* : Pl.

vidŭō, āre [viduus], *to deprive or bereave of.* **a.** In gen. With ABL. : urbem civibus, Verg. ; ornos foliis, Hor. With GEN. : manuum viduata, Lucr. **b.** *Part.* **vidŭāta**, *left a widow* : Tac., Suet.

vidŭus (-uos), a, um [*cf.* ἠίθεος], *bereft, destitute.* **A.** In gen. With ABL. : Hor., etc. With *ab* : Verg. With GEN. (v. rare) : pectus amoris, Ov. **B.** *bereft or parted from husband or wife.* **1.** Lit. : Pl., Prop., Ov. As Noun, **vidŭa**, ae, *f. a widow* : Pl., Cic., Hor. Also, *an unmarried woman, a spinster* : Liv., Ov. **2.** Transf. **a.** Of trees : *unmarried* (of vines without a treesupport or of trees without vines) : Cat., Hor., etc. **b.** Of other things : torus, Prop. ; domus, cubile, noctes, Ov. ; manus (Penelopes), Ov. ; caelibatus, Sen.

vĭeō, viēre [*cf.* vīmen, vītis, vitta], *to twine, plait, weave* : Varr.

vĭētor, ōris, *m.* [vieō], *a cooper* : Pl.

vĭētus (disyl., Hor.), a, um. **I.** *Part.* vieō. **II.** Adj. *shrivelled* : senex, Ter. ; aliquid vietum et caducum, Cic. ; vestis (of a spider's web), *shrivelled*, Lucr. ; membra, Hor.

vĭgeō, ēre, uī, *to be lively or vigorous; to flourish, thrive.* **1.** Lit. : quae a terrā stirpibus continentur, arte naturae vivunt et vigent, Cic. ; integris vobis ac vigentibus, Liv. ; Hor. ; corpore, Liv. ; animus, Cic. ; animus laetitiā, Lucr. ; vegetum ingenium in vivido pectore, Liv. ; memoriā, Cic. ; fama mobilitate, Verg. Also perh. : legiones Caesaris, Cic. **2.** Transf. : quoius facta viva nunc vigent, Naev. ; studia rei militaris, Cic. ; audacia, largitio, avaritia, Sall. ; (Philonem) in Academiā maxime vigere audio, Cic. ; regum conciliis, Verg.

vĭgēscō, ere [vigeō], *to become lively or vigorous.* **1.** Lit. : copia rerum, Lucr. ; laeti studio pedes, Cat. **2.** Transf. : summis honoribus, Tac.

vĭgēnsimus (-ēs-), *v.* vīcēnsimus.

vĭgĭl, ilis, *adj. awake, wakeful.* **1.** Lit. : amore vigil torquebere, Hor. ; ales, Ov. **2.** Transf. of things : oculi, Verg. ; lucernae, Hor. ; ignis, Verg. ; cura (i.e. *that keeps one awake*, Ov. As Noun, **vigil**, ilis, *m. a watchman, sentinel* : Pl., Cic., Liv., Ov. Esp. of the nightpolice in Rome: Suet. **2.** Transf. : mundi (sol et luna), Lucr.

vĭgĭlāns, antis. **I.** *Part.* vigilō. **II.** Adj. *watchful* : Cic. ; oculi, Verg. Also, curae, Cic. *Comp.* : Cic.

vĭgĭlanter, *adv. watchfully, vigilantly* : Cic. *Comp.* and *Sup.* : Cic.

vĭgĭlantĭa, ae, *f.* [vigilō], *wakefulness.* **1.** Lit. : Cic. Ep., Plin. Ep. **2.** Transf. : Ter., Cic., Quint.

vĭgĭlāx, ācis, *adj.* [vigilō], *watchful (by nature).* **1.** Lit. : Subura, Prop. **2.** Transf. : curae, Ov.

vĭgĭlĭa, ae, *f.* [vigil], *wakefulness, sleeplessness, a lying awake.* **1.** Lit. **a.** In gen. : patiens vigiliae, Sall. In *pl.* : Demosthenis vigiliae, Cic. **b.** *a keeping awake for the security of a place, a night-watching, watch, guard* : vigiles scutum in vigiliam ferre vetuit, Liv. ; vigilias agere ad aedis sacras, Cic. ; stationibus vigiliisque fessus, Liv. **2.** Transf. **a.** *a watch* (a fourth part of the night) : prima, secunda, tertia, quarta, Caes. ; Liv. ; de tertiā vigiliā, Caes. ; tertiā vigiliā, Caes. **b.** *the watch,* i.e. those standing on guard : vigilias ponere, Sall. ; milites disponit perpetuis vigiliis stationibusque, Caes. ; per urbem disponere, Liv. **c.** In *pl.* At religious festivals, *nightly vigils* : Cereris vigiliae, Pl. **d.** *watchfulness, vigilance* : vigilia et prospicientia, Cic.

vĭgĭlō, āre. **A.** Without ACC. : *to keep awake, to watch.* **1.** Lit. **a.** usque ad lucem, Ter. ; ad multam noctem, Cic. ; de nocte, Cic. Ep. ; ad ipsum mane, Hor. ; hic vigilans somniat, Pl. ; vigilans stertis, Lucr. **b.** Of a sentinel : Liv. **2.** Transf. **a.** lumina vigilantia (of a lighthouse), Ov. **b.** *to be watchful, vigilant* : vigilandum est semper, Acc. ; pro vobis, Cic. With *ut* or *ne* and *Subj.* : Cic., Hor. **c.** *to be attentive to* : studiis severis, Prop. **B.** In *Pass.* : *to be spent or done in wakefulness* : noctes vigilantur amarae, Ov. ; mollior aetas vigilanda viris, Verg. ; carmen, labores, Ov. [It. *vegliare* ; Sp. *velar* ; Fr. *veiller*.]

vīgintī, *indecl. adj.* [*cf.* εἴκοσι], *twenty* : Pl., Cic., Hor., etc. [It. *venti* ; Sp. *veinte* ; Fr. *vingt*.]

vīgintīvĭrātus, ūs, *m.* [vigintīvirī], *the office of* vigintivir : Cic., Tac.

vīgintī-vĭri, ōrum, *m. pl. a commission or board of twenty men.* **a.** Appointed by Caesar for distributing the Campanian lands : Cic. Ep., Suet. *Sing.* : Plin. **b.** *a board* one-half of whose members assisted the praetor, while the other half presided over the roads, the mint, and public executions : Tac.

vĭgor, ōris, *m.* [vigeō], *liveliness, activity, force, vigour* : Verg., Hor. ; animi, Ov. ; mentis, Quint. ; in libro, Sen. Ep.

vīlĭcō (vīll-), āre [vīlicus], *to act as a steward or overseer.* Transf. : in ro publicā, Cic.

vīlĭcus (vīll-), a, um [villa], *of a countryhouse.* As Noun, **vīlĭcus**, ī, *m. an overseer or manager of a farm or estate* ; *a farmbailiff, steward* : Cato, Cic., Hor., etc. ; silvarum, Hor. Transf. : Juv. **vīlĭca**, ae, *f. the wife of a farm-bailiff* : Cato, Cat., Juv.

vilis, e, *adj. of small price* or *value, cheap.* **1.** Lit.: Pl., Ter.; istuc verbum vile est viginti minis, Pl. *Comp.* and *Sup.* : Cic. Abl. *Neut.* as Noun, **vili**, *at a cheap price* : Pl., Mart. **2.** Transf.: mores mali, Pl.; Cic.; poma, Verg.; fidem fortunas pericula vilia habere, Sall.; nec adeo vilis tibi vita esset nostra, Liv.; quorum tibi auctoritas est cara, vita vilissima, Cic.; honor noster vobis vilior, Cic.; vilior algā, Hor.; est tibi vile mori, Ov. *Neut. pl.* as Noun : tu poscis vilia rerum, Hor.

vilitās, ātis, *f.* [vilis], *lowness of price, cheapness.* **1.** Lit.: offerre aliquid vilitati, Pl.; cum alter annus in vilitate, alter in summā caritate fuerit, Cic. : annonae, Cic. **2.** Transf. **a.** *worthlessness, baseness* : nominum, Plin.; Quint. **b.** *low esteem, contempt* : sui, Sen.

viliter, *adv. cheaply. Comp.* : Pl. *Sup.* : Plin.

villa (**vēlla**, Varr.), ae, *f.* [for vīcula fr. vicus], *a country-house, country-seat, farm.* **A.** Ter., Cato, Cic., Hor. **B.** villa publica, in the Campus Martius. **a.** As a gathering-place for recruits, and of the people for the census, etc. : Cic. Ep., Liv. **b.** As quarters for foreign ambassadors : Liv.

villic-, *v.* vīlic-.

villōsus, a, um [villus], *hairy, shaggy, rough* : leo, Verg.; pectora saetis, Verg.; guttura colubris, Ov. *Comp.* : Plin. [Fr. *velours.*]

villula, ae, *f.* [dim. villa], *a poor little country-house* : Cic. Ep., Hor.

villum, i, *n.* [contr. fr. vīnulum, fr. vīnum], *a sup of wine* : Ter.

villus, i, *m.* [cf. vellus], *shaggy hair, fleece.* **1.** Lit.: Cic., Verg., etc. **2.** Transf. (in *pl.*), *the nap* of cloth : tonsis villis, Verg.

vimen, inis, *n.* [v. vieō], *a switch, withe, osier.* **1.** Lit. : Caes., Verg., Ov., etc. **2.** Transf. **a.** *the wand of Mercury* : Lethaeum, Stat. **b.** *a basket* : Ov., Mart.

vimentum, i, *n.* [vimen], *an osier, withy* : Tac.

Vimināus collis, *one of the seven hills of Rome.*

vimineus, a, um [vimen], *made of osiers* : tegimenta, Caes.; crates, Verg.

vin or **vin'** ? for visne ? from volō.

vināceus, a, um [vinum], *of a grape* : acinus, *a grapestone* : Cic.; so, **vināceus** alone, *a grapestone* : Cato ; *a grapeskin* : Varr.

Vinālia, ium and iōrum, *n. pl.* [vinum], *the name of two wine-festivals, the former* (priora) *celebrated on the 23rd of April, and the latter* (rustica) *on the 19th of August* : Varr., Ov.

vinārius, a, um [vinum], *of or for wine, wine-* : lacus, Cato; vasculum, cella, Pl.; vas, Cic.; crimen (i.e. relating to the duty on wine), Cic. As a Noun, **vinārius**, i, *m. a wine-dealer, vintner* : Pl., Sall., Suet. **vināria**, ōrum, *n. pl. wine-pots, wine-flasks* : Pl., Hor.

vincibilis, e, *adj.* [vincō], *that can be easily gained* : causa, Ter.

vinciō, vincire, vinxi, vinctum, *to bind, twine.* **1.** Lit. : aliquem, Pl., Cic.; trinis catenis vinctus, Caes.; post terga manūs, Verg.; alto suras cothurno, Verg.; tempora floribus, Hor.; boves vincti cornua vittis, Ov. **2.** Transf. **a.** *to encircle, surround* : loca praesidiis, Cic. Ep. **b.** *to bind, secure, restrain* : vi Veneris vinctus, Pl.; religione vinctus, Cic.; somno vinctus, Liv., Ov., Tac.; mentem multo Lyaeo, Prop.; tuam numine teste fidem, Ov.; aliquem pacto matrimonio, Tac.; membra orationis numeris, Cic.; hence, verba vincta, oratio vincta, Quint.

vincō, vincere, vici, victum, *to overcome, defeat, subdue, conquer, vanquish.* **1.** Lit. **a.** Milit.: Pl., Caes.; vi militum oppidum victum, Pl.; Galliam bello, Caes.; Carthaginiensis navalibus pugnis, Cic. **b.** In gen. *to be successful, to prevail ;* and with Acc. of Direct Object, *to prevail over, to get the better of, to beat, defeat, surpass* : equōs spatio supremo vicit Olympia (*Intern.* Acc.), Enn.; in dicing, Suet.; virgam (i.e. *to gain, win*), Verg.; iudicio, sponsione, Cic.; sponsionem (*Intern.* Acc.), Cic.; so, causam suam, Ov.; haec sententia in consilio, Caes.; Liv.; in senatu pars illa, Sall.; Liv.; respectu rerum privatarum Appius, Liv.; aliquem carminibus, Verg.; Ov.; competitorem in suffragiis, Quint; navitae aequora, Hor. **2.** Transf. **a.** Of inanimate Subjects : eam (noctem) multo haec (nox) vicit longitudine, Pl.; labor omnia vicit, Verg.; iter durum pietas, Verg.; noctem funalia flammis, Verg.; querna glans victa est utiliore cibo, Ov.; stellarum globi terreae magnitudinem, Cic. Of outlasting : multa virum (Gen.) durando saecula vincit, Verg. **b.** Mentally and morally : *to prevail (over), defeat, convince, persuade* : argumentis, Pl.; naturam studio, Caes.; animum, Pl., Cic.; vinci a voluptate, Cic.; victus patris precibus lacrimisque, Liv.; Hor.; filia victa in lacrimas, Tac.; pietas victa furore, Hor.; victus amore pudor, Ov.; victus animi respexit, Verg.; vincor ut credam, Hor. With Acc. and *Inf.* : Pl., Cic., Hor. With *ut* and *Subj.* : nec vincet ratio hoc ut etc., Hor. **c.** *to prevail (over), surpass* : exspectationem omnium, Cic.; morum immanitate beluas, Cic.; Hor. [Sp. *vencer* ; Fr. *vaincre.*]

vinctus, a, um, *Part.* vinciō.

vinculum (contr. **vinclum**), i, *n.* [vinciō], *a band, bond, cord, fetter, chain.* **1.** Lit. **a.** In gen. : Cic., Verg.; of a sandal, Verg.; of a letter, Nep.; of a ship, Verg.; of the caestus, Verg.; of dress, Ov. **b.** *prison-fetters* ; hence, *prison* (usually in *pl.*): in vincula abripi, Cic.; aliquem vinculis mandare, Cic.; in vincula coniecti, Caes.; in vincula duci, Liv.; ex vinculis causam dicere, Caes.; publica, Cic. **2.** Transf.: corporum vincula, Cic.; concordiae, Cic.; propinquitatis, adfinitatis, utilitatis, vitae communis, Cic.; fidei, Liv.; sponsionis vinculum levare, Liv.; ad adstringendam fidem, Cic.; iugale, Verg.; mercennaria, Hor. With *Obj.* Gen. : immodicae cupiditatis, Liv.; fugae (i.e. checks upon flight), Liv.

vindēmia, ae, *f.* [vinum dēmō], *a grape-gathering, vintage.* **1.** Lit. : Pl., Varr. In *pl.* : Plin. Ep., Suet. **2.** Transf.

grapes, wine : arboribus pendet vindemia, Verg. ; Plin. [Fr. *vendange.*]

vindēmiātor (quadrisyl., Hor.), ōris, *m.* [vindēmia], *a grape gatherer, vintager.* 1. Lit.: Varr., Hor. 2. Transf. in form **vindēmitor**, *a star in the constellation Virgo* : Ov.

vindēmiŏla, ae, *f.* [dim. vindēmia], *a little vintage.* Transf. *of minor sources of income* : Cic.

vindex, icis, *m. f.* [vim dicō]. In law, *a claimant ; hence, a champion, protector.* 1. Lit.: tabellam quasi vindicem libertatis, Cic. : Liv. ; terrae Hercules, Ov. ; maiestatis imperi, Liv. ; aeris alieni, Cic. Ep. ; iniuriae, Liv. ; honori posterorum tuorum ut vindex fieres, Pl. 2. Transf. **a.** *a deliverer* : dignus vindice nodus, Hor. **b.** *an avenger, punisher, revenger :* coniurationis, Cic. Ep. ; parentis, Ov. ; *Fem. :* deae vindices scelerum, Cic. In apposition : poena, Cat. ; flamma. Ov.

vindicātiō. ōnis. *f.* [vindicō], *a laying claim in law.* 1. Lit.: intestatorum civium bonorum, Traj. ap. Plin. Ep. 2. Transf. *an avenging, punishing :* Cic.

vindiciae, ārum, *f. pl.* [vindicō]. 1. Lit. **a.** *things or persons claimed or disputed :* postulare, Liv. With dare, dicere, or decernere, *to hand over an object claimed :* vindicias ab libertate in servitutem dare, Liv. ; vindiciae nuper a libertate dictae, Liv. ; Cato: decresse vindicias secundum servitutem, Liv. **b.** *an act of claiming, a claim :* iniustis vindiciis alienos fundos petere, Cic. ; Liv. 2. Transf. *championship, protection :* cum vindicias amisisset ipsa libertas, Cic.

vindicō, āre [vim dicō], *to lay legal claim to a thing.* 1. Lit.: sponsam (or puellam) in libertatem, Liv. ; also, ita vindicatur Verginia spondentibus propinquis, Liv. 2. Transf. **a.** *to assert or champion the freedom of a person* (with or without in libertatem or libertatem): Galliam in libertatem, Caes. ; ex dominatu Ti. Gracchi in libertatem rem publicam, Cic. Hence, *to protect, defend, deliver :* libertatem, Caes. ; sapientia nos a formidinum terrore vindicat, Cic. ; Liv. ; aliquem a miseriis morte, Cic. ; se ex suspicione sceleris, Cic. ; quam dura ad saxa revinctam vindicat Alcides, Ov. **b.** *to make a claim upon ; to arrogate, appropriate :* omnia pro suis, Cic. ; Homerum Chii suum vindicant, Cic. ; ad se, Liv. ; decus belli, Liv. ; prospera omnes sibi vindicant, Tac. **c.** *to avenge, punish; to take vengeance on or for :* maleficium in aliis, Cic. ; in quos vindicandum statuit, Caes. ; mortem, Sall. ; Ov. ; iniurias, Liv. Also, se de or ab aliquo, Sen., Plin. Ep. [It. *vengiare* ; Sp. *vengar* ; Fr. *venger.*]

vindicta, ae, *f.* [vim dicō], *the claiming or asserting of liberty ;* hence, ceremonially of the *liberating-rod* used in manumitting a slave. 1. Lit.: Pl., Cic., Ov., etc. 2. Transf. **a.** *a championing, defending, defence, deliverance (from) :* civitas in ipsā vindictā libertatis peritura, Liv. ; petatur a virtute invisae huius vitae vindicta, Liv. ; mors una vindicta est, Liv.; legis severae, Ov. **b.** *vengeance, punishment :* Liv., Juv., Tac.

vīnĕa, ae, *f.* [vīnum], *a plantation of vines, a vineyard.* 1. Lit.: Pl., Cic., Verg., etc. 2. Transf. **a.** *a vine :* Cato, Varr., Phaedr. **b.** Milit. *a kind of pent-house, shed,* or *mantlet,* for sheltering besiegers : Caes., Cic. [Fr. *vigne.*]

vīnētum, i, *n.* [vīnum], *a plantation of vines, a vineyard :* Cic., ,Verg., etc. Prov. : vineta ut egomet caedam mea (i.e. be severe against myself), Hor.

vīnitor, ōris, *m.* [vīnum], *a vine-dresser :* Cic., Verg.

vinnŭlus, a, um [porh. fr. venus], *charming, sweet :* oratio, Pl.

vīnŏlentia, ae, *f.* [vīnolentus], *wine-bibbing, intoxication from wine :* Cic., Suet.

vīnŏlentus, a, um [vīnum]. I. *drunk with wine, intoxicated :* Ter., Cic. Masc. pl. as Noun : Cic. II. *mixed with wine :* medicamina, Cic.

vīnōsus, a, um [vīnum]. I. *full of wine, drunk with wine :* Liv. II. *fond of wine, wine-bibbing :* Hor. Comp. : aetas, Ov. Sup. : lena, Pl. III. *having the flavour of wine :* pomum succi vinosioris, Suet.

vīnum, i, *n.* [cf. Gk. ϝοῖνος], *wine.* 1. Lit.: Pl., Cic., Verg., etc. In pl. : Lucr., Verg., etc. 2. Transf. **a.** *grapes :* Pl., Cato. **b.** *vines :* vinum conserere, Cato, Plin. **c.** Of the effects of wine : vini plenus, Cic. ; vino sepulta urbs, Verg. ; per vinum, Cic.

viŏla, ae, *f.* [dim. fr. root seen in Gk. ϝίον], *the violet* and also *the stock.* 1. Lit.: Cic., Verg. 2. Transf. of colour : Hor., Plin.

viŏlābilis, e, adj. [violō], *that can be harmed or profaned :* non violabile numen, Verg. ; cor levibus telis, Ov.

viŏlārium, i, *n.* [viola], *a bed or bank of violets :* Varr., Verg., Hor., Ov.

viŏlārius, i, *m.* [viola], *a dyer of violet colour :* Pl.

viŏlātiō, ōnis, *f.* [violō], *an injury, profanation :* templi, Liv. ; religionum, Sen. Ep.

viŏlātor, ōris, *m.* [violō], *an outrager, profaner :* templi, Ov. ; iuris gentium, Liv. ; foederis, Tac.

viŏlens, entis, adj. [vis], *impetuous, vehement :* Aufidus, Hor. ; equus, Hor.

viŏlenter, adv. *impetuously, vehemently :* Ter., Hor., Liv., Tac., etc. Comp. : Suet. Sup. : Col.

viŏlentia, ae, *f.* [violentus], *vehemence, impetuosity, ferocity :* vinolentorum, Cic. ; leonum, Lucr. Of things : vultūs, Ov. ; vini, Lucr. ; fortunae, Sall.

viŏlentus, a, um [vis], *forcible, vehement, impetuous, boisterous.* 1. Lit.: homo, Cic. ; Liv. ; in aliquem, Liv. ; in armis, Ov. ; vis leonum, Lucr. ; ventus, Lucr. ; opes, Cic. ; ingenium, Liv. ; ingenio violentus, Tac. ; imperium, Liv. Comp. : violentior Eurus, Verg. ; amnis, Verg. ; pars violentior natalis horae, Hor. Sup. : violentissimae tempestates, Cic. ; Liv. 2. Transf. of style : nimis violentum est dicere etc., Cic.

viŏlō, āre [vis], *to harm or injure by violence, to outrage.* 1. Lit. (physically). **a.** hospites, Caes. ; aliquem, Liv. ; qui stupris aut caedibus violati sunt, Liv. ; violatus ab arcu, Ov. Impiously **or** unnaturally:

parentis, Cic. ; matres familias, Cic. ; (virginem), Tib. ; sacrum vulnere corpus, Verg. **b.** Of territory : finis. Caes. ; agros ferro, Verg. ; loca religiosa, Cic. ; Cereale nemus securi, Ov. **2.** T r a n s f. (morally) *to outrage, violate, break :* indutias per scelus, Caes. ; officium, ius, religionem, amicitiam, etc., Cic. ; foedera, Liv. ; Tib. ; nominis nostri famam tuis probris, Cic. ; virginitatem filiae, Cic.

vipĕra, ae, *f.* [contr. fr. vivi-pera, from vivus pariō, because supposed to bring forth its young living], *a viper.* **1.** L i t. : Plin. **2.** T r a n s f. **a.** *an adder, snake :* Verg., Hor., Ov. P r o v. : in sinu viperam habere (of treachery), Cic. **b.** As a term of re-proach : Juv. [Fr. *guivre.*]

vipĕrĕus, a, um [vipĕra], *of a viper or snake :* dentes, Ov. ; crinis, Verg. ; monstrum (i.e. the head of Medusa), Ov. ; anima (i.e. poisonous), Verg. ; genus, Verg.

vipĕrīnus, a, um [vipĕra], *of a viper or snake :* morsus, Acc. ; sanguis, Hor. ; Plin.

Vipsānius, a, *the name of a Roman gens.* Esp. M. Vipsanius Agrippa, *the son-in-law of Augustus.*

vir, viri, *m. a male person, a man.* **1.** L i t. **a.** In gen. : Ter., Lucr., Cic., Verg., etc. **b.** *a husband :* Pl., Cic., Ov., etc. Of animals : vir gregis, Verg. ; Ov. **c.** *a man* (opp. to a boy) : pueri hoc possunt, viri non potuerunt ? Cic. ; Ov. **d.** *a man,* i.e. *a real man, who deserves the name :* cum is iam se conroboravisset ac vir inter viros esset, Cic. ; Liv. ; Hor. **e.** M i l i t. : Pl., Liv. E s p. *an infantryman :* equites virique, Liv. P r o v. : equis viris or viris equisque (i.e. with might and main), Cic., Liv. **f.** D i s-t r i b u t i v e l y : vir cum viro congrediaris, Liv. ; legitque virum vir, Verg., Cic., Liv., Suet. **2.** T r a n s f. *manhood, virility :* Cat., Luc.

virāgō, inis, *f.* [vir], *a manlike, heroic maiden, a female warrior :* Pl., Verg., Ov.

Virbius, i, *m.* **I.** *a surname of Hippolytus.* **II.** *a son of Hippolytus.*

viridĭcāta, ae, *f. adj.* unknown and dub. [perh. fr. viridis, hence, *green*], silva, Cic. Ep.

virēcta, ōrum, *n. pl.* [virēscō], *green places, green spots, greensward :* nemorum, Verg.

virĕō, ēre, *to be green or verdant.* **1.** L i t. : Cic., Verg., etc. **2.** T r a n s f. : *to be fresh, vigorous :* ingenium, Liv. ; Hor. ; Ov.

virēs, ium, *f. pl., v.* vis.

virēscō, ere [virĕō], *to grow green or verdant :* rami arboribus, Lucr. ; gramina, Verg. ; Plin.

virētum, *v.* virēcta.

virga, ae, *f.* [perh. fr. same root as virgō], *a twig, sprout, switch.* **1.** L i t. **a.** Cato, Varr., Verg., Ov. E s p. *a graft, scion, set :* Ov. ; also, *a limed twig :* Ov. **b.** *a rod, switch* for flogging : Pl., Juv. ; esp. *the rods in the fasces :* Cic. Hence, poet. for fasces : Ov., etc. **c.** *a staff, walking-stick :* Liv., Ov. **d.** *a magic wand :* Verg., Ov. **2.** T r a n s f. **a.** *a coloured stripe* in a garment : purpureae, Ov. **b.** *a branch* in a family tree or pedigree : Juv. [It. Sp. *verga ;* Fr. *verge.*]

virgātor, ōris, *m.* [virga], *one who beats with rods, a flogger :* Pl.

virgātus, a, um [virga]. **I.** *made of twigs* or *osiers :* calathisci, Cat. **II.** *striped :* sagula, Verg.

virgētum, i, *n.* [virga], *a thicket of rods* or *osiers :* Cic.

virgĕus, a. um [virga], *of rods* or *twigs, of brushwood :* scopae, Cato ; flamma, Verg.

virgĭdēmia, ae, *f.* [virgō ; *cf.* vindēmia], *a harvest of birches* (i.e. of blows) : Pl.

Virgĭliae, *v.* Vergiliae.

virgĭnālis, e, *adj.* (and **virgĭnārius,** a, um, Pl.) [virgō], *of a maiden, maidenly, maiden's :* habitus atque vestitus, Cic. ; feles, Pl. As Noun, **virgĭnāle,** is, *n.* (*sc.* membrum) : Phaedr.

virgĭnĕus, a, um [virgō], *of a maiden, maid-enly, maiden's, maiden- :* comptus, Lucr. ; rubor, Verg. ; pudor, Tib. ; forma, Ov. ; sagitta (i.e. of Diana), Hor. ; ara (of Vesta), Ov. ; urnae (of the Danaides), Prop. ; volucres (the Harpies), Ov. ; Helicon (as the home of the Muses), Ov.

Virgĭnēsvēndōnĭdēs, is, *m.* [virgō vēndō], *Virgin-seller's-son :* Pl.

virgĭnĭtās, ātis, *f.* [virgō], *maidenhood, virginity :* Cic., Verg., Ov.

virgō, inis, *f. a maiden, virgin, girl, young woman.* **1.** L i t. : Cic., Ov., etc. ; bellica (i.e. Pallas), Ov. Of a Vestal : Cic., Hor. In apposition : virgo filia, Cic. ; dea (i.e. Diana), Ov. **2.** T r a n s f. **a.** *a young married woman :* Verg., Ov. **b.** *the con-stellation Virgo :* Cic. poet. **c.** Aqua Virgo, or simply Virgo, *an aqueduct constructed by M. Agrippa,* Ov., Plin. [It. *vergine ;* Sp. *virgen ;* Fr. *vierge.*]

virgŭla, ae, *f.* [dim. virga], *a little twig, a small rod, a wand :* Cic. ; divina, *a divining-rod,* Cic. ; censoria (i.e. an obelus in reject-ing a passage in an author), Quint.

virgulta, ōrum, *n. pl.* [virgula]. **I.** *thickets, copses, brushwood :* Caes., Cic., Liv., Ov. **II.** *slips, cuttings of trees :* Lucr., Verg.

virguncula, ae, *f.* [dim. virgō], *a little maid, young girl :* Curt., Juv.

Viriāthus (-ātus), i, *m., a famous leader of the Lusitanians in their war against the Romans* (149 B.C.) : **Viriāthinus (Viriā-tinus),** a, um.

viridāns, antis [viridis], *growing green, green :* herbae, Lucr. ; Plin. ; laurus, torus, Verg ; color, Lucr. Hence, **virĭdor,** āri, *to become green :* vada ab herbis, Ov.

viridārium, i, *n.* [viridis], *a plantation of trees, a pleasure-garden :* Cic. Ep. [It. *verziere ;* Fr. *verger.*]

viridĭcātus, *v.* viridicāta.

viridis, e, *adj.* [virĕō], *green* (of every shade). **1.** L i t. : Lucr., Cic., Hor., Ov. As Noun, **viridia,** ium, *n. pl. green plants or trees :* Sen. Ep. ; Phaedr., Plin. Ep. **2.** T r a n s f. *fresh, young :* iuventa, senectus, Juv. ; aevum, Ov. ; viridis ' animo, Sen. Ep. ; usque ad novissimam valetudinem viridis, Plin. Ep. ; fructus studiorum, Quint. *Comp.* : praemiorum genera, Cic. [It. Sp. *verde ;* Fr. *vert.*]

virĭdĭtās, ātis, *f.* [viridis], *greenness, verdure.* **1.** L i t. : pratorum, Cic. ; herbescens, Cic. **2.** T r a n s f. *freshness, vigour :* Cic.

viridō, virĭdor, *v.* viridāns.

virilis, e, *adj.* [vir], *of a man.* **1.** L i t. **a.** With ref. to sex]: *male, masculine :* secus, Pl., Sall.; genus, Lucr.; stirps fratris, Liv.; vox, vultus, Ov.; nomen (in grammar), Varr. **b.** With ref. to age : *arrived at manhood, fully grown :* aetas animusque, Hor.; partes (in plays), Hor.; toga (*of a fully grown man*), Cic., Liv. **2.** T r a n s f. of character, etc.: *manly, vigorous, bold, etc. :* oratio, Cic.; ratio atque sententia, Cic.; acta illa res est animo virili, consilio puerili, Cic. Ep.; ingenium, Sall. **P h r.** pars virilis, *a man's share,* hence, *one's part or duty :* est aliqua mea pars virilis, Cic.; plus quam pars virilis postulat, Cic.; cum illius gloriae pars virilis apud omnis milites sit, Liv.; pro virili parte *or* portione, *in proportion to* or *to the best of one's ability,* Cic., Liv., Tac. As Noun, **virilia**, ium, *n. pl. manly deeds :* Sall.

virilitās, ātis, *f.* [virilis], *the age* or *power of manhood, manhood, virility.* **1.** L i t.: Plin., Tac. **2.** T r a n s f. **a,** C o n c r. *the manly parts :* Plin., Quint. **b.** sanctitas et, ut sic dicam, virilitas ab his (veteribus Latinis) petenda, Quint.

viriliter, *adv. manfully, courageously :* Cic., Ov. C o m p. : Sen.

viri-potēns, entis, *adj.* [virēs (*v.* vis), potēns], *all-powerful, almighty :* Iuppiter, Pl.

viritim, *adv.* [vir], *man by man, (to) each one separately :* aliquid dispertire, Pl.; pecus distribuere, Caes.; agrum dividere, Cic.; commonefacere benefici sui, Sall.; Hor.; Tac.

virōsus, a, um [virus]. **I.** *slimy :* loci, Cato. **II.** *strong-smelling, rank :* Verg.

virtūs, ūtis, *f.* [vir], *manliness, manhood* (including all that is best in the physical and moral nature of man), *strength and vigour, bravery, courage, ability, capacity, worth, virtue, etc.* **A.** Of social excellence in gen. **1.** L i t.: ut animi virtus corporis virtuti anteponatur, Cic.; virtus clara aeternaque habetur, Sall.; oratoris vis divina virtusque, Cic.; virtutes continentiae, gravitatis, iustitiae. fidei, Cic.; propter multas virtutes cum dignitate vixit, Nep. **2.** T r a n s f. of animals and things: *good quality, excellence, worth, etc. :* merci pretium statui, pro virtute ut veneat, Pl.; praedium solo bono, suā virtute valeat, Cato; arboris, equi, Cic.; navium, Liv.; herbarum, Ov.; dicendi, facundiae, Quint.; oratoriae virtutes, Cic. **B.** Of military, etc., qualities : *bravery, courage, valour :* Caes., Sall., Hor., etc. **C.** *moral excellence, virtue :* Cic., Sall.; aliquem ad virtutem a luxuriā revocare, Nep. **D.** P e r s o n i f i e d : aedes Virtutis, Liv.; Pl.; Cic.

virus, i, *n.* [*cf.* Gk. ἰός]. **I.** *a slimy liquid, slime* (of animals and plants) : Verg., Plin., etc. **II.** *a poisonous liquid, poison.* **1.** L i t.: Cic. poët., Verg., Ov., Plin. **2.** T r a n s f.: evomere virus acerbitatis suae, Cic. **III.** *strong smell, pungency :* Lucr., Plin. **IV.** *a sharp, salt taste.* Of seawater : Lucr. Of wine : Plin.

vis, N o m.; vim, A c c.; vi, A b l.; and *pl.* **virēs** (vis, Lucr.), N o m.; viris or virēs (vis, Lucr.), A c c.; virium, G e n.; viribus, D a t. and A b l.; *f.* [*cf.* Gk. ἴς]. **I.** S i n g.

force, vigour. **1.** L i t. (physical). **a.** In gen.: equorum, Cic.; venti, solis, teli, Lucr.; tempestatis, fluminis, Caes.; virium, Liv.; vini, Lucr.; veneni, Cic.; genitalis, Tac. **b.** *hostile force, violence :* Pl.; facere in aliquem, Ter.; alicui adferre, Cic., Nep.; matribus familias vim adferre, Cic.; Ov.; praesidio tam valido vim adferre, Liv.; adhibere, Cic.; vi possidere, Cic.; iter per vim temptare, Caes.; vi vis inlata defenditur, Cic.; nec vi nec munimento capi poterat, Liv.; vim viribus exit, Verg.; de vi reus, de vi condemnatus, Cic. **2.** T r a n s f. **a,** *quantity, number :* hominum, Pl., Liv.; servorum, Cic.; vis magna pulveris, Caes.; magna vis auri argentique, Cic. **b.** Mental or legal : *power, energy, vigour : ·* vis ac facultas oratoris, Cic.; ingeni, etc., Cic.; vim ac ius magistratui (*office*) demere, Liv. **c,** Of abstract things : *force, meaning, import, essence :* amicitiae, eloquentiae, honesti, verbi, Cic. **II.** Plural. **virēs**, *strength, force.* **1.** L i t. (physical) : hoc ali viris nervosque confirmari putant, Caes.; corporis, Cic., Liv.; adulescentis, Cic.; me iam sanguis viresque deficiunt, Caes.; validis viribus hastam contorquere, Verg.; agere pro viribus, Cic.; supra viris, Hor.; nec mihi sunt vires (with *Inf.*), Ov.; oleae, Cato; neglecta solent incendia sumere viris, Hor.; viris habet herba ? Ov.; viris alias flumina concipiunt, Ov. **2.** T r a n s f. **a.** M i l i t. *forces, troops :* ut viris ad coercendum haberet, Caes.; exiguae, Verg.; satis virium ad certamen, Liv.; undique contractis viribus signa cum Papirio conferre, Liv.; Ov. **b.** Mental : *power, energy, vigour :* mentis, Ov.; ingeni, orationis, eloquentiae, Quint.

viscātus, a, um [viscum], *smeared with bird-lime, limed :* Varr. Ov. T r a n s f.: Plin. Ep.

viscerātiō, ōnis, *f.* [viscera], *a public distribution of flesh* or *meat :* Cic., Liv.

viscum, i, *n.* (**viscus**, i, *m.*, Pl.) [*cf.* Gk. ἰξός]. **I.** *mistletoe :* Verg., Plin. *birdlime* made from mistletoe-berries. **1.** L i t.: Cic., Verg. **2.** T r a n s f.: viscus merus vostra est blanditia, Pl.

viscus, visceris, and more freq. *pl.* **viscera**, um, *n.* [perh. fr. same root as viscum; lit. the soft parts], *the flesh and all parts* (of the animal body) *below the skin.* **1.** L i t. **a.** In gen.: (exta is the usual word in prose): *the internal organs, the viscera* (the heart, lungs, liver, and also the stomach, entrails). *Sing.* : Lucr., Tib., Ov. *Plur.* : Lucr., Cic., Ov. **b.** *the flesh, the carcase :* boum visceribus vesci, Cic.; solida taurorum viscera, Verg. **2.** T r a n s f. **a.** In *pl., the womb :* Ov., Quint. Also *the offspring,* ' *one's own flesh and blood* ' : Ov., Curt. **b.** In *pl., the heart, vitals, bowels* (i.e. the inmost parts): montis (Aetnae), Verg.; terrae, Ov.; in venis atque in visceribus rei publicae, Cic.; patriae, Verg.; aerari, Cic.; magnarum domuum (i.e. the heart or the favourite, so ' bosomfriends '), Juv.

visendus, a, um. **I.** *Gerund.* visō. **II.** A d j. *worthy of being seen, admirable, remarkable :* Cic. *Neut. pl.* as Noun : Liv.

visĭō, ōnis, f. [vidĕŏ], *a seeing*. Transf. **a.** *a thing seen, an appearance, apparition* : Cic. **b.** *an idea, notion :* veri falsique, Cic.

visĭtō, āre [*freq.* vĭsŏ]. **I.** *to see frequently or habitually :* aliquem, Pl. **II.** *to go to see, to visit :* aliquem, Cic., Suet.

visō, visere, visi, visum [*freq.* videŏ], *to look at attentively, to view*. **1.** Lit.: Pl., Cic., Verg. With Acc.: ex muris visite agros vestros ferro vastatos, Liv.; Pl.; Tac. **2.** Transf. **a.** *to go or come in order to look at, to see to or find (out)*. With Acc.: Pl. With *Indir. Quest.* : Pl., Ter., Hor., Liv. With *Indir. Deliberative :* Liv. With *ad :* vise ad portum, Pl.; Varr. **b.** *to go to see, to visit*. With Acc. (of person or thing): Ter., Cic. Ep., Hor.; in *Pass. :* Thespiae visuntur, Cic. With *ad* (esp. of visiting a sick person) : Ter., Lucr., Ov.

vīsus, a, um. **I.** *Part.* videŏ. **II.** Noun, **visum**, i, n. *something seen, a sight, appearance, vision :* visa somniorum, Cic.; Prop.; Ov.

vīsus, ūs, m. [vidĕŏ], *a seeing, the faculty or act of seeing, sight*. **1.** Lit.: oculorum visus, Lucr.; corpus visu tactuque manifestum, Lucr. In *pl. :* Ov. **2.** Transf. **a.** *a thing seen, a sight, vision :* rite secundarent visūs, Verg.; augustior humano visu, Liv.; inopino territa visu, Ov.; nocturni visūs, Liv. **b.** perh. *the capability of being seen :* Cic.

vita, ae (GEN. *sing.* vitāi, Lucr.), f. (v. vīvŏ), *life*. **1.** Lit. **a.** vitae necisque potestas, Caes.; nae ego hodie tibi bonam vitam feci, Pl.; vitam alicui dare, adimere, auferre, Cic.; vitā aliquem privare, expellere, Cic.; vitam agere honestissime, Cic.; vitam in egestate degere, Cic.; degere miserrimam, Cic.; tutiorem vivere, Cic.; in vitā esse, manere, Cic. Ep.; de vitā decedere, Cic.; vitā cedere, Cic.; e vitā discedere, Cic. Ep.; vitam profundere pro aliquo, Cic.; amittere per summum dedecus, Cic. **b.** *life* as a period of time: XXXVII annos vitae explevit, Tac.; periit anno vitae septimo et quinquagensimo, Suet. **2.** Transf. **a.** *a livelihood :* sibi reperire, Pl. **b.** *a way or mode of life :* rustica, Cic.; utriusque vita et mores, Liv.; Ov.; communis, Cic.; omni vitā atque victu excultus, Cic. **c.** Of a very dear object : mea vita, or simply vita, Pl., Ter., Cic. Ep., Prop. **d.** *a life*, i.e. *a course of life, career*, as the subject of biography : Nep., Tac. **e.** *a form of existence, a ghostly being* or *life :* tenues sine corpore vitae, Verg. [Sp. *vida ;* Fr. *vie.*]

vitābĭlis, e, *adj.* [vĭtŏ], *that can be or ought to be shunned :* Ov.

vītābundus, a, um [vĭtŏ], *shunning, avoiding, evading :* Sall., Tac. With Acc.: castra hostium, Liv.; Sall.

vītālis, e, *adj.* [vīta]. **I.** *of life, vital :* aevom, Pl.; motus, saecla, Lucr.; vis, spiritus, Cic.; viae (i.e. air-passages), Ov. As Noun, **vitāle**, is, n. *the means of life :* Liv. **vītālia**, ium, n. *pl. the vital parts, vitals :* Sen., Plin., Luc.; rerum, Lucr. **II.** *likely to live, remaining alive :* Pl., Hor., Sen.

vītālĭter, *adv. vitally :* animata, Lucr.

vĭtātĭō, ōnis, f. [vĭtŏ], *a shunning, avoidance :* oculorum, lucis, urbis, fori, doloris, Cic.

Vĭtellĭus, a, *the name of a Roman gens*. Esp. A. Vitellius, *Roman emperor*, A.D. 69 ; **Vĭtellĭus, Vĭtellĭānus**, a, um ; **Vĭtelliāni**, ōrum, m. *pl. soldiers of Vitellius ;* also, *a kind of writing-tablet :* Mart.

vitellus, i, m. [*dim.* vitulus]. **1.** Lit. *a little calf*, as a term of endearment : Pl. **2.** Transf. *the yolk* of an egg : Cic., Hor., etc. [Fr. *veau.*]

vīteus, a, um [vītis], *of the vine :* Varr.; pocula (i.e. wine), Verg.

vĭtĭātus, a, um. **I.** *Part.* vitiŏ. **II.** Adj. *forged :* Cic.

vīticula, ae, f. [*dim.* vītis], *a little vine :* Cic.

vītĭfer, fera, ferum [vītis ferŏ], *vine-bearing :* colles, Plin.; Mart.

vītĭgĕnus, a, um [vītis and *gen* in gignŏ], *produced from the vine :* liquor, Lucr.

vĭtĭlēna, ae, f. [vitium lēna], *a bawd, procuress :* Pl.

vĭtĭō, āre [vitium], *to make faulty, to spoil, mar, taint, corrupt, etc.* **1.** Lit.: lues vitiaverat auras, Ov.; oculos, Ov.; vina, Hor. Esp. of outrage : aliquam in occulto, Cato; virginem, Ter., Suet.; vitiati pondera ventris, Ov. **2.** Transf. *to falsify :* senatūs consulta, Liv.; vitiandis diebus, Cic. Ep.; pectora limo malorum, Ov.

vĭtĭōsē, *adv. faultily, defectively, badly, corruptly*. **1.** Lit.: Cic. **2.** Transf.: concludere, Cic. Sup. : Col.

vĭtĭōsĭtās, ātis, f. [vitiōsus], *a faulty or corrupt condition*. Transf.: Cic.

vĭtĭōsus, a, um [vitium], *faulty, defective, bad, corrupt*. **1.** Lit.: nux, Pl.; pecus, Varr. **2.** Transf. **a.** vitiosissimus orator, Cic. **b.** *defective, informal :* suffragium, Cic.; consul (i.e. elected contrary to the auspices), Cic. Neut. *pl.* as Noun (opp. to sinistra): Cic. **b.** *morally faulty, vicious :* Pl., Cic.; vita, Cic.; cura, Hor. Comp. : progenies vitiosior, Hor. Sup. : Vell.

vītis, is, f. [v. vieŏ], *a vine, grape-vine*. **1.** Lit.: Cic., Verg., etc. **2.** Transf. **a.** *a vine-branch :* Cato, Varr., Ov. **b.** *a centurion's switch* or *staff*, made of a vine-branch : Ov., Tac., etc. Transf. *the office of a centurion, centurionship :* Juv.

vīti-sātor, ōris, m. [vītis, sator fr. serŏ], *a vine-planter :* Verg. Of Bacchus : Acc.

vĭtĭum, i, n. *a fault, defect, blemish, flaw*. **1.** Lit.: corporis, Pl.; in parietibus aut in tecto, Cic.; animadverso vitio castrorum, Caes.; aëris, Verg.; of the soil : omne per ignem excoquitur vitium, Verg. **2.** Transf. **a.** In gen. *the fault :* vini vitio atque amoris feci, Pl.; honorem vitio civitatis, non suo, non sunt adsecuti, Cic.; quamvis fortunae vitio, non suo, decoxisset, Cic.; milites conflictati et tempestatis et sentinae vitiis, Caes. **b.** In morals, etc. : illud mihi vitiumst maxumum, Ter.; non dicam vitium sed erratum, Cic.; in vitio esse, Cic.; virtus est vitium fugere, Hor.; vitio parentum rara iuventus, Hor.; legibus et praemia proposita virtutibus et supplicia vitiis, Cic. Of outrage : pudicitiae (Alcumenae) vitium addere, adferre,

Pl. ; alicui per vim offerre, Ter. ; virginis, Ter. ; redimere, Ov. **c.** In style : Cic. ; orationis, sermonis, Quint. **d.** In mind : mentis, ingeni, Quint. ; Stoicae sectae, Quint. **e.** In auspices or augury : comitiorum, Cic. ; vitio creatus, Liv. ; id obvenit vitium, Cic. ; tabernaculum vitio captum, Cic. [It. *vizio* ; Sp. *vicio* ; Fr. *vice*.]

vĭtō, āre, *to avoid, shun, seek to escape, evade.* **1.** L i t. : tela, Caes. ; Hor. ; lacum, Caes. ; forum, balnea, Hor. ; Ov. ; aliquem, Hor. **2.** T r a n s f. : vitia, Cic. ; suspiciones, periculum, Caes. : mortem fugā, Caes. ; culpam, Hor. With DAT. : infortunio, Pl. With *ne* and *Subj.* : erit vitandum ne etc., Cic. ; Liv. With *Inf.* : Hor.

vĭtrĕus, a, um [vitrum], *of glass, glass-.* **1.** L i t. : hostis (a piece in draughts), Ov. ; latro, Mart. As a Noun, **vitrea,** ōrum, *n. pl. glass vessels, glass-ware* : Stat., Mart. **2.** T r a n s f. *like glass, glassy* (in colour, transparency, or brilliance) : togae, Varr. ; unda, Verg. ; Circe, Hor. T r a n s f. : fama (perh. brilliant and brittle), Hor.

vĭtrĭcus, i, *m. a stepfather* : Cic., Ov., Tac.

vĭtrum, i, *n.* **I.** *glass* : Lucr., Cic., Hor. etc. **II.** *woad, a plant used for dyeing blue* : Caes. [It. *vetro* ; Sp. *vidrio* ; Fr. *verre*.]

Vĭtrūvĭus, i, *m.* : M. Pollio, *a contemporary of Augustus, author of a work on architecture.*

vitta, ae, *f.* [*v.* vieŏ], *a ribbon, band,* esp. worn round the head ; in relig. lang. *a head-band, a sacrificial or sacerdotal fillet* : Verg., Ov., etc. Worn by brides and Vestals : Pl., Tib., Ov., etc. Bound around the altar, etc., Verg., Ov. ; and upon the branches borne by suppliants for protection or pardon : Verg., Hor., Ov.

vittātus, a, um [vitta], *bound with a fillet* or *chaplet* : capilli, Ov. ; navis, Plin.

vĭtŭlīnus, a, um [vitulus], *of a calf* : caruncula, Cic. ; assum, Cic. Ep. As a Noun, **vĭtŭlīna,** ae, *f.* (*sc.* caro), *veal* : Pl., Nep. [Fr. *vélin*.]

vĭtŭlor, āri [Vitula, the goddess of victory, of joy], *to celebrate a festival, keep holiday, be thankful and joyful* : Iovi lubens vitulor, Pl. ; Varr.

vĭtŭlus, i, *m.* and **vitula,** ae, *f. a calf, bull-calf, cow-calf.* **1.** L i t. : Cic., Verg., etc. **2.** T r a n s f. in gen. **a.** *a calf, foal* : Verg. ; of the elephant or whale : Plin. **b.** vitulus marinus, *a sea-calf, seal* : Juv., Suet.

vĭtŭpĕrābĭlis, e, *adj.* [vituperŏ], *blameworthy, blameable, censurable* : Cic.

vĭtŭpĕrātĭō, ōnis, *f.* [vituperŏ], *blaming, censuring ; blame, censure.* **1.** L i t. : in vituperationem venire, adduci, cadere, Cic. In *pl.* : Cic., Quint. **2.** T r a n s f. *a subject or cause for blame* : alicui esse vituperationi, Cic. Ep. **b.** *blameworthiness, scandalous conduct* : Cic.

vĭtŭpĕrātor, ōris, *m.* [vituperŏ], *a blamer, censurer, vituperator* : Cic ; philosophiae, Cic.

vĭtŭpĕrō, āre [vitium parŏ]. **I.** R e l i g. *to render defective, spoil* an omen : omen mihi, Pl. **II.** *to censure, blame* : Cic. ; deos, Pl. ; Cic. ; tuum consilium, Cic. P r o v. : qui caelum vituperant (i.e. nothing can satisfy them), Phaedr.

vīvācĭtās, ātis, *f.* [vīvāx], *tenacity of life* : Plin., Plin. Ep.

vīvārĭum, i, *n.* [vīvus], *a preserve, fish-pond,* etc. **1.** L i t. : Plin., Juv. **2.** T r a n s f. : excipiant senes, quos in vivaria mittant, Hor.

vīvātus, a, um [vīvus], *quickened, animated* : potestas animi, Lucr.

vīvāx, ācis, *adj.* [vīvŏ], *tenacious of life, long-lived.* **1.** L i t. : Verg., Hor., Ov. *Comp.* : Hor. **2.** T r a n s f. **a.** *Of things, lasting long, enduring* : oliva, Verg. ; gratia, Hor. ; carmine fit vivax virtus, Ov. **b.** *brisk in burning* : sulpura, Ov. **c.** *brisk in learning* : discipuli vivaciores, Quint.

vīvēscō (vīvīscō), vīvēscere, vixī [vīvŏ], *to become alive, get life.* **1.** L i t. : Plin. **2.** T r a n s f. *to grow lively, strong* : ulcus. Lucr.

vīvĭdus, a, um [vīvus], *full of life, teeming with life.* **1.** L i t. : tellus, Lucr. **2.** T r a n s f. **a.** Of statuary : Prop. **b.** Of mental or physical powers : vis animi, Lucr. ; ingenium, pectus, Liv. ; corpus, Plin. Ep. ; senectus, Tac. ; Umber (canis), Verg. ; dextra bello, Verg. ; bello vivida virtus, Verg. ; odia, eloquentia, Tac.

vīvĭ-rādix, īcis, *f. a rooted cutting* (i.e. having a root) : Cato, Varr., Cic.

vīvĭscō, *v.* vīvēscō.

vīvŏ, vīvere, vixī, victum. (*Aor. Subj.* vixet, Verg.) [*cf.* βιόω], *to live, be alive.* **1.** L i t. of animal life. **a.** In gen. : Pl., Cic., Ov., etc. ; alicui vivere, Ter., Cic. ; ad summam senectutem, Cic. (Also of plants : Cic.) With *Intern.* Acc. : vitam, Pl., Cic., etc. ; in *Pass.* : nunc tertia vivitur aetas, Ov. **b.** *to be still alive, survive* : Cic., Liv. **c.** In *Perf.* : *to have done with life* : Pl., Cic. **d.** *to live well, enjoy life* : sed quando vivemus ? Cic. Ep. ; Cat. But usually with an *Adv.* : Pl., Cic., Hor. (*Impers. Pass.* : negat Epicurus iucunde posse vivi nisi cum virtute vivatur, Cic.) Hence, in bidding farewell, vive valeque, Hor. ; vivite, silvae, Verg. **e.** *to live (on), support life (on)* : de suo, Pl. ; piscibus atque ovis avium, Caes. ; Cic. ; Hor. ; rapto, Verg. (*Impers. Pass.* : vivitur ex rapto, Ov.) ; misere, Pl. ; parcius, Hor. ; in diem (i.e. from hand to mouth), Cic. **f.** *to pass one's life, to reside, dwell* : extra urbem, Cic. ; vixit Syracusis, Nep. ; in maximā celebritate atque in oculis civium, Cic. ; in paupertate, Cic. ; e naturā, Cic. ; familiariter cum aliquo, Cic. Ep. ; secum (i.e. for oneself alone), Cic. **2.** T r a n s f. **a.** Of things : saepes, Varr. ; cinis, ignes, Ov. ; sub pectore vulnus, Verg. **b.** Of fame, etc. : calores Aeoliae puellae, Ov. ; Scipio vivit semperque vivet, Cic. ; per omnia saecula famā vivam, Ov.

vīvus (-os), a, um [*v.* vīvŏ], *alive, living.* **1.** L i t. : me vivo, Pl. ; Cic. ; (simulacrorum) membra vivos hominibus complent, Caes. ; ut eam (curiam) mortuus incenderet quam vivus everterat, Cic. Esp. in phrase, vivus vidensque, *before one's very eyes* : huic vivo videntique funus ducitur, Cic. ; vivos vidensque pereo, Ter. **2.** T r a n s f. **a.** Of things : caespes (i.e. fresh cut), Hor.,

Ov.; flumen (i.e. *running*), Liv.; ros (i.e. *fresh*), Ov.; lucernae (i.e. *burning*), Hor.; saxum (i.e. *natural*), Verg.; vivos ducent de marmore vultūs, Verg.; vox (i.e. *speaking*), Cic., Quint., etc. *Neut.* as Noun, *the quick:* ad vivum resecare, Col.; calor ad vivum adveniens, Liv. Of money, *the capital:* de vivo aliquid detrahere, resecare, Cic. **b.** In fame: vivo' per ora virum (GEN.), Enn. **c.** *lively:* animus, Plin. Ep.

vix, *adv.* [v. vincō], *with difficulty, with much ado, hardly.* **a.** carros ducere, Caes.; Pl., etc.; vix teneor quin etc., Cic. Ep. Strengthened with *aegre:* vix et aegre, Pl. **b.** Of time, *scarcely, only just:* vix tandem legi litteras, Cic. Ep.; Ter.; Cat. With *cum* or (poet. *et*) to denote immediate succession: vix agmen processerat cum Galli etc., Caes.; Cic.; Verg. With *dum* (usually in one word, **vixdum**), *hardly then, scarcely yet:* (Hannibalem) vixdum puberem, Liv.; haec vixdum coetu dimisso comperi, Cic.; Ter.

vixet, *v.* vivō.

vocābulum, i, *n.* [vocō], *an appellation, designation, name.* **a.** In gen.: Chaldaei ex gentis vocabulo nominati, Cic.; Ter.; imponens cognata vocabula rebus, Hor.; liberta cui vocabulum Acte fuit, Tac.; artifex vocabulo Locusta, Tac. **b.** Gramm. *a noun:* Varr., Quint.

vōcālis, e, *adj.* [vōx], *having a voice or utterance, gifted with speech or song, tuneful, etc.:* Cic.; boves, Tib.; suā terram Dodonida quercu, Ov.; Orpheus, Hor.; chordae, Tib.; carmen, Ov. *Comp.:* Sen., Quint. *Sup.:* Plin. Ep. As Noun, **vōcālis,** is, *f.* (*sc.* littera), *a vowel:* Cic., Quint. [Fr. *voyelle.*]

vocāmen, inis, *n.* [vocō], *an appellation, designation, name:* Lucr.

vocātiō, ōnis, *f.* [vocō]. **I.** *a citing before a court, a summons:* Varr. **II.** *an invitation to dinner:* Cat.

vocātor, ōris, *m.* [vocō], *an inviter to dinner, etc.:* Sen., Mart., Suet.

vocātus, ūs, *m.* [vocō]. **I.** *a summoning:* senatus vocatu Drusi in curiam venit, Cic. In *pl.:* Verg. **II.** *an invitation* to dinner: (in ABL.): Suet.

vōciferātiō, ōnis, *f.* [vōciferor], *a loud calling, outcry:* Cic., Quint.

vōciferor, āri (and **vōciferō,** āre, Varr.) [vōx ferō], *to cry out, cry aloud, shout out.* **1.** Lit.: Cic.; talia, Verg.; pauca in senatu, Liv.; hoc (with *Indir. Quest.*), Cic. With *Acc.* and *Inf.:* Cic., Liv. With *ne* and *Juss. Subj.:* Liv. With *Indir. Quest.* and *Indir. Deliberative:* Liv. With quoted words: Liv., Suet. *Impers. Pass.:* Liv. **2.** Transf. of things. **a.** res ipsa per se, Lucr.; ratio naturam rerum, Lucr. **b.** Of resounding noise: aera, Lucr.

vocitō, āre [*freq.* vocō]. **I.** *to be accustomed to call, name:* Demetrius qui Phalereus vocitatus est, Cic.; Lucr.; Tac. **II.** *to call or shout out again and again:* Tac.

vocō, āre [*cf.* Gk. Ϝεῖπον, Ϝέπος], *to call; to call upon, summon.* **1.** Lit. **a.** In gen.: Pl.; fortuna vocat, Verg.; spes vocat,

Liv. With *Acc.:* nutu vocibusque host[?] Caes.; ad bellum, Liv.; populum R. [?] arma, Caes.; milites ad concilium, Liv[?] aliquem in contionem, Cic.; patres, Verg[?] concilium, Verg.; contionem, Tac.; pop[?] lum auxilio, Tac.; ventos, Lucr., Ver[?] votis imbrem, Verg. With *Inf.:* (Char[?] levare pauperem vocatus, Hor. *Imp[?] Pass.:* in contionem vocari placuit, L[?] **b.** *to summon* into court: in ius, Cic.; [?] dictator, Liv.; te ex iure manum consert[?] Cic. **c.** *to invite* to dinner, etc.: aliqu[?] Pl., Cic.; aliquem ad cenam, Ter.; [?] prandium, Cic.; convivam, Pl.; voc[?] res est and vocata est opera nunc quid[?] *I have an engagement,* Pl. **d.** *to call* u[?] the gods: patrios voce deos, Verg.; T[?] auxilio deos, Verg.; divos in vota, Ve[?] Ov. **e.** *to call, name:* certabant ur[?] Romam Remoramne vocarent, E[?] Cic.; ad Spelaeum quod vocant mor[?] Liv.; patrioque vocant de nomine [?] sem, Ov.; ego vocor Lyconides, Pl.; [?] Hor. **2.** Transf. **a.** *to call, invite,* [?] me ad vitam, Cic. Ep.; in spem me, [?] Ep.; fessos nox imberque ad quie[?] Liv.; Auster in altum, Verg. With *In[?]* sedare sitim fluvii vocabant, Lucr. [?] *call,* i.e. *to bring, draw, put, etc., in* [?] position or condition: me apud mi[?] in invidiam, Cic.; aliquem in partem [?] rum, Tac.; aliquid in iudicium, [?] verba sub iudicium, Ov.; aliquid i[?] bium, Cic.; vitam omnem civiu[?] exitum, Cic.

vōcula, ae, *f.* [*dim.* vōx], *a small or feeble voice.* **1.** Lit.: Cic. Ep., Prop. **2.** Transf. **a.** *a soft note or tone:* Cic. **b.** *a petty jeer:* Cic. Ep.

volaema (pira), *n. pl. a kind of large pear:* Cato, Verg.

volāns, antis. **I.** Part. volō. **II.** Noun, **volantēs,** ium, *f. pl. birds:* Verg.

volāticus, a, um [volō], *flying, wing[?]* Lit.: Pl. **2.** Transf. *fleeting, trans[?]* Academia, Cic. Ep.; impetūs, Cic. [Fr. *volage.*]

volātilis, e, *adj.* [volō], *flying, wing[?]* Lit.: Cic., Ov. **2.** Transf. **a.** *swift, rapid:* telum, Lucr.; ferrum, Verg. **b.** *fleeting, transitory:* aetas, Ov.; Sen. Ep.

volātus, ūs, *m.* [volō], *a flying, flight:* lae, Cic.; Pegaseo volatu, Cat. in *pl.:* Cic.

Volcānus (Vulc-), i, *m. the fire-god,* s. of Jupiter and Juno. **1.** Lit.: Caes. Ov., etc.; **Volcānius,** a, um; **Volcānalia,** ium, *n. pl. his festival, celebrated* Aug. 23.

volēns, entis. **I.** Part. volō. **II.** Adj. A. Attributively: *willing, permitting:* cum dis volentibus, Pl., Cato; volenti animo, animis volentibus, Sall. B. Predicatively **a.** *willing, ready:* volentes in amicitiam non veniebant, Liv.; Verg., Cic., etc. **b.** *favourable, well-disposed:* precantes Iovem ut volens propitius prae[?]: beat sacra arma pro patriā, Liv.; Pl.; uti militibus exaequata cum imperatore labos volentibus esset, Sall.; Liv. **III.** Noun. **a.** *Masc., one who wishes, is willing, well-disposed, etc.:* Sall., Liv., Verg., Ov., etc. **b.** *Neut. pl., acceptable or suitable* *things :* vole.. plebi facere, Sall. ; Muciano volentia scripsere, Tac.

volg-, *v.* vulg-.

volĭtāns, antis. [. *Part.* volitō. **II.** *Masc.* Noun, *a winged insect :* Verg.

volito, āre [*freq.* volō], *to fly to and fro, flit, or float about.* **1.** Lit. **a.** Of birds and insects : Cic., Ov., Plin. **b.** *rerum simulacra ultro citroque per auras,* Lucr. ; Cic. ; favilla in nimbo, Verg. ; umbrae inter vivos, Lucr. ; (umbrae) circum litora, Verg. **2.** Transf. **a.** Of excited persons : Clodius, Cic. Ep. in foro, Cic. ; totā acie, Liv. ; mediis in milibus ductores, Verg. ; per mare navita Hor. **b.** voces per auras, Lucr. ; volito vivo' (= vivus) per ora virum (GEN.), Enn. ; nostrum nomen latissime, Cic. ; nec volitabo in hoc insolentius (i.e. fly into a passion), Cic.

voln-, *v.* vuln-.

volo, āre [*cf.* velō], *to fly.* **1.** Lit. : Pl., Lucr., Cic., Ov., etc. ; supra nubem, Verg. ; per aëra remigio alarum, Verg. **2.** Transf. of swift or hurried movement : vola curriculo, Pl. ; per summa aequora curru, Verg. ; currus, Verg. ; nubes, tempestates, fulmina, Lucr. ; solum, Lucr., Sall., Verg., Liv. ; fama, Verg. ; aetas, Cic.

volo, velle, volui (contr. forms : vln or vln' for vis-ne ? Pl., Ter. ; sis, sultis, for sī vis, si vultis) [*cf.* Gk. βούλομαι], *to be willing, to want, wish, desire, be disposed.* **A.** In gen. **a.** Pl., Cic., Liv., Verg., etc. ; hactenus, Tac. With *Inf.* : Pl., Cic., Ov., etc. With Acc. and *Inf.* : Pl., Cic., Hor., etc. With Acc. of thing or person : Pl., Cic., Verg., etc. With Subj. : volunt haec ut infecta faciant, Pl. ; Ter. ; quam vellem Panaetium nostrum nobiscum haberemus ! Cic. **b.** Elliptically. deinde Arpinum (sc. ire) volebamus, Cic. Ep. ; si quid ille se velit, *if he wanted him for anything,* Caes. ; num quid me vis ? (politely ' can I do anything more for you ?'), Pl., Ter., Hor. ; tibi bene (male) ex animo volo, *good (ill) befall you !* Pl., Ter. **b.** In partic. **a.** *to will, determine, ordain* : sic di voluistis, Verg. ; maiores vos sententiam ferre voluerunt, Cic. Hence, on proposing a new law to the people : velitis, iubeatis haec sic fieri ! Liv. ; so, with *ut* and *Subj.* : Liv. **b.** *to suppose, be of opinion ; to maintain* : quod cum volunt, declarant quaedam esse vera, Cic. ; Mars alter, ut isti volunt, Liv. With Acc. and *Inf.* : Cic. **c.** *to mean, signify* : quid vult concursus ? Verg. Usually with *sibi* (or *tibi*) : nec satis intellexi, quid sibi lex, aut quid verba ista vellent, Cic. ; quid tibi vis, insane ? Cic. **d.** *to wish rather, to prefer* : malae rei esse quam nullius duces esse volunt, Liv. ; Cic. ; Ov.

volōnēs, um, *m. pl.* [volō], *volunteers* (of the slaves who enlisted after Cannae) : Liv.

volpēs, *v.* vulpes.

Volsci, ōrum, *m. pl. an ancient people in the south of Latium ;* **Volscus,** a, um.

volsella, ae, *f.* [vellō], *a kind of pincers for pulling out hairs, tweezers :* Pl.

volsus, a, um, *Part.* vellō.

Voltinia tribus, *a Roman tribe, of unknown locality ;* **Voltiniēnsēs,** ium, *m. pl. the people of the Voltinian tribe.*

Voltumna, ae, *f. an Etruscan goddess, in whose temple the Etrurian States assembled.*

voltus, *v.* vultus.

volūbilis, e, *adj.* [volvō], *turning or being turned, spinning, revolving.* **1.** Lit. : buxum, Verg. ; amnis, Hor. ; caelum, Cic. **2.** Transf. **a.** Of speech, *rapid, fluent,* voluble : Cic. ; of the speaker : Cic. **b.** *changeable, mutable :* fortuna, Cic.

volūbilĭtās, ātis, *f.* [volūbilis], *a rapid, whirling motion.* **1.** Lit. : mundi, Cic. **2.** Transf. **a.** *roundness :* capitis, Ov. **b.** Of speech, *fluency, volubility :* Ov. ; nimia vocis, Quint. **c.** *changeableness, mutability :* fortunae, Cic.

volūbiliter, *adv.* of speech, *rapidly, fluently, volubly :* Cic.

volucer (volucris, Tib.), cris, e, *adj.* [volō], *flying, winged.* **1.** Lit. : Cic., Ov. As Noun, **volucris,** is, *f.* (*sc.* avis : once masc., *sc.* ales : Cic. poet.) **a.** *a bird :* Lucr., Cic., Verg., Hor., etc. **b.** *an insect :* Ov. ; of bees : Ov. **2.** Transf. *flying, fleet.* **a.** lumen, Lucr. ; sagitta, aurae, fumi, Verg. ; equi, procellae, etc., Ov. **b.** male dictum, Cic. ; Somnus, Verg. **c.** Of *transitory things :* fortuna, Cic. ; dies, Hor. ; fama, Ov. ; gaudium, Tac.

volūmen, inis, *n.* [volvō]. **I.** *a roll of writing, a roll, book.* **a.** Of a (whole) book : evolvere, explicare, Cic. ; annosa vatum, Hor. **b.** Of a separate portion of a work, *a part, book :* Cic., Nep., Ov., etc. **II.** *a roll, whirl, fold, eddy, etc. :* (anguis) sinuat immensa volumine terga, Verg. ; fumi, Ov. ; alterna volumina crurum, Verg.

voluntārius, a, um [voluntās], *of one's own free will, voluntary.* **1.** Lit. : milites, Caes., Liv. ; exercitus, Liv. ; auxilia, Cic. As Noun, **voluntāriī,** ōrum, *m. pl.* (*sc.* milites), *volunteers :* Caes., Liv. **2.** Transf. of things : *done of one's free will, voluntary :* mors, Cic. ; accusationes, Tac.

volūntās, ātis, *f.* [volēns], *will, wish, choice, inclination.* **1.** Lit. **a.** In gen. : quid esset suae voluntatis ostendere, Caes. ; multitudinis, Cic. ; mentem voluntatemque suscipere, Cic. Adv. phr. : (i) voluntate alone or with *Possess.* Pron. or GEN., *of one's own accord, willingly, voluntarily :* Ter. ; suā voluntate descendere, Cic. ; voluntate omnium concedi, Cic. ; aliae civitates voluntate in dicionem venerunt, Liv. ; Cic. (ii) ad voluntatem ; de, ex voluntate, *according to the will, at the desire of :* ad voluntatem loqui, Cic. ; ex Caesaris voluntate, Cic. Ep. (iii) praeter legem et sui voluntatem patris studeat, Ter. **b.** *a disposition, attitude* (good or bad) : populum esse in alia voluntate, Cic. ; celans quā voluntate esset in regem, Nep. ; bona voluntas erga nos, Liv. ; summa in se voluntas, Caes. ; gens dubiae ad id voluntatis, Liv. ; aliena a te, Cic. ; mutua, Cic. Ep. **2.** Transf. **a.** *a last will, testament :* Cic., Tac. **b.** Of speech : *meaning, sense :* Quint. [Fr. *volonté*.]

volup, *adv.* [*cf.* Gk. ἔλπομαι], *agreeably, delightfully, to one's satisfaction, etc. :* si illis aegrest mihi quod volup est, Pl. ; Ter.

voluptābilis, e, *adj.* [voluptās], *pleasant, agreeable :* Pl.

voluptārius, a, um. **I.** *giving pleasure, pleasant, agreeable* to the senses : res, locus, Pl. ; possessiones, Cic. Ep. ; gustatus, Cic. **II.** *concerned with the pleasures of the senses :* disputationes, Cic. **III.** *devoted to sensual pleasures :* Cic. *Masc. pl.* as Noun : Pl.

voluptās, ātis, *f.* [volup], *satisfaction, enjoyment, pleasure, delight* of any kind. **1.** Lit. : Cic. ; percipere ex libidine, Cic. ; ex tuis litteris cepi, Cic. Ep. ; fictas fabulas cum voluptate legere, Cic. In *pl.*, mostly *of sensual gratifications :* frui voluptatibus, Cic. ; a voluptatibus (servus), *master of the revels*, Suet. **2.** Transf. **a.** Of persons, as a term of endearment : mea voluptas, Pl., Verg. **b.** In *pl.*, *sports, shows*, given to the people : Cic., Tac. **c.** Personified : Cic. [Fr. *volupté.*]

voluptuōsus, a, um [voluptās], *pleasant, agreeable :* Plin. Ep.

volūtābrum, ī, *n.* [volūtō], *a wallowing-place* for swine : Verg.

volūtābundus, a, um [volūtō], *wallowing about :* in voluptatibus, Cic.

volūtātiō, ōnis, *f.* [volūtō], *a rolling about, wallowing.* **1.** Lit. : (in *pl.*) : corporis, Cic. **2.** Transf. *restlessness, disquiet :* animi, Sen. ; rerum humanarum, Sen. Ep.

volūtō, āre [*freq.* volvō], *to roll over and over* or *about,* (and in *Mid.*) *to flounder, wallow.* **1.** Lit. : se in pulvere, Plin. In *Mid. :* in luto, Cic. ; animi corporibus elapsi circum terram ipsam volutantur, Cic. ; amnis per cava saxa, Ov. ; genua amplexus genibusque volutans haerebat, Verg. ; in glacie, Liv. **2.** Transf. **a.** vocem per atria, Verg. ; confusa verba, Ov. ; murmura, Verg. In *Mid. :* omnes in omne genere scelerum, Cic. ; inter mala plurima, Sen. **b.** In the mind, *to turn over, revolve :* rem in pectore, Pl. ; aliquid mente, Lucr. ; haec secum in animo, Liv. ; multa secum animo, Liv. ; secum corde, Verg. ; suo cum corde, Verg. ; mecum ipse, Verg. ; aliquid in secreto cum amicis, Liv. ; consilia de bello, Liv. **c.** *to engross :* animum cogitationibus, Liv. In *Mid. :* in veteribus scriptis studiose, Cic.

volūtus, a, um, *Part.* volvō.

volva (**vulva**), ae, *f.* [volvō] *a wrapper, covering.* **a.** fungorum, Plin. **b.** *the womb, matrix :* Juv. Esp. *a sow's womb* (as a favourite dish) : Hor.

volvō, volvere, volvī, volūtum [*cf.* Gk. ἐλύω, εἰλύω, root Ϝελ], *to roll, wind, turn about, tumble.* **1.** Lit. **a.** In gen. : amnis sub undis saxa, Lucr. ; Verg. ; fumum caligine ventus, Lucr. ; filum, Varr. (*cf.* sic volvere Parcas, Verg.) ; huc illuc oculos, Verg. ; volvendi sunt libri, Cic. ; sub naribus ignem, Verg. Also, *to form by rolling up :* volvere orbem, (milit.) *to form circle*, Liv. **b.** In *Mid. :* (anguis) inter vestis et levia pectora lapsus volvitur, Verg. ; stellarum cursūs, Cic. ; lacrimae, Verg. ; volvi humi, Verg. ; Euryalus leto, Verg. ; volventia plaustra, Verg. **2.** Transf. **a.** satis diu hoc saxum volvo, Ter. ; (lunam) celerem pronos volvere mensis, Hor. ; volvendis mensibus, Verg. ; volventibus annis, Verg. ; celeriter verba, Cic. ; tot casūs, Verg. **b.** In the mind : *to turn over* or *revolve :* multa secum,

Sall. ; multa cum animo suo, Sall. ; immensa omnia animo, Liv. ; bellum in animo, Liv. ; iras in pectore, Liv. ; cogitationes, Liv. ; sub pectore sortis, Verg. ; bellum adversus nos, Tac. ; intra me ipsum, Tac.

vōmer (**vōmis**, Cato, Verg.), eris, *m.* *a ploughshare.* **1.** Lit. : Cic., Verg., etc. **2.** Transf. of the penis : Lucr.

vomica, ae, *f.* [vomō], *a sore, boil, ulcer, abscess.* **1.** Lit. : Pl., Cic., Juv. **2.** Transf. *an annoyance, plague, curse* (rare, and censured by Quint.) : Liv. (old prophecy).

vōmis, eris, *v.* vōmer.

vomitiō, ōnis, *f.* [vomō], *a vomiting :* Cic.

vomitō, āre [*freq.* vomō], *to vomit often* or *regularly :* Sen. Ep., Suet.

vomitus, ūs, *m.* [vomō], *a vomiting.* **1.** Lit. : Pl., Curt., Sen. Ep., etc. **2.** Transf. as term of abuse : Pl., Lucil.

vomō, ere, uī, itum [*cf.* Gk. ἐμέω, root Ϝεμ], *to throw up, vomit.* **1.** Lit. : post cenam, Cic. With *Intern.* Acc. : vomitum, Pl. *Impers. Pass. :* Cic. **2.** Transf. : quā largius vomit (Padus), Plin. With *Intern.* Acc. : vitam, Lucr. ; undam, fumum, flammas, Verg. ; Charybdis fluctūs, Ov. Comic. : argentum, Pl.

vorāgō, inis, *f.* [vorō], *an abyss, chasm, deep hole.* **1.** Lit. Of watery depths : Cic., Cat., Verg., Liv. Of *a gulf* or *chasm* in the earth : Liv. Of a deep stomach : ventris, Ov. **2.** Transf. : gurges et vorago patrimoni. Cic. ; rei publicae, Cic. ; vitiorum, Cic. ; Liv.

vorāx, ācis, *adj.* [vorō], *swallowing, devouring :* Charybdis, Cic. ; venter, Ov. *Comp. :* ignis, Ov.

vorō, āre [*cf.* Gk. βιβρώσκω and perh. gurges], *to swallow up, eat greedily, devour.* **1.** Lit. : ambabus mālis, Pl. ; vitulum balaena, Pl. ; animalium alia vorant, alia mandunt, Cic. Prov. : meus hic est, hamum vorat, Pl. **2.** Transf. **a.** (navem) rapidus vorat aequore vortex, Verg. ; Ov. **b.** Of eager action : viam, Cat. ; litteras, Cic. Ep.

vors-, vort-, *v.* vers-, vert-.

vorsōria, ae, *f.* [vorsō (versō)], *a turning round, return ;* or perh. *the sheet* (' sailrope '). Transf. : vorsoriam capere, *to tack* (i.e. change one's course), Pl.

vōs, *v.* tū.

voster, tra, trum, *v.* vester.

vōtīvus, a, um [vōtum], *promised by a vow, given in consequence of a vow, votive :* ludi, Cic. ; tabula, Hor. ; legatio, Cic. Ep.

votō, āre, *v.* vetō.

vōtum, ī, *n.* [voveō]. **1.** Lit. **a.** *a solemn promise* made to a deity ; *a vow :* quam multi votis vim tempestatis effugerint, Cic. ; obstringi religione voti, Cic. Ep. ; voto teneri, Cic. Ep. ; nuncupare (usually of a magistrate), suscipere, facere, Cic. ; debere diis, Cic. ; solvere, reddere, Cic. ; exsequi, Verg. ; persolvere, Plin. Ep. ; voti reus, Verg. ; voti damnari, Cic. ; so, votis, Verg. **b.** *a votive offering :* Cic. ; votis incendimus aras, Verg. ; pro reditu, Verg. **2.** Transf. *a wish, desire, prayer :* Cic., Liv. ; audivere di mea vota, Hor. ; quod omnibus votis petendum erat, Liv. ;

hoc erat in votis, Hor. ; ea esse vota ut etc., Liv. ; contra spem votaque, Liv. ; supra votum, Plin. Ep. [Fr. *voeu*.]

voveō, vovēre, vōvī, vōtum, *to vow, to promise solemnly, to devote something to a deity.* **1.** Lit. : iaientaculum, Pl. ; sua capita, pro salute patriae, Cic. ; Herculi decumam, Cic. ; voti ludi, Liv. ; victimam pro reditu Ov. ; Salios fanaque Pavori, Liv. With Acc. and *Fut. Inf.* : Caes., Liv. With Acc. and *Pres. Inf.* : Pl. **2.** Transf. *to wish, wish for* : elige, quid voveas, Ov. ; Hor. With *ut* and *Subj.* : ut tua sim voveo, Ov.

vōx, vōcis, *f.* [*cf.* vocō], *a voice, tone, cry, call* of living creatures. **1.** Lit. : exercere, comprimere, Pl. ; inclinatā ululantique voce canere, Cic. ; vox inflexa ad miserabilem sonum, Cic. ; magnā voce dicere, Cic. ; vocem late nemora alta remittunt, Verg. ; summa, magna, Hor. ; acuta, Cic. ; cornix plenā improba voce, Verg. **2.** Transf. **a.** Of things : sonus et vox omnis, Lucr. ; fractae ad litora voces, Verg. ; bucina litore voce replet, Ov. **b.** Of any *utterance* of words : nulla vox audiebatur nisi haec ' civis Romanus sum,' Cic. ; ex percontatione nostrorum vocibusque Gallorum, Caes. ; vocem pro aliquo mittere, Cic. ; nescit vox missa reverti, Hor. ; illius nefari gladiatoris voces, Cic. ; contumeliosae, Caes. ; cultūs hominum recentum voce formasti catus (Mercurius), Hor. [It. *voce* ; Sp. *voz* ; Fr. *voix*.]

Vulcānus, *v.* Volcānus.

vulgāris (volg-), e, *adj.* [vulgus], *general, usual, common* : (artis) usus, Cic. ; consuetudo, Cic. ; liberalitas, opinio, Cic. ; vulgaris popularisque sensus, Cic. ; vulgari et pervagatā declamatione contendere, Cic. *Neut. pl.* as Noun : ieiunus raro stomachus vulgaria temnit, Hor.

vulgāriter (volg-), *adv. after the ordinary* or *common manner* : scribere, Cic. Ep.

vulgātor (volg-), ōris, *m.* [vulgō], *a divulger* : taciti, Ov.

vulgātus (volg-), a, um. **I.** *Part.* vulgō. **II.** Adj. **a.** *general, common* : vulgatissimi sensūs, Quint. **b.** *commonly* or *generally known, notorious* : vulgatior fama est, Liv. ; amores, Ov. *Sup.* : Suet.

vulgi-vagus (volg-), a, um [vulgus, vagus], *that wanders about everywhere, roving, inconstant* : mos ferarum, Lucr. ; Venus, Lucr.

vulgō (volg-), āre [vulgus], *to make general* or *common*, *to spread, publish, broadcast.* **a.** In gen. : morbos, Liv. ; contagium in alios, Curt. ; rem, Liv. ; librum, Quint. **b.** By words : dolorem verbis, Verg. ; vulgatur rumor, Liv. ; facinus per omnis, Liv. ; vulgare aliquem vulgo, Pl. **c.** Of prostitution : corpus, Liv. **d.** *to level* (by getting rid of distinctions), *to confound* : concubitūs plebis patrumque, Liv. In *Mid.* : vulgari cum privatis, Liv.

vulgus (volg-), i, n. (*masc.* Acc., freq. in Lucr., and sometimes in Verg., Liv.). **I.** *masses, the multitude, the people, public* : non est consilium in vulgo, non ratio, Cic. ; Verg. ; in vulgo notus, Liv. ; in vulgus notus, Cic. Ep. **II.** *any crowd,*

throng, herd : servorum, Ter. ; patronorum, Cic. ; inane (animarum), Ov. Of deer : Verg. **III.** Esp. contemptuously, *the crowd, rabble, populace* : Cic., Sall., Verg. ; gratiam ad vulgum quaesierat, Liv. ; profanum, malignum, infidum, Hor. ; mobile, Stat. So, vulgus militum, *the soldiery* : Curt. ABL. *neut.* **vulgō** as *Adv., before everybody, generally, everywhere, publicly* : Ter. ; vulgo totis castris testamenta obsignabantur, Caes. ; aliquid vulgo ostendere ac proferre, Cic. ; vulgo nascetur amomum, Verg.

vulnerātiō (voln-), ōnis, *f.* [vulnerō], *a wounding, wound.* **1.** Lit. : Cic. **2.** Transf. : famae, salutis, Cic.

vulnerō (voln-), āre [vulnus], *to wound.* **1.** Lit. : corpus ferro, Cic. ; eum in adversum os fundā, Caes. Of things : *to damage* : navis, Liv. **2.** Transf. : aliquem voce, Cic. ; gravior nuntius auris, Verg. ; virorum animos, Liv. ; crimine vulnerari, Ov. ; fortunae vulneror ictu, Ov.

vulnificus, a, um [vulnus faciō], *wound-making* : sus, Ov. ; chalybs, Verg.

vulnus (voln-), eris, n. *a wound.* **1.** Lit. : alicui facere, Pl. ; Ov. ; in latere, Cic. ; (alicui) inferre, Caes. ; alicui infligere, Cic. ; accipere, sustinere, Caes. ; excipere, Cic. ; gravi vulnere ictus, Liv. ; vulneribus defessus, Caes. ; vulneribus confectus, Liv. ; ex vulnere claudicare, Cic. ; ex vulnere recreari, Cic. ; mortiferum, Cic. Of things : *a blow, stroke, etc.* : vulneribus evicta (ornus), Verg. **2.** Transf. **a.** *a loss* in battle : Caes., Liv., Tac. **b.** In gen. : *a blow, disaster* : fortunae gravissimo percussus vulnere, Cic. ; inusta rei publicae, Cic. ; quae hio rei publicae vulnera imponebat, eadem ille sanabat, Cic. Of private or personal grief : Lucr., Verg., Ov. Of the wounds of love : Lucr., Verg., Hor.

vulpēcula (volp-), ae, *f.* [*dim.* vulpēs], *a (sly) little fox* : Cic., Phaedr.

vulpēs (volpēs), is, *f. a fox.* **1.** Lit. : Hor., Plin. **2.** Transf. *cunning, craftiness* : Hor. Prov. : (i) iungere vulpes (*to harness foxes,* of any absurd undertaking), Verg. (ii) vulpes pilum mutat, non mores (of a hypocrite), Suet.

vulsus (vols-), a, um. **I.** *Part.* vellō. **II.** Adj. *plucked, beardless, effeminate.* Lit. : Pl., Prop., Quint. **2.** Transf. : mens, Mart.

vulticulus (volt-), i, *m.* [*dim.* vultus], *a (mere) look* : Cic. Ep.

vultum (volt-), i, *v.* vultus.

vultuōsus (volt-), a, um [vultus], *full of airs* or *grimaces.* Transf. of style, *affected* : Cic., Quint.

vultur (volt-), uris, *m. a vulture.* **1.** Lit. : Verg., Liv. **2.** Transf. of a grasping, avaricious person : Sen., Mart.

Vultur (Volt-), uris, *m. a mountain in Apulia near Venusia, now Monte Vulture.*

vulturīnus (volt-), a, um, *of a vulture, like a vulture's* : species, Plin. ; collum, Mart.

vulturius (volt-), i, *m.* [vultur], *a vulture, bird of prey.* **1.** Lit. : Pl., Lucr., Liv. **2.** Transf. **a.** Of a rapacious or extortionate person : Pl., Cic. **b.** The name of an unlucky throw at dice : Pl. [Fr. *vautour*.]

Vulturnum (Volt-), i, *n. a town in Campania, on the river Vulturnus, now Castel Volturno.*

Vulturnus (Volt-), i, *m. the principal river of Campania, now Volturno.*

vultus (volt-), ūs, *m.* (*n. pl.* volta, Lucr.), *the countenance, visage,* as to features and expression : hence, *features, looks, mien, expression.* **1.** L i t. **a.** In gen. : imago animi vultus est, Cic. ; Verg. ; vultus acer in hostem, Hor. ; macatus, torvus, Hor. ; hilari vultu esse, Cic. In *pl. :* Cic., Hor. ; ficti simulatique, Cic. ; vultūs sumit acerbos, Ov. **b.** *a stern, grim look :* instantis tyranni, Hor. **2.** T r a n s f. **a.** *the face :* simiae vultum subire, Cael. ap. Cic. Ep. ; petamque vultūs umbra curvis unguibus, Hor., Ov. **b.** Of things, *the face, look, appearance :* unus erat toto naturae vultus in orbe, Ov. ; salis placidi, Verg.

vulva, *v.* volva.

X

X, x, is found in the oldest Latin inscriptions known to us. **I.** It is a double consonant, like the Greek ξ, being substituted for *cs* ; e.g. pax = pac-s, dixi = dic-si. As the other gutturals, *g, q,* and *h,* become *c* before *s, x* takes the place of the combinations *gs, qs,* and *hs ;* e.g. rex = reg-s, coxi = coq-si, traxi = trah-si. The sibilant element of *x* was very strongly pronounced ; hence *s* sometimes remains alone before *c* and *t,* as in sescenti, Sestius. **II.** In Italian, *x* becomes *s, ss,* or *sci,* as in esempio, testo, tessere, lasciare from exemplum, textus, texere, laxare. In French it commonly changes to *ss,* as in aisselle, laisser from axilla, laxare ; or, less frequently, *s,* as in buis from buxus, frêne (through fresne) from fraxinus, setier (through sestier) from sextarius. **III.** As an abbreviation, X stands for denarius and also for the number ten.

Xanthō, ūs, *f. a sea-nymph, d. of Nereus and Doris.*

Xanthus, i, *m.* **I.** *a river in Troas.* **II.** *a river in Lycia.* **III.** *a stream in Epirus.*

xenium, i, *n.* [ξένιον], *a gift made to guests.* **1.** L i t. : Plin. Ep., Mart. **2.** T r a n s f. *any gift :* Plin. Ep.

Xenophanēs, is, *m.* an early Greek philosopher of Colophon (b. c. 556 B.C.).

Xenophōn, ōntis, *m. a Greek historian (b. 445 B.C.), a pupil of Socrates, and leader in the famous retreat of the 10,000 Greeks (400 B.C.):* **Xenophōntēus (-ius)**, a, um.

xērampelinae, arum, *f. pl.* (*sc.* vestes) [ξηραμπέλιναι (of the colour of dry vine-leaves)], *dark-red or dark-coloured clothes :* Juv.

Xerxēs, is (ī, Nep.), *m. king of Persia, who invaded Greece and was defeated by the Greeks at Salamis* (B.C. 490).

xiphiās, ae, *m.* [ξιφίας], *a sword-fish :* Ov.

xystici, orum, *m. pl.* [ξυστικός], *athletes :* Suet.

xystus, i, *m.* and **xystum**, i, *n.* [ξυστός]. Among the Romans, *an open colonnade or portico,* or *a walk planted with trees,* etc., for recreation, conversation, philosophic discussion, etc. : Cic., Phaedr., Plin. Ep., etc.

Y

Y, y, was adopted into the later Roman alphabet as representative of Greek υ. It appears to have been already in use in Cicero's time ; but its application was restricted to foreign words.

Z

Z, z, had a place in the oldest Roman alphabet, and occurred in the Carmen Saliare, but afterwards ceased to be written. In Cicero's time it again came into use, but only to represent ζ in words borrowed from the Greek.

Zaleucus, i, *m. a lawgiver of the Locrians, about* B.C. 660.

Zama, ae, *f. a small town in Numidia, celebrated for the victory gained there by Scipio over Hannibal,* B.C. 201 ; *now Zamra;* **Zamēnsēs,** ium, *m. its inhabitants.*

zāmia, ae, *f.* [ζημία], *hurt, damage, loss :* Pl.

Zanclē, ēs, *f. an older name of Messana, in Sicily;* **Zanclaeus, Zanclēius,** a, um.

zēlotypus, a, um [ζηλότυπος], *jealous :* Iarbas, Juv. *Masc.* as Noun, *a jealous man :* Quint., Mart.

Zēnō or **Zēnōn**, ōnis, *m.* **I.** *the founder of the Stoic philosophy, a native of Citium in Cyprus (3rd century* B.C.). **II.** *a philosopher of Elea ("the Eleatic"), in Magna Graecia; born* B.C. 488. **III.** *an Epicurean philosopher, the teacher of Cicero and Atticus.*

Zephyritis, idis, *f. Arsinoe, wife of Ptolemaeus Philadelphus, who was honoured as a goddess.*

Zephyrus, i, *m.* [Ζέφυρος], *a gentle west wind, the western breeze, zephyr (pure Latin,* Favonius). **1.** L i t. : Verg., Hor., Ov. **2.** T r a n s f. *wind, in gen. :* Verg.

Zērynthius, a, um, *belonging to the Thracian town of Zerynthus.*

Zētēs, ae, *m. brother of Calais and son of Boreas, one of the Argonauts.*

Zēthus, i, *m. son of Jupiter by Antiope, and brother of Amphion.*

Zeuxis, is and idis, *m.* (Acc. -im or -in), *a famous Greek painter of Heraclea.*

xmaragdus (smar-), i, *f.* (rarely *m.*) [σμάραγδος], *a transparent green precious stone (emerald, beryl, jasper, etc.) :* Lucr., Ov., etc.

zōdiacus, i, *m.* [ζωδιακός], *the zodiac ; pure Lat.,* orbis signifer : Cic. poet.

Zōilus, i, *m. a proverbially severe Alexandrine critic of Homer; (hence called Homeromastix, scourge of Homer).*

zōna, ae, *f.* [ζώνη], *a belt, girdle worn by women.* **1.** L i t. : Cat., Ov. **2.** T r a n s f. **a.** *a belt for money, worn by men :* Hor. **b.** *the girdle or belt of Orion, a constellation :* Ov. **c.** *one of the imaginary belts which divide the earth into five climates, a zone :* Verg., Ov.

zōnārius, a, um [zōna], *of a belt or girdle :* sector, *a cut-purse,* Pl. *Masc.* as Noun, *a maker of girdles :* Lucil., Cic.

zōnula, ae, *f.* [dim. zōna], *a little girdle :* Cat.

Zōroastrēs, is, *m. a lawgiver of the Medes.*

zōthēca, ae, *f.* [ζωθήκη], *a small room in which to rest during the day :* Plin. Ep.

zōthēcula, ae, *f.* [dim. zōthēca] : Plin. Ep.

ROMAN CALENDAR

Our days of the Month.	March, May, July, October, have 31 days.	January, August, December, have 31 days.	April, June, September, November, have 30 days.	February has 28 days and in Leap Year 29.
1.	KALENDIS.*	KALENDIS.	KALENDIS.	KALENDIS.
2.	VI. ⎤	IV. ⎤ ante Nonas.	IV. ⎤ ante Nonas.	IV. ⎤ ante Nonas.
3.	V. ⎟	III. ⎦	III. ⎦	III. ⎦
4.	IV. ⎟ ante Nonas.	pridie Nonas.	pridie Nonas.	pridie Nonas.
5.	III. ⎦	NONIS.	NONIS.	NONIS.
6.	pridie Nonas.	VIII. ⎤	VIII. ⎤	VIII. ⎤
7.	NONIS.	VII. ⎟	VII. ⎟	VII. ⎟
8.	VIII. ⎤	VI. ⎟ ante Idus.	VI. ⎟ ante Idus.	VI. ⎟ ante Idus.
9.	VII. ⎟	V. ⎟	V. ⎟	V. ⎟
10.	VI. ⎟ ante Idus.	IV. ⎟	IV. ⎟	IV. ⎟
11.	V. ⎦	III. ⎦	III. ⎦	III. ⎦
12.	IV. ⎟	pridie Idus.	pridie Idus.	pridie Idus.
13.	III. ⎦	IDIBUS.	IDIBUS.	IDIBUS.
14.	pridie Idus.	XIX. ⎤	XVIII. ⎤	XVI. ⎤
15.	IDIBUS.	XVIII. ⎟	XVII. ⎟	XV. ⎟
16.	XVII. ⎤	XVII. ⎟	XVI. ⎟	XIV. ⎟
17.	XVI. ⎟	XVI. ⎟	XV. ⎟	XIII. ⎟
18.	XV. ⎟	XV. ⎟	XIV. ⎟	XII. ⎟
19.	XIV. ⎟ ante Kalendas (of the month following)	XIV. ⎟ ante Kalendas (of the month following)	XIII. ⎟ ante Kalendas (of the month following)	XI. ⎟ ante Kalendas Martias
20.	XIII. ⎟	XIII. ⎟	XII. ⎟	X. ⎟
21.	XII. ⎟	XII. ⎟	XI. ⎟	IX. ⎟
22.	XI. ⎟	XI. ⎟	X. ⎟	VIII. ⎟
23.	X. ⎟	X. ⎟	IX. ⎟	VII. ⎟
24.	IX. ⎟	IX. ⎟	VIII. ⎟	VI. ⎟
25.	VIII. ⎟	VIII. ⎟	VII. ⎟	V. ⎟
26.	VII. ⎟	VII. ⎟	VI. ⎟	IV. ⎟
27.	VI. ⎟	VI. ⎟	V. ⎟	III. ⎦
28.	V. ⎟	V. ⎟	IV. ⎟	pridie Kalendas
29.	IV. ⎟	IV. ⎟	III. ⎦	Martias.
30.	III. ⎦	III. ⎦	pridie Kalendas (Maias, Quinctilis, Octobris, Decembris).	In Leap-Year, Feb. 24 (a.d.vi. Kal. Mart.) was reckoned twice. Hence this day was called bis-sextus, and the year annus bissextus.
31.	pridie Kalendas (Aprilis, Iunias, Sextilis, Novembris).	pridie Kalendas (Februarias, Septembris, Ianuarias).		

* The words are given in the Ablative Case, the form employed in assigning a date.

TABLES OF ROMAN MEASURES, WEIGHTS AND MONEY

Modern British and metric equivalents are given to as great an accuracy as is known; the right hand figures in each column are rough equivalents, in the same units as the column heading except where otherwise shown.

TABLE I

LENGTH I—smaller measures

							inches		centimetres	
digitus							0·728		1·85	
1½	UNCIA (' *inch* ') or pollex						0·971		2·47	2½
4	3	palmus					2·91		7·40	
12	9	3	palmus maior (of late times)				8·74		22·2	
16	12	4	1⅓	PES			11·6	1 ft	29·6	30
20	15	5	1⅔	1¼	palmipes		14·6		37·0	
24	18	6	2	1½	1⅕	CUBITUS	17·5	1½ ft	44·4	⁴⁄₉ m

TABLE II

LENGTH II—larger measures—land and itinerary

							feet		metres	
PES							0·971	1	0·296	30 cm
1½	cubitus						1·46	1½	0·444	
2½	1⅔	gradus, or pes sestertius					2·43		0·740	¾ m
5	3⅓	2	PASSUS				4·85	5	1·48	1½ m
10	6⅔	4	2	decempeda, or pertica			9·71	10	2·96	3 m
120	80	48	24	12	actus (in length)		116		35·5	
5000	3333⅓	2000	1000	500	41⅔	MILLE PASSUUM	4850	⁹⁄₁₀ mile	1480	1½ km

Modern British and metric equivalents are given to as great an accuracy as is known; the right hand figures in each column are rough equivalents, in the same units as the column heading except otherwise shown.

TABLE III

Surface AREA of land

										sq yards		sq metres	
PES QUADRATUS										0·105	1 sq ft	0·0876	1/11
100	scrupulum, or decempeda quadrata									10·5	10	8·76	
480	4⅘	ACTUS SIMPLEX								50·2	50	42·1	40
2400	24	5	uncia*							251	250	210	
3600	36	7½	1½	clima						377			
										acres		hectares	
14,400	144	30	6	4	ACTUS QUADRATUS					0·312	⅓	0·126	⅛
28,800	288	60	12	8	2	TUGERUM				0·623	⅝	0·252	¼
57,600	576	120	24	16	4	2	heredium			1·25	1¼	0·504	½
5,760,000	57,600	12,000	2400	1600	400	200	100	centuria		125		50·4	50
23,040,000	230,400	48,000	9600	6400	1600	800	400	4	saltus	500		202	200

* The *as* or unit to which this *uncia* and the above *scrupulum* belong is the *iugerum*. The other uncial divisions of the *iugerum* may be easily calculated from the *uncia*. The *semissis* is, of course, the *actus quadratus*.

TABLE IV

CAPACITY—liquid

									pints		litres	
ligula	.	.	.	.	.	.	.	.	0·02	$\frac{1}{50}$	0·0114	
4	CYATHUS*	.	.	.	.	.	.	.	0·08	$\frac{1}{12}$	0·0455	45 ml
6	1½	acetabulum	.	.	.	.	.	.	0·12		0·0682	
12	3	2	quartarius, *ie* ¼ of the sextarius	.	.		.	.	0·24	¼	0·136	
24	6	4	2	hemina, or cotyla	.	.		.	0·48	½	0·273	¼
48	12	8	4	2	SEXTARIUS, *ie* ⅛ of the congius	.		0·96	1	0·546	½
288	72	48	24	12	6	CONGIUS	.	.	5·76		3·27	
1152	288	192	96	48	24	4	urna	.	2·30	3 gall	13·1	
2304	576	384	192	96	48	8	2	AMPHORA QUADRANTAL	46·1	6 gall	26·2	25
46,080	11,520	7680	3840	1920	960	160	40	20 culleus .	922	115 gall	524	

* According to the uncial division, the *sextarius* was the *as* or unit, and the *cyathus* the *uncia* or twelfth part.

TABLE V

CAPACITY—dry

								pints		litres	
ligula	.	.	.	.	.	.	.	0·02	$\frac{1}{50}$	0·0114	
4	CYATHUS*	.	.	.	.	.	.	0·08	$\frac{1}{12}$	0·0455	45 ml
6	1½	acetabulum	.	.	.	.	.	0·12		0·0682	
12	3	2	quartarius, *ie* ¼ of the sextarius	.		.	.	0·24	¼	0·136	
24	6	4	2	hemina, or cotyla	.	.	.	0·48	½	0·273	¼
48	12	8	4	2	SEXTARIUS, *ie* ⅛ of the congius	.		0·96	1	0·546	½
384	96	64	32	16	8	semimodius	.	7·68	1 gall	4·36	
768	192	128	64	32	16	2	MODIUS .	15·4	2 gall	8·73	9

* See note to Table IV.

TABLE VI

WEIGHT I—the Uncial divisions of the pound

	ounces		grams	
UNCIA	0·957	1	27·3	30
1½ sescuncia, or sescunx	1·44		40·9	
2 sextans	1·91		54·6	
3 quadrans, or teruncius	2·88		81·8	
4 triens	3·84	⅓ lb	109	
5 quincunx	4·79		136	
6 SEMIS, or semissis	5·75	⅜ lb	164	⅛ kg
7 septunx	6·71		191	
8 bes, or bessis	7·67	½ lb	218	
9 dodrans	8·62		245	¼ kg
10 dextans	9·57		273	
11 deunx	10·5		300	
12 AS, or LIBRA	11·5	¾ lb	327	⅓ kg

TABLE VII

WEIGHT II—subdivisions of the Uncia

										ounces		grams	
siliqua										0·007		0·189	
	3	obolus								0·02		0·569	
	6	2	SCRUPULUM							0·04	$\frac{1}{24}$	1·14	1½
	12	4	2	semisextula						0·08		2·28	
	24	8	4	2	SEXTULA					0·16	⅙	4·55	4½
	36	12	6	3	1½	sicilicus				0·24	¼	6·83	
	48	16	8	4	2	1½	duella			0·32	⅓	9·11	
	72	24	12	6	3	2	1½	semi-uncia		0·48	½	13·7	
	144	48	24	12	6	4	3	2	UNCIA	0·96	1	27·3	30
1728	576	288	144	72	48	36	24	12	AS, or LIBRA	11·5	¾ lb	327	⅛ kg

TABLE VIII

MONEY

COPPER and SILVER coins

Before the time of Augustus: the denarius was ½ uncia of silver; the sestertius and higher value of coin were silver, but lower values were copper, except for a few silver coins with special names (marked * in table).

After the time of Augustus: the denarius was ⅛ uncia of silver and all coins were made of silver.

									pence
sextula									⅓
1½	quadrans, teruncius*								½
2	1½	triens							¾
3	2	1½	semissis, sembella*						1
6	4	3	2	AS, libella*					2
12	8	6	4	2	dupondius				4
24	16	12	8	4	2	SESTERTIUS			8
48	32	24	16	8	4	2	quinarius, or victoriatus		16
96	64	48	32	16	8	4	2	denarius	32

GOLD coin

	pence
AUREUS, reckoned as 25 denarii	£8

MONEY of ACCOUNT
(not a coin)

SESTERTIUM, or mille nummi, reckoned as 1000 sestertii	£80

The equivalents are given as a rough guide to values in modern currency, but it should be borne in mind that absolute values both in Roman times and nowadays fluctuate rapidly.

TABLE VIII

MONEY

COPPER and SILVER coins

Before the time of Augustus, the denarius was ¼ uncia of silver; the asterius and higher value of coin were silver, but lower values were copper, except for a few silver coins with special names (marked * in table).

After the time of Augustus, the denarius was ⅛ uncia of silver and all coins were made of silver.

GOLD coin

aureus, reckoned as 25 denarii

MONEY of ACCOUNT
(not a coin)

sestertium, or unit number, reckoned as 1000 sesterces

The equivalents are given as a rough guide to values in modern currency, but it should be borne in mind that absolute values both in Roman times and nowadays fluctuate rapidly.